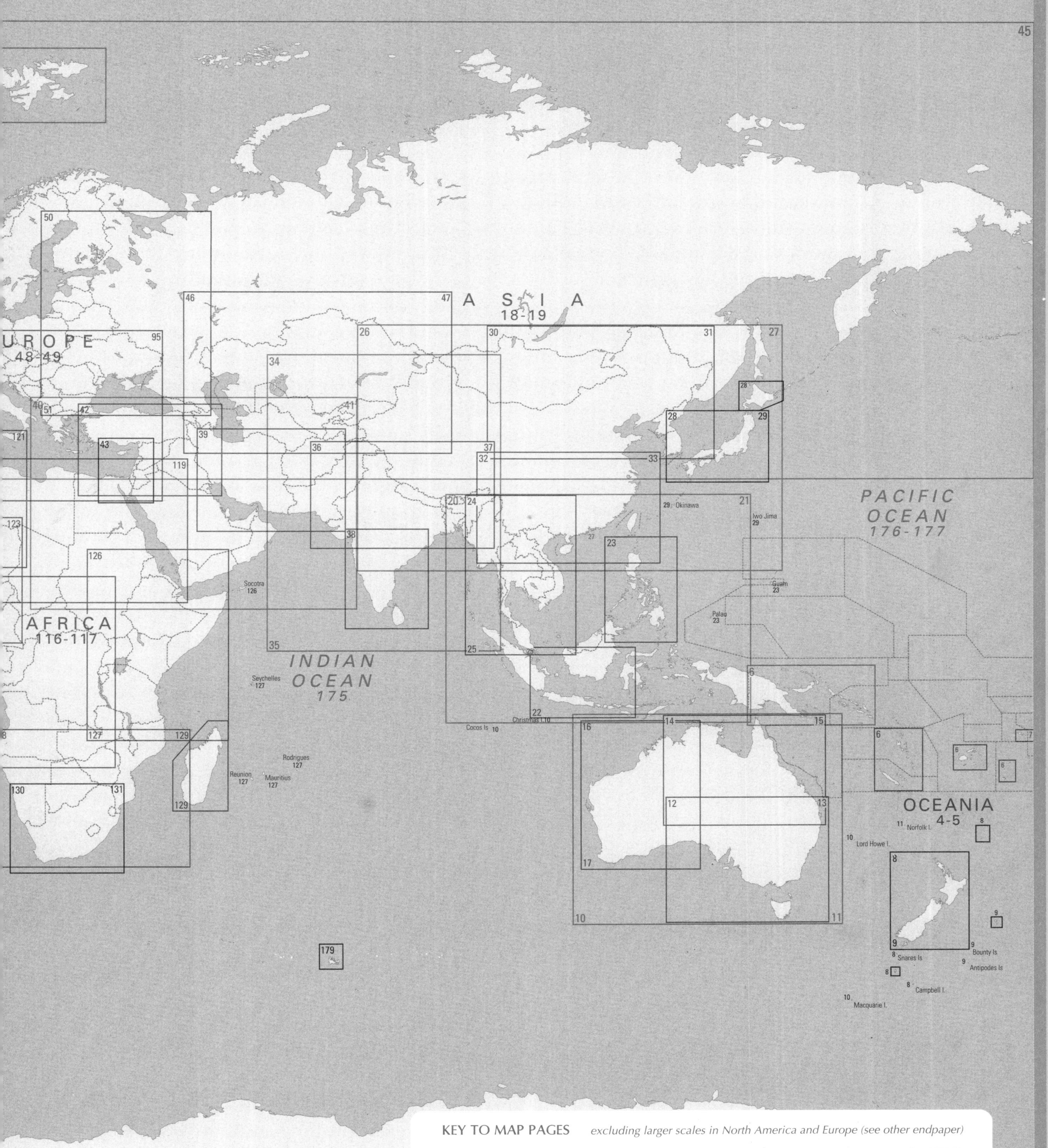

ARCTIC OCEAN
178

45

EUROPE
48-49

ASIA
18-19

AFRICA
116-117

PACIFIC
OCEAN
176-177

INDIAN
OCEAN
175

Socotra
126

Seychelles
127

Rodrigues
127

Reunion
127

Mauritius
127

Okinawa

Iwo Jima
29

Guam
23

Palau
23

Cocos Is
10

Christmas I. 10

OCEANIA
4-5

Norfolk I.

Lord Howe I.

Snares Is

Bounty Is

Antipodes Is

Campbell I.

Macquarie I.

179

ANTARCTIC
179

KEY TO MAP PAGES   *excluding larger scales in North America and Europe (see other endpaper)*

10 11	128 129	168 169
1:10 000 000 to 1:18 000 000	1:5 000 000 to 1:9 000 000	**1:3 000 000 to 1:3 750 000 & larger scales for inset maps**

THE TIMES
ATLAS
OF THE
WORLD

THE TIMES

ATLAS OF THE WORLD

CONCISE EDITION

BCA

LONDON   NEW YORK   SYDNEY   TORONTO

This edition published 1996
by BCA by arrangement with
Times Books, London
77–85 Fulham Palace Road
Hammersmith
London W6 8JB

First Edition 1972
Second Edition 1975
Third Edition 1978
Fourth Edition 1980
Fifth Edition 1986
Sixth Edition 1992

Seventh Edition 1995
Reprinted with changes 1996

Geographical Consultants

Mr H A G Lewis OBE
Geographical Consultant to The Times and
Chairman of The Permanent Committee of
Geographical Place Names

Mr B L D Winkleman

Printed in the UK:
Maps printed by
The Edinburgh Press Limited
Index printed by Scotprint, Musselburgh
Books bound by The Bath Press

Physical Earth Maps pages 34–47:
Duncan Mackay

Picture credits pages 50–51:
Science Photo Library

The maps in this product are also available
for purchase in digital format, from
Bartholomew Data Sales.
Tel: +44 (0) 181 307 4065.
Fax: +44 (0) 181 307 4813

CN 1072

The publishers would like to thank all National Survey
Departments, Road, Rail and National Park authorities,
Statistical Offices and national Place-Name Committees
throughout the World for their valuable assistance, and
in particular the following:

Antarctic Place-Names Committee, London

Australian Surveying & Land Information Group,
Belconnen, Australia

Automobile Association of South Africa,
Johannesburg, Republic of South Africa

Mr John C. Bartholomew, Edinburgh

British Antarctic Survey, Cambridge

British Geological Survey,
Keyworth, Nottinghamshire

The British Petroleum Company Ltd., London

Bureau of Coast and Geodetic Survey, Manila,
Republic of the Philippines

Chief Directorate: Surveys and Land Information,
Mowbray, Republic of South Africa

Commission de toponymie du Québec, Québec, Canada

Defense Mapping Agency, Aerospace Center,
St Louis, Missouri, USA

Department of Survey and Land Information,
Wellington, New Zealand

Department of National Development,
Director of National Mapping, Canberra,
Australia

Federal Survey Division, Lagos, Nigeria

Food and Agriculture Organisation of the
United Nations, Rome, Italy

Foreign and Commonwealth Office, London

French Railways, London

Mr P J M Geelan, London

General Directorate of Highways, Ankara, Turkey

General Bathymetric Chart of the Oceans (GEBCO),
International Hydrographic Organisation, Monaco

HM Stationery Office, London

Hydrographic Office, Ministry of Defence, Taunton

Institut Géographique National, Brussels, Belgium

Institut Géographique National, Paris, France

Instituto Brasileiro de Geografia e Estatistica,
Rio de Janeiro, Brazil

Instituto Geografico e Cadastral, Lisbon, Portugal

Instituto Geografico Nacional, Lima, Peru

Instituto Geografico Nacional, Madrid, Spain

International Atomic Energy Agency, Vienna, Austria

International Boundaries Research Unit, Durham

International Road Federation, Geneva, Switzerland

International Union for the Conservation of Nature,
Gland, Switzerland and Cambridge, UK

Kort- og Matrikelstyrelsen, Copenhagen, Denmark

Lands and Surveys Department, Kampala, Uganda

The Meteorological Office, Bracknell, Berkshire

National Geographic Society, Washington, DC, USA

National Library of Scotland, Edinburgh

Permanent Committee of Geographical Names, London

Royal Geographical Society, London

Royal Scottish Geographical Society, Glasgow

Scott Polar Research Institute, Cambridge

Scottish Development Department, Edinburgh

Statens Kartverket, Hønefoss, Norway

Survey of Israel, Tel Aviv, Israel

Survey Department, Singapore

Survey of India, Dehra Dun, India

Survey of Kenya, Nairobi, Kenya

Surveyor General, Harare, Zimbabwe

Surveyor General,
Ministry of Lands and Natural Resources,
Lusaka, Zambia

Surveys and Mapping Branch,
Department of Energy, Mines and Resources,
Ottawa, Canada

Surveys and Mapping Division,
Dar-es-Salaam, Tanzania

The United States Board on Geographic Names,
Washington, DC, USA

The United States Department of State,
Washington, DC, USA

The United States Geological Survey,
Earth Science Information Center, Reston,
Virginia, USA

United Nations, specialised agencies, New York, USA

Marcel Vârlan, University 'Al. I. Cuza', Iaşi, Romania

THE ⚜ TIMES
ATLAS
OF THE
WORLD

IN ITS VARIOUS editions the Times Atlas of the World has been established for many years, as amongst the most authoritative in the world. The Atlas was described, in 1944, by Lord Shackleton, then President of the Royal Geographical Society, as 'the finest reference atlas ever produced'.

In 1972 the first Concise Edition of the Times Atlas of the World was published in the form of an abridged version of the Comprehensive Edition. Since then there have been six editions of the Concise, each extensively up-dated, but each containing essentially the same selection of maps, and the map scales and areas covered remained the same. This new seventh Edition, however, is a completely new atlas.

The methods employed by cartographers to create maps and atlases have evolved gradually over the centuries. Some of the changes have been small and others have been significant leaps, but none have compared with the revolution brought about by computer cartography.

Extensive databases, covering the world at a variety of scales, and computer cartography have allowed the creation of this new edition of the Concise with substantial changes in the selection of the areas mapped, the map scales and the design of the maps. The content of this seventh Edition reflects the world at the end of the 20th century.

In contrast to these radical changes in map production technology, the extensive editorial research, the accuracy and depth of detail, the effort to ensure the maps are as up-to-date as possible remain the same. The Introduction to the Atlas, located at the beginning of the reference map section, explains the sequence of the maps, the scales and projections used, the editorial policies on name forms and on international boundaries.

CONTENTS

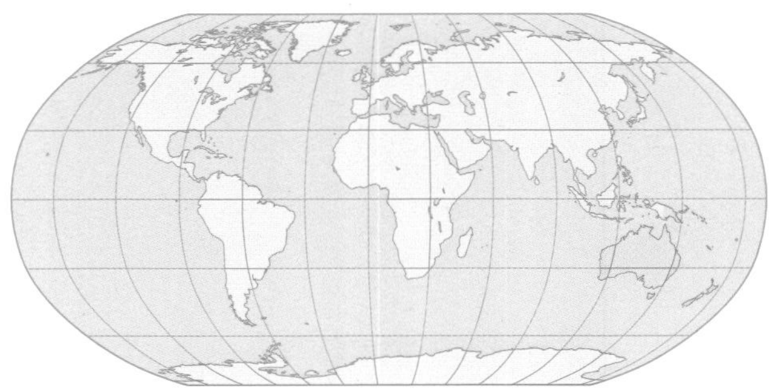

THE WORLD
1:66M **2–3**

OCEANIA
1:30M **4–5**

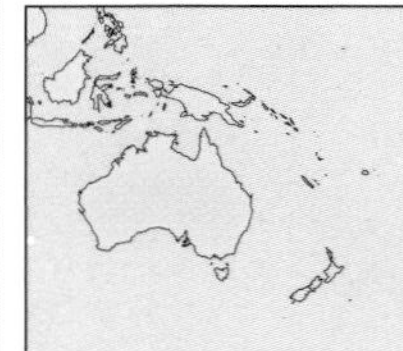

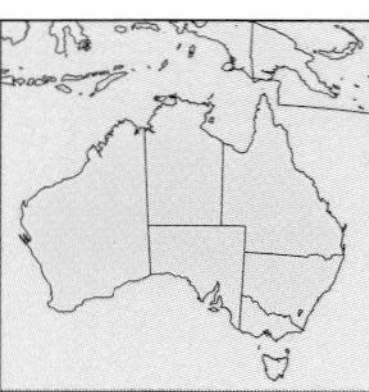

COUNTRYFINDER

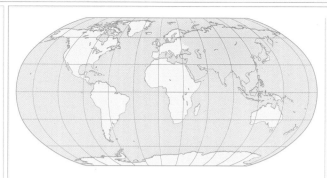

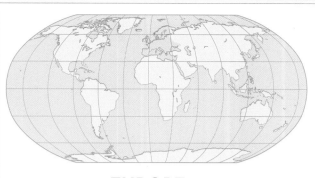

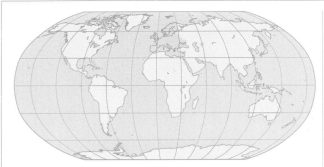

EUROPE continued

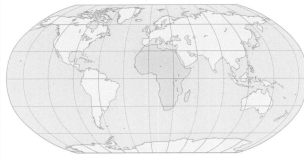

AFRICA
1:24M **116–117**

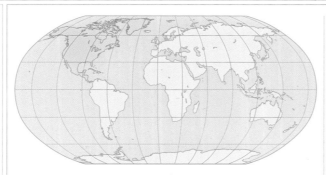

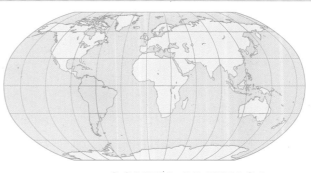

IN THIS GUIDE to States and Territories all independent states and all major territories appear. The states and territories are arranged in alphabetical order using the same English-language conventional name form as is used on the maps. The name of the capital city is also given in its English-language form, while on the maps it is given in its local form with the English-language form in brackets.

The statistics used for the area and population, and as the basis for languages and religions, are from the latest available sources. The information for the internal divisions in federal states may be for a less recent date than that for the entire country, but are the latest available.

The order of the different languages and religions reflects their relative importance within the country; generally all languages and religions with over one or two per cent speakers or adherents are mentioned.

For independent states membership of the following international organizations is shown by the abbreviations below. Territories are not shown as having seperate membership of these international organizations.

ASEAN   Association of Southeast Asian Nations

CARICOM Caribbean Community

CIS   Commonwealth of Independent States
COMM.   Commonwealth
EU   European Union
NAFTA   North American Free Trade Area
OAU   Organization of African Unity
OECD   Organization for Economic Cooperation and Development
OPEC   Organization of Petroleum Exporting Countries
SADC   Southern African Development Community
UN   United Nations

AFGHANISTAN
Status : REPUBLIC
Area : 652,225 sq km (251,825 sq mls)
Population : 17,691,000
Capital : KABUL
Language : DARI, PUSHTU, UZBEK, TURKMEN
Religion : SUNNI MUSLIM, SHI'A MUSLIM
Currency : AFGHANI
Organizations : UN

MAP PAGE: 39

A LANDLOCKED COUNTRY in central Asia, Afghanistan borders Pakistan, Iran, Turkmenistan, Uzbekistan, Tajikistan and China. Its central highlands are bounded by the Hindu Kush to the north and desert to the south and west. Most farming is on the plains round Kabul, the most populated area, and in the far northeast. The climate is dry, with extreme temperatures. Civil war has disrupted the rural-based economy. Exports included dried fruit, nuts, carpets, wool, hides and cotton.

ALBANIA
Status : REPUBLIC
Area : 28,748 sq km (11,100 sq mls)
Population : 3,389,000
Capital : TIRANA
Language : ALBANIAN (GHEG, TOSK DIALECTS), GREEK
Religion : SUNNI MUSLIM, GREEK ORTHODOX, R.CATHOLIC
Currency : LEK
Organizations : UN

MAP PAGE: 112-113

A LBANIA LIES IN the western Balkans of south Europe, on the Adriatic Sea. It is mountainous, with coastal plains which support half the population. The economy is based mainly on agriculture and mining, chiefly chromite. The fall of communism brought reform and foreign aid for the ailing economy.

ALGERIA
Status : REPUBLIC
Area : 2,381,741 sq km (919,595 sq mls)
Population : 26,722,000
Capital : ALGIERS
Language : ARABIC, FRENCH, BERBER
Religion : SUNNI MUSLIM, R.CATHOLIC
Currency : DINAR
Organizations : OAU, OPEC, UN

MAP PAGE: 120-121

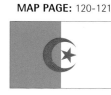

A LGERIA IS ON the Mediterranean coast of North Africa. The second largest country in Africa, it extends southwards from the coast into the Sahara Desert. Over 85 per cent of the land area is a dry sandstone plateau, cut by valleys and rocky mountains, including the Hoggar Massif in the southeast. Though hot, arid and largely uninhabited, the region contains oil and gas reserves. To the north lie the Atlas Mountains, enclosing the grassland of the Chott Plateau. The mountains separate the arid south from the narrow coastal plain which has a Mediterranean climate and is well suited to agriculture. Most people live on the plain and on the fertile northern slopes of the Atlas. Hydrocarbons have been the mainstay of the economy. Though reserves are dwindling, oil, natural gas and related products still account for over 90 per cent of export earnings. Other industries produce building materials, food products, iron, steel and vehicles. Agriculture employs a quarter of the workforce, producing mainly food crops. Political unrest including Islamic militancy in the early 1990s weakened the economy.

AMERICAN SAMOA
Status : US TERRITORY
Area : 197 sq km (76 sq mls)
Population : 53,000
Capital : PAGO PAGO
Language : SAMOAN, ENGLISH
Religion : PROTESTANT, R.CATHOLIC
Currency : US DOLLAR

MAP PAGE: 7

L YING IN THE South Pacific Ocean, American Samoa consists of five islands and two coral atolls. The main island is Tutuila.

ANDORRA
Status : PRINCIPALITY
Area : 465 sq km (180 sq mls)
Population : 61,000
Capital : ANDORRA LA VELLA
Language : CATALAN, SPANISH, FRENCH
Religion : R.CATHOLIC
Currency : FRENCH FRANC, SPANISH PESETA
Organizations : UN

MAP PAGE: 102

A LANDLOCKED STATE in southwest Europe, Andorra nestles in the Pyrenees between France and Spain. It consists of deep valleys and gorges, surrounded by mountains. Winter lasts six months, with heavy snowfalls; spring and summer are warm. One-third of the population lives in the capital. Tourism (about 12 million visitors a year), trade and banking are the main activities. Livestock, tobacco and timber are also important. Exports include clothing, mineral water, cattle, electrical equipment, and paper and paper products.

ANGOLA
Status : REPUBLIC
Area : 1,246,700 sq km (481,354 sq mls)
Population : 10,276,000
Capital : LUANDA
Language : PORTUGUESE, MANY LOCAL LANGUAGES
Religion : R.CATHOLIC, PROTESTANT, TRAD.BELIEFS
Currency : KWANZA
Organizations : OAU, SADC, UN

MAP PAGE: 125

A NGOLA LIES ON the Atlantic coast of southern central Africa. Its northern province, Cabinda, is separated from the rest of the country by part of Zaire. Much of Angola is high plateau, with a fertile coastal plain where most people live. The climate is equatorial in the north but desert in the south. Over half the workforce are farmers, growing cassava, maize, bananas, coffee, cotton and sisal. Angola is rich in minerals. Oil and diamonds account for 90 per cent of exports. Civil war has slowed economic development.

ANGUILLA
Status : UK TERRITORY
Area : 155 sq km (60 sq mls)
Population : 9,000
Capital : THE VALLEY
Language : ENGLISH

Religion : PROTESTANT, R.CATHOLIC
Currency : E. CARIB. DOLLAR

MAP PAGE: 159

A NGUILLA LIES AT the northern end of the Leeward Islands in the Caribbean Sea. Tourism and fishing are the basis of the economy.

ANTIGUA AND BARBUDA
Status : MONARCHY
Area : 442 sq km (171 sq mls)
Population : 65,000
Capital : ST JOHN'S
Language : ENGLISH, CREOLE
Religion : PROTESTANT, R.CATHOLIC
Currency : E. CARIB. DOLLAR
Organizations : CARICOM, COMM., UN

MAP PAGE: 159

T HE STATE COMPRISES Antigua, Barbuda and Redonda, three of the Leeward Islands in the eastern Caribbean. Antigua, the largest and most populous, is mainly hilly scrubland, with many beaches and a warm, dry climate. The economy relies heavily on tourism.

ARGENTINA
Status : REPUBLIC
Area : 2,766,889 sq km (1,068,302 sq mls)
Population : 33,778,000
Capital : BUENOS AIRES
Language : SPANISH, ITALIAN, AMERINDIAN LANGUAGES
Religion : R.CATHOLIC, PROTESTANT, JEWISH
Currency : PESO
Organizations : UN

MAP PAGE: 170-171

A RGENTINA OCCUPIES ALMOST the whole of the southern part of South America, from Bolivia to Cape Horn and from the Andes to the Atlantic Ocean. The second largest South American state has four geographical regions: the subtropical forests and swampland of the Chaco in the north; the temperate fertile plains or Pampas in the centre, which support most of the farming and the bulk of the population; the wooded foothills and valleys of the Andes in the west; and the cold, semi-arid plateaux of Patagonia, south of the Colorado river. Farming was the making of Argentina and still plays an important part in terms of export earnings. Beef, mutton and wool are the main produce but grains, sugarcane, soybeans, oilseeds and cotton are also important. Industry now makes the biggest contribution to the economy. Oil and gas are being produced and some mineral resources, chiefly iron ore, are being exploited. Manufacturing has expanded to include not only food processing but also textiles, motor vehicles, steel products, iron and steel, industrial chemicals and machinery.

ARMENIA
Status : REPUBLIC
Area : 29,800 sq km (11,506 sq mls)
Population : 3,732,000
Capital : YEREVAN
Language : ARMENIAN, AZERI, RUSSIAN
Religion : ARMENIAN ORTHODOX, R.CATHOLIC, SHI'A MUSLIM
Currency : DRAM
Organizations : CIS, UN

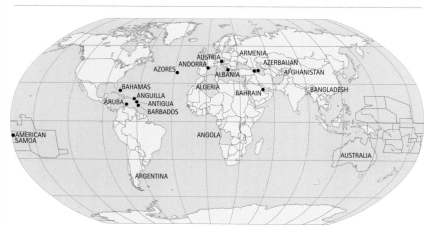

MAP PAGE: 42

A LANDLOCKED STATE in southwest Asia, Armenia is in southwest Transcaucasia and borders Georgia, Azerbaijan, Iran and Turkey. It is mountainous, with a central plateau-basin, and dry, with warm summers and cold winters. One-third of the population lives in Yerevan. War over Nagorno-Karabakh, the majority-Armenian enclave in Azerbaijan, has crippled the economy. Manufacturing and mining were the main activities. Agriculture was also important, producing mostly grapes (for brandy), vegetables, wheat and tobacco.

ARUBA
Status : NETHERLANDS TERRITORY
Area : 193 sq km (75 sq mls)
Population : 69,000
Capital : ORANJESTAD
Language : DUTCH, PAPIAMENTO, ENGLISH
Religion : R.CATHOLIC, PROTESTANT
Currency : FLORIN

MAP PAGE: 158

T HE MOST SOUTHWESTERLY of the islands in the Lesser Antilles, Aruba lies just off the coast of Venezuela. Tourism and offshore finance are the most important activities.

AUSTRALIA
Status : FEDERATION
Area : 7,682,300 sq km (2,966,153 sq mls)
Population : 17,663,000
Capital : CANBERRA
Language : ENGLISH, ITALIAN, GREEK, ABORIGINAL LANGUAGES
Religion : PROTESTANT, R.CATHOLIC, ORTHODOX, ABORIGINAL
Currency : DOLLAR
Organizations : COMM., OECD, UN

MAP PAGE: 10-11

A USTRALIA, THE WORLD'S sixth largest country, occupies the smallest, flattest and driest continent. The western half of the continent is mostly arid plateaux, ridges and vast deserts. The central-eastern area comprises lowlands of river systems draining into Lake Eyre, while to the east is the Great Dividing Range, a belt of ridges and plateaux running from Queensland to Tasmania. Climatically more than two-thirds of the country is arid or semi-arid. The north is tropical monsoon: the south is subtropical in the west, temperate in the east. A majority of Australia's highly urbanized population lives in cities along on the east, southeast and southwest coasts. Australia is richly endowed with natural resources. It has vast mineral deposits and various sources of energy. Over 50 per cent of the land is suitable for livestock rearing, though only 6 per cent can be used for crop growing. Forests cover 18 per cent of the land and fishing grounds off the coasts are teeming with marine life. Agriculture was the main sector of the economy, but its contribution to national income has fallen in recent years, as other sectors have grown. Sheep-rearing is still the main activity and Australia is the world's leading wool producer. It is also a major beef exporter and wheat grower. Wool, wheat, meat (beef and mutton), sugar and dairy products account for a third of export earnings. Minerals have overtaken agricultural produce as an export earner. As well as being among the world's leading producers of iron ore, bauxite, nickel and uranium, Australia also exploits lead, gold, silver, zinc and copper ores, tungsten and gems. Its is a major producer of coal; petroleum and natural gas are also being exploited. Manufacturing and processing has shifted from being based on agricultural pro-

duce (chiefly food processing and textiles) to being based on mineral production. The main products are: iron and steel, construction materials, petrochemicals, motor vehicles, electrical goods. Along with manufacturing, trade and services are the key growth sectors of the economy. Tourism is a major foreign exchange earner, with 1.5 million visitors a year.

AUSTRALIAN CAPITAL TERRITORY
Status: FEDERAL TERRITORY
Area: 2,400 sq km (927 sq mls)
Population: 299,000
Capital: CANBERRA

NEW SOUTH WALES
Status: STATE
Area: 801,600 sq km (309,499 sq mls)
Population: 6,009,000
Capital: SYDNEY

NORTHERN TERRITORY
Status: TERRITORY
Area: 1,346,200 sq km (519,771 sq mls)
Population: 168,000
Capital: DARWIN

QUEENSLAND
Status: STATE
Area: 1,727,200 sq km (666,876 sq mls)
Population: 3,113,000
Capital: BRISBANE

SOUTH AUSTRALIA
Status: STATE
Area: 984,000 sq km (379,925 sq mls)
Population: 1,462,000
Capital: ADELAIDE

TASMANIA
Status: STATE
Area: 67,800 sq km (26,178 sq mls)
Population: 472,000
Capital: HOBART

VICTORIA
Status: STATE
Area: 227,600 sq km (87,877 sq mls)
Population: 4,462,000
Capital: MELBOURNE

WESTERN AUSTRALIA
Status: STATE
Area: 2,525,000 sq km (974,908 sq mls)
Population: 1,678,000
Capital: PERTH

AUSTRIA
Status : REPUBLIC
Area : 83,855 sq km (32,377 sq mls)
Population : 7,988,000
Capital : VIENNA
Language : GERMAN, SERBO-CROAT, TURKISH
Religion : R.CATHOLIC, PROTESTANT
Currency : SCHILLING
Organizations : EU, OECD, UN

MAP PAGE: 80-81

A LANDLOCKED STATE in central Europe, Austria borders the Czech Republic, Italy, Slovenia, Hungary, Germany, Switzerland and Liechtenstein. Two-thirds of the country, from the Swiss border to eastern Austria, lies within the Alps, with the low mountains of the Bohemian Massif to the north. The only lowlands are in the east. The Vienna Basin and Danube river valley in the northeast contain almost all the agricultural land and most of the population. Austria also has a large forested area, minerals, chiefly iron ore, and fast-flowing rivers for hydroelectric power. The climate varies according to altitude, but in general summers are warm and winters cold with

heavy snowfalls. Industry is the mainstay of the economy. Manufactures include machinery, iron and steel, electrical goods, chemicals, food products, vehicles, and paper products. Agricultural output covers 90 per cent of food needs. Crops include cereals, fruit (chiefly grapes) and vegetables as well as silage, sugar beet and rapeseed. Dairy and timber products are exported. With 15 million visitors a year, tourism is a major industry.

AZERBAIJAN
Status : REPUBLIC
Area : 86,600 sq km (33,436 sq mls)
Population : 7,392,000
Capital : BAKU
Language : AZERI, ARMENIAN, RUSSIAN, LEZGIAN
Religion : SHI'A MUSLIM, SUNNI MUSLIM, RUSSIAN AND ARMENIAN
Currency : MANAT
Organizations : CIS, UN

MAP PAGE: 42

A ZERBAIJAN IS IN east Transcaucasia, southwest Asia, on the Caspian Sea. Its region of Nakhichevan is separated from the rest of the country by part of Armenia. It has mountains in the northeast and west, valleys in the centre and a coastal plain. The climate is continental. It is rich in energy and mineral resources. Oil production onshore and offshore is the main industry and the basis of heavy industries. Agriculture is still important, with cotton and tobacco the main cash crops. War with Armenia has reduced output.

AZORES
Status : PORTUGUESE TERRITORY
Area : 2,247 sq km (868 sq mls)
Population : 236,700
Capital : PONTA DELGADA
Language : PORTUGUESE
Religion : R.CATHOLIC, PROTESTANT
Currency : PORT. ESCUDO

MAP PAGE: 100

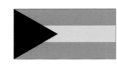

A GROUP OF islands in the Atlantic Ocean around 1500 kilometres (1000 miles) west of Portugal.

THE BAHAMAS
Status : MONARCHY
Area : 13,939 sq km (5,382 sq mls)
Population : 269,000
Capital : NASSAU
Language : ENGLISH, CREOLE, FRENCH CREOLE
Religion : PROTESTANT, R.CATHOLIC
Currency : DOLLAR
Organizations : CARICOM, COMM., UN

MAP PAGE: 145

T HE BAHAMAS IS an archipelago of about 700 islands and 2,400 cays in the northern Caribbean between the Florida coast of the USA and Haiti. Twenty-two islands are inhabited, and two thirds of the population live on the main island of New Providence. The climate is warm for much of the year, with heavy rainfall in the summer. Tourism is the islands' main industry. Banking, insurance and ship registration are also major foreign exchange earners. Exports include oil transhipments, chemicals, pharmaceuticals, crayfish and rum.

BAHRAIN
Status : MONARCHY
Area : 691 sq km (267 sq mls)
Population : 539,000
Capital : MANAMA
Language : ARABIC, ENGLISH
Religion : SHI'A MUSLIM, SUNNI MUSLIM, CHRISTIAN
Currency : DINAR
Organizations : UN

MAP PAGE: 39

B AHRAIN'S 33 ARID islands lie in a bay in The Gulf, southwest Asia, off the coasts of Saudi Arabia and Qatar. Bahrain Island, the largest, has irrigated areas in the north where most people live. Oil is the main sector of the economy. Banking is also strong.

BANGLADESH
Status : REPUBLIC
Area : 143,998 sq km (55,598 sq mls)
Population : 115,203,000
Capital : DHAKA
Language : BENGALI, BIHARI, HINDI, ENGLISH, LOCAL LANGUAGES
Religion : SUNNI MUSLIM, HINDU, BUDDHIST, CHRISTIAN
Currency : TAKA
Organizations : COMM., UN

MAP PAGE: 37

T HE SOUTH ASIAN state of Bangladesh is in the northeast of the Indian subcontinent, on the Bay of Bengal. It consists almost entirely of the low-lying alluvial plains and deltas of the Ganges and Brahmaputra rivers. The southwest is swampy, with mangrove forests in the delta area. The north, northeast and southeast have low forested hills. With a cultivable area of 70 per cent and few other natural resources, Bangladesh has a strong agricultural base, engaging two-thirds of the workforce. Food crops include rice, wheat, fruit and pulses; cash crops include jute, sugar cane, oilseeds, spices and tea. The main industries produce fertilizers, iron and steel, paper and glass as well as agricultural, marine and timber products. Exports include garments, raw and manufactured jute, fish and prawns, leather and tea. Bangladesh faces problems of overpopulation, low world commodity prices and the vagaries of climate. Floods and cyclones during the summer monsoon season often cause destroy crops. As a result, the country relies on foreign aid and remittances from its workers abroad.

BARBADOS
Status : MONARCHY
Area : 430 sq km (166 sq mls)
Population : 260,000
Capital : BRIDGETOWN
Language : ENGLISH, CREOLE (BAJAN)
Religion : PROTESTANT, R.CATHOLIC
Currency : DOLLAR
Organizations : UN, COMM., CARICOM

MAP PAGE: 159

T HE MOST EASTERLY of the Caribbean islands, Barbados is small and densely populated, with a fairly flat terrain, white-sand beaches and a tropical climate. The economy is based on tourism, financial services, light industries and sugar production.

BELARUS

Status: REPUBLIC
Area: 207,600 sq km (80,155 sq mls)
Population: 10,188,000
Capital: MINSK
Language: BELORUSSIAN, RUSSIAN, UKRAINIAN
Religion: BELORUSSIAN ORTHODOX, R.CATHOLIC
Currency: ROUBLE
Organizations: CIS, UN

MAP PAGE: 50-51

BELARUS IS A landlocked state in east Europe, bounded by Lithuania, Latvia, Russia, Ukraine and Poland. Belarus consists of low hills and forested plains, with many lakes, rivers and, in the south, extensive marshes. It has a continental climate. Agriculture contributes a third of national income, with beef cattle and grains as the major products. Manufacturing produces a range of items, from machinery and crude steel to computers and watches. Output has fallen since the ending of cheap Soviet energy supplies and raw materials.

BELGIUM

Status: MONARCHY
Area: 30,520 sq km (11,784 sq mls)
Population: 10,046,000
Capital: BRUSSELS
Language: DUTCH (FLEMISH), FRENCH, GERMAN (ALL OFFICIAL), ITALIAN
Religion: R.CATHOLIC, PROTESTANT
Currency: FRANC
Organizations: EU, OECD, UN

MAP PAGE: 69

BELGIUM LIES ON the North Sea coast of west Europe. Beyond low sand dunes and a narrow belt of reclaimed land are fertile plains which extend to the Sambre-Meuse river valley from where the land rises to the forested Ardennes plateau in the southeast. Belgium has mild winters and cool summers. It is densely populated and has a highly urbanized population. The economy is based on trade, industry and services. With few mineral resources, Belgium imports raw materials for processing and manufacture, and exports semi-finished and finished goods. Metal working, machine building, food processing and brewing, chemical production, iron and steel, and textiles are the major industries. External trade is equivalent to over 70 per cent of national income. Exports include cars, machinery, chemicals, foodstuffs and animals, iron and steel, diamonds, textiles and petroleum products. The agricultural sector is small, but provides for most food needs and a tenth of exports. A large services sector reflects Belgium's position as the home base for over 800 international institutions.

BELIZE

Status: MONARCHY
Area: 22,965 sq km (8,867 sq mls)
Population: 205,000
Capital: BELMOPAN
Language: ENGLISH, CREOLE, SPANISH, MAYAN
Religion: R.CATHOLIC, PROTESTANT, HINDU
Currency: DOLLAR
Organizations: CARICOM, COMM., UN

MAP PAGE: 157

BELIZE IS ON the Caribbean coast of central America and includes cays and a large barrier reef offshore. Belize's coastal areas are flat and swampy; the north and west are hilly, and the southwest contains the Maya mountain range. Jungle covers about half of the country. The climate is tropical, but tempered by sea breezes. A third of the population lives in the capital. The economy is based primarily on agriculture, forestry and fishing. Exports include sugar, clothing, citrus concentrates, bananas and lobsters.

BENIN

Status: REPUBLIC
Area: 112,620 sq km (43,483 sq mls)
Population: 5,215,000
Capital: PORTO NOVO
Language: FRENCH, FON, YORUBA, ADJA, LOCAL LANGUAGES
Religion: TRAD.BELIEFS, R.CATHOLIC, SUNNI MUSLIM
Currency: CFA FRANC
Organizations: OAU, UN

MAP PAGE: 123

BENIN IS IN west Africa, on the Gulf of Guinea. The Atakora range lies in the northwest; the Niger plains in the northeast. To the south are plateaux, then a fertile plain and finally an area of lagoons and sandy coast. The climate is tropical in the north, but equatorial in the south. The economy is based mainly on agriculture and transit trade. Agricultural products, chiefly cotton, coffee, cocoa beans and oil palms, account for two thirds of export earnings. Oil, produced offshore, is also a major export.

BERMUDA

Status: UK TERRITORY
Area: 54 sq km (21 sq mls)
Population: 63,000
Capital: HAMILTON
Language: ENGLISH
Religion: PROTESTANT, R.CATHOLIC
Currency: DOLLAR

MAP PAGE: 145

IN THE ATLANTIC Ocean to the east of the USA, Bermuda is a group of small islands. The climate is warm and humid. The economy is based on tourism, insurance and shipping.

BHUTAN

Status: MONARCHY
Area: 46,620 sq km (18,000 sq mls)
Population: 1,596,000
Capital: THIMPHU
Language: DZONGKHA, NEPALI, ASSAMESE, ENGLISH
Religion: BUDDHIST, HINDU
Currency: NGULTRUM, INDIAN RUPEE
Organizations: UN

MAP PAGE: 37

BHUTAN NESTLES IN the eastern Himalayas of south Asia, between China and India. It is mountainous in the north, with fertile valleys in the centre, where most people live, and forested lowlands in the south. The climate ranges between permanently cold in the far north and subtropical in the south. Most of the working population is involved in livestock raising and subsistence farming, though fruit and cardamon are exported. Electricity, minerals, timber and cement are the main exports. Bhutan relies heavily on aid.

BOLIVIA

Status: REPUBLIC
Area: 1,098,581 sq km (424,164 sq mls)
Population: 7,065,000
Capital: LA PAZ
Language: SPANISH, QUECHUA, AYMARA
Religion: R.CATHOLIC, PROTESTANT, BAHA'I
Currency: BOLIVIANO
Organizations: UN

MAP PAGE: 164-165

A LANDLOCKED STATE in central South America, Bolivia borders Brazil, Paraguay, Argentina, Chile and Peru. Most Bolivians live in the high plateau within the Andes ranges. The lowlands range between dense Amazon forest in the northeast and semi-arid grasslands in the southeast. Bolivia is rich in minerals, and sales (chiefly zinc, tin, silver and gold) generate half of export income. Natural gas and timber are also exported. Subsistence farming predominates, though sugar, soya beans and, unofficially, coca are exported.

BOSNIA–HERZEGOVINA

Status: REPUBLIC
Area: 51,130 sq km (19,741 sq mls)
Population: 3,707,000
Capital: SARAJEVO
Language: SERBO-CROAT
Religion: SUNNI MUSLIM, SERBIAN ORTHODOX, R.CATHOLIC, PROTESTANT
Currency: DINAR
Organizations: UN

MAP PAGE: 104

BOSNIA-HERZEGOVINA LIES IN the western Balkans of south Europe, on the Adriatic Sea. It is mountainous, with ridges crossing the country northwest-southeast. The main lowlands are around the Sava valley in the north. Summers are warm, but winters can be very cold. Civil war has ruined the economy, which was based on agriculture, sheep rearing and forestry. All production has ceased, the currency is worthless and only the black economy operates. Much of the population relies on UN relief.

BOTSWANA

Status: REPUBLIC
Area: 581,370 sq km (224,468 sq mls)
Population: 1,443,000
Capital: GABORONE
Language: ENGLISH (OFFICIAL), SETSWANA, SHONA, LOCAL LANGUAGES
Religion: TRAD.BELIEFS, PROTESTANT, R.CATHOLIC
Currency: PULA
Organizations: COMM., OAU, SADC, UN

MAP PAGE: 128-129

BOTSWANA, A LANDLOCKED state in south Africa, borders South Africa, Namibia, Zambia and Zimbabwe. Over half of the country lies within the upland Kalahari desert, with swamps to the north and salt-pans to the northeast. Most people live near the eastern border. The climate is subtropical, but drought-prone. The economy was founded upon cattle rearing, and beef is an important export, but now it is based on mining and industry. Diamonds account for 80 per cent of export earnings. Copper-nickel matte is also exported.

BRAZIL

Status: REPUBLIC
Area: 8,511,965 sq km (3,286,488 sq mls)
Population: 151,534,000
Capital: BRASÍLIA
Language: PORTUGUESE, GERMAN, JAPANESE, ITALIAN, AMERINDIAN LANGUAGES
Religion: R.CATHOLIC, SPIRITIST, PROTESTANT
Currency: REAL
Organizations: UN

MAP PAGE: 162-167

BRAZIL, IN EASTERN South America, covers almost half of the continent - making it the world's fifth largest country - and borders ten countries and the Atlantic Ocean. The northwest contains the vast Amazon Basin, backed by the Guiana Highlands. The centre west is largely a vast plateau of savannah and rock escarpments. The northeast is mostly semi-arid plateaux, while the east and south contain the rugged mountains and fertile valleys of the Brazilian Highlands and narrow, fertile coastal plains. The Amazon basin is hot, humid and wet; the rest of Brazil is cooler and drier, with seasonal variations. The northeast is drought-prone. Most Brazilians live in urban areas along the coast and on the central plateau, chiefly São Paulo, Rio de Janeiro and Salvador. Brazil is well endowed with minerals and energy resources. Over 50 per cent of the land is forested and 7 per cent is cultivated. Agriculture employs a quarter of the workforce. Brazil is the world's largest producer of coffee and a leading producer of sugar, cocoa, soya beans and beef. Timber production and fish catches are also important. Brazil is a major producer of iron, bauxite and manganese ores, zinc, copper, tin, gold and diamonds as well as oil and coal. Manufacturing contributes a quarter of national income. Industrial products include food, machinery, iron and steel, textiles, cars, pharmaceuticals, chemicals, refined oil, metal products and paper products. The main exports are machinery, metallic ores, cars, metal products, coffee beans, soya products, electrical and electronic

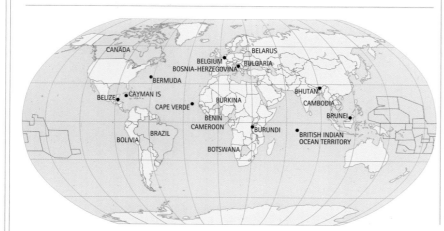

goods, and orange juice. Despite its natural wealth and one of the largest economies in the world, Brazil has a large external debt and growing poverty gap.

BRITISH INDIAN OCEAN TERRITORY
Status: UK TERRITORY
Population: 2,000

MAP PAGE: 175

THE TERRITORY CONSISTS of the Chagos Archipelago in the middle of the Indian Ocean. The islands are uninhabited apart from the US military base on Diego Garcia.

BRUNEI
Status: MONARCHY
Area: 5,765 sq km (2,226 sq mls)
Population: 274,000
Capital: BANDAR SERI BEGAWAN
Language: MALAY, ENGLISH, CHINESE
Religion: SUNNI MUSLIM, BUDDHIST, CHRISTIAN
Currency: DOLLAR (RINGGIT)
Organizations: ASEAN, COMM., UN

MAP PAGE: 21

THE SOUTHEAST ASIAN state of Brunei lies on the northwest coast of the island of Borneo, on the South China Sea. Its two enclaves are surrounded inland by Malaysia. The western part is hilly with a narrow coastal plain which supports some crops and most of the population. The eastern part is mountainous and more forested. Tropical rainforest covers over two thirds of Brunei. The economy is dominated by the oil and gas industries.

BULGARIA
Status: REPUBLIC
Area: 110,994 sq km (42,855 sq mls)
Population: 8,469,000
Capital: SOFIA
Language: BULGARIAN, TURKISH, ROMANY, MACEDONIAN
Religion: BULGARIAN ORTHODOX, SUNNI MUSLIM
Currency: LEV
Organizations: UN

MAP PAGE: 112

BULGARIA, IN SOUTH Europe, borders Romania, Yugoslavia, Macedonia, Greece, Turkey and the Black Sea. The Balkan Mountains separate the Danube plains in the north from the Rhodope massif and the lowlands in the south. The climate is subject to regional variation. The economy is based on agriculture and manufacturing, chiefly machinery, consumer goods, chemicals and metals. Disruption of Soviet-dominated trade has reduced output.

BURKINA
Status: REPUBLIC
Area: 274,200 sq km (105,869 sq mls)
Population: 9,682,000
Capital: OUAGADOUGOU
Language: FRENCH, MORE (MOSSI), FULANI, LOCAL LANGUAGES
Religion: TRAD.BELIEFS, SUNNI MUSLIM, R.CATHOLIC
Currency: CFA FRANC
Organizations: OAU, UN

MAP PAGE: 122-123

BURKINA, A LANDLOCKED country in west Africa, borders Mali, Niger, Benin, Togo, Ghana and Côte d'Ivoire. The north of Burkina lies in the Sahara and is arid. The south is mainly semi-arid savannah. Rainfall is erratic and droughts are common. Settlements centre on the country's rivers. Livestock rearing and farming are the main activities. Cotton, livestock, groundnuts and some minerals are exported. Burkina relies heavily on aid.

BURUNDI
Status: REPUBLIC
Area: 27,835 sq km (10,747 sq mls)
Population: 5,958,000
Capital: BUJUMBURA
Language: KIRUNDI (HUTU, TUTSI), FRENCH
Religion: R.CATHOLIC, TRAD.BELIEFS, PROTESTANT, SUNNI MUSLIM
Currency: FRANC
Organizations: OAU, UN

MAP PAGE: 127

THE DENSELY POPULATED east African state of Burundi borders Rwanda, Zaire, Tanzania and Lake Tanganyika. It is hilly with high plateaux and a tropical climate. Burundi depends upon subsistence farming, coffee exports and foreign aid.

CAMBODIA
Status: MONARCHY
Area: 181,000 sq km (69,884 sq mls)
Population: 9,308,000
Capital: PHNOM PENH
Language: KHMER, VIETNAMESE
Religion: BUDDHIST, R.CATHOLIC, SUNNI MUSLIM
Currency: RIEL
Organizations: UN

MAP PAGE: 25

CAMBODIA LIES IN southeast Asia, on the Gulf of Thailand. It consists of the Mekong river basin, with the Tonle Sap (Great Lake) at its centre. To the north, northeast and east are plateaux and to the southwest are mountains. The climate is tropical monsoon, with forests covering half the land. Most people live on the plains and are engaged in farming (chiefly rice growing), fishing and forestry. Devastated by civil war, Cambodia is dependent on aid.

CAMEROON
Status: REPUBLIC
Area: 475,442 sq km (183,569 sq mls)
Population: 12,522,000
Capital: YAOUNDÉ
Language: FRENCH, ENGLISH, FANG, BAMILEKE, MANY LOCAL LANGUAGES
Religion: TRAD.BELIEFS, R.CATHOLIC, SUNNI MUSLIM, PROTESTANT
Currency: CFA FRANC
Organizations: OAU, UN

MAP PAGE: 124

CAMEROON IS IN west Africa, on the Gulf of Guinea. The coastal plains, southern and central plateaux are covered with tropical forest. The northern lowlands are semi-arid savannah, and the western highlands, around Mount Cameroon, support a range of crops. A majority of Cameroonians are farmers. Cocoa, coffee and cotton are the main cash crops, though crude oil, sawn wood and logs account for over half of export earnings.

CANADA
Status: FEDERATION
Area: 9,970,610 sq km (3,849,674 sq mls)
Population: 28,436,000
Capital: OTTAWA
Language: ENGLISH, FRENCH, AMERINDIAN LANGUAGES, INUKTITUT (ESKIMO)
Religion: R.CATHOLIC, PROTESTANT, GREEK ORTHODOX, JEWISH
Currency: DOLLAR
Organizations: COMM., NAFTA, OECD, UN

MAP PAGE: 134-135

THE WORLD'S SECOND largest country, Canada covers the northern two-fifths of North America and has coastlines on the Atlantic, Arctic and Pacific Oceans. On the west coast, the Cordilleran region contains coastal mountains, interior plateaux and the Rocky Mountains. To the east lie the fertile prairies. Further east, covering about half the total land area, is the Canadian, or Laurentian, Shield, fairly flat U-shaped lowlands around the Hudson Bay extending to Labrador. The Shield is bordered to the south by the fertile Great Lakes-St Lawrence lowlands. In the far north climatic conditions are polar. In general, however, Canada has a continental climate. Winters are long and cold with heavy snowfalls, while summers are hot with light to moderate rainfall. Most Canadians live in the south, chiefly in the southeast, in the urban areas of the Great Lakes-St Lawrence basin, principally Toronto and Montreal. Canada is well endowed with minerals, energy resources, forests and rich coastal waters. Only 5 per cent of land is classified as arable, but that is still a large area. Canada is among the world's leading exporter of wheat. Other major agricultural exports are apples, beef cattle, potatoes, oilseeds and feed grain. Canada is also a leading exporter of wood from its vast coniferous forests, and fish and seafood from its rich Atlantic and Pacific fishing grounds. It is a top producer of iron ore, uranium, nickel, copper, zinc and other minerals, as well as crude oil and natural gas. Its abundant raw materials are the basis of for manufacturing industries. The principal ones are car manufacture, food processing, chemical production, lumber, woodpulp and paper making, oil refining, iron and steel, and metal refining, Canada is an important trading nation. External trade is equivalent to about 30 per cent of national income. Exports include cars, crude materials, minerals fuels (chiefly oil and gas), food (chiefly wheat), newsprint, lumber, wood pulp, industrial machinery and aluminium. Canada has an important banking and insurance sector.

ALBERTA
Status: PROVINCE
Area: 661,190 sq km (255,287 sq mls)
Population: 2,672,000
Capital: EDMONTON

BRITISH COLUMBIA
Status: PROVINCE
Area: 947,800 sq km (365,948 sq mls)
Population: 3,570,000
Capital: VICTORIA

MANITOBA
Status: PROVINCE
Area: 649,950 sq km (250,947 sq mls)
Population: 1,117,000
Capital: WINNIPEG

NEW BRUNSWICK
Status: PROVINCE
Area: 73,440 sq km (28,355 sq mls)
Population: 751,000
Capital: FREDERICTON

NEWFOUNDLAND
Status: PROVINCE
Area: 405,720 sq km (156,649 sq mls)
Population: 581,000
Capital: ST JOHN'S

NORTHWEST TERRITORIES
Status: TERRITORY
Area: 3,426,320 sq km (1,322,910 sq mls)
Population: 63,000
Capital: YELLOWKNIFE

NOVA SCOTIA
Status: PROVINCE
Area: 55,490 sq km (21,425 sq mls)
Population: 925,000
Capital: HALIFAX

ONTARIO
Status: PROVINCE
Area: 1,068,580 sq km (412,581 sq mls)
Population: 10,795,000
Capital: TORONTO

PRINCE EDWARD ISLAND
Status: PROVINCE
Area: 5,660 sq km (2,158 sq mls)
Population: 132,000
Capital: CHARLOTTETOWN

QUEBEC
Status: PROVINCE
Area: 1,540,680 sq km (594,860 sq mls)
Population: 7,226,000
Capital: QUÉBEC

SASKATCHEWAN
Status: PROVINCE
Area: 652,330 sq km (251,866 sq mls)
Population: 1,002,000
Capital: REGINA

YUKON TERRITORY
Status: TERRITORY
Area: 483,450 sq km (186,661 sq mls)
Population: 33,000
Capital: WHITEHORSE

CAPE VERDE
Status: REPUBLIC
Area: 4,033 sq km (1,557 sq mls)
Population: 370,000
Capital: PRAIA
Language: PORTUGUESE, PORTUGUESE CREOLE
Religion: R.CATHOLIC, PROTESTANT, TRAD.BELIEFS
Currency: ESCUDO
Organizations: OAU, UN

MAP PAGE: 122

CAPE VERDE COMPRISES ten semi-arid volcanic islands and five islets off the coast of west Africa. The economy is based on fishing and mainly subsistence farming, but relies on workers' remittances and foreign aid.

CAYMAN ISLANDS
Status: UK TERRITORY
Area: 259 sq km (100 sq mls)
Population: 29,000
Capital: GEORGE TOWN
Language: ENGLISH
Religion: PROTESTANT, R.CATHOLIC
Currency: DOLLAR

MAP PAGE: 158

LYING IN THE Caribbean, northwest of Jamaica, there are three main islands: Grand Cayman, Little Cayman and Cayman Brac. The islands are one of the world's most important offshore financial centres, though tourism is also important.

CENTRAL AFRICAN REPUBLIC

Status: REPUBLIC
Area: 622,436 sq km (240,324 sq mls)
Population: 3,156,000
Capital: BANGUI
Language: FRENCH, SANGO, BANDA, BAYA, LOCAL LANGUAGES
Religion: PROTESTANT, R.CATHOLIC, TRAD. BELIEFS, SUNNI MUSLIM
Currency: CFA FRANC
Organizations: OAU, UN

MAP PAGE: 124

THE LANDLOCKED CENTRAL African Republic borders Chad, Sudan, Zaire, Congo and Cameroon. Most of the country is savannah plateaux, drained by the Ubangi and Chari river systems, with mountains to the north and west. The climate is hot with high rainfall. Most of the population live in the south and west, and a majority of the workforce is involved in subsistence farming. Some cotton, coffee, tobacco and timber are exported. However, diamonds and some gold account for more than half of export earnings.

CHAD

Status: REPUBLIC
Area: 1,284,000 sq km (495,755 sq mls)
Population: 6,098,000
Capital: NDJAMENA
Language: ARABIC, FRENCH, MANY LOCAL LANGUAGES
Religion: SUNNI MUSLIM, TRAD.BELIEFS, R.CATHOLIC
Currency: CFA FRANC
Organizations: OAU, UN

MAP PAGE: 118

CHAD IS A landlocked state of central Africa, bordered by Libya, Sudan, Central African Republic, Niger, Nigeria and Cameroon. It consists of plateaux, the Tibesti massif in the north and Lake Chad basin in the west. Climatic conditions range between desert in the north and tropical forest in the southwest. Most people live in the south and near Lake Chad. Farming and cattle herding are the main activities, cattle and raw cotton the chief exports. Impoverished by civil war and drought, Chad relies upon foreign aid.

CHILE

Status: REPUBLIC
Area: 756,945 sq km (292,258 sq mls)
Population: 13,813,000
Capital: SANTIAGO
Language: SPANISH, AMERINDIAN LANGUAGES
Religion: R.CATHOLIC, PROTESTANT
Currency: PESO
Organizations: UN

MAP PAGE: 170 -171

CHILE HUGS THE Pacific coast of the southern half of South America. Between the High Andes in the east and the lower coastal ranges is a central valley, with a mild climate, where most Chileans live. To the north is arid desert, to the south is cold, wet forested grassland. Chile is a leading exporter of copper, and is rich in other minerals and nitrates. Agriculture, forestry and fishing are important activities. Timber products, chemicals products and other manufactures account for a third of exports.

CHINA

Status: REPUBLIC
Area: 9,560,900 sq km (3,691,484 sq mls)
Population: 1,196,360,000
Capital: BEIJING
Language: CHINESE (MANDARIN OFFICIAL), MANY REGIONAL LANGUAGES
Religion: CONFUCIAN, TAOIST, BUDDHIST, SUNNI MUSLIM, R.CATHOLIC
Currency: YUAN
Organizations: UN

MAP PAGE: 26-27

CHINA, THE WORLD'S third largest country, occupies almost the whole of east Asia, borders fourteen states and has coastlines on the Yellow, East China and South China seas. It has an amazing variety of landscapes. The southwest contains the high Tibetan plateau, flanked by the Himalayas and Kunlun mountains. The northwest is mountainous with arid basins and extends from the Tien Shan and Altai ranges and vast Taklimakan desert in the west to the Mongolian plateau and Gobi desert in the centre-east. Eastern China is predominantly lowland and is divided broadly into the basins of the Huang He (Yellow River) in the north, Chang Jiang (Yangtze) in the centre and Xi Jiang (Pearl River) in the southeast. The main exceptions are the Manchurian uplands, loess plateau, Qin Ling range, southeast mountains and the Yunnan plateau in the far south. Climatic conditions and vegetation are as diverse as the topography. Northern China has an extreme continental climate, much of the country experiences temperate conditions, while the southwest enjoys a moist, warm subtropical climate. More than 70 per cent of China's huge population live in rural areas, chiefly in the northern part of the eastern lowlands and along the coast. Agriculture and livestock rearing involves two thirds of the working population. China is the world's largest producer of rice, wheat, soya beans and sugar and is self-sufficient in cereals, fish and livestock. Cotton, soya bean and oilseeds are the major cash crops. China is rich in coal, oil, natural gas and many minerals, chiefly iron ore, wolfram (tungsten ore), tin and phosphates. Industrial and agricultural production were given a boost by the economic reforms of the 1980s which introduced a degree of private enterprise. Industry also benefited from the setting up of joint ventures and the inflow of foreign investment. The major industries produce iron and steel, machinery, textiles, processed foods, chemicals and building materials. China's chief exports are textiles and clothing, petroleum and products, machinery and transport equipment, agricultural products, metal products, iron and steel.

ANHUI (ANHWEI)

Status: PROVINCE
Area: 139,000 sq km (53,668 sq miles)
Population: 58,340,000
Capital: HEFEI

BEIJING (PEKING)

Status: MUNICIPALITY
Area: 16,800 sq km (6,487 sq miles)
Population: 11,020,000
Capital: BEIJING

FUJIAN (FUKIEN)

Status: PROVINCE
Area: 121,400 sq km (46,873 sq miles)
Population: 31,160,000
Capital: FUZHOU

GANSU (KANSU)

Status: PROVINCE
Area: 453,700 sq km (175,175 sq miles)
Population: 23,140,000
Capital: LANZHOU

GUANGDONG (KWANGTUNG)

Status: PROVINCE
Area: 178,000 sq km (68,726 sq miles)
Population: 65,250,000
Capital: GUANGZHOU

GUANGXI ZHUANG (KWANGSI CHUANG)

Status: AUTONOMOUS REGION
Area: 236,000 sq km (91,120 sq miles)
Population: 43,800,000
Capital: NANNING

GUIZHOU (KWEICHOW)

Status: PROVINCE
Area: 176,000 sq km (67,954 sq miles)
Population: 33,610,000
Capital: GUIYANG

HAINAN

Status: PROVINCE
Area: 34,000 sq km (13,127 sq miles)
Population: 6,860,000
Capital: HAIKOU

HEBEI (HOPEI)

Status: PROVINCE
Area: 187,700 sq km (72,471 sq miles)
Population: 62,750,000
Capital: SHIJIAZHUANG

HEILONGJIANG (HEILUNGKIANG)

Status: PROVINCE
Area: 454,600 sq km (175,522 sq miles)
Population: 36,080,000
Capital: HARBIN

HENAN (HONAN)

Status: PROVINCE
Area: 167,000 sq km (64,479 sq miles)
Population: 88,620,000
Capital: ZHENGZHOU

HUBEI (HUPEI)

Status: PROVINCE
Area: 185,900 sq km (71,776 sq miles)
Population: 55,800,000
Capital: WUHAN

HUNAN

Status: PROVINCE
Area: 210,000 sq km (81,081 sq miles)
Population: 62,670,000
Capital: CHANGSHA

JIANGSU (KIANGSU)

Status: PROVINCE
Area: 102,600 sq km (39,614 sq miles)
Population: 69,110,000
Capital: NANJING

JIANGXI (KIANGSI)

Status: PROVINCE
Area: 166,900 sq km (64,440 sq miles)
Population: 39,130,000
Capital: NANCHANG

JILIN (KIRIN)

Status: PROVINCE
Area: 187,000 sq km (72,201 sq miles)
Population: 25,320,000
Capital: CHANGCHUN

LIAONING

Status: PROVINCE
Area: 147,400 sq km (56,911 sq miles)
Population: 40,160,000
Capital: SHENYANG

NEI MONGGOL (INNER MONGOLIA)

Status: AUTONOMOUS REGION
Area: 1,183,000 sq km (456,759 sq miles)
Population: 22,070,000
Capital: HOHHOT

NINGXIA HUI (NINGHSIA HUI)

Status: AUTONOMOUS REGION
Area: 66,400 sq km (25,637 sq miles)
Population: 4,870,000
Capital: YINCHUAN

QINGHAI (TSINGHAI)

Status: PROVINCE
Area: 721,000 sq km (278,380 sq miles)
Population: 4,610,000
Capital: XINING

SHAANXI (SHENSI)

Status: PROVINCE
Area: 205,600 sq km (79,383 sq miles)
Population: 34,050,000
Capital: XI'AN

SHANDONG (SHANTUNG)

Status: PROVINCE
Area: 153,300 sq km (59,189 sq miles)
Population: 86,100,000
Capital: JINAN

SHANGHAI

Status: MUNICIPALITY
Area: 6,300 sq km (2,432 sq miles)
Population: 13,450,000
Capital: SHANGHAI

SHANXI (SHANSI)

Status: PROVINCE
Area: 156,300 sq km (60,348 sq miles)
Population: 29,790,000
Capital: TAIYUAN

SICHUAN (SZECHWAN)

Status: PROVINCE
Area: 569,000 sq km (219,692 sq miles)
Population: 109,980,000
Capital: CHENGDU

TIANJIN (TIENTSIN)

Status: MUNICIPALITY
Area: 11,300 sq km (4,363 sq miles)
Population: 9,200,000
Capital: TIANJIN

XIZANG (TIBET)

Status: AUTONOMOUS REGION
Area: 1,228,400 sq km (474,288 sq miles)
Population: 2,280,000
Capital: LHASA

XINJIANG UYGUR (SINKIANG UIGHUR)

Status: AUTONOMOUS REGION
Area: 1,600,000 sq km (617,763 sq miles)
Population: 15,810,000
Capital: ÜRÜMQI

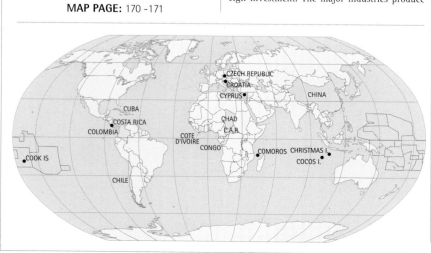

YUNNAN
Status: PROVINCE
Area: 394,000 sq km (152,124 sq miles)
Population: 38,320,000
Capital: KUNMING

ZHEJIANG (CHEKIANG)
Status: PROVINCE
Area: 101,800 sq km (39,305 sq miles)
Population: 42,360,000
Capital: HANGZHOU

CHRISTMAS ISLAND
Status: AUSTRALIAN TERRITORY
Area: 135 sq km (52 sq mls)
Population: 2,000
Capital: THE SETTLEMENT
Language: ENGLISH
Religion: BUDDHIST, SUNNI MUSLIM,
PROTESTANT, R.CATHOLIC
Currency: AUSTR. DOLLAR

MAP PAGE: 10 -11

THE ISLAND IS situated in the east of the Indian Ocean, to the south of Indonesia. The economy is based on phosphate mining, but tourism is also being developed.

COCOS ISLANDS
Status: AUSTRALIAN TERRITORY
Area: 14 sq km (5 sq mls)
Population: 1,000
Capital: HOME ISLAND
Language: ENGLISH
Religion: SUNNI MUSLIM, CHRISTIAN
Currency: AUSTR. DOLLAR

MAP PAGE: 10 -11

THE COCOS, OR Keeling Islands, are two separate coral atolls in the east of the Indian Ocean between Sri Lanks and Australia. Most of the population live on West Island and Home Island.

COLOMBIA
Status: REPUBLIC
Area: 1,141,748 sq km (440,831 sq miles)
Population: 33,951,000
Capital: BOGOTÁ
Language: SPANISH,
AMERINDIAN LANGUAGES
Religion: R.CATHOLIC, PROTESTANT
Currency: PESO
Organizations: UN

MAP PAGE: 162

A STATE IN northwest South America, Colombia has coastlines on the Pacific Ocean and the Caribbean Sea. Behind coastal plains lie three ranges of the Andes, separated by high valleys and plateaus where most Colombians live. To the southeast are the prairies and then the jungle of the Amazon. Colombia has a tropical climate, though temperatures vary with altitude. Only 5 per cent of land can be cultivated, but a range of crops are grown. Coffee (Colombia is the world's second largest producer), sugar, bananas, cotton and flowers are exported. Petroleum and its products are the main export. Coal, nickel, gold, silver, platinum and emeralds (Colombia is the world's largest producer) are mined. Industry involves mainly processing minerals and agricultural produce. In spite of government efforts to stop the drugs trade, coca growing and cocaine smuggling are rife.

COMOROS
Status: REPUBLIC
Area: 1,862 sq km (719 sq mls)
Population: 607,000
Capital: MORONI
Language: COMORIAN, FRENCH, ARABIC
Religion: SUNNI MUSLIM, R.CATHOLIC
Currency: FRANC
Organizations: OAU, UN

MAP PAGE: 126 -127

THE STATE COMPRISES three volcanic islands Grande Comore, Anjouan and Mohéil and some coral atolls in the Indian Ocean, off the east African coast. The tropical islands are mountainous, with poor soil. Subsistence farming predominates, but vanilla, cloves and ylang-ylang (an essential oil) are exported.

CONGO
Status: REPUBLIC
Area: 342,000 sq km (132,047 sq mls)
Population: 2,443,000
Capital: BRAZZAVILLE
Language: FRENCH (OFFICIAL), KONGO,
MONOKUTUBA, LOCAL LANGUAGES
Religion: R.CATHOLIC, PROTESTANT,
TRAD. BELIEFS, SUNNI MUSLIM
Currency: CFA FRANC
Organizations: OAU, UN

MAP PAGE: 124 -125

CONGO, IN CENTRAL Africa, is for the most part forest or savannah-covered plateaux drained by the Oubangui-Zaire river systems. Sand dunes and lagoons line the short Atlantic coast. The climate is hot and tropical. Most Congolese live in the southern third of the country. Oil is the main source of export revenue. Diamonds, lead, zinc and gold are also mined. Hardwoods are the second biggest export earner. Half of the workforce are farmers, growing food crops and cash crops including sugar, coffee, cocoa and oil palms.

COOK ISLANDS
Status: NEW ZEALAND TERRITORY
Area: 293 sq km (113 sq mls)
Population: 19,000
Capital: AVARUA
Language: ENGLISH, MAORI
Religion: PROTESTANT, R.CATHOLIC
Currency: DOLLAR

MAP PAGE: 4-5

A GROUP OF coral atolls and volcanic islands in the southwest Pacific Ocean. The main island is Rarotonga. Tourism is important to the economy.

COSTA RICA
Status: REPUBLIC
Area: 51,100 sq km (19,730 sq mls)
Population: 3,199,000
Capital: SAN JOSÉ
Language: SPANISH
Religion: R.CATHOLIC, PROTESTANT
Currency: COLÓN
Organizations: UN

MAP PAGE: 157

COSTA RICA IS in central America, with coastlines on the Caribbean Sea and Pacific Ocean. From the tropical coastal plains the land rises to rugged mountains and a temperate central plateau where most people live. Rainfall is heaviest on the east coast. Farming is the main activity and exports include bananas, coffee, sugar, flowers and beef. There is some mining and a strong manufacturing sector, producing a range of goods from clothing (the main export) and electrical components to food products and cement.

CÔTE D'IVOIRE
Status: REPUBLIC
Area: 322,463 sq km (124,504 sq mls)
Population: 13,316,000
Capital: YAMOUSSOUKRO
Language: FRENCH (OFFICIAL), AKAN,
KRU, GUR, LOCAL LANGUAGES
Religion: TRAD.BELIEFS,
SUNNI MUSLIM, R.CATHOLIC
Currency: CFA FRANC
Organizations: OAU, UN

MAP PAGE: 122

COTE D'IVOIRE (IVORY Coast) is in west Africa, on the Gulf of Guinea. In the north are plateaux and savannah, in the south are low undulating plains and rainforest, with sand-bars and lagoons on the coast. Temperatures are warm, and rainfall is heavier in the south. Most of the workforce is engaged in farming. Côte d'Ivoire is a major producer of cocoa and coffee, and agricultural products (including cotton and timber) are the main export. Gold and diamonds are mined and some oil is produced offshore.

CROATIA
Status: REPUBLIC
Area: 56,538 sq km (21,829 sq mls)
Population: 4,511,000
Capital: ZAGREB
Language: SERBO-CROAT
Religion: R.CATHOLIC, ORTHODOX,
SUNNI MUSLIM
Currency: KUNA
Organizations: UN

MAP PAGE: 104 -105

THE SOUTH EUROPEAN state of Croatia, in the northwest Balkans, has a long coastline on the Adriatic Sea and many offshore islands. The coastal strip has limestone ridges, central parts around Zagreb are hilly, while in the east Slavonia is a lowland plain. Coastal areas have a Mediterranean climate, inland is colder and wetter. Croatia had a strong agricultural and industrial base, but secessionist and ethnic conflict, the loss of markets and, particularly, loss of tourist revenue have caused severe economic difficulties.

CUBA
Status: REPUBLIC
Area: 110,860 sq km (42,803 sq mls)
Population: 10,905,000
Capital: HAVANA
Language: SPANISH
Religion: R.CATHOLIC, PROTESTANT
Currency: PESO
Organizations: UN

MAP PAGE: 158

CUBA COMPRISES THE island of Cuba, the largest island in the Caribbean, and many islets and cays. Cuba itself consists of plains interrupted by three mountain ranges and has a tropical climate modified by trade winds. A fifth of Cubans live in and around Havana. Sugar, with molasses and rum, account for two thirds of export earnings. Nickel, citrus fruits, tobacco and fish products are also exported. Severe recession followed the disruption of traditional trade with east Europe and the ending of Russian subsidies.

CYPRUS
Status: REPUBLIC
Area: 9,251 sq km (3,572 sq mls)
Population: 726,000
Capital: NICOSIA
Language: GREEK, TURKISH, ENGLISH
Religion: GREEK (CYPRIOT) ORTHODOX,
SUNNI MUSLIM
Currency: POUND
Organizations: COMM., UN

MAP PAGE: 43

THE MEDITERRANEAN ISLAND of Cyprus in southwest Asia is dominated by the Troödos mountains in the centre-west. To the east is the fertile plain of Messaoria, flanked by the Kyrenian hills to the northeast. Cyprus has a typically Mediterranean climate, with hot summers and mild winters. The economy of the Greek south is based mainly on specialist agriculture and tourism, though shipping and offshore banking are also major sources of income. The Turkish north depends upon agriculture, tourism and aid from Turkey.

CZECH REPUBLIC
Status: REPUBLIC
Area: 78,864 sq km (30,450 sq mls)
Population: 10,328,000
Capital: PRAGUE
Language: CZECH, MORAVIAN, SLOVAK
Religion: R.CATHOLIC, PROTESTANT
Currency: KORUNA
Organizations: UN

MAP PAGE: 78

THE LANDLOCKED CZECH Republic, in central Europe, borders Slovakia, Poland, Germany and Austria. It is a land of rolling countryside, wooded hills and fertile valleys. Bohemia, the western part, consists of the upper basin of the river Elbe system surrounded by mountain ranges. Moravia, the eastern part, is a lowland area, separated from Bohemia by the Moravian Heights. The climate is temperate, but summers are warm and winters fairly cold. The Czech Republic possesses substantial reserves of coal and lignite, timber and some minerals, chiefly iron ore, graphite, garnets and silver. It is highly industrialized and major manufactures include industrial machinery, consumer goods, cars, iron and steel, chemicals, fertilizers, glass, ceramics and clothing. Bohemia is also the home of the Skoda armaments plant. Since separation from Slovakia in January 1993, trade between the two countries has declined, exacerbating the difficulties the economy was already experiencing from the introduction of a free-market economy. There is, however, a growing tourist industry.

DENMARK
Status: MONARCHY
Area: 43,075 sq km (16,631 sq mls)
Population: 5,189,000
Capital: COPENHAGEN
Language: DANISH
Religion: PROTESTANT, R.CATHOLIC
Currency: KRONE
Organizations: EU, OECD, UN

MAP PAGE: 55

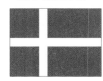

THE KINGDOM OF Denmark in north Europe occupies the Jutland Peninsula and nearly 500 islands in between the North and Baltic seas. The country is low-lying, with a mixture of fertile and sandy soils, and long, indented coastlines. The climate is cool and temperate, with rainfall throughout the year. A fifth of the population lives in Greater Copenhagen on the largest of the islands, Zealand. Denmark's main natural resource is its agricultural potential; two thirds of the total area is fertile farmland or pasture. Agriculture, forestry and fishing are all important sectors of the economy. The chief agricultural products are cheese and other dairy products, beef and bacon, much of which is exported. Some oil and natural gas is produced from fields in the North Sea. Manufacturing, largely based on imported raw materials, now accounts for over half of exports. The main industries are iron and metal working, food processing and brewing, chemicals and engineering. Exports include machinery, food, chemicals, furniture, fuels and energy, and transport equipment.

DJIBOUTI
Status: REPUBLIC
Area: 23,200 sq km (8,958 sq mls)
Population: 557,000
Capital: DJIBOUTI
Language: SOMALI, FRENCH, ARABIC, ISSA, AFAR
Religion: SUNNI MUSLIM, R.CATHOLIC
Currency: FRANC
Organizations: OAU, UN

MAP PAGE: 119

DJIBOUTI LIES IN northeast Africa, on the Gulf of Aden. It consists mostly of low-lying desert, with some areas below sea level and a mountainous area to the north. Temperatures are high and rainfall is low. Most people live in the coastal strip. There is some camel, sheep and goat herding, and cattle, hides and skins are the main exports. With few natural resources, the economy is based on services and trade. The deep-water port and the railway line to Addis Ababa account for about two thirds of national income.

DOMINICA
Status: REPUBLIC
Area: 750 sq km (290 sq mls)
Population: 71,000
Capital: ROSEAU

Language: ENGLISH, FRENCH CREOLE
Religion: R.CATHOLIC, PROTESTANT
Currency: E. CARIB. DOLLAR, POUND STERLING, FRENCH FRANC
Organizations: CARICOM, COMM., UN

MAP PAGE: 159

DOMINICA IS THE most northerly of the Windward Islands in the eastern Caribbean. It is mountainous and forested, with a coastline of steep cliffs, and features geysers and hot springs. The climate is tropical and rainfall abundant. A quarter of Dominicans live in the capital. The economy is based on agriculture, with bananas (the major export), coconuts and citrus fruits the most important crops. There is some forestry, fishing and mining. Manufactured exports include soap, coconut oil, rum and bottled water. Tourism is growing.

DOMINICAN REPUBLIC
Status: REPUBLIC
Area: 48,442 sq km (18,704 sq mls)
Population: 7,608,000
Capital: SANTO DOMINGO
Language: SPANISH, FRENCH CREOLE
Religion: R.CATHOLIC, PROTESTANT
Currency: PESO
Organizations: UN

MAP PAGE: 159

THE STATE OCCUPIES the eastern two thirds of the Caribbean island of Hispaniola. It has a series of mountain ranges, fertile valleys and a large coastal plain in the east. The climate is hot tropical, with heavy rainfall. A third of the population lives in the capital. Sugar, coffee and cocoa are the main cash crops. Bauxite, nickel (the main export), gold and silver are mined, and there is some light industry. Tourism is the main foreign exchange earner.

ECUADOR
Status: REPUBLIC
Area: 272,045 sq km (105,037 sq mls)
Population: 10,981,000
Capital: QUITO
Language: SPANISH, QUECHUA, AMERINDIAN LANGUAGES
Religion: R.CATHOLIC, PROTESTANT
Currency: SUCRE
Organizations: UN

MAP PAGE: 162

ECUADOR IS IN northwest South America, on the Pacific coast. It consists of a broad coastal plain, the high ranges of the Andes and the forested upper Amazon basin to the east. The climate is tropical, moderated by altitude. Most people live on the coast or in the mountain valleys. Ecuador is one of the continent's

leading oil producers. Mineral reserves include gold, silver, zinc and copper. Most of the workforce depends on agriculture. Ecuador is the world's leading producer of bananas. Shrimps, coffee and cocoa are also exported.

EGYPT
Status: REPUBLIC
Area: 1,000,250 sq km (386,199 sq mls)
Population: 56,488,000
Capital: CAIRO
Language: ARABIC, FRENCH
Religion: SUNNI MUSLIM, COPTIC CHRISTIAN
Currency: POUND
Organizations: OAU, UN

MAP PAGE: 118-119

EGYPT, ON THE eastern Mediterranean coast of North Africa, is low-lying, with areas below sea level in the west, and in the Qattara depression, and mountain ranges along the Red Sea coast and in the Sinai peninsula. It is a land of desert and semi-desert, except for the Nile valley, where 99 per cent of Egyptians live, about half of them in towns. The summers are hot, the winters mild and rainfall is negligible. Less than 4 per cent of land (chiefly around the Nile floodplain and delta) is cultivated, but farming employs half the workforce and contributes a sixth of exports. Cotton is the main cash crop. Rice, fruit and vegetables are exported, but Egypt imports over half its food needs. It has major reserves of oil and natural gas, phosphates, iron ore, manganese and nitrates. Oil and its products account for half of export earnings. Manufactures include cement, fertilizers, textiles, electrical goods, cars and processed foods. Workers' remittances, Suez canal tolls and tourist receipts are major sources of income, though attacks on tourists by Islamic militants has reduced the latter.

EL SALVADOR
Status: REPUBLIC
Area: 21,041 sq km (8,124 sq mls)
Population: 5,517,000
Capital: SAN SALVADOR
Language: SPANISH
Religion: R.CATHOLIC, PROTESTANT
Currency: COLÓN
Organizations: UN

MAP PAGE: 157

A DENSELY POPULATED state on the Pacific coast of central American, El Salvador has a coastal plain and volcanic mountain ranges that enclose a plateau where most people live. The coast is hot, with heavy summer rainfall, the highlands are cooler. Coffee (the chief export), sugar and cotton are main cash crops. Shrimps are also exported. Manufactures include processed foods, cosmetics, pharmaceuticals, textiles and clothing.

EQUATORIAL GUINEA
Status: REPUBLIC
Area: 28,051 sq km (10,831 sq mls)
Population: 379,000
Capital: MALABO
Language: SPANISH, FANG
Religion: R.CATHOLIC, TRAD.BELIEFS
Currency: CFA FRANC
Organizations: OAU, UN

MAP PAGE: 124

THE STATE CONSISTS of Rio Muni, an enclave on the Atlantic coast of central Africa, and the islands of Bioco, Annobón and Corisco group. Most people live on the coastal plain and upland plateau of the mainland; the capital is on the fertile volcanic island of Bioco. The climate is hot, humid and wet. Cocoa and timber are the main exports, but the economy depends heavily upon foreign aid.

ERITREA
Status: REPUBLIC
Area: 117,400 sq km (45,328 sq mls)
Population: 3,345,000
Capital: ASMARA
Language: TIGRINYA, ARABIC, TIGRE, ENGLISH
Religion: SUNNI MUSLIM, COPTIC CHRISTIAN
Currency: ETHIOPIAN BIRR
Organizations: OAU, UN

MAP PAGE: 126

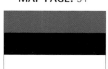

ERITREA, ON THE Red Sea coast of north-east Africa, consists of high plateau in the north and a coastal plain that widens to the south. The coast is hot, inland is cooler. Rainfall is unreliable. The agricultural-based economy has suffered from 30 years of war and occasional poor rains. Coffee and cotton were the main cash crops, though food crops were important to reduce food aid.

ESTONIA
Status: REPUBLIC
Area: 45,200 sq km (17,452 sq mls)
Population: 1,517,000
Capital: TALLINN
Language: ESTONIAN, RUSSIAN
Religion: PROTESTANT, RUSSIAN ORTHODOX
Currency: KROON
Organizations: UN

MAP PAGE: 54

ESTONIA IS IN north Europe, on the Gulf of Finland and Baltic Sea. The land, one third of which is forested, is generally low-lying, with many lakes. The climate is temperate. About one third of Estonians live in Tallinn. Forests and oil-shale deposits are the main natural resources. Agriculture is limited to livestock and dairy farming. Industries include timber, furniture production, shipbuilding, leather, fur and food processing.

ETHIOPIA
Status: REPUBLIC
Area: 1,133,880 sq km (437,794 sq mls)
Population: 51,859,000
Capital: ADDIS ABABA
Language: AMHARIC (OFFICIAL), OROMO, LOCAL LANGUAGES
Religion: ETHIOPIAN ORTHODOX, SUNNI MUSLIM, TRAD.BELIEFS
Currency: BIRR
Organizations: OAU, UN

MAP PAGE: 126

ETHIOPIA, IN NORTHEAST Africa, borders Eritrea, Djibouti, Somalia, Kenya and Sudan. The western half is a mountainous region traversed by the Great Rift Valley. To the east is mostly arid plateaux. The highlands are warm with summer rainfall, though droughts occur; the east is hot and dry. Most people live in the centre-north. Secessionist wars have hampered economic development. Subsistence farming is the main activity, though droughts have led to famine. Coffee is the main export and there is some light industry.

FAEROES

Status: DANISH TERRITORY
Area: 1,399 sq km (540 sq mls)
Population: 47,000
Capital: TÓRSHAVN
Language: DANISH, FAEROESE
Religion: PROTESTANT
Currency: DANISH KRONE

MAP PAGE: 55

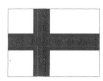

A SELF GOVERNING territory, the Faeroes lie in the north Atlantic Ocean between the UK and Iceland. The islands benefit from the Gulf Stream which has a moderating effect on the climate. The economy is based on deep-sea fishing and sheep farming.

FALKLAND ISLANDS

Status: UK TERRITORY
Area: 12,170 sq km (4,699 sq mls)
Population: 2,000
Capital: STANLEY
Language: ENGLISH
Religion: PROTESTANT, R.CATHOLIC
Currency: POUND

MAP PAGE: 170

L YING IN THE southwest Atlantic Ocean, northeast of Cape Horn, the Falklands consists of two main islands, West Falkland and East Falkland, where most of the population live and many smaller islands. The economy is based on sheep farming and the sale of fishing licences, though oil has been discovered offshore.

FIJI

Status: REPUBLIC
Area: 18,330 sq km (7,077 sq mls)
Population: 762,000
Capital: SUVA
Language: ENGLISH, FIJIAN, HINDI
Religion: PROTESTANT, HINDU, R.CATHOLIC, SUNNI MUSLIM
Currency: DOLLAR
Organizations: UN

MAP PAGE: 6

F IJI COMPRISES TWO main islands, of volcanic origin and mountainous, and over 300 smaller islands in the South Pacific Ocean. The climate is tropical and the economy is based on agriculture (chiefly sugar, the main export), fishing, forestry, gold mining and tourism.

FINLAND

Status: REPUBLIC
Area: 338,145 sq km (130,559 sq mls)
Population: 5,067,000
Capital: HELSINKI
Language: FINNISH, SWEDISH
Religion: PROTESTANT, FINNISH (GREEK) ORTHODOX
Currency: MARKKA
Organizations: EU, OECD, UN

MAP PAGE: 56-57

F INLAND IS IN north Europe, on the Gulf of Bothnia and the Gulf of Finland. It is low-lying apart from mountainous areas in the northwest. Forests cover 70 per cent of the land area, lakes and tundra over 20 per cent. Only 8 per cent is cultivated. Summers are short and warm, and winters are long and severe, particularly in the north. Most people live in the southern third of the country, along the coast or near the many lakes. Timber is the main resource and products of the forest-based industries account for a third of exports. Finland has a large fishing industry and its agricultural sector produces enough cereals and dairy products to cover domestic needs. It has some mineral deposits, chiefly zinc, copper, nickel, gold and silver. Finland is a highly industrialised country, though it must import most of the raw materials. Apart from the timber and related industries, it has important metal working, shipbuilding and engineering industries. Other industries produce chemicals, pharmaceuticals, plastics, rubber, textiles, electronic equipment, glass and ceramics.

F.Y.R.O.M. (MACEDONIA)

Status: REPUBLIC
Area: 25,713 sq km (9,928 sq mls)
Population: 2,060,000
Capital: SKOPJE
Language: MACEDONIAN, ALBANIAN, SERBO-CROAT, TURKISH, ROMANY
Religion: MACEDONIAN ORTHODOX, SUNNI MUSLIM, R.CATHOLIC
Currency: DENAR
Organizations: UN

MAP PAGE: 112-113

F YROM, FORMERLY THE Yugoslav republic of Macedonia, is a landlocked state of south Europe, bordered by Yugoslavia, Bulgaria, Greece and Albania. Lying within the south Balkans, it is a rugged country, traversed north-south by the Vardar valley. It has fine, hot summers, but very cold winters. The economy is based on industry, mining and, to a lesser degree, agriculture. But conflict with Greece and UN sanctions against Yugoslavia have reduced trade, caused economic difficulties and discouraged investment.

FRANCE

Status: REPUBLIC
Area: 543,965 sq km (210,026 sq mls)
Population: 57,660,000
Capital: PARIS
Language: FRENCH, FRENCH DIALECTS, ARABIC, GERMAN (ALSATIAN), BRETON
Religion: R.CATHOLIC, PROTESTANT, SUNNI MUSLIM
Currency: FRANC
Organizations: EU, OECD, UN

MAP PAGE: 84-85

F RANCE LIES IN southwest Europe, with coastlines on the North Sea, Atlantic Ocean and Mediterranean Sea; it includes the Mediterranean island of Corsica. Northern and western regions consist mostly of flat or rolling countryside, and include the major lowlands of the Paris basin, the Loire valley and the Aquitaine basin, drained by the Seine, Loire and Garonne river systems respectively. The centre-south is dominated by the Massif Central. Eastwards, beyond the fourth major lowland area of the Rhône-Saône valley, are the Alps and the Jura mountains. In the south-west, the Pyrenees form a natural border with Spain. The climate of northern parts is temper-

ate and wet, but in the centre and east it is continental, with warmer summers and milder winters. Along the south coast a Mediterranean climate prevails, with hot, dry summers and mild winters with some rainfall. Some 75 per cent of the population live in towns, but Greater Paris is the only major conurbation, with a sixth of the French population. Rich soil, a large cultivable area and contrasts in temperature and relief have given France a strong and varied agricultural base. It is a major producer of both fresh and processed food and the world's second largest exporter of agricultural products, after the USA. Major exports include cereals (chiefly wheat), dairy products, wines and sugar. France has relatively few mineral resources, though iron ore, potash salts, zinc and uranium are mined. It has coal reserves, some oil and natural gas, but it relies mainly for its energy needs on nuclear and hydroelectric power and imported fuels. France is the world's fourth largest industrial power after the USA, Japan and Germany. Heavy industries include iron, steel and aluminium production and oil refining. Other major industries are food processing, motor vehicles, aerospace, chemicals and pharmaceuticals, telecommunications, computers and armaments as well as luxury goods, fashion and perfumes. The main exports are machinery, agricultural products, cars and other transport equipment. France has a strong services sector and tourism is a major source of revenue and employment.

FRENCH GUIANA

Status: FRENCH TERRITORY
Area: 90,000 sq km (34,749 sq mls)
Population: 135,000
Capital: CAYENNE
Language: FRENCH, FRENCH CREOLE
Religion: R.CATHOLIC, PROTESTANT
Currency: FRENCH FRANC

MAP PAGE: 163

F RENCH GUIANA, ON the northeast coast of South America, is densely forested and is mountainous in the south. The climate is tropical with high rainfall. Most people live in the coastal strip and most workers are involved in subsistence farming, though sugar is exported. Livestock rearing and fishing are also important. Timber and mineral resources are largely unexploited and industry is limited. French Guiana depends upon French aid.

FRENCH POLYNESIA

Status: FRENCH TERRITORY
Area: 3,265 sq km (1,261 sq mls)
Population: 213,000
Capital: PAPEETE
Language: FRENCH, POLYNESIAN LANGUAGES
Religion: PROTESTANT, R.CATHOLIC, MORMON
Currency: PACIFIC FRANC

MAP PAGE: 7

E XTENDING OVER A vast area of the south-east Pacific Ocean, French Polynesia comprises more than 130 islands and coral atolls. The main island groups are the Marquesas, the Tuamotu Archipelago and the Society Islands. The capital, Papeete, is on Tahiti in the Society Islands. The climate is subtropical and the economy is based on tourism.

FRENCH SOUTHERN AND ANTARCTIC LANDS

Status: FRENCH TERRITORY
Area: 7,781 sq km (3,004 sq mls)

MAP PAGE: 175

T HIS TERRITORY INCLUDES Crozet Island, Kerguelen, Amsterdam Island and St Paul Island. All are uninhabited apart from scientific research staff. In accordance with the Antarctic Treaty, French territorial claims in Antarctica have been suspended.

GABON

Status: REPUBLIC
Area: 267,667 sq km (103,347 sq mls)
Population: 1,012,000
Capital: LIBREVILLE
Language: FRENCH, FANG, LOCAL LANGUAGES
Religion: R.CATHOLIC, PROTESTANT, TRAD.BELIEFS
Currency: CFA FRANC
Organizations: OAU, OPEC, UN

MAP PAGE: 124-125

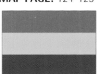

G ABON, ON THE Atlantic coast of central consists of low plateaux, with a coastal plain lined by lagoons and mangrove swamps. The climate is tropical and rainforests cover 75 per cent of the land. Half of the population lives in towns, chiefly Libreville and Port Gentil. The economy is heavily dependent on mineral resources, mainly oil but also manganese and uranium. Timber, chiefly okoumé, is exported. Agriculture is mainly at subsistence level, but oil palms, bananas, sugarcane and rubber are grown.

THE GAMBIA

Status: REPUBLIC
Area: 11,295 sq km (4,361 sq mls)
Population: 1,026,000
Capital: BANJUL
Language: ENGLISH (OFFICIAL), MALINKE, FULANI, WOLOF
Religion: SUNNI MUSLIM, PROTESTANT
Currency: DALASI
Organizations: COMM., OAU, UN

MAP PAGE: 122

T HE GAMBIA, ON the coast of west Africa, occupies a strip of land along the lower Gambia River. Sandy beaches are backed by mangrove swamps, beyond which is savannah. The climate is tropical, with rainfall in the summer. Over 70 per cent of Gambians are farmers, growing chiefly groundnuts (the main export) but also seed cotton, oil palms and food crops. Livestock rearing and fishing are important, while manufacturing is limited. Re-exports, mainly from Senegal, and tourism are major sources of income.

GAZA

Status: AUTONOMOUS REGION
Area: 363 sq km (140 sq mls)
Population: 712,000
Language: ARABIC
Religion: SUNNI MUSLIM, SHI'A MUSLIM

MAP PAGE: 43

G AZA IS A narrow strip of land on the southwest corner of the Mediterranean Sea, between Egypt and Israel. The territory has limited autonomy from Israel. The economy is based on agriculture and remittances from work in Israel.

GEORGIA

Status: REPUBLIC
Area: 69,700 sq km (26,911 sq mls)
Population: 5,493,000
Capital: TBILISI
Language: GEORGIAN, RUSSIAN, ARMENIAN, AZERI, OSSETIAN, ABKHAZ
Religion: GEORGIAN ORTHODOX, RUSSIAN ORTHODOX, SHI'A MUSLIM
Currency: COUPON
Organizations: CIS, UN

MAP PAGE: 51

GEORGIA IS IN northwest Transcaucasia, southwest Asia, on the Black Sea. Mountain ranges in the north and south flank the Kura and Rioni valleys. The climate is generally mild, but subtropical along the coast. Agriculture is important, with tea, grapes, citrus fruits and tobacco the major crops. Mineral resources include manganese, coal and oil, and the main industries are iron and steel, oil refining and machine building. However, economic activity has been seriously affected by separatist wars and political unrest.

GERMANY

Status: REPUBLIC
Area: 357,868 sq km (138,174 sq mls)
Population: 81,409,530
Capital: BERLIN
Language: GERMAN, TURKISH
Religion: PROTESTANT, R.CATHOLIC, SUNNI MUSLIM
Currency: MARK
Organizations: EU, OECD, UN

MAP PAGE: 70

THE WEST EUROPEAN state of Germany borders nine countries and has coastlines on the North and Baltic seas. It includes the southern part of the Jutland peninsula and Frisian islands. Behind the indented coastline and covering about one third of the country is the north German plain, a region of fertile farmland and sandy heaths drained by the country's major rivers. The central highlands are a belt of forested hills and plateaux which stretches from the Eifel region in the west to the Erzgebirge (Ore mountains) along the border with the Czech Republic. Farther south the land rises to the Swabian and Jura mountains, with the high rugged and forested Black Forest in the southwest and the Bavarian plateau and Alps to the southeast. The climate is temperate, with continental conditions in eastern areas where winters are colder. Rainfall is evenly spread throughout the year. Divided in 1945 after defeat in the second world war, Germany was reunified in 1990, barely a year after the collapse of communism in eastern Europe. It had been thought that west Germany, the world's third largest industrial economy and second largest exporter, would easily absorb east Germany, less than half the size and with a quarter of the population. But the initial cost of unification was high. The overhaul of east

German industry led to 30 per cent unemployment there, while the high level of investment and the rising social security bill led to tax increases in the west. In addition unification coincided with recession in the west German economy and rising unemployment, which created social tensions. However, by 1994 there were signs that the economy was pulling out of the recession. Germany lacks minerals and other industrial raw materials, with the exception of lignite and potash. It has a small agricultural base, though a few products (chiefly wines and beers) enjoy an international reputation. It is predominantly an industrial economy, dominated by the mechanical and engineering, iron and steel, chemical, pharmaceutical, motor, textile and high-tech industries. It also has a large service sector, with tourism, banking and finance being important.

BADEN-WÜRTTEMBERG

Status: STATE
Area: 35,751 sq km (13,804 sq miles)
Population: 10,247,515
Capital: STUTTGART

BAYERN (BAVARIA)

Status: STATE
Area: 70,554 sq km (27,241 sq miles)
Population: 11,888,925
Capital: MÜNCHEN

BERLIN

Status: STATE
Area: 889 sq km (343 sq miles)
Population: 3,477,916
Capital: BERLIN

BRANDENBURG

Status: STATE
Area: 29,056 sq km (11,219 sq miles)
Population: 2,533,241
Capital: POTSDAM

BREMEN

Status: STATE
Area: 404 sq km (156 sq miles)
Population: 682,148
Capital: BREMEN

HAMBURG

Status: STATE
Area: 755 sq km (292 sq miles)
Population: 1,703,802
Capital: HAMBURG

HESSEN (HESSE)

Status: STATE
Area: 21,114 sq km (8,152 sq miles)
Population: 5,969,442
Capital: WIESBADEN

MECKLENBURG-VORPOMMERN (MECKLENBURG-WEST POMERANIA)

Status: STATE
Area: 23,559 sq km (9,096 sq miles)
Population: 1,836,996
Capital: SCHWERIN

NIEDERSACHSEN (LOWER SAXONY)

Status: STATE
Area: 47,351 sq km (18,282 sq miles)
Population: 7,680,426
Capital: HANNOVER

NORDRHEIN-WESTFALEN (NORTH RHINE-WESTPHALIA)

Status: STATE
Area: 34,070 sq km (13,155 sq miles)
Population: 17,779,202
Capital: DÜSSELDORF

RHEINLAND-PFALZ (RHINELAND-PALATINATE)

Status: STATE
Area: 19,849 sq km (7,664 sq miles)
Population: 3,937,555
Capital: MAINZ

SAARLAND

Status: STATE
Area: 2,570 sq km (992 sq miles)
Population: 1,083,199
Capital: SAARBRÜCKEN

SACHSEN (SAXONY)

Status: STATE
Area: 18,341 sq km (7,081 sq miles)
Population: 4,595,847
Capital: DRESDEN

SACHSEN-ANHALT (SAXONY-ANHALT)

Status: STATE
Area: 20,607 sq km (7,956 sq miles)
Population: 2,769,312
Capital: MAGDEBURG

SCHLESWIG-HOLSTEIN

Status: STATE
Area: 15,731 sq km (6,074 sq miles)
Population: 2,699,167
Capital: KIEL

THÜRINGEN (THURINGIA)

Status: STATE
Area: 16,251 sq km (6,275 sq miles)
Population: 2,524,837
Capital: ERFURT

GHANA

Status: REPUBLIC
Area: 238,537 SQ KM (92,100 SQ MLS)
Population: 16,446,000
Capital: ACCRA
Language: ENGLISH (OFFICIAL), HAUSA, AKAN, LOCAL LANGUAGES
Religion: PROTESTANT, R.CATHOLIC, SUNNI MUSLIM, TRAD. BELIEFS
Currency: CEDI
Organizations: COMM., OAU, UN

MAP PAGE: 122

A WEST AFRICAN STATE on the Gulf of Guinea, Ghana is a land of plains and low plateaux covered with savannah and, in the west, rainforest. In the east is the Volta basin. The climate is tropical, with high rainfall in the south, where most people live. Ghana is a major producer of cocoa. Timber is also an important commodity. Bauxite, gold, diamonds and manganese ore are mined, and there are a number of industries around Tema.

GIBRALTAR

Status: UK TERRITORY
Area: 6.5 sq km (2.51 sq mls)
Population: 28,000
Capital: GIBRALTAR
Language: ENGLISH, SPANISH
Religion: R.CATHOLIC, PROTESTANT, SUNNI MUSLIM
Currency: POUND

MAP PAGE: 101

GIBRALTAR LIES ON the south coast of Spain at the western entrance to the Mediterranean Sea. The economy depends on tourism, offshore banking and entrepôt trade.

GREECE

Status: REPUBLIC
Area: 131,957 sq km (50,949 sq mls)
Population: 10,350,000
Capital: ATHENS
Language: GREEK, MACEDONIAN
Religion: GREEK ORTHODOX, SUNNI MUSLIM
Currency: DRACHMA
Organizations: EU, OECD, UN

MAP PAGE: 114-115

GREECE OCCUPIES THE southern part of the Balkan Peninsula of south Europe and many islands in the Ionian, Aegean and Mediterranean Seas. The islands make up over one fifth of its area. Mountains and hills cover much of the country. The most important lowlands are the plains of Thessaly in the centre-east and Salonica in the northeast. Summers are hot and dry. Winters are mild and wet, colder in the north with heavy snowfalls in the mountains. One third of Greeks live in the Athens area. Agriculture involves one quarter of the workforce and exports include citrus fruits, raisins, wine, olives and olive oil. A variety of ores and minerals are mined and a wide range of manufactures are produced including food and tobacco products, textiles, clothing, chemical products and metal products. Tourism is an important industry and there is a large services sector. Tourism, shipping and remittances from Greeks abroad are major foreign exchange earners. The war in former Yugoslavia and UN embargo on trade to Serbia have lost Greece an important market and regular trade route.

GREENLAND

Status: DANISH TERRITORY
Area: 2,175,600 sq km (840,004 sq mls)
Population: 55,000
Capital: NUUK
Language: GREENLANDIC, DANISH
Religion: PROTESTANT
Currency: DANISH KRONE

MAP PAGE: 135

SITUATED TO THE northeast of North America between the Atlantic and Arctic Oceans, Greenland is the largest island in the world. It has a polar climate and over 80 per cent of the land area is permanent ice-cap. The economy is based on fishing and fish processing.

GRENADA

Status: MONARCHY
Area: 378 sq km (146 sq mls)
Population: 92,000
Capital: ST GEORGE'S
Language: ENGLISH, CREOLE
Religion: R.CATHOLIC, PROTESTANT
Currency: E. CARIB. DOLLAR
Organizations: CARICOM, COMM., UN

MAP PAGE: 159

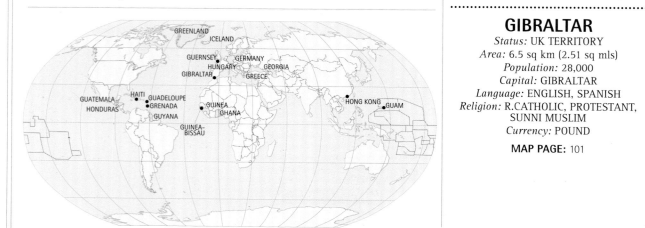

THE CARIBBEAN STATE comprises Grenada, the most southerly of the Windward Islands, and the southern Grenadines. Grenada has wooded hills, beaches in the southwest, a warm climate and good rainfall. Agriculture is the main activity, with bananas, nutmeg and cocoa the main exports. Tourism and manufacturing are important. Grenada relies on grant aid.

GUADELOUPE

Status: FRENCH TERRITORY
Area: 1,780 sq km (687 sq mls)
Population: 413,000
Capital: BASSE-TERRE
Language: FRENCH, FRENCH CREOLE
Religion: R.CATHOLIC, HINDU
Currency: FRENCH FRANC

MAP PAGE: 159

GUADELOUPE, IN THE Caribbean's Leeward group, consists of two main islands, Basse-Terre and Grande Terre, connected by a bridge, and a few outer islands. The climate is tropical, but moderated by trade winds. Bananas, sugar and rum, tourism and French aid are the main sources of foreign exchange.

GUAM

Status: US TERRITORY
Area: 541 sq km (209 sq mls)
Population: 143,000
Capital: AGANA
Language: CHAMORRO, ENGLISH, TAGALOG
Religion: R.CATHOLIC
Currency: US DOLLAR

MAP PAGE: 21

LYING AT THE south end of the North Mariana Islands in the Western Pacific Ocean, Guam has a humid tropical climate. The island has a large US military base and the economy relies on that and tourism which is beginning to develop.

GUATEMALA

Status: REPUBLIC
Area: 108,890 sq km (42,043 sq mls)
Population: 10,029,000
Capital: GUATEMALA CITY
Language: SPANISH, MAYAN LANGUAGES
Religion: R.CATHOLIC, PROTESTANT
Currency: QUETZAL
Organizations: UN

MAP PAGE: 157

THE MOST POPULOUS country in Central America after Mexico, Guatemala has a long Pacific and a short Caribbean coastline. Northern areas are lowland tropical forests. To the south lie mountain ranges with some active volcanoes, then the Pacific coastal plain. The climate is hot tropical in the lowlands, cooler in the highlands, where most people live. Farming is the main activity, coffee, sugar and bananas are the main exports. There is some mining and manufacturing (chiefly clothing and textiles). Tourism is important. Guerrilla activity is rife in certain areas.

GUERNSEY

Status: UK TERRITORY
Area: 79 sq km (31 sq mls)
Population: 64,000
Capital: ST PETER PORT
Language: ENGLISH, FRENCH
Religion: PROTESTANT, R.CATHOLIC
Currency: POUND

MAP PAGE: 63

ONE OF THE Channel Islands lying off the west coast of the Cherbourg peninsula in northern France.

GUINEA

Status: REPUBLIC
Area: 245,857 sq km (94,926 sq mls)
Population: 6,306,000
Capital: CONAKRY
Language: FRENCH, FULANI, MALINKE, LOCAL LANGUAGES
Religion: SUNNI MUSLIM, TRAD.BELIEFS, R.CATHOLIC
Currency: FRANC
Organizations: OAU, UN

MAP PAGE: 122

GUINEA IS IN west Africa, on the Atlantic Ocean. The coastal plains are lined with mangrove swamps. Inland are the Fouta Djallon mountains and plateaux. To the east are savannah plains drained by the upper Niger river system, while to the southeast are mountains. The climate is tropical, with high coastal rainfall. Agriculture is the main activity, with coffee, bananas and pineapples the chief cash crops. Bauxite, alumina, iron ore, gold and diamonds are the main exports, but Guinea relies upon foreign aid.

GUINEA-BISSAU

Status: REPUBLIC
Area: 36,125 sq km (13,948 sq mls)
Population: 1,028,000
Capital: BISSAU
Language: PORTUGUESE, PORTUGUESE CREOLE, LOCAL LANGUAGES
Religion: TRAD.BELIEFS, SUNNI MUSLIM, R.CATHOLIC
Currency: PESO
Organizations: OAU, UN

MAP PAGE: 122

GUINEA-BISSAU, ON THE Atlantic coast of west Africa, includes the Bijagos Archipelago. The mainland coast is swampy and contains many estuaries. Inland are forested plains and to the east are savannah plateaux. The climate is tropical. The economy is based mainly on subsistence farming. There is some fishing, but little industry. Forestry and mineral resources are largely unexploited. The main exports are cashews, groundnuts, oil palms and their products. Donors largely suspended support in 1991 because of payment arrears.

GUYANA

Status: REPUBLIC
Area: 214,969 sq km (83,000 sq mls)
Population: 816,000
Capital: GEORGETOWN
Language: ENGLISH, CREOLE, HINDI, AMERINDIAN LANGUAGES
Religion: PROTESTANT, HINDU, R.CATHOLIC, SUNNI MUSLIM
Currency: DOLLAR
Organizations: CARICOM, COMM., UN

MAP PAGE: 163

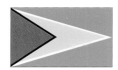

GUYANA, ON THE northeast coast of South America, consists of the densely forested highlands in the west, and the savannah uplands in the south. A lowland coastal belt supports crops and most of the population. The generally hot, humid and wet conditions are modified along the coast by sea breezes. The economy is based on agriculture, mining, forestry and fishing. Sugar, bauxite, gold and rice are the main exports. Other exports are shrimps and timber.

HAITI

Status: REPUBLIC
Area: 27,750 sq km (10,714 sq mls)
Population: 6,903,000
Capital: PORT-AU-PRINCE
Language: FRENCH, FRENCH CREOLE
Religion: R.CATHOLIC, PROTESTANT, VOODOO
Currency: GOURDE
Organizations: UN

MAP PAGE: 159

HAITI, OCCUPYING THE western third of the Caribbean island of Hispaniola, is a mountainous state, with small coastal plains and a central valley. The climate is tropical, hottest in coastal areas. Haiti has few natural resources, is overpopulated and relies on exports of local manufactures and coffee, and remittances from workers abroad. Political unrest and UN sanctions from 1991 to 1994 hit the economy badly.

HONDURAS

Status: REPUBLIC
Area: 112,088 sq km (43,277 sq mls)
Population: 5,595,000
Capital: TEGUCIGALPA
Language: SPANISH, AMERINDIAN LANGUAGES
Religion: R.CATHOLIC, PROTESTANT
Currency: LEMPIRA
Organizations: UN

MAP PAGE: 159

HONDURAS, IN CENTRAL America, is a mountainous and forested country with lowland areas along its long Caribbean and short Pacific coasts. Coastal areas are hot and humid with heavy summer rainfall, inland is cooler and drier. Most people live in the central valleys. Coffee and bananas are the main exports, along with shrimps, lead, zinc and timber. Industry involves mainly agricultural processing. Honduras depends on foreign aid.

HONG KONG

Status: UK TERRITORY
Area: 1,075 sq km (415 sq mls)
Population: 5,919,000
Capital:
Language: CHINESE (CANTONESE OFFICIAL, MANDARIN), ENGLISH (OFFICIAL)
Religion: BUDDHIST, TAOIST, PROTESTANT
Currency: DOLLAR

MAP PAGE: 27

LYING ON THE southeast coast of China, Hong Kong comprises the New Territories, which are part of the mainland, Hong Kong and Lantau Islands and many smaller islands. In 1997 when the UK's 99-year lease expires, Hong Kong will revert to China. Hong Kong is a major port for south and southeast Asia and an important financial centre.

HUNGARY

Status: REPUBLIC
Area: 93,030 sq km (35,919 sq mls)
Population: 10,294,000
Capital: BUDAPEST
Language: HUNGARIAN, ROMANY, GERMAN, SLOVAK
Religion: R.CATHOLIC, PROTESTANT
Currency: FORINT
Organizations: UN

MAP PAGE: 78-79

A LANDLOCKED COUNTRY in central Europe, Hungary borders Austria, Slovakia, Ukraine, Romania, Yugoslavia, Croatia and Slovenia. The Danube river flows north-south through central Hungary. To the east lies a great plain, flanked by highlands in the north. To the west low mountains and Lake Balaton separate a small plain and southern uplands. The climate is continental, with warm summers and cold winters. Rainfall is fairly evenly distributed throughout the year. Half the population lives in urban areas, and one fifth lives in Budapest. Hungary has a predominantly industrial economy. The main industries produce metals, machinery, transport equipment (chiefly buses), textiles, chemicals and food products. Some minerals and energy resources are exploited, chiefly bauxite, coal and natural gas. Farming remains important, though output has fallen. Fruit, vegetables, cigarettes and wine are the main agricultural exports. Tourism is an important foreign exchange earner. Progress towards creating a market economy has been proved slow.

ICELAND

Status: REPUBLIC
Area: 102,820 sq km (39,699 sq mls)
Population: 263,000
Capital: REYKJAVIK
Language: ICELANDIC
Religion: PROTESTANT, R.CATHOLIC
Currency: KRÓNA
Organizations: OECD, UN

MAP PAGE: 56

THE NORTHWEST EUROPEAN island of Iceland lies in the Atlantic Ocean, near the Arctic Circle. It consists mainly of a plateau of basalt lava flows. Some of its 200 volcanoes are active, and there are geysers and hot springs, but one tenth of the country is covered by ice caps. Only coastal lowlands can be cultivated and settled, and over half the population lives in the Reykjavik area. The climate is fairly mild, moderated by the North Atlantic Drift and southwesterly winds. The mainstay of the economy is fishing and fish processing, which account for 80 per cent of exports. Agriculture involves mainly sheep and dairy farming. Iceland is self-sufficient in meat and dairy products, and exports wool and sheepskins. Diatomite is the only mineral resource but hydro-electric and geothermal energy resources are considerable. The main industries produce aluminium, ferro-silicon, electrical equipment, books, fertilizers, textiles and clothing. Tourism is growing in importance.

INDIA

Status: REPUBLIC
Area: 3,287,263 sq km (1,269,219 sq mls)
Population: 901,459,000
Capital: NEW DELHI
Language: HINDI, ENGLISH (OFFICIAL), MANY REGIONAL LANGUAGES
Religion: HINDU, SUNNI MUSLIM, SIKH, CHRISTIAN, BUDDHIST, JAIN
Currency: RUPEE
Organizations: COMM., UN

MAP PAGE: 34-35

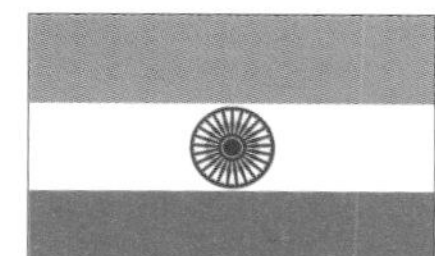

MOST OF THE South Asian state of India occupies a peninsula that juts out into the Indian Ocean between the Arabian Sea and Bay of Bengal. The heart of the peninsula is the Deccan plateau, bordered on either side by ranges of hills, the Western Ghats and the lower Eastern Ghats, which fall away to narrow coastal plains. To the north is a broad plain, drained by the Indus, Ganges and Brahmaputra rivers and their tributaries. The plain is intensively farmed and is the most populous region. In the west is the Thar Desert. The Himalayas form India's northern border, together with parts of the Karakoram and Hindu Kush ranges in the northwest. The climate shows marked seasonal variation: the hot season from March to June; the monsoon season from June to October; and the cold season from November to February. Rainfall ranges between heavy in the northeast Assam region and negligible in the Thar Desert, while temperatures range from very cold in the Himayalas to tropical heat over much of the south. India is among the ten largest economies in the world. It has achieved a high degree of self-sufficiency and its involvement in world trade is relatively small, though growing. Agriculture, forestry and fishing account for one third of national output and two thirds of employment. Much of the farming is on a subsistence basis and involves mainly rice and wheat growing. India is a major world producer of tea, sugar, jute, cotton and tobacco. Livestock is raised mainly for dairy products and hides. India has substantial reserves of coal, oil and natural gas and many minerals including iron, manganese and copper ores, bauxite, diamonds and gold. The manufacturing sector is large and diverse. The main manufactures are chemicals and chemical products, textiles, iron and steel, food products, electrical goods and transport equipment. The main exports are diamonds, clothing, chemicals and chemical products, textiles, leather and leather goods, iron ore, fish products, electronic goods and tea. However, with a huge population - the second largest in the world - India receives foreign aid to support its balance of payments.

INDONESIA

Status: REPUBLIC
Area: 1,919,445 sq km (741,102 sq mls)
Population: 189,921,000
Capital: JAKARTA
Language: INDONESIAN (OFFICIAL), MANY LOCAL LANGUAGES
Religion: SUNNI MUSLIM, PROTESTANT, R.CATHOLIC, HINDU, BUDDHIST
Currency: RUPIAH
Organizations: ASEAN, OPEC, UN

MAP PAGE: 20-21

INDONESIA, THE LARGEST and most populous country in southeast Asia, consists of 13,677 islands extending along the Equator between the Pacific and Indian oceans. Sumatra, Java, Sulawesi, Kalimantan (two thirds of Borneo) and Irian Jaya (western New Guinea) make up 90 per cent of the land area. Most of Indonesia is mountainous and covered with rainforest or mangrove swamps, and there are over 300 volcanoes, some still active. Two thirds of the population live in the lowland areas of Java and Madura. In general the climate is tropical monsoon. Indonesia is rich in energy resources, minerals, forests and fertile soil. It is among the world's top producers of rice, palm oil, tea, coffee, rubber and tobacco. It is the world's leading exporter of natural gas and a major exporter of oil and timber. In recent years manufacturing output has risen. A range of goods are produced including textiles, clothing, cement, fertilizer and vehicles. Tourism has also increased. However, given its huge population, Indonesia remains a relatively poor country.

IRAN

Status: REPUBLIC
Area: 1,648,000 sq km (636,296 sq mls)
Population: 64,169,000
Capital: TEHRAN
Language: FARSI (PERSIAN), AZERI, KURDISH, REGIONAL LANGUAGES
Religion: SHI'A MUSLIM, SUNNI MUSLIM, BAHA'I, CHRISTIAN, ZOROASTRIAN
Currency: RIAL
Organizations: OPEC, UN

MAP PAGE: 39

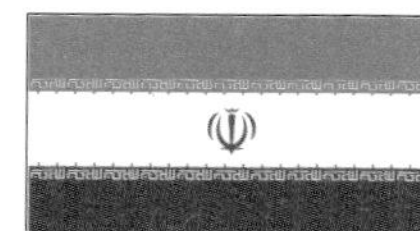

IRAN IS IN southwest Asia, on The Gulf, the Gulf of Oman and Caspian Sea. Eastern Iran is high plateaux country, with large salt pans and a vast sand desert. In the west the Zagros Mountains form a series of ridges, while to the north lie the Elburz Mountains. Most farming and settlement is on the narrow plain along the Caspian Sea and the foothills of the north and west. The climate is one of extremes, with hot summers and very cold winters. Most of the light rainfall is in the winter months. Agriculture involves one quarter of the workforce. Wheat is the main crop but fruit (chiefly dates) and pistachio nuts are grown for export. Fishing in the Caspian Sea is important and caviar is exported. Petroleum (the main export) and natural gas are Iran's leading natural resources. There are also reserves of coal, iron ore, copper ore and other minerals. Manufactures include carpets, clothing, food products, construction materials, chemicals, vehicles, leather goods and metal products. The 1979 revolution and 1980-88 war with Iraq slowed economic development.

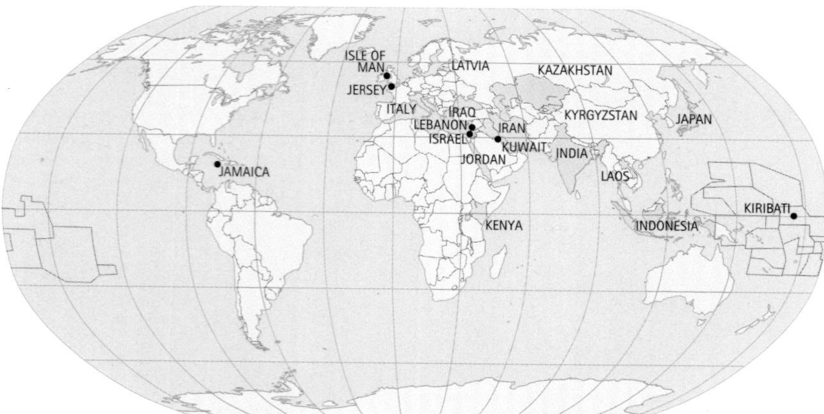

IRAQ

Status: REPUBLIC
Area: 438,317 sq km (169,235 sq mls)
Population: 19,454,000
Capital: BAGHDAD
Language: ARABIC, KURDISH, TURKMEN
Religion: SHI'A MUSLIM, SUNNI MUSLIM, R.CATHOLIC
Currency: DINAR
Organizations: OPEC, UN

MAP PAGE: 42

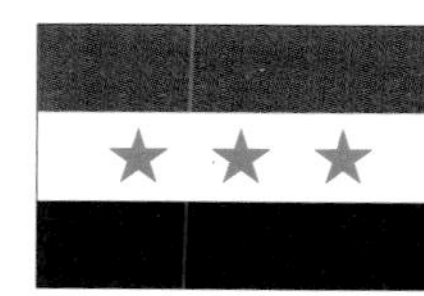

IRAQ, WHICH LIES on the northwest shores of The Gulf in southwest Asia, has at its heart the lowland valley of the Tigris and Euphrates rivers. In the southeast where the two rivers join are marshes and the Shatt al Arab waterway. Northern Iraq is hilly, rising to the Zagros Mountains, while western Iraq is desert. Summers are hot and dry, while winters are mild with light though unreliable rainfall. The Tigris-Euphrates valley contains most of the arable land and population, including one in five who live in Baghdad. One third of the workforce is involved in agriculture, with dates, cotton, wool, hides and skins exported in normal times. However, the 1980-88 war with Iraq, defeat in the 1991 Gulf war and international sanctions have ruined the economy and caused considerable hardship. Petroleum and natural gas sales, which had accounted for 98 per cent of export earnings, were severely restricted. Much of the infrastructure was damaged and industrial output - which had included petroleum products, cement, steel, textiles, bitumen and pharmaceuticals - was reduced.

ISLE OF MAN

Status: UK TERRITORY
Area: 572 sq km (221 sq mls)
Population: 71,000
Capital: DOUGLAS
Language: ENGLISH
Religion: PROTESTANT, R.CATHOLIC
Currency: POUND

MAP PAGE: 64

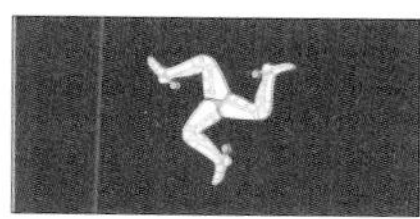

ISRAEL

Status: REPUBLIC
Area: 20,770 sq km (8,019 sq mls)
Population: 5,256,000
Capital: JERUSALEM
Language: HEBREW, ARABIC, YIDDISH, ENGLISH
Religion: JEWISH, SUNNI MUSLIM, CHRISTIAN, DRUZE
Currency: SHEKEL
Organizations: UN

MAP PAGE: 43

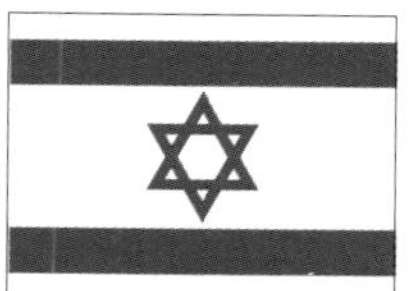

ISRAEL LIES ON the Mediterranean coast of southwest Asia. Beyond the coastal plain of Sharon are the hills and valleys of Judea and Samaria with the Galilee highlands to the north. In the east is the rift valley, which extends from Lake Tiberias to the Gulf of Aqaba and contains the Jordan river and Dead Sea. In the south is the Negev, a triangular semi-desert plateau. Most people live on the coastal plain or in northern and central areas. Much of Israel has warm summers and mild winters, during which most rain falls. Southern Israel is hot and dry. Agricultural production was boosted by the inclusion of the West Bank of the Jordan in 1967. Citrus fruit, vegetables and flowers are exported. Mineral resources are few but potash, bromine and some oil and gas are produced. Manufacturing makes the largest contribution to the economy. Israel produces finished diamonds, textiles, clothing and food products as well as chemical and metal products, military and transport equipment, electrical and electronic goods. Tourism and foreign aid are important to the economy.

ITALY

Status: REPUBLIC
Area: 301,245 sq km (116,311 sq mls)
Population: 57,057,000
Capital: ROME
Language: ITALIAN, ITALIAN DIALECTS
Religion: R.CATHOLIC
Currency: LIRA
Organizations: EU, OECD, UN

MAP PAGE: 104-105

MOST OF THE south European state of Italy occupies a peninsula that juts out into the Mediterranean Sea. It includes the main islands of Sicily and Sardinia and about 70 smaller islands in the surrounding seas. Italy is mountainous and dominated by two high ranges: the Alps, which form its northern border; and the Apennines, which run almost the full length of the peninsula. Many of Italy's mountains are of volcanic origin and its two active volcanoes are Vesuvius near Naples and Etna on Sicily. The main lowland area is the Po river valley in the northeast, which is the main agricultural and industrial area and is the most populous region. Italy has a Mediterranean climate with warm, dry summers and mild winters. Sicily and Sardinia are warmer and drier than the mainland. Northern Italy experiences colder, wetter winters, with heavy snow in the Alps. Italy's natural resources are limited. Only about 20 per cent of the land is suitable for cultivation. Some oil, natural gas and coal are produced, but most fuels and minerals used by industry must be imported. Italy has a fairly diversified economy. Agriculture flourishes, with cereals, wine, fruit (including olives) and vegetables the main crops. Italy is the world's largest wine producer. Cheese is also an important product. However, Italy is a net food importer. The north is the centre of Italian industry, especially around Turin, Milan and Genoa, while the south is largely agricultural with production based on smaller, less mechanized farms. Thus average income in the north is much higher than that in the south. Another feature of the Italian economy is the size of the state sector, which is much larger than that of other European Union countries. Italy's leading manufactures include industrial and office equipment, domestic appliances, cars, textiles, clothing, leather goods, chemicals and metal products and its famous brand names include Olivetti, Fiat and Benetton. Italy has a strong service sector. With over 25 million visitors a year, tourism is a major employer and accounts for 5 per cent of national income. Finance and banking are also important.

JAMAICA

Status: MONARCHY
Area: 10,991 sq km (4,244 sq mls)
Population: 2,411,000
Capital: KINGSTON
Language: ENGLISH, CREOLE
Religion: PROTESTANT, R.CATHOLIC, RASTAFARIAN
Currency: DOLLAR
Organizations: CARICOM, COMM., UN

MAP PAGE: 159

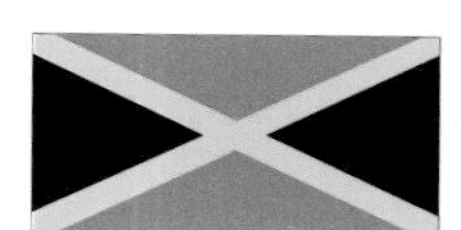

JAMAICA, THE THIRD largest Caribbean island, has beaches and densely populated coastal plains traversed by hills and plateaux rising to the forested Blue Mountains in the east. The climate is tropical, cooler and wetter on high ground. The economy is based on tourism, agriculture, mining and light manufacturing. Bauxite, alumina, sugar and bananas are the main exports. Jamaica depends on foreign aid.

JAPAN
Status: MONARCHY
Area: 377,727 sq km (145,841 sq mls)
Population: 124,536,000
Capital: TOKYO
Language: JAPANESE
Religion: SHINTOIST, BUDDHIST, CHRISTIAN
Currency: YEN
Organizations: OECD, UN

MAP PAGE: 28-29

JAPAN, WHICH LIES in the Pacific Ocean off the coast of east Asia, consists of four main islands - Hokkaido, Honshu, Shikoku and Kyushu - which extend northeast-southwest over 1,600 km (995 miles). It includes more than 3,000 smaller volcanic islands in the surrounding Sea of Japan, East China Sea and Pacific Ocean. The central island of Honshu occupies 60 per cent of the total land area and contains 80 per cent of the population, mostly in the east-central Kanto plain which includes Tokyo, Kawasaki and Yokohama. Behind the long and deeply indented coastline, nearly three quarters of Japan is mountainous and heavily forested. The most rugged range crosses Honshu and includes the country's highest point, Mount Fuji, which reaches a height of 3,776 m (12,388 ft). Japan has over 60 active volcanoes, and is subject to frequent major earthquakes, monsoons, typhoons and tidal waves. The climate is generally temperate maritime, with warm summers and mild winters, except in western Hokkaido and northwest Honshu, where the winters are very cold with heavy snow. Rain falls mainly in June and July, and typhoons sometimes occur in September. Japan has few natural resources. It has a limited land area of which only 14 per cent is suitable for cultivation, and production of its few industrial raw materials (chiefly coal, oil, natural gas and copper) is insufficient for its industry. Most raw materials must be imported, including about 90 per cent of energy requirements. Yet, in a fairly short space of time, Japan has become the world's second largest industrial economy. Its economic success is based on manufacturing, which employs one third of the workforce and accounts for one third of national output. Japan has a range of heavy and light industries centred mainly round the major ports of Yokohama, Osaka and Tokyo. It is the world's largest manufacturer of cars, motorcycles and merchant ships, and a major producer of steel, textiles, chemicals and cement. It is a leading producer of many consumer durables, such as washing machines, and electronic equipment, chiefly office equipment and computers. Recent years have seen the spread of Japanese business overseas, with many industrial plants sited in the European Union and the USA. Japan has a strong service sector, banking and finance are particularly important and Tokyo is one of the world's major stock exchanges. Owing to intensive agricultural production, Japan is 70 per cent self-sufficient in food. The main food crops are rice, barley, fruit, wheat and soya beans. Livestock raising (chiefly cattle, pigs and chickens) and fishing are also important. Japan has one of the largest fishing fleets in the world. In spite of its forestry resources, Japan has to import timber as well as food.

JERSEY
Status: UK TERRITORY
Area: 116 sq km (45 sq mls)
Population: 86,000
Capital: ST HELIER
Language: ENGLISH, FRENCH
Religion: PROTESTANT, R.CATHOLIC
Currency: POUND

MAP PAGE: 63

ONE OF THE Channel Islands lying off the west coast of the Cherbourg peninsula in northern France.

JORDAN
Status: MONARCHY
Area: 89,206 sq km (34,443 sq mls)
Population: 4,936,000
Capital: AMMAN
Language: ARABIC
Religion: SUNNI MUSLIM, CHRISTIAN, SHI'A MUSLIM
Currency: DINAR
Organizations: UN

MAP PAGE: 43

JORDAN, IN SOUTHWEST Asia, has a short coastline on the Gulf of Aqaba. Much of Jordan is rocky desert plateaux. In the west, behind a belt of hills, the land falls below sea level to the Dead Sea and Jordan river. Much of Jordan is hot and dry, the west is cooler and wetter and most people live in the northwest. Phosphates, potash, fertilizers, pharmaceuticals, fruit and vegetables are the main exports. Jordan relies upon tourism, workers' remittances and foreign aid, all of which were affected by the 1991 Gulf crisis.

KAZAKHSTAN
Status: REPUBLIC
Area: 2,717,300 sq km (1,049,155 sq mls)
Population: 16,956,000
Capital: ALMA-ATA
Language: KAZAKH, RUSSIAN, GERMAN, UKRAINIAN, UZBEK, TATAR
Religion: SUNNI MUSLIM, RUSSIAN ORTHODOX, PROTESTANT
Currency: TANGA
Organizations: CIS, UN

MAP PAGE: 46-47

STRETCHING ACROSS CENTRAL Asia, Kazakhstan covers a vast area of steppe land and semi-desert. The land is flat in the west rising to mountains in the southeast. The climate is continental and mainly dry. Agriculture and livestock rearing are the main activities, with cotton and tobacco the main cash crops. Kazakhstan is very rich in minerals, such as oil, natural gas, coal, iron ore, chromium, gold, lead and zinc. Mining, metallurgy, machine building and food processing are major industries.

KENYA
Status: REPUBLIC
Area: 582,646 sq km (224,961 sq mls)
Population: 28,113,000
Capital: NAIROBI
Language: SWAHILI (OFFICIAL), ENGLISH, MANY LOCAL LANGUAGES
Religion: R.CATHOLIC, PROTESTANT, TRAD.BELIEFS
Currency: SHILLING
Organizations: COMM., OAU, UN

MAP PAGE: 126-127

KENYA IS IN east Africa, on the Indian Ocean. Beyond the coastal plains the land rises to plateaux interrupted by volcanic mountains. The Rift Valley runs northwest of Nairobi to Lake Turkana. Most people live in central Kenya. Conditions are tropical on the coast, semi-desert in the north and savannah in the south. Agricultural products, chiefly tea and coffee, provide half export earnings. Light industry is important. Tourism is the main foreign exchange earner; oil refining and re-exports for landlocked neighbours are others.

KIRIBATI
Status: REPUBLIC
Area: 717 sq km (277 sq mls)
Population: 77,000
Capital: BAIRIKI
Language: I-KIRIBATI (GILBERTESE), ENGLISH
Religion: R.CATHOLIC, PROTESTANT, BAHA'I, MORMON
Currency: AUSTR. DOLLAR
Organizations: COMM.

MAP PAGE: 4-5

KIRIBATI COMPRISES 32 coral islands in the Gilbert, Phoenix and Line groups and the volcanic island of Banaba, which straddle the Equator in the Pacific Ocean. Most people live on the Gilbert islands, and the capital, Bairiki, is on Tarawa, one of the Gilbert Islands. The climate is hot, wetter in the north. Kiribati depends on subsistence farming and fishing. Copra and fish exports and licences for foreign fishing fleets are the main foreign exchange earners.

KUWAIT
Status: MONARCHY
Area: 17,818 sq km (6,880 sq mls)
Population: 1,433,000
Capital: KUWAIT CITY
Language: ARABIC
Religion: SUNNI MUSLIM, SHI'A MUSLIM, OTHER MUSLIM, CHRISTIAN, HINDU
Currency: DINAR
Organizations: OPEC, UN

MAP PAGE: 42

KUWAIT LIES ON the northwest shores of The Gulf in southwest Asia. It is mainly low-lying desert, with irrigated areas along the Bay of Kuwait where most people live. Summers are hot and dry, winters are cool with some rainfall. The oil industry, which accounts for 80 per cent of exports, has largely recovered from the damage caused by Iraq in 1991. Income is also derived from extensive overseas investments.

KYRGYZSTAN
Status: REPUBLIC
Area: 198,500 sq km (76,641 sq mls)
Population: 4,528,000
Capital: BISHKEK
Language: KIRGHIZ, RUSSIAN, UZBEK
Religion: SUNNI MUSLIM, RUSSIAN ORTHODOX
Currency: SOM
Organizations: CIS, UN

MAP PAGE: 47

A LANDLOCKED CENTRAL Asian state, Kyrgyzstan is rugged and mountainous, lying in the western Tien Shan range. Most people live in the valleys of the north and west. Summers are hot and winters cold. Agriculture (chiefly livestock farming) is the main activity. Coal, gold, antimony and mercury are produced. Manufactures include machinery, metals and food products. Disruption of Russian-dominated trade has caused economic problems.

LAOS
Status: REPUBLIC
Area: 236,800 sq km (91,429 sq mls)
Population: 4,605,000
Capital: VIENTIANE
Language: LAO, LOCAL LANGUAGES
Religion: BUDDHIST, TRAD.BELIEFS, R.CATHOLIC, SUNNI MUSLIM
Currency: KIP
Organizations: UN

MAP PAGE: 24-25

A LANDLOCKED COUNTRY in southeast Asia, Laos borders Vietnam, Cambodia, Thailand, Myanmar and China. Forested mountains and plateaux predominate. The climate is tropical monsoon. Most people live in the Mekong valley and the low plateau in the south, and grow food crops, chiefly rice. Electricity, timber, coffee and tin are exported. Foreign aid and investment and the opium trade are important.

LATVIA
Status: REPUBLIC
Area: 63,700 sq km (24,595 sq mls)
Population: 2,586,000
Capital: RIGA
Language: LATVIAN, RUSSIAN
Religion: PROTESTANT, R.CATHOLIC, RUSSIAN ORTHODOX
Currency: LAT
Organizations: UN

MAP PAGE: 54

LATVIA IS IN north Europe, on the Baltic Sea and Gulf of Riga. The land is flat near the coast but hilly with woods and lakes inland. Latvia has a modified continental climate. One third of the people live in Riga. Crop and livestock farming are important. Industry is varied but specialist products include telephones, diesel trains, buses and paper. Latvia has few natural resources. Economic priorities are creating a market economy and reducing economic dependence on Russia.

LEBANON
Status: REPUBLIC
Area: 10,452 sq km (4,036 sq mls)
Population: 2,806,000
Capital: BEIRUT
Language: ARABIC, FRENCH, ARMENIAN
Religion: SHI'A, SUNNI AND OTHER MUSLIM, PROTESTANT, R.CATHOLIC
Currency: POUND
Organizations: UN

MAP PAGE: 43

LEBANON LIES ON the Mediterranean coast of southwest Asia. Beyond the coastal strip, where most people live, are two parallel mountain ranges, separated by the Bekaa Valley. In general the climate is Mediterranean. Civil war crippled the traditional sectors of banking, commerce and tourism, but some fruit production and light industry survived. Reconstruction is under way.

LESOTHO
Status: MONARCHY
Area: 30,355 sq km (11,720 sq mls)
Population: 1,943,000
Capital: MASERU
Language: SESOTHO, ENGLISH, ZULU
Religion: R.CATHOLIC, PROTESTANT, TRAD.BELIEFS
Currency: LOTI
Organizations: COMM., OAU, SADC, UN

MAP PAGE: 131

LESOTHO IS A landlocked state surrounded by the Republic of South Africa. It is a mountainous country lying within the Drakensberg range. Most people live in the western lowlands and southern Orange and Caledon river valleys. In general Lesotho has hot moist summers and cool, dry winters, with lower temperatures in the mountains. Subsistence farming and herding are the main activities. Exports include livestock, vegetables, wool and mohair. The economy depends heavily on South Africa for transport links and employment.

LIBERIA
Status: REPUBLIC
Area: 111,369 sq km (43,000 sq mls)
Population: 2,640,000
Capital: MONROVIA
Language: ENGLISH, CREOLE, MANY LOCAL LANGUAGES
Religion: TRAD. BELIEFS, SUNNI MUSLIM, PROTESTANT, R.CATHOLIC
Currency: DOLLAR
Organizations: OAU, UN

MAP PAGE: 122

LIBERIA IS ON the Atlantic coast of west Africa. Beyond the coastal belt of sandy beaches and mangrove swamps the land rises to a forested plateau, with highlands along the Guinea border. A quarter of the population lives along the coast. The climate is hot with heavy rainfall. The 1989-93 civil war ruined the economy. Before the war exports included iron ore, diamonds and gold along with rubber, timber and coffee. Ship registration was a major foreign exchange earner. Liberia now relies on foreign aid.

LIBYA
Status: REPUBLIC
Area: 1,759,540 sq km (679,362 sq mls)
Population: 4,700,000
Capital: TRIPOLI
Language: ARABIC, BERBER
Religion: SUNNI MUSLIM, R.CATHOLIC
Currency: DINAR
Organizations: OAU, OPEC, UN

MAP PAGE: 118

LIBYA LIES ON the Mediterranean coast of north Africa. The desert plains and hills of the Sahara dominate the landscape and the climate is hot and dry. Most people live in cities near the coast, where the climate is cooler with moderate rainfall. Farming and herding, chiefly in the northwest, are important but the main industry is oil, which accounts for about 95 per cent of export earnings. There is some heavy industry. In 1993 the UN imposed economic sanctions because of alleged sponsorship of terrorism.

LIECHTENSTEIN
Status: MONARCHY
Area: 160 sq km (62 sq mls)
Population: 30,000
Capital: VADUZ
Language: GERMAN
Religion: R.CATHOLIC, PROTESTANT
Currency: SWISS FRANC
Organizations: UN

MAP PAGE: 83

A LANDLOCKED STATE between Switzerland and Austria in central Europe, Liechtenstein occupies the floodplains of the upper Rhine valley and part of the Austrian Alps. It has a temperate climate with cool winters. Dairy farming is important, but manufacturing is dominant. Major products include precision instruments, dentistry equipment, pharmaceuticals, ceramics and textiles. There is also some metal working. Finance, chiefly banking, is very important. Tourism and postal stamps provide additional revenue.

LITHUANIA
Status: REPUBLIC
Area: 65,200 sq km (25,174 sq mls)
Population: 3,730,000
Capital: VILNIUS
Language: LITHUANIAN, RUSSIAN, POLISH
Religion: R.CATHOLIC, PROTESTANT, RUSSIAN ORTHODOX
Currency: LITAS
Organizations: UN

MAP PAGE: 54

LITHUANIA IS IN north Europe, on the eastern shores of the Baltic Sea. It is mainly lowland with many lakes, small rivers and marshes. The climate is generally temperate. About 15 per cent of people live in Vilnius. Agriculture, fishing and forestry are important, but manufacturing dominates the economy. The main products are processed foods, light industrial goods, machinery and metalworking equipment. Progress towards a market economy is slow. The economy remains heavily dependent on Russia.

LUXEMBOURG
Status: MONARCHY
Area: 2,586 sq km (998 sq mls)
Population: 395,000
Capital: LUXEMBOURG
Language: LETZEBURGISH, GERMAN, FRENCH, PORTUGUESE
Religion: R.CATHOLIC, PROTESTANT
Currency: FRANC
Organizations: EU, OECD, UN

MAP PAGE: 69

LUXEMBOURG, A LANDLOCKED country in west Europe, borders Belgium, France and Germany. The hills and forests of the Ardennes dominate the north, with rolling pasture to the south, where the main towns, farms and industries are found. Summers are warm and winters mild, though colder in the north. The iron and steel industry is still important, but light industries (including textiles, chemicals and food products) are growing. Luxembourg is a major banking centre and the home base of key European Union institutions.

MACAU
Status: PORTUGUESE TERRITORY
Area: 17 sq km (7 sq mls)
Population: 388,000
Capital: MACAU
Language: CANTONESE, PORTUGUESE
Religion: BUDDHIST, R.CATHOLIC, PROTESTANT
Currency: PATACA

MAP PAGE: 33

AN ENCLAVE ON the south coast of China, Macau consists of an area of the mainland and the two islands of Taipa and Coloane. The territory is scheduled to revert to China in 1999.

MADAGASCAR
Status: REPUBLIC
Area: 587,041 sq km (226,658 sq mls)
Population: 13,854,000
Capital: ANTANANARIVO
Language: MALAGASY, FRENCH
Religion: TRAD.BELIEFS, R.CATHOLIC, PROTESTANT, SUNNI MUSLIM
Currency: FRANC
Organizations: OAU, UN

MAP PAGE: 129

MADAGASCAR AND ADJACENT islets lie off the east coast of south Africa. The world's fourth largest island is in the main a high plateau with a coastal strip to the east and scrubby plain to the west. The climate is tropical with heavy rainfall in the north and east. Most people live on the plateau. Exports include coffee, vanilla, cloves, sugar and shrimps. The main industries are agricultural processing, textile manufacturing, oil refining and mining (chiefly chromite). Tourism and foreign aid are important.

MADEIRA
Status: PORTUGUESE TERRITORY
Area: 794 sq km (307 sq mls)
Population: 253,000
Capital: FUNCHAL
Language: PORTUGUESE
Religion: R.CATHOLIC, PROTESTANT
Currency: PORT. ESCUDO

MAP PAGE: 96

AN ISLAND GROUP in the Atlantic Ocean to the southwest of Portugal. Tourism is important to the economy.

MALAWI
Status: REPUBLIC
Area: 118,484 sq km (45,747 sq mls)
Population: 9,135,000
Capital: LILONGWE
Language: ENGLISH (OFFICIAL), CHICHEWA, LOMWE
Religion: PROTESTANT, R.CATHOLIC, TRAD. BELIEFS, SUNNI MUSLIM
Currency: KWACHA
Organizations: COMM., OAU, SADC, UN

MAP PAGE: 127

LANDLOCKED MALAWI IN central Africa is a narrow hilly country at the southern end of the East African Rift Valley. One fifth of the country is covered by Lake Malawi, which lies above sea level. Most people live in the southern regions. The climate is mainly subtropical with varying rainfall. The economy is predominantly agricultural. Tobacco, tea and sugar are the main exports. Manufacturing involves mainly chemicals, textiles and agricultural products. Malawi relies heavily on foreign aid.

MALAYSIA
Status: FEDERATION
Area: 332,665 sq km (128,442 sq mls)
Population: 19,247,000
Capital: KUALA LUMPUR
Language: MALAY, ENGLISH, CHINESE, TAMIL, LOCAL LANGUAGES
Religion: SUNNI MUSLIM, BUDDHIST, HINDU, CHRISTIAN, TRAD. BELIEFS
Currency: DOLLAR (RINGGIT)
Organizations: ASEAN, COMM., UN

MAP PAGE: 20-21

THE FEDERATION OF Malaysia, in southeast Asia, comprises two regions, separated by the South China Sea. Peninsular Malaysia occupies the southern Malay peninsula, which has a chain of mountains dividing the eastern coastal strip from the wider plains to the west. To the east, the states of Sabah and Sarawak in the north of the island of Borneo are mainly rainforest-covered hills and mountains with mangrove swamps along the coast. Both regions have a tropical climate with heavy rainfall. About 80 per cent of the population lives in Peninsular Malaysia, mainly on the coasts. The country is rich in natural resources. It is the world's largest producer of tin, palm oil, pepper and tropical hardwoods, and a major producer of natural rubber, coconut and cocoa. It also has vast reserves of minerals and fuels. However high economic growth in recent years has come from manufacturing which now provides most exports and involves mainly processing industries, electronics assembly and engineering (chiefly car production). With over 7 million visitors a year, tourism is also a major industry.

PENINSULAR MALAYSIA
Status: STATE
Area: 131,585 sq km (50,805 sq mls)
Population: 14,942,697
Capital: KUALA LUMPUR

SABAH
Status: STATE
Area: 76,115 sq km (29,388 sq mls)
Population: 1,583,726
Capital: KOTA KINABALU

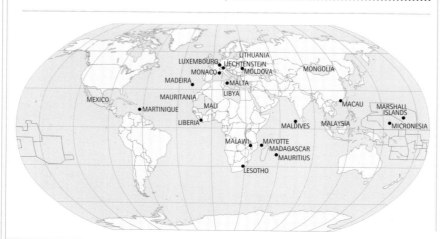

SARAWAK
Status: STATE
Area: 124,965 sq km (48,249 sq mls)
Population: 1,708,737
Capital: KUCHING

MALDIVES
Status: REPUBLIC
Area: 298 sq km (115 sq mls)
Population: 238,000
Capital: MALE
Language: DIVEHI (MALDIVIAN)
Religion: SUNNI MUSLIM
Currency: RUFIYAA
Organizations: COMM., UN

MAP PAGE: 135

THE MALDIVE ARCHIPELAGO comprises 1,190 coral atolls (202 of which are inhabited), in the Indian Ocean, southwest of India. The climate is hot, humid and monsoonal. The islands depend mainly on fishing and fish processing, light manufacturing (chiefly clothing) and tourism.

MALI
Status: REPUBLIC
Area: 1,240,140 sq km (478,821 sq mls)
Population: 10,135,000
Capital: BAMAKO
Language: FRENCH, BAMBARA, MANY LOCAL LANGUAGES
Religion: SUNNI MUSLIM, TRAD.BELIEFS, R.CATHOLIC
Currency: CFA FRANC
Organizations: OAU, UN

MAP PAGE: 122

A LANDLOCKED STATE in west Africa, Mali is low-lying, rising to mountains in the northeast. Northern regions lie within the Sahara desert. To the south, around the Niger river, are marshes and savannah grassland. Rainfall is unreliable. Most people live along the Niger and Senegal rivers. Exports include cotton and groundnuts. Some gold is produced. Mali relies heavily on foreign aid.

MALTA
Status: REPUBLIC
Area: 316 sq km (122 sq mls)
Population: 361,000
Capital: VALLETTA
Language: MALTESE, ENGLISH
Religion: R.CATHOLIC
Currency: LIRA
Organizations: COMM., UN

MAP PAGE: 111

THE ISLANDS OF Malta and Gozo lie in the Mediterranean Sea, off the coast of south Italy. Malta, the main island, has low hills and an indented coastline. Two thirds of the population lives in the Valletta area. The islands have hot, dry summers and mild winters. The main industries are tourism, ship building and repair, and export manufacturing (chiefly clothing). Vegetables, flowers, wine and tobacco are also exported.

MARSHALL ISLANDS
Status: REPUBLIC
Area: 181 sq km (70 sq mls)
Population: 52,000
Capital: DALAP-ULIGA-DARRIT

Language: MARSHALLESE, ENGLISH
Religion: PROTESTANT, R.CATHOLIC
Currency: US DOLLAR
Organizations: UN

MAP PAGE: 4

THE MARSHALL ISLANDS consist of over 1,000 atolls, islands and islets, within two chains, in the North Pacific Ocean. The main atolls are Majuro (home to half the population), Kwajalein, Jaluit, Enewetak and Bikini. The climate is tropical with heavy autumn rainfall. The islands depend on farming, fishing, tourism, financial services, and US aid and rent for a missile base.

MARTINIQUE
Status: FRENCH TERRITORY
Area: 1,079 sq km (417 sq mls)
Population: 371,000
Capital: FORT-DE-FRANCE
Language: FRENCH, FRENCH CREOLE
Religion: R.CATHOLIC, PROTESTANT, HINDU, TRAD.BELIEFS
Currency: FRENCH FRANC

MAP PAGE: 159

MARTINIQUE, ONE OF the Caribbean's Windward Islands, has volcanic peaks in the north, a populous central plain, and hills and beaches in the south. The tropical island depends on fruit growing (chiefly bananas), oil refining, rum distilling, tourism and French aid.

MAURITANIA
Status: REPUBLIC
Area: 1,030,700 sq km (397,955 sq mls)
Population: 2,161,000
Capital: NOUAKCHOTT
Language: ARABIC, FRENCH, LOCAL LANGUAGES
Religion: SUNNI MUSLIM
Currency: OUGUIYA
Organizations: OAU, UN

MAP PAGE: 122

MAURITANIA IS ON the Atlantic coast of northwest Africa and lies almost entirely within the Sahara desert. Oases and a fertile strip along the Senegal river to the south are the only areas suitable for cultivation. The climate is generally hot and dry. A quarter of Mauritanians live in Nouakchott. Livestock rearing and subsistence farming are important. The economy is heavily dependent on iron ore mining and fishing, which together account for 90 per cent of export earnings, and foreign aid.

MAURITIUS
Status: REPUBLIC
Area: 2,040 sq km (788 sq mls)
Population: 1,098,000
Capital: PORT LOUIS
Language: ENGLISH, FRENCH CREOLE, HINDI, INDIAN LANGUAGES
Religion: HINDU, R.CATHOLIC, SUNNI MUSLIM, PROTESTANT
Currency: RUPEE
Organizations: COMM., OAU, UN

MAP PAGE: 127

THE STATE COMPRISES Mauritius, Rodrigues and some 20 small islands in the Indian Ocean, east of Madagascar. The main island of Mauritius is volcanic in origin and has a coral coast rising to a central plateau. Most people live on the west side of the island. The climate is warm and humid. Mauritius depends mainly on sugar production, light manufacturing (chiefly clothing) and tourism.

MAYOTTE
Status: FRENCH TERRITORY
Area: 373 sq km (144 sq mls)
Population: 104,000
Capital: DZAOUDZI
Language: MAHORIAN (SWAHILI), FRENCH
Religion: SUNNI MUSLIM, R.CATHOLIC
Currency: FRENCH FRANC

MAP PAGE: 127

LYING IN THE Indian Ocean off the east coast of Central Africa, Mayotte is part of the Comoros Archipelago, but remains a French Territory.

MEXICO
Status: REPUBLIC
Area: 1,972,545 sq km (761,604 sq mls)
Population: 91,261,000
Capital: MEXICO CITY
Language: SPANISH, MANY AMERINDIAN LANGUAGES
Religion: R.CATHOLIC, PROTESTANT
Currency: PESO
Organizations: NAFTA, OECD, UN

MAP PAGE: 156-157

THE LARGEST COUNTRY in central America, Mexico extends southwards from the USA to Guatemala and Belize, and from the Pacific Ocean to the Gulf of Mexico. The greater part of the country is high plateaus flanked by the western and eastern Sierra Madre mountain ranges. The principal lowland is the Yucatán peninsula in the southeast. The climate varies with latitude and altitude: hot and humid in the lowlands, warm in the plateaux and cool with cold winters in the mountains. The north is arid, while the far south has heavy rainfall. Mexico City is one of the world's largest conurbations and the centre of trade and industry. Agriculture involves a quarter of the workforce and exports include coffee, fruit and vegetables. Shrimps are also exported and timber production is important for allied industries. Mexico is rich in minerals, including copper, zinc, lead and sulphur, and is the world's leading producer of silver. It is one of the world's largest producers of oil, from vast oil and gas resources in the Gulf of Mexico. The oil and petrochemical industries are still the mainstay, but a variety of manufactures are now produced including iron and steel, motor vehicles, textiles and electronic goods. Tourism is growing in importance.

FEDERATED STATES OF MICRONESIA
Status: REPUBLIC
Area: 701 sq km (271 sq mls)
Population: 105,000
Capital: PALIKIR
Language: ENGLISH, TRUKESE, POHNPEIAN, LOCAL LANGUAGES
Religion: PROTESTANT, R.CATHOLIC
Currency: US DOLLAR
Organizations: UN

MAP PAGE: 4

MICRONESIA COMPRISES 607 atolls and islands in the Carolines group in the North Pacific Ocean. A third of the population lives on Pohnpei. The climate is tropical with

heavy rainfall. Fishing and subsistence farming are the main activities. Copra and fish are the main exports. Income also derives from tourism and the licensing of foreign fishing fleets. The islands depend on US aid.

MOLDOVA
Status: REPUBLIC
Area: 33,700 sq km (13,012 sq mls)
Population: 4,356,000
Capital: CHIŞINĂU
Language: ROMANIAN, RUSSIAN, UKRAINIAN, GAGAUZ
Religion: MOLDOVAN ORTHODOX, RUSSIAN ORTHODOX
Currency: LEU
Organizations: CIS, UN

MAP PAGE: 51

MOLDOVA IS IN east Europe, sandwiched between Romania and Ukraine. It consists of hilly steppe land, drained by the Prut and Dnestr rivers; the latter provides access to the Black Sea through Ukrainian territory. Moldova has long hot summers and mild winters. The economy is mainly agricultural, with tobacco, wine and fruit the chief products. Food processing and textiles are the main industries. Ethnic tension, which erupted into civil war in 1992, has slowed economic reform.

MONACO
Status: MONARCHY
Area: 2 sq km (1 sq mls)
Population: 31,000
Capital: MONACO
Language: FRENCH, MONEGASQUE, ITALIAN
Religion: R.CATHOLIC
Currency: FRENCH FRANC
Organizations: UN

MAP PAGE: 91

THE PRINCIPALITY, IN south Europe, occupies a rocky peninsula and a strip of land on France's Mediterranean coast. It depends on service industries (chiefly tourism, banking and finance) and light industry.

MONGOLIA
Status: REPUBLIC
Area: 1,565,000 sq km (604,250 sq mls)
Population: 2,318,000
Capital: ULAN BATOR
Language: KHALKA (MONGOLIAN), KAZAKH, LOCAL LANGUAGES
Religion: BUDDHIST, SUNNI MUSLIM, TRAD.BELIEFS
Currency: TUGRIK
Organizations: UN

MAP PAGE: 26-27

MONGOLIA IS A landlocked country in east Asia between Russia and China. Much of it is high steppe land, with mountains and lakes in the west and north. In the south is the Gobi desert. Mongolia has long, cold winters and short, mild summers. A quarter of the population lives in the capital. Mongolia is rich in minerals and fuels. Copper accounts for half export earnings. Livestock breeding and agricultural processing are important. The demise of the Soviet Union caused economic problems and Mongolia depends on foreign aid.

MONTSERRAT

Status: UK TERRITORY
Area: 100 sq km (39 sq mls)
Population: 11,000
Capital: PLYMOUTH
Language: ENGLISH
Religion: PROTESTANT, R.CATHOLIC
Currency: E. CARIB. DOLLAR
Organizations: CARICOM

MAP PAGE: 159

MOROCCO

Status: MONARCHY
Area: 446,550 sq km (172,414 sq mls)
Population: 26,069,000
Capital: RABAT
Language: ARABIC, BERBER, FRENCH, SPANISH
Religion: SUNNI MUSLIM, R.CATHOLIC
Currency: DIRHAM
Organizations: UN

MAP PAGE: 120

L YING IN THE northwest corner of Africa, Morocco has both Atlantic and Mediterranean coasts. The Atlas ranges separate the arid south and disputed Western Sahara from the fertile regions of the west and north, which have a milder climate. Most Moroccans live on the Atlantic coastal plain. The economy is based mainly on agriculture, phosphate mining and tourism. Manufacturing (chiefly textiles and clothing) and fishing are important.

MOZAMBIQUE

Status: REPUBLIC
Area: 799,380 sq km (308,642 sq mls)
Population: 15,583,000
Capital: MAPUTO
Language: PORTUGUESE, MAKUA, TSONGA, MANY LOCAL LANGUAGES
Religion: TRAD.BELIEFS, R.CATHOLIC, SUNNI MUSLIM
Currency: METICAL
Organizations: OAU, SADC, UN

MAP PAGE: 129

M OZAMBIQUE LIES ON the east coast of southern Africa. The land is mainly a savannah plateau drained by the Zambezi and other rivers, with highlands to the north. Most people live on the coast or in the river valleys. In general the climate is tropical with winter rainfall, but droughts occur. Reconstruction began in 1992 after 16 years of civil war. The economy is based on agriculture and trade. Exports include shrimps, cashews, cotton and sugar, but Mozambique relies heavily on aid.

MYANMAR

Status: REPUBLIC
Area: 676,577 sq km (261,228 sq mls)
Population: 44,596,000
Capital: RANGOON
Language: BURMESE, SHAN, KAREN, LOCAL LANGUAGES
Religion: BUDDHIST, SUNNI MUSLIM, PROTESTANT, R.CATHOLIC
Currency: KYAT
Organizations: UN

MAP PAGE: 24-25

M YANMAR IS IN southeast Asia, on the Bay of Bengal and Andaman Sea. Most people live in the valley and delta of the Irrawaddy river, which is flanked on three sides by mountains and high plateaux. The climate is hot and monsoonal, and rainforest covers much of the land. Most people depend on agriculture. Exports include teak and rice. Myanmar is rich in oil and gemstones. Political unrest has affected economic development.

NAMIBIA

Status: REPUBLIC
Area: 824,292 sq km (318,261 sq mls)
Population: 1,461,000
Capital: WINDHOEK
Language: ENGLISH, AFRIKAANS, GERMAN, OVAMBO
Religion: PROTESTANT, R.CATHOLIC
Currency: DOLLAR
Organizations: COMM., OAU, SADC, UN

MAP PAGE: 128

N AMIBIA LIES ON the Atlantic coast of southern Africa. Mountain ranges separate the coastal Namib Desert from the interior plateau, bordered to the south and east by the Kalahari desert. Namibia is hot and dry, but some summer rain falls in the north which supports crops, herds and most of the population. The economy is based mainly on agriculture and diamond and uranium mining. Fishing is increasingly important.

NAURU

Status: REPUBLIC
Area: 21 sq km (8 sq mls)
Population: 10,000
Capital: YAREN
Language: NAURUAN, GILBERTESE, ENGLISH
Religion: PROTESTANT, R.CATHOLIC
Currency: AUSTR. DOLLAR
Organizations: COMM.

MAP PAGE: 4

N AURU IS A coral island in the South Pacific Ocean, with a fertile coastal strip, a barren central plateau and a tropical climate. The economy is based on phosphate mining, but reserves are near exhaustion.

NEPAL

Status: MONARCHY
Area: 147,181 sq km (56,827 sq mls)
Population: 20,812,000
Capital: KATHMANDU
Language: NEPALI, MAITHILI, BHOJPURI, ENGLISH, MANY LOCAL LANGUAGES
Religion: HINDU, BUDDHIST, SUNNI MUSLIM
Currency: RUPEE
Organizations: UN

MAP PAGE: 37

T HE SOUTH ASIAN country of Nepal lies in the southern Himalayas between India and China. High mountains (including Everest) dominate northern Nepal. Most people live in the temperate central valleys and subtropical southern plains. The economy is based largely on agriculture and forestry. Manufacturing (chiefly textiles) and tourism are important. Nepal relies upon foreign aid.

NETHERLANDS

Status: MONARCHY
Area: 41,526 sq km (16,033 sq mls)
Population: 15,287,000
Capital: AMSTERDAM
Language: DUTCH, FRISIAN, TURKISH
Religion: R.CATHOLIC, PROTESTANT, SUNNI MUSLIM
Currency: GUILDER
Organizations: EU, OECD, UN

MAP PAGE: 68-69

T HE NETHERLANDS LIES on the North Sea coast of west Europe. Apart from hills in the far southeast, the land is flat and low-lying, much of it below sea level. The coastal region contains the delta of five rivers and polders (reclaimed land), protected by sand dunes, dikes and canals. The climate is temperate, with cool summers and mild winters. Rainfall is spread evenly throughout the year. The Netherlands is a densely populated country, with the majority of people living in the western Amsterdam-Rotterdam-The Hague area. Horticulture and dairy farming are important activities, with exports of eggs, butter and cheese. The Netherlands is Europe's leading producer and exporter of natural gas from reserves in the North Sea, but otherwise lacks raw materials. The economy is based mainly on international trade and manufacturing industry. Industrial sites are centred mainly around the port of Rotterdam. The chief industries produce food products, chemicals, machinery, electric and electronic goods and transport equipment. Financial services and tourism are important.

NETHERLANDS ANTILLES

Status: NETHERLANDS TERRITORY
Area: 800 sq km (309 sq mls)
Population: 195,000
Capital: WILLEMSTAD
Language: DUTCH, PAPIAMENTO
Religion: R.CATHOLIC, PROTESTANT
Currency: GUILDER

MAP PAGE: 159

T HE TERRITORY COMPRISES two separate island groups: Curacao and Bonaire off the coast of the northern coast of South America, and Saba, Sint Eustatius and the southern part of Sint Maarten in the northern Lesser Antilles.

NEW CALEDONIA

Status: FRENCH TERRITORY
Area: 19,058 sq km (7,358 sq mls)
Population: 179,000
Capital: NOUMÉA
Language: FRENCH, LOCAL LANGUAGES
Religion: R.CATHOLIC, PROTESTANT, SUNNI MUSLIM
Currency: PACIFIC FRANC

MAP PAGE: 6

A N ISLAND GROUP, lying in the southwest Pacific, with a sub-tropical climate. The economy is based on nickel mining, tourism and agriculture.

NEW ZEALAND

Status: MONARCHY
Area: 270,534 sq km (104,454 sq mls)
Population: 3,451,000
Capital: WELLINGTON
Language: ENGLISH, MAORI
Religion: PROTESTANT, R.CATHOLIC
Currency: DOLLAR
Organizations: COMM., OECD, UN

MAP PAGE: 8-9

N EW ZEALAND, IN Australasia, comprises two main islands separated by the narrow Cook Strait, and a number of smaller islands. North Island, where three quarters of the population lives, has mountain ranges, broad fertile valleys and a volcanic central plateau with hot springs and two active volcanoes. South Island is also mountainous, the Southern Alps running its entire length. The only major lowland area is the Canterbury Plains in the east. The climate is generally temperate, though South Island has cooler winters with upland snow. Rainfall is distributed throughout the year. Farming is the mainstay of the economy. New Zealand is one of the world's leading producers of meat (beef, lamb and mutton), wool and dairy products. Specialist foods, such as kiwi fruit, and fish are also important. Coal, oil and natural gas are produced, but hydroelectric and geothermal power provide much of the country's energy needs. Other industries produce timber, wood pulp, iron, aluminium, machinery and chemicals. Tourism is the largest foreign exchange earner.

NICARAGUA

Status: REPUBLIC
Area: 130,000 sq km (50,193 sq mls)
Population: 4,265,000
Capital: MANAGUA
Language: SPANISH, AMERINDIAN LANGUAGES
Religion: R.CATHOLIC, PROTESTANT
Currency: CÓRDOBA
Organizations: UN

MAP PAGE: 157

N ICARAGUA LIES AT the heart of Central America, with both Pacific and Caribbean coasts. Mountain ranges separate the east, which is largely jungle, from the more developed western regions, which include Lake Nicaragua and some active volcanoes. The highest land is in the north. The climate is tropical. The economy is largely agricultural.

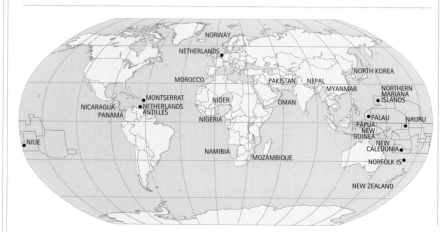

Traditional exports include cotton, coffee, bananas and gold. The aid-dependent economy has suffered from civil war (1978-89) and US sanctions.

NIGER
Status: REPUBLIC
Area: 1,267,000 sq km (489,191 sq mls)
Population: 8,361,000
Capital: NIAMEY
Language: FRENCH (OFFICIAL), HAUSA, FULANI, LOCAL LANGUAGES
Religion: SUNNI MUSLIM, TRAD.BELIEFS
Currency: CFA FRANC
Organizations: OAU, UN

MAP PAGE: 123

A LANDLOCKED STATE of west Africa, Niger lies mostly within the Sahara desert, but with savannah land in the south and Niger valley. The Air massif dominates central regions. Much of the country is hot and dry. The south has some summer rainfall, though droughts occur. The economy depends on subsistence farming and herding, uranium exports and foreign aid.

NIGERIA
Status: REPUBLIC
Area: 923,768 sq km (356,669 sq mls)
Population: 105,264,000
Capital: ABUJA
Language: ENGLISH, CREOLE, HAUSA, YORUBA, IBO, FULANI
Religion: SUNNI MUSLIM, PROTESTANT, R.CATHOLIC, TRAD. BELIEFS
Currency: NAIRA
Organizations: COMM., OAU, OPEC, UN

MAP PAGE: 123

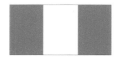

N IGERIA IS IN west Africa, on the Gulf of Guinea, and is the most populous country in the African continent. The Niger delta dominates coastal areas, fringed with sandy beaches, mangrove swamps and lagoons. Inland is a belt of rainforest that gives way to woodland or savannah on high plateaux. The far north is the semi-desert edge of the Sahara. The climate is tropical with heavy summer rainfall in the south but low rainfall in the north. Most people live in the coastal lowlands or in western Nigeria. About half the workforce is involved in agriculture, mainly growing subsistence crops, and Nigeria is virtually self-sufficient in food. Cocoa and rubber are the only significant export crops. The economy is heavily dependent on vast oil resources in the Niger delta and shallow offshore waters, which account for about 90 per cent of export earnings. Nigeria also has natural gas reserves and some mineral deposits, but these are as yet largely undeveloped. Industry involves mainly oil refining, chemicals (chiefly fertilizer), agricultural processing, textiles, steel manufacture and vehicle assembly. Economic mismanagement in the oil boom of the 1970s and political instability have left Nigeria with a heavy debt, poverty and rising unemployment.

NIUE
Status: NEW ZEALAND TERRITORY
Area: 258 sq km (100 sq mls)
Population: 2,000
Capital: ALOFI
Language: ENGLISH, POLYNESIAN (NIUEAN)
Religion: PROTESTANT, R.CATHOLIC
Currency: NZ DOLLAR

MAP PAGE: 5

NORFOLK ISLAND
Status: AUSTRALIAN TERRITORY
Area: 35 sq km (14 sq mls)
Population: 2,000
Capital: KINGSTON
Language: ENGLISH
Religion: PROTESTANT, R.CATHOLIC
Currency: AUSTR. DOLLAR

MAP PAGE: 11

NORTH KOREA
Status: REPUBLIC
Area: 120,538 sq km (46,540 sq mls)
Population: 23,048,000
Capital: PYONGYANG
Language: KOREAN
Religion: TRAD.BELIEFS, CHONDOIST, BUDDHIST, CONFUCIAN, TAOIST
Currency: WON
Organizations: UN

MAP PAGE: 31

O CCUPYING THE NORTHERN half of the Korean peninsula in east Asia, North Korea is a rugged and mountainous country. The principal lowlands and the main agricultural areas are the Pyongyang and Chaeryong plains in the southwest. More than half the population lives in urban areas, mainly on the coastal plains, which are wider along the Yellow Sea to the west than the Sea of Japan to the east. North Korea has a continental climate, with cold, dry winters and hot, wet summers. About half the workforce is involved in agriculture, mainly growing food crops on cooperative farms. A variety of minerals and ores, chiefly iron ore, are mined and are the basis of the country's heavy industry. Exports include minerals (chiefly lead, magnesite and zinc) and metal products (chiefly iron and steel). North Korea depends heavily on aid, but has suffered since support from Russia and China was ended in in 1991 and 1993 respectively. Agricultural, mining and maufacturing output have fallen. Living standards are much lower than in South Korea from which it was separated in 1945.

NORTHERN MARIANA ISLANDS
Status: US TERRITORY
Area: 477 sq km (184 sq mls)
Population: 53,000
Capital: SAIPAN
Language: ENGLISH, CHAMORRO, TAGALOG, LOCAL LANGUAGES
Religion: R.CATHOLIC, PROTESTANT
Currency: US DOLLAR

MAP PAGE: 21

A CHAIN OF islands in the Western Pacific Ocean, tourism is increasingly important to the economy.

NORWAY
Status: MONARCHY
Area: 323,878 sq km (125,050 sq mls)
Population: 4,312,000
Capital: OSLO
Language: NORWEGIAN
Religion: PROTESTANT, R.CATHOLIC
Currency: KRONE
Organizations: OECD, UN

MAP PAGE: 56-57

A COUNTRY OF NORTH Europe, Norway stretches along the north and west coasts of Scandinavia, from the Arctic Ocean to the North Sea. Its extensive coastline is indented

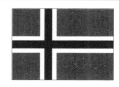

with fjords and fringed with many islands. Inland, the terrain is mountainous, with coniferous forests and lakes in the south. The only major lowland areas are along the southern North Sea and Skagerrak coasts, where most people live. The climate on the west coast is modified by the North Atlantic Drift. Inland, summers are warmer but winters are colder. Norway has vast petroleum and natural gas resources in the North Sea. It is west Europe's leading producer of oil and gas, which account for over 40 per cent of export earnings. Related industries include engineering (such as oil and gas platforms) and petrochemicals. More traditional industries process local raw materials: fish, timber and minerals. Agriculture is limited, but fishing and fish farming are important. Norway is the world's leading exporter of salmon. Merchant shipping and tourism are major sources of foreign exchange.

OMAN
Status: MONARCHY
Area: 271,950 sq km (105,000 sq mls)
Population: 1,992,000
Capital: MUSCAT
Language: ARABIC, BALUCHI, FARSI, SWAHILI, INDIAN LANGUAGES
Religion: IBADHI MUSLIM, SUNNI MUSLIM
Currency: RIAL
Organizations: UN

MAP PAGE: 41

T HE SULTANATE OF southwest Asia occupies the southeast coast of Arabia and an enclave north of the United Arab Emirates. Oman is a desert land, with mountains in the north and south. The climate is hot and mainly dry. Most people live on the coastal strip on the Gulf of Oman. The majority depends on farming and fishing, but the oil and gas industries dominate the economy. Copper is mined.

PAKISTAN
Status: REPUBLIC
Area: 803,940 sq km (310,403 sq mls)
Population: 122,802,000
Capital: ISLAMABAD
Language: URDU (OFFICIAL), PUNJABI, SINDHI, PUSHTU, ENGLISH
Religion: SUNNI MUSLIM, SHI'A MUSLIM, CHRISTIAN, HINDU
Currency: RUPEE
Organizations: COMM., UN

MAP PAGE: 39

P AKISTAN IS IN the northwest part of the Indian subcontinent in south Asia, on the Arabian Sea. Eastern and southern Pakistan are dominated by the great basin drained by the Indus river system. It is the main agricultural area and contains most of the population. To the north the land rises to the mountains of the Karakoram and part of the Hindu Kush and Himalayas. The west is semi-desert plateaux and mountain ranges. The climate ranges between dry desert and polar ice cap. However, temperatures are generally warm and rainfall is monsoonal. Agriculture is the main sector of the economy, employing about half the workforce and accounting for over two thirds of export earnings. Cultivation is based on extensive irrigation schemes. Pakistan is one of the world's leading producers of cotton and an important exporter of rice. However, much of the country's food needs must be imported. Pakistan produces natural gas and has a variety of mineral deposits including coal and

gold, but they are little developed. The main industries are textiles and clothing manufacture and food processing, with fabrics and ready-made clothing the leading exports. Pakistan also produces leather goods, fertilizers, chemicals, paper and precision instruments. The country depends heavily upon foreign aid and remittances from Pakistanis working abroad.

PALAU
Status: REPUBLIC
Area: 497 sq km (192 sq mls)
Population: 16,000
Capital: KOROR
Language: PALAUAN, ENGLISH
Religion: R.CATHOLIC, PROTESTANT, TRAD.BELIEFS
Currency: US DOLLAR
Organizations: UN

MAP PAGE: 23

P ALAU COMPRISES OVER 300 islands in the western Carolines group of the North Pacific Ocean. Two thirds of the people live on Koror. The climate is tropical. Palau depends on farming, fishing, tourism and US aid.

PANAMA
Status: REPUBLIC
Area: 77,082 sq km (29,762 sq mls)
Population: 2,563,000
Capital: PANAMA CITY
Language: SPANISH, ENGLISH CREOLE, AMERINDIAN LANGUAGES
Religion: R.CATHOLIC, PROTESTANT, SUNNI MUSLIM, BAHA'I
Currency: BALBOA
Organizations: UN

MAP PAGE: 157

P ANAMA IS THE most southerly state in Central America and has Pacific and Caribbean coasts. It is hilly, with mountains in the west and jungle near the Colombian border. The climate is tropical. Most people live on the drier Pacific side. The economy is based mainly on services related to the canal, shipping, banking and tourism. Exports include bananas, shrimps, sugar and petroleum products.

PAPUA NEW GUINEA
Status: MONARCHY
Area: 462,840 sq km (178,704 sq mls)
Population: 3,922,000
Capital: PORT MORESBY
Language: ENGLISH, TOK PISIN (PIDGIN), LOCAL LANGUAGES
Religion: PROTESTANT, R.CATHOLIC, TRAD.BELIEFS
Currency: KINA
Organizations: COMM., UN

MAP PAGE: 6

P APUA NEW GUINEA, in Australasia, occupies the eastern half of New Guinea and includes many island groups. Papua New Guinea has a forested and mountainous interior, bordered by swampy plains, and a tropical monsoon climate. Most of the workforce are farmers. Timber, copra, coffee and cocoa are important, but exports are dominated by minerals, chiefly copper and gold. The country depends on foreign aid.

PARAGUAY

Status: REPUBLIC
Area: 406,752 sq km (157,048 sq mls)
Population: 4,643,000
Capital: ASUNCIÓN
Language: SPANISH, GUARANÍ
Religion: R.CATHOLIC, PROTESTANT
Currency: GUARANÍ
Organizations: UN

MAP PAGE: 165

PARAGUAY IS A landlocked country in central South America, bordering Bolivia, Brazil and Argentina. The river Paraguay separates a sparsely populated western zone of marsh and flat alluvial plains from a more developed, hilly and forested region to the east. The climate is subtropical. The mainstay of the economy is agriculture and agricultural processing. Exports include cotton, soya bean and edible oil products, timber and meat. The largest hydro-electric dam in the world is at Itaipú on the river Paraná.

PERU

Status: REPUBLIC
Area: 1,285,216 sq km (496,225 sq mls)
Population: 22,454,000
Capital: LIMA
Language: SPANISH, QUECHUA, AYMARA
Religion: R.CATHOLIC, PROTESTANT
Currency: SOL
Organizations: UN

MAP PAGE: 162, 164

PERU LIES ON the Pacific coast of South America. Most people live on the coastal strip and the slopes of the high Andes. East of the Andes is high plateau country and the Amazon rainforest. The coast is temperate with low rainfall, while the east is hot, humid and wet. Agriculture involves one third of the workforce. Sugar, cotton, coffee and, illegally, coca are the main cash crops. Fishmeal and timber are also important, but copper, zinc, lead, gold, silver, petroleum and its products are the main exports.

PHILIPPINES

Status: REPUBLIC
Area: 300,000 sq km (115,831 sq mls)
Population: 65,649,000
Capital: MANILA
Language: ENGLISH, FILIPINO (TAGALOG), CEBUANO
Religion: R.CATHOLIC, AGLIPAYAN, SUNNI MUSLIM, PROTESTANT
Currency: PESO
Organizations: ASEAN, UN

MAP PAGE: 23

THE PHILIPPINES, IN southeast Asia, consists of 7,100 islands and atolls lying between the South China Sea and the Pacific

Ocean. The islands of Luzon and Mindanao occupy two thirds of the land area. They and nine other fairly large islands are mountainous and forested. There are ten active volcanoes and earthquakes are common. Most people live in the intermontane plains on the larger islands or on the coastal strips. The climate is hot and humid with heavy monsoonal rainfall. Coconuts, sugar, pineapples and bananas are the main agricultural exports. Fish and timber are also important. The Philippines produces copper, gold, silver, chromium and nickel as well as oil, though geothermal power is also used. The main industries process raw materials and manufacture electrical and electronic equipment and components, footwear and clothing, textiles and furniture. Tourism is being encouraged. Foreign aid and remittances from workers abroad are important to the economy, which faces problems of high population growth rate and high unemployment.

PITCAIRN ISLAND

Status: UK TERRITORY
Area: 45 sq km (17 sq mls)
Population: 71
Capital: ADAMSTOWN
Language: ENGLISH
Religion: PROTESTANT
Currency: DOLLAR

MAP PAGE: 7

AN ISLAND IN the southeast Pacific Ocean, originally settled by mutineers from HMS Bounty. Three uninhabited islands are included in the territory.

POLAND

Status: REPUBLIC
Area: 312,683 sq km (120,728 sq mls)
Population: 38,459,000
Capital: WARSAW
Language: POLISH, GERMAN
Religion: R.CATHOLIC, POLISH ORTHODOX
Currency: ZŁOTY
Organizations: UN

MAP PAGE: 76–77

POLAND LIES ON the Baltic coast of central Europe. The Oder and Vistula deltas dominate the coast, fringed with sand dunes. Inland much of Poland is low-lying (part of the North European plain), with woods and lakes. In the south the land rises to the Sudeten and western Carpathian mountains which form the borders with the Czech Republic and Slovakia respectively. The climate is continental, with warm summers and cold winters. Conditions are milder in the west and on the coast. A third of the workforce is involved in agriculture, forestry and fishing. Agricultural exports include livestock products and sugar. The

economy is heavily industrialized, with mining and manufacturing accounting for 40 per cent of national income. Poland is one of the world's major producers of coal. It also produces copper, zinc, lead, nickel, sulphur and natural gas. The main industries are ship building, car manufacture, metal and chemical production. The transition to a market economy has resulted in 15 per cent unemployment and economic hardship.

PORTUGAL

Status: REPUBLIC
Area: 88,940 sq km (34,340 sq mls)
Population: 9,860,000
Capital: LISBON
Language: PORTUGUESE
Religion: R.CATHOLIC, PROTESTANT
Currency: ESCUDO
Organizations: EU, OECD, UN

MAP PAGE: 96

PORTUGAL LIES IN the western part of the Iberian peninsula in southwest Europe, has an Atlantic coastline and is flanked by Spain to the north and east. North of the river Tagus are mostly highlands with forests of pine and cork. South of the river is undulating lowland. The climate in the north is cool and moist, influenced by the Atlantic Ocean. The south is warmer, with dry, mild winters. Most Portuguese live near the coast, with one third of the total population in Lisbon and Oporto. Agriculture, fishing and forestry involve 12 per cent of the workforce. Wines, tomatoes, citrus fruit, cork (Portugal is the world's largest producer) and sardines are important exports. Mining and manufacturing are the main sectors of the economy. Portugal produces pyrite, kaolin, zinc, tungsten and other minerals. Export manufactures include textiles, clothing and footwear, electrical machinery and transport equipment, cork and wood products, and chemicals. Service industries, chiefly tourism and banking, are important to the economy as are remittances from workers abroad.

PUERTO RICO

Status: US TERRITORY
Area: 9,104 sq km (3,515 sq mls)
Population: 3,620,000
Capital: SAN JUAN
Language: SPANISH, ENGLISH
Religion: R.CATHOLIC, PROTESTANT
Currency: US DOLLAR

MAP PAGE: 159

THE CARIBBEAN ISLAND of Puerto Rico has a forested, hilly interior, coastal plains and a tropical climate. Half the population lives in the San Juan area. The economy is based on export manufacturing (chiefly chemicals and electronics), tourism and agriculture.

QATAR

Status: MONARCHY
Area: 11,437 sq km (4,416 sq mls)
Population: 559,000
Capital: DOHA
Language: ARABIC, INDIAN LANGUAGES
Religion: SUNNI MUSLIM, CHRISTIAN, HINDU
Currency: RIYAL
Organizations: OPEC, UN

MAP PAGE: 39

THE EMIRATE OCCUPIES a peninsula that extends northwards from east-central Arabia into The Gulf in southwest Asia. The

peninsula is flat and barren with sand dunes and salt pans. The climate is hot and mainly dry. Most people live in the Doha area. The economy is heavily dependent on petroleum, natural gas and the oil-refining industry. Income also comes from overseas investment.

REPUBLIC OF IRELAND

Status: REPUBLIC
Area: 70,282 sq km (27,136 sq mls)
Population: 3,563,000
Capital: DUBLIN
Language: ENGLISH, IRISH
Religion: R.CATHOLIC, PROTESTANT
Currency: PUNT
Organizations: EU, OECD, UN

MAP PAGE: 67

A STATE IN northwest Europe, the Irish republic occupies some 80 per cent of the island of Ireland in the Atlantic Ocean. It is a lowland country of wide valleys, lakes and peat bogs, with isolated mountain ranges around the coast. The west coast is rugged and indented with many bays. The climate is mild due to the North Atlantic Drift and rainfall is plentiful, though highest in the west. Nearly 60 per cent of people live in urban areas, Dublin and Cork being the main cities. Agriculture, the traditional mainstay, involves mainly the production of livestock, meat and dairy products, which account for about 20 percent of exports. Manufactured goods form the bulk of exports. The main industries are electronics, pharmaceuticals and engineering as well as food processing, brewing and textiles. Natural resources include petroleum, natural gas, peat, lead and zinc. Services industries are expanding, with tourism a major foreign exchange earner. The economy could benefit from peace in Northern Ireland, which is part of the United Kingdom.

RÉUNION

Status: FRENCH TERRITORY
Area: 2,551 sq km (985 sq mls)
Population: 634,000
Capital: ST-DENIS
Language: FRENCH, FRENCH CREOLE
Religion: R.CATHOLIC
Currency: FRENCH FRANC

MAP PAGE: 127

THE INDIAN OCEAN island of Réunion is mountainous, with coastal lowlands and a warm climate. It depends heavily on sugar, tourism and French aid. Some uninhabited islets to the east are administered from Réunion.

ROMANIA

Status: REPUBLIC
Area: 237,500 sq km (91,699 sq mls)
Population: 22,755,000
Capital: BUCHAREST
Language: ROMANIAN, HUNGARIAN
Religion: ROMANIAN ORTHODOX, R.CATHOLIC, PROTESTANT
Currency: LEU
Organizations: UN

MAP PAGE: 112

ROMANIA LIES ON the Black Sea coast of east Europe. Mountains separate the Transylvanian plateau from the populous plains of the east and south and the Danube delta. The climate is continental. Romania is rich in fuels and metallic ores. Mining and manufacturing (chiefly metallurgy and machine building) predominate but agriculture is important. Pre-1989 mismanagement and economic reforms of the 1990s have caused hardship.

RUSSIAN FEDERATION

Status: REPUBLIC
Area: 17,075,400 sq km (6,592,849 sq mls)
Population: 147,760,000
Capital: MOSCOW
Language: RUSSIAN, TATAR, UKRAINIAN, LOCAL LANGUAGES
Religion: RUSSIAN ORTHODOX, SUNNI MUSLIM, OTHER CHRISTIAN, JEWISH
Currency: ROUBLE
Organizations: CIS, UN

MAP PAGE: 44-45

RUSSIA OCCUPIES MUCH of east Europe and all of north Asia, and is the world's largest state, nearly twice the size of the USA. It borders thirteen countries to the west and south and has long coastlines on the Arctic and Pacific oceans to the north and east. European Russia, which lies west of the Ural mountains, is part of the North European plain. To the south the land rises to uplands and the Caucasus Mountains on the border with Georgia and Azerbaijan. East of the Urals lies the flat Siberian plain. Much of central Siberia is plateaux. In the south is Lake Baikal, the world's deepest lake, and the Altai and Sayan ranges on the border with Azerbaijan and Mongolia. Eastern Siberia is rugged and mountainous with active volcanoes, notably in the Kamchatka peninsula. Russia's major rivers are the Volga in the west and the Ob, Yenisey, Lena and Amur in Siberia. The climate and vegetation range between Arctic tundra in the north and semi-arid steppe towards the Black and Caspian Sea coasts in the south. In general, the climate is continental with extreme temperatures. The majority of the population (the sixth largest in the world), industry and agriculture are concentrated in European Russia, but there has been increased migration to Siberia to exploit its vast natural resources. The economy is heavily dependent on exploitation of its raw materials and heavy industry. Russia has a wealth of mineral resources, though they are often difficult to exploit because of the climate. It is one of the world's leading producers of petroleum, natural gas and coal as well as iron and manganese ores, platinum, potash, asbestos and many precious and rare metals. Mining provides important exports and is the basis of heavy industry. Russia is a major producer of steel and machinery such as tractors, motor vehicles and generators, as well as chemicals and textiles. Other light industries are less important to the economy. Forests cover about 40 per cent of the land area and supply an important timber, paper and pulp industry. About 8 per cent of land is suitable for cultivation. However farming is generally inefficient and much of food needs, especially grains, must be imported. Fishing is important and Russia operates a large fleet throughout the world. Economic reforms begun in the late 1980s to liberalize the economy met with mixed success, largely because of political unrest. The transition to a free market economy, which was speeded up in the 1990s has been painful, with rising unemployment.

RWANDA

Status: REPUBLIC
Area: 26,338 sq km (10,169 sq mls)
Population: 7,554,000
Capital: KIGALI
Language: KINYARWANDA, FRENCH
Religion: R.CATHOLIC, TRAD.BELIEFS, PROTESTANT, SUNNI MUSLIM
Currency: FRANC
Organizations: OAU, UN

MAP PAGE: 127

A DENSELY POPULATED and landlocked state in east Africa, Rwanda consists mainly of mountains and plateaux to the east of the Rift Valley. The climate is warm with a summer dry season. Rwanda depends upon subsistence farming, coffee and tea exports, light industry and foreign aid, but the 1990-93 civil war and ethnic conflict have devastated the country.

ST HELENA

Status: UK TERRITORY
Area: 411 sq km (159 sq mls)
Population: 7,000
Capital: JAMESTOWN
Language: ENGLISH
Religion: PROTESTANT, R.CATHOLIC
Currency: POUND STERLING

MAP PAGE: 128

ST HELENA AND its dependencies, Ascension and Tristan da Cunha are isolated island groups lying in the south Atlantic Ocean. Ascension is over 1000 kilometres (620 miles) northwest of St Helena and Tristan da Cunha over 2000 kilometres (1240 miles) to the south.

ST KITTS-NEVIS

Status: MONARCHY
Area: 261 sq km (101 sq mls)
Population: 42,000
Capital: BASSETERRE
Language: ENGLISH, CREOLE
Religion: PROTESTANT, R.CATHOLIC
Currency: E. CARIB. DOLLAR
Organizations: CARICOM, COMM., UN

MAP PAGE: 157

ST KITTS-NEVIS are in the Leeward group in the Caribbean Sea. Both volcanic islands are mountainous and forested with sandy beaches and a warm, wet climate. Some 75 per cent of the population lives on St Kitts. Agriculture is the main activity, with sugar, molasses and sea island cotton the main products. Tourism and manufacturing (chiefly garments and electronic components) are important.

ST LUCIA

Status: MONARCHY
Area: 616 sq km (238 sq mls)
Population: 139,000
Capital: CASTRIES
Language: ENGLISH, FRENCH CREOLE
Religion: R.CATHOLIC, PROTESTANT
Currency: E. CARIB. DOLLAR
Organizations: CARICOM, COMM., UN

MAP PAGE: 157

ST LUCIA, PART OF the Windward group in the Caribbean Sea, is a volcanic island with forested mountains, hot springs, sandy beaches and a wet tropical climate. Agriculture is the main activity, with bananas accounting for over half export earnings. Tourism, agricultural processing and manufacturing (chiefly garments, cardboard boxes and electronic components) are increasingly important.

ST PIERRE AND MIQUELON

Status: FRENCH TERRITORY
Area: 242 sq km (93 sq mls)
Population: 6,000
Capital: ST-PIERRE
Language: FRENCH
Religion: R.CATHOLIC
Currency: FRENCH FRANC

MAP PAGE: 139

A GROUP OF islands off the south coast of Newfoundland in eastern Canada.

ST VINCENT AND THE GRENADINES

Status: MONARCHY
Area: 389 sq km (150 sq mls)
Population: 110,000
Capital: KINGSTOWN
Language: ENGLISH, CREOLE
Religion: PROTESTANT, R.CATHOLIC
Currency: E. CARIB. DOLLAR
Organizations: CARICOM, COMM., UN

MAP PAGE: 157

ST VINCENT, WHOSE TERRITORY includes 32 islets and cays in the Grenadines, is in the Windward Islands group in the Caribbean Sea. St Vincent is forested and mountainous, with an active volcano, Mount Soufrière. The climate is tropical and wet. The economy is based mainly on agriculture and tourism. Bananas account for about half export earnings. Arrowroot is also important.

SAN MARINO

Status: REPUBLIC
Area: 61 sq km (24 sq mls)
Population: 24,000
Capital: SAN MARINO
Language: ITALIAN
Religion: R.CATHOLIC
Currency: ITALIAN LIRA
Organizations: UN

MAP PAGE: 107

LANDLOCKED SAN MARINO lies on the slopes of Mt Titano in northeast Italy. It has a mild climate. A third of the people live in the capital. There is some agriculture and light industry, but most income comes from tourism and postage stamp sales.

SÃO TOMÉ AND PRÍNCIPE

Status: REPUBLIC
Area: 964 sq km (372 sq mls)
Population: 122,000
Capital: SÃO TOMÉ
Language: PORTUGUESE, PORTUGUESE CREOLE
Religion: R.CATHOLIC, PROTESTANT
Currency: DOBRA
Organizations: OAU, UN

MAP PAGE: 125

THE TWO MAIN islands and adjacent islets lie off the coast of west Africa in the Gulf of Guinea. São Tomé is the larger island and supports over 90 per cent of the population. Both São Tomé and Príncipe are mountainous and tree-covered, and have a hot and humid climate. The economy is heavily dependent on cocoa, which accounts for over 90 per cent of export earnings.

SAUDI ARABIA

Status: MONARCHY
Area: 2,200,000 sq km (849,425 sq mls)
Population: 17,119,000
Capital: RIYADH
Language: ARABIC
Religion: SUNNI MUSLIM, SHI'A MUSLIM
Currency: RIYAL
Organizations: OPEC, UN

MAP PAGE: 40-41

SAUDI ARABIA OCCUPIES most of the Arabian peninsula in southwest Asia. The terrain is desert or semi-desert plateaux, which rise to mountains running parallel to the Red Sea in the west and slope down to plains in the southeast and along The Gulf in the east. Most people live in urban areas, one third in the cities of Riyadh, Jiddah and Mecca. Summers are hot, winters are warm and rainfall is low. Saudi Arabia has the world's largest reserves of oil and gas, located in the northeast, both onshore and in The Gulf. Crude oil and refined products account for over 90 per cent of export earnings. Other industries and irrigated agriculture are being encouraged, but most food and raw materials are imported. Saudi Arabia has important banking and commercial interests. Each year 2 million pilgrims visit Islam's holiest cities, Mecca and Medina, in the west.

SENEGAL

Status: REPUBLIC
Area: 196,720 sq km (75,954 sq mls)
Population: 7,902,000
Capital: DAKAR
Language: FRENCH (OFFICIAL), WOLOF, FULANI, LOCAL LANGUAGES
Religion: SUNNI MUSLIM, R.CATHOLIC, TRAD.BELIEFS
Currency: CFA FRANC
Organizations: OAU, UN

MAP PAGE: 122

SENEGAL LIES ON the Atlantic coast of west Africa. The north is arid semi-desert, while the south is mainly fertile savannah bushland. The climate is tropical with summer rains, though droughts occur. One fifth of the population lives in Dakar. Groundnuts, phosphates and fish are the main resources. There is some oil refining and Dakar is a major port. Senegal relies heavily on aid.

SEYCHELLES

Status: REPUBLIC
Area: 455 sq km (176 sq mls)
Population: 72,000
Capital: VICTORIA
Language: SEYCHELLOIS (SESELWA, FRENCH CREOLE), ENGLISH
Religion: R.CATHOLIC, PROTESTANT
Currency: RUPEE
Organizations: COMM., OAU, UN

MAP PAGE: 127

THE SEYCHELLES COMPRISES an archipelago of 115 granitic and coral islands in the western Indian Ocean. The main island, Mahé, contains about 90 per cent of the population. The climate is hot and humid with heavy rainfall. The economy is based mainly on tourism, transit trade, and light manufacturing, with fishing and agriculture (chiefly copra, cinnamon and tea) also important.

SIERRA LEONE

Status: REPUBLIC
Area: 71,740 sq km (27,699 sq mls)
Population: 4,297,000
Capital: FREETOWN
Language: ENGLISH, CREOLE, MENDE, TEMNE, LOCAL LANGUAGES
Religion: TRAD. BELIEFS, SUNNI MUSLIM, PROTESTANT, R.CATHOLIC
Currency: LEONE
Organizations: COMM., OAU, UN

MAP PAGE: 122

SIERRA LEONE LIES on the Atlantic coast of west Africa. Its coast is heavily indented and lined with mangrove swamps. Inland is a forested area rising to savannah plateaux, with the mountains to the northeast. The climate is tropical and rainfall is heavy. Most of the workforce is involved in subsistence farming. Cocoa and coffee are the main cash crops, but rutile (titanium ore), bauxite and diamonds are the main exports. Civil war and economic decline have caused serious difficulties.

SINGAPORE

Status: REPUBLIC
Area: 639 sq km (247 sq mls)
Population: 2,874,000
Capital: SINGAPORE
Language: CHINESE, ENGLISH, MALAY, TAMIL
Religion: BUDDHIST, TAOIST, SUNNI MUSLIM, CHRISTIAN, HINDU
Currency: DOLLAR
Organizations: ASEAN, COMM., UN

MAP PAGE: 25

THE STATE COMPRISES the main island of Singapore and 57 other islands, lying off the southern tip of the Malay Peninsula in southeast Asia. A causeway links Singapore to the mainland across the Johor Strait. Singapore is generally low-lying and includes land reclaimed from swamps. It is hot and humid, with heavy rainfall throughout the year. There are fish farms and vegetable gardens in the north and east of the island, but most food needs must be imported. Singapore also lacks mineral and energy resources. Manufacturing industries and services are the main sectors of the economy. Their rapid development has fuelled the nation's impressive economic growth over the last three decades to become the richest of Asia's four 'little dragons'. The main industries include electronics, oil refining, chemicals, pharmaceuticals, ship building and repair, iron and steel, food processing and textiles. Singapore is a major financial centre. Its port is one of the world's largest and busiest and acts as an entrepot for neighbouring states. Tourism is also important.

SLOVAKIA

Status: REPUBLIC
Area: 49,035 sq km (18,933 sq mls)
Population: 5,318,000
Capital: BRATISLAVA
Language: SLOVAK, HUNGARIAN, CZECH
Religion: R.CATHOLIC, PROTESTANT, ORTHODOX
Currency: KORUNA
Organizations: UN

MAP PAGE: 79

A LANDLOCKED COUNTRY in central Europe, Slovakia borders the Czech Republic, Poland, Ukraine, Hungary and Austria. Slovakia is mountainous along the border with Poland in the north, but low-lying along the plains of the Danube in the southwest. The climate is continental. Slovakia is the smaller, less populous and less developed part of former Czechoslovakia. With few natural resources, uncompetitive heavy industry and loss of federal subsidies, the economy has suffered economic difficulties.

SLOVENIA

Status: REPUBLIC
Area: 20,251 sq km (7,819 sq mls)
Population: 1,990,000
Capital: LJUBLJANA
Language: SLOVENE, SERBO-CROAT
Religion: R.CATHOLIC, PROTESTANT
Currency: TÓLAR
Organizations: UN

MAP PAGE: 104

SLOVENIA LIES IN the northwest Balkans of south Europe and has a short coastline on the Adriatic Sea. It is mountainous and hilly, with lowlands on the coast and in the Sava and Drava river valleys. The climate is generally continental, but Mediterranean nearer the coast. Dairy farming, mercury mining, light manufacturing and tourism are the main activities. Conflict in the other former Yugoslav states, which has affected tourism and international trade, has caused serious economic problems.

SOLOMON ISLANDS

Status: MONARCHY
Area: 28,370 sq km (10,954 sq mls)
Population: 355,000
Capital: HONIARA
Language: ENGLISH, SOLOMON ISLANDS PIDGIN, MANY LOCAL LANGUAGES
Religion: PROTESTANT, R.CATHOLIC
Currency: DOLLAR
Organizations: COMM., UN

MAP PAGE: 6

THE STATE CONSISTS of the southern Solomon, Santa Cruz and Shortland islands in Australasia. The six main islands are volcanic, mountainous and forested, though Guadalcanal, the most populous, has a large area of flat land. The climate is generally hot and humid. Subsistence farming and fishing predominate. Exports include fish, timber, copra and palm oil. The islands depend on foreign aid.

SOMALIA

Status: REPUBLIC
Area: 637,657 sq km (246,201 sq mls)
Population: 8,954,000
Capital: MOGADISHU
Language: SOMALI, ARABIC (OFFICIAL)
Religion: SUNNI MUSLIM
Currency: SHILLING
Organizations: OAU, UN

MAP PAGE: 126-127

SOMALIA IS IN the Horn of northeast Africa, on the Gulf of Aden and Indian Ocean. It consists of a dry scrubby plateau, rising to highlands in the north. The climate is hot and dry, but coastal areas and the Jubba and Shebele river valleys support crops and the bulk of the population. Subsistence farming and herding are the main activities. Exports include livestock and bananas. Drought and war have ruined the economy.

SOUTH AFRICA

Status: REPUBLIC
Area: 1,225,815 sq km (473,290 sq mls)
Population: 39,659,000
Capital: PRETORIA/CAPE TOWN
Language: AFRIKAANS, ENGLISH, NINE LOCAL LANGUAGES (ALL OFFICIAL)
Religion: PROTESTANT, R.CATHOLIC, SUNNI MUSLIM, HINDU
Currency: RAND
Organizations: COMM., OAU, SADC, UN

MAP PAGE: 130-131

SOUTH AFRICA OCCUPIES most of the southern part of Africa. It borders five states, surrounds Lesotho and has a long coastline on the Atlantic and Indian oceans. Much of the land is a vast plateau, covered with grassland or bush and drained by the Orange and Limpopo river systems. A fertile coastal plain rises to mountain ridges in the south and east, including Table Mountain near Cape Town and the Drakensberg range in the east. Gauteng is the most populous province, with Johannesburg and Pretoria its main cities. South Africa has warm summers and mild winters. Most of the country has rainfall in summer, but the coast around Cape Town has winter rains. South Africa is the largest and most developed economy in Africa, though wealth is unevenly distributed. Agriculture provides one third of exports, including fruit, wine, wool and maize. South Africa is rich in minerals. It is the world's leading producer of gold, which accounts for one third of export earnings. Coal, diamonds, platinum, uranium, chromite and other minerals are also mined. The main industries process minerals and agricultural produce, and manufacture chemical products, motor vehicles, electrical equipment and textiles. Financial services are also important.

SOUTH KOREA

Status: REPUBLIC
Area: 99,274 sq km (38,330 sq mls)
Population: 44,056,000
Capital: SEOUL
Language: KOREAN
Religion: BUDDHIST, PROTESTANT, R.CATHOLIC, CONFUCIAN, TRADITIONAL
Currency: WON
Organizations: UN

MAP PAGE: 31

THE STATE CONSISTS of the southern half of the Korean Peninsula in east Asia and many islands lying off the western and southern coasts in the Yellow Sea. The terrain is mountainous, though less rugged than that of North Korea. Population density is high and most people live on the western coastal plains and in the Han basin in the northwest and Naktong basin in the southeast. South Korea has a continental climate, with hot, wet summers and dry, cold winters. Arable land is limited by the mountainous terrain, but because of intensive farming South Korea is nearly self-sufficient in food. Sericulture is important as is fishing, which contributes to exports. South Korea has few mineral resources, except for coal and tungsten. It is one of Asia's four 'little dragons' (Hong Kong, Singapore and Taiwan being the others), which have achieved high economic growth based mainly on export manufacturing. In South Korea industry is dominated by a few giant conglomerates, such as Hyundai and Samsung. The main manufactures are cars, electronic and electrical goods, ships, steel, chemicals, and toys as well as textiles, clothing, footwear and food products. Banking and other financial services are increasingly important.

SPAIN

Status: MONARCHY
Area: 504,782 sq km (194,897 sq mls)
Population: 39,143,000
Capital: MADRID
Language: SPANISH, CATALAN, GALICIAN, BASQUE
Religion: R.CATHOLIC
Currency: PESETA
Organizations: EU, OECD, UN

MAP PAGE: 96-97

SPAIN OCCUPIES THE greater part of the Iberian peninsula in southwest Europe, with coastlines on the Atlantic Ocean (Bay of Biscay and Gulf of Cadiz) and Mediterranean Sea. It includes the Balearic and Canary island groups in the Mediterranean and Atlantic, and two enclaves in north Africa. Much of the mainland is a high plateau, the Meseta, drained by the Duero, Tagus and Guadiana rivers. The plateau is interrupted by a low mountain range and bounded to the east and north also by mountains, including the Pyrenees which form the border with France and Andorra. The main lowland areas are the Ebro basin in the northeast, the eastern coastal plains and the Guadalquivir basin in the southwest. Three quarters of the population lives in urban areas, chiefly Madrid and Barcelona, which alone contain one quarter of the population. The plateau experiences hot summers and cold winters. Conditions are cooler and wetter to the north, though warmer and drier to the south. Agriculture involves about 10 per cent of the workforce and fruit, vegetables and wine are exported. Fishing is an important industry and Spain has a large fishing fleet. Mineral resources include iron, lead, copper and mercury. Some oil is produced, but Spain has to import most energy needs. The economy is based mainly on manufacturing and services. Manufacturing industries account for one third of national income and are based mainly around Madrid and Barcelona. The principal products are machinery and transport equip-

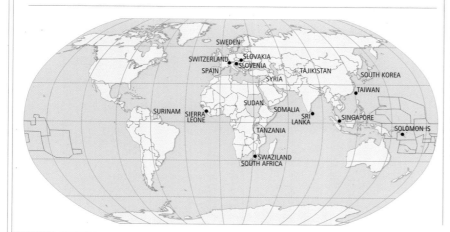

ment. Spain is a leading manufacturer of motor vehicles (SEAT). Other manufactures are agricultural products, chemicals, steel and other metals, paper products, wood and cork products, clothing and footwear, and textiles. With some 50 million visitors a year, tourism is a major industry, accounting for 10 per cent of national income and employing about the same percentage of the workforce. Banking and commerce are also important.

SRI LANKA

Status: REPUBLIC
Area: 65,610 sq km (25,332 sq mls)
Population: 17,619,000
Capital: COLOMBO
Language: SINHALESE, TAMIL, ENGLISH
Religion: BUDDHIST, HINDU, SUNNI MUSLIM, R.CATHOLIC
Currency: RUPEE
Organizations: COMM., UN

MAP PAGE: 38

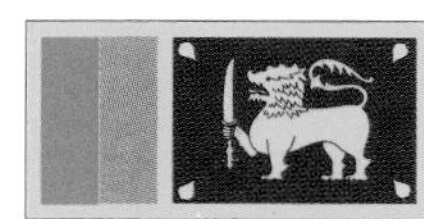

SRI LANKA LIES in the Indian Ocean off the southeast coast of India in south Asia. It has rolling coastal plains with mountains in the centre-south. The climate is hot and monsoonal and most people live on the west coast. Manufactures (chiefly textiles and clothing), tea, rubber, copra and gems are exported. The economy relies on aid and workers' remittances. Tourism has been damaged by separatist activities.

SUDAN

Status: REPUBLIC
Area: 2,505,813 sq km (967,500 sq mls)
Population: 28,129,000
Capital: KHARTOUM
Language: ARABIC, DINKA, NUBIAN, BEJA, NUER, LOCAL LANGUAGES
Religion: SUNNI MUSLIM, TRAD. BELIEFS, R.CATHOLIC, PROTESTANT
Currency: DINAR
Organizations: OAU, UN

MAP PAGE: 118-119

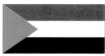

AFRICA'S LARGEST COUNTRY, Sudan is in northeast Africa, on the Red Sea. It lies within the Upper Nile basin, much of which is arid plain but with swamps to the south. Mountains lie to the northeast and south. The climate is hot and arid with light summer rainfall, though droughts occur. Most people live along the Nile and are farmers and herders. Cotton, gum arabic, livestock and other agricultural products are exported. In southern Sudan civil war has ruined the economy.

SURINAM

Status: REPUBLIC
Area: 163,820 sq km (63,251 sq mls)
Population: 414,000
Capital: PARAMARIBO
Language: DUTCH, SURINAMESE (SRANAN TONGO), ENGLISH, HINDI, JAVANESE
Religion: HINDU, R.CATHOLIC, PROTESTANT, SUNNI MUSLIM
Currency: GUILDER
Organizations: CARICOM, UN

MAP PAGE: 163

SURINAM, ON THE Atlantic coast of northern South America, consists of a swampy coastal plain (where most people live), central plateaux and the Guiana Highlands. The climate is tropical and rainforest covers much of the land. Bauxite mining is the main industry. Alumina and aluminium are the chief exports, with shrimps, rice, bananas and timber. Surinam depends on Dutch aid.

SWAZILAND

Status: MONARCHY
Area: 17,364 sq km (6,704 sq mls)
Population: 809,000
Capital: MBABANE
Language: SWAZI (SISWATI), ENGLISH
Religion: PROTESTANT, R.CATHOLIC, TRAD.BELIEFS
Currency: EMALANGENI
Organizations: COMM., OAU, SADC, UN

MAP PAGE: 131

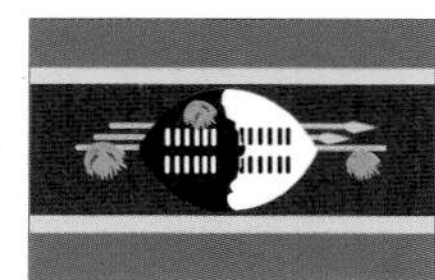

LANDLOCKED SWAZILAND IN southern Africa lies between Mozambique and South Africa. Savannah plateaux descend from mountains in the west towards hill country in the east. The climate is subtropical, temperate in the mountains. Subsistence farming predominates. Asbestos, coal and diamonds are mined. Exports include sugar, fruit and wood pulp. Tourism and workers' remittances are important.

SWEDEN

Status: MONARCHY
Area: 449,964 sq km (173,732 sq mls)
Population: 8,716,000
Capital: STOCKHOLM
Language: SWEDISH
Religion: PROTESTANT, R.CATHOLIC
Currency: KRONA
Organizations: EU, OECD, UN

MAP PAGE: 56-57

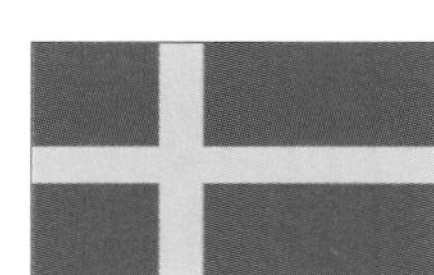

SWEDEN, THE LARGEST and most populous of the Scandinavian countries, occupies the eastern part of the peninsula in north Europe and borders the North and Baltic Seas and Gulf of Bothnia. Forested mountains cover the northern half of the country, part of which lies within the Arctic Circle. Southwards is a lowland lake region, where most of the population lives. Farther south is an upland region, and then a fertile plain at the tip of the peninsula. Sweden has warm summers and cold winters, though the latter are longer and more severe in the north and milder in the far south. Sweden's natural resources include coniferous forests, mineral deposits and water resources. There is little agriculture, though some dairy products, meat, cereals and vegetables are produced in the south. The forests supply timber for export and for the important pulp, paper and furniture industries. Sweden is one of the world's leading producers of iron ore. Copper, zinc, lead, uranium and other metallic ores are also mined. Mineral industries, chiefly iron and steel, are the basis for the production of a range of products, but chiefly machinery and transport equipment of which cars and trucks (Volvo and Saab) are the most important export. Sweden also manufactures chemicals, electrical goods (Electrolux) and telecommunications equipment (Ericsson). Like their Scandinavian neighbours, Swedes enjoy a high standard of living.

SWITZERLAND

Status: FEDERATION
Area: 41,293 sq km (15,943 sq mls)
Population: 6,938,000
Capital: BERN
Language: GERMAN, FRENCH, ITALIAN, ROMANSCH
Religion: R.CATHOLIC, PROTESTANT
Currency: FRANC
Organizations: OECD

MAP PAGE: 82-83

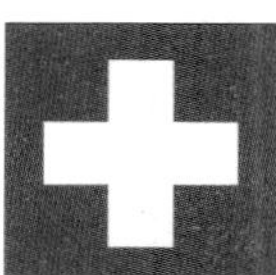

SWITZERLAND IS A landlocked country of southwest Europe that is surrounded by France, Germany, Austria, Liechtenstein and Italy. It is also Europe's most mountainous country. The southern half of the nation lies within the Alps, while the northwest is dominated by the Jura mountains. The rest of the land is a high plateau, which contains the bulk of the population and economic activity. The climate varies greatly, depending on altitude and relief, but in general summers are mild and winters are cold with heavy snowfalls. Switzerland has one of the highest standards of living in the world. Yet it has few mineral resources and, owing to its mountainous terrain, agriculture is based mainly on dairy and stock farming. Most food and industrial raw materials have to be imported. Manufacturing makes the largest contribution to the economy and though varied is specialist in certain products. Engineering is the most important industry, producing precision instruments such as scientific and optical instruments, watches and clocks, and heavy machinery such as turbines and generators. Other industries produce chemicals, pharmaceuticals, metal products, textiles, clothing and food products (cheese and chocolate). Banking and other financial services are very important and Zurich is one of the world's leading banking cities. Tourism and international organisations based in Switzerland are also major foreign currency earners.

SYRIA

Status: REPUBLIC
Area: 185,180 sq km (71,498 sq mls)
Population: 13,393,000
Capital: DAMASCUS
Language: ARABIC, KURDISH, ARMENIAN
Religion: SUNNI MUSLIM, OTHER MUSLIM, CHRISTIAN
Currency: POUND
Organizations: UN

MAP PAGE: 42

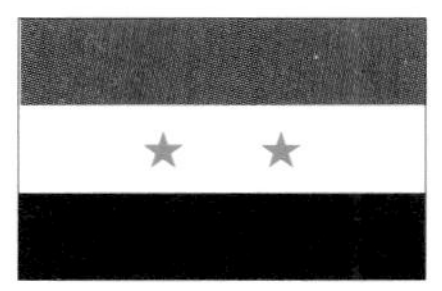

SYRIA IS IN southwest Asia, on the Mediterranean Sea. Behind the coastal plain lies a range of hills and then a plateau cut by the Euphrates river. Mountains flank the borders with Lebanon and Israel, east of which is desert. The climate is Mediterranean in coastal regions, hotter and drier inland. Most Syrians live on the coast or in the river valleys. Cotton, cereals and fruit are important, but the main exports are petroleum and its products, textiles and chemicals. Syria receives support from Gulf states.

TAIWAN

Status: REPUBLIC
Area: 36,179 sq km (13,969 sq mls)
Population: 20,300,000
Capital: TAIPEI
Language: CHINESE (MANDARIN OFFICIAL, FUKIEN, HAKKA), LOCAL LANGUAGES
Religion: BUDDHIST, TAOIST, CONFUCIAN, CHRISTIAN
Currency: DOLLAR

MAP PAGE: 33

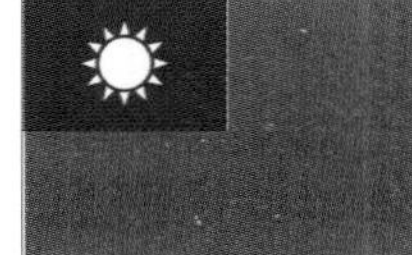

THE EAST ASIAN state consists of the island of Taiwan, separated from mainland China by the Taiwan Strait, and several much smaller islands. Much of Taiwan itself is mountainous and forested. Densely populated coastal plains in the west contain the bulk of the population and most economic activity. Taiwan has a tropical monsoon climate, with warm, wet summers and mild winters. Agriculture is highly productive. Taiwan is virtually self-sufficient in food and exports some products. Coal, oil and natural gas are produced and a few minerals are mined but none of them are of great significance to the economy. Taiwan depends heavily on imports of raw materials and exports of manufactured goods. The latter is equivalent to 50 per cent of national income. The country's main manufactures are electrical and electronic goods, including television sets, watches, personal computers and calculators. Other products include clothing, footwear (chiefly track shoes), textiles and toys. In contrast to mainland China, Taiwan has enjoyed considerable prosperity.

TAJIKISTAN

Status: REPUBLIC
Area: 143,100 sq km (55,251 sq mls)
Population: 5,767,000
Capital: DUSHANBE
Language: TAJIK, UZBEK, RUSSIAN
Religion: SUNNI MUSLIM
Currency: ROUBLE
Organizations: CIS, UN

MAP PAGE: 47

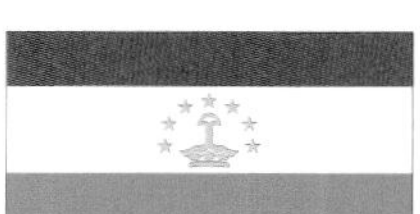

LANDLOCKED TAJIKISTAN IN central Asia is a mountainous country, occupying the western Tien Shan and part of the Pamir ranges. In less mountainous western areas summers are warm though winters are cold. Most activity is in the Fergana basin. Agriculture is the main sector of the economy, chiefly cotton growing and cattle breeding. Mineral and fuel deposits include lead, zinc, uranium and oil. Textiles and clothing are the main manufactures. Civil war has damaged the economy, which depends heavily on Russian support.

TANZANIA

Status: REPUBLIC
Area: 945,087 sq km (364,900 sq mls)
Population: 28,019,000
Capital: DODOMA
Language: SWAHILI, ENGLISH, NYAMWEZI, MANY LOCAL LANGUAGES
Religion: R.CATHOLIC, SUNNI MUSLIM, TRAD. BELIEFS, PROTESTANT
Currency: SHILLING
Organizations: COMM., OAU, SADC, UN

MAP PAGE: 127

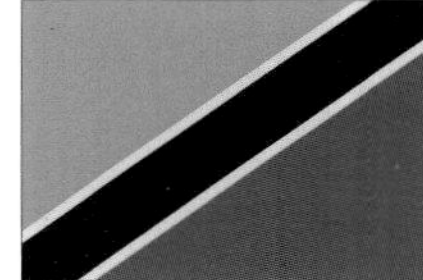

TANZANIA LIES ON the coast of east Africa and includes Zanzibar in the Indian Ocean. Most of the mainland is a savannah plateau lying east of the great Rift Valley. In the north are Mount Kilimanjaro and the Serangeti National Park. The climate is tropical and most people live on the narrow coastal plain or in the north. The economy is mainly agricultural. Coffee, cotton and sisal are the main exports, with cloves from Zanzibar. Agricultural processing and diamond mining are the main industries, though tourism is growing. Tanzania depends heavily on aid.

THAILAND

Status: MONARCHY
Area: 513,115 sq km (198,115 sq mls)
Population: 58,584,000
Capital: BANGKOK
Language: THAI, LAO, CHINESE, MALAY, MON-KHMER LANGUAGES
Religion: BUDDHIST, SUNNI MUSLIM
Currency: BAHT
Organizations: ASEAN, UN

MAP PAGE: 24-25

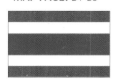

A COUNTRY IN southeast Asia, Thailand borders Myanmar, Laos, Cambodia and Malaysia and has coastlines on the Gulf of Thailand and Andaman Sea. Central Thailand is dominated by the Chao Phraya river basin, which contains Bangkok, the only major urban centre, and most economic activity. To the east is a dry plateau drained by tributaries of the Mekong river, while to the north, west and south, extending halfway down the Malay peninsula, are forested hills and mountains. Many small islands line the coast. The climate is hot, humid and monsoonal. About half the workforce is involved in agriculture. Thailand is the world's leading exporter of rice and rubber, and a major exporter of maize and tapioca. Fish and fish processing are important. Thailand produces natural gas, some oil and lignite, metallic ores (chiefly tin and tungsten) and gemstones. Manufacturing is the largest contributor to national income, with electronics, textiles, clothing and footwear, and food processing the main industries. With over 5 million visitors a year, tourism is the major source of foreign exchange.

TOGO

Status: REPUBLIC
Area: 56,785 sq km (21,925 sq mls)
Population: 3,885,000
Capital: LOMÉ
Language: FRENCH, EWE, KABRE, MANY LOCAL LANGUAGES
Religion: TRAD. BELIEFS, R.CATHOLIC, SUNNI MUSLIM, PROTESTANT
Currency: CFA FRANC
Organizations: OAU, UN

MAP PAGE: 123

T OGO IS A long narrow country in west Africa with a short coastline on the Gulf of Guinea. The interior consists of plateaux rising to mountainous areas. The climate is tropical, drier inland. Agriculture is the mainstay of the economy. Cotton, coffee and cocoa are exported, but phosphates are the main exports. Oil refining and food processing are the main industries. Lomé is an entrepot trade centre.

TOKELAU

Status: NEW ZEALAND TERRITORY
Area: 10 sq km (4 sq mls)
Population: 2,000
Language: ENGLISH, TOKELAUAN

Religion: PROTESTANT, R.CATHOLIC
Currency: NZ DOLLAR

MAP PAGE: 5

TONGA

Status: MONARCHY
Area: 748 sq km (289 sq mls)
Population: 98,000
Capital: NUKU'ALOFA
Language: TONGAN, ENGLISH
Religion: PROTESTANT, R.CATHOLIC, MORMON
Currency: PA'ANGA
Organizations: COMM.

MAP PAGE: 6

T ONGA COMPRISES SOME 170 islands in the South Pacific Ocean, northeast of New Zealand. The three main groups are Tongatapu (where 60 per cent of Tongans live), Ha'apai and Vava'u. The climate is warm with good rainfall and the economy relies heavily on agriculture. Exports include coconut products, root crops, bananas and vanilla. Fishing, tourism and light industry are increasingly important.

TRINIDAD AND TOBAGO

Status: REPUBLIC
Area: 5,130 sq km (1,981 sq mls)
Population: 1,260,000
Capital: PORT OF SPAIN
Language: ENGLISH, CREOLE, HINDI
Religion: R.CATHOLIC, HINDU, PROTESTANT, SUNNI MUSLIM
Currency: DOLLAR
Organizations: CARICOM, COMM., UN

MAP PAGE: 159

T RINIDAD, THE MOST southerly Caribbean island, lies off the Venezuelan coast. It is hilly in the north, with a populous central plain. Tobago, to the northeast, is smaller, more mountainous and less developed. The climate is tropical. Oil and petrochemicals dominate the economy. Asphalt is also important. Sugar, fruit, cocoa and coffee are produced. Tourism is important on Tobago.

TUNISIA

Status: REPUBLIC
Area: 164,150 sq km (63,379 sq mls)
Population: 8,570,000
Capital: TUNIS
Language: ARABIC, FRENCH
Religion: SUNNI MUSLIM
Currency: DINAR
Organizations: OAU, UN

MAP PAGE: 121

T UNISIA IS ON the Mediterranean coast of north Africa. The north is mountanous with valleys and coastal plains, where most people live. Beyond a central area of salt pans are Saharan plains. The north has a Mediterranean climate, the south is hot and arid. Oil and phosphates are the main resources. Olive oil, citrus fruit and textiles are also exported. Tourism is important.

TURKEY

Status: REPUBLIC
Area: 779,452 sq km (300,948 sq mls)
Population: 60,227,000
Capital: ANKARA
Language: TURKISH, KURDISH
Religion: SUNNI MUSLIM, SHI'A MUSLIM
Currency: LIRA
Organizations: OECD, UN

MAP PAGE: 42

T URKEY OCCUPIES THE Asia Minor peninsula of southwest Asia and has coastlines on the Black, Mediterranean and Aegean seas. It includes eastern Thrace, which is in south Europe and separated from the rest of the country by the Bosporus, Sea of Marmara and Dardanelles. The Asian mainland consists of the semi-arid Anatolian plateau, flanked to the north, south and east by mountains. Over 40 per cent of Turks live in central Anatolia and the Marmara and Aegean coastal plains. The coast has a Mediterranean climate, but inland conditions are more extreme with hot, dry summers and cold, snowy winters. Agriculture involves about half the workforce and exports include cotton, tobacco, fruit, nuts and livestock. Turkey is one of the world's major producers of chrome. Coal and lignite, petroleum, iron ore and boron are also exploited. Apart from food products, the main manufactures are textiles (the chief export), iron and steel, vehicles and chemicals. With over 7 million visitors a year, tourism is a major industry. Remittances by workers aboard are also important.

TURKMENISTAN

Status: REPUBLIC
Area: 488,100 sq km (188,456 sq mls)
Population: 3,921,000
Capital: ASHKHABAD
Language: TURKMEN, RUSSIAN
Religion: SUNNI MUSLIM
Currency: MANAT
Organizations: CIS, UN

MAP PAGE: 46

T URKMENISTAN, IN CENTRAL Asia, lies mainly within the desert plains of the Kara Kum. Most people live on the fringes: the foothills of the Kopet Dag in the south, Amudarya valley in the north and Caspian Sea plains in the west. The climate is dry with extreme temperatures. The economy is based mainly on irrigated agriculture, chiefly cotton growing. Turkmenistan is rich in oil, natural gas (the main export) and minerals.

TURKS AND CAICOS ISLANDS

Status: UK TERRITORY
Area: 430 sq km (166 sq mls)
Population: 13,000
Capital: GRAND TURK
Language: ENGLISH
Religion: PROTESTANT
Currency: US DOLLAR

MAP PAGE: 159

T HE STATE CONSISTS of 40 or so low-lying islands and cays in the northern Caribbean. Only eight islands are inhabited, two fifths of people living on Grand Turk and Salt Cay. The climate is tropical. The islands depend on fishing, tourism and offshore banking.

TUVALU

Status: MONARCHY
Area: 25 sq km (10 sq mls)
Population: 9,000
Capital: FUNAFUTI
Language: TUVALUAN, ENGLISH (OFFICIAL)
Religion: PROTESTANT
Currency: DOLLAR
Organizations: COMM.

MAP PAGE: 4

T UVALU COMPRISES NINE coral atolls in the South Pacific Ocean. One third of the population lives on Funafuti and most people depend on subsistence farming and fishing. The islands export copra, stamps and clothing, but rely heavily on UK aid.

UGANDA

Status: REPUBLIC
Area: 241,038 sq km (93,065 sq mls)
Population: 19,940,000
Capital: KAMPALA
Language: ENGLISH, SWAHILI (OFFICIAL), LUGANDA, MANY LOCAL LANGUAGES
Religion: R.CATHOLIC, PROTESTANT, SUNNI MUSLIM, TRAD. BELIEFS
Currency: SHILLING
Organizations: COMM., OAU, UN

MAP PAGE: 126-127

A LANDLOCKED COUNTRY in east Africa, Uganda consists of a savannah plateau with mountains and lakes. It includes part of Lake Victoria from which the Nile flows northwards to Sudan. The climate is warm and wet. Most people live in the southern half of the country. Agriculture dominates the economy. Coffee is the main export, with some cotton and tea. Uganda relies heavily on aid.

UKRAINE

Status: REPUBLIC
Area: 603,700 sq km (233,090 sq mls)
Population: 52,179,000
Capital: KIEV
Language: UKRAINIAN, RUSSIAN, REGIONAL LANGUAGES
Religion: UKRAINIAN ORTHODOX, R.CATHOLIC
Currency: KARBOVANETS
Organizations: CIS, UN

MAP PAGE: 53

U KRAINE LIES ON the Black Sea coast of east Europe. Much of the land is steppe, generally flat and treeless, but with rich black soil and drained by the river Dnieper. Along the border with Belarus are forested, marshy plains. The only uplands are the Carpathian mountains in the west and smaller ranges on the Crimean peninsula. Summers are warm and

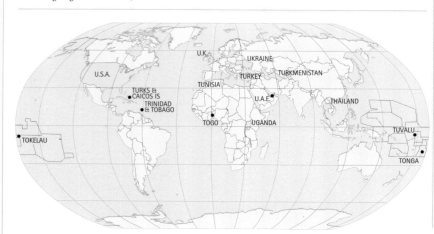

winters are cold, with milder conditions in the Crimea. About a quarter of the population lives in the mainly industrial provinces of Donetsk, Kiev and Dnepropetrovsk. The Ukraine is rich in natural resources: fertile soil, substantial mineral deposits and forests. Agriculture, livestock raising and viticulture are important, but mining and manufacturing predominate, contributing over 40 per cent of national income. Coal mining, iron and steel production, engineering and chemicals are the main industries. Output has fallen and few state enterprises have been privatized since Ukraine became independent in 1991.

....

UNITED ARAB EMIRATES
(UAE)
Status: FEDERATION
Area: 77,700 sq km (30,000 sq mls)
Population: 1,910,000
Capital: ABU DHABI
Language: ARABIC (OFFICIAL), ENGLISH, HINDI, URDU, FARSI
Religion: SUNNI MUSLIM, SHI'A MUSLIM, CHRISTIAN
Currency: DIRHAM
Organizations: OPEC, UN

MAP PAGE: 39

THE UAE IS in east-central Arabia, southwest Asia. Six emirates lie on The Gulf while the seventh, Fujairah, fronts the Gulf of Oman. Most of the land is flat desert with sand dunes and salt pans. The only hilly area is in the northeast. Three emirates - Abu Dhabi, Dubai and Sharjah - contain 85 per cent of the population. Summers are hot and winters are mild with occasional rainfall in coastal areas. Fruit and vegetables are grown in oases and irrigated areas. The state's wealth is based on hydrocarbons, mainly within Abu Dhabi, but with smaller supplies in Dubai, Sharjah and Ras al Khaimah. Dubai is a thriving entrepot trade centre.

ABU DHABI
Status: EMIRATE
Area: 64,750 sq km (25,000 sq miles)
Population: 800,000

AJMAN
Status: EMIRATE
Area: 260 sq km (100 sq miles)
Population: 76,000

DUBAI
Status: EMIRATE
Area: 3,900 sq km (1,506 sq miles)
Population: 500,000

FUJAIRAH
Status: EMIRATE
Area: 1,170 sq km (452 sq miles)
Population: 63,000

RAS AL KHAIMAH
Status: EMIRATE
Area: 1,690 sq km (653 sq miles)
Population: 130,000

SHARJAH
Status: EMIRATE
Area: 2,600 sq km (1,004 sq miles)
Population: 314,000

UMM AL QAIWAIN
Status: EMIRATE
Area: 780 sq km (301 sq miles)
Population: 27,000

....

UNITED KINGDOM
(UK)
Status: MONARCHY
Area: 242,534 sq km (93,643 sq mls)
Population: 58,191,000
Capital: LONDON
Language: ENGLISH, SOUTH INDIAN LANGUAGES, CHINESE, WELSH, GAELIC
Religion: PROTESTANT, R.CATHOLIC, MUSLIM, SIKH, HINDU, JEWISH
Currency: POUND
Organizations: COMM., EU, OECD, UN

MAP PAGE: 60-61

A COUNTRY OF northwest Europe, the United Kingdom occupies the island of Great Britain, part of Ireland and many small adjacent islands in the Atlantic Ocean. Great Britain comprises the countries of England, Scotland and Wales. England covers over half the land area and supports over four-fifths of the population, chiefly in the southeast region. The landscape is flat or rolling with some uplands, notably the Cheviot Hills on the Scottish border, the Pennines in the centre-north and the Cumbrian mountains in the northwest. Scotland consists of southern uplands, central lowlands, highlands (which include the UK's highest peak) and islands. Wales is a land of mountains and river valleys. Northern Ireland contains uplands, plains and the UK's largest lake, Lough Neagh. The climate is mild, wet and variable. The UK has few mineral deposits, but has important energy resources. Over 40 per cent of land is suitable for grazing, over 25 per cent is cultivated, and 10 per cent is forested. Agriculture involves mainly sheep and cattle raising and dairy farming, with crop and fruit growing in the east and southeast. Productivity is high, but about one third of food needs must be imported. Both forestry and fishing are also important. The UK produces petroleum and natural gas from reserves in the North Sea and is self-sufficient in energy in net terms. It also has reserves of coal, though the coal industry has contracted in recent years. Manufacturing accounts for over 20 per cent of national income and relies heavily on imported raw materials. Major manufactures are food and drinks, motor vehicles and parts, aerospace equipment, machinery, electronic and electrical equipment, and chemicals and chemical products. However, the economy is dominated by service industries, including banking, insurance, finance, business services, retail and catering. London is one of the world's major banking, financial and insurance capitals. Tourism is a major industry, with over 18 million visitors a year. International trade is also important, equivalent to a third of national income and the UK has a large merchant fleet.

ENGLAND
Status: CONSTITUENT COUNTRY
Area: 130,423 sq km (50,357 sq miles)
Population: 48,532,700
Capital: LONDON

NORTHERN IRELAND
Status: CONSTITUENT REGION
Area: 14,121 sq km (5,452 sq miles)
Population: 1,631,800
Capital: BELFAST

SCOTLAND
Status: CONSTITUENT COUNTRY
Area: 78,772 sq km (30,414 sq miles)
Population: 5,120,200
Capital: EDINBURGH

WALES
Status: PRINCIPALITY
Area: 20,766 sq km (8,018 sq miles)
Population: 2,906,500
Capital: CARDIFF

....

UNITED STATES OF AMERICA
(USA)
Status: REPUBLIC
Area: 9,372,610 sq km (3,618,785 sq mls)
Population: 258,233,000
Capital: WASHINGTON
Language: ENGLISH, SPANISH, AMERINDIAN LANGUAGES
Religion: PROTESTANT, R.CATHOLIC, SUNNI MUSLIM, JEWISH, MORMON
Currency: DOLLAR
Organizations: NAFTA, OECD, UN

MAP PAGE: 142-143

THE USA COMPRISES 48 contiguous states in North America, bounded by Canada and Mexico, and the states of Alaska, to the northwest of Canada, and Hawaii, in the Pacific Ocean. The populous eastern states consist of the Atlantic coastal plain (which includes the Florida peninsula and the Gulf of Mexico coast) and the Appalachian mountains. The central states form a vast interior plain drained by the Mississippi-Missouri river system. To the west lie the Rocky Mountains, separated from the Pacific coastal ranges by the intermontane plateaux. The coastal ranges, which are prone to earthquakes, extend northwards into Alaska. Hawaii is a group of some 20 volcanic islands. Climatic conditions range between arctic in Alaska to desert in the intermontane plateaux. Most of the USA is temperate, though the interior has continental conditions. The USA has abundant natural resources. It has major reserves minerals and energy resources. About 20 per cent of the land can be used for crops, over 25 per cent is suitable for livestock rearing and over 30 per cent is forested. The USA has the largest economy in the world, which is based mainly on manufacturing and services. Though agriculture accounts for only about 2 per cent national income, productivity is high and the USA is a net exporter of food, chiefly grains and fruit. Major industrial crops include cotton, tobacco and sugarbeet. Livestock rearing, forestry and fishing are also important. Mining is well developed. The USA produces iron ore, bauxite, copper, lead, zinc, phosphate and many other minerals. It is a major producer of coal, petroleum and natural gas, though being the world's biggest energy user it must import significant quanities of petroleum and its products. Manufacturing is well diversified. The main products are: iron, steel and aluminium metals and products, machinery, transport equipment (chiefly motor vehicles and aircraft), electrical and electronic goods, food products, chemicals, textiles and clothing. Tourism is a major foreign currency earner. Other important service industries are banking and finance, and Wall Street in New York is a major stock exchange.

ALABAMA
Status: STATE
Area: 135,775 sq km (52,423 sq miles)
Population: 4,136,000
Capital: MONTGOMERY

ALASKA
Status: STATE
Area: 1,700,130 sq km (656,424 sq miles)
Population: 587,000
Capital: JUNEAU

ARIZONA
Status: STATE
Area: 295,274 sq km (114,006 sq miles)
Population: 3,832,000
Capital: PHOENIX

ARKANSAS
Status: STATE
Area: 137,741 sq km (53,182 sq miles)
Population: 2,399,000
Capital: LITTLE ROCK

CALIFORNIA
Status: STATE
Area: 423,999 sq km (163,707 sq miles)
Population: 30,867,000
Capital: SACRAMENTO

COLORADO
Status: STATE
Area: 269,618 sq km (104,100 sq miles)
Population: 3,470,000
Capital: DENVER

CONNECTICUT
Status: STATE
Area: 14,359 sq km (5,544 sq miles)
Population: 3,281,000
Capital: HARTFORD

DISTRICT OF COLUMBIA
Status: FEDERAL DISTRICT
Area: 176 sq km (68 sq miles)
Population: 589,000
Capital: WASHINGTON

DELAWARE
Status: STATE
Area: 6,446 sq km (2,489 sq miles)
Population: 689,000
Capital: DOVER

FLORIDA
Status: STATE
Area: 170,312 sq km (65,758 sq miles)
Population: 13,488,000
Capital: TALLAHASSEE

GEORGIA
Status: STATE
Area: 153,951 sq km (59,441 sq miles)
Population: 6,751,000
Capital: ATLANTA

HAWAII
Status: STATE
Area: 28,314 sq km (10,932 sq miles)
Population: 1,160,000
Capital: HONOLULU

IDAHO
Status: STATE
Area: 216,456 sq km (83,574 sq miles)
Population: 1,067,000
Capital: BOISE

ILLINOIS
Status: STATE
Area: 150,007 sq km (57,918 sq miles)
Population: 11,631,000
Capital: SPRINGFIELD

INDIANA
Status: STATE
Area: 94,327 sq km (36,420 sq miles)
Population: 5,662,000
Capital: INDIANAPOLIS

IOWA
Status: STATE
Area: 145,754 sq km (56,276 sq miles)
Population: 2,812,000
Capital: DES MOINES

KANSAS
Status: STATE
Area: 213,109 sq km (82,282 sq miles)
Population: 2,523,000
Capital: TOPEKA

KENTUCKY
Status: STATE
Area: 104,664 sq km (40,411 sq miles)
Population: 3,755,000
Capital: FRANKFORT

LOUISIANA
Status: STATE
Area: 134,273 sq km (51,843 sq miles)
Population: 4,287,000
Capital: BATON ROUGE

USA
continued

MAINE
Status: STATE
Area: 91,652 sq km (35,387 sq miles)
Population: 1,235,000
Capital: AUGUSTA

MARYLAND
Status: STATE
Area: 32,134 sq km (12,407 sq miles)
Population: 4,908,000
Capital: ANNAPOLIS

MASSACHUSETTS
Status: STATE
Area: 27,337 sq km (10,555 sq miles)
Population: 5,998,000
Capital: BOSTON

MICHIGAN
Status: STATE
Area: 250,737 sq km (96,810 sq miles)
Population: 9,437,000
Capital: LANSING

MINNESOTA
Status: STATE
Area: 225,181 sq km (86,943 sq miles)
Population: 4,480,000
Capital: ST PAUL

MISSISSIPPI
Status: STATE
Area: 125,443 sq km (48,434 sq miles)
Population: 2,614,000
Capital: JACKSON

MISSOURI
Status: STATE
Area: 180,545 sq km (69,709 sq miles)
Population: 5,193,000
Capital: JEFFERSON CITY

MONTANA
Status: STATE
Area: 380,847 sq km (147,046 sq miles)
Population: 824,000
Capital: HELENA

NEBRASKA
Status: STATE
Area: 200,356 sq km (77,358 sq miles)
Population: 1,606,000
Capital: LINCOLN

NEVADA
Status: STATE
Area: 286,367 sq km (110,567 sq miles)
Population: 1,327,000
Capital: CARSON CITY

NEW HAMPSHIRE
Status: STATE
Area: 24,219 sq km (9,351 sq miles)
Population: 1,111,000
Capital: CONCORD

NEW JERSEY
Status: STATE
Area: 22,590 sq km (8,722 sq miles)
Population: 7,789,000
Capital: TRENTON

NEW MEXICO
Status: STATE
Area: 314,937 sq km (121,598 sq miles)
Population: 1,581,000
Capital: SANTA FE

NEW YORK
Status: STATE
Area: 141,090 sq km (54,475 sq miles)
Population: 18,119,000
Capital: ALBANY

NORTH CAROLINA
Status: STATE
Area: 139,396 sq km (53,821 sq miles)
Population: 6,843,000
Capital: RALEIGH

NORTH DAKOTA
Status: STATE
Area: 183,123 sq km (70,704 sq miles)
Population: 638,000
Capital: BISMARCK

OHIO
Status: STATE
Area: 116,104 sq km (44,828 sq miles)
Population: 11,016,000
Capital: COLUMBUS

OKLAHOMA
Status: STATE
Area: 181,048 sq km (69,903 sq miles)
Population: 3,212,000
Capital: OKLAHOMA CITY

OREGON
Status: STATE
Area: 254,819 sq km (98,386 sq miles)
Population: 2,977,000
Capital: SALEM

PENNSYLVANIA
Status: STATE
Area: 119,290 sq km (46,058 sq miles)
Population: 12,009,000
Capital: HARRISBURG

RHODE ISLAND
Status: STATE
Area: 4,002 sq km (1,545 sq miles)
Population: 1,005,000
Capital: PROVIDENCE

SOUTH CAROLINA
Status: STATE
Area: 82,898 sq km (32,007 sq miles)
Population: 3,603,000
Capital: COLUMBIA

SOUTH DAKOTA
Status: STATE
Area: 199,742 sq km (77,121 sq miles)
Population: 711,000
Capital: PIERRE

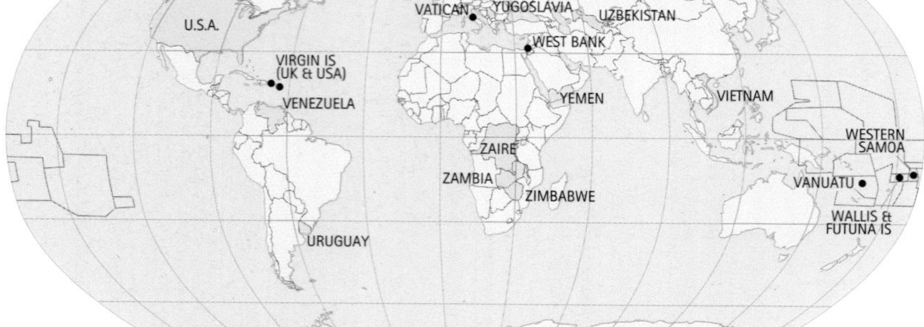

TENNESSEE
Status: STATE
Area: 109,158 sq km (42,146 sq miles)
Population: 5,024,000
Capital: NASHVILLE

TEXAS
Status: STATE
Area: 695,673 sq km (268,601 sq miles)
Population: 17,656,000
Capital: AUSTIN

UTAH
Status: STATE
Area: 219,900 sq km (84,904 sq miles)
Population: 1,813,000
Capital: SALT LAKE CITY

VERMONT
Status: STATE
Area: 24,903 sq km (9,615 sq miles)
Population: 570,000
Capital: MONTPELIER

VIRGINIA
Status: STATE
Area: 110,771 sq km (42,769 sq miles)
Population: 6,377,000
Capital: RICHMOND

WASHINGTON
Status: STATE
Area: 184,674 sq km (71,303 sq miles)
Population: 5,136,000
Capital: OLYMPIA

WEST VIRGINIA
Status: STATE
Area: 62,758 sq km (24,231 sq miles)
Population: 1,812,000
Capital: CHARLESTON

WISCONSIN
Status: STATE
Area: 169,652 sq km (65,503 sq miles)
Population: 5,007,000
Capital: MADISON

WYOMING
Status: STATE
Area: 253,347 sq km (97,818 sq miles)
Population: 466,000
Capital: CHEYENNE

URUGUAY
Status: REPUBLIC
Area: 176,215 sq km (68,037 sq mls)
Population: 3,149,000
Capital: MONTEVIDEO
Language: SPANISH
Religion: R.CATHOLIC, PROTESTANT,
JEWISH
Currency: PESO
Organizations: UN

MAP PAGE: 173

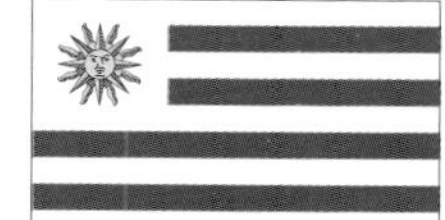

URUGUAY, ON THE Atlantic coast of central South America, is a low-lying land of prairies. The coast and the River Plate estuary in the south are fringed with lagoons and sand dunes. Almost half the population lives in Montevideo. Uruguay has warm summers and mild winters. The economy was founded on cattle and sheep ranching, and meat, wool and hides are major exports. The main industries produce food products, textiles, petroleum products, chemicals and transport equipment. Offshore banking and tourism are important.

UZBEKISTAN
Status: REPUBLIC
Area: 447,400 sq km (172,742 sq mls)
Population: 21,860,000
Capital: TASHKENT
Language: UZBEK, RUSSIAN, TAJIK,
KAZAKH
Religion: SUNNI MUSLIM,
RUSSIAN ORTHODOX
Currency: SOM
Organizations: CIS, UN

MAP PAGE: 46-47

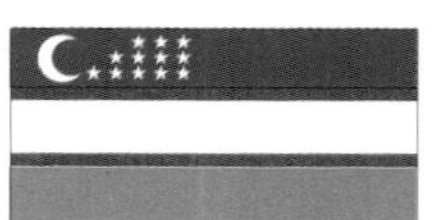

A REPUBLIC OF central Asia, Uzbekistan borders the Aral Sea and five countries. It consists mainly of the flat desert of the Kyzyl Kum, which rises eastwards towards the mountains of the western Pamirs. Most settlement is in the Fergana basin. The climate is dry and arid. The economy is based mainly on irrigated agriculture, chiefly cotton production. Industry specializes in fertilizers and machinery for cotton harvesting and textile manufacture. Uzbekistan is rich in minerals and has the largest gold mine in the world.

VANUATU
Status: REPUBLIC
Area: 12,190 sq km (4,707 sq mls)
Population: 156,000
Capital: PORT-VILA
Language: ENGLISH, BISLAMA
(ENGLISH CREOLE), FRENCH
(ALL OFFICIAL)
Religion: PROTESTANT, R.CATHOLIC,
TRAD.BELIEFS
Currency: VATU
Organizations: COMM., UN

MAP PAGE: 6

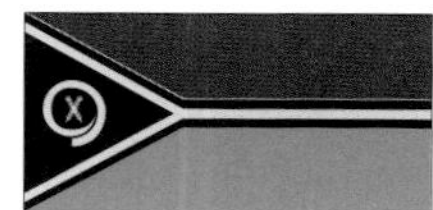

VANUATU OCCUPIES AN archipelago of some 80 islands in Oceania. Many of the islands are mountainous, of volcanic origin and densely forested. The climate is tropical with heavy rainfall. Half the population lives on the main islands of Efate, Santo and Tafea, and the majority of people live by farming. Copra, beef, seashells, cocoa and timber are the main exports. Tourism is growing and foreign aid is important.

VATICAN CITY
Status: ECCLESIASTICAL STATE
Area: .44 sq km (.17 sq mls)
Population: 1,000
Language: ITALIAN
Religion: R.CATHOLIC
Currency: ITALIAN LIRA

MAP PAGE: 109

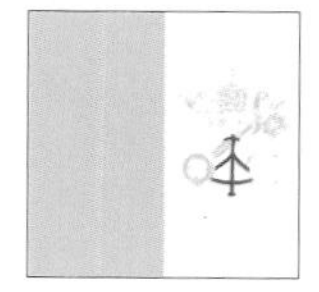

THE WORLD'S SMALLEST sovereign state, the Vatican City occupies a hill to the west of the river Tiber in the Italian capital, Rome. It is the headquarters of the Roman Catholic church and income comes from investments, voluntary contributions and tourism.

VENEZUELA
Status: REPUBLIC
Area: 912,050 sq km (352,144 sq mls)
Population: 20,712,000
Capital: CARACAS
Language: SPANISH, AMERINDIAN
LANGUAGES
Religion: R.CATHOLIC, PROTESTANT
Currency: BOLÍVAR
Organizations: OPEC, UN

MAP PAGE: 162-163

VENEZUELA IS IN northern South America, on the Caribbean Sea. Its coast is much indented, with the oil-rich area of Lake Maracaibo at the western end and the swampy Orinoco delta in the east. Mountain ranges run parallel to the coast then turn southwestwards to form the northern extension of the Andes chain. Central Venezuela is lowland grasslands drained by the Orinoco river system, while to the south are the Guiana Highlands which contain the Angel Falls, the world's highest waterfall. About 85 per cent of the population lives in towns, mostly in the coastal mountain areas. The climate is tropical, with summer rainfall. Temperatures are lower in the mountains. Venezuela is an important oil producer, and sales account for about 75 per cent of export earnings. Bauxite, iron ore and gold are also mined and manufactures include aluminium, iron and steel, textiles, timber and wood products, and petrochemicals. Farming is important, particularly cattle ranching and dairy farming. Coffee, cotton, maize, rice and sugarcane are major crops.

VIETNAM
Status: REPUBLIC
Area: 329,565 sq km (127,246 sq mls)
Population: 71,324,000
Capital: HANOI
Language: VIETNAMESE, THAI, KHMER, CHINESE, MANY LOCAL LANGUAGES
Religion: BUDDHIST, TAOIST, R.CATHOLIC, CAO DAI, HOA HAO
Currency: DONG
Organizations: UN

MAP PAGE: 24-25

VIETNAM EXTENDS ALONG the east coast of the Indochina peninsula in southeast Asia, with the South China Sea to the east and south. The Red River (Song-koi) delta lowlands in the north are separated from the huge Mekong delta in the south by narrow coastal plains backed by the generally rough mountainous and forested terrain of the Annam highlands. Most people live in the river deltas. The climate is tropical, with summer monsoon rains. Over three quarters of the workforce is involved in agriculture, forestry and fishing. Rice growing is the main activity, and Vietnam is the world's third largest rice exporter, after the USA and Thailand. Coffee, tea and rubber are the main cash crops. The north is fairly rich in minerals including some oil, coal, iron ore, manganese, apatite and gold. The food processing and textile industries are important, but the steel, oil and gas and car industries are growing rapidly. The 1992 economic reform programme, inflow of foreign investment and the 1994 lifting of the US trade embargo are boosting an economy which suffered from decades of war and strife.

VIRGIN ISLANDS (UK)
Status: UK TERRITORY
Area: 153 sq km (59 sq mls)
Population: 18,000
Capital: ROAD TOWN
Language: ENGLISH
Religion: PROTESTANT, R.CATHOLIC
Currency: US DOLLAR

MAP PAGE: 159

THE CARIBBEAN TERRITORY comprises four main islands and some 36 islets at the eastern end of the Virgin Islands group. Apart from the flat coral atoll of Anegada, the islands are volcanic in origin and hilly. The climate is subtropical and tourism is the main industry.

VIRGIN ISLANDS (USA)
Status: US TERRITORY
Area: 352 sq km (136 sq mls)
Population: 104,000
Capital: CHARLOTTE AMALIE
Language: ENGLISH, SPANISH
Religion: PROTESTANT, R.CATHOLIC
Currency: US DOLLAR

MAP PAGE: 159

THE TERRITORY CONSISTS of three main islands and some 50 islets in the Caribbean's western Virgin Islands. The islands are mostly hilly and of volcanic origin and the climate is subtropical. The economy is based on tourism, with some manufacturing on St Croix.

WALLIS AND FUTUNA
Status: FRENCH TERRITORY
Area: 274 sq km (106 sq mls)
Population: 14,000
Capital: MATA-UTU
Language: FRENCH, POLYNESIAN (WALLISIAN, FUTUNIAN)
Religion: R.CATHOLIC
Currency: PACIFIC FRANC

MAP PAGE: 4-5

THE SOUTH PACIFIC territory comprises the volcanic islands of the Wallis archipelago and Hoorn Islands. The climate is tropical. The islands depend upon subsistence farming, the sale of licences to foreign fishing fleets, workers' remittances and French aid.

WEST BANK
Status: TERRITORY
Area: 5,860 sq km (2,263 sq mls)
Population: 1,054,000
Language: ARABIC, HEBREW
Religion: SUNNI MUSLIM, JEWISH, SHI'A MUSLIM, CHRISTIAN

MAP PAGE: 43

THE TERRITORY CONSISTS of the west bank of the river Jordan and parts of Judea and Samaria in southwest Asia. The land was annexed by Israel in 1967, but the Jericho area was granted self-government under an agreement between Israel and the PLO in 1993.

WESTERN SAHARA
Status: TERRITORY
Area: 266,000 sq km (102,703 sq mls)
Population: 261,000
Capital: LAÂYOUNE
Language: ARABIC
Religion: SUNNI MUSLIM
Currency: MOROCCAN DIRHAM

MAP PAGE: 120

SITUATED ON THE northwest coast of Africa, the territory of Western Sahara is controlled by Morocco.

WESTERN SAMOA
Status: MONARCHY
Area: 2,831 sq km (1,093 sq mls)
Population: 163,000
Capital: APIA
Language: SAMOAN, ENGLISH
Religion: PROTESTANT, R.CATHOLIC, MORMON
Currency: TALA
Organizations: COMM., UN

MAP PAGE: 7

WESTERN SAMOA CONSISTS of two main mountainous and forested islands and seven small islands in the South Pacific Ocean. Seventy per cent of people live on Upolu. The climate is tropical. The economy is based on agriculture, with some fishing and light manufacturing. Traditional exports are coconut products, timber, taro, cocoa and fruit, but cyclones in recent years devastated the coconut palms. Tourism is increasing, but the islands depend upon workers' remittances and foreign aid.

YEMEN
Status: REPUBLIC
Area: 527,968 sq km (203,850 sq mls)
Population: 12,302,000
Capital: SANA
Language: ARABIC
Religion: SUNNI MUSLIM, SHI'A MUSLIM
Currency: DINAR, RIAL
Organizations: UN

MAP PAGE: 40-41

YEMEN OCCUPIES THE southwestern Arabian Peninsula, on the Red Sea and Gulf of Aden. Beyond the Red Sea coastal plain the land rises to a mountain range then descends to desert plateaux. Much of Yemen is hot and arid, but rainfall in the west supports crops and most settlement. Farming and fishing are the main activities, with cotton the main cash crop. Oil production is increasingly important. Remittances from workers abroad are the main foreign exchange earner.

YUGOSLAVIA
Status: REPUBLIC
Area: 102,173 sq km (39,449 sq mls)
Population: 10,485,000
Capital: BELGRADE
Language: SERBO-CROAT, ALBANIAN, HUNGARIAN
Religion: SERBIAN ORTHODOX, MONTENEGRIN ORTHODOX, SUNNI MUSLIM
Currency: DINAR
Organizations: UN

MAP PAGE: 112

THE SOUTH EUROPEAN state comprises only two of the former Yugoslav republics: the large and populous but landlocked Serbia and the much smaller Montenegro on the Adriatic Sea. The landscape is for the most part rugged, mountainous and forested. Northern Serbia (including the formerly autonomous province of Vojvodina) is low-lying, drained by the Danube river system. The climate is Mediterranean on the coast, continental inland. War and economic sanctions have ruined Serbia's economy and damaged that of Montenegro.

ZAIRE
Status: REPUBLIC
Area: 2,345,410 sq km (905,568 sq mls)
Population: 41,231,000
Capital: KINSHASA
Language: FRENCH, LINGALA, SWAHILI, KONGO, MANY LOCAL LANGUAGES
Religion: R.CATHOLIC, PROTESTANT, SUNNI MUSLIM, TRAD. BELIEFS
Currency: ZAÏRE
Organizations: OAU, UN

MAP PAGE: 124-125

THE CENTRAL AFRICAN state of Zaire consists of the basin of the Zaire river flanked by plateaux, with high mountain ranges to the north and east and a short Atlantic coastline to the west. The climate is tropical with rainforest close to the Equator and savannah to the north and south. Zaire has fertile land that grows a range of food crops and cash crops, chiefly coffee. It has vast mineral resources, copper and diamonds being the most important. However economic mismanagement and political turmoil have ruined the economy.

ZAMBIA
Status: REPUBLIC
Area: 752,614 sq km (290,586 sq mls)
Population: 8,936,000
Capital: LUSAKA
Language: ENGLISH, BEMBA, NYANJA, TONGA, MANY LOCAL LANGUAGES
Religion: PROTESTANT, R.CATHOLIC, TRAD. BELIEFS, SUNNI MUSLIM
Currency: KWACHA
Organizations: COMM., OAU, SADC, UN

MAP PAGE: 124-125

A LANDLOCKED STATE in central Africa, Zambia borders seven countries. It is dominated by high savannah plateaux and flanked by the Zambezi river in the south. Most people live in the central Copperbelt. The climate is tropical with a rainy season from November to May. Agriculture, which involves 70 per cent of the workforce, is mainly at subsistence level. Copper is still the mainstay of the economy, though reserves are declining. Lead, zinc, cobalt and tobacco are also exported. Manufacturing and tourism are important.

ZIMBABWE
Status: REPUBLIC
Area: 390,759 sq km (150,873 sq mls)
Population: 10,739,000
Capital: HARARE
Language: ENGLISH (OFFICIAL), SHONA, NDEBELE
Religion: PROTESTANT, R.CATHOLIC, TRAD.BELIEFS
Currency: DOLLAR
Organizations: COMM., OAU, SADC, UN

MAP PAGE: 128-129

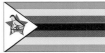

ZIMBABWE, A LANDLOCKED state in southern central Africa, consists of high plateaux flanked by the Zambezi river valley and Lake Kariba in the north and the Limpopo in the south. Climatic conditions are temperate because of altitude. Most people live in central Zimbabwe. Tobacco, cotton, sugar, tea, coffee and beef are produced for export as are a variety of minerals including gold, nickel, asbestos and copper. Manufacturing provides a wide range of goods. Tourism is a major foreign exchange earner.

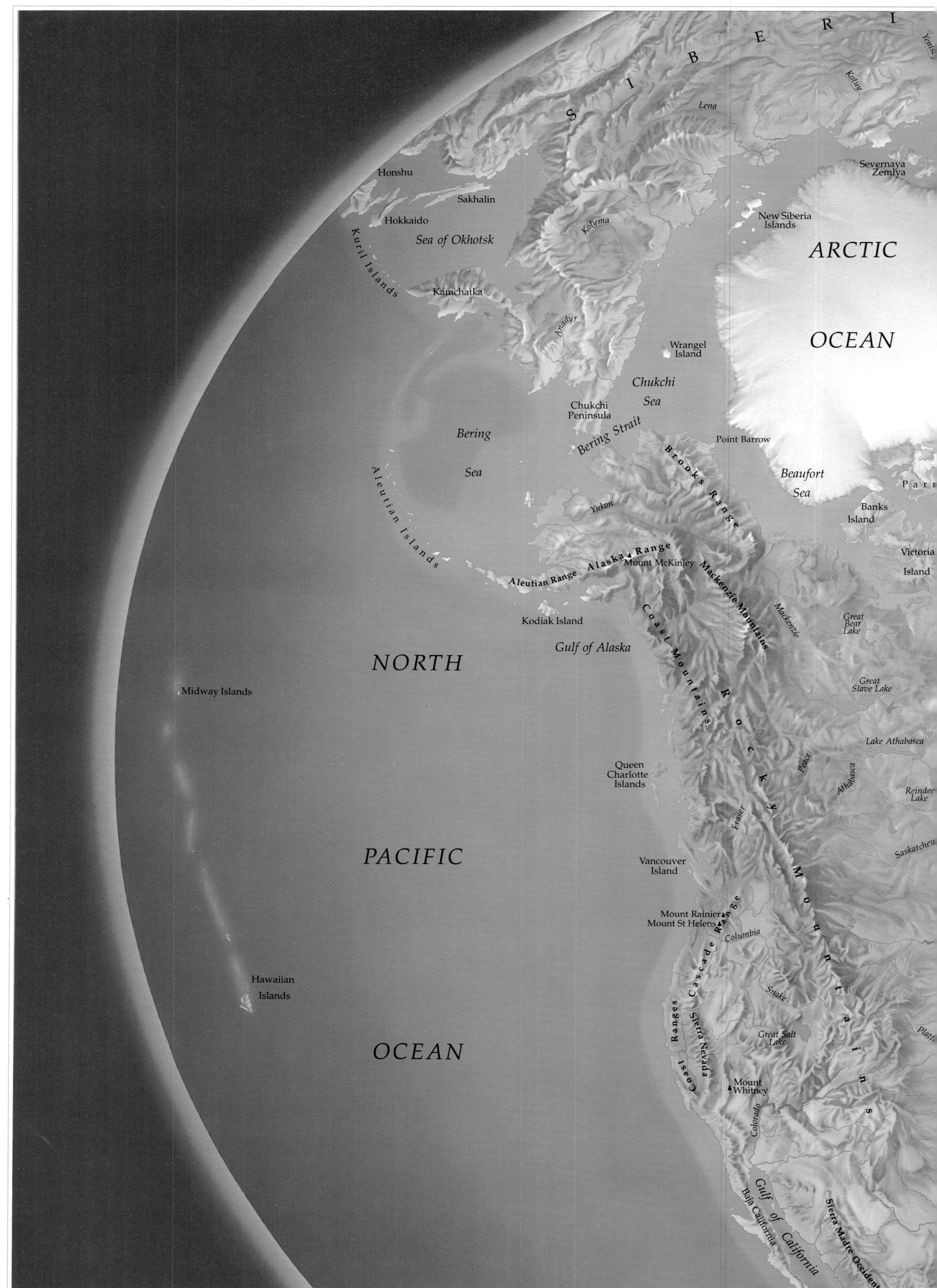

S I B E R I

Yenise

Kotuy

Lena

SIBERIA

Severnaya
Zemlya

Honshu

Sakhalin

New Siberia
Islands

ARCTIC

Hokkaido

Sea of Okhotsk

Kolyma

OCEAN

Kuril Islands

Kamchatka

Anadyr

Wrangel
Island

Chukchi

Sea

Chukchi
Peninsula

Bering

Point Barrow

Beaufort

Par

Bering Strait

Brooks Range

Sea

Sea

Banks
Island

Yukon

Aleutian Islands

Victoria

Alaska Range

Mount McKinley

Mackenzie Mountains

Island

Aleutian Range

Mackenzie

*Great
Bear
Lake*

Kodiak Island

Coast Mountains

Gulf of Alaska

NORTH

*Great
Slave Lake*

Midway Islands

R
o
c
k
y

Lake Athabasca

Queen
Charlotte
Islands

Peace

Athabasca

*Reindeer
Lake*

Fraser

Saskatchewan

PACIFIC

Vancouver
Island

M
o
u
n
t
a
i
n
s

Mount Rainier
Mount St Helens

Columbia

Cascade Range

Snake

Hawaiian
Islands

C
o
a
s
t

R
a
n
g
e
s

Sierra Nevada

*Great Salt
Lake*

Platte

OCEAN

Mount
Whitney

Colorado

Gulf of California

Baja California

Sierra Madre Occidental

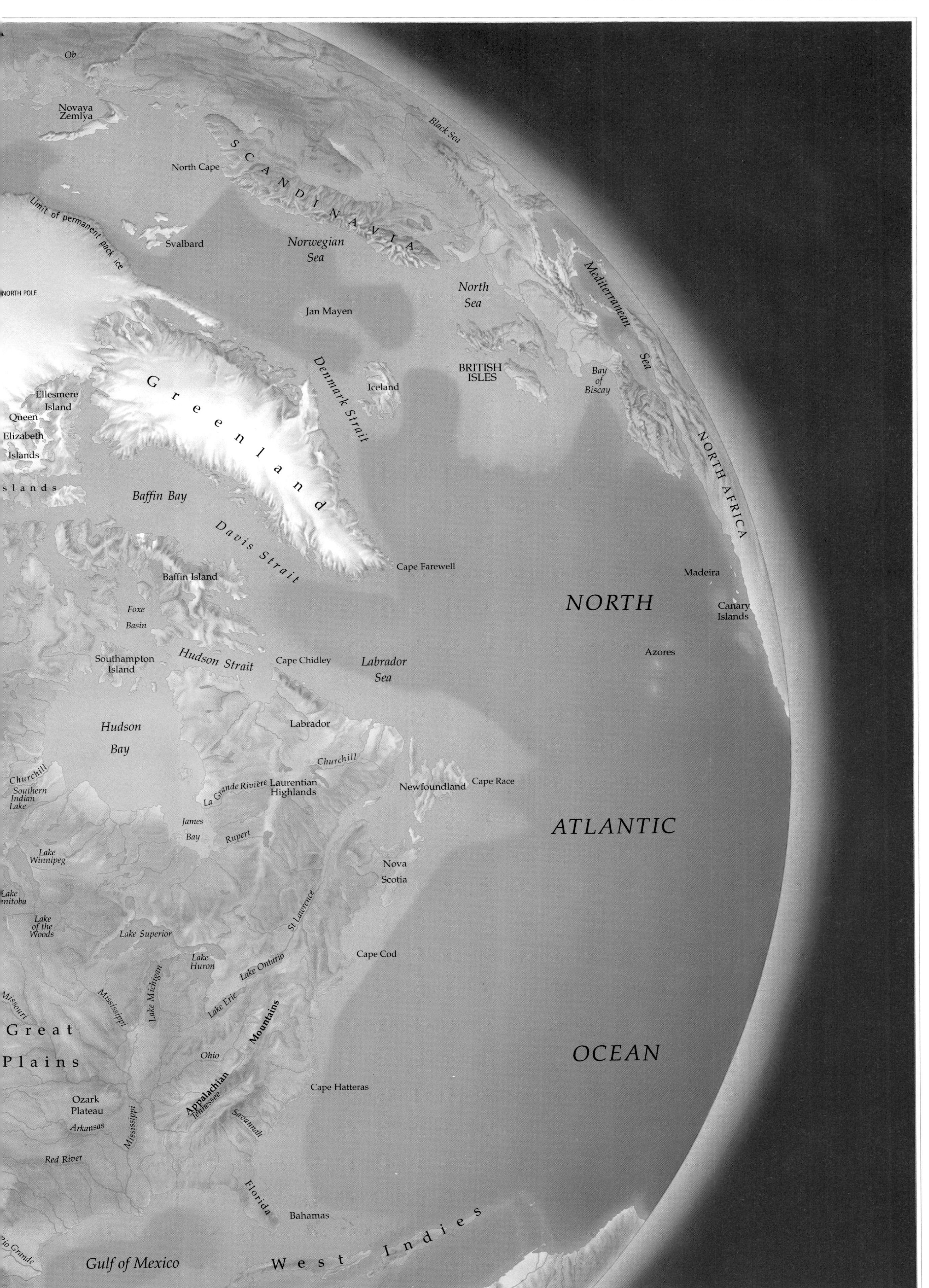

Ob

Novaya
Zemlya

North Cape

S C A N D I N A V I A

Black Sea

Svalbard

Norwegian
Sea

North
Sea

Limit of permanent pack ice

Jan Mayen

Mediterranean Sea

NORTH POLE

Denmark Strait

Iceland

BRITISH
ISLES

Bay
of
Biscay

Ellesmere
Island

G r e e n l a n d

Queen

Elizabeth

Islands

slands

Baffin Bay

NORTH AFRICA

Davis Strait

Cape Farewell

Madeira

Baffin Island

NORTH

Canary
Islands

Foxe
Basin

Azores

Southampton
Island

Hudson Strait

Cape Chidley

Labrador
Sea

Hudson
Bay

Labrador

Churchill

Churchill

La Grande Rivière

Laurentian
Highlands

Newfoundland

Cape Race

ATLANTIC

Southern
Indian
Lake

James
Bay

Rupert

Lake
Winnipeg

Nova
Scotia

Lake
nitoba

Lake
of the
Woods

St Lawrence

Lake Superior

Cape Cod

Lake
Huron

Lake Michigan

Lake Ontario

Mississippi

Lake Erie

Cape Hatteras

G r e a t

Mountains

Ohio

OCEAN

P l a i n s

Appalachian

Ozark
Plateau

Tennessee

Arkansas

Savannah

Missouri

Mississippi

Red River

Florida

o Grande

Bahamas

Gulf of Mexico

W e s t   I n d i e s

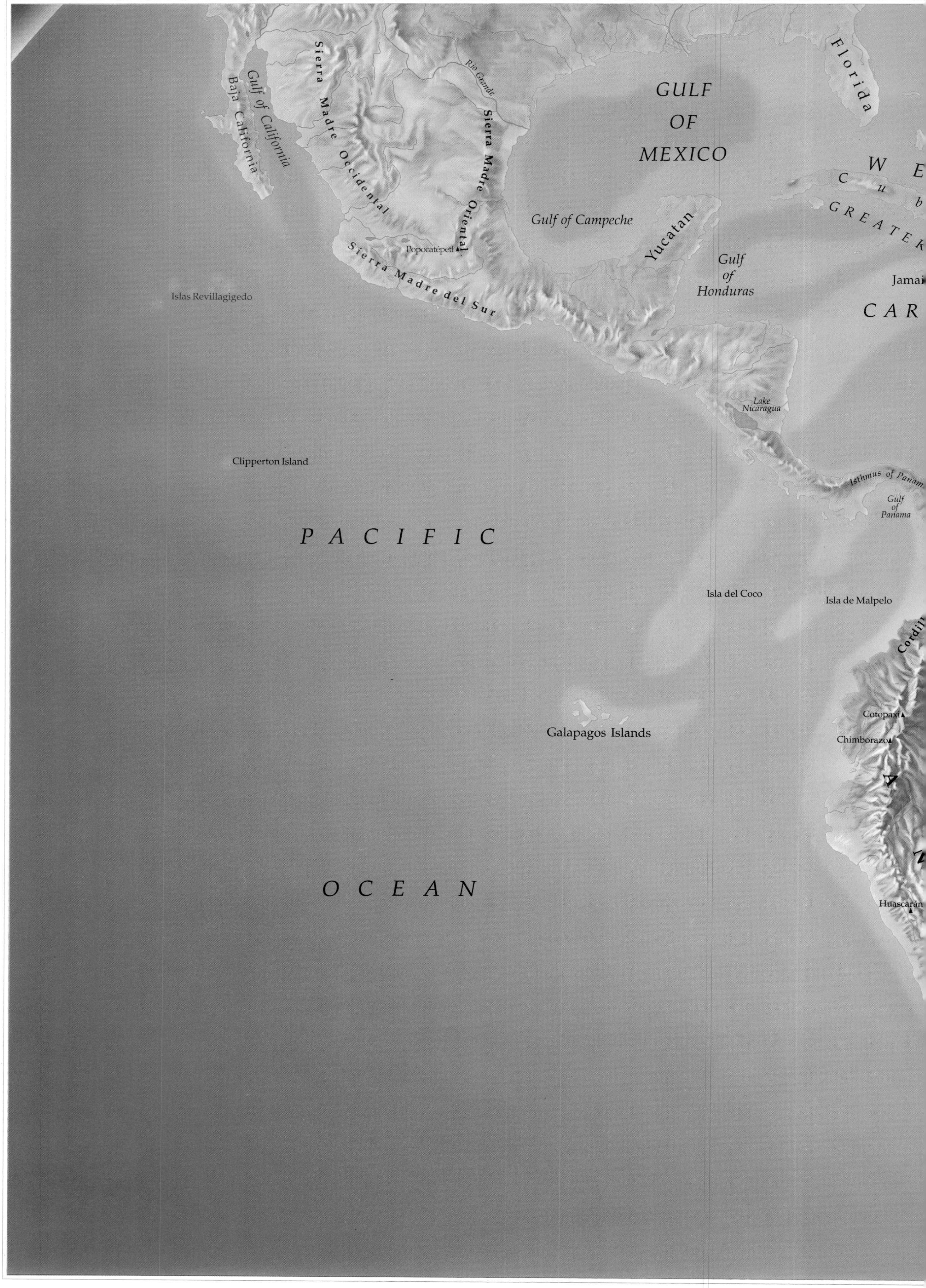

Florida

Sierra Madre

Río Grande

Gulf of California

Baja California

Sierra Madre Occidental

Sierra Madre Oriental

GULF
OF
MEXICO

Gulf of Campeche

Yucatan

Popocatépetl

W E

C
u
b

GREATER

Jamai

CAR

Sierra Madre del Sur

Gulf
of
Honduras

Islas Revillagigedo

Lake
Nicaragua

Isthmus of Panama

Gulf
of
Panama

Clipperton Island

PACIFIC

Isla del Coco

Isla de Malpelo

Cordi

Cotopaxi

Chimborazo

Galapagos Islands

OCEAN

Huascarán

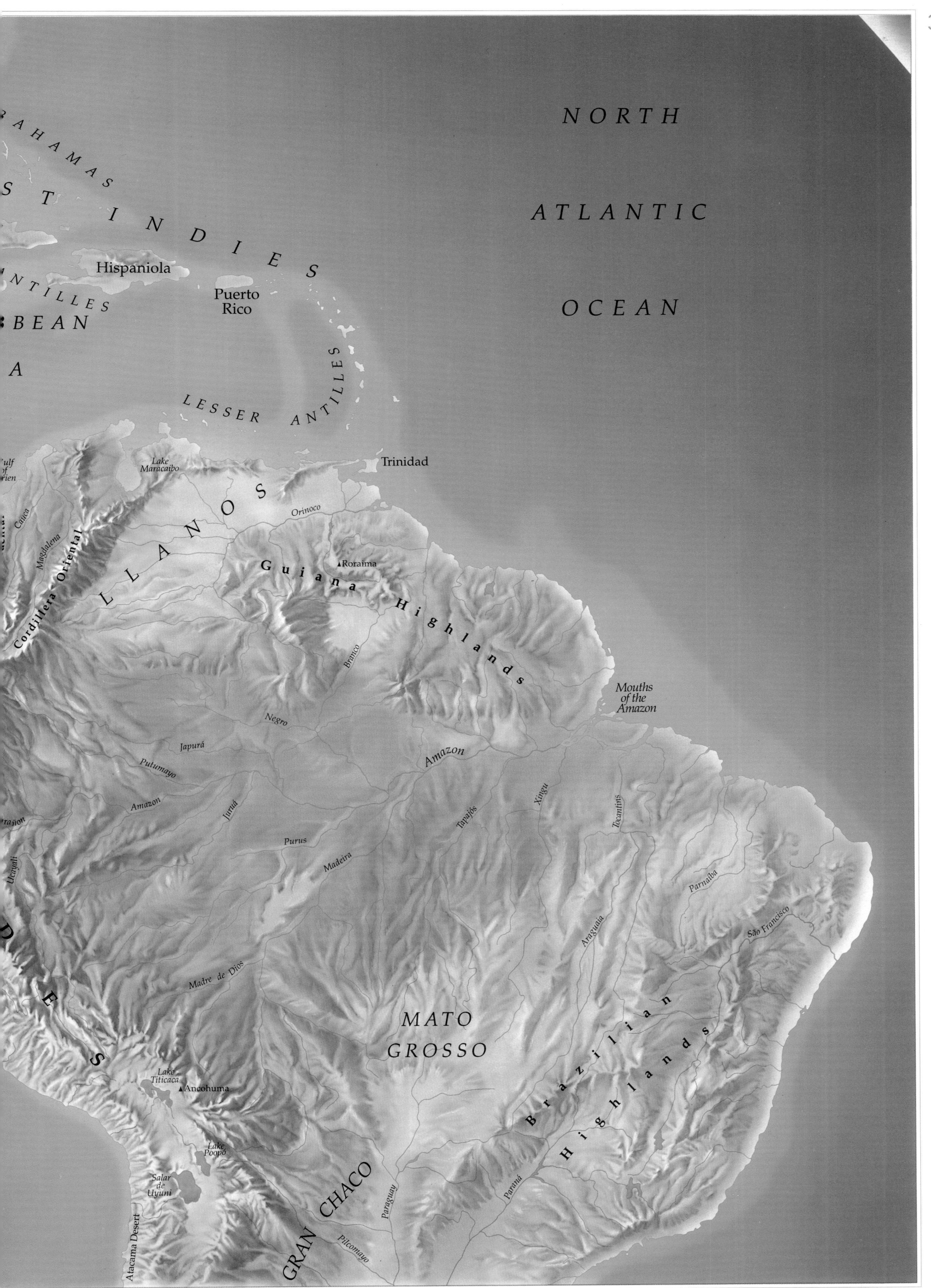

NORTH

ATLANTIC

OCEAN

BAHAMAS

ST INDIES

Hispaniola

Puerto
Rico

NTILLES

BEAN

A

LESSER ANTILLES

Trinidad

Gulf
of
rien

Lake
Maracaibo

LLANOS

Orinoco

Cauca

Magdalena

Cordillera Oriental

Guiana Highlands

▲Roraima

Branco

Mouths
of the
Amazon

Negro

Japurá

Amazon

Putumayo

Amazon

Juruá

Tapajós

Xingu

Tocantins

rajon

Ucayali

Purus

Madeira

Madre de Dios

Parnaíba

Araguaia

São Francisco

Lake
Titicaca

▲Ancohuma

MATO
GROSSO

Brazilian Highlands

Lake
Poopó

Salar
de
Uyuni

GRAN CHACO

Paraguay

Paraná

Atacama Desert

Pilcomayo

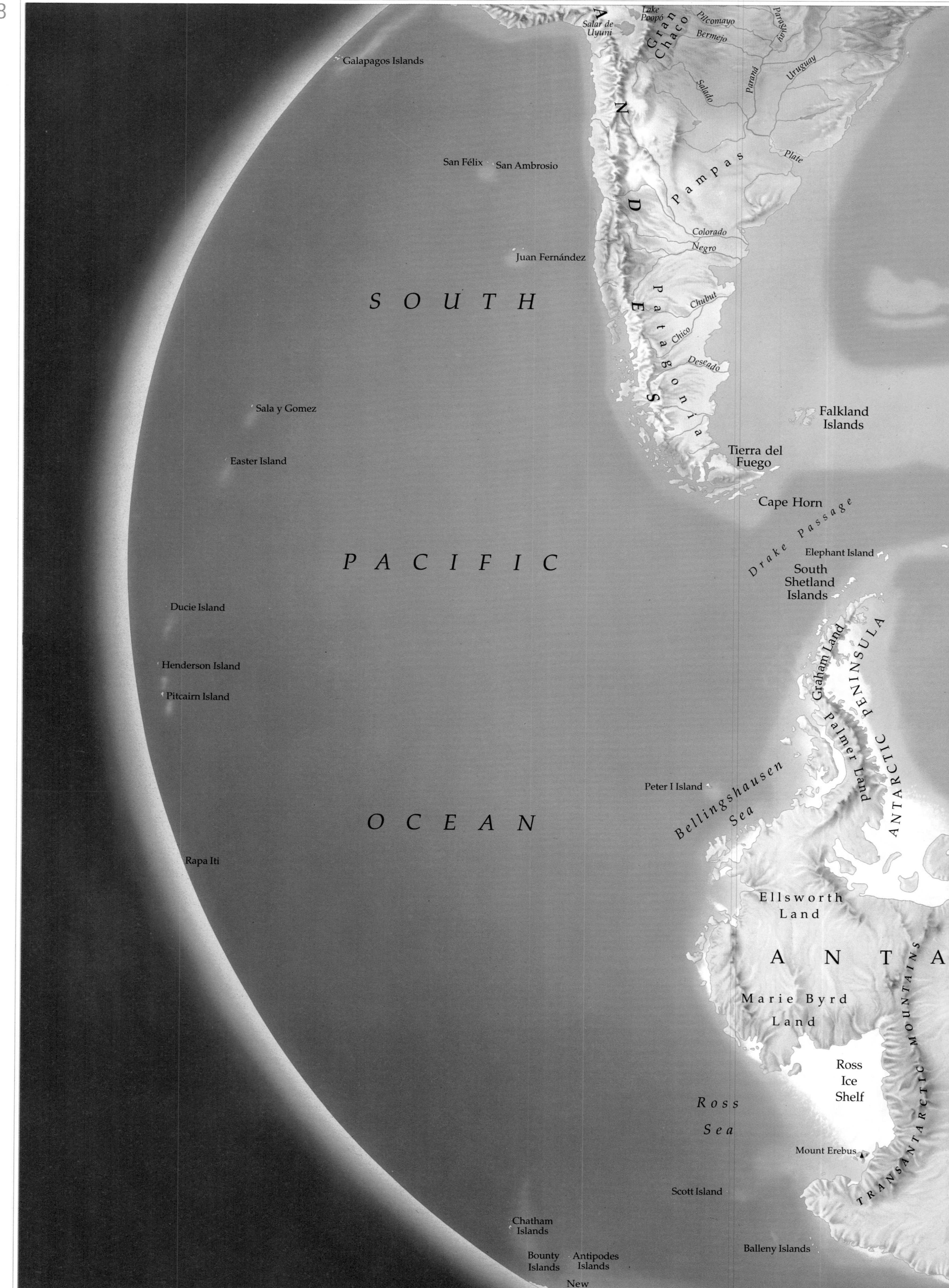

Galapagos Islands

Salar de Uyuni Lake Poopó *Gran Chaco* *Pilcomayo* *Bermejo* *Paraguay*

A N D *Saludo* *Paraná* *Uruguay*

Pampas *Plate*

San Félix   San Ambrosio

Colorado

Negro

S O U T H   *E* *Chubut*

Juan Fernández   *Chico*

S *Deseado*

Patagonia

Sala y Gomez

Falkland Islands

Easter Island

Tierra del Fuego

Cape Horn   *Drake Passage*

P A C I F I C   Elephant Island   South Shetland Islands

Ducie Island   *Graham Land*   *Palmer Land*   PENINSULA

ANTARCTIC

Henderson Island

Pitcairn Island

Peter I Island   *Bellingshausen*   *Sea*

O C E A N

Ellsworth Land

Rapa Iti   A N T A

TRANSANTARCTIC MOUNTAINS

M a r i e   B y r d   L a n d

Ross Ice Shelf

R o s s

S e a

Mount Erebus

Scott Island

Chatham Islands

Bounty Islands   Antipodes Islands   Balleny Islands

New Zealand   Campbell Island   I N D I A N

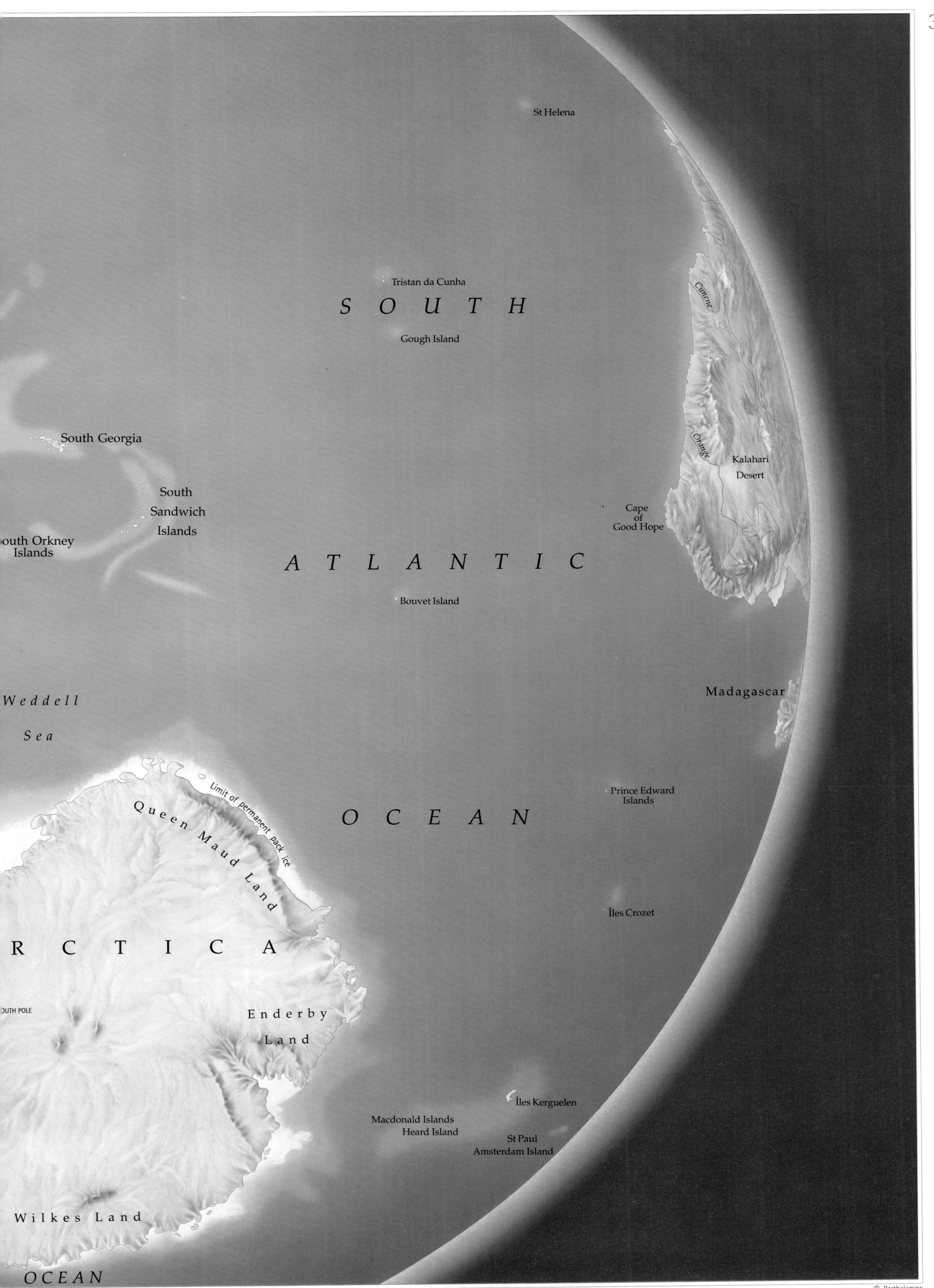

St Helena

S O U T H

Tristan da Cunha

Gough Island

Cunene

South Georgia

Orange

Kalahari
Desert

South
Sandwich
Islands

Cape
of
Good Hope

outh Orkney
Islands

A T L A N T I C

Bouvet Island

Madagascar

W e d d e l l

S e a

Prince Edward
Islands

O C E A N

Limit of permanent pack ice

Queen Maud Land

Îles Crozet

R C T I C A

OUTH POLE

E n d e r b y
L a n d

Îles Kerguelen

Macdonald Islands
Heard Island

St Paul
Amsterdam Island

W i l k e s L a n d

OCEAN

© Bartholomew

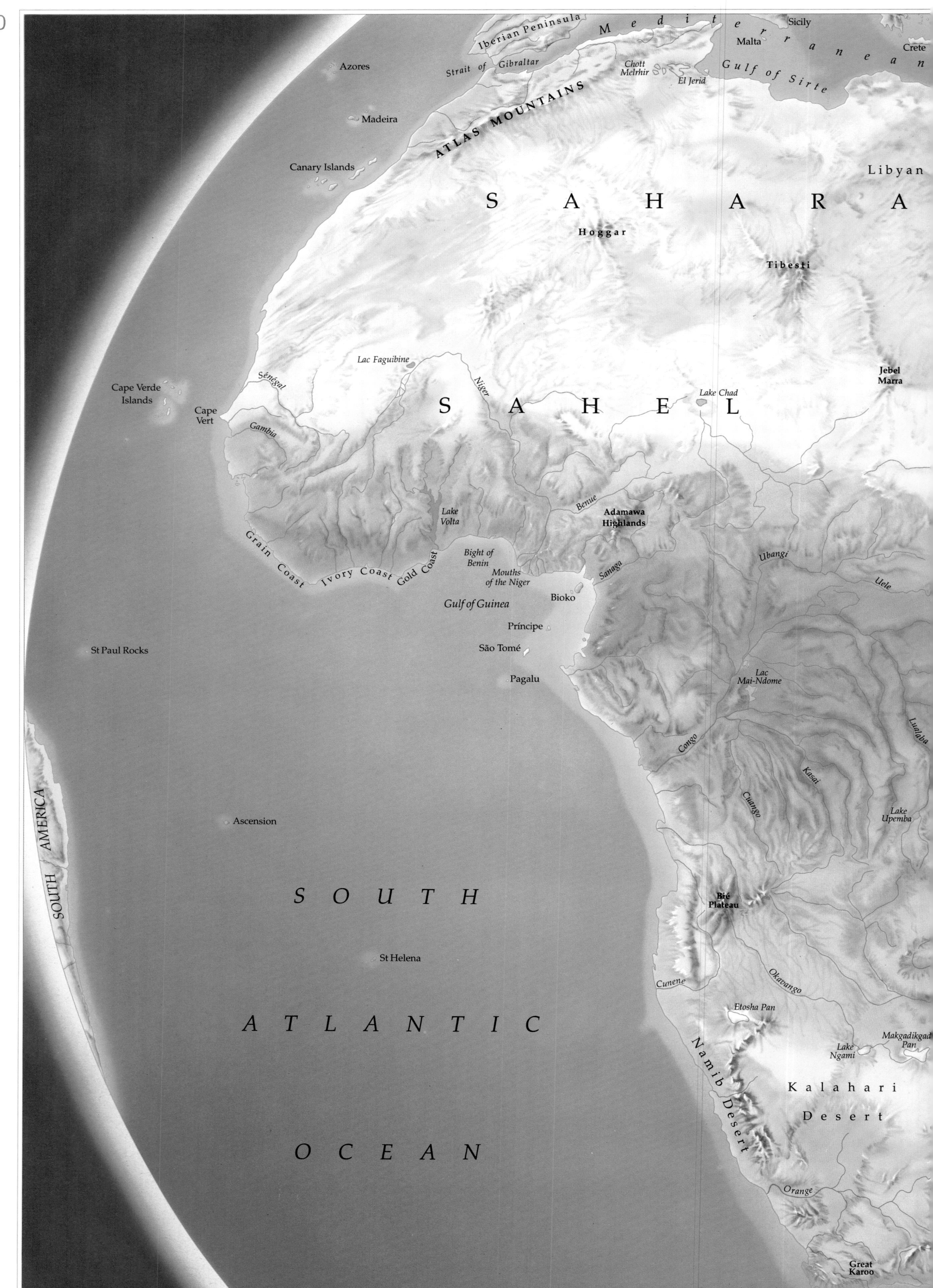

Iberian Peninsula

Azores

Strait of Gibraltar

Madeira

ATLAS MOUNTAINS

Canary Islands

Mediterranean

Sicily

Malta

Crete

Gulf of Sirte

Chott
Melrhir

El Jerid

S A H A R A

Libyan

Hoggar

Tibesti

Jebel
Marra

Cape Verde
Islands

Sénégal

Lac Faguibine

Niger

S A H E L

Lake Chad

Cape
Vert

Gambia

Grain Coast

Ivory Coast

Gold Coast

Lake
Volta

Bight of
Benin

Mouths
of the Niger

Gulf of Guinea

Benue

Adamawa
Highlands

Sanaga

Ubangi

Uele

Bioko

Príncipe

St Paul Rocks

São Tomé

Pagalu

Lac
Mai-Ndome

Congo

Kasai

Cuango

Luaiaba

Lake
Upemba

SOUTH AMERICA

Ascension

S O U T H

Bié
Plateau

St Helena

A T L A N T I C

Cunene

Okavango

Namib Desert

Etosha Pan

Lake
Ngami

Makgadikgadi
Pan

K a l a h a r i

O C E A N

D e s e r t

Orange

Great
Karoo

Cape of Good Hope

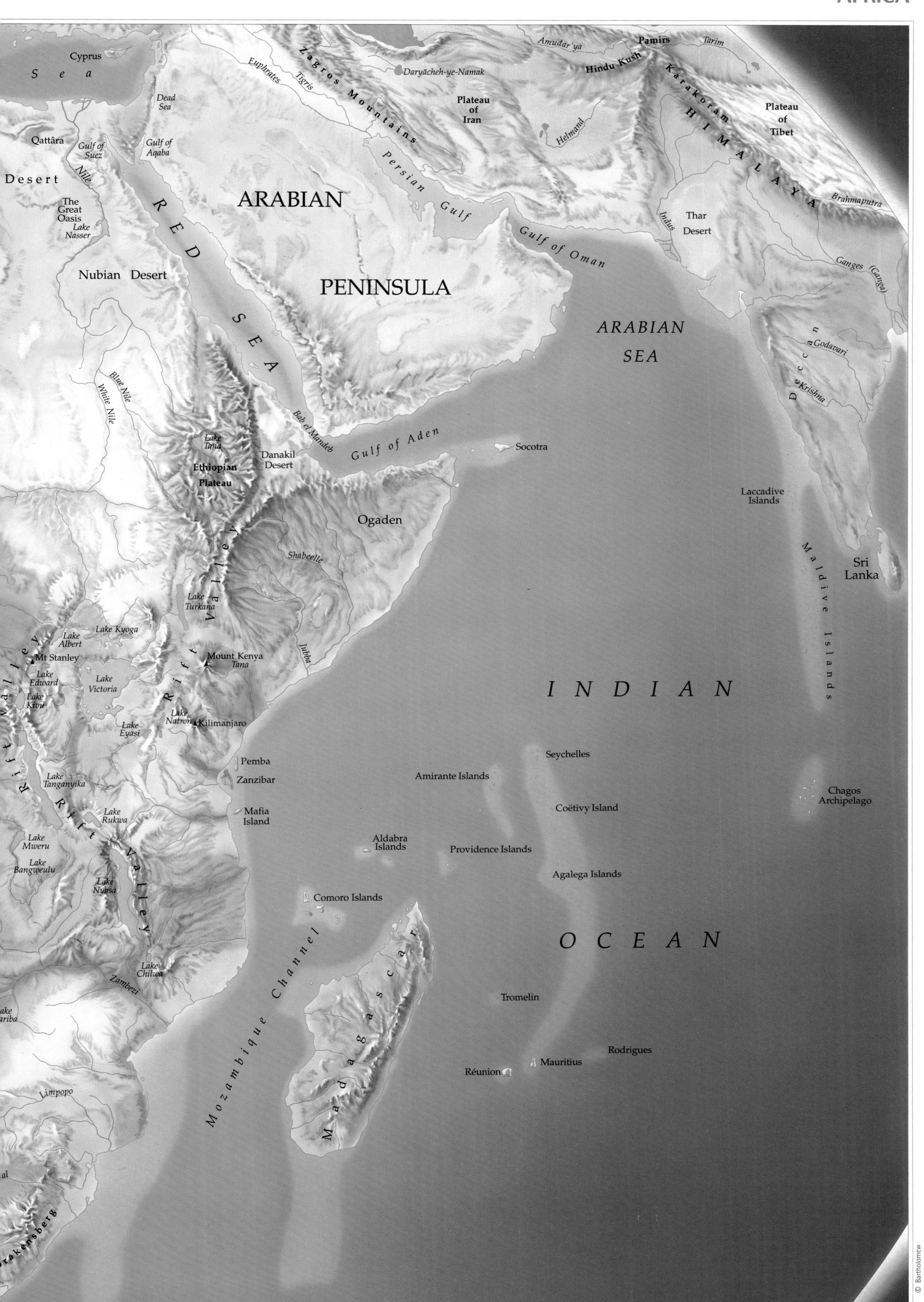

Cyprus

Sea

Qattâra

Gulf of
Suez

Gulf of
Aqaba

Dead
Sea

Euphrates

Zagros Mountains

Tigris

Daryācheh-ye-Namak

Amudar'ya

Pamirs

Hindu Kush

Tarim

Karakoram

Plateau
of Iran

HIMALAYA

Plateau
of
Tibet

Helmand

Brahmaputra

Nile

Desert

The
Great
Oasis

Lake
Nasser

Nubian Desert

ARABIAN

PENINSULA

RED SEA

Blue Nile

White Nile

Lake
Tana

Danakil
Desert

Bab el Mandeb

Ethiopian
Plateau

Ogaden

Shabeelle

Lake
Turkana

Juba

Rift Valley

Lake Kyoga

Lake
Albert

Mt Stanley

Mount Kenya
Tana

Lake
Edward

Lake
Kivu

Lake
Victoria

Lake
Eyasi

Lake
Natron

Kilimanjaro

Rift Valley

Lake
Tanganyika

Pemba

Zanzibar

Mafia
Island

Lake
Rukwa

Lake
Mweru

Lake
Bangweulu

Lake
Nyasa

Comoro Islands

Lake
Chilwa

Zambezi

Limpopo

Drakensberg

Persian Gulf

Gulf of Oman

Indus

Thar
Desert

Ganges (Ganga)

Deccan

Godavari

Krishna

ARABIAN
SEA

Gulf of Aden

Socotra

Laccadive
Islands

Maldive Islands

Sri
Lanka

INDIAN

Seychelles

Amirante Islands

Coëtivy Island

Aldabra
Islands

Providence Islands

Agalega Islands

Chagos
Archipelago

OCEAN

Mozambique Channel

Madagascar

Tromelin

Réunion

Mauritius

Rodrigues

© Bartholomew

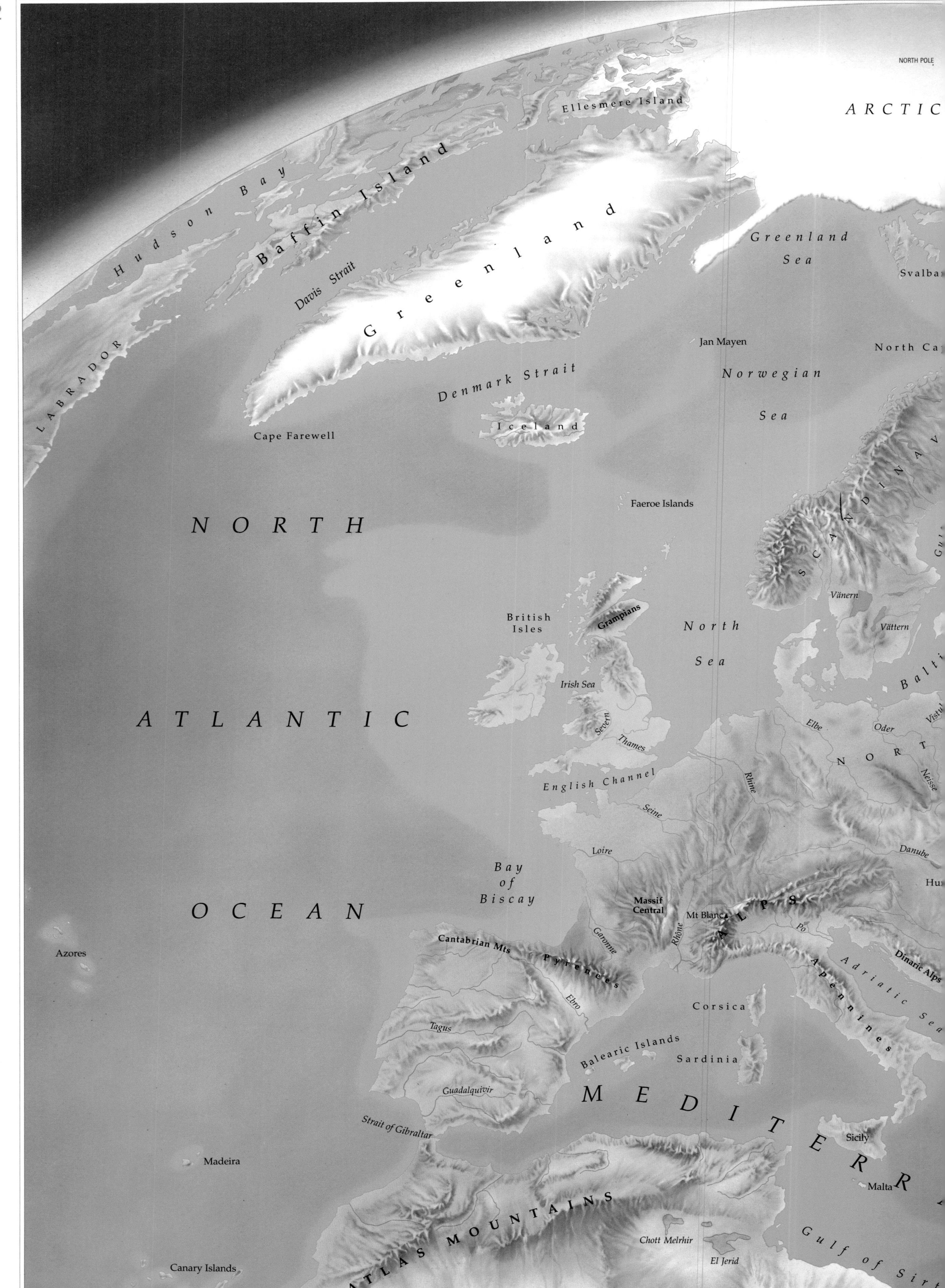

NORTH POLE

ARCTIC

Ellesmere Island

Greenland
Sea

Svalba

Hudson Bay

Baffin Island

Greenland

Jan Mayen

North Ca

Davis Strait

LABRADOR

Norwegian

Sea

Denmark Strait

Cape Farewell

Iceland

Faeroe Islands

NORTH

SCANDINAV

GU

Vänern

Vättern

British
Isles

Grampians

North

Sea

Balti

ATLANTIC

Irish Sea

Severn

Thames

Elbe

Oder

Vistu

Neisse

N O R T

Rhine

English Channel

Seine

Loire

Danube

Hu

OCEAN

Bay
of
Biscay

Massif
Central

Mt Blanc

A L P S

Po

Azores

Cantabrian Mts

Pyrenees

Garonne

Rhône

Apennines

Adriatic Sea

Dinaric Alps

Corsica

Ebro

Tagus

Balearic Islands

Sardinia

M E D I T E R R

Guadalquivir

Strait of Gibraltar

Sicily

Madeira

Malta

ATLAS MOUNTAINS

Chott Melrhir

Gulf of Sirt

Canary Islands

El Jerid

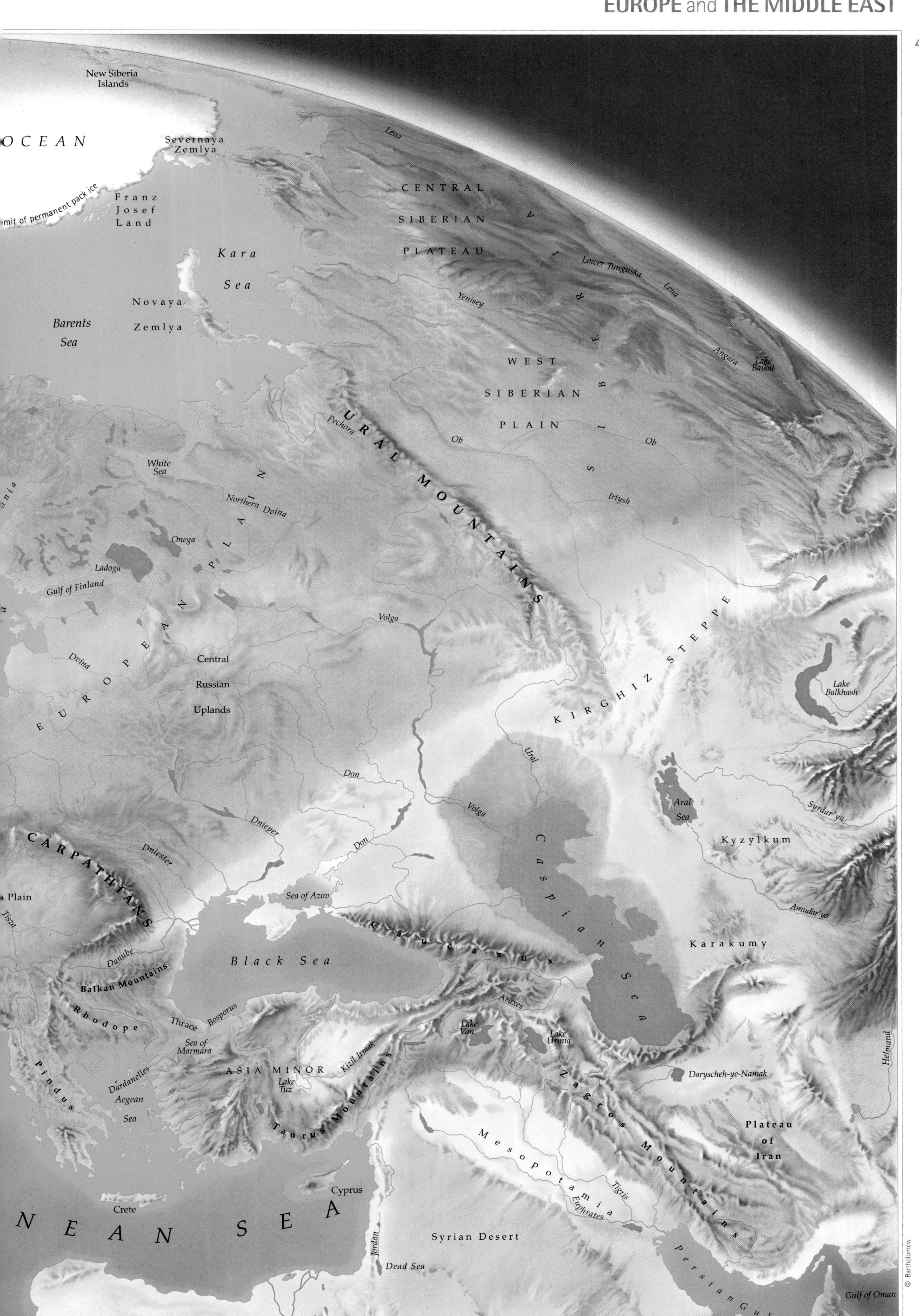

New Siberia
Islands

OCEAN

Severnaya
Zemlya

Limit of permanent pack ice

Franz
Josef
Land

*Kara
Sea*

Novaya
Zemlya

*Barents
Sea*

C E N T R A L

S I B E R I A N

P L A T E A U

Lena

Lower Tunguska

Lena

Yenisey

W E S T

S I B E R I A N

P L A I N

S
I
B
E
R
I
A

Angara

*Lake
Baikal*

*White
Sea*

Northern Dvina

Pechora

U
R
A
L

M
O
U
N
T
A
I
N
S

Ob

Ob

Irtysh

Onega

Ladoga

Gulf of Finland

E
U
R
O
P
E
A
N

P
L
A
I
N

Volga

Central

Russian

Uplands

Dvina

K I R G H I Z   S T E P P E

*Lake
Balkhash*

Don

Ural

Volga

*Aral
Sea*

Syrdar'ya

K y z y l k u m

C A R P A T H I A N S

Dnieper

Dniester

Don

Plain

Tisza

Sea of Azov

C
a
s
p
i
a
n

S
e
a

Amudar'ya

Danube

Balkan Mountains

*C
a
u
c
a
s
u
s*

K a r a k u m y

Rhodope

Thrace

Bosporus

Black Sea

Araxes

*P
i
n
d
u
s*

*Sea of
Marmara*

Dardanelles

*Aegean
Sea*

Crete

A S I A   M I N O R

Kizil Irmak

T
a
u
r
u
s

M
o
u
n
t
a
i
n
s

*Lake
Van*

*Lake
Urmia*

Daryacheh-ye-Namak

Z
a
g
r
o
s

M
o
u
n
t
a
i
n
s

Helmand

**Plateau
of
Iran**

Cyprus

*Lake
Tuz*

N E A N   S E A

Jordan

Dead Sea

Syrian Desert

M
e
s
o
p
o
t
a
m
i
a

Euphrates

Tigris

*P
e
r
s
i
a
n

G
u
l
f*

Gulf of Oman

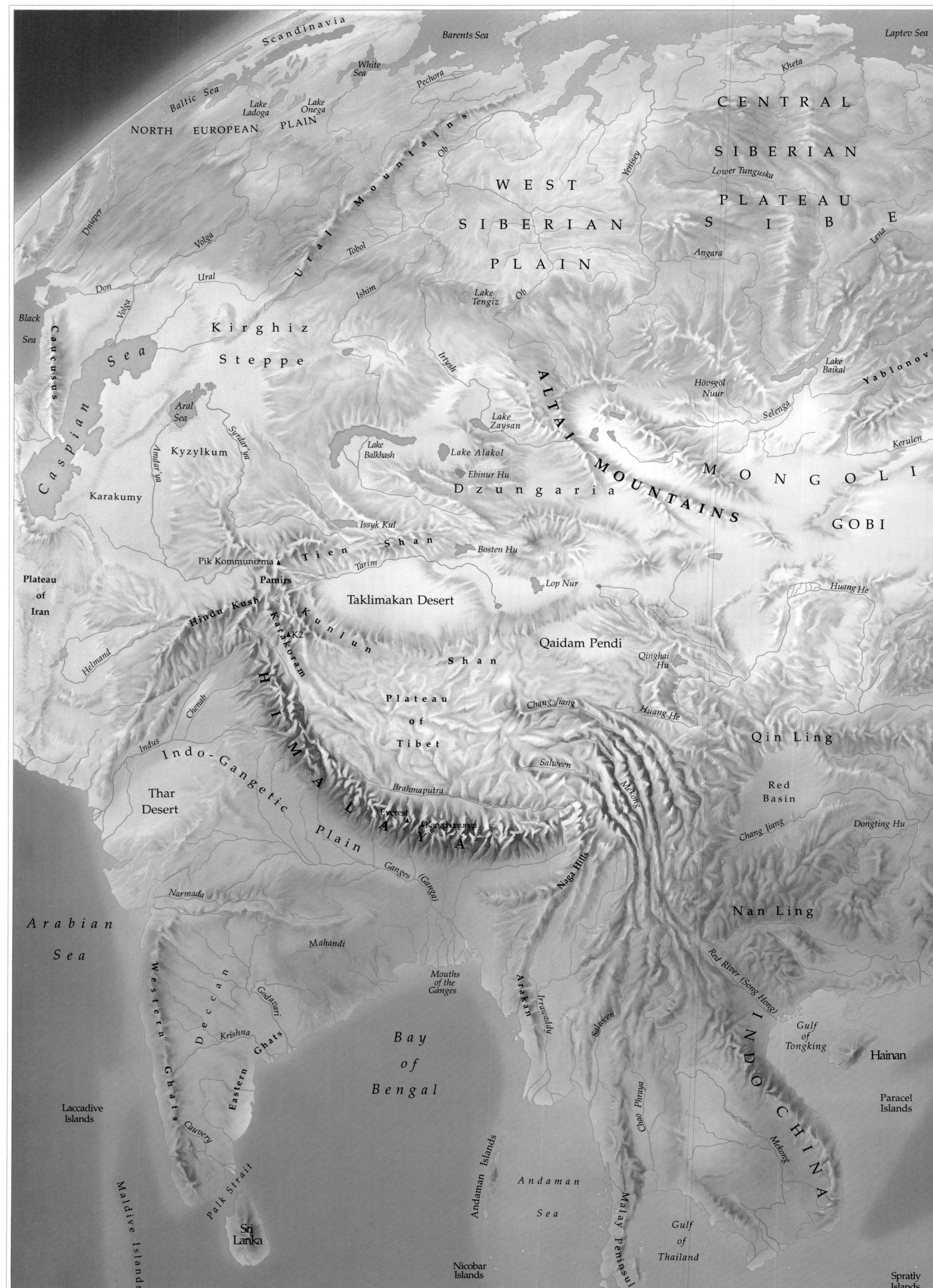

Barents Sea

Laptev Sea

Scandinavia

White
Sea

Pechora

Kheta

CENTRAL

Baltic Sea

Lake
Ladoga

Lake
Onega

SIBERIAN

Dnieper

NORTH EUROPEAN PLAIN

Ob

Lower Tunguska

PLATEAU

Yenisey

S I B E

Volga

Ural Mountains

WEST

Tobol

SIBERIAN

Lena

Angara

Don

Ural

Ishim

PLAIN

Volga

Black
Sea

Caspian Sea

Caucusus

Kirghiz

Steppe

Lake
Tengiz

Ob

Lake
Baikal

Hövsgöl
Nuur

Yablonovy

Aral
Sea

Irtysh

Selenga

Kerulen

Kyzylkum

Syrdar'ya

Lake
Zaysan

ALTAI MOUNTAINS

M O N G O L I

Amdar'ya

Lake
Balkhash

Lake Alakol

Karakumy

Ebinur Hu

Dzungaria

GOBI

Issyk Kul

Bosten Hu

Plateau
of
Iran

Pik Kommunizma ▲

Tien   Shan

Pamirs

Tarim

Lop Nur

Huang He

Hindu Kush

Kunlun

Taklimakan Desert

Helmand

K2

Karakoram

Shan

Qaidam Pendi

Qinghai
Hu

Qin Ling

HIMALAYA

Chenab

Plateau

of

Tibet

Chang Jiang

Huang He

Indus

Indo-Gangetic

Tibet

Salween

Red
Basin

Thar
Desert

Brahmaputra

Mekong

Chang Jiang

Dongting Hu

Everest

Plain

Kangchanjunga

Narmada

Ganges (Ganga)

Naga Hills

Nan Ling

Arabian

Sea

Mahandi

Red River (Song Hong)

Deccan

Godavari

Mouths
of the
Ganges

Arakan

Gulf
of
Tongking

Hainan

Western Ghats

Krishna

Irrawaddy

Salween

Bay

of

Bengal

Eastern Ghats

INDO CHINA

Paracel
Islands

Laccadive
Islands

Cauvery

Chao Phraya

Mekong

Palk Strait

Andaman
Islands

Andaman

Sea

Malay Peninsula

Maldive Islands

Sri
Lanka

Nicobar
Islands

Gulf
of
Thailand

Spratly
Islands

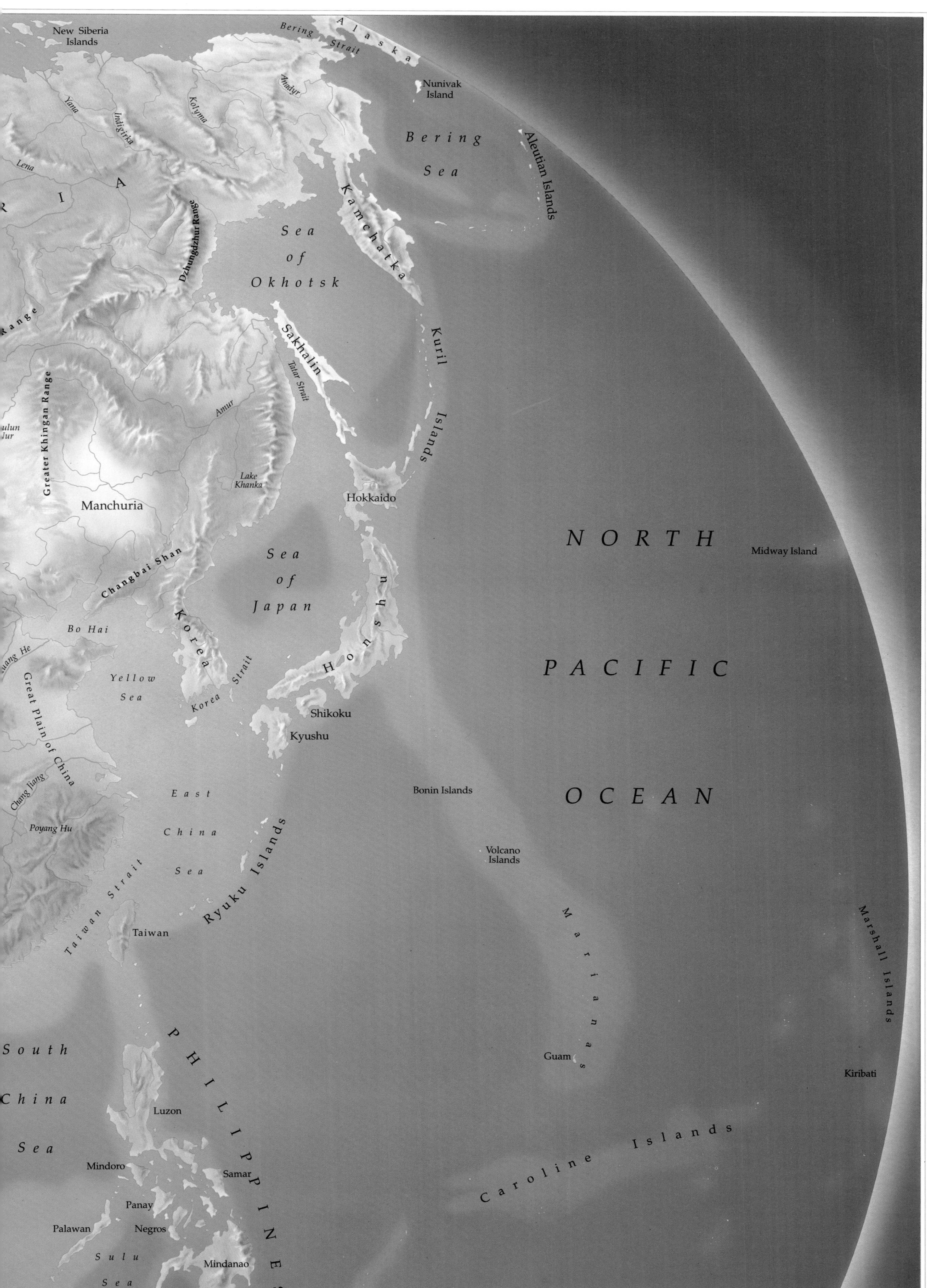

New Siberia
Islands

Yana

Indigirka

Kolyma

Lena

R I A

Anadyr

Bering Strait

Alaska

Nunivak
Island

B e r i n g

S e a

Aleutian Islands

Dzhungdzhur Range

Kamchatka

*Sea
of
Okhotsk*

Range

Greater Khingan Range

Amur

Sakhalin

Tatar Strait

Kuril

Islands

*ulun
ur*

Manchuria

*Lake
Khanka*

Hokkaido

N O R T H

Midway Island

Changbai Shan

*Sea
of
Japan*

Korea

Honshu

P A C I F I C

Bo Hai

uang He

*Yellow
Sea*

Korea Strait

Shikoku

Kyushu

O C E A N

Great Plain of China

Chang Jiang

Poyang Hu

*East

China

Sea*

Bonin Islands

Ryuku Islands

Volcano
Islands

Marianas

Marshall Islands

Taiwan Strait

Taiwan

South

China

Sea

P H I L I P P I N E S

Guam

Kiribati

Luzon

Mindoro

Samar

Caroline   Islands

Panay

Palawan   Negros

*Sulu
Sea*

Mindanao

© Bartholomew

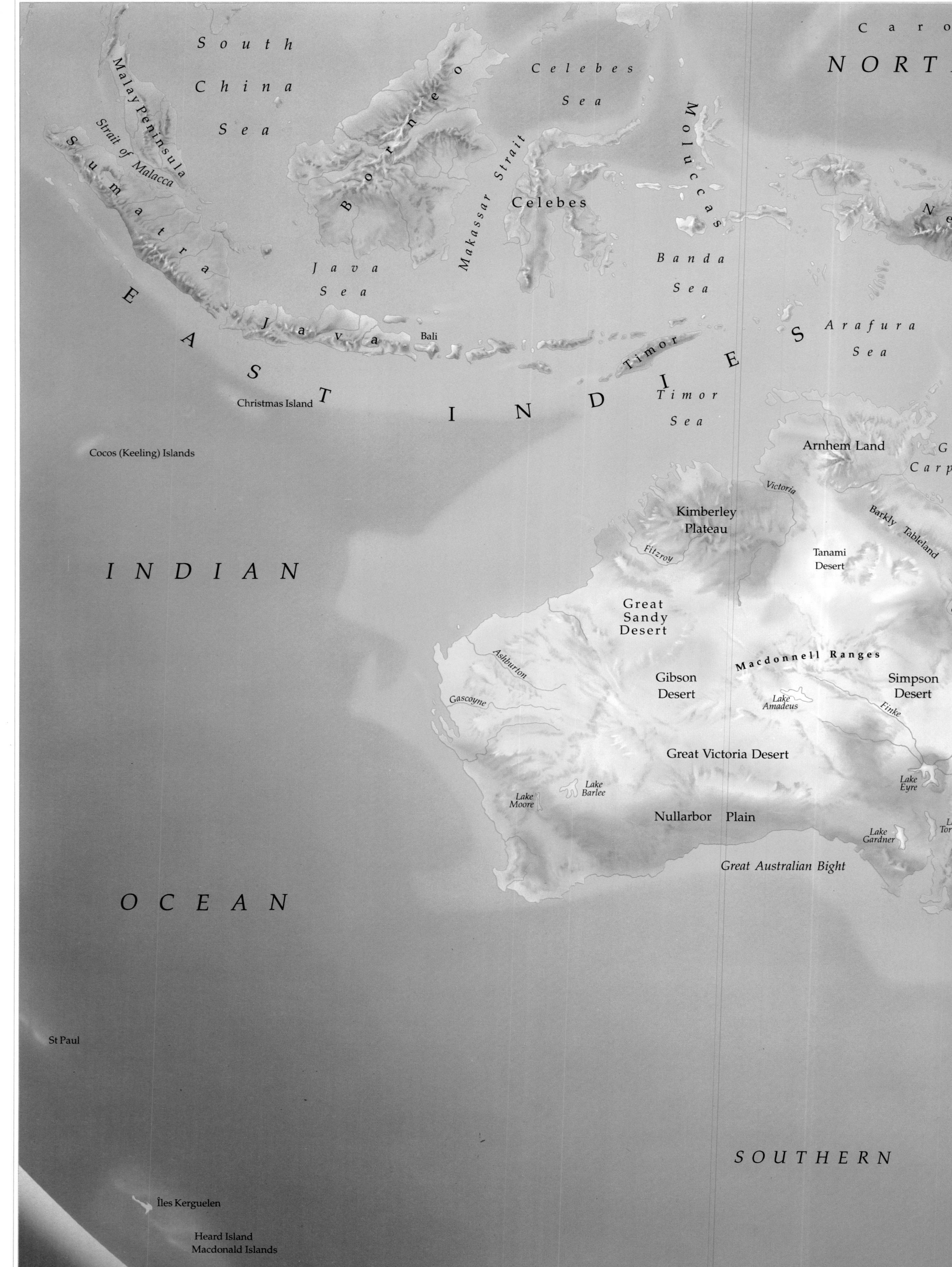

South China Sea

Celebes Sea

Borneo

Celebes

Moluccas

Makassar Strait

Java Sea

Banda Sea

Java

Bali

Timor

Timor Sea

Arafura Sea

E A S T   I N D I E S

Christmas Island

Cocos (Keeling) Islands

Malay Peninsula

Strait of Malacca

Sumatra

C a r o

N O R T H

Ne

Arnhem Land

Gu
Carp

Victoria

Kimberley
Plateau

Fitzroy

Barkly Tableland

Tanami
Desert

I N D I A N

Great
Sandy
Desert

Ashburton

Gascoyne

Macdonnell Ranges

Gibson
Desert

*Lake
Amadeus*

Finke

Simpson
Desert

Gr

Great Victoria Desert

*Lake
Eyre*

*Lake
Moore*

*Lake
Barlee*

Nullarbor   Plain

*Lake
Gardner*

*Lak
Torre*

Great Australian Bight

O C E A N

St Paul

S O U T H E R N

Îles Kerguelen

Heard Island
Macdonald Islands

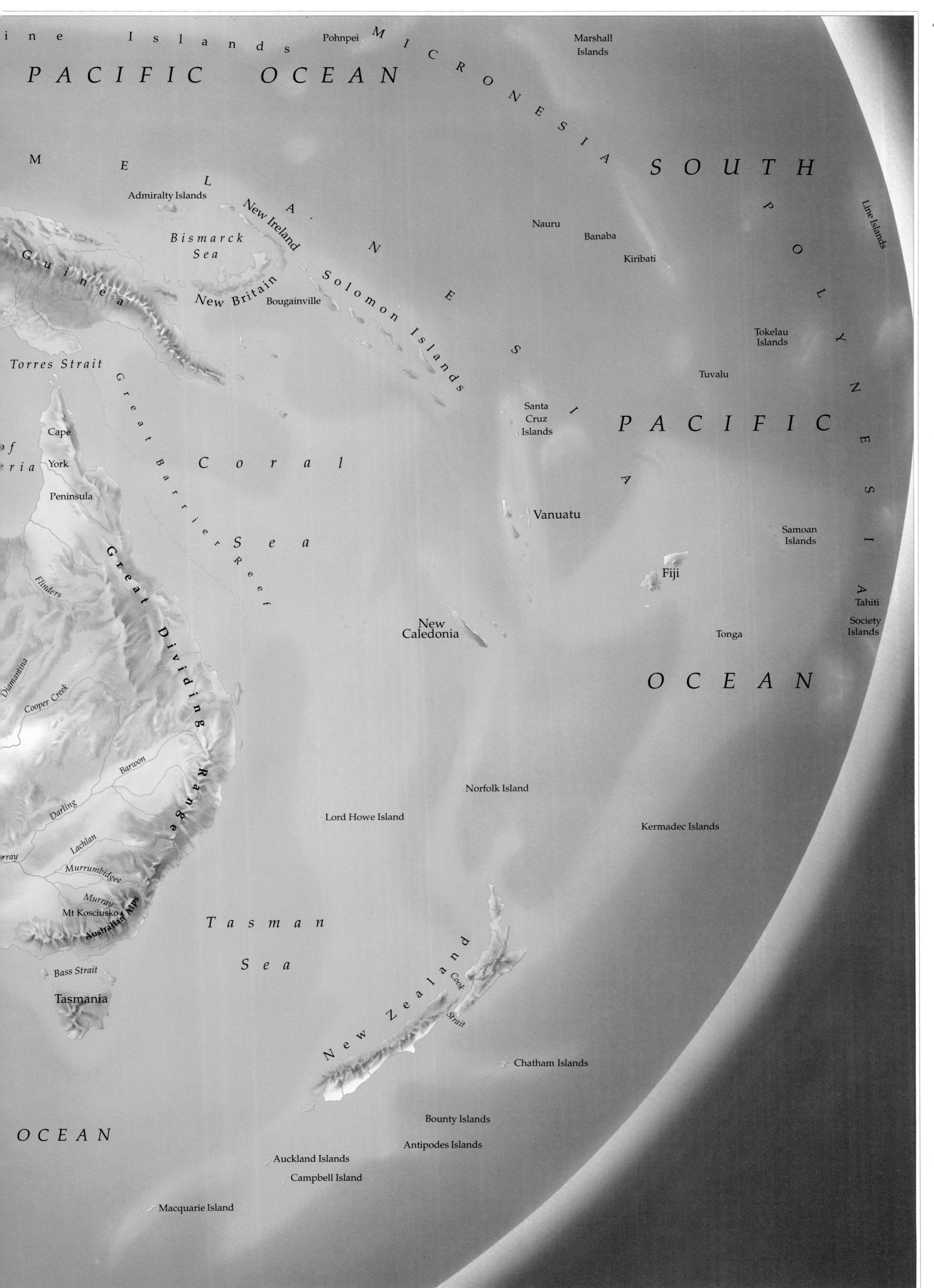

ine Islands
Pohnpei
MICRONESIA
Marshall Islands

PACIFIC OCEAN

M E L A N E S I A
Admiralty Islands

SOUTH

Nauru
Banaba
Kiribati

Line Islands

New Ireland
Bismarck Sea
New Britain
Bougainville
Solomon Islands

Guinea

Tokelau Islands

P O L Y N E S I A

Torres Strait

Great Barrier Reef

Coral

Cape
York
Peninsula

Sea

Santa Cruz Islands

Tuvalu

PACIFIC

Vanuatu

Samoan Islands

Flinders

Great Dividing Range

Fiji

Tahiti
Society Islands

Diamantina

Cooper Creek

New Caledonia

Tonga

OCEAN

Barwon

Darling

Lachlan
Murrumbidgee
Murray
Mt Kosciusko
Australian Alps

Bass Strait

Tasmania

Tasman

Sea

Norfolk Island

Lord Howe Island

Kermadec Islands

New Zealand

Cook Strait

Chatham Islands

OCEAN

Bounty Islands

Antipodes Islands

Auckland Islands

Campbell Island

Macquarie Island

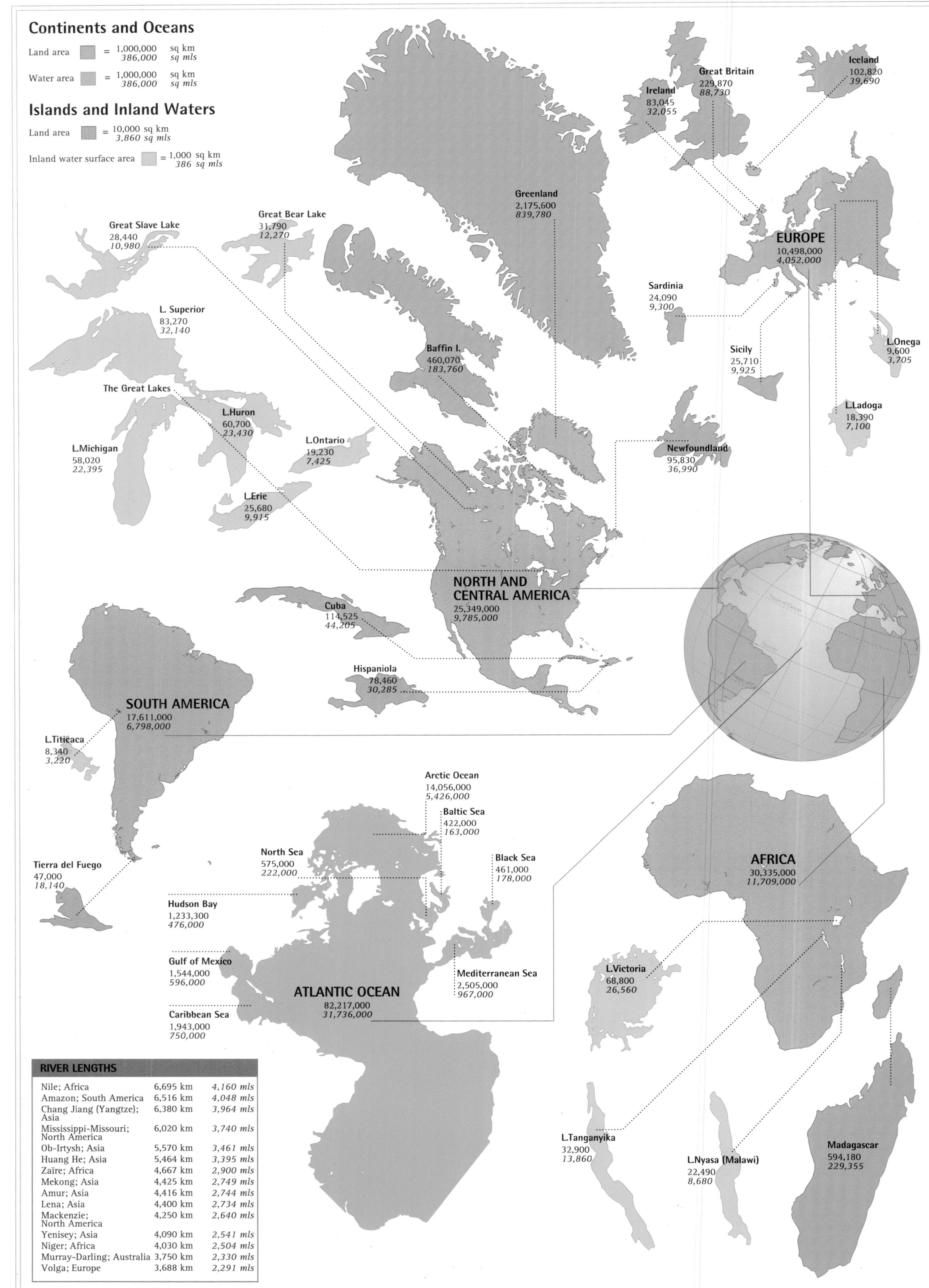

48

Continents and Oceans

Land area = 1,000,000 sq km
             386,000 sq mls

Water area = 1,000,000 sq km
             386,000 sq mls

Islands and Inland Waters

Land area = 10,000 sq km
             3,860 sq mls

Inland water surface area = 1,000 sq km
                            386 sq mls

Ireland
83,045
32,055

Great Britain
229,870
88,730

Iceland
102,820
39,690

Greenland
2,175,600
839,780

EUROPE
10,498,000
4,052,000

Sardinia
24,090
9,300

L.Onega
9,600
3,705

Great Slave Lake
28,440
10,980

Great Bear Lake
31,790
12,270

L. Superior
83,270
32,140

Baffin I.
460,070
183,760

Sicily
25,710
9,925

L.Ladoga
18,390
7,100

The Great Lakes

L.Huron
60,700
23,430

L.Ontario
19,230
7,425

Newfoundland
95,830
36,990

L.Michigan
58,020
22,395

L.Erie
25,680
9,915

Cuba
114,525
44,205

NORTH AND
CENTRAL AMERICA
25,349,000
9,785,000

Hispaniola
78,460
30,285

SOUTH AMERICA
17,611,000
6,798,000

L.Titicaca
8,340
3,220

Arctic Ocean
14,056,000
5,426,000

Baltic Sea
422,000
163,000

Black Sea
461,000
178,000

AFRICA
30,335,000
11,709,000

North Sea
575,000
222,000

Tierra del Fuego
47,000
18,140

Hudson Bay
1,233,300
476,000

Gulf of Mexico
1,544,000
596,000

ATLANTIC OCEAN
82,217,000
31,736,000

Mediterranean Sea
2,505,000
967,000

L.Victoria
68,800
26,560

Caribbean Sea
1,943,000
750,000

RIVER LENGTHS		
Nile; Africa	6,695 km	4,160 mls
Amazon; South America	6,516 km	4,048 mls
Chang Jiang (Yangtze); Asia	6,380 km	3,964 mls
Mississippi-Missouri; North America	6,020 km	3,740 mls
Ob-Irtysh; Asia	5,570 km	3,461 mls
Huang He; Asia	5,464 km	3,395 mls
Zaïre; Africa	4,667 km	2,900 mls
Mekong; Asia	4,425 km	2,749 mls
Amur; Asia	4,416 km	2,744 mls
Lena; Asia	4,400 km	2,734 mls
Mackenzie; North America	4,250 km	2,640 mls
Yenisey; Asia	4,090 km	2,541 mls
Niger; Africa	4,030 km	2,504 mls
Murray-Darling; Australia	3,750 km	2,330 mls
Volga; Europe	3,688 km	2,291 mls

L.Tanganyika
32,900
13,860

L.Nyasa (Malawi)
22,490
8,680

Madagascar
594,180
229,355

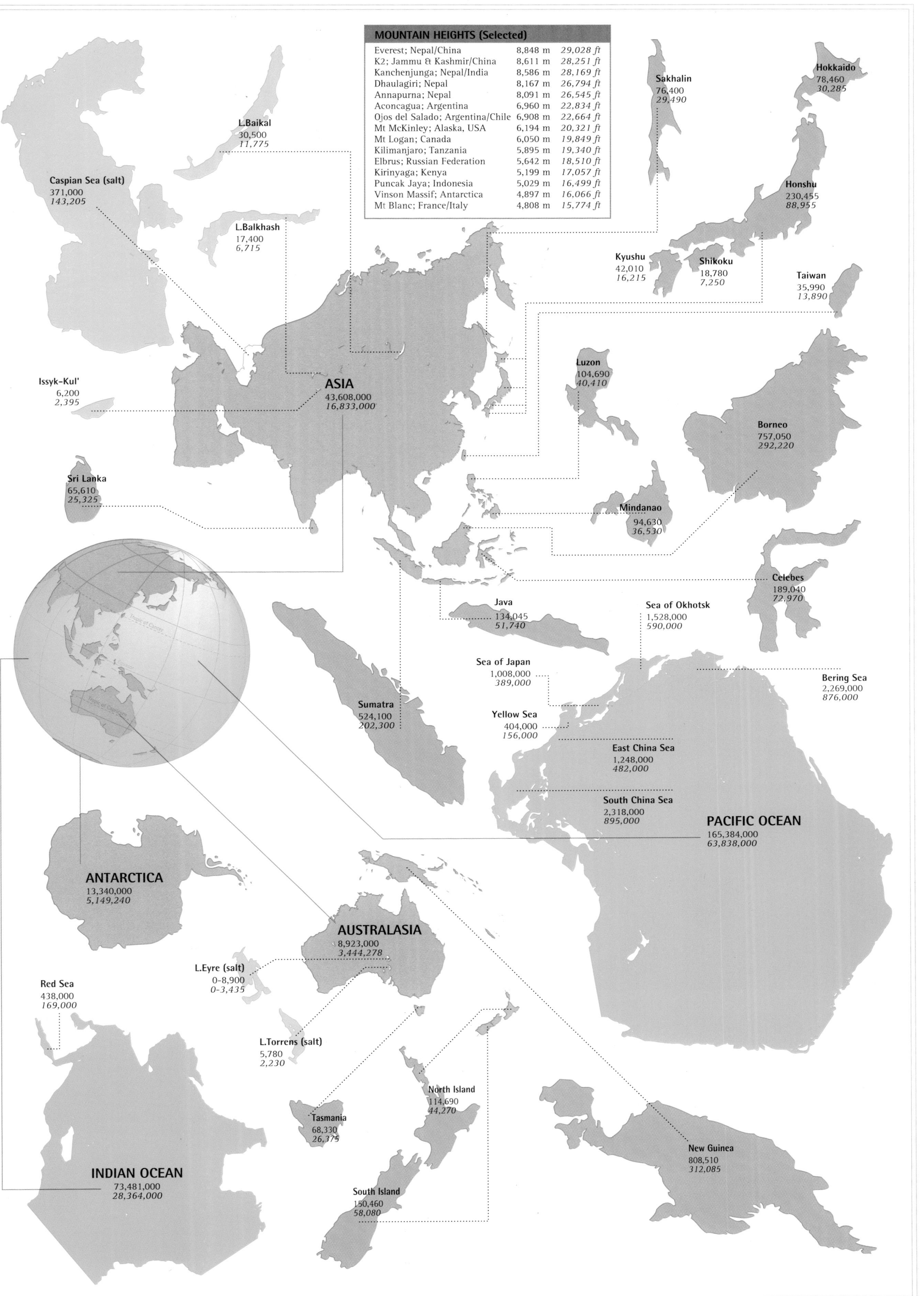

MOUNTAIN HEIGHTS (Selected)

Everest; Nepal/China	8,848 m	29,028 ft
K2; Jammu & Kashmir/China	8,611 m	28,251 ft
Kanchenjunga; Nepal/India	8,586 m	28,169 ft
Dhaulagiri; Nepal	8,167 m	26,794 ft
Annapurna; Nepal	8,091 m	26,545 ft
Aconcagua; Argentina	6,960 m	22,834 ft
Ojos del Salado; Argentina/Chile	6,908 m	22,664 ft
Mt McKinley; Alaska, USA	6,194 m	20,321 ft
Mt Logan; Canada	6,050 m	19,849 ft
Kilimanjaro; Tanzania	5,895 m	19,340 ft
Elbrus; Russian Federation	5,642 m	18,510 ft
Kirinyaga; Kenya	5,199 m	17,057 ft
Puncak Jaya; Indonesia	5,029 m	16,499 ft
Vinson Massif; Antarctica	4,897 m	16,066 ft
Mt Blanc; France/Italy	4,808 m	15,774 ft

L.Baikal
30,500
11,775

Caspian Sea (salt)
371,000
143,205

L.Balkhash
17,400
6,715

Sakhalin
76,400
29,490

Hokkaido
78,460
30,285

Honshu
230,455
88,955

Kyushu
42,010
16,215

Shikoku
18,780
7,250

Taiwan
35,990
13,890

Issyk-Kul'
6,200
2,395

ASIA
43,608,000
16,833,000

Luzon
104,690
40,410

Borneo
757,050
292,220

Sri Lanka
65,610
25,325

Mindanao
94,630
36,530

Celebes
189,040
72,970

Java
134,045
51,740

Sea of Okhotsk
1,528,000
590,000

Sea of Japan
1,008,000
389,000

Bering Sea
2,269,000
876,000

Sumatra
524,100
202,300

Yellow Sea
404,000
156,000

East China Sea
1,248,000
482,000

South China Sea
2,318,000
895,000

PACIFIC OCEAN
165,384,000
63,838,000

ANTARCTICA
13,340,000
5,149,240

AUSTRALASIA
8,923,000
3,444,278

L.Eyre (salt)
0-8,900
0-3,435

Red Sea
438,000
169,000

L.Torrens (salt)
5,780
2,230

North Island
114,690
44,270

Tasmania
68,330
26,375

New Guinea
808,510
312,085

INDIAN OCEAN
73,481,000
28,364,000

South Island
150,460
58,080

© Bartholomew

NEPTUNE

URANUS

SATURN

JUPITER   VENUS

Asteroid belt

EARTH

1000

500 million miles

MARS   MERCURY

CURRENT THEORY SUGGESTS that the solar system condensed from a primitive solar nebula of gas and dust during an interval of a few tens of millions of years about 4600 million years ago. Gravity caused this nebula to contract, drawing most of its mass into the proto-sun at the centre. Turbulence gave the original cloud a tendency to rotate, and as it contracted, conservation of angular momentum caused the proto-sun to spin faster and faster, forcing the remainder of the cloud into a disc shape. The centre of the cloud heated up as it compressed, and so became hot enough for the Sun to begin to shine, through nuclear energy released at its core. Meanwhile the surrounding disc cooled, allowing

material to condense into solid form. Particles stuck together as they collided and progressively larger bodies were built up. These swept up most of the debris to form the planets, which orbit the Sun close to the plane of the now vanished disc. The first materials to condense were the least volatile refractory compounds such as oxides of iron, nickel and aluminium. Decreasing temperature allowed rocky silicate material to appear followed by more volatile compounds such as water and methane. Thus composition of the planets progressed from less refractory cores to more volatile outer layers.

The planets nearest to the Sun are dense with metallic cores mantled by rocky silicate materials; planets

farther from the Sun accreted and retained large volumes of volatiles and are thus much more massive. They may have cores of rock and ice, surrounded by solid or liquid hydrogen enveloped in thick gassy atmospheres. These gas giants are accompanied by captured rocky and icy satellites which are mostly too small to have accreted and held atmospheres.

The subsequent evolution of the solar system was dominated by chemical segregation within the planets and surface bombardment by smaller bodies. This bombardment was over by 3 to 4 million years ago, although minor impacts still occur. Traces of these events remain on the surfaces of planets which have insufficient internal heat to drive resurfacing processes.

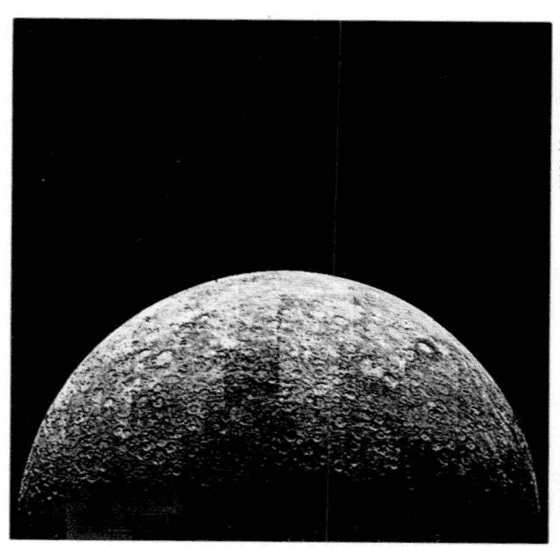

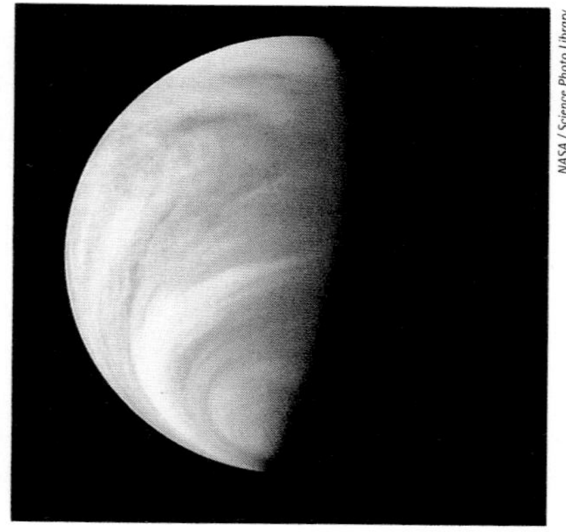

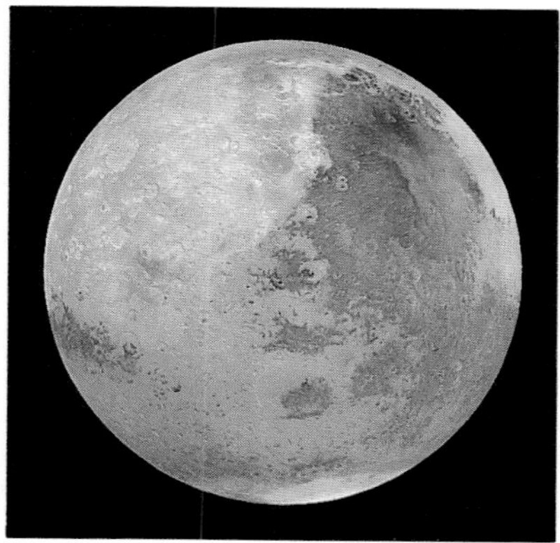

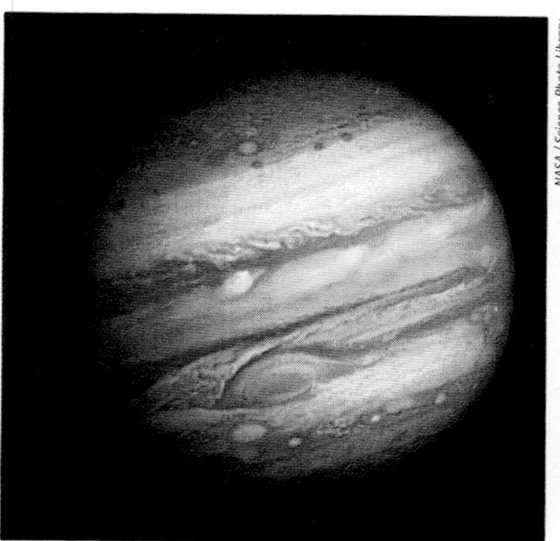

MERCURY is the nearest planet to the Sun, spinning three times for every two orbits around the Sun. It has an exceptionally large metallic core which may be responsible for Mercury's weak magnetic field. Mercury is an airless world subject to vast extremes of temperature, from -180°C at night to 430°C near the middle of its long day. Photographs taken from the Mariner 10 spacecraft probe during the mid-1970s, revealed the surface to be dominated by heavily cratered areas dating from the early meteorite bombardment of the inner solar system. As the bombardment was tailing off Mercury's radius contracted by between one and two kilometres, forming compressional features (lobate scarps) which may have been caused by a change in the core from liquid to solid. The image above is a mosaic made from photographs taken as Mariner 10 approached the planet.

VENUS has a dense atmosphere of 96 per cent carbon dioxide mixed with nitrogen, oxygen, suphur dioxide and water vapour which hides the surface under permanent cloud and maintains a mean surface temperature of about 480°C. The planet's slow rotation means that weather systems are driven mostly by solar heat, rather than by spin. As a result, beyond 10 kilometres above the surface, westerly winds at speeds up to 100 metres per second cause a bulk rotation of the atmosphere in about four days. Imaging radar has been used to map most of the planet from orbiting spacecraft. The most recent survey by the Magellan probe began in the 1990s. Mountains, valleys, impact craters and other features have been mapped and three dimensional simulations generated by computer from the Magellan data. The false-colour image above, made at ultraviolet wavelengths, shows the upper cloud layers.

MARS has a thin atmosphere of about 95 per cent carbon dioxide mixed with other minor constituents. Day and night surface temperatures vary between about -120°C and -20°C. A variety of landscapes has been identified, including ancient heavily cratered terrains and plains. The large dark area on the right of the image above is Syrtis Major Planitia, this dark material is thought to have originated in eruptions from ancient shield volcanoes. There are several large volcanoes; the best preserved of these, Olympus Mons, rises 26 kilometres above the surface and is 550 kilometres across at its base. Mars shows evidence of erosional processes. Dust storms frequently obscure the surface. The large channels, such as the 5000 kilometre long Valles Marineris, may have been cut by flowing water. Water is abundant in the polar caps and may be widespread held in as perma-frost below the surface.

JUPITER has at least 16 satellites and a debris ring system. The outer atmosphere is all that can be directly observed. It is mostly hydrogen with lesser amounts of helium, ammonia, methane, water vapour and more exotic compounds. Jupiter's rapid rotation causes it to be flattened towards the poles. This rotation, and heat flow convection from the interior, cause complex weather patterns. Where cloud systems interact vast storms can occur. Some last only a few days, but the most persistent of these is the Great Red Spot which can be seen at the lower left centre in the image above. The internal structure of Jupiter can be deduced. At about 1000 kilometres below the cloud tops hydrogen and helium may liquify to form a 10,000 kilometre layer. Convection currents in this region generate the planet's intense magnetic field. The denser core, about 4 per cent of the planet's mass, is mostly of rock and ice, with a little iron near the centre.

PLUTO

4000 million kilometres

3000

2500

2000

distance from the Sun

2000

1500

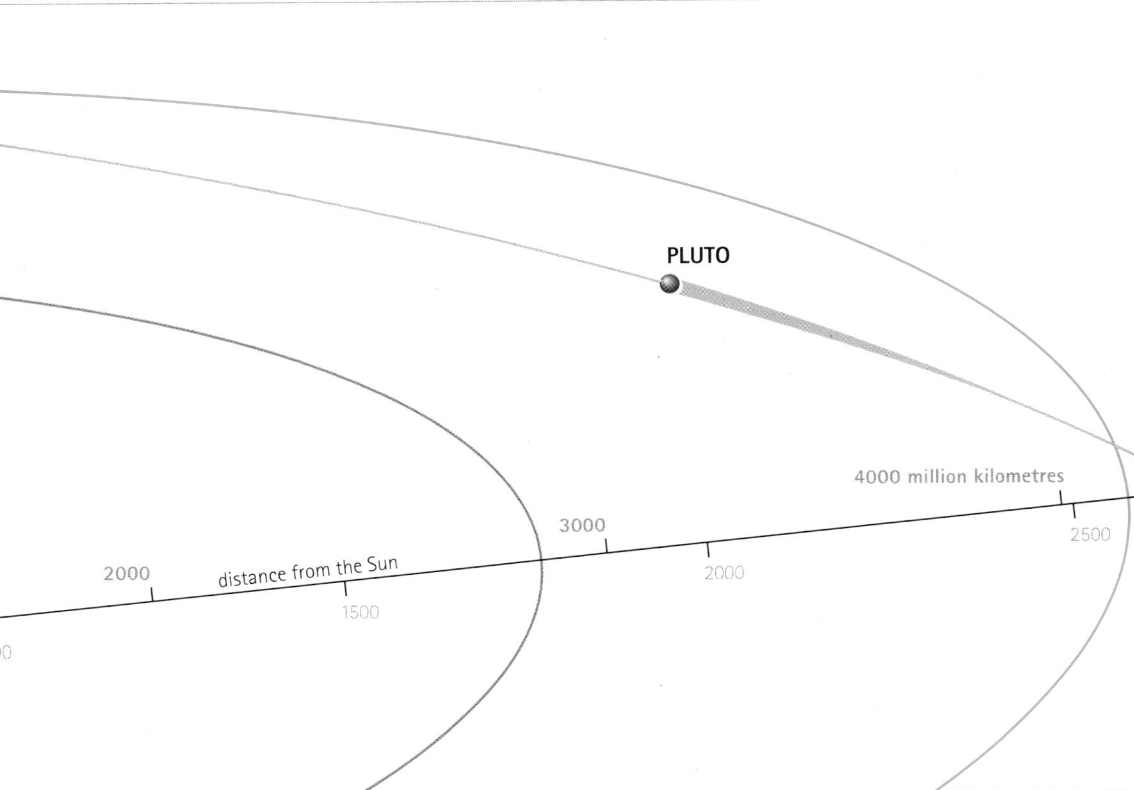

The Sun is seen above, in an x-ray image taken by the YOHKOH satellite in 1992. The image shows the activity of the outer layer of the solar atmosphere, the corona. The brightest areas are solar active regions where sunspots would be seen in visible light; the dark areas are coronal holes where gas density is extremely low and from which the solar wind, a stream of charged particles, is ejected into space.

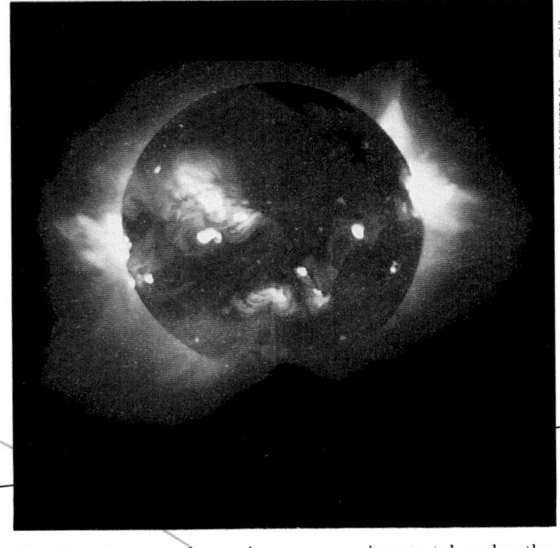

	SUN	MERCURY	VENUS	EARTH	(MOON)	MARS	JUPITER	SATURN	URANUS	NEPTUNE	PLUTO
Mass (Earth=1)	333 400	0.055	0.815	1 (5.97 10^{24}kg)	0.012	0.107	317.8	95.2	14.5	17.2	0.003
Volume (Earth=1)	1 306 000	0.06	0.88	1	0.020	0.150	1 323	752	64	54	0.007
Density (water=1)	1.41	5.43	5.24	5.52	3.34	3.94	1.33	0.70	1.30	1.64	2.0
Equatorial diameter (km)	1 392 000	4 878	12 104	12 756	3 476	6 794	142 800	120 000	52 000	48 400	2 302
Polar flattening	0	0	0	0.003	0	0.005	0.065	0.108	0.060	0.021	0
'Surface' gravity (Earth=1)	27.9	0.37	0.88	1	0.16	0.38	2.69	1.19	0.93	1.22	0.05
Number of satellites greater than 100km in diameter	–	0	0	1	–	0	7	13	7	6	1
Total number of satellites	–	0	0	1	–	2	16	17	15	8	1
Period of rotation (in Earth days)	25.38	58.65	-243 (retrograde)	23hr 56m 4 secs	27.32	1.03	0.414	0.426	-0.74 (retrograde)	0.67	-6.39 (retrograde)
Length of year (in Earth days and years)	–	88 days	224.7 days	365.26 days	–	687 days	11.86 years	29.46 years	84.01 years	164.8 years	247.7 years
Distance from Sun (max) Mkm	–	69.7	109	152.1	–	249.1	815.7	1 507	3 004	4 537	7 375
Distance from Sun (min) Mkm	–	45.9	107.4	147.1	–	206.7	740.9	1 347	2 735	4 456	4 425
Distance from Sun (mean) Mkm	–	57.9	108.9	149.6	–	227.9	778.3	1 427	2 870	4 497	5 900
Mean orbital velocity km/sec	–	47.9	35.0	29.8	–	24.1	13.1	9.6	6.8	5.4	4.7
Inclination of equator to orbit plane	7.25°	0.0°	177.3°	23.45°	6.68°	25.19°	3.12°	26.73°	97.86°	29.56°	122°
Inclination of orbit to ecliptic	–	7.01°	3.39°	0°	5.15°	1.85°	1.30°	2.48°	0.77°	1.77°	17.13°

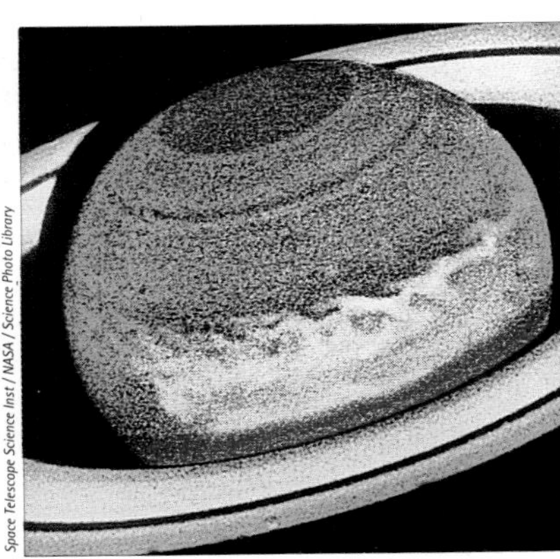

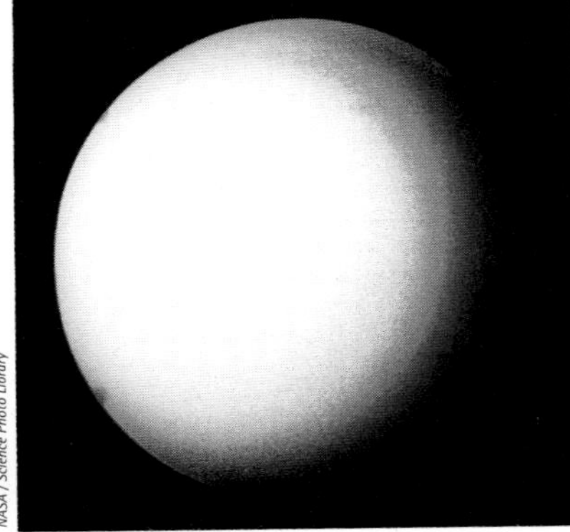

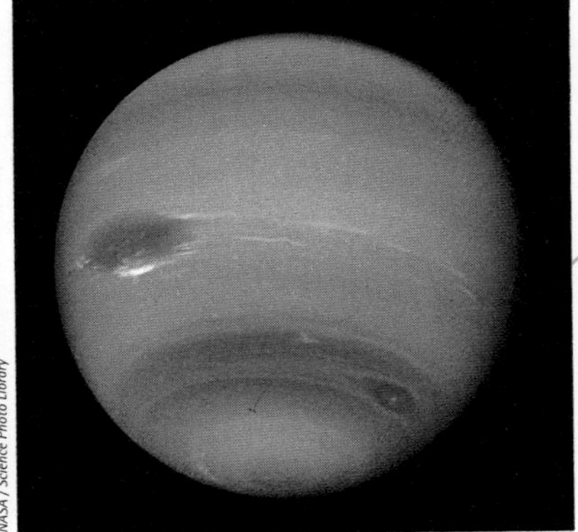

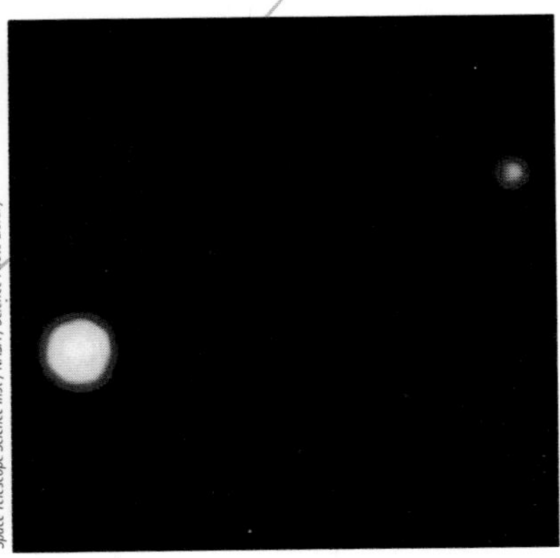

SATURN is the least dense of the planets. It has a stormy atmosphere situated above a 30,000 km layer of liquid molecular hydrogen and helium distorted by the planet's rotation. Below is a thin shell of liquid metallic hydrogen wrapped around a rock and ice core containing 25 per cent of Saturn's mass. The rings of Saturn are thought to be mostly made of icy debris, from 10 metres down to a few microns in size, derived from the break-up of one of its satellites. The rings are less than one kilometre thick but extend from above the cloud layer out to about 170,000 kilometres from the centre. The rings are divided by gaps swept clear by complex gravitational interaction. The Hubble Telescope image above shows an unusual, long-lived storm which first appeared in 1990. The storm is the elongated reddish-white region along the planet's equator.

URANUS was little known until Voyager 2 flew past it in January 1986. It has a cloud cover even more featureless than either Jupiter or Saturn, and consists mostly of hydrogen. Unique among the planets, its axis is tilted almost into the plane of its orbit, with the south pole presently facing towards the Sun. Voyager 2 discovered ten more satellites and povided detailed images of the planet's eleven rings of icy debris. The above composite false-coloured image was taken from Voyager 2, 2.7 million kilometres from the planet. The pink areas centred on the poles are due to the presence of hazes high in the atmosphere. The blue areas at mid-latitudes are the most haze-free.

NEPTUNE provided a number of surprises when Voyager 2 flew past in August 1989, travelling within 5000 kilometres of the planet's north pole. It was discovered the planet rotates in 16 hours 3 minutes, one hour faster than was believed to be the rate. Six new satellites were discovered, all irregular in shape, and with impact craters little changed since soon after their formation. Neptune has four rings. The magnetic axis is inclined 50° to the axis of rotation and displaced 10,000 kilometres from the centre. Neptune's atmosphere, a mixture of hydrogen, helium and methane, exhibits great turbulence. The above, virtually true-colour, image, shows two prominent cloud features of this highly active atmosphere. To the left is the Great Dark Spot, a giant storm, which circuits the planet every 18.3 hours. A second, smaller dark spot (lower right) circuits the planet every 16.1 hours.

PLUTO, usually the most distant planet, is temporarily within the orbit of Neptune. The atmosphere is thought to be composed mostly of methane. The above image of Pluto (left) and its satellite, Charon, was taken by the Hubble Space Telescope in February 1994. Astronomers were able to see the two bodies clearly for the first time and to measure directly and accurately their diameters. When the image was taken Pluto was 4.4 billion kilometres from the Earth and 19,640 kilometres from Charon.

NORTHERN SKY

Star Magnitude

Each unit of magnitude indicates
a difference of brightness of
2.512 times. The brightest star
is Sirius (mag. −1.45)

| 0 |
| 1 |
| 2 |
| 3 |
| 4 |
| 5 |

0 h R.A.

PISCES

CETUS

ARIES

Markab

Enif

EQUULEUS

PEGASUS

Scheat

Alpheratz

Menkar

Hamal

DELPHINUS

ANDROMEDA

Mirach

TRIANGULUM

M31

Almach

TAURUS

Algol

Pleiades

Altair

LACERTA

PERSEUS

Hyades

AQUILA

Schedar

Ruchbah H VI 33 34

Mirfak

Aldebaran

M

Deneb

Capella

CASSIOPEIA

Galactic Equator

CYGNUS

CEPHEUS

ORION

Bellatrix

LYRA

Vega

DRACO

Polaris

CAMELOPARDALIS

Capella

Elnath

Betelgeuse

Eltanin

URSA

AURIGA

HERCULES

MINOR

Kochab

M92

MONOCEROS

Rasalhague

OPHIUCHUS

M13

GEMINI

Castor

LYNX

Pollux

CORONA
BOREALIS

Dubhe

CANIS

Procyon

MINOR

Alphecca

Mizar

Merak

URSA

CANCER

Alkaid

Alioth

M44

Phecda

SERPENS CAPUT

MAJOR

CANES
VENATICI

LEO
MINOR

HYDRA

BOOTES

M3

N. Galactic Pole

COMA

Arcturus

BERENICES

LEO

Regulus

M5

Denebola

SEXTANS

Ecliptic

VIRGO

Link Line

Variable star

Open star cluster

Globular star cluster

EQUATORIAL ZONE

CANES VENATICI

ANDROMEDA

CYGNUS

LYRA

CORONA
BOREALIS

Alpheratz

Scheat

VULPECULA

HERCULES

Alphecca

N. Galactic
Pole

COMA
BERENICES

PEGASUS

SAGITTA

BOOTES

Markab

Enif

DELPHINUS

Arcturus

Altair

EQUULEUS

Rasalhague

SERPENS
CAPUT

PISCES

Spring Equinox

AQUILA

OPHIUCHUS

VIRGO

Equator

SCUTUM
SOBIESKI

CETUS

AQUARIUS

SERPENS
CAUDA

LIBRA

Oct 16

Sabik

Spica

Diphda

Zubenelgenubi

Gienah

CORVUS

CAPRICORNUS

Ecliptic

S Galactic Pole

SAGITTARIUS

Antares

PISCIS

SCORPIUS

HYDRA

Fomalhaut

AUSTRINUS

MICROSCOPIUM

Nunki

LUPUS

SCULPTOR

Kaus Australis

CENTAURUS

Right 18 h Ascension

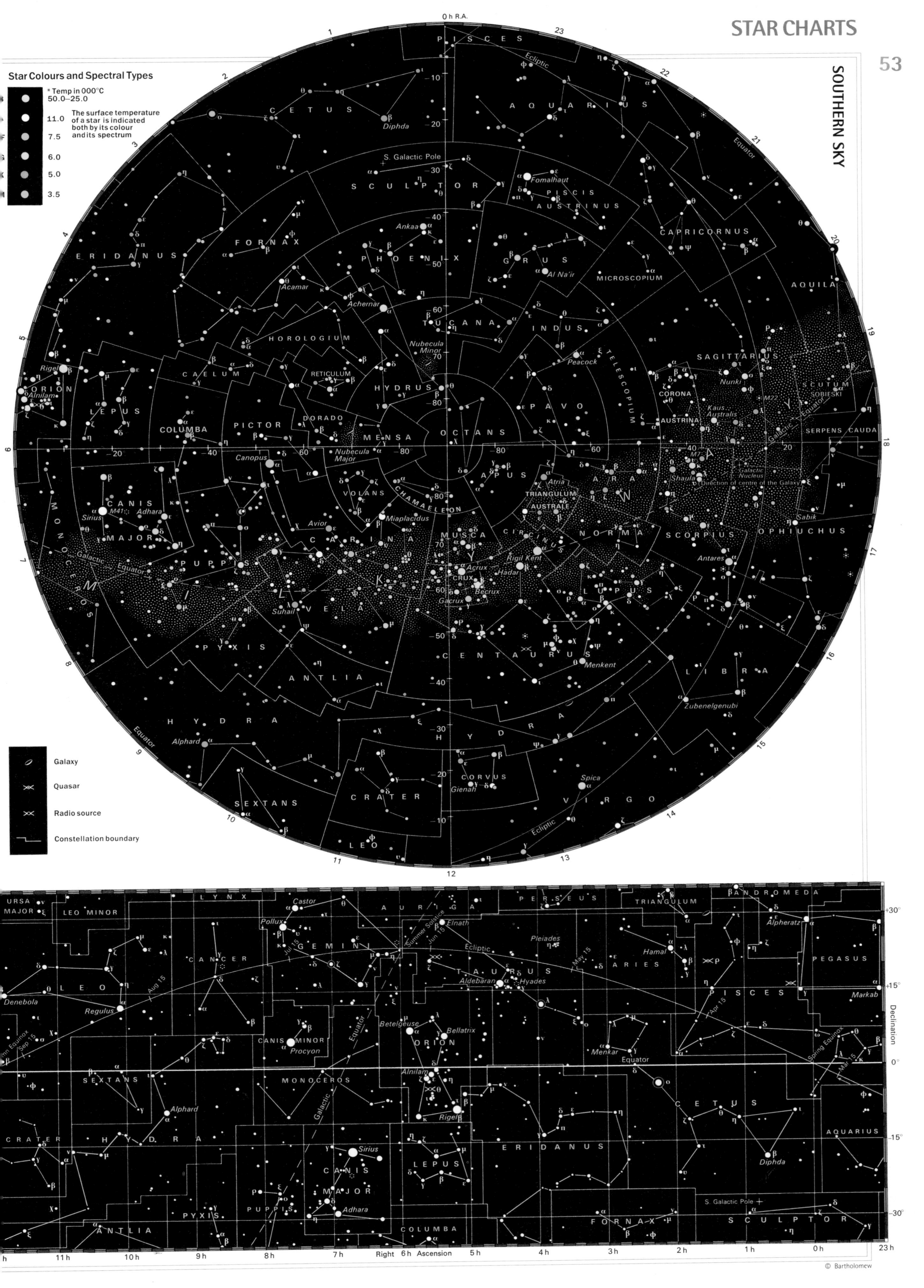

Star Colours and Spectral Types

* Temp in 000°C
50.0–25.0

The surface temperature of a star is indicated both by its colour and its spectrum

11.0
7.5
6.0
5.0
3.5

Galaxy

Quasar

Radio source

Constellation boundary

© Bartholomew

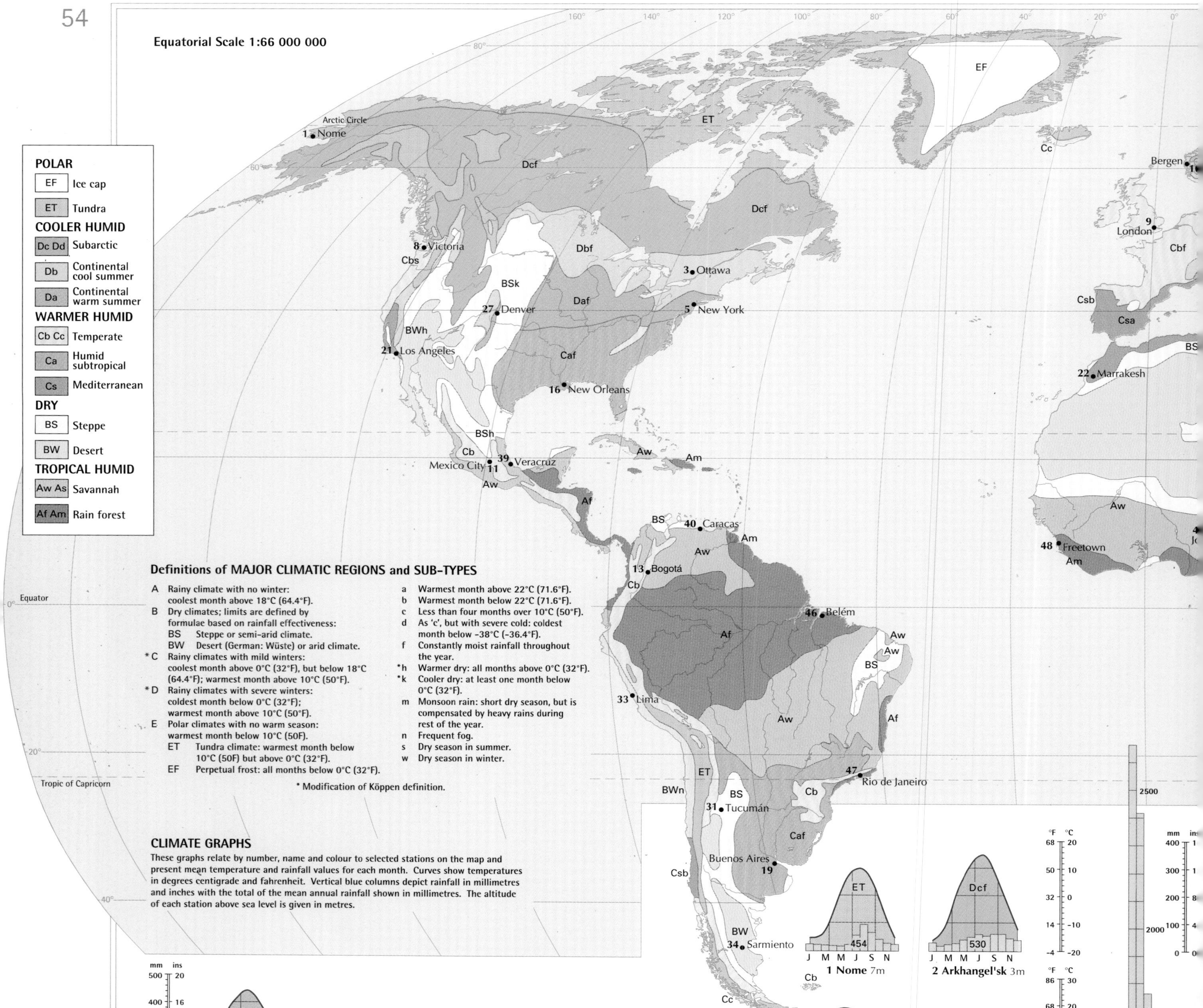

Equatorial Scale 1:66 000 000

POLAR

| EF | Ice cap |
| ET | Tundra |

COOLER HUMID

Dc Dd	Subarctic
Db	Continental cool summer
Da	Continental warm summer

WARMER HUMID

Cb Cc	Temperate
Ca	Humid subtropical
Cs	Mediterranean

DRY

| BS | Steppe |
| BW | Desert |

TROPICAL HUMID

| Aw As | Savannah |
| Af Am | Rain forest |

Definitions of MAJOR CLIMATIC REGIONS and SUB-TYPES

A   Rainy climate with no winter:
    coolest month above 18°C (64.4°F).
B   Dry climates; limits are defined by
    formulae based on rainfall effectiveness:
    BS   Steppe or semi-arid climate.
    BW   Desert (German: Wüste) or arid climate.
*C   Rainy climates with mild winters:
    coolest month above 0°C (32°F), but below 18°C
    (64.4°F); warmest month above 10°C (50°F).
*D   Rainy climates with severe winters:
    coldest month below 0°C (32°F);
    warmest month above 10°C (50°F).
E   Polar climates with no warm season:
    warmest month below 10°C (50F).
    ET   Tundra climate: warmest month below
          10°C (50F) but above 0°C (32°F).
    EF   Perpetual frost: all months below 0°C (32°F).

    * Modification of Köppen definition.

a   Warmest month above 22°C (71.6°F).
b   Warmest month below 22°C (71.6°F).
c   Less than four months over 10°C (50°F).
d   As 'c', but with severe cold: coldest
    month below –38°C (–36.4°F).
f   Constantly moist rainfall throughout
    the year.
*h   Warmer dry: all months above 0°C (32°F).
*k   Cooler dry: at least one month below
    0°C (32°F).
m   Monsoon rain: short dry season, but is
    compensated by heavy rains during
    rest of the year.
n   Frequent fog.
s   Dry season in summer.
w   Dry season in winter.

CLIMATE GRAPHS

These graphs relate by number, name and colour to selected stations on the map and
present mean temperature and rainfall values for each month. Curves show temperatures
in degrees centigrade and fahrenheit. Vertical blue columns depict rainfall in millimetres
and inches with the total of the mean annual rainfall shown in millimetres. The altitude
of each station above sea level is given in metres.

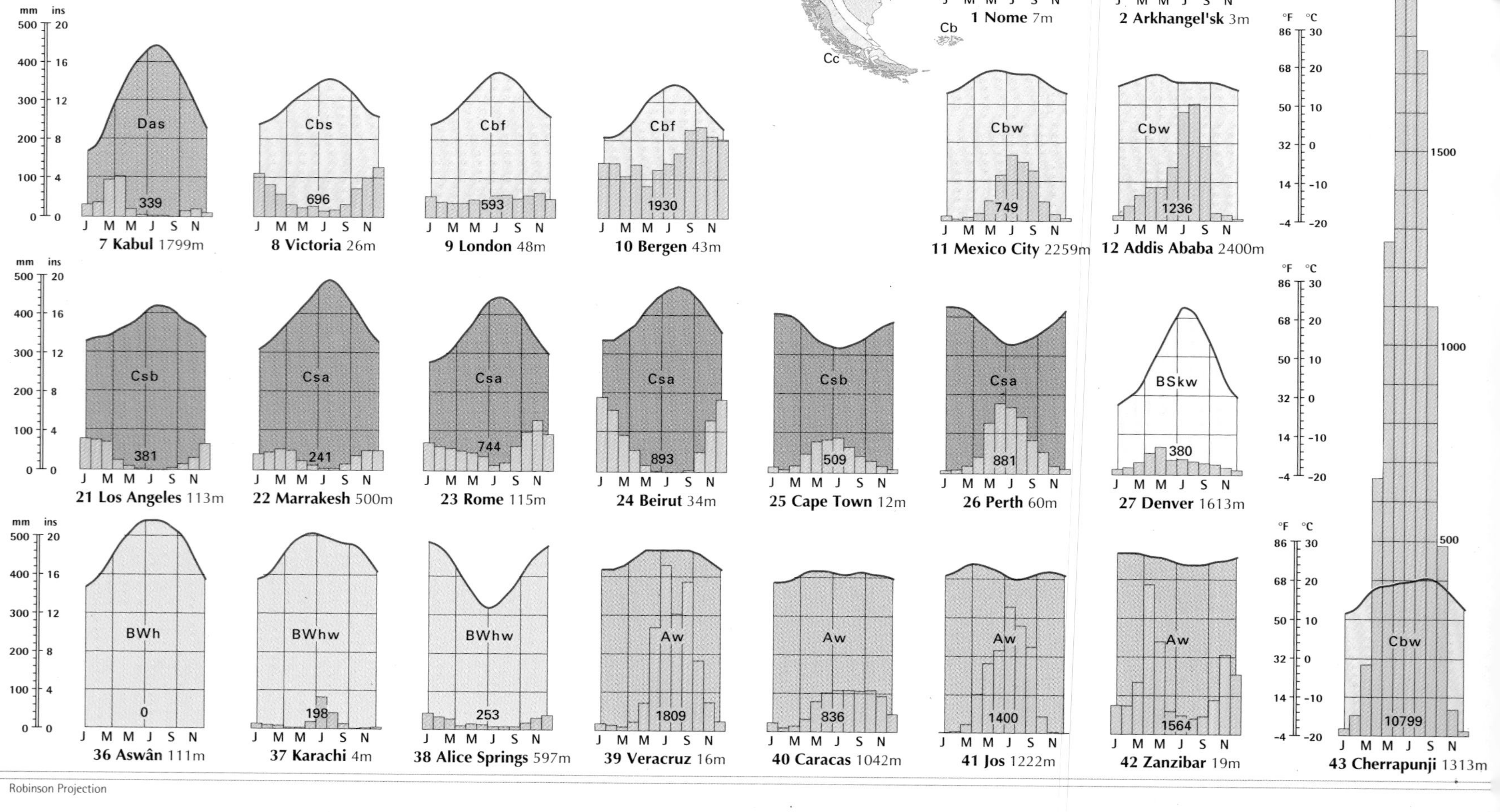

1 Nome 7m — ET 454
2 Arkhangel'sk 3m — Dcf 530
7 Kabul 1799m — Das 339
8 Victoria 26m — Cbs 696
9 London 48m — Cbf 593
10 Bergen 43m — Cbf 1930
11 Mexico City 2259m — Cbw 749
12 Addis Ababa 2400m — Cbw 1236
21 Los Angeles 113m — Csb 381
22 Marrakesh 500m — Csa 241
23 Rome 115m — Csa 744
24 Beirut 34m — Csa 893
25 Cape Town 12m — Csb 509
26 Perth 60m — Csa 881
27 Denver 1613m — BSkw 380
36 Aswân 111m — BWh 0
37 Karachi 4m — BWhw 198
38 Alice Springs 597m — BWhw 253
39 Veracruz 16m — Aw 1809
40 Caracas 1042m — Aw 836
41 Jos 1222m — Aw 1400
42 Zanzibar 19m — Aw 1564
43 Cherrapunji 1313m — Cbw 10799

Robinson Projection

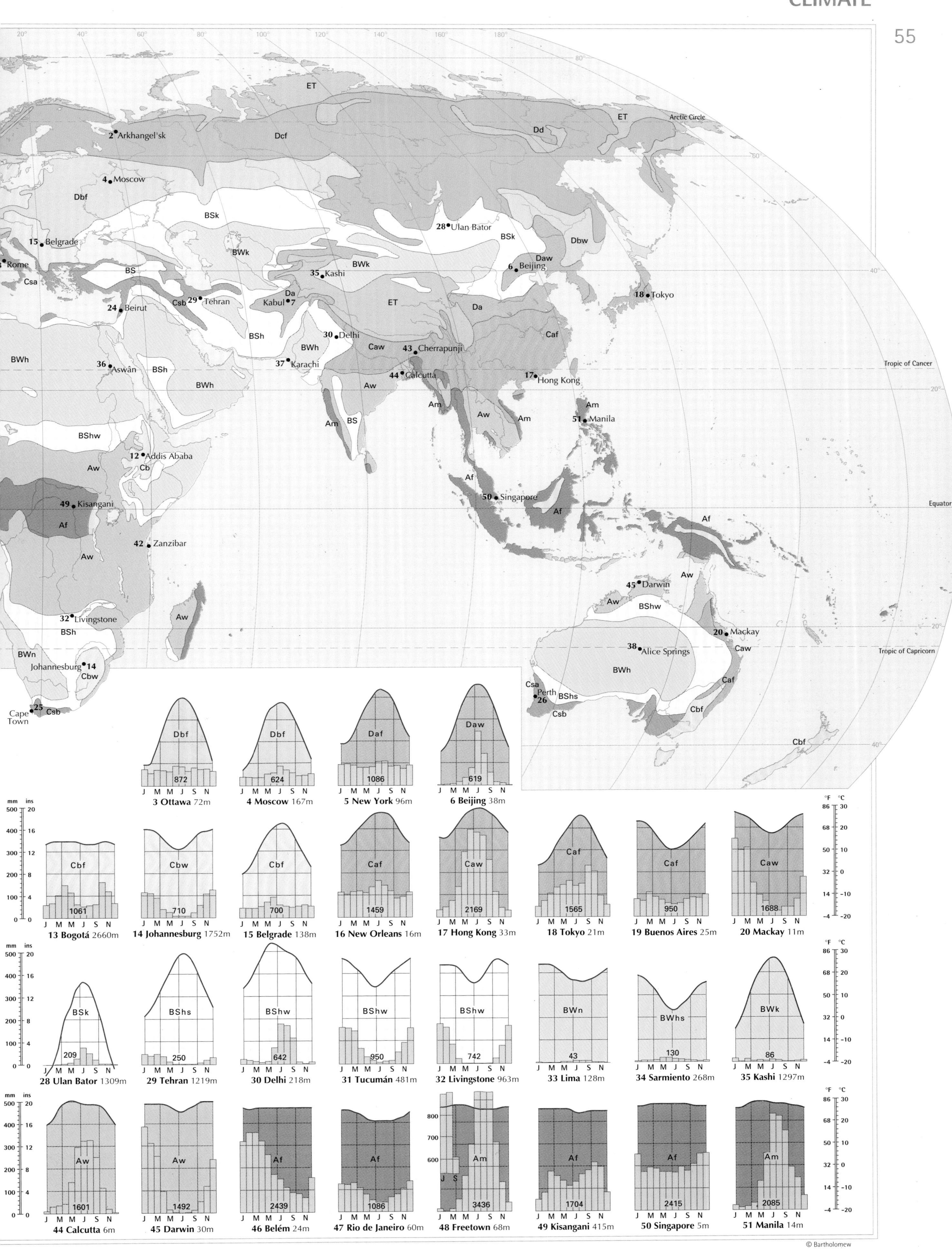

ET

2 ● Arkhangel'sk

Dcf

Dd

ET

Arctic Circle

4 ● Moscow

Dbf

BSk

15 ● Belgrade

28 ● Ulan Bator

BSk

Dbw

● Rome

BWk

35 ● Kashi

6 ● Beijing

Daw

Csa

BS

Da

18 ● Tokyo

24 ● Beirut

Csb 29 ● Tehran

Kabul ● 7

Da

BWh

BSh

30 ● Delhi

Caw

43 ● Cherrapunji

Caf

Tropic of Cancer

36 ● Aswân

BSh

37 ● Karachi

BWh

44 ● Calcutta

17 ● Hong Kong

Aw

Am

Am

BShw

Aw

51 ● Manila

12 ● Addis Ababa

Aw

Cb

Af

49 ● Kisangani

50 ● Singapore

Af

Af

Af

42 ● Zanzibar

Aw

Aw

Equator

Aw

45 ● Darwin

32 ● Livingstone

Aw

BShw

BSh

20 ● Mackay

BWn

38 ● Alice Springs

Caw

Johannesburg ● 14

Tropic of Capricorn

Cbw

BWh

Caf

25 ● Csb

Csa

Perth

Cbf

Cape

26

BShs

Town

Csb

Cbf

© Bartholomew

Dbf 872	Dbf 624	Daf 1086	Daw 619
3 Ottawa 72m	**4 Moscow** 167m	**5 New York** 96m	**6 Beijing** 38m

mm ins °F °C
500 20 86 30
400 16 68 20
300 12 50 10
200 8 32 0
100 4 14 -10
0 -4 -20

Cbf 1061	Cbw 710	Cbf 700	Caf 1459	Caw 2169	Caf 1565	Caf 950	Caw 1688
13 Bogotá 2660m	**14 Johannesburg** 1752m	**15 Belgrade** 138m	**16 New Orleans** 16m	**17 Hong Kong** 33m	**18 Tokyo** 21m	**19 Buenos Aires** 25m	**20 Mackay** 11m

BSk 209	BShs 250	BShw 642	BShw 950	BShw 742	BWn 43	BWhs 130	BWk 86
28 Ulan Bator 1309m	**29 Tehran** 1219m	**30 Delhi** 218m	**31 Tucumán** 481m	**32 Livingstone** 963m	**33 Lima** 128m	**34 Sarmiento** 268m	**35 Kashi** 1297m

Aw 1601	Aw 1492	Af 2439	Af 1086	Am 3436	Af 1704	Af 2415	Am 2085
44 Calcutta 6m	**45 Darwin** 30m	**46 Belém** 24m	**47 Rio de Janeiro** 60m	**48 Freetown** 68m	**49 Kisangani** 415m	**50 Singapore** 5m	**51 Manila** 14m

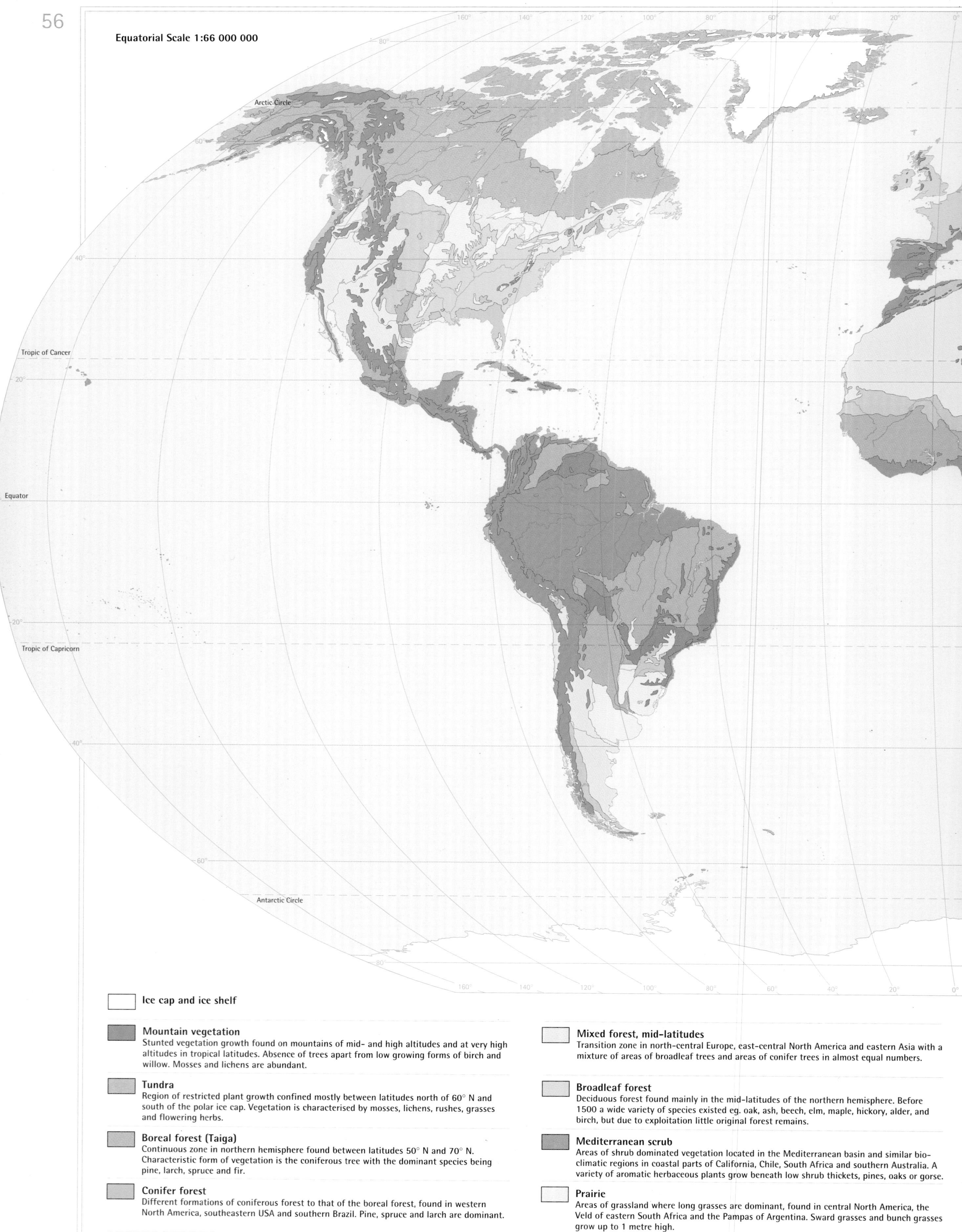

56

Equatorial Scale 1:66 000 000

Arctic Circle

Tropic of Cancer

Equator

Tropic of Capricorn

Antarctic Circle

Robinson Projection

Ice cap and ice shelf

Mountain vegetation
Stunted vegetation growth found on mountains of mid- and high altitudes and at very high altitudes in tropical latitudes. Absence of trees apart from low growing forms of birch and willow. Mosses and lichens are abundant.

Tundra
Region of restricted plant growth confined mostly between latitudes north of 60° N and south of the polar ice cap. Vegetation is characterised by mosses, lichens, rushes, grasses and flowering herbs.

Boreal forest (Taiga)
Continuous zone in northern hemisphere found between latitudes 50° N and 70° N. Characteristic form of vegetation is the coniferous tree with the dominant species being pine, larch, spruce and fir.

Conifer forest
Different formations of coniferous forest to that of the boreal forest, found in western North America, southeastern USA and southern Brazil. Pine, spruce and larch are dominant.

Mixed forest, mid-latitudes
Transition zone in north-central Europe, east-central North America and eastern Asia with a mixture of areas of broadleaf trees and areas of conifer trees in almost equal numbers.

Broadleaf forest
Deciduous forest found mainly in the mid-latitudes of the northern hemisphere. Before 1500 a wide variety of species existed eg. oak, ash, beech, elm, maple, hickory, alder, and birch, but due to exploitation little original forest remains.

Mediterranean scrub
Areas of shrub dominated vegetation located in the Mediterranean basin and similar bio-climatic regions in coastal parts of California, Chile, South Africa and southern Australia. A variety of aromatic herbaceous plants grow beneath low shrub thickets, pines, oaks or gorse.

Prairie
Areas of grassland where long grasses are dominant, found in central North America, the Veld of eastern South Africa and the Pampas of Argentina. Sward grasses and bunch grasses grow up to 1 metre high.

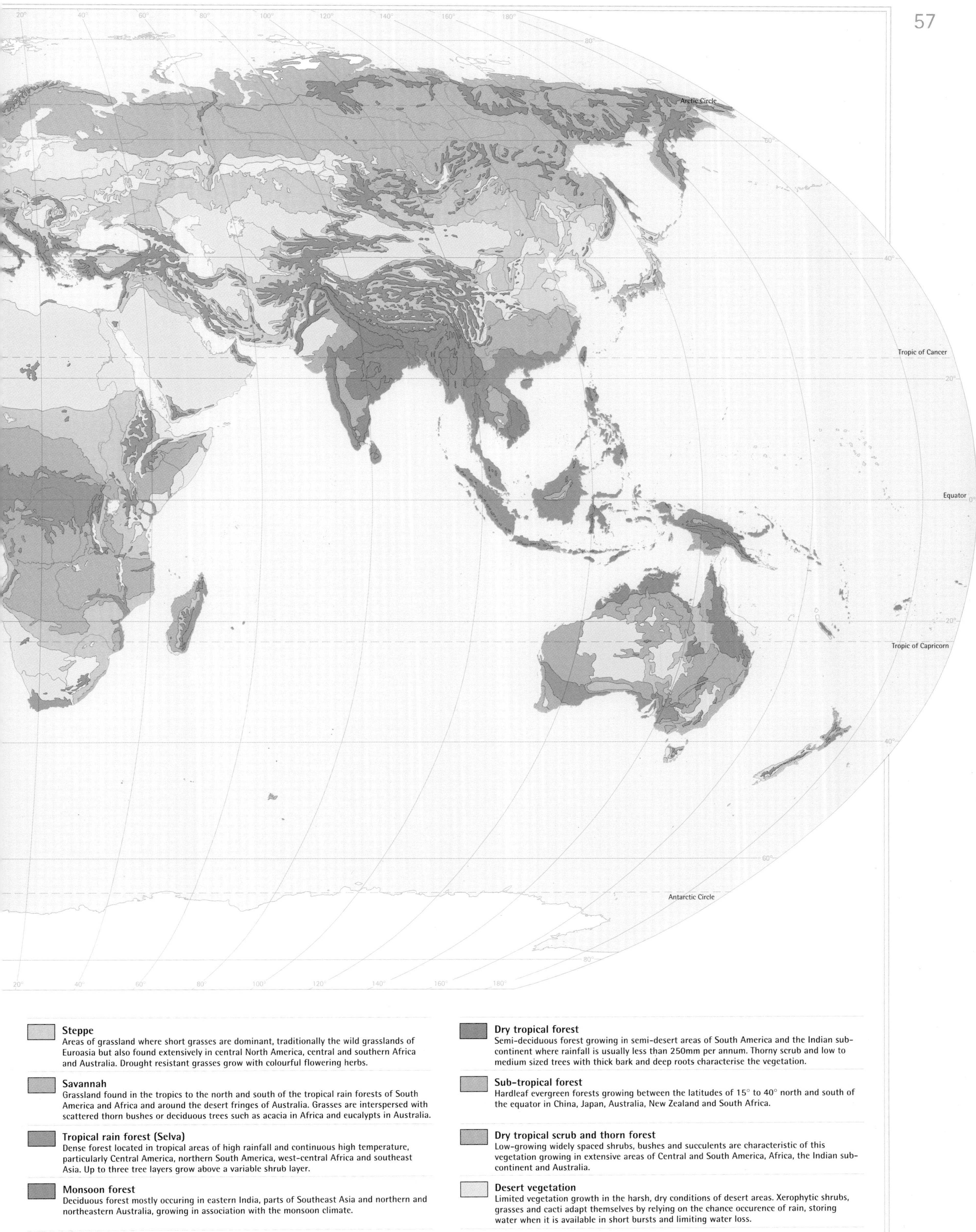

Steppe
Areas of grassland where short grasses are dominant, traditionally the wild grasslands of Euroasia but also found extensively in central North America, central and southern Africa and Australia. Drought resistant grasses grow with colourful flowering herbs.

Savannah
Grassland found in the tropics to the north and south of the tropical rain forests of South America and Africa and around the desert fringes of Australia. Grasses are interspersed with scattered thorn bushes or deciduous trees such as acacia in Africa and eucalypts in Australia.

Tropical rain forest (Selva)
Dense forest located in tropical areas of high rainfall and continuous high temperature, particularly Central America, northern South America, west-central Africa and southeast Asia. Up to three tree layers grow above a variable shrub layer.

Monsoon forest
Deciduous forest mostly occuring in eastern India, parts of Southeast Asia and northern and northeastern Australia, growing in association with the monsoon climate.

Dry tropical forest
Semi-deciduous forest growing in semi-desert areas of South America and the Indian sub-continent where rainfall is usually less than 250mm per annum. Thorny scrub and low to medium sized trees with thick bark and deep roots characterise the vegetation.

Sub-tropical forest
Hardleaf evergreen forests growing between the latitudes of 15° to 40° north and south of the equator in China, Japan, Australia, New Zealand and South Africa.

Dry tropical scrub and thorn forest
Low-growing widely spaced shrubs, bushes and succulents are characteristic of this vegetation growing in extensive areas of Central and South America, Africa, the Indian sub-continent and Australia.

Desert vegetation
Limited vegetation growth in the harsh, dry conditions of desert areas. Xerophytic shrubs, grasses and cacti adapt themselves by relying on the chance occurence of rain, storing water when it is available in short bursts and limiting water loss.

© Bartholomew

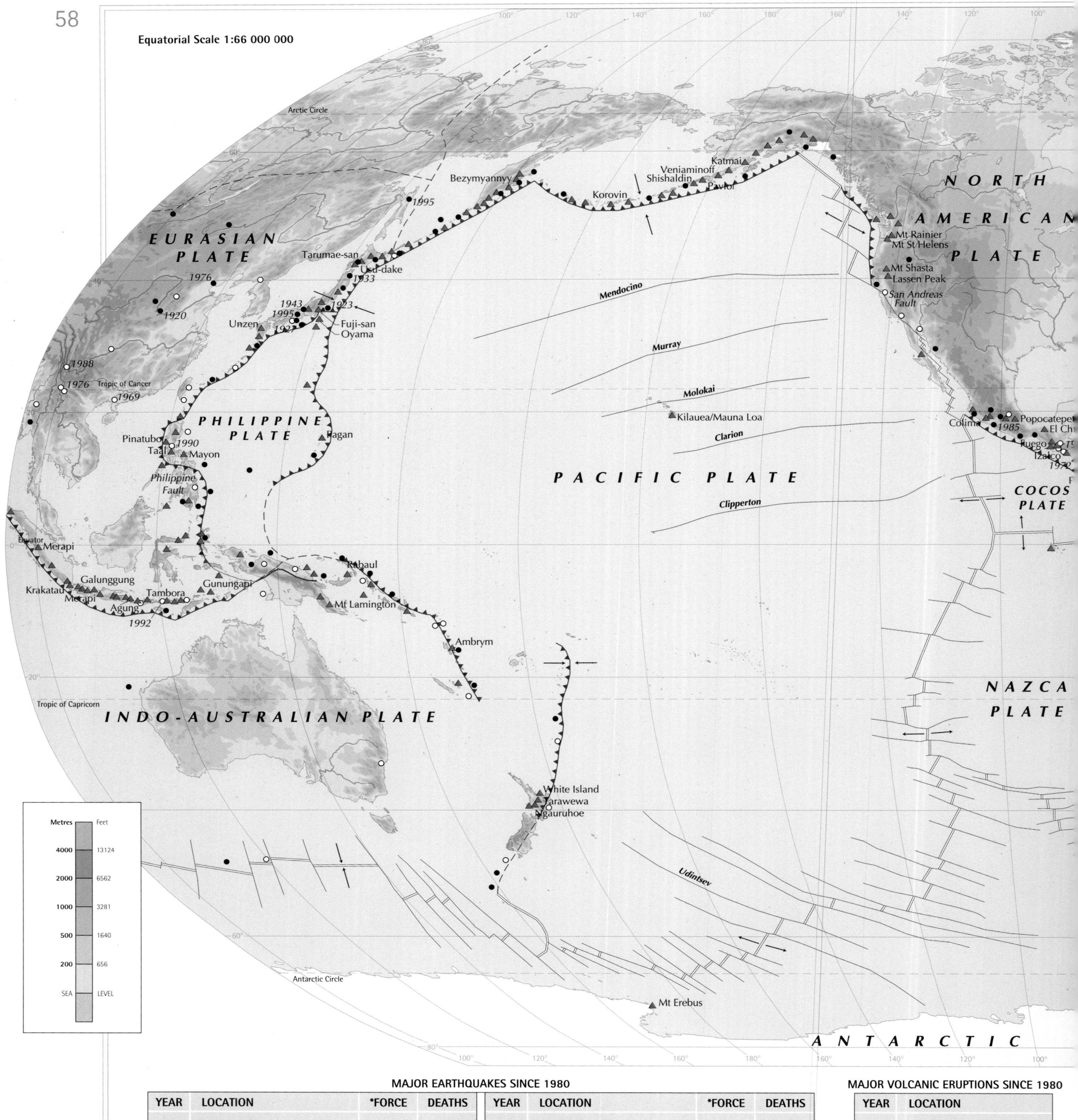

Equatorial Scale 1:66 000 000

Robinson Projection

MAJOR EARTHQUAKES SINCE 1980

YEAR	LOCATION	*FORCE	DEATHS	YEAR	LOCATION	*FORCE	DEATHS
1980	El Asnam, Algeria	7.7	4000	1990	Northwestern Iran	7.7	50 000
1980	Southern Italy	6.9	3000	1990	Luzon, Philippines	7.7	1600
1981	Kerman, Iran	7.3	2500	1991	Costa Rica / Panama	7.4	82
1982	El Salvador	7.4	16	1991	Georgia	7.1	114
1982	Dhamar, Yemen	6.0	3000	1991	Uttar Pradesh, India	6.1	1600
1983	Eastern Turkey	7.1	1500	1992	Kyrgyzstan	7.5	50
1985	Santiago, Chile	7.8	177	1992	Flores, Indonesia	7.5	2500
1985	Xinjiang Uygur, China	7.4	63	1992	Erzincan, Turkey	6.8	500
1985	Michoacán, Mexico	8.1	20 000	1992	Cairo, Egypt	5.9	550
1986	El Salvador	7.5	1000	1993	Northern Japan	7.8	185
1987	Ecuador	7.0	2000	1993	Maharashtra, India	6.4	9700
1988	Yunnan, China	7.6	1000	1994	Northern Bolivia	8.3	10
1988	Armenia	6.9	25 000	1994	Kuril Islands, Japan	8.3	10
1988	Nepal / India	6.9	1000	1995	Kobe, Japan	7.2	5200
1989	San Francisco Bay, USA	7.1	67	1995	Sakhalin, Russian Fed	7.6	2500

* Richter scale

MAJOR VOLCANIC ERUPTIONS SINCE 1980

YEAR	LOCATION
1980	Mt St Helens, USA
1981	Hekla, Iceland
1982	El Chichón, Mexico
1982	Galunggung, Indonesia
1983	Kilauea, Hawaii
1983	Oyama, Japan
1985	Nevado del Ruiz, Colombia
1986	Lake Nyos, Cameroon
1988	Gunungapi, Indonesia
1991	Pinatubo, Philippines
1991	Unzen, Japan
1993	Mayon, Philippines
1993	Galeras, Colombia
1994	El Llaima, Chile
1994	Rabaul, PNG

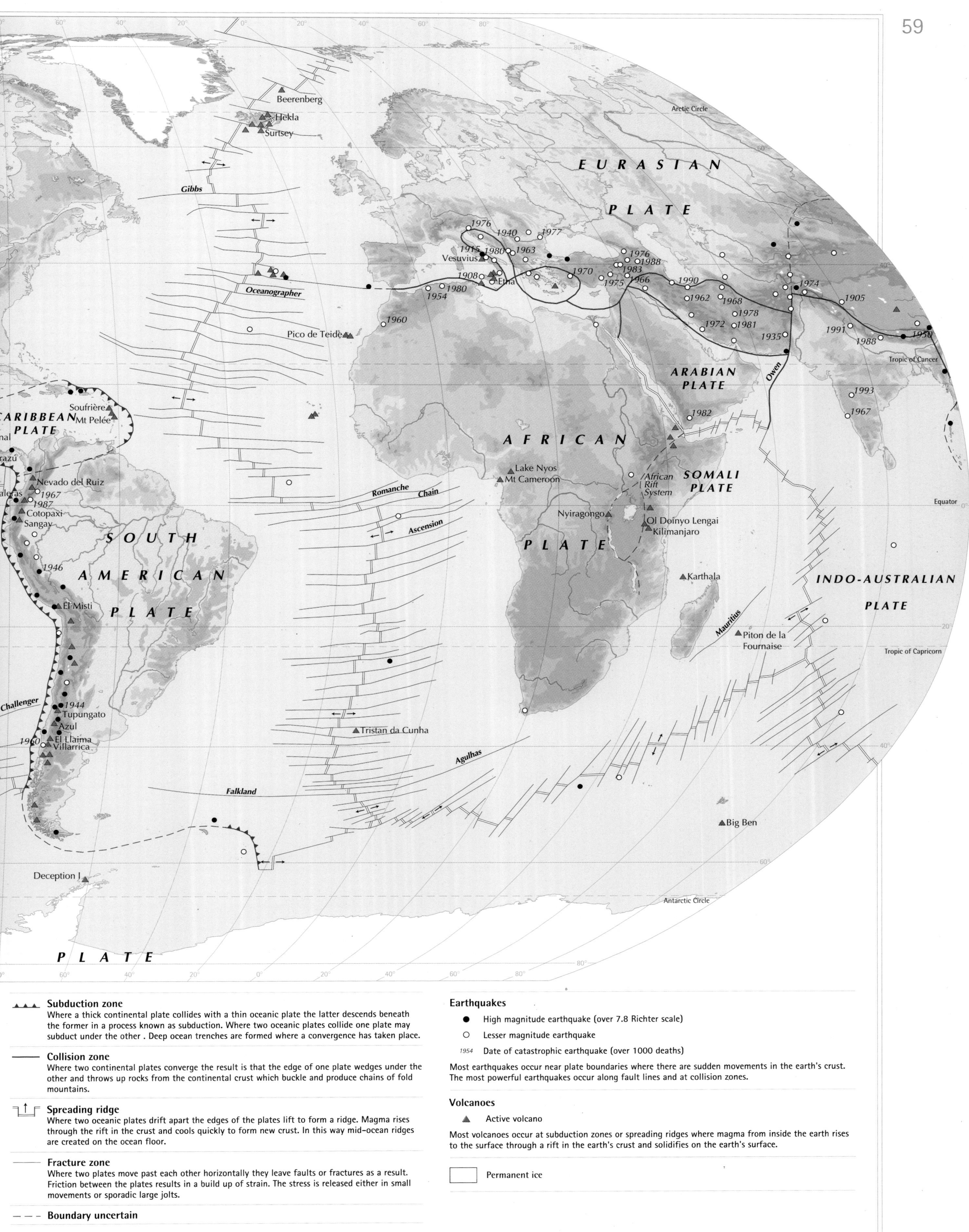

Beerenberg
Hekla
Surtsey
Gibbs
Oceanographer
Pico de Teide
Soufrière
Mt Pelée
CARIBBEAN PLATE
Nevado del Ruiz
Cotopaxi
Sangay
SOUTH AMERICAN PLATE
El Misti
Challenger
Tupungato
Azul
El Llaima
Villarrica
Deception I.
PLATE

EURASIAN PLATE

1976 *1940* *1977*
1915 *1980* *1963*
Vesuvius *1976*
1988
1908 *1970*
Etna *1983*
1954 *1980* *1975* *1966* *1990* *1974* *1905*
1960 *1962* *1968*
1978
ARABIAN PLATE *1972* *1981* *1991* *1958*
1935 *1988*
Owen Tropic of Cancer
1993
1982 *1967*

AFRICAN
Lake Nyos
Mt Cameroon
SOMALI PLATE
African Rift System
Nyiragongo Ol Doinyo Lengai
Kilimanjaro
PLATE Equator

Romanche Chain
Ascension
Karthala
INDO-AUSTRALIAN
PLATE
Mauritius Piton de la Fournaise
Tropic of Capricorn

Tristan da Cunha
1944
1946
1960

Agulhas
Falkland
Big Ben

Antarctic Circle

Arctic Circle

Subduction zone
Where a thick continental plate collides with a thin oceanic plate the latter descends beneath the former in a process known as subduction. Where two oceanic plates collide one plate may subduct under the other . Deep ocean trenches are formed where a convergence has taken place.

Collision zone
Where two continental plates converge the result is that the edge of one plate wedges under the other and throws up rocks from the continental crust which buckle and produce chains of fold mountains.

Spreading ridge
Where two oceanic plates drift apart the edges of the plates lift to form a ridge. Magma rises through the rift in the crust and cools quickly to form new crust. In this way mid–ocean ridges are created on the ocean floor.

Fracture zone
Where two plates move past each other horizontally they leave faults or fractures as a result. Friction between the plates results in a build up of strain. The stress is released either in small movements or sporadic large jolts.

Boundary uncertain

Earthquakes

● High magnitude earthquake (over 7.8 Richter scale)

○ Lesser magnitude earthquake

1954 Date of catastrophic earthquake (over 1000 deaths)

Most earthquakes occur near plate boundaries where there are sudden movements in the earth's crust. The most powerful earthquakes occur along fault lines and at collision zones.

Volcanoes

▲ Active volcano

Most volcanoes occur at subduction zones or spreading ridges where magma from inside the earth rises to the surface through a rift in the earth's crust and solidifies on the earth's surface.

Permanent ice

© Bartholomew

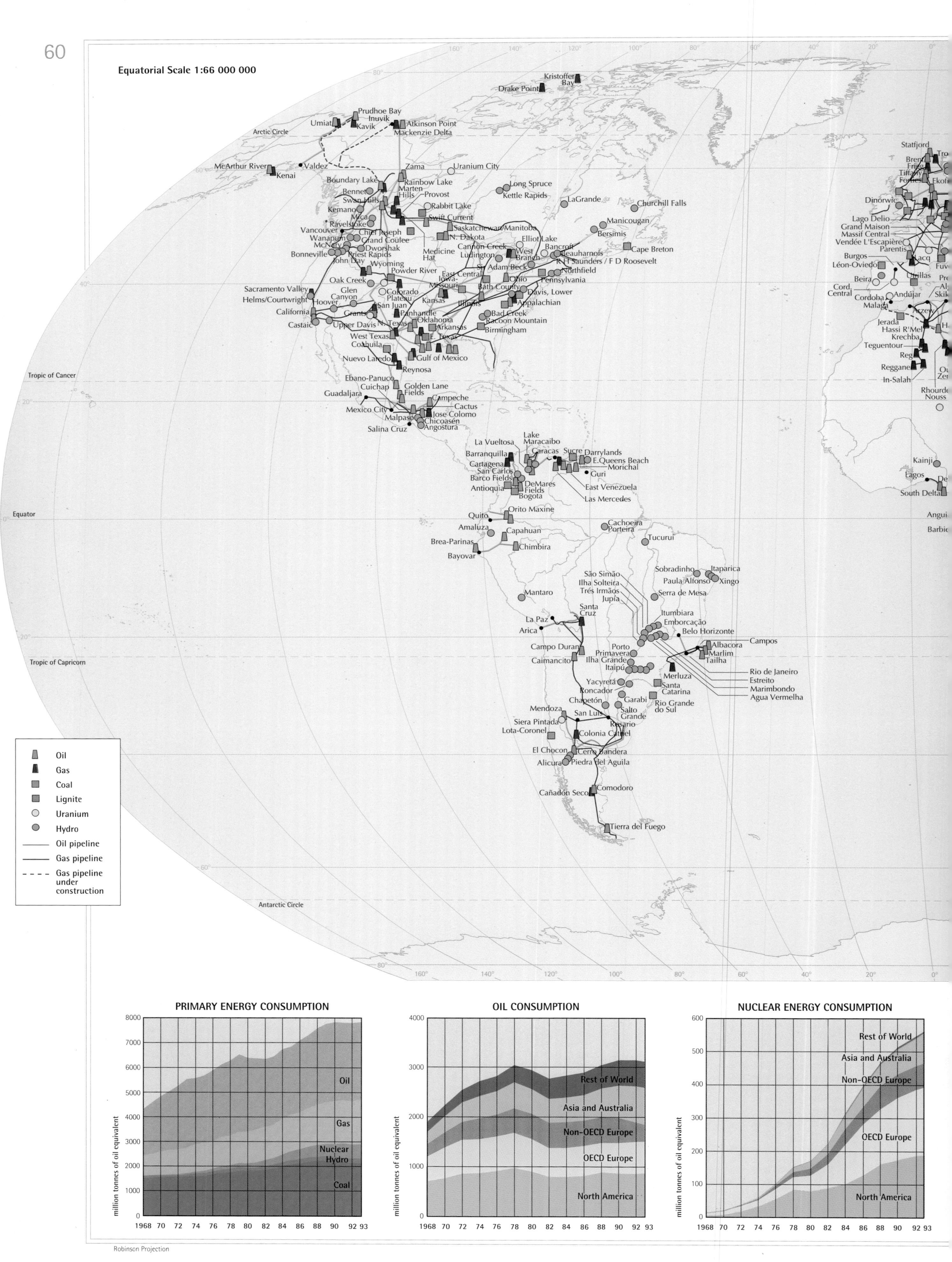

Equatorial Scale 1:66 000 000

Kristoffer Bay
Drake Point

Prudhoe Bay
Inuvik
Umiat Kavik
Atkinson Point
Mackenzie Delta
Arctic Circle
McArthur River
Valdez
Kenai
Zama
Uranium City
Boundary Lake
Rainbow Lake
Bennet
Marten Hills
Provost
Swan Hills
Rabbit Lake
Long Spruce
Kemano
Mica
Kettle Rapids
LaGrande
Revelstoke
Swift Current
Manicougan
Vancouver
Chief Joseph
Churchill Falls
Wanapum
Grand Coulee
Saskatchewan Manitoba
Bersimis
McNary
Dworshak
N. Dakota
Bonneville
Priest Rapids
Canyon Creek
Elliot Lake
John Day
Medicine Hat
Ludington
West Branch
Bancroft
Cape Breton
Wyoming
Powder River
Adam Beck
Beauharnois
R H Saunders / F D Roosevelt
Oak Creek
East Central
Iowa-Missouri
Ohio
Northfield
Sacramento Valley
Glen Canyon
Colorado Plateau
Kansas
St
Davis, Lower
Pennsylvania
Helms/Courtwright
Hoover
San Juan
Illinois
Bath County
Appalachian
California
Grants
Panhandle
Bad Creek
Racoon Mountain
Castaic
Upper Davis
N Texas
Oklahoma
Birmingham
West Texas
Arkansas
Coahuila
Texas
Nuevo Laredo
Gulf of Mexico
Reynosa
Ebano-Panuco
Cuichap
Golden Lane Fields
Guadaljara
Campeche
Cactus
Mexico City
Jose Colomo
Malpaso
Chicoasén
Salina Cruz
Angostura

La Vueltosa
Lake Maracaibo
Barranquilla
Caracas
Sucre Darrylands
Cartagena
San Carlos
E.Queens Beach
Morichal
Barco Fields
DeMares Fields
Guri
Antioquia
Bogota
East Venezuela
Las Mercedes
Orito Maxine
Quito
Amaluza
Capahuan
Cachoeira
Porteira
Tucurui
Brea-Parinas
Chimbira
Bayovar
Sobradinho
Itaparica
São Simão
Paula Alfonso
Xingo
Ilha Solteira
Trés Irmãos
Serra de Mesa
Mantaro
Jupía
Santa
Itumbiara
La Paz
Cruz
Emborcação
Arica
Belo Horizonte
Campo Duran
Porto
Albacora
Campos
Caimancito
Primavera
Marlim
Ilha Grande
Tailha
Itaipú
Merluza
Rio de Janeiro
Yacyretá
Santa
Estreito
Roncador
Catarina
Marimbondo
Chapetón
Garabi
Rio Grande
Agua Vermelha
Mendoza
Salto Grande
do Sul
San Luis
Siera Pintada
Rosario
Lota-Coronel
Colonia Catriel
El Chocon
Cerro Bandera
Alicura
Piedra del Aguila
Comodoro
Cañadón Seco
Tierra del Fuego

Statfjord
Brent
Troll
Tiffa
Frigg
Ekofi
Forti
Dinorwic
Lago Delio
Grand Maison
Massif Central
Vendée L'Escapière
Parentis
Burgos
Léon-Oviedo
Acq
Fuv
Beira
Pro
Cord.
Central
Cordoba
Andújar
Al
Skik
Malaga
Jerada
Hassi R'Mel
Krechba
Teguentour
Reg
Reggane
Ou
In-Salah
Zer
Rhourde
Nouss
Kainji
Lagos
De
South Delta
Angui
Barbie

Oil
Gas
Coal
Lignite
Uranium
Hydro
Oil pipeline
Gas pipeline
Gas pipeline under construction

Arctic Circle
Tropic of Cancer
Equator
Tropic of Capricorn
Antarctic Circle

Robinson Projection

PRIMARY ENERGY CONSUMPTION

million tonnes of oil equivalent

Oil
Gas
Nuclear
Hydro
Coal

1968 70 72 74 76 78 80 82 84 86 88 90 92 93

OIL CONSUMPTION

million tonnes of oil equivalent

Rest of World
Asia and Australia
Non-OECD Europe
OECD Europe
North America

1968 70 72 74 76 78 80 82 84 86 88 90 92 93

NUCLEAR ENERGY CONSUMPTION

Rest of World
Asia and Australia
Non-OECD Europe
OECD Europe
North America

1968 70 72 74 76 78 80 82 84 86 88 90 92 93

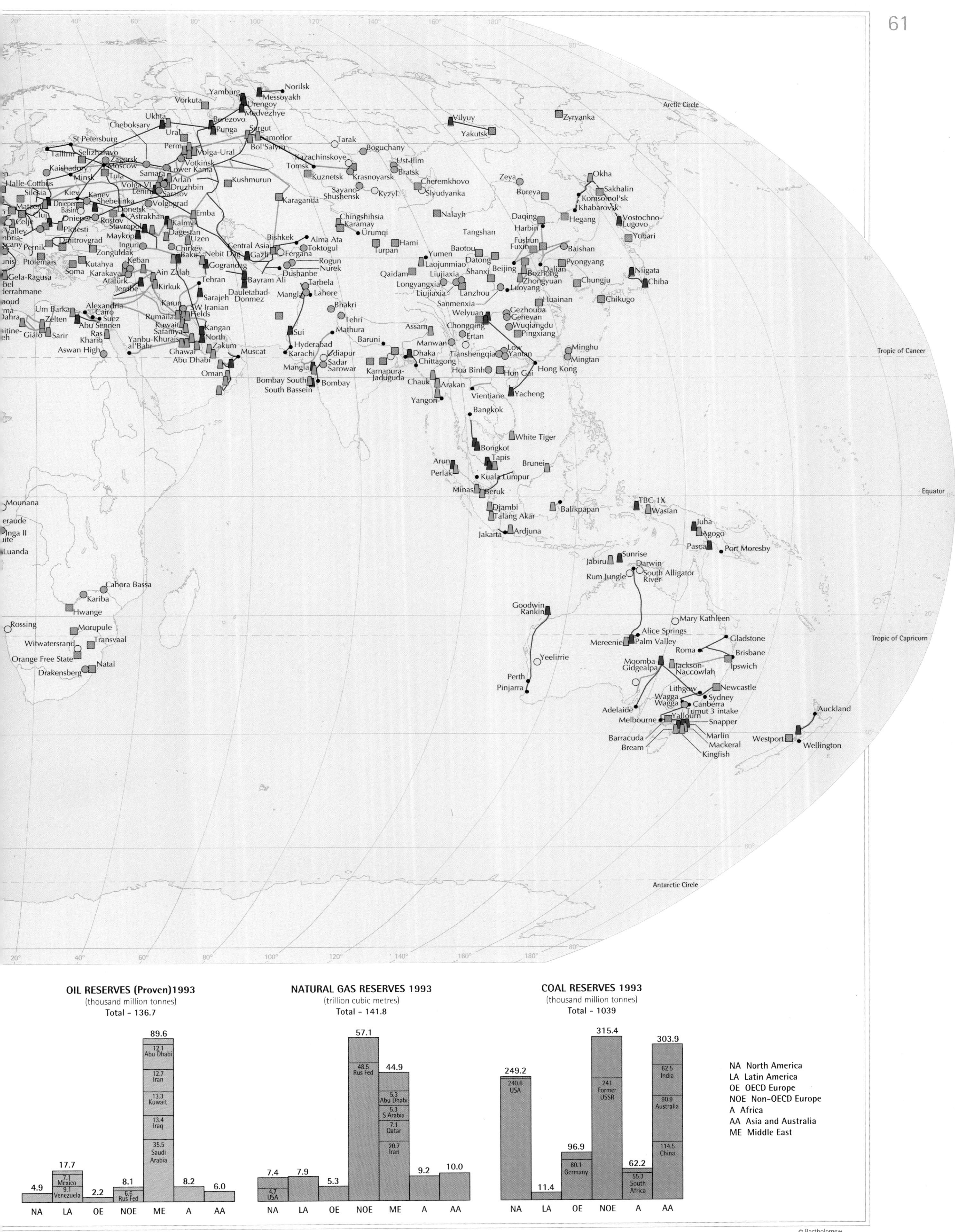

OIL RESERVES (Proven)1993
(thousand million tonnes)
Total – 136.7

NA	LA	OE	NOE	ME	A	AA
4.9	17.7	2.2	8.1	89.6	8.2	6.0
	7.1 Mexico		6.6 Rus Fed	12.1 Abu Dhabi		
	9.1 Venezuela			12.7 Iran		
				13.3 Kuwait		
				13.4 Iraq		
				35.5 Saudi Arabia		

NATURAL GAS RESERVES 1993
(trillion cubic metres)
Total – 141.8

NA	LA	OE	NOE	ME	A	AA
7.4	7.9	5.3	57.1	44.9	9.2	10.0
4.7 USA			48.5 Rus Fed	5.3 Abu Dhabi		
				5.3 S Arabia		
				7.1 Qatar		
				20.7 Iran		

COAL RESERVES 1993
(thousand million tonnes)
Total – 1039

NA	LA	OE	NOE	A	AA
249.2	11.4	96.9	315.4	62.2	303.9
240.6 USA		80.1 Germany	241 Former USSR	55.3 South Africa	62.5 India
					90.9 Australia
					114.5 China

NA North America
LA Latin America
OE OECD Europe
NOE Non-OECD Europe
A   Africa
AA Asia and Australia
ME Middle East

© Bartholomew

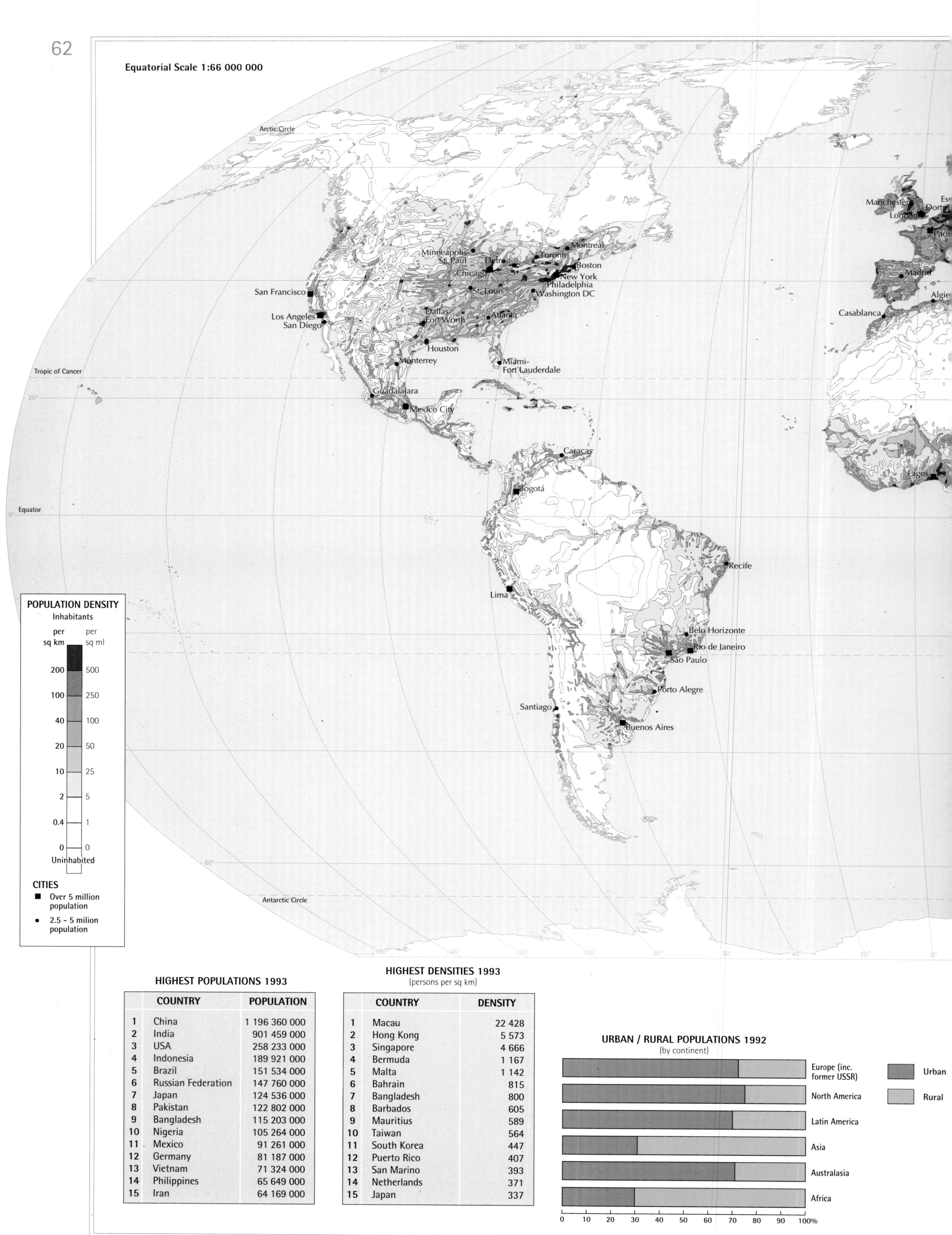

Equatorial Scale 1:66 000 000

Arctic Circle

Tropic of Cancer

Equator

Antarctic Circle

POPULATION DENSITY
Inhabitants

per sq km	per sq ml
200	500
100	250
40	100
20	50
10	25
2	5
0.4	1
0	0

Uninhabited

CITIES
■ Over 5 million population
● 2.5 – 5 milion population

Robinson Projection

HIGHEST POPULATIONS 1993

	COUNTRY	POPULATION
1	China	1 196 360 000
2	India	901 459 000
3	USA	258 233 000
4	Indonesia	189 921 000
5	Brazil	151 534 000
6	Russian Federation	147 760 000
7	Japan	124 536 000
8	Pakistan	122 802 000
9	Bangladesh	115 203 000
10	Nigeria	105 264 000
11	Mexico	91 261 000
12	Germany	81 187 000
13	Vietnam	71 324 000
14	Philippines	65 649 000
15	Iran	64 169 000

HIGHEST DENSITIES 1993
(persons per sq km)

	COUNTRY	DENSITY
1	Macau	22 428
2	Hong Kong	5 573
3	Singapore	4 666
4	Bermuda	1 167
5	Malta	1 142
6	Bahrain	815
7	Bangladesh	800
8	Barbados	605
9	Mauritius	589
10	Taiwan	564
11	South Korea	447
12	Puerto Rico	407
13	San Marino	393
14	Netherlands	371
15	Japan	337

URBAN / RURAL POPULATIONS 1992
(by continent)

Europe (inc. former USSR)
North America
Latin America
Asia
Australasia
Africa

Urban
Rural

0 10 20 30 40 50 60 70 80 90 100%

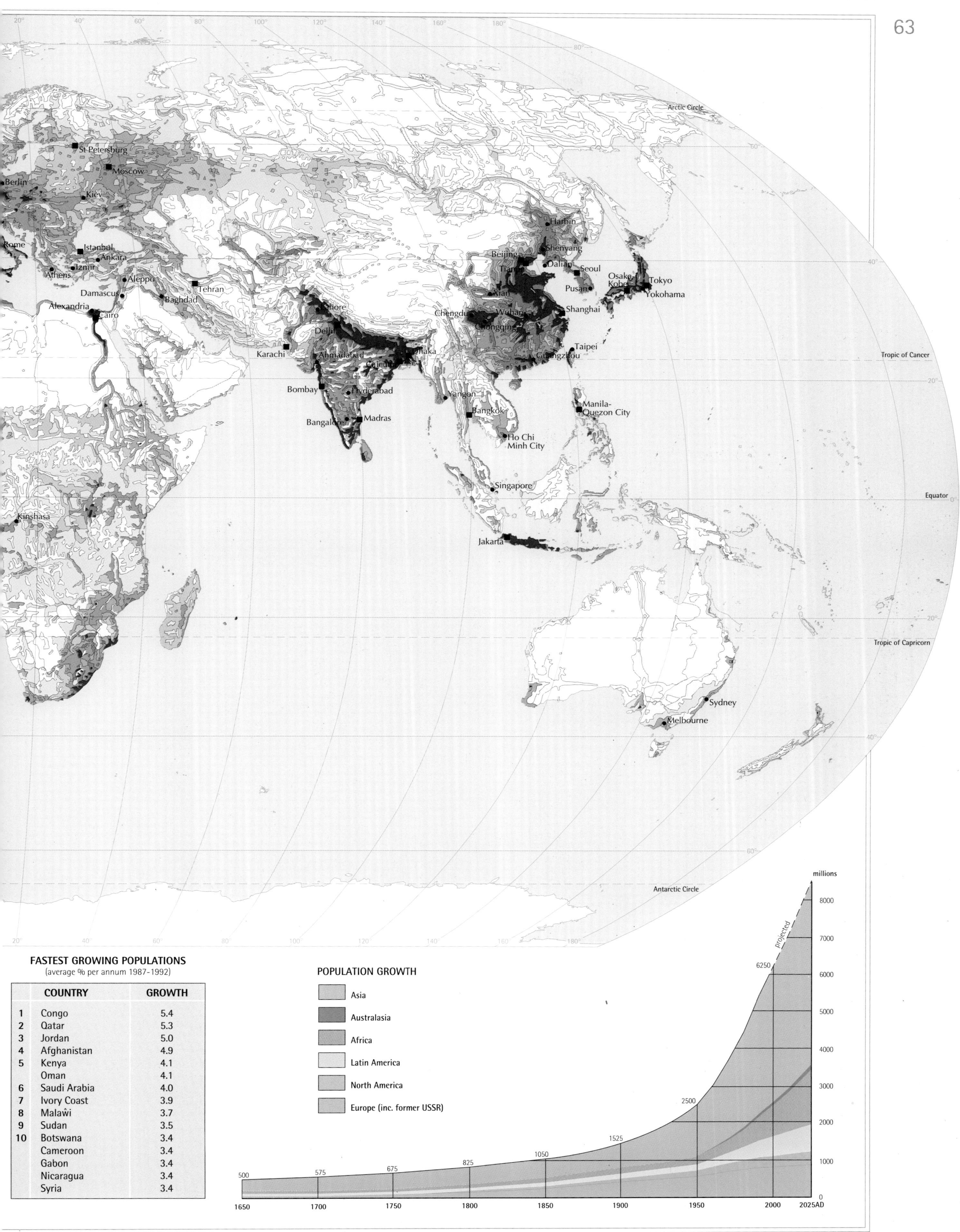

FASTEST GROWING POPULATIONS
(average % per annum 1987-1992)

	COUNTRY	GROWTH
1	Congo	5.4
2	Qatar	5.3
3	Jordan	5.0
4	Afghanistan	4.9
5	Kenya	4.1
	Oman	4.1
6	Saudi Arabia	4.0
7	Ivory Coast	3.9
8	Malawi	3.7
9	Sudan	3.5
10	Botswana	3.4
	Cameroon	3.4
	Gabon	3.4
	Nicaragua	3.4
	Syria	3.4

POPULATION GROWTH

- Asia
- Australasia
- Africa
- Latin America
- North America
- Europe (inc. former USSR)

© Bartholomew

A metropolitan area is a continuous built-up area which may include a number of cities and towns. The population given for the selected metropolitan areas below is from the latest available sources.

POPULATIONS OVER 10 MILLION

Population	Metropolitan area and country
20,200,000	MEXICO CITY MEXICO
16,972,000	NEW YORK USA
15,199,423	SÃO PAULO BRAZIL
13,341,896	SHANGHAI CHINA
12,571,720	BOMBAY INDIA
12,200,000	BUENOS AIRES ARGENTINA
11,642,000	CAIRO EGYPT
11,609,735	TOKYO JAPAN
11,420,000	LOS ANGELES USA
10,916,272	CALCUTTA INDIA
10,819,407	BEIJING CHINA
10,627,000	SEOUL SOUTH KOREA

Population — Metropolitan areas by country

AFGHANISTAN
2,000,000 KABUL

ALGERIA
3,033,000 ALGIERS

ANGOLA
1,717,000 LUANDA

ARGENTINA
12,200,000 BUENOS AIRES
1,179,067 CORDOBA
1,078,374 ROSARIO

ARMENIA
1,200,000 YEREVAN

AUSTRALIA
1,065,000 ADELAIDE
1,386,000 BRISBANE
3,178,000 MELBOURNE
1,215,000 PERTH
3,700,000 SYDNEY

AUSTRIA
1,565,800 VIENNA

AZERBAIJAN
1,779,500 BAKU

BANGLADESH
2,040,663 CHITTAGONG
6,105,160 DHAKA

BELARUS
1,633,600 MINSK

BOLIVIA
1,234,000 LA PAZ

BRAZIL
1,334,460 BELEM
3,461,905 BELO HORIZONTE
1,596,274 BRASILIA
1,975,624 CURITIBA
2,294,524 FORTALEZA
3,015,960 PORTO ALEGRE
2,859,469 RECIFE
9,600,528 RIO DE JANEIRO
2,472,131 SALVADOR
15,199,423 SÃO PAULO

BULGARIA
1,221,000 SOFIA

CANADA
3,127,000 MONTREAL
3,893,000 TORONTO
1,603,000 VANCOUVER

CHILE
4,628,320 SANTIAGO

CHINA
1,370,000 ANSHAN
1,257,000 BAOTOU
10,819,407 BEIJING
2,214,000 CHANGCHUN
1,362,000 CHANGSHA
3,004,000 CHENGDU
3,151,000 CHONGQING
2,543,000 DALIAN
1,420,000 FUSHUN
1,361,000 FUZHOU
3,671,000 GUANGZHOU
1,587,000 GUIYANG
1,412,000 HANGZHOU
2,966,000 HARBIN
1,170,000 HUAINAN
1,327,000 JILIN
2,415,000 JINAN
1,718,000 KUNMING
1,566,000 LANZHOU
1,227,000 LUOYANG
1,415,000 NANCHANG
2,265,000 NANJING
2,040,000 QINGDAO
1,460,000 QIQIHAR
13,341,896 SHANGHAI
4,763,000 SHENYANG
1,352,000 SHIJIAZHUANG
2,199,000 TAIYUAN
1,590,000 TANGSHAN
9,371,000 TIANJIN
3,921,000 WUHAN
2,859,000 XIAN
1,759,000 ZHENGZHOU
2,430,000 ZIBO

COLOMBIA
1,033,951 BARRANQUILLA
5,025,989 BOGOTA
1,655,699 CALI
1,594,967 MEDELLIN

CÔTE D'IVOIRE
2,168,000 ABIDJAN

CUBA
2,099,000 HAVANA

CZECH REPUBLIC
1,214,174 PRAGUE

DENMARK
1,342,679 COPENHAGEN

DOMINICAN REPUBLIC
2,055,000 SANTO DOMINGO

ECUADOR
1,508,444 GUAYAQUIL
1,100,847 QUITO

EGYPT
3,380,000 ALEXANDRIA
11,642,000 CAIRO
2,096,000 EL GIZA

EL SALVADOR
1,522,126 SAN SALVADOR

ETHIOPIA
1,891,000 ADDIS ABABA

FRANCE
1,230,936 MARSEILLES
9,318,821 PARIS

GEORGIA
1,400,000 TBILISI

GERMANY
3,447,916 BERLIN
2,720,400 ESSEN-DORTMUND
1,669,000 HAMBURG
1,236,500 MUNICH

GREECE
3,097,000 ATHENS

GUATEMALA
1,132,730 GUATEMALA CITY

HAITI
1,402,000 PORT-AU-PRINCE

HONG KONG
2,016,700 KOWLOON

HUNGARY
1,992,343 BUDAPEST

INDIA
3,297,655 AHMADABAD
4,086,548 BANGALORE
12,571,720 BOMBAY
10,916,272 CALCUTTA
8,375,188 DELHI
4,280,261 HYDERABAD
1,514,425 JAIPUR
2,111,284 KANPUR
1,642,134 LUCKNOW
5,361,468 MADRAS
1,661,409 NAGPUR
2,485,014 PUNE

INDONESIA
2,056,915 BANDUNG
9,253,000 JAKARTA
1,730,052 MEDAN
1,249,230 SEMARANG
2,473,272 SURABAYA

IRAN
1,484,000 ISFAHAN
1,882,000 MASHHAD
6,773,000 TEHRAN

IRAQ
4,044,000 BAGHDAD

ISRAEL
1,135,800 TEL AVIV

ITALY
1,358,627 MILAN
1,071,744 NAPLES
2,723,327 ROME

JAPAN
1,214,122 FUKUOKA
1,071,898 HIROSHIMA
1,167,604 KAWASAKI
1,015,431 KITAKYUSHU
1,394,964 KYOTO
2,095,393 NAGOYA
8,520,000 OSAKA-KOBE
1,704,135 SAPPORO
11,609,735 TOKYO
3,250,548 YOKOHAMA

JORDAN
1,272,000 AMMAN

KAZAKHSTAN
1,151,300 ALMA-ATA

KENYA
1,503,000 NAIROBI

LEBANON
1,500,000 BEIRUT

LIBYA
1,500,000 TRIPOLI

MALAYSIA
1,711,000 KUALA LUMPUR

MEXICO
2,846,720 GUADALAJARA
20,200,000 MEXICO CITY
2,521,697 MONTERREY
1,267,000 PUEBLA

MOROCCO
3,210,000 CASABLANCA
1,472,000 RABAT

MOZAMBIQUE
1,098,000 MAPUTO

MYANMAR
3,295,000 RANGOON

NETHERLANDS
1,091,338 AMSTERDAM
1,069,356 ROTTERDAM

NIGERIA
5,689,000 LAGOS

NORTH KOREA
2,230,000 PYONGYANG

PAKISTAN
1,507,000 FAISALABAD
7,702,000 KARACHI
4,092,000 LAHORE
1,099,000 RAWALPINDI

PERU
6,483,901 LIMA

PHILIPPINES
7,832,000 MANILA - QUEZON CITY

POLAND
1,655,700 WARSAW

PORTUGAL
1,742,000 LISBON
1,314,794 OPORTO

PUERTO RICO
1,390,000 SAN JUAN

REP OF SOUTH AFRICA
2,350,157 CAPE TOWN
1,137,378 DURBAN
1,916,063 JOHANNESBURG

ROMANIA
2,350,984 BUCHAREST

RUSSIAN FEDERATION
1,143,000 CHELYABINSK
1,104,000 KAZAN
8,957,000 MOSCOW
1,441,000 NIZHNIY NOVGOROD
1,442,000 NOVOSIBIRSK
1,269,000 OMSK
1,099,000 PERM
1,027,000 ROSTOV-ON-DON
1,239,000 SAMARA
5,004,000 ST PETERSBURG
1,097,000 UFA
1,006,000 VOLGOGRAD
1,371,000 YEKATERINBURG

SAUDI ARABIA
1,800,000 JEDDAH
1,500,000 RIYADH

SENEGAL
1,492,000 DAKAR

SINGAPORE
2,874,000 SINGAPORE

SOUTH KOREA
1,818,293 INCHON
3,797,566 PUSAN
10,627,000 SEOUL
2,228,834 TAEGU

SPAIN
1,625,542 BARCELONA
2,909,792 MADRID

SUDAN
1,947,000 KHARTOUM

SWEDEN
1,669,840 STOCKHOLM

SYRIA
2,768,000 ALEPPO
2,913,000 DAMASCUS

TAIWAN
1,400,000 KAOHSIUNG
2,720,000 TAIPEI

TANZANIA
1,657,000 DAR-ES-SALAAM

THAILAND
5,876,000 BANGKOK

TUNISIA
1,636,000 TUNIS

TURKEY
3,022,236 ANKARA
6,407,215 ISTANBUL
2,665,105 IZMIR

UK
2,329,600 BIRMINGHAM
1,784,000 LEEDS
1,440,900 LIVERPOOL
9,227,687 LONDON
2,578,900 MANCHESTER

UKRAINE
1,187,000 DNEPROPETROVSK
1,117,000 DONETSK
1,618,000 KHARKOV
2,616,000 KIEV
1,106,000 ODESSA

URUGUAY
1,383,660 MONTEVIDEO

USA
3,051,000 ATLANTA
2,414,000 BALTIMORE
4,497,000 BOSTON
1,193,000 BUFFALO
7,498,000 CHICAGO
1,539,000 CINCINNATI
2,213,000 CLEVELAND
1,370,000 COLUMBUS
4,135,000 DALLAS - FORT WORTH
1,668,000 DENVER
4,285,000 DETROIT
3,437,000 HOUSTON
1,406,000 INDIANAPOLIS
1,602,000 KANSAS CITY
11,420,000 LOS ANGELES
3,264,000 MIAMI - FORT LAUDERDALE
1,446,000 MILWAUKEE
2,583,000 MINNEAPOLIS -ST PAUL
1,295,000 NEW ORLEANS
16,972,000 NEW YORK
4,941,000 PHILADELPHIA
2,287,000 PHOENIX
2,404,000 PITTSBURG
1,570,000 PORTLAND
1,073,000 ROCHESTER
1,388,000 SACRAMENTO
1,348,000 SAN ANTONIO
2,549,000 SAN DIEGO
5,240,000 SAN FRANCISCO
2,078,000 SEATTLE
2,507,000 ST LOUIS
2,101,000 TAMPA-ST PETERSBURG
4,293,000 WASHINGTON DC

UZBEKISTAN
2,094,000 TASHKENT

VENEZUELA
4,092,000 CARACAS
1,400,643 MARACAIBO
1,274,354 VALENCIA

VIETNAM
1,447,523 HAIPHONG
1,056,146 HANOI
3,924,435 HO CHI MINH

YUGOSLAVIA
1,168,454 BELGRADE

ZAIRE
3,505,000 KINSHASA

ZIMBABWE
1,000,000 HARARE

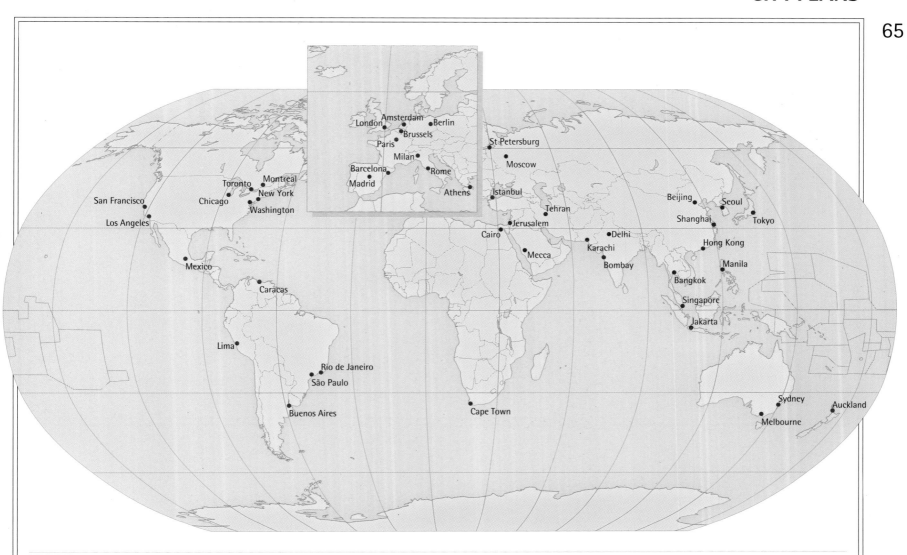

Contents

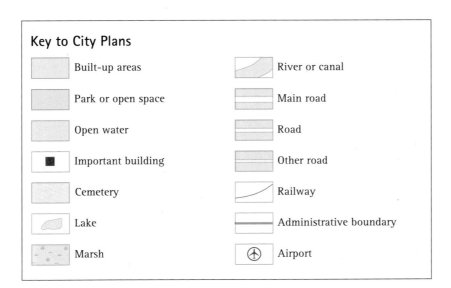

Key to City Plans

Built-up areas

Park or open space

Open water

■ Important building

Cemetery

Lake

Marsh

River or canal

Main road

Road

Other road

Railway

Administrative boundary

✈ Airport

© Bartholomew

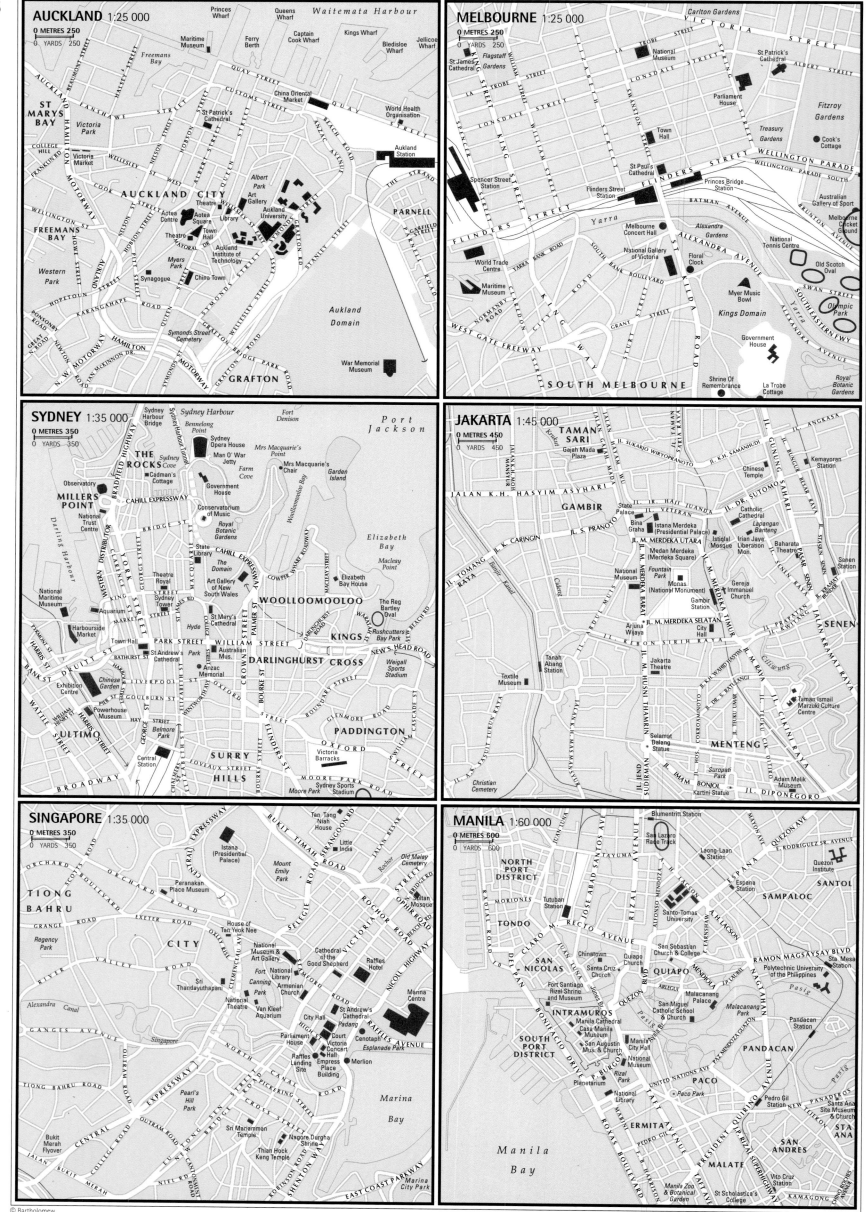

© Bartholomew

AUCKLAND 1:25 000
0 METRES 250
0 YARDS 250
MELBOURNE 1:25 000
0 METRES 250
0 YARDS 250
SYDNEY 1:35 000
0 METRES 350
0 YARDS 350
JAKARTA 1:45 000
0 METRES 450
0 YARDS 450
SINGAPORE 1:35 000
0 METRES 350
0 YARDS 350
MANILA 1:60 000
0 METRES 600
0 YARDS 600

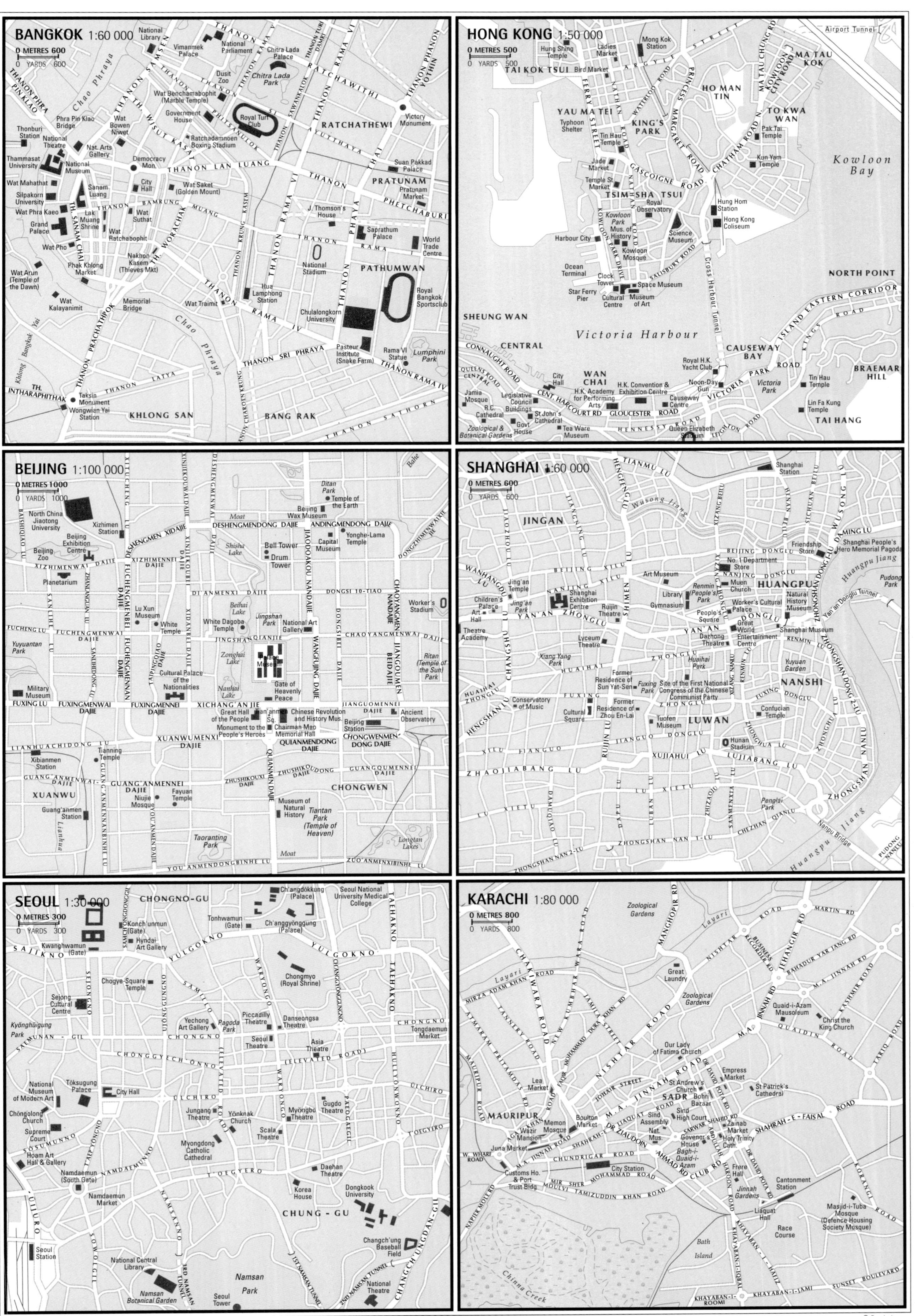

© Bartholomew

BANGKOK 1:60 000
0 METRES 600
0 YARDS 600
National Library
Vimanmek Palace
National Parliament
Chitra Lada Palace
Chitra Lada Park
Dusit Zoo
Wat Benchamabophit (Marble Temple)
Royal Turf Club
Government House
Wat Bowen Niwet
Phra Pin Klao Bridge
Thonburi Station
National Theatre
Nat. Arts Gallery
Ratchadamnoen Boxing Stadium
Thammasat University
National Museum
Democracy Mon.
RATCHATHEWI
Victory Monument
Suan Pakkad Palace
PRATUNAM
Pratunam Market
Wat Mahathat
Sanam Luang
City Hall
Wat Saket (Golden Mount)
Silpakorn University
Wat Phra Kaeo
Lak Muang Shrine
Wat Suthat
J. Thomson's House
Grand Palace
Wat Ratchabophit
Saprathum Palace
World Trade Centre
Wat Pho
Nakhon Kasem (Thieves Mkt)
National Stadium
PATHUMWAN
Phak Khlong Market
Wat Arun (Temple of the Dawn)
Hua Lamphong Station
Royal Bangkok Sportsclub
Wat Kalayanimit
Memorial Bridge
Wat Traimit
Chulalongkorn University
Chao Phraya
Pasteur Institute (Snake Farm)
Rama VI Statue
Lumphini Park
Taksin Monument
Wongwien Yai Station
KHLONG SAN
BANG RAK
THANON LAN LUANG
THANON RAMA IV
THANON SRI PHRAYA
THANON SATHORN
HONG KONG 1:50 000
0 METRES 500
0 YARDS 500
Airport Tunnel
Mong Kok Station
Ladies Market
Hung Shing Temple
TAI KOK TSUI
Bird Market
MA TAU KOK
HO MAN TIN
YAU MA TEI
KING'S PARK
TO KWA WAN
Typhoon Shelter
Tin Hau Temple
Pak Tai Temple
Jade Market
Kun Yam Temple
Kowloon Bay
Temple St. Market
TSIM SHA TSUI
Royal Observatory
Hung Hom Station
Hong Kong Coliseum
Harbour City
Kowloon Park
Mus. of History
Science Museum
Kowloon Mosque
Ocean Terminal
Clock Tower
Space Museum
Star Ferry Pier
Cultural Centre
Museum of Art
NORTH POINT
SHEUNG WAN
Victoria Harbour
CENTRAL
CAUSEWAY BAY
Royal H.K. Yacht Club
WAN CHAI
City Hall
H.K. Convention & Exhibition Centre
H.K. Academy for Performing Arts
Noon-Day Gun
Victoria Park
Tin Hau Temple
BRAEMAR HILL
Jamia Mosque
Legislative Council Buildings
Causeway Centre
R.C. Cathedral
St John's Cathedral
Lin Fa Kung Temple
TAI HANG
Zoological & Botanical Gardens
Govt House
Tea Ware Museum
Queen Elizabeth Stadium
Cross Harbour Tunnel
BEIJING 1:100 000
0 METRES 1000
0 YARDS 1000
Ditan Park
Temple of the Earth
North China Jiaotong University
Xizhimen Station
Beijing Wax Museum
DESHENGMENDONG DAJIE
ANDINGMENDONG DAJIE
Yonghe-Lama Temple
Beijing Exhibition Centre
Beijing Zoo
Shisha Lake
Bell Tower
Drum Tower
Capital Museum
Planetarium
DONGSI 10-TIAO
Lu Xun Museum
Beihai Lake
Jingshan Park
Worker's Stadium
White Temple
White Dagoba Temple
National Art Gallery
CHAOYANGMENWAI DAJIE
Yuyuantan Park
Zonghai Lake
Palace Museum
Ritan (Temple of the Sun) Park
Cultural Palace of the Nationalities
Military Museum
Nanhai Lake
Gate of Heavenly Peace
FUXING LU
XICHANG'AN JIE
JIANGUOMENNEI DAJIE
Great Hall of the People
Tian'anmen Sq.
Chinese Revolution and History Mus.
Ancient Observatory
Monument to the People's Heroes
Chairman Mao Memorial Hall
Beijing Station
XUANWUMENXI DAJIE
QUIANMENDONG DAJIE
CHONGWENMEN-DONG DAJIE
Tianning Temple
Xibianmen Station
XUANWU
CHONGWEN
Niujie Mosque
Fayuan Temple
Guang'anmen Station
Museum of Natural History
Tiantan Park (Temple of Heaven)
Taoranting Park
Longtan Lakes
Moat
SHANGHAI 1:60 000
0 METRES 600
0 YARDS 600
TIANMU LU
Shanghai Station
Wusong Jiang
JINGAN
Shanghai People's Hero Memorial Pagoda
Friendship Store
BEIJING DONGLU
No. 1 Department Store
Art Museum
NANJING DONGLU
Muen Church
HUANGPU
Huangpu Jiang
Pudong Park
Jing'an Temple
Shanghai Exhibition Centre
Renmin (People's) Park
Library
Children's Palace
Jing'an Park
Ruijin Theatre
Gymnasium
Worker's Cultural Palace
Natural History Museum
Yan'an Donglu Tunnel
Art Hall
YAN'AN ZHONGLU
People's Square
Great World Entertainment Centre
Theatre Academy
Dazhong Theatre
Shanghai Museum
Lyceum Theatre
Xiang Yang Park
Huaihai Park
Yuyuan Garden
Former Residence of Sun Yat-Sen
Fuxing Park
Site of the First National Congress of the Chinese Communist Party
NANSHI
Conservatory of Music
Cultural Square
Former Residence of Zhou En-Lai
Confucian Temple
Tuofen Museum
LUWAN
Hunan Stadium
XUJIAHUI LU
LUJIABANG LU
ZHAOJIABANG LU
Penglai Park
ZHONGSHAN NAN 1-LU
ZHONGSHAN NAN 2-LU
Nanpu Bridge
PUDONG NANLU
SEOUL 1:30 000
0 METRES 300
0 YARDS 300
CHONGNO-GU
Ch'angdŏkkung (Palace)
Seoul National University Medical College
Konch'unmun (Gate)
Tonhwamun (Gate)
Ch'anggyŏnggung (Palace)
Hyndai Art Gallery
Kwanghwamun (Gate)
SAJIKNO
YULGOKNO
Chongmyo (Royal Shrine)
Chogye-Square Temple
Sejong Cultural Centre
Yechong Art Gallery
Pagoda Park
Piccadilly Theatre
Danseongsa Theatre
Kyŏnghŭigung Park
Tongdaemun Market
Seoul Theatre
Asia Theatre
CHONGGYECH'ONNO (ELEVATED ROAD)
National Museum of Modern Art
Tŏksugung Palace
City Hall
ULCHIRO
Gugdo Theatre
Chŏngdong Church
Jungang Theatre
Yŏnknak Church
Myŏngbo Theatre
Supreme Court
Scala Theatre
Myongdong Catholic Cathedral
Hoam Art Hall & Gallery
Namdaemun (South Gate)
Daehan Theatre
Namdaemun Market
Korea House
Dongkook University
CHUNG-GU
Changch'ung Baseball Field
Seoul Station
National Central Library
Namsan Park
Namsan Botanical Garden
Seoul Tower
National Theatre
KARACHI 1:80 000
0 METRES 800
0 YARDS 800
Zoological Gardens
MARTIN RD
Great Laundry
Zoological Gardens
Quaid-i-Azam Mausoleum
Christ the King Church
Our Lady of Fatima Church
Empress Market
Lea Market
St Andrew's Church
St Patrick's Cathedral
SADR
Bohri Bazaar
MAURIPUR
Boulton Market
Memon Mosque
Wazir Mansion
Sind Assembly
Sind High Court
Zainab Market
SHAHRAH-E-FAISAL
Nat. Mus.
Holy Trinity Cath.
Juna Market
Govenor's House
Bagh-i-Quaid-i-Azam
City Station
Frere Hall
Customs Ho. & Port Trust Bldg
Cantonment Station
Jinnah Gardens
Liaquat Hall
Masjid-i-Tuba Mosque (Defence Housing Society Mosque)
Race Course
Bath Island
Chinna Creek
KHAYABAN-I-ROOMI
KHAYABAN-I-JAMI
SUNSET BOULEVARD

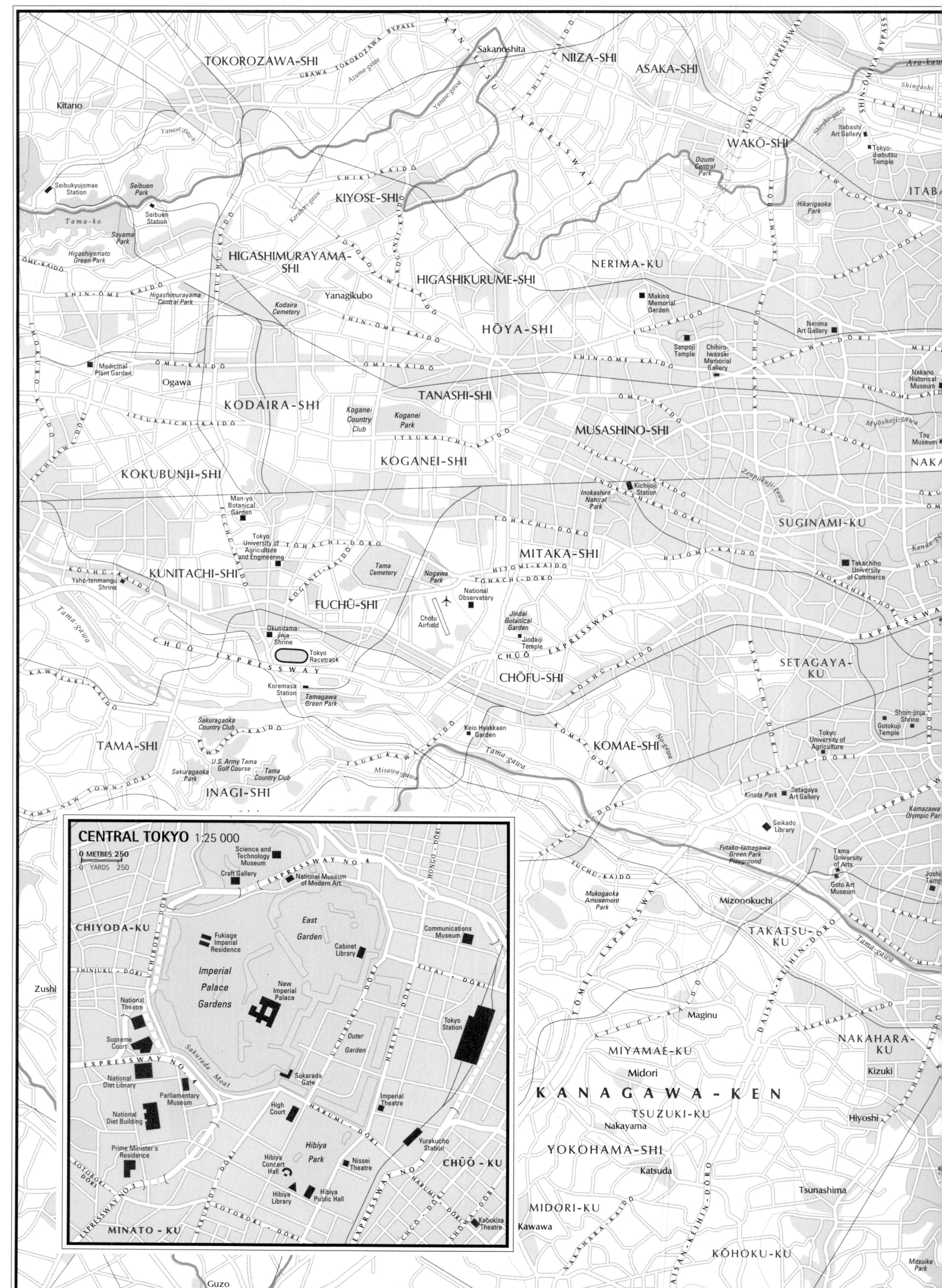
TOKOROZAWA-SHI
Sakanoshita
NIIZA-SHI
ASAKA-SHI
Kitano
WAKŌ-SHI
Oizumi Central Park
Itabashi Art Gallery
Tokyo-daibutsu Temple
Seibukyujomae Station
Seibuen Park
Seibuen Station
Tama-ko
Sayama Park
Higashiyamato Green Park
KIYOSE-SHI
Hikarigaoka Park
HIGASHIMURAYAMA-SHI
NERIMA-KU
Higashimurayama Central Park
Kodaira Cemetery
Yanagikubo
HIGASHIKURUME-SHI
Makino Memorial Garden
HŌYA-SHI
Nerima Art Gallery
Sanpoji Temple
Chihiro-Iwasaki Memorial Gallery
Medicinal Plant Garden
Ogawa
KODAIRA-SHI
Koganei Country Club
Koganei Park
TANASHI-SHI
Nakano Historical Museum
MUSASHINO-SHI
Toy Museum
KOGANEI-SHI
KOKUBUNJI-SHI
Kichijoji Station
Inokashira Natural Park
Man-yo Botanical Garden
SUGINAMI-KU
Tokyo University of Agriculture and Engineering
MITAKA-SHI
Tama Cemetery
Nogawa Park
KUNITACHI-SHI
Yaho-tenmangu Shrine
National Observatory
Takachiho University of Commerce
FUCHŪ-SHI
Chofu Airfield
Okunitama-jinja Shrine
Jindai Botanical Garden
Jindaiji Temple
Tokyo Racetrack
CHŌFU-SHI
SETAGAYA-KU
Koremasa Station
Tamagawa Green Park
Sakuragaoka Country Club
Keio Hyakkaen Garden
Shoin-jinja Shrine
Gotokuji Temple
Tokyo University of Agriculture
TAMA-SHI
KOMAE-SHI
U.S. Army Tama Golf Course
Tama Country Club
Sakuragaoka Park
INAGI-SHI
Kinuta Park
Setagaya Art Gallery
Komazawa Olympic Park
Seikado Library
Futako-tamagawa Green Park Playground
Tama University of Arts
Goto Art Museum
Mukogaoka Amusement Park
Mizonokuchi
TAKATSU-KU
Zushi
Maginu
MIYAMAE-KU
NAKAHARA-KU
Midori
Kizuki
KANAGAWA-KEN
TSUZUKI-KU
Nakayama
Hiyoshi
YOKOHAMA-SHI
Katsuda
Tsunashima
MIDORI-KU
Kawawa
KŌHOKU-KU
Mitsuike Park
Guzo
CENTRAL TOKYO 1:25 000
0 METRES 250
0 YARDS 250
Science and Technology Museum
Craft Gallery
National Museum of Modern Art
EXPRESSWAY NO. 4
CHIYODA-KU
East Garden
Fukiage Imperial Residence
Communications Museum
Cabinet Library
Imperial Palace Gardens
New Imperial Palace
National Theatre
Supreme Court
Tokyo Station
Outer Garden
Sakurada Moat
National Diet Library
Sakurada Gate
Parliamentary Museum
National Diet Building
High Court
Imperial Theatre
Hibiya Park
Yurakucho Station
Prime Minister's Residence
Hibiya Concert Hall
Nissei Theatre
CHŪŌ-KU
Hibiya Library
Hibiya Public Hall
Kabukiza Theatre
MINATO-KU

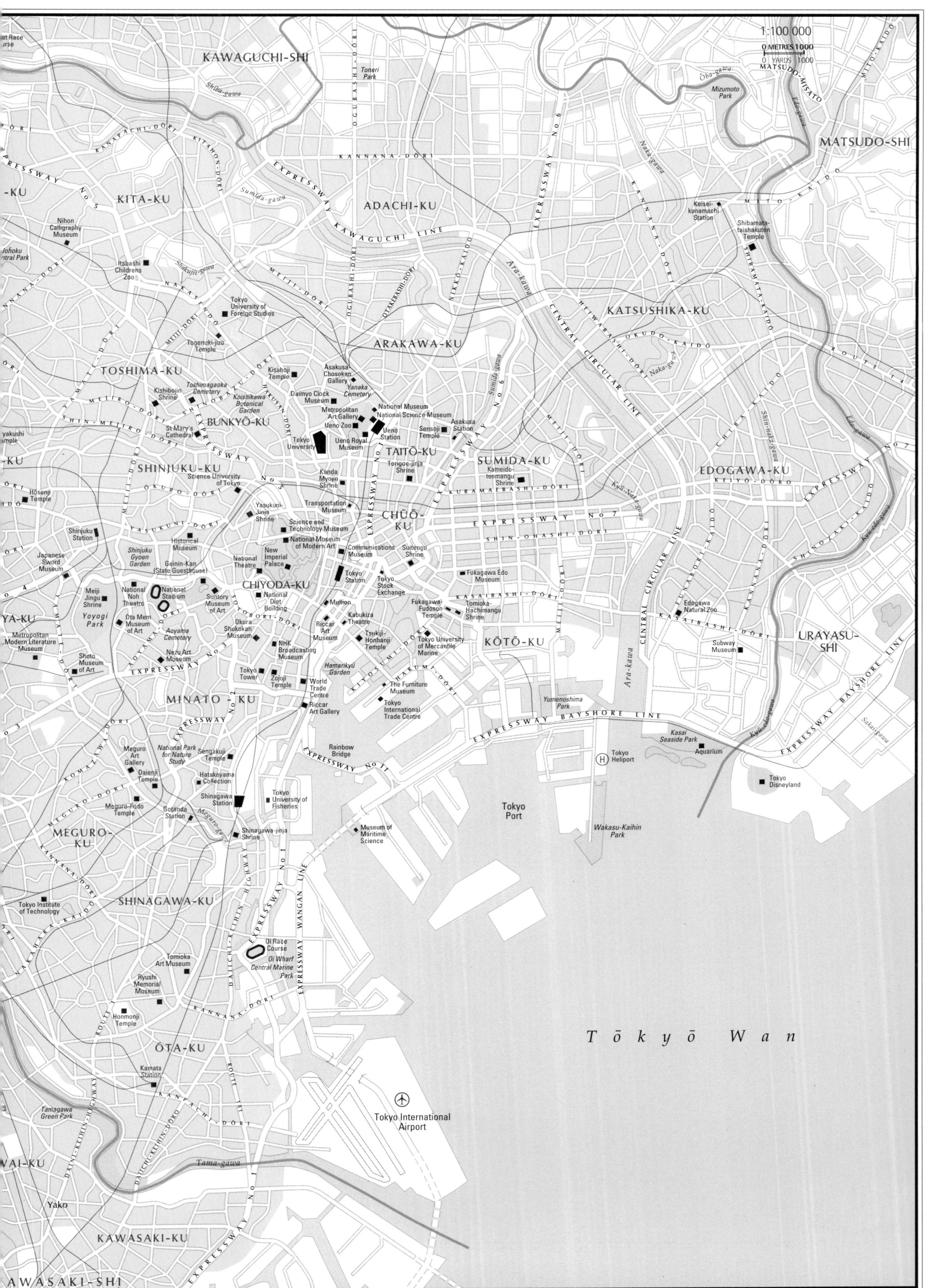

1:100 000

0 METRES 1000
0 YARDS 1000

KAWAGUCHI-SHI

Toneri Park

Shiba-gawa

MATSUDO-MISATO

Ōba-gawa

Mizumoto Park

MATSUDO-SHI

KITA-KU

Shakujii-gawa

Sumida-gawa

ADACHI-KU

Keisei-kanamachi Station

Shibamata-taishakuten Temple

Nihon Calligraphy Museum

Jōhoku Central Park

Itabashi Childrens Zoo

KATSUSHIKA-KU

CENTRAL CIRCULAR LINE

Tokyo University of Foreign Studies

ARAKAWA-KU

Naka-gawa

Togenuki-jizo Temple

TOSHIMA-KU

Kisshōji Temple

Asakusa-Chosokan Gallery

Yanaka Cemetery

Toshimagaoka Cemetery

Koishikawa Botanical Garden

Daimyo Clock Museum

National Museum

National Science Museum

Kishibojin Shrine

BUNKYŌ-KU

Metropolitan Art Gallery

Ueno Zoo

Sensōji Temple

Asakusa Station

SUMIDA-KU

St Mary's Cathedral

Tokyo University

Ueno Station

Ueno Royal Museum

EDOGAWA-KU

Yakushi Temple

SHINJUKU-KU

Science University of Tokyo

Kanda Myojin Shrine

TAITŌ-KU

Torigoe-jinja Shrine

Kameido-tenmangu Shrine

Hōsenji Temple

Yasukuni-jinja Shrine

Transportation Museum

Science and Technology Museum

CHŪŌ-KU

EXPRESSWAY NO 7

URAYASU-SHI

Shinjuku Station

National Museum of Modern Art

Communications Museum

Suitengu Shrine

Japanese Sword Museum

Shinjuku Gyoen Garden

Historical Museum

Geinin-kan (State Guesthouse)

National Theatre

New Imperial Palace

Tokyo Station

Tokyo Stock Exchange

Fukagawa Edo Museum

Edogawa Natural Zoo

Tomioka-Hachimangu Shrine

Meiji Jingu Shrine

National Noh Theatre

National Stadium

Suntory Museum of Art

CHIYODA-KU

National Diet Building

Mullion

Kabukiza Theatre

Fukagawa-Fudoson Temple

Subway Museum

Metropolitan Modern Literature Museum

Yoyogi Park

Ota Mem Museum of Art

Aoyama Cemetery

Okura Shukokan Museum

Riccar Art Museum

Tsukiji-Honganji Temple

Tokyo University of Mercantile Marine

KŌTŌ-KU

Shoto Museum of Art

Nezu Art Museum

NHK Broadcasting Museum

Hamarikyū Garden

Tokyo Tower

Zojoji Temple

World Trade Centre

MINATO-KU

Riccar Art Gallery

The Furniture Museum

Tokyo International Trade Centre

Yumenoshima Park

Kasai Seaside Park

Aquarium

Meguro Art Gallery

National Park for Nature Study

Sengakuji Temple

Hatakeyama Collection

Daienji Temple

Rainbow Bridge

Tokyo Heliport

Tokyo Disneyland

Meguro-Fudo Temple

Gotanda Station

Shinagawa Station

Tokyo University of Fisheries

Tokyo Port

Wakasu-Kaihin Park

MEGURO-KU

Shinagawa-jinja Shrine

Museum of Maritime Science

Tokyo Institute of Technology

SHINAGAWA-KU

Oi Race Course

Oi Wharf Central Marine Park

Tomioka Art Museum

Tōkyō Wan

Ryushi Memorial Museum

Honmonji Temple

ŌTA-KU

Kamata Station

Tamagawa Green Park

Yako

Tama-gawa

Tokyo International Airport

KAWASAKI-KU

KAWASAKI-SHI

© Bartholomew

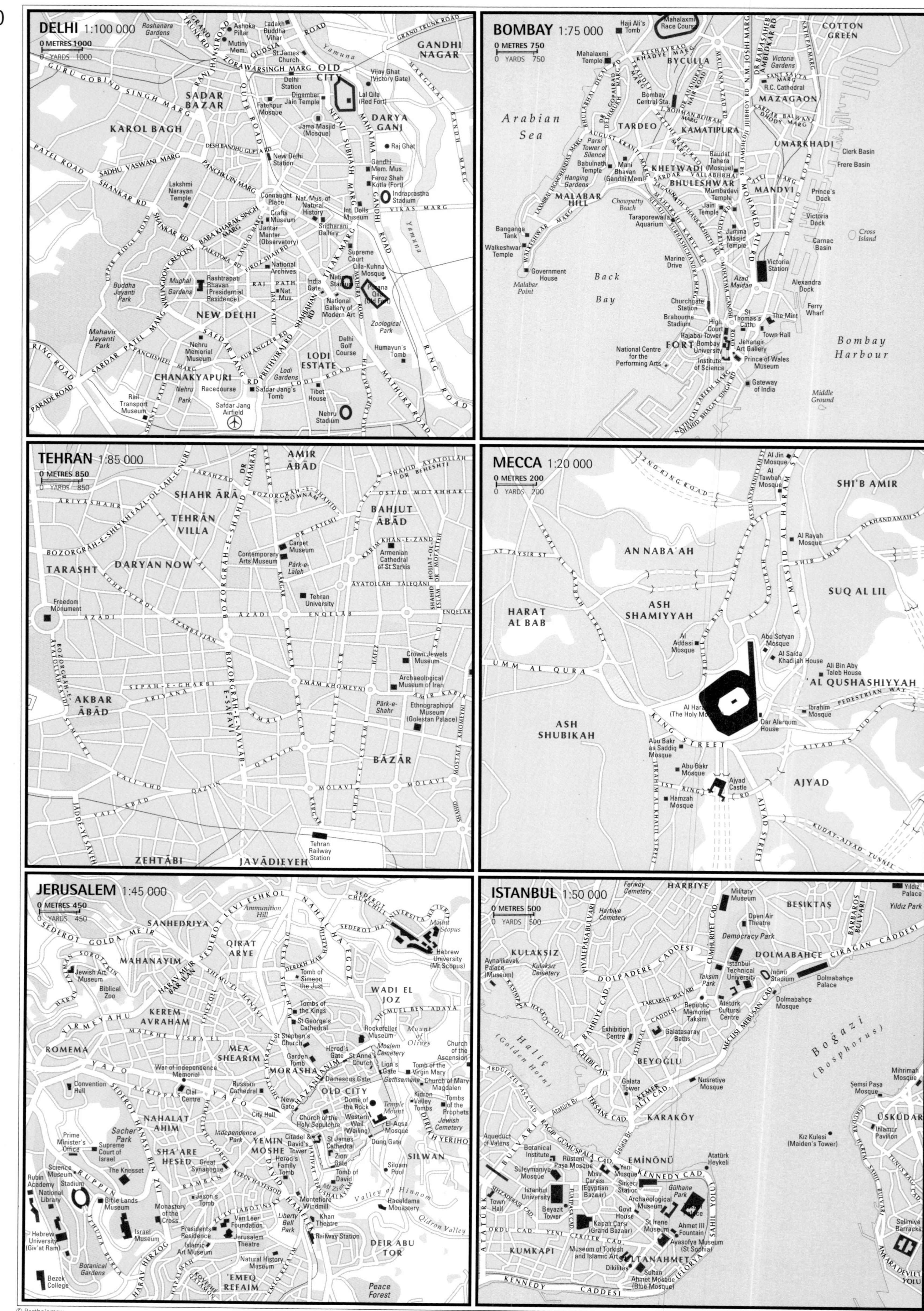

© Bartholomew

DELHI 1:100 000
0 METRES 1000
0 YARDS 1000
Roshanara Gardens
Ashoka Pillar
Ladakh Buddha Vihar
Mutiny Mem.
St James Church
GANDHI NAGAR
OLD CITY
Delhi Station
Vijay Ghat (Victory Gate)
Digamber Jain Temple
Lal Qila (Red Fort)
SADAR BAZAR
Fatehpur Mosque
DARYA GANJ
KAROL BAGH
Jama Masjid (Mosque)
Raj Ghat
New Delhi Station
Gandhi Mem. Mus.
Feroz Shah Kotla (Fort)
Lakshmi Narayan Temple
Connaught Place
Nat. Mus. of Natural History
Indraprastha Stadium
Crafts Museum
Int. Dolls Museum
Jantar Mantar (Observatory)
Sridharani Gallery
Supreme Court
Qila-Kuhna Mosque
National Archives
Rashtrapati Bhavan (Presidential Residence)
Mughal Gardens
Nat. Mus.
India Gate
National Stadium
Purana Qila (Old Fort)
Buddha Jayanti Park
National Gallery of Modern Art
NEW DELHI
Zoological Park
Mahavir Jayanti Park
Nehru Memorial Museum
Delhi Golf Course
Humayun's Tomb
LODI ESTATE
Lodi Gardens
CHANAKYAPURI
Nehru Park
Racecourse
Safdar Jang's Tomb
Tibet House
Rail Transport Museum
Safdar Jang Airfield
Nehru Stadium
GRAND TRUNK ROAD
RING ROAD
MATHURA ROAD
PATEL ROAD
SHANKAR RD
PARADE ROAD
Yamuna
BOMBAY 1:75 000
0 METRES 750
0 YARDS 750
Haji Ali's Tomb
Mahalaxmi Race Course
COTTON GREEN
Mahalaxmi Temple
BYCULLA
Victoria Gardens
St Saviour's R.C. Cathedral
MAZAGAON
Bombay Central Sta.
Arabian Sea
TARDEO
KAMATIPURA
UMARKHADI
Parsi Tower of Silence
Babulnath Temple
Mani Bhavan (Gandhi Mem.)
Baudat Tahera (Mosque)
Clerk Basin
Frere Basin
KHETWADI
BHULESHWAR
Hanging Gardens
MALABAR HILL
Mumbadevi Temple
MANDVI
Prince's Dock
Chowpatty Beach
Jain Temple
Victoria Dock
Taraporewala Aquarium
Banganga Tank
Jumma Masjid
Cross Island
Walkeshwar Temple
Carnac Basin
Marine Drive
Victoria Station
Government House
Malabar Point
Back Bay
Azad Maidan
Alexandra Dock
Churchgate Station
Brabourne Stadium
St Thomas's Cath.
The Mint
Ferry Wharf
High Court
Rajabai Tower
Bombay University
Town Hall
Bombay Harbour
FORT
Jehangir Art Gallery
National Centre for the Performing Arts
Institute of Science
Prince of Wales Museum
Gateway of India
Middle Ground
TEHRAN 1:85 000
0 METRES 850
0 YARDS 850
AMIR ĀBĀD
SHAHR ĀRĀ
BAHJUT ĀBĀD
TEHRĀN VILLA
Carpet Museum
Contemporary Arts Museum
Armenian Cathedral of St Sarkis
Pārk-e-Lāleh
TARASHT
DARYAN NOW
Tehran University
Freedom Monument
Crown Jewels Museum
Archaeological Museum of Iran
AKBAR ĀBĀD
Pārk-e-Shahr
Ethnographical Museum (Golestan Palace)
BĀZĀR
Tehran Railway Station
ZEHTĀBĪ
JAVĀDIEYEH
MECCA 1:20 000
0 METRES 200
0 YARDS 200
Al Jin Mosque
Al Tawbah Mosque
SHI'B AMIR
AN NABA'AH
Al Rayah Mosque
SUQ AL LIL
HARAT AL BAB
ASH SHAMIYYAH
Al Addasi Mosque
Abu Sofyan Mosque
Al Saida Khadijah House
Ali Bin Aby Taleb House
AL QUSHASHIYYAH
Al Haram (The Holy Mosque)
Ibrahim Mosque
ASH SHUBIKAH
Dar Alarqum House
Abu Bakr as Saddiq Mosque
Abu Bakr Mosque
Ajyad Castle
AJYAD
Hamzah Mosque
KING STREET
AJYAD STREET
JERUSALEM 1:45 000
0 METRES 450
0 YARDS 450
Ammunition Hill
SANHEDRIYA
Mount Scopus
QIRAT ARYE
Hebrew University (Mt Scopus)
MAHANAYIM
Jewish Art Museum
Tomb of Simeon the Just
Biblical Zoo
WADI EL JOZ
KEREM AVRAHAM
Tombs of the Kings
St George's Cathedral
Rockefeller Museum
Mount of Olives
ROMEMA
St Stephen's Church
MEA SHEARIM
Herod's Gate
St Anne's Church
Church of the Ascension
Garden Tomb
Moslem Cemetery
MORASHA
Lion's Gate
Tomb of the Virgin Mary
War of Independence Memorial
Damascus Gate
Gethsemane
Church of Mary Magdalen
Convention Hall
Clal Centre
Russian Cathedral
OLD CITY
Kidron Valley Tombs
New Gate
Dome of the Rock
Temple Mount
Tombs of the Prophets
City Hall
Church of the Holy Sepulchre
Western Wall (Wailing)
El-Aqsa Mosque
Jewish Cemetery
NAHALAT AHIM
Sacher Park
Independence Park
Citadel & David's Tower
St James Cathedral
Dung Gate
Prime Minister's Office
Supreme Court of Israel
YEMIN MOSHE
Zion Gate
SILWAN
SHA'ARE HESED
Great Synagogue
Herod's Family Tomb
Siloam Pool
Science Museum
The Knesset
Tomb of David
Rubin Academy
Stadium
Mt Zion
Valley of Hinnom
National Library
Bible Lands Museum
Jason's Tomb
Montefiore Windmill
Haceldama Monastery
Monastery of the Cross
Van Leer Foundation
Khan Theatre
Qidron Valley
Hebrew University (Giv'at Ram)
Israel Museum
President's Residence
Liberty Bell Park
Jerusalem Theatre
Railway Station
Islamic Art Museum
DEIR ABU TOR
Natural History Museum
Botanical Gardens
'EMEQ REFAIM
Bezek College
Peace Forest
ISTANBUL 1:50 000
0 METRES 500
0 YARDS 500
Ferikoy Cemetery
HARBIYE
Military Museum
Yildiz Palace
Yildiz Park
Harbiye Cemetery
BEŞIKTAŞ
Open Air Theatre
Democracy Park
KULAKSIZ
DOLMABAHÇE
Aynalıkavak Palace (Museum)
Kulaksız Cemetery
Istanbul Technical University
İnönü Stadium
Dolmabahçe Palace
Taksim Park
Dolmabahçe Mosque
Republic Memorial Taksim
Atatürk Cultural Centre
Exhibition Centre
Galatasaray Baths
Haliç (Golden Horn)
Boğazi (Bosphorus)
BEYOĞLU
Galata Tower
Nusretiye Mosque
Mihrimah Mosque
Şemsi Paşa Mosque
KARAKÖY
ÜSKÜDAR
İhlamur Pavilion
Aqueduct of Valens
Kız Kulesi (Maiden's Tower)
Botanical Institute
Rüstem Paşa Mosque
EMİNÖNÜ
Atatürk Heykeli
Süleymaniye Mosque
Yeni Mosque
Mısır Çarşısı (Egyptian Bazaar)
Sirkeci Station
Gülhane Park
Istanbul University
Archaeological Museum
Topkapı Palace
Town Hall
Beyazit Tower
Govt House
Ahmet III Fountain
Kapalı Çarşı (Grand Bazaar)
St Irene Museum
Selimiye Barracks
Ayasofya Museum (St Sophia)
KUMKAPI
Museum of Turkish and Islamic Art
SULTANAHMET
Dikilitaş
Sultan Ahmet Mosque (Blue Mosque)
KENNEDY CADDESI

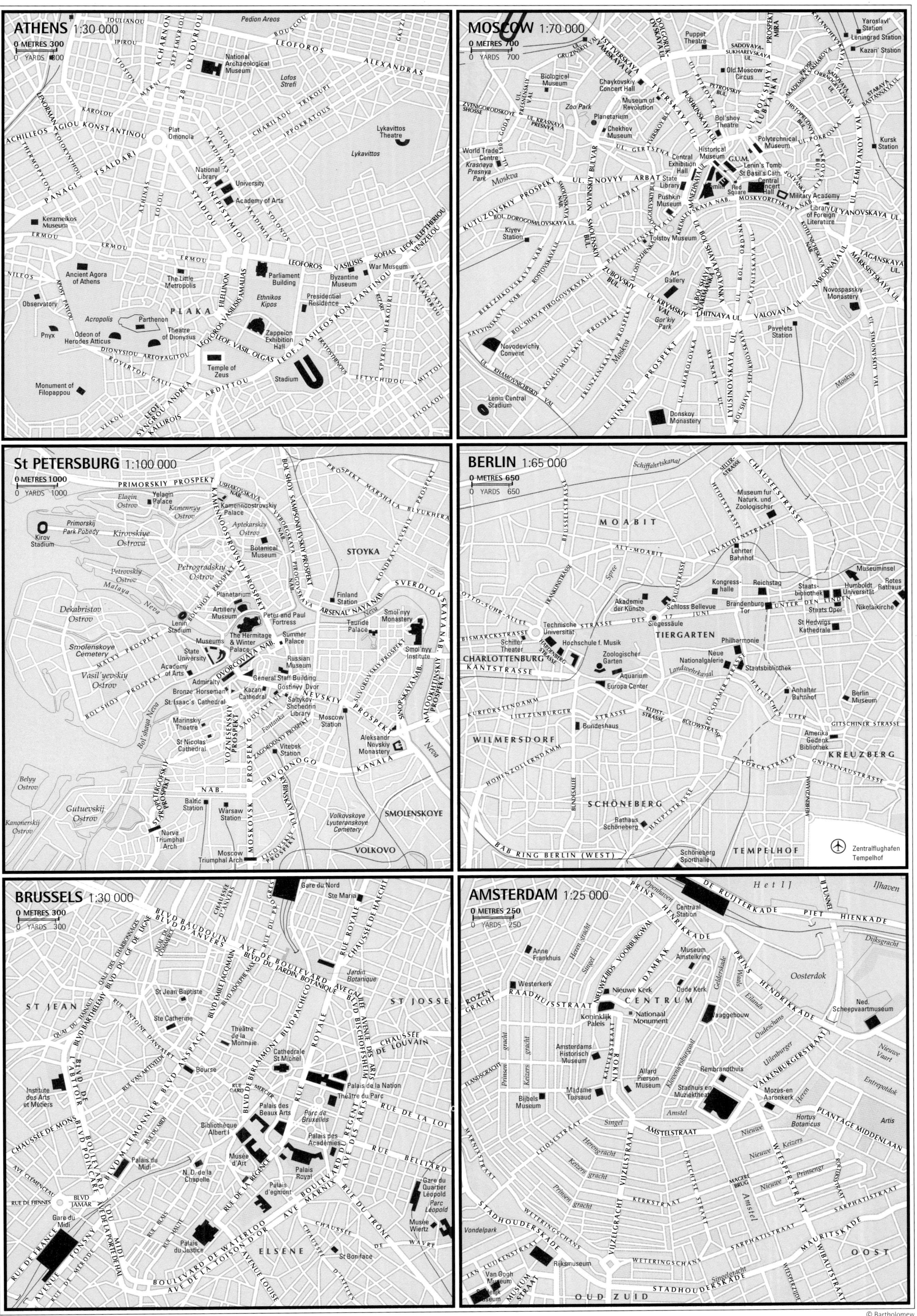
ATHENS 1:30 000
0 METRES 300
0 YARDS 300
National Archaeological Museum
Lofos Strefi
Lykavittos Theatre
Lykavittos
Plat Omonoia
National Library
University
Academy of Arts
Kerameikos Museum
Ancient Agora of Athens
The Little Metropolis
Parliament Building
Byzantine Museum
War Museum
Ethnikos Kipos
Presidential Residence
Observatory
Acropolis
Parthenon
PLAKA
Pnyx
Odeon of Herodes Atticus
Theatre of Dionysus
Zappeion Exhibition Hall
Temple of Zeus
Stadium
Monument of Filopappou
MOSCOW 1:70 000
0 METRES 700
0 YARDS 700
Puppet Theatre
Yaroslavl' Station
Leningrad Station
Kazan' Station
Old Moscow Circus
Biological Museum
Chaykovskiy Concert Hall
Zoo Park
Planetarium
Museum of Revolution
Bol'shoy Theatre
Chekhov Museum
Polytechnical Museum
Kursk Station
World Trade Centre
Krasnaya Presnya Park
Historical Museum
Central Exhibition Hall
G.U.M.
Lenin's Tomb
St Basil's Cath.
Red Square
Central Concert Hall
Military Academy
State Library
Kremlin
Pushkin Museum
Library of Foreign Literature
Kiyev Station
Tolstoy Museum
Art Gallery
Gor'kiy Park
Novospasskiy Monastery
Novodevichiy Convent
Pavelets Station
Lenin Central Stadium
Donskoy Monastery
St PETERSBURG 1:100 000
0 METRES 1000
0 YARDS 1000
Elagin Ostrov
Yelagin Palace
Kamennyy Ostrov
Kamennoostrovskiy Palace
Aptekarskiy Ostrov
Primorskij Park Pobedy
Kirov Stadium
Kirovskiye Ostrova
Botanical Museum
STOYKA
Petrovskiy Ostrov
Petrogradskiy Ostrov
Finland Station
Planetarium
Artillery Museum
Peter and Paul Fortress
Smol'nyy Monastery
Dekabristov Ostrov
Lenin Stadium
Tauride Palace
Smolenskoye Cemetery
Museums
The Hermitage & Winter Palace
Summer Palace
State University
Smol'nyy Institute
Russian Museum
Academy of Arts
General Staff Building
Vasil'yevskiy Ostrov
Admiralty
Gostinyy Dvor
Bronze Horseman
Kazan Cathedral
Saltykov-Shchedrin Library
St Isaac's Cathedral
Moscow Station
Mariinskiy Theatre
St Nicolas' Cathedral
Vitebsk Station
Aleksandr Nevskiy Monastery
Belyy Ostrov
Baltic Station
Warsaw Station
Gutuevskij Ostrov
SMOLENSKOYE
Volkovskoye Lyuteranskoye Cemetery
Kanonerskij Ostrov
Narva Triumphal Arch
Moscow Triumphal Arch
VOLKOVO
BERLIN 1:65 000
0 METRES 650
0 YARDS 650
Schiffahrtskanal
Museum fur Naturk. und Zoologischer
MOABIT
Lehrter Bahnhof
Museuminsel
Kongress-halle
Reichstag
Staats-bibliothek
Humboldt Universität
Rotes Rathaus
Akademie der Künste
Schloss Bellevue
Brandenburg Tor
Nikolaikirche
Siegessäule
Staats Oper
Technische Universität
TIERGARTEN
St Hedwigs Kathedrale
Schiller Theater
Hochschule f. Musik
Philharmonie
CHARLOTTENBURG
Zoologischer Garten
Neue Nationalgalerie
Staatsbibliothek
Aquarium
Europa Center
Anhalter Bahnhof
Berlin Museum
Bundeshaus
WILMERSDORF
Amerika Gedenk Bibliothek
KREUZBERG
SCHÖNEBERG
Rathaus Schöneberg
Schöneberg Sporthalle
TEMPELHOF
Zentralflughafen Tempelhof
BRUSSELS 1:30 000
0 METRES 300
0 YARDS 300
Gare du Nord
Ste Marie
Jardin Botanique
ST JEAN
ST JOSSE
St Jean Baptiste
Ste Catherine
Théatre de la Monnaie
Cathedrale St Michel
Bourse
Institute des Arts et Metiers
Palais de la Nation
Théatre du Parc
Palais des Beaux Arts
Parc de Bruxelles
Bibliothèque Albert I
Palais des Académies
Musée d'Art
Palais du Midi
N. D. de la Chapelle
Palais Royal
Palais d'egmont
Gare du Quartier Leopold
Parc Léopold
Gare du Midi
Musée Wiertz
Palais du Justice
ELSENE
St Boniface
AMSTERDAM 1:25 000
0 METRES 250
0 YARDS 250
Het IJ
IJhaven
Centraal Station
Anne Frankhuis
Museum Amstelkring
Oosterdok
Westerkerk
Nieuwe Kerk
Oude Kerk
CENTRUM
Waaggebouw
Koninklijk Paleis
Nationaal Monument
Ned. Scheepvaartmuseum
Amsterdams Historisch Museum
Rembrandthuis
Allard Pierson Museum
Stadhuis en Muziektheater
Madame Tussaud
Mozes-en Aaronkerk
Bijbels Museum
Hortus Botanicus
Artis
Vondelpark
Rijksmuseum
Van Gogh Museum
OUD ZUID
OOST

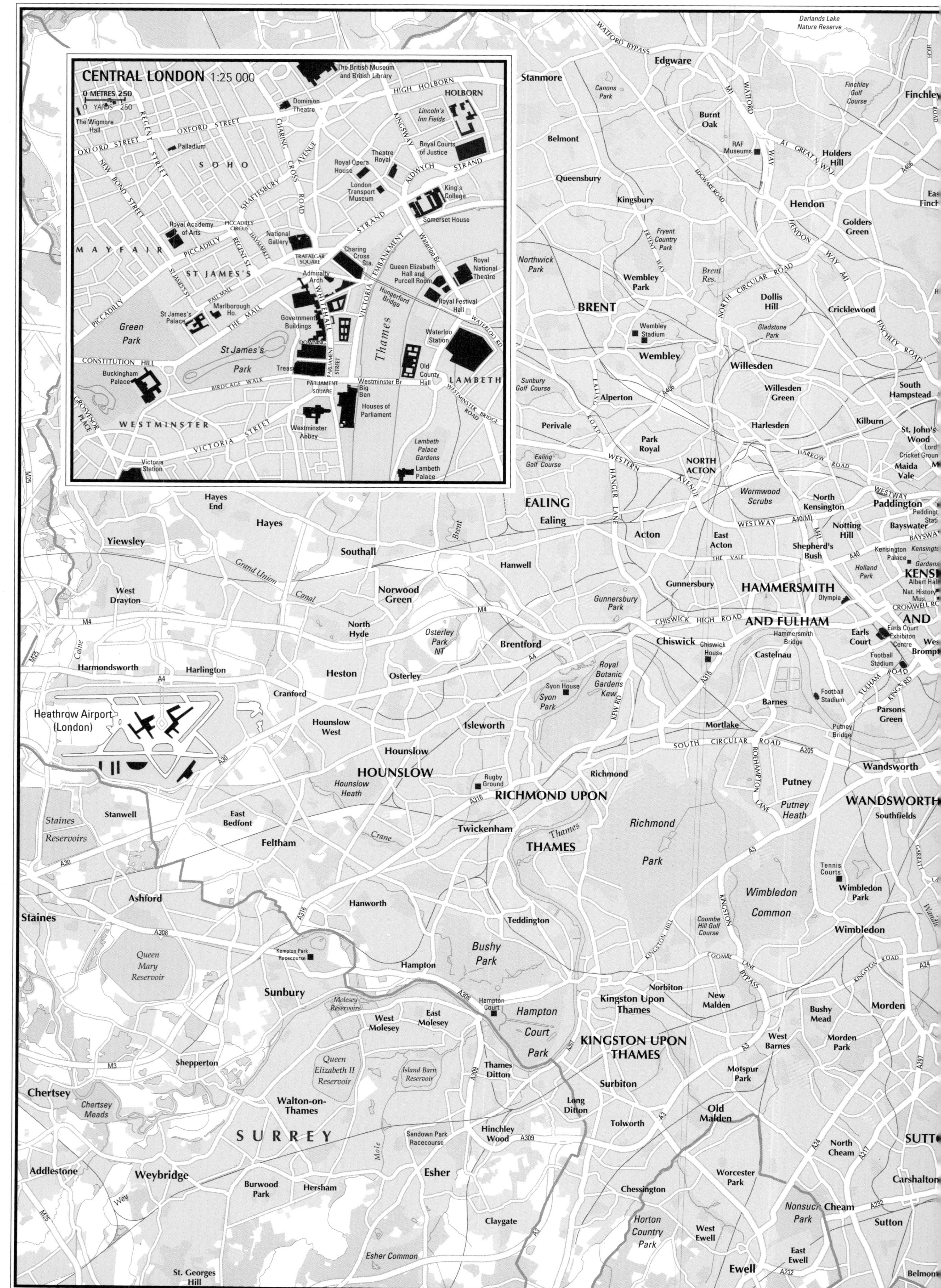

CENTRAL LONDON 1:25 000

0 METRES 250
0 YARDS 250

The British Museum and British Library

HIGH HOLBORN

HOLBORN

Dominion Theatre

Lincoln's Inn Fields

The Wigmore Hall

OXFORD STREET

SOHO

Royal Courts of Justice

STRAND

OXFORD STREET

REGENT STREET

Palladium

Theatre Royal

CHARING CROSS ROAD

KINGSWAY

Royal Opera House

London Transport Museum

ADWYCH

King's College

NEW BOND STREET

SHAFTESBURY AVENUE

Somerset House

Royal Academy of Arts

PICCADILLY CIRCUS

National Gallery

STRAND

MAYFAIR

PICCADILLY

REGENT ST

HAYMARKET

TRAFALGAR SQUARE

Charing Cross Sta.

WATERLOO BRIDGE

ST JAMES'S

Admiralty Arch

VICTORIA EMBANKMENT

Queen Elizabeth Hall and Purcell Room

Royal National Theatre

PICCADILLY

ST JAMES'S ST

Royal Festival Hall

Hungerford Bridge

WATERLOO RD

Green Park

PALL MALL

St James's Palace

Marlborough Ho.

THE MALL

Government Buildings

Thames

Waterloo Station

CONSTITUTION HILL

St James's Park

DOWNING

Treasury

Old County Hall

LAMBETH

Buckingham Palace

BIRDCAGE WALK

PARLIAMENT STREET

PARLIAMENT SQUARE

Westminster Br

Big Ben

WESTMINSTER

WHITEHALL

CROSVENOR PLACE

VICTORIA STREET

Westminster Abbey

Houses of Parliament

WESTMINSTER BRIDGE ROAD

M25

Victoria Station

Lambeth Palace Gardens

Lambeth Palace

Darlands Lake Nature Reserve

WATFORD BYPASS

Edgware

Stanmore

Canons Park

Finchley Golf Course

Finchley

Burnt Oak

MI

WATFORD

A1 GREAT WAY

Holders Hill

Belmont

RAF Museums

EDGWARE ROAD

East Finch

Queensbury

Hendon

Golders Green

Kingsbury

HENDON

WAY A41

Fryent Country Park

Northwick Park

Brent Res.

Wembley Park

NORTH CIRCULAR ROAD

BRENT

Dollis Hill

Cricklewood

Wembley Stadium

Gladstone Park

FINCHLEY ROAD

Wembley

Willesden

South Hampstead

Sunbury Golf Course

EALING ROAD

Alperton

A406

Willesden Green

Kilburn

St. John's Wood

Perivale

Harlesden

Lord's Cricket Ground

Park Royal

HARROW ROAD

Maida Vale

M

Ealing Golf Course

WESTERN AVENUE

NORTH ACTON

WESTWAY

Paddington

Paddington Stati

EALING

HANGER LANE

Wormwood Scrubs

North Kensington

Notting Hill

Bayswater

BAYSWAT

Hayes End

Ealing

WESTWAY

A40(M)

Shepherd's Bush

Kensington Palace

Kensingto Gardens

KENS

Hayes

Acton

East Acton

A40

THE VALE

Holland Park

Albert Hall

Yiewsley

Southall

Hanwell

Gunnersbury

HAMMERSMITH

Nat. History Mus.

Olympia

West Drayton

Grand Union Canal

Norwood Green

M4

Gunnersbury Park

CHISWICK HIGH ROAD

AND FULHAM

Nat. History Mus.

CROMWELL RO

North Hyde

Osterley Park NT

Brentford

Chiswick

Chiswick House

Hammersmith Bridge

Earls Court

Earls Court Exhibiton Centre

Wes

Harmondsworth

Harlington

Heston

Osterley

A4

Royal Botanic Gardens Kew

Castelnau

Football Stadium

Bromp

Coline

Cranford

Syon House

Syon Park

KEW RD

Barnes

Football Stadium

Parsons Green

Heathrow Airport (London)

Hounslow West

Isleworth

Mortlake

Putney Bridge

M4

Hounslow

SOUTH CIRCULAR ROAD

A205

Wandsworth

A30

HOUNSLOW

Rugby Ground

Richmond

Putney

WANDSWORTH

Stanwell

Hounslow Heath

A316

RICHMOND UPON

Richmond Park

Putney Heath

Southfields

Staines Reservoirs

East Bedfont

Twickenham

Crane

Thames

THAMES

ROEHAMPTON LANE

A3

Ashford

Feltham

Tennis Courts

Wimbledon Park

Staines

A316

Hanworth

Teddington

Wimbledon Common

KINGSTON HILL

Wimbledon

A308

Kempton Park Racecourse

Bushy Park

Coombe Hill Golf Course

COOMBE LANE

Queen Mary Reservoir

Hampton

A308

Hampton Court

Norbiton

Kingston Upon Thames

New Malden

KINGSTON ROAD

M3

Sunbury

Molesey Reservoirs

West Molesey

East Molesey

Hampton Court Park

KINGSTON UPON THAMES

Bushy Mead

Morden

Shepperton

Queen Elizabeth II Reservoir

Island Barn Reservoir

A309

Thames Ditton

A3

West Barnes

Motspur Park

Morden Park

Chertsey

Walton-on-Thames

Surbiton

Long Ditton

Old Malden

Chertsey Meads

SURREY

Mole

Sandown Park Racecourse

Hinchley Wood

A309

Tolworth

North Cheam

SUTT

Addlestone

Weybridge

Hersham

Esher

A3

Worcester Park

Carshalton

Wey

Burwood Park

Chessington

Nonsuch Park

Cheam

Sutton

M25

Claygate

Horton Country Park

West Ewell

East Ewell

Belmon

St. Georges Hill

Esher Common

Ewell

A232

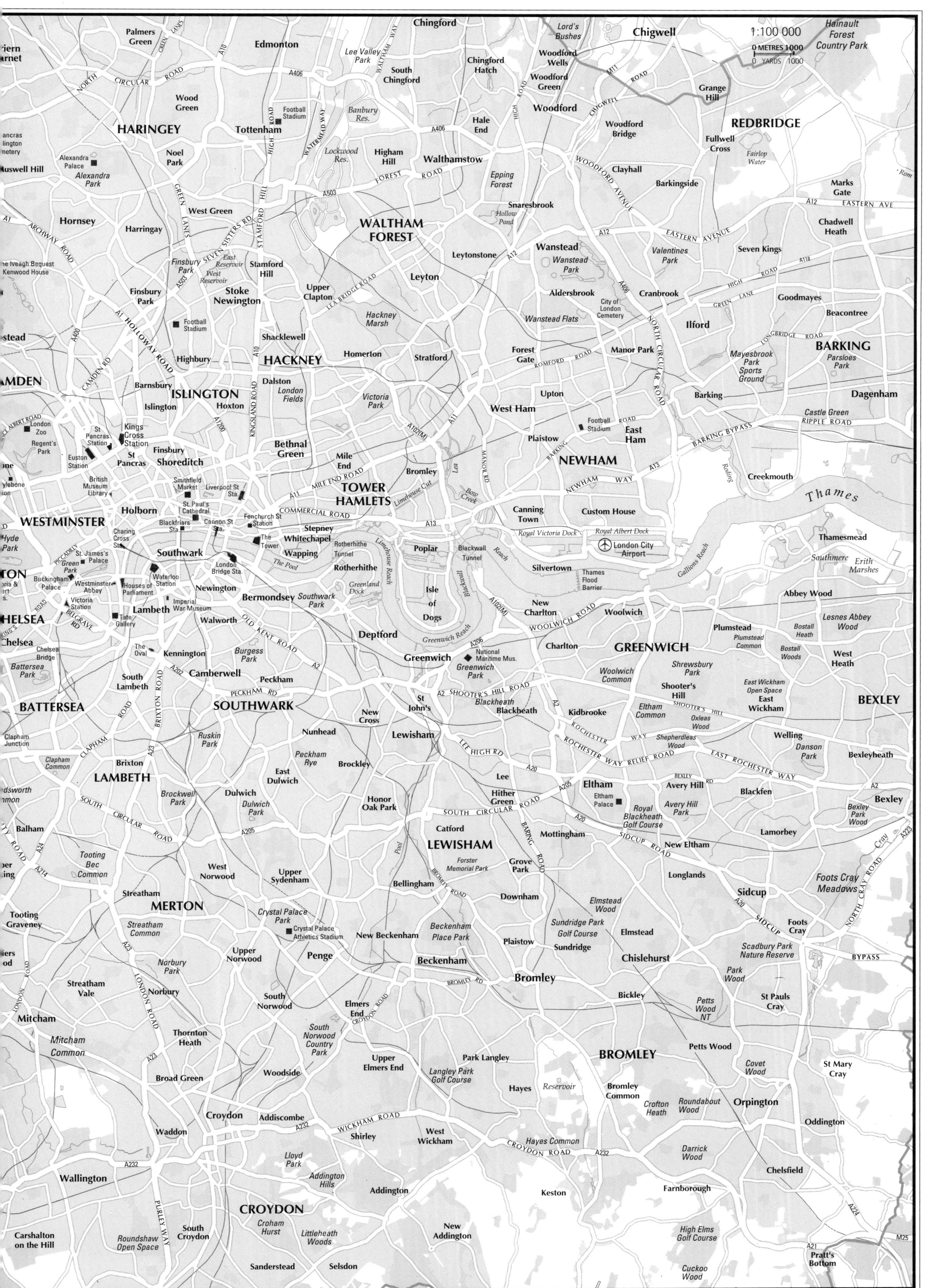
1:100 000
METRES 1000
YARDS 1000
Palmers Green
Edmonton
Chingford
Lee Valley Park
South Chingford
Chingford Hatch
Lord's Bushes
Woodford Wells
Woodford Green
Chigwell
Hainault Forest Country Park
Grange Hill
NORTH CIRCULAR ROAD
A406
A10
Wood Green
Football Stadium
Banbury Res.
Hale End
Woodford
HARINGEY
Tottenham
Woodford Bridge
REDBRIDGE
Fullwell Cross
Fairlop Water
Alexandra Palace
Alexandra Park
Noel Park
Lockwood Res.
Higham Hill
Walthamstow
FOREST ROAD
Epping Forest
Clayhall
Barkingside
Marks Gate
Muswell Hill
A503
Snaresbrook
Hollow Pond
A12
EASTERN AVE
Hornsey
West Green
Harringay
WALTHAM FOREST
Chadwell Heath
ARCHWAY ROAD
SEVEN SISTERS RD
STAMFORD HILL
EASTERN AVENUE
Leytonstone
Wanstead
Wanstead Park
Valentines Park
Seven Kings
The Iveagh Bequest Kenwood House
Finsbury Park
East Reservoir
West Reservoir
Stamford Hill
Upper Clapton
LEA BRIDGE ROAD
Leyton
Aldersbrook
Cranbrook
HIGH ROAD
GREEN LANE
Goodmayes
Stoke Newington
Hackney Marsh
City of London Cemetery
Wanstead Flats
Ilford
Beacontree
Football Stadium
A1 HOLLOWAY ROAD
Shacklewell
LONGBRIDGE ROAD
BARKING
Highbury
HACKNEY
Homerton
Stratford
Forest Gate
ROMFORD ROAD
Manor Park
NORTH CIRCULAR ROAD
Mayesbrook Park Sports Ground
Parsloes Park
CAMDEN
CAMDEN RD
Barnsbury
ISLINGTON
Dalston
London Fields
Victoria Park
Upton
Barking
Dagenham
Islington
Hoxton
KINGSLAND ROAD
West Ham
Castle Green
RIPPLE ROAD
London Zoo
Regent's Park
St Pancras Station
Kings Cross Station
A1200
A102(M)
A11
Football Stadium
East Ham
BARKING BYPASS
Euston Station
Finsbury
St Pancras
Shoreditch
Bethnal Green
Mile End
Plaistow
MANOR RD
NEWHAM
Roding
British Museum Library
Smithfield Market
Liverpool St Sta.
MILE END ROAD
Bromley
Lea
A13
Creekmouth
NEWHAM WAY
Thames
WESTMINSTER
Holborn
St. Paul's Cathedral
TOWER HAMLETS
Limehouse Cut
Bow Creek
Canning Town
Custom House
COMMERCIAL ROAD
Blackfriars Sta.
Cannon St Sta.
Fenchurch St Station
Stepney
Whitechapel
Royal Victoria Dock
Royal Albert Dock
London City Airport
Thamesmead
Hyde Park
Charing Cross Sta.
The Tower
Wapping
Rotherhithe Tunnel
Poplar
Blackwall Tunnel
Southwark
The Pool
Rotherhithe
Limehouse Reach
Gallions Reach
Southmere
Erith Marshes
PICCADILLY
St. James's Palace
Green Park
London Bridge Sta.
Silvertown
Thames Flood Barrier
Buckingham Palace
Westminster Abbey
Waterloo Station
Houses of Parliament
Newington
Greenland Dock
Isle of Dogs
Blackwall Reach
Abbey Wood
Victoria Station
Imperial War Museum
Bermondsey
Southwark Park
A102(M)
New Charlton
Woolwich
CHELSEA
Tate Gallery
Lambeth
Walworth
WOOLWICH ROAD
Lesnes Abbey Wood
Chelsea
OLD KENT ROAD
Deptford
Greenwich Reach
Plumstead
Plumstead Common
Bostall Heath
Chelsea Bridge
The Oval
Kennington
Burgess Park
Greenwich
National Maritime Mus.
Charlton
GREENWICH
Bostall Woods
West Heath
Battersea Park
Camberwell
Greenwich Park
Woolwich Common
Shrewsbury Park
South Lambeth
Peckham
A2
Shooter's Hill
East Wickham Open Space
East Wickham
BATTERSEA
BRIXTON ROAD
PECKHAM RD
SOUTHWARK
New Cross
St John's
A2 SHOOTER'S HILL ROAD
Blackheath
Kidbrooke
Eltham Common
SHOOTER'S HILL
Oxleas Wood
BEXLEY
Clapham Junction
Ruskin Park
Nunhead
Lewisham
LEE HIGH RD
ROCHESTER WAY
Shepherdleas Wood
Welling
Danson Park
Clapham Common
Brixton
Peckham Rye
Brockley
ROCHESTER WAY RELIEF ROAD
EAST ROCHESTER WAY
Bexleyheath
LAMBETH
East Dulwich
Lee
Eltham
Avery Hill
Blackfen
Wandsworth Common
Brockwell Park
Dulwich
Honor Oak Park
Hither Green
Eltham Palace
Royal Blackheath Golf Course
Avery Hill Park
Bexley
Dulwich Park
SOUTH CIRCULAR ROAD
Bexley Park Wood
Balham
A205
Catford
Mottingham
SIDCUP ROAD
Lamorbey
LEWISHAM
New Eltham
Tooting Bec Common
West Norwood
Upper Sydenham
Forster Memorial Park
Grove Park
BARING ROAD
Longlands
Foots Cray Meadows
Bellingham
BROMLEY ROAD
NORTH CRAY ROAD
Streatham
Downham
Sidcup
MERTON
Elmstead Wood
Tooting Graveney
Crystal Palace Park
Crystal Palace Athletics Stadium
Sundridge Park Golf Course
Foots Cray
Streatham Common
New Beckenham
Beckenham Place Park
Elmstead
Plaistow
Sundridge
Scadbury Park Nature Reserve
Upper Norwood
Penge
Beckenham
Chislehurst
BYPASS
Norbury Park
Bromley
Park Wood
Streatham Vale
LONDON ROAD
Norbury
BROMLEY RD
Bickley
St Pauls Cray
Mitcham
South Norwood
Elmers End
Petts Wood NT
Thornton Heath
South Norwood Country Park
Mitcham Common
Petts Wood
Upper Elmers End
Park Langley
BROMLEY
Covet Wood
St Mary Cray
Broad Green
Woodside
Langley Park Golf Course
Hayes
Reservoir
Bromley Common
Crofton Heath
Roundabout Wood
Orpington
Croydon
Addiscombe
Waddon
WICKHAM ROAD
Shirley
West Wickham
Oddington
Hayes Common
CROYDON ROAD
A232
Darrick Wood
Lloyd Park
Chelsfield
Wallington
Addington Hills
Addington
Keston
Farnborough
CROYDON
PURLEY WAY
New Addington
High Elms Golf Course
A224
Carshalton on the Hill
South Croydon
Croham Hurst
Littleheath Woods
Roundshaw Open Space
M25
A21
Pratt's Bottom
Sanderstead
Selsdon
Cuckoo Wood

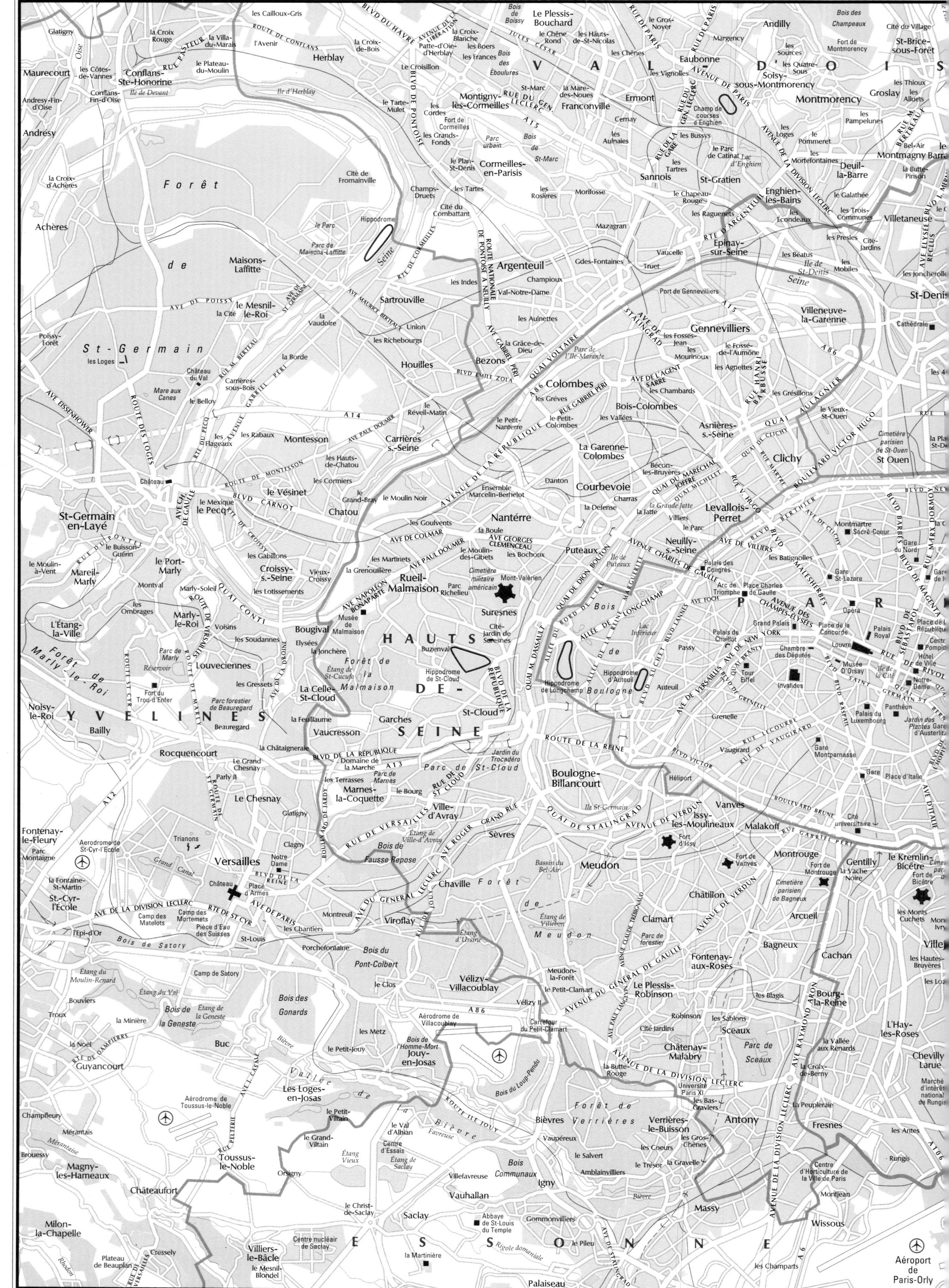

V A L - D ' O I S E
Y V E L I N E S
H A U T S - D E - S E I N E
E S S O N N E
P A R I S
Forêt de St-Germain
Forêt de Marly-le-Roi
Forêt de la Malmaison
Forêt de Meudon
Forêt de Verrières
Bois de Boulogne
Parc de St-Cloud
Seine
Oise
Glatigny
la Croix Rouge
la Villa-du-Marais
les Cailloux-Gris
l'Avenir
Herblay
Maurecourt
les Côtes-de-Vannes
Conflans-Ste-Honorine
le Plateau-du-Moulin
Andresy-Fin-d'Oise
Conflans-Fin-d'Oise
Ile de Devant
Ile d'Herblay
Andresy
la Croix-d'Achères
Achères
Maisons-Laffitte
Hippodrome
Parc de Maisons-Laffitte
le Mesnil-le-Roi
la Cité
Sartrouville
la Vaudoire
Union
les Richebourgs
Poissy-Forêt
les Loges
la Borde
Château du Val
Carrières-sous-Bois
Mare aux Canes
le Belloy
Houilles
Bezons
Montesson
les Rabaux
les Flageaux
Carrières-s.-Seine
le Réveil-Matin
les Hauts-de-Chatou
le Vésinet
les Cormiers
le Grand-Bray
le Moulin Noir
Chatou
Château
St-Germain en-Laye
le Mexique
le Pecq
le Buisson-Guérin
le Port-Marly
Mareil-Marly
le Moulin-à-Vent
Montval
Marly-Soleil
Marly-le-Roi
les Ombrages
L'Étang-la-Ville
Louveciennes
Voisins
les Soudannes
Bougival
Croissy-s.-Seine
les Gabillons
les Lotissements
Vieux-Croissy
la Grenouillère
Rueil-Malmaison
Musée de Malmaison
Parc Richelieu
Cimetière militaire américain
Mont-Valérien
Suresnes
Cité-Jardin de Suresnes
Buzenval
Hippodrome de St-Cloud
la Jonchère
Étang de St-Cucufa
les Gressets
La Celle-St-Cloud
Fort du Trou-d'Enfer
Parc forestier de Beauregard
Beauregard
Noisy-le-Roi
Bailly
Rocquencourt
la Feuillaume
Vaucresson
Garches
St-Cloud
la Châtaigneraie
Domaine de la Marche
le Grand Chesnay
Parly II
Le Chesnay
les Terrasses
Parc de Marnes
Marnes-la-Coquette
le Bourg
Ville-d'Avray
Glatigny
Clagny
Trianons
Versailles
Notre Dame
Château
Place d'Armes
Grand Canal
Fontenay-le-Fleury
Parc Montaigne
Aerodrome de St-Cyr-l'École
la Fontaine-St-Martin
St.-Cyr-l'École
Camp des Matelots
Camp des Mortemets
Pièce d'Eau des Suisses
l'Epi-d'Or
Bois de Satory
Montreuil
St-Louis
les Chantiers
Viroflay
Chaville
Porchefontaine
Bois du Pont-Colbert
Camp de Satory
Étang du Moulin-Renard
Étang du Val
Bois des Gonards
le Clos
Vélizy-Villacoublay
Bouviers
Troux
la Minière
Bois de la Geneste
Étang de la Geneste
Buc
la Noël
Guyancourt
les Metz
le Petit-Jouy
Bois de l'Homme-Mort
Jouy-en-Josas
Aérodrome de Villacoublay
Vélizy II
Les Loges-en-Josas
Aérodrome de Toussus-le-Noble
Champfleury
Mérantais
Brouessy
Magny-les-Hameaux
Toussus-le-Noble
le Petit-Viltain
le Grand-Viltain
le Val d'Albian
Centre d'Essais
Étang de Saclay
Étang Vieux
Orsigny
Châteaufort
le Christ-de-Saclay
Saclay
Villefavreuse
Vauhallan
Bois Communaux
Abbaye de St-Louis du Temple
Milon-la-Chapelle
Plateau de Beauplan
Cressely
Villiers-le-Bâcle
le Mesnil-Blondel
Centre nucléaire de Saclay
la Martinière
Rigole domaniale
Palaiseau
Bois de Boissy
Le Plessis-Bouchard
le Chêne Rond
les Hauts-de-St-Nicolas
la Croix-Blanche
Patte-d'Oie-d'Herblay
la Croix-de-Bois
les Boers
les Frances
Bois des Éboulures
les Chênes
Le Croisillon
le Tarte-Mulet
Montigny-les-Cormeilles
St-Marc
la Mare-des-Noues
Franconville
les Cordes
Fort de Cormeilles
les Grands-Fonds
Parc urbain
Bois de St-Marc
le Plan-St-Denis
Cormeilles-en-Parisis
Cité de Fromainville
Champs-Druets
les Tartes
Cité du Combattant
Argenteuil
les Indes
Val-Notre-Dame
Champioux
Gdes-Fontaines
Mazagran
les Rosières
Morifosse
les Aulnettes
la Grâce-de-Dieu
Parc de l'Ile-Marante
Colombes
les Grèves
le Petit-Nanterre
le Petit-Colombes
Bois-Colombes
les Vallées
Nanterre
les Goulvents
la Boule
les Martinets
le Moulin-des-Gibets
les Bochoux
Ensemble Marcelin-Berthelot
Danton
Courbevoie
Charras
La Garenne-Colombes
la Défense
Puteaux
Ile de Puteaux
Eaubonne
Margency
le Gros-Noyer
Andilly
Ermont
Cernay
les Aulnaies
Sannois
Champ de courses d'Enghien
les Bussys
le Parc de Catinat
Lac d'Enghien
Soisy-sous-Montmorency
Montmorency
les Tartres
St-Gratien
le Chapeau-Rouge
les Raguenets
Enghien-les-Bains
Epinay-sur-Seine
Vaucelle
Truet
Port de Gennevilliers
Gennevilliers
les Fosses-Jean
les Mourinoux
le Fossé-de-l'Aumône
les Agnettes
les Chambards
Asnières-s.-Seine
les Grésillons
Bécon-les-Bruyères
Clichy
Levallois-Perret
La Grande Jatte
Neuilly-s.-Seine
Villiers
le Parc
Palais des Congrès
Bois des Champeaux
Cité du Village
St-Brice-sous-Forêt
Fort de Montmorency
Groslay
les Thioux
les Alluets
les Pampelunes
le Pommeret
Bel-Air
Montmagny
Deuil-la-Barre
la Butte-Pinson
les Mortefontaines
le Galathée
les Trois-Communes
Villetaneuse
les Écondeaux
les Presles
Cité-Jardins
les Béatus
Ile de St-Denis
les Mobiles
St-Denis
Villeneuve-la-Garenne
Cathédrale
le Vieux-St-Ouen
Cimetière parisien de St-Ouen
St Ouen
Montmartre
Sacré-Cœur
Gare du Nord
les Batignolles
Gare St-Lazare
Arc de Triomphe
Place Charles de Gaulle
Opéra
Palais Royal
Grand Palais
Place de la Concorde
Palais de Chaillot
Louvre
Hôtel de Ville
Ile de la Cité
Notre-Dame
Chambre des Députés
Musée d'Orsay
Tour Eiffel
Invalides
Passy
Lac Inférieur
Hippodrome de Longchamp
Hippodrome d'Auteuil
Auteuil
Grenelle
Panthéon
Palais du Luxembourg
Jardin des Plantes
Gare d'Austerlitz
Vaugirard
Gare Montparnasse
Gare
Place d'Italie
Héliport
Cité universitaire
Jardin du Trocadéro
Boulogne-Billancourt
Ile St-Germain
Issy-les-Moulineaux
Fort d'Issy
Vanves
Malakoff
Fort de Vanves
Montrouge
Sèvres
Meudon
Bassin du Bel-Air
Étang de Villebon
Clamart
Parc de forestier
Châtillon
Cimetière parisien de Bagneux
Fort de Montrouge
Gentilly
la Vache Noire
le Kremlin-Bicêtre
Fort de Bicêtre
Arcueil
les Monts Cuchets
Bagneux
Cachan
Meudon-la-Forêt
le Petit-Clamart
Carrefour du Petit-Clamart
Fontenay-aux-Roses
Le Plessis-Robinson
les Blagis
Bourg-la-Reine
Robinson
les Sablons
Cité Jardins
Sceaux
Parc de Sceaux
Châtenay-Malabry
la Butte-Rouge
L'Hay-les-Roses
la Vallée aux Renards
la Croix-de-Berny
Chevilly Larue
Université Paris XI
les Bas-Graviers
Antony
la Peupleraie
Bièvres
Vaupéreux
Verrières-le-Buisson
les Gros-Chênes
les Coeurs
le Salvert
Amblainvilliers
le Trésor
la Gravelle
Fresnes
les Antes
Rungis
Centre d'Horticulture de la Ville de Paris
Montjean
Igny
Gommonvilliers
Massy
Wissous
le Pileu
les Champarts
Aéroport de Paris-Orly
A14
A13
A12
A15
A86
A6
A106

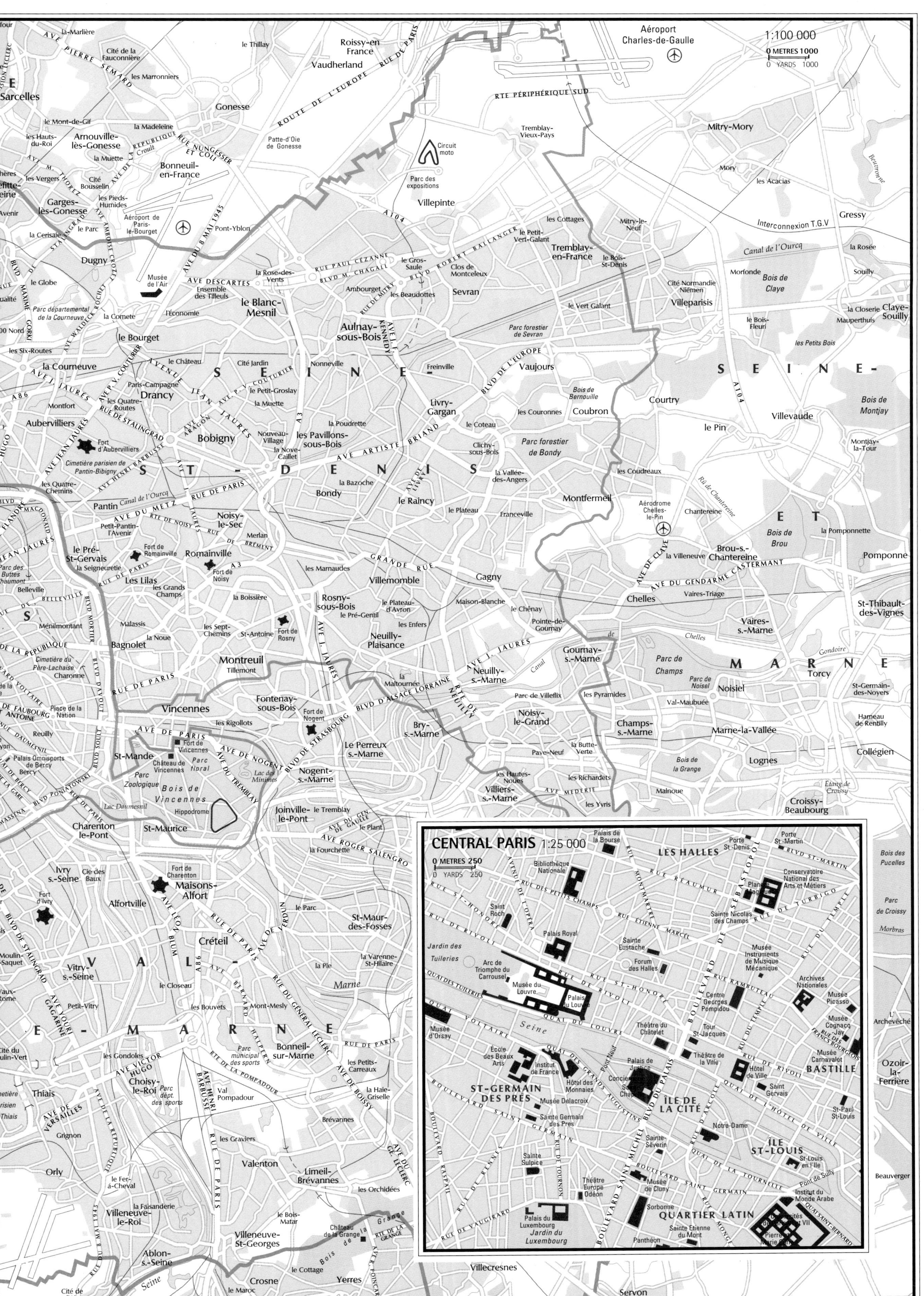
1:100 000
0 METRES 1000
0 YARDS 1000
Aéroport Charles-de-Gaulle
RTE PÉRIPHÉRIQUE SUD
Roissy-en France
Vaudherland
le Thillay
ROUTE DE L'EUROPE
RUE DE PARIS
Sarcelles
la Marlière
Cité de la Fauconnière
les Marronniers
AVE PIERRE SEMARD
Gonesse
le Mont-de-Gif
la Madeleine
les Hauts-du-Roi
Arnouville-lès-Gonesse
Patte-d'Oie de Gonesse
Tremblay-Vieux-Pays
Mitry-Mory
Circuit moto
la Muette
Bonneuil-en-France
Cité Bousselin
les Vergers
Parc des expositions
Mory
les Acacias
Garges-lès-Gonesse
les Pieds-Humides
Aéroport de Paris-le-Bourget
Villepinte
A104
Gressy
la Cerisaie
le Parc
Pont-Yblon
les Cottages
Mitry-le-Neuf
Interconnexion T.G.V
Dugny
AVE DU 8 MAI 1945
le Petit-Vert-Galant
Tremblay-en-France
Canal de l'Ourcq
la Rosée
le Globe
Musée de l'Air
la Rose-des-Vents
le Gros-Saule
les Bois-St-Denis
Morfonde
Bois de Claye
Souilly
AVE DESCARTES
Ensemble des Tilleuls
Clos de Montceleux
Ambourget
les Beaudottes
Sevran
Cité Normandie Niémen
Villeparisis
Parc départemental de la Courneuve
la Comete
le Blanc-Mesnil
l'Économie
le Vert Galant
la Closerie
Claye-Souilly
Mauperthuis
le Bourget
Aulnay-sous-Bois
Parc forestier de Sevran
le Bois-Fleuri
les Petits Bois
les Six-Routes
la Courneuve
le Château
Cité Jardin
Nonneville
Freinville
Vaujours
BLVD DE L'EUROPE
SEINE-ST-DENIS
SEINE-ET-MARNE
Paris-Campagne
Drancy
le Petit-Groslay
Bois de Bernouille
Courtry
les Quatre-Routes
la Muette
Livry-Gargan
les Couronnes
Coubron
Bois de Montjay
Villevaude
Montfort
Aubervilliers
la Poudrette
le Coteau
le Pin
A104
Fort d'Aubervilliers
Bobigny
Nouveau-Village
les Pavillons-sous-Bois
la Nove-Caillet
AVE ARTISTE BRIAND
Clichy-sous-Bois
Parc forestier de Bondy
Montjay-la-Tour
Cimetière parisien de Pantin-Bibigny
les Quatre-Chemins
la Bazoche
Bondy
le Raincy
les Vallée-des-Angers
les Coudreaux
Montfermeil
Pantin
Canal de l'Ourcq
RUE DE PARIS
AVE DU METZ
le Plateau
Franceville
Aérodrome Chelles-le-Pin
Chantereine
Bois de Brou
la Pomponnette
Noisy-le-Sec
Petit-Pantin-l'Avenir
Merlan
le Pré-St-Gervais
Fort de Romainville
Romainville
Fort de Noisy
la Seigneurie
GRANDE RUE
la Villeneuve
Brou-s.-Chantereine
Pomponne
Les Lilas
les Grands Champs
les Marnaudes
Villemomble
Gagny
AVE DU GENDARME CASTERMANT
Parc des Buttes Chaumont
Belleville
la Boissière
Chelles
Vaires-Triage
Maison-Blanche
St-Thibault-des-Vignes
Rosny-sous-Bois
le Plateau-d'Avron
le Chênay
Ménilmontant
Malassis
le Pré-Gentil
les Sept-Chemins
St-Antoine
Fort de Rosny
Pointe-de-Gournay
les Enfers
Neuilly-Plaisance
Vaires-s.-Marne
la Noue
Bagnolet
Chelles
Gondoire
Cimetière du Père-Lachaise
Charonne
Montreuil
Tillemont
AVE J. JAURES
Gournay-s.-Marne
Parc de Champs
Torcy
Neuilly-s.-Marne
Canal
la Maltournée
BLVD D'ALSACE LORRAINE
Parc de Noisel
Noisiel
St-Germain-des-Noyers
RUE DE PARIS
Place de la Nation
Vincennes
Fontenay-sous-Bois
Parc de Villeflix
les Pyramides
Val-Maubuée
Hameau de Renbilly
Fort de Nogent
Noisy-le-Grand
Reuilly
les Rigollots
Bry-s.-Marne
Champs-s.-Marne
Marne-la-Vallée
AVE DE PARIS
Fort de Vincennes
Le Perreux s.-Marne
la Butte-Verte
Palais Omnisports de Bercy
St-Mande
Château de Vincennes
Parc floral
BLVD DE STRASBOURG
Pave-Neuf
Bois de la Grange
Lognes
Collégien
Parc Zoologique
Bois de Vincennes
Lac des Minimes
Nogent-s.-Marne
les Hautes-Noues
les Richardets
Villiers-s.-Marne
AVE MEDERIC
Malnoue
Étang de Croissy
Lac Daumesnil
Hippodrome
Joinville-le-Pont
le Tremblay
les Yvris
Croissy-Beaubourg
Charenton le-Pont
St-Maurice
le Plant
AVE ROGER SALENGRO
la Fourchette
Bois des Pucelles
Fort de Charenton
Ivry s.-Seine
Cité des Baux
Maisons-Alfort
Fort d'Ivry
Alfortville
le Parc
St-Maur-des-Fosses
Parc de Croissy
Morbras
Créteil
la Varenne-St-Hilaire
Vitry-s.-Seine
la Pie
Marne
VAL-DE-MARNE
le Closeau
Petit-Vitry
les Bouvets
Mont-Mesly
L'Archevéché
Bonneuil-sur-Marne
Ozoir-la-Ferrière
les Gondoles
Parc municipal des sports
les Petits-Carreaux
Choisy-le-Roi
Parc dépt. des sports
Val Pompadour
la Haie-Griselle
Thiais
Grignon
Brévannes
les Graviers
Valenton
Orly
Limeil-Brévannes
le Fer-à-Cheval
les Orchidées
la Faisanderie
Villeneuve-le-Roi
le Bois-Matar
Château de la Grange
Villeneuve-St-Georges
Ablon-s.-Seine
le Cottage
Yerres
Seine
Crosne
le Maroc
Cité de l'Air
Villecresnes
Servon
Beauverger
CENTRAL PARIS 1:25 000
0 METRES 250
0 YARDS 250
Palais de la Bourse
LES HALLES
Porte St-Denis
Porte St-Martin
Bibliothèque Nationale
RUE REAUMUR
Conservatoire National des Arts et Métiers
Saint Roch
Sainte Nicolas des Champs
Palais Royal
Sainte Eustache
Jardin des Tuileries
Forum des Halles
Musée Instruments de Musique Mécanique
Arc de Triomphe du Carrousel
Musée du Louvre
Palais du Louvre
Centre Georges Pompidou
Archives Nationales
Musée Picasso
Seine
QUAI DU LOUVRE
Théâtre du Châtelet
Tour St-Jacques
Musée Cognacq-Jay
Musée d'Orsay
Musée Carnavalet
École des Beaux Arts
Institut de France
Hôtel des Monnaies
Palais de Justice
Théâtre de la Ville
Hôtel de Ville
BASTILLE
Saint Gervais
ST-GERMAIN DES PRES
Musée Delacroix
ÎLE DE LA CITÉ
Sainte Germain des Pres
Notre-Dame
St-Paul St-Louis
ÎLE ST-LOUIS
Sainte-Séverin
Sainte Sulpice
St-Louis en l'Ile
Musée de Cluny
Théâtre Europe Odéon
Institut du Monde Arabe
Palais du Luxembourg
Jardin du Luxembourg
Sorbonne
QUARTIER LATIN
Sainte Etienne du Mont
Panthéon
BOULEVARD SAINT MICHEL
BOULEVARD SAINT GERMAIN
BOULEVARD DE SÉBASTOPOL
RUE DE RIVOLI
RUE DE RENNES
RUE DE VAUGIRARD

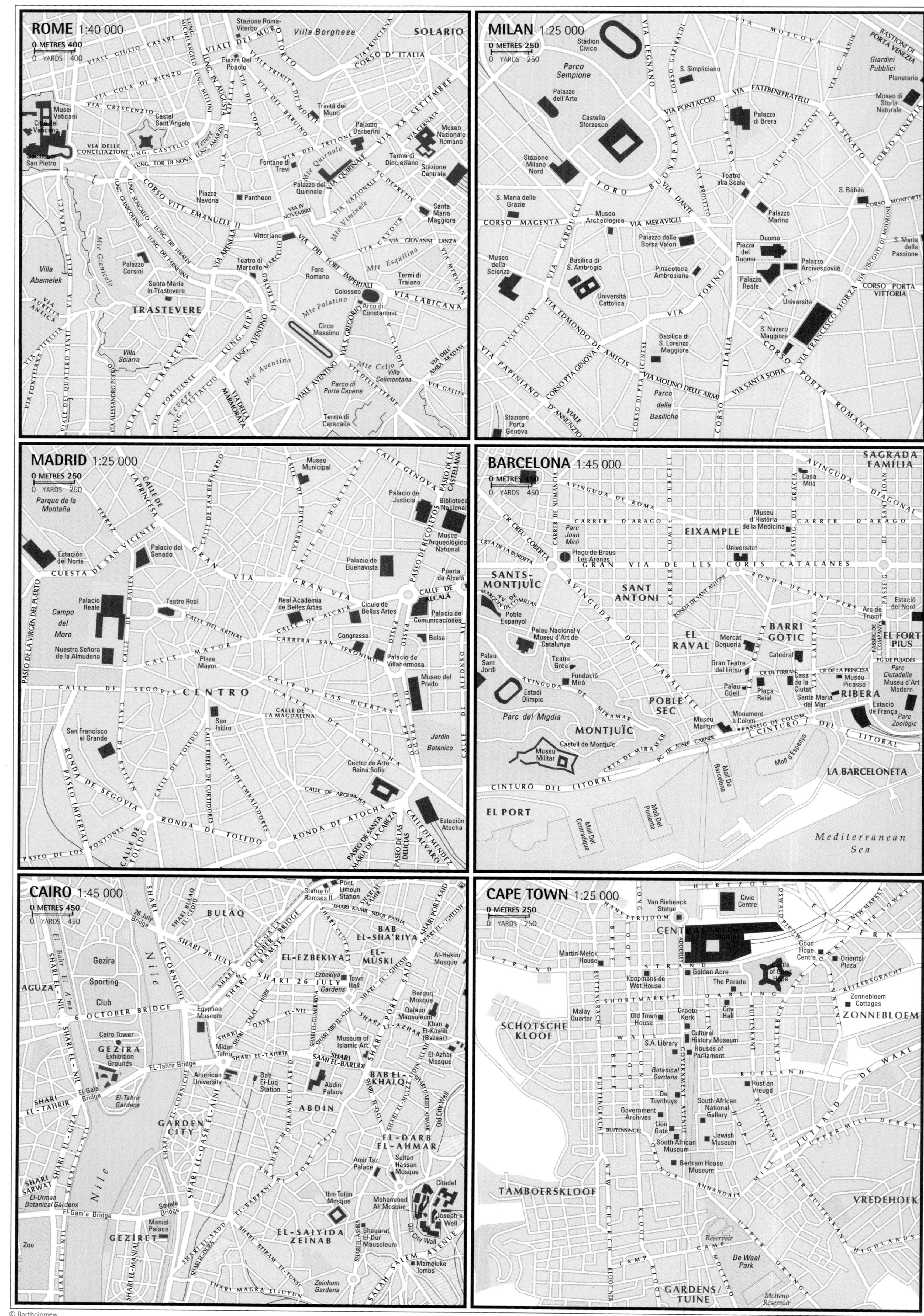

© Bartholomew

ROME 1:40 000
0 METRES 400
0 YARDS 400
SOLARIO
Villa Borghese
Musei Vaticani
Città del Vaticano
Basilica di San Pietro
Castel Sant'Angelo
Piazza Navona
Pantheon
Fontana di Trevi
Palazzo del Quirinale
Palazzo Barberini
Museo Nazionale Romano
Stazione Centrale
Termi di Diocleziano
Santa Maria Maggiore
Vittoriano
Teatro di Marcello
Foro Romano
Colosseo
Arco di Constantino
Circo Massimo
Mte Palatino
Mte Aventino
Mte Celio
Villa Celimontana
Parco di Porta Capena
Terme di Caracalla
TRASTEVERE
Santa Maria in Trastevere
Palazzo Corsini
Villa Abamelek
Villa Sciarra
Mte Gianicolo
Tevere
CORSO VITT. EMANUELE II
VIA XX SETTEMBRE
VIA CAVOUR
VIA LABICANA
CORSO D' ITALIA
MILAN 1:25 000
0 METRES 250
0 YARDS 250
Stàdion Civico
Parco Sempione
Palazzo dell'Arte
Castello Sforzesco
S. Simpliciano
Palazzo di Brera
Stazione Milano Nord
Teatro alla Scala
S. Maria delle Grazie
Museo Archeologico
Palazzo Marino
Palazzo della Borsa Valori
Duomo
Palazzo Arcivescovile
Palazzo Reale
Museo della Scienza
Basilica di S. Ambrogio
Università Cattolica
Pinacoteca Ambrosiana
Università
Basilica di S. Lorenzo Maggiore
S. Nazaro Maggiore
Parco della Basiliche
Stazione Porta Genova
Giardini Pubblici
Planetario
Museo di Storia Naturale
S. Bàbila
S. Maria della Passione
BASTIONI DI PORTA VENEZIA
CORSO PORTA VITTORIA
CORSO PORTA ROMANA
FORO BUONAPARTE
CORSO MAGENTA
VIA TORINO
MADRID 1:25 000
0 METRES 250
0 YARDS 250
Parque de la Montaña
Estación del Norte
Palacio del Senado
Museo Municipal
Palacio de Justicia
Biblioteca Nacional
Museo Arqueológico Nacional
Palacio de Buenavista
Puerta de Alcalá
Palacio Real
Teatro Real
Campo del Moro
Nuestra Señora de la Almudena
Real Academia de Belles Artes
Circulo de Bellas Artes
Palacio de Comunicaciones
Congresso
Bolsa
Palacio de Villahermosa
Plaza Mayor
Museo del Prado
CENTRO
San Isidro
Jardin Botanico
San Francisco el Grande
Centro de Arte Reina Sofia
Estación Atocha
GRAN VIA
CALLE DE ALCALÁ
CALLE MAYOR
RONDA DE TOLEDO
RONDA DE ATOCHA
PASEO DE LA CASTELLANA
PASEO DEL PRADO
BARCELONA 1:45 000
0 METRES 450
0 YARDS 450
SAGRADA FAMÍLIA
Casa Milà
Museu d'Història de la Medicina
EIXAMPLE
Universitat
Parc Joan Miró
Plaça de Braus Les Arenes
GRAN VIA DE LES CORTS CATALANES
SANTS-MONTJUÏC
SANT ANTONI
Poble Espanyol
Palau Nacional y Museu d'Art de Catalunya
Teatre Grec
Fundació Miró
Palau Sant Jordi
Estadi Olímpic
Parc del Migdia
MONTJUÏC
Castell de Montjuïc
Museu Militar
EL RAVAL
Mercat Boqueria
BARRI GÒTIC
Catedral
Gran Teatre del Liceu
Palau Güell
Plaça Reial
Casa de la Ciutat
Santa Maria del Mar
POBLE SEC
Museu Marítim
Monument a Colom
Arc de Triomf
Estació del Nord
EL FORT PIUS
Parc Ciutadella
Museu d'Art Modern
Museu Picasso
RIBERA
Estació de França
Parc Zoològic
Moll d'Espanya
LA BARCELONETA
EL PORT
Moll De Barcelona
Moll Del Contradique
Moll Del Poniente
Mediterranean Sea
AVINGUDA DIAGONAL
AVINGUDA DEL PARAL·LEL
CINTURÓ DEL LITORAL
CAIRO 1:45 000
0 METRES 450
0 YARDS 450
BULÂQ
Statue of Ramses II
Pont Limoun Station
26 July Bridge
BAB EL-SHA'RIYA
EL-EZBEKIYA
EL-MÛSKI
Al-Hakim Mosque
Gezira Sporting Club
Nile
AGUZA
6 OCTOBER BRIDGE
Ezbekiya Gardens
Town Hall
Barquq Mosque
Qalaun Mausoleum
Khan El-Khalili (Bazaar)
Egyptian Museum
Cairo Tower
GEZIRA
Exhibition Grounds
Midan Tahrir
Museum of Islamic Art
El-Azhar Mosque
El-Tahrir Bridge
American University
Bab El-Luq Station
Abdin Palace
BAB EL-KHALQ
El-Gala Bridge
El-Tahrir Gardens
ABDIN
GARDEN CITY
EL-DARB EL-AHMAR
Amir Taz Palace
Sultan Hassan Mosque
Citadel
Ibn-Tulûn Mosque
Mohammed Ali Mosque
Joseph's Well
El-Urman Botanical Gardens
El-Gam'a Bridge
Savala Bridge
Manial Palace
GEZÎRET
EL-SAIYIDA ZEINAB
Shagarat El-Dur Mausoleum
City Wall
Mameluke Tombs
Zoo
Zeinhom Gardens
SALAH SALEM AVENUE
CAPE TOWN 1:25 000
0 METRES 250
0 YARDS 250
HERTZOG
Civic Centre
Van Riebeeck Statue
CENTRAL
Good Hope Centre
Oriental Plaza
Martin Melck House
Golden Acre
Castle of Good Hope
Koopmans de Wet House
The Parade
Zonnebloem Cottages
ZONNEBLOEM
Malay Quarter
Groote Kerk
City Hall
Old Town House
SCHOTSCHE KLOOF
S.A. Library
Cultural History Museum
Houses of Parliament
Botanical Gardens
Rust en Vreugd
De Tuynhuys
South African National Gallery
Government Archives
Lion Gate
Jewish Museum
South African Museum
Bertram House Museum
TAMBOERSKLOOF
VREDEHOEK
Reservoir
De Waal Park
GARDENS/TUINE
Molteno Reservoir
STRAND
DE WAAL

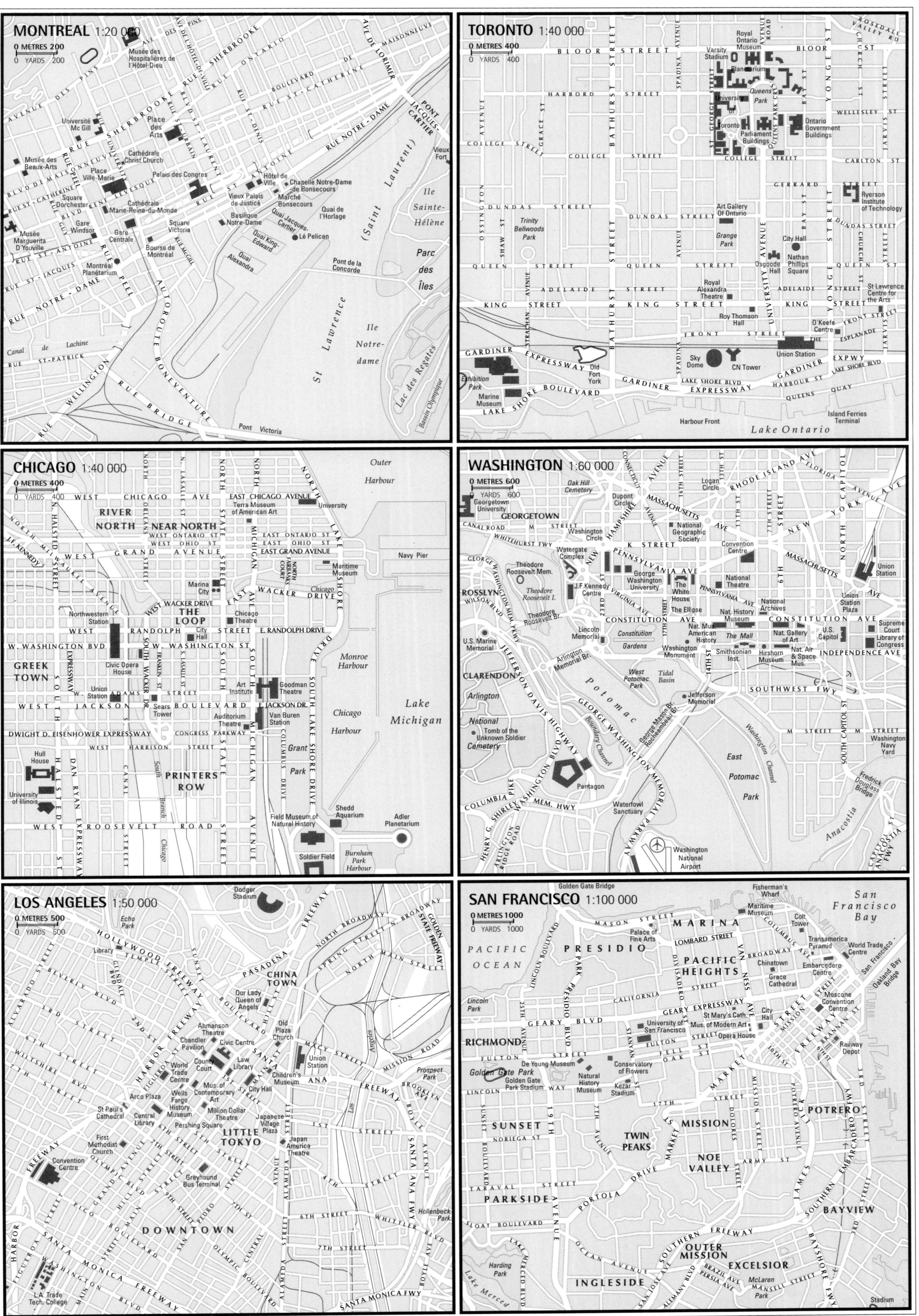
MONTREAL 1:20 000
0 METRES 200
0 YARDS 200
Musée des Hospitalières de l'Hôtel-Dieu
Université Mc Gill
Place des Arts
Cathédrale Christ Church
Musée des Beaux-Arts
Place Ville-Marie
Palais des Congres
Hôtel de Ville
Chapelle Notre-Dame de Bonsecours
Marché Bonsecours
Vieux Palais de Justice
Basilique Notre-Dame
Square Dorchester
Cathédrale Marie-Reine-du-Monde
Gare Windsor
Gare Centrale
Square Victoria
Musée Marguerita D'Youville
Bourse de Montréal
Montréal Planétarium
Quai King-Edward
Quai Alexandra
Quai Jacques-Cartier
Quai de l'Horlage
Lé Pelican
Pont de la Concorde
Pont Jacques-Cartier
Vieux Fort
Ile Sainte-Hélène
Parc des Îles
Ile Notre-dame
Lac des Regates
Bassin Olympique
St Lawrence
(Saint Laurent)
Canal de Lachine
Autoroute Boneventure
Rue Bridge
Pont Victoria
Rue Sherbrooke
Rue Notre-Dame
Rue Ste-Catherine
Boulevard René Lévesque
Rue St-Antoine
Rue St-Jacques
Rue Peel
Rue University
Rue St-Denis
Rue Wellington
Rue St-Patrick
Avenue des Pins
Avenue de Lorimer
Boulevard de Maisonneuve
TORONTO 1:40 000
0 METRES 400
0 YARDS 400
Royal Ontario Museum
Varsity Stadium
Planetarium
University of Toronto
Queens Park
Parliament Buildings
Ontario Government Buildings
Ryerson Institute of Technology
Art Gallery Of Ontario
Grange Park
Trinity Bellwoods Park
City Hall
Osgoode Hall
Nathan Phillips Square
Royal Alexandra Theatre
Roy Thomson Hall
St Lawrence Centre for the Arts
O'Keefe Centre
Union Station
Sky Dome
CN Tower
Old Fort York
Exhibition Park
Marine Museum
Harbour Front
Island Ferries Terminal
Lake Ontario
Bloor Street
Harbord Street
College Street
Gerrard Street
Dundas Street
Queen Street
Adelaide Street
King Street
Front Street
Gardiner Expressway
Lake Shore Boulevard
Queens Quay
Bathurst Street
Spadina Avenue
University Avenue
Yonge Street
Bay Street
Church Street
Jarvis Street
Wellesley Street
Carlton Street
Esplanade
CHICAGO 1:40 000
0 METRES 400
0 YARDS 400
River North
Near North
Terra Museum of American Art
University
Navy Pier
Maritime Museum
Marina City
The Loop
Northwestern Station
Chicago Theatre
City Hall
Civic Opera House
Greek Town
Union Station
Sears Tower
Art Institute
Goodman Theatre
Auditorium Theatre
Van Buren Station
Grant Park
Monroe Harbour
Chicago Harbour
Lake Michigan
Outer Harbour
Hull House
University of Illinois
Printers Row
Field Museum of Natural History
Shedd Aquarium
Adler Planetarium
Soldier Field
Burnham Park Harbour
West Chicago Ave
Grand Avenue
Wacker Drive
Randolph Street
W. Washington Blvd
Jackson Boulevard
Dwight D. Eisenhower Expressway
Congress Parkway
Harrison Street
Roosevelt Road
Michigan Avenue
Lake Shore Drive
Dan Ryan Expressway
Halsted Street
State Street
WASHINGTON 1:60 000
0 METRES 600
0 YARDS 600
Oak Hill Cemetery
Georgetown University
Georgetown
Dupont Circle
Logan Circle
Washington Circle
National Geographic Society
Convention Centre
Watergate Complex
Theodore Roosevelt Mem.
Theodore Roosevelt I.
J.F. Kennedy Centre
George Washington University
The White House
The Ellipse
National Theatre
National Archives
Nat. History Museum
Nat. Mus. American History
The Mall
Nat. Gallery of Art
U.S. Capitol
Supreme Court
Library of Congress
Union Station
Union Station Plaza
Rosslyn
Lincoln Memorial
Constitution Gardens
Washington Monument
Smithsonian Inst.
Hirshorn Museum
Nat. Air & Space Mus.
U.S. Marine Memorial
Arlington Memorial Br.
Clarendon
Arlington
National Cemetery
Tomb of the Unknown Soldier
West Potomac Park
Tidal Basin
Jefferson Memorial
Potomac
East Potomac Park
Washington Channel
Pentagon
Waterfowl Sanctuary
Washington National Airport
Washington Navy Yard
Fredrick Douglass Bridge
Anacostia
Pennsylvania Ave
Constitution Ave
Independence Ave
Southwest Fwy
Massachusetts Ave
Rhode Island Ave
New York Ave
Virginia Ave
K Street
M Street
George Washington Memorial Parkway
Jefferson Davis Highway
Columbia Pike
LOS ANGELES 1:50 000
0 METRES 500
0 YARDS 500
Dodger Stadium
Echo Park
Library
China Town
Our Lady Queen of Angels
Old Plaza Church
Union Station
Ahmanson Theatre
Chandler Pavilion
Civic Centre
County Court
Law Library
City Hall
Children's Museum
World Trade Centre
Mus. of Contemporary Art
Wells Fargo History Museum
Million Dollar Theatre
Arco Plaza
St Paul's Cathedral
Central Library
Pershing Square
Japanese Village Plaza
Little Tokyo
Japan America Theatre
First Methodist Church
Convention Centre
Greyhound Bus Terminal
Downtown
Prospect Park
Brooklyn Ave
Hollenbeck Park
L.A. Trade Tech. College
Hollywood Freeway
Harbor Freeway
Santa Monica Freeway
Santa Ana Freeway
Golden State Freeway
Pasadena Freeway
Sunset Blvd
Wilshire Blvd
Olympic Blvd
Pico Blvd
Mission Road
Whittier Blvd
SAN FRANCISCO 1:100 000
0 METRES 1000
0 YARDS 1000
Golden Gate Bridge
Fisherman's Wharf
San Francisco Bay
Maritime Museum
Coit Tower
Marina
Palace of Fine Arts
Presidio
Pacific Ocean
Pacific Heights
Transamerica Pyramid
World Trade Centre
Chinatown
Embarcadero Centre
Grace Cathedral
Oakland Bay Bridge
Lincoln Park
Richmond
Moscone Convention Centre
St Mary's Cath.
City Hall
Mus. of Modern Art
Opera House
University of San Francisco
Railway Depot
De Young Museum
Conservatory of Flowers
Golden Gate Park
Golden Gate Park Stadium
Natural History Museum
Kezar Stadium
Potrero
Sunset
Mission
Twin Peaks
Noe Valley
Parkside
Bayview
Outer Mission
Excelsior
Ingleside
Harding Park
Lake Merced
McLaren Park
Stadium
Lombard Street
Geary Expressway
Geary Blvd
California Street
Market Street
Portola Drive
Southern Freeway
Bayshore Fwy
Sloat Boulevard
19th Avenue
Van Ness Ave

© Bartholomew

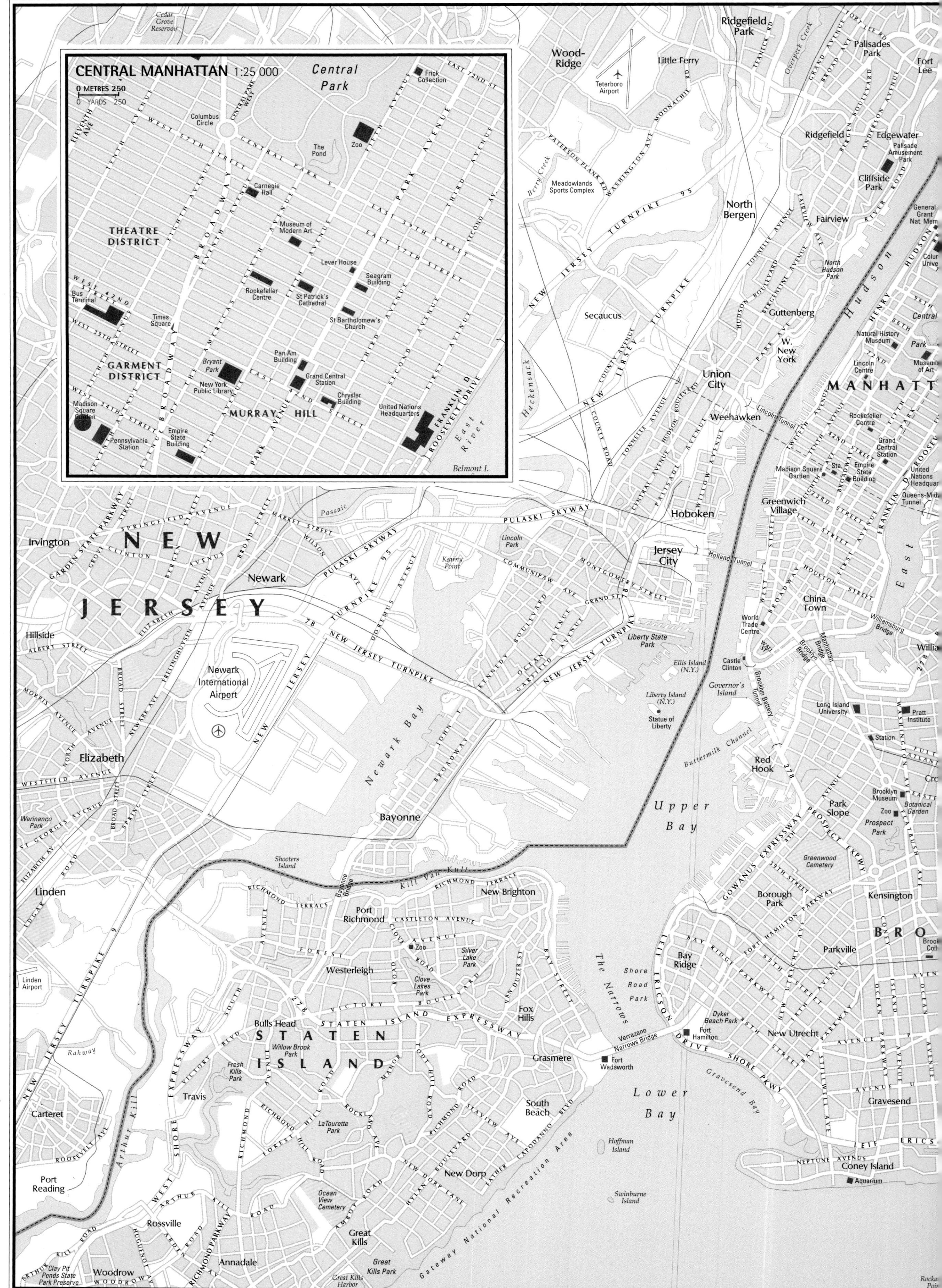

78

CENTRAL MANHATTAN 1:25 000

0 METRES 250
0 YARDS 250

Central Park

Frick Collection

Columbus Circle

THEATRE DISTRICT

Carnegie Hall

Museum of Modern Art

Lever House

Seagram Building

Rockefeller Centre

St Patrick's Cathedral

St Bartholomew's Church

Bus Terminal

Times Square

Pan Am Building

GARMENT DISTRICT

Bryant Park

New York Public Library

Grand Central Station

Chrysler Building

MURRAY HILL

United Nations Headquarters

Madison Square Garden

Pennsylvania Station

Empire State Building

East River

Belmont I.

Cedar Grove Reservoir

Ridgefield Park

Wood-Ridge

Little Ferry

Palisades Park

Fort Lee

Teterboro Airport

Ridgefield

Edgewater

Berry Creek

Meadowlands Sports Complex

Cliffside Park

Palisade Amusement Park

North Bergen

Fairview

General Grant Nat. Mem

NEW JERSEY TURNPIKE 95

Secaucus

North Hudson Park

Guttenberg

Natural History Museum

W. New York

Union City

Weehawken

Lincoln Tunnel

Rockefeller Centre

MANHATT

Hackensack

Hoboken

Greenwich Village

Grand Central Station

Empire State Building

United Nations Headquar

Madison Square Garden

Queens-Mid Tunnel

NEW

Irvington

PULASKI SKYWAY

Lincoln Park

Jersey City

Holland Tunnel

China Town

JERSEY

Newark

PULASKI SKYWAY 95

Kearny Point

Communipaw Ave

Grand St

Montgomery Street

Williamsburg Bridge

Hillside

Liberty State Park

World Trade Centre

Wall

Newark International Airport

Ellis Island (N.Y.)

Castle Clinton

Willi

Governor's Island

Long Island University

Pratt Institute

Elizabeth

Liberty Island (N.Y.)

Statue of Liberty

Buttermilk Channel

Station

Crc

Warinanco Park

Red Hook

Brooklyn Museum

Botanical Garden

Linden

Upper Bay

Park Slope

Zoo

Prospect Park

Bayonne

Greenwood Cemetery

GOWANUS EXPRESSWAY

Kensington

BRO

Linden Airport

Shooters Island

Bayonne Bridge

Kill Van Kull

New Brighton

Borough Park

Brook Colf

Parkville

Port Richmond

CASTLETON AVENUE

BAY RIDGE PARKWAY

Bay Ridge

Rahway

Westerleigh

Zoo

Silver Lake Park

Clove Lakes Park

The Narrows

Shore Road Park

New Utrecht

Bulls Head

STATEN

Willow Brook Park

Fresh Kills Park

STATEN ISLAND EXPRESSWAY

Fox Hills

Dyker Beach Park

Fort Hamilton

Travis

ISLAND

Verrazano Narrows Bridge

Gravesend

Carteret

LaTourette Park

Grasmere

Fort Wadsworth

Lower Bay

Port Reading

Ocean View Cemetery

New Dorp

South Beach

Hoffman Island

Coney Island

Clay Pit Ponds State Park Preserve

Woodrow

Annadale

Great Kills

Great Kills Park

Great Kills Harbor

Gateway National Recreation Area

Swinburne Island

Aquarium

Rossville

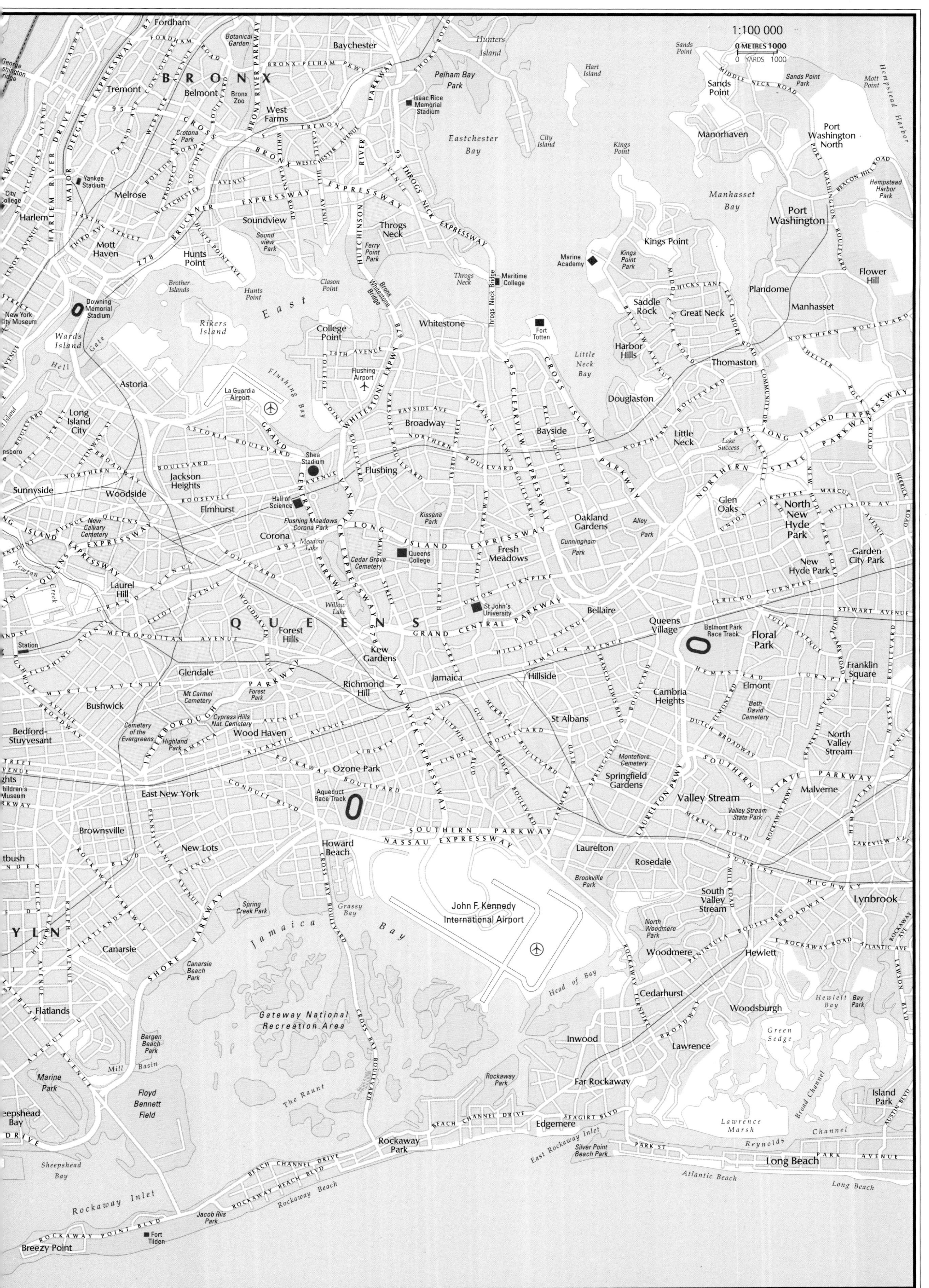
1:100 000
BRONX
QUEENS
Fordham
Baychester
Tremont
Belmont
Bronx Zoo
West Farms
Melrose
Harlem
Mott Haven
Soundview
Throgs Neck
Hunts Point
Rikers Island
Wards Island
Astoria
Long Island City
College Point
Whitestone
La Guardia Airport
Flushing
Jackson Heights
Woodside
Sunnyside
Elmhurst
Corona
Bayside
Douglaston
Little Neck
Kings Point
Great Neck
Manhasset
Port Washington
Sands Point
Manorhaven
Plandome
Flower Hill
Thomaston
Glen Oaks
North New Hyde Park
New Hyde Park
Garden City Park
Oakland Gardens
Fresh Meadows
Bellaire
Queens Village
Floral Park
Franklin Square
Elmont
Forest Hills
Kew Gardens
Jamaica
Hillside
Richmond Hill
Glendale
Bushwick
Bedford-Stuyvesant
Wood Haven
Ozone Park
East New York
Brownsville
New Lots
Howard Beach
St Albans
Cambria Heights
Springfield Gardens
Valley Stream
North Valley Stream
Malverne
Laurelton
Rosedale
South Valley Stream
Lynbrook
John F. Kennedy International Airport
Jamaica Bay
Canarsie
Flatlands
Gateway National Recreation Area
Floyd Bennett Field
Woodmere
Hewlett
Cedarhurst
Woodsburgh
Inwood
Lawrence
Far Rockaway
Edgemere
Rockaway Park
Long Beach
Atlantic Beach
Rockaway Inlet
Breezy Point
Sheepshead Bay
Island Park

© Bartholomew

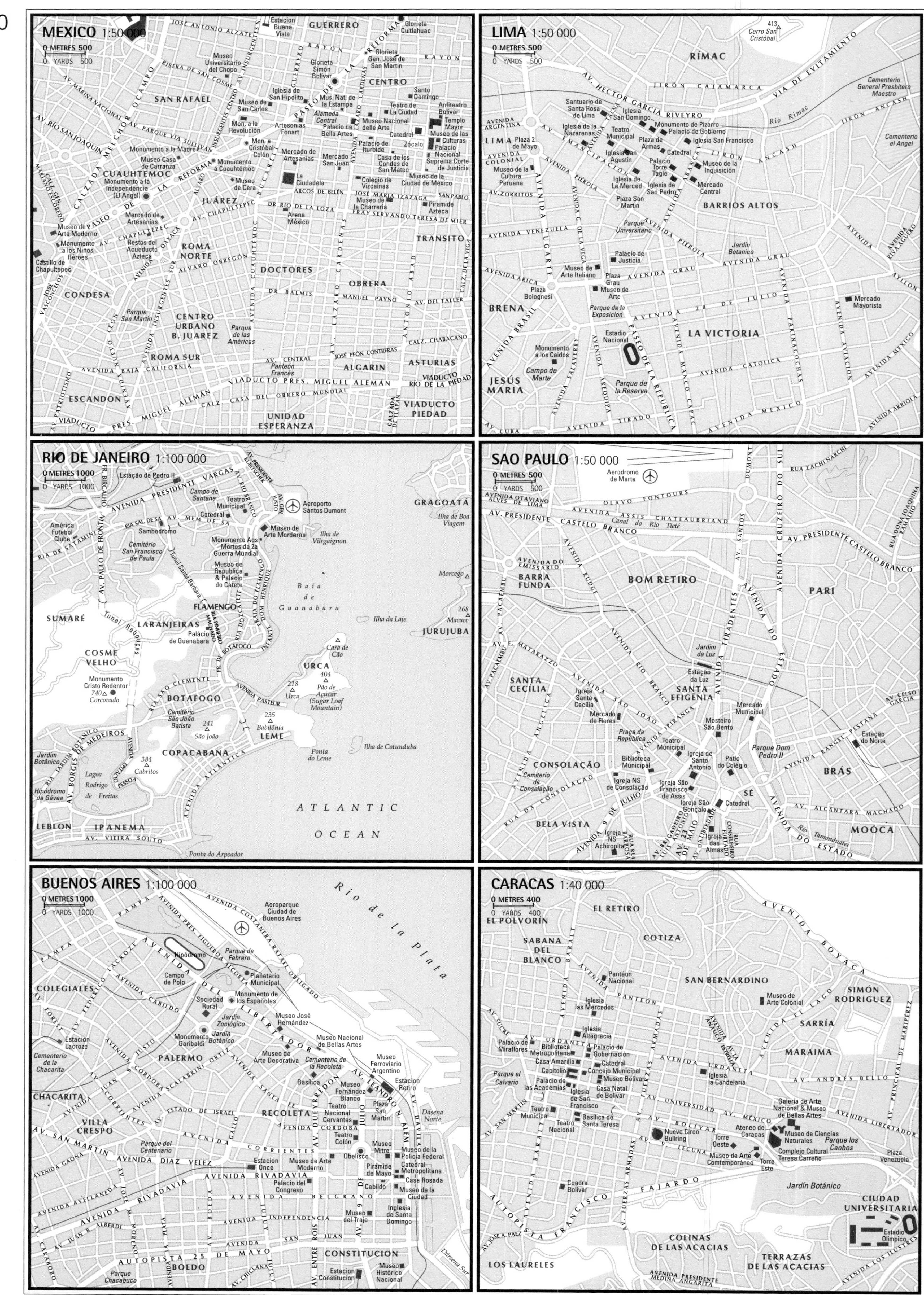

© Bartholomew

MEXICO 1:50 000
0 METRES 500
0 YARDS 500
GUERRERO
SAN RAFAEL
CENTRO
CUAUHTEMOC
JUÁREZ
TRANSITO
ROMA NORTE
DOCTORES
OBRERA
CONDESA
CENTRO URBANO B. JUAREZ
ROMA SUR
ASTURIAS
ALGARIN
ESCANDON
VIADUCTO PIEDAD
UNIDAD ESPERANZA
Zócalo
Catedral
Palacio de Bellas Artes
Monumento a la Independencia (El Angel)
Castillo de Chapultepec
VIADUCTO PRES. MIGUEL ALEMÁN
LIMA 1:50 000
0 METRES 500
0 YARDS 500
RÍMAC
BARRIOS ALTOS
BREÑA
LA VICTORIA
JESÚS MARIA
Plaza de Armas
Catedral
Palacio de Gobierno
Estadio Nacional
Parque de la Reserva
Campo de Marte
Mercado Mayorista
Cerro San Cristóbal
RIO DE JANEIRO 1:100 000
0 METRES 1000
0 YARDS 1000
GRAGOATÁ
FLAMENGO
SUMARÉ
LARANJEIRAS
COSME VELHO
BOTAFOGO
URCA
LEME
COPACABANA
JURUJUBA
LEBLON
IPANEMA
Aeroporto Santos Dumont
Monumento Cristo Redentor
740 Corcovado
404 Pão de Açúcar (Sugar Loaf Mountain)
Baía de Guanabara
Lagoa Rodrigo de Freitas
Jardim Botânico
Ilha da Laje
Ilha de Cotunduba
Ponta do Arpoador
ATLANTIC OCEAN
SAO PAULO 1:50 000
0 METRES 500
0 YARDS 500
Aerodromo de Marte
BARRA FUNDA
BOM RETIRO
PARI
SANTA CECÍLIA
SANTA EFIGÊNIA
CONSOLAÇÃO
BRÁS
SÉ
BELA VISTA
MOÓCA
Estação da Luz
Jardim da Luz
Catedral
Parque Dom Pedro II
Estação do Norte
BUENOS AIRES 1:100 000
0 METRES 1000
0 YARDS 1000
Aeroparque Ciudad de Buenos Aires
Rio de la Plata
COLEGIALES
PALERMO
CHACARITA
VILLA CRESPO
RECOLETA
BOEDO
CONSTITUCION
Hipódromo
Campo de Polo
Jardín Zoológico
Obelisco
Casa Rosada
Catedral Metropolitana
Palacio del Congreso
Estacion Retiro
Dársena Norte
Dársena Sur
AVENIDA DEL LIBERTADOR
AVENIDA RIVADAVIA
AVENIDA 9 DE JULIO
CARACAS 1:40 000
0 METRES 400
0 YARDS 400
EL RETIRO
EL POLVORÍN
SABANA DEL BLANCO
COTIZA
SAN BERNARDINO
SIMÓN RODRIGUEZ
SARRÍA
MARAIMA
CIUDAD UNIVERSITARIA
COLINAS DE LAS ACACIAS
TERRAZAS DE LAS ACACIAS
LOS LAURELES
Panteón Nacional
Capitolio
Catedral
Jardín Botánico
Estadio Olímpico
Parque Los Caobos
Nuevo Circo Bullring
Plaza Venezuela
AUTOPISTA FRANCISCO FAJARDO

THE FIRST CONCISE Edition of the Times Atlas of the World used mapping developed for the larger Comprehensive Edition. This mapping had been compiled using traditional cartographic techniques which placed restrictions on what was possible when planning the Concise Edition pages. While some new mapping was specifically developed, compromises had to be made on many of the derived pages.

This new Seventh Edition of the Concise has been completely redeveloped from Bartholomew digital databases. In planning the map pages, these databases allow the freedom to select the optimum scale and coverage for each region or continent which best suits the format and extent of the new atlas. In order to portray the correct geographical relationships within each map, the use of continuation insets have been avoided wherever possible. Map areas have been selected with historic, cultural, political and economic links in mind as well as their physical geography.

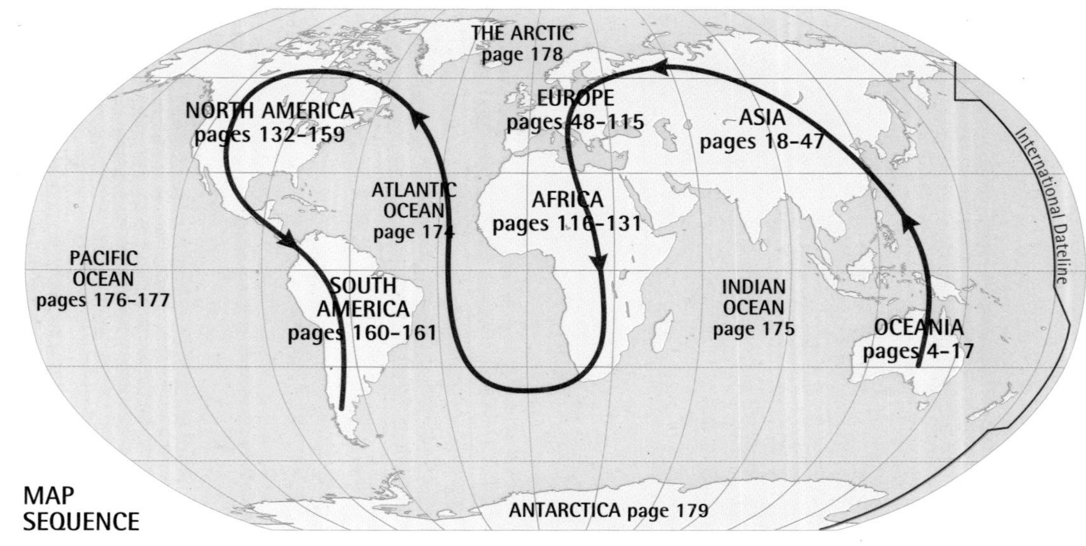

MAP SEQUENCE
In the tradition of the Times Atlas of the World the sequence of coverage starts at the International Date Line in the Pacific Ocean and broadly works westwards, moving from Oceania through Asia, Europe, Africa, North America and finally to South America. Each continent section is prefaced by a politically coloured map highlighting the states and territories within that particular continent. This is followed by reference maps of sub-continent regions, and within each of these in turn, more detailed reference mapping of the relevant individual countries.

While Europe and North America are still well represented in this new edition there is more balanced coverage with much more extensive mapping of Africa, Asia and South America. The new atlas also reflects the changed world scene in the post Cold War era, with new mapping of the re-unified Germany and the now independent Baltic States, for example. A completely new suite of maps covering the World's Oceans concludes the main reference map section.

SCALE
In order to compare like with like throughout the world it would obviously be necessary to maintain a common set of map scales throughout the atlas. However, the desirability of mapping the more densely populated areas of the world at larger scales and practical considerations, such as the need to fit a homogeneous physical region within a uniform rectangular page format, mean that a set of scale bands, as have been used in this atlas, pro-

vide the best practical solution. Scales for continental maps range between 1:15.5 million and 1:30 million, depending on the size of the continental land mass being covered. Scales for regional maps are typically in the range 1:7.5 million to 1:12.6 million, though smaller scales are used for remoter parts of Asia and North America. Detailed local mapping for most of the world is at scales between 1:3 million and 1:6.6 million, though for the most densely populated area of Europe this increases to a maximum scale of 1:1 million. Island insets are covered at a variety of scales.

PROJECTIONS
The creation of the new computer generated maps in this atlas presented the opportunity to review the map projections used and to create projections specifically designed for the area and scale of each map, or suite of maps. As the only way to show the earth with absolute accuracy is on a globe, all map projections are compromises. Some projections seek to maintain correct area relationships (equal area projections) or correct angles and shapes (conformal projections), others attempt to achieve a balance between these properties. The choice of projections used in this atlas has been made on an individual continent and regional basis.

For world maps in the atlas, the Robinson projection is used. This projection combines elements of conformality with that of equal area, and shows, over the earth as a whole, relatively true shapes and resonably equal areas. For the continental maps, different projections were selected according to the latitude and longitude and the overall shape of each continent. The projection used for Asia, the Two-Point Equidistant was chosen for its conformal qualities, while for North and South America

the Bi-Polar Oblique projection, originally specifically designed for these continents, has been used. For Oceania, Europe and Africa, Lambert Azimuthal Equal Area, Chamberlin Trimetric and Stereographic projections resepctively are used.

As with the continental maps, the selection of projections for the series on regional maps within each continent has been made on an individual basis for that region. Oblique Mercator projections have been selected for the regional maps of southeast Asia along the equator, while in higher latitudes in Europe, Conic Equidistant projections have been used extensively. In North America Lambert Conformal Conic projections have been used for regional mapping, while Lambert Azimuthal Equal Area projections have been employed in both South America and Australia. The projection used is indicated at the bottom left of each map.

MAP PRESENTATION
The map pages include a map title, location map showing the position of the region within the continent or, for larger scale maps, the position within the region. A scale bar and a key to the relief colouring are also included on each map. The measurements on the scale bar and the relief key are given in both metric and imperial measures. The symbols used on the maps are fully explained on page 84 of this introductory section. The reference system used in the index is based on the latitude and longitude grid, and the number and letter for each grid square is shown along the sides, top and bottom of each map, within the map frame. The red numbers located within the arrows show the page number for the ajoining map.

MAP SEQUENCE

THE ARCTIC
page 178

NORTH AMERICA
pages 132–159

EUROPE
pages 48–115

ASIA
pages 18–47

ATLANTIC
OCEAN
page 174

AFRICA
pages 116–131

PACIFIC
OCEAN
pages 176–177

SOUTH
AMERICA
pages 160–161

INDIAN
OCEAN
page 175

OCEANIA
pages 4–17

International Dateline

ANTARCTICA page 179

One of the criteria used to classify projections is their geometric characteristics. The diagrams on the right show projections based on an open cylinder, a cone and a plane, the groups are known as cylindrical, conic and azimuthal projections respectively.

Diagram A in each group illustrates the patterns of deformation or distortion when the cylinder, cone or plane is at a tangent to the globe, and diagram B illustrates these patterns when the cylinder, cone or plane intersects the globe. The lines or points of intersection may or may not be lines of latitude.

The patterns of deformation are parallel to the lines of intersection on cylindrical and conic projections, and concentric with the point or plane of intersection on azimuthal projections.

CYLINDRICAL   **CONIC**   **AZIMUTHAL**

A   A   A

B   B   B

increasing distortion

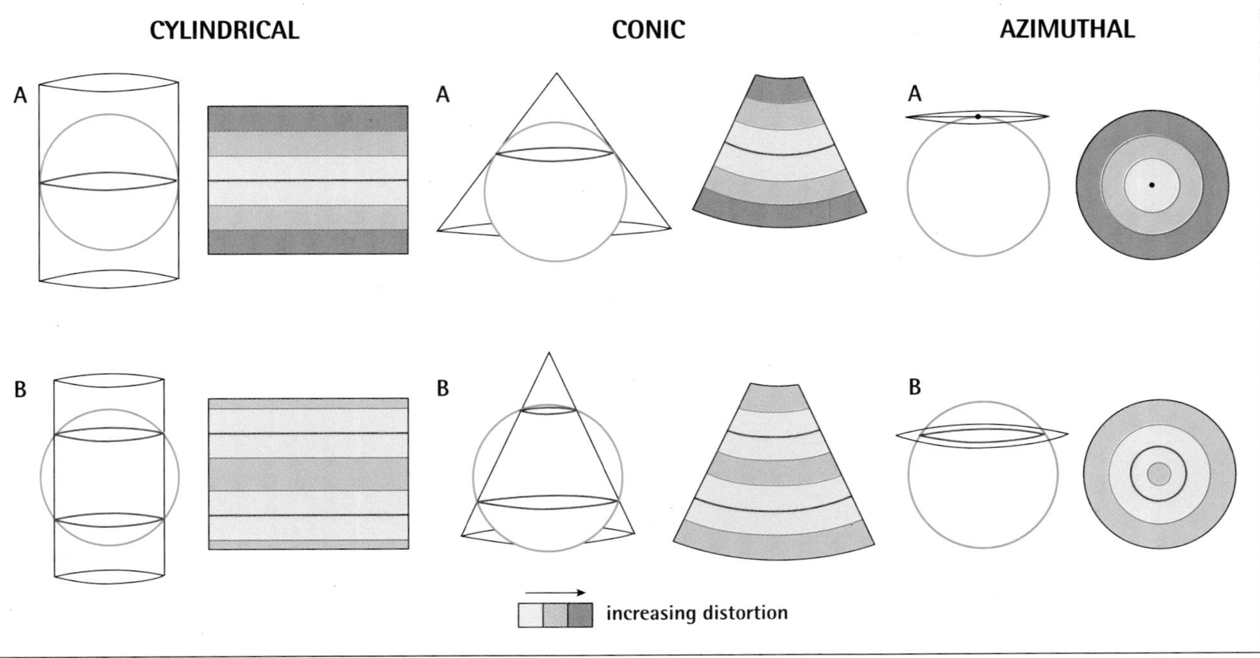

THE SPELLING OF place names on maps has always been a matter of great complexity, because of the variety of the world's languages and of the systems used to write them down. There is no single standard way of spelling names or of converting them from one alphabet, or symbol set, to another. Instead, conventional ways of spelling have evolved in each of the world's major languages, and the results often differ significantly from the name as it is spelt in the original. Familiar examples in English include Munich (München in German), Florence (Firenze in Italian) and Moscow (Moskva from Russian).

Continuing changes in official languages, and in writing systems, have to be taken into account by cartographers when creating maps and databases. Other factors also stand in the way of achieving a single standard. In many countries different languages are in use in different regions, or side-by-side in the same region. Sometimes the problem is dealt with in the country concerned by the use of a 'lingua franca' such as English to provide a mutually intelligible standard. In many cases the most-spoken language takes precedence, but there is still the potential for widely varying name forms even within a single country. A worldwide trend towards national, regional and ethnic self-determination is operating at the same time as an inevitable pressure towards more international standardization. There are other complications for the cartographer. For instance, more than one form is often in use for international feature names, such as extensive mountain ranges or long rivers which are shared by two or more countries.

Place names are, to an extent, a mirror for the changes that continue to transform the political globe. As could naturally be expected, changes of territorial control have an effect on name form usage. Yet even in countries where name forms have long been largely standardized, there are still some continuing issues for the cartographer to address: in the UK for example, the relative prominence (and spelling) of Gaelic and Welsh name forms versus anglicized names. Name spelling issues are, in fact, likely to emerge in any part of the world. A close watch is kept on areas where changes might be expected, although sometimes they crop up in unexpected places.

Reflecting trends across the world, systematic alterations have been made in this edition of the atlas compared with previous editions, involving all name forms for the ex-Soviet republics of Belarus, the Ukraine, Moldova, Armenia, Georgia, Azerbaijan, Tajikistan and Kyrgyzstan. A new romanization system is now used for Greece and Cyprus, and name forms in Cambodia, Laos and Vietnam have also been systematically altered.

These changes result, for example, in Kyyiv for Kiyev; Athina for Athínai; Phnum Penh for Phnom Penh; and Ha Nôi for Hanoi. New mapping of Spain takes full account of the official prominence now given to Catalan, Galician and main Basque names, which results in name forms such as Eivissa for Ibiza; A Coruña for La Coruña; and San Sebastián amended to Donostia - San Sebastián.

The local name forms used in this atlas are those which are officially recognised by the government of the country concerned, usually as represented by its official mapping agency. This is a basic principle laid down by the United Kingdom government's Permanent Committee on Geographical Names (PCGN). PCGN and the US Board on Geographic Names (BGN) for the most part use shared romanization principles for non-Roman alphabets and syllabaries. For example, Russian-language names are spelt using the standard BGN/PCGN system, which gives names such as Lipetsk and Yoshkar-Ola as opposed to a system used in eastern Europe which gives Lipeck and Joškar-Ola. However, for Arabic-speaking countries in particular, US policy is to use a single standard system for romanizing names, where PCGN prefers to follow local versions as one would find in the country itself or in its official mapping; an example from Tunisia is Sfax (local usage) as opposed to Şafāqis (strict romanization). In this atlas PCGN usage is followed.

Cartographers are sometimes criticised for giving undue prominence to local name forms instead of using plain English. It is, in fact, impossible to provide English names for the majority of mappable features, and translating names into English is fraught with linguistic hazards. Consequently a

ABBREVIATIONS AND GLOSSARY

A.	Alp Alpen Alpi *alp*		Cach.	Cachoeira Cachoeiro *waterfall*	G.	Golfe Golfo Gulf *gulf, bay*	Jap.	Japan Japanese
	Alt *upper*		Can.	Canal Canale *canal, channel*		Góra *mountain*		
Abbe	Abbaye *abbey*			Cañon Canyon *canyon*		Guba *bay*	K.	Kaap Kap Kapp *cape*
A.C.T.	Australian Capital Territory		Cat.	Cataract		Gunung *mountain*		Kaikyō *strait*
Afghan.	Afghanistan			Catena *mountains*	-g.	-gawa *river*		Kato Káto *lower*
Afr.	Africa African		Cd	Ciudad *town city*	Gd	Grand *big*		Kiang *river or stream*
Ag.	Agia Agioi Agion Agios *saint*		Ch.	Chaung *stream*	Gde	Grande *big*		Ko *island, lake, inlet*
				Chott *salt lake, marsh*	Geb.	Gebergte *mountain range*		Koh Kūh Kūhha *island*
Aig.	Aiguille *peak*		Chan.	Channel		Gebirge *mountains*		Kolpos *gulf*
Akr.	Ákra Akrotírion Akrotirion *cape, point*		Che	Chaîne *mountain chain*	Gen.	General		Kopf *hill*
			Cma	Cima *summit*	Gez.	Geziran *island*		Kuala *estuary*
Anch.	Anchorage		Cno	Corno *peak*	Ger.	Germany		Kyst *coast*
Appno	Appennino *mountains*		Co	Cerro *hill, peak*	Ghub.	Ghubbat *bay*	Kan.	Kanal Kanaal *canal*
Aqued.	Aqueduct		Cor.	Coronel *colonel*	Gl.	Glacier	Kazakh.	Kazakhstan
Ar.	Arroyo *watercourse*		Cord.	Cordillera *mountain chain*	Gob.	Gobernador *governor*	Kep.	Kepulauan *archipelago, islands*
Arch.	Archipel Archipelago		Cr.	Creek	Grp	Group		
	Archipiélago *archipelago*		Cuch.	Cuchilla *chain of mountains*	Gr.	Graben *trench, ditch*	Kg	Kampong *village*
Arg.	Argentina Argentinian					Gross Grosse Grande *big*		Kompong *landing place*
Arr.	Arrecife *reef*		Czo	Cozzo *mountain*	Gt	Great Groot Groote *big*		Kong *king*
Aust.	Australia Australian				Gy	Góry Gory *mountains*	Kh.	Khawr *inlet*
Ay.	Áyioi Áyion Áyios *saint*		D.	Da *big, river*				Khirbet *ruins*
Azer.	Azerbaijan			Dag Dagh Dağı *mountain*	H.	Hawr *lake*	Khr	Khrebet *mountain range*
				Dağları *mountains*		Hill	Kl.	Klein Kleine *small*
B.	Baai Bahía Baía Baie			Danau *lake*		Hoch *high*	Kör.	Körfez Körfezi *bay, gulf*
	Baja Bay Bucht Bukhta			Darreh *valley*		Hora *mountain*	K.	Küçük *small*
	Bukt *bay*			Daryācheh *lake*		Hory *mountains*	Kyrgyz.	Kyrgyzstan
	Bad *spa*			Diavlos *hill*	Halv.	Halvøy *peninsula*		
	Ban *village*		-d.	-dake *peak*	Harb.	Harbour	L.	Lac Lago Lake Liman
	Bayou *inlet*		D.C.	District of Columbia	Hd	Head		Limni Liqen Loch Lough *lake, loch*
	Bir *well*		Den.	Denmark	Hg.	Hegység *mountains*		
Bc	Banc *(sand) bank*		Dj.	Djebel *mountain*	Hgts	Heights		Lam *stream*
Bca	Boca *mouth*		Dr	Doctor	Hist.	Historic	Lag.	Lagoon Laguna Lagôa *lagoon*
Bel.	Belgium Belgian		Dz.	Dzong *castle, fort*	Hond.	Honduras		
Bg	Berg *mountain*				Ht	Haut *high*	Ldg	Landing
Bge	Barrage		E.	East Eastern	Hte	Haute *high*	Liech.	Liechtenstein
Bge.	Barragem *reservoir*		Eil.	Eiland *island*			Lit.	Little
Bgt	Bight Bugt *bay*			Eilanden *islands*	I.	Île Ilha Insel Isla Island	Lith.	Lithuania
Bi	Bani Beni *tribe (sons of)*		Emb.	Embalse *reservoir*		Isle *island, isle*	Lux.	Luxembourg
Bj	Burj *hills*		Equat.	Equatorial		Isola Isole *island*		
Bk	Bank		Escarp.	Escarpment	im	imeni *in the name of*	M.	Mae *river*
Bn	Basin		Est.	Estuary	In.	Inder Indre Inner Inre *inner*		Me *great, chief, mother*
Bol.	Bol'shoy Bol'shoye		Etg	Etang *lake, lagoon*				Meer *lake, sea*
	Bol'shaya Bol'shiye *big*					Inlet *inlet*		Muang *kingdom, province, town*
Bos.	Bosanski *town*		F.	Firth	Ind.	India Indian		
Br.	Bredning *bay*		F.D.	Federal District	Indon.	Indonesia		Muong *town*
	Brüke *bridge*		Fed.	Federation	Inf.	Inferior Infrieure *lower*		Mys *cape*
	British Britain		Fj.	Fjell *mountain*	Is	Islas Îles Ilhas Islands	Mal.	Malyy Malaya Maloye *small*
	Burun Burnu *point, cape*			Fjord Fjördur *fjord*		Isles *islands, isles*		
Bt	Bukit *bay*		Fk	Fork	Isr.	Israel	Mex.	Mexico Mexican
Bü.	Büyük *big*		Fl.	Fleuve *river*	Isth.	Isthmus	Mf	Massif *mountains, upland*
			Fr.	France French			Mgna	Montagna *mountain*
C.	Cabo Cap *cape, headland*		Fte	Fonte *well*	J.	Jabal Jebel *mountain*	Mgne	Montagne *mountain*
	Cape					Jibāl *mountains*	Mgnes	Montagnes *mountains*
	Col *high pass*		G.	Gebel *mountain*		Jrvi Jaure Jezero Jezioro *lake*	Mon.	Monasterio Monastery *monastery*
Ç.	Çay *river*			Göl Gölö Gól *lake*				
Cabo	Cabeço *summit*					Jökull *glacier*		Monument *monument*
							Moz.	Mozambique

local name form map is more internally consistent than a partly-anglicized one; it reflects more closely name forms found in the country itself, and it has the added advantage of being more accessible to readers whose first language is not English. Local name form mapping such as is found in this atlas is the nearest that the cartographer can achieve to an international standard.

However, prominent English-language conventional names and historic names are not neglected; along with significant superseded names, they are included in brackets on the map where space permits and are cross-referenced in the index, while the Guide to States and Territories on pages 10 to 32 and small-scale continental maps use only these familiar forms. Continents, oceans, seas and underwater features in international waters appear in English throughout the atlas, as do other international features where such a name exists in common use. Country names are also shown in English but include recent policy changes promulgated by some national governments and adopted by the United Nations - Myanmar (replacing Burma), Belarus (replacing Belorussia and a variety of other versions as well as the traditional White Russia), Kyrgyzstan (for Kirghizia or Kirgizia), Moldova (Moldavia), and Côte d'Ivoire (Ivory Coast). Many of these alternate name forms are also cross-referenced in the index. In the case of these country names, and with certain cities such as Beijing (replacing Peking), the gradual incorporation of local forms in to the English language can be seen

at work. This atlas reflects that process but does not attempt to lead it.

NAME CHANGES

Unequivocal renamings are far more common, particularly affecting towns and cities. The dissolution of the Soviet Union in particular has given rise to a series of reversions away from communist-inspired names. Russian-language spellings are now occasionally being amended for other reasons: eg Ashkhabad is now Ashgabat, which is closer to the Turkmen form. Some name changes have attracted international interest - most notably, perhaps, the reversion of Leningrad to Sankt-Peterburg in the Russian form, and St. Petersburg in the English form; but this atlas also represents the latest state of knowledge as regards less famous names, based on a continuously updated collection of reference sources and on contacts with geographical consultants and authorities around the world.

BOUNDARIES

The status of nations and their boundaries, and the names associated with these, are shown in this atlas as they are in reality at the time of going to press, as far as can be ascertained. The atlas naturally includes the recent change of the status of nations and their boundaries which have included the reunification of Germany, and the partition of the Soviet Union, Yugoslavia and Czechoslovakia. Although many former dependent territories are

now independent, new nations such as Eritrea and Palau have also emerged as separate entities quite apart from the above-mentioned schisms.

Where international boundaries are the subject of dispute it may be that no protrayal of them will meet with the approval of the countries involved, but it is not seen as the function of this atlas to try to adjudicate between the rights and wrongs of political issues. Although reference mapping is not a suitable medium for indicating the claims of many separatist and irredentist movements that are active in the world, every reasonable attempt is made to show where a territorial dispute exists, and where there is an important difference between 'de facto' (existing on the ground) and 'de jure' (according to law) boundaries. The territories occupied by Israel are clearly indicated as such rather than simply being incorporated into Israel itself, but at the same time no political entity of 'Palestine' is mentioned. In Kashmir, the long-standing dispute between India and Pakistan is represented by giving prominence to the de facto situation, while suitable boundary symbols also indicate that this is not a settled issue. The atlas aims to take a strictly neutral viewpoint of all such cases, based on advice from expert consultants.

In this atlas changes to the internal administrative divisions of countries are also regarded as being of prime importance, and some attract international interest, such as the changes in the provincial structure in the Republic of South Africa.

Mt	Mont Mount *mountain*		P.P.	Pulau-pulau *islands*		Rte	Route		Tk	Teluk *bay*
Mt.	Mountain		Pak.	Pakistan		Rus. Fed.	Russian Federation		Tmt	Tablemount
Mte	Monte *mountain*		Para.	Paraguay					Tr.	Trench Trough
Mtes	Montes *mountains*		Pass.	Passage		S.	Salar Salina *salt pan*		Tre	Torre *tower, fortress*
Mti	Monti Munţi		Peg.	Pegunungan			San São *saint*		Tte	Teniente *lieutenant*
	mountains			*mountain range*			See *lake*		Turkmen.	Turkmenistan
Mtii	Munţii *mountains*		Pen.	Peninsula Penisola			Seto *strait, channel*			
Mtn	Mountain			*peninsula*			Sjö *lake*		U.A.E.	United Arab Emirates
Mth	Mouth		Per.	Pereval *pass*			Sör South Süd Sud Syd		Ug	Ujung *point, cape*
Mths	Mouths		Phn.	Phnom *hill, mountain*			*south*		U.K.	United Kingdom
Mts	Monts Mountains		Pgio	Poggio *hill*			sur *on*		U.S.A.	United States of America
			Pl.	Planina Planinski		Sa	Serra Sierra		Unt.	Unter *lower*
N.	Nam *south(ern), river*			*mountain(s)*			*mountain range*		Upr	Upper
	Neu Ny *new*		Pla	Playa *beach*		Sab.	Sabkhat *salt flat*		Uzbek.	Uzbekistan
	Nevado *peak*		Plat.	Plateau		Sc.	Scoglio *rock, reef*			
	Nudo *mountain*		Plosk.	Ploskogor'ye *plateau*		Sd	Sound Sund *sound*		V.	Val Valle Valley *valley*
	Noord Nord Nörre Nørre		Pno	Pantano *reservoir, swamp*		S.E.	Southeast			Väster Vest Vester
	North *north*		Pol.	Poland Polish		Seb.	Sebjet Sebkhat Sebkra			*west(ern)*
	Nos *spit, point*		Por.	Porog *rapids*			*salt flat*			Vatn *lake*
Nac.	Nacional *national*		Port.	Portugal Portuguese		Serr.	Serrania *mountain range*			Ville *town*
Nat.	National		P-ov	Poluostrov *peninsula*		Sev.	Severnaya Severnyy			Vorder *near*
N.E.	Northeast		Pr.	Proliv *strait*			*north(ern)*		Va	Vila *small town*
Neth.	Netherlands		Przl.	Przlądek *cape*		Sh.	Sha'ib *watercourse*		Vol.	Volcán Volcan Volcano
Nic.	Nicaragua		Pres.	Presidente *president*			Shaţţ *river (-mouth)*			*volcano*
Nizh.	Nizhneye Nizhniy		Presq.	Presqu'ile *peninsula*			Shima *island*		Vdkhr.	Vodokhranilishche
	Nizhnyaya *lower*		Prom.	Promontory			Shankou *pass*			*reservoir*
Nizm.	Nizmennost' *lowland*		Prov.	Province Provincial		Si	Sidi *lord, master*		Vdskh.	Vodoskhovshche
N.O.	Noord Oost Nord Ost		Psa	Presa *dam*		Sk.	Shuiku *reservoir*			Vodaskhovishcha *reservoir*
	northeast		Pso	Passo *dam*		Skt	Sankt *saint*		Vel.	Velikiy Velikaya Velikiye
Nor.	Norway Norwegian		Pt	Point		Smt	Seamount			*big*
Nov.	Novyy Novaya Noviye			Pont *bridge*		Snra	Senhora *Mrs, lady*		Ven.	Venezuela Venezuelan
	Novoye *new*			Petit *small*		Snro	Senhoro *Mr, gentleman*		Verkh.	Verkhniy Verkhneye
Nr	Nether		Pta	Ponta Punta *cape, point*		Sp.	Spain Spanish			Verkhne *upper*
N.W.	Northwest			Puerta *narrow pass*			Spitze *peak*			Verkhnyaya *upper*
N.Z.	New Zealand		Pte	Pointe *cape, point*		Sr	Sönder Sønder *southern*		Vost.	Vostochnyy *eastern*
Nva	Nueva *new*			Ponte Puente *bridge*		Sr.	Sredniy Srednyaya		Vozv.	Vozvyshennost'
			Pto	Porto Puerto *harbour,*			*middle*			*hills, upland*
O.	Oost Ost *east*			*port*		St	Saint Sint			
	Ostrov *island*		Pzo	Pizzo *mountain peak,*			Staryy *old*		W.	Wadi *watercourse*
Ø	Østre *east*			*mountain*		St.	Stor Store *big*			Wald *forest*
Ob.	Ober *upper, higher*						Stung *river*			Wan *bay*
Oc.	Ocean		Q	Qala *castle, fort*		Sta	Santa *saint*			Water *water*
Ode	Oude *old*					Ste	Sainte *saint*			Well *well*
Ogl.	Oglat *well*		R.	Reshteh *mountain range*		Sto	Santo *saint*			West *west*
Or.	Óri Óros Ori *mountains*			Rūd *river*		Str.	Strait Stretta *strait*		Wr	Wester
	Oros *mountain*		Ra.	Range		Sv.	Sväty Sveti *holy, saint*			
Orm.	Ormos *bay*		Rca	Rocca *rock, fortress*		Switz.	Switzerland		-y	-yama *mountain*
O-va	Ostrova *islands*		Reg.	Region		S.W.	Southwest		Yt.	Ytre Ytter Ytri *outer*
Ot	Olet *mountain*		Rep.	Republic					Yugo.	Yugoslavia
Öv.	Över Övre *upper*		Res.	Reserve		T.	Tal *valley*		Yuzh.	Yuzhnaya Yuzhno
Oz.	Ozero *lake*			Reservoir			Tall Tell *hill*			Yuzhnyy *southern*
	Ozera *lakes*		Resp.	Respublika *republic*			Tepe Tepesi *hill, peak*			
			Rf	Reef		Tajik.	Tajikistan		Zal.	Zaliv *bay*
P.	Pass		Rge	Ridge		Terr.	Territory		Zap.	Zapadnyy Zapadnaya
	Pic Pico Piz *peak, summit*		Riba	Ribeira *coast, bottom of*		Tg	Tanjung Tanjong			Zapadno Zapadnoye
	Pulau *island*			*the river valley*			*cape, point*			*western*
	Pou *mountain*		Rom.	Romania Romanian					Zem.	Zemlya *land*

SYMBOLS

RELIEF

Contour intervals used in layer colouring at scales greater than 1:4 million

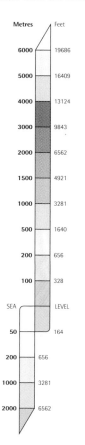

At scales of 1:3m, additional bathymetric contour lines are shown at 1000 and 3000 metres below sea level.

Contour intervals used in layer colouring at scales of 1:4 million and smaller

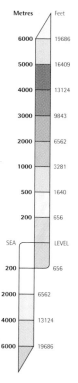

213
△ Summit
height in metres

PHYSICAL FEATURES

	Freshwater lake
	Seasonal freshwater lake
	Saltwater lake *or* Lagoon
	Seasonal saltwater lake
	Dry salt lake *or* Salt pan
	Marsh
	River
	Waterfall
	Dam *or* Barrage
	Seasonal river or Wadi
	Canal
	Flood dyke
	Reef
▲	Volcano
	Lava field
	Sandy desert
	Rocky desert
˘	Oasis
	Escarpment
≍	Mountain pass
	Ice cap *or* Glacier

COMMUNICATIONS

═══	Motorway
⋯⋯	Motorway tunnel

Motorways are classified separately at scales greater than 1:4 million, at smaller scales motorways are classified with main roads.

─────	Main road
─ ─ ─	Main road *under construction*
⋯⋯	Main road tunnel
─────	Other road
─ ─ ─	Other road *under construction*
⋯⋯	Other road tunnel
─ ─ ─	Track
⋯⋯	Car ferry
═══	Main railway
─ ─ ─	Main railway *under construction*
⋯⋯	Main railway tunnel
─────	Other railway
─ ─ ─	Other railway *under construction*
⋯⋯	Other railway tunnel
⋯⋯	Train ferry
✈	Main airport
✦	Other airport

BOUNDARIES

	International
	International *through water*
	International *disputed*
	Ceasefire line
	Main administrative
	Main administrative *through water*
	Other administrative
	Other administrative *through water*
	Main administrative *at scales of 1:4 million and smaller*

Other administrative boundaries are not shown at scales of 1:4 million and smaller

	National park
	Reserve

OTHER FEATURES

	Ancient wall
∴	Historic *or* Tourist site

SETTLEMENTS

POPULATION	NATIONAL CAPITAL	ADMINISTRATIVE CAPITAL	CITY OR TOWN
Over 5 million	▣ **Beijing**	◉ **Tianjin**	◉ **New York**
1 to 5 million	▣ **Sŏul**	◉ **Lagos**	◉ **Barranquilla**
500000 to 1 million	▣ **Bangui**	◉ **Douala**	◉ **Memphis**
100000 to 500000	▢ **Wellington**	○ **Mansa**	○ **Mara**
50000 to 100000	▢ Port of Spain	○ Lubango	○ Arecibo
10000 to 50000	▫ Malabo	○ Chinhoyi	○ El Tigre
Less than 10000	▫ Roseau	○ Áti	○ Soledad

	Urban area

STYLES OF LETTERING

Country name	**ZAIRE**	**BARBADOS**	
Main administrative name	**PORTO**	Main administrative names *at scales of 1:4 million and smaller*	AGADEZ
Other administrative name	M A N C H E	Area name	ARTOIS
Physical feature	ISLAND	LAKE	MOUNTAIN	RIVER
	Gran Canaria	LAKE ERIE	*SOUTHERN ALPS*	*Niger*

© Bartholomew

ATLAS
OF THE
WORLD

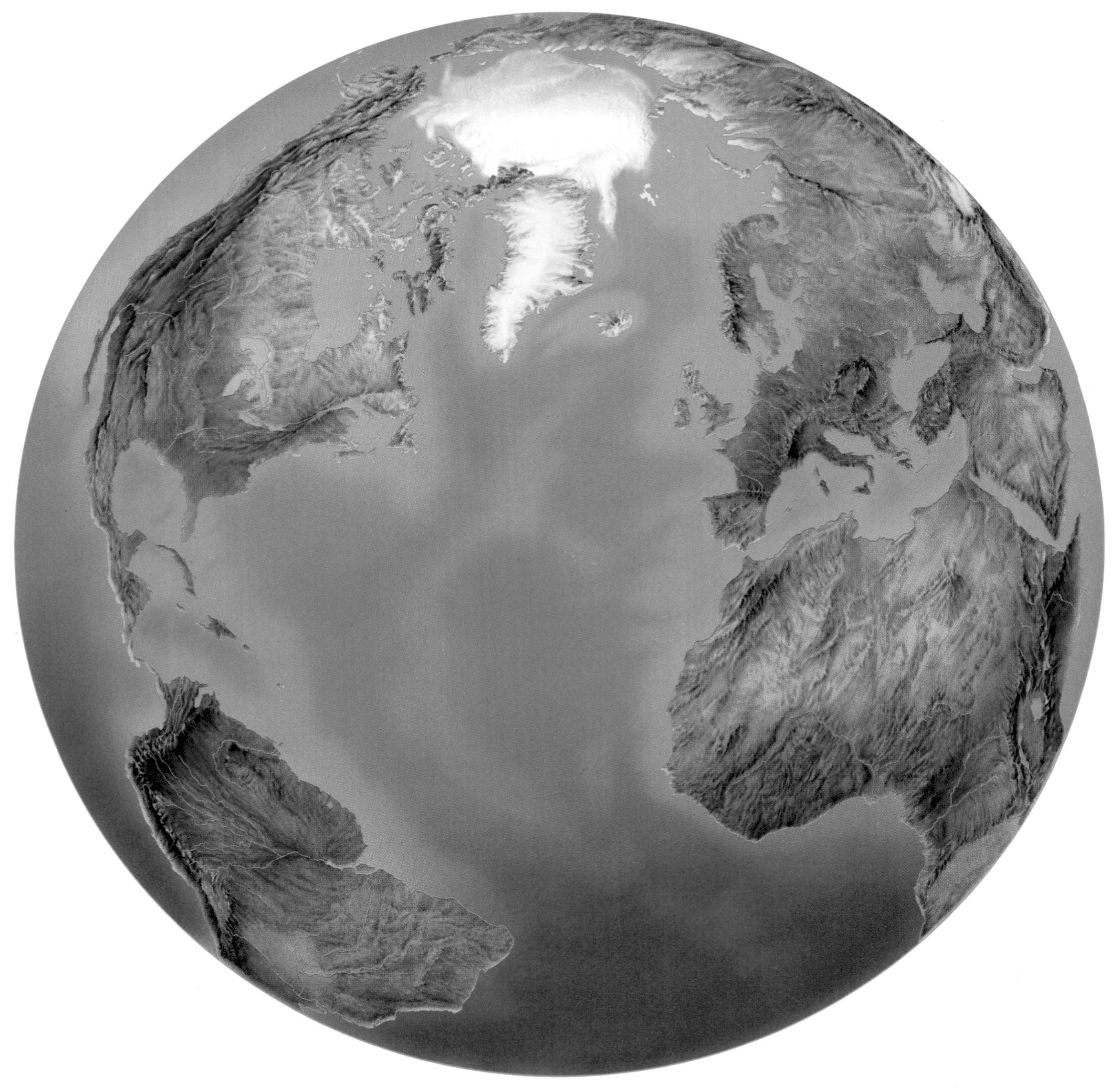

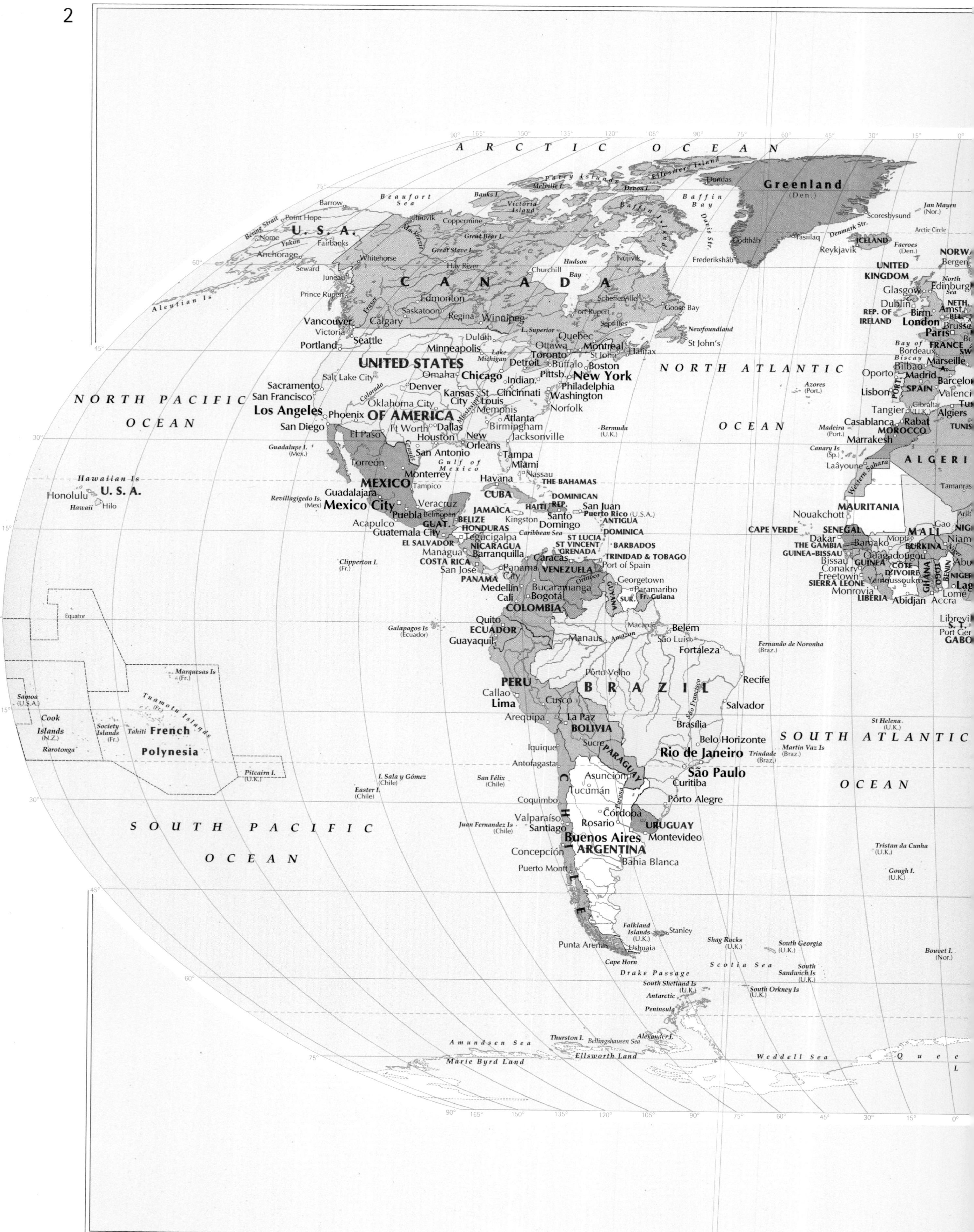

ARCTIC OCEAN

Parry Islands
Melville I.
Banks I.
Devon I.
Dundas
Ellesmere Island
Greenland
(Den.)
Jan Mayen
(Nor.)

Barrow
Beaufort Sea
Victoria Island
Baffin Island
Baffin Bay
Scoresbysund
Arctic Circle

Point Hope
Inuvik
Coppermine
Davis Str.
Denmark Str.
ICELAND
Faeroes
(Den.)
NORW

Bering Strait
Nome
Fairbanks
Great Bear L.
Godthåb
Tasiilaq
Reykjavik
Bergen

U.S.A.
Anchorage
Mackenzie
Great Slave L.
C A N A D A
Frederikshåb
UNITED KINGDOM
North Sea
Glasgow
Edinburgh

Seward
Whitehorse
Hay River
Churchill
Hudson Bay
Schefferville
Goose Bay
Dublin
REP. OF IRELAND
NETH.
Amst.
London
Brusse

Prince Rupert
Fraser
Edmonton
Saskatoon
Regina
Winnipeg
Fort Rupert
Sept-Iles
Newfoundland
Paris
FRANCE
Bay of Biscay
Be

Vancouver
Victoria
Calgary
L. Superior
Quebec
St John
Halifax
St John's
Bordeaux
SW

Portland
Seattle
Minneapolis
Lake Michigan
Ottawa
Montreal
NORTH ATLANTIC
Oporto
Bilbao
Marseille
Bilbao

UNITED STATES
Omaha
Chicago
Detroit
Toronto
Buffalo
Boston
Madrid
SPAIN
Barcelo

Sacramento
Salt Lake City
Denver
St. Louis
Cincinnati
Pittsb.
New York
Philadelphia
Lisbon
Valencia

San Francisco
Colorado
Oklahoma City
Kansas City
Indian.
Washington
OCEAN
Tangier
Gibraltar
Tur

Los Angeles
Phoenix
OF AMERICA
Memphis
Atlanta
Norfolk
Azores
(Port.)
Casablanca
Rabat
Algiers

San Diego
El Paso
Ft Worth
Houston
Birmingham
Jacksonville
Bermuda
(U.K.)
MOROCCO
TUNIS

NORTH PACIFIC OCEAN

Guadalupe I.
(Mex.)
Torreón
Monterrey
New Orleans
Tampa
Miami
Madeira
(Port.)
Marrakesh
ALGERI

Gulf of Mexico
MEXICO
Tampico
Havana
Nassau
THE BAHAMAS
Canary Is
(Sp.)
Laâyoune

Hawaiian Is
Honolulu
U.S.A.
Hilo
Guadalajara
CUBA
DOMINICAN REP.
San Juan
Western Sahara
Tamanras

Hawaii
Revillagigedo Is.
(Mex)
Mexico City
Veracruz
JAMAICA
HAITI
Puerto Rico (U.S.A.)
ANTIGUA
MAURITANIA
Arli

Acapulco
Puebla
Belmopan
BELIZE
Kingston
Santo Domingo
DOMINICA
CAPE VERDE
Nouakchott
SENEGAL
NIG

Guatemala City
GUAT.
HONDURAS
Caribbean Sea
ST LUCIA
BARBADOS
Dakar
Bamako
Mopti
MALI
Niam

EL SALVADOR
Tegucigalpa
ST VINCENT
GRENADA
TRINIDAD & TOBAGO
THE GAMBIA
BURKINA
Ouagadougou

Clipperton I.
(Fr.)
Managua
NICARAGUA
Barranquilla
Caracas
Port of Spain
GUINEA-BISSAU
Bissau
GUINEA
CÔTE D'IVOIRE
GHANA
BENIN
NIGER

COSTA RICA
San José
PANAMA
Panama City
VENEZUELA
Georgetown
Paramaribo
Fr. Guiana
Conakry
Freetown
Yamoussoukro
Lag

Medellin
Bucaramanga
GUYANA
SUR.
SIERRA LEONE
Monrovia
LIBERIA
Abidjan
Accra
Lome

Cali
Bogotá
Orinoco
Macapá
Librevil
S.T.
Port Ger
GABO

COLOMBIA
Quito
ECUADOR
Guayaquil
Manaus
Amazon
São Luís
Belém
Fernando de Noronha
(Braz.)

Galapagos Is
(Ecuador)
Pôrto Velho
Fortaleza
Equator

Marquesas Is
(Fr.)
PERU
Callao
Lima
Cusco
BRAZIL
São Francisco
Recife

Tuamotu Islands
(Fr.)
Arequipa
La Paz
Brasília
Salvador
St Helena
(U.K.)

Cook Islands
(N.Z.)
Society Islands
(Fr.)
Tahiti
French
BOLIVIA
Sucre
Belo Horizonte
Martin Vaz Is
(Braz.)
SOUTH ATLANTIC

Rarotonga
Iquique
PARAGUAY
Rio de Janeiro
Trindade
(Braz.)

I. Sala y Gómez
(Chile)
San Félix
(Chile)
Antofagasta
Asunción
São Paulo
OCEAN

Pitcairn I.
(U.K.)
Easter I.
(Chile)
Coquimbo
Tucumán
Curitiba
Pôrto Alegre

Valparaíso
Córdoba
URUGUAY

Juan Fernandez Is
(Chile)
Santiago
Rosario
Montevideo
Tristan da Cunha
(U.K.)

SOUTH PACIFIC
Buenos Aires
ARGENTINA

Concepción
Bahía Blanca
Gough I.
(U.K.)

OCEAN
Puerto Montt

Falkland Islands
(U.K.)
Stanley
Shag Rocks
(U.K.)
South Georgia
(U.K.)
Bouvet I.
(Nor.)

Punta Arenas
Ushuaia

Cape Horn
Drake Passage
Scotia Sea
South Sandwich Is
(U.K.)

South Shetland Is
(U.K.)
South Orkney Is
(U.K.)

Antarctic Peninsula

Amundsen Sea
Thurston I.
Bellingshausen Sea
Alexander I.
Weddell Sea
Que
L

Marie Byrd Land
Ellsworth Land

Robinson Projection

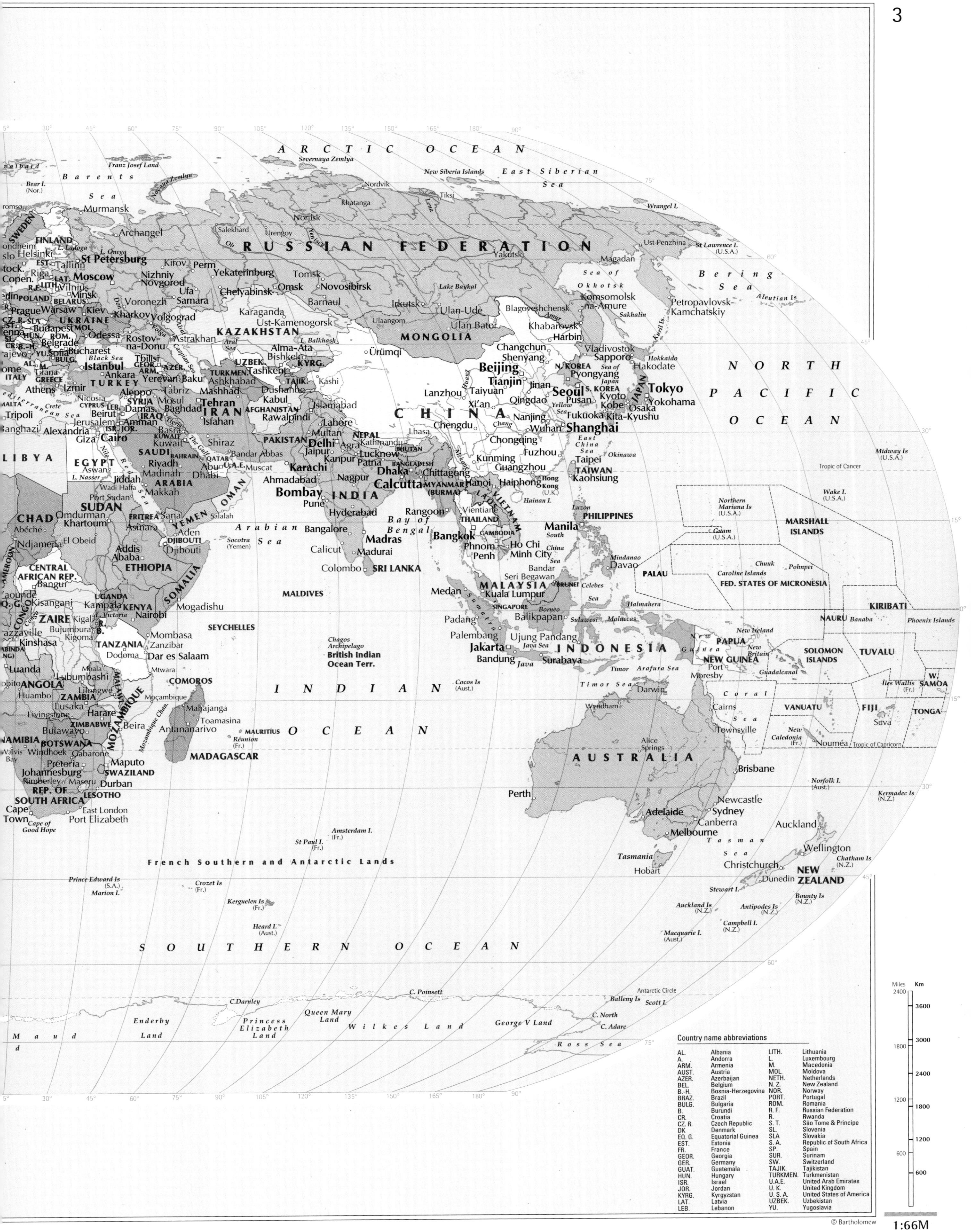

ARCTIC OCEAN

Svalbard
Bear I. (Nor.)
Franz Josef Land
Severnaya Zemlya
New Siberia Islands
East Siberian Sea
Nordvik
Tiksi
Wrangel I.

Barents Sea
Murmansk
Khatanga
Ust-Penzhina
St Lawrence I. (U.S.A.)

SWEDEN
FINLAND
ondheim
oslo Helsinki
stock.
Copen.
L. Ladoga
L. Onega
EST. Tallinn
St Petersburg
Kirov
Perm
Yekaterinburg
Tomsk
Magadan
Sea of Okhotsk
Bering Sea

RUSSIAN FEDERATION

Riga
LAT. LITH.
Vilnius
Moscow
Nizhniy Novgorod
Ufa
Samara
Chelyabinsk
Omsk
Novosibirsk
Yakutsk
Komsomolsk-na-Amure
Petropavlovsk-Kamchatskiy
Aleutian Is

POLAND BELARUS
R.F. Minsk
Voronezh
Volgograd
Barnaul
Irkutsk
Ulan-Ude
Blagoveshchensk
Khabarovsk
Sakhalin

CZ. R. SLA.
Prague Warsaw
UKRAINE
Kharkov
Rostov-na-Donu
KAZAKHSTAN
Karaganda
Ust-Kamenogorsk
Ulaangom
Ulan Bator
Harbin
Kuril Is

HUN. ROM.
Budapest
Kiev
Odessa
Astrakhan
Aral Sea
Alma-Ata
L. Balkhash
MONGOLIA
Changchun
Shenyang
Vladivostok
Hokkaido
Hakodate
NORTH PACIFIC OCEAN

Belgrade
Bucharest
Black Sea
GEOR.
Tbilisi
AZER. ARM.
UZBEK.
Bishkek
KYRG.
Ürümqi
Beijing
N. KOREA
Pyongyang
Sapporo
Japan

Istanbul
Sofia
Ankara
Yerevan
Baku
TURKMEN.
Tashkent
Kashi
Lanzhou
Taiyuan
Tianjin
Jinan
Seoul
S. KOREA
Kyoto
Tokyo
Yokohama

TURKEY
Izmir
Aleppo
SYRIA
Mosul
Tehran
Ashkhabad
Dushanbe
TAJIK.
Xi'an
Qingdao
Pusan
Fukuoka
Kita-Kyushu
Osaka
Kobe

Athens
Nicosia
CYPRUS LEB.
Beirut
Damas.
IRAQ
Baghdad
IRAN
Mashhad
Kabul
AFGHANISTAN
Islamabad
Rawalpindi
Lahore
Chengdu
CHINA
Chang
Wuhan
Shanghai
Yellow Sea
East China Sea
Okinawa

Jerusalem
ISR. JOR.
Amman
Basra
Isfahan
Multan
PAKISTAN
Delhi
Agra
Lucknow
Kanpur
Patna
NEPAL
Kathmandu
BHUTAN
Lhasa
Chongqing
Kunming
Fuzhou
Taipei
TAIWAN

Alexandria
Giza Cairo
KUWAIT
Kuwait
Shiraz
Bandar Abbas
Jaipur
BANGLADESH
Dhaka
Chittagong
Guangzhou
Kaohsiung
Hong Kong (U.K.)

LIBYA
EGYPT
SAUDI
Riyadh
BAHRAIN
QATAR
Abu Dhabi
U.A.E.
Muscat
Karachi
Ahmadabad
Nagpur
Calcutta
MYANMAR (BURMA)
Hanoi
Haiphong
Hainan I.

Tripoli
anghazi
Aswan
L. Nasser
Madinah
ARABIA
OMAN
Bombay
Pune
INDIA
Hyderabad
Rangoon
LAOS
Vientiane
VIETNAM
Tropic of Cancer

Wadi Halfa
Jiddah
Makkah
Bangalore
Madras
Bay of Bengal
Bangkok
THAILAND
CAMBODIA
Manila
PHILIPPINES
Northern Mariana Is (U.S.A.)
Wake I. (U.S.A.)
Midway Is (U.S.A.)

Port Sudan
Omdurman
Khartoum
CHAD
Abéché
YEMEN
Sana
Aden
Salalah
Arabian Sea
Calicut
Madurai
Colombo
SRI LANKA
Phnom Penh
Ho Chi Minh City
South China Sea
Davao
Mindanao
Guam (U.S.A.)
MARSHALL ISLANDS

Ndjamena
El Obeid
SUDAN
ERITREA
Asmara
DJIBOUTI
Djibouti
Socotra (Yemen)
MALDIVES
Medan
MALAYSIA
Kuala Lumpur
Bandar Seri Begawan
BRUNEI
Celebes Sea
PALAU
Caroline Islands
Pohnpei
FED. STATES OF MICRONESIA

CAMEROON
CENTRAL AFRICAN REP.
Bangui
ETHIOPIA
Addis Ababa
SOMALIA
Mogadishu
Padang
SINGAPORE
Borneo
Sulawesi
Moluccas
Chuuk

Yaounde
CONGO
UGANDA
Kampala
KENYA
Nairobi
SEYCHELLES
Chagos Archipelago
British Indian Ocean Terr.
Palembang
Ujung Pandang
Balikpapan
Halmahera
KIRIBATI
Phoenix Islands

ZAIRE
Kisangani
Kigali
R.
B.
Bujumbura
Kigoma
L. Victoria
TANZANIA
Zanzibar
Dodoma
Mombasa
Jakarta
Bandung
Surabaya
INDONESIA
New Guinea
PAPUA NEW GUINEA
NAURU
Banaba

Kinshasa
Luanda
Lubumbashi
Mtwara
Dar es Salaam
Java
Java Sea
Port Moresby
New Ireland
New Britain
SOLOMON ISLANDS
Guadalcanal
TUVALU

ANGOLA
Huambo
ZAMBIA
MALAWI
Lilongwe
INDIAN OCEAN
Cocos Is (Aust.)
Timor
Timor Sea
Arafura Sea
Darwin
New Caledonia (Fr.)
Iles Wallis (Fr.)
W. SAMOA

Livingstone
Lusaka
Harare
Beira
Mahajanga
MAURITIUS
Réunion (Fr.)
Wyndham
New Caledonia
Coral Sea
VANUATU
FIJI
Suva
TONGA

NAMIBIA
BOTSWANA
ZIMBABWE
Bulawayo
MOZAMBIQUE
Moçambique
Antananarivo
Toamasina
Cairns
Townsville
Norfolk I. (Aust.)

Windhoek
Walvis Bay
Gaborone
Maputo
SWAZILAND
MADAGASCAR
Perth
AUSTRALIA
Alice Springs
Brisbane
Kermadec Is (N.Z.)

Pretoria
Johannesburg
Kimberley
Maseru
LESOTHO
Durban
Newcastle
Sydney
Canberra
Auckland

REP. OF SOUTH AFRICA
Cape Town
Cape of Good Hope
East London
Port Elizabeth
Perth
Adelaide
Melbourne
Tasmania
Hobart
Tasman Sea
Christchurch
Wellington
NEW ZEALAND
Dunedin
Chatham Is (N.Z.)
Bounty Is (N.Z.)

Amsterdam I. (Fr.)
St Paul I. (Fr.)
Stewart I.
Antipodes Is (N.Z.)

French Southern and Antarctic Lands
Prince Edward Is (S.A.)
Marion I.
Crozet Is (Fr.)
Kerguelen Is (Fr.)
Auckland Is (N.Z.)
Campbell I. (N.Z.)
Macquarie I. (Aust.)

Heard I. (Aust.)

SOUTHERN OCEAN

Antarctic Circle
C. Darnley
C. Poinsett
Balleny Is
Scott I.

Enderby Land
Princess Elizabeth Land
Queen Mary Land
Wilkes Land
George V Land
C. North
C. Adare

Maud Land
Ross Sea

Country name abbreviations

AL.	Albania	LITH.	Lithuania
A.	Andorra	L.	Luxembourg
ARM.	Armenia	M.	Macedonia
AUST.	Austria	MOL.	Moldova
AZER.	Azerbaijan	NETH.	Netherlands
BEL.	Belgium	N. Z.	New Zealand
B.-H.	Bosnia-Herzegovina	NOR.	Norway
BRAZ.	Brazil	PORT.	Portugal
BULG.	Bulgaria	ROM.	Romania
B.	Burundi	R. F.	Russian Federation
CR.	Croatia	R.	Rwanda
CZ. R.	Czech Republic	S. T.	São Tome & Principe
DK	Denmark	SL.	Slovenia
EQ. G.	Equatorial Guinea	SLA.	Slovakia
EST.	Estonia	S. A.	Republic of South Africa
FR.	France	SP.	Spain
GEOR.	Georgia	SUR.	Surinam
GER.	Germany	SW.	Switzerland
GUAT.	Guatemala	TAJIK.	Tajikistan
HUN.	Hungary	TURKMEN.	Turkmenistan
ISR.	Israel	U.A.E.	United Arab Emirates
JOR.	Jordan	U.K.	United Kingdom
KYRG.	Kyrgyzstan	U.S.A.	United States of America
LAT.	Latvia	UZBEK.	Uzbekistan
LEB.	Lebanon	YU.	Yugoslavia

Miles Km
2400 3600
3000
1800 2400
1200 1800
600 1200
600

© Bartholomew

1:66M

Nanchong
Nanjing
Shanghai
Fukuoka
Kita-Kyushu
Nagasaki
Kyushu
JAPAN
Hachijo-jima (Japan)
Chang
Wuhan
Hangzhou
CHINA
Ningbo
East China Sea
Kagoshima
Changsha
Nanchang
Wenzhou
Tori-shima (Japan)
Amami O-shima
Hengyang
Ryukyu Islands
Ogasawara-shoto (Japan)
Fuzhou
Okinawa (Japan)
Daito-jima (Japan)
Xiamen
Taiwan Strait
Taipei
Kazan-retto (Japan)
Guangzhou
TAIWAN
Macau (Port.)
Hong Kong (U.K.)
Kaohsiung
Batan Is
Luzon Strait
C. Engaño
Wake I. (U.S.A.)
Laoag
Pagan
Northern Mariana Islands (U.S.A.)
Luzon
PHILIPPINES
Saipan
Tinian
Rota
Guam (U.S.A.)
Manila
Quezon City
Naga
MARSHALL ISLANDS
Ratak Chain
South China Sea
Mindoro
Masbate
Samar
Bikini
Panay
Cebu
Leyte
Gaferut
Pikelot
Hall Is
Ralik Chain
Iloilo
Negros
Yap
Palawan
Surigao
Chuuk
Pohnpei
Palikir
Dalap-Uliga-Darrit
Sulu Sea
Dipolog
PALAU
Caroline Islands
Mindanao
Zamboanga
Davao
Nomoi Is
Kosrae
Kota Kinabalu
Sandakan
Sulu Arch.
FED. STATES OF MICRONESIA
MALAYSIA
Talaud Is
BRUNEI
Tarawa
Celebes Sea
Sangir
Nauru
NAURU
Banaba
Nonouti
Beru
Tabiteuea
Nukunau
Manado
Halmahera
Gilbert Islands
Onotoa
Arorae
Molucca Sea
Biak
Admiralty Is
New Hanover
Borneo
Manokwari
Yapen
New Ireland
Jayapura
Wewak
Bismarck Sea
Rabaul
Peleng
Moluccas
Tauu Is
Nukumanu Is
Balikpapan
Palu
Obi
Misoöl
Sula Is
Seram Sea
Bougainville
Ontong Java Atoll
Nanumea
Niutao
Makassar Strait
Sulawesi
Buru
Fakfak
Pk Jaya 5029
Madang
Nanumanga
TUVALU
Nui
Vaitupu
Seram
New Guinea
PAPUA
New Britain
Choiseul
SOLOMON ISLANDS
Nukufetau
Funafuti
Fongafale
Parepare
Kai Is
Wokam
Aru Is
Lae
Banda Sea
Buton
Santa Isabel
Nukulaelae
Banjarmasin
G. of Bone
Kikori
NEW GUINEA
Solomon Sea
New Georgia
Malaita
C. Selatan
Ujung Padang
Trangan
Woodlark I.
Java Sea
INDONESIA
Yamdena
Dolak I.
Duff Is
Damar
Tanimbar Is
G. of Papua
D'Entrecasteaux Is
Guadalcanal
Honiara
Niulakita
Babar
Daru
Port Moresby
Santa Cruz Is
Madura
Flores Sea
Wetar
San Cristobal
Cherry I.
Mitre I.
Surabaya
Alor
Dili
Leti Is
Arafura Sea
Torres Strait
C. York
Rennell
Tikopia
Rotuma
Bali
Sumbawa
Flores
Louisiade Arch.
Lombok
Raba
Endeh
Timor
Banks Is
Sawu Sea
C. Arnhem
Coral Sea Islands Territory
Sumba
Kupang
Melville I.
Espiritu Santo
Ambrym
Vanua Levu
Sawu
Roti
Bathurst I.
Gulf of Carpentaria
Groote Eylandt
Darwin
Malakula
FIJI
Koro
Timor Sea
Katherine
Cooktown
VANUATU
Éfaté
Vila
Viti Levu
Suva
C. Londonderry
Larrimah
Daly Waters
Wellesley Is
Cairns
Great Barrier Reef
Coral Sea
Erromango
Kadavu
Wyndham
Normanton
Tanna
Anatom
Townsville
Loyalty Is
C. Levêque
Derby
Halls Creek
NORTHERN TERRITORY
New Caledonia (Fr.)
Nouméa
Hunter I.
Mount Isa
Cloncurry
Mackay
Île des Pins
Tennant Creek
QUEENSLAND
Broome
Great Dividing Range
Rockhampton
Gladstone
Great Sandy Desert
Longreach
Port Hedland
Alice Springs
Bundaberg
Maryborough
AUSTRALIA
Dampier
Barrow I.
Charleville
Brisbane
Onslow
Toowoomba
Gold Coast
Paraburdoo
Ipswich
Norfolk I. (Aust.)
North West C.
Newman
Cunnamulla
Lismore
Grafton
Oodnadatta
Walgett
Armidale
Carnarvon
WESTERN AUSTRALIA
SOUTH AUSTRALIA
Bourke
Tamworth
Lord Howe I. (Aust.)
Leigh Creek
Darling
NEW SOUTH WALES
Newcastle
Meekatharra
Broken Hill
Dubbo
C. Maria van Diemen
Kaitaia
Mt Magnet
Leonora
Woomera
Orange
Bathurst
Sydney
Great Barrier I.
Whyalla
Port Augusta
Wollongong
Auckland
Hamilton
Geraldton
Kalgoorlie
Ceduna
Port Pirie
Wagga Wagga
A.C.T.
Canberra
Rotorua
Coolgardie
Great Australian Bight
Adelaide
Murray
Albury
North Island
Gisborne
Moora
Merredin
Norseman
Port Lincoln
New Plymouth
Wanganui
Napier
Northam
VICTORIA
Melbourne
TASMAN SEA
Palmerston North
Perth
Esperance
Kangaroo I.
Ballarat
Wellington
Fremantle
Mount Gambier
Geelong
Nelson
Warrnambool
Flinders I.
Blenheim
Bunbury
Bass Strait
Greymouth
King I.
Augusta
Albany
Launceston
Christchurch
C. Leeuwin
TASMANIA
Southern Alps
Hobart
South Island
Timaru
NEW ZEALAND
South East C.
Kingston
Oamaru
Dunedin
West C.
Invercargill
Stewart I.
Bounty I.
Snares Is
Antipodes Is
Auckland Is
Campbell I. (NZ)
Macquarie I. (Aust.)

Metres | Feet
0 | 0
200 | 656
3000 | 9843

Lambert Azimuthal Equal Area Projection

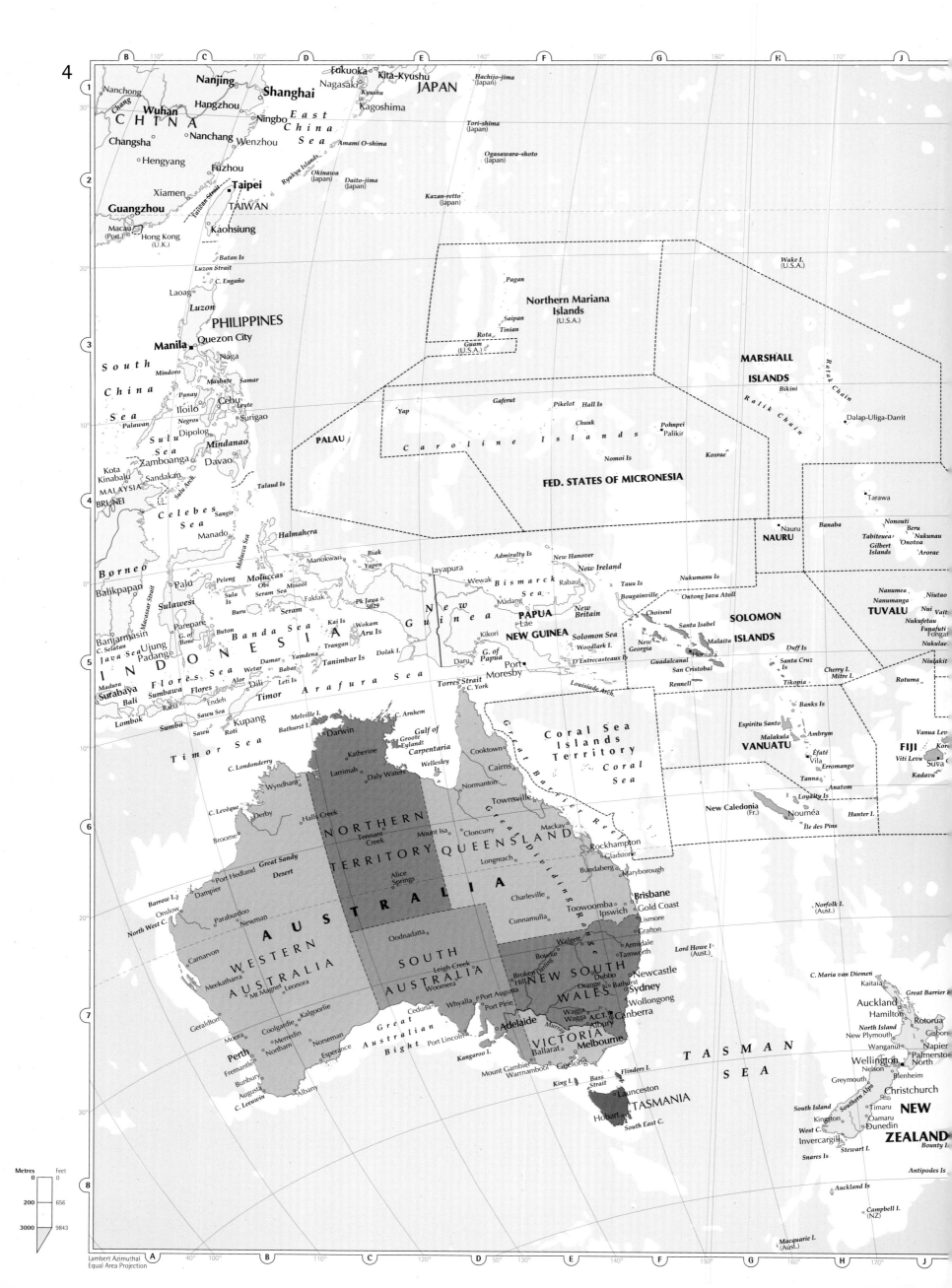

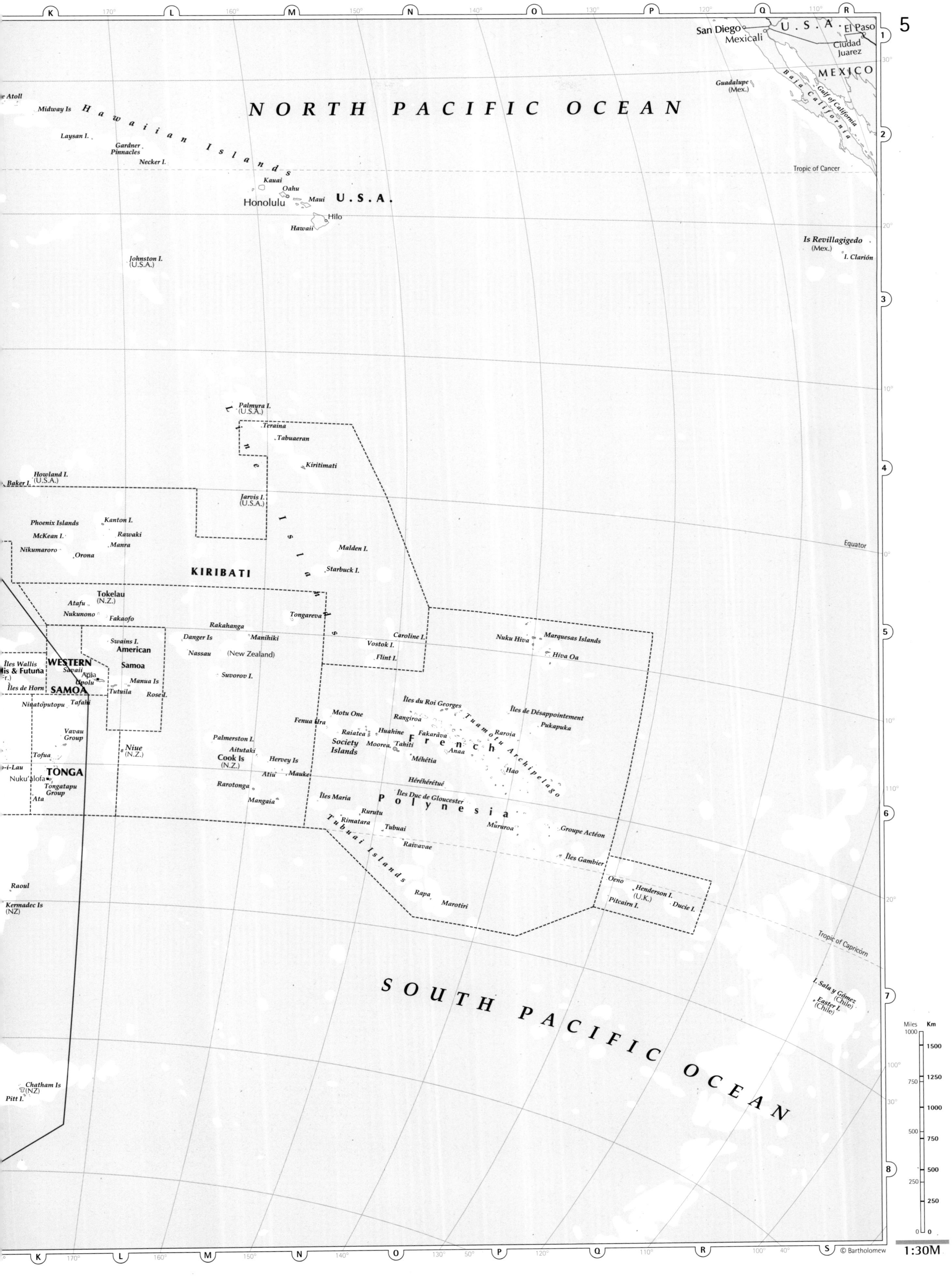

NORTH PACIFIC OCEAN

U.S.A.
San Diego
Mexicali
El Paso
Ciudad Juarez

MEXICO
Baja California
Gulf of California

Guadalupe (Mex.)

Tropic of Cancer

Is Revillagigedo (Mex.)
I. Clarión

e Atoll
Midway Is
Laysan I.
Gardner Pinnacles
Necker I.
Hawaiian Islands

Kauai
Oahu
Honolulu
Maui
Hilo
Hawaii
U.S.A.

Johnston I. (U.S.A.)

Palmyra I. (U.S.A.)
Teraina
Tabuaeran
Kiritimati

The Line Islands

Howland I. (U.S.A.)
Baker I. (U.S.A.)

Jarvis I. (U.S.A.)

Phoenix Islands
Kanton I.
McKean I.
Rawaki
Nikumaroro
Manra
Orona

Malden I.
Starbuck I.

KIRIBATI

Equator

Tokelau (N.Z.)
Atafu
Nukunono
Fakaofo

Rakahanga
Danger Is
Manihiki
Nassau
(New Zealand)
Suvorov I.

Tongareva
Caroline I.
Vostok I.
Flint I.

Nuku Hiva
Marquesas Islands
Hiva Oa

Îles Wallis & Futuna (Fr.)
Îles de Horn

WESTERN
Swains I.
American
Samoa
Savaii
Apia
Upolu
SAMOA
Tutuila
Manua Is
Rose I.

Ninatoputopu
Tafahi

Vavau Group

Tofua
o-i-Lau
Nuku alofa
TONGA
Tongatapu Group
Ata

Niue (N.Z.)

Palmerston I.
Aitutaki
Cook Is (N.Z.)
Atiu
Mauke
Hervey Is

Rarotonga
Mangaia

Îles Maria

Motu One
Femua Ura
Rangiroa
Huahine
Raiatea
Tahiti
Moorea
Society Islands
Mëhëtia

Îles du Roi Georges
Fakaräva
Anaa
French
Hao
Hérëhérëtué
Îles Duc de Gloucester
Polynesia

Îles de Désappointement
Raroia
Pukapuka
Tuamotu Archipelago

Groupe Actéon
Mururoa

Rurutu
Rimatara
Tubuai
Tubuai Islands
Raivavae

Îles Gambier

Rapa
Marotiri

Oeno
Henderson I. (U.K.)
Pitcairn I.
Ducie I.

Raoul

Kermadec Is (NZ)

Tropic of Capricorn

I. Sala y Gómez (Chile)
Easter I. (Chile)

SOUTH PACIFIC OCEAN

Chatham Is (NZ)
Pitt I.

1:30M

Miles / Km
1000 / 1500
750 / 1250 / 1000
500 / 750
250 / 500 / 250
0 / 0

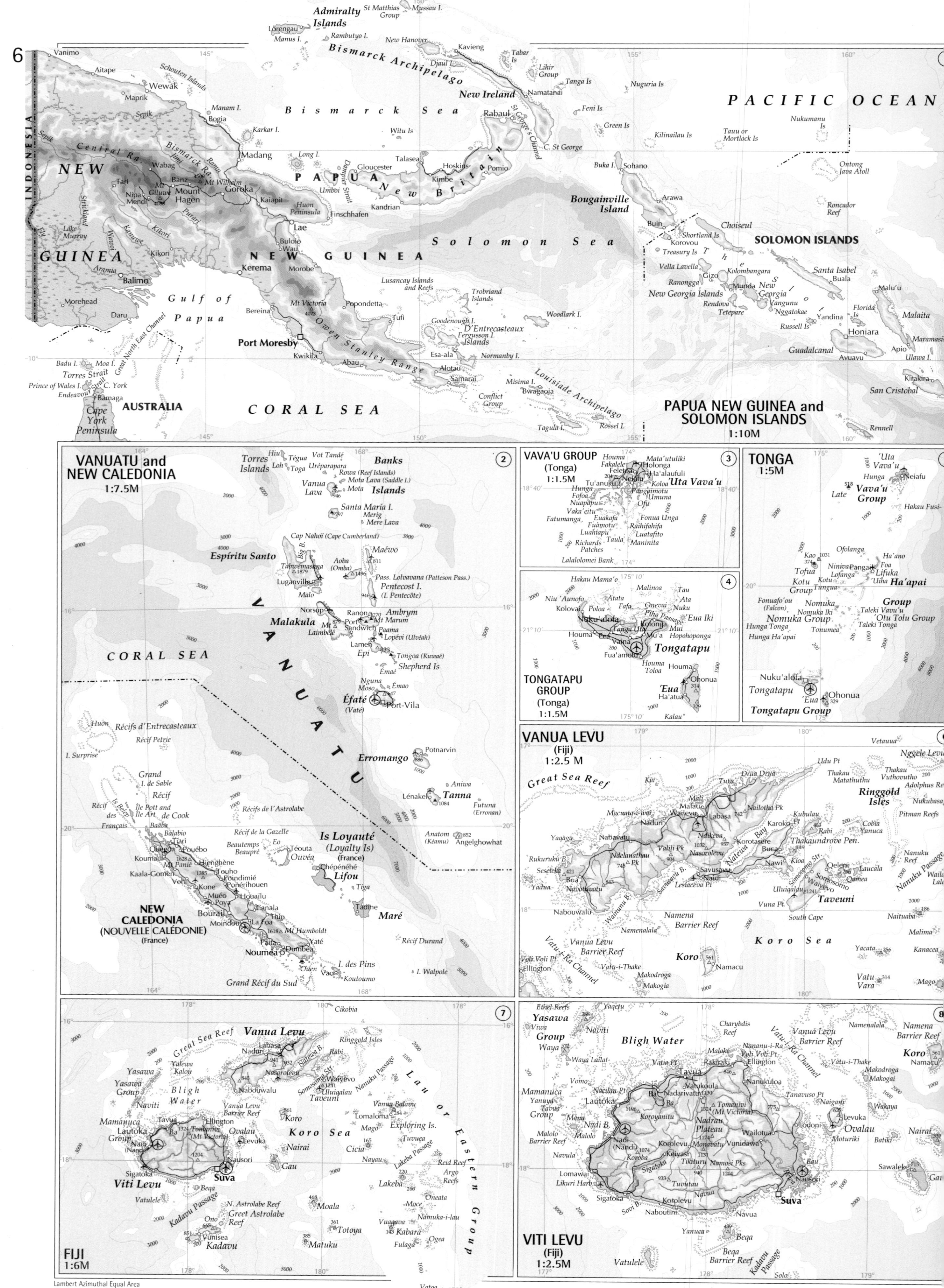
PAPUA NEW GUINEA and SOLOMON ISLANDS
1:10M
PACIFIC OCEAN
Bismarck Sea
Bismarck Archipelago
Admiralty Islands
New Ireland
New Britain
PAPUA NEW GUINEA
Solomon Sea
Bougainville Island
SOLOMON ISLANDS
Gulf of Papua
Port Moresby
Owen Stanley Range
CORAL SEA
AUSTRALIA
Cape York Peninsula
Torres Strait
Louisiade Archipelago
D'Entrecasteaux Islands
New Georgia Islands
Santa Isabel
Malaita
Guadalcanal
Honiara
San Cristobal
Choiseul
INDONESIA
VANUATU and NEW CALEDONIA
1:7.5M
VANUATU
Espíritu Santo
Malakula
Éfaté
Port-Vila
Erromango
Tanna
Banks Islands
Torres Islands
CORAL SEA
Is Loyauté (Loyalty Is) (France)
Lifou
Maré
NEW CALEDONIA (NOUVELLE CALÉDONIE) (France)
Nouméa
Grand Récif du Sud
VAVA'U GROUP (Tonga)
1:1.5M
Uta Vava'u
TONGA
1:5M
Vava'u Group
Ha'apai Group
Nomuka Group
Tongatapu Group
TONGATAPU GROUP (Tonga)
1:1.5M
Tongatapu
Nuku'alofa
'Eua
VANUA LEVU (Fiji)
1:2.5M
Great Sea Reef
Koro Sea
Taveuni
Ringgold Isles
Koro
Namena Barrier Reef
FIJI
1:6M
Vanua Levu
Viti Levu
Suva
Bligh Water
Kadavu
Lau or Eastern Group
VITI LEVU (Fiji)
1:2.5M
Yasawa Group
Lautoka
Nadi
Ovalau
Beqa
Lambert Azimuthal Equal Area

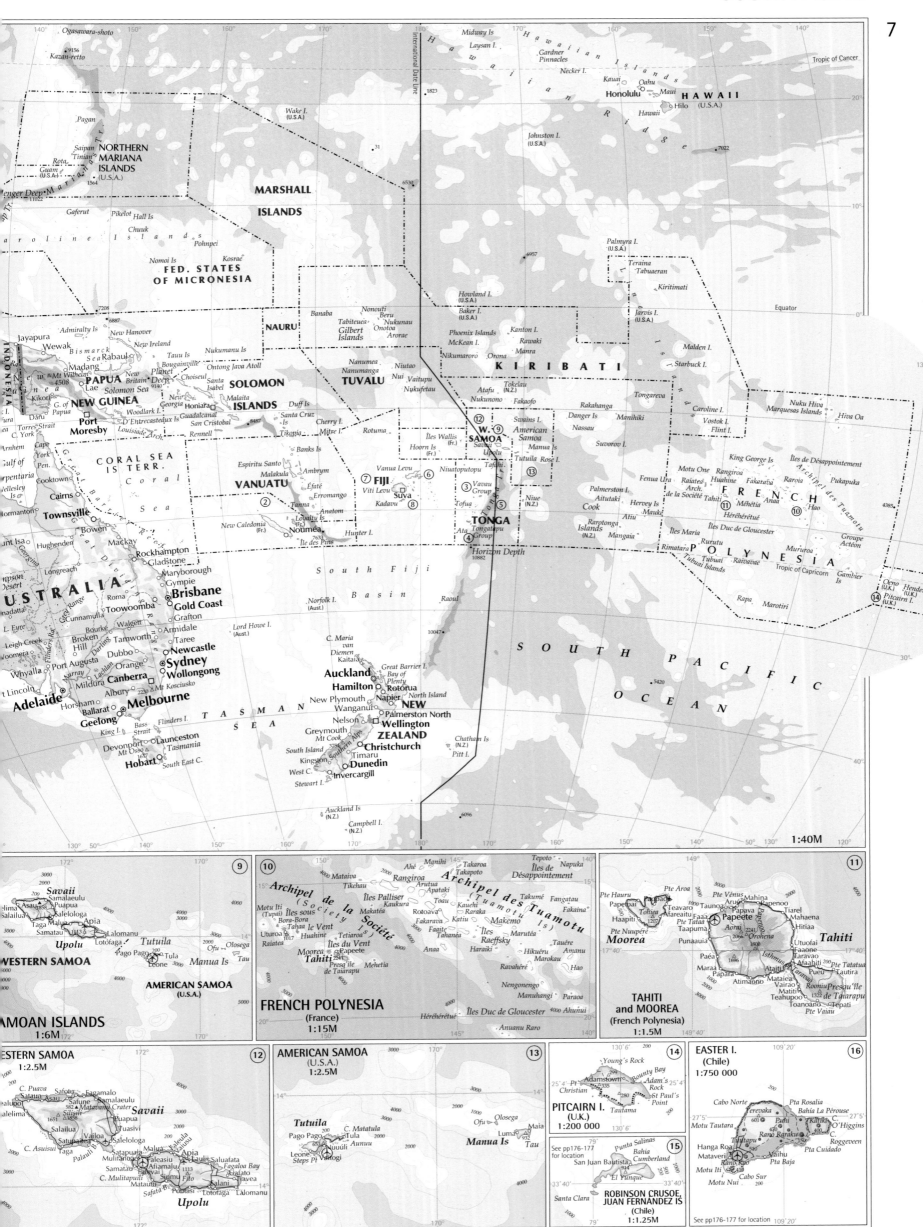

SOUTH PACIFIC OCEAN

1:40M

SAMOAN ISLANDS
1:6M

Savaii · Samalaeulu · Puapua · Asau · Salelologa · Apia
Upolu
Tutuila
Manua Is
WESTERN SAMOA
AMERICAN SAMOA (U.S.A.)

WESTERN SAMOA
1:2.5M
Savaii
Upolu

AMERICAN SAMOA (U.S.A.)
1:2.5M
Tutuila
Pago Pago
Manua Is

FRENCH POLYNESIA
(France)
1:15M
Archipel de la Société
Archipel des Tuamotu
Tahiti
Îles Duc de Gloucester

TAHITI and MOOREA
(French Polynesia)
1:1.5M
Moorea · Papeete · Tahiti

PITCAIRN I.
(U.K.)
1:200 000
Adamstown
See pp176-177 for location

EASTER I.
(Chile)
1:750 000
Hanga Roa · Mataveri

ROBINSON CRUSOE, JUAN FERNANDEZ IS
(Chile)
1:1.25M
San Juan Bautista
See pp176-177 for location

© Bartholomew

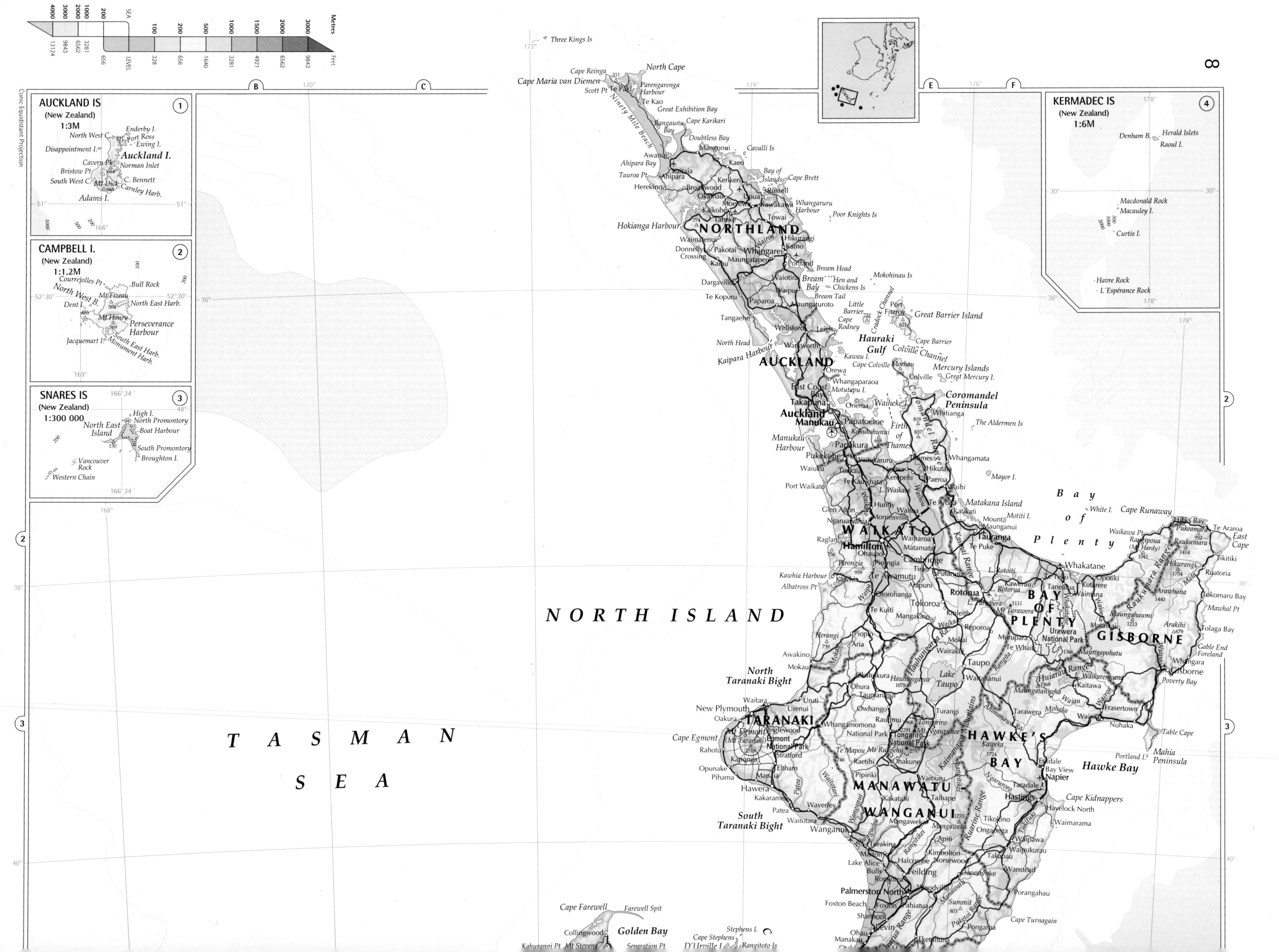

8

KERMADEC IS
(New Zealand)
1:6M

Denham B.
Herald Islets
Raoul I.

Macdonald Rock
Macauley I.
Curtis I.

Havre Rock
L'Esperance Rock

AUCKLAND IS
(New Zealand)
1:3M

Enderby I.
Ewing I.
Port Ross
Auckland I.
North West C.
Norman Inlet
Disappointment I.
Cavern Pk.
C. Bennett
Bristow Pt.
Carnley Harb.
South West C.
Adams I.

CAMPBELL I.
(New Zealand)
1:1.2M

Courrejolles Pt.
Bull Rock
North West B.
Mt Paris
Perseverance
Harbour
Dent I.
North East Harb.
South East Harb.
Jacquemart I.
Monument Harb.

SNARES IS
(New Zealand)
1:300 000

High I.
North Promontory
North East
Island
Boat Harbour
South Promontory
Vancouver
Rock
Broughton I.
Western Chain

Metres | Feet

3000 | 9843
2000 | 6562
1500 | 4921
1000 | 3281
500 | 1640
200 | 656
100 | 328

SEA | LEVEL

200 | 656
1000 | 3281
2000 | 6562
3000 | 9843
4000 | 13124

NORTHLAND

AUCKLAND

WAIKATO

BAY OF PLENTY

GISBORNE

HAWKE'S BAY

TARANAKI

MANAWATU

WANGANUI

NORTH ISLAND

TASMAN SEA

Golden Bay

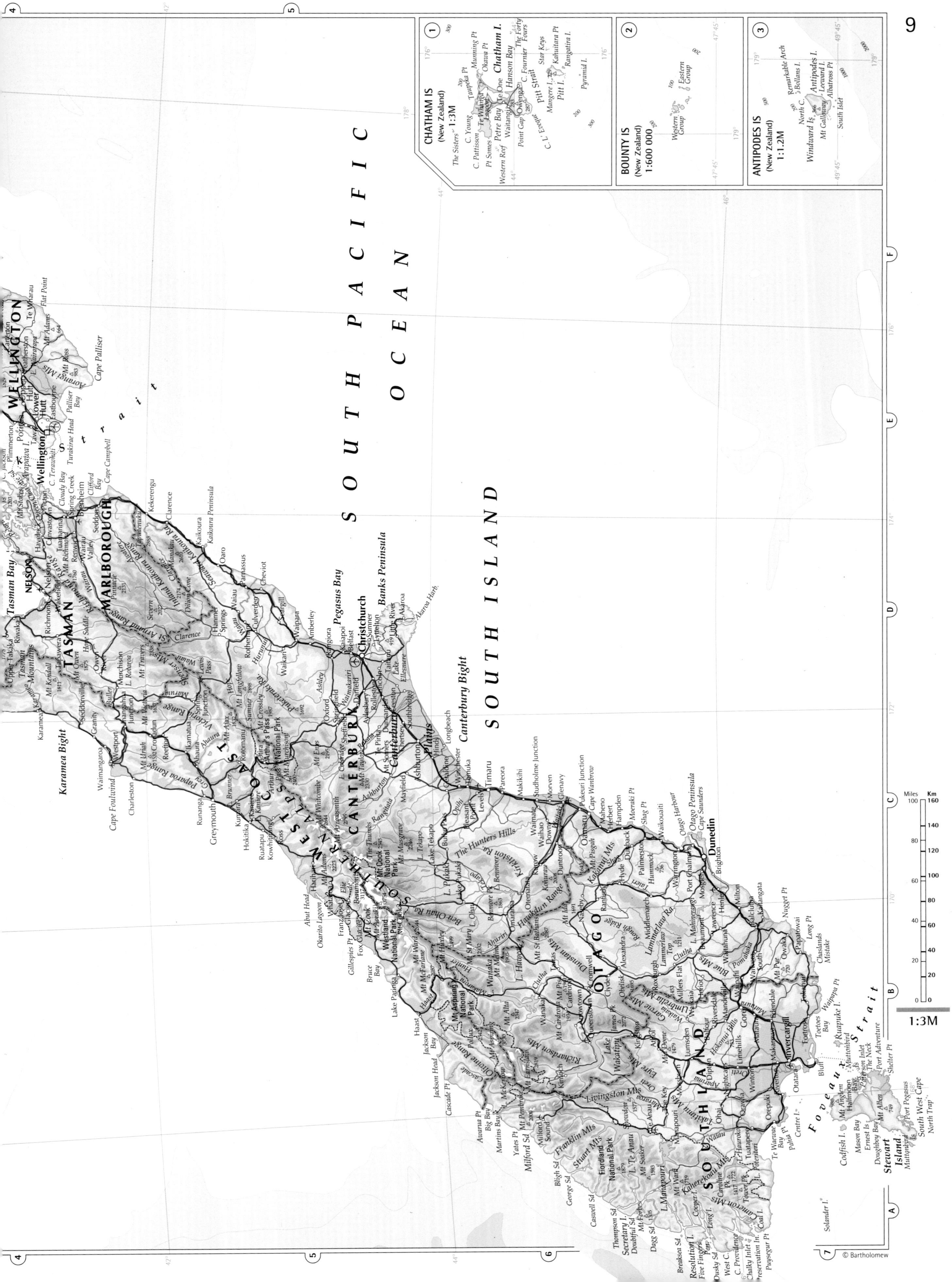

CHATHAM IS
(New Zealand) 1:3M

The Sisters
C. Young
C. Pattisson
Pt Somes
Te Whanga Lagoon
Western Reef
Petre Bay
Waitangi
Point Gap
Owenga
C. L'Eveque
Maunganui Pt
Taupeka Pt
Te One
Kaingaroa
C. Fournier
Mangere I.
Pitt I.
Okawa Pt
Chatham I.
Hanson Bay
The Forty Fours
Star Keys
Pitt Strait
Kahutara Pt
Rangatira I.
Pyramid I.

BOUNTY IS
(New Zealand)
1:600 000

Western Group
Eastern Group

ANTIPODES IS
(New Zealand)
1:1.2M

Remarkable Arch
North C.
Bollans I.
Windward Is.
Mt Galloway
Antipodes I.
Leeward I.
Albatross Pt
South Islet

SOUTH PACIFIC OCEAN

SOUTH ISLAND

WELLINGTON
Wellington
Lower Hutt
Cape Palliser
Cape Campbell

TASMAN
NELSON
MARLBOROUGH
Tasman Bay
Blenheim

WEST COAST
CANTERBURY
SOUTHERN ALPS

Christchurch
Belfast
Pegasus Bay
Banks Peninsula
Akaroa
Canterbury Bight

Greymouth
Hokitika
Westland National Park
Mt Cook National Park

Timaru
The Hunters Hills

OTAGO
Dunedin
Otago Peninsula
Oamaru

SOUTHLAND
Fiordland National Park
Invercargill
Foveaux Strait

Stewart Island

Karamea Bight
Cape Foulwind

Km
Miles
100
80
60
40
20
0
160
140
120
100
80
60
40
20
0

1:3M

© Bartholomew

① COCOS IS.
(Australia)
1:1.2M

N. Keeling I.

Horsburgh I.
(Luar)
Direction I.
Home I.
Bantam
West I.
(Panjang)
Kambling I.
South I.
(Atas)

CHRISTMAS I.
(Australia)
1:1.2M ②

N.W. Point
Flying Fish
Cove
N.E. Point
Headridge
Hill
Low Pt.
Murray Hill △ 357
Jones Pt
Ross
Hill
Phosphate Works
Stubbings Pt
Medwin Pt
2000

INDIAN

OCEAN

INDONESIA
Savu
(Sawu)
Tg Bua
Rote
(Roti)

Timor Sea

Bathurst
Island
Melville
Island
Coburg
Pen.
Croker I.
Arafur
Van Diemen
Gulf
Goulburn Is
Beagle Gulf
Darwin
Jabiru
Rum Jungle
Batchelor
Adelaide River
Arnhem Lan
C. Londonderry
Joseph
Bonaparte
Gulf
Pine
Creek
Katherine
Katherine
Admiralty
Gulf
Wyndham
Ord
Kununurra
Daly
Mataranka
Bonaparte
Archipelago
Drysdale
Lake
Argyle
Victoria
River
Larrimah
Daly Waters
C. Lévêque
Collier
Bay
King
Sound
Derby
Mt Ord △
936
*Kimberley
Plateau*
Ord
Kalkaringi
Lake
Woods
Lombardina
King Leopold Ranges
Halls Creek
Lajamanu
N O R T H E
Broome
Roebuck Bay
Fitzroy
Crossing
Liveringa
Sturt Creek
Gregory
Lake
*Tanami
Desert*
Tennant Creek
Lagrange
Eighty Mile Beach
Sandfire Roadhouse
T E R R I T O
Port Hedland
Goldsworthy
GREAT SANDY DESERT
Lake
Wills
Lake
White
Dampier
Roebourne
Shay Gap
Warrawagine
Barrow C
Karratha
Marble Bar
Lake
Mackay
Yuendumu
Barrow I.
Nullagine
Onslow
Pannawonica
Fortescue
Chichester Range
Mt Liebig △
1524
Alice
Spring
North West C.
Hamersley Range
Lake
Macdonald
Macdonnell Ranges
Exmouth
Tom Price
△1235
Mt Bruce
△1250
Mt Meharry
Newman
Lake
Disappointment
Nanutarra
Roadhouse
Paraburdoo
Ashburton
A
Lake
Hopkins
Lake Neale
Cardabia
Mt Augustus
1106
Gibson Desert
Petermann Ranges
Erlunda
Lake
Macleod
W E S T E R N
Yulara
△862
Ayers Rock (Uluru)
Kulgera
Bernier I.
Gascoyne
Carnarvon
Gascoyne
Junction
Robinson Ranges
Lake Carnegie
Warburton
Musgrave Ranges
Mt Woodroffe △ 1440
Dorre I.
Murchison
Shark Bay
Denham
Everard Range
Marla
Dirk Hartog I.
Overlander
Roadhouse
Wiluna
A U S T R A L I A
Lake Wells
Meekatharra
Albe
Kalbarri
Mount Magnet
Laverton
GREAT VICTORIA
Coober Ped
Northampton
Leonora
Lake
Carey
Lake
Maurice
S o
Houtman
Abrolhos
Lake
Barlee
Lake
Ballard
Kookynie
DESERT
Maralinga
A U S T
Geraldton
Menzies
Lake Marmion
Dongara
Lake
Moore
Nullarbor Plain
Bonnie Rock
Kalgoorlie
Penong
Ceduna
Mooral
Mukinbudin
Coolgardie
Mundrabilla
Eucla
Fowlers
Bay
Streaky Bay
Yanchep
Merredin
Kambalda
Streaky Bay
Northam
Southern Cross
Perth
York
Lake
Cowan
Norseman
Anxious Bay
Fremantle
Rockingham
Mandurah
Hyden
Balladonia
GREAT AUSTRALIAN
Pinjarra
Narrogin
BIGHT
Harvey
Wagin
Ravensthorpe
Bunbury
Collie
Geographe Bay
Donnybrook
Katanning
Jerramungup
Esperance
Busselton
Bridgetown
Kojonup
Hood Pt
*Archipelago of
the Recherche*
Margaret River
Manjimup
Mount Barker
C. Leeuwin
Augusta
Flinders
Bay
Denmark
Albany
Pt d'Entrecasteaux

Metres / Feet scale

Metres	Feet
4000	13124
3000	9843
2000	6562
1000	3281
500	1640
200	656
SEA	LEVEL
200	656
1000	3281
2000	6562
3000	9843
4000	13124
5000	16409
6000	19686

MACQUARIE I.
(Australia)
1:900 000

Hasselborough Bay
Elliot Reef
North Hd
Handspike Pt
Buckles Bay
Anare Station
Langdon Pt
△371
Mt. Elder
Bauer Bay
Prion Lake
Sandy Bay
△341
Sandell Bay
△422
Mt Waite
Victoria Pt
Major Lake
Mt Hamilton
△433
Lusitania
Bay
Mt Fletcher △ 428
Caroline Cove
South West Pt
Hurd Pt
South East Reef

LORD HOWE I. ④
(Australia)
1:900 000

North I.
Sugarloaf
Admiralty Is.
Phillip Pt
Gov. Ho.
Blinkenthorpe B.
Mutton Bird I.
East Pt
Mt Gower △
Lord Howe I.
King Pt
Ball's
Pyramid
Observatory Rock
Wheatsheaf I.
S.E. Rock ⑦

Lambert Azimuthal Equal Area Projection

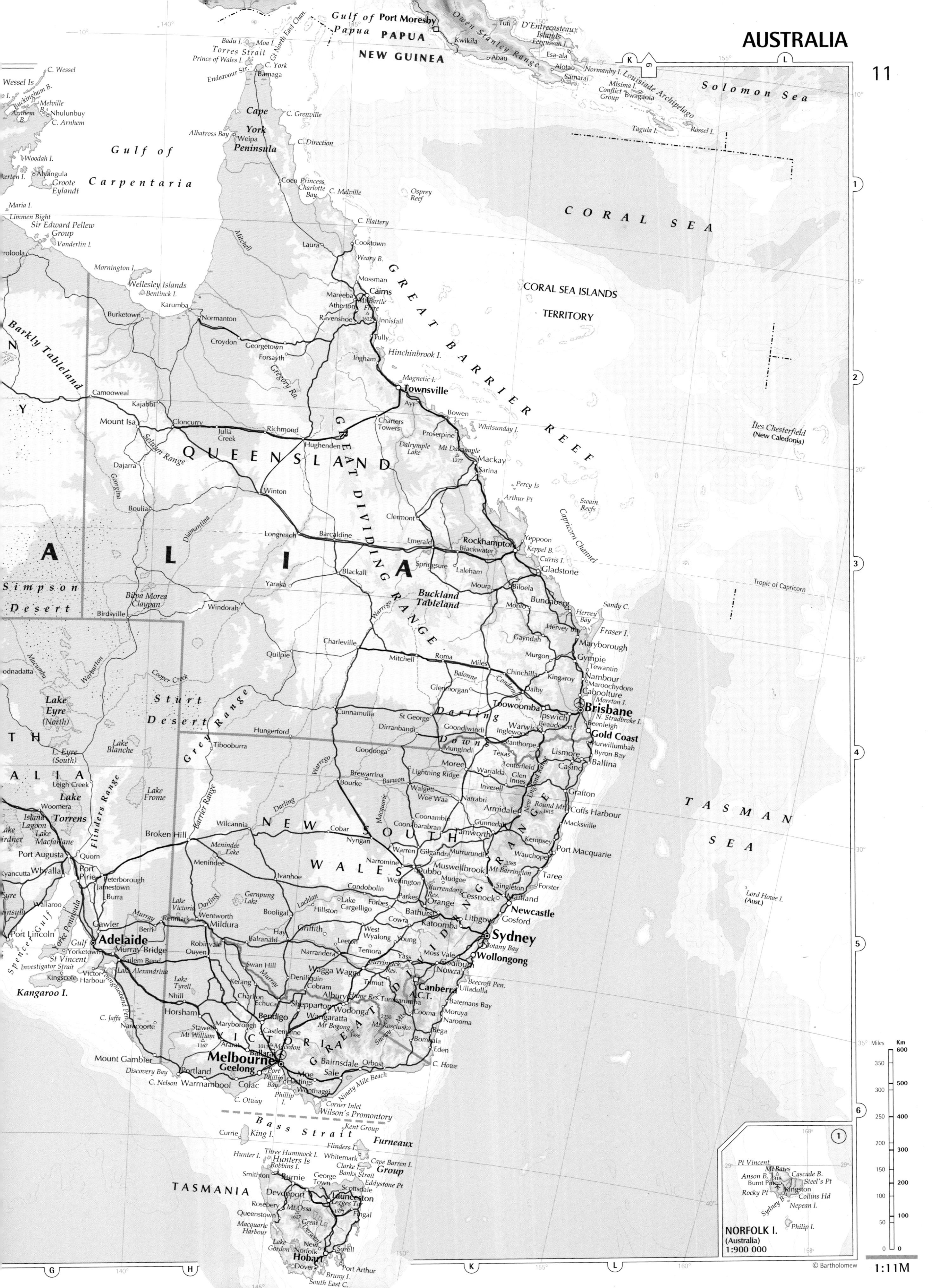
Gulf of Port Moresby
Papua
PAPUA
NEW GUINEA
Port Moresby
Owen Stanley Range
D'Entrecasteaux Islands
Louisiade Archipelago
Solomon Sea
Torres Strait
Cape York Peninsula
Gulf of Carpentaria
CORAL SEA
CORAL SEA ISLANDS TERRITORY
GREAT BARRIER REEF
Îles Chesterfield
(New Caledonia)
Tropic of Capricorn
QUEENSLAND
GREAT DIVIDING RANGE
Cairns
Townsville
Mackay
Rockhampton
Gladstone
Bundaberg
Brisbane
Gold Coast
Toowoomba
Buckland Tableland
Darling Downs
Simpson Desert
Sturt Desert
Lake Eyre (North)
Lake Eyre (South)
Lake Torrens
Lake Frome
Flinders Ranges
NEW SOUTH WALES
Newcastle
Sydney
Wollongong
Canberra
A.C.T.
TASMAN SEA
Lord Howe I.
(Aust.)
Adelaide
Kangaroo I.
VICTORIA
Melbourne
Geelong
Bass Strait
Furneaux Group
TASMANIA
Launceston
Hobart
NORFOLK I.
(Australia)
1:900 000
Miles
Km
© Bartholomew
1:11M

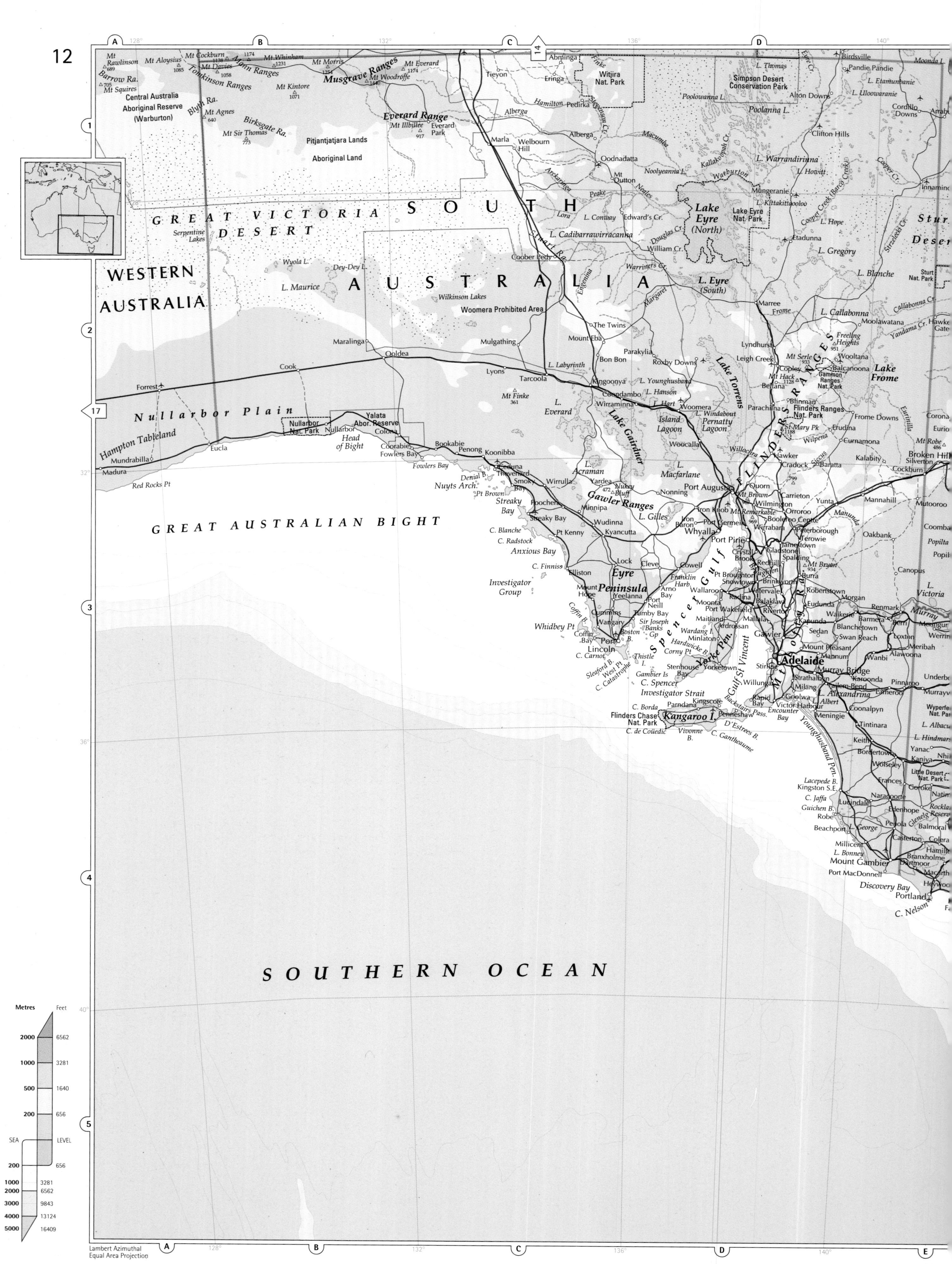
A
B
C
D
E
128°
132°
136°
140°
14
17
1
2
3
4
5
Mt Rawlinson
Mt Aloysius
Mt Cockburn
Mt Davies
Mann Ranges
Mt Whinham
Mt Morris
Mt Everard
Barrow Ra.
Mt Squires
Tomkinson Ranges
Musgrave Ranges
Mt Woodroffe
Mt Kintore
Central Australia Aboriginal Reserve (Warburton)
Blyth Ra.
Mt Agnes
Birksgate Ra.
Mt Sir Thomas
Everard Range
Mt Illbillee
Everard Park
Pitjantjatjara Lands Aboriginal Land
Tieyon
Abminga
Finke
Eringa
Witjira Nat. Park
Hamilton
Pedirka
Alberga
Marla
Welbourn Hill
Oodnadatta
Macumba
Mt Dutton
Arckaringa
Neales
Peake
Noolyeanna L.
L. Thomas
Simpson Desert Conservation Park
Poolowanna L.
Poolanna L.
Alton Downs
Birdsville
Pandie Pandie
L. Etamunbanie
L. Ulloowaranie
Cordillo Downs
Clifton Hills
Kallakoopah Cr.
L. Warrandirinna
L. Howitt
Warburton
Mungeranie
L. Kittakittaooloo
Lake Eyre (North)
Lake Eyre Nat. Park
Cooper Creek (Barco Creek)
Innamincka
Etadunna
L. Hope
L. Gregory
Sturt Desert
L. Blanche
Sturt Nat. Park
Strzelecki Cr.
GREAT VICTORIA DESERT
Serpentine Lakes
SOUTH AUSTRALIA
WESTERN AUSTRALIA
Lora
L. Conway
Edward's Cr.
L. Cadibarrawirracanna
Douglas Cr.
William Cr.
Coober Pedy
Stuart Ra.
Warriners Cr.
L. Eyre (South)
Wyola L.
Dey-Dey L.
L. Maurice
Wilkinson Lakes
Woomera Prohibited Area
Ergenina
Margaret
Marree
Frome
L. Callabonna
Moolawatana
Freeling Heights
Maralinga
Ooldea
Mulgathing
The Twins
Mount Eba
Parakylia
Bon Bon
Roxby Downs
Lyndhurst
Leigh Creek
Mt Serle
Copley
Wooltana
Balcanoona
Gammon Ranges Nat. Park
Lake Frome
Mt Hack
Beltana
Cook
Lyons
Forrest
Tarcoola
L. Labyrinth
Kingoonya
L. Younghusband
L. Hanson
Lake Torrens
Mt Finke
Coondambo
Wirraminna
L. Hart
Woomera
L. Windabout
Pernatty Lagoon
Parachilna
Blinman
Flinders Ranges Nat. Park
Frome Downs
Nullarbor Plain
Yalata Abor. Reserve
Nullarbor Nat. Park
Nullarbor
Colona
Hampton Tableland
Eucla
Mundrabilla
Madura
Head of Bight
Coorabie
Fowlers Bay
Bookabie
Penong
Koonibba
L. Everard
Lake Gairdner
Island Lagoon
Woocalla
St Mary Pk
Wilpena
Edudina
Curnamona
FLINDERS RANGES
Hawker
Cradock
Kalabity
Broken Hill
Silverton
Cockburn
Red Rocks Pt
Denial B.
Ceduna
Thevenard
Smoky Bay
Nuyts Arch.
Pt Brown
Wirrulla
L. Acraman
Yardea
Nukey Bluff
L. Macfarlane
Nonning
Port Augusta
Quorn
Carrieton
Yunta
Mannahill
Mutooroo
Streaky Bay
Poochera
Gawler Ranges
Minnipa
L. Gilles
Iron Knob
Mt Brown
Wilmington
Mt Remarkable
Orroroo
Booleroo Centre
Wirrabara
Peterborough
Terowie
Oakbank
GREAT AUSTRALIAN BIGHT
C. Blanche
C. Radstock
Anxious Bay
Wudinna
Kyancutta
Pt Kenny
Iron Baron
Port Germein
Whyalla
Port Pirie
Crystal Brook
Jamestown
Gladstone
Spalding
Mt Bryan
Burra
C. Finniss
Elliston
Lock
Cleve
Cowell
Franklin Harb.
Redhill
Pt Broughton
Snowtown
Canopus
L. Victoria
Investigator Group
Eyre Peninsula
Mount Hope
Yeelanna
Arno Bay
Port Neill
Wallaroo
Moonta
Kadina
Balaklava
Robertstown
Morgan
Eudunda
Renmark
Murray
Coffin B.
Cummins
Tumby Bay
Sir Joseph Banks Gp
Spencer Gulf
Port Wakefield
Maitland
Ardrossan
Mallala
Riverton
Kapunda
Waikerie
Blanchetown
Barmera
Berri
Loxton
Whidbey Pt
Wangary
Coffin Bay
Port Lincoln
C. Carnot
Boston B.
Wardang I.
Minlaton
Hardwicke B.
Corny Pt
Yorke Pen.
Gulf St Vincent
Gawler
Sedan
Swan Reach
Mount Pleasant
Mannum
Meribah
Alawoona
Wanbi
Thistle I.
Sleaford B.
West Pt
C. Catastrophe
Gambier Is
Stenhouse Bay
Yorketown
Stirling
Adelaide
Murray Bridge
Karoonda
Pinnaroo
C. Spencer
Investigator Strait
Willunga
Strathalbyn
Milang
Tailem Bend
Lameroo
Goolwa
L. Alexandrina
Albert
C. Borda
Parndana
Kingscote
Rapid Bay
Victor Harbour
Encounter Bay
Meningie
Coonalpyn
Flinders Chase Nat. Park
Kangaroo I.
Penneshaw
Backstairs Pass.
C. de Couëdic
Vivonne B.
C. Gantheaume
D'Estrees B.
Tintinara
Youngusband Pen.
Keith
Bordertown
Kaniva
Wolseley
Lacepede B.
Kingston S.E.
Frances
C. Jaffa
Guichen B.
Robe
Lucindale
Naracoorte
Edenhope
Penola
Glenelg R.
Beachport
L. George
Casterton
Millicent
L. Bonney
Mount Gambier
Port MacDonnell
Discovery Bay
Portland
C. Nelson
Dartmoor
SOUTHERN OCEAN
32°
36°
40°
Metres
Feet
2000
6562
1000
3281
500
1640
200
656
SEA
LEVEL
200
656
1000
3281
2000
6562
3000
9843
4000
13124
5000
16409
Lambert Azimuthal Equal Area Projection

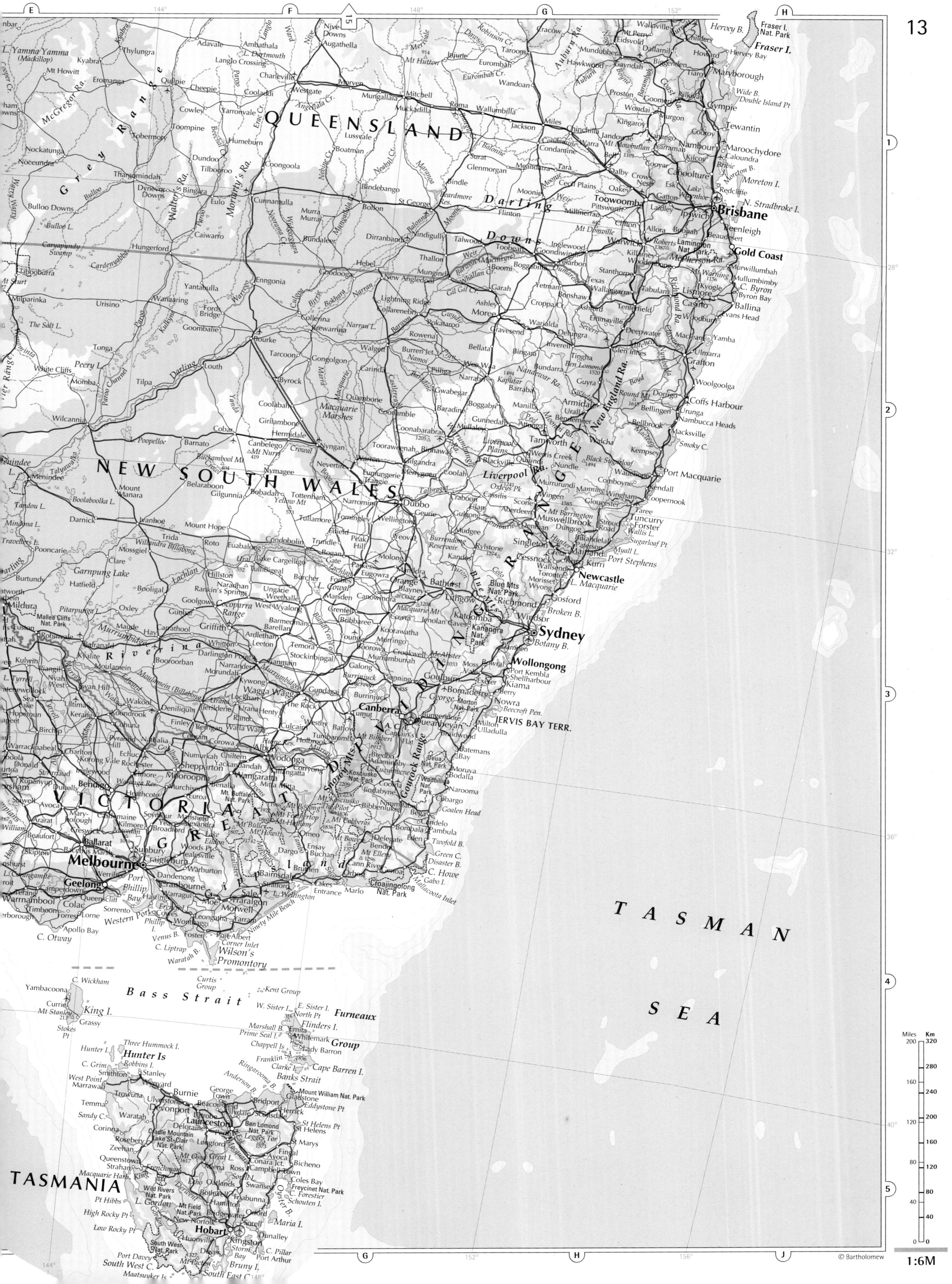

QUEENSLAND

NEW SOUTH WALES

VICTORIA

TASMANIA

Brisbane
Gold Coast
Toowoomba
Ipswich
Maryborough
Gympie
Maroochydore
Caloundra

Newcastle
Sydney
Wollongong
Canberra
A.C.T.

Tamworth
Armidale
Dubbo
Orange
Bathurst
Broken Hill
Bourke
Wagga Wagga
Albury
Wodonga

Melbourne
Geelong
Ballarat
Bendigo

Hobart
Launceston
Devonport
Burnie

Port Macquarie
Coffs Harbour
Grafton
Lismore
Casino
Byron Bay
Ballina

Fraser I.
Hervey Bay

Moreton I.
N. Stradbroke I.

JERVIS BAY TERR.

TASMAN

SEA

Bass Strait

King I.
Furneaux Group
Flinders I.
Cape Barren I.

Wilson's Promontory

Darling
Downs

GREAT DIVIDING RANGE

New England Ra.

Liverpool Ra.

Blue Mts Nat. Park

Snowy Mts

Mt Kosciusko

Miles 200   Km 320

1:6M

© Bartholomew

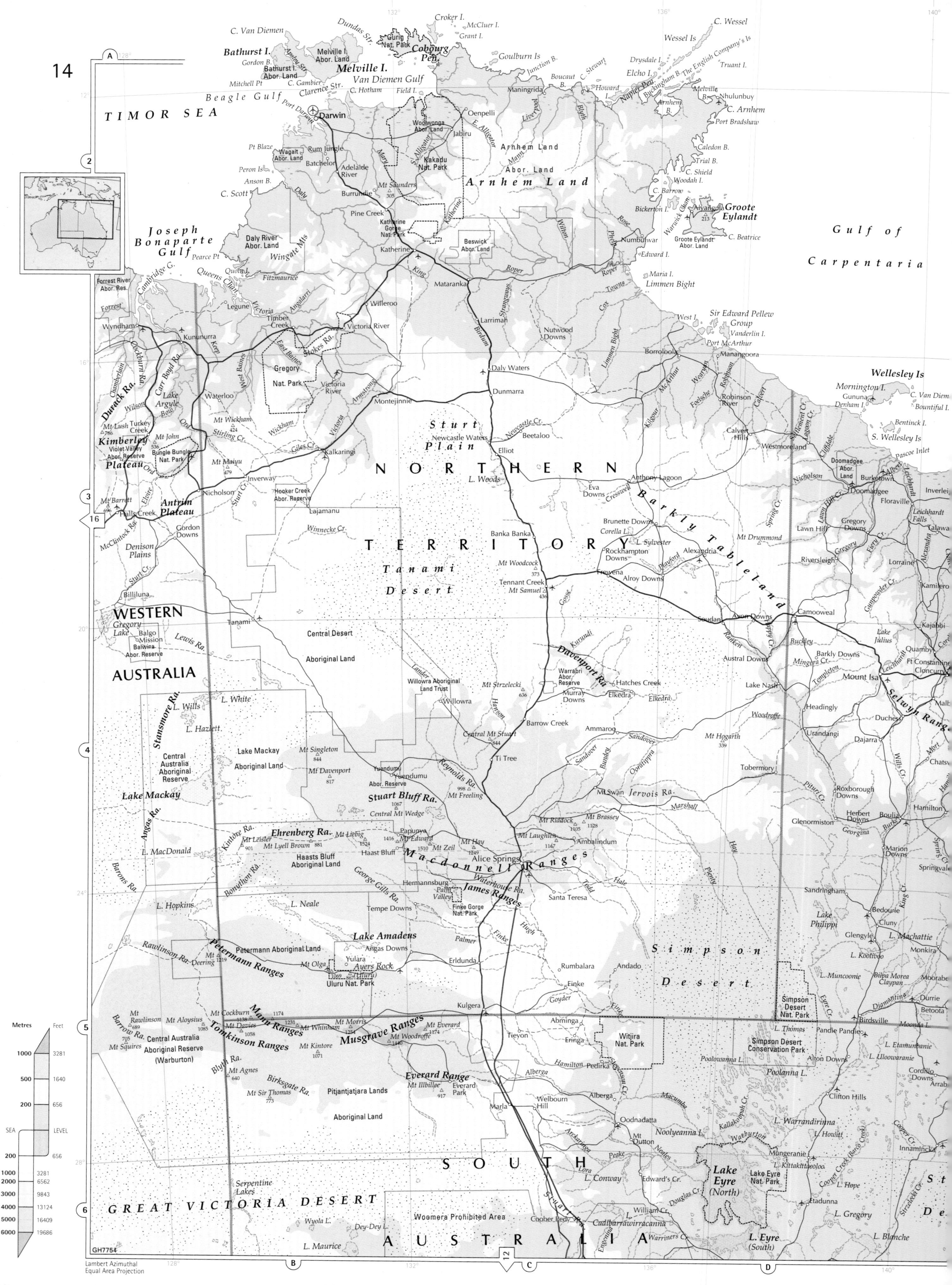
TIMOR SEA
Beagle Gulf
Joseph Bonaparte Gulf
Gulf of Carpentaria
Bathurst I.
Melville I.
Van Diemen Gulf
Cobourg Pen.
Darwin
Arnhem Land
Groote Eylandt
Limmen Bight
Sir Edward Pellew Group
Wellesley Is
Mornington I.
Kakadu Nat. Park
Katherine
Mataranka
Daly Waters
Dunmarra
Borroloola
Victoria River
Timber Creek
Gregory Nat. Park
Kununurra
Wyndham
Durack Ra.
Kimberley Plateau
Bungle Bungle Nat. Park
Halls Creek
Antrim Plateau
Sturt Plain
NORTHERN TERRITORY
Barkly Tableland
Tanami Desert
Tennant Creek
Elliot
Camooweal
Mount Isa
Selwyn Range
Davenport Ra.
Barrow Creek
Central Mt Stuart
Ti Tree
Tanami
Central Desert Aboriginal Land
WESTERN AUSTRALIA
Lake Mackay
Stuart Bluff Ra.
Macdonnell Ranges
Alice Springs
Hermannsburg
James Ranges
Finke Gorge Nat. Park
Lake Amadeus
Petermann Ranges
Ayers Rock
Uluru Nat. Park
Mann Ranges
Musgrave Ranges
Tomkinson Ranges
Everard Range
Kulgera
Simpson Desert
Simpson Desert Nat. Park
Witjira Nat. Park
Simpson Desert Conservation Park
Birdsville
Oodnadatta
Marla
Coober Pedy
Lake Eyre (North)
Lake Eyre Nat. Park
L. Eyre (South)
SOUTH AUSTRALIA
GREAT VICTORIA DESERT
Woomera Prohibited Area
Metres
Feet
SEA LEVEL
GH7754
Lambert Azimuthal Equal Area Projection

CORAL SEA

CORAL SEA ISLANDS
TERRITORY

Cape
York
Peninsula

Great Barrier Reef
Marine Park
(Far North Section)

Great Barrier Reef
Marine Park
(Cairns Section)

GREAT BARRIER REEF

Cairns

Townsville

Q U E E N S L A N D

G R E A T   D I V I D I N G   R A N G E

Great Barrier Reef
Marine Park
(Central Section)

Mackay

Great Barrier Reef
Marine Park
(Capricorn Section)

Rockhampton

Gladstone

Tropic of Capricorn

Bundaberg

Fraser I.

Maryborough

Toowoomba

Brisbane

Gold Coast

Miles 200
Km 320

1:6M

© Bartholomew

TIMOR SEA
INDIAN OCEAN
Joseph Bonaparte Gulf
Bonaparte Archipelago
Buccaneer Archipelago
King Sound
Eighty Mile Beach
GREAT SANDY DESERT
NORTHERN TERRITORY
Tanami Desert
Sturt Plain
Kimberley Plateau
King Leopold Ranges
Durack Range
Princess May Ra.
South Esk Tableland
Antrim Plateau
Percival Lakes
Lake Mackay
Stansmore Ra.
Hamersley Ra.
Chichester Range
Dampier Arch.
Monte Bello Is
Barrow I.
Rowley Shoals
Mermaid Reef
Clerke Reef
Imperieuse Reef
Ashmore Reef
Cartier I.
Hibernia Reef
Scott Reef
Seringapatam Reef
Browse I.
Lynher Reef
Bathurst I.
Melville I.
Cobourg Pen.
Van Diemen Gulf
Beagle Gulf
Darwin
Katherine
Kununurra
Wyndham
Derby
Broome
Roebuck Bay
Port Hedland
Karratha
Roebourne
Dampier
Onslow
Halls Creek
Fitzroy Crossing
Tanami
Lajamanu
Kalkaringi
Victoria River
Lake Argyle
Christmas Creek
Sandfire Roadhouse
Marble Bar
Nullagine
Wittenoom
Metres
Feet
3000
9843
2000
6562
1000
3281
500
1640
200
656
SEA
LEVEL
4000
13124
5000
16409
Lambert Azimuthal Equal Area Projection

WESTERN AUSTRALIA
SOUTH AUSTRALIA
GREAT VICTORIA DESERT
Gibson Desert
Nullarbor Plain
GREAT AUSTRALIAN BIGHT
Hampton Tableland
Archipelago of the Recherche
Perth
Fremantle
Rockingham
Mandurah
Bunbury
Geographe Bay
Busselton
Augusta
C. Leeuwin
Albany
King George Sound
Esperance
Kalgoorlie
Boulder
Coolgardie
Norseman
Southern Cross
Geraldton
Dongara
Kalbarri
Carnarvon
Shark Bay
Geelvink Channel
Houtman Abrolhos
Meekatharra
Wiluna
Leonora
Laverton
Warburton
Eucla
Madura
Balladonia
Forrest
Cook
Ooldea
Maralinga
Nullarbor Nat. Park
Stirling Ra.
Darling Range
Robinson Ranges
Petermann Ranges
Musgrave Ranges
Mann Ranges
Tomkinson Ranges
Lake Amadeus
Ayers Rock
Uluru Nat. Park
L. Carnegie
L. Disappointment
L. Dundas
L. Cowan
L. Lefroy
L. Moore
Lake Macleod
Tropic of Capricorn
Miles
Km
1:6M
© Bartholomew

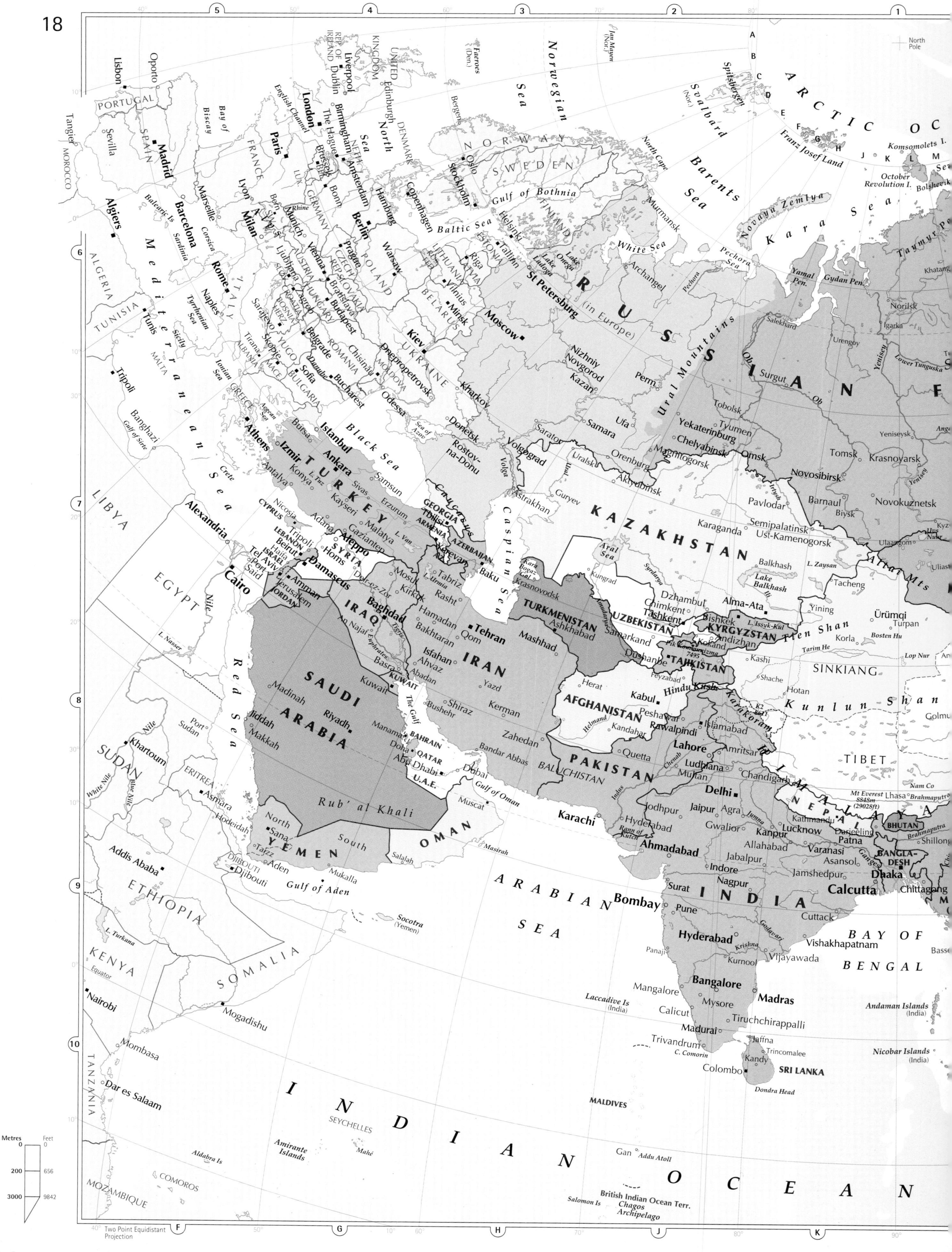

North Pole

ARCTIC OC

A
B
C
D
E
F
G
H
J
K
L
M

Komsomolets I.
October Revolution I.
Bolshevik

Franz Josef Land

Spitsbergen (Nor.)

Svalbard (Nor.)

Jan Mayen (Nor.)

Novaya Zemlya

Kara Sea

Taymyr

Lisboa
Oporto
PORTUGAL
Sevilla
SPAIN
Madrid
Barcelona
Balearic Is
Sardinia
Corsica
Tangier
MOROCCO
Algiers
ALGERIA
Mediterranean Sea
TUNISIA
Tunis
Tripoli
Sicily
Malta
LIBYA

Bay of Biscay
FRANCE
Paris
Lyon
Marseille
Alps
Milan
Rome
ITALY
Naples
Tyrrhenian Sea
Ionian Sea

REP. OF IRELAND
Dublin
Liverpool
Birmingham
London
UNITED KINGDOM
Edinburgh
English Channel
The Hague
Brussels
Amsterdam
NETH.
LUX.
Bonn
GERMANY
Munich
Rhine
Bern
AUSTRIA
Vienna
Zurich
Ljubljana
SWITZ.
SLOVENIA
CROATIA
Zagreb
BOSNIA
Sarajevo
YUGO.
Tirana
ALBANIA
MACE.
Skopje
GREECE
Athens
Aegean Sea
Crete

Faeroes (Den.)

North Cape

Norwegian Sea

NORWAY
Oslo
Bergen
SWEDEN
Stockholm
DENMARK
Copenhagen
Hamburg
Berlin
Prague
CZECH REP.
SLOVAKIA
Bratislava
HUNGARY
Budapest
ROMANIA
Belgrade
Sofia
BULGARIA
Bucharest
Danube
Warsaw
POLAND

North Sea
Baltic Sea
Helsinki
FINLAND
Gulf of Bothnia
Tallinn
ESTONIA
Riga
LATVIA
LITHUANIA
Vilnius
BELARUS
Minsk
Kiev
UKRAINE
Dnepropetrovsk
Chisinau
MOLDOVA
Odessa
Black Sea

Murmansk
White Sea
Archangel
Lake Ladoga
Lake Onega
St Petersburg
RUSSIA (in Europe)
Moscow
Nizhniy Novgorod
Kazan
Perm
Ufa
Samara
Saratov
Volgograd
Volga
Rostov-na-Donu
Donetsk
Kharkov
Sea of Azov

Barents Sea
Pechora Sea
Pechora
Yamal Pen.
Gydan Pen.
Salekhard
Ob
Surgut
Urengoy
Norilsk
Igarka
Yenisey
Lower Tunguska

Ural Mountains
RUSSIAN F
Yekaterinburg
Tyumen
Chelyabinsk
Magnitogorsk
Tobolsk
Omsk
Novosibirsk
Tomsk
Krasnoyarsk
Novokuznetsk
Biysk
Barnaul

Istanbul
Bursa
Ankara
Izmir
Konya
Antalya
TURKEY
Sivas
Kayseri
Erzurum
Malatya
Gaziantep
Adana
Samsun
L. Van
CYPRUS
Nicosia
LEBANON
Beirut
Tripoli
Homs
Aleppo
SYRIA
Damascus
Haifa
Tel Aviv
Jerusalem
ISRAEL
Amman
JORDAN
Port Said

GEORGIA
Tbilisi
ARMENIA
Yerevan
AZERBAIJAN
Baku
Caucasus
Tabriz
L. Urmia
Rasht

Caspian Sea
Astrakhan
Guryev
Uralsk
Aktyubinsk

Aral Sea
KAZAKHSTAN
Karaganda
Semipalatinsk
Ust-Kamenogorsk
Pavlodar
L. Zaysan
Tacheng
Ulaangom
Altai Mts
Uliastay

Alexandria
Cairo
EGYPT
Nile
L. Nasser

Mosul
Kirkuk
Der-ez-Zor
Baghdad
IRAQ
Euphrates
Tigris
An Najaf
Basra
Hamadan
Bakhtaran
Isfahan
Ahvaz
Abadan
KUWAIT
Kuwait
Shiraz
Bushehr
The Gulf
BAHRAIN
Manama
Doha
QATAR
Abu Dhabi
U.A.E.
Dubai
Gulf of Oman
Muscat
OMAN

Tehran
Qom
Mashhad
IRAN
Yazd
Kerman
Zahedan
Bandar Abbas

TURKMENISTAN
Krasnovodsk
Kungrad
Ashkhabad
Kara Bogaz Gol
UZBEKISTAN
Chimkent
Tashkent
Samarkand
Bishkek
KYRGYZSTAN
L. Issyk-Kul
Andizhan
Dushanbe
TAJIKISTAN
Pik Kommunizma 7495
Feyzabad

Syrdarya
Amudarya
Kokand
Yining
Ürümqi
Turpan
Bosten Hu
Korla
Tarim He
Tien Shan
Kashi
Shache
SINKIANG
Lop Nur
Hotan
Kunlun Shan
Golmud

Herat
Kabul
AFGHANISTAN
Hindu Kush
Kandahar
Helmand
Quetta
BALUCHISTAN
Peshawar
Rawalpindi
Islamabad
PAKISTAN
Lahore
Multan
Indus
Karachi

K2
Karakoram
Amritsar
Chandigarh
Ludhiana
HIMALAYA
TIBET
Nam Co
Mt Everest 8848m (29028ft)
Lhasa
Brahmaputra
NEPAL
Kathmandu
Darjeeling
BHUTAN
Shillong

SUDAN
Khartoum
White Nile
Blue Nile
ERITREA
Asmara
ETHIOPIA
Addis Ababa
DJIBOUTI
Djibouti
L. Turkana
KENYA
Equator
Nairobi
Mogadishu
SOMALIA
TANZANIA
Mombasa
Dar es Salaam

SAUDI ARABIA
Madinah
Jiddah
Makkah
Riyadh
Rub' al Khali
Red Sea
North Yemen
Sana
Taizz
Aden
YEMEN
South Yemen
Mukalla
Gulf of Aden
Salalah
Masirah

ARABIAN SEA
Socotra (Yemen)

Delhi
Jodhpur
Jaipur
Agra
Jumna
Gwalior
Kanpur
Lucknow
Allahabad
Varanasi
INDIA
Ahmadabad
Indore
Jabalpur
Nagpur
Surat
Bombay
Pune
Hyderabad
Bangalore
Mysore
Mangalore
Calicut
Madurai
Trivandrum
C. Comorin
Laccadive Is (India)
Krishna
Godavari
Kurnool
Vijayawada
Madras
Tiruchchirappalli
SRI LANKA
Jaffna
Kandy
Colombo
Dondra Head
Trincomalee

Jamshedpur
Asansol
Patna
Ganges
BANGLA-DESH
Dhaka
Calcutta
Chittagong
Cuttack
Vishakhapatnam
BAY OF BENGAL
Andaman Islands (India)
Nicobar Islands (India)

INDIAN OCEAN
MALDIVES
SEYCHELLES
Amirante Islands
Mahé
Aldabra Is
COMOROS
MOZAMBIQUE
Gan
Addu Atoll
British Indian Ocean Terr.
Chagos Archipelago
Salomon Is

Metres / Feet
0 / 0
200 / 656
3000 / 9842

Two Point Equidistant Projection

5   4   3   2   1
6
7
8
9
10
F   G   H   J   K

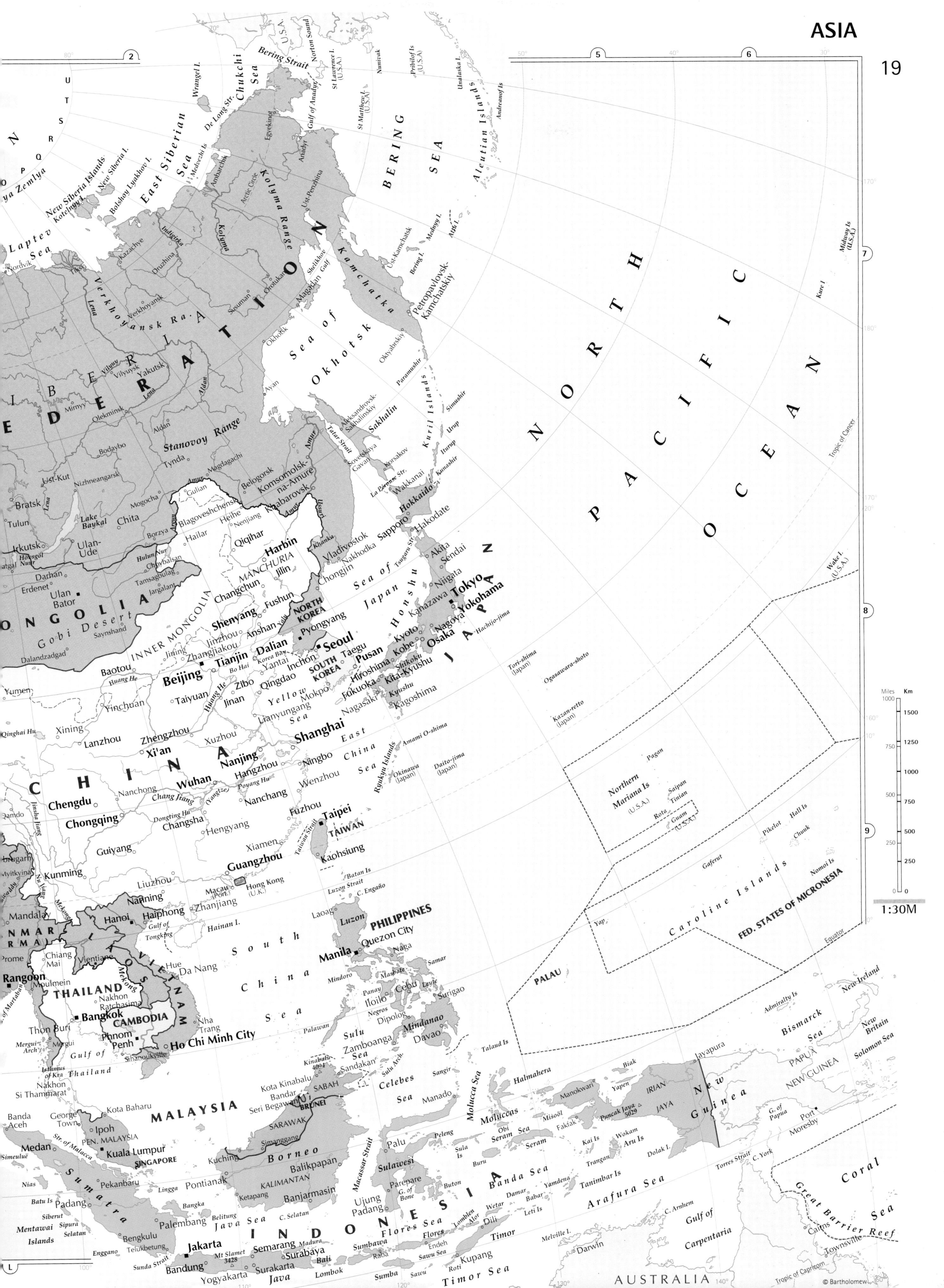

AUSTRALIA

© Bartholomew

1:30M

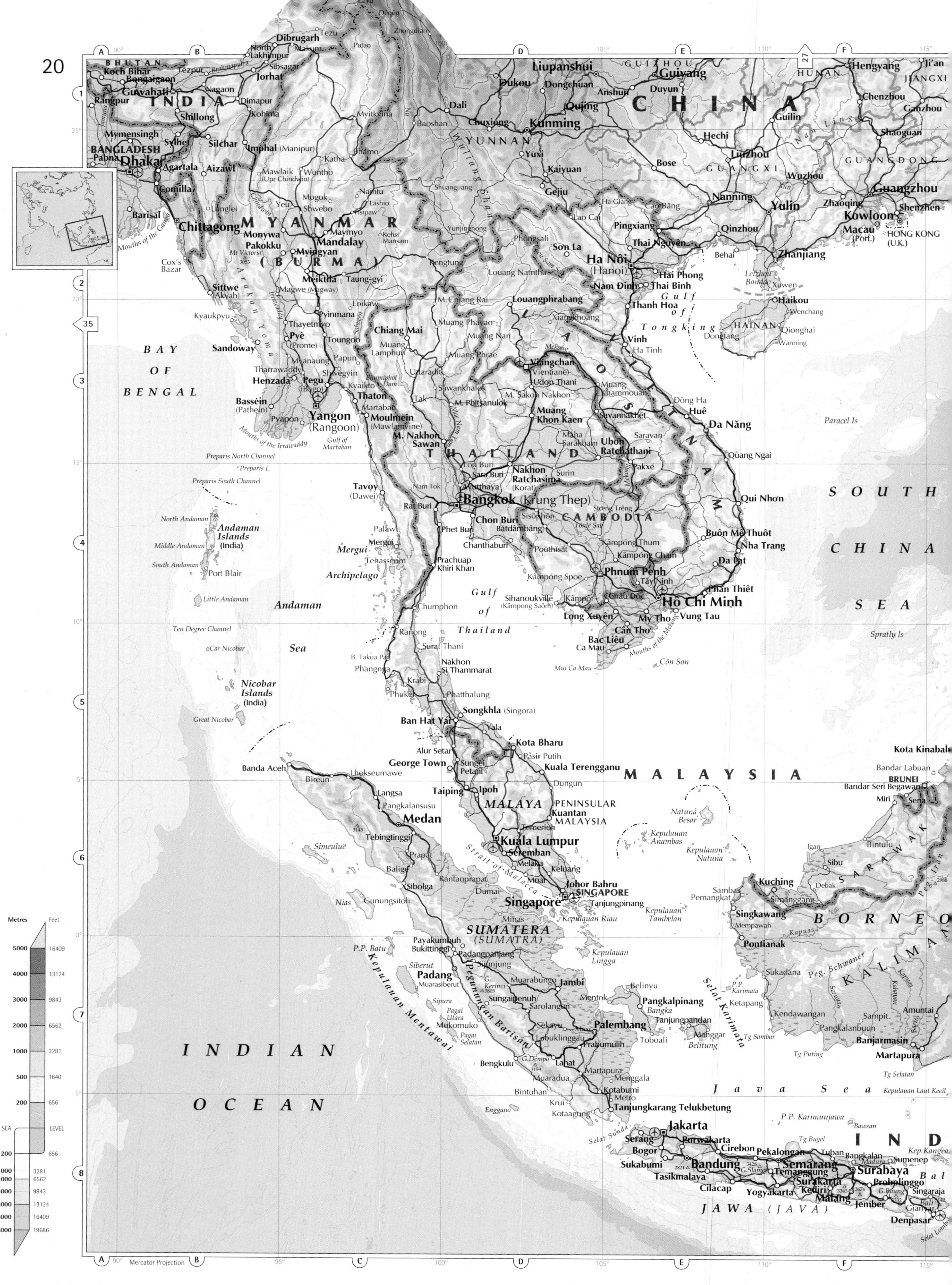

BHUTAN
INDIA
BANGLADESH
Dhaka
Chittagong
Cox's Bazar
MYANMAR (BURMA)
Mandalay
Yangon (Rangoon)
Moulmein (Mawlamyine)
Sittwe (Akyab)
Pyè (Prome)
Pegu (Bago)
Bassein (Pathein)
Tavoy (Dawei)
CHINA
Kunming
YUNNAN
Guiyang
GUIZHOU
HUNAN
JIANGXI
GUANGXI
GUANGDONG
Nanning
Guangzhou
Kowloon
Macau (Port.)
HONG KONG (U.K.)
Zhanjiang
Haikou
HAINAN
LAOS
Vientiane
Louangphrabang
VIETNAM
Ha Nôi (Hanoi)
Hai Phong
Huê
Đa Năng
Qui Nhơn
Nha Trang
Hô Chi Minh
THAILAND
Bangkok (Krung Thep)
Chiang Mai
CAMBODIA
Phnum Penh
Gulf of Tongking
Gulf of Thailand
BAY OF BENGAL
Andaman Sea
Andaman Islands (India)
Nicobar Islands (India)
Mergui Archipelago
SOUTH CHINA SEA
Paracel Is
Spratly Is
MALAYSIA
MALAYA
PENINSULAR MALAYSIA
Kuala Lumpur
George Town
Ipoh
Kota Bharu
Kuala Terengganu
Kuantan
Johor Bahru
Singapore
SINGAPORE
Strait of Malacca
SUMATERA (SUMATRA)
Medan
Banda Aceh
Padang
Palembang
Jambi
Bengkulu
Tanjungkarang Telukbetung
Kepulauan Mentawai
Pegunungan Barisan
INDIAN OCEAN
BRUNEI
Bandar Seri Begawan
Kota Kinabalu
SARAWAK
Kuching
BORNEO
KALIMANTAN
Pontianak
Banjarmasin
Selat Karimata
Java Sea
JAWA (JAVA)
Jakarta
Bandung
Semarang
Surabaya
Yogyakarta
Malang
Denpasar
Bali
Selat Sunda
Metres
Feet
5000
4000
3000
2000
1000
500
200
SEA
LEVEL
16409
13124
9843
6562
3281
1640
656
19686
6000
Mercator Projection

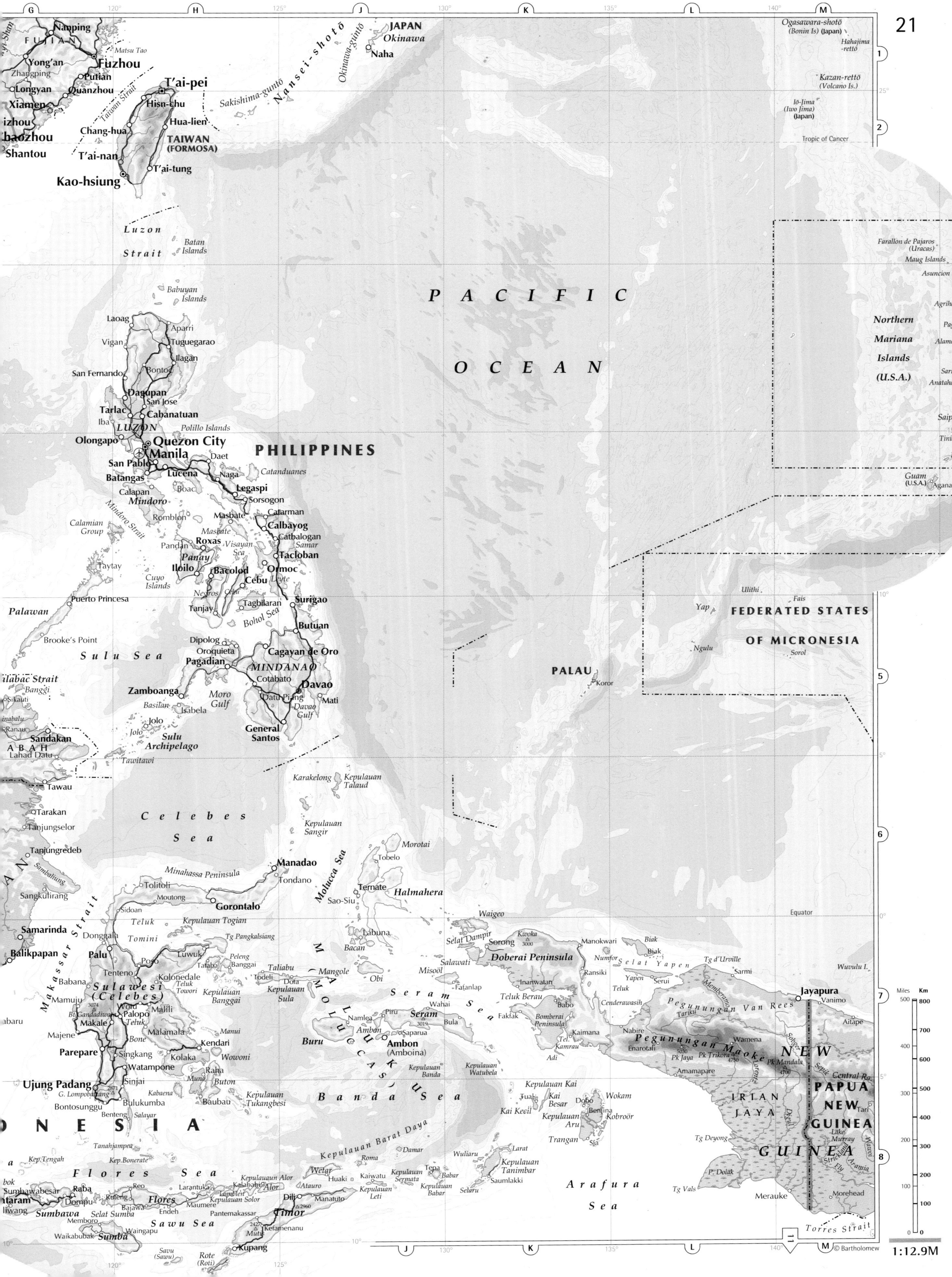

G | 120° | H | 125° | J | 130° | K | 135° | L | 140° | M

FUJIAN
Namping
Yong'an
Zhangping
Longyan
Putian
Fuzhou
Quanzhou
Xiamen
izhou
baozhou
Shantou

Matsu Tao

T'ai-pei
Hisn-chu
Hua-lien
Chang-hua
TAIWAN
(FORMOSA)
T'ai-nan
T'ai-tung
Kao-hsiung

Taiwan Strait

Sakishima-guntō
Nansei-shotō
Okinawa-guntō

JAPAN
Okinawa
Naha

*Ogasawara-shotō
(Bonin Is) (Japan)*
Hahajima-rettō

*Kazan-rettō
(Volcano Is.)*

*Iō-Jima
(Iwo Jima)
(Japan)*

Tropic of Cancer

1

25°

2

*Luzon
Strait*

*Batan
Islands*

*Babuyan
Islands*

Laoag
Vigan
San Fernando
Dagupan
Tarlac
Iba
LUZON
Olongapo
Quezon City
Manila
San Pablo
Batangas
Lucena
Calapan
Mindoro

Aparri
Tuguegarao
Ilagan
Bontoc
San Jose
Cabanatuan

Polillo Islands

Daet
Naga
Boac

PHILIPPINES

Catanduanes

Legaspi
Sorsogon
Catarman
Calbayog
Catbalogan
Samar
Tacloban

Romblon
Masbate
Masbate
Roxas
Pandan
Panay
Iloilo
*Visayan
Sea*
Leyte
Ormoc
Cebu
Bacolod
Cebu

*Calamian
Group*
Mindoro Strait

Taytay

*Cuyo
Islands*
Tanjay
Tagbilaran
Bohol Sea
Surigao
Butuan

P A C I F I C

O C E A N

Palawan

Puerto Princesa

Brooke's Point

Sulu Sea

Dipolog
Oroquieta
Pagadian
Cagayan de Oro
MINDANAO
Cotabato
Davao
*Davao
Gulf*
Mati

Zamboanga
*Moro
Gulf*
Dato Piang
*Davao
Gulf*

Basilan
Isabela
Jolo
Jolo
**General
Santos**

*Sulu
Archipelago*

*Northern
Mariana
Islands
(U.S.A.)*

*Farallon de Pajaros
(Uracas)*
Maug Islands
Asuncion
Agrihan
Pagan
Alamagan
Sarigan
Anatahan
Saipan
Tinian
Rota

*Guam
(U.S.A.)* Agana

20°

15°

3

4

Ulithi
Fais
Yap
Yap
Ngulu
Ngulu
Sorol

FEDERATED STATES

OF MICRONESIA

PALAU
Koror

10°

5

ilabac Strait
Banggi
Sikauti
inabalu
Ranau
ABAH
Sandakan
Lahad Datu

Tawitawi

Tawau

Tarakan

Tanjungselor

Tanjungredeb

*Celebes
Sea*

Karakelong
*Kepulauan
Talaud*

5°

6

AN

Sangkulirang

Simbaliung

Samarinda

Balikpapan

Makassar Strait

Donggala
Palu

Babana
Gandadiwata
*Sulawesi
(Celebes)*
Mamuju
Makale
Majene
Parepare

Ujung Padang

G. Lompobatang

Bontosunggu

Bulukumba

Benteng
Salayar

NESIA

Kep. Tengah

Flores Sea

Tanahjampea

Kep. Bonerate

Kepulauan Sangir

Manadao
Tondano
Tolitoli
Moutong
Sidoan
Gorontalo

Minahassa Peninsula

*Molucca
Sea*

Tobelo
Morotai

Halmahera

Ternate
Sao-Siu

*Teluk
Tomini*
Kepulauan Togian
Tg Pangkalsiang
Luwuk
Poso
Tenteno
Kolonedale
Tataba
Peleng
*Kepulauan
Banggai*
Teluk
Towori
Todeli
Dora
*Kepulauan
Sula*
Mangole
Obi
Obi

Malili
Wotu
Palopo
Teluk
Malamala
Bone
Kendari

Singkang
Watampone
Sinjai
Kolaka
Raha
Wowoni
Buton
Kabaena
*Kepulauan
Tukangbesi*

Baubau
Buru

Banda Sea

Waigeo

Selat Dampir
Sorong

Bacan
Labuna

*Seram
Sea*

Taliabu
Manui

Muna

M O L U C C A S

Mangole

Salawati
Misool

Fatanlan
Piru
Seram
Ambon
(Amboina)
Namlea
Wahai
Bula
Saparua

*Kepulauan
Banda*

Kepulauan Kai

Kwoka
3000
Manokwari
Numfor
Biak
Biak
Ransiki
Yapen

Doberai Peninsula
Inanwatan

Teluk Berau
Babo
Faklak
Bomberai
Peninsula
Kaimana

Tel.
Kamrau
Adi

Namatota
Kobroör
*Kepulauan
Aru*
*Kai
Besar*
Bengina

*Kepulauan
Watubela*
Kai Keeil

Wokam

Equator

Selat Yapen
Serui
Cenderawasih
Nabire
Enarotali

Tg d'Urville
Sarmi

Pegunungan Van Rees

Pegunungan Maoke
Pk Jaya
Pk Trikora
Wamena

Amamapare

*New
Guinea*

Jayapura
Vanimo

Wuvulu I.

Aitape

**PAPUA
NEW
GUINEA**

**IRIAN
JAYA**

Central Ra.
Pk Mandala
Tari

*Lake
Murray*

G U I N E A

*Arafura
Sea*

Merauke

Morehead

Torres Strait

7

0°

8

5°

Trangan
Sia

*Kepulauan
Tanimbar*
Larat
Wuliaru
Tepa
*Kepulauan
Sermata*
*Kepulauan
Babar*
Saumlakki

Damar
Roma
Wetar
Huaki
Kaiwatu
Kisar
Atauro
Dili
Timor
Manatuto

Kepulauan Barat Daya
Kepulauan Alor
Pantar
Alor
Larantuka
Maumere
Pantemakassar
Kefamenanu

Mutis
*Savu
(Sawu)*
Rote (Roti)
Kupang

Flores Sea

Raba
Reo
Ruteng
Flores
Endeh

Dompu

Bajawa
Sawu Sea

bok
Sumbawabesar
Sumbawa
Membora
Selat Sumba
Waikabubak
Sumba
Waingapu

Mataram
liwang

© Bartholomew

1:12.9M

Miles Km
500 800
700
400 600
300 500
400
200 300
100 200
100
0 0

Miles Km

1:6M

Metres Feet

3000 9843
2000 6562
1000 3281
500 1640
200 656
SEA LEVEL
200 656
1000 3281
2000 6562
3000 9843
4000 13124
5000 16409
6000 19686

Mercator Projection

© Bartholomew

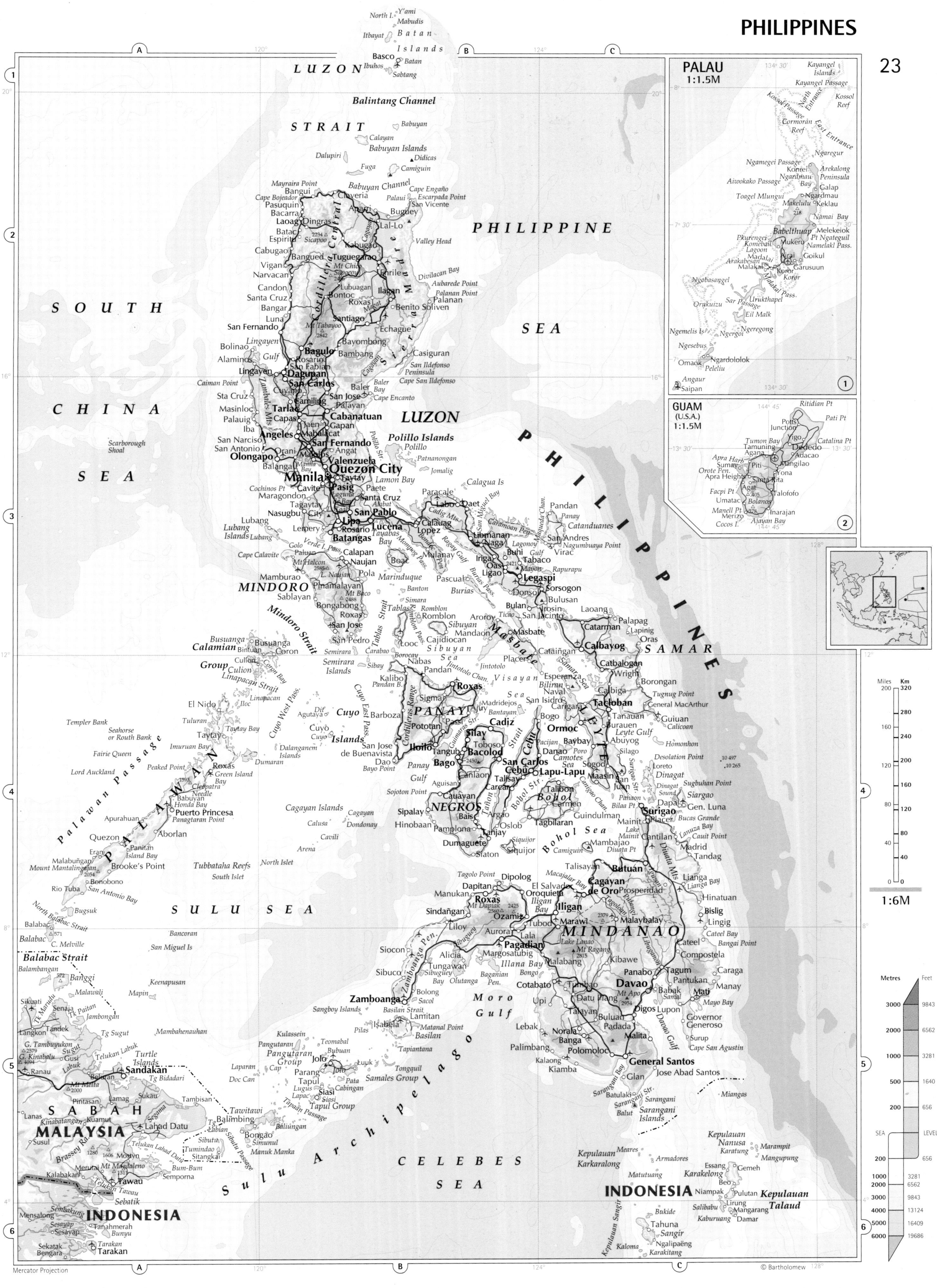

PALAU
1:1.5M

GUAM
(U.S.A.)
1:1.5M

LUZON STRAIT

South China Sea

PHILIPPINE SEA

PHILIPPINES

LUZON

Cordillera Central

Sierra Madre

Manila
Quezon City
Pasig
Valenzuela
Cavite
San Fernando
Angeles
Olongapo
Tarlac
Cabanatuan
Dagupan
San Carlos
Baguio
Laoag
Vigan
Tuguegarao
Ilagan

MINDORO

Calapan
Batangas
Lipa
San Pablo
Lucena
Naga
Legaspi
Sorsogon

PANAY

Roxas
Iloilo
Bacolod
Silay
Cadiz
Bago

NEGROS

Dumaguete
Bais

CEBU
Cebu
Lapu-Lapu
San Carlos

BOHOL
Tagbilaran

SAMAR

Calbayog
Catbalogan
Tacloban
Ormoc

LEYTE

MINDANAO

Cagayan de Oro
Iligan
Ozamiz
Dipolog
Pagadian
Zamboanga
Butuan
Surigao
Davao
Digos
General Santos

Sulu Archipelago

SULU SEA

CELEBES SEA

MALAYSIA
SABAH
Sandakan
Tawau

INDONESIA

Tarakan

Mt Apo 2954

Lake Lanao

Mt Ragang 2815

Palawan Passage

PALAWAN

Puerto Princesa

Calamian Group

Cuyo Islands

Miles / Km
200 / 320

1:6M

1:6,000,000

Metres / Feet
3000 / 9843
2000 / 6562
1000 / 3281
500 / 1640
200 / 656
SEA / LEVEL
200 / 656
1000 / 3281
2000 / 6562
3000 / 9843
4000 / 13124
5000 / 16409
6000 / 19686

Mercator Projection

© Bartholomew

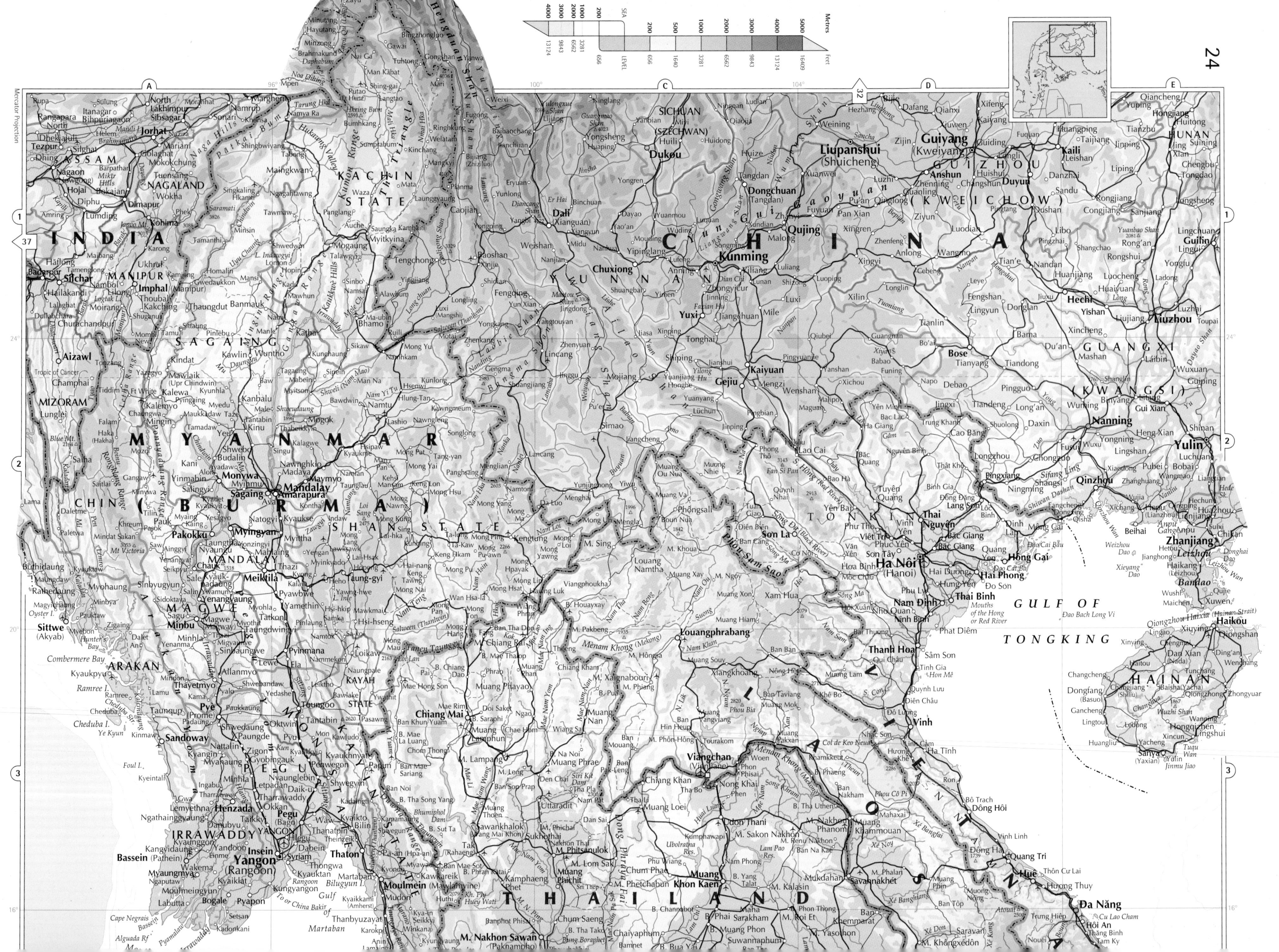
CHINA
INDIA
MYANMAR (BURMA)
THAILAND
LAOS
VIETNAM
YUNNAN
GUIZHOU (KWEICHOW)
GUANGXI (KWANGSI)
SICHUAN (SZECHWAN)
HAINAN
GULF OF TONGKING
KACHIN STATE
SHAN STATE
SAGAING
MANDALAY
MAGWE
ARAKAN
PEGU
IRRAWADDY
YANGON
KAYAH STATE
KAYIN STATE
MON STATE
CHIN
ASSAM
NAGALAND
MANIPUR
MIZORAM
TONKIN
Kunming
Guiyang (Kweiyang)
Liupanshui (Shuicheng)
Nanning
Hà Nôi (Hanoi)
Hai Phong
Mandalay
Yangon (Rangoon)
Chiang Mai
Viangchan (Vientiane)
Louangphrabang
Haikou
Zhanjiang
Đa Năng
Mercator Projection
Metres
Feet

CAMBODIA

THAILAND

GULF OF THAILAND

ANDAMAN SEA

INDONESIA

MALAYSIA

PENINSULAR MALAYSIA

STRAIT OF MALACCA

TENASSERIM

Mergui Archipelago

ANDAMAN & NICOBAR ISLANDS
(India)

Andaman Islands

Nicobar Islands

Ten Degree Channel

Sombrero Channel

Car Nicobar

Great Nicobar

Little Nicobar

Port Blair

Qui Nhon · Ninh Hoa · Nha Trang · Cam Ranh · Phan Rang · Da Lat · Buon Me Thuot · Phan Thiet · Bien Hoa · Ho Chi Minh · Vung Tau · Long Xuyen · Can Tho · Bac Lieu · Ca Mau

Phnum Penh · Battdambang · Kampong Cham · Kracheh · Stoeng Treng

Bangkok · Krung Thep · Nonthaburi · Nakhon Ratchasima (Korat) · Chon Buri · Pattaya · Rayong · Chanthaburi · Prachuap Khiri Khan · Chumphon · Surat Thani (Ban Don) · Nakhon Si Thammarat · Songkhla (Singora) · Ban Hat Yai · Narathiwat · Yala · Pattani

Tavoy (Dawei) · Mergui

Ko Samui · Ko Phangan · Ko Phuket · Thalang

Kuala Terengganu · Kota Bharu · Kuantan · Kuala Lumpur · Kelang · Seremban · Ipoh · Taiping · George Town · Pinang · Butterworth · Alur Setar · Sungei Petani · Melaka · Johor Bahru · Singapore

KELANTAN · **TERENGGANU** · **PAHANG** · **PERAK** · **KEDAH** · **PERLIS** · **SELANGOR** · **NEGERI SEMBILAN** · **JOHOR**

INDONESIA

Natuna Besar

Charlotte Bank

SINGAPORE
1:375 000

Johor Bahru · WOODLANDS · SEMBAWANG · YISHUN · SELETAR · CHANGI · JURONG · SINGAPORE · BUKIT TIMAH · TUAS

MALAYSIA

Strait of Singapore

Selat Johor

Miles	Km
200	320
160	280
120	240
80	200
40	160
40	120
	80
	40
0	0

© Bartholomew

1:6M

KAZAKHSTAN
RUSSIAN FEDERATION
MONGOLIA
CHINA
INDIA
NEPAL
BHUTAN
BANGLADESH
MYANMAR (BURMA)
THAILAND
LAOS
KYRGYZSTAN
TAJIKISTAN
XINJIANG UYGUR ZIZHIQU (SINKIANG UIGHUR AUT. REGION)
XIZANG ZIZHIQU (TIBET AUT. REGION)
QINGHAI
GANSU
SICHUAN
YUNNAN
GUIZHOU
NINGXIA
JAMMU AND KASHMIR
HIMACHAL PRADESH
UTTAR PRADESH
MADHYA PRADESH
BIHAR
WEST BENGAL
ORISSA
SIKKIM
ARUNACHAL PRADESH
ASSAM
MEGHALAYA
NAGALAND
MANIPUR
MIZORAM
TRIPURA
AKSAI CHIN
CHINESE TURKESTAN
TIEN SHAN
KUNLUN SHAN
KARAKORAM
HIMALAYA
ALTAI MTS
Tarim Pendi (Tarim Basin)
Taklimakan Shamo (Taklimakan Desert)
Xizang Gaoyuan (Plateau of Tibet)
Junggar Pendi (Dzungarian Basin)
Qaidam Pendi
Sichuan Pendi
Altun Shan (Astin Tagh)
Qilian Shan
Bayan Har Shan
Hengduan Shan
Gangdisê Shan (Kailas Range)
Nyainqêntanglha Shan
Tanggula (Dangla) Shan
Hoh Xil Shan
Khrebet Tarbagatay
Khrebet Tannu Ola
Zapadnyy Sayan
Vostochnyy Sayan
Hangayn Nuruu
Gobi
Badain Jaran Shamo
Tengger Shamo
Melkosopochnik
Betpak-Dala
Ozero Balkhash
Kaimur Range
Eastern Ghats
Arakan Yoma
BAY OF BENGAL
Mouths of the Ganga
Mt Everest (Qomolangma Feng)
Lop Nur
Qinghai Hu
Karaganda
Temirtau
Semipalatinsk
Rubtsovsk
Ust'-Kamenogorsk
Biysk
Abakan
Mezhdurechensk
Kyzyl
Irkutsk
Angarsk
Ulan-Ude
Ulaanbaatar
Almaty
Bishkek
Zhambyl
Taldykorgan
Namangan
Andizhan
Osh
Ürümqi (Urumchi)
Shihezi
Kuytun
Karamay
Tacheng
Altay
Aksu
Korla
Kashi (Kashgar)
Hotan
Hami
Turpan
Dunhuang
Golmud
Xining
Lanzhou
Tianshui
Baoji
Linxia
Lhasa
Xigazê
Chengdu
Mianyang
Deyang
Leshan
Yibin
Zigong
Chongqing
Zhaotong
Liupanshui
Guiyang
Kunming
Qujing
Dali
Gejiu
Kaiyuan
Ha Nôi
Haiphong
Nam Đinh
Thanh Hoa
Vinh
Luang Prabang
Chiang Mai
Mandalay
Monywa
Meiktila
Pyinmana
Sittwe
Chittagong
Dhaka
Khulna
Calcutta
Patna
Varanasi
Allahabad
Kanpur
Lucknow
Agra
Delhi
Meerut
Chandigarh
Dehra Dun
Bareilly
Gorakhpur
Kathmandu
Thimphu
Shillong
Guwahati
Imphal
Dibrugarh
Jamshedpur
Ranchi
Dhanbad
Asansol
Cuttack
Bhubaneshwar
Brahmapur
Vishakhapatnam (Vizagapatam)
Rajahmundry
Kakinada (Cocanada)
Raipur
Jabalpur
Gwalior
Jhansi
Albers Equal Area Conic Projection

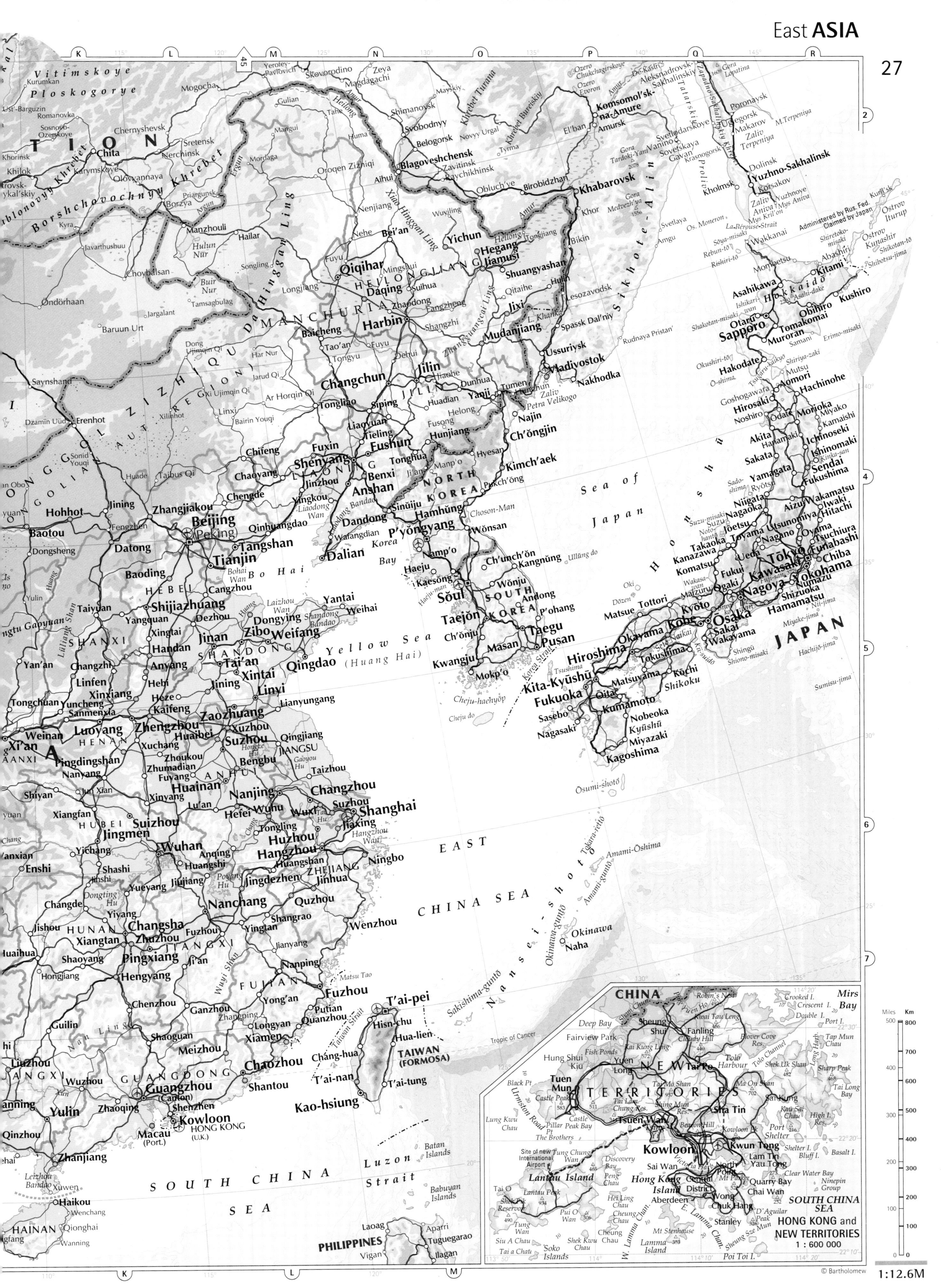
Sea of Japan
Yellow Sea (Huang Hai)
EAST CHINA SEA
SOUTH CHINA SEA
JAPAN
NORTH KOREA
SOUTH KOREA
TAIWAN (FORMOSA)
PHILIPPINES
MANCHURIA
Beijing (Peking)
Shanghai
Tōkyō
Sŏul
P'yŏngyang
HONG KONG and NEW TERRITORIES
1 : 600 000
1:12.6M
© Bartholomew

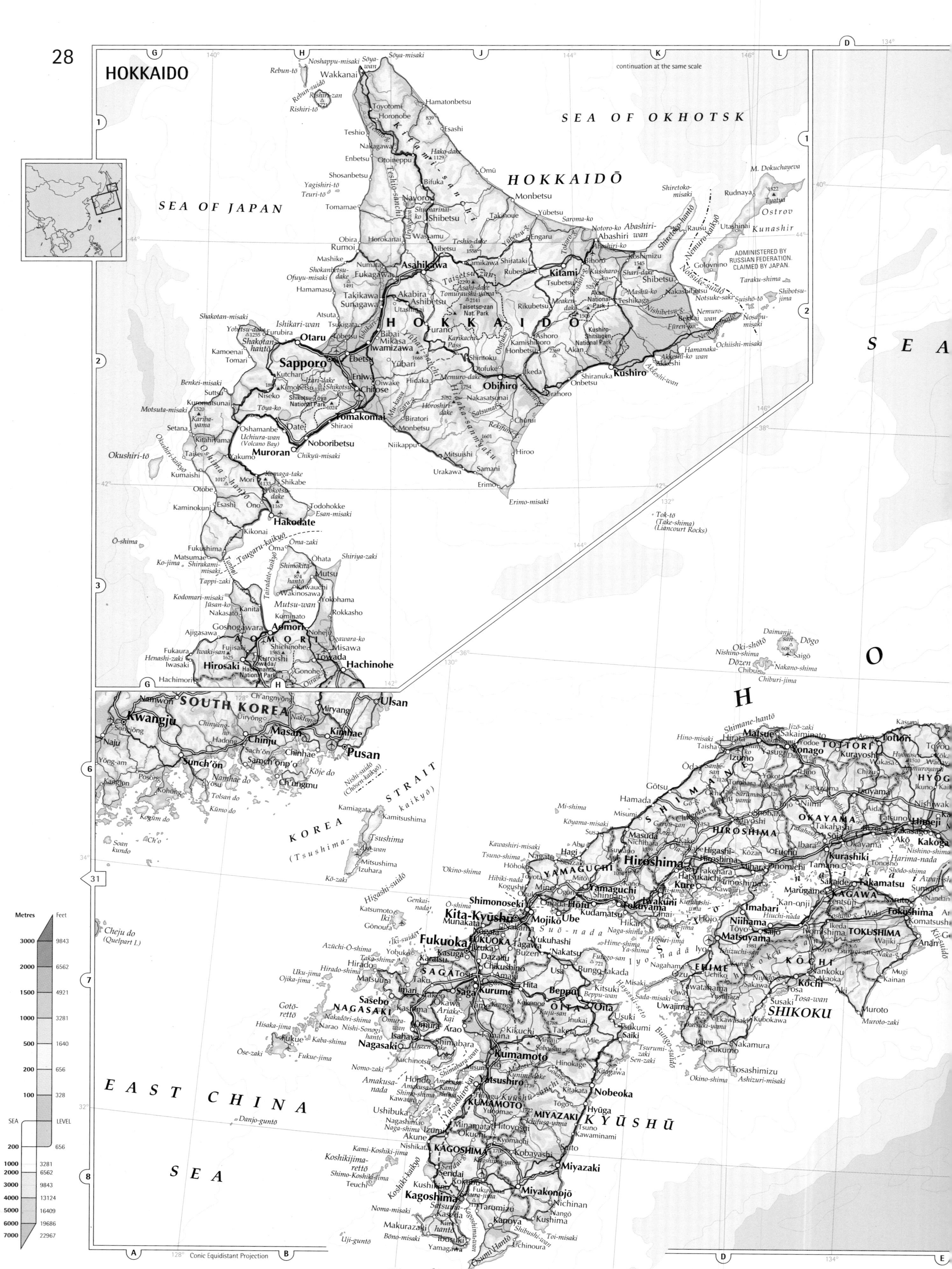
HOKKAIDO
continuation at the same scale
SEA OF OKHOTSK
SEA OF JAPAN
HOKKAIDŌ
ADMINISTERED BY RUSSIAN FEDERATION. CLAIMED BY JAPAN.
Kunashir
Sapporo
Asahikawa
Hakodate
Kushiro
Obihiro
Aomori
Hachinohe
Hirosaki
Tsugaru-kaikyō
SOUTH KOREA
Pusan
Ulsan
Kwangju
KOREA STRAIT
(Tsushima-kaikyō)
Tsushima
Tok-tō
(Take-shima)
(Liancourt Rocks)
Oki-shotō
SHIMANE
HIROSHIMA
OKAYAMA
YAMAGUCHI
Hiroshima
Fukuoka
Kita-Kyūshū
Shimonoseki
Nagasaki
Kumamoto
Kagoshima
Miyazaki
Ōita
SHIKOKU
EHIME
KŌCHI
TOKUSHIMA
KAGAWA
Matsuyama
Takamatsu
Kōchi
KYŪSHŪ
EAST CHINA SEA
Cheju do
(Quelpart I.)
Metres
Feet
3000
9843
2000
6562
1500
4921
1000
3281
500
1640
200
656
100
328
SEA
LEVEL
200
656
1000
3281
2000
6562
3000
9843
4000
13124
5000
16409
6000
19686
7000
22967
Conic Equidistant Projection

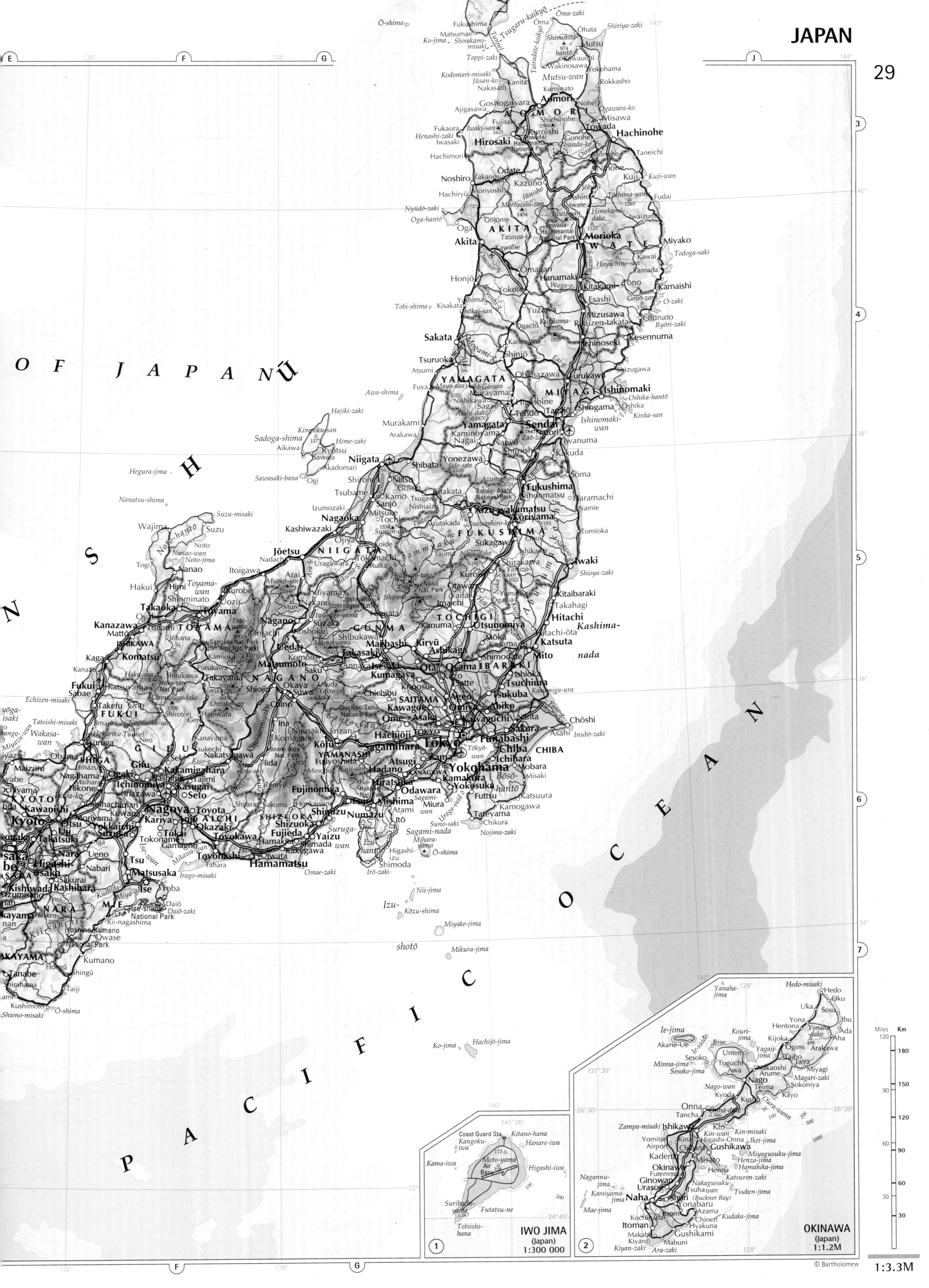
SEA OF JAPAN (EAST SEA)
PACIFIC OCEAN
AOMORI
AKITA
IWATE
YAMAGATA
MIYAGI
FUKUSHIMA
NIIGATA
TOYAMA
ISHIKAWA
FUKUI
GIFU
NAGANO
GUNMA
TOCHIGI
IBARAKI
SAITAMA
CHIBA
YAMANASHI
SHIZUOKA
AICHI
MIE
NARA
KYOTO
SHIGA
KANAGAWA
Hachinohe
Hirosaki
Aomori
Noshiro
Akita
Morioka
Miyako
Kamaishi
Sakata
Ishinomaki
Sendai
Yamagata
Niigata
Fukushima
Kōriyama
Iwaki
Nagaoka
Jōetsu
Kanazawa
Toyama
Takaoka
Nagano
Matsumoto
Utsunomiya
Mito
Hitachi
Maebashi
Takasaki
Tōkyō
Yokohama
Kawasaki
Chiba
Funabashi
Hachiōji
Sagamihara
Shizuoka
Hamamatsu
Toyohashi
Nagoya
Gifu
Fukui
Kyoto
Ōsaka
Nara
Tsu
Kashima-nada
Sagami-nada
Izu-shotō
Sado-shima
Hachijō-jima
IWO JIMA
(Japan)
1:300 000
OKINAWA
(Japan)
1:1.2M
Naha
Okinawa
Nago
1:3.3M
© Bartholomew

RUSSIAN FEDERATION
MONGOLIA
CHINA
TYVA
IRKUTSK
BURYATIYA
HÖVSGÖL
DZAVHAN
ARHANGAY
BULGAN
SELENGE
TÖV
HENTIY
GOVĬALTAY
BAYAN-HONGOR
ÖVÖR-HANGAY
DUNDGOVĬ
DORNGOVĬ
SÜHBAATAR
ÖMNÖGOVĬ
GOBI
GANSU (KANSU)
QINGHAI (TSINGHAI)
NINGXIA (NINGSIA)
SHAANXI (SHENSI)
SHANXI
Ulaanbaatar (Ulan Bator)
Ulan-Ude
Irkutsk
Angarsk
Chita
Hohhot (Huhehot)
Baotou
Datong
Yinchuan
Lanzhou (Lanchow)
Xining
Taiyuan
Shijiazhuang
Yan'an
Jinchang
Wuhai
Erenhot
Ozero Baykal (Lake Baykal)
Hangayn Nuruu
Govĭaltay Nuruu
Badain Jaran Shamo
Tengger Shamo
Mu Us Shamo
Yin Shan
Qilian Shan
Huang (Yellow River)
Metres
Feet
6000 19686
5000 16409
4000 13124
3000 9843
2000 6562
1000 3281
500 1640
200 656
SEA LEVEL
200 656
1000 3281
2000 6562
3000 9843
4000 13124
GH7754
Albers Equal Area Conic Projection
32

CHITA
KHABAROVSK
YEVREYSKAYA AVTONOMNAYA OBLAST'
HEILONGJIANG
MANCHURIA
JILIN
LIAONING
NEI MONGGOL ZIZHIQU
(INNER MONGOLIAN AUT. REGION)
DORNOD
NORTH KOREA
SOUTH KOREA
HEBEI
TIANJIN
SHANDONG
(SHANTUNG)
Da Hinggan Ling
Xiao Hinggan Ling
Changbai Shan
Blagoveshchensk
Khabarovsk
Vladivostok
Ussuriysk
Qiqihar
(Tsitsihar)
Harbin
Daqing
(Anda)
Yichun
Jiamusi
Hegang
(Hokang)
Mudanjiang
Jixi
Changchun
Jilin
Siping
Tonghua
Shenyang
(Mukden)
Fushun
Benxi
Anshan
Dalian
(Dairen) (Lüda)
Dandong
Beijing
(Peking)
Tianjin
(Tientsin)
Tangshan
Qinhuangdao
Jinan (Tsinan)
Zibo
Weifang
Yantai
(Chefoo)
Qingdao (Tsingtao)
Zhangjiakou (Kalgan)
Chifeng
(Ulanhad)
Hailar
(Hulun)
Manzhouli
Xilinhot
P'yŏngyang
Hamhŭng
Ch'ŏngjin
Kaesŏng
Sŏul (Seoul)
Inch'ŏn
Taejŏn
Taegu
Kwangju
Pusan
Ulsan
BO HAI
(GULF OF CHIHLI)
Liaodong Wan
Korea Bay
(So-chaoson-man)
Sea of Japan
YELLOW SEA
(HUANG HAI)
Korea Strait
Miles
Km
1:6M
© Bartholomew

Map (China, Tibet, Myanmar, Laos, Thailand, Vietnam region)

Grid references: A · B · 30 · C · D (top), 96° · 100° · 104° · 108°

Major regions and countries

QINGHAI (TSINGHAI)
XIZANG ZIZHIQU (TIBET AUT. REGION)
GANSU (KANSU)
NINGXIA (NINGSIA)
SHAANXI (SHENSI)
SICHUAN (SZECHWAN)
C H I N A
GUIZHOU (KWEICHOW)
YUNNAN
ARUNACHAL PRADESH
INDIA
NAGALAND
KACHIN STATE
SAGAING
MANDALAY
MYANMAR (BURMA)
SHAN STATE
KAYAH STATE
KAYIN STATE
PEGU
THAILAND
LAOS
VIETNAM
TONKIN
GULF OF TONKIN

Selected towns and cities

Linxia, Tianshui, Baoji, Xianyang, Hanzhong, Guangyuan, Mianyang, Deyang, Daxian, Wanxi, Nanchong, Chengdu (Chengtu), Ya'an, Leshan, Neijiang, Zigong, Yibin, Luzhou, Chongqing (Chungking), Fuling, Zunyi, Guiyang (Kweiyang), Liupanshui (Shuicheng), Anshun, Duyun, Kaili, Hechi, Bose, Nannin, Xichang, Dukou, Zhaotong, Dali (Xiaguan), Chuxiong, Kunming, Qujing, Yuxi, Gejiu, Kaiyuan, Mengzi, Baoshan, Pingxiang, Lang Son, Thai Nguyen, Ha Noi (Hanoi), Hai Phong, Hong Gai, Nam Dinh, Thai Binh, Thanh Hoa, Vinh, Mandalay, Amarapura, Sagaing, Meiktila, Pyinmana, Toungoo, Chiang Mai, Chiang Rai, Louangphrabang (Luang Prabang), Son La, Viet Tri, Hoa Binh

Scale (Metres / Feet)

Metres	Feet
6000	19686
5000	16409
4000	13124
3000	9843
2000	65621
1000	3281
500	1640
200	656
SEA	LEVEL
200	656
1000	3281
2000	6562
3000	9843
4000	13124
5000	16409

Albers Equal Area Conic Projection

South CHINA

YELLOW SEA (HUANG HAI)

SHANXI
SHANDONG (SHANTUNG)
HENAN
HUBEI (HUPEH)
ANHUI (ANHWEI)
JIANGSU (KIANGSU)
HUNAN
JIANGXI
ZHEJIANG (HEKIANG)
FUJIAN (FUKIEN)
GUANGDONG (KWANGTUNG)
GUANGXI
TAIWAN (FORMOSA)

SOUTH CHINA SEA

Taiwan Strait (Taiwan Haixia)

PHILIPPINES

Luzon Strait

Balintang Channel

Babuyan Islands

Babuyan Channel

Tropic of Cancer

Major cities and places (selection):
Linfen, Jincheng, Zhengzhou (Zhengchow), Luoyang (Loyang), Kaifeng, Jining (Tsining), Zaozhuang, Linyi, Xuzhou (Tongshan), Huaibei, Lianyungang, Huaiyin, Qingjiang, Yancheng, Shiyan, Laohekou, Xiangfan, Suizhou (Sui Xian), Nanyang, Pingdingshan, Zhoukou, Fuyang, Bengbu, Huainan, Hefei, Nanjing (Nanking), Changzhou, Wuxi, Changshu, Shanghai, Suzhou (Soochow), Jingmen, Xiaogan, Wuhan, Huangshi, Anqing, Tongling, Wuhu, Ma'anshan, Huzhou (Wuxing), Jiaxing, Hangzhou (Hangchow), Ningbo, Shaoxing, Yichang, Jingzhou, Shashi, Xianning, Jiujiang, Jingdezhen, Jinhua, Quzhou (Qu Xian), Wenzhou, Changde, Yiyang, Changsha, Xiangtan, Zhuzhou, Nanchang, Yingtan, Fuzhou (Foochow), Wenzhou, Jishou, Huaihua, Lengshuijiang, Shaoyang, Hengyang, Hengshan, Ji'an, Nanping, Sanming, Yong'an, Putian, Quanzhou, Xiamen (Amoy), Guilin, Chenzhou, Ganzhou, Longyan, Zhangzhou, Shantou, Chaozhou, Wuzhou, Zhaoqing, Guangzhou (Canton), Foshan, Dongguan, Shenzhen, HONG KONG (U.K.), Kowloon, Macau (Portugal), Zhongshan, Zhuhai, Jiangmen, Yangjiang, Maoming, Zhanjiang, Leizhou, Haikou, Qionghai, Sanya
T'ai-pei (Taibei), Chi-lung (Jilong), Hsin-chu, T'ai-chung (Taizhong), Hua-lien, Chia-i (Jiayi), T'ai-nan (Tainan), Kao-hsiung (Gaoxiong), P'ing-tung (Pingdong), T'ai-tung

Scale 1:6M
Miles 0–200
Km 0–320

© Bartholomew

Metres
Feet
6000
19685
5000
16409
4000
13124
3000
9843
2000
6562
1000
3281
500
1640
200
656
SEA
LEVEL
200
656
1000
3281
2000
6562
3000
9843
4000
13124
5000
16409
Transverse Mercator Projection
KAZAKHSTAN
UZBEKISTAN
TURKMENISTAN
KYRGYZSTAN
TAJIKISTAN
AFGHANISTAN
IRAN
PAKISTAN
MONGOLIA
CHINA
XINJIANG UYGUR ZIZHIQU
(SINKIANG UIGHUR AUT. REGION)
XIZANG ZIZHIQU
(TIBET AUT. REGION)
NEI MONGOL ZIZHIQU
(INNER MONGOLIAN AUT. REGION)
Tarim Pendi
(Tarim Basin)
Taklimakan Shamo
(Taklimakan Desert)
KUNLUN SHAN
TIEN SHAN
Xizang Gaoyuan
(Plateau of Tibet)
NEPAL
BHUTAN
JAMMU AND KASHMIR
Tashkent
Almaty
Bishkek
Dushanbe
Kābul
Delhi
Karachi
Lahore
Ürümqi

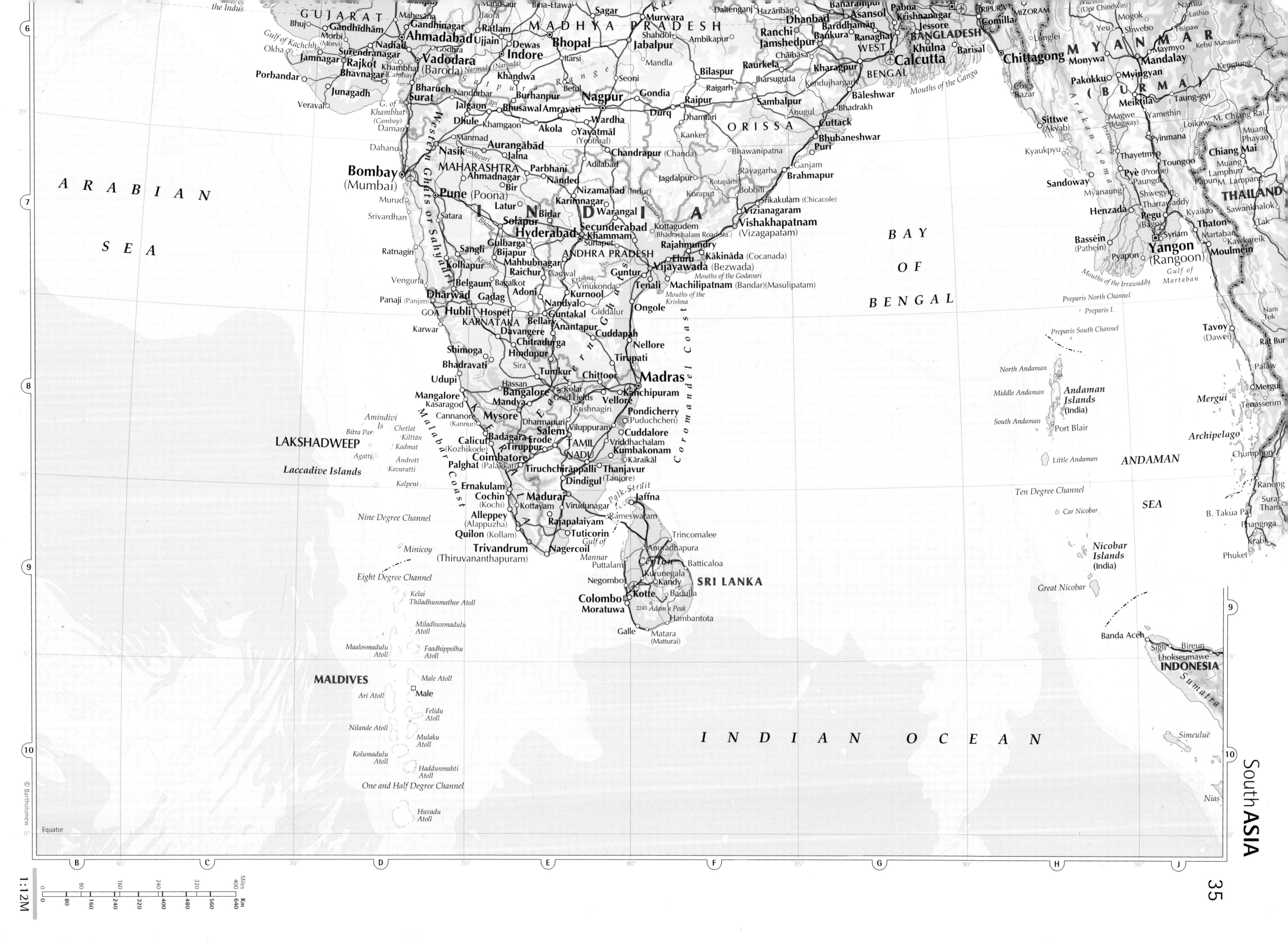

THAILAND
MYANMAR (BURMA)
Chiang Mai
Mandalay
Yangon (Rangoon)
Moulmein
Tavoy (Dawei)
Mergui
Mergui Archipelago
INDONESIA
Sumatra
Nias
Banda Aceh
Simeulué
Lhokseumawe
Sigli

ANDAMAN SEA

Bassein (Pathein)
Sandoway
Sittwe (Akyab)
Kyaukpyu

Nicobar Islands (India)
Great Nicobar
Car Nicobar
Little Andaman
Ten Degree Channel
South Andaman
Middle Andaman
North Andaman
Andaman Islands (India)
Port Blair
Preparis South Channel
Preparis North Channel

Chittagong
BANGLADESH
Khulna
Calcutta
WEST BENGAL
Mouths of the Ganga

BAY OF BENGAL

ORISSA
Bhubaneshwar
Puri
Cuttack
Brahmapur
Ganjam

MADHYA PRADESH
Nagpur
MAHARASHTRA
Hyderabad
ANDHRA PRADESH
Vishakhapatnam (Vizagapatam)
Kakinada (Cocanada)
Rajahmundry
Vijayawada (Bezwada)
Machilipatnam (Bandar)(Masulipatam)
Mouths of the Godavari
Mouths of the Krishna
Coromandel Coast
Madras
Nellore
Ongole
Guntur

INDIA

Bombay (Mumbai)

ARABIAN SEA

GUJARAT

Western Ghats or Sahyadri

Pune (Poona)

GOA
KARNATAKA
Bangalore
Mysore
Coimbatore
TAMIL NADU
Tiruchchirappalli
Madurai
Trivandrum (Thiruvananthapuram)
Nagercoil
Tuticorin
Cochin (Kochi)
Malabar Coast

Mangalore

LAKSHADWEEP
Laccadive Islands
Amindivi Is.
Minicoy

SRI LANKA
Jaffna
Trincomalee
Batticaloa
Colombo
Kotte
Kandy
Galle
Adam's Peak
Matara (Mattrai)
Palk Strait
Gulf of Mannar
Rameswaram

INDIAN OCEAN

MALDIVES
Male
Male Atoll
Ari Atoll
Nine Degree Channel
Eight Degree Channel
Equator

Miles 400
Km 640

© Bartholomew
1:12M

AFGHANISTAN
PAKISTAN
INDIA
BALOCHISTAN
SINDH
PUNJAB
HARYANA
RAJASTHAN
GUJARAT
MADHYA PRADESH
UTTAR PRADESH
MAHARASHTRA
HIMACHAL PRADESH
JAMMU AND KASHMIR
NORTHERN AREAS
NORTH-WEST FRONTIER
TRIBAL AREAS
XINJIANG (SINKIANG)
AKSAI CHIN
CLAIMED BY INDIA UNDER CHINESE ADMINISTRATION
ARABIAN SEA
Gulf of Kachchh
Gulf of Khambhat (Gulf of Cambay)
Rann of Kachchh
Thar or Indian Desert
Mouths of the Indus
Tropic of Cancer
Kābul
Islamabad
Delhi
Karachi
Lahore
Ahmadabad
Bhopal
Indore
Nagpur
Jaipur
Lucknow
Kanpur
Metres
Feet
6000
19686
5000
16409
4000
13124
3000
9843
2000
6562
1000
3281
500
1640
200
656
SEA
LEVEL
200
656
1000
3281
2000
6562
3000
9843
Indian states not named on map
1. Dadra & Nagar Haveli (C5)
2. Daman & Diu (C5)
Conic Equidistant Projection
A
B
C
D
1
2
5
6
39
47
38
68°
72°
76°
80°
36°
32°
28°
20°

1:6M

© Bartholomew

CHINA
XIZANG GAOYUAN (PLATEAU OF TIBET)
XIZANG ZIZHIQU (TIBET AUT. REGION)
QINGHAI (TSINGHAI)
NEPAL
BHUTAN
SIKKIM
BANGLADESH
MYANMAR (BURMA)
ARUNACHAL PRADESH
ASSAM
MEGHALAYA
NAGALAND
MANIPUR
MIZORAM
TRIPURA
BIHAR
WEST BENGAL
ORISSA
BAY OF BENGAL
Mouths of the Ganga

BAY OF BENGAL

MADHYA PRADESH

MAHARASHTRA

ANDHRA PRADESH

KARNATAKA

TAMIL NADU

ORISSA

BIHAR

GUJARAT

GOA

LAKSHADWEEP

MALDIVES

SRI LANKA

Ceylon

Laccadive Islands

Amindivi Is

Cannanore Is

Gulf of Khambhat (Gulf of Cambay)

Mouths of the Godavari

Mouths of the Krishna

Coromandel Coast

Malabar Coast

Palk Strait

Palk Bay

Gulf of Mannar

Adam's Bridge

Major cities and towns (selection):
Bombay (Mumbai), Pune (Poona), Nagpur, Hyderabad, Secunderabad, Bangalore, Madras, Vishakhapatnam (Vizagapatam), Kakinada (Cocanada), Vijayawada (Bezwada), Mangalore, Mysore, Coimbatore, Madurai, Tiruchchirappalli, Thanjavur (Tanjore), Salem, Pondicherry (Puducheri), Cochin (Kochi), Ernakulam, Trivandrum (Thiruvananthapuram), Quilon (Kollam), Calicut (Kozhikode), Cape Comorin (Kanniya Kumari), Nagercoil

Sri Lanka: Jaffna, Trincomalee, Anuradhapura, Colombo, Kotte, Dehiwala-Mount Lavinia, Moratuwa, Kandy, Galle, Matara, Dondra Head, Hambantota, Batticaloa

Scale 1:6M

Miles / Km scale: 0 40 80 120 160 200 miles / 0 40 80 120 160 200 240 280 320 km

Metres / Feet:
Metres	Feet
2000	6562
1000	3281
500	1640
200	656
SEA LEVEL	LEVEL
200	656
1000	3281
2000	6562
3000	9843
4000	13124

Conic Equidistant Projection

© Bartholomew '84

Indian states not named on map
1. Dadra & Nagar Haveli (A1)
2. Daman & Diu (A1)

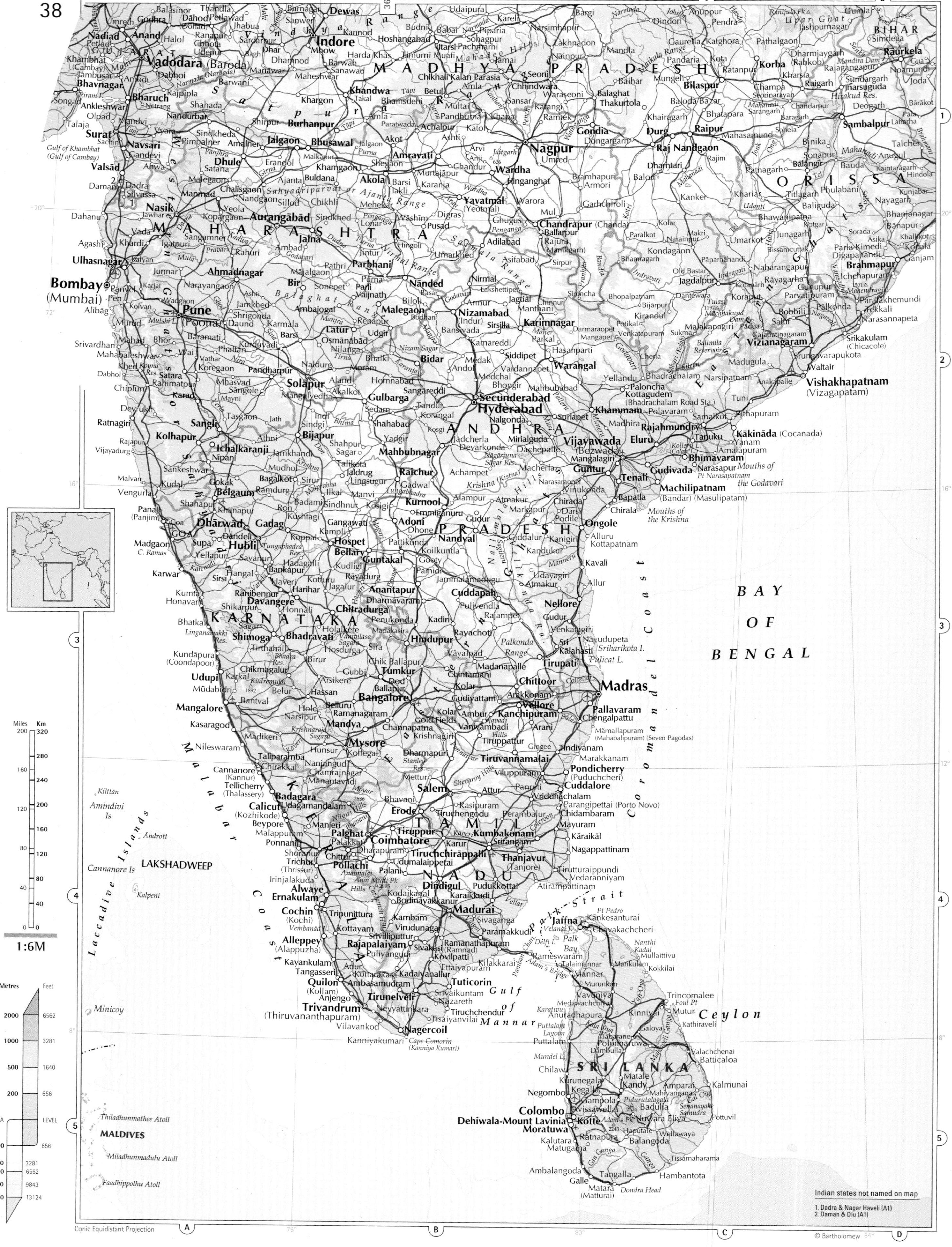

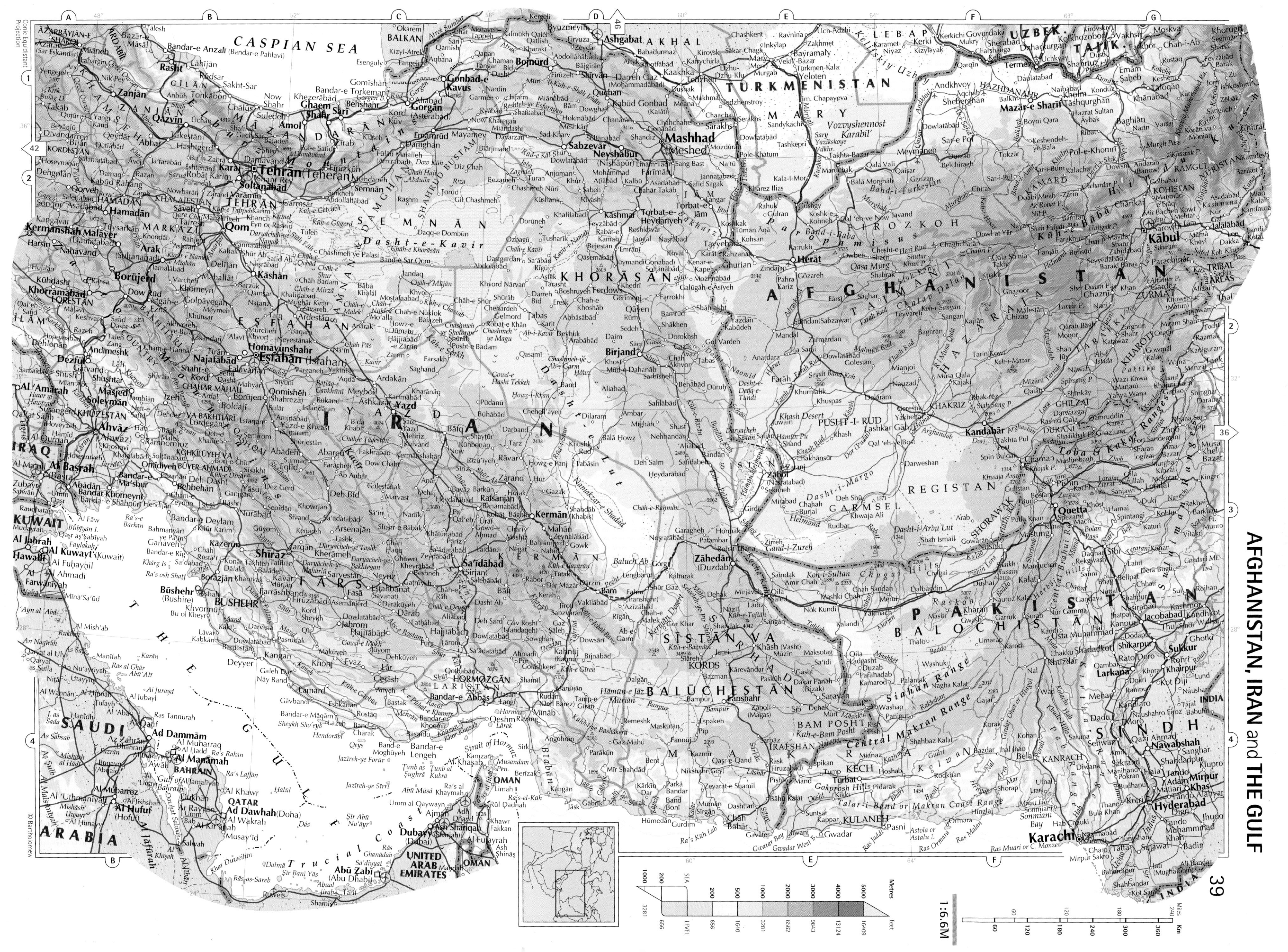

Miles Km
240 360
180 300
120 240
180
120
60 60

1:6.6M

Metres Feet
5000 16409
4000 13124
3000 9843
2000 6562
1000 3281
500 1640
200 656
SEA LEVEL
200 656
1000 3281

Conic Equidistant
Projection

© Bartholomew

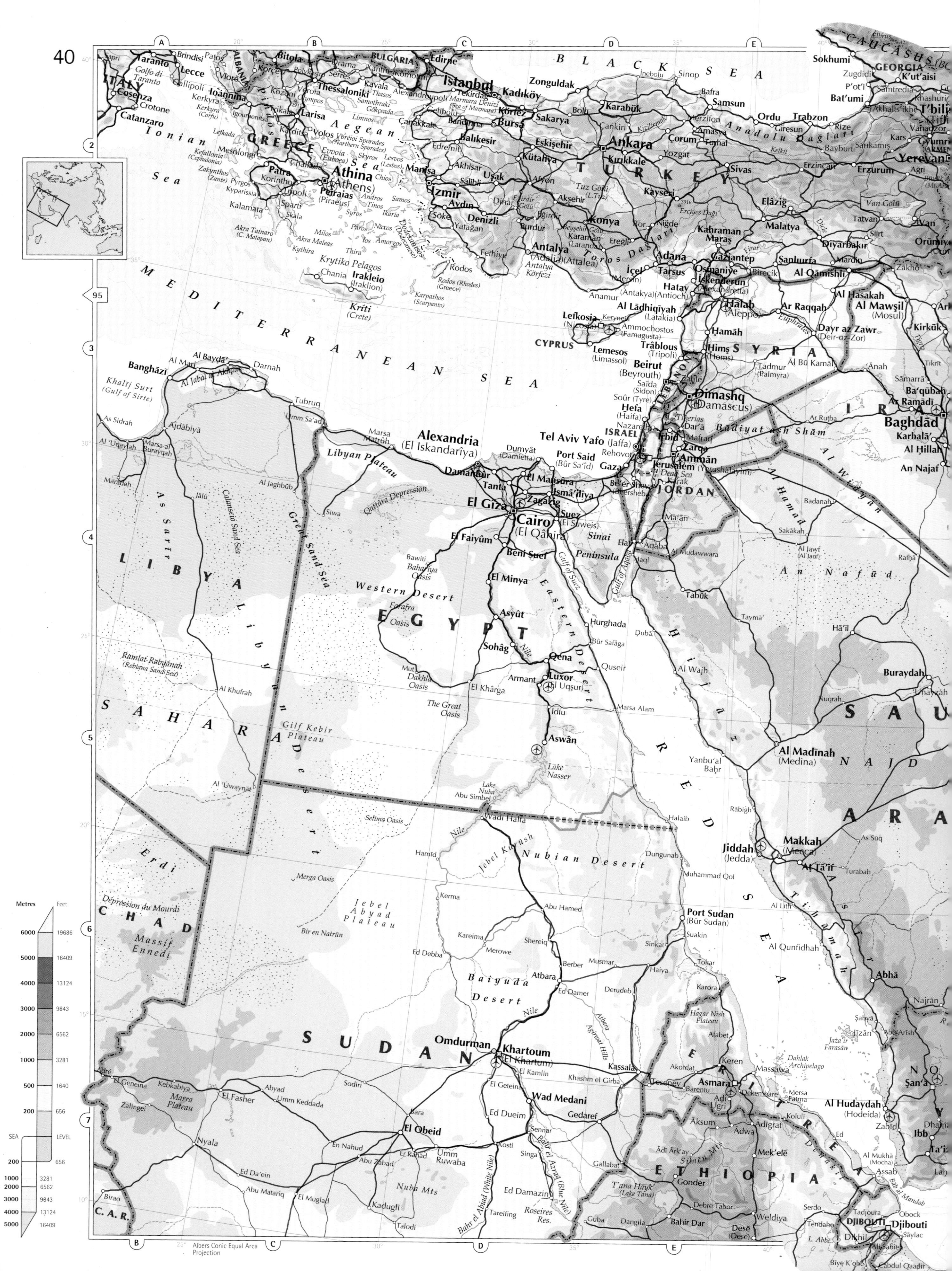

A
B
C
D
E
BLACK SEA
CAUCASUS
Sokhumi
GEORGIA
K'ut'aisi
Zugdidi
P'ot'i
Bat'umi
T'bilisi
Yerevan
ARMENIA
Taranto
Brindisi
Lecce
Golfo di Taranto
Gallipoli
ITALY
Cosenza
Crotone
Catanzaro
ALBANIA
Vlorë
Bitola
Ioánnina
Kerkyra (Corfu)
Igoumenitsa
Trikala
Larisa
Volos
Thessaloniki
Kavala
Thasos
Drama
Serres
Xanthi
Komotini
BULGARIA
Edirne
Alexandroupoli
Samothraki
Gökçeada
Limnos
Istanbul
Tekirdağ
Marmara Denizi (Sea of Marmara)
Kadıköy
Körfez
Bursa
Sakarya
Bandırma
Çanakkale
Gelibolu
Zonguldak
İnebolu
Sinop
Bafra
Samsun
Karabük
Bolu
Çankiri
Kızılırmak
Merzifon
Amasya
Tokat
Çorum
Ordu
Giresun
Trabzon
Rize
Bayburt
Kars
Sarıkamış
Erzincan
Erzurum
Ağri
Anadolu Dağları
Ankara
Kırıkkale
Eskişehir
Kütahya
Balıkesir
Edremit
Yozgat
Sivas
Kayseri
Erciyes Dağı
3916
Niğde
Nevşehir
TURKEY
Tuz Gölü (L. Tuz)
Akşehir
Konya
Karaman
Ereğli
Eğirdir Gölü
Beyşehir Gölü
Afyon
Uşak
Akhisar
Manisa
Salihli
İzmir
Aydın
Söke
Denizli
Yatağan
Dinar
Burdur
Fethiye
Antalya (Adalia)
Antalya Körfezi
Toros Dağları
Adana
Tarsus
İçel (Mersin)
Osmaniye
Gaziantep
İskenderun (Alexandretta)
Hatay (Antakya) (Antioch)
Kahraman Maraş
Malatya
Elâzığ
Diyarbakır
Tatvan
Van Gölü
Van
Siirt
Mardin
Şanlıurfa
Birecik
Al Qāmishlī
Zākhō
Al Hasakah
Al Mawşil (Mosul)
Kirkūk
Dayr az Zawr (Deir-oz-Zor)
Ar Raqqah
Euphrates
Ḩalab (Aleppo)
Ḩamāh
Ḩimş (Homs)
SYRIA
Tadmur (Palmyra)
Al Bū Kamāl
'Ānah
Tikrit
Sāmarrā'
Ba'qūbah
Ar Ramādī
Baghdād
Karbalā'
Al Ḩillah
An Najaf
IRAQ
Ar Rutba
Bādiyat ash Shām
Al Wiḏyān
Al Ḩamād
Al Lādhiqīyah (Latakia)
Trâblous (Tripoli)
Beirut (Beyrouth)
LEBANON
Saïda (Sidon)
Soûr (Tyre)
Zahle
Dimashq (Damascus)
Ḩefa (Haifa)
Tiberias
Dar'ā
Irbid
Mafraq
Zarqa
'Ammān
ISRAEL
Tel Aviv Yafo (Jaffa)
Rehovot
Jerusalem (Yerushalayim)
Dead Sea
Karak
Gaza
Be'er Sheva (Beersheba)
JORDAN
Ma'ān
Aqaba
Elat
Al Mudawwara
Ḩaql
Badanah
Sakākah
Al Jawf (Al Jauf)
Rafḩā
An Nafūd
Tabūk
Taymā'
Ḩā'il
Buraydah
'Unayzah
Nuqrah
SAUDI ARABIA
NAJD
Al Madīnah (Medina)
Yanbu'al Baḩr
Rābigh
Jiddah (Jedda)
Makkah (Mecca)
Aţ Ţā'if
As Sūq
Turabah
Al Līth
Al Qunfidhah
Tihāmah
'Asīr
Abhā
Najrān
Şabyā
Jīzān
Abū 'Arīsh
Jazā'ir Farasān
Şan'ā'
Al Ḩudaydah (Hodeida)
Zabīd
Ibb
Ta'izz
Al Mukhā (Mocha)
Bab el Mandab
Assab
Ḑubā
Al Wajh
Ḩijāz
Lefkosia (Nicosia)
Kyrenia
Ammochostos (Famagusta)
Lemesos (Limassol)
CYPRUS
Anamur
Rodos
Rodos (Rhodes) (Greece)
Karpathos (Scarpanto)
Dodekanisos (Dodecanese)
Kriti (Crete)
Chania
Irakleio (Iraklion)
Krytiko Pelagos
Thira
Milos
Akra Maleas
Kythira
Akra Tainaro (C. Matapan)
Kalamata
Pyrgos
Kyparissia
Sparti
Skala
Tripoli
Korinthos
Patra
Athina (Athens)
Peiraias (Piraeus)
Chalkida
Evvoia (Euboea)
Voreioi Sporades (Northern Sporades)
Skyros
Lesvos (Lesbos)
Chios
Samos
Ikaria
Naxos
Paros
Ios
Amorgos
Andros
Tinos
Syros
Aegean Sea
GREECE
Pindos
Mesolongi
Lefkada
Kefallonia (Cephalonia)
Zakynthos (Zante)
Ionian Sea
Kozani
Veroia
Olympos
Karditsa
MEDITERRANEAN SEA
Al Bayḑā'
Al Marj
Darnah
Banghāzī
Al Jabal al Akhḑar
Khalīj Surt (Gulf of Sirte)
As Sidrah
Ajdābiyā
Marsa al Burayqah
Al 'Uqaylah
Tubruq
Umm Sa'ad
Al Jaghbūb
Jālū
Marādah
As Sarīr
Calanscio Sand Sea
LIBYA
Libyan Desert
Great Sand Sea
Ramlat Rabyānah (Rebiana Sand Sea)
Al Khufrah
SAHARA
Al 'Uwaynāt
Erdi
Dépression du Mourdi
CHAD
Massif Ennedi
Marsa Matrûh
Libyan Plateau
Alexandria (El Iskandarîya)
Damanhûr
Tanta
Dumyât (Damietta)
Port Said (Bûr Sa'îd)
El Mansûra
Ismâ'ilîya
Zagazig
El Giza
Cairo (El Qâhira)
Suez (El Suweis)
Sinai Peninsula
Gulf of Suez
Gulf of Aqaba
Qattâra Depression
Siwa
El Faiyûm
Beni Suef
Bawiti
Bahariya Oasis
El Minya
Western Desert
Farafra Oasis
EGYPT
Asyût
Eastern Desert
Hurghada
Bûr Safâga
Sohâg
Nile
Qena
Quseir
Armant
Luxor (El Uqsur)
Mut
Dakhla Oasis
El Khârga
The Great Oasis
Idfu
Marsa Alam
Aswân
Gilf Kebir Plateau
Lake Nasser
Lake Nuba
Abu Simbel
Wadi Halfa
Halaib
Selima Oasis
Hamîd
Jebel Kurûsh
Nubian Desert
Dungunab
Muhammad Qol
RED SEA
Merga Oasis
Kerma
Jebel Abyad Plateau
Abu Hamed
Bir en Natrûn
Port Sudan (Bûr Sudan)
Suakin
Kareima
Merowe
Shereiq
Sinkat
Ed Debba
Berber
Musmar
Tokar
Haiya
Atbara
Baiyuda Desert
Ed Damer
Derudeb
Karora
Atbara
Agrawit Hills
SUDAN
Omdurman
Khartoum (El Khartum)
El Kamlin
Kassala
Khashm el Girba
Adré
El Geneina
Kebkabiya
Marra Plateau
Zalingei
El Fasher
Abyad
Umm Keddada
Sodiri
Bara
El Obeid
En Nahud
Er Rahad
Umm Ruwaba
Abu Zabad
Nyala
Ed Da'ein
Abu Matariq
El Muglad
Nuba Mts
Kadugli
Talodi
El Geteina
Wad Medani
Gedaref
Ed Dueim
Sennar
Kosti
Singa
Bahr el Azraq (Blue Nile)
Bahr el Abiad (White Nile)
Ed Damazin
Tareifing
Roseires Res.
Gallabat
Birao
C. A. R.
ERITREA
Hagar Nish Plateau
Afabet
Keren
Akordat
Tesenney
Barentu
Asmara
Adi Ugri
Dekemhare
Massawa
Dahlak Archipelago
Mersa Fatma
Aksum
Adwa
Adigrat
Koluli
Denakil
Adi Ark'ay
Simen Mts
Mek'ele
ETHIOPIA
Gonder
T'ana Hayk' (Lake Tana)
Debre Tabor
Bahir Dar
Weldiya
Dese (Dese)
Dangila
Guba
Serdo
Tendaho
Dikhil
L. Abbe
Tadjoura
Obock
DJIBOUTI
Djibouti
Saylac
Ali Sabieh
Biye K'obe
Cabdul Qaadir
Metres
Feet
6000
19686
5000
16409
4000
13124
3000
9843
2000
6562
1000
3281
500
1640
200
656
SEA
LEVEL
200
656
1000
3281
2000
6562
3000
9843
4000
13124
5000
16409
95
Albers Conic Equal Area Projection

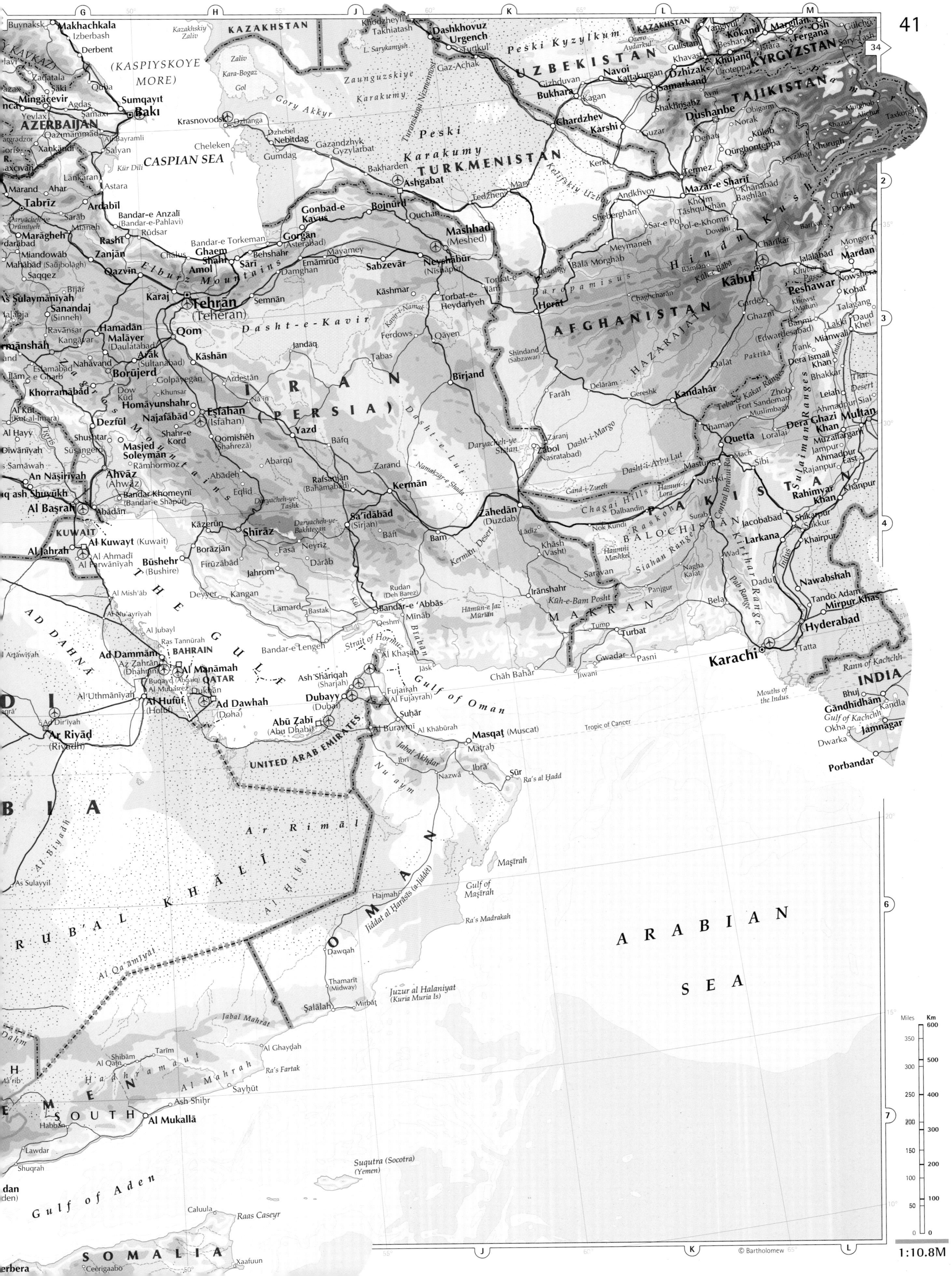

KAZAKHSTAN

Buynaksk Makhachkala Izberbash
Derbent Kazakhskiy Zaliv
(KAVKAZ) Khodzheyli Takhiatash Dashkhovuz Urgench Turtkul' Peski Kyzylkum KAZAKHSTAN Yangiyul Kokand Margilan Osh Gülcho
Zaqatala Quba (KASPIYSKOYE MORE) Takhiatash UZBEKISTAN Besharyk Chirara Khūjand KYRGYZSTAN Sary-Tash
Şäki Agdaş Sumqayıt Krasnovodsk L. Sarykamysh Gaz-Achak Khavasi Navoi Kattakurgan Ozhizak Samarkand Uratteppa Fergana
Mingäçevir Yevlax Şamaxı Bakı Kara-Bogaz Gol Zaungutskiye Gizhduvan Bukhara Kagan TAJIKISTAN Dushanbe
Yevlax Qazımämmäd Baki Gory Akkyr Karakumy Chardzhev Karshi Guzar Shakhrisabz Obigarm Norak
AZERBAIJAN Bayramli CASPIAN SEA Cheleken Nebitdag Gazandzhyk Peski TURKMENISTAN Kerki Dehau Qürghonteppa Khorugh
Salyan Kür Dili Gumdag Bakharden Kizil Keloo
Marand Ahar Astara Ländkäran Ashgabat Tedzhen Andkhvoy Mazar-e Sharif Khānābād Baghlān HINDU KUSH
Tabrīz Ardabīl Bandar-e Anzalī (Bandar-e-Pahlavī) Gonbad-e Kavus Bojnūrd Quchan Mashhad (Meshed) Sheberghan Sar-e Pol Pol-e-Khomri Chārikār Jalālābād Mardan
Sarab Mianeh Rasht Rūdsar Bandar-e Torkeman Gorgān (Asterābād) Mayamey Neyshābūr (Nishāpur) Torbat-e Jām Meymaneh Bālā Morghāb AFGHANISTAN Bāmiān Kūh-i Bābā Kābul Peshawar
Marāgheh Zanjān Ghaem Shahr Sārī Behshahr Sabzevār Kāshmar HAZARAJAT Chaghcharān Ghazni Cardez Khyber Pass
Miandowāb Mahābād Amol Damghan Emāmrūd Torbat-e Heydariyeh Herat Paropamisus Gereshk Qalāt Mianwali
Saqqez Qazvin Karaj Elburz Mountains Semnān Damghan Ferdows Qāyen Shindand (Sabzawar) Delārām Kandahār Quetta
Bījār Sanandaj (Sinneh) Tehrān (Teheran) Dasht-e Kavir Kāshmar Tabas Bīrjand Farāh Gand-i Zureh Spin Baldak
Sulaymāniyah Hamadān Qom Kavir-e Namak Zarand IRAN (PERSIA) Zābol Dasht-i-Margo (Nasrābād) Zaranj Lorālai Fort Sandeman (Zhob) Dera Ghazi Khan Multan
Ravānsar Malāyer (Daulatabad) Eşfahān (Isfahan) Yazd Dasht-e-Lut Chagai Hills Dera Ismail Khan
Kermānshāh Kangāvar Arāk (Sultanabad) Najafābād Qomisheh (Shahrezā) Abarqū Namakzār-e Shāda Zāhedān (Duzdab) Nushki Kīkar Range
Eslāmābād e Gharb Borūjerd Golpayegān Ardestān Bāfq Rafsanjān (Bahramabad) Bam Khāsh (Vasht) Dalbandin PAKISTAN Sibi
Khorramābād Dezfūl Shahr-e Kord Kermān Irānshahr Saravan BALOCHISTAN Mastung Jacobabad Sukkur
Shushtar Masjed Soleymān Kāzerūn Daryācheh-ye Tashk Sa'īdābād (Sirjan) Kermān Siahan Range Panjgur Kalat Rahimyar Khan Shikarpur Khairpur
Ahvāz (Ahwāz) Rāmhormoz Shīrāz Daryācheh-ye Bakhtegān Kūh-e Bam Posht Bela Larkana Nawabshah
An Nāşirīyah Bandar-e Khomeynī (Bandar-e Shapur) Fasa Neyrīz Dārāb Bakran Tump Turbat Gwadar Pasni Hyderabad Mirpur Khas Tando Adam
Al Başrah Abādān KUWAIT Eqlid Jahrom Bam Rudan (Deh Barez) Hamūn-e Jaz Mūriān Gwadar Karachi Tatta INDIA
Al Kuwayt (Kuwait) Borāzjan Firūzābād Bandar-e 'Abbās Mīnāb Chāh Bahār Jiwani Rann of Kachchh
Al Jahrah Būshehr (Bushire) Deyyer Kangan Qeshm Jāsk Gulf of Oman Bhuj Gāndhīdhām Gulf of Kachchh
Al Ahmadī Al Parwānīyah THE GULF Lamard Bastak Bandar-e Lengeh Al Khaşab Strait of Hormuz Mouths of the Indus Kandla Jamnagar
AD DAHNA Al Mish'āb Deyyer Ash Shāriqah (Sharjah) Fujairah (Al Fujayrah) Okha Dwarka
Al Nu'ayrīyah Ras Tannūrah BAHRAIN Dubayy (Dubai) Suhār Suhār Masqaţ (Muscat) Tropic of Cancer Porbandar
Ad Dammām Al Manāmah QATAR Abū Zabī (Abu Dhabi) Al Buraymī Al Khāburah Matrah
Az Zahrān (Dhahran) Ad Dawhah (Doha) Dukhan UNITED ARAB EMIRATES Al Khāburah Jabal Akhdar Nazwā Ibrā Sūr Ra's al Hadd
Al Hufūf (Hofuf) Buqayq (Abqaiq) Al Mubarrez OMAN Ibrī
Al Uthmānīyah Al Hufūf Ar Rimāl Nu'aym Masīrah
SAUDI ARABIA Ad Dir'īyah Al Biyāḍ Ar Riyāḍ (Riyadh) Al Hibak Gulf of Masīrah
As Sulayyil RUB' AL KHĀLĪ Al Qa'āmīyāt Jiddat al Harāsīs (al Jiddah) Ra's Madrakah ARABIAN SEA
Hajmah Dawqah
Al Qa'āmīyāt Shibām Tarīm Thamarīt (Midway) Juzur al Halaniyat (Kuria Muria Is)
Jabal Mahrāt Şalālah Mirbāţ
YEMEN SOUTH Ḥaḍramaut Al Mahrah Al Ghaydah Suqutra (Socotra) (Yemen)
Habban Lawdar Al Qaţn Ash Shihr Sayhūt Ra's Fartak
Shuqrah Al Mukallā Raas Caseyr
Gulf of Aden Caluula
SOMALIA Xaafuun
Berbera

1:10.8M © Bartholomew

Miles / Km
600 / 350 / 500 / 300 / 400 / 250 / 300 / 200 / 150 / 100 / 100 / 50 / 0

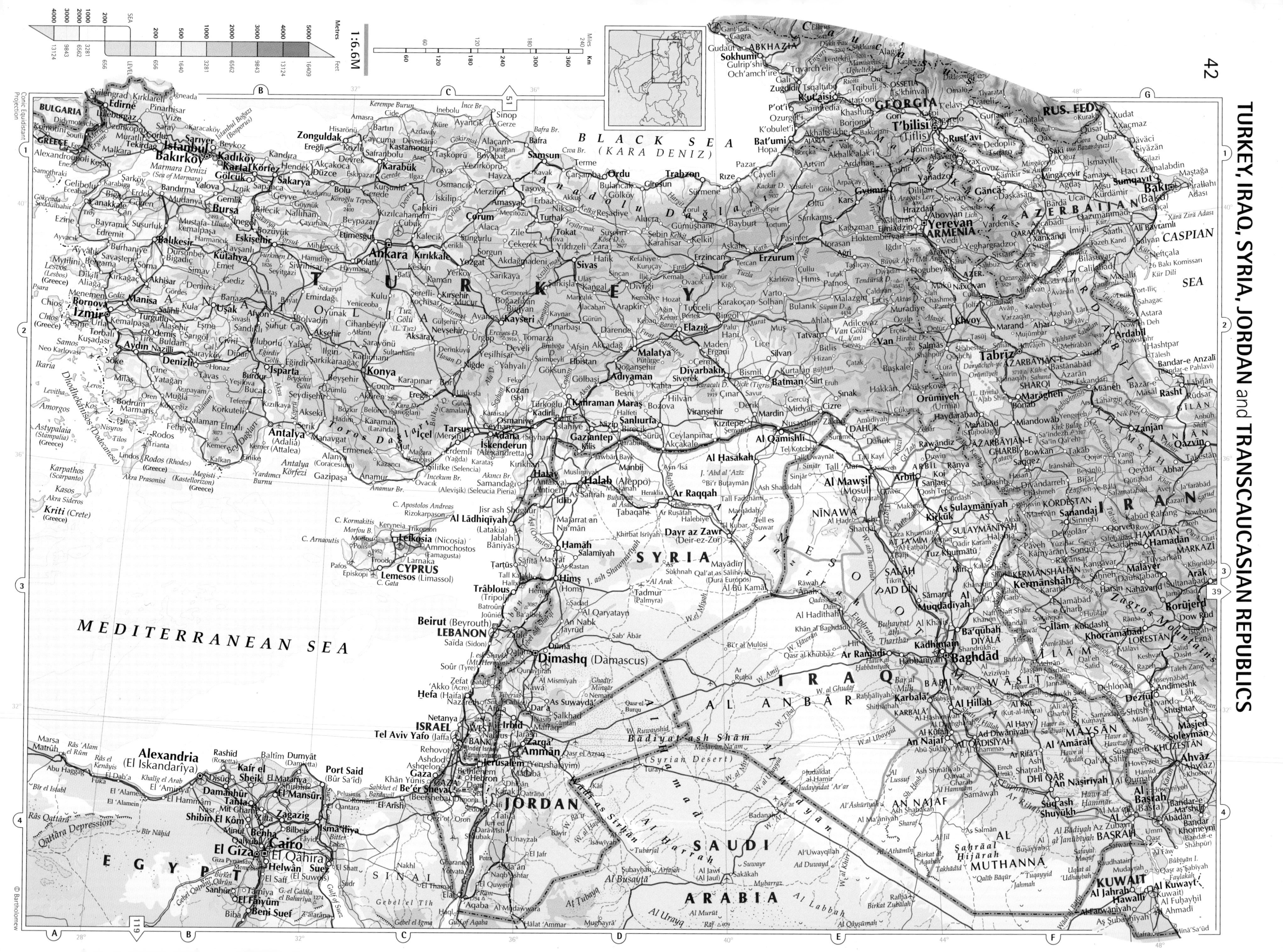

1:6.6M

© Bartholomew

Conic Equidistant Projection

1:3.3M

Conic Equidistant Projection

© Bartholomew

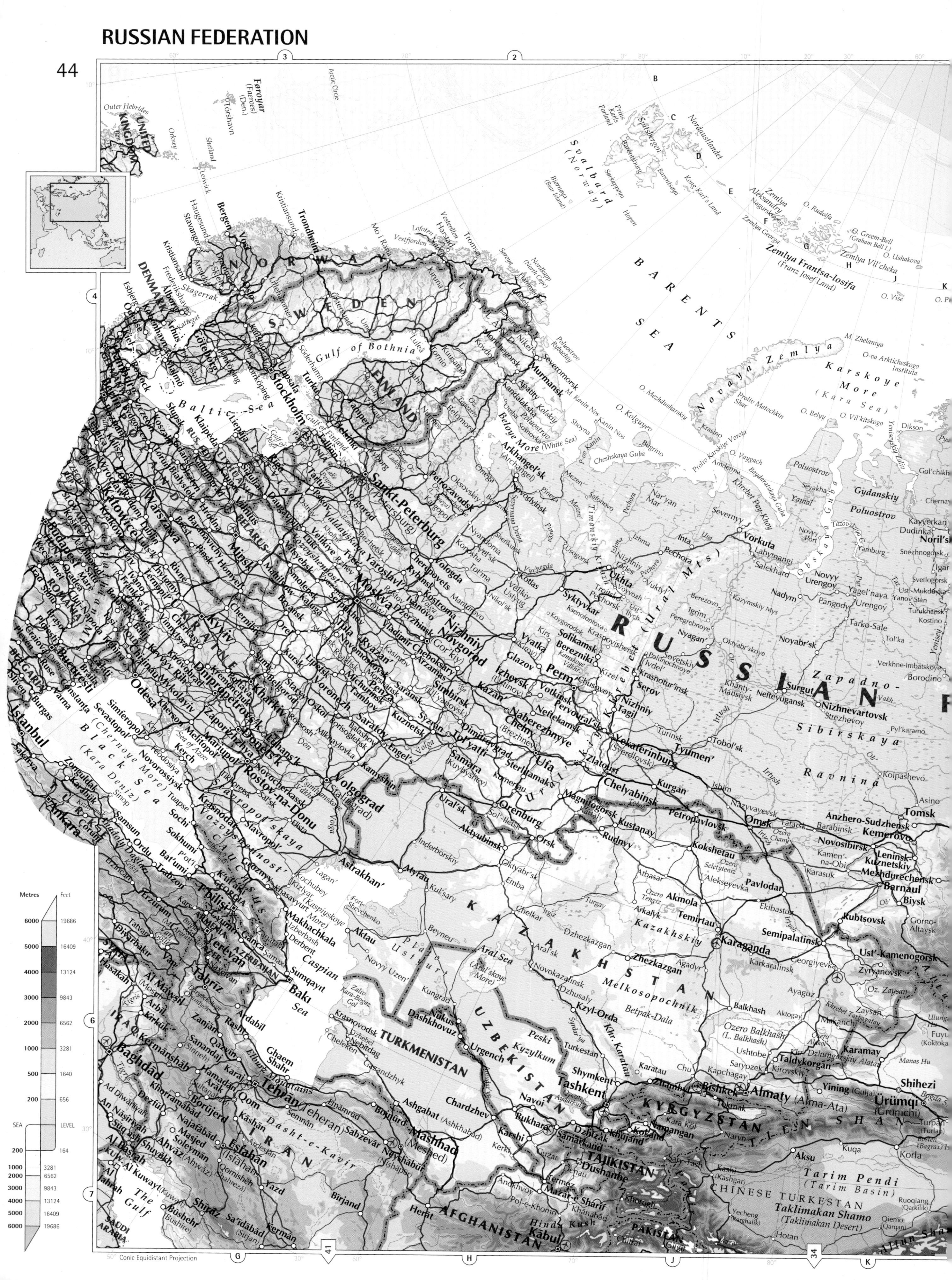

RUSSIAN FEDERATION
Conic Equidistant Projection
Metres
Feet
6000
19686
5000
16409
4000
13124
3000
9843
2000
6562
1000
3281
500
1640
200
656
SEA
LEVEL
164
B A R E N T S
S E A
Karskoye More
(Kara Sea)
Svalbard
(Norway)
Zemlya Frantsa-Iosifa
(Franz Josef Land)
Novaya Zemlya
Beloye More (White Sea)
Gulf of Bothnia
Baltic Sea
Black Sea
(Chernoye More)
(Kara Deniz)
Caspian Sea
Aral Sea
(Aral'skoye More)
The Gulf
NORWAY
SWEDEN
FINLAND
DENMARK
UNITED KINGDOM
BELARUS
UKRAINE
ROMANIA
BULGARIA
KAZAKHSTAN
UZBEKISTAN
TURKMENISTAN
KYRGYZSTAN
TAJIKISTAN
AFGHANISTAN
PAKISTAN
IRAN
IRAQ
SYRIA
SAUDI ARABIA
GEORGIA
ARMENIA
AZERBAIJAN
RUSSIAN F
Khrebet (Ural Mts)
Zapadno-Sibirskaya Ravnina
Kazakhskiy Melkosopochnik
Betpak-Dala
Tarim Pendi
(Tarim Basin)
Taklimakan Shamo
(Taklimakan Desert)
CHINESE TURKESTAN
TIEN SHAN
Dasht-e-Kavir
Elburz Mountains
Hindu Kush
Moskva
Sankt-Peterburg
Nizhniy Novgorod
Yekaterinburg
Chelyabinsk
Omsk
Novosibirsk
Tomsk
Barnaul
Volgograd
Rostov-na-Donu
Samara
Kazan'
Perm'
Ufa
Orenburg
Murmansk
Arkhangel'sk
Vorkuta
Surgut
Nizhnevartovsk
Noril'sk
Stockholm
Helsinki
Warszawa
Minsk
Kyyiv
Bucuresti
Istanbul
Ankara
Tbilisi
Yerevan
Baki
Tehran
Baghdad
Esfahan
Mashhad
Ashgabat
Tashkent
Bishkek
Almaty
Dushanbe
Kabul
Ürümqi
Karaganda
Akmola
Pavlodar
Semipalatinsk

RUSSIAN FEDERATION
MONGOLIA
CHINA
JAPAN
NORTH KOREA
SOUTH KOREA
U.S.A.
Vostochno-Sibirskaye More (East Siberian Sea)
More Laptevykh (Laptev Sea)
OKHOTSKOYE MORE (SEA OF OKHOTSK)
BERING SEA
Sea of Japan
Yellow Sea (Huang Hai)
EAST CHINA SEA
Bo Hai
Bering Strait
Chukchi Sea
Severnaya Zemlya
Novosibirskiye Ostrova (New Siberian Islands)
O. Vrangelya (Wrangel I.)
O. Sakhalin
Kuril'skiye Ostrova (Kuril Is)
SREDNE-SIBIRSKOYE PLOSKOGOR'YE
GOBI
MANCHURIA
Verkhoyanskiy Khrebet
Khrebet Cherskogo
Khrebet Kolymskiy
Koryakskiy Khrebet
Sredinnyy Khrebet
Stanovoy Khrebet
Stanovoye Nagor'ye
Khrebet Dzhugdzhur
Sikhote-Alin'
Yablonovyy Khrebet
Da Hinggan Ling
Xiao Hinggan Ling
Honshū
Hokkaidō
Yakutsk
Magadan
Petropavlovsk-Kamchatskiy
Irkutsk
Krasnoyarsk
Bratsk
Chita
Ulan-Ude
Khabarovsk
Vladivostok
Yuzhno-Sakhalinsk
Ulaanbaatar
Harbin
Changchun
Shenyang
Beijing (Peking)
Tianjin
Dalian
Qingdao
Shanghai
Nanjing
P'yŏngyang
Sŏul (Seoul)
Taegu
Sapporo
Sendai
Tōkyō
Yokohama
Nagoya
Ōsaka
Kōbe
Hiroshima
Fukuoka
Kagoshima
Miles
Km
1:18M
© Bartholomew

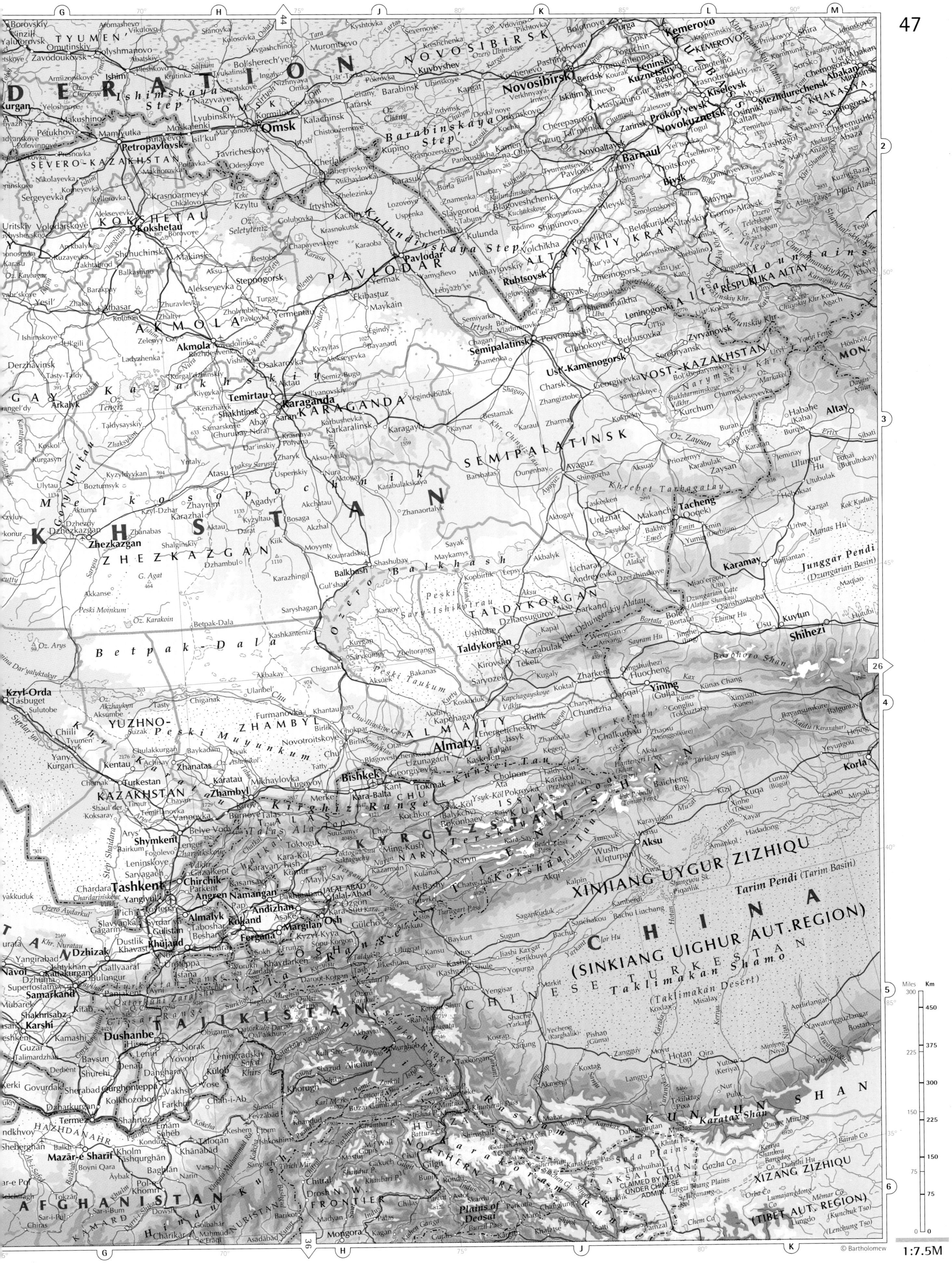

Central ASIA

RUSSIAN FEDERATION

TYUMEN'
SEVERO-KAZAKHSTAN
Omsk
Petropavlovsk
NOVOSIBIRSK
Novosibirsk
Kemerovo
KEMEROVO
Kuznetsk
Novokuznetsk
Prokop'yevsk
Kiselevsk
HAKASYA
Barabinskaya Step
Barnaul
Biysk
ALTAYSKIY KRAY
RESPUBLIKA ALTAY
Gorno-Altaysk
MON.

KOKSHETAU
Kokshetau
AKMOLA
Akmola
Temirtau
KARAGANDA
Shakhtinsk
Saran

Semipalatinsk
Ust-Kamenogorsk
VOST-KAZAKHSTAN
Altay

KAZAKHSTAN

Zhezkazgan
ZHEZKAZGAN

SEMIPALATINSK

Balkhash
Oz. Balkhash
TALDYKORGAN
Taldykorgan

Betpak-Dala
Peski Moinkum
Peski Taukum

Karamay
Junggar Pendi
(Dzungarian Basin)
Shihezi
Borohoro Shan

Kzyl-Orda

YUZHNO-
ZHAMBYL
ALMATY
Almaty
Bishkek
Ysyk-Köl
Yining (Gulja)

Korla
Aksu

KAZAKHSTAN
Turkestan
Shymkent

KYRGYZSTAN
TIEN SHAN
NARYN

XINJIANG UYGUR ZIZHIQU
XINJIANG UIGHUR AUT.REGION
(SINKIANG UIGHUR AUT.REGION)
CHINESE TURKESTAN
Tarim Pendi (Tarim Basin)
Taklimakan Shamo
(Taklimakan Desert)

Tashkent
Chirchik
Angren Namangan
Andizhan
Almalyk
Kokand
Margilan Osh
Fergana
Khujand

Samarkand
Karshi

Dushanbe
TAJIKISTAN

PAMIR

KUNLUN SHAN
XIZANG ZIZHIQU
(TIBET AUT. REGION)

CLAIMED BY INDIA
ADMIN. UNDER CHINESE
ARAS
AKSAI CHIN
Karataf Shan

Mazar-e Sharif
AFGHANISTAN
HINDU KUSH
Plains of Deosai

1:7.5M

Miles 300 / 225 / 150 / 75 / 0
Km 450 / 375 / 300 / 225 / 150 / 75 / 0

© Bartholomew

Labrador Sea
Frederikshåb
Greenland (Den.)
King Christian X Land
King Christian IX Land
King Frederick VI Coast
C. Farewell
Shannon I.
Traill I.
Scoresbysund
Greenland Sea
Spitsbergen
Longyearbyen
Svalbard (Nor.)
Bear I. (Nor.)
Denmark Strait
Jan Mayen (Nor.)
Ísafjörður
Húnaflói
Siglufjörður
ICELAND
Keflavík
Reykjavík
Vatnajökull
Höfn
Vesterålen
Lofoten
Tromsø
Narvik
Kiruna
Mo i Rana
NORWEGIAN SEA
Faeroes (Den.)
Tórshavn
Trondheim
Kristiansund
NORWAY
SWEDEN
Östersund
Härnösand
Shetland
Orkney
Bergen
Voss
Lillehammer
Falun
Uppsala
Oslo
Drammen
Karlstad
Stockholm
Stavanger
Egersund
Arendal
Larvik
Kristiansand
Vänern
Örebro
Vättern
Norrköping
Skagerrak
Skagen
Kattegat
Outer Hebrides
Inverness
SCOTLAND
Aberdeen
UNITED KINGDOM
Glasgow
Dundee
Edinburgh
Londonderry
N. IRELAND
Belfast
NORTH SEA
Ålborg
Århus
Borås
Jönköping
Göteborg
Gotland
Sligo
REP. OF IRELAND
L. of Man
Manchester
Newcastle
DENMARK
Esbjerg
Copenhagen
Helsingborg
Malmö
Kalmar
Öland
Tralee
Limerick
Irish Sea
Dublin
York
Leeds
Liverpool
Odense
Bornholm
Baltic
Cork
WALES
ENGLAND
Swansea
Cardiff
Birmingham
Norwich
Groningen
NETHERLANDS
Amsterdam
Hamburg
Kiel
Rostock
Lübeck
Gdańsk
Szczecin
Bydgoszcz
Toruń
Plymouth
London
Bristol
Dover
Rotterdam
The Hague
Bremen
Elbe
Hannover
Berlin
POLAND
Poznań
Płock
Isles of Scilly
Southampton
English Channel
Essen
GERMANY
Düsseldorf
Cologne
Frankfurt
Kalisz
Legnica
Łódź
Wrocław
ATLANTIC OCEAN
Channel Is
Cherbourg
Calais
Lille
Brussels
BELGIUM
Bonn
Koblenz
Rhine
Leipzig
Dresden
Brest
Caen
Amiens
Rouen
Seine
Reims
Luxembourg
LUXEMBOURG
Frankfurt
Prague
Rennes
Le Mans
Paris
Saarbrücken
Mannheim
CZECH REP.
Katowice
Ostrava
São Jorge
Terceira
Pico
Azores (Port.)
São Miguel
Santa Maria
St-Nazaire
Angers
Orléans
Nancy
Nürnberg
Plzeň
České Budějovice
Brno
Nantes
Tours
Loire
Strasbourg
Stuttgart
SLOVAKIA
Bay of Biscay
La Rochelle
FRANCE
Mulhouse
Dijon
Freiburg
Zürich
Munich
Danube
Vienna
Bratislava
Limoges
Lausanne
Bern
SWITZERLAND
LIECHTENSTEIN
Innsbruck
Salzburg
AUSTRIA
Budapest
HUNGARY
A Coruña
C. Finisterre
Gijón
Oviedo
Santander
Clermont-Ferrand
Lyon
Geneva
Mt Blanc 4808
Bolzano
Graz
Maribor
Balaton
Kecskemét
Szeged
Vigo
Bilbao
Bordeaux
St-Étienne
Grenoble
Rhône
Milan
Brescia
Trieste
Ljubljana
SLOV.
Zagreb
CROATIA
Ourense
León
Donostia-San Sebastián
Turin
Venice
Oporto
Braga
Douro
Burgos
Pyrenees
Toulouse
Nîmes
Montpellier
Genoa
Parma
Bologna
Pula
Rijeka
Coimbra
Valladolid
Logroño
Pamplona
Ebro
Andorra
ANDORRA
Nice
MONACO
Marseille
La Spezia
Pisa
SAN MARINO
Florence
Zadar
BOSNIA-HERZ.
Sarajevo
PORTUGAL
Salamanca
Zaragoza
Perpignan
Toulon
Livorno
Adriatic Sea
Ancona
Split
Lisbon
Setúbal
Tajo
SPAIN
Madrid
Toledo
Lleida
Barcelona
Corsica
Ajaccio
Perugia
Apennines
Dubrovnik
Podgorica
Castelló de la Plana
Tarragona
Civitavecchia
VATICAN CITY
Rome
ITALY
Badajoz
Ciudad Real
Balearic Islands
Menorca
Tirana
C. St Vincent
Huelva
Sevilla
Córdoba
Valencia
Palma
Mallorca
Ibiza
Sardinia
Naples
Salerno
Foggia
Bari
ALBANIA
Madeira (Port.)
Funchal
Cádiz
Málaga
Granada
Alicante
Murcia
Taranto
Algeciras
Gibraltar (U.K.)
Str. of Gibraltar
Ceuta (Sp.)
Tangier
Tétouan
Almería
Cartagena
Cagliari
Cosenza
Corfu
Melilla (Sp.)
Oran
Algiers
MEDITERRANEAN
Palermo
Messina
Reggio di Calabria
Ionian Sea
Rabat
Casablanca
Meknès
Fez
Sidi Bel Abbès
Sétif
Annaba
Tunis
Sicilian Channel
Sicily
Mount Etna 3323
Catania
Siracusa
Marrakesh
MOROCCO
Sousse
MALTA
Valletta
La Palma
Canary Islands (Spain)
Tenerife
Santa Cruz
Lanzarote
Fuerteventura
Gran Canaria
Las Palmas
Béchar
TUNISIA
Gabès
Tripoli
ALGERIA
Banghazi
Gulf of Sirte
LIBYA
SEA LEVEL
200
656
3000
9843
Chamberlin Trimetric Projection
60°
50°
40°
30°
20°
10°
0°
80°
2
3
4
5
6
B
C
D
E
F
G

BARENTS SEA

Nordaustlandet

Novaya Zemlya

Belyy I. O

KARA Sea

Vaygach I.

L

M

Kolguyev I.

North Cape *Nøroya*

K

J

H

Gulf of Ob

2

3

Yenisey

Arctic Circle

Lesosibirsk

Achinsk

Novy Urengoy

Nadym

Novobirsk

Tomsk

Kemerovo

Novosibirsk

Vorkuta

Inta

Pechora

Pechora

Surgut

Nizhnevartovsk

Barnaul

Ob

Murmansk

Severomorsk

Monchegorsk

Apatity

Kandalaksha

White Sea

Mezen

Mezen

Ukhta

Nyagan

Ob

Nefteyugansk

Ob

R U S S I A N   F E D E R A T I O N

(in Asia)

Irtysh

Tobolsk

Pavlodar

FINLAND

Tampere

Turku

Helsinki

Tallinn

ESTONIA

Tartu

Lappland

Lap.

Gulf of Bothnia

Archangel

Severodvinsk

Northern Dvina

Kotlas

Syktyvkar

Serov

Solikamsk

Berezniki

Pervoural'sk

Yekaterinburg

Tyumen

Omsk

Nizhniy Tagil

Chelyabinsk

Kurgan

Petropavlovsk

Kokshetau

Akmola

Temirtau

Karaganda

Petrozavodsk

Lake Onega

Lake Ladoga

St Petersburg

Novgorod

Cherepovets

Vologda

Rybinsk Res.

Kostroma

Yaroslavl

Vyatka

Glazov

Perm

Izhevsk

Volga

Kazan

Naberezhnyye Chelny

Oktyabrskiy

Magnitogorsk

Zlatoust

Zhezkazgan

K A Z A K H S T A N

Kustanay

Aktyubinsk

Gulf of Riga

Riga

LATVIA

Pskov

Lake Peipus

Velikiye Luki

Tver

Ivanovo

Nizhniy Novgorod

Cheboksary

Simbirsk

Arzamas

Samara

Orenburg

Orsk

Šiauliai

LITHUANIA

Klaipéda

Kaunas

Vitsyebsk

Smolensk

Moscow

Kaluga

Vladimir

Ryazan

Saransk

Penza

Kuznetsk

Saratov

Uralsk

RUS. FED.

Kaliningrad

Minsk

Mahilyow

Tula

Novomoskovsk

Tambov

K A Z A K H S T A N

Hrodna

Vilnius

BELARUS

Bryansk

Orel

Yelets

Voronezh

Kamyshin

ND

Warsaw

Baranavichy

Pinsk

Homyel'

Kursk

Staryy Oskol

Belgorod

Volgograd

Atyrau

Aral Sea

Białystok

Brest

Chernihiv

Sumy

Don

Tsimlyansk Res.

Nukus

Dashkhovuz

Navoi

raków

Radom

Lublin

Luts'k

Rivne

Zhytomyr

Kiev

Kharkov

Lugansk

Volga

Astrakhan

U Z B E K I S T A N

Urgench

Amudarya

Bukhara

Lvov

Ternopil'

Cherkasy

Poltava

Kramators'k

Donetsk

Novocherkassk

Rostov-na-Donu

Caspian Sea

Makhachkala

Syrdarya

Kzyl-Orda

Turkestan

Chardzhev

KIA

Ivano-Frankivs'k

Chernivtsi

U K R A I N E

Kirovohrad

Dnepropetrovsk

Zaporozhye

Berdyans'k

Aktau

Kara-Bogaz-Gol

T U R K M E N I S T A N

Košice

Mare

Krivoy Rog

MOLDOVA

Chişinău

Mykolayiv

Melitopol'

Stavropol

Miskolc

Satu

Botoşani

Iaşi

Kherson

Dnieper

Odessa

Sea of Azov

Krasnodar

Armavir

Groznyy

Ashgabat

Debrecen

Oradea

Cluj-Napoca

ROMANIA

Sibiu

Galaţi

Simferopol'

Crimea

Kerch

Novorossiysk

Tuapse

Sochi

Caucasus

Elbrus

Mashhad

Timişoara

Braşov

Brăila

Sevastopol

Black Sea

Sokhumi

Bat'umi

GEORGIA

Tbilisi

Sumqayit

Baku

elgrade

Ploieşti

Bucharest

Constanţa

K'ut'aisi

AZERBAIJAN

YUGO-LAVIA

Craiova

Ruse

Pleven

Varna

Samsun

Ordu

Trabzon

AZER.

Mashhad

Vranje

Niš

BULGARIA

Sliven

Burgas

Zonguldak

Karabük

ARMENIA

Yerevan

Tabriz

Rasht

Skopje

Sofia

Plovdiv

Edirne

Istanbul

Sea of Marmara

Sakarya

Çorum

Erzurum

Lake Van

Van

Tehran

MACEDONIA

A

Thessaloniki

Bursa

Eskişehir

Ankara

Sivas

Malatya

Diyarbakır

Larisa

Volos

Balıkesir

Kütahya

Lake Tuz

Kayseri

T U R K E Y

Şanlıurfa

Mosul

Kirkuk

Qom

Isfahan

Yazd

GREECE

Euboea

Lesvos

Manisa

Konya

Adana

Gaziantep

I R A N

Patra

Korinthos

Athens

Peiraias

Samos

Izmir

Aydın

Aegean Sea

İskenderun

Aleppo

Deir ez-Zor

Euphrates

Tigris

Ahvaz

Shiraz

Busheher

Cyclades

Thira

Antalya

Hama

Homs

S Y R I A

Baghdad

Kirkuk

Crete

Rhodes

Rhodes

CYPRUS

Nicosia

I R A Q

An Najaf

Basra

KUWAIT

Kuwait

Busheher

Beirut

LEBANON

Damascus

Haifa

ISRAEL

Tel Aviv

Amman

Jerusalem

Dubai

THE GULF

A

MEDITERRANEAN SEA

JORDAN

SAUDI ARABIA

Alexandria

Port Said

EGYPT

Giza

Cairo

J

K

L

Miles 500

Km 800

© Bartholomew

1:15.5M

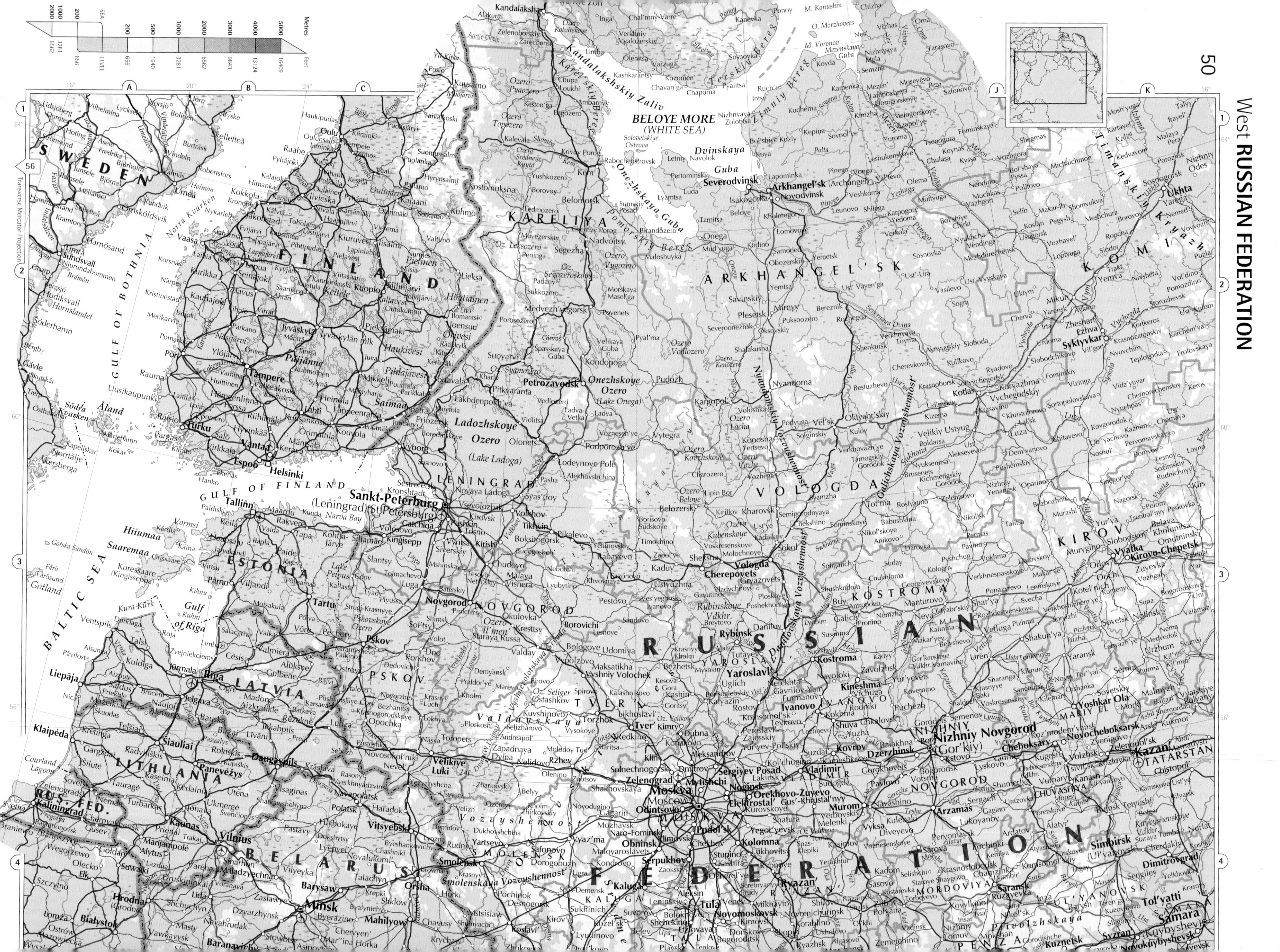
Metres
Feet
5000
16409
4000
13124
3000
9843
2000
6562
1000
3281
500
1640
200
656
SEA
LEVEL
200
656
1000
3281
2000
6562
Transverse Mercator Projection
SWEDEN
FINLAND
ESTONIA
LATVIA
LITHUANIA
BELARUS
RUS. FED.
RUSSIAN
FEDERATION
KARELIYA
ARKHANGEL'SK
VOLOGDA
KOMI
KIROV
KOSTROMA
LENINGRAD
NOVGOROD
PSKOV
TVER'
GULF OF BOTHNIA
GULF OF FINLAND
BALTIC SEA
Gulf of Riga
BELOYE MORE
(WHITE SEA)
Dvinskaya Guba
Onezhskaya Guba
Kandalakshskiy Zaliv
Ladozhskoye Ozero
(Lake Ladoga)
Onezhskoye Ozero
(Lake Onega)
Moskva
Moscow
Sankt-Peterburg
(Leningrad) (St Petersburg)
Helsinki
Tallinn
Riga
Vilnius
Minsk
Arkhangel'sk
Severodvinsk
Petrozavodsk
Vologda
Cherepovets
Kostroma
Yaroslavl'
Ivanovo
Nizhniy Novgorod
Gor'kiy
Kazan'
Syktyvkar
Ukhta
Kotlas
Tver'
Novgorod
Pskov
Smolensk
Tula
Ryazan'
Kaluga
Samara
Tol'yatti
Simbirsk
Kaliningrad
Klaipėda
Liepāja
Tartu
Tampere
Turku
Oulu
Vaasa
Umeå
Sundsvall
Gävle

CASPIAN SEA

(KASPIYSKOYE MORE)

(CHERNOYE MORE)

BLACK SEA

(KARA DENIZ)

Sea of Azov

UKRAINE

MOLDOVA (MOLDAVIA)

ROMANIA

BULGARIA

GREECE

TURKEY

GEORGIA

ARMENIA

AZERBAIJAN

KAZAKHSTAN

POLAND

Miles 0 40 80 120 160 200
Km 0 40 80 120 160 200 240 280 320

1:6M

MOSCOW REGION

52

53

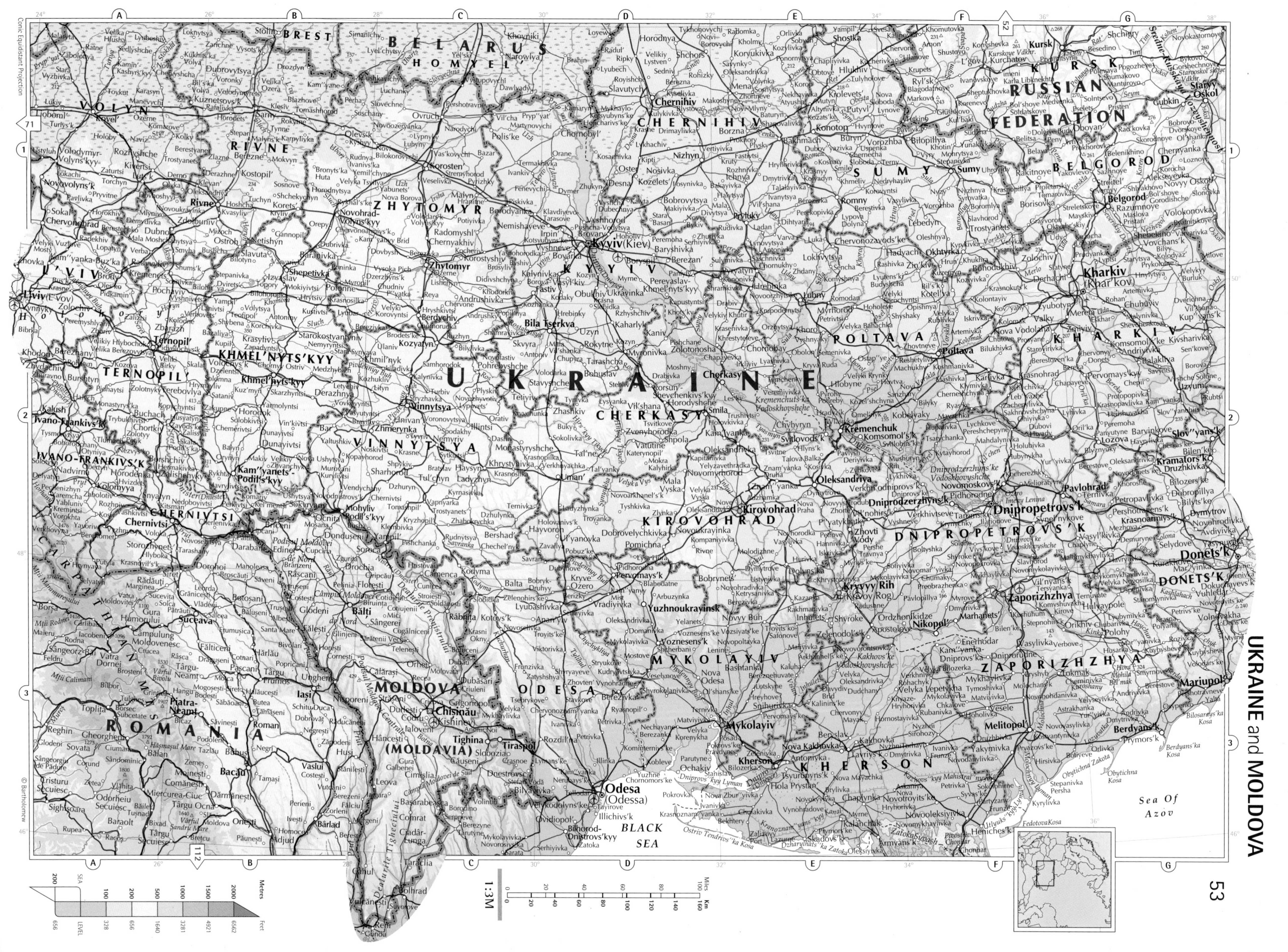
UKRAINE
MOLDOVA
(MOLDAVIA)
RUSSIAN FEDERATION
BELARUS
ROMANIA
BLACK SEA
Sea Of Azov
Kyyiv (Kiev)
Kharkiv
Odesa (Odessa)
Dnipropetrovs'k
Donets'k
Chişinău
Miles
Km
1:3M
Metres
Feet
SEA LEVEL
Conic Equidistant Projection
© Bartholomew
52
71
112

LATVIA, LITHUANIA and ESTONIA

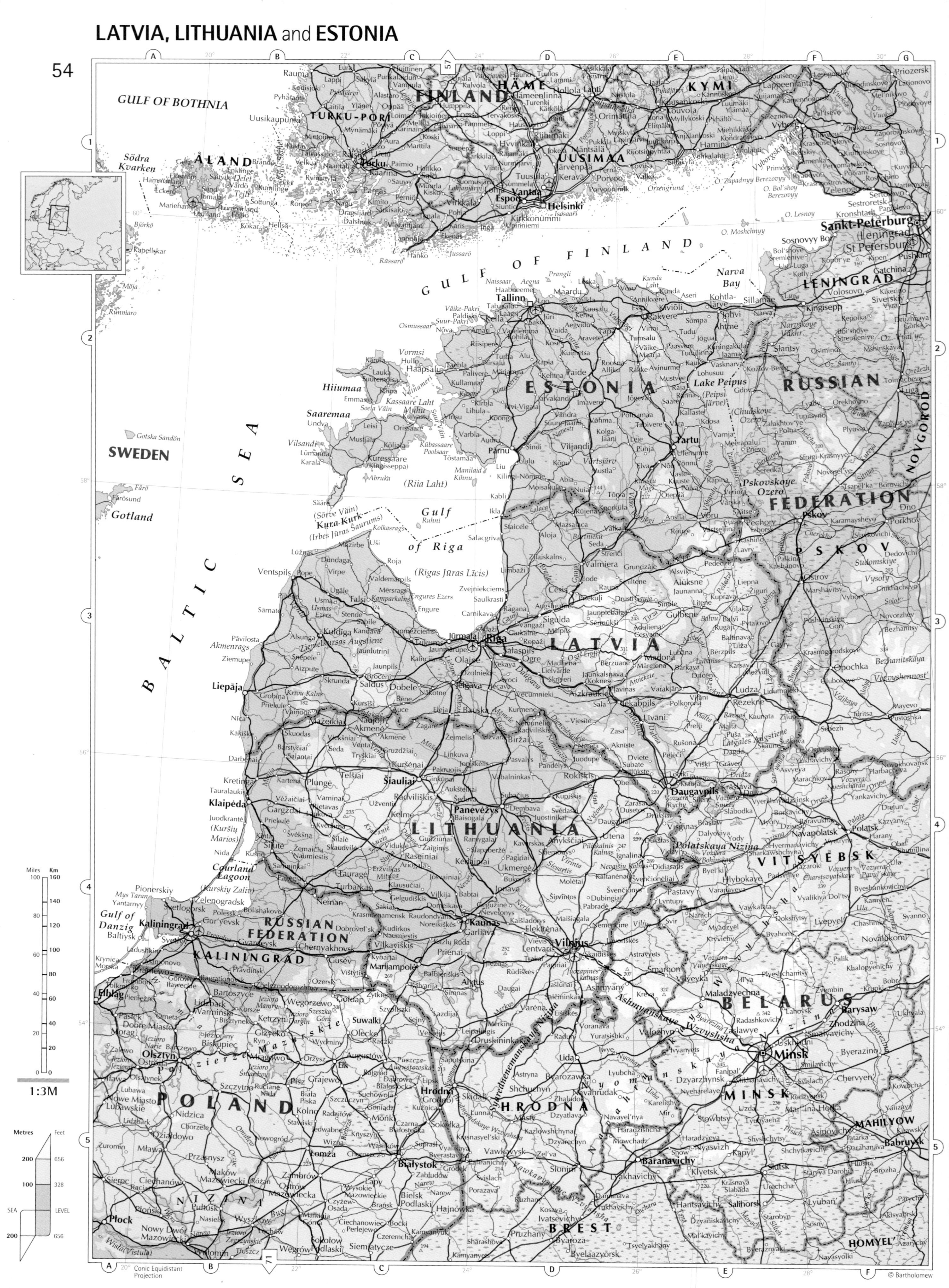
GULF OF BOTHNIA
ÅLAND
FINLAND
TURKU-PORI
HÄME
KYMI
UUSIMAA
Helsinki
GULF OF FINLAND
Sankt-Peterburg
(Leningrad)
St Petersburg
LENINGRAD
Tallinn
ESTONIA
Lake Peipus
RUSSIAN FEDERATION
NOVGOROD
PSKOV
Pskov
Tartu
Pärnu
Hiiumaa
Saaremaa
SWEDEN
Gotland
BALTIC SEA
Gulf of Riga
(Rīgas Jūras Līcis)
(Riia Laht)
LATVIA
Rīga
Liepāja
Ventspils
Daugavpils
LITHUANIA
Klaipėda
Šiauliai
Panevėžys
Kaunas
Vilnius
Courland Lagoon
(Kurskiy Zaliv)
Gulf of Danzig
Kaliningrad
RUSSIAN FEDERATION
KALININGRAD
VITSYEBSK
BELARUS
Minsk
MINSK
HRODNA
Hrodna
BREST
MAHILYOW
HOMYEL'
POLAND
Olsztyn
Białystok
Miles
Km
1:3M
Metres
Feet
SEA
LEVEL
Conic Equidistant Projection
© Bartholomew

FAEROES
(Denmark)
1:2.5M

FØROYAR

1:1.5M

BORNHOLM
(Denmark)

at the same scale

Miles / Km

Metres / Feet

500 / 1640
200 / 656
100 / 328
SEA / LEVEL
50 / 164
200 / 656

© Bartholomew

Conic Equidistant
Projection

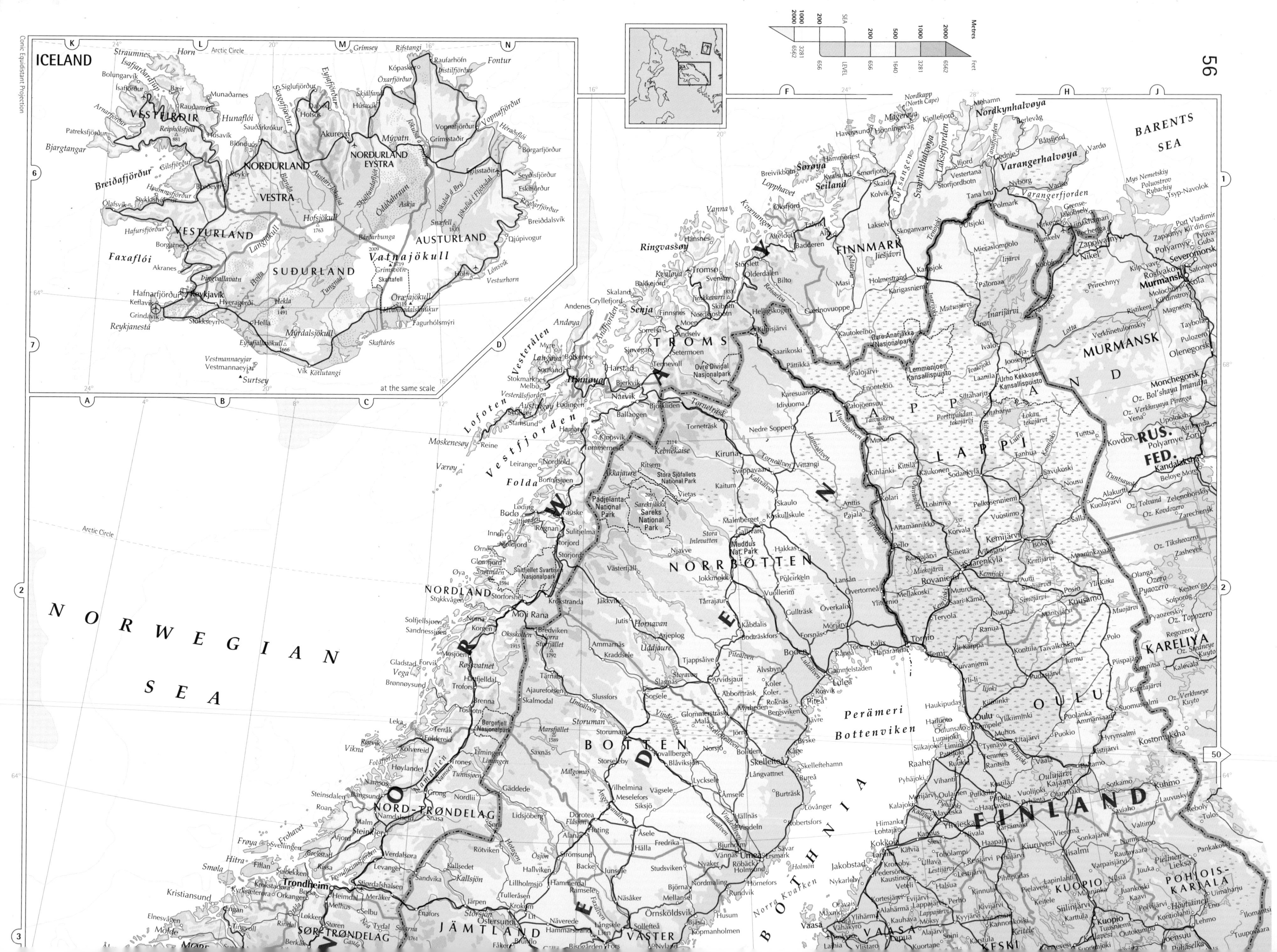

ICELAND

Conic Equidistant Projection

VESTFIRÐIR
NORÐURLAND VESTRA
NORÐURLAND EYSTRA
VESTURLAND
SUÐURLAND
AUSTURLAND
Vatnajökull
Reykjavík
Akureyri
Faxaflói
Breiðafjörður
Húnaflói
Arctic Circle
at the same scale
Metres
Feet
BARENTS SEA
NORWEGIAN SEA
MURMANSK
RUS. FED.
KARELIYA
LAPPI
OULU
FINLAND
KUOPIO
POHJOIS-KARJALA
VAASA
FINNMARK
TROMS
NORDLAND
NORRBOTTEN
VÄSTERBOTTEN
JÄMTLAND
NORD-TRØNDELAG
SØR-TRØNDELAG
Perämeri
Bottenviken
Vestfjorden
Lofoten
Vesterålen
Trondheim
Tromsø
Narvik
Kiruna
Luleå
Umeå
Oulu
Rovaniemi
Murmansk

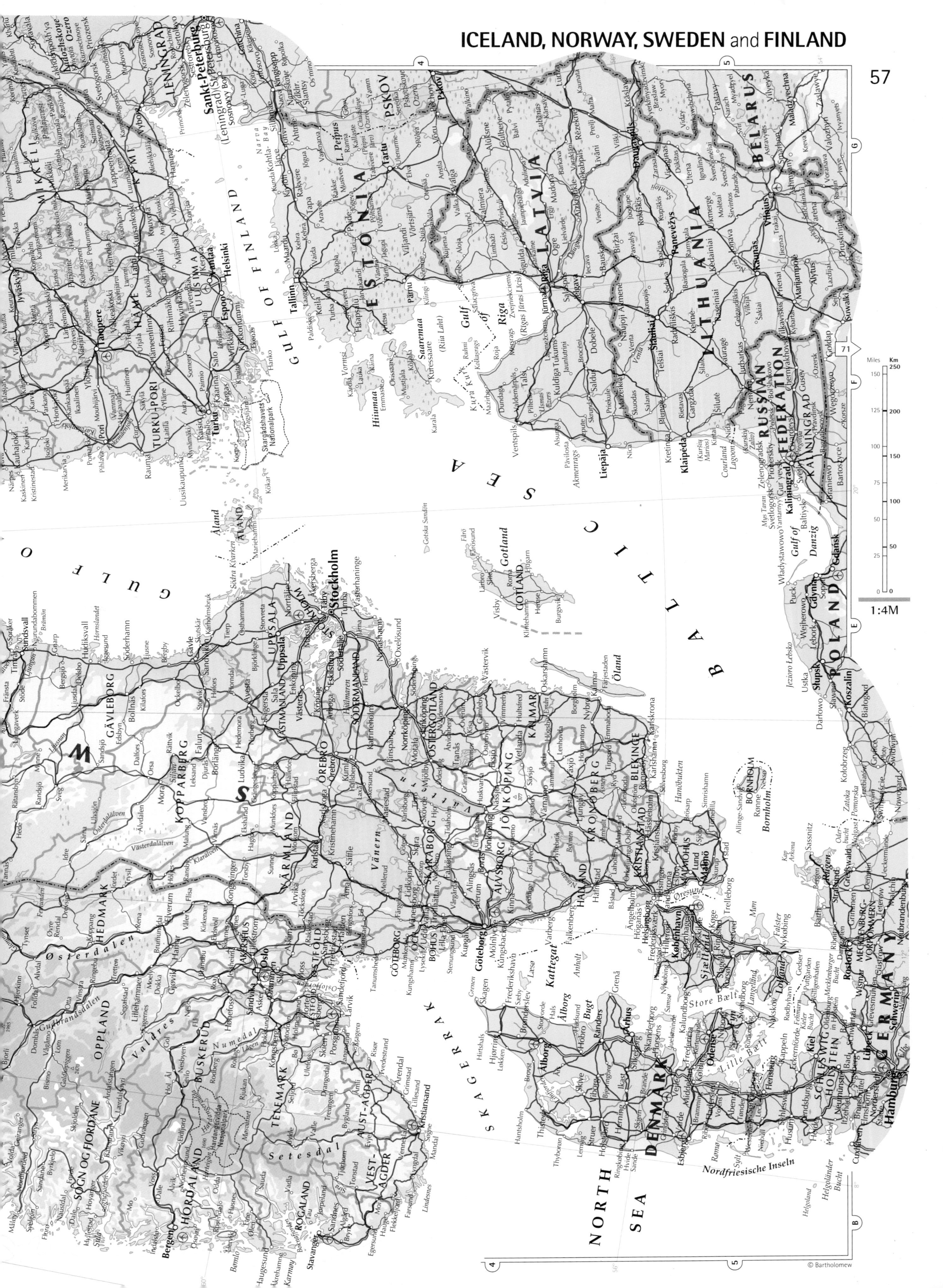

Miles   Km
250

150
200

125

100   150

75   100

50

25   50

0   0

1:4M

© Bartholomew

SOGN OG FJORDANE
OPPLAND
HEDMARK
HORDALAND
NORWAY
BUSKERUD
AKERSHUS
TELEMARK
ØSTFOLD
VESTFOLD
ROGALAND
AUST-AGDER
VEST-AGDER
Bergen
Stavanger
Oslo
Kristiansand
Arendal
Drammen
Haugesund
Sandnes
Skien
Larvik
Fredrikstad
Sarpsborg
Hamar
Gjøvik
Lillehammer
Kongsberg
Hardangervidda
Jotunheimen Nasjonalpark
Hardangervidda Nasjonalpark
Sognefjorden
Hardangerfjorden
Oslofjorden
S K A G E R R A K
N O R T H
S E A
K A T T E G A T
DENMARK
NORDJYLLAND
VIBORG
ÅRHUS
RINGKØBING
VEJLE
RIBE
VESTSJÆLLAND
FYN
Ålborg
Århus
Randers
Viborg
Silkeborg
Herning
Horsens
Vejle
Kolding
Esbjerg
Odense
Fredericia
Frederikshavn
Hjørring
Skagen
Hirtshals
Holstebro
Skive
Grenå
Kalundborg
Læsø
Anholt
Samsø
Jammerbugten
Ålborg Bugt
Limfjorden
Göteborg
Strömstad
Uddevalla
Newcastle upon Tyne
Tórshavn
Lerwick
Amsterdam
Metres
Feet
2000
6562
1500
4921
1000
3281
500
1640
200
656
100
328
SEA
LEVEL
50
164
200
656
Conic Equidistant Projection
A
B
C
D
1
2
3
4
55

GULF OF BOTHNIA

FINLAND

ÅLAND

KOPPARBERG

GÄVLEBORG

VÄRMLAND

VÄSTMANLAND

UPPSALA

Uppsala

ÖREBRO

STOCKHOLM

Stockholm

SÖDERMANLAND

VÄNERN

Dalbosjön

S W E D E N

SKARABORG

ÖSTERGÖTLAND

Norrköping

VÄTTERN

ÄLVSBORG

Borås

Jönköping

JÖNKÖPING

GOTLAND

Visby

Gotland

KALMAR

HALLAND

KRONOBERG

Växjö

Öland

Kalmar

BLEKINGE

Ronneby

Karlshamn

Karlskrona

KRISTIANSTAD

Helsingborg

Kristianstad

B A L T I C

S E A

Hanöbukten

MALMÖHUS

KØBENHAVN

Malmö

København

Öresund

Köge Bugt

© Bartholomew

1:2M

Miles   Km

80   120

100

60   80

40   60

20   40

20

0   0

FAEROES
(FØROYAR)
(Denmark)
Tórshavn
Streymoy
Eysturoy
Vágar
Sandoy
Suðuroy
Sumba
Shetland Is
Unst
Yell
Fetlar
Mainland
Whalsay
Out Skerries
Lerwick
Bressay
Sumburgh Head
Fair Isle
Foula
Papa Stour
Orkney Is
Westray
Sanday
Stronsay
Rousay
Kirkwall
Stromness
Hoy
South Ronaldsay
Pentland Firth
Dunnet Head
Duncansby Head
Wick
Thurso
Cape Wrath
Sule Skerry
Rona
Sula Sgeir
NORWAY
SOGN OG FJORDANE
HORDALAND
Bergen
Store Sotra
Stord
Haugesund
Karmøy
Butt of Lewis
Stornoway
Lewis
(Eilean Leodhais)
South Harris
North Uist
Benbecula
South Uist
Barra
Flannan Is
St Kilda
Outer Hebrides
The Minch
Little Minch
Skye
Rum
Mull
Tiree
Coll
Colonsay
Islay
Jura
Moray Firth
Lossiemouth
Fraserburgh
Peterhead
Aberdeen
Stonehaven
Montrose
Arbroath
Dundee
St Andrews
Firth of Forth
Kirkcaldy
Dunfermline
Edinburgh
Berwick-upon-Tweed
Glasgow
Paisley
Greenock
Inverness
Nairn
Elgin
Ullapool
Fort William
Oban
Perth
Stirling
GRAMPIAN MOUNTAINS
Cairngorm Mts
SCOTLAND
Loch Ness
NORTH SEA
ATLANTIC OCEAN
Rockall
at the same scale
Metres
Feet
1000
3281
500
1640
200
656
100
328
SEA
LEVEL
200
656
1000
3281
Conic Equidistant Projection

1:3M

© Bartholomew

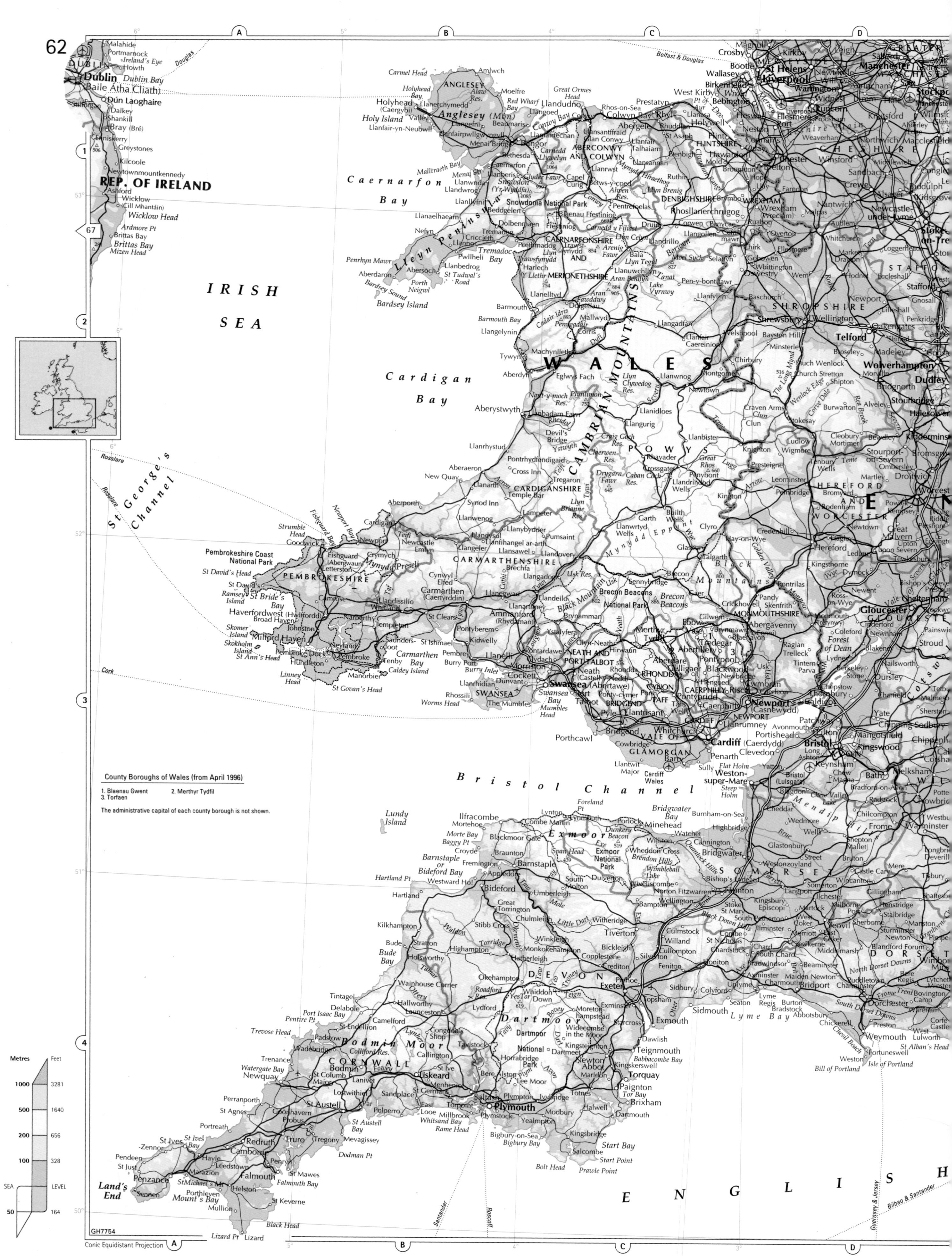
REP. OF IRELAND
IRISH SEA
WALES
CAMBRIAN MOUNTAINS
Caernarfon Bay
Cardigan Bay
St George's Channel
Bristol Channel
ENGLISH
Dublin
Baile Átha Cliath
Dún Laoghaire
Wicklow Head
Anglesey (Môn)
Holyhead (Caergybi)
Bangor
Caernarfon
Snowdonia National Park
Lleyn Peninsula
Bardsey Island
Aberystwyth
POWYS
CARDIGANSHIRE
CARMARTHENSHIRE
PEMBROKESHIRE
Pembrokeshire Coast National Park
Milford Haven
Swansea (Abertawe)
Cardiff (Caerdydd)
Newport (Casnewydd)
Brecon Beacons National Park
Black Mountains
MONMOUTHSHIRE
Lundy Island
Exmoor National Park
Dartmoor National Park
Bodmin Moor
CORNWALL
DEVON
SOMERSET
Plymouth
Exeter
Torquay
Land's End
Penzance
Lizard Pt
Lyme Bay
Bristol
Gloucester
Hereford
Shrewsbury
Telford
Wolverhampton
Liverpool
Manchester
Chester
Wrexham
Bath
Weymouth
Isle of Portland
County Boroughs of Wales (from April 1996)
1. Blaenau Gwent
2. Merthyr Tydfil
3. Torfaen
The administrative capital of each county borough is not shown.
Metres
Feet
1000
3281
500
1640
200
656
100
328
SEA
LEVEL
50
164
GH7754
Conic Equidistant Projection

NORTH SEA

ENGLAND

ENGLISH CHANNEL

CHANNEL ISLANDS (ÎLES NORMANDES) (To United Kingdom)

Isles of Scilly

at the same scale

at the same scale

1:1.2M

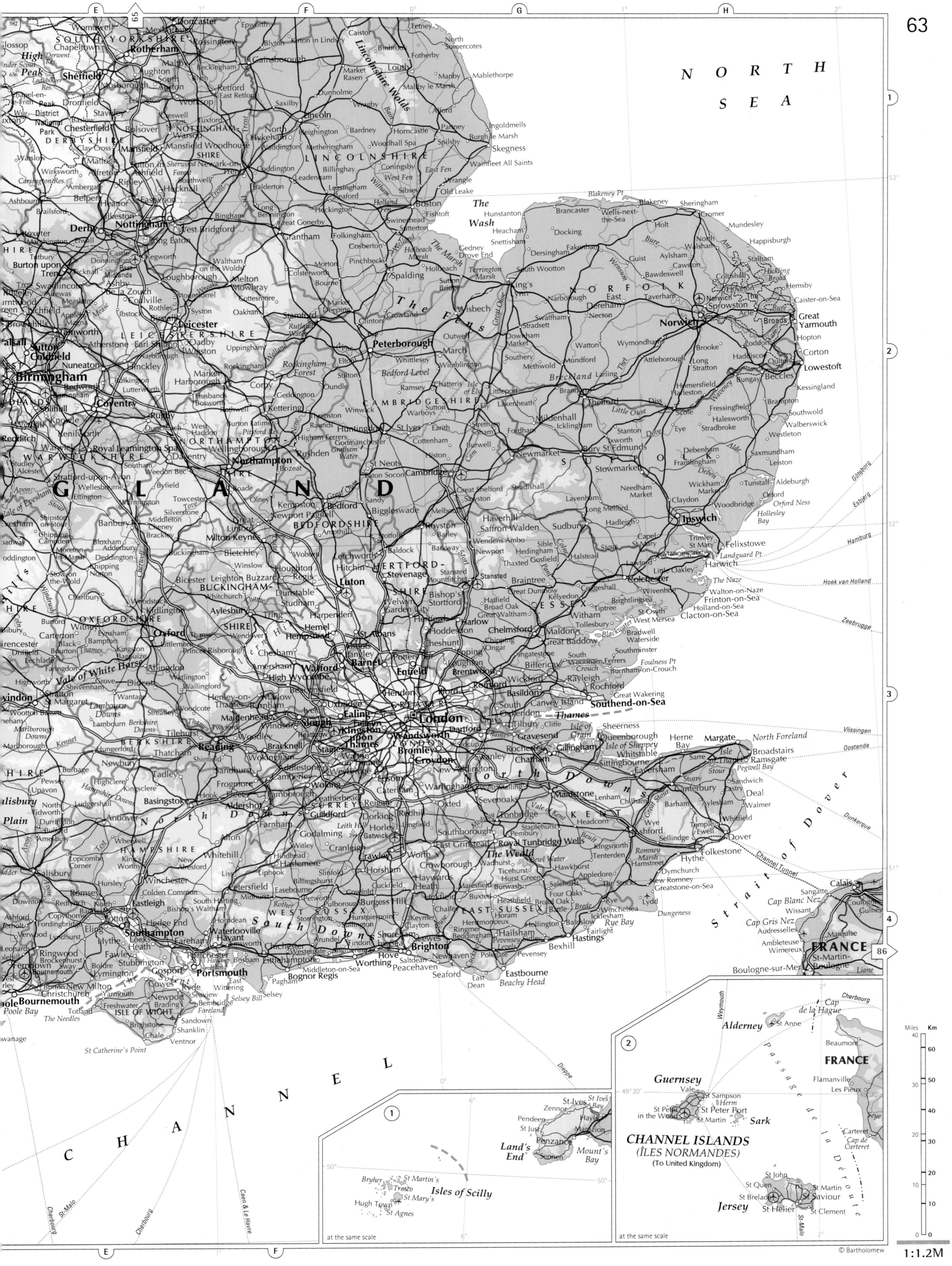

Councils of Scotland (from April 1996)
1. City of Dundee
2. City of Edinburgh
3. City of Glasgow
4. Clackmannan
5. Dumbarton & Clydebank
6. East Dunbartonshire
7. East Lothian
8. East Renfrewshire
9. Falkirk
10. Inverclyde
11. Lothian
12. North Lanarkshire
13. Renfrewshire
14. West Lothian
The administrative capital of each council is not shown.
Counties and County Boroughs of Wales (from April 1996)
15. Aberconwy & Colwyn
16. Anglesey
17. Caernarfonshire & Merionethshire
18. Denbighshire
19. Flintshire
The administrative capital of each county or county borough is not shown.
Metres
Feet
1000
3281
500
1640
200
656
100
328
SEA
LEVEL
50
164
200
656
Conic Equidistant Projection
SCOTLAND
NORTHERN IRELAND
REPUBLIC OF IRELAND
ISLE OF MAN (To U.K.)
IRISH SEA
North Channel
Firth of Lorn
Firth of Clyde
ULSTER
LEINSTER
ARGYLL & BUTE
DONEGAL
LONDONDERRY
ANTRIM
TYRONE
FERMANAGH
ARMAGH
DOWN
MONAGHAN
CAVAN
LEITRIM
LONGFORD
LOUTH
MEATH
WESTMEATH
OFFALY
KILDARE
Lough Neagh
Belfast
Dublin (Baile Átha Cliath)
Londonderry (Derry)
Glasgow
Douglas
Holyhead (Caergybi)
Anglesey (Môn)
66
67

NORTH SEA

ENGLAND

SCOTLAND

Edinburgh

Dundee

Perth

Newcastle upon Tyne

Sunderland

Middlesbrough

Carlisle

Leeds & Bradford

Liverpool

Manchester

Sheffield

Kingston upon Hull

York

Blackpool

Berwick-upon-Tweed

SOUTHERN UPLANDS

CHEVIOT HILLS

NORTHUMBERLAND

CUMBRIA

DURHAM

CLEVELAND

NORTH YORKSHIRE

WEST YORKSHIRE

SOUTH YORKSHIRE

HUMBERSIDE

LANCASHIRE

MERSEYSIDE

GREATER MANCHESTER

DERBYSHIRE

LINCOLNSHIRE

NOTTINGHAMSHIRE

CHESHIRE

TYNE AND WEAR

Firth of Forth

Solway Firth

Lake District National Park

Yorkshire Dales National Park

North York Moors National Park

Northumberland National Park

Peak District National Park

1:1.2M

Miles / Km

© Bartholomew

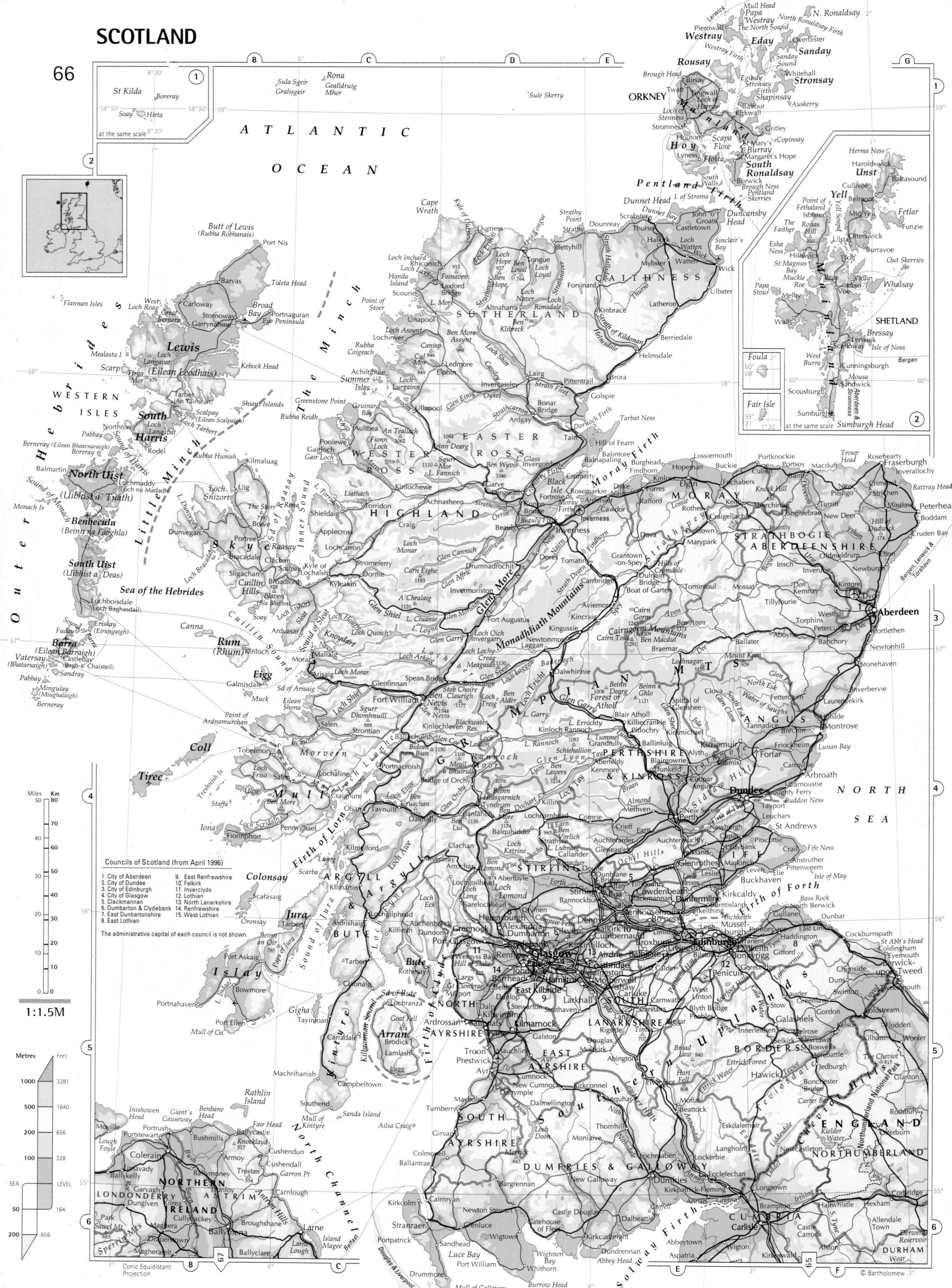
SCOTLAND
ATLANTIC OCEAN
NORTH SEA
ORKNEY
SHETLAND
Councils of Scotland (from April 1996)
1. City of Aberdeen
2. City of Dundee
3. City of Edinburgh
4. City of Glasgow
5. Clackmannan
6. Dumbarton & Clydebank
7. East Dunbartonshire
8. East Lothian
9. East Renfrewshire
10. Falkirk
11. Inverclyde
12. Lothian
13. North Lanarkshire
14. Renfrewshire
15. West Lothian
The administrative capital of each council is not shown.
Miles
Km
1:1.5M
Metres
Feet
SEA
LEVEL
at the same scale
Conic Equidistant Projection
© Bartholomew

A
B
C
D
E
F
10°
9°
8°
7°
6°
55°
54°
53°
52°
1
2
3
4
5
69
64
62
ATLANTIC
OCEAN
NORTHERN
IRELAND
REPUBLIC
OF
IRELAND
SCOTLAND
ULSTER
CONNAUGHT
LEINSTER
MUNSTER
North Channel
St George's Channel
Port Ellen
Mull of Oa
Islay
Tayinloan
Carradale
Machrihanish
Campbeltown
Southend
Sanda Island
Mull of Kintyre
Ailsa Craig
Colmonell
Ballantrae
Kirkcolm
Cairnryan
Stranraer
Portpatrick
Sandhead
Drummore
Inishtrahull
Inishtrahull Sound
Malin Head
Ballygorman
Glengad Head
Tory Island
Tory Sound
Fanad Head
Dunaff Head
Inishowen
Inishowen Head
Giant's Causeway
Benbane Head
Rathlin Island
Fair Head
Ballycastle
Sheep Haven
Portsalon
Carndonagh
Moville
Slieve Snaght
Buncrana
Lough Swilly
Magilligan Pt
Portrush
Portstewart
Bushmills
Knocklayd
Cushendun
Cushendall
Garron Pt
Bloody Foreland
Inishbofin
Gortahork
Creeslough
Carrowkeel
Lough Foyle
Coleraine
Armoy
Trostan
Aran Island
Bunbeg
Gweedore
Derryveagh Mts
Errigal
Glenveagh National Park
Milford
Kilmacrenan
Letterkenny
Londonderry
(Derry)
Limavady
Ballykelly
Eglinton
Ballymoney
Dunloy
ANTRIM
Antrim Hills
Carnlough
Burtonport
Dungloe
DONEGAL
LONDONDERRY
Garvagh
Dungiven
Kilrea
Cullybackey
Fintown
Cark Mtn
Claudy
Park
Ballymena
Broughshane
Larne
Gweebarra Bay
Aghla Mtn
Raphoe
Sawel Mt.
Sperrin Mts
Island Magee
Dawros Head
Loughros More Bay
Glenties
Finn
Stranorlar
Deele
Strabane
Sion Mills
Draperstown
Larne Lough
Whitehead
Ballyclare
Blue Stack Mts
Ballybofey
Maghera
Magherafelt
Randalstown
Antrim
Carrickfergus
Belfast Lough
Newtownabbey
Bangor
Donaghadee
Rossan Pt
Malin More
Slieve League
Killybegs
Lough Eske
Ardara
Castlederg
Newtownstewart
Cookstown
Moneymore
Lough Neagh
Belfast
Dundonald
Newtownards
Muckross Head
St John's Pt
Donegal
Lough Derg
Pettigo
Omagh
TYRONE
Pomeroy
Sixmilecross
Beragh
Dunmurry
Comber
Ards Pen.
Kircubbin
Portavogie
Killinchy
Donegal Bay
Bundoran
Ballyshannon
Erne
Dromore
Fintona
Donaghmore
Dungannon
Lisburn
Lurgan
Craigavon
Saintfield
Strangford Lough
Portaferry
Strangford
Ballyquintin Pt
Inishmurray
Cliffony
Lower Lough Erne
Lisnarrick
Tully
Augher
Ballygawley
Aughnacloy
Benburb
Portadown
Tandragee
Annahilt
Dromore
Ballynahinch
DOWN
Crossgar
Downpatrick
Ballyward
Ardglass
St John's Pt
Banbridge
Benwee Head
Downpatrick Head
Roskeeragh Pt
Benbulben
Truskmore
Lough Melvin
Dartry Mts
LEITRIM
Belcoo
Fivemiletown
Enniskillen
Lisbellaw
Slieve Beagh
Armagh
ARMAGH
Markethill
Newry Canal
Rathfriland
Mourne Mts
Slieve Donard
Newcastle
Dundrum
Erris Head
Broad Haven
Belderg
Ballycastle
Killala Bay
Sligo Bay
Dromore West
Sligo
(Sligeach)
Manorhamilton
FERMANAGH
Upper Lough Erne
Lisnaskea
Middletown
Keady
Ulster Canal
Monaghan
(Muineachán)
Bessbrook
Newry
Annalong
Kilkeel
Belmullet
Maumakeogh
Killala
Knockalongy
Collooney
Lough Gill
Glengavlen
Cuncagh
Newtownbutler
Clones
MONAGHAN
The Mullet
Carrowmore Lake
Inishkea North
Inishkea South
Bangor Erris
Ballina
(Béal an Átha)
Ox Mts
Slieve Gamph
Drumkeeran
Lough Allen
Iron Mts
Slieve Anierin
Ballyconnell
Ballinamore
Butlers Bridge
Ballybay
Castleblayney
Crossmaglen
Warrenpoint
Carlingford
Greenore
Greencastle
Carlingford Lough
Blacksod Bay
Ballycroy
Slieve Car
Lough Conn
Nephin
Nephin Beg Range
Mullanys Cross
Ballymote
Lough Gara
Lough Arrow
Ballinafad
Lough Key
Carrick-on-Shannon
Carrigallen
Lough Oughter
Annalee
Cootehill
Dundalk
Dún Dealgan
Slieve More
Achill Head
Dooagh
Achill Island
Corraun Pen.
Tubbercurry
Foxford
Charlestown
Boyle
Cavan
Shercock
Carrickmacross
Castlebellingham
Dundalk Bay
Dunany Pt
Beltra Lough
Lough Feeagh
Pontoon
Swinford
Ballaghaderreen
Frenchpark
Urlaur Lough
Dromod
Mohill
Arvagh
Lough Gowna
Ballieborough
Kingscourt
Nobber
Ardee
LOUTH
Dunleer
Clew Bay
Mulrany
Newport
Castlebar
(Caisleán an Bharraigh)
Bohola
Kiltimagh
Knock
Cloonfeagh
Ballyjamesduff
Virginia
Lough Ramor
Clogher Head
Clare Island
Croagh Patrick
Louisburgh
Westport
Ballyhaunis
ROSCOMMON
Strokestown
Granard
Lough Sheelin
Kells
(Ceanannus Mór)
Drogheda
(Droichead Átha)
Bettystown
Caher Island
Inishturk
Cregganbaun
MAYO
Lough Carra
Claremorris
Castlerea
LONGFORD
Longford
Oldcastle
Slieve na Calliagh
Slane
Inishbofin
Inishark
Killary Harbour
Mweelrea
Partry Mts
Partry
Connemara National Park
Benwee
Lough Mask
Ballinrobe
Ballindine
Dunmore
Glenamaddy
Roscommon
Lanesborough
Lough Ree
Edgeworthstown
Castlepollard
Lough Derravaragh
Ballinalack
Inny
Lough Owel
Delvin
Athboy
Navan
(An Uaimh)
Boyne
MEATH
Balbriggan
Skerries
Omey Island
Aasleagh
Benbaun
Joyce's Country
Maumturk Mts
Kilmaine
Cong
Clonbern
Tuam
Athleague
Ballymahon
WESTMEATH
Mullingar
Trim
Rush
Lambay Island
Mannin Bay
Clifden
Connemara
Lough Corrib
Horseleap
Ballygar
Mount Bellew
Athlone
(Baile Átha Luain)
Moate
Lough Ennell
Kinnegad
Moyvalley
Dunboyne
Ashbourne
Swords
Portrane
Malahide
Ireland's Eye
Howth
Slyne Head
Recess
Headford
Clare
Clara
Royal Canal
Dublin
Baile Átha Cliath
Leixlip
Lucan
Dún Laoghaire
Holyhead
Ballyconneely Bay
Bertraghboy Bay
GALWAY
Iar Connaught
Monivea
Athenry
Galway
(Gaillimh)
Oranmore
Kiltullagh
Ballinasloe
(Béal Átha na Sluaighe)
Brosna
Kilbeggan
Tullamore
(Tulach Mhór)
Edenderry
Bog of Allen
Celbridge
Newcastle
Clane
KILDARE
Rathangan
Naas
(An Nás)
Bray (Bré)
Enniskerry
Gorumna Island
Galway Bay
Inishmore
Aran Islands
Inisheer
Inishmaan
Murroogh
Black Head
Ballyvaughan
Burren Nat. Park
Kinvara
Gort
Loughrea
Killimor
Banagher
OFFALY
Clonygowan
Portarlington
Monasterevan
Newbridge
Droichead Nua
Kilcullen
Blessington Lakes
Wicklow Mts National Park
Kilcoole
Newtownmountkennedy
Wicklow
(Cill Mhantáin)
Wicklow Head
Slieve Elva
Lisdoonvarna
Cliffs of Moher
Hag's Head
Liscannor Bay
Corofin
Ennistymon
Slieve Aughty Mts
Lough Cutra
Lough Graney
Scalp
Mountshannon
Portumna
Shannon
Birr
Slieve Bloom Mts
Kilcormac
Mountmellick
Portlaoise
Mountrath
Castletown
Stradbally
LAOIS
Ballylynan
Athy
Dunlavin
Timolin
Baltinglass
WICKLOW
Wicklow Mts
Lugnaquilla Mtn
Rathdrum
Brittas Bay
Mizen Head
Milltown Malbay
Mal Bay
Slievecallan
CLARE
Ennis
(Inis)
Crusheen
Tulla
Lough Derg
Borrisokane
Roscrea
IRELAND
Castledermot
Carlow
(Ceatharlach)
Rathvilly
Aughrim
Avoca
Arklow (An tInbhear Mór)
Kilmichael Pt
Mutton Island
Clarecastle
Slieve Bernagh
Arra Mts
Killaloe
Nenagh
(An tAonach)
Devils Bit Mtn
Templemore
Rathdowney
Durrow
Castlecomer
Graigue
CARLOW
Tullow
Shillelagh
Donegal Pt
Moore Bay
Knockalough
Newmarket on-Fergus
Hurler's Cross
Castleconnell
Silvermine Mts
Borrisoleigh
Newport
Templetuohy
Ballyragget
Leighlinbridge
Johnstown
Urlingford
Suir
Whitehall
Muine Bheag
Derry
Inch
Gorey
Kilkee
Doonbeg
Shannon
Shannon
Limerick
(Luimneach)
Slievefelim Mtns
Milestone
Thurles
(Durlas)
Holycross
KILKENNY
Kilkenny
(Cill Chainnigh)
Mt Leinster
Blackstairs Mts
Bunclody
Courtown
Ballycanew
Cahore Pt
Kilrush
Foynes
Tarbert
Loop Head
Mouth of the Shannon
Ballybunnion
Cashen
Adare
Rathkeale
Croom
Pallas Green
Golden Vale
TIPPERARY
Slieveardagh Hills
Callan
Kells
Ballymurphy
Dungarvan
Thomastown
Ferns
WEXFORD
Enniscorthy
(Inis Córthaidh)
Blackwater
Kerry Head
Listowel
LIMERICK
Newcastle West
Hospital
Tipperary
Cashel
Killenaule
Ninemilehouse
Fethard
Slievenamon
Knocktopher
Ballyhale
Brandon Hill
Nore
Drummin
Clonroche
Killurin
Castlebridge
Wexford Bay
Wexford (Loch Garman)
Wexford Harbour
Rosslare
Ballyheigue Bay
Ballyheigue
Abbeyfeale
Mullaghareirk Mts
Glanaruddery Mts
Broadford
Galbally
Kilmallock
Galtymore
Galtee Mts
Cahir
Newin
Clonmel
(Cluain Meala)
Kilcommon
Lukeswell
New Ross
Booley Hills
Wellington Bridge
Taghmon
Killinick
Rosslare Harbour
Fishguard
Brandon Head
Brandon Bay
Brandon Mtn
Beenoskee
Tralee Bay
Tralee
(Trá Lí)
Castlegregory
Rathluirc
(Charleville)
Newtown
Ballyhoura Mts
Mitchelstown
Tar
Comeragh Mts
Ballymacarberry
Carrick-on-Suir
Portlaw
Cheekpoint
Duncannon
Duncormick
Carnsore Pt
Smerwick Harb.
Sybil Pt
Slievanea
Dingle
Slieve Mish Mts
Castleisland
Knockacummer
Newmarket
Buttevant
Knockmealdown Mts
Seefin
Waterford
(Port Láirge)
Ballyteige Bay
Kilmore Quay
Saltee Islands
Inishtooskert
Great Blasket I.
Dunquin
Slea Head
Dingle Bay
Inch
Castlemaine
Killorglin
KERRY
Killarney
(Cill Airne)
Ballydesmond
Cloonbannin
Kanturk
Mallow
(Mala)
Fermoy
Blackwater
Tallow
WATERFORD
Cappoquin
Lismore
Ballymacmague
Tramore
(Trá Mhór)
Dunmore East
Hook Head
Waterford Harb.
Laune
Lough Caragh
Lough Leane
Millstreet
Boggeragh Mts
Banteer
Nagles Mts
Bride
Dungarvan
(Dún Garbhán)
Clashmore
Helvick Head
Pembroke Dock
Doulus Head
Valentia Island
Coomacarrea
Macgillycuddy's Reeks
Killarney Nat. Park
Mangerton Mt
The Paps
Musheramore
CORK
Watergrasshill
Grange
Mine Head
Ardmore Bay
Bray Head
Cahersiveen
Foilclough
The Pocket
Poulgorm Bridge
Ballymakeery
Macroom
Kilmona
Tower
Blarney
Carrigtwohill
Midleton
Youghal
(Eochaill)
Castlemartyr
Portmagee
Lough Currane
Sneem
Kenmare
Carrigadrohid Reservoir
Cork
(Corcaigh)
Cobh
(An Cóbh)
St Finan's Bay
Ballybrack
Ballinskelligs Bay
Knockaboy
Shanacrane
Halfway
Crosshaven
Youghal Bay
Skellig Rocks
Caherdaniel
Scariff I.
Kenmare River
Lauragh
Caha Mts
Glengarriff
Enniskean
Bandon
Kinsale
Cod's Head
Slieve Miskish Mts
Castletown Bere
Bear I.
Dunmanway
Drimoleague
Clonakilty
Courtmacsherry
Old Head of Kinsale
Dursey Island
Dursey Head
Cahermore
Bantry
Bantry Bay
Leap
Ross Carbery
Seven Heads
Clonakilty Bay
Sheep's Head
Dunmanus Bay
Schull
Skibbereen
Galley Head
Crookhaven
Roaringwater Bay
Toe Head
Mizen Head
Cape Clear
Clear Island
Fastnet Rock
Cherbourg, Le Havre, Roscoff, St-Malo & Swansea
Cherbourg & Le Havre
Douglas
Liverpool
10° Conic Equidistant Projection
© Bartholomew
Miles
Km
1:1.5M
Metres
Feet
500
1640
200
656
100
328
SEA
LEVEL
50
164
200
656

NORTH
SEA
NETHERLANDS
GERMANY
NIEDERSACHSEN
GRONINGEN
FRIESLAND
DRENTHE
OVERIJSSEL
FLEVOLAND
GELDERLAND
UTRECHT
NOORD-HOLLAND
ZUID-HOLLAND
NOORD-BRABANT
MÜNSTER
Waddenzee
Waddeneilanden
IJsselmeer
Markermeer
Noordoost Polder
Wieringermeer Polder
Texel
Vlieland
Terschelling
Ameland
Schiermonnikoog
Borkum
Amsterdam
Rotterdam
's-Gravenhage (Den Haag)(The Hague)
Utrecht
Haarlem
Leiden
Groningen
Leeuwarden
Zwolle
Arnhem
Nijmegen
Apeldoorn
Enschede
Almelo
Hengelo
Dordrecht
Breda
Hertogenbosch
Emden
Den Helder
Alkmaar
Hoorn
Lelystad
Zandvoort
Hull
Harwich
Metres
Feet
500
1640
200
656
100
328
SEA LEVEL
50
164
Conic Equidistant Projection

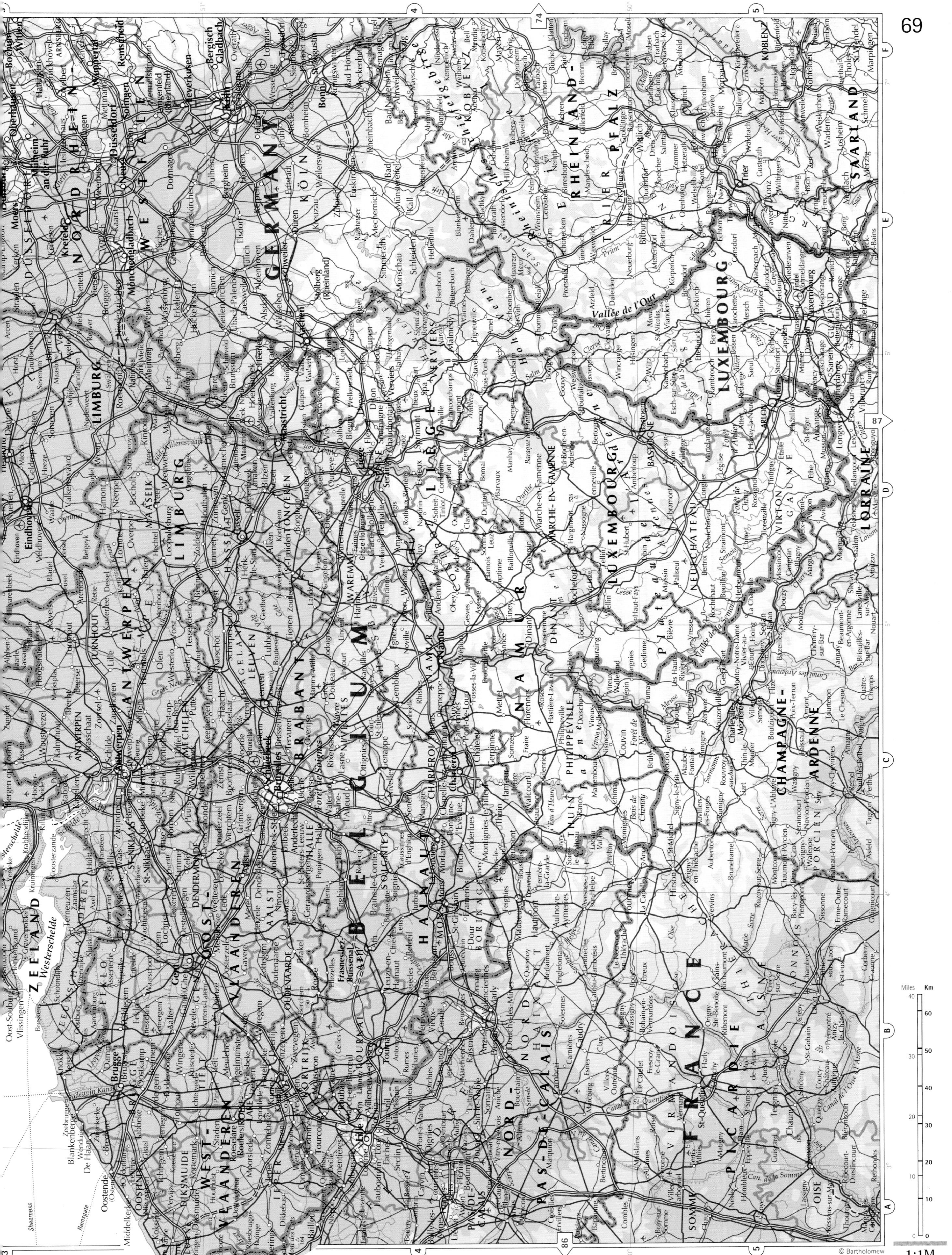

NORD-RHEIN-WESTFALEN

GERMANY

RHEINLAND-PFALZ

TRIER

SAARLAND

LUXEMBOURG

Luxembourg

LORRAINE

LIMBURG

BELGIUM

ANTWERPEN

BRABANT

LIÈGE

NAMUR

LUXEMBOURG

HAINAUT

OOST-VLAANDEREN

WEST-VLAANDEREN

ZEELAND

Brugge

Gent

Bruxelles/Brussel

Antwerpen

Eindhoven

Maastricht

Köln

Düsseldorf

Koblenz

BASTOGNE

DINANT

MARCHE-EN-FAMENNE

NEUFCHÂTEAU

VIRTON

ARLON

ARDENNE

CHAMPAGNE-ARDENNE

PICARDIE

FRANCE

NORD-PAS-DE-CALAIS

AISNE

OISE

SOMME

Vallée de l'Our

Westerschelde

Vlissingen

Oostende

1:1M

Miles 40   Km 60

© Bartholomew

NORTH SEA
DENMARK
NETHERLANDS
BELGIUM
GERMANY
FRANCE
SWITZERLAND
AUSTRIA
ITALY
LUXEMBOURG
LIECHTENSTEIN
SCHLESWIG-HOLSTEIN
MECKLENBURG-VORPOMMERN
NIEDERSACHSEN
SACHSEN-ANHALT
NORDRHEIN-WESTFALEN
HESSEN
THÜRINGEN
RHEINLAND-PFALZ
SAARLAND
BADEN-WÜRTTEMBERG
BAYERN
LORRAINE
ALSACE
CHAMPAGNE-ARDENNE
BOURGOGNE
FRANCHE-COMTÉ
RHÔNE-ALPES
TIROL
SALZBURG
VORARLBERG
TRENTINO-ALTO ADIGE
LOMBARDIA
FRIULI-VENEZIA GIULIA
VENETO
Helgoländer Bucht
Ostfriesische Inseln
Nordfriesische Inseln
Waddenzee
Hamburg
Bremen
Hannover
Berlin
Leipzig
Dresden
Köln
Düsseldorf
Frankfurt am Main
Stuttgart
München (Munich)
Nürnberg
Amsterdam
Rotterdam
's-Gravenhage (Den Haag) (The Hague)
Antwerpen
Bruxelles
Luxembourg
Strasbourg
Zürich
Bern
Basel
Genève
Lausanne
Innsbruck
Salzburg
Bolzano
Metres
Feet
4000
13124
3000
9843
2000
6562
1500
4921
1000
3281
500
1640
200
656
100
656
SEA
LEVEL
200
656
85
104
Conic Equidistant Projection

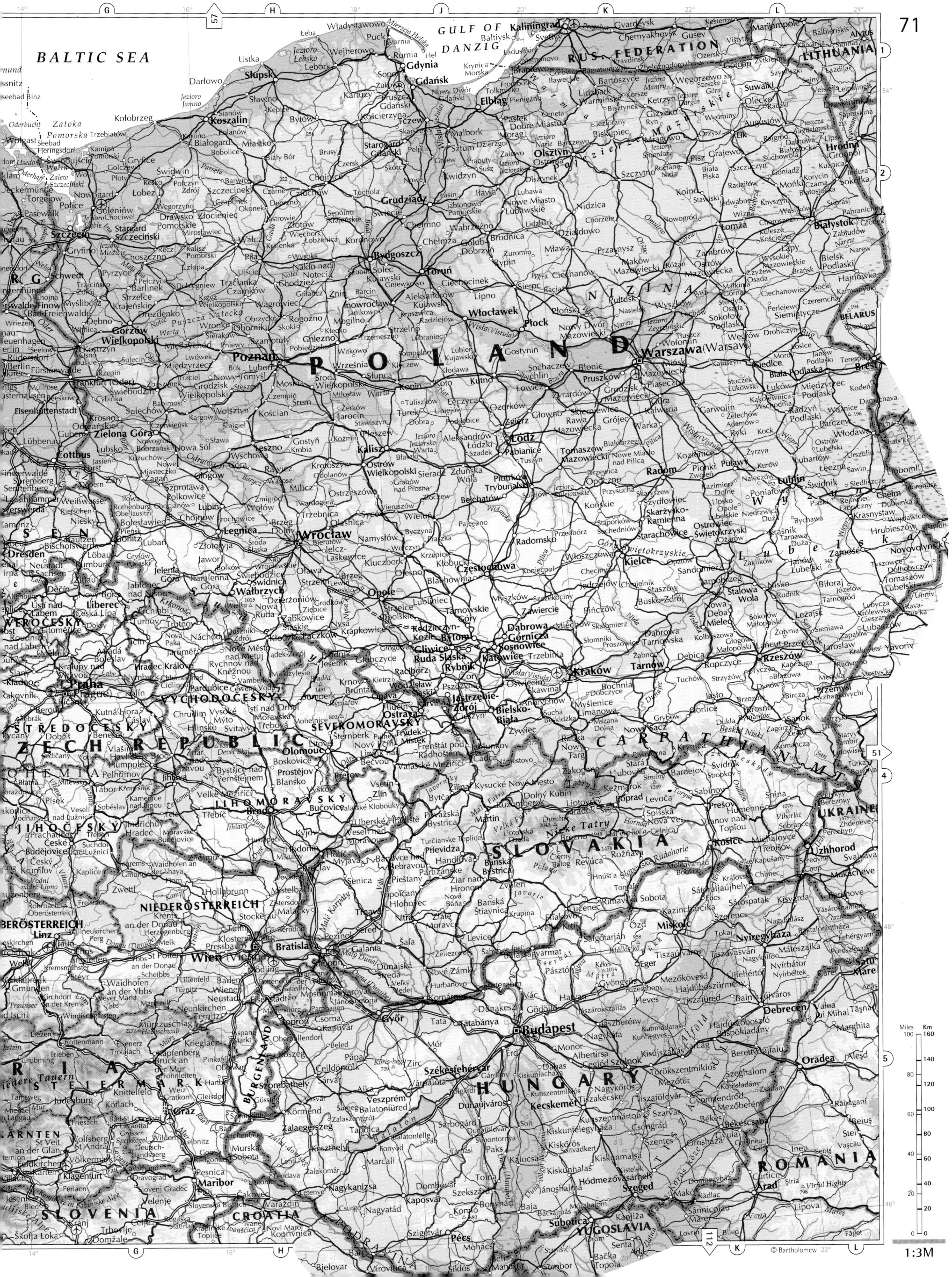

BALTIC SEA

GULF OF DANZIG

RUS. FEDERATION

LITHUANIA

BELARUS

P O L A N D

Warszawa (Warsaw)

Gdańsk · Gdynia · Słupsk · Koszalin · Kołobrzeg · Szczecin · Stargard Szczeciński · Gorzów Wielkopolski · Poznań · Bydgoszcz · Toruń · Włocławek · Płock · Łódź · Kalisz · Wrocław · Legnica · Opole · Częstochowa · Radom · Kielce · Lublin · Kraków · Tarnów · Rzeszów · Przemyśl · Katowice · Gliwice · Bytom · Sosnowiec · Dąbrowa Górnicza · Ruda Śląska · Rybnik · Bielsko-Biała

CZECH REPUBLIC

BOHEMIA · VYCHODOČESKÝ · STŘEDOČESKÝ · JIHOČESKÝ · JIHOMORAVSKÝ · SEVEROMORAVSKÝ

Praha (Prague) · Dresden · Liberec · Ústí nad Labem · Hradec Králové · Pardubice · Olomouc · Ostrava · Brno · Zlín · Jihlava

SLOVAKIA

Bratislava · Žilina · Košice · Prešov · Poprad · Martin · Banská Bystrica · Nitra · Trnava

CARPATHIAN MTS

NIEDERÖSTERREICH · OBERÖSTERREICH · STEIERMARK · KÄRNTEN · BURGENLAND

Wien (Vienna) · Linz · Graz · Klagenfurt

HUNGARY

Budapest · Miskolc · Debrecen · Nyíregyháza · Szeged · Győr · Pécs · Székesfehérvár · Kecskemét · Eger

UKRAINE · Uzhhorod

SLOVENIA · CROATIA · Maribor

YUGOSLAVIA · ROMANIA · Oradea · Arad

1:3M

© Bartholomew

NORTH SEA
Newcastle upon Tyne
Harwich
Nordfriesische Inseln
Helgoländer Bucht
Ostfriesische Inseln
Nationalpark Schleswig-Holsteinisches Wattenmeer
Nationalpark Hamburgisches Wattenmeer
Nationalpark Niedersächsisches Wattenmeer
Waddenzee
IJsselmeer
Noordoost Polder
DENMARK
SCHLESWIG-HOLSTEIN
NIEDERSACHSEN
NETHERLANDS
GERMANY
GRONINGEN
FRIESLAND
DRENTHE
OVERIJSSEL
GELDERLAND
NOORD-BRABANT
LIMBURG
BELGIUM
NORDRHEIN-WESTFALEN
HESSEN
WESER-EMS
HANNOVER
LÜNEBURG
BRAUNSCHWEIG
DETMOLD
MÜNSTER
DÜSSELDORF
ARNSBERG
KÖLN
KASSEL
OSTFRIESLAND
AMMERLAND
MÜNSTERLAND
SAUERLAND
BERGISCHES LAND
Teutoburger Wald
Wiehengebirge
Rothaargebirge
Bourtanger Moor
Sylt
Föhr
Amrum
Pellworm
Helgoland
Borkum
Juist
Norderney
Langeoog
Spiekeroog
Wangerooge
Terschelling
Ameland
Schiermonnikoog
Hamburg
Bremen
Bremerhaven
Hannover
Kiel
Flensburg
Lübeck
Cuxhaven
Oldenburg
Osnabrück
Münster
Bielefeld
Emden
Wilhelmshaven
Groningen
Leeuwarden
Zwolle
Enschede
Apeldoorn
Arnhem
Nijmegen
Eindhoven
Maastricht
Dortmund
Essen
Duisburg
Düsseldorf
Köln
Bonn
Aachen
Wuppertal
Hagen
Bochum
Gelsenkirchen
Krefeld
Mönchengladbach
Paderborn
Hamm
Siegen
Marburg
Kassel
Göttingen
Hildesheim
Celle
Lüneburg
Neumünster
Schleswig
Husum
Rendsburg
Heide
Itzehoe
Stade
Verden (Aller)
Nienburg (Weser)
Minden
Herford
Detmold
Gütersloh
Lippstadt
Arnsberg
Leverkusen
Solingen
Remscheid
Recklinghausen
Oberhausen
Mülheim an der Ruhr
Moers
Conic Equidistant Projection
Metres
Feet
1000
3281
500
1640
200
656
100
328
SEA LEVEL
50
164
68
74
55

BALTIC SEA

Bornholm (Denmark)

Kaliningrad, Klaipeda, Riga & Sankt Peterburg

DANMARK

Kieler Bucht

Mecklenburger Bucht

Lübeck

Rostock

Rügen

Stralsund

Greifswald

KOSZALIN

MECKLENBURG-VORPOMMERN

Schwerin

Neubrandenburg

Szczecin

SZCZECIN

SZCZECINSKIE

GORZÓW

PRIGNITZ

WENDLAND

ALTMARK

BRANDENBURG

Berlin

Potsdam

Frankfurt (Oder)

POLAND

ZIELONA GÓRA

GÓRA

Wolfsburg

SACHSEN-ANHALT

Magdeburg

Dessau

Halle

Leipzig

Cottbus

NIEDERLAUSITZ

OBERLAUSITZ

Hoyerswerda

JELENIA GÓRA

THÜRINGEN

Erfurt

Weimar

Jena

Gera

SACHSEN

Chemnitz

Dresden

Görlitz

Liberec

CZECH REPUBLIC

Miles Km

1:1.5M

© Bartholomew

NETHERLANDS
BELGIUM
LUXEMBOURG
FRANCE
GERMANY
SWITZERLAND

NORDRHEIN-WESTFALEN
HESSEN
RHEINLAND-PFALZ
SAARLAND
BADEN-WÜRTTEMBERG
LORRAINE
ALSACE
FRANCHE-COMTÉ
VORARLBERG
LIECHTENSTEIN

Metres	Feet
3000	9843
2000	6562
1500	4921
1000	3281
500	1640
200	656
100	328
SEA	LEVEL

Conic Equidistant Projection

POLAND

CZECH REPUBLIC

AUSTRIA

ITALY

SACHSEN-ANHALT

THÜRINGEN

SACHSEN

DRESDEN

SEVEROČESKÝ

STŘEDOČESKÝ

ZÁPADOČESKÝ

BOHEMIA

JIHOČESKÝ

BAYERN

OBERFRANKEN

OBERPFALZ

NIEDERBAYERN

OBERBAYERN

SCHWABEN

MÜHLVIERTEL

OBERÖSTERREICH

NIEDER-ÖSTERREICH

STEIERMARK

KÄRNTEN

TIROL

SALZBURG

Leipzig · Dresden · Görlitz · Praha Prague · Erfurt · Jena · Gera · Zwickau · Chemnitz · Karl-Marx-Stadt · Liberec · Plzeň · České Budějovice · Bamberg · Bayreuth · Nürnberg · Fürth · Erlangen · Regensburg · Ingolstadt · Landshut · Passau · Linz · München Munich · Augsburg · Salzburg · Innsbruck · Garmisch-Partenkirchen · Rosenheim

1:1.5M

© Bartholomew

Miles 50 40 30 20 10 0
Km 80 70 60 50 40 30 20 10 0

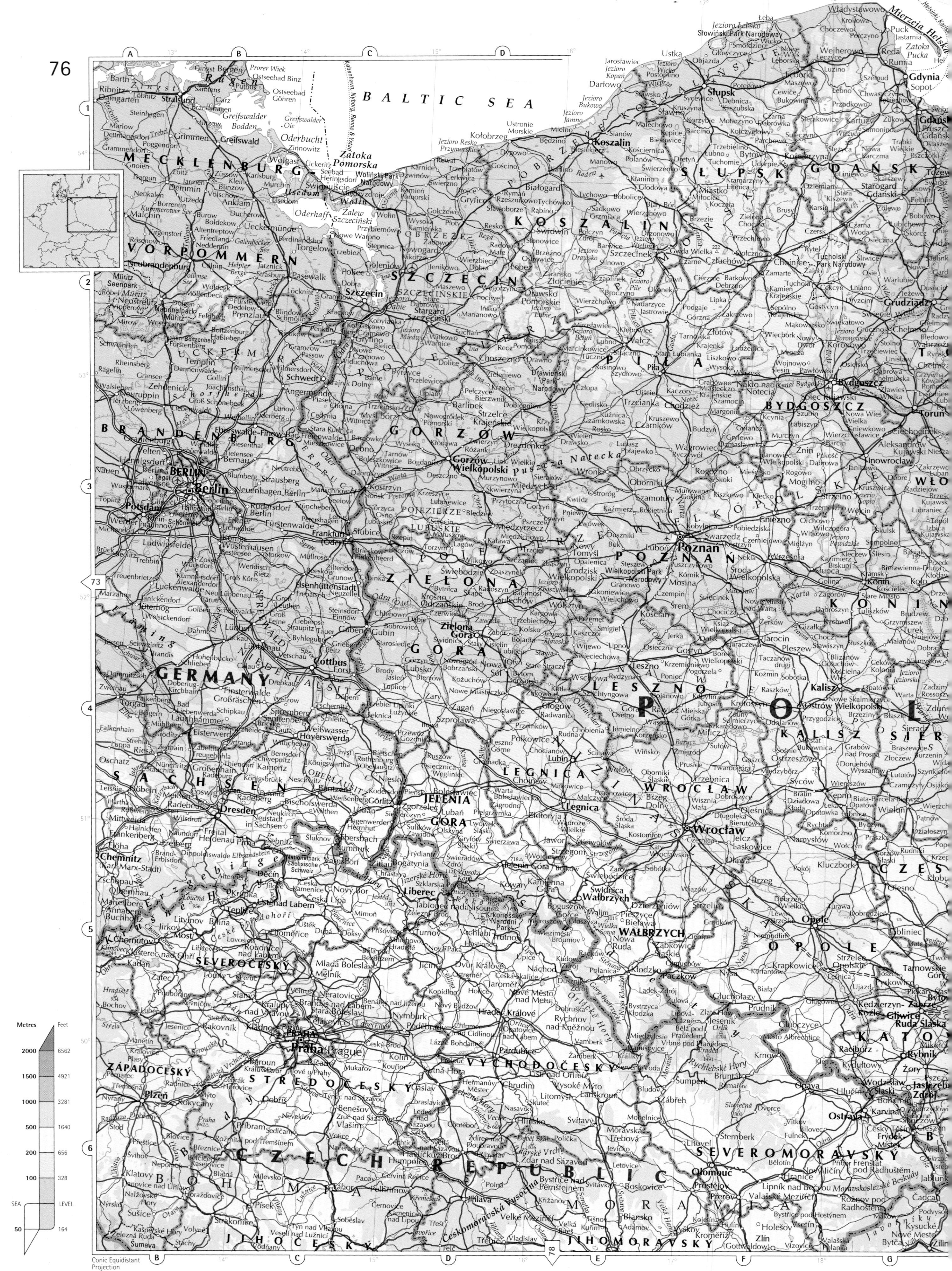
BALTIC SEA
MECKLENBURG-
VORPOMMERN
BRANDENBURG
GERMANY
SACHSEN
KOSZALIN
SŁUPSK
GDAŃSK
SZCZECIN
GORZÓW
PIŁA
BYDGOSZCZ
POZNAŃ
ZIELONA GÓRA
LESZNO
KALISZ
KONIN
LEGNICA
WROCŁAW
JELENIA GÓRA
WAŁBRZYCH
OPOLE
SEVEROČESKÝ
VÝCHODOČESKÝ
ZÁPADOČESKÝ
STŘEDOČESKÝ
JIHOČESKÝ
JIHOMORAVSKÝ
SEVEROMORAVSKÝ
CZECH REPUBLIC
BOHEMIA
MORAVIA
Berlin
Szczecin
Poznań
Wrocław
Dresden
Praha
Prague
Gdynia
Bydgoszcz
Toruń
Opole
Ostrava
Olomouc
Metres
Feet
2000
6562
1500
4921
1000
3281
500
1640
200
656
100
328
SEA LEVEL
50
164
73
78
Conic Equidistant
Projection

GULF OF DANZIG
RUSSIAN FEDERATION
LITHUANIA
BELARUS
UKRAINE
SLOVAKIA
ELBLĄG
OLSZTYN
SUWAŁKI
ŁOMŻA
BIAŁYSTOK
CIECHANÓW
OSTROŁĘKA
PŁOCK
WARSZAWA
SIEDLCE
BIAŁA PODLASKA
SKIERNIEWICE
ŁÓDŹ
RADOM
LUBLIN
CHEŁM
PIOTRKÓW
KIELCE
TARNOBRZEG
ZAMOŚĆ
KRAKÓW
TARNÓW
RZESZÓW
PRZEMYŚL
KROSNO
NOWY SĄCZ
HRODNA
BREST
VOLYNS'K
L'VIV
CARPATHIAN MTS
Warszawa (Warsaw)
Kaliningrad
Białystok
Lublin
Kraków
Rzeszów
Hrodna (Grodno)
Brest
L'viv (L'vov)
© Bartholomew
1:1.8M

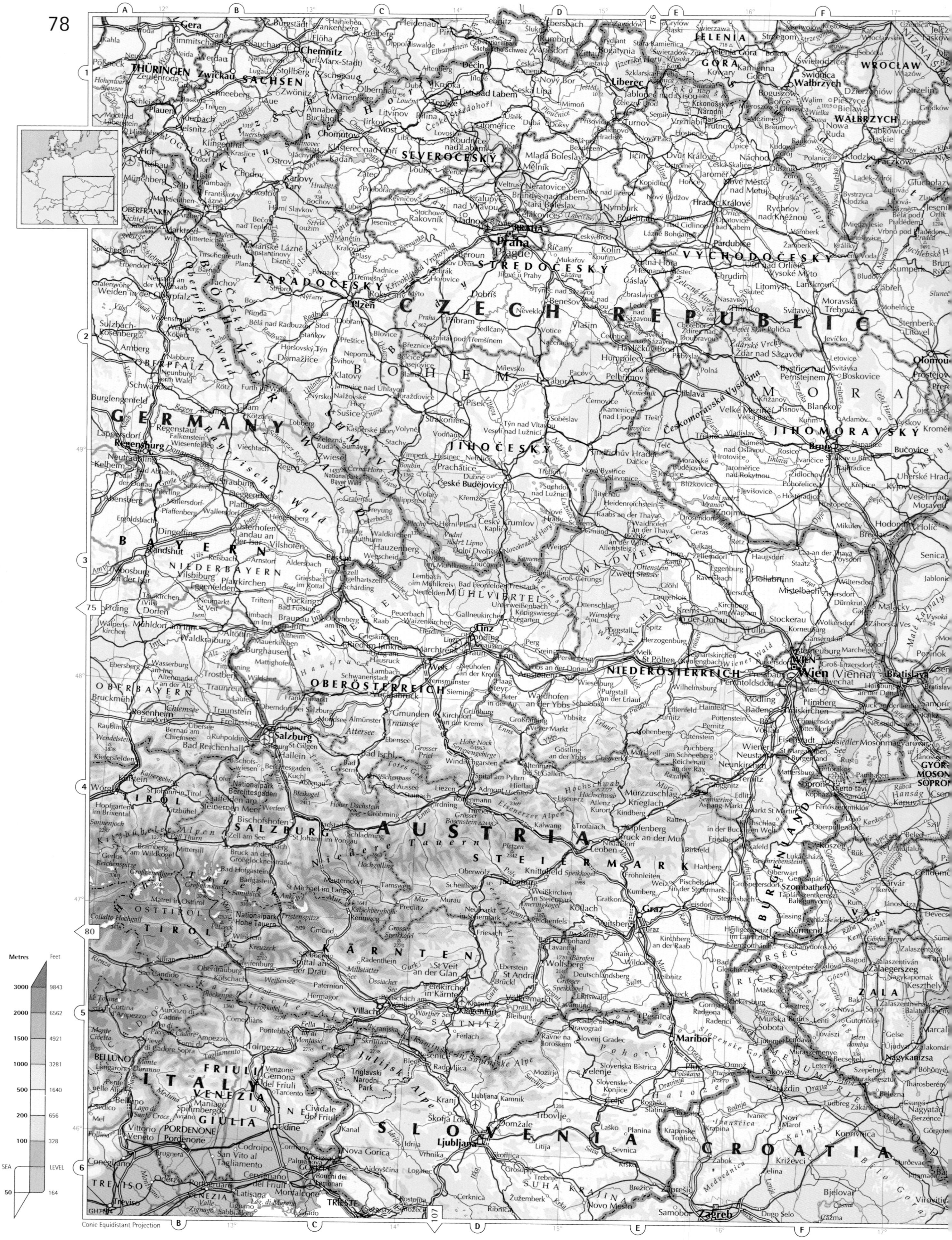

GERMANY

CZECH REPUBLIC

AUSTRIA

SLOVENIA

CROATIA

ITALIA

THÜRINGEN
SACHSEN
OBERFRANKEN
OBERPFALZ
BAYERN
NIEDERBAYERN
OBERBAYERN
TIROL
OSTTIROL
SALZBURG
KÄRNTEN
STEIERMARK
NIEDERÖSTERREICH
OBERÖSTERREICH
BURGENLAND
BÖHMERWALD

ZÁPADOČESKÝ
SEVEROČESKÝ
STŘEDOČESKÝ
VÝCHODOČESKÝ
JIHOČESKÝ
JIHOMORAVSKÝ
MORAVA
MÜHLVIERTEL
WALDVIERTEL
WACHAU
BOHEM

FRIULI
VENEZIA
GIULIA

Gera
Chemnitz
Zwickau
Plauen
Hof
Regensburg
Landshut
Plzeň
Praha (Prague)
Karlovy Vary
Mariánské Lázně
České Budějovice
Jihlava
Brno
Linz
Salzburg
Wien (Vienna)
Bratislava
Graz
Klagenfurt
Villach
Maribor
Ljubljana
Zagreb
Trieste
Treviso
BELLUNO
PORDENONE
Udine
WROCŁAW
WAŁBRZYCH
JELENIA GÓRA

Conic Equidistant Projection

Metres / Feet
3000 / 9843
2000 / 6562
1500 / 4921
1000 / 3281
500 / 1640
200 / 656
100 / 328
SEA LEVEL
50 / 164

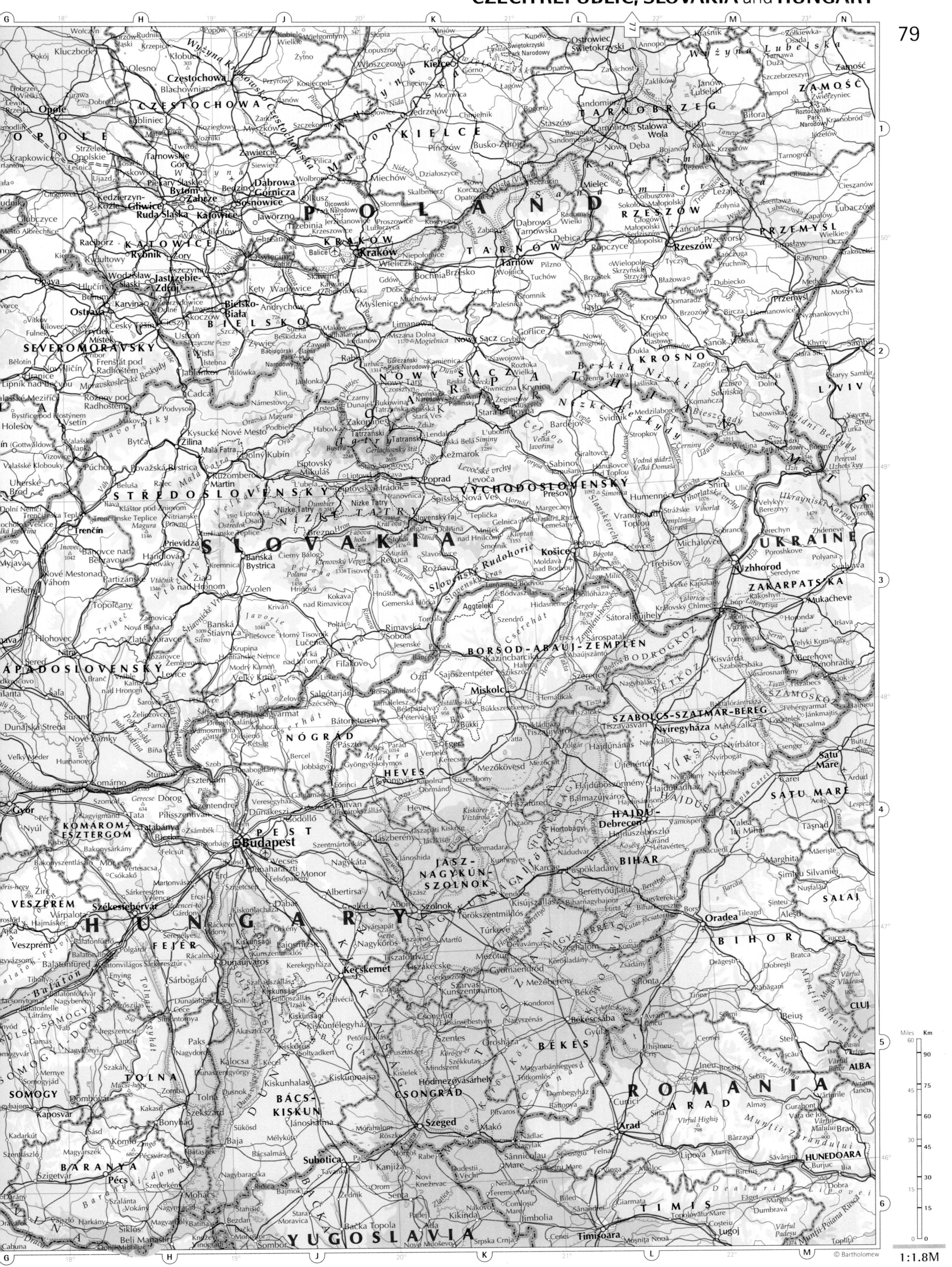
POLAND
SLOVAKIA
HUNGARY
ROMANIA
UKRAINE
YUGOSLAVIA
CZESTOCHOWA
OPOLE
KIELCE
TARNOBRZEG
ZAMOŚĆ
KATOWICE
KRAKÓW
TARNÓW
RZESZÓW
PRZEMYŚL
BIELSKO
NOWY SĄCZ
KROSNO
SEVEROMORAVSKÝ
STŘEDOSLOVENSKÝ
VÝCHODOSLOVENSKÝ
ZÁPADOSLOVENSKÝ
L'VIV
ZAKARPATS'KA
BORSOD-ABAÚJ-ZEMPLÉN
SZABOLCS-SZATMÁR-BEREG
NÓGRÁD
HEVES
PEST
KOMÁROM-ESZTERGOM
HAJDÚ-BIHAR
JÁSZ-NAGYKUN-SZOLNOK
VESZPRÉM
FEJÉR
TOLNA
SOMOGY
BARANYA
BÁCS-KISKUN
CSONGRÁD
BÉKÉS
SATU MARE
SALAJ
BIHOR
CLUJ
ALBA
ARAD
HUNEDOARA
TIMIŞ
Budapest
Kraków
Katowice
Ostrava
Košice
Miskolc
Debrecen
Szeged
Oradea
Arad
Timişoara
Uzhhorod
Győr
Pécs
Kecskemét
Szolnok
Miles
Km
© Bartholomew

1:1.8M

GERMANY
BAYERN
OBERPFALZ
MITTELFRANKEN
NIEDERBAYERN
OBERBAYERN
SCHWABEN
BADEN-WÜRTTEMBERG
STUTTGART
TÜBINGEN
ALLGÄU
SALZBURG
TIROL
INNSBRUCK
IMST
LANDECK
KUFSTEIN
KITZBÜHEL
SCHWAZ
ZELL AM SEE
OSTTIROL
LIENZ
SPITTAL
VORARLBERG
BREGENZ
BLUDENZ
REUTTE
LIECHTENSTEIN
SWITZERLAND
ALPS
ITALY
TRENTINO
ALTO ADIGE
BOLZANO
BELLUNO
TRENTO
LOMBARDIA
SONDRIO
BERGAMO
BRESCIA
VICENZA
TREVISO
PORDENONE
UDINE
FRIULI
VENEZIA GIULIA
München (Munich)
Augsburg
Regensburg
Ingolstadt
Landshut
Salzburg
Innsbruck
Bolzano
Trento
Ulm
Kempten (Allgäu)
Bodensee
Metres
Feet
4000
13124
3000
9843
2000
6562
1500
4921
1000
3281
500
1640
200
656
100
328
SEA
LEVEL
50
164
Conic Equidistant Projection
75
83

1:1.2M

Metres	Feet
4000	13124
3000	9843
2000	6562
1500	4921
1000	3281
500	1640
200	656
100	328
SEA	LEVEL

Conic Equidistant Projection

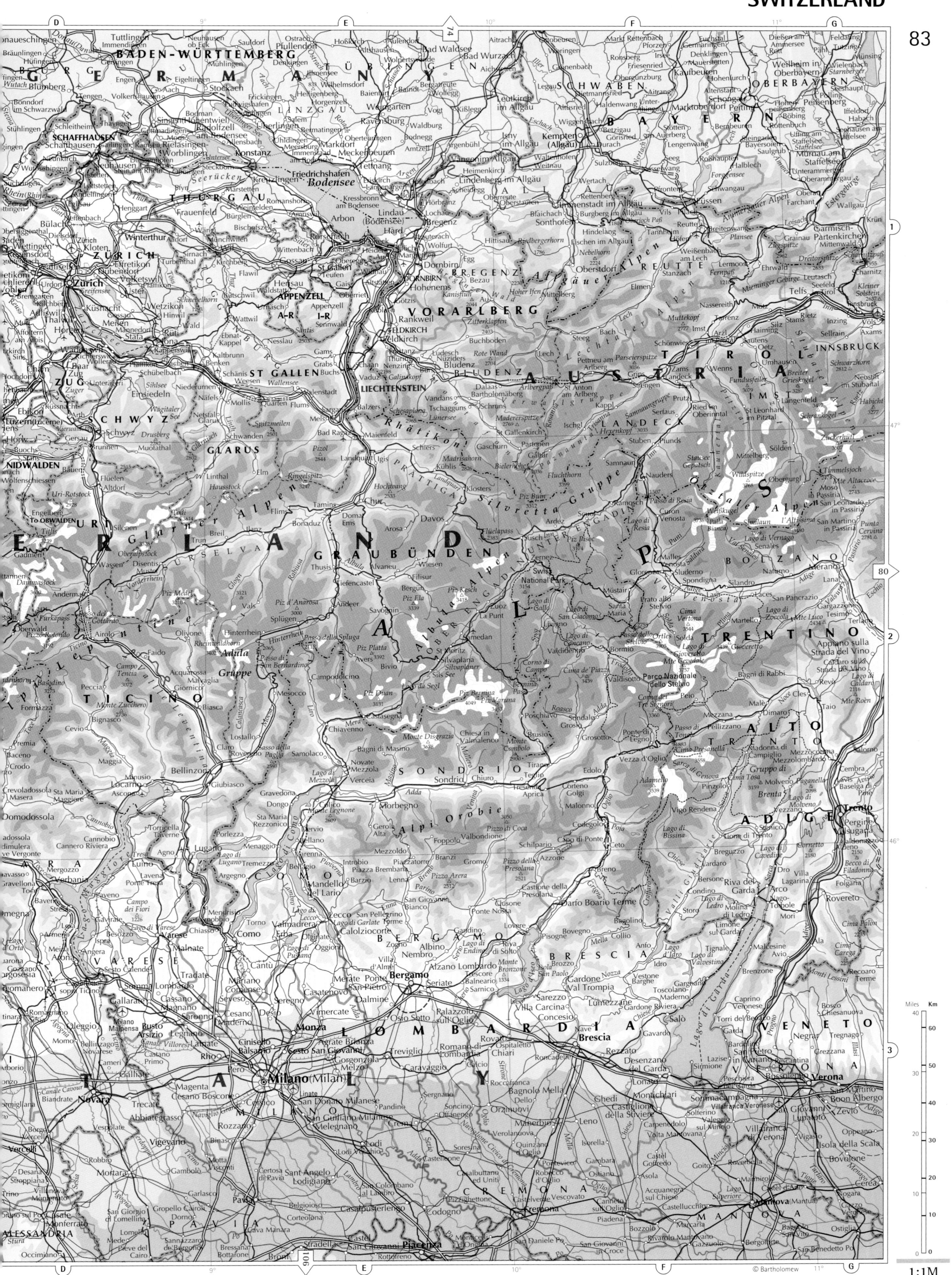
BADEN-WÜRTTEMBERG
GERMANY
TÜBINGEN
SCHWABEN
OBERBAYERN
BAYERN
LINZGAU
THURGAU
Bodensee
ZÜRICH
Zürich
SCHAFFHAUSEN
APPENZELL
A-R
I-R
ST GALLEN
LIECHTENSTEIN
VORARLBERG
BREGENZ
Allgäuer Alpen
Lechtaler Alpen
TIROL
INNSBRUCK
AUSTRIA
LANDECK
IMST
REUTTE
ZUG
SCHWYZ
GLARUS
NIDWALDEN
URI
Glarner Alpen
Rhätikon
Silvretta Gruppe
GRAUBÜNDEN
SWITZERLAND
Swiss National Park
Ötztaler Alpen
BOLZANO
TRENTINO
ALPS
TICINO
Lepontine Alpen
SONDRIO
Alpi Orobie
ALTO ADIGE
COMO
BERGAMO
BRESCIA
VARESE
LOMBARDIA
MILANO
Milano (Milan)
ITALY
PAVIA
CREMONA
MANTOVA
VERONA
VENETO
Lago di Garda
Lago Maggiore
Lago di Como
Bergamo
Brescia
Verona
Trento
Novara
Piacenza
Cremona
Mantova
Miles
Km
1:1M
© Bartholomew

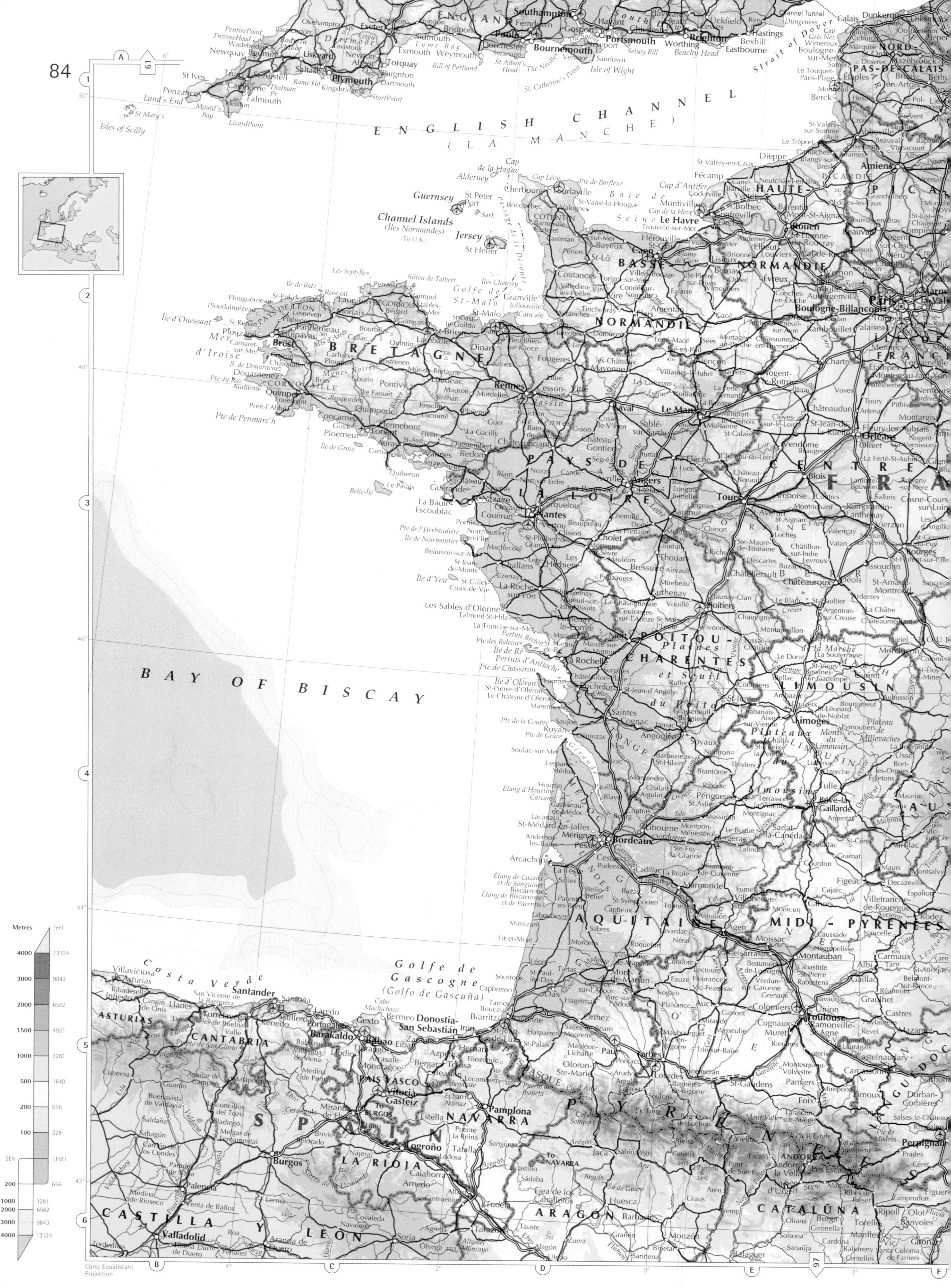

ENGLISH CHANNEL
(LA MANCHE)
BAY OF BISCAY
Golfe de Gascogne
(Golfo de Gascuña)
Costa Verde
Strait of Dover
Channel Tunnel
Channel Islands
(Îles Normandes)
(To U.K.)
Guernsey
Jersey
Alderney
St Peter Port
St Helier
Isles of Scilly
Land's End
Penzance
St Ives
Newquay
Falmouth
Plymouth
Torquay
Exeter
Weymouth
Bournemouth
Poole
Southampton
Portsmouth
Isle of Wight
Brighton
Hastings
Eastbourne
Worthing
Calais
Dunkerque
Boulogne-sur-Mer
NORD-PAS-DE-CALAIS
HAUTE-NORMANDIE
BASSE-NORMANDIE
PICARDIE
ÎLE-DE-FRANCE
BRETAGNE
PAYS DE LA LOIRE
CENTRE
POITOU-CHARENTES
LIMOUSIN
AQUITAINE
MIDI-PYRÉNÉES
Amiens
Rouen
Le Havre
Dieppe
Fécamp
Cherbourg
Caen
Évreux
Paris
Boulogne-Billancourt
Versailles
Chartres
Orléans
Blois
Tours
Le Mans
Laval
Angers
Nantes
Rennes
St-Malo
St-Brieuc
Brest
Quimper
Lorient
Vannes
St-Nazaire
La Baule-Escoublac
Cholet
La Roche-sur-Yon
Les Sables-d'Olonne
Niort
La Rochelle
Rochefort
Poitiers
Châtellerault
Limoges
Angoulême
Cognac
Saintes
Royan
Périgueux
Bordeaux
Mérignac
Arcachon
Libourne
Bergerac
Brive-la-Gaillarde
Agen
Montauban
Toulouse
Mont-de-Marsan
Dax
Biarritz
Bayonne
Pau
Tarbes
Lourdes
Carcassonne
Perpignan
Bourges
Vierzon
Châteauroux
Montluçon
PYRÉNÉES
ANDORRA
Donostia-San Sebastián
Bilbao
Barakaldo
Vitoria Gasteiz
Pamplona
Logroño
Santander
Burgos
Palencia
Valladolid
Huesca
ASTURIAS
CANTABRIA
PAÍS VASCO
NAVARRA
LA RIOJA
ARAGÓN
CATALUÑA
CASTILLA Y LEÓN
SPAIN
Metres
Feet
4000
3000
2000
1500
1000
500
200
100
SEA
LEVEL
13124
9843
6562
4921
3281
1640
656
328
Conic Equidistant Projection

BELGIUM

HAINAUT LIÈGE

RHEINLAND-PFALZ

Namur LUXEMBOURG LUXEMBOURG

Frankfurt am Main Wiesbaden Offenbach

Mainz Darmstadt

Koblenz

SAARLAND Saarbrücken Ludwigshafen am Rhein Mannheim Heidelberg

Trier

Metz Verdun

LORRAINE

Nancy St-Nicolas-de-Port

Strasbourg Karlsruhe Stuttgart Heilbronn

BADEN

ALSACE

CHAMPAGNE-ARDENNE

Reims Épernay Châlons-sur-Marne Bar-le-Duc

WÜRTTEMBERG

GERMANY

BAYERN

Nürnberg Regensburg

München (Munich)

Augsburg

Reutlingen Tübingen

Freiburg im Breisgau Donau

Mulhouse Belfort Basel

FRANCHE-COMTÉ

Besançon Dijon

BOURGOGNE

Chalon-sur-Saône Mâcon

Zürich Bern

SWITZERLAND

Lausanne Genève (Geneva)

Innsbruck

TIROL

VORARLBERG LIECHTEN-STEIN

AUSTRIA

ALPS

TRENTINO ALTO ADIGE

Bolzano Trento VENETO

LOMBARDIA

Bergamo Brescia

Milano (Milan) Monza

Verona Padova

Lyon Villeurbanne

Grenoble Chambéry Annecy

Mont Blanc

VALLE D'AOSTA

RHÔNE-ALPES PIEMONTE

Torino (Turin)

ITALY

Novara Vercelli

EMILIA ROMAGNA

Parma Modena Bologna

Reggio nell'Emilia

Piacenza

St-Étienne Valence

MASSIF CENTRAL

Cuneo

Genova (Genoa) La Spezia

Savona

Privas Gap

Dauphiné

PROVENCE-ALPES-CÔTE-D'AZUR

Digne Draguignan

Avignon Aix-en-Provence Cannes Antibes Nice MONACO

Grasse

Nîmes Arles Toulon

Montpellier Marseille Hyères Îles d'Hyères

Golfe du Lion

LIGURIAN SEA

Golfo di Genova

Livorno (Leghorn) Pisa

Viareggio

TOSCANA

Firenze (Florence)

Siena

CORSE (CORSICA) (France)

Calvi L'Île-Rousse Bastia

Ajaccio Corte Porto-Vecchio Bonifacio

Isola d'Elba Piombino Grosseto

LIGURIAN SEA

Costa Brava

Roses Palamós

Miles Km

1:3M

© Bartholomew

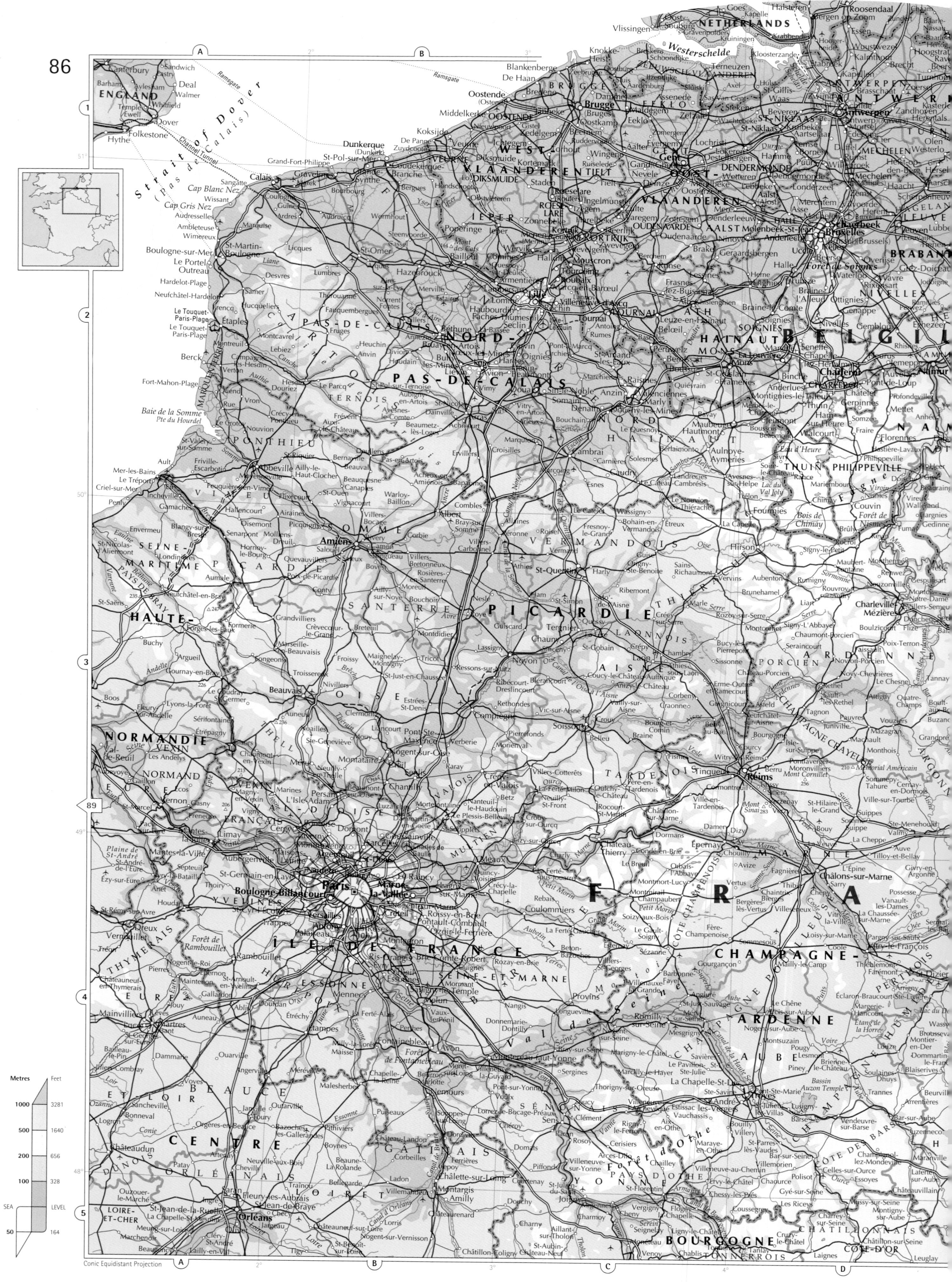

NETHERLANDS
Westerschelde
ENGLAND
Strait of Dover
(Pas de Calais)
Channel Tunnel
Canterbury
Sandwich
Deal
Walmer
Dover
Folkestone
Hythe
Vlissingen
Goes
Bergen op Zoom
Roosendaal
Knokke-Heist
Blankenberge
De Haan
Oostende
Middelkerke
Brugge
Gent
Antwerpen
Mechelen
Bruxelles (Brussel)
Schaerbeek
Anderlecht
Uccle
Ieper
Kortrijk
Roeselare
Oudenaarde
Aalst
Dendermonde
St-Niklaas
Eeklo
Nivelles
Waterloo
Charleroi
Mons
La Louvière
Namur
Tournai
Mouscron
Dunkerque
Calais
Gravelines
Boulogne-sur-Mer
Le Portel
Le Touquet-Paris-Plage
Étaples
Berck
Montreuil
St-Omer
Hazebrouck
Lille
Roubaix
Tourcoing
Villeneuve-d'Ascq
Béthune
Lens
Arras
Douai
Valenciennes
Cambrai
Maubeuge
Abbeville
St-Valery-sur-Somme
Le Tréport
Amiens
Albert
Péronne
St-Quentin
Laon
Soissons
Reims
Épernay
Châlons-sur-Marne
Vitry-le-François
Charleville-Mézières
Beauvais
Compiègne
Noyon
Creil
Senlis
Chantilly
Pontoise
Cergy
Mantes-la-Jolie
Versailles
Paris
Boulogne-Billancourt
Marne-la-Vallée
Créteil
Évry
Melun
Fontainebleau
Meaux
Provins
Sens
Montereau-faut-Yonne
Nemours
Montargis
Pithiviers
Étampes
Rambouillet
Chartres
Dreux
Châteaudun
Orléans
Troyes
Auxerre
Joigny
Romilly-sur-Seine
Nogent-sur-Seine
Bar-sur-Seine
Bar-sur-Aube
Château-Thierry
Coulommiers
NORD-PAS-DE-CALAIS
PAS-DE-CALAIS
NORD
PICARDIE
SOMME
AISNE
OISE
HAUTE-NORMANDIE
SEINE-MARITIME
EURE
ÎLE-DE-FRANCE
SEINE-ET-MARNE
ESSONNE
YVELINES
VAL-D'OISE
CENTRE
LOIRET
EURE-ET-LOIR
LOIR-ET-CHER
CHAMPAGNE-ARDENNE
MARNE
AUBE
ARDENNES
BOURGOGNE
YONNE
CÔTE-D'OR
BELGIË
WEST-VLAANDEREN
OOST-VLAANDEREN
HAINAUT
BRABANT
FRANCE
Conic Equidistant Projection
Metres
Feet
1000
3281
500
1640
200
656
100
328
SEA
LEVEL
50
164

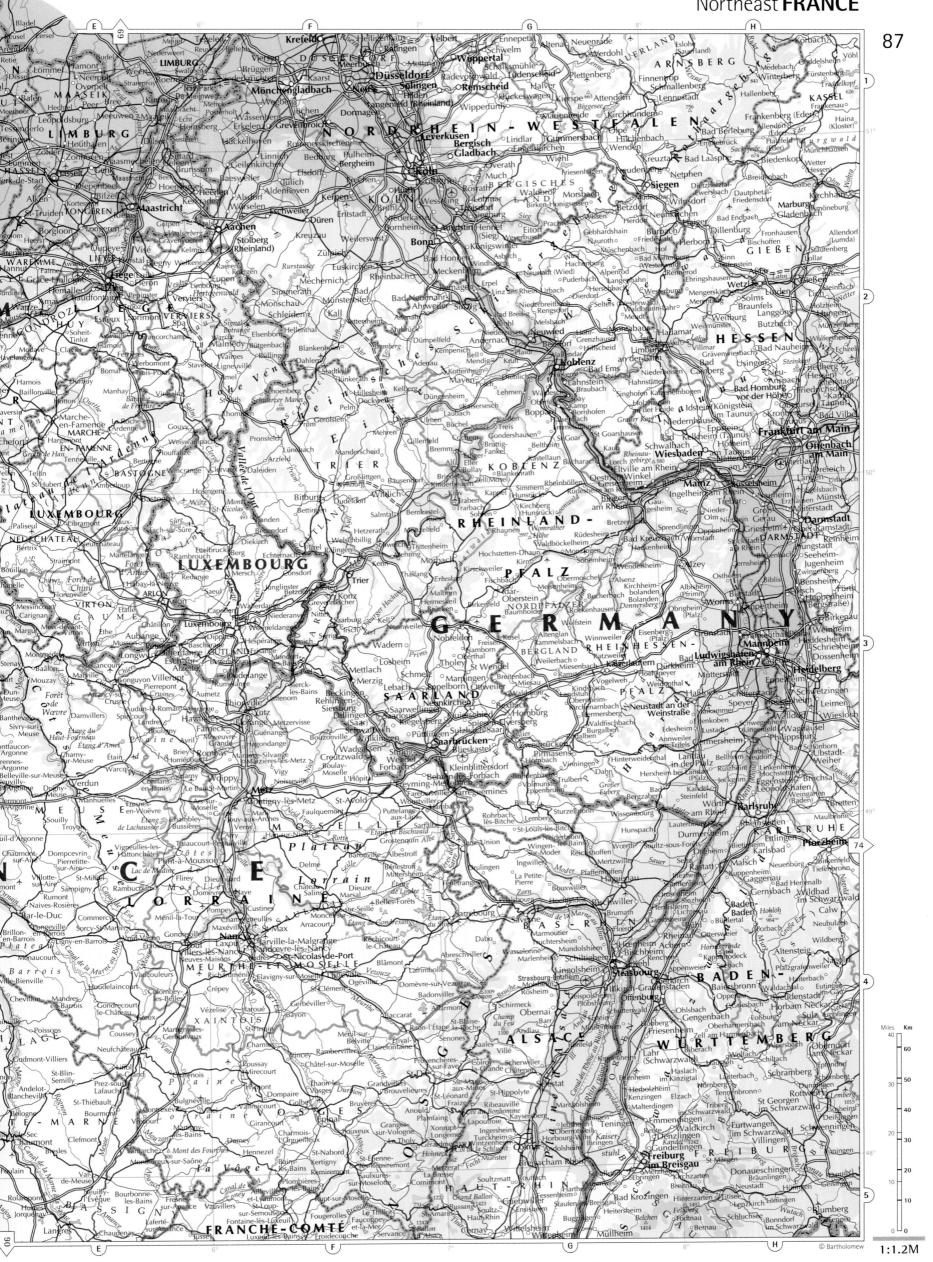

1:1.2M

© Bartholomew

ENGLISH CHANNEL
(LA MANCHE)
CHANNEL ISLANDS
(ÎLES NORMANDES)
(To United Kingdom)
Alderney
Guernsey
Sark
Jersey
Herm
St Peter Port
St Helier
St Anne
Cap de la Hague
Passage de la Déroute
Les Minquiers
Golfe de St-Malo
Cherbourg
COTENTIN
MANCHE
Granville
Coutances
Les Sept-Îles
Les Triagoz
Île de Batz
Roscoff
Morlaix
Lannion
TRÉGORROIS
Île de Bréhat
Paimpol
St-Brieuc
Baie de St-Brieuc
Dinard
St-Malo
Dinan
Lamballe
Île d'Ouessant
Passage du Fromveur
Île Molène
PAYS DE LÉON
Brest
Landerneau
Plouzané
Pte de St-Mathieu
Mer d'Iroise
Monts d'Arrée
FINISTÈRE
CÔTES-D'ARMOR
Guingamp
Loudéac
BRETAGNE
Montagnes Noires
Baie de Douarnenez
Douarnenez
Île de Sein
Pte du Raz
Quimper
CORNOUAILLE
Concarneau
Quimperlé
Pte de Penmarc'h
Îles de Glénan
Île de Groix
Lorient
Pontivy
MORBIHAN
Landes de Lanvaux
Vannes
Auray
Quiberon
Presq. de Quiberon
Belle-Île
Le Palais
Île de Houat
Île de Hœdic
Île Dumet
Rennes
ILLE-ET-VILAINE
Bassin de Rennes
Redon
Châteaubriant
Guérande
La Baule-Escoublac
St-Nazaire
GRANDE BRIÈRE
LOIRE-ATLANTIQUE
Loire
Nantes
PAYS DE RETZ
Lac de Grand-Lieu
Pornic
Baie de Bourgneuf
Noirmoutier-en-l'Île
Île de Noirmoutier
Challans
Marais Breton
Île d'Yeu
Port-Joinville
La Roche-sur-Yon
VENDÉE
BOCAGE VE
BAY OF BISCAY
Cork & Rosslare
Cork
Plymouth
Weymouth
Portsmouth
Metres
Feet
200
656
100
328
SEA
LEVEL
50
164
200
656
Conic Equidistant Projection
A
B
C
D
1
2
3
4
5
62

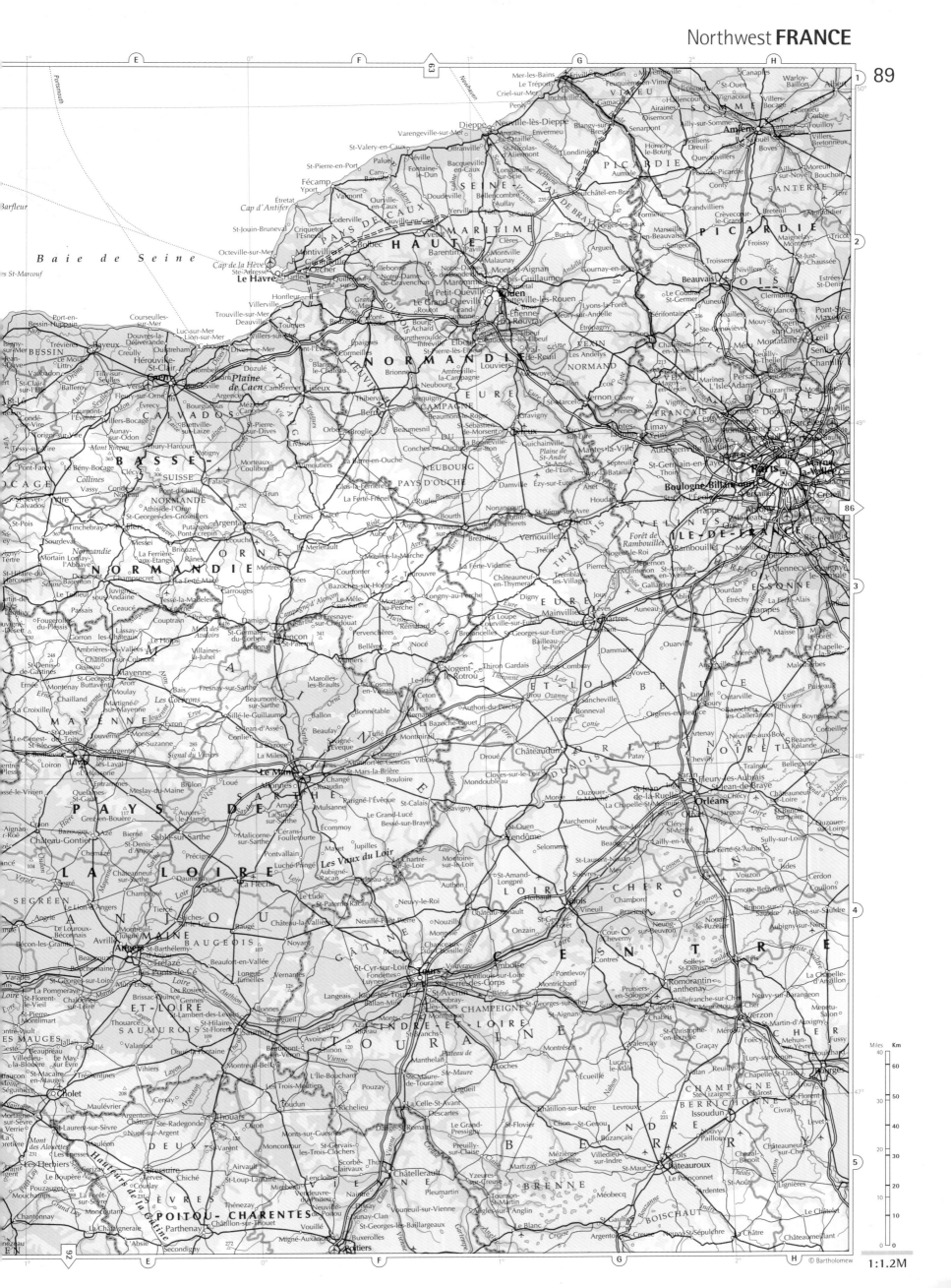

1:1.2M

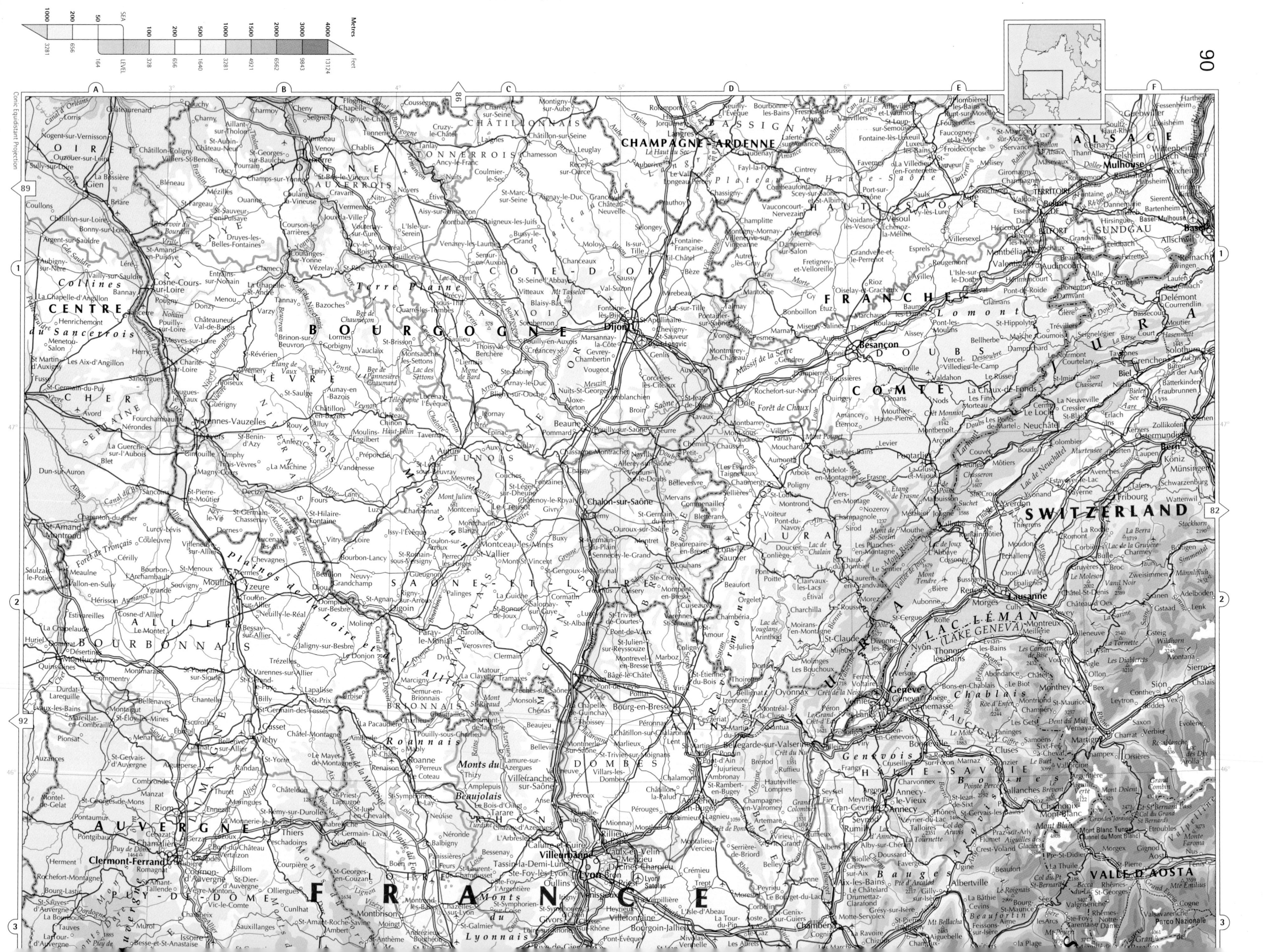
SWITZERLAND
ALSACE
FRANCHE-COMTÉ
BOURGOGNE
CHAMPAGNE-ARDENNE
AUVERGNE
CENTRE
FRANCE
VALLE D'AOSTA
LAC LÉMAN (LAKE GENEVA)
JURA
Dijon
Besançon
Genève
Lausanne
Bern
Basel
Mulhouse
Lyon
Clermont-Ferrand
Metres
Feet
4000
13124
3000
9843
2000
6562
1500
4921
1000
3281
500
1640
200
656
100
328
SEA
LEVEL
50
164
200
656
1000
3281
Conic Equidistant Projection

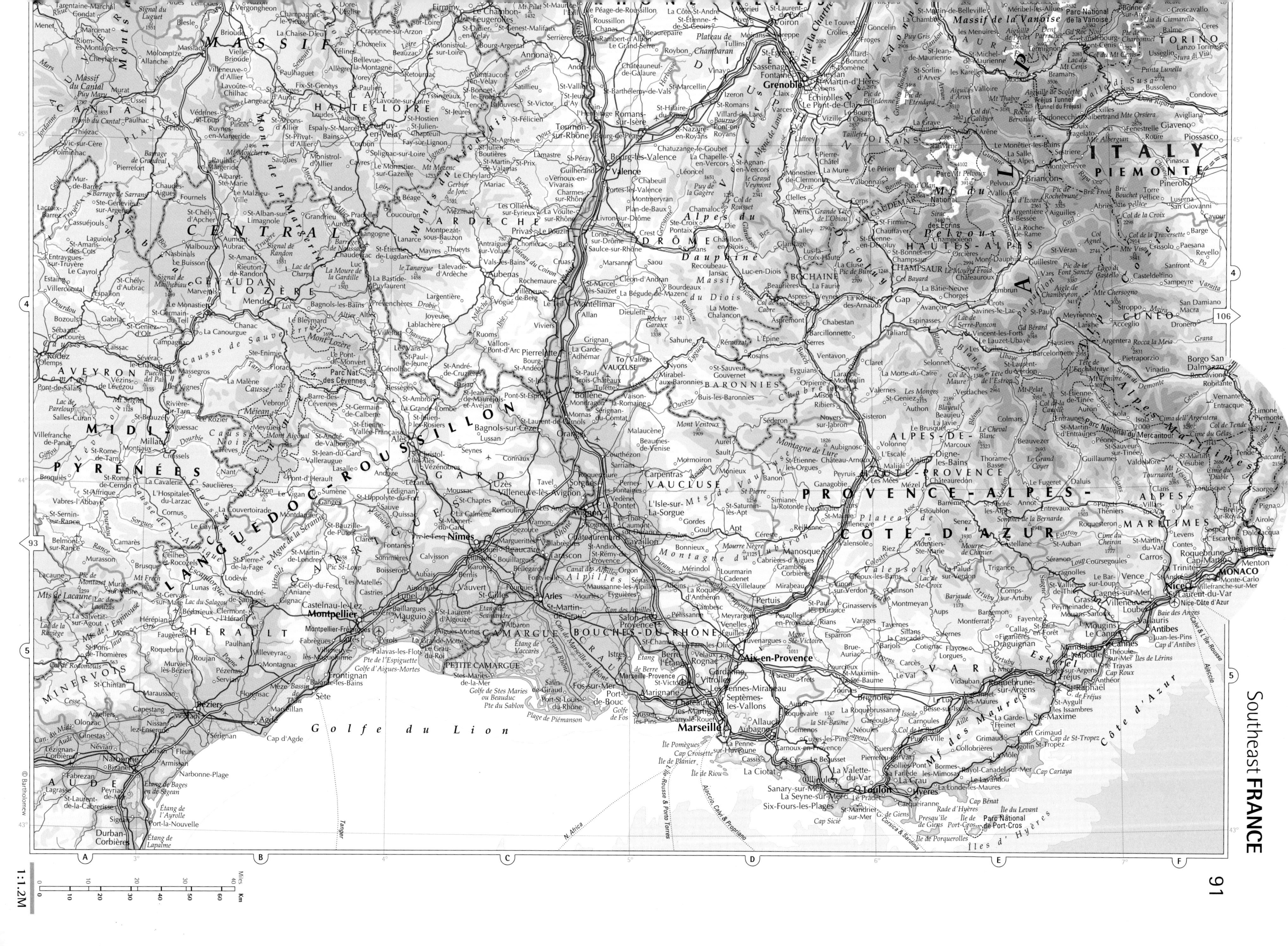
ITALY
PIEMONTE
TORINO
CUNEO
MONACO
Nice
Marseille
Toulon
Grenoble
Valence
Avignon
Nîmes
Montpellier
Béziers
Narbonne
Aix-en-Provence
Golfe du Lion
PROVENCE-ALPES-CÔTE-D'AZUR
LANGUEDOC-ROUSSILLON
MIDI-PYRÉNÉES
MASSIF CENTRAL
Miles
Km
1:1.2M
© Bartholomew

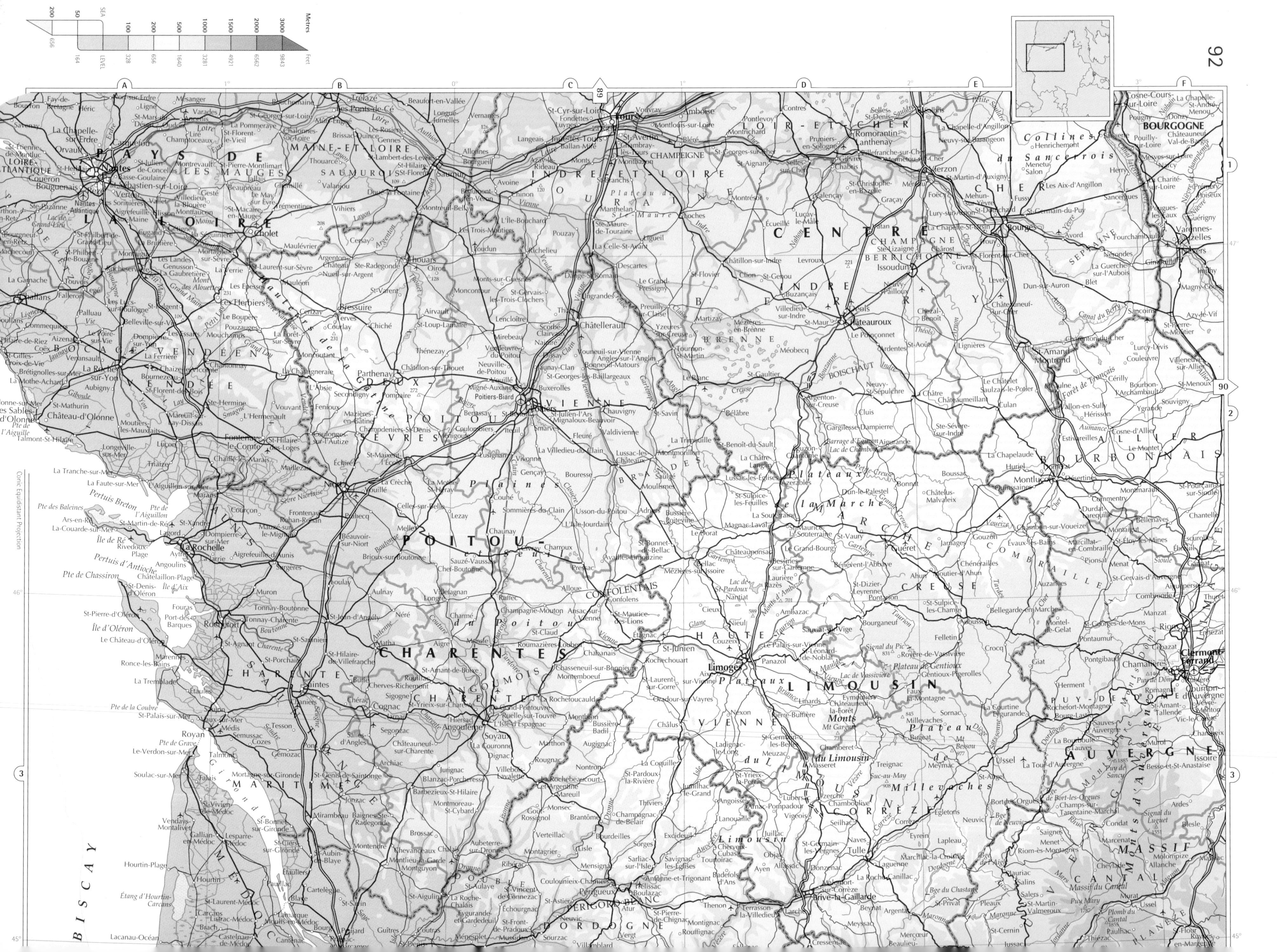
Metres
Feet
3000
9843
2000
6562
1500
4921
1000
3281
500
1640
200
656
100
328
SEA
LEVEL
50
164
200
656
PAYS DE LA LOIRE
CENTRE
POITOU-CHARENTES
LIMOUSIN
AUVERGNE
BOURGOGNE
BISCAY
Conic Equidistant Projection
89
90

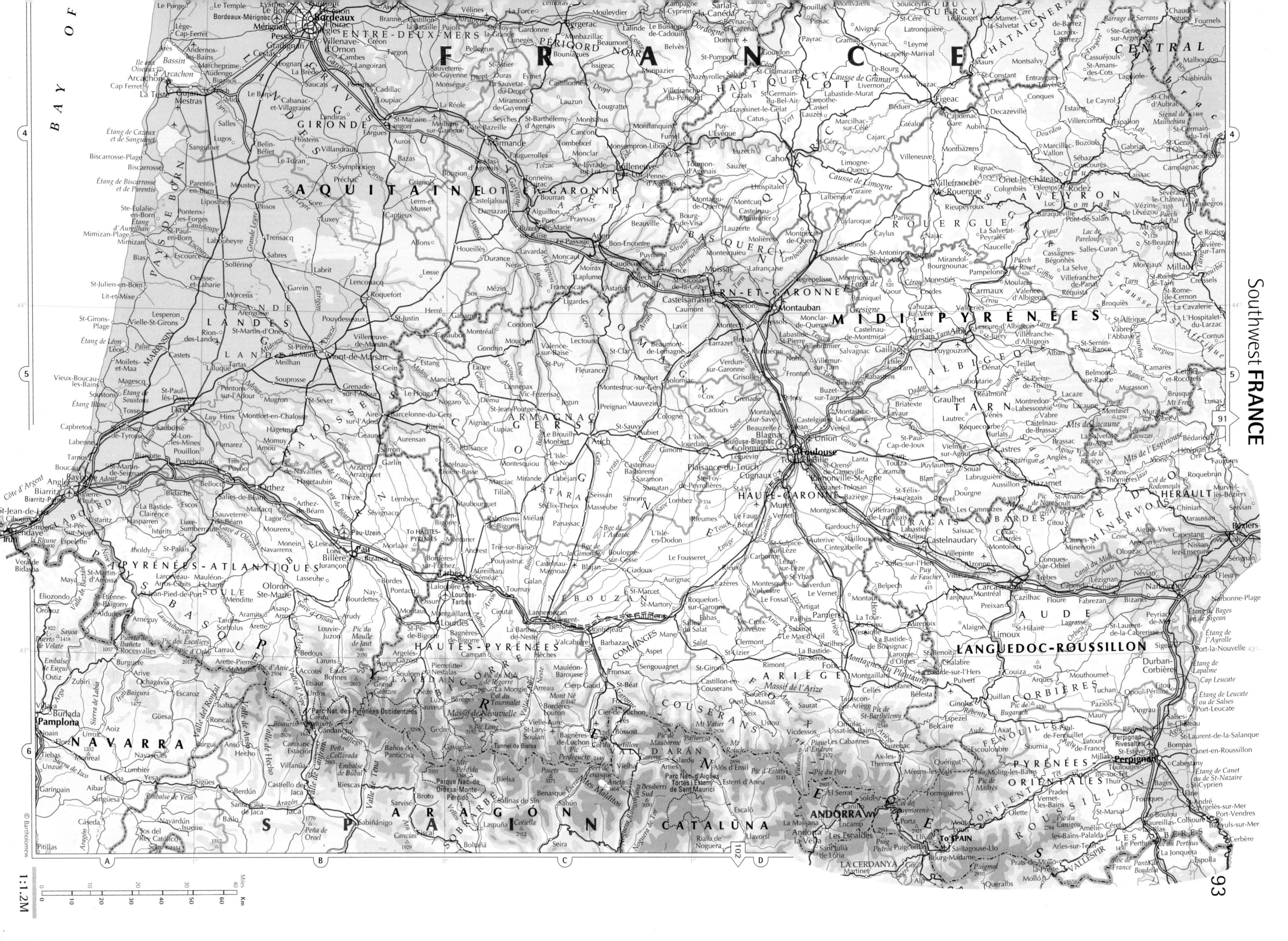
BAY OF
FRANCE
AQUITAINE
MIDI-PYRÉNÉES
LANGUEDOC-ROUSSILLON
ANDORRA
CATALUNA
ARAGÓN
NAVARRA
SPAIN
Bordeaux
Toulouse
Perpignan
Pamplona
1:1.2M
© Bartholomew

REPUBLIC OF IRELAND
Cork
Waterford
Wexford
St George's Channel
Cardigan Bay
WALES
Swansea
Cardiff
Bristol Channel
Birmingham
Wolverhampton
Derby
Nottingham
Lincoln
Leicester
Norwich
ENGLAND
Northampton
Gloucester
Cambridge
Luton
Hereford
Newport
Bristol
Taunton
London
Southend-on-Sea
Reading
Margate
Great Yarmouth
Southampton
Bournemouth
Brighton
Dover
Portsmouth
Exeter
Plymouth
Penzance
Land's End
Isles of Scilly
I. of Wight
English Channel
Strait of Dover
Channel Islands (Îles Normandes) (To U.K.)
Guernsey
Jersey
Île d'Ouessant
Den Helder
Leeuwarden
Groningen
NETHERLANDS
Haarlem
Amsterdam
's-Gravenhage (Den Haag) (The Hague)
Rotterdam
Utrecht
Arnhem
Breda
Dordrecht
Eindhoven
Dunkerque (Dunkirk)
Calais
Brugge
Antwerpen
Bruxelles (Brussel) (Brussels)
BELGIUM
Lille
Charleroi
LUX.
Luxembourg
Wilhelmshaven
Cuxhaven
Hamburg
Lübeck
Bremerhaven
Bremen
Oldenburg
Schwerin
Berlin
Hannover
Wolfsburg
Potsdam
Osnabrück
Münster
Magdeburg
Salzgitter
Dortmund
Essen
Düsseldorf
Göttingen
Halle
Leipzig
Kassel
Köln (Cologne)
Bonn
Erfurt
Jena
Dresden
Chemnitz
GERMANY
Koblenz
Frankfurt am Main
Offenbach
Würzburg
Mainz
Darmstadt
Ludwigshafen
Mannheim
Heidelberg
Saarbrücken
Heilbronn
Nürnberg
Erlangen
Bayreuth
Praha (Prague)
Plzeň
Karlsruhe
Pforzheim
Stuttgart
Regensburg
Strasbourg
Ulm
Augsburg
Freiburg im Breisgau
München (Munich)
Landshut
Passau
Salzburg
Innsbruck
Basel
Zürich
Bern
LIECH.
Vaduz
SWITZERLAND
Lausanne
Genève
Luzern
Chur
Cherbourg
Le Havre
Dieppe
Abbeville
Amiens
Rouen
Caen
Beauvais
Reims
Arras
Charleville-Mézières
Laon
Brest
St-Malo
St-Brieuc
Rennes
Quimper
Lorient
Vannes
Alençon
Évreux
Dreux
Chartres
Paris
Versailles
Châlons-sur-Marne
Metz
Nancy
Troyes
St-Dizier
Épinal
Colmar
Mulhouse
Besançon
Dijon
Laval
Le Mans
Orléans
Angers
Nantes
St-Nazaire
Tours
Blois
Bourges
Vierzon
Châtellerault
Poitiers
La Roche-sur-Yon
Niort
La Rochelle
Saintes
Angoulême
Limoges
Montluçon
Vichy
Clermont-Ferrand
Moulins
Mâcon
Autun
Chalon-sur-Saône
Lyon
St-Étienne
Annecy
Chambéry
Grenoble
FRANCE
Bordeaux
Périgueux
Brive-la-Gaillarde
Massif Central
Le-Puy-en-Velay
Valence
Cahors
Rodez
Mende
Millau
Albi
Agen
Montauban
Toulouse
Nîmes
Avignon
Arles
Montpellier
Béziers
Carcassonne
Narbonne
Perpignan
Marseille
Aix-en-Provence
Toulon
Cannes
Nice
MONACO
Monte-Carlo
Golfe du Lion
Bay of Biscay
Golfe de Gascogne (Golfo de Gascuña)
Bayonne
Pau
Tarbes
Donostia-San Sebastián
Pyrénées
ANDORRA
Andorra la Vella
Torino (Turin)
Cuneo
Aosta
Novara
Milano (Milan)
Bergamo
Monza
Como
Verona
Padova (Padua)
Venezia (Venice)
Vicenza
Trento
Bolzano
Trieste
Ljubljana
Udine
Genova (Genoa)
Golfo di Genova
Savona
San Remo
Parma
Modena
Bologna
Ferrara
Ravenna
Rimini
SAN MARINO
Forlì
Firenze (Florence)
La Spezia
Pisa
Livorno (Leghorn)
Arezzo
Perugia
Ancona
Grosseto
ITALY
Terni
Viterbo
Civitavecchia
Pescara
Roma (Rome)
Latina
Napoli (Naples)
Benevento
Salerno
Ligurian Sea
Bastia
Calvi
Corse (Corsica) (France)
Ajaccio
Bonifacio
Strait of Bonifacio
Sassari
Olbia
Sardegna (Sardinia) (Italy)
Nuoro
Oristano
Iglesias
Cagliari
Sant'Antioco
C. Carbonara
C. Spartivento
Tyrrhenian Sea
Sicilia (Sicily)
Trapani
Marsala
Palermo
Caltanissetta
Agrigento
Sicilian Channel
Isola di Pantelleria (Italy)
MALTA
Valletta
A Coruña
Cabo Fisterra (Cape Finisterre)
Santiago
Lugo
Oviedo
Gijón
Cordillera Cantábrica (Cantabrian Mountains)
Santander
Bilbao
Vitoria-Gasteiz
Pontevedra
Vigo
Ourense
León
Ponferrada
Miranda de Ebro
Burgos
Logroño
Pamplona
Palencia
Valladolid
Soria
Zaragoza
Lleida
Sabadell
Girona
Figueres
Barcelona
Tarragona
Porto
Braga
Bragança
Zamora
Salamanca
Coimbra
Covilhã
Ciudad Rodrigo
Segovia
Ávila
Madrid
Guadalajara
Alcalá de Henares
Calatayud
SPAIN
PORTUGAL
Lisboa (Lisbon)
Setúbal
Sines
Portalegre
Plasencia
Talavera de la Reina
Toledo
Aranjuez
Tortosa
Castelló de la Plana
Mérida
Badajoz
Villanueva de la Serena
Évora
Beja
Puertollano
Ciudad Real
Valdepeñas
Villarrobledo
Albacete
Sagunto
Valencia
Golfo de Valencia
Gandía
Sierra Morena
Zafra
Sevilla (Seville)
Córdoba (Cordova)
Andújar
Linares
Jaén
Alicante
Elche
Murcia
Lorca
Cartagena
Huelva
Faro
Lagos
Cabo de São Vicente (Cape St Vincent)
Cádiz
Jerez de la Frontera
Antequera
Granada
Guadix
Sierra Nevada
Mulhacén
Málaga
Almería
Adra
Algeciras
Gibraltar (U.K.)
Strait of Gibraltar
Palma de Mallorca
Mallorca
Menorca
Mahón
Manacor
Alcúdia
Eivissa (Ibiza)
Formentera
Islas Baleares (Balearic Islands)
MEDITERRANEAN SEA
Tanger (Tangier)
Ceuta (Sp.)
Tétouan (Tetuán)
Larache
Chaouèn
Al Hoceima
Melilla (Sp.)
Nador
Ksar el Kebir
Ouezzane
Kénitra
Rabat
Sidi Kacem
Meknès
Fès (Fez)
Taza
Oujda
Taourirt
El Jadida
Casablanca
Settat
Khouribga
Oued Zem
Moyen Atlas
Azrou
Khenifra
Kasba Tadla
MOROCCO
Beni Mellal
HAUT ATLAS (HIGH ATLAS)
Er Rachidia
Bouârfa
Figuig
Ouarzazate
Béchar
Abadla
Hammada du Drâa
Alger (Algiers)
Blida
Tizi Ouzou
Bejaïa
Skikda
Annaba
Oran
Mostaganem
Relizane
Ech Chélif
Beni-Saf
Mascara
Ghazaouet
Sidi Bel Abbès
Tlemcen
Naret
Ksar El Boukhari
Sétif
Constantine
Guelma
Souk Ahras
El Eulma
Aïn Beïda
Tébessa
Batna
Khenchela
Biskra
Bou Saâda
Chott el Hodna
Hauts Plateaux
Chott ech Chergui
Mecheria
El Bayadh
Djelfa
Atlas Saharien
Aïn Sefra
Laghouat
El Meghaïer
Chott Melrhir
Touggourt
El Oued
Ghardaïa
Ouargla
Hassi Messaoud
Beni-Abbès
Grand Erg Occidental
ALGERIA
El Goléa
Timimoun
El Homr
Ksabi
Tabelbala
Erg Iguidi
Sbaa
Adrar
Plateau du Tademaït (Tademaït Plateau)
Grand Erg Oriental
Plateau du Tinrhert
Bordj Messaouda
Ghadamis
Bordj Omar Driss
In Aménas
In Salah
Reggane
El Eglab
Chenachane
Bizerte
Menzel Bourguiba
Tunis
C. Bon
Béja
Jendouba
Nabeul
Golfe de Hammamet
Kairouan
Sousse
M'Saken
Sbeïtla
Kasserine
TUNISIA
Sfax
Gafsa
Tozeur
Chott el Jerid
G. de Gabès
Gabès
Zarzis
Medenine
Zuwārah
Ṭarābulus (Tripoli)
Al Khums
Al Jawsh
Gharyān
Nālūt
Jādū
Mizdah
Daraj
TRIPOLITANIA
Al Hamādah al Ḥamrā'
Idhān Awbārī
Metres
Feet
4000
13124
3000
9843
2000
6562
1000
3281
500
1640
200
656
SEA
LEVEL
5000
16409
GH 7754
Lambert Conformal Conic Projection

121

POLAND
BELARUS
RUSSIAN FEDERATION
UKRAINE
SLOVAKIA
HUNGARY
ROMANIA
MOLDOVA
CROATIA
BOSNIA-HERZEGOVINA
YUGOSLAVIA
BULGARIA
MACEDONIA (F.Y.R.O.M.)
ALBANIA
GREECE
TURKEY
GEORGIA
SYRIA
LEBANON
CYPRUS
ISRAEL
WEST BANK
GAZA
JORDAN
EGYPT
LIBYA
CYRENAICA
Warszawa (Warsaw)
Kyyiv (Kiev)
Budapest
Wien (Vienna)
Bratislava
București (Bucharest)
Beograd (Belgrade)
Sofiya (Sofia)
Skopje
Tiranë (Tirana)
Athina (Athens)
İstanbul
Ankara
Chișinău (Kishinev)
Odesa (Odessa)
Kharkiv (Khar'kov)
Dnipropetrovs'k
Donets'k
Rostov-na-Donu
Sevastopol'
Simferopol'
Izmir
Bursa
Konya
Adana
Antalya (Adalia)
Halab (Aleppo)
Dimashq (Damascus)
Beirut (Beyrouth)
Lefkosia (Nicosia)
Tel Aviv Yafo (Jaffa)
Jerusalem
'Ammān
Alexandria (El Iskandarîya)
Cairo (El Qâhira)
El Giza
Port Said (Bûr Sa'îd)
Suez (El Suweis)
Banghāzī
Tubruq
BLACK SEA
(CHERNOYE MORE)
(KARA DENIZ)
Sea of Azov
Aegean Sea
Ionian Sea
Adriatic Sea
Kriti (Crete)
Rodos (Rhodes)
Khalīj Surt (Gulf of Sirte)
Libyan Plateau
Qattara Depression
Western Desert
Eastern Desert
SINAI
RED SEA
Carpathian Mts
Stara Planina
Rodopi Pl.
Anadolu Dağları
Toros Dağları
Great Sand Sea
Calanscio Sand Sea
Nile
Miles
Km
© Bartholomew
1:9M

ATLANTIC

OCEAN

BAY OF BISCAY
(MAR CANTÁBRICO)

Costa Verde

GALICIA

CANTABRIAN MOUNTAINS

ASTURIAS

CANTABRIA

CASTILLA Y LEÓN

MINHO

BRAGA

VILA REAL

BRAGANÇA

TRÁS-OS-MONTES

Valladolid

PORTO

VISEU

AVEIRO

GUARDA

Salamanca

COIMBRA

CASTELO BRANCO

SPA

MADRID

Madrid

LEIRIA

SANTARÉM

PORTALEGRE

EXTREMADURA

CASTILLA

Toledo

LISBOA

Lisboa

ÉVORA

Badajoz

Mérida

SETÚBAL

Sevilla

FARO

ANDALUCÍA

Córdoba

SIERRA MORENA

Huelva

Jaén

Cabo de São Vicente
(Cape St Vincent)

Granada

GOLFO DE CÁDIZ

Jeréz de la Frontera

Cádiz

Málaga

Costa del Sol

Strait of Gibraltar

Gibraltar (U.K.)

Tanger (Tanger)

Ceuta (Spain)

Tétouan (Tetuán)

MOROCCO

MADEIRA ISLANDS
(Portugal)

Ilha de
Porto Santo

Porto
Santo

Porto Moniz

Ilha da
Madeira

Câmara de Lobos   Funchal

Ilhas Desertas

Deserta Grande

Bugio

at the same scale

Conic Equidistant Projection

Golfe de Gascogne
(Golfo de Gascuña)

AQUITAINE

FRANCE

MIDI-PYRÉNÉE

Toulouse

PYRÉNÉES

LANGUEDOC-ROUSSILLON

Perpignan

Golfe du Lion

Donostia-San Sebastián

NAVARRA

Pamplona

ANDORRA
Andorra la Vella

Figueres

Cap de Creus

LA RIOJA

Logroño

Zaragoza

ARAGÓN

Huesca

Lleida

CATALUÑA

Manresa

Sabadell

Girona

Costa Brava

Soria

Barcelona
El Prat de Llobregat

Teruel

Tarragona

Costa Dorada

Costa del Azahar

Castelló de la Plana

MENORCA
Ciutadella de Menorca
Mahón

MALLORCA

Palma de Mallorca

Cuenca

VALENCIA

Valencia

Golfo de Valencia

LA MANCHA

Albacete

Alicante

Costa Blanca

EIVISSA
(IBIZA)
Eivissa (Ibiza)

Formentera

ISLAS BALEARES
(BALEARIC ISLANDS)

Cabrera

MURCIA

Murcia

Cartagena

M E D I T E R R A N E A N

S E A

Almería
Cabo de Gata

ALGERIA

Beni-Saf

Ghazaouet

CANARY ISLANDS
(Spain)

I S L A S   C A N A R I A S

Alegranza

Graciosa

Lanzarote

Arrecife

La Palma

San Cristóbal de la Laguna
Sta Cruz de Tenerife

Fuerteventura

Puerto del Rosario

Tenerife

La Gomera

Las Palmas de Gran Canaria

El Hierro

Gran Canaria

at the same scale

Miles 100   Km 160

1:3M

© Bartholomew

BAY OF
(MAR CANT
ATLANTIC
OCEAN
PORTUGAL
GALICIA
LA CORUÑA
LUGO
ORENSE
ASTURI
CORDILLERA CANTA
CANTABRIAN MOU
EL BIERZO
MARAGATERÍA
SANABRIA
ZAMORA
SAYAGO
SALAMANCA
EXTREMADURA
CÁCERES
VIANA DO CASTELO
MINHO
BRAGA
VILA REAL
BRAGANÇA
TRÁS-OS-MONTES
PORTO
AVEIRO
VISEU
BEIRA ALTA
GUARDA
COIMBRA
BEIRA LITORAL
CASTELO BRANCO
BEIRA BAIXA
LEIRIA
SANTARÉM
A Coruña
Ferrol
Santiago
Santiago de Compostela
Pontevedra
Vigo
Lugo
Ourense
Oviedo
Gijón
Avilés
Mieres
Ponferrada
Zamora
Salamanca
Porto
Vila Nova de Gaia
Braga
Guimarães
Viana do Castelo
Aveiro
Coimbra
Viseu
Guarda
Covilhã
Castelo Branco
Leiria
Figueira da Foz
Plasencia
Ciudad-Rodrigo
Cabo Ortegal
Pta da Estaca de Bares
Cabo Fisterra (Cape Finisterre)
Cabo Touriñán
Cabo Mondego
Serra da Estrela
Sierra de la Culebra
Sierra de la Cabrera
Montes de León
Metres
Feet
2000
1500
1000
500
200
100
SEA
LEVEL
50
6562
4921
3281
1640
656
328
164
Conic Equidistant Projection
100

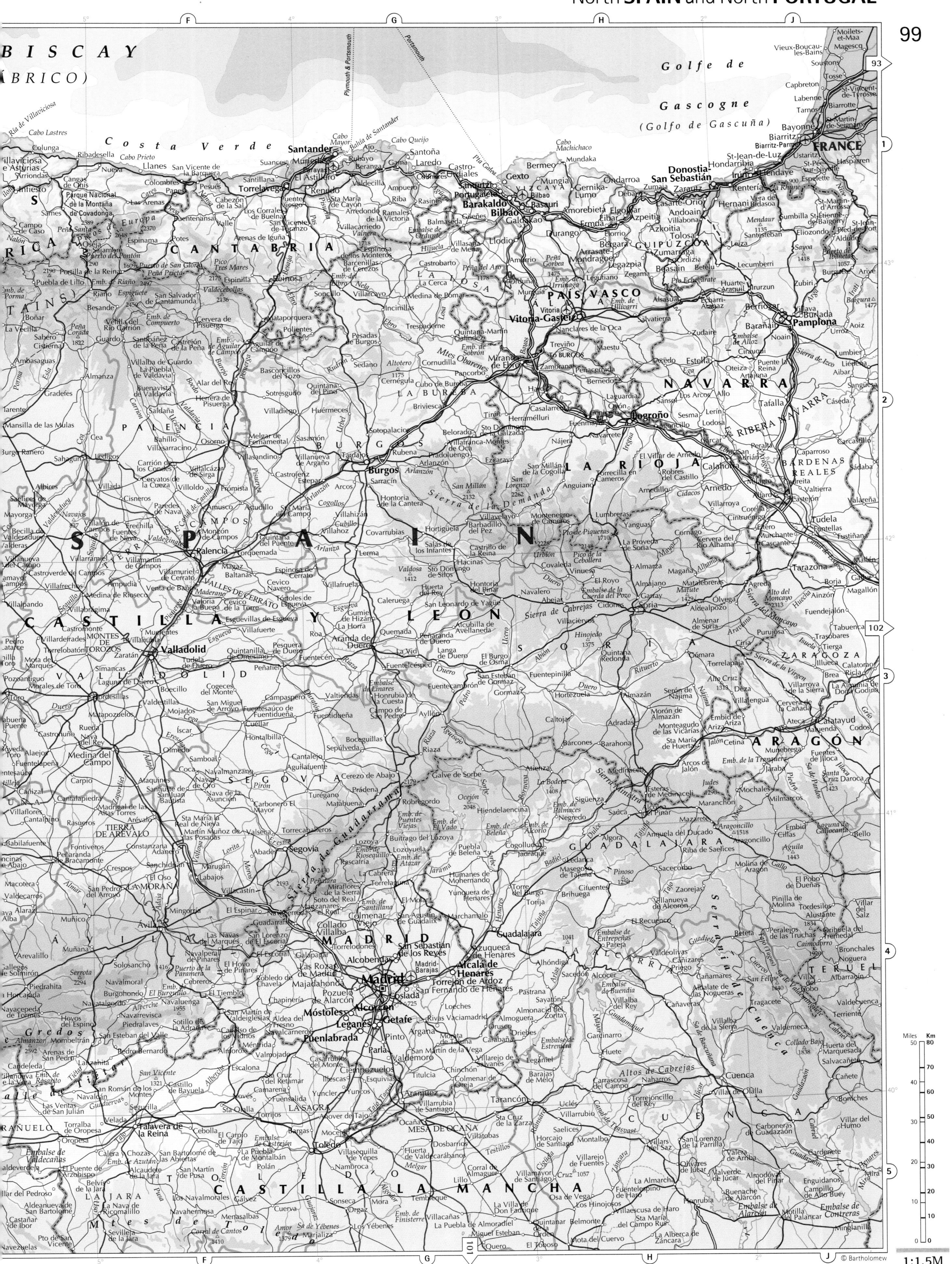
F
G
H
J
BISCAY
Golfe de Gascogne
(Golfo de Gascuña)
Costa Verde
FRANCE
Santander
Bilbao
Donostia-San Sebastián
Vitoria-Gasteiz
Pamplona
Logroño
Burgos
Palencia
Valladolid
Segovia
Ávila
Madrid
Toledo
Guadalajara
Cuenca
Soria
CANTABRIA
PAÍS VASCO
NAVARRA
LA RIOJA
CASTILLA Y LEÓN
SPAIN
ARAGÓN
CASTILLA-LA MANCHA
MADRID
PALENCIA
BURGOS
SORIA
VALLADOLID
SEGOVIA
ÁVILA
GUADALAJARA
CUENCA
ZARAGOZA
TERUEL
VIZCAYA
GUIPÚZCOA
ÁLAVA
Picos de Europa
Sierra de Guadarrama
Sierra de la Demanda
Serranía de Cuenca
Sierra de Gredos
Alcalá de Henares
Torrejón de Ardoz
Móstoles
Leganés
Getafe
Alcorcón
Fuenlabrada
Aranjuez
Talavera de la Reina
Calatayud
Tudela
Tarazona
Miranda de Ebro
Aranda de Duero
Medina del Campo
Torrelavega
Barakaldo
Irun
Bayonne
Biarritz
Hendaye
93
102
101
Miles
Km
1:1.5M

98
CASTELO BRANCO
LEIRIA
SANTARÉM
PORTALEGRE
PORTUGAL
ÉVORA
SETÚBAL
BEJA
FARO
ALGARVE
LISBOA
EXTREMADURA
CÁCERES
BADAJOZ
HUELVA
CÁDIZ
CAMPO
TIERRA DE BARROS
LLANOS DE OLIVENZA
EL ANDÉVALO
EL ALJARAFE
CONDADO DE NIEBLA
Las Marismas
Parque Nacional de Doñana
Sierra de San Pedro
Sierra de Aracena
Serra de Monchique
Serra do Caldeirão
Serra de Grândola
Sierra Morena
Baía de Setúbal
Costa Bela
Costa da Galé
Costa de la Luz
Playa de Castilla
GOLFO DE CÁDIZ
ATLANTIC OCEAN
Strait of
Cabo da Roca
Cabo Espichel
Cabo de Sines
Cabo Sardão
Cabo de São Vicente (Cape St Vincent)
Pta de Sagres
Cabo de Santa Maria
Cabo Trafalgar
Leiria
Marinha Grande
Nazaré
Alcobaça
Caldas da Rainha
Peniche
Torres Vedras
Santarém
Tomar
Abrantes
Castelo Branco
Portalegre
Elvas
Badajoz
Mérida
Cáceres
Estremoz
Évora
Amadora
Lisboa (Lisbon)
Almada
Barreiro
Setúbal
Sines
Beja
Serpa
Moura
Mértola
Lagos
Portimão
Faro
Olhão
Tavira
Vila Real de Santo António
Ayamonte
Lepe
Huelva
Moguer
Almonte
Sevilla
Alcalá de Guadaira
Dos Hermanas
Utrera
Lebrija
Sanlúcar de Barrameda
Chipiona
Jeréz de la Frontera
El Puerto de Santa María
Puerto Real
Cádiz
San Fernando
Chiclana de la Frontera
Conil de la Frontera
Barbate de Franco
Tarifa
Tanger
MOROCCO
Santa Cruz de Tenerife
Las Palmas
ARQUIPÉLAGO DOS AÇÔRES
Corvo
Flores
Santa Cruz das Flores
Graciosa
Terceira
Vila da Praia da Vitória
Angra do Heroismo
São Jorge
Faial
Horta
Madalena
Pico
São Miguel
Ribeira Grande
Ponta Delgada
Lagoa
Povoação
Santa Maria
Vila do Porto
AZORES
(Portugal)
1:5M
Metres
Feet
3000 9843
2000 6562
1500 4921
1000 3281
500 1640
200 656
100 328
SEA LEVEL
50 164
200 656
1000 3281
2000 6562
Conic Equidistant Projection

© Bartholomew

1:1.5M

GIBRALTAR
(United Kingdom)
1:75 000

NEUTRAL ZONE

Bay of Gibraltar
(Bahía de Algeciras)

The Rock

Europa Point

F R A N C E
S P A I N
ANDORRA
LANGUEDOC-ROUSSILLON
MIDI-PYRÉNÉES
AQUITAINE
PYRÉNÉES-ORIENTALES
HAUTE-GARONNE
HAUTES-PYRÉNÉES
PAÍS VASCO
NAVARRA
LA RIOJA
ARAGÓN
CATALUÑA
CASTILLA Y LEÓN
Barcelona
Zaragoza
Pamplona
Lleida
Tarragona
Perpignan
Donostia-San Sebastián
Logroño
Metres
Feet
3000
9843
2000
6562
1500
4921
1000
3281
500
1640
200
656
100
328
SEA LEVEL
50
164
Conic Equidistant Projection

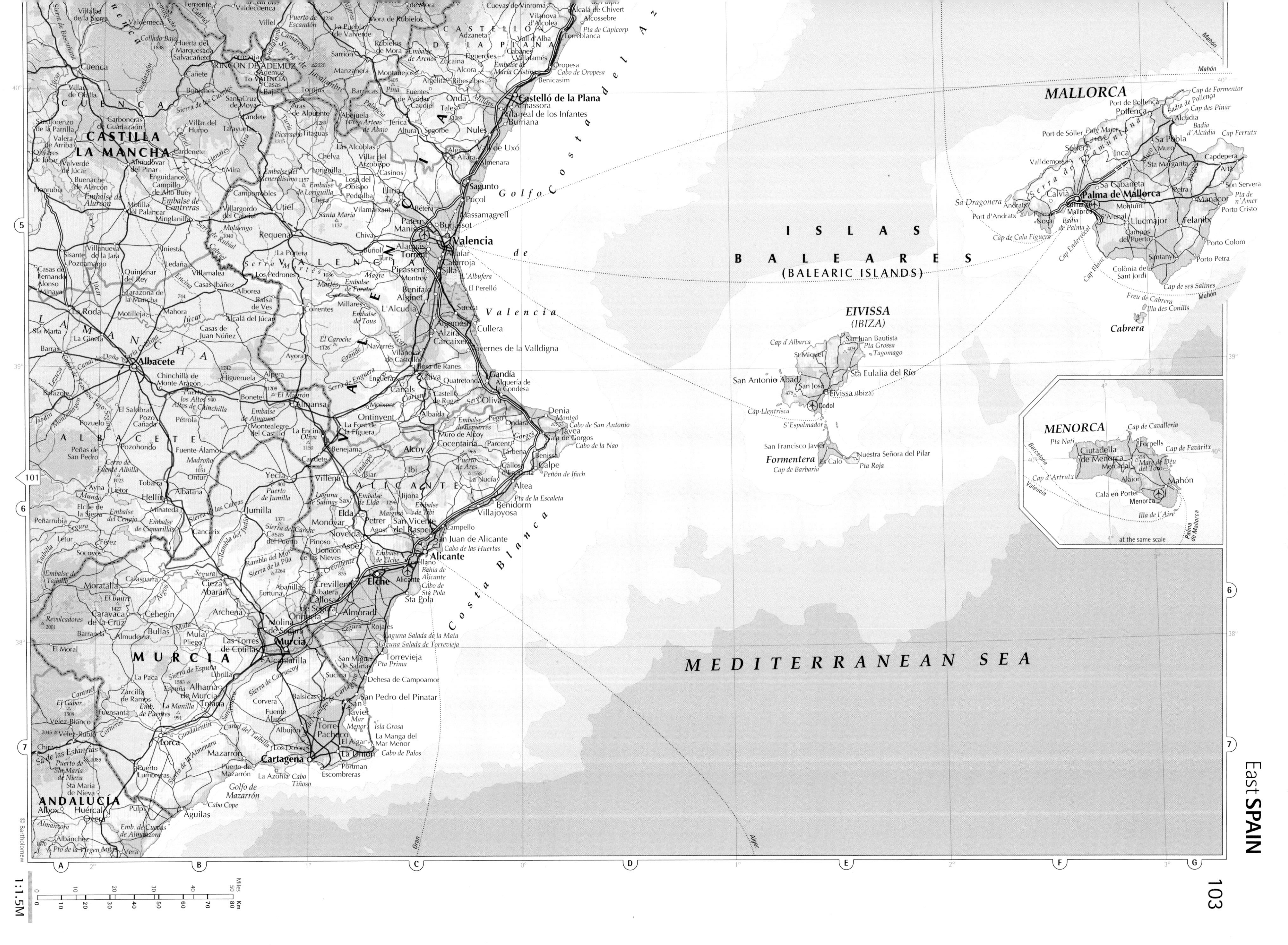

MALLORCA

MENORCA

ISLAS BALEARES
(BALEARIC ISLANDS)

EIVISSA
(IBIZA)

Formentera

M E D I T E R R A N E A N   S E A

Alger

CASTILLA
LA MANCHA

CASTELLÓ
DE LA PLANA

Castelló de la Plana

VALÈNCIA

València

ALACANT

Alicante

Elche

MURCIA

Murcia

Cartagena

ANDALUCÍA

Costa Blanca

Costa del Azahar

Albacete

Miles	Km
50	80
40	70
	60
30	50
	40
20	30
10	20
	10
0	0

© Bartholomew

1:1.5M

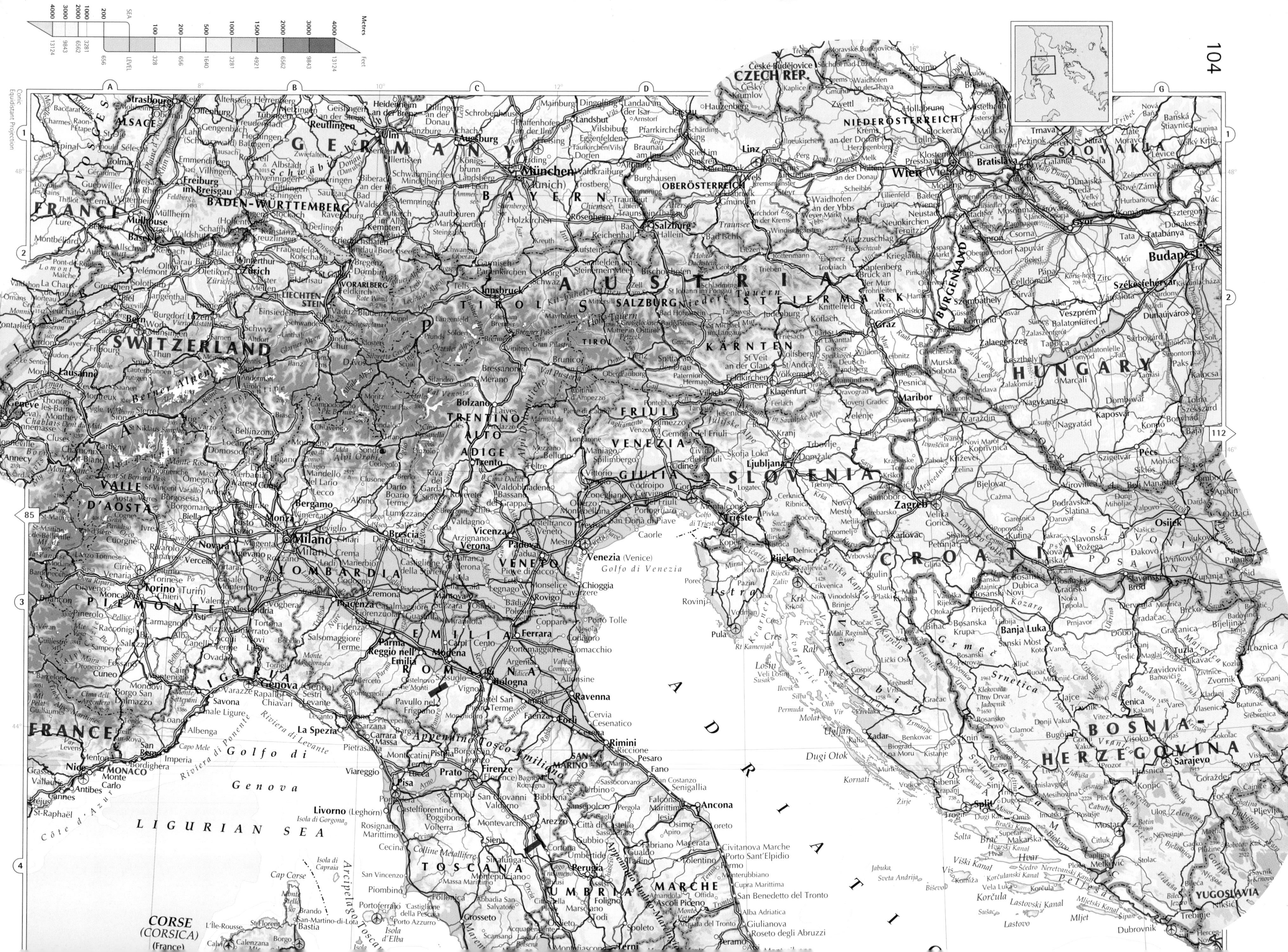

GERMANY
AUSTRIA
SWITZERLAND
HUNGARY
CROATIA
SLOVENIA
BOSNIA-HERZEGOVINA
FRANCE
CZECH REP.
SLOVAKIA
YUGOSLAVIA
ADRIATIC
LIGURIAN SEA
CORSE (CORSICA) (France)
MONACO
SAN MARINO
Metres
Feet
4000
13124
3000
9843
2000
6562
1500
4921
1000
3281
500
1640
200
656
100
328
SEA
LEVEL
Conic Equidistant Projection

TYRRHENIAN SEA
IONIAN SEA
Sicilian Channel
Malta Channel
Canal de la Galite
Golfo di Taranto
Golfo di Salerno
Golfo di Gaeta
Golfo di Squillace
Golfo di Manfredonia
Strait of Bonifacio
SARDEGNA (SARDINIA) (Italy)
SICILIA (SICILY)
CORSE
MALTA
TUNISIA
ALGERIA
PUGLIA
BASILICATA
CAMPANIA
CALABRIA
MOLISE
LAZIO
ABRUZZO
Roma (Rome)
Napoli (Naples)
Bari
Taranto
Brindisi
Lecce
Foggia
Salerno
Potenza
Cosenza
Catanzaro
Crotone
Reggio di Calabria
Messina
Palermo
Catania
Siracusa (Syracuse)
Trapani
Marsala
Agrigento
Ragusa
Cagliari
Sassari
Oristano
Nuoro
Olbia
Ajaccio
Tunis
Bizerte
Annaba
Isole Lipari
Isola di Ustica
Isole Pelagie
Isola di Lampedusa
Isola di Linosa
Isola di Pantelleria
Monte Etna (Etna)
Miles
Km
1:3M
© Bartholomew

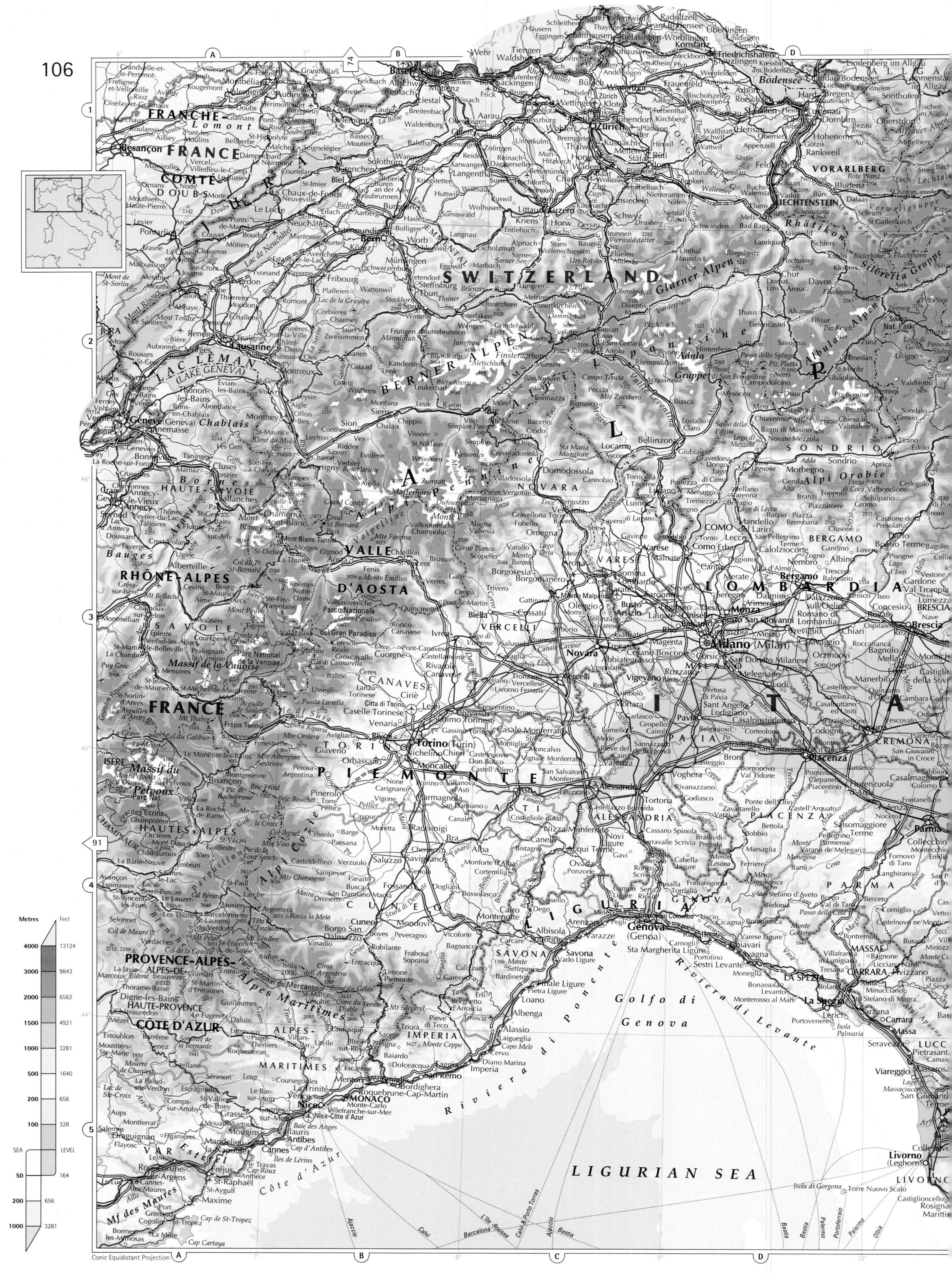

A
B
C
D
74
91
1
2
3
4
5
FRANCHE-COMTÉ
FRANCE
DOUBS
SWITZERLAND
VORARLBERG
LIECHTENSTEIN
BERNER ALPEN
Glarner Alpen
Lac Léman (Lake Geneva)
Chablais
HAUTE-SAVOIE
RHÔNE-ALPES
SAVOIE
Massif de la Vanoise
FRANCE
ISÈRE
Massif du Pelvoux
HAUTES-ALPES
PROVENCE-ALPES-CÔTE D'AZUR
ALPES-DE-HAUTE-PROVENCE
ALPES-MARITIMES
VAR
Alpes Maritimes
MONACO
VALLE D'AOSTA
PIEMONTE
TORINO
CUNEO
ASTI
ALESSANDRIA
VERCELLI
NOVARA
VARESE
COMO
LOMBARDIA
BERGAMO
SONDRIO
MILANO
PAVIA
PIACENZA
PARMA
CREMONA
LIGURIA
GENOVA
SAVONA
IMPERIA
LA SPEZIA
MASSA-CARRARA
ITALIA
Golfo di Genova
Riviera di Ponente
Riviera di Levante
LIGURIAN SEA
Côte d'Azur
Torino (Turin)
Milano (Milan)
Genova (Genoa)
Genève (Geneva)
Zürich
Bern
Lausanne
Nice
Cannes
Livorno (Leghorn)
Bodensee
Metres
Feet
4000
13124
3000
9843
2000
6562
1500
4921
1000
3281
500
1640
200
656
100
328
SEA
LEVEL
50
164
200
656
1000
3281
Conic Equidistant Projection

AUSTRIA
SLOVENIA
CROATIA
ADRIATIC SEA
Golfo di Venezia
Golfo di Trieste
SALZBURG
TIROL
OSTTIROL
KÄRNTEN
STEIERMARK
BOLZANO
TRENTINO
ALTO ADIGE
TRENTO
FRIULI VENEZIA GIULIA
UDINE
PORDENONE
BELLUNO
VENETO
VERONA
VICENZA
TREVISO
PADOVA
ROVIGO
EMILIA ROMAGNA
FERRARA
MODENA
BOLOGNA
RAVENNA
FORLÌ
TOSCANA
SIENA
AREZZO
PISTOIA
MARCHE
PESARO E URBINO
ANCONA
MACERATA
PERUGIA
SAN MARINO
MONTEFELTRO
GORSKI KOTAR
Istra
Innsbruck
Bolzano
Trento
Verona
Vicenza
Padova (Padua)
Venezia (Venice)
Treviso
Udine
Trieste
Ljubljana
Rijeka
Klagenfurt
Villach
Ferrara
Modena
Bologna
Ravenna
Rimini
Pesaro
Ancona
Firenze (Florence)
Prato
Arezzo
Siena
Pula
Koper
Chioggia
Krk
Cres
Lošinj
Rab
Pag
Dubrovnik, Durrës, Igoumenitsa & Split
Alexandria, Antalya, Bari, Cesme & Izmir
Durrës, Kusadasi & Patra
Split
Miles
Km
1:1.5M
© Bartholomew

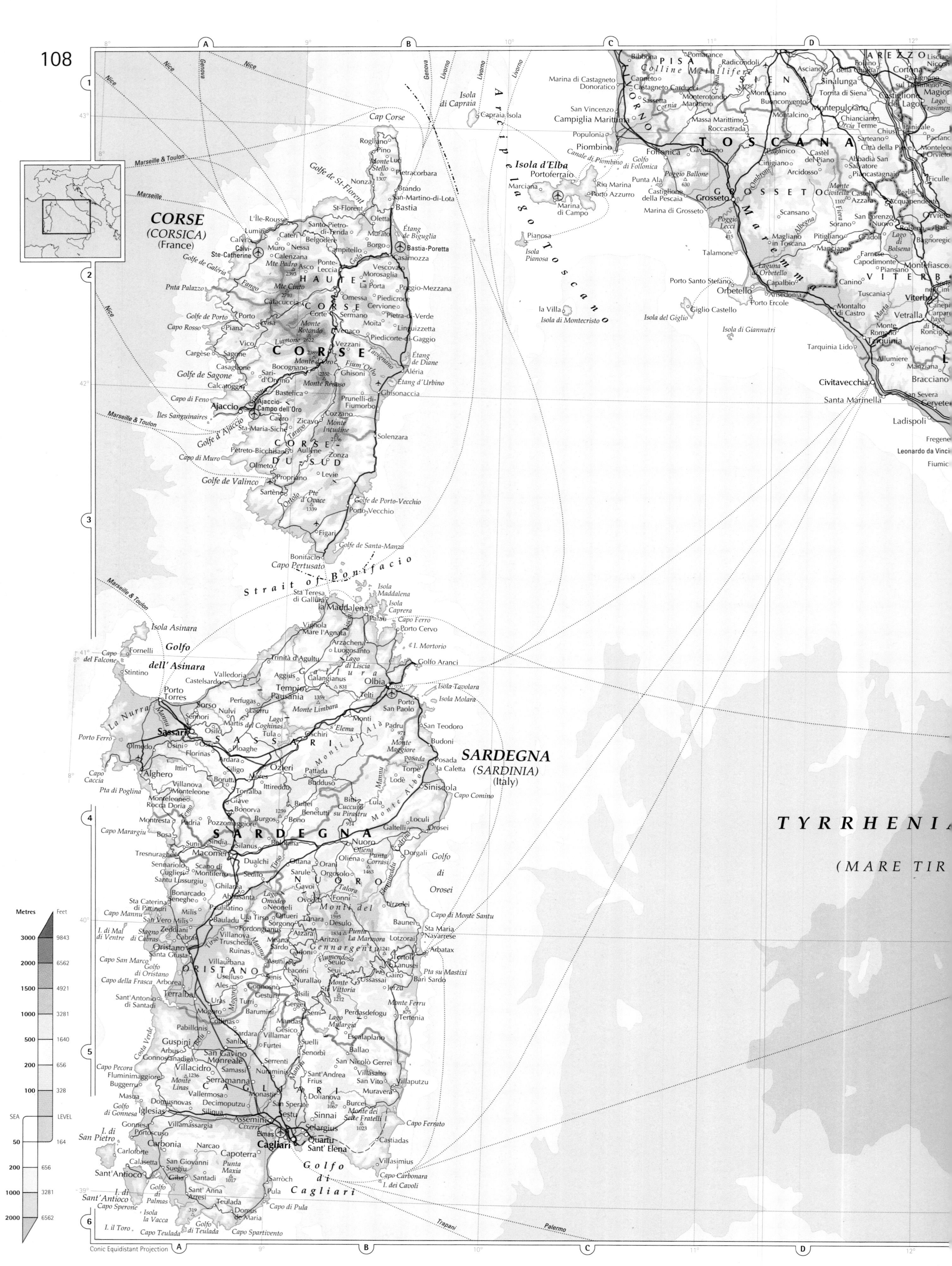
CORSE
(CORSICA)
(France)
SARDEGNA
(SARDINIA)
(Italy)
TOSCANA
TYRRHENIA
(MARE TIR
Strait of Bonifacio
Arcipelago Toscano
Golfo dell' Asinara
Golfo di Cagliari
Ajaccio
Bastia
Sassari
Olbia
Nuoro
Oristano
Cagliari
Civitavecchia
Grosseto
Metres
Feet
3000
9843
2000
6562
1500
4921
1000
3281
500
1640
200
656
100
328
SEA LEVEL
50
164
Conic Equidistant Projection

CROATIA

ADRIATIC SEA

MARCHE
MACERATA
ASCOLI PICENO
TERAMO
ABRUZZO
PESCARA
CHIETI
LAZIO
Roma (Rome)
FROSINONE
LATINA
MOLISE
CAMPOBASSO
ISERNIA
CASERTA
BENEVENTO
CAMPANIA
AVELLINO
Napoli (Naples)
PUGLIA
Foggia
FOGGIA
Promontorio del Gargano
Golfo di Manfredonia
POTENZA
BASILICATA
MATERA
SALERNO
Golfo di Salerno
Golfo di Gaeta
Golfo di Napoli
Isola d'Ischia
Isola di Capri
Isole Ponziane
Golfo di Policastro
COSENZA
CALABRIA
Cosenza
SEA

Pescara
L'Aquila
Terni
Latina
Salerno
Potenza
Barletta
Trani
Andria

Isole Tremiti
I. Pianosa

1:1.5M

Miles Km
50   80
      70
40   60
      50
30
20   40
      30
10   20
      10
0   0

© Bartholomew

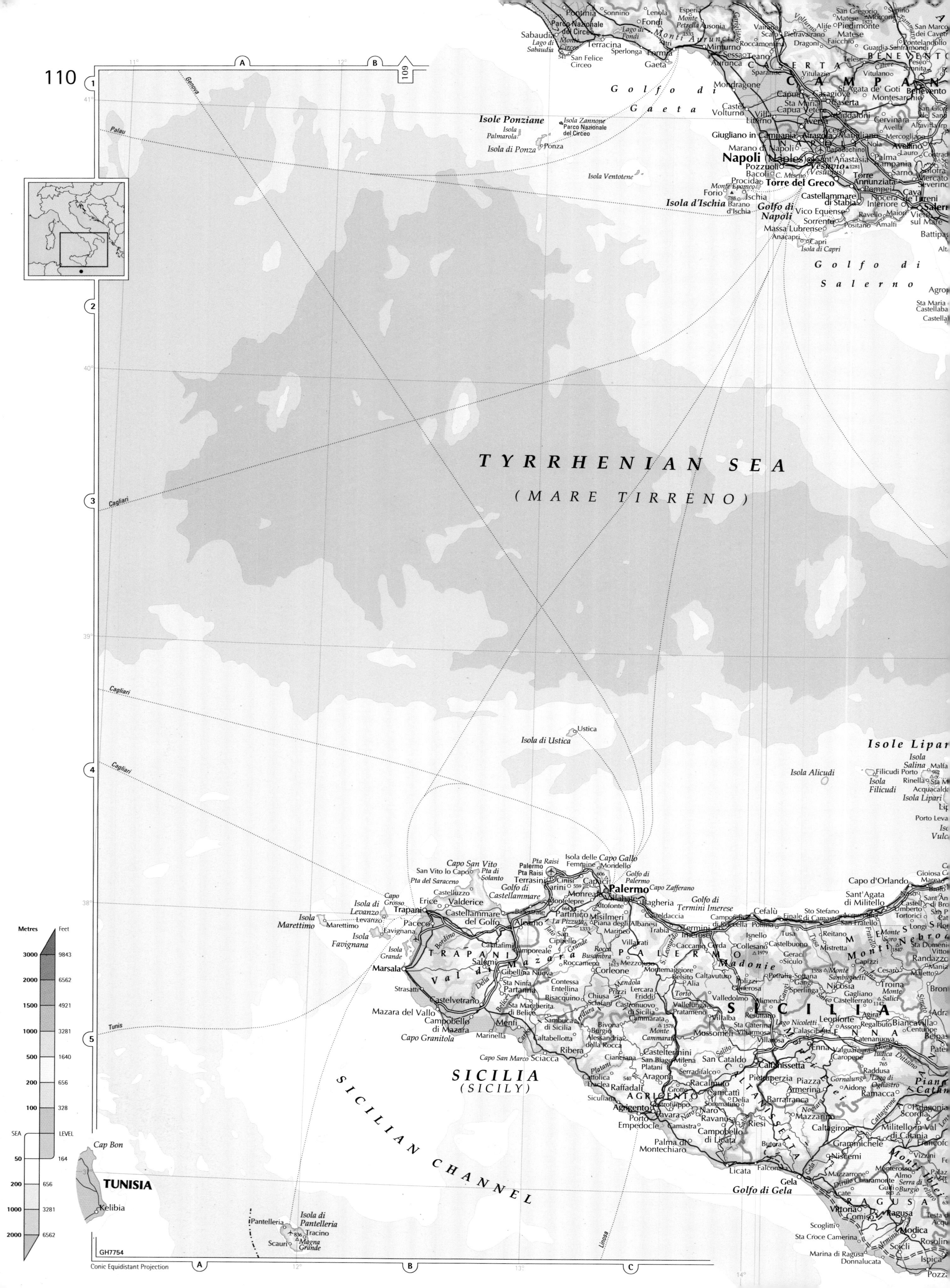

109

1

A   11°   B   12°

41°

Gennaro
Palau

Isole Ponziane
Isola
Palmarola
Isola di Ponza   Ponza
Parco Nazionale
del Circeo

Isola Zannone

2

40°

3

Cagliari

Cagliari

TYRRHENIAN SEA

(MARE TIRRENO)

39°

Cagliari

Cagliari

4

Isola di Ustica
Ustica

Isole Lipari

*Isola
Salina* Malfa
Filicudi Porto
Isola Rinella Sta M
Filicudi Acquacalde
Isola Lipari Lip

Isola Alicudi

Porto Leva

Isc
Vulca

5

Tunis

Capo San Vito
San Vito lo Capo
Pta del Saraceno
Pta di
Solanto
Terrasini

Isola delle Capo Gallo
Femmine

Mondello
Capo
Grosso
Castelluzzo
Erice Valderice
Trapani
Isola di
Levanzo Levanzo
*Isola
Marettimo* Marettimo
*Isola
Favignana* Favignana
Paceco

Pta di Raisi
Palermo
Pta Raisi
Cinisi
Carini 559
Capaci
Monreale
Monfelepre
Altofonte
La Pizzuta
1333

Golfo di
Palermo
Palermo Capo Zafferano
Bagheria
Golfo di
Termini Imerese
Aldaccia

Capo d'Orlando
Sant'Agata
di Militello

Gioiosa C
Marea

Castel Sant'An
di Bro

Capo
San
Piano degli Albanesi
Marineo Trabia Termini Imerese Cefalù Sto Stefano Finale di Castas
Campofel
San Fratello

Sto Longi S Flor
Tortorici

Isola di
Levanzo

Bordino
TRAPANI Imporeale Roccamena
Val di Mazara
Calatafimi
Busambra
Corleone Montemaggiore Isnello Tusa Reitano Mistretta
Belsito Caccamo Corda Castelbuono Geraci
Siculo Fratello
Monte S Domeni
1847 Vittor

Madonie 1979

Montri Nebros
Monte Capizzi
Salici Cesarò Randazz

Marsala

Strasatti
Castelvetrano

Salemi
Delia
Gibellina Nuova
Contessa
Entellina
Partanna
Sta Ninfa
Sta Margherita
di Belice

San
Cipirello
Roccamena
Kendola
Lercara Friddi
Sperlinga
Valledolmo 1558 Monte
Sambughetti
Gangi Monte
Troina Maletto
Bron

Nicosia Gagliano

Mazara del Vallo
Campobello
di Mazara

Menfi
Sambuca
di Sicilia
Bisacquino
Chiusa
Sclafani
Castronuovo
di Sicilia Vallelunga
Pratameno Castelverrato **SICILIA** 765

Calascibetta ENNA Centurip
Assaro Belpa

Capo Granitola

Marinella

Menfi
Alessandria
della Rocca
Bivona Burgio
Monte
Cammarata
1578 Cammarata
Villalba
Mussomeli Villarosa

ENNA
Enna Valguarnera
Caropepe
Leonforte
Bianca villa
Agira

Capo San Marco Sciacca

Ciancana
San Biago Milena San Cataldo **Caltanissetta**
Platani Raffadali Serradifalco Pietraperzia Piazza 765 Dittaino Piano
Caropepe Raddusa Cath

Cianciana
San Biago
Platani
Grotte Milena
Aragona 540
Racalmuto
Barrafranca
Mazzarino
Aidone
Mazzarino Militello in Val Franco
Grammichele

Platani

SICILIA

(SICILY)

Comitini
Porto
Empedocle
Favara
Agrigento
Canicattì
Naro Delia Riesi
Campobello
di Licata

Aragona
AGRIGENTO Ravanusa
Camastra

Butera Vizzini
Caltagirone

Metres Feet

3000 9843

2000 6562

1500 4921

1000 3281

500 1640

200 656

100 328

SEA LEVEL

50 164

200 656

1000 3281

2000 6562

Cap Bon

TUNISIA

Kelibia

Palma di
Montechiaro

SICILIAN CHANNEL

Licata
Golfo di Gela Gela Niscemi
Falcone Piazza
Mazzarrone Serra di Be

Monte di Catania
RAGUSA
Vittoria Santo
Comiso Ragusa

GH7754

Pantelleria
*Isola di
Pantelleria* Tracino
Scauri Magna
Grande 836

Limosa

Scoglitti
Sta Croce Camerina
Marina di Ragusa Donnalucata

Modica
Scicli Rosolin

A 12° B 13° C 14°

Conic Equidistant Projection

ADRIATIC SEA
Strait of Otranto
Golfo di Taranto
IONIAN SEA
Golfo di Policastro
Golfo di Sta Eufemia
Golfo di Squillace
Golfo di Gioia
Golfo di Catania
Golfo di Noto
PUGLIA
Basilicata
CALABRIA
FOGGIA
BARI
TARANTO
BRINDISI
LECCE
POTENZA
MATERA
COSENZA
CATANZARO
REGGIO DI CALABRIA
Barletta
Trani
Bisceglie
Molfetta
Bari
Monopoli
Brindisi
Lecce
Taranto
Gallipoli
Otranto
Capo Sta Maria di Leuca
Potenza
Matera
Altamura
Cosenza
Crotone
Capo Colonna
Catanzaro
Vibo Valentia
Reggio di Calabria
Messina
Catania
Siracusa
Capo Spartivento
Capo Rizzuto
Punta Stilo
Monti Peloritani
Stretto di Messina
Isola Stromboli
MALTA and GOZO
1:500 000
MALTA
Gozo
Victoria
Valletta
Sliema
Marsaxlokk
MEDITERRANEAN SEA
Filfla
Comino
1:1.5M
© Bartholomew

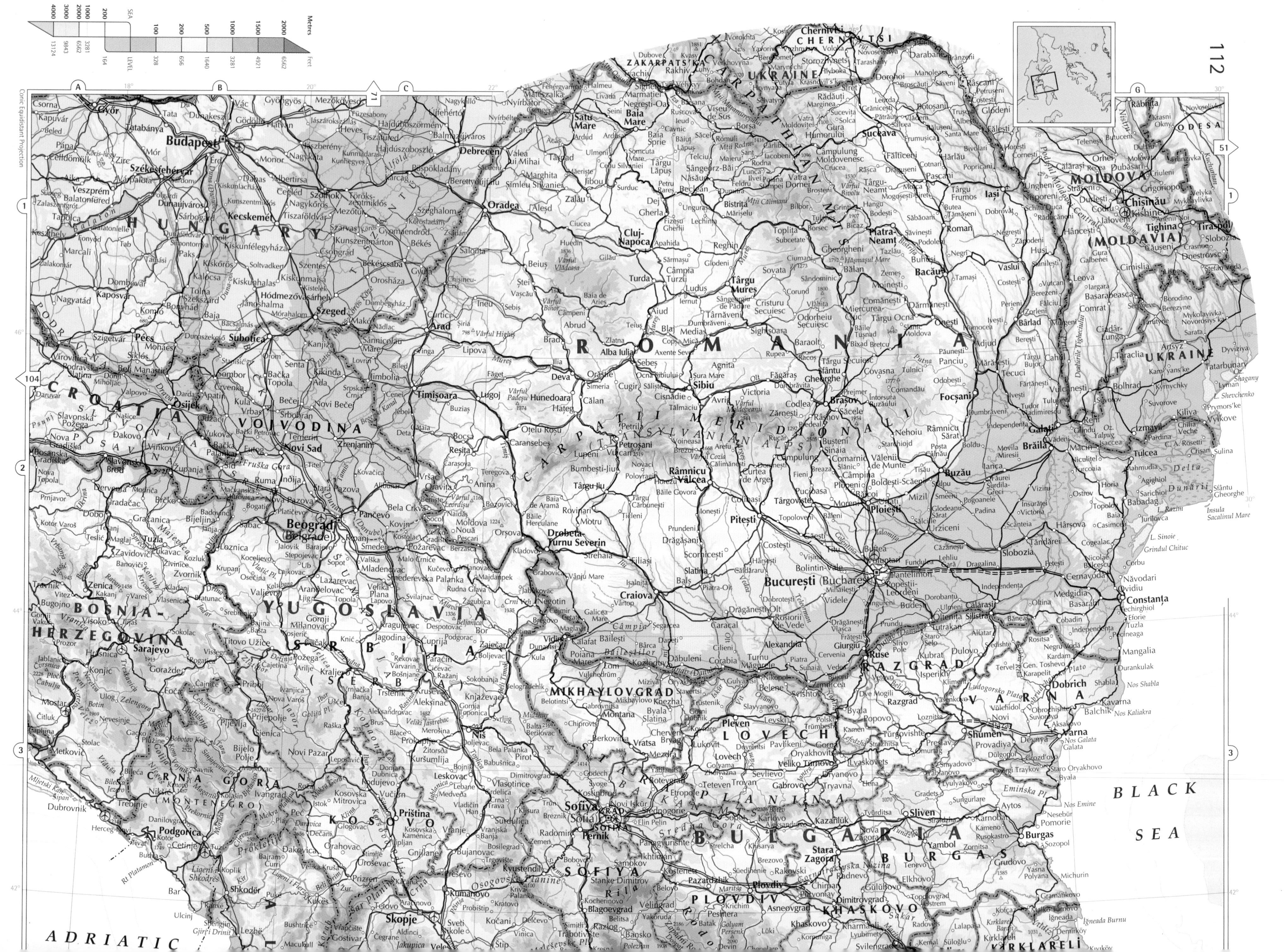
BLACK SEA
ROMANIA
BULGARIA
YUGOSLAVIA
HUNGARY
MOLDOVA
UKRAINE
CROATIA
BOSNIA-HERZEGOVINA
SERBIA
VOJVODINA
KOSOVO
CRNA GORA
ADRIATIC
CARPATHIAN MTS
STARA PLANINA
București (Bucharest)
Beograd (Belgrade)
Budapest
Sofiya (Sofia)
Chișinău
Sarajevo
Skopje
Constanța
Varna
Burgas
Cluj-Napoca
Timișoara
Iași
Metres
Feet
2000
6562
1500
4921
1000
3281
500
1640
200
656
100
328
SEA
LEVEL
200
164
1000
3281
2000
6562
3000
9843
4000
13124
Conic Equidistant Projection

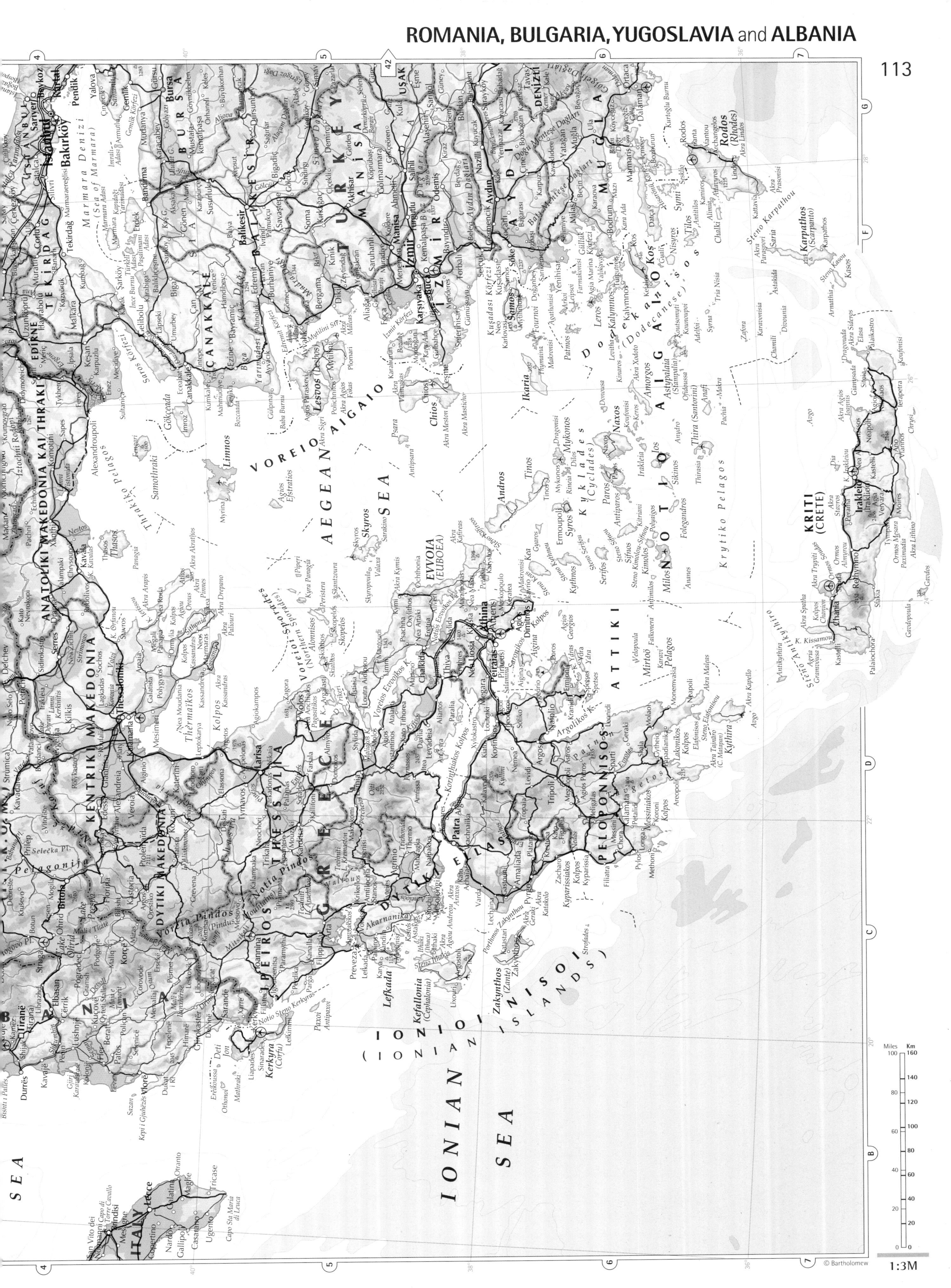

AEGEAN SEA
VOREIO AIGAIO
IONIAN SEA
IONIOI NISOI
(IONIAN ISLANDS)
GREECE
TURKEY
KRITI
(CRETE)
Rodos
(Rhodes)
Karpathos
(Skarpanto)
Kythira
Peloponnisos
Kyklades
(Cyclades)
Dodekanisos
(Dodecanese)
Lesvos
(Lesbos)
Limnos
Chios
Samos
Ikaria
Naxos
Andros
Tinos
Thira (Santorini)
Skyros
EVVOIA
(EUBOEA)
Kerkyra
(Corfu)
Kefallonia
(Cephalonia)
Zakynthos
(Zante)
Lefkada
Athina
(Athens)
Peiraias
(Piraeus)
Thessaloniki
Patra
Larisa
Izmir
Istanbul
Bursa
Balıkesir
Manisa
Aydın
Muğla
Denizli
Uşak
Çanakkale
Edirne
Tekirdağ
Irakleio
THESSALIA
IPEIROS
ATTIKI
KENTRIKI MAKEDONIA
DYTIKI MAKEDONIA
ANATOLIKI MAKEDONIA KAI THRAKI
Marmara Denizi
(Sea of Marmara)
Tirana
Durrës
Vlorë
Elbasan
Korçë
Bitola
Ohrid
Lecce
Brindisi
ITALY
Miles
Km
© Bartholomew
1:3M

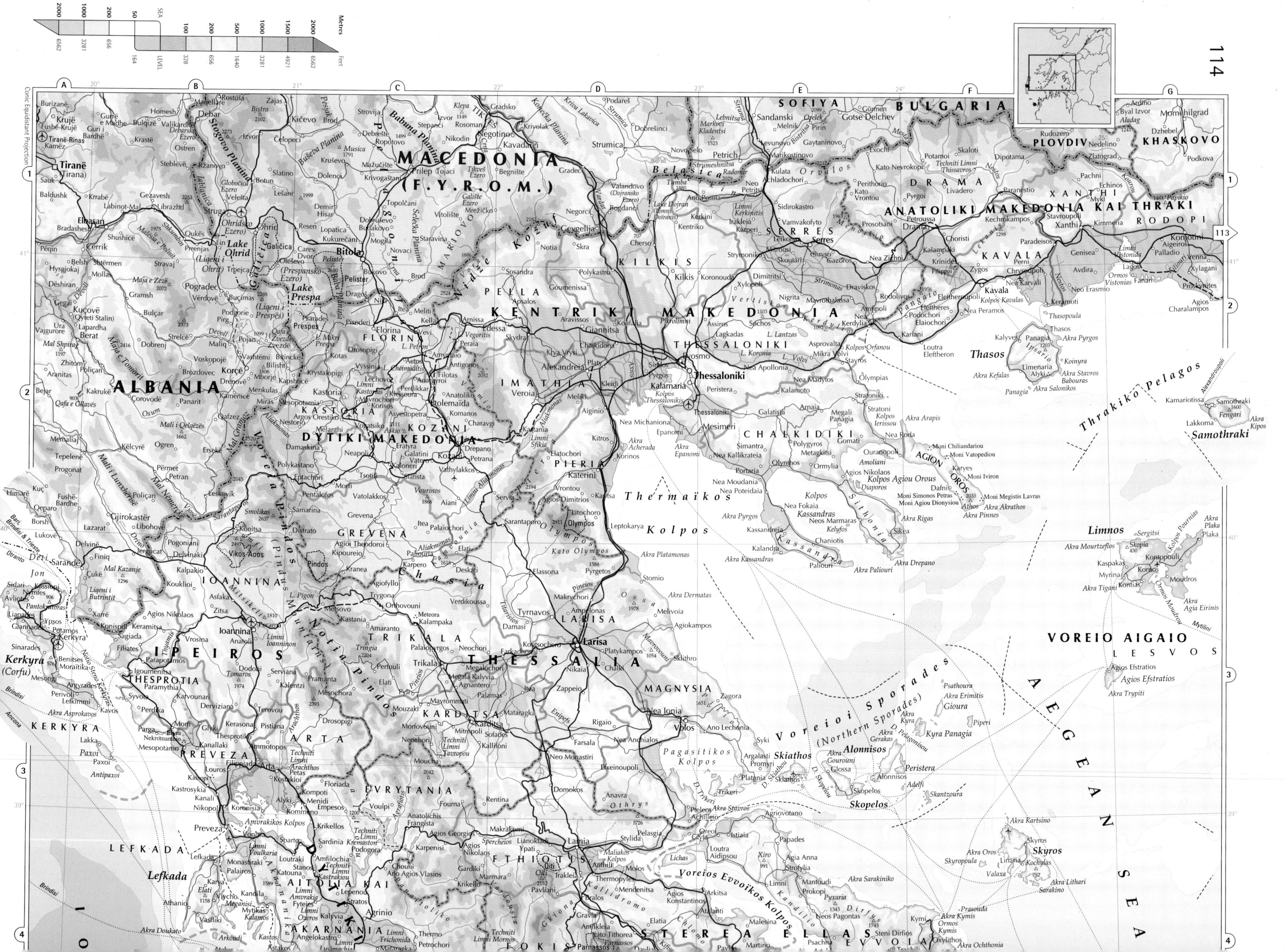
BULGARIA
SOFIYA
PLOVDIV
KHASKOVO
MACEDONIA (F.Y.R.O.M.)
ALBANIA
Tiranë (Tirana)
AEGEAN SEA
VOREIO AIGAIO
LESVOS
Thessaloniki
KENTRIKI MAKEDONIA
ANATOLIKI MAKEDONIA KAI THRAKI
DYTIKI MAKEDONIA
THESSALIA
IPEIROS
STEREA ELLAS
CHALKIDIKI
Thermaïkos Kolpos
Thrakiko Pelagos
Limnos
Thasos
Samothraki
Skyros
Skopelos
Skiathos
Alonnisos
Lefkada
Kerkyra (Corfu)
Lake Ohrid
Lake Prespa
Voreioi Sporades (Northern Sporades)
Voreia Pindos (Pindus Mountains)
Larisa
Ioannina
Kavala
Volos
Lamia
113
Conic Equidistant Projection
Metres
Feet
SEA
LEVEL

IONIAN SEA
IONIOI NISOI (IONIAN ISLANDS)
KEFALLONIA
Kefallonia (Cephalonia)
ZAKYNTHOS
Zakynthos (Zante)
PELOPONNISOS
ACHAIA
ILIA
MESSINIA
ARKADIA
KORINTHIA
ARGOLIS
LAKONIA
KYTHIRA
ATTIKI
EVVOIA (EUBOEA)
VOIOTIA
CHIOS
Korinthiakos Kolpos
Saronikos Kolpos
Argolikos Kolpos
Kyparissiakos Kolpos
Lakonikos Kolpos
Messiniakos Kolpos
MIRTOÖ PELAGOS
Krytiko Pelagos
NOTIO AIGAIO
KYKLADES (Cyclades)
Athina (Athens)
Peiraias
Patra
Korinthos
Tripoli
Kalamata
Sparti
Naxos
Paros
Mykonos
Tinos
Andros
Syros
Kea
Kythnos
Serifos
Sifnos
Milos
Ios
Thira (Santorini)
Aigina
Ydra
KRITI (Crete)
CHANIA
RETHYMNO
IRAKLEIO
LASITHI
Irakleio (Iraklion)
Chania
Rethymno
Lefka Ori
RHODES (Greece) at the same scale
RODOS
TURKEY
Symi
CRETE (Greece) continuation at the same scale
Miles
Km

© Bartholomew
1:1.5M

K A Z A K H S T A N
RUSSIAN FEDERATION
UZBEKISTAN
TURKMENISTAN
I R A N
I R A Q
SYRIA
TURKEY
SAUDI ARABIA
Rub' al Khali
YEMEN
OMAN
U.A.E.
QATAR
BAHRAIN
KUWAIT
JORDAN
ISRAEL
LEBANON
CYPRUS
EGYPT
SUDAN
ERITREA
DJIBOUTI
CHAD
LIBYA
NIGER
ALGERIA
TUNISIA
MOROCCO
WESTERN SAHARA
MAURITANIA
MALI
BURKINA
SENEGAL
THE GAMBIA
GUINEA BISSAU
GUINEA
S A H A R A
Libyan Desert
Tibesti
Hoggar
Atlas Mountains
GEORGIA
ARM.
AZERBAIJAN
AZ.
UKRAINE
BELARUS
MOLDOVA
ROMANIA
BULGARIA
GREECE
MACE.
ALBANIA
YUGO.
BOSNIA HERZ.
CROATIA
SLOV.
HUNGARY
SLOVAKIA
CZECH REP.
POLAND
LITHUANIA
LATVIA
ESTONIA
FINLAND
SWEDEN
NORWAY
DENMARK
RUS. FED.
GERMANY
NETH.
BEL.
LUX.
FRANCE
SWITZ.
AUSTRIA
ITALY
SPAIN
PORTUGAL
UNITED KINGDOM
REP. OF IRELAND
Caspian Sea
Aral Sea
Kara Bogaz Gol
Black Sea
Sea of Azov
Caucasus
Mediterranean Sea
Red Sea
Gulf of Aden
Gulf of Oman
The Gulf
G. of Suez
G. of 'Aqaba
Aegean Sea
Ionian Sea
Tyrrhenian Sea
Adriatic Sea
Baltic Sea
Gulf of Bothnia
North Sea
English Channel
Bay of Biscay
Str. of Gibraltar
Gulf of Sirte
G. of Gabès
Pyrenees
Alps
Balearic Is
Corsica
Sardinia
Sicily
Crete
MALTA
Canary Is (Sp.)
Madeira (Port.)
Azores (Port.)
São Miguel
Gibraltar (U.K.)
Socotra (Yemen)
Volga
Syrdarya
Amudarya
Kyzylkum
Danube
Rhine
Tigris
Euphrates
Nile
Blue Nile
White Nile
L. Nasser
L. Tana
L. Chad
Niger
Senegal
Fouta Djallon
Tropic of Cancer
Karaganda
Chelyabinsk
Yekaterinburg
Samara
Nizhniy Novgorod
Volgograd
Astrakhan
Moscow
St Petersburg
Helsinki
Tallinn
Riga
Vilnius
Minsk
Kiev
Kharkov
Donetsk
Dnepropetrovsk
Odessa
Chişinău
Bucharest
Sofia
Skopje
Tirana
Belgrade
Sarajevo
Zagreb
Ljubljana
Budapest
Bratislava
Vienna
Prague
Warsaw
Berlin
Hamburg
Copenhagen
Stockholm
Oslo
Bergen
Amsterdam
The Hague
Brussels
Bonn
Munich
Bern
Milan
Rome
Naples
Athens
Istanbul
Izmir
Ankara
Tbilisi
Yerevan
Baku
Tabriz
Tehran
Mashhad
Ashkhabad
Samarkand
Chimkent
Isfahan
Shiraz
Bandar Abbas
Muscat
Abu Dhabi
Doha
Manama
Kuwait
Basra
Baghdad
Riyadh
Jiddah
Sana
Aden
Mukalla
Hodeidah
Asmara
Massawa
Assab
Djibouti
Berbera
Dese
Aleppo
Damascus
Beirut
Amman
Jerusalem
Aqaba
Elat
Nicosia
Tanta
Port Said
Suez
Cairo
Giza
Alexandria
Asyut
Aswan
Wadi Halfa
Port Sudan
Khartoum
Omdurman
Wad Medani
El Obeid
Abéché
Ndjamena
Maiduguri
Kano
Zaria
Sokoto
Zinder
Arlit
Niamey
Gao
Mopti
Ségou
Bamako
Kayes
Ouagadougou
Bobo Dioulasso
Conakry
Bissau
Kaolack
Dakar
Nouakchott
Nouâdhibou
Fdérik
Laâyoune
Las Palmas
Sta Cruz
Gran Canaria
Marrakesh
Casablanca
Rabat
Meknès
Fez
Tangier
Tétouan
Oujda
Béchar
Oran
Sidi-bel-Abbès
Algiers
Sétif
Constantine
Annaba
Bizerte
Tunis
Sousse
Sfax
Gabès
Tripoli
Banghazi
Al Bayda
Touggourt
Djanet
Ghat
Tamanrasset
Lisbon
Oporto
Madrid
Sevilla
Barcelona
Marseille
Lyon
Paris
London
Birmingham
Liverpool
Edinburgh
Dublin
Metres
Feet
0
200
3000
656
9842
Oblated Stereographic Projection

SOMALIA

ETHIOPIA

Addis Ababa

Wau

I N D I A N

O C E A N

SEYCHELLES

Praslin

Mahé

Desroches

Cöetivy

Amirante Islands

Farquhar Group (Sey.)

Aldabra Is (Sey.)

COMOROS

Grande Comore

Mayotte (Fr.)

Anjouan

MAURITIUS

Port Louis

Réunion (Fr.)

St-Denis

I. Tromelin (Fr.)

Agalega Is (Maur.)

C. Bobaomby

Antsiranana

Marromsetra

Tsaratanana 2876

MADAGASCAR

Antananarivo

Toamasina

Antsirabe

Mananjary

Fianarantsoa

Farafangana

Tôlanaro

C. Vohimena

Toliara

Morondava

Maintirano

Mahajanga

Mogadishu

KENYA

Mt Kenya 5199

Nairobi

Turkana

Nakuru

UGANDA

Kampala

Lake Victoria

Entebbe

L. Albert

RWANDA

Kigali

Bujumbura

BURUNDI

L. Edward

L. Kivu

Bukavu

Mwanza

Mombasa

Kismaayo

Voi

Tanga

Zanzibar

Pemba

Dar es Salaam

Kilwa Masoko

Mafia

TANZANIA

Arusha

Kilimanjaro 5895

Dodoma

Iringa

Mbeya

Tabora

Kigoma

Lake Tanganyika

Mbala

Songea

Rufiji

Lindi

Mtwara

Ruvuma

MOZAMBIQUE

Nampula

Mozambique

Pemba

Lichinga

L. Nyasa

MALAWI

Lilongwe

Blantyre

Zomba

Chipata

Quelimane

M o z a m b i q u e   C h a n n e l

Bassas da India (Fr.)

Europa (Fr.)

CENTRAL AFRICAN REPUBLIC

Bangassou

Bangui

Sarh

Chari

Bossangoa

Ubangi

Uele

ZAIRE

Kisangani

Lomami

Lualaba

Ubundu

Kindu

Kalémié

Kasai

Kananga

Kamina

Kaniama

Mbuji-Mayi

Kabalo

Manono

Mwene-Ditu

Kabinda

L. Mweru

Lubumbashi

Likasi

Kolwezi

ZAMBIA

Kabwe

Lusaka

Kitwe

Ndola

Chililabombwe

Kasama

Mpika

Mongu

Kariba

L. Kariba

Zambezi

Luangwa

CONGO

Brazzaville

Kinshasa

Owando

Djambala

Boma

Matadi

Maquela do Zombo

CABINDA (ANG.)

Pointe Noire

Tchibanga

GABON

Libreville

Lambaréné

Franceville

Port Gentil

EQUAT. GUINEA

Bata

Bioco

SAO TOME & PRINCIPE

Principe

São Tomé

Annobón

CAMEROON

Yaoundé

Douala

Ngaoundéré

Benue

NIGERIA

Lagos

Ibadan

Ogbomoso

Onitsha

Port Harcourt

Bight of Benin

BENIN

TOGO

Porto Novo

Lomé

Accra

GHANA

Kumasi

Takoradi

L. Volta

CÔTE D'IVOIRE

Bouaké

Yamoussoukro

Abidjan

LIBERIA

Monrovia

LEONE

G u l f   o f   G u i n e a

ANGOLA

Luanda

Malanje

Saurimo

Luau

Dondo

Cuanza

Sumbe

Lobito

Benguela

Namibe

Tombua

Kuito

Huambo

Menongue

Lubango

Ondjiva

Cubango

Cuito

Cunene

Cubango

NAMIBIA

Windhoek

Tsumeb

Grootfontein

Gobabis

Mariental

Keetmanshoop

Lüderitz

Swakopmund

Walvis Bay

N a m i b   D e s e r t

K a l a h a r i   D e s e r t

Okavango Delta

BOTSWANA

Gaborone

Francistown

Serowe

Kanye

Victoria Falls

ZIMBABWE

Harare

Bulawayo

Gweru

Mutare

Masvingo

Hwange

Limpopo

Messina

Pietersburg

Pretoria

Johannesburg

Vereeniging

Witbank

Springs

SWAZILAND

Mbabane

Maputo

Xai-Xai

Inhambane

Beira

Inharrime

Vilanculos

Gwelo

MOZAMBIQUE

Pietermaritzburg

Durban

Ladysmith

Kroonstad

LESOTHO

Maseru

Kokstad

Bloemfontein

Kimberley

De Aar

Upington

Vryburg

Rustenburg

Mafikeng

REPUBLIC OF SOUTH AFRICA

Queenstown

East London

Port Elizabeth

Grahamstown

Beaufort West

Great Karoo

Oudtshoorn

Mossel Bay

Worcester

Cape Town

Cape of Good Hope

C. Agulhas

Karasburg

Springbok

Port Nolloth

Orange

Beaufort

S O U T H

A T L A N T I C

O C E A N

St Helena I. (U.K.)

Ascension I. (U.K.)

Tristan da Cunha (U.K.)

Equator

Tropic of Capricorn

© Bartholomew

1:24M

Miles   Km
800   1280
         1020
640   960
         800
480   640
         480
320
         320
160   160
0   0

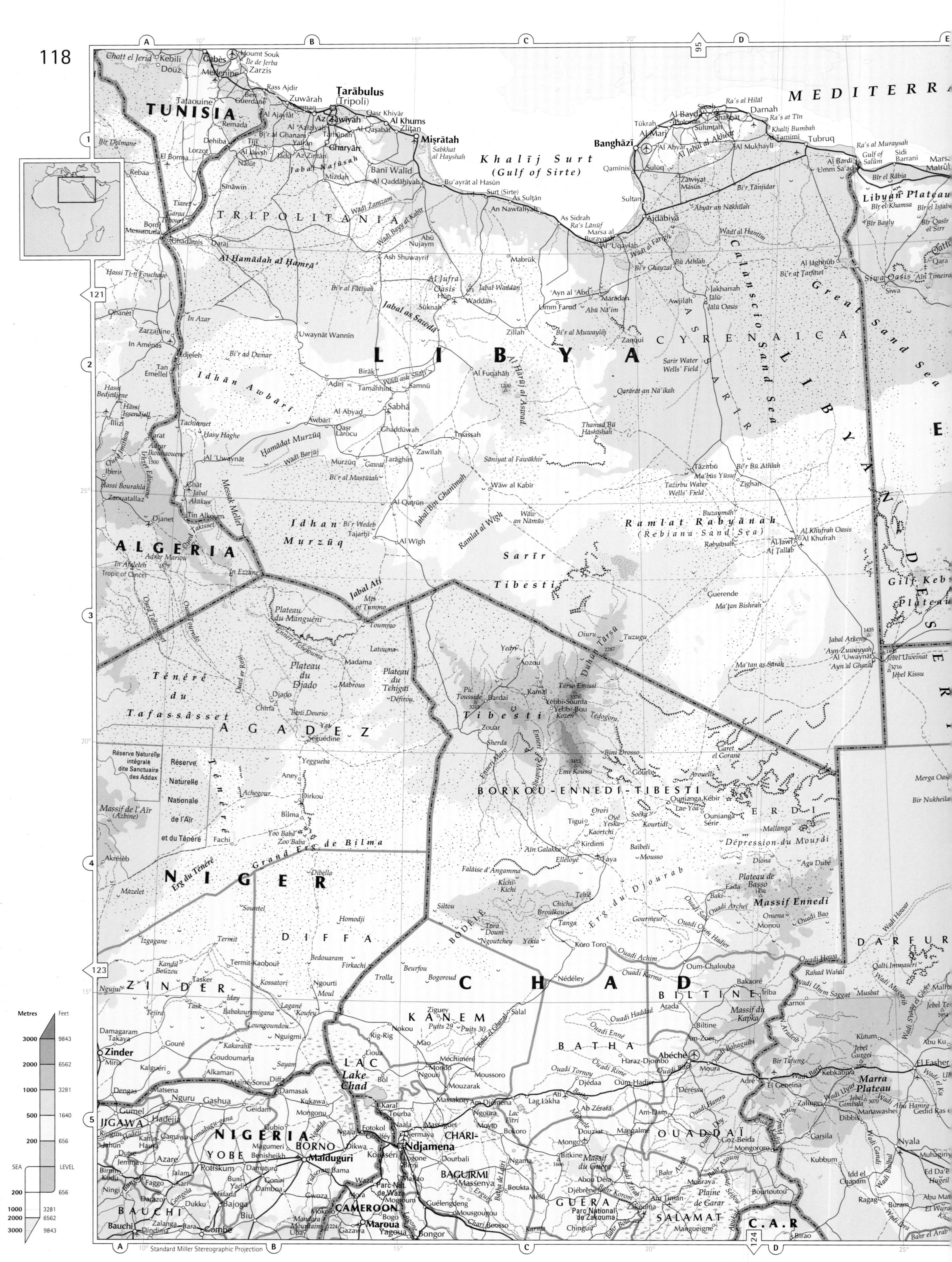

MEDITERRA
TUNISIA
LIBYA
ALGERIA
NIGER
CHAD
NIGERIA
CAMEROON
C.A.R
Khalīj Surt
(Gulf of Sirte)
TRIPOLITANIA
CYRENAICA
LIBYAN DESERT
Great Sand Sea
Calanscio Sand Sea
Ramlat Rabyānah
(Rebiana Sand Sea)
Idhān Awbārī
Idhan Murzūq
Al Hamādah al Hamrā'
Ḥamādat Murzūq
Sarīr Tibesti
Tibesti
AGADEZ
DIFFA
ZINDER
Ténéré du Tafassâsset
Grand Erg de Bilma
Erg du Ténéré
Erg du Djourab
BORKOU-ENNEDI-TIBESTI
KANEM
BATHA
BILTINE
OUADDAÏ
GUERA
SALAMAT
BAGUIRMI
CHARI-
BORNO
YOBE
JIGAWA
BAUCHI
LAC
Lake Chad
DARFUR
Massif Ennedi
Massif de l'Aïr (Azbine)
Plateau du Djado
Plateau du Manguéni
Ţarābulus (Tripoli)
Mişrātah
Banghāzī
Sabhā
Ghadāmis
Tubruq
Darnah
Al Khums
Ajdābiyā
Al Kufrah
Ndjamena
Abéché
Faya
Bardaï
Emi Koussi
Maiduguri
Zinder
Maroua
Réserve Naturelle intégrale dite Sanctuaire des Addax
Réserve Naturelle Nationale de l'Aïr et du Ténéré
Tropic of Cancer
Metres
Feet
3000
2000
1000
500
200
SEA
LEVEL
9843
6562
3281
1640
656
121
123
124
95
Standard Miller Stereographic Projection

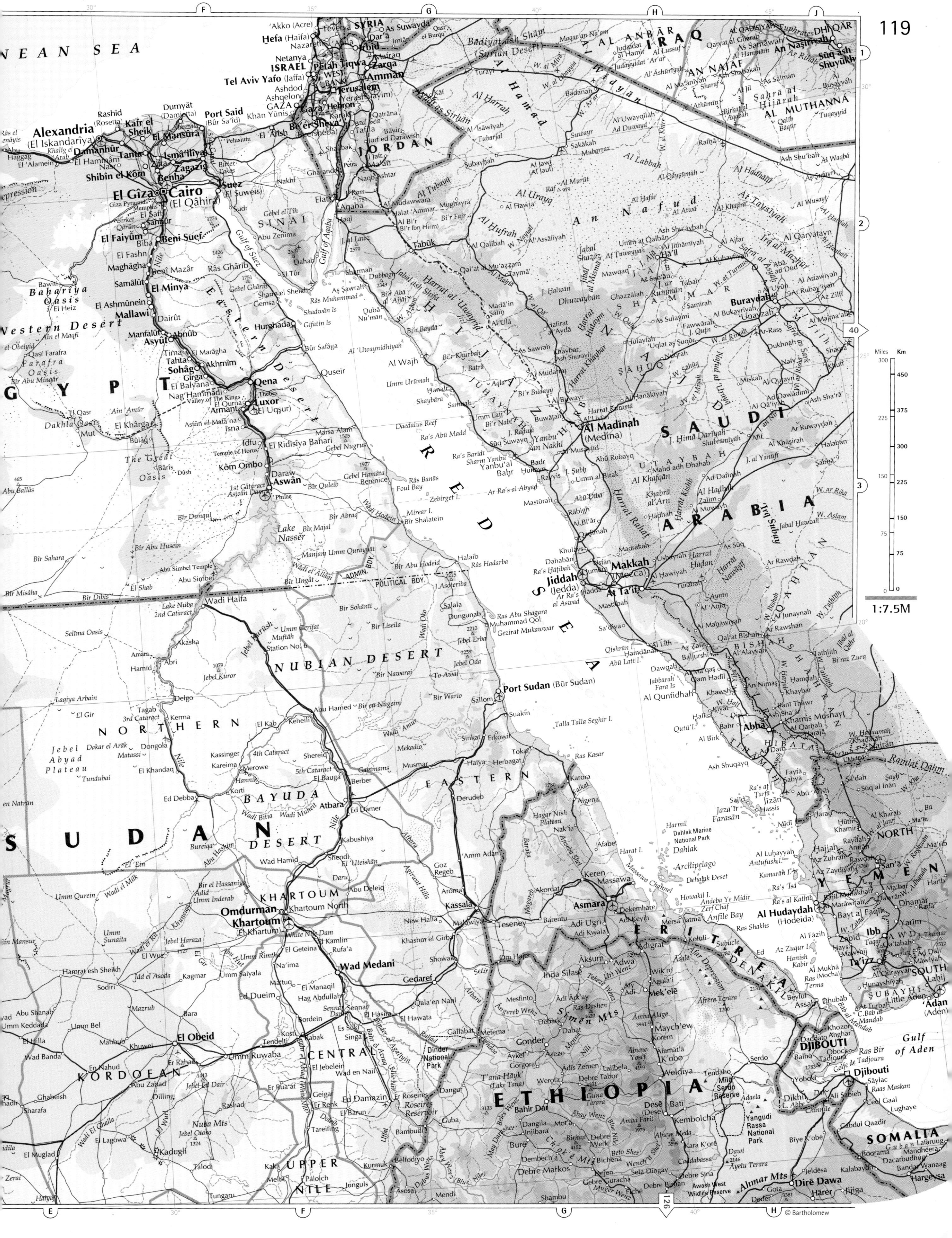

NEAN SEA

SYRIA
Hefa (Haifa)
Nazareth
Netanya
Tel Aviv Yafo (Jaffa)
ISRAEL
Petáh Tiqwa
Jerusalem
WEST BANK
GAZA
Gaza / Hebron
Bér Sheva (Beersheba)
Ashdod
Ashqelon

JORDAN
Amman
Zarqa
Irbid
Dar'a
As Suwaydá

IRAQ
AL ANBAR
AN NAJAF
An Nasiriyah
Suq ash Shuyukh
AL MUTHANNA
AL QADISIYAH
DHI QAR
Euphrates

Alexandria (El Iskandariya)
Rashid (Rosetta)
Dumyât (Damietta)
Port Said (Bûr Sa'îd)
Damanhûr
Kafr el Sheikh
El Mansûra
Tanta
Isma'îliya
Zagazig
Benha
Shibîn el Kôm
El Gîza
Cairo (El Qâhira)
Suez (El Suweis)

SINAI

EGYPT

El Faiyûm
Beni Suef
El Fashn
Maghâgha
Beni Mazâr
Samalût
El Minya
El Ashmûnein
Mallawi
Manfalût
Abnûb
Asyût
Sohâg
Akhmîm
Girga
El Balyana
Qena
Nag' Hammâdi
Luxor (El Uqsur)
Armant
Isna
Idfu
Kôm Ombo
Daraw
Aswân
Aswân Dam

Western Desert
Bahariya Oasis
Farafra Oasis
Dakhla Oasis
The Great Oasis
Kharga

Eastern Desert

Hurghada
Ras Gharib
Marsa Alam

RED SEA

Lake Nasser

SAUDI ARABIA

Tabûk
Al Madinah (Medina)
Yanbu' al Bahr
Jiddah (Jedda)
Makkah (Mecca)
At Ta'if
Ha'il
Buraydah
Unayzah
Abha
Khamis Mushayt

An Nafud

HIJAZ

Ar Rawdah

SUDAN

Wadi Halfa
NORTHERN
Dongola
Ed Debba
Korti
Merowe
Berber
Atbara
Ed Damer

NUBIAN DESERT
BAYUDA DESERT

Port Sudan (Bûr Sudan)
Suakin
Tokar

EASTERN

Kassala
KHARTOUM
Omdurman
Khartoum (El Khartum)
Khartoum North
Wad Medani
Gedaref
Kosti
El Obeid
KORDOFAN
CENTRAL
El Gedaref

ERITREA
Asmara
Massawa
Keren
Agordat
Adi Ugri
Adi Keyih

DENAKIL

ETHIOPIA
Gonder
Bahir Dar
Lake Tana
Mek'elê
Aksum
Adwa
Adigrat
Debre Markos
Dese
Simën Mts

YEMEN
San'a
Al Hudaydah (Hodeida)
Ta'izz
Ibb
Zabid
Adan (Aden)
SOUTH

DJIBOUTI
Djibouti
Obock
Dikhil
Ali Sabieh

SOMALIA
Dirê Dawa
Hargeysa

Gulf of Aden

© Bartholomew

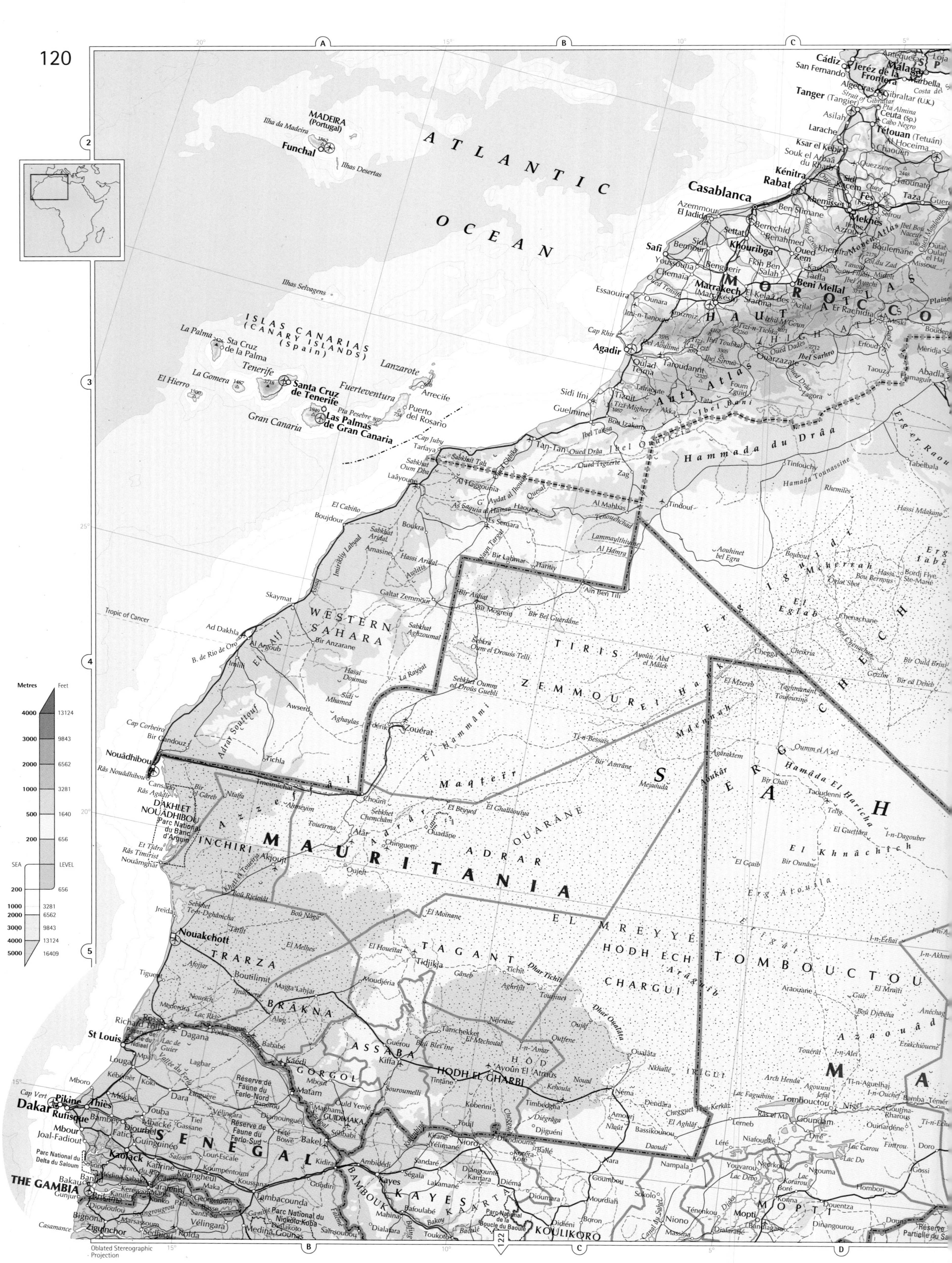

ATLANTIC OCEAN
MADEIRA (Portugal)
Ilha da Madeira
Funchal
Ilhas Desertas
Ilhas Selvagens
ISLAS CANARIAS (CANARY ISLANDS) (Spain)
La Palma
Sta Cruz de la Palma
Tenerife
Santa Cruz de Tenerife
La Gomera
El Hierro
Gran Canaria
Las Palmas de Gran Canaria
Lanzarote
Fuerteventura
Arrecife
Puerto del Rosario
MOROCCO
HAUT ATLAS
Anti Atlas
Cádiz
San Fernando
Jeréz de la Frontera
Málaga
Marbella
Algeciras
Gibraltar (U.K.)
Strait of Gibraltar
Tanger (Tangier)
Ceuta (Sp.)
Tétouan (Tetuán)
Asilah
Larache
Ksar el Kebir
Souk el Arbaâ du Rharb
Chaouèn
Al Hoceima
Ouezzane
Kénitra
Rabat
Casablanca
Fès
Meknès
Taza
Taounate
Khemisset
Sidi Kacem
Azemmour
El Jadida
Ben Slimane
Settat
Berrechid
Benahmed
Oued Zem
Khouribga
Safi
Youssoufia
Chemaïa
Benguerir
Fkih Ben Salah
Kasba Tadla
Beni Mellal
Khenifra
Azrou
Boulemane
Midelt
Missour
Essaouira
Marrakech (Marrakesh)
Ounara
Imi-n-Tanoute
Amizmiz
Azilal
Er Rachidia
Erfoud
Cap Rhir
Agadir
Taroudannt
Oulad Teïma
Ouarzazate
Jbel Sarhro
Zagora
Taouz
Tafraoute
Tiznit
Sidi Ifni
Guelmine
Foum Zguid
Tata
Akka
Bou Izakarn
Tan-Tan
Cap Juby
Tarfaya
Oued Drâa
Hammada du Drâa
Jbel Bani
Tindouf
Hamada Tounassine
Tinfouchy
Tabelbala
Erg er Raoui
Laâyoune
Al Haggounia
As Saquia al Hamra
Es Semara
Al Mahbas
Boujdour
El Cabiño
Boukra
Hassi Aridal
Amasine
Bir Lahmar
Haritiy
Galtat Zemmour
Aïn Ben Tili
Skaymat
WESTERN SAHARA
Ad Dakhla
B. de Rio de Oro
Bir Anzarane
Awserd
Aghaylas
Tropic of Cancer
Cap Corbeiro
Bir Gandouz
Adrar Souttouf
Tichla
Nouâdhibou
Râs Nouâdhibou
DAKHLET NOUÂDHIBOU
Parc National du Banc d'Arguin
Râs Timirist
Nouâmghâr
Bir Mogreïn
Bir Bel Guerdâne
TIRIS ZEMMOUR
Zouérat
F'dérik
Erg Iguidi
Erg Chech
Chegga
Hamâda El Haricha
Taoudenni
El Khnâchîch
Erg Atouïla
MAURITANIA
INCHIRI
Akjoujt
ADRAR
Atâr
Chinguetti
Ouadâne
Choûm
Ouarâne
Maqteïr
El Mreyyé
Ouarâne
Mejaouda
HODH ECH CHARGUI
TAGANT
Tidjikja
Tichît
Dhar Tichît
TRARZA
Nouakchott
Boutilimit
Tiguent
BRAKNA
Aleg
Magta Lahjar
Moudjéria
ASSABA
Kiffa
Guérou
Tâmchekket
Ayoûn El Atroûs
HODH EL GHARBI
Oualâta
Néma
Timbedgha
Kaédi
GORGOL
GUIDIMAKA
Sélibabi
St Louis
Richard Toll
Dagana
Louga
Lac de Guier
Podor
Matam
Linguère
Réserve de Faune du Ferlo-Nord
Réserve de Faune du Ferlo-Sud
Dara
Mboro
Cap Vert
Dakar
Pikine
Thiès
Rufisque
Mbour
Joal-Fadiout
Diourbel
Fatick
Kaolack
Bakel
SENEGAL
Parc National du Delta du Saloum
THE GAMBIA
Banjul
Tambacounda
Parc National du Niokolo Koba
Kédougou
Ziguinchor
Kolda
Vélingara
Bignona
Casamance
Kayes
KAYES
BAMBOUK
KAARTA
Nioro
Diéma
Bafoulabé
KOULIKORO
Parc National de la Boucle du Baoulé
Nara
Niono
Mopti
MOPTI
TOMBOUCTOU
Tombouctou
Goundam
Araouane
Lac Faguibine
Niafunké
Douentza
Hombori
Gossi
Azaouâd
Oblated Stereographic Projection

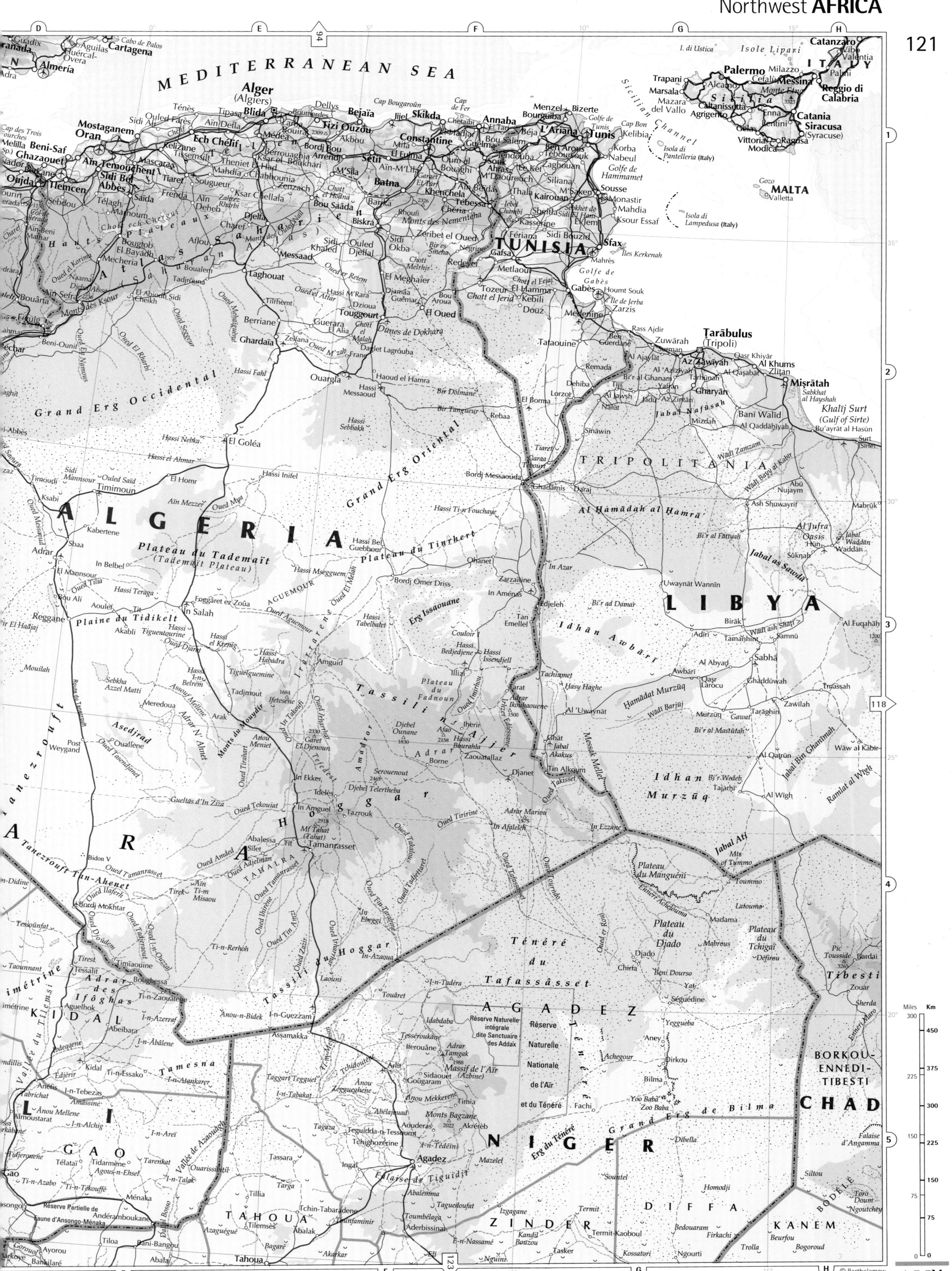
MEDITERRANEAN SEA
ALGERIA
TUNISIA
LIBYA
NIGER
CHAD
ITALY
MALTA
Alger (Algiers)
Tunis
Tarābulus (Tripoli)
Grand Erg Occidental
Grand Erg Oriental
Ténéré du Tafassâsset
AGADEZ
Réserve Naturelle intégrale dite Sanctuaire des Addax
Réserve Naturelle Nationale de l'Aïr et du Ténéré
BORKOU-ENNEDI-TIBESTI
1:7.5M
© Bartholomew

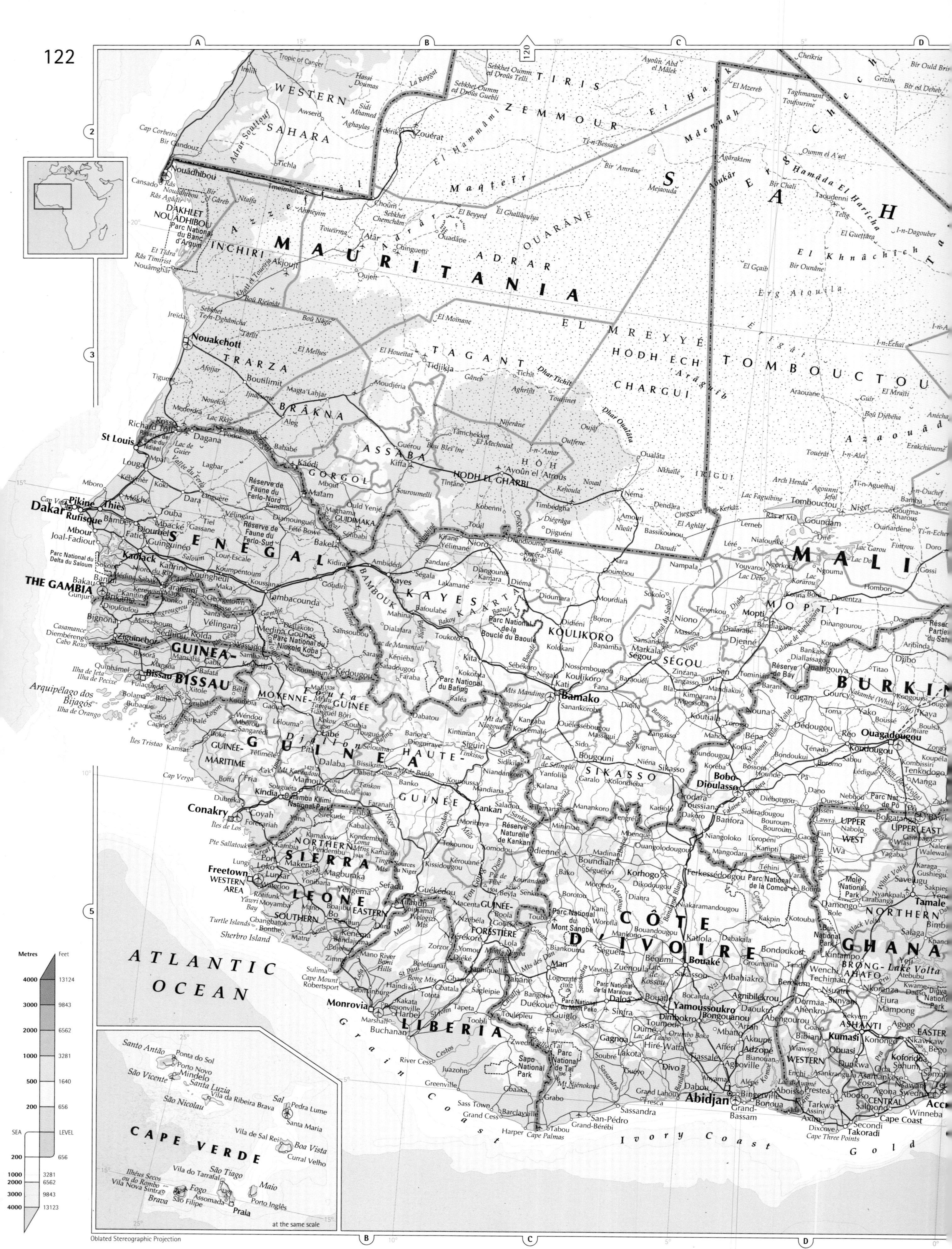
A
B
C
D
120
WESTERN SAHARA
MAURITANIA
SENEGAL
THE GAMBIA
GUINEA-BISSAU
GUINEA
SIERRA LEONE
LIBERIA
CÔTE D'IVOIRE
MALI
BURKINA
GHANA
ATLANTIC OCEAN
CAPE VERDE
TIRIS ZEMMOUR
INCHIRI
ADRAR
TRARZA
BRAKNA
TAGANT
ASSABA
GORGOL
GUIDIMAKA
HODH EL GHARBI
HODH ECH CHARGUI
TOMBOUCTOU
KAYES
KOULIKORO
SÉGOU
MOPTI
SIKASSO
MOYENNE-GUINÉE
HAUTE-GUINÉE
GUINÉE-MARITIME
GUINÉE-FORESTIÈRE
NORTHERN
SOUTHERN
EASTERN
WESTERN AREA
UPPER WEST
UPPER EAST
BRONG-AHAFO
ASHANTI
CENTRAL
Nouâdhibou
Nouakchott
Dakar
St Louis
Banjul
Bissau
Conakry
Freetown
Monrovia
Bamako
Yamoussoukro
Abidjan
Ouagadougou
Bobo Dioulasso
Praia
Tropic of Cancer
Grain Coast
Ivory Coast
Gold Coast
Lake Volta
Santo Antão
São Vicente
Santa Luzia
São Nicolau
Sal
Boa Vista
Maio
São Tiago
Fogo
Brava
Metres
Feet
4000
13124
3000
9843
2000
6562
1000
3281
500
1640
200
656
SEA
LEVEL
13123
at the same scale
Oblated Stereographic Projection

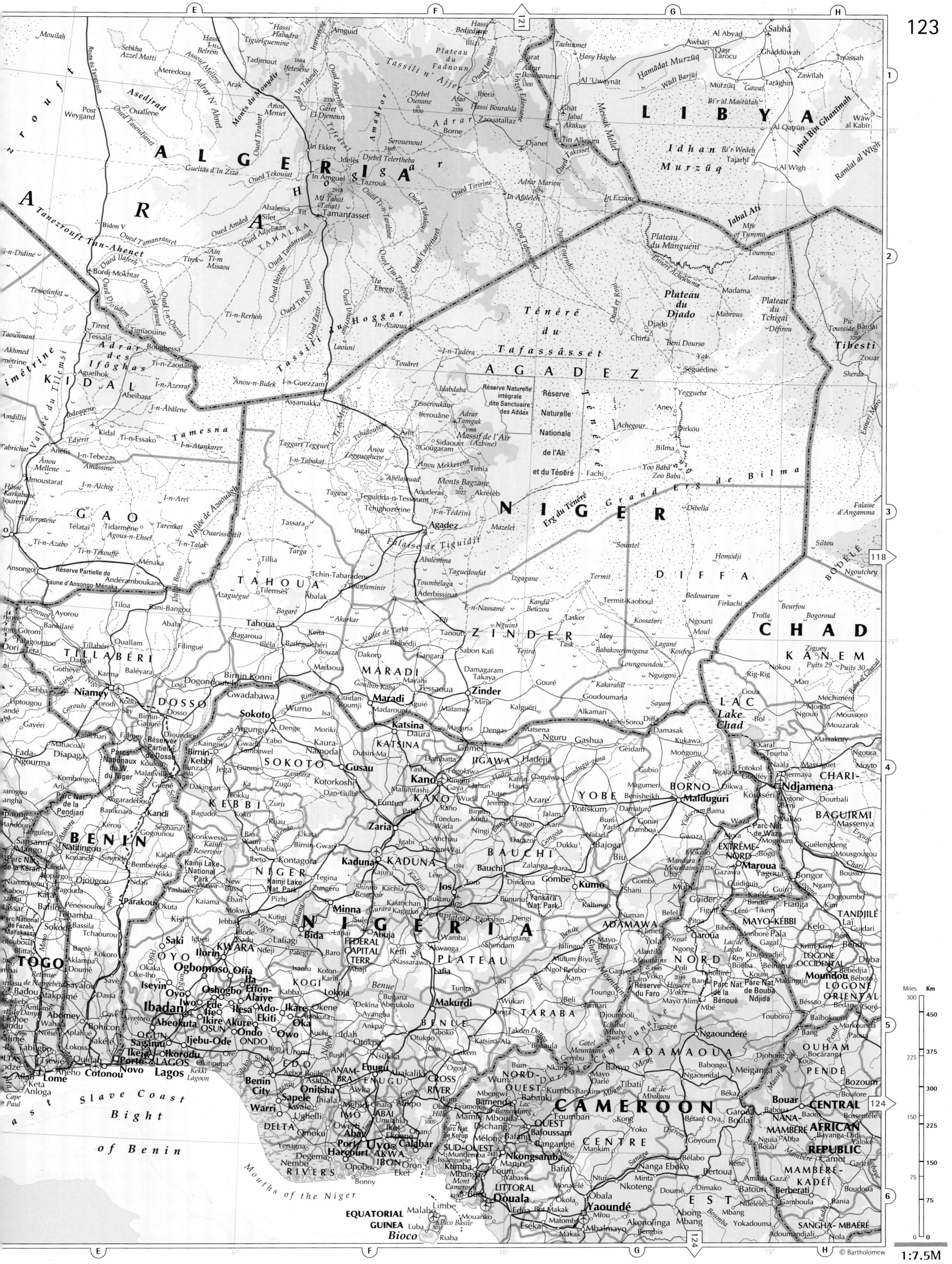

ALGERIA

LIBYA

NIGER

CHAD

NIGERIA

BENIN

TOGO

CAMEROON

CENTRAL AFRICAN REPUBLIC

EQUATORIAL GUINEA

Bioco

Lake Chad

Slave Coast

Bight of Benin

Mouths of the Niger

Niamey

Lagos

Ibadan

Abuja

Kano

Kaduna

Zaria

Sokoto

Katsina

Maradi

Zinder

Agadez

Maiduguri

Ndjamena

Maroua

Yaoundé

Douala

Cotonou

Lomé

Porto Novo

Tamanrasset

Tibesti

1:7.5M

© Bartholomew

NIGER
SUDAN
CHAD
DARFUR
KORDOFAN
BAHR EL GHAZAL
UPPER NILE
EQUATORIA
CENTRAL AFRICAN REPUBLIC
CAMEROON
NIGERIA
EQUATORIAL GUINEA
GABON
CONGO
ZAIRE
UGANDA
RWANDA
KAGERA
HAUT-ZAIRE
EQUATEUR
KIVU
El Obeid
Ndjamena
Bangui
Yaoundé
Douala
Libreville
Kisangani
Mbandaka
Maiduguri
Kano
Abéché
Kigali
Port-Gentil
Bioco
Zinder
Bouar
Bossangoa
Moundou
Sarh
Wau
Garoua
Maroua
Makurdi
Jos
Bauchi
Gombe
Kumo
Calabar
Lake Chad
Metres
Feet
4000
13124
3000
9843
2000
6562
1000
3281
500
1640
200
656
SEA
LEVEL
200
656
1000
3281
2000
6562
3000
9843
4000
13124
5000
16409
118
126
123
Oblated Stereographic Projection

TANZANIA
BURUNDI
ZAMBIA
ANGOLA
NAMIBIA
BOTSWANA
ZIMBABWE
MOZAMBIQUE
ATLANTIC
OCEAN
SAO TOME and PRINCIPE
Príncipe
São Tomé
Kinshasa
Brazzaville
Luanda
Lusaka
Harare
Lubumbashi
Benguela
Lobito
Huambo
Pointe-Noire
CABINDA (Angola)
Miles
Km
at the same scale
© Bartholomew
1:7.5M

SOCOTRA (Yemen)
Socotra
continuation at the same scale
YEMEN
GULF OF ADEN
RED SEA
ERITREA
DJIBOUTI
ETHIOPIA
SUDAN
SOMALIA
Ādīs Ābeba (Addis Ababa)
Asmara
Djibouti
Khartoum (El Khartum)
Omdurman
Muqdisho (Mogadishu)
Berbera
Hargeysa
Dirē Dawa
San'a
'Adan (Aden)
Lake Turkana
Metres
Feet
5000
16405
4000
13124
3000
9843
2000
6562
1000
3281
500
1640
200
656
SEA
LEVEL
200
656
1000
3281
2000
6562
3000
9843
4000
13124
5000
16409
6000
19686
GH7754
Oblated Stereographic Projection
119
124

UGANDA
KENYA
TANZANIA
RWANDA
BURUNDI
ZAIRE
ZAMBIA
MALAWI
MOZAMBIQUE
INDIAN
OCEAN
LAKE VICTORIA
Lake Nyasa
(L. Niassa)
(L. Malawi)
Kampala
Nairobi
Mombasa
Dar es Salaam
Dodoma
Zanzibar
Kigali
Bujumbura
Lilongwe
COMOROS
MAYOTTE
(France)
Aldabra Is
(Seychelles)
SEYCHELLES
1:3M
MAHÉ
1:1.5M
RODRIGUES I.
(Mauritius)
1:1.5M
MAURITIUS
1:1.5M
Port Louis
RÉUNION
(France)
1:1.5M
St-Denis
Miles
Km
1:7.5M
© Bartholomew

ANGOLA
NAMIBIA
BOTSWANA
REPUBLIC OF SOUTH AFRICA
ATLANTIC OCEAN
Windhoek
Gaborone
Cape Town
Port Elizabeth
Bloemfontein
Kimberley
Maseru
Livingstone
Lubango
Namibe
Walvis Bay
Swakopmund
Lüderitz
Keetmanshoop
Kalahari Desert
Great Karoo
Little Karoo
Cape of Good Hope
Cape Agulhas
Okavango Delta
Etosha Pan
Tropic of Capricorn
ASCENSION (U.K.) 1:500 000
ST HELENA (U.K.) 1:500 000
TRISTAN DA CUNHA (U.K.) 1:1.5M
Metres
Feet
Oblated Stereographic Projection

1:7.5M

© Bartholomew

ZAIRE
ZAMBIA
LUSAKA
Lusaka
EASTERN
MALAWI
Lilongwe
SOUTHERN
Blantyre
NIASSA
CABO DELGADO
Pemba
NAMPULA
Nampula
Nacala
TETE
ZAMBÉZIA
Quelimane
MOZAMBIQUE
Harare
MASHONALAND CENTRAL
MASHONALAND EAST
MASHONALAND WEST
MIDLANDS
MANICALAND
MANICA
Chimoio
SOFALA
Beira
ZIMBABWE
Bulawayo
MASVINGO
MATABELELAND SOUTH
INHAMBANE
Inhambane
GAZA
Xai Xai
MAPUTO
Maputo
NORTHERN TRANSVAAL
Pietersburg
EASTERN TRANSVAAL
Pretoria
SWAZILAND
KWAZULU-NATAL
Pietermaritzburg
Durban
MOZAMBIQUE CHANNEL
Juan de Nova (Fr.)
ANTSIRANANA
Antsiranana
MAHAJANGA
Mahajanga
TOAMASINA
Toamasina
ANTANANARIVO
Antananarivo
MADAGASCAR
Antsirabe
FIANARANTSOA
Fianarantsoa
TOLIARA
Toliara
Tropic of Capricorn
continuation at the same scale
Miles
Km

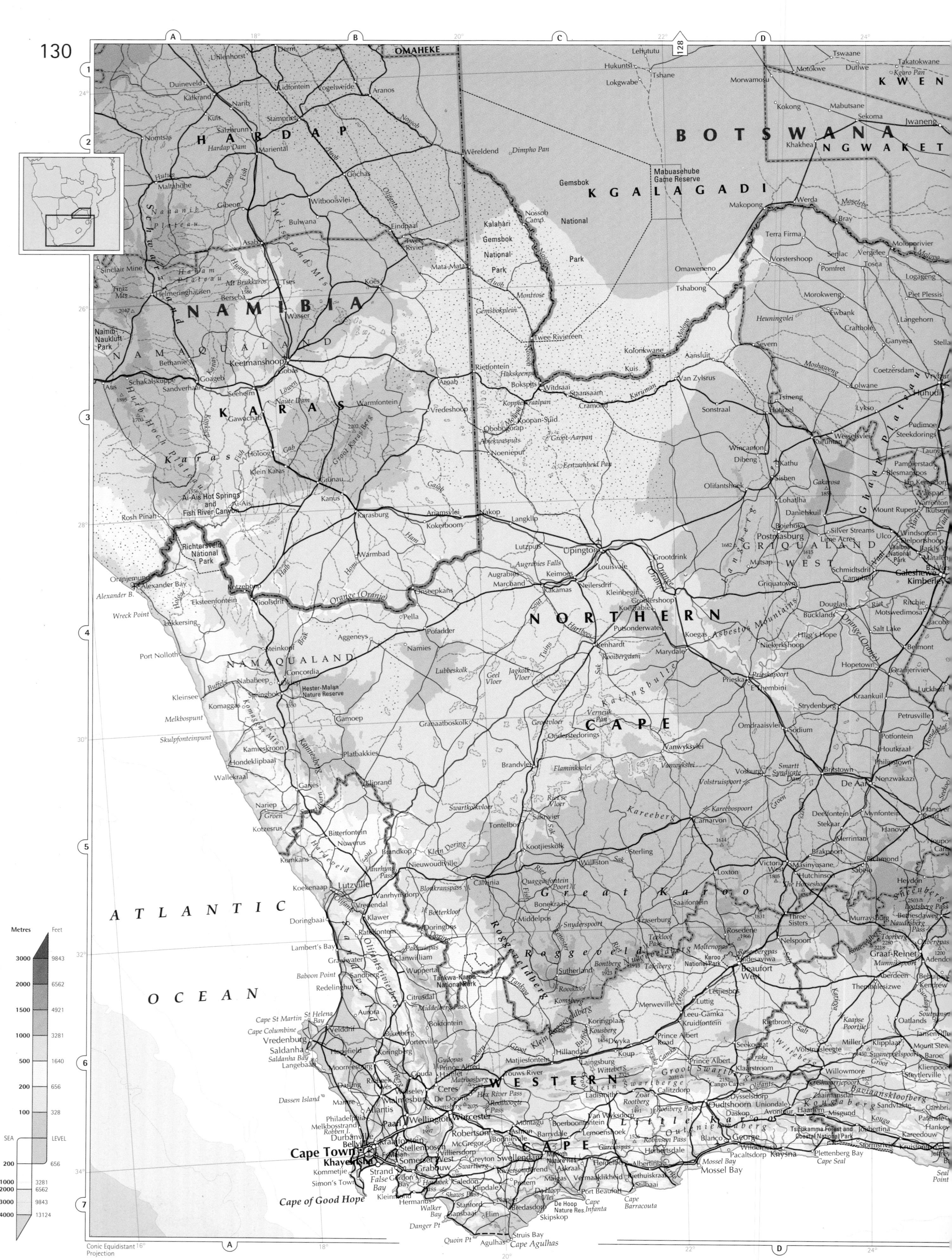
NAMIBIA
BOTSWANA
HARDAP
KARAS
OMAHEKE
KGALAGADI
NGWAKETSE
NAMAQUALAND
NORTHERN CAPE
WESTERN CAPE
GRIQUALAND WEST
ATLANTIC OCEAN
Great Karoo
Little Karoo
Roggeveld
Kalahari Gemsbok National Park
Gemsbok National Park
Mabuasehube Game Reserve
Richtersveld National Park
Ai-Ais Hot Springs and Fish River Canyon
Tankwa-Karoo National Park
Orange (Oranje)
Cape Town
Khayelitsha
Cape of Good Hope
Cape Agulhas
Keetmanshoop
Mariental
Upington
Kimberley
Beaufort West
Mossel Bay
George
Worcester
Springbok
Vredenburg
Saldanha
Karasburg
De Aar
Graaff-Reinet
Knysna
Oudtshoorn
Kuruman
Metres
Feet
3000
9843
2000
6562
1500
4921
1000
3281
500
1640
200
656
100
328
SEA
LEVEL
4000
13124
Conic Equidistant Projection

NORTHERN TRANSVAAL
continuation at the same scale

INDIAN

OCEAN

1:3.75M

© Bartholomew

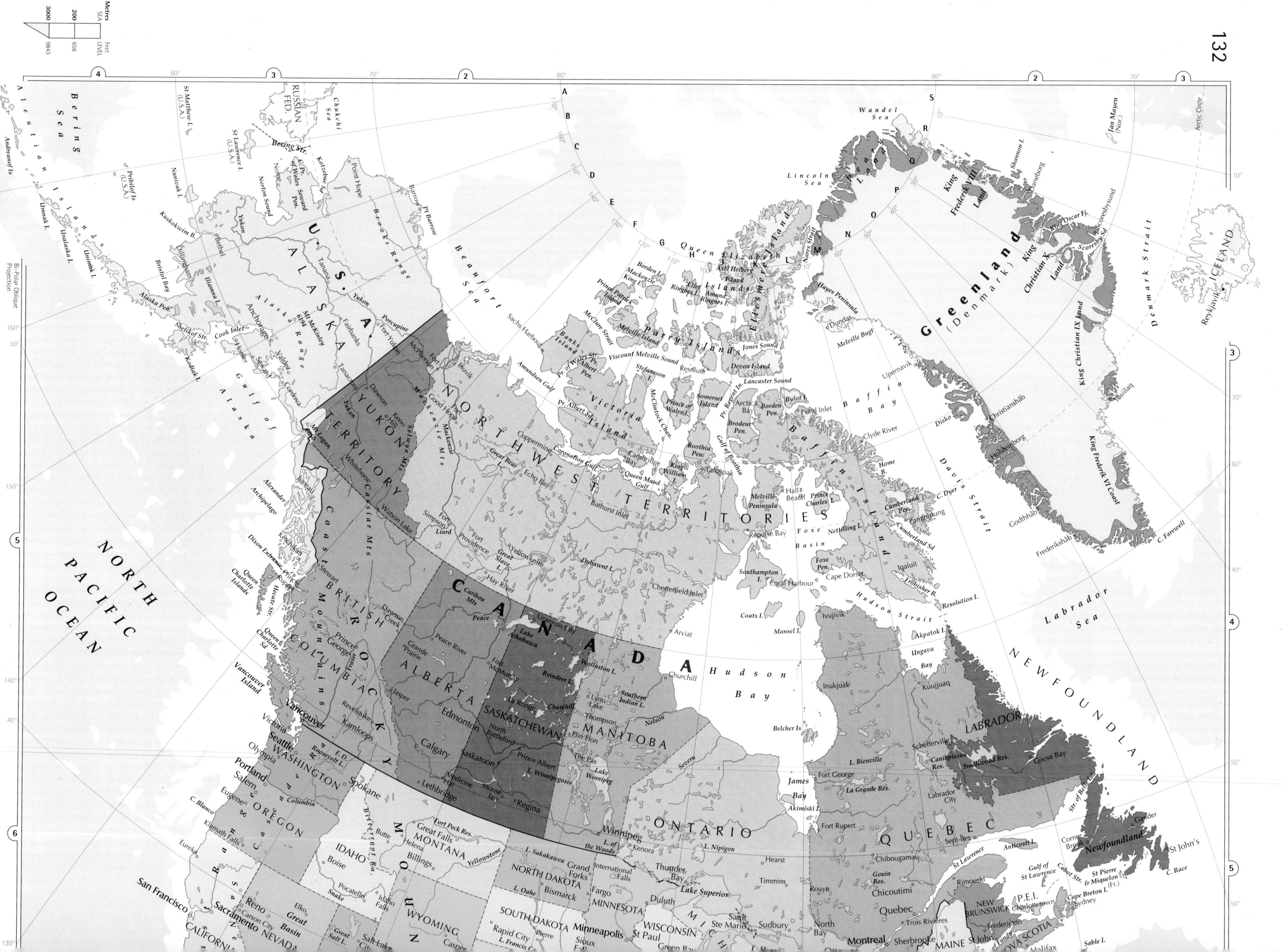

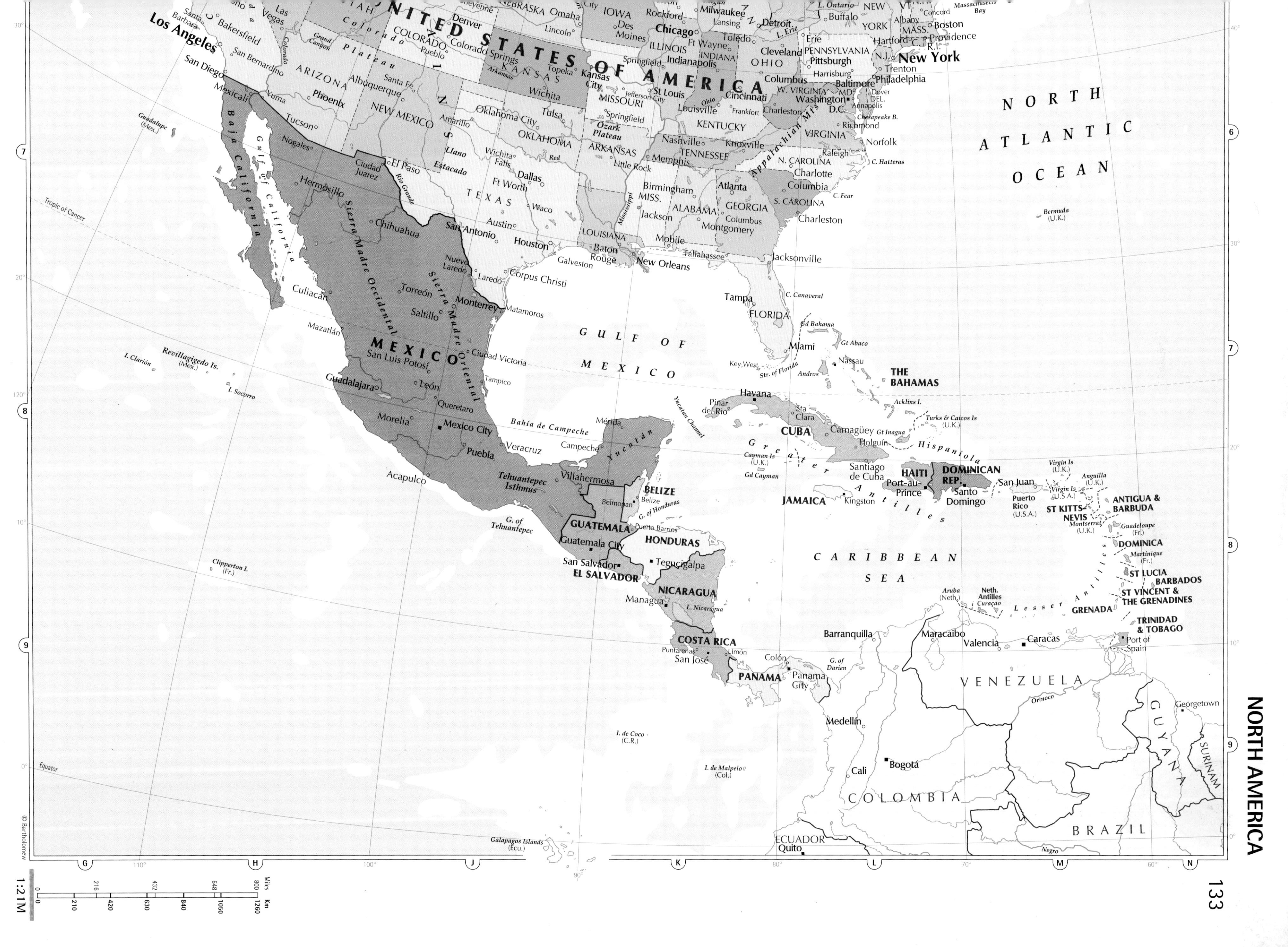

1:21M

© Bartholomew

Miles Km

800 1260

648 1050

432 840

216 630

210 420

0 0

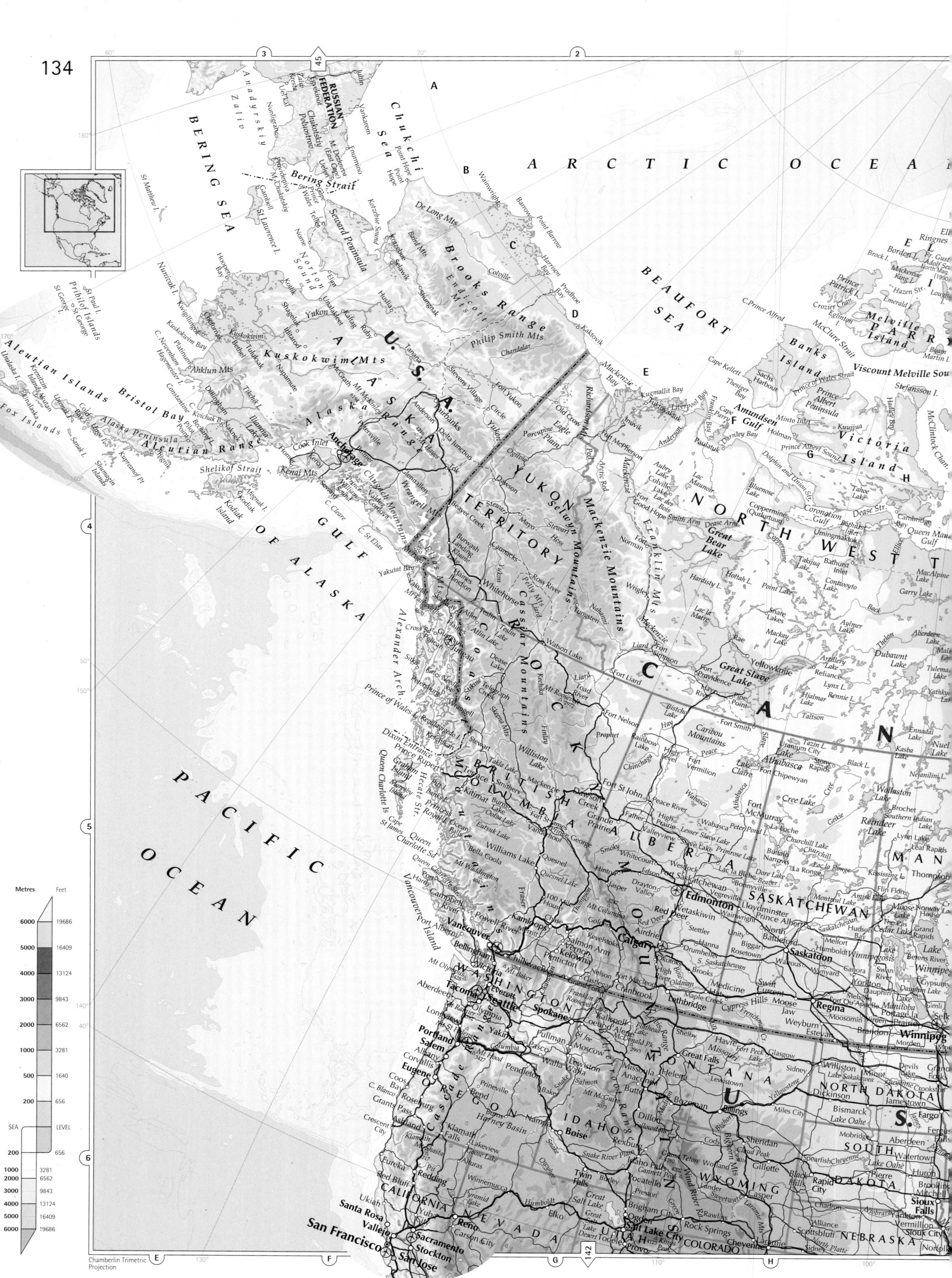
ARCTIC OCEAN
BERING SEA
Chukchi Sea
BEAUFORT SEA
Bering Strait
RUSSIAN FEDERATION
U.S.A.
ALASKA
Brooks Range
Alaska Range
Kuskokwim Mts
Aleutian Islands
Aleutian Range
Bristol Bay
Fox Islands
Pribilof Islands
Seward Peninsula
Norton Sound
Kodiak Island
GULF OF ALASKA
Anchorage
Fairbanks
YUKON TERRITORY
Mackenzie Mountains
Selwyn Mountains
NORTHWEST T
Great Bear Lake
Great Slave Lake
Banks Island
Victoria Island
Melville Island
PARRY
Viscount Melville Sou
Amundsen Gulf
Lake Athabasca
CAN
ROCKY MOUNTAINS
Cassiar Mountains
Coast Mountains
BRITISH COLUMBIA
ALBERTA
SASKATCHEWAN
MAN
Whitehorse
Prince George
Edmonton
Calgary
Saskatoon
Regina
Winnipeg
Vancouver
Vancouver Island
Queen Charlotte Is
Alexander Arch
PACIFIC OCEAN
WASHINGTON
Seattle
Tacoma
Spokane
Portland
Salem
OREGON
IDAHO
Boise
MONTANA
Helena
Billings
WYOMING
NORTH DAKOTA
SOUTH DAKOTA
NEBRASKA
NEVADA
UTAH
Salt Lake City
COLORADO
CALIFORNIA
San Francisco
Sacramento
San Jose
Reno
Metres
Feet
SEA LEVEL
Chamberlin Trimetric Projection

GREENLAND SEA

KALAALLIT NUNAAT
(GREENLAND)
(Denmark)

ICELAND

Denmark Strait

BAFFIN BAY

DAVIS STRAIT

Ellesmere Island

Devon Island

Baffin Peninsula

BAFFIN ISLAND

Lancaster Sound

Boothia Peninsula

Melville Peninsula

Gulf of Boothia

Foxe Basin

Foxe Channel

Southampton Island

Cumberland Peninsula

Cumberland Sound

Frobisher Bay

Hall Pen.

Resolution Island

Labrador Sea

HUDSON STRAIT

Ungava Bay

Péninsule d'Ungava

HUDSON BAY

James Bay

Belcher Islands

Labrador Sea

ATLANTIC OCEAN

NEWFOUNDLAND

LABRADOR

QUÉBEC

ONTARIO

MANITOBA

Churchill

Cape Churchill

Schefferville

Smallwood Reservoir

Churchill Falls

Happy Valley-Goose Bay

Réservoir Caniapiscau

Réservoir Manicouagan

Gulf of St Lawrence
(Golfe du St-Laurent)

Cabot Strait

Gaspé

PRINCE EDWARD ISLAND

Charlottetown

Cape Breton Island

Sydney

NEW BRUNSWICK

NOVA SCOTIA

Halifax

Saint John

Bay of Fundy

MAINE

St Lawrence

Québec

Montréal

Ottawa

Toronto

Lake Superior

Lake Michigan

Lake Huron

Lake Ontario

Lake Erie

Thunder Bay

MINNESOTA

WISCONSIN

MICHIGAN

Chicago

Milwaukee

Detroit

Cleveland

Buffalo

Rochester

NEW YORK

PENNSYLVANIA

Boston

New York

Providence

Hartford

Syracuse

Albany

Atlantic Ocean

Miles
500
400
300
200
100
0

Km
800
700
600
500
400
300
200
100
0

1:15M

© Bartholomew

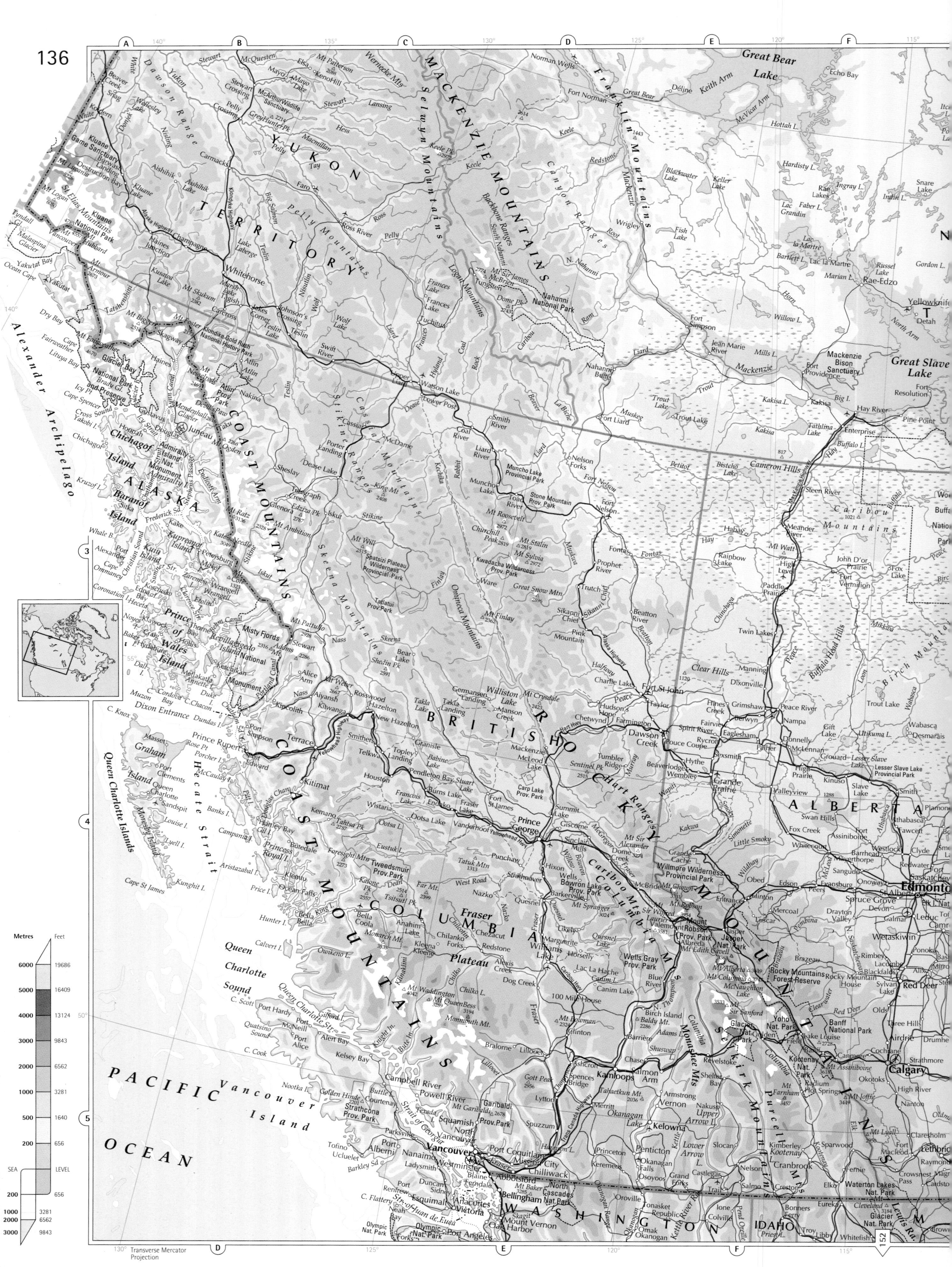

A
B
C
D
E
F
YUKON TERRITORY
MACKENZIE MOUNTAINS
Selwyn Mountains
Pelly Mountains
Franklin Mountains
Great Bear Lake
Great Slave Lake
Alexander Archipelago
ALASKA
COAST MOUNTAINS
BRITISH COLUMBIA
ROCKY MOUNTAINS
ALBERTA
Fraser Plateau
Queen Charlotte Islands
Queen Charlotte Sound
Hecate Strait
Dixon Entrance
Vancouver Island
PACIFIC OCEAN
WASHINGTON
IDAHO
Skeena Mountains
Cassiar Mountains
Omineca Mountains
Cariboo Mts
Columbia Mts
Monashee Mts
Selkirk Mountains
Purcell Mts
Caribou Mountains
Birch Mountains
Whitehorse
Juneau
Prince Rupert
Prince George
Vancouver
Victoria
Kamloops
Kelowna
Edmonton
Calgary
Red Deer
Yellowknife
Hay River
Fort Nelson
Fort St John
Dawson Creek
Grande Prairie
Metres
Feet
6000
19686
5000
16409
4000
13124
3000
9843
2000
6562
1000
3281
500
1640
200
656
SEA
LEVEL
200
656
1000
3281
2000
6562
3000
9843
Transverse Mercator Projection
152

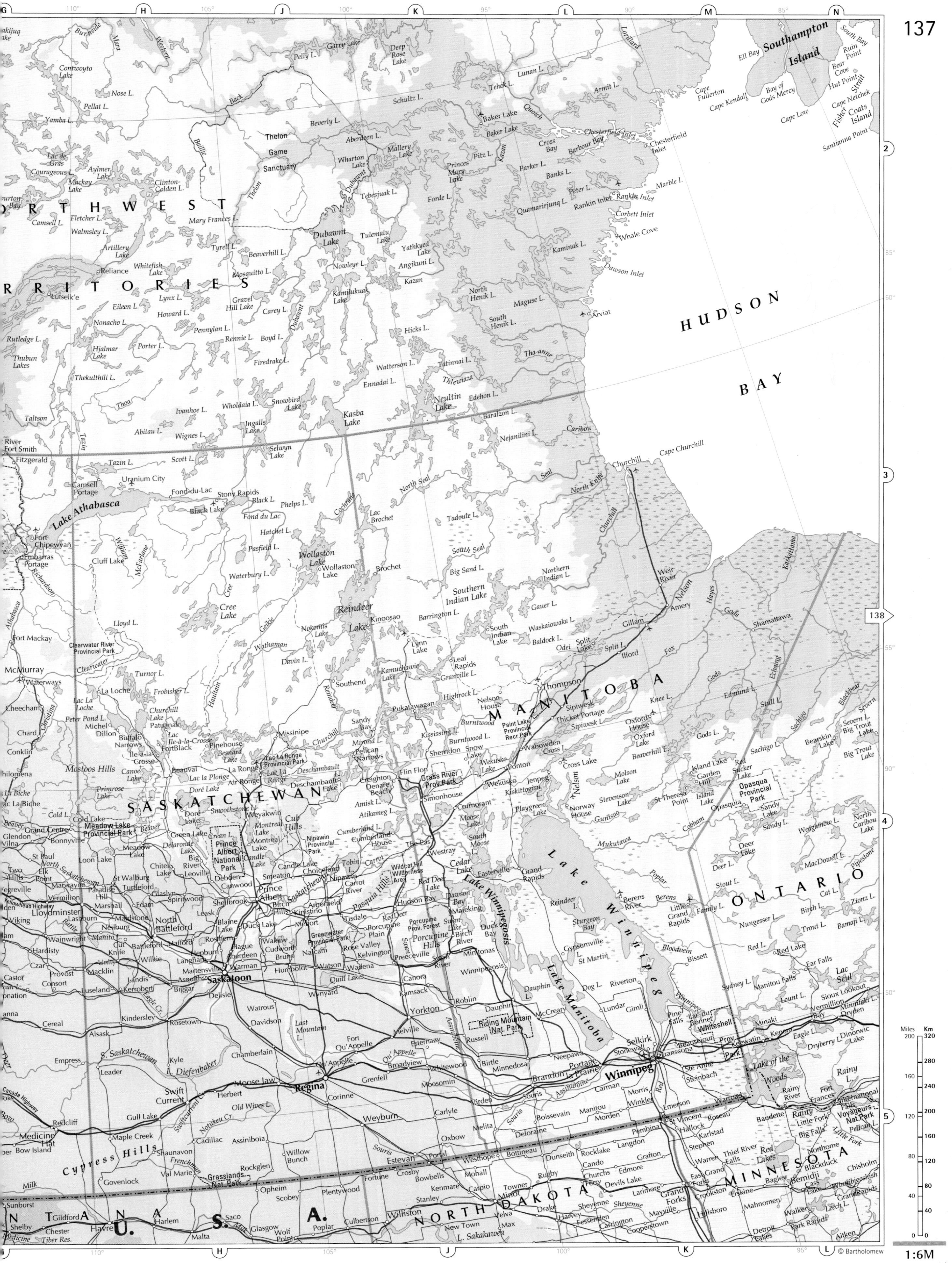

HUDSON

BAY

Southampton
Island

NORTHWEST

TERRITORIES

MANITOBA

SASKATCHEWAN

ONTARIO

ALBERTA

Lake Athabasca

Reindeer
Lake

Lake
Winnipeg

Lake
Winnipegosis

Lake
Manitoba

Cree
Lake

Wollaston
Lake

Dubawnt
Lake

Thelon
Game
Sanctuary

Saskatoon

Regina

Winnipeg

Prince
Albert

Thompson

Churchill

Flin Flon

The Pas

Moose Jaw

Swift
Current

Medicine
Hat

Brandon

Selkirk

Yorkton

Dauphin

Melville

Prince
Albert
National
Park

Riding Mountain
Nat. Park

Grasslands
Nat. Park

Cypress Hills

M O N T A N A

U. S. A.

NORTH DAKOTA

MINNESOTA

Lloydminster

North
Battleford

U. S. A.

Miles	Km
200	320
	280
160	240
	200
120	160
80	120
40	80
	40
0	0

© Bartholomew

1:6M

137
HUDSON BAY
JAMES BAY
MANITOBA
ONTARIO
MICHIGAN
WISCONSIN
U. S. A.
NEW YORK
LAKE SUPERIOR
LAKE MICHIGAN
LAKE HURON
LAKE ONTARIO
LAKE ERIE
Georgian Bay
North Channel
Belcher Islands
Akimiski Island
Polar Bear Provincial Park
Opasqua Provincial Park
Winisk River Provincial Park
Pukaskwa Nat. Park
Isle Royale Nat. Park
Voyageurs Nat. Park
Algonquin Prov. Park
La Vérendrye
Réserve faunique
Adirondack Mountains
Churchill
Cape Churchill
Gillam
Shamattawa
Fort Severn
Peawanuck
Cape Henrietta Maria
Attawapiskat
Kashechewan
Fort Albany
Moosonee
Moose Factory
Chisasibi
Radisson
Rés. de La Grande 2
Rés. de La Grande 3
Rés. de La Grande 4
Rés. Opinaca
Wemindji
Eastmain
Waskaganish
Mistassini
Chibougamau
Matagami
Inukjuak (Port Harrison)
Umiujaq
Sanikiluaq
Whapmagoostui
Lac Seul
Lake of the Woods
Lake Nipigon
Kenora
Dryden
Sioux Lookout
Fort Frances
International Falls
Atikokan
Thunder Bay
Marathon
Terrace Bay
Nakina
Hearst
Kapuskasing
Cochrane
Timmins
Kirkland Lake
Rouyn
Noranda
Val-d'Or
Amos
Chapleau
Wawa
Sault Ste Marie
Sudbury
North Bay
Lake Nipissing
Mattawa
Pembroke
Deep River
Gatineau
Hull
Ottawa
Montreal
Laval
Kingston
Peterborough
Barrie
Orillia
Oshawa
Scarborough
Toronto
Mississauga
Brampton
Hamilton
Kitchener
Guelph
London
Sarnia
Windsor
Detroit
Sterling Heights
Warren
Livonia
Ann Arbor
Flint
Lansing
Grand Rapids
Saginaw
Toledo
St Catharines
Niagara Falls
Buffalo
Rochester
Syracuse
Albany
Schenectady
Erie
Milwaukee
Madison
Green Bay
Appleton
Oshkosh
Rockford
Chicago
Gary
South Bend
Duluth
Superior
Marquette
Escanaba
Metres
Feet
SEA LEVEL
Transverse Mercator Projection
144

Labrador Sea
ATLANTIC OCEAN
UNGAVA BAY
Akpatok I.
Kangirsuk (Bellin)
C. Chidley
Killiniq
Gray Str.
William Smith Cap
North Aulatsivik I.
Seven Islands Bay
Torngat Mts
Mt Eliot
Cirque Mtn
Ramah
Mt Caubvick
Saglek Bay
Cape Uivak
Baie Hopes Advance
Aupaluk
Gyrfalcon Is
Cap Kattaktoc
Baie de Kegla
Pte Hubbard
Lac Tassialuijjuaq
Lac Peters
Lac Faribault
Kangiqsualujjuaq (Port-Nouveau-Québec)
Hebron
HebronFiord
Cap Kernertut
Tasiujaq
Lac Bérard
Rivière aux Feuilles
Koksoak
Kuujjuaq (Fort-Chimo)
Rivière à la Baleine
Ford
George
Kaumajet Mts
Cod I.
Nutak
Okak Is
Kiglapait Mts
Port Manvers
South Aulatsivik I.
Dog I.
Paul I.
Nain
Fraser
Lac Duvert
Rivière aux Mélèzes
Lac Le Moyne
Lac Guerard
Tunungayualok I.
Davis Inlet
Nunaksaluk I.
Kogaluk
Lac Cananée
Mistastin L.
Lac Castignon
Lac Jeannin
Lac Cambrien
Hopedale
Cape Makkovik
Makkovik
Cape Harrison
Adlavik Is
Mt Benedict
Indian Harbour
Lac aux Goélands
Harp L.
Postville
Kaipokok Bay
Lac Wakuach
Caniapiscau
Lac Sérigny
Lac Talon
Kawawachikamach
Schefferville
Matimekosh
Snegamook L.
Groswater Bay
West Bay
Rigolet
Cape Porcupine
Sandwich Bay
Cartwright
Spotted Island
Island of Ponds
LABRADOR
Nipishish L.
Hamilton Inlet
Lac Chaigneau
Menihek
Seal L.
Red Wine
Grand L.
L. Melville
Dove Brook
Paradise River
Hawke I.
Snug Harbour
St Michaels Bay
Fontanges
Brisay
Rés. Caniapiscau
Menihek Lakes
Smallwood Res.
Hope Mts
Mealy Mts
North West River
Esker
Flour L.
Churchill Falls
Goose
Happy Valley-Goose Bay
Parke L.
Eagle
Alexis
Port Hope Simpson
St Lewis
Mary's Harbour
Cape Charles
Belle Isle
Lac Muntviel
Lac Chambeaux
Twin Falls
Ossokmanuan Lake
Churchill
Saint Lewis
Lac Roundeyed
Opiscotéo L.
Wabush L.
Emeril
Shabogamo L.
Labrador City
Wabush
Ross Bay Junction
Minipi L.
Nitchequon
Lac Nichicun
Lac Naococane
Lac Raimbault
Atikonak L.
Little Mecatina
Red Bay
Cook's Harbour
C. Bauld
St Anthony
Strait of Belle Isle
Fermont
Lac Joseph
Lac du Sommet
Burnt L.
Pitaga
Ashuanipi Lake
Monts Otish
Blanc-Sablon
Main Brook
Petit Mécatina
St-Augustin
Roddickton
Englee
Grey Is
Petit Lac Manicouagan
Gagnon
Réservoir Manicouagan
Plétipi L.
Moisie
Romaine
Natashquan
Tabatière
Port aux Choix
Long Range Mts
White Bay
Horse Is
La Scie
Baie Verte
Notre Dame Bay
Twillingate
Fogo I.
Summerford
Wesleyville
Magpie L.
Harrington Harbour
Ste Marguerite
Outardes
Manouane L.
Manicouagan
Magpie
Mingan
Havre-St-Pierre
Natashquan
Springdale
Botwood
Gander
Bonavista Bay
Bonavista
Gros Morne Nat. Pk
Moisie
Sept-Îles
Sheldrake
Détroit de Jacques-Cartier
Lac Péribonca
L. Ste Anne
Deer Lake
Badger
Windsor
Grand Falls
Gambo
Terra Nova Nat. Pk
Trinity Bay
Île d'Anticosti
Port-Menier
Corner Brook
Grand Lake
Buchans
Red Indian L.
NEWFOUNDLAND
Clarenville
Old Perlican
C. St Francis
Pouch Cove
Chute des Passes
Réservoir Pipmuacan
Godbout
Mont Louis
Grand Vallée
Détroit d'Honguedo
Lourdes
Stephenville
Meelpaeg Res.
Upr Salmon Res.
Carbonear
St John's
Conception Bay South
Pte des Monts
Baie Comeau
Hauterive
Betsiamites
Parc de la Gaspésie
Murdochville
C. Gaspé
Gaspé
Gulf of St Lawrence
(Golfe du St-Laurent)
Cape St George
St George's B.
Victoria L.
Granite L.
St Alban's
Terrenceville
Placentia B.
Avalon Peninsula
Mistassini
Dolbeau
St-Félicien
Lac St-Jean
Alma
Arvida
Jonquière
Chicoutimi
Saguenay
Les Escoumins
Forestville
Mt Jacques Cartier
Matane
Peninsule de Gaspé
Percé
Price
Mont Joli
Rimouski
St Lawrence
Causapscal
New Richmond
Grande-Rivière
Long Range Mts
Rose Blanche
Burgeo
Harbour Breton
Fortune B.
Burin Peninsula
Marystown
Placentia
Branch
Trepassey
Tadoussac
Monts Notre Dame
Matapédia
Dalhousie
Chaleur Bay
New Carlisle
Miscou I.
I. Lamèque
Shippegan
Caraquet
Jacquet River
Campbellton
C. Ray
Channel-Port-aux-Basques
Île Brion
Îles de la Madeleine
Île de l'Est
Cap-aux-Meules
Île du Havre Aubert
Cabot Strait
Grand Bank
Miquelon
St-Pierre
St Lawrence
C. St Mary's
C. Pine
C. Race
St-Pierre & Miquelon (France)
Réserve faunique des Laurentides
St Siméon
Rivière-du-Loup
L. Témiscouata
Cabano
Kedgwick
Bathurst
St Pascal
Baie St Paul
Edmundston
Ste-Anne-de-Beaupré
Fort Kent
Van Buren
St-Léonard
Grand Falls
Newcastle
Chatham
North Cape
Tignish
PRINCE EDWARD ISLAND
East Pt
Cape Breton Highlands Nat. Pk
C. North
Ingonish
Chéticamp
Montmorency
Québec
Île d'Orléans
Montmagny
Lévis
Eagle Lake
Caribou
Presque Isle
NEW BRUNSWICK
Miramichi
Rexton
Northumberland Strait
Summerside
Borden
Charlottetown
Souris
Inverness
Baddeck
Sydney Mines
Glace Bay
Sydney
Cap-de-la-Madeleine
Thetford Mines
St Joseph
Eagle L.
Peaked Mt.
Bath
Hartland
Woodstock
Bouctouche
Shediac
Moncton
Tormentine
Cape
L. Ainslie
Bras d'Or L.
Cape Breton Island
Victoriaville
St Georges
Chesuncook L.
Mt Katahdin
Houlton
Fredericton
Minto
Marysville
Riverview
Sackville
Amherst
Pictou
Antigonish
Port Hawkesbury
Canso
C. Canso
Drummondville
Lac Mégantic
Asbestos
Jackman
Millinocket
Oromocto
Grand L.
Sussex
Norton
Hampton
Fundy Nat. Park
Chignecto B.
Springhill
New Glasgow
Truro
NOVA SCOTIA
Sherbrooke
Rockwood
Moosehead L.
Penobscot
Topsfield
St Croix
Grand Bay
Milltown
St John
Parrsboro
Minas Basin
Sheet Harbour
Magog
Flagstaff
Lincoln
MAINE
Calais
Eastport
Kentville
Wolfville
Windsor
Lower Sackville
Dartmouth
Halifax
Stratton
Sugarloaf Mt.
Guildford
Dover-Foxcroft
W. Grand L.
Old Town
Bingham
Bangor
Brewer
Machias
Bay of Fundy
Digby
Annapolis Royal
Colebrook
Norton
Errol
Farmington
Skowhegan
Bucksport
Ellsworth
Jonesport
Grand Manan I.
Sable I.
Berlin
Waterville
Bar Harbor
Mt Desert I.
Bridgewater
Kejimkujik National Park
L. Rossignol
Lancaster
Bethel
Rumford
Norway
Augusta
Belfast
Camden
Thomaston
Mt Washington
Littleton
Auburn
Lewiston
Brunswick
Bath
Isle au Haut
Liverpool
Conway
Plymouth
Sebago L.
Falmouth
Yarmouth
Shelburne
Westbrook
Portland
NEW HAMPSHIRE
Laconia
Saco
Biddeford
Cape Sable
Claremont
Rochester
Concord
Dover
Exeter
Kittery
Portsmouth
Keene
Manchester
Nashua
Haverhill
Lawrence
Lowell
Miles
Km
1:6M
© Bartholomew

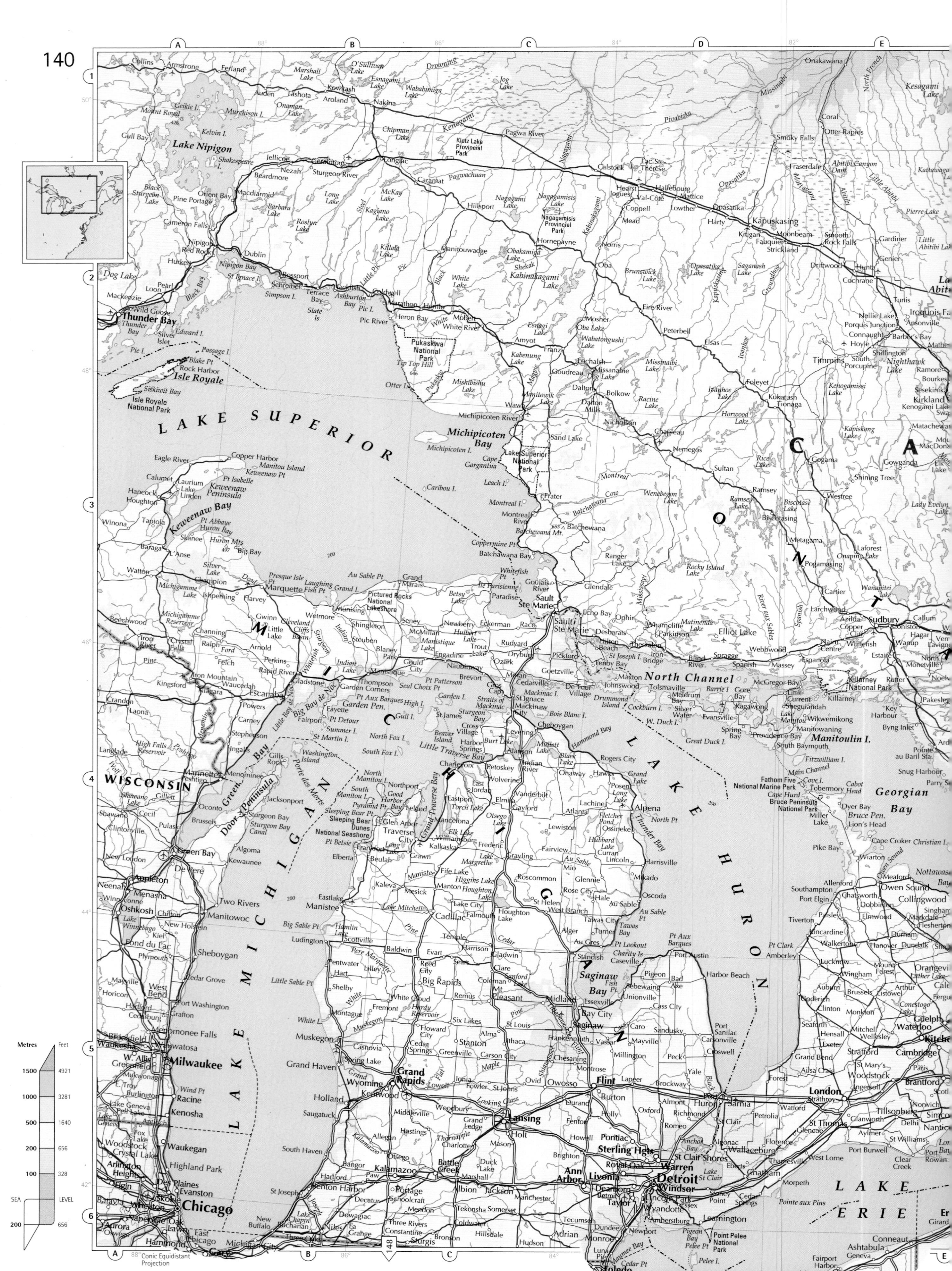
LAKE SUPERIOR
LAKE MICHIGAN
LAKE HURON
LAKE ERIE
MICHIGAN
WISCONSIN
ONTARIO
CANADA
Georgian Bay
North Channel
Saginaw Bay
Michipicoten Bay
Keweenaw Bay
Green Bay
Lake Nipigon
Isle Royale
Isle Royale National Park
Pukaskwa National Park
Lake Superior National Park
Pictured Rocks National Lakeshore
Sleeping Bear Dunes National Seashore
Fathom Five National Marine Park
Bruce Peninsula National Park
Killarney National Park
Point Pelee National Park
Klotz Lake Provincial Park
Nagagamisis Provincial Park
Manitoulin I.
Keweenaw Peninsula
Door Peninsula
Bruce Pen.
Thunder Bay
Sault Ste Marie
Sudbury
Timmins
Kapuskasing
Hearst
Marquette
Escanaba
Green Bay
Appleton
Oshkosh
Fond du Lac
Sheboygan
Manitowoc
Milwaukee
Racine
Kenosha
Waukegan
Chicago
Evanston
Gary
Hammond
Muskegon
Grand Rapids
Kalamazoo
Battle Creek
Lansing
Flint
Saginaw
Bay City
Midland
Ann Arbor
Detroit
Windsor
Toledo
Port Huron
Sarnia
London
Traverse City
Petoskey
Alpena
Cheboygan
Owen Sound
Conic Equidistant Projection
Metres
Feet
1500
4921
1000
3281
500
1640
200
656
100
328
SEA
LEVEL
200
656
148

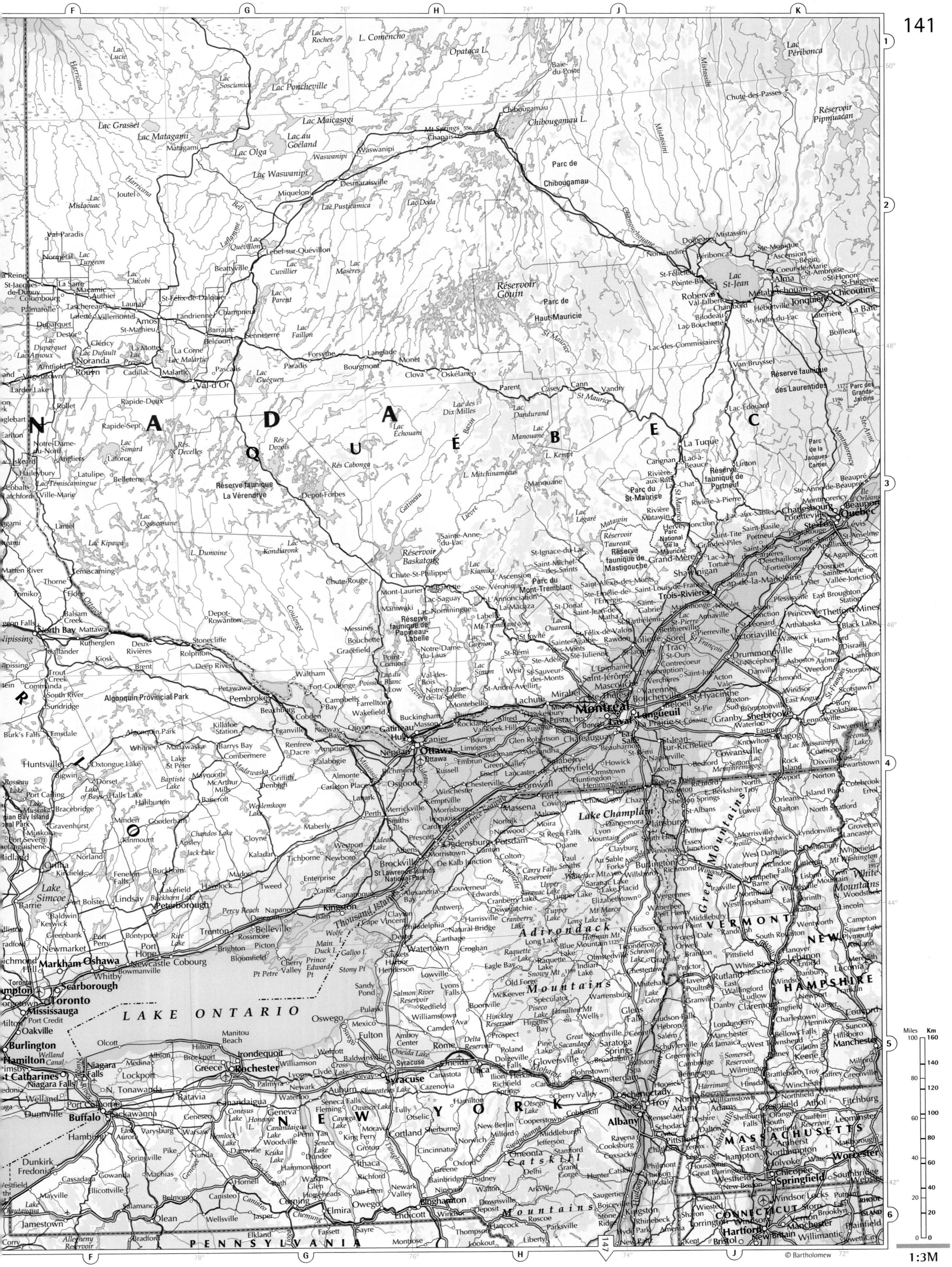

LAKE ONTARIO

N E W   Y O R K

PENNSYLVANIA

VERMONT

NEW HAMPSHIRE

MASSACHUSETTS

CONNECTICUT

Lake Champlain

Adirondack Mountains

Green Mountains

Catskill Mountains

Algonquin Provincial Park

Réservoir Gouin

Lac St-Jean

Montréal

Ottawa

Toronto

Québec

Buffalo

Rochester

Syracuse

Albany

Hartford

Springfield

Worcester

Scale 1:3M

Miles 100   Km 160

© Bartholomew

BRITISH COLUMBIA
ALBERTA
SASKATCHEWAN
CANADA
WASHINGTON
OREGON
IDAHO
MONTANA
WYOMING
NORTH DAKOTA
SOUTH DAKOTA
NEBRASKA
NEVADA
UTAH
COLORADO
CALIFORNIA
ARIZONA
NEW MEXICO
KANSAS
OKLAHOMA
TEXAS
MEXICO
SONORA
CHIHUAHUA
COAHUILA
DURANGO
SINALOA
NUEVO LEÓN
BAJA CALIFORNIA NORTE
BAJA CALIFORNIA SUR
PACIFIC OCEAN
Golfo de California
ROCKY MOUNTAINS
Great Basin
Colorado Plateau
Columbia Plateau
Snake River Plain
Sierra Madre Occidental
Bolson de Mapimi
Llano Estacado
Edwards Plateau
Smoky Hills
Cascade Range
Coast Ranges
Sierra Nevada
Edmonton
Calgary
Vancouver
Victoria
Seattle
Tacoma
Spokane
Portland
Salem
Eugene
Boise
Helena
Great Falls
Billings
Missoula
Butte
Salt Lake City
Ogden
Provo
Reno
Sacramento
San Francisco
Oakland
San Jose
Stockton
Fresno
Bakersfield
Los Angeles
Long Beach
San Diego
Las Vegas
Phoenix
Tucson
Albuquerque
Santa Fe
El Paso
Ciudad Juárez
Denver
Colorado Springs
Pueblo
Cheyenne
Casper
Rapid City
Bismarck
Amarillo
Lubbock
Oklahoma City
San Antonio
Tijuana
Mexicali
Hermosillo
Chihuahua
Monterrey
Saltillo
Torreón
Culiacán
Los Mochis
Saskatoon
Regina
Lethbridge
Medicine Hat
Guadalupe (Mexico)
Tropic of Cancer
Metres
Feet
4000
13124
3000
9843
2000
6562
1000
3281
500
1640
200
656
SEA
LEVEL
5000
16409
GH7754
Lambert Conformal Conic Projection
A
B
C
D
E
F
1
2
3
4
5
6
7
134
156
130°
125°
120°
115°
110°
105°
100°
50°
45°
40°
35°
30°
25°

CANADA

QUÉBEC

ONTARIO

NEW BRUNSWICK

NOVA SCOTIA

MAINE

VERMONT

NEW HAMP.

MASS.

CONN.

NEW YORK

PENNSYLVANIA

NEW JERSEY

MARYLAND

DELAWARE

WEST VIRGINIA

VIRGINIA

OHIO

INDIANA

ILLINOIS

MICHIGAN

WISCONSIN

MINNESOTA

IOWA

MISSOURI

KENTUCKY

TENNESSEE

NORTH CAROLINA

SOUTH CAROLINA

GEORGIA

ALABAMA

MISSISSIPPI

ARKANSAS

LOUISIANA

FLORIDA

KANSAS

OKLAHOMA

TEXAS

LAKE SUPERIOR

LAKE MICHIGAN

LAKE HURON

LAKE ERIE

Lake Ontario

James Bay

ATLANTIC OCEAN

GULF OF MEXICO

THE BAHAMAS

Major cities: Minneapolis, St Paul, Milwaukee, Madison, Chicago, Detroit, Cleveland, Columbus, Cincinnati, Indianapolis, Louisville, Nashville, Memphis, Little Rock, St Louis, Kansas City, Topeka, Tulsa, Dallas, Houston, New Orleans, Baton Rouge, Jackson, Birmingham, Montgomery, Atlanta, Savannah, Jacksonville, Tallahassee, Orlando, Tampa, St Petersburg, Miami, Fort Lauderdale, Hollywood, Charlotte, Raleigh, Greensboro, Durham, Richmond, Norfolk, Virginia Beach, Washington D.C., Baltimore, Philadelphia, Wilmington, Pittsburgh, Buffalo, Rochester, Syracuse, Albany, New York, Newark, Boston, Providence, Hartford, New Haven, Portland, Montreal, Ottawa, Toronto, Québec

Montreal, Ottawa, Toronto, Hamilton, Kitchener, London, Windsor, Sudbury, Thunder Bay, Sault Ste Marie

Scale 1:10M

Miles 0 100 200 300

Km 0 100 200 300 400 500

© Bartholomew

135 158

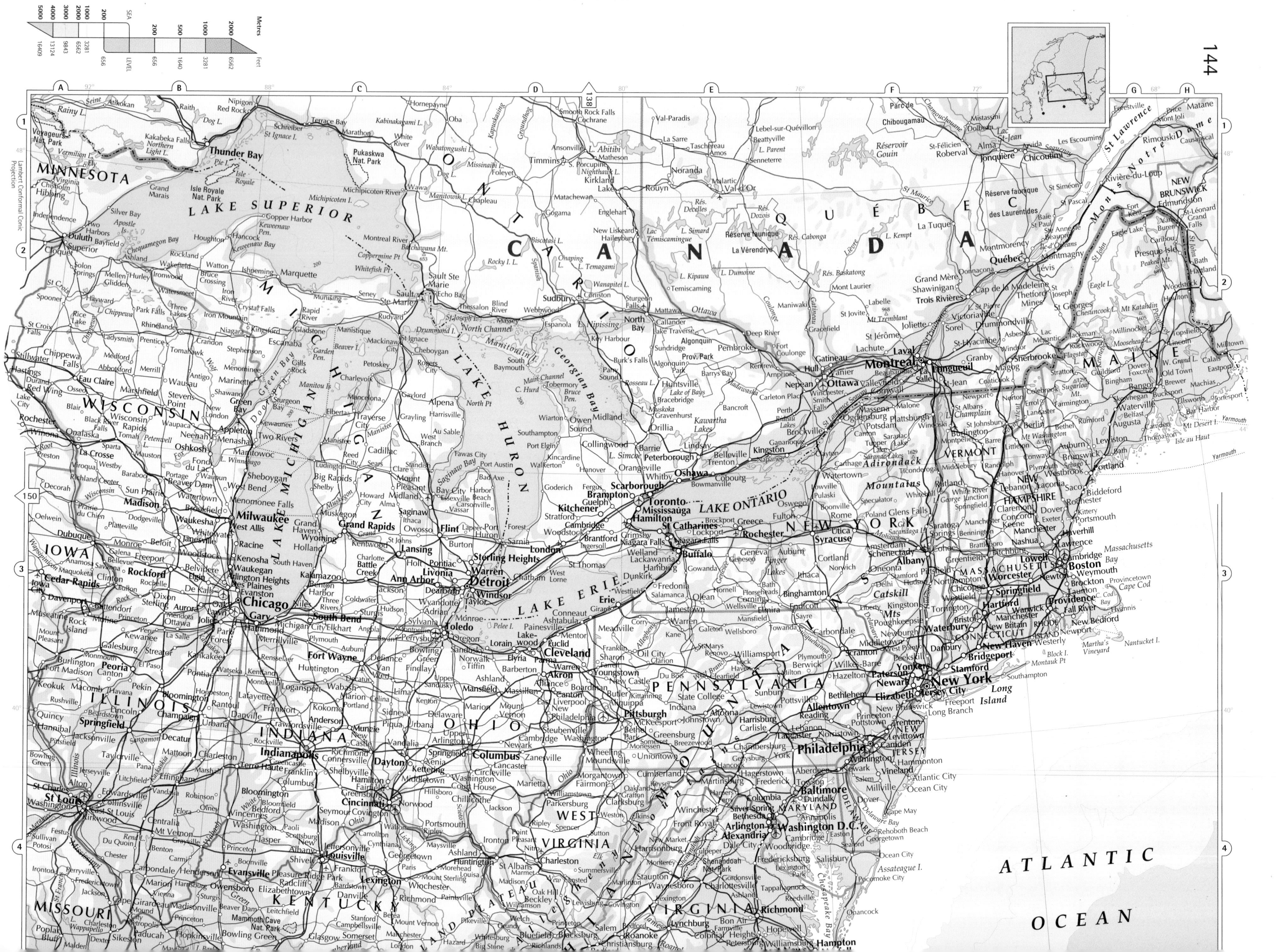
ATLANTIC OCEAN
CANADA
ONTARIO
QUEBEC
LAKE SUPERIOR
LAKE HURON
LAKE MICHIGAN
LAKE ERIE
LAKE ONTARIO
Georgian Bay
MINNESOTA
WISCONSIN
MICHIGAN
IOWA
ILLINOIS
INDIANA
OHIO
KENTUCKY
WEST VIRGINIA
VIRGINIA
PENNSYLVANIA
NEW YORK
VERMONT
NEW HAMPSHIRE
MAINE
MASSACHUSETTS
CONNECTICUT
NEW JERSEY
MARYLAND
DELAWARE
MISSOURI
NEW BRUNSWICK
Chesapeake Bay
Long Island
Metres
Feet
2000
6562
1000
3281
500
1640
200
656
SEA
LEVEL
200
656
1000
3281
2000
6562
3000
9843
4000
13124
5000
16409
Lambert Conformal Conic Projection
138
150

BERMUDA
(United Kingdom)
1:500 000

NEW PROVIDENCE
(The Bahamas)
1:600 000

PUERTO RICO and VIRGIN ISLANDS
1:3M

© Bartholomew

1:6M

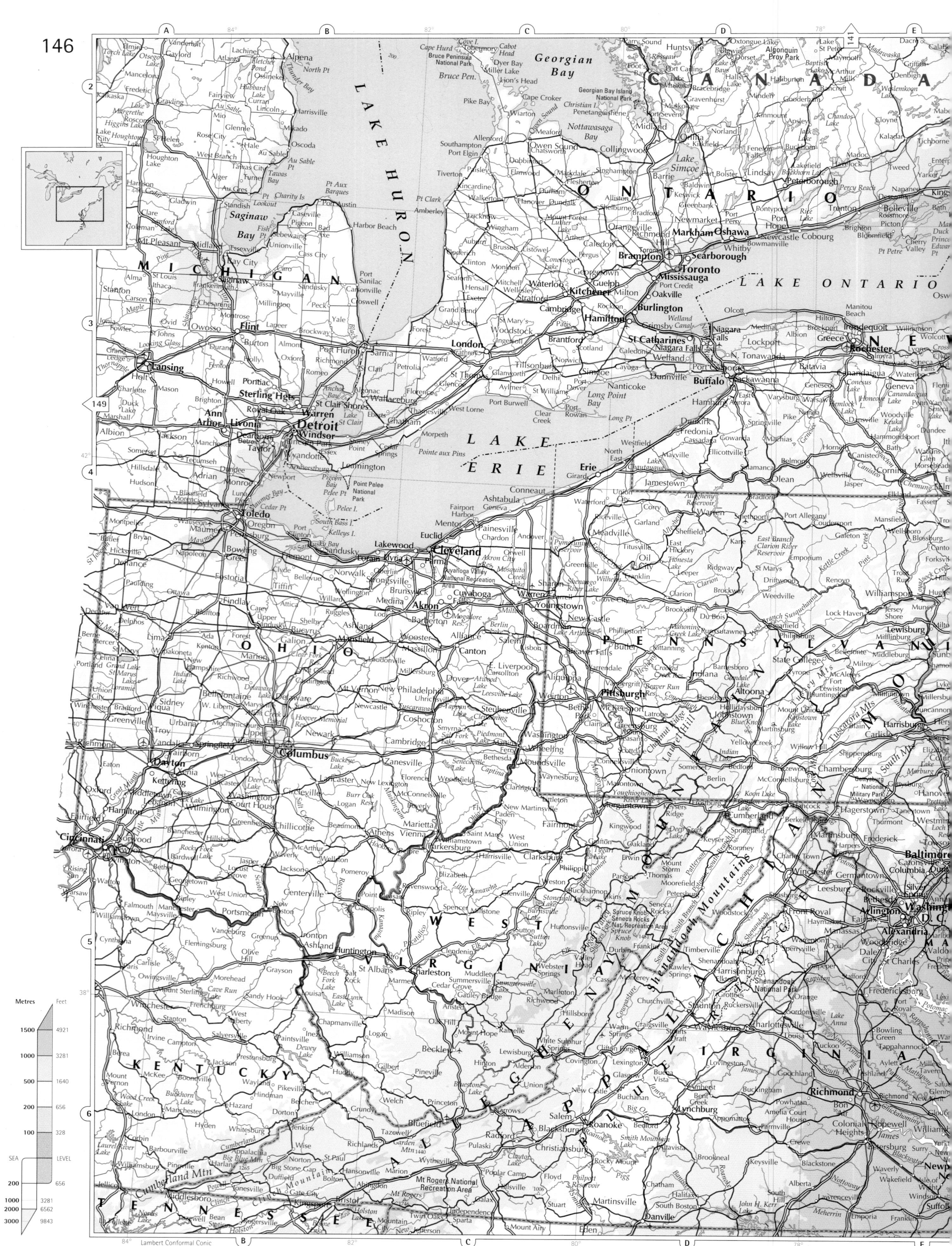
LAKE HURON
Georgian Bay
LAKE ONTARIO
LAKE ERIE
CANADA
ONTARIO
MICHIGAN
OHIO
PENNSYLVANIA
WEST VIRGINIA
VIRGINIA
KENTUCKY
TENNESSEE
NEW
APPALACHIAN MOUNTAINS
ALLEGHENY MOUNTAINS
BLUE RIDGE
Detroit
Cleveland
Pittsburgh
Toronto
Columbus
Cincinnati
Buffalo
Richmond
Washington
Baltimore
Metres
Feet
1500
4921
1000
3281
500
1640
200
656
100
328
SEA
LEVEL
200
656
1000
3281
2000
6562
3000
9843
141
149
Lambert Conformal Conic Projection

ATLANTIC

OCEAN

continuation at the same scale

1:3M

© Bartholomew

LAKE SUPERIOR
LAKE MICHIGAN
MINNESOTA
WISCONSIN
MICHIGAN
IOWA
ILLINOIS
INDIANA
MISSOURI
Isle Royale
Isle Royale National Park
Apostle Islands National Lakeshore
Pictured Rocks National Lakeshore
Pukaskwa National Park
Quetico Provincial Park
Sleeping Bear Dunes National Seashore
Lake Superior National Park
Keweenaw Peninsula
Keweenaw Bay
Green Bay
Door Peninsula
Little Traverse Bay
Grand Traverse Bay
Michipicoten Bay
Thunder Bay
Sawtooth Mountains
Mesabi Range
Gogebic Range
Duluth
Superior
St Paul
Minneapolis
Rochester
La Crosse
Eau Claire
Wausau
Green Bay
Appleton
Oshkosh
Madison
Milwaukee
Racine
Kenosha
Rockford
Chicago
Gary
South Bend
Fort Wayne
Peoria
Bloomington
Springfield
Decatur
Champaign
Indianapolis
Cedar Rapids
Iowa City
Davenport
Dubuque
Waterloo
Grand Rapids
Kalamazoo
Lansing
Muskegon
Marquette
Sault Ste Marie
Metres
Feet
500
1640
200
656
100
328
SEA
LEVEL
200
656
Lambert Conformal Conic Projection
A
B
C
D
E
1
2
3
4
5
6
48°
46°
44°
42°
40°
92°
90°
88°
86°

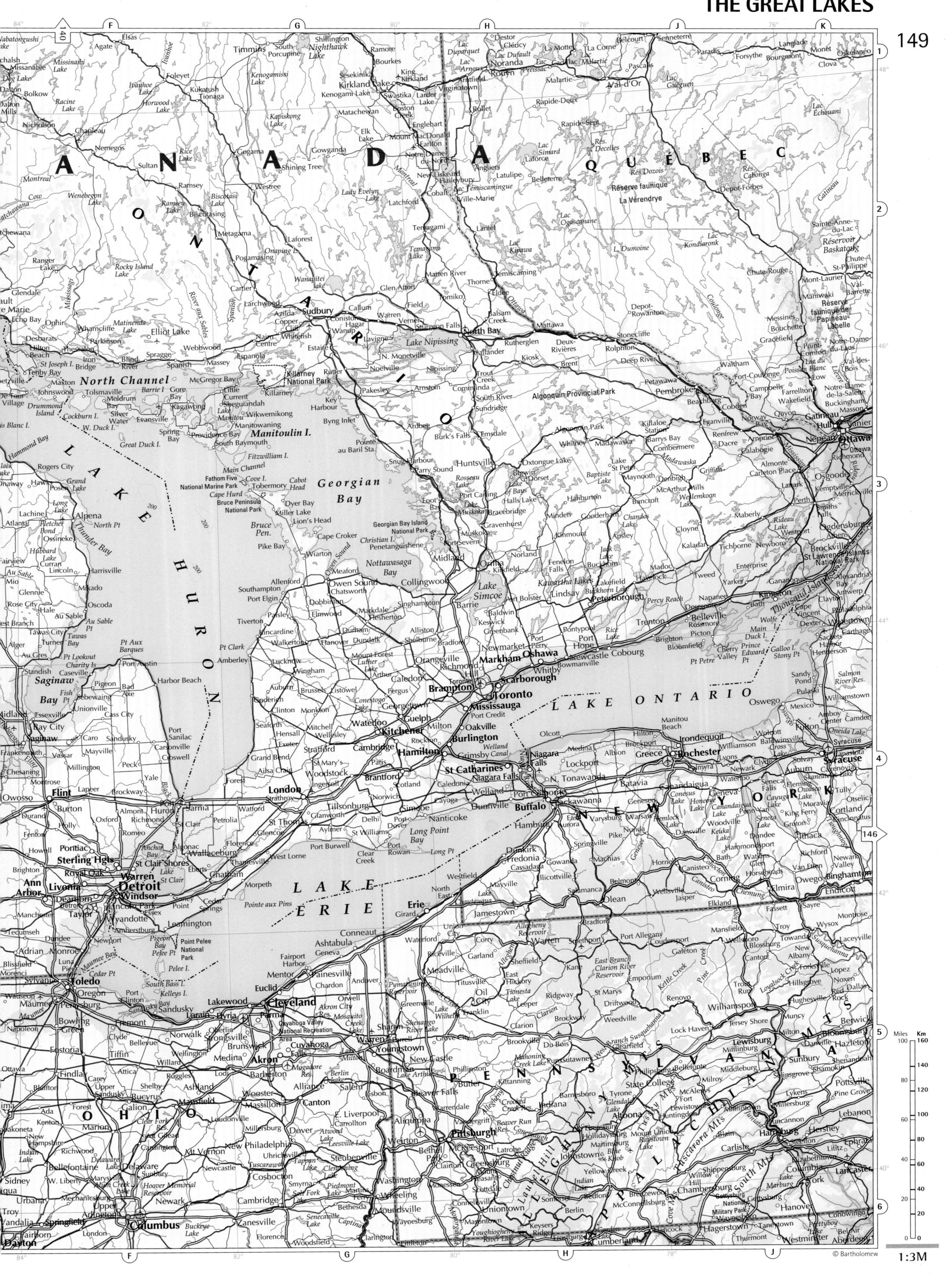

CANADA
ONTARIO
QUÉBEC
NEW YORK
PENNSYLVANIA
OHIO
APPALACHIAN MTS
LAKE HURON
LAKE ONTARIO
LAKE ERIE
Georgian Bay
North Channel
Manitoulin I.
Lake Nipissing
Lake Simcoe
Saginaw Bay
Thunder Bay
Nottawasaga Bay
Long Point Bay
Algonquin Provincial Park
Réserve faunique La Verendrye
Thousand Islands
Sudbury
North Bay
Ottawa
Toronto
Scarborough
Mississauga
Brampton
Hamilton
Burlington
Kitchener
London
St Catharines
Niagara Falls
Buffalo
Rochester
Syracuse
Detroit
Windsor
Toledo
Cleveland
Akron
Youngstown
Pittsburgh
Erie
Columbus
Flint
Saginaw
Sarnia
Kingston
Peterborough
Oshawa
Binghamton
Harrisburg
Timmins
Rouyn-Noranda
Val-d'Or
Pembroke
Barrie
Orillia
Guelph
Cambridge
Brantford
Oakville
Markham
Sterling Hgts
Warren
Ann Arbor
Livonia
Dearborn
Lakewood
Canton
Mansfield
Johnstown
Altoona
State College
Williamsport
Elmira
Oswego
Belleville
Cornwall
Gatineau
Hull
Nepean
Kenogamissi Lake
Lake Timiskaming
Bruce Peninsula National Park
Fathom Five National Marine Park
Georgian Bay Island National Park
Point Pelee National Park
St Lawrence Islands National Park
Cuyahoga Valley National Recreation Area
Allegheny Reservoir
1:3M
Miles
Km
© Bartholomew
146
140

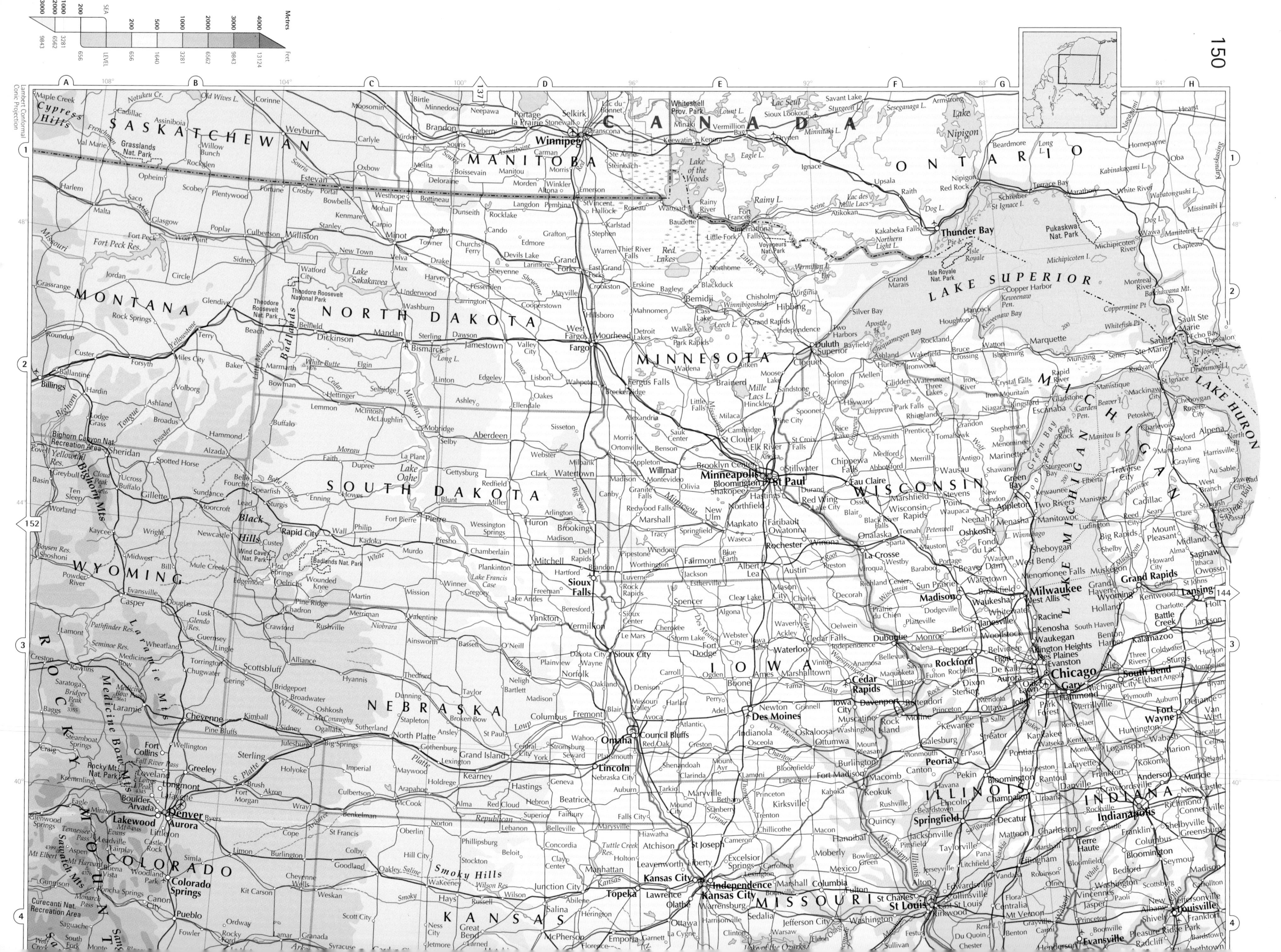

CANADA
ONTARIO
MANITOBA
SASKATCHEWAN
LAKE SUPERIOR
LAKE HURON
LAKE MICHIGAN
MICHIGAN
WISCONSIN
MINNESOTA
NORTH DAKOTA
SOUTH DAKOTA
IOWA
ILLINOIS
INDIANA
MISSOURI
NEBRASKA
KANSAS
MONTANA
WYOMING
COLORADO
ROCKY MOUNTAINS
Bighorn Mts
Laramie Mts
Medicine Bow Mts
Black Hills
Badlands
Smoky Hills
Cypress Hills
Lake of the Woods
Red Lakes
Winnipeg
Thunder Bay
Duluth
Minneapolis
St Paul
Milwaukee
Chicago
Madison
Des Moines
Omaha
Lincoln
Kansas City
St Louis
Indianapolis
Denver
Aurora
Colorado Springs
Cheyenne
Billings
Sioux Falls
Sioux City
Fargo
Bismarck
Pierre
Rapid City
Topeka
Grand Rapids
Lansing
Peoria
Springfield
Rockford
Cedar Rapids
Council Bluffs
Metres
Feet
4000
13124
3000
9843
2000
6562
1000
3281
500
1640
200
656
SEA
LEVEL
137
144
152
Lambert Conformal
Conic Projection

GULF OF MEXICO

KENTUCKY
TENNESSEE
ALABAMA
FLORIDA
MISSISSIPPI
ARKANSAS
LOUISIANA
OKLAHOMA
TEXAS
NEW MEXICO
MEXICO
CHIHUAHUA
COAHUILA
NUEVO LEON
DURANGO

Nashville
Memphis
Birmingham
Montgomery
Mobile
New Orleans
Baton Rouge
Jackson
Little Rock
North Little Rock
Shreveport
Springfield
Tulsa
Oklahoma City
Norman
Wichita
Amarillo
Lubbock
Midland
Odessa
El Paso
Ciudad Juárez
Dallas
Fort Worth
Plano
Garland
Mesquite
Arlington
Waco
Austin
San Antonio
Houston
Pasadena
Baytown
Beaumont
Galveston
Corpus Christi
Laredo
Nuevo Laredo
Brownsville
Matamoros
Monterrey
Saltillo
Torreón
Gómez Palacio
Cd Delicias
Santa Fe
Albuquerque

Edwards Plateau
Llano Estacado
Sacramento Mts
Guadalupe Mts Nat. Park
Big Bend Nat. Park
Ouachita Mts
Boston Mts
Red Hills

Miles 200
Km 320

© Bartholomew

1:6M

CANADA
BRITISH COLUMBIA
ALBERTA
SASKATCHEWAN
NORTH DAKOTA
SOUTH DAKOTA
NEBRASKA
MONTANA
WYOMING
IDAHO
WASHINGTON
OREGON
ROCKY MOUNTAINS
BITTERROOT RANGE
COAST MOUNTAINS
Cascade Range
Columbia Plateau
Snake River Plain
Bighorn Mountains
Absaroka Range
Medicine Bow Mts
Great Salt Lake
Selkirk Mountains
Purcell Mountains
Monashee Mountains
Salmon River Mountains
Cypress Hills
Vancouver Island
OCEAN
Lambert Conformal Conic Projection
Metres
Feet
SEA
LEVEL
136
150

COLORADO
NEW MEXICO
TEXAS
ARIZONA
NEVADA
UTAH
CALIFORNIA
SONORA MEXICO
CHIHUAHUA
BAJA CALIFORNIA NORTE

GREAT BASIN

COLORADO PLATEAU

Sangre de Cristo Range
Sacramento Mountains
San Andres Mts
Sawatch Mts
San Juan Mts
Sierra Nevada
Shoshone Mountains
Panamint Range
Mojave Desert
San Joaquin Valley
Santa Lucia Range
Death Valley Nat. Mon.
Grand Canyon
Painted Desert
Golfo de California
Desierto de Vizcaíno

Colorado Springs
Pueblo
Santa Fe
Albuquerque
Las Cruces
El Paso
Ciudad Juárez
Chihuahua
Roswell
Silver City
Tucson
Phoenix
Scottsdale
Mesa
Chandler
Glendale
Avondale
Flagstaff
Prescott
Yuma
San Luis Río Colorado
Mexicali
Calexico
El Centro
Brawley
San Diego
Tijuana
Chula Vista
Escondido
Oceanside
Carlsbad
Ensenada
Los Angeles
Long Beach
Santa Ana
Anaheim
Riverside
San Bernardino
Pasadena
Torrance
Glendale
Sta Clarita
Lancaster
Bakersfield
Santa Barbara
Ventura
Oxnard
Fresno
Modesto
Stockton
Sacramento
San Jose
Sunnyvale
Hayward
Oakland
Berkeley
San Francisco
Redwood City
Santa Rosa
Reno
Las Vegas
Henderson
Hermosillo
Guaymas
Ciudad Obregón
Nogales
Agua Prieta
Douglas
Bisbee

OAHU (Hawaii) 1:1.5M
Honolulu
Pearl Harbor
Waikiki Beach
Diamond Hd

HAWAIIAN ISLANDS (Main group) (U.S.A.)
Kauai
Oahu
Molokai
Maui
Lanai
Kahoolawe
Hawaii
Honolulu
Hilo
Mauna Kea
Mauna Loa
Kilauea
Hawaii Volcanoes National Park

PACIFIC OCEAN

Miles 200 / Km 320
1:6M

© Bartholomew

CALIFORNIA
NEVADA
SIERRA NEVADA
PACIFIC OCEAN
Channel Islands
Mojave Desert
Death Valley
Red Bluff
Chico
Oroville
Reno
Sparks
Carson City
Sacramento
Santa Rosa
Napa
Vallejo
Concord
Berkeley
Oakland
San Francisco
Hayward
Stockton
Modesto
Sunnyvale
San Jose
Merced
Salinas
Fresno
Visalia
Bakersfield
Santa Maria
Santa Barbara
Oxnard
Thousand Oaks
Simi Valley
Santa Clarita
Pasadena
Glendale
Los Angeles
Long Beach
Anaheim
Santa Ana
Irvine
Huntington Beach
Riverside
San Bernardino
Moreno Valley
Oceanside
Escondido
San Diego
Chula Vista
Tijuana
Ensenada
Lake Tahoe
Mono Lake
Yosemite National Park
Kings Canyon National Park
Sequoia National Park
Mt Whitney 4418
San Joaquin Valley
Coast Ranges
Santa Barbara Channel
Gulf of Santa Catalina
Santa Catalina I.
San Clemente I.
San Nicolas I.
Lambert Conformal Conic Projection
Metres
Feet
4000 13124
3000 9843
2000 6562
1500 4921
1000 3281
500 1640
200 656
100 328
SEA LEVEL

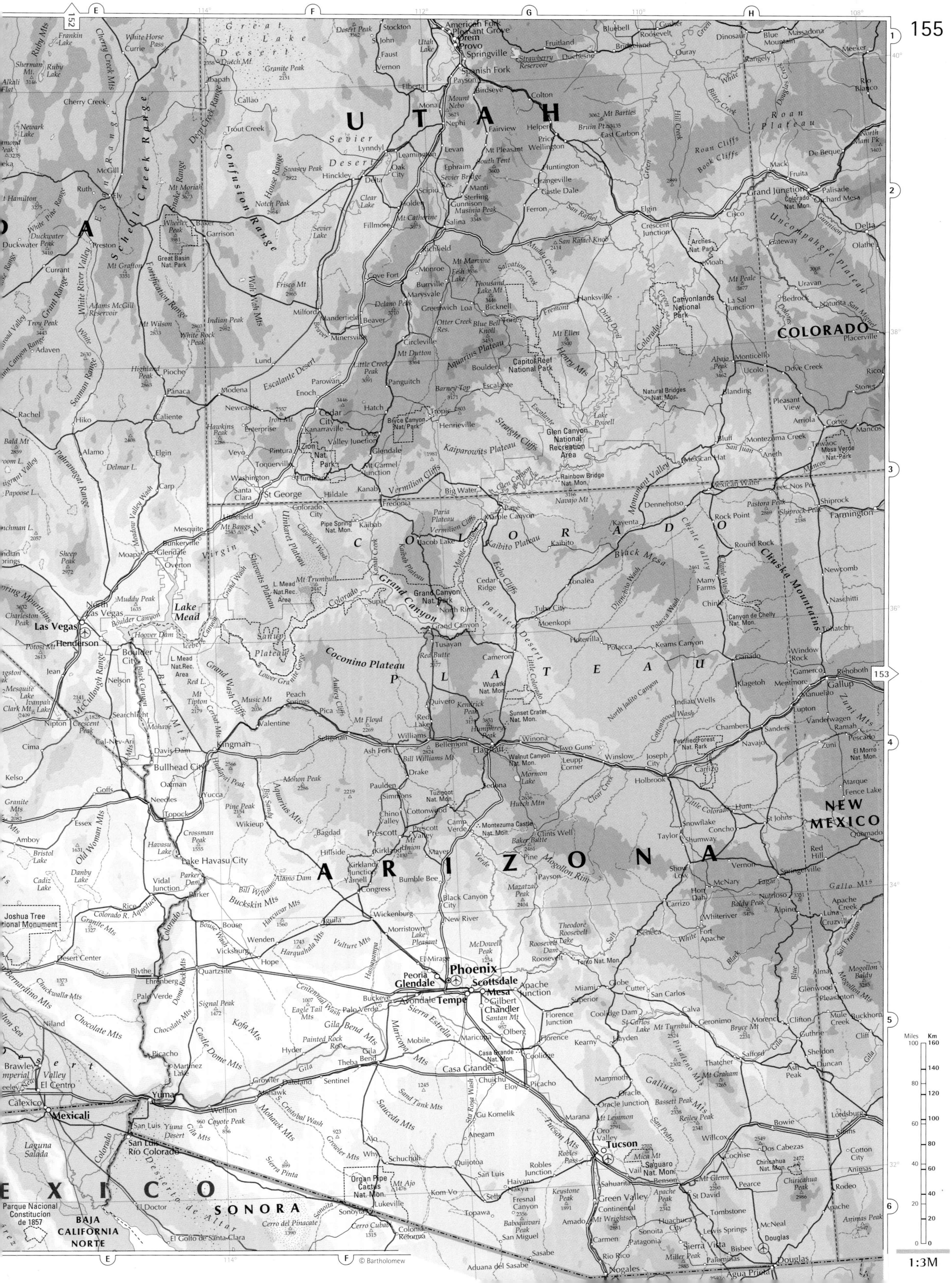

UTAH

COLORADO

ARIZONA

NEW MEXICO

C O L O R A D O   P L A T E A U

Grand Canyon

Lake Mead

Las Vegas

Phoenix
Glendale
Scottsdale
Mesa
Tempe
Chandler
Gilbert
Peoria
Avondale

Tucson

Yuma

Mexicali

Calexico
El Centro

Flagstaff

Kingman

Lake Havasu City

Coconino Plateau

Kaiparowits Plateau

Glen Canyon National Recreation Area

Canyonlands National Park

Capitol Reef National Park

Bryce Canyon Nat. Park

Zion Nat. Park

Grand Canyon Nat. Park

Joshua Tree National Monument

Organ Pipe Cactus Nat. Mon.

Chuska Mountains

Black Mesa

Painted Desert

Mogollon Rim

Sonoran Desert

Hoover Dam

Lake Powell

Grand Junction

Farmington

Gallup

Provo
Orem
Spanish Fork
Springville

Nogales

Douglas

Bisbee

M E X I C O

SONORA

BAJA CALIFORNIA NORTE

Miles / Km scale

ARIZONA
NEW MEXICO
UNITED
SONORA
CHIHUAHUA
COAHUILA
SINALOA
DURANGO
ZACATECAS
NAYARIT
JALISCO
MEXICO
BAJA CALIFORNIA NORTE
BAJA CALIFORNIA SUR
GOLFO DE CALIFORNIA
PACIFIC
SIERRA MADRE OCCIDENTAL
Tijuana
Chula Vista
Mexicali
Calexico
Yuma
Ensenada
Tucson
Ciudad Juárez
El Paso
Las Cruces
Hermosillo
Guaymas
Ciudad Obregón
Los Mochis
Culiacán
Mazatlán
Chihuahua
Durango
Torreón
Tepic
Guadalajara
La Paz
Guadalupe (Mex.)
Islas Revillagigedo (Mexico)
at the same scale
HONDURAS
NICARAGUA
COSTA RICA
PANAMA
EL SALVADOR
CARIBBEAN SEA
PACIFIC OCEAN
Tegucigalpa
San Salvador
Managua
San José
Panamá
Colón
Metres
Feet
SEA LEVEL
continuation at the same scale
Lambert Conformal Conic Projection
153
162

United States of America

STATES OF AMERICA

TEXAS
Edwards Plateau

Dallas · Fort Worth · Irving · Garland · Mesquite
Shreveport
Jackson
MISSISSIPPI
ALABAMA
Montgomery
Selma
Meridian
Baton Rouge
New Orleans
Houston · Pasadena · Galveston
Beaumont
Austin
San Antonio
Waco
Corpus Christi
Laredo
Nuevo Laredo
Monterrey · Guadalupe
Saltillo
Monclova

COAHUILA
TAMAULIPAS
NUEVO LEÓN
Reynosa · Matamoros
Brownsville
Ciudad Victoria

GULF OF MEXICO

Tropic of Cancer

158

Arrecife Alacrán
Cayo Nuevo
Cayos Arcas

Tampico
Ciudad Madero
SAN LUIS POTOSÍ
San Luis Potosí
GUANAJUATO
León · Guanajuato
QUERÉTARO
Querétaro
HIDALGO
Pachuca
Poza Rica
Tuxpan
Papantla

Mérida
YUCATÁN
Progreso
Valladolid
Cancún
Cozumel
Puerto Morelos

Campeche
CAMPECHE
QUINTANA ROO
Chetumal

BAHÍA DE CAMPECHE

Veracruz
Jalapa
Ciudad del Carmen
TABASCO
Villahermosa
Coatzacoalcos
Minatitlán

México
Toluca
Puebla
Cuernavaca
Orizaba
Córdoba
MORELOS
PUEBLA
TLAXCALA
Acapulco
GUERRERO
SIERRA MADRE DEL SUR
OAXACA
Oaxaca
Tuxtla Gutiérrez
CHIAPAS

Golfo de Tehuantepec

BELIZE
Belmopan
Golfo de Honduras
Pto Barrios
S. Pedro Sula

GUATEMALA
Guatemala
Quezaltenango
EL SALVADOR
San Salvador
Nueva San Salvador
Santa Ana
S. Miguel
Sipacate

OCEAN

Miles / Km
240 / 360
300
180 / 240
120 / 180
60 / 120
60

© Bartholomew

1:6.6M

ARUBA (Neth.)
1:1.5M
Kudarebe
Arasji
Alto Vista
Druif
Paradera
Oranjestad
Prinses Beatrix
Barcadera
Jamanota
Sint Nicolaas
Seroe Colorado
Punt Basora
CURAÇAO
(Neth.)
1:1.5M
Noord Punt
Westpunt
St Christoffelberg
St Kruis
St Jozefsdal
Ascension
Bocht van Hato
St Willebrordus
Hato
Curaçao
Bullen Baai
St Michiel
Otrabanda
Willemstad
Brakmastad
Sta Catharina
St Anna-baai
Spaanse Baai
Punt Kanon
New Port
BONAIRE
(Neth.)
1:1.5M
Malmok
Gotomeer
Rincon
Barcadera
Kralendijk
Klein Bonaire
Wanapa
Witte Pan
Lacre Pt
Tropic of Cancer
Gulf of Mexico
Port Charlotte
Punta Gorda
Lake Okeechobee
Hobe Sound
West Palm Beach
Pahokee
Clewiston
Palm Beach
Cape Coral
Fort Myers
Belle Glade
U.S.A.
FLORIDA
The Everglades
Delray Beach
Naples
Plantation
Fort Lauderdale
Big Cypress Nat. Preserve
Hollywood
Marco
Hialeah
Miami Beach
Ten Thousand Islands
Coral Gables
Miami
Everglades
Biscayne Nat. Park
Homestead
Nat. Park
Florida City
Cape Sable
Florida Bay
Key Largo
Islamorada
Dry Tortugas
Marathon
Marquesas Keys
Pine Is
Key West
Straits of Florida
Little Bahama Bank
Little Abaco
Coopers Town
West End Pt
Freeport City
Grand Bahama
Great Guana Cay
Marsh Harbour
High Rock
Elbow Cay
Cherokee Sound
Great Abaco
Northwest Providence Chan.
Northeast Providence Chan.
Bimini Is
Alice Town
Cat Cays
Gt Harbour Cay
Berry Is
Whale Cay
The Bluff
Eleuthera
Nicholl's Town
New Providence
Nassau
Hatchet Bay
Tarpum Bay
Powell Pt
Great Bahama Bank
Stafford Ck
Williams I.
Ship Chan Cay
Andros Town
Bannerman Town
Andros
Mangrove Cay
Kemp's Bay
Tongue of the Ocean
Exuma Sound
North End Pt
Arthur's Town
Cat I.
Devil's Pt
Columbus Pt
San Salvador
Victoria Hill
Fowl Cay
Green Cay
Cay Sal
Cay Sal Bank
Santaren Channel
Anguilla Cays
Water Cays
Snap Pt
Cape Sta Marie
Rum Cay
Port Nelson
Great Exuma
George Town
Long I.
THE BAHAMAS
Samana Cay
Nicholas Channel
Arch. de Sabana
Old Bahama Channel
Clarence Town
Channel Rock
Crooked I. Passage
Crooked I.
Northeast Pt
South Pt
Colonel Hill
Snug Corner
Acklins I.
Salina Pt
Mayaguana Passage
Ragged I.
Columbus Bank
Duncan Town
Habana
(Havana)
Marianao
Guanabacoa
Matanzas
Artemisa
Güines
Cárdenas
Isabela de Sagua
Sagua la Grande
Matahambre
Los Palacios
Surgidero de Batabanó
Ensenada de la Broa
Colón
Caibarién
Arch. de Camagüey
B. de Buena Vista
B. de Guadiana
Guane
Pinar del Río
Golfo de Batabanó
Jagüey Grande
Sta Clara
Pen. de Zapata
Cienfuegos
Pen. de Guanahacabibes
Laf
Nueva Gerona
C. San Antonio
Cabo Corrientes
B. de Cochinos
San Juan
Cabaiguán
Morón
Cunagua
Cayo Romano
Sancti Spíritus
Ciego de Ávila
Esmeralda
Trinidad
Tunas de Zaza
Júcaro
Cayo Sabinal
Nuevitas
Arch. de los Canarreos
Pta Francés
Cayo del Rosario
Cayo Largo
Isla de la Juventud
CUBA
Vertientes
Camagüey
Puerto Manatí
Puerto Padre
Puerto Samá
Cabo Lucrecia
Banes
Gibara
Guáimaro
Cayo Breton
Cayo Cinco-Balas
Cayo Gde
Cayo Ancliras
Jardines de la Reina
San Pedro
Santa Cruz del Sur
Victoria de las Tunas
Holguín
Cauto
Golfo de Guacanayabo
Bayamo
Manzanillo
Niquero
Sierra Maestra
Palma Soriano
Guantánamo
Baracoa
Cabo Maisí
Maisí
Jauco
Sagua de Tánamo
Turquino
Cabo Cruz
Pilón
Santiago de Cuba
B. de Guantánamo
Windward Passage
Pickle Bank
Brown Bank
Great Inagua
Matthew Town
Lake Windsor
Le Môle St Nicolas
Cap-à-Foux
C. Catoche
I. Contoy
Puerto Juárez
Cancún
Yucatan Channel
Puerto de Morelos
Cozumel
I. de Cozumel
MEXICO
Vigía Chico
B. de la Ascensión
Felipe C. Puerto
B. del Espíritu Santo
Pta Herrero
Bacalar
Chetumal
Banco Chinchorro
Corozal
Boca Bacalar Chico
Orange Walk
S. Pedro
St George's Cay
Turneffe Is
Belize
Belmopan
Middlesex
BELIZE
Dangriga
Golfo de Honduras
Punta Gorda
Pto Cortés
Pto Barrios
CAYMAN ISLANDS
(U.K.)
Little Cayman
Cayman Brac
Georgetown
Grand Cayman
Bodden Town
Misteriosa Bank
Rosario Bank
CAYMAN TRENCH
Swan Is (Hond.)
GREATER ANTILLES
CARIBBEAN
Montego Bay
Falmouth
St Ann's Bay
South Negril Point
Savanna la Mar
JAMAICA
Port Antonio
Mandeville
Kingston
Spanish Town
Morant Pt
Portland Pt
Jamaica Channel
Île de la Gonâve
Cap Dame-Marie
Dame Marie
Jérémie
Navassa I.
(U.S.A.)
Mf de la Hotte
Port-à-Piment
Pte-à-Gravois
Les Cayes
Pedro Bank
Pedro Cays
Southwest Rock
Thunder Knoll
Rosalind Bank
Alice Shoal
Islas de la Bahía
Roatán
Guanaja
Tela
La Ceiba
Trujillo
Limón
C. Camarón
S. Pedro Sula
Nva Armenia
Sa de la Esperanza
Pta Patuca
Cayos Becerro
Banco Gorda
Progreso
Olanchito
Caratasca
Laguna Caratasca
Puerto Lempira
Dulce Nombre de Dios
HONDURAS
MOSQUITIA
Santa Bárbara
Victoria
Pito Solo
Siguatepeque
Salamá
Patuca
Pto Cabo Gracias á Dios
Arrecife de la Media Luna
Comayagua
Guaimaca
Juticalpa
Azacualpa
Waspán
Bilwascarma
Cayos Miskitos
(Nic.)
Tegucigalpa
Danlí
Jalapa
Coco
Pta Gorda
Pto Cabezas
Quita Sueño Bank
(Col.)
Serrana Bank
(Col.)
Bonanza
Siuna
Choluteca
Somoto
Condega
Cordillera Isabelia
COSTA DE MOSQUITOS
Estelí
Jinotega
Matagalpa
Prinzapolca
Roncador Cay
(Col.)
I. de Providencia (Col.)
Grande
La Cruz
León
Darío
NICARAGUA
Laguna de Perlas
Pta de Perlas
Managua
Tipitapa
Boaco
Sto Domingo
Masaya
Juigalpa
I. de San Andrés (Col.)
Masachapa
Granada
Acoyapa
Paso del Cascal
Bluefields
Is del Maíz
(Corn Is)
(Col.)
Cayes de Albuquerque (Col.)
Jinotepe
Lago de Nicaragua
Rivas
I. de Ometepe
San Juan del Sur
Peñas Blancas
San Carlos
Pta Gorda
Bahía de San Juan del Norte
San Juan del Norte
C. Sta Elena
San Juan
Liberia
Altamira
Rio Frio
Filadelfia
Guápiles
COSTA RICA
Pto Jesus
Puntarenas
Alajuela
Heredia
San José
Limón
Pen. de Nicoya
G. de Nicoya
Santamaría
Cartago
C. Blanco
Parrita
Chirripó
Suretka
Changuinola
Almirante
Bocas del Toro
Dominical
Pta Cortés
B. de Coronado
PACIFIC OCEAN
Golfito
Pen. de Osa
El Hato del Volcán
Volcán Barú
Laguna de Chiriquí
Golfo de los Mosquitos
Bajo Boquete
Concepción
David
Cordillera Central
C. Matapalo
Golfo Dulce
Pto Armuelles
Pta Burica
Golfo de Chiriquí
Portobelo
Pta Manzanillo
Colón
Cristóbal
Gatún L.
El Porvenir
Arch. de San Blas
Cord. de San Blas
Ailigandi
Miguel de la Borda
Coclé del Norte
Sta Catalina
La Chorrera
Panamá
Chepo
San Miguelito
B. de Panamá
PANAMA
Penonomé
Antón
Aguadulce
Chimán
Santiago
San Francisco
Soná
Santiago
Parita
Chitré
Río de Jesús
Atalaya
Las Tablas
I. Pedro González
I. San José
San Miguel
G. de S. Miguel
Isla del Rey
Garachiné
La Palma
El Real
Pto Obaldía
Golfo del Darién
Golfo de Urabá
Acandí
Tacarcuna
Turbo
Parque Nac. Los Katíos
Parque Nac. de Darién
Jaqué
Riosucio
Chigorodó
Pto Letras
Serranía del Darién
Serranía del Sapo
Golfo de Panamá
Coiba
I. Cebaco
Pen. de Azuero
Tonosí
Pedasí
Pta Mala
I. Jicarón
Pta Mariato
Cabo de La Aguja
Ríohacha
Santa Marta
Parque Nac. Sierra Nevada de Santa Marta
Barranquilla
Ciénaga
P. Cristóbal Colón
Baranoa
Sabanalarga
Soledad
Sta Catalina
Aracataca
Pivijay
Fundación
Valledupar
Cartagena
Turbaco
Calamar
Arjona
San Jacinto
I. de San Bernardo
Carmen
G. de Morrosquillo
Tolú
Plato
El Difícil
COLOMBIA
Sincelejo
Corozal
Chimichagua
Mompós
Lorica
Chinú
Sincé
Magangué
El Banco
Puerto Rey
Cga Grande
Montería
Cereté
Ciénaga de Oro
Sahagún
Sucre
Necoclí
Planeta Rica
Majagual
Alto de Quimarí
Tierra Alta
Ayapel
Caucasia
Nechí
Ocaña
Magdalena
Simití
Pedro Pt
Green Island
N Negril Pt
Long Bay
Negril
S Negril Pt
Glasgow
Grange Hill
Lucea
S.W. Pt
Metres
Feet
SEA
LEVEL
Lambert Conformal Conic Projection

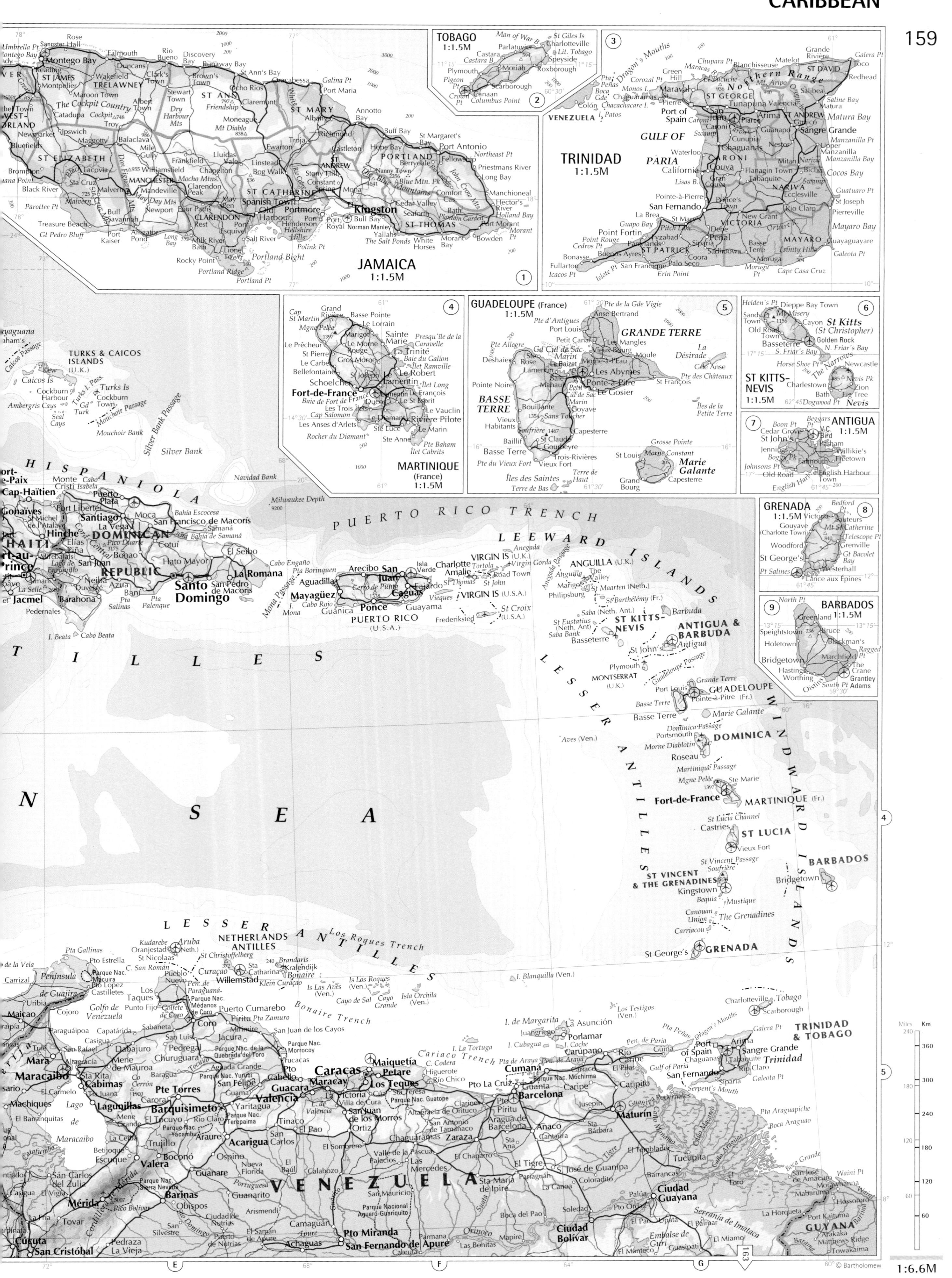

TOBAGO 1:1.5M

TRINIDAD 1:1.5M

JAMAICA 1:1.5M

GUADELOUPE (France) 1:1.5M

MARTINIQUE (France) 1:1.5M

ST KITTS-NEVIS 1:1.5M

ANTIGUA 1:1.5M

GRENADA 1:1.5M

BARBADOS 1:1.5M

CARIBBEAN SEA

HISPANIOLA

HAITI

DOMINICAN REPUBLIC

PUERTO RICO (U.S.A.)

LEEWARD ISLANDS

LESSER ANTILLES

WINDWARD ISLANDS

NETHERLANDS ANTILLES

VENEZUELA

GUYANA

TRINIDAD & TOBAGO

TURKS & CAICOS ISLANDS (U.K.)

Miles 240

Km 360

1 2 3 4 5

J

H

G

F

E

Fernando de Noronha
(Brazil)

Natal
João Pessoa
RIO GRANDE
DO NORTE
PARAÍBA
Campina Grande
Olinda
Recife
Maceió
Aracaju
Salvador

Fortaleza

CEARÁ

PERNAMBUCO
ALAGOAS
SERGIPE

PIAUÍ

MARANHÃO

Teresina

BAHIA

São Luís

B R A Z I L

Belém

Mouths of the Amazon

PARÁ

TOCANTINS
Palmas

Araguaia

São Francisco

Cayenne

French
Guiana

AMAPÁ

Macapá

GOIÁS
Brasília
(F. D.)

Paramaribo

MATO GROSSO

Cuiabá

SURINAM

Amazon

Georgetown

GUYANA

Manaus

Boa Vista

RORAIMA

AMAZONAS

S e l v a s

RONDÔNIA

Trinidad

Cumaná

Ciudad
Bolívar

Pôrto Velho

BOLIVIA

Caracas
Maracay

VENEZUELA

Orinoco

Puerto
Ayacucho

Negro

Río
Branco

Cobija

L. Titicaca

Puno

Port of
Spain

TRINIDAD
& TOBAGO

GRENADA

ST VINCENT &
THE GRENADINES

BARBADOS

ST LUCIA

Martinique
(Fr.)

DOMINICA

Guadeloupe
(Fr.)

ANTIGUA &
BARBUDA

Montserrat
(U.K.)

NEVIS

ST KITTS

Virgin Is
(U.S.A.)

Virgin Is
(U.K.)

Anguilla
(U.K.)

L e s s e r   A n t i l l e s

NETH.
ANTILLES
Curaçao

Aruba
(Neth.)

Coro

Valencia
Barquisimeto

Maracaibo

San Cristóbal

Cúcuta

Bucaramanga

Tunja

COLOMBIA

L l a n o s

ACRE

Madeira

Puerto
Maldonado

Cusco

N

Puerto
Rico
(U.S.A.)

San Juan

Santo
Domingo

DOMINICAN
REP.

Hispaniola

HAITI

Port-au-
Prince

A n t i l l e s

G r e a t e r

Turks & Caicos Is
(U.K.)

Acklins I.

Gt Inagua

Holguín

Camagüey

Santiago
de Cuba

CUBA

Sta Clara

Kingston

JAMAICA

Cayman Is
(U.K.)

Gd Cayman

C A R I B B E A N   S E A

Sta
Marta

Barranquilla

Cartagena

G. of
Darién

Medellín

Manizales

Ibagué

Bogotá

Cali

Neiva

Popayán

Pasto

Buenaventura

Montería

Quito
Ambato

ECUADOR

Cuenca

Guayaquil

G. of
Guayaquil

Manta

Esmeraldas

PERU

Iquitos

Marañón

Amazon

Moyobamba

Cajamarca

Huánuco

Chiclayo

Trujillo

Chimbote

Huaraz

Callao Lima

Huancayo

Ayacucho

Ica

Pucallpa

Piura

Tampa

U.S.A.

Miami

C. Canaveral

Key West

Piñar
del Río

Havana

Gd Bahama

Gt Abaco

Nassau

THE
BAHAMAS

Gd Bahama

Andros

Straits of Florida

Yucatan Channel

GULF OF MEXICO

Tropic of Cancer

Bahía de Campeche

Veracruz

Tampico

Matamoros

Mérida

Campeche

MEXICO
Villahermosa

Isthmus

Yucatan

G. of
Tehuantepec

Tehuantepec

BELIZE

Belmopan

Belize

Puerto Barrios

GUATEMALA
City

GUAT.

San Salvador

EL SALVADOR

HONDURAS

Tegucigalpa

G. of Honduras

Honduras

NICARAGUA

Managua

L. Nicaragua

L. Managua

COSTA RICA

San José

Limón

Puntarenas

PANAMA
Panama
City

Colón

I. de Malpelo
(Col.)

I. de Coco
(C. R.)

Galapagos Islands
(Ecu.)

Equator

Bi-Polar Oblique
Projection

Metres   Feet
0   0
200   656
3000   9843

SOUTH ATLANTIC OCEAN

SOUTH PACIFIC OCEAN

MINAS GERAIS
ESPÍRITO SANTO
Vitória
Campos
RIO DE JANEIRO
Niterói
Rio de Janeiro
Belo Horizonte
Juiz de Fora
Volta Redonda
Uberaba
São Paulo
SÃO PAULO
Ribeirão Prêto
Campinas
Santos
Curitiba
PARANÁ
Florianópolis
SANTA CATARINA
Pôrto Alegre
RIO GRANDE DO SUL
Sta Maria
Rio Grande
Pelotas

MATO GROSSO DO SUL
Campo Grande
Concepción
PARAGUAY
Paraguay
Asunción
Villarrica
Encarnación
Posadas
Corrientes
Resistencia
Formosa
Paraná
Sucre
Potosí
Tarija
S. Salvador de Jujuy
Salta
Catamarca
Tucumán
Santiago del Estero
Santa Fé
Paraná
Rosario
Córdoba
S. Luis
Mendoza
S. Juan
S. Rafael
Sta Rosa
Neuquén
Buenos Aires
La Plata
Río de la Plata
Paysandú
Salto
URUGUAY
Montevideo
Mar del Plata
Bahía Blanca
Viedma
Golfo San Matías

A R G E N T I N A

Gran Chaco

Arica
Iquique
Antofagasta
Atacama
Ojos del Saldo 6880
Aconcagua 6960
Coquimbo
Valparaíso
Viña del Mar
Santiago
Talca
Chillán
Talcahuano
Concepción
Temuco
Valdivia
Puerto Montt
I. de Chiloé
Arch. de los Chonos
Golfo de Penas
Cochrane
Puerto Aisén
Golfo de San Jorge
Comodoro Rivadavia
Deseado
Ravson

P A T A G O N I A

I. Wellington
Puerto Natales
Punta Arenas
Str. of Magellan
Bahía Grande
Río Gallegos
Tierra del Fuego
Ushuaia
Cape Horn
I. de los Estados

Stanley
Falkland Islands (U.K.)

Drake Passage

San Félix (Chile)
San Ambrosio (Chile)
Juan Fernández Is (Chile)

Tropic of Capricorn

Martin Vaz Is Trindade (Brazil)

Scotia Sea

Shag Rocks
South Georgia (U.K.)

Coronation I.
South Orkney Is (U.K.)

Traversay Is
Candlemas I.
Saunders I.
Montagu I.
South Sandwich Islands (U.K.)
Southern Thule I.
Bristol I.

Elephant I.
King George I.
South Shetland Is (U.K.)
Livingston I.
Bransfield Str.
Joinville I.
Anvers I.
Biscoe Islands
Antarctic Peninsula
Graham Land

Miles	Km
800	1280
	1020
640	960
480	800
	640
320	480
	320
160	160
0	0

© Bartholomew

1:21M

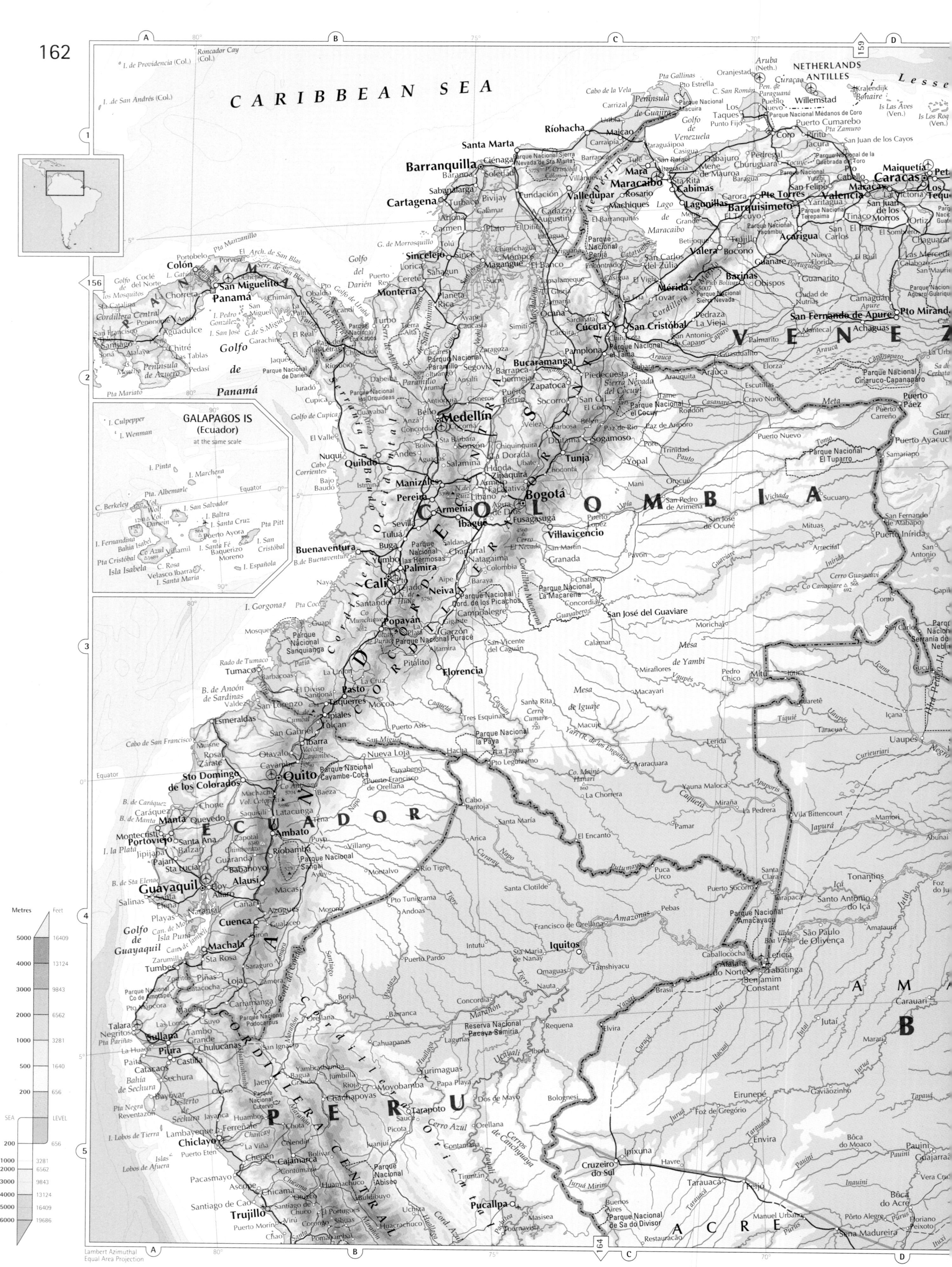
CARIBBEAN SEA
GALAPAGOS IS
(Ecuador)
at the same scale
NETHERLANDS ANTILLES
PANAMA
COLOMBIA
VENEZ
ECUADOR
PERU
CORDILLERA CENTRAL
ACRE
Golfo de Panamá
Golfo del Darién
Golfo de Venezuela
Lago de Maracaibo
Golfo de Guayaquil
Bahía de Sechura
Barranquilla
Cartagena
Santa Marta
Ríohacha
Maracaibo
Cabimas
Valledupar
Caracas
Valencia
Maracay
Barquisimeto
Mérida
Barinas
San Cristóbal
Cúcuta
Bucaramanga
Medellín
Bogotá
Manizales
Pereira
Armenia
Ibagué
Cali
Palmira
Neiva
Popayán
Pasto
Buenaventura
Tumaco
Villavicencio
Florencia
Montería
Sincelejo
Tunja
Sogamoso
Colón
Panamá
San Miguelito
Quito
Guayaquil
Cuenca
Ambato
Riobamba
Machala
Esmeraldas
Manta
Portoviejo
Sto Domingo de los Colorados
Iquitos
Leticia
Tabatinga
Benjamim Constant
Sullana
Piura
Chiclayo
Trujillo
Cajamarca
Tarapoto
Moyobamba
Pucallpa
Cruzeiro do Sul
Puerto Inírida
San Fernando de Apure
Puerto Ayacucho
Amazonas
Equator
Metres
Feet
5000
16409
4000
13124
3000
9843
2000
6562
1000
3281
500
1640
200
656
SEA
LEVEL
200
656
1000
3281
2000
6562
3000
9843
4000
13124
5000
16409
6000
19686
Lambert Azimuthal
Equal Area Projection
A
B
C
D
1
2
3
4
5
156
159
164

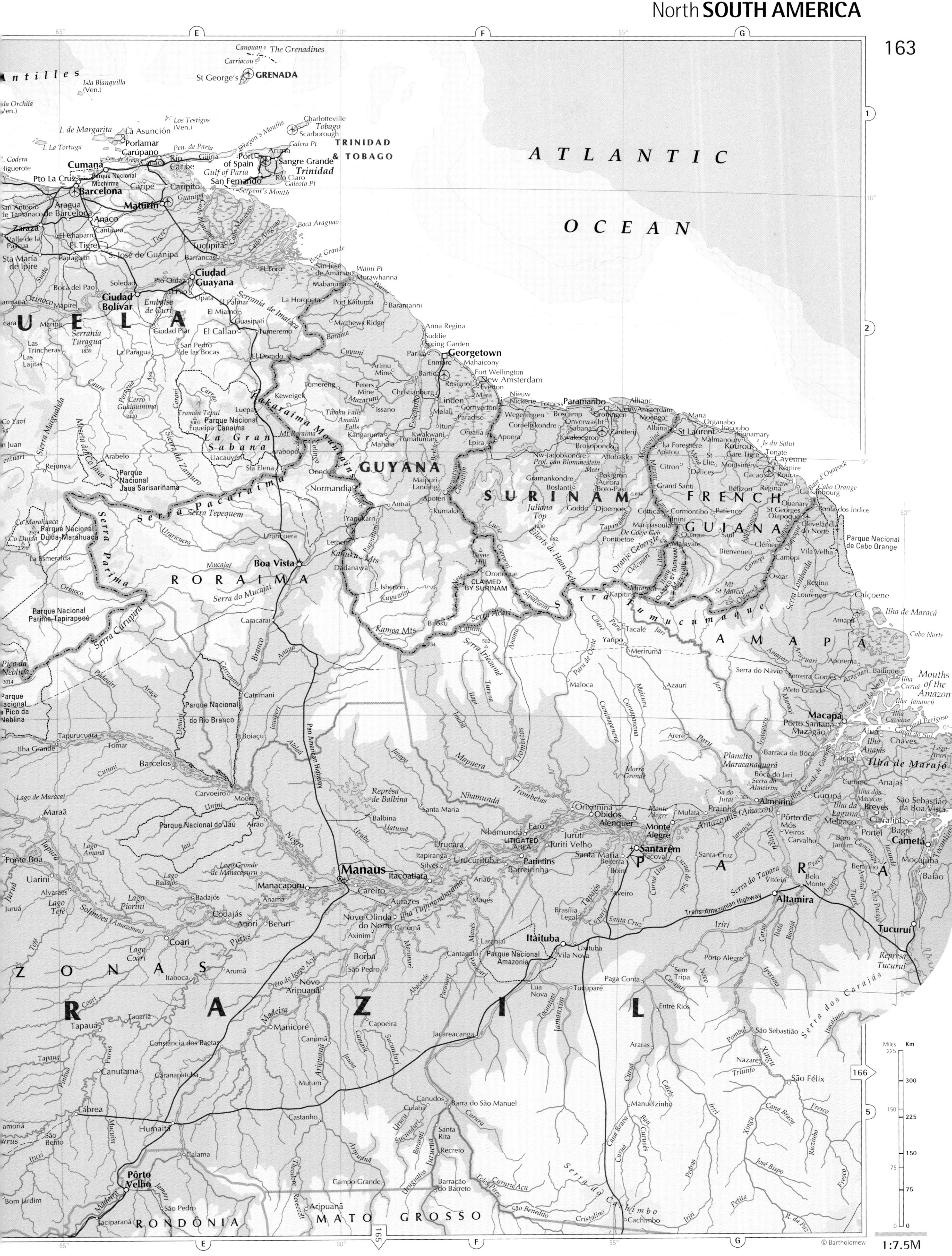

Antilles

Canouan *The Grenadines*
Carriacou
St George's ⊙ **GRENADA**

Isla Blanquilla
(Ven.)

I. de Margarita
La Asunción (Ven.)
Los Testigos
(Ven.)

Charlotteville
Tobago
Scarborough
Galera Pt

I. La Tortuga
Porlamar
Pen. de Paria

Pto La Cruz
Caribe

**TRINIDAD
& TOBAGO**

Pen. de Araya
Arima
Port
of Spain
Sangre Grande
Trinidad

Cumaná
Río
Caribe
Güiria
Dragon's Mouths
San Fernando
Río Claro
Galeota Pt

Gulf of Paria

Serpent's Mouth

A T L A N T I C

O C E A N

Barcelona
Maturín

Tucupita

Boca Araguao

Caño Araguao

Boca Grande

Waini Pt
Morawhanna

**Ciudad
Guayana**

**Ciudad
Bolívar**

Barrancas
San José de Amacuro
Mabaruma
Baramanni

Anna Regina
Spring Garden
Suddie

Georgetown

New Amsterdam

Fort Wellington
Everton

Paramaribo
Nieuw Amsterdam

Mana

St Laurent

Organabo
Iracoubo
Sinnamary

Kourou

Cayenne

**FRENCH
GUIANA**

SURINAM

GUYANA

Juliana
Top

Domy
Hill

Serra
Tumucumaque

A M A P A

Parque Nacional
de Cabo Orange

Cabo Orange

R O R A I M A

Boa Vista

Serra
Acari

Serra
Irioume

Mouths
of the
Amazon

Cabo Norte

Ilha de Maracá

Pico da
Neblina

Macapá

Ilha de Marajó

Manaus

Represa
de Balbina

Óbidos

Santarém

P A R Á

Almeirim

Cametá

Tucuruí

Altamira

**Pôrto
Velho**

R O N D Ô N I A

M A T O   G R O S S O

B R A Z I L

A M A Z O N A S

Miles   Km
225
300

150   225

150

75
75

© Bartholomew

1:7.5M

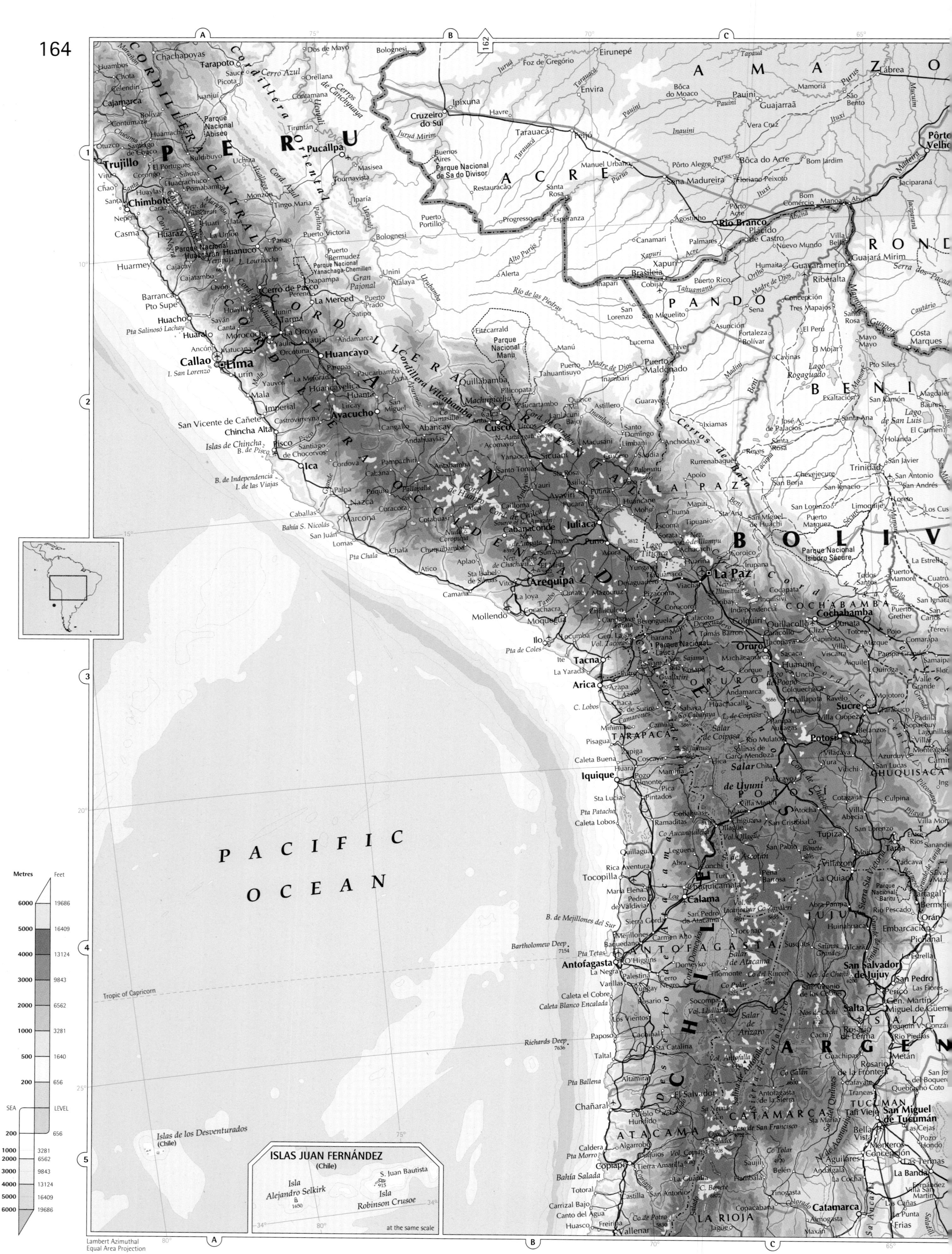
PERU
BOLIVIA
CHILE
ARGENTINA
AMAZONAS
ACRE
RONDÔNIA
PANDO
BENI
LA PAZ
COCHABAMBA
ORURO
POTOSÍ
CHUQUISACA
TARAPACA
ANTOFAGASTA
ATACAMA
CATAMARCA
TUCUMAN
JUJUY
SALTA
LA RIOJA
PACIFIC OCEAN
CORDILLERA CENTRAL
CORDILLERA OCCIDENTAL
CORDILLERA ORIENTAL
Cordillera Oriental
Cordillera Vilcabamba
Desierto de Atacama
Lima
Callao
Trujillo
Chimbote
Chachapoyas
Tarapoto
Cajamarca
Pucallpa
Huánuco
Cerro de Pasco
Huancayo
Ayacucho
Cusco
Ica
Pisco
Nazca
Arequipa
Juliaca
Puno
Moquegua
Tacna
Arica
Iquique
Tocopilla
Calama
Antofagasta
Taltal
Chañaral
Copiapó
Vallenar
La Paz
Lago Titicaca
Oruro
Cochabamba
Sucre
Potosí
Salar de Uyuni
Tupiza
Trinidad
Riberalta
Guayaramerín
Cobija
Rio Branco
Cruzeiro do Sul
Pôrto Velho
Sena Madureira
Puerto Maldonado
San Salvador de Jujuy
Salta
San Miguel de Tucumán
Catamarca
Santiago del Estero
La Banda
Tropic of Capricorn
Bartholomew Deep 7154
Richards Deep 7636
Islas de los Desventurados (Chile)
ISLAS JUAN FERNÁNDEZ (Chile)
Isla Alejandro Selkirk
Isla Robinson Crusoe
S. Juan Bautista
at the same scale
Metres
Feet
6000 19686
5000 16409
4000 13124
3000 9843
2000 6562
1000 3281
500 1640
200 656
SEA LEVEL
Lambert Azimuthal Equal Area Projection
A
B
C
1
2
3
4
5
162
75°
70°
65°
80°
10°
15°
20°
25°

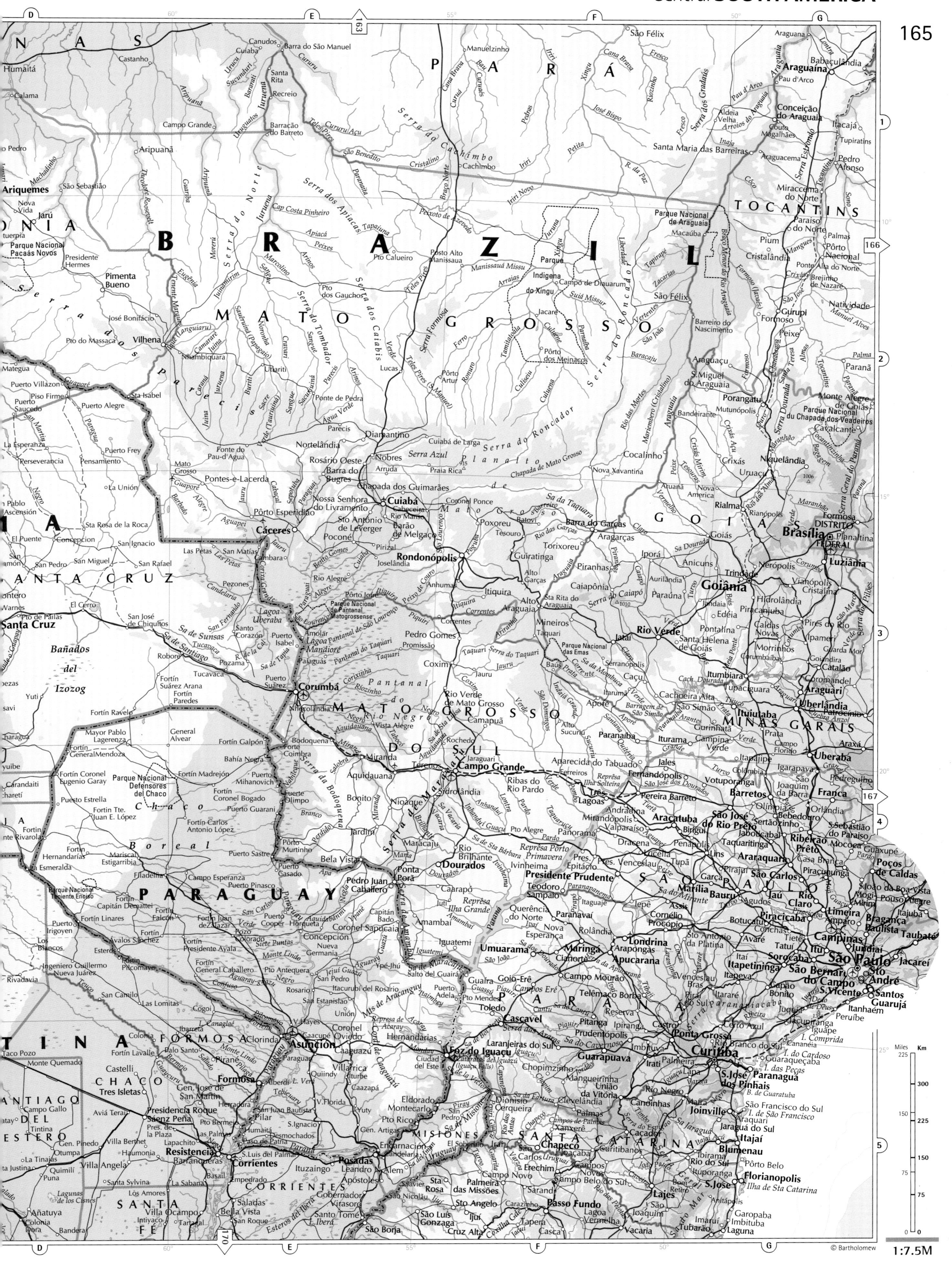
BRAZIL
PARÁ
TOCANTINS
MATO GROSSO
MATO GROSSO DO SUL
GOIÁS
DISTRITO FEDERAL
MINAS GERAIS
SÃO PAULO
PARANÁ
SANTA CATARINA
PARAGUAY
SANTA CRUZ
FORMOSA
CHACO
CORRIENTES
MISIONES
SANTA FÉ
Brasília
Goiânia
Cuiabá
Campo Grande
Corumbá
Cáceres
Rondonópolis
Araguaína
Conceição do Araguaia
Vilhena
Ariquemes
Santa Cruz
Asunción
Formosa
Resistencia
Corrientes
Posadas
Foz do Iguaçu
Curitiba
Ponta Grossa
Londrina
Maringá
Cascavel
São Paulo
Santos
Campinas
Ribeirão Prêto
Uberlândia
Uberaba
Florianopolis
Joinville
Blumenau
Passo Fundo
Pantanal
Serra do Roncador
Serra dos Parecis
Planalto de Mato Grosso
Bañados del Izozog
Chaco Boreal
Paraná
Paraguay
Araguaia
Tocantins
Xingu
Teles Pires
Juruena
Miles
Km
1:7.5M
© Bartholomew

Metres
Feet
2000
6562
1000
3281
500
1640
200
656
SEA
LEVEL
200
656
1000
3281
2000
6562
3000
9843
4000
13124
5000
16409
6000
19686
Lambert Azimuthal Equal Area Projection
B R A Z I L
M A R A N H Ã O
P I A U Í
C E A R Á
B A H I A
T O C A N T I N S
P A R Á
M A T O G R O S S O
RIO GRANDE DO NORTE
SERGIPE
ALAGOAS
Natal
João Pessoa
Recife
Olinda
Maceió
Aracaju
Salvador
Fortaleza
Teresina
São Luís
Belém
Macapá
Santarém
Altamira
Marabá
Imperatriz
Araguaína
Petrolina
Juazeiro
Feira de Santana
Campina Grande
Mossoró
Parnaíba
Caxias
Bacabal
Barra do Corda
Tucuruí
Itaituba
Ilha de Marajó
Serra Geral de Goiás
Serra do Roncador
Serra dos Carajás
Chapada Diamantina
Trans-Amazonian Highway
LITIGATED AREA
Equator

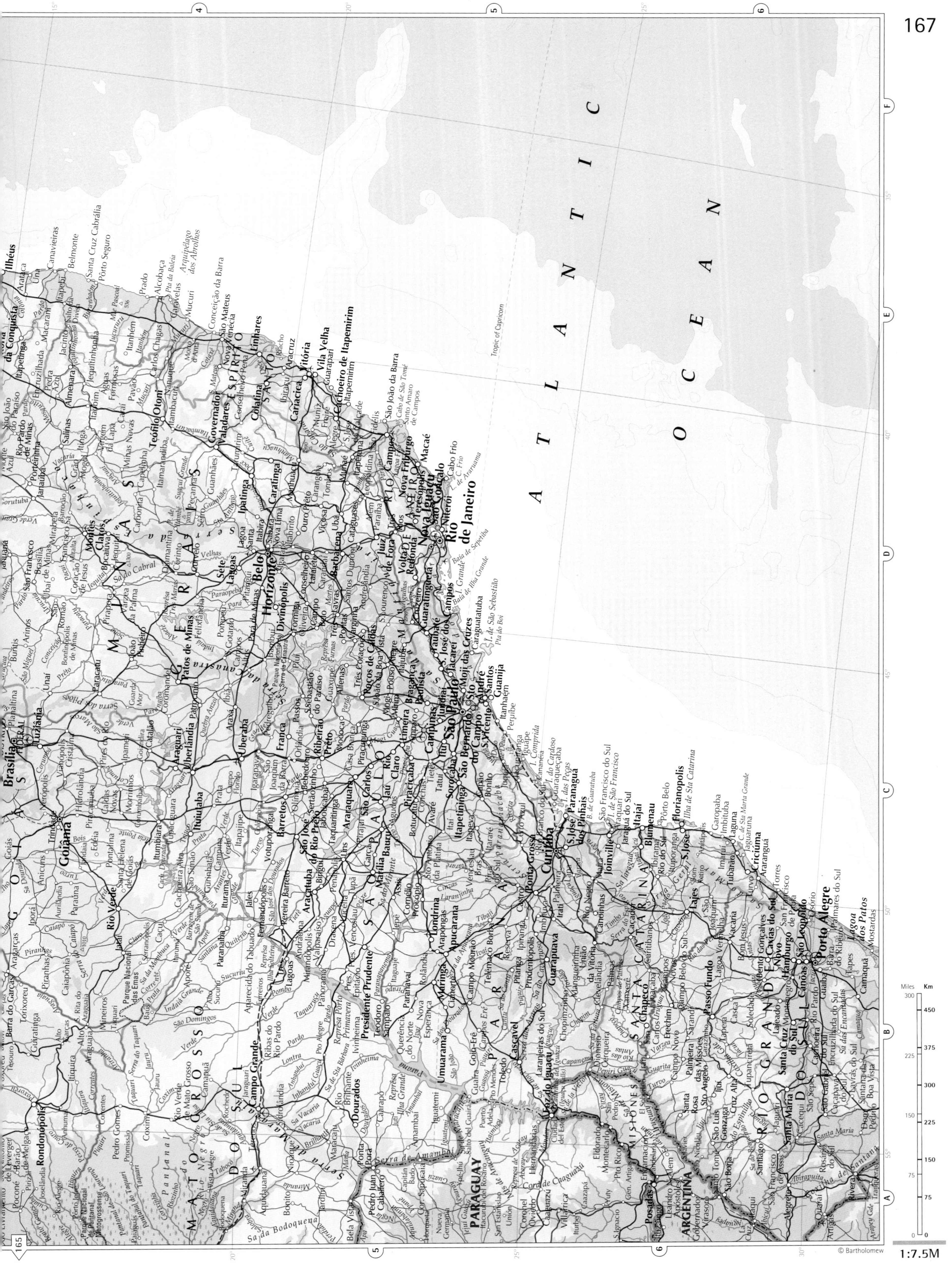

ATLANTIC OCEAN

Tropic of Capricorn

MINAS GERAIS

GOIÁS

MATO GROSSO DO SUL

SÃO PAULO

PARANÁ

SANTA CATARINA

RIO GRANDE DO SUL

PARAGUAY

ARGENTINA

MISIONES

ESPÍRITO SANTO

RIO DE JANEIRO

DISTRITO FEDERAL

Illhéus
da Conquista
Belmonte
Santa Cruz Cabrália
Pôrto Seguro
Prado
Alcobaça
Arquipélago dos Abrolhos
Conceição da Barra
São Mateus
Venécia
Linhares
Vitória
Vila Velha
Guarapari
Cachoeiro de Itapemirim
Itapemirim
São João da Barra
Campos
Macaé
Cabo Frio
Teófilo Otoni
Governador Valadares
Caratinga
Nova Friburgo
Teresópolis
São Gonçalo
Niterói
Rio de Janeiro
Nova Iguaçu
Montes Claros
Sete Lagoas
Belo Horizonte
Divinópolis
Juiz de Fora
Volta Redonda
Barra Mansa
Guaratinguetá
Taubaté
São José dos Campos
Mogi das Cruzes
Sto. André
São Bernardo do Campo
São Vicente
Santos
Guarujá
Itanhaém
Patos de Minas
Uberaba
Uberlândia
Araguari
Franca
Ribeirão Prêto
Poços de Caldas
Três Corações
Varginha
Barretos
São José do Rio Prêto
Araraquara
São Carlos
Araçatuba
Marília
Bauru
Jaú
Piracicaba
Limeira
Rio Claro
São Paulo
Jundiaí
Campinas
Sorocaba
Itu
Itapetininga
Presidente Prudente
Umuarama
Maringá
Apucarana
Londrina
Dourados
Campo Grande
Rondonópolis
Cascavel
Guarapuava
Ponta Grossa
Curitiba
S.José dos Pinhais
Paranaguá
Joinville
Jaraguá do Sul
Blumenau
Itajaí
Florianópolis
Lajes
Chapecó
Passo Fundo
Caxias do Sul
Bento Gonçalves
Novo Hamburgo
São Leopoldo
Canoas
Pôrto Alegre
Criciúma
Tubarão
Araranguá
Torres
Posadas
Rio Verde
Goiânia
Brasília
Luziânia
Ciudad del Este
PARAGUAY
ARGENTINA
Santa Maria
Santana do Livramento

Lagoa dos Patos
Lagoa Mirim
Baía de Guanabara
Baía da Ilha Grande

1:7.5M

© Bartholomew

Miles / Km
300 / 450
225 / 375
     / 300
150 / 225
     / 150
75 / 75
0 / 0

165

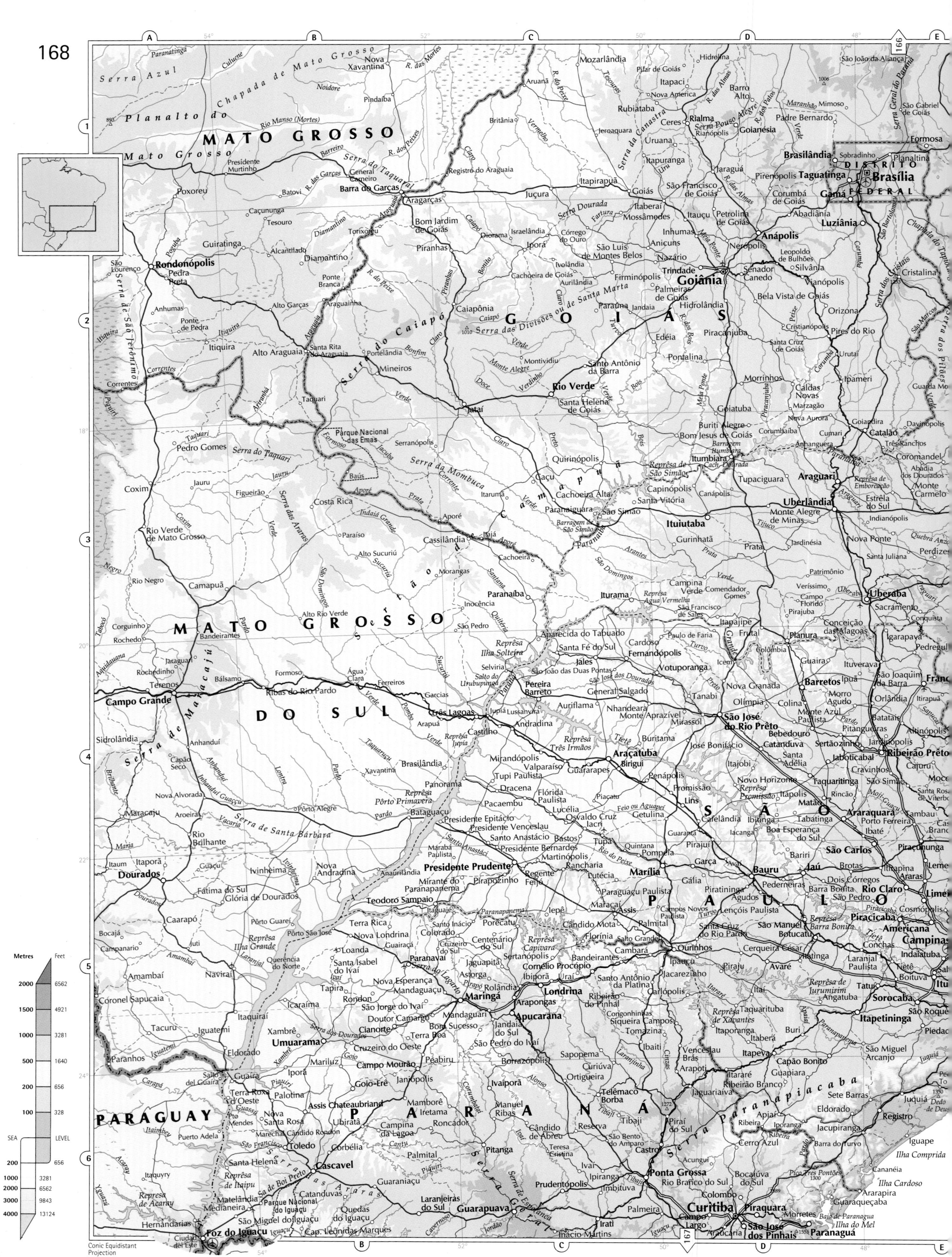
MATO GROSSO
MATO GROSSO DO SUL
GOIÁS
SÃO PAULO
PARANÁ
PARAGUAY
DISTRITO FEDERAL
Brasília
Planalto do Mato Grosso
Chapada de Mato Grosso
Serra Azul
Serra do Taquaral
Serra do Caiapó
Serra das Divisões ou de Santa Marta
Serra da Mombuca
Serra do Taquari
Serra das Araras
Serra de Maracajú
Serra de Santa Bárbara
Serra de São Jerônimo
Serra Geral
Serra Paranapiacaba
Serra da Canastra
Serra Dourada
Parque Nacional das Emas
Parque Nacional do Iguaçu
Represa de Itaipu
Represa Ilha Solteira
Represa Três Irmãos
Represa Pôrto Primavera
Represa de Furnas
Represa Capivara
Represa de Xavantes
Represa de Jurumirim
Represa Barra Bonita
Represa de Emborcação
Represa São Simão
Represa Água Vermelha
Goiânia
Anápolis
Rondonópolis
Campo Grande
Dourados
Três Lagoas
Barra do Garças
Rio Verde
Jataí
Itumbiara
Uberlândia
Uberaba
Araguari
Ribeirão Prêto
São José do Rio Prêto
Araçatuba
Presidente Prudente
Marília
Bauru
Londrina
Maringá
Apucarana
Umuarama
Campo Mourão
Cascavel
Foz do Iguaçu
Guarapuava
Ponta Grossa
Curitiba
Paranaguá
São José dos Pinhais
Sorocaba
Campinas
Piracicaba
Araraquara
São Carlos
Jaú
Americana
Rio Claro
Itapetininga
Ourinhos
Assis
Ituiutaba
Catalão
Luziânia
Taguatinga
Gama
Brasilândia
Formosa
Coxim
Camapuã
Paranaíba
Cassilândia
Costa Rica
Aquidauana
Maracaju
Ponta Porã
Amambai
Guaíra
Toledo
Hernandarias
Ciudad del Este
Sobradinho
Planaltina
Inset: South America
Metres
Feet
SEA
LEVEL
2000
1500
1000
500
200
100
200
1000
2000
3000
4000
6562
4921
3281
1640
656
328
656
3281
6562
9843
13124
Conic Equidistant Projection
A
B
C
D
E
1
2
3
4
5
6
166
167
54°
52°
50°
48°
18°
20°
22°
24°

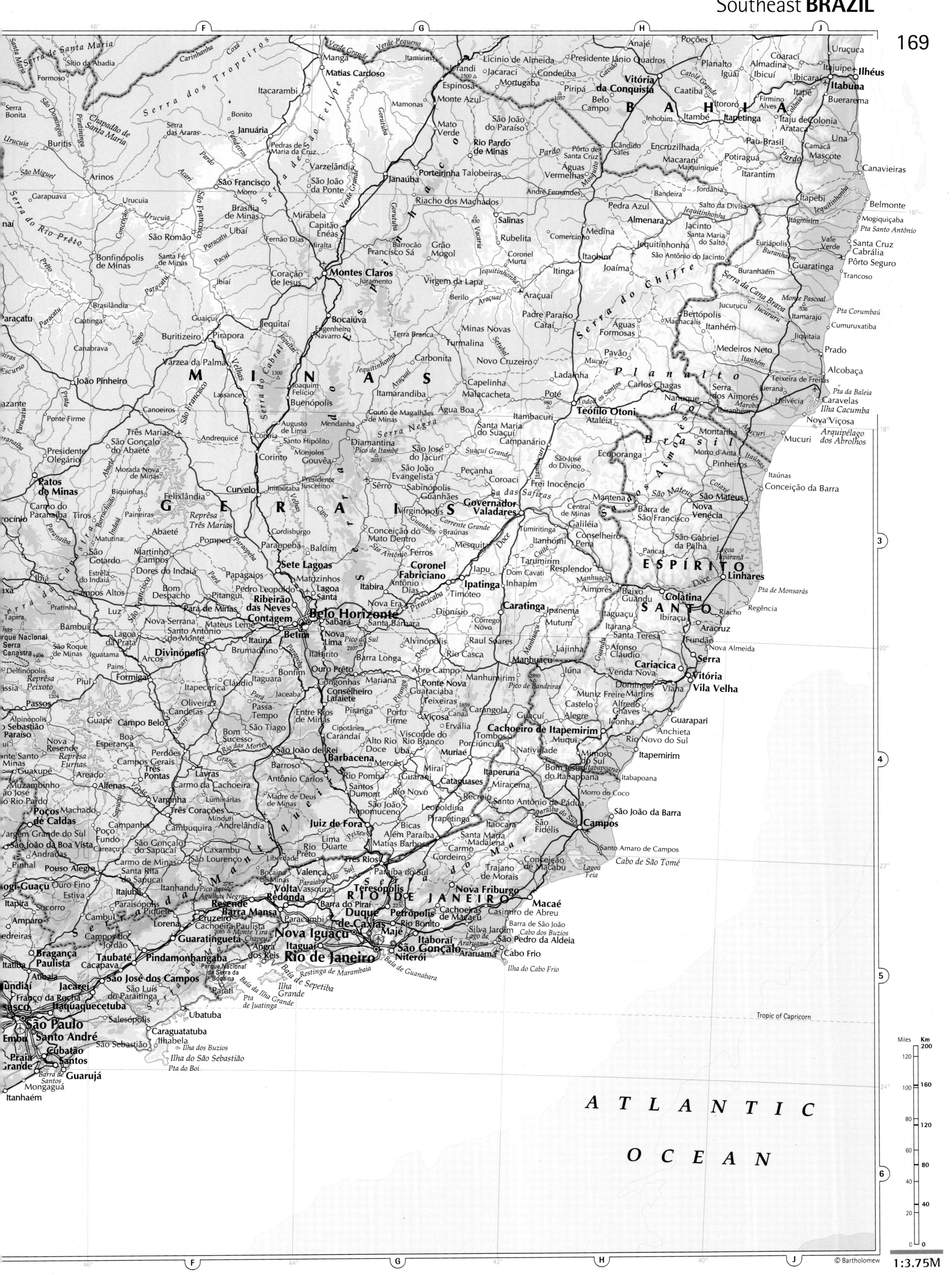
F
G
H
J
B A H I A
M I N A S
G E R A I S
E S P Í R I T O
S A N T O
R I O D E J A N E I R O
A T L A N T I C
O C E A N
Serra dos Tropeiros
Serra do Espinhaço
Serra do Cabral
Serra Negra
Serra do Chifre
Serra dos Aimorés
Serra da Mantiqueira
Serra do Mar
Planalto do Brasil
Serra da Canastra
Chapadão de Santa Maria
Represa Três Marias
Tropic of Capricorn
Arquipélago dos Abrolhos
Cabo de São Tomé
Cabo Frio
Ilha do Cabo Frio
Ilha Grande
Baía de Sepetiba
Baía da Ilha Grande
Baía de Guanabara
Ilha do São Sebastião
Vitória da Conquista
Ilhéus
Itabuna
Canavieiras
Belmonte
Santa Cruz Cabrália
Pôrto Seguro
Trancoso
Prado
Alcobaça
Caravelas
Nova Viçosa
Mucuri
Teixeira de Freitas
Itamaraju
Guaratinga
Eunápolis
Montes Claros
Janaúba
Porteirinha
Januária
Manga
Matias Cardoso
Salinas
Araçuaí
Teófilo Otoni
Governador Valadares
Diamantina
Curvelo
Pirapora
Bocaiúva
Buritizeiro
Várzea da Palma
João Pinheiro
Paracatu
Unaí
Patos de Minas
Três Marias
Sete Lagoas
Belo Horizonte
Contagem
Betim
Ribeirão das Neves
Itabira
Coronel Fabriciano
Ipatinga
Timóteo
Caratinga
Manhuaçu
Divinópolis
Ouro Prêto
Mariana
Conselheiro Lafaiete
Barbacena
São João del Rei
Lavras
Juiz de Fora
Varginha
Três Corações
Pouso Alegre
Poços de Caldas
Cataguases
Muriaé
Ubá
Leopoldina
Linhares
Colatina
São Mateus
Nova Venécia
Aracruz
Serra
Cariacica
Vitória
Vila Velha
Guarapari
Anchieta
Cachoeiro de Itapemirim
Itapemirim
Campos
Macaé
Nova Friburgo
Teresópolis
Petrópolis
Duque de Caxias
Nova Iguaçu
Rio de Janeiro
Niterói
São Gonçalo
Itaboraí
Araruama
Cabo Frio
Volta Redonda
Barra Mansa
Resende
Guaratinguetá
Pindamonhangaba
Taubaté
São José dos Campos
Jacareí
Bragança Paulista
São Paulo
Santo André
Cubatão
Santos
Guarujá
Itanhaém
Ubatuba
Caraguatatuba
Ilhabela
Parati
Angra dos Reis
Miles
Km
© Bartholomew
1:3.75M

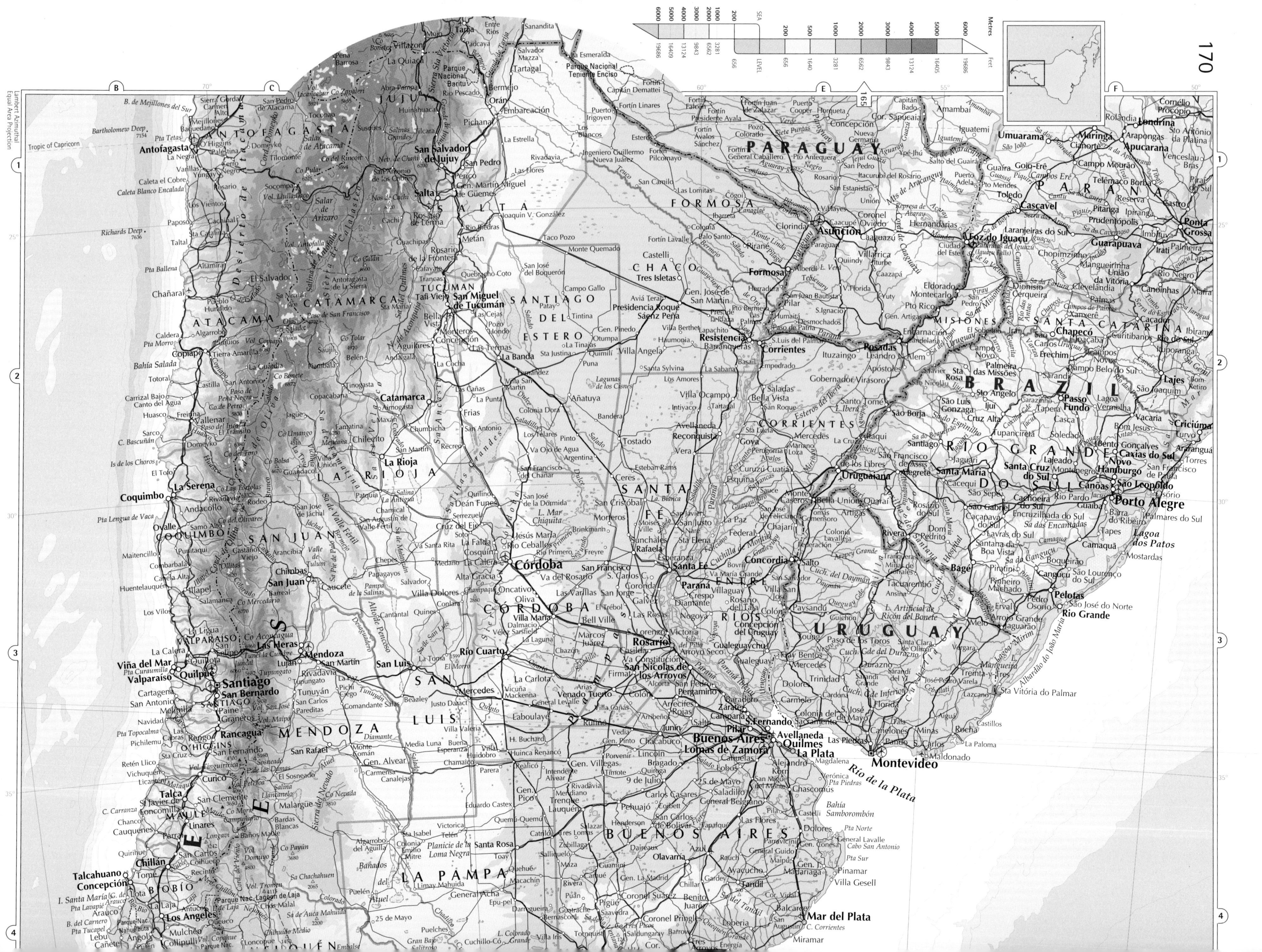
Metres
Feet
6000
19686
5000
16405
4000
13124
3000
9843
2000
6562
1000
3281
500
1640
200
656
SEA
LEVEL
200
656
Lambert Azimuthal
Equal Area Projection
Tropic of Capricorn
165
PARAGUAY
URUGUAY
BRAZIL
RIO GRANDE DO SUL
SANTA CATARINA
PARANÁ
BUENOS AIRES
LA PAMPA
CÓRDOBA
SANTA FE
ENTRE RÍOS
CORRIENTES
MISIONES
CHACO
FORMOSA
SALTA
JUJUY
TUCUMÁN
CATAMARCA
LA RIOJA
SANTIAGO DEL ESTERO
SAN JUAN
SAN LUIS
MENDOZA
ANTOFAGASTA
ATACAMA
COQUIMBO
VALPARAISO
O'HIGGINS
MAULE
BIOBÍO
Asunción
Montevideo
Buenos Aires
Santiago
Porto Alegre
Córdoba
Rosario
Mendoza
La Plata
Río de la Plata
Mar del Plata
Antofagasta
Valparaíso
Concepción
Pelotas
Rio Grande
Lagoa dos Patos
Corrientes
Resistencia
Posadas
Formosa
Santa Fe
Paraná
San Miguel de Tucumán
Salta
San Salvador de Jujuy
Catamarca
La Rioja
San Luis
San Juan
Santa Rosa
Coquimbo
La Serena
Copiapó
Talca
Chillán
Los Angeles

SOUTH ATLANTIC OCEAN
ARGENTINA
CHILE
RIO NEGRO
CHUBUT
SANTA CRUZ
LOS LAGOS
AISÉN
MAGALLANES & ANTARTICA CHILENA
TIERRA DEL FUEGO
FALKLAND ISLANDS
(ISLAS MALVINAS)
(U.K.)
West Falkland
East Falkland
Stanley
SOUTH GEORGIA
(U.K.)
at the same scale
Golfo San Matías
Golfo de San Jorge
Estrecho de Magallanes
Bahía Blanca
Bahía Grande
Comodoro Rivadavia
Río Gallegos
Punta Arenas
Puerto Montt
Osorno
Valdivia
Temuco
Neuquén
Trelew
Rawson
Ushuaia
Isla Grande de Tierra del Fuego
Archipiélago de los Chonos
Archipiélago de la Reina Adelaida
Cabo de Hornos
(C. Horn)
Miles
Km
© Bartholomew
1:7.5M

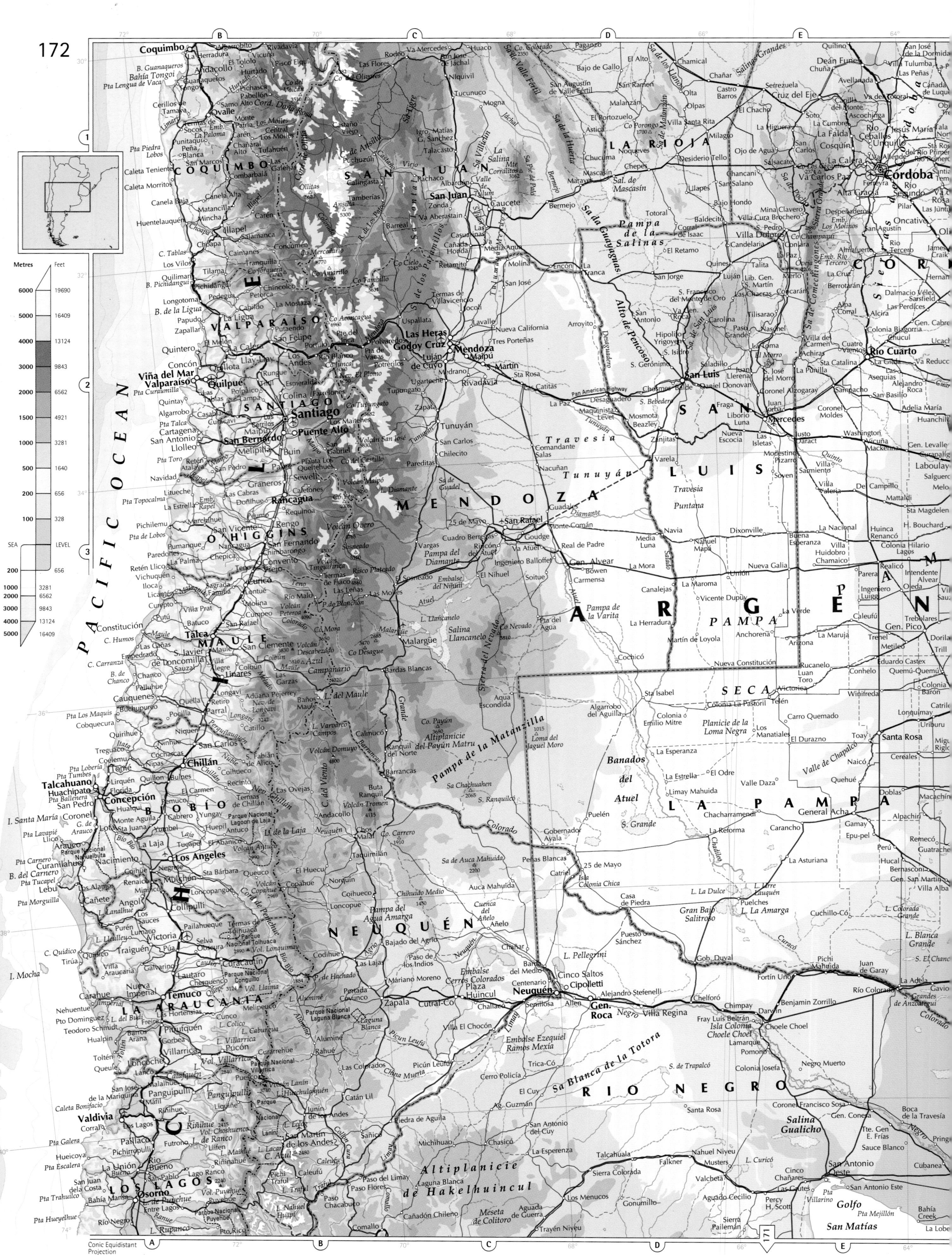
B
C
D
E
72°
70°
68°
66°
64°
30°
32°
34°
36°
38°
40°
1
2
3
Metres
Feet
6000
19690
5000
16409
4000
13124
3000
9843
2000
6562
1500
4921
1000
3281
500
1640
200
656
100
328
SEA
LEVEL
200
656
1000
3281
2000
6562
3000
9843
4000
13124
5000
16409
PACIFIC OCEAN
COQUIMBO
VALPARAÍSO
SANTIAGO
O'HIGGINS
MAULE
BIOBÍO
LA ARAUCANÍA
LOS LAGOS
SAN JUAN
LA RIOJA
MENDOZA
SAN LUIS
LA PAMPA
NEUQUÉN
RÍO NEGRO
Coquimbo
Ovalle
Illapel
Viña del Mar
Valparaíso
Quilpué
Santiago
Puente Alto
San Bernardo
Rancagua
Curicó
Talca
Linares
Chillán
Talcahuano
Huachipato
Concepción
Los Angeles
Temuco
Valdivia
Osorno
San Juan
Mendoza
Godoy Cruz
Las Heras
San Luis
San Rafael
Mercedes
Córdoba
Río Cuarto
Santa Rosa
Neuquén
Cipolletti
Gen. Roca
Pampa de la Matanzilla
Altiplanicie de Hakelhuincul
Golfo San Matías
Salina Gualicho
Conic Equidistant Projection
A
B
C
D
E
72°
70°
68°
66°
64°
171

F
G
H
J
K
L
62°
60°
58°
56°
54°
30°
34°
36°
38°
40°
1
4
5
6
170
ATLANTIC
OCEAN
B R A Z I L
U R U G U A Y
ARTIGAS
SALTO
RIVER
PAYSANDU
TACUAREMBÓ
CERRO LARGO
RIO NEGRO
DURAZNO
TREINTA-Y-TRES
SORIANO
FLORES
FLORIDA
LAVALLEJA
ROCHA
COLONIA
S. JOSÉ
CANELONES
MALDONADO
SANTA FE
ENTRE RÍOS
BUENOS AIRES
HUMEDA
Buenos Aires
Montevideo
Rosario
Santa Fe
Paraná
Concordia
Salto
Paysandú
La Plata
Mar del Plata
Bahía Blanca
Río de la Plata
Bahía Samborombón
Bahía Blanca
Bahía Anegada
Delta del Paraná
Delta del R.Colorado
Lago Artificial de Rincón del Bonete
Cuch. Gde del Durazno
Cuch. Gde Inferior
Cuch. del Daymán
Cuch. de Haedo
L. Mar Chiquita
Necochea
Tandil
Olavarria
Azul
Junín
Pergamino
San Nicolás de los Arroyos
Gualeguaychú
Fray Bentos
Mercedes
Colonia del Sacramento
Tacuarembó
Rivera
Melo
Punta del Este
Maldonado
Rocha
Chuy
Viedma
Punta Alta
Coronel Pringles
Tres Arroyos
Miramar
Pinamar
Villa Gesell
Dolores
Chascomús
Miles
Km
120
100
80
60
40
20
0
200
160
120
80
40
0
© Bartholomew
1:3.75M

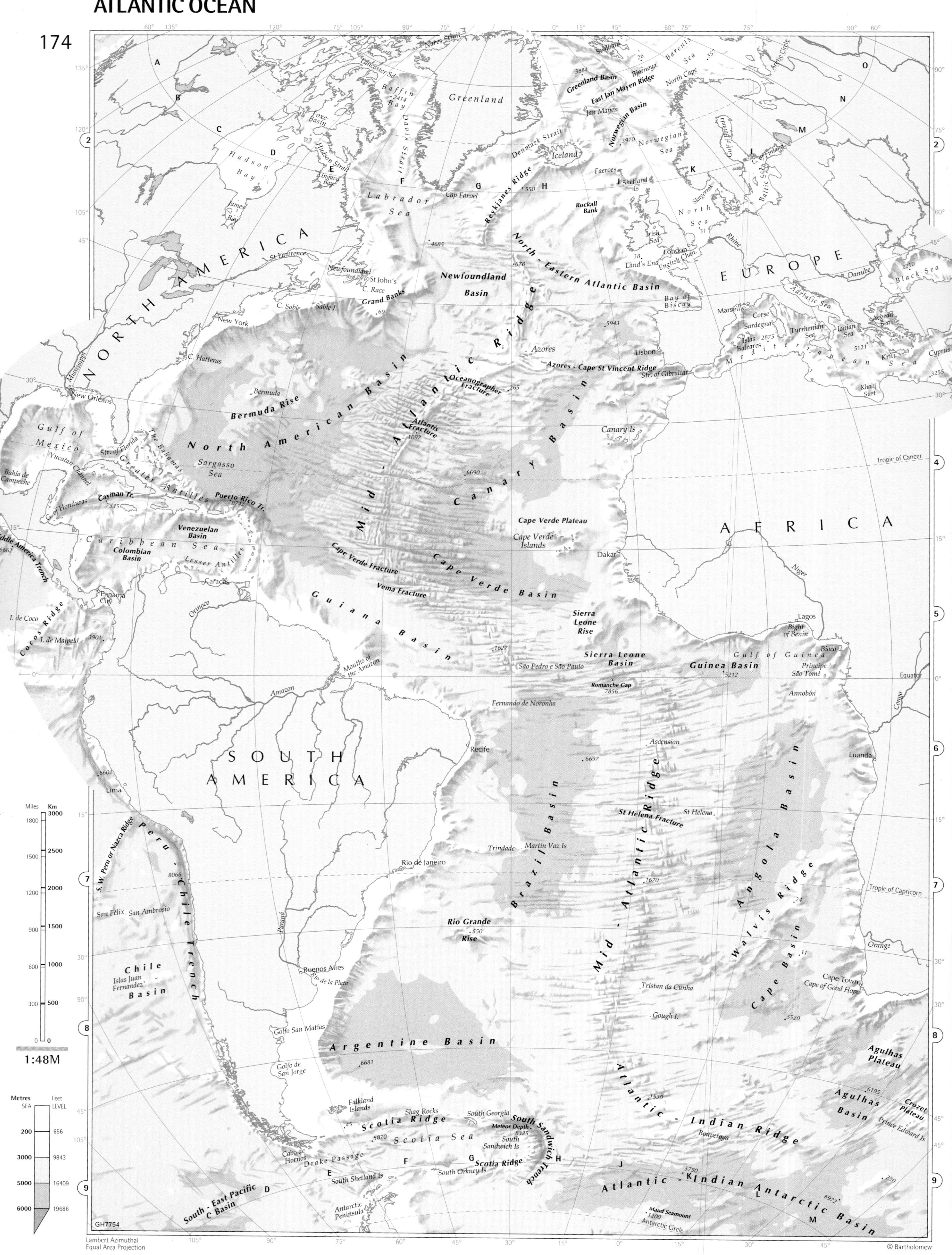

ATLANTIC OCEAN

NORTH AMERICA

SOUTH AMERICA

EUROPE

AFRICA

Greenland

Greenland Basin
East Jan Mayen Ridge
Jan Mayen
Norwegian Basin
Norwegian Sea
Iceland
Reykjanes Ridge
Denmark Strait
Cap Farvel
Labrador Sea
Baffin Bay
Davis Strait
Hudson Bay
Foxe Basin
Ungava Bay
James Bay
Hudson Strait
St Lawrence
Newfoundland
St John's
C. Race
C. Sable
Sable I.
Grand Banks
Newfoundland Basin
New York
C. Hatteras
Bermuda
Bermuda Rise
North American Basin
Sargasso Sea
Gulf of Mexico
New Orleans
Mississippi
Str. of Florida
Yucatan Channel
Bahía de Campeche
G. of Honduras
The Bahamas
Greater Antilles
Cayman Tr.
7535
Puerto Rico Tr.
Venezuelan Basin
Caribbean Sea
Colombian Basin
Middle America Trench
6662
Lesser Antilles
Caracas
Panama City
I. de Coco
Cocos Ridge
I. de Malpelo
3901
Mid-Atlantic Ridge
Oceanographer Fracture
265
Atlantis Fracture
1092
6690
Azores
Azores - Cape St Vincent Ridge
5943
Lisbon
Str. of Gibraltar
Marseille
Corse
Sardegna
Islas Baleares
2875
Tyrrhenian Sea
Mediterranean Sea
Ionian Sea
Aegean Sea
5121
Kriti
Cyprus
3255
Khalij Surt
North - Eastern Atlantic Basin
Bay of Biscay
Land's End
London
English Chan.
Irish Sea
Rhine
Rockall Bank
Faeroes
Shetland Is
North Sea
31
550
678
4685
Skagerrak
Baltic Sea
Gulf of Bothnia
Greenland
Barents Sea
North Cape
Bjørnøya
26
357
3884
Spitsbergen
Arctic Circle
3970
38.
Danube
2210
Black Sea
Adriatic Sea
Tropic of Cancer
Canary Is
Canary Basin
Cape Verde Plateau
Cape Verde Islands
Dakar
Cape Verde Fracture
Vema Fracture
Cape Verde Basin
Sierra Leone Rise
Sierra Leone Basin
São Pedro e São Paulo
1627
Guinea Basin
5212
Gulf of Guinea
Principe
São Tomé
Bioco I.
Lagos
Bight of Benin
Niger
Annobón
Guiana Basin
Mouth of the Amazon
Amazon
Orinoco
Fernando de Noronha
Recife
6697
Romanche Gap
7856
Equator
Ascension
Congo
Luanda
Brazil Basin
Mid - Atlantic Ridge
St Helena Fracture
St Helena
1670
Angola Basin
Rio de Janeiro
Trindade
Martin Vaz Is
Rio Grande Rise
550
Tristan da Cunha
Gough I.
Walvis Ridge
24
Tropic of Capricorn
Orange
11
Cape Basin
Cape Town
Cape of Good Hope
5520
Argentine Basin
6681
Buenos Aires
Río de la Plata
Golfo San Matías
Golfo de San Jorge
Paraná
Peru - Chile Trench
S.W. Peru or Nazca Ridge
8066
San Félix
San Ambrosio
Lima
6601
Islas Juan Fernandez
Chile Basin
South - East Pacific Basin
Cabo de Hornos
Drake Passage
South Shetland Is
Antarctic Peninsula
Falkland Islands
45
Scotia Ridge
Shag Rocks
South Georgia
Scotia Sea
5870
South Orkney Is
South Sandwich Is
Meteor Depth
8325
South Sandwich Trench
Scotia Ridge
Atlantic - Indian Ridge
7538
Bouvetøya
Agulhas Plateau
6195
Agulhas Basin
Crozet Plateau
Prince Edward Is
5750
Atlantic - Indian Antarctic Basin
6972
Maud Seamount
1200
Antarctic Circle
230

Miles   Km
1800   3000
1500   2500
        2000
1200
900   1500
600   1000
300   500
0   0

1:48M

Metres   Feet
SEA   LEVEL
200   656
3000   9843
5000   16409
6000   19686

A B C D E F G H J K L M N O

2 4 5 6 7 8 9

60° 135° 120° 105° 90° 75° 60° 45° 30° 15° 0° 15° 30° 45° 60° 75° 90° 60°

GH7754

Lambert Azimuthal Equal Area Projection

© Bartholomew

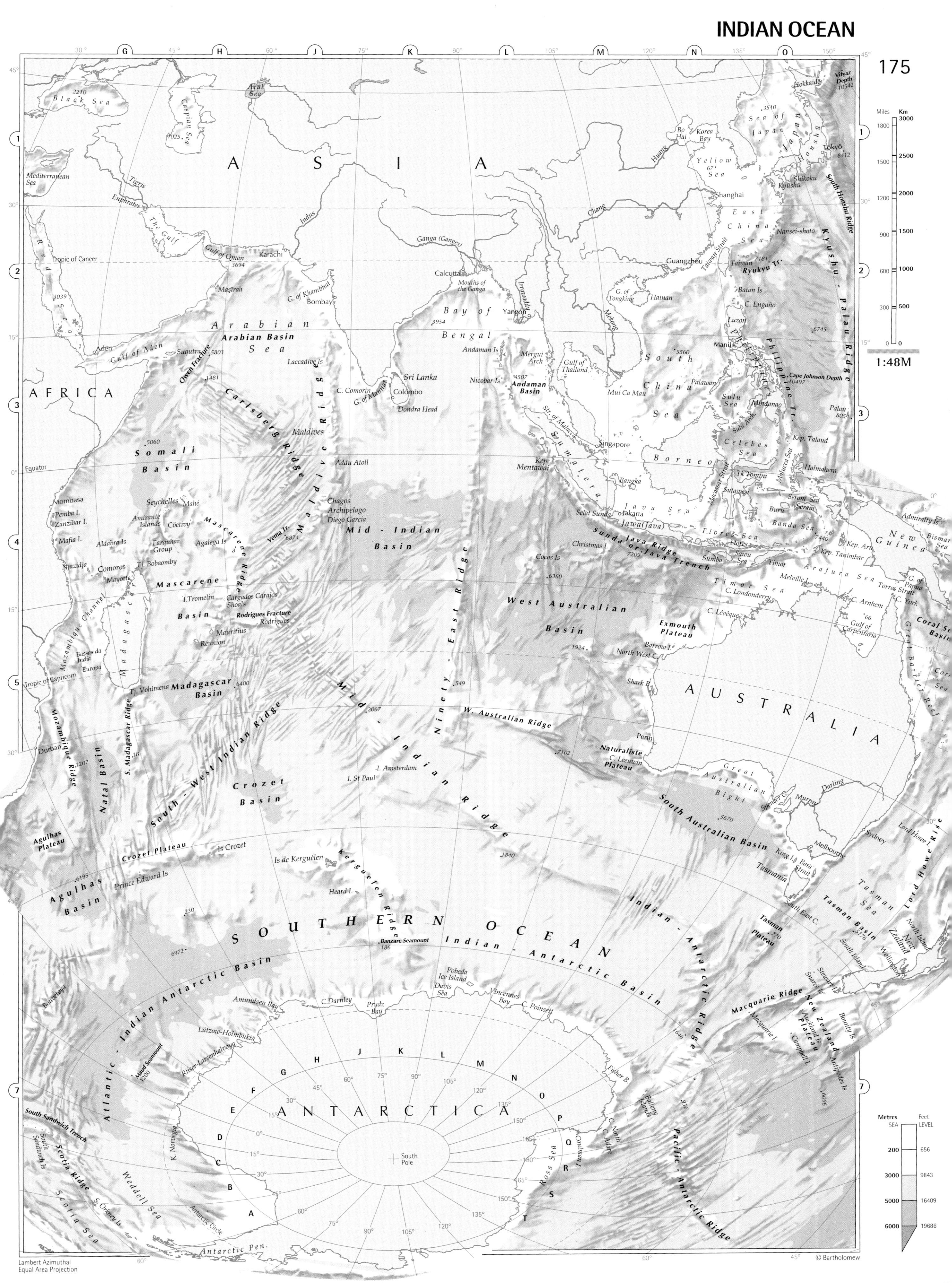

Miles Km
1:48M

Metres Feet
SEA LEVEL
200 656
3000 9843
5000 16409
6000 19686

Lambert Azimuthal
Equal Area Projection

© Bartholomew

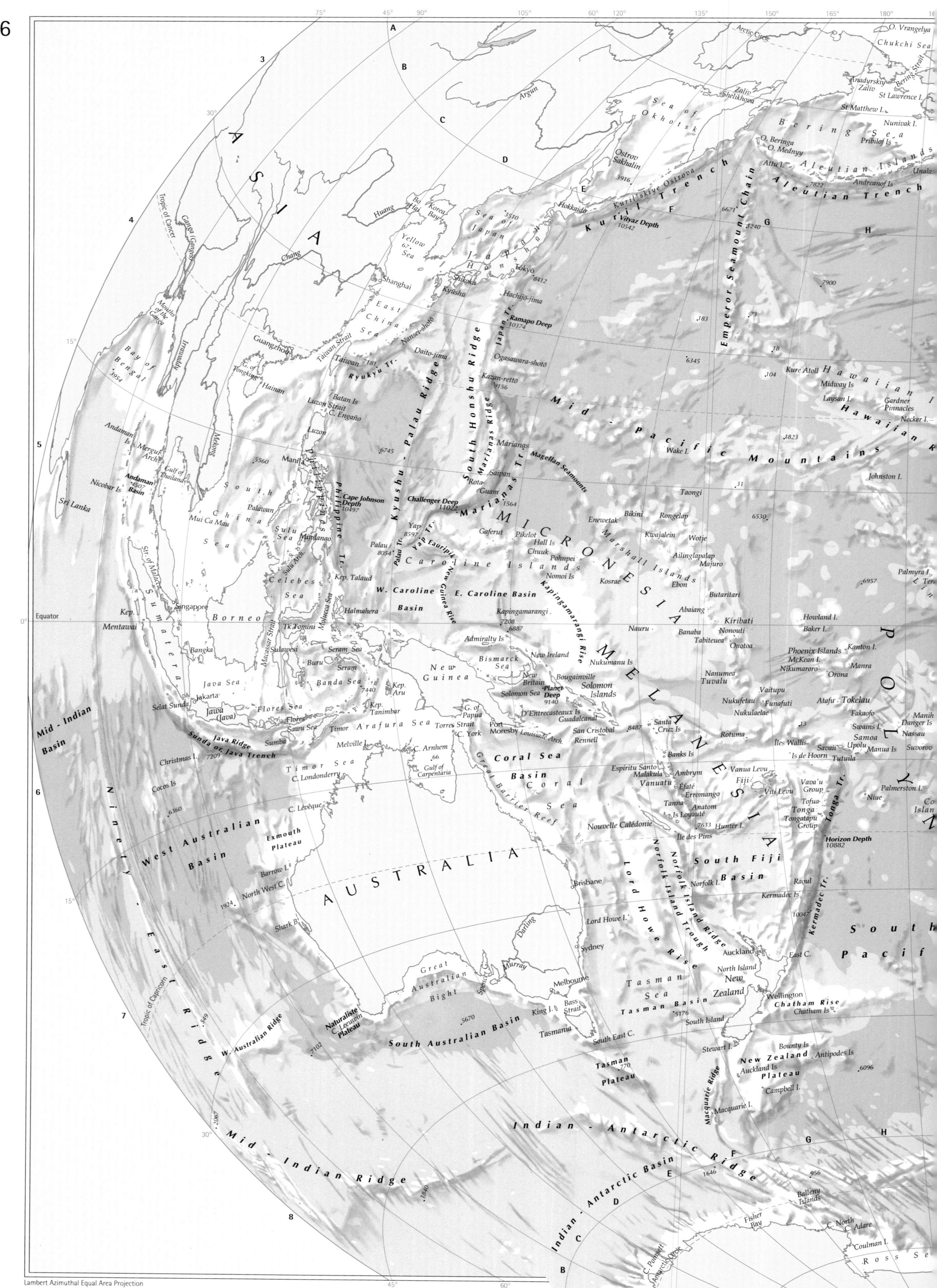

176

Lambert Azimuthal Equal Area Projection

Barrow
Mackenzie
Gulf of Alaska
Kodiak I.
Alexander Archipelago
Queen Charlotte Islands
Vancouver Island · Vancouver
Columbia
Hudson Bay
Amundsen Bay

NORTH AMERICA

Mendocino Seascarp
C. Mendocino 2733
San Francisco
Erben Tablemount 412
Los Angeles
Murray Seascarp
6217
Molokai Fracture Zone
Guadalupe
Golfo de California
Colorado
Missouri
Mississippi
New Orleans
Gulf of Mexico
Bahía de Campeche
G. of Honduras
Yucatan Channel
Str. of Florida
The Bahamas
Greater Antilles
Cayman Tr. -7535
Colombian Basin
Panama City
Venezuelan Basin
Caribbean Sea
Lesser Antilles
Puerto Rico Tr. -8742
Margarita

New York
C. Sable I.
C. Hatteras
Bermuda Rise
Bermuda
North American Basin

Mid-Atlantic Ridge
Atlantis Fracture
Hudson Basin
Cape Verde Fracture
Vema Fracture
Guiana Basin

Maui
Hawaii
7022
Kiritimati
Clarion Fracture Zone
Is Revillagigedo
I. Clarión · I. Socorro
Clipperton Fracture Zone
Clipperton I.
.20
.10
East Pacific Rise
Tehuantepec Ridge
Middle America Trench
G. de Tehuantepec -6662
I. de Coco
Cocos Ridge
I. de Malpelo
Islas Galápagos
Carnegie Ridge
G. de Guayaquil
Orinoco
Amazon
Mouths of the Amazon

Malden I.
Starbuck I.
Flint I.
Tongareva
Caroline I.
Nuku Hiva
Is Marquises
Hiva Oa
Is du Roi Georges
Îles de Désappointement
1929
Is Tuamotu
4385.
SOUTH AMERICA

Rarotonga
Raiatea
Is de la Société
Tahiti
Anaa
Hao
Héréhérétué
Îles Duc de Gloucester
Mangaia
Îles Maria
Tubuai
Raivavae
Mururoa
Groupe Actéon
Is Gambier
Henderson I.
Pitcairn I.
Ducie I.
Is Tubuai
Rapa
3344
East Pacific Ridge
Easter Island Fracture Zone
Easter I.
I. Sala y Gómez
San Félix · San Ambrosio
Is Juan Fernández
Robinson Crusoe
Peru Basin
S.W. Peru or Nazca Ridge
.5470
Peru
Chile Trench
Lima
.6601
Callao

West Basin
.5420
Challenger Fracture Zone
.2743
Chile Basin
Santiago
Río de Janeiro
Paraná
Río de la Plata
Buenos Aires

POLYNESIA
Antarctic Ridge
Eltanin Fracture Zone
Pacific
J · K · L · M · N · O · P
.5210
South-East Pacific Basin
Amundsen Sea
Peter I Oy
Antarctic Peninsula
South Shetland Is
Drake Passage
Cabo de Hornos
Golfo San Jorge
Golfo de San Matías
Scotia Sea
Scotia Ridge
Falkland Is
Argentine Basin
.6681

© Bartholomew

Miles | Km
1800 | 3000
1500 | 2500
1200 | 2000
900 | 1500
600 | 1000
300 | 500
0 | 0

1:48M

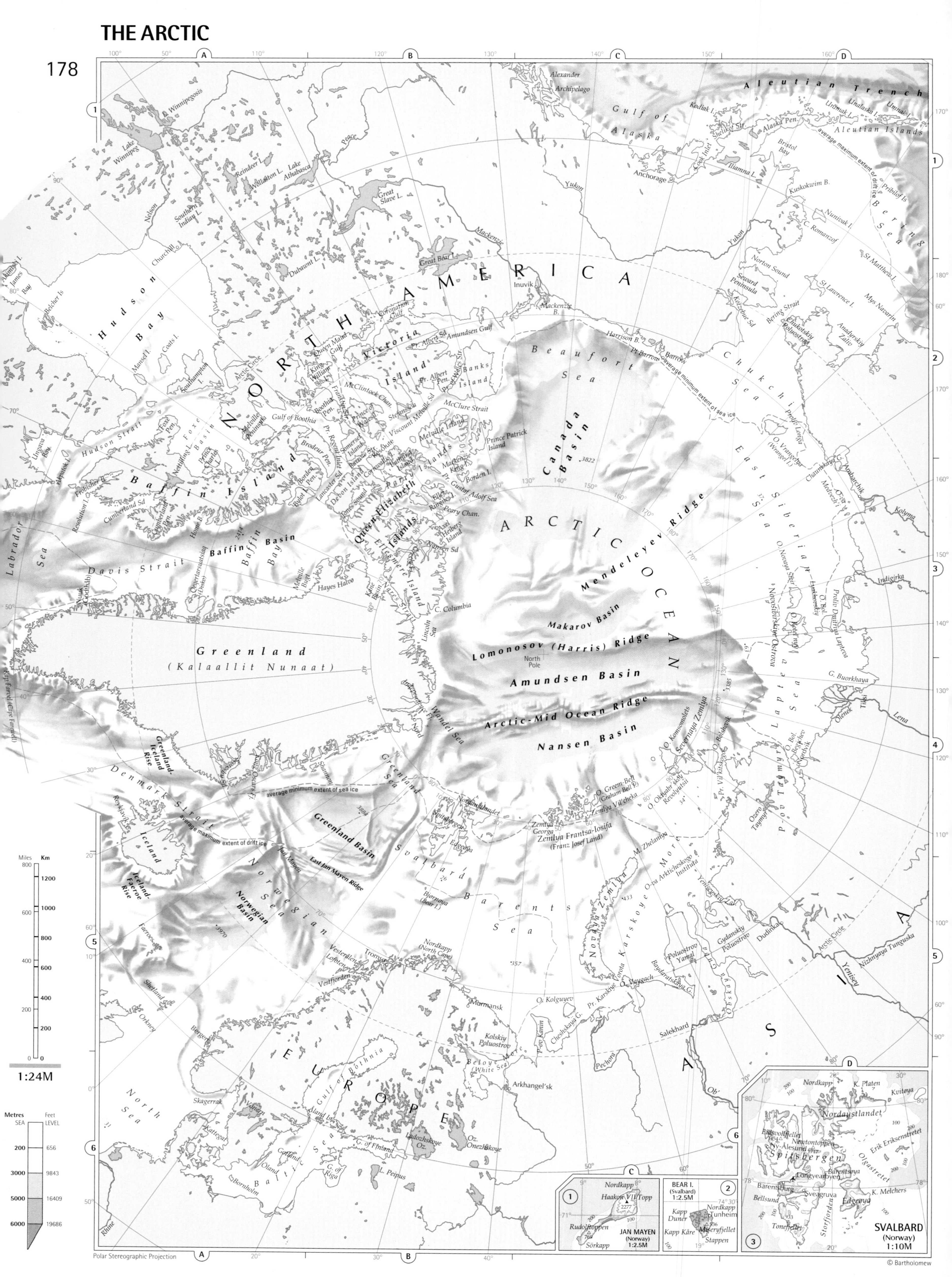

1:24M

Polar Stereographic Projection

© Bartholomew

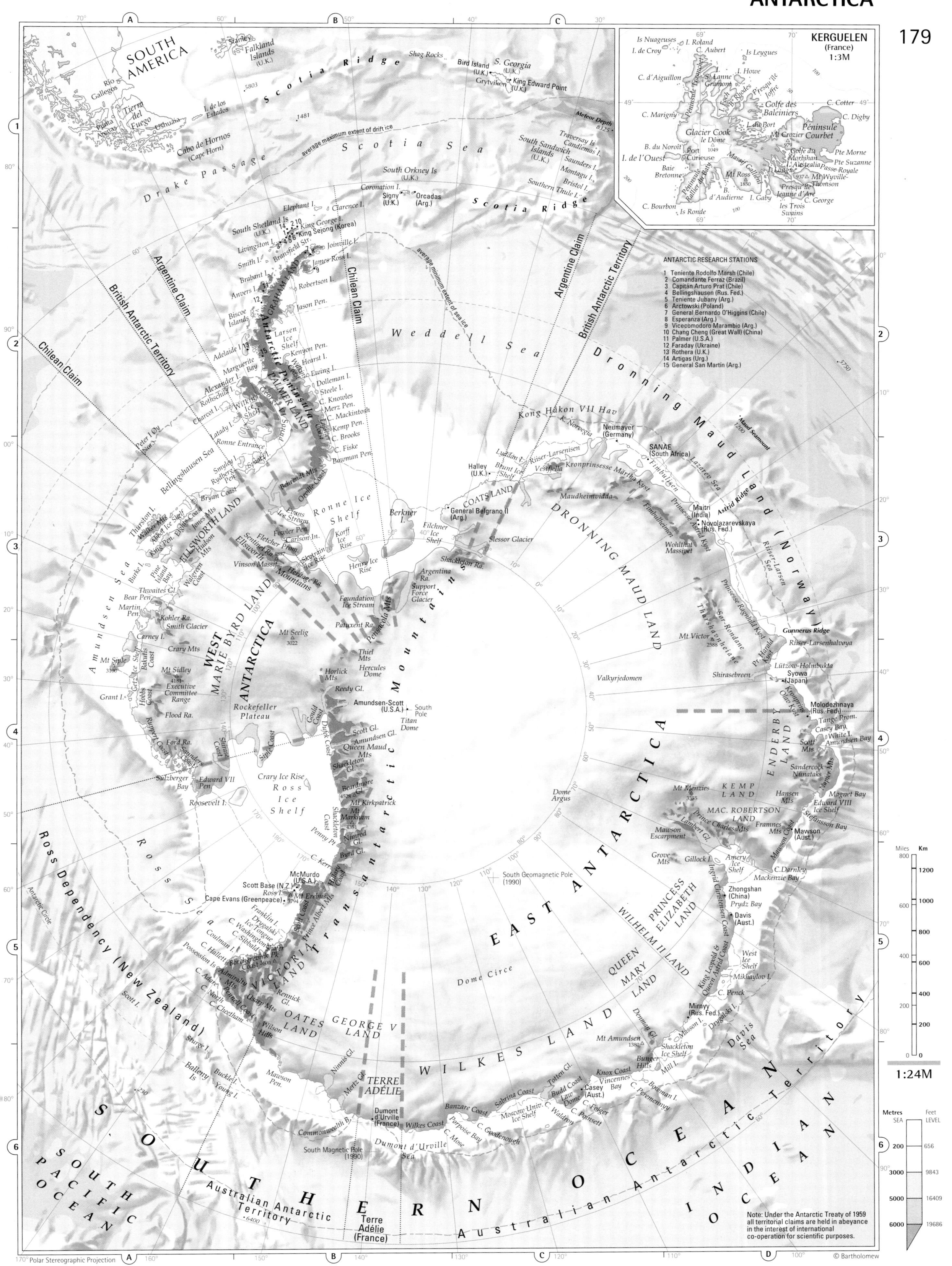

KERGUELEN
(France) 1:3M

ANTARCTIC RESEARCH STATIONS
1 Teniente Rodolfo Marsh (Chile)
2 Comandante Ferraz (Brazil)
3 Capitán Arturo Prat (Chile)
4 Bellingshausen (Rus. Fed.)
5 Teniente Jubany (Arg.)
6 Arctowski (Poland)
7 General Bernardo O'Higgins (Chile)
8 Esperanza (Arg.)
9 Viceacomodoro Marambio (Arg.)
10 Chang Cheng (Great Wall) (China)
11 Palmer (U.S.A.)
12 Faraday (Ukraine)
13 Rothera (U.K.)
14 Artigas (Uru.)
15 General San Martin (Arg.)

Miles   Km
800   1200

600   1000
         800

400   600

200   400
         200

0   0

1:24M

Metres   Feet
SEA   LEVEL

200   656

3000   9843

5000   16409

6000   19686

Note: Under the Antarctic Treaty of 1959
all territorial claims are held in abeyance
in the interest of international
co-operation for scientific purposes.

© Bartholomew

Polar Stereographic Projection

THE INDEX INCLUDES the names on the maps in the ATLAS of the WORLD section. The names are indexed to the largest scale map on which they appear, and can be located using the grid reference letters and numbers around the map frame. Names on insets have a symbol: □, followed by the inset number.

Abbreviations used to describe features in the index, and for country names in the index, are explained on the right. Abbreviations used in feature names on the maps, and within feature names in the index, are explained on pages 82 and 83 of the Introduction to the Atlas.

A.C.T.	Australian Capital Territory
b.	bay
B.C.	British Columbia
Bos.-Herz.	Bosnia-Herzegovina
c.	cape
chan.	channel
div.	division
est.	estuary
g.	gulf
gl.	glacier
h.	hill, hills
i., I.	island
is, Is	islands
l.	lake
lag.	lagoon
mt.	mountain
mts	mountains
N.	North
nat. park	national park
N.W.T.	Northwest Territories
pen.	peninsula
plat.	plateau
P.N.G.	Papua New Guinea
pt	point
r.	river
reg.	region
Rep.	Republic
res.	reserve
resr	reservoir
Rus. Fed.	Russian Federation
S.	South
Str.	Strait
Terr.	Territory
U.A.E.	United Arab Emirates
U.K.	United Kingdom
U.S.A.	United States of America
v.	valley

A

86 B2 **Aa r.** France
83 E1 **Aach r.** Germany
74 D5 **Aach** Germany
74 B2 **Aachen** Germany
83 D1 **Aadorf** Switzerland
74 F4 **Aalen** Germany
68 C2 **Aalsmeer** Netherlands
69 B4 **Aalst div.** *Oost-Vlaanderen* Belgium
69 C4 **Aalst** Belgium
68 E3 **Aalten** Netherlands
69 B3 **Aalter** Belgium
130 D3 **Aansluit** South Africa
82 D1 **Aarau** Switzerland
82 C1 **Aarberg** Switzerland
82 C1 **Aarburg** Switzerland
69 B3 **Aardenburg** Netherlands
82 D1 **Aare r.** Switzerland
82 D1 **Aargau div.** Switzerland
69 C4 **Aarschot** Belgium
69 C3 **Aartselaar** Belgium
82 C1 **Aarwangen** Switzerland
67 B3 **Aasleagh** Rep. of Ireland
32 C1 **Aba** China
123 F5 **Aba** Nigeria
124 F3 **Aba** Zaire
119 H2 **Abā ad Dūd** Saudi Arabia
163 F5 **Abacaxis r.** Brazil
39 B3 **Abādān** Iran
39 C3 **Abādeh** Iran
98 D4 **Abadengo reg.** Spain
99 F4 **Abades** Spain
168 E3 **Abadia dos Dourados** Brazil
168 D2 **Abadiânia** Brazil
98 C1 **Abadín** Spain
120 D2 **Abadla** Algeria
169 F3 **Abaeté r.** Brazil
169 F3 **Abaeté** Brazil
166 C1 **Abaetetuba** Brazil
31 F2 **Abagaytuy** Rus. Fed.
31 E4 **Abag Qi** China
123 F5 **Abai div.** Nigeria
98 B1 **A Baiuca** Spain
123 F5 **Abaji** Nigeria
153 E4 **Abajo Pk summit** *Utah* U.S.A.
123 F5 **Abakaliki** Nigeria
47 L2 **Abakan r.** Rus. Fed.
47 M2 **Abakan** Rus. Fed.
47 L2 **Abakanskiy Khrebet mountain range** Rus. Fed.
124 C4 **Abala** Congo
123 E4 **Abala** Niger
123 F3 **Abalak** Niger
123 F3 **Abalemma well** Niger
121 E4 **Abalessa** Algeria
39 C3 **Āb Anbār** Iran
164 B2 **Abancay** Peru
124 B3 **Abanga r.** Gabon
103 B6 **Abanilla** Spain
103 B6 **Abarán** Spain
39 C3 **Abarqū** Iran
98 C2 **A Barrela** Spain
28 K1 **Abashiri** Japan
28 K2 **Abashiri-gawa r.** Japan
28 K2 **Abashiri-ko l.** Japan
28 K1 **Abashiri-wan b.** Japan
127 C5 **Abasula waterhole** Kenya
47 H1 **Abatskiy** Rus. Fed.
6 □1 **Abau** P.N.G.
79 L3 **Abaújszántó** Hungary
47 H3 **Abay** Kazakhstan
126 C3 **Ābaya Hāyk' l.** Ethiopia
Ābay Wenz *see* **Blue Nile**
47 M2 **Abaza** Rus. Fed.
124 C2 **Abba** Central African Rep.
108 D2 **Abbadia San Salvatore** Italy
39 D2 **Abbāsābād** Iran
108 A4 **Abbasanta** *Sardegna* Italy
148 C2 **Abbaye, Pt pt** *Michigan* U.S.A.
59 E4 **Abbekås** Sweden
126 D2 **Abbe, L. l.** Ethiopia
151 E6 **Abbeville** *Louisiana* U.S.A.
145 D5 **Abbeville** *S. Carolina* U.S.A.
86 A2 **Abbeville** France
67 B4 **Abbeyfeale** Rep. of Ireland
66 E6 **Abbey Head headland** *Scotland* U.K.
15 F2 **Abbey Peak h.** *Queensland* Australia
65 E3 **Abbeytown** *England* U.K.
106 C3 **Abbiategrasso** Italy
56 E2 **Abborrträsk** Sweden
179 A3 **Abbot Ice Shelf ice feature** Antarctica
15 F4 **Abbot, Mt mt.** *Queensland* Australia
62 D4 **Abbotsbury** *England* U.K.
136 E5 **Abbotsford** *B.C.* Canada
148 B3 **Abbotsford** *Wisconsin* U.S.A.
63 F3 **Abbots Langley** *England* U.K.
153 F4 **Abbott** *New Mexico* U.S.A.
36 C2 **Abbottabad** Pakistan
42 D2 **'Abd al 'Azīz, J. h.** Syria
126 □ **'Abd al Kūrī i.** *Socotra* Yemen
50 J4 **Abdi** Rus. Fed.
39 D2 **Abdolabād** Iran
39 D1 **Abdollāhābād** Iran
39 C2 **Abdollāhābād** Iran
46 D2 **Abdulino** Rus. Fed.
118 D5 **Abéché** Chad
39 D3 **Āb-e Garm** Iran
123 E3 **Abeïbara well** Mali
99 H3 **Abejar** Spain
103 C5 **Abejuela** Spain
123 F5 **Abejukolo** Nigeria
100 B2 **Abela** Portugal
123 F3 **Abélajouad well** Niger
69 A4 **Abele** Belgium
9 D4 **Abel Tasman National Park nat. park** New Zealand
122 D5 **Abengourou** Côte d'Ivoire
101 F2 **Abenójar** Spain
55 B4 **Åbenrå** Denmark
55 B4 **Åbenrå Fjord inlet** Denmark
75 G4 **Abens r.** Germany
75 G4 **Abensberg** Germany
123 E5 **Abeokuta** Nigeria
62 B2 **Aberaeron** *Wales* U.K.
66 F3 **Aberchirder** *Scotland* U.K.
62 C1 **Aberconwy and Colwyn div.** *Wales* U.K.
62 C3 **Aberdare** *Wales* U.K.
62 B2 **Aberdaron** *Wales* U.K.
147 E5 **Aberdeen** *Maryland* U.S.A.
151 F5 **Aberdeen** *Mississippi* U.S.A.
13 G3 **Aberdeen** *New South Wales* Australia
137 H4 **Aberdeen** *Saskatchewan* Canada
66 F3 **Aberdeen** *Scotland* U.K.
150 D2 **Aberdeen** *S. Dakota* U.S.A.
152 B2 **Aberdeen** *Washington* U.S.A.
27 □ **Aberdeen** Hong Kong
130 E6 **Aberdeen** South Africa
66 F3 **Aberdeen, City of div.** *Scotland* U.K.
137 J2 **Aberdeen Lake l.** *N.W.T.* Canada
66 F3 **Aberdeenshire div.** *Scotland* U.K.
62 B2 **Aberdyfi** *Wales* U.K.
66 E4 **Aberfeldy** *Scotland* U.K.
65 G4 **Aberford** *England* U.K.
66 D4 **Aberfoyle** *Scotland* U.K.
62 C3 **Abergavenny** *Wales* U.K.
62 C1 **Abergele** *Wales* U.K.
Abergwaun *see* **Fishguard**
65 F1 **Aberlady** *Scotland* U.K.
151 C5 **Abernathy** *Texas* U.S.A.
65 E1 **Abernethy** *Scotland* U.K.
62 B2 **Aberporth** *Wales* U.K.
62 B2 **Abersoch** *Wales* U.K.
75 H2 **Abertamy** Czech Rep.
Abertawe *see* **Swansea**
62 C3 **Abertillery** *Wales* U.K.
65 E1 **Aberuthven** *Scotland* U.K.
62 B2 **Aberystwyth** *Wales* U.K.
107 E4 **Abetone** Italy
119 H4 **Abhā** Saudi Arabia
39 B1 **Abhar r.** Iran
39 B1 **Abhar** Iran
54 D2 **Abia** Estonia
126 C3 **Ābīata Hāyk' l.** Ethiopia
39 B2 **Ab-i Bazuft r.** Iran
122 D5 **Abidjan** Côte d'Ivoire
102 C2 **Abiego** Spain
130 C3 **Abiekwasputs salt pan** South Africa
39 G2 **Ab-i-Istada l.** Afghanistan
126 C3 **Abijatta-Shalla National Park nat. park** Ethiopia
39 D2 **Ab-i-Kavir salt flat** Iran
29 H6 **Abiko** Japan
150 D4 **Abilene** *Kansas* U.S.A.
151 D5 **Abilene** *Texas* U.S.A.
63 E3 **Abingdon** *England* U.K.
148 B5 **Abingdon** *Illinois* U.S.A.
146 C6 **Abingdon** *Virginia* U.S.A.
66 E5 **Abington** *Scotland* U.K.
15 G3 **Abington Reef reef** *Coral Sea Islands Terr.* Pacific Ocean
51 F6 **Abinsk** Rus. Fed.
99 H3 **Abión r.** Spain
39 E2 **Ab-i-Rahuk** Afghanistan
39 F1 **Ab-i-Safed r.** Afghanistan
164 A1 **Abiseo, Parque Nacional nat. park** Peru
137 H2 **Abitau Lake l.** *N.W.T.* Canada
140 E2 **Abitibi r.** *Ontario* Canada
140 E2 **Abitibi Canyon Dam dam** *Ontario* Canada
140 E2 **Abitibi, Lake l.** *Ontario/Québec* Canada
51 G7 **Abkhazia div.** Georgia
Abkhazskaya Respublika *see* **Abkhazia**
101 H3 **Abla** Spain
89 G3 **Ablis** France
12 C1 **Abminga** *S. Australia* Australia
119 F2 **Abnûb** Egypt
122 D5 **Aboisso** Côte d'Ivoire
126 B3 **Aboke** Sudan
123 E5 **Abomey** Benin
36 C3 **Abonar** India
90 E2 **Abondance** France
124 B3 **Abong Mbang** Cameroon
79 K4 **Abony** Hungary
122 D5 **Abooso** Ghana
23 A4 **Aborlan** Philippines
124 C1 **Abou Déia** Chad
42 F1 **Abovyan** Armenia
66 F3 **Aboyne** *Scotland* U.K.
Abqaiq *see* **Buqayq**
164 C4 **Abra** Chile
126 E1 **Abrād, W. watercourse** Yemen
159 D2 **Abraham's Bay** The Bahamas
100 B1 **Abrantes** Portugal
170 C1 **Abra Pampa** Argentina
98 C4 **Abraveses** Portugal
169 G4 **Abre Campo** Brazil
98 C3 **Abreiro** Portugal
87 G4 **Abreschviller** France
119 F3 **'Abri** Sudan
91 E4 **Abriès** France
173 K3 **Abril, 19 de** Uruguay
112 D1 **Abrud** Romania
54 C2 **Abruka i.** Estonia
109 F2 **Abruzzo div.** Italy
109 F3 **Abruzzo, Parco Nazionale d' nat. park** Italy
80 C3 **Absam** Austria
152 E2 **Absaroka Range mountain range** *Montana/Wyoming* U.S.A.
81 G2 **Absdorf** Austria
41 H1 **Abşeron Yarımdası pen.** Azerbaijan
75 J5 **Abtenau** Austria
74 E4 **Abtsgmünd** Germany
28 C6 **Abu** Japan
43 D2 **Abū aḑ Ḑuhūr** Syria
39 B4 **Abū'Alī i.** Saudi Arabia
39 C4 **Abual Jirab i.** U.A.E.
43 D5 **Abu 'Amūd, W. watercourse** Jordan
119 H4 **Abū 'Arīsh** Saudi Arabia
43 C4 **Abu 'Aweigîla well** Egypt
119 E3 **Abu Ballûs h.** Egypt
119 F4 **Abu Deleiq** Sudan
Abu Dhabi *see* **Abū Ẓabī**
119 G3 **Abū Ḑībā'** Saudi Arabia
43 B5 **Abu Durba** Egypt
43 B5 **Abu Hâd, W. watercourse** Egypt
43 D3 **Abu Hafrah, W. watercourse** Jordan
119 E1 **Abu Haggag** Egypt
43 D4 **Abū Hallūfa, J. h.** Jordan
119 F4 **Abu Hamed** Sudan
119 F4 **Abu Hashim watercourse** Sudan
119 F5 **Abu Hut watercourse** Sudan
123 F5 **Abuja** Nigeria
43 A4 **Abu Kebîr** Egypt
77 N2 **Abukhava** Belarus
118 E5 **Abu Ku** Sudan
29 H5 **Abukuma-gawa r.** Japan
29 H5 **Abukuma-kochi plat.** Japan
119 G4 **Abū Latt I. i.** Saudi Arabia
124 E1 **Abu Matariq** Sudan
124 D3 **Abumombazi** Zaire
39 C4 **Abū Mūsá i.** U.A.E.
164 C1 **Abunã r.** Bolivia
164 C1 **Abunã** Brazil
162 D4 **Abunai** Brazil
118 C2 **Abū Nā'im well** Libya
126 C2 **Ābune Yosēf mt.** Ethiopia
118 C1 **Abū Nujaym** Libya
43 D2 **Abū Qa'ţūr** Syria
43 A6 **Abu Qurqâs** Egypt
124 F3 **Aburo mt.** Zaire
36 C4 **Abu Road** India
119 G3 **Abū Rubayq** Saudi Arabia
43 B5 **Abu Rudeis** Egypt
43 D5 **Abu Sallah watercourse** Saudi Arabia
119 E5 **Abu Shanab** Sudan
119 F3 **Abu Simbel** Egypt
119 F3 **Abu Simbel Temple** Egypt
42 F4 **Abū Şukhayr** Iraq
9 C5 **Abut Head headland** New Zealand
43 D5 **Abū Ujayyijāt well** Saudi Arabia
126 C2 **Abuye Meda mt.** Ethiopia
23 C4 **Abuyog** Philippines
119 E5 **Abu Zabad** Sudan
39 C4 **Abū Ẓabī** U.A.E.
119 F2 **Abu Zenîma** Egypt
59 F3 **Åby** Sweden
119 E5 **Abyad** Sudan
119 E4 **Abyad Plateau, Jebel plat.** Sudan
118 D1 **Abyār an Nākhīlah well** Libya
43 C5 **Abyār Banī Murr well** Saudi Arabia
55 B2 **Åbybro** Denmark
16 B4 **Abydos** *Western Australia* Australia
124 E2 **Abyei** Sudan
118 C5 **Ab Zérafa** Chad
162 C1 **A. Cadazzi** Colombia
147 J2 **Acadia Nat. Park nat. park** *Maine* U.S.A.
157 E4 **Acambaro** Mexico
157 H4 **Acancéh** Mexico
162 B2 **Acandí** Colombia
98 B2 **A Cañiza** Spain
156 D4 **Acaponeta** Mexico
157 F5 **Acapulco** Mexico
166 C1 **Acará r.** Brazil
166 C1 **Acará** Brazil
166 C1 **Acará Miri r.** Brazil
166 D1 **Acaraú r.** Brazil
166 D1 **Acaraú** Brazil
165 E5 **Acaray r.** Paraguay
169 F1 **Acari r.** Brazil
166 E2 **Acarí** Brazil
162 D2 **Acarigua** Venezuela
79 M4 **Acâş** Romania
110 D5 **Acate** *Sicilia* Italy
157 F5 **Acatlan** Mexico
157 G5 **Acayucán** Mexico
109 H3 **Accadia** Italy
91 E4 **Acceglio** Italy
109 J4 **Accettura** Italy
109 H4 **Acciaroli** Italy
93 B6 **Accous** France
122 D5 **Accra** Ghana
65 F4 **Accrington** *England* U.K.
109 F2 **Accumoli** Italy
173 G2 **Aceba** Argentina
100 E1 **Acedera** Spain
99 H2 **Acedo** Spain
173 K1 **Aceguá** Brazil
109 H4 **Acerenza** Italy
109 H4 **Acerno** Italy
109 G4 **Acerra** Italy
80 C3 **Ach r.** Germany
80 D2 **Ach** Austria
164 C3 **Achacachi** Bolivia
162 D2 **Achaguas** Venezuela
115 C4 **Achaïa div.** Greece
36 D5 **Achalpur** India
38 B2 **Achampet** India
173 J2 **Achar** Uruguay
45 T3 **Achayvayam** Rus. Fed.
123 G3 **Achegour well** Niger
115 C4 **Acheloös r.** Greece
31 H3 **Acheng** China
80 C3 **Achensee l.** Austria
74 D4 **Achern** Germany
86 B2 **Acheux-en-Amiénois** France
86 B2 **Achicourt** France
51 H6 **Achikulak** Rus. Fed.
67 B3 **Achill** Rep. of Ireland
114 D4 **Achilleio** Greece
67 A3 **Achill Head headland** Rep. of Ireland
67 A3 **Achill Island i.** Rep. of Ireland
66 C2 **Achiltibuie** *Scotland* U.K.
72 E2 **Achim** Germany
45 L4 **Achinsk** Rus. Fed.
172 E2 **Achiras** Argentina
47 G4 **Achisay** Kazakhstan
46 E1 **Achit** Rus. Fed.
114 E1 **Achladochori** Greece
64 C1 **Achnacroish** *Scotland* U.K.
66 C3 **Achnasheen** *Scotland* U.K.
43 B2 **Achno** Cyprus
66 C3 **A'Chralaig mt.** *Scotland* U.K.
80 D2 **Achslach** Germany
74 E4 **Achstetten** Germany
111 E5 **Aci Castello** *Sicilia* Italy
111 E5 **Aci Catena** *Sicilia* Italy
42 B2 **Acıpayam** Turkey
111 E5 **Acireale** *Sicilia* Italy
150 E3 **Ackley** *Iowa* U.S.A.
158 D2 **Acklins I. i.** The Bahamas
63 H2 **Acle** *England* U.K.
90 B2 **Acolin r.** France
164 B2 **Acomayo** Peru
172 B2 **Aconcagua, Co mt.** Argentina
166 E2 **Acopiara** Brazil
164 C3 **Acora** Peru
100 □ **Açores, Arquipélago dos is** Portugal
131 H2 **Acornhoek** South Africa
98 B1 **A Coruña** Spain
156 J7 **Acoyapa** Nicaragua
110 D4 **Acquacalda** Italy
107 G5 **Acqualagna** Italy
83 F3 **Acquanegra sul Chiese** Italy
108 D2 **Acquapendente** Italy
83 D2 **Acquarossa** Switzerland
109 F2 **Acquasanta Terme** Italy
109 E2 **Acquasparta** Italy
109 F2 **Acquaviva Picena** Italy
110 D4 **Acquedolci** *Sicilia* Italy
106 C4 **Acqui Terme** Italy
12 C3 **Acraman, L. salt flat** *S. Australia* Australia
164 B1 **Acre div.** Brazil
164 C2 **Acre r.** Brazil
Acre *see* **'Akko**
111 F3 **Acri** Italy
98 C2 **A Cruz de Incio** Spain
A.C.T. div. *see* **Australian Capital Territory**
141 J4 **Acton Vale** *Québec* Canada
166 E2 **Açu** Brazil
166 E2 **Açude Banabuiu resr** Brazil
166 D2 **Açude Boa Esperança resr** Brazil
166 E2 **Açude Orós resr** Brazil
168 D6 **Acungui** Brazil
124 B3 **Acurenam** Equatorial Guinea
146 B4 **Ada** *Ohio* U.S.A.
151 D5 **Ada** *Oklahoma* U.S.A.
29 □2 **Ada** Japan
79 K6 **Ada** Yugoslavia
23 □2 **Adacao** *Guam* Pacific Ocean
126 D2 **Adaela well** Ethiopia
99 F3 **Adaja r.** Spain
126 E3 **Adale well** Ethiopia
Adalia *see* **Antalya**
124 B2 **Adamaoua div.** Cameroon
115 F6 **Adamas** Greece
123 G5 **Adamawa div.** Nigeria
80 B4 **Adamello mt.** Italy
13 G4 **Adaminaby** *New South Wales* Australia
171 E7 **Adam, Mt h.** Falkland Is.
78 F2 **Adamov** Czech Rep.
46 F2 **Adamovka** Rus. Fed.
77 L4 **Adamów** Poland
147 G3 **Adams** *Massachusetts* U.S.A.
148 C4 **Adams** *Wisconsin* U.S.A.
38 B4 **Adam's Bridge reef** India/Sri Lanka
8 □1 **Adams I. i.** *Auckland Is* New Zealand
136 F4 **Adams L. l.** *B.C.* Canada
155 E2 **Adams McGill Reservoir resr** *Nevada* U.S.A.
9 E4 **Adams, Mt h.** New Zealand
136 C3 **Adams Mt. mt.** *Alaska* U.S.A.
152 B2 **Adams, Mt mt.** *Washington* U.S.A.
9 C5 **Adams, Mt mt.** New Zealand
154 B2 **Adams Peak mt.** *California* U.S.A.
38 C5 **Adam's Pk** Sri Lanka
7 □14 **Adam's Rock rock** *Pitcairn I.* Pacific Ocean
7 □14 **Adamstown** *Pitcairn I.* Pacific Ocean
101 F2 **Adamuz** Spain
126 D2 **'Adan** Yemen
43 C1 **Adana div.** Turkey
42 C2 **Adana** Turkey
99 F4 **Adanero** Spain
22 D2 **Adang, Tk b.** Indonesia
98 C4 **Adão** Portugal
67 C4 **Adare** Rep. of Ireland
179 A5 **Adare, C. c.** Antarctica
15 F5 **Adavale** *Queensland* Australia
155 E2 **Adaven** *Nevada* U.S.A.
54 D3 **Ādaži** Latvia
106 D3 **Adda r.** Italy
124 D2 **Adda watercourse** Central African Rep./Sudan
119 H3 **Ad Dafīnah** Saudi Arabia
41 G4 **Ad Dahnā reg.** Saudi Arabia
120 A4 **Ad Dakhla** *Western Sahara*
126 D2 **Aḑ Ḑāli'** Yemen
39 B4 **Ad Dammām** Saudi Arabia
119 H4 **Ad Darb** Saudi Arabia
119 H3 **Ad Dawādimī** Saudi Arabia
39 B4 **Ad Dawhah** Qatar
43 D2 **Ad Daww plain** Syria
123 F3 **Addax, Réserve Naturelle intégrale dite Sanctuaire des res.** Niger
63 E2 **Adderbury** *England* U.K.
41 G5 **Ad Dir'īyah** Saudi Arabia
147 K2 **Addison** *Maine* U.S.A.
42 F4 **Ad Dīwānīyah** Iraq
63 F3 **Addlestone** *England* U.K.
131 E6 **Addo** South Africa
175 J4 **Addu Atoll atoll**
43 D2 **Ad Duraykīsh** Syria
119 H1 **Ad Duwayd well** Saudi Arabia
145 D6 **Adel** *Georgia* U.S.A.
150 E3 **Adel** *Iowa* U.S.A.
12 D3 **Adelaide** *S. Australia* Australia
145 □2 **Adelaide** The Bahamas
179 B2 **Adelaide I i.** Antarctica
14 B2 **Adelaide River** *Northern Terr.* Australia
154 D4 **Adelanto** *California* U.S.A.
82 C2 **Adelboden** Switzerland
114 E3 **Adelfi i.** Greece
111 F1 **Adelfia** Italy
113 F6 **Adelfoi i.** Greece
172 E2 **Adelia María** Argentina
75 F3 **Adelsdorf** Germany
74 E3 **Adelsheim** Germany
103 B4 **Ademuz** Spain
Aden *see* **'Adan**
74 B2 **Adenau** Germany
72 F2 **Adendorf** Germany
130 E6 **Adendorp** South Africa
41 G7 **Aden, Gulf of g.** Somalia/Yemen
123 F3 **Aderbissinat** Niger
126 D1 **Adhanah, W. watercourse** Yemen
39 C4 **Adh Dhayd** U.A.E.
21 K7 **Adi i.** Indonesia
126 C2 **Ādī Ārk'ay** Ethiopia
100 C3 **Adiça, Serra da h.** Portugal
119 F4 **'Adid Umm Inderab well** Sudan
107 G3 **Adige r.** Italy
126 C2 **Ādīgrat** Ethiopia
126 C2 **Adi Keyih** Eritrea
126 C2 **Adi Kwala** Eritrea
38 B2 **Adilabad** India
126 B4 **Adilanga** Uganda
42 E2 **Adilcevaz** Turkey
152 B3 **Adin** *California* U.S.A.
118 B2 **Adīrī** Libya
147 F2 **Adirondack Mountains mountain range** *New York* U.S.A.
126 C3 **Ādīs Ābeba** Ethiopia
126 C3 **Ādīs Alem** Ethiopia
126 C2 **Ādīs Zemen** Ethiopia
126 C2 **Adi Ugri** Eritrea
42 D2 **Adıyaman** Turkey
112 F1 **Adjud** Romania
145 □3 **Adjuntas** Puerto Rico
157 F4 **Adjuntas, Presa de las resr** Mexico
139 J3 **Adlavik Islands is** *Newfoundland* Canada
51 F7 **Adler** Rus. Fed.
83 D1 **Adliswil** Switzerland
16 D2 **Admiralty Gulf b.** *Western Australia* Australia
16 D2 **Admiralty Gulf Abor. Reserve res.** *Western Australia* Australia
135 K2 **Admiralty Inlet inlet** *N.W.T.* Canada
10 □4 **Admiralty Is is** *Lord Howe I.* Pacific Ocean
136 C3 **Admiralty Island i.** *Alaska* U.S.A.
136 C3 **Admiralty Island Nat. Monument** *Alaska* U.S.A.
6 □1 **Admiralty Islands is** P.N.G.
179 A5 **Admiralty Mts mountain range** Antarctica
81 F3 **Admont** Austria
123 F5 **Ado-Ekiti** Nigeria
126 B3 **Adok** Sudan
173 G5 **Adolfo Gon. Chaves** Argentina
6 □6 **Adolphus Reef reef** Fiji
38 B3 **Adoni** India
79 H4 **Adony** Hungary
75 H2 **Adorf** Germany
124 C3 **Adoumandjali** Central African Rep.
93 A5 **Adour r.** France
101 H4 **Adra r.** Spain
101 G4 **Adra** Spain
99 H3 **Adradas** Spain
124 F3 **Adranga** Zaire
110 D5 **Adrano** *Sicilia* Italy
120 B4 **Adrar div.** Mauritania
120 B4 **Adrâr h.** Mauritania
121 F4 **Adrar mts** Algeria
121 D3 **Adrar** Algeria
123 E3 **Adrar des Ifôghas reg.** Mali
121 F3 **Adrar Ikouhaouene mt.** Algeria
121 F4 **Adrar Mariou mt.** Algeria
121 E3 **Adrar N'Ahnet mts** Algeria
120 A4 **Adrar Souttouf mts** *Western Sahara*
123 F3 **Adrar Tamgak mt.** Niger
43 B1 **Adras D. mt.** Turkey
39 E2 **Adraskand r.** Afghanistan
118 D5 **Adré** Chad
107 G3 **Adria** Italy
149 E5 **Adrian** *Michigan* U.S.A.
151 C5 **Adrian** *Texas* U.S.A.
95 F3 **Adriatic Sea sea** Mediterranean Sea
92 C2 **Adriers** France
155 G6 **Aduana del Sasabe** Mexico
172 B4 **Aduana Pejerrey** Chile
68 E1 **Aduard** Netherlands
83 E2 **Adula Gruppe mt.** Switzerland
54 E3 **Aduliena** Latvia
38 B4 **Adur** India
124 E3 **Adusa** Zaire
126 C2 **Ādwa** Ethiopia
45 P3 **Adycha r.** Rus. Fed.
51 F6 **Adygeya div.** Rus. Fed.
51 F6 **Adygeysk** Rus. Fed.
51 H6 **Adyk** Rus. Fed.
103 C4 **Adzaneta** Spain
53 E2 **Adzhamka** Ukraine
Adzharskaya Respublika *see* **Ajaria**
122 D5 **Adzopé** Côte d'Ivoire
55 C4 **Æbelø i.** Denmark
114 □ **Aegean Sea sea** Greece/Turkey
54 D2 **Aegna i.** Estonia
54 D2 **Aegvidu** Estonia
55 C5 **Ærø i.** Denmark
62 B2 **Aeron r.** *Wales* U.K.
55 C5 **Ærøskøbing** Denmark
72 E3 **Aerzen** Germany
98 B2 **A Estrada** Spain
114 C2 **Aetos** *Dytiki Makedonia* Greece
115 C5 **Aetos** *Peloponnisos* Greece
7 □11 **Afaahiti** *French Polynesia* Pacific Ocean
126 C1 **Afabet** Eritrea
126 D3 **Afaf Badane well** Ethiopia
Afal watercourse *see* **'Ifāl, W.**
115 □ **Afantou** Greece
121 F3 **Afao mt.** Algeria
126 D2 **Afar Depression depression** Eritrea/Ethiopia
7 □11 **Afareaitu** *French Polynesia* Pacific Ocean
88 C4 **Aff r.** France
122 D5 **Afféri** Côte d'Ivoire
80 B2 **Affing** Germany
163 F2 **Affobakka** Surinam
83 D1 **Affoltern am Albis** Switzerland
18 H6 **Afghanistan country** Asia
126 E4 **Afgooye** Somalia
131 F1 **Afguns** South Africa
7 □12 **Afiamalu** Western Samoa
119 H3 **'Afīf** Saudi Arabia
98 B3 **Afife** Portugal
123 F5 **Afikpo** Nigeria
52 B1 **Afim'ino** Rus. Fed.
56 C3 **Åfjord** Norway
123 E5 **Aflao** Ghana
81 G3 **Aflenz Kurort** Austria
121 E2 **Aflou** Algeria
127 D4 **Afmadow** Somalia
134 C4 **Afognak I. i.** *Alaska* U.S.A.
120 A5 **Afojjar well** Mauritania
98 C1 **A Fonsagrada** Spain
169 H4 **Afonso Cláudio** Brazil
98 C2 **A Forxa** Spain
58 C2 **Åfoss** Norway
109 G4 **Afragola** France
166 D2 **Afrânio** Brazil
126 D2 **Āfrēra Terara mt.** Ethiopia
56 J2 **Afrikanda** Rus. Fed.
42 D3 **'Afrīn r.** Syria
43 D1 **'Afrīn r.** Syria/Turkey
42 D2 **Afşin** Turkey
68 D2 **Afsluitdijk dam** Netherlands
126 D3 **Aftol well** Ethiopia
152 E3 **Afton** *Wyoming* U.S.A.
166 B1 **Afuá** Brazil
43 C3 **'Afula** Israel
42 B2 **Afyon** Turkey
31 E2 **Aga r.** Rus. Fed.
43 A4 **Aga** Egypt
75 H2 **Aga** Germany
31 E2 **Aga** Rus. Fed.
123 F2 **Agadez div.** Niger
123 F3 **Agadez** Niger
120 C2 **Agadir** Morocco
118 D4 **Aga Dubé well** Chad
47 H3 **Agadyr'** Kazakhstan
117 K7 **Agalega Islands is**
23 □2 **Agana** *Guam* Pacific Ocean
36 D5 **Agar** India
122 C2 **Agâraktem well** Mali
126 C3 **Āgaro** Ethiopia
37 G5 **Agartala** India
58 D1 **Agåsen h.** Norway
38 A2 **Agashi** India
23 □2 **Agat** *Guam* Pacific Ocean
149 F2 **Agate** *Ontario* Canada
47G3 **Agat, G. h.** Kazakhstan
113 F6 **Agathonisi i.** Greece
35 D8 **Agatti i.** India
123 F5 **Agbor Bojiboji** Nigeria
122 D5 **Agboville** Côte d'Ivoire
42 F1 **Ağcabädi** Azerbaijan
42 F1 **Agdaş** Azerbaijan
Agdash *see* **Agdaş**
91 B5 **Agde** France
Agdzhabedi *see* **Ağcabädi**
93 C4 **Agen** France
93 C4 **Agenais reg.** France
29 G5 **Ageo** Japan
102 D2 **Àger** Spain
55 A4 **Agerbæk** Denmark
126 C3 **Āgere Maryam** Ethiopia
74 D5 **Ägerisee l.** Switzerland
55 C4 **Agernæs pt** Denmark
55 D4 **Agersø i.** Denmark
52 C2 **Ageyevo** Rus. Fed.
81 H3 **Ágfalva** Hungary
130 B4 **Aggeneys** South Africa
74 C2 **Agger r.** Germany
55 B2 **Aggersund** Denmark
108 B4 **Aggius** *Sardegna* Italy
81 G2 **Aggsbach Markt** Austria
79 K3 **Aggteleki nat. park** Hungary
172 C5 **Ag. Guzmán** Argentina
64 B3 **Aghalee** *Northern Ireland* U.K.
64 B2 **Aghanloo** *Northern Ireland* U.K.
120 B4 **Aghaylas well** *Western Sahara*
36 D1 **Aghil Pass pass** China
67 C2 **Aghla Mountain h.** Rep. of Ireland
120 C5 **Aghrîjît well** Mauritania
114 E4 **Agia Anna** Greece
115 F7 **Agia Galini** Greece
115 F4 **Agia Marina** *Attiki* Greece
113 F6 **Agia Marina** *Notio Aiyaion* Greece
115 D6 **Agia Pelagia** Greece
115 C5 **Agia Triada** Greece
115 G7 **Agia Vervara** Greece
112 G2 **Agighiol** Romania
42 D2 **Ağin** Turkey
30 E2 **Aginskiy-Buryatskiy Avt. Okr.** Rus. Fed.
30 E2 **Aginskoye** Rus. Fed.
114 C3 **Agiofyllo** Greece
115 E4 **Agioi Apostoloi** Greece
115 F7 **Agioi Deka** Greece
114 C3 **Agioi Theodoroi** *Dytiki Makedonia* Greece
115 E5 **Agioi Theodoroi** *Pelopónnisos* Greece
114 D3 **Agiokampos** Greece
114 F2 **Agion Oros div.** Greece
114 G2 **Agios Charalampos** Greece
115 E5 **Agios Dimitrios** *Attiki* Greece
114 D2 **Agios Dimitrios** *Kentriki Makedonia* Greece
115 D6 **Agios Dimitrios** *Peloponnisos* Greece
114 G3 **Agios Efstratios i.** Greece
114 F3 **Agios Efstratios** Greece
115 E5 **Agios Georgios i.** Greece
114 C4 **Agios Georgios** *Stereá Ellás* Greece
115 D6 **Agios Ioannis** Greece
115 D5 **Agios Konstantinos** *Peloponnisos* Greece
114 D4 **Agios Konstantinos** *Stereá Ellás* Greece
115 G7 **Agios Myron** Greece
115 B5 **Agios Nikolaos** *Ionioi Nisoi* Greece
114 B3 **Agios Nikolaos** *Ípeiros* Greece
114 E2 **Agios Nikolaos** *Kentriki Makedonia* Greece
115 G7 **Agios Nikolaos** *Kriti* Greece
115 D6 **Agios Nikolaos** *Peloponnisos* Greece

100 C3 **Alcaria Ruiva** Portugal
100 C2 **Alcarrache r.** Portugal/Spain
102 D3 **Alcarràs** Spain
101 F3 **Alcaudete** Spain
99 F5 **Alcaudete de la Jara** Spain
100 D2 **Alcazaba r.** Spain
101 G1 **Alcázar de San Juan** Spain
63 E2 **Alcester** England U.K.
51 F5 **Alchevs'k** Ukraine
172 E2 **Alcira** Argentina
101 F1 **Alcoba** Spain
169 J2 **Alcobaça** Brazil
100 B1 **Alcobaça** Portugal
99 G4 **Alcobendas** Spain
99 H4 **Alcocer** Spain
100 B2 **Alcochete** Portugal
100 B1 **Alcoentre** Portugal
101 F3 **Alcolea** Spain
102 D3 **Alcolea de Cinca** Spain
99 H3 **Alcolea del Pinar** Spain
100 E3 **Alcolea del Río** Spain
100 E1 **Alcollarín** Spain
100 C2 **Alconchel** Spain
103 C4 **Alcora** Spain
99 G4 **Alcorcón** Spain
102 C4 **Alcorisa** Spain
99 H3 **Alcorlo, Emb. de resr** Spain
100 C1 **Alcorneo r.** Portugal/Spain
173 G2 **Alcorta** Argentina
103 D4 **Alcossebre** Spain
100 C3 **Alcoutim** Portugal
102 E3 **Alcover** Spain
103 C6 **Alcoy** Spain
102 C3 **Alcubierre** Spain
99 G3 **Alcubilla de Avellaneda** Spain
101 F2 **Alcudia r.** Spain
103 G5 **Alcúdia** Spain
101 G3 **Alcudia de Guadix** Spain
101 F2 **Alcudia, Sierra de mountain range** Spain
101 F2 **Alcudia, Valle de reg.** Spain
100 D1 **Alcuéscar** Spain
117 J6 **Aldabra Islands is** Seychelles
42 F3 **Al Daghghārah** Iraq
156 D2 **Aldama** Chihuahua Mexico
157 F4 **Aldama** Tamaulipas Mexico
45 P3 **Aldan r.** Rus. Fed.
45 O4 **Aldan** Rus. Fed.
65 H4 **Aldbrough** England U.K.
63 H2 **Alde r.** England U.K.
98 D3 **Aldeadávila de la Ribera** Spain
100 D1 **Aldea del Cano** Spain
99 F4 **Aldea del Fresno** Spain
101 G2 **Aldea del Rey** Spain
99 H3 **Aldealpozo** Spain
98 E4 **Aldeanueva del Camino** Spain
101 E1 **Aldeanueva de San Bartolomé** Spain
98 E3 **Aldearrodrigo** Spain
63 H2 **Aldeburgh** England U.K.
98 C4 **Aldeia de João Pires** Portugal
166 B2 **Aldeia Velha** Brazil
69 E4 **Aldenhoven** Germany
83 G3 **Aldeno** Italy
63 E4 **Alderholt** England U.K.
62 D1 **Alderley Edge** England U.K.
8 F2 **Aldermen Is, The is** New Zealand
63 □2 **Alderney i.** Channel Is.
154 B4 **Alder Peak summit** California U.S.A.
75 J4 **Aldersbach** Germany
63 F3 **Aldershot** England U.K.
146 C6 **Alderson** W. Virginia U.S.A.
112 C4 **Aldinci** Macedonia
65 E3 **Aldingham** England U.K.
80 C3 **Aldrans** Austria
93 A5 **Aldudes** France
148 B5 **Aledo** Illinois U.S.A.
120 B5 **Aleg** Mauritania
97 □ **Alegranza i.** Canary Is Spain
165 E3 **Alegre r.** Brazil
169 H4 **Alegre** Espírito Santo Brazil
166 C1 **Alegre** Pará Brazil
166 B1 **Alegre, Monte h.** Brazil
168 C2 **Alegre, Monte r.** Brazil
125 □ **Alegre, Pto pt** Sao Tome and Principe
167 A6 **Alegrete** Brazil
173 K2 **Alejandro Gallinal** Uruguay
172 F2 **Alejandro Roca** Argentina
172 D5 **Alejandro Stefenelli** Argentina
50 E2 **Alekhovshchina** Rus. Fed.
46 D4 **Aleksandra Bekovicha-Cherkassogo, Zaliv bay** Kazakhstan
52 E3 **Aleksandro-Nevskiy** Rus. Fed.
52 D1 **Aleksandrov** Rus. Fed.
112 C3 **Aleksandrovac** Yugoslavia
51 J5 **Aleksandrov Gay** Rus. Fed.
112 E3 **Aleksandrovo** Bulgaria
51 H6 **Aleksandrovskoye** Rus. Fed.
77 H4 **Aleksandrów** Poland
76 G3 **Aleksandrów Kujawski** Poland
77 H4 **Aleksandrów Łódzki** Poland
47 L3 **Alekseyevka** Kazakhstan
47 H2 **Alekseyevka** Kazakhstan
47 G2 **Alekseyevka** Kazakhstan
47 J2 **Alekseyevka** Kazakhstan
51 F5 **Alekseyevka** Rus. Fed.
53 G1 **Alekseyevka** Rus. Fed.
52 H3 **Alekseyevka** Rus. Fed.
52 F4 **Alekseyevka** Rus. Fed.
52 C2 **Aleksin** Rus. Fed.
112 C3 **Aleksinac** Yugoslavia
52 D2 **Aleksino-Shatur** Rus. Fed.
27 Q1 **Aleksnadrovsk-Sakhalinskiy** Rus. Fed.
59 G3 **Ålem** Sweden
157 F5 **Alemán, Presa, M. resr** Mexico
124 B4 **Alèmbé** Gabon
169 G4 **Além Paraíba** Brazil
56 C3 **Ålen** Norway
89 F3 **Alençon** France
90 B2 **Alène r.** France
100 A1 **Alenquer r.** Portugal
166 B1 **Alenquer** Brazil
100 B1 **Alenquer** Portugal
100 C2 **Alentejo reg.** Portugal
153 □2 **Alenuihaha Channel chan.** Hawaii U.S.A.
122 D5 **Alépé** Côte d'Ivoire
Aleppo see **Ḩalab**
108 B2 **Aléria** Corse France
135 M1 **Alert** N.W.T. Canada
164 B2 **Alerta** Peru
136 D4 **Alert Bay** B.C. Canada
108 A5 **Ales** Sardegna Italy
91 C4 **Alès** France
79 M4 **Aleşd** Romania
106 C4 **Alessandria div.** Piemonte Italy
106 C4 **Alessandria** Alessandria Italy
110 C5 **Alessandria della Rocca** Sicilia Italy
111 H3 **Alessano** Italy
55 B3 **Ålestrup** Denmark
56 B3 **Ålesund** Norway
82 C2 **Aletschhorn mt.** Switzerland
134 B4 **Aleutian Islands** Alaska U.S.A.
134 C4 **Aleutian Range mountain range** Alaska U.S.A.
178 D1 **Aleutian Trench sea feature** Pacific Ocean
45 R4 **Alevina, M. c.** Rus. Fed.
Alevisik see **Samandağı**
147 K2 **Alexander** Maine U.S.A.
134 E4 **Alexander Archipelago is** Alaska U.S.A.
130 A4 **Alexander B. b.** Namibia/South Africa
130 A4 **Alexander Bay** South Africa
145 C5 **Alexander City** Alabama U.S.A.
179 A2 **Alexander I. i.** Antarctica
14 E3 **Alexandra r.** Queensland Australia
13 F4 **Alexandra** Victoria Australia
9 B6 **Alexandra** New Zealand
171 □ **Alexandra, C. c.** S. Georgia Atlantic Ocean
114 D2 **Alexandreia** Greece
Alexandretta see **İskenderun**
148 E5 **Alexandria** Indiana U.S.A.
151 E6 **Alexandria** Louisiana U.S.A.
150 E2 **Alexandria** Minnesota U.S.A.
14 D3 **Alexandria** Northern Terr. Australia
141 H4 **Alexandria** Ontario Canada
66 D5 **Alexandria** Scotland U.K.
146 E5 **Alexandria** Virginia U.S.A.
119 E1 **Alexandria** Egypt
112 E3 **Alexandria** Romania
131 F6 **Alexandria** South Africa
147 F2 **Alexandria Bay** New York U.S.A.
12 D3 **Alexandrina, L. l.** S. Australia Australia
113 E4 **Alexandroupoli** Greece
139 J3 **Alexis r.** Newfoundland Canada
148 B5 **Alexis** Illinois U.S.A.
136 E4 **Alexis Creek** B.C. Canada
47 K2 **Aley r.** Rus. Fed.
43 C3 **'Āley** Lebanon
47 K2 **Aleysk** Rus. Fed.
74 C2 **Alf** Germany
103 C5 **Alfafar** Spain
98 D4 **Alfaiates** Portugal
102 C3 **Alfajarín** Spain
102 C4 **Alfambra r.** Spain
100 B3 **Alfambra** Portugal
102 B4 **Alfambra** Spain
98 D3 **Alfândega da Fé** Portugal
102 D3 **Alfántega** Spain
98 B4 **Alfarelos** Portugal
102 B2 **Alfaro** Spain
102 D3 **Alfarràs** Spain
42 F4 **Al Farwānīyah** Kuwait
112 F3 **Alfatar** Bulgaria
42 E3 **Al Fatḩah** Iraq
42 G4 **Al Fāw** Iraq
126 D2 **Al Fāzih** Yemen
80 A2 **Alfdorf** Germany
109 G3 **Alfedena** Italy
115 C5 **Alfeios r.** Greece
100 A1 **Alfeizerão** Portugal
72 E4 **Alfeld (Leine)** Germany
169 F4 **Alfenas** Brazil
79 K4 **Alföld plain** Hungary
107 G4 **Alfonsine** Italy
63 G1 **Alford** England U.K.
147 H3 **Alfred** Maine U.S.A.
141 H4 **Alfred** Ontario Canada
169 H4 **Alfredo Chaves** Brazil
63 E1 **Alfreton** England U.K.
42 G4 **Al Fuḩayḩil** Kuwait
39 D4 **Al Fujayrah** U.A.E.
Al-Fujayrah see **Fujairah**
118 C2 **Al Fuqahā'** Libya
46 E3 **Alga** Kazakhstan
46 D2 **Algabas** Kazakhstan
58 A2 **Algård** Norway
101 F3 **Algarinejo** Spain
173 F5 **Algarroba** Argentina
172 B1 **Algarrobito** Chile
170 B2 **Algarrobo** Atacama Chile
172 B2 **Algarrobo** Valparaíso Chile
172 D4 **Algarrobo del Aguilla** Argentina
173 F6 **Algarrobo, S. del salt pan** Argentina
100 B3 **Algarve reg.** Portugal
52 E3 **Algasovo** Rus. Fed.
101 E4 **Algeciras** Spain
Algeciras, Bahía de b. see **Gibraltar, Bay of**
103 C5 **Algemesi** Spain
126 C1 **Algena** Eritrea
149 E3 **Alger** Michigan U.S.A.
121 E1 **Alger** Algeria
116 D3 **Algeria country** Africa
42 F4 **Al Ghammas** Iraq
41 H6 **Al Ghayḑah** Yemen
108 A4 **Alghero** Sardegna Italy
59 F3 **Älghult** Sweden
Algiers see **Alger**
103 C5 **Algimia de Alfara** Spain
103 C5 **Alginet** Spain
131 E6 **Algoa Bay b.** South Africa
101 E4 **Algodonales** Spain
99 G5 **Algodor r.** Spain
148 D3 **Algoma** Wisconsin U.S.A.
150 E3 **Algona** Iowa U.S.A.
149 F4 **Algonac** Michigan U.S.A.
141 F4 **Algonquin Park** Ontario Canada
141 F4 **Algonquin Provincial Park res.** Ontario Canada
99 H4 **Algora** Spain
173 J2 **Algorta** Uruguay
98 D3 **Algoso** Portugal
100 B3 **Algoz** Portugal
87 F3 **Algrange** France
24 A4 **Alguada Reef reef** Myanmar
102 D3 **Alguaire** Spain
119 H3 **Al Haḑbah reg.** Saudi Arabia
39 B4 **Al Ḩadd** Bahrain
119 H2 **Al Hadhālīl plat.** Saudi Arabia
43 D2 **Al Ḩadīdīyah** Syria
42 E3 **Al Hadīthah** Iraq
43 D4 **Al Hadīthah** Saudi Arabia
42 E3 **Al Ḩaḑr** Iraq
119 H2 **Al Ḩafár well** Saudi Arabia
120 B3 **Al Haggounia** Western Sahara
101 G3 **Alhama r.** Spain
99 H3 **Alhama r.** Spain
42 D3 **Al Hamad plain** Jordan/Saudi Arabia
118 B2 **Al Ḩamādah al Ḩamrā' plat.** Libya
101 H4 **Alhama de Almería** Spain
101 G3 **Alhama de Granada** Spain
103 B7 **Alhama de Murcia** Spain
101 G2 **Alhambra** Spain
43 C2 **Al Ḩamīdīyah** Syria
101 H4 **Alhamilla, Sierra h.** Spain
42 F4 **Al Hammām well** Iraq
120 C3 **Al Hamra watercourse** Western Sahara
43 D2 **Al Ḩamrāt** Syria
119 H3 **Al Ḩanākīyah** Saudi Arabia
119 J2 **Al Ḩanbalī plain** Saudi Arabia
119 G1 **Al Ḩarrah h.** Saudi Arabia
118 C2 **Al Harūj al Aswad mountain range** Libya
42 E2 **Al Ḩasakah** Syria
42 F3 **Al Hāshimīyah** Iraq
119 J2 **Al Ḩatīfah plain** Saudi Arabia
101 F4 **Alhaurín de la Torre** Spain
119 H3 **Al Ḩawīyah** Saudi Arabia
119 G2 **Al Hawja'** Saudi Arabia
42 F3 **Al Ḩayy** Iraq
43 D5 **Al Hazm** Saudi Arabia
42 F3 **Al Ḩillah** Iraq
39 B4 **Al Ḩinnāh** Saudi Arabia
43 D4 **Al Ḩinw mt.** Saudi Arabia
43 C5 **Al Ḩismā plain** Saudi Arabia
120 D1 **Al Hoceima** Morocco
96 E5 **Al Hoceima, Baie d' b.** Morocco
99 H4 **Alhóndiga** Spain
126 D2 **Al Hudaydah** Yemen
119 G2 **Al Ḩufrah reg.** Saudi Arabia
39 B4 **Al Hufuf** Saudi Arabia
43 C5 **Al Ḩumayḑah** Saudi Arabia
126 E2 **Al Ḩumayshah** Yemen
39 B4 **Al Ḩunayy** Saudi Arabia
43 D2 **Al Ḩuwayz** Syria
111 E4 **Alì** Sicilia Italy
36 D2 **Ali** China
110 C5 **Alia** Sicilia Italy
101 E1 **Alía** Spain
39 E3 **'Alīābād** Iran
39 D2 **Aliabad** Iran
39 C1 **Alīābad** Iran
39 C3 **Aliabad** Iran
102 C4 **Aliaga** Spain
42 A2 **Aliağa** Turkey
114 D2 **Aliakmonas r.** Greece
42 F3 **'Alī al Gharbī** Iraq
109 J4 **Aliano** Italy
115 E4 **Aliartos** Greece
38 A2 **Alībāg** India
36 B4 **Ali Bandar** Pakistan
42 G2 **Äli Bayramlı** Azerbaijan
113 F5 **Alibey Adası i.** Turkey
123 E4 **Alibori r.** Benin
112 C2 **Alibunar** Yugoslavia
103 C6 **Alicante airport** Spain
103 C6 **Alicante div.** Valencia Spain
103 C6 **Alicante** Alicante Spain
103 C6 **Alicante, Bahía de b.** Spain
15 E2 **Alice r.** Queensland Australia
15 F4 **Alice watercourse** Queensland Australia
15 F4 **Alice** Queensland Australia
151 D7 **Alice** Texas U.S.A.
131 F6 **Alice** South Africa
136 D3 **Alice Arm** B.C. Canada
131 F6 **Alicedale** South Africa
111 G3 **Alice, Punta pt** Italy
158 C3 **Alice Shoal sea feature** Caribbean
14 C4 **Alice Springs** Northern Terr. Australia
158 C1 **Alice Town** The Bahamas
47 H5 **Alichur** Tajikistan
173 F1 **Alicia** Argentina
23 B5 **Alicia** Philippines
15 E4 **Alick Cr. r.** Queensland Australia
110 D4 **Alicudi, Isola i.** Italy
101 G3 **Alicún de Ortega** Spain
109 G3 **Alife** Italy
36 D4 **Aligarh** India
98 C3 **Alijó** Portugal
126 □ **Al Ikhwān is** Socotra Yemen
52 H2 **Alikovo** Rus. Fed.
124 C4 **Alima r.** Congo
110 D5 **Alimena** Sicilia Italy
115 □ **Alimia i.** Greece
98 C2 **A Limia reg.** Spain
124 D2 **Alindao** Central African Rep.
22 D2 **Alindau** Indonesia
39 G2 **Alinghar r.** Afghanistan
59 E3 **Alingsås** Sweden
113 G5 **Aliova r.** Turkey
37 G4 **Alipur Duar** India
146 C4 **Aliquippa** Pennsylvania U.S.A.
126 D2 **Ali Sabieh** Djibouti
43 D4 **'Al 'Īsāwīyah** Saudi Arabia
100 D1 **Aliseda** Spain
153 E6 **Alisos r.** Mexico
98 D3 **Aliste r.** Spain
111 E4 **Alì Terme** Sicilia Italy
115 F4 **Aliveri** Greece
131 F5 **Aliwal North** South Africa
136 G4 **Alix** Alberta Canada
36 B2 **Alizai** Pakistan
118 D1 **Al Jabal al Akhéar mts** Libya
39 B4 **Al Jāfūrah desert** Saudi Arabia
118 D2 **Al Jaghbūb** Libya
42 F4 **Al Jahrah** Kuwait
39 B4 **Al Jamalīyah** Qatar
Al Jauf see **Al Jawf**
118 D3 **Al Jawf** Libya
119 G2 **Al Jawf** Saudi Arabia
118 B1 **Al Jawsh** Libya
42 E3 **Al Jazīrah reg.** Iraq/Syria
39 B4 **Al Jībān reg.** Saudi Arabia
42 F4 **Al Jil well** Iraq
119 H2 **Al Jilh escarpment** Saudi Arabia
39 B4 **Al Jishshah** Saudi Arabia
119 H2 **Al Jithāmīyah** Saudi Arabia
39 B4 **Al Jubayl** Saudi Arabia
100 D1 **Aljucén r.** Spain
100 D1 **Aljucén** Spain
118 C2 **Al Jufra Oasis oasis** Libya
119 G3 **Al Jumūm** Saudi Arabia
119 H3 **Al Junaynah** Saudi Arabia
39 B4 **Al Jurayd i.** Saudi Arabia
100 B3 **Aljustrel** Portugal
43 D3 **Al Juwayf depression** Syria
43 D5 **Al Kabid waterhole** Jordan
154 D2 **Alkali Flat salt flat** Nevada U.S.A.
154 D1 **Alkali Flat salt flat** Nevada U.S.A.
155 E1 **Alkali Flat salt flat** Nevada U.S.A.
123 G4 **Alkamari** Niger
69 D4 **Alken** Belgium
41 J5 **Al Khābūrah** Oman
119 H2 **Al Khaḑrā' well** Saudi Arabia
119 H3 **Al Khafqān salt pan** Saudi Arabia
42 F3 **Al Khālis** Iraq
126 D1 **Al Kharāb** Yemen
39 D4 **Al Khaşab** Oman
119 H3 **Al Khāşirah** Saudi Arabia
39 B4 **Al Khawr** Qatar
39 B4 **Al Khīşah well** Saudi Arabia
118 D3 **Al Khufrah** Libya
118 D3 **Al Khufrah Oasis oasis** Libya
118 B1 **Al Khums** Libya
43 C3 **Al Khushnīyah** Syria
39 B4 **Al Kir'ānah** Qatar
43 D3 **Al Kiswah** Syria
68 C2 **Alkmaar** Netherlands
68 C2 **Alkmaarder-meer l.** Netherlands
42 F3 **Al Kūfah** Iraq
119 H2 **Al Kuhayfīyah** Saudi Arabia
42 F3 **Al Kumayt** Iraq
42 F3 **Al Kūt** Iraq
42 F4 **Al Kuwayt** Kuwait
119 H2 **Al Labbah plain** Saudi Arabia
42 C3 **Al Lādhiqīyah** Syria
147 J1 **Allagash r.** Maine U.S.A.
147 J1 **Allagash** Maine U.S.A.
147 J1 **Allagash Lake l.** Maine U.S.A.
37 E4 **Allahabad** India
86 B3 **Allaines** France
88 C4 **Allaire** France
43 D3 **Al Lajā lava** Syria
45 P3 **Allakh-Yun'** Rus. Fed.
91 C4 **Allan** France
92 E3 **Allanche** France
24 A3 **Allanmyo** Myanmar
131 F3 **Allanridge** South Africa
98 C2 **Allariz** Spain
87 G4 **Allarmont** France
92 D3 **Allassac** France
91 D5 **Allauch** France
131 G1 **Alldays** South Africa
82 C1 **Alle** Switzerland
148 E4 **Allegan** Michigan U.S.A.
107 G2 **Alleghe** Italy
146 D4 **Allegheny r.** Pennsylvania U.S.A.
146 C6 **Allegheny Mountains mountain range** U.S.A.
146 D4 **Allegheny Reservoir resr** New York/Pennsylvania U.S.A.
91 B3 **Allègre** France
159 □5 **Allegre, Pte pt** Guadeloupe Caribbean
91 D5 **Alleins** France
131 F4 **Allemanskraaldam resr** South Africa
82 B3 **Allemond** France
172 D5 **Allen** Argentina
145 D5 **Allendale** S. Carolina U.S.A.
65 F3 **Allendale Town** England U.K.
157 E2 **Allende** Coahuila Mexico
157 E3 **Allende** Nuevo León Mexico
72 D4 **Allendorf (Eder)** Germany
74 D2 **Allendorf (Lumda)** Germany
140 E4 **Allenford** Ontario Canada
65 F3 **Allenheads** England U.K.
67 C2 **Allen, Lough l.** Rep. of Ireland
9 A7 **Allen, Mt h.** New Zealand
83 E1 **Allensbach** Germany
147 F4 **Allentown** Pennsylvania U.S.A.
81 G2 **Allentsteig** Austria
38 B4 **Alleppey** India
102 C4 **Allepuz** Spain
72 F3 **Aller r.** Germany
90 C2 **Allerey-sur-Saône** France
75 G3 **Allersberg** Germany
75 G4 **Allershausen** Germany
91 E3 **Allevard** France
91 C4 **Allex** France
74 F5 **Allgäu reg.** Germany
80 B3 **Allgäuer Alpen mountain range** Austria/Germany
59 F3 **Allgunnen l.** Sweden
163 G2 **Allianc** Surinam
150 C3 **Alliance** Nebraska U.S.A.
146 C4 **Alliance** Ohio U.S.A.
90 B2 **Allier div.** Auvergne France
90 B2 **Allier r.** France
159 □1 **Alligator Pond** Jamaica
55 C3 **Allingåbro** Denmark
82 B2 **Allinges** France
55 □2 **Allinge-Sandvig** Denmark
141 F4 **Alliston** Ontario Canada
119 H3 **Al Līth** Saudi Arabia
74 E4 **Allmendingen** Germany
99 H2 **Allo** Spain
66 E4 **Alloa** Scotland U.K.
89 F4 **Allonnes** Maine-et-Loire France
89 F4 **Allonnes** Sarthe France
93 B4 **Allons** France
15 H5 **Allora** Queensland Australia
92 C2 **Alloue** France
131 G5 **All Saints Nek pass** South Africa
82 C1 **Allschwil** Switzerland
73 G4 **Allstedt** Germany
22 D3 **Allu** Indonesia
126 D1 **Al Luḩayyah** Yemen
108 D2 **Allumiere** Italy
38 C3 **Allur** India
38 C3 **Alluru Kottapatnam** India
42 E4 **Al Lussuf well** Iraq
90 B1 **Alluy** France
148 E4 **Alma** Michigan U.S.A.
150 D3 **Alma** Nebraska U.S.A.
155 H5 **Alma** New Mexico U.S.A.
141 K2 **Alma** Québec Canada
Alma Ata see **Almaty**
42 E4 **Al Ma'ānīyah** Iraq
102 D3 **Almacelles** Spain
100 A2 **Almada** Portugal
43 D5 **Al Madāfi' plat.** Saudi Arabia
126 D1 **Al Maḑāyā** Saudi Arabia
15 F3 **Almaden** Queensland Australia
101 F2 **Almadén** Spain
100 D3 **Almadén de la Plata** Spain
169 J1 **Almadina** Brazil
119 G3 **Al Madīnah** Saudi Arabia
172 E2 **Almafuerte** Argentina
101 G2 **Almagro** Spain
119 H3 **Al Maḩāwiyah** Saudi Arabia
120 C3 **Al Mahbas** Western Sahara
119 G2 **Al Maḩiā depression** Saudi Arabia
99 H3 **Almajano** Spain
119 J2 **Al Majma'ah** Saudi Arabia
39 B4 **Al Malsūnīyah reg.** Saudi Arabia
47 G4 **Almalyk** Uzbekistan
39 B4 **Al Manāmah** Bahrain
154 B1 **Almanor, Lake l.** California U.S.A.
103 B6 **Almansa** Spain
100 B3 **Almansil** Portugal
99 E2 **Almanza** Spain
99 E4 **Almanzor mt.** Spain
101 H3 **Almanzora r.** Spain
119 H4 **Al Ma'qaş** Saudi Arabia
42 F4 **Al Ma'qil** Iraq
99 E4 **Almar r.** Spain
126 D2 **Al Marāwi'ah** Yemen
98 E5 **Almaraz** Spain
101 E3 **Almargen** Spain
118 D1 **Al Marj** Libya
99 H3 **Almarza** Spain
166 C3 **Almas r.** Brazil
166 C3 **Almas** Brazil
79 M5 **Almaş** Romania
79 H4 **Almásfüzitő** Hungary
168 D1 **Almas, R. das r.** Brazil
103 C5 **Almassora** Spain
47 J4 **Almaty div.** Kazakhstan
47 J4 **Almaty** Kazakhstan
42 E2 **Al Mawşil** Iraq
99 H3 **Almazán** Spain
45 N3 **Almaznyy** Rus. Fed.
101 H2 **Almedina** Spain
101 F3 **Almedinilla** Spain
98 D4 **Almeida** Portugal
98 D3 **Almeida de Sayago** Spain
166 B1 **Almeirim** Brazil
100 B1 **Almeirim** Portugal
68 E2 **Almelo** Netherlands
169 H2 **Almenara** Brazil
103 C5 **Almenara** Spain
101 H2 **Almenaras mt.** Spain
103 B7 **Almenara, Sierra de la h.** Spain
99 H3 **Almenar de Soria** Spain
100 D2 **Almendral** Spain
100 D2 **Almendralejo** Spain
68 D2 **Almere** Netherlands
101 H4 **Almería airport** Spain
101 H3 **Almería div.** Andalucía Spain
101 H4 **Almería** Almería Spain
101 H4 **Almería, Golfo de b.** Spain
101 H4 **Almerimar** Spain
46 D2 **Al'met'yevsk** Rus. Fed.
59 F3 **Älmhult** Sweden
101 G4 **Almijara, Sierra de mountain range** Spain
101 E5 **Almina, Pta pt** Ceuta Spain
55 B4 **Almind** Denmark
171 C7 **Almirantazgo, S. del chan.** Chile
156 K7 **Almirante** Panama
39 B3 **Al Mish'āb** Saudi Arabia
42 D3 **Al Mismīyah** Syria
100 E4 **Almodóvar r.** Spain
100 B3 **Almodôvar** Portugal
101 F2 **Almodóvar del Campo** Spain
103 B5 **Almodóvar del Pinar** Spain
101 F4 **Almogía** Spain
99 H4 **Almoguera** Spain
100 D1 **Almoharín** Spain
99 H4 **Almonacid del Zorita** Spain
66 E4 **Almond r.** Scotland U.K.
149 F4 **Almont** Michigan U.S.A.
100 D1 **Almonte r.** Spain
141 G4 **Almonte** Ontario Canada
100 D3 **Almonte** Spain
36 D3 **Almora** India
103 C6 **Almoradí** Spain
99 F4 **Almorox** Spain
100 B1 **Almoster r.** Portugal
123 E3 **Almoustarat** Mali
59 H2 **Älmsta** Sweden
39 B4 **Al Mubarrez** Saudi Arabia
119 G2 **Al Mudarraj** Saudi Arabia
42 C4 **Al Mudawwara** Jordan
103 B6 **Almudema** Spain
102 C2 **Almudévar** Spain
39 B4 **Al Muharraq** Bahrain
43 D5 **Al Muḩtaţab depression** Saudi Arabia
41 G7 **Al Mukallā** Yemen
126 D2 **Al Mukhā** Yemen
118 D1 **Al Mukhaylī** Libya
101 G4 **Almuñécar** Spain
59 H2 **Almunge** Sweden
81 E3 **Almünster** Austria
42 F3 **Al Muqdādīyah** Iraq
101 G2 **Almuradiel** Spain
100 C1 **Almuro r.** Portugal
119 G2 **Al Murūt well** Saudi Arabia
119 G3 **Al Musayjīd** Saudi Arabia
42 F3 **Al Musayyib** Iraq
42 F4 **Al Muthanná div.** Iraq
119 H3 **Al Muwayh** Saudi Arabia
59 G3 **Almvik** Sweden
115 F4 **Almyropotamos** Greece
113 D5 **Almyros** Greece
153 □1 **Alna Haina** Hawaii U.S.A.
36 B3 **Alnnadpur East** Pakistan
65 G2 **Alnwick** England U.K.
54 D3 **Aloja** Latvia
54 F3 **Alolya r.** Rus. Fed.
24 A2 **Alon** Myanmar
37 H3 **Along** India
31 G2 **Alongshan** China
114 E3 **Alonnisos i.** Greece
114 E3 **Alonnisos** Greece
168 C6 **Alonso r.** Brazil
21 H8 **Alor i.** Indonesia
101 F4 **Álora** Spain
102 E2 **Alós d'Ensil** Spain
100 C3 **Alosno** Spain
Alost see **Aalst**
36 C5 **Alot** India
6 □1 **Alotau** P.N.G.
92 B2 **Alouettes, Mont des h.** France
90 C1 **Aloxe-Corton** France
17 E5 **Aloysius, Mt mt.** Western Australia Australia
101 F4 **Alozaina** Spain
102 E2 **Alp** Spain
172 F4 **Alpachiri** Argentina
172 E2 **Alpa Corral** Argentina
154 C4 **Alpaugh** California U.S.A.
98 C4 **Alpedrinha** Portugal
68 E3 **Alpen** Germany
149 F3 **Alpena** Michigan U.S.A.
87 G2 **Alpenrod** Germany
103 B6 **Alpera** Spain
166 C2 **Alpercatas r.** Brazil
91 E4 **Alpes-de-Haute-Provence div.** France
91 D4 **Alpes du Dauphiné mts** France
91 F5 **Alpes-Maritimes div.** France
91 E4 **Alpes Maritimes mountain range** France/Italy
15 F4 **Alpha** Queensland Australia
69 C3 **Alphen** Netherlands
68 C2 **Alphen aan den Rijn** Netherlands
106 E4 **Alpi Apuane mountain range** Italy
100 B1 **Alpiarça** Portugal
106 A4 **Alpi Cozie mountain range** France/Italy
107 F2 **Alpi Dolomitiche mountain range** Italy
83 D2 **Alpi Lepontine mountain range** Italy/Switzerland
91 C5 **Alpilles h.** France
155 H5 **Alpine** Arizona U.S.A.
151 C6 **Alpine** Texas U.S.A.
152 E3 **Alpine** Wyoming U.S.A.
169 E4 **Alpinópolis** Brazil
106 D2 **Alpi Orobie mountain range** Italy
82 C3 **Alpi Pennine mountain range** Italy/Switzerland
87 H4 **Alpirsbach** Germany
83 D2 **Alpnach** Switzerland
94 E2 **Alps**
41 G6 **Al Qa'āmīyāt reg.** Saudi Arabia
118 C1 **Al Qaddāḩīyah** Libya
42 F4 **Al Qādisīyah div.** Iraq
43 D2 **Al Qadmūs** Syria
119 H3 **Al Qā'īyah** Saudi Arabia
119 G2 **Al Qalībah** Saudi Arabia
42 E2 **Al Qāmishlī** Syria
119 H4 **Al Qarḩah** Saudi Arabia
43 D4 **Al Qarqar** Saudi Arabia
42 D3 **Al Qaryatayn** Syria
118 B1 **Al Qaşabāt** Libya
39 B4 **Al Qaţīf** Saudi Arabia
41 G6 **Al Qaţn** Yemen
118 B3 **Al Qaţrūn** Libya
119 H2 **Al Qâyşūmah well** Saudi Arabia
103 C6 **Alquería de la Condesa** Spain
43 C3 **Al Qunayţirah div.** Syria
42 C3 **Al Qunayţirah** Syria
119 H4 **Al Qunfidhah** Saudi Arabia
119 H3 **Al Qurayn** Saudi Arabia
126 D2 **Al Qurayyah** Yemen
42 F4 **Al Qurnah** Iraq
43 D2 **Al 'Quşayr** Syria
43 D3 **Al Quţayfah** Syria
63 E2 **Alrewas** England U.K.
55 C4 **Alrø i.** Denmark
14 D3 **Alroy Downs** Northern Terr. Australia
55 B4 **Als i.** Denmark
55 C3 **Als** Denmark
87 G4 **Alsace div.** France
62 D1 **Alsager** England U.K.
137 H4 **Alsask** Saskatchewan Canada
99 H2 **Alsasua** Spain
74 B2 **Alsdorf** Germany
74 C3 **Alsenz** Germany
74 E2 **Alsfeld** Germany
55 B4 **Als Fjord inlet** Denmark
52 G3 **Al'shanka** Rus. Fed.
173 H2 **Alsina** Argentina
73 G4 **Alsleben** Germany
59 F3 **Alsterbro** Sweden
65 F3 **Alston** England U.K.
54 B3 **Alsunga** Latvia
54 E3 **Alsviķi** Latvia
56 F1 **Alta** Norway
83 G2 **Altacroce, Monte mt.** Italy
56 F1 **Altaelva r.** Norway
172 E1 **Alta Gracia** Argentina
162 C1 **Altagracía** Venezuela
159 F5 **Altagracía de Orituco** Venezuela
26 E2 **Altai Mountains mountain range** Asia
145 D6 **Altamaha r.** Georgia U.S.A.
166 B1 **Altamira** Brazil
170 C2 **Altamira** Chile
162 B3 **Altamira** Colombia
156 J7 **Altamira** Costa Rica
173 H3 **Altamirano** Argentina
101 E1 **Altamira, Sierra de mountain range** Spain
102 F2 **Alt Amporda reg.** Spain
9 B6 **Alta, Mt mt.** New Zealand
109 J4 **Altamura** France
30 D2 **Altan** Rus. Fed.
30 C3 **Altanbulag** Mongolia
30 C2 **Altanbulag** Mongolia
156 C2 **Altar** Mexico
156 D3 **Altata** Mexico
81 E3 **Altaussee** Austria
109 G4 **Altavilla Irpina** Italy
109 H4 **Altavilla Silentina** Italy
146 D6 **Altavista** Virginia U.S.A.
47 L3 **Altay** China
30 A3 **Altay** Mongolia
47 L2 **Altay, Respublika** Rus. Fed.
47 L2 **Altayskiy** Rus. Fed.
47 K2 **Altayskiy Kray** Rus. Fed.
75 H4 **Altdorf** Germany
83 D2 **Altdorf** Switzerland
75 G3 **Altdorf bei Nürnberg** Germany
103 C6 **Altea** Spain
73 J1 **Altefähr** Germany
56 F1 **Alteidet** Norway
72 C4 **Altena** Germany
69 E4 **Altenahr** Germany
72 F4 **Altenau** Germany
75 J2 **Altenberg** Germany
72 C3 **Altenberge** Germany
75 H2 **Altenburg** Germany
87 G3 **Altenglan** Germany
72 F1 **Altenholz** Germany
73 J1 **Altenkirchen** Germany
75 H4 **Altenmarkt an der Alz** Germany
81 G2 **Altenmarkt an der Triesting** Austria
81 F3 **Altenmarkt bei St Gallen** Austria
73 F2 **Altenmedingen** Germany
80 B2 **Altenmünster** Germany
37 H1 **Altenqoke** China
74 F4 **Altenstadt** Baden-Württemberg Germany
83 F1 **Altenstadt** Bayern Germany
74 D2 **Altenstadt** Hessen Germany
74 D4 **Altensteig** Germany
73 J2 **Altentreptow** Germany
73 K3 **Alte Oder r.** Germany
100 C1 **Alter do Chão** Portugal
80 D2 **Altfraunhofen** Germany
80 E2 **Altheim** Austria
91 B4 **Altier r.** France
91 B4 **Altier** France
39 G2 **Altimur P. pass** Afghanistan
113 F5 **Altınoluk** Turkey
168 E4 **Altinópolis** Brazil
113 F5 **Altınova** Turkey
42 B2 **Altıntaş** Turkey
172 C6 **Altiplanicie de Hakelhuincul plat.** Argentina
172 C4 **Altiplanicie del Payún Matru plat.** Argentina
164 C3 **Altiplano plain** Bolivia
83 G2 **Altissima, l' mt.** Austria/Italy
90 F1 **Altkirch** France
75 G4 **Altmannstein** Germany
73 G3 **Altmark reg.** Germany
75 G4 **Altmühl r.** Germany
66 D2 **Altnaharra** Scotland U.K.
173 F2 **Alto Alegre** Argentina
168 B2 **Alto Araguaia** Brazil
125 C6 **Alto Chicapa** Angola
99 H3 **Alto Cruz mt.** Spain
102 B3 **Alto del Moncayo mt.** Spain
172 D2 **Alto de Pencoso h.** Argentina
158 C5 **Alto de Quimari mt.** Colombia
101 G3 **Alto de San Juan mt.** Spain
110 C4 **Altofonte** Sicilia Italy
168 B2 **Alto Garças** Brazil
166 D2 **Alto Longá** Brazil
129 F2 **Alto Molócuè** Mozambique
111 F3 **Altomonte** Italy
75 G4 **Altomünster** Germany
63 F3 **Alton** England U.K.
144 B4 **Alton** Illinois U.S.A.
151 F4 **Alton** Missouri U.S.A.
147 H3 **Alton** New Hampshire U.S.A.
12 D1 **Alton Downs** S. Australia Australia
146 D4 **Altoona** Pennsylvania U.S.A.
166 B1 **Alto Pacajá r.** Brazil
166 C2 **Alto Parnaíba** Brazil
107 E5 **Altopascio** Italy
164 B2 **Alto Purús r.** Peru
98 C3 **Alto Rabagao, Barragem do resr** Portugal
169 G4 **Alto Rio Doce** Brazil
168 B3 **Alto Rio Verde** Brazil
102 D3 **Altorricón** Spain
166 D2 **Altos** Brazil
99 H4 **Altos de Cabrejas mountain range** Spain
103 B6 **Altos de Chinchilla mountain range** Spain
173 F1 **Altos de Chipión** Argentina
168 B3 **Alto Sucuriú** Brazil
99 G2 **Altotero mt.** Spain
75 H4 **Altötting** Germany
158 □1 **Alto Vista h.** Aruba Caribbean
69 E5 **Altrich** Germany
65 F4 **Altrincham** England U.K.
73 H3 **Alt Ruppin** Germany
74 E5 **Altshausen** Germany
83 E1 **Altstätten** Switzerland
52 B3 **Altukhovo** Rus. Fed.
157 H5 **Altun Ha** Belize
26 E4 **Altun Shan mountain range** China
103 C5 **Altura** Spain
152 B3 **Alturas** California U.S.A.
151 D5 **Altus** Oklahoma U.S.A.
74 F5 **Altusried** Germany
46 F3 **Altynasar** Kazakhstan
53 E1 **Altynivka** Ukraine
52 H2 **Altyshevo** Rus. Fed.
54 D2 **Alu** Estonia
42 D1 **Alucra** Turkey
54 E3 **Alūksne** Latvia
119 G2 **Al'Ulā** Saudi Arabia
126 E2 **Al'ulah reg.** Yemen
146 B4 **Alum Creek Lake l.** Ohio U.S.A.
172 B5 **Aluminé r.** Argentina
172 B5 **Aluminé** Argentina
172 B5 **Aluminé, L. l.** Argentina
59 H1 **Alunda** Sweden
51 E6 **Alupka** Ukraine
118 C1 **Al 'Uqaylah** Libya
39 B4 **Al 'Uqayr** Saudi Arabia
119 G2 **Al Urayq desert** Saudi Arabia
25 C6 **Alur Setar** Malaysia
51 E6 **Alushta** Ukraine
102 B4 **Alustante** Spain
43 D5 **Al Uthaylī** Saudi Arabia
39 B4 **Al 'Uthmānīyah** Saudi Arabia
118 D3 **Al 'Uwaynāt** Libya
118 B2 **Al 'Uwaynāt** Libya

67 E2 **Armagh** Northern Ireland U.K.
93 C5 **Armagnac** reg. France
98 C3 **Armamar** Portugal
45 R4 **Arman'** Rus. Fed.
86 C4 **Armance** r. France
90 C1 **Armançon** r. France
119 F2 **Armant** Egypt
113 F7 **Armathia** i. Greece
Oktemberyan see **Hoktemberyan**
51 G6 **Armavir** Rus. Fed.
18 F5 **Armenia** country Asia
162 B3 **Armenia** Colombia
83 D3 **Armeno** Italy
115 F7 **Armenoi** Greece
86 B2 **Armentières** France
162 C3 **Armero** Colombia
111 E5 **Armi, Capo dell'** c. Italy
13 G2 **Armidale** New South Wales Australia
101 G3 **Armilla** Spain
173 G2 **Arminda** Argentina
91 B5 **Armissan** France
137 L2 **Armit Lake** l. N.W.T. Canada
47 G1 **Armizonskoye** Rus. Fed.
36 E5 **Armori** India
136 B3 **Armour, Mt** mt. Canada/U.S.A.
67 E1 **Armoy** Northern Ireland U.K.
14 B3 **Armstrong** r. Northern Terr. Australia
136 F4 **Armstrong** B.C. Canada
140 A1 **Armstrong** Ontario Canada
173 G2 **Armstrong** Argentina
38 B2 **Armur** India
113 G4 **Armutlu** Turkey
53 E3 **Armyans'k** Ukraine
55 B4 **Arnå** r. Denmark
92 D3 **Arnac-Pompadour** France
89 F4 **Arnage** France
114 E2 **Arnaia** Greece
43 B2 **Arnaoutis, C.** headland Cyprus
56 K6 **Arnarfjörður** b. Iceland
139 F1 **Arnaud** r. Québec Canada
36 B2 **Arnawai** Pakistan
90 C1 **Arnay-le-Duc** France
73 H3 **Arneburg** Germany
99 H2 **Arnedillo** Spain
99 H2 **Arnedo** Spain
98 B2 **Arnego** r. Spain
173 H2 **Ar Negro** r. Uruguay
93 A5 **Arnéguy** France
69 B3 **Arnemuiden** Netherlands
58 D1 **Årnes** Norway
102 D4 **Arnes** Spain
151 D4 **Arnett** Oklahoma U.S.A.
68 D3 **Arnhem** Netherlands
14 D2 **Arnhem Bay** b. Northern Terr. Australia
14 D2 **Arnhem, C.** c. Northern Terr. Australia
14 C2 **Arnhem Land** reg. Northern Terr. Australia
14 C2 **Arnhem Land Abor. Land** res. Northern Terr. Australia
114 C2 **Arnissa** Greece
106 E5 **Arno** r. Italy
12 D3 **Arno Bay** S. Australia Australia
98 B2 **Arnoia** r. Spain
148 D2 **Arnold** Michigan U.S.A.
81 E4 **Arnoldstein** Austria
92 E2 **Arnon** r. France
141 F2 **Arnoux, Lac** l. Québec Canada
141 G4 **Arnprior** Ontario Canada
64 D1 **Arnprior** Scotland U.K.
72 D4 **Arnsberg** div. Nordrhein-Westfalen Germany
72 D4 **Arnsberg** Nordrhein-Westfalen Germany
75 F2 **Arnstadt** Germany
141 F4 **Arnstein** Ontario Canada
74 E3 **Arnstein** Germany
75 H4 **Arnstorf** Germany
141 F2 **Arntfield** Québec Canada
55 B4 **Årø** i. Denmark
128 B4 **Aroab** Namibia
7 □11 **Aroa, Pte** pt French Polynesia Pacific Ocean
173 G2 **Arocena** Argentina
168 A4 **Aroeira** Brazil
140 B1 **Aroland** Ontario Canada
82 C2 **Arolla** Switzerland
72 E4 **Arolsen** Germany
119 G4 **Aroma** Sudan
47 G1 **Aromashevo** Rus. Fed.
90 B1 **Aron** r. France
89 E3 **Aron** France
97 □ **Arona** Canary Is Spain
106 C3 **Arona** Italy
147 J1 **Aroostook** r. Maine Canada/U.S.A.
147 K1 **Aroostook** New Brunswick Canada
4 J5 **Arorae** i. Kiribati
23 B3 **Aroroy** Philippines
83 E2 **Arosa** Switzerland
98 B4 **Arouca** Portugal
118 D4 **Arouelli** well Chad
42 E1 **Arpaçay** Turkey
42 E1 **Arpa** r. Turkey
93 E4 **Arpajon-sur-Cère** France
109 F3 **Arpino** Italy
107 F3 **Arquà Petrarca** Italy
109 F2 **Arquata del Tronto** Italy
106 C4 **Arquata Scrivia** Italy
93 E6 **Arques** Languedoc-Roussillon France
86 B2 **Arques** Nord - Pas-de-Calais France
89 G2 **Arques-la-Bataille** France
101 G2 **Arquillos** Spain
169 J2 **Arquipélago dos Abrolhos** is Brazil
36 A4 **Arra** r. Pakistan
14 E5 **Arrabury** Queensland Australia
87 F4 **Arracourt** France
88 C4 **Arradon** France
122 D5 **Arrah** Côte d'Ivoire
166 B3 **Arraias** r. Brazil
166 C3 **Arraias, Sa da** h. Brazil
100 C2 **Arraiolos** Portugal
42 E3 **Ar Ramādī** Iraq
43 C5 **Ar Ramlah** Jordan
67 C4 **Arra Mountains** h. Rep. of Ireland
66 C5 **Arran** i. Scotland U.K.
87 E3 **Arrancy-sur-Crusne** France
42 D3 **Ar Raqqah** Syria
86 B2 **Arras** France
119 G3 **Ar Ra's al Abyaḍ** pt Saudi Arabia
119 G3 **Ar Ra's al Aswad** pt Saudi Arabia
99 H1 **Arrasate-Mondragoe** Spain
119 H2 **Ar-Rass** Saudi Arabia
42 D3 **Ar Rastan** Syria
93 C5 **Arrats** r. France
119 H3 **Ar Rawḍah** Saudi Arabia
119 H3 **Ar Rawshan** Saudi Arabia
43 D6 **Ar Rawwafah** Saudi Arabia
39 B4 **Ar Rayyān** Qatar
93 C6 **Arreau** France
162 D3 **Arrecifal** Colombia
97 □ **Arrecife** Canary Is Spain
157 H4 **Arrecife Alacrán** atoll Mexico
156 K6 **Arrecife de la Media Luna** is Caribbean Sea
173 G3 **Arrecifes** Argentina
99 G1 **Arredondo** Spain
86 D4 **Arrentières** France
157 G5 **Arriaga** Chiapas Mexico
157 E4 **Arriaga** San Luis Potosí Mexico
173 G3 **Arribeños** Argentina
42 F4 **Ar Rifā'ī** Iraq
98 B4 **Arrifana** Portugal
86 D4 **Arrigny** France
42 F4 **Ar Rihāb** salt flat Iraq
41 H5 **Ar Rimāl** reg. Saudi Arabia
17 A6 **Arrino** Western Australia Australia
155 H3 **Arriola** Colorado U.S.A.
99 E1 **Arriondas** Spain
41 G5 **Ar Riyāḍ** Saudi Arabia
101 F1 **Arroba de los Montes** Spain
66 D4 **Arrochar** Scotland U.K.
170 F3 **Arroio Grande** Brazil
166 B2 **Arroios do Araguaia** r. Brazil
166 C3 **Arrojado** r. Brazil
100 C1 **Arronches** Portugal
109 E3 **Arrone** r. Italy
93 C5 **Arros** r. France
106 B4 **Arroscia** r. Italy
90 C2 **Arroux** r. France
62 C2 **Arrow** r. England U.K.
148 B1 **Arrow Lake** l. Ontario Canada
67 C2 **Arrow, Lough** l. Rep. of Ireland
152 D3 **Arrowrock Res.** resr Idaho U.S.A.
9 C5 **Arrowsmith, Mt** mt. New Zealand
9 B6 **Arrowtown** New Zealand
173 G3 **Arroy Dulce** Argentina
173 F1 **Arroyito** Cordoba Argentina
172 D2 **Arroyito** Mendoza Argentina
145 □3 **Arroyo** Puerto Rico
100 D1 **Arroyo de la Luz** Spain
157 E4 **Arroyo, Dr** Mexico
173 H4 **Arroyo Gde** r. Argentina
154 B4 **Arroyo Grande** California U.S.A.
100 D2 **Arroyomolinos de León** Spain
173 G2 **Arroyo Seco** Argentina
157 F4 **Arroyo Seco** Mexico
119 H2 **Ar Rubay'iyah** Saudi Arabia
166 A3 **Arruda** Brazil
100 A2 **Arruda dos Vinhos** Portugal
173 G1 **Arrufó** Argentina
42 D3 **Ar Ruṣāfah** Syria
42 E3 **Ar Ruṭba** Iraq
119 H3 **Ar Ruwayḍah** Saudi Arabia
88 B3 **Arree, Mont d'** h. France
87 F3 **Arry** France
55 B3 **Års** Denmark
39 A1 **Ars** Iran
102 E2 **Arsèguel** Spain
39 C3 **Arsenajān** Iran
92 A2 **Ars-en-Ré** France
52 C3 **Arsen'yevo** Rus. Fed.
115 E5 **Arsida** i. Greece
107 F3 **Arsiero** Italy
38 B3 **Arsikere** India
50 J3 **Arsk** Rus. Fed.
55 C4 **Årslev** Denmark
109 F2 **Arsoli** Italy
87 F3 **Ars-sur-Moselle** France
43 C1 **Arsuz** Turkey
114 C3 **Arta** div. Greece
114 B3 **Arta** Greece
103 G5 **Artà** Spain
102 B2 **Artajona** Spain
156 E5 **Arteaga** Mexico
103 C5 **Arteas de Abajo** mt. Spain
31 K4 **Artem** Rus. Fed.
90 D3 **Artemare** France
158 B2 **Artemisa** Cuba
53 G2 **Artemivka** Kharkivs'ka Oblast' Ukraine
53 F2 **Artemivka** Poltavs'ka Oblast' Ukraine
51 F5 **Artemivs'k** Ukraine
109 E3 **Artena** Italy
89 G3 **Artenay** France
73 G4 **Artern** Germany
102 E3 **Artesa de Segre** Spain
153 F5 **Artesia** New Mexico U.S.A.
83 D1 **Arth** Switzerland
141 K3 **Arthabaska** Québec Canada
93 B5 **Arthez-de-Béarn** France
88 D4 **Arthon-en-Retz** France
140 E5 **Arthur** Ontario Canada
131 E6 **Arthur, L.** l. South Africa
146 C4 **Arthur, Lake** l. Pennsylvania U.S.A.
15 G4 **Arthur Pt** pt Queensland Australia
9 C5 **Arthur's Pass** pass New Zealand
9 C5 **Arthur's Pass National Park** nat. park New Zealand
158 D1 **Arthur's Town** The Bahamas
46 E1 **Arti** Rus. Fed.
102 D2 **Arties** Spain
179 B1 **Artigas** Uruguay Base Antarctica
173 J1 **Artigas** div. Uruguay
173 J1 **Artigas** Uruguay
93 D5 **Artigat** France
42 E1 **Art'ik** Armenia
6 □2 **Art, Île** i. New Caledonia Pacific Ocean
137 H2 **Artillery Lake** l. N.W.T. Canada
86 A2 **Artois** reg. France
42 D1 **Artova** Turkey
103 □ **Artrutx, Cap d'** pt Spain
30 B3 **Arts Bogd Uul** mts Mongolia
112 G2 **Artsyz** Ukraine
91 E5 **Artuby** r. France
47 J5 **Artux** China
42 E1 **Artvin** Turkey
39 D1 **Artyk** Turkmenistan
124 F3 **Aru** Zaire
98 C2 **A Rúa** Spain
126 B4 **Arua** Uganda
168 C1 **Aruanã** Brazil
159 E4 **Aruba** territory Caribbean
97 □ **Arucas** Canary Is Spain
93 B5 **Arudy** France
163 E4 **Arumã** Brazil
29 □2 **Arume** Japan
31 G2 **Arun** r. China
37 F4 **Arun** r. Nepal
37 H4 **Arunachal Pradesh** div. India
63 F4 **Arundel** England U.K.
31 G2 **Arun Qi** China
7 □11 **Aruó** French Polynesia Pacific Ocean
55 C4 **Årup** Denmark
166 C1 **Arurandéua** r. Brazil
127 C5 **Arusha** div. Tanzania
127 C5 **Arusha** Tanzania
22 E1 **Arus, Tg** pt Indonesia
22 B2 **Arut** r. Indonesia
7 □10 **Arutua** i. French Polynesia Pacific Ocean
124 E3 **Aruwimi** r. Zaire
150 B4 **Arvada** Colorado U.S.A.
67 D3 **Arvagh** Rep. of Ireland
91 E3 **Arvan** r. France
30 B3 **Arvayheer** Mongolia
90 E2 **Arve** r. France
93 B4 **Arveyres** France
36 D5 **Arvi** India
137 L2 **Arviat** N.W.T. Canada
139 F4 **Arvida** Quebec Canada
56 E2 **Arvidsjaur** Sweden
59 E2 **Arvika** Sweden
154 C4 **Arvin** California U.S.A.
111 F3 **Arvo, Lago** l. Italy
31 F3 **Arxan** China
45 O2 **Ary** Rus. Fed.
47 G2 **Arykbalyk** Kazakhstan
47 G4 **Arys'** r. Kazakhstan
47 G4 **Arys'** Kazakhstan
47 G3 **Arys, Oz.** salt lake Kazakhstan
108 B3 **Arzachena** Sardegna Italy
93 B5 **Arzacq-Arraziguet** France
52 F2 **Arzamas** Rus. Fed.
75 H2 **Arzberg** Germany
74 B2 **Arzfeld** Germany
51 H6 **Arzgir** Rus. Fed.
107 F3 **Arzignano** Italy
80 B3 **Arzl im Pitztal** Austria
91 B3 **Arzon** r. France
98 B2 **Arzúa** Spain
69 D3 **As** Belgium
78 B1 **Aš** Czech Rep.
163 E2 **Asa** r. Venezuela
127 C5 **Asa** waterhole Kenya
55 C2 **Aså** Denmark
55 E2 **Åsa** Sweden
130 A2 **Asab** Namibia
123 F5 **Asaba** Nigeria
39 B2 **Asadābād** Hamadan Iran
39 E2 **Asadābād** Khorāsan Iran
39 G2 **Asadābād** Afghanistan
25 B7 **Asahan** r. Indonesia
29 H6 **Asahi** Japan
29 G4 **Asahi-dake** mt. Japan
28 J2 **Asahi-dake** volcano Japan
28 D6 **Asahi-gawa** r. Japan
28 J2 **Asahikawa** Japan
29 G6 **Asaka** Japan
47 H4 **Asake** Uzbekistan
126 D2 **Āsalē** l. Ethiopia
122 D5 **Asamankese** Ghana
29 G5 **Asama-yama** volcano Japan
122 D5 **Asankranguaa** Ghana
31 H5 **Asan Man** b. South Korea
37 F5 **Asansol** India
113 F3 **Asar** China
59 E2 **Åsarp** Sweden
93 B5 **Asasp-Arros** France
7 □12 **Asau** Western Samoa
87 G2 **Asbach** Germany
75 F4 **Asbach-Bäumenheim** Germany
46 F1 **Asbest** Rus. Fed.
141 K4 **Asbestos** Québec Canada
130 D4 **Asbestos Mountains** mts South Africa
126 D3 **Āsbe Teferi** Ethiopia
109 H4 **Ascea** Italy
128 □1 **Ascension** i. Atlantic Ocean
158 □2 **Ascension** Curaçao Netherlands Ant.
165 D3 **Ascensión** Bolivia
156 C2 **Ascensión** Mexico
157 J5 **Ascensión, B. de la** b. Mexico
174 J6 **Ascension Island** i. Atlantic Ocean
78 B2 **Asch** r. Germany
80 D1 **Ascha** Germany
81 F2 **Aschach an der Donau** Austria
74 E3 **Aschaffenburg** Germany
75 H4 **Aschau am Inn** Germany
81 F2 **Aschbach Markt** Austria
72 C4 **Ascheberg** Germany
72 F1 **Ascheberg (Holstein)** Germany
80 E2 **Aschenstein** h. Germany
73 G4 **Aschersleben** Germany
107 F5 **Asciano** Italy
108 B2 **Asco** Corse France
102 D3 **Ascó** Spain
172 E1 **Ascochinga** Argentina
109 F2 **Ascoli Piceno** div. Marche Italy
109 F2 **Ascoli Piceno** Ascoli Piceno Italy
109 H3 **Ascoli Satriano** Italy
83 D2 **Ascona** Switzerland
162 B5 **Ascope** Peru
164 C4 **Ascotán, S. de** mt. Chile
126 D3 **Āsebot** mt. Ethiopia
59 F3 **Åseda** Sweden
121 E4 **Asedjrad** plat. Algeria
126 C3 **Āsela** Ethiopia
56 E2 **Åsele** Sweden
39 C3 **Asemānjerd** Iran
58 B2 **Åseral** Norway
54 F2 **Aseri** Estonia
39 D2 **Asfāk** Iran
114 B3 **Asfaka** Greece
86 D3 **Asfeld** France
119 F2 **Asfûn el Matâ'na** Egypt
58 D2 **Asgårstrand** Norway
46 E2 **Asha** Rus. Fed.
122 D5 **Ashanti** div. Ghana
63 E1 **Ashbourne** England U.K.
67 E3 **Ashbourne** Rep. of Ireland
17 B5 **Ashburton** r. Western Australia Australia
9 C5 **Ashburton** r. New Zealand
9 C5 **Ashburton** New Zealand
140 B2 **Ashburton Bay** b. Ontario Canada
147 F4 **Ashbury Park** New Jersey U.S.A.
63 E2 **Ashby de la Zouch** England U.K.
47 H4 **Ashchikol', Oz.** salt lake Kazakhstan
136 E4 **Ashcroft** B.C. Canada
43 C4 **Ashdod** Israel
151 E5 **Ashdown** Arkansas U.S.A.
145 E5 **Asheboro** N. Carolina U.S.A.
145 D5 **Asheville** N. Carolina U.S.A.
63 E4 **Ashford** England U.K.
63 G3 **Ashford** England U.K.
13 G2 **Ashford** New South Wales Australia
62 A1 **Ashford** Rep. of Ireland
155 F4 **Ash Fork** Arizona U.S.A.
46 E5 **Ashgabat** Turkmenistan
28 J2 **Ashibetsu** Japan
29 G5 **Ashikaga** Japan
65 G2 **Ashington** England U.K.
29 H3 **Ashiro** Japan
50 J3 **Ashit** r. Rus. Fed.
28 D7 **Ashizuri-misaki** pt Japan
39 C3 **Ashkazar** Iran
65 F2 **Ashkirk** Scotland U.K.
36 B2 **Ashkun** reg. Afghanistan
151 D4 **Ashland** Kansas U.S.A.
146 B5 **Ashland** Kentucky U.S.A.
147 J1 **Ashland** Maine U.S.A.
152 F2 **Ashland** Montana U.S.A.
147 H3 **Ashland** New Hampshire U.S.A.
146 B4 **Ashland** Ohio U.S.A.
152 B3 **Ashland** Oregon U.S.A.
146 E6 **Ashland** Virginia U.S.A.
148 B2 **Ashland** Wisconsin U.S.A.
9 D5 **Ashley** r. New Zealand
150 D2 **Ashley** N. Dakota U.S.A.
13 G2 **Ashley** New South Wales Australia
16 C2 **Ashmore Reef** reef Western Australia Australia
43 B5 **Ashmūn** Egypt
54 E4 **Ashmyanskaye Wzvyshsha** reg. Belarus
54 D4 **Ashmyany** Belarus
36 D4 **Ashoknagar** India
28 J2 **Ashoro** Japan
155 H5 **Ash Peak** Arizona U.S.A.
43 C4 **Ashqelon** Israel
119 H4 **Ash Sha'ār** Saudi Arabia
42 E4 **Ash Shabakah** Iraq
42 E2 **Ash Shadādah** Syria
119 H3 **Ash Sha'rā'** Saudi Arabia
126 D1 **Ash Sharafah** Yemen
39 C4 **Ash Shāriqah** U.A.E.
42 E3 **Ash Sharqāṭ** Iraq
42 F4 **Ash Shaṭrah** Iraq
126 D2 **Ash Shaykh 'Uthman** Yemen
41 G7 **Ash Shiḥr** Yemen
42 F4 **Ash Shināfīyah** Iraq
39 D4 **Ash Shināṣ** Oman
119 H2 **Ash Shu'āybah** Saudi Arabia
119 H2 **Ash Shu'bah** Saudi Arabia
119 H4 **Ash Shuqayq** Saudi Arabia
Ash Shurayf see **Khaybar**
118 B2 **Ash Shuwayrif** Libya
146 C4 **Ashtabula** Ohio U.S.A.
42 F1 **Ashtarak** Armenia
36 D5 **Ashti** India
38 A2 **Ashti** India
39 B2 **Ashtiān** Iran
152 E2 **Ashton** Idaho U.S.A.
130 C6 **Ashton** South Africa
65 F4 **Ashton-under-Lyne** England U.K.
135 M4 **Ashuanipi L.** l. Newfoundland Canada
145 C5 **Ashville** Alabama U.S.A.
43 D2 **'Āṣī** r. Lebanon/Syria
43 D1 **Asi** r. Turkey
107 F3 **Asiago** Italy
156 E4 **Asientos** Mexico
38 B2 **Asifabad** India
38 D2 **Āsika** India
54 D1 **Asikkala** Finland
120 C1 **Asilah** Morocco
164 B2 **Asillo** Peru
102 B2 **Asín** Spain
108 A4 **Asinara, Golfo dell'** b. Sardegna Italy
108 A3 **Asinara, Isola** i. Sardegna Italy
36 C4 **Asind** India
44 K4 **Asino** Rus. Fed.
54 F5 **Asipovichy** Belarus
119 H4 **Asīr** div. Saudi Arabia
42 E2 **Aşkale** Turkey
53 E3 **Askaniya Nova** Ukraine
58 D2 **Asker** Norway
65 G4 **Askern** England U.K.
59 F2 **Askersund** Sweden
64 A3 **Askill** Rep. of Ireland
58 D2 **Askim** Norway
58 D3 **Askims fjord** chan. Sweden
46 E1 **Askino** Rus. Fed.
114 C2 **Askio** mt. Greece
115 □ **Askipeio** Greece
55 D5 **Askø** i. Denmark
59 G2 **Askö** i. Sweden
59 G2 **Asköping** Sweden
36 E3 **Askot** India
58 A1 **Askøy** i. Norway
130 C7 **Askraal** South Africa
60 K1 **Askvoll** Norway
43 B5 **Asl** Egypt
119 H3 **Aslam, W.** watercourse Saudi Arabia
43 C1 **Aslanköy** r. Turkey
126 C1 **Asmara** Eritrea
98 B1 **As Mariñas** reg. Spain
55 C4 **Asnæs** pen. Denmark
55 D4 **Asnæs** Denmark
59 F3 **Åsnen** l. Sweden
112 E3 **Asenovgrad** Bulgaria
98 B2 **As Neves** Spain
106 E3 **Asola** Italy
107 F3 **Asolo** Italy
36 C4 **Asop** India
115 E4 **Asopia** Greece
115 E4 **Asopos** r. Greece
126 B2 **Asosa** Ethiopia
119 G3 **Asoteriba, J.** mt. Sudan
28 B6 **Asō-wan** b. Japan
92 G2 **Aspa** Sweden
81 H3 **Aspang-Markt** Austria
81 H2 **Aspam an der Zaya** Austria
65 E3 **Aspatria** England U.K.
103 C6 **Aspe** Spain
153 F4 **Aspen** Colorado U.S.A.
43 A1 **Aspendos** Turkey
58 D2 **Asperen** l. Norway
74 E4 **Asperg** Germany
151 C5 **Aspermont** Texas U.S.A.
93 C5 **Aspet** France
93 B6 **Aspe, Vallée d'** v. France
9 B6 **Aspiring, Mt** mt. New Zealand
98 C1 **As Pontes de García Rodríguez** Spain
91 D4 **Aspremont** France
91 D4 **Aspres-sur-Buëch** France
114 E2 **Asprovalta** Greece
137 H4 **Asquith** Saskatchewan Canada
80 C5 **Assa** r. Italy
43 D2 **As Sa'an** Syria
126 D2 **Assab** Eritrea
120 B5 **Assaba** div. Mauritania
119 H2 **Aš Sab'ān** Saudi Arabia
39 B4 **As Sabsab** well Saudi Arabia
42 D2 **As Safīrah** Syria
39 B4 **As Saji** well Saudi Arabia
46 E4 **Assake-Audan, Vpadina** basin Uzbekistan
42 F4 **As Salmān** Iraq
24 1 **Assam** div. India
123 F3 **Assamakka** Niger
42 F4 **As Samāwah** Iraq
120 B4 **Assaq** watercourse Western Sahara
120 B3 **As Saquia al Hamra** watercourse Western Sahara
118 D2 **As Sarīr** reg. Libya
147 F5 **Assateague I.** i. Maryland U.S.A.
147 F6 **Assateague Island National Seashore** res. Virginia U.S.A.
119 G2 **As Sawrah** Saudi Arabia
119 G2 **As Şawrah** Saudi Arabia
43 C6 **As Sawrah** Saudi Arabia
91 E5 **Asse** r. France
69 C4 **Asse** Belgium
108 B5 **Assemini** Sardegna Italy
68 E1 **Assen** Netherlands
131 F2 **Assen** South Africa
69 B3 **Assenede** Belgium
55 C3 **Assens** Århus Denmark
55 B4 **Assens** Fyn Denmark
109 F2 **Assergi** Italy
69 D4 **Assesse** Belgium
37 F5 **Assia Hills** h. India
118 C1 **As Sidrah** Libya
93 D4 **Assier** France
137 H5 **Assiniboia** Saskatchewan Canada
137 K5 **Assiniboine** r. Manitoba Canada
136 F4 **Assiniboine, Mt** mt. Alberta/B.C. Canada
114 E2 **Assiros** Greece
168 C5 **Assis** Brazil
168 B6 **Assis Chateaubriand** Brazil
109 E1 **Assisi** Italy
74 D2 **Aßlar** Germany
80 D3 **Aßling** Germany
122 □ **Assomada** Cape Verde
110 D5 **Assoro** Sicilia Italy
121 E3 **Assouf Mellene** watercourse Algeria
42 F4 **Aş Şubayḥīyah** Kuwait
119 J2 **Aş Şufayrī** well Saudi Arabia
119 H3 **As Sūq** Saudi Arabia
42 D3 **As Sukhnah** Syria
42 F3 **As Sulaymānīyah** div. Iraq
42 F3 **As Sulaymānīyah** Iraq
119 H2 **As Sulaymī** Saudi Arabia
39 B4 **Aş Şulb** reg. Saudi Arabia
118 C1 **As Sulṭān** Libya
119 H3 **As Sūq** Saudi Arabia
43 D3 **As Suwaydā'** Syria
42 D3 **As Suwaydā'** Syria
126 E2 **As Suwādīyah** Yemen
66 C2 **Assynt, Loch** l. Scotland U.K.
58 D1 **Åsta** r. Norway
58 D1 **Åsta** Norway
80 C4 **Asta, Cima d'** mt. Italy
93 C4 **Astaffort** France
113 F7 **Astakida** i. Greece
114 C4 **Astakos** Greece
Astalu I. i. see **Astola I.**
42 G2 **Astara** Azerbaijan
93 C5 **Astarac** reg. France
93 C5 **Astarac, Barrage de l'** dam France
59 E1 **Åsteby** Sweden
81 F2 **Asten** Austria
69 D3 **Asten** Netherlands
Asterabad see **Gorgān**
106 C4 **Asti** div. Piemonte Italy
106 C4 **Asti** Asti Italy
154 A2 **Asti** California U.S.A.
172 D1 **Astica** Argentina
107 F3 **Astico** r. Italy
164 C2 **Astillero** Peru
Astin Tagh mountain range see **Altun Shan**
39 E4 **Astola I.** i. Pakistan
141 J3 **Aston-Jonction** Québec Canada
36 C2 **Astor** r. Pakistan
47 J5 **Astor** Jammu and Kashmir
36 C2 **Astor** Pakistan
168 C5 **Astorga** Brazil
98 D2 **Astorga** Spain
152 B2 **Astoria** Oregon U.S.A.
59 E3 **Åstorp** Sweden
52 H2 **Astradamovka** Rus. Fed.
51 J6 **Astrakhan'** Rus. Fed.
51 H6 **Astrakhan'** Rus. Fed.
Astrakhan' Bazar see **Cälilabad**
53 F3 **Astrakhanka** Ukraine
59 E1 **Åstrand** Sweden
54 D4 **Astravyets** Belarus
179 D3 **Astrid Ridge** sea feature Antarctica
115 D5 **Astros** Greece
77 N2 **Astryna** Belarus
99 F2 **Astudillo** Spain
109 E3 **Astura** r. Italy
98 D1 **Asturias** airport Spain
98 D1 **Asturias** div. Spain
173 G4 **Asturias** Argentina
113 F6 **Astypalaia** i. Greece
7 □12 **Asuisui, C.** c. Western Samoa
21 M3 **Asuncion** i. Northern Mariana Is Pacific Ocean
164 C2 **Asunción** Bolivia
165 E5 **Asunción** Paraguay
59 E3 **Åsunden** l. Sweden
59 F3 **Åsunden** l. Sweden
108 A5 **Asuni** Sardegna Italy
114 C2 **Asvestopetra** Greece
55 C4 **As Vig** b. Denmark
54 F3 **Asvyeya** Belarus
126 B4 **Aswa** r. Uganda
119 F3 **Aswân** Egypt
119 F3 **Aswân Dam** dam Egypt
119 F2 **Asyût** Egypt
79 J4 **Aszód** Hungary
6 □4 **Ata** i. Tonga
170 B2 **Atacama** div. Chile
176 H6 **Atafu** i.
43 B5 **Atairtîr el Dahami, G.** mt. Egypt
43 C4 **Atā'ita, J. el** mt. Jordan
7 □11 **Ataiti** French Polynesia Pacific Ocean
32 B2 **Ata Kang La** pass China
123 E5 **Atakpamé** Togo
100 B2 **Atalaia** mt. Portugal
166 E2 **Atalaia** Brazil
162 C4 **Atalaia do Norte** Brazil
100 B3 **Atalaia, Pta da** pt Portugal
114 E4 **Atalanti** Greece
156 K8 **Atalaya** Panama
164 B2 **Atalaya** Peru
169 H3 **Ataléia** Brazil
30 E2 **Atamanovka** Rus. Fed.
29 G6 **Atami** Japan
126 E2 **'Ataq** Yemen
43 B5 **'Ataqa, G.** h. Egypt
173 K1 **Ataques** Uruguay
99 F3 **Ataquines** Spain
24 B3 **Ataran** r. Myanmar
101 G3 **Atarfe** Spain
155 H4 **Atarque** New Mexico U.S.A.
154 B4 **Atascadero** California U.S.A.
Atas I. i. see **South I.**
47 H3 **Atasu** Kazakhstan
6 □4 **Atata** i. Tonga
21 J8 **Atauro** i. Indonesia
119 G4 **Atbara** r. Sudan
119 F4 **Atbara** Sudan
47 G2 **Atbasar** Kazakhstan
47 J4 **At-Bashy** Kyrgyzstan
151 F6 **Atchafalaya Bay** b. Louisiana U.S.A.
150 E4 **Atchison** Kansas U.S.A.
122 D5 **Atebubu** Ghana
102 B3 **Ateca** Spain
156 D4 **Atenguillo** Mexico
109 F2 **Aterno** r. Italy
109 G3 **Atessa** Italy
69 B4 **Ath** div. Hainaut Belgium
69 B4 **Ath** Belgium
134 G4 **Athabasca** r. Alberta Canada
136 G4 **Athabasca** Alberta Canada
137 G3 **Athabasca, Lake** l. Saskatchewan Canada
37 F5 **Āthagarh** India
114 B4 **Athanio** Greece
67 E3 **Athboy** Rep. of Ireland
67 C3 **Athenry** Rep. of Ireland
145 C5 **Athens** Alabama U.S.A.
145 D5 **Athens** Georgia U.S.A.
146 B5 **Athens** Ohio U.S.A.
141 H4 **Athens** Ontario Canada
145 C5 **Athens** Tennessee U.S.A.
151 E5 **Athens** Texas U.S.A.
Athens see **Athina**
63 E2 **Atherstone** England U.K.
15 F3 **Atherton** Queensland Australia
127 C5 **Athi** r. Kenya
86 B3 **Athies** France
86 C3 **Athies-sous-Laon** France
115 E5 **Athina** Greece
127 C5 **Athi River** Kenya
89 E3 **Athis-de-l'Orne** France
67 C3 **Athleague** Rep. of Ireland
67 D3 **Athlone** Rep. of Ireland
38 A2 **Athni** India
147 G3 **Athol** Massachusetts U.S.A.
9 B6 **Athol** New Zealand
145 □2 **Athol I.** i. The Bahamas
66 E4 **Atholl, Forest of** forest Scotland U.K.
114 F2 **Athos** mt. Greece
43 D5 **Ath Thāyat** mt. Saudi Arabia
67 E4 **Athy** Rep. of Ireland
118 C5 **Ati** Chad
39 D2 **Aṭīābād** Iran
169 E5 **Atibaia** Brazil
164 B3 **Atico** Peru
124 E2 **Atiedo** Sudan
99 H3 **Atienza** Spain
118 B3 **Ati, Jabal** mountain range Libya
137 J4 **Atikameg L.** l. Saskatchewan Canada
138 B4 **Atikokan** Ontario Canada
139 H3 **Atikonak L.** l. Labrador Canada
7 □11 **Atimaono** French Polynesia Pacific Ocean
109 F3 **Atina** Italy
38 B4 **Atirampattinam** India
5 M7 **Atiu** i.
45 R3 **Atka** Rus. Fed.
52 G4 **Atkara** r. Rus. Fed.
52 G4 **Atkarsk** Rus. Fed.
157 F5 **Atlacomulco** Mexico
145 C5 **Atlanta** Georgia U.S.A.
148 C5 **Atlanta** Illinois U.S.A.
148 E3 **Atlanta** Michigan U.S.A.
148 A6 **Atlanta** Missouri U.S.A.
42 C2 **Atlantı** Turkey
150 E3 **Atlantic** Iowa U.S.A.
147 F5 **Atlantic City** New Jersey U.S.A.
175 M6 **Atlantic-Indian Antarctic Basin** sea feature Atlantic Ocean
174 K9 **Atlantic-Indian Ridge** sea feature Indian Ocean
130 B6 **Atlantis** South Africa
174 G3 **Atlantis Fracture** sea feature Atlantic Ocean
121 E2 **Atlas Saharien** mountain range Algeria
121 E1 **Atlas Tellien** mountain range Algeria
136 C3 **Atlin** B.C. Canada
136 C3 **Atlin Lake** l. B.C. Canada
136 C3 **Atlin Prov. Park** res. B.C. Canada
157 F5 **Atlixco** Mexico
38 B3 **Atmakur** India
38 B3 **Atmakur** India
52 F3 **Atmis** r. Rus. Fed.
151 G6 **Atmore** Alabama U.S.A.
28 C6 **Atō** Japan
164 C4 **Atocha** Bolivia
151 D5 **Atoka** Oklahoma U.S.A.
114 B4 **Atokos** i. Greece
24 D3 **Atouat** mt. Laos
100 A1 **Atouguia da Baleia** Portugal
157 E5 **Atoyac de Alvarez** Mexico
37 G4 **Atrai** r. India
39 D1 **Atrak** r. Iran
59 E3 **Ätran** r. Sweden
59 E3 **Ätran** Sweden
162 B3 **Atrato** r. Colombia
39 C1 **Atrek** r. Iran/Turkmenistan
109 F2 **Atri** Italy
147 F5 **Atsion** New Jersey U.S.A.
29 G6 **Atsugi** Japan
29 G4 **Atsumi** Japan
28 H2 **Atsuta** Japan
119 H3 **Aṭ Ṭā'if** Saudi Arabia
Adalia see **Antalya**
145 C5 **Attalla** Alabama U.S.A.
118 D3 **Aṭ Ṭallāb** oasis Libya
42 E3 **At Ta'mīm** div. Iraq
118 D1 **At Tamīmī** Libya
25 D4 **Attapu** Laos
115 □ **Attavyros** mt. Greece
138 C3 **Attawapiskat** r. Ontario Canada
138 D3 **Attawapiskat** Ontario Canada
138 C3 **Attawapiskat L.** l. Ontario Canada
119 H2 **At Taysīyah** plat. Saudi Arabia
72 C4 **Attendorn** Germany
80 C2 **Attenkirchen** Germany
131 G2 **Atteridgeville** South Africa
81 E3 **Attersee** l. Austria
81 E3 **Attersee** Austria
69 D5 **Attert** r. Luxembourg
69 D5 **Attert** Belgium
148 D5 **Attica** Indiana U.S.A.
146 B4 **Attica** Ohio U.S.A.
109 E2 **Attigliano** Italy
86 D3 **Attigny** France
115 E5 **Attiki** div. Greece
147 H3 **Attleboro** Massachusetts U.S.A.
63 H2 **Attleborough** England U.K.
81 E2 **Attnang** Austria
36 C2 **Attock** Pakistan
119 G2 **Aṭ Ṭubayq** reg. Saudi Arabia
176 G2 **Attu Island** i. Alaska U.S.A.
13 G2 **Attunga** New South Wales Australia
38 B4 **Attur** India
126 D2 **At Turbah** Yemen
119 H2 **Aṭ Ṭuwayyah** well Saudi Arabia
172 D3 **Atuel** r. Argentina
92 C3 **Atur** France
59 F2 **Åtvidaberg** Sweden
146 C4 **Atwood Lake** l. Ohio U.S.A.
52 H2 **Atyashevo** Rus. Fed.
46 D3 **Atyrau** div. Kazakhstan
46 D3 **Atyrau** Kazakhstan
52 F2 **Atyur'yevo** Rus. Fed.
53 E1 **Atyusha** Ukraine
108 B5 **Atzara** Sardegna Italy
80 A3 **Au** Austria
83 E1 **Au** Switzerland
74 F3 **Aub** Germany
91 D5 **Aubagne** France
91 C5 **Aubais** France
69 D5 **Aubange** Belgium
23 B2 **Aubarede Point** pt Philippines
86 D4 **Aube** div. France
86 D5 **Aube** r. France
91 C4 **Aubenas** France
86 D3 **Aubenton** France
89 G3 **Aubergenville** France
90 D1 **Auberive** France
179 □ **Aubert, C.** c. Kerguelen Indian Ocean
92 C3 **Aubeterre-sur-Dronne** France
86 C4 **Aubetin** r. France
89 G2 **Aubevoye** France
90 B3 **Aubière** France
93 C5 **Aubiet** France
89 F4 **Aubigné-Racan** France
91 D4 **Aubignosc** France
92 A2 **Aubigny** France
86 B2 **Aubigny-en-Artois** France
89 H4 **Aubigny-sur-Nère** France
93 E4 **Aubin** France
82 B2 **Aubonne** Switzerland
87 E3 **Auboué** France
93 E4 **Aubrac** mts France
155 F4 **Aubrey Cliffs** cliff Arizona U.S.A.
134 F3 **Aubry Lake** l. N.W.T. Canada
15 G5 **Auburn** r. Queensland Australia
145 C5 **Auburn** Alabama U.S.A.
154 B2 **Auburn** California U.S.A.
148 E5 **Auburn** Indiana U.S.A.
147 H2 **Auburn** Maine U.S.A.
150 E3 **Auburn** Nebraska U.S.A.
146 E3 **Auburn** New York U.S.A.
140 E5 **Auburn** Ontario Canada
152 B2 **Auburn** Washington U.S.A.
15 G5 **Auburn Ra.** h. Queensland Australia
92 E3 **Aubusson** France
69 B4 **Auby** France
172 C4 **Auca Mahuida** Argentina
172 C4 **Auca Mahuida, Sa de** mt. Argentina
164 C4 **Aucanquilcha, Co** mt. Chile
54 C3 **Auce** Latvia
93 C5 **Auch** France
24 B1 **Auche** Myanmar
66 C5 **Auchenbreck** Scotland U.K.
123 F5 **Auchi** Nigeria
66 E4 **Auchterarder** Scotland U.K.
66 E4 **Auchtermuchty** Scotland U.K.
8 E2 **Auckland** div. New Zealand
8 E2 **Auckland** New Zealand
8 □1 **Auckland I.** i. Auckland Is New Zealand
8 □1 **Auckland Is** is New Zealand
93 B6 **Aucun** France
93 E5 **Aude** div. Languedoc-Roussillon France
93 E5 **Aude** r. France
140 B1 **Auden** Ontario Canada
93 A4 **Audenge** France
147 H2 **Audet** Québec Canada
90 D1 **Audeux** France
88 A3 **Audierne** France

B

122 B4 **Banora** Guinea
98 C2 **Baños de Molgas** Spain
98 E4 **Baños de Montemayor** Spain
102 C2 **Baños de Panticosa** Spain
172 B4 **Baños Maule** Chile
79 H3 **Bánovce nad Bebravou** Slovakia
104 G3 **Banoviči** Bos.-Herz.
Banow *see* **Andarāb**
24 C3 **Ban Pak-Leng** Laos
25 C5 **Ban Pak Phanang** Thailand
24 B4 **Banphot Phisai** Thailand
25 B4 **Ban Pong** Thailand
79 K3 **Bánréve** Hungary
25 B5 **Ban Sawi** Thailand
37 E4 **Bansi** India
25 B5 **Ban Sichon** Thailand
25 C4 **Ban Si Racha** Thailand
79 J3 **Banská Bystrica** Slovakia
79 H3 **Banská Štiavnica** Slovakia
112 D4 **Bansko** Bulgaria
24 B3 **Ban Sop Prap** Thailand
38 B2 **Banswada** India
36 C5 **Banswara** India
22 D3 **Bantaeng** Indonesia
10 □1 **Bantam** *Cocos Is* Indian Ocean
24 C3 **Ban Taviang** Laos
23 B4 **Bantayan i.** Philippines
123 E5 **Bantè** Benin
67 C4 **Banteer** Rep. of Ireland
24 B2 **Ban Tha Don** Thailand
24 C4 **Ban Tha Tum** Thailand
87 E3 **Bantheville** France
23 B3 **Banton i.** Philippines
24 D3 **Ban Tôp** Laos
67 B5 **Bantry** Rep. of Ireland
67 B5 **Bantry Bay b.** Rep. of Ireland
22 B3 **Bantul** Indonesia
38 A3 **Bantval** India
24 C3 **Ban Woen** Laos
25 D4 **Ban Xepian** Laos
124 B2 **Banyo** Cameroon
102 F2 **Banyoles** Spain
22 A2 **Banyuasin r.** Indonesia
93 F6 **Banyuls-sur-Mer** France
22 C4 **Banyuwangi** Indonesia
6 □1 **Banz** P.N.G.
179 C6 **Banzare Coast coastal area** Antarctica
175 K7 **Banzare Seamount sea feature** Indian Ocean
73 G2 **Banzkow** Germany
Ba'oan *see* **Shenzhen**
30 B6 **Bao'an** China
31 E5 **Baoding** China
33 F1 **Baofeng** China
24 D2 **Bao Hà** Vietnam
32 D1 **Baoji** China
32 D1 **Baoji** China
33 E2 **Baojing** China
33 E2 **Baokang** China
25 D5 **Bao Lôc** Vietnam
31 K3 **Baoqing** China
124 C2 **Baoro** Central African Rep.
32 B3 **Baoshan** China
30 D4 **Baotou** China
122 C4 **Baoulé r.** Mali
32 C2 **Baoxing** China
33 G1 **Baoying** China
36 C4 **Bap** India
38 C3 **Bapatla** India
86 B2 **Bapaume** France
141 F4 **Baptiste Lake l.** *Ontario* Canada
39 C2 **Baqam** Iran
37 H2 **Baqêm** China
37 H3 **Baqên** China
43 C5 **Bāqir, J. mt.** Jordan
42 F3 **Ba'qūbah** Iraq
164 C4 **Baquedano** Chile
162 □ **Baquerizo Moreno** *Galapagos Is* Ecuador
86 D3 **Bar r.** France
30 C2 **Bar** Rus. Fed.
53 B2 **Bar** Ukraine
112 B3 **Bar** Yugoslavia
37 E4 **Bara** India
123 G4 **Bara** Nigeria
119 F5 **Bara** Sudan
126 D4 **Baraawe** Somalia
22 C2 **Barabai** Indonesia
36 E4 **Bara Banki** India
47 J1 **Barabinsk** Rus. Fed.
47 J2 **Barabinskaya Step' plain** Rus. Fed.
126 D4 **Bar Abir well** Ethiopia
148 B4 **Baraboo r.** *Wisconsin* U.S.A.
148 C4 **Baraboo** *Wisconsin* U.S.A.
166 B3 **Baracaju r.** Brazil
Baracaldo *see* **Barakaldo**
158 D2 **Baracoa** Cuba
43 D3 **Barada r.** Syria
43 D2 **Baradah** Syria
173 H2 **Baradero** Argentina
13 G2 **Baradine r.** *New South Wales* Australia
13 G2 **Baradine** *New South Wales* Australia
148 C2 **Baraga** *Michigan* U.S.A.
37 E5 **Baragarh** India
162 D1 **Baragua** Venezuela
159 E3 **Barahona** Dominican Rep.
99 H3 **Barahona** Spain
37 H4 **Barail Range mountain range** India
99 H4 **Barajas de Melo** Spain
112 C2 **Barajevo** Yugoslavia
37 H4 **Barak r.** India
39 G1 **Barak** Afghanistan
Barak *see* **Kargamiş**
126 C1 **Baraka watercourse** Eritrea/Sudan
99 H1 **Barakaldo** Spain
39 G2 **Barakī Barak** Afghanistan
37 F5 **Bārākot** India
52 D2 **Barakovo** Rus. Fed.
47 G2 **Barakpay** Kazakhstan
15 G5 **Baralaba** *Queensland* Australia
36 D2 **Bara Lacha Pass pass** India
98 C2 **Baralla** Spain
42 E3 **Barˌ al Milḩ l.** Iraq
137 K3 **Baralzon Lake l.** *Manitoba* Canada
163 F2 **Barama r.** Guyana
163 F2 **Baramanni** Guyana
38 A2 **Baramati** India
15 G5 **Barambah r.** *Queensland* Australia
36 C2 **Baramula** India
36 A4 **Baran r.** Pakistan
36 D4 **Baran** India
102 B2 **Barañain** Spain
54 E5 **Baranavichy** Belarus
122 D4 **Barani** Burkina
45 S3 **Baranikha** Rus. Fed.
53 B1 **Baranivka** Ukraine
39 E2 **Bārān, Kūh-e mountain range** Iran
162 C1 **Baranoa** Colombia
109 F4 **Barano d'Ischia** Italy
136 B3 **Baranof Island i.** *Alaska* U.S.A.
52 H3 **Baranovka** Rus. Fed.
77 L4 **Baranów** Poland
77 K5 **Baranów Sandomierska** Poland
79 H5 **Baranya div.** Hungary
79 H6 **Baranyai-dombság h.** Hungary
167 A4 **Barão de Melgaço** Brazil
112 E1 **Baraolt** Romania
122 C4 **Baraouéli** Mali
69 D4 **Baraque de Fraiture h.** Belgium
93 E4 **Baraqueville** France
163 F5 **Bararati r.** Brazil
52 F2 **Barashevo** Rus. Fed.
12 D3 **Baratta** *S. Australia* Australia
36 D3 **Baraut** India
54 F4 **Baravukha** Belarus
162 B3 **Baraya** Colombia
169 G4 **Barbacena** Brazil
162 B3 **Barbacoas** Colombia
99 G2 **Barbadillo del Pez** Spain
165 E3 **Barbado r.** Brazil
133 N8 **Barbados country** Caribbean
107 J3 **Barban** Croatia
140 B2 **Barbara Lake l.** *Ontario* Canada
43 B5 **Barbar, G. el mt.** Egypt
103 E6 **Barbaria, Cap de pt** Spain
102 D2 **Barbastro** Spain
107 J4 **Barbat** Croatia
100 E4 **Barbate r.** Spain
100 E4 **Barbate de Franco** Spain
93 C5 **Barbazan** France
107 F4 **Barberino di Mugello** Italy
140 E2 **Barber's Bay** *Ontario* Canada
153 □1 **Barbers Pt pt** *Hawaii* U.S.A.
146 C4 **Barberton** *Ohio* U.S.A.
131 H2 **Barberton** South Africa
92 B3 **Barbezieux-St-Hilaire** France
86 C4 **Barbonne-Fayel** France
162 C2 **Barbosa** Colombia
137 L2 **Barbour Bay b.** *N.W.T.* Canada
146 B6 **Barbourville** *Kentucky* U.S.A.
23 B4 **Barboza** Philippines
25 C4 **Bar Bua Chum** Thailand
24 C4 **Bar Bua Yai** Thailand
159 G3 **Barbuda i.** Antigua
73 G4 **Barby** Germany
112 D3 **Bârca** Romania
98 D3 **Barca de Alva** Portugal
158 □1 **Barcadera** *Aruba* Caribbean
158 □3 **Barcadera** *Bonaire* Netherlands Ant.
15 F4 **Barcaldine** *Queensland* Australia
100 D2 **Barcarrota** Spain
79 M4 **Barcău r.** Romania
111 E4 **Barcellona Pozzo di Gotto** *Sicilia* Italy
102 F3 **Barcelona airport** Spain
102 E3 **Barcelona div.** Spain
102 F3 **Barcelona** *Barcelona* Spain
163 E1 **Barcelona** Venezuela
145 □3 **Barceloneta** Puerto Rico
93 B5 **Barcelonne-du-Gers** France
91 E4 **Barcelonnette** France
163 E4 **Barcelos** Brazil
98 B3 **Barcelos** Portugal
99 G1 **Barcenillas de Cerezos** Spain
24 C3 **Bar Channabot** Thailand
74 F2 **Barchfeld** Germany
24 B3 **Bar Chiang Dao** Thailand
77 K1 **Barciany** Poland
91 D4 **Barcillonnette** France
76 F3 **Barcin** Poland
76 E1 **Barcino** Poland
122 C6 **Barclayville** Liberia
Barco Creek watercourse *see* **Cooper Cr.**
99 H3 **Barcones** Spain
15 E5 **Barcoo watercourse** *Queensland* Australia
78 G6 **Barcs** Hungary
77 J2 **Barczewo** Poland
42 F1 **Bärdä** Azerbaijan
172 C5 **Barda del Medio** Argentina
118 C3 **Bardai** Chad
56 M6 **Bárðarbunga mt.** Iceland
172 C3 **Bardas Blancas** Argentina
37 F5 **Barddhamān** India
79 L2 **Bardejov** Slovakia
102 B2 **Bárdenas Reales reg.** Spain
55 C4 **Bårdesø** Denmark
39 B4 **Bardestān** Iran
37 E4 **Bardi** India
106 D4 **Bardi** Italy
106 C4 **Bardineto** Italy
90 C1 **Bard, Montagne de h.** France
63 F1 **Bardney** *England* U.K.
107 E3 **Bardolino** Italy
25 D4 **Bar Đôn** Vietnam
106 A3 **Bardonecchia** Italy
62 B2 **Bardsey Island i.** *Wales* U.K.
62 B2 **Bardsey Sound chan.** *Wales* U.K.
144 C4 **Bardstown** *Kentucky* U.S.A.
146 B5 **Bardwell** *Ohio* U.S.A.
93 C6 **Barèges** France
36 D3 **Bareilly** India
13 F3 **Barellan** *New South Wales* Australia
73 F2 **Barendorf** Germany
68 C3 **Barendrecht** Netherlands
89 F2 **Barentin** France
89 E3 **Barenton** France
178 □3 **Barentsburg** *Svalbard* Arctic Ocean
178 □3 **Barentsøya i.** *Svalbard* Arctic Ocean
44 E2 **Barents Sea sea** Arctic Ocean
126 C1 **Barentu** Eritrea
88 D2 **Barfleur** France
88 D2 **Barfleur, Pte de pt** France
36 E3 **Barga** China
106 E4 **Barga** Italy
126 F2 **Bargaal** Somalia
15 H5 **Bargara** *Queensland* Australia
99 F5 **Bargas** Spain
106 B4 **Barge** Italy
91 E5 **Bargemon** France
83 F3 **Barghe** Italy
36 D5 **Bargi** India
77 L2 **Bargłów Kościelny** Poland
66 D5 **Bargrennan** *Scotland* U.K.
72 F2 **Bargteheide** Germany
93 C4 **Barguelonne r.** France
37 G5 **Barguna** Bangladesh
37 E4 **Barhalganj** India
63 H3 **Barham** *England* U.K.
147 J2 **Bar Harbor** *Maine* U.S.A.
24 C2 **Bar Houayxay** Laos
25 B4 **Bar Hua Hin** Thailand
109 J3 **Bari div.** *Puglia* Italy
126 F2 **Bari div.** Somalia
111 F1 **Bari** *Bari* Italy
36 D4 **Bari** India
124 C3 **Bari** Zaire
25 D5 **Ba Ria** Vietnam
121 F1 **Barika** Algeria
39 G2 **Barikot** Afghanistan
37 E3 **Barikot** Nepal
159 H6 **Barima r.** Guyana
162 C2 **Barinas** Venezuela
124 D3 **Baringa** Zaire
127 C4 **Baringo, L. l.** Kenya
55 B4 **Båring Vig b.** Denmark
111 F1 **Bari Palese airport** Italy
168 D5 **Bariri** Brazil
119 F3 **Bârîs** Egypt
37 G5 **Barisal** Bangladesh
108 B5 **Barì Sardo** *Sardegna* Italy
109 F2 **Barisciano** Italy
22 C2 **Barito r.** Indonesia
170 D1 **Baritu, Parque Nacional nat. park** Argentina
91 C4 **Barjac** France
91 E5 **Barjaude mt.** France
91 E5 **Barjols** France
32 C2 **Barkam** China
39 B3 **Barkan, Ra's-e pt** Iran
54 E3 **Barkava** Latvia
136 E4 **Barkerville** *B.C.* Canada
36 B3 **Barkhan** Pakistan
25 B4 **Bar Khao Yoi** Thailand
37 F4 **Barki Saraiya** India
144 C4 **Barkley, L. l.** *Kentucky* U.S.A.
136 D5 **Barkley Sd inlet** *B.C.* Canada
14 D4 **Barkly Downs** *Queensland* Australia
131 F5 **Barkly East** South Africa
131 F5 **Barkly Pass** South Africa
14 D3 **Barkly Tableland reg.** *Northern Terr.* Australia
130 E4 **Barkly West** South Africa
26 F3 **Barkol** China
76 F2 **Barkowo** Poland
39 D3 **Barkūh** Iran
63 G2 **Barkway** *England* U.K.
112 F1 **Bârlad** Romania
73 G3 **Barleben** Germany
87 E4 **Bar-le-Duc** France
17 B6 **Barlee, L. salt flat** *Western Australia* Australia
17 B4 **Barlee Ra. h.** *Western Australia* Australia
109 J3 **Barletta** Italy
63 G2 **Barley** *England* U.K.
76 D3 **Barlinek** Poland
24 B3 **Bar Mae La Luang** Thailand
24 B3 **Bar Mae Thalop** Thailand
13 F3 **Barmedman** *New South Wales* Australia
36 B4 **Barmer** India
12 E3 **Barmera** *S. Australia* Australia
62 B2 **Barmouth** *Wales* U.K.
62 B2 **Barmouth Bay b.** *Wales* U.K.
24 C4 **Bar Muang Phon** Thailand
36 C5 **Barnagar** India
36 C3 **Barnala** India
24 C3 **Bar Na Noi** Thailand
65 G3 **Barnard Castle** *England* U.K.
13 F2 **Barnato** *New South Wales* Australia
78 B2 **Bärnau** Germany
47 K2 **Barnaul** Rus. Fed.
81 G3 **Barnbach** Austria
73 G3 **Barneberg** Germany
147 F5 **Barnegat** *New Jersey* U.S.A.
147 F5 **Barnegat Bay b.** *New Jersey* U.S.A.
146 D4 **Barnesboro** *Pennsylvania* U.S.A.
135 L2 **Barnes Icecap ice cap** *N.W.T.* Canada
63 F3 **Barnet** *England* U.K.
68 D2 **Barneveld** Netherlands
88 D2 **Barneville-Carteret** France
73 H3 **Barnewitz** Germany
155 G3 **Barney Top mt.** *Utah* U.S.A.
151 C6 **Barnhart** *Texas* U.S.A.
128 □2 **Barn Long Pt pt** *St Helena* Atlantic Ocean
65 F4 **Barnoldswick** *England* U.K.
76 C3 **Barnowko** Poland
65 G4 **Barnsley** *England* U.K.
73 G4 **Barnstädt** Germany
62 B3 **Barnstaple** *England* U.K.
62 B3 **Barnstaple Bay b.** *England* U.K.
72 D3 **Barnstorf** Germany
72 E4 **Barntrup** Germany
145 D5 **Barnwell** *S. Carolina* U.S.A.
123 F5 **Baro** Nigeria
Baroda *see* **Vadodara**
131 E5 **Baroda** South Africa
130 E6 **Baroe** South Africa
81 F4 **Bärofen mt.** Austria
106 C3 **Barone, Monte mt.** Italy
32 B2 **Barong** China
91 D4 **Baronnies reg.** France
17 D4 **Barons Ra. h.** *Western Australia* Australia
87 F4 **Baronville** France
126 B3 **Baro Wenz r.** Ethiopia
25 C4 **Bar Pak Thong Chai** Thailand
37 H4 **Barpathar** India
37 G4 **Barpeta** India
24 D3 **Bar Phaeng** Thailand
24 C4 **Bar Phai** Thailand
25 C4 **Bar Phanat Nikhom** Thailand
24 D4 **Bar Phon** Laos
24 C3 **Bar Phon Thong** Thailand
24 B3 **Bar Phran Katai** Thailand
Bar Pla Soi *see* **Chon Buri**
24 C3 **Bar Pua** Thailand
43 D5 **Barqā 'Damaj well** Saudi Arabia
43 C5 **Barqa, G. mt.** Egypt
148 D3 **Barques, Pt Aux pt** *Michigan* U.S.A.
149 F3 **Barques, Pt Aux pt** *Michigan* U.S.A.
162 D1 **Barquisimeto** Venezuela
87 G4 **Barr** France
66 A4 **Barra i.** *Scotland* U.K.
166 D3 **Barra** Brazil
13 G2 **Barraba** *New South Wales* Australia
168 D5 **Barra Bonita** Brazil
166 B1 **Barraca da Bôca** Brazil
165 E1 **Barracão do Barreto** Brazil
103 C4 **Barracas** Spain
130 C7 **Barracouta, Cape headland** South Africa
169 E6 **Barra de Santos inlet** Brazil
169 H3 **Barra de São Francisco** Brazil
169 G5 **Barra de São João** Brazil
166 A4 **Barra do Bugres** Brazil
166 C2 **Barra do Corda** Brazil
125 B5 **Barra do Cuanza** Angola
168 B1 **Barra do Garças** Brazil
169 G5 **Barra do Piraí** Brazil
173 J1 **Barra do Quaraí** Brazil
167 B7 **Barra do Ribeiro** Brazil
163 F5 **Barra do São Manuel** Brazil
168 D6 **Barra do Turvo** Brazil
129 F3 **Barra Falsa, Pta da pt** Mozambique
110 D5 **Barrafranca** *Sicilia* Italy
169 G4 **Barra Longa** Brazil
169 F5 **Barra Mansa** Brazil
162 B4 **Barranca** Peru
164 A2 **Barranca** Peru
162 C2 **Barranca-bermeja** Colombia
172 B4 **Barrancas r.** Argentina
172 C4 **Barrancas** *Neuquen* Argentina
173 G2 **Barrancas** *Santa Fe* Argentina
162 C1 **Barrancas** Colombia
163 E2 **Barrancas** Venezuela
100 D2 **Barrancos** Portugal
100 C3 **Barranco Velho** Portugal
103 B6 **Barranda** Spain
170 E2 **Barranqueras** Argentina
162 C1 **Barranquilla** Colombia
129 F3 **Barra, Pta da pt** Mozambique
166 D1 **Barras** Brazil
66 A3 **Barra, Sound of chan.** *Scotland* U.K.
141 G2 **Barraute** *Québec* Canada
101 H1 **Barrax** Spain
147 G2 **Barre** *Vermont* U.S.A.
172 C1 **Barreal** Argentina
91 B4 **Barre-des-Cévennes** France
166 D3 **Barreiras** Brazil
166 A1 **Barreirinha** Brazil
166 D1 **Barreirinhas** Brazil
168 B1 **Barreiro r.** Brazil
100 A2 **Barreiro** Portugal
166 B3 **Barreiro do Nascimento** Brazil
166 E2 **Barreiros** Brazil
91 E5 **Barrême** France
25 A4 **Barren I. i.** *Andaman and Nicobar Is* India
13 G5 **Barren I., Cape i.** *Tasmania* Australia
168 D4 **Barretos** Brazil
16 D3 **Barrett, Mt h.** *Western Australia* Australia
136 G4 **Barrhead** *Alberta* Canada
66 D5 **Barrhead** *Scotland* U.K.
64 D2 **Barrhill** *Scotland* U.K.
141 F4 **Barrie** *Ontario* Canada
98 B2 **Barrié de la Maza, Emb. de resr** Spain
140 D4 **Barrie I i.** *Ontario* Canada
8 E2 **Barrier, Cape c.** New Zealand
136 E4 **Barrière** *B.C.* Canada
13 E2 **Barrier Range h.** *New South Wales* Australia
137 J3 **Barrington Lake l.** *Manitoba* Canada
13 G3 **Barrington, Mt mt.** *New South Wales* Australia
168 D1 **Barro Alto** Brazil
169 G2 **Barrocão** Brazil
148 B3 **Barron** *Wisconsin* U.S.A.
15 F3 **Barron Falls waterfall** *Queensland* Australia
172 A5 **Barros Arana** Chile
169 G4 **Barroso** Brazil
151 C7 **Barroterán** Mexico
67 D4 **Barrow r.** Rep. of Ireland
134 C2 **Barrow** *Alaska* U.S.A.
173 G5 **Barrow** Argentina
14 C2 **Barrow, C. c.** *Northern Terr.* Australia
14 C4 **Barrow Creek** *Northern Terr.* Australia
16 A4 **Barrow I. i.** *Western Australia* Australia
65 E3 **Barrow-in-Furness** *England* U.K.
17 D5 **Barrow Ra. h.** *Western Australia* Australia
135 J2 **Barrow Strait str.** *N.W.T.* Canada
17 C5 **Barr Smith Ra. h.** *Western Australia* Australia
98 D3 **Barruecopardo** Spain
62 C3 **Barry** *Wales* U.K.
130 C6 **Barrydale** South Africa
141 G4 **Barrys Bay** *Ontario* Canada
46 E3 **Barsa-Kel'mes, O. i.** Kazakhstan
36 C3 **Barsalpur** India
112 E1 **Bârsana** Romania
24 B3 **Bar Saraphi** Thailand
25 C4 **Bar Sattahip** Thailand
72 F2 **Barsbüttel** Germany
47 J3 **Barshatas** Kazakhstan
38 A2 **Barsi** India
36 D5 **Barsi lakli** India
72 E3 **Barsinghausen** Germany
55 B4 **Barsø i.** Denmark
72 C2 **Barßel** Germany
154 D4 **Barstow** *California* U.S.A.
54 B3 **Barstyčiai** Lithuania
52 C2 **Barsuki** Rus. Fed.
86 D4 **Bar-sur-Aube** France
86 D4 **Bar-sur-Seine** France
24 B3 **Bar Sut Ta** Thailand
24 C4 **Bar Ta Khli** Thailand
25 B5 **Bar Takua Pa** Thailand
90 F1 **Bartenheim** France
73 H1 **Barth** Germany
25 B5 **Bar Tha Chang** Thailand
25 B5 **Bar Thai Muang** Thailand
25 B5 **Bar Tha Kham** Thailand
24 B3 **Bar Tha Song Yang** Thailand
24 C4 **Bar Tha Tako** Thailand
24 D3 **Bar Tha Uthen** Thailand
80 A3 **Bartholomäberg** Austria
164 B4 **Bartholomew Deep depth** Chile
25 B4 **Bar Thung Luang** Thailand
163 F2 **Bartica** Guyana
42 C1 **Bartın** Turkey
15 F3 **Bartle Frere, Mt mt.** *Queensland* Australia
155 G2 **Bartles, Mt mt.** *Utah* U.S.A.
150 D3 **Bartlett** *Nebraska* U.S.A.
147 H2 **Bartlett** *New Hampshire* U.S.A.
136 F2 **Bartlett Lake l.** *N.W.T.* Canada
77 M1 **Bartninkai** Lithuania
129 F3 **Bartolomeu Dias** Mozambique
147 G2 **Barton** *Vermont* U.S.A.
65 H4 **Barton-upon-Humber** *England* U.K.
77 J1 **Bartoszyce** Poland
77 H3 **Baruchowo** Poland
108 B5 **Barumini** *Sardegna* Italy
22 C4 **Barung i.** Indonesia
73 J3 **Baruth** Germany
30 C2 **Baruunharaa** Mongolia
30 C4 **Baruunsuu** Mongolia
30 E3 **Baruun Urt** Mongolia
66 B2 **Barvas** *Scotland* U.K.
69 D4 **Barvaux** Belgium
53 G2 **Barvinkove** Ukraine
36 D5 **Barwah** India
36 C3 **Barwala** India
36 C5 **Barwani** India
36 D4 **Barwa Sagar** India
76 E2 **Barwice** Poland
13 G2 **Barwon r.** *New South Wales* Australia
24 C3 **Bar Yang Talat** Thailand
52 B2 **Baryatino** Rus. Fed.
76 F4 **Barycz r.** Poland
54 F4 **Barysaw** Belarus
52 H3 **Barysh r.** Rus. Fed.
52 H3 **Barysh** Rus. Fed.
53 D1 **Baryshivka** Ukraine
79 M5 **Bârzava** Romania
106 D3 **Barzio** Italy
39 B2 **Barzūk** Iran
39 C4 **Basaidu** Iran
170 E2 **Basail** Argentina
15 F3 **Basalt r.** *Queensland* Australia
154 C2 **Basalt** *Nevada* U.S.A.
27 □ **Basalt I. i.** Hong Kong
124 C3 **Basankusu** Zaire
38 B2 **Basar** India
53 C3 **Basarabeasca** Moldova
112 G2 **Basarabi** Romania
99 H1 **Basauri** Spain
173 H2 **Basavilbaso** Argentina
102 F2 **Bàscara** Spain
69 D5 **Bascharage** Luxembourg
108 E2 **Baschi** Italy
62 D2 **Baschurch** *England* U.K.
23 B1 **Basco** Philippines
99 G2 **Basconcillos del Tozo** Spain
99 H4 **Bascuñana, Sa de mountain range** Spain
170 B2 **Bascuñán, C. c.** Chile
69 B4 **Basècles** Belgium
82 C1 **Basel** Switzerland
83 G2 **Baselga di Pinè** Italy
82 C1 **Basellandschaft div.** Switzerland
90 F1 **Basel-Mulhouse airport** France
111 F2 **Basentello r.** Italy
111 F2 **Basento r.** Italy
148 B1 **Basewood Lake l.** *Minnesota* U.S.A.
39 D4 **Bashākerd, Kūhhā-ye mountain range** Iran
136 G4 **Bashaw** *Alberta* Canada
131 G6 **Bashee r.** South Africa
39 G2 **Bashgul r.** Afghanistan
46 E1 **Bashkortostan** Rus. Fed.
52 F3 **Bashmakovo** Rus. Fed.
39 B3 **Bāsht** Iran
53 E3 **Bashtanka** Ukraine
37 F5 **Basia** India
23 B5 **Basilan i.** Philippines
23 B5 **Basilan Strait chan.** Philippines
63 G3 **Basildon** *England* U.K.
107 H2 **Basiliano** Italy
109 H4 **Basilicata div.** Italy
111 E4 **Basiluzzo, Isola i.** Italy
152 E2 **Basin** *Wyoming* U.S.A.
174 K8 **Basin, Cape sea feature** Atlantic Ocean
63 E3 **Basingstoke** *England* U.K.
37 G5 **Basirhat** India
107 J4 **Baška** Croatia
147 K2 **Baskahegan Lake l.** *Maine* U.S.A.
52 B2 **Baskakovka** Rus. Fed.
42 F2 **Başkale** Turkey
141 H3 **Baskatong, Réservoir resr** *Québec* Canada
43 B1 **Başköy** Turkey
Basle *see* **Basel**
63 E1 **Baslow** *England* U.K.
22 A2 **Baso i.** Indonesia
36 D5 **Basoda** India
83 D2 **Basodino mt.** Italy/Switzerland
124 D3 **Basoko** Zaire
Basque Country div. *see* **País Vasco**
93 D4 **Bas Quercy reg.** France
Basra *see* **Al Başrah**
87 G4 **Bas-Rhin div.** France
107 F3 **Bassano del Grappa** Italy
123 E5 **Bassar** Togo
117 J8 **Bassas da India is**
82 C1 **Bassecourt** Switzerland
88 D4 **Basse-Goulaine** France
24 A4 **Bassein r.** Myanmar
24 A3 **Bassein** Myanmar
124 D3 **Basse-Kotto div.** Central African Rep.
69 D4 **Bassenge** Belgium
89 E3 **Basse-Normandie div.** France
93 B4 **Bassens** France
65 E3 **Bassenthwaite Lake l.** *England* U.K.
159 □4 **Basse Pointe** *Martinique* Caribbean
122 B4 **Basse Santa Su** The Gambia
159 □5 **Basse Terre i.** *Guadeloupe* Caribbean
159 □5 **Basse Terre** *Guadeloupe* Caribbean
159 □6 **Basseterre** *St Kitts-Nevis* Caribbean
159 □3 **Basse Terre** Trinidad and Tobago
150 D3 **Bassett** *Nebraska* U.S.A.
155 G5 **Bassett Peak summit** *Arizona* U.S.A.
147 J2 **Bass Harbor** *Maine* U.S.A.
87 E5 **Bassigny reg.** France
120 C5 **Bassikounou** Mauritania
123 E5 **Bassila** Benin
86 D4 **Bassin Auzon Temple resr** France
93 A4 **Bassin d'Arcachon inlet** France
88 D3 **Bassin de Rennes basin** France
91 B5 **Bassin de Thau lag.** France
66 F4 **Bass Rock i.** *Scotland* U.K.
13 F4 **Bass Strait str.** Australia
72 D3 **Bassum** Germany
82 A3 **Bassy** France
59 E3 **Båstad** Sweden
39 C4 **Bastak** Iran
42 F2 **Bastānābād** Iran
109 E2 **Bastardo** Italy
108 B2 **Bastelica** *Corse* France
70 E3 **Bastheim** Germany
37 E4 **Basti** India
108 B2 **Bastia** *Corse* France
109 E1 **Bastia** Italy
108 B2 **Bastia-Poretta airport** *Corse* France
166 E2 **Bastioes r.** Brazil
69 D5 **Bastogne div.** *Luxembourg* Belgium
69 D4 **Bastogne** Belgium
168 C4 **Bastos** Brazil
151 F5 **Bastrop** *Louisiana* U.S.A.
151 D6 **Bastrop** *Texas* U.S.A.
59 F1 **Basttjärn** Sweden
39 F4 **Basul r.** Pakistan
Basuo *see* **Dongfang**
22 A2 **Basu, Tg pt** Indonesia
125 B5 **Bas-Zaire div.** Zaire
124 A3 **Bata** Equatorial Guinea
158 B2 **Batabanó, Golfo de b.** Cuba
23 B2 **Batac** Philippines
45 P3 **Batagay** Rus. Fed.
45 P3 **Batagay-Alyta** Rus. Fed.
30 B1 **Batagol** Rus. Fed.
168 B4 **Bataguaçu** Brazil
112 E4 **Batak** Bulgaria
22 C3 **Batakan** Indonesia
36 C3 **Batala** India
100 B1 **Batalha** Portugal
22 A1 **Batam i.** Indonesia
124 E3 **Batama** Zaire
45 O3 **Batamay** Rus. Fed.
46 E2 **Batamshinskiy** Kazakhstan
23 B1 **Batan i.** Philippines
32 B2 **Batang** China
124 A4 **Batanga** Gabon
124 C2 **Batangafo** Central African Rep.
23 B3 **Batangas** Philippines
22 2 **Batanghari r.** Indonesia
23 B1 **Batan Islands is** Philippines
79 H5 **Bátaszék** Hungary
168 E4 **Batatais** Brazil
148 C5 **Batavia** *Illinois* U.S.A.
146 D3 **Batavia** *New York* U.S.A.
52 A3 **Batayeva** Rus. Fed.
51 F6 **Bataysk** Rus. Fed.
140 C3 **Batchawana r.** *Ontario* Canada
140 C3 **Batchawana Bay** *Ontario* Canada
138 D4 **Batchawana Mt. h.** *Ontario* Canada
14 B2 **Batchelor** *Northern Terr.* Australia
140 C3 **Batchewana** *Ontario* Canada
140 C3 **Batchewana Mt mt.** *Ontario* Canada
25 C4 **Bătdâmbâng** Cambodia
102 D3 **Batea** Spain
13 G3 **Batemans Bay** *New South Wales* Australia
29 □2 **Baten** Japan
11 □1 **Bates, Mt h.** *Norfolk I.* Pacific Ocean
17 C5 **Bates Ra. h.** *Western Australia* Australia
151 F5 **Batesville** *Arkansas* U.S.A.
151 F5 **Batesville** *Mississippi* U.S.A.
50 D3 **Batetskiy** Rus. Fed.
62 D3 **Bath** *England* U.K.
147 J3 **Bath** *Maine* U.S.A.
139 G4 **Bath** *New Brunswick* Canada
146 E3 **Bath** *New York* U.S.A.
141 G4 **Bath** *Ontario* Canada
159 □6 **Bath** *St Kitts-Nevis* Caribbean
118 C5 **Batha div.** Chad
118 C5 **Batha watercourse** Chad
124 C1 **Batha de Laïri watercourse** Chad
66 E5 **Bathgate** *Scotland* U.K.
36 C3 **Bathinda** India
68 E2 **Bathmen** Netherlands
139 G4 **Bathurst** *New Brunswick* Canada
13 G3 **Bathurst** *New South Wales* Australia
173 G4 **Bathurst** Argentina
131 F6 **Bathurst** South Africa
14 B1 **Bathurst I. i.** *Northern Terr.* Australia
135 J2 **Bathurst I. i.** *N.W.T.* Canada
14 B1 **Bathurst I. Abor. Land res.** *Northern Terr.* Australia
134 H3 **Bathurst Inlet inlet** *N.W.T.* Canada
134 H3 **Bathurst Inlet** *N.W.T.* Canada
126 C2 **Batī** Ethiopia
122 D5 **Batié** Burkina
22 E2 **Batikala, Tg pt** Indonesia
6 □8 **Batiki i.** Fiji
113 F6 **Batı Menteşe Dağları mountain range** Turkey
79 H6 **Batina** Croatia
141 J3 **Batiscan** *Québec* Canada
39 C2 **Bāţlāq-e Gavkhūnī salt marsh** Iran
65 G4 **Batley** *England* U.K.
13 G3 **Batlow** *New South Wales* Australia
42 E2 **Batman** Turkey
52 F1 **Batmany** Rus. Fed.
121 F1 **Batna** Algeria
151 F6 **Baton Rouge** *Louisiana* U.S.A.
79 J3 **Bátonyterenye** Hungary
156 D3 **Batopilas** Mexico
124 B3 **Batouri** Cameroon
168 B1 **Batovi** Brazil
119 G2 **Batrā, J. mt.** Saudi Arabia
43 C5 **Batrā, J. el mt.** Jordan
43 C2 **Batroûn** Lebanon
56 H1 **Båtsfjord** Norway
115 F5 **Batsi** Greece
30 A2 **Bat-Sot** Rus. Fed.
82 C1 **Bätterkinden** Switzerland
36 C3 **Batti** India
38 C5 **Batticaloa** Sri Lanka
25 A5 **Batti Malv i.** *Andaman and Nicobar Is* India
109 G4 **Battipaglia** Italy
137 G4 **Battle r.** *Alberta* Canada
63 G4 **Battle** *England* U.K.
148 E4 **Battle Creek** *Michigan* U.S.A.
137 H4 **Battleford** *Saskatchewan* Canada
152 C3 **Battle Mountain** *Nevada* U.S.A.
79 L5 **Battonya** Hungary
47 H5 **Battura Gl. gl.** *Jammu and Kashmir*
36 C1 **Battura Gl. gl.** Pakistan
126 C3 **Batu mt.** Ethiopia
22 A2 **Batubetumbang** Indonesia
172 B3 **Batuco** Chile
25 C6 **Batu Gajah** Malaysia
22 C4 **Batukau, G. volcano** Indonesia
23 C5 **Batulaki** Philippines
22 D4 **Batulanteh mt.** Indonesia
22 C2 **Batulicin** Indonesia
22 C1 **Batulilangmebang, G. mt.** Indonesia
Batum *see* **Bat'umi**
51 G7 **Bat'umi** Georgia
25 C7 **Batu Pahat** Malaysia
20 C7 **Batu, P.P. is** Indonesia
25 C6 **Batu Puteh, Gunung mt.** Malaysia
22 A3 **Baturaja** Indonesia
22 B3 **Baturetno** Indonesia
166 E1 **Baturité** Brazil
166 E1 **Baturite, Sa h.** Brazil
53 E1 **Baturyn** Ukraine
52 H2 **Batyrevo** Rus. Fed.
88 A3 **Batz, Île de i.** France
88 C4 **Batz-sur-Mer** France
6 □8 **Bau i.** Fiji
166 B2 **Bau r.** Brazil
21 H8 **Baubau** Indonesia
123 G4 **Bauchi div.** Nigeria
123 F4 **Bauchi** Nigeria
88 B4 **Baud** France
37 F5 **Bauda** India
150 E1 **Baudette** *Minnesota* U.S.A.
137 L5 **Baudette** *Minnesota* U.S.A.
83 D2 **Bauen** Switzerland
10 □3 **Bauer Bay b.** *Macquarie I.* Pacific Ocean
126 E3 **Bauet well** Ethiopia
89 E4 **Baugé** France
89 E4 **Baugeois reg.** France
90 E3 **Bauges mts** France
15 G5 **Bauhinia Downs** *Queensland* Australia
108 A4 **Bauladu** *Sardegna* Italy
74 E3 **Bauland reg.** Germany
139 K3 **Bauld, C. headland** *Newfoundland* Canada
90 E1 **Baume-les-Dames** France
87 G3 **Baumholder** Germany
75 F2 **Baunach r.** Germany
108 B4 **Baunei** *Sardegna* Italy
164 D2 **Baures** Bolivia
168 D5 **Bauru** Brazil
168 B3 **Baús** Brazil
74 B2 **Bausendorf** Germany
54 D3 **Bauska** Latvia
73 K4 **Bautzen** Germany
Bavaria div. *see* **Bayern**
86 C2 **Bavay** France
59 G2 **Båven l.** Sweden
106 C3 **Baveno** Italy
130 D6 **Baviaanskloofberg mts** South Africa
82 B1 **Bavilliers** France
156 C2 **Bavispe r.** Mexico
52 D1 **Bavleny** Rus. Fed.
46 D2 **Bavly** Rus. Fed.
81 F1 **Bavorov** Czech Rep.
124 C3 **Bavula** Zaire
24 A2 **Baw** Myanmar
22 B2 **Bawal i.** Indonesia
22 B2 **Bawang, Tg pt** Indonesia
63 H2 **Bawdeswell** *England* U.K.
24 B2 **Bawdwin** Myanmar
22 C3 **Bawean i.** Indonesia
72 C3 **Bawinkel** Germany
119 E2 **Bawiti** Egypt
122 D4 **Bawku** Ghana
24 B3 **Bawlake** Myanmar
32 C2 **Bawolung** China
32 C1 **Baxi** China
32 D2 **Ba Xian** China
31 F5 **Ba Xian** China
145 D6 **Baxley** *Georgia* U.S.A.
32 B2 **Baxoi** China
126 D4 **Bay div.** Somalia
Bay *see* **Baicheng**
158 C2 **Bayamo** Cuba
145 □3 **Bayamón** Puerto Rico
31 H3 **Bayan** China
22 D4 **Bayan** Indonesia
30 D2 **Bayan** Mongolia
30 B3 **Bayan** Mongolia
36 D4 **Bayana** India
47 J2 **Bayanaul** Kazakhstan
30 D3 **Bayanbulag** Mongolia
30 A3 **Bayanbulag** Mongolia
30 D3 **Bayandelger** Mongolia
124 C3 **Bayanga** Central African Rep.
124 C2 **Bayanga-Didi** Central African Rep.
30 B2 **Bayangol** Rus. Fed.
32 A1 **Bayan Har Shan mountain range** China
32 B1 **Bayan Har Shankou pass** China
30 A3 **Bayan- Hongor div.** Mongolia
30 B3 **Bayanhongor** Mongolia
30 B3 **Bayanhushuu** Mongolia
30 C4 **Bayan Mod** China
30 D4 **Bayan Obo** China
30 E3 **Bayan-Ovoo** Mongolia
31 G3 **Bayan Qagan** China
30 A3 **Bayansayr** Mongolia
47 K4 **Bayansumküre** China
31 F2 **Bayan Ta** China
99 H2 **Bayas r.** Spain
30 E3 **Bayasgalant** Mongolia
42 B2 **Bayat** Turkey

39 C3 Bayāz Iran
23 C4 Baybay Philippines
42 E1 Bayburt Turkey
149 F4 Bay City Michigan U.S.A.
151 D6 Bay City Texas U.S.A.
44 H3 Baydaratskaya Guba b. Rus. Fed.
126 D4 Baydhabo Somalia
30 A3 Baydrag Gol r. Mongolia
75 J3 Bayerisch Eisenstein Germany
75 H3 Bayerischer Wald mountain range Germany
75 G4 Bayern div. Germany
83 G1 Bayersoien Germany
75 J4 Bayer Wald, Nationalpark nat. park Germany
89 E2 Bayeux France
47 K2 Bayevo Rus. Fed.
148 B2 Bayfield Wisconsin U.S.A.
47 E3 Bayganin Kazakhstan
173 J2 Baygorria, Lago Artificial de resr Uruguay
126 E2 Bayḥan al Qiṣab Yemen
113 F5 Bayındır Turkey
42 D4 Bāyir Jordan
47 H4 Baykadam Kazakhstan
30 C2 Baykal Rus. Fed.
30 C1 Baykal, Ozero l. Rus. Fed.
30 C2 Baykal'sk Rus. Fed.
47 G3 Baykonur Kazakhstan
47 J5 Baykurt China
23 B3 Bay, Laguna de lag. Philippines
46 E2 Baymak Rus. Fed.
8 F3 Bay of Plenty div. New Zealand
23 B2 Bayombong Philippines
87 F4 Bayon France
93 A5 Bayonne France
23 B4 Bayo Point pt Philippines
162 A5 Bayóvar Peru
46 F5 Bayramaly Turkmenistan
42 A2 Bayramiç Turkey
122 D4 Bay, Réserve de res. Mali
75 G3 Bayreuth Germany
151 F6 Bay St Louis Mississippi U.S.A.
119 H4 Baysh watercourse Saudi Arabia
147 G4 Bay Shore New York U.S.A.
62 D2 Bayston Hill England U.K.
47 G5 Baysun Uzbekistan
126 D2 Bayt al Faqīh Yemen
151 E6 Baytown Texas U.S.A.
119 F4 Bayuda Desert desert Sudan
22 A2 Bayunglincir Indonesia
8 F3 Bay View New Zealand
101 H3 Baza r. Spain
101 H3 Baza Spain
81 H4 Bázakerettye Hungary
53 B2 Bazaliya Ukraine
53 C1 Bazar Ukraine
39 B1 Bāzār-e Māsāl Iran
52 H3 Bazarnaya Ken'sha Rus. Fed.
52 H3 Bazarnyy Karabulak Rus. Fed.
52 H3 Bazarnyy Syzgan Rus. Fed.
46 D3 Bazartobe Kazakhstan
129 F3 Bazaruto, Ilha do i. Mozambique
93 B4 Bazas France
101 H3 Baza, Sierra de mountain range Spain
39 F4 Bazdar Pakistan
69 C5 Bazeilles France
32 D2 Bazhong China
93 D5 Baziège France
141 H3 Bazin r. Québec Canada
39 E4 Bazman Iran
39 E3 Bazmān, Kūh-e mt. Iran
90 B1 Bazoches France
86 B4 Bazoches-les-Gallerandes France
89 F3 Bazoches-sur-Hoëne France
90 B1 Bazois reg. France
89 E4 Bazouges France
93 A5 Baztán, Valle de v. France/Spain
107 F4 Bazzano Italy
171 C6 B. Bustamante Argentina
179 □ B. d'Audierne b. Kerguelen Indian Ocean
25 D5 Be r. Vietnam
150 C2 Beach N. Dakota U.S.A.
141 G4 Beachburg Ontario Canada
147 F5 Beach Haven New Jersey U.S.A.
12 E4 Beachport S. Australia Australia
147 F5 Beachwood New Jersey U.S.A.
63 G4 Beachy Head headland England U.K.
147 G4 Beacon New York U.S.A.
17 B6 Beacon Western Australia Australia
131 F6 Beacon Bay South Africa
27 □ Beacon Hill h. Hong Kong
63 F3 Beaconsfield England U.K.
13 F5 Beaconsfield Tasmania Australia
65 G2 Beadnell Bay b. England U.K.
16 C3 Beagle Bay Abor. Reserve res. Western Australia Australia
14 B2 Beagle Gulf b. Northern Terr. Australia
129 H1 Bealanana Madagascar
Béal an Átha see Ballina
Béal Átha na Sluaighe see Ballinasloe
62 D4 Beaminster England U.K.
129 H3 Beampingaratra mts Madagascar
146 B6 Bean Station Tennessee U.S.A.
152 E3 Bear r. Idaho U.S.A.
137 N2 Bear Cove b. N.W.T. Canada
140 B2 Beardmore Ontario Canada
179 B4 Beardmore Gl. gl. Antarctica
15 G5 Beardmore Res. resr Queensland Australia
148 B5 Beardstown Illinois U.S.A.
138 D3 Bear Island i. Ontario Canada
Bear Island i. see Bjørnøya
67 B5 Bear Island i. Rep. of Ireland
98 B2 Beariz Spain
152 E3 Bear L. l. Idaho/Utah U.S.A.
136 D3 Bear Lake B.C. Canada
36 D5 Bearma r. India
93 B5 Béarn reg. France
152 E1 Bear Paw Mt. mt. Montana U.S.A.
179 A3 Bear Pen. pen. Antarctica
64 D2 Bearsden Scotland U.K.
138 B3 Bearskin Lake Ontario Canada
154 B2 Bear Valley California U.S.A.
99 H1 Beasain Spain
159 E3 Beata, Cabo c. Dominican Rep.
159 E3 Beata, I. i. Dominican Rep.
150 D3 Beatrice Nebraska U.S.A.
14 D2 Beatrice, C. c. Northern Terr. Australia
66 E5 Beattock Scotland U.K.
136 E3 Beatton r. B.C. Canada
136 E3 Beatton River B.C. Canada
154 D3 Beatty Nevada U.S.A.
141 G2 Beattyville Québec Canada
127 □4 Beau Bassin Mauritius
91 C5 Beaucaire France
89 G3 Beauce reg. France
171 E7 Beauchene I. i. Falkland Is.
90 E1 Beaucourt France
89 E4 Beaucouzé France
15 H5 Beaudesert Queensland Australia
89 F3 Beaufay France
90 D2 Beaufort Franche-Comté France
90 E3 Beaufort Rhône-Alpes France
145 D5 Beaufort S. Carolina U.S.A.
13 E4 Beaufort Victoria Australia
43 C3 Beaufort Castle Lebanon
89 E4 Beaufort-en-Vallée France
90 E3 Beaufortin mts France
134 D2 Beaufort Sea sea Canada/U.S.A.
130 D6 Beaufort West South Africa
89 G4 Beaugency France
141 J4 Beauharnois Québec Canada
91 E4 Beaujeu Provence - Alpes - Côte-d'Azur France
90 C2 Beaujeu Rhône-Alpes France
90 C2 Beaujolais, Monts du mts France
92 D4 Beaulieu-sur-Dordogne France
90 B2 Beaulon France
66 D3 Beauly Scotland U.K.
66 D3 Beauly Firth est. Scotland U.K.
62 B1 Beaumaris Wales U.K.
91 D4 Beaumes-de-Venise France
89 F2 Beaumesnil France
86 B2 Beaumetz-lès-Loges France
93 C4 Beaumont Aquitaine France
151 F6 Beaumont Mississippi U.S.A.
145 B6 Beaumont Mississippi U.S.A.
146 B5 Beaumont Ohio U.S.A.
88 D2 Beaumont Picardie France
151 E6 Beaumont Texas U.S.A.
69 C4 Beaumont Belgium
9 B6 Beaumont New Zealand
93 C5 Beaumont-de-Lomagne France
69 D5 Beaumont-en-Argonne France
89 F4 Beaumont-en-Véron France
89 F2 Beaumont-le-Roger France
86 B3 Beaumont-sur-Oise France
89 F3 Beaumont-sur-Sarthe France
90 C1 Beaune France
86 B4 Beaune-La Rolande France
141 K3 Beauport Québec Canada
6 □2 Beaupré i. New Caledonia Pacific Ocean
141 K3 Beaupré Québec Canada
89 E4 Beaupréau France
86 B2 Beauquesne France
69 C4 Beauraing Belgium
91 D3 Beaurepaire France
90 D2 Beaurepaire-en-Bresse France
91 D4 Beaurières France
137 K4 Beausejour Manitoba Canada
6 □2 Beautemps i. New Caledonia Pacific Ocean
69 B5 Beautor France
86 B3 Beauvais France
137 H3 Beauval Saskatchewan Canada
86 B2 Beauval France
91 E4 Beauvezer France
93 C4 Beauville France
88 C5 Beauvoir-sur-Mer France
92 B2 Beauvoir-sur-Niort France
91 C3 Beauzac France
93 D5 Beauzelle France
136 H4 Beaver r. Alberta Canada
136 D2 Beaver r. B.C./Yukon Canada
138 C2 Beaver r. Ontario Canada
155 F2 Beaver r. Utah U.S.A.
155 F2 Beaver Utah U.S.A.
136 A2 Beaver Creek Yukon Terr. Canada
144 C4 Beaver Dam Kentucky U.S.A.
148 C4 Beaver Dam Wisconsin U.S.A.
146 C4 Beaver Falls Pennsylvania U.S.A.
152 D2 Beaverhead Mts mountain range Montana U.S.A.
137 K4 Beaverhill L. l. Manitoba Canada
137 J2 Beaverhill L. l. N.W.T. Canada
148 E3 Beaver Island i. Michigan U.S.A.
151 E4 Beaver L. resr Arkansas U.S.A.
136 F3 Beaverlodge Alberta Canada
146 D4 Beaver Run Reservoir resr Pennsylvania U.S.A.
36 C4 Beawar India
172 D2 Beazley Argentina
172 D2 Bebedero, S. salt pan Argentina
124 C2 Bébédjia Chad
168 D4 Bebedouro Brazil
73 G3 Bebertal Germany
65 E4 Bebington England U.K.
124 C2 Béboto Chad
74 E2 Bebra Germany
138 F1 Bécard, Lac l. Québec Canada
90 E3 Becca du Lac mt. France
63 H2 Beccles England U.K.
83 G3 Becco di Filadonna mt. Italy
98 E4 Becedas Spain
112 B2 Bečej Yugoslavia
98 C2 Becerreá Spain
121 D2 Béchar Algeria
134 C4 Becharof L. l. Alaska U.S.A.
87 G3 Becherbach Germany
88 D3 Bécherel France
75 F3 Bechhofen Germany
75 K3 Bechyně Czech Rep.
99 E2 Becilla de Valderaduey Spain
113 F6 Beçin Turkey
74 B3 Beckingen Germany
65 H4 Beckingham England U.K.
146 C6 Beckley W. Virginia U.S.A.
72 D4 Beckum Germany
112 E1 Beclean Romania
89 E4 Bécon-les-Granits France
78 B1 Bečov nad Teplou Czech Rep.
78 F5 Becsehely Hungary
81 H4 Becsvölgye Hungary
65 G3 Bedale England U.K.
124 C2 Bédan Chad
91 B5 Bédarieux France
74 B2 Bedburg Germany
68 E3 Bedburg-Hau Germany
62 B1 Beddgelert Wales U.K.
63 G4 Beddingham England U.K.
147 J2 Beddington Maine U.S.A.
126 C3 Bedelē Ethiopia
47 J4 Bedel Pass pass China/Kyrgyzstan
72 D2 Bederkesa Germany
126 D3 Bedēsa Ethiopia
63 F2 Bedford England U.K.
144 C4 Bedford Indiana U.S.A.
147 H3 Bedford Massachusetts U.S.A.
146 D4 Bedford Pennsylvania U.S.A.
141 J4 Bedford Québec Canada
146 D6 Bedford Virginia U.S.A.
131 F6 Bedford South Africa
15 F2 Bedford, C. c. Queensland Australia
63 F2 Bedford Level reg. England U.K.
159 □8 Bedford Pt pt Grenada Caribbean
63 F2 Bedfordshire div. England U.K.
77 H4 Będków Poland
65 G2 Bedlington England U.K.
77 H3 Bedlno Poland
101 G3 Bedmar Spain
78 F5 Bednja r. Croatia
52 F3 Bednodem'yanovsk Rus. Fed.
25 □ Bedok Singapore
25 □ Bedok Res. resr Singapore
80 C4 Bedollo Italy
106 D4 Bedonia Italy
123 G3 Bedouaram well Niger
14 D5 Bedourie Queensland Australia
93 B5 Bedous France
155 H2 Bedrock Colorado U.S.A.
55 A3 Bedsted Stationsby Denmark
93 D4 Béduer France
68 E1 Bedum Netherlands
63 E2 Bedworth England U.K.
77 H5 Będzin Poland
76 D1 Będzino Poland
15 F5 Beechal Cr. watercourse Queensland Australia
146 B5 Beech Fork Lake l. W. Virginia U.S.A.
148 C2 Beechwood Michigan U.S.A.
13 G3 Beecroft Pen. pen. New South Wales Australia
68 D3 Beek Gelderland Netherlands
69 D4 Beek Limburg Netherlands
69 D3 Beek Noord-Brabant Netherlands
68 D2 Beekbergen Netherlands
73 H3 Beelitz Germany
15 H5 Beenleigh Queensland Australia
67 A4 Beenoskee h. Rep. of Ireland
73 J2 Beenz Germany
17 B6 Beeringgnurding, Mt h. Western Australia Australia
43 C4 Beer Menuha Israel
69 B3 Beernem Belgium
43 C5 Beer Ora Israel
69 C3 Beerse Belgium
69 C4 Beersel Belgium
Beersheba see Be'ér Sheva'
43 C4 Be'ér Sheva' Israel
68 F1 Beerta Netherlands
73 K3 Beeskow Germany
131 F2 Beestekraal South Africa
14 C3 Beetaloo Northern Terr. Australia
68 E1 Beetsterzwaag Netherlands
73 G3 Beetzendorf Germany
73 H3 Beetzsee l. Germany
151 D6 Beeville Texas U.S.A.
124 D3 Befale Zaire
129 H2 Befandriana Avaratra Madagascar
124 D3 Befori Zaire
129 H3 Befotaka Madagascar
13 G4 Bega New South Wales Australia
37 G5 Begamganj Bangladesh
88 B3 Bégard France
112 C2 Begejski Kanal canal Romania/Yugoslavia
159 □7 Beggars Pt pt Antigua Caribbean
101 G3 Begíjar Spain
141 K2 Bégin Québec Canada
93 B4 Bègles France
64 B3 Beg, Lough l. Northern Ireland U.K.
58 D1 Begna r. Norway
58 C1 Begnadal Norway
114 D1 Begnište Macedonia
122 D5 Begoro Ghana
52 H3 Beguch Rus. Fed.
36 C4 Begun India
102 G3 Begur Spain
102 G3 Begur, Cap de pt Spain
37 F4 Begusarai India
39 D2 Behābād Iran
39 B3 Behbehān Iran
37 G1 Behleg China
136 C3 Behm Canal inlet Alaska U.S.A.
179 B3 Behrendt Mts mts Antarctica
87 F3 Behren-lès-Forbach France
39 C1 Behshahr Iran
39 F2 Behsūd Afghanistan
130 E6 Behulpsaam South Africa
33 F4 Bei r. China
31 H2 Bei'an China
32 D1 Beiba China
32 D2 Beibei China
32 D2 Beichuan China
126 B3 Beigi Ethiopia
33 E4 Beihai China
31 F4 Beijing div. China
31 F5 Beijing China
68 E2 Beilen Netherlands
33 E4 Beiliu China
75 G3 Beilngries Germany
124 C2 Béinamar Chad
66 E4 Beinn a' Ghlo mt. Scotland U.K.
66 B5 Beinn an Oir h. Scotland U.K.
64 C2 Beinn an Tuirc h. Scotland U.K.
64 B2 Beinn Bheigeir h. Scotland U.K.
64 C2 Beinn Bhreac h. Scotland U.K.
64 C1 Beinn Bhreac h. Scotland U.K.
64 C1 Beinn Chapull h. Scotland U.K.
66 E4 Beinn Dearg mt. Scotland U.K.
66 D3 Beinn Dearg mt. Scotland U.K.
66 D4 Beinn Heasgarnich mt. Scotland U.K.
64 D1 Beinn Ime mt. Scotland U.K.
64 C1 Beinn Mhor h. Scotland U.K.
Beinn na Faoghla i. see Benbecula
64 C1 Beinn Sgulaird mt. Scotland U.K.
82 D1 Beinwil Switzerland
31 G4 Beipiao China
129 E2 Beira Mozambique
98 C4 Beira Alta reg. Portugal
98 C5 Beira Baixa reg. Portugal
98 B4 Beira Litoral reg. Portugal
33 F1 Beiru r. China
43 C3 Beirut Lebanon
30 A4 Beishan China
131 H1 Beitbridge Zimbabwe
66 D5 Beith Scotland U.K.
79 M5 Beiuș Romania
31 G4 Beizhen China
100 B3 Beja div. Portugal
100 C2 Beja Portugal
121 F1 Béja Tunisia
121 F1 Bejaïa Algeria
114 A2 Bejar Albania
98 E4 Béjar Spain
39 D2 Bejestān Iran
36 B3 Beji r. Pakistan
124 B2 Béka Cameroon
23 A3 Bekasi Indonesia
46 D4 Bekdash Turkmenistan
79 L5 Békés div. Hungary
79 L5 Békés Hungary
79 L5 Békéscsaba Hungary
53 E3 Bekhtery Ukraine
129 H3 Bekily Madagascar
28 K2 Bekkai Japan
52 D1 Beklemishevo Rus. Fed.
52 F3 Bekovo Rus. Fed.
122 D5 Bekyem Ghana
37 E4 Bela India
36 A4 Bela Pakistan
130 G2 Bela-Bela South Africa
124 B3 Bélabo Cameroon
92 D2 Bélâbre France
112 C2 Bela Crkva Yugoslavia
47 K2 Bel'agash Kazakhstan
88 C3 Bel Air h. France
147 E5 Bel Air Maryland U.S.A.
101 E2 Belalcázar Spain
78 B2 Bělá nad Radbuzou Czech Rep.
112 D3 Bela Palanka Yugoslavia
79 K3 Bélapátfalva Hungary
78 D1 Bělá pod Bezdězem Czech Rep.
78 G1 Bělá pod Pradědem Czech Rep.
13 F3 Belaraboon New South Wales Australia
49 H3 Belarus country Europe
114 D1 Belasica mts Bulgaria/Macedonia
52 G1 Belasovka Rus. Fed.
167 A5 Bela Vista Brazil
129 E4 Bela Vista Mozambique
168 D2 Bela Vista de Goiás Brazil
45 T3 Belaya r. Rus. Fed.
52 F1 Belaya Rus. Fed.
52 A3 Belaya Berezka Rus. Fed.
51 G6 Belaya Glina Rus. Fed.
53 G2 Belaya Kalitva Rus. Fed.
50 J3 Belaya Kholunitsa Rus. Fed.
22 C1 Belayan r. Indonesia
52 G1 Belbazh Rus. Fed.
123 F4 Belbédji Niger
106 C4 Belbo r. Italy
93 D6 Belcaire France
77 H4 Bełchatów Poland
82 C1 Belchen mt. Germany
146 B6 Belcher Kentucky U.S.A.
135 L4 Belcher Islands is Québec Canada
39 F2 Belchiragh Afghanistan
102 C3 Belchite Spain
78 C2 Bělčice Czech Rep.
67 D2 Belcoo Northern Ireland U.K.
141 G2 Belcourt Québec Canada
154 B1 Belden California U.S.A.
67 B2 Belderg Rep. of Ireland
55 C4 Beldringe-Odense airport Denmark
47 D2 Belebey Rus. Fed.
78 G4 Beled Hungary
126 E4 Beledweyne Somalia
122 C5 Belefuanai Liberia
107 J4 Belej Croatia
46 D5 Belek Turkmenistan
123 G5 Belel Nigeria
166 C1 Belém Brazil
166 E2 Belém de S. Francisco Brazil
153 F5 Belen New Mexico U.S.A.
170 C2 Belén Argentina
162 C2 Belén Colombia
173 J1 Belén Uruguay
99 G4 Beleña, Emb. de resr Spain
173 J1 Belén, Cuch. de h. Uruguay
112 E3 Belene Bulgaria
53 G1 Belenikhino Rus. Fed.
93 D6 Bélesta France
126 C2 Beles Wenz r. Ethiopia
46 E4 Beleuli Uzbekistan
47 G3 Beleutty r. Kazakhstan
52 C3 Belev Rus. Fed.
113 F5 Belevi Turkey
78 F5 Belezna Hungary
67 E2 Belfast airport Northern Ireland U.K.
147 J2 Belfast Maine U.S.A.
67 F2 Belfast Northern Ireland U.K.
9 D5 Belfast New Zealand
131 H2 Belfast South Africa
67 F2 Belfast Lough inlet Northern Ireland U.K.
69 E3 Belfeld Netherlands
150 C2 Belfield N. Dakota U.S.A.
126 B2 Bēlfodiyo Ethiopia
65 G2 Belford England U.K.
90 E1 Belfort France
90 E1 Belfort, Territoire de div. France
38 A3 Belgaum India
52 G4 Belgaza r. Rus. Fed.
73 J4 Belgern Germany
73 H4 Belgershain Germany
106 D3 Belgioioso Italy
48 F3 Belgium country Europe
108 B2 Belgodère Corse France
53 G1 Belgorod div. Rus. Fed.
53 G1 Belgorod Rus. Fed.
152 E2 Belgrade Montana U.S.A.
Belgrade see Beograd
122 B4 Béli Guinea-Bissau
123 G5 Beli Nigeria
102 E3 Belianes Spain
110 B5 Belice r. Sicilia Italy
100 C3 Beliche r. Portugal
112 C3 Beli Drim r. Albania/Yugoslavia
112 F3 Beli Lom r. Bulgaria
79 H6 Beli Manastir Croatia
93 B4 Belin-Béliet France
52 F3 Belinskiy Rus. Fed.
22 A2 Belinyu Indonesia
112 D3 Beli Timok r. Yugoslavia
112 D4 Belitsa Bulgaria
53 F1 Belitsa Rus. Fed.
22 B2 Belitung i. Indonesia
133 K8 Belize country Central America
125 B4 Belize Cabinda Angola
157 H5 Belize Belize
163 G3 Bélizon French Guiana
112 C2 Beljanica mt. Yugoslavia
45 P2 Bel'kovskiy, O. i. Rus. Fed.
141 G2 Bell r. Québec Canada
15 G5 Bell Queensland Australia
69 F4 Bell Germany
131 F6 Bell South Africa
109 H4 Bella Italy
136 D4 Bella Bella B.C. Canada
92 D2 Bellac France
90 E3 Bellachat, Mont mt. France
136 D4 Bella Coola B.C. Canada
106 D3 Bellagio Italy
151 E6 Bellaire Texas U.S.A.
106 D2 Bellano Italy
109 F2 Bellante Italy
107 G4 Bellaria Italy
38 B3 Bellary India
13 G2 Bellata New South Wales Australia
173 J1 Bella Unión Uruguay
170 E2 Bella Vista Corrientes Argentina
171 B7 Bella Vista Santa Cruz Argentina
170 C2 Bella Vista Tucumán Argentina
13 H2 Bellbrook New South Wales Australia
15 G4 Bell Cay reef Queensland Australia
102 D3 Bellclaire d'Urgell Spain
91 D3 Belledonne mts France
91 D3 Belledonne, Pic de mt. France
64 A3 Belleek Northern Ireland U.K.
159 □4 Bellefontaine Martinique Caribbean
146 B4 Bellefontaine Ohio U.S.A.
146 E4 Bellefonte Pennsylvania U.S.A.
150 C2 Belle Fourche r. S. Dakota U.S.A.
150 C2 Belle Fourche S. Dakota U.S.A.
86 B5 Bellegarde Centre France
91 C5 Bellegarde Languedoc-Roussillon France
92 E3 Bellegarde-en-Marche France
90 D2 Bellegarde-sur-Valserine France
145 D7 Belle Glade Florida U.S.A.
88 B4 Belle-Île i. France
139 K3 Belle Isle i. Newfoundland Canada
88 B3 Belle-Isle-en-Terre France
139 J3 Belle Isle, Strait of str. Newfoundland Canada
89 F3 Bellême France
155 G4 Bellemont Arizona U.S.A.
90 B2 Bellenaves France
89 G2 Bellencombre France
148 A5 Belle Plaine Iowa U.S.A.
90 B2 Bellerive-sur-Allier France
87 F4 Belles-Forêts France
141 F3 Belleterre Québec Canada
86 C3 Belleu France
82 B2 Bellevaux France
90 D2 Bellevesvre France
150 D4 Belleville Kansas U.S.A.
141 G4 Belleville Ontario Canada
90 C2 Belleville France
87 E3 Belleville-sur-Meuse France
92 A2 Belleville-sur-Vie France
152 D3 Bellevue Idaho U.S.A.
148 B4 Bellevue Iowa U.S.A.
146 B4 Bellevue Ohio U.S.A.
152 B2 Bellevue Washington U.S.A.
91 B3 Bellevue-la-Montagne France
90 D3 Belley France
74 D3 Bellheim Germany
90 E1 Bellherbe France
90 D2 Bellignat France
Bellin see Kangirsuk
55 C4 Bellinge Denmark
13 H2 Bellingen New South Wales Australia
65 F2 Bellingham England U.K.
152 B1 Bellingham Washington U.S.A.
179 B2 Bellingshausen Rus. Fed. Base Antarctica
179 A3 Bellingshausen Sea sea Antarctica
68 F1 Bellingwolde Netherlands
106 C3 Bellinzago Novarese Italy
83 E2 Bellinzona Switzerland
102 D3 Bell-Lloc d'Urgell Spain
162 B2 Bello Colombia
102 B4 Bello Spain
93 B5 Bellocq France
147 G3 Bellows Falls Vermont U.S.A.
36 B3 Bellpat Pakistan
102 E3 Bellpuig d'Urgell Spain
178 □3 Bellsund inlet Svalbard Arctic Ocean
147 F5 Belltown Delaware U.S.A.
107 F2 Belluno div. Veneto Italy
107 G2 Belluno Italy
38 B3 Belluru India
173 F2 Bell Ville Argentina
130 B6 Bellville South Africa
72 D3 Belm Germany
101 E2 Bélmez Spain
101 G3 Bélmez de la Moraleda Spain
146 D3 Belmont New York U.S.A.
66 □2 Belmont Scotland U.K.
130 E4 Belmont South Africa
90 C2 Belmont-de-la-Loire France
98 D1 Belmonte Asturias Spain
101 H1 Belmonte Castilla - La Mancha Spain
169 J1 Belmonte Brazil
98 C4 Belmonte Portugal
93 E5 Belmont-sur-Rance France
157 H5 Belmopan Belize
15 E3 Belmore Cr. r. Queensland Australia
67 B2 Belmullet Rep. of Ireland
169 H1 Belo Campo Brazil
141 J4 Beloeil Québec Canada
69 B4 Belœil Belgium
31 J2 Belogorsk Rus. Fed.
112 D3 Belogradchik Bulgaria
129 H3 Beloha Madagascar
169 G3 Belo Horizonte Brazil
150 D4 Beloit Kansas U.S.A.
148 C4 Beloit Wisconsin U.S.A.
166 E2 Belo Jardim Brazil
47 K2 Belokurikha Rus. Fed.
127 □4 Bel Ombre Mauritius
166 B1 Belo Monte Brazil
50 E1 Belomorsk Rus. Fed.
37 G5 Belonia India
52 D2 Beloomut Rus. Fed.
52 D2 Beloozerskiy Rus. Fed.
22 E2 Belopa Indonesia
99 G4 Belorado Spain
51 F6 Belorechensk Rus. Fed.
42 C1 Belören Turkey
46 E2 Beloretsk Rus. Fed.
Belorussia see Belarus
79 G2 Bělotín Czech Rep.
112 D3 Belotintsi Bulgaria
129 G2 Belo Tsiribihina Madagascar
47 K2 Belousovka Kazakhstan
52 C2 Belousovo Rus. Fed.
112 D3 Belovo Bulgaria
47 L2 Belovo Rus. Fed.
52 H2 Belovod'ye Rus. Fed.
50 F1 Beloye Rus. Fed.
44 E3 Beloye More g. Rus. Fed.
56 J2 Beloye More Rus. Fed.
50 F2 Beloye, Ozero l. Rus. Fed.
50 F2 Belozersk Rus. Fed.
82 C2 Belp Switzerland
110 D5 Belpasso Sicilia Italy
93 D5 Belpech France
63 E1 Belper England U.K.
146 C5 Belpre Ohio U.S.A.
65 G2 Belsay England U.K.
114 A2 Belsh Albania
77 J4 Bełsk Duży Poland
52 E2 Bel'skoye Rus. Fed.
152 E2 Belt Montana U.S.A.
12 D2 Beltana S. Australia Australia
154 D3 Belted Range mts Nevada U.S.A.
166 B1 Belterra Brazil
30 A2 Beltes Gol r. Mongolia
87 G2 Beltheim Germany
81 H4 Beltinci Slovenia
151 D6 Belton Texas U.S.A.
67 B3 Beltra Lough l. Rep. of Ireland
108 A5 Belu r. Sardegna Italy
38 A3 Belur India
23 A5 Beluran Malaysia
79 H2 Beluša Slovakia
111 E3 Belvedere Marittimo Italy
93 D4 Belvès France
148 C4 Belvidere Illinois U.S.A.
99 F5 Belvís de la Jara Spain
15 F4 Belyando r. Queensland Australia
47 G4 Belye Vody Kazakhstan
50 H3 Belyshevo Rus. Fed.
52 A2 Belyy Rus. Fed.
52 B3 Belyye Berega Rus. Fed.
52 C1 Belyy Gorodok Rus. Fed.
44 H2 Belyy, O. i. Rus. Fed.
88 B4 Belz France
77 N5 Belz Ukraine
77 M5 Bełżec Poland
73 H3 Belzig Germany
77 L4 Bełżyce Poland
129 G2 Bemaraha, Plateau du plat. Madagascar
129 H1 Bemarivo r. Madagascar
125 B5 Bembe Angola
123 E4 Bembéréké Benin
101 E2 Bembézar r. Spain
98 D2 Bembibre Spain
63 E4 Bembridge England U.K.
148 C6 Bement Illinois U.S.A.
150 E2 Bemidji Minnesota U.S.A.
68 D3 Bemmel Netherlands
100 B1 Bemposta Portugal
65 H3 Bempton England U.K.
122 D4 Bèna Burkina
102 D2 Benabarre Spain
125 D4 Bena Dibele Zaire
22 C2 Benagin Indonesia
101 H4 Benahadux Spain
120 C2 Benahmed Morocco
66 D4 Ben Alder mt. Scotland U.K.
13 F4 Benalla Victoria Australia
101 F4 Benalmádena Spain
101 G3 Benalúa de Guadix Spain
101 G3 Benalúa de las Villas Spain
100 E4 Benalup de Sidonia Spain
101 F4 Benamargosa Spain
101 H3 Benamaurel Spain
127 □4 Benares Mauritius
121 G1 Ben Arous Tunisia
103 C4 Benasal Spain
102 D2 Benasque Spain
92 C2 Benassay France
125 D4 Bena-Sungu Zaire
91 E5 Bénat, Cap c. France
78 D1 Benátky nad Jizerou Czech Rep.
100 B2 Benavente Portugal
98 E2 Benavente Spain
98 E2 Benavides de Órbigo Spain
100 C1 Benavila Portugal
66 E3 Ben Avon mt. Scotland U.K.
67 E1 Benbane Head headland Northern Ireland U.K.
67 B3 Benbaun h. Rep. of Ireland
66 A3 Benbecula i. Scotland U.K.
64 C1 Ben Buie h. Scotland U.K.
67 C2 Benbulben h. Rep. of Ireland
67 E2 Benburb Northern Ireland U.K.
64 E1 Ben Chonzie mt. Scotland U.K.
66 C4 Ben Cruachan mt. Scotland U.K.
17 B6 Bencubbin Western Australia Australia
152 B2 Bend Oregon U.S.A.
131 G5 Bendearg mt. South Africa
125 C4 Bendela Zaire
13 G2 Bendemeer New South Wales Australia
126 F3 Bender-Bayla Somalia
13 F4 Bendigo Victoria Australia
13 G4 Bendoc Victoria Australia
74 C2 Bendorf Germany
54 C3 Bēne Latvia
129 E2 Bene Mozambique
68 D3 Beneden-Leeuwen Netherlands
147 J2 Benedicta Maine U.S.A.
80 C3 Benediktbeuren Germany
100 B1 Benedita Portugal
103 C6 Benejama Spain
129 H3 Benenitra Madagascar
78 D2 Benešov Czech Rep.
81 F2 Benešov nad Černou Czech Rep.
75 K2 Benešov nad Ploučnicí Czech Rep.
87 F4 Bénestroff France
108 B4 Benetutti Sardegna Italy
92 D2 Bénévent-l'Abbaye France
109 G3 Benevento div. Campania Italy
109 G3 Benevento Benevento Italy
87 G4 Benfeld France
100 B1 Benfica do Ribatejo Portugal
33 G1 Beng r. China
37 G5 Bengal, Bay of sea Asia
124 E3 Bengamisa Zaire
124 B3 Bengbis Cameroon
33 G1 Bengbu China
25 C7 Bengkalis Indonesia
22 B1 Bengkayang Indonesia
22 A3 Bengkulu div. Indonesia
20 D7 Bengkulu Indonesia
22 D2 Bengkung Indonesia
125 B5 Bengo div. Angola
59 E2 Bengtsfors Sweden
125 B6 Benguela div. Angola
125 B6 Benguela Angola
121 G2 Ben Guerdane Tunisia
120 C2 Benguerir Morocco
43 A4 Benha Egypt
66 D2 Ben Hope mt. Scotland U.K.
164 D2 Beni div. Bolivia
164 C2 Beni r. Bolivia
124 E3 Beni Zaire
121 D2 Beni-Abbès Algeria
96 D5 Beni Boufrah Morocco
102 D4 Benicarló Spain
103 D4 Benicasim Spain
103 C6 Benidorm Spain
123 G2 Beni Dourso well Niger
103 C5 Benifaio Spain
88 A3 Beniguet, Île de i. France
43 A6 Beni Hasan Egypt
119 F2 Benī Mazār Egypt
120 C2 Beni Mellal Morocco
117 E5 Benin country Africa
123 F5 Benin r. Nigeria
123 F5 Benin, Bight of g. Africa
123 F5 Benin City Nigeria
121 D2 Beni-Ounif Algeria
121 D1 Beni-Saf Algeria
123 G4 Benisheikh Nigeria
103 D6 Benissa Spain
119 F2 Beni Suef Egypt
43 A5 Beni Suef Egypt
156 B2 Benito, Islas is Mexico
173 H4 Benito Juárez Argentina
23 B2 Benito Soliven Philippines
114 A3 Benitses Greece
162 D4 Benjamim Constant Brazil
156 C2 Benjamín Hill Mexico
171 B5 Benjamin, I. i. Chile
172 E5 Benjamín Zorrillo Argentina
21 K8 Benjina Indonesia
28 H2 Benkei-misaki pt Japan
150 C3 Benkelman Nebraska U.S.A.
83 E1 Benken Switzerland
66 D2 Ben Klibreck mt. Scotland U.K.
104 E3 Benkovac Croatia
131 G1 Ben Lavin Nature Reserve res. South Africa
66 D4 Ben Lawers mt. Scotland U.K.
64 D1 Ben Ledi h. Scotland U.K.
13 G2 Ben Lomond mt. New South Wales Australia
66 D4 Ben Lomond mt. Scotland U.K.
13 F5 Ben Lomond Nat. Park nat. park Tasmania Australia

69 B4 **Boué** France
125 B4 **Bouenza div.** Congo
124 C2 **Boufore** Central African Rep.
98 B3 **Bougado** Portugal
16 D2 **Bougainville, C. c.** *Western Australia* Australia
6 □1 **Bougainville Island i.** P.N.G.
15 F2 **Bougainville Reef reef** *Coral Sea Islands Terr.* Pacific Ocean
121 F1 **Bougaroûn, Cap headland** Algeria
123 E3 **Boughessa** Mali
93 C4 **Bougion** France
122 C4 **Bougouni** Mali
121 E2 **Bougtob** Algeria
88 D4 **Bouguenais** France
159 □5 **Bouillante** *Guadeloupe* Caribbean
91 C5 **Bouillargues** France
69 D5 **Bouillon** Belgium
86 C4 **Bouilly** France
88 C5 **Bouin** France
121 E1 **Bouira** Algeria
120 C3 **Bou Izakarn** Morocco
82 B2 **Boujailles** France
120 B3 **Boujdour** *Western Sahara*
120 B3 **Boukra** *Western Sahara*
124 C1 **Boukta** Chad
87 F3 **Boulay-Moselle** France
92 C3 **Boulazac** France
152 F3 **Boulder** *Colorado* U.S.A.
152 D2 **Boulder** *Montana* U.S.A.
155 G3 **Boulder** *Utah* U.S.A.
17 C6 **Boulder** *Western Australia* Australia
155 E3 **Boulder Canyon** *Nevada* U.S.A.
155 E4 **Boulder City** *Nevada* U.S.A.
120 D2 **Boulemane** Morocco
154 D5 **Boulevard** *California* U.S.A.
173 H5 **Boulevard Atlántico** Argentina
14 D4 **Boulia** *Queensland* Australia
87 E3 **Bouligny** France
92 A2 **Boulogne r.** France
86 B4 **Boulogne-Billancourt** France
93 C5 **Boulogne-sur-Gesse** France
86 A2 **Boulogne-sur-Mer** France
89 F4 **Bouloire** France
124 D2 **Boulouba** Central African Rep.
122 D4 **Boulsa** Burkina
65 F4 **Boulsworth Hill h.** *England* U.K.
86 D3 **Boult-aux-Bois** France
86 D3 **Boulzicourt** France
124 B4 **Boumango** Gabon
124 B3 **Boumba r.** Cameroon
102 E2 **Boumort mt.** Spain
102 E2 **Boumort, Serra del mountain range** Spain
122 D5 **Bouna** Côte d'Ivoire
120 D2 **Bou Naceur, Jbel mt.** Morocco
120 B5 **Boû Nâga** Mauritania
147 H2 **Boundary Mountains mountain range** *Maine* U.S.A.
154 C3 **Boundary Peak summit** *Nevada* U.S.A.
122 C5 **Boundiali** Côte d'Ivoire
124 C4 **Boundji** Congo
24 E4 **Boung r.** Vietnam
124 D2 **Boungou r.** Central African Rep.
93 C4 **Bouniagues** France
24 C2 **Boun Nua** Laos
152 E3 **Bountiful** *Utah* U.S.A.
14 D3 **Bountiful I. i.** *Queensland* Australia
7 □14 **Bounty Bay b.** *Pitcairn I.* Pacific Ocean
9 □2 **Bounty Is is** New Zealand
173 G2 **Bouquet** Argentina
55 □1 **Bøur** Faeroes
6 □2 **Bourail** *New Caledonia* Pacific Ocean
90 C2 **Bourbince r.** France
179 □ **Bourbon, C. c.** *Kerguelen* Indian Ocean
90 B2 **Bourbon-Lancy** France
90 B2 **Bourbon-l'Archambault** France
92 E2 **Bourbonnais reg.** France
87 E5 **Bourbonne-les-Bains** France
86 B2 **Bourbourg** France
90 D3 **Bourbre r.** France
88 B3 **Bourbriac** France
91 D4 **Bourdeaux** France
92 C3 **Bourdeilles** France
90 B1 **Bourdon, Réservoir du resr** France
123 D3 **Bourem** Mali
92 C2 **Bouresse** France
92 B3 **Bourg** France
89 F2 **Bourg-Achard** France
92 D3 **Bourganeuf** France
91 C3 **Bourg-Argental** France
91 D3 **Bourg-de-Péage** France
93 C4 **Bourg-de-Visa** France
90 D2 **Bourg-en-Bresse** France
89 H4 **Bourges** France
141 H4 **Bourget** *Ontario* Canada
86 C3 **Bourg-et-Comin** France
90 D3 **Bourget, Lac du l.** France
92 E3 **Bourg-Lastic** France
91 C4 **Bourg-lès-Valence** France
93 D6 **Bourg-Madame** France
141 H2 **Bourgmont** *Québec* Canada
88 C4 **Bourgneuf, Baie de b.** France
88 D4 **Bourgneuf-en-Retz** France
90 B1 **Bourgogne div.** France
86 D3 **Bourgogne** France
90 D3 **Bourgoin-Jallieu** France
91 C4 **Bourg-St-Andéol** France
90 E3 **Bourg-St-Maurice** France
89 F2 **Bourgtheroulde-Infreville** France
89 E2 **Bourguébus** France
89 F4 **Bourgueil** France
120 A5 **Boû Rjeimât well** Mauritania
13 F2 **Bourke** *New South Wales* Australia
140 E2 **Bourkes** *Ontario* Canada
121 E1 **Bourmerdes** Algeria
87 E4 **Bourmont** France
91 D3 **Bourne r.** France
63 F2 **Bourne** *England* U.K.
63 E4 **Bournemouth airport** *England* U.K.
63 E4 **Bournemouth** *England* U.K.
92 A2 **Bournezeau** France
82 B1 **Bourogne** France
122 D4 **Bouroum-Bouroum** Burkina
93 C4 **Bourran** France
86 B4 **Bourron-Marlotte** France
68 F1 **Bourtange** Netherlands
72 C3 **Bourtanger Moor reg.** Germany
89 F3 **Bourth** France
124 D1 **Bourtoutou** Chad
121 E1 **Bou Saâda** Algeria
121 F1 **Bou Salem** Tunisia
155 E5 **Bouse** *Arizona* U.S.A.
155 E5 **Bouse Wash r.** *Arizona* U.S.A.
92 E2 **Boussac** France
122 D4 **Boussé** Burkina
90 D1 **Boussières** France
124 C1 **Bousso** Chad
86 D2 **Boussois** France
69 B4 **Boussu** Belgium
69 C4 **Boutersem** Belgium
120 B5 **Boutilimit** Mauritania
92 B3 **Boutonne r.** France
82 B2 **Bouveret** Switzerland
174 K9 **Bouvetøya i.** Atlantic Ocean
88 D4 **Bouvron** France
87 G4 **Bouxwiller** France
86 D3 **Bouy** France
123 F4 **Bouza** Niger
92 D2 **Bouzanne r.** France
87 F3 **Bouzonville** France
111 E5 **Bova** Italy
111 F4 **Bovalino** Italy
58 D2 **Bovallstrand** Sweden
111 E5 **Bova Marina** Italy
81 E4 **Bovec** Slovenia
98 C2 **Bóveda** Spain
83 F3 **Bovegno** Italy
72 E4 **Bovenden** Germany
22 C1 **Boven Kapuas Mts mountain range** Malaysia
68 D2 **Bovenkarspel** Netherlands
68 E2 **Bovensmilde** Netherlands
86 B3 **Boves** France
106 B4 **Boves** Italy
62 C4 **Bovey r.** *England* U.K.
69 D4 **Bovigny** Belgium
62 D4 **Bovington Camp** *England* U.K.
109 H3 **Bovino** Italy
107 F3 **Bovolone** Italy
173 H1 **Bovril** Argentina
53 E2 **Bovtyshka** Ukraine
137 G4 **Bow r.** *Alberta* Canada
16 E3 **Bow r.** *Western Australia* Australia
150 C1 **Bowbells** *N. Dakota* U.S.A.
159 □1 **Bowden** Jamaica
15 F4 **Bowen r.** *Queensland* Australia
148 B5 **Bowen** *Illinois* U.S.A.
15 G3 **Bowen** *Queensland* Australia
172 D3 **Bowen** Argentina
15 F4 **Bowen Downs** *Queensland* Australia
13 G4 **Bowen, Mt mt.** *Victoria* Australia
65 F3 **Bowes** *England* U.K.
155 H5 **Bowie** *Arizona* U.S.A.
15 F4 **Bowie** *Queensland* Australia
151 D5 **Bowie** *Texas* U.S.A.
137 G5 **Bow Island** *Alberta* Canada
42 F2 **Bowkan** Iran
65 F3 **Bowland, Forest of forest** *England* U.K.
144 C4 **Bowling Green** *Kentucky* U.S.A.
150 F4 **Bowling Green** *Missouri* U.S.A.
146 B4 **Bowling Green** *Ohio* U.S.A.
146 E5 **Bowling Green** *Virginia* U.S.A.
15 F3 **Bowling Green B. b.** *Queensland* Australia
15 F3 **Bowling Green, C. c.** *Queensland* Australia
150 C2 **Bowman** *N. Dakota* U.S.A.
179 C6 **Bowman I. i.** Antarctica
136 E4 **Bowman, Mt mt.** *B.C.* Canada
179 B3 **Bowman Pen. pen.** Antarctica
141 F5 **Bowmanville** *Ontario* Canada
66 B5 **Bowmore** *Scotland* U.K.
65 E3 **Bowness-on-Solway** *England* U.K.
Bowo *see* **Bomi**
32 B2 **Bowo** China
13 G3 **Bowral** *New South Wales* Australia
136 E4 **Bowron r.** *B.C.* Canada
136 E4 **Bowron Lake Provincial Park** *B.C.* Canada
74 E3 **Boxberg** Germany
59 F2 **Boxholm** Sweden
33 F1 **Bo Xian** China
31 F5 **Boxing** China
68 D3 **Boxmeer** Netherlands
68 D3 **Boxtel** Netherlands
42 C1 **Boyabat** Turkey
33 G2 **Boyang** China
53 D1 **Boyarka** Ukraine
13 H2 **Boyd r.** *New South Wales* Australia
137 J2 **Boyd Lake l.** *N.W.T.* Canada
124 C3 **Boyellé** Congo
136 G4 **Boyle** *Alberta* Canada
67 C3 **Boyle** Rep. of Ireland
15 G5 **Boyne r.** *Queensland* Australia
67 E3 **Boyne r.** Rep. of Ireland
131 G1 **Boyne** South Africa
86 B4 **Boynes** France
39 F1 **Boyni Qara** Afghanistan
145 D7 **Boynton Beach** *Florida* U.S.A.
124 E3 **Boyoma Falls waterfall** Zaire
152 E3 **Boysen Res. resr** *Wyoming* U.S.A.
165 D4 **Boyuibe** Bolivia
17 B7 **Boyup Brook** *Western Australia* Australia
113 G6 **Bozburun** Turkey
43 A1 **Bozburun Dağ mt.** Turkey
113 E5 **Bozcaada i.** Turkey
113 F5 **Bozdağ mt.** Turkey
43 D1 **Bozdağ mt.** Turkey
113 F5 **Boz Dağlari mountain range** Turkey
113 G6 **Bozdoğan** Turkey
63 F2 **Bozeat** *England* U.K.
82 B3 **Bozel** France
152 E2 **Bozeman** *Montana* U.S.A.
81 H2 **Božíce** Czech Rep.
81 H5 **Božjakovina** Croatia
42 C2 **Bozkır** Turkey
93 E4 **Bozouls** France
124 C2 **Bozoum** Central African Rep.
43 A1 **Bozova** *Antalya* Turkey
42 D2 **Bozova** *Şanlıurfa* Turkey
112 D2 **Bozovici** Romania
47 G3 **Boztumsyk** Kazakhstan
42 B2 **Bozüyük** Turkey
Bozyaka *see* **Beskonak**
106 E3 **Bozzolo** Italy
172 B2 **B. Pichidangui b.** Chile
106 B4 **Bra** Italy
66 E4 **Braan r.** *Scotland* U.K.
69 C4 **Brabant div.** Belgium
179 B2 **Brabant I. i.** Antarctica
104 F4 **Brač i.** Croatia
66 B3 **Bracadale** *Scotland* U.K.
66 B3 **Bracadale, Loch b.** *Scotland* U.K.
108 E2 **Bracciano** Italy
109 E2 **Bracciano, Lago di l.** Italy
141 F4 **Bracebridge** *Ontario* Canada
92 B3 **Brach** France
89 G4 **Bracieux** France
57 D3 **Bracke** Sweden
74 E3 **Brackenheim** Germany
104 F4 **Brački Kanal chan.** Croatia
63 E2 **Brackley** *England* U.K.
63 F3 **Bracknell** *England* U.K.
64 E1 **Braco** *Scotland* U.K.
166 B3 **Braço Menor do Rio Araguaia r.** Brazil
166 A2 **Braço Norte r.** Brazil
79 M5 **Brad** Romania
111 F2 **Bradano r.** Italy
114 B1 **Bradashesh** Albania
145 D7 **Bradenton** *Florida* U.S.A.
65 G4 **Bradford** *England* U.K.
146 A4 **Bradford** *Ohio* U.S.A.
141 F4 **Bradford** *Ontario* Canada
146 D4 **Bradford** *Pennsylvania* U.S.A.
147 G3 **Bradford** *Vermont* U.S.A.
62 D3 **Bradford-on-Avon** *England* U.K.
63 E4 **Brading** *England* U.K.
16 D2 **Bradshaw, Mt h.** *Western Australia* Australia
63 G3 **Bradwell Waterside** *England* U.K.
151 D6 **Brady** *Texas* U.S.A.
136 B3 **Brady Gl. gl.** *Alaska* U.S.A.
66 □2 **Brae** *Scotland* U.K.
55 B4 **Brædstrup** Denmark
66 E3 **Braemar** *Scotland* U.K.
98 B3 **Braga div.** Portugal
98 B3 **Braga** *Braga* Portugal
173 G3 **Bragado** Argentina
98 D3 **Bragança div.** Portugal
98 D3 **Bragança** *Bragança* Portugal
166 C1 **Bragança** Brazil
169 E5 **Bragança Paulista** Brazil
53 D1 **Brahin** Belarus
37 H4 **Brahmakund** India
37 G5 **Brahman Baria** Bangladesh
37 F5 **Brahmani r.** India
38 D2 **Brahmapur** India
37 G4 **Brahmaputra r.** Bangladesh/ India
13 G3 **Braidwood** *New South Wales* Australia
112 F2 **Brăila** Romania
63 E2 **Brailsford** *England* U.K.
86 C3 **Braine** France
69 C4 **Braine-l'Alleud** Belgium
69 C4 **Braine-le-Comte** Belgium
150 E2 **Brainerd** *Minnesota* U.S.A.
63 G3 **Braintree** *England* U.K.
69 D4 **Braives** Belgium
131 G1 **Brak r.**
130 B4 **Brak watercourse** South Africa
69 B4 **Brakel** Belgium
72 E4 **Brakel** Germany
72 D2 **Brake (Unterweser)** Germany
120 B5 **Brâkna div.** Mauritania
59 F3 **Bräkneån r.** Sweden
130 D5 **Brakpoort** South Africa
131 F3 **Brakspruit** South Africa
59 E2 **Brålanda** Sweden
76 F4 **Bralin** Poland
106 D4 **Brallo di Pregola** Italy
136 E4 **Bralorne** *B.C.* Canada
114 D4 **Bralos** Greece
91 E3 **Bramans** France
80 D3 **Bramberg am Wildkogel** Austria
36 D5 **Bramhapuri** India
55 A4 **Bramming** Denmark
57 E3 **Brämön i.** Sweden
65 F3 **Brampton** *England* U.K.
63 H2 **Brampton** *England* U.K.
141 F5 **Brampton** *Ontario* Canada
72 D3 **Bramsche** Germany
59 G1 **Bramsö-Fjärden l.** Sweden
72 D2 **Bramstedt** Germany
15 E2 **Bramwell** *Queensland* Australia
79 H3 **Branč** Slovakia
111 F5 **Brancaleone** Italy
63 G2 **Brancaster** *England* U.K.
139 K4 **Branch** *Newfoundland* Canada
170 C2 **Branco r.** Argentina
163 E3 **Branco r.** Brazil
165 E4 **Branco r.** Brazil
159 E4 **Brandaris h.** Netherlands Ant.
128 A3 **Brandberg mt.** Namibia
58 D1 **Brandbu** Norway
131 H2 **Branddraai** South Africa
55 B4 **Brande** Denmark
80 C3 **Brandenberg** Austria
73 J3 **Brandenburg div.** Germany
73 H3 **Brandenburg** *Brandenburg* Germany
75 J2 **Brand-Erbisdorf** Germany
92 C2 **Brandes reg.** France
65 H4 **Brandesburton** *England* U.K.
131 F4 **Brandfort** South Africa
73 J4 **Brandis** Germany
130 B5 **Brandkop** South Africa
108 B2 **Brando** *Corse* France
59 J1 **Brändö** Finland
63 G2 **Brandon** *England* U.K.
137 K5 **Brandon** *Manitoba* Canada
15 F3 **Brandon** *Queensland* Australia
150 D3 **Brandon** *S. Dakota* U.S.A.
147 G3 **Brandon** *Vermont* U.S.A.
67 A4 **Brandon Bay b.** Rep. of Ireland
67 A4 **Brandon Head headland** Rep. of Ireland
67 E4 **Brandon Hill h.** Rep. of Ireland
67 A4 **Brandon Mountain mt.** Rep. of Ireland
73 J1 **Brandshagen** Germany
55 B4 **Brandsø i.** Denmark
130 C5 **Brandvlei** South Africa
78 D1 **Brandýs nad Labem-Stará Boleslav** Czech Rep.
145 D6 **Branford** *Florida* U.S.A.
81 E5 **Branica r.** Slovenia
77 H1 **Braniewo** Poland
81 E5 **Branik** Slovenia
90 B1 **Branlin r.** France
59 E2 **Bränna** Sweden
93 B4 **Branne** France
75 H5 **Brannenburg** Germany
179 B2 **Bransfield Str. str.** Antarctica
77 L3 **Brańsk** Poland
140 E5 **Brantford** *Ontario* Canada
92 C3 **Brantôme** France
12 E4 **Branxholme** *Victoria* Australia
53 D1 **Branytsya** Ukraine
53 B2 **Brânzeni** Moldova
106 D2 **Branzi** Italy
139 H4 **Bras d'Or L. l.** *Nova Scotia* Canada
162 C4 **Brasil** Brazil
168 D1 **Brasilândia** *Goiás* Brazil
168 B4 **Brasilândia** *Mato Gross do Sul* Brazil
169 E2 **Brasilândia** *Minas Gerais* Brazil
164 C2 **Brasileia** Brazil
168 E1 **Brasília** Brazil
169 F2 **Brasília de Minas** Brazil
166 A1 **Brasília Legal** Brazil
58 D1 **Braskereidfoss** Norway
54 D3 **Brasla r.** Latvia
54 E4 **Braslaw** Belarus
112 E2 **Brașov** Romania
52 B3 **Brasovo** Rus. Fed.
127 □5 **Bras-Panon** *Réunion* Indian Ocean
93 E5 **Brassac** France
69 C3 **Brasschaat** Belgium
14 C4 **Brassey, Mt mt.** *Northern Terr.* Australia
17 C5 **Brassey Ra. h.** *Western Australia* Australia
23 A5 **Brassey Range mountain range** Malaysia
147 J2 **Brassua Lake l.** *Maine* U.S.A.
75 J3 **Břasy** Czech Rep.
76 G4 **Brąszewice** Poland
79 M5 **Bratca** Romania
78 G3 **Bratislava airport** Slovakia
78 G3 **Bratislava** Slovakia
45 M4 **Bratsk** Rus. Fed.
53 D3 **Brats'ke** Ukraine
53 C2 **Bratslav** Ukraine
147 G3 **Brattleboro** *Vermont* U.S.A.
59 E1 **Brattmon** Sweden
104 G3 **Bratunac** Bos.-Herz.
74 C2 **Braubach** Germany
169 G3 **Braúnas** Brazil
80 E2 **Braunau am Inn div.** Austria
80 E2 **Braunau am Inn** Austria
74 D2 **Braunfels** Germany
73 F4 **Braunlage** Germany
83 D1 **Bräunlingen** Germany
74 E3 **Braunsbach** Germany
73 G4 **Braunsbedra** Germany
72 E4 **Braunschweig div.** *Niedersachsen* Germany
73 F3 **Braunschweig** *Braunschweig* Germany
62 B3 **Braunton** *England* U.K.
122 □ **Brava i.** Cape Verde
101 H3 **Bravatas r.** Spain
59 G2 **Bråviken inlet** Sweden
156 D2 **Bravo del Norte r.** Mexico/U.S.A.
100 B3 **Bravura, Barragem da resr** Portugal
155 E5 **Brawley** *California* U.S.A.
62 C3 **Bray r.** *England* U.K.
130 D2 **Bray** Botswana
67 E3 **Bray** Rep. of Ireland
89 F4 **Braye r.** France
67 A5 **Bray Head headland** Rep. of Ireland
53 C2 **Brayiliv** Ukraine
86 C4 **Bray-sur-Seine** France
86 B3 **Bray-sur-Somme** France
101 F2 **Brazatortas** Spain
136 F4 **Brazeau r.** *Alberta* Canada
136 F4 **Brazeau** *Alberta* Canada
82 A1 **Brazey-en-Plaine** France
160 G5 **Brazil country** South America
174 H7 **Brazil Basin sea feature** Atlantic Ocean
151 D5 **Brazos r.** *Texas* U.S.A.
125 C4 **Brazzaville** Congo
104 G3 **Brčko** Bos.-Herz.
76 F2 **Brda r.** Poland
78 C2 **Brdy h.** Czech Rep.
Bré *see* **Bray**
102 B3 **Brea** Spain
64 D1 **Breadalbane mts** *Scotland* U.K.
9 A6 **Breaksea Sd inlet** New Zealand
8 E1 **Bream Bay b.** New Zealand
8 E1 **Bream Head headland** New Zealand
8 E2 **Bream Tail c.** New Zealand
112 E2 **Breaza** Romania
22 B3 **Brebes** Indonesia
89 D3 **Brécey** France
88 C4 **Brech** France
86 B3 **Brêche r.** France
62 B3 **Brechfa** *Wales* U.K.
66 F4 **Brechin** *Scotland* U.K.
69 C3 **Brecht** Belgium
150 D2 **Breckenridge** *Minnesota* U.S.A.
151 D5 **Breckenridge** *Texas* U.S.A.
63 G2 **Breckland reg.** *England* U.K.
78 F3 **Břeclav** Czech Rep.
62 C3 **Brecon** *Wales* U.K.
62 C3 **Brecon Beacons h.** *Wales* U.K.
62 C3 **Brecon Beacons National Park nat. park** *Wales* U.K.
68 C3 **Breda** Netherlands
59 E3 **Bredaryd** Sweden
130 C7 **Bredasdorp** South Africa
13 G3 **Bredbo** *New South Wales* Australia
73 H3 **Breddin** Germany
63 G4 **Brede r.** *England* U.K.
55 A4 **Brede r.** Denmark
55 A4 **Bredebro** Denmark
69 A3 **Bredene** Belgium
72 D1 **Bredstedt** Germany
56 D2 **Bredviken** Sweden
46 F2 **Bredy** Rus. Fed.
69 D3 **Bree** Belgium
68 C2 **Breezand** Netherlands
146 D5 **Breezewood** *Pennsylvania* U.S.A.
74 D5 **Breg r.** Germany
81 G5 **Bregana** Croatia
80 A3 **Bregenz div.** Austria
80 A3 **Bregenz** Austria
80 A3 **Bregenzer Wald forest** Austria
55 C5 **Bregninge** Denmark
112 D2 **Bregovo** Bulgaria
83 F3 **Breguzzo** Italy
88 D3 **Bréhal** France
88 C3 **Bréhan** France
88 C3 **Bréhat, Île de i.** France
73 H4 **Brehna** Germany
56 K6 **Breiðafjörður b.** Iceland
56 N6 **Breiðalsvík** Iceland
87 G3 **Breidenbach** France
74 D2 **Breidenbach** Germany
83 E2 **Breil** Switzerland
91 F5 **Breil-sur-Roya** France
131 F5 **Breipaal** South Africa
74 C4 **Breisach am Rhein** Germany
74 C5 **Breisgau reg.** Germany
87 G3 **Breitenbach** Germany
82 C1 **Breitenbach** Switzerland
80 C3 **Breitenbach am Inn** Austria
81 E2 **Breitenberg** Germany
80 C1 **Breitenbrunn** *Bayern* Germany
80 B2 **Breitenbrunn** *Bayern* Germany
73 F2 **Breitenfelde** Germany
75 F3 **Breitengüßbach** Germany
80 B3 **Breitenwang** Austria
83 G1 **Breiter Grieskogel mt.** Austria
82 D1 **Breitnau** Germany
74 F2 **Breitungen** Germany
56 F1 **Breivikbotn** Norway
100 B3 **Brejeira, Serra da mountain range** Portugal
166 C3 **Brejinho de Nazaré** Brazil
166 D2 **Brejo r.** Brazil
166 D1 **Brejo** Brazil
166 C2 **Brejo da Porta** Brazil
56 C3 **Brekstad** Norway
83 E3 **Brembo r.** Italy
72 D2 **Bremen div.** Germany
72 D2 **Bremen** *Bremen* Germany
145 C5 **Bremen** *Georgia* U.S.A.
148 D5 **Bremen** *Indiana* U.S.A.
17 B7 **Bremer B. b.** *Western Australia* Australia
72 D2 **Bremerhaven** Germany
17 C7 **Bremer Ra. h.** *Western Australia* Australia
152 B2 **Bremerton** *Washington* U.S.A.
72 E2 **Bremervörde** Germany
83 D1 **Bremgarten** Switzerland
74 C2 **Bremm** Germany
58 A2 **Bremnes** Norway
62 C3 **Brendon Hills h.** *England* U.K.
100 E3 **Brenes** Spain
151 D6 **Brenham** *Texas* U.S.A.
100 C2 **Brenhas r.** Portugal
62 C1 **Brenig, Llyn l.** *Wales* U.K.
56 D2 **Brenna** Norway
89 F4 **Brenne r.** France
90 D2 **Brenne r.** France
92 D2 **Brenne reg.** France
107 F2 **Brennero** Italy
80 C3 **Brenner Pass pass** Austria/Italy
106 E3 **Breno** Italy
90 D2 **Brénod** France
141 F3 **Brent** *Ontario* Canada
107 F3 **Brenta r.** Italy
154 B3 **Brentwood** *California* U.S.A.
63 G3 **Brentwood** *England* U.K.
147 G4 **Brentwood** *New York* U.S.A.
107 E3 **Brenzone** Italy
106 E3 **Brescia div.** *Lombardia* Italy
106 E3 **Brescia** *Brescia* Italy
69 B3 **Breskens** Netherlands
89 G2 **Bresle r.** France
83 E3 **Bressana Bottarone** Italy
107 F2 **Bressanone** Italy
66 □2 **Bressay i.** *Scotland* U.K.
90 D2 **Bresse reg.** France
93 D5 **Bressols** France
92 B2 **Bressuire** France
77 N3 **Brest div.** Belarus
88 A3 **Brest** *Finistère* France
77 M3 **Brest** Belarus
81 G5 **Brestanica** Slovenia
81 G4 **Bresternica** Slovenia
88 C2 **Bretagne div.** France
58 D2 **Bretangen b.** Norway
112 F1 **Brețcu** Romania
93 D4 **Bretenoux** France
89 F3 **Breteuil** *Haute-Normandie* France
86 B3 **Breteuil** *Picardie* France
92 A2 **Brétignolles-sur-Mer** France
89 F3 **Bretoncelles** France
179 □ **Bretonne, Baie b.** *Kerguelen* Indian Ocean
151 F6 **Breton Sound b.** *Louisiana* U.S.A.
8 E1 **Brett, Cape c.** New Zealand
74 D3 **Bretten** Germany
62 D1 **Bretton** *Wales* U.K.
89 E2 **Brettville-sur-Laize** France
87 G3 **Bretzenheim** Germany
74 E3 **Breuberg-Neustadt** Germany
87 F5 **Breuchin r.** France
82 C3 **Breuil-Cervinia** Italy
145 D5 **Brevard** *N. Carolina* U.S.A.
90 E3 **Brévent, Le mt.** France
166 B1 **Breves** Brazil
58 C2 **Brevik** Norway
59 E2 **Breviken** Sweden
90 E2 **Brévon r.** France
148 E2 **Brevort** *Michigan* U.S.A.
13 F2 **Brewarrina** *New South Wales* Australia
147 J2 **Brewer** *Maine* U.S.A.
152 C1 **Brewster** *Washington* U.S.A.
Brewster, Kap c. *see* **Kangikajik**
151 G6 **Brewton** *Alabama* U.S.A.
131 G3 **Breyten** South Africa
50 F3 **Breytovo** Rus. Fed.
Brezhnev *see* **Naberezhnyye Chelny**
81 H2 **Březí** Czech Rep.
81 G5 **Brežice** Slovenia
81 H4 **Breznica** Croatia
78 C2 **Březnice** Czech Rep.
112 D3 **Breznik** Bulgaria
79 J3 **Brezno** Slovakia
112 E2 **Brezoi** Romania
89 G3 **Brézolles** France
112 E3 **Brezovo** Bulgaria
179 □ **B. Rhodes b.** *Kerguelen* Indian Ocean
124 D2 **Bria** Central African Rep.
92 D3 **Briance r.** France
91 E4 **Briançon** France
62 C2 **Brianne, Llyn resr** *Wales* U.K.
90 A1 **Briare** France
93 D5 **Briatexte** France
111 F4 **Briatico** Italy
13 F3 **Bribbaree** *New South Wales* Australia
15 H5 **Bribie I. i.** *Queensland* Australia
53 B2 **Briceni** Moldova
106 B4 **Bric Bouchet mt.** France/Italy
91 E4 **Bric Froid mt.** France/Italy
88 D2 **Bricquebec** France
67 C4 **Bride r.** Rep. of Ireland
91 E3 **Brides-les-Bains** France
155 G1 **Bridgeland** *Utah* U.S.A.
62 C3 **Bridgend div.** *Wales* U.K.
64 B2 **Bridgend** *Scotland* U.K.
62 C3 **Bridgend** *Wales* U.K.
66 E4 **Bridge of Allan** *Scotland* U.K.
64 D1 **Bridge of Balgie** *Scotland* U.K.
65 E1 **Bridge of Cally** *Scotland* U.K.
65 E1 **Bridge of Earn** *Scotland* U.K.
66 D4 **Bridge of Orchy** *Scotland* U.K.
64 D2 **Bridge of Weir** *Scotland* U.K.
154 C2 **Bridgeport** *California* U.S.A.
147 G4 **Bridgeport** *Connecticut* U.S.A.
150 C3 **Bridgeport** *Nebraska* U.S.A.
152 E2 **Bridger** *Montana* U.S.A.
152 F3 **Bridger Peak summit** *Wyoming* U.S.A.
147 F5 **Bridgeton** *New Jersey* U.S.A.
159 □9 **Bridgetown** *Barbados* Caribbean
17 B7 **Bridgetown** *Western Australia* Australia
147 K1 **Bridgewater** *Maine* U.S.A.
139 H5 **Bridgewater** *Nova Scotia* Canada
13 F5 **Bridgewater** *Tasmania* Australia
131 G1 **Bridgewater** South Africa
62 D2 **Bridgnorth** *England* U.K.
147 H2 **Bridgton** *Maine* U.S.A.
62 C3 **Bridgwater** *England* U.K.
62 C3 **Bridgwater Bay b.** *England* U.K.
65 H3 **Bridlington** *England* U.K.
65 H3 **Bridlington Bay b.** *England* U.K.
62 D4 **Bridport** *England* U.K.
13 F5 **Bridport** *Tasmania* Australia
86 B4 **Brie reg.** France
88 B3 **Briec** France
86 B4 **Brie-Comte-Robert** France
69 F4 **Briedel** Germany
68 C3 **Brielle** Netherlands
86 D4 **Brienne-le-Château** France
82 D2 **Brienz** Switzerland
109 H4 **Brienza** Italy
82 D2 **Brienzer Rothorn mt.** Switzerland
82 C2 **Brienzer See l.** Switzerland
73 K3 **Briesen** Germany
73 J4 **Brieske** Germany
73 K3 **Brieskow-Finkenheerd** Germany
69 C5 **Brieuilles-sur-Bar** France
87 E3 **Briey** France
82 C2 **Brig** Switzerland
87 H4 **Brigach r.** Germany
173 J1 **Brigadier General Diego Lamas** Uruguay
65 H4 **Brigg** *England* U.K.
152 D3 **Brigham City** *Utah* U.S.A.
63 E4 **Brighstone** *England* U.K.
63 H3 **Brightlingsea** *England* U.K.
63 F4 **Brighton** *England* U.K.
149 F4 **Brighton** *Michigan* U.S.A.
141 G4 **Brighton** *Ontario* Canada
9 C6 **Brighton** New Zealand
15 E4 **Brighton Downs** *Queensland* Australia
166 E2 **Brigida, R. da r.** Brazil
91 E5 **Brignoles** France
99 H4 **Brihuega** Spain
107 H4 **Brijuni nat. park** Croatia
122 A4 **Brikama** The Gambia
168 A4 **Brilhante r.** Brazil
87 E4 **Brillon-en-Barrois** France
72 D4 **Brilon** Germany
52 F1 **Brilyakovo** Rus. Fed.
58 B1 **Brimnes** Norway
111 G2 **Brindisi div.** *Puglia* Italy
111 G2 **Brindisi** *Brindisi* Italy
104 E3 **Brinje** Croatia
173 F1 **Brinkmann** Argentina
12 D3 **Brinkworth** *S. Australia* Australia
90 B1 **Brinon-sur-Beuvron** France
89 H4 **Brinon-sur-Sauldre** France
139 H4 **Brion, Île i.** *Québec* Canada
90 C2 **Brionnais reg.** France
89 F2 **Brionne** France
91 B3 **Brioude** France
92 B2 **Brioux-sur-Boutonne** France
89 E3 **Briouze** France
139 F3 **Brisay** *Québec* Canada
15 H5 **Brisbane** *Queensland* Australia
107 F4 **Brisighella** Italy
89 E4 **Brissac-Quince** France
62 D3 **Bristol airport** *England* U.K.
147 G4 **Bristol** *Connecticut* U.S.A.
62 D3 **Bristol** *England* U.K.
147 K1 **Bristol** *New Brunswick* Canada
147 F4 **Bristol** *Pennsylvania* U.S.A.
146 B6 **Bristol** *Tennessee* U.S.A.
134 B4 **Bristol Bay b.** *Alaska* U.S.A.
62 B3 **Bristol Channel est.** *England/Wales* U.K.
179 C1 **Bristol I. i.** *S. Sandwich Is* Atlantic Ocean
155 E4 **Bristol Lake l.** *California* U.S.A.
155 D4 **Bristol Mts mts** *California* U.S.A.
8 □1 **Bristow Pt pt** *Auckland Is* New Zealand
62 D4 **Brit r.** *England* U.K.
168 C1 **Britânia** Brazil
98 B3 **Britelo** Portugal
179 A2 **British Antarctic Territory reg.** Antarctica
136 D3 **British Columbia div.** Canada
135 L1 **British Empire Range mountain range** *N.W.T.* Canada
131 F2 **Brits** South Africa
130 D5 **Britstown** South Africa
Brittany div. *see* **Bretagne**
67 E4 **Brittas Bay b.** Rep. of Ireland
62 A2 **Brittas Bay** Rep. of Ireland
92 D3 **Brive-la-Gaillarde** France
99 G2 **Briviesca** Spain
88 D2 **Brix** France
62 C4 **Brixham** *England* U.K.
80 C3 **Brixlegg** Austria
47 H4 **Brlik** Kazakhstan
78 F2 **Brno** *Jihomoravsk* Czech Rep.
59 H3 **Bro** *Gotland* Sweden
59 G2 **Bro** *Uppsala* Sweden
145 D5 **Broad r.** *S. Carolina* U.S.A.
147 F3 **Broadalbin** *New York* U.S.A.
17 C6 **Broad Arrow** *Western Australia* Australia
138 E3 **Broadback r.** *Québec* Canada
66 B2 **Broad Bay b.** *Scotland* U.K.
66 C3 **Broadford** *Scotland* U.K.
13 F4 **Broadford** *Victoria* Australia
67 C4 **Broadford** Rep. of Ireland
67 B2 **Broad Haven b.** Rep. of Ireland
62 A3 **Broad Haven** *Wales* U.K.
66 E5 **Broad Law h.** *Scotland* U.K.
63 G4 **Broad Oak** *England* U.K.
15 G4 **Broad Sound Channel chan.** *Queensland* Australia
15 G4 **Broadsound Ra. h.** *Queensland* Australia
63 H3 **Broadstairs** *England* U.K.
63 H2 **Broads, The reg.** *England* U.K.
152 F2 **Broadus** *Montana* U.S.A.
137 J4 **Broadview** *Saskatchewan* Canada
150 C3 **Broadwater** *Nebraska* U.S.A.
63 E2 **Broadway** *England* U.K.
62 D4 **Broadwindsor** *England* U.K.
8 D1 **Broadwood** New Zealand
55 B5 **Broager** Denmark
59 F3 **Broby** Sweden
82 C2 **Broc** Switzerland
54 C3 **Brocēni** Latvia
137 J3 **Brochet** *Manitoba* Canada
137 J3 **Brochet, Lac l.** *Manitoba* Canada
73 F4 **Brocken mt.** Germany
63 E4 **Brockenhurst** *England* U.K.
134 G2 **Brock I. i.** *N.W.T.* Canada
146 E3 **Brockport** *New York* U.S.A.
147 H3 **Brockton** *Massachusetts* U.S.A.
141 H4 **Brockville** *Ontario* Canada
149 F4 **Brockway** *Michigan* U.S.A.
146 D4 **Brockway** *Pennsylvania* U.S.A.
62 D3 **Brockworth** *England* U.K.
76 E2 **Broczyno** Poland
114 C1 **Brod** Macedonia
114 C2 **Brod** Macedonia
58 D2 **Brodalen** Sweden
73 H1 **Broderstorf** Germany
53 C2 **Brodets'ke** Ukraine
135 K2 **Brodeur Peninsula pen.** *N.W.T.* Canada
148 C4 **Brodhead** *Wisconsin* U.S.A.
66 C5 **Brodick** *Scotland* U.K.
77 H2 **Brodnica** Poland
81 J2 **Brodské** Slovakia
76 C4 **Brody** Poland
76 D3 **Brody** *Zielona Góra* Poland
53 A1 **Brody** Ukraine
131 E3 **Broedersput** South Africa
131 F5 **Broekpoort r.** South Africa
89 F2 **Broglie** France
87 G2 **Brohl** Germany
90 D1 **Broin** France
76 D2 **Brojce** Poland
151 E4 **Broken Arrow** *Oklahoma* U.S.A.
13 G3 **Broken B. b.** *New South Wales* Australia
150 D3 **Broken Bow** *Nebraska* U.S.A.
151 E5 **Broken Bow** *Oklahoma* U.S.A.
12 E2 **Broken Hill** *New South Wales* Australia
163 F2 **Brokopondo** Surinam
72 E2 **Brokstedt** Germany
110 D4 **Brolo** *Sicilia* Italy
73 F3 **Brome** Germany
63 G3 **Bromley** *England* U.K.
59 G2 **Bromma airport** Sweden

59 E2 Brommo i. Sweden
159 □1 Brompton Jamaica
141 K4 Bromptonville Québec Canada
59 G3 Brömsebro Sweden
62 D2 Bromsgrove England U.K.
62 D2 Bromyard England U.K.
90 C3 Bron France
102 B4 Bronchales Spain
55 B2 Brønderslev Denmark
122 D5 Brong-Ahafo div. Ghana
106 D3 Broni Italy
131 G2 Bronkhorstspruit South Africa
56 D2 Brønnøysund Norway
55 A4 Brøns Denmark
148 E5 Bronson Michigan U.S.A.
110 D5 Bronte Sicilia Italy
53 B1 Bronyts'ka Huta Ukraine
83 E3 Bronzone, Monte mt. Italy
63 H2 Brooke England U.K.
64 A3 Brookeborough Northern Ireland U.K.
23 A4 Brooke's Point Philippines
148 C4 Brookfield Wisconsin U.S.A.
151 F6 Brookhaven Mississippi U.S.A.
152 A3 Brookings Oregon U.S.A.
150 D2 Brookings S. Dakota U.S.A.
147 H3 Brookline Massachusetts U.S.A.
148 B5 Brooklyn Illinois U.S.A.
148 A5 Brooklyn Iowa U.S.A.
148 A3 Brooklyn Center Minnesota U.S.A.
146 D6 Brookneal Virginia U.S.A.
137 G4 Brooks Alberta Canada
154 A2 Brooks California U.S.A.
147 J2 Brooks Maine U.S.A.
179 B3 Brooks, C. c. Antarctica
134 C3 Brooks Range mountain range Alaska U.S.A.
145 D6 Brooksville Florida U.S.A.
17 B7 Brookton Western Australia Australia
146 D4 Brookville Pennsylvania U.S.A.
131 G1 Broombeek South Africa
16 C3 Broome Western Australia Australia
17 B7 Broome Hill Western Australia Australia
66 C3 Broom, Loch inlet Scotland U.K.
88 C3 Broons France
93 E4 Broquiès France
66 E2 Brora Scotland U.K.
55 B4 Brørup Denmark
59 F4 Brösarp Sweden
112 F1 Broscăuţi Romania
62 D2 Broseley England U.K.
67 D3 Brosna r. Rep. of Ireland
92 B3 Brossac France
112 E1 Broşteni Romania
168 D5 Brotas Brazil
100 B2 Brotas Portugal
25 A5 Brothers i. Andaman and Nicobar Is India
152 B3 Brothers Oregon U.S.A.
Brothers, The is see Al Ikhwān
27 □ Brothers, The is Hong Kong
93 B6 Broto Spain
59 H2 Brottby Sweden
65 H3 Brotton England U.K.
89 G3 Brou France
65 F3 Brough England U.K.
65 H4 Brough England U.K.
66 E1 Brough Head headland Scotland U.K.
66 F2 Brough Ness pt Scotland U.K.
67 E2 Broughshane Northern Ireland U.K.
12 D3 Broughton r. S. Australia Australia
65 E2 Broughton Scotland U.K.
62 D1 Broughton Wales U.K.
8 □3 Broughton I. i. Snares Is New Zealand
135 M3 Broughton Island N.W.T. Canada
66 F4 Broughty Ferry Scotland U.K.
118 C4 Broulkou well Chad
78 F1 Broumov Czech Rep.
86 D4 Brousseval France
87 F4 Brouvelieures France
68 B3 Brouwershaven Netherlands
53 D1 Brovary Ukraine
55 B2 Brovst Denmark
158 D2 Brown Bank sea feature The Bahamas
151 C5 Brownfield Texas U.S.A.
63 E2 Brownhills England U.K.
152 D1 Browning Montana U.S.A.
17 B6 Brown, L. salt flat Western Australia Australia
12 D3 Brown, Mt mt. S. Australia Australia
12 C3 Brown, Pt headland S. Australia Australia
148 D6 Brownsburg Indiana U.S.A.
147 F5 Browns Mills New Jersey U.S.A.
159 □1 Brown's Town Jamaica
145 B5 Brownsville Tennessee U.S.A.
151 D7 Brownsville Texas U.S.A.
147 J2 Brownville Maine U.S.A.
147 J2 Brownville Junction Maine U.S.A.
151 D6 Brownwood Texas U.S.A.
16 C2 Browse I. i. Western Australia Australia
66 E5 Broxburn Scotland U.K.
82 B2 Broye r. Switzerland
100 D1 Brozas Spain
114 B2 Brozdovec Albania
54 F5 Brozha Belarus
83 F3 Brozzo Italy
86 B2 Bruay-en-Artois France
159 □9 Bruce Barbados Caribbean
9 B5 Bruce Bay b. New Zealand
148 C2 Bruce Crossing Michigan U.S.A.
16 B4 Bruce, Mt mt. Western Australia Australia
140 E4 Bruce Pen. pen. Ontario Canada
140 E4 Bruce Peninsula National Park nat. park Ontario Canada
17 B6 Bruce Rock Western Australia Australia
87 G4 Bruche r. France
72 E3 Bruchhausen-Vilsen Germany
74 D3 Bruchsal Germany
73 H3 Brück Germany
80 D3 Bruck an der Großglocknerstraße Austria
81 H2 Bruck an der Leitha div. Austria
81 H2 Bruck an der Leitha Austria
81 G3 Bruck an der Mur div. Austria
81 G3 Bruck an der Mur Austria
69 F5 Brücken Germany
81 F4 Brückl Austria
75 G5 Bruckmühl Germany
111 E5 Brucoli Sicilia Italy
76 G3 Brudzew Poland
62 D3 Brue r. England U.K.
91 D5 Brue-Auriac France
69 B4 Brugelette Belgium
Bruges see Brugge
82 D1 Brugg Switzerland
69 B3 Brugge div. West-Vlaanderen Belgium
69 B3 Brugge Brugge Belgium
72 B4 Brüggen Germany
107 G3 Brugnera Italy
74 B2 Brühl Germany
68 C3 Bruinisse Netherlands
155 G2 Bruin Pt summit Utah U.S.A.
37 H3 Bruint India
130 A2 Brukkaros, Mt mt. Namibia
43 B4 Brûk, W. el watercourse Egypt
148 B2 Brule Wisconsin U.S.A.
89 E4 Brûlon France
69 C5 Brûly Belgium
169 F4 Brumadinho Brazil
166 D3 Brumado Brazil
87 G4 Brumath France
68 E2 Brummen Netherlands
58 D1 Brumunddal Norway
73 G3 Brunau Germany
152 D3 Bruneau r. Idaho U.S.A.
152 D3 Bruneau Idaho U.S.A.
86 D3 Brunehamel France
19 N9 Brunei country Asia
14 C3 Brunette Downs Northern Terr. Australia
56 D3 Brunflo Sweden
107 F2 Brunico Italy
93 D4 Bruniquel France
59 G2 Brunna Sweden
81 H2 Brunn am Gebirge Austria
83 D2 Brunnen Switzerland
9 C5 Brunner, L. l. New Zealand
137 H4 Bruno Saskatchewan Canada
59 E2 Brunsberg Sweden
72 E2 Brunsbüttel Germany
69 D4 Brunssum Netherlands
82 C1 Brunstatt France
145 D6 Brunswick Georgia U.S.A.
147 J3 Brunswick Maine U.S.A.
146 C4 Brunswick Ohio U.S.A.
16 D2 Brunswick Bay b. Western Australia Australia
17 A7 Brunswick Jct. Western Australia Australia
140 D2 Brunswick Lake l. Ontario Canada
171 B7 Brunswick, Peninsula de pen. Chile
78 G2 Bruntál Czech Rep.
179 C3 Brunt Ice Shelf ice feature Antarctica
13 F5 Bruny I. i. Tasmania Australia
112 C3 Brus Yugoslavia
58 A2 Brusand Norway
50 G2 Brusenets Rus. Fed.
152 G3 Brush Colorado U.S.A.
83 F2 Brusio Switzerland
93 E5 Brusque France
Brussel see Bruxelles
140 E5 Brussels Ontario Canada
148 D3 Brussels Wisconsin U.S.A.
Brussels see Bruxelles
106 B3 Brusson Italy
73 K2 Brüssow Germany
76 F2 Brusy Poland
53 C1 Brusyliv Ukraine
13 F4 Bruthen Victoria Australia
62 D3 Bruton England U.K.
87 G2 Bruttig-Fankel Germany
86 D2 Bruxelles airport Belgium
69 C4 Bruxelles Brabant Belgium
87 F4 Bruyères France
88 D3 Bruz France
59 F3 Bruzaholm Sweden
111 F4 Bruzzano, Capo c. Italy
77 J3 Brwinów Poland
146 A4 Bryan Ohio U.S.A.
151 D6 Bryan Texas U.S.A.
179 A3 Bryan Coast coastal area Antarctica
12 D3 Bryan, Mt h. S. Australia Australia
52 A3 Bryansk div. Rus. Fed.
52 B3 Bryansk Rus. Fed.
51 H6 Bryanskoye Rus. Fed.
155 F3 Bryce Canyon Nat. Park nat. park Utah U.S.A.
155 H5 Bryce Mt mt. Arizona U.S.A.
63 □1 Bryher i. England U.K.
53 E3 Brylivka Ukraine
62 C1 Brymbo Wales U.K.
62 C3 Brynamman Wales U.K.
58 A2 Bryne Norway
62 C3 Brynmawr Wales U.K.
51 F6 Bryukhovetskaya Rus. Fed.
76 F5 Brzeg Poland
76 E4 Brzeg Dolny Poland
76 G3 Brześc Kujawski Poland
77 J6 Brzesko Poland
76 E2 Brzezie Poland
76 G4 Brzeziny Kalisz Poland
77 H4 Brzeziny Skierniewice Poland
73 L4 Brzeźnica Poland
76 D2 Brzeźno Poland
77 K6 Brzostek Poland
77 K4 Brzóza Poland
77 L6 Brzozów Krosno Poland
77 J3 Brzozów Plock Poland
156 B2 Sebastián Vizcaíno, B b. Mexico
22 C2 Bt Baka mt. Indonesia
22 C1 Bt Batuayau mt. Indonesia
22 C1 Bt Batuesambang mt. Indonesia
22 D2 Bt Gandadiwata mt. Indonesia
22 E2 Bt Kambuno mt. Indonesia
22 B1 Bt Lanjak mt. Malaysia
22 C1 Bt Liangpran mt. Indonesia
22 A3 Bt Nanti mt. Indonesia
22 C1 Bt Pancingapan mt. Indonesia
22 C2 Bt Raya mt. Indonesia
22 B2 Bt Raya mt. Indonesia
22 A3 Bt Ridingan mt. Indonesia
22 B2 Bt Tukung mt. Indonesia
22 C1 Bt Tungun mt. Indonesia
119 J4 Bū well Yemen
127 B7 Bua r. Malawi
6 □6 Bua Fiji
59 E3 Bua Sweden
126 D4 Bu'aale Somalia
6 □1 Buala Solomon Is.
98 B4 Buarcos Portugal
10 D1 Bua, Tg pt Indonesia
118 D2 Bū Athlah well Libya
118 C1 Bu'ayrāt al Hasūn Libya
122 A4 Buba Guinea-Bissau
127 A5 Bubanza Burundi
111 □ Bubaqra Malta
122 A4 Bubaque Guinea-Bissau
129 E3 Bubi r. Zimbabwe
42 G4 Būbīyān I. i. Kuwait
88 B4 Bubry France
23 B5 Bubuan i. Philippines
65 H4 Bubwith England U.K.
6 □6 Buca Fiji
113 F5 Buca Turkey
42 B2 Bucak Turkey
43 B1 Bucakkışla Turkey
162 C2 Bucaramanga Colombia
23 C4 Bucas Grande i. Philippines
16 C3 Buccaneer Archipelago is Western Australia Australia
109 G2 Bucchianico Italy
109 H4 Buccino Italy
100 A2 Bucelas Portugal
82 B2 Buch Germany
53 A2 Buchach Ukraine
13 G4 Buchan Victoria Australia
148 D5 Buchanan Michigan U.S.A.
146 D6 Buchanan Virginia U.S.A.
122 B5 Buchanan Liberia
151 D6 Buchanan, L. l. Texas U.S.A.
15 F4 Buchanan, L. salt flat Queensland Australia
17 C5 Buchanan, L. salt flat Western Australia Australia
135 L2 Buchan Gulf b. N.W.T. Canada
139 J4 Buchans Newfoundland Canada
Bucharest see Bucureşti
75 H4 Buchbach Germany
80 D3 Buchboden Austria
69 F4 Büchel Germany
73 F2 Büchen Germany
74 E3 Buchen (Odenwald) Germany
73 H2 Buchholz Germany
75 F4 Buchloe Germany
72 E2 Bucholz in der Nordheide Germany
83 E1 Buchs Switzerland
172 A4 Buchupureo Chile
89 G2 Buchy France
114 B2 Buçimas Albania
107 F5 Bucine Italy
13 F2 Buckambool Mt h. New South Wales Australia
72 E3 Bückeburg Germany
72 E3 Bücken Germany
155 F5 Buckeye Arizona U.S.A.
146 B5 Buckeye Lake l. Ohio U.S.A.
146 C5 Buckhannon r. W. Virginia U.S.A.
146 C5 Buckhannon W. Virginia U.S.A.
66 E4 Buckhaven Scotland U.K.
155 H5 Buckhorn New Mexico U.S.A.
141 F4 Buckhorn Ontario Canada
146 B6 Buckhorn Lake l. Kentucky U.S.A.
141 F4 Buckhorn Lake l. Ontario Canada
66 F3 Buckie Scotland U.K.
63 F3 Buckingham England U.K.
141 H4 Buckingham Québec Canada
146 D6 Buckingham Virginia U.S.A.
14 C2 Buckingham B. b. Northern Terr. Australia
63 F3 Buckinghamshire div. England U.K.
130 D4 Bucklands South Africa
15 G5 Buckland Tableland reg. Queensland Australia
179 A6 Buckle I. i. Antarctica
10 □3 Buckles Bay b. Macquarie I. Pacific Ocean
14 D4 Buckley watercourse Queensland Australia
81 G3 Bucklige Welt h. Austria
155 F4 Buckskin Mts mts Arizona U.S.A.
154 B2 Bucks Mt mt. California U.S.A.
147 J2 Bucksport Maine U.S.A.
73 H3 Bückwitz Germany
78 G2 Bučovice Czech Rep.
125 B4 Buco-Zau Cabinda Angola
112 E2 Bucureşti Romania
86 C3 Bucy-lès-Pierrepont France
146 B4 Bucyrus Ohio U.S.A.
77 H4 Buczek Poland
52 B3 Buda Rus. Fed.
102 D4 Buda, Illa de i. Spain
114 C1 Budakovo Macedonia
24 A2 Budalin Myanmar
79 J4 Budapest Hungary
36 D3 Budaun India
126 E4 Bud Bud Somalia
179 C6 Budd Coast coastal area Antarctica
126 D3 Buddi Ethiopia
66 F4 Buddon Ness pt Scotland U.K.
108 B4 Buddusò Sardegna Italy
62 B4 Bude England U.K.
151 F6 Bude Mississippi U.S.A.
62 B4 Bude Bay b. England U.K.
69 D3 Budel Netherlands
72 E1 Büdelsdorf Germany
51 H6 Budennovsk Rus. Fed.
112 F2 Budeşti Romania
36 B4 Budhapur Pakistan
43 B5 Budhiya, G. mountain range Egypt
36 C3 Budhlada India
172 A5 Budi, L. del l. Chile
74 E2 Büdingen Germany
81 H4 Budinšćina Croatia
124 C3 Budjala Zaire
36 D5 Budni India
50 E3 Budogoshch' Rus. Fed.
80 D4 Budoia Italy
37 H2 Budongquan China
108 B4 Budoni Sardegna Italy
107 F4 Budrio Italy
112 B3 Budva Yugoslavia
76 E3 Budzyń Poland
124 A3 Buea Cameroon
91 D4 Buëch r. France
58 A1 Buefjorden b. Norway
154 B4 Buellton California U.S.A.
99 H5 Buenache de Alarcón Spain
172 E3 Buena Esperanza Argentina
162 B3 Buenaventura Colombia
156 D2 Buenaventura Mexico
162 B3 Buenaventure, B. de b. Colombia
153 F4 Buena Vista Colorado U.S.A.
146 D6 Buena Vista Virginia U.S.A.
101 □ Buena Vista Gibraltar
158 C2 Buena Vista, B. de b. Cuba
99 F2 Buenavista de Valdavia Spain
125 C5 Buenga r. Angola
172 A6 Bueno r. Chile
169 F2 Buenópolis Brazil
173 G4 Buenos Aires div. Argentina
173 H3 Buenos Aires Argentina
164 B1 Buenos Aires Brazil
171 B6 Buenos Aires, L. l. Argentina/Chile
159 □3 Buenos Ayres Trinidad and Tobago
171 C6 Buen Pasto Argentina
171 C7 Buen Tiempo, C. headland Argentina
169 J1 Buerarema Brazil
90 E2 Buet, Le mt. France
98 B2 Bueu Spain
156 D3 Búfalo Mexico
136 G3 Buffalo r. Alberta Canada
148 B3 Buffalo r. Wisconsin U.S.A.
146 D3 Buffalo New York U.S.A.
151 D4 Buffalo Oklahoma U.S.A.
150 C2 Buffalo S. Dakota U.S.A.
151 D6 Buffalo Texas U.S.A.
148 B3 Buffalo Wisconsin U.S.A.
152 F2 Buffalo Wyoming U.S.A.
136 F3 Buffalo Head Hills h. Yukon Terr. Canada
136 F2 Buffalo Lake l. N.W.T. Canada
137 H3 Buffalo Narrows Saskatchewan Canada
159 □1 Buff Bay Jamaica
130 C6 Buffels r. South Africa
131 H3 Buffels r. South Africa
130 A4 Buffels watercourse South Africa
145 D5 Buford Georgia U.S.A.
112 E2 Buftea Romania
77 K3 Bug r. Europe
162 B3 Buga Colombia
79 J5 Bugac reg. Hungary
123 F5 Bugana Nigeria
30 C2 Bugant Mongolia
93 E6 Bugarach, Pic de mt. France
92 D3 Bugeat France
22 B3 Bugel, Tg pt Indonesia
90 D3 Bugey reg. France
108 A5 Buggerru Sardegna Italy
74 C5 Buggingen Germany
111 □ Bugibba Malta
96 □ Bugio i. Madeira Portugal
104 F3 Bugojno Bos.-Herz.
44 F3 Bugrino Rus. Fed.
23 A4 Bugsuk i. Philippines
31 G2 Bugt China
23 B2 Buguey Philippines
30 C1 Bugul'deyka Rus. Fed.
46 D2 Bugul'ma Rus. Fed.
46 F3 Bugun' Kazakhstan
Bügür see Luntai
46 D2 Buguruslan Rus. Fed.
30 A5 Buh r. China
39 C3 Būhābād Iran
113 G6 Buharkent Turkey
42 C3 Buḩayrat al Asad resr Syria
43 D3 Buhayrat al Hījānah l. Syria
42 E3 Buḩayrat ath Tharthār l. Iraq
129 E2 Buhera Zimbabwe
23 B3 Buhi Philippines
152 D3 Buhl Idaho U.S.A.
148 A2 Buhl Minnesota U.S.A.
74 D4 Bühl Germany
87 H4 Bühlertal Germany
74 E3 Bühlertann Germany
42 E2 Bühtan r. Turkey
127 C6 Buhu r. Tanzania
112 F1 Buhuşi Romania
107 H2 Buia Italy
62 C2 Builth Wells Wales U.K.
172 B2 Buin Chile
6 □1 Buin P.N.G.
122 D5 Bui National Park nat. park Ghana
50 J4 Buinsk Rus. Fed.
52 H2 Buinsk Rus. Fed.
39 B2 Bu'in Zahrā Iran
31 F3 Buir Nur l. Mongolia
91 D4 Buis-les-Baronnies France
68 E1 Buitenpost Netherlands
128 B3 Buitepos Namibia
99 G4 Buitrago del Lozoya Spain
101 F3 Bujalance Spain
112 C3 Bujanovac Yugoslavia
102 C3 Bujaraloz Spain
107 H3 Buje Croatia
112 E3 Bujoru Romania
127 A5 Bujumbura Burundi
78 F4 Bük Hungary
76 E3 Buk Poland
31 F1 Bukachacha Rus. Fed.
77 N6 Bukachivtsi Ukraine
6 □1 Buka I. i. P.N.G.
128 C2 Bukalo Namibia
125 E5 Bukama Zaire
52 B3 Bukan' Rus. Fed.
39 C3 Būkand Iran
125 E4 Bukavu Zaire
46 F5 Bukhara Uzbekistan
47 K3 Bukhtarminskoye Vdkhr. resr Kazakhstan
23 C6 Bukide i. Indonesia
25 □ Bukit Batok Singapore
25 C7 Bukit Fraser Malaysia
25 □ Bukit Gombak h. Singapore
22 C2 Bukitlidi Indonesia
25 □ Bukit Panjang Singapore
25 □ Bukit Timah Singapore
20 D7 Bukittinggi Indonesia
79 K3 Bükk mts Hungary
43 C4 Bukka, J. el mt. Jordan
79 K3 Bükki nat. park Hungary
79 K3 Bükkszentkereszt Hungary
127 B5 Bukoba Tanzania
127 B5 Bukombekombe Tanzania
54 D4 Bukonys Lithuania
114 C2 Bukovo Macedonia
73 L3 Bukowiec h. Poland
76 F1 Bukowina Poland
77 J6 Bukowina Tatrzańska Poland
76 G4 Bukownica Poland
52 D2 Bukrino Rus. Fed.
25 □ Bukum, P. i. Singapore
123 F5 Bukuru Nigeria
22 A2 Buku, Tg pt Indonesia
53 D2 Buky Ukraine
21 K7 Bula Indonesia
83 D1 Bülach Switzerland
30 D2 Bulag Mongolia
30 C2 Bulagtay Mongolia
13 H3 Bulahdelal New South Wales Australia
23 B3 Bulan Philippines
42 D1 Bulancak Turkey
36 D3 Bulandshahr India
42 E2 Bulanık Turkey
119 F2 Bûlâq Egypt
129 D3 Bulawayo Zimbabwe
47 H2 Bulayevo Kazakhstan
114 B2 Bulçar Albania
42 B2 Buldan Turkey
36 D5 Buldana India
164 A1 Buldibuyo Peru
126 D3 Bulei well Ethiopia
131 H2 Bulembu Swaziland
63 E3 Bulford England U.K.
30 B2 Bulgan div. Mongolia
30 B3 Bulgan Mongolia
30 B2 Bulgan Mongolia
49 H4 Bulgaria country Europe
87 E4 Bulgnéville France
63 E2 Bulkington England U.K.
64 B4 Bullagon Point pt Rep. of Ireland
101 F1 Bullaque r. Spain
103 B6 Bullas Spain
69 F4 Bullay Germany
159 □1 Bull Bay Jamaica
82 C2 Bulle Switzerland
158 □2 Bullen Baai b. Curaçao Netherlands Ant.
9 D4 Buller r. New Zealand
13 F4 Buller, Mt mt. Victoria Australia
155 E4 Bullhead City Arizona U.S.A.
69 E4 Büllingen Belgium
154 D4 Bullion Mts mts California U.S.A.
15 E6 Bulloo watercourse Queensland Australia
15 E6 Bulloo Downs Queensland Australia
15 E6 Bulloo L. salt flat Queensland Australia
8 □2 Bull Rock i. Campbell I. New Zealand
8 E4 Bulls New Zealand
159 □1 Bull Savannah Jamaica
86 B2 Bully-les-Mines France
172 A4 Bulnes Chile
25 □ Buloh, P. i. Singapore
6 □1 Bulolo P.N.G.
114 B1 Bulqizë Albania
108 B4 Bultei Sardegna Italy
131 F4 Bultfontein South Africa
23 C5 Buluan Philippines
22 E3 Bulubulu Indonesia
126 C4 Buluk well Kenya
22 E3 Bulukumba Indonesia
124 D4 Bulukutu Zaire
45 O2 Bulun Rus. Fed.
125 C4 Bulungu Bandundu Zaire
125 D5 Bulungu Kasai-Occidental Zaire
47 G5 Bulungur Uzbekistan
23 C3 Bulusan Philippines
130 B2 Bulwana Namibia
131 G4 Bulwer South Africa
124 B2 Bum Cameroon
125 C5 Bumba Bandundu Zaire
124 D3 Bumba Équateur Zaire
30 C3 Bumbat Mongolia
30 C4 Bumbat Sum China
112 D2 Bumbeşti-Jiu Romania
127 B5 Bumbire I. i. Tanzania
155 F4 Bumble Bee Arizona U.S.A.
23 A5 Bum-Bum i. Malaysia
24 B1 Bumhkang Myanmar
126 C4 Buna Kenya
125 C4 Buna Zaire
127 B5 Bunazi Tanzania
67 C1 Bunbeg Rep. of Ireland
17 A7 Bunbury Western Australia Australia
67 E4 Bunclody Rep. of Ireland
67 D1 Buncrana Rep. of Ireland
127 B5 Bunda Tanzania
15 H5 Bundaberg Queensland Australia
15 F6 Bundaleer Queensland Australia
13 G2 Bundarra New South Wales Australia
68 F1 Bunde Germany
72 D3 Bünde Germany
14 C4 Bundey watercourse Northern Terr. Australia
36 C4 Bundi India
127 B4 Bundibugyo Uganda
67 C2 Bundoran Rep. of Ireland
37 F5 Bundu India
126 B3 Bunduqiya Sudan
123 F4 Bunga watercourse Nigeria
63 H2 Bungay England U.K.
24 C4 Bung Boraphet l. Thailand
13 G3 Bungendore New South Wales Australia
179 C6 Bunger Hills h. Antarctica
15 G5 Bungil Cr. r. Queensland Australia
16 E3 Bungle Bungle Nat. Park nat. park Western Australia Australia
125 C5 Bungo Angola
28 D7 Bungo-suidō chan. Japan
28 C7 Bungo-takada Japan
124 F3 Bunia Zaire
125 D4 Buniangu Zaire
123 G4 Buni-Yadi Nigeria
36 C2 Bunji Jammu and Kashmir
55 E4 Bunkeflostrand Sweden
15 H4 Bunker Group atolls Queensland Australia
155 E3 Bunkerville Nevada U.S.A.
125 E6 Bunkeya Zaire
151 E6 Bunkie Louisiana U.S.A.
145 D6 Bunnell Florida U.S.A.
68 D2 Bunnik Netherlands
103 C5 Buñol Spain
68 D2 Bunschoten-Spakenburg Netherlands
22 C2 Buntok Indonesia
22 C2 Buntokecil Indonesia
123 F5 Bununu Nigeria
42 C2 Bünyan Turkey
23 A6 Bunyu i. Indonesia
123 E4 Bunza Nigeria
104 F3 Buoač Bos.-Herz.
83 D2 Buochs Switzerland
39 B3 Bu ol Kheyr Iran
109 H4 Buonabitacolo Italy
108 D1 Buonconvento Italy
25 E4 Buôn Hô Vietnam
25 E4 Buôn Mê Thuột Vietnam
39 B4 Buqayq Saudi Arabia
127 C5 Bura Kenya
126 E2 Buraan Somalia
124 E1 Buram Sudan
47 L3 Buran Kazakhstan
36 E3 Burang China
169 J2 Buranhaém r. Brazil
169 H2 Buranhaém Brazil
107 G5 Burano r. Italy
126 E3 Burao Somalia
43 D3 Burāq Syria
52 H3 Burasy Rus. Fed.
23 C4 Burauen Philippines
119 H2 Buraydah Saudi Arabia
74 D2 Burbach Germany
63 E3 Burbage England U.K.
102 B3 Burbáguena Spain
154 C4 Burbank California U.S.A.
108 B5 Burcei Sardegna Italy
13 F3 Burcher New South Wales Australia
15 F4 Burdekin r. Queensland Australia
15 F4 Burdekin Falls waterfall Queensland Australia
69 D4 Burdinne Belgium
43 A1 Burdur div. Turkey
42 B2 Burdur Turkey
63 H2 Bure r. England U.K.
126 C2 Burē Ethiopia
126 B3 Burē Ethiopia
56 F2 Bureå Sweden
31 K2 Bureinskiy Khrebet mountain range Rus. Fed.
119 F4 Bureiqa well Sudan
99 F2 Burejo r. Spain
98 C1 Burela, Cabo pt Spain
72 D4 Büren Germany
68 D3 Buren Netherlands
82 C1 Büren an der Aare Switzerland
30 A2 Buren-Khem Rus. Fed.
30 D3 Bürentsogt Mongolia
91 D4 Bure, Pic de mt. France
31 J2 Bureya r. Rus. Fed.
31 J2 Bureya Rus. Fed.
63 E3 Burford England U.K.
73 K4 Burg Brandenburg Germany
73 G1 Burg Sachsen-Anhalt Germany
112 F3 Burgas div. Bulgaria
112 F3 Burgas Bulgaria
81 H3 Burgau Austria
74 F4 Burgau Germany
100 B3 Burgau Portugal
145 E5 Burgaw N. Carolina U.S.A.
73 G3 Burg bei Magdeburg Germany
83 F1 Burgberg im Allgäu Germany
74 F3 Burgbernheim Germany
72 F3 Burgdorf Germany
82 C1 Burgdorf Switzerland
75 F3 Burgebrach Germany
81 H3 Burgenland div. Austria
139 J4 Burgeo Newfoundland Canada
131 F5 Burgersdorp South Africa
131 H2 Burgersfort South Africa
17 C6 Burges, Mt h. Western Australia Australia
63 F4 Burgess Hill England U.K.
68 B3 Burgh Netherlands
74 F2 Burghaun Germany
75 H4 Burghausen Germany
66 E3 Burghead Scotland U.K.
75 G4 Burgheim Germany
63 G1 Burgh le Marsh England U.K.
110 C5 Burgio Sicilia Italy
75 H4 Burgkirchen an der Alz Germany
75 G2 Burgkunstadt Germany
83 E1 Bürglen Switzerland
75 H3 Burglengenfeld Germany
99 F4 Burgohondo Spain
99 G2 Burgos div. Spain
99 G2 Burgos Burgos Spain
108 A4 Burgos Sardegna Italy
74 E2 Burgsinn Germany
75 H2 Burgstädt Germany
73 J2 Burg Stargard Germany
59 H3 Burgsvik Sweden
102 B2 Burguete Spain
102 B2 Burgui Spain
100 D2 Burguillos del Cerro Spain
Burgundy div. see Bourgogne
74 D2 Burgwald forest Germany
26 G4 Burhan Budai Shan mountain range China
42 A2 Burhaniye Turkey
36 D5 Burhanpur India
37 E5 Burhar-Dhanpuri India
37 F4 Burhi Gandak r. India
168 D5 Buri Brazil
23 B3 Burias i. Philippines
23 B3 Burias Pass. chan. Philippines
46 E2 Buribay Rus. Fed.
156 K7 Burica, Pta pt Costa Rica
92 B3 Burie France
127 B5 Burigi, Lake l. Tanzania
139 J4 Burin Peninsula pen. Newfoundland Canada
25 C4 Buriram Thailand
168 C4 Buritama Brazil
165 E2 Buriti r. Brazil
166 D1 Buriti Brazil
168 D3 Buriti Alegre Brazil
166 D2 Buriti Bravo Brazil
166 C2 Buriticupu r. Brazil
166 D1 Buriti dos Lopes Brazil
166 D3 Buritirama Brazil
169 E1 Buritis Brazil
169 F2 Buritizeiro Brazil
114 A1 Burizanë Albania
36 A3 Burj Pakistan
103 C5 Burjassot Spain
79 M6 Burjuc Romania
80 B1 Burk Germany
14 D4 Burke watercourse Queensland Australia
179 A3 Burke I. i. Antarctica
9 C6 Burke Pass New Zealand
14 D3 Burketown Queensland Australia
116 D4 Burkina country Africa
141 F4 Burk's Falls Ontario Canada
47 J2 Burla r. Rus. Fed.
47 J2 Burla Rus. Fed.
102 B2 Burlada Spain
74 E4 Burladingen Germany
93 E5 Burlats France
15 E4 Burleigh Queensland Australia
152 D3 Burley Idaho U.S.A.
46 D2 Burlin Kazakhstan
153 G4 Burlington Colorado U.S.A.
148 D5 Burlington Indiana U.S.A.
148 B5 Burlington Iowa U.S.A.
147 J2 Burlington Maine U.S.A.
141 F5 Burlington Ontario Canada
147 G2 Burlington Vermont U.S.A.
148 C4 Burlington Wisconsin U.S.A.
Burma see Myanmar
52 E3 Burminka Rus. Fed.
151 D6 Burnet Texas U.S.A.
15 H5 Burnett r. Queensland Australia
152 B3 Burney California U.S.A.
63 F3 Burnham England U.K.
147 J2 Burnham Maine U.S.A.
63 G3 Burnham-on-Crouch England U.K.
62 D3 Burnham-on-Sea England U.K.
13 F5 Burnie Tasmania Australia
65 H3 Burniston England U.K.
65 F4 Burnley England U.K.
47 H4 Burnoye Kazakhstan
152 C3 Burns Oregon U.S.A.
137 H1 Burnside r. N.W.T. Canada
17 C5 Burnside, L. salt flat Western Australia Australia
134 F4 Burns Lake B.C. Canada
146 C5 Burnsville Lake l. W. Virginia U.S.A.
145 F7 Burnt Ground The Bahamas
66 E4 Burntisland Scotland U.K.
139 H3 Burnt Lake l. Labrador/Québec Canada
11 □1 Burnt Pine Norfolk I. Pacific Ocean
137 K3 Burntwood r. Manitoba Canada
63 E2 Burntwood Green England U.K.
137 J3 Burnt Wood Lake l. Manitoba Canada
106 C3 Buronzo Italy
73 J2 Burow Germany
47 L3 Burqin China
12 D3 Burra S. Australia Australia
66 □2 Burravoe Scotland U.K.
66 F2 Burray i. Scotland U.K.
112 C4 Burrel Albania
13 G3 Burrendong Reservoir resr New South Wales Australia
13 G2 Burren Jct. New South Wales Australia
67 B3 Burren National Park nat. park Rep. of Ireland
103 C5 Burriana Spain
13 G3 Burrinjuck New South Wales Australia
13 G3 Burrinjuck Reservoir resr New South Wales Australia
146 B5 Burr Oak Reservoir resr Ohio U.S.A.
66 D6 Burrow Head headland Scotland U.K.
14 B2 Burrundie Northern Terr. Australia
155 G2 Burrville Utah U.S.A.
62 B3 Burry Inlet inlet Wales U.K.
62 B3 Burry Port Wales U.K.
80 A3 Bürs Austria
113 G4 Bursa div. Turkey
42 B1 Bursa Turkey
119 F2 Bûr Safâga Egypt
Bûr Sa'îd see Port Said
65 F4 Burscough Bridge England U.K.
53 A2 Burshtyn Ukraine
74 D3 Bürstadt Germany
Bûr Sudan see Port Sudan
43 B5 Bûr Taufiq Egypt
80 B2 Burtenbach Germany
148 E3 Burt Lake l. Michigan U.S.A.
54 D3 Burtnieku l. Latvia
63 E4 Burton England U.K.
149 F4 Burton Michigan U.S.A.
62 D4 Burton Bradstock England U.K.
65 F3 Burton-in-Kendal England U.K.
138 E3 Burton, Lac l. Québec Canada
63 F2 Burton Latimer England U.K.
67 C2 Burtonport Rep. of Ireland
63 E2 Burton upon Trent England U.K.
56 F2 Burträsk Sweden
147 K1 Burtts Corner New Brunswick Canada
13 E3 Burtundy New South Wales Australia
21 J7 Buru i. Indonesia
Burultokay see Fuhai
117 G6 Burundi country Africa
127 A5 Bururi Burundi
62 D2 Burwarton England U.K.
63 G4 Burwash England U.K.
136 B2 Burwash Landing Yukon Terr. Canada
63 G2 Burwell England U.K.
66 F2 Burwick Scotland U.K.
65 F4 Bury England U.K.
141 K4 Bury Québec Canada
30 B2 Buryatiya div. Rus. Fed.
53 E1 Buryn' Ukraine
46 D3 Burynshyk Kazakhstan
63 G2 Bury St Edmunds England U.K.
76 G4 Burzenin Poland
36 C2 Burzil Pass pass Jammu & Kashmir
106 C4 Busalla Italy
106 E4 Busana Italy
124 D4 Busanga Zaire

106 B4 Busca Italy
72 E1 Busdorf Germany
114 C1 Buševa Planina mountain range Macedonia
67 E1 Bush r. Northern Ireland U.K.
53 C2 Busha Ukraine
127 D5 Bushbush r. Kenya/Somalia
53 B1 Bushcha Ukraine
39 B3 Büshehr div. Iran
39 B3 Büshehr Iran
37 E2 Bushêngcaka China
127 B5 Bushenyi Uganda
Bushire see Büshehr
67 E1 Bushmills Northern Ireland U.K.
148 B5 Bushnell Illinois U.S.A.
112 C4 Bushtricë Albania
31 F1 Bushuley Rus. Fed.
69 B4 Busigny France
124 D3 Businga Zaire
25 □ Busing, P. i. Singapore
124 C4 Busira r. Zaire
53 A2 Bus'k Ukraine
58 C1 Buskerud div. Norway
77 J5 Busko-Zdrój Poland
43 D3 Buşrá ash Shām Syria
82 B1 Bussang France
31 H2 Busse Rus. Fed.
17 A7 Busselton Western Australia Australia
124 E2 Busseri watercourse Sudan
106 E3 Busseto Italy
92 C3 Bussière-Badil France
92 C2 Bussière-Poitevine France
82 B2 Bussigny Switzerland
109 F2 Bussi sul Tirino Italy
83 F3 Bussolengo Italy
82 C3 Bussoleno Italy
68 D2 Bussum Netherlands
90 C1 Bussy-le-Grand France
151 C7 Bustamante Mexico
171 C6 Bustamante, B. b. Argentina
112 E2 Buşteni Romania
156 D2 Bustillos, L. l. Mexico
106 C3 Busto Arsizio Italy
98 D1 Busto, Cabo pt Spain
23 A3 Busuanga i. Philippines
23 A3 Busuanga Philippines
72 D1 Büsum Germany
80 E4 But r. Italy
124 D3 Buta Zaire
126 C3 Butajīra Ethiopia
25 B6 Butang Group is Thailand
172 C4 Buta Ranquil Argentina
127 A5 Butare Rwanda
66 C5 Bute i. Scotland U.K.
112 F1 Butea Romania
136 D4 Butedale B.C. Canada
136 D4 Bute In. inlet B.C. Canada
124 E3 Butembo Zaire
110 D5 Butera Sicilia Italy
66 C5 Bute, Sound of chan. Scotland U.K.
69 E4 Bütgenbach Belgium
131 G4 Butha-Buthe Lesotho
24 A2 Buthidaung Myanmar
79 M4 Butiz Romania
72 D2 Butjadingen reg. Germany
148 E5 Butler Indiana U.S.A.
146 D4 Butler Pennsylvania U.S.A.
67 D2 Butlers Bridge Rep. of Ireland
21 H8 Buton i. Indonesia
53 G1 Butovo Rus. Fed.
73 H2 Bütow Germany
100 D2 Butrera mt. Spain
77 O1 Butrimonys Lithuania
77 J2 Butryny Poland
83 E1 Bütschwil Switzerland
77 N4 Butsyn Ukraine
152 D2 Butte Montana U.S.A.
73 G4 Buttelstedt Germany
154 B1 Butte Meadows California U.S.A.
75 G3 Buttenheim Germany
65 E3 Buttermere England U.K.
25 C6 Butterworth Malaysia
131 G6 Butterworth South Africa
67 C4 Buttevant Rep. of Ireland
136 D5 Buttle L. l. B.C. Canada
66 B2 Butt of Lewis headland Scotland U.K.
135 M3 Button Is is Newfoundland Canada
154 C4 Buttonwillow California U.S.A.
17 C7 Butty Hd pt Western Australia Australia
23 C4 Butuan Philippines
53 C3 Butuceni Moldova
32 C3 Butuo China
52 G2 Buturlino Rus. Fed.
51 G5 Buturlinovka Rus. Fed.
37 E4 Butwal Nepal
52 E2 Butylitsy Rus. Fed.
74 D2 Butzbach Germany
73 G2 Bützow Germany
126 E4 Buulobarde Somalia
127 D5 Buur Gaabo Somalia
126 D4 Buurhabaka Somalia
126 B4 Buvuma I. i. Uganda
43 C5 Buwārah, J. mt. Saudi Arabia
119 G3 Buwāṭah Saudi Arabia
37 F4 Buxar India
92 C2 Buxerolles France
74 F5 Buxheim Germany
63 G4 Buxted England U.K.
72 E2 Buxtehude Germany
63 E1 Buxton England U.K.
90 C2 Buxy France
50 G3 Buy Rus. Fed.
30 D3 Buyant Mongolia
30 A3 Buyant Mongolia
30 A3 Buyant Gol r. Mongolia
30 C3 Buyant-Ovoo Mongolia
30 D3 Buyant-Uhaa Mongolia
148 A1 Buyck Minnesota U.S.A.
51 H7 Buynaksk Rus. Fed.
122 C5 Buyo, Lac de l. Côte d'Ivoire
131 G1 Buysdorp South Africa
32 C4 Buyuan r. China
42 E2 Büyük Ağri mt. Turkey
43 B1 Büyük Egri D. mt. Turkey
113 F4 Büyükkarıştıran Turkey
113 G6 Büyükmenderes r. Turkey
113 G5 Büyükorhan Turkey
31 G4 Buyun Shan mt. China
46 D4 Buzachi, Pov. pen. Kazakhstan
92 D2 Buzançais France
86 D3 Buzancy France
112 F2 Buzău Romania
118 D3 Buzaymah oasis Libya
28 C7 Buzen Japan
107 H3 Buzet Croatia
93 C4 Buzet-sur-Baïse France
93 D5 Buzet-sur-Tarn France
52 E2 Buzha r. Rus. Fed.
129 E3 Búzi r. Mozambique
129 E2 Buzi Mozambique
112 C2 Buziaş Romania
169 H5 Buzios, Cabo dos headland Brazil
169 F5 Buzios, Ilha dos i. Brazil
52 G3 Buzovlevo Rus. Fed.
51 G5 Buzuluk r. Rus. Fed.
46 D2 Buzuluk Rus. Fed.
147 H4 Buzzards Bay b. Massachusetts U.S.A.
6 □1 Bwagaoia P.N.G.
54 F4 Byahoml' Belarus
37 G4 Byakar Bhutan
112 F3 Byala Burgas Bulgaria
112 E3 Byala Razgrad Bulgaria
112 D3 Byala Slatina Bulgaria
114 G1 Byal Izvor Bulgaria
50 D4 Byalynichy Belarus
134 H2 Byam Martin I. i. N.W.T. Canada
54 E4 Byarezina r. Belarus
77 N3 Byaroza Belarus
54 D5 Byarozawka Belarus
77 N3 Byarozna Belarus
77 L4 Bychawa Poland
52 E3 Bychki Rus. Fed.
76 G4 Byczyna Poland
76 F2 Bydgoszcz div. Poland
76 G2 Bydgoszcz Poland
77 O3 Byelaazyorsk Belarus
77 M3 Byelavyezhski Belarus
54 E4 Byel'ki Belarus
77 O1 Byenyakoni Belarus
54 F5 Byerazino Belarus
54 E5 Byeraznyaki Belarus
152 F4 Byers Colorado U.S.A.
77 N2 Byershty Belarus
54 F4 Byeshankovichy Belarus
63 E2 Byfield England U.K.
58 C1 Bygdin l. Norway
58 B2 Bygland Norway
58 B2 Byglandsfjord Norway
58 B2 Byglandsfjorden l. Norway
58 A1 Bygstad Norway
73 K4 Byhleguhre Germany
54 D4 Bykhaw Belarus
58 B2 Bykle Norway
58 B2 Bykleheiane reg. Norway
51 H5 Bykovo Rus. Fed.
135 L2 Bylot Island i. N.W.T. Canada
131 G1 Bylsteel South Africa
140 E4 Byng Inlet Ontario Canada
179 B5 Byrd Gl. gl. Antarctica
31 F2 Byrka Rus. Fed.
58 B2 Byrkjedal Norway
56 B3 Byrkjelo Norway
58 A1 Byrknesøy i. Norway
53 E1 Byrlivka Ukraine
13 F2 Byrock New South Wales Australia
148 C4 Byron Illinois U.S.A.
147 H2 Byron Maine U.S.A.
13 H2 Byron Bay New South Wales Australia
13 H2 Byron, C. headland New South Wales Australia
55 C2 Byrum Denmark
52 A3 Byryne Ukraine
53 C1 Byshiv Ukraine
75 K2 Byšice Czech Rep.
56 F2 Byske Sweden
79 J2 Bystrá mt. Slovakia
75 K3 Bystřice Czech Rep.
78 F2 Bystřice nad Pernštejnem Czech Rep.
79 G2 Bystřice pod Hostýnem Czech Rep.
30 D2 Bystrinskiy Golets, G. mt. Rus. Fed.
76 E5 Bystrzyca Kłodzka Poland
78 F1 Bystrzyckie, Góry mountain range Czech Rep./Poland
45 P3 Bytantay r. Rus. Fed.
79 H2 Bytča Slovakia
76 D3 Bytnica Poland
76 G5 Bytom Poland
76 D4 Bytom Odrzański Poland
52 B3 Bytosh' Rus. Fed.
76 F1 Bytów Poland
127 B5 Byumba Rwanda
46 E5 Byuzmeyin Turkmenistan
59 G3 Byxelkrok Sweden
77 J3 Bzura r. Poland

C

165 E5 Caacupé Paraguay
165 E5 Caaguazú Paraguay
125 C6 Caála Angola
168 A5 Caarapó Brazil
169 H1 Caatiba Brazil
169 F2 Caatinga Brazil
165 E5 Caazapá Paraguay
165 E3 Cabaçal r. Brazil
158 C2 Cabaiguán Cuba
164 A2 Caballas Peru
162 C4 Caballococha Peru
156 D2 Caballos Mesteños, Llano de los plain Mexico
164 B2 Cabana Peru
93 B4 Cabanac-et-Villagrains France
164 B3 Cabanaconde Peru
98 E1 Cabañaquinta Spain
101 H3 Cabañas mt. Spain
23 B3 Cabanatuan Philippines
62 C2 Caban Coch Res. resr Wales U.K.
103 D4 Cabanes Spain
139 G4 Cabano Québec Canada
107 J3 Čabar Croatia
164 C3 Cabaraya, Co mt. Bolivia
93 E5 Cabardès reg. France
126 D2 Cabdul Qaadir Somalia
167 A4 Abeceira Rio Manso Brazil
98 C3 Cabeceiras de Basto Portugal
100 C1 Cabeço de Vide Portugal
98 C5 Cabeço Rainha mt. Portugal
166 F2 Cabedelo Brazil
106 D4 Cabella Ligure Italy
93 E6 Cabestany France
101 G2 Cabeza de Buey mt. Spain
101 E2 Cabeza del Buey Spain
101 F2 Cabezarados Spain
165 D3 Cabezas Bolivia
145 □3 Cabezas de San Juan pt Puerto Rico
100 C3 Cabezas Rubias Spain
100 C3 Cabezo Gordo h. Spain
99 F1 Cabezón de la Sal Spain
98 E4 Cabezuela del Valle Spain
173 G5 Cabildo Argentina
172 B2 Cabildo Chile
162 C1 Cabimas Venezuela
125 B5 Cabinda div. Angola
125 B5 Cabinda Cabinda Angola
152 C1 Cabinet Mts mountain range Montana U.S.A.
23 B5 Cabingan i. Philippines
145 □2 Cable Beach The Bahamas
171 C6 Cabo Blanco Argentina
101 H4 Cabo de Gata, Sierra del h. Spain
127 C7 Cabo Delgado div. Mozambique
169 G5 Cabo Frio Brazil
169 H5 Cabo Frio, Ilha do c. Brazil
141 G3 Cabonga, Réservoir resr Québec Canada
151 E4 Cabool Missouri U.S.A.
15 H5 Caboolture Queensland Australia
163 G3 Cabo Orange, Parque Nacional de nat. park Brazil
162 B4 Cabo Pantoja Peru
156 B2 Caborca Mexico
145 □3 Cabo Rojo Puerto Rico
140 E4 Cabot Head pt Ontario Canada
139 J4 Cabot Strait str. Newfoundland/Nova Scotia Canada
89 E2 Cabourg France
101 F3 Cabra r. Spain
101 F3 Cabra Spain
101 G3 Cabra del Santo Cristo Spain
108 A5 Cabras Sardegna Italy
103 B6 Cabras, Sierra de las mountain range Spain
100 B2 Cabrela r. Portugal
103 F5 Cabrera i. Spain
101 J3 Cabrera, Sierra mountain range Spain
98 D2 Cabrera, Sierra de la mountain range Spain
172 A4 Cabrero Chile
103 B5 Cabriel r. Spain
91 D5 Cabrières-d'Aigues France
98 D4 Cabrillas Spain
159 □4 Cabrits, Îlet i. Martinique Caribbean
166 E2 Cabrobó Brazil
162 D2 Cabruta Venezuela
23 B2 Cabugao Philippines
104 F4 Čabulja mt. Bos.-Herz.
79 G6 Cabuna Croatia
172 B5 Caburgua, L. l. Chile
98 D2 Cacabelos Spain
167 B6 Caçador Brazil
157 F5 Cacahuatepec Mexico
112 C3 Čačak Yugoslavia
163 G3 Cacao French Guiana
169 F5 Caçapava Brazil
167 B7 Caçapava do Sul Brazil
146 D5 Cacapon r. W. Virginia U.S.A.
162 B2 Cácares Colombia
110 C5 Caccamo Sicilia Italy
108 A4 Caccia, Capo pt Sardegna Italy
111 F3 Caccuri Italy
100 A2 Cacém Portugal
167 B6 Cacequi Brazil
100 D1 Cáceres div. Spain
100 D1 Cáceres Cáceres Spain
165 E3 Cáceres Brazil
173 H4 Cachari Argentina
152 D3 Cache Peak summit Idaho U.S.A.
122 A4 Cacheu Guinea-Bissau
170 C2 Cachi Argentina
166 B2 Cachimbo Brazil
125 D5 Cachimo Angola
164 C4 Cachinal Chile
125 C6 Cachingues Angola
162 C2 Cáchira Colombia
166 C2 Cachoeira r. Brazil
166 E3 Cachoeira Bahia Brazil
168 C3 Cachoeira Mato Grosso do Sul Brazil
168 C3 Cachoeira Alta Brazil
168 C2 Cachoeira de Goiás Brazil
166 C1 Cachoeira do Arari Brazil
167 B7 Cachoeira do Sul Brazil
169 F5 Cachoeira Paulista Brazil
169 G5 Cachoeiras de Macacu Brazil
169 H4 Cachoeiro de Itapemirim Brazil
100 C3 Cachopo Portugal
101 G3 Cacín r. Spain
122 A4 Cacine Guinea-Bissau
125 C6 Cacolo Angola
125 C6 Caconda Angola
125 B5 Cacongo Cabinda Angola
154 D3 Cactus Range mts Nevada U.S.A.
168 C3 Caçu Brazil
125 B5 Cacuaco Angola
166 D3 Caculé Brazil
169 J2 Cacumba, Ilha i. Brazil
168 B2 Caçununga Brazil
62 B2 Cadair Idris h. Wales U.K.
99 F4 Cadalso de los Vidrios Spain
100 A1 Cadaval Portugal
79 H2 Čadca Slovakia
126 D2 Caddabassa I. Ethiopia
107 E4 Cadelbosco di Sopra Italy
72 E2 Cadenberge Germany
91 D5 Cadenet France
157 E3 Cadereyta Mexico
12 C2 Cadibarrawirracanna, L. salt flat S. Australia Australia
23 B3 Cadig Mts mountain range Philippines
148 E3 Cadillac Michigan U.S.A.
141 F2 Cadillac Québec Canada
137 H5 Cadillac Saskatchewan Canada
93 B4 Cadillac France
100 E4 Cádiz div. Spain
100 D4 Cádiz Spain
23 B4 Cadiz Philippines
100 D4 Cádiz, B. de b. Spain
100 C4 Cádiz, Golfo de g. Spain
155 E4 Cadiz Lake l. California U.S.A.
107 G2 Cadore reg. Italy
93 D5 Cadours France
17 B6 Cadoux Western Australia Australia
102 B2 Cadreita Spain
89 E2 Caen Calvados France
Caerdydd see Cardiff
Caerfyrddin see Carmarthen
Caergybi see Holyhead
62 D3 Caerleon Wales U.K.
62 B1 Caernarfon Wales U.K.
62 B1 Caernarfon Bay b. Wales U.K.
62 C2 Caernarfonshire and Merionethshire div. Wales U.K.
62 C3 Caerphilly div. Wales U.K.
62 C3 Caerphilly Wales U.K.
146 B5 Caesar Creek Lake l. Ohio U.S.A.
43 C3 Caesarea Israel
166 D3 Caetité Brazil
170 C2 Cafayate Argentina
168 D4 Cafelândia Brazil
163 F3 Cafuini r. Brazil
23 B4 Cagayan i. Philippines
23 B2 Cagayan r. Philippines
23 C4 Cagayan de Oro Philippines
23 B4 Cagayan Islands is Philippines
107 G5 Cagli Italy
108 A5 Cagliari div. Sardegna Italy
108 B5 Cagliari Sardegna Italy
108 B5 Cagliari, Golfo di b. Sardegna Italy
109 H3 Cagnano Varano Italy
91 F5 Cagnes-sur-Mer France
162 C3 Caguán r. Colombia
145 □3 Caguas Puerto Rico
67 B5 Caha h. Rep. of Ireland
145 C5 Cahaba r. Alabama U.S.A.
125 B7 Cahama Angola
67 B5 Caha Mts h. Rep. of Ireland
67 A3 Caher Island i. Rep. of Ireland
67 A5 Cahermore Rep. of Ireland
67 A5 Cahersiveen Rep. of Ireland
67 D4 Cahir Rep. of Ireland
129 E2 Cahora Bassa, Barragem de barrage Mozambique
129 E2 Cahora Bassa, Lago de l. Mozambique
67 E4 Cahore Point pt Rep. of Ireland
93 D4 Cahors France
162 B5 Cahuapanas Peru
53 C3 Cahul Moldova
93 D5 Cahuzac-sur-Vère France
100 C1 Caia r. Portugal
129 F2 Caia Mozambique
100 C1 Caia, Barragem do resr Portugal
125 D6 Caianda Angola
168 C2 Caiapó r. Brazil
168 C2 Caiapônia Brazil
158 C2 Caibarién Cuba
25 D5 Cai Be Vietnam
163 D2 Caicara Venezuela
166 E2 Caicó Brazil
159 D2 Caicos Is is Turks and Caicos Is Caribbean
159 D2 Caicos Passage chan. The Bahamas/Turks and Caicos Is Caribbean
164 B3 Cailloma Peru
172 B1 Caimanes Chile
23 A3 Caiman Point pt Philippines
102 B4 Caimodorro mt. Spain
25 D5 Cai Nước Vietnam
66 E3 Cairn Gorm mt. Scotland U.K.
66 E3 Cairngorm Mts mountain range Scotland U.K.
66 C6 Cairnryan Scotland U.K.
15 F3 Cairns Queensland Australia
64 D2 Cairnsmore of Carsphairn h. Scotland U.K.
64 D3 Cairnsmore of Fleet h. Scotland U.K.
66 E3 Cairn Toul mt. Scotland U.K.
145 C6 Cairo Georgia U.S.A.
43 A4 Cairo Egypt
106 C4 Cairo Montenotte Italy
Caisléan an Bharraigh see Castlebar
64 C2 Caisteal Abhail h. Scotland U.K.
63 H2 Caister-on-Sea England U.K.
65 H4 Caistor England U.K.
66 E2 Caithness reg. Scotland U.K.
125 B6 Caitou Angola
125 C7 Caiundo Angola
15 F6 Caiwarro Queensland Australia
33 G2 Caizi Hu l. China
164 A2 Cajacay Peru
145 □3 Caja de Muertos, I. i. Puerto Rico
162 B5 Cajamarca Peru
93 D4 Cajarc France
166 C1 Cajari Brazil
164 A2 Cajatambo Peru
166 E2 Cajàzeiras Brazil
112 B3 Čajetina Yugoslavia
23 B3 Cajidiocan Philippines
104 G4 Čajniče Bos.-Herz.
168 E4 Cajuru Brazil
30 A5 Caka China
30 A5 Caka Yanhu salt lake China
43 A1 Çakırlar Turkey
43 C1 Çakit r. Turkey
78 F5 Čakovec Croatia
42 B2 Çal Turkey
165 E3 Cal, R. de la r. Bolivia
100 D3 Cala r. Spain
131 F5 Cala South Africa
100 D3 Cala Spain
123 F6 Calabar Nigeria
141 G4 Calabogie Ontario Canada
162 D2 Calabozo Venezuela
111 F4 Calabria div. Italy
111 E4 Calabria, Parco Nazionale della nat. park Italy
101 F4 Calaburra, Punta de pt Spain
102 D3 Calaceite Spain
164 C3 Calacoto Bolivia
108 B2 Calacuccia Corse France
103 □ Cala en Porter Spain
102 E3 Calaf Spain
112 D3 Calafat Romania
171 B7 Calafate Argentina
103 F5 Cala Figuera, Cap de pt Spain
172 A5 Calafquén, L. l. Chile
23 B3 Calagua Islands is Philippines
102 B2 Calahorra Spain
125 C7 Calai Angola
147 K2 Calais Maine U.S.A.
86 A2 Calais France
170 C2 Calalasteo, Sierra de mountain range Argentina
107 G2 Calalzo di Cadore Italy
165 D1 Calama Brazil
164 C4 Calama Chile
162 C1 Calamar Bolívar Colombia
162 C3 Calamar Guaviare Colombia
23 A3 Calamian Group is Philippines
102 B4 Calamocha Spain
112 D2 Călan Romania
100 D3 Calañas Spain
83 E2 Calancasca r. Switzerland
102 C4 Calanda Spain
125 C5 Calandula Angola
108 B4 Calangianus Sardegna Italy
118 D2 Calanscio Sand Sea desert Libya
23 B3 Calapan Philippines
131 F5 Calapas pass South Africa
101 H3 Calar Alta mt. Spain
53 C3 Călăraşi Moldova
112 F2 Călăraşi Romania
101 H2 Calar del Mundo mountain range Spain
110 D5 Calascibetta Sicilia Italy
108 A5 Calasetta Sardegna Italy
103 B6 Calasparra Spain
110 B5 Calatafimi Sicilia Italy
102 B3 Calatayud Spain
102 B3 Calatorao Spain
73 J4 Calau Germany
23 B3 Calauag Philippines
110 D4 Calavà, Capo c. Sicilia Italy
23 B3 Calavite, Cape c. Philippines
23 B2 Calayan i. Philippines
23 C3 Calbayog Philippines
73 G4 Calbe Germany
23 C4 Calbiga Philippines
171 B5 Calbuco Chile
164 B2 Calca Peru
166 E1 Calcanhar, Ponta do pt Brazil
151 E6 Calcasieu L. l. Louisiana U.S.A.
108 A2 Calcatoggio Corse France
83 E3 Calcio Italy
163 G3 Calçoene Brazil
37 G5 Calcutta India
112 E2 Căldăraru Romania
83 G2 Caldaro, Lago di l. Italy
83 G2 Caldaro sulla Strada del Vino Italy
100 A1 Caldas da Rainha Portugal
98 B3 Caldas de Vizela Portugal
168 D2 Caldas Novas Brazil
100 B3 Caldeirão, Serra de mountain range Portugal
72 E4 Calden Germany
170 B2 Caldera Chile
64 E2 Caldercruix Scotland U.K.
101 G1 Calderina, Sierra de la mountain range Spain
15 F5 Caldervale Queensland Australia
102 F3 Caldes de Montbui Spain
65 E3 Caldew r. England U.K.
62 B3 Caldey Island i. Wales U.K.
62 D3 Caldicot Wales U.K.
42 E2 Çaldıran Turkey
83 G2 Caldonazzo Italy
107 F2 Caldonazzo, Lago di l. Italy
152 C3 Caldwell Idaho U.S.A.
131 F5 Caledon r. Lesotho/South Africa
140 E5 Caledon Ontario Canada
130 B7 Caledon South Africa
14 D2 Caledon B. b. Northern Terr. Australia
148 B4 Caledonia Minnesota U.S.A.
141 F5 Caledonia Ontario Canada
102 F3 Calella Spain
15 G4 Calen Queensland Australia
108 A2 Calenzana Corse France
156 E4 Calera Mexico
99 E5 Calera y Chozas Spain
99 G3 Caleruega Spain
164 B4 Caleta Blanco Encalada b. Chile
172 A5 Caleta Bonifacio pt Chile
164 B3 Caleta Buena Chile
171 B7 Caleta Clarencia Chile
171 C7 Caleta Coig inlet Argentina
164 B4 Caleta el Cobre Chile
171 B7 Caleta Josefina Chile
164 B4 Caleta Lobos Chile
172 B1 Caleta Morritos Chile
171 C6 Caleta Olivia Argentina
172 B1 Caleta Teniente Chile
172 B3 Caletones Chile
172 B6 Caleufu r. Argentina
172 B6 Caleufú Neuquen Argentina
172 E3 Caleufú Pampas Argentina
155 E5 Calexico California U.S.A.
64 D3 Calf of Man i. Isle of Man
65 F3 Calf, The h. England U.K.
136 G4 Calgary Alberta Canada
64 B1 Calgary Scotland U.K.
96 □ Calheta Madeira Portugal
145 C5 Calhoun Georgia U.S.A.
162 B3 Cali Colombia
23 C4 Calicoan i. Philippines
38 A4 Calicut India
154 C4 Caliente California U.S.A.
155 E3 Caliente Nevada U.S.A.
154 B3 California div. U.S.A.
159 □3 California Trinidad and Tobago
154 B3 California Aqueduct canal California U.S.A.
156 B2 California, Golfo de g. Mexico
154 C4 California Hot Springs California U.S.A.
42 G2 Cälilabad Azerbaijan
112 E2 Călimăneşti Romania
172 C1 Calingasta Argentina
153 D5 Calipatria California U.S.A.
154 A2 Calistoga California U.S.A.
109 H4 Calitri Italy
130 C6 Calitzdorp South Africa
106 C4 Calizzano Italy
157 H4 Calkiní Mexico
12 E2 Callabonna Cr. watercourse S. Australia Australia
12 D2 Callabonna, L. salt flat S. Australia Australia
88 B3 Callac France
154 D2 Callaghan, Mt mt. Nevada U.S.A.
145 D6 Callahan Florida U.S.A.
64 B3 Callan r. Northern Ireland U.K.
67 D4 Callan Rep. of Ireland
141 F3 Callander Ontario Canada
66 D4 Callander Scotland U.K.
68 C2 Callantsoog Netherlands
155 F2 Callao Utah U.S.A.
164 A2 Callao Peru
91 E5 Callas France
157 F4 Calles Mexico
147 F4 Callicoon New York U.S.A.
15 G5 Callide Queensland Australia
62 B4 Callington England U.K.
15 G5 Calliope Queensland Australia
103 C6 Callosa d'En Sarrià Spain
103 C6 Callosa de Segura Spain
140 E3 Callum Ontario Canada
136 G4 Calmar Alberta Canada
148 B4 Calmar Iowa U.S.A.
172 C4 Calmucó Argentina
62 D3 Calne England U.K.
155 E4 Cal-Nev-Ari Nevada U.S.A.
106 D3 Calolziocorte Italy
145 D7 Caloosahatchee r. Florida U.S.A.
109 G3 Calore r. Italy
157 H4 Calotmul Mexico
15 H5 Caloundra Queensland Australia
103 D6 Calpe Spain
43 A1 Çalpınar Turkey
154 B2 Calpine California U.S.A.
157 F5 Calpulálpan Mexico
140 C2 Calstock Ontario Canada
110 C5 Caltabellotta Sicilia Italy
110 D5 Caltagirone r. Sicilia Italy
110 D5 Caltagirone Sicilia Italy
110 D5 Caltanissetta div. Italy
110 C5 Caltanissetta i. Sicilia Italy
110 C5 Caltavuturo Sicilia Italy
99 H3 Caltojar Spain
125 C6 Calucinga Angola
90 C3 Caluire-et-Cuire France
125 B5 Calulo Angola
148 C2 Calumet Michigan U.S.A.
125 D6 Calunda Angola
125 C7 Calunga Angola
125 B6 Caluquembe Angola
23 B4 Calusa i. Philippines
82 C3 Caluso Italy
126 F2 Caluula Somalia
155 G5 Calva Arizona U.S.A.
89 E2 Calvados div. France
98 B4 Calvão Portugal
109 H4 Calvello Italy
14 D3 Calvert r. Northern Terr. Australia
14 D3 Calvert Hills Northern Terr. Australia
136 D4 Calvert I. i. B.C. Canada
17 C4 Calvert Ra. h. Western Australia Australia
108 A2 Calvi Corse France
103 F5 Calvià Spain
156 E4 Calvillo Mexico
130 B5 Calvinia South Africa
91 C5 Calvisson France
108 A2 Calvi-Ste-Catherine airport Corse France
98 E4 Calvitero mt. Spain
109 H3 Calvo, Monte mt. Italy
73 G3 Calvörde Germany
98 C3 Calvos Spain
74 D4 Calw Germany
101 G2 Calzada de Calatrava Spain
98 E3 Calzada de Valdunciel Spain
63 G2 Cam r. England U.K.
125 C5 Camabatela Angola
169 J1 Camacã Brazil
166 E3 Camaçari Brazil
154 B2 Camache Reservoir resr California U.S.A.
156 E3 Camacho Mexico
125 B6 Camacuio Angola
125 C6 Camacupa Angola
162 D2 Camaguán Venezuela
158 C2 Camagüey Cuba
158 C2 Camagüey, Arch. de is Cuba
25 C6 Camah, Gunung mt. Malaysia
106 E5 Camaiore Italy
163 F5 Camaiú r. Brazil
Çamalan see Gülek
156 B2 Camalli, Sa de mt. Mexico
164 B3 Camana Peru
125 D6 Camanongue Angola
168 A3 Camapuã Brazil
167 B7 Camaquã r. Brazil
167 B7 Camaquã Brazil
96 □ Câmara de Lobos Madeira Portugal
166 B1 Camaraipi r. Brazil
165 E2 Camararé r. Brazil
103 B4 Camarena r. Spain
99 F4 Camarena Spain
93 E5 Camarès France
88 A3 Camaret-sur-Mer France
157 F3 Camargo Mexico
91 C5 Camargue reg. France
102 C4 Camarillas Spain
100 E4 Camarinal, Pta pt Spain
98 A1 Camariñas Spain
158 A4 Camarón, C. c. Honduras
156 D4 Camaronero, L. del lag. Mexico
164 C3 Camarones r. Chile
171 C5 Camarones Argentina
171 C5 Camarones, Bahía b. Argentina
98 D2 Camarzana de Tera Spain
152 B2 Camas Washington U.S.A.
100 D3 Camas Spain
110 C5 Camastra Sicilia Italy
25 D5 Ca Mau Vietnam
98 B2 Cambados Spain
168 C5 Cambará Brazil
165 E3 Cambara Brazil
Cambay see Khambhat
Cambay, Gulf of g. see Khambhat, Gulf of
63 F3 Camberley England U.K.
93 B4 Cambes France
19 M8 Cambodia country Asia
125 B6 Cambongo r. Angola
62 A4 Camborne England U.K.
86 C2 Cambrai France
98 B1 Cambre Spain
154 B4 Cambria California U.S.A.
130 E6 Cambria South Africa
62 C2 Cambrian Mountains mountain range Wales U.K.
63 G2 Cambridge England U.K.
148 B5 Cambridge Illinois U.S.A.
147 E5 Cambridge Maryland U.S.A.
147 H3 Cambridge Massachusetts U.S.A.
148 A3 Cambridge Minnesota U.S.A.
147 G3 Cambridge New York U.S.A.
146 C4 Cambridge Ohio U.S.A.
140 E5 Cambridge Ontario Canada
8 E2 Cambridge New Zealand
134 H3 Cambridge Bay N.W.T. Canada
16 E2 Cambridge Gulf b. Western Australia Australia
63 F2 Cambridgeshire div. England U.K.
139 G2 Cambrien, Lac l. Québec Canada
102 E3 Cambrils de Mar Spain
69 A4 Cambrin France
169 F5 Cambuí Brazil
125 D5 Cambulo Angola
125 C6 Cambundi-Catembo Angola
169 F4 Cambuquira Brazil
73 G4 Camburg Germany
145 C5 Camden Alabama U.S.A.
151 G5 Camden Alabama U.S.A.
147 J2 Camden Maine U.S.A.
147 F5 Camden New Jersey U.S.A.
13 G3 Camden New South Wales Australia
147 F3 Camden New York U.S.A.
145 D5 Camden S. Carolina U.S.A.
171 B7 Camden, Is i. Chile
16 D2 Camden Sd chan. Western Australia Australia
125 D6 Cameia Angola
125 D6 Cameia, Parque Nacionalm da nat. park Angola
62 B4 Camelford England U.K.
53 C2 Camenca Moldova
107 F5 Camerano Italy
83 D3 Cameri Italy
109 F1 Camerino Italy
155 G4 Cameron Arizona U.S.A.
151 E6 Cameron Louisiana U.S.A.
150 E4 Cameron Missouri U.S.A.
151 D6 Cameron Texas U.S.A.
148 B3 Cameron Wisconsin U.S.A.
140 A2 Cameron Falls Ontario Canada
25 C6 Cameron Highlands Malaysia
136 F3 Cameron Hills h. Yukon Terr. Canada
9 A7 Cameron Mts mts New Zealand
154 B2 Cameron Park California U.S.A.
117 F5 Cameroon country Africa
109 H4 Camerota Italy
124 A3 Cameroun, Mont mt. Cameroon
173 J4 Camet Argentina
166 C1 Cametá Brazil
23 C4 Camiguin i. Philippines
23 B2 Camiguin i. Philippines
23 B3 Camiling Philippines
145 C6 Camilla Georgia U.S.A.
164 C3 Camiña Chile
98 B3 Caminha Portugal
98 D4 Caminomorisco Spain
102 B4 Caminreal Spain
166 C1 Camiranga Brazil
164 D4 Camiri Bolivia
125 D5 Camissombo Angola
43 C1 Çamlıyayla Turkey
110 C5 Cammarata Sicilia Italy
110 C5 Cammarata, Monte mt. Sicilia Italy
156 C3 Camoa Mexico
166 D1 Camocim Brazil
106 D4 Camogli Italy
86 B3 Camon France
14 D3 Camooweal Queensland Australia
163 G3 Camopi r. French Guiana
163 G3 Camopi Brazil
88 C3 Camors France
25 A5 Camorta i. Andaman and Nicobar Is India
23 C4 Camotes Sea g. Philippines
109 H4 Campagna Italy
91 B4 Campagnac France
109 E2 Campagnano di Roma Italy
93 C4 Campagne France
89 F3 Campagne d'Alençon plain France
89 F2 Campagne du Neubourg reg. France
86 A2 Campagne-lès-Hesdin France
173 J1 Campamento Uruguay
93 C5 Campan France
173 H3 Campana Argentina
111 F3 Campana Italy
173 J3 Campana Uruguay
171 A6 Campana, I. i. Chile
173 G3 Campanario mt. Argentina/Chile
168 A5 Campanario Brazil
169 H3 Campanário Brazil
100 E2 Campanario Spain
169 F4 Campanha Brazil
109 G3 Campania div. Italy
136 D4 Campania I. i. B.C. Canada
99 F3 Campaspero Spain
130 D4 Campbell South Africa
9 E4 Campbell, Cape c. New Zealand
25 B5 Campbell I. i. Myanmar
8 □2 Campbell I. i. New Zealand
36 C2 Campbellpore Pakistan
136 D4 Campbell River B.C. Canada
141 G4 Campbells Bay Québec Canada

144 C4 **Campbellsville** Kentucky U.S.A.
139 G4 **Campbellton** New Brunswick Canada
13 F5 **Campbell Town** Tasmania Australia
66 C5 **Campbeltown** Scotland U.K.
88 D4 **Campbon** France
102 F2 **Campdevànol** Spain
157 H5 **Campeche div.** Mexico
157 H5 **Campeche** Mexico
157 G5 **Campeche, Bahía de g.** Mexico
103 C6 **Campello** Spain
88 C4 **Campénéac** France
13 E4 **Camperdown** Victoria Australia
131 H4 **Camperdown** South Africa
145 □2 **Camperdown** The Bahamas
112 D2 **Câmpia Băileştilor plain** Romania
79 M4 **Câmpia Carei plain** Romania
53 B3 **Câmpia Moldovei de Nord plain** Moldova
53 C3 **Câmpia Moldovei de Sud plain** Moldova
112 D1 **Câmpia Turzii** Romania
107 F5 **Campi Bisenzio** Italy
108 C1 **Campiglia Marittima** Italy
82 C3 **Campiglia Soana** Italy
100 B3 **Campilhas r.** Portugal
103 B5 **Campillo de Alto Buey** Spain
100 E2 **Campillo de Llerena** Spain
101 F3 **Campillos** Spain
101 E3 **Campiña reg.** Spain
112 E2 **Câmpina** Romania
168 B6 **Campina da Lagoa** Brazil
166 E2 **Campina Grande** Brazil
168 E5 **Campinas** Brazil
168 D3 **Campina Verde** Brazil
111 H2 **Campi Salentina** Italy
108 B2 **Campitello** Corse France
109 F2 **Campli** Italy
124 A3 **Campo** Cameroon
102 D2 **Campo** Spain
162 B3 **Campoalegre** Colombia
98 E5 **Campo Arañuelo reg.** Spain
109 G3 **Campobasso div.** Molise Italy
109 G3 **Campobasso** Campobasso Italy
110 C5 **Campobello di Licata** Sicilia Italy
110 B5 **Campobello di Mazara** Sicilia Italy
169 F4 **Campo Belo** Brazil
167 B6 **Campo Belo do Sul** Brazil
98 B1 **Campo da Feira** Spain
107 F3 **Campodarsego** Italy
101 G2 **Campo de Calatrava reg.** Spain
102 B3 **Campo de Cariñena reg.** Spain
99 E1 **Campo de Caso** Spain
101 G1 **Campo de Criptana** Spain
101 H4 **Campo de Dalías reg.** Spain
166 B3 **Campó de Diauarum** Brazil
100 E4 **Campo de Gibraltar reg.** Spain
83 D3 **Campo dei Fiori mt.** Italy
101 H2 **Campo de Montiel reg.** Spain
101 H4 **Campo de Níjar reg.** Spain
99 G3 **Campo de San Pedro** Spain
80 C4 **Campo di Trens** Italy
106 D2 **Campodolcino** Italy
165 E4 **Campo Esperanza** Paraguay
110 C5 **Campofelice di Roccella** Sicilia Italy
168 D3 **Campo Florido** Brazil
107 H2 **Campoformido** Italy
166 D3 **Campo Formoso** Brazil
100 D3 **Campofrío** Spain
170 D2 **Campo Gallo** Argentina
165 E1 **Campo Grande** Amazonas Brazil
168 A4 **Campo Grande** Mato Grosso do Sul Brazil
98 B2 **Campo Lameiro** Spain
168 D6 **Campo Largo** Brazil
111 E5 **Campolato, Capo c.** Sicilia Italy
106 C4 **Campo Ligure** Italy
166 D1 **Campo Maior** Brazil
100 C1 **Campo Maior** Portugal
109 H3 **Campomarino** Molise Italy
111 G2 **Campomarino** Puglia Italy
168 B6 **Campo Mourão** Brazil
167 B6 **Campo Novo** Brazil
111 F3 **Campora San Giovanni** Italy
110 C5 **Camporeale** Sicilia Italy
124 B3 **Campo, Reserva de res.** Cameroon
103 B5 **Camporrobles** Spain
169 H4 **Campos** Brazil
169 E3 **Campos Altos** Brazil
166 C3 **Campos Belos** Brazil
103 G5 **Campos del Puerto** Spain
167 B6 **Campos de Palmas reg.** Brazil
169 F5 **Campos do Jordão** Brazil
167 B5 **Campos Eré reg.** Brazil
169 F4 **Campos Gerais** Brazil
167 B6 **Campos Novos** Brazil
168 D5 **Campos Novos Paulista** Brazil
166 D2 **Campos Sales** Brazil
101 G3 **Campotéjar** Spain
83 D2 **Campo Tencia mt.** Switzerland
109 F2 **Campotosto** Italy
109 F2 **Campotosto, Lago di l.** Italy
107 F2 **Campo Tures** Italy
102 F2 **Camprodon** Spain
66 D4 **Campsie Fells h.** Scotland U.K.
146 B6 **Campton** Kentucky U.S.A.
147 H3 **Campton** New Hampshire U.S.A.
112 E2 **Câmpulung** Romania
112 E1 **Câmpulung Moldovenesc** Romania
155 G4 **Camp Verde** Arizona U.S.A.
25 E5 **Cam Ranh** Vietnam
136 G4 **Camrose** Alberta Canada
62 A3 **Camrose** Wales U.K.
137 G2 **Camsell Lake l.** N.W.T. Canada
137 H3 **Camsell Portage** Saskatchewan Canada
101 G1 **Camuñas** Spain
145 □3 **Camuy** Puerto Rico
42 A1 **Çan** Turkey
169 G4 **Canaã** Brazil
147 G3 **Canaan** Connecticut U.S.A.
159 □2 **Canaan** Tobago Trinidad and Tobago
166 A2 **Cana Brava r.** Brazil
169 F2 **Canabrava** Brazil
132 G4 **Canada country** North America
178 C2 **Canada Basin sea feature** Arctic Ocean
173 G2 **Cañada de Gómez** Argentina
172 F1 **Cañada de Luque** Argentina
147 H2 **Canada Falls Lake l.** Maine U.S.A.
172 C1 **Cañada Honda** Argentina
173 G2 **Cañada Rosquin** Argentina
173 F3 **Cañada Seca** Argentina
151 C5 **Canadian r.** Texas U.S.A.
172 B6 **Cañadón Chileno** Argentina
170 E2 **Canaglaé, L. l.** Argentina
163 E2 **Canaima, Parque Nacional nat. park** Venezuela
147 F3 **Canajoharie** New York U.S.A.
113 F5 **Çanakkale div.** Turkey
42 A1 **Çanakkale** Turkey
113 F4 **Çanakkale Boğazı str.** Turkey
173 H4 **Canal 1 canal** Argentina
173 J4 **Canal 2 canal** Argentina
173 H4 **Canal 9 canal** Argentina
173 H4 **Canal 11 canal** Argentina
173 H4 **Canal 12 canal** Argentina
173 H3 **Canal 16 canal** Argentina
6 □2 **Canala** New Caledonia Pacific Ocean
171 C7 **Canal Beagle chan.** Argentina
171 A7 **Canal Concepción chan.** Chile
86 B2 **Canal d'Aire canal** France
90 C1 **Canal de Bourgogne canal** France
86 B4 **Canal de Briare canal** France
99 F2 **Canal de Castilla canal** Spain
102 D2 **Canal de Cinca r.** Spain
91 D5 **Canal de Craponne canal** France
103 B5 **Canal de Doña María Cristina canal** Spain
86 C4 **Canal de la Haute Seine canal** France
90 D1 **Canal de la Marne à la Saône canal** France
87 E4 **Canal de la Marne au Rhin canal** France
86 B3 **Canal de la Somme canal** France
100 E3 **Canal del Bajo canal** Spain
103 C7 **Canal del Campo de Cartagena canal** Spain
87 F4 **Canal de l'Est canal** France
101 G1 **Canal del Guadiana canal** Spain
102 B3 **Canal de Lodosa canal** Spain
86 C3 **Canal de l'Oise à l'Aisne canal** France
103 B7 **Canal del Taibilla canal** Spain
91 C5 **Canal de Marseille au Rhône canal** France
102 C3 **Canal de Monegros canal** Spain
88 C3 **Canal de Nantes à Brest canal** France
100 E4 **Canal de Riego canal** Spain
90 B2 **Canal de Roanne à Digoin canal** France
86 C2 **Canal de St-Quentin canal** France
91 C5 **Canal des Alpilles canal** France
86 D3 **Canal des Ardennes canal** France
87 F4 **Canal des Houillères de la Sarve canal** France
99 H5 **Canal de Trasvase canal** Spain
101 H1 **Canal de Trasvase Tajo-Segura canal** Spain
88 D3 **Canal d'Ille-et-Rance canal** France
163 G3 **Canal do Norte chan.** Brazil
86 B5 **Canal d'Orléans canal** France
100 B3 **Canal do Sado Morgavel canal** Portugal
166 B1 **Canal do Sul chan.** Brazil
92 E2 **Canal du Berry canal** France
90 C2 **Canal du Centre canal** France
93 E5 **Canal du Midi canal** France
90 B1 **Canal du Nivernais canal** France
86 C2 **Canal du Nord canal** France
102 D3 **Canal d'Urgell canal** Spain
87 G4 **Canal du Rhône au Rhin canal** France
122 C4 **Canal du Sahel canal** Mali
106 B4 **Canale** Italy
107 F3 **Canale Bianco canal** Italy
106 C3 **Canale Cavour canal** Italy
108 C2 **Canale di Piombino chan.** Italy
172 D3 **Canalejas** Argentina
107 F5 **Canale Maestro canal** Italy
111 G2 **Canale Reale r.** Italy
83 D3 **Canale Villoresi canal** Italy
102 B3 **Canal Imperial de Aragón canal** Spain
90 A1 **Canal latéral à la Loire canal** France
90 B2 **Canal Latéral à la Loire canal** France
171 B5 **Canal Moraleda chan.** Chile
166 C1 **Canal Perigoso chan.** Brazil
173 F2 **Canals** Argentina
103 C6 **Canals** Spain
171 B7 **Canal Smyth chan.** Chile
101 H2 **Cañamares r.** Spain
99 H4 **Cañamares** Spain
164 C2 **Canamari** Brazil
101 E1 **Cañamero** Spain
146 E3 **Canandaigua** New York U.S.A.
146 E3 **Canandaigua Lake l.** New York U.S.A.
156 C2 **Cananea** Mexico
139 H2 **Cananée, Lac l.** Québec Canada
168 E6 **Cananéia** Brazil
162 D3 **Canapiare, Co h.** Colombia
86 B2 **Canaples** France
168 D3 **Canápolis** Brazil
162 B4 **Cañar** Ecuador
97 □ **Canarias, Islas div.** Spain
120 A3 **Canarias, Islas is** Atlantic Ocean
158 B2 **Canarreos, Arch. de los is** Cuba
174 H4 **Canary Basin sea feature** Atlantic Ocean
Canary Islands is see **Canarias, Islas**
147 F3 **Canastota** New York U.S.A.
166 D2 **Canastra r.** Brazil
156 D3 **Canatlán** Mexico
98 D5 **Cañaveral** Spain
145 D6 **Canaveral, Cape c.** Florida U.S.A.
99 H4 **Cañaveras** Spain
106 B3 **Canavese reg.** Italy
169 J1 **Canavieiras** Brazil
107 F2 **Canazei** Italy
13 F2 **Canbelego** New South Wales Australia
13 G3 **Canberra** A.C.T. Australia
152 B3 **Canby** California U.S.A.
150 D2 **Canby** Minnesota U.S.A.
88 D3 **Cancale** France
83 F2 **Cancano, Lago di l.** Italy
103 B6 **Cancarix** Spain
91 C3 **Cance r.** France
86 A2 **Canche r.** France
102 C2 **Cancias mt.** Spain
93 C4 **Cancon** France
157 J4 **Cancún** Mexico
93 B6 **Candanchú** Spain
164 B3 **Candarave** Peru
98 E1 **Candás** Spain
89 D4 **Candé** France
169 F4 **Candeias** Brazil
109 H3 **Candela** Italy
165 E3 **Candelaria r.** Bolivia
157 H5 **Candelaria** Campeche Mexico
153 F6 **Candelaria** Chihuahua Mexico
170 E2 **Candelaria** Misiones Argentina
172 E2 **Candelaria** San Luis Argentina
98 B1 **Candelaria, Pta pt** Spain
98 E4 **Candelario, Sa de mountain range** Spain
109 H3 **Candelaro r.** Italy
99 E4 **Candeleda** Spain
13 G4 **Candelo** New South Wales Australia
82 C3 **Candia, Lago di l.** Italy
168 C6 **Cândido de Abreu** Brazil
166 C1 **Cândido Mendes** Brazil
168 C5 **Cândido Mota** Brazil
169 H1 **Cândido Sales** Brazil
137 H4 **Candle Lake l.** Saskatchewan Canada
137 H4 **Candle Lake** Saskatchewan Canada
179 C1 **Candlemas I. i.** S. Sandwich Is Atlantic Ocean
147 G4 **Candlewood, Lake l.** Connecticut U.S.A.
150 D1 **Cando** N. Dakota U.S.A.
23 B2 **Candon** Philippines
100 D4 **Candor, Pta pt** Spain
131 H3 **Candover** South Africa
16 A4 **Cane r.** Western Australia Australia
172 B1 **Canela Alta** Chile
172 B1 **Canela Baja** Chile
106 C4 **Canelli** Italy
173 J3 **Canelones div.** Uruguay
173 J3 **Canelones** Uruguay
101 G2 **Canena** Spain
108 E2 **Canepina** Italy
91 B5 **Canet** France
102 F3 **Canet de Mar** Spain
172 A4 **Cañete** Chile
103 B4 **Cañete** Spain
101 F3 **Cañete de las Torres** Spain
93 F6 **Canet-en-Roussillon** France
102 C2 **Canfranc-Estación** Spain
93 B6 **Canfranc, Valle de v.** Spain
164 B2 **Cangallo** Peru
125 C6 **Cangamba** Angola
125 C5 **Cangandala** Angola
98 B2 **Cangas** Spain
98 D1 **Cangas del Narcea** Spain
99 E1 **Cangas de Onís** Spain
130 D6 **Cango Caves caves** South Africa
125 D6 **Cangombe** Angola
33 G1 **Cangshan** China
166 E2 **Canguaretama** Brazil
170 F3 **Canguçu** Brazil
170 F3 **Canguçu, Sa do h.** Brazil
33 E4 **Cangwu** China
31 F5 **Cangzhou** China
100 B2 **Canha r.** Portugal
100 B2 **Canha** Portugal
139 G2 **Caniapiscau r.** Québec Canada
139 G3 **Caniapiscau** Québec Canada
139 G3 **Caniapiscau, Rés. resr** Québec Canada
98 B3 **Canicada, Barragem de resr** Portugal
110 C5 **Canicattì** Sicilia Italy
111 E5 **Canicattini Bagni** Sicilia Italy
23 C4 **Canigao Channel chan.** Philippines
93 E6 **Canigou, Pic du mt.** France
101 H3 **Caniles** Spain
93 D6 **Canillo** Andorra
136 E4 **Canim L. l.** B.C. Canada
136 E4 **Canim Lake** B.C. Canada
166 D2 **Canindé r.** Brazil
166 C1 **Canindé** Pará Brazil
166 E1 **Caninde** Brazil
108 D2 **Canino** Italy
66 C2 **Canisp h.** Scotland U.K.
146 E3 **Canisteo r.** New York U.S.A.
146 E3 **Canisteo** New York U.S.A.
88 D2 **Canisy** France
156 E4 **Cañitas de Felipe Pescador** Mexico
99 E3 **Cañizal** Spain
99 H4 **Cañizares** Spain
42 C1 **Çankiri** Turkey
127 B5 **Cankuzo** Burundi
23 B4 **Canlaon** Philippines
136 F4 **Canmore** Alberta Canada
141 J3 **Cann** Québec Canada
66 B3 **Canna i.** Scotland U.K.
17 A6 **Canna** Western Australia Australia
38 A4 **Cannanore** India
38 A4 **Cannanore Islands is** India
90 B2 **Canne r.** France
83 D2 **Cannero Riviera** Italy
91 F5 **Cannes** France
108 C1 **Canneto** Italy
83 F3 **Canneto sull'Oglio** Italy
17 B6 **Canning Hill h.** Western Australia Australia
62 C3 **Cannington** England U.K.
83 D2 **Cannobio r.** Italy
106 C2 **Cannobio** Italy
62 D2 **Cannock** England U.K.
148 A3 **Cannon r.** Minnesota U.S.A.
127 □4 **Cannoniers Pt pt** Mauritius
15 G4 **Cannonvale** Queensland Australia
13 G4 **Cann River** Victoria Australia
163 E2 **Caño Araguao r.** Venezuela
167 B6 **Canõas** Brazil
169 F3 **Canoeiros** Brazil
137 H3 **Canoe L. l.** Saskatchewan Canada
167 B6 **Canoinhas** Brazil
111 F4 **Canolo** Italy
163 E2 **Caño Macareo r.** Venezuela
163 E2 **Caño Manamo r.** Venezuela
65 F2 **Canonbie** Scotland U.K.
153 F4 **Canon City** Colorado U.S.A.
15 G4 **Canoona** Queensland Australia
12 E3 **Canopus** S. Australia Australia
137 J4 **Canora** Saskatchewan Canada
109 J3 **Canosa di Puglia** Italy
159 G4 **Canouan i.** St Vincent
13 G3 **Canowindra** New South Wales Australia
120 A4 **Cansado** Western Sahara
139 H4 **Canso, C. headland** Nova Scotia Canada
164 A2 **Canta** Peru
99 F1 **Cantabria div.** Spain
Cantabrian Mountains mountain range see **Cantábrica, Cordillera**
98 D1 **Cantábrica, Cordillera mountain range** Spain
Cantábrico, Mar see **Biscay, Bay of**
163 F4 **Cantagalo** Brazil
92 E3 **Cantal div.** France
99 E3 **Cantalapiedra** Spain
99 G3 **Cantalejo** Spain
99 E3 **Cantalpino** Spain
98 B4 **Cantanhede** Portugal
170 C3 **Cantantal** Argentina
163 E2 **Cantaura** Venezuela
93 A4 **Canteloupe r.** France
92 B3 **Cantenac** France
101 H1 **Canteras mt.** Spain
9 C5 **Canterbury div.** New Zealand
63 H3 **Canterbury** England U.K.
147 K2 **Canterbury** New Brunswick Canada
9 C6 **Canterbury Bight b.** New Zealand
9 C5 **Canterbury Plains plain** New Zealand
25 D5 **Cân Thơ** Vietnam
107 G5 **Cantiano** Italy
23 C4 **Cantilan** Philippines
100 E3 **Cantillana** Spain
170 B2 **Canto del Agua** Chile
166 D2 **Canto do Buriti** Brazil
148 B5 **Canton** Illinois U.S.A.
147 H2 **Canton** Maine U.S.A.
151 F5 **Canton** Mississippi U.S.A.
147 F2 **Canton** New York U.S.A.
146 C4 **Canton** Ohio U.S.A.
146 E4 **Canton** Pennsylvania U.S.A.
Canton see **Guangzhou**
168 B6 **Cantu r.** Brazil
106 D3 **Cantù** Italy
167 B5 **Cantú, Sa do h.** Brazil
163 F5 **Canudos** Brazil
173 H3 **Cañuelas** Argentina
163 F4 **Canumã** Amazonas Brazil
163 E5 **Canumã** Amazonas Brazil
163 E5 **Canutama** Brazil
9 D4 **Canvastown** New Zealand
63 G3 **Canvey Island** England U.K.
89 F2 **Cany-Barville** France
151 C5 **Canyon** Texas U.S.A.
152 C2 **Canyon City** Oregon U.S.A.
155 H3 **Canyon de Chelly National Monument nat. park** Arizona U.S.A.
152 D2 **Canyon Ferry L. l.** Montana U.S.A.
155 H2 **Canyonlands National Park nat. park** Utah U.S.A.
136 D2 **Canyon Ranges mountain range** N.W.T. Canada
152 B3 **Canyonville** Oregon U.S.A.
125 D5 **Canzar** Angola
24 D2 **Cao Băng** Vietnam
47 K4 **Caohu** China
32 B3 **Caojian** China
64 C2 **Caolisport, Loch inlet** Scotland U.K.
125 C5 **Caombo** Angola
25 E4 **Cao Nguyên Đăc Lăc plat.** Vietnam
107 G3 **Caorle** Italy
31 H4 **Caoshi** China
33 F1 **Cao Xian** China
23 B5 **Cap i.** Philippines
109 H4 **Capaccio** Italy
110 C4 **Capaci** Sicilia Italy
158 D3 **Cap-à-Foux c.** Haiti
125 D5 **Capaia** Angola
108 D2 **Capalbio** Italy
162 D2 **Capanaparo r.** Venezuela
167 B6 **Capanema r.** Brazil
166 C1 **Capanema** Pará Brazil
168 D6 **Capão Bonito** Brazil
168 A4 **Capão Seco** Brazil
167 D5 **Caparaó, Sa do mountain range** Brazil
162 C2 **Caparo r.** Venezuela
98 B4 **Caparrosa** Portugal
102 B2 **Caparroso** Spain
23 B3 **Capas** Philippines
159 E5 **Capatárida** Venezuela
139 H4 **Cap-Aux-Meules** Québec Canada
173 G2 **Cap. Bermudez** Argentina
93 A5 **Capbreton** France
91 B5 **Cap d'Agde** France
141 J3 **Cap-de-la-Madeleine** Québec Canada
93 E4 **Capdenac-Gare** France
103 G5 **Capdepera** Spain
15 F4 **Cape r.** Queensland Australia
17 C7 **Cape Arid Nat. Park nat. park** Western Australia Australia
16 D2 **Cape Bougainville Abor. Land res.** Western Australia Australia
139 H4 **Cape Breton Highlands Nat. Pk nat. park** Nova Scotia Canada
139 H4 **Cape Breton Island i.** Nova Scotia Canada
139 J3 **Cape Charles** Newfoundland Canada
147 E6 **Cape Charles** Virginia U.S.A.
122 D5 **Cape Coast** Ghana
147 J4 **Cape Cod National Seashore res.** Massachusetts U.S.A.
145 D7 **Cape Coral** Florida U.S.A.
140 E4 **Cape Croker** Ontario Canada
135 L3 **Cape Dorset** N.W.T. Canada
179 B5 **Cape Evans Antarctic Base** Antarctica
151 F4 **Cape Girardeau** Missouri U.S.A.
175 N3 **Cape Johnson Depth sea feature** "
62 C1 **Capel Curig** Wales U.K.
17 C7 **Cape Le Grand Nat. Park nat. park** Western Australia Australia
169 G2 **Capelinha** Brazil
15 G4 **Capella** Queensland Australia
69 E5 **Capellen** Luxembourg
63 H3 **Capel St Mary** England U.K.
147 F5 **Cape May** New Jersey U.S.A.
147 F5 **Cape May Court House** New Jersey U.S.A.
147 F5 **Cape May Pt pt** New Jersey U.S.A.
125 C5 **Capenda-Camulemba** Angola
93 E5 **Capendu** France
16 A4 **Cape Range Nat. Park nat. park** Western Australia Australia
135 H5 **Cape Sable Island i.** Nova Scotia Canada
139 J4 **Cape St George** Newfoundland Canada
91 B5 **Capestang** France
159 □5 **Capesterre** Guadeloupe Caribbean
109 F2 **Capestrano** Italy
139 H4 **Cape Tormentine** New Brunswick Canada
130 B6 **Cape Town** South Africa
122 □ **Cape Verde country** Africa
174 G5 **Cape Verde Basin sea feature** Atlantic Ocean
174 F5 **Cape Verde Fracture sea feature** Atlantic Ocean
174 H4 **Cape Verde Plateau sea feature** Atlantic Ocean
147 E2 **Cape Vincent** New York U.S.A.
15 E2 **Cape York pen.** Queensland Australia
93 A4 **Cap Ferret** France
159 D3 **Cap-Haïtien** Haiti
162 D3 **Capibara** Venezuela
166 E2 **Capiberibe r.** Brazil
103 D4 **Capicorp, Pta de pt** Spain
173 K2 **Capilia del Sauce** Uruguay
101 E2 **Capilla** Spain
172 E1 **Capilla del Monte** Argentina
166 C1 **Capim r.** Brazil
166 C1 **Capim** Brazil
98 C4 **Capinha** Portugal
168 D3 **Capinópolis** Brazil
164 C3 **Capinota** Bolivia
109 F3 **Capistrello** Italy
179 B2 **Capitán Arturo Prat Chile Base** Antarctica
165 E4 **Capitán Bado** Paraguay
153 F5 **Capitan Peak mt.** New Mexico U.S.A.
169 G2 **Capitão Enéas** Brazil
155 G2 **Capitol Reef National Park nat. park** Utah U.S.A.
166 D2 **Capivara, Parque Nacional da Serra da nat. park** Brazil
166 D3 **Capivari r.** Brazil
166 D3 **Capixaba** Brazil
110 D5 **Capizzi** Sicilia Italy
88 A3 **Cap, Le headland** France
168 B6 **Cap. Leônidas Marques** Brazil
104 F4 **Čapljina** Bos.-Herz.
129 E1 **Capoche r.** Mozambique/Zambia
108 D2 **Capodimonte** Italy
106 E2 **Capo di Ponte** Italy
109 G4 **Capodochino airport** Italy
110 D4 **Capo d'Orlando** Sicilia Italy
163 F5 **Capoeira** Brazil
111 E6 **Capo Passero, Isola i.** Sicilia Italy
108 A5 **Capoterra** Sardegna Italy
109 F2 **Cappadocia** Italy
72 D3 **Cappeln (Oldenburg)** Germany
67 D4 **Cappoquin** Rep. of Ireland
108 B1 **Capraia Isola** Italy
108 B1 **Capraia, Isola di i.** Italy
108 B3 **Caprera, Isola i.** Sardegna Italy
109 G4 **Capri** Italy
15 G4 **Capricorn, C. c.** Queensland Australia
15 H4 **Capricorn Channel chan.** Queensland Australia
15 H4 **Capricorn Group atolls** Queensland Australia
15 G4 **Capricorn Section nat. park** Queensland Australia
109 G4 **Capri, Isola di i.** Italy
83 F3 **Caprino Veronese** Italy
128 C2 **Caprivi div.** Namibia
128 C2 **Caprivi Strip reg.** Namibia
153 □2 **Captain Cook** Hawaii U.S.A.
13 G3 **Captain's Flat** New South Wales Australia
93 B4 **Captieux** France
146 C5 **Captina r.** Ohio U.S.A.
109 G3 **Capua** Italy
127 □2 **Capucin Pt pt** Seychelles
73 H3 **Caputh** Germany
162 C4 **Caquetá r.** Colombia
99 G4 **Carabaña** Spain
23 B3 **Carabao i.** Philippines
164 B2 **Carabay, Cord. de mountain range** Peru
112 E2 **Caracal** Romania
163 E3 **Caracarai** Brazil
162 D1 **Caracas** Venezuela
166 D2 **Caracol** Brazil
164 C3 **Caracollo** Bolivia
157 E5 **Carácuaro** Mexico
101 F2 **Caracuel de Calatrava** Spain
23 C5 **Caraga** Philippines
67 B4 **Caragh, Lough l.** Rep. of Ireland
173 K2 **Caraguatá r.** Uruguay
169 F5 **Caraguatatuba** Brazil
172 A5 **Carahue** Chile
169 H2 **Caraí** Brazil
64 C2 **Cara Island i.** Scotland U.K.
166 B1 **Carajari r.** Brazil
93 D5 **Caraman** France
109 G2 **Caramanico Terme** Italy
140 B2 **Caramat** Ontario Canada
101 H3 **Caramel r.** Spain
23 B3 **Caramoan Pen. pen.** Philippines
98 B4 **Caramulo, Sa do mountain range** Portugal
165 E2 **Caraná r.** Brazil
163 E5 **Càranapatuba** Brazil
172 E4 **Carancho** Argentina
169 G4 **Carandaí** Brazil
165 D4 **Carandaiti** Bolivia
98 D1 **Caranga** Spain
169 G4 **Carangola** Brazil
100 B1 **Caranguejeira** Portugal
112 D2 **Caransebeş** Romania
168 A6 **Carapá r.** Paraguay
109 H3 **Carapelle r.** Italy
139 H4 **Caraquet** New Brunswick Canada
162 A4 **Caráquez** Ecuador
162 A4 **Caráquez, B. de b.** Ecuador
112 C2 **Caraşova** Romania
156 K6 **Caratasca** Honduras
156 K6 **Caratasca, Laguna lag.** Honduras
169 G3 **Caratinga** Brazil
162 D4 **Carauari** Brazil
103 B6 **Caravaca de la Cruz** Spain
106 D3 **Caravaggio** Italy
169 J2 **Caravelas** Brazil
164 A1 **Caraz** Peru
167 B6 **Carazinho** Brazil
98 E3 **Carbajales de Alba** Spain
98 B2 **Carballiño** Spain
98 B1 **Carballo** Spain
150 D1 **Carberry** Manitoba Canada
173 H2 **Carbo** Argentina
156 C2 **Carbo** Mexico
110 B5 **Carboi r.** Sicilia Italy
108 B5 **Carbonara, Capo pt** Sardegna Italy
144 B4 **Carbondale** Illinois U.S.A.
147 F4 **Carbondale** Pennsylvania U.S.A.
139 K4 **Carbonear** Newfoundland Canada
101 J4 **Carboneras** Spain
103 B5 **Carboneras de Guadazaón** Spain
99 F3 **Carbonero El Mayor** Spain
108 A5 **Carbonia** Sardegna Italy
80 D4 **Carbonìn** Italy
169 G2 **Carbonita** Brazil
93 D5 **Carbonne** France
64 B4 **Carbury** Rep. of Ireland
98 D4 **Carcaboso** Spain
103 C5 **Carcaixent** Spain
92 A3 **Carcans** France
23 B4 **Carcar** Philippines
102 B2 **Cárcar** Spain
173 F2 **Carcaraña r.** Argentina
106 C4 **Carcare** Italy
93 E5 **Carcassonne** France
102 B2 **Carcastillo** Spain
91 E5 **Carcès** France
103 B6 **Carche, Sierra del mountain range** Spain
13 G3 **Carcoar** New South Wales Australia
82 D3 **Carcoforo** Italy
136 C2 **Carcross** Yukon Terr. Canada
17 A4 **Cardabia** Western Australia Australia
38 B4 **Cardamon Hills mts** India
101 F2 **Cardeña** Spain
173 F6 **Cardenal Cagliero** Argentina
157 F4 **Cárdenas** San Luis Potosí Mexico
157 G5 **Cárdenas** Tabasco Mexico
158 B2 **Cárdenas** Cuba
65 E1 **Cardenden** Scotland U.K.
103 B5 **Cardenete** Spain
13 E2 **Cardenyabba watercourse** New South Wales Australia
111 E4 **Cardeto** Italy
171 B6 **Cardiel, L. l.** Argentina
62 C3 **Cardiff div.** Wales U.K.
62 C3 **Cardiff** Wales U.K.
62 C3 **Cardiff Wales airport** Wales U.K.
62 B2 **Cardigan** Wales U.K.
62 B2 **Cardigan Bay b.** Wales U.K.
62 B2 **Cardiganshire div.** Wales U.K.
141 H4 **Cardinal** Ontario Canada
146 B4 **Cardington** Ohio U.S.A.
102 E3 **Cardona** Spain
173 J2 **Cardona** Uruguay
102 E3 **Cardoner r.** Spain
168 C4 **Cardoso** Brazil
168 E6 **Cardoso, Ilha i.** Brazil
9 B6 **Cardrona** New Zealand
9 B6 **Cardrona, Mt mt.** New Zealand
136 G5 **Cardston** Alberta Canada
15 F3 **Cardwell** Queensland Australia
169 F5 **Careaçu** Brazil
107 F3 **Carega, Cima mt.** Italy
79 M4 **Carei** Romania
163 F4 **Careiro** Brazil
172 B1 **Carén** Coquimbo Chile
88 D2 **Carentan** France
88 C4 **Carentoir** France
99 F1 **Cares r.** Spain
81 H4 **Carevdar** Croatia
114 C1 **Carev Dvor** Macedonia
146 B4 **Carey** Ohio U.S.A.
17 A5 **Carey Downs** Western Australia Australia
17 C6 **Carey, L. salt flat** Western Australia Australia
137 J2 **Carey Lake l.** N.W.T. Canada
175 J5 **Cargados Carajos sand bank**
108 A2 **Cargèse** Corse France
88 B3 **Carhaix-Plouguer** France
173 F4 **Carhué** Argentina
98 C4 **Caria** Portugal
166 E3 **Cariacá r.** Brazil
169 H4 **Cariacica** Brazil
163 E1 **Cariaco** Venezuela
166 B1 **Cariaí r.** Brazil
162 B4 **Cariamanga** Ecuador
125 C6 **Cariango** Angola
111 F3 **Cariati** Italy
158 B3 **Caribbean Sea sea**
136 E4 **Cariboo Mts mountain range** B.C. Canada
137 K3 **Caribou r.** Manitoba Canada
136 D2 **Caribou r.** N.W.T. Canada
147 K1 **Caribou** Maine U.S.A.
140 C3 **Caribou I. i.** Ontario Canada
136 F3 **Caribou Mountains mts** Alberta Canada
156 D3 **Carichic** Mexico
23 C4 **Carigara** Philippines
141 J3 **Carignan** Québec Canada
87 E3 **Carignan** France
106 B4 **Carignano** Italy
13 F2 **Carinda** New South Wales Australia
102 B3 **Cariñena** Spain
166 C3 **Carinhanha r.** Brazil
166 D3 **Carinhanha** Brazil
110 C4 **Carini** Sicilia Italy
98 C1 **Cariño** Spain
163 E1 **Caripe** Venezuela
163 E1 **Caripito** Venezuela
166 D1 **Cariré** Brazil
67 D2 **Cark Mtn h.** Rep. of Ireland
64 B4 **Carlanstown** Rep. of Ireland
111 E5 **Carlentini** Sicilia Italy
141 G4 **Carleton Place** Ontario Canada
131 F3 **Carletonville** South Africa
112 E1 **Cârlibaba** Romania
152 C3 **Carlin** Nevada U.S.A.
67 E2 **Carlingford** Rep. of Ireland
67 E2 **Carlingford Lough inlet** Rep. of Ireland/U.K.
65 F3 **Carlisle** England U.K.
146 A5 **Carlisle** Kentucky U.S.A.
146 E4 **Carlisle** Pennsylvania U.S.A.
108 A5 **Carloforte** Sardegna Italy
111 F3 **Carlopoli** Italy
168 D5 **Carlópolis** Brazil
65 E2 **Carlops** Scotland U.K.
173 G3 **Carlos Casares** Argentina
169 H2 **Carlos Chagas** Brazil
173 J2 **Carlos Reyles** Uruguay
173 G3 **Carlos Salas** Argentina
173 F3 **Carlos Tejedor** Argentina
67 E4 **Carlow div.** Rep. of Ireland
67 E4 **Carlow** Rep. of Ireland
131 G1 **Carlow** South Africa
66 B2 **Carloway** Scotland U.K.
154 D5 **Carlsbad** California U.S.A.
153 F5 **Carlsbad** New Mexico U.S.A.
151 C6 **Carlsbad** Texas U.S.A.
153 F5 **Carlsbad Caverns Nat. Park** New Mexico U.S.A.
175 J3 **Carlsberg Ridge sea feature** Indian Ocean
179 B3 **Carlson In. inlet** Antarctica
130 E5 **Carlton** South Africa
66 E5 **Carluke** Scotland U.K.
93 D4 **Carlux** France
137 J5 **Carlyle** Saskatchewan Canada
136 B2 **Carmacks** Yukon Terr. Canada
106 B4 **Carmagnola** Italy
137 K5 **Carman** Manitoba Canada
62 B3 **Carmarthen** Wales U.K.
62 B3 **Carmarthen Bay b.** Wales U.K.
62 B3 **Carmarthenshire div.** Wales U.K.
93 E4 **Carmaux** France
147 J2 **Carmel** Maine U.S.A.
62 B1 **Carmel Head headland** Wales U.K.
157 H5 **Carmelita** Guatemala
173 H3 **Carmelo** Uruguay
156 C3 **Carmen i.** Mexico
155 G6 **Carmen** Arizona U.S.A.
173 G2 **Carmen** Argentina
162 B2 **Carmen** Colombia
23 C4 **Carmen** Philippines
173 J2 **Carmen** Uruguay
164 C4 **Carmen Alto** Chile
173 H3 **Carmen de Areco** Argentina
157 H5 **Carmen, I. del i.** Mexico
172 D3 **Carmensa** Argentina
144 B4 **Carmi** Illinois U.S.A.
154 B2 **Carmichael** California U.S.A.
145 □2 **Carmichael** The Bahamas
15 G4 **Carmila** Queensland Australia
169 G4 **Carmo** Brazil
169 F4 **Carmo da Cachoeira** Brazil
169 F5 **Carmo de Minas** Brazil
169 E3 **Carmo do Paranaíba** Brazil
100 E3 **Carmona** Spain
66 F4 **Carmyllie** Scotland U.K.
88 B4 **Carnac** France
17 A5 **Carnarvon** Western Australia Australia

148 A4 Cedar Falls *Iowa* U.S.A.
159 □7 Cedar Grove *Antigua* Caribbean
148 D4 Cedar Grove *Wisconsin* U.S.A.
146 C5 Cedar Grove *W. Virginia* U.S.A.
147 F6 Cedar I. i. *Virginia* U.S.A.
137 J4 Cedar L. l. *Manitoba* Canada
148 D5 Cedar Lake l. *Indiana* U.S.A.
146 B4 Cedar Pt pt *Ohio* U.S.A.
148 B5 Cedar Rapids *Iowa* U.S.A.
155 G3 Cedar Ridge *Arizona* U.S.A.
147 F5 Cedar Run *New Jersey* U.S.A.
148 E4 Cedar Springs *Michigan* U.S.A.
140 D5 Cedar Springs *Ontario* Canada
145 C5 Cedartown *Georgia* U.S.A.
159 □1 Cedar Valley Jamaica
148 E3 Cedarville *Michigan* U.S.A.
131 G5 Cedarville South Africa
106 E2 Cedegolo Italy
98 B1 Cedeira h. Spain
98 B1 Cedeira Spain
102 C4 Cedrillas Spain
108 B4 Cedrino r. *Sardegna* Italy
156 B2 Cedros i. Mexico
159 □3 Cedros Pt pt *Trinidad* Trinidad and Tobago
12 C3 Ceduna *S. Australia* Australia
76 C3 Cedynia Poland
98 A2 Cée Spain
126 E4 Ceelbuur Somalia
126 E4 Ceeldheere Somalia
126 F2 Ceel Gaal *Bari* Somalia
126 D2 Ceel Gaal *Woqooyi Galbeed* Somalia
126 D4 Ceel Garas well Somalia
126 D4 Ceel Qoondhato well Somalia
126 D4 Ceel Walaaq well Somalia
126 E2 Ceerigaabo Somalia
110 D4 Cefalù *Sicilia* Italy
62 C2 Cefn-mawr *Wales* U.K.
99 F3 Cega r. Spain
107 G3 Ceggia Italy
79 J4 Cegléd Hungary
111 G2 Ceglie Messapica Italy
112 C4 Čegrane Macedonia
103 B6 Cehegín Spain
32 D3 Ceheng China
112 B3 Čehotina r. Yugoslavia
112 D1 Cehu Silvaniei Romania
145 □3 Ceiba Puerto Rico
173 H2 Ceibas Argentina
91 B5 Ceilhes-et-Rocozels France
98 B4 Ceira r. Portugal
78 F3 Čejč Czech Rep.
76 G2 Cekcyn Poland
42 C1 Çekerek Turkey
76 G4 Ceków-Kolonia Poland
25 C6 Celah, Gunung mt. Malaysia
78 D1 Čelákovice Czech Rep.
109 F2 Celano Italy
98 C2 Celanova Spain
157 E4 Celaya Mexico
67 E3 Celbridge Rep. of Ireland
Celebes i. *see* Sulawesi
21 H6 Celebes Sea sea Indonesia/Philippines
162 B5 Celendín Peru
146 A4 Celina *Ohio* U.S.A.
81 G4 Celje Slovenia
78 G4 Celldömölk Hungary
72 F3 Celle *Niedersachsen* Germany
69 B4 Celles Belgium
93 D6 Celles France
92 B2 Celles-sur-Belle France
86 D4 Celles-sur-Ource France
80 D4 Cellina r. Italy
111 G2 Cellino San Marco Italy
109 H3 Celone r. Italy
114 C1 Čelopeci Macedonia
98 C4 Celorico da Beira Portugal
98 B3 Celorico de Basto Portugal
61 D6 Celtic Sea Rep. of Ireland/U.K.
62 C2 Celyn, Llyn l. *Wales* U.K.
107 F2 Cembra Italy
79 K6 Cenei Romania
99 H2 Cenicero Spain
106 D4 Ceno r. Italy
93 B4 Cenon France
22 D2 Cenrana Philippines
131 G6 Centani South Africa
102 F3 Centelles Spain
172 C5 Centenario Argentina
168 C5 Centenário do Sul Brazil
129 E2 Centenary Zimbabwe
155 F5 Centennial Wash r. *Arizona* U.S.A.
151 E6 Center *Texas* U.S.A.
147 G4 Centereach *New York* U.S.A.
145 C5 Center Point *Alabama* U.S.A.
146 B5 Centerville *Ohio* U.S.A.
107 F4 Cento Italy
128 D3 Central div. Botswana
122 D5 Central div. Ghana
127 C5 Central div. Kenya
127 B7 Central div. Malawi
119 F5 Central div. Sudan
125 E6 Central div. Zambia
117 F5 Central African Republic country Africa
16 E4 Central Australia Aboriginal Reserve res. *Western Australia* Australia
17 E5 Central Australia Aboriginal Reserve (Warburton) res. *Western Australia* Australia
36 A3 Central Brahui Ra. mountain range Pakistan
148 B4 Central City *Iowa* U.S.A.
150 D3 Central City *Nebraska* U.S.A.
162 B3 Central, Cord. mountain range Colombia
159 E3 Central, Cord. mountain range Dominican Rep.
164 C3 Central, Cordillera mountain range Bolivia
156 K7 Central, Cordillera mountain range Panama
164 A1 Central, Cordillera mountain range Peru
23 B2 Central, Cordillera mountain range Philippines
169 H3 Central de Minas Brazil
14 B4 Central Desert Aboriginal Land res. *Northern Terr.* Australia
27 □ Central District reg. Hong Kong
144 B4 Centralia *Illinois* U.S.A.
152 B2 Centralia *Washington* U.S.A.
128 C3 Central Kalahari Game Reserve res. Botswana
148 A2 Central Lakes *Minnesota* U.S.A.
172 B1 Central Los Molles Chile
39 E4 Central Makran Range mountain range Pakistan
14 C4 Central Mt Stuart h. *Northern Terr.* Australia
14 B4 Central Mt Wedge mt. *Northern Terr.* Australia
152 B3 Central Point *Oregon* U.S.A.
6 □1 Central Ra. mountain range P.N.G.
131 G4 Central Range mountain range Lesotho
124 B2 Centre div. Cameroon
89 G4 Centre div. France
127 □4 Centre de Flacq Mauritius
9 A7 Centre I. i. New Zealand
145 C5 Centreville *Alabama* U.S.A.
173 L2 Centurión Uruguay
110 D5 Centuripe *Sicilia* Italy
33 E4 Cenxi China
93 D4 Céou r. France
109 G2 Cepagatti Italy
Cephalonia i. *see* Kefallonia
81 E4 Čepovan Slovenia
86 B4 Cepoy France
106 B5 Ceppo, Monte mt. Italy
82 D3 Ceppo Morelli Italy
109 F3 Ceprano Italy
77 L3 Cerańow Poland
89 F4 Cérans-Foulletourte France
109 H4 Ceraso Italy
162 D2 Cerbatana, Sa de la mt. Venezuela
155 E4 Cerbat Mts mts *Arizona* U.S.A.
93 F6 Cerbère France
102 G2 Cerbère, Cap pt France/Spain
100 B3 Cercal Portugal
100 B3 Cercal, Sa do mountain range Portugal
75 K3 Čerčany Czech Rep.
98 B2 Cercedo Spain
110 C5 Cerda *Sicilia* Italy
102 F3 Cerdanyola del Vallès Spain
89 H4 Cerdon France
93 E4 Cère r. France
107 F3 Cerea Italy
137 G4 Cereal *Alberta* Canada
172 F4 Cereales Argentina
107 F3 Ceregnano Italy
88 D3 Cérences France
170 D2 Ceres Argentina
168 D1 Ceres Brazil
106 B3 Ceres Italy
130 B6 Ceres South Africa
106 B3 Ceresole Reale Italy
91 D5 Céreste France
93 E6 Céret France
162 B2 Cereté Colombia
99 G3 Cerezo de Abajo Spain
127 □2 Cerf I. i. Seychelles
127 □4 Cerfs, Is aux is Mauritius
79 L2 Čergov mts Slovakia
86 B3 Cergy France
109 H3 Cerignola Italy
42 C2 Çerikli Turkey
172 B1 Cerillos de Tamaya Chile
92 E2 Cérilly France
111 F3 Cerisano Italy
86 C4 Cerisiers France
88 D2 Cerisy-la-Salle France
92 B2 Cerizay France
51 E7 Çerkeş Turkey
113 G4 Çerkezköy Turkey
81 G5 Cerklje Slovenia
81 F4 Cerklje Slovenia
81 F5 Cerknica Slovenia
81 E4 Cerkno Slovenia
76 D1 Cerkwica Poland
79 L5 Cermei Romania
42 D2 Çermik Turkey
98 B5 Cernache de Bonjardim Portugal
98 D3 Cernadilla, Emb. de resr Spain
78 C3 Černá Hora mt. Czech Rep.
112 G2 Cernavodă Romania
90 F1 Cernay France
86 D3 Cernay-en-Dormois France
75 J2 Černčice Czech Rep.
99 G2 Cernégula Spain
82 B1 Cernier Switzerland
79 M2 Černiny h. Slovakia
106 D3 Cernobbio Italy
75 K3 Černošice Czech Rep.
75 H3 Černošín Czech Rep.
78 D2 Černovice Czech Rep.
93 D4 Cérou r. France
107 J3 Cerovlje Croatia
168 D5 Cerqueira César Brazil
98 D4 Cerralbo Spain
157 F3 Cerralvo Mexico
99 F3 Cerrato, Valles de v. Spain
114 A1 Cërrik Albania
173 K1 Cerrillada Uruguay
157 E4 Cerritos Mexico
168 D6 Cerro Azul Brazil
173 K2 Cerro Chato Uruguay
162 A4 Cerro de Amotape, Parque Nacional nat. park Peru
164 A2 Cerro de Pasco Peru
101 G4 Cerrón mt. Spain
159 E5 Cerrón, Co mt. Venezuela
170 C1 Cerro Negro Chile
172 C5 Cerro Policía Argentina
164 C2 Cerros de Bala mountain range Bolivia
162 C5 Cerros de Canchyuaya h. Peru
89 E4 Cersay France
109 J4 Cersosimo Italy
107 F5 Certaldo Italy
106 D3 Certosa di Pavia Italy
109 H3 Cervaro r. Italy
109 H4 Cervati, Monte mt. Italy
99 F2 Cervatos de la Cueza Spain
78 F1 Červená Voda Czech Rep.
112 E3 Cervenia Romania
102 E3 Cervera Spain
102 B3 Cervera de la Cañada Spain
102 B2 Cervera del Río Alhama Spain
99 F2 Cervera de Pisuerga Spain
108 E3 Cerveteri Italy
107 G4 Cervia Italy
107 H3 Cervignano del Friuli Italy
107 F2 Cervina, Punta mt. Italy
109 G3 Cervinara Italy
78 E2 Červiná Řečice Czech Rep.
108 B2 Cervione *Corse* France
106 C3 Cervo r. Italy
106 C5 Cervo Italy
98 C1 Cervo Spain
111 F3 Cerzeto Italy
106 D3 Cesano Boscone Italy
83 E3 Cesano Maderno Italy
110 D5 Cesarò *Sicilia* Italy
107 G4 Cesena Italy
107 G4 Cesenatico Italy
108 D1 Cesina r. Italy
54 D3 Cēsis Latvia
78 D1 Česká Kamenice Czech Rep.
78 D1 Česká Lípa Czech Rep.
78 F1 Česká Skalice Czech Rep.
78 D3 České Budějovice Czech Rep.
78 C1 České Středohoří h. Czech Rep.
81 F2 České Velenice Czech Rep.
78 E2 Českomoravská Vysočina reg. Czech Rep.
78 D1 Český Brod Czech Rep.
78 D3 Český Krumlov Czech Rep.
78 B2 Český Les mts Czech Rep./Germany
79 H2 Český Těšín Czech Rep.
78 F6 Česma r. Croatia
42 A2 Çeşme Turkey
93 E5 Cesse r. France
13 G3 Cessnock *New South Wales* Australia
88 D3 Cesson-Sévigné France
93 B4 Cestas France
122 C5 Cestos r. Liberia
54 E3 Cesvaine Latvia
112 D2 Cetate Romania
104 F4 Cetina r. Croatia
102 B3 Cetina Spain
112 B3 Cetinje Yugoslavia
83 F2 Ceto Italy
89 F3 Ceton France
111 E3 Cetraro Italy
101 E5 Ceuta Spain
106 C4 Ceva Italy
107 E2 Cevedale, Monte mt. Italy
91 B5 Cévennes mts France
91 B4 Cévennes, Parc National des nat. park France
99 F3 Cevico de la Torre Spain
99 F3 Cevico Navero Spain
90 E3 Cevins France
83 D2 Cevio Switzerland
43 A1 Cevizli Turkey
76 F1 Cewice Poland
42 D2 Ceyhan r. Turkey
42 C2 Ceyhan Turkey
42 D2 Ceylanpinar Turkey
90 D2 Ceyzériat France
91 B4 Cèze r. France
39 E1 Chaacha Turkmenistan
52 G3 Chaadayevka Rus. Fed.
52 F2 Chaadayevo Rus. Fed.
69 C3 Chaam Netherlands
92 C3 Chabanais France
173 G2 Chabas Argentina
91 D4 Chabestan France
91 D4 Chabeuil France
77 H4 Chabielice Poland
90 E2 Chablais mts France
90 B1 Chablis France
91 D4 Chabre ridge France
90 B3 Chabreloche France
89 G4 Chabris France
164 B3 Chaca Chile
173 G3 Chacabuco Argentina
159 □3 Chacachacare I. i. *Trinidad* Trinidad and Tobago
171 B5 Chacao Chile
170 C4 Chachahuen, Sa mt. Argentina
162 B5 Chachapoyas Peru
172 E4 Chacharramendi Argentina
51 D4 Chachersk Belarus
25 C4 Chachoengsao Thailand
36 B4 Chachro Pakistan
172 C4 Chachuahen, Sa mt. Argentina
170 D2 Chaco div. Argentina
165 E4 Chaco Boreal reg. Paraguay
136 C4 Chacon, C. c. *Alaska* U.S.A.
116 F4 Chad country Africa
26 F1 Chadan Rus. Fed.
172 D4 Chadileo r. Argentina
118 B5 Chad, Lake l. Africa
150 C3 Chadron *Nebraska* U.S.A.
24 B3 Chae Hom Thailand
47 H4 Chaek Kyrgyzstan
31 H5 Chaeryŏng North Korea
162 C3 Chafurray Colombia
39 F3 Chagai Pakistan
39 E3 Chagai Hills mountain range Afghanistan/Pakistan
47 J2 Chagan Kazakhstan
37 F2 Chagdo Kangri China
39 F2 Chaghcharān Afghanistan
47 G2 Chaglinka r. Kazakhstan
90 C2 Chagny France
50 E3 Chagoda Rus. Fed.
175 J4 Chagos Archipelago Indian Ocean
31 J1 Chagoyan Rus. Fed.
46 E3 Chagrayskoye Plato plat. Kazakhstan
159 □3 Chaguanas Trinidad and Tobago
159 □3 Chaguaramas Trinidad and Tobago
162 D2 Chaguaramas Venezuela
46 E4 Chagyl Turkmenistan
37 G3 Cha'gyüngoinba China
39 E3 Chahah Burjal Afghanistan
39 D2 Chāh Ākhvor Iran
39 B2 Chahār Maḩāll va Bakhtīārī div. Iran
39 D2 Chahār Takāb Iran
39 C2 Chāh Badam Iran
39 E4 Chāh Bahār Iran
121 E1 Chahbounia Algeria
39 E1 Chahchaheh Iran
39 D2 Chāh-e Kavīr well Iran
39 C2 Chāh-e Khorāsān well Iran
39 D2 Chāh-e Khoshāb Iran
39 C2 Chāh-e Malek well Iran
39 D3 Chāh-e Malek Iran
39 C2 Chāh-e Mirzā well Iran
39 C2 Chāh-e Mūjān well Iran
39 C2 Chāh-e Nūklok well Iran
39 C2 Chāh-e Nūklok Iran
39 C3 Chāh-e Qeyşar well Iran
39 C2 Chāh-e Qobād well Iran
39 C3 Chāh-e Rāh Iran
39 D3 Chāh-e-Raḩmān well Iran
39 C2 Chāh-e Shur well Iran
39 C2 Chāh-e Shūr Iran
39 C3 Chāh-e Ţāqestān well Iran
39 C2 Chah Haji Abdulla well Iran
39 C3 Chāh Ḩaqq Iran
39 G1 Chah-i-Ab Afghanistan
42 F3 Chah-i-Shurkh Iraq
39 C2 Chāh Pās well Iran
39 B3 Chāh Rūstā'ī Iran
39 E3 Chah Sandan Pakistan
127 D7 Chai Mozambique
37 F5 Chāībāsa India
139 G3 Chaigneau, Lac l. *Québec* Canada
63 F4 Chailey *England* U.K.
89 E3 Chailland France
92 A2 Chaillé-les-Marais France
86 C4 Chailley France
123 E4 Chaîne de l'Atakora mountain range Benin
125 E6 Chaine des Mitumba mountain range Zaire
86 D4 Chaintrix-Bierges France
25 C4 Chai Si r. Thailand
171 B5 Chaitén Chile
27 □ Chai Wan Hong Kong
25 B5 Chaiya Thailand
24 C4 Chaiyaphum Thailand
173 J1 Chajarí Argentina
129 D2 Chakari Zimbabwe
36 C2 Chakdarra Pakistan
127 C6 Chake Chake Tanzania
39 E3 Chakhānsūr Afghanistan
36 A4 Chakku Pakistan
36 C1 Chakmaktin L. l. Afghanistan
37 F5 Chakradharpur India
36 C2 Chakwal Pakistan
164 B3 Chala Peru
127 B6 Chala Tanzania
93 E6 Chalabre France
90 D2 Chalain, Lac de l. France
92 C3 Chalais France
82 C2 Chalais Switzerland
102 D3 Chalamera Spain
90 D2 Chalamont France
82 C1 Chalampé France
115 C4 Chalandritsa Greece
39 F2 Chalap Dalan mountain range Afghanistan
164 B3 Chala, Pta pt Peru
90 C2 Chalaronne r. France
156 H6 Chalatenango El Salvador
129 F2 Chaláua Mozambique
32 B1 Chalaxung China
126 C4 Chalbi Desert desert Kenya
63 E4 Chale *England* U.K.
86 B4 Châlette-sur-Loing France
139 G4 Chaleur Bay inlet *New Brunswick* Canada
171 B6 Chalía r. Argentina
82 A1 Chalindrey France
33 F3 Chaling China
127 C6 Chalinze Tanzania
36 C5 Chalisgaon India
115 □ Chalki i. Greece
114 D3 Chalki *Thessalia* Greece
115 E4 Chalkida Greece
114 E2 Chalkidiki div. Greece
114 D2 Chalkidona Greece
47 J4 Chalkudysu Kazakhstan
9 A7 Chalky Inlet inlet New Zealand
172 C5 Challacó Argentina
92 A2 Challans France
164 C3 Challapata Bolivia
177 M8 Challenger Fracture Zone sea feature Pacific Ocean
82 A3 Challes-les-Eaux France
152 D2 Challis *Idaho* U.S.A.
89 E4 Challones-sur-Loire France
50 F1 Chal'mny Varre Rus. Fed.
37 G5 Chalna India
90 C1 Chaloire r. France
86 D4 Châlons-sur-Marne France
90 C2 Chalon-sur-Saône France
93 B5 Chalosse reg. France
36 C1 Chalt *Jammu and Kashmir*
31 H4 Chaluhe China
92 C3 Châlus France
39 B1 Chālūs Iran
75 H3 Cham Germany
83 D1 Cham Switzerland
153 F4 Chama *New Mexico* U.S.A.
127 B7 Chama Zambia
172 E3 Chamaico Argentina
90 B3 Chamalières France
91 D4 Chamaloc France
36 A3 Chaman Pakistan
39 D1 Chaman Bid Iran
75 H3 Chamb r. Germany
36 D2 Chamba India
127 C7 Chamba Tanzania
36 D4 Chambal r. India
139 G3 Chambeaux, Lac l. *Québec* Canada
92 D3 Chamberet France
90 D2 Chambéria France
16 D3 Chamberlain r. *Western Australia* Australia
137 H4 Chamberlain *Saskatchewan* Canada
150 D3 Chamberlain *S. Dakota* U.S.A.
173 J2 Chamberlain Uruguay
147 J1 Chamberlain Lake l. *Maine* U.S.A.
155 H4 Chambers *Arizona* U.S.A.
146 E5 Chambersburg *Pennsylvania* U.S.A.
90 D3 Chambéry France
127 B7 Chambeshi r. Zambia
127 B7 Chambeshi Zambia
121 F1 Chambi, Jebel mt. Tunisia
87 E3 Chambley-Bussières France
92 D2 Chambon, Lac de l. France
92 E2 Chambon-sur-Voueize France
141 J2 Chambord *Québec* Canada
89 G4 Chambord France
92 D3 Chamboulive France
89 F4 Chambray-lès-Tours France
86 C3 Chambry France
39 B2 Cham-e Ḩannā Iran
90 C1 Chamesson France
39 B3 Cham-e Zeydun Iran
172 D1 Chamical Argentina
113 F7 Chamili i. Greece
37 F4 Chamlang mt. Nepal
25 C5 Châmnar Cambodia
126 C3 Ch'amo Hāyk' l. Ethiopia
36 D3 Chamoli India
90 E3 Chamonix-Mont-Blanc France
141 J2 Chamouchouane r. *Québec* Canada
90 E3 Chamoux-sur-Gelon France
37 E5 Champa India
92 C3 Champagnac-de-Belair France
91 B3 Champagnac-le-Vieux France
136 B2 Champagne *Yukon Terr.* Canada
86 D4 Champagne-Ardenne div. France
89 G4 Champagne Berrichonne reg. France
131 G4 Champagne Castle mt. South Africa
86 D3 Champagne Crayeuse reg. France
90 D3 Champagne-en-Valromey France
86 D4 Champagne Humide reg. France
92 C3 Champagne-Mouton France
86 D4 Champagne Pouilleuse reg. France
90 E1 Champagney France
90 D2 Champagnole France
148 C5 Champaign *Illinois* U.S.A.
172 E1 Champaqui, Co mt. Argentina
25 D4 Champasak Laos
86 C4 Champaubert France
92 B2 Champdeniers-St-Denis France
87 G4 Champ du Feu mt. France
89 F4 Champeigne reg. France
90 B3 Champeix France
82 B2 Champéry Switzerland
82 C2 Champex Switzerland
37 H5 Champhai India
91 D3 Champier France
89 E4 Champigné France
87 F4 Champigneulles France
86 D4 Champignol-lez-Mondeville France
148 D2 Champion *Michigan* U.S.A.
147 G2 Champlain *New York* U.S.A.
144 F2 Champlain, L. l. *New York/Vermont* U.S.A.
147 G2 Champlain, L. l. U.S.A.
90 D1 Champlitte France
141 G2 Champneuf *Québec* Canada
91 E4 Champoléon France
106 B3 Champoluc Italy
157 H5 Champotón Mexico
91 E4 Champsaur reg. France
89 E3 Champsecret France
92 E3 Champs-sur-Tarentaine-Marchal France
90 B1 Champs-sur-Yonne France
88 D4 Champtoceaux France
82 A1 Champvans France
38 B4 Chamrajnagar India
52 H2 Chamzinka Rus. Fed.
52 G2 Chamzinka Rus. Fed.
25 C6 Chana Thailand
36 D2 Chanab r. India
166 C3 Chanabrava r. Brazil
91 B4 Chanac France
173 H1 Chañar *Entre Ríos* Argentina
172 E1 Chañar *La Rioja* Argentina
172 C5 Chañar *Neuquen* Argentina
170 B2 Chañaral Chile
172 B1 Chañaral Alto Chile
39 D1 Chanārān Iran
173 F2 Chañar Ladeado Argentina
91 C3 Chanas France
172 E1 Chancani Argentina
162 B5 Chancay r. Peru
90 C1 Chanceaux France
89 F4 Chanceaux-sur-Choisille France
172 A3 Chanco Chile
172 A3 Chanco, B. de b. Chile
Chanda *see* Chandrapur
134 D3 Chandalar r. *Alaska* U.S.A.
37 E5 Chandarpur India
36 D3 Chandausi India
37 F5 Chandbali India
151 F6 Chandeleur Islands is *Louisiana* U.S.A.
36 D4 Chanderi India
36 E5 Chandia India
36 D3 Chandigarh India
155 G5 Chandler *Arizona* U.S.A.
30 A2 Chandmany Mongolia
141 G4 Chandos Lake l. *Ontario* Canada
37 G5 Chandpur Bangladesh
36 D3 Chandpur India
37 H5 Chandraghana Bangladesh
38 B2 Chandrapur India
115 C6 Chandrinos Greece
36 D5 Chandur India
32 G2 Chang r. China
131 J3 Changalane Mozambique
129 E3 Changane r. Mozambique
129 E2 Changara Mozambique
31 H4 Changbai Shan mts China
32 E5 Changcheng China
179 B1 Chang Cheng (Great Wall) China Base Antarctica
31 H4 Changchun China
31 G5 Changdao China
33 E2 Changde China
89 E3 Changé *Mayenne* France
89 F4 Changé *Sarthe* France
33 G1 Changfeng China
31 J5 Changgi Gap pt South Korea
31 G5 Changhai China
31 H6 Changhang South Korea
33 F2 Chang Hu l. China
33 E5 Changhua China
33 H3 Chang-hua Taiwan
25 □ Changi airport Singapore
25 □ Changi Singapore
33 E5 Changjiang China
33 H2 Changjiang Kou river mouth China
31 H4 Changjin North Korea
33 G3 Changle China
31 F5 Changli China
31 G3 Changling China
30 C5 Changliushui China
36 D2 Changlung *Jammu and Kashmir*
33 F3 Changning China
28 B6 Ch'angnyŏng South Korea
31 F4 Changping China
31 F5 Changqing China
31 H5 Changsan-got pt North Korea
33 F2 Changsha China
33 G2 Changshan China
31 G5 Changshan Qundao is China
32 D2 Changshou China
33 F2 Changshoujie China
33 H2 Changshu China
32 D3 Changshun China
31 H6 Changsŏng South Korea
33 G3 Changtai China
33 G3 Changting China
31 J3 Changting China
31 H4 Changtu China
156 K7 Changuinola Panama
31 J6 Ch'angwŏn South Korea
32 D1 Changwu China
33 G2 Changxing China
31 G5 Changxing Dao i. China
33 E2 Changyang China
31 F5 Changyi China
33 F1 Changyuan China
30 E5 Changzhi China
33 G2 Changzhou China
30 E6 Changzi China
115 E7 Chania div. Greece
115 F7 Chania Greece
92 B3 Chaniers France
114 E2 Chaniotis Greece
31 H4 Chanjin r. North Korea
30 C6 Chankou China
38 B3 Channapatna India
154 C5 Channel Islands is *California* U.S.A.
63 □2 Channel Islands is English Channel
154 B5 Channel Is Nat. Park nat. park *California* U.S.A.
139 J4 Channel-Port-aux-Basques *Newfoundland* Canada
17 B7 Channel Pt pt *Western Australia* Australia
158 C2 Channel Rock i. The Bahamas
63 H3 Channel Tunnel tunnel France/U.K.
148 C2 Channing *Michigan* U.S.A.
98 C2 Chantada Spain
90 B2 Chantelle France
88 D3 Chantepie France
25 C4 Chanthaburi Thailand
86 B3 Chantilly France
92 A2 Chantonnay France
82 B1 Chantrans France
25 A5 Chanumla *Andaman and Nicobar Is* India
151 E4 Chanute *Kansas* U.S.A.
47 J1 Chany Rus. Fed.
47 J2 Chany, Oz. salt lake Rus. Fed.
100 C3 Chanza r. Portugal/Spain
164 A1 Chao Peru
98 C1 Chao Spain
33 G2 Chao Hu l. China
25 C4 Chao Phraya r. Thailand
31 G3 Chaor r. China
31 G2 Chaor China
120 C1 Chaouèn Morocco
86 D4 Chaource France
32 A1 Chaowula Shan mts China
33 G2 Chao Xian China
33 G4 Chaoyang China
31 G4 Chaoyang China
31 G2 Chaozhong China
33 G4 Chaozhou China
166 D3 Chapada de Maracás reg. Brazil
168 B1 Chapada de Mato Grosso plat. Brazil
166 D3 Chapada Diamantina plat. Brazil
166 D3 Chapada Diamantina, Parque Nacional nat. park Brazil
166 D2 Chapada do Araripe reg. Brazil
166 A4 Chapada dos Guimarães Brazil
166 C3 Chapada Dos Veadeiros, Parque Nacional Du nat. park Brazil
168 E2 Chapada do Tapiocanga mts Brazil
169 F1 Chapadão de Santa Maria reg. Brazil
166 D1 Chapadinha Brazil
141 H2 Chapais *Québec* Canada
156 E4 Chapala Mexico
156 E4 Chapala, L. de l. Mexico
172 E4 Chapalcó, Valle de v. Argentina
173 H4 Chapaleofú Argentina
90 D3 Chapareillan France
162 B3 Chaparral Colombia
46 D2 Chapayev Kazakhstan
53 F2 Chapayeve Ukraine
53 E2 Chapayevka Ukraine
50 J4 Chapayevsk Rus. Fed.
47 H2 Chapayevskoye Kazakhstan
167 B6 Chapecó r. Brazil
167 B6 Chapecó Brazil
63 E1 Chapel-en-le-Frith *England* U.K.
65 F3 Chapelfell Top h. *England* U.K.
145 E5 Chapel Hill *N. Carolina* U.S.A.
69 C4 Chapelle-lez-Herlaimont Belgium
159 □1 Chapelton Jamaica
65 G4 Chapeltown *England* U.K.
173 J1 Chapicuy Uruguay
99 F4 Chapinería Spain
148 D5 Chapin, Lake l. *Michigan* U.S.A.
140 D3 Chapleau *Ontario* Canada
53 E1 Chapliyivka Ukraine
52 D3 Chaplygin Rus. Fed.
53 G2 Chaplyne Ukraine
53 E3 Chaplynka Ukraine
146 B6 Chapmanville *W. Virginia* U.S.A.
50 F1 Chapoma Rus. Fed.
13 F5 Chappell Is is *Tasmania* Australia
39 F2 Chapri P. pass Afghanistan
173 G2 Chapuy Argentina
164 C3 Chaqui Bolivia
36 D2 Char India
165 D3 Charagua Bolivia
36 B5 Charakra Doi India
164 C3 Charana Bolivia
129 D2 Charara Safari Area res. Zimbabwe
114 C2 Charavgi Greece
90 C2 Charbonnat France
91 F3 Charbonnel, Pte de mt. France
157 E4 Charcas Mexico
90 D2 Charchilla France
37 H3 Char Chu r. China
179 A2 Charcot I. i. Antarctica
137 G3 Chard *Alberta* Canada
62 D4 Chard *England* U.K.
47 G4 Chardara Kazakhstan
146 C4 Chardon *Ohio* U.S.A.
62 D4 Chardstock *England* U.K.
46 F5 Chardzhev Turkmenistan
121 E2 Charef Algeria
92 C3 Charente div. *Poitou-Charentes* France
92 B3 Charente r. France
92 B3 Charente-Maritime div. France
92 E2 Charenton-du-Cher France
89 F2 Charentonne r. France
62 D3 Charfield *England* U.K.
82 A1 Chargey-lès-Gray France
124 C2 Chari r. Cameroon/Chad
39 D3 Chārī Iran
124 C1 Chari-Baguirmi div. Chad
39 G2 Chārīkār Afghanistan
150 E3 Chariton r. *Iowa* U.S.A.
149 F3 Charity Is i. *Michigan* U.S.A.
36 D4 Charkhari India
63 E3 Charlbury *England* U.K.
69 C4 Charleroi div. *Hainaut* Belgium
69 C4 Charleroi *Charleroi* Belgium
141 K3 Charlesbourg *Québec* Canada
148 A4 Charles City *Iowa* U.S.A.
86 B3 Charles de Gaulle airport France
151 E6 Charles, Lake *Louisiana* U.S.A.
17 C7 Charles Pk h. *Western Australia* Australia
144 B4 Charleston *Illinois* U.S.A.
147 J2 Charleston *Maine* U.S.A.
151 F4 Charleston *Missouri* U.S.A.
145 E5 Charleston *S. Carolina* U.S.A.
146 C5 Charleston *W. Virginia* U.S.A.
9 C4 Charleston New Zealand
155 E3 Charleston Peak summit *Nevada* U.S.A.
147 G3 Charlestown *New Hampshire* U.S.A.
147 H4 Charlestown *Rhode Island* U.S.A.
159 □6 Charlestown *St Kitts-Nevis* Caribbean
146 E5 Charles Town *W. Virginia* U.S.A.
67 C3 Charlestown Rep. of Ireland
131 G3 Charlestown South Africa
15 F5 Charleville *Queensland* Australia
Charleville *see* Rathluirc
86 D3 Charleville-Mézières France
148 E3 Charlevoix *Michigan* U.S.A.
136 E3 Charlie Lake *B.C.* Canada
90 C2 Charlieu France
148 E4 Charlotte *Michigan* U.S.A.
145 D5 Charlotte *N. Carolina* U.S.A.
145 □3 Charlotte Amalie *Virgin Is* Caribbean
25 D6 Charlotte Bank sand bank Vietnam
145 D7 Charlotte Harbour harbour *Florida* U.S.A.
59 E2 Charlottenberg Sweden
146 D5 Charlottesville *Virginia* U.S.A.
Charlotte Town *see* Gouyave
139 H4 Charlottetown *Prince Edward I.* Canada
159 □2 Charlotteville *Tobago* Trinidad and Tobago
13 E4 Charlton *Victoria* Australia
138 E3 Charlton I. i. *Québec* Canada
86 C4 Charly France
92 C3 Charmé France
87 F4 Charmes France
91 C4 Charmes-sur-Rhône France
82 C2 Charmey Switzerland
62 D4 Charminster *England* U.K.
87 F4 Charmois-l'Orgueilleux France
62 D4 Charmouth *England* U.K.
86 C5 Charmoy France
16 D3 Charnley r. *Western Australia* Australia
90 B1 Charny France
77 N4 Charnyany Belarus
87 E3 Charny-sur-Meuse France
115 C6 Charokopeio Greece
90 C2 Charollais reg. France
90 C2 Charolles France
92 E2 Chârost France
50 F2 Charozero Rus. Fed.
91 B4 Charpal, Lac de l. France
82 B1 Charquemont France
82 C2 Charrat Switzerland
86 D5 Charrey-sur-Seine France
92 C2 Charroux France
36 B2 Charsadda Pakistan
39 F1 Charshanga Turkmenistan
47 K3 Charsk Kazakhstan
54 F4 Charstsvyatskaye, Vozyera l. Belarus
15 F4 Charters Towers *Queensland* Australia
89 G3 Chartres France
88 D3 Chartres-de-Bretagne France

47 G4 Charvakskoye Vdkhr. resr Kazakhstan/Uzbekistan
90 E2 Charvonnex France
6 □8 Charybdis Reef reef Fiji
47 J4 Charyn r. Kazakhstan
47 J4 Charyn Kazakhstan
47 K2 Charysh r. Rus. Fed.
47 K2 Charyshskoye Rus. Fed.
73 L1 Charzyno Poland
98 B4 Chãs mt. Portugal
173 H3 Chas Argentina
173 H3 Chascomús Argentina
173 H3 Chascomús, L. l. Argentina
136 F4 Chase B.C. Canada
39 E1 Chashkent Turkmenistan
42 F3 Chāshmeh Iran
39 D2 Chashmeh Nūrī Iran
39 D2 Chashmeh-ye Ab-e Garm spring Iran
39 D2 Chashmeh-ye Magu well Iran
39 C2 Chashmeh ye Palasi Iran
39 C2 Chashmeh ye Shotoran well Iran
54 F4 Chashniki Belarus
114 C3 Chasia reg. Greece
173 F5 Chasicó Buenos Aires Argentina
172 C6 Chasicó Rio Negro Argentina
173 F5 Chasicó, L. l. Argentina
9 B7 Chaslands Mistake c. New Zealand
31 H4 Chasŏng North Korea
90 C2 Chassagne-Montrachet France
125 C4 Chasse de la Léfini, Réserve de res. Congo
92 C3 Chasseneuil-sur-Bonnieure France
82 C1 Chasseral mt. Switzerland
82 B2 Chasseron mt. Switzerland
90 C3 Chasse-sur-Rhône France
91 C4 Chassezac r. France
90 D1 Chassigny-Aisey France
92 A2 Chassiron, Pte de pt France
39 C2 Chastab, Kūh-e mountain range Iran
92 E3 Chastang, Barrage du dam France
52 H3 Chasy Rus. Fed.
39 C1 Chāt Iran
93 E4 Châtaigneraie reg. France
91 D4 Château-Arnoux France
88 D3 Châteaubourg France
173 G2 Chateaubriand Argentina
88 D4 Châteaubriant France
90 B1 Château-Chinon France
82 C2 Château-d'Oex Switzerland
92 A2 Château-d'Olonne France
89 F4 Château-du-Loir France
89 G3 Châteaudun France
147 F2 Chateaugay New York U.S.A.
88 D3 Châteaugiron France
89 E4 Château-Gontier France
141 J4 Châteauguay Québec Canada
86 B4 Château-Landon France
89 F4 Château-la-Vallière France
88 A3 Châteaulin France
92 E2 Châteaumeillant France
91 C3 Châteauneuf-de-Galaure France
88 D3 Châteauneuf-d'Ille-et-Vilaine France
88 B3 Châteauneuf-du-Faou France
89 G3 Châteauneuf-en-Thymerais France
92 D3 Châteauneuf-la-Forêt France
91 D5 Châteauneuf-les-Martigues France
92 B3 Châteauneuf-sur-Charente France
92 E2 Châteauneuf-sur-Cher France
86 B5 Châteauneuf-sur-Loire France
89 E4 Châteauneuf-sur-Sarthe France
90 B1 Châteauneuf-Val-de-Bargis France
92 D2 Châteauponsac France
86 D3 Château-Porcien France
88 B3 Château, Pte du pt France
91 E4 Châteauredon France
86 B5 Châteaurenard Centre France
91 C5 Châteaurenard Provence-Alpes-Côte-d'Azur France
89 F4 Château-Renault France
92 D2 Châteauroux Centre France
91 E4 Châteauroux Provence-Alpes-Côte-d'Azur France
87 F4 Château-Salins France
86 C3 Château-Thierry France
86 D4 Châteauvillain France
159 □5 Châteaux, Pte des pt Guadeloupe Caribbean
90 E2 Châtel France
92 A2 Châtelaillon-Plage France
88 C3 Châtelaudren France
90 B3 Châteldon France
69 C4 Châtelet Belgium
92 C2 Châtellerault France
90 B2 Châtel-Montagne France
82 B2 Châtel-St-Denis Switzerland
87 F4 Châtel-sur-Moselle France
92 E2 Châtelus-Malvaleix France
87 G4 Châtenois Alsace France
87 E4 Châtenois Lorraine France
90 E1 Châtenois-les-Forges France
90 C2 Châtenoy-le-Royal France
148 A4 Chatfield Minnesota U.S.A.
63 G3 Chatham England U.K.
147 H4 Chatham Massachusetts U.S.A.
139 G4 Chatham New Brunswick Canada
147 G3 Chatham New York U.S.A.
140 D5 Chatham Ontario Canada
146 D6 Chatham Virginia U.S.A.
9 □1 Chatham I. i. Chatham Is New Zealand
9 □1 Chatham Is is New Zealand
136 C4 Chatham Sd chan. B.C. Canada
136 C3 Chatham Strait chan. Alaska U.S.A.
69 D5 Châtillon Belgium
106 B3 Châtillon Italy
90 A1 Châtillon-Coligny France
90 B1 Châtillon-en-Bazois France
91 D4 Châtillon-en-Diois France
82 A2 Châtillon-en-Michaille France
90 D3 Châtillon-la-Palud France
86 D5 Châtillonnais reg. France
90 C2 Châtillon-sur-Chalaronne France
89 E3 Châtillon-sur-Colmont France
92 D2 Châtillon-sur-Indre France
90 A1 Châtillon-sur-Loire France
86 C3 Châtillon-sur-Marne France
90 C1 Châtillon-sur-Seine France
92 B2 Châtillon-sur-Thouet France
47 H4 Chatkal mountain range Kyrgyzstan
47 H4 Chatkal r. Kyrgyzstan
171 B5 Chato mt. Chile
37 F4 Chatra India
148 C5 Chatsworth Illinois U.S.A.
140 E4 Chatsworth Ontario Canada
14 E4 Chatsworth Queensland Australia
115 C5 Chatsys Greece
145 C5 Chattanooga Tennessee U.S.A.
63 G2 Chatteris England U.K.
24 C4 Chatturat Thailand
91 D3 Chatuzange-le-Goubet France
47 J4 Chatyrkel, Oz. l. Kyrgyzstan
47 J4 Chatyr-Tash Kyrgyzstan
90 D1 Chaudenay France
91 B4 Chaudes-Aigues France
91 B4 Chaudeyrac France
69 D4 Chaudfontaine Belgium
25 D5 Châu Đôc Vietnam
90 C2 Chauffailles France
91 E4 Chauffayer France
36 B4 Chauhtan India
24 A2 Chauk Myanmar
36 E4 Chauka r. India
69 A5 Chaulnes France
90 B1 Chaumeçon, Barrage de dam France
90 D2 Chaumergy France
87 E4 Chaumont France
89 G2 Chaumont-en-Vexin France
86 D3 Chaumont-Porcien France
87 E4 Chaumont-sur-Aire France
92 C2 Chaunay France
24 A2 Chaungwa Myanmar
25 B4 Chaungwabyin Myanmar
45 S3 Chaunskaya G. b. Rus. Fed.
86 C3 Chauny France
90 D2 Chaussin France
88 D3 Chausey, Îles is France
146 D3 Chautauqua, Lake l. New York U.S.A.
92 C2 Chauvigny France
38 C4 Chavakachcheri Sri Lanka
50 F1 Chavan'ga Rus. Fed.
42 F3 Chavār Iran
166 C1 Chaves Brazil
98 C3 Chaves Portugal
138 E2 Chavigny, Lac l. Québec Canada
125 D6 Chavuma Zambia
50 D4 Chavusy Belarus
36 A3 Chawal r. Pakistan
24 D2 Chây r. Vietnam
47 G4 Chayan Kazakhstan
Chayek see Chaek
90 C3 Chazay-d'Azergues France
90 C3 Chazelles-sur-Lyon France
173 F2 Chazón Argentina
147 G2 Chazy New York U.S.A.
146 D5 Cheat r. W. Virginia U.S.A.
78 B1 Cheb Czech Rep.
52 H2 Cheboksarskoye Vdkhr. resr Rus. Fed.
52 H1 Cheboksary Rus. Fed.
148 E3 Cheboygan Michigan U.S.A.
53 E2 Checheliyivka Ukraine
53 C2 Chechel'nyk Ukraine
Chechenia div. see Chechnya
51 H7 Chechen', O. i. Rus. Fed.
51 H7 Chechnya div. Rus. Fed.
31 J5 Chech'ŏn South Korea
77 J5 Chęciny Poland
151 E5 Checotah Oklahoma U.S.A.
86 B5 Chécy France
89 H4 Checy France
62 D3 Cheddar England U.K.
24 A3 Cheduba Myanmar
24 A3 Cheduba I. i. Myanmar
24 A3 Cheduba Str. chan. Myanmar
86 D4 Chée r. France
137 G3 Cheecham Alberta Canada
67 E4 Cheekpoint Rep. of Ireland
15 F5 Cheepie Queensland Australia
179 B5 Cheetham, C. c. Antarctica
92 B2 Chef-Boutonne France
Chefoo see Yantai
134 B3 Chefornak Alaska U.S.A.
31 K2 Chegdomyn Rus. Fed.
120 C3 Chegga Mauritania
120 C5 Chegguè watercourse Mauritania
120 C5 Chegguet Ti-n-Kerkâz sand dunes Mauritania
129 E2 Chegutu Zimbabwe
152 B2 Chehalis Washington U.S.A.
39 G2 Chehardar P. pass Afghanistan
39 D2 Chehardeh Iran
39 D3 Chehell'āyeh Iran
120 C3 Cheikria well Algeria
114 C2 Cheimaditis, L. l. Greece
91 E5 Cheiron, Cime du mt. France
28 A7 Cheju Do i. China
27 N5 Cheju-haehyŏp chan. South Korea
52 C2 Chekalin Rus. Fed.
52 C2 Chekhov Rus. Fed.
Chekiang see Zhejiang
50 G3 Chekshino Rus. Fed.
31 K2 Chekunda Rus. Fed.
152 B2 Chelan, L. l. Washington U.S.A.
125 B7 Chela, Serra da mts Angola
46 D5 Cheleken Turkmenistan
100 C2 Cheles Spain
172 D5 Chelforó Argentina
121 E1 Chélif r. Algeria
46 E3 Chelkar Kazakhstan
77 M4 Chełm div. Poland
77 M4 Chełm Poland
63 G3 Chelmer r. England U.K.
76 G2 Chełmno Poland
63 G3 Chelmsford England U.K.
147 H3 Chelmsford Massachusetts U.S.A.
131 G4 Chelmsford Dam dam South Africa
76 G2 Chełmża Poland
62 D3 Cheltenham England U.K.
103 C5 Chelva Spain
46 F1 Chelyabinsk Rus. Fed.
46 F2 Chelyabinsk Rus. Fed.
45 M2 Chelyuskin Rus. Fed.
45 M2 Chelyuskin, M. c. Rus. Fed.
120 C2 Chemaïa Morocco
89 E4 Chemazé France
129 E2 Chemba Mozambique
52 G2 Chembiley Rus. Fed.
36 D2 Chem Co l. China
53 B2 Chemerivtsi Ukraine
69 C5 Chémery-sur-Bar France
89 E4 Chemillé France
90 D2 Chemin France
127 □4 Chemin Grenier Mauritius
75 H2 Chemnitz div. Germany
75 H2 Chemnitz Germany
52 G3 Chemodanovka Rus. Fed.
146 E3 Chemung r. New York U.S.A.
120 D3 Chenachane Algeria
147 F3 Chenango r. New York U.S.A.
90 C2 Chênas France
31 F2 Chen Barag Qi China
126 C3 Ch'ench'a Ethiopia
82 A1 Chenecey-Buillon France
92 E2 Chénérailles France
152 C2 Cheney Washington U.S.A.
151 D4 Cheney Res. resr Kansas U.S.A.
38 C3 Chengalpattu India
31 E5 Cheng'an China
33 E3 Chengbu China
33 E1 Chengcheng China
Chengchow see Zhengzhou
31 F4 Chengde China
32 D2 Chengdu China
26 C3 Chengel'dy Kazakhstan
32 D1 Chenggu China
33 G4 Chenghai China
32 E2 Chengkou China
33 E5 Chengmai China
Chengtu see Chengdu
32 D1 Cheng Xian China
33 G1 Cheniu Shan i. China
148 C5 Chenoa Illinois U.S.A.
31 H2 Chenqingqiao China
30 C2 Chentejn Nuruu mountain range Mongolia
33 E3 Chenxi China
86 C5 Cheny France
33 F3 Chenzhou China
25 E4 Cheo Reo Vietnam
112 E4 Chepelare Bulgaria
162 B5 Chepén Peru
6 □2 Chépénéhé New Caledonia Pacific Ocean
172 D1 Chepes Argentina
172 B3 Chepica Chile
53 G2 Chepil' Ukraine
156 L7 Chepo Panama
62 D3 Chepstow Wales U.K.
86 D4 Chepy France
148 B2 Chequamegon Bay b. Michigan U.S.A.
89 H4 Cher div. Centre France
89 G4 Cher r. France
103 C5 Chera Spain
92 B3 Chérac France
111 G2 Cheradi, Isole i. Italy
90 E3 Chéran r. France
106 B4 Cherasco Italy
145 E5 Cheraw S. Carolina U.S.A.
88 D2 Cherbourg France
50 J4 Cherdakly Rus. Fed.
88 D4 Chère r. France
54 F3 Cherekha r. Rus. Fed.
52 C4 Cheremisinovo Rus. Fed.
26 H1 Cheremkhovo Rus. Fed.
47 M2 Cheremushki Rus. Fed.
47 K2 Cherepanovo Rus. Fed.
50 F3 Cherepovets Rus. Fed.
50 H2 Cherevkovo Rus. Fed.
121 F1 Chéria Algeria
83 E3 Cherio r. Italy
53 G2 Cherkas'ke Ukraine
52 H3 Cherkasskoye Rus. Fed.
53 D2 Cherkasy div. Ukraine
53 E2 Cherkasy Ukraine
51 G6 Cherkessk Rus. Fed.
52 D1 Cherkutino Rus. Fed.
38 C2 Cherla India
47 H2 Cherlak Rus. Fed.
30 D3 Cherlen Gol r. Mongolia
53 B2 Cherlenivka Ukraine
52 C3 Chern' Rus. Fed.
47 G4 Chernak Kazakhstan
52 D3 Chernava Rus. Fed.
52 D3 Chernava Rus. Fed.
52 F3 Chernavka Rus. Fed.
54 E2 Chernaya r. Rus. Fed.
44 K2 Chernaya Rus. Fed.
53 E1 Chernecha Sloboda Ukraine
53 F2 Cherneshchyna Ukraine
50 D2 Chernevo Rus. Fed.
31 K3 Chernigovka Rus. Fed.
53 D1 Chernihiv Ukraine
53 G3 Cherninivka Ukraine
53 A2 Chernivtsi div. Ukraine
53 A2 Chernivtsi Chernivets'ka Oblast' Ukraine
53 C2 Chernivtsi Vinnyts'ka Oblast' Ukraine
52 D1 Chernogolovka Rus. Fed.
47 M2 Chernogorsk Rus. Fed.
50 K2 Chernorechenskiy Rus. Fed.
30 E2 Chernovskiye Rus. Fed.
52 F3 Chernoyar Rus. Fed.
47 G1 Chernoye, Oz. l. Rus. Fed.
52 F2 Chernukha Rus. Fed.
46 E1 Chernushka Rus. Fed.
53 C1 Chernyakhiv Ukraine
54 B4 Chernyakhovsk Rus. Fed.
53 G1 Chernyanka Rus. Fed.
31 H1 Chernyayeve Rus. Fed.
31 F1 Chernyshevsk Rus. Fed.
51 H6 Chernyye Zemli reg. Rus. Fed.
50 E2 Chernyy Porog Rus. Fed.
51 H5 Chernyy Yar Rus. Fed.
150 E3 Cherokee Iowa U.S.A.
151 D4 Cherokee Oklahoma U.S.A.
151 E4 Cherokees, Lake O' The l. Oklahoma U.S.A.
158 C1 Cherokee Sound The Bahamas
86 C4 Chéroy France
172 A5 Cherquenco Chile
37 G4 Cherrapunji India
155 E2 Cherry Creek Nevada U.S.A.
155 E1 Cherry Creek Mts mts Nevada U.S.A.
147 K2 Cherryfield Maine U.S.A.
4 J6 Cherry Island i. Solomon Islands
147 F3 Cherry Valley New York U.S.A.
141 G5 Cherry Valley Ontario Canada
45 S3 Cherskiy Rus. Fed.
45 Q3 Cherskogo, Khrebet mountain range Rus. Fed.
114 D1 Cherso Greece
106 B4 Chersogno, Monte mt. Italy
115 G7 Chersonisos Spinalogka pen. Greece
51 G5 Chertkovo Rus. Fed.
9 C5 Chertsey New Zealand
50 J2 Cherva Rus. Fed.
92 D3 Cherveix-Cubas France
112 E3 Cherven Bryag Bulgaria
92 B3 Cherves-Richemont France
52 B4 Chervone Rus. Fed.
53 C2 Chervone Ukraine
53 C1 Chervonoarmiys'k Ukraine
53 A1 Chervonohrad Ukraine
53 D3 Chervonozam"yanka Ukraine
53 E1 Chervonozavods'ke Ukraine
53 G2 Chervonyy Donets' Ukraine
53 E3 Chervonyy Mayak Ukraine
54 F5 Chervyen' Belarus
63 E3 Cherwell r. England U.K.
149 E4 Chesaning Michigan U.S.A.
147 E6 Chesapeake Virginia U.S.A.
147 E5 Chesapeake Bay b. U.S.A.
63 F3 Chesham England U.K.
62 D1 Cheshire div. England U.K.
147 G3 Cheshire Massachusetts U.S.A.
62 D1 Cheshire Plain lowland England U.K.
46 F5 Cheshme 2-y Turkmenistan
44 F3 Cheshskaya Guba b. Rus. Fed.
39 E2 Chesht-e Sharīf Afghanistan
63 F3 Cheshunt England U.K.
62 D4 Chesil Beach beach England U.K.
46 F2 Chesma Rus. Fed.
86 C4 Chessy-les-Prés France
147 E5 Chester r. Maryland U.S.A.
154 B1 Chester California U.S.A.
62 D1 Chester England U.K.
144 B4 Chester Illinois U.S.A.
152 E1 Chester Montana U.S.A.
147 F5 Chester Pennsylvania U.S.A.
145 D5 Chester S. Carolina U.S.A.
159 □1 Chester Cas. Jamaica
63 E1 Chesterfield England U.K.
11 L2 Chesterfield, Îles is New Caledonia Pacific Ocean
137 L2 Chesterfield Inlet inlet N.W.T. Canada
137 L2 Chesterfield Inlet N.W.T. Canada
65 G3 Chester-le-Street England U.K.
147 E5 Chestertown Maryland U.S.A.
147 G3 Chestertown New York U.S.A.
141 H4 Chesterville Ontario Canada
146 D4 Chestnut Ridge ridge Pennsylvania U.S.A.
147 J1 Chesuncook Maine U.S.A.
147 J1 Chesuncook Lake l. Maine U.S.A.
121 F1 Chetaïbi Algeria
25 A5 Chetamale Andaman and Nicobar Is India
129 D2 Chete Safari Area res. Zimbabwe
139 H4 Chéticamp Nova Scotia Canada
32 B2 Cheti La pass China
35 D8 Chetlat i. India
157 H5 Chetumal Mexico
9 E4 Chetwode Is is New Zealand
136 E3 Chetwynd B.C. Canada
31 J2 Cheugda Rus. Fed.
27 □ Cheung Chau i. Hong Kong
27 □ Cheung Chau Hong Kong
90 B2 Chevagnes France
91 E4 Cheval Blanc, Le mt. France
91 E3 Cheval Noir, Le mt. France
92 B3 Chevanceaux France
164 C2 Chevejecure Bolivia
90 D1 Chevigny-St-Sauveur France
87 E4 Chevillon France
89 G3 Chevilly France
9 D5 Cheviot New Zealand
65 F2 Cheviot Hills h. England/Scotland U.K.
15 E5 Cheviot Ra. h. Queensland Australia
65 F2 Cheviot, The h. England U.K.
88 A3 Chèvre, Cap de la pt France
82 B3 Chevril, Lac du l. France
126 C4 Che'w Bahir salt lake Ethiopia
126 C3 Che'w Bahir Wildlife Reserve res. Ethiopia
152 C1 Chewelah Washington U.S.A.
62 D3 Chew Magna England U.K.
129 D2 Chewore Safari Area res. Zimbabwe
62 D3 Chew Valley Lake l. England U.K.
150 C3 Cheyenne r. S. Dakota U.S.A.
151 D5 Cheyenne Oklahoma U.S.A.
152 F3 Cheyenne Wyoming U.S.A.
153 G4 Cheyenne Wells Colorado U.S.A.
92 E3 Cheylade France
17 B7 Cheyne B. b. Western Australia Australia
136 E4 Chezacut B.C. Canada
92 E2 Chezal-Benoît France
93 B6 Chèze France
36 D4 Chhabra India
37 F4 Chhapra India
36 D4 Chhata India
37 G4 Chhatak Bangladesh
36 D4 Chhatarpur India
36 B3 Chhatr Pakistan
36 D5 Chhindwara India
25 D4 Chhlong, P. r. Cambodia
38 A1 Chhota Udepur India
37 G4 Chhukha Bhutan
33 H4 Chi-a-i Taiwan
107 F3 Chiampo Italy
108 D1 Chianciano Terme Italy
125 B7 Chiange Angola
24 C3 Chiang Kham Thailand
24 C3 Chiang Khan Thailand
24 B3 Chiang Mai Thailand
157 G5 Chiapas div. Mexico
110 D5 Chiaramonte Gulfi Sicilia Italy
111 F4 Chiaravalle Centrale Italy
106 D3 Chiari Italy
109 J4 Chiaromonte Italy
109 E1 Chiascio r. Italy
83 E3 Chiasso Italy
157 F5 Chiautla Mexico
106 D4 Chiavari Italy
106 D2 Chiavenno Italy
29 H6 Chiba div. Japan
29 H6 Chiba Japan
29 □2 Chibana Japan
125 B7 Chibemba Angola
125 B7 Chibia Angola
129 E3 Chiboma Mozambique
141 H2 Chibougamau Québec Canada
141 H2 Chibougamau L. l. Québec Canada
141 J2 Chibougamau, Parc de res. Québec Canada
28 D5 Chibu Japan
28 D6 Chiburi-jima i. Japan
29 F5 Chibu-Sangaku Nat. Park Japan
131 J2 Chibuto Mozambique
37 G2 Chibuzhang Hu salt lake China
Chicacole see Srikakulam
148 D5 Chicago airport Illinois U.S.A.
148 D5 Chicago Illinois U.S.A.
148 D5 Chicago Heights Illinois U.S.A.
148 C5 Chicago Ship Canal canal Illinois U.S.A.
125 D6 Chicaluege r. Angola
162 B5 Chicama r. Peru
162 B5 Chicama Peru
129 E2 Chicamba Real, Barragem de dam Mozambique
125 C6 Chicapa r. Angola
118 C4 Chicha well Chad
131 J1 Chichacuare r. Mozambique
136 B3 Chichagof Alaska U.S.A.
136 B3 Chichagof Island i. Alaska U.S.A.
164 C4 Chichas, Cord. de mountain range Bolivia
92 B2 Chiché France
31 E4 Chicheng China
157 H4 Chichén Itza Mexico
63 F4 Chichester England U.K.
16 B4 Chichester Ra. Nat. Park nat. park Western Australia Australia
16 B4 Chichester Range mountain range Western Australia Australia
29 G6 Chichibu Japan
29 G6 Chichibu-Tama National Park nat. park Japan
146 E6 Chickahominy r. Virginia U.S.A.
145 C5 Chickamauga L. l. Tennessee U.S.A.
151 D5 Chickasha Oklahoma U.S.A.
62 D4 Chickerell England U.K.
100 D4 Chiclana de la Frontera Spain
162 B5 Chiclayo Peru
171 C6 Chico r. Argentina
173 G5 Chico r. Argentina
171 B7 Chico r. Argentina/Chile
154 B2 Chico California U.S.A.
129 E2 Chicoa Mozambique
141 F2 Chicobi, Lac l. Québec Canada
125 B6 Chicomba Angola
157 G6 Chicomucelo Mexico
147 G3 Chicopee Massachusetts U.S.A.
23 B2 Chico Sapocoy, Mt mt. Philippines
127 □5 Chicots, Pl. des plain Réunion Indian Ocean
141 K2 Chicoutimi Québec Canada
131 H1 Chicualacuala Mozambique
125 C6 Chicupo Angola
38 B4 Chidambaram India
129 E3 Chidenguele Mozambique
139 H1 Chidley, C. c. Québec Canada
145 D6 Chiefland Florida U.S.A.
75 H5 Chiemgauer Alpen mts Germany
80 D3 Chieming Germany
75 H5 Chiemsee l. Germany
80 C4 Chienes Italy
125 E5 Chiengi Zambia
109 E1 Chienti r. Italy
106 B3 Chieri Italy
87 E3 Chiers r. France
106 D2 Chiesa in Valmalenco Italy
107 E3 Chiese r. Italy
109 G2 Chieti div. Abruzzo Italy
109 G2 Chieti Chieti Italy
157 F5 Chietla Mexico
109 H3 Chieuti Italy
69 B4 Chièvres Belgium
31 F4 Chifeng China
47 H4 Chiganak Kazakhstan
47 H3 Chiganak Kazakhstan
139 G4 Chignecto B. b. New Brunswick/Nova Scotia Canada
134 C4 Chignik Alaska U.S.A.
90 E3 Chignin France
162 B2 Chigorodó Colombia
164 C4 Chiguana Bolivia
129 E3 Chigubo Mozambique
37 G3 Chigu Co l. China
Chihli, Gulf of g. see Bo Hai
156 D2 Chihuahua div. Mexico
156 D2 Chihuahua Mexico
172 C5 Chihuido Medio mt. Argentina
47 G4 Chiili Kazakhstan
33 E4 Chikan China
38 B3 Chik Ballapur India
54 F3 Chikhachevo Rus. Fed.
36 D5 Chikhali Kalan Parasia India
36 D5 Chikhli India
38 A3 Chikmagalur India
30 C2 Chikoy r. Rus. Fed.
30 C2 Chikoy Rus. Fed.
29 G5 Chikuma-gawa r. Japan
29 G6 Chikura Japan
28 C7 Chikushino Japan
127 B7 Chikwa Zambia
129 E2 Chikwawa Malawi
28 H2 Chikyū-misaki pt Japan
125 B6 Chila Angola
136 E4 Chilanko Forks B.C. Canada
157 F5 Chilapa Mexico
36 C2 Chilas Jammu and Kashmir
38 B5 Chilaw Sri Lanka
164 B3 Chilca, Cord. de mountain range Peru
62 D3 Chilcompton England U.K.
154 B2 Chilcoot California U.S.A.
136 E4 Chilcotin r. B.C. Canada
15 G3 Chilcott I. i. Coral Sea Islands Terr. Pacific Ocean
15 H5 Childers Queensland Australia
151 C5 Childress Texas U.S.A.
161 E8 Chile country South America
174 D8 Chile Basin sea feature Pacific Ocean
171 B6 Chile Chico Chile
170 C2 Chilecito La Rioja Argentina
172 C2 Chilecito Mendoza Argentina
125 B6 Chilengue, Serra do mts Angola
63 G3 Chilham England U.K.
112 G2 Chilia Veche Romania
148 C5 Chillicothe Illinois U.S.A.
47 J4 Chilik Kazakhstan
37 F6 Chilika Lake l. India
125 E6 Chililabombwe Zambia
115 D5 Chiliomodi Greece
136 E4 Chilko r. B.C. Canada
136 E4 Chilko L. l. B.C. Canada
15 F3 Chillagoe Queensland Australia
172 B4 Chillán r. Chile
172 A4 Chillán Chile
173 H4 Chillar Argentina
150 E4 Chillicothe Missouri U.S.A.
146 B5 Chillicothe Ohio U.S.A.
164 C3 Chilliculco Peru
36 C1 Chillinji Pakistan
136 E5 Chilliwack B.C. Canada
129 E3 Chiloane, Ilha i. Mozambique
171 B5 Chiloé, Isla De i. Chile
171 B5 Chiloé, Parque Nacional nat. park Chile
152 B3 Chiloquin Oregon U.S.A.
157 F5 Chilpancingo Mexico
36 C1 Chilpi Pakistan
13 F4 Chiltern Victoria Australia
63 F3 Chiltern Hills h. England U.K.
148 C3 Chilton Wisconsin U.S.A.
125 E6 Chilubi Zambia
127 B7 Chilumba Malawi
33 H3 Chi-lung Taiwan
36 D2 Chilung P. pass India
129 F2 Chilwa, Lake l. Malawi
127 B6 Chimala Tanzania
157 H6 Chimaltenango Guatemala
156 L7 Chimán Panama
129 E2 Chimanimani Zimbabwe
129 E2 Chimanimani Mountains mts Mozambique/Zimbabwe
69 C4 Chimay Belgium
172 B3 Chimbarongo Chile
170 C3 Chimbas Argentina
46 E4 Chimbay Uzbekistan
162 B4 Chimborazo mt. Ecuador
164 A1 Chimbote Peru
45 S3 Chimchememel' Rus. Fed.
162 C2 Chimichaguá Colombia
127 □1 Chimney Rocks i. Seychelles
129 E2 Chimoio Mozambique
101 F2 Chimorra, Sierra mountain range Spain
172 D5 Chimpay Argentina
24 A2 Chin div. Myanmar
19 L6 China country Asia
157 F3 China Mexico
162 C2 Chinácota Colombia
157 H5 Chinajá Guatemala
154 D4 China Lake l. California U.S.A.
147 J2 China Lake l. Maine U.S.A.
172 B5 China Muerta r. Argentina
156 J6 Chinandega Nicaragua
154 C5 China Pt pt California U.S.A.
164 A2 Chincha Alta Peru
136 F3 Chinchaga r. Yukon Terr. Canada
164 A2 Chincha, Islas de is Peru
15 G5 Chinchilla Queensland Australia
103 B6 Chinchilla de Monte Aragón Spain
99 G4 Chinchón Spain
172 B2 Chincolco Chile
147 F6 Chincoteague B. b. U.S.A.
129 F2 Chinde Mozambique
31 H6 Chin Do i. South Korea
82 A3 Chindrieux France
32 B1 Chindu China
24 A2 Chindwin r. Myanmar
29 □2 Chinen Japan
36 C2 Chineni India
47 J5 Chinese Turkestan reg. China
31 H5 Chinghwa North Korea
46 D2 Chingirlau Rus. Fed.
47 J3 Chingiz-Tau, Khr. mountain range Kazakhstan
125 E6 Chingola Zambia
125 C6 Chinguar Angola
120 B4 Chinguețți Mauritania
124 C1 Chinguil Chad
31 J6 Chinhae South Korea
129 E2 Chinhoyi Zimbabwe
36 C3 Chiniot Pakistan
156 C3 Chinipas Mexico
31 J6 Chinju South Korea
46 E4 Chink Kaplankyr h. Asia
124 D2 Chinko r. Central African Rep.
155 H3 Chinle Arizona U.S.A.
155 H3 Chinle Valley v. Arizona U.S.A.
155 H3 Chinle Wash r. Arizona U.S.A.
33 G3 Chinmen Taiwan
126 D2 Chinnile well Djibouti
38 B2 Chinnur India
29 G6 Chino Japan
89 F4 Chinon France
155 F4 Chino Valley Arizona U.S.A.
127 B7 Chinsali Zambia
38 B3 Chintamani India
158 D5 Chinú Colombia
69 D5 Chiny Belgium
28 A6 Chinyang-ho l. South Korea
46 D4 Chin Zap. escarpment Kazakhstan
107 G3 Chioggia Italy
82 B3 Chiomonte Italy
115 C4 Chiona Greece
115 B4 Chionata Greece
115 G4 Chios div. Greece
113 E5 Chios i. Greece
113 F5 Chios Greece
127 B7 Chipata Zambia
171 C5 Chipchihua, Sa de mountain range Argentina
125 E6 Chipili Zambia
125 C6 Chipindo Angola
31 F5 Chiping China
129 E3 Chipinge Zimbabwe
100 D4 Chipiona Spain
38 A2 Chiplun India
140 B2 Chipman Lake l. Ontario Canada
125 C6 Chipoia Angola
63 D3 Chippenham England U.K.
148 B3 Chippewa r. Wisconsin U.S.A.
148 B3 Chippewa Falls Wisconsin U.S.A.
148 B3 Chippewa, Lake l. Wisconsin U.S.A.
63 E2 Chipping Campden England U.K.
63 E3 Chipping Norton England U.K.
63 G3 Chipping Ongar England U.K.
62 D3 Chipping Sodbury England U.K.
82 C2 Chippis Switzerland
112 D3 Chiprovtsi Bulgaria
147 K2 Chiputneticook Lakes lakes Maine U.S.A.
157 H6 Chiquimula Guatemala
162 C2 Chiquinquira Colombia
51 G5 Chir r. Rus. Fed.
38 C3 Chirada India
129 F2 Chiradzulu Malawi
38 A4 Chirakkal India
38 C3 Chirala India
129 E2 Chiramba Mozambique
39 F2 Chiras Afghanistan
62 C2 Chirbury England U.K.
47 G4 Chirchik Uzbekistan
129 E3 Chiredzi Zimbabwe
123 G2 Chirfa Niger
30 A2 Chirgalandy Rus. Fed.
155 H5 Chiricahua National Monument nat. park Arizona U.S.A.
155 H6 Chiricahua Peak summit Arizona U.S.A.
162 C2 Chiriguaná Colombia
37 H5 Chiringa Bangladesh
156 K7 Chiriquí, Golfo de b. Panama
156 K7 Chiriquí, L. de b. Panama
129 D2 Chirisa Safari Area res. Zimbabwe
101 H3 Chirivel Spain
62 C2 Chirk Wales U.K.
66 F5 Chirnside Scotland U.K.
129 F2 Chiromo Malawi
112 E3 Chirpan Bulgaria
156 K7 Chirripo mt. Costa Rica
125 E7 Chirundu Zambia
125 E6 Chisamba Zambia
138 E3 Chisasibi Québec Canada
173 J3 Chis Chis, L. l. Argentina
157 H6 Chisec Guatemala
46 E2 Chishmy Rus. Fed.
148 A2 Chisholm Minnesota U.S.A.
36 C3 Chishtian Mandi Pakistan
32 D2 Chishur China
53 C3 Chişinău Moldova
79 L5 Chişineu-Criș Romania
106 B4 Chisone r. Italy
47 J2 Chistoozernoye Rus. Fed.
50 J4 Chistopol' Rus. Fed.
77 L1 Chistye-Prudy Rus. Fed.
31 F1 Chita div. Rus. Fed.
164 C4 Chita Bolivia
30 E2 Chita Rus. Fed.
125 B7 Chitado Angola
127 B7 Chitambo Zambia
30 D2 Chitanga Rus. Fed.
125 D5 Chitato Angola
50 J2 Chitayevo Rus. Fed.
137 H4 Chitek Lake Saskatchewan Canada
125 C6 Chitembo Angola
127 B6 Chitipa Malawi
129 E3 Chitobe Mozambique
28 H2 Chitose Japan
38 B3 Chitradurga India
36 E4 Chitrakut India
36 B2 Chitral r. Pakistan
36 B2 Chitral Pakistan

156 K8 **Chitré** Panama
37 G5 **Chittagong** Bangladesh
37 G5 **Chittagong div.** Bangladesh
36 C4 **Chittaurgarh** India
38 B3 **Chittoor** India
38 B4 **Chittur** India
127 B7 **Chitungulu** Zambia
129 E2 **Chitungwiza** Zimbabwe
157 H5 **Chiuchanhá** Mexico
127 C7 **Chiulezi r.** Mozambique
125 D5 **Chiumbe r.** Angola/Zaire
125 D7 **Chiume** Angola
127 C7 **Chiúre Novo** Mozambique
83 E2 **Chiuro** Italy
107 F2 **Chiusa** Italy
107 H2 **Chiusaforte** Italy
110 C5 **Chiusa Sclafani** *Sicilia* Italy
82 C3 **Chiusella r.** Italy
108 D1 **Chiusi** Italy
107 F5 **Chiusi della Verna** Italy
129 F1 **Chiuta, Lake l.** Malawi/Mozambique
103 C5 **Chiva** Spain
106 B3 **Chivasso** Italy
164 C2 **Chive** Bolivia
129 E2 **Chivhu** Zimbabwe
129 E3 **Chivi** Zimbabwe
173 H3 **Chivilcoy** Argentina
33 F4 **Chixi** China
128 D2 **Chizarira National Park nat. park** Zimbabwe
50 H1 **Chizha** Rus. Fed.
28 E6 **Chizu** Japan
53 F3 **Chkalove** Ukraine
47 H2 **Chkalovo** Kazakhstan
52 F1 **Chkalovsk** Rus. Fed.
76 C3 **Chlebowo** Poland
79 L3 **Chlmec r.** Slovakia
114 D4 **Chlomo mts** Greece
75 J3 **Chlumčany** Czech Rep.
75 J2 **Chlumec** Czech Rep.
78 E1 **Chlumec nad Cidlinou** Czech Rep.
81 F2 **Chlum u Třeboně** Czech Rep.
77 J5 **Chmielnik** Poland
31 H6 **Ch'o i.** South Korea
25 □ **Choa Chu Kang h.** Singapore
25 □ **Choa Chu Kang** Singapore
25 D4 **Chŏâm Khsant** Cambodia
172 B1 **Choapa r.** Chile
172 B1 **Choapa** Chile
128 C2 **Chobe div.** Botswana
128 C2 **Chobe National Park nat. park** Botswana
76 E4 **Chobienia** Poland
79 G3 **Chocholná-Velčice** Slovakia
76 D4 **Chocianów** Poland
76 F3 **Chocicza** Poland
76 D2 **Chociwel** Poland
155 E5 **Chocolate Mts mts** *California* U.S.A.
162 C2 **Chocontá** Colombia
76 F4 **Chocz** Poland
76 F1 **Choczewo** Poland
77 H3 **Chodecz** Poland
77 L4 **Chodel** Poland
78 B1 **Chodov** Czech Rep.
75 H3 **Chodová Planá** Czech Rep.
77 L3 **Chodów** Poland
76 E3 **Chodzież** Poland
172 E5 **Choele Choel** Argentina
129 E1 **Chofombo** Mozambique
36 C2 **Chogo Lungma Gl. gl.** Pakistan
51 H6 **Chograyskoye Vdkhr. resr** Rus. Fed.
137 J4 **Choiceland** *Saskatchewan* Canada
173 F5 **Choique** Argentina
6 □1 **Choiseul i.** Solomon Is.
171 E7 **Choiseul Sound chan.** Falkland Is.
82 B3 **Choisy** France
156 C3 **Choix** Mexico
76 C3 **Chojna** Poland
76 F2 **Chojnice** Poland
76 D4 **Chojnów** Poland
29 H4 **Chōkai-san volcano** Japan
151 D6 **Choke Canyon L. l.** *Texas* U.S.A.
126 C2 **Ch'ok'ē Mountains mountain range** Ethiopia
126 E3 **Chokola mt.** China
47 H4 **Chokpar** Kazakhstan
37 F3 **Choksum** China
45 Q2 **Chokurdakh** Rus. Fed.
129 E3 **Chókwé** Mozambique
32 B1 **Chola Shan mountain range** China
89 E4 **Cholet** France
171 B5 **Cholila** Argentina
47 J4 **Cholpon-Ata** Kyrgyzstan
156 J6 **Choluteca** Honduras
125 E7 **Choma** Zambia
91 B3 **Chomelix** France
91 C4 **Chomérac** France
37 G4 **Chomo Lhari mt.** Bhutan
24 B3 **Chom Thong** Thailand
36 C4 **Chomun** India
78 C1 **Chomutov** Czech Rep.
78 C1 **Chomutovka r.** Czech Rep.
45 M3 **Chona r.** Rus. Fed.
31 H5 **Ch'ŏnan** South Korea
25 C4 **Chon Buri** Thailand
162 A4 **Chone** Ecuador
33 G3 **Chong'an** China
31 H5 **Chongchon r.** North Korea
Chonggye *see* **Qonggyai**
31 J4 **Ch'ŏngjin** North Korea
31 H5 **Chŏngju** North Korea
31 H5 **Ch'ŏngju** South Korea
25 C4 **Chông Kal** Cambodia
32 B2 **Chongkü** China
33 H2 **Chongming Dao i.** China
125 B6 **Chongoroi** Angola
31 H5 **Chŏngp'yŏng** North Korea
32 D2 **Chongqing** China
32 C2 **Chongqing** China
33 F3 **Chongren** China
31 H6 **Chŏngŭp** South Korea
125 E7 **Chongwe** Zambia
32 D1 **Chongxin** China
33 F2 **Chongyang** China
33 G3 **Chongyang Xi r.** China
33 F3 **Chongyi** China
32 D4 **Chongzuo** China
53 F3 **Chonhar** Ukraine
31 H6 **Ch'ŏnju** South Korea
31 E3 **Chonogol** Mongolia
25 D5 **Chơn Thanh** Vietnam
37 F3 **Cho Oyu mt.** China
69 C4 **Chooz** France
79 M3 **Chop** Ukraine
37 E4 **Chopan** India
25 D5 **Chợ Phước Hai** Vietnam
167 B6 **Chopim r.** Brazil
167 B6 **Chopimzinho** Brazil
53 C1 **Chopovychi** Ukraine
147 F5 **Choptank r.** *Maryland* U.S.A.
36 B4 **Chor** Pakistan
115 C5 **Chora** Greece
91 E4 **Chorges** France
114 F1 **Choristi** Greece
101 F1 **Chorito, Sierra del mountain range** Spain
65 F4 **Chorley** *England* U.K.
77 N5 **Chorniyiv** Ukraine
53 E2 **Chornobay** Ukraine
53 D1 **Chornobyl'** Ukraine
53 D3 **Chornomors'ke** *Odes'ka Oblast'* Ukraine
51 E6 **Chornomors'ke** *Respublika Krym* Ukraine
53 C2 **Chornorudka** Ukraine
53 E1 **Chornukhy** Ukraine
53 B2 **Chornyy Ostriv** Ukraine
170 B2 **Choros, Is de los is** Chile
77 L2 **Choroszcz** Poland
166 E2 **Chorrochó** Brazil
53 A2 **Chortkiv** Ukraine
31 H5 **Ch'ŏrwŏn** South Korea
77 J2 **Chorzele** Poland
31 H4 **Ch'osan** North Korea
Chōsen-kaikyō chan. *see* **Nishi-suidō**
29 H6 **Chōshi** Japan
172 B4 **Chos Malal** Argentina
172 D2 **Chosmes** Argentina
27 N4 **Choson-Man b.** North Korea
76 D2 **Choszczno** Poland
162 B5 **Chota** Peru
37 E5 **Chota Nagpur reg.** India
152 D2 **Choteau** *Montana* U.S.A.
78 E2 **Chotěboř** Czech Rep.
36 B3 **Choti** Pakistan
121 D2 **Chott ech Chergui salt lake** Algeria
121 F2 **Chott el Fejaj salt lake** Tunisia
121 E1 **Chott el Hodna salt lake** Algeria
121 F2 **Chott el Jerid salt lake** Tunisia
121 F2 **Chott el Malah salt lake** Algeria
121 F2 **Chott Melrhir salt lake** Algeria
86 D3 **Chouilly** France
120 B4 **Choûm** Mauritania
114 C4 **Chouni** Greece
100 B1 **Chouto** Portugal
154 B3 **Chowchilla** *California* U.S.A.
136 F4 **Chown, Mt mt.** *Alberta* Canada
30 E3 **Choybalsan** Mongolia
82 A1 **Choye** France
30 D3 **Choyr** Mongolia
75 J3 **Chrást** Czech Rep.
78 D1 **Chrastava** Czech Rep.
78 G2 **Chřiby h.** Czech Rep.
148 D6 **Chrisman** *Illinois* U.S.A.
131 H3 **Chrissiesmeer** South Africa
63 E4 **Christchurch** *England* U.K.
9 D5 **Christchurch** New Zealand
131 E3 **Christiana** South Africa
163 F2 **Christianburg** Guyana
135 M2 **Christian, C. pt** *N.W.T.* Canada
140 E4 **Christian I. i.** *Ontario* Canada
7 □14 **Christian, Pt pt** *Pitcairn I.* Pacific Ocean
146 C6 **Christiansburg** *Virginia* U.S.A.
55 B4 **Christiansfeld** Denmark
Christianshåb *see* **Qasigiannguit**
136 C3 **Christian Sound chan.** *Alaska* U.S.A.
145 □3 **Christiansted** *Virgin Is* Caribbean
137 G3 **Christina r.** *Alberta* Canada
16 D3 **Christmas Cr. r.** *Western Australia* Australia
16 D3 **Christmas Creek** *Western Australia* Australia
175 M4 **Christmas Island i.** Indian Ocean
65 G2 **Christon Bank** *England* U.K.
78 E2 **Chrudim** Czech Rep.
115 G8 **Chrysi i.** Greece
114 E1 **Chryso** Greece
114 F2 **Chrysoupoli** Greece
77 H5 **Chrzanów** Poland
47 J4 **Chu div.** Kyrgyzstan
47 H4 **Chu r.** Kazakhstan
47 H4 **Chu** Kazakhstan
37 G5 **Chuadanga** Bangladesh
129 E3 **Chuali, L. l.** Mozambique
33 H2 **Chuansha** China
32 B2 **Chubalung** China
53 G3 **Chubarivka** Ukraine
152 D3 **Chubbuck** *Idaho* U.S.A.
171 C5 **Chubut div.** Argentina
171 C5 **Chubut r.** Argentina
52 E2 **Chuchkovo** Rus. Fed.
155 E5 **Chuckwalla Mts mts** *California* U.S.A.
172 E2 **Chucul** Argentina
172 D1 **Chucuma** Argentina
53 C1 **Chudniv** Ukraine
50 D3 **Chudovo** Rus. Fed.
134 D3 **Chugach Mountains mountain range** *Alaska* U.S.A.
28 D6 **Chūgoku-sanchi mountain range** Japan
152 F3 **Chugwater** *Wyoming* U.S.A.
53 G2 **Chuhuyiv** Ukraine
155 G5 **Chuichu** *Arizona* U.S.A.
47 H4 **Chu-Iliyskiye Gory mountain range** Kazakhstan
27 P1 **Chukchagirskoye, Ozero l.** Rus. Fed.
134 A3 **Chukchi Sea sea** Rus. Fed./U.S.A.
50 G3 **Chukhloma** Rus. Fed.
45 T3 **Chukotskiy Khrebet mountain range** Rus. Fed.
134 A3 **Chukotskiy Poluostrov pen.** Rus. Fed.
53 E3 **Chulakivka** Ukraine
47 G4 **Chulakkurgan** Kazakhstan
50 H1 **Chulasa** Rus. Fed.
154 D5 **Chula Vista** *California* U.S.A.
52 F1 **Chulkovo** Rus. Fed.
101 E4 **Chullera, Pta de la pt** Spain
62 C4 **Chulmleigh** *England* U.K.
162 A5 **Chulucanas** Peru
30 B2 **Chuluut Gol r.** Mongolia
47 L2 **Chulyshmanskiy Khr. mountain range** Rus. Fed.
164 C3 **Chuma** Bolivia
53 F3 **Chumaky** Ukraine
36 D2 **Chumar** India
126 C4 **Chumba** Ethiopia
37 G4 **Chumbi** China
170 C2 **Chumbicha** Argentina
47 L3 **Chumek** Kazakhstan
45 P4 **Chumikan** Rus. Fed.
24 C3 **Chum Phae** Thailand
25 B5 **Chumphon** Thailand
24 C4 **Chum Saeng** Thailand
47 K2 **Chumysh r.** Rus. Fed.
172 E1 **Chuña** Argentina
33 G2 **Chun'an** China
31 H5 **Ch'unch'ŏn** South Korea
47 J4 **Chundzha** Kazakhstan
125 E7 **Chunga** Zambia
31 H5 **Ch'ungju** South Korea
Chungking *see* **Chongqing**
31 J6 **Ch'ungmu** South Korea
127 C7 **Chungu** Tanzania
157 H5 **Chunhuhub** Mexico
131 G2 **Chuniespoort pass** South Africa
37 F3 **Chunit Tso l.** China
45 M3 **Chunya r.** Rus. Fed.
127 B6 **Chunya** Tanzania
25 D5 **Chuŏr Phnum Dâmrei mountain range** Cambodia
25 D4 **Chuŏr Phnum Dângrêk mountain range** Cambodia/Thailand
25 C4 **Chuor Phnum Krâvanh mountain range** Cambodia
32 C2 **Chuosijia** China
50 E1 **Chupa** Rus. Fed.
52 F2 **Chupaleyka** Rus. Fed.
159 □3 **Chupara Pt pt** *Trinidad* Trinidad and Tobago
53 D2 **Chupyra** Ukraine
164 B3 **Chuquibamba** Peru
164 C4 **Chuquicamata** Chile
164 D4 **Chuquisaca div.** Bolivia
83 E2 **Chur** Switzerland
37 H4 **Churachandpur** India
52 H2 **Churachiki** Rus. Fed.
45 P3 **Churapcha** Rus. Fed.
46 E1 **Churayevo** Rus. Fed.
137 K3 **Churchill r.** *Manitoba/Saskatchewan* Canada
139 H3 **Churchill r.** *Newfoundland* Canada
137 L3 **Churchill** *Manitoba* Canada
137 L3 **Churchill, Cape c.** *Manitoba* Canada
139 H3 **Churchill Falls** *Newfoundland* Canada
137 H3 **Churchill Lake l.** *Saskatchewan* Canada
136 D3 **Churchill Peak summit** *B.C.* Canada
138 E2 **Churchill Sound chan.** *Québec* Canada
150 D1 **Churchs Ferry** *N. Dakota* U.S.A.
62 D2 **Church Stretton** *England* U.K.
146 D5 **Churchville** *Virginia* U.S.A.
37 F4 **Churia Ghati Hills mountain range** Nepal
36 C3 **Churu** India
Churubay Nura *see* **Abay**
162 D1 **Churuguara** Venezuela
28 J2 **Chūrui** Japan
36 D2 **Chushul** India
155 H3 **Chuska Mountains mts** *New Mexico* U.S.A.
44 G4 **Chusovoy** Rus. Fed.
141 K2 **Chute-des-Passes** *Québec* Canada
141 G3 **Chute-Rouge** *Québec* Canada
141 H3 **Chute-St-Philippe** *Québec* Canada
53 F2 **Chutove** Ukraine
33 H3 **Chu-tung** Taiwan
4 G4 **Chuuk is** Fed. States of Micronesia
52 H2 **Chuvashia div.** Rus. Fed.
33 G1 **Chu Xian** China
32 C3 **Chuxiong** China
173 L2 **Chuy** Brazil
25 E4 **Chư Yang Sin mt.** Vietnam
76 G1 **Chwaszczyno** Poland
53 D3 **Chychykliya r.** Ukraine
53 E2 **Chyhyryn** Ukraine
77 K4 **Chynów** Poland
127 C5 **Chyulu Range mountain range** Kenya
53 C3 **Ciadâr-Lunga** Moldova
93 C5 **Ciadoux** France
111 E3 **Ciagola, Monte mt.** Italy
22 B3 **Ciamis** Indonesia
109 E3 **Ciampino airport** Italy
110 C5 **Cianciana** *Sicilia* Italy
22 A3 **Cianjur** Indonesia
168 B5 **Cianorte** Brazil
91 F4 **Cians** France
76 F3 **Ciążeń** Poland
22 A3 **Cibadak** Indonesia
22 B3 **Cibatu** Indonesia
22 A3 **Cibinong** Indonesia
100 B2 **Ciborro** Portugal
93 A5 **Ciboure** France
153 E6 **Cibuta** Mexico
106 D4 **Cicagna** Italy
107 H3 **Čićarija mountain range** Croatia
113 G5 **Çiçekli** Turkey
112 C3 **Ćićevac** Yugoslavia
6 □7 **Cicia i.** Fiji
77 M3 **Cicibór duży** Poland
99 H2 **Cidacos r.** Spain
42 C1 **Cide** Turkey
78 E1 **Cidlina r.** Czech Rep.
99 H3 **Cidones** Spain
77 J3 **Ciechanów div.** Poland
77 J3 **Ciechanów** Poland
77 L3 **Ciechanowiec** Poland
76 G3 **Ciechocinek** Poland
158 C2 **Ciego de Avila** Cuba
172 C2 **Cielo, Co mt.** Argentina
99 G4 **Ciempozuelos** Spain
162 C1 **Ciénaga** Colombia
158 D5 **Ciénaga de Oro** Colombia
158 D5 **Ciénaga Grande l.** Colombia
151 C7 **Ciénega de Flores** Mexico
153 E6 **Cieneguita** Mexico
158 B2 **Cienfuegos** Cuba
77 K4 **Ciepielów** Poland
93 C6 **Cier-de-Luchon** France
79 J3 **Čierny Balog** Slovakia
93 C6 **Cierp-Gaud** France
76 F2 **Cierznie** Poland
98 B2 **Cíes, Illas is** Spain
77 M5 **Cieszanów** Poland
76 G6 **Cieszyn** Poland
93 C5 **Cieutat** France
92 D3 **Cieux** France
103 B6 **Cieza** Spain
113 G4 **Çiftlikköy** Turkey
99 H4 **Cifuentes** Spain
106 C3 **Cigliano** Italy
101 G1 **Cigüela r.** Spain
42 C2 **Cihanbeyli** Turkey
156 D5 **Cihuatlán** Mexico
112 B3 **Cijevna r.** Albania
22 B3 **Cikalong** Indonesia
6 □7 **Cikobia i.** Fiji
104 F4 **Čikola r.** Croatia
22 B3 **Cilacap** Indonesia
127 □5 **Cilaog** *Réunion* Indian Ocean
51 G7 **Çıldır** Turkey
51 G7 **Çıldır Gölü l.** Turkey
22 B3 **Ciledug** Indonesia
33 E2 **Cili** China
43 B1 **Cilicia reg.** Turkey
43 C1 **Cilician Gates pass** Turkey
112 E3 **Cilieni** Romania
Cill Airne *see* **Killarney**
102 B4 **Cillas** Spain
Cill Chainnigh *see* **Kilkenny**
Cill Mhantáin *see* **Wicklow**
46 D4 **Çiloy Adası i.** Azerbaijan
155 E4 **Cima** *California* U.S.A.
22 A3 **Cimahi** Indonesia
151 D4 **Cimarron r.** *Oklahoma* U.S.A.
153 F4 **Cimarron** *New Mexico* U.S.A.
53 C3 **Cimişlia** Moldova
107 G2 **Cimolais** Italy
112 D1 **Cîmpeni** Romania
42 E2 **Çınar** Turkey
113 G4 **Çınarcık** Turkey
162 D2 **Cinaruco-Capanaparo, Parque Nacional nat. park** Venezuela
102 D3 **Cinca r.** Spain
146 A5 **Cincinnati** *Ohio* U.S.A.
147 F3 **Cincinnatus** *New York* U.S.A.
172 E6 **Cinco Chañares** Argentina
172 C5 **Cinco Saltos** Argentina
102 B2 **Cinco Villas reg.** Spain
102 C4 **Cinctorres** Spain
62 D3 **Cinderford** *England* U.K.
42 B2 **Çine** Turkey
69 D4 **Ciney** Belgium
98 B3 **Cinfães** Portugal
107 H5 **Cingoli** Italy
108 D2 **Cinigiano** Italy
106 D3 **Cinisello Balsamo** Italy
110 C4 **Cinisi** *Sicilia* Italy
111 F4 **Cinquefrondi** Italy
25 A5 **Cinque I. i.** *Andaman and Nicobar Is* India
157 G5 **Cintalapa** Mexico
93 D5 **Cintegabelle** France
108 A2 **Cinto, Mte mt.** France
173 F2 **Cintra** Argentina
90 D1 **Cintrey** France
102 B2 **Cintruénigo** Spain
168 D5 **Cinzas r.** Brazil
169 G3 **Cipo r.** Brazil
172 D5 **Cipolletti** Argentina
169 G4 **Cipotânea** Brazil
102 B2 **Cirauqui** Spain
109 F3 **Circeo, Monte h.** Italy
109 F4 **Circeo, Parco Nazionale del nat. park** Italy
134 D3 **Circle** *Alaska* U.S.A.
152 F2 **Circle** *Montana* U.S.A.
146 B5 **Circleville** *Ohio* U.S.A.
155 F2 **Circleville** *Utah* U.S.A.
22 B3 **Cirebon** Indonesia
22 B3 **Ciremay, G. volcano** Indonesia
63 E3 **Cirencester** *England* U.K.
102 B3 **Ciria** Spain
106 B3 **Ciriè** Italy
109 J4 **Cirigliano** Italy
53 C2 **Ciripcău** Moldova
111 G3 **Cirò** Italy
79 M3 **Cirocha r.** Slovakia
111 G3 **Cirò Marina** Italy
93 B4 **Ciron r.** France
139 H2 **Cirque Mtn mt.** *Newfoundland* Canada
106 D4 **Cisa, Passo della pass** Italy
148 C6 **Cisco** *Illinois* U.S.A.
151 D5 **Cisco** *Texas* U.S.A.
155 H2 **Cisco** *Utah* U.S.A.
77 L6 **Cisna** Poland
112 E2 **Cisnădie** Romania
162 B2 **Cisneros** Colombia
99 F2 **Cisneros** Spain
171 B5 **Cisnes r.** Chile
109 E3 **Cisterna di Latina** Italy
111 G2 **Cisternino** Italy
99 E2 **Cistierna** Spain
163 F3 **Citaré r.** Brazil
157 F5 **Citlaltépetl, Vol. volcano** Mexico
104 F4 **Čitluk** Bos.-Herz.
93 E5 **Citou** France
163 G3 **Citron** French Guiana
130 B6 **Citrusdal** South Africa
107 F3 **Cittadella** Italy
111 E3 **Cittadella del Capo c.** Italy
108 E2 **Città della Pieve** Italy
107 G5 **Città di Castello** Italy
106 B3 **Città di Torino airport** Italy
109 E2 **Cittaducale** Italy
111 F4 **Cittanova** Italy
79 M5 **Ciucea** Romania
157 E2 **Ciudad Acuña** Mexico
163 E2 **Ciudad Bolívar** Venezuela
156 D3 **Ciudad Camargo** Mexico
157 H6 **Ciudad Cuauhtémoc** Mexico
157 H5 **Ciudad del Carmen** Mexico
165 F5 **Ciudad del Este** Paraguay
162 D2 **Ciudad de Nutrias** Venezuela
163 E2 **Ciudad Guayana** Venezuela
156 D2 **Ciudad Juárez** Mexico
156 E3 **Ciudad Lerdo** Mexico
157 F4 **Ciudad Madero** Mexico
157 F4 **Ciudad Mante** Mexico
156 C3 **Ciudad Obregón** Mexico
163 E2 **Ciudad Piar** Venezuela
101 G2 **Ciudad Real div.** *Castilla - La Mancha* Spain
101 G2 **Ciudad Real** Spain
98 D4 **Ciudad-Rodrigo** Spain
157 F4 **Ciudad Victoria** Mexico
112 E1 **Ciumani** Romania
103 □ **Ciutadella de Menorca** Spain
42 D1 **Cıva Br. pt** Turkey
107 G2 **Civetta, Monte mt.** Italy
107 H2 **Cividale del Friuli** Italy
109 E2 **Civita Castellana** Italy
107 H5 **Civitanova Marche** Italy
108 D2 **Civitavecchia** Italy
109 F2 **Civitella del Tronto** Italy
107 F4 **Civitella di Romagna** Italy
107 F5 **Civitella in Val di Chiana** Italy
108 D2 **Civitella, Monte mt.** Italy
109 F3 **Civitella Roveto** Italy
92 E2 **Civray** *Centre* France
92 C2 **Civray** *Poitou-Charentes* France
42 B2 **Çivril** Turkey
108 A5 **Cixerri r.** *Sardegna* Italy
33 H2 **Cixi** China
30 E5 **Ci Xian** China
42 E2 **Cizre** Turkey
75 J3 **Čkyně** Czech Rep.
66 D4 **Clachan** *Scotland* U.K.
66 B3 **Clachan** *Scotland* U.K.
66 E4 **Clackmannan div.** *Scotland* U.K.
66 E4 **Clackmannan** *Scotland* U.K.
63 H3 **Clacton-on-Sea** *England* U.K.
64 C1 **Cladich** *Scotland* U.K.
64 A3 **Clady** *Northern Ireland* U.K.
62 C2 **Claerwen Res. resr** *Wales* U.K.
92 C2 **Clain r.** France
93 C4 **Clairac** France
137 G3 **Claire, Lake l.** *Alberta* Canada
152 B3 **Clair Engle L. resr** *California* U.S.A.
146 D4 **Clairton** *Pennsylvania* U.S.A.
90 D2 **Clairvaux-les-Lacs** France
92 C2 **Claise r.** France
91 D3 **Claix** France
90 B1 **Clamecy** France
154 D2 **Clan Alpine Mts mts** *Nevada* U.S.A.
67 E3 **Clane** Rep. of Ireland
145 C5 **Clanton** *Alabama* U.S.A.
130 B6 **Clanwilliam** South Africa
66 C5 **Claonaig** *Scotland* U.K.
65 F3 **Clapham** *England* U.K.
15 E3 **Clara r.** *Queensland* Australia
173 H1 **Clara** Argentina
67 D3 **Clara** Rep. of Ireland
25 B5 **Clara I. i.** Myanmar
15 E3 **Claraville** *Queensland* Australia
173 H4 **Claraz** Argentina
67 B4 **Clare div.** Rep. of Ireland
67 C3 **Clare r.** Rep. of Ireland
148 E4 **Clare** *Michigan* U.S.A.
13 E3 **Clare** *New South Wales* Australia
67 C4 **Clarecastle** Rep. of Ireland
67 A3 **Clare Island i.** Rep. of Ireland
147 G3 **Claremont** *New Hampshire* U.S.A.
159 □1 **Claremont** Jamaica
151 E4 **Claremore** *Oklahoma* U.S.A.
67 C3 **Claremorris** Rep. of Ireland
13 H2 **Clarence r.** *New South Wales* Australia
9 D5 **Clarence r.** New Zealand
9 D5 **Clarence** New Zealand
128 □1 **Clarence Bay b.** *Ascension* Atlantic Ocean
179 B1 **Clarence I. i.** Antarctica
171 B7 **Clarence, I. i.** Chile
136 C3 **Clarence Str. chan.** *Alaska* U.S.A.
14 B1 **Clarence Str. chan.** *Northern Terr.* Australia
158 D2 **Clarence Town** The Bahamas
159 □1 **Clarendon div.** Jamaica
151 C5 **Clarendon** *Texas* U.S.A.
159 □1 **Clarendon Peak** Jamaica
139 K4 **Clarenville** *Newfoundland* Canada
136 G5 **Claresholm** *Alberta* Canada
91 B5 **Claret** *Languedoc-Roussillon* France
91 D4 **Claret** *Provence - Alpes - Côte-d'Azur* France
103 C6 **Clariano r.** Spain
150 E3 **Clarinda** *Iowa* U.S.A.
159 F5 **Clarines** Venezuela
146 C5 **Clarington** *Ohio* U.S.A.
146 D4 **Clarion r.** *Pennsylvania* U.S.A.
146 D4 **Clarion** *Pennsylvania* U.S.A.
177 L4 **Clarion Fracture Zone sea feature** Pacific Ocean
156 □ **Clarión, I. i.** Mexico
150 D2 **Clark** *S. Dakota* U.S.A.
15 F3 **Clarke r.** *Queensland* Australia
131 G5 **Clarkebury** South Africa
13 G5 **Clarke I. i.** *Tasmania* Australia
15 F4 **Clarke Ra. mountain range** *Queensland* Australia
15 F3 **Clarke River** *Queensland* Australia
15 E3 **Clarkes Cr. r.** *Queensland* Australia
145 D5 **Clark Hill Res. resr** *Georgia/S. Carolina* U.S.A.
155 E4 **Clark Mt mt.** *California* U.S.A.
140 E4 **Clark, Pt pt** *Ontario* Canada
146 C5 **Clarksburg** *W. Virginia* U.S.A.
151 F5 **Clarksdale** *Mississippi* U.S.A.
147 F4 **Clarks Summit** *Pennsylvania* U.S.A.
152 C2 **Clarkston** *Washington* U.S.A.
159 □1 **Clark's Town** Jamaica
151 E5 **Clarksville** *Arkansas* U.S.A.
148 A4 **Clarksville** *Iowa* U.S.A.
145 C4 **Clarksville** *Tennessee* U.S.A.
168 C1 **Claro r.** Brazil
83 E2 **Claro** Switzerland
173 G5 **Claromecó** Argentina
69 B4 **Clary** France
67 D4 **Clashmore** Rep. of Ireland
169 F4 **Cláudio** Brazil
173 G5 **Claudio Molina** Argentina
67 D2 **Claudy** *Northern Ireland* U.K.
72 F4 **Clausthal-Zellerfeld** Germany
23 B2 **Claveria** Philippines
69 D4 **Clavier** Belgium
147 G2 **Clayburg** *New York* U.S.A.
150 D4 **Clay Center** *Kansas* U.S.A.
63 E1 **Clay Cross** *England* U.K.
63 H2 **Claydon** *England* U.K.
155 F3 **Clayhole Wash r.** *Arizona* U.S.A.
63 F4 **Clayton** *England* U.K.
145 D5 **Clayton** *Georgia* U.S.A.
153 G4 **Clayton** *New Mexico* U.S.A.
147 E2 **Clayton** *New York* U.S.A.
147 J1 **Clayton Lake** *Maine* U.S.A.
146 C6 **Claytor Lake l.** *Virginia* U.S.A.
173 H2 **Clé r.** Argentina
67 B5 **Clear, Cape c.** Rep. of Ireland
155 G4 **Clear Creek r.** *Arizona* U.S.A.
140 E5 **Clear Creek** *Ontario* Canada
134 D4 **Cleare, C. c.** *Alaska* U.S.A.
146 D4 **Clearfield** *Pennsylvania* U.S.A.
152 E3 **Clearfield** *Utah* U.S.A.
146 B4 **Clear Fork Reservoir resr** *Ohio* U.S.A.
136 F3 **Clear Hills mts** *Yukon Terr.* Canada
67 B5 **Clear Island i.** Rep. of Ireland
154 A2 **Clear Lake l.** *California* U.S.A.
155 F2 **Clear Lake l.** *Utah* U.S.A.
150 E3 **Clear Lake** *Iowa* U.S.A.
148 A3 **Clear Lake** *Wisconsin* U.S.A.
152 B3 **Clear L. Res. resr** *California* U.S.A.
136 F4 **Clearwater r.** *Alberta* Canada
137 H3 **Clearwater r.** *Saskatchewan* Canada
145 D7 **Clearwater** *Florida* U.S.A.
27 □ **Clear Water Bay b.** Hong Kong
152 D2 **Clearwater Mountains mts** *Idaho* U.S.A.
137 H3 **Clearwater River Provincial Park** *Saskatchewan* Canada
65 E3 **Cleator Moor** *England* U.K.
151 D5 **Cleburne** *Texas* U.S.A.
89 E3 **Clécy** France
88 A3 **Cléder** France
152 B2 **Cle Elum** *Washington* U.S.A.
65 H4 **Cleethorpes** *England* U.K.
87 E4 **Clefmont** France
88 B4 **Cléguer** France
88 B3 **Cléguérec** France
91 D4 **Clelles** France
69 D5 **Clémency** Luxembourg
163 G3 **Clément** French Guiana
25 □ **Clementi** Singapore
146 C5 **Clendenin** *W. Virginia* U.S.A.
146 C4 **Clendening Lake l.** *Ohio* U.S.A.
62 D2 **Cleobury Mortimer** *England* U.K.
89 G2 **Cléon** France
91 C4 **Cléon-d'Andran** France
23 A4 **Cleopatra Needle mt.** Philippines
89 G2 **Clères** France
141 F2 **Cléricy** *Québec* Canada
16 B3 **Clerke Reef reef** *Western Australia* Australia
90 C2 **Clermain** France
145 D6 **Clermont** *Florida* U.S.A.
93 D5 **Clermont** *Midi-Pyrénées* France
86 B3 **Clermont** *Picardie* France
15 F4 **Clermont** *Queensland* Australia
131 H4 **Clermont** South Africa
87 E3 **Clermont-en-Argonne** France
90 B3 **Clermont-Ferrand** *Puy-de-Dôme* France
91 B5 **Clermont-l'Hérault** France
90 E1 **Clerval** France
69 E4 **Clervaux** Luxembourg
69 E4 **Clervé r.** Luxembourg
89 G4 **Cléry-St-André** France
107 F2 **Cles** Italy
12 D3 **Cleve** *S. Australia* Australia
62 D3 **Clevedon** *England* U.K.
65 G3 **Cleveland div.** *England* U.K.
151 F5 **Cleveland** *Mississippi* U.S.A.
146 C4 **Cleveland** *Ohio* U.S.A.
145 C5 **Cleveland** *Tennessee* U.S.A.
15 F3 **Cleveland, C. headland** *Queensland* Australia
148 D2 **Cleveland Cliffs Basin l.** *Michigan* U.S.A.
65 G3 **Cleveland Hills h.** *England* U.K.
167 B6 **Clevelândia** Brazil
163 G3 **Clevelândia do Norte** Brazil
136 G5 **Cleveland, Mt mt.** *Montana* U.S.A.
65 E4 **Cleveleys** *England* U.K.
67 B3 **Clew Bay b.** Rep. of Ireland
145 D7 **Clewiston** *Florida* U.S.A.
67 A3 **Clifden** Rep. of Ireland
155 H5 **Cliff** *New Mexico* U.S.A.
14 D3 **Cliffdale r.** *Queensland* Australia
63 G3 **Cliffe** *England* U.K.
67 C2 **Cliffonoy** Rep. of Ireland
131 F5 **Clifford** South Africa
9 E4 **Clifford Bay b.** New Zealand
67 B4 **Cliffs of Moher cliff** Rep. of Ireland
155 H5 **Clifton** *Arizona* U.S.A.
15 G5 **Clifton** *Queensland* Australia
145 □2 **Clifton** The Bahamas
146 D6 **Clifton Forge** *Virginia* U.S.A.
12 D1 **Clifton Hills** *S. Australia* Australia
145 □2 **Clifton Pt pt** The Bahamas
146 B6 **Clinch r.** *Tennessee* U.S.A.
146 B6 **Clinch Mountain mountain range** *Virginia* U.S.A.
136 E4 **Clinton** *B.C.* Canada
147 G4 **Clinton** *Connecticut* U.S.A.
148 C5 **Clinton** *Illinois* U.S.A.
148 B5 **Clinton** *Iowa* U.S.A.
147 J2 **Clinton** *Maine* U.S.A.
147 H3 **Clinton** *Massachusetts* U.S.A.
145 B5 **Clinton** *Mississippi* U.S.A.
151 F5 **Clinton** *Mississippi* U.S.A.
150 E4 **Clinton** *Missouri* U.S.A.
145 E5 **Clinton** *N. Carolina* U.S.A.
151 D5 **Clinton** *Oklahoma* U.S.A.
140 E5 **Clinton** *Ontario* Canada
137 H2 **Clinton-Colden Lake l.** *N.W.T.* Canada
148 C5 **Clinton Lake l.** *Illinois* U.S.A.
148 C3 **Clintonville** *Wisconsin* U.S.A.
155 G4 **Clints Well** *Arizona* U.S.A.
92 D2 **Clion** France
177 K5 **Clipperton Fracture Zone sea feature** Pacific Ocean
177 M5 **Clipperton I. i.** France
88 D4 **Clisson** France
65 F4 **Clitheroe** *England* U.K.
164 C3 **Cliza** Bolivia
17 A4 **Cloates, Pt pt** *Western Australia* Australia
64 A3 **Cloghan** *Donegal* Rep. of Ireland
64 A4 **Cloghan** *Offaly* Rep. of Ireland
64 A3 **Clogher** *Northern Ireland* U.K.
67 E3 **Clogher Head headland** Rep. of Ireland
64 B4 **Clogherhead** Rep. of Ireland
64 B2 **Clogh Mills** *Northern Ireland* U.K.
64 C3 **Cloghy** *Northern Ireland* U.K.
67 C5 **Clonakilty** Rep. of Ireland
67 C5 **Clonakilty Bay b.** Rep. of Ireland
67 C3 **Clonbern** Rep. of Ireland
64 A4 **Clonbulloge** Rep. of Ireland
14 E3 **Cloncurry r.** *Queensland* Australia
14 E4 **Cloncurry** *Queensland* Australia
67 D2 **Clones** Rep. of Ireland
67 D4 **Clonmel** Rep. of Ireland
64 A4 **Clonmellon** Rep. of Ireland
67 E4 **Clonroche** Rep. of Ireland
67 D3 **Clonygowan** Rep. of Ireland
67 B4 **Cloonbannin** Rep. of Ireland
67 D3 **Clooneagh** Rep. of Ireland
72 D3 **Cloppenburg** Germany
148 A2 **Cloquet** *Minnesota* U.S.A.
170 E2 **Clorinda** Argentina
152 F2 **Cloud Peak summit** *Wyoming* U.S.A.
9 E4 **Cloudy Bay b.** New Zealand
27 □ **Cloudy Hill h.** Hong Kong
92 C2 **Clouère r.** France
64 C3 **Clough** *Northern Ireland* U.K.
141 H2 **Clova** *Québec* Canada
66 E4 **Clova** *Scotland* U.K.
154 A2 **Cloverdale** *California* U.S.A.
153 G5 **Clovis** *New Mexico* U.S.A.
89 G4 **Cloyes-sur-le-Loir** France
141 G4 **Cloyne** *Ontario* Canada
Cluain Meala *see* **Clonmel**
66 C3 **Cluanie, Loch l.** *Scotland* U.K.
137 H3 **Cluff Lake** *Saskatchewan* Canada
92 D2 **Cluis** France
79 M5 **Cluj div.** Romania
112 D1 **Cluj-Napoca** Romania
62 D2 **Clun r.** *England* U.K.
62 C2 **Clun** *England* U.K.
14 D5 **Cluny** *Queensland* Australia
90 C2 **Cluny** France
90 D3 **Cluse des Hôpitaux gorge** France
90 E2 **Cluses** France
106 D3 **Clusone** Italy
9 B6 **Clutha r.** New Zealand
62 C1 **Clwydian Range h.** *Wales* U.K.
62 C3 **Clydach** *Wales* U.K.
66 E5 **Clyde r.** *Scotland* U.K.
136 G4 **Clyde** *Alberta* Canada
146 E3 **Clyde** *New York* U.S.A.
146 B4 **Clyde** *Ohio* U.S.A.
9 B6 **Clyde** New Zealand
66 D5 **Clydebank** *Scotland* U.K.
66 C5 **Clyde, Firth of est.** *Scotland* U.K.
135 M2 **Clyde River** *N.W.T.* Canada
64 E2 **Clydesdale v.** *Scotland* U.K.
62 C2 **Clyro** *Wales* U.K.
62 C2 **Clywedog, Llyn resr** *Wales* U.K.
64 C2 **Cnoc Moy h.** *Scotland* U.K.
98 C4 **Côa r.** Portugal
153 C5 **Coachella** *California* U.S.A.
64 B3 **Coagh** *Northern Ireland* U.K.
157 E5 **Coahuayutla de Guerrero** Mexico
156 E3 **Coahuila div.** Mexico
136 D2 **Coal r.** *Yukon Terr.* Canada
148 C5 **Coal City** *Illinois* U.S.A.
156 E5 **Coalcomán** Mexico
154 D3 **Coaldale** *Nevada* U.S.A.
151 D5 **Coalgate** *Oklahoma* U.S.A.
9 A7 **Coal I. i.** New Zealand
154 B3 **Coalinga** *California* U.S.A.
136 D3 **Coal River** *B.C.* Canada
63 E2 **Coalville** *England* U.K.
145 □3 **Coamo** Puerto Rico
98 D1 **Coaña** Spain
169 J1 **Coaraci** Brazil
163 E5 **Coari r.** Brazil

134 G3 **Coppermine r.** *N.W.T.* Canada
134 G3 **Coppermine** *N.W.T.* Canada
140 C3 **Coppermine Pt pt** *Ontario* Canada
62 C4 **Copplestone** *England* U.K.
112 E1 **Copşa Mică** Romania
63 E4 **Copythorne** *England* U.K.
37 F3 **Coqên** China
65 G2 **Coquet Island i.** *England* U.K.
172 B1 **Coquimbo div.** Chile
172 B1 **Coquimbo** Chile
112 E3 **Corabia** Romania
169 F2 **Coração de Jesus** Brazil
111 F4 **Corace r.** Italy
Coracesium *see* **Alanya**
164 B2 **Coracora** Peru
140 E1 **Coral** *Ontario* Canada
145 D7 **Coral Gables** *Florida* U.S.A.
135 K3 **Coral Harbour** *N.W.T.* Canada
145 □2 **Coral Harbour** The Bahamas
176 F7 **Coral Sea sea** Pacific Ocean
175 P4 **Coral Sea Basin sea feature**
4 G6 **Coral Sea Islands Territory div.** Pacific Ocean
148 B5 **Coralville Reservoir resr** *Iowa* U.S.A.
13 E4 **Corangamite, L. l.** *Victoria* Australia
163 F3 **Corantijn r.** Surinam
109 J3 **Corato** Italy
88 B3 **Coray** France
102 C4 **Corbalán** Spain
86 B4 **Corbeil-Essonnes** France
86 B4 **Corbeilles** France
120 A4 **Corbeiro, Cap pt** *Western Sahara*
168 B6 **Corbélia** Brazil
90 D3 **Corbelin** France
86 C3 **Corbeny** France
173 G3 **Corbett** Argentina
137 L2 **Corbett Inlet inlet** *N.W.T.* Canada
86 B3 **Corbie** France
93 E6 **Corbières reg.** France
91 D5 **Corbières** France
82 C2 **Corbières** Switzerland
90 B1 **Corbigny** France
146 A6 **Corbin** *Kentucky* U.S.A.
101 E3 **Corbones r.** Spain
65 F3 **Corbridge** *England* U.K.
112 G2 **Corbu** Romania
63 F2 **Corby** *England* U.K.
102 G3 **Corça** Spain
Corcaigh *see* **Cork**
90 D1 **Corcelles-lès-Cîteaux** France
109 E2 **Corchiano** Italy
101 H1 **Córcoles r.** Spain
154 C3 **Corcoran** *California* U.S.A.
171 B5 **Corcovado** Argentina
171 B5 **Corcovado, G. de chan.** Chile
171 B5 **Corcovado, V. volcano** Chile
98 A2 **Corcubión** Spain
166 C2 **Corda r.** Brazil
165 E5 **Cord de Caaguazú h.** Paraguay
172 B4 **Cord de Pemehue mountain range** Chile
169 G5 **Cordeiro** Brazil
145 D6 **Cordele** *Georgia* U.S.A.
80 D5 **Cordenòns** Italy
93 D4 **Cordes** France
162 C3 **Cordillera de los Picachos, Parque Nacional nat. park** Colombia
23 B4 **Cordilleras Range mountain range** Philippines
12 E1 **Cordillo Downs** *S. Australia* Australia
169 F3 **Cordisburgo** Brazil
172 F2 **Córdoba div.** Argentina
101 F2 **Córdoba div.** Spain
101 F3 **Córdoba** *Córdoba* Spain
171 C5 **Córdoba** Argentina
172 E1 **Córdoba** Argentina
157 F5 **Córdoba** Mexico
156 E3 **Córdoba** Mexico
101 F3 **Córdoba, Sierra de h.** Spain
170 D3 **Cordoba, Sierras de mountain range** Argentina
173 K2 **Cordobes r.** Uruguay
134 D3 **Cordova** *Alaska* U.S.A.
Cordova *see* **Córdoba**
164 A2 **Cordova** Peru
136 C4 **Cordova Bay b.** *Alaska* U.S.A.
147 K2 **Corea** *Maine* U.S.A.
166 D1 **Coreaú** Brazil
14 E4 **Corella r.** *Queensland* Australia
102 B2 **Corella** Spain
14 C3 **Corella L. salt flat** *Northern Terr.* Australia
62 D4 **Corfe Castle** *England* U.K.
15 E4 **Corfield** *Queensland* Australia
109 F2 **Corfinio** Italy
Corfu i. *see* **Kerkyra**
98 C3 **Corgo r.** Portugal
168 A3 **Corguinho** Brazil
109 E3 **Cori** Italy
98 D5 **Coria** Spain
100 D3 **Coria del Río** Spain
111 F3 **Corigliano Calabro** Italy
107 H5 **Corinaldo** Italy
15 G3 **Coringa Is is** *Coral Sea Islands Terr.* Pacific Ocean
147 J2 **Corinna** *Maine* U.S.A.
13 F5 **Corinna** *Tasmania* Australia
137 J4 **Corinne** *Saskatchewan* Canada
151 F5 **Corinth** *Mississippi* U.S.A.
147 G3 **Corinth** *New York* U.S.A.
169 F3 **Corinto** Brazil
101 E4 **Coripe** Spain
165 E3 **Corixa Grande r.** Bolivia
165 E3 **Corixinha r.** Brazil
67 C5 **Cork airport** Rep. of Ireland
67 C4 **Cork div.** Rep. of Ireland
67 C5 **Cork** Rep. of Ireland
88 B3 **Corlay** France
110 C5 **Corleone** *Sicilia* Italy
109 J4 **Corleto Perticara** Italy
42 A1 **Çorlu** Turkey
90 C2 **Cormatin** France
89 F2 **Cormeilles** France
107 H3 **Cormòns** Italy
163 G3 **Cormontibo** French Guiana
86 D3 **Cormontreuil** France
23 □1 **Cormoran Reef reef** Palau
137 J4 **Cormorant** *Manitoba* Canada
109 H3 **Cornacchia, Monte mt.** Italy
99 H2 **Cornago** Spain
131 G3 **Cornelia** South Africa
168 C5 **Cornélio Procópio** Brazil
163 F2 **Corneliskondre** Surinam
148 B3 **Cornell** *Wisconsin* U.S.A.
102 F3 **Cornellá de Llobregat** Spain
98 D1 **Cornellana** Spain
139 J4 **Corner Brook** *Newfoundland* Canada
13 F4 **Corner Inlet b.** *Victoria* Australia
103 B7 **Corneros r.** Spain
53 C3 **Cornești** Moldova
82 B2 **Cornettes de Bise, Les mts** France/Switzerland
107 F3 **Cornetto mt.** Italy
108 C1 **Cornia r.** Italy
106 E4 **Corniglio** Italy
86 D3 **Cornillet, Mont h.** France
87 F5 **Cornimont** France
154 A2 **Corning** *California* U.S.A.
146 E3 **Corning** *New York* U.S.A.
Corn Is i. *see* **Maíz, Is del**
106 B3 **Corno Bianco mt.** Italy
83 F2 **Corno dei Tre Signori mt.** Italy
83 F2 **Corno di Campo mt.** Italy/Switzerland
109 F2 **Corno, Monte mt.** Italy
88 A3 **Cornouaille reg.** France
107 G3 **Cornuda** Italy
99 G2 **Cornudilla** Spain
91 B5 **Cornus** France
62 B4 **Cornwall div.** *England* U.K.
141 H4 **Cornwall** *Ontario* Canada
135 J2 **Cornwall I. i.** *N.W.T.* Canada
135 J2 **Cornwallis I. i.** *N.W.T.* Canada
12 D3 **Corny Pt pt** *S. Australia* Australia
162 D1 **Coro** Venezuela
169 G3 **Coroaci** Brazil
166 D1 **Coroatá** Brazil
164 C3 **Corocoro** Bolivia
67 B4 **Corofin** Rep. of Ireland
164 C3 **Coroico** Bolivia
168 E3 **Coromandel** Brazil
38 C4 **Coromandel Coast coastal area** India
8 E2 **Coromandel Peninsula pen.** New Zealand
8 E2 **Coromandel Range h.** New Zealand
23 B3 **Coron** Philippines
100 B2 **Corona r.** Portugal
154 D5 **Corona** *California* U.S.A.
12 E2 **Corona** *New South Wales* Australia
154 D5 **Coronado** *California* U.S.A.
156 K7 **Coronado, B. de b.** Panama
171 B5 **Coronados, G. de los inlet** Chile
137 G4 **Coronation** *Alberta* Canada
134 G3 **Coronation Gulf b.** *N.W.T.* Canada
179 B1 **Coronation I. i.** *S. Orkney Is* Atlantic Ocean
16 D2 **Coronation Is is** *Western Australia* Australia
136 C3 **Coronation Island i.** *Alaska* U.S.A.
23 B4 **Coron Bay b.** Philippines
173 G1 **Coronda** Argentina
172 A4 **Coronel** Chile
172 E2 **Coronel Alzogaray** Argentina
173 H3 **Coronel Brandsen** Argentina
173 G5 **Coronel Dorrego** Argentina
169 G3 **Coronel Fabriciano** Brazil
172 E6 **Coronel Francisco Sosa** Argentina
172 E2 **Coronel Moldes** Argentina
169 G2 **Coronel Murta** Brazil
165 E5 **Coronel Oviedo** Paraguay
166 B4 **Coronel Ponce** Brazil
173 G4 **Coronel Pringles** Argentina
168 A5 **Coronel Sapucaia** Brazil
173 G4 **Coronel Suárez** Argentina
173 J4 **Coronel Vidal** Argentina
164 A1 **Corongo** Peru
173 K1 **Coronilla** Uruguay
114 B2 **Çorovodë** Albania
13 F3 **Corowa** *New South Wales* Australia
157 H5 **Corozal** Belize
158 D5 **Corozal** Colombia
159 □3 **Corozal Pt pt** *Trinidad* Trinidad and Tobago
91 D4 **Corps** France
151 D7 **Corpus Christi** *Texas* U.S.A.
151 D6 **Corpus Christi, L. l.** *Texas* U.S.A.
164 C3 **Corque** Bolivia
172 A5 **Corral** Chile
99 G5 **Corral de Almaguer** Spain
173 F2 **Corral de Bustos** Argentina
101 F1 **Corral de Cantos mt.** Spain
172 D1 **Corral de Isaac** Argentina
97 □ **Corralejo** *Canary Is* Spain
172 D1 **Corralitos, Mte mt.** Argentina
108 B4 **Corrasi, Punta mt.** *Sardegna* Italy
67 B3 **Corraun Peninsula pen.** Rep. of Ireland
82 A1 **Corre** France
107 E4 **Correggio** Italy
168 C2 **Córrego do Ouro** Brazil
169 G3 **Córrego Novo** Brazil
168 C3 **Corrente r.** Brazil
166 D3 **Corrente r.** Brazil
166 C3 **Corrente** Brazil
168 C3 **Corrente Grande r.** Brazil
167 B4 **Correntes r.** Brazil
168 A2 **Correntes** Brazil
Correntina r. *see* **Éguas**
166 D3 **Correntina** Brazil
92 D3 **Corrèze div.** *Limousin* France
92 D3 **Corrèze r.** France
92 D3 **Corrèze** France
67 B3 **Corrib, Lough l.** Rep. of Ireland
107 H5 **Corridonia** Italy
170 E2 **Corrientes div.** Argentina
170 E2 **Corrientes r.** Argentina
170 E2 **Corrientes** Argentina
173 J5 **Corrientes, C. c.** Argentina
156 D4 **Corrientes, C. c.** Mexico
162 B2 **Corrientes, Cabo pt** Colombia
158 A2 **Corrientes, Cabo pt** Cuba
151 E6 **Corrigan** *Texas* U.S.A.
17 B7 **Corrigin** *Western Australia* Australia
62 C2 **Corris** *Wales* U.K.
163 F2 **Corriverton** Guyana
146 D4 **Corry** *Pennsylvania* U.S.A.
13 F4 **Corryong** *Victoria* Australia
106 B4 **Corsaglia r.** Italy
108 B2 **Corse div.** France
108 A2 **Corse i.** France
108 B1 **Corse, Cap c.** *Corse* France
108 A3 **Corse-du-Sud div.** *Corse* France
64 D2 **Corserine h.** *Scotland* U.K.
62 D3 **Corsham** *England* U.K.
Corsica i. *see* **Corse**
151 D5 **Corsicana** *Texas* U.S.A.
108 D3 **Corsico** Italy
64 E2 **Corsock** *Scotland* U.K.
Cort Adelaer, Kap headland *see* **Kangeq**
108 B2 **Corte** *Corse* France
100 D2 **Corte de Peleas** Spain
98 B2 **Cortegada** Spain
100 D3 **Cortegana** Spain
106 C4 **Cortemilia** Italy
83 F2 **Corteno Golgi** Italy
106 D3 **Corteolona** Italy
102 C4 **Cortes de Aragón** Spain
101 H3 **Cortes de Baza** Spain
155 H3 **Cortez** *Colorado* U.S.A.
154 D1 **Cortez Mts mts** *Nevada* U.S.A.
102 D3 **Cortiella r.** Spain
101 F1 **Cortijo de Arriba** Spain
101 H2 **Cortijos Nuevos** Spain
107 G2 **Cortina d'Ampezzo** Italy
147 E3 **Cortland** *New York* U.S.A.
107 F3 **Corto, Lago del l.** Italy
63 H2 **Corton** *England* U.K.
107 F5 **Cortona** Italy
100 B2 **Coruche** Portugal
42 E1 **Çoruh r.** Turkey
42 C1 **Çorum** Turkey
168 D2 **Corumbá r.** Brazil
165 E3 **Corumbá** Brazil
168 D1 **Corumbá de Goiás** Brazil
168 D3 **Corumbaíba** Brazil
168 C6 **Corumbataí r.** Brazil
169 J2 **Corumbaú, Pta pt** Brazil
112 E1 **Corund** Romania
166 E3 **Coruripe** Brazil
152 B2 **Corvallis** *Oregon* U.S.A.
107 F2 **Corvara in Badia** Italy
62 D2 **Corve Dale v.** *England* U.K.
103 B7 **Corvera** Spain
100 □ **Corvo i.** *Azores* Portugal
62 C2 **Corwen** *Wales* U.K.
102 B4 **Cosa** Spain
156 D3 **Cosalá** Mexico
164 C3 **Cosapa** Bolivia
164 C3 **Coscaya** Chile
111 E3 **Coscile r.** Italy
111 F3 **Cosenza div.** *Calabria* Italy
111 F3 **Cosenza** *Cosenza* Italy
64 E1 **Coshieville** *Scotland* U.K.
146 C4 **Coshocton** *Ohio* U.S.A.
99 G4 **Coslada** Spain
168 E5 **Cosmópolis** Brazil
92 E1 **Cosne-Cours-sur-Loire** France
92 E2 **Cosne-d'Allier** France
172 E1 **Cosquín** Argentina
106 C3 **Cossato** Italy
89 E4 **Cossé-le-Vivien** France
89 G4 **Cosson r.** France
82 B2 **Cossonay** Switzerland
100 A2 **Costa Bela coastal area** Portugal
103 C6 **Costa Blanca coastal area** Spain
103 G3 **Costa Brava coastal area** France/Spain
100 B2 **Costa da Galé coastal area** Portugal
102 D4 **Costa de Fora coastal area** Spain
100 C3 **Costa de la Luz reg.** Spain
103 C5 **Costa del Azahar coastal area** Spain
101 F4 **Costa del Sol coastal area** Spain
156 K6 **Costa de Mosquitos reg.** Nicaragua
102 F3 **Costa Dorada coastal area** Spain
173 G2 **Costa Grande** Argentina
164 D2 **Costa Marques** Brazil
165 E2 **Costa Pinheiro, Cap r.** Brazil
133 K8 **Costa Rica country** Central America
168 B3 **Costa Rica** Brazil
156 D3 **Costa Rica** Mexico
108 A5 **Costa Verde coastal area** *Sardegna* Italy
99 F1 **Costa Verde reg.** Spain
79 L6 **Coşteiu** Romania
53 B3 **Costești** Moldova
112 F1 **Costești** Romania
147 J2 **Costigan** *Maine* U.S.A.
106 C2 **Costigliole d'Asti** Italy
73 H4 **Coswig** *Sachsen-Anhalt* Germany
73 J4 **Coswig** *Sachsen* Germany
23 C5 **Cotabato** Philippines
164 C4 **Cotagaita** Bolivia
164 B3 **Cotahuasi** Peru
169 H3 **Cotaxé r.** Brazil
86 C4 **Côte Champenoise reg.** France
93 A5 **Côte d'Argent reg.** France
91 F5 **Côte d'Azur reg.** France
86 D4 **Côte des Bars reg.** France
117 D5 **Côte d'Ivoire country** Africa
90 C1 **Côte-d'Or div.** France
90 C2 **Côte d'Or reg.** France
166 D3 **Cotegipe** Brazil
136 C3 **Cote, Mt mt.** *Alaska* U.S.A.
88 D2 **Cotentin reg.** France
88 C5 **Côtes-d'Armor div.** France
87 E3 **Côtes de Meuse ridge** France
87 E4 **Côtes de Moselle reg.** France
112 E2 **Coteşti** Romania
68 D2 **Cothen** Netherlands
62 B3 **Cothi r.** *Wales* U.K.
102 D2 **Cotiella mt.** Spain
91 E5 **Cotignac** France
163 E3 **Cotingo r.** Brazil
53 C3 **Cotiujeni** Moldova
53 C3 **Cotiujenii Mici** Moldova
112 F1 **Cotnari** Romania
123 E5 **Cotonou** Benin
127 □3 **Coton, Pt pt** *Rodrigues I.* Mauritius
162 B4 **Cotopaxi, Vol. volcano** Ecuador
111 F3 **Cotronei** Italy
62 D3 **Cotswold Hills h.** *England* U.K.
152 B3 **Cottage Grove** *Oregon* U.S.A.
109 E2 **Cottanello** Italy
73 K4 **Cottbus** Germany
38 B3 **Cotteliar r.** India
63 G2 **Cottenham** *England* U.K.
179 □ **Cotter, C. c.** *Kerguelen* Indian Ocean
63 F2 **Cottesmore** *England* U.K.
163 G3 **Cottica** Surinam
155 H5 **Cotton City** *New Mexico* U.S.A.
155 F4 **Cottonwood** *Arizona* U.S.A.
155 G4 **Cottonwood Wash r.** *Arizona* U.S.A.
159 E3 **Cotuí** Dominican Rep.
151 D6 **Cotulla** *Texas* U.S.A.
91 B3 **Coubon** France
92 A3 **Coubre, Pte de la pt** France
90 C2 **Couches** France
91 B4 **Coucouron** France
86 C3 **Coucy-le-Château-Auffrique** France
86 B1 **Coudekerque-Branche** France
146 D4 **Coudersport** *Pennsylvania* U.S.A.
12 D4 **Couëdic, C. de c.** *S. Australia* Australia
88 D4 **Couëron** France
88 D3 **Couesnon r.** France
92 C2 **Couhé** France
93 E6 **Couiza** France
89 F3 **Coulaines** France
90 B1 **Coulanges-la-Vineuse** France
90 B1 **Coulanges-sur-Yonne** France
92 E2 **Couleuvre** France
89 H4 **Coullons** France
179 B1 **Coulman I. i.** Antarctica
90 C1 **Coulmier-le-Sec** France
86 A2 **Coulogne** France
121 F3 **Couloir 1 well** Algeria
92 C2 **Coulombiers** France
86 C4 **Coulommiers** France
91 D5 **Coulon r.** France
141 G3 **Coulonge r.** *Québec* Canada
92 B2 **Coulonges-sur-l'Autize** France
92 C3 **Couloumieix-Chamiers** France
64 B2 **Coul Point pt** *Scotland* U.K.
64 D1 **Coulport** *Scotland* U.K.
154 B3 **Coulterville** *California* U.S.A.
152 C2 **Council** *Idaho* U.S.A.
150 E3 **Council Bluffs** *Iowa* U.S.A.
66 E4 **Coupar Angus** *Scotland* U.K.
89 E3 **Couptrain** France
137 G2 **Courageous Lake l.** *N.W.T.* Canada
163 F3 **Courantyne r.** Guyana
179 □ **Courbet, Péninsule pen.** *Kerguelen* Indian Ocean
82 B1 **Courchaton** France
91 E3 **Courchevel** France
89 G4 **Cour-Cheverny** France
82 B2 **Courçon** France
86 D3 **Courcy** France
82 C1 **Courgenay** Switzerland
54 B4 **Courland Lagoon lag.** Lithuania/Rus. Fed.
92 B2 **Courlay** France
82 B3 **Courmayeur** Italy
90 B3 **Cournon-d'Auvergne** France
90 B3 **Courpière** France
8 □2 **Courrejolles Pt pt** *Campbell I.* New Zealand
82 C1 **Courrendlin** Switzerland
69 A4 **Courrières** France
85 B5 **Coursan** France
91 F5 **Coursegoules** France
89 E2 **Courseulles-sur-Mer** France
90 B1 **Courson-les-Carrières** France
82 C1 **Court** Switzerland
82 C1 **Courtelary** Switzerland
136 E5 **Courtenay** *B.C.* Canada
86 C4 **Courtenay** France
91 C4 **Courthézon** France
67 C5 **Courtmacsherry** Rep. of Ireland
89 F3 **Courtomer** France
67 E4 **Courtown** Rep. of Ireland
Courtrai *see* **Kortrijk**
69 C4 **Court-St-Etienne** Belgium
89 G3 **Courville-sur-Eure** France
82 A2 **Cousance** France
93 C6 **Couserans reg.** France
151 E5 **Coushatta** *Louisiana* U.S.A.
90 C1 **Cousin r.** France
127 □1 **Cousin Is is** Seychelles
86 D5 **Coussegrey** France
87 E4 **Coussey** France
125 B5 **Coutada do Ambriz res.** Angola
125 D7 **Coutada Pública do Longa-Mavinga res.** Angola
125 D7 **Coutada Pública do Luengué res.** Angola
125 D7 **Coutada Pública do Luiana res.** Angola
125 D7 **Coutada Pública do Mucusso res.** Angola
88 D2 **Coutances** France
89 E3 **Couterne** France
169 G3 **Couto de Magalhães de Minas** Brazil
166 C2 **Couto Magalhães** Brazil
92 B3 **Coutras** France
92 B3 **Couture r.** France
138 E2 **Couture, Lac l.** *Québec* Canada
159 □3 **Couva** Trinidad and Tobago
82 B2 **Couvet** Switzerland
69 C4 **Couvin** Belgium
93 C4 **Couze r.** France
92 D3 **Couzeix** France
99 H3 **Covaleda** Spain
99 G2 **Covarrubias** Spain
112 F2 **Covasna** Romania
123 E5 **Covè** Benin
155 F2 **Cove Fort** *Utah* U.S.A.
140 E4 **Cove I. i.** *Ontario* Canada
173 H4 **Covello** Argentina
146 E5 **Cove Mts h.** *Pennsylvania* U.S.A.
63 E2 **Coventry** *England* U.K.
147 E5 **Cove Point** *Maryland* U.S.A.
65 G3 **Cover r.** *England* U.K.
98 C4 **Covilhã** Portugal
145 D5 **Covington** *Georgia* U.S.A.
148 D5 **Covington** *Indiana* U.S.A.
146 A5 **Covington** *Kentucky* U.S.A.
145 B5 **Covington** *Tennessee* U.S.A.
146 D6 **Covington** *Virginia* U.S.A.
140 D3 **Cow r.** *Ontario* Canada
13 F3 **Cowal, L. l.** *New South Wales* Australia
17 C6 **Cowan, L. salt flat** *Western Australia* Australia
141 J4 **Cowansville** *Québec* Canada
32 B1 **Cowargarze** China
62 C3 **Cowbridge** *Wales* U.K.
17 B6 **Cowcowing Lakes salt flat** *Western Australia* Australia
66 E4 **Cowdenbeath** *Scotland* U.K.
12 D3 **Cowell** *S. Australia* Australia
63 E4 **Cowes** *England* U.K.
13 F4 **Cowes** *Victoria* Australia
64 F4 **Cowfold** *England* U.K.
65 F3 **Cow Green Res. resr** *England* U.K.
15 F5 **Cowley** *Queensland* Australia
146 D5 **Cowpasture r.** *Virginia* U.S.A.
13 G3 **Cowra** *New South Wales* Australia
93 D5 **Cox** France
166 D3 **Coxá r.** Brazil
173 K1 **Coxilha de Santana h.** Brazil/Uruguay
167 A7 **Coxilha de Santana** Brazil
167 B6 **Coxilha Gde** Brazil
168 A3 **Coxim r.** Brazil
168 A3 **Coxim** Brazil
14 C2 **Cox R. r.** *Northern Terr.* Australia
147 G3 **Coxsackie** *New York* U.S.A.
37 G5 **Cox's Bazar** Bangladesh
65 G3 **Coxwold** *England* U.K.
122 B5 **Coyah** Guinea
171 C7 **Coy Aike** Argentina
154 D4 **Coyote Lake l.** *California* U.S.A.
155 E5 **Coyote Peak summit** *Arizona* U.S.A.
154 C3 **Coyote Peak summit** *California* U.S.A.
156 C3 **Coyote, Pta pt** Mexico
156 D4 **Coyotitán** Mexico
155 F5 **Coyuca de Benitez** Mexico
92 B3 **Cozes** France
37 F2 **Cozhê** China
153 D6 **Cozón, Co mt.** Mexico
157 J4 **Cozumel** Mexico
157 J4 **Cozumel, I. de i.** Mexico
108 B3 **Cozzano** *Corse* France
111 F3 **Cozzo del Pellegrino mt.** Italy
67 E4 **Craanford** Rep. of Ireland
15 E1 **Crab I. i.** *Queensland* Australia
127 □3 **Crab I. i.** *Rodrigues I.* Mauritius
13 G3 **Craboon** *New South Wales* Australia
88 B4 **Crach** France
15 G5 **Cracow** *Queensland* Australia
13 F5 **Cradle Mountain Lake St Clair Nat. Park nat. park** *Tasmania* Australia
12 D2 **Cradock** *S. Australia* Australia
131 E6 **Cradock** South Africa
8 E2 **Cradock Channel chan.** New Zealand
83 F3 **Craffaro r.** Italy
130 E3 **Crafthole** South Africa
136 C3 **Craig** *Alaska* U.S.A.
152 F3 **Craig** *Colorado* U.S.A.
66 C3 **Craig** *Scotland* U.K.
67 E2 **Craigavon** *Northern Ireland* U.K.
66 E3 **Craigellachie** *Scotland* U.K.
62 C2 **Craig Goch Res. resr** *Wales* U.K.
13 F4 **Craigieburn** *Victoria* Australia
66 C4 **Craignure** *Scotland* U.K.
146 D5 **Craigsville** *Virginia* U.S.A.
66 F4 **Crail** *Scotland* U.K.
74 F3 **Crailsheim** Germany
112 D2 **Craiova** Romania
65 G2 **Cramlington** *England* U.K.
130 C3 **Cramond** South Africa
64 A2 **Crana r.** Rep. of Ireland
147 F2 **Cranberry L. l.** *New York* U.S.A.
147 F2 **Cranberry Lake** *New York* U.S.A.
62 D4 **Cranborne Chase forest** *England* U.K.
13 F4 **Cranbourne** *Victoria* Australia
136 F5 **Cranbrook** *B.C.* Canada
17 B7 **Cranbrook** *Western Australia* Australia
148 C3 **Crandon** *Wisconsin* U.S.A.
152 C3 **Crane** *Oregon* U.S.A.
151 C6 **Crane** *Texas* U.S.A.
148 A1 **Crane Lake** *Minnesota* U.S.A.
159 □9 **Crane, The** *Barbados* Caribbean
64 B3 **Cranfield Point pt** *Northern Ireland* U.K.
90 E3 **Cran-Gevrier** France
63 F3 **Cranleigh** *England* U.K.
82 C2 **Crans-sur-Sierre** Switzerland
147 H4 **Cranston** *Rhode Island* U.S.A.
89 E4 **Craon** France
86 C3 **Craonne** France
91 B3 **Craponne-sur-Arzon** France
179 B4 **Crary Ice Rise ice feature** Antarctica
179 A4 **Crary Mts mts** Antarctica
79 M4 **Crasna r.** Romania
53 C3 **Crasnoe** Moldova
152 B3 **Crater L. l.** *Oregon* U.S.A.
152 B3 **Crater Lake Nat. Pk** *Oregon* U.S.A.
152 D3 **Craters of the Moon Nat. Mon. nat. park** *Idaho* U.S.A.
166 D2 **Crateús** Brazil
111 F3 **Crati r.** Italy
166 E2 **Crato** Brazil
100 C1 **Crato** Portugal
91 C5 **Crau reg.** France
90 B1 **Cravant** France
165 E2 **Cravari r.** Brazil
62 D2 **Craven Arms** *England* U.K.
168 E4 **Cravinhos** Brazil
162 C2 **Cravo Norte** Colombia
150 C3 **Crawford** *Nebraska* U.S.A.
64 E2 **Crawfordjohn** *Scotland* U.K.
148 D5 **Crawfordsville** *Indiana* U.S.A.
145 C6 **Crawfordville** *Florida* U.S.A.
63 F3 **Crawley** *England* U.K.
145 □1 **Crawl, The pt** Bermuda
152 E2 **Crazy Mts mountain range** *Montana* U.S.A.
66 D4 **Creag Meagaidh mt.** *Scotland* U.K.
88 D2 **Créances** France
90 C1 **Créancey** France
137 H4 **Crean L. l.** *Saskatchewan* Canada
90 C2 **Crèches-sur-Saône** France
131 G2 **Crecy** South Africa
86 A2 **Crécy-en-Ponthieu** France
86 B4 **Crécy-la-Chapelle** France
86 C3 **Crécy-sur-Serre** France
62 D2 **Credenhill** *England* U.K.
62 C4 **Crediton** *England* U.K.
137 H3 **Cree r.** *Saskatchewan* Canada
156 D3 **Creel** Mexico
137 H3 **Cree Lake l.** *Saskatchewan* Canada
67 D1 **Creeslough** Rep. of Ireland
67 B3 **Cregganbaun** Rep. of Ireland
74 F3 **Creglingen** Germany
137 J4 **Creighton** *Saskatchewan* Canada
131 G5 **Creighton** South Africa
86 B3 **Creil** France
91 B4 **Creissels** France
106 D3 **Crema** Italy
90 D3 **Crémieu** France
73 F3 **Cremlingen** Germany
106 E3 **Cremona div.** *Lombardia* Italy
106 E3 **Cremona** *Cremona* Italy
81 H4 **Črenšovci** Slovenia
93 B4 **Créon** France
87 E4 **Crépey** France
86 C3 **Crépy** France
86 B3 **Crépy-en-Valois** France
107 J4 **Cres i.** Croatia
107 J4 **Cres** Croatia
152 A3 **Crescent City** *California* U.S.A.
27 □ **Crescent I. i.** Hong Kong
106 C3 **Crescentino** Italy
155 H2 **Crescent Junction** *Utah* U.S.A.
154 B1 **Crescent Mills** *California* U.S.A.
155 E4 **Crescent Peak summit** *Nevada* U.S.A.
148 A4 **Cresco** *Iowa* U.S.A.
173 G2 **Crespo** Argentina
99 F4 **Crespos** Spain
92 D3 **Cressensac** France
82 C1 **Cressier** Switzerland
14 C3 **Cresswell watercourse** *Northern Terr.* Australia
91 D4 **Crest** France
136 F5 **Creston** *B.C.* Canada
150 E3 **Creston** *Iowa* U.S.A.
152 F3 **Creston** *Wyoming* U.S.A.
145 C6 **Crestview** *Florida* U.S.A.
151 G6 **Crestview** *Florida* U.S.A.
90 E3 **Crest-Voland** France
147 F5 **Crestwood Village** *New Jersey* U.S.A.
63 E1 **Creswell** *England* U.K.
13 E4 **Creswick** *Victoria* Australia
80 D4 **Creta Forata, Mte mt.** Italy
90 D2 **Crêt de la Neige mt.** France
90 D3 **Crêt de Pont mt.** France
90 D2 **Crêt du Nu mt.** France
Crete i. *see* **Kriti**
86 B4 **Créteil** France
90 E1 **Crêt Monniot mt.** France
102 D4 **Creu de Santos, La mt.** Spain
89 E2 **Creully** France
102 G2 **Creus, Cap de pt** Spain
92 E2 **Creuse div.** *Limousin* France
92 C2 **Creuse r.** France
75 G3 **Creußen** Germany
87 F3 **Creutzwald** France
72 F4 **Creuzburg** Germany
107 F4 **Crevalcore** Italy
86 B3 **Crèvecœur-le-Grand** France
103 C6 **Crevillente** Spain
103 C6 **Crevillente, Sa de mountain range** Spain
106 C2 **Crevoladossola** Italy
62 D1 **Crewe** *England* U.K.
146 D6 **Crewe** *Virginia* U.S.A.
62 D4 **Crewkerne** *England* U.K.
66 D4 **Crianlarich** *Scotland* U.K.
62 B2 **Criccieth** *Wales* U.K.
167 C6 **Criciúma** Brazil
62 C3 **Crickhowell** *Wales* U.K.
53 C3 **Cricova** Moldova
66 E4 **Crieff** *Scotland* U.K.
89 G1 **Criel-sur-Mer** France
66 E6 **Criffell h.** *Scotland* U.K.
107 J3 **Crikvenica** Croatia
51 E6 **Crimea pen.** Ukraine
75 H2 **Crimmitschau** Germany
66 G3 **Crimond** *Scotland* U.K.
64 C1 **Crinan** *Scotland* U.K.
89 F2 **Criquetot-l'Esneval** France
112 G2 **Crişan** Romania
147 F6 **Crisfield** *Maryland* U.S.A.
106 B4 **Crissolo** Italy
166 C3 **Cristalândia** Brazil
168 E2 **Cristalina** Brazil
163 F5 **Cristalino r.** Brazil
Cristalino r. *see* **Mariembero**
80 D4 **Cristallo mt.** Italy
124 B3 **Cristal, Monts de mountain range** Equatorial Guinea/Gabon
168 D2 **Cristianópolis** Brazil
159 E3 **Cristi, Monte** Dominican Rep.
166 D2 **Cristino Castro** Brazil
156 L7 **Cristóbal** Panama
162 C1 **Cristóbal Cólon, P. mt.** Colombia
162 □ **Cristóbal, Pta pt** *Galapagos Is* Ecuador
106 C4 **Cristoforo Colombo airport** Italy
112 E1 **Cristuru Secuiesc** Romania
53 C3 **Criuleni** Moldova
73 G2 **Crivitz** Germany
166 C3 **Crixás r.** Brazil
166 C3 **Crixás** Brazil
166 C3 **Crixás Açu r.** Brazil
166 B3 **Crixás Mirim r.** Brazil
114 C1 **Crna r.** Macedonia
81 F4 **Črna** Slovenia
112 B3 **Crna Gora div.** Yugoslavia
112 C3 **Crna Gora mts** Macedonia/Yugoslavia
112 D3 **Crna Trava** Yugoslavia
112 D2 **Crni Vrh mt.** Yugoslavia
104 E3 **Črnomelj** Slovenia
67 B3 **Croagh Patrick h.** Rep. of Ireland
13 G4 **Croajingolong Nat. Park nat. park** *Victoria* Australia
48 G4 **Croatia country** Europe
107 F2 **Croce, Monte mt.** Italy
64 E2 **Crocketford** *Scotland* U.K.
151 E6 **Crockett** *Texas* U.S.A.
131 F2 **Crocodile r.** South Africa
92 E3 **Crocq** France
107 G2 **Croda dei Toni mt.** Italy
107 G2 **Croda Rossa mt.** Italy
106 C2 **Crodo** Italy
147 F3 **Croghan** *New York* U.S.A.
91 D5 **Croisette, Cap c.** France
88 C4 **Croisic, Pte de pt** France
86 B2 **Croisilles** France
14 C1 **Croker I. i.** *Northern Terr.* Australia
91 D3 **Crolles** France
66 D3 **Cromarty** *Scotland* U.K.
66 D3 **Cromarty Firth est.** *Scotland* U.K.
66 E3 **Cromdale, Hills of h.** *Scotland* U.K.
63 H2 **Cromer** *England* U.K.
9 B6 **Cromwell** New Zealand
9 C5 **Cronadun** New Zealand
64 A3 **Cronamuck Mtn h.** Rep. of Ireland
91 B3 **Cronce r.** France
65 G3 **Crook** *England* U.K.
146 D4 **Crooked Creek Reservoir resr** *Pennsylvania* U.S.A.
27 □ **Crooked I. i.** Hong Kong
158 D2 **Crooked I. i.** The Bahamas
158 D2 **Crooked I. Passage chan.** The Bahamas
148 B1 **Crooked Lake l.** Canada/U.S.A.
65 F2 **Crookham** *England* U.K.
67 B5 **Crookhaven** Rep. of Ireland
150 D2 **Crookston** *Minnesota* U.S.A.
13 G3 **Crookwell** *New South Wales* Australia
67 C4 **Croom** Rep. of Ireland
111 F3 **Cropalati** Italy
111 F4 **Cropani** Italy
13 G2 **Croppa Cr.** *New South Wales* Australia
15 E2 **Crosbie r.** *Queensland* Australia
65 E4 **Crosby** *England* U.K.
137 J5 **Crosby** *N. Dakota* U.S.A.
123 F5 **Cross r.** Nigeria
64 A4 **Crossakeel** Rep. of Ireland
137 L2 **Cross Bay b.** *N.W.T.* Canada
65 E3 **Crosscanonby** *England* U.K.
145 D6 **Cross City** *Florida* U.S.A.
147 K1 **Cross Creek** *New Brunswick* Canada
151 E5 **Crossett** *Arkansas* U.S.A.
65 F3 **Cross Fell h.** *England* U.K.
67 F2 **Crossgar** *Northern Ireland* U.K.
62 C2 **Crossgates** *Wales* U.K.
64 D2 **Crosshands** *Scotland* U.K.
67 C5 **Crosshaven** Rep. of Ireland
62 B2 **Cross Inn** *Wales* U.K.
137 K4 **Cross Lake l.** *Manitoba* Canada
146 E3 **Cross Lake l.** *New York* U.S.A.
137 K4 **Cross Lake** *Manitoba* Canada
9 D5 **Crossley, Mt mt.** New Zealand
67 E2 **Crossmaglen** *Northern Ireland* U.K.
155 E4 **Crossman Peak summit** *Arizona* U.S.A.
123 F5 **Cross River div.** Nigeria
136 B3 **Cross Sound chan.** *Alaska* U.S.A.
134 E4 **Cross Sound** *Alaska* U.S.A.
148 E3 **Cross Village** *Michigan* U.S.A.
145 C5 **Crossville** *Tennessee* U.S.A.
149 F4 **Croswell** *Michigan* U.S.A.
111 G3 **Crotone** Italy
91 E4 **Crots** France
75 H2 **Crottendorf** Germany
173 G4 **Crotto** Argentina
63 G3 **Crouch r.** *England* U.K.
86 C3 **Crouy** France
86 C3 **Crouy-sur-Ourcq** France
13 F2 **Crowal watercourse** *New South Wales* Australia
63 G3 **Crowborough** *England* U.K.
13 F2 **Crowl watercourse** *New South Wales* Australia
63 F2 **Crowland** *England* U.K.
65 H4 **Crowle** *England* U.K.
151 E6 **Crowley** *Louisiana* U.S.A.
154 C3 **Crowley, Lake l.** *California* U.S.A.
148 D5 **Crown Point** *Indiana* U.S.A.
147 G3 **Crown Point** *New York* U.S.A.

24 D2 Đao Cai Bâu i. Vietnam
24 D2 Đao Cat Ba i. Vietnam
32 C2 Daocheng China
25 C5 Đao Phu Quôc i. Vietnam
30 B5 Daotanghe China
25 C5 Đao Thô Chư i. Vietnam
120 C5 Daoudi well Mauritania
122 D5 Daoukro Côte d'Ivoire
25 C5 Đao Vây i. Vietnam
33 E3 Dao Xian China
32 D2 Daozhen China
23 C4 Dapa Philippines
123 E4 Dapaong Togo
37 H4 Daphabum mt. India
43 B4 Daphnae Egypt
23 B4 Dapiak, Mt mt. Philippines
23 B4 Dapitan Philippines
26 G4 Da Qaidam China
31 H3 Daqing China
39 C2 Daqq-e Dombūn Iran
30 D4 Daquing Shan mountain range China
42 F3 Dāqūq Iraq
33 H2 Daqu Shan i. China
122 A3 Dara Senegal
42 D3 Dar'ā Syria
43 D3 Dar'a Syria
39 C3 Dārāb Iran
36 B3 Daraban Pakistan
112 F1 Darabani Romania
54 F5 Darahanava Belarus
118 B1 Daraj Libya
39 C3 Dārākūyeh Iran
41 H3 Dārān Iran
79 G6 Darány Hungary
47 H3 Darat Kazakhstan
112 C3 Daravica mt. Yugoslavia
119 F3 Daraw Egypt
123 G4 Darazo Nigeria
39 D3 Darband Iran
36 B1 Darband Pakistan
54 B3 Darbėnai Lithuania
96 D5 Dar Ben Karricha el Behri Morocco
37 F4 Darbhanga India
32 B1 Darcang China
96 D5 Dar Chaoui Morocco
104 G3 Darda Croatia
154 C2 Dardanelle California U.S.A.
151 E5 Dardanelle, Lake l. Arkansas U.S.A.
Dardanelles str. see Çanakkale Boğazı
73 F4 Dardesheim Germany
Dardo see Kangding
42 D2 Darende Turkey
127 C6 Dar es Salaam Tanzania
9 D5 Darfield New Zealand
106 E3 Darfo Boario Terme Italy
118 D4 Darfur div. Sudan
36 B2 Dargai Pakistan
46 F4 Dargan-Ata Turkmenistan
8 D1 Dargaville New Zealand
13 F4 Dargo Victoria Australia
123 E4 Dargol Niger
73 H2 Dargun Germany
30 C2 Darhan Mongolia
30 D4 Darhan Muminggan Lianheqi China
145 D6 Darien Georgia U.S.A.
162 B2 Darién, Golfo del g. Colombia
156 L8 Darién, Parque Nacional de nat. park Panama
47 H3 Dar'inskiy Kazakhstan
156 J6 Darío Nicaragua
37 G4 Dārjiling India
17 B7 Darkan Western Australia Australia
32 B1 Darlag China
13 E3 Darling r. New South Wales Australia
130 B6 Darling South Africa
15 G5 Darling Downs reg. Queensland Australia
17 B7 Darling Range h. Western Australia Australia
65 G3 Darlington England U.K.
148 B4 Darlington Wisconsin U.S.A.
13 F3 Darlington Point New South Wales Australia
17 C5 Darlot, L. salt flat Western Australia Australia
76 E1 Darłowo Poland
112 F1 Dărmănești Romania
36 E3 Darma Pass pass China/India
38 B2 Darmaraopet India
39 D3 Dar Mazār Iran
74 D2 Darmstadt div. Hessen Germany
74 D3 Darmstadt Darmstadt Germany
38 A2 Darna r. India
118 D1 Darnah Libya
131 H4 Darnall South Africa
89 G2 Darnétal France
87 F4 Darney France
13 E3 Darnick New South Wales Australia
134 F3 Darnley Bay b. N.W.T. Canada
179 D5 Darnley, C. c. Antarctica
102 B3 Daroca Spain
47 H5 Daroot-Korgan Kyrgyzstan
50 G3 Darovka Rus. Fed.
50 H3 Darovskoy Rus. Fed.
98 B3 Darque Portugal
15 E4 Darr watercourse Queensland Australia
173 F4 Darregueira Argentina
39 D2 Darreh Bīd Iran
39 D1 Darreh Gaz Iran
39 G2 Darri-i-Shikar r. Afghanistan
126 □ Darsa i. Socotra Yemen
38 B3 Darsi India
73 H1 Darß pen. Germany
73 H1 Darßer Ort c. Germany
62 C4 Dart r. England U.K.
63 G3 Dartford England U.K.
62 C4 Dartmeet England U.K.
62 B4 Dartmoor reg. England U.K.
12 E4 Dartmoor Victoria Australia
62 C4 Dartmoor National Park England U.K.
62 C4 Dartmouth England U.K.
139 H5 Dartmouth Nova Scotia Canada
15 F5 Dartmouth, L. salt flat Queensland Australia
65 G4 Darton England U.K.
67 C2 Darty Mts h. Rep. of Ireland
119 F4 Daru waterhole Sudan
6 □1 Daru P.N.G.
122 B5 Daru Sierra Leone
37 G3 Darum Tso l. China
104 F3 Daruvar Croatia
46 E4 Darvaza Turkmenistan
39 B3 Darvīsla Iran
39 F3 Darwazgai Afghanistan
65 F4 Darwen England U.K.
39 F3 Darweshan Afghanistan
14 B2 Darwin Northern Terr. Australia
172 E5 Darwin Argentina
171 E7 Darwin Falkland Is.
171 C7 Darwin, Mte mt. Chile
162 □ Darwin, Vol. volcano Galapagos Is Ecuador
39 C3 Daryacheh-ye Bakhtegan salt lake Iran
39 C3 Daryācheh-ye Mahārlū salt lake Iran
39 B2 Daryācheh-ye Namak salt flat Iran
42 F2 Daryācheh-ye Orūmīyeh salt lake Iran
39 E3 Daryacheh-ye Sīstan marsh Afghanistan
39 C3 Daryacheh-ye Tashk salt lake Iran
39 D3 Dārzīn Iran
39 C4 Dās i. U.A.E.
77 N6 Dashava Ukraine
30 E2 Dashbalbar Mongolia
33 E2 Dashennongjia mt. China
53 C2 Dashiv Ukraine
31 G3 Dashizhai China
Dashkesan see Daşkäsän
46 E4 Dashkhovuz div. Turkmenistan
46 E4 Dashkhovuz Turkmenistan
39 E4 Dasht r. Pakistan
39 D1 Dasht Iran
39 D3 Dasht Āb Iran
39 D3 Dasht-e-Daqq-e-Tundi depression Afghanistan
39 C2 Dasht-e-Kavir salt flat Iran
39 D2 Dasht-e-Lut desert Iran
39 E2 Dasht-e-Naomid plain Afghanistan/Iran
39 B3 Dasht-e Palang r. Iran
39 F3 Dasht-i-Arbu Lut desert Afghanistan
39 E4 Dashtiari Iran
39 E3 Dasht-i-Margo desert Afghanistan
30 C5 Dashuikeng China
30 C5 Dashuitou China
80 C2 Dasing Germany
36 C2 Daska Pakistan
42 F1 Daşkäsän Azerbaijan
130 D6 Daskop South Africa
36 C1 Daspar mt. Pakistan
123 E5 Dassa Benin
72 E4 Dassel Germany
130 B6 Dassen Island i. South Africa
73 F2 Dassow Germany
39 D2 Dastgardān Iran
31 J4 Da Suife r. China
36 C3 Dasuya India
131 G3 Dasville South Africa
77 H3 Daszyna Poland
22 C1 Datadian Indonesia
42 A2 Datça Turkey
28 H2 Date Japan
155 F5 Dateland Arizona U.S.A.
36 D4 Datia India
33 G3 Datian China
30 A5 Datong r. China
30 B5 Datong China
30 E4 Datong China
31 H3 Datong China
30 A5 Datong Shan mountain range China
72 C4 Datteln Germany
22 B1 Datu i. Indonesia
22 A2 Datuk, Tg pt Indonesia
23 C5 Datu Piang Philippines
22 B1 Datu, Tg c. Indonesia/Malaysia
36 B2 Daud Khel Pakistan
37 F4 Daudnagar India
50 C3 Dauga r. Latvia
77 N1 Daugai Lithuania
54 D4 Daugailiai Lithuania
54 D3 Daugava r. Europe
54 E4 Daugavpils Latvia
39 F1 Daulatabad Afghanistan
Daulatabad see Malāyer
89 E4 Daumeray France
74 B2 Daun Germany
38 A2 Daund India
25 B4 Daung Kyun i. Myanmar
24 A2 Daungyu r. Myanmar
137 J4 Dauphin Manitoba Canada
91 D3 Dauphiné reg. France
151 F6 Dauphin I. i. Alabama U.S.A.
137 K4 Dauphin L. l. Manitoba Canada
123 F4 Daura Nigeria
17 A5 Daurie Cr. r. Western Australia Australia
31 F2 Dauriya Rus. Fed.
30 D2 Daurskiy Khrebet mountain range Rus. Fed.
36 D4 Dausa India
87 H2 Dautphetal-Friedensdorf Germany
66 E3 Dava Scotland U.K.
42 G1 Däväçi Azerbaijan
38 A3 Davangere India
23 C5 Davao Philippines
23 C5 Davao Gulf b. Philippines
39 E4 Dāvar Panāh Iran
39 D1 Dāvarzan Iran
131 G3 Davel South Africa
154 A3 Davenport California U.S.A.
148 B5 Davenport Iowa U.S.A.
15 E5 Davenport Downs Queensland Australia
14 B4 Davenport, Mt h. Northern Terr. Australia
14 C4 Davenport Ra. h. Northern Terr. Australia
63 E2 Daventry England U.K.
131 G3 Daveyton South Africa
156 K7 David Panama
137 H4 Davidson Saskatchewan Canada
12 B1 Davies, Mt mt. S. Australia Australia
137 J3 Davin Lake l. Saskatchewan Canada
168 E3 Davinópolis Brazil
179 D5 Davis Australia Base Antarctica
154 B2 Davis California U.S.A.
155 E4 Davis Dam Arizona U.S.A.
139 H2 Davis Inlet Newfoundland Canada
179 D5 Davis Sea sea Antarctica
135 N3 Davis Strait str. Canada/Greenland
46 D2 Davlekanovo Rus. Fed.
114 D4 Davlia Greece
83 E2 Davos Graubünden Switzerland
77 N6 Davydiv Ukraine
53 E3 Davydiv Brid Ukraine
52 D1 Davydovo Rus. Fed.
30 A4 Dawan China
126 D4 Dawa Wenz r. Ethiopia
37 F3 Dawaxung China
32 C2 Dawe China
Dawei see Tavoy
39 B4 Dawḩat Salwah b. Qatar/Saudi Arabia
126 D2 Dawi well Ethiopia
62 C4 Dawlish England U.K.
53 C1 Dawlyady Belarus
24 B3 Dawna Range mountain range Myanmar/Thailand
41 H6 Dawqah Oman
119 H4 Dawqah Saudi Arabia
126 D2 Ḑawrān Yemen
67 C2 Dawros Head headland Rep. of Ireland
15 G5 Dawson r. Queensland Australia
145 C6 Dawson Georgia U.S.A.
150 D2 Dawson N. Dakota U.S.A.
134 E3 Dawson Yukon Terr. Canada
137 J4 Dawson Bay b. Manitoba Canada
136 E3 Dawson Creek B.C. Canada
137 L2 Dawson Inlet inlet N.W.T. Canada
136 B2 Dawson Range mountain range N.W.T. Canada
32 C2 Dawu China
33 F2 Dawu China
Dawukou see Shizuishan
93 A5 Dax France
32 D2 Daxian China
32 D4 Daxin China
31 F5 Daxing China
32 C2 Daxue Shan mountain range China
37 H4 Dayang r. India
31 H2 Dayangshu China
47 L3 Dayan Nuur l. Mongolia
32 C3 Dayao China
33 E4 Dayao Shan mountain range China
33 F2 Daye China
32 C2 Dayi China
154 D3 Daylight Pass pass Nevada U.S.A.
173 J1 Daymán r. Uruguay
173 J1 Daymán Uruguay
173 J1 Dayman, Cuch. del h. Uruguay
33 E2 Dayong China
43 D2 Dayr 'Aṭīyah Syria
42 E3 Dayr az Zawr Syria
146 A5 Dayton Ohio U.S.A.
145 C5 Dayton Tennessee U.S.A.
152 C2 Dayton Washington U.S.A.
145 D6 Daytona Beach Florida U.S.A.
33 F3 Dayu China
22 C2 Dayu Indonesia
33 F3 Dayu Ling mountain range China
33 G1 Da Yunhe r. China
152 C2 Dayville Oregon U.S.A.
28 C7 Dazaifu Japan
32 D2 Dazhu China
32 D2 Dazu China
130 D5 De Aar South Africa
148 D2 Dead r. Michigan U.S.A.
145 F7 Deadman's Cay The Bahamas
155 E4 Dead Mts mts Nevada U.S.A.
147 H2 Dead River r. Maine U.S.A.
43 C4 Dead Sea salt lake Israel/Jordan
63 H3 Deal England U.K.
131 E4 Dealesville South Africa
79 M6 Dealurile Lipovei mountain range Romania
53 C3 Dealurile Prenistrului h. Moldova
53 C3 Dealurile Tigheciului h. Moldova
136 D4 Dean r. B.C. Canada
33 F2 De'an China
62 D3 Dean, Forest of forest England U.K.
172 E1 Deán Funes Argentina
65 F1 Dean Water r. Scotland U.K.
149 F4 Dearborn Michigan U.S.A.
136 D3 Dease r. B.C. Canada
134 F3 Dease Arm b. N.W.T. Canada
136 C3 Dease Lake B.C. Canada
134 H3 Dease Strait chan. N.W.T. Canada
154 D3 Death Valley v. California U.S.A.
154 D3 Death Valley Junction California U.S.A.
154 D3 Death Valley National Monument nat. park California U.S.A.
89 F2 Deauville France
99 H1 Deba Spain
22 B1 Debak Malaysia
32 D4 Debao China
114 B1 Debar Macedonia
126 C2 Debark Ethiopia
114 B1 Debarsko Ezero l. Macedonia
137 H4 Debden Saskatchewan Canada
159 □3 Debe Trinidad and Tobago
131 G4 De Beers Pass pass South Africa
63 H2 Deben r. England U.K.
63 H2 Debenham England U.K.
155 H2 De Beque Colorado U.S.A.
77 K5 Dębica Poland
68 D2 De Bilt Netherlands
45 R3 Debin Rus. Fed.
77 K4 Dęblin Poland
147 J2 Deblois Maine U.S.A.
76 F1 Dębnica Kaszubska Poland
76 C3 Dębno Poland
122 D3 Débo, Lac l. Mali
17 B6 Deborah, L. salt flat Western Australia Australia
77 J4 Dęborzeczka Poland
77 M4 Dębowa Kłoda Poland
126 C3 Debre Birhan Ethiopia
79 L4 Debrecen Hungary
126 C2 Debre Markos Ethiopia
126 C3 Debre Sīna Ethiopia
114 C1 Debrešte Macedonia
126 C2 Debre Tabor Ethiopia
126 C2 Debre Werk' Ethiopia
126 C3 Debre Zeyit Ethiopia
76 F2 Debrzno Poland
112 C3 Dečani Yugoslavia
145 C5 Decatur Alabama U.S.A.
145 C5 Decatur Georgia U.S.A.
148 C6 Decatur Illinois U.S.A.
148 E5 Decatur Indiana U.S.A.
148 E4 Decatur Michigan U.S.A.
93 E4 Decazeville France
141 G3 Decelles, Réservoir resr Québec Canada
128 C3 Deception watercourse Botswana
128 C3 Deception Pans salt pan Botswana
32 C3 Dechang China
108 A5 Decimoputzu Sardegna Italy
78 D1 Děčín Czech Rep.
90 C3 Décines-Charpieu France
90 B2 Decize France
68 C1 De Cocksdorp Netherlands
111 F3 Decollatura Italy
148 B4 Decorah Iowa U.S.A.
63 E3 Deddington England U.K.
23 □2 Dededo Guam Pacific Ocean
73 F3 Dedeleben Germany
73 J2 Dedelow Germany
68 E2 Dedemsvaart Netherlands
126 D3 Deder Ethiopia
52 D2 Dedinovo Rus. Fed.
171 B5 Dedo, Co mt. Chile
168 E6 Dedo de Deus mt. Brazil
130 B6 De Doorns South Africa
51 H7 Dedoplis Tsqaro Georgia
122 D4 Dédougou Burkina
54 F3 Dedovichi Rus. Fed.
31 H2 Dedu China
129 E1 Dedza Malawi
129 E1 Dedza Mountain mt. Malawi
62 C1 Dee est. England/Wales U.K.
62 D2 Dee r. England/Wales U.K.
66 F3 Dee r. Scotland U.K.
64 B4 Dee r. Rep. of Ireland
36 D4 Deeg India
67 C4 Deel r. Rep. of Ireland
67 D2 Deele r. Rep. of Ireland
130 D5 Deelfontein South Africa
27 □ Deep Bay b. Hong Kong China
146 D5 Deep Creek Lake l. Maryland U.S.A.
155 F2 Deep Creek Range mts Utah U.S.A.
147 G4 Deep River Connecticut U.S.A.
141 G3 Deep River Ontario Canada
137 K1 Deep Rose Lake l. N.W.T. Canada
154 D3 Deep Springs California U.S.A.
128 □2 Deep Valley B. b. St Helena Atlantic Ocean
13 G2 Deepwater New South Wales Australia
146 B5 Deer Creek Lake l. Ohio U.S.A.
147 J2 Deer I. i. Maine U.S.A.
147 K2 Deer I. i. New Brunswick Canada
126 E4 Deeri Somalia
17 E5 Deering, Mt mt. Western Australia Australia
147 J2 Deer Isle Maine U.S.A.
138 B3 Deer L. l. Ontario Canada
139 J4 Deer Lake Newfoundland Canada
138 B3 Deer Lake Ontario Canada
69 B4 Deerlijk Belgium
152 D2 Deer Lodge Montana U.S.A.
165 D4 Defensores del Chaco, Parque Nacional nat. park Paraguay
173 H5 Defferrari Argentina
146 A4 Defiance Ohio U.S.A.
123 G2 Défirou well Niger
145 C6 De Funiak Springs Florida U.S.A.
98 D2 Degaña Spain
80 D4 Degano r. Italy
32 B2 Dêgê China
100 C2 Degebe r. Portugal
59 F4 Degeberga Sweden
126 D3 Degeh Bur Ethiopia
123 F6 Degema Nigeria
37 G3 Dêgên China
59 F2 Degerfors Sweden
75 H4 Deggendorf Germany
106 C4 Dego Italy
126 D4 Degodia reg. Ethiopia
163 G3 De Goeje Geb h. Surinam
16 C4 De Grey r. Western Australia Australia
16 B4 De Grey Western Australia Australia
52 E3 Degtyanka Rus. Fed.
69 B3 De Haan Belgium
39 C3 Dehaj Iran
39 E3 Dehak Iran
39 E4 Dehak Iran
126 D1 Dehalak Desēt i. Eritrea
Deh Barez see Rudan
39 C3 Deh Bīd Iran
39 B3 Deh-Dasht Iran
39 B3 Dehdez Iran
39 B3 Deh-e Khalīfeh Iran
103 C7 Dehesa de Campoamor Spain
39 A2 Dehgolān Iran
121 G2 Dehiba Tunisia
38 B5 Dehiwala-Mount Lavinia Sri Lanka
39 C4 Dehkūyeh Iran
39 A2 Dehlonān Iran
130 C7 De Hoop Vlei l. South Africa
36 D3 Dehra Dun India
37 F4 Dehri India
39 D3 Deh Salm Iran
39 B3 Deh Sard Iran
39 E3 Deh Shū Afghanistan
33 G3 Dehua China
31 H3 Dehui China
101 G3 Deifontes Spain
124 E2 Deim Zubeir Sudan
69 B4 Deinze Belgium
Deir-ez-Zor see Dayr az Zawr
87 H4 Deißlingen Germany
112 D1 Dej Romania
59 E2 Deje Sweden
126 C2 Dejen Ethiopia
32 E2 Dejiang China
128 D2 Deka Drum r. Zimbabwe
148 C5 De Kalb Illinois U.S.A.
151 E5 De Kalb Texas U.S.A.
147 F2 De Kalb Junction New York U.S.A.
107 H3 Dekani Slovenia
27 Q1 De-Kastri Rus. Fed.
126 C1 Dekemhare Eritrea
125 D4 Dekese Zaire
123 F5 Dekina Nigeria
124 C2 Dékoa Central African Rep.
68 C1 De Koog Netherlands
62 B4 Delabole England U.K.
173 G4 De la Garma Argentina
154 C4 Delano California U.S.A.
155 F2 Delano Peak summit Utah U.S.A.
39 E2 Delārām Afghanistan
131 E3 Delareyville South Africa
137 H4 Delaronde Lake l. Saskatchewan Canada
59 E3 Delary Sweden
148 C5 Delavan Illinois U.S.A.
148 C4 Delavan Wisconsin U.S.A.
147 F5 Delaware div. U.S.A.
147 F4 Delaware r. New York U.S.A.
146 B4 Delaware Ohio U.S.A.
147 F5 Delaware Bay b. U.S.A.
146 B4 Delaware Lake l. Ohio U.S.A.
147 F4 Delaware Water Gap National Recreational Area res. U.S.A.
72 D4 Delbrück Germany
172 E3 Del Campillo Argentina
112 D4 Delčevo Macedonia
68 E2 Delden Netherlands
13 G4 Delegate New South Wales Australia
82 C1 Delémont Switzerland
59 J1 Delet Teili b. Finland
169 E4 Delfinópolis Brazil
115 D4 Delfoi Greece
68 C2 Delft Netherlands
38 B4 Delft I. i. Sri Lanka
68 E1 Delfzijl Netherlands
127 D7 Delgado, Cabo pt Mozambique
30 A2 Delger Mörön r. Mongolia
119 F3 Delgo Sudan
153 F4 Delhi Colorado U.S.A.
147 F3 Delhi New York U.S.A.
140 E5 Delhi Ontario Canada
36 D3 Delhi India
22 A3 Deli i. Indonesia
110 B5 Delia r. Sicilia Italy
110 C5 Delia Sicilia Italy
42 C1 Delice r. Turkey
163 G3 Délices French Guiana
109 H3 Deliceto Italy
39 B2 Delījān Iran
111 □ Delimara Pt pt Malta
136 E1 Délįne N.W.T. Canada
26 G4 Delingha China
137 H4 Delisle Saskatchewan Canada
73 H4 Delitzsch Germany
80 E4 Dellach Austria
90 F1 Delle France
72 E4 Delligsen Germany
83 F3 Dello Italy
150 D3 Dell Rapids S. Dakota U.S.A.
121 E1 Dellys Algeria
154 D5 Del Mar California U.S.A.
155 E3 Delmar L. l. Nevada U.S.A.
87 F4 Delme France
72 D2 Delmenhorst Niedersachsen Germany
107 J3 Delnice Croatia
45 R2 De-Longa, O-va i. Rus. Fed.
134 B3 De Long Mts mountain range Alaska U.S.A.
137 J5 Deloraine Manitoba Canada
13 F5 Deloraine Tasmania Australia
148 D5 Delphi Indiana U.S.A.
146 A4 Delphos Ohio U.S.A.
130 E4 Delportshoop South Africa
145 D7 Delray Beach Florida U.S.A.
151 C6 Del Rio Texas U.S.A.
153 E6 Del Río Mexico
57 E3 Delsbo Sweden
123 F5 Delta div. Nigeria
155 H2 Delta Colorado U.S.A.
148 A5 Delta Iowa U.S.A.
155 F2 Delta Utah U.S.A.
173 H3 Delta del Paraná delta Argentina
173 F5 Delta del R.Colorado delta Argentina
171 D4 Delta del R. Colorado delta Argentina
15 E3 Delta Downs Queensland Australia
112 G2 Delta Dunării delta Romania
122 A4 Delta du Saloum, Parc National du nat. park Senegal
134 D3 Delta Junction Alaska U.S.A.
147 F3 Delta Reservoir resr New York U.S.A.
145 D6 Deltona Florida U.S.A.
13 G2 Delungra New South Wales Australia
68 F2 De Lutte Netherlands
173 G3 Del Valle Argentina
67 D3 Delvin Rep. of Ireland
114 B3 Delvinaki Greece
114 B3 Delvinë Albania
53 A2 Delyatyn Ukraine
46 E2 Dema r. Rus. Fed.
99 G2 Demanda, Sierra de la mountain range Spain
125 D5 Demba Zaire
54 D4 Dembava Lithuania
126 C2 Dembech'a Ethiopia
124 D2 Dembia Central African Rep.
126 B3 Dembī Dolo Ethiopia
69 C4 Demer r. Belgium
50 D4 Demidov Rus. Fed.
52 E2 Demidovo Rus. Fed.
153 F5 Deming New Mexico U.S.A.
163 E4 Demini r. Brazil
42 B2 Demirci Turkey
114 C1 Demir Hisar Macedonia
113 G5 Demirköprü Barajı resr Turkey
112 F4 Demirköy Turkey
73 J2 Demmin Germany
145 C5 Demopolis Alabama U.S.A.
148 D5 Demotte Indiana U.S.A.
20 D7 Dempo, G. volcano Indonesia
17 C7 Dempster, Pt pt Western Australia Australia
36 D2 Dêmqog Jammu and Kashmir
93 C5 Dému France
53 G2 Demuryne Ukraine
52 A2 Demyakhi Rus. Fed.
50 H2 Dem'yanovo Rus. Fed.
50 E3 Demyansk Rus. Fed.
53 A1 Demydivka Ukraine
86 C2 Denain France
126 D2 Denakil reg. Eritrea
126 D3 Denan Ethiopia
137 J4 Denare Beach Saskatchewan Canada
93 E5 Dénat France
47 G5 Denau Uzbekistan
141 G4 Denbigh Ontario Canada
62 C1 Denbigh Wales U.K.
62 C1 Denbighshire div. Wales U.K.
68 C1 Den Burg Netherlands
24 C3 Den Chai Thailand
22 A2 Dendang Indonesia
120 C5 Dendâra Mauritania
69 C4 Denderleeuw Belgium
69 B3 Dendermonde div. Oost-Vlaanderen Belgium
69 C3 Dendermonde Belgium
126 C3 Dendi mt. Ethiopia
69 B4 Dendre r. Belgium
131 G1 Dendron South Africa
68 D3 Den Dungen Netherlands
68 F2 Denekamp Netherlands
123 F4 Dengas Niger
123 F4 Denge Nigeria
123 F5 Dengi Nigeria
30 C4 Dengkou China
32 A2 Dêngqên China
33 F1 Deng Xian China
Den Haag see 's-Gravenhage
17 A5 Denham Western Australia Australia
68 E2 Den Ham Netherlands
8 □4 Denham B. b. Kermadec Is New Zealand
14 D3 Denham I. i. Queensland Australia
15 F4 Denham Ra. mountain range Queensland Australia
17 A5 Denham Sound chan. Western Australia Australia
68 C2 Den Helder Netherlands
65 F2 Denholm Scotland U.K.
103 D6 Denia Spain
12 C3 Denial B. b. S. Australia Australia
13 F3 Deniliquin New South Wales Australia
152 C3 Denio Nevada U.S.A.
127 □1 Denis I. i. Seychelles
150 E3 Denison Iowa U.S.A.
151 D5 Denison Texas U.S.A.
16 E3 Denison Plains plain Western Australia Australia
113 G6 Denizli div. Turkey
42 B2 Denizli Turkey
75 G4 Denkendorf Germany
83 E1 Denkingen Germany
83 F1 Denklingen Germany
13 G3 Denman New South Wales Australia
179 C5 Denman Glacier gl. Antarctica
48 F3 Denmark country Europe
17 B7 Denmark Western Australia Australia
135 Q3 Denmark Strait str. Greenland/Iceland
155 H3 Dennehotso Arizona U.S.A.
147 H4 Dennis Port Massachusetts U.S.A.
66 E4 Denny Scotland U.K.
147 K2 Dennysville Maine U.S.A.
68 D2 Den Oever Netherlands
22 C4 Denpasar Indonesia
82 C2 Dent Blanche mt. Switzerland
82 B2 Dent du Midi mt. Switzerland
8 □2 Dent I. i. Campbell I. New Zealand
147 F5 Denton Maryland U.S.A.
151 D5 Denton Texas U.S.A.
91 E3 Dent Parrachée mt. France
6 □1 D'Entrecasteaux Islands is P.N.G.
17 A7 D'Entrecasteaux, Pt pt Western Australia Australia
152 F4 Denver Colorado U.S.A.
74 C4 Denzlingen Germany
36 D3 Deoband India
37 E5 Deogarh mt. India
36 C4 Deogarh India
37 F5 Deogarh India
37 F4 Deoghar India
92 D2 Déols France
36 D5 Deori India
37 E4 Deoria India
36 C2 Deosai, Plains of plain Pakistan
37 E5 Deosil India
69 A3 De Panne Belgium
68 D3 De Peel reg. Netherlands
148 C3 De Pere Wisconsin U.S.A.
147 F3 Deposit New York U.S.A.
141 G3 Depot-Forbes Québec Canada
141 G3 Depot-Rowanton Québec Canada
118 D4 Dépression du Mourdi depression Chad
148 C5 Depue Illinois U.S.A.
45 P3 Deputatskiy Rus. Fed.
32 B2 Dêqên China
33 H2 Deqing China
33 E4 Deqing China
33 G3 Deqiu China
151 E5 De Queen Arkansas U.S.A.
36 B3 Dera Bugti Pakistan
36 B3 Dera Ghazi Khan Pakistan
36 B3 Dera Ismail Khan Pakistan
36 B3 Derajat reg. Pakistan
36 B3 Derawar Fort Pakistan
53 B1 Derazhne Ukraine
53 B2 Derazhnya Ukraine
51 J7 Derbent Rus. Fed.
113 G5 Derbent Turkey
47 G5 Derbent Uzbekistan
124 D2 Derbissaka Central African Rep.
147 G4 Derby Connecticut U.S.A.
63 E2 Derby England U.K.
151 D4 Derby Kansas U.S.A.
16 C3 Derby Western Australia Australia
63 E1 Derbyshire div. England U.K.
131 F2 Derdepoort South Africa
73 F4 Derenburg Germany
118 D5 Déréssa Chad
67 D2 Derg r. Northern Ireland U.K.
51 J5 Dergachi Rus. Fed.
67 D2 Derg, Lough l. Rep. of Ireland
67 C4 Derg, Lough l. Rep. of Ireland
53 G1 Derhachi Ukraine
151 E6 De Ridder Louisiana U.S.A.
68 C2 De Rijp Netherlands
42 E2 Derik Turkey
42 C2 Derinkuyu Turkey
126 D3 Derio well Ethiopia
53 E2 Deriyivka Ukraine
126 D4 Derkali well Kenya
51 F5 Derkul r. Rus. Fed.
86 D4 Der, Lac du l. France
130 B1 Derm Namibia
74 F2 Dermbach Germany
128 B4 Dernberg, Cape c. Namibia
53 A1 Derno Ukraine
32 B2 Dêrong China
67 D3 Derravaragh, Lough l. Rep. of Ireland
129 F2 Derre Mozambique
67 E4 Derry r. Rep. of Ireland
147 H3 Derry New Hampshire U.S.A.
Derry see Londonderry
64 A3 Derrygonnelly Northern Ireland U.K.
67 C2 Derryveagh Mts h. Rep. of Ireland
63 G2 Dersingham England U.K.
30 B4 Derstei China
72 C3 Dersum Germany
119 G4 Derudeb Sudan
109 E2 Deruta Italy
88 D4 Derval France
115 D5 Dervenakia Greece
104 F3 Derventa Bos.-Herz.
83 E2 Dervio Italy
114 B3 Derviziana Greece
64 B2 Dervock Northern Ireland U.K.
65 H3 Derwent r. England U.K.
13 F5 Derwent r. Tasmania Australia
65 G3 Derwent Res. resr England U.K.
65 G4 Derwent Res. resr England U.K.
65 E3 Derwent Water l. England U.K.
52 B1 Derza r. Rus. Fed.
47 G2 Derzhavinsk Kazakhstan
172 D2 Desaguadero r. Argentina
164 C3 Desaguadero r. Bolivia
172 D2 Desaguadero Argentina
164 C3 Desaguadero Peru
172 C3 Desague, Co mt. Argentina
83 D3 Desana Italy
7 □10 Désappointement, Îles de islands French Polynesia Pacific Ocean
154 D2 Desatoya Mts mts Nevada U.S.A.
140 E5 Desbarats Ontario Canada
134 F3 Des Bois, Lac l. N.W.T. Canada
98 D4 Descargamaría Spain
92 C2 Descartes France
141 J3 Deschaillons Québec Canada
137 J3 Deschambault L. l. Saskatchewan Canada
137 J4 Deschambault Lake Saskatchewan Canada
152 B2 Deschutes r. Oregon U.S.A.
126 C2 Desē Ethiopia
171 C6 Deseado r. Argentina
171 C6 Deseado Argentina
145 □3 Desecheo, I. i. Puerto Rico
156 B2 Desemboque Mexico
171 C6 Desengaño, Pta pt Argentina
107 E3 Desenzano del Garda Italy
141 G4 Deseronto Ontario Canada
96 □ Deserta Grande i. Madeira Portugal
96 □ Desertas, Ilhas is Madeira Portugal
155 E5 Desert Center California U.S.A.
92 E2 Désertines France
155 F1 Desert Peak summit Utah U.S.A.
101 G2 Desfiladero de Despeñaperros pass Spain
159 □5 Deshaies Guadeloupe Caribbean
114 A2 Dëshiran Albania
36 C4 Deshnok India
172 D1 Desiderio Tello Argentina
156 B2 Desierto de Altar desert Mexico
170 C2 Desierto de Atacama desert Chile
102 C3 Desierto de Calanda reg. Spain
162 A5 Desierto de Sechura desert Peru
156 B3 Desierto de Vizcaíno desert Mexico
106 D3 Desio Italy
114 C3 Deskati Greece
81 E4 Deskle Slovenia
136 G3 Desmarais Alberta Canada
141 G2 Desmaraisville Québec Canada
165 E5 Desmochados Paraguay
148 A5 Des Moines r. Iowa U.S.A.
150 E3 Des Moines Iowa U.S.A.
153 G4 Des Moines New Mexico U.S.A.
52 A3 Desna r. Rus. Fed.
53 D1 Desna Ukraine
52 A2 Desnogorsk Rus. Fed.
171 B5 Desnudo, Co mt. Argentina
171 A7 Desolación, I. i. Chile
23 C4 Desolation Point pt Philippines
131 E6 Despatch South Africa
172 E1 Despeñaderos Argentina
148 D4 Des Plaines Illinois U.S.A.
115 F6 Despotiko i. Greece
112 C2 Despotovac Yugoslavia
117 K6 Desroches i. Seychelles
73 H4 Dessau Sachsen-Anhalt Germany
69 D3 Dessel Belgium
90 E1 Dessoubre r. France
69 B3 Destelbergen Belgium
75 K3 Deštná Czech Rep.
141 F2 Destor Québec Canada

123 G5 **Donga r.** Cameroon/Nigeria
123 G5 **Donga** Nigeria
33 E3 **Dong'an** China
17 A6 **Dongara** *Western Australia* Australia
36 E5 **Dongargarh** India
32 C3 **Dongchuan** China
37 F2 **Dongco** China
24 D2 **Đông Đăng** Vietnam
31 F5 **Dong'e** China
68 C3 **Dongen** Netherlands
88 C4 **Donges** France
32 E5 **Dongfang** China
31 K3 **Dongfanghong** China
31 H4 **Dongfeng** China
33 F1 **Dongfeng** China
22 D2 **Donggala** Indonesia
32 B1 **Donggi Cona l.** China
31 H5 **Donggou** China
33 F3 **Donggu** China
33 F4 **Dongguan** China
31 F5 **Dongguang** China
24 D3 **Đông Ha** Vietnam
33 G1 **Donghai** China
33 E4 **Donghai Dao** China
24 D3 **Dông Hôi** Vietnam
31 J3 **Dongjingcheng** China
37 H3 **Dongjug** China
22 D2 **Dongkait, Tg pt** Indonesia
21 H6 **Dongkalang** Indonesia
33 E3 **Dongkou** China
37 G4 **Dongkya La** India
32 D3 **Donglan** China
30 B5 **Dongle** China
31 G4 **Dongliao r.** China
31 G3 **Dongminzhutun** China
31 J4 **Dongning** China
125 C6 **Dongo** Angola
106 D2 **Dongo** Italy
124 C3 **Dongo** Zaire
124 D3 **Dongobe** Zaire
119 F4 **Dongola** Sudan
126 B4 **Dongotona Mts mt.** Sudan
124 C3 **Dongou** Congo
24 C3 **Dong Phraya Fai mountain range** Thailand
25 C4 **Dong Phraya Yen escarpment** Thailand
31 F6 **Dongping** China
33 F4 **Dongping** China
37 G3 **Dongqiao** China
33 G4 **Dongshan** China
33 G4 **Dongshan Dao i.** China
30 D5 **Dongsheng** China
33 H1 **Dongtai r.** China
33 H1 **Dongtai** China
33 F2 **Dongting Hu l.** China
33 H3 **Dongtou** China
31 F3 **Dong Ujimqin Qi** China
33 G2 **Dongxiang** China
30 B6 **Dongxiangzu** China
32 D4 **Dongxing** China
33 H2 **Dongyang** China
31 F5 **Dongying** China
30 B5 **Dongzhen** China
33 G2 **Dongzhi** China
172 B3 **Doñihue** Chile
98 E4 **Doñinos de Salamanca** Spain
112 C3 **Donja Dubnica** Yugoslavia
81 H4 **Donja Konjšćina** Croatia
81 G5 **Donja Stubica** Croatia
81 H4 **Donja Višnjica** Croatia
81 H5 **Donja Zelina** Croatia
136 B2 **Donjek r.** *Yukon Terr.* Canada
79 H6 **Donji Miholjac** Croatia
112 D2 **Donji Milanovac** Yugoslavia
104 F3 **Donji Vakuf** Bos.-Herz.
68 E1 **Donkerbroek** Netherlands
131 E5 **Donkerpoort** South Africa
37 G5 **Donmanick Is. is** Bangladesh
151 C7 **Don Martín** Mexico
139 F4 **Donnacona** *Québec* Canada
110 D6 **Donnalucata** *Sicilia* Italy
82 C3 **Donnas** Italy
136 F3 **Donnelly** *Alberta* Canada
8 D1 **Donnellys Crossing** New Zealand
86 C4 **Donnemarie-Dontilly** France
154 B2 **Donner Pass pass** *California* U.S.A.
87 G3 **Donnersberg h.** Germany
17 A7 **Donnybrook** *Western Australia* Australia
87 G4 **Donon mt.** France
102 B1 **Donostia-San Sebastián** *Guipúzcoa* Spain
113 E6 **Donousa i.** Greece
53 G3 **Dons'ke** Ukraine
50 F4 **Donskoy** Rus. Fed.
52 D3 **Donskoye** Rus. Fed.
51 G6 **Donskoye** Rus. Fed.
23 B3 **Donsol** Philippines
88 D3 **Donville-les-Bains** France
80 A2 **Donzdorf** Germany
107 G4 **Donzella, Isola della i.** Italy
92 D3 **Donzenac** France
90 B1 **Donzy** France
67 A3 **Dooagh** Rep. of Ireland
16 B4 **Dooleena h.** *Western Australia* Australia
14 D3 **Doomadgee** *Queensland* Australia
14 D3 **Doomadgee Abor. Land res.** *Queensland* Australia
66 D5 **Doon r.** *Scotland* U.K.
67 B4 **Doonbeg r.** Rep. of Ireland
66 D5 **Doon, Loch l.** *Scotland* U.K.
130 B6 **Doorn r.** South Africa
68 D2 **Doorn** Netherlands
68 D2 **Doornspijk** Netherlands
148 D3 **Door Peninsula pen.** *Michigan* U.S.A.
126 E3 **Dooxo Nugaaleed v.** Somalia
32 C1 **Do Qu r.** China
39 E3 **Dor watercourse** Afghanistan
52 B2 **Dor** Rus. Fed.
153 G5 **Dora** *New Mexico* U.S.A.
106 B3 **Dora Baltea r.** Italy
16 C4 **Dora, L. salt flat** *Western Australia* Australia
106 B3 **Dora Riparia r.** Italy
Dorbiljin *see* **Emin**
31 H3 **Dorbod** China
Dorbod Qi *see* **Siziwang Qi**
62 D4 **Dorchester** *England* U.K.
128 B3 **Dordabis** Namibia
86 B4 **Dordives** France
92 C3 **Dordogne div.** *Aquitaine* France
93 C4 **Dordogne r.** France
68 C3 **Dordrecht** Netherlands
131 F5 **Dordrecht** South Africa
90 B3 **Dore r.** France
137 H4 **Doré L. l.** *Saskatchewan* Canada
137 H4 **Doré Lake** *Saskatchewan* Canada
91 B3 **Dore-l'Église** France
92 E3 **Dore, Monts mts** France
66 D3 **Dores** *Scotland* U.K.
169 F3 **Dores do Indaiá** Brazil
75 H4 **Dorfen** Germany
80 E3 **Dorfgastein** Austria
73 G2 **Dorf Mecklenburg** Germany
108 B4 **Dorgali** *Sardegna* Italy
39 F3 **Dori r.** Afghanistan
123 D4 **Dori** Burkina
172 F3 **Dorila** Argentina
130 B6 **Doring r.** South Africa
130 B5 **Doringbaai** South Africa
130 B5 **Doringbos** South Africa
63 F3 **Dorking** *England* U.K.
122 D5 **Dormaa-Ahenkro** Ghana
72 B4 **Dormagen** *Nordrhein-Westfalen* Germany
79 K4 **Dormánd** Hungary
86 C3 **Dormans** France
31 K3 **Dormidontovka** Rus. Fed.
82 C1 **Dornach** Switzerland
81 G4 **Dornava** Slovenia
83 E1 **Dornbirn div.** Austria
80 A3 **Dornbirn** Austria
73 G4 **Dornburg** Germany
74 F2 **Dorndorf** Germany
90 B2 **Dornes** France
30 D3 **Dorngovĭ div.** Mongolia
66 C3 **Dornie** *Scotland* U.K.
83 D3 **Dorno** Italy
66 D3 **Dornoch Firth est.** *Scotland* U.K.
31 E3 **Dornod div.** Mongolia
74 E4 **Dornstadt** Germany
72 C2 **Dornum** Germany
122 D3 **Doro** Mali
112 F2 **Dorobanțu** Romania
52 C3 **Dorobino** Rus. Fed.
79 H4 **Dorog** Hungary
52 A2 **Dorogobuzh** Rus. Fed.
50 H1 **Dorogorskoye** Rus. Fed.
52 G1 **Dorogucha** Rus. Fed.
112 F1 **Dorohoi** Romania
77 M4 **Dorohusk** Poland
52 C2 **Dorokhovo** Rus. Fed.
39 D2 **Dorokhsh** Iran
26 F2 **Döröö Nuur salt lake** Mongolia
77 N5 **Dorosyni** Ukraine
56 E2 **Dorotea** Sweden
68 F2 **Dörpen** Germany
17 A5 **Dorre I. i.** *Western Australia* Australia
13 H2 **Dorrigo** *New South Wales* Australia
152 B3 **Dorris** *California* U.S.A.
124 B2 **Dorsale Camerounaise slope** Cameroon/Nigeria
62 D4 **Dorset** *England* U.K.
141 F4 **Dorset** *Ontario* Canada
72 B4 **Dorsten** *Nordrhein-Westfalen* Germany
90 D2 **Dortan** France
72 C4 **Dortmund** Germany
72 C4 **Dortmund-Ems-Kanal canal** Germany
146 B6 **Dorton** *Kentucky* U.S.A.
43 D1 **Dörtyol** Turkey
76 G4 **Doruchów** Poland
72 D2 **Dorum** Germany
124 E3 **Doruma** Zaire
39 D2 **Dorūneh** Iran
141 J4 **Dorval** *Québec* Canada
72 E3 **Dörverden** Germany
74 E3 **Dörzbach** Germany
31 F2 **Dosatuy** Rus. Fed.
171 C5 **Dos Bahías, C. c.** Argentina
99 G5 **Dosbarrios** Spain
155 H5 **Dos Cabezas** *Arizona* U.S.A.
52 F2 **Doschatoye** Rus. Fed.
162 B5 **Dos de Mayo** Peru
100 E3 **Dos Hermanas** Spain
24 D2 **Đo Son** Vietnam
154 B3 **Dos Palos** *California* U.S.A.
112 D4 **Dospat r.** Bulgaria
112 E4 **Dospat** Bulgaria
141 K3 **Dosquet** *Québec* Canada
73 H2 **Dosse r.** Germany
74 D3 **Dossenheim** Germany
123 E4 **Dosso div.** Niger
123 E4 **Dosso** Niger
46 D3 **Dossor** Kazakhstan
123 E4 **Dosso, Réserve Partielle de res.** Niger
145 C6 **Dothan** *Alabama* U.S.A.
83 D1 **Döttingen** Switzerland
86 C2 **Douai** France
124 A3 **Douala** Cameroon
88 A3 **Douarnenez** France
88 A3 **Douarnenez, Baie de b.** France
92 C3 **Double reg.** France
27 □ **Double I. i.** Hong Kong
15 H5 **Double Island Pt pt** *Queensland* Australia
154 C4 **Double Peak summit** *California* U.S.A.
15 F3 **Double Pt pt** *Queensland* Australia
78 E2 **Doubrava r.** Czech Rep.
90 E1 **Doubs div.** France
90 D2 **Doubs r.** France/Switzerland
9 A6 **Doubtful Sound inlet** New Zealand
8 D1 **Doubtless Bay b.** New Zealand
86 C5 **Douchy** France
86 C2 **Douchy-les-Mines** France
90 D2 **Doucier** France
89 F2 **Doudeville** France
89 E4 **Doué-la Fontaine** France
122 D4 **Douentza** Mali
9 A7 **Doughboy Bay b.** New Zealand
155 H6 **Douglas airport** *Arizona* U.S.A.
136 C3 **Douglas** *Alaska* U.S.A.
155 H6 **Douglas** *Arizona* U.S.A.
145 D6 **Douglas** *Georgia* U.S.A.
66 E5 **Douglas** *Scotland* U.K.
152 F3 **Douglas** *Wyoming* U.S.A.
64 D3 **Douglas** Isle of Man
130 D4 **Douglas** South Africa
136 D4 **Douglas Chan. chan.** *B.C.* Canada
12 D2 **Douglas Cr. watercourse** *S. Australia* Australia
155 H2 **Douglas Creek r.** *Colorado* U.S.A.
86 B2 **Doullens** France
67 A5 **Doulus Head headland** Rep. of Ireland
123 E5 **Doumè** Benin
124 B3 **Doumé** Cameroon
122 D4 **Douna** Mali
115 C5 **Dounaiika** Greece
66 D4 **Doune** *Scotland* U.K.
64 D1 **Doune Hill h.** *Scotland* U.K.
66 E2 **Dounreay** *Scotland* U.K.
75 J2 **Doupovské Hory mts** Czech Rep.
69 B4 **Dour** Belgium
167 B4 **Dourada, Cach. waterfall** Brazil
168 D3 **Dourada, Cach. waterfall** Brazil
168 A5 **Dourados r.** Brazil
168 A5 **Dourados** Brazil
124 C1 **Dourbali** Chad
91 B4 **Dourbie r.** France
86 B4 **Dourdan** France
93 E4 **Dourdou r.** France
93 E5 **Dourgne** France
86 A2 **Douriez** France
98 C3 **Douro r.** Portugal
90 E3 **Doussard** France
168 B5 **Doutor Camargo** Brazil
82 B2 **Douvaine** France
88 D2 **Douve r.** France
89 E2 **Douvres-la-Déliverande** France
91 C3 **Doux r.** France
121 F2 **Douz** Tunisia
93 B5 **Douze r.** France
118 C5 **Douziat** Chad
87 E3 **Douzy** France
53 C1 **Dovbysh** Ukraine
63 E1 **Dove r.** *England* U.K.
63 H2 **Dove r.** *England* U.K.
65 H3 **Dove r.** *England* U.K.
139 J3 **Dove Brook** *Newfoundland* Canada
155 H3 **Dove Creek** *Colorado* U.S.A.
147 F5 **Dover** *Delaware* U.S.A.
63 H3 **Dover** *England* U.K.
147 H3 **Dover** *New Hampshire* U.S.A.
147 F4 **Dover** *New Jersey* U.S.A.
146 C4 **Dover** *Ohio* U.S.A.
13 F5 **Dover** *Tasmania* Australia
147 J2 **Dover-Foxcroft** *Maine* U.S.A.
17 D7 **Dover, Pt pt** *Western Australia* Australia
42 F3 **Doveyrīch r.** Iran/Iraq
53 A1 **Dovhoshyyi** Ukraine
55 C5 **Dovnsklint cliff** Denmark
47 J2 **Dovol'noye** Rus. Fed.
148 D5 **Dowagiac** *Michigan* U.S.A.
39 C3 **Dow Chāhī** Iran
39 D1 **Dowgha'ī** Iran
39 C2 **Dow Kūh mt.** Iran
39 E2 **Dowlatābād** Afghanistan
39 F1 **Dowlatābād** Afghanistan
39 C3 **Dowlatābād** Iran
39 E1 **Dowlatābād** Iran
39 D3 **Dowlatābād** Iran
39 D1 **Dowlatābād** Iran
39 C3 **Dowlatābād** Iran
39 F2 **Dowl at Yār** Afghanistan
67 E2 **Down div.** *Northern Ireland* U.K.
63 G2 **Downham Market** *England* U.K.
154 B2 **Downieville** *California* U.S.A.
67 F2 **Downpatrick** *Northern Ireland* U.K.
67 B2 **Downpatrick Head headland** Rep. of Ireland
147 F3 **Downsville** *New York* U.S.A.
63 E4 **Downton** *England* U.K.
39 B2 **Dow Rūd** Iran
39 D3 **Dowsārī** Iran
39 G2 **Dowshī** Afghanistan
154 B1 **Doyle** *California* U.S.A.
173 H2 **Doyle** Argentina
147 F4 **Doylestown** *Pennsylvania* U.S.A.
112 E3 **Doyrentsi** Bulgaria
39 D3 **Dozdān r.** Iran
28 D5 **Dōzen i.** Japan
141 G3 **Dozois, Réservoir resr** *Québec* Canada
89 E2 **Dozulé** France
53 E2 **Drabiv** Ukraine
53 D2 **Drabivka** Ukraine
91 D4 **Drac r.** France
168 C4 **Dracena** Brazil
52 E2 **Drachevo** Rus. Fed.
75 J3 **Drachselsried** Germany
68 E1 **Drachten** Netherlands
112 F2 **Dragalina** Romania
112 E2 **Drăgănești-Olt** Romania
112 E2 **Drăgănești-Vlașca** Romania
112 E2 **Drăgășani** Romania
79 M5 **Drăgești** Romania
115 H7 **Dragonada i.** Greece
109 G3 **Dragoni** Italy
115 G5 **Dragonisi i.** Greece
159 □3 **Dragon's Mouths str.** *Trinidad* Trinidad and Tobago
55 E4 **Dragør** Denmark
114 C2 **Dragoš** Macedonia
57 F3 **Dragsfjärd** Finland
91 E5 **Draguignan** France
112 F1 **Drăgușeni** Romania
77 O3 **Drahichyn** Belarus
155 F4 **Drake** *Arizona* U.S.A.
137 J5 **Drake** *N. Dakota* U.S.A.
131 G5 **Drakensberg mountain range** Lesotho/South Africa
131 H2 **Drakensberg mountain range** South Africa
131 G5 **Draken's Rock mt.** South Africa
179 A1 **Drake Passage str.** Antarctica
114 F1 **Drama div.** Greece
114 F1 **Drama** Greece
58 D2 **Drammen** Norway
58 D2 **Dramsfjorden inlet** Norway
58 C2 **Drangedal** Norway
90 E2 **Dranse r.** France
72 E4 **Dransfeld** Germany
67 E2 **Draperstown** *Northern Ireland* U.K.
36 C2 **Dras** India
36 C1 **Drasan** Pakistan
81 H2 **Drasenhofen** Austria
81 F4 **Drau r.** Austria
78 E5 **Drava r.** Croatia/Hungary
79 G6 **Drávafok** Hungary
78 E5 **Dravinja r.** Slovenia
114 E2 **Draviskos** Greece
81 G4 **Dravograd** Slovenia
76 D3 **Drawa r.** Poland
76 D2 **Drawienski Park Narodowy nat. park** Poland
76 D2 **Drawno** Poland
76 E3 **Drawsko** Poland
76 D2 **Drawsko Pomorskie** Poland
136 G4 **Drayton Valley** *Alberta* Canada
105 A7 **Dréan** Algeria
73 K4 **Drebkau** Germany
90 C1 **Drée r.** France
79 J3 **Drégelypalánk** Hungary
74 D2 **Dreieich** Germany
69 E5 **Dreis** Germany
87 G4 **Dreisam r.** Germany
81 E2 **Dreisesselberg mt.** Germany
74 E2 **Dreistelzberge h.** Germany
80 C3 **Dreitorspitze mt.** Germany
55 C5 **Drejø i.** Denmark
107 H2 **Drenchia** Italy
114 B2 **Drenovë** Albania
72 C4 **Drensteinfurt** Germany
68 E2 **Drenthe div.** Netherlands
68 E2 **Drentse Hoofdvaart canal** Netherlands
114 C2 **Drepano** Greece
76 B4 **Dresden airport** Germany
73 J4 **Dresden** Germany
102 D4 **Dreta de l'Ebre, La delta** Spain
54 F4 **Dretun'** Belarus
76 E1 **Dretyń** Poland
89 G3 **Dreux** France
56 D3 **Drevsjø** Norway
73 H3 **Drewitz** Germany
73 H2 **Drewitzer See l.** Germany
76 D3 **Drezdenko** Poland
32 B2 **Dri** China
54 E3 **Driceni** Latvia
54 E4 **Dridža l.** Latvia
68 D2 **Driebergen** Netherlands
99 G4 **Driebes** Spain
68 E1 **Driesum** Netherlands
63 E3 **Driffield** *England* U.K.
140 E2 **Driftwood** *Ontario* Canada
146 D4 **Driftwood** *Pennsylvania* U.S.A.
53 D1 **Drimaylivka** Ukraine
64 C1 **Drimnin** *Scotland* U.K.
67 B5 **Drimoleague** Rep. of Ireland
112 B2 **Drina r.** Bos.-Herz./Yugoslavia
113 C4 **Drino r.** Albania
81 F1 **Dříteň** Czech Rep.
81 H2 **Drnholec** Czech Rep.
104 F4 **Drniš** Croatia
81 H4 **Drnje** Croatia
83 F3 **Dro** Italy
58 D2 **Drøbak** Norway
112 D2 **Drobeta-Turnu Severin** Romania
91 C4 **Drobie r.** France
77 H3 **Drobin** Poland
53 B2 **Drochia** Moldova
72 E2 **Drochtersen** Germany
68 E1 **Drogeham** Netherlands
67 E3 **Drogheda** Rep. of Ireland
77 L3 **Drohiczyn** Poland
77 M6 **Drohobych** Ukraine
Droichead Átha *see* **Drogheda**
Droichead Nua *see* **Newbridge**
62 D2 **Droitwich** *England* U.K.
37 G4 **Drokung** India
91 D4 **Drôme div.** *Rhône-Alpes* France
91 D4 **Drôme r.** France
73 F3 **Drömling reg.** Germany
67 D3 **Dromod** Rep. of Ireland
67 E2 **Dromore** *Northern Ireland* U.K.
67 D2 **Dromore** *Northern Ireland* U.K.
67 C2 **Dromore West** Rep. of Ireland
106 B4 **Dronero** Italy
63 E1 **Dronfield** *England* U.K.
92 C3 **Dronne r.** France
135 Q2 **Dronning Louise Land reg.** Greenland
55 C2 **Dronninglund** Denmark
179 C3 **Dronning Maud Land reg.** Antarctica
68 D2 **Dronten** Netherlands
93 C4 **Dropt r.** France
81 G2 **Drosendorf** Austria
36 B2 **Drosh** Pakistan
81 H2 **Drösing** Austria
53 C3 **Droskovo** Rus. Fed.
114 C2 **Drosopigi** *Dytiki Makedonia* Greece
114 C3 **Drosopigi** *Ipeiros* Greece
89 G3 **Droué** France
30 E2 **Drovyanaya** Rus. Fed.
140 B1 **Drowning r.** *Ontario* Canada
53 B1 **Drozdyn'** Ukraine
6 □6 **Drua Drua i.** Fiji
62 C2 **Druid** *Wales* U.K.
158 □1 **Druif** *Aruba* Caribbean
64 C2 **Druimdrishaig** *Scotland* U.K.
37 H3 **Druk La** China
54 E4 **Drūkšiai l.** Belarus/Lithuania
87 G4 **Drulingen** France
64 A3 **Drumcard** *Northern Ireland* U.K.
90 D3 **Drumettaz-Clarafond** France
64 A2 **Drumfree** Rep. of Ireland
136 G4 **Drumheller** *Alberta* Canada
67 C2 **Drumkeeran** Rep. of Ireland
67 E4 **Drummin** Rep. of Ireland
152 D2 **Drummond** *Montana* U.S.A.
148 B2 **Drummond** *Wisconsin* U.S.A.
149 F3 **Drummond Island i.** *Michigan* U.S.A.
131 G2 **Drummondlea** South Africa
14 D3 **Drummond, Mt h.** *Northern Terr.* Australia
15 F4 **Drummond Range h.** *Queensland* Australia
141 J4 **Drummondville** *Québec* Canada
66 D6 **Drummore** *Scotland* U.K.
66 D3 **Drumnadrochit** *Scotland* U.K.
64 A3 **Drumquin** *Northern Ireland* U.K.
68 D3 **Drunen** Netherlands
83 D1 **Drusberg mt.** Switzerland
87 G4 **Drusenheim** France
54 D5 **Druskininkai** Lithuania
54 D3 **Drusti** Latvia
68 D3 **Druten** Netherlands
54 E4 **Druya** Belarus
90 B1 **Druyes-les-Belles-Fontaines** France
77 K1 **Druzhba** Rus. Fed.
52 A3 **Druzhba** Ukraine
53 F3 **Druzhbivka** Ukraine
45 Q3 **Druzhina** Rus. Fed.
53 G2 **Druzhkivka** Ukraine
54 G2 **Druzhnaya Gorka** Rus. Fed.
77 H2 **Drwęca r.** Poland
112 E3 **Dryanovo** Bulgaria
52 D3 **Dryazgi** Rus. Fed.
136 B3 **Dry Bay b.** *Alaska* U.S.A.
138 B4 **Dryberry L. l.** *Ontario* Canada
148 E2 **Dryburg** *Michigan* U.S.A.
138 B4 **Dryden** *Ontario* Canada
179 D5 **Drygalski I. i.** Antarctica
179 B5 **Drygalski Ice Tongue ice feature** Antarctica
62 C2 **Drygarn Fawr h.** *Wales* U.K.
159 □1 **Dry Harbour Mts mts** Jamaica
154 D2 **Dry Lake l.** *Nevada* U.S.A.
66 D4 **Drymen** *Scotland* U.K.
54 F4 **Drysa r.** Belarus
16 D2 **Drysdale r.** *Western Australia* Australia
14 C1 **Drysdale I. i.** *Northern Terr.* Australia
16 D2 **Drysdale River Nat. Park nat. park** *Western Australia* Australia
158 B1 **Dry Tortugas is** *Florida* U.S.A.
76 G2 **Dryzcim** Poland
76 G3 **Drzewce** Poland
77 J4 **Drzewica** Poland
76 E2 **Drzonowo** Poland
124 B2 **Dschang** Cameroon
33 E1 **Du r.** China
124 D3 **Dua r.** Zaire
39 B2 **Dūāb r.** Iran
108 A4 **Dualchi** *Sardegna* Italy
32 E4 **Du'an** China
147 F2 **Duane** *New York* U.S.A.
15 G4 **Duaringa** *Queensland* Australia
37 G4 **Duars reg.** India
78 D1 **Dubá** Czech Rep.
119 G2 **Ḍubā** Saudi Arabia
Dubai *see* **Dubayy**
53 C3 **Dubăsari** Moldova
53 C3 **Dubău** Moldova
137 J2 **Dubawnt r.** *N.W.T.* Canada
137 J2 **Dubawnt Lake l.** *N.W.T.* Canada
39 C4 **Dubayy** U.A.E.
119 G2 **Dubbāgh, J. mt.** Saudi Arabia
43 C6 **Dubbagh, J. ad mt.** Saudi Arabia
13 G3 **Dubbo** *New South Wales* Australia
77 N4 **Dubechne** Ukraine
73 H4 **Düben** Germany
83 D1 **Dübendorf** Switzerland
73 H4 **Dübener Heide forest** Germany
77 L1 **Dubeniki** Poland
52 H2 **Dubenki** Rus. Fed.
52 D1 **Dubets** Rus. Fed.
78 C1 **Dubí** Czech Rep.
77 N1 **Dubičiai** Lithuania
77 M3 **Dubicze Cerkiewne** Poland
77 L6 **Dubiecko** Poland
77 M4 **Dubienka** Poland
54 D4 **Dubingiai** Lithuania
52 H4 **Dubki** Rus. Fed.
67 E3 **Dublin div.** Rep. of Ireland
145 D5 **Dublin** *Georgia* U.S.A.
140 B2 **Dublin** *Ontario* Canada
67 E3 **Dublin** Rep. of Ireland
64 B4 **Dublin Bay b.** Rep. of Ireland
75 K3 **Dublovice** Czech Rep.
77 M6 **Dublyany** Ukraine
77 N6 **Dublyany** Ukraine
54 E3 **Dubna r.** Latvia
52 C1 **Dubna r.** Rus. Fed.
77 N2 **Dubna** Belarus
52 C2 **Dubna** Rus. Fed.
52 C1 **Dubna** Rus. Fed.
81 J2 **Dubňany** Czech Rep.
78 D3 **Dubné** Czech Rep.
53 A1 **Dubno** Ukraine
152 D2 **Dubois** *Idaho* U.S.A.
146 D4 **Du Bois** *Pennsylvania* U.S.A.
152 E3 **Dubois** *Wyoming* U.S.A.
52 C3 **Dubovaya Roshcha** Rus. Fed.
112 D1 **Dubove** Ukraine
53 F2 **Dubovi Hryady** Ukraine
52 D3 **Dubovka** Rus. Fed.
51 H5 **Dubovka** Rus. Fed.
51 G5 **Dubovka** Rus. Fed.
51 G6 **Dubovskoye** Rus. Fed.
53 E1 **Dubov"yazivka** Ukraine
81 H5 **Dubrava** Croatia
81 G5 **Dubravica** Croatia
122 B5 **Dubréka** Guinea
53 B1 **Dubrivka** Ukraine
52 A3 **Dubrovka** Rus. Fed.
52 F3 **Dubrovki** Rus. Fed.
104 G4 **Dubrovnik** Croatia
53 B1 **Dubrovytsya** Ukraine
50 D4 **Dubrowna** Belarus
124 D3 **Dubulu** Zaire
148 B4 **Dubuque** *Iowa* U.S.A.
53 D2 **Dubynove** Ukraine
54 C4 **Dubysa r.** Lithuania
7 □10 **Duc de Gloucester, Îles is** *French Polynesia* Pacific Ocean
88 D3 **Ducey** France
33 G2 **Duchang** China
73 J2 **Ducherow** Germany
155 G1 **Duchesne** *Utah* U.S.A.
14 D4 **Duchess** *Queensland* Australia
177 L7 **Ducie Island i.** Pacific Ocean
145 C5 **Duck r.** *Tennessee* U.S.A.
137 J4 **Duck Bay** *Manitoba* Canada
16 B4 **Duck Cr. r.** *Western Australia* Australia
148 E4 **Duck Lake** *Michigan* U.S.A.
137 H4 **Duck Lake** *Saskatchewan* Canada
155 E2 **Duckwater** *Nevada* U.S.A.
155 E2 **Duckwater Peak summit** *Nevada* U.S.A.
159 □4 **Ducos** *Martinique* Caribbean
25 E4 **Đưc Pho** Vietnam
25 E5 **Đưc Trong** Vietnam
53 E3 **Dudchany** Ukraine
69 E5 **Dudelange** Luxembourg
74 B3 **Dudeldorf** Germany
72 F4 **Duderstadt** Germany
79 K5 **Dudestii Vechi** Romania
37 E4 **Dudhi** India
37 G4 **Dudhnai** India
36 E3 **Dudhwa** India
44 K3 **Dudinka** Rus. Fed.
62 D2 **Dudley** *England* U.K.
38 B2 **Dudna r.** India
52 B3 **Dudorovskiy** Rus. Fed.
66 F3 **Dudwick, Hill of h.** *Scotland* U.K.
122 C5 **Duékoué** Côte d'Ivoire
98 D2 **Duerna r.** Spain
98 D3 **Duero r.** Spain
107 F3 **Dueville** Italy
141 F2 **Dufault, Lac l.** *Québec* Canada
179 B4 **Dufek Coast coastal area** Antarctica
69 C3 **Duffel** Belgium
138 E2 **Dufferin, Cape headland** *Québec* Canada
146 B6 **Duffield** *Virginia* U.S.A.
4 H5 **Duff Is is** Solomon Is.
66 E3 **Dufftown** *Scotland* U.K.
82 C3 **Dufourspitze summit** Italy/Switzerland
138 E1 **Dufrost, Pte pt** *Québec* Canada
43 D5 **Dughdash mountain range** Saudi Arabia
104 E4 **Dugi Otok i.** Croatia
104 F4 **Dugi Rat** Croatia
52 C2 **Dugna** Rus. Fed.
87 E3 **Dugny-sur-Meuse** France
104 F4 **Dugopolje** Croatia
78 F6 **Dugo Selo** Croatia
30 D5 **Dugui Qarag** China
118 C3 **Duhūn Tārsū mts** Chad/Libya
163 D3 **Duida, Co mt.** Venezuela
162 D3 **Duida-Marahuaca, Parque Nacional nat. park** Venezuela
15 E2 **Duifken Pt pt** *Queensland* Australia
130 A1 **Duineveld** Namibia
72 E3 **Duingen** Germany
107 H3 **Duino** Italy
72 B4 **Duisburg** Germany
162 C2 **Duitama** Colombia
68 E3 **Duiven** Netherlands
131 H1 **Duiwelskloof** South Africa
45 R3 **Dukat** Rus. Fed.
131 F5 **Dukathole** South Africa
113 B4 **Dukat i Ri** Albania
136 C4 **Duke I. i.** *Alaska* U.S.A.
Duke of Gloucester Is is *see* **Îles Duc de Gloucester**
126 B3 **Duk Fadiat** Sudan
126 B3 **Duk Faiwil** Sudan
39 B4 **Dukhān** Qatar
119 H2 **Dukhnah** Saudi Arabia
52 A2 **Dukhovshchina** Rus. Fed.
36 B3 **Duki** Pakistan
123 G4 **Dukku** Nigeria
77 K6 **Dukla** Poland
32 C3 **Dukou** China
54 E4 **Dūkštas** Lithuania
30 C2 **Dulaanhaan** Mongolia
26 G4 **Dulan** China
170 D2 **Dulce r.** Argentina
99 H4 **Dulce r.** Spain
156 K7 **Dulce, Golfo b.** Costa Rica
156 J6 **Dulce Nombre de Dios** Honduras
30 E2 **Dul'durga** Rus. Fed.
64 B4 **Duleek** Rep. of Ireland
112 F3 **Dŭlgopol** Bulgaria
15 E1 **Dulhunty r.** *Queensland* Australia
37 E2 **Dulishi Hu salt lake** China
37 H4 **Dullabchara** India
131 H2 **Dullstroom** South Africa
72 C4 **Dülmen** Germany
66 E3 **Dulnain Bridge** *Scotland* U.K.
112 F3 **Dulovo** Bulgaria
148 A2 **Duluth** *Minnesota* U.S.A.
148 A2 **Duluth/Superior airport** *Minnesota* U.S.A.
62 C3 **Dulverton** *England* U.K.
52 E1 **Dulyapino** Rus. Fed.
42 D3 **Dūmā** Syria
23 B4 **Dumaguete** Philippines
25 C7 **Dumai** Indonesia
23 B4 **Dumaran i.** Philippines
13 G2 **Dumaresq r.** *New South Wales* Australia
151 F5 **Dumas** *Arkansas* U.S.A.
151 C5 **Dumas** *Texas* U.S.A.
43 D3 **Ḑumayr** Syria
43 D3 **Ḑumayr, J. mountain range** Syria
66 D5 **Dumbarton** *Scotland* U.K.
66 D4 **Dumbarton and Clydebank div.** *Scotland* U.K.
131 H3 **Dumbe** South Africa
6 □2 **Dumbéa** *New Caledonia* Pacific Ocean
79 J3 **Ďumbier mt.** Slovakia
79 M6 **Dumbrava** Romania
112 E1 **Dumbrăveni** *Sibiu* Romania
112 F2 **Dumbrăveni** *Vrancea* Romania
112 E2 **Dumbrăvița** Romania
98 A1 **Dumbría** Spain
36 D2 **Dumchele** India
22 A1 **Dumdum i.** Indonesia
37 H4 **Dum Duma** India
88 C4 **Dumet, Île i.** France
66 E5 **Dumfries** *Scotland* U.K.
66 E5 **Dumfries and Galloway div.** *Scotland* U.K.
52 B3 **Duminichi** Rus. Fed.
112 E1 **Dumitra** Romania
37 F4 **Dumka** India
72 D3 **Dümmer l.** Germany
73 H2 **Dummerstorf** Germany
141 G3 **Dumoine, L. l.** *Québec* Canada
179 □ **Dumont d'Urville France Base** Antarctica
179 B6 **Dumont d'Urville Sea sea** Antarctica
74 B2 **Dümpelfeld** Germany
43 A4 **Dumyât** Egypt
72 F4 **Dün ridge** Germany
79 H5 **Duna r.** Hungary
79 J4 **Dunabogdány** Hungary
67 D1 **Dunaff Head headland** Rep. of Ireland
79 H5 **Dunaföldvár** Hungary
79 J4 **Dunaharaszti** Hungary
112 B1 **Dunaj r.** Hungary
77 J5 **Dunajec r.** Poland
79 G4 **Dunajská Streda** Slovakia
79 J4 **Dunakeszi** Hungary
13 F5 **Dunalley** *Tasmania* Australia
67 E3 **Dunany Point pt** Rep. of Ireland
112 B1 **Dunaszekcső** Hungary
79 H5 **Dunaszentgyörgy** Hungary
79 J5 **Duna-Tisza Köze reg.** Hungary
79 H5 **Dunaújváros** Hungary
112 F3 **Dunav r.** Bulgaria/Romania
79 J5 **Duna-völgyi-főcsatorna canal** Hungary
112 D3 **Dunavtsi** Bulgaria
53 B2 **Dunayivtsi** *Khmel'nyts'ka Oblast'* Ukraine
53 B2 **Dunayivtsi** *Khmel'nyts'ka Oblast'* Ukraine
9 C6 **Dunback** New Zealand
15 E3 **Dunbar** *Queensland* Australia
66 F4 **Dunbar** *Scotland* U.K.
66 E4 **Dunblane** *Scotland* U.K.
67 E3 **Dunboyne** Rep. of Ireland
155 H5 **Duncan** *Arizona* U.S.A.
136 E5 **Duncan** *B.C.* Canada
151 D5 **Duncan** *Oklahoma* U.S.A.
138 D3 **Duncan, Cape c.** *Ontario* Canada
138 E3 **Duncan, L. l.** *Québec* Canada
146 E4 **Duncannon** *Pennsylvania* U.S.A.
67 E4 **Duncannon** Rep. of Ireland
25 A5 **Duncan Passage chan.** *Andaman and Nicobar Is* India
159 □1 **Duncans** Jamaica
66 E2 **Duncansby Head headland** *Scotland* U.K.
148 B5 **Duncans Mills** *Illinois* U.S.A.
158 D2 **Duncan Town** The Bahamas
63 E2 **Dunchurch** *England* U.K.
67 E4 **Duncormick** Rep. of Ireland
54 C3 **Dundaga** Latvia
146 E5 **Dundalk** *Maryland* U.S.A.
140 E4 **Dundalk** *Ontario* Canada
67 E2 **Dundalk** Rep. of Ireland
67 E3 **Dundalk Bay b.** Rep. of Ireland
Dundas *see* **Uummannaq**
136 C4 **Dundas I. i.** *B.C.* Canada
17 C7 **Dundas, L. salt flat** *Western Australia* Australia
14 B1 **Dundas Str. chan.** *Northern Terr.* Australia
30 D3 **Dundbürd** Mongolia
Dún Dealgan *see* **Dundalk**
149 F5 **Dundee** *Michigan* U.S.A.
146 E3 **Dundee** *New York* U.S.A.
66 F4 **Dundee** *Scotland* U.K.
131 H4 **Dundee** South Africa
66 E4 **Dundee, City of div.** *Scotland* U.K.
30 C3 **Dundgovĭ div.** Mongolia
67 F2 **Dundonald** *Northern Ireland* U.K.
15 F5 **Dundoo** *Queensland* Australia
66 E6 **Dundrennan** *Scotland* U.K.
67 F2 **Dundrum** *Northern Ireland* U.K.
64 C3 **Dundrum Bay b.** *Northern Ireland* U.K.
37 E4 **Dundwa Ra. mountain range** Nepal
145 D6 **Dunedin** *Florida* U.S.A.
9 C6 **Dunedin** New Zealand
138 F2 **Dune, Lac l.** *Québec* Canada
47 J3 **Dunenbay** Kazakhstan
121 F2 **Dunes de Dokhara sand dunes** Algeria
64 A2 **Dunfanaghy** Rep. of Ireland
66 E4 **Dunfermline** *Scotland* U.K.
67 E2 **Dungannon** *Northern Ireland* U.K.
Dún Garbhán *see* **Dungarvan**
36 C3 **Dungargarh** India
36 C5 **Dungarpur** India
67 D4 **Dungarvan** Rep. of Ireland
80 D2 **Dungau reg.** Germany
63 G4 **Dungeness headland** *England* U.K.
171 C7 **Dungeness, Pta pt** Argentina
74 C2 **Düngenheim** Germany
67 E2 **Dungiven** *Northern Ireland* U.K.
67 C2 **Dungloe** Rep. of Ireland
13 G3 **Dungog** *New South Wales* Australia
124 E3 **Dungu** Zaire
25 C6 **Dungun** Malaysia
119 G3 **Dungunab** Sudan
63 F1 **Dunholme** *England* U.K.
31 J4 **Dunhua** China
26 F3 **Dunhuang** China
66 E4 **Dunkeld** *Scotland* U.K.
81 G2 **Dunkelsteiner Wald forest** Austria
86 B1 **Dunkerque** France
62 C3 **Dunkery Beacon h.** *England* U.K.
146 D3 **Dunkirk** *New York* U.S.A.
Dunkirk *see* **Dunkerque**
122 D5 **Dunkwa** Ghana
67 E3 **Dún Laoghaire** Rep. of Ireland
67 E3 **Dunlavin** Rep. of Ireland
67 E3 **Dunleer** Rep. of Ireland
92 D2 **Dun-le-Palestel** France
66 D5 **Dunlop** *Scotland* U.K.
67 E1 **Dunloy** *Northern Ireland* U.K.
67 B5 **Dunmanus Bay b.** Rep. of Ireland
67 B5 **Dunmanway** Rep. of Ireland
14 C3 **Dunmarra** *Northern Terr.* Australia

67 C3 **Dunmore** Rep. of Ireland
67 E4 **Dunmore East** Rep. of Ireland
145 E7 **Dunmore Town** The Bahamas
154 D3 **Dunmovin** *California* U.S.A.
67 F2 **Dunmurry** *Northern Ireland* U.K.
145 E5 **Dunn** *N. Carolina* U.S.A.
64 A3 **Dunnamanagh** *Northern Ireland* U.K.
66 E2 **Dunnet Bay b.** *Scotland* U.K.
66 E2 **Dunnet Head headland** *Scotland* U.K.
154 B2 **Dunnigan** *California* U.S.A.
150 C3 **Dunning** *Nebraska* U.S.A.
87 H4 **Dunningen** Germany
141 F5 **Dunnville** *Ontario* Canada
89 G4 **Dunois reg.** France
13 E4 **Dunolly** *Victoria* Australia
66 D5 **Dunoon** *Scotland* U.K.
67 A4 **Dunquin** Rep. of Ireland
65 E2 **Dun Rig h.** *Scotland* U.K.
66 F5 **Duns** *Scotland* U.K.
9 D5 **Dunsandel** New Zealand
150 C1 **Dunseith** *N. Dakota* U.S.A.
64 B4 **Dunshaughlin** Rep. of Ireland
152 B3 **Dunsmuir** *California* U.S.A.
63 F3 **Dunstable** *England* U.K.
9 B6 **Dunstan Mts mountain range** New Zealand
92 E2 **Dun-sur-Auron** France
87 E3 **Dun-sur-Meuse** France
9 C6 **Duntroon** New Zealand
62 B3 **Dunvant** *Wales* U.K.
66 B3 **Dunvegan** *Scotland* U.K.
66 B3 **Dunvegan, Loch inlet** *Scotland* U.K.
36 B3 **Dunyapur** Pakistan
31 H2 **Duobukur r.** China
31 F4 **Duolon** China
33 E3 **Dupang Ling mountain range** China
141 F2 **Duparquet** *Québec* Canada
141 F2 **Duparquet, Lac l.** *Québec* Canada
150 C2 **Dupree** *S. Dakota* U.S.A.
16 A4 **Dupuy, C. c.** *Western Australia* Australia
169 G5 **Duque de Caxias** Brazil
171 A7 **Duque de York, I. i.** Chile
144 B4 **Du Quoin** *Illinois* U.S.A.
43 C4 **Dura** Israel
74 F5 **Durach** Germany
16 D3 **Durack r.** *Western Australia* Australia
16 D3 **Durack Range h.** *Western Australia* Australia
Dura Europos *see* **Qal'at as Sālihīyah**
42 C1 **Durağan** Turkey
91 D5 **Durance r.** France
93 C4 **Durance** France
149 F4 **Durand** *Michigan* U.S.A.
148 B3 **Durand** *Wisconsin* U.S.A.
101 F2 **Duranes h.** Spain
156 D3 **Durango div.** Mexico
153 F4 **Durango** *Colorado* U.S.A.
156 D3 **Durango** *Durango* Mexico
99 H1 **Durango** Spain
39 F3 **Durani reg.** Afghanistan
112 G3 **Durankulak** Bulgaria
107 G2 **Duranno, Monte mt.** Italy
173 G4 **Durañona** Argentina
151 D5 **Durant** *Oklahoma* U.S.A.
93 C4 **Duras** France
99 G3 **Duratón r.** Spain
173 J2 **Durazno div.** Uruguay
173 J2 **Durazno** Uruguay
173 J2 **Durazno, Cuch. Gde del h.** Uruguay
131 H4 **Durban** South Africa
93 E6 **Durban-Corbières** France
130 B6 **Durbanville** South Africa
146 D5 **Durbin** *W. Virginia* U.S.A.
87 F4 **Durbion r.** France
69 D4 **Durbuy** Belgium
101 G3 **Dúrcal r.** Spain
101 G4 **Dúrcal** Spain
92 E2 **Durdat-Larequille** France
89 F2 **Durdent r.** France
78 G5 **Đurđevac** Croatia
74 B2 **Düren** Germany
37 E5 **Durg** India
37 G4 **Durgapur** Bangladesh
37 F5 **Durgapur** India
65 F3 **Durham div.** *England* U.K.
154 B2 **Durham** *California* U.S.A.
65 G3 **Durham** *England* U.K.
145 E4 **Durham** *N. Carolina* U.S.A.
147 H3 **Durham** *New Hampshire* U.S.A.
140 E4 **Durham** *Ontario* Canada
15 E5 **Durham Downs** *Queensland* Australia
126 D3 **Durhi well** Ethiopia
Durlas *see* **Thurles**
53 C3 **Durleşti** Moldova
81 G4 **Durmanec** Croatia
69 C3 **Durme r.** Belgium
74 D4 **Durmersheim** Germany
66 D2 **Durness** *Scotland* U.K.
66 D2 **Durness, Kyle of inlet** *Scotland* U.K.
81 H2 **Dürnkrut** Austria
31 F2 **Duroy** Rus. Fed.
113 B4 **Durrës** Albania
14 E5 **Durrie** *Queensland* Australia
63 E3 **Durrington** *England* U.K.
67 D4 **Durrow** Rep. of Ireland
67 A5 **Dursey Head headland** Rep. of Ireland
67 A5 **Dursey Island i.** Rep. of Ireland
62 D3 **Dursley** *England* U.K.
42 B2 **Dursunbey** Turkey
89 E4 **Durtal** France
39 F2 **Dūruḥ** Iran
126 E3 **Durukhsi** Somalia
43 D3 **Durūz, Jabal ad mt.** Syria
8 D4 **D'Urville Island i.** New Zealand
39 F2 **Durzab** Afghanistan
54 D4 **Dusetos** Lithuania
119 F3 **Dûsh** Egypt
36 A3 **Dushai** Pakistan
39 D1 **Dushak** Turkmenistan
32 D3 **Dushan** China
47 G5 **Dushanbe** Tajikistan
77 M1 **Dusia l.** Lithuania
9 A6 **Dusky Sound inlet** New Zealand
79 H5 **Dusnok** Hungary
76 G2 **Dusocin** Poland
72 B4 **Düsseldorf div.** *Nordrhein-Westfalen* Germany
72 B4 **Düsseldorf** *Düsseldorf* Germany
39 G1 **Dusti** Tajikistan
47 G4 **Dustlik** Uzbekistan
76 E3 **Duszniki** Poland
76 E5 **Duszniki-Zdrój** Poland
155 F1 **Dutch Mt mt.** *Utah* U.S.A.
130 D1 **Dutlwe** Botswana
81 E5 **Dutovlje** Slovenia
123 F4 **Dutsan-Wai** Nigeria
123 F4 **Dutse** Nigeria
123 F4 **Dutsin-Ma** Nigeria
15 E4 **Dutton r.** *Queensland* Australia
155 F3 **Dutton, Mt mt.** *Utah* U.S.A.
46 E1 **Duvan** Rus. Fed.
159 E3 **Duvergé** Dominican Rep.
139 F2 **Duvert, Lac l.** *Québec* Canada
42 F2 **Duwin** Iraq
32 D3 **Duyun** China
39 E4 **Duzab** Pakistan
42 B1 **Düzce** Turkey
Duzdab *see* **Zāhedān**
112 E3 **Dve Mogili** Bulgaria
54 E3 **Dviete** Latvia
50 F1 **Dvinskaya Guba** Rus. Fed.
53 B1 **Dvirets'** Ukraine
77 N5 **Dvirtsi** Ukraine
79 G2 **Dvorce** Czech Rep.
53 G2 **Dvorichna** Ukraine
52 D2 **Dvoyni** Rus. Fed.
78 E1 **Dvůr Králové** Czech Rep.
131 F2 **Dwaalboom** South Africa
36 B5 **Dwarka** India
131 F2 **Dwarsberg** South Africa
17 B7 **Dwellingup** *Western Australia* Australia
148 C5 **Dwight** *Illinois* U.S.A.
68 E2 **Dwingeloo** Netherlands
152 C2 **Dworshak Res. resr** *Idaho* U.S.A.
130 C6 **Dwyka r.** South Africa
130 C6 **Dwyka** South Africa
64 B3 **Dyan** *Northern Ireland* U.K.
52 B3 **Dyat'kovo** Rus. Fed.
55 D4 **Dybsø Fjord lag.** Denmark
66 F3 **Dyce** *Scotland* U.K.
73 L4 **Dychów** Poland
148 D5 **Dyer** *Indiana* U.S.A.
154 C3 **Dyer** *Nevada* U.S.A.
140 E4 **Dyer Bay** *Ontario* Canada
135 M3 **Dyer, C. c.** *N.W.T.* Canada
145 B4 **Dyersburg** *Tennessee* U.S.A.
148 B4 **Dyersville** *Iowa* U.S.A.
62 C2 **Dyfi r.** *Wales* U.K.
76 D1 **Dygowo** Poland
78 F3 **Dyje r.** Austria/Czech Rep.
53 F2 **Dykan'ka** Ukraine
66 E3 **Dyke** *Scotland* U.K.
51 G7 **Dykh Tau mt.** Georgia
78 B2 **Dyleň h.** Czech Rep.
77 H2 **Dylewska Góra h.** Poland
63 G3 **Dymchurch** *England* U.K.
53 D1 **Dymer** Ukraine
62 D3 **Dymock** *England* U.K.
53 G2 **Dymytrov** Ukraine
53 E2 **Dymytrove** *Kirovohrads'ka Oblast'* Ukraine
58 C1 **Dyna mt.** Norway
15 F6 **Dynevor Downs** *Queensland* Australia
77 L6 **Dynów** Poland
90 C2 **Dyo** France
131 G5 **Dyoki** South Africa
148 A4 **Dysart** *Iowa* U.S.A.
130 D6 **Dysselsdorp** South Africa
114 C4 **Dytiki Ellas div.** Greece
114 C2 **Dytiki Makedonia div.** Greece
46 F3 **Dyurmen'tyube** Kazakhstan
46 D1 **Dyurtyuli** Rus. Fed.
112 G2 **Dyviziya** Ukraine
77 J2 **Dywity** Poland
30 B3 **Dzaanhushuu** Mongolia
30 A3 **Dzag Gol r.** Mongolia
30 A3 **Dzalaa** Mongolia
30 D4 **Dzamïn Üüd** Mongolia
127 E7 **Dzaoudzi** *Mayotte* Africa
30 A2 **Dzavhan div.** Mongolia
78 C1 **Džbán mts** Czech Rep.
30 B3 **Dzegstey** Mongolia
53 B2 **Dzelentsi** Ukraine
30 C2 **Dzelter** Mongolia
52 F1 **Dzerzhinsk** Rus. Fed.
47 K3 **Dzerzhinskoye** Kazakhstan
53 B1 **Dzerzhyns'k** Ukraine
46 F3 **Dzhalagash** Kazakhstan
Dzhalal-Abad *see* **Jalal-Abad**
31 G1 **Dzhalinda** Rus. Fed.
46 D2 **Dzhambeyty** Kazakhstan
47 H3 **Dzhambul** Kazakhstan
46 D4 **Dzhanga** Turkmenistan
46 D3 **Dzhangala** Kazakhstan
46 F4 **Dzhankel'dy** Uzbekistan
51 E6 **Dzhankoy** Ukraine
47 J3 **Dzhansugurov** Kazakhstan
51 H5 **Dzhanybek** Rus. Fed.
47 G5 **Dzharkurgan** Uzbekistan
53 E3 **Dzharylhats"ka Zatoka b.** Ukraine
114 G1 **Dzhebel** Bulgaria
46 D5 **Dzhebel** Turkmenistan
46 F2 **Dzhetygara** Kazakhstan
47 G3 **Dzhezdy** Kazakhstan
47 G3 **Dzhezkazgan** Kazakhstan
30 C2 **Dzhida** Rus. Fed.
30 C2 **Dzhida** Rus. Fed.
30 B2 **Dzhidinskiy, Khrebet mountain range** Mongolia/Rus. Fed.
45 R3 **Dzhigudzhak** Rus. Fed.
47 G4 **Dzhizak** Uzbekistan
39 E1 **Dzhu-Dzhu-Klu** Turkmenistan
45 P4 **Dzhugdzhur, Khrebet mountain range** Rus. Fed.
Dzhul'fa *see* **Culfa**
53 C2 **Dzhulynka** Ukraine
47 G5 **Dzhuma** Uzbekistan
47 J4 **Dzhungarskiy Alatau, Khr. mountain range** China/Kazakhstan
46 E3 **Dzhurun** Kazakhstan
53 C2 **Dzhuryn** Ukraine
46 F3 **Dzhusaly** Kazakhstan
77 L3 **Dziadkowice** Poland
76 F4 **Dziadowa Kłoda** Poland
77 J2 **Działdowo** Poland
77 J5 **Działoszyce** Poland
76 G4 **Działoszyn** Poland
76 G2 **Działyń** Poland
157 H5 **Dzibalchén** Mexico
76 F1 **Dziemiany** Poland
77 H2 **Dzierzgoń** Poland
77 J2 **Dzierzgowo** Poland
76 E5 **Dzierżoniów** Poland
157 H4 **Dzilam de Bravo** Mexico
121 F2 **Dzioua** Algeria
54 E4 **Dzisna r.** Belarus/Lithuania
54 F4 **Dzisna** Belarus
77 O2 **Dzitva r.** Belarus
77 N4 **Dzivin** Belarus
76 C2 **Dziwna r.** Poland
77 M3 **Dzmitravichy** Belarus
123 E5 **Dzodze** Ghana
30 C3 **Dzogsool** Mongolia
30 A2 **Dzöölön** Mongolia
77 N1 **Dzūkija nat. park** Lithuania
Dzungarian Basin basin *see* **Junggar Pendi**
47 K3 **Dzungarian Gate pass** China/Kazakhstan
30 A2 **Dzur** Mongolia
30 D3 **Dzüünbayan** Mongolia
30 C2 **Dzüünharaa** Mongolia
30 C3 **Dzuunmod** Mongolia
77 J2 **Dźwierzuty** Poland
76 C1 **Dzwinów** Poland
54 E5 **Dzyaniskavichy** Belarus
77 N2 **Dzyarechyn** Belarus
54 E5 **Dzyarzhynsk** Belarus
54 D5 **Dzyatlava** Belarus

E

138 C3 **Eabamet L. l.** *Ontario* Canada
155 H4 **Eagar** *Arizona* U.S.A.
139 J3 **Eagle r.** *Newfoundland* Canada
153 F4 **Eagle** *Colorado* U.S.A.
147 F3 **Eagle Bay** *New York* U.S.A.
137 H4 **Eagle Cr. r.** *Saskatchewan* Canada
154 D4 **Eagle Crags summit** *California* U.S.A.
152 B3 **Eagle L. l.** *California* U.S.A.
138 B4 **Eagle L. l.** *Ontario* Canada
147 J1 **Eagle Lake l.** *Maine* U.S.A.
147 J1 **Eagle Lake** *Maine* U.S.A.
148 B2 **Eagle Mtn h.** *Minnesota* U.S.A.
151 C6 **Eagle Pass** *Texas* U.S.A.
134 E3 **Eagle Plain plain** *Yukon Terr.* Canada
148 C2 **Eagle River** *Michigan* U.S.A.
148 C3 **Eagle River** *Wisconsin* U.S.A.
136 F3 **Eaglesham** *Alberta* Canada
155 F5 **Eagle Tail Mts mts** *Arizona* U.S.A.
29 H4 **Eai-gawa r.** Japan
63 F3 **Ealing** *England* U.K.
17 C5 **Earaheedy** *Western Australia* Australia
138 B3 **Ear Falls** *Ontario* Canada
63 G2 **Earith** *England* U.K.
154 C4 **Earlimart** *California* U.S.A.
63 E2 **Earl Shilton** *England* U.K.
65 F2 **Earlston** *Scotland* U.K.
141 F3 **Earlton** *Ontario* Canada
66 E4 **Earn r.** *Scotland* U.K.
66 D4 **Earn, L. l.** *Scotland* U.K.
9 B6 **Earnslaw, Mt mt.** New Zealand
151 C5 **Earth** *Texas* U.S.A.
64 C1 **Easdale** *Scotland* U.K.
63 F4 **Easebourne** *England* U.K.
65 G3 **Easington** *England* U.K.
65 J4 **Easington** *England* U.K.
65 G3 **Easingwold** *England* U.K.
145 D5 **Easley** *S. Carolina* U.S.A.
14 C2 **East Alligator r.** *Northern Terr.* Australia
141 K4 **East Angus** *Québec* Canada
179 C5 **East Antarctica reg.** Antarctica
147 F4 **East Ararat** *Pennsylvania* U.S.A.
146 D3 **East Aurora** *New York* U.S.A.
66 D5 **East Ayrshire div.** *Scotland* U.K.
14 B2 **East Baines r.** *Northern Terr.* Australia
151 F6 **East Bay b.** *Louisiana* U.S.A.
147 G2 **East Berkshire** *Vermont* U.S.A.
63 G4 **Eastbourne** *England* U.K.
9 E4 **Eastbourne** New Zealand
146 D4 **East Branch Clarion River Reservoir resr** *Pennsylvania* U.S.A.
147 H4 **East Brooklyn** *Connecticut* U.S.A.
141 K3 **East Broughton Station** *Québec* Canada
8 G2 **East Cape c.** New Zealand
East Cape c. *see* **M. Dezhneva**
155 G2 **East Carbon** *Utah* U.S.A.
148 D5 **East Chicago** *Indiana* U.S.A.
27 M6 **East China Sea sea** Asia
8 E2 **East Coast Bays** New Zealand
62 D4 **East Coker** *England* U.K.
147 G2 **East Corinth** *Vermont* U.S.A.
63 G4 **East Dean** *England* U.K.
63 G2 **East Dereham** *England* U.K.
66 D5 **East Dunbartonshire div.** *Scotland* U.K.
145 □2 **East End Pt pt** The Bahamas
23 □1 **East Entrance chan.** Palau
7 □16 **Easter I. i.** Chile
177 M7 **Easter Island Fracture Zone sea feature** Pacific Ocean
122 D5 **Eastern div.** Ghana
126 C4 **Eastern div.** Kenya
122 B5 **Eastern div.** Sierra Leone
119 G4 **Eastern div.** Sudan
127 B7 **Eastern div.** Zambia
101 □ **Eastern Beach beach** Gibraltar
131 F5 **Eastern Cape div.** South Africa
119 F2 **Eastern Desert desert** Egypt
38 B3 **Eastern Ghats mountain range** India
9 □2 **Eastern Group is** *Bounty Is* New Zealand
Eastern Group is *see* **Lau Group**
131 G2 **Eastern Transvaal div.** South Africa
66 D3 **Easter Ross reg.** *Scotland* U.K.
137 K4 **Easterville** *Manitoba* Canada
171 E7 **East Falkland i.** Falkland Is.
147 H4 **East Falmouth** *Massachusetts* U.S.A.
63 G1 **East Fen reg.** *England* U.K.
65 H3 **Eastfield** *England* U.K.
154 D2 **Eastgate** *Nevada* U.S.A.
150 D2 **East Grand Forks** *Minnesota* U.S.A.
63 F3 **East Grinstead** *England* U.K.
147 G3 **Easthampton** *Massachusetts* U.S.A.
147 G4 **East Hampton** *New York* U.S.A.
146 D4 **East Hickory** *Pennsylvania* U.S.A.
147 G3 **East Jamaica** *Vermont* U.S.A.
178 B5 **East Jan Mayen Ridge sea feature** Atlantic Ocean
148 E3 **East Jordan** *Michigan* U.S.A.
66 D5 **East Kilbride** *Scotland* U.K.
148 D3 **East Lake** *Michigan* U.S.A.
27 □ **East Lamma Channel chan.** *Hong Kong*
63 E4 **Eastleigh** *England* U.K.
66 F5 **East Linton** *Scotland* U.K.
146 C4 **East Liverpool** *Ohio* U.S.A.
66 B3 **East Loch Tarbert b.** *Scotland* U.K.
131 F6 **East London** South Africa
62 B4 **East Looe** *England* U.K.
66 F5 **East Lothian div.** *Scotland* U.K.
146 B5 **East Lynn Lake l.** *W. Virginia* U.S.A.
138 F3 **Eastmain r.** *Québec* Canada
138 E3 **Eastmain** *Québec* Canada
145 D5 **Eastman** *Georgia* U.S.A.
141 J4 **Eastman** *Québec* Canada
15 F4 **Eastmere** *Queensland* Australia
63 E2 **East Midlands airport** *England* U.K.
147 J2 **East Millinocket** *Maine* U.S.A.
148 B5 **East Moline** *Illinois* U.S.A.
148 C5 **Easton** *Illinois* U.S.A.
147 E5 **Easton** *Maryland* U.S.A.
147 F4 **Easton** *Pennsylvania* U.S.A.
177 M8 **East Pacific Ridge sea feature** Pacific Ocean
177 N5 **East Pacific Rise sea feature** Pacific Ocean
154 A2 **East Park Res. resr** *California* U.S.A.
145 C5 **East Point** *Georgia* U.S.A.
147 K2 **Eastport** *Maine* U.S.A.
148 E3 **Eastport** *Michigan* U.S.A.
10 □4 **East Pt pt** *Lord Howe I.* Pacific Ocean
139 H4 **East Pt pt** *Prince Edward I.* Canada
128 □3 **East Pt pt** *Tristan da Cunha* Atlantic Ocean
145 □3 **East Pt pt** *Virgin Is* Caribbean
145 □3 **East Pt pt** *Virgin Is* Caribbean
154 D1 **East Range mts** *Nevada* U.S.A.
66 D5 **East Renfrewshire div.** *Scotland* U.K.
East Retford *see* **Retford**
63 H3 **Eastry** *England* U.K.
144 B4 **East St Louis** *Illinois* U.S.A.
East Siberian Sea sea *see* **Vostochno-Sibirskoye More**
13 G4 **East Sister I. i.** *Tasmania* Australia
63 G4 **East Sussex div.** *England* U.K.
37 E4 **East Tons r.** India
148 C4 **East Troy** *Wisconsin* U.S.A.
147 F6 **Eastville** *Virginia* U.S.A.
154 C2 **East Walker r.** *Nevada* U.S.A.
147 G3 **East Wallingford** *Vermont* U.S.A.
65 E1 **East Wemyss** *Scotland* U.K.
63 F4 **East Wittering** *England* U.K.
63 E1 **Eastwood** *England* U.K.
146 A5 **Eaton** *Ohio* U.S.A.
63 F2 **Eaton Socon** *England* U.K.
145 D5 **Eatonton** *Georgia* U.S.A.
148 B3 **Eau Claire r.** *Wisconsin* U.S.A.
148 B3 **Eau Claire** *Wisconsin* U.S.A.
138 F2 **Eau Claire, Lac á l' l.** *Québec* Canada
86 D2 **Eau d'Heure, l' l.** Belgium
89 G2 **Eaulne r.** France
176 E5 **Eauripik - New Guinea Rise sea feature** Pacific Ocean
93 B6 **Eaux-Bonnes** France
93 C5 **Eauze** France
15 E2 **Ebagoola** *Queensland* Australia
123 E5 **Eban** Nigeria
157 F4 **Ebano** Mexico
80 D3 **Ebbs** Austria
62 C3 **Ebbw Vale** *Wales* U.K.
124 B3 **Ebebiyin** Equatorial Guinea
73 F4 **Ebeleben** Germany
55 C3 **Ebeltoft** Denmark
55 C3 **Ebeltoft Vig b.** Denmark
81 E4 **Ebene Reichenau** Austria
131 G1 **Ebenezer Dam dam** South Africa
81 H3 **Ebenfurth** Austria
81 E3 **Eben im Pongau** Austria
146 D4 **Ebensburg** *Pennsylvania* U.S.A.
81 E3 **Ebensee** Austria
75 F2 **Ebensfeld** Germany
81 F4 **Ebental** Austria
74 D3 **Eberbach** Germany
72 F4 **Ebergötzen** Germany
75 F2 **Ebern** Germany
81 F4 **Eberndorf** Austria
73 K4 **Ebersbach** Germany
75 G4 **Ebersberg** Germany
81 E2 **Eberschwang** Austria
81 G3 **Ebersdorf** Austria
72 E2 **Ebersdorf** Germany
75 G2 **Ebersdorf bei Coburg** Germany
81 F4 **Eberstein** Austria
73 J3 **Eberswalde-Finow** Germany
140 D5 **Eberts** *Ontario* Canada
28 H2 **Ebetsu** Japan
32 C2 **Ebian** China
83 D1 **Ebikon** Switzerland
47 K4 **Ebinur Hu salt lake** China
43 D2 **Ebla** Syria
83 E1 **Ebnat-Kappel** Switzerland
124 D3 **Ebola r.** Zaire
109 H4 **Eboli** Italy
124 B3 **Ebolowa** Cameroon
128 B3 **Ebony** Namibia
81 H3 **Ebreichsdorf** Austria
90 B2 **Ébreuil** France
82 C1 **Ebringen** Germany
102 D4 **Ebro r.** Spain
99 G1 **Ebro, Emb. del resr** Spain
72 F2 **Ebstorf** Germany
69 C4 **Écaussinnes-d'Enghien** Belgium
66 E5 **Ecclefechan** *Scotland* U.K.
62 D2 **Eccleshall** *England* U.K.
159 □3 **Ecclesville** Trinidad and Tobago
42 A1 **Eceabat** Turkey
23 B2 **Echague** Philippines
82 B2 **Echallens** Switzerland
99 H2 **Echarri-Aranaz** Spain
121 E1 **Ech Chélif** Algeria
99 H2 **Echegárate, Pto pass** Spain
33 F2 **Echeng** China
90 E1 **Échenoz-la-Méline** France
114 B4 **Echinades i.** Greece
75 G4 **Eching** Germany
114 F1 **Echinos** Greece
92 B2 **Échiré** France
91 D3 **Échirolles** France
29 E6 **Echizen-misaki pt** Japan
Echmiadzin *see* **Ejmiadzin**
136 F1 **Echo Bay** *N.W.T.* Canada
140 C3 **Echo Bay** *Ontario* Canada
155 G3 **Echo Cliffs cliff** *Arizona* U.S.A.
138 B3 **Echoing r.** *Manitoba* Canada
13 F5 **Echo, L. l.** *Tasmania* Australia
141 H3 **Échouani, Lac l.** *Québec* Canada
92 C3 **Échourgnac** France
81 G2 **Echsenbach** Austria
69 D3 **Echt** Netherlands
69 E5 **Echternach** Luxembourg
13 F4 **Echuca** *Victoria* Australia
74 D2 **Echzell** Germany
101 E3 **Ecija** Spain
173 J3 **Ecilda Paullier** Uruguay
75 G3 **Eckental** Germany
148 E2 **Eckerman** *Michigan* U.S.A.
72 E1 **Eckernförde** Germany
72 F1 **Eckernförder Bucht b.** Germany
59 H1 **Eckerö** Finland
62 D2 **Eckington** *England* U.K.
63 E1 **Eckington** *England* U.K.
66 D4 **Eck, Loch l.** *Scotland* U.K.
86 D4 **Éclaron-Braucourt-Ste-Livière** France
135 L2 **Eclipse Sound chan.** *N.W.T.* Canada
89 F4 **Écommoy** France
169 H3 **Ecoporanga** Brazil
89 G2 **Écos** France
89 E3 **Écouché** France
91 E4 **Ecrins, Parc National des nat. park** France
87 E4 **Écrouves** France
160 E4 **Ecuador country** South America
89 G4 **Écueillé** France
138 E2 **Écueils, Pte aux pt** *Québec* Canada
126 D2 **Ed** Eritrea
58 D2 **Ed** Sweden
137 H4 **Edam** *Saskatchewan* Canada
68 D2 **Edam** Netherlands
66 F1 **Eday i.** *Scotland* U.K.
124 E1 **Ed Da'ein** Sudan
119 F5 **Ed Dair, Jebel mt.** Sudan
126 B2 **Ed Damazin** Sudan
119 F4 **Ed Damer** Sudan
119 F4 **Ed Debba** Sudan
65 E2 **Eddleston** *Scotland* U.K.
119 F5 **Ed Dueim** Sudan
13 G5 **Eddystone Pt pt** *Tasmania* Australia
148 A5 **Eddyville** *Iowa* U.S.A.
68 D2 **Ede** *Gelderland* Netherlands
123 E5 **Ede** Nigeria
124 B3 **Edéa** Cameroon
69 C3 **Edegem** Belgium
137 K2 **Edehon Lake l.** *N.W.T.* Canada
168 D2 **Edéia** Brazil
72 F3 **Edemissen** Germany
65 F3 **Eden r.** *England* U.K.
146 D6 **Eden** *N. Carolina* U.S.A.
13 G4 **Eden** *New South Wales* Australia
151 D6 **Eden** *Texas* U.S.A.
131 E4 **Edenburg** South Africa
9 B7 **Edendale** New Zealand
131 H4 **Edendale** South Africa
67 D3 **Edenderry** Rep. of Ireland
12 E4 **Edenhope** *Victoria* Australia
87 H3 **Edenkoben** Germany
145 E4 **Edenton** *N. Carolina* U.S.A.
131 F3 **Edenville** South Africa
72 D4 **Eder r.** Germany
72 E4 **Edermünde-Grifte** Germany
64 A3 **Ederny** *Northern Ireland* U.K.
74 D3 **Edesheim** Germany
114 D2 **Edessa** Greece
72 C2 **Edewecht** Germany
16 C4 **Edgar, Mt h.** *Western Australia* Australia
16 C3 **Edgar Ra. h.** *Western Australia* Australia
147 H4 **Edgartown** *Massachusetts* U.S.A.
150 D2 **Edgeley** *N. Dakota* U.S.A.
150 C3 **Edgemont** *S. Dakota* U.S.A.
178 □3 **Edgeøya i.** *Svalbard* Arctic Ocean
148 C4 **Edgerton** *Wisconsin* U.S.A.
67 D3 **Edgeworthstown** Rep. of Ireland
69 F4 **Ediger-Eller** Germany
148 A5 **Edina** *Missouri* U.S.A.
148 C6 **Edinburg** *Illinois* U.S.A.
151 D7 **Edinburg** *Texas* U.S.A.
66 E5 **Edinburgh** *Scotland* U.K.
66 E5 **Edinburgh, City of div.** *Scotland* U.K.
53 B2 **Edineţ** Moldova
113 F4 **Edirne div.** Turkey
42 A1 **Edirne** Turkey
136 F4 **Edith Cavell, Mt mt.** *Alberta* Canada
118 A2 **Edjeleh** Libya
123 E3 **Édjérir watercourse** Mali
17 C6 **Edjudina** *Western Australia* Australia
58 B2 **Edland** Norway
65 G2 **Edlingham** *England* U.K.
81 H3 **Edlitz** Austria
152 B2 **Edmonds** *Washington* U.S.A.
136 G4 **Edmonton** *Alberta* Canada
137 K5 **Edmore** *N. Dakota* U.S.A.
148 B4 **Edmund** *Wisconsin* U.S.A.
65 G3 **Edmundbyres** *England* U.K.
137 L4 **Edmund L. l.** *Manitoba* Canada
139 G4 **Edmundston** *New Brunswick* Canada
151 D6 **Edna** *Texas* U.S.A.
136 C3 **Edna Bay** *Alaska* U.S.A.
123 F5 **Edo div.** Nigeria
106 E2 **Edolo** Italy
43 C4 **Edom reg.** Israel/Jordan
42 A2 **Edremit** Turkey
113 F5 **Edremit Körfezi b.** Turkey
30 A3 **Edrengiyn Nuruu mountain range** Mongolia
98 D3 **Edrosa** Portugal
59 H2 **Edsbro** Sweden
59 G2 **Edsbruk** Sweden
57 D3 **Edsbyn** Sweden
136 F4 **Edson** *Alberta* Canada
59 E2 **Edsvalla** Sweden
172 E3 **Eduardo Castex** Argentina
13 F3 **Edward r.** *New South Wales* Australia
15 E2 **Edward r.** *Queensland* Australia
Edwardesabad *see* **Banmi**
14 C2 **Edward I. i.** *Northern Terr.* Australia
140 A2 **Edward I. i.** *Ontario* Canada
127 A5 **Edward, Lake l.** Uganda/Zaire
14 B4 **Edward, Mt mt.** *Northern Terr.* Australia
15 E2 **Edward River** *Queensland* Australia
15 E2 **Edward River Abor. Land res.** *Queensland* Australia
147 F2 **Edwards** *New York* U.S.A.
12 C2 **Edward's Cr.** *S. Australia* Australia
151 C6 **Edwards Plateau plat.** *Texas* U.S.A.
144 B4 **Edwardsville** *Illinois* U.S.A.
179 D4 **Edward VIII Ice Shelf ice feature** Antarctica
179 A4 **Edward VII Pen. pen.** Antarctica
136 C3 **Edziza Pk mt.** *B.C.* Canada
124 B4 **Edzouga** Congo
69 B3 **Eeklo div.** *Oost-Vlaanderen* Belgium
69 B3 **Eeklo** Belgium
154 A1 **Eel r.** *California* U.S.A.
68 E1 **Eelde** Netherlands
68 D2 **Eem r.** Netherlands
68 E1 **Eemshaven** Netherlands
68 E1 **Eemskanaal canal** Netherlands
130 C3 **Eenzamheid Pan l.** South Africa
68 E2 **Eerbeek** Netherlands
69 B3 **Eernegem** Belgium
69 D3 **Eersel** Netherlands
6 □2 **Éfaté i.** Vanuatu
81 E2 **Eferding div.** Austria
81 F2 **Eferding** Austria
144 B4 **Effingham** *Illinois* U.S.A.
123 E5 **Effon-Alaiye** Nigeria
83 D1 **Effretikon** Switzerland
112 G2 **Eforie** Romania
115 C4 **Efpali** Greece
74 C5 **Efringen-Kirchen** Germany
114 D3 **Efxeinoupoli** Greece
114 B3 **Efyra Nekromanteio** Greece
30 D2 **Eg** Mongolia
102 B2 **Ega r.** Spain
155 E2 **Egan Range mts** *Nevada* U.S.A.
141 G4 **Eganville** *Ontario* Canada
73 G4 **Egeln** Germany
87 H3 **Egelsbach** Germany
55 C3 **Egense** Denmark
75 H2 **Eger r.** Germany
79 K4 **Eger** Hungary
79 K4 **Eger-patak r.** Hungary
58 B2 **Egersund** Norway
81 H4 **Egervár** Hungary
72 F2 **Egestorf** Germany
80 A3 **Egg** Austria
58 C1 **Eggedøla r.** Norway
72 D4 **Eggegebirge h.** Germany
81 G2 **Eggenburg** Austria
75 H4 **Eggenfelden** Germany
74 D3 **Eggenstein-Leopoldshafen** Germany
73 K2 **Eggesin** Germany
74 D5 **Eggingen** Germany
82 C2 **Eggiwil** Switzerland
75 J4 **Egglham** Germany
75 G3 **Eggolsheim** Germany
69 C4 **Eghezée** Belgium
55 B2 **Egholm i.** Denmark
55 D4 **Egholm i.** Denmark
66 F1 **Egilsay i.** *Scotland* U.K.
56 N6 **Egilsstaðir** Iceland
16 B4 **Eginbah** *Western Australia* Australia
47 J2 **Egindy** Kazakhstan
80 E2 **Eging am See** Germany
42 B2 **Eğirdir** Turkey
42 B2 **Eğirdir Gölü l.** Turkey
30 B2 **Egiyn Gol r.** Mongolia
92 E3 **Égletons** France
80 C3 **Egling** Germany
65 G2 **Eglingham** *England* U.K.
67 D1 **Eglinton** *Northern Ireland* U.K.
134 G2 **Eglinton I. i.** *N.W.T.* Canada
83 D1 **Eglisau** Switzerland
62 C2 **Eglwys Fach** *Wales* U.K.
68 C2 **Egmond aan Zee** Netherlands
8 D3 **Egmont, Cape c.** New Zealand
8 E3 **Egmont, Mt volcano** New Zealand
8 E3 **Egmont National Park nat. park** New Zealand
107 F2 **Egna** Italy
65 E3 **Egremont** *England* U.K.
113 G5 **Eğrigöz Dağı mts** Turkey
65 H3 **Egton** *England* U.K.
55 B4 **Egtved** Denmark
166 C3 **Éguas r.** Brazil
91 D5 **Eguilles** France
92 D2 **Éguzon, Barrage d' dam** France
92 D2 **Éguzon-Chantôme** France
134 A3 **Egvekinot** Rus. Fed.
81 H3 **Egyházasfalu** Hungary
78 F4 **Egyházasrádóc** Hungary
116 G3 **Egypt country** Africa
15 E3 **E. Haydon** *Queensland* Australia
28 D7 **Ehime div.** Japan
75 F3 **Ehingen** Germany
74 E4 **Ehingen (Donau)** Germany
73 H3 **Ehle r.** Germany
73 F3 **Ehra-Lessien** Germany
155 E5 **Ehrenberg** *Arizona* U.S.A.
14 B4 **Ehrenberg Ra. h.** *Northern Terr.* Australia
87 H2 **Ehringshausen** Germany
80 B3 **Ehrwald** Austria
99 H1 **Eibar** Spain
74 F3 **Eibelstadt** Germany
75 H2 **Eibenstock** Germany
68 E2 **Eibergen** Netherlands
81 G4 **Eibiswald** Austria
73 G3 **Eichenbarleben** Germany
75 H4 **Eichendorf** Germany
74 E2 **Eichenzell** Germany
81 G2 **Eichgraben** Austria
72 F4 **Eichsfeld reg.** Germany
75 G4 **Eichstätt** Germany
73 J3 **Eichwalde** Germany
72 E1 **Eider r.** Germany
58 B1 **Eidfjord** Norway
55 □1 **Eiði** Faeroes
59 E1 **Eidskog** Norway
58 A2 **Eidsund** Norway
15 G5 **Eidsvold** *Queensland* Australia
58 D1 **Eidsvoll** Norway
178 □3 **Eidsvollfjellet mt.** *Svalbard* Arctic Ocean
74 B2 **Eifel reg.** Germany
83 D1 **Eigeltingen** Germany
82 D2 **Eiger mt.** Switzerland
58 A2 **Eigerøya i.** Norway
66 B4 **Eigg i.** *Scotland* U.K.
35 D9 **Eight Degree Channel chan.** India/Maldives
179 A3 **Eights Coast coastal area** Antarctica
16 C3 **Eighty Mile Beach beach** *Western Australia* Australia
69 D4 **Eijsden** Netherlands
58 A1 **Eikelandsosen** Norway
13 F4 **Eildon, Lake l.** *Victoria* Australia
Eilean Barraigh i. *see* **Barra**
Eilean Bhearnaraigh i. *see* **Berneray**
Eilean Leodhais i. *see* **Lewis**
Eilean Scalpaigh i. *see* **Scalpay**
66 C4 **Eilean Shona i.** *Scotland* U.K.
137 H2 **Eileen Lake l.** *N.W.T.* Canada
73 H4 **Eilenburg** Germany
163 F3 **Eilerts de Haan Geb mountain range** Surinam
23 □1 **Eil Malk i.** Palau
73 G3 **Eilsleben** Germany
72 F3 **Eimke** Germany
15 E3 **Einasleigh r.** *Queensland* Australia
15 F3 **Einasleigh** *Queensland* Australia
58 D1 **Einavatnet l.** Norway
72 E4 **Einbeck** Germany
69 D3 **Eindhoven** Netherlands
130 B2 **Eindpaal** Namibia
119 E4 **Ein Mansur well** Sudan
24 A3 **Einme** Myanmar
83 D1 **Einsiedeln** Switzerland
Eiriosgaigh i. *see* **Eriskay**
162 D5 **Eirunepé** Brazil
72 E4 **Eisberg h.** Germany
69 E5 **Eisch r.** Luxembourg
128 C3 **Eiseb watercourse** Botswana/Namibia
75 H4 **Eiselfing** Germany
74 F2 **Eisenach** Germany
75 G2 **Eisenberg** Germany
74 D3 **Eisenberg (Pfalz)** Germany
81 F3 **Eisenerz** Austria
81 F3 **Eisenerzer Alpen mts** Austria
81 E4 **Eisenhut mt.** Austria
73 K3 **Eisenhüttenstadt** Germany
81 F4 **Eisenkappel** Austria
81 H3 **Eisenstadt** Austria
81 H3 **Eisenstadt-Umgebung div.** Austria
81 F3 **Eisenwurzen reg.** Austria
75 F2 **Eisfeld** Germany
66 B3 **Eishort, Loch inlet** *Scotland* U.K.
54 D4 **Eišiškės** Lithuania
80 A2 **Eislingen (Fils)** Germany
80 C2 **Eitensheim** Germany
74 E2 **Eiterfeld** Germany
87 G2 **Eitorf** Germany
58 A1 **Eivinvik** Norway
103 E5 **Eivissa i.** *Islas Baleares* Spain
103 E6 **Eivissa** Spain
55 B4 **Ejby** *Fyn* Denmark
55 D4 **Ejby** *Roskilde* Denmark
102 B2 **Ejea de los Caballeros** Spain
129 G3 **Ejeda** Madagascar
156 C3 **Ejido Insurgentes** Mexico
30 D5 **Ejin Horo Qi** China
30 B4 **Ejin Qi** China
42 F1 **Ejmiadzin** Armenia
55 B4 **Ejstrupholm** Denmark
102 C4 **Ejulve** Spain
122 D5 **Ejura** Ghana
157 F5 **Ejutla** Mexico
57 F4 **Ekenäs** Finland
59 G2 **Ekerö** Sweden

89 E2 Évrecy France
89 G2 Évreux France
89 E3 Évron France
113 F4 Evros r. Greece/Turkey
115 D5 Evrotas r. Greece
86 B4 Évry France
114 C3 Evrytania div. Greece
114 E4 Evvoia div. Greece
115 F4 Evvoia i. Greece
153 □1 Ewa Beach Hawaii U.S.A.
159 □1 Ewarton Jamaica
127 C5 Ewaso Ngiro r. Kenya
130 D3 Ewbank South Africa
66 C3 Ewe, Loch inlet Scotland U.K.
31 F2 Ewenkizu Zizhiqi China
8 □1 Ewing I. i. Auckland Is New Zealand
179 B2 Ewing I. i. Antarctica
124 B4 Ewo Congo
164 C2 Exaltación Bolivia
131 F4 Excelsior South Africa
154 C2 Excelsior Mt mt. California U.S.A.
154 C2 Excelsior Mts mts Nevada U.S.A.
150 E4 Excelsior Springs Missouri U.S.A.
92 D3 Excideuil France
62 C4 Exe r. England U.K.
179 A4 Executive Committee Range mountain range Antarctica
154 C3 Exeter California U.S.A.
62 C4 Exeter England U.K.
147 H3 Exeter New Hampshire U.S.A.
13 G3 Exeter New South Wales Australia
140 E5 Exeter Ontario Canada
82 B3 Exilles Italy
89 F3 Exmes France
62 C4 Exminster England U.K.
62 C3 Exmoor reg. England U.K.
62 C3 Exmoor National Park nat. park England U.K.
147 F6 Exmore Virginia U.S.A.
62 C4 Exmouth England U.K.
16 A4 Exmouth Western Australia Australia
16 A4 Exmouth Gulf b. Western Australia Australia
175 M5 Exmouth Plateau sea feature Indian Ocean
114 E1 Exochi Greece
15 G5 Expedition Range mountain range Queensland Australia
6 □7 Exploring Is is Fiji
100 D1 Extremadura div. Spain
124 B1 Extrême-Nord div. Cameroon
98 B3 Extremo Portugal
166 E2 Exú Brazil
158 C1 Exuma Sound chan. The Bahamas
124 D4 Eyangu Zaire
127 B5 Eyasi, Lake salt lake Tanzania
91 D3 Eybens France
63 H2 Eye England U.K.
63 F2 Eye England U.K.
66 F5 Eyemouth Scotland U.K.
66 B2 Eye Peninsula pen. Scotland U.K.
91 D4 Eygues r. France
91 D4 Eyguians France
91 D5 Eyguières France
92 E3 Eygurande France
92 C3 Eygurande-et-Gardedeuil France
56 M6 Eyjafjörður b. Iceland
126 E3 Eyl Somalia
93 C4 Eymet France
92 D3 Eymoutiers France
Eynihal see Kale
39 C2 Eyn or Rashid Iran
63 E3 Eynsham England U.K.
93 B4 Eyre r. France
14 D5 Eyre Cr. watercourse Queensland Australia
92 D3 Eyrein France
9 B6 Eyre Mountains mountain range New Zealand
12 D2 Eyre (North), Lake salt flat S. Australia Australia
12 C3 Eyre Peninsula pen. S. Australia Australia
12 D2 Eyre (South), L. salt flat S. Australia Australia
91 C4 Eyrieux r. France
93 B4 Eysines France
72 E3 Eystrup Germany
55 □1 Eysturoy i. Faeroes
127 C5 Eyuku waterhole Kenya
124 A2 Eyumojok Cameroon
131 H4 Ezakheni South Africa
99 H2 Ezcaray Spain
91 F5 Èze France
50 J2 Ezhva Rus. Fed.
42 A2 Ezine Turkey
68 E1 Ezinge Netherlands
89 G3 Ézy-sur-Eure France

F

7 □11 Faaa French Polynesia Pacific Ocean
35 D9 Faadhippolhu Atoll atoll Maldives
126 D4 Faafxadhuun Somalia
7 □10 Faaite i. French Polynesia Pacific Ocean
7 □11 Faaone French Polynesia Pacific Ocean
93 D5 Fabas France
151 B6 Fabens Texas U.S.A.
136 F2 Faber Lake l. N.W.T. Canada
25 □ Faber, Mt h. Singapore
98 D2 Fabero Spain
77 H3 Fabianki Poland
79 K5 Fábiánsebestyén Hungary
55 C4 Fåborg Denmark
79 J3 Fabova hoľa mt. Slovakia
91 B5 Fabrègues France
93 E5 Fabrezan France
107 G5 Fabriano Italy
101 H2 Fábricas de San Juan de Alcaraz Spain
111 F4 Fabrizia Italy
162 C3 Facatativá Colombia
86 C2 Faches-Thumesnil France
123 G3 Fachi Niger
100 E4 Fachinas Spain
15 G4 Facing I. i. Queensland Australia
23 □2 Facpi Pt pt Guam Pacific Ocean
147 F4 Factoryville Pennsylvania U.S.A.
171 B6 Facundo Argentina
118 D4 Fada Chad
123 E4 Fada-Ngourma Burkina
126 E2 Faḍli reg. Yemen
55 B4 Fænø i. Denmark
107 F4 Faenza Italy
Færingehavn see Kangerluarsoruseq
55 □1 Faeroes is Atlantic Ocean
109 H3 Faeto Italy
6 □4 Fafa i. Tonga
124 C2 Fafa r. Central African Rep.
21 K7 Fafanlap Indonesia
98 B3 Fafe Portugal
126 D3 Fafen Shet' watercourse Ethiopia
7 □12 Fagaloa Bay b. Western Samoa
7 □12 Fagamalo Western Samoa
112 E2 Făgăraş Romania
59 F3 Fågelfors Sweden
59 F3 Fagerhult Sweden
58 C1 Fagernes Norway
59 F2 Fagersta Sweden
79 M6 Făget Romania
107 F4 Faggeta, Monte la mt. Italy
123 F4 Faggo Nigeria
111 F3 Fagnano Castello Italy
171 C7 Fagnano, L. l. Argentina
69 C4 Fagne reg. Belgium
86 D4 Fagnières France
122 D3 Faguibine, Lac l. Mali
56 M7 Fagurhólsmýri Iceland
126 B3 Fagwir Sudan
39 D3 Fahraj Iran
100 □ Faial i. Azores Portugal
96 □ Faial Madeira Portugal
109 G3 Faicchio Italy
69 F4 Faid Germany
83 D2 Faido Switzerland
141 G2 Faillon, Lac l. Québec Canada
69 D4 Faimes Belgium
134 D3 Fairbanks Alaska U.S.A.
146 B5 Fairborn Ohio U.S.A.
150 D3 Fairbury Nebraska U.S.A.
146 E5 Fairfax Virginia U.S.A.
154 A2 Fairfield California U.S.A.
148 B5 Fairfield Iowa U.S.A.
146 A5 Fairfield Ohio U.S.A.
151 D6 Fairfield Texas U.S.A.
147 G3 Fair Haven Vermont U.S.A.
67 E1 Fair Head headland Northern Ireland U.K.
23 A4 Fairie Queen sand bank Philippines
66 □1 Fair Isle i. Scotland U.K.
63 G4 Fairlight England U.K.
15 F2 Fairlight Queensland Australia
150 E3 Fairmont Minnesota U.S.A.
146 C5 Fairmont W. Virginia U.S.A.
153 F4 Fairplay Colorado U.S.A.
148 D3 Fairport Michigan U.S.A.
146 C4 Fairport Harbor Ohio U.S.A.
136 F3 Fairview Alberta Canada
149 E3 Fairview Michigan U.S.A.
151 D4 Fairview Oklahoma U.S.A.
15 F2 Fairview Queensland Australia
155 G2 Fairview Utah U.S.A.
27 □ Fairview Park Hong Kong
136 B3 Fairweather, Cape c. Alaska U.S.A.
136 B3 Fairweather, Mt mt. Alaska/British Columbia Canada/U.S.A.
64 A3 Fairy Water r. Northern Ireland U.K.
21 M5 Fais i. Fed. States of Micronesia
36 C3 Faisalabad Pakistan
86 D3 Faissault France
115 F7 Faistos Greece
150 C2 Faith S. Dakota U.S.A.
66 □2 Faither, The pt Scotland U.K.
37 E4 Faizabad India
145 □3 Fajardo Puerto Rico
77 L4 Fajsławice Poland
7 □10 Fakaina i. French Polynesia Pacific Ocean
6 □3 Fakalele i. Tonga
5 K5 Fakaofo i. Tokelau
7 □10 Fakarava i. French Polynesia Pacific Ocean
63 G2 Fakenham England U.K.
56 D3 Fåker Sweden
21 K7 Fakfak Indonesia
39 C3 Fakhrabad Iran
55 E4 Fakse Denmark
55 E4 Fakse Bugt b. Denmark
55 E4 Fakse Ladeplads Denmark
31 G4 Faku China
62 B4 Fal r. England U.K.
122 B5 Falaba Sierra Leone
123 E4 Falagountou Burkina
89 E3 Falaise France
118 C4 Falaise d'Angamma cliff Chad
122 D4 Falaise de Bandiagara escarpment Mali
122 D4 Falaise de Banfora escarpment Burkina
123 F3 Falaise de Tiguidit escarpment Niger
37 G4 Falakata India
24 A2 Falam Myanmar
39 B2 Falavarjan Iran
107 F2 Falcade Italy
64 A2 Falcarragh Rep. of Ireland
112 G1 Fălciu Romania
107 F5 Falco, Monte mt. Italy
Falcon i. see Fonuafo'ou
110 D5 Falconara Sicilia Italy
107 H5 Falconara Marittima Italy
111 E4 Falcone Sicilia Italy
108 A4 Falcone, Capo del pt Sardegna Italy
151 D7 Falcon Lake l. Mexico/U.S.A.
55 C4 Faldsled Denmark
7 □12 Falealupo Western Samoa
7 □12 Faleasiu Western Samoa
7 □12 Falelima Western Samoa
122 B4 Falémé r. Mali/Senegal
50 J3 Falenki Rus. Fed.
7 □12 Falerai Western Samoa
111 F3 Falerna Italy
53 B3 Făleşti Moldova
7 □12 Faleula Western Samoa
151 D7 Falfurrias Texas U.S.A.
136 F3 Falher Alberta Canada
126 C1 Falkat r. Eritrea
73 J4 Falkenberg Germany
59 E3 Falkenberg Sweden
73 H2 Falkenhagen Germany
76 A4 Falkenhain Germany
73 J3 Falkensee Germany
75 H3 Falkenstein Bayern Germany
75 H2 Falkenstein Sachsen Germany
66 E5 Falkirk div. Scotland U.K.
66 E5 Falkirk Scotland U.K.
66 E4 Falkland Scotland U.K.
171 E7 Falkland Islands is Atlantic Ocean
171 D7 Falkland Sound chan. Falkland Is.
172 D6 Falkner Argentina
115 E6 Falkonera i. Greece
59 E2 Falköping Sweden
77 J4 Fałków Poland
154 D5 Fallbrook California U.S.A.
92 A2 Falleron France
72 E3 Fallingbostel Germany
154 C2 Fallon Nevada U.S.A.
147 H4 Fall River Massachusetts U.S.A.
152 F3 Fall River Pass Colorado U.S.A.
150 E3 Falls City Nebraska U.S.A.
59 E1 Falltorp Sweden
123 E4 Falmey Niger
159 □7 Falmouth Antigua Caribbean
62 A4 Falmouth England U.K.
146 A5 Falmouth Kentucky U.S.A.
147 H3 Falmouth Maine U.S.A.
148 E3 Falmouth Michigan U.S.A.
159 □1 Falmouth Jamaica
62 A4 Falmouth Bay b. England U.K.
130 B7 False Bay b. South Africa
103 D3 Falset Spain
55 E5 Falster i. Denmark
65 F2 Falstone England U.K.
112 F1 Fălticeni Romania
59 F1 Falun Sweden
80 D4 Falzarego, Passo di pass Italy
Famagusta see Ammochostos
170 C2 Famatina Argentina
170 C2 Famatina, Sa de mountain range Argentina
125 C4 Fambono Zaire
87 F3 Fameck France
69 C4 Famenne v. Belgium
137 K4 Family L. l. Manitoba Canada
122 C4 Fana Mali
67 D1 Fanad Head Northern Ireland U.K.
129 H2 Fanandrana Madagascar
114 G2 Fanari Greece
33 G2 Fanchang China
129 H3 Fandriana Madagascar
67 E3 Fane r. Rep. of Ireland
24 B3 Fang Thailand
7 □10 Fangatau i. French Polynesia Pacific Ocean
6 □4 Fanga Uta lag. Tonga
33 F1 Fangcheng China
32 E4 Fangcheng China
32 E2 Fangdou Shan mountain range China
33 H4 Fang-liao Taiwan
59 G2 Fångö i. Sweden
108 A2 Fango r. Corse France
30 D5 Fangshan China
32 E1 Fangshan China
33 H4 Fangshan Taiwan
33 E1 Fang Xian China
31 J3 Fangzheng China
53 E1 Fanipal' Belarus
93 E5 Fanjeaux France
27 □ Fanling Hong Kong
66 C3 Fannich, Loch l. Scotland U.K.
39 D4 Fannūj Iran
55 A4 Fanø i. Denmark
107 H5 Fano Italy
55 A4 Fanø Bugt b. Denmark
33 H3 Fanshan China
30 E5 Fanshi China
24 C2 Fan Si Pan mt. Vietnam
59 F2 Fanthyttan Sweden
31 E6 Fan Xian China
46 F5 Farab Turkmenistan
122 B4 Faraba Mali
179 B2 Faraday Ukraine Base Antarctica
124 E3 Faradje Zaire
129 H3 Farafangana Madagascar
122 A4 Farafenni The Gambia
119 E2 Farafra Oasis oasis Egypt
39 C3 Farāgheh Iran
39 E2 Farah watercourse Afghanistan
39 E2 Farāh Afghanistan
39 E2 Farah Rud r. Afghanistan
39 G2 Farakhulm Afghanistan
21 M2 Farallon de Pajaros i. Northern Mariana Is Pacific Ocean
122 B4 Faranah Guinea
109 G2 Fara San Martino Italy
59 G3 Fårbo Sweden
83 G1 Farchant Germany
69 C4 Farciennes Belgium
109 J4 Fardella Italy
101 G3 Fardes r. Spain
87 F3 Farébersviller France
63 E4 Fareham England U.K.
8 D4 Farewell, Cape c. New Zealand
8 D4 Farewell Spit spit New Zealand
150 D2 Fargo N. Dakota U.S.A.
93 B4 Fargues France
150 E2 Faribault Minnesota U.S.A.
139 F2 Faribault, Lac l. Québec Canada
36 D3 Faridabad India
36 C3 Faridkot India
37 G5 Faridpur Bangladesh
36 D3 Faridpur India
129 H2 Farihy Alaotra l. Madagascar
129 G3 Farihy Ihotry l. Madagascar
129 H2 Farihy Kinkony l. Madagascar
129 H2 Farihy Tsiazompaniry l. Madagascar
129 G3 Farihy Tsimanampetsotsa l. Madagascar
100 A1 Farilhões i. Portugal
39 D2 Farīmān Iran
63 E3 Faringdon England U.K.
166 C2 Farinha r. Brazil
43 A4 Fâriskûr Egypt
98 D3 Fariza de Sayago Spain
114 D3 Farkadhon Greece
47 G5 Farkhor Tajikistan
113 F6 Farmakonisi i. Greece
148 C5 Farmer City Illinois U.S.A.
138 D2 Farmer Island i. Québec Canada
136 E3 Farmington B.C. Canada
148 B5 Farmington Illinois U.S.A.
148 B5 Farmington Iowa U.S.A.
147 H2 Farmington Maine U.S.A.
147 H3 Farmington New Hampshire U.S.A.
155 H3 Farmington New Mexico U.S.A.
152 E3 Farmington Utah U.S.A.
136 D4 Far Mt. mt. B.C. Canada
146 D6 Farmville Virginia U.S.A.
79 H3 Farná Slovakia
59 F2 Färna Sweden
59 F1 Färnäs Sweden
63 F3 Farnborough England U.K.
62 D1 Farndon England U.K.
59 G1 Färnebo-fjärden l. Sweden
65 G2 Farne Islands is England U.K.
108 D2 Farnese Italy
63 F3 Farnham England U.K.
136 F4 Farnham, Mt mt. B.C. Canada
73 G4 Farnstädt Germany
100 C3 Faro airport Portugal
100 B3 Faro div. Portugal
59 H3 Fårö i. Sweden
100 C3 Faro Portugal
136 C2 Faro Yukon Terr. Canada
173 G5 Faro Argentina
166 A1 Faro Brazil
106 B3 Faroma, Monte mt. Italy
124 B2 Faro, Réserve du res. Cameroon
98 C2 Faro, Serra do mountain range Spain
59 H3 Fårösund Sweden
117 K7 Farquhar Group is Seychelles
15 E5 Farrars Cr. watercourse Queensland Australia
39 C3 Farrāshband Iran
146 C4 Farrell Pennsylvania U.S.A.
141 H4 Farrellton Québec Canada
172 B2 Farrelones Chile
58 C2 Farris l. Norway
39 D2 Farrokhī Iran
Farrukhabad see Fatehgarh
39 C3 Fārs div. Iran
39 C2 Farsakh Iran
114 D3 Farsala Greece
39 E2 Fārsī Afghanistan
55 B3 Farsø Denmark
152 E3 Farson Wyoming U.S.A.
58 B2 Farsund Norway
125 B6 Baia Farta Angola
112 F2 Fârţăneşti Romania
168 C2 Fartura r. Brazil
167 B6 Fartura, Sa da mountain range Brazil
55 B3 Fårvang Denmark
Farvel, Kap c. see Uummannarsuaq
151 C5 Farwell Texas U.S.A.
39 C3 Fasā Iran
111 G2 Fasano Italy
72 F3 Faßberg Germany
146 E4 Fassett Pennsylvania U.S.A.
53 C1 Fastiv Ukraine
53 E1 Fastivtsi Ukraine
67 B5 Fastnet Rock i. Rep. of Ireland
124 F3 Fataki Zaire
36 C3 Fatehabad India
36 D4 Fatehgarh India
36 C3 Fatehjang Pakistan
36 C4 Fatehnagar India
36 E4 Fatehpur India
36 E4 Fatehpur India
36 C4 Fatehpur India
36 B3 Fatehpur Pakistan
36 D4 Fatehpur Sikri India
100 E4 Fates, Sierra de mountain range Spain
52 B3 Fateyevka Rus. Fed.
52 B3 Fatezh Rus. Fed.
39 C3 Fatḥābād Iran
140 E4 Fathom Five National Marine Park nat. park Ontario Canada
122 A4 Fatick Senegal
100 B1 Fátima Santarém Portugal
168 A5 Fátima do Sul Brazil
6 □3 Fatumanga i. Tonga
125 C4 Fatundu Zaire
90 E2 Faucigny reg. France
90 E1 Faucogney-et-la-Mer France
91 B5 Faugères France
64 A3 Faughan r. Northern Ireland U.K.
93 C4 Fauguerolles France
65 E2 Fauldhouse Scotland U.K.
73 H2 Faulenrost Germany
87 F3 Faulquemont France
86 B2 Fauquembergues France
140 D2 Fauquier Ontario Canada
17 A5 Faure I. i. Western Australia Australia
112 F2 Făurei Romania
56 D2 Fauske Norway
155 F1 Faust Utah U.S.A.
173 H2 Faustino M. Parera Argentina
89 F2 Fauville-en-Caux France
92 D3 Faux-la-Montagne France
98 C3 Favaios Portugal
107 G5 Favalto, Monte mt. Italy
110 C5 Favara Sicilia Italy
103 □ Favàritx, Cap de pt Spain
90 E3 Faverges France
90 E1 Faverney France
63 G3 Faversham England U.K.
110 B5 Favignana Sicilia Italy
110 B5 Favignana, Isola i. Sicilia Italy
136 G4 Fawcett Alberta Canada
63 E4 Fawley England U.K.
138 C3 Fawn r. Ontario Canada
119 H2 Fawwārah Saudi Arabia
56 K6 Faxaflói b. Iceland
56 E3 Faxälven r. Sweden
32 C3 Faxian Hu l. China
118 C4 Faya Chad
88 D4 Fay-de-Bretagne France
91 E5 Fayence France
148 D3 Fayette Michigan U.S.A.
151 E4 Fayetteville Arkansas U.S.A.
145 E5 Fayetteville N. Carolina U.S.A.
145 C5 Fayetteville Tennessee U.S.A.
119 H4 Fayfā Saudi Arabia
43 B4 Fâyid Egypt
42 G4 Faylakah i. Kuwait
90 D1 Fayl-la-Forêt France
102 D3 Fayón Spain
91 C4 Fay-sur-Lignon France
43 D5 Fazair al Ghrazi watercourse Saudi Arabia
107 H4 Fažana Croatia
123 E5 Fazao Malfakassa, Parc National de nat. park Togo
63 E2 Fazeley England U.K.
36 C3 Fazilka India
36 B3 Fazilpur Pakistan
39 B4 Fazrān, J. h. Saudi Arabia
120 B4 Fdérik Mauritania
67 B4 Feale r. Rep. of Ireland
145 E5 Fear, Cape c. N. Carolina U.S.A.
145 E5 Fear, Cape r. N. Carolina U.S.A.
154 B2 Feather Falls California U.S.A.
9 E4 Featherston New Zealand
13 F4 Feathertop, Mt mt. Victoria Australia
89 F2 Fécamp France
87 G4 Fecht r. France
173 J1 Federación Argentina
173 H1 Federal Argentina
123 F5 Federal Capital Territory div. Nigeria
58 A1 Fedje Norway
46 D2 Fedorovka Kazakhstan
46 F2 Fedorovka Kazakhstan
47 J2 Fedorovka Kazakhstan
53 F3 Fedotova Kosa spit Ukraine
67 B3 Feeagh, Lough l. Rep. of Ireland
64 A3 Feeny Northern Ireland U.K.
59 E3 Fegen l. Sweden
59 E3 Fegen Sweden
79 M4 Fehérgyarmat Hungary
73 G1 Fehmarn i. Germany
73 F1 Fehmarnsund chan. Germany
169 H5 Feia, Lagoa lag. Brazil
33 G2 Feidong China
69 B4 Feignies France
33 H1 Feihuanghe Kou river mouth China
164 B1 Feijó Brazil
8 E4 Feilding New Zealand
75 G2 Feilitzsch Germany
168 C4 Feio ou Aguapei r. Brazil
166 E3 Feira de Santana Brazil
98 C1 Feira do Monte Spain
43 B5 Feirân well Egypt
43 B5 Feirân, W. watercourse Egypt
90 E3 Feissons-sur-Isère France
33 G2 Feixi China
33 G1 Fei Xian China
79 H4 Fejér div. Hungary
55 D5 Fejø i. Denmark
42 C2 Feke Turkey
79 L5 Fekete-Körös r. Hungary
103 G5 Felanitx Spain
148 D3 Felch Michigan U.S.A.
79 H4 Felcsút Hungary
83 G1 Feldafing Germany
81 E4 Feld am See Austria
81 G4 Feldbach div. Austria
81 G4 Feldbach Austria
90 F1 Feldbach France
74 D5 Feldberg mt. Germany
82 C1 Feldberg Baden-Württemberg Germany
73 J2 Feldberg Mecklenburg-Vorpommern Germany
80 A3 Feldkirch div. Austria
80 A3 Feldkirch Austria
81 E4 Feldkirchen div. Austria
81 G3 Feldkirchen bei Graz Austria
81 F4 Feldkirchen in Kärnten Austria
75 G5 Feldkirchen-Westerham Germany
112 E1 Feldru Romania
6 □3 Felea i. Tonga
98 B3 Felgueiras Portugal
173 H1 Feliciano r. Argentina
127 □1 Félicité I. i. Seychelles
35 D10 Felidu Atoll atoll Maldives
91 B3 Félines France
157 H5 Felipe C. Puerto Mexico
169 F3 Felixlândia Brazil
63 H3 Felixstowe England U.K.
156 D2 Félix U. Gómez Mexico
106 C4 Felizzano Italy
69 E5 Fell Germany
107 H2 Fella r. Italy
92 E3 Felletin France
59 F2 Fellingsbro Sweden
159 □1 Fellowship Jamaica
79 L5 Felnac Romania
72 E4 Felsberg Germany
79 J4 Felsőpakony Hungary
81 H4 Felső-Válicka r. Hungary
55 B5 Felsted Denmark
107 F2 Feltre Italy
166 C3 Femeas r. Brazil
73 F1 Femer Bælt str. Denmark/Germany
111 F3 Femminamorta, Monte mt. Italy
55 D5 Femø i. Denmark
58 D2 Femsjøen l. Norway
57 C3 Femunden l. Norway
30 D5 Fen r. China
129 G4 Fenambosy, Lohatanjona pt Madagascar
155 H4 Fence Lake New Mexico U.S.A.
141 F4 Fenelon Falls Ontario Canada
Fener Br. c. see Karataş Br.
106 B3 Fenestrelle Italy
87 G4 Fénétrange France
53 D1 Fenevychi Ukraine
114 G2 Fengari mt. Greece
31 H4 Fengcheng China
33 F2 Fengcheng China
32 D2 Fengdu China
32 D3 Fenggang China
33 H2 Fenghua China
33 E3 Fenghuang China
33 E2 Fengjie China
33 E4 Fengkai China
33 H4 Fenglin Taiwan
31 F5 Fengnan China
31 F4 Fengning China
32 B3 Fengqing China
33 F1 Fengqiu China
31 F5 Fengrun China
32 D3 Fengshan China
33 G4 Fengshun China
33 G1 Fengtai China
32 D1 Feng Xian China
33 F2 Fengxin China
33 G1 Fengyang China
30 E4 Fengzhen China
37 G5 Feni Bangladesh
6 □1 Feni Is is P.N.G.
92 B2 Fenioux France
106 B3 Fenis Italy
62 C4 Feniton England U.K.
5 M6 Fenua Ura is French Polynesia Pacific Ocean
148 B4 Fennimore Wisconsin U.S.A.
129 H2 Fenoarivo Atsinanana Madagascar
129 H2 Fenoarivo Be Madagascar
108 A3 Feno, Capo di pt Corse France
93 E6 Fenouillet reg. France
58 A1 Fensfjorden chan. Norway
55 D4 Fensmark Denmark
63 F2 Fens, The reg. England U.K.
149 F4 Fenton Michigan U.S.A.
177 J7 Fenua Ura is
65 G2 Fenwick England U.K.
30 D5 Fenxi China
30 D5 Fenyang China
51 E6 Feodosiya Ukraine
64 B2 Feolin Ferry Scotland U.K.
69 C4 Fépin France
64 A4 Ferbane Rep. of Ireland
121 F1 Fer, Cap de headland Algeria
111 F4 Ferdinandea Italy
73 J2 Ferdinandshof Germany
39 D2 Ferdows Iran
86 C4 Fère-Champenoise France
86 C3 Fère-en-Tardenois France
88 C4 Férel France
109 E2 Ferentillo Italy
109 F3 Ferentino Italy
113 F4 Feres Greece
103 B6 Férez Spain
47 H4 Fergana Uzbekistan
Fergana Range mountain range see Fergana Too Tizmegi
47 H4 Fergana Too Tizmegi mountain range Kyrgyzstan
140 E5 Fergus Ontario Canada
150 D2 Fergus Falls Minnesota U.S.A.
6 □1 Fergusson I. i. P.N.G.
121 F2 Fériana Tunisia
100 D2 Feria, Sierra de h. Spain
122 C5 Ferkessédougou Côte d'Ivoire
110 D5 Ferla Sicilia Italy
81 F4 Ferlach Austria
140 A1 Ferland Ontario Canada
122 B3 Ferlo-Nord, Réserve de Faune du res. Senegal
122 B4 Ferlo Sud, Réserve de Faune du res. Senegal
122 A3 Ferlo, Vallée du watercourse Senegal
67 D2 Fermanagh div. Northern Ireland U.K.
107 G5 Fermignano Italy
109 F1 Fermo Italy
139 G3 Fermont Québec Canada
98 D3 Fermoselle Spain
67 C4 Fermoy Rep. of Ireland
101 G1 Fernáncaballero Spain
170 D2 Fernández Argentina
145 D6 Fernandina Beach Florida U.S.A.
162 □ Fernandina, I. i. Galapagos Is Ecuador
171 B7 Fernando de Magallanes, Parque Nacional nat. park Chile
174 G6 Fernando de Noronha i. Atlantic Ocean
168 C4 Fernandópolis Brazil
169 F2 Fernão Dias Brazil
129 G1 Fernão Veloso, Baia de b. Mozambique
152 B1 Ferndale Washington U.S.A.
63 E4 Ferndown England U.K.
90 E2 Ferney-Voltaire France
136 F5 Fernie B.C. Canada
154 C2 Fernley Nevada U.S.A.
80 B3 Fernpaß Austria
147 F4 Fernridge Pennsylvania U.S.A.
67 E4 Ferns Rep. of Ireland
152 C2 Fernwood Idaho U.S.A.
109 J4 Ferrandina Italy
107 F4 Ferrara div. Emilia-Romagna Italy
107 F4 Ferrara Ferrara Italy
108 B5 Ferrato, Capo pt Sardegna Italy
109 G3 Ferrazzano Italy
98 C1 Ferreira Spain
100 B2 Ferreira do Alentejo Portugal
100 B1 Ferreira do Zêzere Portugal
163 G3 Ferreira-Gomes Brazil
168 B4 Ferreiros Brazil
162 B5 Ferreñafe Peru
102 B3 Ferreruela de Huerva Spain
90 F1 Ferrette France
172 E1 Ferreyra Argentina
151 F6 Ferriday Louisiana U.S.A.
106 D4 Ferriere Italy
69 C4 Ferrière-la-Grande France
69 D4 Ferrières Belgium
86 B4 Ferrières France
55 A3 Ferring Sø l. Denmark
166 B3 Ferro r. Brazil
108 B3 Ferro, Capo pt Sardegna Italy
98 B1 Ferrol Spain
155 G2 Ferron Utah U.S.A.
169 G3 Ferros Brazil
108 B5 Ferru, Monte h. Sardegna Italy
103 G5 Ferrutx, Cap pt Spain
65 G3 Ferryhill England U.K.
78 F4 Fertő l. Austria/Hungary
81 H3 Fertőd Hungary
78 F4 Fertőrákos Hungary
78 F4 Fertőszentmiklós Hungary
78 F4 Fertő-tavi nat. park Hungary
68 D1 Ferwerd Netherlands
52 C2 Ferzikovo Rus. Fed.
120 D2 Fès Morocco
125 C5 Feshi Zaire
137 K5 Fessenden N. Dakota U.S.A.
87 G5 Fessenheim France
69 B5 Festieux France
150 F4 Festus Missouri U.S.A.
122 B4 Fété Bowé Senegal
112 F2 Feteşti Romania
66 □2 Fethaland, Point of pt Scotland U.K.
67 D4 Fethard Rep. of Ireland
42 B2 Fethiye Turkey
66 □2 Fetlar i. Scotland U.K.
66 F4 Fettercairn Scotland U.K.
75 G3 Feucht Germany
74 F3 Feuchtwangen Germany
89 G1 Feuquières-en-Vimeu France
90 C3 Feurs France
43 D1 Fevzipaşa Turkey
39 G1 Feyzābād Afghanistan
39 D2 Feyẓābād Iran
Fez see Fès
62 C2 Ffestiniog Wales U.K.
170 C2 Fiambalá Argentina
109 F2 Fiamignano Italy
122 D4 Fian Ghana
129 H3 Fianarantsoa div. Madagascar
129 H3 Fianarantsoa Madagascar
124 C2 Fianga Chad
82 C3 Fiano Italy
109 E2 Fiano Romano Italy
100 C3 Ficalho h. Portugal
126 C3 Fichē Ethiopia
75 H2 Fichtelgebirge h. Germany
75 H3 Fichtelnaab r. Germany
131 F4 Ficksburg South Africa
108 E2 Ficulle Italy
166 D2 Fidalgo r. Brazil
106 E4 Fidenza Italy
58 B2 Fidjeland Norway
80 D3 Fieberbrunn Austria
136 F4 Field B.C. Canada
140 E3 Field Ontario Canada
14 C2 Field I. i. Northern Terr. Australia
112 E2 Fieni Romania
90 D3 Fier r. France
113 B4 Fier Albania
107 F2 Fiera di Primiero Italy
14 D3 Fiery Cr. r. Queensland Australia
82 D2 Fiesch Switzerland
66 F4 Fife div. Scotland U.K.
148 E3 Fife Lake Michigan U.S.A.
66 F4 Fife Ness pt Scotland U.K.
13 F3 Fifield New South Wales Australia
148 B3 Fifield Wisconsin U.S.A.
119 F4 5th Cataract rapids Sudan
91 E5 Figanières France
108 B3 Figari Corse France
93 E4 Figeac France
59 G3 Figeholm Sweden
159 □6 Fig Tree St Kitts-Nevis Caribbean
100 B2 Figueira r. Portugal
98 B4 Figueira da Foz Portugal
98 D4 Figueira de Castelo Rodrigo Portugal
168 B3 Figueirão Brazil
100 C1 Figueiró r. Portugal
98 B5 Figueiró dos Vinhos Portugal
102 F2 Figueres Spain
103 C4 Figueroles Spain
121 D2 Figuig Morocco
124 B2 Figuil Cameroon
43 D5 Fiha al 'Ināb reg. Saudi Arabia
126 E2 Fi'i reg. Yemen
4 J6 Fiji country Pacific Ocean
101 H3 Filabres, Sa de los mountain range Spain
129 D3 Filabusi Zimbabwe
156 J7 Filadelfia Costa Rica
111 F4 Filadelfia Italy
165 D4 Filadélfia Paraguay
79 J3 Fiľakovo Slovakia
122 C4 Filamana Mali
179 B3 Filchner Ice Shelf ice feature Antarctica
109 F3 Filettino Italy
65 H3 Filey England U.K.
112 D2 Filiaşi Romania
114 B3 Filiates Greece
115 C5 Filiatra Greece
110 D4 Filicudi, Isola i. Italy
110 D4 Filicudi Porto Italy
123 E4 Filingué Niger
52 F2 Filinskoye Rus. Fed.
114 G2 Filiouri r. Greece
77 L1 Filipów Poland
114 B3 Filippiada Greece
114 F2 Filippoi Greece
59 F2 Filipstad Sweden
83 E2 Filisur Switzerland
56 C3 Fillan Norway
154 C4 Fillmore California U.S.A.
155 F2 Fillmore Utah U.S.A.
114 C2 Filotas Greece
115 G5 Filoti Greece
107 H5 Filottrano Italy
74 E4 Fils r. Germany
62 D3 Filton England U.K.
126 D3 Fīltu Ethiopia
156 E3 F. I. Madero Mexico
179 C3 Fimbulheimen mountain range Antarctica
179 C3 Fimbulisen ice feature Antarctica
110 D4 Finale Sicilia Italy
107 F4 Finale Emilia Italy
106 C4 Finale Ligure Italy
141 H4 Finch Ontario Canada
126 C3 Finch'a'ā Hāyk' l. Ethiopia
69 E5 Findel airport Luxembourg
66 E3 Findhorn r. Scotland U.K.
66 E3 Findhorn Scotland U.K.
43 C1 Findıkpınarı Turkey
146 B4 Findlay Ohio U.S.A.

63 F4 Findon England U.K.
13 G5 Fingal Tasmania Australia
138 E5 Finger Lakes lakes New York U.S.A.
129 E2 Fingoè Mozambique
93 D5 Finhan France
42 B2 Finike Turkey
43 A1 Finike Kör. b. Turkey
114 B3 Finiq Albania
88 A3 Finistère div. France
Finisterre, Cape c. see Fisterra, Cabo
59 E3 Finjasjön l. Sweden
14 C5 Finke watercourse Northern Terr. Australia
14 C5 Finke Northern Terr. Australia
14 C5 Finke Gorge Nat. Park Northern Terr. Australia
12 C2 Finke, Mt h. S. Australia Australia
81 E4 Finkenstein Austria
49 H2 Finland country Europe
54 C2 Finland, Gulf of g. Europe
136 D3 Finlay r. B.C. Canada
136 D3 Finlay, Mt mt. B.C. Canada
13 F3 Finley New South Wales Australia
67 D2 Finn r. Rep. of Ireland
59 F1 Finnbodarna Sweden
73 G4 Finne ridge Germany
64 A4 Finnea Rep. of Ireland
87 G1 Finnentrop Germany
59 F2 Finnerödja Sweden
15 F2 Finnigan, Mt h. Queensland Australia
12 C3 Finniss, C. c. S. Australia Australia
44 D3 Finnland Finland
56 F1 Finnmark div. Norway
59 G2 Finnö i. Sweden
58 A2 Finnøy i. Norway
59 E1 Finnskog Norway
56 E1 Finnsnes Norway
73 J3 Finowfurt Germany
6 □1 Finschhafen P.N.G.
59 F2 Finspång Sweden
82 D2 Finsteraarhorn mt. Switzerland
73 J4 Finsterwalde Germany
68 F1 Finsterwolde Netherlands
59 H1 Finström Finland
67 D2 Fintona Northern Ireland U.K.
67 C2 Fintown Rep. of Ireland
122 D3 Fintrou well Mali
15 E4 Finucane Ra. h. Queensland Australia
66 C3 Fionn Loch l. Scotland U.K.
66 B4 Fionnphort Scotland U.K.
108 D2 Fiora r. Italy
9 A6 Fiordland National Park nat. park New Zealand
106 D4 Fiorenzuola d'Arda Italy
42 D2 Fırat r. Turkey
95 L4 Firat Turkey
154 B3 Firebaugh California U.S.A.
137 J2 Firedrake Lake l. N.W.T. Canada
147 G4 Fire Island National Seashore res. New York U.S.A.
107 F5 Firenze div. Toscana Italy
107 F5 Firenze Firenze Italy
107 F4 Firenzuola Italy
140 D2 Fire River Ontario Canada
123 G3 Firkachi well Niger
77 L4 Firlrj Poland
173 G2 Firmat Argentina
169 J1 Firmino Alves Brazil
168 C2 Firminópolis Brazil
91 C3 Firminy France
74 F4 Firngrund reg. Germany
50 E3 Firovo Rus. Fed.
36 B3 Firoza Pakistan
36 D4 Firozabad India
39 F2 Firozkoh reg. Afghanistan
36 D4 Firozpur India
36 C3 Firozpur India
119 F3 1st Cataract rapids Egypt
147 H2 First Connecticut L. l. New Hampshire U.S.A.
15 F2 1st Three Mile Opening chan. Queensland Australia
8 E2 Firth of Thames b. New Zealand
Firuzabad see Rāsk
39 C3 Firūzābād Iran
39 D1 Firūzeh Iran
39 C2 Fīrūzkūh Iran
39 D1 Firyuza Turkmenistan
93 B6 Fiscal Spain
81 H2 Fischamend Markt Austria
74 C3 Fischbach Germany
80 C3 Fischbachau Germany
81 G3 Fischbacher Alpen mts Austria
73 H3 Fischbeck Germany
74 F5 Fischen im Allgäu Germany
128 B4 Fish watercourse Namibia
130 C5 Fish watercourse South Africa
176 E10 Fisher Bay b. Antarctica
147 F6 Fisherman I. i. Virginia U.S.A.
147 H4 Fishers I. i. New York U.S.A.
137 N2 Fisher Strait chan. N.W.T. Canada
62 B3 Fishguard Wales U.K.
62 B2 Fishguard Bay b. Wales U.K.
148 A2 Fish Lake l. Minnesota U.S.A.
136 E2 Fish Lake l. N.W.T. Canada
155 G2 Fish Lake l. Utah U.S.A.
27 □ Fish Ponds lakes Hong Kong
149 F4 Fish Pt pt Michigan U.S.A.
63 G2 Fishtoft England U.K.
115 B4 Fiskardo Greece
55 D1 Fiskebäckskil Sweden
179 B3 Fiske, C. c. Antarctica
Fiskenæsset see Qeqertarsuatsiaat
59 H2 Fisksätra Sweden
86 C3 Fismes France
98 A2 Fisterra Spain
98 A2 Fisterra, Cabo c. Spain
147 H3 Fitchburg Massachusetts U.S.A.
102 B2 Fitero Spain
58 A2 Fitjar Norway
7 □12 Fito mt. Western Samoa
93 E6 Fitou France
118 C5 Fitri, Lac l. Chad
164 B2 Fitzcarrald Peru
137 G3 Fitzgerald Alberta Canada
145 D6 Fitzgerald Georgia U.S.A.
17 B7 Fitzgerald River Nat. Park nat. park Western Australia Australia
14 B2 Fitzmaurice r. Northern Terr. Australia
15 G4 Fitzroy r. Queensland Australia
16 C3 Fitzroy r. Western Australia Australia
171 C6 Fitz Roy Argentina
171 B6 Fitz Roy, Co mt. Argentina
16 D3 Fitzroy Crossing Western Australia Australia
140 E4 Fitzwilliam I. i. Ontario Canada
109 F3 Fiuggi Italy
111 F3 Fiumefreddo Bruzio Italy
111 E5 Fiumefreddo di Sicilia Sicilia Italy
108 E3 Fiumicino Italy
108 B2 Fium'Orbo r. Corse France
9 A6 Five Fingers Peninsula pen. New Zealand
67 D2 Fivemiletown Northern Ireland U.K.
106 E4 Fivizzano Italy
91 B3 Fix-St-Geneys France
8 □2 Fizeau, Mt h. Campbell I. New Zealand
112 D1 Fizeşu Gherlii Romania
125 E4 Fizi Zaire
58 D2 Fjällbacka Sweden
59 G2 Fjärdhundra Sweden
58 A1 Fjell Norway
55 C3 Fjellerup Denmark
55 B2 Fjerritslev Denmark
59 F2 Fjugesta Sweden
120 C2 Fkih Ben Salah Morocco
58 C1 Flå Norway
81 E3 Flachau Austria
55 A4 Fladså r. Denmark
155 G4 Flagstaff Arizona U.S.A.
131 G5 Flagstaff South Africa
128 □2 Flagstaff Bay b. St Helena Atlantic Ocean
147 H2 Flagstaff L. l.
147 H2 Flagstaff Lake l. Maine U.S.A.
138 E2 Flaherty Island i. Québec Canada
58 B1 Flåm Norway
88 D2 Flamanville France
148 B3 Flambeau r. Wisconsin U.S.A.
65 H3 Flamborough England U.K.
65 H3 Flamborough Head headland England U.K.
173 F6 Flamenco, I. i. Argentina
73 H3 Fläming h. Germany
152 E3 Flaming Gorge Res. l. Utah/Wyoming U.S.A.
130 C5 Flaminksvlei l. South Africa
159 □3 Flanagin Town Trinidad and Tobago
86 B2 Flandre reg. France
124 C4 Flandria Zaire
66 A2 Flannan Isles is Scotland U.K.
56 D2 Flåsjön l. Sweden
148 E4 Flat r. Michigan U.S.A.
152 D2 Flathead L. l. Montana U.S.A.
62 C3 Flat Holm i. England U.K.
127 □4 Flat I. i. Mauritius
9 E4 Flat Point pt New Zealand
80 E4 Flattach Austria
15 F2 Flattery, C. c. Queensland Australia
152 A1 Flattery, C. c. Washington U.S.A.
145 □1 Flatts Village Bermuda
58 C2 Flåvatnet l. Norway
87 F4 Flavigny-sur-Moselle France
83 E1 Flawil Switzerland
91 E5 Flayosc France
73 G3 Flechtingen Germany
73 H2 Flecken Zechlin Germany
145 □2 Fleeming Pt pt The Bahamas
73 H2 Fleesensee l. Germany
63 F3 Fleet England U.K.
73 G3 Fleetmark Germany
65 E4 Fleetwood England U.K.
147 F4 Fleetwood Pennsylvania U.S.A.
58 B2 Flekkefjord Norway
58 C2 Flekkerøy i. Norway
69 D4 Flémalle Belgium
146 E3 Fleming New York U.S.A.
146 B5 Flemingsburg Kentucky U.S.A.
59 G2 Flen Sweden
72 E1 Flensborg Fjord inlet Denmark/Germany
72 E1 Flensburg Germany
55 B5 Flensburger Förde inlet Denmark/Germany
69 D4 Fléron Belgium
89 E3 Flers France
58 C2 Flesberg Norway
140 E4 Flesherton Ontario Canada
58 A1 Flesland airport Norway
137 H2 Fletcher Lake l. N.W.T. Canada
10 □3 Fletcher, Mt h. Macquarie I. Pacific Ocean
149 F3 Fletcher Pond l. Michigan U.S.A.
179 B3 Fletcher Prom. headland Antarctica
93 C5 Fleurance France
92 C2 Fleuré France
82 B2 Fleurier Switzerland
69 C4 Fleurus Belgium
91 B5 Fleury France
89 G4 Fleury-les-Aubrais France
89 G2 Fleury-sur-Andelle France
89 E2 Fleury-sur-Orne France
125 E5 Fleuve Zaire r. Zaire
115 E5 Fleves i. Greece
68 D2 Flevoland div. Netherlands
74 E2 Flieden Germany
83 F1 Fließ Austria
65 E3 Flimby England U.K.
83 E2 Flims Switzerland
15 E3 Flinders r. Queensland Australia
17 A7 Flinders B. b. Western Australia Australia
12 D3 Flinders Chase Nat. Park nat. park S. Australia Australia
15 F2 Flinders Grp is Queensland Australia
13 G4 Flinders I. i. Tasmania Australia
15 G3 Flinders Passage chan. Australia
12 D2 Flinders Ranges mountain range S. Australia Australia
12 D2 Flinders Ranges Nat. Park nat. park S. Australia Australia
15 G3 Flinders Reefs reef Coral Sea Islands Terr. Pacific Ocean
137 J4 Flin Flon Manitoba Canada
145 C6 Flint r. Georgia U.S.A.
149 F4 Flint r. Michigan U.S.A.
149 F4 Flint Michigan U.S.A.
62 C1 Flint Wales U.K.
72 F1 Flintbek Germany
5 M6 Flint Island i. Kiribati
15 G5 Flinton Queensland Australia
62 C1 Flintshire div. Wales U.K.
87 E4 Flirey France
59 E1 Flisa r. Norway
59 E1 Flisa Norway
58 B2 Fliseggi mt. Norway
59 G3 Fliseryd Sweden
102 D3 Flix Spain
86 B2 Flixecourt France
86 D3 Flize France
59 E3 Floda Sweden
65 F2 Flodden England U.K.
86 C5 Flogny-la-Chapelle France
72 F5 Floh Germany
75 J2 Flöha r. Germany
75 J2 Flöha Germany
69 C5 Floing France
93 B4 Floirac France
179 A4 Flood Ra. mountain range Antarctica
148 A2 Floodwood Minnesota U.S.A.
144 B4 Flora Illinois U.S.A.
91 B4 Florac France
87 F3 Florange France
15 F3 Flora Reef reef Coral Sea Islands Terr. Pacific Ocean
14 D3 Floraville Queensland Australia
69 C4 Floreffe Belgium
145 C5 Florence Alabama U.S.A.
155 G5 Florence Arizona U.S.A.
150 D4 Florence Kansas U.S.A.
146 C5 Florence Ohio U.S.A.
140 D5 Florence Ontario Canada
152 A3 Florence Oregon U.S.A.
145 E5 Florence S. Carolina U.S.A.
Florence see Firenze
155 G5 Florence Junction Arizona U.S.A.
147 K1 Florenceville New Brunswick Canada
162 B3 Florencia Colombia
69 C4 Florennes Belgium
91 B5 Florensac France
171 C5 Florentino Ameghino Argentina
69 D5 Florenville Belgium
173 J2 Flores div. Uruguay
100 □ Flores i. Azores Portugal
22 E4 Flores i. Indonesia
173 H3 Flores r. Argentina
166 D2 Flores r. Brazil
166 E2 Flores Pernambuco Brazil
166 D2 Flores Piauí Brazil
157 H5 Flores Guatemala
22 D3 Flores Sea sea Indonesia
110 D5 Floresta Sicilia Italy
166 E2 Floresta Brazil
53 C3 Floreşti Moldova
114 C3 Floriada Greece
166 D2 Floriano Brazil
164 C1 Floriano Peixoto Brazil
167 C6 Florianopolis Brazil
145 D6 Florida div. U.S.A.
173 J3 Florida div. Uruguay
164 D3 Florida Bolivia
172 A4 Florida Chile
173 J3 Florida Uruguay
145 D7 Florida Bay b. Florida U.S.A.
145 D7 Florida City Florida U.S.A.
6 □1 Florida Is is Solomon Is.
168 C4 Flórida Paulista Brazil
111 E5 Floridia Sicilia Italy
114 C2 Florina div. Greece
114 C2 Florina Greece
108 A4 Florinas Sardegna Italy
168 C5 Florínia Brazil
57 B3 Florø Norway
75 H3 Flossenbürg Germany
66 E2 Flotta i. Scotland U.K.
93 E5 Floure France
139 H3 Flour Lake l. Newfoundland Canada
148 A4 Floyd Iowa U.S.A.
146 C6 Floyd Virginia U.S.A.
151 C5 Floydada Texas U.S.A.
155 F4 Floyd, Mt mt. Arizona U.S.A.
83 F2 Fluchthorn mt. Austria/Switzerland
83 E2 Flüelapass Switzerland
83 D2 Flüelen Switzerland
68 D2 Fluessen l. Netherlands
102 C3 Flúmen r. Spain
108 B5 Flumendosa r. Sardegna Italy
90 E3 Flumet France
108 B4 Flumineddu r. Sardegna Italy
108 A5 Fluminimaggiore Sardegna Italy
83 E1 Flums Switzerland
102 F2 Fluvià r. Spain
6 □1 Fly r. P.N.G.
146 C5 Fly Ohio U.S.A.
10 □2 Flying Fish Cove Christmas I. Indian Ocean
6 □5 Foa i. Tonga
106 C3 Fobello Italy
104 G4 Foča Bos.-Herz.
113 F5 Foça Turkey
69 D4 Focant Belgium
66 E3 Fochabers Scotland U.K.
179 □ Foch, I. i. Kerguelen Indian Ocean
112 F2 Focşani Romania
124 D2 Fodé Central African Rep.
89 H4 Foëcy France
14 D3 Foelsche r. Northern Terr. Australia
6 □3 Fofoa i. Tonga
33 F4 Fogang China
47 G4 Fogelevo Kazakhstan
121 E3 Foggâret ez Zoûa Algeria
109 H3 Foggia div. Puglia Italy
109 H3 Foggia Foggia Italy
107 G5 Foglia r. Italy
109 E3 Fogliano, Lago di lag. Italy
59 J1 Föglö Finland
122 □ Fogo i. Cape Verde
139 K4 Fogo I. i. Newfoundland Canada
123 F4 Fogolawa Nigeria
81 F3 Fohnsdorf Austria
72 D1 Föhr i. Germany
69 E5 Föhren Germany
107 F5 Foiano della Chiana Italy
67 A5 Foilclough h. Rep. of Ireland
66 D2 Foinaven h. Scotland U.K.
115 C6 Foinikountas Greece
93 D6 Foix reg. France
93 D6 Foix France
52 B3 Fokino Rus. Fed.
114 D4 Fokis div. Greece
123 E4 Fokku Nigeria
58 B1 Folarskarnuten mt. Norway
56 D2 Folda chan. Norway
56 D2 Foldereid Norway
56 C2 Foldfjorden chan. Norway
115 F6 Folegandros i. Greece
115 F6 Folegandros Greece
140 D2 Foleyet Ontario Canada
107 F3 Folgarìa Italy
58 C1 Folgefonn l. Norway
109 E2 Foligno Italy
63 H3 Folkestone England U.K.
63 F2 Folkingham England U.K.
145 D6 Folkston Georgia U.S.A.
57 C3 Folldal Norway
107 G3 Follina Italy
108 C2 Follonica Italy
108 C2 Follonica, Golfo di b. Italy
58 C2 Follsjå l. Norway
154 B2 Folsom Lake l. California U.S.A.
127 D7 Fomboni Comoros
52 F2 Fominki Rus. Fed.
50 J1 Fominskaya Rus. Fed.
50 J2 Fominskiy Rus. Fed.
50 G3 Fominskoye Rus. Fed.
137 J3 Fond du Lac r. Saskatchewan Canada
137 H3 Fond-du-Lac Saskatchewan Canada
148 C4 Fond du Lac Wisconsin U.S.A.
127 □4 Fond du Sac Mauritius
89 F4 Fondettes France
98 B3 Fondevila Spain
109 F3 Fondi Italy
109 F3 Fondi, Lago di l. Italy
101 H4 Fondón Spain
102 B3 Fonfría Aragón Spain
98 D3 Fonfría Castilla y León Spain
122 C5 Fon Going ridge Guinea
108 B4 Fonni Sardegna Italy
156 H6 Fonseca, G. de b. Central America
90 F1 Fontaine Franche-Comté France
91 D3 Fontaine Rhône-Alpes France
86 B4 Fontainebleau France
90 D1 Fontaine-Française France
89 F2 Fontaine-le-Dun France
90 D1 Fontaine-lès-Dijon France
90 E1 Fontaine-lès-Luxeuil France
69 C4 Fontaine-l'Evêque Belgium
90 C2 Fontaines France
106 E4 Fontanellato Italy
91 C5 Fontanès France
139 F3 Fontanges Québec Canada
106 D4 Fontanigorda Italy
136 E3 Fontas r. B.C. Canada
136 E3 Fontas B.C. Canada
163 D4 Fonte Boa Brazil
165 E2 Fonte do Pau-d'Agua Brazil
102 B2 Fontellas Spain
92 B2 Fontenay-le-Comte France
82 B1 Fontenoy-le-Château France
107 F3 Fonti, Cima mt. Italy
99 F4 Fontiveros Spain
91 E4 Font Sancte, Pic de la mt. France
56 N6 Fontur pt Iceland
91 C5 Fontvieille France
6 □5 Fonuafo'ou i. Tonga
6 □3 Fonua Unga i. Tonga
79 G5 Fonyód Hungary
102 D2 Fonz Spain
107 F2 Fonzaso Italy
Foochow see Fuzhou
141 F4 Foot's Bay Ontario Canada
32 E1 Foping China
106 D2 Foppolo Italy
109 E2 Forano Italy
87 F3 Forbach France
74 D4 Forbach Germany
13 G3 Forbes New South Wales Australia
37 F4 Forbesganj India
152 C1 Forbes, Mt mt. Alberta Canada
9 A6 Forbes, Mt mt. New Zealand
131 H3 Forbes Reef Swaziland
102 C4 Forcall Spain
91 D5 Forcalquier France
98 B2 Forcarei Spain
75 G3 Forchheim Germany
81 H3 Forchtenstein Austria
148 D2 Ford r. Michigan U.S.A.
139 G2 Ford r. Québec Canada
57 B3 Førde Norway
137 K2 Forde Lake l. N.W.T. Canada
63 G2 Fordham England U.K.
63 E4 Fordingbridge England U.K.
108 A5 Fordongianus Sardegna Italy
179 A4 Ford Ra. mountain range Antarctica
13 F2 Fords Bridge New South Wales Australia
151 E5 Fordyce Arkansas U.S.A.
122 B5 Forécariah Guinea
63 E4 Foreland headland England U.K.
62 C3 Foreland Point pt England U.K.
109 H4 Forenza Italy
136 D4 Foresight Mtn mt. B.C. Canada
151 F5 Forest Mississippi U.S.A.
146 B4 Forest Ohio U.S.A.
140 E5 Forest Ontario Canada
147 G3 Forest Dale Vermont U.S.A.
154 B2 Foresthill California U.S.A.
13 G5 Forestier, C. headland Tasmania Australia
148 A3 Forest Lake Minnesota U.S.A.
145 C5 Forest Park Georgia U.S.A.
139 G4 Forestville Québec Canada
58 A2 Føresvik Norway
69 D5 Forêt d'Anlier forest Belgium
90 D1 Forêt de Chaux woodland France
69 D5 Forêt de Chiny forest Belgium
86 B4 Forêt de Fontainebleau forest France
93 D4 Forêt de Gresigne reg. France
90 E2 Forêt de la Joux forest France
69 C4 Forét de Nismes forest Belgium
88 C3 Forêt de Paimpont forest France
89 G3 Forêt de Rambouillet forest France
69 C4 Forêt de Soignes forest Belgium
92 E2 Forêt de Tronçais forest France
87 E3 Forêt de Wœvre forest France
86 C4 Forêt d'Othe forest France
90 B3 Forez, Monts du mountain range France
66 F4 Forfar Scotland U.K.
89 G2 Forges-les-Eaux France
75 F5 Forggensee l. Germany
109 F4 Forio Italy
152 A2 Forks Washington U.S.A.
147 J2 Forks, The Maine U.S.A.
146 E4 Forksville Pennsylvania U.S.A.
107 F5 Forlì div. Italy
107 G4 Forlì Forlì Italy
107 G4 Forlimpopoli Italy
106 C2 Formazza Italy
65 E4 Formby England U.K.
103 E6 Formentera i. Spain
103 G5 Formentor, Cap de pt Spain
89 G2 Formerie France
109 F3 Formia Italy
169 F4 Formiga Brazil
107 E4 Formigine Italy
83 D3 Formigliana Italy
93 E6 Formiguères France
170 D1 Formosa div. Argentina
170 E2 Formosa Argentina
168 E1 Formosa Brazil
Formosa see Taiwan
166 C3 Formosa do R. Prêto Brazil
166 C3 Formoso r. Brazil
168 B3 Formoso r. Brazil
169 E1 Formoso Goiás Brazil
168 B4 Formoso Mato Grosso do Sul Brazil
166 C3 Formoso Tocantins Brazil
55 C3 Fornæs c. Denmark
58 D2 Fornebu airport Norway
108 A3 Fornelli Sardegna Italy
103 □ Fornells Spain
107 G2 Forni Avoltri Italy
107 G2 Forni di Sopra Italy
80 D4 Forni di Sotto Italy
82 C3 Forno Alpi Graie Italy
107 G2 Forno di Zoldo Italy
98 D3 Fornos Portugal
98 C4 Fornos de Algodres Portugal
106 E4 Fornovo di Taro Italy
66 E3 Forres Scotland U.K.
16 D2 Forrest r. Western Australia Australia
148 C5 Forrest Illinois U.S.A.
13 E4 Forrest Victoria Australia
17 E6 Forrest Western Australia Australia
151 F5 Forrest City Arkansas U.S.A.
148 C4 Forreston Illinois U.S.A.
16 D2 Forrest River Abor. Reserve res. Western Australia Australia
56 E3 Fors Sweden
58 B2 Forsand Norway
15 E3 Forsayth Queensland Australia
59 E2 Forshaga Sweden
66 E2 Forsinard Scotland U.K.
56 F2 Forsnäs Sweden
57 F3 Forssa Finland
73 K4 Forst Germany
13 H3 Forster New South Wales Australia
151 E4 Forsyth Missouri U.S.A.
152 F2 Forsyth Montana U.S.A.
141 G2 Forsythe Québec Canada
15 E4 Forsyth Ra. h. Queensland Australia
36 C3 Fort Abbas Pakistan
138 D3 Fort Albany Ontario Canada
164 C2 Fortaleza Bolivia
166 E1 Fortaleza Brazil
102 C4 Fortanete Spain
155 H5 Fort Apache Arizona U.S.A.
136 G4 Fort Assiniboine Alberta Canada
148 C4 Fort Atkinson Wisconsin U.S.A.
66 D3 Fort Augustus Scotland U.K.
131 F6 Fort Beaufort South Africa
152 E2 Fort Benton Montana U.S.A.
137 H3 Fort Black Saskatchewan Canada
154 A2 Fort Bragg California U.S.A.
Fort-Chimo see Kuujjuaq
137 G3 Fort Chipewyan Alberta Canada
151 D5 Fort Cobb Res. resr Oklahoma U.S.A.
152 F3 Fort Collins Colorado U.S.A.
14 E4 Fort Constantine Queensland Australia
141 G4 Fort-Coulonge Québec Canada
147 F2 Fort Covington New York U.S.A.
151 C6 Fort Davis Texas U.S.A.
159 □4 Fort-de-France Martinique Caribbean
159 □4 Fort de France, Baie de b. Martinique Caribbean
145 C5 Fort Deposit Alabama U.S.A.
150 E3 Fort Dodge Iowa U.S.A.
165 E3 Forte Coimbra Brazil
16 B4 Fortescue r. Western Australia Australia
107 F2 Fortezza Italy
150 E1 Fort Frances Minnesota U.S.A.
138 E3 Fort George Québec Canada
134 F3 Fort Good Hope N.W.T. Canada
66 D4 Forth r. Scotland U.K.
65 E2 Forth Scotland U.K.
Fort Hertz see Putao
66 F4 Forth, Firth of est. Scotland U.K.
141 J3 Fortierville Québec Canada
155 E2 Fortification Range mts Nevada U.S.A.
165 D4 Fortín Ávalos Sánchez Paraguay
165 D4 Fortín Capitán Demattei Paraguay
165 E4 Fortín Carlos Antonio López Paraguay
165 E4 Fortín Coronel Bogado Paraguay
165 D4 Fortín Coronel Eugenio Garay Paraguay
165 E4 Fortín Falcón Paraguay
165 E3 Fortín Galpón Paraguay
165 E4 Fortín General Caballero Paraguay
165 D4 Fortín General Mendoza Paraguay
165 D4 Fortín Hernandarías Paraguay
165 D4 Fortín Infante Rivarola Paraguay
165 E4 Fortín Juan deZalazar Paraguay
170 D2 Fortín Lavalle Argentina
165 D4 Fortín Linares Paraguay
165 E4 Fortín Madrejón Paraguay
173 F3 Fortín Olavarría Argentina
165 E3 Fortín Paredes Bolivia
170 D1 Fortín Pilcomayo Argentina
165 E4 Fortín Presidente Ayala Paraguay
165 D3 Fortín Ravelo Bolivia
165 D3 Fortín Suárez Arana Bolivia
165 D4 Fortín Tte. Juan E. López Paraguay
172 E5 Fortín Uno Argentina
147 J1 Fort Kent Maine U.S.A.
145 D7 Fort Lauderdale Florida U.S.A.
136 E2 Fort Liard N.W.T. Canada
159 E3 Fort Liberté Haiti
137 G3 Fort Mackay Alberta Canada
136 G5 Fort Macleod Alberta Canada
148 B5 Fort Madison Iowa U.S.A.
86 A2 Fort-Mahon-Plage France
148 B3 Fort McCoy Wisconsin U.S.A.
137 G3 Fort McMurray Alberta Canada
134 E3 Fort McPherson N.W.T. Canada
152 G3 Fort Morgan Colorado U.S.A.
36 B3 Fort Munro Pakistan
145 D7 Fort Myers Florida U.S.A.
136 E3 Fort Nelson r. B.C. Canada
136 E3 Fort Nelson B.C. Canada
136 D2 Fort Norman N.W.T. Canada
109 H3 Fortore r. Italy
145 C5 Fort Payne Alabama U.S.A.
152 F1 Fort Peck Montana U.S.A.
152 F2 Fort Peck Res. resr Montana U.S.A.
145 D7 Fort Pierce Florida U.S.A.
150 C2 Fort Pierre S. Dakota U.S.A.
127 B4 Fort Portal Uganda
136 F2 Fort Providence N.W.T. Canada
137 J4 Fort Qu'Appelle Saskatchewan Canada
136 G2 Fort Resolution N.W.T. Canada
129 D2 Fort Rixon Zimbabwe
66 D3 Fortrose Scotland U.K.
9 B7 Fortrose New Zealand
154 A2 Fort Ross California U.S.A.
138 E3 Fort Rupert Québec Canada
136 E4 Fort St James B.C. Canada
136 E3 Fort St John B.C. Canada
Fort Sandeman see Zhob
136 G4 Fort Saskatchewan Alberta Canada
151 E4 Fort Scott Kansas U.S.A.
138 C2 Fort Severn Ontario Canada
136 E2 Fort Simpson N.W.T. Canada
151 E5 Fort Smith Arkansas U.S.A.
137 G2 Fort Smith N.W.T. Canada
151 C6 Fort Stockton Texas U.S.A.
153 F5 Fort Sumner New Mexico U.S.A.
152 A3 Fortuna California U.S.A.
103 B6 Fortuna Spain
150 C1 Fortune N. Dakota U.S.A.
139 J4 Fortune B. b. Newfoundland Canada
62 D4 Fortuneswell England U.K.
136 F3 Fort Vermilion Alberta Canada
145 C6 Fort Walton Beach Florida U.S.A.
148 E5 Fort Wayne Indiana U.S.A.
163 F2 Fort Wellington Guyana
24 A2 Fort White Myanmar
66 C4 Fort William Scotland U.K.
151 D5 Fort Worth Texas U.S.A.
9 □1 Forty Fours, The is Chatham Is New Zealand
131 G4 42nd Hill South Africa
134 D3 Fort Yukon Alaska U.S.A.
56 D2 Forvik Norway
111 E5 Forza d'Agrò Sicilia Italy
93 C6 Fos France
91 C5 Fos, Golfe de b. France
33 F4 Foshan China
122 D5 Foso Ghana
109 G2 Fossacesia Italy
106 B4 Fossano Italy
58 D2 Fossby Norway
58 D2 Fosser Norway
69 C4 Fosses-la-Ville Belgium
107 G5 Fossombrone Italy
91 C5 Fos-sur-Mer France
13 F4 Foster Victoria Australia
136 B3 Foster, Mt mt. Canada/U.S.A.
146 B4 Fostoria Ohio U.S.A.
129 H3 Fotadrevo Madagascar
65 H4 Fotherby England U.K.
124 B1 Fotokol Cameroon
127 □3 Fouce, Pte de la pt Rodrigues I. Mauritius
82 A1 Foucherans France
88 A4 Fouesnant France
124 B4 Fougamou Gabon
88 D3 Fougères France
90 E1 Fougerolles France
89 E3 Fougerolles-du-Plessis France
89 H2 Fouilloy France
66 □2 Foula i. Scotland U.K.
87 E4 Foulain France
119 G3 Foul Bay b. Egypt
124 A4 Foulenzem Gabon
24 A3 Foul I. i. Myanmar
63 G3 Foulness Point pt England U.K.
38 C4 Foul Pt pt Sri Lanka
9 C4 Foulwind, Cape c. New Zealand
124 B2 Foumban Cameroon
120 C2 Foum Zguid Morocco
179 B3 Foundation Ice Stream ice feature Antarctica
148 A4 Fountain Minnesota U.S.A.
100 C3 Foupana r. Portugal
92 A3 Fouras France
90 B1 Fourchambault France
87 E4 Fourches, Mont des h. France
154 D4 Four Corners California U.S.A.
131 G4 Fouriesburg South Africa
86 D2 Fourmies France
114 C3 Fourna Greece
91 B4 Fournels France
9 □1 Fournier, C. c. Chatham Is New Zealand
113 F6 Fournoi i. Greece
63 G4 Four Oaks England U.K.
159 □1 Four Paths Jamaica
93 E6 Fourques Languedoc-Roussillon France
91 C5 Fourques Languedoc-Roussillon France
90 B2 Fours France
148 C2 Fourteen Mile Pt pt Michigan U.S.A.
119 F4 4th Cataract rapids Sudan
122 B4 Fouta Djallon reg. Guinea
9 A7 Foveaux Strait str. New Zealand
62 B4 Fowey r. England U.K.
158 C1 Fowl Cay i. The Bahamas
153 F4 Fowler Colorado U.S.A.
148 D5 Fowler Indiana U.S.A.
148 E4 Fowler Michigan U.S.A.
179 B3 Fowler Pen. pen. Antarctica
12 C3 Fowlers B. b. S. Australia Australia
12 C2 Fowlers Bay S. Australia Australia
137 L3 Fox r. Manitoba Canada
148 C4 Fox r. Wisconsin U.S.A.
98 B1 Foxas Spain
136 F4 Fox Creek Alberta Canada
64 D3 Foxdale Isle of Man
135 L3 Foxe Basin g. N.W.T. Canada
135 K3 Foxe Channel str. N.W.T. Canada
58 D2 Foxen l. Sweden
135 L3 Foxe Peninsula pen. N.W.T. Canada
67 B3 Foxford Rep. of Ireland
9 C5 Fox Glacier New Zealand
134 B4 Fox Islands is Alaska U.S.A.
136 G3 Fox Lake Alberta Canada
148 C4 Fox Lake Illinois U.S.A.
8 E4 Foxton New Zealand
8 E4 Foxton Beach New Zealand
67 D2 Foyle r. Rep. of Ireland/U.K.
67 D1 Foyle, Lough inlet Rep. of Ireland/U.K.
67 B4 Foynes Rep. of Ireland
98 C1 Foz Spain
162 C5 Foz de Gregório Brazil
98 B3 Foz de Sousa Portugal
100 A1 Foz do Arelho Portugal
125 B7 Foz do Cunene Angola
167 B6 Foz do Iguaçu Brazil
162 D4 Foz do Jutaí Brazil
98 C5 Foz Giraldo Portugal
106 B4 Frabosa Soprana Italy
77 M2 Frącki Poland
98 E4 Frades de la Sierra Spain
172 E2 Fraga Argentina
102 D3 Fraga Spain
111 G2 Fragagnano Italy
81 F2 Fraham Austria
173 K2 Fraile Muerto Uruguay
69 C4 Fraire Belgium
82 A1 Fraisans France
87 G4 Fraize France
69 B4 Frameries Belgium
55 C3 Framlev Denmark
63 H2 Framlingham England U.K.
59 G1 Främlingshem Sweden
74 E2 Frammersbach Germany
179 D4 Framnes Mts mts Antarctica
77 L5 Frampol Poland
168 E4 Franca Brazil
109 G2 Francavilla al Mare Italy
111 E5 Francavilla di Sicilia Sicilia Italy
111 G2 Francavilla Fontana Italy

109 J4 Francavilla in Sinni Italy
48 F4 France country Europe
135 R2 France, Île de i. Greenland
136 D2 Frances r. Yukon Terr. Canada
12 E4 Frances S. Australia Australia
93 C4 Francescas France
136 D2 Frances Lake l. Yukon Terr. Canada
136 D2 Frances Lake Yukon Terr. Canada
158 B2 Francés, Pta pt Cuba
148 D5 Francesville Indiana U.S.A.
124 B4 Franceville Gabon
90 E1 Franche-Comté div. France
150 D3 Francis Case, Lake l. S. Dakota U.S.A.
162 C4 Francisco de Orellana Peru
156 D3 Francisco I. Madero Mexico
169 G2 Francisco Sá Brazil
147 H2 Francis, Lake l. New Hampshire U.S.A.
128 D3 Francistown Botswana
169 E5 Franco da Rocha Brazil
110 D5 Francofonte Sicilia Italy
136 D4 Francois Lake l. B.C. Canada
102 E3 Francolí r. Spain
69 D4 Francorchamps Belgium
152 E3 Francs Peak summit Wyoming U.S.A.
121 F2 Frane Algeria
68 D1 Franeker Netherlands
90 D2 Frangy France
87 H1 Frankenau Germany
75 J2 Frankenberg Germany
72 D4 Frankenberg (Eder) Germany
81 E2 Frankenburg am Hausruck Austria
81 G3 Frankenfels Austria
74 F2 Frankenheim Germany
81 E3 Frankenmarkt Austria
149 F4 Frankenmuth Michigan U.S.A.
74 D3 Frankenthal (Pfalz) Germany
75 G2 Frankenwald forest Germany
159 □1 Frankfield Jamaica
148 D5 Frankfort Indiana U.S.A.
144 C4 Frankfort Kentucky U.S.A.
148 D3 Frankfort Michigan U.S.A.
131 G3 Frankfort South Africa
87 H2 Frankfurt am Main airport Germany
74 D2 Frankfurt am Main Hessen Germany
73 K3 Frankfurt (Oder) Germany
155 E1 Frankin Lake l. Nevada U.S.A.
75 F4 Frankische Alb h. Germany
74 E2 Fränkische Saale r. Germany
75 G3 Fränkische Schweiz reg. Germany
17 B7 Frankland r. Western Australia Australia
152 E3 Franklin Idaho U.S.A.
144 C4 Franklin Indiana U.S.A.
151 F6 Franklin Louisiana U.S.A.
147 H3 Franklin Massachusetts U.S.A.
145 D5 Franklin N. Carolina U.S.A.
147 H3 Franklin New Hampshire U.S.A.
147 F4 Franklin New Jersey U.S.A.
146 D4 Franklin Pennsylvania U.S.A.
145 C5 Franklin Tennessee U.S.A.
146 E6 Franklin Virginia U.S.A.
146 D5 Franklin W. Virginia U.S.A.
131 G5 Franklin South Africa
134 F2 Franklin Bay b. N.W.T. Canada
152 C1 Franklin D. Roosevelt Lake l. Washington U.S.A.
12 D3 Franklin Harb. harbour S. Australia Australia
179 B5 Franklin I. i. Antarctica
136 E2 Franklin Mountains mountain range N.W.T. Canada
9 A6 Franklin Mts mts New Zealand
13 F5 Franklin Sd chan. Tasmania Australia
135 J2 Franklin Str. chan. N.W.T. Canada
90 D1 Franois France
56 E3 Fränsta Sweden
78 B1 Františkovy Lázně Czech Rep.
140 C2 Franz Ontario Canada
9 C5 Franz Josef Glacier New Zealand
Franz Josef Land is see Zemlya Frantsa-Iosifa
108 A5 Frasca, Capo della pt Sardegna Italy
109 E3 Frascati Italy
111 F3 Frascineto Italy
80 D3 Frasdorf Germany
136 E4 Fraser r. B.C. Canada
139 H2 Fraser r. Newfoundland Canada
130 C5 Fraserburg South Africa
66 F3 Fraserburgh Scotland U.K.
140 E2 Fraserdale Ontario Canada
15 H5 Fraser I. i. Queensland Australia
15 H5 Fraser I. Nat. Park Queensland Australia
136 E4 Fraser Lake B.C. Canada
17 B5 Fraser, Mt h. Western Australia Australia
136 E4 Fraser Plateau plat. B.C. Canada
8 F3 Frasertown New Zealand
90 E2 Frasne France
69 B4 Frasnes-lez-Buissenal Belgium
107 E4 Frassinoro Italy
80 A3 Frastanz Austria
100 C1 Fratel Portugal
110 D5 Fratello r. Sicilia Italy
140 C3 Frater Ontario Canada
112 E3 Frăteşti Romania
107 F3 Fratta r. Italy
82 C1 Fraubrunnen Switzerland
83 D1 Frauenfeld Switzerland
81 H3 Frauenkirchen Austria
75 J2 Frauenstein Germany
80 D2 Fraunberg Germany
173 H2 Fray Bentos Uruguay
172 E5 Fray Luís Beltrán Argentina
173 K3 Fray Marcos Uruguay
93 D4 Frayssinet-le-Gélat France
98 B3 Freamunde Portugal
74 B2 Frechen Germany
99 F2 Frechilla Spain
91 B5 Frech, Mt mt. France
65 F4 Freckleton England U.K.
55 E4 Fredensborg Denmark
148 E3 Frederic Michigan U.S.A.
148 A3 Frederic Wisconsin U.S.A.
55 B4 Fredericia Denmark
17 B5 Frederick r. Western Australia Australia
146 E5 Frederick Maryland U.S.A.
151 D5 Frederick Oklahoma U.S.A.
135 Q1 Frederick E. Hyde Fjord inlet Greenland
15 H4 Frederick Reef reef Coral Sea Islands Terr. Pacific Ocean
151 D6 Fredericksburg Texas U.S.A.
146 E5 Fredericksburg Virginia U.S.A.
136 C3 Frederick Sound chan. Alaska U.S.A.
151 F4 Fredericktown Missouri U.S.A.
139 G4 Fredericton New Brunswick Canada
55 E4 Frederiksberg Denmark
55 E4 Frederiksborg div. Denmark
Frederikshåb see Paamiut
55 C2 Frederikshavn Denmark
55 E4 Frederikssund Denmark
145 □3 Frederiksted Virgin Is Caribbean
159 F3 Frederiksted Virgin Is Caribbean
55 E4 Frederiksværk Denmark
73 J3 Fredersdorf Germany
155 F3 Fredonia Arizona U.S.A.
146 D3 Fredonia New York U.S.A.
56 E2 Fredrika Sweden
59 F1 Fredriksberg Sweden
58 D2 Fredrikstad Norway
147 F4 Freehold New Jersey U.S.A.
147 F4 Freeland Pennsylvania U.S.A.
12 D2 Freeling Heights mt. S. Australia Australia
14 C4 Freeling, Mt mt. Northern Terr. Australia
154 C2 Freel Peak summit California U.S.A.
150 D3 Freeman S. Dakota U.S.A.
148 D5 Freeman, Lake l. Indiana U.S.A.
148 C4 Freeport Illinois U.S.A.
147 H3 Freeport Maine U.S.A.
147 G4 Freeport New York U.S.A.
151 E6 Freeport Texas U.S.A.
158 C1 Freeport City The Bahamas
151 D7 Freer Texas U.S.A.
159 □7 Freetown Antigua Caribbean
122 B5 Freetown Sierra Leone
100 D2 Fregenal de la Sierra Spain
108 E3 Fregene Italy
88 C3 Fréhel France
88 C3 Fréhel, Cap pt France
75 J2 Freiberg Germany
75 J2 Freiberger Mulde r. Germany
74 D5 Freiburg div. Germany
72 E2 Freiburg (Elbe) Germany
72 E2 Freiburg (Elbe) Germany
74 C4 Freiburg im Breisgau Germany
74 F2 Freiensteinau Germany
75 G3 Freihung Germany
169 H3 Frei Inocêncio Brazil
75 H5 Freilassing Germany
172 A5 Freire Chile
170 B2 Freirina Chile
74 C3 Freisen Germany
75 G4 Freising Germany
81 F2 Freistadt div. Austria
81 F2 Freistadt Austria
75 J2 Freital Germany
98 C4 Freixedas Portugal
98 B3 Freixo Portugal
98 D3 Freixo de Espada à Cinta Portugal
91 E5 Fréjus France
91 E5 Fréjus, G. de b. France
91 E3 Fréjus Tunnel France/Italy
58 A1 Frekhaug Norway
17 A7 Fremantle Western Australia Australia
74 F4 Fremdingen Germany
62 B3 Fremington England U.K.
155 G2 Fremont r. Utah U.S.A.
148 E4 Fremont Michigan U.S.A.
150 D3 Fremont Nebraska U.S.A.
146 B4 Fremont Ohio U.S.A.
146 B6 Frenchburg Kentucky U.S.A.
146 C4 French Creek r. Pennsylvania U.S.A.
160 G3 French Guiana territory South America
13 F4 French I. i. Victoria Australia
137 H5 Frenchman r. Canada/U.S.A.
154 C2 Frenchman Nevada U.S.A.
13 F5 Frenchman Cap mt. Tasmania Australia
154 B2 Frenchman L. l. California U.S.A.
155 E3 Frenchman L. l. Nevada U.S.A.
67 C3 Frenchpark Rep. of Ireland
9 D4 French Pass New Zealand
5 N6 French Polynesia territory Pacific Ocean
147 J1 Frenchville Maine U.S.A.
86 A2 Frencq France
121 E1 Frenda Algeria
89 G2 Freneuse France
79 H2 Frenštát pod Radhoštěm Czech Rep.
109 G2 Frentani, Monti dei mts Italy
131 G4 Frere South Africa
72 C3 Freren Germany
81 E4 Fresach Austria
122 C5 Fresca Côte d'Ivoire
166 B2 Fresco r. Brazil
63 E4 Freshwater England U.K.
155 G6 Fresnal Canyon Arizona U.S.A.
89 F3 Fresnay-sur-Sarthe France
101 G2 Fresnedas r. Spain
87 E3 Fresnes-en-Woëvre France
87 E5 Fresnes-sur-Apance France
82 A1 Fresne-St-Mamès France
156 E4 Fresnillo Mexico
154 C3 Fresno r. California U.S.A.
154 C3 Fresno California U.S.A.
98 E4 Fresno Alhándiga Spain
98 E3 Fresno de la Ribera Spain
98 E3 Fresno de Sayago Spain
86 C3 Fresnoy-le-Grand France
63 H2 Fressingfield England U.K.
58 B1 Fresvikbreen mt. Norway
90 D1 Fretigney-et-Velloreille France
97 H3 Freu, Cap des pt Spain
103 F5 Freu de Cabrera chan. Spain
74 C2 Freudenberg Germany
69 E5 Freudenburg Germany
74 D4 Freudenstadt Germany
86 B2 Frévent France
14 C3 Frewena Northern Terr. Australia
73 G4 Freyburg Germany
17 A5 Freycinet Est. b. Western Australia Australia
13 G5 Freycinet Nat. Park nat. park Tasmania Australia
73 H2 Freyenstein Germany
87 F3 Freyming-Merlebach France
173 F1 Freyre Argentina
75 G3 Freystadt Germany
75 J4 Freyung Germany
152 B4 Fria Guinea
128 A2 Fria, Cape c. Namibia
154 C3 Friant California U.S.A.
170 D2 Frías Argentina
82 C2 Fribourg div. Switzerland
82 C2 Fribourg Fribourg Switzerland
82 D1 Frick Switzerland
83 E1 Frickingen Germany
65 H3 Fridaythorpe England U.K.
81 H3 Friedberg Austria
75 F4 Friedberg Germany
74 D2 Friedberg (Hessen) Germany
72 C2 Friedeburg Germany
74 E2 Friedewald Hessen Germany
87 G2 Friedewald Rheinland-Pfalz Germany
73 K3 Friedland Brandenburg Germany
73 J2 Friedland Mecklenburg-Vorpommern Germany
72 E4 Friedland Niedersachsen Germany
75 F2 Friedrichroda Germany
74 D2 Friedrichsdorf Germany
74 E5 Friedrichshafen Germany
72 D1 Friedrichskoog Germany
73 G2 Friedrichsruhe Germany
72 E1 Friedrichstadt Germany
73 J2 Friedrichswalde Germany
75 F2 Friemar Germany
159 □1 Friendship h. Jamaica
147 J3 Friendship Maine U.S.A.
81 F4 Friesach Austria
73 H3 Friesack Germany
87 G2 Friesenhagen Germany
74 C4 Friesenheim Germany
83 F1 Friesenried Germany
68 D1 Friese Wad tidal flats Netherlands
68 D1 Friesland div. Netherlands
72 C2 Friesoythe Germany
127 □1 Frigate I. i. Seychelles
107 E4 Frignano reg. Italy
59 E3 Frillesås Sweden
59 F3 Frinnaryd Sweden
63 H3 Frinton-on-Sea England U.K.
151 D6 Frio r. Texas U.S.A.
66 F4 Friockheim Scotland U.K.
98 C1 Friol Spain
66 B4 Frisa, Loch l. Scotland U.K.
69 E5 Frisange Luxembourg
155 F2 Frisco Mt mt. Utah U.S.A.
59 E3 Fristad Sweden
59 E3 Fritsla Sweden
72 E4 Fritzlar Germany
107 G2 Friuli - Venezia Giulia div. Italy
89 G1 Friville-Escarbotin France
135 M3 Frobisher Bay b. N.W.T. Canada
137 H3 Frobisher Lake l. Saskatchewan Canada
55 C4 Frøbjerg Bavnehøj h. Denmark
80 B4 Frodolfo r. Italy
62 D1 Frodsham England U.K.
91 D3 Froges France
63 F3 Frogmore England U.K.
56 C3 Frohavet b. Norway
75 F3 Frohburg Germany
81 G3 Frohnleiten Austria
90 E1 Froideconche France
86 B3 Froissy France
58 C2 Froland Norway
52 F1 Frolishchi Rus. Fed.
51 G5 Frolovo Rus. Fed.
50 K2 Frolovskaya Rus. Fed.
77 H1 Frombork Poland
62 D4 Frome r. England U.K.
12 D2 Frome watercourse S. Australia Australia
62 D3 Frome England U.K.
159 □1 Frome Jamaica
12 D2 Frome Downs S. Australia Australia
12 D2 Frome, Lake salt flat S. Australia Australia
99 F2 Frómista Spain
72 C4 Fröndenberg Germany
74 D2 Fronhausen Germany
93 B4 Fronsac Aquitaine France
93 C6 Fronsac Midi-Pyrénées France
100 C1 Fronteira Portugal
93 B2 Frontenay-Rohan-Rohan France
75 H4 Frontenhausen Germany
97 □ Frontera Canary Is Spain
157 G5 Frontera Mexico
157 G5 Frontera, Pta pt Mexico
156 C2 Fronteras Mexico
91 B5 Frontignan France
93 D5 Fronton France
146 D5 Front Royal Virginia U.S.A.
109 F3 Frosinone div. Lazio Italy
109 F3 Frosinone Italy
109 G3 Frosolone Italy
146 D5 Frostburg Maryland U.S.A.
59 F2 Frövi Sweden
56 C3 Frøya i. Norway
86 B2 Fruges France
155 H2 Fruita Colorado U.S.A.
155 G1 Fruitland Utah U.S.A.
52 D2 Fruktovaya Rus. Fed.
112 F1 Frumuşica Romania
53 F3 Frunze Khersons'ka Oblast' Ukraine
53 F3 Frunze Khersons'ka Oblast' Ukraine
47 H4 Frunze Kyrgyzstan
Frunze see Bishkek
53 C3 Frunzivka Ukraine
112 B2 Fruška Gora h. Yugoslavia
168 D4 Frutal Brazil
82 C2 Frutigen Switzerland
79 H2 Frýdek-Místek Czech Rep.
78 E1 Frýdlant Czech Rep.
147 H2 Fryeburg Maine U.S.A.
77 J2 Frygnowo Poland
81 F2 Frymburk Czech Rep.
77 K6 Frysztak Poland
114 D4 Fthiotis div. Greece
32 D1 Fu r. China
6 □4 Fua'amotu Tonga
6 □3 Fuamotu i. Tonga
33 G3 Fu'an China
64 C1 Fuar Bheinn h. Scotland U.K.
107 E5 Fucecchio Italy
83 F1 Fuchstal Germany
28 D6 Fuchū Japan
33 E3 Fuchuan China
29 H3 Fudai Japan
66 A3 Fuday i. Scotland U.K.
33 G3 Fude China
33 H3 Fuding China
101 F2 Fuencaliente Spain
102 B3 Fuendejalón Spain
101 F4 Fuengirola Spain
99 G4 Fuenlabrada Spain
99 H2 Fuenmayor Spain
99 F4 Fuensalida Spain
103 B7 Fuensanta Spain
103 B7 Fuente Álamo Spain
103 B6 Fuente-Álamo Spain
103 B6 Fuente Albilla, Cerro de mt. Spain
99 G3 Fuentecambrón Spain
99 G3 Fuentecén Spain
100 D2 Fuente de Cantos Spain
100 D2 Fuente del Maestre Spain
101 F3 Fuente de Piedra Spain
101 F3 Fuente de Piedra, Laguna de l. Spain
101 G1 Fuente el Fresno Spain
98 D4 Fuenteguinaldo Spain
99 E3 Fuentelapeña Spain
99 G3 Fuentelcésped Spain
101 H1 Fuentelespino de Haro Spain
101 E2 Fuente Obejuna Spain
101 E3 Fuente Palmera Spain
99 H3 Fuentepinilla Spain
102 C3 Fuenterodos Spain
99 E3 Fuentesaúco Spain
99 F3 Fuentesaúco de Fuentidueña Spain
103 C4 Fuentes de Ayódar Spain
102 C3 Fuentes de Ebro Spain
102 B3 Fuentes de Jiloca Spain
100 D2 Fuentes de León Spain
99 F2 Fuentes de Nava Spain
98 D4 Fuentes de Oñoro Spain
102 D4 Fuentespalda Spain
100 D1 Fuentes, Sierra de Spain
99 G3 Fuentidueña Spain
171 B7 Fuerte Bulnes Chile
101 G3 Fuerte del Rey Spain
165 E4 Fuerte Olimpo Paraguay
97 □ Fuerteventura i. Canary Is Spain
23 B2 Fuga i. Philippines
80 C3 Fügen Austria
55 □1 Fuglafjørður Faeroes
55 D4 Fuglebjerg Denmark
32 B3 Fugong China
33 F1 Fugou China
30 D5 Fugu China
47 L3 Fuhai China
72 E2 Fuhlsbüttel airport Germany
73 H4 Fuhne r. Germany
41 J4 Fujairah U.A.E.
29 G6 Fuji Japan
33 G3 Fujian div. China
29 G6 Fujieda Japan
29 G6 Fuji-Hakone-Izu National Park Japan
31 J3 Fujin China
29 G6 Fujinomiya Japan
28 H3 Fujisaki Japan
29 G6 Fuji-san volcano Japan
29 G6 Fujiyoshida Japan
42 A4 Fūka Egypt
28 J2 Fukagawa Japan
28 G3 Fukaura Japan
Fukien see Fujian
28 E6 Fukuchiyama Japan
28 B7 Fukue Japan
28 B7 Fukue-jima i. Japan
29 F6 Fukui div. Japan
29 F5 Fukui Japan
28 C7 Fukuoka div. Japan
28 C7 Fukuoka Japan
29 H5 Fukushima div. Japan
29 H5 Fukushima Japan
28 H3 Fukushima Japan
28 C8 Fukuyama Japan
122 A4 Fulacunda Guinea-Bissau
39 C1 Fūlād Maïalleh Iran
6 □7 Fulaga i. Fiji
72 E4 Fulda r. Germany
74 E2 Fulda Hessen Germany
65 G4 Fulford England U.K.
63 F3 Fulham England U.K.
33 G1 Fuliji China
32 D2 Fuling China
159 □3 Fullarton Trinidad and Tobago
137 M2 Fullerton, Cape headland N.W.T. Canada
79 G2 Fulnek Czech Rep.
79 J5 Fülöpszállás Hungary
80 C3 Fulpmes Austria
148 B5 Fulton Illinois U.S.A.
144 B4 Fulton Kentucky U.S.A.
150 F4 Fulton Missouri U.S.A.
147 E3 Fulton New York U.S.A.
173 H4 Fulton Argentina
86 D3 Fumay France
93 C4 Fumel France
29 H6 Funabashi Japan
4 J5 Funafuti i. Tuvalu
96 □ Funchal Madeira Portugal
162 C1 Fundación Colombia
169 H3 Fundão Brazil
98 C4 Fundão Portugal
156 C3 Fundición Mexico
112 F2 Fundulea Romania
80 B3 Fundusfeiler mt. Austria
139 G5 Fundy, Bay of b. New Brunswick/Nova Scotia Canada
139 G4 Fundy Nat. Park nat. park New Brunswick Canada
154 D3 Funeral Peak summit California U.S.A.
129 E3 Funhalouro Mozambique
32 D4 Funing China
33 G1 Funing China
33 E1 Funiu Shan mountain range China
123 F4 Funtua Nigeria
66 □2 Funzie Scotland U.K.
30 E5 Fuping China
33 G3 Fuqing China
32 D3 Fuquan China
55 B3 Fur i. Denmark
129 E1 Furancungo Mozambique
28 J2 Furano Japan
28 K2 Füren-ko l. Japan
55 E4 Furesø l. Denmark
39 C3 Fürg Iran
59 H3 Furilden i. Sweden
83 D2 Furkapass Switzerland
55 E1 Furmanov Rus. Fed.
47 H4 Furmanovka Kazakhstan
46 C3 Furmanovo Kazakhstan
154 D3 Furnace Creek California U.S.A.
13 G5 Furneaux Group is Tasmania Australia
43 D2 Furqlus Syria
72 C3 Fürstenau Germany
73 J2 Fürstenberg Brandenburg Germany
72 D4 Fürstenberg Nordrhein-Westfalen Germany
81 G3 Fürstenfeld div. Austria
81 H3 Fürstenfeld Austria
75 G4 Fürstenfeldbruck Germany
73 K3 Fürstenwalde Germany
73 J2 Fürstenwerder Germany
75 J4 Fürstenzell Germany
79 L4 Furta Hungary
59 E2 Furtan Sweden
108 A5 Furtei Sardegna Italy
75 F3 Fürth Bayern Germany
74 D3 Fürth Hessen Germany
75 H3 Furth im Wald Germany
74 D4 Furtwangen im Schwarzwald Germany
28 H2 Furubira Japan
59 F1 Furudal Sweden
29 F5 Furukawa Japan
29 H4 Furukawa Japan
135 K3 Fury and Hecla Strait str. N.W.T. Canada
162 C3 Fusagasugá Colombia
111 F3 Fuscaldo Italy
114 B2 Fushë-Bardhe Albania
114 A1 Fushë-Krujë Albania
31 G4 Fushun China
32 D2 Fushun China
107 H2 Fusine in Valromana Italy
31 H4 Fusong China
75 F5 Füssen Germany
89 H4 Fussy France
102 B2 Fustiñana Spain
32 D4 Fusui China
28 C7 Futago-san volcano Japan
171 B5 Futaleufú Chile
107 F4 Futa, Passo della pass Italy
29 □1 Futatsu-ne is Japan
29 □2 Futemma Japan
112 B2 Futog Yugoslavia
172 A6 Futrono Chile
29 G6 Futtsu Japan
6 □2 Futuna i. Vanuatu
33 G3 Futun Xi r. China
91 D5 Fuveau France
30 D6 Fu Xian China
Fuxian see Wafangdian
31 G4 Fuxin China
29 G4 Fuya Japan
31 E5 Fuyang r. China
33 G2 Fuyang China
33 F1 Fuyang China
31 H3 Fuyu China
31 K2 Fuyuan China
32 D3 Fuyuan China
26 E2 Fuyun China
79 K4 Füzesabony Hungary
33 G3 Fuzhou Fujian China
33 G3 Fuzhou Jiangxi China
107 J3 Fužine Croatia
55 C4 Fyn i. Denmark
64 D1 Fyne r. Scotland U.K.
66 C5 Fyne, Loch inlet Scotland U.K.
55 C4 Fyns Hoved headland Denmark
58 C2 Fyresdal Norway
58 C2 Fyresvatn l. Norway
59 G1 Fyrisån r. Sweden
114 C4 Fyteies Greece
159 □3 Fyzabad Trinidad and Tobago

G

105 B7 Gaâfour Tunisia
81 F3 Gaal Austria
126 E3 Gaalkacyo Somalia
130 B3 Gab watercourse Namibia
126 D3 Gabangab well Ethiopia
93 C5 Gabarret France
93 B5 Gabas r. France
154 D2 Gabbs Nevada U.S.A.
154 C2 Gabbs Valley Range mts Nevada U.S.A.
125 B6 Gabela Angola
121 G2 Gabès Tunisia
121 G2 Gabès, Golfe de g. Tunisia
101 G3 Gabia la Grande Spain
107 G5 Gabicce Mare Italy
77 H3 Gąbin Poland
8 G3 Gable End Foreland headland New Zealand
81 H2 Gablitz Austria
13 G4 Gabo I. i. Victoria Australia
117 F6 Gabon country Africa
128 D3 Gaborone Botswana
173 G2 Gaboto Argentina
93 E4 Gabriac France
127 □4 Gabriel I. i. Mauritius
39 D4 Gābrīk watercourse Iran
39 D4 Gābrīk Iran
112 D3 Gabrovnitsa Bulgaria
112 E3 Gabrovo Bulgaria
122 B4 Gabú Guinea-Bissau
106 B3 Gaby Italy
179 □ Gaby, I. i. Kerguelen Indian Ocean
89 F3 Gacé France
39 B1 Gach Sār Iran
104 G4 Gacko Bos.-Herz.
38 A3 Gadag India
56 D2 Gäddede Sweden
32 B1 Gadê China
73 G2 Gadebusch Germany
80 C4 Gadera r. Italy
36 B5 Gadhra India
83 D2 Gadmen Switzerland
108 B5 Gadoni Sardegna Italy
101 H4 Gádor Spain
101 H4 Gádor, Sierra de mountain range Spain
36 B4 Gadra Pakistan
145 C5 Gadsden Alabama U.S.A.
38 B2 Gadwal India
124 C3 Gadzi Central African Rep.
56 F1 Gædnovuoppe Norway
62 C3 Gaer Wales U.K.
112 E2 Găeşti Romania
109 F3 Gaeta Italy
109 F3 Gaeta, Golfo di g. Italy
98 B4 Gafanha da Nazare Portugal
4 F4 Gaferut i. Fed. States of Micronesia
100 C1 Gáfete Portugal
145 D5 Gaffney S. Carolina U.S.A.
121 F2 Gafsa Tunisia
124 C2 Gagal Chad
52 B2 Gagarin Rus. Fed.
47 G4 Gagarin Uzbekistan
74 D4 Gaggenau Germany
111 E5 Gaggi Sicilia Italy
107 E4 Gaggio Montano Italy
52 G2 Gagino Rus. Fed.
110 D5 Gagliano Castelferrato Sicilia Italy
111 H3 Gagliano del Capo Italy
122 C5 Gagnoa Côte d'Ivoire
139 G3 Gagnon Québec Canada
141 H3 Gagnon, Lac l. Québec Canada
51 G7 Gagra Georgia
102 E3 Gaià r. Spain
130 B3 Gaiab r. Namibia
37 G4 Gaibanda Bangladesh
80 D4 Gail r. Austria
74 E4 Gaildorf Germany
83 D1 Gailingen Germany
93 D5 Gaillac France
90 E2 Gaillard France
Gaillimh see Galway
89 G2 Gaillon France
171 C5 Gaimán Argentina
75 G4 Gaimersheim Germany
145 D6 Gainesville Florida U.S.A.
145 D5 Gainesville Georgia U.S.A.
151 D5 Gainesville Texas U.S.A.
65 H4 Gainsborough England U.K.
17 B7 Gairdner r. Western Australia Australia
12 C2 Gairdner, Lake salt flat S. Australia Australia
66 C3 Gair Loch inlet Scotland U.K.
66 C3 Gairloch Scotland U.K.
108 B5 Gairo Sardegna Italy
83 E1 Gais Switzerland
81 F3 Gaishorn Austria
31 G4 Gai Xian China
38 C2 Gajapatinagaram India
36 A4 Gajar Pakistan
78 F3 Gajary Slovakia
126 C4 Gajos well Kenya
130 D3 Gakarosa mt. South Africa
123 F5 Gakem Nigeria
36 C1 Gakuch Jammu and Kashmir
37 G3 Gala China
46 F5 Galaasiya Uzbekistan
43 A5 Galâla el Baharîya, G. el plat. Egypt
43 A5 Galâla el Qiblîya, G. el plat. Egypt
93 C5 Galan France
127 C5 Galana r. Kenya
170 C2 Galán, Co mt. Argentina
39 C1 Galand Iran
79 G3 Galanta Slovakia
23 □1 Galap Palau
99 G4 Galapagar Spain
162 □ Galápagos, Islas is Ecuador
66 F5 Galashiels Scotland U.K.
112 F3 Galata Bulgaria
115 E5 Galatas Greece
53 B Galaţi div. Romania
112 F2 Galaţi Romania
111 H2 Galatina Italy
114 C2 Galatini Greece
114 E2 Galatista Greece
111 H2 Galatone Italy
66 F5 Gala Water r. Scotland U.K.
146 C6 Galax Virginia U.S.A.
115 D4 Galaxidi Greece
67 C4 Galbally Rep. of Ireland
15 E3 Galbraith Queensland Australia
99 H1 Galdakao Spain
97 □ Gáldar Canary Is Spain
57 C3 Galdhøpiggen summit Norway
157 E3 Galeana Mexico
99 G1 Galea, Pta pt Spain
39 C4 Galeh Dār Iran
148 B4 Galena Illinois U.S.A.
73 J2 Galenbecker See l. Germany
159 □3 Galeota Pt pt Trinidad Trinidad and Tobago
101 H3 Galera r. Spain
101 H3 Galera Spain
159 □3 Galera Pt pt Trinidad Trinidad and Tobago
157 F6 Galera, Pta pt Mexico
172 A5 Galera, Punta headland Chile
148 B5 Galesburg Illinois U.S.A.
131 F5 Galeshewe South Africa
148 B3 Galesville Wisconsin U.S.A.
146 E4 Galeton Pennsylvania U.S.A.
127 □5 Galets, Pte des pt Réunion Indian Ocean
79 J4 Galgamácsa Hungary
126 E3 Galguduud div. Somalia
166 C3 Galheirão r. Brazil
51 G7 Gali Georgia
168 D5 Gália Brazil
112 D2 Galicea Mare Romania
50 G3 Galich Rus. Fed.
50 G3 Galichskaya Vozvyshennost' lowland Rus. Fed.
98 B2 Galicia div. Spain
114 B2 Galičica mountain range Macedonia
114 B1 Galičica nat. park Macedonia
15 F4 Galilee, L. salt flat Queensland Australia
Galilee, Sea of l. see Tiberias, L.
169 H3 Galiléia Brazil
106 E5 Galileo airport Italy
83 E1 Galinakopf mt. Austria/Liechtenstein
159 □1 Galina Pt pt Jamaica
146 B4 Galion Ohio U.S.A.
159 □4 Galion, Baie du b. Martinique Caribbean
114 C1 Galište Ezero l. Macedonia
98 D5 Galisteo Spain
52 C3 Galitsa Rus. Fed.
155 G5 Galiuro Mts mts Arizona U.S.A.
119 G5 Gallabat Sudan
106 C3 Gallarate Italy
89 G3 Gallardon France
152 E2 Gallatin r. Montana U.S.A.
145 C4 Gallatin Tennessee U.S.A.
38 C5 Galle Sri Lanka
102 C2 Gállego r. Spain
171 B7 Gallegos r. Argentina
99 E4 Gallegos de Solmirón Spain
67 C5 Galley Head headland Rep. of Ireland
92 B3 Gallian-en-Médoc France
106 C3 Galliate Italy
102 E2 Gallina Pelada mt. Spain
162 C1 Gallinas, Pta pt Colombia
107 F3 Gallio Italy
111 H2 Gallipoli Italy
146 B5 Gallipolis Ohio U.S.A.
56 F2 Gällivare Sweden
81 F4 Gallizien Austria
81 F2 Gallneukirchen Austria
99 J4 Gallo r. Spain
56 D3 Gällö Sweden
102 B4 Gallocanta, Laguna de l. Spain
110 C4 Gallo, Capo c. Sicilia Italy
147 E3 Gallo I. i. New York U.S.A.
106 E2 Gallo, Lago di l. Italy
155 H4 Gallo Mts mts New Mexico U.S.A.
9 □3 Galloway, Mt h. Antipodes Is New Zealand
66 D6 Galloway, Mull of c. Scotland U.K.
59 E3 Gällstad Sweden
155 H4 Gallup New Mexico U.S.A.
102 B3 Gallur Spain
108 B4 Gallura reg. Sardegna Italy
47 G5 Gallyaaral Uzbekistan
127 D5 Galma Galla waterhole Kenya
66 B4 Galmisdale Scotland U.K.
13 G3 Galong New South Wales Australia
38 C5 Gal Oya r. Sri Lanka
38 C4 Galoya Sri Lanka
126 E2 Gal Shiikh Somalia
66 D5 Galston Scotland U.K.
154 B2 Galt California U.S.A.
120 B3 Galtat Zemmour Western Sahara
67 C4 Galtee Mountains h. Rep. of Ireland
108 B4 Galtelli Sardegna Italy
59 G2 Galten l. Sweden
55 B3 Galten Denmark
58 D1 Galterud Norway
80 B4 Galtür Austria
67 C4 Galtymore h. Rep. of Ireland
39 D2 Galūgāh-e Āsīyeh Iran
148 B5 Galva Illinois U.S.A.
172 A5 Galvarino Chile
99 G3 Galve de Sorbe Spain
100 C1 Galveias Portugal
151 E6 Galveston Texas U.S.A.
151 E6 Galveston Bay b. Texas U.S.A.
173 G2 Galvez Argentina
101 F1 Gálvez Spain
37 E3 Galwa Nepal
67 B3 Galway div. Rep. of Ireland
67 B3 Galway Rep. of Ireland
67 B3 Galway Bay g. Rep. of Ireland
24 D2 Gâm r. Vietnam
168 D2 Gamá Brazil
99 G1 Gama Spain
89 G2 Gamaches France
29 F6 Gamagōri Japan
173 F6 Gama, I. i. Argentina
131 H5 Gamalakhe South Africa
162 C2 Gamarra Colombia
79 G5 Gamás Hungary
123 G4 Gamawa Nigeria
172 E4 Gamay Argentina
37 G3 Gamba China
125 A4 Gamba Gabon
122 D4 Gambaga Ghana
106 E3 Gambara Italy
111 E4 Gambarie Italy
126 B3 Gambēla Ethiopia
126 B3 Gambela National Park nat. park Ethiopia
134 A3 Gambell Alaska U.S.A.
107 G4 Gambettola Italy
122 A4 Gambia r. The Gambia
116 C4 Gambia, The country Africa
122 B4 Gambie r. Senegal
14 B1 Gambier, C. c. Northern Terr. Australia
5 O7 Gambier, Îles is French Polynesia Pacific Ocean
12 D3 Gambier Is is S. Australia Australia
145 □2 Gambier Village The Bahamas
139 K4 Gambo Newfoundland Canada
124 D3 Gambo Central African Rep.
106 C3 Gambolò Italy
124 C4 Gamboma Congo
15 E3 Gamboola Queensland Australia
124 C3 Gamboula Central African Rep.

87 G4 **Gambsheim** France
155 H4 **Gamerco** *New Mexico* U.S.A.
81 G3 **Gaming** Austria
130 C6 **Gamka r.** South Africa
59 G3 **Gamleby** Sweden
119 F4 **Gammams well** Sudan
56 F2 **Gammelstaden** Sweden
74 E4 **Gammertingen** Germany
12 D2 **Gammon Ranges Nat. Park nat. park** *S. Australia* Australia
131 H1 **Ga-Modjadji** South Africa
130 B4 **Gamoep** South Africa
98 E1 **Gamonal mt.** Spain
38 C5 **Gampola** Sri Lanka
83 E1 **Gams** Switzerland
32 B2 **Gamtog** China
126 C4 **Gamud mt.** Ethiopia
33 F3 **Gan r.** China
31 H2 **Gan r.** China
32 C1 **Gana** China
155 H4 **Ganado** *Arizona* U.S.A.
91 D4 **Ganagobie** France
141 G4 **Gananoque** *Ontario* Canada
39 B3 **Ganāveh** Iran
42 F1 **Gäncä** Azerbaijan
32 E5 **Gancheng** China
Gand *see* **Gent**
125 B6 **Ganda** Angola
37 G3 **Gandaingoin** China
125 D5 **Gandajika** Zaire
98 B1 **Gándara** *Galicia* Spain
36 B3 **Gandari Mt. mt.** Pakistan
36 A3 **Gandava** Pakistan
139 K4 **Gander** *Newfoundland* Canada
72 D2 **Ganderkesee** Germany
102 D3 **Gandesa** Spain
36 C5 **Gandevi** India
36 B5 **Gāndhīdhām** India
36 C5 **Gandhinagar** India
36 C4 **Gāndhi Sāgar resr** India
103 C6 **Gandía** Spain
106 D3 **Gandino** Italy
39 E3 **Gand-i-Zureh depression** Afghanistan
166 E3 **Gandu** Brazil
Gandzha *see* **Gäncä**
120 B5 **Gâneb well** Mauritania
36 F4 **Ganga r.** India
38 C5 **Ganga r.** Sri Lanka
124 E3 **Gangala Na Bodia** Zaire
37 G5 **Ganga, Mouths of the river mouth** Bangladesh
171 C5 **Gangán** Argentina
36 C3 **Ganganagar** India
36 C4 **Gangapur** India
36 D4 **Gangapur** India
123 F4 **Gangara** Niger
24 A2 **Gangaw** Myanmar
38 B3 **Gangawati** India
24 B1 **Gangaw Range mountain range** Myanmar
30 B5 **Gangca** China
37 E3 **Gangdisê Shan mountain range** China
37 F4 **Ganges r.** India
91 B5 **Ganges** France
110 D5 **Gangi r.** *Sicilia* Italy
110 D5 **Gangi** *Sicilia* Italy
75 H4 **Gangkofen** Germany
36 D3 **Gangotri mt.** India
37 G4 **Gangtok** India
32 D1 **Gangu** China
38 D2 **Ganjam** India
39 B3 **Ganjgān** Iran
31 E3 **Ganjur Sum** China
32 C2 **Ganluo** China
13 F3 **Ganmain** *New South Wales* Australia
31 G3 **Gannan** China
90 B2 **Gannat** France
152 E3 **Gannett Peak summit** *Wyoming* U.S.A.
53 B1 **Gannopil'** Ukraine
36 C5 **Ganora** India
30 D5 **Ganquan** China
130 B7 **Gansbaai** South Africa
81 H2 **Gänserndorf div.** Austria
81 H2 **Gänserndorf** Austria
69 C4 **Ganshoren** Belgium
30 B5 **Gansu div.** China
126 D4 **Gantamaa** Somalia
30 C5 **Gantang** China
12 D4 **Gantheaume, C. headland** *S. Australia* Australia
51 G7 **Gant'iadi** Georgia
82 C2 **Gantrisch mt.** Switzerland
22 B2 **Gantung** Indonesia
37 F4 **Ganwan** India
33 F3 **Gan Xian** China
123 G5 **Ganye** Nigeria
130 E3 **Ganyesa** South Africa
33 G1 **Ganyu** China
46 C3 **Ganyushkino** Kazakhstan
33 F3 **Ganzhou** China
126 B4 **Ganzi** Sudan
73 H2 **Ganzlin** Germany
123 E3 **Gao div.** Mali
123 D3 **Gao** Mali
33 F2 **Gao'an** China
31 E5 **Gaocheng** China
33 G2 **Gaochun** China
33 G2 **Gaohebu** China
30 B5 **Gaolan** China
32 B3 **Gaoligong Shan mountain range** China
31 F5 **Gaomi** China
33 E3 **Gaomutang** China
30 E6 **Gaoping** China
31 F5 **Gaoqing** China
30 A5 **Gaotai** China
31 F5 **Gaotang** China
30 D4 **Gaotouyao** China
122 D4 **Gaoua** Burkina
122 B4 **Gaoual** Guinea
32 D2 **Gao Xian** China
Gaoxiong *see* **Kao-hsiung**
31 E5 **Gaoyang** China
31 E5 **Gaoyi** China
33 G1 **Gaoyou** China
33 G1 **Gaoyou Hu l.** China
33 E4 **Gaozhou** China
91 E4 **Gap** France
23 B3 **Gapan** Philippines
91 D5 **Gapeau r.** France
36 E2 **Gar** China
121 F2 **Garaa Tebourt well** Tunisia
126 E3 **Garacad** Somalia
156 L7 **Garachiné** Panama
126 E3 **Garadag** Somalia
121 F1 **Garaet Et Tarf salt pan** Algeria
39 E3 **Garagheh** Iran
109 J4 **Garaguso** Italy
13 G2 **Garah** *New South Wales* Australia
122 C4 **Garalo** Mali
67 C3 **Gara, Lough l.** Rep. of Ireland
124 E3 **Garamba r.** Zaire
124 E3 **Garamba, Parc National de la nat. park** Zaire
166 E2 **Garanhuns** Brazil
131 F2 **Ga-Rankuwa** South Africa
169 E2 **Garapuava** Brazil
124 D2 **Garba** Central African Rep.
126 D4 **Garbahaarey** Somalia
77 K4 **Garbatka-Letnisko** Poland
127 C4 **Garba Tula** Kenya
101 F1 **Garbayuela** Spain
154 A1 **Garberville** *California* U.S.A.
77 L4 **Garbów** Poland
72 E3 **Garbsen** *Niedersachsen* Germany
168 D5 **Garça** Brazil
166 D2 **Garças r.** Brazil
168 B1 **Garças, R. das r.** Brazil
75 H4 **Garching an der Alz** Germany
75 G4 **Garching bei München** Germany
102 D3 **Garcia** Spain
168 B4 **Garcias** Brazil
130 C6 **Garciaspas pass** South Africa
100 E1 **Garciaz** Spain
99 H4 **Garcinarro** Spain
37 G2 **Garco** China
91 C4 **Gard div.** *Languedoc-Roussillon* France
91 C5 **Gard r.** France
107 E3 **Garda** Italy
107 E3 **Garda, Lago di l.** Italy
91 D5 **Gardanne** France
105 A7 **Garde, Cap de c.** Algeria
76 G2 **Gardeja** Poland
73 G3 **Gardelegen** Germany
80 C4 **Gardena r.** Italy
150 C4 **Garden City** *Kansas* U.S.A.
148 D3 **Garden Corners** *Michigan* U.S.A.
154 C5 **Garden Grove** *California* U.S.A.
137 L4 **Garden Hill** *Manitoba* Canada
148 E3 **Garden I. i.** *Michigan* U.S.A.
144 C2 **Garden Pen. pen.** *Michigan* U.S.A.
173 H4 **Gardey** Argentina
39 G2 **Gardēz** Afghanistan
114 C4 **Gardiki** Greece
147 J2 **Gardiner** *Maine* U.S.A.
152 E2 **Gardiner** *Montana* U.S.A.
140 E2 **Gardiner** *Ontario* Canada
147 G4 **Gardiners I. i.** *New York* U.S.A.
72 D1 **Garding** Germany
148 C5 **Gardner** *Illinois* U.S.A.
147 K2 **Gardner Lake l.** *Maine* U.S.A.
176 H4 **Gardner Pinnacles is** *Hawaii* U.S.A.
154 C2 **Gardnerville** *Nevada* U.S.A.
83 F3 **Gardone Riviera** Italy
106 E3 **Gardone Val Trompia** Italy
93 C4 **Gardonne** France
79 H4 **Gárdony** Hungary
93 D5 **Gardouch** France
59 E4 **Gårdstånga** Sweden
93 B4 **Garein** France
66 D4 **Garelochhead** *Scotland* U.K.
91 E5 **Garéoult** France
104 F3 **Garešnica** Croatia
106 C4 **Garessio** Italy
121 F4 **Garet El Djenoun mt.** Algeria
118 D3 **Garet el Gorane depression** Chad
163 G3 **Gare Tigre** French Guiana
65 G4 **Garforth** *England* U.K.
115 C5 **Gargalianoi** Greece
101 E1 **Gargáligas r.** Spain
92 D3 **Gargan, Mont h.** France
140 C3 **Gargantua, Cape c.** *Ontario* Canada
83 G2 **Gargazzone** Italy
92 D2 **Gargilesse-Dampierre** France
107 E3 **Gargnano** Italy
64 D1 **Gargunnock Hills h.** *Scotland* U.K.
Gargunsa *see* **Gar**
54 B4 **Gargždai** Lithuania
36 D5 **Garhakota** India
36 E5 **Garhchiroli** India
39 F3 **Garhi Khairo** Pakistan
36 D4 **Garhi Malehra** India
136 E5 **Garibaldi, Mt mt.** *B.C.* Canada
136 E5 **Garibaldi Prov. Park nat. park** *B.C.* Canada
131 E5 **Gariep Dam dam** South Africa
131 E5 **Gariep Dam Nature Reserve res.** South Africa
130 A5 **Garies** South Africa
109 F3 **Garigliano r.** Italy
68 D1 **Garijp** Netherlands
93 A6 **Garinoain** Spain
127 C5 **Garissa** Kenya
54 D3 **Garkalne** Latvia
146 D4 **Garland** *Pennsylvania* U.S.A.
151 D5 **Garland** *Texas* U.S.A.
106 C3 **Garlasco** Italy
83 E3 **Garlate, Lago di l.** Italy
81 F3 **Garlenz** Austria
54 C4 **Garliava** Lithuania
93 B5 **Garlin** France
39 D1 **Garmeh** Iran
75 G5 **Garmisch-Partenkirchen** Germany
39 C2 **Garmsar** Iran
39 E3 **Garmsel reg.** Afghanistan
150 E4 **Garnett** *Kansas* U.S.A.
13 E3 **Garnpung Lake l.** *New South Wales* Australia
37 G4 **Gāro Hills** India
102 D2 **Garona r.** Spain
93 B4 **Garonne r.** France
91 C5 **Garons** France
126 E3 **Garoowe** Somalia
167 C6 **Garopaba** Brazil
124 B2 **Garoua** Cameroon
124 B2 **Garoua Boulai** Cameroon
122 D3 **Garou, Lac l.** Mali
98 E2 **Garrafe de Torio** Spain
99 H3 **Garray** Spain
173 F4 **Garré** Argentina
72 D3 **Garrel** Germany
91 B5 **Garrigues reg.** France
64 A3 **Garrison** *Northern Ireland* U.K.
155 E2 **Garrison** *Utah* U.S.A.
64 B4 **Garristown** Rep. of Ireland
67 F1 **Garron Pt pt** *Northern Ireland* U.K.
100 D1 **Garrovillas** Spain
101 J3 **Garrucha** Spain
102 C4 **Garrucha, Sierra de la mountain range** Spain
36 A3 **Garruk** Pakistan
137 J1 **Garry Lake l.** *N.W.T.* Canada
66 D4 **Garry, Loch l.** *Scotland* U.K.
66 B2 **Garrynahine** *Scotland* U.K.
81 G2 **Gars am Kamp** Austria
59 F1 **Garsås** Sweden
127 D5 **Garsen** Kenya
118 D5 **Garsila** Sudan
65 F4 **Garstang** *England* U.K.
81 F2 **Garsten** Austria
Gartar *see* **Qianning**
92 C2 **Gartempe r.** France
62 C2 **Garth** *Wales* U.K.
Gartok *see* **Garyarsa**
73 G2 **Gartow** Germany
74 D4 **Gärtringen** Germany
73 K2 **Gartz** Germany
23 □1 **Garusuun** Palau
22 A3 **Garut** Indonesia
67 E2 **Garvagh** *Northern Ireland* U.K.
64 A4 **Garvagh** Rep. of Ireland
65 F2 **Garvald** *Scotland* U.K.
100 B3 **Garvão** Portugal
66 D3 **Garve** *Scotland* U.K.
64 C1 **Garvellachs i.** *Scotland* U.K.
9 B6 **Garvie Mts mts** New Zealand
37 E4 **Garwa** India
77 K4 **Garwolin** Poland
148 D5 **Gary** *Indiana* U.S.A.
36 E3 **Garyarsa** China
32 B2 **Garyi** China
28 D6 **Garyū-zan mt.** Japan
73 J1 **Garz** Germany
36 E2 **Gar Zangbo r.** China
32 B2 **Garzê** China
162 B3 **Garzón** Colombia
173 K3 **Garzón, L. l.** Uruguay
80 B4 **Gaschurn** Austria
93 B5 **Gascogne reg.** France
99 H1 **Gascogne, Golfe de g.** France
150 E4 **Gasconade r.** *Missouri* U.S.A.
17 A5 **Gascoyne r.** *Western Australia* Australia
17 A5 **Gascoyne Junction** *Western Australia* Australia
17 B5 **Gascoyne, Mt h.** *Western Australia* Australia
Gascuña, Golfo de g. *see* **Gascogne, Golfe de**
131 F1 **Gaseleka** South Africa
36 D2 **Gasherbrum mt.** China/Jammu and Kashmir
39 E4 **Gasht** Iran
123 G4 **Gashua** Nigeria
39 D2 **Gask** Iran
77 L2 **Gąski** Poland
89 G2 **Gasny** France
139 H4 **Gaspé** *Québec* Canada
139 H4 **Gaspé, C. c.** *Québec* Canada
139 G4 **Gaspé, Péninsule de pen.** *Québec* Canada
139 G4 **Gaspésie, Parc de la nat. park** *Québec* Canada
81 E2 **Gaspoltshofen** Austria
29 H4 **Gassan volcano** Japan
122 A4 **Gassane** Senegal
68 E2 **Gasselte** Netherlands
106 B3 **Gassino Torinese** Italy
80 E3 **Gasteiner Tal v.** Austria
99 H2 **Gasteiz-Vitoria** Spain
145 D5 **Gastonia** *N. Carolina* U.S.A.
115 C5 **Gastouni** Greece
171 C5 **Gastre** Argentina
98 D4 **Gata** Spain
43 B2 **Gata, C. c.** Cyprus
101 H4 **Gata, Cabo de c.** Spain
103 D6 **Gata de Gorgos** Spain
112 C2 **Gătaia** Romania
98 D4 **Gata, Sierra de mountain range** Spain
54 G2 **Gatchina** Rus. Fed.
146 B6 **Gate City** *Virginia* U.S.A.
66 D6 **Gatehouse of Fleet** *Scotland* U.K.
65 G3 **Gateshead** *England* U.K.
151 D6 **Gatesville** *Texas* U.S.A.
155 H2 **Gateway** *Colorado* U.S.A.
147 F4 **Gateway National Recreational Area res.** *New Jersey* U.S.A.
86 B4 **Gâtinais reg.** France
89 F4 **Gâtine reg.** France
141 H3 **Gatineau r.** *Québec* Canada
141 H4 **Gatineau** *Québec* Canada
39 C3 **Gaţrūyeh** Iran
107 G4 **Gatteo a Mare** Italy
106 C3 **Gattinara** Italy
15 H5 **Gatton** *Queensland* Australia
156 K7 **Gatún L. l.** Panama
39 B2 **Gatvand** Iran
63 F3 **Gatwick airport** *England* U.K.
6 □8 **Gau i.** Fiji
74 D3 **Gau-Algesheim** Germany
69 B5 **Gauchy** France
101 E4 **Gaucín** Spain
137 K3 **Gauer Lake l.** *Manitoba* Canada
54 D3 **Gauja r.** Latvia
56 C3 **Gaula r.** Norway
146 C5 **Gauley Bridge** *W. Virginia* U.S.A.
69 D5 **Gaume reg.** Belgium
58 B2 **Gaupefjellet mt.** Norway
58 B1 **Gaupne** Norway
37 E5 **Gaurella** India
58 C2 **Gausta mt.** Norway
131 F2 **Gauteng div.** South Africa
75 G4 **Gauting** Germany
102 C3 **Gautizalema r.** Spain
39 F2 **Gauzan** Afghanistan
102 F3 **Gavà** Spain
83 F3 **Gavardo** Italy
93 B6 **Gavarnie** France
39 E4 **Gavāter** Iran
39 C4 **Gāvbandī** Iran
39 C4 **Gāvbūs, Kūh-e mountain range** Iran
115 F8 **Gavdopoula i.** Greece
115 F8 **Gavdos i.** Greece
93 B5 **Gave r.** France
93 B5 **Gave d'Aspe r.** France
93 B5 **Gave d'Oloron r.** France
93 B5 **Gave d'Ossau r.** France
42 F3 **Gaveh r.** Iran
69 B4 **Gavere** Belgium
106 C4 **Gavi** Italy
166 D3 **Gavião r.** Brazil
100 C1 **Gavião** Portugal
162 D5 **Gaviãozinho** Brazil
154 B4 **Gaviota** *California* U.S.A.
172 F5 **Gaviotas** Argentina
106 C3 **Gavirate** Italy
39 D3 **Gāv Koshī** Iran
59 G1 **Gävle** Sweden
59 G1 **Gävleborg div.** Sweden
59 G1 **Gävlebukten b.** Sweden
108 B4 **Gavoi** *Sardegna* Italy
108 C2 **Gavorrano** Italy
88 D3 **Gavray** France
52 F3 **Gavrilovka Vtoraya** Rus. Fed.
52 E1 **Gavrilov Posad** Rus. Fed.
52 D1 **Gavrilov-Yam** Rus. Fed.
115 C4 **Gavrolimni** Greece
54 E3 **Gavry** Latvia
130 A3 **Gawachab** Namibia
24 B1 **Gawai** Myanmar
118 B2 **Gawat well** Libya
81 H2 **Gaweinstal** Austria
12 D3 **Gawler** *S. Australia* Australia
12 C3 **Gawler Ranges h.** *S. Australia* Australia
30 B4 **Gaxun Nur salt lake** China
46 E2 **Gay** Rus. Fed.
31 J4 **Gaya r.** China
37 F4 **Gaya** India
123 E4 **Gaya** Niger
123 F4 **Gaya** Nigeria
36 C2 **Gayal Gah** Pakistan
22 C3 **Gayam** Indonesia
120 B3 **G'Aydat al Jhoucha ridge** *Western Sahara*
123 E4 **Gayéri** Burkina
148 E3 **Gaylord** *Michigan* U.S.A.
15 G5 **Gayndah** *Queensland* Australia
52 C1 **Gaynovo** Rus. Fed.
114 E1 **Gaytaninovo** Bulgaria
50 F3 **Gayutino** Rus. Fed.
129 E3 **Gaza div.** Mozambique
43 C4 **Gaza territory** Asia
43 C4 **Gaza** *Gaza*
46 F4 **Gaz-Achak** Turkmenistan
39 D3 **Gazak** Iran
47 G4 **Gazalkent** Uzbekistan
46 E5 **Gazandzhyk** Turkmenistan
124 B1 **Gazawa** Cameroon
43 D1 **Gaziantep div.** Turkey
42 D2 **Gaziantep** Turkey
39 E2 **Gazīk** Iran
31 F2 **Gazimur r.** Rus. Fed.
30 D2 **Gazimuro-Ononskiy Khrebet mountain range** Rus. Fed.
31 F2 **Gazimurskiy Khr. mountain range** Rus. Fed.
31 F2 **Gazimurskiy Zavod** Rus. Fed.
42 C2 **Gazipaşa** Turkey
46 F4 **Gazli** Uzbekistan
39 D4 **Gaz Māhū** Iran
114 E1 **Gazoros** Greece
39 D3 **Gaz Şāleḩ** Iran
83 G3 **Gazzo Veronese** Italy
107 E3 **Gazzuolo** Italy
122 C5 **Gbaaka** Liberia
124 D3 **Gbadolite** Zaire
122 B5 **Gbangbatok** Sierra Leone
122 C5 **Gbarnga** Liberia
122 C5 **Gbatala** Liberia
81 J2 **Gbely** Slovakia
123 F5 **Gboko** Nigeria
124 D3 **Gbwado** Zaire
76 G1 **Gdańsk div.** Poland
76 G1 **Gdańsk** Poland
159 □5 **Gde Vigie, Pte de la pt** *Guadeloupe* Caribbean
54 E2 **Gdov** Rus. Fed.
77 J6 **Gdów** Poland
159 E2 **Gd Turk i.** *Turks and Caicos Is* Caribbean
76 G1 **Gdynia** Poland
66 C1 **Gealldruig Mhor i.** *Scotland* U.K.
93 B5 **Geaune** France
73 F4 **Gebesee** Germany
87 G2 **Gebhardshain** Germany
43 A1 **Gebiz** Turkey
126 C3 **Gebre Guracha** Ethiopia
119 G5 **Gedaref** Sudan
63 F2 **Geddington** *England* U.K.
74 E2 **Gedern** Germany
118 E5 **Gedid Ras el Fil** Sudan
69 C5 **Gedinne** Belgium
42 A2 **Gediz r.** Turkey
42 B2 **Gediz** Turkey
126 D3 **Gedlegubē** Ethiopia
63 G2 **Gedney Drove End** *England* U.K.
56 H1 **Gednje** Norway
126 D4 **Gedo div.** Somalia
93 C6 **Gèdre** France
55 D5 **Gedser** Denmark
55 D5 **Gedser Odde pt** Denmark
55 B3 **Gedsted** Denmark
55 B4 **Gedved** Denmark
13 F4 **Geelong** *Victoria* Australia
17 A6 **Geelvink Channel chan.** *Western Australia* Australia
130 C4 **Geel Vloer l.** South Africa
69 D4 **Geer r.** Belgium
68 C3 **Geertruidenberg** Netherlands
126 F2 **Geesaley** Somalia
72 C3 **Geeste** Germany
72 F2 **Geesthacht** Germany
69 D4 **Geetbets** Belgium
126 C3 **Gefersa** Ethiopia
114 A2 **Gegai** Albania
54 D4 **Gegužinė** Lithuania
36 E2 **Gê'gyai** China
33 G2 **Ge Hu l.** China
123 G4 **Geidam** Nigeria
126 B2 **Geigar** Sudan
137 J3 **Geikie r.** *Saskatchewan* Canada
140 A1 **Geikie I. i.** *Ontario* Canada
15 E2 **Geikie Ra. h.** *Queensland* Australia
74 B2 **Geilenkirchen** Germany
58 C1 **Geilo** Norway
56 B3 **Geiranger** Norway
75 H4 **Geiselhöring** Germany
75 G4 **Geisenfeld** Germany
75 H4 **Geisenhausen** Germany
74 C3 **Geisenheim** Germany
83 D1 **Geisingen** Germany
74 E4 **Geislingen an der Steige** Germany
72 F4 **Geismar** Germany
87 G4 **Geispolsheim** France
148 E6 **Geist Reservoir resr** *Indiana* U.S.A.
81 G3 **Geistthal** Austria
127 B5 **Geita** Tanzania
73 H4 **Geithain** Germany
32 C4 **Gejiu** China
124 E2 **Gel watercourse** Sudan
110 D5 **Gela r.** *Sicilia* Italy
110 D5 **Gela** *Sicilia* Italy
126 E3 **Geladī** Ethiopia
110 D5 **Gela, Golfo di g.** *Sicilia* Italy
22 B2 **Gelam i.** Indonesia
25 C6 **Gelang, Tanjung pt** Malaysia
91 F4 **Gélas, Cime du mt.** France/Italy
68 E2 **Gelderland div.** Netherlands
68 D3 **Geldermalsen** Netherlands
72 B4 **Geldern** Germany
69 D3 **Geldrop** Netherlands
69 D4 **Geleen** Netherlands
51 F6 **Gelendzhik** Rus. Fed.
54 C4 **Gelgaudiškis** Lithuania
42 A1 **Gelibolu** Turkey
113 F4 **Gelibolu Yarımadası pen.** Turkey
93 C5 **Gelise r.** France
81 H4 **Gellénháza** Hungary
62 C3 **Gelligaer** *Wales* U.K.
39 D2 **Gelmord** Iran
74 E2 **Gelnhausen** Germany
79 K3 **Gelnica** Slovakia
55 B4 **Gels r.** Denmark
102 C3 **Gelsa** Spain
78 G5 **Gelse** Hungary
72 C4 **Gelsenkirchen** Germany
72 E1 **Gelting** Germany
25 C7 **Gemas** Malaysia
69 C4 **Gembloux** Belgium
123 G5 **Gembu** Nigeria
23 C5 **Gemeh** Indonesia
124 C3 **Gemena** Zaire
91 D5 **Gémenos** France
42 C2 **Gemerek** Turkey
79 K3 **Gemerská Hôrka** Slovakia
68 D3 **Gemert** Netherlands
42 B1 **Gemlik** Turkey
113 G4 **Gemlik Körfezi b.** Turkey
107 H2 **Gemona del Friuli** Italy
92 B3 **Gémozac** France
119 F2 **Gemsa** Egypt
128 C4 **Gemsbok National Park nat. park** Botswana
130 C3 **Gemsbokplein well** South Africa
74 E2 **Gemünden am Main** Germany
31 G2 **Gen r.** China
101 E4 **Genal r.** Spain
126 D3 **Genalē Wenz r.** Ethiopia
69 C4 **Genappe** Belgium
109 E3 **Genazzano** Italy
92 C2 **Gençay** France
78 F4 **Gencsapáti** Hungary
171 B7 **Gendarme Barreto** Argentina
126 C2 **Gendoa r.** Ethiopia
90 D1 **Gendrey** France
68 E3 **Gendringen** Netherlands
68 E2 **Genemuiden** Netherlands
172 E4 **General Acha** Argentina
173 G4 **General Alvear** *Buenos Aires* Argentina
172 D3 **General Alvear** *Mendoza* Argentina
173 G3 **General Arenales** Argentina
165 E5 **General Artigas** Paraguay
173 H3 **General Belgrano** Argentina
179 B3 **General Belgrano II Argentina Base** Antarctica
179 B2 **General Bernardo O'Higgins Chile Base** Antarctica
151 D7 **General Bravo** Mexico
172 F2 **General Cabrera** Argentina
173 H1 **General Campos** Argentina
168 B1 **General Carneiro** Brazil
171 B6 **General Carrera, L. l.** Chile
157 E3 **General Cepeda** Mexico
173 J4 **General Conesa** *Buenos Aires* Argentina
172 E6 **General Conesa** *Río Negro* Argentina
173 F5 **General D. Cerri** Argentina
173 L2 **General Enrique Martinez** Uruguay
173 H2 **General Galarza** Argentina
173 J4 **General Guido** Argentina
173 J4 **General J. Madariaga** Argentina
170 E2 **General José de San Martin** Argentina
164 C3 **General Lagos** Chile
173 G4 **General La Madrid** Argentina
173 H3 **General Las Heras** Argentina
173 J4 **General Lavalle** Argentina
172 F3 **General Levalle** Argentina
23 C4 **General MacArthur** Philippines
170 D1 **General Martín Miguel de Güemes** Argentina
173 G3 **General O'Brien** Argentina
171 B5 **General Paz, L. l.** Argentina/Chile
172 F3 **General Pico** Argentina
170 D2 **General Pinedo** Argentina
173 G3 **General Pinto** Argentina
173 J4 **General Pirán** Argentina
172 D5 **General Roca** Argentina
168 C4 **General Salgado** Brazil
172 F4 **General San Martín** Argentina
173 H3 **General San Martin** Argentina
179 B2 **General San Martín Argentina Base** Antarctica
23 C5 **General Santos** Philippines
157 F3 **General Terán** Mexico
112 F3 **General Toshevo** Bulgaria
173 F3 **General Villegas** Argentina
146 D3 **Genesee r.** *New York* U.S.A.
148 B5 **Geneseo** *Illinois* U.S.A.
146 E3 **Geneseo** *New York* U.S.A.
126 C3 **Genet** Ethiopia
148 C5 **Geneva** *Illinois* U.S.A.
150 D3 **Geneva** *Nebraska* U.S.A.
146 E3 **Geneva** *New York* U.S.A.
146 C4 **Geneva** *Ohio* U.S.A.
Geneva *see* **Genève**
148 C4 **Geneva, Lake l.** *Wisconsin* U.S.A.
82 B2 **Genève div.** Switzerland
82 B2 **Genève** *Genève* Switzerland
90 E2 **Genevois mts** France
107 G5 **Genga** Italy
74 D4 **Gengenbach** Germany
32 B4 **Gengma** China
125 D4 **Gengwa** Zaire
77 M1 **Geniai** Lithuania
140 E2 **Genier** *Ontario* Canada
101 E3 **Genil r.** Spain
114 F1 **Genisea** Greece
69 D4 **Genk** *Limburg* Belgium
28 B7 **Genkai-nada b.** Japan
90 D1 **Genlis** France
23 C4 **Gen. Luna** Philippines
115 □ **Gennadio** Greece
108 B5 **Gennargentu, Monti del mountain range** *Sardegna* Italy
68 D3 **Gennep** Netherlands
89 E4 **Gennes** France
171 B5 **Genoa r.** Argentina
13 G4 **Genoa** *Victoria* Australia
Genoa *see* **Genova**
106 B4 **Genola** Italy
91 B4 **Génolhac** France
106 D4 **Genova div.** *Liguria* Italy
106 C4 **Genova** *Genova* Italy
106 C4 **Genova, Golfo di g.** Italy
69 B3 **Gent div.** *Oost-Vlaanderen* Belgium
69 B3 **Gent** *Gent* Belgium
22 C3 **Genteng i.** Indonesia
22 A3 **Genteng** Indonesia
73 H3 **Genthin** Germany
92 D3 **Gentioux-Pigerolles** France
173 G3 **Gen. Viamonte** Argentina
109 J4 **Genzano di Lucania** Italy
109 E3 **Genzano di Roma** Italy
17 A7 **Geographe Bay b.** *Western Australia* Australia
17 A5 **Geographe Channel chan.** *Western Australia* Australia
139 G2 **George r.** *Québec* Canada
16 B4 **George r.** *Western Australia* Australia
130 D6 **George** South Africa
179 □ **George, C. c.** *Kerguelen* Indian Ocean
14 B4 **George Gills Ra. mountain range** *Northern Terr.* Australia
145 D6 **George, L. l.** *Florida* U.S.A.
13 G3 **George, L. l.** *New South Wales* Australia
12 D4 **George, L. l.** *S. Australia* Australia
16 C4 **George, L. salt flat** *Western Australia* Australia
127 B4 **George, Lake l.** Uganda
75 G3 **Georgensgmünd** Germany
73 F5 **Georgenthal** Germany
9 A6 **George Sd inlet** New Zealand
128 □1 **Georgetown** *Ascension* Atlantic Ocean
158 B3 **Georgetown** *Cayman Is* Caribbean
147 F5 **Georgetown** *Delaware* U.S.A.
148 D6 **Georgetown** *Illinois* U.S.A.
144 C4 **Georgetown** *Kentucky* U.S.A.
146 B5 **Georgetown** *Ohio* U.S.A.
141 F5 **Georgetown** *Ontario* Canada
15 E3 **Georgetown** *Queensland* Australia
145 E5 **Georgetown** *S. Carolina* U.S.A.
13 F5 **George Town** *Tasmania* Australia
151 D6 **Georgetown** *Texas* U.S.A.
163 F2 **Georgetown** Guyana
25 C6 **George Town** Malaysia
158 D2 **George Town** The Bahamas
122 B4 **Georgetown** The Gambia
179 B2 **George VI Sd chan.** Antarctica
179 B5 **George V Land reg.** Antarctica
151 D6 **George West** *Texas* U.S.A.
18 F5 **Georgia country** Asia
145 D5 **Georgia div.** U.S.A.
140 E4 **Georgian Bay l.** *Ontario* Canada
141 F4 **Georgian Bay Island National Park nat. park** *Ontario* Canada
14 D4 **Georgina watercourse** *Queensland* Australia
115 F7 **Georgioupoli** Greece
112 F3 **Georgi Traykov** Bulgaria
47 H4 **Georgiyevka** Kazakhstan
47 K3 **Georgiyevka** Kazakhstan
51 G6 **Georgiyevsk** Rus. Fed.
50 H3 **Georgiyevskoye** Rus. Fed.
68 F2 **Georgsdorf** Germany
72 D3 **Georgsmarienhütte** Germany
102 E2 **Ger** Spain
75 H2 **Gera** Germany
69 B4 **Geraardsbergen** Belgium
111 F4 **Gerace** Italy
110 D5 **Geraci Siculo** Italy
115 D6 **Geraki** Greece
9 C6 **Geraldine** New Zealand
140 B2 **Geraldton** *Ontario* Canada
17 A6 **Geraldton** *Western Australia* Australia
115 D5 **Geraneia mts** Greece
43 C4 **Gerar watercourse** Israel
87 F4 **Gérardmer** France
81 G2 **Geras** Austria
81 H2 **Gerasdorf bei Wien** Austria
39 C4 **Gerāsh** Iran
87 F4 **Gerbéviller** France
91 C4 **Gerbier de Jonc mt.** France
73 G4 **Gerbstedt** Germany
42 E2 **Gercüş** Turkey
131 F3 **Gerdau** South Africa
79 H4 **Gerecse mt.** Hungary
42 C1 **Gerede r.** Turkey
42 C1 **Gerede** Turkey
39 F3 **Gereshk** Afghanistan
98 C3 **Gerês, Serra do mountain range** Portugal
80 D2 **Geretsberg** Austria
75 G5 **Geretsried** Germany
101 H3 **Gérgal** Spain
108 B5 **Gergei** *Sardegna* Italy
79 L3 **Gergely-hegy mt.** Hungary
122 B5 **Gerihun** Sierra Leone
25 C6 **Gerik** Malaysia
39 D2 **Gerīmenj** Iran
150 C3 **Gering** *Nebraska* U.S.A.
79 J4 **Gerje r.** Hungary
152 C3 **Gerlach** *Nevada* U.S.A.
79 K2 **Gerlachovský štit mt.** Slovakia
80 D3 **Gerlos** Austria
80 D3 **Gerlospaß** Austria
173 F3 **Germania** Argentina
135 Q2 **Germania Land reg.** Greenland
136 E3 **Germansen Landing** *B.C.* Canada
146 E5 **Germantown** *Maryland* U.S.A.
48 F3 **Germany country** Europe
75 F5 **Germaringen** Germany
113 F6 **Germencik** Turkey
75 G4 **Germering** Germany
74 D3 **Germersheim** Germany
99 H1 **Gernika-Lumo** Spain
73 G4 **Gernrode** Germany
74 D4 **Gernsbach** Germany
74 D3 **Gernsheim** Germany
29 F6 **Gero** Japan
106 D2 **Gerola Alta** Italy
115 D6 **Gerolimenas** Greece
74 B2 **Gerolstein** Germany
Gerona *see* **Girona**
155 G5 **Geronimo** *Arizona* U.S.A.
115 F7 **Geropotamos r.** Greece
107 J3 **Gerovo** Croatia
69 C4 **Gerpinnes** Belgium
93 C5 **Gers div.** *Midi-Pyrénées* France
93 C5 **Gers r.** France
83 D1 **Gersau** Switzerland
74 E2 **Gersfeld (Rhön)** Germany
73 J4 **Gerste r.** Germany
80 B2 **Gerstetten** Germany
75 F4 **Gersthofen** Germany
74 F2 **Gerstungen** Germany
73 J2 **Gerswalde** Germany
91 D4 **Gervanne r.** France
73 G3 **Gerwisch** Germany
90 B3 **Gerzat** France
37 F2 **Gêrzê** China
42 C1 **Gerze** Turkey
58 D2 **Gesäter** Sweden
72 C4 **Gescher** Germany
81 H3 **Geschriebenstein h.** Austria
108 B5 **Gesico** *Sardegna* Italy
86 D3 **Gespunsart** France
173 G1 **Gessler** Argentina
106 B4 **Gesso r.** Italy
89 D4 **Gesté** France
108 B5 **Gesturi** *Sardegna* Italy
32 B1 **Gesu** China
109 H3 **Gesualdo** Italy
59 F1 **Gesunda** Sweden
69 D4 **Gesves** Belgium
59 H1 **Geta** Finland
99 G4 **Getafe** Spain
39 C2 **Getcheh, Kūh-e h.** Iran
69 D4 **Gete r.** Belgium
92 A1 **Gétigné** France
72 E1 **Gettorf** Germany
146 E5 **Gettysburg** *Pennsylvania* U.S.A.
150 D2 **Gettysburg** *S. Dakota* U.S.A.
146 E5 **Gettysburg National Military Park res.** *Pennsylvania* U.S.A.
32 D3 **Getu r.** China
168 D4 **Getulina** Brazil
179 A4 **Getz Ice Shelf ice feature** Antarctica
69 D4 **Geul r.** Netherlands
13 G3 **Geurie** *New South Wales* Australia
42 E2 **Gevaş** Turkey
91 B4 **Gévaudan reg.** France
72 C4 **Gevelsberg** Germany
88 D3 **Gévezé** France
114 D1 **Gevgelija** Macedonia
90 C1 **Gevrey-Chambertin** France
90 E2 **Gex** France
99 H1 **Gexto** Spain
Gey *see* **Nikshahr**
43 A1 **Geydik D. mts** Turkey
43 B1 **Geyik Dağ mt.** Turkey
113 F5 **Geyikli** Turkey
25 □ **Geylang** Singapore
131 E3 **Geysdorp** South Africa
42 B1 **Geyve** Turkey
114 B1 **Gezavesh** Albania
33 E2 **Gezhouba** China
119 G3 **Gezirat Mukawwar i.** Sudan
81 G2 **Gföhl** Austria
130 D3 **Ghaap Plateau plat.** South Africa
43 D3 **Ghabāghib** Syria
119 E5 **Ghabeish** Sudan
43 D4 **Ghadaf, W. el watercourse** Jordan
118 A1 **Ghadāmis** Libya
118 B2 **Ghaddūwah** Libya
43 D3 **Ghadīr Minqār l.** Syria
39 C1 **Ghaem Shahr** Iran
47 G4 **Ghafurov** Tajikistan
37 E4 **Ghaghara r.** India
37 F5 **Ghaghra** India
111 □ **Ghajn Tuffieha Bay b.** Malta
117 D5 **Ghana country** Africa
39 C4 **Ghanādah, Rās pt** U.A.E.
36 C4 **Ghanliala** India
128 C3 **Ghanzi div.** Botswana
128 C3 **Ghanzi** Botswana
42 C4 **Gharandal** Jordan
121 E2 **Ghardaïa** Algeria
119 F2 **Ghârib, Gebel mt.** Egypt
36 A4 **Gharo** Pakistan
39 B4 **Ghār, Ras al pt** Saudi Arabia
118 B1 **Gharyān** Libya
118 B2 **Ghāt** Libya
36 E4 **Ghatampur** India
121 D1 **Ghazaouet** Algeria
36 D3 **Ghaziabad** India
37 E4 **Ghazipur** India
36 A3 **Ghazluna** Pakistan
39 G2 **Ghazni r.** Afghanistan
39 G2 **Ghaznī** Afghanistan
39 F2 **Ghazoor** Afghanistan
119 H2 **Ghazzālah** Saudi Arabia
106 E3 **Ghedi** Italy
53 B **Ghelinta** Romania

81 F4 **Gorenja vas** Slovenia
52 B2 **Goretovo** Rus. Fed.
67 E4 **Gorey** Rep. of Ireland
39 D3 **Gorg** Iran
39 C1 **Gorgān** Iran
39 C1 **Gorgan B. b.** Iran
39 C1 **Gorgān, Rūd-e r.** Iran
15 F3 **Gorge Ra., The mountain range** Queensland Australia
78 G5 **Görgeteg** Hungary
120 B5 **Gorgol div.** Mauritania
162 B3 **Gorgona, I. i.** Colombia
106 D5 **Gorgona, Isola di i.** Italy
106 D3 **Gorgonzola** Italy
126 C2 **Gorgora** Ethiopia
103 C6 **Gorgos r.** Spain
147 H2 **Gorham** New Hampshire U.S.A.
51 H7 **Gori** Georgia
81 H4 **Goričan** Croatia
81 H4 **Goričko reg.** Slovenia
68 C3 **Gorinchem** Netherlands
107 G4 **Gorino** Italy
42 F2 **Goris** Armenia
83 F1 **Görisried** Germany
52 C1 **Goritsy** Rus. Fed.
107 H3 **Gorizia div.** Friuli - Venezia Giulia Italy
107 H3 **Gorizia** Italy
52 D1 **Gorka** Rus. Fed.
37 F4 **Gorkhā** Nepal
Gor'kiy see **Nizhniy Novgorod**
51 H5 **Gor'ko-Solenoye, Ozero l.** Rus. Fed.
47 H1 **Gor'kovskoye** Rus. Fed.
50 G3 **Gor'kovskoye Vdkhr. resr** Rus. Fed.
55 D4 **Gørlev** Denmark
77 K6 **Gorlice** Poland
73 K4 **Görlitz** Germany
99 H3 **Gormaz** Spain
73 J2 **Görmin** Germany
64 B2 **Gorm, Loch l.** Scotland U.K.
110 D5 **Gornalunga r.** Sicilia Italy
112 E3 **Gorna Oryakhovitsa** Bulgaria
112 E3 **Gorni Dŭbnik** Bulgaria
81 G4 **Gornja Radgona** Slovenia
112 C3 **Gornja Toponica** Yugoslavia
107 J3 **Gornje Jelenje** Croatia
81 H4 **Gornje Vratno** Croatia
81 F4 **Gornji Grad** Slovenia
112 C2 **Gornji Milanovac** Yugoslavia
81 H5 **Gornji Tkalec** Croatia
104 F4 **Gornji Vakuf** Bos.-Herz.
77 J5 **Górno** Poland
47 L2 **Gorno-Altaysk** Rus. Fed.
112 E3 **Gornotrakiyska Nizina lowland** Bulgaria
47 K2 **Gornyak** Rus. Fed.
31 K3 **Gornye Klyuchi** Rus. Fed.
31 F2 **Gornyy Zerentuy** Rus. Fed.
124 D2 **Goro r.** Central African Rep.
52 F1 **Gorodets** Rus. Fed.
52 G3 **Gorodishche** Rus. Fed.
51 H5 **Gorodishche** Rus. Fed.
51 F5 **Gorodishche** Rus. Fed.
51 G6 **Gorodovikovsk** Rus. Fed.
6 □1 **Goroka** P.N.G.
12 E4 **Goroke** Victoria Australia
52 F1 **Gorokhovets** Rus. Fed.
123 D4 **Gorom Gorom** Burkina
129 E2 **Gorongosa mt.** Mozambique
129 E2 **Gorongosa** Mozambique
129 E2 **Gorongosa, Parque Nacional de nat. park** Mozambique
21 H6 **Gorontalo** Indonesia
123 E4 **Goroubi watercourse** Niger
123 E4 **Gorouol r.** Burkina/Niger
77 J1 **Górowo Iławeckie** Poland
68 E2 **Gorredijk** Netherlands
89 E3 **Gorron** France
51 F5 **Gorshechnoye** Rus. Fed.
107 J3 **Gorski Kotar reg.** Croatia
68 E2 **Gorssel** Netherlands
67 C3 **Gort** Rep. of Ireland
67 C1 **Gortahork** Rep. of Ireland
64 A3 **Gortin** Northern Ireland U.K.
67 B3 **Gorumna Island i.** Rep. of Ireland
169 G1 **Gorutuba r.** Brazil
82 D1 **Görwihl** Germany
51 F6 **Goryachiy Klyuch** Rus. Fed.
46 D4 **Gory Akkyr h.** Turkmenistan
47 G5 **Gory Baysuntau mountain range** Uzbekistan
45 L2 **Gory Byrranga mountain range** Rus. Fed.
76 E5 **Góry Bystrzyckie mountain range** Czech Rep./Poland
46 E4 **Gory Koymatdag h.** Turkmenistan
77 J5 **Góry Świętokrzyskie h.** Poland
47 G3 **Gory Ulutau mountain range** Kazakhstan
109 F2 **Gorzano, Monte mt.** Italy
87 F3 **Gorze** France
73 H3 **Görzke** Germany
76 E2 **Górzna** Poland
77 K4 **Górzno** Siedlce Poland
77 H2 **Górzno** Toruń Poland
76 D3 **Gorzów div.** Poland
76 G4 **Gorzów Śląski** Poland
76 D3 **Gorzów Wielkopolski** Gorzów Poland
73 L2 **Górzyca** Szczecin Poland
76 C3 **Górzyca** Poland
76 D3 **Gorzyń** Poland
76 C4 **Górzyn** Poland
107 F2 **Gosaldo** Italy
81 E3 **Gosau** Austria
63 F2 **Gosberton** England U.K.
76 D1 **Gościno** Poland
73 L4 **Gósciszów** Poland
29 G5 **Gosen** Japan
78 F5 **Gősfai Hegy h.** Hungary
63 G3 **Gosfield** England U.K.
13 G3 **Gosford** New South Wales Australia
65 G2 **Gosforth** England U.K.
65 E3 **Gosforth** England U.K.
74 D4 **Gosheim** Germany
148 E5 **Goshen** Indiana U.S.A.
147 F4 **Goshen** New York U.S.A.
28 H3 **Goshogawara** Japan
72 F4 **Goslar** Germany
77 H3 **Goślice** Poland
104 E3 **Gospić** Croatia
63 E4 **Gosport** England U.K.
83 E1 **Gossau** St Gallen Switzerland
83 D1 **Gossau** Zürich Switzerland
14 C3 **Gosse watercourse** Northern Terr. Australia
122 D3 **Gossi** Mali
81 E3 **Gößl** Austria
75 H2 **Gößnitz** Germany
112 C4 **Gostivar** Macedonia
81 F3 **Göstling an der Ybbs** Austria
76 F2 **Gostycyn** Poland
76 F4 **Gostyń** Leszno Poland
73 K1 **Gostyń** Szczecin Poland
77 H3 **Gostynin** Poland
76 F4 **Goszcz** Poland
126 D3 **Gota** Ethiopia
55 E1 **Göta** Sweden
59 E2 **Göta älv r.** Sweden
59 G2 **Göta Kanal canal** Sweden
58 D3 **Göteborg** Sweden
58 D2 **Göteborg och Bohus div.** Sweden
124 B2 **Gotel Mountains mountain range** Cameroon/Nigeria
59 E2 **Götene** Sweden
75 F2 **Gotha** Germany
59 H3 **Gothem** Sweden
59 H3 **Gothemån r.** Sweden
150 C3 **Gothenburg** Nebraska U.S.A.
123 E4 **Gothèye** Niger
59 H3 **Gotland div.** Sweden
59 H3 **Gotland i.** Sweden
59 F2 **Götlunda** Sweden
158 □3 **Gotomeer l.** Bonaire Netherlands Ant.
28 B7 **Gotō-rettō is** Japan
114 E1 **Gotse Delchev** Bulgaria
59 H2 **Gotska Sandön i.** Sweden
59 H2 **Gotska Sandön Nationalpark** Sweden
28 D6 **Gōtsu** Japan
106 D4 **Gottero, Monte mt.** Italy
72 E4 **Göttingen** Niedersachsen Germany
83 D1 **Gottmadingen** Germany
136 E4 **Gott Peak summit** B.C. Canada
Gottwaldow see **Zlín**
80 A3 **Götzis** Austria
122 C5 **Gouan r.** Côte d'Ivoire
88 B3 **Gouarec** France
30 C5 **Gouchengyi** China
68 C2 **Gouda** Netherlands
130 B6 **Gouda** South Africa
172 C3 **Goudge** Argentina
122 B4 **Goudiri** Senegal
123 G4 **Goudoumaria** Niger
140 C2 **Goudreau** Ontario Canada
122 C5 **Gouéké** Guinea
88 A3 **Gouesnou** France
88 C3 **Gouet r.** France
123 F3 **Goûgaram** Niger
174 J8 **Gough Island i.**
82 B1 **Gouhenans** France
141 H2 **Gouin, Réservoir resr** Québec Canada
93 E4 **Goul r.** France
140 C3 **Goulais River** Ontario Canada
123 F4 **Goulbin Kaba watercourse** Niger
13 G3 **Goulburn r.** New South Wales Australia
13 F4 **Goulburn r.** Victoria Australia
13 G3 **Goulburn** New South Wales Australia
14 C1 **Goulburn Is is** Northern Terr. Australia
148 E2 **Gould City** Michigan U.S.A.
179 B4 **Gould Coast coastal area** Antarctica
88 A3 **Goulet de Brest chan.** France
124 B1 **Goulféy** Cameroon
91 D5 **Goult** France
122 C4 **Goumbou** Mali
114 D2 **Goumenissa** Greece
90 E1 **Goumois** France
122 D3 **Goundam** Mali
124 C2 **Goundi** Chad
159 □5 **Gourbeyre** Guadeloupe Caribbean
122 D4 **Gourcy** Burkina
93 D4 **Gourdon** France
123 G4 **Gouré** Niger
102 C2 **Gourette** France
86 D4 **Gourgançon** France
88 B3 **Gourin** France
37 G4 **Gouripur** Bangladesh
130 C7 **Gourits r.** South Africa
122 D3 **Gourma-Rharous** Mali
118 D4 **Gourmeur well** Chad
89 G2 **Gournay-en-Bray** France
118 C4 **Gouro** Chad
13 G4 **Gourock Range mountain range** New South Wales Australia
86 B3 **Goussainville** France
92 C3 **Gout-Rossignol** France
68 D1 **Goutum** Netherlands
169 G3 **Gouvêa** Brazil
98 C4 **Gouveia** Portugal
147 F2 **Gouverneur** New York U.S.A.
69 D4 **Gouvy** Belgium
159 □8 **Gouyave** Grenada Caribbean
92 E2 **Gouzon** France
45 S4 **Govena, M. headland** Rus. Fed.
137 H5 **Govenlock** Saskatchewan Canada
169 H3 **Governador Valadares** Brazil
23 C5 **Governor Generoso** Philippines
145 E7 **Governor's Harbour** The Bahamas
30 A3 **Govĭaltay div.** Mongolia
30 B4 **Govĭaltay Nuruu mountain range** Mongolia
37 E4 **Govind Ballash Pant Sāgar resr** India
47 G5 **Govurdak** Turkmenistan
146 D3 **Gowanda** New York U.S.A.
15 F5 **Gowan Ra. h.** Queensland Australia
39 F3 **Gowārān** Afghanistan
77 J4 **Gowarczów** Poland
39 C3 **Gowd-e Aḥmad** Iran
39 D2 **Gowd-e Hasht Tekkeh waterhole** Iran
39 C3 **Gowd-e Mokh salt lake** Iran
10 □4 **Gower, Mt h.** Lord Howe I. Pacific Ocean
140 E3 **Gowganda** Ontario Canada
73 K2 **Gowienica r.** Poland
39 D3 **Gowk** Iran
39 G2 **Gowmal Kalay** Afghanistan
67 D3 **Gowna, Lough l.** Rep. of Ireland
65 H4 **Goxhill** England U.K.
170 E2 **Goya** Argentina
159 □5 **Goyave** Guadeloupe Caribbean
41 G1 **Göyçay** Azerbaijan
14 C5 **Goyder watercourse** Northern Terr. Australia
173 F4 **Goyena** Argentina
42 B1 **Göynük** Turkey
113 G5 **Göynükbelen** Turkey
124 B2 **Goyoum** Cameroon
29 H4 **Goyō-zan mt.** Japan
39 E2 **Gōzareh** Afghanistan
118 D5 **Goz-Beïda** Chad
77 K4 **Gózd** Poland
76 D4 **Gozdnica** Poland
77 H3 **Gozdowo** Poland
36 E2 **Gozha Co salt lake** China
43 C1 **Gözne** Turkey
111 □ **Gozo i.** Malta
119 G4 **Goz Regeb** Sudan
83 D3 **Gozzano** Italy
130 E6 **Graaf-Reinet** South Africa
130 B6 **Graafwater** South Africa
80 B2 **Graben** Germany
87 H3 **Graben-Neudorf** Germany
80 D3 **Grabenstätt** Germany
74 F2 **Grabfeld plain** Germany
122 C6 **Grabo** Côte d'Ivoire
130 B7 **Grabouw** South Africa
112 D2 **Grabovica** Yugoslavia
52 G3 **Grabovo** Rus. Fed.
73 H1 **Grabow inlet** Germany
73 G2 **Grabow** Germany
77 M2 **Grabówka** Poland
77 K4 **Grabów nad Pilicą** Poland
76 G4 **Grabów nad Prosną** Poland
76 F2 **Grabówno** Poland
77 L2 **Grabowo** Poland
83 E1 **Grabs** Switzerland
104 E3 **Gračac** Croatia
104 G3 **Gračanica** Bos.-Herz.
89 G4 **Graçay** France
141 G3 **Gracefield** Québec Canada
69 D4 **Grâce-Hollogne airport** Belgium
69 D4 **Grâce-Hollogne** Belgium
17 B7 **Grace, L. salt flat** Western Australia Australia
52 E3 **Grachevka** Rus. Fed.
46 D2 **Grachevka** Rus. Fed.
156 H6 **Gracías** Honduras
100 □ **Graciosa i.** Azores Portugal
97 □ **Graciosa i.** Canary Is Spain
81 H4 **Grad** Slovenia
104 G3 **Gradačac** Bos.-Herz.
107 G5 **Gradara** Italy
81 H5 **Gradec** Croatia
114 D1 **Gradec** Macedonia
99 E2 **Gradefes** Spain
112 F3 **Gradets** Bulgaria
93 B4 **Gradignan** France
107 H3 **Grado** Italy
98 D1 **Grado** Spain
166 C2 **Grado Bravo, Sa do h.** Brazil
81 E5 **Grado, Laguna di lag.** Italy
108 D2 **Gradoli** Italy
114 C1 **Gradsko** Macedonia
112 D3 **Grad Sofiya div.** Bulgaria
55 E3 **Græsted** Denmark
75 G4 **Gräfelfing** Germany
75 J4 **Grafenau** Germany
75 G3 **Gräfenberg** Germany
73 H4 **Gräfenhainichen** Germany
75 F2 **Gräfenroda** Germany
75 G3 **Grafenwöhr** Germany
63 F2 **Grafham Water resr** England U.K.
75 G4 **Grafing bei München** Germany
58 C1 **Gråfjell mt.** Norway
80 D2 **Grafling** Germany
80 C2 **Grafrath** Germany
55 E1 **Gräfsnäs** Sweden
150 D1 **Grafton** N. Dakota U.S.A.
13 H2 **Grafton** New South Wales Australia
148 D4 **Grafton** Wisconsin U.S.A.
146 C5 **Grafton** W. Virginia U.S.A.
15 F3 **Grafton, C. c.** Queensland Australia
171 B7 **Grafton, Islas is** Chile
155 E2 **Grafton, Mt mt.** Nevada U.S.A.
15 F3 **Grafton Passage chan.** Queensland Australia
58 C1 **Grågalten mt.** Norway
151 D5 **Graham** Texas U.S.A.
Graham Bell I. i. see **Greem-Bell, O.**
135 J2 **Graham I. i.** N.W.T. Canada
136 C4 **Graham Island i.** B.C. Canada
147 J2 **Graham Lake l.** Maine U.S.A.
179 B2 **Graham Land reg.** Antarctica
155 H5 **Graham, Mt mt.** Arizona U.S.A.
131 F6 **Grahamstown** South Africa
81 E4 **Grahovo** Slovenia
67 E4 **Graigue** Rep. of Ireland
83 G1 **Grainau** Germany
122 B5 **Grain Coast coastal area** Liberia
63 G3 **Grain, Isle of i.** England U.K.
22 C4 **Grajagan** Indonesia
166 C2 **Grajaú r.** Brazil
166 C2 **Grajaú** Maranhão Brazil
77 L2 **Grajewo** Poland
66 B1 **Gralisgeir i.** Scotland U.K.
59 G2 **Grällsta** Sweden
55 B4 **Gram** Denmark
163 F3 **Gramankondre** Surinam
93 D4 **Gramat** France
112 F3 **Gramatikovo** Bulgaria
91 D5 **Grambois** France
73 K2 **Grambow** Germany
73 H1 **Grammendorf** Germany
110 D5 **Grammichele** Sicilia Italy
47 L2 **Gramoteino** Rus. Fed.
66 D4 **Grampian Mts mountain range** Scotland U.K.
13 E4 **Grampians mountain range** Victoria Australia
68 E2 **Gramsbergen** Netherlands
114 B2 **Gramsh** Albania
73 K2 **Gramzow** Germany
91 F4 **Grana r.** Italy
130 B5 **Granaatboskolk** South Africa
101 G3 **Granada div.** Spain
153 G4 **Granada** Colorado U.S.A.
101 G3 **Granada** Spain
162 C3 **Granada** Colombia
156 J7 **Granada** Nicaragua
97 □ **Granadilla de Abona** Canary Is Spain
100 C3 **Granado h.** Spain
171 C6 **Gran Altiplanicie Central Seco reg.** Argentina
67 D3 **Granard** Rep. of Ireland
80 D3 **Granatspitze mt.** Austria
101 G2 **Granátula de Calatrava** Spain
170 C4 **Gran Bajo Salitroso salt marsh** Argentina
141 J4 **Granby** Québec Canada
97 □ **Gran Canaria i.** Canary Is Spain
90 D1 **Grancey-le-Château-Nouvelle** France
161 F6 **Gran Chaco reg.** Argentina
159 □3 **Gran Couva** Trinidad and Tobago
144 C3 **Grand r.** Michigan U.S.A.
150 E3 **Grand r.** Missouri U.S.A.
98 D1 **Grandas de Salime** Spain
158 C1 **Grand Bahama i.** The Bahamas
87 G5 **Grand Ballon mt.** France
139 J4 **Grand Bank** Newfoundland Canada
174 F2 **Grand Banks sea feature** Atlantic Ocean
122 D5 **Grand-Bassam** Côte d'Ivoire
127 □5 **Grand Bassin** Réunion Indian Ocean
139 G4 **Grand Bay** New Brunswick Canada
140 E5 **Grand Bend** Ontario Canada
91 E4 **Grand Bérard mt.** France
122 C6 **Grand-Bérébi** Côte d'Ivoire
159 □5 **Grand Bourg** Guadeloupe Caribbean
127 □5 **Grand Brûlé mt.** Réunion Indian Ocean
64 A4 **Grand Canal canal** Rep. of Ireland
155 F3 **Grand Canyon gorge** Arizona U.S.A.
155 F3 **Grand Canyon** Arizona U.S.A.
155 F3 **Grand Canyon Nat. Park nat. park** Arizona U.S.A.
158 B3 **Grand Cayman i.** Cayman Is Caribbean
137 G4 **Grand Centre** Alberta Canada
122 C6 **Grand Cess** Liberia
88 C4 **Grand-Champ** France
82 B1 **Grand-Charmont** France
90 D3 **Grand Colombier mt.** France
82 C3 **Grand Combin mt.** Switzerland
Grand Comore i. see **Njazidja**
152 C2 **Grand Coulee** Washington U.S.A.
89 G2 **Grand-Couronne** France
91 E4 **Grand Coyer, Le mt.** France
90 D2 **Grand-Crêt-d'Eau, Le mt.** France
159 □5 **Grand Cul de Sac Marin b.** Guadeloupe Caribbean
173 K2 **Grande h.** Uruguay
110 C5 **Grande r.** Sicilia Italy
172 C4 **Grande r.** Argentina
164 D3 **Grande r.** Bolivia
166 D3 **Grande r.** Brazil
168 D4 **Grande r.** Brazil
156 D2 **Grande r.** Mexico/U.S.A.
156 J6 **Grande r.** Nicaragua
164 A2 **Grande r.** Peru
101 G2 **Grande r.** Spain
103 C5 **Grande r.** Spain
138 E3 **Grande 2, Réservoir de La resr** Québec Canada
138 E3 **Grande 3, Réservoir de La resr** Québec Canada
138 F3 **Grande 4, Réservoir de La resr** Québec Canada
159 □5 **Grande Anse** Guadeloupe Caribbean
171 C7 **Grande, Bahía b.** Argentina
127 □4 **Grande Baie** Mauritius
88 C4 **Grande Brière reg.** France
136 F4 **Grande Cache** Alberta Canada
91 E3 **Grande Casse, Pte de la mt.** France
92 D2 **Grande-Creuse r.** France
166 B1 **Grande de Gurupa, Ilha g.** Brazil
164 C4 **Grande de Jujuy r.** Argentina
163 E4 **Grande de Manacapuru, Lago l.** Brazil
156 D4 **Grande de Santiago r.** Mexico
164 D4 **Grande de Tarija r.** Argentina/Bolivia
88 B3 **Grande, Île i.** France
169 F5 **Grande, Ilha i.** Brazil
110 B5 **Grande, Isola i.** Sicilia Italy
93 B4 **Grande Lande reg.** France
93 B4 **Grande Leyre r.** France
89 F2 **Grande Mare l.** France
165 D3 **Grande o'Guapay r.** Bolivia
136 F3 **Grande Prairie** Alberta Canada
123 G3 **Grand Erg de Bilma sand dunes** Niger
121 D2 **Grand Erg Occidental desert** Algeria
121 F3 **Grand Erg Oriental desert** Algeria
159 □3 **Grande Rivère** Trinidad Trinidad and Tobago
139 H4 **Grande-Rivière** Québec Canada
138 F3 **Grande Rivière de la Baleine r.** Québec Canada
82 C3 **Grande Rochère mt.** Italy
152 C2 **Grande Ronde r.** Oregon U.S.A.
172 D4 **Grande, S. salt flat** Argentina
90 A1 **Grande Sauldre r.** France
82 C3 **Grandes Jorasses mts** France/Italy
141 J3 **Grandes-Piles** Québec Canada
91 E3 **Grandes Rousses mts** France
86 B1 **Grande-Synthe** France
159 □5 **Grande Terre i.** Guadeloupe Caribbean
91 D4 **Grande Tête de l'Obiou mt.** France
88 D5 **Grand Etier r.** France
82 C3 **Grand Eyvia r.** Italy
139 G4 **Grand Falls** New Brunswick Canada
139 J4 **Grand Falls** Newfoundland Canada
136 F5 **Grand Forks** B.C. Canada
150 D2 **Grand Forks** N. Dakota U.S.A.
86 B1 **Grand-Fort-Philippe** France
88 D4 **Grand-Fougeray** France
93 B6 **Grand Gabizos mt.** France
147 F3 **Grand Gorge** New York U.S.A.
147 K2 **Grand Harbour** New Brunswick Canada
148 D4 **Grand Haven** Michigan U.S.A.
148 D2 **Grand I. i.** Michigan U.S.A.
136 F2 **Grandin, Lac l.** N.W.T. Canada
150 D3 **Grand Island** Nebraska U.S.A.
151 F6 **Grand Isle** Louisiana U.S.A.
147 J1 **Grand Isle** Maine U.S.A.
155 H2 **Grand Junction** Colorado U.S.A.
151 E6 **Grand L. l.** Louisiana U.S.A.
139 G4 **Grand L. l.** New Brunswick Canada
122 C5 **Grand Lahou** Côte d'Ivoire
147 K2 **Grand Lake l.** Maine U.S.A.
149 F3 **Grand Lake l.** Michigan U.S.A.
139 J4 **Grand Lake l.** Newfoundland Canada
139 H3 **Grand Lake l.** Newfoundland Canada
147 J1 **Grand Lake Matagamon l.** Maine U.S.A.
146 A4 **Grand Lake St Marys l.** Ohio U.S.A.
147 J1 **Grand Lake Seboeis l.** Maine U.S.A.
147 K2 **Grand Lake Stream** Maine U.S.A.
92 B2 **Grand Lay r.** France
148 E4 **Grand Ledge** Michigan U.S.A.
88 D4 **Grand-Lieu, Lac de l.** France
92 A2 **Grand Maine r.** France
139 G5 **Grand Manan I. i.** New Brunswick Canada
148 E2 **Grand Marais** Michigan U.S.A.
148 B2 **Grand Marais** Minnesota U.S.A.
141 J3 **Grand-Mère** Québec Canada
86 C4 **Grand Morin r.** France
100 B2 **Grândola r.** Portugal
100 B2 **Grândola** Portugal
100 B2 **Grândola, Serra de mountain range** Portugal
148 C2 **Grand Portage** Minnesota U.S.A.
86 D3 **Grandpré** France
137 K4 **Grand Rapids** Manitoba Canada
148 E4 **Grand Rapids** Michigan U.S.A.
150 E2 **Grand Rapids** Minnesota U.S.A.
6 □2 **Grand Récif de Cook reef** New Caledonia Pacific Ocean
6 □2 **Grand Récif du Sud reef** New Caledonia Pacific Ocean
88 D4 **Grand Réservoir de Vioreau resr** France
91 C5 **Grand Rhône r.** France
91 B4 **Grandrieu** France
159 □4 **Grand Rivère** Martinique Caribbean
91 E3 **Grand Roc Noir mt.** France
127 □4 **Grand R. S.E. r.** Mauritius
163 G3 **Grand Santi** French Guiana
141 K3 **Grands-Jardins, Parc des res.** Québec Canada
152 E3 **Grand Teton mt.** Wyoming U.S.A.
152 E3 **Grand Teton Nat. Park** Wyoming U.S.A.
148 E3 **Grand Traverse Bay b.** Michigan U.S.A.
66 E4 **Grandtully** Scotland U.K.
91 B4 **Grandval, Barrage de dam** France
139 G4 **Grand Vallée** Québec Canada
90 E1 **Grandvelle-et-le-Perrenot** France
91 D4 **Grand Veymont, le mt.** France
152 C2 **Grandview** Washington U.S.A.
90 E1 **Grandvillars** France
87 F4 **Grandvillers** France
89 G2 **Grandvilliers** France
155 F3 **Grand Wash r.** Arizona U.S.A.
155 E4 **Grand Wash Cliffs cliff** Arizona U.S.A.
91 C4 **Grane** France
102 C3 **Grañén** Spain
172 B3 **Graneros** Chile
67 C4 **Graney, Lough l.** Rep. of Ireland
59 E1 **Granfjället h.** Sweden
67 D5 **Grange** Rep. of Ireland
159 □1 **Grange Hill** Jamaica
65 E1 **Grangemouth** Scotland U.K.
152 E3 **Granger** Wyoming U.S.A.
59 F1 **Grängesberg** Sweden
87 F4 **Granges-sur-Vologne** France
152 C2 **Grangeville** Idaho U.S.A.
112 F1 **Grănicești** Romania
136 D3 **Granisle** B.C. Canada
150 E2 **Granite Falls** Minnesota U.S.A.
139 J4 **Granite Lake l.** Newfoundland Canada
155 E4 **Granite Mts mts** California U.S.A.
152 E2 **Granite Peak summit** Montana U.S.A.
155 F1 **Granite Peak summit** Utah U.S.A.
110 B5 **Granitola, Capo c.** Sicilia Italy
9 C4 **Granity** New Zealand
166 D1 **Granja** Brazil
100 E2 **Granja de Torrehermosa** Spain
171 C5 **Gran Laguna Salada l.** Argentina
59 F2 **Gränna** Sweden
102 F3 **Granollers** Spain
59 G1 **Granön** Sweden
76 E3 **Granowo** Poland
164 B2 **Gran Pajonal plain** Peru
106 B3 **Gran Paradiso mt.** Italy
106 B3 **Gran Paradiso, Parco Nazionale del nat. park** Italy
107 F2 **Gran Pilastro mt.** Austria/Italy
109 F2 **Gran Sasso d'Italia mts** Italy
73 J2 **Gransee** Germany
59 G2 **Gransö i.** Sweden
63 F2 **Grantham** England U.K.
14 C1 **Grant I. i.** Northern Terr. Australia
179 A4 **Grant I. i.** Antarctica
159 □9 **Grantley Adams airport** Barbados Caribbean
154 C2 **Grant, Mt mt.** Nevada U.S.A.
154 D2 **Grant, Mt mt.** Nevada U.S.A.
66 E3 **Grantown-on-Spey** Scotland U.K.
155 E2 **Grant Range mts** Nevada U.S.A.
153 F5 **Grants** New Mexico U.S.A.
65 F2 **Grantshouse** Scotland U.K.
152 B3 **Grants Pass** Oregon U.S.A.
59 F2 **Granvik** Sweden
148 C5 **Granville** Illinois U.S.A.
147 G3 **Granville** New York U.S.A.
88 D3 **Granville** France
137 J3 **Granville Lake l.** Manitoba Canada
58 B1 **Granvin** Norway
169 G2 **Grão Mogol** Brazil
154 C4 **Grapevine** California U.S.A.
154 D3 **Grapevine Mts mts** Nevada U.S.A.
147 G3 **Graphite** New York U.S.A.
59 G3 **Gräsgård** Sweden
131 H2 **Graskop** South Africa
137 G2 **Gras, Lac de l.** N.W.T. Canada
73 G3 **Grasleben** Germany
65 E3 **Grasmere** England U.K.
59 H1 **Gräsö i.** Sweden
147 F2 **Grass r.** New York U.S.A.
109 J4 **Grassano** Italy
75 H5 **Grassau** Germany
91 E5 **Grasse** France
141 F2 **Grasset, Lac l.** Québec Canada
65 G3 **Grassington** England U.K.
137 H5 **Grasslands Nat. Park nat. park** Saskatchewan Canada
152 E2 **Grassrange** Montana U.S.A.
131 E5 **Grassridgedam l.** South Africa
137 J4 **Grass River Prov. Park res.** Manitoba Canada
154 B2 **Grass Valley** California U.S.A.
13 F5 **Grassy** Tasmania Australia
145 E **Grassy Cr. r.** The Bahamas
55 B5 **Gråsten** Denmark
59 E2 **Grästorp** Sweden
102 D3 **Gratallops** Spain
148 B4 **Gratiot** Wisconsin U.S.A.
81 G3 **Gratkorn** Austria
81 G3 **Gratwein** Austria
83 E2 **Graubünden div.** Switzerland
87 G2 **Grauer Kopf h.** Germany
93 D5 **Graulhet** France
102 D2 **Graus** Spain
166 E2 **Gravata r.** Brazil
166 E2 **Gravata** Brazil
68 D3 **Grave** Netherlands
106 D2 **Gravedona** Italy
137 J2 **Gravel Hill Lake l.** N.W.T. Canada
86 B2 **Gravelines** France
106 C3 **Gravellona Toce** Italy
131 H1 **Gravelotte** South Africa
141 F4 **Gravenhurst** Ontario Canada
55 B4 **Gravens** Denmark
87 H2 **Grävenwiesbach** Germany
92 A3 **Grave, Pte de pt** France
54 E3 **Grāveri** Latvia
93 B4 **Graves reg.** France
63 G3 **Gravesend** England U.K.
13 G2 **Gravesend** New South Wales Australia
114 D4 **Gravia** Greece
89 G2 **Gravigny** France
111 F2 **Gravina di Matera r.** Italy
109 J4 **Gravina in Puglia** Italy
108 A3 **Gravona r.** Corse France
148 E3 **Grawn** Michigan U.S.A.
147 H3 **Gray** Maine U.S.A.
90 D1 **Gray** France
148 E3 **Grayling** Michigan U.S.A.
63 G3 **Grays** England U.K.
152 A2 **Grays Harbor harbour** Washington U.S.A.
152 E3 **Grays L. l.** Idaho U.S.A.
146 B5 **Grayson** Kentucky U.S.A.
139 H1 **Gray Strait chan.** Newfoundland Canada
144 B4 **Grayville** Illinois U.S.A.
53 F1 **Grayvoron** Rus. Fed.
81 G4 **Graz airport** Austria
81 G3 **Graz** Steiermark Austria
52 F3 **Grazhdanovka** Rus. Fed.
81 G3 **Graz-Umgebung div.** Austria
112 D3 **Grdelica** Yugoslavia
93 D4 **Gréalou** France
159 □1 **Great r.** Jamaica
158 C1 **Great Abaco i.** The Bahamas
6 □7 **Great Astrolabe Reef reef** Fiji
12 B3 **Great Australian Bight g.** S. Australia Australia
159 □8 **Great Bacolet Bay b.** Grenada Caribbean
63 G3 **Great Baddow** England U.K.
158 C1 **Great Bahama Bank sea feature** The Bahamas
8 E2 **Great Barrier Island i.** New Zealand
15 G3 **Great Barrier Reef reef** Queensland Australia
15 F3 **Great Barrier Reef Marine Park (Cairns Section) nat. park** Queensland Australia
15 G4 **Great Barrier Reef Marine Park (Capricorn Section) nat. park** Queensland Australia
15 G3 **Great Barrier Reef Marine Park (Central Section) nat. park** Queensland Australia
15 F2 **Great Barrier Reef Marine Park (Far North Section) nat. park** Queensland Australia
147 G3 **Great Barrington** Massachusetts U.S.A.
153 C4 **Great Basin basin** Nevada U.S.A.
155 E2 **Great Basin Nat. Park nat. park** Nevada U.S.A.
147 F5 **Great Bay b.** New Jersey U.S.A.
136 E1 **Great Bear r.** N.W.T. Canada
134 F3 **Great Bear Lake l.** N.W.T. Canada
150 D4 **Great Bend** Kansas U.S.A.
130 B6 **Great Berg r.** South Africa
66 B2 **Great Bernera i.** Scotland U.K.
67 A4 **Great Blasket I. i.** Rep. of Ireland
25 A4 **Great Coco I. i.** Cocos Is Indian Ocean
66 D5 **Great Cumbrae i.** Scotland U.K.
13 F4 **Great Dividing Range mountain range** Australia
65 H3 **Great Driffield** England U.K.
140 D4 **Great Duck I. i.** Ontario Canada
63 G3 **Great Dunmow** England U.K.
147 F5 **Great Egg Harbor harbour** New Jersey U.S.A.
158 B2 **Greater Antilles is** Caribbean
63 F3 **Greater London div.** England U.K.
65 F4 **Greater Manchester div.** England U.K.
8 D1 **Great Exhibition Bay b.** New Zealand
158 C2 **Great Exuma i.** The Bahamas
152 E2 **Great Falls** Montana U.S.A.
131 F6 **Great Fish r.** South Africa
131 F6 **Great Fish Pt pt** South Africa
37 F4 **Great Gandak r.** India
63 F2 **Great Gonerby** England U.K.
158 C1 **Great Guana Cay i.** The Bahamas
65 G3 **Greatham** England U.K.
145 E7 **Great Harbour Cay i.** The Bahamas
65 F4 **Great Harwood** England U.K.
37 D2 **Great Himalaya mountain range** India
158 D2 **Great Inagua i.** The Bahamas
130 C5 **Great Karoo plat.** South Africa
131 G6 **Great Kei r.** South Africa
13 F5 **Great L. l.** Tasmania Australia
63 F2 **Great Linford** England U.K.
62 D2 **Great Malvern** England U.K.
8 E2 **Great Mercury I. i.** New Zealand
146 A5 **Great Miami r.** Ohio U.S.A.
25 A6 **Great Nicobar i.** Andaman and Nicobar Is India
6 □1 **Great North East Channel chan.** Australia/P.N.G.
119 F3 **Great Oasis, The oasis** Egypt
62 C1 **Great Ormes Head headland** Wales U.K.
63 G2 **Great Ouse r.** England U.K.
15 F3 **Great Palm Is. is** Queensland Australia
147 G4 **Great Peconic Bay b.** New York U.S.A.
159 □1 **Great Pedro Bluff headland** Jamaica
147 H4 **Great Pt pt** Massachusetts U.S.A.
62 C2 **Great Rhos h.** Wales U.K.
127 C6 **Great Ruaha r.** Tanzania
147 F3 **Great Sacandaga L. l.**
82 C3 **Great St Bernard Pass pass** Italy/Switzerland
145 E7 **Great Sale Cay i.** The Bahamas
152 D3 **Great Salt Lake l.** Utah U.S.A.
155 F1 **Great Salt Lake Desert desert** Utah U.S.A.
118 D2 **Great Sand Sea desert** Egypt/Libya
16 C4 **Great Sandy Desert desert** Western Australia Australia
122 B5 **Great Scarcies r.** Guinea/Sierra Leone
6 □6 **Great Sea Reef reef** Fiji
63 G2 **Great Shelford** England U.K.
136 G2 **Great Slave Lake l.** N.W.T. Canada
145 D5 **Great Smoky Mts mountain range** N. Carolina/Tennessee U.S.A.
145 D5 **Great Smoky Mts Nat. Park** N. Carolina U.S.A.

32 D3 Guiyang China
33 F3 Guiyang China
32 D3 Guizhou div. China
93 A4 Gujan-Mestras France
36 B5 Gujarat India
36 C2 Gujar Khan Pakistan
36 C2 Gujranwala Pakistan
36 C2 Gujrat Pakistan
155 G5 Gu Komelik Arizona U.S.A.
36 D2 Gulabgarh India
30 B5 Gulang China
113 F5 Gülbahçe Turkey
38 B2 Gulbarga India
54 E3 Gulbene Latvia
47 H4 Gülchö Kyrgyzstan
43 C1 Gülcihan Turkey
55 D5 Guldborg Denmark
55 D5 Guldborg Sund str. Denmark
42 C2 Gülek Turkey
52 G3 Gulenovka Rus. Fed.
57 E3 Gulf of Bothnia g. Finland/Sweden
145 B6 Gulfport Mississippi U.S.A.
151 F6 Gulfport Mississippi U.S.A.
39 B3 Gulf, The g. Asia
13 G3 Gulgong New South Wales Australia
31 G1 Gulin China
32 D3 Gulin China
36 A3 Gulistan Pakistan
47 G4 Gulistan Uzbekistan
73 G2 Glitz Germany
31 G2 Guliya Shan mt. China
Gulja see Yining
59 F3 Gullabo Sweden
66 F4 Gullane Scotland U.K.
140 A2 Gull Bay Ontario Canada
58 B1 Gullbrå Norway
59 E3 Gullbrandstorp Sweden
148 E3 Gull I. I. Michigan U.S.A.
137 H4 Gull Lake Saskatchewan Canada
59 F2 Gullspång Sweden
56 F2 Gullträsk Sweden
113 F6 Güllük Körfezi b. Turkey
43 B1 Gülnar Turkey
69 D4 Gulpen Netherlands
73 H3 Gülper See l. Germany
113 F5 Gülpınar Turkey
39 E2 Gulran Afghanistan
51 G7 Gülrip'shi Georgia
42 C2 Gülşehir Turkey
47 H3 Gul'shad Kazakhstan
126 B4 Gulu Uganda
112 E3 Gülübovo Bulgaria
127 C6 Gulwe Tanzania
112 E3 Gulyantsi Bulgaria
Guma see Pishan
36 B2 Gumal r. Pakistan
128 C2 Gumare Botswana
126 B4 Gumbiri, J. mt. Sudan
46 D5 Gumdag Turkmenistan
123 F4 Gumel Nigeria
37 F5 Gumia India
99 G3 Gumiel de Hizán Spain
37 F5 Gumla India
72 C4 Gummersbach Germany
42 D1 Gümüşhane Turkey
113 F5 Gümüşsuyu Turkey
36 D4 Guna India
126 C2 Guna Terara mt. Ethiopia
13 F3 Gunbar New South Wales Australia
37 H3 Güncang China
47 H5 Gund r. Tajikistan
13 G3 Gundagai New South Wales Australia
74 C4 Gundelfingen Germany
74 F4 Gundelfingen an der Donau Germany
74 E3 Gundelsheim Germany
43 A1 Gündoğmuş Turkey
113 G5 Güney Denizli Turkey
113 G5 Güney Kütahya Turkey
125 C5 Gungu Zaire
51 H7 Gunib Rus. Fed.
137 K4 Gunisao r. Manitoba Canada
122 A4 Gunjur The Gambia
29 C6 Gunma div. Japan
29 G5 Gunmi Nigeria
64 B1 Gunna i. Scotland U.K.
43 C5 Gunna, G. mts Egypt
15 F3 Gunnawarra Queensland Australia
135 Q3 Gunnbjørn Fjeld mt. Greenland
13 G2 Gunnedah New South Wales Australia
127 □4 Gunners Quoin i. Mauritius
179 D3 Gunnerus Ridge sea feature Antarctica
13 G3 Gunning New South Wales Australia
153 E4 Gunnison r. Colorado U.S.A.
153 F4 Gunnison Colorado U.S.A.
155 G2 Gunnison Utah U.S.A.
14 D3 Gunpowder Cr. r. Queensland Australia
38 B3 Guntakal India
38 B3 Güntersberge Germany
81 H2 Guntersdorf Austria
145 C5 Guntersville Alabama U.S.A.
145 C5 Guntersville L. l. Alabama U.S.A.
38 C2 Guntur India
14 D3 Gunuma Queensland Australia
22 D2 Gunungbatubesar Indonesia
20 C6 Gunungsitoli Indonesia
22 A3 Gunungsugih Indonesia
38 C2 Gunupur India
74 F4 Günz r. Germany
74 F4 Günzburg Germany
75 F3 Gunzenhausen Germany
31 H4 Guojiatun China
33 G1 Guoyang China
47 H5 Gupis Jammu and Kashmir
36 A3 Gupis Pakistan
53 C3 Gura Galbenei Moldova
79 M5 Gurahonţ Romania
112 E1 Gura Humorului Romania
36 C2 Gurais Jammu and Kashmir
123 F5 Gurara r. Nigeria
124 E3 Gurba r. Zaire
30 B5 Gurban Hudag China
30 C4 Gurban Obo China
36 C2 Gurdaspur India
39 E4 Gurdim Iran
Gurdzhaani see Gurjaani
113 G5 Güre Turkey
30 D3 Gurgan, Jebel mt. Sudan
118 D5 Gurgei, Jebel mt. Sudan
166 D2 Gurgueia r. Brazil
36 B4 Gurha India

14 C1 Gurig Nat. Park nat. park Northern Terr. Australia
114 B1 Guri i Bardhë Albania
168 D3 Gurinhatã Brazil
112 F1 Gurjaani Georgia
51 H7 Gurjaani Georgia
81 F4 Gurk r. Austria
81 F4 Gurk Austria
39 D3 Gur Khar Iran
36 E3 Gurla Mandhata mt. China
46 F4 Gurlen Uzbekistan
114 E1 Gürmen Bulgaria
129 E2 Guro Mozambique
114 B1 Gurrë e Madhe Albania
113 G4 Gürsu Turkey
37 G3 Guru China
129 F2 Gurué Mozambique
42 D2 Gürün Turkey
166 B1 Gurupá Brazil
166 C1 Gurupi r. Brazil
166 C3 Gurupi Brazil
36 C2 Guru Sikhar mt. India
129 E2 Guruve Zimbabwe
47 L2 Gur'yevsk Rus. Fed.
54 B4 Gur'yevsk Rus. Fed.
52 E2 Gus' r. Rus. Fed.
123 F4 Gusau Nigeria
73 G3 Güsen Germany
54 C4 Gusev Rus. Fed.
31 G5 Gushan China
155 H1 Gusher Utah U.S.A.
39 E2 Gushgy Afghanistan
46 F5 Gushgy Turkmenistan
33 F1 Gushi China
122 D5 Gushiegu Ghana
29 □3 Gushikami Japan
29 □2 Gushikawa Japan
23 A5 Gusi Malaysia
45 M2 Gusika Rus. Fed.
30 C2 Gusinoozersk Rus. Fed.
30 C2 Gusinoye, Ozero l. Rus. Fed.
30 E2 Gusinoye Ozero Rus. Fed.
52 E2 Gus'-Khrustal'nyy Rus. Fed.
108 A5 Guspini Sardegna Italy
81 H3 Güssing div. Austria
81 H3 Güssing Austria
106 E3 Gussola Italy
81 G3 Gußwerk Austria
135 P3 Gustav Holm, Kap c. Greenland
59 H2 Gustavsberg Sweden
134 E4 Gustavus Alaska U.S.A.
136 B3 Gustavus Alaska U.S.A.
63 G4 Güsten Germany
69 E4 Gusterath Germany
154 B3 Gustine California U.S.A.
73 H2 Güstrow Germany
52 E2 Gus'-Zheleznyy Rus. Fed.
32 A2 Gutang China
81 F2 Gutau Austria
81 G3 Gutenstein Austria
72 D4 Gütersloh Germany
155 H5 Guthrie Arizona U.S.A.
144 C4 Guthrie Kentucky U.S.A.
151 D5 Guthrie Oklahoma U.S.A.
151 E5 Guthrie Texas U.S.A.
33 G3 Gutian China
74 B3 Gutland reg. Germany/Luxembourg
78 F5 Gutorfölde Hungary
37 F3 Gutsuo China
83 D2 Guttannen Switzerland
148 B4 Guttenberg Iowa U.S.A.
129 E2 Gutu Zimbabwe
37 G4 Guwahati India
42 E2 Guwēr Iraq
72 E4 Guxhagen Germany
30 D5 Gu Xian China
160 D3 Guyana country South America
30 D4 Guyang China
90 C2 Guye r. France
93 B4 Guyenne reg. France
151 C4 Guymon Oklahoma U.S.A.
39 D3 Güyom Iran
13 G2 Guyra New South Wales Australia
30 C6 Guyuan China
31 E4 Guyuan China
47 G5 Guzar Uzbekistan
113 F5 Güzelhisar Barajı resr Turkey
43 A1 Güzelsu Turkey
33 E2 Guzhang China
33 G1 Guzhen China
156 D2 Guzmán Mexico
156 D2 Guzmán, L. de l. Mexico
54 B4 Gvardeysk Rus. Fed.
58 C2 Gvarv Norway
24 A3 Gwa Myanmar
13 G2 Gwabegar New South Wales Australia
123 F4 Gwadabawa Nigeria
39 E4 Gwadar Pakistan
39 E4 Gwadar West B. b. Pakistan
123 E4 Gwadu Nigeria
36 D3 Gwalam India
36 D4 Gwalior India
129 D3 Gwanda Zimbabwe
124 E3 Gwane Zaire
36 A3 Gwash Pakistan
39 E4 Gwatar Bay b. Pakistan
124 E3 Gwawele Zaire
128 D2 Gwayi r. Zimbabwe
76 E2 Gwda r. Poland
76 E2 Gwda Wielka Poland
24 A1 Gwedaukkon Myanmar
67 C2 Gweebarra Bay b. Rep. of Ireland
67 C1 Gweedore Rep. of Ireland
129 D2 Gweru r. Zimbabwe
129 D2 Gweru Zimbabwe
127 A5 Gweshe Zaire
128 D3 Gweta Botswana
148 D2 Gwinn Michigan U.S.A.
123 D4 Gwoza Nigeria
13 G2 Gwydir r. New South Wales Australia
90 D1 Gy France
37 H3 Gyaca China
32 C1 Gyagartang China
Gyaisi see Jiulong
113 F6 Gyali i. Greece
37 F3 Gyangrang China
Gyangtse see Gyangzê
37 G3 Gyangzê China
32 B1 Gyaring China
32 C1 Gyaring Co l. China
32 B1 Gyaring Hu l. China
115 F5 Gyaros i. Greece
115 F5 Gyaros Greece
37 F3 Gyarubtang China
46 F4 Gy Auminzatau h. Uzbekistan
46 F4 Gy Bukantau h. Uzbekistan
44 J2 Gydanskiy Poluostrov pen. Rus. Fed.
130 B6 Gydopas pass South Africa

86 D4 Gyé-sur-Seine France
72 E2 Gyhum Germany
37 H3 Gyimda China
37 F3 Gyirong China
37 F3 Gyirong China
32 B2 Gyitang China
32 A1 Gyiza China
46 F4 Gy Kul'dzhuktau h. Uzbekistan
135 O3 Gyldenløves Fjord inlet Greenland
55 D4 Gyldenløveshøj h. Denmark
55 C4 Gylling Denmark
15 H5 Gympie Queensland Australia
24 A3 Gyobingauk Myanmar
79 K5 Gyomaendrőd Hungary
78 F4 Gyöngyös r. Hungary
79 J4 Gyöngyös Hungary
79 J4 Gyöngyössolymos Hungary
79 G4 Győr Hungary
78 G4 Győr-Moson-Sopron div. Hungary
79 M4 Győrtelek Hungary
137 K4 Gypsumville Manitoba Canada
139 O2 Gyrfalcon Is i. Québec Canada
58 C1 Gyrinos-vatnet l. Norway
59 G1 Gysinge Sweden
115 D6 Gytheio Greece
59 F2 Gyttorp Sweden
79 L5 Gyula Hungary
42 E1 Gyumri Armenia
47 H2 Gy Yerementau h. Kazakhstan
46 E5 Gyzylarbat Turkmenistan
52 B2 Gzhat' r. Rus. Fed.
111 □ Gzira Malta
77 J3 Gzy Poland

H

54 D2 Haabneeme Estonia
69 C4 Haacht Belgium
81 F2 Haag Austria
81 E2 Haag am Hausruck Austria
75 H4 Haag in Oberbayern Germany
178 □1 Haakon VII Topp volcano Jan Mayen Arctic Ocean
68 E2 Haaksbergen Netherlands
6 □3 Ha'alaufuli Tonga
6 □5 Ha'ano i. Tonga
6 □5 Ha'apai Group is Tonga
56 G3 Haapajärvi Finland
56 G2 Haapavesi Finland
7 □11 Haapiti French Polynesia Pacific Ocean
54 C2 Haapsalu Estonia
75 G4 Haar r. Germany
81 F3 Haardt h. Germany
68 C2 Haarlem Netherlands
130 D6 Haarlem South Africa
72 C4 Haarstrang ridge Germany
9 B3 Haast r. New Zealand
9 B5 Haast New Zealand
14 B4 Haast Bluff Northern Terr. Australia
14 B4 Haasts Bluff Aboriginal Land res. Northern Terr. Australia
36 A4 Hab r. Pakistan
83 G1 Habach Germany
47 L3 Habahe China
158 B2 Habana Cuba
38 C4 Habarane Sri Lanka
126 E4 Habar Cirir Somalia
75 H2 Habartov Czech Rep.
127 C4 Habaswein Kenya
119 H4 Habawnah, W. watercourse Saudi Arabia
136 F3 Habay Alberta Canada
69 D5 Habay-la-Neuve Belgium
41 G7 Habbān Yemen
42 E3 Habbānīyah Iraq
36 A4 Hab Chauki Pakistan
43 C4 Habesor watercourse Israel
80 D2 Habicht mt. Austria
37 G4 Habiganj Bangladesh
31 E4 Habirag China
43 C4 Habis, W. el watercourse Jordan
59 F3 Habo Sweden
79 J2 Habovka Slovakia
90 F1 Habsheim France
162 B4 Hacha Colombia
172 B5 Hachado, P. de pass Argentina/Chile
74 C2 Hachenburg Germany
29 G7 Hachijō-jima i. Japan
29 C7 Hachiman Japan
28 H3 Hachinohe Japan
29 G6 Hachiōji Japan
29 G3 Hachiryū Japan
99 G5 Hacinas Spain
42 G1 Hacı Zeynalabidin Azerbaijan
87 G4 Hackenheim Germany
12 D2 Hack, Mt mt. S. Australia
65 H3 Hackness England U.K.
129 F3 Hacufera Mozambique
47 K4 Hadadong China
38 A3 Hadagali India
74 D2 Hadamar Germany
26 H2 Hadano Japan
31 H2 Hadayang China
119 G3 Haddah Saudi Arabia
66 F5 Haddington Scotland U.K.
63 H2 Haddiscoe England U.K.
127 □1 Haddon Pt pt Seychelles
35 D10 Haddunmahti Atoll atoll Maldives
123 F4 Hadejia watercourse Nigeria
123 G4 Hadejia Nigeria
43 C3 Hadera Israel
55 A3 Haderslev Denmark
55 D5 Haderup Denmark
119 H3 Hadh Banī Saudi Arabia
126 □ Hadiboh Socotra Yemen
43 D4 Hādī, J. el mts Jordan
42 C2 Hadım Turkey
63 G2 Hadleigh England U.K.

134 H2 Hadley Bay b. N.W.T. Canada
28 A6 Hadong South Korea
81 J6 Hadres Austria
55 C3 Hadsten Denmark
55 C3 Hadsund Denmark
31 H5 Haeju North Korea
31 H5 Haeju North Korea
31 H6 Haenam South Korea
137 H4 Hafford Saskatchewan Canada
42 D2 Hafik Turkey
119 G2 Hafirat al'Aydā Saudi Arabia
43 D4 Hafira, W. watercourse Jordan
36 C2 Hafizabad Pakistan
37 H4 Häflong India
56 L6 Hafnarfjörður Iceland
39 B3 Haft Gel Iran
56 L6 Hafursfjörður b. Iceland
119 F5 Hag Abdullah Sudan
131 G6 Haga-Haga South Africa
81 H5 Haganj Croatia
140 E3 Hagar Ontario Canada
38 B3 Hagari r. India
126 C1 Hagar Nish Plateau plat. Eritrea
59 G3 Hagbyån r. Sweden
68 F1 Hage Germany
69 C4 Hageland reg. Belgium
73 H3 Hagelberg h. Germany
134 B4 Hagemeister I. i. Alaska U.S.A.
72 C4 Hagen Germany
80 E2 Hagenbeirge mts Austria
73 G2 Hagenow Germany
73 K4 Hagenwerder Germany
126 C3 Hägere Hiywet Ethiopia
126 C3 Hägere Selam Ethiopia
146 E5 Hagerstown Maryland U.S.A.
93 B5 Hagetaubin France
93 B5 Hagetmau France
59 E1 Hagfors Sweden
28 C6 Hagi Japan
24 D2 Ha Giang Vietnam
29 F6 Hagiwara Japan
62 D2 Hagley England U.K.
87 F3 Hagondange France
111 □ Hagoromo pt Malta
67 B4 Hag's Head headland Rep. of Ireland
137 H4 Hague Saskatchewan Canada
88 D2 Hague, Cap de la pt France
87 G4 Haguenau France
Hague, The see 's-Gravenhage
21 M1 Hahajima-rettō is Japan
74 D2 Hahnbach Germany
74 D2 Hahnstätten Germany
81 H4 Hahót Hungary
31 F5 Hai r. China
33 H1 Hai'an China
130 A4 Haib watercourse Namibia
37 G4 Haidargarh India
75 G3 Haidenaab r. Germany
81 F2 Haidershofen Austria
81 E2 Haidmühle Germany
24 D2 Hai Duong Vietnam
Haifa see Hefa
43 C3 Haifa, B. of b. Israel
33 F4 Haifeng China
74 D2 Haiger Germany
33 E4 Haikang China
119 H2 Ha'il Saudi Arabia
37 H4 Hailakandi India
31 F2 Hailar r. China
141 F3 Haileybury Ontario Canada
31 J3 Hailin China
31 H4 Hailong China
64 G4 Hailsham England U.K.
31 H3 Hailun China
56 G3 Hailuoto Finland
33 H2 Haimen China
80 C2 Haimhausen Austria
80 B3 Haiming Austria
87 H1 Haina (Kloster) Germany
33 E5 Hainan i. China
24 B2 Hai-nang Myanmar
Hainan Strait see Qiongzhou Haixia
69 B4 Hainaut reg. Belgium
81 H2 Hainburg an der Donau Austria
122 B5 Haindi Liberia
136 B3 Haines Alaska U.S.A.
134 E4 Haines Alaska U.S.A.
136 B2 Haines Junction Yukon Terr. Canada
81 G2 Hainfeld Austria
72 F4 Hainich ridge Germany
75 J2 Hainichen Germany
73 H4 Hainleite ridge Germany
24 D2 Hai Phong Vietnam
31 K3 Haiqing Rus. Fed.
30 B5 Hairag China
31 G4 Hairhan Namag China
33 G3 Haitan Dao i. China
43 D4 Haiterbach Germany
133 L8 Haiti country Caribbean
158 D3 Haitou China
155 G5 Haivana Nakya Arizona U.S.A.
154 D3 Haiwee Reservoir California U.S.A.
31 F5 Haixing China
119 G4 Haiya Sudan
124 E1 Haiyaf pool Sudan
33 H4 Haiyan China
30 B5 Haiyan China
33 H1 Haiyang China
31 G5 Haiyang Dao i. China
30 C5 Haiyuan China
33 G1 Haizhou Wan b. China
79 L4 Hajdú-Bihar div. Hungary
79 L4 Hajdúböszörmény Hungary
79 L4 Hajdúdorog Hungary
79 L4 Hajdúhadház Hungary
79 L4 Hajdúnánás Hungary
79 L4 Hajdúsámson Hungary
79 L4 Hajdúszoboszló Hungary
39 G2 Hajigak P. pass Afghanistan
29 C6 Hajiki-zaki pt Japan
37 E4 Hajipur India
41 F5 Hajjah Yemen
126 D1 Hajjah Yemen

39 C3 Hajjīābād Iran
39 C3 Hajjīābād Iran
39 C2 Hajjīābād-e Zarrīn Iran
41 J6 Hajmah Oman
79 G4 Hajmáskér Hungary
77 M3 Hajnówka Poland
30 C3 Hajuu-Us Mongolia
24 A2 Haka Myanmar
126 □ Hakabi Socotra Yemen
153 □2 Hakalau Hawaii U.S.A.
125 E5 Hakansson, Monts mts Zaire
6 □5 Hakau Fusi reef Tonga
55 D2 Hakefjord chan. Sweden
Hakha see Haka
42 E2 Hakkâri Turkey
56 F2 Hakkas Sweden
29 E6 Hakken-zan mt. Japan
28 J1 Hako-dake mt. Japan
29 H3 Hakodate Japan
29 F5 Haku-san volcano Japan
29 F5 Haku-san National Park Japan
29 F5 Hakui Japan
36 B4 Hala Pakistan
43 D1 Halab div. Syria
42 D2 Halab Syria
119 H3 Halabān Saudi Arabia
42 F3 Halabja Iraq
31 H3 Halahai China
119 G3 Halaib Sudan
43 B4 Halâl, G. h. Egypt
119 G2 Hālat 'Ammār Saudi Arabia
43 D5 Hālat 'Ammār Saudi Arabia
153 D5 Halawa Hawaii U.S.A.
153 □2 Halawa Hawaii U.S.A.
72 C4 Halba Lebanon
80 E2 Halberg Austria
73 G3 Halberstadt Germany
62 C4 Halberton England U.K.
23 B3 Halcon, Mt mt. Philippines
131 G5 Halcyon Drift South Africa
58 D2 Halden Norway
73 G3 Haldensleben Germany
83 F1 Haldenwang Germany
37 G5 Haldi r. India
37 G5 Haldia India
37 G4 Haldibari India
14 C4 Hale watercourse Northern Terr. Australia
65 G4 Hale England U.K.
149 E3 Hale Michigan U.S.A.
42 D3 Halebiye Syria
153 □1 Haleiwa Hawaii U.S.A.
69 D4 Halen Belgium
62 D2 Halesowen England U.K.
63 H2 Halesworth England U.K.
122 D5 Half Assini Ghana
42 D2 Halfeti Turkey
75 H5 Halfing Germany
9 B7 Halfmoon Bay New Zealand
136 E3 Halfway r. B.C. Canada
67 C5 Halfway Rep. of Ireland
81 F1 Halgan Mongolia
58 E1 Halgan v. Norway
81 F1 Halghoh Mongolia
119 H4 Halhal Germany
141 F3 Haliburton Ontario Canada
146 D6 Halifax Virginia U.S.A.
15 F3 Halifax Bay b. Queensland Australia
15 F3 Halifax, Mt mt. Queensland Australia
15 F3 Halifax Queensland Australia
139 H5 Halifax Nova Scotia Canada
65 F4 Halifax England U.K.
54 C1 Halikko Finland
43 D2 Halīmah mt. Lebanon
77 K3 Halinów Poland
119 H4 Halī, W. watercourse Saudi Arabia
66 E5 Halkirk Scotland U.K.
59 H1 Hall Sweden
59 G1 Hälla Sweden
59 F3 Hallabro Sweden
59 E3 Halland div. Sweden
55 A3 Hallandsås h. Sweden
59 E3 Hallands Väderö i. Sweden
59 F3 Hälläryd Sweden
69 C4 Halle Belgium
73 G4 Halle Germany
73 G4 Halle (Westfalen) Germany
73 G4 Halle-Neustadt Germany
75 G3 Hallertau reg. Germany
179 A5 Hallett, C. c. Antarctica
59 D2 Hällevadsholm Sweden
58 D2 Hälleviksstrand Sweden
72 D3 Halle (Westfalen) Germany
179 B3 Halley U.K. Base Antarctica
72 D2 Halligen is Germany
150 D1 Halliste Estonia
135 M3 Hall Pen. pen. N.W.T. Canada
135 K3 Hall Beach N.W.T. Canada
69 D4 Halle Belgium
73 G4 Halle Germany
58 C1 Hallingdal v. Norway
58 C1 Hallingskarvet mt. Norway
80 D3 Hall in Tirol Austria
4 □ Hall Is is Fed. States of Micronesia
56 E2 Hällnäs Sweden
150 D1 Hallock Minnesota U.S.A.
16 D2 Hall Pt pt Western Australia Australia
120 C3 Hammada du Drâa plat. Algeria
105 □ Hammamet Tunisia
121 G1 Hammamet, Golfe de g. Tunisia
131 G2 Hammanskraal South Africa
59 H1 Hammar Sweden
59 G1 Hallsberg Sweden
148 D2 Hallstadt Germany
59 H1 Hallstavik Sweden
62 B4 Hallworthy England U.K.

79 L3 Halmaj Hungary
79 N4 Halmeu Romania
59 E3 Halmstad Sweden
38 A1 Halol India
77 N3 Halowchytsy Belarus
81 G4 Haloze h. Slovenia
30 C3 Hals Mongolia
87 G2 Halsenbach Germany
58 A2 Halsnøy i. Norway
55 C4 Halsskov Denmark
63 G3 Halstead England U.K.
72 E2 Halstenbek Germany
69 D3 Halsteren Netherlands
56 G3 Halsua Finland
72 C4 Haltern Germany
65 F3 Haltwhistle England U.K.
39 C4 Hālūl i. Qatar
22 E4 Halura i. Indonesia
36 B5 Halvad India
36 B5 Halver Germany
178 □3 Halvmåneøya i. Svalbard Arctic Ocean
119 G2 Halwān, J. mt. Saudi Arabia
62 C4 Halwell England U.K.
53 A2 Halych Ukraine
53 E1 Halytsya Ukraine
130 B4 Ham watercourse Namibia
86 C3 Ham France
28 D6 Hamada Japan
122 D2 Hamâda El Haricha desert Mali
39 B2 Hamadān div. Iran
39 B2 Hamadān Iran
118 B4 Hamādat Murzuq plat. Libya
120 C3 Hamada Tounassine desert Algeria
120 D2 Hamaguir Algeria
43 D3 Hamāh div. Syria
42 D3 Hamāh Syria
29 □2 Hamahika-jima i. Japan
29 F6 Hamakita Japan
43 D1 Hamam Turkey
29 H2 Hamamasu Japan
29 F6 Hamamatsu Japan
28 K2 Hamanaka-wan b. Japan
29 F6 Hamana-ko l. Japan
100 E2 Hamapega h. Spain
58 D1 Hamar Norway
56 D1 Hamarøy Norway
119 F3 Hamāta, Gebel mt. Egypt
28 J1 Hamatonbetsu Japan
87 G3 Hambach France
38 C5 Hambantota Sri Lanka
73 G3 Hamberg Germany
65 G3 Hambleton Hills h. England U.K.
145 □3 Ham Bluff pt Virgin Is Caribbean
72 F2 Hamburg div. Germany
151 F5 Hamburg Arkansas U.S.A.
72 F2 Hamburg Hamburg Germany
147 F4 Hamburg Pennsylvania U.S.A.
131 G2 Hamburg South Africa
72 Hamburgisches Wattenmeer, Nationalpark nat. park Germany
58 D2 Hamburgsund Sweden
88 D3 Hambye France
119 H4 Hamdah Saudi Arabia
119 H4 Hamdānah Saudi Arabia
147 G4 Hamden Connecticut U.S.A.
113 G5 Hamdibey Turkey
54 D1 Häme div. Finland
57 G3 Hämeenlinna Finland
17 A5 Hamelin Western Australia Australia
17 A5 Hamelin Pool b. Western Australia Australia
72 E3 Hameln Germany
17 B4 Hamersley Ra. Nat. Park nat. park Western Australia Australia
16 B4 Hamersley Range mountain range Western Australia Australia
26 H5 Hamhŭng North Korea
26 F3 Hami China
39 B3 Hāmī, W. watercourse Saudi Arabia
66 D5 Hamilton Scotland U.K.
13 F5 Hamilton Tasmania Australia
12 E4 Hamilton Victoria Australia
145 □1 Hamilton Bermuda
8 E2 Hamilton New Zealand
154 A2 Hamilton City California U.S.A.
10 □3 Hamilton, Mt h. Macquarie I. Pacific Ocean
141 H5 Hamilton Mt mt. New York U.S.A.
154 B3 Hamilton, Mt mt. California U.S.A.
145 C5 Hamilton Alabama U.S.A.
148 B5 Hamilton Illinois U.S.A.
152 D2 Hamilton Montana U.S.A.
147 F4 Hamilton New York U.S.A.
146 A5 Hamilton Ohio U.S.A.
141 F5 Hamilton Ontario Canada
12 C1 Hamilton watercourse S. Australia Australia
14 E4 Hamilton watercourse Queensland Australia
139 J3 Hamilton Inlet inlet Newfoundland Canada
58 B1 Hamlagrovatnet l. Norway
148 D3 Hamlin Lake l. Michigan U.S.A.
57 G3 Hammarland Finland
59 F1 Hammarö i. Sweden
56 E3 Hammarstrand Sweden
74 E2 Hammelburg Germany
73 J2 Hammelspring Germany
69 C3 Hamme Belgium

69 C4 Hamme-Mille Belgium
59 F4 Hammenhög Sweden
56 D3 Hammerdal Sweden
56 F1 Hammerfest Norway
72 B4 Hamminkeln Germany
148 D5 Hammond Indiana U.S.A.
151 F6 Hammond Louisiana U.S.A.
152 F2 Hammond Montana U.S.A.
149 E3 Hammond Bay b. Michigan U.S.A.
146 E3 Hammondsport New York U.S.A.
147 F5 Hammonton New Jersey U.S.A.
141 K4 Ham-Nord Québec Canada
69 D4 Hamoir Belgium
69 D1 Hamont Belgium
9 C6 Hampden New Zealand
63 E3 Hampshire div. England U.K.
63 E3 Hampshire Downs h. England U.K.
151 E5 Hampton Arkansas U.S.A.
139 G4 Hampton New Brunswick Canada
147 H3 Hampton New Hampshire U.S.A.
147 E6 Hampton Virginia U.S.A.
17 D6 Hampton Tableland reg. Western Australia Australia
59 G1 Hamrångefjärden Sweden
119 E5 Hamrat esh Sheikh Sudan
111 □ Hamrun Malta
63 G3 Hamstreet England U.K.
69 C4 Ham-sur-Heure Belgium
25 D5 Ham Tân Vietnam
36 D2 Hamta P. pass India
39 D4 Hāmūn-e Jaz Mūriān salt marsh Iran
39 E3 Hāmūn Helmand marsh Iran
41 L4 Hamun-i-Lora salt flat Pakistan
39 E3 Hāmūn Pu salt lake Afghanistan
153 □2 Hana Hawaii U.S.A.
124 C3 Hanahai watercourse Botswana/Namibia
119 G2 Hanak Saudi Arabia
153 □2 Hanalei Hawaii U.S.A.
29 H4 Hanamaki Japan
130 A2 Hanam Plateau plat. Namibia
29 □1 Hanare-iwa is Japan
74 D2 Hanau Germany
53 C3 Hâncești Moldova
33 E1 Hancheng China
33 F2 Hanchuan China
146 D5 Hancock Maryland U.S.A.
148 C2 Hancock Michigan U.S.A.
147 F4 Hancock New York U.S.A.
66 C2 Handa Island i. Scotland U.K.
30 E5 Handan China
127 C6 Handeni Tanzania
72 F1 Handewitt Germany
79 H3 Handlová Slovakia
145 □2 Handover Sd chan. The Bahamas
10 □3 Handspike Pt pt Macquarie I. Pacific Ocean
154 □3 Hanford California U.S.A.
38 A1 Hangal India
31 H5 Hangang r. South Korea
7 □16 Hanga Roa Easter I. Chile
30 A3 Hangayn Nuruu mountain range Mongolia
Hangchow see Hangzhou
30 C4 Hanggin Houqi China
30 D5 Hanggin Qi China
31 F5 Hangu China
36 B2 Hangu Pakistan
112 F1 Hangu Romania
33 F3 Hanguang China
33 H2 Hangzhou Wan b. China
33 H2 Hangzhou China
42 C2 Hani Turkey
39 B4 Hanīdh Saudi Arabia
113 G4 Hanife r. Turkey
126 D2 Hanish Kabir i. Eritrea
33 F2 Hanjiang China
30 C4 Hanjiaoshui China
73 H3 Hankensbüttel Germany
130 E6 Hankey South Africa
57 F4 Hanko Finland
155 G5 Hanksville Utah U.S.A.
36 D2 Hanle India
9 D5 Hanmer Springs New Zealand
41 K4 Hanmni Mashkel salt flat Pakistan
15 E2 Hann r. Queensland Australia
16 D3 Hann r. Western Australia Australia
137 G4 Hanna Alberta Canada
77 M4 Hanna Poland
138 D3 Hannah Bay b. Ontario Canada
148 B6 Hannibal Missouri U.S.A.
119 F4 Hannik well Sudan
53 C2 Hannivka Ukraine
16 D2 Hann, Mt h. Western Australia Australia
72 E3 Hannover div. Niedersachsen Germany
72 E3 Hannover Hannover Germany
69 D4 Hannut Belgium
59 F4 Hanö i. Sweden
59 F4 Hanöbukten b. Sweden
Hanoi see Ha Nôi
25 D5 Ha Nôi Vietnam
159 □1 Hanover Jamaica
147 G3 Hanover New Hampshire U.S.A.
140 E4 Hanover Ontario Canada
146 E5 Hanover Pennsylvania U.S.A.
130 E5 Hanover South Africa
130 E5 Hanover Road South Africa
79 H3 Hanság h. Hungary
179 D4 Hansen Mts mts Antarctica
33 E2 Hanshou China
33 F2 Han Shui r. China
36 D3 Hansi India
131 H1 Hans Merensky Nature Reserve res. South Africa
56 E1 Hansnes Norway
14 C4 Hanson watercourse Northern Terr. Australia
9 □1 Hanson Bay b. Chatham Is New Zealand

69 C4 Hamme-Mille Belgium
59 F4 Hammenhög Sweden
56 D3 Hammerdal Sweden
56 F1 Hammerfest Norway
72 B4 Hamminkeln Germany
148 D5 Hammond Indiana
151 F6 Hammond Louisiana
152 F2 Hammond Montana
149 E3 Hammond Bay b. Michigan U.S.A.
146 E3 Hammondsport New York
147 F5 Hammonton New Jersey
141 K4 Ham-Nord Québec Canada
69 D4 Hamoir Belgium
59 F4 Hamont Belgium
9 C6 Hampden New Zealand
63 E3 Hampshire div. England U.K.
63 E3 Hampshire Downs h. England U.K.
151 E5 Hampton Arkansas U.S.A.
139 G4 Hampton New Brunswick Canada
147 H3 Hampton New Hampshire U.S.A.
147 E6 Hampton Virginia U.S.A.
17 D6 Hampton Tableland reg. Western Australia Australia
59 G1 Hamrångefjärden Sweden
119 E5 Hamrat esh Sheikh Sudan
111 □ Hamrun Malta
63 G3 Hamstreet England U.K.
69 C4 Ham-sur-Heure Belgium
25 D5 Ham Tân Vietnam
36 D2 Hamta P. pass India
39 D4 Hāmūn-e Jaz Mūriān salt marsh Iran
39 E3 Hāmūn Helmand marsh Iran
41 L4 Hamun-i-Lora salt flat Pakistan
39 E3 Hāmūn Pu salt lake Afghanistan
153 □2 Hana Hawaii U.S.A.
124 C3 Hanahai watercourse Botswana/Namibia
29 □1 Hanare-iwa is Japan
74 D2 Hanau Germany
29 H4 Hanamaki Japan
130 A2 Hanam Plateau plat. Namibia
33 E1 Hancheng China
33 F2 Hanchuan China
146 D5 Hancock Maryland U.S.A.
148 C2 Hancock Michigan U.S.A.
147 F4 Hancock New York U.S.A.
66 C2 Handa Island i. Scotland U.K.
30 E5 Handan China
127 C6 Handeni Tanzania
79 H3 Handlová Slovakia
154 □3 Hanford California U.S.A.
38 A1 Hangal India
31 H5 Hangang r. South Korea
7 □16 Hanga Roa Easter I. Chile
30 A3 Hangayn Nuruu mountain range Mongolia
Hangchow see Hangzhou
30 C4 Hanggin Houqi China
30 D5 Hanggin Qi China
31 F5 Hangu China
36 B2 Hangu Pakistan
112 F1 Hangu Romania
33 F3 Hanguang China
33 H2 Hangzhou Wan b. China
33 H2 Hangzhou China
42 C2 Hani Turkey
39 B4 Hanīdh Saudi Arabia
113 G4 Hanife r. Turkey
126 D2 Hanish Kabir i. Eritrea
33 F2 Hanjiang China
30 C4 Hanjiaoshui China
73 H3 Hankensbüttel Germany
130 E6 Hankey South Africa
57 F4 Hanko Finland
155 G5 Hanksville Utah U.S.A.
36 D2 Hanle India
9 D5 Hanmer Springs New Zealand
41 K4 Hanmni Mashkel salt flat Pakistan
15 E2 Hann r. Queensland Australia
16 D3 Hann r. Western Australia Australia
137 G4 Hanna Alberta Canada
77 M4 Hanna Poland
138 D3 Hannah Bay b. Ontario Canada
148 B6 Hannibal Missouri U.S.A.
119 F4 Hannik well Sudan
53 C2 Hannivka Ukraine
16 D2 Hann, Mt h. Western Australia Australia
72 E3 Hannover div. Niedersachsen Germany
72 E3 Hannover Hannover Germany
69 D4 Hannut Belgium
59 F4 Hanö i. Sweden
59 F4 Hanöbukten b. Sweden
Hanoi see Ha Nôi
25 D5 Ha Nôi Vietnam
159 □1 Hanover Jamaica
147 G3 Hanover New Hampshire U.S.A.
140 E4 Hanover Ontario Canada
146 E5 Hanover Pennsylvania U.S.A.
130 E5 Hanover South Africa
130 E5 Hanover Road South Africa
179 D4 Hansen Mts mts Antarctica
33 E2 Hanshou China
33 F2 Han Shui r. India
131 H1 Hans Merensky Nature Reserve res. South Africa
56 E1 Hansnes Norway
14 C4 Hanson watercourse Northern Terr. Australia
9 □1 Hanson Bay b. Chatham Is New Zealand

63 F3 **Henley-on-Thames** England U.K.
147 F5 **Henlopen, Cape** pt Delaware U.S.A.
29 □2 **Henna** Japan
88 B4 **Hennebont** France
74 C2 **Hennef (Sieg)** Germany
131 F3 **Hennenman** South Africa
55 A4 **Henne Stationsby** Denmark
87 F4 **Hennezel** France
73 J3 **Hennigsdorf Berlin** Germany
147 H3 **Henniker** New Hampshire U.S.A.
58 C2 **Hennseid** Norway
92 E1 **Henrichemont** France
151 D5 **Henrietta** Texas U.S.A.
138 D2 **Henrietta Maria, Cape** c. Ontario Canada
155 G3 **Henrieville** Utah U.S.A.
148 C5 **Henry** Illinois U.S.A.
179 B3 **Henry Ice Rise** ice feature Antarctica
135 M3 **Henry Kater, C.** headland N.W.T. Canada
25 A4 **Henry Lawrence I.** i. Andaman and Nicobar Is India
155 G2 **Henry Mts** mts Utah U.S.A.
140 E5 **Hensall** Ontario Canada
72 E2 **Henstedt-Ulzburg** Germany
62 D4 **Henstridge** England U.K.
128 A3 **Hentiesbaai** Namibia
30 D3 **Hentiy** div. Mongolia
29 □2 **Hentona** Japan
13 F3 **Henty** New South Wales Australia
24 A3 **Henzada** Myanmar
29 □2 **Henza-jima** i. Japan
137 H4 **Hepburn** Saskatchewan Canada
33 F3 **Heping** China
74 D3 **Heppenheim (Bergstraße)** Germany
33 E4 **Hepu** China
30 D5 **Hequ** China
56 N6 **Héraðsflói** b. Iceland
42 D3 **Heraklia** Syria
15 G3 **Herald Cays** atolls Coral Sea Islands Terr. Pacific Ocean
8 □4 **Herald Islets** is Kermadec Is New Zealand
8 E3 **Herangi** h. New Zealand
39 E2 **Herāt** Afghanistan
91 B5 **Hérault** div. Languedoc-Roussillon France
91 B5 **Hérault** r. France
119 G4 **Herbagat** Sudan
91 D3 **Herbasse** r. France
89 G4 **Herbault** France
15 F3 **Herbert** r. Queensland Australia
137 H4 **Herbert** Saskatchewan Canada
9 C6 **Herbert** New Zealand
25 A5 **Herbertabad** Andaman and Nicobar Is India
14 D4 **Herbert Downs** Queensland Australia
74 E4 **Herbertingen** Germany
15 F3 **Herberton** Queensland Australia
130 C7 **Herbertsdale** South Africa
69 D5 **Herbeumont** Belgium
88 C4 **Herbignac** France
74 C4 **Herbolzheim** Germany
74 D2 **Herborn** Germany
74 F4 **Herbrechtingen** Germany
74 E2 **Herbstein** Germany
112 B3 **Herceg-Novi** Yugoslavia
179 B4 **Hercules Dome** ice feature Antarctica
72 C4 **Herdecke** Germany
87 G2 **Herdorf** Germany
156 J7 **Heredia** Costa Rica
62 D2 **Hereford** England U.K.
151 C5 **Hereford** Texas U.S.A.
173 F3 **Hereford** Argentina
62 D2 **Hereford and Worcester** div. England U.K.
131 H2 **Herefords** Swaziland
58 C2 **Herefoss** Norway
7 □10 **Héréhérétué** i. French Polynesia Pacific Ocean
8 D1 **Herekino** New Zealand
101 G1 **Herencia** Spain
69 C4 **Herent** Belgium
69 C3 **Herentals** Belgium
91 B5 **Hérépian** France
72 D3 **Herford** Germany
100 E1 **Herguijuela** Spain
88 D4 **Héric** France
90 E1 **Héricourt** France
90 E1 **Hérimoncourt** France
74 F2 **Heringen (Werra)** Germany
73 G1 **Heringsdorf** Germany
150 D4 **Herington** Kansas U.S.A.
9 B6 **Heriot** New Zealand
83 E1 **Herisau** Switzerland
92 E2 **Hérisson** France
179 B3 **Heritage Ra.** mountain range Antarctica
69 D4 **Herk** r. Belgium
69 D4 **Herk-de-Stad** Belgium
147 F3 **Herkimer** New York U.S.A.
31 E2 **Herlen** r. China
30 D3 **Herlen** Mongolia
Herlen Gol r. see **Kerulen**
72 F4 **Herleshausen** Germany
63 □2 **Herm** i. Channel Is.
80 E2 **Hermagor** div. Austria
81 E4 **Hermagor** Austria
53 B2 **Hermakivka** Ukraine
157 E3 **Hermanas** Mexico
66 □2 **Herma Ness** headland Scotland U.K.
14 C4 **Hermannsburg** Northern Terr. Australia
72 F3 **Hermannsburg** Germany
77 L6 **Hermanowice** Poland
58 B1 **Hermansverk** Norway
130 B7 **Hermanus** South Africa
78 E2 **Heřmanův Městec** Czech Rep.
43 D2 **Hermel** Lebanon
92 E3 **Herment** France
74 C3 **Hermersberg** Germany
131 G5 **Hermes, Cape** c. South Africa
74 B3 **Hermeskeil** Germany
13 F2 **Hermidale** New South Wales Australia
97 □ **Hermigua** Canary Is Spain
152 C2 **Hermiston** Oregon U.S.A.
171 C7 **Hermite, Is** is Chile
Hermon, Mt mt. see **Shaykh, Jabal esh**
162 B3 **Hermosas, Parque Nacional las** nat. park Colombia
171 C6 **Hermosa, Valle** Argentina
156 C2 **Hermosillo** Mexico
157 F3 **Hermoso, Valle** Mexico
75 G2 **Hermsdorf** Germany
79 L3 **Hernád** r. Hungary
79 K3 **Hernádkak** Hungary
173 H1 **Hernandarias** Argentina
165 F5 **Hernandarias** Paraguay
173 G2 **Hernández** Argentina
172 F2 **Hernando** Argentina
102 B1 **Hernani** Spain
69 C4 **Herne** Belgium
72 C4 **Herne** Germany
63 H3 **Herne Bay** England U.K.
55 A3 **Herning** Denmark
69 D4 **Héron** Belgium
140 B2 **Heron Bay** Ontario Canada
89 E2 **Hérouville-St-Clair** France
78 G4 **Herpenyő** r. Hungary
170 E2 **Herradura** Argentina
157 E4 **Herradura** Mexico
99 G2 **Herramélluri** Spain
93 B5 **Herré** France
74 D4 **Herrenberg** Germany
102 B3 **Herrera** mt. Spain
101 F3 **Herrera** Spain
101 E1 **Herrera del Duque** Spain
102 B3 **Herrera de los Navarros** Spain
99 F2 **Herrera de Pisuerga** Spain
156 D3 **Herreras** Mexico
173 G4 **Herrera Vegas** Argentina
157 J5 **Herrero, Pta** pt Mexico
100 D1 **Herreruela** Spain
13 F5 **Herrick** Tasmania Australia
75 F3 **Herrieden** Germany
87 G4 **Herrlisheim** France
59 E2 **Herrljunda** Sweden
73 K4 **Herrnhut** Germany
75 G5 **Herrsching am Ammersee** Germany
59 H3 **Herrvik** Sweden
92 E1 **Herry** France
93 D5 **Hers** r. France
75 G3 **Hersbruck** Germany
87 G2 **Herschbach** Germany
131 F5 **Herschel** South Africa
69 C3 **Herselt** Belgium
146 E4 **Hershey** Pennsylvania U.S.A.
69 D4 **Herstal** Belgium
63 G4 **Herstmonceux** England U.K.
72 C4 **Herten** Germany
63 F3 **Hertford** England U.K.
63 F3 **Hertfordshire** div. England U.K.
69 E4 **Hertogenwald** forest Belgium
131 E4 **Hertzogville** South Africa
98 E4 **Hervás** Spain
69 D4 **Herve** Belgium
15 H5 **Hervey B.** b. Queensland Australia
15 H5 **Hervey Bay** Queensland Australia
177 J7 **Hervey Islands** is Cook Is Pacific Ocean
141 J3 **Hervey-Jonction** Québec Canada
15 F3 **Hervey Ra.** mountain range Queensland Australia
74 D3 **Herxheim bei Landau (Pfalz)** Germany
73 H3 **Herzberg** Brandenburg Germany
73 J4 **Herzberg** Brandenburg Germany
72 F4 **Herzberg am Harz** Germany
72 D4 **Herzebrock-Clarholz** Germany
69 B4 **Herzele** Belgium
72 C3 **Herzlake** Germany
43 C3 **Herzliyya** Israel
75 F3 **Herzogenaurach** Germany
82 C1 **Herzogenbuchsee** Switzerland
81 G2 **Herzogenburg** Austria
73 H2 **Herzsprung** Germany
69 C4 **Hesbaye** reg. Belgium
86 B2 **Hesdin** France
72 C2 **Hesel** Germany
24 E2 **Heshan** China
33 F2 **Heshengqiao** China
30 D6 **Heshui** China
30 E5 **Heshun** China
69 E5 **Hespérange** Luxembourg
154 D4 **Hesperia** California U.S.A.
136 C2 **Hess** r. Yukon Terr. Canada
73 F5 **Heßdorf** Germany
80 B1 **Hesselberg** h. Germany
55 D3 **Hesselø** i. Denmark
74 E2 **Hessen** div. Germany
72 E4 **Hessisch Lichtenau** Germany
72 E3 **Hessisch Oldendorf** Germany
130 B4 **Hester-Malan Nature Reserve** res. South Africa
62 C1 **Heswall** England U.K.
24 C2 **Het** r. Laos
154 B3 **Hetch Hetchy Aqueduct** canal California U.S.A.
81 H4 **Hetés** h. Hungary
33 E4 **Hetou** China
80 C2 **Hettens-hausen** Germany
74 E4 **Hettingen** Germany
150 C2 **Hettinger** N. Dakota U.S.A.
65 F3 **Hetton** England U.K.
73 G4 **Hettstedt** Germany
74 B3 **Hetzerath** Germany
68 F3 **Heubach** r. Germany
86 B2 **Heuchin** France
130 D3 **Heuningvlei** salt pan South Africa
74 F2 **Heustreu** Germany
89 F2 **Hève, Cap de la** pt France
79 K4 **Heves** div. Hungary
79 K4 **Heves** Hungary
81 H2 **Hevlín** Czech Rep.
80 B3 **Hexenkopf** mt. Austria
65 F3 **Hexham** England U.K.
33 E3 **He Xian** China
33 G2 **He Xian** China
30 B5 **Hexibao** China
31 F4 **Hexigten Qi** China
130 B6 **Hex River Pass** South Africa
33 E1 **Heyang** China
39 C3 **Ḥeydarābād** Iran
39 E3 **Ḥeydarābād** Iran
130 E5 **Heydon** South Africa
126 E3 **Heygali** well Ethiopia
90 D3 **Heyrieux** France
65 F3 **Heysham** England U.K.
131 H3 **Heyshope Dam** dam South Africa
65 F4 **Heywood** England U.K.
12 E4 **Heywood** Victoria Australia
148 C5 **Heyworth** Illinois U.S.A.
33 F1 **Heze** China
32 D3 **Hezhang** China
32 C1 **Hezheng** China
32 C1 **Hezuozhen** China
131 E7 **H. F. Verwoerd** airport South Africa
131 H3 **Hhohho** reg. Swaziland
145 D7 **Hialeah** Florida U.S.A.
150 E4 **Hiawatha** Kansas U.S.A.
119 H4 **Hibata** reg. Saudi Arabia
148 A2 **Hibbing** Minnesota U.S.A.
13 F5 **Hibbs, Pt** headland Tasmania Australia
16 C2 **Hibernia Reef** reef Western Australia Australia
28 C6 **Hibiki-nada** b. Japan
63 H2 **Hickling Broad** l. England U.K.
145 D5 **Hickory** N. Carolina U.S.A.
8 G2 **Hicks Bay** New Zealand
137 K2 **Hicks L.** l. N.W.T. Canada
146 A4 **Hicksville** Ohio U.S.A.
151 D5 **Hico** Texas U.S.A.
28 J2 **Hidaka** Japan
28 J2 **Hidaka-sanmyaku** mountain range Japan
157 F4 **Hidalgo** div. Mexico
157 F3 **Hidalgo** Coahuila Mexico
156 D3 **Hidalgo del Parral** Mexico
156 C3 **Hidalgo, Psa M.** resr Mexico
79 L3 **Hidasnémeti** Hungary
73 J1 **Hiddensee** i. Germany
15 F3 **Hidden Valley** Queensland Australia
168 D2 **Hidrolândia** Brazil
168 D1 **Hidrolina** Brazil
81 F3 **Hieflau** Austria
99 H3 **Hiendelaencina** Spain
6 □2 **Hienghène** New Caledonia Pacific Ocean
89 E4 **Hière** r. France
92 B3 **Hiersac** France
28 D6 **Higashi-Hiroshima** Japan
29 □1 **Higashi-iwa** is Japan
29 G6 **Higashi-izu** Japan
29 H4 **Higashine** Japan
29 □2 **Higashi-Onna** Japan
29 E6 **Higashi-ōsaka** Japan
28 B7 **Higashi-suidō** chan. Japan
147 F3 **Higgins Bay** New York U.S.A.
148 E3 **Higgins Lake** l. Michigan U.S.A.
130 D4 **Higg's Hope** South Africa
63 F2 **Higham Ferrers** England U.K.
62 B4 **Highampton** England U.K.
High Atlas mountain range see **Haut Atlas**
62 D3 **Highbridge** England U.K.
63 E3 **Highclere** England U.K.
152 B3 **High Desert** desert Oregon U.S.A.
148 C3 **High Falls Reservoir** resr Wisconsin U.S.A.
65 F3 **High Hesket** England U.K.
148 E3 **High I.** i. Michigan U.S.A.
8 □3 **High I.** i. Snares Is New Zealand
27 □ **High Island Res.** resr Hong Kong
66 C3 **Highland** div. Scotland U.K.
148 D4 **Highland Park** Illinois U.S.A.
154 C2 **Highland Peak** summit California U.S.A.
155 E3 **Highland Peak** summit Nevada U.S.A.
136 F3 **High Level** Alberta Canada
65 G4 **High Peak** h. England U.K.
128 □2 **High Pk** h. St Helena Atlantic Ocean
145 E5 **High Point** N. Carolina U.S.A.
136 F3 **High Prairie** Alberta Canada
136 G4 **High River** Alberta Canada
158 C1 **High Rock** The Bahamas
137 J3 **Highrock Lake** l. Manitoba Canada
13 F5 **High Rocky Pt** headland Tasmania Australia
65 F3 **High Seat** h. England U.K.
147 F4 **Hightstown** New Jersey U.S.A.
63 E3 **Highworth** England U.K.
63 F3 **High Wycombe** England U.K.
126 D3 **Higlale** well Ethiopia
126 E3 **Higlokadhacday** well Somalia
100 E2 **Higuera de la Serena** Spain
100 D3 **Higuera de la Sierra** Spain
100 D2 **Higuera de Vargas** Spain
156 C3 **Higuera de Zaragoza** Mexico
100 D2 **Higuera La Real** Spain
145 □3 **Higuero, Pta** pt Puerto Rico
163 D1 **Higuerote** Venezuela
103 B6 **Higueruela** Spain
43 A4 **Hihya** Egypt
126 E4 **Hiiraan** div. Somalia
54 C2 **Hiiumaa** i. Estonia
102 C3 **Híjar** Spain
119 G2 **Ḥijāz** reg. Saudi Arabia
99 G1 **Hijuela** r. Spain
28 C7 **Hikari** Japan
155 E3 **Hiko** Nevada U.S.A.
29 F6 **Hikone** Japan
7 □10 **Hikuéru** i. French Polynesia Pacific Ocean
8 G2 **Hikurangi** mt. New Zealand
8 E1 **Hikurangi** New Zealand
8 E3 **Hikutaia** New Zealand
87 H2 **Hilchenbach** Germany
155 F3 **Hildale** Utah U.S.A.
75 F2 **Hildburghausen** Germany
72 B4 **Hilden** Germany
74 F2 **Hilders** Germany
72 E3 **Hildesheim** Germany
131 H1 **Hildreth Ridge** South Africa
80 C2 **Hilgertshausen** Germany
37 G4 **Hili** Bangladesh
130 C6 **Hillandale** South Africa
179 B5 **Hillary Coast** coastal area Antarctica
150 D4 **Hill City** Kansas U.S.A.
155 H2 **Hill Creek** r. Utah U.S.A.
68 C2 **Hillegom** Netherlands
55 E4 **Hillerød** Denmark
74 B2 **Hillesheim** Germany
15 F3 **Hillgrove** Queensland Australia
66 E3 **Hill of Fearn** Scotland U.K.
150 D2 **Hillsboro** N. Dakota U.S.A.
147 H3 **Hillsboro** New Hampshire U.S.A.
146 B5 **Hillsboro** Ohio U.S.A.
151 D5 **Hillsboro** Texas U.S.A.
148 B4 **Hillsboro** Wisconsin U.S.A.
146 C5 **Hillsboro** W. Virginia U.S.A.
64 B3 **Hillsborough** Northern Ireland U.K.
15 G4 **Hillsborough, C.** c. Queensland Australia
87 G2 **Hillscheid** Germany
148 E5 **Hillsdale** Michigan U.S.A.
147 G3 **Hillsdale** New York U.S.A.
146 E4 **Hillsgrove** Pennsylvania U.S.A.
155 F4 **Hillside** Arizona U.S.A.
66 F4 **Hillside** Scotland U.K.
140 C2 **Hillsport** Ontario Canada
13 F3 **Hillston** New South Wales Australia
146 C6 **Hillsville** Virginia U.S.A.
66 □2 **Hillswick** Scotland U.K.
64 B3 **Hilltown** Northern Ireland U.K.
153 □2 **Hilo** Hawaii U.S.A.
75 G3 **Hilpoltstein** Germany
65 E3 **Hilpsford Point** pt England U.K.
146 E3 **Hilton** New York U.S.A.
140 D3 **Hilton Beach** Ontario Canada
145 D5 **Hilton Head Island** S. Carolina U.S.A.
42 D2 **Hilvan** Turkey
69 D3 **Hilvarenbeek** Netherlands
68 D2 **Hilversum** Netherlands
36 D3 **Himachal Pradesh** India
119 H3 **Ḥimā Ḍarīyah, J.** mt. Saudi Arabia
37 F3 **Himalchul** mt. Nepal
56 F2 **Himanka** Finland
114 A2 **Himarë** Albania
36 C5 **Himatnagar** India
81 H2 **Himberg** Austria
28 E6 **Himeji** Japan
29 H4 **Himekami-dake** mt. Japan
28 C7 **Hime-shima** i. Japan
29 G4 **Hime-zaki** pt Japan
29 F5 **Himi** Japan
81 F4 **Himmelberg** Austria
55 B3 **Himmelbjerget** h. Denmark
72 E2 **Himmelpforten** Germany
55 B3 **Himmerland** reg. Denmark
43 D2 **Ḥimṣ** div. Syria
43 D3 **Ḥimṣ** Syria
28 C7 **Hinagu** Japan
23 C4 **Hinatuan** Philippines
159 D3 **Hinche** Haiti
15 F3 **Hinchinbrook I.** i. Queensland Australia
63 E2 **Hinckley** England U.K.
148 A2 **Hinckley** Minnesota U.S.A.
155 F2 **Hinckley** Utah U.S.A.
147 F3 **Hinckley Reservoir** resr New York U.S.A.
125 B4 **Hinda** Congo
36 D3 **Hindan** r. India
59 E3 **Hindås** Sweden
36 D4 **Hindaun** India
83 F1 **Hindelang** Germany
63 H5 **Hinderwell** England U.K.
63 F3 **Hindhead** England U.K.
65 F4 **Hindley** England U.K.
146 B6 **Hindman** Kentucky U.S.A.
12 E4 **Hindmarsh, L.** l. Victoria Australia
37 F5 **Hindola** India
9 C6 **Hinds** New Zealand
55 C4 **Hindsholm** pen. Denmark
39 G2 **Hindu Kush** mountain range Asia
38 B3 **Hindupur** India
43 C5 **Hind, W. al** watercourse Saudi Arabia
136 F3 **Hines Creek** Alberta Canada
145 D6 **Hinesville** Georgia U.S.A.
36 D5 **Hinganghat** India
39 F4 **Hinglaj** Pakistan
Hingol r. see **Girdar Dhor**
38 B2 **Hingoli** India
42 E2 **Hinis** Turkey
154 D4 **Hinkley** California U.S.A.
55 C3 **Hinnerup** Denmark
56 D1 **Hinnøya** i. Norway
28 D6 **Hino** Japan
23 B4 **Hinobaan** Philippines
100 D3 **Hinojales, Sierra de** h. Spain
101 H3 **Hinojares** Spain
99 H3 **Hinojedo** mt. Spain
173 G4 **Hinojo** Argentina
98 D4 **Hinojosa de Duero** Spain
101 E2 **Hinojosa del Duque** Spain
28 C7 **Hinokage** Japan
28 D6 **Hino-misaki** pt Japan
147 G3 **Hinsdale** New Hampshire U.S.A.
59 G1 **Hinsen** i. Sweden
72 C2 **Hinte** Germany
80 C3 **Hinteres Sonnenwendjoch** mt. Austria
75 F2 **Hinternah** Germany
83 E2 **Hinterrhein** r. Switzerland
83 E2 **Hinterrhein** Switzerland
80 E3 **Hintersee** Austria
87 G3 **Hinterweidenthal** Germany
74 D5 **Hinterzarten** Germany
136 F4 **Hinton** Alberta Canada
146 C6 **Hinton** W. Virginia U.S.A.
83 D1 **Hinwil** Switzerland
93 B5 **Hinx** France
172 D2 **Hipolito Yrigoyen** Argentina
80 C3 **Hippach** Austria
68 C2 **Hippolytushoef** Netherlands
125 C4 **Hippopotames de Mangai, Réserve de Faune de la** res. Zaire
125 E6 **Hippopotames de Sakania, Réserve de** res. Zaire
125 E4 **Hippopotames, Réserve de** res. Zaire
42 F2 **Hirabit Dağ** mt. Turkey
28 B7 **Hirado** Japan
28 B7 **Hirado-shima** i. Japan
37 E5 **Hirakud Reservoir** resr India
127 C5 **Hiraman** watercourse Kenya
36 D4 **Hirapur** India
28 D6 **Hirata** Japan
29 G6 **Hiratsuka** Japan
122 C5 **Hiré-Watta** Côte d'Ivoire
77 N5 **Hirnyk** Ukraine
28 J2 **Hiroo** Japan
28 H3 **Hirosaki** Japan
28 D6 **Hiroshima** div. Japan
28 D6 **Hiroshima** Japan
75 G3 **Hirschaid** Germany
75 G3 **Hirschau** Germany
80 C3 **Hirschberg** mt. Germany
75 G2 **Hirschberg** Germany
75 K2 **Hirschfelde** Germany
55 C2 **Hirsholmene** is Denmark
90 F1 **Hirsingue** France
53 F3 **Hirsivka** Ukraine
53 D2 **Hirs'kyy Tikych** r. Ukraine
86 D3 **Hirson** France
66 □1 **Hirta** i. Scotland U.K.
81 H3 **Hirtenberg** Austria
55 B2 **Hirtshals** Denmark
62 C3 **Hirwaun** Wales U.K.
28 B7 **Hisaka-jima** i. Japan
42 C1 **Hisarönü** Turkey
113 F6 **Hisarönü Körfezi** b. Turkey
47 G5 **Hisor** Tajikistan
159 E2 **Hispaniola** i. Caribbean
36 C1 **Hispur Gl** gl. Pakistan
36 C3 **Hissar** India
63 G2 **Histon** England U.K.
37 F4 **Hisua** India
43 D2 **Hisyah** Syria
42 E3 **Hīt** Iraq
28 C7 **Hita** Japan
29 H5 **Hitachi** Japan
29 H5 **Hitachi-ōta** Japan
63 F3 **Hitchin** England U.K.
7 □11 **Hitiaa** French Polynesia Pacific Ocean
28 C7 **Hitoyoshi** Japan
56 C3 **Hitra** i. Norway
55 E3 **Hittarp** Sweden
80 A3 **Hittisau** Austria
73 G2 **Hitzacker** Germany
81 G3 **Hitzendorf** Austria
83 D1 **Hitzkirch** Switzerland
6 □2 **Hiu** i. Vanuatu
29 G5 **Hiuchiga-take** volcano Japan
28 D6 **Hiuchi-nada** b. Japan
177 K6 **Hiva Oa** i.
136 E4 **Hixon** B.C. Canada
43 C4 **Hiyon** watercourse Israel
42 E2 **Hizan** Turkey
55 C2 **Hjallerup** Denmark
59 F2 **Hjälmaren** l. Sweden
137 H2 **Hjalmar Lake** l. N.W.T. Canada
59 F3 **Hjältevad** Sweden
58 C2 **Hjartdal** Norway
58 C2 **Hjartdøld** r. Norway
58 A1 **Hjellestad** Norway
55 B3 **Hjelm** i. Denmark
55 E5 **Hjelm Bugt** b. Denmark
58 B2 **Hjelmeland** Norway
58 A1 **Hjeltefjorden** chan. Norway
56 C3 **Hjerkinn** Norway
59 F2 **Hjo** Sweden
55 B4 **Hjordkær** Denmark
55 C2 **Hjørring** Denmark
59 G3 **Hjorted** Sweden
59 F2 **Hjortkvarn** Sweden
58 D3 **Hjuvik** Sweden
24 B2 **Hkok** r. Myanmar
24 B1 **Hkring Bum** mt. Myanmar
131 H4 **Hlabisa** South Africa
24 A3 **Hlaing** r. Myanmar
37 F3 **Hlako Kangri** mt. China
131 H3 **Hlatikulu** Swaziland
52 A3 **Hlazove** Ukraine
24 B3 **Hlegu** Myanmar
131 F4 **Hlhlolwane** South Africa
78 E2 **Hlinsko** Czech Rep.
53 E2 **Hlobyne** Ukraine
79 G3 **Hlohovec** Slovakia
131 G4 **Hlotse** Lesotho
81 F1 **Hluboká nad Vltavou** Czech Rep.
79 H2 **Hlučín** Czech Rep.
131 J4 **Hluhluwe** South Africa
131 J4 **Hluhluwe Game Reserve** res. South Africa
53 E1 **Hlukhiv** Ukraine
24 B2 **Hlung-Tan** Myanmar
54 F5 **Hlusha** Belarus
53 B1 **Hlushkavichy** Belarus
54 F5 **Hlusk** Belarus
53 A2 **Hlyboka** Ukraine
54 E4 **Hlybokaye** Belarus
53 E2 **Hlyns'k** Ukraine
77 N6 **Hlynyany** Ukraine
53 C2 **Hnivan'** Ukraine
77 N6 **Hnizdychiv** Ukraine
79 J3 **Hnúšťa** Slovakia
53 G1 **Hnylytsya** Ukraine
53 D2 **Hnylyy Tikych** r. Ukraine
123 E5 **Ho** Ghana
24 D2 **Hoa Binh** Vietnam
128 B3 **Hoachanas** Namibia
128 A2 **Hoanib** watercourse Namibia
128 A2 **Hoarusib** watercourse Namibia
151 D5 **Hobart** Oklahoma U.S.A.
13 F5 **Hobart** Tasmania Australia
153 G5 **Hobbs** New Mexico U.S.A.
179 A4 **Hobbs Coast** coastal area Antarctica
145 D7 **Hobe Sound** Florida U.S.A.
131 F4 **Hobhouse** South Africa
47 L3 **Hoboksar** China
Hobot Xar Qi see **Xianghuang Qi**
55 B3 **Hobro** Denmark
55 A4 **Ho Bugt** inlet Denmark
59 H3 **Hoburg** Sweden
59 H3 **Hoburgen** pt Sweden
126 E3 **Hobyo** Somalia
74 E3 **Höchberg** Germany
81 F2 **Hochbira** h. Austria
72 E1 **Hochdonn** Germany
83 D1 **Hochdorf** Switzerland
82 D1 **Höchenschwand** Germany
80 C4 **Hochfeiler** mt. Austria/Italy
81 E3 **Hochfeind** mt. Austria
128 B3 **Hochfeld** Namibia
87 G4 **Hochfelden** France
72 D4 **Hochfläche** reg. Germany
81 E3 **Hochgolling** mt. Austria
74 F2 **Höchheim** Germany
25 D5 **Hô Chi Minh** Vietnam
81 F3 **Hochschwab** mountain range Austria
81 G3 **Hochschwab** mt. Austria
87 G3 **Hochspeyer** Germany
80 A3 **Höchst** Austria
75 F3 **Höchstadt an der Aisch** Germany
87 G3 **Hochstetten-Dhaun** Germany
80 A2 **Hochsträß** reg. Germany
81 F3 **Hochtor** mt. Austria
80 C3 **Hochunnutz** mt. Austria
83 E2 **Hochwang** mt. Switzerland
74 D3 **Hockenheim** Germany
146 B5 **Hocking** r. Ohio U.S.A.
157 H4 **Hoctún** Mexico
120 C5 **Hôd** reg. Mauritania
126 F2 **Hodda** mt. Somalia
65 F4 **Hodder** r. England U.K.
63 F3 **Hoddesdon** England U.K.
Hodeida see **Al Hudaydah**
147 K1 **Hodgdon** Maine U.S.A.
120 C5 **Hodh Ech Chargui** div. Mauritania
120 C5 **Hodh El Gharbi** div. Mauritania
79 K5 **Hódmezővásárhely** Hungary
126 E2 **Hodmo** watercourse Somalia
62 D2 **Hodnet** England U.K.
78 G3 **Hodonín** Czech Rep.
30 A2 **Hödrögö** Mongolia
88 C4 **Hœdic, Île de** i. France
131 H2 **Hoedspruit** South Africa
68 C3 **Hoek van Holland** Netherlands
87 G4 **Hœnheim** France
69 D4 **Hoensbroek** Netherlands
87 G4 **Hœrdt** France
31 J4 **Hoeryŏng** North Korea
69 D4 **Hoeselt** Belgium
31 H5 **Hoeyang** North Korea
75 G2 **Hof** Bayern Germany
87 H2 **Hof** Rheinland-Pfalz Germany
83 F1 **Höfen** Austria
141 H5 **Hoffman Mt** mt. New York U.S.A.
72 E4 **Hofgeismar** Germany
74 D2 **Hofheim am Taunus** Germany
75 F2 **Hofheim in Unterfranken** Germany
131 E5 **Hofmeyr** South Africa
56 N6 **Höfn** Austurland Iceland
135 R3 **Höfn** Iceland
59 G1 **Hofors** Sweden
56 M6 **Hofsjökull** ice cap Iceland
56 M6 **Hofsós** Iceland
28 C6 **Hōfu** Japan
Hofuf see **Al Hufuf**
59 E3 **Höganäs** Sweden
15 F5 **Hoganthulla Cr.** r. Queensland Australia
14 D4 **Hogarth, Mt** h. Northern Terr. Australia
59 G1 **Högbacka** Sweden
68 D2 **Hoge Vaart** canal Netherlands
68 D2 **Hoge Veluwe, Nationaal Park De** Netherlands
121 E4 **Hoggar** plat. Algeria
147 F6 **Hog I.** i. Virginia U.S.A.
59 E2 **Högsäter** Sweden
59 G3 **Högsby** Sweden
59 F2 **Högsjö** Sweden
87 G4 **Hohberg** Germany
81 E4 **Hohe Leier** mt. Austria
80 E4 **Hohe Leiten** mt. Austria
80 B2 **Hohen-altheim** Germany
75 J4 **Hohenau** Germany
81 G3 **Hohenberg** Austria
73 J4 **Hohenbucko** Germany
80 A3 **Hohenems** Austria
75 G3 **Hohenfels** Germany
75 F5 **Hohenfurch** Germany
72 E2 **Hohenlockstedt** Germany
74 E3 **Hohenloher Ebene** plain Germany
73 H4 **Hohenmölsen** Germany
73 H3 **Hohennauen** Germany
81 F3 **Hohe Nock** mt. Austria
83 G1 **Hohenpeißenberg** Germany
73 K3 **Hohensaaten** Germany
75 H2 **Hohenstein-Ernstthal** Germany
73 H2 **Hohen Wangelin** Germany
80 C2 **Hohenwart** Germany
75 G2 **Hohenwarte-Stausee** resr Germany
72 E1 **Hohenwestedt** Germany
81 E2 **Hohenzell** Austria
81 E3 **Hoher Dachstein** mt. Austria
74 E2 **Hohe Rhön** mountain range Germany
80 B3 **Hoher Ifen** mt. Austria/Germany
80 D3 **Hohe Tauern** mountain range Austria
80 D3 **Hohe Tauern, Nationalpark** nat. park Austria
69 E4 **Hohe Venn** moorland Belgium
82 C2 **Hohgant** mt. Switzerland
30 D4 **Hohhot** China
87 H4 **Hohloh** h. Germany
72 F3 **Hohne** Germany
87 G4 **Hohneck** mt. France
123 E5 **Hohoe** Ghana
28 C6 **Hōhoku** Japan
53 E2 **Hoholeve** Ukraine
53 D1 **Hoholiv** Ukraine
53 F3 **Hoholivka** Ukraine
87 G2 **Höhr-Grenzhausen** Germany
73 F1 **Hohwachter Bucht** b. Germany
37 G2 **Hoh Xil Hu** salt lake China
37 G2 **Hoh Xil Shan** mountain range China
24 E4 **Hôi An** Vietnam
127 B4 **Hoima** Uganda
24 D2 **Hôi Xuân** Vietnam
37 H4 **Hojai** India
55 D4 **Højby** Denmark
55 A5 **Højer** Denmark
28 D7 **Hōjo** Japan
55 B3 **Højslev Stationsby** Denmark
32 B4 **Hok** r. Myanmar
59 F3 **Hok** Sweden
Hokang see **Hegang**
59 G3 **Hökhallen** b. Sweden
59 H1 **Hökhuvud** Sweden
8 D1 **Hokianga Harbour** harbour New Zealand
29 G5 **Hōki-gawa** r. Japan
9 C5 **Hokitika** New Zealand
28 J2 **Hokkaidō** div. Japan
28 J2 **Hokkaidō** i. Japan
58 C2 **Hokksund** Norway
39 D1 **Hokmābād** Iran
9 B6 **Hokonui Hills** h. New Zealand
42 F1 **Hoktemberyan** Armenia
29 F6 **Hokuriku Tunnel** tunnel Japan
58 C1 **Hol** Norway
38 B3 **Holalkere** India
164 D2 **Holanda** Bolivia
53 E3 **Hola Prystan'** Ukraine
55 C3 **Holbæk** Århus Denmark
55 D4 **Holbæk** Vestsjælland Denmark
131 H3 **Holbank** South Africa
63 G2 **Holbeach** England U.K.
63 F2 **Holbeach Marsh** marsh England U.K.
15 G3 **Holborne I.** i. Queensland Australia
155 G4 **Holbrook** Arizona U.S.A.
13 F3 **Holbrook** New South Wales Australia
148 B3 **Holcombe Flowage** resr Wisconsin U.S.A.
137 G4 **Holden** Alberta Canada
155 F2 **Holden** Utah U.S.A.
151 D5 **Holdenville** Oklahoma U.S.A.
65 H4 **Holderness** pen. England U.K.
72 D3 **Holdorf** Germany
150 D3 **Holdrege** Nebraska U.S.A.
55 D5 **Holeby** Denmark
38 B3 **Hole Narsipur** India
79 G2 **Holešov** Czech Rep.
159 □9 **Holetown** Barbados Caribbean
130 A4 **Holgat** watercourse South Africa
158 C2 **Holguín** Cuba
78 G3 **Holíč** Slovakia
59 E1 **Höljan** r. Sweden
59 E1 **Höljes** Sweden
81 H2 **Hollabrunn** div. Austria
81 H2 **Hollabrunn** Austria
148 D4 **Holland** Michigan U.S.A.
159 □1 **Holland Bay** b. Jamaica
63 F2 **Holland Fen** reg. England U.K.
63 H3 **Holland-on-Sea** England U.K.
68 C3 **Hollands Diep** est. Netherlands
68 E2 **Hollandse Veld** Netherlands
69 D5 **Hollange** Belgium
75 G4 **Hollenbach** Germany
81 E3 **Höllengebirge** h. Austria
81 F3 **Hollenstein an der Ybbs** Austria
63 H2 **Hollesley Bay** b. England U.K.
75 G3 **Hollfeld** Germany
146 D4 **Hollidaysburg** Pennsylvania U.S.A.
63 G4 **Hollington** England U.K.
136 C3 **Hollis** Alaska U.S.A.
151 D5 **Hollis** Oklahoma U.S.A.
154 B3 **Hollister** California U.S.A.
79 L3 **Hollóháza** Hungary
54 D1 **Hollola** Finland
149 F4 **Holly** Michigan U.S.A.
151 F5 **Holly Springs** Mississippi U.S.A.
145 D7 **Hollywood** Florida U.S.A.
134 G2 **Holman** N.W.T. Canada
55 B4 **Holme** r. Denmark
131 G3 **Holmedene** South Africa
65 H4 **Holme-on-Spalding-Moor** England U.K.
15 F3 **Holmes Reef** reef Coral Sea Islands Terr. Pacific Ocean
58 D2 **Holmestrand** Vestfold Norway
56 G1 **Holmestrand** Finnmark Norway
65 G4 **Holmfirth** England U.K.
56 F3 **Holmön** i. Sweden
59 F3 **Holmsjö** Sweden
55 A4 **Holmsland Klit** spit Denmark
135 N2 **Holms Ø** i. Greenland
59 G1 **Holmsveden** Sweden
53 A1 **Holoby** Ukraine
53 A2 **Holohory** h. Ukraine
43 C3 **Holon** Israel
6 □3 **Holonga** Tonga
128 B4 **Holoog** Namibia
53 D2 **Holovanivs'k** Ukraine
77 L6 **Holovets'ko** Ukraine
53 E2 **Holovkivka** Ukraine
77 N4 **Holovne** Ukraine
53 C1 **Holovyne** Ukraine
15 E2 **Holroyd** r. Queensland Australia
58 B1 **Holskarvatnet** l. Norway
58 A1 **Holsnøy** i. Norway
131 G3 **Holspruit** r. South Africa
55 A3 **Holstebro** Denmark
55 A4 **Holsted** Denmark
82 C1 **Holstein** Switzerland
Holsteinsborg see **Sisimiut**
145 D4 **Holston** r. Tennessee U.S.A.
146 C6 **Holston Lake** l. Tennessee U.S.A.
62 B4 **Holsworthy** England U.K.
63 H2 **Holt** England U.K.
148 E4 **Holt** Michigan U.S.A.
68 E2 **Holten** Netherlands
150 E4 **Holton** Kansas U.S.A.
53 F2 **Holubivka** Ukraine
68 D1 **Holwerd** Netherlands
67 D4 **Holycross** Rep. of Ireland
62 B1 **Holyhead** Wales U.K.
62 B1 **Holyhead Bay** b. Wales U.K.
65 G2 **Holy Island** i. England U.K.
62 B1 **Holy Island** i. Wales U.K.
152 G3 **Holyoke** Colorado U.S.A.
147 G3 **Holyoke** Massachusetts U.S.A.
62 C1 **Holywell** Wales U.K.
64 C3 **Holywood** Northern Ireland U.K.
73 H4 **Holzhausen** Germany
74 C2 **Holzhausen an der Haide** Germany
80 B2 **Holzheim** Bayern Germany
87 H2 **Holzheim** Hessen Germany
75 G5 **Holzkirchen** Germany
72 E4 **Holzminden** Germany

73 F4 Holzthaleben Germany
72 C4 Holzwickede Germany
130 B4 Hom watercourse Namibia
127 B5 Homa Bay Kenya
24 A1 Homalin Myanmar
39 B2 Homāyunshahr Iran
72 E4 Homberg (Efze) Germany
74 D2 Homberg (Ohm) Germany
69 A5 Hombleux France
122 D3 Hombori Mali
74 C3 Homburg Germany
135 M3 Home Bay b. N.W.T. Canada
87 E3 Homécourt France
15 F3 Home Hill Queensland Australia
10 □1 Home I. i. Cocos Is Indian Ocean
98 B3 Homem r. Portugal
134 C4 Homer Alaska U.S.A.
151 E5 Homer Louisiana U.S.A.
63 H2 Homersfield England U.K.
146 D6 Homerville Georgia U.S.A.
114 B1 Homesh Albania
145 D7 Homestead Florida U.S.A.
15 F4 Homestead Queensland Australia
145 C5 Homewood Alabama U.S.A.
38 B2 Homnabad India
112 F1 Homocea Romania
123 G3 Homodji well Niger
129 F3 Homoine Mozambique
23 C4 Homonhon pt Philippines
Homs see Ḩimş
54 F5 Homyel' div. Belarus
51 D4 Homyel' Homyel'skaya Voblasts' Belarus
38 A3 Honavar India
42 B2 Honaz Turkey
28 J2 Honbetsu Japan
53 D1 Honcharivs'ke Ukraine
162 C2 Honda Colombia
23 A4 Honda Bay b. Philippines
155 H4 Hon Dah Arizona U.S.A.
102 B1 Hondarribia Spain
130 E5 Hondeblaf r. South Africa
130 A5 Hondeklipbaai South Africa
30 D4 Hondlon Ju China
151 D6 Hondo Texas U.S.A.
28 C7 Hondo Japan
103 C6 Hondón de las Nieves Spain
86 B2 Hondschoote France
68 E1 Hondsrug reg. Netherlands
133 K8 Honduras country Central America
157 H5 Honduras, Golfo de g. Mexico
58 D1 Hønefoss Norway
147 F4 Honesdale Pennsylvania U.S.A.
154 B1 Honey Lake l. California U.S.A.
8 □2 Honey, Mt h. Campbell I. New Zealand
147 E3 Honeyoye Lake l. New York U.S.A.
89 F2 Honfleur France
33 F1 Hong r. China
55 D4 Høng Denmark
33 F2 Hong'an China
31 H5 Hongch'ŏn South Korea
24 D2 Hông Gai Vietnam
33 F4 Honghai Wan b. China
32 C4 Honghe China
33 F2 Honghu China
33 E3 Hongjiang China
27 □ Hong Kong territory Asia
27 □ Hong Kong Island i. Hong Kong
30 D5 Hongliu r. China
30 A4 Hongliu Daquan China
30 A4 Hongliugou China
30 A4 Hongliujing China
30 B5 Hongliuyuan China
25 D5 Hông Ngư Vietnam
30 E3 Hongor China
30 E3 Hongor Mongolia
24 D2 Hong or Red River, Mouths of the river mouth Vietnam
33 E5 Hongqizhen China
30 C5 Hongshansi China
31 H4 Hongshi China
32 D3 Hongshui r. China
30 D5 Hongtong China
29 E7 Hongū Japan
31 H4 Hongwŏn North Korea
31 G3 Hongxing China
32 C1 Hongyuan China
33 G1 Hongze China
33 G1 Hongze Hu l. China
6 □1 Honiara Solomon Is.
62 C4 Honiton England U.K.
29 H4 Honjō Japan
57 F3 Honkajoki Finland
29 G6 Honkawane Japan
25 D5 Hon Khoai i. Vietnam
65 G4 Honley England U.K.
25 E4 Hon Lon i. Vietnam
24 D3 Hon Mê i. Vietnam
38 A3 Honnali India
131 H1 Honnet Nature Reserve res. South Africa
56 G1 Honningsvåg Norway
153 □2 Honokaa Hawaii U.S.A.
153 □1 Honolulu Hawaii U.S.A.
73 J3 Hönow Germany
25 D5 Hon Rai i. Vietnam
99 H5 Honrubia Spain
99 G3 Honrubia de la Cuesta Spain
28 D6 Honshū i. Japan
99 F3 Hontalbilla Spain
79 H3 Hontianske Nemce Slovakia
99 G2 Hontoria de la Cantera Spain
99 G3 Hontoria del Pinar Spain
152 B2 Hood, Mt volcano Oregon U.S.A.
17 B7 Hood Pt pt Western Australia Australia
68 C2 Hoofddorp Netherlands
72 D1 Hooge i. Germany
72 D1 Hooge Germany
69 C3 Hoogerheide Netherlands
68 E2 Hoogersmilde Netherlands
68 E2 Hoogeveen Netherlands
68 E1 Hoogezand-Sappemeer Netherlands
68 E2 Hooghalen Netherlands
68 D2 Hoogkarspel Netherlands
68 E1 Hoogkerk Netherlands
73 E3 Hoogstede Germany
69 C3 Hoogstraten Belgium
63 F3 Hook England U.K.
151 C4 Hooker Oklahoma U.S.A.
14 B3 Hooker Creek Abor. Reserve res. Northern Terr. Australia
67 E4 Hook Head headland Rep. of Ireland
15 G4 Hook I. i. Queensland Australia
Hook of Holland see Hoek van Holland
15 G3 Hook Rf reef Queensland Australia
136 B3 Hoonah Alaska U.S.A.
134 B3 Hooper Bay Alaska U.S.A.
147 E5 Hooper I. i. Maryland U.S.A.
148 D5 Hoopeston Illinois U.S.A.
131 E3 Hoopstad South Africa
59 E4 Höör Sweden
68 D2 Hoorn Netherlands
176 H6 Hoorn, Îles de Wallis & Futuna Pacific Ocean
147 G3 Hoosick New York U.S.A.
155 E3 Hoover Dam dam Arizona U.S.A.
146 B4 Hoover Memorial Reservoir resr Ohio U.S.A.
30 B3 Höövör Mongolia
42 E1 Hopa Turkey
147 F4 Hop Bottom Pennsylvania U.S.A.
9 D5 Hope r. New Zealand
155 F5 Hope Arizona U.S.A.
151 E5 Hope Arkansas U.S.A.
142 B2 Hope B.C. Canada
62 C1 Hope Wales U.K.
159 □1 Hope Bay Jamaica
139 J2 Hopedale Newfoundland Canada
130 B6 Hopefield South Africa
12 D2 Hope, L. salt flat S. Australia Australia
17 C7 Hope, L. salt flat Western Australia Australia
157 H5 Hopelchén Mexico
66 D2 Hope, Loch l. Scotland U.K.
66 E3 Hopeman Scotland U.K.
139 H3 Hope Mountains mountain range Newfoundland Canada
44 D2 Hopen i. Svalbard Arctic Ocean
9 D4 Hope Saddle pass New Zealand
139 G2 Hopes Advance, Baie b. Québec Canada
13 E3 Hopetoun Victoria Australia
17 C7 Hopetoun Western Australia Australia
130 E4 Hopetown South Africa
15 F2 Hope Vale Queensland Australia
146 E6 Hopewell Virginia U.S.A.
138 E2 Hopewell Islands is Québec Canada
80 D3 Hopfgarten im Brixental Austria
24 B1 Hopin Myanmar
13 E4 Hopkins r. Victoria Australia
17 E5 Hopkins, L. salt flat Western Australia Australia
144 C4 Hopkinsville Kentucky U.S.A.
154 A2 Hopland California U.S.A.
24 B2 Hopong Myanmar
69 F5 Hoppstädten Germany
72 C3 Hopsten Germany
63 H2 Hopton England U.K.
55 B4 Hoptrup Denmark
152 B2 Hoquiam Washington U.S.A.
32 C1 Hor China
42 F2 Horadiz Azerbaijan
63 G4 Horam England U.K.
53 G3 'Hora Mohila Bel'mak h. Ukraine
42 E1 Horasan Turkey
78 C2 Horažďovice Czech Rep.
74 D4 Horb am Neckar Germany
55 E5 Horbelev Denmark
87 G4 Horbourg-Wihr France
83 E1 Hörbranz Austria
59 E4 Hörby Sweden
101 F1 Horcajo de los Montes Spain
99 H5 Horcajo de Santiago Spain
156 D2 Horcasitas Mexico
58 B2 Horda Norway
58 A1 Hordaland div. Norway
53 B3 Horeşti Moldova
112 D2 Horezu Romania
83 D1 Horgen Switzerland
83 E1 Horgenzell Germany
30 A2 Horgo Mongolia
79 J5 Horgoš Yugoslavia
53 A2 Horhany r. Ukraine
30 C4 Hörh Uul mts Mongolia
112 G2 Horia Romania
78 E1 Hořice Czech Rep.
148 C4 Horicon Wisconsin U.S.A.
30 D4 Horinger China
81 H3 Horitschon Austria
30 B3 Horiult Mongolia
73 K4 Horka Germany
50 D4 Horki Belarus
63 F3 Horley England U.K.
179 B4 Horlick Mts mts Antarctica
51 F5 Horlivka Ukraine
39 E3 Hormak Iran
39 D4 Hormoz i. Iran
39 D4 Hormozgan div. Iran
39 D4 Hormuz, Strait of str. Iran/Oman
56 L6 Horn c. Iceland
81 G2 Horn div. Austria
136 F2 Horn r. N.W.T. Canada
81 G2 Horn Austria
59 F3 Horn Sweden
100 D2 Hornachos Spain
101 E3 Hornachuelos Spain
79 K3 Hornád r. Slovakia
56 E2 Hornavan l. Sweden
87 G3 Hornbach Germany
151 E6 Hornbeck Louisiana U.S.A.
74 D4 Hornberg Germany
73 F3 Hornburg Germany
65 F3 Hornby England U.K.
Horn, C. c. see Hornos, Cabo de
63 F1 Horncastle England U.K.
59 G1 Horndal Sweden
63 E4 Horndean England U.K.
72 E2 Horneburg Germany
56 E3 Hörnefors Sweden
146 E3 Hornell New York U.S.A.
140 C2 Hornepayne Ontario Canada
55 D2 Hornfiskrøn i. Denmark
67 C1 Horn Head headland Rep. of Ireland
145 B6 Horn I. i. Mississippi U.S.A.
15 E1 Horn I. i. Queensland Australia
75 J3 Horní Bříza Czech Rep.
75 J2 Horní Jiřetín Czech Rep.
55 C3 Hørning Denmark
78 D3 Horní Planá Czech Rep.
74 D4 Hornisgrinde mt. Germany
78 B1 Horní Slavkov Czech Rep.
58 B2 Hornnes Norway
151 C7 Hornos Mexico
101 H2 Hornos Spain
171 C7 Hornos, Cabo de c. Chile
171 C7 Hornos, Parque Nacional de nat. park Chile
53 E3 Hornostayivka Ukraine
89 G2 Hornoy-le-Bourg France
65 H4 Hornsea England U.K.
57 E3 Hornslandet pen. Sweden
55 C3 Hornslet Denmark
59 G3 Hornsviken l. Sweden
55 B3 Hornum Denmark
72 D1 Hörnum Germany
79 J3 Horný Tisovník Slovakia
53 A2 Horodenka Ukraine
53 B1 Horodets' Ukraine
53 D1 Horodnya Ukraine
53 B1 Horodnytsya Ukraine
53 B2 Horodok Khmel'nyts'ka Oblast' Ukraine
77 M6 Horodok L'vivs'ka Oblast' Ukraine
53 D2 Horodyshche Ukraine
28 J1 Horokanai Japan
53 A1 Horokhiv Ukraine
79 M3 Horonda Ukraine
28 H1 Horonobe Japan
28 J2 Horoshiri-dake mt. Japan
78 C2 Hořovice Czech Rep.
31 G4 Horqin Shadi reg. China
31 G3 Horqin Youyi Qianqi China
31 G3 Horqin Youyi Zhongqi China
31 G4 Horqin Zuoyi Houqi China
31 G3 Horqin Zuoyi Zhongqi China
165 E4 Horqueta Paraguay
62 B4 Horrabridge England U.K.
55 E5 Horreby Denmark
59 E3 Horred Sweden
17 A6 Horrocks Western Australia Australia
37 G3 Horru China
10 □1 Horsburgh I. i. Cocos Is Indian Ocean
81 F2 Hörsching Austria
136 E4 Horsefly B.C. Canada
146 E3 Horseheads New York U.S.A.
139 J3 Horse Is is Newfoundland Canada
67 C3 Horseleap Rep. of Ireland
55 B4 Horsens Denmark
55 C4 Horsens Fjord inlet Denmark
152 C3 Horseshoe Bend Idaho U.S.A.
159 □6 Horse Shoe Pt pt St Kitts-Nevis Caribbean
130 D5 Horseshoe, The mt. South Africa
65 G4 Horsforth England U.K.
63 F3 Horsham England U.K.
13 E4 Horsham Victoria Australia
55 E4 Hørsholm Denmark
55 D5 Horslunde Denmark
78 B2 Horšovský Týn Czech Rep.
69 E3 Horst Netherlands
73 G3 Hörstel Germany
72 C3 Horstmar Germany
100 □ Horta Azores Portugal
58 D2 Horten Norway
103 B6 Hortezuela Spain
99 G2 Hortigüela Spain
79 L4 Hortobágy reg. Hungary
79 K4 Hortobágy-Berettyó canal Hungary
79 L4 Hortobágyi nat. park Hungary
55 B5 Hørup Denmark
119 F3 Horus, Temple of Egypt
55 D4 Hørve Denmark
59 F3 Hörvik Sweden
83 D1 Horw Switzerland
65 F4 Horwich England U.K.
140 D2 Horwood Lake l. Ontario Canada
53 B1 Horyn' r. Ukraine
37 H2 Ho Sai Hu salt lake China
126 C3 Hosa'ina Ethiopia
74 E2 Hösbach Germany
38 B3 Hosdurga India
39 B2 Ḩoseynābād Iran
39 A2 Ḩoseynābād Iran
39 B3 Ḩoseynīyeh Iran
39 E4 Hoshab Pakistan
36 D5 Hoshangabad India
31 B3 Hoshcha Ukraine
36 C3 Hoshiarpur India
47 L3 Höshööt Mongolia
30 B2 Höshööt Mongolia
69 E4 Hosingen Luxembourg
6 □1 Hoskins P.N.G.
38 B3 Hospet India
67 C4 Hospital Rep. of Ireland
173 K2 Hospital, Cuch. del h. Uruguay
124 B2 Hosséré Vokre mt. Cameroon
83 E1 Hoßkirch Germany
159 H5 Hossororo Guyana
102 B3 Hostalric Spain
171 C7 Hoste, I. i. Chile
93 B4 Hostens France
78 F3 Hostěradice Czech Rep.
78 E1 Hostinné Czech Rep.
75 K2 Hostivice Czech Rep.
56 D3 Hotagen r. Sweden
47 K5 Hotan watercourse China
36 E1 Hotan China
130 D3 Hotazel South Africa
155 G4 Hotevilla Arizona U.S.A.
17 B7 Hotham r. Western Australia Australia
14 B2 Hotham, C. c. Northern Terr. Australia
13 F4 Hotham, Mt mt. Victoria Australia
56 E2 Hoting Sweden
151 E5 Hot Springs Arkansas U.S.A.
150 C3 Hot Springs S. Dakota U.S.A.
136 F1 Hottah Lake l. N.W.T. Canada
128 A4 Hottentots Bay b. Namibia
69 D4 Hotton Belgium
74 D5 Hotzenwald reg. Germany
55 C2 Hou Denmark
6 □2 Houaïlu New Caledonia Pacific Ocean
88 C4 Houat, Île de i. France
86 B2 Houdain France
89 G3 Houdan France
87 E4 Houdelaincourt France
93 C4 Houeillès France
69 D4 Houffalize Belgium
25 □ Hougang Singapore
148 C2 Houghton Michigan U.S.A.
148 E3 Houghton Lake l. Michigan U.S.A.
148 E3 Houghton Lake Michigan U.S.A.
65 G3 Houghton le Spring England U.K.
63 F3 Houghton Regis England U.K.
130 B7 Houhoek Pass pass South Africa
55 B3 Houlbjerg Denmark
147 K1 Houlton Maine U.S.A.
6 □3 Houma i. Tonga
151 F6 Houma Louisiana U.S.A.
30 D6 Houma China
6 □4 Houma Tonga
6 □4 Houma Tonga
6 □4 Houma Toloa pt Tonga
121 G2 Houmt Souk Tunisia
122 D4 Houndé Burkina
86 A2 Hourdel, Pte du pt France
66 C3 Hourn, Loch inlet Scotland U.K.
92 A3 Hourtin France
92 A3 Hourtin-Plage France
147 G3 Housatonic Massachusetts U.S.A.
155 F2 House Range mts Utah U.S.A.
136 D4 Houston B.C. Canada
151 F5 Houston Mississippi U.S.A.
151 F4 Houston Missouri U.S.A.
151 E6 Houston Texas U.S.A.
68 D2 Houten Netherlands
69 D3 Houthalen Belgium
69 A4 Houthulst Belgium
130 E5 Houtkraal South Africa
17 A6 Houtman Abrolhos is Western Australia Australia
66 E2 Houton Scotland U.K.
59 J1 Houtskär Finland
55 C4 Hov Denmark
58 D1 Hov Norway
59 F2 Hova Sweden
30 B3 Hovd Mongolia
26 F2 Hovd Mongolia
58 C2 Hovdefjell h. Norway
58 B2 Hovden Norway
63 F4 Hove England U.K.
72 D4 Hövelhof Germany
55 A4 Hoven Denmark
55 A3 Hover r. Denmark
63 H2 Hoveton England U.K.
39 B3 Hoveyzeh Iran
65 H3 Hovingham England U.K.
59 F3 Hovmantorp Sweden
81 H2 Hovorany Czech Rep.
30 A2 Hövsgöl div. Mongolia
30 D4 Hövsgöl Mongolia
30 B2 Hövsgöl Nuur l. Mongolia
53 F2 Hovtva r. Ukraine
53 E2 Hovtva Ukraine
30 B4 Hövüün Mongolia
126 D1 Howakil I. i. Eritrea
15 H5 Howard Queensland Australia
148 E4 Howard City Michigan U.S.A.
14 C2 Howard I. i. Northern Terr. Australia
137 H2 Howard Lake l. N.W.T. Canada
65 H4 Howden England U.K.
13 G4 Howe, C. headland Victoria Australia
179 □ Howe, I. i. Kerguelen Indian Ocean
149 F4 Howell Michigan U.S.A.
150 C2 Howes S. Dakota U.S.A.
141 J4 Howick Québec Canada
131 H4 Howick South Africa
12 D1 Howitt, L. salt flat S. Australia Australia
13 F4 Howitt, Mt mt. Victoria Australia
147 J2 Howland Maine U.S.A.
176 H5 Howland I. Pacific Ocean
67 E3 Howth Rep. of Ireland
39 D2 Ḩowz well Iran
39 C2 Ḩowz-e Dūmatu Iran
39 D3 Ḩowz-e Panj Iran
39 D2 Ḩowz-i-Khan well Iran
72 E4 Höxter Germany
66 E2 Hoy i. Scotland U.K.
72 E3 Hoya Germany
58 B1 Hoyanger Norway
73 K4 Hoyerswerda Germany
56 D2 Høylandet Norway
140 E2 Hoyle Ontario Canada
73 G4 Hoym Germany
98 D4 Hoyos Spain
99 E4 Hoyos del Espino Spain
56 H3 Höytiäinen l. Finland
42 D2 Hozat Turkey
101 E4 Hozgarganta r. Spain
77 M2 Hozha Belarus
Hpa-an see Pa-an
78 E1 Hradec Králové Czech Rep.
75 K2 Hrádek nad Nisou Czech Rep.
75 J3 Hradešice Czech Rep.
78 C1 Hradiště h. Czech Rep.
53 E2 Hradyz'k Ukraine
77 M2 Hrandzichy Belarus
79 G2 Hranice Severomoravsk Czech Rep.
75 H2 Hranice Západočesk Czech Rep.
53 C1 Hranitne Ukraine
79 H3 Hranovnica Slovakia
104 G4 Hrasnica Bos.-Herz.
81 G4 Hrastnik Slovenia
42 F1 Hrazdan Armenia
53 E1 Hrebinka Ukraine
53 D2 Hrebinky Ukraine
52 A3 Hrem"yach Ukraine
53 E3 Hreyhove Ukraine
79 J3 Hriňová Slovakia
53 C2 Hristovaia Moldova
77 O2 Hrodna div. Belarus
77 M2 Hrodna Belarus
77 M2 Hrodnyendskaye Wzvyshsha reg. Belarus
79 H4 Hron r. Slovakia
78 F2 Hrotovice Czech Rep.
77 M5 Hrubieszów Poland
53 F1 Hrun' r. Ukraine
53 F1 Hrun' Ukraine
53 G2 Hrushuvakha Ukraine
81 H2 Hrušovany nad Jevišovkou Czech Rep.
53 E1 Hryhorivka Chernihivs'ka Oblast' Ukraine
53 E3 Hryhorivka Khersons'ka Oblast' Ukraine
53 B2 Hrymayliv Ukraine
53 A3 Hrynyava Ukraine
53 C2 Hryshkivtsi Ukraine
53 B2 Hrytsiv Ukraine
24 B2 Hsenwi Myanmar
24 B2 Hsi-hkip Myanmar
24 B2 Hsi-hseng Myanmar
33 G4 Hsi-hsu-p'ing Hsü i. Taiwan
33 H3 Hsin-chu Taiwan
24 B2 Hsipaw Myanmar
33 H3 Hsueh Shan mt. Taiwan
33 G3 Hua'an China
128 A3 Huab watercourse Namibia
164 C3 Huachacalla Bolivia
30 D5 Huachi China
172 A4 Huachipato Chile
164 A2 Huacho Peru
31 J3 Huachuan China
155 G6 Huachuca City Arizona U.S.A.
172 C1 Huaco Argentina
164 A1 Huacrachuco Peru
30 E4 Huade China
31 H4 Huadian China
7 □10 Huahine i. French Polynesia Pacific Ocean
33 F1 Huai r. China
30 E4 Huai'an China
33 G1 Huai'an China
33 G1 Huaibei China
33 F1 Huaibin China
31 H4 Huaidezhen China
33 E3 Huaihua China
33 F4 Huaiji China
31 E4 Huailai China
24 C3 Huai Luang r. Thailand
33 G1 Huainan China
33 G2 Huaining China
30 E5 Huairen China
33 F1 Huaiyang China
33 G1 Huaiyin China
32 E3 Huaiyuan China
33 G1 Huaiyuan China
32 D1 Huajialing China
157 F5 Huajuápan de León Mexico
21 J8 Huaki Indonesia
155 F4 Hualapai Peak summit Arizona U.S.A.
33 H3 Hua-lien Taiwan
162 B5 Huallaga r. Peru
30 B5 Hualong China
172 A5 Hualpin Chile
172 A4 Hualqui Chile
164 A1 Huamachuco Peru
125 C6 Huambo div. Angola
125 C6 Huambo Angola
162 B5 Huambos Peru
130 A2 Huams watercourse Namibia
30 C5 Huan r. China
31 J3 Huanan China
162 B5 Huancabamba r. Peru
171 C5 Huancache, Sa mountain range Argentina
164 C3 Huancane Peru
164 A2 Huancavelica Peru
164 A2 Huancayo Peru
172 F2 Huanchilla Argentina
31 F5 Huang r. China
30 B5 Huangcheng China
33 F1 Huangchuan China
33 F2 Huanggang China
Huang Hai sea see Yellow Sea
31 F5 Huanghe Kou river mouth China
32 A1 Huanghetan China
31 F5 Huanghua China
33 H1 Huangjiajian China
30 D6 Huangling China
32 E5 Huangliu China
33 F2 Huangmei China
31 H4 Huangnihe China
33 F2 Huangpi China
32 D3 Huangping China
30 E4 Huangqi Hai l. China
33 F2 Huangshajie China
33 G2 Huang Shan mt. China
33 G2 Huangshan China
33 F2 Huangshi China
30 B5 Huang Shui r. China
30 C5 Huangtu Gaoyuan mountain range China
173 G4 Huanguelén Argentina
31 G5 Huang Xian China
33 H2 Huangyan China
30 B5 Huangyuan China
32 E3 Huanjiang China
31 H4 Huanren China
164 B2 Huanta Peru
31 F5 Huantai China
164 A1 Huanuco Peru
164 C3 Huanuni Bolivia
30 C5 Huan Xian China
30 C5 Huan Xian China
164 B2 Huanzo, Cord. de mountain range Peru
32 C3 Huaping China
33 H3 Hua-p'ing Hsü i. Taiwan
164 C3 Huar Bolivia
164 C4 Huara Chile
164 A2 Huaral Peru
164 A1 Huaráz Peru
164 A1 Huari Peru
164 C3 Huarina Bolivia
164 A2 Huarmey Peru
33 F2 Huarong China
102 B2 Huarte-Araquil Spain
164 A1 Huascarán, Parque Nacional nat. park Peru
170 B2 Huasco r. Chile
170 B2 Huasco Chile
33 E1 Hua Shan mt. China
33 F1 Huashixia China
156 C3 Huatabampo Mexico
32 D1 Huating China
157 F5 Huatusco Mexico
157 F4 Huauchinango Mexico
157 F5 Huautla Mexico
30 E6 Hua Xian China
33 E1 Hua Xian China
164 A2 Huayhuash, Cord. mountain range Peru
164 A1 Huaylas Peru
164 A2 Huayllay Peru
33 E2 Huayuan China
33 F2 Huayuan China
32 D2 Huayun China
33 E4 Huazhou China
77 J4 Huba Poland
149 F3 Hubbard Lake l. Michigan U.S.A.
136 B2 Hubbard, Mt mt. Alaska/Yukon Territory Canada/U.S.A.
139 G2 Hubbard, Pointe headland Québec Canada
33 E2 Hubei div. China
38 A3 Hubli India
77 N5 Hubyn Ukraine
53 F2 Hubynykha Ukraine
172 E4 Hucal Argentina
31 H4 Huch'ang North Korea
72 B4 Hückelhoven Germany
72 C4 Hückeswagen Germany
63 E1 Hucknall England U.K.
86 A2 Hucqueliers France
65 G4 Huddersfield England U.K.
59 G2 Huddinge Sweden
146 B6 Huddy Kentucky U.S.A.
72 D2 Hude (Oldenburg) Germany
31 G2 Huder China
57 E3 Hudiksvall Sweden
144 F3 Hudson r. New York U.S.A.
148 E5 Hudson Michigan U.S.A.
147 G3 Hudson New York U.S.A.
148 A3 Hudson Wisconsin U.S.A.
138 D2 Hudson Bay sea Canada
137 J4 Hudson Bay Saskatchewan Canada
147 G3 Hudson Falls New York U.S.A.
135 Q2 Hudson Land reg. Greenland
179 A3 Hudson Mts mts Antarctica
136 E3 Hudson's Hope B.C. Canada
135 L3 Hudson Strait str. Québec/N.W.T. Canada
24 D3 Huê Vietnam
98 D4 Huebra r. Spain
102 B3 Huecha r. Spain
171 B5 Huechucuicui, Pta pt Chile
172 B5 Huechulafquén, L. l. Argentina
112 D1 Huedin Romania
157 H6 Huehuetenango Guatemala
156 D3 Huehueto, Co mt. Mexico
172 A6 Hueicoya Chile
157 F5 Huejotzingo Mexico
157 F4 Hujutla Mexico
101 G3 Huelago Spain
88 B3 Huelgoat France
101 G3 Huelma Spain
100 D3 Huelva div. Andalucia Spain
100 D3 Huelva r. Spain
100 D3 Huelva Spain
172 B1 Huentelauquén Chile
172 B4 Huepil Chile
103 B7 Huércal-Overa Spain
99 G2 Huérmeces Spain
103 B4 Huerta del Marquesada Spain
99 G3 Huerta del Rey Spain
99 G5 Huerta de Valdecarábanos Spain
172 D1 Huerta, Sa de la mountain range Argentina
103 C6 Huertas, Cabo de las pt Spain
102 C3 Huerva r. Spain
101 G3 Huesa Spain
102 C2 Huesca div. Aragón Spain
102 C2 Huesca Spain
101 H3 Huéscar Spain
157 E5 Huétamo Mexico
99 H4 Huete Spain
101 F3 Huétor-Tájar Spain
101 G3 Huétor-Vega Spain
157 F5 Huexotla Mexico
172 A6 Hueyelhue, Punta pt Chile
100 E3 Huezna r. Spain
74 D5 Hüfingen Germany
58 A1 Huftarøy i. Norway
124 E1 Hugeilig pool Sudan
14 C5 Hugh watercourse Northern Terr. Australia
15 F4 Hughenden Queensland Australia
173 G2 Hughes Argentina
146 E4 Hughesville Pennsylvania U.S.A.
63 □1 Hugh Town England U.K.
37 F5 Hugli inlet India
37 G5 Hugli-Chunchura India
151 E5 Hugo Oklahoma U.S.A.
151 C4 Hugoton Kansas U.S.A.
30 E5 Huguan China
Huhehot see Hohhot
130 E3 Huhudi South Africa
33 G3 Hui'an China
30 C5 Hui'anbu China
8 F3 Huiarau Range mountain range New Zealand
128 B4 Huib-Hoch Plateau Namibia
33 F3 Huichang China
31 H4 Huich'ŏn North Korea
33 F4 Huidong China
32 C3 Huidong China
31 H4 Huifa r. China
31 F2 Huihe China
33 F1 Huiji r. China
125 B6 Huíla div. Angola
33 G4 Huilai China
125 C7 Huíla Plateau plat. Angola
32 C3 Huili China
157 G5 Huimanguillo Mexico
31 F5 Huimin China
170 C1 Huinahuaca Argentina
31 H4 Huinan China
172 E3 Huinca Renancó Argentina
30 C6 Huining China
80 B2 Huisheim Germany
32 D3 Huishui China
89 F3 Huisne r. France
68 D3 Huissen Netherlands
37 G2 Huiten Nur l. China
33 E3 Huitong China
57 F3 Huittinen Finland
157 F5 Huitzuco Mexico
33 F1 Hui Xian China
32 D1 Hui Xian China
157 G6 Huixtla Mexico
Huiyang see Huizhou
32 C3 Huize China
68 D2 Huizen Netherlands
33 F4 Huizhou China
30 C3 Hujirt Mongolia
24 B1 Hukawng Valley v. Myanmar
33 G2 Hukou China
128 C3 Hukuntsi Botswana
31 H3 Hulan r. China
31 H3 Hulan China
31 G3 Hulan Ergi China
119 H2 Ḩulayfah Saudi Arabia
148 E2 Hulbert Lake l. Michigan U.S.A.
39 A2 Hulilan Iran
31 G3 Hulin r. China
31 K3 Hulin China
78 G2 Hulín Czech Rep.
Hulin Rocks is see Maidens, The
141 H4 Hull Québec Canada
72 D3 Hüllhorst Germany
54 C2 Hullo Estonia
69 C3 Hulst Netherlands
59 F3 Hultsfred Sweden
31 G4 Huludao China
Hulun see Hailar
31 F2 Hulun Nur l. China
53 G3 Hulyaypole Ukraine
31 G1 Huma r. China
31 H2 Huma China
145 □3 Humacao Puerto Rico
164 C2 Humaita Bolivia
165 D1 Humaitá Brazil
165 E5 Humaitá Paraguay
99 G4 Humanes de Mohernando Spain
125 B7 Humbe Angola
65 H4 Humber, Mouth of the river mouth England U.K.
65 H4 Humberside airport England U.K.
65 H4 Humberside div. England U.K.
125 B6 Humbe, Serra do mts Angola
55 C5 Humble Denmark
152 C3 Humboldt r. Nevada U.S.A.
137 H4 Humboldt Saskatchewan Canada
173 G1 Humboldt Argentina
152 A3 Humboldt Bay b. California U.S.A.
154 C1 Humboldt Lake l. Nevada U.S.A.
6 □2 Humboldt, Mt mt. New Caledonia Pacific Ocean
154 C1 Humboldt Range mts Nevada U.S.A.
154 D2 Humbolt Salt Marsh marsh Nevada U.S.A.
15 F5 Humeburn Queensland Australia
173 G4 Humeda plain Argentina
39 D4 Hūmedān Iran
33 F4 Hu Men chan. China
79 L3 Humenné Slovakia
13 F3 Hume Res. resr New South Wales Australia
87 E5 Humes-Jorquenay France
55 E4 Humlebæk Denmark
55 A3 Humlum Denmark
59 G2 Hummelsta Sweden
9 C6 Hummock h. New Zealand
81 G4 Hum na Sutli Croatia
172 A3 Humos, C. headland Chile
125 B7 Humpata Angola
154 C3 Humphreys, Mt mt. California U.S.A.
155 G4 Humphreys Peak summit Arizona U.S.A.
78 E2 Humpolec Czech Rep.
54 C1 Humppila Finland
65 F2 Humshaugh England U.K.
31 J4 Hun r. China
31 H4 Hun r. China
118 C2 Hūn Libya
56 L6 Húnaflói b. Iceland
33 E3 Hunan div. China
126 D2 Ḩunayshīyah Yemen
31 J4 Hunchun r. China
73 H4 Hundeluft Germany
75 H4 Hunderdorf Germany
55 D4 Hundested Denmark
62 B3 Hundleton Wales U.K.
136 E4 100 Mile House B.C. Canada
79 M5 Hunedoara div. Romania
112 D2 Hunedoara Romania
74 E2 Hünfeld Germany
6 □3 Hunga i. Tonga
6 □5 Hunga Ha'apai i. Tonga
48 G4 Hungary country Europe
6 □5 Hunga Tonga i. Tonga
74 D2 Hungen Germany
63 E3 Hungerford England U.K.
15 F6 Hungerford Queensland Australia
31 H5 Hŭngnam North Korea
152 D1 Hungry Horse Res. resr Montana U.S.A.
27 □ Hung Shui Kiu Hong Kong
24 D2 Hưng Yên Vietnam
90 F1 Huningue France
31 H4 Hunjiang China
65 H3 Hunmanby England U.K.
59 F2 Hunn l. Sweden
58 D2 Hunnebostrand Sweden
68 E1 Hunsingo reg. Netherlands
87 G4 Hunspach France
63 G2 Hunstanton England U.K.
38 B3 Hunsur India
155 H4 Hunt Arizona U.S.A.
140 E2 Hunta Ontario Canada
72 D2 Hunte r. Germany
13 G3 Hunter r. New South Wales Australia
9 B6 Hunter r. New Zealand
147 F3 Hunter New York U.S.A.
136 D4 Hunter I. i. B.C. Canada
176 G7 Hunter I. i. New Caledonia Pacific Ocean
13 F5 Hunter I. i. Tasmania Australia
24 A3 Hunter's Bay b. Myanmar
9 C6 Hunters Hills, The h. New Zealand
13 F5 Hunters Is is Tasmania Australia
63 F2 Huntingdon England U.K.
146 E4 Huntingdon Pennsylvania U.S.A.
141 H4 Huntingdon Québec Canada
148 E5 Huntington Indiana U.S.A.
155 G2 Huntington Utah U.S.A.
146 B5 Huntington W. Virginia U.S.A.
154 D5 Huntington Beach California U.S.A.
131 G1 Huntleigh South Africa
66 F3 Huntly Scotland U.K.
8 E2 Huntly New Zealand
145 C5 Huntsville Alabama U.S.A.
141 F4 Huntsville Ontario Canada
151 E6 Huntsville Texas U.S.A.
30 E5 Hunyuan China
47 H5 Hunza reg. Jammu and Kashmir
36 C1 Hunza Pakistan

68 E1 **Hunze r.** Netherlands
47 K4 **Huocheng** China
33 F1 **Huojia** China
31 G3 **Huolin r.** China
31 H2 **Huolongmen** China
6 □2 **Huon i.** *New Caledonia* Pacific Ocean
24 D3 **Hương Khê** Vietnam
24 D3 **Hương Thuy** Vietnam
6 □1 **Huon Peninsula pen.** P.N.G.
13 F5 **Huonville** *Tasmania* Australia
33 G1 **Huoqiu** China
33 G2 **Huo Shan mt.** China
33 G2 **Huoshan** China
33 H4 **Huo-shao Tao i.** Taiwan
30 D5 **Huo Xian** China
53 F2 **Hupalivka** Ukraine
Hupeh *see* **Hubei**
43 D1 **Hupnik r.** Turkey
39 D3 **Hūr** Iran
79 H4 **Hurbanovo** Slovakia
58 D1 **Hurdalssjøen l.** Norway
140 E4 **Hurd, Cape headland** *Ontario* Canada
10 □3 **Hurd Pt pt** *Macquarie I.* Pacific Ocean
30 C4 **Hure Jadgai** China
30 B2 **Hüremt** Mongolia
89 H3 **Hurepoix reg.** France
31 G4 **Hure Qi** China
119 F2 **Hurghada** Egypt
92 E2 **Huriel** France
53 E2 **Hurivka** Ukraine
140 A2 **Hurkett** *Ontario* Canada
67 C4 **Hurler's Cross** Rep. of Ireland
148 B2 **Hurley** *Wisconsin* U.S.A.
150 D2 **Huron** *S. Dakota* U.S.A.
148 C2 **Huron Bay b.** *Michigan* U.S.A.
149 F3 **Huron, Lake l.** Canada/U.S.A.
148 D2 **Huron Mts h.** *Michigan* U.S.A.
155 F3 **Hurricane** *Utah* U.S.A.
63 E3 **Hursley** *England* U.K.
63 G3 **Hurst Green** *England* U.K.
63 F4 **Hurstpierpoint** *England* U.K.
172 B1 **Hurtado r.** Chile
172 B1 **Hurtado** Chile
74 B2 **Hürth** Germany
22 C1 **Hurung, G. mt.** Indonesia
129 D2 **Hurungwe Safari Area res.** Zimbabwe
9 D5 **Hurunui r.** New Zealand
55 A3 **Hurup** Denmark
36 B3 **Husain Nika** Pakistan
53 G3 **Husarka** Ukraine
56 L6 **Húsavík** *Norðurland eystra* Iceland
56 M6 **Húsavík** *Vestfirðir* Iceland
55 □1 **Húsavík** Faeroes
63 E2 **Husbands Bosworth** *England* U.K.
72 E1 **Husby** Germany
59 G1 **Husby** Sweden
112 G1 **Huşi** Romania
78 C2 **Husinec** Czech Rep.
59 F3 **Huskvarna** Sweden
134 C3 **Huslia** *Alaska* U.S.A.
43 C3 **Husn** Jordan
126 E1 **Ḥusn Āl 'Abr** Yemen
58 A2 **Husnes** Norway
58 A1 **Husøy i.** Norway
37 F4 **Hussainabad** India
78 F3 **Hustopeče** Czech Rep.
72 E1 **Husum** Germany
56 E3 **Husum** Sweden
53 B2 **Husyatyn** Ukraine
77 L3 **Huszlew** Poland
30 B2 **Hutag** Mongolia
39 D3 **Hūtak** Iran
150 D4 **Hutchinson** *Kansas* U.S.A.
130 D5 **Hutchinson** South Africa
155 G4 **Hutch Mtn mt.** *Arizona* U.S.A.
126 D1 **Ḥūth** Yemen
24 B3 **Huthi** Myanmar
31 K3 **Hutou** China
137 N2 **Hut Point pt** *N.W.T.* Canada
80 E3 **Hüttau** Austria
81 F4 **Hüttenberg** Austria
75 J4 **Hutthurm** Germany
80 A2 **Hüttisheim** Germany
74 F4 **Hüttlingen** Germany
15 G5 **Hutton, Mt h.** *Queensland* Australia
65 G3 **Hutton Rudby** *England* U.K.
146 D5 **Huttonsville** *W. Virginia* U.S.A.
80 E3 **Hüttschlag** Austria
82 C1 **Huttwil** Switzerland
47 L4 **Hutubi** China
30 E5 **Hutuo r.** China
130 A2 **Hutup watercourse** Namibia
53 F1 **Huty** Ukraine
35 D10 **Huvadu Atoll atoll** Maldives
32 E1 **Hu Xian** China
9 B6 **Huxley, Mt mt.** New Zealand
69 D4 **Huy div.** Belgium
69 D4 **Huy** Belgium
31 G2 **Huzhong** China
33 H2 **Huzhou** China
30 B5 **Huzhu** China
55 □1 **Hvalba** Faeroes
58 D2 **Hvaler i.** Norway
55 D4 **Hvalsø** Denmark
56 L6 **Hvammsfjörður b.** Iceland
56 M7 **Hvannadalshnúkur mt.** Iceland
55 □1 **Hvannasund** Faeroes
104 F4 **Hvar i.** Croatia
109 J1 **Hvar** Croatia
51 E6 **Hvardiys'ke** Ukraine
104 F4 **Hvarski Kanal chan.** Croatia
56 L6 **Hveragerði** Iceland
55 A3 **Hvidbjerg** Denmark
55 A3 **Hvide Sande** Denmark
56 L6 **Hvíta r.** Iceland
58 C2 **Hvittingfoss** Norway
53 A2 **Hvizdets'** Ukraine
55 B3 **Hvorslev** Denmark
53 E1 **Hvyntove** Ukraine
128 D2 **Hwange** Zimbabwe
128 D2 **Hwange National Park nat. park** Zimbabwe
129 E2 **Hwedza** Zimbabwe
Hwlffordd *see* **Haverfordwest**
29 □2 **Hyakuna** Japan
147 H4 **Hyannis** *Massachusetts* U.S.A.
150 C3 **Hyannis** *Nebraska* U.S.A.
26 F2 **Hyargas Nuur salt lake** Mongolia
136 C3 **Hydaburg** *Alaska* U.S.A.
9 C6 **Hyde** New Zealand
146 B6 **Hyden** *Kentucky* U.S.A.
17 B7 **Hyden** *Western Australia* Australia
147 G4 **Hyde Park** *New York* U.S.A.
155 F5 **Hyder** *Arizona* U.S.A.
38 B2 **Hyderabad** India
36 B4 **Hyderabad** Pakistan
91 E5 **Hyères** France
91 E **Hyères, Îles d' is** France
54 E4 **Hyermanavichy** Belarus
31 J4 **Hyesan** North Korea
136 D2 **Hyland r.** *Yukon Terr.* Canada
58 B2 **Hylestad** Norway
55 D5 **Hyllekrog i.** Denmark
58 A1 **Hyllestad** Norway
59 E3 **Hyltebruk** Sweden
87 F4 **Hymont** France
28 E6 **Hyōgo div.** Japan
28 E6 **Hyōnosen mt.** Japan
56 H2 **Hyrynsalmi** Finland
114 A2 **Hysgjokaj** Albania
136 F3 **Hythe** *Alberta* Canada
63 E4 **Hythe** *England* U.K.
63 H3 **Hythe** *England* U.K.
59 G1 **Hyttön** Sweden
28 C7 **Hyūga** Japan
57 G3 **Hyvinkää** Finland

I

168 D4 **Iacanga** Brazil
112 E1 **Iacobeni** Romania
168 C4 **Iacri** Brazil
166 D3 **Iaçu** Brazil
129 H3 **Iakora** Madagascar
112 F2 **Ialomiţa r.** Romania
53 C3 **Ialoveni** Moldova
112 F2 **Ianca** Romania
169 G3 **Iapu** Brazil
67 B3 **Iar Connaught reg.** Rep. of Ireland
53 C3 **Iargara** Moldova
112 F1 **Iaşi** Romania
23 A3 **Iba** Philippines
123 E5 **Ibadan** Nigeria
162 B3 **Ibagué** Colombia
168 C5 **Ibaiti** Brazil
155 F1 **Ibapah** *Utah* U.S.A.
112 C3 **Ibar r.** Yugoslavia
28 D6 **Ibara** Japan
29 H5 **Ibaraki div.** Japan
173 K1 **Ibare** Brazil
162 B3 **Ibarra** Ecuador
170 E2 **Ibarreta** Argentina
168 E4 **Ibaté** Brazil
126 D2 **Ibb** Yemen
124 E2 **Ibba watercourse** Sudan
124 E3 **Ibba** Sudan
72 C3 **Ibbenbüren** Germany
123 E3 **Ibdeqqene watercourse** Mali
170 E2 **Iberá, L. l.** Argentina
162 C5 **Iberia** Peru
123 F4 **Ibeto** Nigeria
123 F5 **Ibi** Nigeria
103 C6 **Ibi** Spain
169 E3 **Ibiá** Brazil
169 F2 **Ibiaí** Brazil
98 D2 **Ibias r.** Spain
169 J1 **Ibicaraí** Brazil
167 A6 **Ibicuí r.** Brazil
169 J1 **Ibicuí** Brazil
173 K1 **Ibicuí da Cruz r.** Brazil
91 C4 **Ibie r.** France
166 E2 **Ibimirim** Brazil
168 C5 **Ibiporã** Brazil
169 H3 **Ibiraçu** Brazil
167 C6 **Ibirama** Brazil
169 H2 **Ibiranhém** Brazil
167 A6 **Ibirapuitã** Brazil
166 D3 **Ibitiara** Brazil
168 D4 **Ibitinga** Brazil
Ibiza i. *see* **Eivissa**
Ibiza *see* **Eivissa**
110 D5 **Iblei, Monti mts** *Sicilia* Italy
124 E4 **Ibonga** Zaire
166 D3 **Ibotirama** Brazil
124 B4 **Iboundji, Mont mt.** Gabon
41 J5 **Ibrā'** Oman
52 H2 **Ibresi** Rus. Fed.
41 J5 **'Ibrī** Oman
43 A5 **Ibshawāi** Egypt
63 E3 **Ibstock** *England* U.K.
29 □2 **Ibu** Japan
23 B1 **Ibuhos i.** Philippines
28 C8 **Ibusuki** Japan
162 D4 **Içá r.** Brazil
164 A2 **Ica** Peru
159 □3 **Icacos Pt pt** *Trinidad* Trinidad and Tobago
162 D3 **Içana r.** Brazil
162 D3 **Içana** Brazil
168 B5 **Icaraíma** Brazil
162 D1 **Icatu** Brazil
155 E3 **Iceberg Canyon** *Nevada* U.S.A.
43 B1 **İçel div.** Turkey
42 C2 **İçel** Turkey
48 C2 **Iceland country** Europe
168 D4 **Icem** Brazil
38 A2 **Ichalkaranji** India
52 G2 **Ichalki** Rus. Fed.
38 D2 **Ichchapuram** India
74 F4 **Ichenhausen** Germany
28 C7 **Ichifusa-yama mt.** Japan
29 H6 **Ichihara** Japan
164 D3 **Ichilo r.** Bolivia
29 F6 **Ichinomiya** Japan
29 H4 **Ichinoseki** Japan
53 E1 **Ichnya** Ukraine
31 H5 **Ich'ŏn** South Korea
69 B3 **Ichtegem** Belgium
75 F2 **Ichtershausen** Germany
80 C3 **Icking** Germany
63 G4 **Icklesham** *England* U.K.
63 G2 **Icklingham** *England* U.K.
113 G6 **İçmeler** Turkey
166 E2 **Icó** Brazil
97 □ **Icod de Los Vinos** *Canary Is* Spain
169 H4 **Iconha** Brazil
136 B3 **Icy Pt pt** *Alaska* U.S.A.
136 B3 **Icy Strait chan.** *Alaska* U.S.A.
123 F3 **Idabdaba well** Niger
151 E5 **Idabel** *Oklahoma* U.S.A.
123 F5 **Idah** Nigeria
152 D2 **Idaho div.** U.S.A.
152 D3 **Idaho City** *Idaho* U.S.A.
152 D3 **Idaho Falls** *Idaho* U.S.A.
43 C2 **Idaidet Ghazir** Lebanon
43 B2 **Idalion** Cyprus
9 C6 **Ida, Mt mt.** New Zealand
98 C5 **Idanha-a-Nova** Portugal
74 C3 **Idar-Oberstein** Germany
75 F5 **Idarwald forest** Germany
123 G4 **Iday well** Niger
119 E5 **Idd el Asoda well** Sudan
124 D1 **Idd el Chanam** Sudan
58 D2 **Idefjorden inlet** Norway/Sweden
121 F4 **Idelès** Algeria
30 A2 **Ider** Mongolia
30 A2 **Ideriyn Gol r.** Mongolia
119 F3 **Idfu** Egypt
118 B2 **Idhān Awbārī desert** Libya
118 B3 **Idhan Murzūq desert** Libya
115 F7 **Idi mts** Greece
107 F4 **Idice r.** Italy
125 C4 **Idiofa** Zaire
134 C3 **Iditarod** *Alaska* U.S.A.
56 F1 **Idivuoma** Sweden
43 D2 **Idlib div.** Syria
42 D3 **Idlib** Syria
52 G4 **Idolga r.** Rus. Fed.
57 D3 **Idre** Sweden
81 F4 **Idrija** Slovenia
81 E4 **Idrijca r.** Slovenia
47 M2 **Idrinskoye** Rus. Fed.
54 F3 **Idritsa** Rus. Fed.
106 E3 **Idro** Italy
81 F3 **Idro, Lago d' l.** Italy
74 D2 **Idstein** Germany
131 G6 **Idutywa** South Africa
54 D3 **Iecava** Latvia
29 □2 **Ie-jima i.** Japan
168 C5 **Iepê** Brazil
69 A4 **Ieper div.** Belgium
69 A4 **Ieper** Belgium
115 G7 **Ierapetra** Greece
112 E1 **Iermut** Romania
29 □2 **Ie-suido str.** Japan
127 C6 **Ifakara** Tanzania
43 C5 **'Ifāl, W. watercourse** Saudi Arabia
129 H3 **Ifanadiana** Madagascar
123 E5 **Ife** Nigeria
123 F3 **Iferouâne** Niger
121 E3 **Ifetesene mt.** Algeria
83 C1 **Iffeldorf** Germany
87 H4 **Iffezheim** Germany
15 E3 **Iffley** *Queensland* Australia
56 G1 **Ifjord** Norway
123 F5 **Ifon** Nigeria
120 C2 **Ifrane** Morocco
89 E2 **Ifs** France
81 F5 **Ig** Slovenia
29 F6 **Iga** Japan
123 F4 **Igabi** Nigeria
127 B6 **Igalula** Tanzania
20 F6 **Igan** Malaysia
127 B4 **Iganga** Uganda
166 F2 **Igaraçu** Brazil
168 E4 **Igarapava** Brazil
167 D5 **Igarapé** Brazil
166 C1 **Igarapé Açu** Brazil
166 D1 **Igarapé Grande** Brazil
44 K3 **Igarka** Rus. Fed.
173 F5 **Igarzabal** Argentina
38 A2 **Igatpuri** India
123 E5 **Igbeti** Nigeria
42 F2 **Iğdır** Turkey
75 J4 **Iggensbach** Germany
56 E3 **Iggesund** Sweden
59 G1 **Iggön i.** Sweden
83 E2 **Igis** Switzerland
108 A5 **Iglesias** *Sardegna* Italy
120 D2 **Igli** Algeria
80 B2 **Igling** Germany
135 K3 **Igloolik** *N.W.T.* Canada
42 C4 **'Igma, Gebel el mts** Egypt
43 B5 **'Igma, Gebel el plat.** Egypt
138 B4 **Ignace** *Ontario* Canada
156 D2 **Ignacio Zaragosa** Mexico
54 E4 **Ignalina** Lithuania
31 G1 **Ignashino** Rus. Fed.
42 B1 **İğneada** Turkey
112 G4 **İğneada Burnu pt** Turkey
25 A5 **Ignoitijala** *Andaman and Nicobar Is* India
90 C1 **Ignon r.** France
127 B6 **Igoma** Tanzania
127 B5 **Igombe r.** Tanzania
90 C1 **Igornay** France
114 B3 **Igoumenitsa** Greece
98 B2 **Igrexario** Spain
44 H3 **Igrim** Rus. Fed.
167 B6 **Iguaçu r.** Brazil
Iguaçu Falls rapids *see* **Cataratas del Iguazú**
168 B6 **Iguaçu, Parque Nacional do nat. park** Argentina
169 H1 **Iguaí** Brazil
157 F5 **Iguala** Mexico
102 E3 **Igualada** Spain
168 E6 **Iguape** Brazil
166 D1 **Iguará r.** Brazil
169 F4 **Iguatama** Brazil
166 A5 **Iguatemi r.** Brazil
168 A5 **Iguatemi** Brazil
166 E2 **Iguatu** Brazil
124 A4 **Iguéla** Gabon
98 D2 **Igueña** Spain
127 B5 **Igunga** Tanzania
129 H1 **Iharaña** Madagascar
78 G5 **Iharosberény** Hungary
30 C4 **Ihbulag** Mongolia
121 F3 **Iherir** Algeria
30 C3 **Ihhayrhan** Mongolia
123 F5 **Ihiala** Nigeria
43 A5 **Ihnâsya el Madîna** Egypt
93 A5 **Iholdy** France
129 H3 **Ihosy** Madagascar
74 C4 **Ihringen** Germany
30 C2 **Ihsuuj** Mongolia
31 G4 **Ih Tal** China
29 F6 **Iida** Japan
29 G5 **Iide-san mt.** Japan
169 F5 **Ilhabela** Brazil
56 H1 **Iijärvi l.** Finland
56 G2 **Iijoki r.** Finland
56 G3 **Iisalmi** Finland
54 E1 **Iitti** Finland
29 G5 **Iiyama** Japan
28 C7 **Iizuka** Japan
123 E5 **Ijebu-Ode** Nigeria
68 D1 **IJlst** Netherlands
68 C2 **IJmuiden** Netherlands
120 B5 **Ijnâouene well** Mauritania
68 D2 **IJssel r.** Netherlands
68 D2 **IJsselmeer l.** Netherlands
68 D2 **IJsselmuiden** Netherlands
68 D2 **IJsselstein** Netherlands
167 B6 **Ijuí r.** Brazil
167 B6 **Ijuí** Brazil
69 B3 **IJzendijke** Netherlands
69 A3 **Ijzer r.** Belgium
57 F3 **Ikaalinen** Finland
131 F2 **Ikageleng** South Africa
131 F3 **Ikageng** South Africa
129 H2 **Ikahavo h.** Madagascar
129 H3 **Ikalamavony** Madagascar
124 D4 **Ikali** Zaire
9 C5 **Ikamatua** New Zealand
125 D4 **Ikanda-Nord** Zaire
123 F5 **Ikare** Nigeria
125 C4 **Ikari** Zaire
113 F6 **Ikaria i.** Greece
55 B3 **Ikast** Denmark
28 D6 **Ikeda** Japan
28 J2 **Ikeda** Japan
29 □2 **Ikei-jima i.** Japan
123 E5 **Ikeja** Nigeria
124 D4 **Ikela** Zaire
124 C3 **Ikelemba r.** Zaire
78 F4 **Ikervár** Hungary
112 D3 **Ikhtiman** Bulgaria
130 E4 **Ikhutseng** South Africa
28 B7 **Iki i.** Japan
51 H6 **Iki-Burul** Rus. Fed.
127 B5 **Ikimba, Lake l.** Tanzania
123 E5 **Ikire** Nigeria
28 B7 **Iki-suidō chan.** Japan
54 D3 **Ikla** Estonia
123 F5 **Ikom** Nigeria
129 H3 **Ikongo** Madagascar
129 H2 **Ikopa r.** Madagascar
123 E5 **Ikorodu** Nigeria
125 E4 **Ikosi** Zaire
123 F5 **Ikot Ekpene** Nigeria
51 H6 **Ikryanoye** Rus. Fed.
127 B6 **Ikungu** Tanzania
28 E6 **Ikuno** Japan
53 A1 **Ikva r.** Ukraine
123 E5 **Ila** Nigeria
23 B2 **Ilagan** Philippines
126 C4 **Ilaisamis** Kenya
39 A2 **Īlām div.** Iran
42 F3 **Īlām** Iran
37 F4 **Ilam** Nepal
33 H3 **I-lan** Taiwan
129 H3 **Ilanana r.** Madagascar
73 K3 **Iłanka r.** Poland
83 E2 **Ilanz** Switzerland
53 F2 **Ilarionove** Ukraine
79 H3 **Ilava** Slovakia
77 H2 **Iława** Poland
39 D3 **Ilazārān, Kūh-e mt.** Iran
62 D4 **Ilchester** *England* U.K.
137 H3 **Île-à-la-Crosse** *Saskatchewan* Canada
137 H3 **Île-à-la-Crosse, Lac l.** *Saskatchewan* Canada
125 D4 **Ilebo** Zaire
86 B4 **Île-de-France div.** France
127 B6 **Ileje** Tanzania
42 E2 **Ilek r.** Rus. Fed.
46 D2 **Ilek** Rus. Fed.
126 C4 **Ileret** Kenya
123 E5 **Ilesa** Nigeria
46 C1 **Ilet' r.** Rus. Fed.
73 F4 **Ilfeld** Germany
63 G3 **Ilford** *England* U.K.
137 K3 **Ilford** *Manitoba* Canada
62 B3 **Ilfracombe** *England* U.K.
15 F4 **Ilfracombe** *Queensland* Australia
42 C1 **Ilgaz** Turkey
42 B2 **Ilgın** Turkey
163 D4 **Ilha Grande** Brazil
169 F5 **Ilha Grande, Baia da b.** Brazil
98 B4 **Ílhavo** Portugal
169 J1 **Ilhéus** Brazil
122 □ **Ilhéus Secos ou do Rombo i.** Cape Verde
115 C5 **Ilia div.** Greece
79 M6 **Ilia** Romania
134 C4 **Iliamna Lake l.** *Alaska* U.S.A.
42 D2 **İliç** Turkey
47 G4 **Il'ich** Kazakhstan
Il'ichevsk *see* **Şărur**
23 C4 **Iligan** Philippines
23 C4 **Iligan Bay b.** Philippines
104 G4 **Ilijaš** Bos.-Herz.
52 G1 **Il'ino-Zaborskoye** Rus. Fed.
30 E2 **Il'inskiy** Rus. Fed.
52 C1 **Il'inskoye** Rus. Fed.
52 D1 **Il'inskoye** Rus. Fed.
52 B3 **Il'inskoye** Rus. Fed.
52 D1 **Il'inskoye-Khovanskoye** Rus. Fed.
147 F3 **Ilion** *New York* U.S.A.
107 J3 **Ilirska Bistrica** Slovenia
38 B3 **Ilkal** India
63 E2 **Ilkeston** *England* U.K.
52 E2 **Il'kino** Rus. Fed.
65 G4 **Ilkley** *England* U.K.
111 □ **Il-Kullana pt** Malta
87 G4 **Ill r.** France
23 B5 **Illana Bay b.** Philippines
172 B1 **Illapel r.** Chile
172 B1 **Illapel** Chile
101 H4 **Illar** Spain
83 G3 **Illasi r.** Italy
12 C1 **Illbillee, Mt h.** *S. Australia* Australia
88 D3 **Ille r.** France
88 D3 **Ille-et-Vilaine div.** France
123 F4 **Illéla** Niger
74 F4 **Iller r.** Germany
74 F4 **Illertissen** Germany
99 G4 **Illescas** Spain
173 K2 **Illescas** Uruguay
93 E6 **Ille-sur-Têt** France
53 D3 **Illichivs'k** Ukraine
89 G3 **Illiers-Combray** France
53 D3 **Illinka** Ukraine
148 C5 **Illinois div.** U.S.A.
148 C5 **Illinois r.** *Illinois* U.S.A.
148 B5 **Illinois and Mississippi Canal canal** *Illinois* U.S.A.
53 C2 **Illintsi** Ukraine
121 F3 **Illizi** Algeria
87 G4 **Illkirch-Graffenstaden** France
83 E1 **Illmensee** Germany
81 H3 **Illmitz** Austria
101 G3 **Illora** Spain
102 B3 **Illueca** Spain
90 F1 **Illzach** France
73 G5 **Ilm r.** Germany
73 F2 **Ilmenau r.** Germany
75 F2 **Ilmenau** Germany
50 D3 **Il'men', Ozero l.** Rus. Fed.
62 D4 **Ilminster** *England* U.K.
75 G4 **Ilmmünster** Germany
164 B3 **Ilo** Peru
23 B4 **Iloc i.** Philippines
172 A3 **Iloca** Chile
23 B4 **Iloilo** Philippines
57 H3 **Ilomantsi** Finland
123 E5 **Ilorin** Nigeria
51 F6 **Ilovays'k** Ukraine
107 J4 **Ilovik i.** Croatia
51 H5 **Ilovlya r.** Rus. Fed.
51 G5 **Ilovlya** Rus. Fed.
76 D4 **Iłowa** Poland
77 J2 **Iłowo Osada** Poland
45 S3 **Il'pyrskiy** Rus. Fed.
111 □ **Il Qala Ta San Blas b.** Malta
72 F3 **Ilsede** Germany
73 F4 **Ilsenburg** Germany
74 E3 **Ilshofen** Germany
51 F6 **Il'skiy** Rus. Fed.
54 E4 **Ilūkste** Latvia
135 N3 **Ilulissat** Greenland
123 F5 **Ilushi** Nigeria
54 E4 **Il'ya** Belarus
46 E4 **Il'yaly** Turkmenistan
52 F1 **Il'ya-Vysokovo** Rus. Fed.
75 J4 **Ilz r.** Germany
81 G3 **Ilz** Austria
77 K4 **Iłża** Poland
28 D6 **Imabari** Japan
163 F3 **Imabú r.** Brazil
29 G5 **Imaichi** Japan
29 F6 **Imajō** Japan
129 F1 **Imala** Mozambique
56 J2 **Imandra** Rus. Fed.
44 E3 **Imandra, Ozero l.** Rus. Fed.
129 H3 **Imanombo** Madagascar
170 E2 **Iman, Sa del h.** Argentina
28 B7 **Imari** Japan
167 C6 **Imaruí** Brazil
164 B3 **Imata** Peru
114 D2 **Imathia div.** Greece
57 H3 **Imatra** Finland
54 D2 **Imavere** Estonia
29 F6 **Imazu** Japan
167 C6 **Imbituba** Brazil
168 C6 **Imbituva** Brazil
46 F5 **im. Chapayeva** Turkmenistan
imeni 26 Bakinskikh Komissarov *see* **Bakı Komissarı, 26**
50 G3 **Imeni Babushkina** Rus. Fed.
53 F1 **Imeni Karla Libknekhta** Rus. Fed.
50 H3 **Imeni M.I. Kalinina** Rus. Fed.
52 G2 **Imeni Stepana Razina** Rus. Fed.
52 E2 **Imeni Vorovskogo** Rus. Fed.
53 F2 **Imeny Lenina, Ozero l.** Ukraine
126 D3 **Īmī** Ethiopia
120 C2 **Imi-n-Tanoute** Morocco
120 B3 **Imirikliy Labyad reg.** *Western Sahara*
Imishli *see* **İmişli**
42 G2 **İmişli** Azerbaijan
31 H6 **Imja Do i.** South Korea
120 A4 **Imlili** *Western Sahara*
83 D1 **Immendingen** Germany
83 E1 **Immenstaad am Bodensee** Germany
74 F5 **Immenstadt im Allgäu** Germany
65 H4 **Immingham** *England* U.K.
123 F5 **Imo div.** Nigeria
123 F5 **Imo r.** Nigeria
107 F4 **Imola** Italy
104 F4 **Imotski** Croatia
131 G4 **Impendle** South Africa
166 C2 **Imperatriz** Brazil
106 B5 **Imperia div.** *Liguria* Italy
106 C5 **Imperia** Italy
172 A5 **Imperial r.** Chile
150 C3 **Imperial** *Nebraska* U.S.A.
164 A2 **Imperial** Peru
154 D5 **Imperial Beach** *California* U.S.A.
155 E5 **Imperial Valley v.** *California* U.S.A.
16 B3 **Imperieuse Reef** *Western Australia* Australia
124 C3 **Impfondo** Congo
37 H4 **Imphal** India
90 B2 **Imphy** France
107 F5 **Impruneta** Italy
113 G4 **İmralı Adası i.** Turkey
113 E4 **İmroz** Turkey
80 B3 **Imst div.** Austria
80 B3 **Imst** Austria
42 D3 **Imtān** Syria
156 C2 **Imuris** Mexico
23 A4 **Imuruan Bay b.** Philippines
77 N3 **Imyanin** Belarus
52 G2 **Imza r.** Rus. Fed.
96 E5 **Imzouren** Morocco
76 C2 **Ina r.** Poland
29 F6 **Ina** Japan
123 E3 **I-n-Âbâlene well** Mali
128 □3 **Inaccessible I. i.** *Tristan da Cunha* Atlantic Ocean
168 C6 **Inácio Martins** Brazil
121 F4 **In Afaleleh well** Algeria
29 G5 **Ina-gawa r.** Japan
166 B2 **Inajá r.** Brazil
166 E2 **Inajá** Brazil
123 D3 **I-n-Akhmed well** Mali
122 D2 **I-n-Alchi well** Mali
123 E3 **I-n-Alchig well** Mali
122 D3 **I-n-Aleï well** Mali
120 C5 **I-n-'Amar well** Mauritania
164 B2 **Inambari r.** Peru
164 C2 **Inambari** Peru
121 F3 **In Aménas** Algeria
121 F4 **In Amguel** Algeria
131 H4 **Inanda** South Africa
9 C4 **Inangahua Junction** New Zealand
21 K7 **Inanwatan** Indonesia
164 C2 **Iñapari** Peru
23 □2 **Inarajan** *Guam* Pacific Ocean
123 E3 **I-n-Areï well** Mali
56 G1 **Inari** Finland
56 G1 **Inarijärvi l.** Finland
56 G1 **Inarijoki r.** Finland
123 E3 **I-n-Atankarer well** Mali
162 D5 **Inauini r.** Brazil
29 H5 **Inawashiro-ko l.** Japan
123 F2 **In-Azaoua well** Niger
118 B2 **In Azar well** Libya
29 F6 **Inazawa** Japan
123 E3 **I-n-Azerraf well** Mali
121 E3 **In Belbel** Algeria
103 F5 **Inca** Spain
113 F4 **İnce Burnu pt** Turkey
42 C1 **İnce Burun headland** Turkey
42 C2 **Incekum Burun pt** Turkey
67 B4 **Inch** *Kerry* Rep. of Ireland
67 E4 **Inch** *Wicklow* Rep. of Ireland
66 C2 **Inchard, Loch b.** *Scotland* U.K.
89 G1 **Incheville** France
126 C4 **Inch'īni Terara mt.** Ethiopia
120 A5 **Inchiri div.** Mauritania
64 A2 **Inch Island i.** Rep. of Ireland
66 E4 **Inchkeith i.** *Scotland* U.K.
31 H5 **Inch'ŏn** South Korea
99 G2 **Incinillas** Spain
107 F5 **Incisa in Val d'Arno** Italy
131 J2 **Incomati r.** Mozambique
69 C4 **Incourt** Belgium
66 B5 **Indaal, Loch inlet** *Scotland* U.K.
122 D2 **I-n-Dagouber well** Mali
169 F3 **Indaiá r.** Brazil
168 B3 **Indaiá Grande r.** Brazil
168 E5 **Indaiatuba** Brazil
57 E3 **Indalsälven r.** Sweden
58 A1 **Indalstø** Norway
126 C2 **Inda Silasē** Ethiopia
24 B2 **Indaw** Myanmar
24 B1 **Indawgyi, L. l.** Myanmar
156 D3 **Indé** Mexico
154 C3 **Independence** *California* U.S.A.
148 B4 **Independence** *Iowa* U.S.A.
151 E4 **Independence** *Kansas* U.S.A.
148 A2 **Independence** *Minnesota* U.S.A.
150 E4 **Independence** *Missouri* U.S.A.
146 C6 **Independence** *Virginia* U.S.A.
148 B3 **Independence** *Wisconsin* U.S.A.
135 P1 **Independence Fj. inlet** Greenland
152 C3 **Independence Mts mountain range** *Nevada* U.S.A.
164 C3 **Independencia** Bolivia
164 A2 **Independencia, B. de b.** Peru
112 F2 **Independenţa** *Călăraşi* Romania
112 G3 **Independenţa** *Constanţa* Romania
112 F2 **Independenţa** *Galaţi* Romania
126 C3 **Inderacha** Ethiopia
46 D3 **Inderborskiy** Kazakhstan
46 D3 **Inder, Oz. salt lake** Kazakhstan
38 B2 **Indi** India
18 J7 **India country** Asia
148 D2 **Indian r.** *Michigan* U.S.A.
148 D5 **Indiana div.** U.S.A.
146 D4 **Indiana** *Pennsylvania* U.S.A.
148 D5 **Indiana Dunes National Lakeshore res.** *Indiana* U.S.A.
175 O7 **Indian-Antarctic Ridge sea feature** Pacific Ocean
148 D6 **Indianapolis airport** *Indiana* U.S.A.
148 D6 **Indianapolis** *Indiana* U.S.A.
139 J3 **Indian Harbour** *Newfoundland* Canada
148 D3 **Indian Lake l.** *Michigan* U.S.A.
146 B4 **Indian Lake l.** *Ohio* U.S.A.
146 D4 **Indian Lake l.** *Pennsylvania* U.S.A.
147 F3 **Indian Lake** *New York* U.S.A.
150 E3 **Indianola** *Iowa* U.S.A.
151 F5 **Indianola** *Mississippi* U.S.A.
168 E3 **Indianópolis** Brazil
155 F2 **Indian Peak summit** *Utah* U.S.A.
148 E3 **Indian River** *Michigan* U.S.A.
155 E3 **Indian Springs** *Nevada* U.S.A.
155 G4 **Indian Wells** *Arizona* U.S.A.
166 B3 **Indígena Do Xingu, Parque nat. park** Brazil
45 Q2 **Indigirka r.** Rus. Fed.
112 C2 **Inđija** Yugoslavia
136 F2 **Indin Lake l.** *N.W.T.* Canada
154 D5 **Indio** *California* U.S.A.
173 G5 **Indio Rico** Argentina
19 N10 **Indonesia country** Asia
36 C5 **Indore** India
22 B3 **Indramayu** Indonesia
22 B3 **Indramayu, Tg pt** Indonesia
38 C2 **Indravati r.** India
92 D2 **Indre div.** *Centre* France
92 D1 **Indre r.** France
58 A1 **Indre Arna** Norway
89 F4 **Indre-et-Loire div.** France
Indur *see* **Nizamabad**
77 M2 **Indura** Belarus
36 B4 **Indus r.** Pakistan
36 A4 **Indus, Mouths of the river mouth** Pakistan
131 F5 **Indwe r.** South Africa
131 F5 **Indwe** South Africa
121 F4 **In Ebeggi well** Algeria
42 C1 **İnebolu** Turkey
122 D2 **I-n-Échaï well** Mali
42 B1 **İnegöl** Turkey
121 F4 **In Ekker** Algeria
22 E4 **Inerie volcano** Indonesia
79 L5 **Ineu** Romania
146 B6 **Inez** *Kentucky* U.S.A.
121 G4 **In Ezzane well** Algeria
130 C7 **Infanta, Cape headland** South Africa
157 E5 **Infiernillo, L. l.** Mexico
99 E1 **Infiesto** Spain
54 D1 **Ingå** Finland
50 E1 **Inga** Rus. Fed.
24 A3 **Ingabu** Myanmar
123 F3 **Ingal** Niger
148 D3 **Ingalls** *Michigan* U.S.A.
137 J2 **Ingalls Lake l.** *N.W.T.* Canada
154 B2 **Ingalls, Mt mt.** *California* U.S.A.
47 H1 **Ingaly** Rus. Fed.
63 G3 **Ingatestone** *England* U.K.
59 F3 **Ingatorp** Sweden
74 D3 **Ingelheim am Rhein** Germany
69 B4 **Ingelmunster** Belgium
124 C4 **Ingende** Zaire
172 D3 **Ingeniero Balloffet** Argentina
170 D1 **Ingeniero Guillermo Nueva Juárez** Argentina
171 C5 **Ingeniero Jacobacci** Argentina
172 E3 **Ingeniero Luiggi** Argentina
172 C1 **Ingeniero Matías G. Sánchez** Argentina
173 F5 **Ingeniero White** Argentina
97 □ **Ingenio** *Canary Is* Spain
87 G4 **Ingersheim** France
140 E5 **Ingersoll** *Ontario* Canada
30 B2 **Ingettolgoy** Mongolia
15 F3 **Ingham** *Queensland* Australia
65 F3 **Ingleborough h.** *England* U.K.
135 L2 **Inglefield Land reg.** Greenland
65 F3 **Ingleton** *England* U.K.
15 G6 **Inglewood** *Queensland* Australia
13 E4 **Inglewood** *Victoria* Australia
8 E3 **Inglewood** New Zealand
65 F3 **Inglewood Forest forest** *England* U.K.
30 E2 **Ingoda r.** Rus. Fed.
63 G1 **Ingoldmells** *England* U.K.
75 G4 **Ingolstadt** Germany
139 H4 **Ingonish** *Nova Scotia* Canada
37 G4 **Ingrāj Bāzār** India
92 C2 **Ingrandes** France
136 F2 **Ingray Lake l.** *N.W.T.* Canada
164 D4 **Ingre** Bolivia
89 G4 **Ingré** France
179 D5 **Ingrid Christensen Coast coastal area** Antarctica
121 F5 **I-n-Guezzam** Algeria
88 B4 **Inguiniel** France
Inguri r. *see* **Enguri**
51 H7 **Ingushetiya div.** Rus. Fed.
131 J3 **Ingwavuma** South Africa
87 G4 **Ingwiller** France
131 J3 **Inhaca e dos Portugueses, Ilhas da is** Mozambique
131 J3 **Inhaca Peninsula pen.** Mozambique
129 E3 **Inhambane div.** Mozambique
129 F3 **Inhambane** Mozambique
129 F3 **Inhambane, Baia de b.** Mozambique
166 E3 **Inhambupe** Brazil
129 F2 **Inhaminga** Mozambique
169 G3 **Inhapim** Brazil
129 F3 **Inharrime** Mozambique
166 D3 **Inhaúmas** Brazil
169 H1 **Inhobim** Brazil
53 E3 **Inhul r.** Ukraine
53 E3 **Inhulets' r.** Ukraine
53 E3 **Inhulets'** Ukraine
168 D2 **Inhumas** Brazil
103 B5 **Iniesta** Spain
169 F3 **Inimutaba** Brazil
163 G3 **Inini** French Guiana
59 J1 **Iniö** Finland
162 D3 **Inírida r.** Colombia
Inis *see* **Ennis**
Inis Córthaidh *see* **Enniscorthy**
67 A3 **Inishark i.** Rep. of Ireland
67 A3 **Inishbofin i.** Rep. of Ireland
67 C1 **Inishbofin** Rep. of Ireland
67 B3 **Inisheer i.** Rep. of Ireland
67 A2 **Inishkea North i.** Rep. of Ireland
67 A2 **Inishkea South i.** Rep. of Ireland
67 B3 **Inishmaan i.** Rep. of Ireland
67 B3 **Inishmore i.** Rep. of Ireland
67 C2 **Inishmurray i.** Rep. of Ireland
67 D1 **Inishowen pen.** Rep. of Ireland
67 E1 **Inishowen Head headland** Rep. of Ireland
67 A4 **Inishtooskert i.** Rep. of Ireland
67 D1 **Inishtrahull i.** Rep. of Ireland
67 D1 **Inishtrahull Sound chan.** Rep. of Ireland
67 A3 **Inishturk i.** Rep. of Ireland
47 J3 **Injgan Sum** China
126 C2 **Injibara** Ethiopia
15 G5 **Injune** *Queensland* Australia
15 E3 **Inkerman** *Queensland* Australia
39 E1 **Inkylap** Turkmenistan
9 D5 **Inland Kaikoura Range mountain range** New Zealand
24 B2 **Inle, L. l.** Myanmar
80 D2 **Inn r.** Europe
12 E1 **Innamincka** *S. Australia* Australia
56 D2 **Inndyr** Norway
66 E5 **Innerleithen** *Scotland* U.K.
Inner Mongolian Aut. Region div. *see* **Nei Monggol Zizhiqu**
66 C3 **Inner Sound chan.** *Scotland* U.K.
82 D2 **Innertkirchen** Switzerland
80 D4 **Innervillgraten** Austria
15 F3 **Innisfail** *Queensland* Australia
31 J2 **Innokent'yevka** Rus. Fed.
28 D6 **Innoshima** Japan
80 C3 **Innsbruck div.** Austria
80 C3 **Innsbruck** Austria
81 E2 **Innviertel reg.** Austria
67 D3 **Inny r.** Rep. of Ireland
168 C3 **Inocência** Brazil
124 C4 **Inongo** Zaire
122 D3 **I-n-Ouchef well** Mali
79 H3 **Inovec mt.** Slovakia
76 G3 **Inowrocław** Poland
164 C3 **Inquisivi** Bolivia
82 C1 **Ins** Switzerland
121 E3 **In Salah** Algeria
52 G2 **Insar r.** Rus. Fed.
52 G3 **Insar** Rus. Fed.
66 F3 **Insch** *Scotland* U.K.
17 A5 **Inscription, C. c.** *Western Australia* Australia
24 B3 **Insein** Myanmar
76 D2 **Ińsko** Poland
112 G2 **Insula Sacalinul Mare i.** Romania
112 F2 **Însurăţei** Romania
129 D2 **Insuza r.** Zimbabwe
44 H3 **Inta** Rus. Fed.
123 F3 **I-n-Tabakat well** Niger
123 F2 **I-n-Tadéra well** Niger
123 E3 **I-n-Talak well** Mali
123 E3 **I-n-Tebezas** Mali
123 F3 **I-n-Tédéini well** Niger
172 F3 **Intendente Alvear** Argentina
113 F4 **İntepe** Turkey
82 C2 **Interlaken** Switzerland
150 E1 **International Falls** *Minnesota* U.S.A.
25 A4 **Interview I. i.** *Andaman and Nicobar Is* India

156 J6 Jalapa Nicaragua
57 F3 Jalasjärvi Finland
36 D4 Jalaun India
37 G4 Jaldhaka r. Bangladesh
38 B2 Jaldrug India
168 C4 Jales Brazil
36 D4 Jalesar India
37 F5 Jaleshwar India
36 C5 Jalgaon India
36 D5 Jalgaon India
69 D4 Jalhay Belgium
90 B2 Jaligny-sur-Besbre France
123 G5 Jalingo Nigeria
156 D5 Jalisco div. Mexico
36 C2 Jalkot Pakistan
89 E4 Jallais France
38 A2 Jalna India
39 E4 Jālo Iran
102 B3 Jalón r. Spain
36 C4 Jalor India
156 E4 Jalostotitlán Mexico
112 B2 Jalovik Yugoslavia
77 M2 Jałówka Poland
156 E4 Jalpa Mexico
37 G4 Jalpaiguri India
157 F4 Jalpan Mexico
118 D2 Jālū Libya
42 F3 Jalūlā Iraq
118 D2 Jālū Oasis oasis Libya
39 E2 Jām r. Iran
39 E2 Jām reg. Iran
36 D5 Jamai India
133 L8 Jamaica country Caribbean
158 D3 Jamaica Channel chan. Jamaica
39 B2 Jamālābād Iran
37 G4 Jamalpur Bangladesh
37 F4 Jamalpur India
158 □1 Jamanota mt. Aruba Caribbean
163 F5 Jamanxim r. Brazil
165 D1 Jamari r. Brazil
162 A4 Jambeli, Can. de chan. Ecuador
22 A2 Jambi div. Indonesia
22 A2 Jambi Indonesia
15 G5 Jambin Queensland Australia
36 C4 Jambo India
23 A5 Jambongan i. Malaysia
36 C5 Jambusar India
150 D2 James r. N. Dakota U.S.A.
146 D6 James r. Virginia U.S.A.
138 D3 James Bay b. Ontario/Québec Canada
172 F2 James Craik Argentina
171 B6 James, I. i. Chile
135 Q2 Jameson Land reg. Greenland
9 B6 James Pk mt. New Zealand
14 C5 James Ranges mountain range Northern Terr. Australia
179 B2 James Ross I. i. Antarctica
150 D2 Jamestown N. Dakota U.S.A.
146 D3 Jamestown New York U.S.A.
12 D3 Jamestown S. Australia Australia
128 □2 Jamestown St Helena Atlantic Ocean
131 F5 Jamestown South Africa
59 F3 Jämjö Sweden
38 A2 Jamkhandi India
38 A2 Jamkhed India
38 B3 Jammalamadugu India
55 B2 Jammerbugten b. Denmark
55 C4 Jammerland Bugt b. Denmark
36 C2 Jammu India
36 D1 Jammu and Kashmir
36 B5 Jamnagar India
36 D4 Jamni r. India
22 A3 Jampang Kulon Indonesia
41 M4 Jampur Pakistan
57 G3 Jämsä Finland
57 G3 Jämsänkoski Finland
37 F5 Jamshedpur India
123 G5 Jamtari Nigeria
56 D3 Jämtland div. Sweden
37 F4 Jamui India
37 G4 Jamuna r. Bangladesh
126 D4 Janaale Somalia
37 F4 Janakpur Nepal
169 G1 Janaúba Brazil
163 G3 Janaucú, Ilha i. Brazil
36 C2 Jand Pakistan
168 C2 Jandaia Brazil
168 C5 Jandaia do Sul Brazil
39 C2 Jandaq Iran
97 □ Jandía, Pta de pt Canary Is Spain
36 B2 Jandola Pakistan
124 D3 Jandongi Zaire
15 G5 Jandowae Queensland Australia
101 G2 Jándula r. Spain
101 G3 Jandulilla r. Spain
166 C3 Janeiro r. Brazil
154 B1 Janesville California U.S.A.
148 C4 Janesville Wisconsin U.S.A.
39 D2 Jangal Iran
37 G4 Jangipur India
22 A2 Jang, Tg pt Indonesia
73 J3 Jänickendorf Germany
36 B2 Jani Khel Pakistan
76 G3 Janikowo Poland
168 B6 Janiópolis Brazil
104 G3 Janja Bos.-Herz.
130 E3 Jan Kempdorp South Africa
79 M4 Jánkmajtis Hungary
178 A4 Jan Mayen i. Svalbard Arctic Ocean
42 F3 Jannah Iraq
39 B2 Jannatābād Iran
39 E2 Jannatabad Iran
156 C2 Janos Mexico
79 J5 Jánoshalma Hungary
78 G4 Jánosháza Hungary
79 K4 Jánoshida Hungary
78 G4 Jánossomorja Hungary
78 C2 Janovice nad Úhlavou Czech Rep.
77 M2 Janów Białystok Poland
77 H5 Janów Czestochowa Poland
76 F3 Janowiec Wlelkopolski Poland
77 L5 Janów Lubelski Poland
77 J2 Janowo Poland
77 M3 Janów Podlaski Poland
130 E6 Jansenville South Africa
131 G3 Jan Smuts airport South Africa
112 E3 Jantra r. Bulgaria
169 F1 Januária Brazil
89 G3 Janville France
88 D4 Janzé France
36 C5 Jaora India
19 P6 Japan country Asia
Japan Alps Nat. Park see Chibu-Sangaku Nat. Park
29 E4 Japan, Sea of sea Asia
176 E4 Japan Tr. sea feature Pacific Ocean
163 D4 Japurá r. Brazil
37 H4 Japvo Mt. mt. India
156 L8 Jaqué Panama
102 B3 Jaraba Spain
42 D2 Jarābulus Syria
76 F4 Jaraczewa Poland
168 D1 Jaraguá Brazil
167 C6 Jaraguá do Sul Brazil
168 A4 Jaraguari Brazil
167 C6 Jaraguá, Sa mountain range Brazil
100 E1 Jaraicejo Spain
98 E4 Jaraiz de la Vera Spain
99 G4 Jarama r. Spain
98 E4 Jarandilla de la Vera Spain
42 C3 Jarash Jordan
166 B1 Jarauçu r. Brazil
59 G1 Järbo Sweden
167 A5 Jardim Brazil
101 H2 Jardín r. Spain
15 E1 Jardine River Nat. Park nat. park Queensland Australia
158 C2 Jardines de la Reina is Cuba
168 D3 Jardinésia Brazil
168 E4 Jardinópolis Brazil
30 A3 Jargalant Mongolia
31 E3 Jargalant Mongolia
30 B3 Jargalant Mongolia
30 A3 Jargalant Mongolia
30 D3 Jargalthaan Mongolia
86 B5 Jargeau France
163 G3 Jari r. Brazil
73 J2 Jarmen Germany
59 F1 Järna Kopparberg Sweden
59 G2 Järna Södermanland Sweden
92 B3 Jarnac France
92 E2 Jarnages France
59 F3 Järnforsen Sweden
87 E3 Jarny France
76 F4 Jarocin Poland
78 E1 Jaroměř Czech Rep.
78 E2 Jaroměřice nad Rokytnou Czech Rep.
81 H2 Jaroslavice Czech Rep.
77 L5 Jarosław Poland
76 E1 Jarosławiec Poland
81 G1 Jarošov nad Nežárkou Czech Rep.
56 D3 Järpen Sweden
72 E1 Jarplund-Weding Germany
39 B3 Jarrāhi watercourse Iran
173 F6 Jarrillas Argentina
30 C5 Jartai China
165 D2 Jarú Brazil
31 G3 Jarud Qi China
54 D2 Jarvakandi Estonia
57 G3 Järvenpää Finland
87 F4 Jarville-la-Malgrange France
177 J6 Jarvis Island i.
59 G1 Järvsta Sweden
37 E4 Jarwa India
36 B5 Jasdan India
37 F5 Jashpurnagar India
76 D4 Jasień Poland
77 J4 Jasieniec Poland
127 D5 Jasiired Jofay i. Somalia
77 K6 Jasiołka r. Poland
77 M2 Jasionówka Poland
39 D4 Jāsk Iran
77 K6 Jaśliska Poland
77 K6 Jasło Poland
54 D4 Jašlūnai Lithuania
73 J1 Jasmund pen. Germany
73 J1 Jasmund, Naturschutzgebiet res. Germany
171 D7 Jason Is is Falkland Is.
179 B2 Jason Pen. pen. Antarctica
145 C5 Jasper Alabama U.S.A.
136 F4 Jasper Alberta Canada
151 E4 Jasper Arkansas U.S.A.
145 D6 Jasper Florida U.S.A.
144 C4 Jasper Indiana U.S.A.
146 E3 Jasper New York U.S.A.
146 B5 Jasper Ohio U.S.A.
151 E6 Jasper Texas U.S.A.
136 F4 Jasper Nat. Park nat. park Alberta Canada
42 F3 Jaşşān Iraq
82 A2 Jasseron France
76 G1 Jastarnia Poland
104 E3 Jastrebarsko Croatia
76 E2 Jastrowie Poland
77 K4 Jastrzębia Poland
76 G6 Jastrzębie-Zdrój Poland
79 K4 Jászapáti Hungary
79 J4 Jászárokszállás Hungary
79 J4 Jászberény Hungary
79 K4 Jászkisér Hungary
79 K4 Jász-Nagykún-Szolnok div. Hungary
168 C2 Jataí Brazil
163 F4 Jatapu r. Brazil
36 D4 Jatara India
38 A2 Jath India
36 B4 Jati Pakistan
22 B3 Jatibarang Indonesia
110 C5 Jato r. Sicilia Italy
36 B3 Jatoi Pakistan
73 J2 Jatznick Germany
163 E4 Jaú r. Brazil
168 D5 Jaú Brazil
163 E4 Jauaperi r. Brazil
163 E3 Jaua Sarisariñama, Parque Nacional nat. park Venezuela
158 D2 Jauco Cuba
164 A2 Jauja Peru
82 C2 Jaun Switzerland
163 F5 Jauna r. Brazil
54 E3 Jaunanna Latvia
92 A2 Jaunay r. France
92 C2 Jaunay-Clan France
54 D3 Jaunkalsnava Latvia
54 C3 Jaunlutriṇi Latvia
54 C3 Jaunmārupe Latvia
54 E3 Jaunpiebalga Latvia
54 C3 Jaunpils Latvia
37 E4 Jaunpur India
163 E4 Jaú, Parque Nacional do nat. park Brazil
93 E5 Jaur r. France
39 E3 Jauri Iran
165 E3 Jauru r. Brazil
168 A3 Jauru Brazil
91 E4 Jausiers France
Java i. see Jawa
38 B3 Javadi Hills mts India
Javaés r. see Formoso
103 B4 Javalambre, Sierra de mountain range Spain
39 F2 Javand Afghanistan
175 M4 Java Ridge sea feature Indian Ocean
30 E2 Javarthushuu Mongolia
22 B3 Java Sea sea Indonesia
103 D6 Jávea Spain
73 G3 Jävenitz Germany
101 F3 Javerero mt. Spain
173 J1 Javier de Viana Uruguay
171 B6 Javier, I. i. Chile
112 C3 Javor mts Yugoslavia
78 E2 Javořice h. Czech Rep.
79 J3 Javorie mt. Slovakia
79 H2 Javorníky mts Slovakia
56 F2 Jävre Sweden
22 B4 Jawa i. Indonesia
22 A3 Jawa Barat div. Indonesia
36 C4 Jawad India
36 C4 Jawai r. India
22 B3 Jawa Tengah div. Indonesia
22 C4 Jawa Timur div. Indonesia
42 D2 Jawbān Bayk Syria
119 H4 Jawf, W. al watercourse Yemen
38 A2 Jawhar India
126 E4 Jawhar Somalia
76 E4 Jawor Poland
77 K4 Jawor Solecki Poland
79 H2 Jaworze Poland
77 H5 Jaworzno Poland
162 B5 Jayanca Peru
37 G4 Jayanti India
21 L7 Jaya, Pk mt. Indonesia
21 M7 Jayapura Indonesia
37 F4 Jaynagar India
42 D3 Jayrūd Syria
119 H4 Jaza'ir Farasān is Saudi Arabia
39 C4 Jazīreh-ye Forūr i. Iran
39 C4 Jazīreh-ye Sīrrī i. Iran
43 C2 Jbail Lebanon
131 F4 J. B. M. Hertzog airport South Africa
148 D5 J.C. Murphey Lake l. Indiana U.S.A.
42 D3 Jdaide Syria
155 E4 Jean Nevada U.S.A.
136 E2 Jean Marie River N.W.T. Canada
139 G2 Jeannin, Lac l. Québec Canada
39 D3 Jebāl Bārez, Kūh-e mountain range Iran
123 E5 Jebba Nigeria
112 C2 Jebel Romania
96 D5 Jebha Morocco
55 B3 Jebjerg Denmark
87 G4 Jebsheim France
22 A2 Jebus Indonesia
66 F5 Jedburgh Scotland U.K.
Jedda see Jiddah
105 B7 Jedeida Tunisia
77 L4 Jedlanka Poland
77 K4 Jedlińsk Poland
77 K4 Jedlnia-Letnisko Poland
77 J5 Jędrzejów Poland
77 L2 Jedwabne Poland
77 J2 Jedwabno Poland
73 G2 Jeetze r. Germany
152 D2 Jefferson r. Montana U.S.A.
146 C6 Jefferson N. Carolina U.S.A.
147 F3 Jefferson New York U.S.A.
148 C4 Jefferson Wisconsin U.S.A.
150 E4 Jefferson City Missouri U.S.A.
154 D2 Jefferson, Mt mt. Nevada U.S.A.
152 B2 Jefferson, Mt volcano Oregon U.S.A.
144 C4 Jeffersonville Indiana U.S.A.
130 E7 Jeffrey's Bay South Africa
123 E4 Jega Nigeria
55 A3 Jegindo i. Denmark
93 C5 Jegun France
43 C4 Jeib, W. el watercourse Israel/Jordan
165 E4 Jejuí Guazú r. Paraguay
54 D3 Jēkabpils Latvia
76 F4 Jelcz-Laskowice Poland
126 D3 Jeldēsa Ethiopia
76 D4 Jelenia Góra div. Poland
76 D5 Jelenia Góra Jelenia Góra Poland
77 L1 Jeleniewa Poland
37 G4 Jelep La China
54 C3 Jelgava Latvia
112 C3 Jelica mts Yugoslavia
146 A6 Jellico Tennessee U.S.A.
140 B2 Jellicoe Ontario Canada
55 B4 Jelling Denmark
55 B4 Jels Denmark
109 G3 Jelsi Italy
25 D7 Jemaja i. Indonesia
22 C4 Jember Indonesia
69 C4 Jemeppe Belgium
72 C2 Jemgum Germany
76 E4 Jemielno Poland
47 L3 Jeminay China
123 F4 Jemma Nigeria
78 E2 Jemnice Czech Rep.
22 D2 Jempang, D. l. Indonesia
75 G2 Jena Germany
80 C3 Jenbach Austria
121 F1 Jendouba Tunisia
76 D2 Jenikowo Poland
43 C3 Jenin West Bank
146 B6 Jenkins Kentucky U.S.A.
154 A2 Jenner California U.S.A.
81 H4 Jennersdorf Austria
159 □7 Jennings Antigua Caribbean
151 E6 Jennings Louisiana U.S.A.
13 G3 Jenolan Caves New South Wales Australia
137 K4 Jenpeg Manitoba Canada
22 B3 Jepara Indonesia
13 E4 Jeparit Victoria Australia
166 D3 Jequié Brazil
169 F2 Jequitaí r. Brazil
169 F2 Jequitaí Brazil
169 J1 Jequitinhonha r. Brazil
169 H2 Jequitinhonha Brazil
121 D2 Jerada Morocco
25 C7 Jerantut Malaysia
121 G2 Jerba, Île de i. Tunisia
126 B3 Jerbar Sudan
158 D3 Jérémie Haiti
166 E3 Jeremoabo Brazil
126 D3 Jerer Shet' watercourse Ethiopia
22 D4 Jereweh Indonesia
156 E4 Jerez Mexico
100 D4 Jeréz de la Frontera Spain
100 D2 Jeréz de los Caballeros Spain
114 B3 Jergucat Albania
103 C5 Jerica Spain
15 F4 Jericho Queensland Australia
73 H3 Jerichow Germany
13 F3 Jerilderie New South Wales Australia
76 E4 Jerka Poland
168 C1 Jeroaquara Brazil
152 D3 Jerome Idaho U.S.A.
173 G1 Jeronimo Norte Argentina
17 B7 Jerramungup Western Australia Australia
36 B4 Jerruck Pakistan
63 □2 Jersey i. Channel Is.
147 F4 Jersey City New Jersey U.S.A.
146 E4 Jersey Shore Pennsylvania U.S.A.
144 B4 Jerseyville Illinois U.S.A.
98 E4 Jerte r. Spain
98 E4 Jerte Spain
166 D2 Jerumenha Brazil
43 C4 Jerusalem Israel
14 C4 Jervois Ra. h. Northern Terr. Australia
77 H5 Jerzmanowice Poland
108 B5 Jerzu Sardegna Italy
78 C1 Jesenice Středočesk Czech Rep.
81 F4 Jesenice Slovenia
78 G1 Jeseník Czech Rep.
79 K3 Jesenské Slovakia
73 H3 Jeserig Brandenburg Germany
107 H5 Jesi Italy
73 L2 Jesionowo Poland
73 H4 Jessen Germany
131 J3 Jesser Point pt South Africa
58 D1 Jessheim Norway
73 H4 Jeßnitz Germany
37 G5 Jessore Bangladesh
72 E2 Jesteburg Germany
78 D1 Ještěd mt. Czech Rep.
83 D1 Jestetten Germany
145 D6 Jesup Georgia U.S.A.
157 G5 Jesús Carranza Mexico
172 E1 Jesús María Argentina
122 A4 Jeta, Ilha de i. Guinea-Bissau
36 B5 Jetalsar India
Jethro see Maghā'ir Shu'ayb
150 D4 Jetmore Kansas U.S.A.
80 C2 Jetzendorf Germany
86 D2 Jeumont France
72 C2 Jever Germany
78 F2 Jevíčko Czech Rep.
78 F3 Jevišovice Czech Rep.
81 H2 Jevišovka r. Czech Rep.
58 D1 Jevnaker Norway
141 K6 Jewett City Connecticut U.S.A.
76 G3 Jezerio Gopło l. Poland
77 L2 Jeżewo Białystok Poland
76 G2 Jeżewo Toruń Poland
77 J2 Jeziorany Poland
76 E2 Jezioro Betyń l. Poland
76 E1 Jezioro Bukowo lag. Poland
76 C2 Jezioro Dąbie l. Poland
77 K1 Jezioro Dargin l. Poland
76 E2 Jezioro Drawsko l. Poland
76 E1 Jezioro Jamno lag. Poland
77 H2 Jezioro Jeziorak l. Poland
76 G4 Jezioro Jeziorsko l. Poland
76 E1 Jezioro Kopań lag. Poland
76 G2 Jezioro Koronowskie l. Poland
77 J2 Jezioro Łańskie l. Poland
76 F1 Jezioro Łebsko lag. Poland
76 D2 Jezioro Lubie l. Poland
77 J2 Jezioro Luterskie l. Poland
77 K1 Jezioro Mamry l. Poland
76 C2 Jezioro Miedwie l. Poland
73 K3 Jezioro Myśliborskie l. Poland
77 J2 Jezioro Narie l. Poland
76 E2 Jezioro Pile l. Poland
73 L2 Jezioro Płoń l. Poland
76 G3 Jezioro Powidzkie l. Poland
76 D1 Jezioro Resko Przymorskie lag. Poland
77 K2 Jezioro Roś l. Poland
77 M3 Jezioro Siemianowskie l. Poland
76 E4 Jezioro Sławskie l. Poland
77 K2 Jezioro Śniardwy l. Poland
77 L6 Jezioro Solińskie l. Poland
77 H4 Jezioro Sulejowskie l. Poland
76 E1 Jezioro Wicko lag. Poland
76 E2 Jezioro Wielimie l. Poland
77 M1 Jezioro Wigry l. Poland
73 L2 Jezioro Woświn l. Poland
76 D3 Jezioro Zbąszyńskie l. Poland
77 K3 Jezioro Zegrzyńskie l. Poland
77 H4 Jeżów Poland
77 L5 Jeżowe Poland
43 C3 Jezzine Lebanon
36 C5 Jhabua India
37 F4 Jha Jha India
36 C4 Jhajju India
36 A3 Jhal Pakistan
37 G5 Jhalakati Bangladesh
36 D4 Jhalawar India
36 A4 Jhal Jhao Pakistan
36 D4 Jhalrapatan India
36 C3 Jhang Maghiana Pakistan
36 D4 Jhansi India
37 F5 Jharsuguda India
36 B3 Jhatpat Pakistan
37 F4 Jhawani Nepal
36 C2 Jhelum Pakistan
37 G5 Jhenida Bangladesh
39 G4 Jhimpir Pakistan
36 B4 Jhudo Pakistan
37 F4 Jhumritilaiya India
36 C3 Jhunjhunūn India
32 D1 Jiachuan China
33 H2 Jiading China
33 F3 Jiahe China
Jiaji see Qionghai
32 C2 Jiajiang China
31 J3 Jiamusi China
31 H4 Ji'an China
33 F3 Ji'an China
33 F3 Ji'an China
31 F4 Jianchang China
32 B3 Jianchuan China
33 G2 Jiande China
32 D2 Jiang r. China
32 D2 Jiang'an China
32 D2 Jiangbei China
32 C4 Jiangcheng China
32 C3 Jiangchuan China
32 D2 Jiange China
33 E4 Jianghong China
33 E3 Jianghua China
32 D2 Jiangjin China
32 E3 Jiangkou China
33 G3 Jiangle China
33 F2 Jiangling China
32 D1 Jiangluozhen China
33 F4 Jiangmen China
33 G2 Jiangshan China
33 G1 Jiangsu div. China
30 C6 Jiangtaibu China
33 F3 Jiangxi div. China
33 E1 Jiang Xian China
30 B5 Jiangxigou China
33 H2 Jiangyin China
33 E3 Jiangyong China
32 D2 Jiangyou China
33 G1 Jianhu China
33 F2 Jianli China
33 G3 Jianning China
33 G3 Jian'ou China
31 F4 Jianping China
31 F4 Jianping China
33 F2 Jianshan China
33 E2 Jianshi China
32 C4 Jianshui China
32 D2 Jianyang China
33 G3 Jianyang China
30 E5 Jiaocheng China
31 H4 Jiaohe China
31 F5 Jiaohe China
33 H2 Jiaojiang China
30 D5 Jiaokou China
31 F5 Jiaolai r. China
31 G4 Jiaolai r. China
33 G3 Jiaoling China
31 F6 Jiaonan China
31 G5 Jiao Xian China
31 G5 Jiaozhou Wan b. China
33 F1 Jiaozuo China
32 C3 Jiasa China
33 G1 Jiashan China
33 H2 Jiashan China
47 J5 Jiashi China
30 D5 Jia Xian China
33 H2 Jiaxing China
Jiayi see Chia-i
31 J2 Jiayin China
33 F2 Jiayu China
30 A5 Jiayuguan China
33 G4 Jiazi China
112 D1 Jibou Romania
156 K8 Jicarón, I. i. Panama
78 E1 Jičín Czech Rep.
119 G3 Jiddah Saudi Arabia
41 J6 Jiddat al Ḩarāsīs gravel area Oman
30 B5 Jiehebe China
56 E1 Jiehkkevarri mt. Norway
33 F4 Jieshi China
33 F4 Jieshi Wan b. China
33 F1 Jieshou China
56 G1 Iešjávri l. Norway
33 F4 Jiexi China
30 D5 Jiexiu China
33 G4 Jieyang China
54 D4 Jieznas Lithuania
123 F4 Jigawa div. Nigeria
17 C4 Jiggalong Western Australia Australia
32 C1 Jigzhi China
43 D2 Jiḩār, W. al watercourse Syria
78 F2 Jihlava r. Czech Rep.
78 E2 Jihlava Czech Rep.
78 D2 Jihočeský div. Czech Rep.
78 F2 Jihomoravský div. Czech Rep.
39 E2 Jija Sarai Afghanistan
121 F1 Jijel Algeria
126 D3 Jijiga Ethiopia
103 C6 Jijona Spain
32 C2 Jiju China
39 G2 Jilga r. Afghanistan
47 J6 Jilganang Kol, S. salt lake China/Jammu and Kashmir
127 D4 Jilib Somalia
31 H4 Jilin div. China
31 H4 Jilin China
30 B5 Jiling China
31 H4 Jilin Handa Ling mountain range China
31 G2 Jiliu r. China
102 B3 Jiloca r. Spain
Jilong see Chi-lung
78 D1 Jílové Czech Rep.
78 D2 Jílové u Prahy Czech Rep.
126 C3 Jīma Ethiopia
159 E3 Jimani Haiti
79 K6 Jimbolia Romania
32 C2 Jimda China
101 E4 Jimena de la Frontera Spain
156 D3 Jiménez Chihuahua Mexico
157 E2 Jiménez Coahuila Mexico
157 F3 Jiménez Tamaulipas Mexico
123 G5 Jimeta Nigeria
6 □1 Jimi r. P.N.G.
31 G5 Jimo China
26 E3 Jimsar China
147 F4 Jim Thorpe Pennsylvania U.S.A.
33 F2 Jin r. China
31 F5 Jinan China
75 J3 Jince Czech Rep.
30 B5 Jinchang China
33 F1 Jincheng China
32 C2 Jinchuan China
36 D3 Jind India
13 G4 Jindabyne New South Wales Australia
78 E2 Jindřichův Hradec Czech Rep.
30 A5 Jinfosi China
32 E1 Jing r. China
Jing see Jinghe
33 F2 Jing'an China
30 D5 Jingbian China
32 D1 Jingchuan China
33 G2 Jingde China
33 G2 Jingdezhen China
32 C3 Jingdong China
33 F3 Jinggangshan China
33 G2 Jinggongqiao China
32 C4 Jinggu China
31 F5 Jinghai China
47 K4 Jinghe China
30 E5 Jingle China
33 F2 Jingmen China
32 D1 Jingning China
31 J4 Jingpo China
31 J4 Jingpo Hu resr China
30 B5 Jingtai China
32 D4 Jingxi China
33 E3 Jing Xian China
31 H4 Jingyu China
30 C5 Jingyuan China
32 D1 Jingyuan China
31 G2 Jinhe China
33 G1 Jinhu China
33 G2 Jinhua China
31 F6 Jining China
33 G1 Jining China
127 B4 Jinja Uganda
33 G3 Jinjiang China
126 C3 Jinka Ethiopia
32 C2 Jinkouhe China
31 G4 Jinlingsi China
33 E5 Jinmu Jiao China
32 C3 Jinning China
156 J6 Jinotega Nicaragua
156 J7 Jinotepe Nicaragua
32 C4 Jinping China
33 E3 Jinping China
32 C2 Jinping Shan r. China
32 C3 Jinsha r. China
32 D3 Jinsha China
33 H2 Jinshan China
33 E2 Jinshi China
30 A5 Jinta China
32 D2 Jintang China
23 B4 Jintotolo i. Philippines
23 B4 Jintotolo Channel chan. Philippines
38 B2 Jintur India
33 G3 Jinxi China
31 G4 Jinxi China
31 G5 Jin Xian China
33 G2 Jinxian China
33 G1 Jinxiang China
33 H3 Jinxiang China
32 C3 Jinyang China
33 H2 Jinyun China
33 F2 Jinzhai China
31 G4 Jinzhou China
127 C5 Jipe, L. l. Tanzania
162 A4 Jipijapa Ecuador
169 J2 Jiquitaia Brazil
47 H5 Jirgatol Tajikistan
31 F3 Jirin Gol China
78 C1 Jirkov Czech Rep.
75 K2 Jirny Czech Rep.
39 D3 Jīroft Iran
126 E3 Jirriiban Somalia
30 D6 Jishan China
33 E2 Jishou China
33 F3 Jishui China
42 D3 Jisr ash Shughūr Syria
75 K3 Jistebnice Czech Rep.
25 C6 Jitra Malaysia
112 D3 Jiu r. Romania
30 C5 Jiudengkou China
32 C2 Jiuding Shan mt. China
32 D1 Jiufoping China
33 F2 Jiujiang China
33 G2 Jiujiang China
33 F2 Jiuling Shan mountain range China
32 C2 Jiulong China
31 G4 Jiumiao China
30 A5 Jiuquan China
31 H3 Jiutai China
32 D3 Jiuxu China
39 E4 Jiwani Pakistan
31 G2 Jiwen China
31 J3 Jixi China
33 G2 Jixi China
30 D5 Ji Xian China
31 E5 Ji Xian China
31 J3 Jixian China
33 F1 Ji Xian China
33 F1 Jiyuan China
119 H4 Jīzān Saudi Arabia
78 D1 Jizera r. Czech Rep.
78 E1 Jizerské Hory mts Czech Rep.
119 G2 Jizl watercourse Saudi Arabia
28 D6 Jizō-zaki pt Japan
167 B6 Joaçaba Brazil
73 J3 Joachimsthal Germany
169 H2 Joaíma Brazil
122 A4 Joal-Fadiout Senegal
167 B6 João Paulo r. Brazil
166 F2 João Pessoa Brazil
169 E2 João Pinheiro Brazil
169 F2 Joaquim Felício Brazil
170 D2 Joaquin V. González Argentina
79 J4 Jobbágyi Hungary
154 C2 Job Peak summit Nevada U.S.A.
80 D3 Jochberg Austria
75 H2 Jocketa Germany
87 H3 Jockgrim Germany
172 C2 Jocoli Argentina
37 F5 Joda India
101 G3 Jódar Spain
36 C4 Jodhpur India
69 C4 Jodoigne Belgium
56 H3 Joensuu Finland
29 G5 Jōetsu Japan
129 E3 Jofane Mozambique
136 F4 Joffre, Mt mt. B.C. Canada
37 F4 Jogbani India
54 E2 Jõgeva Estonia
46 E5 Joghatāy India
36 D3 Jogindarnagar India
140 C1 Jog Lake l. Ontario Canada
54 E2 Jõgua Estonia
140 D2 Jogues Ontario Canada
29 F5 Jōhana Japan
58 B1 Johannesberg mt. Norway
154 D4 Johannesburg California U.S.A.
131 G3 Johannesburg South Africa
80 D2 Johanniskirchen Germany
28 D7 Jōhen Japan
38 C1 Johilla r. India
159 □1 John Crow Mts mts Jamaica
152 B2 John Day r. Oregon U.S.A.
152 C2 John Day Oregon U.S.A.
136 F3 John D'or Prairie Alberta Canada
146 D6 John H. Kerr Lake resr Virginia U.S.A.
16 E3 John, Mt h. Western Australia Australia
66 E2 John o' Groats Scotland U.K.
145 D4 Johnson City Tennessee U.S.A.
171 B5 Johnson, I. i. Chile
136 C2 Johnson's Crossing Yukon Terr. Canada
159 □7 Johnsons Pt pt Antigua Caribbean
145 D5 Johnston S. Carolina U.S.A.
62 B3 Johnston Wales U.K.
66 D5 Johnstone Scotland U.K.
176 H4 Johnston I. Pacific Ocean
17 C7 Johnston, L. salt flat Western Australia Australia
147 F3 Johnstown New York U.S.A.
146 D4 Johnstown Pennsylvania U.S.A.
67 D4 Johnstown Rep. of Ireland
149 F3 Johnswood Michigan U.S.A.
29 H3 Jōhōji Japan
25 C7 Johor div. Malaysia
25 C7 Johor Bahru Malaysia
54 E2 Jõhvi Estonia
86 C5 Joigny France
167 C6 Joinville Brazil
87 E4 Joinville France
179 B2 Joinville I. i. Antarctica
54 D1 Jokela Finland
54 C1 Jokioinen Finland
56 E2 Jokkmokk Sweden
56 N6 Jökulsá á Brú r. Iceland
56 M6 Jökulsá á Fjöllum r. Iceland
56 N6 Jökulsá í Fljótsdal r. Iceland
107 F4 Jolanda di Savoia Italy
42 F2 Jolfa Iran
148 C5 Joliet Illinois U.S.A.
141 J3 Joliette Québec Canada
23 B5 Jolo i. Philippines
23 B5 Jolo Philippines
82 B3 Joly, Mont mt. France
59 H1 Jomala Finland
23 B3 Jomalig i. Philippines
22 C3 Jombang Indonesia
58 C2 Jomfruland i. Norway
58 D1 Jømna Norway
83 D1 Jona Switzerland
54 D4 Jonava Lithuania
58 B1 Jondal Norway
32 C1 Jonê China
151 F5 Jonesboro Arkansas U.S.A.
147 K2 Jonesboro Maine U.S.A.
64 B3 Jonesborough Northern Ireland U.K.
179 A3 Jones Mts mts Antarctica
147 K2 Jonesport Maine U.S.A.
10 □2 Jones Pt pt Christmas I. Indian Ocean
135 K2 Jones Sound chan. N.W.T. Canada
146 B6 Jonesville Virginia U.S.A.
126 B3 Jonglei Sudan
126 B3 Jonglei Canal canal Sudan
54 D3 Joniškėlis Lithuania
37 E5 Jonk r. India
59 F3 Jönköping div. Sweden
59 F3 Jönköping Sweden
77 J2 Jonkowo Poland
141 K2 Jonquière Québec Canada
157 G5 Jonuta Mexico
92 B3 Jonzac France
151 E4 Joplin Missouri U.S.A.
147 E5 Joppatowne Maryland U.S.A.
111 E4 Joppolo Italy
36 D4 Jora India
18 E6 Jordan country Asia
152 E3 Jordan r. Utah U.S.A.
43 C3 Jordan r. Asia
152 F2 Jordan Montana U.S.A.
15 F4 Jordan Cr. watercourse Queensland Australia
169 H1 Jordânia Brazil
92 E3 Jordanne r. France
77 H6 Jordanów Poland
152 C3 Jordan Valley Oregon U.S.A.
167 B6 Jordão r. Brazil
73 H2 Jördenstorf Germany
57 D3 Jordet Norway
37 H4 Jorhat India
47 J5 Jor Hu l. China
72 E2 Jork Germany
58 D3 Jörlanda Sweden
39 G1 Jorm Afghanistan
56 F2 Jörn Sweden
56 G3 Joroinen Finland
58 B2 Jørpeland Norway
172 B2 Jorquera, Co mt. Chile
58 D1 Jørstadmoen Norway
123 F5 Jos Nigeria
23 C5 Jose Abad Santos Philippines
164 C2 José A de Palacios Bolivia
173 K2 José Battle-y-Ordonez Uruguay
173 F6 José B. Casas Argentina
166 B2 José Bispo r. Brazil
165 D2 José Bonifácio Rondônia Brazil
168 D4 José Bonifácio São Paulo Brazil
157 F5 José Cardel Mexico
171 B5 José de San Martin Argentina
173 J2 José Enrique Rodó Uruguay
173 K3 Jose Ignacio, L. l. Uruguay
167 A4 Joselândia Brazil
173 K1 José Otávio Brazil
173 K2 José Pedro Varela Uruguay
16 E2 Joseph Bonaparte Gulf g. Western Australia Australia
155 G4 Joseph City Arizona U.S.A.
139 G3 Joseph, Lac l. Newfoundland Canada
36 D3 Joshimath India
29 G5 Jōshin'etsu-kōgen National Park Japan
155 E5 Joshua Tree National Monument nat. park California U.S.A.
123 F5 Jos Plateau plat. Nigeria
88 C4 Josselin France
58 B1 Jostedalsbreen Nasjonalpark nat. park Norway
145 □3 Jost Van Dyke I. i. Virgin Is Caribbean
54 C4 Josvainiai Lithuania
58 B1 Jotunheimen Nasjonalpark nat. park Norway
89 E3 Jouanne r. France
130 D6 Joubertina South Africa
131 F3 Jouberton South Africa
89 F4 Joué-lès-Tours France
90 E2 Jougne France
43 C3 Joûnié Lebanon
68 D2 Joure Netherlands
141 F2 Joutel Québec Canada

K

Kampuchea *see* Cambodia
137 J4 Kamsack *Saskatchewan* Canada
122 B4 Kamsar Guinea
50 J4 Kamskoye Ust'ye Rus. Fed.
44 G4 Kamskoye Vdkhr. resr Rus. Fed.
127 D4 Kamsuuma Somalia
137 J3 Kamuchawie Lake l. *Manitoba* Canada
127 B4 Kamuli Uganda
114 C3 Kamvounia mountain range Greece
53 B1 Kam"yane *Rivens'ka Oblast'* Ukraine
53 F1 Kam"yane *Sums'ka Oblast'* Ukraine
53 B2 Kam"yanets'-Podil's'kyy Ukraine
53 E2 Kam"yanka *Cherkas'ka Oblast'* Ukraine
53 G2 Kam"yanka *Kharkivs'ka Oblast'* Ukraine
53 D3 Kam"yanka *Odes'ka Oblast'* Ukraine
53 A1 Kam"yanka-Buz'ka Ukraine
53 F3 Kam"yanka-Dniprovs'ka Ukraine
112 G2 Kam"yans'ke Ukraine
77 M3 Kamyanyets Belarus
77 M3 Kamyanyuki Belarus
53 B1 Kam"yanyy Brid Ukraine
53 D3 Kam"yanyy Mist Ukraine
42 F3 Kāmyārān Iran
54 F4 Kamyen' Belarus
77 N2 Kamyenka Belarus
51 F6 Kamyshevatskaya Rus. Fed.
51 H5 Kamyshin Rus. Fed.
46 F3 Kamyshlybash Kazakhstan
46 F3 Kamyslybas, Oz. l. Kazakhstan
51 J6 Kamyzyak Rus. Fed.
39 D4 Kamzar Oman
126 B3 Kan Sudan
129 D2 Kana r. Zimbabwe
124 F3 Kana Zaire
138 F3 Kanaaupscow r. *Québec* Canada
155 F3 Kanab *Utah* U.S.A.
155 F3 Kanab Creek r. *Arizona* U.S.A.
6 □6 Kanacea i. Fiji
29 G6 Kanagawa div. Japan
36 A3 Kanak Pakistan
81 E4 Kanal Slovenia
115 F5 Kanala Greece
77 M2 Kanał Augustowski canal Poland
76 F2 Kanał Bydgoski canal Poland
77 N3 Kanal Dnyaprowska-Buhski canal Belarus
114 B3 Kanali Greece
114 B3 Kanallaki Greece
76 E4 Kanał Obry canal Poland
107 J3 Kanal Srednja Vrata chan. Croatia
107 J3 Kanal Vela Vrata chan. Croatia
77 M4 Kanał Wieprz-Krzna canal Poland
131 F3 Kanana South Africa
125 D5 Kananga Zaire
13 G3 Kanangra Nat. Park nat. park *New South Wales* Australia
155 F3 Kanarraville *Utah* U.S.A.
130 A3 Kanas watercourse Namibia
52 H2 Kanash Rus. Fed.
146 C5 Kanawha r. *W. Virginia* U.S.A.
29 F6 Kanayama Japan
29 F5 Kanazawa Japan
29 F5 Kanazu Japan
24 A2 Kanbalu Myanmar
25 B4 Kanchanaburi Thailand
38 B3 Kanchipuram India
77 L6 Kańczuga Poland
44 F3 Kand mt. Pakistan
39 F3 Kandahār Afghanistan
56 J2 Kandalaksha Rus. Fed.
50 E1 Kandalakshskiy Zaliv Rus. Fed.
22 C2 Kandangan Indonesia
54 C3 Kandava Latvia
123 E5 Kandé Togo
87 H4 Kandel mt. Germany
74 D3 Kandel Germany
73 J1 Kandelin Germany
82 C2 Kander r. Switzerland
74 C5 Kandern Germany
82 C2 Kandersteg Switzerland
36 B3 Kandhkot Pakistan
36 B2 Kandhura Pakistan
123 E4 Kandi Benin
36 A3 Kandi Pakistan
36 B4 Kandiaro Pakistan
115 D5 Kandila *Peloponnisos* Greece
114 B4 Kandila *Stereá Ellás* Greece
123 G3 Kandil Bouzou well Niger
114 E4 Kandilio mts Greece
42 B1 Kandıra Turkey
41 M5 Kandla India
13 G3 Kandos *New South Wales* Australia
129 H2 Kandreho Madagascar
6 □1 Kandrian P.N.G.
38 B3 Kandukur India
38 C5 Kandy Sri Lanka
146 D4 Kane *Pennsylvania* U.S.A.
135 M2 Kane Basin b. Greenland
39 C4 Kaneh watercourse Iran
118 C5 Kanem div. Chad
153 □1 Kaneohe *Hawaii* U.S.A.
153 □1 Kaneohe Bay b. *Hawaii* U.S.A.
50 F1 Kanevka Rus. Fed.
51 F6 Kanevskaya Rus. Fed.
29 H4 Kaneyama Japan
128 C3 Kang Botswana
37 G5 Kanga r. Bangladesh
124 F3 Kanga Zaire
135 N3 Kangaatsiaq Greenland
122 C4 Kangaba Mali
42 D2 Kangal Turkey
39 D4 Kangān Iran
39 C4 Kangan Iran
25 C6 Kangar Malaysia
12 D3 Kangaroo I. i. *S. Australia* Australia
163 F2 Kangaruma Guyana
57 H3 Kangaslampi Finland
56 G3 Kangasniemi Finland
39 A2 Kangāvar Iran
31 E4 Kangbao China
37 G4 Kangchenjunga mt. Nepal
32 C2 Kangding China
31 H5 Kangdong North Korea
22 C3 Kangean i. Indonesia
22 C3 Kangean, Kep. is Indonesia
126 B3 Kangen r. Sudan
135 O3 Kangeq headland Greenland
135 N3 Kangerluarsoruseq Greenland
135 P3 Kangerlussuaq inlet Greenland
135 N3 Kangerlussuaq Greenland
135 N2 Kangersuatsiaq Greenland
135 P3 Kangertittivatsiaq inlet Greenland
126 C4 Kangetet Kenya
31 H4 Kanggye North Korea
135 O2 Kangikajik c. Greenland
31 F1 Kangil Rus. Fed.
139 G2 Kangiqsualujjuaq *Québec* Canada
135 L3 Kangiqsujuaq *Québec* Canada
139 G1 Kangirsuk *Québec* Canada
28 A6 Kangjon South Korea
32 C1 Kangle China
Kang-ma *see* Kangmar
37 F3 Kangmar China
37 G3 Kangmar China
31 J5 Kangnŭng South Korea
124 B3 Kango Gabon
29 □1 Kangoku-iwa i. Japan
31 G4 Kangping China
36 D2 Kangra India
37 H3 Kangri Karpo Pass India
37 E3 Kangrinboqê Feng mt. China
37 H4 Kangto mt. China
37 F2 Kangtog China
32 D1 Kang Xian China
36 D1 Kangxiwar China
24 A3 Kangyidaung Myanmar
38 B1 Kanhan r. India
37 E4 Kanhar r. India
122 C5 Kani Côte d'Ivoire
24 A2 Kani Myanmar
125 D5 Kaniama Zaire
9 C5 Kaniere New Zealand
9 C5 Kaniere, L. l. New Zealand
122 A4 Kanifing The Gambia
38 B3 Kanigiri India
36 B2 Kaniguram Pakistan
44 F3 Kanin Nos Rus. Fed.
44 F3 Kanin Nos, M. c. Rus. Fed.
44 F3 Kanin, P-ov pen. Rus. Fed.
83 E1 Kanisfluh mt. Austria
28 H3 Kanita Japan
53 D2 Kaniv Ukraine
12 E4 Kaniva *Victoria* Australia
79 K5 Kanjiža Yugoslavia
56 F3 Kankaanpää Finland
148 C5 Kankakee r. *Illinois* U.S.A.
148 D5 Kankakee *Illinois* U.S.A.
122 C4 Kankan Guinea
122 C5 Kankan, Réserve Naturelle de res. Guinea
37 E5 Kanker India
38 C4 Kankesanturai Sri Lanka
36 C1 Kankhun P. pass Afghanistan/Pakistan
25 B5 Kanmaw Kyun i. Myanmar
59 E3 Kånna Sweden
36 D4 Kannanj India
145 D5 Kannapolis *N. Carolina* U.S.A.
Kanniya Kumari c. *see* Comorin, Cape
38 B4 Kanniyakumari India
36 D5 Kannod India
56 G3 Kannonkoski Finland
Kannur *see* Cannanore
56 F3 Kannus Finland
54 E1 Kannuskoski Finland
123 F4 Kano div. Nigeria
28 C6 Kano Japan
123 F4 Kano Nigeria
28 D6 Kan-onji Japan
22 C1 Kanowit Malaysia
28 C8 Kanoya Japan
36 E4 Kanpur India
36 B3 Kanpur Pakistan
36 A4 Kanrach reg. Pakistan
150 D4 Kansas div. U.S.A.
150 D4 Kansas r. *Kansas* U.S.A.
150 E4 Kansas City *Kansas* U.S.A.
150 E4 Kansas City *Missouri* U.S.A.
45 L4 Kansk Rus. Fed.
Kansu div. *see* Gansu
47 J5 Kansu China
47 H4 Kant Kyrgyzstan
126 C3 Kanta mt. Ethiopia
115 E7 Kantanos Greece
25 D4 Kantaralak Thailand
123 E4 Kantchari Burkina
51 F5 Kantemirovka Rus. Fed.
68 E1 Kantens Netherlands
37 F5 Kānthi India
37 F4 Kanti India
115 D5 Kantia Greece
176 H6 Kanton Island i. *Kiribati*
29 G6 Kanto-sanchi mountain range Japan
67 C4 Kanturk Rep. of Ireland
163 F3 Kanuku Mts mountain range Guyana
29 G5 Kanuma Japan
128 B4 Kanus Namibia
6 □1 Kanuwe r. P.N.G.
131 H2 KaNyamazane South Africa
128 D3 Kanye Botswana
52 A2 Kanyutino Rus. Fed.
6 □5 Kao i. Tonga
25 C5 Kaôh Kŏng i. Cambodia
25 C5 Kaôh Rŭng i. Cambodia
33 H4 Kao-hsiung Taiwan
25 C5 Kaôh Smăch i. Cambodia
128 A2 Kaokoveld plat. Namibia
122 A4 Kaolack Senegal
125 D6 Kaoma Zambia
118 C4 Kaortchi well Chad
124 D2 Kaouadja Central African Rep.
153 □2 Kapaa *Hawaii* U.S.A.
153 □2 Kapaau *Hawaii* U.S.A.
47 J3 Kapal Kazakhstan
125 D5 Kapanga Zaire
127 B6 Kapatu Zambia
47 J4 Kapchagay Kazakhstan
47 J4 Kapchagayskoye Vdkhr. resr Kazakhstan
126 B4 Kapchorwa Uganda
77 M2 Kapčiamiestis Lithuania
69 B3 Kapelle Netherlands
69 C3 Kapellen Belgium
59 H2 Kapellskär Sweden
81 G3 Kapfenberg Austria
37 H4 Kapili r. India
176 F5 Kapingamarangi Rise sea feature Pacific Ocean
36 B3 Kapip Pakistan
125 E6 Kapiri Mposhi Zambia
135 N3 Kapisigdlit Greenland
138 D3 Kapiskau r. *Ontario* Canada
138 D3 Kapiskau *Ontario* Canada
140 E3 Kapiskong Lake l. *Ontario* Canada
22 C1 Kapit Malaysia
53 D2 Kapitanivka Ukraine
8 E4 Kapiti I. i. New Zealand
163 F3 Kapiting Brazil
78 D3 Kaplice Czech Rep.
25 B5 Kapoe Thailand
126 B4 Kapoeta Sudan
79 K4 Kápolna Hungary
8 E3 Kaponga New Zealand
79 G5 Kaposvár Hungary
131 H2 Kappamuiden South Africa
39 E4 Kappar Pakistan
178 □2 Kapp Duner c. *Bjørnøya* Arctic Ocean
74 C3 Kappel Germany
72 E1 Kappeln Germany
87 H4 Kappelrodeck Germany
59 H3 Kappelshamns-viken b. Sweden
178 □2 Kapp Kåre c. *Bjørnøya* Arctic Ocean
80 B3 Kappl Austria
178 □3 Kapp Platen c. *Svalbard* Arctic Ocean
69 B3 Kaprijke Belgium
127 C4 Kapsabet Kenya
31 J4 Kapsan North Korea
115 D5 Kapsas Greece
114 C2 Kapshticë Albania
31 F2 Kaptsegaytuy Rus. Fed.
77 M2 Kaptsyowka Belarus
22 B1 Kapuas r. Indonesia
12 D3 Kapunda *S. Australia* Australia
36 D4 Kapūriya India
36 C3 Kapurthala India
79 L2 Kapušany Slovakia
140 D2 Kapuskasing r. *Ontario* Canada
140 D2 Kapuskasing *Ontario* Canada
51 H5 Kapustin Yar Rus. Fed.
53 D1 Kapustyntsi Ukraine
13 G2 Kaputar mt. *New South Wales* Australia
126 C4 Kaputir Kenya
79 G4 Kapuvár Hungary
54 E5 Kapyl' Belarus
52 A2 Kapyrevshchina Rus. Fed.
42 E2 Kara r. Turkey
123 E5 Kara Togo
113 F6 Kara Ada i. Turkey
113 F5 Kara Ada i. Turkey
47 H4 Kara-Balta Kyrgyzstan
52 D1 Karabanovo Rus. Fed.
46 F5 Karabekaul Turkmenistan
42 A1 Karabiga Turkey
46 D4 Kara-Bogaz-Gol Turkmenistan
42 C1 Karabük Turkey
52 E2 Karabukhino Rus. Fed.
47 J4 Karabulak Kazakhstan
47 K3 Karabulak Kazakhstan
47 J3 Karabulakskaya Kazakhstan
113 F5 Karaburun Turkey
46 F3 Karabutak Kazakhstan
113 G4 Karacabey Turkey
42 B1 Karacaköy Turkey
42 D2 Karacalı Dağlari mt. Turkey
43 B1 Karaçal T. mt. Turkey
113 G6 Karacasu Turkey
51 G7 Karachayevo-Cherkesiya div. Rus. Fed.
51 G7 Karachayevsk Rus. Fed.
52 B3 Karachev Rus. Fed.
36 A4 Karachi Pakistan
42 C2 Kara D. mt. Turkey
38 A2 Karad India
42 C2 Kara Dağ mt. Turkey
47 H4 Kara-Darya r. Kyrgyzstan
Kara Deniz sea *see* Black Sea
122 D5 Karaga Ghana
47 H3 Karaganda Kazakhstan
47 J3 Karagayly Kazakhstan
45 S4 Karaginskiy, O. i. Rus. Fed.
45 S4 Karaginskiy Zaliv b. Rus. Fed.
127 B5 Karagwe Tanzania
112 F4 Karahalil Turkey
113 G6 Karahisar Turkey
38 B4 Kāraikāl India
38 B4 Karaikkudi India
47 K3 Kara Irtysh r. Kazakhstan
42 C2 Karaisalı Turkey
39 B2 Karaj Iran
42 C4 Karak Jordan
46 E5 Kara Kala Turkmenistan
46 E4 Karakalpakiya Uzbekistan
47 J5 Karakax r. China
23 C5 Karakelong i. Indonesia
23 C6 Karakitang i. Indonesia
Kirovakan *see* Vanadzor
42 E2 Karakoçan Turkey
47 G3 Karakoin, Oz. salt lake Kazakhstan
46 D3 Karakol' Kazakhstan
47 H4 Kara-Köl Kyrgyzstan
47 J4 Karakol Kyrgyzstan
36 D2 Karakoram Pass pass China/Jammu and Kashmir
36 C1 Karakoram Range mountain range Pakistan
126 C2 Kara K'orē Ethiopia
31 E2 Karaksar Rus. Fed.
47 G5 Karakul' Uzbekistan
47 H5 Karakul', Ozero l. Tajikistan
124 B1 Karal Chad
54 B2 Karala Estonia
22 D2 Karama r. Indonesia
43 B1 Karaman div. Turkey
42 C2 Karaman *Karaman* Turkey
47 K3 Karamay China
54 F3 Karamyshevo Rus. Fed.
47 H5 Karambar Pass pass Afghanistan/Pakistan
22 D2 Karambu Indonesia
9 D4 Karamea New Zealand
9 C4 Karamea Bight b. New Zealand
9 D4 Karamea River r. New Zealand
39 F1 Karamet-Niyaz Turkmenistan
22 C3 Karamian i. Indonesia
37 F1 Karamiran China
37 F1 Karamiran Shankou China
77 L1 Karamyshevo Rus. Fed.
39 B4 Karān i. Saudi Arabia
39 G1 Karan r. Afghanistan
42 F3 Karand Iran
22 A2 Karangagung Indonesia
22 A3 Karangan Indonesia
22 C4 Karangasem Indonesia
22 B4 Karangbolong, Tg pt Indonesia
22 D2 Karang, Tg pt Indonesia
38 B2 Karanja r. India
36 D5 Karanja India
37 F5 Karanjia India
47 J2 Karaoba Kazakhstan
113 F6 Karaova Turkey
47 H3 Karaoy Kazakhstan
112 F3 Karapelit Bulgaria
42 C2 Karapınar Turkey
113 G5 Karapürçek Turkey
128 B4 Karas div. Namibia
130 A3 Karas mts Namibia
37 E1 Karasay China
47 J4 Kara-Say Kyrgyzstan
128 B4 Karasburg Namibia
Kara Sea sea *see* Karskoye More
52 D1 Karash Rus. Fed.
56 G1 Karasjok Norway
47 H2 Karasu r. Kazakhstan
43 D1 Karasu r. Turkey
46 F2 Karasu Kazakhstan
47 G2 Karasu Kazakhstan
42 B1 Karasu Turkey
51 D7 Karasu Turkey
47 K2 Karasuk r. Rus. Fed.
47 J2 Karasuk Rus. Fed.
47 H4 Kara-Suu Kyrgyzstan
53 A1 Karasyn Ukraine
39 E2 Karāt Iran
47 L3 Karatan Kazakhstan
42 C2 Karataş Turkey
42 C1 Karataş Br. c. Turkey
47 H4 Karatau Kazakhstan
47 G4 Karatau, Khr. mountain range Kazakhstan
36 E2 Karatax Shan mountain range China
25 B5 Karathuri Myanmar
38 B4 Karativu i. Sri Lanka
46 D3 Karatobe Kazakhstan
47 J3 Karatol r. Kazakhstan
46 D3 Karaton Kazakhstan
115 C5 Karatoulas Greece
37 G4 Karatoya r. Bangladesh
28 B7 Karatsu Japan
23 C5 Karatung i. Indonesia
47 G2 Karaturgay r. Kazakhstan
47 J3 Karaul Kazakhstan
36 D4 Karauli India
46 E4 Karauzyak Uzbekistan
47 H4 Karavan Kyrgyzstan
115 E6 Karavi i. Greece
113 F7 Karavonisia i. Greece
43 B2 Karavostasi Cyprus
22 A3 Karawang Indonesia
81 F4 Karawanken mountain range Austria
Karaxahar r. *see* Kaidu
52 F4 Karay r. Rus. Fed.
47 K4 Karayulgan China
47 H3 Karazhal Kazakhstan
46 E4 Karazhar Uzbekistan
47 H3 Karazhingil Kazakhstan
42 E3 Karbalā' div. Iraq
42 F3 Karbalā' Iraq
87 H2 Karben Germany
47 J3 Karbushevka Kazakhstan
55 A3 Karby Denmark
79 K4 Karcag Hungary
77 K3 Karczew Poland
77 L4 Karczmiska Poland
115 B4 Kardakata Greece
112 G3 Kardam Bulgaria
115 D6 Kardamyli Greece
74 C2 Karden Germany
115 G6 Kardiotissa i. Greece
114 D3 Karditsa div. Greece
114 C3 Karditsa Greece
54 C2 Kärdla Estonia
78 F4 Kardos-ér r. Hungary
52 A2 Kardymovo Rus. Fed.
131 F4 Karee South Africa
130 C5 Kareeberg mts South Africa
130 D5 Kareebospoort pass South Africa
130 E6 Kareedouw South Africa
119 F4 Kareima Sudan
36 D5 Kareli India
54 E5 Karelichy Belarus
50 D1 Kareliya div. Rus. Fed.
50 E1 Karel'skiy Bereg Rus. Fed.
127 B6 Karema Tanzania
36 D4 Karera India
56 F1 Karesuando Sweden
39 E4 Kārevāndar Iran
51 H7 Kargalinskaya Rus. Fed.
46 E2 Kargalinskoye Kazakhstan
43 D1 Kargamiş Turkey
46 F1 Kargapol'ye Rus. Fed.
47 K1 Kargat r. Rus. Fed.
47 K1 Kargat Rus. Fed.
Karghalik *see* Yecheng
51 E7 Kargı Turkey
36 D2 Kargil *Jammu and Kashmir*
52 H3 Kargino Rus. Fed.
50 F2 Kargopol' Rus. Fed.
76 D3 Kargowa Poland
59 G1 Karholmsbruk Sweden
123 G4 Kari Nigeria
52 E3 Karian Rus. Fed.
114 E2 Kariani Greece
129 D2 Kariba Zimbabwe
129 D2 Kariba, Lake l. Zambia/Zimbabwe
28 G2 Kariba-yama volcano Japan
128 B3 Karibib Namibia
130 D6 Kariega watercourse South Africa
56 G1 Karigasniemi Finland
57 F3 Karijoki Finland
28 J2 Karikachi Pass pass Japan
8 D1 Karikari, Cape c. New Zealand
39 C2 Karīmābād Iran
22 B2 Karimata i. Indonesia
22 B2 Karimata, P.P. is Indonesia
39 B2 Karim Khanch Iran
38 B2 Karimnagar India
22 B3 Karimunjawa i. Indonesia
22 B3 Karimunjawa, P.P. is Indonesia
126 E2 Karin Somalia
54 C1 Karinainen Finland
54 C1 Karis Finland
39 D2 Karit Iran
115 D5 Karitaina Greece
114 D2 Karitsa Greece
29 F6 Kariya Japan
38 A2 Karjat India
37 F5 Karkai India
38 A3 Karkal India
115 D5 Karkalou Greece
47 J3 Karkaralinsk Kazakhstan
6 □1 Karkar I. i. P.N.G.
39 B3 Karkheh r. Iran
39 D4 Kārkīn Dar Iran
51 E6 Karkinits'ka Zatoka Ukraine
54 D1 Karkkila Finland
57 G3 Kärkölä Finland
59 J2 Karlby Finland
76 D1 Karlino Poland
42 E2 Karlıova Turkey
53 F2 Karlivka Ukraine
47 H5 Karl Marks mt. Tajikistan
Karl-Marx-Stadt *see* Chemnitz
104 E3 Karlovac Croatia
112 E3 Karlovo Bulgaria
78 B1 Karlovy Vary Czech Rep.
87 H4 Karlsbad Germany
59 F2 Karlsborg Sweden
73 J2 Karlsburg Germany
75 G4 Karlsfeld Germany
59 F3 Karlshamn Sweden
80 C2 Karlshuld Germany
59 F2 Karlskoga Sweden
75 G4 Karlskron Germany
59 F3 Karlskrona Sweden
74 D4 Karlsruhe div. *Baden-Württemberg* Germany
74 D3 Karlsruhe *Karlsruhe* Germany
150 D1 Karlstad *Minnesota* U.S.A.
59 E2 Karlstad Sweden
74 E3 Karlstadt Germany
81 G2 Karlstetten Austria
124 C1 Karma r. Chad
51 D4 Karma Belarus
123 E4 Karma Niger
38 A2 Karmala India
52 B2 Karmanovo Rus. Fed.
58 A2 Karmøy i. Norway
37 H5 Karnafuli Reservoir resr Bangladesh
36 D3 Karnal India
37 E3 Karnali r. Nepal
36 D3 Karnaprayag India
38 A3 Karnataka div. India
76 D1 Karnice Poland
77 J3 Karniewa Poland
80 D4 Karnische Alpen mountain range Austria
112 F3 Karnobat Bulgaria
118 D4 Karnoi Sudan
58 D2 Kärnsjön l. Sweden
81 E4 Kärnten div. Austria
36 A4 Karodi Pakistan
129 D2 Karoi Zimbabwe
107 H3 Karojba Croatia
6 □6 Karoko Fiji
24 B4 Karokpi Myanmar
37 G3 Karo La China
37 H4 Karong India
127 B6 Karonga Malawi
127 A5 Karonje mt. Rwanda
130 D6 Karoo National Park nat. park South Africa
12 D3 Karoonda *S. Australia* Australia
36 B3 Karor Pakistan
126 C1 Karora Eritrea
22 D2 Karossa Indonesia
22 D4 Karossa, Tg pt Indonesia
73 H2 Karow Germany
113 F7 Karpathos i. Greece
113 F7 Karpathos Greece
77 K6 Karpaty mountain range Poland/Slovakia
114 C4 Karpenisi Greece
114 E1 Karperi Greece
114 C3 Karpero Greece
50 H1 Karpogory Rus. Fed.
43 A1 Karpuz r. Turkey
113 F6 Karpuzlu *Aydın* Turkey
113 F4 Karpuzlu *Edirne* Turkey
53 B1 Karpylivka Ukraine
16 B4 Karratha *Western Australia* Australia
55 D4 Karrebæksminde Denmark
55 D4 Karrebæksminde Bugt b. Denmark
131 F5 Karringmelkspruit South Africa
39 E2 Karrukh Afghanistan
39 E1 Karrychirla Turkmenistan
42 E1 Kars Turkey
56 G3 Kärsämäki Finland
54 E3 Kārsava Latvia
46 D4 Karshi Turkmenistan
47 G5 Karshi Uzbekistan
76 F2 Karsin Poland
113 F5 Karşıyaka Turkey
44 J2 Karskoye More sea Rus. Fed.
73 G2 Karstädt Germany
56 G3 Karstula Finland
52 H2 Karsun Rus. Fed.
42 B1 Kartal Turkey
127 D7 Kartala crater Comoros
46 F2 Kartaly Rus. Fed.
50 K1 Kartayel' Rus. Fed.
54 B4 Kartena Lithuania
56 G3 Karttula Finland
76 G1 Kartuzy Poland
15 E3 Karumba *Queensland* Australia
39 B3 Kārūn r. Iran
127 B5 Karungu Bay b. Kenya
22 D4 Karuni Indonesia
55 B3 Karup r. Denmark
55 B3 Karup Denmark
38 B4 Karur India
57 F3 Karvia Finland
57 F3 Karvianjoki r. Finland
79 H2 Karviná Czech Rep.
114 B3 Karvounari Greece
38 A3 Karwar India
80 C3 Karwendelgebirge mts Austria
114 B4 Karya Greece
114 F2 Karyes Greece
30 E2 Karymskoye Rus. Fed.
115 F4 Karystos Greece
52 G3 Karzhimant Rus. Fed.
55 B2 Kås Denmark
138 C3 Kasabonika *Ontario* Canada
138 C3 Kasabonika Lake l. *Ontario* Canada
125 C4 Kasai r. Zaire
28 E6 Kasai Japan
125 D5 Kasai Occidental div. Zaire
125 D5 Kasai Oriental div. Zaire
125 D6 Kasaji Zaire
29 H5 Kasama Japan
127 B7 Kasama Zambia
47 G5 Kasan Uzbekistan
128 D2 Kasane Botswana
125 C4 Kasangulu Zaire
47 H4 Kasansay Uzbekistan
38 A3 Kasaragod India
54 C2 Kasari r. Estonia
137 J2 Kasba Lake l. *N.W.T.* Canada
120 C2 Kasba Tadla Morocco
28 C8 Kaseda Japan
78 C2 Kasejovice Czech Rep.
125 E6 Kasempa Zambia
75 G2 Kasendorf Germany
125 E6 Kasenga Zaire
125 E5 Kasengu Zaire
124 F3 Kasenye Zaire
127 B4 Kasese Uganda
124 E4 Kasese Zaire
36 D4 Kasganj India
39 C3 Kāshān Iran
51 G5 Kashary Rus. Fed.
138 D3 Kashechewan *Ontario* Canada
Kashgar *see* Kashi
47 J5 Kashi China
29 E6 Kashihara Japan
28 C7 Kashima Japan
29 H5 Kashima-nada b. Japan
52 C1 Kashin Rus. Fed.
52 C1 Kashinka r. Rus. Fed.
54 E3 Kashino Rus. Fed.
36 D3 Kashipur India
52 D2 Kashira Rus. Fed.
51 F5 Kashirskoye Rus. Fed.
29 G5 Kashiwazaki Japan
47 H3 Kashkanteniz Kazakhstan
50 F1 Kashkarantsy Rus. Fed.
53 G3 Kashlahach r. Ukraine
52 F3 Kashma r. Rus. Fed.
39 D2 Kāshmar Iran
36 B3 Kashmor Pakistan
39 G2 Kashmund reg. Afghanistan
125 E5 Kashyukulu Zaire
37 E4 Kasia India
52 A3 Kasilovo Rus. Fed.
22 D2 Kasimbar Indonesia
52 E2 Kasimov Rus. Fed.
81 H5 Kašina Croatia
144 B4 Kaskaskia r. *Illinois* U.S.A.
137 L3 Kaskattama r. *Manitoba* Canada
47 J4 Kaskelen Kazakhstan
57 F3 Kaskinen Finland
46 F1 Kasli Rus. Fed.
22 C2 Kasongan Indonesia
125 E4 Kasongo Zaire
125 C5 Kasongo-Lunda Zaire
113 F7 Kasos i. Greece
114 G3 Kaspakas Greece
78 C2 Kašperské Hory Czech Rep.
51 H7 Kaspi Georgia
51 H7 Kaspiysk Rus. Fed.
Kaspiyskoye More sea *see* Caspian Sea
54 C2 Kassaare Laht b. Estonia
119 G4 Kassala Sudan
114 E2 Kassandra pen. Greece
114 E2 Kassandreia Greece
72 E4 Kassel div. *Hessen* Germany
72 E4 Kassel *Kassel* Germany
121 F1 Kasserine Tunisia
119 F4 Kassinger Sudan
114 A3 Kassiopi Greece
148 A3 Kasson *Minnesota* U.S.A.
114 B3 Kassopi Greece
42 C1 Kastamonu Turkey
114 D2 Kastania *Kentriki Makedonia* Greece
114 C3 Kastania *Thessalia* Greece
74 C2 Kastellaun Germany
115 E7 Kastelli *Kriti* Greece
115 G7 Kastelli *Kriti* Greece
69 C3 Kasterlee Belgium
80 D2 Kastl *Bayern* Germany
75 G3 Kastl *Bayern* Germany
59 G3 Kastlösa Sweden
114 C2 Kastoria div. Greece
114 C2 Kastoria Greece
52 D4 Kastornoye Rus. Fed.
114 B4 Kastos i. Greece
114 B3 Kastrosykia Greece
28 C7 Kasuga Japan
29 F6 Kasugai Japan
124 E4 Kasuku Zaire
127 B5 Kasulu Tanzania
125 E6 Kasumbalesa Zaire
28 E6 Kasumi Japan
29 H5 Kasumiga-ura l. Japan
51 J7 Kasumkent Rus. Fed.
127 B7 Kasungu Malawi
127 B7 Kasungu National Park nat. park Malawi
36 C3 Kasur Pakistan
76 E4 Kaszczor Poland
147 J2 Katahdin, Mt mt. *Maine* U.S.A.
36 D2 Kataklik *Jammu and Kashmir*
125 D4 Katako-Kombe Zaire
115 C5 Katakolo Greece
126 B4 Katakwi Uganda
36 D5 Katangi India
17 B7 Katanning *Western Australia* Australia
124 E4 Katanti Zaire
115 B5 Katastari Greece
127 B6 Katavi National Park nat. park Tanzania
46 E2 Katav Ivanovsk Rus. Fed.
39 G2 Katawaz Afghanistan
46 F1 Kataysk Rus. Fed.
25 A6 Katchall i. *Andaman and Nicobar Is* India
125 E5 Katea Zaire
125 D5 Katenge Zaire
114 D2 Katerini Greece
53 D2 Katerynopil' Ukraine
127 C5 Katesh Tanzania
136 C3 Kate's Needle mt. *Alaska/British Columbia* Canada/U.S.A.
127 B7 Katete Zambia
37 E5 Katghora India
24 B1 Katha Myanmar
43 B5 Katherîna, G. mt. Egypt
14 C2 Katherine r. *Northern Terr.* Australia
14 C2 Katherine *Northern Terr.* Australia
15 E4 Katherine Cr. watercourse *Queensland* Australia
14 C2 Katherine Gorge Nat. Park nat. park *Northern Terr.* Australia
36 B5 Kathiawar India
43 B4 Kathīb el Henu h. Egypt
43 B4 Kathīb el Makhāzin sand dunes Egypt
38 C4 Kathiraveli Sri Lanka
131 G3 Kathlehong South Africa
73 K4 Kathlow Germany
37 F4 Kathmandu Nepal
130 D3 Kathu South Africa
127 C5 Kathua watercourse Kenya
36 C2 Kathua India
122 C4 Kati Mali
37 F4 Katihar India
8 E2 Katikati New Zealand
131 F6 Kati-Kati South Africa
7 □16 Katiki h. *Easter I.* Chile
128 C2 Katima Mulilo Namibia
122 C5 Katiola Côte d'Ivoire
7 □10 Katiu i. *French Polynesia* Pacific Ocean
115 C4 Kato Achaïa Greece
115 E4 Kato Alepochori Greece
115 C4 Katochi Greece
115 C5 Kato Figaleia Greece
115 G6 Kato Koufonisi i. Greece
36 D5 Katol India
114 C4 Kato Makrinou Greece
114 E1 Kato Nevrokopi Greece
25 □ Katong Singapore
127 B4 Katonga r. Uganda
114 D3 Kato Olympos mt. Greece
13 G3 Katoomba *New South Wales* Australia
114 D4 Kato Tithorea Greece
114 C4 Katouna Greece
75 J3 Katovice Czech Rep.
114 E1 Kato Vrontou Greece
76 G5 Katowice div. Poland
77 H5 Katowice Poland
37 G5 Katoya India
115 H7 Kato Zakros Greece
59 G2 Katrineholm Sweden
66 D4 Katrine, Loch l. *Scotland* U.K.
115 D5 Katsaros Greece
81 E3 Katschberghöhe pass Austria
81 F2 Katsdorf Austria
129 H2 Katsepy Madagascar
123 F4 Katsina div. Nigeria
123 F4 Katsina Nigeria
123 F5 Katsina-Ala Nigeria
28 B7 Katsumoto Japan
29 □2 Katsuren-zaki c. Japan
29 H5 Katsuta Japan
29 H6 Katsuura Japan
28 D6 Katsuyama Japan
29 F5 Katsuyama Japan
139 G2 Kattaktoc, Cap headland *Québec* Canada
47 G5 Kattakurgan Uzbekistan
115 □ Kattavia Greece
140 E2 Kattawagami Lake l. *Ontario* Canada
59 F1 Kattbo Sweden
55 C3 Kattegat str. Denmark
59 E2 Kättilstorp Sweden
47 L2 Katun' r. Rus. Fed.
52 F1 Katunki Rus. Fed.
47 L2 Katunskiy Khrebet mountain range Rus. Fed.
36 B3 Katuri Pakistan
68 C2 Katwijk aan Zee Netherlands
76 E4 Kąty Wrocławskie Poland
74 C2 Katzenelnbogen Germany
74 C3 Katzweiler Germany
153 □2 Kauai i. *Hawaii* U.S.A.
153 □2 Kauai Channel chan. *Hawaii* U.S.A.
74 F3 Kaub Germany
128 C2 Kaudom Game Park res. Namibia
7 □10 Kauehi i. *French Polynesia* Pacific Ocean
75 F5 Kaufbeuren Germany
75 F4 Kaufering Germany
72 E4 Kaufungen Germany
57 F3 Kauhajoki Finland
56 F3 Kauhava Finland
24 B1 Kaukkwè Hills mountain range Myanmar
56 G2 Kaukonen Finland
54 E2 Kauksi Estonia
7 □10 Kaukura i. *French Polynesia* Pacific Ocean
153 □2 Kaula i. *Hawaii* U.S.A.
153 □2 Kaulakahi Channel chan. *Hawaii* U.S.A.
75 G2 Kaulsdorf Germany
139 H2 Kaumajet Mts mountain range *Newfoundland* Canada
153 □2 Kaunakakai *Hawaii* U.S.A.
54 C4 Kaunas Lithuania
54 E3 Kaunata Latvia
80 B4 Kaunertal v. Austria
58 B1 Kaupanger Norway
123 F4 Kaura-Namoda Nigeria
27 □ Kau Sai Chau i. Hong Kong
56 F3 Kaustinen Finland
69 E5 Kautenbach Luxembourg
56 F1 Kautokeino Norway
81 G2 Kautzen Austria
25 B5 Kau-ye Kyun i. Myanmar
114 D1 Kavadarci Macedonia
114 B4 Kavajë Albania
113 F4 Kavak *Çanakkale* Turkey
42 C1 Kavak *Samsun* Turkey
113 G6 Kavaklıdere Turkey
114 F1 Kavala div. Greece
114 F2 Kavala *Kavála* Greece
38 C3 Kavali India
39 C3 Kavār Iran
35 D8 Kavaratti i. India
112 G3 Kavarna Bulgaria
54 D4 Kavarskas Lithuania
52 A2 Kavel'shchino Rus. Fed.
73 H2 Kavelstorf Germany
122 B4 Kavendou, Mt mt. Guinea
38 B4 Kāveri r. India
52 E2 Kaverino Rus. Fed.
6 □1 Kavieng P.N.G.
128 C2 Kavimba Botswana
39 C3 Kavīr salt flat Iran
39 C2 Kavir salt flat Iran
39 B2 Kavir e Namak-e Miqhān salt flat Iran
39 D2 Kavīr-i-Namak salt flat Iran
55 F4 Kävlinge Sweden
114 B3 Kavos Greece
77 M6 Kavs'ke Ukraine
46 D3 Kavzshanbas Kazakhstan
163 G3 Kaw French Guiana
29 H4 Kawabe Japan
29 G6 Kawagoe Japan
29 G6 Kawaguchi Japan
29 H4 Kawai Japan
153 □2 Kawaihae *Hawaii* U.S.A.
28 D6 Kawajiri Japan
8 E1 Kawakawa New Zealand
125 E5 Kawambwa Zambia
28 C7 Kawaminami Japan
29 E6 Kawanishi Japan

75 H3 **Kötzting** Germany
123 E4 **Kouandé** Benin
124 D3 **Kouango** Central African Rep.
122 B4 **Koubia** Guinea
122 D4 **Koudougou** Burkina
68 D2 **Koudum** Netherlands
130 D6 **Koueveldberg mts** South Africa
114 D2 **Koufalia** Greece
123 G4 **Koufey well** Niger
115 G6 **Koufonisi i.** Greece
115 H8 **Koufonisi i.** Greece
130 E6 **Kouga r.** South Africa
130 D6 **Kougaberg mts** South Africa
124 C2 **Koui** Central African Rep.
125 B4 **Kouilou div.** Congo
122 D4 **Kouka** Burkina
114 B3 **Kouklioi** Greece
124 D2 **Koukourou r.** Central African Rep.
124 B4 **Koulamoutou** Gabon
122 C4 **Koulikoro div.** Mali
122 C4 **Koulikoro** Mali
123 E4 **Koulou** Niger
122 B4 **Koulountou r.** Guinea/Senegal
124 B2 **Koum** Cameroon
124 C2 **Kouma r.** Central African Rep.
6 □2 **Koumac** *New Caledonia* Pacific Ocean
15 G4 **Koumala** *Queensland* Australia
122 B4 **Koumbia** Guinea
124 C2 **Koumogo** Chad
122 B4 **Koumpentoum** Senegal
124 C2 **Koumra** Chad
122 B4 **Koundâra** Guinea
122 D4 **Koundougou** Burkina
122 B4 **Koungheul** Senegal
113 F6 **Kounoupoi i.** Greece
47 H3 **Kounradskiy** Kazakhstan
130 C6 **Koup** South Africa
122 D4 **Koupéla** Burkina
47 K2 **Kourak** Rus. Fed.
122 C5 **Kourandou mt.** Guinea
124 C2 **Kourayadjé** Chad
122 C4 **Kourémalé** Mali
29 □2 **Kouri-jima i.** Japan
78 D2 **Kouřim** Czech Rep.
114 G1 **Kourou r.** Greece
163 G2 **Kourou** French Guiana
122 C4 **Kouroussa** Guinea
118 D4 **Kourtidi well** Chad
130 C6 **Kousberg mt.** South Africa
122 B4 **Koussanar** Senegal
124 C1 **Kousséri** Cameroon
122 C4 **Koutiala** Mali
6 □2 **Koutoumo i.** *New Caledonia* Pacific Ocean
114 D3 **Koutsochero** Greece
113 F6 **Koutsomyti i.** Greece
115 D5 **Koutsopodi** Greece
57 G3 **Kouvola** Finland
124 C4 **Kouyou r.** Congo
112 C2 **Kovačica** Yugoslavia
56 E2 **Kovallberget** Sweden
75 J2 **Kovářská** Czech Rep.
56 H2 **Kovdor** Rus. Fed.
56 H2 **Kovdozero, Oz. l.** Rus. Fed.
53 A1 **Kovel'** Ukraine
52 F1 **Kovernino** Rus. Fed.
38 B4 **Kovilpatti** India
112 C2 **Kovin** Yugoslavia
52 E1 **Kovrov** Rus. Fed.
53 F2 **Kov"yahy** Ukraine
52 F2 **Kovylkino** Rus. Fed.
50 F2 **Kovzhskoye, Ozero l.** Rus. Fed.
77 H3 **Kowal** Poland
77 L1 **Kowale Oleckie** Poland
76 G2 **Kowalewo Pomorskie** Poland
73 K3 **Kowalów** Poland
15 E2 **Kowanyama** *Queensland* Australia
128 A2 **Kowares waterhole** Namibia
76 D5 **Kowary** Poland
54 F5 **Kowbcha** Belarus
9 C5 **Kowhitirangi** New Zealand
77 J4 **Kowiesy** Poland
140 B1 **Kowkash** *Ontario* Canada
27 □ **Kowloon** Hong Kong
27 □ **Kowloon Pk h.** Hong Kong
47 K5 **Koxlax** China
47 J5 **Koxtag** China
28 C6 **Kōyama-misaki pt** Japan
25 B5 **Ko Yao Yai i.** Thailand
42 B2 **Köyceğiz** Turkey
113 G6 **Köyceğiz Gölü l.** Turkey
50 G1 **Koyda** Rus. Fed.
50 J2 **Koygorodok** Rus. Fed.
112 E3 **Koynare** Bulgaria
38 A2 **Koyna Res. resr** India
50 H1 **Koynas** Rus. Fed.
29 H4 **Koyoshi-gawa r.** Japan
53 G1 **Kozacha Lopan'** Ukraine
28 B6 **Kō-zaki pt** Japan
28 D6 **Kōzan** Japan
42 C2 **Kozan** Turkey
114 C2 **Kozani div.** Greece
114 C2 **Kozani** Greece
104 F3 **Kozara mountain range** Bos.-Herz.
79 H3 **Kozárovce** Slovakia
53 E1 **Kozats'ke** Ukraine
53 D1 **Kozelets'** Ukraine
53 E2 **Kozel'shchyna** Ukraine
52 B2 **Kozel'sk** Rus. Fed.
118 C3 **Kozen well** Chad
46 F3 **Kozhabakhy** Kazakhstan
53 C2 **Kozhanka** Ukraine
45 N2 **Kozhevnikovo** Rus. Fed.
Kozhikode *see* **Calicut**
53 B2 **Kozhukliv** Ukraine
77 H5 **Koziegłowy** Poland
73 K2 **Kozielice** Poland
77 K4 **Kozienice** Poland
52 G1 **Kozikovo** Rus. Fed.
107 H3 **Kozina** Slovenia
53 F1 **Koziyivka** Ukraine
75 J3 **Kožlany** Czech Rep.
112 D3 **Kozloduy** Bulgaria
54 F2 **Kozlov-Bereg** Rus. Fed.
52 E4 **Kozlovka** Rus. Fed.
52 G2 **Kozlovka** Rus. Fed.
50 J4 **Kozlovka** Rus. Fed.
52 C1 **Kozlovo** Rus. Fed.
77 J3 **Kozłów Biskupi** Poland
77 J2 **Kozłowo** Poland
42 B1 **Kozlu** Turkey
104 G3 **Kozluk** Bos.-Herz.
76 F4 **Koźmin** Poland
52 H1 **Koz'modem'yansk** Rus. Fed.
53 A2 **Kozova** Ukraine
76 D4 **Kożuchów** Poland
114 D1 **Kožuf mts** Greece/Macedonia
29 G6 **Kōzu-shima i.** Japan
53 C2 **Kozyatyn** Ukraine
53 E1 **Kozylivka** Ukraine
53 D2 **Kozyn** *Kyyivs'ka Oblast'* Ukraine
53 D1 **Kozyn** *Kyyivs'ka Oblast'* Ukraine
113 F4 **Kozyörük** Turkey
123 E5 **Kpalimé** Togo
122 D5 **Kpandae** Ghana
123 E5 **Kpandu** Ghana
25 B5 **Kra, Isthmus of isth.** Thailand
131 F5 **Kraai r.** South Africa
130 B6 **Kraaifontein** South Africa
130 E4 **Kraankuil** South Africa
173 G4 **Krabbé** Argentina
69 C3 **Krabbendijke** Netherlands
25 B5 **Krabi** Thailand
25 B5 **Kra Buri** Thailand
25 D4 **Krâcheh** Cambodia
73 K2 **Krackow** Germany
56 E2 **Kraddsele** Sweden
22 B3 **Kragan** Indonesia
58 C2 **Kragerø** Norway
112 C2 **Kragujevac** Yugoslavia
80 D2 **Kraiburg am Inn** Germany
87 H3 **Kraichbach r.** Germany
74 D3 **Kraichgau reg.** Germany
76 F2 **Krajenka** Poland
76 C2 **Krajnik Dolny** Poland
22 A3 **Krakatau i.** Indonesia
58 A1 **Krakhella** Norway
25 D4 **Krâkôr** Cambodia
77 M6 **Krakovets'** Ukraine
77 J5 **Kraków div.** Poland
77 H5 **Kraków** Poland
73 H2 **Krakower See l.** Germany
25 C4 **Krâlănh** Cambodia
158 □3 **Kralendijk** *Bonaire* Netherlands Ant.
78 F1 **Králíky** Czech Rep.
107 J3 **Kraljevica** Croatia
112 C3 **Kraljevo** Yugoslavia
79 K3 **Kráľova hoľa mt.** Slovakia
78 C2 **Kralovice** Czech Rep.
79 L3 **Kráľovský Chlmec** Slovakia
78 D1 **Kralupy nad Vltavou** Czech Rep.
78 D2 **Králův Dvůr** Czech Rep.
76 F1 **Kramarzyny** Poland
53 G2 **Kramators'k** Ukraine
56 E3 **Kramfors** Sweden
68 C3 **Krammer est.** Netherlands
76 G3 **Kramsk** Poland
114 C3 **Kranea** Greece
72 B4 **Kranenburg** Germany
73 G5 **Kranichfeld** Germany
115 E5 **Kranidi** Greece
81 F4 **Kranj** Slovenia
25 □ **Kranji Res. resr** Singapore
81 E4 **Kranjska Gora** Slovenia
53 E3 **Kranoznam"yans'kyy Kanal canal** Ukraine
131 G4 **Kransfontein** South Africa
131 G3 **Kranskop mt.** South Africa
131 H4 **Kranskop** South Africa
104 E4 **Krapanj** Croatia
73 L2 **Krąpiel** Poland
78 E5 **Krapina** Croatia
78 E5 **Krapinske Toplice** Croatia
47 L1 **Krapivinskiy** Rus. Fed.
52 A2 **Krapivna** Rus. Fed.
76 F5 **Krapkowice** Poland
50 H2 **Krasavino** Rus. Fed.
53 E2 **Krasenivka** Ukraine
44 G2 **Krasino** Rus. Fed.
77 M6 **Krasiv** Ukraine
52 F3 **Krasivka** Rus. Fed.
54 E4 **Krāslava** Latvia
78 B1 **Kraslice** Czech Rep.
75 K3 **Krásná Hora nad Vltavou** Czech Rep.
75 K2 **Krásná Lípa** Czech Rep.
53 G3 **Krasna Polyana** Ukraine
53 D2 **Krasna Slobidka** Ukraine
77 N2 **Krasnasyel'ski** Belarus
51 D4 **Krasnaya Gora** Rus. Fed.
52 E2 **Krasnaya Gorbatka** Rus. Fed.
47 H3 **Krasnaya Polyana** Kazakhstan
51 G7 **Krasnaya Polyana** Rus. Fed.
54 E5 **Krasnaya Slabada** Belarus
53 F1 **Krasnaya Yaruga** Rus. Fed.
52 C3 **Krasnaya Zarya** Rus. Fed.
52 F3 **Krasnaya Znamya** Rus. Fed.
53 D1 **Krasne** *Chernihivs'ka Oblast'* Ukraine
53 A2 **Krasne** *L'vivs'ka Oblast'* Ukraine
77 N6 **Krasne** *L'vivs'ka Oblast'* Ukraine
53 C2 **Krasne** *Vinnyts'ka Oblast'* Ukraine
77 J3 **Krasne** Poland
77 M5 **Kraśniczyn** Poland
77 L5 **Kraśnik** Poland
53 C3 **Krasni Okny** Ukraine
47 H2 **Krasnoarmeysk** Kazakhstan
51 H5 **Krasnoarmeysk** Rus. Fed.
52 D1 **Krasnoarmeysk** Rus. Fed.
51 F6 **Krasnoarmeyskaya** Rus. Fed.
45 T3 **Krasnoarmeyskiy** Rus. Fed.
52 H2 **Krasnoarmeyskoye** Rus. Fed.
53 G2 **Krasnoarmiys'k** Ukraine
50 H2 **Krasnoborsk** Rus. Fed.
77 M5 **Krasnobród** Poland
47 L2 **Krasnobrodskiy** Rus. Fed.
51 F6 **Krasnodar div.** Rus. Fed.
51 F6 **Krasnodar** Rus. Fed.
51 F5 **Krasnodon** Ukraine
54 F3 **Krasnogorodskoye** Rus. Fed.
52 C2 **Krasnogorsk** Rus. Fed.
27 Q2 **Krasnogorsk** Rus. Fed.
46 F2 **Krasnogorskiy** Rus. Fed.
52 E1 **Krasnogvardeyskiy** Rus. Fed.
51 G6 **Krasnogvardeyskoye** Rus. Fed.
53 F2 **Krasnohrad** Ukraine
51 E6 **Krasnohvardiys'ke** Ukraine
31 F2 **Krasnokamensk** Rus. Fed.
47 J2 **Krasnokutsk** Kazakhstan
53 F1 **Krasnokuts'k** Ukraine
52 D4 **Krasnolesnyy** Rus. Fed.
77 L1 **Krasnoles'ye** Rus. Fed.
52 H1 **Krasnooktyabr'skiy** Rus. Fed.
54 F1 **Krasnoostrovskiy** Rus. Fed.
53 G2 **Krasnopavlivka** Ukraine
51 E6 **Krasnoperekops'k** Ukraine
53 D2 **Krasnopilka** Ukraine
53 F1 **Krasnopillya** Ukraine
77 M1 **Krasnopol** Poland
54 F1 **Krasnosel'skoye** Rus. Fed.
50 F1 **Krasnoshchel'ye** Rus. Fed.
77 K2 **Krasnosielc** Poland
53 B2 **Krasnosilka** Ukraine
46 B2 **Krasnoslobodsk** Rus. Fed.
52 F2 **Krasnoslobodsk** Rus. Fed.
52 E3 **Krasnosvobodnoye** Rus. Fed.
44 H4 **Krasnotur'insk** Rus. Fed.
46 E1 **Krasnoufimsk** Rus. Fed.
46 E2 **Krasnousol'skiy** Rus. Fed.
44 G3 **Krasnovishersk** Rus. Fed.
46 D4 **Krasnovodsk** Turkmenistan
46 D5 **Krasnovodsk, M pt** Turkmenistan
46 D5 **Krasnovodskiy Zaliv b.** Turkmenistan
46 D4 **Krasnovodskoye Plato plat.** Turkmenistan
46 E2 **Krasnoyar** Kazakhstan
31 J2 **Krasnoyarovo** Rus. Fed.
45 L4 **Krasnoyarsk** Rus. Fed.
47 M2 **Krasnoyarskoye Vdkhr. resr** Rus. Fed.
52 D3 **Krasnoye** Rus. Fed.
52 A3 **Krasnoye** Rus. Fed.
52 E2 **Krasnoye Ekho** Rus. Fed.
52 E1 **Krasnoye-na-Volge** Rus. Fed.
52 D1 **Krasnoye Plamya** Rus. Fed.
52 B1 **Krasnoye Znamya** Rus. Fed.
53 A2 **Krasnoyil's'k** Ukraine
50 J2 **Krasnozatonskiy** Rus. Fed.
52 D1 **Krasnozavodsk** Rus. Fed.
47 J2 **Krasnozerskoye** Rus. Fed.
54 C4 **Krasnoznamensk** Rus. Fed.
53 E3 **Krasnoznam"yanka** Ukraine
77 M5 **Krasnystaw** Poland
50 D4 **Krasnyy** Rus. Fed.
52 E1 **Krasnyy Bogatyr'** Rus. Fed.
30 D2 **Krasnyy Chikoy** Rus. Fed.
52 G1 **Krasnyye Baki** Rus. Fed.
51 H6 **Krasnyye Barrikady** Rus. Fed.
52 H2 **Krasnyye Chetai** Rus. Fed.
52 D1 **Krasnyye Tkachi** Rus. Fed.
52 C1 **Krasnyy Kholm** Rus. Fed.
53 E1 **Krasnyy Kolyadyn** Ukraine
51 H5 **Krasnyy Kut** Rus. Fed.
50 D3 **Krasnyy Luch** Rus. Fed.
51 F5 **Krasnyy Lyman** Ukraine
52 H1 **Krasnyy Most** Rus. Fed.
52 D1 **Krasnyy Oktyabr'** Rus. Fed.
52 E1 **Krasnyy Oktyabr'** Rus. Fed.
52 G4 **Krasnyy Oktyabr'** Rus. Fed.
52 E1 **Krasnyy Profintern** Rus. Fed.
52 A3 **Krasnyy Rog** Rus. Fed.
52 G1 **Krasnyy Yar** Rus. Fed.
52 H4 **Krasnyy Yar** Rus. Fed.
51 J6 **Krasnyy Yar** Rus. Fed.
50 J4 **Krasnyy-Yar** Rus. Fed.
51 H5 **Krasnyy Yar** Rus. Fed.
114 B1 **Krastë** Albania
53 B2 **Krasyliv** Ukraine
79 M4 **Kraszna r.** Hungary
112 D3 **Kratovo** Macedonia
74 E4 **Krauchenwies** Germany
54 E4 **Krauja** Latvia
51 H7 **Kraynovka** Rus. Fed.
54 C4 **Kražantė r.** Lithuania
72 B4 **Krefeld** Germany
72 E4 **Kreiensen** Germany
115 □ **Kremasti** Greece
53 E2 **Kremenchuk** Ukraine
53 E2 **Kremenchuts'ka Vodoskhovshche resr** Ukraine
53 A1 **Kremenets'** Ukraine
52 C2 **Kremenki** Rus. Fed.
52 F2 **Kremenki** Rus. Fed.
52 B2 **Kremenskoye** Rus. Fed.
78 E2 **Křemešník h.** Czech Rep.
53 A2 **Kremintsi** Ukraine
152 F3 **Kremmling** *Colorado* U.S.A.
79 H3 **Kremnica** Slovakia
72 E2 **Krempe** Germany
81 G2 **Krems div.** Austria
81 G2 **Krems r.** Austria
81 G2 **Krems an der Donau** Austria
81 F2 **Kremsmünster** Austria
78 D3 **Křemže** Czech Rep.
134 B4 **Krenitzin Islands is** *Alaska* U.S.A.
78 F3 **Křepice** Czech Rep.
47 J1 **Kreshchenka** Rus. Fed.
112 D4 **Kresna** Bulgaria
81 F4 **Kresnice** Slovenia
74 E5 **Kressbronn am Bodensee** Germany
115 C5 **Krestena** Greece
50 E3 **Kresttsy** Rus. Fed.
52 D3 **Kresty** Rus. Fed.
54 B4 **Kretinga** Lithuania
75 G5 **Kreuth** Germany
74 B2 **Kreuzau** Germany
80 E4 **Kreuzeck mt.** Austria
83 E1 **Kreuzlingen** Switzerland
74 C2 **Kreuztal** Germany
54 E4 **Kreva** Belarus
124 A3 **Kribi** Cameroon
112 E3 **Krichim** Bulgaria
81 G3 **Krieglach** Austria
82 C1 **Kriegstetten** Switzerland
131 G3 **Kriel** South Africa
83 D1 **Kriens** Switzerland
114 C4 **Krikello** Greece
114 C4 **Krikellos** Greece
124 C2 **Krim-Krim** Chad
80 D3 **Krimmler Wasserfälle waterfall** Austria
68 C3 **Krimpen aan de IJssel** Netherlands
75 L2 **Křinec** Czech Rep.
114 F1 **Krinides** Greece
81 E3 **Krippenstein mt.** Austria
38 B2 **Krishna r.** India
38 B3 **Krishnagiri** India
38 C3 **Krishna, Mouths of the river mouth** India
37 G5 **Krishnanagar** India
38 B3 **Krishnaraja Sagara l.** India
59 G3 **Kristdala** Sweden
58 C2 **Kristiansand airport** Norway
58 B2 **Kristiansand** Norway
59 E3 **Kristianstad div.** Sweden
59 F3 **Kristianstad** Sweden
56 B3 **Kristiansund** Norway
59 F2 **Kristinehamn** Sweden
57 F3 **Kristinestad** Finland
115 F7 **Kriti i.** Greece
115 □ **Kritinia** Greece
52 D2 **Kriusha** Rus. Fed.
52 F2 **Kriusha** Rus. Fed.
104 G3 **Krivaja r.** Bos.-Herz.
114 D1 **Kriva Lakavica r.** Macedonia
79 J3 **Kriváň** Slovakia
112 D3 **Kriva Palanka** Macedonia
114 C1 **Krivogaštani** Macedonia
78 C2 **Křivoklátská Vrchovina h.** Czech Rep.
114 D1 **Krivolak** Macedonia
50 E1 **Krivoy Porog** Rus. Fed.
Krivoy Rog *see* **Kryvyy Rih**
52 F3 **Krivozer'ye** Rus. Fed.
54 B3 **Krīvu Kalns h.** Latvia
78 F2 **Křižanov** Czech Rep.
78 F5 **Križevci** Croatia
107 J3 **Krk i.** Croatia
107 J3 **Krk** Croatia
104 F3 **Krka r.** Croatia
81 F5 **Krka r.** Slovenia
81 F5 **Krka** Slovenia
78 E1 **Krkonoše mountain range** Czech Rep.
78 E1 **Krkonošský Narodní Park nat. park** Czech Rep.
81 E4 **Krn mt.** Slovenia
79 G1 **Krnov** Czech Rep.
112 B3 **Krnovo** Yugoslavia
71 H3 **Krobia** Poland
58 C1 **Krøderen l.** Norway
58 C1 **Krøderen** Norway
115 D6 **Krokees** Greece
56 D3 **Krokom** Sweden
22 B1 **Krokong** Malaysia
76 G1 **Krokowa** Poland
56 C3 **Krokstadøra** Norway
53 E1 **Krolevets'** Ukraine
52 B3 **Kroma r.** Rus. Fed.
131 F2 **Kromellenboog Dam dam** South Africa
78 G2 **Kroměříž** Czech Rep.
68 C2 **Krommenie** Netherlands
52 B3 **Kromy** Rus. Fed.
75 G2 **Kronach** Germany
87 H2 **Kronberg im Taunus** Germany
25 C5 **Krŏng Kaôh Kŏng** Cambodia
59 F3 **Kronoberg div.** Sweden
56 F3 **Kronoby** Finland
135 Q1 **Kronprins Christian Ld reg.** Greenland
135 P3 **Kronprins Frederik Bjerge nunatak** Greenland
72 F1 **Kronshagen** Germany
54 F2 **Kronshtadt** Rus. Fed.
24 B4 **Kronwa** Myanmar
131 F3 **Kroonstad** South Africa
73 G1 **Kröpelin** Germany
51 G6 **Kropotkin** Rus. Fed.
73 H4 **Kropstädt** Germany
53 C1 **Kropyvnya** Ukraine
77 M1 **Krosna** Lithuania
77 H3 **Krośniewice** Poland
77 K6 **Krosno div.** Poland
77 K6 **Krosno** Poland
76 D3 **Krosno Odrzańskie** Poland
58 C2 **Krossen** Norway
73 H4 **Krostitz** Germany
76 F4 **Krotoszyn** Poland
81 G3 **Krottendorf** Austria
74 C3 **Kröv** Germany
22 B3 **Kroya** Indonesia
114 A1 **Krrabë** Albania
107 J3 **Kršan** Croatia
81 G5 **Krško** Slovenia
52 G3 **Kruchi** Rus. Fed.
87 G2 **Kruft** Germany
131 F4 **Krugerdrifdam resr** South Africa
131 H2 **Kruger National Park nat. park** South Africa
131 F3 **Krugersdorp** South Africa
131 H2 **Krugerspos** South Africa
22 A3 **Krui** Indonesia
69 C3 **Kruibeke** Belgium
130 C6 **Kruidfontein** South Africa
69 C3 **Kruiningen** Netherlands
130 E7 **Kruisfontein** South Africa
114 A1 **Krujë** Albania
77 M6 **Krukenychi** Ukraine
77 K2 **Krukowo** Poland
81 H3 **Krumbach** Austria
74 F4 **Krumbach (Schwaben)** Germany
113 E4 **Krumovgrad** Bulgaria
83 G1 **Krün** Germany
Krungkao *see* **Ayutthaya**
Krung Thep *see* **Bangkok**
112 B2 **Krupanj** Yugoslavia
52 B4 **Krupets** Rus. Fed.
79 J3 **Krupina** Slovakia
79 J3 **Krupinská Planina plat.** Slovakia
78 C1 **Krupka** Czech Rep.
54 F4 **Krupki** Belarus
53 E2 **Krupodernytsi** Ukraine
55 B5 **Kruså** Denmark
112 C3 **Kruševac** Yugoslavia
114 C1 **Kruševo** Macedonia
78 B1 **Krušné Hory mountain range** Czech Rep.
76 E3 **Kruszewo** Poland
76 G3 **Kruszwica** Poland
76 F1 **Kruszyna** Poland
47 K2 **Krutikha** Rus. Fed.
47 H1 **Krutinka** Rus. Fed.
52 C3 **Krutoye** Rus. Fed.
53 E1 **Kruty** Ukraine
136 B3 **Kruzof I. i.** *Alaska* U.S.A.
114 D2 **Krya Vrysi** Greece
50 D4 **Krychaw** Belarus
53 B1 **Kryliv** Ukraine
51 E6 **Krym' pen.** Ukraine
77 N4 **Krymne** Ukraine
51 F6 **Krymsk** Rus. Fed.
51 E6 **Kryms'ki Hori** Ukraine
77 J6 **Krynica** Poland
71 J1 **Krynica Morska** Poland
77 M2 **Krynki** Poland
53 F2 **Krynychky** Ukraine
77 L2 **Krypno Kościelne** Poland
114 C2 **Krystalopigi** Greece
115 F6 **Krytiko Pelagos sea** Greece
53 E2 **Kryva Ruda** Ukraine
53 C2 **Kryvchunka** Ukraine
53 D3 **Kryve Ozero l.** Ukraine
54 E4 **Kryvichy** Belarus
53 E3 **Kryvyy Rih** Ukraine
53 C2 **Kryzhopil'** Ukraine
76 D2 **Krzęcin** Poland
76 E4 **Krzemieniewo** Poland
76 G5 **Krzepice** Poland
77 L3 **Krzesk-Królowa Niwa** Poland
77 L5 **Krzeszów** Poland
77 H5 **Krzeszowice** Poland
76 D3 **Krzeszyce** Poland
77 M3 **Krzna r.** Poland
77 J2 **Krzynowłoga Mała** Poland
73 L4 **Krzystkowice** Poland
77 L4 **Krzywwda** Poland
77 H3 **Krzyżanów** Poland
76 E3 **Krzyż Wielkopolski** Poland
121 D3 **Ksabi** Algeria
121 E1 **Ksar Chellala** Algeria
121 E1 **Ksar el Boukhari** Algeria
120 C1 **Ksar el Kebir** Morocco
100 E5 **Ksar Sghir** Morocco
44 G3 **Ksenofontova** Rus. Fed.
52 C4 **Kshen' r.** Rus. Fed.
52 C4 **Kshenskiy** Rus. Fed.
77 H2 **Książki** Poland
76 F3 **Książ Wielkopolski** Poland
121 G1 **Ksour Essaf** Tunisia
121 D2 **Ksour, Monts des mts** Algeria
52 G1 **Kstovo** Rus. Fed.
52 B3 **Ktsyn'** Rus. Fed.
25 B6 **Kuah** Malaysia
22 B2 **Kualajelai** Indonesia
25 C6 **Kuala Kangsar** Malaysia
22 C2 **Kualakapuas** Indonesia
25 C6 **Kuala Kerai** Malaysia
22 C2 **Kualakuayan** Indonesia
25 C7 **Kuala Kubu Baharu** Malaysia
25 C6 **Kuala Lipis** Malaysia
25 C7 **Kuala Lumpur** Malaysia
25 C6 **Kuala Nerang** Malaysia
22 C2 **Kualapembuang** Indonesia
25 C7 **Kuala Pilah** Malaysia
25 C7 **Kuala Rompin** Malaysia
25 B6 **Kualasimpang** Indonesia
25 C6 **Kuala Terengganu** Malaysia
22 A2 **Kualatungkai** Indonesia
23 A5 **Kuamut** Malaysia
31 F4 **Kuancheng** China
31 H4 **Kuandian** China
33 H4 **Kuanshan** Taiwan
25 C7 **Kuantan** Malaysia
Kuba *see* **Quba**
51 F6 **Kuban' r.** Rus. Fed.
54 C2 **Kübassaare Poolsaar pen.** Estonia
43 D2 **Kubaybāt** Syria
124 D1 **Kubbum** Sudan
50 F3 **Kubenskoye, Ozero l.** Rus. Fed.
73 J1 **Kubitzer Bodden b.** Germany
83 E2 **Küblis** Switzerland
50 H4 **Kubnya r.** Rus. Fed.
28 D7 **Kubokawa** Japan
112 F3 **Kubrat** Bulgaria
22 C4 **Kubu** Indonesia
6 □6 **Kubulau Pt pt** Fiji
22 C1 **Kubumesaäi** Indonesia
114 A2 **Kuç** Albania
112 C2 **Kučevo** Yugoslavia
36 C4 **Kuchāman** India
50 G1 **Kuchema** Rus. Fed.
80 A2 **Kuchen** Germany
52 B4 **Kucherivka** Rus. Fed.
22 B1 **Kuching** Malaysia
28 C7 **Kuchinotsu** Japan
80 E3 **Kuchl** Austria
47 J2 **Kuchukskoye, Oz. salt lake** Rus. Fed.
53 C3 **Kuchurhan r.** Ukraine
77 M1 **Kučiūnai** Lithuania
73 K2 **Kückelsberg h.** Germany
114 A2 **Kuçovë** Albania
77 J2 **Kuczbork-Osada** Poland
29 □2 **Kudaka-jima i.** Japan
38 A3 **Kudal** India
28 C7 **Kudamatsu** Japan
25 C7 **Kudap** Malaysia
30 C1 **Kudara** Rus. Fed.
158 □1 **Kudarebe pt** *Aruba* Caribbean
54 C4 **Kudirkos Naumiestis** Lithuania
38 B3 **Kudligi** India
52 G1 **Kud'ma r.** Rus. Fed.
76 E5 **Kudowa-Zdrój** *Wałbrzych* Poland
38 A3 **Kudremukh mt.** India
52 B2 **Kudrinskaya** Rus. Fed.
53 D3 **Kudryavtsivka** Ukraine
22 B3 **Kudus** Indonesia
33 H3 **Kuei-shan Tao i.** Taiwan
80 D3 **Kufstein div.** Austria
80 D3 **Kufstein** Austria
47 J4 **Kugaly** Kazakhstan
52 H1 **Kugesi** Rus. Fed.
134 E3 **Kugmallit Bay b.** *N.W.T.* Canada
39 E4 **Kūhak** Iran
75 G4 **Kühbach** Germany
73 H2 **Kuhbier** Germany
39 D3 **Kūhbonān** Iran
39 A2 **Kūhdasht** Iran
46 E5 **Kūh-e-Bīnālūd mountain range** Iran
42 F2 **Kūh-e Sahand mt.** Iran
42 F2 **Kūhhaye Sabalan mountain range** Iran
39 E4 **Kūhlab, Ra's pt** Iran
56 H2 **Kuhmo** Finland
57 G3 **Kuhmoinen** Finland
39 D4 **Kūh, Ra's-al pt** Iran
54 D2 **Kuimetsa** Estonia
68 D2 **Kuinre** Netherlands
130 A2 **Kuis** Namibia
128 B3 **Kuiseb watercourse** Namibia
128 B3 **Kuiseb Pass** Namibia
125 C6 **Kuito** Angola
136 C3 **Kuiu Island i.** *Alaska* U.S.A.
56 G2 **Kuivaniemi** Finland
54 C2 **Kuivastu** Estonia
37 F5 **Kujang** India
31 H5 **Kujang-Dong** North Korea
29 H3 **Kuji** Japan
29 H5 **Kuji-gawa r.** Japan
29 H3 **Kuji-wan b.** Japan
28 C7 **Kujū-san volcano** Japan
31 K2 **Kukan** Rus. Fed.
140 D2 **Kukatush** *Ontario* Canada
123 G4 **Kukawa** Nigeria
17 B7 **Kukerin** *Western Australia* Australia
112 C3 **Kukës** Albania
53 A1 **Kukhits'ka Volya** Ukraine
54 E3 **Kukhva r.** Latvia/Rus. Fed.
50 J3 **Kukmor** Rus. Fed.
22 A1 **Kukup** Malaysia
114 C1 **Kukurečani** Macedonia
39 C4 **Kūl r.** Iran
112 D3 **Kula** Bulgaria
42 B2 **Kula** Turkey
112 B2 **Kula** Yugoslavia
36 B3 **Kulachi** Pakistan
46 D3 **Kulagino** Kazakhstan
37 G3 **Kula Kangri mt.** Bhutan
46 D4 **Kulaly, O. i.** Kazakhstan
47 J4 **Kulanak** Kyrgyzstan
46 E3 **Kulandy** Kazakhstan
39 E4 **Kulaneh reg.** Pakistan
39 F3 **Kulao r.** Pakistan
45 P2 **Kular** Rus. Fed.
23 B5 **Kulassein i.** Philippines
114 E1 **Kulata** Bulgaria
22 D1 **Kulat, G. mt.** Indonesia
37 H4 **Kulaura** Bangladesh
22 D2 **Kulawi** Indonesia
53 F1 **Kul'baki** Rus. Fed.
54 B3 **Kuldīga** Latvia
31 J2 **Kul'dur** Rus. Fed.
52 F2 **Kulebaki** Rus. Fed.
25 D4 **Kulen** Cambodia
52 C3 **Kuleshi** Rus. Fed.
77 L2 **Kulesze Kościelne** Poland
52 E3 **Kulevatovo** Rus. Fed.
14 C4 **Kulgera** *Northern Terr.* Australia
50 H2 **Kulikovo** Rus. Fed.
25 C6 **Kulim** Malaysia
17 B7 **Kulin** *Western Australia* Australia
47 H5 **Kuli Sarez l.** Tajikistan
17 B6 **Kulja** *Western Australia* Australia
46 F4 **Kulkuduk** Uzbekistan
13 F2 **Kulkyne watercourse** *New South Wales* Australia
54 D2 **Kullamaa** Estonia
36 D3 **Kullu** India
75 G2 **Kulmbach** Germany
47 G5 **Kŭlob** Tajikistan
50 G1 **Kuloy r.** Rus. Fed.
50 G2 **Kuloy** Rus. Fed.
147 F4 **Kulpsville** *Pennsylvania* U.S.A.
46 D3 **Kul'sary** Kazakhstan
74 E3 **Külsheim** Germany
30 D1 **Kul'skiy** Rus. Fed.
79 G5 **Kolső-Somogy reg.** Hungary
42 C2 **Kulu** Turkey
47 K2 **Kulunda r.** Rus. Fed.
47 J2 **Kulunda** Rus. Fed.
47 J2 **Kulundinskaya Step' plain** Kazakhstan/Rus. Fed.
47 J2 **Kulundinskoye, Oz. salt lake** Rus. Fed.
31 E2 **Kulusutay** Rus. Fed.
39 C3 **Kūlvand** Iran
13 E3 **Kulwin** *Victoria* Australia
52 F4 **Kulyabovka** Rus. Fed.
77 N6 **Kulykiv** Ukraine
53 D1 **Kulykivka** Ukraine
31 H5 **Kŭm r.** South Korea
51 H6 **Kuma r.** Rus. Fed.
28 D7 **Kuma** Japan
29 G5 **Kumagaya** Japan
22 B2 **Kumai** Indonesia
28 G2 **Kumaishi** Japan
22 B2 **Kumai, Tk b.** Indonesia
46 E2 **Kumak r.** Rus. Fed.
163 F3 **Kumaka** Guyana
31 F1 **Kumakanda** Rus. Fed.
28 C7 **Kumamoto div.** Japan
28 C7 **Kumamoto** Japan
29 F7 **Kumano** Japan
112 C3 **Kumanovo** Macedonia
9 C5 **Kumara** New Zealand
31 H2 **Kumara** Rus. Fed.
122 D5 **Kumasi** Ghana
124 A3 **Kumba** Cameroon
113 F4 **Kumbağ** Turkey
38 B4 **Kumbakonam** India
81 G3 **Kumberg** Austria
124 B2 **Kumbo** Cameroon
39 C2 **Kumel well** Iran
50 J3 **Kumeny** Rus. Fed.
46 E2 **Kumertau** Rus. Fed.
37 G4 **Kumguri** India
75 H4 **Kumhausen** Germany
31 J6 **Kŭmho r.** South Korea
31 J5 **Kumi** South Korea
126 B4 **Kumi** Uganda
113 F5 **Kumkale** Turkey
59 F2 **Kumla** Sweden
59 J1 **Kumlinge** Finland
43 A1 **Kumluca** Turkey
73 H2 **Kummerower See l.** Germany
75 G3 **Kümmersbruck** Germany
73 J3 **Kummersdorf-Alexanderdorf** Germany
123 G4 **Kumo** Nigeria
31 H6 **Kŭmo Do i.** South Korea
24 B1 **Kumon Range mountain range** Myanmar
24 C3 **Kumphawapi** Thailand
81 G4 **Kumrovec** Croatia
38 A3 **Kumta** India
124 E3 **Kumu** Zaire
43 C4 **Kumub** Israel
51 H7 **Kumukh** Rus. Fed.
52 H1 **Kum'ya** Rus. Fed.
51 G5 **Kumylzhenskiy** Rus. Fed.
24 B3 **Kun r.** Myanmar
39 G2 **Kunar r.** Afghanistan
47 K4 **Künas Chang** China
46 F1 **Kunashak** Rus. Fed.
28 L1 **Kunashir, Ostrov i.** Rus. Fed.
24 B2 **Kunchaung** Myanmar
37 F3 **Kunchha** Nepal
36 E2 **Kunchuk Tso l.** China
54 E2 **Kunda** Estonia
37 E4 **Kunda** India
125 C5 **Kunda-dia-Baze** Angola
54 E2 **Kunda Laht b.** Estonia
38 A3 **Kundāpura** India
36 B3 **Kundar r.** Afghanistan/Pakistan
125 E6 **Kundelungu, Monts mts** Zaire
125 E6 **Kundelungu Ouest, Parc National de nat. park** Zaire
125 E6 **Kundelungu, Parc National de nat. park** Zaire
36 B2 **Kundian** Pakistan
80 C3 **Kundl** Austria
46 F2 **Kundravy** Rus. Fed.
22 A1 **Kundur i.** Indonesia
39 G1 **Kunduz r.** Afghanistan
128 A2 **Kunene div.** Namibia
128 A2 **Kunene r.** Namibia
47 K4 **Künes r.** China
Künes *see* **Xinyuan**
58 D3 **Kungälv** Sweden
47 J4 **Kungei-Tau mountain range** Kazakhstan/Kyrgyzstan
136 C4 **Kunghit I. i.** *B.C.* Canada
46 E4 **Kungrad** Uzbekistan
59 G2 **Kungsängen** Sweden
59 E3 **Kungsbacka** Sweden
55 E2 **Kungsbacka fjorden b.** Sweden
58 D2 **Kungshamn** Sweden
59 G2 **Kungsör** Sweden
124 C3 **Kungu** Zaire
127 B6 **Kunguta** Tanzania
24 A3 **Kungyangon** Myanmar
79 K4 **Kunhegyes** Hungary
24 B2 **Kunhing** Myanmar
28 C7 **Kunimi-dake mt.** Japan
54 E2 **Kuningaküla** Estonia
22 B3 **Kuningan** Indonesia
37 F5 **Kunjabar** India
24 B2 **Kunlong** Myanmar
37 F4 **Kunlui r.** India
37 E2 **Kunlun Shan mountain range** China
79 K4 **Kunmadaras** Hungary
32 C3 **Kunming** China
16 D3 **Kunmunya Abor. Reserve res.** *Western Australia* Australia
16 D2 **Kunmunya Abor. Reserve res.** *Western Australia* Australia
36 D4 **Kuno r.** India
77 K5 **Kunów** Poland
73 K3 **Kunowice** Poland
31 H6 **Kunsan** South Korea
33 H2 **Kunshan** China
79 K5 **Kunszentmárton** Hungary
79 J4 **Kunszentmiklós** Hungary
16 E2 **Kununurra** *Western Australia* Australia
31 G5 **Kunyu Shan h.** China
81 G1 **Kunžak** Czech Rep.
74 E2 **Künzell** Germany
74 E3 **Künzelsau** Germany
73 G4 **Künzels-Berg h.** Germany
75 J4 **Künzing** Germany
125 C4 **Kunzulu** Zaire
33 H2 **Kuocang Shan mountain range** China
57 G3 **Kuohijärvi l.** Finland
56 H2 **Kuolayarvi** Rus. Fed.
56 G3 **Kuopio div.** Finland
56 G3 **Kuopio** Finland
56 F3 **Kuortane** Finland
104 E3 **Kupa r.** Croatia/Slovenia
21 H8 **Kupang** Indonesia
53 B2 **Kupil'** Ukraine
47 J2 **Kupino** Rus. Fed.
54 D4 **Kupiškis** Lithuania
107 J3 **Kupjak** Croatia
87 H4 **Kuppenheim** Germany
54 E3 **Kuprava** Latvia
136 C3 **Kupreanof Island i.** *Alaska* U.S.A.
134 C4 **Kupreanof Pt pt** *Alaska* U.S.A.
52 E2 **Kupreyevo** Rus. Fed.
75 G2 **Küps** Germany
53 G2 **Kup"yans'k** Ukraine
77 N5 **Kupychiv** Ukraine
47 K4 **Kuqa** China
42 G2 **Kür r.** Azerbaijan
31 K2 **Kur r.** Rus. Fed.
Kura r. *see* **Kür**
51 G7 **Kura r.** Azerbaijan/Georgia
17 B4 **Kurabuka r.** *Western Australia* Australia
28 D6 **Kurahashi-jima i.** Japan
42 F1 **Kurakh** Rus. Fed.
53 G3 **Kurakhove** Ukraine
52 G3 **Kurakino** Rus. Fed.
52 H2 **Kurakino** Rus. Fed.
54 C3 **Kura Kurk chan.** Estonia
28 D6 **Kurashiki** Japan
37 E5 **Kurasia** India
28 D6 **Kurayoshi** Japan
47 L2 **Kurayskiy Khr. mountain range** Rus. Fed.
30 D1 **Kurba r.** Rus. Fed.
30 D2 **Kurba, Nov.** Rus. Fed.
59 F1 **Kurbergets fab h.** Sweden
52 B4 **Kurchatov** Rus. Fed.
47 K3 **Kurchum** Kazakhstan
42 G1 **Kürdämir** Azerbaijan
42 G2 **Kür Dili pen.** Azerbaijan
38 A2 **Kurduvadi** India
52 F1 **Kurdyum** Rus. Fed.
112 E4 **Kŭrdzhali** Bulgaria
28 D6 **Kure** Japan
42 C1 **Küre** Turkey
5 K2 **Kure Atoll atoll** *Hawaii* U.S.A.
54 C2 **Kuressaare** Estonia
54 F2 **Kureya r.** Rus. Fed.
47 H2 **Kurgal'dzhinskiy** Kazakhstan
47 G1 **Kurgan** Rus. Fed.
51 G6 **Kurganinsk** Rus. Fed.
47 G3 **Kurgasyn** Kazakhstan
39 G1 **Kuri** Afghanistan
36 B4 **Kuri** India
57 F3 **Kurikka** Finland
29 H4 **Kurikoma-yama volcano** Japan
Kuril Is is *see* **Kuril'skiye Ostrova**
51 J5 **Kurilovka** Rus. Fed.
27 R2 **Kuril'sk** Japan
45 Q5 **Kuril'skiye Ostrova is** Rus. Fed.
78 F2 **Kuřim** Czech Rep.
Kurinskaya Kosa pen. *see* **Kür Dili**
52 D3 **Kurkino** Rus. Fed.
31 F1 **Kurleya** Rus. Fed.
52 E2 **Kurlovskiy** Rus. Fed.
46 D2 **Kurmanayevka** Rus. Fed.
54 D3 **Kurmene** Latvia
126 B2 **Kurmuk** Sudan
52 H2 **Kurmysh** Rus. Fed.
38 B3 **Kurnool** India
29 F5 **Kurobe** Japan
28 C7 **Kurogi** Japan
28 H3 **Kuroishi** Japan
29 H5 **Kuroiso** Japan
28 H2 **Kuromatsunai** Japan
119 F3 **Kuror, Jebel mt.** Sudan
75 J2 **Kurort Bad Gottleuba** Germany
30 E2 **Kurort-Darasun** Rus. Fed.
74 F2 **Kurort Schmalkalden** Germany
73 G4 **Kurort Wippra** Germany

173 H4 **Las Flores** *Buenos Aires* Argentina
172 C1 **Las Flores** *San Juan* Argentina
170 D1 **Las Flores** Argentina
172 B1 **Las Galenas** Chile
172 B3 **Las Garzas** Chile
172 E6 **Las Grutes** Argentina
39 E4 **Lāshār r.** Iran
137 H4 **Lashburn** *Saskatchewan* Canada
172 C2 **Las Heras** Argentina
24 B2 **Lashio** Myanmar
39 F3 **Lashkar Gāh** Afghanistan
52 E2 **Lashma** Rus. Fed.
171 B6 **Las Horquetas** Argentina
172 A5 **Las Hortensias** Chile
98 D4 **Las Hurdes reg.** Spain
111 F3 **La Sila reg.** Italy
77 H2 **Łasin** Poland
172 E2 **Las Isletas** Argentina
115 G7 **Lasithi div.** Greece
172 F1 **Las Junturas** Argentina
77 H4 **Łask** Poland
77 K4 **Łaskarzew** Poland
53 A2 **Laskivtsi** Ukraine
81 G4 **Laško** Slovenia
172 B5 **Las Lajas** Argentina
163 D2 **Las Lajitas** Venezuela
172 B3 **Las Leñas** Argentina
162 A4 **Las Lomas** Peru
170 D1 **Las Lomitas** Argentina
100 D3 **Las Marismas marsh** Spain
171 C6 **Las Martinetas** Argentina
162 D2 **Las Mercedes** Venezuela
172 C3 **Las Molles** Argentina
99 F4 **Las Navas del Marqués** Spain
69 C4 **Lasne** Belgium
101 J4 **Las Negras** Spain
151 B7 **Las Nieves** Mexico
101 G2 **La Solana** Spain
98 D2 **Las Omañas reg.** Spain
92 D2 **La Souterraine** France
172 B4 **Las Ovejas** Argentina
154 D5 **Las Palmas r.** Mexico
170 E2 **Las Palmas** Argentina
97 □ **Las Palmas de Gran Canaria** *Canary Is* Spain
101 H1 **Las Pedroñeras** Spain
102 C2 **Las Pedrosas** Spain
172 F1 **Las Peñas** Argentina
172 F2 **Las Perdices** Argentina
165 E3 **Las Petas r.** Bolivia
165 E3 **Las Petas** Bolivia
106 D4 **La Spezia div.** *Liguria* Italy
106 D4 **La Spezia** *La Spezia* Italy
173 J3 **Las Piedras** Uruguay
171 C5 **Las Plumas** Argentina
93 C6 **Laspuña** Spain
36 C1 **Laspur** Pakistan
157 H6 **Las Quebradas** Guatemala
173 G2 **Las Rosas** Argentina
99 G4 **Las Rozas de Madrid** Spain
169 F2 **Lassance** Brazil
89 E3 **Lassay-les-Châteaux** France
152 B3 **Lassen Pk volcano** *California* U.S.A.
152 B3 **Lassen Volcanic Nat. Park nat. park** *California* U.S.A.
93 B5 **Lasseube** France
86 B3 **Lassigny** France
81 F3 **Lassing** Austria
179 B2 **Lassiter Coast coastal area** Antarctica
81 G3 **Laßnitzhöhe** Austria
141 J4 **L'Assomption** *Québec* Canada
172 B2 **Las Tablas** Chile
156 K8 **Las Tablas** Panama
80 C4 **Lastè delle Sute mt.** Italy
170 D2 **Las Termas** Argentina
137 H4 **Last Mountain L. l.** *Saskatchewan* Canada
103 B6 **Las Torres de Cotillas** Spain
124 B4 **Lastoursville** Gabon
104 F4 **Lastovo i.** Croatia
104 F4 **Lastovski Kanal chan.** Croatia
99 E1 **Lastres, Cabo headland** Spain
163 E2 **Las Trincheras** Venezuela
72 C3 **Lastrup** Germany
89 F4 **La Suze-sur-Sarthe** France
153 F6 **Las Varas** *Chihuahua* Mexico
156 D4 **Las Varas** *Nayarit* Mexico
173 F1 **Las Varillas** Argentina
155 E3 **Las Vegas** *Nevada* U.S.A.
153 F5 **Las Vegas** *New Mexico* U.S.A.
98 E4 **Las Veguillas** Spain
99 E4 **Las Ventas de San Julián** Spain
101 E1 **Las Villuercas mt.** Spain
77 M5 **Łaszczów** Poland
162 B4 **Latacunga** Ecuador
179 A2 **Latady I. i.** Antarctica
162 C4 **La Tagua** Colombia
Latakia *see* **Al Lādhiqīyah**
90 C3 **La Talaudière** France
141 F3 **Latchford** *Ontario* Canada
6 □5 **Late i.** Tonga
37 F5 **Latehar** India
107 F2 **Latemar mt.** Italy
141 K2 **Laterrière** *Québec* Canada
111 F2 **Laterza** Italy
93 A4 **La Teste** France
54 E3 **Latgales Augstiene reg.** Latvia
17 B6 **Latham** *Western Australia* Australia
72 C3 **Lathen** Germany
66 E2 **Latheron** *Scotland* U.K.
106 A3 **La Thuile** Italy
111 G2 **Latiano** Italy
109 E3 **Latina div.** *Lazio* Italy
109 E3 **Latina** Italy
170 D2 **La Tinajas** Argentina
107 H3 **Latisana** Italy
52 D4 **Latnaya** Rus. Fed.
172 E2 **La Toma** Argentina
79 L3 **Latorica r.** Slovakia
102 D2 **La Torre de Cabdella** Spain
163 D1 **La Tortuga, I. i.** Venezuela
79 M3 **Latorytsya r.** Ukraine
16 C3 **Latouche Treville, C. c.** *Western Australia* Australia
123 G2 **Latouma well** Niger
92 E3 **La Tour-d'Auvergne** France
93 E6 **Latour-de-France** France
93 D5 **La Tour-du-Crieu** France
90 D3 **La Tour-du-Pin** France
77 K3 **Latowicz** Poland
172 D2 **La Tranca** Argentina
92 A2 **La Tranche-sur-Mer** France
79 G5 **Látrány** Hungary
92 A3 **La Tremblade** France
92 D2 **La Trimouille** France
159 □4 **La Trinité** *Martinique* Caribbean
91 F5 **La Trinité** France
88 C3 **La Trinité-Porhoët** France
146 D4 **Latrobe** *Pennsylvania* U.S.A.
13 F5 **Latrobe** *Tasmania* Australia
109 J4 **Latronico** Italy
93 E4 **Latronquière** France
170 C2 **La Troy r.** Argentina
52 D1 **Latskoye** Rus. Fed.
91 B5 **Lattes** France
141 F3 **Latulipe** *Québec* Canada
141 J3 **La Tuque** *Québec* Canada
38 B2 **Latur** India
88 C4 **La Turballe** France
49 H3 **Latvia country** Europe
126 B3 **Lau r.** Sudan
126 B3 **Lau** Sudan
37 F5 **Laua** India
74 D2 **Laubach** *Hessen* Germany
69 F4 **Laubach** *Rheinland-Pfalz* Germany
128 C2 **Lauban waterhole** Namibia
6 □6 **Laucala i.** Fiji
164 C3 **Lauca, Parque Nacional nat. park** Chile
73 J4 **Lauchhammer** Germany
74 D5 **Lauchringen** Germany
74 E3 **Lauda-Königshofen** Germany
58 B2 **Laudal** Norway
66 F5 **Lauder** *Scotland* U.K.
72 E2 **Lauenbrück** Germany
73 F2 **Lauenburg (Elbe)** Germany
75 G3 **Lauf an der Pegnitz** Germany
75 H5 **Laufen** Germany
82 C1 **Laufen** Switzerland
82 D1 **Laufenberg** Switzerland
74 E3 **Lauffen am Neckar** Germany
148 D2 **Laughing Fish Pt pt** *Michigan* U.S.A.
14 C4 **Laughlen, Mt mt.** *Northern Terr.* Australia
6 □7 **Lau Group is** Fiji
74 F4 **Lauingen (Donau)** Germany
54 C2 **Lauka** Estonia
54 C4 **Laukuva** Lithuania
7 □12 **Laulii** Western Samoa
25 B5 **Laun** Thailand
141 F2 **Launay** *Québec* Canada
62 B4 **Launceston** *England* U.K.
13 F5 **Launceston** *Tasmania* Australia
67 B4 **Laune r.** Rep. of Ireland
24 B1 **Launggyaung** Myanmar
25 B4 **Launglon** Myanmar
25 B4 **Launglon Bok Is is** Myanmar
165 D3 **La Unión** Bolivia
172 A6 **La Unión** Chile
162 B3 **La Uníon** Colombia
156 J6 **La Unión** El Salvador
157 E5 **La Unión** Mexico
164 A1 **La Unión** Peru
103 C7 **La Unión** Spain
82 C2 **Laupen** Switzerland
74 E4 **Laupheim** Germany
15 F2 **Laura** *Queensland* Australia
93 D5 **Lauragais reg.** France
67 B5 **Lauragh** Rep. of Ireland
162 D2 **La Urbana** Venezuela
111 F4 **Laureana di Borrello** Italy
147 F5 **Laurel** *Delaware* U.S.A.
151 F6 **Laurel** *Mississippi* U.S.A.
152 E2 **Laurel** *Montana* U.S.A.
146 D4 **Laurel Hill h.** *Pennsylvania* U.S.A.
146 A6 **Laurel River Lake l.** *Kentucky* U.S.A.
66 F4 **Laurencekirk** *Scotland* U.K.
141 K3 **Laurentides, Réserve faunique des res.** *Québec* Canada
109 H4 **Laurenzana** Italy
93 A5 **Laurhibar r.** France
36 E4 **Lauri** India
109 H4 **Lauria** Italy
92 D2 **Laurière** France
64 D3 **Laurieston** *Scotland* U.K.
145 E5 **Laurinburg** *N. Carolina* U.S.A.
109 H4 **Laurino** Italy
148 C2 **Laurium** *Michigan* U.S.A.
109 G4 **Lauro** Italy
82 B2 **Lausanne** Switzerland
59 H3 **Lausholmar is** Sweden
73 K4 **Lausitzer Gebirge h.** Germany
73 J4 **Laußnitz** Germany
25 E6 **Laut i.** Indonesia
22 B2 **Laut i.** Indonesia
22 D2 **Laut i.** Indonesia
73 K4 **Lauta** Germany
172 A5 **Lautaro** Chile
74 D3 **Lauter r.** France/Germany
80 A3 **Lauterach** Austria
87 H4 **Lauterbach** Germany
87 H4 **Lauterbourg** France
82 C2 **Lauterbrunnen** Switzerland
74 E2 **Lautersbach (Hessen)** Germany
80 A2 **Lauterstein** Germany
6 □8 **Lautoka** Fiji
93 E5 **Lautrec** France
56 H3 **Lauvuskylä** Finland
68 E1 **Lauwersmeer l.** Netherlands
93 D4 **Lauzerte** France
93 D4 **Lauzès** France
93 C4 **Lauzun** France
77 K1 **Lava r.** Rus. Fed.
128 □1 **Lava Fields lava** *Ascension* Atlantic Ocean
106 D4 **Lavagna** Italy
106 D4 **Lavagne r.** Italy
141 J4 **Laval** *Québec* Canada
89 E3 **Laval** France
91 D5 **La Valette-du-Var** France
172 C2 **Lavalle** Argentina
80 C4 **La Valle** Italy
173 K2 **Lavalleja div.** Uruguay
81 F4 **Lavamünd** Austria
81 F4 **Lavant r.** Austria
172 A4 **Lavapié, Pta headland** Chile
93 C4 **Lavardac** France
39 B3 **Lāvar Kabkān** Iran
93 D5 **Lavaur** France
99 E2 **La Vecilla** Spain
93 B6 **Lavedan reg.** France
159 E3 **La Vega** Dominican Rep.
93 D6 **Lavelanet** France
98 E3 **La Vellés** Spain
109 H3 **Lavello** Italy
83 D3 **Lavena Ponte Tresa** Italy
63 G2 **Lavenham** *England* U.K.
106 C3 **Laveno** Italy
157 G5 **La Venta** Mexico
69 A4 **Laventie** France
98 E4 **La Vera reg.** Spain
172 E3 **La Verde** Argentina
90 D3 **La Verpillière** France
92 B2 **La Verrie** France
17 C6 **Laverton** *Western Australia* Australia
86 D3 **La Veuve** France
156 E3 **La Víbora** Mexico
162 D1 **La Victoria** Venezuela
99 G3 **La Vid** Spain
140 E3 **Lavigne** *Ontario* Canada
108 C2 **la Villa** Italy
101 G1 **La Villa de Don Fadrique** Spain
92 C2 **La Villedieu-du-Clain** France
90 E1 **La Villedieu-en-Fontenette** France
152 E2 **Lavina** *Montana* U.S.A.
162 B5 **La Viña** Peru
109 E3 **Lavinio-Lido di Enea** Italy
173 G2 **La Violeta** Argentina
82 B1 **Laviron** France
107 F2 **Lavìs** Italy
93 C5 **Lavit** France
54 D4 **Lavoriškės** Lithuania
91 C4 **La Voulte-sur-Rhône** France
91 B3 **Lavoûte-Chilhac** France
91 B3 **Lavoûte-sur-Loire** France
169 F4 **Lavras** Brazil
167 B7 **Lavras do Sul** Brazil
100 B2 **Lavre r.** Portugal
100 B2 **Lavre** Portugal
115 F5 **Lavrio** Greece
54 E3 **Lavry** Rus. Fed.
131 H3 **Lavumisa** Swaziland
127 B7 **Lavushi-Manda Nat. Park nat. park** Zambia
163 G3 **Lawa r.** Surinam
126 E2 **Lawdar** Yemen
179 C6 **Law Dome ice feature** Antarctica
64 D1 **Lawers** *Scotland* U.K.
63 H3 **Lawford** *England* U.K.
22 C1 **Lawit, G. mt.** Indonesia/Malaysia
25 C6 **Lawit, Gunung mt.** Malaysia
24 B2 **Lawksawk** Myanmar
14 D3 **Lawn Hill** *Queensland* Australia
14 D3 **Lawn Hill Cr. r.** *Queensland* Australia
122 D4 **Lawra** Ghana
150 E4 **Lawrence** *Kansas* U.S.A.
147 H3 **Lawrence** *Massachusetts* U.S.A.
9 B6 **Lawrence** New Zealand
145 C5 **Lawrenceburg** *Tennessee* U.S.A.
147 K2 **Lawrence Station** *New Brunswick* Canada
64 B3 **Lawrencetown** *Northern Ireland* U.K.
146 E6 **Lawrenceville** *Virginia* U.S.A.
151 D5 **Lawton** *Oklahoma* U.S.A.
119 G2 **Lawz, J. al mt.** Saudi Arabia
59 F2 **Laxå** Sweden
64 D3 **Laxey** Isle of Man
66 C2 **Laxford Bridge** *Scotland* U.K.
66 C2 **Laxford, Loch inlet** *Scotland* U.K.
66 □2 **Laxo** *Scotland* U.K.
87 F4 **Laxou** France
92 A2 **Lay r.** France
164 B3 **La Yarada** Peru
22 D3 **Layar, Tg pt** Indonesia
89 E4 **Layon r.** France
5 K2 **Laysan I.** *Hawaii* U.S.A.
154 A2 **Laytonville** *California* U.S.A.
173 F4 **La Zanja** Argentina
114 B2 **Lazarat** Albania
112 C2 **Lazarevac** Yugoslavia
46 E4 **Lazareva, Oz. l.** Uzbekistan
52 C3 **Lazarevo** Rus. Fed.
179 D3 **Lazarev Sea sea** Antarctica
51 F7 **Lazarevskoye** Rus. Fed.
153 D6 **Lázaro Cárdenas** *Baja California* Mexico
156 E5 **Lázaro Cárdenas** *Michoacán* Mexico
156 D3 **Lázaro Cardénas, Presa resr** Mexico
156 C4 **Lázaro, Sa de S. mountain range** Mexico
173 K2 **Lazcano** Uruguay
77 M1 **Lazdijai** Lithuania
39 C4 **Lāzeh** Iran
52 B2 **Lazinki** Rus. Fed.
109 E2 **Lazio div.** Italy
107 E3 **Lazise** Italy
78 E1 **Lázně Bohdaneč** Czech Rep.
75 H2 **Lázně Kynžvart** Czech Rep.
173 H2 **Lazo** Argentina
45 P3 **Lazo** Rus. Fed.
53 E3 **Lazurne** Ukraine
173 H4 **Lazzarino** Argentina
25 C4 **Leach** Cambodia
140 C3 **Leach I. i.** *Ontario* Canada
150 C2 **Lead** *S. Dakota* U.S.A.
65 E2 **Leadburn** *Scotland* U.K.
63 F1 **Leadenham** *England* U.K.
137 H4 **Leader** *Saskatchewan* Canada
65 F2 **Leader Water r.** *Scotland* U.K.
153 F4 **Leadville** *Colorado* U.S.A.
151 F6 **Leaf r.** *Mississippi* U.S.A.
137 J3 **Leaf Rapids** *Manitoba* Canada
151 D6 **Leakey** *Texas* U.S.A.
140 D5 **Leamington** *Ontario* Canada
155 F2 **Leamington** *Utah* U.S.A.
63 E2 **Leamington Spa, Royal** *England* U.K.
33 F3 **Le'an** China
131 G3 **Leandra** South Africa
170 E2 **Leandro N. Alem** Argentina
67 B4 **Leane, Lough l.** Rep. of Ireland
129 H2 **Leanja** Madagascar
67 B5 **Leap** Rep. of Ireland
16 A4 **Learmonth** *Western Australia* Australia
63 F1 **Leasingham** *England* U.K.
137 H4 **Leask** *Saskatchewan* Canada
63 F3 **Leatherhead** *England* U.K.
69 C4 **L'Eau d'Heure r.** Belgium
150 E4 **Leavenworth** *Kansas* U.S.A.
152 B2 **Leavenworth** *Washington* U.S.A.
154 C2 **Leavitt Peak summit** *California* U.S.A.
76 F1 **Łeba** Poland
74 B3 **Lebach** Germany
22 A3 **Lebak** Indonesia
23 C5 **Lebak** Philippines
131 E3 **Lebaleng** South Africa
124 B4 **Lébamba** Gabon
112 C3 **Lebane** Yugoslavia
18 E6 **Lebanon country** Asia
148 D5 **Lebanon** *Indiana* U.S.A.
150 D4 **Lebanon** *Kansas* U.S.A.
151 E4 **Lebanon** *Missouri* U.S.A.
147 G3 **Lebanon** *New Hampshire* U.S.A.
147 F4 **Lebanon** *New Jersey* U.S.A.
146 A5 **Lebanon** *Ohio* U.S.A.
152 B2 **Lebanon** *Oregon* U.S.A.
147 E4 **Lebanon** *Pennsylvania* U.S.A.
145 C4 **Lebanon** *Tennessee* U.S.A.
87 F3 **Le Ban-St-Martin** France
46 F5 **Lebap div.** Turkmenistan
46 F4 **Lebap** Turkmenistan
93 B4 **Le Barp** France
91 E5 **Le Bar-sur-Loup** France
69 C4 **Lebbeke** Belgium
91 C4 **Le Béage** France
91 D5 **Le Beausset** France
52 D3 **Lebedyan'** Rus. Fed.
53 F1 **Lebedyn** Ukraine
141 G2 **Lebel-sur-Quévillon** *Québec* Canada
89 E3 **Le Bény-Bocage** France
86 A2 **Lebiez** France
90 E2 **Le Biot** France
92 D2 **Le Blanc** France
91 B4 **Le Bleymard** France
114 E1 **Lebnitsa r.** Bulgaria
76 G1 **Łebno** Poland
124 D3 **Lebo** Zaire
131 G3 **Lebohang** South Africa
90 C3 **Le Bois-d'Oingt** France
76 F1 **Lębork** Poland
93 E6 **Le Boulou** France
92 B2 **Le Boupère** France
93 D4 **Le Bourg** France
91 E3 **Le Bourg-d'Oisans** France
90 D3 **Le Bourget-du-Lac** France
93 B4 **Le Bouscat** France
131 G2 **LebowaKgomo** South Africa
86 C4 **Le Breuil** France
100 D4 **Lebrija** Spain
93 C5 **Le Brouilh-Monbert** France
127 □5 **Le Brûlé** *Réunion* Indian Ocean
91 E4 **Le Brusquet** France
172 A4 **Lebu** Chile
93 C4 **Le Bugue** France
91 B4 **Le Buisson** France
93 C4 **Le Buisson-de-Cadouin** France
73 K3 **Lebus** Germany
73 J4 **Lebusa** Germany
53 F2 **Leb"yazhe** Ukraine
47 J2 **Lebyazh'ye** Kazakhstan
47 G1 **Lebyazh'ye** Rus. Fed.
52 D3 **Lebyazh'ye** Rus. Fed.
50 J3 **Lebyazh'ye** Rus. Fed.
98 B3 **Leça da Palmeira** Portugal
91 F5 **Le Cannet** France
91 E5 **Le Cannet-des-Maures** France
159 □4 **Le Carbet** *Martinique* Caribbean
86 C2 **Le Cateau-Cambrésis** France
86 C2 **Le Catelet** France
91 B5 **Le Caylar** France
93 E4 **Le Cayrol** France
111 H2 **Lecce div.** *Puglia* Italy
111 H2 **Lecce** *Lecce* Italy
106 D3 **Lecco** Italy
106 D3 **Lecco, Lago di l.** Italy
102 C3 **Lécera** Spain
75 F4 **Lech r.** Austria/Germany
80 B3 **Lech** Austria
115 C5 **Lechaina** Greece
91 C3 **Le Chambon-Feugerolles** France
33 F3 **Lechang** China
92 A3 **Le Château-d'Oléron** France
90 E3 **Le Châtelard** France
92 E2 **Le Châtelet** France
86 D4 **Le Chêne** France
86 D3 **Le Chesne** France
91 C4 **Le Cheylard** France
112 E1 **Lechința** Romania
63 E3 **Lechlade** *England* U.K.
114 C2 **Lechovo** Greece
80 B3 **Lechtaler Alpen mountain range** Austria
102 C3 **Leciñena** Spain
72 D1 **Leck** Germany
90 C2 **Le Coteau** France
89 G2 **Le Coudray-St-Germer** France
88 D3 **Lécousse** France
91 B5 **Le Crès** France
90 C2 **Le Creusot** France
86 A2 **Le Crotoy** France
93 C5 **Lectoure** France
102 B1 **Lecumberri** Spain
77 L4 **Łęczna** Poland
77 H3 **Łęczyca** Poland
76 F1 **Łęczyce** Poland
72 C2 **Leda r.** Germany
103 B5 **Ledaña** Spain
99 H4 **Ledanca** Spain
25 C7 **Ledang, Gunung mt.** Malaysia
78 F5 **Ledava r.** Slovenia
62 D2 **Ledbury** *England* U.K.
93 C4 **Lède r.** France
69 B4 **Lede** Belgium
78 E2 **Ledeč nad Sázavou** Czech Rep.
81 F2 **Ledenice** Czech Rep.
98 E3 **Ledesma** Spain
159 □4 **Le Diamant** *Martinique* Caribbean
91 C5 **Lédignan** France
99 F2 **Ledigos** Spain
122 D4 **Lédigué** Burkina
66 D2 **Ledmore** *Scotland* U.K.
50 E1 **Ledmozero** Rus. Fed.
81 H2 **Lednice** Czech Rep.
22 B1 **Ledo** Indonesia
179 □ **le Dôme summit** *Kerguelen* Indian Ocean
33 E5 **Ledong** China
90 B2 **Le Donjon** France
92 D2 **Le Dorat** France
83 F3 **Ledro, Lago di l.** Italy
30 B5 **Ledu** China
136 G4 **Leduc** *Alberta* Canada
73 L1 **Lędzin** Poland
147 G3 **Lee** *Massachusetts* U.S.A.
150 E2 **Leech L. l.** *Minnesota* U.S.A.
65 G4 **Leeds** *England* U.K.
65 G4 **Leeds & Bradford airport** *England* U.K.
147 H2 **Leeds Junction** *Maine* U.S.A.
62 A4 **Leedstown** *England* U.K.
62 D1 **Leek** *England* U.K.
68 E1 **Leek** Netherlands
65 G3 **Leeming** *England* U.K.
62 B4 **Lee Moor** *England* U.K.
146 D4 **Leeper** *Pennsylvania* U.S.A.
68 D3 **Leerdam** Netherlands
72 C2 **Leer (Ostfriesland)** Germany
68 D2 **Leersum** Netherlands
145 D6 **Leesburg** *Florida* U.S.A.
146 E5 **Leesburg** *Virginia* U.S.A.
72 E3 **Leese** Germany
9 D5 **Leeston** New Zealand
151 E6 **Leesville** *Louisiana* U.S.A.
146 C4 **Leesville Lake l.** *Ohio* U.S.A.
13 F3 **Leeton** *New South Wales* Australia
131 F3 **Leeudoringstad** South Africa
130 C6 **Leeu-Gamka** South Africa
131 E4 **Leeukop mt.** South Africa
131 F2 **Leeupoort** South Africa
130 C6 **Leeuw r.** South Africa
68 D1 **Leeuwarden** *Friesland* Netherlands
17 A7 **Leeuwin, C. c.** *Western Australia* Australia
154 C3 **Lee Vining** *California* U.S.A.
9 □3 **Leeward I. i.** *Antipodes Is* New Zealand
159 G3 **Leeward Islands is** Caribbean
88 A3 **Le Faou** France
88 B3 **Le Faouët** France
93 D5 **Le Fauga** France
112 E3 **Lefedzha r.** Bulgaria
88 D5 **Le Fenouiller** France
69 A3 **Leffinge** Belgium
43 B2 **Lefka** Cyprus
114 B4 **Lefkada div.** Greece
114 B4 **Lefkada i.** Greece
114 B4 **Lefkada** Greece
115 E7 **Lefka Ori mountain range** Greece
43 B2 **Lefkara** Cyprus
114 B3 **Lefkimmi** Greece
114 E1 **Lefkonas** Greece
43 B2 **Lefkonikon** Cyprus
43 B2 **Lefkosia** Cyprus
69 B4 **Leforest** France
93 D5 **Le Fossat** France
93 D5 **Le Fousseret** France
159 □4 **Le François** *Martinique* Caribbean
17 C6 **Lefroy, L. salt flat** *Western Australia* Australia
91 E4 **Le Fugeret** France
99 G4 **Leganés** Spain
99 H4 **Leganiel** Spain
141 J3 **Légaré, Lac l.** *Québec* Canada
23 B3 **Legaspi** Philippines
83 F1 **Legau** Germany
86 C4 **Le Gault-Soigny** France
99 H1 **Legazpia** Spain
72 C3 **Legden** Germany
92 A2 **Legé** France
93 A4 **Lège-Cap-Ferret** France
16 B4 **Legendre I. i.** *Western Australia* Australia
89 E3 **Le Genest-St-Isle** France
13 F5 **Legges Tor mt.** *Tasmania* Australia
154 A2 **Leggett** *California* U.S.A.
Leghorn *see* **Livorno**
131 G1 **Legkraal** South Africa
69 D5 **Léglise** Belgium
107 F3 **Legnago** Italy
106 C3 **Legnano** Italy
76 E4 **Legnica div.** Poland
76 E4 **Legnica** *Legnica* Poland
106 D2 **Legnone, Monte mt.** Italy
92 C3 **Le Gond-Pontouvre** France
159 □5 **Le Gosier** *Guadeloupe* Caribbean
81 H4 **Legrad** Croatia
82 B3 **Le Grand-Bornand** France
92 D2 **Le Grand-Bourg** France
82 A3 **Le Grand-Lemps** France
89 F4 **Le Grand-Lucé** France
92 C2 **Le Grand-Pressigny** France
89 G2 **Le Grand-Quevilly** France
91 D3 **Le Grand-Serre** France
91 C5 **Le Grau-du-Roi** France
82 A3 **Le Gua** France
164 C4 **Leguena** Chile
88 B3 **Léguer r.** France
93 D5 **Léguevin** France
124 E3 **Leguga** Zaire
14 B2 **Legune** *Northern Terr.* Australia
99 H2 **Legutiano** Spain
36 D2 **Leh** India
89 F2 **Le Havre** *Seine-Maritime* France
147 F4 **Lehighton** *Pennsylvania* U.S.A.
112 F2 **Lehliu Gară** Romania
173 G1 **Lehmann** Argentina
74 C2 **Lehmen** Germany
56 H3 **Lehmo** Finland
73 H3 **Lehnin** Germany
88 C3 **Léhon** France
89 E3 **Le Horps** France
93 B5 **Le Houga** France
75 F3 **Lehrberg** Germany
73 F3 **Lehre** Germany
72 E3 **Lehrte** Germany
56 F3 **Lehtimäki** Finland
128 C3 **Lehututu** Botswana
36 B3 **Leiah** Pakistan
80 D2 **Leiblfing** Germany
81 G4 **Leibnitz div.** Austria
81 G4 **Leibnitz** Austria
63 E2 **Leicester** *England* U.K.
63 F2 **Leicestershire div.** *England* U.K.
14 D3 **Leichhardt r.** *Queensland* Australia
14 D3 **Leichhardt Falls waterfall** *Queensland* Australia
15 F4 **Leichhardt Range mountain range** *Queensland* Australia
68 C2 **Leiden** Netherlands
68 C2 **Leiderdorp** Netherlands
68 C2 **Leidschendam** Netherlands
69 B4 **Leie r.** Belgium
54 E2 **Leie** Estonia
65 F4 **Leigh** *England* U.K.
8 E2 **Leigh** New Zealand
12 D2 **Leigh Creek** *S. Australia* Australia
67 E4 **Leighlinbridge** Rep. of Ireland
63 F3 **Leighton Buzzard** *England* U.K.
58 B1 **Leikanger** Norway
24 B3 **Leiktho** Myanmar
74 D3 **Leimen** Germany
72 E3 **Leine r.** Germany
72 F4 **Leinefelde** Germany
106 B3 **Leinì** Italy
67 D3 **Leinster div.** Rep. of Ireland
80 A2 **Leinzell** Germany
77 M1 **Leipalingis** Lithuania
113 F6 **Leipsoi i.** Greece
73 H4 **Leipzig airport** Germany
73 H4 **Leipzig div.** Germany
73 H4 **Leipzig** *Sachsen-Anhalt* Germany
58 C1 **Leira** Norway
56 D2 **Leiranger** Norway
100 B1 **Leiria div.** Portugal
98 B5 **Leiria** Portugal
98 B2 **Leiro** Spain
32 E3 **Leishan** China
33 F3 **Lei Shui r.** China
54 C2 **Leisi** Estonia
14 B4 **Leisler, Mt h.** *Northern Terr.* Australia
73 H4 **Leisnig** Germany
63 H2 **Leiston** *England* U.K.
144 C4 **Leitchfield** *Kentucky* U.S.A.
66 E5 **Leith** *Scotland* U.K.
63 F3 **Leith Hill h.** *England* U.K.
67 C2 **Leitrim div.** Rep. of Ireland
73 G3 **Leitzkau** Germany
69 E5 **Leiwen** Germany
67 E3 **Leixlip** Rep. of Ireland
33 F3 **Leiyang** China
102 B1 **Leiza** Spain
Leizhou *see* **Haikang**
33 E4 **Leizhou Bandao pen.** China
33 E4 **Leizhou Wan** China
59 F1 **Lejberget h.** Sweden
55 D4 **Lejre** Denmark
68 C3 **Lek r.** Netherlands
56 C2 **Leka** Norway
124 B4 **Lékana** Congo
114 F1 **Lekanis mts** Greece
76 G4 **Łeka Opatowka** Poland
124 D4 **Lekatero** Zaire
121 F1 **Le Kef** Tunisia
59 F3 **Lekeryd** Sweden
124 B4 **Lékila** Gabon
130 A4 **Lekkersing** South Africa
76 C4 **Łęknica** Poland
124 B4 **Lékoni** Gabon
125 B4 **Lékoumou div.** Congo
73 L2 **Lekowo** Poland
59 F1 **Leksand** Sweden
50 D2 **Leksozero, Oz. l.** Rus. Fed.
159 □4 **Le Lamentin** *Martinique* Caribbean
148 E3 **Leland** *Michigan* U.S.A.
151 F5 **Leland** *Mississippi* U.S.A.
59 E2 **Lelång l.** Sweden
91 E4 **Le Lauzet-Ubaye** France
91 E5 **Le Lavandou** France
77 H3 **Lelice** Poland
31 F5 **Leling** China
89 E4 **Le Lion-d'Angers** France
77 J1 **Lelkowo** Poland
82 B1 **Le Locle** Switzerland
159 □4 **Le Lorrain** *Martinique* Caribbean
122 B4 **Lélouma** Guinea
89 E4 **Le Louroux-Béconnais** France
91 E5 **Le Luc** France
89 F4 **Le Lude** France
68 D2 **Lelystad** Netherlands
55 A3 **Lem** Denmark
91 B4 **Le Malzieu-Ville** France
82 B2 **Léman, Lac l.** France/Switzerland
89 F3 **Le Mans** *Sarthe* France
159 □4 **Le Marin** *Martinique* Caribbean
82 C1 **le Markstein** France
150 D3 **Le Mars** *Iowa* U.S.A.
93 C4 **Le Mas-d'Agenais** France
93 D5 **Le Mas-d'Azil** France
91 B4 **Le Massegros** France
90 B2 **Le Mayet-de-Montagne** France
89 E4 **Le May-sur Èvre** France
81 E2 **Lembach im Mühlkreis** Austria
74 D4 **Lemberg mt.** Germany
87 G3 **Lemberg** France
93 B5 **Lembeye** France
93 D4 **Lemboulas r.** France
93 C4 **Lembras** France
72 D3 **Lembruch** Germany
168 E5 **Leme** Brazil
68 E2 **Lemelerveld** Netherlands
89 F3 **Le Mêle-sur-Sarthe** France
126 D3 **Lemem Bar YeWha Gudgwad well** Ethiopia
89 F3 **Le Merlerault** France
23 B3 **Lemery** Philippines
79 L3 **Lemešany** Slovakia
43 B2 **Lemesos** Cyprus
72 D3 **Lemgo** Germany
57 G3 **Lemi** Finland
73 K3 **Lemierzyce** Poland
135 M3 **Lemieux Islands is** *N.W.T.* Canada
59 J1 **Lemland** Finland
56 G1 **Lemmenjoen Kansallispuisto nat. park** Finland
68 D2 **Lemmer** Netherlands
150 C2 **Lemmon** *S. Dakota* U.S.A.
155 G5 **Lemmon, Mt mt.** *Arizona* U.S.A.
130 C6 **Lemoenshoek** South Africa
89 E2 **Le Molay-Littry** France
158 D3 **Le Môle St Nicolas** Haiti
82 C2 **Le Moleson mt.** Switzerland
91 B4 **Le Monastier** France
91 B4 **Le Monastier-sur-Gazeille** France
91 E4 **Le Monêtier-les-Bains** France
90 B2 **Le Montet** France
154 C3 **Lemoore** *California* U.S.A.
159 □4 **Le Morne Rouge** *Martinique* Caribbean
156 H6 **Lempa r.** El Salvador
91 B3 **Lempdes** *Auvergne* France
90 B3 **Lempdes** *Auvergne* France
24 A2 **Lemro r.** Myanmar
25 B5 **Lem Tom Chob pt** Thailand
22 B1 **Lemukutan i.** Indonesia
109 H3 **Le Murge reg.** Italy
91 E5 **Le Muy** France
55 A3 **Lemvig** Denmark
24 A3 **Lemyethna** Myanmar
100 B1 **Lena r.** Portugal
45 M4 **Lena r.** Rus. Fed.
148 C4 **Lena** *Illinois* U.S.A.
58 D1 **Lena** Norway
6 □2 **Lénakel** Vanuatu
22 D4 **Lenangguar** Indonesia
81 G4 **Lenart** Slovenia
36 E2 **Lenchung Tso l.** China
92 C2 **Lencloître** France
166 D3 **Lencóis** Brazil
167 A4 **Lençóis Maranhenses, Parque Nacional dos nat. park** Brazil
168 D5 **Lençóis Paulista** Brazil
93 B4 **Lencouacq** France
80 E3 **Lend** Austria
124 E3 **Lenda r.** Zaire
79 K2 **Lendak** Slovakia
81 H4 **Lendava** Slovenia
69 B4 **Lendelede** Belgium
107 F3 **Lendinara** Italy
81 E4 **Lendorf** Austria
75 J2 **Lenešice** Czech Rep.
89 F2 **Le Neubourg** France
80 E2 **Lengau** Austria
39 D3 **Lengbarūt** Iran
75 J2 **Lengefeld** Germany
83 F1 **Lengenwang** Germany
47 G4 **Lenger** Kazakhstan
72 C3 **Lengerich** Germany
75 G5 **Lenggries** Germany
30 B5 **Lenglong Ling mountain range** China
82 C1 **Lengnau** Switzerland
124 C3 **Lengoué r.** Congo
33 E3 **Lengshuijiang** China
33 E3 **Lengshuitan** China
172 B1 **Lengua de Vaca, Pta headland** Chile
63 G3 **Lenham** *England* U.K.
59 F3 **Lenhovda** Sweden
47 G5 **Lenin** Tajikistan
46 E4 **Leninabad** Uzbekistan
Leninakan *see* **Gyumri**
53 E3 **Lenine** *Mykolayivs'ka Oblast'* Ukraine
51 E6 **Lenine** *Respublika Krym* Ukraine
54 F2 **Leningrad div.** Rus. Fed.
51 F6 **Leningradskaya** Rus. Fed.
45 T3 **Leningradskiy** Rus. Fed.
47 H5 **Leningradskiy** Tajikistan
47 K2 **Leninogorsk** Kazakhstan
46 D2 **Leninogorsk** Rus. Fed.
46 F3 **Leninsk** Kazakhstan
51 H5 **Leninsk** Rus. Fed.
46 E4 **Leninsk** Turkmenistan
52 C2 **Leninskiy** Rus. Fed.
47 L2 **Leninsk-Kuznetskiy** Rus. Fed.
47 G2 **Leninskoye** Kazakhstan
47 G4 **Leninskoye** Kazakhstan
31 K3 **Leninskoye** Rus. Fed.
50 H3 **Leninskoye** Rus. Fed.
82 C2 **Lenk** Switzerland
83 E3 **Lenna** Italy
87 G1 **Lenne r.** Germany
72 D4 **Lennestadt** Germany
74 E4 **Lenningen** Germany
171 C7 **Lennox, I. i.** Chile
141 K4 **Lennoxville** *Québec* Canada
106 E3 **Leno** Italy
145 D5 **Lenoir** *N. Carolina* U.S.A.
82 B1 **Le Noirmont** Switzerland
109 F3 **Lenola** Italy
86 C2 **Le Nouvion-en-Thiérache** France
147 G3 **Lenox** *Massachusetts* U.S.A.
69 B4 **Lens** Belgium
86 B2 **Lens** France
73 F1 **Lensahn** Germany
45 N3 **Lensk** Rus. Fed.
90 D2 **Lent** France
42 E1 **Lentekhi** Georgia
78 F5 **Lenti** Hungary
107 G2 **Lentiai** Italy
80 C2 **Lenting** Germany
110 D5 **Lentini r.** *Sicilia* Italy
54 D4 **Lentvaris** Lithuania
82 D1 **Lenzburg** Switzerland
73 G2 **Lenzen** Germany
81 E3 **Lenzing** Austria
74 D5 **Lenzkirch** Germany
107 E4 **Leo r.** Italy
122 D4 **Léo** Burkina
81 F3 **Leoben div.** Austria
81 G3 **Leoben** *Steiermark* Austria
95 G2 **Leoben** Austria
80 D3 **Leogang** Austria
93 B4 **Léognan** France
62 D2 **Leominster** *England* U.K.
147 H3 **Leominster** *Massachusetts* U.S.A.
98 E2 **León div.** Spain
98 E2 **León** *León* Spain
93 A5 **Léon** France
157 E4 **León** Mexico
156 J6 **León** Nicaragua
108 E3 **Leonardo da Vinci airport** Italy
128 B3 **Leonardville** Namibia
43 C2 **Leonarisson** Cyprus
74 E4 **Leonberg** Germany
91 D4 **Léoncel** France
81 F2 **Leonding** Austria
7 □13 **Leone** *American Samoa* Pacific Ocean

82 D2 Leone, Monte mt. Italy/Switzerland
173 F2 Leones Argentina
109 E2 Leonessa Italy
110 D5 Leonforte *Sicilia* Italy
13 F4 Leongatha *Victoria* Australia
115 D5 Leonidi Greece
100 D4 León, Isla de i. Spain
98 D2 León, Montes de mountain range Spain
17 C6 Leonora *Western Australia* Australia
173 J1 León, Paso del pass Brazil
115 D5 Leontario Greece
16 D3 Leopold r. *Western Australia* Australia
169 G4 Leopoldina Brazil
69 B3 Leopold Kanaal canal Belgium
168 D2 Leopoldo de Bulhões Brazil
69 D3 Leopoldsburg Belgium
87 G4 Leopoldskanal canal Germany
112 F1 Leorda Romania
53 C3 Leova Moldova
137 H4 Leoville *Saskatchewan* Canada
88 B4 Le Palais France
92 D3 Le Palais-sur-Vienne France
22 A2 Lepar i. Indonesia
86 B2 Le Parcq France
93 C4 Le Passage France
86 C4 Le Pavillon-Ste-Julie France
100 C3 Lepe Spain
91 C3 Le Péage-de-Roussillon France
114 C4 Lepenou Greece
91 D4 Le Périer France
93 E6 Le Perthus France
89 G2 Le Petit-Quevilly France
128 D3 Lephepe Botswana
131 E5 Lephoi South Africa
92 B4 Le Pian-Médoc France
86 D4 L'Épine *Champagne-Ardenne* France
91 D4 L'Épine *Provence - Alpes - Côte-d'Azur* France
33 G2 Leping China
141 J4 L'Épiphanie *Québec* Canada
86 B3 Le Plessis-Belleville France
91 D4 Le Poët France
81 H4 Lepoglava Croatia
92 D2 Le Poinçonnet France
92 A2 Le Poiré-sur-Vie France
91 D3 Le Pont-de-Claix France
91 B4 Le Pont-de-Monvert France
91 C5 Le Pontet France
93 A4 Le Porge France
127 □5 Le Port *Réunion* Indian Ocean
86 A2 Le Portel France
112 C3 Leposavić Yugoslavia
88 C4 Le Pouliguen France
115 F4 Lepoura Greece
91 C4 Le Pouzin France
56 G3 Leppävirta Finland
91 E5 Le Pradet France
47 J3 Lepsy Kazakhstan
114 D2 Leptokarya Greece
91 B3 Le-Puy-en-Velay France
86 C2 Le Quesnoy France
111 H2 Lequile Italy
86 B4 Le Raincy France
159 □5 Le Raizet airport *Guadeloupe* Caribbean
110 C5 Lercara Friddi *Sicilia* Italy
124 B2 Léré Chad
90 A1 Léré France
123 F4 Lere Nigeria
88 A3 Le Relecq-Kerhuon France
98 B2 Lérez r. Spain
106 D4 Lerici Italy
162 C4 Lerida Colombia
Lérida *see* Lleida
42 G2 Lerik Azerbaijan
102 B2 Lerín Spain
91 F5 Lérins, Îles de is France
99 G2 Lerma Spain
93 B4 Lerm-et Musset France
51 G6 Lermontov Rus. Fed.
31 K3 Lermontovka Rus. Fed.
80 B3 Lermoos Austria
122 D3 Lerneb Mali
159 □4 Le Robert *Martinique* Caribbean
90 E3 Le Roignais mt. France
113 F6 Leros i. Greece
93 E4 Le Rouget France
148 C5 Le Roy *Illinois* U.S.A.
91 B4 Le Rozier France
59 E3 Lerum Sweden
90 E1 Le Russey France
66 □2 Lerwick *Scotland* U.K.
124 E1 Ler Zerai well Sudan
93 C6 Lés Spain
83 D3 Lesa Italy
90 D3 Les Abrets France
159 □5 Les Abymes *Guadeloupe* Caribbean
159 □4 Le St Esprit *Martinique* Caribbean
92 E1 Les Aix-d'Angillon France
93 E6 Les Albères reg. France
89 G2 Les Andelys France
91 C5 Les Angles France
114 B1 Lešani Macedonia
159 □4 Les Anses d'Arlets *Martinique* Caribbean
90 E3 Les Arcs France
127 C5 Lesatima mt. Kenya
82 A3 Les Avenières France
127 □5 Les Avirons *Réunion* Indian Ocean
102 D3 Les Borges Blanques Spain
Lesbos i. *see* Lesvos
90 D2 Les Bouchoux France
65 G2 Lesbury *England* U.K.
93 D6 Les Cabannes France
102 G2 L'Escala Spain
91 E4 L'Escale France
127 □4 L'Escalier Mauritius
93 E5 Les Cammazes France
93 B5 Lescar France
91 F5 L'Escarène France
158 D3 Les Cayes Haiti
81 F4 Lesce Slovenia
89 E3 Les Coëvrons h. France
82 B3 Les Contamines-Montjoie France
93 E5 Lescure-d'Albigeois France
111 F3 Lese r. Italy
91 D3 Les Échelles France
88 D4 Le Sel-de-Bretagne France
82 B2 Le Sentier Switzerland
92 B2 Les Epesses France
93 D6 Les Escaldes Andorra
139 G4 Les Escoumins *Québec* Canada
90 D2 Les Essards-Taignevaux France
92 A2 Les Essarts France
147 J1 Les Étroits *Québec* Canada
93 D4 Les Eyzies-de-Tayac-Sireuil France
90 E1 Les Fins France
82 B2 Les Fourgs France
90 E2 Les Gets France
32 C2 Leshan China
69 C5 Les Hautes-Rivières France
92 A2 Les Herbiers France
82 B3 Les Houches France
50 H1 Leshukonskoye Rus. Fed.
124 E2 Lesi watercourse Sudan
6 □6 Lesiaceva Pt pt Fiji
106 D4 Lesima, Monte mt. Italy
109 H3 Lesina Italy
109 H3 Lesina, Lago di lag. Italy
91 E5 les Issambres France
59 F2 Lesjöfors Sweden
91 E3 les Karellis France
77 L6 Lesko Poland
112 C3 Leskovac Yugoslavia
114 B2 Leskovik Albania
53 E2 Les'ky Ukraine
92 A2 Les Landes-Genusson France
66 E4 Leslie *Scotland* U.K.
92 A2 Les Lucs-sur-Boulogne France
64 E2 Lesmahagow *Scotland* U.K.
159 □5 Les Mangles *Guadeloupe* Caribbean
90 E3 Les Marches France
91 B5 Les Matelles France
89 E4 Les Mauges reg. France
91 D4 Les Mées France
91 E3 Les Menuires France
88 C3 Les Minquiers is Channel Is.
86 D4 Lesmont France
73 L4 Leśna Poland
52 D1 Lesnaya Polyana Rus. Fed.
88 A3 Lesneven France
76 G5 Leśnica Poland
73 L4 Leśniów Wielki Poland
52 E2 Lesnoy Rus. Fed.
50 K3 Lesnoy Rus. Fed.
53 E2 Lesnoye Rus. Fed.
54 F1 Lesnoy, O. i. Rus. Fed.
52 F2 Lesogorsk Rus. Fed.
54 F1 Lesogorskiy Rus. Fed.
91 C4 Les Ollières-sur-Eyrieux France
44 L4 Lesosibirsk Rus. Fed.
117 G8 Lesotho country Africa
131 G4 Lesotho Highlands Water Scheme Lesotho
31 K3 Lesozavodsk Rus. Fed.
92 B3 Lesparre-Médoc France
91 D5 Les Pennes-Mirabeau France
93 A5 Lesperon France
79 N4 Lespezi h. Romania
88 D2 Les Pieux France
90 E2 Les Planches-en-Montagne France
89 E4 Les Ponts-de-Cé France
82 B1 Les Ponts-de-Martel Switzerland
86 D5 Les Riceys France
89 E4 Les Rosiers France
90 E2 Les Rousses France
92 A2 Les Sables-d'Olonne France
81 E3 Lessach Austria
88 D2 Lessay France
69 D4 Lesse r. Belgium
159 G3 Lesser Antilles is Caribbean
162 D1 Lesser Antilles is Venezuela
Lesser Caucasus mountain range *see* Malyy Kavkaz
136 F3 Lesser Slave Lake l. *Yukon Terr.* Canada
136 G3 Lesser Slave Lake Provincial Park nat. park *Alberta* Canada
86 C2 Lessines Belgium
131 F4 Lessingskop mt. South Africa
83 G3 Lessini, Monti mts Italy
88 D4 Les Sorinières France
91 E4 Les Thuiles France
56 G3 Lestijärvi l. Finland
56 G3 Lestijärvi Finland
159 □4 Les Trois Îlets is *Martinique* Caribbean
89 F4 Les Trois-Moutiers France
179 □ les Trois Swains is *Kerguelen* Indian Ocean
16 D2 Lesueur I. i. *Western Australia* Australia
17 A6 Lesueur, Mt h. *Western Australia* Australia
91 C4 Les Vans France
91 B4 Les Vignes France
114 G3 Lesvos div. Greece
113 E5 Lesvos i. Greece
73 L2 Leszczyn Poland
77 L4 Leszkowice Poland
76 E4 Leszno div. Poland
76 E4 Leszno *Leszno* Poland
76 E4 Leszno Górne Poland
131 H1 Letaba South Africa
59 F2 Letälven r. Sweden
127 □5 Le Tampon *Réunion* Indian Ocean
79 L4 Létavértes Hungary
63 F3 Letchworth *England* U.K.
93 A4 Le Teich France
91 C4 Le Teil France
89 E3 Le Teilleul France
93 E4 Le Temple France
78 F5 Letenye Hungary
36 D4 Leteri India
131 F2 Lethabile South Africa
24 A2 Letha Range mountain range Myanmar
136 G5 Lethbridge *Alberta* Canada
89 F3 Le Theil France
163 F3 Lethem Guyana
87 F5 Le Thillot France
87 F4 Le Tholy France
91 C5 Le Thor France
162 D4 Leticia Colombia
31 F5 Leting China
109 G3 Letino Italy
130 D6 Letjiesbos South Africa
128 D3 Letlhakane Botswana
128 D3 Letlhakeng Botswana
50 F1 Letniy Navolok Rus. Fed.
52 F1 Letnyaya Baza Rus. Fed.
80 D4 Le Tofane mt. Italy
111 E5 Letojanni *Sicilia* Italy
86 A2 Le Touquet-Paris-Plage airport France
86 A2 Le Touquet-Paris-Plage France
91 D3 Le Touvet France
78 F2 Letovice Czech Rep.
24 A3 Letpadan Myanmar
91 E5 le Trayas France
89 G1 Le Tréport France
73 K3 Letschin Germany
131 H1 Letsitele South Africa
25 B5 Letsok-aw Kyun i. Myanmar
131 E3 Letsopa South Africa
67 D2 Letterkenny Rep. of Ireland
62 B3 Letterston *Wales* U.K.
25 D7 Letung Indonesia
101 H2 Letur Spain
93 B4 Le Tuzan France
53 B2 Letychiv Ukraine
73 G3 Letzlingen Germany
125 D6 Léua Angola
93 F6 Leucate, Cap pt France
66 F4 Leuchars *Scotland* U.K.
112 E1 Leud Romania
90 C1 Leuglay France
82 C2 Leuk Switzerland
82 C2 Leukerbad Switzerland
73 H4 Leuna Germany
50 G1 Leunovo Rus. Fed.
155 G4 Leupp Corner *Arizona* U.S.A.
15 G4 Leura *Queensland* Australia
68 D2 Leusden Netherlands
80 C3 Leutasch Austria
74 F3 Leutershausen Germany
74 F5 Leutkirch im Allgäu Germany
69 C4 Leuven div. Belgium
69 C4 Leuven *Leuven* Belgium
69 B4 Leuze-en-Hainaut Belgium
115 D4 Levadeia Greece
91 E5 Le Val France
90 D1 Le Vallinot-Longeau-Percey France
155 G2 Levan *Utah* U.S.A.
113 B4 Levan Albania
56 C3 Levanger Norway
91 E5 Levant, Île du i. France
106 D4 Levanto Italy
110 B5 Levanzo *Sicilia* Italy
110 B4 Levanzo, Isola di i. *Sicilia* Italy
51 H7 Levashi Rus. Fed.
159 □4 Le Vauclin *Martinique* Caribbean
151 C5 Levelland *Texas* U.S.A.
9 C6 Levels New Zealand
65 H4 Leven *England* U.K.
66 F4 Leven *Scotland* U.K.
66 E4 Leven, Loch l. *Scotland* U.K.
131 J3 Leven Pt l. South Africa
65 F3 Levens *England* U.K.
91 F5 Levens France
16 C3 Lévêque, C. c. *Western Australia* Australia
111 H2 Leverano Italy
92 A3 Le-Verdon-sur-Mer France
148 E3 Levering *Michigan* U.S.A.
72 B4 Leverkusen Germany
93 D5 Le Vernet France
93 C3 Lèves France
92 E2 Levet France
93 E4 Lévézou mts France
79 H3 Levice Slovakia
107 F2 Levico Terme Italy
115 D5 Levidi Greece
108 B3 Levie *Corse* France
92 E2 Levier France
91 B5 Le Vigan France
8 E4 Levin New Zealand
141 K3 Lévis *Québec* Canada
113 F6 Levitha i. Greece
147 G4 Levittown *New York* U.S.A.
147 F4 Levittown *Pennsylvania* U.S.A.
79 K2 Levoča Slovakia
79 K2 Levočské vrchy mountain range Slovakia
92 D2 Levroux France
112 E3 Levski Bulgaria
52 D3 Lev Tolstoy Rus. Fed.
6 □8 Levuka Fiji
112 E1 Levunovo Bulgaria
88 D2 Lévy, Cap pt France
22 D4 Lewa Indonesia
24 B3 Lewe Myanmar
130 A2 Lewer watercourse Namibia
147 F5 Lewes *Delaware* U.S.A.
63 G4 Lewes *England* U.K.
76 F5 Lewin Brzeski Poland
66 B2 Lewis i. *Scotland* U.K.
146 E4 Lewisburg *Pennsylvania* U.S.A.
146 C6 Lewisburg *W. Virginia* U.S.A.
9 D5 Lewis Pass pass New Zealand
16 E4 Lewis Ra. h. *Western Australia* Australia
152 D1 Lewis Range mountain range *Montana* U.S.A.
145 C5 Lewis Smith, L. l. *Alabama* U.S.A.
155 G6 Lewis Springs *Arizona* U.S.A.
152 C2 Lewiston *Idaho* U.S.A.
147 H2 Lewiston *Maine* U.S.A.
140 C4 Lewiston *Michigan* U.S.A.
148 B4 Lewiston *Minnesota* U.S.A.
148 B5 Lewistown *Illinois* U.S.A.
152 E2 Lewistown *Montana* U.S.A.
146 E4 Lewistown *Pennsylvania* U.S.A.
151 E5 Lewisville *Arkansas* U.S.A.
151 D5 Lewisville, Lake l. *Texas* U.S.A.
148 C5 Lexington *Illinois* U.S.A.
144 C4 Lexington *Kentucky* U.S.A.
150 E4 Lexington *Missouri* U.S.A.
145 D5 Lexington *N. Carolina* U.S.A.
150 D3 Lexington *Nebraska* U.S.A.
145 B5 Lexington *Tennessee* U.S.A.
146 D6 Lexington *Virginia* U.S.A.
146 E5 Lexington Park *Maryland* U.S.A.
69 D5 Lexy France
65 G3 Leyburn *England* U.K.
131 H1 Leydsdorp South Africa
32 D3 Leye China
179 □ Leygues, Is is *Kerguelen* Indian Ocean
65 F4 Leyland *England* U.K.
93 D4 Leyme France
82 C2 Leysin Switzerland
23 C4 Leyte i. Philippines
23 C4 Leyte Gulf g. Philippines
82 C2 Leytron Switzerland
77 L5 Leżajsk Poland
91 C4 Lézan France
93 D5 Lézat-sur-Lèze France
82 B2 Lezay France
93 D5 Lèze r. France
112 B4 Lezhë Albania
32 D2 Lezhi China
52 E1 Lezhnevo Rus. Fed.
93 E5 Lézignan-Corbières France
90 B3 Lezoux France
101 H2 Lezuza r. Spain
101 H2 Lezuza Spain
147 G3 L George l. *New York* U.S.A.
52 B4 L'gov Rus. Fed.
37 H3 Lhari China
37 G4 Lhasa *Tibet* China
86 B4 L'Hay-les-Roses France
37 F3 Lhazê China
37 F3 Lhazhong China
81 F1 Lhenice Czech Rep.
88 C4 l'Herbaudière, Pte de pt France
92 B2 L'Hermenault France
88 D3 L'Hermitage France
87 F3 L'Hôpital France
20 C5 Lhokseumawe Indonesia
32 A2 Lhorong China
93 D4 Lhospitalet France
102 D4 L'Hospitalet de l'Infant Spain
102 F3 L'Hospitalet de Llobregat Spain
91 B5 L'Hospitalet-du-Larzac France
102 D4 L'Hostal del Alls Spain
82 A3 Lhuis France
89 E3 L'Huisserie France
37 H3 Lhünzê China
37 G3 Lhünzhub China
33 E3 Li r. China
128 C2 Liambezi, Lake l. Namibia
108 A2 Liamone r. *Corse* France
33 G3 Liancheng China
86 B3 Liancourt France
Liancourt Rocks is *see* Tok-tō
86 A2 Liane r. France
23 C4 Lianga Philippines
23 C4 Lianga Bay b. Philippines
33 F2 Liangaz Hu l. China
30 E4 Liangcheng China
32 D1 Liangdang China
32 D1 Lianghekou China
32 D2 Liangping China
31 E6 Liangshan China
33 E4 Liangtian China
32 C3 Liangwang Shan mountain range China
30 D5 Liangzhen China
33 F3 Lianhua China
33 F4 Lianhua Shan mountain range China
33 G3 Lianjiang China
33 E4 Lianjiang China
33 F3 Liannan China
114 D4 Lianokladi Greece
33 F3 Lianping China
33 F3 Lianshan China
33 G1 Lianshui China
25 C4 Liant, C. c. Thailand
33 F3 Lian Xian China
31 G1 Lianyin China
33 E3 Lianyuan China
33 G1 Lianyungang China
33 G1 Lianyungang China
Lianzhou *see* Hepu
31 J3 Lianzhushan China
31 G4 Liao r. China
31 E5 Liaocheng China
31 G4 Liaodong h. China
31 G4 Liaodong Wan b. China
31 G4 Liaoning div. China
31 G4 Liaoyang China
31 H4 Liaoyuan China
31 G4 Liaozhong China
114 A3 Liapades Greece
36 B2 Liaqatabad Pakistan
134 E3 Liard r. *B.C.* Canada
136 E2 Liard r. *B.C./N.W.T.* Canada
136 D3 Liard River *B.C.* Canada
36 A4 Liari Pakistan
86 D3 Liart France
66 C3 Liathach mt. *Scotland* U.K.
59 E3 Liatorp Sweden
75 L2 Libáň Czech Rep.
43 C3 Liban, Jebel mountain range Lebanon
173 G4 Libano Argentina
162 B3 Libano Colombia
101 E4 Libar, Sierra de mountain range Spain
152 D1 Libby *Montana* U.S.A.
78 C1 Libčeves Czech Rep.
124 C3 Libenge Zaire
77 J2 Liberadz Poland
151 C4 Liberal *Kansas* U.S.A.
166 B3 Liberdade r. Brazil
169 F5 Liberdade *Minas Gerais* Brazil
78 E1 Liberec Czech Rep.
117 D5 Liberia country Africa
156 J7 Liberia Costa Rica
173 J3 Libertad Uruguay
156 B2 Libertad, Pto Mexico
131 F4 Libertase South Africa
148 B6 Liberty *Illinois* U.S.A.
147 J2 Liberty *Maine* U.S.A.
150 E4 Liberty *Missouri* U.S.A.
147 F4 Liberty *New York* U.S.A.
151 E6 Liberty *Texas* U.S.A.
172 E2 Lib. Gen. S. Martín Argentina
77 H5 Libiąż Poland
69 D5 Libin Belgium
23 B3 Libmanan Philippines
32 D3 Libo China
131 G5 Libode South Africa
114 B2 Libohovë Albania
131 G4 Libono Lesotho
172 E2 Liborio Luna Argentina
75 K2 Libouchec Czech Rep.
93 B4 Libourne France
69 D5 Libramont Belgium
114 B1 Librazhd Albania
124 A3 Libreville Gabon
103 B7 Librilla Spain
23 C5 Libuganon r. Philippines
116 F3 Libya country Africa
118 D2 Libyan Desert desert Egypt/Libya
118 E1 Libyan Plateau plat. Egypt
164 C4 Licancabur, Vol. volcano Chile
172 A3 Licantén Chile
110 C5 Licata *Sicilia* Italy
106 E4 Licciana Nardi Italy
42 E2 Lice Turkey
74 D2 Lich Germany
114 D4 Lichas pen. Greece
30 E5 Licheng China
63 E2 Lichfield *England* U.K.
127 C7 Lichinga Mozambique
70 E3 Lichte Germany
74 D4 Lichtenau *Baden-Württemberg* Germany
75 F3 Lichtenau *Bayern* Germany
72 D4 Lichtenau *Nordrhein-Westfalen* Germany
75 G2 Lichtenberg Germany
131 F3 Lichtenburg South Africa
75 G2 Lichtenfels Germany
75 H2 Lichtenstein Germany
68 E3 Lichtenvoorde Netherlands
81 H3 Lichtenwörth Austria
69 B3 Lichtervelde Belgium
33 E2 Lichuan China
33 G3 Lichuan China
169 G1 Licinio de Almeida Brazil
146 B5 Licking r. *Kentucky* U.S.A.
104 E3 Lički Osik Croatia
86 A2 Licques France
154 D3 Lida *Nevada* U.S.A.
77 O2 Lida Belarus
59 E2 Lidan r. Sweden
65 F2 Liddel r. *England/Scotland* U.K.
66 F5 Liddesdale v. *Scotland* U.K.
130 B2 Lidfontein Namibia
59 E3 Lidhult Sweden
59 H2 Lidingö Sweden
59 E2 Lidköping Sweden
107 G3 Lido Italy
107 G4 Lido Adriano Italy
107 G4 Lido di Classe Italy
107 G3 Lido di Jesolo Italy
111 F2 Lido di Metaponto Italy
109 E3 Lido di Ostia Italy
107 G4 Lido di Spina Italy
56 D2 Lidsjöberg Sweden
54 E3 Lidumnieki Latvia
77 H2 Lidzbark Poland
77 J1 Lidzbark Warmiński Poland
81 F2 Liebenau Austria
72 E3 Liebenau Germany
72 F3 Liebenburg Germany
73 J3 Liebenwalde Germany
73 K4 Lieberose Germany
14 B4 Liebig, Mt mt. *Northern Terr.* Australia
81 G4 Lieboch Austria
48 F4 Liechtenstein country Europe
102 B2 Liédena Spain
69 D4 Liège div. Belgium
69 D4 Liège Belgium
56 H3 Lieksa Finland
54 C3 Lielupe r. Latvia
54 D3 Lielvārde Latvia
56 E3 Lien Sweden
124 E3 Lienart Zaire
80 D4 Lienz div. Austria
80 D4 Lienz Austria
54 B3 Liepāja Latvia
73 J2 Liepen Germany
54 E3 Liepna Latvia
77 N1 Lieponys Lithuania
69 C3 Lier Belgium
90 C1 Liernais France
69 D4 Lierneux Belgium
58 A2 Liervik Norway
81 F3 Liesing r. Austria
82 C1 Liestal Switzerland
54 C1 Lieto Finland
103 B6 Liétor Spain
59 F2 Lieuvin reg. France
86 B2 Liévin France
141 H3 Lièvre r. *Québec* Canada
81 F3 Liezen div. Austria
81 F3 Liezen Austria
124 D3 Lifanga Zaire
67 E3 Liffey r. Rep. of Ireland
87 E4 Liffol-le-Grand France
67 D2 Lifford Rep. of Ireland
88 D3 Liffré France
171 C5 Lifi Mahuida mt. Argentina
6 □2 Lifou i. *New Caledonia* Pacific Ocean
6 □5 Lifuka i. Tonga
23 B3 Ligao Philippines
93 C4 Ligardes France
57 G4 Līgatne Latvia
13 F2 Lightning Ridge *New South Wales* Australia
107 H3 Lignano Sabbiadoro Italy
88 D4 Ligné France
92 A2 Ligneron r. France
69 E4 Ligneuville Belgium
92 E2 Lignières France
90 B3 Lignon r. France
87 E4 Ligny-en-Barrois France
90 B1 Ligny-le-Châtel France
129 F2 Ligonha r. Mozambique
148 E5 Ligonier *Indiana* U.S.A.
77 H3 Ligowo Poland
172 B2 Ligua, B. de la b. Chile
89 F4 Ligueil France
156 C3 Ligui Mexico
106 C4 Liguria div. Italy
106 C5 Ligurian Sea sea Italy
127 C7 Lihehe Tanzania
6 □1 Lihir Group is P.N.G.
55 A3 Lihme Denmark
15 G3 Lihou Reef & Cays reef *Coral Sea Islands Terr.* Pacific Ocean
153 □2 Lihue *Hawaii* U.S.A.
54 C2 Lihula Estonia
32 C3 Lijiang China
31 F5 Lijin China
125 E6 Likasi Zaire
124 D3 Likati r. Zaire
124 D3 Likati Zaire
136 E4 Likely *B.C.* Canada
59 E1 Likenäs Sweden
52 B1 Likhoslavl' Rus. Fed.
124 D4 Likolia Zaire
124 D4 Likoto Zaire
124 C3 Likouala div. Congo
124 C3 Likouala r. Congo
124 C3 Likouala aux Herbes r. Congo
22 B1 Liku Indonesia
6 □8 Likuri Harb. b. Fiji
89 F4 L'Île-Bouchard France
108 A2 L'Île-Rousse *Corse* France
81 G3 Lilienfeld div. Austria
81 G2 Lilienfeld Austria
72 D2 Lilienthal Germany
33 F3 Liling China
36 C2 Lilla Pakistan
59 E2 Lilla Edet Sweden
59 H3 Lilla Karlsö i. Sweden
86 C2 Lille *Nord* France
69 C3 Lille Belgium
55 A3 Lilleå r. Denmark
55 B4 Lille Bælt chan. Denmark
89 F2 Lillebonne France
58 D1 Lillehammer Norway
86 C2 Lille-Lesquin airport France
86 B2 Lillers France
58 C2 Lillesand Norway
62 D2 Lilleshall *England* U.K.
55 E4 Lille Skensved Denmark
58 D2 Lillestrom Norway
148 E4 Lilley *Michigan* U.S.A.
56 D3 Lillholmsjö Sweden
17 D5 Lillian, Pt h. *Western Australia* Australia
65 F2 Lilliesleaf *Scotland* U.K.
101 G1 Lillo Spain
136 E4 Lillooet r. *B.C.* Canada
136 E4 Lillooet *B.C.* Canada
37 H4 Lilong India
129 E1 Lilongwe r. Malawi
127 B7 Lilongwe Malawi
127 □1 L'Îlot i. Seychelles
23 B4 Liloy Philippines
171 B5 Lilpela, P. pass Argentina/Chile
13 F5 Lilydale *Tasmania* Australia
152 D2 Lima *Montana* U.S.A.
146 A4 Lima *Ohio* U.S.A.
173 H3 Lima Argentina
164 A2 Lima Peru
169 G4 Lima Duarte Brazil
90 B3 Limagne reg. France
39 D4 Limah Oman
Lima Is is *see* Wanshan Qundao
51 H6 Liman Rus. Fed.
23 B3 Liman, G. mt. Indonesia
76 J6 Limanowa Poland
172 B1 Limarí r. Chile
37 E2 Lima Ringma Tso l. China
22 A1 Limas Indonesia
Limassol *see* Lemesos
67 E1 Limavady *Northern Ireland* U.K.
172 C5 Limay r. Argentina
89 G2 Limay France
172 D4 Limay Mahuida Argentina
75 H2 Limbach-Oberfrohna Germany
164 C2 Limbani Peru
108 B4 Limbara, Monte mountain range *Sardegna* Italy
54 D3 Limbaži Latvia
124 A3 Limbe Cameroon
69 D4 Limbourg Belgium
22 C2 Limbungan Indonesia
69 D3 Limburg div. Belgium
69 D3 Limburg div. Netherlands
131 G1 Limburg South Africa
74 D2 Limburg an der Lahn Germany
25 □ Lim Chu Kang h. Singapore
25 □ Lim Chu Kang Singapore
130 D4 Lime Acres South Africa
59 E1 Limedsforsen Sweden
9 B7 Limehills New Zealand
168 E5 Limeira Brazil
114 F2 Limenaria Greece
67 B4 Limerick div. Rep. of Ireland
67 C4 Limerick Rep. of Ireland
148 A4 Lime Springs *Iowa* U.S.A.
147 K1 Limestone *Maine* U.S.A.
55 A3 Limfjorden chan. Denmark
98 C2 Limia r. Spain
56 D2 Limingen l. Norway
56 D2 Limingen *Nord-Trøndelag* Norway
147 H3 Limington *Maine* U.S.A.
56 G2 Liminka Finland
14 D2 Limmen Bight b. *Northern Terr.* Australia
14 C3 Limmen Bight R. r. *Northern Terr.* Australia
114 E4 Limni Greece
114 C2 Limni Aliakmonas l. Greece
114 C4 Limni Amvrakia l. Greece
115 F4 Limni Distos l. Greece
Limni Doïranis l. *see* Dojran, Lake
114 B3 Limni Ioanninon l. Greece
114 C2 Limni Kastorias l. Greece
114 E1 Limni Kerkinitis l. Greece
114 C4 Limni Lysimachia l. Greece
114 C2 Limni Mikri Prespa l. Greece
114 C4 Limni Ozeros l. Greece
114 D2 Limni Sfikia resr Greece
115 D5 Limni Stymfalia l. Greece
114 C4 Limni Trichonida l. Greece
114 G1 Limni Vistonida lag. Greece
114 B4 Limni Voulkaria l. Greece
115 E4 Limni Yliki l. Greece
114 G3 Limnos i. Greece
166 E2 Limoeiro Brazil
92 D3 Limoges *Haute-Vienne* France
141 H4 Limoges *Ontario* Canada
93 D4 Limogne-en-Quercy France
153 G4 Limon *Colorado* U.S.A.
156 K7 Limón Costa Rica
156 J6 Limón Honduras
106 B4 Limone Piemonte Italy
107 E3 Limone sul Garda Italy
100 D2 Limonetes r. Spain
127 □3 Limon, Mt h. *Rodrigues I.* Mauritius
164 D3 Limoquije Bolivia
92 D3 Limousin div. France
92 D3 Limousin reg. France
92 D3 Limousin, Monts du h. France
93 E5 Limoux France
129 E3 Limpopo r. Africa
33 E3 Limu China
114 B1 Lin Albania
131 G4 Linakeng Lesotho
56 H1 Linakhamari Rus. Fed.
33 G2 Lin'an China
23 A4 Linapacan i. Philippines
23 A4 Linapacan Strait chan. Philippines
92 D3 Linards France
172 B3 Linares Chile
157 F3 Linares Mexico
101 G2 Linares Spain
103 C4 Linares de Mora Spain
98 E4 Linares de Riofrío Spain
114 F4 Linaria Greece
108 A5 Linas, Monte mt. *Sardegna* Italy
106 D3 Linate airport Italy
32 C4 Lincang China
69 D4 Lincent Belgium
30 E5 Lincheng China
33 G3 Linchuan China
154 B2 Lincoln *California* U.S.A.
63 F1 Lincoln *England* U.K.
148 C5 Lincoln *Illinois* U.S.A.
147 J2 Lincoln *Maine* U.S.A.
149 F3 Lincoln *Michigan* U.S.A.
150 D3 Lincoln *Nebraska* U.S.A.
147 H2 Lincoln *New Hampshire* U.S.A.
173 G3 Lincoln Argentina
9 D5 Lincoln New Zealand
152 A2 Lincoln City *Oregon* U.S.A.
149 F4 Lincoln Park *Michigan* U.S.A.
135 M1 Lincoln Sea sea Canada/Greenland
63 F1 Lincolnshire div. *England* U.K.
65 H4 Lincolnshire Wolds reg. *England* U.K.
147 J2 Lincolnville *Maine* U.S.A.
55 A3 Lind Denmark
52 F1 Linda r. Rus. Fed.
52 G1 Linda Rus. Fed.
58 A1 Lindas Norway
166 D3 Linda, Sa h. Brazil
73 H3 Lindau Germany
74 E5 Lindau (Bodensee) Germany
55 A3 Linde Denmark
145 C5 Linden *Alabama* U.S.A.
151 G5 Linden *Alabama* U.S.A.
145 C5 Linden *Tennessee* U.S.A.
74 D2 Linden Germany
163 F2 Linden Guyana
74 E5 Lindenberg im Allgäu Germany
148 A2 Linden Grove *Minnesota* U.S.A.
135 O3 Lindenow Fjord inlet Greenland
72 C3 Lindern (Oldenburg) Germany
59 E4 Linderödsåsen h. Sweden
17 B7 Lindesay, Mt h. *Western Australia* Australia
59 F2 Lindesberg Sweden
58 B2 Lindesnes c. Norway
127 C6 Lindi div. Tanzania
124 E4 Lindi r. Zaire
127 C6 Lindi Tanzania
31 H3 Lindian China
Lindisfarne i. *see* Holy Island
87 G1 Lindlar Germany
131 F3 Lindley South Africa
55 E2 Lindome Sweden
165 E4 Lindo, Monte r. Paraguay
65 E1 Lindores *Scotland* U.K.
115 □ Lindos Greece
154 C3 Lindsay *California* U.S.A.
147 K1 Lindsay *New Brunswick* Canada
141 F4 Lindsay *Ontario* Canada
59 G3 Lindsdal Sweden
75 J3 Líně Czech Rep.
5 M5 Line Islands is Pacific Ocean
47 K2 Linevo Rus. Fed.
30 D5 Linfen China
38 A3 Linganamakki Reservoir resr India
33 E5 Lingao China
23 B2 Lingayen Philippines
23 B2 Lingayen Gulf b. Philippines
33 E1 Lingbao China
33 G1 Lingbi China
30 E6 Lingchuan China
33 E3 Lingchuan China
131 F6 Lingelethu South Africa
131 E6 Lingelihle South Africa
72 C3 Lingen (Ems) Germany
87 H3 Lingenfeld Germany
63 F3 Lingfield *England* U.K.
22 A2 Lingga i. Indonesia
22 B1 Lingga Malaysia
23 C4 Lingig Philippines
152 F3 Lingle *Wyoming* U.S.A.
87 G4 Lingolsheim France
124 D3 Lingomo Zaire
30 E5 Lingqiu China
33 E4 Lingshan China
31 G6 Lingshan Dao i. China
30 D5 Lingshi China
33 E5 Lingshui China
38 B2 Lingsugur India
32 D1 Lingtai China
32 E5 Lingtou China
111 E5 Linguaglossa *Sicilia* Italy
122 A3 Linguère Senegal
33 E3 Lingui China
108 B2 Linguizzetta *Corse* France
30 C5 Lingwu China
33 F3 Ling Xian China
31 F4 Lingyuan China
32 D3 Lingyun China
36 D2 Lingzi Thang Plains plain China/Jammu and Kashmir
33 H2 Linhai China
169 H3 Linhares Brazil
24 D3 Linh Cam Vietnam
30 C4 Linhe China
147 H1 Linière *Québec* Canada
76 G1 Liniewo Poland
31 H4 Linjiang China
87 H3 Linkenheim-Hochstetten Germany
59 F2 Linköping Sweden
31 J3 Linkou China
54 C3 Linkuva Lithuania
33 E2 Linli China
66 E5 Linlithgow *Scotland* U.K.
62 A3 Linney Head headland *Wales* U.K.
66 C4 Linnhe, Loch est. *Scotland* U.K.
74 B2 Linnich Germany
154 A1 Linn, Mt mt. *California* U.S.A.
105 D7 Linosa, Isola di i. Italy
77 N3 Linova Belarus
31 E5 Linqing China
31 F5 Linqu China
33 F1 Linquan China
33 F1 Linru China
168 D4 Lins Brazil
33 G1 Linshu China
32 D2 Linshui China
159 □1 Linstead Jamaica
129 G3 Linta r. Madagascar
32 C1 Lintan China
32 C1 Lintao China
83 E1 Linth r. Switzerland
83 E2 Linthal Switzerland

31 H2 **Longzhen** China
32 D4 **Longzhou** China
107 F3 **Lonigo** Italy
72 C3 **Löningen** Germany
78 F6 **Lonja r.** Croatia
104 F3 **Lonjsko Polje plain** Croatia
89 E3 **Lonlay-l'Abbaye** France
68 E2 **Lonneker** Netherlands
172 F4 **Lonquimay** Argentina
93 B5 **Lons** France
59 F3 **Lönsboda** Sweden
90 D2 **Lons-le-Saunier** France
55 B2 **Lønstrup** Denmark
56 N6 **Lónsvík b.** Iceland
24 B1 **Lonton** Myanmar
168 B4 **Lontra r.** Brazil
166 C2 **Lontra r.** Brazil
172 B3 **Lontué** Chile
69 E4 **Lontzen** Belgium
54 D2 **Loo** Estonia
23 B3 **Looc** Philippines
148 E4 **Looking Glass r.** *Michigan* U.S.A.
147 F4 **Lookout** *Pennsylvania* U.S.A.
145 E5 **Lookout, Cape c.** *N. Carolina* U.S.A.
138 D2 **Lookout, Cape c.** *Ontario* Canada
154 C3 **Lookout Mt mt.** *California* U.S.A.
149 F3 **Lookout, Pt pt** *Michigan* U.S.A.
15 F2 **Lookout Pt pt** *Queensland* Australia
127 C5 **Loolmalasin crater** Tanzania
136 F3 **Loon r.** *Yukon Terr.* Canada
140 A2 **Loon** *Ontario* Canada
147 J1 **Loon Lake l.** *Maine* U.S.A.
137 H4 **Loon Lake** *Saskatchewan* Canada
67 B4 **Loop Head headland** Rep. of Ireland
69 B4 **Loos** France
81 G2 **Loosdorf** Austria
130 E5 **Lootsberg Pass** South Africa
36 E1 **Lop** China
107 J4 **Lopar** Croatia
114 C1 **Lopatica** Macedonia
52 G3 **Lopatino** Rus. Fed.
45 R4 **Lopatka, M. c.** Rus. Fed.
53 A1 **Lopatyn** Ukraine
25 C4 **Lop Buri** Thailand
63 E3 **Lopcombe Corner** *England* U.K.
124 B4 **Lopé-Okanda, Réserve de res.** Gabon
6 □2 **Lopévi i.** Vanuatu
147 E4 **Lopez** *Pennsylvania* U.S.A.
173 H4 **López** Argentina
23 B3 **Lopez** Philippines
124 A4 **Lopez, Cap pt** Gabon
173 F5 **Lopez Lecube** Argentina
68 C3 **Lopik** Netherlands
26 F3 **Lop Nur h.** China
124 D3 **Lopori r.** Zaire
68 E1 **Loppersum** Netherlands
56 F1 **Lopphavet b.** Norway
54 D1 **Loppi** Finland
50 J2 **Loptyuga** Rus. Fed.
52 G4 **Lopukhovka** Rus. Fed.
77 J5 **Łopuszno** Poland
98 C2 **Lor r.** Spain
39 F3 **Lora r.** Afghanistan
12 C2 **Lora watercourse** *S. Australia* Australia
100 E3 **Lora del Río** Spain
146 B4 **Lorain** *Ohio* U.S.A.
36 B3 **Loralai r.** Pakistan
36 B3 **Loralai** Pakistan
146 A4 **Loramie, Lake l.** *Ohio* U.S.A.
179 □ **Loranchet, Péninsule pen.** *Kerguelen* Indian Ocean
103 B7 **Lorca** Spain
74 E4 **Lorch** *Baden-Württemberg* Germany
87 G2 **Lorch** *Hessen* Germany
23 A4 **Lord Auckland sand bank** Philippines
39 B3 **Lordegān** Iran
10 □4 **Lord Howe Island i.** Australia
175 P6 **Lord Howe Rise sea feature** Pacific Ocean
25 B5 **Lord Loughborough I. i.** Myanmar
98 C4 **Lordosa** Portugal
155 H5 **Lordsburg** *New Mexico* U.S.A.
169 F5 **Lorena** Brazil
6 □1 **Lorengau** P.N.G.
58 D2 **Lørenskog** Norway
21 L7 **Lorentz r.** Indonesia
173 J2 **Lorenzo Geyres** Uruguay
107 G3 **Loreo** Italy
39 B2 **Lorestān div.** Iran
164 D3 **Loreto** Bolivia
166 C2 **Loreto** Brazil
107 H5 **Loreto** Italy
156 C3 **Loreto** Mexico
23 C4 **Loreto** Philippines
109 F2 **Loreto Aprutino** Italy
141 K3 **Loretteville** *Québec* Canada
91 E5 **Lorgues** France
162 B2 **Lorica** Colombia
88 B4 **Lorient** France
103 C5 **Loriguilla** Spain
137 L1 **Lorillard r.** *N.W.T.* Canada
79 J4 **Lőrinci** Hungary
91 C4 **Loriol-sur-Drôme** France
99 F4 **Lorita r.** Spain
90 B1 **Lormes** France
93 B4 **Lormont** France
64 C1 **Lorn mts** *Scotland* U.K.
15 F5 **Lorne** *Queensland* Australia
13 E4 **Lorne** *Victoria* Australia
66 C4 **Lorn, Firth of est.** *Scotland* U.K.
37 H3 **Loro r.** China
107 F5 **Loro Ciuffenna** Italy
122 D4 **Loropéni** Burkina
109 F1 **Loro Piceno** Italy
74 C5 **Lörrach** Germany
87 F4 **Lorraine div.** France
14 D3 **Lorraine** *Queensland* Australia
86 B4 **Lorrez-le-Bocage-Préaux** France
90 A1 **Lorris** France
87 H3 **Lorsch** Germany
72 C3 **Lorup** Germany
121 G2 **Lorzot** Tunisia
99 G2 **Losa r.** Spain
103 C5 **Losa del Obispo** Spain
126 C4 **Losai National Reserve res.** Kenya
153 F5 **Los Alamos** *New Mexico* U.S.A.
172 A4 **Los Alamos** Chile
171 B5 **Los Alerces, Parque Nacional nat. park** Argentina
170 D2 **Los Amores** Argentina
172 B2 **Los Andes** Chile
154 C5 **Los Angeles airport** *California* U.S.A.
154 C5 **Los Angeles** *California* U.S.A.
172 A4 **Los Angeles** Chile
154 C4 **Los Angeles Aqueduct canal** *California* U.S.A.
99 H2 **Los Arcos** Spain
154 B3 **Los Banos** *California* U.S.A.
101 H2 **Los Barreros mt.** Spain
170 D1 **Los Blancos** Argentina
156 C3 **Los Burros** Mexico
97 □ **Los Canarios** *Canary Is* Spain
172 B2 **Los Cerrillos airport** Chile
173 H1 **Los Charrúas** Argentina
173 H1 **Los Conquistadores** Argentina
154 D5 **Los Coronados is** Mexico
99 F1 **Los Corrales de Buelna** Spain
164 D3 **Los Cusis** Bolivia
103 B7 **Los Dolores** Spain
51 G5 **Losevo** Rus. Fed.
127 C5 **Loseya well** Tanzania
101 J3 **Los Gallardos** Spain
154 B3 **Los Gatos** *California* U.S.A.
171 B7 **Los Glacieres, Parque Nacional nat. park** Chile
74 B3 **Losheim** Germany
101 H1 **Los Hinojosos** Spain
77 L3 **Łosice** Poland
122 B5 **Los, Îles de is** Guinea
107 J4 **Lošinj i.** Croatia
77 M3 **Łosinka** Poland
54 D2 **Loska** Estonia
162 B2 **Los Katios, Parque Nacional nat. park** Colombia
131 G2 **Loskop Dam dam** South Africa
131 G2 **Loskop Dam Nature Reserve res.** South Africa
172 A6 **Los Lagos div.** Chile
172 A5 **Los Lagos** Chile
97 □ **Los Llanos de Aridane** *Canary Is* Spain
153 F5 **Los Lunas** *New Mexico* U.S.A.
172 B2 **Los Maitenes** Chile
172 E4 **Los Manatiales** Argentina
172 C6 **Los Menucos** Argentina
52 B2 **Los'mino** Rus. Fed.
156 C3 **Los Mochis** Mexico
154 A1 **Los Molinos** *California* U.S.A.
172 B1 **Los Molles r.** Chile
102 C3 **Los Monegros reg.** Spain
101 F1 **Los Navalmorales** Spain
124 C3 **Losombo** Zaire
158 B2 **Los Palacios** Cuba
100 E3 **Los Palacios y Villafranca** Spain
172 C1 **Los Patos, R. de r.** Argentina
101 E2 **Los Pedroches plat.** Spain
103 B5 **Los Pedrones** Spain
156 C2 **Los Pocitos** Mexico
101 G2 **Los Pozuelos de Calatrava** Spain
97 □ **Los Realejos** *Canary Is* Spain
156 E5 **Los Reyes** Mexico
162 D1 **Los Roques, Is is** Venezuela
98 E4 **Los Santos** Spain
100 D2 **Los Santos de Maimona** Spain
97 □ **Los Sauces** *Canary Is* Spain
172 A4 **Los Sauces** Chile
74 D4 **Loßburg** Germany
93 B4 **Losse** France
68 E2 **Losser** Netherlands
66 E3 **Lossie r.** *Scotland* U.K.
66 E3 **Lossiemouth** *Scotland* U.K.
75 H2 **Lößnitz** Germany
83 E2 **Lostallo** Switzerland
162 C1 **Los Taques** Venezuela
170 D2 **Los Telares** Argentina
162 D1 **Los Teques** Venezuela
163 E1 **Los Testigos is** Venezuela
154 C4 **Lost Hills** *California* U.S.A.
152 D2 **Lost Trail Pass pass** *Idaho* U.S.A.
62 B4 **Lostwithiel** *England* U.K.
164 C4 **Los Vientos** Chile
101 G3 **Los Villares** Spain
172 B1 **Los Vilos** Chile
101 G1 **Los Yébenes** Spain
53 D1 **Losynivka** Ukraine
93 D4 **Lot div.** *Midi-Pyrénées* France
93 D4 **Lot r.** France
172 A4 **Lota** Chile
126 B4 **Lotagipi Swamp swamp** Kenya/Sudan
58 D1 **Løten** Norway
93 C4 **Lot-et-Garonne div.** France
39 D1 **Lotfābād** Iran
131 H3 **Lothair** South Africa
66 E5 **Lothian div.** *Scotland* U.K.
126 B4 **Lotikipi Plain plain** Kenya
125 D4 **Loto** Zaire
7 □12 **Lotofaga** Western Samoa
124 C4 **Lotoi r.** Zaire
52 B1 **Lotoshino** Rus. Fed.
128 D3 **Lotsane watercourse** Botswana
53 E3 **Lotskyne** Ukraine
56 H1 **Lotta r.** Rus. Fed.
72 C3 **Lotte** Germany
74 D5 **Lottstetten** Germany
76 E2 **Lotyń** Poland
108 B5 **Lotzorai** *Sardegna* Italy
24 C2 **Louang Namtha** Laos
24 C3 **Louangphrabang** Laos
88 B3 **Louannec** France
125 B4 **Loubomo** Congo
78 C1 **Loučná mt.** Czech Rep.
78 D3 **Loučovice** Czech Rep.
88 C3 **Loudéac** France
91 B3 **Loudes** France
33 E3 **Loudi** China
125 B4 **Loudima** Congo
146 B4 **Loudonville** *Ohio* U.S.A.
89 F4 **Loudun** France
90 D1 **Loue r.** France
89 E4 **Loué** France
125 B4 **Louéssé r.** Congo
179 □ **l'Ouest, I. de i.** *Kerguelen* Indian Ocean
122 A3 **Louga** Senegal
93 D5 **Louge r.** France
63 E2 **Loughborough** *England* U.K.
64 B3 **Loughbrickland** *Northern Ireland* U.K.
134 H2 **Lougheed I. i.** *N.W.T.* Canada
62 B3 **Loughor r.** *Wales* U.K.
67 C3 **Loughrea** Rep. of Ireland
67 C2 **Loughros More Bay b.** Rep. of Ireland
63 G3 **Loughton** *England* U.K.
93 C4 **Lougratte** France
90 D2 **Louhans** France
146 B5 **Louisa** *Kentucky* U.S.A.
146 E5 **Louisa** *Virginia* U.S.A.
131 H4 **Louis Botha airport** South Africa
67 B3 **Louisburgh** Rep. of Ireland
136 C4 **Louise I. i.** *B.C.* Canada
6 □1 **Louisiade Archipelago is** P.N.G.
151 E6 **Louisiana div.** U.S.A.
131 G1 **Louis Trichardt** South Africa
130 C4 **Louisvale** South Africa
145 D5 **Louisville** *Georgia* U.S.A.
144 C4 **Louisville** *Kentucky* U.S.A.
151 F5 **Louisville** *Mississippi* U.S.A.
138 E3 **Louis-XIV, Pointe c.** *Québec* Canada
50 E1 **Loukhi** Rus. Fed.
124 C4 **Loukoléla** Congo
125 B4 **Loukouo** Congo
92 B2 **Loulay** France
100 B3 **Loulé** Portugal
124 A3 **Loum** Cameroon
125 B4 **Louna r.** Congo
123 G4 **Loungoundou well** Niger
138 B3 **Lount L. l.** *Ontario* Canada
78 C1 **Louny** Czech Rep.
150 D3 **Loup r.** *Nebraska* U.S.A.
91 E5 **Loup r.** France
93 B4 **Loupiac** France
138 F2 **Loups Marins, Lacs des l.** *Québec* Canada
139 J4 **Lourdes** *Newfoundland* Canada
93 B5 **Lourdes** France
93 C5 **Lourdes-Tarbes airport** France
163 G3 **Lourenço** Brazil
122 B4 **Lour-Escale** Senegal
98 B4 **Louriçal** Portugal
164 A2 **Louricocha, source of the Amazon, L. river source** Peru
100 A1 **Lourinhã** Portugal
91 D5 **Lourmarin** France
114 B3 **Louros** Greece
98 B4 **Lourosa** Portugal
98 B4 **Lousã** Portugal
98 B3 **Lousada** Portugal
98 B4 **Lousã, Sa da mountain range** Portugal
67 E3 **Louth div.** Rep. of Ireland
65 H4 **Louth** *England* U.K.
13 F2 **Louth** *New South Wales* Australia
114 E4 **Loutra Aidipsou** Greece
114 F2 **Loutra Eleftheron** Greece
114 C4 **Loutraki** *Dytiki Ellas* Greece
115 D5 **Loutraki** *Peloponnisos* Greece
115 C5 **Loutra Kyllinis** Greece
Louvain *see* **Leuven**
89 E3 **Louverné** France
93 B5 **Louvie-Juzon** France
89 G2 **Louviers** France
89 D3 **Louvigné-du-Désert** France
69 B4 **Louvroil** France
131 H3 **Louwsburg** South Africa
86 D4 **Louze** France
76 F2 **Lövånger** Sweden
78 F5 **Lovászi** Hungary
50 D3 **Lovat' r.** Rus. Fed.
112 E3 **Lovech div.** Bulgaria
112 E3 **Lovech** Bulgaria
152 F3 **Loveland** *Colorado* U.S.A.
152 E2 **Lovell** *Wyoming* U.S.A.
154 C1 **Lovelock** *Nevada* U.S.A.
106 E3 **Lovere** Italy
57 G3 **Loviisa** Finland
146 D6 **Lovingston** *Virginia* U.S.A.
148 C6 **Lovington** *Illinois* U.S.A.
153 G5 **Lovington** *New Mexico* U.S.A.
55 B3 **Lovns Bredning b.** Denmark
78 F4 **Lövő** Hungary
78 D1 **Lovosice** Czech Rep.
107 J3 **Lovran** Croatia
79 K6 **Lovrin** Romania
59 F1 **Lövsjön** Sweden
59 G1 **Lövstabukten b.** Sweden
52 D2 **Lovtsy** Rus. Fed.
125 D5 **Lóvua** Angola
125 D6 **Lôvua** Angola
141 H4 **Low** *Québec* Canada
124 E4 **Lowa r.** Zaire
124 E4 **Lowa** Zaire
137 M2 **Low, Cape c.** *N.W.T.* Canada
77 M4 **Łowcza** Poland
147 H3 **Lowell** *Massachusetts* U.S.A.
144 G3 **Lowell** *Massachusetts* U.S.A.
148 E4 **Lowell** *Michigan* U.S.A.
147 G2 **Lowell** *Vermont* U.S.A.
130 B3 **Löwen watercourse** Namibia
73 J3 **Löwenberg** Germany
74 E3 **Löwenstein** Germany
136 F5 **Lower Arrow L. l.** *B.C.* Canada
Lower California pen. *see* **Baja California**
155 F4 **Lower Granite Gorge gorge** *Arizona* U.S.A.
9 E4 **Lower Hutt** New Zealand
154 A2 **Lower Lake** *California* U.S.A.
67 D2 **Lower Lough Erne l.** *Northern Ireland* U.K.
25 □ **Lower Peirce Res. resr** Singapore
136 D3 **Lower Post** *B.C.* Canada
131 H2 **Lower Sabie** South Africa
139 H5 **Lower Sackville** *Nova Scotia* Canada
125 E7 **Lower Zambezi National Park nat. park** Zambia
63 H2 **Lowestoft** *England* U.K.
39 G2 **Lowgar r.** Afghanistan
77 H3 **Łowicz** Poland
138 E3 **Low, Lac l.** *Québec* Canada
10 □2 **Low Pt pt** *Christmas I.* Indian Ocean
13 F5 **Low Rocky Pt headland** *Tasmania* Australia
140 D2 **Lowther** *Ontario* Canada
66 E5 **Lowther Hills h.** *Scotland* U.K.
147 F3 **Lowville** *New York* U.S.A.
76 D3 **Łowyń** Poland
72 D2 **Loxstedt** Germany
12 E3 **Loxton** *S. Australia* Australia
130 D5 **Loxton** South Africa
66 D2 **Loyal, Loch l.** *Scotland* U.K.
146 E4 **Loyalsock Creek r.** *Pennsylvania* U.S.A.
154 B2 **Loyalton** *California* U.S.A.
Loyalty Is is *see* **Loyauté, Îs**
Loyang *see* **Luoyang**
6 □2 **Loyauté, Îs is** *New Caledonia* Pacific Ocean
131 H3 **Loyengo** Swaziland
53 D1 **Loyew** Belarus
66 C3 **Loyne, Loch l.** *Scotland* U.K.
50 K3 **Loyno** Rus. Fed.
91 B4 **Lozère div.** France
91 B4 **Lozère, Mont mt.** France
112 B2 **Loznica** Yugoslavia
112 F3 **Loznitsa** Bulgaria
53 G1 **Loznoye** Rus. Fed.
53 G2 **Lozova** Ukraine
47 J2 **Lozovoye** Kazakhstan
99 G4 **Lozoya** Spain
99 G4 **Lozoyuela** Spain
53 G3 **Lozuvatka r.** Ukraine
124 C3 **Lua r.** Zaire
125 D6 **Luacano** Angola
125 D5 **Luachimo r.** Angola/Zaire
6 □3 **Luahiapu i.** Tonga
129 F2 **Luala r.** Mozambique
125 D6 **Luampa r.** Zambia
31 F4 **Luan r.** China
33 G2 **Lu'an** China
159 □1 **Luana Point pt** Jamaica
33 E1 **Luanchuan** China
98 E1 **Luanco** Spain
125 B5 **Luanda div.** Angola
125 B5 **Luanda** Angola
125 C6 **Luando r.** Angola
125 C6 **Luando** Angola
125 C6 **Luando, Reserva Natural Integral do res.** Angola
125 D6 **Luanginga r.** Zambia
125 D6 **Luanguinga r.** Angola
125 F6 **Luangwa r.** Zambia
37 H2 **Luanhaizi** China
137 L2 **Luan Lake l.** *N.W.T.* Canada
31 F5 **Luannan** China
166 A1 **Lua Nova** Brazil
31 F4 **Luanping** China
125 E6 **Luanshya** Zambia
172 E4 **Luan Toro** Argentina
31 F5 **Luan Xian** China
125 E5 **Luanza** Zaire
125 E6 **Luapula div.** Zambia
98 D1 **Luarca** Spain
22 C1 **Luar, D. l.** Indonesia
Luar I. i. *see* **Horsburgh I.**
125 D5 **Luashi** Zaire
6 □3 **Luatafito i.** Tonga
127 C7 **Luatize r.** Mozambique
125 D6 **Luau** Angola
124 C3 **Lua Vindu r.** Zaire
124 A3 **Luba** Equatorial Guinea
157 H5 **Lubaantum** Belize
77 M5 **Lubaczów** Poland
77 L5 **Lubaczówka r.** Poland
125 C5 **Lubalo** Angola
76 D4 **Lubań** Poland
54 E3 **Lubāna** Latvia
54 E3 **Lubānas I. l.** Latvia
23 B3 **Lubang i.** Philippines
23 B3 **Lubang** Philippines
23 A3 **Lubang Islands is** Philippines
125 B6 **Lubango** Angola
76 G3 **Lubanie** Poland
125 E5 **Lubao** Zaire
73 H3 **Lübars** Germany
77 L4 **Lubartów** Poland
76 E3 **Lubasz** Poland
77 H2 **Lubawa** Poland
72 D3 **Lübbecke** Germany
69 C4 **Lubbeek** Belgium
73 J4 **Lübben** Germany
73 J4 **Lübbenau** Germany
130 B4 **Lubbeskolk l.** South Africa
151 C5 **Lubbock** *Texas* U.S.A.
73 G3 **Lübbow** Germany
73 K2 **Lubczyna** Poland
73 F2 **Lübeck** Germany
73 F1 **Lübecker Bucht b.** Germany
125 D4 **Lubefu** Zaire
77 J2 **L'ubeľa** Slovakia
78 C1 **Lubenec** Czech Rep.
47 D2 **Lubenka** Kazakhstan
124 E4 **Lubero** Zaire
91 D5 **Lubéron, Montagne du ridge** France
92 D3 **Lubersac** France
98 D2 **Lubián** Spain
76 G2 **Lubichowo** Poland
76 G2 **Lubicz Dolny** Poland
76 D4 **Lubięcin** Poland
77 H3 **Lubienka r.** Poland
77 H3 **Lubień Kujawski** Poland
125 D5 **Lubilash r.** Zaire
76 E4 **Lubin** *Legnica* Poland
125 E4 **Lubirizi** Zaire
73 K3 **Lubiszyn** Poland
77 L4 **Lublin div.** Poland
77 L4 **Lublin** Poland
76 G5 **Lubliniec** Poland
66 D4 **Lubnaig, Loch l.** *Scotland* U.K.
76 G4 **Łubnice** Poland
76 D3 **Lubniewice** Poland
76 F1 **Łubno** Poland
76 E2 **Lubno** Poland
53 E1 **Lubny** Ukraine
77 J4 **Lubochnia** Poland
22 B1 **Lubok Antu** Malaysia
77 J1 **Lubomino** Poland
76 E3 **Luboń** Poland
52 E2 **Lubonos** Rus. Fed.
77 J5 **Luborzyca** Poland
79 K2 **L'ubotín** Slovakia
76 G3 **Lubraniec** Poland
101 H3 **Lubrín** Spain
73 L3 **Lubrza** Poland
76 C4 **Lubsko** Poland
73 G2 **Lübstorf** Germany
73 K4 **Lubsza r.** Poland
73 G2 **Lübtheen** Germany
23 B2 **Lubuagan** Philippines
125 E5 **Lubudi** Zaire
22 A2 **Lubukbalang** Indonesia
20 D7 **Lubuklinggau** Indonesia
125 E6 **Lubumbashi** Zaire
125 E6 **Lubungu** Zambia
124 E4 **Lubutu** Zaire
52 B3 **Lubyanki** Rus. Fed.
77 M5 **Lubycza Królewska** Poland
73 H2 **Lübz** Germany
91 B4 **Luc** *Languedoc-Roussillon* France
93 E4 **Luc** *Midi-Pyrénées* France
101 H3 **Lucainena de las Torres** Spain
125 C5 **Lucala** Angola
67 E3 **Lucan** Rep. of Ireland
136 A2 **Lucania, Mt mt.** *N.W.T.* Canada
125 D5 **Lucapa** Angola
101 H3 **Lúcar, Sa de mountain range** Spain
173 H1 **Lucas r.** Argentina
166 A3 **Lucas** Brazil
173 H2 **Lucas González** Argentina
173 H1 **Lucas Sur** Argentina
145 F7 **Lucaya** The Bahamas
89 G4 **Luçay-le-Mâle** France
106 E5 **Lucca div.** Italy
89 G3 **Lucé** France
81 F4 **Luče** Slovenia
159 □1 **Lucea** Jamaica
66 D6 **Luce Bay b.** *Scotland* U.K.
168 C4 **Lucélia** Brazil
23 B3 **Lucena** Philippines
101 F3 **Lucena** Spain
101 G3 **Lucena, Sierra de mountain range** Spain
90 B2 **Lucenay-lès-Aix** France
90 C1 **Lucenay-l'Évêque** France
91 D4 **Luc-en-Diois** France
79 J3 **Lučenec** Slovakia
109 H3 **Lucera** Italy
164 C2 **Lucerna** Peru
Lucerne *see* **Luzern**
53 C1 **Luchanky** Ukraine
31 K3 **Luchegorsk** Rus. Fed.
30 E5 **Lucheng** China
89 F4 **Luché-Pringé** France
127 C7 **Lucheringo r.** Mozambique
52 D1 **Luchki** Rus. Fed.
73 G3 **Lüchow** Germany
33 E4 **Luchuan** China
32 C4 **Lüchun** China
101 F2 **Luciana** Spain
163 F3 **Lucie r.** Surinam
141 F1 **Lucie, Lac l.** *Québec* Canada
107 H3 **Lucija** Slovenia
15 F3 **Lucinda** *Queensland* Australia
12 E4 **Lucindale** *S. Australia* Australia
125 B6 **Lucira** Angola
109 G3 **Lucito** Italy
73 H4 **Lucka** Germany
73 J4 **Luckau** Germany
37 F4 **Luckeesarai** India
73 J3 **Luckenwalde** Germany
130 E4 **Luckhoff** South Africa
140 E5 **Lucknow** *Ontario* Canada
36 E4 **Lucknow** India
107 F2 **Luco, Monte mt.** Italy
92 A2 **Luçon** France
158 D2 **Lucrecia, Cabo headland** Cuba
89 E2 **Luc-sur-Mer** France
125 D6 **Lucusse** Angola
90 B1 **Lucy-le-Bois** France
Lüda *see* **Dalian**
50 F1 **Luda** Rus. Fed.
78 F5 **Ludbreg** Croatia
72 C4 **Lüdenscheid** Germany
128 B4 **Lüderitz** Namibia
73 F2 **Lüdersdorf** Germany
80 A3 **Ludesch** Austria
127 B7 **Ludewa** Tanzania
63 E3 **Ludgershall** *England* U.K.
36 C3 **Ludhiana** India
32 C3 **Ludian** China
72 C4 **Lüdinghausen** Germany
148 D4 **Ludington** *Michigan* U.S.A.
154 D4 **Ludlow** *California* U.S.A.
62 D2 **Ludlow** *England* U.K.
147 J1 **Ludlow** *Maine* U.S.A.
147 G3 **Ludlow** *Vermont* U.S.A.
112 F3 **Ludogorsko Plato plat.** Bulgaria
87 G4 **Ludres** France
112 E1 **Luduş** Romania
59 F1 **Ludvika** Sweden
80 C1 **Ludwig-Donau-Main Kanal canal** Germany
74 E4 **Ludwigsburg** Germany
73 J3 **Ludwigsfelde** Germany
74 E5 **Ludwigshafen** Germany
74 D3 **Ludwigshafen am Rhein** Germany
73 G2 **Ludwigslust** Germany
75 G2 **Ludwigsstadt** Germany
54 E3 **Ludza** Latvia
125 D5 **Luebo** Zaire
125 E4 **Lueki** Zaire
125 E4 **Luemba** Zaire
125 D6 **Luena r.** Zambia
125 C6 **Luena** Angola
125 D6 **Luena Flats plain** Zambia
125 D7 **Luengue r.** Angola
129 E2 **Luenha r.** Mozambique/Zimbabwe
163 E2 **Luepa** Venezuela
102 B2 **Luesia** Spain
32 D1 **Lüeyang** China
33 F4 **Lufeng** China
32 C3 **Lufeng** China
125 E5 **Lufira r.** Zaire
125 E6 **Lufira, Lac de retenue de la l.** Zaire
151 E6 **Lufkin** *Texas* U.S.A.
127 B6 **Lufubu r.** Zambia
54 F2 **Luga r.** Rus. Fed.
54 F2 **Luga** Rus. Fed.
83 D2 **Lugano** *Ticino* Switzerland
83 D3 **Lugano, Lago di l.** Italy/Switzerland
6 □2 **Luganville** Vanuatu
78 B1 **Lugau** Germany
72 E4 **Lügde** Germany
129 F2 **Lugela r.** Mozambique
129 F2 **Lugela** Mozambique
127 C7 **Lugenda r.** Mozambique
62 C2 **Lugg r.** *Wales* U.K.
126 D2 **Lugh Ganane** Somalia
109 E2 **Lugnano in Teverina** Italy
90 C2 **Lugny** France
98 C2 **Lugo div.** *Galicia* Spain
107 F4 **Lugo** Italy
98 C1 **Lugo** Spain
79 L6 **Lugoj** Romania
98 E1 **Lugones** Spain
93 B4 **Lugos** France
47 H4 **Lugovoy** Kazakhstan
47 H4 **Lugovoye** Kazakhstan
23 B5 **Lugus i.** Philippines
51 F5 **Luhans'k** Ukraine
72 F2 **Luhe r.** Germany
33 G1 **Luhe** China
31 F3 **Luhin Sum** China
73 J1 **Lühmannsdorf** Germany
127 C6 **Luhombero** Tanzania
32 C2 **Luhuo** China
112 E1 **Luhy** Ukraine
53 C1 **Luhyny** Ukraine
125 D6 **Luia r.** Angola
129 E2 **Luia r.** Mozambique
125 D7 **Luiana r.** Angola
125 D7 **Luiana** Angola
Luik *see* **Liège**
124 D4 **Luilaka r.** Zaire
Luimneach *see* **Limerick**
66 C4 **Luing i.** *Scotland* U.K.
106 C3 **Luino** Italy
125 D6 **Luio r.** Angola
56 G2 **Luiro r.** Finland
89 G3 **Luisant** France
166 D1 **Luís Correia** Brazil
156 E4 **Luis Moya** Mexico
125 D5 **Luiza** Zaire
173 H3 **Luján** *Buenos Aires* Argentina
172 E2 **Luján** *San Luis* Argentina
172 C2 **Luján de Cuyo** Argentina
33 G2 **Lujiang** China
53 E1 **Luka** Ukraine
78 F4 **Lukácsháza** Hungary
125 B5 **Lukala** Zaire
104 G3 **Lukavac** Bos.-Herz.
17 B5 **Luke, Mt h.** *Western Australia* Australia
125 C4 **Lukenie r.** Zaire
67 D3 **Lukeswell** Rep. of Ireland
155 F6 **Lukeville** *Arizona* U.S.A.
52 F1 **Lukh r.** Rus. Fed.
52 F1 **Lukh** Rus. Fed.
52 D2 **Lukhovitsy** Rus. Fed.
52 G2 **Lukhovka** Rus. Fed.
112 E4 **Lŭki** Bulgaria
125 D4 **Lukibu r.** Zaire
52 F1 **Lukino** Rus. Fed.
53 A1 **Lukiv** Ukraine
124 C4 **Lukolela** Zaire
54 F4 **Lukomka r.** Belarus
114 A3 **Lukovë** Albania
112 E3 **Lukovit** Bulgaria
52 B1 **Lukovnikovo** Rus. Fed.
77 L4 **Łuków** Poland
52 G2 **Lukoyanov** Rus. Fed.
125 E5 **Lukuga r.** Zaire
125 B5 **Lukula** Zaire
127 C7 **Lukuledi r.** Tanzania
127 B7 **Lukulu r.** Zambia
125 D6 **Lukulu** Zambia
127 C6 **Lukumburu** Tanzania
125 F6 **Lukusashi r.** Zambia
127 B7 **Lukusuzi National Park nat. park** Zambia
77 M6 **Luky** Ukraine
108 B4 **Lula** *Sardegna* Italy
56 F2 **Luleå** Sweden
56 F2 **Luleälven r.** Sweden
42 A1 **Lüleburgaz** Turkey
131 H1 **Lulekani** South Africa
32 C3 **Luliang** China
30 D5 **Lüliang Shan mountain range** China
125 E4 **Lulimba** Zaire
151 D6 **Luling** *Texas* U.S.A.
31 F5 **Lulong** China
124 C3 **Lulonga r.** Zaire
124 C3 **Lulonga** Zaire
125 D5 **Lulua r.** Zaire
37 F3 **Lülung** China
17 B5 **Lulworth, Mt h.** *Western Australia* Australia
7 □13 **Luma** *American Samoa* Pacific Ocean
37 F3 **Lumachomo** China
172 A5 **Lumaco** Chile
22 C4 **Lumajang** Indonesia
37 E2 **Lumajangdong Co salt lake** China
54 C2 **Lümanda** Estonia
125 D6 **Lumbala Kaquengue** Angola
125 D6 **Lumbala N'guimbo** Angola
125 D7 **Lumbe r.** Zambia
145 E5 **Lumberton** *N. Carolina* U.S.A.
102 B2 **Lumbier** Spain
98 D4 **Lumbrales** Spain
99 H2 **Lumbreras** Spain
86 B2 **Lumbres** France
37 H4 **Lumding** India
127 C7 **Lumecha** Tanzania
106 E3 **Lumezzane** Italy
56 G2 **Lumijoki** Finland
169 F4 **Luminárias** Brazil
108 A2 **Lumio** *Corse* France
69 D4 **Lummen** Belgium
59 J1 **Lumparland** Finland
59 J1 **Lumparn r.** Finland
25 D4 **Lumphăt** Cambodia
9 B6 **Lumsden** New Zealand
22 C2 **Lumut, G. mt.** Indonesia
22 A2 **Lumut, Tg pt** Indonesia
30 C3 **Lün** Mongolia
100 E4 **Luna h.** Spain
98 E2 **Luna r.** Spain
155 H5 **Luna** *New Mexico* U.S.A.
23 B2 **Luna** Philippines
102 C2 **Luna** Spain
32 C3 **Lunan** China
66 F4 **Lunan Bay b.** *Scotland* U.K.
149 F5 **Luna Pier** *Michigan* U.S.A.
91 B5 **Lunas** France
36 C5 **Lunavada** India
112 E1 **Lunca Ilvei** Romania
155 F2 **Lund** *Utah* U.S.A.
36 B4 **Lund** Pakistan
59 E4 **Lund** Sweden
125 C5 **Lunda Norte div.** Angola
137 K4 **Lundar** *Manitoba* Canada
125 D6 **Lunda Sul div.** Angola
127 B7 **Lundazi** Zambia
55 D4 **Lundby** Denmark
55 B4 **Lunderskov** Denmark
58 B2 **Lundevatn l.** Norway
65 F1 **Lundin Links** *Scotland* U.K.
59 F2 **Lundsfjärden l.** Sweden
62 B3 **Lundy Island i.** *England* U.K.
65 F3 **Lune r.** *England* U.K.
74 B2 **Lünebach** Germany
131 H3 **Luneberg** South Africa
72 E2 **Lüneburg div.** *Niedersachsen* Germany
72 F2 **Lüneburg** *Niedersachsen* Germany
72 F2 **Lüneburger Heide reg.** Germany
91 C5 **Lunel** France
106 B3 **Lunella, Punta mt.** Italy
72 C4 **Lünen** Germany
83 E1 **Lünersee l.** Austria
87 F4 **Lunéville** France
125 E6 **Lunga r.** Zambia
81 E3 **Lungau basin** Austria
37 E2 **Lungdo** China
82 D2 **Lungern** Switzerland
37 E3 **Lunggar** China
122 B5 **Lungi** Sierra Leone
27 □ **Lung Kwu Chau h.** Hong Kong
37 H5 **Lunglei** India
36 E2 **Lungmu Co salt lake** China
67 E4 **Lungnaquilla Mountain mt.** Rep. of Ireland
111 F3 **Lungro** Italy
125 D6 **Lungué-Bungo r.** Angola
125 D6 **Lungwebungu r.** Zambia
36 C4 **Luni r.** India
36 C4 **Luni** India
154 C2 **Luning** *Nevada* U.S.A.
52 G4 **Lunino** Rus. Fed.
51 C4 **Luninyets** Belarus
93 D5 **L'Union** France
36 C3 **Lunkaransar** India
36 C1 **Lunkho mt.** Afghanistan/Pakistan
77 N2 **Lunna** Belarus
73 C3 **Lünne** Germany
73 K3 **Lunow** Germany
122 B5 **Lunsar** Sierra Leone
125 E6 **Lunsemfwa r.** Zambia
47 K4 **Luntai** China
68 D2 **Lunteren** Netherlands
22 D4 **Lunyuk** Indonesia
75 H2 **Lunzenau** Germany
30 D6 **Luo r.** China
31 J3 **Luobei** China
33 E3 **Luocheng** China
30 A5 **Luocheng** China
30 D6 **Luochuan** China
32 D3 **Luodian** China
33 E4 **Luoding** China
33 E4 **Luodou Sha** China
33 E4 **Luog** China
108 B3 **Luogosanto** *Sardegna* Italy
33 F1 **Luohe** China
127 B6 **Luombe r.** Zambia
33 E1 **Luoning** China
32 D3 **Luoping** China
33 F1 **Luoshan** China
33 F2 **Luotian** China
33 F1 **Luoyang** China
33 G3 **Luoyuan** China
125 B4 **Luozi** Zaire
31 J4 **Luozigou** China
128 D2 **Lupane** Zimbabwe
22 B1 **Lupar r.** Malaysia
100 C1 **Lupe r.** Portugal
112 D2 **Lupeni** Romania
93 C5 **Lupiac** France
127 C7 **Lupilichi** Mozambique
107 J3 **Lupoglav** Croatia
23 C5 **Lupon** Philippines
73 H4 **Luppa** Germany
155 H4 **Lupton** *Arizona* U.S.A.
111 □ **Luqa** Malta
32 C1 **Luqu** China
32 C3 **Luquan** China
101 F3 **Luque** Spain
145 □3 **Luquillo** Puerto Rico
42 F2 **Lūrā Shīrīn** Iran
92 E2 **Lurcy-Lévis** France
90 E1 **Lure** France
127 C7 **Lureco r.** Mozambique
125 C5 **Luremo** Angola
91 D4 **Lure, Montagne de mt.** France
66 C2 **Lurgainn, Loch l.** *Scotland* U.K.
67 E2 **Lurgan** *Northern Ireland* U.K.
108 B2 **Luri** *Corse* France
164 C3 **Luribay** Bolivia
164 A2 **Lurín** Peru
129 F1 **Lurio r.** Mozambique
127 D7 **Lúrio** Mozambique
127 D7 **Lúrio, Baía do b.** Mozambique
91 D5 **Lurs** France
89 H4 **Lury-sur-Arnon** France
127 B5 **Lusahunga** Tanzania
125 E7 **Lusaka div.** Zambia
125 E7 **Lusaka** Zambia
125 D4 **Lusambo** Zaire
6 □1 **Lusancay Islands and Reefs is** P.N.G.
125 E4 **Lusangi** Zaire
136 F4 **Luscar** *Alberta* Canada
137 H4 **Luseland** *Saskatchewan* Canada
124 C3 **Lusengo** Zaire
91 F4 **Luserna San Giovanni** Italy
32 C2 **Lushan** China
33 E1 **Lushi** China
16 D3 **Lush, Mt h.** *Western Australia* Australia
113 B4 **Lushnjë** Albania
127 C5 **Lushoto** Tanzania
31 G5 **Lüshun** China
92 C2 **Lusignan** France
86 D4 **Lusigny-sur-Barse** France
124 E4 **Lusika** Zaire
131 G5 **Lusikisiki** South Africa
10 □3 **Lusitania Bay b.** *Macquarie I.* Pacific Ocean
152 F3 **Lusk** *Wyoming* U.S.A.
64 B4 **Lusk** Rep. of Ireland
91 D4 **Lus-la-Croix-Haute** France
92 C2 **Lussac-les-Châteaux** France
92 D2 **Lussac-les-Églises** France
91 C4 **Lussan** France
168 C4 **Lussanvira** Brazil
15 F5 **Lussvale** *Queensland* Australia
87 G3 **Lustadt** Germany
80 A3 **Lustenau** Austria
131 H3 **Lusushwana r.** Swaziland
107 F2 **Lutago** Italy
168 C5 **Lutécia** Brazil
125 D6 **Lutembo** Angola
140 E5 **Luther Lake l.** *Ontario* Canada
73 G4 **Lutherstadt Eisleben** Germany
73 H4 **Lutherstadt Wittenberg** Germany
124 E4 **Lutiba** Zaire
73 F1 **Lütjenburg** Germany
131 H1 **Lutombe** Zimbabwe
63 F3 **Luton** *England* U.K.
77 L6 **Lutowiska** Poland
77 J1 **Lutry** Poland
137 G2 **Lutsel'k'e** *N.W.T.* Canada
125 E5 **Lutshima r.** Zaire
53 A1 **Luts'k** Ukraine
72 F4 **Lutter am Barenberge** Germany

103 B5 Mahora Spain
122 D4 Mahou Mali
121 G2 Mahrès Tunisia
36 B5 Mahuva India
39 B2 Mahyār Iran
7 □13 Maia American Samoa Pacific Ocean
98 B3 Maia Portugal
102 D3 Maials Spain
37 H4 Maibang India
162 C1 Maicao Colombia
141 G2 Maicasagi, Lac l. Québec Canada
90 E1 Maîche France
33 E4 Maichen China
163 G3 Maicuru r. Brazil
111 F4 Maida Italy
63 F3 Maidenhead England U.K.
62 D4 Maiden Newton England U.K.
64 D2 Maidens Scotland U.K.
64 C3 Maidens, The is Rep. of Ireland
63 G3 Maidstone England U.K.
137 H4 Maidstone Saskatchewan Canada
123 G4 Maiduguri Nigeria
83 E1 Maienfeld Switzerland
111 F4 Maierato Italy
112 E1 Maieru Romania
103 C6 Maigmó mt. Spain
86 B3 Maignelay-Montigny France
126 C3 Mai Gudo mt. Ethiopia
67 C4 Maigue r. Rep. of Ireland
29 F6 Maihara Japan
172 A6 Maihué, L. l. Chile
37 E5 Maikala Range India
87 H3 Maikammer Germany
124 E4 Maiko r. Zaire
124 E4 Maiko, Parc National de la nat. park Zaire
37 E5 Mailan Hill h. India
36 E3 Mailani India
124 C1 Maïlao Chad
92 B2 Maillezais France
86 D4 Mailly-le-Camp France
36 C3 Mailsi Pakistan
67 E2 Main r. Northern Ireland U.K.
74 E3 Main r. Germany
119 H4 Ma'īn Yemen
37 G4 Mainaguri India
115 D5 Mainalo mts Greece
139 J3 Main Brook Newfoundland Canada
75 G4 Mainburg Germany
140 E4 Main Channel chan. Ontario Canada
124 C4 Mai-Ndombe, Lac l. Zaire
75 G3 Main-Donau-Kanal canal Germany
141 G5 Main Duck I. i. Ontario Canada
147 J2 Maine div. U.S.A.
89 E4 Maine r. France
89 E3 Maine reg. France
89 E4 Maine-et-Loire div. France
162 C4 Mainé Hanari, Co h. Colombia
123 G4 Maïné-Soroa Niger
24 B1 Maingkwan Myanmar
25 B4 Maingy I. i. Myanmar
74 E3 Mainhardt Germany
23 C4 Mainit Philippines
23 C4 Mainit, Lake l. Philippines
32 B2 Mainkung China
66 E1 Mainland (Orkney) i. Scotland U.K.
66 □2 Mainland (Shetland) i. Scotland U.K.
75 G2 Mainleus Germany
37 E5 Mainpat India
36 D4 Mainpuri India
89 G3 Maintenon France
129 G2 Maintirano Madagascar
89 G3 Mainvilliers France
74 D3 Mainz Germany
122 □ Maio i. Cape Verde
107 H5 Maiolati Spontini Italy
100 B1 Maior r. Portugal
109 G4 Maiori Italy
172 B2 Maipo r. Chile
170 C3 Maipó, Vol. volcano Chile
173 J4 Maipú Buenos Aires Argentina
172 C2 Maipú Mendoza Argentina
172 B2 Maipú Chile
163 F3 Maipuri Landing Guyana
159 F5 Maiquetía Venezuela
169 H1 Maiquinique Brazil
106 B4 Maira r. Italy
75 G4 Maisach Germany
80 D3 Maishofen Austria
158 D2 Maisí Cuba
54 D4 Maišiagala Lithuania
158 D2 Maisí, Cabo c. Cuba
37 G5 Maiskhal I. i. Bangladesh
86 B4 Maisons-Laffitte France
86 B4 Maisse France
69 D5 Maissin Belgium
80 D2 Maitenbeth Germany
170 B3 Maitencillo Chile
128 D3 Maitengwe Botswana
13 G3 Maitland New South Wales Australia
12 D3 Maitland S. Australia Australia
179 D3 Maitri India Base Antarctica
14 B3 Maiyu, Mt h. Northern Terr. Australia
37 G3 Maizhokunggar China
87 F3 Maizières-lès-Metz France
158 B4 Maíz, Is del i. Colombia
29 E6 Maizuru Japan
99 G4 Majadahonda Spain
114 B2 Maja e Tomorit mts Albania
114 B2 Maja e Zezë mt. Albania
158 D5 Majagual Colombia
22 B3 Majalengka Indonesia
38 B2 Mājalgaon India
112 C2 Majdanpek Yugoslavia
169 G5 Majé Brazil
22 D2 Majene Indonesia
104 G3 Majevica mts Bos.-Herz.
126 C3 Majī Ethiopia
31 F5 Majia r. China
33 E4 Majiang China
Majorca i. see Mallorca
10 □3 Major Lake l. Macquarie I. Pacific Ocean
81 G4 Majšperk Slovenia
37 H4 Majuli I. i. India
131 F4 Majwemasweu South Africa
122 B4 Maka Senegal
125 B4 Makabana Congo
29 □2 Makabe Japan
153 □1 Makaha Hawaii U.S.A.
124 B3 Makak Cameroon
22 D2 Makale Indonesia
37 F4 Makalu, Mt mt. China
127 A5 Makamba Burundi
47 K3 Makanchi Kazakhstan
153 □1 Makapuu Hd headland Hawaii U.S.A.
9 B7 Makarewa New Zealand
50 J2 Makar-Ib Rus. Fed.
9 B6 Makarora r. New Zealand
27 Q2 Makarov Rus. Fed.
52 F3 Makarovo Rus. Fed.
104 F4 Makarska Croatia
50 J3 Makar'ye Rus. Fed.
50 G3 Makar'yev Rus. Fed.
46 D3 Makat Kazakhstan
7 □10 Makatéa i. French Polynesia Pacific Ocean
131 J3 Makatini Flats plain South Africa
6 □4 Makau Mama'o i. Tonga
131 F4 Makeleketla South Africa
23 □1 Makelulu h. Palau
7 □10 Makemo i. French Polynesia Pacific Ocean
122 B5 Makeni Sierra Leone
127 B6 Makete Tanzania
128 D3 Makgadikgadi salt pan Botswana
128 C3 Makgadikgadi Pans Game Reserve res. Botswana
51 H7 Makhachkala Rus. Fed.
131 F4 Makhaleng r. Lesotho
52 H3 Makhalino Rus. Fed.
Makharadze see Ozurget'i
39 E1 Makhmal Turkmenistan
42 E3 Makhmūr Iraq
47 G2 Makhorovka Kazakhstan
9 C6 Makikihi New Zealand
127 C5 Makindu Kenya
47 H2 Makinsk Kazakhstan
53 B2 Makiv Ukraine
53 D1 Makiyivka Ukraine
119 G3 Makkah Saudi Arabia
30 E2 Makkaveyevo Rus. Fed.
139 J2 Makkovik Newfoundland Canada
139 J2 Makkovik, Cape c. Newfoundland Canada
68 D1 Makkum Netherlands
55 E4 Måkläppen i. Sweden
79 K5 Makó Hungary
6 □8 Makodroga i. Fiji
6 □8 Makogai i. Fiji
124 B3 Makokou Gabon
131 F3 Makokskraal South Africa
127 B6 Makongolosi Tanzania
130 D2 Makopong Botswana
124 E3 Makoro Zaire
53 E1 Makoshyne Ukraine
124 C4 Makotipoko Congo
124 C4 Makoua Congo
79 H2 Makov Slovakia
76 F2 Mąkowarsko Poland
77 K3 Maków Mazowiecki Poland
77 H6 Maków Podhalański Poland
113 E6 Makra i. Greece
114 D4 Makrakomi Greece
39 E4 Makran reg. Iran/Pakistan
36 C4 Makrana India
Makran Coast Range mountain range see Talar-i-Band
115 C4 Makri i. Greece
38 C2 Makri India
113 F6 Makronisi i. Greece
115 F5 Makronisi i. Greece
114 D3 Makrychori Greece
115 G7 Makrygialos Greece
50 E3 Maksatikha Rus. Fed.
36 D5 Maksi India
52 H3 Maksimovka Rus. Fed.
39 E3 Maksotag Iran
46 E4 M. Aktumsyk pt Uzbekistan
42 F2 Mākū Iran
37 H4 Makum India
127 B6 Makumbako Tanzania
125 D5 Makumbi Zaire
127 C7 Makunguwiro Tanzania
28 C8 Makurazaki Japan
123 F5 Makurdi Nigeria
47 G1 Makushino Rus. Fed.
127 B7 Makutu Mountains mts Zambia
127 D4 Makuungo Somalia
39 C3 Makūyeh Iran
131 F3 Makwassie South Africa
131 F1 Makwate Botswana
37 G4 Mal India
164 A2 Mala r. Peru
164 A2 Mala Peru
Mala see Mallow
101 G3 Malá Spain
56 E2 Malå Sweden
23 C5 Malabang Philippines
38 A3 Malabar Coast coastal area India
124 A3 Malabo Equatorial Guinea
173 J3 Mal Abrigo Uruguay
23 A4 Malabuñgan Philippines
169 G2 Malacacheta Brazil
25 B6 Malacca, Strait of str. Indonesia/Malaysia
78 G3 Malacky Slovakia
152 D3 Malad City Idaho U.S.A.
53 E1 Mala Divytsya Ukraine
54 E4 Maladzyechna Belarus
79 H2 Malá Fatra mts Slovakia
79 J2 Malá Fatra nat. park Slovakia
101 F4 Málaga airport Spain
101 F4 Málaga div. Andalucía Spain
101 F4 Málaga Málaga Spain
147 F5 Malaga New Jersey U.S.A.
153 F5 Malaga New Mexico U.S.A.
101 F4 Málaga, Montes de mountain range Spain
127 A5 Malagarasi r. Burundi/Tanzania
127 B6 Malagarasi Tanzania
100 C3 Malagon r. Spain
101 G1 Malagón Spain
67 E3 Malahide Rep. of Ireland
129 H3 Malaimbandy Madagascar
76 D2 Mała Ina r. Poland
6 □1 Malaita i. Solomon Is.
23 □1 Malakal Palau
126 B3 Malakal Sudan
23 □1 Malakal Passage chan. Palau
38 C2 Malakanagiri India
104 E3 Mala Kapela mts Croatia
6 □8 Malake i. Fiji
104 E3 Mala Kladuša Bos.-Herz.
6 □2 Malakula i. Vanuatu
36 C2 Malakwal Pakistan
107 F4 Malalbergo Italy
172 A5 Malalhue Chile
163 F2 Malali Guyana
22 E2 Malamala Indonesia
131 H2 Mala Mala Game Res. res. South Africa
53 A1 Mala Moshchanytsya Ukraine
124 D3 Malanda Zaire
115 D4 Malandrino Greece
22 C3 Malang Indonesia
22 E2 Malangke Indonesia
37 F4 Malangwa Nepal
125 C5 Malanje div. Angola
125 C5 Malanje Angola
76 G4 Malanów Poland
39 F4 Malan, Ras pt Pakistan
123 E4 Malanville Benin
172 D1 Malanzán Argentina
172 D1 Malanzán, Sa de mountain range Argentina
170 C3 Malanzán, Sa de mountain range Argentina
38 B4 Malappuram India
156 L8 Mala, Pta pt Panama
59 G2 Mälaren l. Sweden
172 C3 Malargüe r. Argentina
172 C3 Malargüe Argentina
141 F2 Malartic Québec Canada
141 F2 Malartic, Lac l. Québec Canada
77 N4 Malaryta Belarus
75 L2 Malá Skála Czech Rep.
136 A3 Malaspina Glacier gl. Alaska U.S.A.
81 H4 Mala Subotica Croatia
42 D2 Malatya Turkey
6 □6 Malau Fiji
91 D4 Malaucène France
89 G2 Malaunay France
36 C3 Malaut India
163 G3 Malavate French Guiana
39 A2 Mālavi Iran
53 D2 Mala Vil'shanka Ukraine
53 D2 Mala Vyska Ukraine
23 A5 Malawali i. Malaysia
117 H7 Malawi country Africa
Malawi, L. l. see Nyasa, Lake
119 G4 Malawiya Sudan
25 C6 Malaya reg. Malaysia
77 M2 Malaya Byerastavitsa Belarus
50 K1 Malaya Pera Rus. Fed.
52 G3 Malaya Serdoba Rus. Fed.
50 E3 Malaya Vishera Rus. Fed.
23 C4 Malaybalay Philippines
39 B2 Malāyer Iran
32 B1 Malayiwan China
19 M9 Malaysia country Asia
42 E2 Malazgirt Turkey
67 B4 Mal Bay b. Rep. of Ireland
14 E4 Malbon Queensland Australia
77 H1 Malbork Poland
74 B3 Malborn Germany
91 B4 Malbouzon France
90 E2 Malbuisson France
107 E3 Malcesine Italy
73 H2 Malchin Germany
73 H2 Malchiner See l. Germany
73 H2 Malchow Germany
17 C7 Malcolm, Pt pt Western Australia Australia
76 E4 Malczyce Poland
69 B3 Maldegem Belgium
151 F4 Malden Missouri U.S.A.
68 D3 Malden Netherlands
5 M5 Malden Island i. Kiribati
108 A5 Mal di Ventre, Isola di i. Sardegna Italy
175 J4 Maldive Ridge sea feature Indian Ocean
35 D9 Maldives Maldives
63 G3 Maldon England U.K.
173 K3 Maldonado div. Uruguay
173 K3 Maldonado Uruguay
77 H2 Małdyty Poland
107 E2 Malè Italy
35 D10 Male Maldives
24 A2 Male Myanmar
35 D10 Male Atoll atoll Maldives
131 E4 Malebogo South Africa
76 E1 Malechowo Poland
36 C5 Malegaon India
38 B2 Malegaon India
78 G3 Malé Karpaty h. Slovakia
124 E4 Malela Zaire
125 C5 Malele Zaire
129 F1 Malema Mozambique
125 E5 Malemba Nkulu Zaire
115 E7 Maleme Greece
92 D3 Malemort-sur-Corrèze France
123 F4 Malendo watercourse Nigeria
73 F1 Malente Germany
59 F3 Målerås Sweden
115 G7 Males Greece
112 D4 Maleševske Planine mts Bulgaria/Macedonia
86 B4 Malesherbes France
114 B1 Malësia e Polisit mts Albania
114 E4 Malesina Greece
39 F2 Mālestān Afghanistan
88 C4 Malestroit France
30 D2 Maleta Rus. Fed.
110 D5 Maletto Sicilia Italy
52 D3 Malevka Rus. Fed.
110 D4 Malfa Italy
130 C7 Malgas South Africa
51 H7 Malgobek Rus. Fed.
30 C1 Mal. Goloustnoye Rus. Fed.
56 E2 Malgomaj l. Sweden
114 B2 Mal Gramoz mt. Albania/Greece
102 F3 Malgrat de Mar Spain
118 E4 Malha Sudan
127 □4 Malheureux, C. c. Mauritius
152 C3 Malheur L. l. Oregon U.S.A.
116 D4 Mali country Africa
6 □6 Mali i. Fiji
122 B4 Mali Guinea
125 E4 Mali Zaire
115 G7 Malia Greece
114 D4 Maliakos Kolpos b. Greece
30 C6 Malian r. China
131 G4 Malibamatso r. Lesotho
89 E4 Malicorne-sur-Sarthe France
24 B1 Mali Hka r. Myanmar
114 B2 Mali i Lunxhërisë ridge Albania
114 B2 Mali i Qelqëzës mt. Albania
113 C4 Mali i Thatë mt. Albania
91 E4 Malijai France
53 E3 Mali Kopani Ukraine
25 B4 Mali Kyun i. Myanmar
22 E2 Malili Indonesia
59 F3 Målilla Sweden
107 J4 Mali Lošinj Croatia
6 □6 Malima i. Fiji
125 E5 Malimba, Mont mts Zaire
77 M6 Mali Mokryany Ukraine
22 A3 Malimping Indonesia
127 D5 Malindi Kenya
Malines see Mechelen
124 B4 Malinga Gabon
67 D1 Malin Head headland Rep. of Ireland
67 C2 Malin More Rep. of Ireland
22 D3 Malino Indonesia
52 D2 Malino Rus. Fed.
6 □4 Malinoa i. Tonga
22 E1 Malino, G. mt. Indonesia
52 E3 Malinovka Rus. Fed.
52 F4 Malinovka Rus. Fed.
107 J3 Malinska Croatia
32 D4 Malipo China
114 B2 Maliq Albania
104 E3 Mali Raginac mt. Croatia
23 C5 Malita Philippines
25 B5 Maliwun Myanmar
36 B5 Maliya India
53 E3 Maliyivka Ukraine
51 G7 Malka r. Rus. Fed.
36 D5 Malkapur India
42 A1 Malkara Turkey
54 E5 Mal'kavichy Belarus
114 B3 Mal Kazanje mt. Albania
30 D2 Malkhanskiy Khr. mountain range Rus. Fed.
77 L3 Małkinia Górna Poland
112 F4 Malko Tŭrnovo Bulgaria
30 C2 Mal. Kunaley Rus. Fed.
13 G4 Mallacoota Inlet b. Victoria Australia
66 C4 Mallaig Scotland U.K.
12 D3 Mallala S. Australia Australia
118 D4 Mallanga well Chad
36 B4 Mallani reg. India
119 F2 Mallawi Egypt
13 E3 Mallee Cliffs Nat. Park nat. park New South Wales Australia
102 B3 Mallén Spain
83 E2 Mallero r. Italy
75 H4 Mallersdorf Germany
137 K2 Mallery Lake l. N.W.T. Canada
107 E2 Malles Venosta Italy
55 C3 Malling Denmark
80 E4 Mallnitz Austria
103 F5 Mallorca i. Spain
67 C4 Mallow Rep. of Ireland
62 B1 Malltraeth Bay b. Wales U.K.
62 C2 Mallwyd Wales U.K.
56 C2 Malm Norway
163 G2 Malmanoury French Guiana
39 E2 Malman Rud r. Afghanistan
59 F3 Malmbäck Sweden
56 F2 Malmberget Sweden
69 E4 Malmédy Belgium
62 D3 Malmesbury England U.K.
130 B6 Malmesbury South Africa
59 G2 Malmköping Sweden
59 E4 Malmö Sweden
58 D2 Malmö fjord b. Sweden
59 E4 Malmöhus div. Sweden
158 □3 Malmok headland Bonaire Netherlands Ant.
50 J3 Malmyzh Rus. Fed.
106 C3 Malnate Italy
114 B2 Mal Nëmerçkë ridge Albania
6 □2 Malo i. Vanuatu
107 F3 Malo Italy
52 C3 Maloarkhangel'sk Rus. Fed.
163 F3 Maloca Brazil
112 C2 Malo Crniće Yugoslavia
6 □8 Malolo i. Fiji
6 □8 Malolo Barrier Reef reef Fiji
23 B3 Malolos Philippines
131 H3 Maloma Swaziland
129 F1 Malombe, Lake l. Malawi
73 L4 Małomice Poland
58 D3 Malön i. Sweden
82 C3 Malone r. Italy
147 F2 Malone New York U.S.A.
32 C3 Malong China
125 D6 Malonga Zaire
83 F2 Malonno Italy
81 F2 Malonty Czech Rep.
50 F2 Maloshuyka Rus. Fed.
57 B3 Måløy Norway
52 C2 Maloyaroslavets Rus. Fed.
52 H1 Maloye Karachkino Rus. Fed.
100 D1 Malpartida de Cáceres Spain
98 D5 Malpartida de Plasencia Spain
62 D1 Malpas England U.K.
177 O5 Malpelo, I. de i. Colombia
98 B1 Malpica Spain
54 D3 Mālpils Latvia
38 A3 Malprabha r. India
36 C4 Malpura India
74 D4 Malsch Germany
81 F2 Malše r. Czech Rep.
114 A2 Mal Shpirag mt. Albania
48 G5 Malta country Europe
54 E3 Malta r. Latvia
152 F1 Malta Montana U.S.A.
54 E3 Malta Latvia
128 B3 Maltahöhe Namibia
65 G4 Maltby England U.K.
63 G1 Maltby le Marsh England U.K.
74 C4 Malterdingen Germany
82 D1 Malters Switzerland
36 D4 Mālthone India
65 H3 Malton England U.K.
7 □12 Malua Western Samoa
102 B3 Maluenda Spain
21 J7 Maluku is. Indonesia
43 D3 Ma'lūlā, J. mountain range Syria
123 F4 Malumfashi Nigeria
59 E1 Malung Sweden
59 E1 Malungsfors Sweden
76 D3 Małuszów Poland
131 G4 Maluti Mts mts Lesotho
6 □1 Malu'u Solomon Is.
83 D2 Malvaglia Switzerland
38 A2 Malvan India
100 A2 Malveira Portugal
159 □1 Malvern r. Jamaica
151 E5 Malvern Arkansas U.S.A.
159 □1 Malvern Jamaica
Malvinas, Islas is see Falkland Islands
36 C5 Malwa reg. India
73 K4 Malxe r. Germany
79 G3 Malý Dunaj r. Slovakia
77 N3 Malyech Belarus
30 A2 Mal Yenisey r. Rus. Fed.
53 C1 Malyn Ukraine
53 G2 Malynivka Ukraine
53 B1 Malyns'k Ukraine
77 L2 Mały Płock Poland
47 L2 Malyy Anzas Rus. Fed.
51 H6 Malyye Derbety Rus. Fed.
51 J4 Malyy Irgiz r. Rus. Fed.
42 E1 Malyy Kavkaz mountain range Asia
51 H5 Malyy Uzen' r. Kazakhstan/Rus. Fed.
50 J4 Mamadysh Rus. Fed.
131 G3 Mamafubedu South Africa
131 F4 Mamahabane South Africa
39 G2 Māmā Kheyl Afghanistan
38 C3 Māmallapuram India
6 □8 Mamanuca Group is Fiji
98 B4 Mamarrosa Portugal
22 D2 Mamasa Indonesia
23 A5 Mambahenauhan i. Philippines
23 C4 Mambajao Philippines
124 E3 Mambasa Zaire
124 C3 Mambéré r. Central African Rep.
124 C3 Mambéré-Kadéï div. Central African Rep.
168 B6 Mamborê Brazil
23 B3 Mamburao Philippines
127 □1 Mamelle I. i. Seychelles
131 G2 Mamelodi South Africa
69 E5 Mamer Luxembourg
89 F3 Mamers France
124 A2 Mamfé Cameroon
164 C4 Mamiña Chile
90 E1 Mamirolle France
42 E1 Mamisonis Ugheltekhili pass Georgia
Mamisonskiy Pereval pass see Mamisonis Ugheltekhili
47 G2 Mamlyutka Kazakhstan
155 G5 Mammoth Arizona U.S.A.
144 C4 Mammoth Cave Nat. Park Kentucky U.S.A.
154 C3 Mammoth Lakes California U.S.A.
169 G1 Mamonas Brazil
54 A4 Mamonovo Rus. Fed.
164 C2 Mamoré r. Bolivia/Brazil
162 D4 Mamori Brazil
164 C1 Mamoriá Brazil
122 B4 Mamou Guinea
129 H2 Mampikony Madagascar
122 D5 Mampong Ghana
130 B6 Mamre South Africa
172 B5 Mamuil Malal, P. pass Argentina/Chile
22 D2 Mamuju Indonesia
127 E7 Mamutzu Mayotte Africa
31 H4 Man r. China
122 C5 Man Côte d'Ivoire
6 □8 Mana i. Fiji
163 G2 Mana r. French Guiana
163 G2 Mana French Guiana
36 D3 Mana India
163 E4 Manacapuru Brazil
103 G5 Manacor Spain
21 J6 Manadao Indonesia
69 C4 Manage Belgium
156 J6 Managua Nicaragua
156 J6 Managua, L. de l. Nicaragua
8 E3 Manaia New Zealand
129 H3 Manakara Madagascar
9 D5 Manakau mt. New Zealand
8 E4 Manakau New Zealand
126 D1 Manākhah Yemen
36 D2 Manali India
129 G2 Manambaho r. Madagascar
129 H1 Manambato r. Madagascar
129 H3 Manambondro Madagascar
129 H3 Manambovo r. Madagascar
6 □1 Manam I. i. P.N.G.
153 □1 Manana i. Hawaii U.S.A.
129 H2 Mananara r. Madagascar
129 H3 Mananara r. Madagascar
129 H2 Mananara Avaratra Madagascar
14 D3 Manangoora Northern Terr. Australia
129 H3 Mananjary Madagascar
129 H3 Manankoliva Madagascar
122 C4 Manankoro Mali
122 B4 Manantali, Lac de l. Mali
38 B4 Mānantavādi India
129 H3 Manantenina Madagascar
129 D2 Mana Pools National Park nat. park Zimbabwe
9 A6 Manapouri New Zealand
9 A6 Manapouri, L. l. New Zealand
129 H2 Manarantsandry Madagascar
47 L3 Manas Hu l. China
37 F3 Manaslu mt. Nepal
146 E5 Manassas Virginia U.S.A.
145 □3 Manatí Puerto Rico
128 □2 Manati Bay b. St Helena Atlantic Ocean
21 J8 Manatuto Indonesia
163 E4 Manaus Brazil
42 B2 Manavgat Turkey
36 C5 Manāwar India
118 D5 Manawashei Sudan
8 E4 Manawatu r. New Zealand
8 E3 Manawatu-Wanganui div. New Zealand
23 C5 Manay Philippines
52 C3 Manayenki Rus. Fed.
42 D2 Manbij Syria
65 J4 Manby England U.K.
148 E3 Mancelona Michigan U.S.A.
98 B3 Mancelos Portugal
101 G3 Mancha Real Spain
88 D3 Manche div. France
La Manche str. see English Channel
31 E5 Mancheng China
65 F4 Manchester airport England U.K.
159 □1 Manchester div. Jamaica
154 A2 Manchester California U.S.A.
147 G4 Manchester Connecticut U.S.A.
65 F4 Manchester England U.K.
148 B4 Manchester Iowa U.S.A.
146 B6 Manchester Kentucky U.S.A.
149 E4 Manchester Michigan U.S.A.
147 H3 Manchester New Hampshire U.S.A.
146 B5 Manchester Ohio U.S.A.
145 C5 Manchester Tennessee U.S.A.
147 G3 Manchester Vermont U.S.A.
36 A4 Manchhar L. l. Pakistan
75 G4 Manching Germany
159 □1 Manchioneal Jamaica
31 G3 Manchuria reg. China
108 D2 Manciano Italy
93 C5 Manciet France
42 D2 Mancılık Turkey
155 H3 Mancos r. Colorado U.S.A.
155 H3 Mancos Colorado U.S.A.
39 B3 Mand r. Iran
39 E4 Mand Pakistan
129 G3 Mandabe Madagascar
168 B5 Mandaguaçu Brazil
168 C5 Mandaguari Brazil
22 A2 Mandah Indonesia
25 □ Mandai Singapore
124 D2 Manda, Jebel mt. Sudan
39 E2 Mandal Afghanistan
36 C4 Mandal India
30 C2 Mandal Mongolia
58 B2 Mandal Norway
21 M7 Mandala, Pk mt. Indonesia
24 A2 Mandalay div. Myanmar
24 B2 Mandalay Myanmar
30 C3 Mandalgovĭ Mongolia
42 F3 Mandalī Iraq
30 E3 Mandalt Sum China
150 C2 Mandan N. Dakota U.S.A.
111 E4 Mandanici Sicilia Italy
23 B3 Mandaon Philippines
124 C2 Manda, Parc National de nat. park Chad
124 B1 Mandara Mountains mts Cameroon/Nigeria
108 B5 Mandas Sardegna Italy
111 F3 Mandatoriccio Italy
91 E5 Mandelieu-la-Napoule France
106 D3 Mandello del Lario Italy
98 C1 Mandeo r. Spain
126 D4 Mandera Kenya
155 F2 Manderfield Utah U.S.A.
74 B2 Manderscheid Germany
82 B1 Mandeure France
159 □1 Mandeville Jamaica
9 B6 Mandeville New Zealand
36 B4 Mandha India
126 D3 Mandheera Somalia
36 D3 Mandi India
122 D4 Mandiakui Mali
122 C4 Mandiana Guinea
36 C3 Mandi Burewala Pakistan
129 E2 Mandié Mozambique
129 F1 Mandimba Mozambique
122 C4 Manding, Mts mts Mali
165 E3 Mandioré, Lagoa l. Bolivia
37 F5 Mandira Dam India
173 H1 Mandiso ví Argentina
124 B4 Mandji Gabon
36 E5 Mandla India
55 A4 Mandø i. Denmark
22 B1 Mandor Indonesia
129 H2 Mandoro Madagascar
123 E4 Mandouri Togo
115 E4 Mandra Greece
129 H3 Mandrare r. Madagascar
87 E4 Mandres-en-Barrois France
115 □ Mandriko Greece
129 H2 Mandritsara Madagascar
36 C4 Mandsaur India
91 C5 Manduel France
17 A7 Mandurah Western Australia Australia
111 G2 Manduria Italy
36 B5 Mandvi India
36 C5 Mandvi India
38 B3 Mandya India
58 C2 Måne r. Norway
93 C5 Mane France
23 □2 Manell Pt pt Guam Pacific Ocean
38 B2 Maner r. India
106 E3 Manerbio Italy
78 C1 Manětín Czech Rep.
53 A1 Manevychi Ukraine
119 F2 Manfalūt Egypt
109 H3 Manfredonia Italy
109 J3 Manfredonia, Golfo di g. Italy
169 G1 Manga Brazil
122 D4 Manga Burkina
125 C4 Mangai Zaire
177 J7 Mangaia i. Cook Islands Pacific Ocean
8 E3 Mangakino New Zealand
38 C2 Mangalagiri India
37 H4 Mangaldai India
112 G3 Mangalia Romania
118 C5 Mangalmé Chad
38 A3 Mangalore India
38 A2 Mangalvedha India
37 G4 Mangan India
38 C2 Mangapet India
23 C6 Mangarang Indonesia
131 F4 Mangaung South Africa
8 F3 Mangaweka mt. New Zealand
8 E3 Mangaweka New Zealand
37 G4 Mangde r. Bhutan
125 E4 Mangembe Zaire
58 A1 Manger Norway
9 □1 Mangere I. i. Chatham Is New Zealand
67 B5 Mangerton Mt h. Rep. of Ireland
80 C3 Mangfall r. Germany
75 G5 Mangfallgebirge mountain range Germany
22 B2 Manggar Indonesia
23 □2 Mangilao Guam Pacific Ocean
46 D4 Mangistau Kazakhstan
46 F4 Mangit Uzbekistan
22 D1 Mangkalihat, Tg pt Indonesia
22 C2 Mangkutup r. Indonesia
24 B1 Mangkyi Myanmar
26 F4 Mangnai China
129 F1 Mangochi Malawi
122 D5 Mangodara Burkina
129 G3 Mangoky r. Madagascar
129 H3 Mangoky r. Madagascar
21 J7 Mangole i. Indonesia
8 D1 Mangonui New Zealand
129 H2 Mangoro r. Madagascar
62 D3 Mangotsfield England U.K.
36 B5 Māngral India
36 D4 Mangrol India
158 C1 Mangrove Cay The Bahamas
59 E1 Mångsbodarna Sweden
Mangshi see Luxi
98 C4 Mangualde Portugal
36 A3 Manguchar Pakistan
124 D1 Mangueigne Chad
170 F3 Mangueira, L. l. Brazil
167 B6 Mangueirinha Brazil
166 C3 Mangues r. Brazil
31 G1 Mangui China
166 E3 Manguinha, Pontal do pt Brazil
23 C5 Mangupung i. Indonesia
30 E2 Mangut Rus. Fed.
46 D4 Mangyshlak Kazakhstan
46 D4 Mangyshlak, Pov. pen. Kazakhstan
46 D4 Mangyshlakskiy Zal. b. Kazakhstan
30 A2 Manhan Mongolia
150 D4 Manhattan Kansas U.S.A.
154 D2 Manhattan Nevada U.S.A.
69 D4 Manhay Belgium
129 E4 Manhiça Mozambique
169 H3 Manhuaçu r. Brazil
169 G4 Manhuaçu Brazil
87 E3 Manhuelles France
169 H4 Manhumirim Brazil
115 D6 Mani pen. Greece
162 C3 Mani Colombia
129 H3 Mania r. Madagascar
110 D5 Maniace Sicilia Italy
107 G2 Maniago Italy
127 B7 Maniamba Mozambique
129 E2 Manica div. Mozambique
129 E2 Manicaland div. Zimbabwe
163 E5 Manicoré Brazil
139 G3 Manicouagan r. Québec Canada
139 G3 Manicouagan Québec Canada
139 G3 Manicougan, Réservoir resr Québec Canada
39 B4 Manīfah Saudi Arabia
15 G4 Manifold, C. pt Queensland Australia
32 B2 Maniganggo China
37 F4 Manihari India
7 □10 Manihi i. French Polynesia Pacific Ocean
176 J6 Manihiki atoll Cook Islands Pacific Ocean
135 N3 Maniitsoq Greenland
37 G5 Manikganj Bangladesh
Manikgarh see Rajura
36 E4 Manikpur India
152 E3 Manila Utah U.S.A.
23 B3 Manila Philippines
23 B3 Manila Bay b. Philippines
54 D2 Manilaid i. Estonia
13 G3 Manildra New South Wales Australia
13 G2 Manilla New South Wales Australia
103 B7 Manilla, La mt. Spain
22 D2 Manimbaya, Tg pt Indonesia
14 C2 Maningrida Northern Terr. Australia
6 □3 Maninita i. Tonga
37 H4 Manipur r. India/Myanmar
37 H4 Manipur India
Manipur see Imphal
113 F5 Manisa div. Turkey
42 A2 Manisa Turkey
103 C5 Manises Spain
64 D3 Man, Isle of territory Europe
22 B2 Manismata Indonesia
166 B3 Manissauá Missu r. Brazil
148 E3 Manistee r. Michigan U.S.A.
148 D3 Manistee Michigan U.S.A.
148 D3 Manistique Michigan U.S.A.
148 E2 Manistique Lake l. Michigan U.S.A.
138 B2 Manitoba div. Canada
137 K4 Manitoba, Lake l. Manitoba Canada
137 H4 Manito L. l. Saskatchewan Canada
137 K5 Manitou Manitoba Canada
146 E3 Manitou Beach New York U.S.A.
138 B3 Manitou Falls Ontario Canada
144 C2 Manitou Is is Michigan U.S.A.
148 D2 Manitou Island i. Michigan U.S.A.
140 E4 Manitou, Lake l. Ontario Canada
140 E4 Manitoulin I. i. Ontario Canada
140 C2 Manitouwadge Ontario Canada
140 E4 Manitowaning Ontario Canada
140 C2 Manitowik Lake l. Ontario Canada
148 D3 Manitowoc Wisconsin U.S.A.
141 H3 Maniwaki Québec Canada
162 B2 Manizales Colombia
129 G3 Manja Madagascar
129 H2 Manjak Madagascar
119 F3 Manjam Umm Qurayyāt waterhole Egypt
38 B4 Manjeri India
39 G4 Manjhand Pakistan
17 B7 Manjimup Western Australia Australia
124 A3 Manjo Cameroon
38 B2 Manjra r. India
81 G2 Mank Austria
24 B1 Man Kabat Myanmar
37 G4 Mankachar India
59 G1 Månkarbo Sweden
150 E2 Mankato Minnesota U.S.A.
36 B3 Mankera Pakistan
124 B2 Mankim Cameroon
53 D2 Man'kivka Ukraine
122 C5 Mankono Côte d'Ivoire
38 C4 Mankulam Sri Lanka
131 G1 Mankweng South Africa
24 B1 Manlc Myanmar
102 F3 Manlleu Spain
36 C5 Manmad India

14 C2 Mann r. Northern Terr. Australia
24 B2 Man Na Myanmar
12 D3 Mannahill S. Australia Australia
38 B4 Mannar Sri Lanka
38 B4 Mannar, Gulf of g. India/Sri Lanka
83 D1 Männedorf Switzerland
58 B3 Mannefjorden b. Norway
81 H3 Mannersdorf am Leithagebirge Austria
38 B3 Manneru r. India
74 D3 Mannheim Germany
67 A3 Mannin Bay b. Rep. of Ireland
13 G2 Manning r. New South Wales Australia
136 F3 Manning Alberta Canada
145 D5 Manning S. Carolina U.S.A.
63 H3 Manningtree England U.K.
82 C2 Männlifluh mt. Switzerland
12 B1 Mann Ranges mountain range S. Australia Australia
108 A4 Mannu r. Sardegna Italy
108 A5 Mannu r. Sardegna Italy
108 B4 Mannu r. Sardegna Italy
108 B5 Mannu r. Sardegna Italy
108 A4 Mannu, Capo pt Sardegna Italy
12 D3 Mannum S. Australia Australia
122 B5 Mano r. Liberia/Sierra Leone
122 B5 Mano Sierra Leone
164 C1 Manoa Bolivia
159 □2 Man of War B. b. Tobago Trinidad and Tobago
36 D4 Manohar Thana India
21 K7 Manokwari Indonesia
112 E1 Manoleasa Romania
129 G3 Manombo Atsimo Madagascar
129 H2 Manompana Madagascar
125 E5 Manono Zaire
109 G2 Manoppello Italy
62 B3 Manorbier Wales U.K.
67 C2 Manorhamilton Rep. of Ireland
122 B5 Mano River Liberia
25 B5 Manoron Myanmar
91 D5 Manosque France
141 H3 Manouane Québec Canada
141 H3 Manouane, Lac l. Québec Canada
76 E1 Manowo Poland
24 B2 Man Pan Myanmar
31 H4 Manp'o North Korea
176 H6 Manra i. Kiribati
102 E3 Manresa Spain
36 C3 Mānsa India
125 E6 Mansa Zambia
122 A4 Mansabá Guinea-Bissau
122 A4 Mansa Konko The Gambia
73 K3 Manschnow Germany
36 C2 Mansehra Pakistan
135 K3 Mansel I. i. Québec Canada
73 G4 Mansfeld Germany
63 E1 Mansfield England U.K.
151 E5 Mansfield Louisiana U.S.A.
146 B4 Mansfield Ohio U.S.A.
146 E4 Mansfield Pennsylvania U.S.A.
13 F4 Mansfield Victoria Australia
63 E1 Mansfield Woodhouse England U.K.
24 A1 Mansi Myanmar
99 E2 Mansilla de las Mulas Spain
92 C3 Mansle France
122 A4 Mansôa Guinea-Bissau
136 E3 Manson Creek B.C. Canada
62 D4 Manston England U.K.
162 A4 Manta Ecuador
162 A4 Manta, B. de b. Ecuador
31 J4 Mantapsan mt. North Korea
154 B3 Manteca California U.S.A.
162 D2 Mantecal Venezuela
98 C4 Manteigas Portugal
169 H3 Mantena Brazil
145 F5 Manteo N. Carolina U.S.A.
69 E5 Manternach Luxembourg
89 G3 Mantes-la-Jolie France
89 G3 Mantes-la-Ville France
38 B2 Manthani India
89 F4 Manthelan France
155 G2 Manti Utah U.S.A.
90 D1 Mantoche France
148 E3 Manton Michigan U.S.A.
114 E4 Mantoudi Greece
107 E3 Mantova div. Lombardia Italy
107 E3 Mantova Mantova Italy
57 G3 Mäntsälä Finland
57 G3 Mänttä Finland
Mantua see Mantova
15 F5 Mantuan Downs Queensland Australia
53 G1 Manturovo Rus. Fed.
50 H3 Manturovo Rus. Fed.
57 G3 Mäntyharju Finland
56 G2 Mäntyjärvi Finland
164 B2 Manú Peru
7 □13 Manua Is is American Samoa Pacific Ocean
166 C3 Manuel Alves r. Brazil
166 C2 Manuel Alves Grande r. Brazil
166 C2 Manuel Alves Pequeno r. Brazil
155 H4 Manuelito New Mexico U.S.A.
173 J3 Manuel J. Cobo Argentina
168 C6 Manuel Ribas Brazil
171 B7 Manuel Rodriguez, I. i. Chile
164 C1 Manuel Urbano Brazil
166 B2 Manuelzinho Brazil
7 □10 Manuhangi i. French Polynesia Pacific Ocean
21 H7 Manui i. Indonesia
39 D4 Manūjān Iran
23 B4 Manukan Philippines
8 E2 Manukau New Zealand
8 E2 Manukau Harbour harbour New Zealand
23 A5 Manuk Manka i. Philippines
12 D3 Manunda watercourse S. Australia Australia
164 B2 Manu, Parque Nacional nat. park Peru
6 □1 Manus I. i. P.N.G.
38 B3 Manvi India
129 E2 Manyame r. Mozambique/Zimbabwe
129 E2 Manyame, Lake l. Zimbabwe
127 C5 Manyara, Lake salt lake Tanzania
113 F4 Manyas Turkey
51 G6 Manych-Gudilo, Ozero l. Rus. Fed.
131 H2 Manyeleti Game Reserve res. South Africa
155 H3 Many Farms Arizona U.S.A.
53 B2 Manykivtsi Ukraine
127 B6 Manyoni Tanzania
129 E3 Manyuchi Dam dam Zimbabwe
36 B2 Manzai Pakistan
119 F1 Manzala, L. l. Egypt
101 G1 Manzanares Spain
99 G4 Manzanares el Real Spain
103 C4 Manzanera Spain
159 □3 Manzanilla Bay b. Trinidad Trinidad and Tobago
159 □3 Manzanilla Pt pt Trinidad Trinidad and Tobago
158 C2 Manzanillo Cuba
156 D5 Manzanillo Mexico
156 L7 Manzanillo, Pta pt Panama
81 E5 Manzano Italy
125 E5 Manzanza Zaire
39 B2 Manzariyeh Iran
92 E3 Manzat France
31 F2 Manzhouli China
108 E2 Manziana Italy
43 D4 Manzil Jordan
131 H3 Manzini Swaziland
118 C5 Mao Chad
Maó see Mahón
30 C5 Maojiachuan China
131 F3 Maokeng South Africa
30 B5 Maomao Shan mt. China
33 E4 Maoming China
27 □ Ma On Shan h. Hong Kong
32 C3 Maotou Shan mt. China
129 E3 Mapai Mozambique
37 E3 Mapam Yumco l. China
22 E2 Mapane Indonesia
131 E5 Maphodi South Africa
156 E3 Mapimí Mexico
23 A5 Mapin i. Philippines
129 F3 Mapinhane Mozambique
163 E2 Mapire Venezuela
164 C3 Mapiri Bolivia
148 E4 Maple r. Michigan U.S.A.
137 H5 Maple Creek Saskatchewan Canada
15 E1 Mapoon Queensland Australia
15 E2 Mapoon Abor. Reserve res. Queensland Australia
22 A1 Mapor i. Indonesia
131 F4 Mapoteng Lesotho
6 □1 Maprik P.N.G.
163 F4 Mapuera r. Brazil
129 E3 Mapulanguene Mozambique
131 H4 Mapumulo South Africa
129 E4 Maputo div. Mozambique
129 E4 Maputo r. Mozambique/South Africa
129 E4 Maputo Mozambique
131 J3 Maputo, Baia de b. Mozambique
131 J3 Maputo Elephant Reserve res. Mozambique
131 F4 Maputsoe Lesotho
42 D4 Maqar an Na'am well Iraq
114 B1 Maqellarë Albania
32 C1 Maqên China
32 B1 Maqên Gangri mt. China
47 L4 Maqiao China
43 C5 Maqla, J. al mt. Saudi Arabia
43 C5 Maqnā Saudi Arabia
120 B4 Maqṭeïr reg. Mauritania
32 C1 Maqu China
37 E3 Maquan r. China
23 C3 Maqueda Channel chan. Philippines
125 C5 Maquela do Zombo Angola
171 C5 Maquinchao r. Argentina
171 C5 Maquinchao Argentina
172 D2 Maquinista Levet Argentina
172 A4 Maquis, Punta Los pt Chile
148 B4 Maquoketa r. Iowa U.S.A.
148 B4 Maquoketa Iowa U.S.A.
58 C1 Mår r. Norway
36 A4 Mar r. Pakistan
127 B5 Mara div. Tanzania
137 H1 Mara r. N.W.T. Canada
163 F2 Mara Guyana
37 E5 Māra India
131 G1 Mara South Africa
162 C1 Mara Venezuela
7 □11 Maraa French Polynesia Pacific Ocean
163 D4 Maraã Brazil
166 C2 Maraba Brazil
168 C5 Marabá Paulista Brazil
22 C3 Marabatua is Indonesia
15 F4 Maraboon, L. resr Queensland Australia
82 A1 Marac France
163 G3 Maracá r. Brazil
166 C1 Maracaçumé r. Brazil
168 C5 Maracaí Brazil
162 C1 Maracaibo Venezuela
162 C2 Maracaibo, Lago de l. Venezuela
163 D4 Maracaí, Lago de l. Brazil
163 G3 Maracá, Ilha de i. Brazil
168 A4 Maracaju Brazil
165 E4 Maracaju, Sa de h. Paraguay
166 C1 Maracanã Brazil
159 □3 Maracas B. b. Trinidad Trinidad and Tobago
162 D1 Maracay Venezuela
54 F4 Marachkova Belarus
118 C2 Marādah Libya
123 F4 Maradi div. Niger
123 F4 Maradi Niger
98 D2 Maragatería reg. Spain
42 F2 Marāgheh Iran
166 E3 Maragogipe Brazil
23 B3 Maragondon Philippines
163 D3 Marahuaca, Co mt. Venezuela
88 C5 Marais Breton marsh France
166 C1 Marajó, Baía de est. Brazil
166 B1 Marajó, Ilha de i. Brazil
131 G4 Marakabeis Lesotho
59 G1 Maråkersbotten b. Sweden
38 B3 Marakkanam India
127 C4 Maralal Kenya
124 C2 Marali Central African Rep.
12 B2 Maralinga S. Australia Australia
6 □1 Maramasike i. Solomon Is.
23 C5 Marampit i. Indonesia
25 C7 Maran Malaysia
155 G5 Marana Arizona U.S.A.
99 H3 Maranchón Spain
42 F2 Marand Iran
107 E4 Maranello Italy
25 C6 Marang Malaysia
25 B5 Marang Myanmar
87 F3 Marange-Silvange France
166 E1 Maranguape Brazil
166 C1 Maranhão div. Brazil
166 C3 Maranhão r. Brazil
100 C1 Maranhão, Barragem do resr Portugal
15 G5 Maranoa r. Queensland Australia
109 G4 Marano di Napoli Italy
107 H3 Marano, Laguna di lag. Italy
162 B4 Marañón r. Peru
92 B2 Marans France
86 D4 Maranville France
98 C3 Marão mt. Portugal
122 C5 Maraoué r. Côte d'Ivoire
122 C5 Maraoue, Parc National de la nat. park Côte d'Ivoire
166 C1 Marapanim Brazil
108 A4 Marargiu, Capo pt Sardegna Italy
162 D5 Marari Brazil
9 A6 Mararoa r. New Zealand
173 L2 Marasco Brazil
22 D3 Marasende i. Indonesia
112 F2 Mărășești Romania
111 E3 Maratea Italy
100 B2 Marateca Portugal
145 D7 Marathon Florida U.S.A.
140 B2 Marathon Ontario Canada
151 C6 Marathon Texas U.S.A.
115 E4 Marathonas Greece
166 E3 Maraú Brazil
22 B2 Marau Indonesia
91 B5 Maraussan France
159 □3 Maraval Trinidad and Tobago
23 C4 Marawi Philippines
86 C4 Maraye-en-Othe France
172 D1 Marayes Argentina
62 A4 Marazion England U.K.
82 C2 Marbach Switzerland
74 E4 Marbach am Neckar Germany
101 F4 Marbella Spain
16 B4 Marble Bar Western Australia Australia
155 G3 Marble Canyon gorge Arizona U.S.A.
155 G3 Marble Canyon Arizona U.S.A.
131 G2 Marble Hall South Africa
147 H3 Marblehead Massachusetts U.S.A.
137 L2 Marble I. i. N.W.T. Canada
90 D2 Marboz France
36 C2 Marbul Pass pass India
74 D2 Marburg Germany
131 H5 Marburg South Africa
146 E5 Marburg, Lake l. Pennsylvania U.S.A.
78 G5 Marcali Hungary
107 H4 Marčana Croatia
125 B7 Marca, Pta do pt Angola
107 E3 Marcaria Italy
173 G1 Marcelino Escalada Argentina
100 B3 Marcello Caetano, Barragem de resr Portugal
92 E3 Marcenat France
81 H2 March r. Austria/Slovakia
63 G2 March England U.K.
36 E3 Marcha India
99 G4 Marchamalo Spain
130 C4 Marchand South Africa
90 E1 Marchaux France
107 G5 Marche div. Italy
92 D2 Marche reg. France
69 D4 Marche-en-Famenne div. Luxembourg Belgium
69 D4 Marche-en-Famenne Belgium
81 H2 Marchegg Austria
101 E3 Marchena Spain
162 □ Marchena, I. i. Galapagos Is Ecuador
89 G4 Marchenoir France
93 B4 Marcheprime France
159 □9 Marchfield Barbados Caribbean
86 C2 Marchiennes France
172 B3 Marchihue Chile
69 D4 Marchin Belgium
63 E2 Marchington England U.K.
173 G3 Mar Chiquita l. Argentina
173 J4 Mar Chiquita Argentina
173 J4 Mar Chiquita, L. l. Buenos Aires Argentina
173 F1 Mar Chiquita, L. l. Cordoba Argentina
170 D3 Mar Chiquita, L. l. Argentina
81 F2 Marchtrenk Austria
93 C5 Marciac France
108 C2 Marciana Italy
54 E3 Mārciena Latvia
90 C2 Marcigny France
93 D4 Marcilhac-sur-Célé France
92 E3 Marcillac-la-Croisille France
93 E4 Marcillac-Vallon France
92 E2 Marcillat-en-Combraille France
86 C4 Marcilly-le-Hayer France
77 N1 Marcinkonys Lithuania
76 E2 Marcinkowice Poland
86 A2 Marck France
87 G4 Marckolsheim France
145 D7 Marco Florida U.S.A.
98 B3 Marco de Canaveses Portugal
86 C2 Marcoing France
165 E2 Marcolino r. Brazil
164 A3 Marcona Peru
138 E2 Marcopeet Islands is Québec Canada
107 G3 Marco Polo airport Italy
173 F2 Marcos Juárez Argentina
91 E4 Marcoux France
86 C2 Marcq-en-Barœul France
147 G2 Marcy, Mt mt. New York U.S.A.
36 C2 Mardan Pakistan
173 J4 Mar de Ajó Argentina
173 J4 Mar del Plata Argentina
16 A4 Mardie Western Australia Australia
42 E2 Mardin Turkey
30 B3 Mardzad Mongolia
6 □2 Maré i. New Caledonia Pacific Ocean
90 C3 Mare r. France
107 F2 Marebbe Italy
107 G5 Marecchia r. Italy
168 A6 Marechal Cândido Rondon Brazil
103 □ Mare de Déu del Toro h. Spain
15 F3 Mareeba Queensland Australia
66 C3 Maree, Loch l. Scotland U.K.
108 D2 Maremma reg. Italy
148 C4 Marengo Illinois U.S.A.
148 A5 Marengo Iowa U.S.A.
92 A3 Marennes France
93 A5 Marensin reg. France
111 G2 Mare Piccolo b. Italy
63 G4 Maresfield England U.K.
Mare Tirreno sea see Tyrrhenian Sea
110 B5 Marettimo Sicilia Italy
110 B5 Marettimo, Isola i. Sicilia Italy
92 C3 Mareuil France
92 A2 Mareuil-sur-Lay-Dissais France
52 A1 Marevo Rus. Fed.
151 B6 Marfa Texas U.S.A.
111 □ Marfa Pt pt Malta
111 □ Marfa Rge ridge Malta
37 F2 Margai Caka salt lake China
16 D3 Margaret r. Western Australia Australia
12 D2 Margaret watercourse S. Australia Australia
17 A7 Margaret River Western Australia Australia
163 E1 Margarita, I. de i. Venezuela
63 H3 Margate England U.K.
131 H5 Margate South Africa
79 L3 Margecany Slovakia
91 B3 Margeride, Monts de la mts France
86 D4 Margerie-Hancourt France
37 H4 Margherita India
109 J3 Margherita di Savoia Italy
79 M4 Marghita Romania
47 H4 Margilan Uzbekistan
79 M6 Margina Romania
112 E1 Marginea Romania
77 N2 Margionys Lithuania
69 A5 Margny-lès-Compiègne France
76 F3 Margonin Poland
23 B5 Margosatubig Philippines
148 E3 Margrethe, Lake l. Michigan U.S.A.
140 C4 Margrethe, Lake l. Michigan U.S.A.
136 E4 Marguerite B.C. Canada
179 B2 Marguerite Bay b. Antarctica
91 C5 Marguerittes France
87 E3 Margut France
37 G3 Margyang China
53 F3 Marhanets' Ukraine
173 K1 Marhinote Uruguay
121 D2 Marhoum Algeria
24 B1 Mari Myanmar
168 A4 Maria r. Brazil
91 C4 Mariac France
156 D4 María Cleofas, I. i. Mexico
164 C4 María Elena Chile
173 G1 Mariá Eugenia Argentina
55 B3 Mariager Denmark
55 C3 Mariager Fjord inlet Denmark
14 C2 Maria I. i. Northern Terr. Australia
13 G5 Maria I. i. Tasmania Australia
173 H4 María Ignacia Argentina
177 J7 Maria, Îles is French Polynesia Pacific Ocean
81 G3 Maria Lankowitz Austria
156 D4 María Madre, I. i. Mexico
156 D4 María Magdalena, I. i. Mexico
15 G4 Marian Queensland Australia
169 G4 Mariana Brazil
158 B2 Marianao Cuba
176 E4 Marianas Ridge sea feature Pacific Ocean
176 E5 Marianas Tr. sea feature Pacific Ocean
37 H4 Mariani India
136 F2 Marian Lake l. N.W.T. Canada
151 F5 Marianna Arkansas U.S.A.
145 C6 Marianna Florida U.S.A.
59 F3 Mariannelund Sweden
83 E3 Mariano Comense Italy
170 E2 Mariano Loza Argentina
172 B5 Mariano Moreno Argentina
173 G4 Mariano Unzué Argentina
76 D2 Marianowo Poland
78 B2 Mariánské Lázně Czech Rep.
81 E3 Mariapfarr Austria
81 F4 Maria Saal Austria
101 H3 María, Sierra de mountain range Spain
156 D4 Marías, Islas is Mexico
156 K8 Mariato, Pta pt Panama
8 D1 Maria van Diemen, Cape c. New Zealand
81 G3 Mariazell Austria
126 E1 Ma'rib Yemen
55 D5 Maribo Denmark
81 G4 Maribor Slovenia
131 F2 Marico r. South Africa
155 F5 Maricopa Arizona U.S.A.
154 C4 Maricopa California U.S.A.
155 F5 Maricopa Mts mts Arizona U.S.A.
124 E2 Maridi watercourse Sudan
124 E3 Maridi Sudan
127 □1 Marie Anne I. i. Seychelles
179 A4 Marie Byrd Land reg. Antarctica
59 G2 Mariefred Sweden
159 □5 Marie Galante i. Guadeloupe Caribbean
57 E3 Mariehamn Finland
59 E4 Marieholm Sweden
52 H1 Mari-El div. Rus. Fed.
166 B3 Mariembero r. Brazil
69 C4 Mariembourg Belgium
75 J2 Marienberg Germany
72 C2 Marienhafe Germany
87 G1 Marienheide Germany
128 B3 Mariental Namibia
59 E2 Mariestad Sweden
145 C5 Marietta Georgia U.S.A.
146 C5 Marietta Ohio U.S.A.
109 G4 Marigliano Italy
91 D5 Marignane France
88 D2 Marigny France
179 □ Marigny, C. c. Kerguelen Indian Ocean
86 C4 Marigny-le-Châtel France
159 G3 Marigot Guadeloupe Caribbean
159 □4 Marigot Martinique Caribbean
54 C4 Marijampolė Lithuania
131 F2 Marikana South Africa
114 E1 Marikostinovo Bulgaria
168 D5 Marília Brazil
16 B4 Marillana Western Australia Australia
168 B6 Mariluz Brazil
163 F4 Marimari r. Brazil
125 C5 Marimba Angola
22 C2 Marimun Indonesia
151 C7 Marin Mexico
98 B2 Marín Spain
109 H4 Marina di Camerota Italy
108 C2 Marina di Campo Italy
108 C1 Marina di Castagneto Donoratico Italy
111 F2 Marina di Ginosa Italy
111 F4 Marina di Gioiosa Ionica Italy
108 C2 Marina di Grosseto Italy
111 H3 Marina di Leuca Italy
111 H3 Marina di Novaglie Italy
111 G2 Marina di Pulsano Italy
110 D6 Marina di Ragusa Sicilia Italy
107 G4 Marina di Ravenna Italy
54 F5 Mar"ina Horka Belarus
101 F3 Marinaleda Spain
107 G4 Marina Romea Italy
23 B3 Marinduque i. Philippines
110 B5 Marinella Sicilia Italy
110 C5 Marineo Sicilia Italy
89 G2 Marines France
148 D3 Marinette Wisconsin U.S.A.
124 D3 Maringa r. Zaire
168 C5 Maringá Brazil
129 E2 Maringué Mozambique
90 B3 Maringues France
98 B4 Marinha das Ondas Portugal
98 B5 Marinha Grande Portugal
100 B1 Marinhais Portugal
144 B4 Marion Illinois U.S.A.
148 E5 Marion Indiana U.S.A.
147 K2 Marion Maine U.S.A.
146 B4 Marion Ohio U.S.A.
145 E5 Marion S. Carolina U.S.A.
146 C6 Marion Virginia U.S.A.
14 D4 Marion Downs Queensland Australia
145 D5 Marion, L. l. S. Carolina U.S.A.
15 H3 Marion Reef reef Coral Sea Islands Terr. Pacific Ocean
114 C2 Mariovo reg. Macedonia
163 D2 Maripa Venezuela
163 G3 Maripasoula French Guiana
154 C3 Mariposa California U.S.A.
173 K3 Mariscala Uruguay
165 D4 Mariscal Estigarribia Paraguay
112 E1 Mărișelu Romania
112 E3 Maritsa r. Bulgaria
115 □ Maritsa Greece
50 J3 Mari Turek Rus. Fed.
53 G3 Mariupol' Ukraine
42 F3 Marīvān Iran
101 G1 Marjaliza Spain
54 D2 Märjamaa Estonia
Marjan see Wazi Khwa
43 C3 Marjayoûn Lebanon
126 D4 Marka Somalia
47 L3 Markakol', Oz. l. Kazakhstan
122 C4 Markala Mali
32 B2 Markam China
38 B3 Markapur India
59 E3 Markaryd Sweden
39 B2 Markazī div. Iran
140 E4 Markdale Ontario Canada
74 E5 Markdorf Germany
68 E2 Markelo Netherlands
73 G1 Markelsdorfer Huk pt Germany
68 D2 Marken i. Netherlands
131 G1 Marken South Africa
68 D2 Markermeer l. Netherlands
63 F2 Market Deeping England U.K.
62 D2 Market Drayton England U.K.
63 F2 Market Harborough England U.K.
67 E2 Markethill Northern Ireland U.K.
65 H4 Market Rasen England U.K.
65 H4 Market Weighton England U.K.
45 O3 Markha r. Rus. Fed.
141 F5 Markham Ontario Canada
179 B4 Markham, Mt mt. Antarctica
77 K3 Marki Poland
66 E4 Markinch Scotland U.K.
73 J3 Märkisch Buchholz Germany
47 J5 Markit China
73 H4 Markkleeberg Germany
80 D2 Marklkofen Germany
72 E3 Marklohe Germany
68 D2 Marknesse Netherlands
75 H2 Markneukirchen Germany
115 E5 Markopoulo Greece
124 C2 Markounda Central African Rep.
81 H5 Markovac Trojstveni Croatia
114 E1 Markovi Kladentsi mt. Bulgaria
53 F1 Markovo Rus. Fed.
45 T3 Markovo Rus. Fed.
52 E1 Markovo Rus. Fed.
123 E4 Markoye Burkina
73 H4 Markranstädt Germany
52 H4 Marks Rus. Fed.
74 F2 Marksuhl Germany
81 H3 Markt Allhau Austria
74 F3 Markt Bibart Germany
75 F3 Markt Erlbach Germany
74 E3 Marktheidenfeld Germany
80 C2 Markt Indersdorf Germany
75 G2 Marktleugast Germany
75 H2 Marktleuthen Germany
75 F5 Marktoberdorf Germany
75 H2 Marktredwitz Germany
83 F1 Markt Rettenbach Germany
75 G2 Marktrodach Germany
81 F2 Markt St Florian Austria
81 H3 Markt St Martin Austria
80 C2 Markt Schwaben Germany
148 B6 Mark Twain Lake l. Missouri U.S.A.
80 B2 Markt Wald Germany
72 C4 Marl Germany
12 C1 Marla S. Australia Australia
9 D4 Marlborough div. New Zealand
63 E3 Marlborough England U.K.
147 H3 Marlborough Massachusetts U.S.A.
15 G4 Marlborough Queensland Australia
63 E3 Marlborough Downs h. England U.K.
62 C4 Marldon England U.K.
86 C3 Marle France
87 G4 Marlenheim France
90 D2 Marlieux France
151 D6 Marlin Texas U.S.A.
146 C5 Marlinton W. Virginia U.S.A.
13 G4 Marlo Victoria Australia
130 C7 Marloth Nature Reserve South Africa
63 F3 Marlow England U.K.
73 H1 Marlow Germany
87 F3 Marly Lorraine France
86 C2 Marly Nord-Pas-de-Calais France
93 C4 Marmande France
114 D4 Marmara Greece
113 F4 Marmara Turkey
42 B1 Marmara Denizi sea Turkey
113 F4 Marmaraereğlisi Turkey
Marmara, Sea of sea see Marmara Denizi
115 F4 Marmari Greece
42 B2 Marmaris Turkey
150 C2 Marmarth N. Dakota U.S.A.
100 B3 Marmelete Portugal
103 C7 Mar Menor lag. Spain
146 C5 Marmet W. Virginia U.S.A.
138 B4 Marmion L. l. Ontario Canada
17 C6 Marmion, Lake salt pan Western Australia Australia
83 F3 Marmirolo Italy
107 F2 Marmolada mt. Italy
101 F2 Marmolejo Spain
82 C3 Marmore r. Italy
87 G4 Marmoutier France
157 G5 Mar Muerto l. Mexico
90 D1 Marnay France
90 E2 Marnaz France
86 D3 Marne div. Champagne-Ardenne France
86 C3 Marne r. France
72 E2 Marne Germany
86 B4 Marne-la-Vallée France
73 G2 Marnitz Germany
131 G1 Marnitz South Africa
124 C2 Maro Chad
129 H2 Maroantsetra Madagascar
169 J2 Maroba r. Brazil
7 □10 Marokau i. French Polynesia Pacific Ocean
36 D2 Marol Jammu and Kashmir
129 H3 Marolambo Madagascar
75 F2 Maroldsweisach Germany
89 F3 Marolles-les-Braults France
89 G2 Maromme France
129 H1 Maromokotro mt. Madagascar
129 H1 Maromony, Lohatanjona headland Madagascar
129 E2 Marondera Zimbabwe
163 G3 Maroni r. French Guiana
92 E3 Maronne r. France
15 H5 Maroochydore Queensland Australia
159 □1 Maroon Town Jamaica
22 D3 Maros Indonesia
129 H2 Maroseranana Madagascar
79 K5 Maros-Körös Köze plain Hungary
107 F3 Marostica Italy
5 N7 Marotiri is French Polynesia Pacific Ocean
129 H1 Marotolana Madagascar
124 B1 Maroua Cameroon
88 C3 Maroué France
163 G3 Marouini r. French Guiana
129 H2 Marovoay Madagascar
163 G2 Marowijne r. Surinam
69 F5 Marpingen Germany
115 G5 Marpissa Greece
65 F4 Marple England U.K.
42 E3 Marqādah Syria
32 C1 Mar Qu r. China
131 F4 Marquard South Africa
86 A2 Marquenterre reg. France
145 D7 Marquesas Keys is Florida U.S.A.
148 D2 Marquette Michigan U.S.A.
86 C2 Marquion France
86 A2 Marquise France
177 K6 Marquises, Îles is French Polynesia Pacific Ocean
13 F2 Marra r. New South Wales Australia
129 E4 Marracuene Mozambique
120 C2 Marrakech Morocco
Marrakesh see Marrakech
129 E3 Marrangua, L. l. Mozambique
118 D5 Marra Plateau plat. Sudan
13 F5 Marrawah Tasmania Australia
166 D2 Marrecas, Sa das h. Brazil
12 D2 Marree S. Australia Australia
151 F6 Marrero Louisiana U.S.A.
129 F2 Marromeu Mozambique
129 F2 Marromeu, Reserva de res. Mozambique
127 C7 Marrupa Mozambique
92 E3 Mars r. France
119 F2 Marsa Alam Egypt
118 C1 Marsa al Burayqah Libya
126 C4 Marsabit Kenya
126 C4 Marsabit National Reserve res. Kenya
90 B3 Marsac-en-Livradois France
88 D4 Marsac-sur-Don France
43 C5 Marsa Dahab b. Egypt
106 D4 Marsaglia Italy
87 F4 Marsal France
110 B5 Marsala Trapani Italy
111 □ Marsalforn Malta
118 E1 Marsa Matrûh Egypt
90 C1 Marsannay-la-Côte France
91 C4 Marsanne France
111 □ Marsaskala Malta
122 A4 Marsassoum Senegal
111 □ Marsaxlokk Malta
111 □ Marsaxlokk B. b. Malta
128 □1 Mars Bay b. Ascension Atlantic Ocean
72 D4 Marsberg Germany
109 E2 Marsciano Italy
13 F3 Marsden New South Wales Australia
68 C2 Marsdiep chan. Netherlands
91 B5 Marseillan France
91 D5 Marseille Bouches-du-Rhône France
89 G2 Marseille-en-Beauvaisis France
91 D5 Marseille-Provence airport France
148 C5 Marseilles Illinois U.S.A.
56 D2 Marsfjället mt. Sweden
14 D4 Marshall watercourse Northern Terr. Australia
151 E5 Marshall Arkansas U.S.A.
144 C4 Marshall Illinois U.S.A.
148 E4 Marshall Michigan U.S.A.
150 E2 Marshall Minnesota U.S.A.
150 E4 Marshall Missouri U.S.A.
137 H4 Marshall Saskatchewan Canada
151 E5 Marshall Texas U.S.A.
122 B5 Marshall Liberia
13 F4 Marshall B. b. Tasmania Australia
4 H3 Marshall Islands country Pacific Ocean
140 B1 Marshall Lake l. Ontario Canada
150 E3 Marshalltown Iowa U.S.A.
54 F3 Marshavitsy Rus. Fed.
148 B3 Marshfield Wisconsin U.S.A.
158 C1 Marsh Harbour The Bahamas
147 K1 Mars Hill Maine U.S.A.
151 F6 Marsh Island i. Louisiana U.S.A.
136 C2 Marsh Lake l. Yukon Terr. Canada
63 G2 Marsh, The reg. England U.K.
109 H4 Marsico Nuovo Italy
152 C3 Marsing Idaho U.S.A.
93 E5 Marssac-sur-Tarn France
59 G2 Märsta Sweden
55 C5 Marstal Denmark
55 C5 Marstal Bugt b. Denmark
83 E1 Märstetten Switzerland
58 D3 Marstrand Sweden
37 F3 Marsyangdi r. Nepal
108 D2 Marta r. Italy
24 B3 Martaban Myanmar
24 B3 Martaban, Gulf of g. Myanmar
59 F1 Mårtanberg Sweden
111 H2 Martano Italy
22 A3 Martapura Indonesia
22 C2 Martapura Indonesia
93 D4 Martel France
69 D5 Martelange Belgium
107 G3 Martellago Italy
83 F2 Martello Italy
141 F3 Marten River Ontario Canada
137 H4 Martensville Saskatchewan Canada
103 C5 Martés mt. Spain
103 B5 Martés, Serra mountain range Spain
72 E3 Martfeld Germany
79 K4 Martfo Hungary
147 H4 Martha's Vineyard i. Massachusetts U.S.A.
92 C3 Marthon France
88 D4 Martigné-Ferchaud France
89 E3 Martigné-sur-Mayenne France
82 C2 Martigny Switzerland
87 E4 Martigny-les-Bains France
87 E4 Martigny-les-Gerbonvaux France
101 E5 Martil Morocco
100 C3 Martim Longo Portugal
102 C3 Martín r. Spain
150 C3 Martin S. Dakota U.S.A.
145 B4 Martin Tennessee U.S.A.
79 H2 Martin Slovakia
111 G2 Martina Franca Italy
173 H3 Martín Chico Uruguay
173 H4 Martin Colman Argentina
101 F3 Martín de la Jara Spain
172 D3 Martín de Loyola Argentina
102 E2 Martinet Spain
157 F4 Martínez Mexico
155 E5 Martinez Lake Arizona U.S.A.
100 B1 Martingança Portugal
173 H3 Martín García, I. i. Argentina
169 F3 Martinho Campos Brazil
133 M8 Martinique territory Caribbean
159 G4 Martinique Passage chan. Dominica/Martinique
145 C5 Martin, L. l. Alabama U.S.A.
99 F3 Martín Muñoz de las Posadas Spain
114 E4 Martino Greece
166 D1 Martinópole Brazil

168 C5 **Martinópolis** Brazil
179 A3 **Martin Pen.** pen. Antarctica
9 A6 **Martins Bay** b. New Zealand
81 G2 **Martinsberg** Austria
146 D4 **Martinsburg** Pennsylvania U.S.A.
146 E5 **Martinsburg** W. Virginia U.S.A.
107 J4 **Martinšćica** Croatia
131 F1 **Martin's Drift** South Africa
146 C4 **Martins Ferry** Ohio U.S.A.
146 D6 **Martinsville** Virginia U.S.A.
174 H7 **Martin Vas, Ilhas** is Atlantic Ocean
108 A4 **Martis** Sardegna Italy
92 D2 **Martizay** France
62 D2 **Martley** England U.K.
62 D4 **Martock** England U.K.
8 E4 **Marton** New Zealand
79 H4 **Martonvásár** Hungary
102 E3 **Martorell** Spain
101 G3 **Martos** Spain
136 F2 **Martre, Lac la** l. N.W.T. Canada
54 C1 **Marttila** Finland
46 E2 **Martuk** Kazakhstan
53 C1 **Martynovychi** Ukraine
39 E2 **Maruchak** Afghanistan
23 A5 **Marudu, Tk** b. Malaysia
28 D6 **Marugame** Japan
99 F4 **Marugán** Spain
9 D5 **Maruia** r. New Zealand
166 E3 **Maruim** Brazil
173 F1 **Marull** Argentina
68 E1 **Marum** Netherlands
6 □2 **Marum, Mt** mt. Vanuatu
36 B4 **Marusthali** reg. India
7 □10 **Marutéa** i. French Polynesia Pacific Ocean
100 C1 **Marvão** Portugal
39 C3 **Marvast** Iran
91 B4 **Marvejols** France
87 E3 **Marville** France
155 G2 **Marvine, Mt** mt. Utah U.S.A.
36 C4 **Marwar Jct** India
137 G4 **Marwayne** Alberta Canada
46 F5 **Mary** div. Turkmenistan
14 B2 **Mary** r. Northern Terr. Australia
46 F5 **Mary** Turkmenistan
77 N5 **Mar''yanivka** Volyns'ka Oblast' Ukraine
53 G3 **Mar''yanivka** Zaporiz'ka Oblast' Ukraine
53 B1 **Mar''yanivka** Zhytomyrs'ka Oblast' Ukraine
47 H2 **Mar'yanovka** Rus. Fed.
15 H5 **Maryborough** Queensland Australia
13 E4 **Maryborough** Victoria Australia
130 D4 **Marydale** South Africa
52 H3 **Mar'yevka** Rus. Fed.
137 H2 **Mary Frances Lake** l. N.W.T. Canada
53 G3 **Mar''yinka** Ukraine
147 E5 **Maryland** div. U.S.A.
112 E1 **Marynychi** Ukraine
66 E3 **Marypark** Scotland U.K.
65 E3 **Maryport** England U.K.
139 J3 **Mary's Harbour** Newfoundland Canada
139 K4 **Marystown** Newfoundland Canada
155 F2 **Marysvale** Utah U.S.A.
154 B2 **Marysville** California U.S.A.
150 D4 **Marysville** Kansas U.S.A.
139 G4 **Marysville** New Brunswick Canada
146 B4 **Marysville** Ohio U.S.A.
15 F3 **Maryvale** Queensland Australia
150 E3 **Maryville** Missouri U.S.A.
107 F4 **Marzabotto** Italy
168 D2 **Marzagão** Brazil
73 H3 **Marzahna** Germany
73 H3 **Marzahne** Germany
111 E6 **Marzamemi** Sicilia Italy
80 C2 **Marzling** Germany
43 A4 **Masabb Dumyât** river mouth Egypt
43 A4 **Masabb Rashîd** river mouth Egypt
156 J7 **Masachapa** Nicaragua
42 D3 **Maşâf** Syria
127 B5 **Masai Mara National Reserve** res. Kenya
127 C5 **Masai Steppe** plain Tanzania
127 B5 **Masaka** Uganda
131 F5 **Masakhane** South Africa
128 C3 **Masalanyane Pan** salt pan Botswana
22 C3 **Masalembu Besar** i. Indonesia
22 C3 **Masalembu Kecil** i. Indonesia
42 G2 **Masallı** Azerbaijan
22 E2 **Masamba** mt. Indonesia
22 E2 **Masamba** Indonesia
31 J6 **Masan** South Korea
147 J1 **Masardis** Maine U.S.A.
115 □ **Masari** Greece
127 C7 **Masasi** Tanzania
165 D3 **Masavi** Bolivia
156 J7 **Masaya** Nicaragua
23 B3 **Masbate** i. Philippines
23 B3 **Masbate** Philippines
111 E5 **Mascalucia** Sicilia Italy
121 E1 **Mascara** Algeria
175 H5 **Mascarene Basin** sea feature Indian Ocean
175 J4 **Mascarene Ridge** sea feature Indian Ocean
172 D1 **Mascasín** Argentina
169 J1 **Mascote** Brazil
141 J4 **Mascouche** Québec Canada
102 C4 **Mas de las Matas** Spain
99 H4 **Masegoso de Tajuña** Spain
131 G1 **Masekwaspoort** South Africa
59 E3 **Mäsen** l. Sweden
127 B4 **Maseno** Kenya
83 D2 **Masera** Italy
80 D5 **Maserada sul Piave** Italy
141 G2 **Masères, Lac** l. Québec Canada
131 F4 **Maseru** Lesotho
90 E1 **Masevaux** France
58 A1 **Masfjorden** Norway
131 G4 **Mashai** Lesotho
65 G3 **Masham** England U.K.
32 E4 **Mashan** China
129 E3 **Mashava** Zimbabwe
36 D2 **Masherbrum** mt. Pakistan
39 D1 **Mashhad** Iran
36 C4 **Mashi** r. India
28 H2 **Mashike** Japan
53 F2 **Mashivka** Ukraine
39 D3 **Mashīz** Iran
39 E4 **Mashket** r. Pakistan
39 E3 **Mashki Chah** Pakistan
39 E4 **Māshkīd** r. Iran
129 E2 **Mashonaland Central** div. Zimbabwe
129 E2 **Mashonaland East** div. Zimbabwe
129 D2 **Mashonaland West** div. Zimbabwe
Mashtagi see **Maştağa**
28 K2 **Mashū-ko** l. Japan
56 F1 **Masi** Norway
156 C3 **Masiáca** Mexico
131 F5 **Masibambane** South Africa
98 B2 **Maside** Spain
131 F4 **Masilo** South Africa
125 C4 **Masi-Manimba** Zaire
22 D2 **Masimbu** Indonesia
126 B4 **Masindi** Uganda
127 C5 **Masinga Res.** resr Kenya
23 A3 **Masinloc** Philippines
83 E2 **Masino** r. Italy
130 D5 **Masinyusane** South Africa
175 H2 **Maşîrah** i.
41 J6 **Maşîrah, Gulf of** b. Oman
164 B1 **Masisea** Peru
131 H1 **Masisi** South Africa
124 F4 **Masisi** Zaire
39 B3 **Masjed Soleymān** Iran
42 D2 **Maskanah** Syria
141 J3 **Maskinongé** Québec Canada
67 B3 **Mask, Lough** l. Rep. of Ireland
54 C1 **Masku** Finland
39 D4 **Maskūtān** Iran
93 B5 **Maslacq** France
79 L5 **Maşloc** Romania
53 G1 **Maslova Pristan'** Rus. Fed.
39 F3 **Maslti** Pakistan
47 K2 **Maslyanino** Rus. Fed.
98 C1 **Masma** r. Spain
80 C4 **Maso** r. Italy
129 J2 **Masoala, Tanjona** c. Madagascar
129 G2 **Masoarivo** Madagascar
173 K1 **Masoller** Uruguay
147 E4 **Mason** Michigan U.S.A.
154 C2 **Mason** Nevada U.S.A.
151 D6 **Mason** Texas U.S.A.
9 A7 **Mason Bay** b. New Zealand
148 C5 **Mason City** Illinois U.S.A.
150 E3 **Mason City** Iowa U.S.A.
146 D5 **Masontown** Pennsylvania U.S.A.
41 J5 **Masqaţ** Oman
106 E4 **Massa** Italy
147 G3 **Massachusetts** div. U.S.A.
147 H3 **Massachusetts Bay** b. U.S.A.
106 E5 **Massaciuccoli, Lago di** l. Italy
155 H1 **Massadona** Colorado U.S.A.
106 D4 **Massa e Carrara** div. Italy
111 G2 **Massafra** Italy
124 C1 **Massaguet** Chad
124 C1 **Massakory** Chad
109 G4 **Massa Lubrense** Italy
103 C5 **Massamagrell** Spain
108 C1 **Massa Marittimo** Italy
109 E2 **Massa Martana** Italy
124 B4 **Massana** Gabon
129 E3 **Massangena** Mozambique
125 C5 **Massango** Angola
127 C7 **Massangulo** Mozambique
166 D1 **Massapê** Brazil
105 E3 **Massarosa** Italy
125 B4 **Massassa-Lewémé** Congo
93 D6 **Massat** France
126 C1 **Massawa** Eritrea
126 C1 **Massawa Channel** chan. Eritrea
141 K4 **Massawippi, Lac** l. Québec Canada
147 F2 **Massena** New York U.S.A.
124 C1 **Massenya** Chad
92 D3 **Masseret** France
136 C4 **Masset** B.C. Canada
93 C5 **Masseube** France
140 D3 **Massey** Ontario Canada
91 B3 **Massiac** France
91 B3 **Massif Central** mts France
122 B4 **Massif de Banko** mt. Guinea
91 D3 **Massif de la Chartreuse** mountain range France
158 D3 **Massif de la Hotte** mountain range Haiti
123 F3 **Massif de l'Aïr** mts Niger
93 D6 **Massif de l'Arize** mt. France
90 D1 **Massif de la Serre** h. France
91 E3 **Massif de la Vanoise** mts France
129 H3 **Massif de L'Isalo** mts Madagascar
93 C6 **Massif de Néouvielle** mts France
124 D2 **Massif des Bongo** mts Central African Rep.
91 E5 **Massif des Maures** reg. France
92 E3 **Massif du Cantal** mts France
124 B4 **Massif du Chaillu** mts Gabon
91 D4 **Massif du Diois** mts France
124 C1 **Massif du Guéra** mts Chad
118 D5 **Massif du Kapka** mts Chad
91 E4 **Massif du Pelvoux** mts France
122 B4 **Massif du Tamgué** mts Guinea
129 H1 **Massif du Tsaratanana** mts Madagascar
124 C2 **Massif du Yadé** mts Central African Rep.
118 D4 **Massif Ennedi** mts Chad
179 □ **Massif Galliéni** mts Kerguelen Indian Ocean
122 C4 **Massigui** Mali
146 C4 **Massillon** Ohio U.S.A.
122 C4 **Massina** Mali
80 D2 **Massing** Germany
129 F3 **Massinga** Mozambique
129 E3 **Massingir** Mozambique
129 E3 **Massingir, Barragem de** resr Mozambique
129 E3 **Massintonto** r. Mozambique/South Africa
179 D3 **Massivet** mts Antarctica
141 H4 **Masson** Québec Canada
179 D5 **Masson I.** i. Antarctica
119 G3 **Mastābah** Saudi Arabia
42 G1 **Maştağa** Azerbaijan
47 G5 **Mastchoh** Tajikistan
46 D3 **Masteksay** Kazakhstan
9 E4 **Masterton** New Zealand
145 E7 **Mastic Point** The Bahamas
141 J3 **Mastigouche, Réserve faunique de** res. Québec Canada
108 B5 **Mastixi, Pta su** pt Sardegna Italy
58 A1 **Mastrevik** Norway
36 C1 **Mastuj** Pakistan
36 A3 **Mastung** Pakistan
119 G3 **Mastūrah** Saudi Arabia
77 N2 **Masty** Belarus
108 A5 **Masua** Sardegna Italy
28 C6 **Masuda** Japan
Masulipatam see **Machilipatnam**
129 E3 **Masvingo** div. Zimbabwe
129 E3 **Masvingo** Zimbabwe
127 B5 **Maswe** Tanzania
127 B5 **Maswe Game Reserve** res. Tanzania
77 M4 **Masyevichy** Belarus
76 F1 **Maszewo** Słupsk Poland
76 D2 **Maszewo** Szczecin Poland
8 G2 **Mata** r. New Zealand
24 B1 **Mata** Myanmar
126 E3 **Matabaan** Somalia
128 D2 **Matabeleland North** div. Zimbabwe
129 D3 **Matabeleland South** div. Zimbabwe
37 G4 **Matabhanga** India
99 G3 **Matabuena** Spain
100 E2 **Matachel** r. Spain
140 E3 **Matachewan** Ontario Canada
153 F6 **Matachic** Mexico
125 B5 **Matadi** Zaire
156 J6 **Matagalpa** Nicaragua
141 G2 **Matagami** Québec Canada
141 F2 **Matagami, Lac** l. Québec Canada
151 D6 **Matagorda I.** i. Texas U.S.A.
158 B2 **Matahambre** Cuba
43 A5 **Matâi** Egypt
7 □11 **Mataiea** French Polynesia Pacific Ocean
7 □10 **Mataiva** i. French Polynesia Pacific Ocean
25 D7 **Matak** i. Indonesia
8 F2 **Matakana Island** i. New Zealand
125 C6 **Matala** Angola
115 F8 **Matala** Greece
38 C5 **Matale** Sri Lanka
99 H3 **Matalebreras** Spain
130 E4 **Mataleng** South Africa
122 B3 **Matam** Senegal
8 E2 **Matamata** New Zealand
130 C2 **Mata-Mata** South Africa
123 F4 **Matamey** Niger
156 E3 **Matamoros** Coahuila Mexico
157 F3 **Matamoros** Tamaulipas Mexico
23 B5 **Matanal Point** pt Philippines
118 D3 **Ma'tan as Sārah** well Libya
118 D3 **Ma'ţan Bishrah** well Libya
172 B1 **Matancilla** Chile
127 C6 **Matandu** r. Tanzania
139 G4 **Matane** Québec Canada
158 B2 **Matanzas** Cuba
168 D4 **Matão** Brazil
173 J1 **Mataojo** Uruguay
156 K7 **Matapalo, C.** c. Costa Rica
Matapan, C. c. see **Akra Tainaro**
76 G5 **Mata Panew** r. Poland
139 G4 **Matapédia** r. Québec Canada
99 F2 **Mataporquera** Spain
99 F3 **Matapozuelos** Spain
172 B3 **Mataquito** r. Chile
38 C5 **Matara** Sri Lanka
114 C4 **Mataragka** Dytiki Ellas Greece
114 D3 **Mataragka** Thessalia Greece
22 D4 **Mataram** Indonesia
14 C2 **Mataranka** Northern Terr. Australia
102 F3 **Mataró** Spain
102 D3 **Matarraña** r. Spain
22 C3 **Matasiri** i. Indonesia
119 E4 **Matassi** well Sudan
131 G5 **Matatiele** South Africa
7 □13 **Matatula, C.** c. American Samoa Pacific Ocean
9 B7 **Mataura** r. New Zealand
9 B7 **Mataura** New Zealand
7 □12 **Matautu** Western Samoa
6 □3 **Mata'utuliki** i. Tonga
7 □12 **Matavanu Crater** crater Western Samoa
7 □16 **Mataveri** Easter I. Chile
131 H1 **Matavhelo** South Africa
8 F3 **Matawai** New Zealand
141 J3 **Matawin** r. Québec Canada
165 D2 **Mategua** Bolivia
157 E4 **Matehuala** Mexico
168 B6 **Matelândia** Brazil
105 H5 **Matelica** Italy
159 □3 **Matelot** Trinidad and Tobago
127 C7 **Matemanga** Tanzania
127 D7 **Matemo, Ilha** i. Mozambique
109 J4 **Matera** div. Basilicata Italy
109 J4 **Matera** Matera Italy
109 G3 **Matese, Monti del** mts Italy
79 M4 **Mátészalka** Hungary
128 D2 **Matetsi** r. Zimbabwe
105 B7 **Mateur** Tunisia
98 C3 **Mateus** Portugal
169 F3 **Mateus Leme** Brazil
92 B3 **Matha** France
126 B4 **Matheniko Game Reserve** res. Uganda
140 E2 **Matheson** Ontario Canada
151 D6 **Mathis** Texas U.S.A.
113 B5 **Mathraki** i. Greece
36 D4 **Mathura** India
23 C5 **Mati** Philippines
123 E4 **Matiacoali** Burkina
37 G4 **Matiali** India
33 F3 **Matianxu** China
36 B4 **Matiari** Pakistan
169 G4 **Matias Barbosa** Brazil
169 G1 **Matias Cardoso** Brazil
157 G5 **Matías Romero** Mexico
88 C3 **Matignon** France
69 B5 **Matigny** France
139 G3 **Matimekosh** Newfoundland Canada
140 D3 **Matinenda Lake** l. Ontario Canada
166 C1 **Matinha** Brazil
147 J3 **Matinicus I.** i. Maine U.S.A.
111 H2 **Matino** Italy
7 □11 **Matiti** French Polynesia Pacific Ocean
130 C6 **Matjiesfontein** South Africa
37 G5 **Matla** r. India
131 F1 **Matlabas** r. South Africa
131 F2 **Matlabas** South Africa
63 E1 **Matlock** England U.K.
131 F3 **Matlwangtlwang** South Africa
129 D3 **Matobo Hills** mts Zimbabwe
166 A3 **Mato Grosso** div. Brazil
165 E3 **Mato Grosso** Brazil
168 B1 **Mato Grosso** Brazil
168 A3 **Mato Grosso do Sul** div. Brazil
129 E4 **Matola** Mozambique
124 B3 **Matomb** Cameroon
98 B3 **Matosinhos** Portugal
90 C2 **Matour** France
169 G1 **Mato Verde** Brazil
169 F3 **Matozinhos** Brazil
79 J4 **Mátra** mts Hungary
41 J5 **Maţraḩ** Oman
58 A1 **Matre** Norway
80 D3 **Matrei in Osttirol** Austria
130 B6 **Matroosberg** mt. South Africa
131 F2 **Matrooster** South Africa
122 B5 **Matru** Sierra Leone
130 D4 **Matsap** South Africa
131 H3 **Matsapha** Swaziland
123 G4 **Matsena** Nigeria
51 F7 **Matsesta** Rus. Fed.
129 H3 **Matsiatra** r. Madagascar
28 D6 **Matsue** Japan
28 H3 **Matsumae** Japan
29 F5 **Matsumoto** Japan
29 F6 **Matsusaka** Japan
33 G3 **Matsu Tao** i. Taiwan
28 C7 **Matsuura** Japan
28 D7 **Matsuyama** Japan
140 E2 **Mattagami** r. Ontario Canada
135 L5 **Mattagami** Québec Canada
172 E3 **Mattaldi** Argentina
141 F3 **Mattawa** Ontario Canada
147 J2 **Mattawamkeag** Maine U.S.A.
152 D3 **Matterhorn** mt. Nevada U.S.A.
82 C3 **Matterhorn** mt. Italy/Switzerland
81 H3 **Mattersburg** div. Austria
81 H3 **Mattersburg** Austria
82 C2 **Mattertal** v. Switzerland
163 E2 **Matthews Ridge** Guyana
158 D2 **Matthew Town** The Bahamas
140 D2 **Mattice** Ontario Canada
80 E2 **Mattighofen** Austria
109 J3 **Mattinata** Italy
29 F5 **Mattō** Japan
144 B4 **Mattoon** Illinois U.S.A.
Matturai see **Matara**
164 A2 **Matucana** Peru
38 C5 **Matugama** Sri Lanka
77 N1 **Matuizos** Lithuania
6 □7 **Matuku** i. Fiji
107 J3 **Matulji** Croatia
125 C6 **Matumbo** Angola
Matun see **Khowst**
119 F5 **Ma'tuq** Sudan
159 □3 **Matura** Trinidad and Tobago
159 □3 **Matura Bay** b. Trinidad Trinidad and Tobago
162 B2 **Maturín** Venezuela
129 D2 **Matusadona National Park** nat. park Zimbabwe
99 H3 **Matute** mt. Spain
169 F3 **Matutina** Brazil
23 C5 **Matutuang** i. Indonesia
52 H1 **Matvinur** Rus. Fed.
53 D3 **Matviyivka** Mykolayivs'ka Oblast' Ukraine
53 F3 **Matviyivka** Zaporiz'ka Oblast' Ukraine
131 F4 **Matwabeng** South Africa
52 E3 **Matyra** r. Rus. Fed.
52 D3 **Matyrskiy** Rus. Fed.
52 D3 **Matyrskoye Vdkhr.** resr Rus. Fed.
127 C5 **Mau** mt. Kenya
37 E4 **Mau** India
36 D4 **Mau** India
127 C7 **Maúa** Mozambique
37 E4 **Mau Aimma** India
102 D2 **Maubermé, Pic de** mt. Spain
86 D3 **Maubert-Fontaine** France
86 C2 **Maubeuge** France
24 B1 **Ma-ubin** Myanmar
93 C5 **Maubourguet** France
66 D5 **Mauchline** Scotland U.K.
36 E4 **Maudaha** India
13 F3 **Maude** New South Wales Australia
179 C3 **Maudheimvidda** mountain range Antarctica
17 A4 **Maud, Pt** pt Western Australia Australia
179 D2 **Maud Seamount** sea feature Antarctica
80 E2 **Mauerkirchen** Austria
75 G4 **Mauern** Germany
83 F1 **Mauerstetten** Germany
163 F4 **Maués** r. Brazil
163 F4 **Maués** Brazil
37 E4 **Mauganj** India
64 D3 **Maughold Head** headland Isle of Man
21 M2 **Maug Islands** is Northern Mariana Is Pacific Ocean
91 C5 **Mauguio** France
153 □2 **Maui** i. Hawaii U.S.A.
5 M7 **Mauke** i. Cook Islands Pacific Ocean
24 A2 **Maukkadaw** Myanmar
87 H4 **Maulbronn** Germany
92 D3 **Maulde** r. France
172 B3 **Maule** div. Chile
172 A3 **Maule** r. Chile
172 B3 **Maule** Chile
172 B4 **Maule, L. del** l. Chile
92 B2 **Mauléon** France
93 C6 **Mauléon-Barousse** France
93 B5 **Mauléon-Licharre** France
89 E4 **Maulévrier** France
171 B5 **Maullín** Chile
37 G4 **Maulvi-Bazar** Bangladesh
67 B2 **Maumakeogh** h. Rep. of Ireland
149 E5 **Maumee** r. Ohio U.S.A.
148 E5 **Maumee** Ohio U.S.A.
149 F5 **Maumee Bay** b. Michigan/Ohio U.S.A.
146 B4 **Maumee Bay** b. Michigan/Ohio U.S.A.
21 H8 **Maumere** Indonesia
67 B3 **Maumturk Mts** h. Rep. of Ireland
128 C2 **Maun** Botswana
153 □2 **Mauna Kea** volcano Hawaii U.S.A.
153 □2 **Mauna Loa** volcano Hawaii U.S.A.
153 □1 **Maunalua B.** b. Hawaii U.S.A.
8 F3 **Maungahaumi** mt. New Zealand
8 F3 **Maungapohatu** mt. New Zealand
8 F3 **Maungataniwha** mt. New Zealand
8 E1 **Maungatapere** New Zealand
8 E2 **Maungaturoto** New Zealand
24 A2 **Maungdaw** Myanmar
25 B4 **Maungmagan Is** is Myanmar
25 B4 **Maungmagon** Myanmar
134 F3 **Maunoir, Lac** l. N.W.T. Canada
36 D4 **Mau Rampur** India
88 D4 **Maure-de-Bretagne** France
93 E6 **Maureillas-las-Illas** France
93 C4 **Maurens** France
164 C3 **Mauri** r. Bolivia
92 E3 **Mauriac** France
12 B2 **Maurice, L.** salt flat S. Australia Australia
141 J3 **Mauricie, Parc National de la** nat. park Québec Canada
91 E3 **Maurienne** reg. France
116 C4 **Mauritania** country Africa
117 K7 **Mauritius** is
109 G3 **Mauro, Monte** mt. Italy
88 C3 **Mauron** France
98 C3 **Mauros** mt. Spain
93 E4 **Maurs** France
93 E6 **Maury** France
91 C5 **Maussanne-les-Alpilles** France
148 B4 **Mauston** Wisconsin U.S.A.
81 E3 **Mauterndorf** Austria
81 F3 **Mautern in Steiermark** Austria
81 F2 **Mauthausen** Austria
80 D4 **Mauthen** Austria
93 C5 **Mauvezin** France
92 B2 **Mauzé-sur-le-Mignon** France
124 E3 **Mava** Zaire
127 C7 **Mavago** Mozambique
131 H1 **Mavamba** South Africa
125 C7 **Mavengue** Angola
125 D7 **Mavinga** Angola
114 C3 **Mavrochori** Greece
114 C2 **Mavrommati** Greece
114 E2 **Mavrothalassa** Greece
114 D2 **Mavrovouni** mts Greece
131 F5 **Mavuya** South Africa
36 D3 **Mawana** India
125 C5 **Mawanga** Zaire
33 F2 **Ma Wang Dui** China
25 B5 **Mawdaung Pass** pass Myanmar/Thailand
8 G3 **Mawhai Pt** pt New Zealand
24 B1 **Mawhun** Myanmar
126 D2 **Māwiyah** Yemen
24 B2 **Mawkmai** Myanmar
24 A2 **Mawlaik** Myanmar
Mawlamyine see **Moulmein**
37 G4 **Mawphlang** India
119 H2 **Mawqaq** Saudi Arabia
126 D2 **Mawshij** Yemen
179 D4 **Mawson** Australia Base Antarctica
179 D5 **Mawson Coast** coastal area Antarctica
179 D4 **Mawson Escarpment** escarpment Antarctica
179 B6 **Mawson Pen.** pen. Antarctica
25 B5 **Maw Taung** mt. Myanmar
150 C2 **Max** N. Dakota U.S.A.
126 E4 **Maxaas** Somalia
170 C2 **Maxán** Argentina
157 H4 **Maxcanú** Mexico
87 F4 **Maxéville** France
75 H3 **Maxhütte-Haidhof** Germany
108 A5 **Maxia, Punta** mt. Sardegna Italy
148 D5 **Maxinkuckee, Lake** l. Indiana U.S.A.
56 F3 **Maxmo** Finland
148 F2 **Maxton** Michigan U.S.A.
154 A2 **Maxwell** California U.S.A.
15 E4 **Maxwelton** Queensland Australia
45 P4 **Maya** r. Rus. Fed.
22 B2 **Maya** Indonesia
93 A5 **Maya** Spain
53 F2 **Mayachka** Ukraine
42 E3 **Mayādīn** Syria
159 D2 **Mayaguana** i. The Bahamas
158 D2 **Mayaguana Passage** chan. The Bahamas
145 □3 **Mayagüez** Puerto Rico
123 F4 **Mayahi** Niger
77 L1 **Mayakovskoye** Rus. Fed.
125 B4 **Mayama** Congo
39 C1 **Mayamey** Iran
157 H5 **Maya Mountains** mountain range Belize
32 D1 **Mayan** China
33 E3 **Mayang** China
159 □3 **Mayaro** div. Trinidad Trinidad and Tobago
29 G4 **Maya-san** mt. Japan
66 D5 **Maybole** Scotland U.K.
126 C2 **Maych'ew** Ethiopia
67 E2 **May Corner** Northern Ireland U.K.
52 E1 **Maydakovo** Rus. Fed.
43 D1 **Maydan Ikbis** Turkey
126 C2 **May Darashet'** r. Ethiopia
39 G2 **Maydā Shahr** Afghanistan
159 □1 **May Day Mts** mts Jamaica
126 E2 **Maydh** Somalia
74 C2 **Mayen** Germany
89 E3 **Mayenne** div. Pays de la Loire France
89 E4 **Mayenne** r. France
89 E3 **Mayenne** France
155 F4 **Mayer** Arizona U.S.A.
136 F4 **Mayerthorpe** Alberta Canada
89 F4 **Mayet** France
54 F3 **Mayevo** Rus. Fed.
144 B4 **Mayfield** Kentucky U.S.A.
9 C5 **Mayfield** New Zealand
30 B3 **Mayhan** Mongolia
153 F5 **Mayhill** New Mexico U.S.A.
31 J3 **Mayi** r. China
66 F4 **May, Isle of** i. Scotland U.K.
47 J2 **Maykain** Kazakhstan
47 J3 **Maykamys** Kazakhstan
51 G6 **Maykop** Rus. Fed.
46 F3 **Maylibash** Kazakhstan
47 H4 **Mayly-Say** Kyrgyzstan
47 L2 **Mayma** Rus. Fed.
24 B2 **Maymyo** Myanmar
50 H4 **Mayna** Rus. Fed.
15 E4 **Mayne** watercourse Queensland Australia
38 A2 **Mayni** India
141 G4 **Maynooth** Ontario Canada
67 B3 **Mayo** div. Rep. of Ireland
171 B6 **Mayo** r. Argentina
136 B2 **Mayo** Yukon Terr. Canada
173 G3 **Mayo, 25 de** Buenos Aires Argentina
172 D4 **Mayo, 25 de** La Pampa Argentina
172 C3 **Mayo, 25 de** Mendoza Argentina
173 J3 **Mayo, 25 de** Uruguay
124 B2 **Mayo Alim** Cameroon
23 C5 **Mayo Bay** b. Philippines
123 G5 **Mayo-Belwa** Nigeria
124 B2 **Mayo Darlé** Cameroon
124 B2 **Mayo-Kébbi** div. Chad
124 B4 **Mayoko** Congo
136 B2 **Mayo Lake** l. Yukon Terr. Canada
164 C2 **Mayo Mayo** Bolivia
23 B3 **Mayon** volcano Philippines
99 H4 **Mayor** r. Spain
173 F5 **Mayor Buratovich** Argentina
99 G1 **Mayor, Cabo** c. Spain
99 E2 **Mayorga** Spain
8 F2 **Mayor I.** i. New Zealand
159 □3 **Mayoro Bay** b. Trinidad Trinidad and Tobago
165 D3 **Mayor Pablo Lagerenza** Paraguay
117 J7 **Mayotte** i. Africa
159 □1 **May Pen** Jamaica
23 B2 **Mayraira Point** pt Philippines
91 C4 **Mayres** France
80 C3 **Mayrhofen** Austria
42 F4 **Maysān** div. Iraq
69 F4 **Mayschoß** Germany
52 H1 **Mayskiy** Rus. Fed.
53 G1 **Mayskiy** Rus. Fed.
27 N1 **Mayskiy** Rus. Fed.
146 B5 **Maysville** Kentucky U.S.A.
125 B4 **Mayumba** Gabon
37 E3 **Mayum La** pass China
38 B4 **Mayuram** India
149 F4 **Mayville** Michigan U.S.A.
150 D2 **Mayville** N. Dakota U.S.A.
146 D3 **Mayville** New York U.S.A.
148 C4 **Mayville** Wisconsin U.S.A.
150 C3 **Maywood** Nebraska U.S.A.
45 P3 **Mayya** Rus. Fed.
173 F4 **Maza** Argentina
125 E7 **Mazabuka** Zambia
166 B1 **Mazagão** Brazil
100 D3 **Mazagón** Spain
86 D3 **Mazagran** France
86 E5 **Mazamet** France
39 B1 **Māzandarān** div. Iran
36 D1 **Mazar** China
43 C4 **Mazār** Jordan
110 B5 **Mazara del Vallo** Sicilia Italy
39 F1 **Mazār-e Sharīf** Afghanistan
99 H4 **Mazarete** Spain
171 C6 **Mazarredo** Argentina
103 B7 **Mazarrón** Spain
103 B7 **Mazarrón, Golfo de** b. Spain
163 F2 **Mazaruni** r. Guyana
47 K5 **Mazartagh** mt. China
156 C2 **Mazatán** Mexico
157 H6 **Mazatenango** Guatemala
156 D4 **Mazatlán** Mexico
155 G4 **Mazatzal Peak** summit Arizona U.S.A.
131 G6 **Mazeepa Bay** South Africa
54 C3 **Mažeikiai** Lithuania
123 F3 **Mazelet** well Niger
131 F4 **Mazelspoort** l. South Africa
93 D4 **Mazeyrolles** France
46 D3 **Mazhambet** Kazakhstan
113 F6 **Mazı** Turkey
92 B2 **Mazières-en-Gâtine** France
131 J2 **Mazimechopes** r. Mozambique
54 C3 **Mazirbe** Latvia
156 C2 **Mazocahui** Mexico
164 C3 **Mazocruz** Peru
127 C6 **Mazomora** Tanzania
129 E2 **Mazowe** r. Zimbabwe
43 C4 **Mazra** Jordan
119 E5 **Mazrub** well Sudan
54 D3 **Mazsalaca** Latvia
114 C1 **Mažučište** Macedonia
129 D3 **Mazunga** Zimbabwe
77 K1 **Mazurskii Kanal** canal Poland/Rus. Fed.
77 K2 **Mazurskii Park Narodowy** nat. park Poland
51 D4 **Mazyr** Belarus
110 D5 **Mazzarino** Sicilia Italy
110 D5 **Mazzarrone** Sicilia Italy
131 H3 **Mbabane** Swaziland
122 A4 **Mbacké** Senegal
122 D5 **Mbahiakro** Côte d'Ivoire
124 C3 **Mbaïki** Central African Rep.
124 B2 **Mbakaou, Lac de** l. Cameroon
127 B6 **Mbala** Zambia
129 D3 **Mbalabala** Zimbabwe
124 B3 **Mbalam** Cameroon
127 B4 **Mbale** Uganda
124 B3 **Mbalmayo** Cameroon
124 B2 **Mbam** r. Cameroon
127 B7 **Mbamba Bay** Tanzania
124 C4 **Mbandaka** Zaire
124 B3 **Mbanga** Cameroon
124 A3 **Mbanga** Cameroon
125 B5 **M'banza Congo** Angola
125 B5 **Mbanza-Ngungu** Zaire
127 B5 **Mbarara** Uganda
124 D3 **Mbari** r. Central African Rep.
127 C6 **Mbarika Mountains** mts Tanzania
131 J3 **Mbaswana** South Africa
124 C3 **Mbata** Central African Rep.
127 B7 **Mbati** Zambia
122 D5 **Mbatto** Côte d'Ivoire
124 B2 **Mbé** Cameroon
127 C6 **Mbemkuru** r. Tanzania
124 B2 **Mbengwi** Cameroon
122 C4 **Mbenqué** Côte d'Ivoire
129 D3 **Mberengwa** Zimbabwe
127 B6 **Mbeya** div. Tanzania
127 B6 **Mbeya** Tanzania
124 C3 **Mbi** r. Central African Rep.
124 B4 **Mbigou** Gabon
124 A4 **Mbilapé** Gabon
124 B4 **Mbinda** Congo
127 C7 **Mbinga** Tanzania
124 A3 **Mbini** Equatorial Guinea
129 E3 **Mbizi** Zimbabwe
127 B6 **Mbizi Mts** mts Tanzania
124 E2 **Mboki** Central African Rep.
124 B3 **Mbomo** Congo
124 D2 **Mbomou** div. Central African Rep.
124 D3 **Mbomou** r. Central African Rep.
114 B2 **Mborje** Albania
122 A3 **Mboro** Senegal
124 B2 **Mbouda** Cameroon
122 A4 **Mbour** Senegal
120 B5 **Mbout** Mauritania
124 C2 **Mbrès** Central African Rep.
125 D5 **Mbuji-Mayi** Zaire
127 C5 **Mbulu** Tanzania
131 H3 **Mbuluzi** r. Swaziland
127 C6 **Mbuyuni** Tanzania
134 H2 **Mc Clintock Channel** chan. N.W.T. Canada
120 D3 **Mcherrah** reg. Algeria
127 C6 **Mchinga** Tanzania
127 B7 **Mchinji** Malawi
134 A3 **M. Chukotskiy** c. Rus. Fed.
127 B6 **Mdandu** Tanzania
131 F6 **Mdantsane** South Africa
121 F1 **M'Daourouch** Algeria
120 C4 **Mdennah** reg. Mali/Mauritania
134 A3 **M. Dezhneva** c. Rus. Fed.
111 □ **Mdina** Malta
101 E5 **Mdiq** Morocco
140 D2 **Mead** Ontario Canada
151 C4 **Meade** Kansas U.S.A.
83 B1 **Meadela** Portugal
155 E3 **Mead, Lake** l. Arizona/Nevada U.S.A.
155 E4 **Mead Nat. Rec. Area, L.** res. Arizona U.S.A.
137 H4 **Meadow Lake** Saskatchewan Canada
137 H4 **Meadow Lake Provincial Park** nat. park Saskatchewan Canada
155 E3 **Meadow Valley Wash** r. Nevada U.S.A.
146 C4 **Meadville** Pennsylvania U.S.A.
140 E4 **Meaford** Ontario Canada
28 K2 **Meaken-dake** volcano Japan
66 A2 **Mealasta Island** i. Scotland U.K.
98 B4 **Mealhada** Portugal
66 D4 **Meall a'Bhuiridh** mt. Scotland U.K.
139 J3 **Mealy Mountains** mountain range Newfoundland Canada
39 E1 **Meana** Turkmenistan
108 B5 **Meana Sardo** Sardegna Italy
15 G5 **Meandarra** Queensland Australia
136 F3 **Meander River** Alberta Canada
23 C5 **Meares** i. Indonesia
166 D1 **Mearim** r. Brazil
63 E2 **Mease** r. England U.K.
63 E2 **Measham** England U.K.
67 E3 **Meath** div. Rep. of Ireland
92 E2 **Meaulne** France
86 B4 **Meaux** France
125 B5 **Mebridege** r. Angola
Mecca see **Makkah**
147 H2 **Mechanic Falls** Maine U.S.A.
146 B4 **Mechanicsburg** Ohio U.S.A.
148 B5 **Mechanicsville** Iowa U.S.A.
69 C3 **Mechelen** div. Antwerpen Belgium
69 C3 **Mechelen** Mechelen Belgium
121 D2 **Mecheria** Algeria
74 B2 **Mechernich** Germany
118 C5 **Mechiméré** Chad
173 H5 **Mechongue** Argentina
73 L2 **Mechowo** Poland
113 F4 **Mecidiye** Turkey
75 J3 **Měčín** Czech Rep.
101 G4 **Mecina-Bombarón** Spain
42 C1 **Mecitözü** Turkey
74 E5 **Meckenbeuren** Germany
74 C2 **Meckenheim** Germany
73 G1 **Mecklenburger Bucht** b. Germany
73 G2 **Mecklenburgische Seenplatte** reg. Germany
73 H2 **Mecklenburg-Vorpommern** div. Germany
129 F1 **Meconta** Mozambique
129 F1 **Mecubúri** r. Mozambique
129 F1 **Mecubúri** Mozambique
127 C7 **Mecula** Mozambique
98 C2 **Meda** mt. Spain
16 D3 **Meda** r. Western Australia Australia

98 C4 Meda Portugal
38 B2 Medak India
22 D4 Medang i. Indonesia
20 C6 Medan Indonesia
170 C3 Medano Argentina
173 H2 Médanos *Entre Ríos* Argentina
173 F5 Médanos Argentina
171 C6 Medanosa, Pta pt Argentina
162 D1 Médanos de Coro, Parque Nacional nat. park Venezuela
38 C4 Medawachchiya Sri Lanka
38 B2 Medchal India
147 K2 Meddybemps L. l. *Maine* U.S.A.
106 C3 Mede Italy
121 E1 Médéa Algeria
72 D4 Medebach Germany
169 H2 Medeiros Neto Brazil
98 C4 Medelim Portugal
162 B2 Medellín Colombia
68 D2 Medemblik Netherlands
63 E1 Meden r. *England* U.K.
121 G2 Medenine Tunisia
77 M6 Medenychi Ukraine
120 A5 Mederdra Mauritania
43 C1 Medetsiz T. mt. Turkey
152 B3 Medford *Oregon* U.S.A.
148 B3 Medford *Wisconsin* U.S.A.
147 F5 Medford Farms *New Jersey* U.S.A.
112 G2 Medgidia Romania
148 B5 Media *Illinois* U.S.A.
172 D3 Media Luna Argentina
102 C3 Mediana Spain
101 J4 Media Naranja, Pta de la headland Spain
168 A6 Medianeira Brazil
112 E1 Mediaş Romania
152 C2 Medical Lake *Washington* U.S.A.
107 F4 Medicina Italy
152 F3 Medicine Bow *Wyoming* U.S.A.
152 F3 Medicine Bow Mts mountain range *Wyoming* U.S.A.
152 F3 Medicine Bow Peak summit *Wyoming* U.S.A.
137 G4 Medicine Hat *Alberta* Canada
151 D4 Medicine Lodge *Kansas* U.S.A.
146 D3 Medina *New York* U.S.A.
146 C4 Medina *Ohio* U.S.A.
169 H2 Medina Brazil
Medina *see* Al Madīnah
99 H3 Medinaceli Spain
99 F3 Medina del Campo Spain
99 G2 Medina de Pomar Spain
99 E3 Medina de Rioseco Spain
122 B4 Médina Gounas Senegal
122 A4 Médina Sabakh Senegal
100 E4 Medina-Sidonia Spain
127 □4 Medine Mauritius
37 F5 Medinīpur India
92 B3 Médis France
94 D4 Mediterranean Sea sea
105 A7 Medjerda, Monts de la mts Algeria
46 E2 Mednogorsk Rus. Fed.
52 B1 Mednoye Rus. Fed.
176 G2 Mednyy, Ostrov i. Rus. Fed.
92 B3 Médoc reg. France
124 B3 Médouneu Gabon
77 J1 Medovoye Rus. Fed.
172 C2 Medrano Argentina
Medu Kongkar *see* Maizhokunggar
107 H4 Medulin Croatia
78 F5 Medumurje reg. Croatia
107 G3 Meduna r. Italy
80 D4 Meduno Italy
112 C3 Medveđa Yugoslavia
52 H1 Medvedevo Rus. Fed.
52 C1 Medveditsa r. Rus. Fed.
52 G3 Medveditsa r. Rus. Fed.
78 E6 Medvednica mts Croatia
50 J3 Medvedok Rus. Fed.
53 G1 Medvenka Rus. Fed.
45 S2 Medvezh'i, O-va is Rus. Fed.
50 E2 Medvezh'yegorsk Rus. Fed.
81 F4 Medvode Slovenia
63 G3 Medway r. *England* U.K.
10 □2 Medwin Pt pt *Christmas I.* Indian Ocean
52 H2 Medyana Rus. Fed.
77 L6 Medyka Poland
52 B2 Medyn' Rus. Fed.
53 B2 Medzhybizh Ukraine
79 L2 Medzilaborce Slovakia
17 A5 Meeberrie *Western Australia* Australia
68 E1 Meeden Netherlands
17 B5 Meekatharra *Western Australia* Australia
155 H1 Meeker *Colorado* U.S.A.
154 B2 Meeks Bay *California* U.S.A.
139 J4 Meelpaeg Res. resr *Newfoundland* Canada
64 A3 Meenanarwa Rep. of Ireland
75 H2 Meerane Germany
54 E2 Meerapalu Estonia
72 B4 Meerbusch Germany
69 D3 Meerhout Belgium
68 C3 Meerkerk Netherlands
74 E5 Meersburg Germany
69 D4 Meerssen Netherlands
36 D3 Meerut India
152 E2 Meeteetse *Wyoming* U.S.A.
69 D3 Meeuwen Belgium
126 C4 Mēga Ethiopia
126 C4 Mega Escarpment escarpment Ethiopia/Kenya
114 C3 Megala Kalyvia Greece
114 E2 Megali Panagia Greece
126 D3 Megalo Ethiopia
114 C3 Megalochori Greece
115 D5 Megalopoli Greece
114 B4 Meganisi i. Greece
147 H2 Mégantic, Lac l. *Québec* Canada
115 E5 Megara Greece
30 B1 Meget Rus. Fed.
82 B3 Megève France
37 G4 Meghalaya India
37 F5 Meghāsani India
43 C3 Megiddo Armageddon Israel
56 G1 Mehamn Norway
36 A4 Mehar Pakistan
17 B4 Meharry, Mt mt. *Western Australia* Australia
59 G1 Mehedeby Sweden
36 D5 Mehekar India
37 G5 Meherpur Bangladesh
146 E6 Meherrin r. *Virginia* U.S.A.
7 □10 Mehetia i. *French Polynesia* Pacific Ocean
37 E4 Mehndawal India
42 F2 Mehrābān Iran
39 C4 Mehrān watercourse Iran
42 F3 Mehrān Iraq
74 B2 Mehren Germany
74 B3 Mehring Germany
39 C3 Mehriz Iran
39 G2 Mehtar Lām Afghanistan
89 H4 Mehun-sur-Yèvre France
33 F3 Mei r. China
168 D3 Meia Ponte r. Brazil
124 B2 Meiganga Cameroon
64 B3 Meigh *Northern Ireland* U.K.
135 J2 Meighen I. i. *N.W.T.* Canada
32 C2 Meigu China
69 D3 Meijel Netherlands
91 E3 Meije, La mt. France
69 D3 Meijnweg, Nationaal Park De Netherlands
65 E1 Meikleour *Scotland* U.K.
65 F2 Meikle Says Law h. *Scotland* U.K.
24 A2 Meiktila Myanmar
83 D1 Meilen Switzerland
93 B5 Meilhan France
93 C4 Meilhan-sur-Garonne France
88 D3 Meillac France
90 E2 Meillerie France
Meilü *see* Wuchuan
98 C4 Meimoa Portugal
106 C3 Meina Italy
73 F3 Meine Germany
72 F3 Meinersen Germany
74 F2 Meiningen Germany
98 C1 Meira Spain
98 C1 Meira, Serra de mountain range Spain
82 D2 Meiringen Switzerland
74 C3 Meisenheim Germany
32 C2 Meishan China
73 J4 Meißen Germany
87 G4 Meißenheim Germany
32 D3 Meitan China
75 F4 Meitingen Germany
69 D5 Meix-devant-Virton Belgium
31 J3 Meixi China
32 D1 Mei Xian China
Mei Xian *see* Meizhou
33 G3 Meizhou China
36 C4 Mej r. India
120 C4 Mejaouda well Mauritania
170 C2 Mejicana mt. Argentina
164 B4 Mejillones Chile
164 B4 Mejillones del Sur, B. de b. Chile
172 E6 Mejillón, Punta pt Argentina
119 G4 Mekadio well Sudan
124 B3 Mékambo Gabon
126 C2 Mek'elē Ethiopia
122 A3 Mékhé Senegal
36 B3 Mekhtar Pakistan
81 F4 Mekinje Slovenia
120 C2 Meknès Morocco
Mekong r. *see* Mènam Khong
25 D5 Mekong, Mouths of the river mouth Vietnam
107 G2 Mel Italy
172 B3 Melado r. Chile
25 C7 Melaka div. Malaysia
25 C7 Melaka Malaysia
129 F2 Melala r. Mozambique
22 A2 Melalo, Tg pt Indonesia
115 F7 Melambes Greece
176 F6 Melanesia is Pacific Ocean
114 C2 Melanthi Greece
22 C2 Melawi r. Indonesia
82 A1 Melay France
63 G2 Melbourn *England* U.K.
145 D6 Melbourne *Florida* U.S.A.
13 F4 Melbourne *Victoria* Australia
66 □2 Melby *Scotland* U.K.
157 H5 Melchor de Mencos Guatemala
171 B6 Melchor, I. i. Chile
107 G4 Meldola Italy
72 E1 Meldorf Germany
140 D4 Meldrum Bay *Ontario* Canada
106 C4 Mele Italy
106 C5 Mele, Capo pt Italy
106 D3 Melegnano Italy
23 □1 Melekeiok Palau
52 E1 Melekhovo Rus. Fed.
111 H2 Melendugno Italy
52 E2 Melenki Rus. Fed.
88 D3 Melesse France
46 E2 Meleuz Rus. Fed.
124 C1 Mélfi Chad
109 H4 Melfi Italy
137 J4 Melfort *Saskatchewan* Canada
166 B1 Melgaço Brazil
98 B2 Melgaço Portugal
101 G1 Melgar r. Spain
99 F2 Melgar de Fernamental Spain
98 D3 Melgar de Tera Spain
88 B4 Melgven France
56 C3 Melhus Norway
22 B2 Meliau Indonesia
69 E3 Melick Netherlands
98 C2 Melide Spain
80 B2 Melides Portugal
115 C5 Meligalas Greece
114 D2 Meliki Greece
168 D6 Mel, Ilha do i. Brazil
121 D1 Melilla Spain
111 E5 Melilli *Sicilia* Italy
171 B5 Melimoyu, Mte mt. Chile
9 B6 Melina, Mt mt. New Zealand
173 G2 Melincué Argentina
173 G2 Melincué, L. l. Argentina
53 F2 Melioratyvne Ukraine
172 B5 Melipeuco Chile
172 B2 Melipilla Chile
90 E1 Mélisey France
137 J5 Melita *Manitoba* Canada
114 C2 Meliti Greece
111 E5 Melito di Porto Salvo Italy
53 F3 Melitopol' Ukraine
114 D3 Melivoia Greece
81 G2 Melk div. Austria
81 G2 Melk r. Austria
81 G2 Melk Austria
126 C4 Melka Guba Ethiopia
130 A4 Melkbospunt pt South Africa
130 B6 Melkbosstrand South Africa
47 H3 Melkosopochnik reg. Kazakhstan
131 G1 Melkrivier South Africa
63 D3 Melksham *England* U.K.
106 E3 Mella r. Italy
88 B4 Mellac France
56 G2 Mellakoski Finland
59 E2 Mellan Fryken l. Sweden
56 E3 Mellansel Sweden
58 B2 Melle France
72 D3 Melle Germany
148 B2 Mellen *Wisconsin* U.S.A.
59 E2 Mellerud Sweden
111 □ Mellieha Malta
111 □ Mellieha Bay b. Malta
54 C1 Mellilä Finland
171 B6 Mellizo Sur, C. mt. Chile
120 B5 Mellousa Morocco
74 F2 Mellrichstadt Germany
72 D2 Mellum i. Germany
118 C5 Melmele watercourse Chad
131 H4 Melmoth South Africa
114 D1 Melnik Bulgaria
78 D1 Mělník Czech Rep.
54 F1 Mel'nikovo Rus. Fed.
172 F3 Melo Argentina
173 K2 Melo Uruguay
127 C7 Meloco Mozambique
131 F4 Meloding South Africa
50 H1 Melogorskoye Rus. Fed.
22 E4 Melolo Indonesia
124 A2 Mélong Cameroon
66 F5 Melrose *Scotland* U.K.
83 E1 Mels Switzerland
87 G2 Melsbach Germany
72 E4 Melsungen Germany
23 A5 Melta, Mt mt. Malaysia
65 G4 Meltham *England* U.K.
63 F2 Melton Mowbray *England* U.K.
52 G2 Mel'tsany Rus. Fed.
22 B1 Meluan Malaysia
127 C7 Meluco Mozambique
86 B4 Melun France
126 B2 Melut Sudan
137 J4 Melville *Saskatchewan* Canada
14 D2 Melville B. b. *Northern Terr.* Australia
135 M2 Melville Bugt b. Greenland
15 F2 Melville, C. c. *Queensland* Australia
23 A5 Melville, C. c. Philippines
14 B1 Melville I. i. *Northern Terr.* Australia
14 B1 Melville I. Abor. Land res. *Northern Terr.* Australia
134 G2 Melville Island i. *N.W.T.* Canada
139 J3 Melville, Lake l. *Newfoundland* Canada
135 K3 Melville Peninsula pen. *N.W.T.* Canada
67 C2 Melvin, Lough l. Rep. of Ireland
79 J5 Mélykút Hungary
45 T3 Melyuveyem Rus. Fed.
106 D3 Melzo Italy
114 A2 Memaliaj Albania
37 E2 Mêmar Co salt lake China
129 G1 Memba Mozambique
129 G1 Memba, Baia de b. Mozambique
21 L7 Memberamo r. Indonesia
22 D4 Memboro Indonesia
90 D1 Membrey France
100 C1 Membrio Spain
131 G3 Memel South Africa
54 D3 Mēmele r. Lithuania
73 F3 Memmelsdorf Germany
74 F5 Memmingen Germany
80 B3 Memmingerberg Germany
86 D3 Mémorial Américain h. France
22 B1 Mempawah Indonesia
148 A5 Memphis *Missouri* U.S.A.
145 B5 Memphis *Tennessee* U.S.A.
151 C5 Memphis *Texas* U.S.A.
119 F2 Memphis Egypt
141 J4 Memphrémagog, Lac l. *Québec* Canada
28 J2 Memuro-dake mt. Japan
151 E5 Mena *Arkansas* U.S.A.
53 E1 Mena Ukraine
129 G3 Menabe mts Madagascar
173 J2 Menafra Uruguay
106 D2 Menaggio Italy
83 G3 Menago r. Italy
62 B1 Menai Bridge *Wales* U.K.
62 B1 Menai Strait chan. *Wales* U.K.
123 E3 Ménaka Mali
68 D1 Menaldum Netherlands
24 C3 Mènam Khong r. Asia
129 G4 Menarandra r. Madagascar
151 D6 Menard *Texas* U.S.A.
71 E5 Menasalbas Spain
148 C3 Menasha *Wisconsin* U.S.A.
92 E2 Menat France
87 E4 Menaucourt France
101 G3 Mencal mt. Spain
22 A4 Mendanau i. Indonesia
169 G3 Mendanha Brazil
22 A1 Mendarik i. Indonesia
102 B1 Mendaur mt. Spain
22 C2 Mendawai r. Indonesia
22 C2 Mendawai Indonesia
91 B4 Mende France
126 C3 Mendebo Mountains mountain range Ethiopia
136 C3 Mendenhall Glacier gl. *Alaska* U.S.A.
114 D4 Mendenitsa Greece
72 C4 Menden (Sauerland) Germany
113 F5 Menderes Turkey
157 F3 Méndez Mexico
126 C3 Mendī Ethiopia
6 □1 Mendi P.N.G.
74 C2 Mendig Germany
62 D3 Mendip Hills h. *England* U.K.
93 B5 Menditte France
173 K2 Mendizabal Uruguay
154 A2 Mendocino *California* U.S.A.
152 A3 Mendocino, C. c. *California* U.S.A.
177 K3 Mendocino Seascarp sea feature Pacific Ocean
111 C5 Mendola r. *Sicilia* Italy
148 E4 Mendon *Michigan* U.S.A.
154 B3 Mendota *California* U.S.A.
148 C5 Mendota *Illinois* U.S.A.
148 C4 Mendota, Lake l. *Wisconsin* U.S.A.
172 C3 Mendoza div. Argentina
172 C2 Mendoza r. Argentina
172 C2 Mendoza Argentina
83 D3 Mendrisio Switzerland
88 C3 Ménéac France
162 C1 Mene de Mauroa Venezuela
106 D4 Menegosa, Monte mt. Italy
162 C2 Mene Grande Venezuela
42 A2 Menemen Turkey
69 B4 Menen Belgium
92 C3 Ménesplet France
92 E3 Menet France
89 H4 Menetou-Salon France
88 B3 Menez Bré h. France
88 A3 Menez Hom h. France
110 B5 Menfi *Sicilia* Italy
124 B2 Meng r. Cameroon
33 G1 Mengcheng China
74 E4 Mengen Germany
51 E7 Mengen Turkey
87 H2 Mengerskirchen Germany
81 F4 Mengeš Slovenia
22 A3 Menggala Indonesia
32 C4 Menghai China
101 G3 Mengíbar Spain
22 C2 Mengkatip Indonesia
80 D2 Mengkofen Germany
22 E2 Mengkoka, G. mt. Indonesia
32 C4 Mengla China
32 B4 Menglian China
33 E3 Mengshan China
31 F6 Mengyin China
32 C4 Mengzi China
62 B4 Menheniot *England* U.K.
114 C3 Menidi Greece
92 B2 Ménigoute France
139 G3 Menihek *Newfoundland* Canada
139 G3 Menihek Lakes lakes *Newfoundland* Canada
87 E4 Ménil-la-Tour France
87 F4 Ménil-sur-Belvitte France
Menin *see* Menen
13 E3 Menindee *New South Wales* Australia
13 E3 Menindee L. l. *New South Wales* Australia
12 D3 Meningie *S. Australia* Australia
45 O3 Menkere Rus. Fed.
112 B2 Menkulas Albania
126 C2 Menna r. Ethiopia
86 B4 Mennecy France
89 G4 Mennetou-sur-Cher France
114 E1 Menoikio mts Greece
148 D3 Menominee r. *Wisconsin* U.S.A.
148 D3 Menominee *Michigan* U.S.A.
148 C4 Menomonee Falls *Wisconsin* U.S.A.
148 B3 Menomonie *Wisconsin* U.S.A.
125 C6 Menongue Angola
103 □ Menorca airport Spain
103 □ Menorca i. *Islas Baleares* Spain
90 B1 Menou France
91 D4 Mens France
23 A6 Mensalong Indonesia
92 C3 Mensignac France
72 C3 Menslage Germany
109 E2 Mentana Italy
22 C2 Mentaya r. Indonesia
25 C7 Mentekab Malaysia
73 F4 Menteroda Germany
100 C2 Menteras h. Portugal
101 H2 Menteras mt. Spain
155 H4 Mentmore *New Mexico* U.S.A.
22 A2 Mentok Indonesia
91 F5 Menton France
146 C4 Mentor *Ohio* U.S.A.
99 F4 Méntrida Spain
22 C2 Menukung Indonesia
22 E1 Menunu Indonesia
52 D2 Menyaka Rus. Fed.
22 D1 Menyapa, G. mt. Indonesia
30 B5 Menyuan China
30 D2 Menza r. Rus. Fed.
30 D2 Menza Rus. Fed.
121 F1 Menzel Bourguiba Tunisia
105 C7 Menzel Temime Tunisia
17 C6 Menzies *Western Australia* Australia
179 D4 Menzies, Mt mt. Antarctica
82 D1 Menznau Switzerland
92 D2 Méobecq France
107 G3 Meolo Italy
156 D2 Meoqui Mexico
127 B7 Meponda Mozambique
68 E2 Meppel Netherlands
72 C3 Meppen Germany
131 F4 Meqheleng South Africa
102 D3 Mequinenza Spain
89 G4 Mer France
106 D2 Mera r. Italy
50 G3 Mera r. Rus. Fed.
107 J4 Merag Croatia
22 D1 Merah Indonesia
22 A3 Merak Indonesia
56 C3 Meråker Norway
150 F4 Meramec r. *Missouri* U.S.A.
107 F2 Merano Italy
106 D3 Merate Italy
128 C3 Meratswe r. Botswana
21 M8 Merauke Indonesia
13 E3 Merbein *Victoria* Australia
69 C4 Merbes-le-Château Belgium
103 □ Mercadal Spain
91 E4 Mercantour, Parc National du nat. park France
107 G5 Mercatino Conca Italy
109 G4 Mercato San Severino Italy
154 B3 Merced *California* U.S.A.
172 B1 Mercedario, Co mt. Argentina
173 H3 Mercedes *Buenos Aires* Argentina
172 E2 Mercedes *San Luis* Argentina
170 E2 Mercedes Argentina
173 H2 Mercedes Uruguay
146 A4 Mercer *Ohio* U.S.A.
148 B2 Mercer *Wisconsin* U.S.A.
169 G4 Mercês Brazil
75 F4 Merching Germany
69 C4 Merchtem Belgium
43 C1 Mercimek Turkey
136 F4 Mercoal *Alberta* Canada
92 D3 Mercœur France
109 G4 Mercogliano Italy
82 B3 Mercury France
8 E2 Mercury Islands is New Zealand
135 M3 Mercy, C. headland *N.W.T.* Canada
88 A3 Mer d'Iroise g. France
88 C3 Merdrignac France
62 D3 Mere *England* U.K.
69 B4 Mere Belgium
89 H4 Méreau France
147 H3 Meredith *New Hampshire* U.S.A.
171 D7 Meredith, C. c. Falkland Is.
151 C5 Meredith, Lake l. *Texas* U.S.A.
151 C5 Meredith Nat. Recreation Area, Lake res. *Texas* U.S.A.
148 B6 Meredosia *Illinois* U.S.A.
121 E3 Meredoua Algeria
53 G2 Merefa Ukraine
6 □2 Mere Lava i. Vanuatu
69 B4 Merelbeke Belgium
74 D2 Merenberg Germany
93 D6 Mérens-les-Vals France
86 B4 Méréville France
118 E4 Merga Oasis oasis Sudan
106 C3 Mergozzo Italy
25 B4 Mergui Myanmar
25 B5 Mergui Archipelago is Myanmar
12 E3 Meribah *S. Australia* Australia
91 E3 Méribel-les-Allues France
113 F4 Meriç r. Greece/Turkey
113 F4 Meriç Turkey
115 F5 Merichas Greece
157 H4 Mérida Mexico
100 D2 Mérida Spain
162 C2 Mérida Venezuela
162 C2 Mérida, Cordillera de mountain range Venezuela
147 G4 Meriden *Connecticut* U.S.A.
154 B2 Meridian *California* U.S.A.
145 B5 Meridian *Mississippi* U.S.A.
151 F5 Meridian *Mississippi* U.S.A.
170 D4 Meridiano Argentina
120 D2 Mèridja Algeria
6 □2 Merig i. Vanuatu
93 B4 Mérignac France
56 G2 Merijärvi Finland
57 F3 Merikarvia Finland
15 G4 Merinda *Queensland* Australia
91 D5 Mérindol France
75 F4 Mering Germany
12 E3 Meringur *Victoria* Australia
163 G3 Merirumã Brazil
15 G5 Merivale r. *Queensland* Australia
23 □2 Merizo *Guam* Pacific Ocean
47 H4 Merke Kazakhstan
151 C5 Merkel *Texas* U.S.A.
75 F3 Merkendorf Germany
77 N1 Merkinė Lithuania
75 J3 Merklín Czech Rep.
80 A2 Merklingen Germany
69 C3 Merksplas Belgium
54 D4 Merkys r. Lithuania
89 G1 Merl-les-Bains France
88 B4 Merlevenez France
25 □ Merlimau, P. i. Singapore
53 F1 Merlo r. Ukraine
172 E1 Merlo Argentina
15 E2 Merluna *Queensland* Australia
16 B3 Mermaid Reef reef *Western Australia* Australia
79 G5 Mernye Hungary
98 B1 Mero r. Spain
112 C3 Merošina Yugoslavia
119 F4 Merowe Sudan
17 B6 Merredin *Western Australia* Australia
66 D5 Merrick h. *Scotland* U.K.
141 H4 Merrickville *Ontario* Canada
148 C3 Merrill *Wisconsin* U.S.A.
148 D5 Merrillville *Indiana* U.S.A.
150 C3 Merriman *Nebraska* U.S.A.
130 D5 Merriman South Africa
62 D4 Merriott *England* U.K.
136 E4 Merritt *B.C.* Canada
145 D6 Merritt Island *Florida* U.S.A.
13 G2 Merrygoen *New South Wales* Australia
126 D2 Mersa Fatma Eritrea
69 E5 Mersch Luxembourg
108 D1 Merse r. Italy
73 G4 Merseburg Germany
65 F4 Mersey est. *England* U.K.
65 E4 Merseyside div. *England* U.K.
Mersin *see* İçel
25 C7 Mersing Malaysia
54 C3 Mērsrags Latvia
36 C4 Merta India
109 F3 Merta, la mt. Italy
69 E5 Mertert Luxembourg
62 C3 Merthyr Tydfil div. *Wales* U.K.
62 C3 Merthyr Tydfil *Wales* U.K.
127 C4 Merti Kenya
80 B2 Mertingen Germany
100 C3 Mértola Portugal
179 B6 Mertz Gl. gl. Antarctica
87 G4 Mertzwiller France
127 C5 Meru crater Tanzania
86 B3 Méru France
127 C4 Meru Kenya
39 E3 Merui Pakistan
23 A5 Merutai Malaysia
Merv *see* Mary
90 D2 Mervans France
86 B2 Merville France
130 C6 Merweville South Africa
86 C4 Méry-sur-Seine France
82 C1 Merzhausen Germany
42 C1 Merzifon Turkey
74 B3 Merzig Germany
179 B2 Merz Pen. pen. Antarctica
102 A3 Mesa r. Spain
155 G5 Mesa *Arizona* U.S.A.
131 F3 Mesa South Africa
148 A2 Mesabi Range h. *Minnesota* U.S.A.
162 C3 Mesa de Iguaje h. Colombia
99 G5 Mesa de Ocaña reg. Spain
153 D6 Mesa de S. Carlos h. Mexico
162 C3 Mesa de Yambi h. Colombia
111 G2 Mesagne Italy
115 E5 Mesagros Greece
115 □ Mesanagros Greece
22 A1 Mesanak i. Indonesia
88 D4 Mésanger France
98 C3 Mesão Frio Portugal
155 H3 Mesa Verde Nat. Park nat. park *Colorado* U.S.A.
171 C5 Mesa Volcánica de Somuncurá plat. Argentina
72 D4 Meschede Germany
56 E2 Meselefors Sweden
172 C6 Meseta de Colitoro plat. Argentina
163 E2 Meseta del Co Jáua plat. Venezuela
171 C5 Meseta de Montemayor plat. Argentina
126 C2 Mesfinto Ethiopia
138 F3 Mesgouez L. l. *Québec* Canada
86 C4 Mesgrigny France
52 D2 Meshcherskaya Nizmennost' lowland Rus. Fed.
52 B2 Meshchovsk Rus. Fed.
50 J2 Meshchura Rus. Fed.
Meshed *see* Mashhad
39 D1 Meshkān Iran
124 E2 Meshra'er Req Sudan
148 E3 Mesick *Michigan* U.S.A.
104 F4 Mesihovina Bos.-Herz.
111 F4 Mesima r. Italy
114 E2 Mesimeri Greece
120 D2 Meski Morocco
89 E4 Meslay-du-Maine France
82 A2 Mesnay France
83 E2 Mesocco Switzerland
114 C3 Mesochora Greece
107 G4 Mesola Italy
115 C4 Mesolongi Greece
98 B1 Mesón do Vento Spain
114 A3 Mesongi Greece
42 E3 Mesopotamia reg. Iraq
114 C2 Mesopotamia Greece
114 B3 Mesopotamo Greece
111 F3 Mesoraca Italy
169 G3 Mesquita Brazil
155 E3 Mesquite *Nevada* U.S.A.
151 D5 Mesquite *Texas* U.S.A.
155 E4 Mesquite Lake l. *California* U.S.A.
121 E2 Messaad Algeria
88 D4 Messac France
118 B2 Messak Mellet h. Libya
127 C7 Messalo r. Mozambique
73 G3 Meßdorf Germany
89 E3 Messei France
110 D5 Messina div. *Sicilia* Italy
111 E4 Messina *Sicilia* Italy
131 H1 Messina South Africa
87 E3 Messincourt France
141 G3 Messines *Québec* Canada
115 D5 Messini Greece
115 C5 Messinia div. Greece
115 D6 Messiniakos Kolpos b. Greece
74 E5 Meßkirch Germany
74 D4 Meßstetten Germany
114 E1 Mesta r. Bulgaria
101 H2 Mesta r. Spain
75 L2 Městec Králové Czech Rep.
135 Q2 Mesters Vig Greenland
73 G2 Mestlin Germany
79 G1 Město Albrechtice Czech Rep.
107 G3 Mestre Italy
22 A2 Mesuji r. Indonesia
92 E1 Mesves-sur-Loire France
90 C2 Mesvres France
90 C2 Mesvrin r. France
162 D2 Meta r. Colombia/Venezuela
141 K2 Métabetchouan *Québec* Canada
90 E2 Métabief France
140 E3 Metagama *Ontario* Canada
114 E2 Metagkitsi Greece
135 L3 Meta Incognita Pen. pen. *N.W.T.* Canada
151 F6 Metairie *Louisiana* U.S.A.
148 C5 Metamora *Illinois* U.S.A.
170 D2 Metán Argentina
22 C2 Metangai Indonesia
127 B7 Metangula Mozambique
129 F1 Metarica Mozambique
107 G5 Metauro r. Italy
68 F2 Metelen Germany
126 C2 Metema Ethiopia
114 C3 Meteora Greece
174 H9 Meteor Depth depth
115 E5 Methana Greece
63 F1 Metheringham *England* U.K.
115 C6 Methoni Greece
147 H3 Methuen *Massachusetts* U.S.A.
66 E4 Methven *Scotland* U.K.
63 G2 Methwold *England* U.K.
172 F3 Metileo Argentina
104 F4 Metković Croatia
136 C3 Metlakatla *Alaska* U.S.A.
121 F2 Metlaoui Tunisia
104 E3 Metlika Slovenia
81 F4 Metnitz r. Austria
81 F4 Metnitz Austria
115 C4 Metochi *Dytiki Ellas* Greece
115 D5 Metochi *Peloponnisos* Greece
127 C7 Metoro Mozambique
22 A3 Metro Indonesia
144 B4 Metropolis *Illinois* U.S.A.
68 E1 Metslawier Netherlands
114 C3 Metsovo Greece
80 D2 Metten Germany
69 E5 Mettendorf Germany
69 C4 Mettet Belgium
72 C3 Mettingen Germany
74 B3 Mettlach Germany
154 C4 Mettler *California* U.S.A.
72 B4 Mettmann Germany
89 F4 Mettray France
38 B4 Mettur India
126 C3 Metu Ethiopia
127 D7 Metundo, Ilha i. Mozambique
87 F3 Metz *Moselle* France
87 G4 Metzeral France
87 F3 Metzervisse France
74 E4 Metzingen Germany
88 C3 Meu r. France
74 C2 Meudt Germany
69 B4 Meulebeke Belgium
89 G4 Meung-sur-Loire France
87 F4 Meurthe r. France
87 F4 Meurthe-et-Moselle div. France
87 E3 Meuse div. France
69 C5 Meuse r. Belgium/France
73 H4 Meuselwitz Germany
92 D3 Meuzac France
90 C1 Meuzin r. France
62 B4 Mevagissey *England* U.K.
32 C1 Mêwa China
65 G4 Mexborough *England* U.K.
151 D6 Mexia *Texas* U.S.A.
166 C1 Mexiana, Ilha i. Brazil
156 B1 Mexicali Mexico
155 H3 Mexican Hat *Utah* U.S.A.
153 F6 Mexicanos, L. de los l. Mexico
155 H3 Mexican Water *Arizona* U.S.A.
133 H7 Mexico country Central America
157 F5 México div. Mexico
147 H2 Mexico *Maine* U.S.A.
150 F4 Mexico *Missouri* U.S.A.
147 E3 Mexico *New York* U.S.A.
157 F5 México Mexico
157 G3 Mexico, Gulf of g. Mexico/U.S.A.
90 D3 Meximieux France
39 C2 Meybod Iran
73 H2 Meyenburg Germany
91 D3 Meylan France
92 E3 Meymac France
39 F2 Meymaneh Afghanistan
39 B2 Meymeh Iran
42 F3 Meymeh r. Iran
45 T3 Meynypil'gyno Rus. Fed.
91 D5 Meyrargues France
91 E4 Meyronnes France
91 B4 Meyrueis France
92 D3 Meyssac France
90 E3 Meythet France
90 C3 Meyzieu France
43 C4 Mezada Israel
157 G5 Mezcalapa r. Mexico
112 D3 Mezdra Bulgaria
91 B5 Mèze France
91 E4 Mézel France
44 F3 Mezen' r. Rus. Fed.
50 H1 Mezen' Rus. Fed.
91 C4 Mezenc, Mt mt. France
50 G1 Mezenskaya Guba Rus. Fed.
52 A1 Mezha r. Rus. Fed.
47 L2 Mezhdurechensk Rus. Fed.
50 J2 Mezhdurechensk Rus. Fed.
44 G2 Mezhdusharskiy, O. i. Rus. Fed.
53 G2 Mezhova Ukraine
75 J2 Meziboří Czech Rep.
81 F4 Mežica Slovenia
89 E2 Mézidon-Canon France
92 D2 Mézières-en-Brenne France
92 C2 Mézières-sur-Issoire France
91 C4 Mézilhac France
90 B1 Mézilles France
78 F1 Mezimĕstí Czech Rep.
93 C4 Mézin France
98 C4 Mezio Portugal
79 L5 Mezőberény Hungary
79 K4 Mezőcsát Hungary
79 K4 Mezőkövesd Hungary
79 H5 Mezőszilas Hungary
79 K5 Mezőtúr Hungary
102 C4 Mezquita de Jarque Spain
156 D4 Mezquital r. Mexico
156 D4 Mezquital Mexico
156 E4 Mezquitic Mexico
54 E3 Mežvidi Latvia
107 E2 Mezzana Italy
107 F2 Mezzano Italy
83 G2 Mezzocorona Italy
110 C5 Mezzojuso *Sicilia* Italy
106 D2 Mezzola, Lago di l. Italy
83 E2 Mezzoldo Italy
107 F2 Mezzolombardo Italy
127 B5 Mfangano I. i. Kenya
124 B3 Mfou Cameroon
127 B7 Mfuwe Zambia
111 □ Mgarr Malta
123 F5 Mgbidi Nigeria
52 A3 Mglin Rus. Fed.
131 F5 Mgwali r. South Africa
129 E2 Mhangura Zimbabwe
38 A2 Mhasvad India
131 H3 Mhlosheni Swaziland
131 H3 Mhlume Swaziland
131 G2 Mhluzi South Africa
36 C5 Mhow India
31 F5 Mi r. China
24 A2 Mi r. Myanmar
77 M5 Miączyn Poland
157 F5 Miahuatlan Mexico
100 E1 Miajadas Spain
155 G5 Miami *Arizona* U.S.A.
145 D7 Miami *Florida* U.S.A.
151 E4 Miami *Oklahoma* U.S.A.
145 D7 Miami Beach *Florida* U.S.A.
39 B3 Mīān Āb Iran
39 D1 Miānābād Iran
39 E4 Mianaz Pakistan
30 A6 Miancaowan China
33 E1 Mianchi China
39 C2 Mīāndarreh Iran
39 D1 Mīāndasht Iran
42 F2 Miandowāb Iran
129 H2 Miandrivazo Madagascar
31 G2 Mianduhe China
39 A1 Mīāneh Iran
23 C5 Miangas i. Philippines
36 A4 Miani Hor b. Pakistan
39 F2 Mianjoi Afghanistan
36 B2 Mian Kalai Pakistan
32 C3 Mianmian Shan mountain range China
32 C2 Mianning China
36 B2 Mianwali Pakistan
32 D1 Mian Xian China
33 F2 Mianyang China
32 D2 Mianyang China
32 D2 Mianzhu China
31 G5 Miao Dao i. China
31 G5 Miaodao Qundao is China
47 K3 Miao'ergou China
33 H3 Miaoli Taiwan
129 H2 Miarinarivo *Antananarivo* Madagascar
129 H2 Miarinarivo *Toamasina* Madagascar
76 F2 Miasteczko Krajeńskie Poland
76 E1 Miastko Poland
77 K4 Miastków Kościelny Poland
77 K2 Miastkowo Poland
131 H2 Mica South Africa
173 G5 Micaela Cascallares Argentina

155 G5 Mica Mt mt. Arizona U.S.A.
32 D1 Micang Shan mountain range China
50 J1 Michaichmon' Rus. Fed.
79 L3 Michalovce Slovakia
77 M2 Michałowa Poland
137 H3 Michel Saskatchewan Canada
75 C2 Michelau in Oberfranken Germany
74 E3 Michelstadt Germany
73 J3 Michendorf Germany
148 C2 Michigamme Lake l. Michigan U.S.A.
148 C2 Michigamme Reservoir resr Michigan U.S.A.
148 D2 Michigan div. U.S.A.
148 D5 Michigan City Indiana U.S.A.
148 D4 Michigan, Lake l. U.S.A.
172 C6 Michihuao Argentina
140 C3 Michipicoten Bay b. Ontario Canada
140 C3 Michipicoten I. i. Ontario Canada
140 C3 Michipicoten River Ontario Canada
156 E5 Michoacán div. Mexico
77 L4 Michów Poland
112 F3 Michurin Bulgaria
52 E3 Michurinsk Rus. Fed.
124 B3 Micomeseng Equatorial Guinea
176 E5 Micronesia is Pacific Ocean
4 G4 Micronesia, Federated States of country Pacific Ocean
25 D7 Midai i. Indonesia
174 G4 Mid-Atlantic Ridge sea feature Atlantic Ocean
130 B6 Middelberg Pass pass South Africa
131 E5 Middelburg Eastern Cape South Africa
131 G2 Middelburg Eastern Transvaal South Africa
69 B3 Middelburg Netherlands
55 B4 Middelfart Denmark
68 C3 Middelharnis Netherlands
69 A3 Middelkerke Belgium
130 C5 Middelpos South Africa
68 E1 Middelstum Netherlands
131 F2 Middelwit South Africa
152 C3 Middle Alkali Lake l. Nevada U.S.A.
174 C5 Middle America Trench sea feature Pacific Ocean
25 A4 Middle Andaman i. Andaman and Nicobar Is India
147 H4 Middleboro Massachusetts U.S.A.
146 E4 Middleburg Pennsylvania U.S.A.
147 F3 Middleburgh New York U.S.A.
147 G2 Middlebury Vermont U.S.A.
15 E3 Middle Cr. r. Queensland Australia
65 G3 Middleham England U.K.
101 □ Middle Hill h. Gibraltar
128 □3 Middle I. i. Tristan da Cunha Atlantic Ocean
Middle Level lowland see Bedford Level
9 C6 Middlemarch New Zealand
62 D4 Middlemarsh England U.K.
146 B6 Middlesboro Kentucky U.S.A.
65 G3 Middlesbrough England U.K.
158 A3 Middlesex Belize
65 F4 Middleton England U.K.
15 E4 Middleton Queensland Australia
131 E6 Middleton South Africa
63 E2 Middleton Cheney England U.K.
63 F4 Middleton-on-Sea England U.K.
65 G3 Middleton St George England U.K.
154 A2 Middletown California U.S.A.
147 G4 Middletown Connecticut U.S.A.
147 F5 Middletown Delaware U.S.A.
147 F4 Middletown New York U.S.A.
67 E2 Middletown Northern Ireland U.K.
146 A5 Middletown Ohio U.S.A.
148 E4 Middleville Michigan U.S.A.
62 D1 Middlewich England U.K.
9 B6 Mid Dome mt. New Zealand
120 D2 Midelt Morocco
126 E2 Midhisho well Somalia
63 F4 Midhurst England U.K.
126 D1 Midī Yemen
93 C6 Midi de Bigorre, Pic du mt. France
175 K4 Mid-Indian Basin sea feature Indian Ocean
175 K6 Mid-Indian Ridge sea feature Indian Ocean
93 D5 Midi-Pyrénées div. France
149 E4 Midland Michigan U.S.A.
141 F4 Midland Ontario Canada
151 C5 Midland Texas U.S.A.
129 D2 Midlands div. Zimbabwe
67 C5 Midleton Rep. of Ireland
72 D2 Midlum Germany
131 H4 Midmar Dam dam South Africa
129 H3 Midongy Atsimo Madagascar
28 C7 Midori-k r. Japan
93 B5 Midou r. France
93 B5 Midouze r. France
176 F4 Mid-Pacific Mountains sea feature Pacific Ocean
32 C3 Midu China
55 □1 Miðvágur Faeroes
Midway see Thamarīt
176 H4 Midway Islands is Pacific Ocean
152 F3 Midwest Wyoming U.S.A.
151 D5 Midwest City Oklahoma U.S.A.
68 F1 Midwolda Netherlands
42 E2 Midyat Turkey
66 □2 Mid Yell Scotland U.K.
112 D3 Midzhur mt. Bulgaria/Yugoslavia
29 F6 Mie div. Japan
28 C7 Mie Japan
77 J5 Miechów Poland
76 D3 Miedzichowo Poland
76 F4 Międzybórz Poland
76 D3 Międzychód Poland
76 G3 Międzylesie Poland
77 L4 Międzyrzec Podlaski Poland
76 D3 Międzyrzecz Poland
76 C2 Międzyzdroje Szczecin Poland
57 G3 Miehikkälä Finland
77 K6 Miejsce Piastowe Poland
76 E4 Miejska-Górka Poland
56 G2 Miekojärvi l. Finland
93 C5 Miélan France
77 K5 Mielec Poland
76 E1 Mielno Poland
76 F3 Mielżyn Poland
127 C6 Miembwe Tanzania
80 B3 Mieminger Gebirge mountain range Austria
59 F3 Mien l. Sweden
13 F5 Miena Tasmania Australia
33 H3 Mien-hua Hsü i. Taiwan
56 G1 Mieraslompolo Finland
112 E1 Miercurea-Ciuc Romania
98 E1 Mieres Spain
69 D3 Mierlo Netherlands
76 F5 Mieroszów Poland
76 G1 Mierzeja Helska pen. Poland
77 H1 Mierzeja Wiślana spit Poland
87 G3 Miesau Germany
75 G5 Miesbach Germany
76 F3 Mieścisko Poland
74 C3 Miesenbach Germany
126 D3 Mī'ēso Ethiopia
73 G3 Mieste Germany
76 C3 Mieszkowice Poland
80 A2 Mietingen Germany
54 B1 Mietoinen Finland
82 B2 Mieussy France
146 E4 Mifflinburg Pennsylvania U.S.A.
146 E4 Mifflintown Pennsylvania U.S.A.
32 D1 Migang Shan mt. China
131 E3 Migdol South Africa
86 C5 Migennes France
39 D3 Mīghān Iran
37 H3 Miging India
107 F4 Migliarino Italy
109 J4 Miglionica Italy
92 C2 Mignaloux-Beauvoir France
92 C2 Migné-Auxances France
82 B2 Mignovillard France
166 D1 Miguel Alves Brazil
156 E3 Miguel Auza Mexico
156 K7 Miguel de la Borda Panama
101 G1 Miguel Esteban Spain
173 J3 Miguelete Uruguay
172 F4 Miguel Riglos Argentina
25 B4 Migyaunglaung Myanmar
24 A3 Migyaunye Myanmar
112 E2 Mihăileşti Romania
42 B2 Mihalıççık Turkey
28 D6 Mihara Japan
29 G6 Mihara-yama volcano Japan
43 C1 Mihmandar Turkey
103 C4 Mijares r. Spain
101 F4 Mijas Spain
101 F4 Mijas, Sierra de mountain range Spain
68 C2 Mijdrecht Netherlands
90 E2 Mijoux France
149 F3 Mikado Michigan U.S.A.
28 H2 Mikasa Japan
29 F6 Mikawa-wan b. Japan
54 E5 Mikhanavichy Belarus
50 F4 Mikhaylov Rus. Fed.
112 D3 Mikhaylovgrad div. Bulgaria
179 D5 Mikhaylov I. i. Antarctica
47 J2 Mikhaylovka Kazakhstan
47 H4 Mikhaylovka Kazakhstan
52 B3 Mikhaylovka Rus. Fed.
51 G5 Mikhaylovka Rus. Fed.
30 D2 Mikhaylovka Rus. Fed.
112 D3 Mikhaylovo Bulgaria
52 F1 Mikhaylovo Rus. Fed.
46 E1 Mikhaylovsk Rus. Fed.
47 J2 Mikhaylovskiy Rus. Fed.
52 G1 Mikhaylovskoye Rus. Fed.
52 C2 Mikhnevo Rus. Fed.
28 E6 Miki Japan
37 H4 Mikīr Hills mountain range India
56 G3 Mikkeli div. Finland
57 G3 Mikkeli Finland
56 G3 Mikkelin mlk Finland
136 G3 Mikkwa r. Alberta Canada
55 □1 Mikladalur Faeroes
81 G4 Miklavž Slovenia
77 K2 Mikołajki Poland
76 G5 Mikołów Poland
114 E2 Mikra Volvi Greece
76 F4 Mikstat Poland
75 L3 Mikuláš Czech Rep.
78 F3 Mikulov Czech Rep.
127 C6 Mikumi Tanzania
127 C6 Mikumi National Park nat. park Tanzania
50 J2 Mikun' Rus. Fed.
29 G5 Mikuni-sammyaku mountain range Japan
29 G7 Mikura-jima i. Japan
121 F1 Mila Algeria
150 E2 Milaca Minnesota U.S.A.
35 D9 Miladhunmadulu Atoll atoll Maldives
166 E2 Milagres Brazil
172 E1 Milagro Argentina
102 B2 Milagro Spain
77 J1 Miłakowo Poland
145 B5 Milan Tennessee U.S.A.
Milan see Milano
125 C5 Milando, Reserva Especial do res. Angola
12 D3 Milang S. Australia Australia
129 F2 Milange Mozambique
106 D3 Milano div. Lombardia Italy
106 D3 Milano Milano Italy
129 H1 Milanoa Madagascar
106 C3 Milano Malpensa airport Italy
77 L4 Milanów Poland
42 A2 Milas Turkey
115 G7 Milatos Greece
111 E4 Milazzo Sicilia Italy
111 E4 Milazzo, Capo di c. Sicilia Italy
111 E4 Milazzo, Golfo di b. Sicilia Italy
150 D2 Milbank S. Dakota U.S.A.
62 D4 Milborne Port England U.K.
63 G2 Mildenhall England U.K.
13 E3 Mildura Victoria Australia
32 C3 Mile China
159 □1 Mile Gully Jamaica
43 B4 Mileiz, W. el watercourse Egypt
110 C5 Milena Sicilia Italy
15 G5 Miles Queensland Australia
152 F2 Miles City Montana U.S.A.
126 D2 Mīlē Serdo Reserve res. Ethiopia
75 J2 Milešovka h. Czech Rep.
67 C4 Milestone Rep. of Ireland
111 F4 Mileto Italy
109 G3 Miletto, Monte mt. Italy
17 B5 Mileura Western Australia Australia
78 D2 Milevsko Czech Rep.
52 B3 Mileyevo Rus. Fed.
154 B1 Milford California U.S.A.
147 G4 Milford Connecticut U.S.A.
147 F5 Milford Delaware U.S.A.
148 D5 Milford Illinois U.S.A.
147 J2 Milford Maine U.S.A.
147 H3 Milford Massachusetts U.S.A.
147 H3 Milford New Hampshire U.S.A.
147 F3 Milford New York U.S.A.
155 F2 Milford Utah U.S.A.
67 D1 Milford Rep. of Ireland
62 A3 Milford Haven Wales U.K.
9 A6 Milford Sd inlet New Zealand
9 A6 Milford Sound New Zealand
15 E3 Milgarra Queensland Australia
17 B5 Milgun Western Australia Australia
98 D3 Milhão Portugal
91 C5 Milhaud France
76 F4 Milicz Poland
17 B6 Miling Western Australia Australia
108 A4 Milis Sardegna Italy
110 D5 Militello in Val di Catania Sicilia Italy
81 G4 Miljana Croatia
152 F1 Milk r. Canada/U.S.A.
77 K2 Miłki Poland
45 R4 Mil'kovo Rus. Fed.
76 E4 Miłkowice Poland
159 □1 Milk River Bath Jamaica
68 D3 Mill Netherlands
15 F3 Millaa Millaa Queensland Australia
103 C5 Millares Spain
103 C5 Millárs r. Spain
145 □2 Millars The Bahamas
93 E6 Millas France
91 B4 Millau France
62 B4 Millbrook England U.K.
154 B1 Mill Creek r. California U.S.A.
145 D5 Milledgeville Georgia U.S.A.
148 C5 Milledgeville Illinois U.S.A.
150 E2 Mille Lacs L. l. Minnesota U.S.A.
138 B4 Mille Lacs, Lac des l. Ontario Canada
150 D2 Miller S. Dakota U.S.A.
130 D6 Miller South Africa
148 B3 Miller Dam Flowage resr Wisconsin U.S.A.
140 E4 Miller Lake Ontario Canada
51 G5 Millerovo Rus. Fed.
155 G6 Miller Peak summit Arizona U.S.A.
146 C4 Millersburg Ohio U.S.A.
146 E4 Millersburg Pennsylvania U.S.A.
9 B6 Millers Flat New Zealand
146 E6 Millers Tavern Virginia U.S.A.
154 C3 Millerton Lake l. California U.S.A.
64 C2 Milleur Point pt Scotland U.K.
92 E3 Millevaches France
179 C6 Mill I. i. Antarctica
12 E4 Millicent S. Australia Australia
68 E3 Millingen ann de Rijn Netherlands
149 F4 Millington Michigan U.S.A.
145 B5 Millington Tennessee U.S.A.
147 J2 Millinocket Maine U.S.A.
64 C3 Millisle Northern Ireland U.K.
15 G5 Millmerran Queensland Australia
65 E3 Millom England U.K.
66 D5 Millport Scotland U.K.
147 F5 Millsboro Delaware U.S.A.
15 E4 Mills Cr. watercourse Queensland Australia
136 F2 Mills Lake l. N.W.T. Canada
81 E4 Millstätter See l. Austria
146 C5 Millstone W. Virginia U.S.A.
67 B4 Millstreet Rep. of Ireland
139 G4 Milltown New Brunswick Canada
67 B4 Milltown Malbay Rep. of Ireland
15 E3 Millungera Queensland Australia
131 F2 Millvale South Africa
147 K1 Millville New Brunswick Canada
147 F5 Millville New Jersey U.S.A.
86 B4 Milly-la-Forêt France
17 B5 Milly Milly Western Australia Australia
102 B3 Milmarcos Spain
73 J2 Milmersdorf Germany
65 E1 Milnathort Scotland U.K.
135 Q2 Milne Land i. Greenland
64 D2 Milngavie Scotland U.K.
65 F3 Milnthorpe England U.K.
122 C5 Milo r. Guinea
147 J2 Milo Maine U.S.A.
111 E5 Milo Sicilia Italy
76 E2 Miłocice Poland
77 H2 Miłomłyn Poland
115 F6 Milos i. Greece
52 D3 Miloslavskoye Rus. Fed.
76 F3 Miłosław Poland
53 G1 Milove Ukraine
77 H6 Milówka Poland
13 E2 Milparinka New South Wales Australia
146 E4 Milroy Pennsylvania U.S.A.
80 D1 Miltach Germany
74 E3 Miltenberg Germany
151 G6 Milton Florida U.S.A.
145 C6 Milton Florida U.S.A.
148 B5 Milton Iowa U.S.A.
13 G3 Milton New South Wales Australia
141 F5 Milton Ontario Canada
146 E4 Milton Pennsylvania U.S.A.
147 G2 Milton Vermont U.S.A.
9 B7 Milton New Zealand
152 C2 Milton-Freewater Oregon U.S.A.
63 F2 Milton Keynes England U.K.
146 C4 Milton, Lake l. Ohio U.S.A.
73 J1 Miltzow Germany
33 F2 Miluo China
148 D4 Milwaukee Wisconsin U.S.A.
159 E3 Milwaukee Depth depth Caribbean
46 F3 Mily Kazakhstan
51 G5 Milyutinskaya Rus. Fed.
124 C3 Mimbelly Congo
93 B5 Mimizan France
93 A4 Mimizan-Plage France
78 D1 Mimoň Czech Rep.
124 B4 Mimongo Gabon
168 D1 Mimoso Brazil
169 H4 Mimoso do Sul Brazil
28 E6 Mimuroyama mt. Japan
32 C2 Min r. China
154 C2 Mina Nevada U.S.A.
157 E3 Mina Mexico
39 D4 Mīnāb Iran
36 B3 Mina Bazar Pakistan
172 E1 Mina Clavero Argentina
21 H6 Minahassa Peninsula pen. Indonesia
138 B3 Minaki Ontario Canada
27 C8 Minamata Japan
29 F6 Minami Alps National Park nat. park Japan
20 D6 Minas Indonesia
173 K3 Minas Uruguay
42 G4 Mīnā'Sa'ūd Kuwait
139 H4 Minas Basin b. Nova Scotia Canada
173 K1 Minas de Corrales Uruguay
169 F2 Minas Gerais div. Brazil
169 G2 Minas Novas Brazil
157 H6 Minas, Sa de las mountain range Guatemala
103 B6 Minateda Spain
157 G5 Minatitlán Mexico
101 H1 Minaya Spain
24 A2 Minbu Myanmar
24 A2 Minbya Myanmar
172 B1 Mincha Chile
171 B5 Minchinmávida volcano Chile
65 E2 Minch Moor h. Scotland U.K.
66 C3 Minch, The str. Scotland U.K.
107 E3 Mincio r. Italy
42 F2 Mincivan Azerbaijan
23 C5 Mindanao i. Philippines
24 A2 Mindat Sakan Myanmar
100 B1 Minde Portugal
74 F4 Mindel r. Germany
75 F4 Mindelheim Germany
122 □ Mindelo Cape Verde
75 G4 Mindelstetten Germany
151 E5 Minden Louisiana U.S.A.
154 C2 Minden Nevada U.S.A.
141 F4 Minden Ontario Canada
72 D3 Minden Germany
24 A3 Mindon Myanmar
13 E3 Mindona L. l. New South Wales Australia
23 B3 Mindoro i. Philippines
23 B3 Mindoro Strait str. Philippines
125 B4 Mindouli Congo
79 K5 Mindszent Hungary
169 F4 Minduri Brazil
Mindzhivan see Mincivan
28 C6 Mine Japan
67 D5 Mine Head headland Rep. of Ireland
62 C3 Minehead England U.K.
168 B2 Mineiros Brazil
151 E5 Mineola Texas U.S.A.
154 B1 Mineral California U.S.A.
154 C3 Mineral King California U.S.A.
51 G6 Mineral'nyye Vody Rus. Fed.
148 B4 Mineral Point Wisconsin U.S.A.
151 D5 Mineral Wells Texas U.S.A.
107 F4 Minerbio Italy
155 F2 Minersville Utah U.S.A.
109 J3 Minervino Murge Italy
93 E5 Minervois reg. France
37 E1 Minfeng China
125 E6 Minga Zaire
42 F1 Mingäçevir Azerbaijan
42 F1 Mingäçevir Su Anbarı resr Azerbaijan
124 D2 Mingala Central African Rep.
139 H3 Mingan Québec Canada
111 E2 Mingardo r. Italy
Mingechaur see Mingäçevir
Mingechaurskoye Vdkhr. l. see Mingäçevir Su Anbarı
15 F3 Mingela Queensland Australia
17 A6 Mingenew Western Australia Australia
14 D4 Mingera Cr. watercourse Queensland Australia
33 F1 Minggang China
24 A2 Mingin Myanmar
24 A1 Mingin Range mountain range Myanmar
47 H4 Ming-Kush Kyrgyzstan
103 B5 Minglanilla Spain
99 F4 Mingorría Spain
127 C7 Mingoyo Tanzania
31 H3 Mingshui China
36 C1 Mingteke China
66 A4 Mingulay i. Scotland U.K.
129 F1 Mingúri Mozambique
33 G3 Mingxi China
30 B5 Minhe China
24 A3 Minhla Myanmar
24 A3 Minhla Myanmar
98 B3 Minho reg. Portugal
38 A4 Minicoy i. India
17 C6 Minigwal, L. salt flat Western Australia Australia
54 B4 Minija r. Lithuania
17 A4 Minilya r. Western Australia Australia
17 A4 Minilya Western Australia Australia
164 C3 Miñimiñe Chile
172 A4 Mininco Chile
122 C4 Minignan Côte d'Ivoire
139 H3 Minipi Lake l. Newfoundland Canada
99 H3 Ministra, Sierra mountain range Spain
137 J4 Minitonas Manitoba Canada
Min-Kush see Ming-Kush
12 D3 Minlaton S. Australia Australia
30 B5 Minle China
123 F5 Minna Nigeria
29 □2 Minna-jima i. Japan
56 D3 Minne Sweden
148 A3 Minneapolis Minnesota U.S.A.
137 K4 Minnedosa Manitoba Canada
148 A2 Minnesota div. U.S.A.
143 G3 Minnesota r. U.S.A.
58 D1 Minnesund Norway
17 A4 Minnie Creek Western Australia Australia
64 D3 Minnigaff Scotland U.K.
12 C3 Minnipa S. Australia Australia
138 B4 Minnitaki L. l. Ontario Canada
98 B3 Miño r. Portugal/Spain
29 G6 Minobu Japan
148 C3 Minocqua Wisconsin U.S.A.
173 H1 Miñones Argentina
148 B2 Minong Wisconsin U.S.A.
148 C5 Minonk Illinois U.S.A.
Minorca i. see Menorca
150 C1 Minot N. Dakota U.S.A.
30 B5 Minqin China
33 G3 Minqing China
32 C1 Min Shan mountain range China
24 A1 Minsin Myanmar
54 E5 Minsk div. Belarus
54 E5 Minsk Belarus
77 K3 Mińsk Mazowiecki Poland
62 D2 Minsterley England U.K.
124 B3 Minta Cameroon
36 C1 Mintaka P. pass China/Jammu and Kashmir
66 G3 Mintlaw Scotland U.K.
139 G4 Minto New Brunswick Canada
134 G2 Minto Inlet inlet N.W.T. Canada
138 F2 Minto, Lac l. Québec Canada
153 F4 Minturn Colorado U.S.A.
109 F3 Minturno Italy
106 E4 Minucciano Italy
43 A4 Minûf Egypt
47 M2 Minusinsk Rus. Fed.
83 D2 Minusio Switzerland
37 H3 Minutang India
124 B3 Minvoul Gabon
32 D1 Min Xian China
43 A4 Minya el Qamh Egypt
Minya Konka mt. see Gongga Shan
46 E1 Minyar Rus. Fed.
24 A2 Minywa Myanmar
37 H4 Minzong India
149 E3 Mio Michigan U.S.A.
90 C3 Mionnay France
93 B4 Mios France
139 J4 Miquelon i. St-Pierre and Miquelon
141 G2 Miquelon Québec Canada
54 E5 Mir Belarus
162 B3 Mira r. Colombia
100 B3 Mira r. Portugal
103 B5 Mira r. Spain
107 G3 Mira Italy
98 B4 Mira Portugal
103 B5 Mira Spain
39 E3 Mirabad Afghanistan
91 D5 Mirabeau France
141 H4 Mirabel airport Québec Canada
141 H4 Mirabel Québec Canada
98 D5 Mirabel Spain
169 F2 Mirabela Brazil
91 D4 Mirabel-aux-Baronnies France
109 H3 Mirabella Eclano Italy
166 C2 Mirador, Parque Nacional de nat. park Brazil
169 G4 Miracema Brazil
166 C2 Miracema Brazil
162 C3 Miraflores Colombia
99 G4 Miraflores de la Sierra Spain
169 G4 Miraí Brazil
169 G2 Miralta Brazil
173 J5 Miramar Buenos Aires Argentina
173 F1 Miramar Cordoba Argentina
107 G4 Miramare Italy
157 H5 Miramar, L. l. Mexico
85 G5 Miramas France
92 B3 Mirambeau France
102 C4 Mirambel Spain
143 N2 Miramichi r. New Brunswick Canada
93 C4 Miramont-de-Guyenne France
36 B2 Miram Shah Pakistan
162 C4 Miraña Colombia
165 E4 Miranda r. Brazil
154 A1 Miranda California U.S.A.
167 A5 Miranda Brazil
99 H2 Miranda de Ebro Spain
98 E4 Miranda del Castañar Spain
98 B4 Miranda do Corvo Portugal
98 D3 Miranda do Douro Portugal
93 C5 Mirande France
98 C3 Mirandela Portugal
107 F4 Mirandola Italy
93 E4 Mirandol-Bourgnounac France
168 C4 Mirandópolis Brazil
107 G3 Mirano Italy
168 C5 Mirante do Paranapanema Brazil
167 B5 Mirante, Sa do h. Brazil
114 B2 Miras Albania
168 D4 Mirassol Brazil
42 E4 Mirā', Wādī al watercourse Iraq/Saudi Arabia
39 G2 Mir Bacheh Kowt Afghanistan
41 H6 Mirbāţ Oman
77 M5 Mircze Poland
119 G3 Mirear I. i. Egypt
159 D3 Mirebalais Haiti
90 D1 Mirebeau Bourgogne France
92 C2 Mirebeau Poitou-Charentes France
87 F4 Mirecourt France
81 E5 Miren Slovenia
93 D5 Mirepoix France
20 F6 Miri Malaysia
123 F4 Miria Niger
38 B2 Mirialguda India
159 E5 Mirimire Venezuela
170 F3 Mirim, Lagoa l. Brazil
170 E2 Miriñay r. Argentina
39 E3 Mīrjāveh Iran
104 D3 Mirna r. Croatia
81 G5 Mirna Slovenia
179 D5 Mirnyy Rus. Fed. Base Antarctica
45 N3 Mirnyy Rus. Fed.
50 G2 Mirnyy Rus. Fed.
137 J3 Mirond L. l. Saskatchewan Canada
77 M1 Miroslavas Lithuania
76 E2 Mirosławiec Poland
75 J3 Mirošov Czech Rep.
75 K3 Mirovice Czech Rep.
73 H2 Mirow Germany
36 C2 Mirpur Pakistan
36 B4 Mirpur Khas Pakistan
36 A4 Mirpur Sakro Pakistan
136 G4 Mirror Alberta Canada
47 L4 Mirsali China
27 □ Mirs Bay b. Hong Kong
39 D4 Mīr Shahdād Iran
75 L2 Mirsk Poland
15 F4 Mirtna Queensland Australia
111 F3 Mirto Crosia Italy
115 E6 Mirtoö Pelagos sea Greece
47 H5 Mir Wali Jammu and Kashmir
36 C1 Mir Wali Pakistan
31 J6 Miryang South Korea
46 F5 Mirzachirla Turkmenistan
37 E4 Mirzapur India
28 D7 Misaki Japan
29 H6 Misaki Japan
32 C3 Misalay China
29 □2 Misato Japan
28 H3 Misawa Japan
82 C2 Mischabel mts Switzerland
81 H3 Mischendorf Austria
139 H4 Miscou I. i. New Brunswick Canada
109 G4 Miseno, Capo c. Italy
90 D1 Miserey-Salines France
178 □2 Miseryfjellet h. Bjørnøya Arctic Ocean
101 □ Misery, Mt h. Gibraltar
159 □6 Misery, Mt mt. St Kitts-Nevis Caribbean
36 C1 Misgar Pakistan
130 D6 Misgund South Africa
25 A6 Misha Andaman and Nicobar Is India
31 J3 Mishan China
39 B4 Mishāsh al Hādī well Saudi Arabia
39 B4 Mishāsh'Uwayr well Saudi Arabia
148 D5 Mishawaka Indiana U.S.A.
52 D2 Misheronskiy Rus. Fed.
140 C2 Mishibishu Lake l. Ontario Canada
28 C6 Mi-shima i. Japan
29 G6 Mishima Japan
46 E1 Mishkino Rus. Fed.
37 H3 Mishmi Hills mountain range India
110 C4 Misilmeri Sicilia Italy
6 □1 Misima I. i. P.N.G.
170 F2 Misiones div. Argentina
170 F2 Misiones, Sa de h. Argentina
171 C7 Misión Fagnano Argentina
43 C1 Misis Dağ h. Turkey
119 H3 Miskah Saudi Arabia
79 K3 Miskolc Hungary
81 G4 Mislinja Slovenia
119 H2 Mismā, Jibāl al mountain range Saudi Arabia
91 D4 Mison France
21 J7 Misoöl i. Indonesia
148 B2 Misquah Hills h. Minnesota U.S.A.
118 C1 Mişrātah Libya
36 E4 Misrikh India
140 C2 Missanabie Ontario Canada
109 J4 Missanello Italy
140 D1 Missinaibi r. Ontario Canada
140 D2 Missinaibi Lake l. Ontario Canada
137 J3 Missinipe Saskatchewan Canada
15 E2 Mission r. Queensland Australia
150 C3 Mission S. Dakota U.S.A.
136 E5 Mission City B.C. Canada
138 D3 Missisa L. l. Ontario Canada
140 D3 Missisagi r. Ontario Canada
141 F5 Mississauga Ontario Canada
148 E5 Mississinewa Lake l. Indiana U.S.A.
151 F5 Mississippi div. U.S.A.
151 F6 Mississippi r. Illinois U.S.A.
141 G4 Mississippi r. Ontario Canada
151 F6 Mississippi Delta delta Louisiana U.S.A.
152 D2 Missoula Montana U.S.A.
120 D2 Missour Morocco
148 A6 Missouri div. U.S.A.
150 C2 Missouri r. S. Dakota U.S.A.
150 E3 Missouri Valley Iowa U.S.A.
15 F4 Mistake Cr. r. Queensland Australia
141 F2 Mistaouac, Lac l. Québec Canada
141 J1 Mistassibi r. Québec Canada
139 F4 Mistassini r. Québec Canada
141 J2 Mistassini Québec Canada
138 F3 Mistassini, L. l. Québec Canada
139 H2 Mistastin Lake l. Newfoundland Canada
81 H2 Mistelbach div. Austria
81 H2 Mistelbach Austria
111 E5 Misterbianco Sicilia Italy
158 B3 Misteriosa Bank sand bank Caribbean
173 F1 Mistolar, L. l. Argentina
110 D5 Mistretta Sicilia Italy
136 C3 Misty Fjords National Monument res. Alaska U.S.A.
28 C6 Misumi Japan
28 C7 Misumi Japan
107 G2 Misurina Italy
159 □3 Mitan Trinidad and Tobago
59 E1 Mitandersfors Sweden
156 D4 Mita, Pta de headland Mexico
163 G3 Mitaraca h. Surinam
13 H2 Mitchell r. New South Wales Australia
15 E2 Mitchell r. Queensland Australia
13 F4 Mitchell r. Victoria Australia
140 E5 Mitchell Ontario Canada
15 F5 Mitchell Queensland Australia
150 D3 Mitchell S. Dakota U.S.A.
148 E3 Mitchell, Lake l. Michigan U.S.A.
145 D5 Mitchell, Mt mt. N. Carolina U.S.A.
14 B1 Mitchell Pt pt Northern Terr. Australia
67 C4 Mitchelstown Rep. of Ireland
141 H3 Mitchinamécus, Lake l. Québec Canada
43 A4 Mît Ghamr Egypt
36 B3 Mithankot Pakistan
36 C2 Mitha Tiwano Pakistan
36 B4 Mithi Pakistan
52 A2 Mitishkovo Rus. Fed.
136 C3 Mitkof I. i. Alaska U.S.A.
29 H5 Mito Japan
28 C6 Mitō Japan
127 C6 Mitole Tanzania
8 E4 Mitre mt. New Zealand
4 J6 Mitre Island i. Solomon Is.
114 C3 Mitropoli Greece
114 E1 Mitrousi Greece
127 D7 Mitsamiouli Comoros
114 B3 Mitsikeli mt. Greece
129 H2 Mitsinjo Madagascar
28 J2 Mitsuishi Japan
29 G5 Mitsuke Japan
28 B6 Mitsushima Japan
13 F4 Mitta Mitta Victoria Australia
80 B4 Mittelberg Tirol Austria
80 B3 Mittelberg Vorarlberg Austria
75 F3 Mittelfranken div. Germany
82 C2 Mittelland reg. Switzerland
72 D3 Mittelland kanal canal Germany
75 G5 Mittenwald Germany
73 J2 Mittenwalde Germany
81 G3 Mitterbach am Erlaufsee Austria
81 E2 Mitterding Austria
87 F4 Mittersheim France
80 D3 Mittersill Austria
75 H3 Mitterteich Germany
75 H2 Mittweida Germany
162 C3 Mitú Colombia
162 D3 Mituas Colombia
124 E4 Mitumba, Monts mountain range Zaire
54 C4 Mituva r. Lithuania
125 E5 Mitwaba Zaire
124 B3 Mitzic Gabon
Miughalaigh i. see Mingulay
29 G6 Miura Japan
29 F6 Miya-gawa r. Japan
29 H4 Miyagi div. Japan
29 □2 Miyagi Japan
29 □2 Miyagusuku-jima i. Japan
42 D3 Miyah, Wādī el watercourse Syria
119 H3 Miyah, W. al watercourse Saudi Arabia
28 C7 Miyaji Japan
29 G6 Miyake-jima i. Japan
29 H4 Miyako Japan
28 C8 Miyakonojō Japan
32 C2 Miyaluo China
46 D3 Miyaly Kazakhstan
36 B5 Miyāni India
28 C7 Miyazaki div. Japan
28 C8 Miyazaki Japan
29 E6 Miyazu Japan
29 E6 Miyazu-wan b. Japan
32 C3 Miyi China
28 D6 Miyoshi Japan
31 F4 Miyun China
31 F4 Miyun Sk. resr China
39 F2 Mīzāni Afghanistan
126 C3 Mīzan Teferī Ethiopia
118 B1 Mizdah Libya
67 B5 Mizen Head headland Rep. of Ireland
67 E4 Mizen Head headland Rep. of Ireland
77 O3 Mizhevichy Belarus
30 D5 Mizhi China
112 F2 Mizil Romania
112 D3 Miziya Bulgaria
53 B1 Mizoch Ukraine
24 A2 Mizoram div. India
43 C4 Mizpe Ramon Israel
164 C3 Mizque Bolivia
29 H4 Mizusawa Japan
59 F2 Mjölby Sweden
58 B1 Mjølfell Norway
58 D2 Mjøndalen Norway
59 E3 Mjörn l. Sweden
58 D1 Mjøsa l. Norway
131 H5 Mkambati Nature Reserve res. South Africa
46 F4 M. Karatobe pt Kazakhstan
127 C6 Mkata Tanzania
131 H3 Mkhondvo r. Swaziland
127 C6 Mkokotoni Tanzania
127 C5 Mkomazi Tanzania
127 C5 Mkomazi Game Reserve res. Tanzania
125 E6 Mkushi Zambia
131 J3 Mkuze r. South Africa
131 J3 Mkuze South Africa
131 J3 Mkuzi Game Reserve res. South Africa
78 D1 Mladá Boleslav Czech Rep.
75 K3 Mladá Vožice Czech Rep.
112 C2 Mladenovac Yugoslavia
127 B6 Mlala Hills h. Tanzania
131 H3 Mlaula r. Swaziland
112 C2 Mlava r. Yugoslavia

77 J2 Mława Poland
104 F4 Mljet i. Croatia
104 F4 Mljetski Kanal chan. Croatia
77 H1 Mlnary Poland
131 H2 Mlumati r. Swaziland
131 F5 Mlungisi South Africa
77 K3 Młynarze Poland
53 A1 Mlyniv Ukraine
77 N6 Mlynys'ka Ukraine
131 E2 Mmabatho South Africa
128 D3 Mmadinare Botswana
131 E2 Mmathethe Botswana
131 G6 Mncwasa Point pt South Africa
75 K3 Mnichovice Czech Rep.
78 D1 Mnichovo Hradiště Czech Rep.
77 J4 Mniów Poland
79 K3 Mnišek nad Hnilcom Slovakia
77 K4 Mniszew Poland
77 J4 Mniszków Poland
131 H3 Mnjoli Dam dam Swaziland
58 A1 Mo Norway
43 C4 Moab reg. Jordan
155 H2 Moab Utah U.S.A.
124 B4 Moabi Gabon
11 H1 Moa I. i. Queensland Australia
6 □7 Moala i. Fiji
39 C2 Mo'alla Iran
129 E4 Moamba Mozambique
98 B2 Moaña Spain
124 B4 Moanda Gabon
155 E3 Moapa Nevada U.S.A.
67 D3 Moate Rep. of Ireland
125 E5 Moba Zaire
29 H6 Mobara Japan
124 D3 Mobaye Central African Rep.
124 D3 Mobayi-Mbongo Zaire
150 E4 Moberly Missouri U.S.A.
140 C2 Mobert Ontario Canada
145 B6 Mobile Alabama U.S.A.
155 F5 Mobile Arizona U.S.A.
145 B6 Mobile Bay b. Alabama U.S.A.
150 C2 Mobridge S. Dakota U.S.A.
Mobutu, Lake l. see Albert, Lake
124 D3 Mobwasa Zaire
159 E3 Moca Dominican Rep.
166 C1 Mocajuba Brazil
129 G2 Moçambique Mozambique
24 D2 Môc Châu Vietnam
6 □7 Moce i. Fiji
99 G5 Mocejón Spain
52 F1 Mocha r. Rus. Fed.
Mocha see Al Mukhā
172 A5 Mocha, I. i. Chile
102 B3 Mochales Spain
163 E1 Mochirma, Parque Nacional nat. park Venezuela
159 □1 Mocho Mts mts Jamaica
77 H3 Mochowo Poland
128 D3 Mochudi Botswana
127 D7 Mocimboa da Praia Mozambique
127 C7 Mocimboa do Rovuma Mozambique
59 F3 Möckeln l. Sweden
73 G3 Möckern Germany
74 E3 Möckmühl Germany
73 H4 Mockrehna Germany
162 B3 Mocoa Colombia
168 E4 Mococa Brazil
173 H1 Mocoretá r. Argentina
156 D2 Moctezuma Chihuahua Mexico
157 E4 Moctezuma San Luis Potosí Mexico
156 C2 Moctezuma Sonora Mexico
129 F2 Mocuba Mozambique
91 E3 Modane France
36 C5 Modasa India
69 D4 Modave Belgium
62 C4 Modbury England U.K.
131 E4 Modder r. South Africa
107 E4 Modena div. Emilia-Romagna Italy
107 E4 Modena Modena Italy
155 F3 Modena Utah U.S.A.
87 G4 Moder r. France
172 E3 Modestino Pizarro Argentina
154 B3 Modesto California U.S.A.
110 D6 Modica Ragusa Italy
107 F4 Modigliana Italy
81 H2 Mödling div. Austria
81 H2 Mödling Austria
30 D3 Modot Mongolia
78 G3 Modra Slovakia
104 G3 Modriča Bos.-Herz.
81 H1 Modřice Czech Rep.
79 J3 Modrý Kameň Slovakia
111 F1 Modugno Italy
32 B2 Modung China
13 F4 Moe Victoria Australia
8 E2 Moehau h. New Zealand
88 B4 Moëlan-sur-Mer France
62 B1 Moelfre Wales U.K.
62 C2 Moel Sych h. Wales U.K.
58 D1 Moely Norway
131 F4 Moemaneng South Africa
56 E1 Moen Norway
80 C4 Moena Italy
163 G2 Moengo Surinam
155 G3 Moenkopi Arizona U.S.A.
9 C6 Moeraki Pt pt New Zealand
69 B3 Moerbeke Belgium
8 E1 Moerewa New Zealand
72 B4 Moers Germany
83 E2 Moesa r. Switzerland
66 E5 Moffat Scotland U.K.
98 D3 Mofreita Portugal
36 C3 Moga India
Mogadishu see Muqdisho
146 C4 Mogadore Reservoir resr Ohio U.S.A.
98 D3 Mogadouro Portugal
98 D3 Mogadouro, Sa do mountain range Portugal
131 G1 Mogalakwena r. South Africa
131 G1 Mogalakwenastroom South Africa
124 C3 Mogalo Zaire
29 G4 Mogami-gawa r. Japan
126 C1 Mogareb watercourse Eritrea
24 B1 Mogaung Myanmar
31 K2 Mogdy Rus. Fed.
55 A5 Møgeltønder Denmark
55 D4 Mogenstrup Denmark
72 E4 Mögglingen Germany
77 J6 Mogielnica mt. Nowy Sacz Poland
77 J4 Mogielnica Radom Poland
169 E5 Mogi-Guaçu Brazil
114 C1 Mogila Macedonia
76 F3 Mogilno Poland
167 C5 Mogi-Mirim Brazil
129 G2 Mogincual Mozambique
169 J2 Mogiquiçaba Brazil
109 F1 Mogliano Italy
107 G3 Mogliano Veneto Italy
172 C1 Mogna Argentina
27 L1 Mogocha Rus. Fed.
128 D3 Mogoditshane Botswana
126 B3 Mogogh Sudan
24 B2 Mogok Myanmar
155 H5 Mogollon Baldy mt. New Mexico U.S.A.
155 H5 Mogollon Mts mts New Mexico U.S.A.
155 G4 Mogollon Rim plat. Arizona U.S.A.
108 A5 Mogoro r. Sardegna Italy
108 A5 Mogoro Sardegna Italy
112 F1 Mogoşeşti-Siret Romania
31 E2 Mogoytuy Rus. Fed.
124 C1 Mogroum Chad
100 D3 Moguer Spain
31 G3 Moguqi China
30 E2 Mogzon Rus. Fed.
79 H6 Mohács Hungary
8 F3 Mohaka r. New Zealand
131 F5 Mohale's Hoek Lesotho
137 J5 Mohall N. Dakota U.S.A.
39 D2 Mohammad Iran
Moḩammadābād see Dareh Gaz
36 E3 Mohan r. India
36 D4 Mohana India
37 G4 Mohanganj Bangladesh
155 E4 Mohave, L. l. Nevada U.S.A.
147 F3 Mohawk r. New York U.S.A.
155 F5 Mohawk Arizona U.S.A.
155 F5 Mohawk Mts mts Arizona U.S.A.
31 G1 Mohe China
Moheli i. see Mwali
78 F2 Mohelnice Czech Rep.
81 H1 Mohelno Czech Rep.
128 C2 Mohembo Botswana
67 D3 Mohill Rep. of Ireland
82 C1 Möhlin Switzerland
72 D4 Möhne r. Germany
164 C3 Moho Peru
155 F4 Mohon Peak summit Arizona U.S.A.
79 J4 Mohora Hungary
127 C6 Mohoro Tanzania
151 C7 Mohovano Ranch Mexico
53 F1 Mohrytsya Ukraine
53 B2 Mohyliv Podil's'kyy Ukraine
58 B2 Moi Norway
102 F3 Moià Spain
93 A5 Moilets-et-Maa France
98 C4 Moimenta da Beira Portugal
36 E3 Moincêr China
6 □2 Moindou New Caledonia Pacific Ocean
89 D4 Moine r. France
131 J2 Moine Mozambique
112 F1 Moineşti Romania
90 C3 Moingt France
147 F2 Moira New York U.S.A.
64 B3 Moira Northern Ireland U.K.
56 D2 Mo i Rana Norway
37 H4 Moirang India
91 D3 Moirans France
90 D2 Moirans-en-Montagne France
93 C4 Moirax France
115 F7 Moires Greece
173 K1 Moirones Uruguay
57 G4 Mõisaküla Estonia
88 D4 Moisdon-la-Rivière France
173 G1 Moisés Ville Argentina
139 G3 Moisie r. Québec Canada
139 G3 Moisie Québec Canada
69 A5 Moislains France
93 D4 Moissac France
124 C2 Moïssala Chad
82 A1 Moissey France
108 B2 Moïta Corse France
100 B2 Moita Portugal
103 C6 Moixent Spain
59 H2 Möja i. Sweden
101 J3 Mojácar Spain
99 F3 Mojados Spain
154 D4 Mojave r. California U.S.A.
154 C4 Mojave California U.S.A.
154 D4 Mojave Desert desert California U.S.A.
32 C4 Mojiang China
167 C5 Moji das Cruzes Brazil
168 E4 Moji-Guaçu r. Brazil
28 C7 Mojikō Japan
112 B3 Mojkovac Yugoslavia
164 C4 Mojo Bolivia
22 C3 Mojokerto Indonesia
101 G3 Mojón Alto mt. Spain
126 D3 Mojo Shet' r. Ethiopia
164 C3 Mojotoro Bolivia
81 E4 Mojstrana Slovenia
166 C1 Moju r. Brazil
29 H5 Mōka Japan
8 E3 Mokai New Zealand
37 F4 Mokāma India
153 □1 Mokapu Pen. pen. Hawaii U.S.A.
124 D3 Mokaria Zaire
8 E3 Mokau r. New Zealand
8 E3 Mokau New Zealand
124 C3 Mokéko Congo
154 B2 Mokelumne r. California U.S.A.
131 G4 Mokhotlong Lesotho
52 C3 Mokhovoye Rus. Fed.
45 O3 Mokhsogollokh Rus. Fed.
53 B1 Mokiyivtsi Ukraine
128 D3 Mokobela Pan salt pan Botswana
8 E1 Mokohinau Is is New Zealand
37 H4 Mokokchung India
131 F2 Mokolo r. South Africa
124 B1 Mokolo Cameroon
131 F1 Mokolo Dam dam South Africa
31 H6 Mokp'o South Korea
112 C3 Mokra Gora mts Yugoslavia
53 D2 Mokra Kalyhirka Ukraine
112 B3 Mokra Planina mts Yugoslavia
52 F3 Mokraya Panda r. Rus. Fed.
51 H5 Mokrous Rus. Fed.
52 C3 Mokroye Rus. Fed.
52 F3 Mokryy Karay r. Rus. Fed.
52 E2 Moksha r. Rus. Fed.
52 G3 Mokshan Rus. Fed.
56 G3 Möksy Finland
153 □1 Mokuaua I. i. Hawaii U.S.A.
153 □1 Mokulua Is is Hawaii U.S.A.
53 B1 Mokvyn Ukraine
123 F5 Mokwa Nigeria
69 D3 Mol Belgium
111 G1 Mola di Bari Italy
157 F4 Molango Mexico
115 D6 Molaoi Greece
108 B4 Molara, Isola i. Sardegna Italy
98 C3 Molares Portugal
107 J4 Molat i. Croatia
81 F4 Mölbling Austria
62 C1 Mold Wales U.K.
79 L3 Moldava nad Bodvou Slovakia
Moldavia see Moldova
56 B3 Molde Norway
56 D2 Moldjord Norway
49 H4 Moldova country Europe
112 C2 Moldova Nouă Romania
55 B3 Møldrup Denmark
62 C4 Mole r. England U.K.
24 B1 Mole Chaung r. Myanmar
90 E2 Mole, Le mt. France
131 G4 Molen r. South Africa
122 D5 Mole National Park nat. park Ghana
69 C4 Molenbeek-St-Jean Belgium
88 A3 Molène, Île i. France
128 D3 Molepolole Botswana
54 D4 Molėtai Lithuania
109 J3 Molfetta Italy
72 F1 Molfsee Germany
93 D4 Molières France
172 C2 Molina Argentina
172 B3 Molina Chile
102 B4 Molina de Aragón Spain
103 B6 Molina de Segura Spain
83 F3 Molina di Ledro Italy
148 B5 Moline Illinois U.S.A.
107 F4 Molinella Italy
90 B2 Molinet France
90 D2 Molinges France
80 C4 Molini di Tures Italy
173 G2 Molinos Doll Argentina
172 E1 Molinos, Emb. Los resr Argentina
102 F3 Molins de Rei Spain
125 F5 Moliro Zaire
109 G3 Molise div. Italy
109 H4 Moliterno Italy
93 E6 Molitg-les-Bains France
59 E2 Molkom Sweden
80 D4 Möll r. Austria
114 B2 Mollas Albania
59 E3 Mölle Sweden
55 B4 Møllebjerg h. Denmark
59 F3 Möllerfjorden b. Sweden
73 J2 Möllenbeck Germany
164 B3 Mollendo Peru
73 H2 Möllenhagen Germany
17 B6 Mollerin, L. salt flat Western Australia Australia
102 D3 Mollerussa Spain
102 F3 Mollet del Vallès Spain
86 B3 Molliens-Dreuil France
83 E1 Mollis Switzerland
81 F3 Mölln Austria
73 F2 Mölln Germany
93 E6 Molló Spain
55 D1 Mölosund Sweden
78 B4 Mölltal v. Austria
59 F2 Mölltorp Sweden
59 E3 Mölnlycke Sweden
53 E3 Molochans'k Ukraine
53 F3 Molochna r. Ukraine
50 F3 Molochnoye Rus. Fed.
56 J1 Molochnyy Rus. Fed.
53 F3 Molochnyy Lyman est. Ukraine
129 F2 Molocue r. Mozambique
179 D4 Molodezhnaya Rus. Fed. Base Antarctica
53 E2 Molodizhne Ukraine
52 A1 Molodoy Tud Rus. Fed.
153 □2 Molokai i. Hawaii U.S.A.
177 K4 Molokai Fracture Zone sea feature Pacific Ocean
50 J3 Moloma r. Rus. Fed.
91 B3 Molompize France
13 G3 Molong New South Wales Australia
130 C3 Molopo watercourse Botswana/South Africa
130 E2 Moloporivier Botswana
114 D4 Molos Greece
124 B3 Moloundou Cameroon
53 C3 Molovata Moldova
90 C1 Moloy France
55 C3 Mols Bjerge h. Denmark
87 G4 Molsheim France
137 K4 Molson L. l. Manitoba Canada
131 F5 Molteno South Africa
130 D6 Moltenopas pass South Africa
Moluccas is see Maluku
21 J6 Molucca Sea g. Indonesia
103 B5 Moluengo mt. Spain
129 F2 Molumbo Mozambique
107 F2 Molveno Italy
83 F2 Molveno, Lago di l. Italy
129 F2 Moma Mozambique
13 E2 Momba New South Wales Australia
166 E2 Mombaça Brazil
127 C5 Mombasa Kenya
99 E4 Mombeltrán Spain
124 C3 Mombenzélé Zaire
37 H4 Mombi New India
55 A3 Mombjerge h. Denmark
124 C3 Momboyo r. Zaire
74 E2 Mömbris Germany
98 D2 Mombuey Spain
114 G1 Momchilgrad Bulgaria
148 D5 Momence Illinois U.S.A.
124 E4 Momi Zaire
100 E4 Momia, Sierra mountain range Spain
69 C4 Momignies Belgium
106 C3 Momo Italy
23 B3 Mompog Pass. chan. Philippines
124 D3 Mompono Zaire
162 C2 Mompós Colombia
93 B5 Momuy France
Mǿn i. see Anglesey
55 E4 Møn i. Denmark
82 B1 Mon Myanmar
155 G2 Mona Utah U.S.A.
159 □1 Mona Jamaica
101 G3 Monachil r. Spain
66 A3 Monach Is is Scotland U.K.
66 A3 Monach, Sound of chan. Scotland U.K.
91 F5 Monaco country Europe
66 D3 Monadhliath Mts mountain range Scotland U.K.
67 D2 Monaghan div. Rep. of Ireland
67 E2 Monaghan Rep. of Ireland
151 C6 Monahans Texas U.S.A.
159 F3 Mona, I. i. Puerto Rico
159 E3 Mona Passage chan. Dominican Rep.
129 G1 Monapo Mozambique
136 D4 Monarch Mt. mt. B.C. Canada
153 F4 Monarch Pass pass Colorado U.S.A.
66 C3 Monar, Loch l. Scotland U.K.
136 F4 Monashee Mts mountain range B.C. Canada
111 F4 Monasterace Italy
67 D3 Monasterevan Rep. of Ireland
108 B5 Monastir Sardegna Italy
121 G1 Monastir Tunisia
114 B4 Monastiraki Greece
77 N6 Monastyrets' Ukraine
53 C2 Monastyrshche Ukraine
53 A2 Monastyrs'ka Ukraine
124 B3 Monatélé Cameroon
6 □8 Monavatu mt. Fiji
93 C4 Monbahus France
93 C4 Monbazillac France
93 D5 Monbéqui France
28 J1 Monbetsu Japan
28 J2 Monbetsu Japan
124 B2 Monboré Cameroon
106 B3 Moncalieri Italy
98 D2 Moncalvo mt. Spain
106 C3 Moncalvo Italy
98 B2 Monção Portugal
100 C3 Moncarapacho Portugal
93 C4 Moncaut France
102 B3 Moncayo, Sierra del mountain range Spain
87 F4 Moncel-sur-Seille France
82 D2 Mönch mt. Switzerland
56 J2 Monchegorsk Rus. Fed.
72 B4 Mönchengladbach Germany
81 H3 Mönchhof Austria
100 B3 Monchique Portugal
100 B3 Monchique, Serra de mountain range Portugal
145 E5 Moncks Corner S. Carolina U.S.A.
93 C4 Monclar France
93 D5 Monclar-de-Quercy France
157 E3 Monclova Mexico
88 C3 Moncontour Bretagne France
92 B2 Moncontour Poitou-Charentes France
92 B2 Moncoutant France
139 H4 Moncton New Brunswick Canada
101 F4 Monda Spain
107 G5 Mondavio Italy
165 E5 Monday r. Paraguay
98 C4 Mondego r. Portugal
98 B4 Mondego, Cabo pt Portugal
110 C4 Mondello Sicilia Italy
89 E2 Mondeville France
124 D3 Mondimbi Zaire
98 C3 Mondim de Basto Portugal
124 D3 Mondjamboli Zaire
124 D4 Mondjuku Zaire
131 H3 Mondlo South Africa
118 C5 Mondo Chad
107 H5 Mondolfo Italy
124 D4 Mondombe Zaire
98 C1 Mondoñedo Spain
69 E5 Mondorf-les-Bains Luxembourg
89 F4 Mondoubleau France
148 B3 Mondovi Wisconsin U.S.A.
106 B4 Mondovì Italy
91 C4 Mondragon France
109 F3 Mondragone Italy
81 E3 Mondsee l. Austria
80 E3 Mondsee Austria
30 B2 Mondy Rus. Fed.
159 □1 Moneague Jamaica
106 D4 Moneglia Italy
102 C3 Monegrillo Spain
93 B5 Monein France
115 E6 Monemvasia Greece
27 P2 Moneron, Ostrov i. Rus. Fed.
146 D4 Monessen Pennsylvania U.S.A.
100 D2 Monesterio Spain
91 D4 Monestier-de-Clermont France
93 E4 Monestiés France
141 H2 Monet Québec Canada
90 B1 Monéteau France
67 E2 Moneymore Northern Ireland U.K.
107 H3 Monfalcone Italy
93 C4 Monflanquin France
93 C5 Monfort France
100 C1 Monforte Portugal
98 C2 Monforte Spain
100 C1 Monforte da Beira Portugal
106 B4 Monforte d'Alba Italy
98 D4 Monfortinho Portugal
100 B2 Monfurado mt. Portugal
124 D3 Monga Zaire
169 E6 Mongaguá Brazil
124 D3 Mongala r. Zaire
124 F3 Mongbwalu Zaire
24 D2 Mông Cai Vietnam
17 B6 Mongers Lake salt flat Western Australia Australia
91 E4 Monges, Les mt. France
Monggolküre see Zhaosu
31 F2 Monggon Qulu China
24 B2 Mong Hang Myanmar
107 F4 Monghidoro Italy
24 B2 Mong Hpayak Myanmar
24 B2 Mong Hsat Myanmar
24 B2 Mong Hsu Myanmar
24 B2 Mong Kung Myanmar
24 B2 Mong Lang Myanmar
24 C2 Mong Lin Myanmar
24 C2 Mong Loi Myanmar
24 B2 Mong Ma Myanmar
24 B3 Mong Mau Myanmar
24 B2 Mong Nai Myanmar
24 B2 Mong Nawng Myanmar
118 C5 Mongo Chad
19 L5 Mongolia country Asia
124 B3 Mongomo Equatorial Guinea
123 G4 Mongonu Nigeria
36 C2 Mongora Pakistan
118 D5 Mongororo Chad
124 C3 Mongoumba Central African Rep.
24 B2 Mong Pan Myanmar
24 B2 Mong Pat Myanmar
24 B2 Mong Ping Myanmar
24 B2 Mong Pu Myanmar
24 B2 Mong Pu-awn Myanmar
82 D3 Mongrando Italy
24 B2 Mong Ton Myanmar
125 D7 Mongu Zambia
107 G2 Monguelfo Italy
24 C2 Mong Un Myanmar
24 B2 Mong Yai Myanmar
24 B2 Mong Yang Myanmar
24 C2 Mong Yawng Myanmar
24 B2 Mong Yu Myanmar
147 J3 Monhegan I. i. Maine U.S.A.
75 F4 Monheim Germany
114 F2 Moni Agiou Dionysiou Greece
66 E5 Moniaive Scotland U.K.
114 F2 Moni Chiliandariou Greece
91 D4 Monieux France
173 G1 Monigotes Argentina
114 F2 Moni Iviron Greece
114 F2 Moni Megistis Lavras Greece
114 F2 Moni Simonos Petras Greece
91 B4 Monistrol-d'Allier France
91 C3 Monistrol-sur-Loire France
154 D2 Monitor Mt mt. Nevada U.S.A.
154 D2 Monitor Range mts Nevada U.S.A.
114 F2 Moni Vatopediou Greece
67 C3 Monivea Rep. of Ireland
169 F3 Monjolos Brazil
129 F1 Monkey Bay Malawi
77 L2 Mońki Poland
14 E5 Monkira Queensland Australia
62 B4 Monkokehampton England U.K.
124 D4 Monkoto Zaire
140 E5 Monkton Ontario Canada
103 C4 Monleón r. Spain
148 B5 Monmouth Illinois U.S.A.
147 H2 Monmouth Maine U.S.A.
62 D3 Monmouth Wales U.K.
136 E4 Monmouth Mt. mt. B.C. Canada
62 C3 Monmouthshire div. Wales U.K.
89 F4 Monnaie France
68 D2 Monnickendam Netherlands
62 D3 Monnow r. England/Wales U.K.
123 E5 Mono r. Benin/Togo
154 C3 Mono Lake l. California U.S.A.
115 □ Monolithos Greece
147 H4 Monomoy Pt pt Massachusetts U.S.A.
148 D5 Monon Indiana U.S.A.
148 B4 Monona Iowa U.S.A.
111 G2 Monopoli Italy
79 J4 Monor Hungary
146 C5 Monorgahela r. Pennsylvania U.S.A.
159 □3 Monos I. i. Trinidad Trinidad and Tobago
118 D4 Monou Chad
103 C6 Monóvar Spain
93 C4 Monpazier France
101 H1 Monreal r. Spain
93 A6 Monreal Spain
102 B4 Monreal del Campo Spain
110 C4 Monreale Sicilia Italy
151 E5 Monroe Louisiana U.S.A.
149 F5 Monroe Michigan U.S.A.
145 D5 Monroe N. Carolina U.S.A.
147 F4 Monroe New York U.S.A.
155 F2 Monroe Utah U.S.A.
148 C4 Monroe Wisconsin U.S.A.
148 B6 Monroe City Missouri U.S.A.
151 G6 Monroeville Alabama U.S.A.
145 C6 Monroeville Alabama U.S.A.
122 B5 Monrovia Liberia
100 D1 Monroy Spain
102 C4 Monroyo Spain
69 B4 Mons div. Hainaut Belgium
69 B4 Mons Mons Belgium
93 E5 Mons France
173 J4 Monsalvo Argentina
74 B2 Monschau Germany
92 C3 Monsec France
93 C4 Monségur France
107 F3 Monselice Italy
93 C4 Monsempron-Libos France
90 C2 Monsols France
68 C2 Monster Netherlands
107 E5 Monsummano Terme Italy
74 C2 Montabaur Germany
91 B5 Montady France
80 A3 Montafon v. Austria
91 B5 Montagnac France
107 F3 Montagnana Italy
93 B4 Montagne France
129 H1 Montagne d'Ambre, Parc National de la nat. park Madagascar
92 C3 Montagrier France
130 C6 Montagu South Africa
148 D4 Montague Michigan U.S.A.
17 B5 Montague Ra. h. Western Australia Australia
16 D2 Montague Sd b. Western Australia Australia
179 C1 Montagu I. i. S. Sandwich Is Atlantic Ocean
92 A2 Montaigu France
93 D4 Montaigu-de-Quercy France
92 E2 Montaigut France
93 D5 Montaigut-sur-Save France
102 C4 Montalbán Spain
111 E4 Montalbano Elicona Sicilia Italy
109 J4 Montalbano Jonico Italy
99 H5 Montalbo Spain
108 D1 Montalcino Italy
98 C3 Montalegre Portugal
90 D3 Montalieu-Vercieu France
111 E4 Montalto mt. Italy
108 D2 Montalto di Castro Italy
111 F3 Montalto Uffugo Italy
100 C1 Montalvão Portugal
162 B4 Montalvo Ecuador
100 B1 Montalvo Portugal
98 E3 Montamarta Spain
152 E2 Montana div. U.S.A.
112 D3 Montana Bulgaria
82 C2 Montana Switzerland
99 E1 Montaña de Covadonga, Parque Nacional de la nat. park Spain
100 D1 Montánchez, Sierra de mountain range Spain
103 C4 Montanejos Spain
93 B5 Montaner France
169 H3 Montanha Brazil
109 H4 Montano Antilia Italy
100 B1 Montargil, Barragem de resr Portugal
86 B5 Montargis France
93 E5 Montaset, Pic de mt. France
93 D5 Montastruc-la-Conseillère France
86 B3 Montataire France
88 C3 Montauban Bretagne France
93 D4 Montauban Midi-Pyrénées France
147 G4 Montauk New York U.S.A.
147 H4 Montauk Pt pt New York U.S.A.
93 B5 Montaut Aquitaine France
93 D5 Montaut Midi-Pyrénées France
90 C1 Montbard France
90 D1 Montbarrey France
93 E4 Montbazens France
89 F4 Montbazon France
90 E1 Montbéliard France
90 E2 Montbenoît France
93 D4 Montbeton France
102 E3 Montblanc Spain
90 E3 Mont Blanc Tunnel France/Italy
82 B1 Montbozon France
90 C3 Montbrison France
92 C3 Montbron France
86 A2 Montcavrel France
90 C2 Montceau-les-Mines France
90 C2 Montcenis France
90 C2 Montchanin France
86 D3 Montcornet France
93 D4 Montcuq France
86 D3 Montcy-Notre-Dame France
91 B5 Montdardier France
91 E4 Mont-Dauphin France
93 B5 Mont-de-Marsan France
86 B3 Montdidier France
111 E3 Montea mt. Italy
164 D3 Monteagudo Bolivia
99 H3 Monteagudo de las Vicarías Spain
172 A4 Monte Aguila Chile
166 B1 Monte Alegre Brazil
166 C3 Monte Alegre de Goiás Brazil
103 B6 Montealegre del Castillo Spain
168 D3 Monte Alegre de Minas Brazil
168 D4 Monte Aprazível Brazil
169 G1 Monte Azul Brazil
168 D4 Monte Azul Paulista Brazil
141 H4 Montebello Québec Canada
111 E5 Montebello Ionico Italy
16 A4 Monte Bello Is is Western Australia Australia
107 G3 Montebelluna Italy
88 D2 Montebourg France
173 F2 Monte Buey Argentina
170 F2 Montecarlo Argentina
106 B5 Monte-Carlo Monaco
168 E3 Monte Carmelo Brazil
173 J1 Monte Caseros Argentina
109 E2 Montecastrilli Italy
107 E5 Montecatini Terme Italy
106 E4 Montecchio Emilia Italy
107 F3 Montecchio Maggiore Italy
93 D5 Montech France
131 F1 Monte Christo South Africa
109 G3 Montecilfone Italy
172 D3 Monte Comán Argentina
109 J4 Monte Cotugna, Lago di l. Italy
107 G2 Montecreale Valcellina Italy
162 A4 Montecristi Ecuador
108 C2 Montecristo, Isola di i. Italy
100 B3 Monte da Rocha, Barragem do resr Portugal
100 C2 Monte das Flores Portugal
171 C7 Monte Dinero Argentina
109 E2 Montefalco Italy
109 H3 Montefalcone di Val Fortore Italy
107 G5 Montefelcino Italy
107 G5 Montefeltro reg. Italy
108 E2 Montefiascone Italy
109 F1 Montefiore dell'Aso Italy
107 E4 Montefiorino Italy
109 F2 Montefortino Italy
101 F3 Montefrío Spain
109 J4 Montegiordano Italy
109 F1 Montegiorgio Italy
159 □1 Montego Bay b. Jamaica
159 □1 Montego Bay Jamaica
107 H5 Montegranaro Italy
107 F3 Montegrotto Terme Italy
173 G5 Monte Hermoso Argentina
98 D4 Montehermoso Spain
101 E4 Montejaque Spain
14 B3 Montejinnie Northern Terr. Australia
92 E3 Montel-de-Gelat France
173 F4 Monte, L. del l. Argentina
109 H3 Monteleone di Puglia Italy
109 E2 Monteleone di Spoleto Italy
108 E2 Monteleone d'Orvieto Italy
108 A4 Monteleone Rocca Doria Sardegna Italy
110 C4 Montelepre Sicilia Italy
91 C4 Montélimar France
170 E2 Monte Lindo r. Argentina
109 H4 Montella Italy
100 E3 Montellano Spain
148 C4 Montello Wisconsin U.S.A.
107 H5 Montelupone Italy
110 C5 Montemaggiore Belsito Sicilia Italy
173 F2 Monte Maíz Argentina
109 H4 Montemarano Italy
101 H2 Montemayor r. Spain
92 C3 Montemboeuf France
111 G2 Montemesola Italy
100 D2 Montemolín Spain
109 F2 Montemonaco Italy
157 F3 Montemorelos Mexico
100 B2 Montemor-o-Novo Portugal
98 B4 Montemor-o-Velho Portugal
107 F5 Montemurlo Italy
98 B3 Montemuro, Serra de mountain range Portugal
89 E3 Montenay France
92 B3 Montendre France
167 B6 Montenegro Brazil
Montenegro div. see Crna Gora
99 H2 Montenegro de Cameros Spain
109 G3 Montenero di Bisaccia Italy
100 C2 Monte Novo, Barragem do resr Portugal
172 B1 Monte Patria Chile
107 H5 Monte Porzio Italy
127 C7 Montepuez r. Mozambique
127 C7 Montepuez Mozambique
108 D1 Montepulciano Italy
170 D2 Monte Quemado Argentina
107 G5 Monterchi Italy
98 B5 Monte Real Portugal
109 F2 Montereale Italy
86 B4 Montereau-faut-Yonne France
98 B5 Monte Redondo Portugal
154 B3 Monterey California U.S.A.
146 D5 Monterey Virginia U.S.A.
154 B3 Monterey Bay b. California U.S.A.
162 B2 Montería Colombia
107 F5 Monteriggioni Italy
165 D3 Montero Bolivia
108 D2 Monte Romano Italy
170 C2 Monteros Argentina
82 C3 Monte Rosa mt. Italy/Switzerland
109 E2 Monterosi Italy
106 D4 Monterosso al Mare Italy
110 D5 Monterosso Almo Sicilia Italy
109 E2 Monterotondo Italy
108 C1 Monterotondo Marittimo Italy
157 E3 Monterrey Mexico
98 C2 Monterroso Spain
101 E2 Monterrubio de la Serena Spain
109 F1 Monterubbiano Italy
166 C2 Montes Altos Brazil
111 H3 Montesano Salentino Italy
109 H4 Montesano sulla Marcellana Italy
107 F5 Monte San Savino Italy
109 H3 Monte Sant'Angelo Italy
166 E3 Monte Santo Brazil
169 E4 Monte Santo de Minas Brazil
108 B4 Monte Santu, Capo di pt Sardegna Italy
107 H5 Monte San Vito Italy
109 G3 Montesarchio Italy
111 F2 Montescaglioso Italy
169 G2 Montes Claros Brazil
107 E5 Montescudaio Italy
101 F1 Montes de Toledo mountain range Spain
109 G2 Montesilvano Italy
102 D2 Montes Malditos mountain range Spain
93 D4 Montesquieu France
93 D5 Montesquieu-Volvestre France
93 C5 Montesquiou France
93 C5 Montestruc-sur-Gers France
107 F5 Montevarchi Italy
109 H3 Monteverde Italy
150 E2 Montevideo Minnesota U.S.A.
173 J3 Montevideo Uruguay
153 F4 Monte Vista Colorado U.S.A.
148 A5 Montezuma Iowa U.S.A.
155 G4 Montezuma Castle National Monument nat. park Arizona U.S.A.
155 H3 Montezuma Creek Utah U.S.A.
154 D3 Montezuma Peak summit Nevada U.S.A.
89 D4 Montfaucon France
87 E3 Montfaucon-d'Argonne France
91 C3 Montfaucon-en-Velay France
91 E5 Montferrat France
68 C2 Montfoort Netherlands
88 D3 Montfort France
93 B5 Montfort-en-Chalosse France
89 F3 Montfort-le-Gesnois France
93 D6 Montgaillard Midi-Pyrénées France
93 C5 Montgaillard Midi-Pyrénées France
91 E4 Montgenèvre France
86 B4 Montgeron France
93 D5 Montgiscard France
103 D6 Montgó h. Spain
145 C5 Montgomery Alabama U.S.A.
62 C2 Montgomery Wales U.K.
92 B3 Montguyon France
86 D3 Monthermé France
82 B2 Monthey Switzerland
86 D3 Monthois France
87 E4 Monthureux-sur-Saône France
108 B4 Monti Sardegna Italy
107 G3 Monticano r. Italy
106 D3 Monticelli d'Ongina Italy
151 F5 Monticello Arkansas U.S.A.
145 D6 Monticello Florida U.S.A.
148 D5 Monticello Indiana U.S.A.
148 B4 Monticello Iowa U.S.A.
147 K1 Monticello Maine U.S.A.
148 B5 Monticello Missouri U.S.A.
147 F4 Monticello New York U.S.A.

122 C4 Mourdiah Mali
91 B4 Moure de la Gardille, La mt. France
93 B5 Mourenx France
91 C5 Mouriès France
115 E4 Mouriki Greece
15 F3 Mourilyan Harbour Queensland Australia
67 D2 Mourne r. Northern Ireland U.K.
67 E2 Mourne Mountains h. Northern Ireland U.K.
91 E5 Mourre de Chanier mt. France
91 E4 Mourre Froid, Le mt. France
91 D5 Mourre Nègre mt. France
66 □2 Mousa i. Scotland U.K.
69 B4 Mouscron Belgium
124 C1 Mousgougou Chad
91 C5 Moussac France
118 C4 Mousso well Chad
118 C5 Moussoro Chad
93 B4 Moustey France
91 E5 Moustiers-Ste-Marie France
125 B4 Moutamba Congo
90 E2 Mouthe France
82 A2 Mouthier-en-Bresse France
90 E1 Mouthier-Haute-Pierre France
93 E6 Mouthoumet France
82 C1 Moutier Switzerland
92 E2 Moutier-d'Ahun France
90 E3 Moûtiers France
92 A2 Moutiers-les-Mauxfaits France
22 E1 Moutong Indonesia
115 G5 Moutsouna Greece
86 B3 Mouy France
121 E4 Mouydir, Monts du plat. Algeria
125 B4 Mouyondzi Congo
114 C3 Mouzaki Greece
118 C5 Mouzarak Chad
87 E3 Mouzay France
87 E4 Mouzon r. France
87 E3 Mouzon France
112 F2 Movila Miresii Romania
67 D1 Moville Rep. of Ireland
15 G5 Mowbullan, Mt mt. Queensland Australia
54 D5 Mowchadz' Belarus
125 C6 Moxico div. Angola
166 E2 Moxotó r. Brazil
67 C2 Moy r. Rep. of Ireland
126 C4 Moyale Ethiopia
122 B5 Moyamba Sierra Leone
38 B4 Moyar r. India
86 C3 Moy-de-l'Aisne France
120 C2 Moyen Atlas mountain range Morocco
124 C2 Moyen-Chari div. Chad
131 F5 Moyeni Lesotho
122 B4 Moyenne-Guinée div. Guinea
89 G1 Moyenneville France
124 B4 Moyen-Ogooué div. Gabon
64 B4 Moyer h. Rep. of Ireland
87 F3 Moyeuvre-Grande France
64 B3 Moygashel Northern Ireland U.K.
64 A4 Moylett Rep. of Ireland
52 B3 Moylovo Rus. Fed.
30 A2 Moynalyk Rus. Fed.
139 G2 Moyne, Lac Le l. Québec Canada
22 D4 Moyo i. Indonesia
126 B4 Moyo Uganda
162 B5 Moyobamba Peru
124 C1 Moyto Chad
47 J5 Moyu China
126 C4 Moyum waterhole Kenya
67 E3 Moyvalley Rep. of Ireland
47 H3 Moyynty Kazakhstan
117 H8 Mozambique country Africa
129 G2 Mozambique Channel str. Africa
175 G5 Mozambique Ridge sea feature Indian Ocean
168 C1 Mozarlândia Brazil
51 H7 Mozdok Rus. Fed.
39 E1 Mozdūrān Iran
52 G2 Mozharov Maydan Rus. Fed.
52 C2 Mozhaysk Rus. Fed.
46 D1 Mozhga Rus. Fed.
39 E2 Mozhnābād Iran
81 F4 Mozirje Slovenia
24 A2 Mozo Myanmar
77 K1 Mozyr' Rus. Fed.
122 A3 Mpal Senegal
125 E5 Mpala Zaire
127 B6 Mpanda Tanzania
128 D2 Mpandamatenga Botswana
125 B4 Mpé Congo
131 H3 Mpemvana South Africa
37 H4 Mpen India
46 D4 M. Peschanyy pt Kazakhstan
122 C4 Mpessoba Mali
127 B4 Mpigi Uganda
127 B7 Mpika Zambia
124 C2 Mpoko r. Central African Rep.
127 B6 Mporokoso Zambia
125 C4 Mpouya Congo
127 B6 Mpulungu Zambia
131 H4 Mpumalanga South Africa
127 C6 Mpwapwa Tanzania
131 G5 Mqanduli South Africa
77 K2 Mrągowo Poland
46 E2 Mrakovo Rus. Fed.
114 C1 Mrežičko Macedonia
104 F3 Mrkonjić-Grad Bos.-Herz.
107 J3 Mrkopalj Croatia
76 F2 Mrocza Poland
77 H2 Mroczno Poland
77 K3 Mrozy Poland
121 G1 M'Saken Tunisia
127 C5 Msambweni Kenya
127 C6 Msata Tanzania
76 E4 Mściwojów Poland
46 D4 M. Sengiri pt Kazakhstan
75 K2 Mšeno Czech Rep.
50 D3 Mshinskaya Rus. Fed.
121 E1 M'Sila Algeria
50 E3 Msta r. Rus. Fed.
52 E1 Mstera Rus. Fed.
52 E1 Mstera Rus. Fed.
50 D4 Mstsislaw Belarus
131 J3 Msunduzi r. South Africa
46 D4 M. Suz pt Kazakhstan
77 J6 Mszana Dolna Poland
77 J4 Mszczonów Poland
127 C7 Mtama Tanzania
127 □4 Mt Blanche Mauritius
155 F3 Mt Carmel Junction Utah U.S.A.
148 C4 Mt Carroll Illinois U.S.A.
91 E3 Mt Cenis, Lac du l. France
9 C5 Mt Cook New Zealand
147 J2 Mt Desert I. i. Maine U.S.A.
153 F4 Mt Elbert mt. U.S.A.
126 C4 Mtelo mt. Kenya
127 C6 Mtera Reservoir resr Tanzania
27 Q2 M. Terpeniya Rus. Fed.
146 B4 Mt Gilead Ohio U.S.A.
134 D3 Mt Hayes mt. Alaska U.S.A.
148 C4 Mt Horeb Wisconsin U.S.A.
112 E1 Mţii Călimani mountain range Romania
112 E1 Mţii Rodnei mountain range Romania
147 G4 Mt Kisco New York U.S.A.
134 C3 Mt McKinley mt. Alaska U.S.A.
148 B5 Mt Pleasant Iowa U.S.A.
148 E4 Mt Pleasant Michigan U.S.A.
155 G2 Mt Pleasant Utah U.S.A.
146 C6 Mt Rogers National Recreation Area res. Virginia U.S.A.
52 C3 Mtsensk Rus. Fed.
9 C5 Mt Somers New Zealand
131 H4 Mtunzini South Africa
144 B4 Mt Vernon Illinois U.S.A.
148 B5 Mt Vernon Iowa U.S.A.
146 B4 Mt Vernon Ohio U.S.A.
127 C7 Mtwara div. Tanzania
127 D7 Mtwara Tanzania
100 B3 Mu mt. Portugal
24 A2 Mu r. Myanmar
6 □4 Mu'a Tonga
127 C7 Muaguide Mozambique
129 F2 Mualama Mozambique
125 B5 Muanda Zaire
25 C4 Muang Chainat Thailand
24 B3 Muang Chiang Rai Thailand
24 C2 Muang Hiam Laos
24 C3 Muang Hôngsa Laos
24 C3 Muang Kalasin Thailand
24 D3 Muang Khammouan Laos
25 D4 Muang Không Laos
24 D4 Muang Khôngxédôn Laos
24 C3 Muang Khon Kaen Thailand
24 C2 Muang Khoua Laos
25 B5 Muang Kirirath r. Thailand
24 B3 Muang Lampang Thailand
24 B3 Muang Lamphun Thailand
24 C3 Muang Loei Thailand
24 C3 Muang Lom Sak Thailand
24 B3 Muang Long Thailand
25 B5 Muang Luang r. Thailand
24 D4 Muang Mai Thailand
24 D3 Muang Mok Laos
24 D3 Muang Nakhon Phanom Thailand
24 C4 Muang Nakhon Sawan Thailand
24 C3 Muang Nan Thailand
24 C2 Muang Ngoy Laos
24 C2 Muang Ou Nua Laos
24 C3 Muang Pakxan Laos
24 B3 Muang Phan Thailand
24 B3 Muang Phayao Thailand
24 C3 Muang Phetchabun Thailand
24 C3 Muang Phichai Thailand
24 C3 Muang Phichit Thailand
24 D3 Muang Phin Laos
24 C3 Muang Phitsanulok Thailand
24 C3 Muang Phrae Thailand
24 D3 Muang Renu Nakhon Thailand
24 C4 Muang Roi Et Thailand
24 D3 Muang Sakon Nakhon Thailand
25 C4 Muang Samut Prakan Thailand
24 C3 Muang Souy Laos
24 B3 Muang Thoen Thailand
24 C4 Muang Uthai Thani Thailand
24 C2 Muang Va Laos
24 C3 Muang Vangviang Laos
24 C2 Muang Xay Laos
24 C2 Muang Xon Laos
24 D4 Muang Yasothon Thailand
25 C7 Muar r. Malaysia
25 C7 Muar Malaysia
22 D1 Muaraatap Indonesia
22 A3 Muarabulian Indonesia
20 D7 Muarabungo Indonesia
22 A3 Muaradua Indonesia
22 A2 Muaraenim Indonesia
22 C2 Muarainu Indonesia
22 D2 Muarajawa Indonesia
22 D2 Muarakaman Indonesia
22 A2 Muaralakitan Indonesia
22 D1 Muaralesan Indonesia
22 D1 Muaramayang Indonesia
22 D1 Muaranawai Indonesia
22 A2 Muarasabak Indonesia
20 C7 Muarasiberut Indonesia
22 C2 Muarateweh Indonesia
22 B1 Muara Tuang Malaysia
22 D1 Muarawahau Indonesia
39 F4 Muari, Ras c. Pakistan
43 C5 Mubārak, J. mt. Jordan/Saudi Arabia
37 E4 Mubarakpur India
47 G5 Mubarek Uzbekistan
119 H2 Mubarraz well Saudi Arabia
127 B4 Mubende Uganda
123 G4 Mubi Nigeria
43 C4 Mubrak, J. mt. Jordan
163 E3 Mucajaí r. Brazil
109 F1 Muccia Italy
74 C2 Much Germany
73 G4 Mücheln Germany
127 B7 Muchinga Escarpment escarpment Zambia
52 F4 Muchkapskiy Rus. Fed.
50 J1 Muchkas Rus. Fed.
77 J6 Muchówka Poland
32 C2 Muchuan China
62 D2 Much Wenlock England U.K.
99 F3 Mucientes Spain
66 B4 Muck i. Scotland U.K.
73 K4 Mücka Germany
15 G5 Muckadilla Queensland Australia
67 C1 Muckish Mountain h. Rep. of Ireland
66 □2 Muckle Roe i. Scotland U.K.
64 B3 Muckno Lake l. Rep. of Ireland
67 C2 Muckross Head headland Rep. of Ireland
127 D7 Mucojo Mozambique
125 D6 Muconda Angola
111 F3 Mucone r. Italy
125 B7 Mucope Angola
79 H5 Mucsi-hegy mt. Hungary
129 F2 Mucubela Mozambique
163 E5 Mucuim r. Brazil
129 E2 Mucumbura Mozambique
42 C2 Mucur Turkey
169 J3 Mucuri r. Brazil
169 J3 Mucuri Brazil
25 C6 Muda r. Malaysia
38 A3 Mūdabidri India
31 J3 Mudan r. China
31 J3 Mudanjiang China
42 B1 Mudanya Turkey
42 F4 Mudayrah Kuwait
146 C5 Muddlety W. Virginia U.S.A.
56 E2 Muddus National Park nat. park Sweden
155 G2 Muddy Creek r. Utah U.S.A.
155 E3 Muddy Peak summit Nevada U.S.A.
39 D2 Mūd-e-Dahanāb Iran
43 D4 Mudeisisat, J. h. Jordan
131 H4 Muden South Africa
72 F3 Müden (Aller) Germany
87 G2 Mudersbach Germany
13 G3 Mudgee New South Wales Australia
38 A2 Mudhol India
154 D3 Mud Lake l. Nevada U.S.A.
24 B3 Mudon Myanmar
126 E3 Mudug div. Somalia
127 C5 Mudukani Tanzania
42 B1 Mudurnu Turkey
50 F2 Mud'yuga Rus. Fed.
129 F1 Muecate Mozambique
127 C7 Mueda Mozambique
102 B3 Muel Spain
98 E3 Muelas del Pan Spain
102 C4 Muela de Ares mt. Spain
16 D3 Mueller Ra. h. Western Australia Australia
6 □2 Mueo New Caledonia Pacific Ocean
64 A2 Muff Rep. of Ireland
119 F3 Muftāh well Sudan
50 H1 Muftyuga Rus. Fed.
125 E6 Mufulira Zambia
125 E6 Mufumbwe Zambia
33 F2 Mufu Shan mountain range China
98 D3 Muga de Sayago Spain
147 K2 Mugaguadavic Lake l. New Brunswick Canada
98 B1 Mugardos Spain
37 F2 Mugarripug China
100 B1 Muge r. Portugal
129 F2 Mugeba Mozambique
73 J4 Mügeln Germany
126 C3 Muger Wenz r. Ethiopia
107 H3 Muggia Italy
Mughalbhin see Jati
37 E4 Mughal Sarai India
39 C2 Mūghār Iran
43 D5 Mughayrā' Saudi Arabia
47 H5 Mughsu r. Tajikistan
28 E7 Mugi Japan
125 E5 Mugila, Monts mountain range Zaire
113 F6 Muğla div. Turkey
42 B2 Muğla Turkey
46 E3 Mugodzhary ridge Kazakhstan
37 H2 Mug Qu r. China
52 F1 Mugreyevskiy Rus. Fed.
93 B5 Mugron France
127 C7 Muguia Mozambique
37 E3 Mugu Karnali r. Nepal
37 H2 Mugxung China
124 E1 Muhagiriya Sudan
119 G3 Muhammad Qol Sudan
74 D4 Mühlacker Germany
73 H4 Mühlanger Germany
73 J4 Mühlberg Germany
75 H4 Mühldorf am Inn Germany
81 G4 Mühldorf bei Feldbach Austria
81 F3 Mühlen Austria
73 J3 Mühlenbeck Germany
80 C1 Mühlhausen Germany
72 F4 Mühlhausen (Thüringen) Germany
74 D2 Mühlheim am Main Germany
83 E1 Mühlingen Germany
75 G2 Mühltroff Germany
81 F2 Mühlviertel reg. Austria
56 G2 Muhos Finland
80 B1 Muhr am See Germany
54 C2 Muhu i. Estonia
124 E4 Muhulu Zaire
127 C7 Muhuwesi r. Tanzania
126 C3 Mui Ethiopia
25 D5 Mui Ca Mau c. Vietnam
68 D2 Muiden Netherlands
25 E5 Mui Dinh headland Vietnam
127 C7 Muidumbe Mozambique
6 □4 Mui Hopohoponga pt Tonga
29 G5 Muika Japan
25 E4 Mui Nây pt Vietnam
Muineachán see Monaghan
67 E4 Muine Bheag Rep. of Ireland
65 F1 Muirdrum Scotland U.K.
65 E1 Muirhead Scotland U.K.
66 D5 Muirkirk Scotland U.K.
154 A3 Muir Woods National Monument nat. park California U.S.A.
162 B3 Muisne Ecuador
129 F1 Muite Mozambique
43 C4 Mujib, W. watercourse Jordan
31 H6 Muju South Korea
42 F2 Mujūmbar Iran
79 M3 Mukacheve Ukraine
37 F3 Mükangsar China
78 D2 Mukařov Czech Rep.
28 J2 Mu-kawa r. Japan
24 D3 Mukdahan Thailand
Mukden see Shenyang
36 C3 Mukerian India
23 □1 Mukeru Palau
77 M3 Mukhavyets Belarus
31 H1 Mukhino Rus. Fed.
30 E1 Mukhor-Konduy Rus. Fed.
30 D2 Mukhorshibir' Rus. Fed.
52 F2 Mukhtolovo Rus. Fed.
17 B6 Mukinbudin Western Australia Australia
37 H3 Mukki India
20 D7 Mukomuko Indonesia
127 B4 Mukono Uganda
47 G5 Mukry Turkmenistan
37 E3 Muktinath Nepal
36 C3 Muktsar India
137 K4 Mukutawa r. Manitoba Canada
148 C4 Mukwonago Wisconsin U.S.A.
36 D5 Mul India
38 A2 Mula r. India
36 A3 Mula r. Pakistan
103 B6 Mula r. Spain
103 B6 Mula Spain
35 D10 Mulaku Atoll atoll Maldives
31 J3 Mulan China
23 B3 Mulanay Philippines
129 F2 Mulanje Malawi
129 F2 Mulanje, Mt mt. Malawi
108 B5 Mulargia, Lago l. Sardegna Italy
166 B1 Mulata Brazil
151 E5 Mulberry Arkansas U.S.A.
172 A4 Mulchén Chile
73 H4 Mulde r. Germany
127 B5 Muleba Tanzania
155 H5 Mule Creek New Mexico U.S.A.
152 F3 Mule Creek Wyoming U.S.A.
156 B3 Mulegé Mexico
22 E4 Mules i. Indonesia
151 C5 Muleshoe Texas U.S.A.
129 F2 Mulevala Mozambique
12 C2 Mulgathing S. Australia Australia
101 G3 Mulhacén mt. Spain
72 B4 Mülheim an der Ruhr Germany
90 F1 Mulhouse Haut-Rhin France
32 C3 Muli China
7 □12 Mulifanua Western Samoa
31 J3 Muling r. China
31 J3 Muling China
31 J3 Muling China
7 □12 Mulitapuili, C. c. Western Samoa
66 B4 Mull i. Scotland U.K.
64 B4 Mullagh Rep. of Ireland
67 B4 Mullaghareirk Mts h. Rep. of Ireland
38 C4 Mullaittivu Sri Lanka
13 G2 Mullaley New South Wales Australia
67 C2 Mullany's Cross Rep. of Ireland
67 A2 Mullet, The b. Rep. of Ireland
148 E3 Mullett Lake l. Michigan U.S.A.
17 A6 Mullewa Western Australia Australia
66 F1 Mull Head headland Scotland U.K.
74 C5 Müllheim Germany
147 F5 Mullica r. New Jersey U.S.A.
67 D3 Mullingar Rep. of Ireland
62 A4 Mullion England U.K.
73 K3 Müllrose Germany
59 E3 Mullsjö Sweden
66 B4 Mull, Sound of chan. Scotland U.K.
13 H2 Mullumbimby New South Wales Australia
125 E7 Mulobezi Zambia
125 D7 Mulonga Plain plain Zambia
67 B3 Mulrany Rep. of Ireland
89 F4 Mulsanne France
38 A2 Mulshi L. l. India
36 D5 Multai India
36 B3 Multan Pakistan
57 G3 Multia Finland
86 B3 Multien reg. France
125 E5 Mulumbe, Monts mts Zaire
124 D3 Muma Zaire
39 E4 Mūmān Iran
Mumbai see Bombay
62 C3 Mumbles Head headland Wales U.K.
62 C3 Mumbles, The Wales U.K.
125 B6 Mumbondo Angola
125 E6 Mumbwa Zambia
82 C1 Mümliswil Switzerland
51 H6 Mumra Rus. Fed.
21 H8 Muna i. Indonesia
157 H4 Muna Mexico
36 B4 Munabao Pakistan
56 L6 Munaðarnes Iceland
28 C7 Munakata Japan
99 E4 Muñana Spain
46 D3 Munayly Kazakhstan
75 G3 Münchberg Germany
73 K3 Müncheberg Germany
75 G4 München airport Germany
75 G4 München Germany
75 G2 Münchenbernsdorf Germany
82 C1 Münchenbuchsee Switzerland
87 H2 Münchhausen Germany
162 B3 Munchique, Co mt. Colombia
136 D3 Muncho Lake B.C. Canada
136 D3 Muncho Lake Provincial Park nat. park B.C. Canada
31 H5 Munch'ŏn North Korea
83 E1 Münchwilen Switzerland
148 E5 Muncie Indiana U.S.A.
14 D5 Muncoonie, L. salt flat Queensland Australia
146 E4 Muncy Pennsylvania U.S.A.
6 □1 Munda Solomon Is.
99 H1 Mundaka Spain
38 B5 Mundel L. l. Sri Lanka
124 A3 Mundemba Cameroon
72 E4 Münden Germany
80 E2 Munderfing Austria
63 H2 Mundesley England U.K.
63 G2 Mundford England U.K.
15 E3 Mundjura Cr. r. Queensland Australia
103 B6 Mundo r. Spain
87 G4 Mundolshiem France
166 D3 Mundo Novo Brazil
36 B5 Mundra India
17 D6 Mundrabilla Western Australia Australia
15 G5 Mundubbera Queensland Australia
36 C4 Mundwa India
102 B3 Munebrega Spain
101 H1 Munera Spain
38 C2 Muneru r. India
15 F5 Mungallala Queensland Australia
15 F6 Mungallala Cr. r. Queensland Australia
15 F3 Mungana Queensland Australia
36 D4 Mungaoli India
129 E2 Mungári Mozambique
124 E3 Mungbere Zaire
37 E5 Mungeli India
37 F4 Munger India
12 D2 Mungeranie S. Australia Australia
22 B1 Mungguresak, Tg pt Indonesia
99 H1 Mungia Spain
13 G2 Mungindi New South Wales Australia
37 G5 Mungla India
127 B7 Mungwi Zambia
125 B6 Munhino Angola
Munich see München
99 E4 Muñico Spain
102 C3 Muniesa Spain
166 D1 Munim r. Brazil
148 D2 Munising Michigan U.S.A.
169 H4 Muniz Freire Brazil
59 E3 Munka-Ljungby Sweden
55 C4 Munkebo Denmark
58 D2 Munkedal Sweden
56 H1 Munkelv Norway
59 E2 Munkfors Sweden
30 B2 Munku-Sardyk, G. mt. Mongolia
74 F2 Münnerstadt Germany
131 G1 Munnik South Africa
130 E6 Munnikspoort pass South Africa
9 □1 Munning Pt pt Chatham Is New Zealand
171 B7 Muñoz Gamero, Pen. de pen. Chile
83 G1 Münsing Germany
74 E4 Münsingen Germany
82 C2 Münsingen Switzerland
72 C3 Münster div. Nordrhein-Westfalen Germany
67 B4 Munster div. Rep. of Ireland
74 D3 Münster Hessen Germany
80 C3 Münster Austria
87 G4 Munster France
72 C4 Münster Germany
72 F3 Munster Germany
106 C2 Münster Switzerland
72 C4 Münsterland reg. Germany
17 B6 Muntadgin Western Australia Australia
22 D1 Munte Indonesia
68 E1 Muntendam Netherlands
112 E1 Munţii Maramureşului mountain range Romania
112 D1 Munţii Oaşului mts Romania
139 F3 Muntviel, Lac l. Québec Canada
111 □ Munxar Malta
129 D2 Munyati r. Zimbabwe
131 G5 Munyu South Africa
87 H2 Münzenberg Germany
81 E2 Münzkirchen Austria
56 H2 Muojärvi l. Finland
24 D3 Mường Lam Vietnam
24 C2 Mường Nhie Vietnam
24 D3 Muong Nong Laos
24 C3 Muong Pakbeng Laos
24 D3 Muong Phalan Laos
24 C3 Muong Phiang Laos
24 D3 Muong Phôn-Hông Laos
24 C2 Muong Sing Laos
24 C3 Muong Xaignabouri Laos
56 F2 Muonio Finland
56 F1 Muonioälven r. Finland/Sweden
82 D2 Muotathal Switzerland
129 F2 Mupa r. Mozambique
125 C7 Mupa, Parque Nacional da nat. park Angola
31 G5 Muping China
126 E4 Muqakoori Somalia
126 E4 Muqdisho Somalia
169 H4 Muqui Brazil
81 G4 Mur r. Austria
78 F5 Mura r. Croatia/Hungary
100 C1 Muradal, Serra do mountain range Portugal
113 F5 Muradiye Manisa Turkey
42 E2 Muradiye Van Turkey
29 G4 Murakami Japan
78 F5 Murakeresztúr Hungary
171 B6 Murallón, Co mt. Chile
127 A5 Muramvya Burundi
79 K3 Muráň r. Slovakia
79 K3 Muráň Slovakia
127 C5 Muranga Kenya
25 □ Mura Res. resr Singapore
50 J3 Murashi Rus. Fed.
93 E5 Murasson France
78 F5 Muraszemenye Hungary
42 E2 Murat r. Turkey
92 E3 Murat France
42 A1 Muratlı Turkey
108 B2 Murato Corse France
93 E5 Murat-sur-Vèbre France
81 F3 Murau div. Austria
81 F3 Murau Austria
108 B5 Muravera Sardegna Italy
52 E3 Muravlyanka Rus. Fed.
29 H4 Murayama Japan
98 C3 Murça Portugal
102 B2 Murchante Spain
39 B2 Murcheh Khvort Iran
73 J2 Murchin Germany
17 A5 Murchison r. Western Australia Australia
13 F4 Murchison Victoria Australia
9 D4 Murchison New Zealand
126 B4 Murchison Falls National Park nat. park Uganda
140 A1 Murchison I. i. Ontario Canada
17 B5 Murchison, Mt h. Western Australia Australia
9 C5 Murchison, Mt mt. New Zealand
103 B7 Murcia div. Spain
103 B7 Murcia Murcia Spain
76 F3 Murczyn Poland
93 E4 Mur-de-Barrez France
88 C3 Mûr-de-Bretagne France
150 C3 Murdo S. Dakota U.S.A.
139 G4 Murdochville Québec Canada
29 G5 Mure Japan
81 G4 Mureck Austria
129 E2 Murehwa Zimbabwe
112 D2 Mureş r. Romania
93 D5 Muret France
145 E4 Murfreesboro N. Carolina U.S.A.
145 C5 Murfreesboro Tennessee U.S.A.
74 D4 Murg r. Germany
74 D5 Murg Germany
46 F5 Murgab r. Turkmenistan
39 E1 Murgab Turkmenistan
112 G1 Murgeni Romania
82 C1 Murgenthal Switzerland
111 G2 Murge Tarantine reg. Italy
39 E2 Murghab r. Afghanistan
36 B3 Murgha Kibzai Pakistan
47 H5 Murghob Tajikistan
39 G2 Murgh Pass pass Afghanistan
109 J4 Murgia Sant'Elia h. Italy
15 G5 Murgon Queensland Australia
17 B5 Murgoo Western Australia Australia
99 H2 Murguía Spain
30 B5 Muri China
30 A5 Muri China
37 F5 Muri India
39 D1 Mūrī Iran
83 D1 Muri Switzerland
169 G4 Muriaé Brazil
99 G1 Muriedas Spain
125 D6 Muriege Angola
30 C2 Murino Rus. Fed.
82 D3 Murisengo Italy
73 H2 Müritz l. Germany
73 J2 Müritz, Nationalpark nat. park Germany
73 H2 Müritz Seenpark nat. park Germany
39 C3 Mūrjān Iran
56 H1 Murmansk div. Rus. Fed.
56 J1 Murmansk Rus. Fed.
52 E2 Murmino Rus. Fed.
75 G5 Murnau am Staffelsee Germany
103 G5 Muro r. Spain
108 A2 Muro Corse France
103 G5 Muro Spain
108 A3 Muro, Capo di pt Corse France
103 C6 Muro de Alcoy Spain
92 E3 Murol France
109 H4 Muro Lucano Italy
52 F2 Murom Rus. Fed.
47 J1 Muromtsevo Rus. Fed.
92 B2 Muron France
127 B5 Murongo Tanzania
28 H2 Muroran Japan
98 A2 Muros Spain
28 E7 Muroto Japan
28 E7 Muroto-zaki pt Japan
77 N5 Murovane Ukraine
53 B2 Murovani Kurylivtsi Ukraine
76 F3 Murowana-Goślina Poland
152 C3 Murphy Idaho U.S.A.
145 D5 Murphy N. Carolina U.S.A.
154 B2 Murphys California U.S.A.
15 F6 Murra Murra Queensland Australia
136 E3 Murray r. B.C. Canada
12 E3 Murray r. Australia
144 B4 Murray Kentucky U.S.A.
152 E3 Murray Utah U.S.A.
12 D3 Murray Bridge S. Australia Australia
14 C4 Murray Downs Northern Terr. Australia
10 □2 Murray Hill h. Christmas I. Indian Ocean
145 D5 Murray, L. l. S. Carolina U.S.A.
6 □1 Murray, Lake l. P.N.G.
130 D5 Murraysburg South Africa
177 L3 Murray Seascarp sea feature Pacific Ocean
12 E3 Murrayville Victoria Australia
36 C2 Murree Pakistan
74 E4 Murrhardt Germany
13 G3 Murringo New South Wales Australia
67 B3 Murrisk reg. Rep. of Ireland
67 B3 Murroogh Rep. of Ireland
13 F3 Murrumbidgee r. New South Wales Australia
13 G3 Murrumburrah New South Wales Australia
129 F2 Murrupula Mozambique
13 G2 Murrurundi New South Wales Australia
89 E4 Mûrs-Erigné France
81 H4 Murska Sobota Slovenia
81 H4 Murska Središće Croatia
39 E4 Mürt Iran
36 D5 Murtajāpur India
101 G4 Murtas Spain
82 C2 Murten Switzerland
82 C2 Murtensee l. Switzerland
104 E4 Murter Croatia
13 E4 Murtoa Victoria Australia
98 B4 Murtosa Portugal
38 A2 Murud India
22 C2 Murui r. Indonesia
31 G4 Muruin Sum Sk. resr China
22 C2 Murung r. Indonesia
38 C4 Murunkan Sri Lanka
8 F3 Murupara New Zealand
177 K7 Mururoa atoll French Polynesia Pacific Ocean
91 B5 Murviel-lès-Béziers France
36 E5 Murwara India
13 H2 Murwillumbah New South Wales Australia
52 A2 Murygino Rus. Fed.
50 J3 Murygino Rus. Fed.
81 G3 Mürz r. Austria
118 B2 Murzūq Libya
76 D3 Murzynowo Poland
81 G3 Mürzzuschlag div. Austria
81 G3 Mürzzuschlag Austria
42 E2 Muş Turkey
54 C3 Mūša r. Latvia/Lithuania
125 D4 Musadi Zaire
36 B3 Musa Khel Bazar Pakistan
31 J4 Musan North Korea
39 D4 Musandam Pen. pen. Oman
39 F2 Musa Qala Afghanistan
39 B4 Musay'īd Qatar
118 D4 Musbat well Sudan
Muscat see Masqaţ
148 B5 Muscatine Iowa U.S.A.
87 G2 Müschenbach Germany
148 B4 Muscoda Wisconsin U.S.A.
147 J3 Muscongus Bay b. Maine U.S.A.
125 D6 Musela Zaire
15 E2 Musgrave Queensland Australia
9 C5 Musgrave, Mt mt. New Zealand
12 B1 Musgrave Ranges mountain range S. Australia Australia
43 D5 Mushash Dabl well Saudi Arabia
43 D4 Musheish watercourse Jordan
67 C4 Musheramore h. Rep. of Ireland
125 C4 Mushie Zaire
55 D4 Musholm i. Denmark
55 D4 Musholm Bugt b. Denmark
53 E2 Mushuryn Rig Ukraine
38 B2 Musi r. India
22 A2 Musi r. Indonesia
114 C1 Musica mt. Macedonia
155 F4 Music Mt mt. Arizona U.S.A.
155 G2 Musinia Peak summit Utah U.S.A.
136 E2 Muskeg r. N.W.T. Canada
147 H4 Muskeget Channel chan. Massachusetts U.S.A.
148 D4 Muskegon r. Michigan U.S.A.
148 D4 Muskegon Michigan U.S.A.
146 C5 Muskingum r. Ohio U.S.A.
59 H2 Muskö i. Sweden
151 E5 Muskogee Oklahoma U.S.A.
141 F4 Muskoka Ontario Canada
141 F4 Muskoka, Lake l. Ontario Canada
136 E3 Muskwa r. B.C. Canada
36 A3 Muslimbagh Pakistan
42 D2 Muslimīyah Syria
119 G4 Musmar Sudan
127 B5 Musoma Tanzania
127 B6 Musombe Tanzania
6 □1 Mussau I. i. P.N.G.
66 E5 Musselburgh Scotland U.K.
68 F2 Mussel-kanaal Netherlands
152 E2 Musselshell r. Montana U.S.A.
125 C6 Mussende Angola
92 C3 Mussidan France
110 C5 Mussomeli Sicilia Italy
69 D5 Musson Belgium
36 D3 Mussoorie India
125 D6 Mussuma r. Angola
86 D5 Mussy-sur-Seine France
42 B1 Mustafa-kemalpaşa Turkey
126 D3 Mustahīl Ethiopia
83 F2 Müstair Switzerland
172 D6 Musters Argentina
171 C6 Musters, L. l. Argentina
159 G4 Mustique i. St Vincent
54 C2 Mustjala Estonia
54 D2 Mustla Estonia
54 E2 Mustvee Estonia
54 D3 Musu r. Latvia/Lithuania
31 J4 Musu-dan pt North Korea
13 G3 Muswellbrook New South Wales Australia
77 J2 Muszaki Poland
77 J6 Muszyna Poland
119 E2 Mut Egypt
42 C2 Mut Turkey
81 G4 Muta Slovenia
131 H1 Mutale r. South Africa
166 E3 Mutá, Pta do pt Brazil
129 E2 Mutare Zimbabwe
126 D1 Mutayyin Yemen
129 E3 Mutirikwi, L. l. Zimbabwe
21 H8 Mutis mt. Indonesia
129 E2 Mutoko Zimbabwe
12 E3 Mutooroo S. Australia Australia
129 E2 Mutorashanga Zimbabwe
127 D7 Mutsamudu Comoros
125 D6 Mutshatsha Zaire
28 H3 Mutsu Japan
28 H3 Mutsu-wan b. Japan
15 F4 Muttaburra Queensland Australia
80 B3 Muttekopf mt. Austria
82 C1 Muttenz Switzerland
74 D3 Mutterstadt Germany
10 □4 Mutton Bird I. i. Lord Howe I. Pacific Ocean
9 B7 Muttonbird Is is New Zealand
9 A7 Muttonbird Islands is New Zealand
67 B4 Mutton Island i. Rep. of Ireland
129 F1 Mutuali Mozambique
163 E5 Mutum Amazonas Brazil
169 H3 Mutum Minas Gerais Brazil
123 G5 Mutum Biyu Nigeria
166 C3 Mutunópolis Brazil
38 C4 Mutur Sri Lanka
56 G1 Mutusjärvi l. Finland
53 E1 Mutyn Ukraine
54 C1 Muurla Finland
56 G2 Muurola Finland
30 D5 Mu Us Shamo desert China
125 B5 Muxaluando Angola
98 A1 Muxía Spain
125 B5 Muxima Angola
50 E2 Muyezerskiy Rus. Fed.
127 B5 Muyinga Burundi
46 E4 Muynak Uzbekistan
125 E5 Muyumba Zaire
33 E2 Muyuping China
36 C2 Muzaffarabad Pakistan
36 B3 Muzaffargarh Pakistan
36 D3 Muzaffarnagar India
37 F4 Muzaffarpur India
169 E4 Muzambinho Brazil
47 K4 Muzat r. China
88 C4 Muzillac France
39 E4 Mūzīn Iran
136 C4 Muzon, C. c. Alaska U.S.A.
157 E3 Múzquiz Mexico
36 E2 Muztag mt. China
37 F1 Muztag mt. China
47 J5 Muztagata mt. China
124 B3 Mvadi Gabon
124 B3 Mvangan Cameroon
124 E2 Mvolo Sudan
127 C6 Mvomero Tanzania
125 B4 Mvouti Congo
129 E2 Mvuma Zimbabwe
127 D7 Mwali i. Comoros
127 B5 Mwanza div. Tanzania
127 B5 Mwanza Tanzania
125 E5 Mwanza Zaire

67 B3 Mweelrea h. Rep. of Ireland
125 D4 Mweka Zaire
125 E6 Mwenda Zambia
125 D5 Mwene-Ditu Zaire
129 E3 Mwenezi r. Zimbabwe
129 E3 Mwenezi Zimbabwe
125 E4 Mwenga Zaire
125 E5 Mweru, Lake l. Zambia
125 E5 Mweru Wantipa, Lake l. Zambia
125 E5 Mweru Wantipa Nat. Park nat. park Zambia
125 D5 Mwimba Zaire
125 D6 Mwinilunga Zambia
54 E4 Myadzyel Belarus
24 A2 Myaing Myanmar
36 B4 Myājlār India
53 B1 M"yakoty Ukraine
13 H3 Myall L. l. New South Wales Australia
24 A3 Myanaung Myanmar
19 L7 Myanmar country Asia
52 B2 Myatlevo Rus. Fed.
24 A3 Myaungmya Myanmar
24 B3 Myawadi Thailand
66 E2 Mybster Scotland U.K.
24 A2 Myebon Myanmar
77 M4 Myedna Belarus
24 A2 Myedu Myanmar
24 A2 Myingyan Myanmar
24 B2 Myinkyado Myanmar
25 B4 Myinmoletkat mt. Myanmar
24 A2 Myinmu Myanmar
24 B1 Myitkyina Myanmar
24 B2 Myitson Myanmar
25 B4 Myitta Myanmar
37 H5 Myittha r. Myanmar
24 B2 Myittha Myanmar
79 G3 Myjava Slovakia
53 F3 Mykhaylivka Zaporiz'ka Oblast' Ukraine
53 F3 Mykhaylivka Zaporiz'ka Oblast' Ukraine
53 D1 Mykhaylo-Kotsyubyns'ke Ukraine
114 F1 Myki Greece
115 D5 Mykines Greece
53 E3 Mykolayiv div. Ukraine
77 M6 Mykolayiv Ukraine
53 E3 Mykolayiv Mykolayivs'ka Oblast' Ukraine
53 F3 Mykolayivka Dnipropetrovs'ka Oblast' Ukraine
53 F3 Mykolayivka Khersons'ka Oblast' Ukraine
53 D3 Mykolayivka Odes'ka Oblast' Ukraine
53 C3 Mykolayivka-Novorosiys'ka Ukraine
115 G5 Mykonos i. Greece
115 G5 Mykonos Greece
54 E1 Myllykoski Finland
115 D5 Myloi Greece
115 D6 Mylopotamos Greece
37 G4 Mymensingh Bangladesh
54 C1 Mynämäki Finland
130 D5 Mynfontein South Africa
62 C2 Mynydd Eppynt h. Wales U.K.
62 C1 Mynydd Hiraethog h. Wales U.K.
62 B3 Mynydd Preseli h. Wales U.K.
24 A2 Myohaung Myanmar
24 B2 Myohla Myanmar
29 G5 Myōkō-san volcano Japan
82 A1 Myon France
31 J4 Myonggan North Korea
54 E4 Myory Belarus
24 A2 Myothit Myanmar
56 M7 Mýrdalsjökull ice cap Iceland
56 D1 Myre Norway
56 F2 Myrheden Sweden
53 E2 Myrhorod Ukraine
114 G3 Myrina Greece
53 E2 Myrivs'ke Ukraine
53 G3 Myrne Donets'ka Oblast' Ukraine
53 E3 Myrne Khersons'ka Oblast' Ukraine
53 D1 Myrne Kyyivs'ka Oblast' Ukraine
77 N5 Myrne Volyns'ka Oblast' Ukraine
53 G2 Myronivka Kharkivs'ka Oblast' Ukraine
53 D2 Myronivka Kyyivs'ka Oblast' Ukraine
53 B1 Myropil' Ukraine
53 F3 Myrove Ukraine
54 D1 Myrskylä Finland
145 E5 Myrtle Beach S. Carolina U.S.A.
152 A3 Myrtle Point Oregon U.S.A.
115 G7 Myrtos Greece
27 Q2 Mys Aniva Rus. Fed.
58 D2 Mysen Norway
31 J4 Mys Gamova c. Rus. Fed.
52 D1 Myshkin Rus. Fed.
113 F5 Mysia reg. Turkey
47 L2 Myski Rus. Fed.
27 Q2 Mys Kril'on Rus. Fed.
73 K3 Myśla r. Poland
77 H6 Myślenice Poland
76 C3 Myślibórz Poland
77 H2 Myślice Poland
56 J1 Mys Nemetskiy c. Rus. Fed.
38 B3 Mysore India
46 D4 Mys Sagyndyk pt Kazakhstan
54 A4 Mys Taran pt Rus. Fed.
147 F5 Mystic Islands New Jersey U.S.A.
46 C4 Mys Tyub-Karagan headland Kazakhstan
77 H5 Myszków Poland
77 K2 Myszyniec Poland
52 F1 Myt Rus. Fed.
25 D5 My Tho Vietnam
114 B4 Mytikas Greece
115 F5 Mytilini Greece
113 F6 Mytilinioi Greece
113 F5 Mytilini Strait chan. Greece
52 C2 Mytishchi Rus. Fed.
78 C2 Mýto Czech Rep.
56 M6 Mývatn l. Iceland
77 N4 Myzove Ukraine
131 F5 Mzamomhle South Africa
75 H3 Mže r. Czech Rep.
127 B7 Mzimba Malawi
131 G4 Mzimkulwana res. South Africa
129 D3 Mzingwani r. Zimbabwe
127 B7 Mzuzu Malawi

N

75 G3 Naab r. Germany
124 C1 Naala Chad
68 C3 Naaldwijk Netherlands
153 □2 Naalehu Hawaii U.S.A.
124 E2 Na'am watercourse Sudan
121 D2 Naama Algeria
57 F3 Naantali Finland
68 D2 Naarden Netherlands
67 E3 Naas Rep. of Ireland
24 B1 Naba Myanmar
130 A4 Nababeep South Africa
98 B5 Nabão r. Portugal
38 C2 Nabarangapur India
29 F6 Nabari Japan
23 B4 Nabas Philippines
43 C3 Nabatiyet et Tahta Lebanon
6 □6 Nabavatu Fiji
75 H3 Nabburg Germany
127 C5 Naberera Tanzania
52 D4 Naberezhnoye Rus. Fed.
46 D1 Naberezhnyye Chelny Rus. Fed.
121 G1 Nabeul Tunisia
36 D3 Nabha India
39 D3 Nabīd Iran
165 E4 Nabileque r. Brazil
21 L7 Nabire Indonesia
43 C3 Nablus West Bank
122 D4 Nabolo Ghana
131 G2 Naboomspruit South Africa
6 □8 Naboutini Fiji
6 □6 Nabouwalu Fiji
43 C5 Nabq Egypt
36 D2 Nabra r. India
25 B4 Nabule Myanmar
129 G1 Nacala Mozambique
156 J6 Nacaome Honduras
129 F1 Nacaroa Mozambique
78 D2 Načeradec Czech Rep.
77 N1 Nacha Belarus
152 B2 Naches Washington U.S.A.
127 C7 Nachingwea Tanzania
36 B4 Nāchna India
78 F1 Náchod Czech Rep.
6 □8 Nacilau Pt pt Fiji
101 H3 Nacimiento r. Spain
172 A4 Nacimiento Chile
154 B4 Nacimiento Reservoir resr California U.S.A.
157 F5 Nacional, Valle Mexico
151 E6 Nacogdoches Texas U.S.A.
156 C2 Nacozari de García Mexico
77 J3 Nacpolsk Poland
172 D3 Nacuñan Argentina
Nada see Dan Xian
29 G5 Nadachi Japan
6 □8 Nadarivatu Fiji
76 E2 Nadarzyce Poland
81 H4 Nádasd Hungary
63 E3 Nadder r. England U.K.
6 □8 Nadi Fiji
36 C5 Nadiad India
6 □8 Nadi B. b. Fiji
39 C3 Nadīk Iran
79 K5 Nădlac Romania
121 D1 Nador Morocco
6 □8 Nadrau Plateau plat. Fiji
79 L4 Nádudvar Hungary
111 □ Nadur Malta
6 □6 Naduri Fiji
111 □ Nadur Tower Malta
53 A2 Nadvirna Ukraine
50 E2 Nadvoitsy Rus. Fed.
44 J3 Nadym Rus. Fed.
36 C4 Naenwa India
55 D4 Næstved Denmark
123 G4 Nafada Nigeria
83 E1 Näfels Switzerland
115 C4 Nafpaktos Greece
115 D5 Nafplio Greece
42 F3 Naft r. Iraq
39 B3 Naft-e Safīd Iran
42 F3 Naft Khanen Iraq
42 F3 Naft Shahr Iran
119 H2 Nafud al 'Urayq sand dunes Saudi Arabia
118 B1 Nafūsah, Jabal h. Libya
119 H2 Nafy Saudi Arabia
23 B3 Naga Philippines
140 C2 Nagagami r. Ontario Canada
140 C2 Nagagami Lake l. Ontario Canada
140 C2 Nagagamisis Lake l. Ontario Canada
140 C2 Nagagamisis Provincial Park res. Ontario Canada
28 D7 Nagahama Japan
29 F6 Nagahama Japan
37 H4 Naga Hills mountain range India
29 H4 Nagai Japan
37 H4 Nagaland India
29 □2 Nagannu-jima i. Japan
29 G5 Nagano div. Japan
29 G5 Nagano Japan
29 G5 Nagaoka Japan
37 H4 Nagaon India
38 B4 Nagappattinam India
34 E4 Nagar India
36 D4 Nagar India
38 B2 Nāgārjuna Sāgar Reservoir resr India
36 B4 Nagar Parkar Pakistan
37 G3 Nagarzê China
28 B7 Nagasaki div. Japan
28 B7 Nagasaki Japan
28 C7 Naga-shima i. Japan
28 D7 Naga-shima i. Japan
28 C7 Nagashima Japan
28 C6 Nagato Japan
36 C4 Nagaur India
38 C2 Nagavali r. India
37 G2 Nag, Co salt lake China
36 C5 Nagda India
68 D2 Nagele Netherlands
38 B4 Nagercoil India
39 F4 Nagha Kalat Pakistan
119 F2 Nag 'Hammâdi Egypt
126 B4 Nagichot Sudan
36 D3 Nagina India
67 C4 Nagles Mts h. Rep. of Ireland
77 J5 Nagłowice Poland
37 E3 Nagma Nepal
29 □2 Nago Japan
36 E4 Nagod India
74 D4 Nagold r. Germany
74 D4 Nagold Germany
32 A2 Nagong Chu r. China
Nagorno-Karabakh div. see Qarabağ
50 J3 Nagorsk Rus. Fed.
52 D1 Nagor'ye Rus. Fed.
30 A2 Nagor'ye Sangilen mountain range Rus. Fed.
107 E3 Nago-Torbole Italy
29 □2 Nago-wan b. Japan
29 F6 Nagoya Japan
36 D5 Nagpur India
37 H3 Nagqu China
54 B1 Nagu Finland
145 □3 Naguabo Puerto Rico
23 C3 Nagumbuaya Point pt Philippines
44 F1 Nagurskoye Rus. Fed.
78 G5 Nagyatád Hungary
79 G5 Nagybajom Hungary
79 H5 Nagybaracska Hungary
79 H5 Nagyberény Hungary
79 H5 Nagydorog Hungary
79 L3 Nagyhalász Hungary
79 H4 Nagyigmánd Hungary
79 L4 Nagykálló Hungary
78 G5 Nagykanizsa Hungary
78 G5 Nagykapornak Hungary
79 J4 Nagykáta Hungary
79 L4 Nagykereki Hungary
79 H5 Nagykónyi Hungary
79 J4 Nagykőrös Hungary
79 K4 Nagykunság reg. Hungary
79 K5 Nagylak Hungary
79 L3 Nagy-Milic mt. Hungary/Slovakia
79 H6 Nagynyárád Hungary
79 L4 Nagy-Sárrét reg. Hungary
79 K5 Nagyszénás Hungary
79 G5 Nagyvázsony Hungary
29 □2 Naha Japan
39 E4 Nahang r. Iran/Pakistan
136 E2 Nahanni Butte N.W.T. Canada
136 D2 Nahanni National Park nat. park N.W.T. Canada
43 C3 Naharayim Israel
43 C3 Nahariyya Israel
99 H4 Naharros Spain
39 B2 Nahāvand Iran
74 C3 Nahe r. Germany
6 □2 Nahoï, Cap c. Vanuatu
89 G4 Nahon r. France
43 D1 Nahr Sājūr r. Syria
172 A4 Nahuelbuta, Parque Nacional nat. park Chile
172 B6 Nahuel Huapí, L. l. Argentina
171 B5 Nahuel Huapi, Parque Nacional nat. park Argentina
172 D3 Nahuel Mapá Argentina
172 D6 Nahuel Niyeu Argentina
173 J4 Nahuel Rucá Argentina
145 D6 Nahunta Georgia U.S.A.
39 F1 Naibabad Afghanistan
156 D3 Naica Mexico
172 E4 Naicó Argentina
112 C2 Naidăș Romania
6 □6 Naidi Fiji
24 B1 Nai Ga Myanmar
6 □8 Naigani i. Fiji
37 H2 Naij Tal China
75 G2 Naila Germany
93 D5 Nailloux France
6 □6 Nailotha Pk h. Fiji
62 D3 Nailsworth England U.K.
119 F5 Na'ima Sudan
31 G4 Naiman Qi China
139 H2 Nain Newfoundland Canada
39 C2 Nā'īn Iran
36 D3 Naini Tal India
36 E5 Nainpur India
92 C2 Naintré France
129 F2 Naiopué Mozambique
6 □8 Nairai i. Fiji
66 D3 Nairn r. Scotland U.K.
66 E3 Nairn Scotland U.K.
140 E3 Nairn Centre Ontario Canada
127 C5 Nairobi Kenya
54 D2 Naissaar i. Estonia
6 □6 Naituaba i. Fiji
Nai-tung see Nêdong
127 C5 Naivasha Kenya
127 C5 Naivasha, L. l. Kenya
87 E4 Naives-Rosières France
31 H4 Naizishan China
93 D4 Najac France
39 B2 Najafābād Iran
119 H2 Najd reg. Saudi Arabia
99 H2 Nájera Spain
36 D3 Najibabad India
99 H3 Nájima r. Spain
31 J4 Najin North Korea
119 H4 Najrān Saudi Arabia
28 A6 Naju South Korea
28 B7 Nakadōri-shima i. Japan
29 H5 Naka-gawa r. Japan
28 E7 Naka-gawa r. Japan
28 J1 Nakagawa Japan
29 □2 Nakagusuku-wan b. Japan
28 C7 Nakama Japan
122 D4 Nakambe watercourse Burkina/Ghana
28 D7 Nakamura Japan
45 M3 Nakanno Rus. Fed.
29 G5 Nakano Japan
28 D5 Nakano-shima i. Japan
28 D6 Nakanoumi lag. Japan
29 □2 Nakaoshi Japan
127 B4 Nakasangola Uganda
28 H3 Nakasato Japan
28 J2 Nakasatsunai Japan
28 K2 Nakashibetsu Japan
28 C7 Nakatsu Japan
29 F6 Nakatsugawa Japan
126 C1 Nak'fa Eritrea
119 F2 Nakhl Egypt
27 O3 Nakhodka Rus. Fed.
37 H4 Nakhola India
25 C4 Nakhon Nayok Thailand
25 C4 Nakhon Pathom Thailand
25 C4 Nakhon Ratchasima Thailand
25 B5 Nakhon Si Thammarat Thailand
24 C3 Nakhon Thai Thailand
36 B5 Nakhtarana India
Nakichevan' see Naxçıvan
136 C3 Nakina B.C. Canada
140 B1 Nakina Ontario Canada
81 F4 Naklo Slovenia
76 F2 Nakło nad Notecią Poland
134 C4 Naknek Alaska U.S.A.
36 C3 Nakodar India
77 K1 Nakomiady Poland
127 B6 Nakonde Zambia
130 B4 Nakop Namibia
54 C3 Nākotne Latvia
79 K6 Nakovo Yugoslavia
55 D5 Nakskov Denmark
31 J6 Naktong r. South Korea
127 C5 Nakuru Kenya
136 F4 Nakusp B.C. Canada
39 F4 Nal r. Pakistan
36 A4 Nal Pakistan
30 C3 Nalayh Mongolia
131 J2 Nalázi Mozambique
37 G4 Nalbari India
51 G7 Nal'chik Rus. Fed.
36 D3 Naldera India
38 B2 Naldurg India
77 L4 Nałęczów Poland
122 D4 Nalerigu Ghana
38 B2 Nalgonda India
37 F4 Nalhati India
38 B3 Nallamala Hills h. India
42 B1 Nallıhan Turkey
99 E1 Nalón r. Spain
118 B1 Nālūt Libya
78 C2 Nalžovské Hory Czech Rep.
131 J2 Namaacha Mozambique
6 □8 Namacu Fiji
125 C7 Namacunde Angola
129 F2 Namacurra Mozambique
131 G3 Namahadi South Africa
23 □1 Namai Bay b. Palau
131 H1 Namakgale South Africa
39 D3 Namakzar-e Shadad salt flat Iran
22 A2 Namang Indonesia
127 C5 Namanga Kenya
47 H4 Namangan Uzbekistan
6 □8 Namanu-i-Ra i. Fiji
127 C7 Namapa Mozambique
128 B4 Namaqualand reg. Namibia
130 A4 Namaqualand reg. South Africa
6 □1 Namatanai P.N.G.
24 C2 Nam Beng r. Laos
37 H4 Nambol India
69 F5 Namborn Germany
15 H5 Nambour Queensland Australia
99 G5 Nambroca Spain
13 H2 Nambucca Heads New South Wales Australia
25 D5 Năm Căn Vietnam
37 H3 Namcha Barwa mt. China
37 F4 Namche Bazar Nepal
31 H5 Namch'ŏn North Korea
37 G3 Nam Co salt lake China
56 D2 Namdalen v. Norway
56 C2 Namdalseid Norway
24 D2 Nam Đinh Vietnam
59 H2 Nämdö i. Sweden
148 B3 Namekagon r. Wisconsin U.S.A.
23 □1 Namelakl Passage chan. Palau
6 □8 Namena Barrier Reef reef Fiji
6 □8 Namenalala i. Fiji
78 F2 Náměšť nad Oslavou Czech Rep.
79 J2 Námestovo Slovakia
31 J6 Namhae Do i. South Korea
24 B2 Nam Hka r. Myanmar
24 B2 Namhkam Myanmar
24 B2 Nam Hsin r. Myanmar
128 A3 Namib Desert desert Namibia
125 B7 Namibe div. Angola
125 B7 Namibe Angola
125 B7 Namibe, Reserva de res. Angola
117 F8 Namibia country Africa
128 B4 Namib-Naukluft Park res. Namibia
129 F2 Namidobe Mozambique
29 H5 Namie Japan
130 B4 Namies South Africa
24 C3 Nam Khan r. Laos
24 B2 Namlan Myanmar
24 B2 Namlang r. Myanmar
21 J7 Namlea Indonesia
24 C3 Nam Lik r. Laos
24 C2 Nam Loi r. Myanmar
Nam Mao r. see Shweli
24 B3 Nammekon Myanmar
24 C2 Nam Na r. China/Vietnam
24 C3 Nam Ngum r. Laos
13 G2 Namoi r. New South Wales Australia
6 □8 Namosi Pks mts Fiji
24 C2 Nam Ou r. Laos
136 F3 Nampa Alberta Canada
152 C3 Nampa Idaho U.S.A.
122 C3 Nampala Mali
24 C3 Nam Pat Thailand
24 C3 Nam Phong Thailand
31 H5 Namp'o North Korea
129 F1 Nampula div. Mozambique
129 F2 Nampula Mozambique
37 G2 Namru Co salt lake China
37 H4 Namrup India
24 B1 Namsai Myanmar
24 D3 Nam Sam r. Laos/Vietnam
37 E3 Namsê La Nepal
56 D2 Namsen r. Norway
37 H4 Namsi India
56 C2 Namsos Norway
24 B2 Nam Teng r. Myanmar
24 C2 Nam Tha r. Laos
24 B3 Namtok Myanmar
25 B4 Nam Tok Thailand
24 B2 Namton Myanmar
45 O3 Namtsy Rus. Fed.
24 B2 Namtu Myanmar
6 □7 Namuka-i-lau i. Fiji
129 F2 Namuli, Monte mt. Mozambique
127 C7 Namuno Mozambique
69 C4 Namur div. Namur Belgium
69 C4 Namur div. Wallonia Belgium
69 C4 Namur Namur Belgium
128 B2 Namutoni Namibia
125 E7 Namwala Zambia
31 H6 Namwŏn South Korea
24 B1 Namya Ra Myanmar
24 B1 Nam Yi Tu r. Myanmar
76 F4 Namysłów Poland
124 C2 Nana Bakassa Central African Rep.
124 C2 Nana Barya r. Central African Rep./Chad
124 C2 Nana-Grébizi div. Central African Rep.
136 E5 Nanaimo B.C. Canada
153 □1 Nanakuli Hawaii U.S.A.
124 C2 Nana-Mambéré div. Central African Rep.
33 G3 Nan'an China
15 H5 Nanango Queensland Australia
130 A2 Nananib Plateau plat. Namibia
29 F5 Nanao Japan
29 F5 Nanao-wan b. Japan
29 F5 Nanatsu-shima i. Japan
32 D2 Nanbu China
172 B3 Nancagua Chile
31 J3 Nancha China
33 F2 Nanchang China
33 F2 Nanchang China
33 G3 Nancheng China
32 D2 Nanchong China
32 D2 Nanchuan China
99 H2 Nanclares de la Oca Spain
25 A6 Nancowry i. Andaman and Nicobar Is India
87 F4 Nancy Meurthe-et-Moselle France
36 E3 Nanda Devi mt. India
36 E3 Nanda Kot mt. India
32 D3 Nandan China
28 E6 Nandan Japan
38 B2 Nānded India
13 G2 Nandewar Range mountain range New South Wales Australia
36 C5 Nandgaon India
Nandi see Nadi
32 B4 Nanding r. China/Myanmar
69 D4 Nandrin Belgium
33 E5 Nandu China
36 C5 Nandurbar India
38 B3 Nandyal India
33 G3 Nanfeng China
33 E4 Nanfeng China
124 B3 Nanga Eboko Cameroon
22 C1 Nangahbunut Indonesia
22 B2 Nangah Dedai Indonesia
22 C1 Nangahembaloh Indonesia
22 B1 Nangahkantuk Indonesia
22 C2 Nangahkemangai Indonesia
22 B1 Nangahketungau Indonesia
22 B1 Nangah Merakai Indonesia
22 B2 Nangahpinoh Indonesia
22 C1 Nangahtempuai Indonesia
31 J4 Nangang Shan mts China
36 C2 Nanga Parbat mt. Jammu and Kashmir
22 B2 Nangatayap Indonesia
25 B5 Nangin Myanmar
86 C4 Nangis France
31 H5 Nangnim Sanmaek mountain range South Korea
28 C8 Nangō Japan
31 E5 Nangong China
32 B1 Nangqên China
127 C6 Nangulangwa Tanzania
37 H3 Nang Xian China
32 C3 Nanhua China
30 A5 Nanhua China
33 H2 Nanhui China
39 G2 Nani Afghanistan
38 B3 Nanjangud India
32 C3 Nanjian China
32 D1 Nanjiang China
33 G3 Nanjing China
33 G1 Nanjing China
32 B4 Nanka r. China
33 F3 Nankang China
Nanking see Nanjing
28 D7 Nankoku Japan
125 C7 Nankova Angola
31 E5 Nanle China
32 B4 Nanlei r. China
33 E3 Nan Ling mountain range China
33 G2 Nanling China
33 E4 Nanliu r. China
32 E4 Nanning China
159 □1 Nanny Town Jamaica
135 O3 Nanortalik Greenland
32 D3 Nanpan r. China
37 E4 Nanpara India
31 G4 Nanpiao China
32 D1 Nanping China
33 G3 Nanping China
33 G3 Nanri Dao i. China
99 F1 Nansa r. Spain
27 N6 Nansei-shotō is Japan
175 N2 Nansei-shotō Trench sea feature Pacific Ocean
135 O1 Nansen Land reg. Greenland
135 J1 Nansen Sound chan. N.W.T. Canada
127 B5 Nansio Tanzania
91 B4 Nant France
86 B4 Nanterre France
88 D4 Nantes Loire-Atlantique France
88 D4 Nantes Atlantique airport France
86 B3 Nanteuil-le-Haudouin France
38 C4 Nanthi Kadal lag. Sri Lanka
92 D2 Nantiat France
147 F5 Nanticoke r. Maryland U.S.A.
140 E5 Nanticoke Ontario Canada
136 G4 Nanton Alberta Canada
33 H1 Nantong China
33 H2 Nantong China
33 H4 Nant'ou Taiwan
90 D2 Nantua France
147 H4 Nantucket Massachusetts U.S.A.
147 H4 Nantucket I. i. Massachusetts U.S.A.
147 H4 Nantucket Sound b. Massachusetts U.S.A.
62 D1 Nantwich England U.K.
62 C2 Nant-y-moch Res. resr Wales U.K.
6 □8 Nanukuloa Fiji
6 □6 Nanuku Passage chan. Fiji
6 □6 Nanuku Reef reef Fiji
4 J5 Nanumanga i. Tuvalu
176 G6 Nanumea i. Tuvalu
169 H2 Nanuque Brazil
17 A4 Nanutarra Roadhouse Western Australia Australia
32 D2 Nanxi China
33 F2 Nan Xian China
33 F3 Nanxiong China
33 F1 Nanyang China
29 H4 Nanyō Japan
127 C5 Nanyuki Kenya
31 H4 Nanzamu China
33 E2 Nanzhang China
33 F1 Nanzhao China
103 D6 Nao, Cabo de la headland Spain
139 F3 Naococane, Lac l. Québec Canada
37 G4 Naogaon Bangladesh
36 C2 Naoshera India
115 G5 Naousa Greece
33 E4 Naozhou Dao China
154 A2 Napa California U.S.A.
147 K1 Napadogan New Brunswick Canada
173 H4 Napaleofú Argentina
134 C3 Napamute Alaska U.S.A.
141 G4 Napanee Ontario Canada
36 C4 Napasar India
135 N3 Napasoq Greenland
148 C5 Naperville Illinois U.S.A.
82 C1 Napf mt. Switzerland
8 F3 Napier New Zealand
130 B7 Napier South Africa
16 D2 Napier Broome B. b. Western Australia Australia
179 D4 Napier Mts mountain range Antarctica
14 C2 Napier Pen. pen. Northern Terr. Australia
141 J4 Napierville Québec Canada
77 J2 Napiwoda Poland
145 D7 Naples Florida U.S.A.
147 H3 Naples Maine U.S.A.
Naples see Napoli
162 C4 Napo r. Ecuador/Peru
32 D4 Napo China
146 A4 Napoleon Ohio U.S.A.
109 G4 Napoli div. Campania Italy
109 G4 Napoli Napoli Italy
109 G4 Napoli, Golfo di b. Italy
173 F5 Naposta r. Argentina
173 F5 Naposta Buenos Aires Argentina
148 E5 Nappanee Indiana U.S.A.
7 □10 Napuka i. French Polynesia Pacific Ocean
42 C4 Naqb Ashtar Jordan
43 B5 Naqb Malha mt. Egypt
126 E2 Naqūb Yemen
29 E6 Nara div. Japan
52 C2 Nara r. Rus. Fed.
29 E6 Nara Japan
122 C3 Nara Mali
54 E4 Narach Belarus
12 E4 Naracoorte S. Australia Australia
13 F3 Naradhan New South Wales Australia
38 C2 Narainpur India
30 E2 Naranbulag Mongolia
162 B4 Naranjal Ecuador
156 C3 Naranjo Mexico
157 F4 Naranjos Mexico
28 B7 Narao Japan
38 D2 Narasannapeta India
38 C2 Narasapatnam, Pt pt India
38 C2 Narasapur India
38 C2 Narasaraopet India
30 E2 Narasun Rus. Fed.
25 C6 Narathiwat Thailand
37 G5 Narayanganj Bangladesh
38 A2 Narayangaon India
37 F4 Narayanghat Nepal
77 N6 Narayiv Ukraine
Narbada r. see Narmada
62 B3 Narberth Wales U.K.
91 B5 Narbonne France
91 B5 Narbonne-Plage France
63 E2 Narborough England U.K.
63 G2 Narborough England U.K.
108 A5 Narcao Sardegna Italy
98 D1 Narcea r. Spain
25 A4 Narcondam I. i. Andaman and Nicobar Is India
90 B1 Narcy France
39 C1 Nardin Iran
111 H2 Nardò Italy
173 G1 Nare Argentina
36 B3 Narechi r. Pakistan
17 B7 Narembeen Western Australia Australia
135 L2 Nares Strait str. Canada/Greenland
77 J3 Narew r. Poland
77 M3 Narew Poland
77 M3 Narewka Poland
39 F3 Nari r. Pakistan
128 B3 Narib Namibia
130 B5 Nariep South Africa
51 H6 Narimanov Rus. Fed.
47 K3 Narimskiy Khr. mountain range Kazakhstan
39 G1 Narin Afghanistan
29 H6 Narita Japan
159 □3 Nariva div. Trinidad Trinidad and Tobago
159 □3 Nariva Swamp swamp Trinidad Trinidad and Tobago
156 C3 Narizon, Pta pt Mexico
37 F4 Narkatiaganj India
43 D1 Narlı Turkey
36 C5 Narmada r. India
36 D3 Narnaul India
109 E2 Narni Italy
110 C5 Naro r. Sicilia Italy
110 C5 Naro Sicilia Italy
53 C1 Narodychi Ukraine
52 C2 Naro-Fominsk Rus. Fed.
127 C5 Narok Kenya
13 G4 Narooma New South Wales Australia
52 F3 Narovchat Rus. Fed.
53 C1 Narowlya Belarus
57 F3 Närpes Finland
13 G2 Narrabri New South Wales Australia
147 H4 Narragansett Bay b. Rhode Island U.S.A.
13 F2 Narran r. New South Wales Australia
13 F3 Narrandera New South Wales Australia
13 F2 Narran L. l. New South Wales Australia
17 B7 Narrogin Western Australia Australia
13 G3 Narromine New South Wales Australia
146 C6 Narrows Virginia U.S.A.
147 F4 Narrowsburg Pennsylvania U.S.A.
159 □6 Narrows, The chan. St Kitts-Nevis Caribbean
132 O3 Narsarsuaq Greenland
36 D5 Narsimhapur India
37 G5 Narsingdi Bangladesh
36 D5 Narsinghgarh India
38 C2 Narsipatnam India
31 E4 Nart China
30 C2 Nart Mongolia
81 H5 Narta Croatia
91 E5 Nartuby r. France
52 G2 Narukosovo Rus. Fed.
77 J3 Naruszewo Poland
28 E6 Naruto Japan
54 E2 Narva r. Estonia/Rus. Fed.
54 E2 Narva Bay b. Estonia/Rus. Fed.
23 B2 Narvacan Philippines
56 E1 Narvik Norway
54 F2 Narvskoye Vdkhr. resr Rus. Fed.
36 D3 Narwana India
36 D4 Narwar India
77 L2 Narwiański Park Narodowy nat. park Poland
44 G3 Nar'yan Mar Rus. Fed.
47 J4 Naryn div. Kyrgyzstan
47 H4 Naryn r. Kyrgyzstan
47 J4 Naryn Kyrgyzstan
30 A2 Naryn Rus. Fed.
52 B3 Naryshkino Rus. Fed.
59 F1 Nås Sweden
56 E3 Näsåker Sweden
112 E1 Năsăud Romania
78 E2 Nasavrky Czech Rep.
91 B4 Nasbinals France
172 E2 Naschel Argentina
155 H3 Naschitti New Mexico U.S.A.
9 C6 Naseby New Zealand
148 A4 Nashua Iowa U.S.A.
147 H3 Nashua New Hampshire U.S.A.
145 C4 Nashville Tennessee U.S.A.
148 A2 Nashwauk Minnesota U.S.A.
42 D3 Nasib Syria
104 G3 Našice Croatia
77 J3 Nasielsk Poland
57 F3 Näsijärvi l. Finland
36 C5 Nasik India
22 B1 Nasilat Indonesia
126 B3 Nasir Sudan
Nasirabad see Mymensingh
36 C4 Nasirabad India
36 B3 Nasirabad Pakistan
37 F4 Nasmganj India
110 D4 Naso Sicilia Italy
125 E6 Nasondoye Zaire
6 □6 Nasorolevu mt. Fiji
Nasosnyy see Hacı Zeynalabdin
119 F1 Nasr Egypt
39 B2 Naṣrābād Iran
39 D2 Naṣrābād Iran
43 D3 Naṣrānī, J. an mountain range Syria
Nasratabad see Zābol
42 F3 Nasrīān-e-Pā'īn Iran
136 D3 Nass r. B.C. Canada
123 F5 Nassarawa Nigeria
145 □2 Nassau airport The Bahamas
176 J6 Nassau i. Cook Is Pacific Ocean
15 E2 Nassau r. Queensland Australia
87 G2 Nassau Germany
145 □2 Nassau The Bahamas
171 C7 Nassau, B. de b. Chile
145 □2 Nassau Village The Bahamas
80 B3 Nassereith Austria
119 F3 Nasser, Lake resr Egypt
59 F3 Nässjö Sweden
69 D4 Nassogne Belgium
138 E2 Nastapoca r. Québec Canada
138 E2 Nastapoka Islands is Québec Canada
54 D1 Nastola Finland
29 G5 Nasu-dake volcano Japan
23 B3 Nasugbu Philippines
59 F3 Näsum Sweden
50 D3 Nasva Rus. Fed.
128 D2 Nata watercourse Botswana/Zimbabwe
128 D3 Nata Botswana
127 B5 Nata Tanzania
162 B3 Natagaima Colombia
166 E2 Natal Brazil
175 G6 Natal Basin sea feature Indian Ocean
39 B2 Naṭanz Iran
139 H3 Natashquan r. Québec Canada
139 H3 Natashquan Québec Canada
151 F6 Natchez Mississippi U.S.A.
151 E6 Natchitoches Louisiana U.S.A.
82 C2 Naters Switzerland
6 □6 Natewa Bay b. Fiji
13 F4 Nathalia Victoria Australia
36 C4 Nathdwara India
12 E4 Natimuk Victoria Australia
154 D5 National City California U.S.A.
8 E3 National Park New Zealand
128 A3 National West Coast Tourist Recreation Area res. Namibia
103 □ Nati, Pta pt Spain
81 E4 Natisone r. Italy
123 E4 Natitingou Benin
169 H4 Natividade Rio de Janeiro Brazil
166 C3 Natividade Tocantins Brazil
24 A2 Natogyi Myanmar
156 C2 Nátora Mexico
29 H4 Natori Japan
127 C5 Natron, Lake salt lake Tanzania
29 H5 Natsui-gawa r. Japan
24 A3 Nattalin Myanmar
59 H2 Nättarö i. Sweden
80 B2 Nattheim Germany
39 E2 Na'tū Iran
25 E6 Natuna Besar i. Indonesia
147 F2 Natural Bridge New York U.S.A.
155 G3 Natural Bridges National Monument nat. park Utah U.S.A.
17 A5 Naturaliste Channel chan. Western Australia Australia
175 M6 Naturaliste Plateau sea feature Indian Ocean
155 H2 Naturita Colorado U.S.A.
107 E2 Naturno Italy
148 E2 Naubinway Michigan U.S.A.
93 E4 Naucelle France
92 E4 Naucelles France
128 B3 Nauchas Namibia
80 B4 Nauders Austria
130 E6 Naudesberg Pass pass South Africa
73 H3 Nauen Germany
147 G4 Naugatuck Connecticut U.S.A.
87 H3 Nauheim Germany
23 B3 Naujan Philippines

67

124 B2 Nord-Ouest div. Cameroon
86 B2 Nord - Pas-de-Calais div. France
74 C3 Nordpfälzer Bergland reg. Germany
55 C2 Nordre Rønner i. Denmark
135 N3 Nordre Strømfjord inlet Greenland
72 C4 Nordrhein-Westfalen div. Germany
72 E3 Nordstemmen Germany
72 D1 Nordstrand i. Germany
56 C2 Nord-Trøndelag div. Norway
56 L6 NorŽurland Vestra div. Iceland
45 N2 Nordvik Rus. Fed.
67 D4 Nore r. Rep. of Ireland
54 C4 Noreikiškės Lithuania
93 E5 Nore, Pic de mt. France
58 C1 Noresund Norway
147 E6 Norfolk airport *Virginia* U.S.A.
63 G2 Norfolk div. *England* U.K.
150 D3 Norfolk *Nebraska* U.S.A.
147 F2 Norfolk *New York* U.S.A.
11 □1 Norfolk I. i. Pacific Ocean
176 G7 Norfolk Island Ridge sea feature Pacific Ocean
176 F7 Norfolk Island Trough sea feature Pacific Ocean
151 E4 Norfork L. l. *Arkansas/Missouri* U.S.A.
68 E1 Norg Netherlands
58 B1 Norheimsund Norway
29 F5 Norikura-dake volcano Japan
44 K3 Noril'sk Rus. Fed.
52 A3 Norino Rus. Fed.
141 F4 Norland *Ontario* Canada
109 E3 Norma Italy
148 C5 Normal *Illinois* U.S.A.
15 E3 Norman r. *Queensland* Australia
151 D5 Norman *Oklahoma* U.S.A.
15 F2 Normanby r. *Queensland* Australia
6 □1 Normanby I. i. P.N.G.
15 G4 Normanby Ra. h. *Queensland* Australia
Normandes, Îles is *see* Channel Islands
163 F3 Normandia Brazil
141 J2 Normandin *Québec* Canada
145 □3 Norman I. i. *Virgin Is* Caribbean
8 □1 Norman Inlet inlet *Auckland Is* New Zealand
145 D5 Norman, L. l. *N. Carolina* U.S.A.
159 □1 Norman Manley airport Jamaica
15 E3 Normanton *Queensland* Australia
136 D1 Norman Wells *N.W.T.* Canada
141 F2 Normétal *Québec* Canada
165 E2 Noronha r. Brazil
82 B1 Noroy-le-Bourg France
172 B4 Norquín Argentina
171 B5 Ñorquinco Argentina
56 F3 Norra Kvarken str. Finland/Sweden
56 D2 Norra Storfjället mts Sweden
59 F1 Norr Barken l. Sweden
56 E2 Norrbotten div. Sweden
55 B3 Nørreå r. Denmark
55 B4 Nørre Åby Denmark
55 D5 Nørre Alslev Denmark
55 C4 Nørre Broby Denmark
55 A4 Nørre Nebel Denmark
86 B2 Norrent-Fontes France
55 B4 Nørre Snede Denmark
55 B2 Nørresundby Denmark
55 A3 Nørre Vorupør Denmark
59 F3 Norrhult-Klavreström Sweden
140 C2 Norris *Ontario* Canada
146 B6 Norris Lake l. *Tennessee* U.S.A.
147 F4 Norristown *Pennsylvania* U.S.A.
59 G2 Norrköping Sweden
59 H2 Norrpada is Sweden
59 G1 Norrsundet Sweden
59 H2 Norrtälje Sweden
17 C7 Norseman *Western Australia* Australia
8 F4 Norsewood New Zealand
59 F2 Norsholm Sweden
58 C2 Norsjø l. Norway
56 E2 Norsjö Sweden
6 □2 Norsup Vanuatu
7 □16 Norte, Cabo c. *Easter I.* Chile
163 G3 Norte, Cabo pt Brazil
166 A3 Nortelândia Brazil
72 E4 Nörten-Hardenberg Germany
173 J4 Norte, Pta pt Argentina
171 D5 Norte, Pta pt Argentina
147 G3 North Adams *Massachusetts* U.S.A.
65 G3 Northallerton *England* U.K.
17 B6 Northam *Western Australia* Australia
131 F2 Northam South Africa
174 F4 North American Basin sea feature Atlantic Ocean
63 F2 Northampton *England* U.K.
147 G3 Northampton *Massachusetts* U.S.A.
17 A6 Northampton *Western Australia* Australia
15 F5 Northampton Downs *Queensland* Australia
63 E2 Northamptonshire div. *England* U.K.
25 A4 North Andaman i. *Andaman and Nicobar Is* India
146 E5 North Anna r. *Virginia* U.S.A.
147 J2 North Anson *Maine* U.S.A.
136 G2 North Arm b. *N.W.T.* Canada
6 □7 North Astrolabe Reef reef Fiji
145 D5 North Augusta *S. Carolina* U.S.A.
139 H2 North Aulatsivik Island i. *Newfoundland* Canada
66 D5 North Ayrshire div. *Scotland* U.K.
63 E4 North Baddesley *England* U.K.
23 A4 North Balabac Strait chan. Philippines
137 H4 North Battleford *Saskatchewan* Canada
141 F3 North Bay *Ontario* Canada
138 E2 North Belcher Islands is *Québec* Canada
152 A3 North Bend *Oregon* U.S.A.
147 H3 North Berwick *Maine* U.S.A.
66 F4 North Berwick *Scotland* U.K.
148 A3 North Branch *Minnesota* U.S.A.
9 □3 North C. c. *Antipodes Is* New Zealand
139 H4 North, C. c. *Nova Scotia* Canada
171 □ North C. c. *S. Georgia* Atlantic Ocean
179 A5 North, C. c. Antarctica
8 D1 North Cape c. New Zealand
139 H4 North Cape pt *Prince Edward I.* Canada
138 B3 North Caribou Lake l. *Ontario* Canada
145 D5 North Carolina div. U.S.A.
152 B1 North Cascades Nat. Park *Washington* U.S.A.
65 H4 North Cave *England* U.K.
145 □2 North Cay i. The Bahamas
140 D3 North Channel chan. *Ontario* Canada
66 C5 North Channel str. *Northern Ireland/Scotland* U.K.
17 B7 Northcliffe *Western Australia* Australia
111 □ North Comino Chan. chan. Malta
147 H2 North Conway *New Hampshire* U.S.A.
150 C2 North Dakota div. U.S.A.
62 D4 North Dorset Downs h. *England* U.K.
63 E3 North Downs h. *England* U.K.
128 D3 North East div. Botswana
146 D3 North East *Pennsylvania* U.S.A.
128 □1 North East Bay b. *Ascension* Atlantic Ocean
126 D4 North-Eastern div. Kenya
174 H2 North-Eastern Atlantic Basin sea feature Atlantic Ocean
8 □2 North East Harb. inlet *Campbell I.* New Zealand
8 □3 North East Island i. *Snares Is* New Zealand
10 □2 North East Point pt *Christmas I.* Indian Ocean
158 C1 Northeast Providence Chan. chan. The Bahamas
159 □1 Northeast Pt pt Jamaica
158 D2 Northeast Pt pt The Bahamas
158 D2 Northeast Pt pt The Bahamas
72 E4 Northeim Germany
158 D1 North End Pt pt The Bahamas
23 □1 North Entrance chan. Palau
122 D5 Northern div. Ghana
127 B7 Northern div. Malawi
122 B5 Northern div. Sierra Leone
119 E4 Northern div. Sudan
127 B7 Northern div. Zambia
36 C1 Northern Areas div. Pakistan
130 C4 Northern Cape div. South Africa
137 K3 Northern Indian Lake l. *Manitoba* Canada
67 □ Northern Ireland div. U.K.
138 B4 Northern Light L. l. *Ontario* Canada
4 F3 Northern Mariana Islands territory Pacific Ocean
10 □2 Northern Plateau plat. *Christmas I.* Indian Ocean
159 □3 Northern Range mountain range *Trinidad* Trinidad and Tobago
Northern Sporades is *see* Voreioi Sporades
14 C3 Northern Territory div. Australia
131 G2 Northern Transvaal div. South Africa
65 E2 North Esk r. *Scotland* U.K.
66 F4 North Esk r. *Scotland* U.K.
147 G3 Northfield *Massachusetts* U.S.A.
148 A3 Northfield *Minnesota* U.S.A.
147 G2 Northfield *Vermont* U.S.A.
63 H3 North Foreland c. *England* U.K.
154 C3 North Fork *California* U.S.A.
154 B2 North Fork American r. *California* U.S.A.
154 B2 North Fork Feather r. *California* U.S.A.
148 E3 North Fox I. i. *Michigan* U.S.A.
140 E1 North French r. *Ontario* Canada
159 □6 North Friar's Bay b. *St Kitts-Nevis* Caribbean
65 H3 North Grimston *England* U.K.
8 E2 North Head headland New Zealand
10 □3 North Head pt *Macquarie I.* Pacific Ocean
147 K2 North Head *New Brunswick* Canada
137 K2 North Henik Lake l. *N.W.T.* Canada
147 G3 North Hudson *New York* U.S.A.
63 F1 North Hykeham *England* U.K.
10 □4 North I. i. *Lord Howe I.* Pacific Ocean
127 □1 North I. i. Seychelles
23 B1 North Is i. Philippines
8 E3 North Island i. New Zealand
23 B4 North Islet reef Philippines
155 G4 North Jadito Canyon *Arizona* U.S.A.
148 D5 North Judson *Indiana* U.S.A.
10 □1 North Keeling I. i. *Cocos Is* Indian Ocean
137 K3 North Knife r. *Manitoba* Canada
19 O5 North Korea country Asia
37 H4 North Lakhimpur India
66 E5 North Lanarkshire div. *Scotland* U.K.
8 E1 Northland div. New Zealand
155 E3 North Las Vegas *Nevada* U.S.A.
151 E5 North Little Rock *Arkansas* U.S.A.
127 B7 North Luangwa National Park nat. park Zambia
155 H2 North Mam Peak summit *Colorado* U.S.A.
148 E5 North Manchester *Indiana* U.S.A.
148 D3 North Manitou I. i. *Michigan* U.S.A.
140 E3 North Monetville *Ontario* Canada
136 D2 North Nahanni r. *N.W.T.* Canada
159 □1 North Negril Pt pt Jamaica
137 L5 Northome *Minnesota* U.S.A.
154 C3 North Pallisade summit *California* U.S.A.
150 C3 North Platte r. *Nebraska* U.S.A.
150 C3 North Platte *Nebraska* U.S.A.
27 □ North Point Hong Kong
148 E3 Northport *Michigan* U.S.A.
8 □3 North Promontory pt *Snares Is* New Zealand
128 □1 North Pt pt *Ascension* Atlantic Ocean
159 □9 North Pt pt *Barbados* Caribbean
144 D2 North Pt pt *Michigan* U.S.A.
13 F4 North Pt pt *Tasmania* Australia
128 □3 North Pt pt *Tristan da Cunha* Atlantic Ocean
127 □2 North Pt pt Seychelles
25 A4 North Reef I. i. *Andaman and Nicobar Is* India
155 F3 North Rim *Arizona* U.S.A.
66 F1 North Ronaldsay i. *Scotland* U.K.
66 F1 North Ronaldsay Firth chan. *Scotland* U.K.
154 B2 North San Juan *California* U.S.A.
137 G4 North Saskatchewan r. *Alberta* Canada
48 F3 North Sea sea Atlantic Ocean
137 J3 North Seal r. *Manitoba* Canada
25 A5 North Sentinel I. i. *Andaman and Nicobar Is* India
65 G2 North Shields *England* U.K.
154 D2 North Shoshone Peak summit *Nevada* U.S.A.
65 J4 North Somercotes *England* U.K.
66 F1 North Sound, The chan. *Scotland* U.K.
15 H5 North Stradbroke I. i. *Queensland* Australia
147 H2 North Stratford *New Hampshire* U.S.A.
65 G2 North Sunderland *England* U.K.
8 E3 North Taranaki Bight b. New Zealand
136 F4 North Thompson r. *B.C.* Canada
63 E3 North Tidworth *England* U.K.
66 A3 Northton *Scotland* U.K.
146 D3 North Tonawanda *New York* U.S.A.
36 D3 North Tons r. India
9 A7 North Trap reef New Zealand
147 G2 North Troy *Vermont* U.S.A.
138 D3 North Twin I. i. *Québec* Canada
65 F2 North Tyne r. *England* U.K.
66 A3 North Uist i. *Scotland* U.K.
65 F2 Northumberland div. *England* U.K.
15 G4 Northumberland Is is *Queensland* Australia
65 F2 Northumberland National Park *England* U.K.
139 H4 Northumberland Strait chan. Canada
136 E5 North Vancouver *B.C.* Canada
147 F3 Northville *New York* U.S.A.
63 H2 North Walsham *England* U.K.
131 E3 North West div. South Africa
8 □2 North West B. b. *Campbell I.* New Zealand
8 □1 North West C. c. *Auckland Is* New Zealand
16 A4 North West C. c. *Western Australia* Australia
125 D6 North-Western div. Zambia
36 C2 North West Frontier Pakistan
10 □2 North West Point pt *Christmas I.* Indian Ocean
158 C1 Northwest Providence Chan. chan. The Bahamas
139 J3 North West River *Newfoundland* Canada
134 H3 Northwest Territories *N.W.T.* Canada
62 D1 Northwich *England* U.K.
147 F5 North Wildwood *New Jersey* U.S.A.
147 H2 North Woodstock *New Hampshire* U.S.A.
65 H3 North York Moors reg. *England* U.K.
65 H3 North York Moors National Park *England* U.K.
65 G3 North Yorkshire div. *England* U.K.
65 H3 Norton *England* U.K.
150 D4 Norton *Kansas* U.S.A.
139 G4 Norton *New Brunswick* Canada
147 H2 Norton *Vermont* U.S.A.
146 B6 Norton *Virginia* U.S.A.
129 E2 Norton Zimbabwe
62 C3 Norton Fitzwarren *England* U.K.
134 B3 Norton Sound b. *Alaska* U.S.A.
72 E1 Nortorf Germany
88 D4 Nort-sur-Erdre France
173 G3 Norumbega Argentina
179 C2 Norvegia, C. c. Antarctica
147 G4 Norwalk *Connecticut* U.S.A.
146 B4 Norwalk *Ohio* U.S.A.
48 F2 Norway country Europe
147 H2 Norway *Maine* U.S.A.
141 G4 Norway Bay *Québec* Canada
137 K4 Norway House *Manitoba* Canada
178 B5 Norwegian Basin sea feature Atlantic Ocean
135 J2 Norwegian Bay b. *N.W.T.* Canada
178 B5 Norwegian Sea sea Atlantic Ocean
63 H2 Norwich airport *England* U.K.
147 G4 Norwich *Connecticut* U.S.A.
63 H2 Norwich *England* U.K.
147 F3 Norwich *New York* U.S.A.
140 E5 Norwich *Ontario* Canada
147 H3 Norwood *Massachusetts* U.S.A.
147 F2 Norwood *New York* U.S.A.
146 A5 Norwood *Ohio* U.S.A.
28 K2 Nosapu-misaki pt Japan
170 C1 Nos de Cachi mt. Argentina
137 H1 Nose Lake l. *N.W.T.* Canada
112 F3 Nos Emine pt Bulgaria
112 F3 Nos Galata pt Bulgaria
28 H1 Noshappu-misaki headland Japan
29 G3 Noshiro Japan
50 J2 Noshul' Rus. Fed.
53 D1 Nosivka Ukraine
112 G3 Nos Kaliakra pt Bulgaria
53 B2 Noskivtsi Ukraine
128 C4 Nosop r. Botswana
52 G1 Nosovaya Rus. Fed.
39 D3 Noşratābād Iran
55 E1 Nossan r. Sweden
100 C1 Nossa Senhora da Graça Póvoa e Meadas Portugal
166 E3 Nossa Senhora das Dores Brazil
167 A4 Nossa Senhora do Livramento Brazil
59 E2 Nossebro Sweden
73 J4 Nossen Germany
73 H2 Nossendorf Germany
112 G3 Nos Shabla pt Bulgaria
66 □2 Noss, Isle of i. *Scotland* U.K.
130 B2 Nossob r. Namibia/South Africa
130 C2 Nossob Camp South Africa
122 C4 Nossombougou Mali
129 H1 Nosy Bé i. Madagascar
129 H2 Nosy Boraha i. Madagascar
129 H1 Nosy Lava i. Madagascar
129 H1 Nosy Radama i. Madagascar
129 H3 Nosy Varika Madagascar
109 F2 Notaresco Italy
155 F2 Notch Peak summit *Utah* U.S.A.
76 D3 Noteć r. Poland
114 D1 Notia Greece
114 C3 Notia Pindos mountain range Greece
115 F5 Notio Aigaio div. Greece
115 E4 Notios Evvoïkos Kolpos chan. Greece
114 B3 Notio Steno Kerkyras chan. Greece
111 E6 Noto *Sicilia* Italy
29 F5 Noto Japan
58 C2 Notodden Norway
111 E6 Noto, Golfo di g. *Sicilia* Italy
29 F5 Noto-hantō pen. Japan
29 F5 Noto-jima i. Japan
28 K1 Notoro-ko l. Japan
81 F5 Notranje Gorice Slovenia
139 K4 Notre Dame Bay b. *Newfoundland* Canada
89 G2 Notre-Dame-de-Bondeville France
89 F2 Notre-Dame-de-Gravenchon France
141 H4 Notre-Dame-de-la-Salette *Québec* Canada
88 C5 Notre-Dame-de-Monts France
147 H2 Notre-Dame-des-Bois *Québec* Canada
141 H3 Notre-Dame-du-Laus *Québec* Canada
141 F3 Notre-Dame-du-Nord *Québec* Canada
139 G4 Notre Dame, Monts mountain range *Québec* Canada
123 E5 Notsé Togo
28 K2 Notsuke-saki pt Japan
28 K2 Notsuke-suidō chan. Japan
140 E4 Nottawasaga Bay b. *Ontario* Canada
138 E3 Nottaway r. *Québec* Canada
63 E2 Nottingham *England* U.K.
131 H4 Nottingham Road South Africa
63 E1 Nottinghamshire div. *England* U.K.
146 E6 Nottoway r. *Virginia* U.S.A.
72 C4 Nottuln Germany
137 H5 Notukeu Cr. r. *Saskatchewan* Canada
120 A4 Nouâdhibou Mauritania
120 A5 Nouakchott Mauritania
120 C5 Noual well Mauritania
120 A5 Nouâmghâr Mauritania
89 H4 Nouan-le-Fuzelier France
87 E3 Nouart France
24 D4 Nouei Vietnam
120 A5 Noueïch well Mauritania
6 □2 Nouméa *New Caledonia* Pacific Ocean
124 B3 Noun r. Cameroon
122 D4 Nouna Burkina
130 E5 Noupoort South Africa
131 G4 Noupoortsnek pass South Africa
56 H2 Nousa Finland
Nouveau-Comptoir *see* Wemindji
Nouvelle Calédonie territory *see* New Caledonia
86 A2 Nouvion France
89 F4 Nouzilly France
86 D3 Nouzonville France
47 G4 Nov Tajikistan
54 C2 Nõva Estonia
78 F5 Nova Hungary
169 H4 Nova Almeida Brazil
168 A4 Nova Alvorada Brazil
168 D1 Nova America Brazil
168 B5 Nova Andradina Brazil
51 F5 Nova Astrakhan' Ukraine
168 D3 Nova Aurora Brazil
79 H3 Nová Baňa Slovakia
53 C1 Nova Borova Ukraine
78 E2 Nová Bystřice Czech Rep.
125 B5 Nova Caipemba Angola
114 C1 Novaci Macedonia
112 D2 Novaci Romania
169 G3 Nova Era Brazil
168 B5 Nova Esperança Brazil
107 G5 Novafeltria Italy
169 G5 Nova Friburgo Brazil
81 E5 Nova Gorica Slovenia
104 F3 Nova Gradiška Croatia
168 D4 Nova Granada Brazil
169 G5 Nova Iguaçu Brazil
53 E3 Nova Kakhovka Ukraine
79 H3 Nováky Slovakia
107 F2 Nova Levante Italy
169 G3 Nova Lima Brazil
107 J4 Novalja Croatia
168 B5 Nova Londrina Brazil
54 F4 Novalukoml' Belarus
129 F3 Nova Mambone Mozambique
53 E3 Nova Mayachka Ukraine
129 F2 Nova Nabúri Mozambique
53 D3 Nova Odesa Ukraine
78 E1 Nová Paka Czech Rep.
112 C2 Nova Pazova Yugoslavia
166 D2 Nova Pilão Arcado Brazil
168 E3 Nova Ponte Brazil
53 E2 Nova Praha Ukraine
106 C2 Novara div. *Piemonte* Italy
106 C3 Novara *Novara* Italy
166 D2 Nova Remanso Brazil
169 E4 Nova Resende Brazil
166 C3 Nova Roma Brazil
168 B6 Nova Santa Rosa Brazil
139 H5 Nova Scotia div. Canada
166 D2 Nova Sento Sé Brazil
169 F3 Nova Serrana Brazil
109 J4 Nova Siri Italy
53 F1 Nova Sloboda Ukraine
166 C3 Nova Soure Brazil
106 D2 Novate Mezzola Italy
154 A2 Novato *California* U.S.A.
104 F3 Nova Topola Bos.-Herz.
53 B2 Nova Ushytsya Ukraine
112 B3 Nova Varoš Yugoslavia
169 H3 Nova Venécia Brazil
169 J2 Nova Viçosa Brazil
165 D2 Nova Vida Brazil
53 F2 Nova Vodolaha Ukraine
168 B1 Nova Xavantina Brazil
52 H3 Novaya Bekshanka Rus. Fed.
46 C3 Novaya Kazanka Kazakhstan
50 E2 Novaya Ladoga Rus. Fed.
52 E3 Novaya Lyada Rus. Fed.
45 R2 Novaya Sibir', O. i. Rus. Fed.
44 G2 Novaya Zemlya i. Rus. Fed.
112 E3 Nova Zagora Bulgaria
53 E3 Nova Zbur"yivka Ukraine
53 E2 Nove Ukraine
78 D3 Nové Hrady Czech Rep.
103 C6 Novelda Spain
107 E4 Novellara Italy
78 F1 Nové Město nad Metuj Czech Rep.
79 G3 Nové Mestonad Váhom Slovakia
99 F4 Novés Spain
75 J2 Nové Strašecí Czech Rep.
79 H4 Nové Zámky Slovakia
50 D3 Novgorod div. Rus. Fed.
50 D3 Novgorod Rus. Fed.
53 E2 Novhorodka Ukraine
52 A4 Novhorod-Sivers'kyy Ukraine
112 C2 Novi Bečej Yugoslavia
53 C1 Novi Bilokorovychi Ukraine
53 D1 Novi Borovychi Ukraine
53 A1 Novi Chervyshcha Ukraine
107 E4 Novi di Modena Italy
107 H3 Novigrad Croatia
112 D3 Novi Iskŭr Bulgaria
79 K5 Novi Kneževac Yugoslavia
106 C4 Novi Ligure Italy
69 C4 Noville Belgium
78 F5 Novi Marof Croatia
53 E1 Novi Mlyny Ukraine
86 D3 Novion-Porcien France
112 F3 Novi Pazar Bulgaria
112 C3 Novi Pazar Yugoslavia
112 B2 Novi Sad Yugoslavia
53 F2 Novi Sanzhary Ukraine
107 J3 Novi Vinodolski Croatia
52 E1 Novki Rus. Fed.
52 E2 Novlyanka Rus. Fed.
166 B1 Novo r. Brazil
51 G6 Novoaleksandrovsk Rus. Fed.
52 B2 Novoaleksandrovskiy Rus. Fed.
46 E2 Novoalekseyevka Kazakhstan
47 K2 Novoaltaysk Rus. Fed.
51 G5 Novoanninskiy Rus. Fed.
163 E5 Novo Aripuanã Brazil
53 D2 Novoarkhanel's'k Ukraine
51 F6 Novoazovs'k Ukraine
53 F3 Novobohdanivka Ukraine
52 E3 Novobokino Rus. Fed.
52 H1 Novocheboksarsk Rus. Fed.
51 G6 Novocherkassk Rus. Fed.
169 H2 Novo Cruzeiro Brazil
53 F3 Novodanylivka Ukraine
52 F2 Novodmitriyevka Rus. Fed.
53 B2 Novodnistrovs'k Ukraine
47 H2 Novodolinka Kazakhstan
53 G2 Novodonets'ke Ukraine
52 F2 Novodugino Rus. Fed.
50 G1 Novodvinsk Rus. Fed.
53 C2 Novofastiv Ukraine
31 H2 Novogeorgiyevka Rus. Fed.
52 B3 Novognezdilovo Rus. Fed.
52 C2 Novogurovskiy Rus. Fed.
167 B6 Novo Hamburgo Brazil
168 D4 Novo Horizonte Brazil
53 E3 Novohradivka Ukraine
78 D3 Novohradské Hory mts Czech Rep.
53 B1 Novohrad-Volyns'kyy Ukraine
53 G2 Novohrodivka Ukraine
30 D2 Novoil'insk Rus. Fed.
53 F3 Novoivanivka Ukraine
52 D4 Novokastornoye Rus. Fed.
46 F3 Novokazalinsk Kazakhstan
54 F4 Novokhovansk Rus. Fed.
31 J2 Novokiyevskiy Uval Rus. Fed.
51 G6 Novokubansk Rus. Fed.
50 J4 Novokuybyshevsk Rus. Fed.
47 L2 Novokuznetsk Rus. Fed.
53 E3 Novokyyivka Ukraine
179 D3 Novolazarevskaya Rus. Fed. Base Antarctica
45 M2 Novoletov'ye Rus. Fed.
53 F2 Novomar"yivka Ukraine
81 G5 Novo mesto Slovenia
104 E3 Novo Mesto Slovenia
52 D2 Novomichurinsk Rus. Fed.
51 F6 Novomikhaylovskiy Rus. Fed.
79 K6 Novo Miloševo Yugoslavia
50 F4 Novomoskovsk Rus. Fed.
53 F2 Novomoskovs'k Ukraine
53 F3 Novomykhaylivka Ukraine
53 F3 Novomykolayivka Ukraine
53 D2 Novomyrhorod Ukraine
53 E3 Novonatalivka Ukraine
51 G5 Novonikolayevskiy Rus. Fed.
51 H5 Novonikol'skoye Rus. Fed.
53 F3 Novooleksiyivka Ukraine
163 F4 Novo Olinda do Norte Brazil
46 E2 Novoorsk Rus. Fed.
53 E1 Novoorzhyts'ke Ukraine
53 C1 Novoozeryanka Ukraine
166 D2 Novo Parnarama Brazil
53 D3 Novopavlivka Ukraine
30 D2 Novopavlovka Rus. Fed.
52 E1 Novopistsovo Rus. Fed.
53 F2 Novopokrovka Ukraine
51 G6 Novopokrovskaya Rus. Fed.
52 F4 Novopokrovskoye Rus. Fed.
53 E3 Novopoltavka Ukraine
52 D3 Novopolyan'ye Rus. Fed.
51 F5 Novopskov Ukraine
31 J1 Novorossiyka Rus. Fed.
51 F6 Novorossiysk Rus. Fed.
45 M2 Novorybnoye Rus. Fed.
54 F3 Novorzhev Rus. Fed.
53 C3 Noviselivka Ukraine
52 F2 Novoselki Rus. Fed.
114 D1 Novo Selo Macedonia
77 J1 Novoselovo Rus. Fed.
54 F2 Novosel'ye Rus. Fed.
53 B2 Novoselytsya Ukraine
46 D2 Novosergiyevka Rus. Fed.
51 F6 Novoshakhtinsk Rus. Fed.
47 K2 Novosibirsk Rus. Fed.
47 K1 Novosibirsk Rus. Fed.
45 P2 Novosibirskiye Ostrova is Rus. Fed.
52 C3 Novosil' Rus. Fed.
52 D4 Novosil'skoye Rus. Fed.
46 F1 Novosineglazovskiy Rus. Fed.
50 D3 Novosokol'niki Rus. Fed.
77 K1 Novostroyevo Rus. Fed.
46 E2 Novotroitsk Rus. Fed.
47 H4 Novotroitskoye Kazakhstan
52 A3 Novotroitskoye Rus. Fed.
52 G2 Novotroitskoye Rus. Fed.
53 F3 Novotroyits'ke Ukraine
53 D2 Novoukrayinka *Kirovohrads'ka Oblast'* Ukraine
53 A1 Novoukrayinka *Rivens'ka Oblast'* Ukraine
51 J5 Novouzensk Rus. Fed.
53 F3 Novovasylivka Ukraine
53 A1 Novovolyns'k Ukraine
51 F5 Novovoronezh Rus. Fed.
53 E3 Novovorontsovka Ukraine
52 F1 Novovyazniki Rus. Fed.
77 M6 Novoyavorivs'ke Ukraine
52 D3 Novoye Dubovoye Rus. Fed.
52 E1 Novoye Leushino Rus. Fed.
52 E3 Novoyur'yevo Rus. Fed.
52 C1 Novozavidovskiy Rus. Fed.
53 C2 Novozhyvotiv Ukraine
51 D4 Novozybkov Rus. Fed.
78 D1 Nový Bor Czech Rep.
78 E1 Nový Bydžov Czech Rep.
86 D3 Novy-Chevrières France
77 N2 Novy Dvor *Hrodna* Belarus
77 N3 Novy Dvor *Hrodna* Belarus
79 G2 Nový Jičín Czech Rep.
45 M2 Novyy Rus. Fed.
53 E3 Novyy Buh Ukraine
53 D1 Novyy Bykiv Ukraine
52 H2 Novyye Aybesi Rus. Fed.
52 H3 Novyye Burasy Rus. Fed.
52 A3 Novyye Ivaytenki Rus. Fed.
52 D1 Novyy Nekouz Rus. Fed.
53 G1 Novyy Oskol Rus. Fed.
44 J3 Novyy Port Rus. Fed.
77 N6 Novyy Rozdil Ukraine
52 C3 Novyy Sinets Rus. Fed.
53 E2 Novyystarodub Ukraine
50 J3 Novyy Tor"yal Rus. Fed.
44 J3 Novyy Urengoy Rus. Fed.
31 K2 Novyy Urgal Rus. Fed.
46 D4 Novyy Uzen' Kazakhstan
77 N5 Novyy Vytkiv Ukraine
77 N6 Novyy Yarychiv Ukraine
39 C3 Now Iran
77 H4 Nowa Brzeźnica Poland
77 M2 Nowa Chodorówka Poland
77 K5 Nowa Dęba Poland
76 G1 Nowa Karczma Poland
76 E5 Nowa Ruda Poland
76 D4 Nowa Sól Poland
151 E4 Nowata *Oklahoma* U.S.A.
77 L2 Nowa Wieś Ełcka Poland
76 G3 Nowa Wieś Wielka Poland
39 B2 Nowbarān Iran
76 G2 Nowe Poland
76 C2 Nowe Czarnowo Poland
77 J4 Nowe Miasło nad Pilicą Poland
76 D4 Nowe Miasteczko Poland
77 J3 Nowe Miasto Poland
77 H2 Nowe Miasto Lubawskie Poland
76 F3 Nowe Miasto nad Wartą Poland
77 H3 Nowe Ostrowy Poland
77 L3 Nowe Piekuty Poland
76 F4 Nowe Skalmierzyce Poland
76 C2 Nowe Warpno Poland
76 F1 Nowe Wieś Lęborska Poland
36 D4 Nowgong India
Nowgong *see* Nagaon
77 L2 Nowinka Poland
42 G2 Nowjeh Deh Iran
39 C1 Now Kharegan Iran
137 J2 Nowleye Lake l. *N.W.T.* Canada
76 D2 Nowogard Poland
77 K2 Nowogród Poland
76 D4 Nowogród Bobrzański Poland
76 D3 Nowogródek Pomorski Poland
73 L4 Nowogrodziec Poland
13 G3 Nowra *New South Wales* Australia
42 G2 Nowshahr Iran
39 B1 Now Shahr Iran
36 C2 Nowshera Pakistan
77 H3 Nowy Duninów Poland
77 M2 Nowy Dwór *Białystok* Poland
76 F2 Nowy Dwór *Toruń* Poland
77 H1 Nowy Dwór Gdański Poland
77 J3 Nowy Dwór Mazowiecki Poland
77 J5 Nowy Korczyn Poland
77 J6 Nowy Sącz div. Poland
77 J6 Nowy Sącz Poland
77 J6 Nowy Targ Poland
76 E3 Nowy Tomyśl Poland
77 K6 Nowy Żmigród Poland
147 E4 Noxen *Pennsylvania* U.S.A.
44 J3 Noyabr'sk Rus. Fed.
88 C3 Noyal-Pontivy France
89 F4 Noyant France
90 B1 Noyers France
91 D4 Noyers-sur-Jabron France
136 C3 Noyes I. i. *Alaska* U.S.A.
86 B3 Noyon France
88 D4 Nozay France
90 E2 Nozeroy France
131 E5 Nozizwe South Africa
83 F3 Nozza r. Italy
131 H5 Nqabeni South Africa
131 H4 Nqutu South Africa
124 C4 Nsambi Zaire
129 F2 Nsanje Malawi
122 D5 Nsawam Ghana
124 B3 Nsoc Equatorial Guinea
131 H3 Nsoko Swaziland
125 E6 Nsombo Zambia
122 D5 Nsuatre Ghana
123 F5 Nsukka Nigeria
120 A4 Ntalfa well Mauritania
124 C4 Ntandembele Zaire
129 E1 Ntcheu Malawi
127 B7 Ntchisi Malawi
124 B3 Ntem r. Africa
131 F3 Ntha South Africa
131 G3 Nthorwane South Africa
124 A3 Ntoum Gabon
124 B3 Ntui Cameroon
127 B5 Ntungamo Uganda
128 D3 Ntwetwe Pan salt pan Botswana
131 G5 Ntywenka South Africa
32 B3 Nu r. China
179 □ Nuageuses, Is is *Kerguelen* Indian Ocean
131 H1 Nuaneteze r. Mozambique
6 □3 Nuapapu i. Tonga
41 J5 Nu'aym reg. Oman
119 F3 Nuba, Lake l. Sudan
126 B2 Nuba Mountains mts Sudan
119 F3 Nubian Desert desert Sudan
172 B4 Nuble r. Chile
98 E1 Nubledo Spain
30 D4 Nüden Mongolia
164 B3 Nudo Coropuna mt. Peru
77 N4 Nudyzhe Ukraine
151 D6 Nueces r. *Texas* U.S.A.
92 B2 Nueil-sur-Argent France
69 D3 Nuenen Netherlands
103 E6 Nuestra Señora del Pilar Spain
99 F1 Nueva Spain
156 J6 Nueva Armenia Honduras
172 C2 Nueva California Argentina
172 D3 Nueva Constitución Argentina
172 E2 Nueva Escocia Argentina
162 D2 Nueva Florida Venezuela
172 E3 Nueva Galia Argentina
165 E4 Nueva Germania Paraguay
158 B2 Nueva Gerona Cuba
173 J3 Nueva Helvecia Uruguay
171 C7 Nueva, I. i. Chile
172 A5 Nueva Imperial Chile
162 B3 Nueva Loja Ecuador
171 B5 Nueva Lubecka Argentina
173 H2 Nueva Palmira Uruguay
157 E3 Nueva Rosita Mexico
157 H6 Nueva San Salvador El Salvador
158 C2 Nuevitas Cuba
173 H2 Nuevo Berlín Uruguay
156 D2 Nuevo Casas Grandes Mexico
171 D5 Nuevo, G. g. Argentina
156 D3 Nuevo Ideal Mexico
157 F3 Nuevo Laredo Mexico
157 F3 Nuevo Leon div. Mexico
164 C2 Nuevo Mundo Bolivia
126 E3 Nugaal div. Somalia
126 E3 Nugaal watercourse Somalia
9 B7 Nugget Pt pt New Zealand
119 F3 Nugrus, Gebel mt. Egypt
6 □1 Nuguria Is is P.N.G.
8 F3 Nuhaka New Zealand
176 G6 Nui i. Tuvalu
54 D2 Nuia Estonia
54 F1 Nuijamaa Finland
90 C1 Nuits France

90 C1 Nuits-St-Georges France
12 C3 Nukey Bluff h. *S. Australia* Australia
6 □4 Nuku i. Tonga
6 □4 Nuku'alofa Tonga
6 □6 Nukubasaga reef Fiji
176 G6 Nukufetau i. Tuvalu
177 K6 Nuku Hiva i. *French Polynesia* Pacific Ocean
176 G6 Nukulaelae i. Tuvalu
6 □1 Nukumanu Is is P.N.G.
5 K5 Nukunono atoll *Tokelau* Pacific Ocean
46 E4 Nukus Uzbekistan
103 C5 Nules Spain
16 C4 Nullagine r. *Western Australia* Australia
16 C4 Nullagine *Western Australia* Australia
12 B2 Nullarbor *S. Australia* Australia
12 B2 Nullarbor Nat. Park nat. park *S. Australia* Australia
12 B2 Nullarbor Plain plain Australia
131 H1 Nulli Zimbabwe
31 F4 Nulu'erhu Shan mountain range China
108 A4 Nulvi *Sardegna* Italy
119 G2 Nu'mān i. Saudi Arabia
123 G5 Numan Nigeria
107 H5 Numana Italy
29 G5 Numata Japan
28 H2 Numata Japan
124 E2 Numatinna watercourse Sudan
29 G6 Numazu Japan
131 H2 Numbi Gate South Africa
14 C2 Numbulwar *Northern Terr.* Australia
58 C1 Numedal v. Norway
21 K7 Numfor i. Indonesia
31 H3 Numin r. China
54 D1 Nummela Finland
13 F4 Numurkah *Victoria* Australia
139 H2 Nunaksaluk Island i. *Newfoundland* Canada
135 O3 Nunarsuit i. Greenland
137 M2 Nunavut reg. *N.W.T.* Canada
73 J4 Nünchritz Germany
146 E3 Nunda *New York* U.S.A.
125 E4 Nunda Zaire
13 G2 Nundle *New South Wales* Australia
63 E2 Nuneaton *England* U.K.
138 B3 Nungesser L. l. *Ontario* Canada
31 F3 Nungnain Sum China
134 B4 Nunivak I. *Alaska* U.S.A.
36 D2 Nunkun mt. India
134 A3 Nunligran Rus. Fed.
98 D4 Nuñomoral Spain
73 J3 Nunsdorf Germany
68 D2 Nunspeet Netherlands
31 G2 Nuomin r. China
108 B4 Nuoro div. *Sardegna* Italy
108 B4 Nuoro *Sardegna* Italy
119 H2 Nuqrah Saudi Arabia
162 B2 Nuquí Colombia
36 E1 Nur China
77 L3 Nur Poland
47 H2 Nura r. Kazakhstan
47 H3 Nura Kazakhstan
39 B3 Nūrābād Iran
46 C5 Nūrābād Iran
108 B5 Nurallao *Sardegna* Italy
108 B5 Nuraminis *Sardegna* Italy
47 G4 Nurata Uzbekistan
47 G4 Nuratau, Khr. mountain range Uzbekistan
43 D1 Nur Dağları mountain range Turkey
106 D4 Nure r. Italy
Nuremberg *see* Nürnberg
39 G2 Nūr Gal Afghanistan
36 A3 Nūr Gamma Pakistan
156 C2 Nuri Mexico
39 G2 Nuristan reg. Afghanistan
22 B2 Nuri, Tk b. Indonesia
36 D2 Nurla India
50 J4 Nurlat Rus. Fed.
56 H3 Nurmes Finland
54 D1 Nurmijärvi Finland
56 F3 Nurmo Finland
75 G3 Nürnberg Germany
36 B3 Nurpur Pakistan
13 F2 Nurri, Mt h. *New South Wales* Australia
74 E4 Nürtingen Germany
37 H1 Nur Turu China
77 L3 Nurzec r. Poland
77 M3 Nurzec-Stacja Poland
82 C3 Nus Italy
22 D4 Nusa Tenggara Barat div. Indonesia
22 D4 Nusa Tenggara Timur div. Indonesia
42 E2 Nusaybin Turkey
43 D2 Nuşayrīyah, Jabal al mountain range Syria
79 M4 Nuşfalău Romania
32 B3 Nu Shan mountain range China
36 A3 Nushki Pakistan
80 D3 Nußdorf am Inn Germany
139 H2 Nutak *Newfoundland* Canada
69 D4 Nuth Netherlands
155 H5 Nutrioso *Arizona* U.S.A.
36 B3 Nuttal Pakistan
14 C2 Nutwood Downs *Northern Terr.* Australia
135 N3 Nuuk Greenland
56 G2 Nuupas Finland
7 □11 Nuupéré, Pte pt *French Polynesia* Pacific Ocean
135 N2 Nuussuaq pen. Greenland
135 N2 Nuussuaq Greenland
7 □13 Nuuúli *American Samoa* Pacific Ocean
38 C5 Nuwara Eliya Sri Lanka
43 C5 Nuweiba el Muzeina Egypt
130 B5 Nuwerus South Africa
130 C6 Nuweveldberg mts South Africa
52 G2 Nuya r. Rus. Fed.
77 N4 Nuyno Ukraine
12 C3 Nuyts Arch. is *S. Australia* Australia
17 B7 Nuyts, Pt pt *Western Australia* Australia
83 E1 Nüziders Austria
163 F3 Nw-Jacobkondre Surinam
17 B7 Nyabing *Western Australia* Australia
129 E2 Nyadire r. Zimbabwe
44 H3 Nyagan' Rus. Fed.
Nyagquka *see* Yajiang
Nyagrong *see* Xinlong
127 C4 Nyahururu Kenya
13 E3 Nyah West *Victoria* Australia
37 G3 Nyainqêntanglha Feng mt. China
37 G3 Nyainqêntanglha Shan mountain range China
37 H2 Nyainrong China
127 B5 Nyakaliro Tanzania
131 F3 Nyakallong South Africa
56 E3 Nyaker Sweden
77 O3 Nyakhachava Belarus
118 D5 Nyala Sudan
37 F3 Nyalam China
178 □3 Ny-Ålesund *Svalbard* Arctic Ocean
129 D2 Nyamandhiovu Zimbabwe
124 E2 Nyamlell Sudan
77 O3 Nyamyerzha Belarus
50 G2 Nyandoma Rus. Fed.
50 F2 Nyandomskiy Vozvyshennost' Rus. Fed.
125 B4 Nyanga div. Gabon
125 B4 Nyanga Congo
129 E2 Nyanga Zimbabwe
37 G3 Nyang Qu r. China
122 D5 Nyankpala Ghana
127 B5 Nyanza div. Kenya
127 A5 Nyanza Rwanda
22 D1 Nyapa, G. mt. Indonesia
79 J4 Nyársapát Hungary
127 B6 Nyasa, Lake l. Africa
54 E5 Nyasvizh Belarus
129 D2 Nyathi Zimbabwe
24 B3 Nyaunglebin Myanmar
24 A2 Nyaungu Myanmar
46 E1 Nyazepetrovsk Rus. Fed.
59 F2 Nybble Sweden
59 E1 Nybergsund Norway
55 C4 Nyborg Denmark
56 H1 Nyborg Norway
59 F3 Nybro Sweden
135 N1 Nyeboe Land reg. Greenland
54 E5 Nyeharelaye Belarus
79 K4 Nyékládháza Hungary
37 G3 Nyêmo China
Nyenchen Tanglha Range mountain range *see* Nyainqêntanglha Shan
127 C5 Nyeri Kenya
54 F4 Nyeshcharda, Vozyera l. Belarus
59 F1 Nyhammar Sweden
127 B7 Nyika National Park nat. park Malawi
37 F3 Nyima China
127 B7 Nyimba Zambia
37 H3 Nyingchi China
79 L4 Nyíradony Hungary
79 L4 Nyírbátor Hungary
79 M4 Nyírbéltek Hungary
79 M4 Nyírbogát Hungary
79 L4 Nyíregyháza Hungary
79 L4 Nyírség reg. Hungary
56 F3 Nykarleby Finland
55 D5 Nykøbing Denmark
55 A3 Nykøbing Mors Denmark
55 D4 Nykøbing S Denmark
59 G2 Nyköping Sweden
59 G1 Nykrogen Sweden
59 F2 Nykroppa Sweden
59 G2 Nykvarn Sweden
59 F2 Nykyrke Sweden
56 E3 Nyland Sweden
131 G2 Nylstroom South Africa
13 F3 Nymagee *New South Wales* Australia
13 H2 Nymboida r. *New South Wales* Australia
78 E1 Nymburk Czech Rep.
114 A3 Nymfes Greece
55 A4 Nymindegab Denmark
59 G2 Nynäshamn Sweden
13 F2 Nyngan *New South Wales* Australia
54 C5 Nyoman r. Belarus/Lithuania
54 E5 Nyomanskaya Nizina lowland Belarus
82 B2 Nyon Switzerland
36 F4 Nyonni Ri mt. China
91 D4 Nyons France
55 D4 Nyråd Denmark
78 C2 Nýřany Czech Rep.
78 C2 Nýrsko Czech Rep.
76 F5 Nysa Poland
76 F5 Nysa Kłodzka r. Poland
73 K4 Nysa Łużycka r. Germany/Poland
59 E2 Nysäter Sweden
55 D5 Nysted Denmark
58 C1 Nystølfjell mt. Norway
50 J2 Nyuchpas Rus. Fed.
29 G4 Nyūdō-zaki pt Japan
50 H2 Nyukhcha Rus. Fed.
50 H2 Nyuksenitsa Rus. Fed.
79 G4 Nyúl Hungary
125 E5 Nyunzu Zaire
45 N3 Nyurba Rus. Fed.
50 J2 Nyuvchim Rus. Fed.
77 N5 Nyvytsi Ukraine
77 L6 Nyzhankovychi Ukraine
53 F3 Nyzhni Sirohozy Ukraine
53 F3 Nyzhni Torhayi Ukraine
79 N3 Nyzhni Vorota Ukraine
53 F1 Nyzhnya Syrovatka Ukraine
53 F1 Nyzy Ukraine
125 B4 Nzambi Congo
124 E3 Nzara Sudan
122 C5 Nzébéla Guinea
127 B5 Nzega Tanzania
122 C5 Nzérékoré Guinea
125 B5 N'zeto Angola
131 H1 Nzhelele Dam dam South Africa
122 D5 Nzi r. Côte d'Ivoire
125 E6 Nzilo, Lac l. Zaire
125 E4 Nzingu Zaire
127 B4 Nzoia r. Kenya
124 E3 Nzoro r. Zaire
127 D7 Nzwani i. Comoros

O

63 E2 Oadby *England* U.K.
150 C2 Oahe, Lake l. *S. Dakota* U.S.A.
153 □1 Oahu i. *Hawaii* U.S.A.
12 E3 Oakbank *S. Australia* Australia
155 F2 Oak City *Utah* U.S.A.
151 E6 Oakdale *Louisiana* U.S.A.
62 D2 Oakengates *England* U.K.
150 D2 Oakes *N. Dakota* U.S.A.
15 G5 Oakey *Queensland* Australia
63 F2 Oakham *England* U.K.
152 B1 Oak Harbor *Washington* U.S.A.
146 C6 Oak Hill *W. Virginia* U.S.A.
154 C3 Oakhurst *California* U.S.A.
148 B2 Oak I. i. *Wisconsin* U.S.A.
154 A3 Oakland airport *California* U.S.A.
154 A3 Oakland *California* U.S.A.
146 D5 Oakland *Maryland* U.S.A.
150 D3 Oakland *Nebraska* U.S.A.
152 B3 Oakland *Oregon* U.S.A.
148 D5 Oak Lawn *Illinois* U.S.A.
150 C4 Oakley *Kansas* U.S.A.
16 C4 Oakover r. *Western Australia* Australia
152 B3 Oakridge *Oregon* U.S.A.
145 C4 Oak Ridge *Tennessee* U.S.A.
8 D3 Oakura New Zealand
141 F5 Oakville *Ontario* Canada
9 C6 Oamaru New Zealand
66 B5 Oa, Mull of headland *Scotland* U.K.
9 D5 Oaro New Zealand
23 B3 Oas Philippines
28 D6 Ōasa Japan
152 D3 Oasis *Nevada* U.S.A.
43 D3 Oasis of Rhube oasis Syria
179 B5 Oates Land reg. Antarctica
13 F5 Oatlands *Tasmania* Australia
130 E6 Oatlands South Africa
155 E4 Oatman *Arizona* U.S.A.
157 F5 Oaxaca div. Mexico
157 F5 Oaxaca Mexico
49 O3 Ob' r. Rus. Fed.
140 C2 Oba *Ontario* Canada
140 C2 Obakamiga Lake l. *Ontario* Canada
54 F4 Obal' r. Belarus
54 F4 Obal' *Vitsyebskaya Voblasts'* Belarus
124 B3 Obala Cameroon
140 C2 Oba Lake l. *Ontario* Canada
29 E6 Obama Japan
66 C4 Oban *Scotland* U.K.
123 F5 Oban Nigeria
29 H4 Obanazawa Japan
123 F5 Oban Hills mt. Nigeria
98 D2 O Barco Spain
99 G2 Obarenes, Mtes mountain range Spain
138 F4 Obatogama L. l. *Québec* Canada
81 F3 Obdach Austria
75 J3 Obecnice Czech Rep.
136 F4 Obed *Alberta* Canada
54 D4 Obeliai Lithuania
9 B6 Obelisk mt. New Zealand
81 G3 Oberaich Austria
83 E1 Oberalm Austria
83 D2 Oberalpstock mt. Switzerland
75 G5 Oberammergau Germany
75 F3 Oberasbach Germany
75 G5 Oberau Germany
72 E5 Oberaula Germany
75 G4 Oberbayern div. Germany
74 D3 Oberderdingen Germany
80 D4 Oberdrauburg Austria
83 E1 Oberegg Switzerland
83 E2 Ober Engadin reg. Switzerland
82 D1 Oberentfelden Switzerland
80 A3 Oberessendorf Germany
87 G2 Oberfell Germany
75 G2 Oberfranken div. Germany
82 C1 Obergösgen Switzerland
81 G2 Ober-Grafendorf Austria
74 F5 Obergünzburg Germany
80 C4 Obergurgl Austria
81 G4 Oberhaag Austria
87 H4 Oberharmersbach Germany
73 F4 Oberharz nat. park Germany
72 B4 Oberhausen Germany
83 F1 Oberjoch Paß Austria/Germany
74 D4 Oberkirch Germany
80 B2 Oberkochen Germany
73 K4 Oberlausitz reg. Germany
150 C4 Oberlin *Kansas* U.S.A.
146 B4 Oberlin *Ohio* U.S.A.
74 E4 Obermarchtal Germany
74 C3 Obermoschel Germany
87 G4 Obernai France
75 J4 Obernberg am Inn Austria
74 D4 Oberndorf am Neckar Germany
80 D3 Oberndorf bei Salzburg Austria
81 F2 Oberneukirchen Austria
87 G3 Obernheim-Kirchenarnbach Germany
72 E3 Obernkirchen Germany
81 E2 Oberösterreich div. Austria
75 G3 Oberpfalz div. Germany
75 H3 Oberpfälzer Wald mts Germany
81 H3 Oberpullendorf div. Austria
81 H3 Oberpullendorf Austria
87 H3 Ober-Ramstadt Germany
83 E1 Oberreute Germany
83 E1 Oberriet Switzerland
87 G4 Oberrotweil Germany
80 D2 Oberschneiding Germany
83 D1 Obersiggenthal Switzerland
74 E2 Obersinn Germany
74 F5 Oberstaufen Germany
74 F5 Oberstdorf Germany
83 E1 Oberteuringen Germany
74 C3 Oberthal Germany
74 E2 Oberthulba Germany
75 H4 Obertraubling Germany
80 E3 Obertrum am See Austria
74 D2 Obertshausen Germany
53 A2 Obertyn Ukraine
73 J2 Oberueckersee l. Germany
87 H2 Oberursel (Taunus) Germany
80 E4 Obervellach Austria
75 H3 Oberviechtach Germany
83 D2 Oberwald Switzerland
72 E4 Oberwälder Land reg. Germany
81 H3 Oberwaltersdorf Austria
81 H3 Oberwart div. Austria
81 H3 Oberwart Austria
75 G2 Oberweißbach Germany
82 C2 Oberwölbling Austria
81 F3 Oberwölz Austria
52 B4 Obesta r. Rus. Fed.
21 J7 Obi i. Indonesia
166 A1 Óbidos Brazil
100 A1 Óbidos Portugal
100 A1 Óbidos, Laguna de lag. Portugal
47 G5 Obigarm Tajikistan
28 J2 Obihiro Japan
51 H6 Obil'noye Rus. Fed.
75 H4 Obing Germany
28 H1 Obira Japan
162 C2 Obispos Venezuela
172 F1 Obispo Trejo Argentina
92 D3 Objat France
76 F1 Objazda Poland
81 E3 Öblarn Austria
51 G5 Oblivskaya Rus. Fed.
31 J2 Obluch'ye Rus. Fed.
52 C2 Obninsk Rus. Fed.
124 E2 Obo Central African Rep.
30 B5 Obo China
130 C3 Obobogorap South Africa
126 D2 Obock Djibouti
124 E4 Obokote Zaire
98 C2 O Bolo Spain
53 E2 Obolon' Ukraine
76 E3 Oborniki Poland
76 E4 Oborniki Śląskie Poland
124 C4 Obouya Congo
53 G1 Oboyan' Rus. Fed.
50 G2 Obozerskiy Rus. Fed.
76 D3 Obra r. Poland
37 E4 Obra India
156 C3 Obregón, Psa resr Mexico
87 H3 Obrigheim (Pfalz) Germany
75 J2 Obrnice Czech Rep.
112 F3 Obrochishte Bulgaria
107 J3 Obrov Slovenia
76 E3 Obrzycko Poland
10 □4 Observatory Rock i. *Lord Howe I.* Pacific Ocean
52 A2 Obsha r. Rus. Fed.
46 D2 Obshchiy Syrt h. Rus. Fed.
44 J3 Obskaya Guba chan. Rus. Fed.
77 L5 Obsza Poland
53 E1 Obtove Ukraine
122 D5 Obuasi Ghana
53 D1 Obukhiv Ukraine
82 D2 Obwalden div. Switzerland
50 J2 Ob"yachevo Rus. Fed.
53 G3 Obytichna Kosa spit Ukraine
53 F3 Obytichna Zakota b. Ukraine
52 F1 Obzherikha Rus. Fed.
98 C1 O Cádabo Spain
145 D6 Ocala *Florida* U.S.A.
156 E3 Ocampo *Coahuila* Mexico
157 E3 Ocampo *Coahuila* Mexico
162 C2 Ocaña Colombia
99 G5 Ocaña Spain
98 B2 O Castelo Spain
107 F4 Occhiobello Italy
109 G3 Occhito, Lago di l. Italy
164 C3 Occidental, Cord. mountain range Chile
162 B3 Occidental, Cordillera mountain range Colombia
164 A2 Occidental, Cordillera mountain range Peru
83 D3 Occimiano Italy
136 B3 Ocean Cape pt *Alaska* U.S.A.
147 F5 Ocean City *Maryland* U.S.A.
147 F5 Ocean City *New Jersey* U.S.A.
136 D4 Ocean Falls *B.C.* Canada
174 G3 Oceanographer Fracture sea feature Atlantic Ocean
154 D5 Oceanside *California* U.S.A.
151 F6 Ocean Springs *Mississippi* U.S.A.
99 G3 Ocejón mt. Spain
93 A6 Ochagavía Spain
53 D3 Ochakiv Ukraine
51 G7 Och'amch'ire Georgia
115 F4 Ochi mt. Greece
28 D6 Ōchi Japan
28 K2 Ochiishi-misaki pt Japan
66 E4 Ochil Hills h. *Scotland* U.K.
64 D2 Ochiltree *Scotland* U.K.
52 A3 Ochkyne Ukraine
159 □1 Ocho Rios Jamaica
74 F3 Ochsenfurt Germany
74 E4 Ochsenhausen Germany
68 D3 Ochten Netherlands
114 F4 Ochthonia Greece
72 C3 Ochtrup Germany
59 G1 Ockelbo Sweden
58 D3 Öckerö Sweden
72 D1 Ockholm Germany
112 D2 Ocna Sibiului Romania
53 B2 Ocniṭa Moldova
157 G5 Ococingo Mexico
148 C4 Oconomowoc *Wisconsin* U.S.A.
148 D3 Oconto *Wisconsin* U.S.A.
98 B2 O Convento Spain
98 C2 O Corgo Spain
156 J6 Ocotal Nicaragua
156 H6 Ocotepeque Honduras
154 D5 Ocotillo Wells *California* U.S.A.
156 E4 Ocotlán Mexico
98 C5 Ocreza r. Portugal
88 D2 Octeville France
89 F2 Octeville-sur-Mer France
122 D5 Oda Ghana
28 D6 Ōda Japan
56 M6 Ódáðahraun lava Iceland
119 G3 Oda, Jebel mt. Sudan
29 H3 Ōdate Japan
29 G6 Odawara Japan
58 B1 Odda Norway
55 C4 Odder Denmark
55 A3 Oddesund chan. Denmark
100 C2 Odearce r. Portugal
100 B3 Odeceixe Portugal
137 K3 Odei r. *Manitoba* Canada
100 C3 Odeleite r. Portugal
148 C5 Odell *Illinois* U.S.A.
100 C2 Odelzhausen Germany
100 B3 Odemira Portugal
42 A2 Ödemiş Turkey
131 F3 Odendaalsrus South Africa
59 F2 Odensbacken Sweden
55 C4 Odense Denmark
55 C4 Odense Fjord b. Denmark
74 D3 Odenwald reg. Germany
Oder r. *see* Odra
73 K3 Oderberg Germany
73 K3 Oderbruch reg. Germany
73 K1 Oderbucht b. Germany
73 K2 Oderhaff b. Germany
73 J3 Oder-Havel-Kanal canal Germany
107 G3 Oderzo Italy
51 D6 Odesa Ukraine
53 C3 Odesa div. Ukraine
170 C2 O de Salado r. Chile
59 F2 Ödeshog Sweden
151 C6 Odessa *Texas* U.S.A.
47 H2 Odesskoye Rus. Fed.
88 B3 Odet r. France
100 D3 Odiel r. Spain
122 C5 Odienné Côte d'Ivoire
52 C2 Odintsovo Rus. Fed.
100 B2 Odivelas *Beja* Portugal
100 A2 Odivelas *Lisboa* Portugal
100 B2 Odivelas, Barragem de resr Portugal
112 F2 Odobeşti Romania
76 F4 Odolanów Poland
89 E2 Odon r. France
25 D5 Ŏdôngk Cambodia
68 E2 Odoorn Netherlands
112 E1 Odorheiu Secuiesc Romania
52 C3 Odoyev Rus. Fed.
76 C2 Odra r. Germany/Poland
44 C4 Odra r. Poland
77 J4 Odrzywół Poland
55 B4 Ødsted Denmark
112 B2 Odžaci Yugoslavia
129 E2 Odzi r. Zimbabwe
73 F3 Oebisfelde Germany
100 C3 Oeiras r. Portugal
166 D2 Oeiras Brazil
100 A2 Oeiras Portugal
163 G3 Oelemari r. Surinam
150 C3 Oelrichs *S. Dakota* U.S.A.
75 H2 Oelsnitz *Sachsen* Germany
75 H2 Oelsnitz *Sachsen* Germany
148 B4 Oelwein *Iowa* U.S.A.
5 P7 Oeno atoll
14 C2 Oenpelli *Northern Terr.* Australia
82 C1 Oensingen Switzerland
69 D5 Oesling h. Luxembourg
72 C2 Oestrich-Winkel Germany
80 B2 Oettingen in Bayern Germany
80 B3 Oetz Austria
72 E1 Oeversee Germany
42 E1 Of Turkey
109 H3 Ofanto r. Italy
43 C4 Ofaqim Israel
131 H2 Ofcolaco South Africa
123 E5 Offa Nigeria
67 D3 Offaly div. Rep. of Ireland
87 G2 Offanengo Italy
82 B1 Offemont France
74 D2 Offenbach am Main Germany
75 H4 Offenberg Germany
74 C4 Offenburg Germany
80 B2 Offingen Germany
124 B4 Offoué r. Gabon
89 G2 Offranville France
71 F6 Ofidoussa i. Greece
123 E5 Ofiki r. Nigeria
6 □5 Ofolanga i. Tonga
7 □13 Ofu i. *American Samoa* Pacific Ocean
6 □3 Ofu i. Tonga
29 H4 Ōfunato Japan
28 H2 Ofuyu-misaki pt Japan
22 C1 Oga r. Indonesia
29 G4 Oga Japan
29 H4 Ogachi Japan
126 E3 Ogadēn reg. Ethiopia
29 G4 Oga-hantō pen. Japan
29 F6 Ōgaki Japan
150 C3 Ogallala *Nebraska* U.S.A.
22 A2 Ogan r. Indonesia
59 E1 Ogan Sweden
21 M1 Ogasawara-shotō is Japan
141 F3 Ogascanane, Lac l. *Québec* Canada
29 H5 Ōgawa Japan
28 H3 Ogawara-ko l. Japan
123 E5 Ogbomoso Nigeria
150 E3 Ogden *Iowa* U.S.A.
152 E3 Ogden *Utah* U.S.A.
136 C3 Ogden, Mt mt. *B.C.* Canada
147 F2 Ogdensburg *New York* U.S.A.
6 □7 Ogea i. Fiji
87 F4 Ogéviller France
58 C2 Ogge l. Norway
106 D3 Oggiono Italy
29 G5 Ogi Japan
52 H1 Ogibnoye Rus. Fed.
134 E3 Ogilvie r. *N.W.T.* Canada
29 □2 Ogimi Japan
120 D3 Oglat Sbot well Algeria
145 C5 Oglethorpe, Mt mt. *Georgia* U.S.A.
109 H4 Ogliastro Cilento Italy
110 D5 Ogliastro, Lago di l. *Sicilia* Italy
106 E3 Oglio r. Italy
15 G4 Ogmore *Queensland* Australia
90 D1 Ognon r. France
22 D1 Ogoamas, G. mt. Indonesia
123 F5 Ogoja Nigeria
138 C3 Ogoki r. *Ontario* Canada
138 C3 Ogoki Res. resr *Ontario* Canada
124 B4 Ogooué r. Gabon
124 B3 Ogooué-Ivindo div. Gabon
124 B4 Ogooué-Lolo div. Gabon
124 A4 Ogooué-Maritime div. Gabon
28 C7 Ogōri Japan
28 C6 Ogōri Japan
54 D3 Ogre r. Latvia
54 D3 Ogre Latvia
114 B2 Ogren Albania
77 K3 Ogrodniki Poland
98 B2 O Grove Spain
104 E3 Ogulin Croatia
123 E5 Ogun div. Nigeria
123 E5 Ogun r. Nigeria
46 D5 Ogurchinskiy, O. i. Turkmenistan
42 F1 Oğuz Azerbaijan
43 D1 Oğuzeli Turkey
123 F5 Ohafia Nigeria
9 A6 Ohai New Zealand
8 E3 Ohakune New Zealand
101 H3 Ohanes Spain
121 F3 Ohanet Algeria
128 B2 Ohangwena div. Namibia
28 H3 Ōhata Japan
8 E4 Ohau New Zealand
9 B6 Ohau, L. l. New Zealand
8 E2 Ohaupo New Zealand
80 E2 Ohe r. Germany
69 D4 Ohey Belgium
172 B3 O'Higgins div. Chile
164 B4 O'Higgins Chile
7 □16 O'Higgins, C. c. *Easter I.* Chile
171 B6 O'Higgins, L. l. Argentina
146 B4 Ohio div. U.S.A.
144 C4 Ohio r. *Indiana* U.S.A.
53 F2 Ohiyivka Ukraine
87 G4 Ohlsbach Germany
74 D2 Ohm r. Germany
83 D1 Öhningen Germany
6 □4 Ohonua Tonga
75 F2 Ohrdruf Germany
78 C1 Ohře r. Czech Rep.
70 E2 Ohre r. Germany
114 B1 Ohrid Macedonia
114 B1 Ohrid, Lake l. Albania/Macedonia
Ohridsko Ezero l. *see* Ohrid, Lake
131 H2 Ohrigstad South Africa
74 E3 Öhringen Germany
8 E3 Ohura New Zealand
115 G6 Oia Greece
98 B4 Oiã Portugal
163 G3 Oiapoque r. Brazil
163 G3 Oiapoque Brazil
66 D3 Oich, Loch l. *Scotland* U.K.
37 H3 Oiga China
86 B2 Oignies France
90 D2 Oignin r. France
146 D4 Oil City *Pennsylvania* U.S.A.
154 C4 Oildale *California* U.S.A.
32 B2 Oi Qu r. China
28 H3 Oirase-gawa r. Japan
92 B2 Oiron France
69 D3 Oirschot Netherlands
91 E3 Oisans reg. France
86 B3 Oise div. *Picardie* France
86 B3 Oise r. France
93 A4 Oiseaux, Île aux i. France
90 D1 Oiselay-et-Grachaux France
89 G2 Oisemont France
89 E3 Oisseau France
89 G2 Oissel France
68 D3 Oisterwijk Netherlands
159 □9 Oistins *Barbados* Caribbean
28 C7 Ōita div. Japan
28 C7 Ōita Japan
98 B2 Oitavén r. Spain
114 D4 Oiti mt. Greece
114 D4 Oiti nat. park Greece
54 D1 Oitti Finland
115 D6 Oitylo Greece
118 C3 Oiuru well Libya
28 H2 Oiwake Japan
154 C4 Ojai *California* U.S.A.
101 G2 Ojailén r. Spain
77 H5 Ojcowski Park Narodowy nat. park Poland
59 E1 Öje Sweden
172 E3 Ojeda Argentina
59 E1 Öjen l. Sweden
148 B3 Ojibwa *Wisconsin* U.S.A.
28 B7 Ojika-jima i. Japan
156 D2 Ojinaga Mexico
157 F5 Ojitlán Mexico
29 G5 Ojiya Japan
172 E1 Ojo de Agua Argentina
170 D2 Ojo de Agua, Va Argentina
156 D2 Ojo de Laguna Mexico
156 B3 Ojo de Liebre, L. b. Mexico
170 C2 Ojos del Salado mt. Argentina
77 J3 Ojrzeń Poland
123 F5 Oju Nigeria
52 F1 Oka r. Rus. Fed.
123 F5 Oka Nigeria
128 B3 Okahandja Namibia
8 E3 Okahukura New Zealand
8 D1 Okaihau New Zealand
123 E5 Okaka Nigeria
128 B3 Okakarara Namibia
139 H2 Okak Islands is *Newfoundland* Canada
77 H2 Okalewo Poland
136 F5 Okanagan Falls *B.C.* Canada
136 F4 Okanagan Lake l. *B.C.* Canada
124 B3 Okano r. Gabon
152 C1 Okanogan r. Canada/U.S.A.
136 F5 Okanogan *Washington* U.S.A.
152 B1 Okanogan Range mountain range *Washington* U.S.A.
124 E3 Okapi, Parc National de la nat. park Zaire
128 B3 Okaputa Namibia
36 C3 Okara Pakistan
46 D5 Okarem Turkmenistan
9 C5 Okarito Lagoon lag. New Zealand
128 B3 Okasise Namibia
128 B2 Okaukuejo Namibia
128 B2 Okavango div. Namibia
128 C2 Okavango r. Botswana/Namibia
128 C2 Okavango Delta swamp Botswana
28 C7 Ōkawa Japan
29 G5 Ō-kawa-gawa r. Japan
9 □1 Okawa Pt pt *Chatham Is* New Zealand
29 G5 Okaya Japan
28 D6 Okayama div. Japan
28 D6 Okayama Japan
29 F6 Okazaki Japan
77 J3 Okęcie airport Poland
145 D7 Okeechobee *Florida* U.S.A.
145 D7 Okeechobee, L. l. *Florida* U.S.A.
145 D6 Okefenokee Swamp swamp *Georgia* U.S.A.
62 B4 Okehampton *England* U.K.
123 E5 Oke-Iho Nigeria
62 B4 Okement r. *England* U.K.
123 F5 Okene Nigeria
72 F3 Oker r. Germany
36 B5 Okha India
45 Q4 Okha Rus. Fed.
37 F4 Okhaldhunga Nepal
36 B5 Okha Rann India
52 C4 Okhochevka Rus. Fed.
52 D1 Okhotino Rus. Fed.
45 Q3 Okhotka r. Rus. Fed.
45 Q4 Okhotsk Rus. Fed.
45 Q4 Okhotsk, More sea Rus. Fed.
Okhotsk, Sea of sea *see* Okhotskoye More
53 F1 Okhtyrka Ukraine
130 A4 Okiep South Africa
27 N6 Okinawa i. Japan
29 □2 Okinawa Japan
27 N6 Okinawa-guntō is Japan
28 D7 Okino-shima i. Japan
28 C6 Okino-shima i. Japan
28 D5 Oki-shotō i. Japan
123 E5 Okitipupa Nigeria
24 A3 Okkan Myanmar
151 D5 Oklahoma div. U.S.A.
151 D5 Oklahoma City *Oklahoma* U.S.A.
151 D5 Okmulgee *Oklahoma* U.S.A.
124 B3 Okola Cameroon
124 B4 Okondja Gabon
76 E2 Okonek Poland
136 G4 Okotoks *Alberta* Canada
128 A2 Okoukuejo Namibia
52 A2 Okovskiy Les forest Rus. Fed.
124 C4 Okoyo Congo
55 A4 Oksbøl Denmark
56 F1 Øksfjord Norway
52 E3 Oksko- Donskaya Ravnina plain Rus. Fed.
50 F2 Oksovskiy Rus. Fed.
56 D2 Oksskolten inlet Greenland
47 H5 Oksu r. Tajikistan
Oktemberyan *see* Hoktemberyan
24 B3 Oktwin Myanmar
52 C1 Oktyabr' Rus. Fed.
46 E3 Oktyabr'sk Kazakhstan
52 F1 Oktyabr'skaya Rus. Fed.
46 D2 Oktyabr'skiy Rus. Fed.
52 D2 Oktyabr'skiy Rus. Fed.
52 G1 Oktyabr'skiy Rus. Fed.
45 R4 Oktyabr'skiy Rus. Fed.
52 E1 Oktyabr'skiy Rus. Fed.
50 H3 Oktyabr'skiy Rus. Fed.
51 G6 Oktyabr'skiy Rus. Fed.
50 G2 Oktyabr'skiy Rus. Fed.
53 G1 Oktyabr'skiy Rus. Fed.
47 G2 Oktyabr'skoye Kazakhstan
44 H3 Oktyabr'skoye Rus. Fed.
45 L2 Oktyabr'skoy Revolyutsii, O. i. Rus. Fed.
29 □2 Oku Japan
104 F3 Okučani Croatia
28 C7 Ōkuchi Japan
50 E3 Okulovka Rus. Fed.
28 G2 Okushiri-kaikyō chan. Japan
28 G2 Okushiri-tō i. Japan
123 E5 Okuta Nigeria
29 E6 Okutango-hantō pen. Japan
128 C3 Okwa watercourse Botswana/Namibia
56 L6 Ólafsvík Iceland
54 C3 Olaine Latvia
154 C3 Olancha *California* U.S.A.
154 C3 Olancha Peak summit *California* U.S.A.
156 J6 Olanchito Honduras
59 G3 Öland i. Sweden
56 H3 Olanga Rus. Fed.
91 E4 Olan, Pic d' mt. France
155 H2 Olathe *Colorado* U.S.A.
150 E4 Olathe *Kansas* U.S.A.
173 G4 Olavarría Argentina
76 F5 Oława Poland
81 H3 Olbendorf Austria
155 G5 Olberg *Arizona* U.S.A.
75 J2 Olbernhau Germany
75 K2 Olbersdorf Germany
108 B4 Olbia *Sardegna* Italy
75 K3 Olbramovice Czech Rep.
75 G4 Olching Germany
146 D3 Olcott *New York* U.S.A.
158 C2 Old Bahama Channel chan. The Bahamas/Cuba
38 C2 Old Bastar India
67 D3 Oldcastle Rep. of Ireland
15 E4 Old Cork *Queensland* Australia
134 E3 Old Crow *Yukon Terr.* Canada
68 E2 Oldeberkoop Netherlands
68 D1 Oldeboorn Netherlands
68 D2 Oldebroek Netherlands
68 E1 Oldehove Netherlands
68 D2 Oldemarkt Netherlands
72 D2 Oldenburg *Niedersachsen* Germany
73 F1 Oldenburg in Holstein Germany
68 E2 Oldenzaal Netherlands
56 F1 Olderdalen Norway
147 F3 Old Forge *New York* U.S.A.
147 F4 Old Forge *Pennsylvania* U.S.A.
145 □2 Old Fort The Bahamas
145 □2 Old Fort Pt pt The Bahamas
65 F4 Oldham *England* U.K.
159 □1 Old Harbour Jamaica
67 C5 Old Head of Kinsale headland Rep. of Ireland
63 G1 Old Leake *England* U.K.
136 G4 Oldman r. *Alberta* Canada
65 E3 Old Man of Coniston, The h. *England* U.K.
66 F3 Oldmeldrum *Scotland* U.K.
147 H3 Old Orchard Beach *Maine* U.S.A.
139 K4 Old Perlican *Newfoundland* Canada
159 □7 Old Road *Antigua* Caribbean
159 □6 Old Road Town *St Kitts-Nevis* Caribbean
136 G4 Olds *Alberta* Canada
147 J2 Old Town *Maine* U.S.A.
137 H4 Old Wives L. l. *Saskatchewan* Canada
155 E4 Old Woman Mts mts *California* U.S.A.
30 B2 Öldziyt Mongolia
30 D3 Öldziyt Mongolia
146 D3 Olean *New York* U.S.A.
77 L1 Olecko Poland
106 C3 Oleggio Italy
98 C5 Oleiros Portugal
45 O3 Olekminsk Rus. Fed.

53 E1 Oleksandrivka Chernihivs'ka Oblast' Ukraine
53 G2 Oleksandrivka Donets'ka Oblast' Ukraine
53 E2 Oleksandrivka Kirovohrads'ka Oblast' Ukraine
53 D2 Oleksandrivka Kirovohrads'ka Oblast' Ukraine
53 D3 Oleksandrivka Mykolayivs'ka Oblast' Ukraine
53 E2 Oleksandriya Kirovohrads'ka Oblast' Ukraine
53 B1 Oleksandriya Rivens'ka Oblast' Ukraine
53 E3 Oleksiyivka Ukraine
50 H1 Olema Rus. Fed.
93 E4 Olemps France
69 C3 Olen Belgium
58 A2 Ølen Norway
56 J1 Olenegorsk Rus. Fed.
45 M3 Olenek r. Rus. Fed.
45 N3 Olenek Rus. Fed.
52 A1 Olenino Rus. Fed.
50 E1 Olenitsa Rus. Fed.
53 E2 Olenivka Ukraine
30 E2 Olentuy Rus. Fed.
47 H2 Olenty r. Kazakhstan
92 A3 Oléron, Île d' i. France
102 E3 Olesa de Montserrat Spain
53 F1 Oleshnya Ukraine
53 A2 Oles'ko Ukraine
76 F4 Oleśnica Poland
76 G5 Olesno Poland
108 B2 Oletta Corse France
93 E6 Olette France
53 B1 Olevs'k Ukraine
141 G2 Olga, Lac l. Québec Canada
14 B5 Olga, Mt mt. Northern Terr. Australia
178 □3 Olgastretet str. Svalbard Arctic Ocean
83 E3 Olginate Italy
55 A4 Ølgod Denmark
100 C3 Olhão Portugal
102 E2 Oliana Spain
107 J4 Olib i. Croatia
108 B4 Oliena r. Sardegna Italy
108 B4 Oliena Sardegna Italy
102 C3 Oliete Spain
130 B5 Olifants r. South Africa
130 D3 Olifantshoek South Africa
130 B6 Olifantsrivierberg mts South Africa
173 K2 Olimar Chico r. Uruguay
173 K2 Olimar Grande r. Uruguay
168 D4 Olímpia Brazil
157 F5 Olinalá Mexico
166 F2 Olinda Brazil
129 F2 Olinda, Pta pt Mozambique
129 F2 Olinga Mozambique
15 E4 Olio Queensland Australia
103 B6 Oliva mt. Spain
172 F2 Oliva Argentina
103 C6 Oliva Spain
170 C2 Oliva, Cord. de mountain range Chile
100 D2 Oliva de la Frontera Spain
100 D2 Oliva de Mérida Spain
172 C1 Olivares, Co del mt. Chile
99 H5 Olivares de Júcar Spain
146 B5 Olive Hill Kentucky U.S.A.
169 F4 Oliveira Brazil
98 B4 Oliveira de Azeméis Portugal
98 B4 Oliveira de Frades Portugal
98 B4 Oliveira do Bairro Portugal
98 B3 Oliveira do Douro Portugal
98 C4 Oliveira do Hospital Portugal
166 D3 Oliveira dos Brejinhos Brazil
100 C2 Olivenza r. Portugal/Spain
100 C2 Olivenza Spain
173 G2 Oliveros Argentina
89 G4 Olivet France
150 E2 Olivia Minnesota U.S.A.
9 B6 Olivine Range mountain range New Zealand
83 D2 Olivone Switzerland
127 C5 Oljoro Wells well Tanzania
58 B1 Øljuvatnet l. Norway
52 E3 Ol'khi Rus. Fed.
51 F5 Ol'khovatka Rus. Fed.
52 D3 Ol'khovets Rus. Fed.
51 H5 Ol'khovka Rus. Fed.
77 H5 Olkusz Poland
164 C4 Ollagüe Chile
164 C4 Ollagüe, Vol. volcano Bolivia
90 B3 Ollergues France
91 D5 Ollioules France
172 B1 Ollita, Cord. de mountain range Argentina
172 B1 Ollitas mt. Argentina
124 C4 Ollombo Congo
82 C2 Ollon Switzerland
108 A4 Olmedo Sardegna Italy
99 F3 Olmedo Spain
108 A3 Olmeto Corse France
173 F2 Olmos Argentina
162 B5 Olmos Peru
147 G3 Olmstedville New York U.S.A.
63 F2 Olney England U.K.
144 C4 Olney Illinois U.S.A.
59 F3 Olofström Sweden
78 G2 Olomouc Czech Rep.
50 E2 Olonets Rus. Fed.
23 B3 Olongapo Philippines
22 C2 Olongliko Indonesia
92 A2 Olonne-sur-Mer France
93 E5 Olonzac France
93 B5 Oloron-Ste-Marie France
7 □13 Olosega i. American Samoa Pacific Ocean
102 F2 Olot Spain
31 E2 Olovyannaya Rus. Fed.
36 C5 Olpad India
172 D1 Olpas Argentina
72 C4 Olpe Germany
80 C3 Olperer mt. Austria
59 E2 Olsätter Sweden
72 D4 Olsberg Germany
79 H2 Olše r. Czech Rep.
53 G1 Ol'shanka Rus. Fed.
53 D3 Ol'shans'ke Ukraine
68 E2 Olst Netherlands
55 E4 Ølstykke Denmark
77 K2 Olszewo-Borki Poland
77 J2 Olsztyn div. Poland
77 J2 Olsztyn Olsztyn Poland
77 J2 Olsztynek Poland
76 D4 Olszyna Poland
112 E2 Olt r. Romania
172 D1 Olta Argentina
58 B2 Oltedal Norway
82 C1 Olten Switzerland
112 F2 Olteniţa Romania
112 F2 Oltina Romania
42 E1 Oltu Turkey
101 H3 Olula del Río Spain
23 B5 Olutanga i. Philippines
102 B3 Ólvega Spain
101 E4 Olvera Spain
53 A1 Olyka Ukraine
52 C3 Olym r. Rus. Fed.
152 B2 Olympia Washington U.S.A.
115 C5 Olympia Greece
114 E2 Olympias Greece
152 A2 Olympic Nat. Park Washington U.S.A.
152 B2 Olympic Nat. Park Washington U.S.A.
114 D2 Olympos mt. Greece
114 E4 Olympos mts Greece
114 D2 Olympos nat. park Greece
43 B2 Olympus mt. Cyprus
152 B2 Olympus, Mt mt. Washington U.S.A.
114 E2 Olynthos Greece
53 D1 Olyshivka Ukraine
45 S3 Olyutorskiy Rus. Fed.
45 T4 Olyutorskiy, M. c. Rus. Fed.
45 S3 Olyutorskiy Zaliv b. Rus. Fed.
47 J1 Om' r. Rus. Fed.
50 H1 Oma r. Rus. Fed.
31 E2 Oma China
28 H3 Ōma Japan
50 H1 Oma Rus. Fed.
29 F5 Ōmachi Japan
29 G6 Omae-zaki pt Japan
29 H4 Ōmagari Japan
67 D2 Omagh Northern Ireland U.K.
162 C4 Omaguas Peru
150 E3 Omaha Nebraska U.S.A.
128 B2 Omaheke div. Namibia
152 C1 Omak Washington U.S.A.
51 H7 Omalo Georgia
18 G8 Oman country Asia
41 J4 Oman, Gulf of g. Asia
23 □1 Omaok Palau
9 B6 Omarama New Zealand
128 B3 Omaruru Namibia
128 B3 Omatako watercourse Namibia
164 B3 Omate Peru
130 D2 Omaweneno Botswana
28 H3 Ōma-zaki c. Japan
Omba i. see Aoba
124 C2 Ombella-Mpoko div. Central African Rep.
62 D2 Ombersley England U.K.
58 A2 Ombo i. Norway
124 A4 Omboué Gabon
108 D2 Ombrone r. Italy
37 F3 Ombu China
173 J2 Ombúes de Lavalle Uruguay
130 D5 Omdraaisvlei South Africa
119 F4 Omdurman Sudan
29 G6 Ōme Japan
106 C3 Omegna Italy
53 E2 Omel'nyk Ukraine
118 D4 Omena well Chad
13 F4 Omeo Victoria Australia
108 B2 Omessa Corse France
156 J7 Ometepe, I. de i. Nicaragua
67 A3 Omey Island i. Rep. of Ireland
126 C2 Om Hajer Eritrea
39 B3 Omīdīyeh Iran
29 F6 Ōmihachiman Japan
Omilo see Omalo
136 D3 Omineca Mountains mountain range B.C. Canada
104 F4 Omiš Croatia
107 J3 Omišalj Croatia
29 G6 Ōmiya Japan
136 C3 Ommaney, Cape headland Alaska U.S.A.
55 A4 Omme r. Denmark
68 E2 Ommen Netherlands
30 B4 Ömnögovĭ div. Mongolia
55 D4 Omø i. Denmark
108 B4 Omodeo, Lago l. Sardegna Italy
123 F5 Omoku Nigeria
45 S2 Omolon r. Rus. Fed.
126 C3 Omo National Park nat. park Ethiopia
29 H4 Omono-gawa r. Japan
69 C5 Omont France
126 C3 Omo Wenz r. Ethiopia
47 H2 Omsk div. Rus. Fed.
47 H2 Omsk Rus. Fed.
45 R3 Omsukchan Rus. Fed.
28 J1 Ōmū Japan
77 K2 Omulew r. Poland
29 B7 Ōmura Japan
28 F7 Ōmura-wan b. Japan
112 F3 Omurtag Bulgaria
128 A2 Omusati div. Namibia
47 G1 Omutinskiy Rus. Fed.
50 K3 Omutninsk Rus. Fed.
140 E1 Onakawana Ontario Canada
148 B4 Onalaska Wisconsin U.S.A.
140 B1 Onaman lake l. Ontario Canada
147 F6 Onancock Virginia U.S.A.
22 D2 Onang Philippines
124 B4 Onangué, Lac l. Gabon
140 E3 Onaping Lake l. Ontario Canada
156 D2 Oñate Mexico
156 C2 Onavas Mexico
149 E3 Onaway Michigan U.S.A.
28 J2 Onbetsu Japan
25 B4 Onbingwin Myanmar
172 F1 Oncativo Argentina
64 D3 Onchan Isle of Man
125 B7 Oncócua Angola
103 C5 Onda Spain
103 D6 Ondara Spain
99 H1 Ondarroa Spain
166 C3 Ondas r. Brazil
79 L3 Ondava r. Slovakia
130 C5 Onderstedorings South Africa
125 C7 Ondjiva Angola
123 F5 Ondo div. Nigeria
123 E5 Ondo Nigeria
30 D3 Öndörhaan Mongolia
31 G3 Ondor Had China
30 E2 Öndörhushuu Mongolia
30 C4 Ondor Mod China
30 E4 Ondor Sum China
75 K3 Ondřejov Czech Rep.
15 F2 One & a Half Mile Opening chan. Queensland Australia
35 D10 One and Half Degree Channel chan. Maldives
6 □7 Oneata i. Fiji
50 F2 Onega r. Rus. Fed.
50 F2 Onega Rus. Fed.
Onega, Lake l. see Onezhskoye Ozero
147 F3 Oneida New York U.S.A.
147 F3 Oneida L. l.
150 D3 O'Neill Nebraska U.S.A.
45 R5 Onekotan, O. i. Rus. Fed.
147 F3 Oneonta New York U.S.A.
8 E2 Oneroa New Zealand
93 A4 Onesse-et-Laharie France
112 F1 Oneşti Romania
93 E4 Onet-le-Château France
6 □4 Onevai i. Tonga
50 E1 Onezhskaya Guba Rus. Fed.
50 E2 Onezhskoye Ozero l. Rus. Fed.
37 E5 Ong r. India
124 B4 Onga Gabon
8 F3 Ongaonga New Zealand
130 D5 Ongers watercourse South Africa
17 B7 Ongerup Western Australia Australia
30 B3 Ongi Mongolia
30 B3 Ongi Mongolia
30 B3 Ongiyn Gol watercourse Mongolia
31 H5 Ongjin North Korea
31 F4 Ongniud Qi China
38 C3 Ongole India
30 B3 Ongon Mongolia
47 L2 Onguday Rus. Fed.
51 G7 Oni Georgia
129 G3 Onilahy r. Madagascar
123 F5 Onitsha Nigeria
128 B3 Onjati Mountain mt. Namibia
29 □2 Onna Japan
29 □2 Onna-dake h. Japan
69 B4 Onnaing France
6 □7 Ono i. Fiji
29 H5 Ono Japan
29 F6 Ono Japan
28 H3 Ōno Japan
28 C7 Onoda Japan
176 H7 Ono-i-Lau i. Fiji
28 D6 Onomichi Japan
31 E2 Onon r. Mongolia/Rus. Fed.
30 D2 Onon Mongolia
176 G6 Onotoa i. Kiribati
136 G4 Onoway Alberta Canada
130 B4 Onseepkans South Africa
131 F1 Ons Hoop South Africa
98 B2 Ons, Illa de i. Spain
55 D5 Ønslev Denmark
16 A4 Onslow Western Australia Australia
145 E5 Onslow Bay b. N. Carolina U.S.A.
31 J4 Onsong North Korea
68 F1 Onstwedde Netherlands
29 F6 Ontake-san volcano Japan
138 B3 Ontario div. Canada
152 C2 Ontario Oregon U.S.A.
149 H4 Ontario, Lake l. Canada/U.S.A.
102 D3 Ontiñena Spain
103 C6 Ontinyent Spain
148 C2 Ontonagon Michigan U.S.A.
6 □1 Ontong Java Atoll atoll Solomon Is.
103 B6 Ontur Spain
53 E2 Onufriyivka Ukraine
163 F2 Onverwacht Surinam
89 G4 Onzain France
98 E2 Onzonilla Spain
12 C1 Oodnadatta S. Australia Australia
126 E3 Oodweyne Somalia
12 B2 Ooldea S. Australia Australia
151 E4 Oologah L. resr Oklahoma U.S.A.
68 C3 Ooltgensplaat Netherlands
14 C4 Ooratippra r. Northern Terr. Australia
15 E4 Oorindi Queensland Australia
131 G1 Oorwinning South Africa
69 B3 Oostburg Netherlands
69 A3 Oostende div. West-Vlaanderen Belgium
69 A3 Oostende Oostende Belgium
68 C1 Oosterend Netherlands
68 E2 Oosterhesseln Netherlands
68 C3 Oosterhout Netherlands
131 F2 Oostermoed South Africa
69 C3 Oosterschelde est. Netherlands
68 E2 Oosterwolde Netherlands
69 B4 Oosterzele Belgium
69 C2 Oosthuizen Netherlands
69 B3 Oostkamp Belgium
69 B3 Oost-Souburg Netherlands
69 B4 Oost-Vlaanderen div. Belgium
69 A4 Oostvleteren Belgium
68 D1 Oost-Vlieland Netherlands
68 C3 Oostvoorne Netherlands
68 E2 Ootmarsum Netherlands
136 D4 Ootsa Lake l. B.C. Canada
136 D4 Ootsa Lake B.C. Canada
146 E5 Opal Virginia U.S.A.
124 D4 Opala Zaire
76 E3 Opalenica Poland
126 B4 Opari Sudan
50 J3 Oparino Rus. Fed.
140 D2 Opasatika r. Ontario Canada
140 D2 Opasatika Ontario Canada
140 D2 Opasatika Lake l. Ontario Canada
138 B3 Opasqua Provincial Park Ontario Canada
138 B3 Opasquia Ontario Canada
141 H1 Opataca L. l. Québec Canada
107 J3 Opatija Croatia
78 E1 Opatovice nad Labem Czech Rep.
76 G4 Opatów Kalisz Poland
77 K5 Opatów Tarnobrzeg Poland
76 G4 Opatówek Poland
77 J5 Opatowiec Poland
79 G2 Opava Czech Rep.
145 C5 Opelika Alabama U.S.A.
151 E6 Opelousas Louisiana U.S.A.
83 E1 Opfenbach Germany
69 D3 Opglabbeek Belgium
152 F1 Opheim Montana U.S.A.
68 D3 Opheusden Netherlands
140 D3 Ophir Ontario Canada
124 E3 Opienge Zaire
9 C6 Opihi r. New Zealand
138 E3 Opinaca r. Québec Canada
138 E3 Opinaca, Réservoir resr Québec Canada
138 D3 Opinnagau r. Ontario Canada
139 G3 Opiscotéo L. l. Québec Canada
53 F2 Opishnya Ukraine
81 G4 Oplotnica r. Slovenia
123 F6 Opobo Nigeria
54 F3 Opochka Rus. Fed.
77 J4 Opoczno Poland
76 F5 Opole div. Poland
76 F5 Opole Poland
77 K4 Opole Lubelskie Poland
46 D3 Opornyy Kazakhstan
Oporto see Porto
8 F3 Opotiki New Zealand
93 E6 Opoul-Périllos France
145 C6 Opp Alabama U.S.A.
73 K4 Oppach Germany
57 C3 Oppdal Norway
83 G5 Oppeano Italy
59 F2 Oppeby Sweden
58 A1 Oppedal Norway
74 D4 Oppenau Germany
74 D3 Oppenheim Germany
109 H4 Oppido Lucano Italy
111 E4 Oppido Mamertina Italy
58 D1 Oppkuven h. Norway
58 C1 Oppland div. Norway
81 F3 Opponitz Austria
107 H3 Oprtalj Croatia
8 D3 Opunake New Zealand
128 A2 Opuwo Namibia
46 D3 Opytnoye Kazakhstan
148 B5 Oquawka Illinois U.S.A.
147 H2 Oquossoc Maine U.S.A.
107 F2 Ora Italy
159 □1 Oracabessa Jamaica
155 G5 Oracle Arizona U.S.A.
155 G5 Oracle Junction Arizona U.S.A.
100 C2 Orada Portugal
79 L4 Oradea Romania
92 C3 Oradour-sur-Vayres France
56 M6 Öræfajökull ice cap Iceland
112 C3 Orahovac Yugoslavia
36 D4 Orai India
90 D2 Orain r. France
121 D1 Oran Algeria
170 D1 Orán Argentina
53 D1 Orane Ukraine
25 D4 O Rang Cambodia
37 H3 Orang China
130 B4 Orange r. Namibia/South Africa
147 G3 Orange Massachusetts U.S.A.
13 G3 Orange New South Wales Australia
151 E6 Orange Texas U.S.A.
146 D5 Orange Virginia U.S.A.
91 C4 Orange France
145 D5 Orangeburg S. Carolina U.S.A.
163 G3 Orange, Cabo pt Brazil
131 F4 Orange Free State div. South Africa
140 E5 Orangeville Ontario Canada
155 G2 Orangeville Utah U.S.A.
157 H5 Orange Walk Belize
122 A4 Orango, Ilha de i. Guinea-Bissau
108 B4 Orani Sardegna Italy
23 B3 Orani Philippines
73 J3 Oranienburg Germany
Oranje r. see Orange
131 F1 Oranjefontein South Africa
163 F3 Oranje Gebergte h. Surinam
68 E2 Oranjekanaal canal Netherlands
128 B4 Oranjemund Namibia
130 E4 Oranjerivier South Africa
158 □1 Oranjestad Aruba Caribbean
131 G3 Oranjeville South Africa
67 C3 Oranmore Rep. of Ireland
128 D3 Orapa Botswana
100 D3 Oraque r. Spain
23 C3 Oras Philippines
112 D2 Orăştie Romania
53 C2 Orativ Ukraine
79 J2 Orava r. Slovakia
57 F3 Oravais Finland
112 C2 Oraviţa Romania
79 J2 Oravská Magura mts Slovakia
9 A7 Orawia New Zealand
91 B5 Orb r. France
106 C4 Orba r. Italy
98 B3 Orbacém Portugal
36 E2 Orba Co l. China
55 C4 Ørbæk Denmark
86 C4 Orbais-l'Abbaye France
106 B3 Orbassano Italy
82 B2 Orbe r. Switzerland
82 B2 Orbe Switzerland
89 F2 Orbec France
108 D2 Orbetello Italy
108 D2 Orbetello, Laguna di lag. Italy
93 E5 Orbieu r. France
98 E2 Orbigo r. Spain
13 G4 Orbost Victoria Australia
59 G1 Örbyhus Sweden
179 B1 Orcadas Argentina Base Antarctica
101 H2 Orcera Spain
101 H3 Orce, Sierra de mountain range Spain
82 B1 Orchamps-Vennes France
155 H2 Orchard Mesa Colorado U.S.A.
92 C2 Orches France
163 D1 Orchila, Isla i. Venezuela
76 G3 Orchowo Poland
108 D1 Orcia r. Italy
91 E4 Orcières France
106 B3 Orco r. Italy
164 A2 Orcotuna Peru
154 B4 Orcutt California U.S.A.
16 E3 Ord r. Western Australia Australia
153 D4 Orderville Utah U.S.A.
98 B1 Ordes Spain
102 D2 Ordesa-Monte-Perdido, Parque Nacional de nat. park Spain
99 H1 Ordizia Spain
16 D3 Ord, Mt h. Western Australia Australia
154 D4 Ord Mt mt. California U.S.A.
173 F2 Ordoñez Argentina
55 D4 Ordrup Næs pt Denmark
42 D1 Ordu Turkey
Ordu see Yayladağı
42 F2 Ordubad Azerbaijan
99 H2 Orduña Spain
153 G4 Ordway Colorado U.S.A.
47 K2 Ordynskoye Rus. Fed.
46 F2 Ordzhonikidze Kazakhstan
Ordzhonikidze see Vladikavkaz
53 F3 Ordzhonikidze Ukraine
123 E5 Ore Nigeria
163 F2 Orealla Guyana
154 C1 Oreana Nevada U.S.A.
59 F2 Örebro div. Sweden
59 F2 Örebro Sweden
81 H1 Ořechov Czech Rep.
54 G2 Oredezh r. Rus. Fed.
152 B3 Oregon div. U.S.A.
148 C4 Oregon Illinois U.S.A.
146 B4 Oregon Ohio U.S.A.
148 C4 Oregon Wisconsin U.S.A.
152 B2 Oregon City Oregon U.S.A.
59 H1 Öregrund Sweden
59 H1 Öregrundsgrepen b. Sweden
55 D5 Orehoved Denmark
52 F1 Orekhovets Rus. Fed.
54 F2 Orekhovno Rus. Fed.
52 D2 Orekhovo-Zuyevo Rus. Fed.
52 C3 Orel div. Rus. Fed.
53 F2 Orel' r. Ukraine
52 C3 Orel Rus. Fed.
114 E1 Orelek mt. Bulgaria
162 B4 Orellana Peru
162 B5 Orellana Peru
100 E1 Orellana la Vieja Spain
155 G1 Orem Utah U.S.A.
42 B2 Ören Turkey
46 E2 Orenburg div. Rus. Fed.
46 E2 Orenburg Rus. Fed.
69 E5 Orenhofen Germany
98 C2 Orense div. Spain
173 H5 Orense Argentina
114 E4 Oreoi Greece
9 A7 Orepuki New Zealand
53 B1 Orepy Ukraine
59 E3 Öresjön l. Sweden
58 D2 Öreskilsälven r. Sweden
113 F4 Orestiada Greece
55 E4 Øresund str. Denmark
9 B7 Oreti r. New Zealand
8 E2 Orewa New Zealand
69 D4 Oreye Belgium
63 H2 Orford England U.K.
13 F5 Orford Tasmania Australia
63 H2 Orford Ness spit England U.K.
163 G2 Organabo French Guiana
158 B2 Organos, Sierra de los h. Cuba
155 F5 Organ Pipe Cactus National Monument nat. park Arizona U.S.A.
102 E2 Organyà Spain
101 G1 Orgaz Spain
86 B4 Orge r. France
90 D2 Orgelet France
89 G3 Orgères-en-Beauce France
107 F3 Orgiano Italy
30 A2 Orgil Mongolia
101 G4 Orgiva Spain
91 D5 Orgon France
108 B4 Orgosolo Sardegna Italy
52 E1 Orgtrud Rus. Fed.
113 G5 Orhaneli Turkey
51 D7 Orhangazi Turkey
53 C3 Orhei Moldova
30 B2 Orhon Gol r. Mongolia
30 C2 Orhontuul Mongolia
102 B2 Orhy, Pic d' mt. France/Spain
111 G2 Oria Italy
101 H3 Oria Spain
50 J3 Orichi Rus. Fed.
147 K2 Orient Maine U.S.A.
164 C3 Oriental, Cordillera mountain range Bolivia
162 B3 Oriental, Cordillera mountain range Colombia
164 B2 Oriental, Cordillera mountain range Peru
140 A2 Orient Bay Ontario Canada
173 G5 Oriente Argentina
69 C5 Origny-en-Thiérache France
86 C3 Origny-Ste-Benoite France
103 C6 Orihuela Spain
102 B4 Orihuela del Tremedal Spain
53 F3 Orikhiv Ukraine
53 G2 Oril'ka r. Ukraine
53 G2 Oril'ka Ukraine
141 F4 Orillia Ontario Canada
57 G3 Orimattila Finland
163 E3 Orinduik Guyana
163 D2 Orinoco r. Colombia/Venezuela
109 J4 Oriolo Italy
54 C1 Oripää Finland
37 F5 Orissa India
54 C2 Orissaare Estonia
108 A5 Oristano div. Sardegna Italy
108 A5 Oristano Sardegna Italy
108 A5 Oristano, Golfo di b. Sardegna Italy
78 F5 Őriszentpéter Hungary
57 G3 Orivesi Finland
50 D2 Orivesi l. Finland
166 A1 Oriximiná Brazil
157 F5 Orizaba Mexico
168 D2 Orizona Brazil
56 C3 Orkanger Norway
59 E3 Örkelljunga Sweden
79 J4 Örkény Hungary
56 C3 Orkla r. Norway
66 E1 Orkney div. Scotland U.K.
131 F3 Orkney South Africa
151 C6 Orla Texas U.S.A.
77 M3 Orla Poland
75 G2 Orlamünde Germany
154 A2 Orland California U.S.A.
168 E4 Orlândia Brazil
145 D6 Orlando Florida U.S.A.
89 G3 Orléanais reg. France
89 G4 Orléans Loiret France
147 J4 Orleans Massachusetts U.S.A.
147 G2 Orleans Vermont U.S.A.
141 K3 Orléans, Île d' i. Québec Canada
59 F2 Orlen l. Sweden
78 E1 Orlice r. Czech Rep.
78 F1 Orlické Hory mountain range Czech Rep.
78 G1 Orlík mt. Czech Rep.
53 E1 Orlivka Chernihivs'ka Oblast' Ukraine
53 G3 Orlivka Zaporiz'ka Oblast' Ukraine
50 J3 Orlov Rus. Fed.
51 J5 Orlov Gay Rus. Fed.
52 D4 Orlovo Rus. Fed.
31 E2 Orlovskiy Rus. Fed.
51 G6 Orlovskiy Rus. Fed.
86 B4 Orly airport France
39 F4 Ormara Pakistan
39 F4 Ormara, Ras headland Pakistan
59 F3 Ormaryd Sweden
65 F2 Ormiston Scotland U.K.
23 C4 Ormoc Philippines
145 D6 Ormond Beach Florida U.S.A.
115 F5 Ormos Greece
115 F7 Ormos Almyrou b. Greece
114 F4 Ormos Kymis b. Greece
115 F7 Ormos Mesara b. Greece
114 G3 Ormos Moudrou b. Greece
115 G5 Ormos Panormou Greece
115 F7 Ormos Soudas b. Greece
114 G2 Ormos Vistonias b. Greece
81 H4 Ormož Slovenia
65 F4 Ormskirk England U.K.
141 J4 Ormstown Québec Canada
58 C1 Ormtjernkampen Nasjonalpark nat. park Norway
114 E2 Ormylia Greece
87 E4 Ornain r. France
90 E1 Ornans France
83 D3 Ornavasso Italy
89 F3 Orne div. Basse-Normandie France
89 E2 Orne r. France
56 D2 Ørnes Norway
77 J1 Orneta Poland
59 H2 Ornö i. Sweden
93 D6 Ornolac-Ussat-les-Bains France
56 E3 Örnsköldsvik Sweden
55 D4 Orø i. Denmark
54 C2 Örö i. Finland
162 C3 Orocué Colombia
122 D4 Orodara Burkina
152 C2 Orofino Idaho U.S.A.
30 B3 Orog Nuur salt lake Mongolia
153 F5 Orogrande New Mexico U.S.A.
7 □11 Orohena mt. French Polynesia Pacific Ocean
107 F3 Orolo r. Italy
79 J6 Orom Yugoslavia
139 G4 Oromocto New Brunswick Canada
108 B2 Oro, Monte d' mt. Corse France
43 C4 Oron Israel
123 F6 Oron Nigeria
176 H6 Orona i. Kiribati
82 B2 Oron-la-Ville Switzerland
147 J2 Orono Maine U.S.A.
163 F3 Oronoque Guyana
93 A5 Oronoz Spain
66 B4 Oronsay i. Scotland U.K.
77 J4 Orońsko Poland
Orontes r. see 'Āṣī
106 B3 Oropa Italy
99 E5 Oropesa Extremadura Spain
103 D4 Oropesa Valencia Spain
103 D4 Oropesa, Cabo de headland Spain
159 □3 Oropuche r. Trinidad Trinidad and Tobago
31 G2 Oroqen Zizhiqi China
23 B4 Oroquieta Philippines
118 C4 Orori well Chad
170 E2 Oro, Río de r. Argentina
108 B4 Orosei Sardegna Italy
108 B4 Orosei, Golfo di b. Sardegna Italy
79 K5 Orosháza Hungary
115 G8 Oros Kofinas mt. Greece
23 □2 Orote Pen. pen. Guam Pacific Ocean
45 R3 Orotukan Rus. Fed.
155 G5 Oro Valley Arizona U.S.A.
154 B2 Oroville California U.S.A.
152 C1 Oroville Washington U.S.A.
154 B2 Oroville, Lake l. California U.S.A.
91 D4 Orpierre France
31 G2 Orqohan China
162 B2 Orquideas, Parque Nacional las nat. park Colombia
54 E1 Orrengrund i. Finland
66 D3 Orrin r. Scotland U.K.
58 D1 Orrkjølen h. Norway
12 D3 Orroroo S. Australia Australia
59 F1 Orsa Sweden
59 F1 Orsasjön l. Sweden
86 B4 Orsay France
59 G2 Örsbacken b. Sweden
78 F5 Őrség reg. Hungary
50 D4 Orsha Belarus
52 C1 Orsha Rus. Fed.
52 H1 Orshanka Rus. Fed.
106 B3 Orsiera, Monte mt. Italy
82 C2 Orsières Switzerland
59 F3 Örsjö Sweden
46 E2 Orsk Rus. Fed.
59 H1 Örskär i. Sweden
55 D4 Orslev Denmark
112 D2 Orşova Romania
56 B3 Ørsta Norway
55 C3 Ørsted Denmark
59 G2 Örsundaån r. Sweden
59 G2 Örsundsbro Sweden
113 G6 Ortaca Turkey
106 C3 Orta, Lago d' l. Italy
109 H3 Orta Nova Italy
109 E2 Orte Italy
98 C1 Ortegal, Cabo c. Spain
74 C4 Ortenau reg. Germany
74 E2 Ortenberg Germany
75 J4 Ortenburg Germany
93 B5 Orthez France
164 C2 Ortho r. Bolivia
114 C3 Orthovouni Greece
100 E2 Ortiga r. Spain
168 C6 Ortigueira Brazil
98 C1 Ortigueira Spain
107 F2 Ortisei Italy
156 C2 Ortiz Mexico
162 D2 Ortiz Venezuela
107 E2 Ortles mt. Italy
159 □3 Ortoire R. r. Trinidad Trinidad and Tobago
108 A3 Ortolo r. Corse France
65 F3 Orton England U.K.
109 G2 Ortona Italy
150 D2 Ortonville Minnesota U.S.A.
73 J4 Ortrand Germany
108 A4 Ortueri Sardegna Italy
72 F3 Örtze r. Germany
23 □1 Orukuizu i. Palau
45 O3 Orulgan, Khrebet mountain range Rus. Fed.
55 B3 Ørum Denmark
122 D5 Orumbo Boka h. Côte d'Ivoire
42 F2 Orūmīyeh Iran
164 C3 Oruro div. Bolivia
164 C3 Oruro Bolivia
99 G4 Orusco Spain
55 D1 Orust i. Sweden
98 C4 Orvalho Portugal
88 D4 Orvault France
108 E2 Orvieto Italy
179 B3 Orville Coast coastal area Antarctica
114 E1 Orvilos mts Greece
109 E2 Orvinio Italy
146 C4 Orwell Ohio U.S.A.
147 G3 Orwell Vermont U.S.A.
31 F2 Orxon Gol r. China
112 D3 Oryakhovo Bulgaria
53 B2 Orynyn Ukraine
53 E2 Orzhytsya r. Ukraine
53 E2 Orzhytsya Ukraine
106 D3 Orzinuovi Italy
77 K2 Orzyc r. Poland
77 K2 Orzysz Poland
57 C3 Os Norway
101 H1 Osa de Vega Spain
150 E4 Osage r. Missouri U.S.A.
148 A4 Osage Iowa U.S.A.
29 E6 Ōsaka div. Japan
29 E6 Ōsaka Japan
47 H2 Osakarovka Kazakhstan
156 K7 Osa, Pen. de pen. Costa Rica
169 E5 Osasco Brazil
69 E5 Osburger Hochwald forest Germany
55 B4 Øsby Denmark
59 E3 Osby Sweden
163 G3 Oscar French Guiana
151 F5 Osceola Arkansas U.S.A.
150 E3 Osceola Iowa U.S.A.
73 J4 Oschatz Germany
73 G3 Oschersleben Germany
108 B4 Oschiri Sardegna Italy
149 F3 Oscoda Michigan U.S.A.
112 B2 Osečina Yugoslavia
98 B3 O Seixo Spain
99 E1 Oseja de Sajambre Spain
75 J2 Osek Czech Rep.
102 C3 Osera Spain
76 E4 Osetno Poland
52 D2 Osetr r. Rus. Fed.
28 B7 Ōse-zaki pt Japan
141 H4 Osgoode Ontario Canada
47 H4 Osh div. Kyrgyzstan
47 H4 Osh Kyrgyzstan
47 H1 Osha r. Rus. Fed.
128 B2 Oshakati Namibia
28 H2 Oshamanbe Japan
128 B2 Oshana div. Namibia
141 F5 Oshawa Ontario Canada
29 H4 Oshika Japan
29 H4 Oshika-hantō pen. Japan
128 B2 Oshikango Namibia
128 B2 Oshikoto div. Namibia
28 G3 Ō-shima i. Japan
28 C7 Ō-shima i. Japan
29 G6 Ō-Shima i. Japan
29 E7 Ō-shima i. Japan
28 H2 Oshima-hantō pen. Japan
150 C3 Oshkosh Nebraska U.S.A.
148 C3 Oshkosh Wisconsin U.S.A.
41 G2 Oshnovīyeh Iran
123 E5 Oshogbo Nigeria
125 C4 Oshwe Zaire
76 G2 Osie Poland
76 G2 Osieczna Gdansk Poland
76 E4 Osieczna Leszno Poland
76 D4 Osiecznica Poland
77 K4 Osiek Siedlce Poland
77 H2 Osiek Toruń Poland
76 G2 Osielsko Poland
95 G2 Osijek Croatia
108 A4 Osilo Sardegna Italy
107 H5 Osimo Italy
73 L2 Osina Poland
47 L2 Osinniki Rus. Fed.
83 E3 Osio Sotto Italy
36 C4 Osiyān India
131 H3 Osizweni South Africa
76 G4 Osjaków Poland
104 F3 Osječenica mts Bos.-Herz.
56 D3 Ösjön l. Sweden
148 A5 Oskaloosa Iowa U.S.A.
59 G3 Oskarshamn Sweden
59 E3 Oskarström Sweden
141 H2 Oskélanéo Québec Canada
53 G1 Oskol r. Rus. Fed.
59 G1 Oslättfors Sweden
78 F2 Oslava r. Czech Rep.
81 H1 Oslavany Czech Rep.
58 D2 Oslo div. Norway
58 D2 Oslo Norway
23 B4 Oslob Philippines
58 D2 Oslofjorden inlet Norway
38 B2 Osmānābād India
42 C1 Osmancık Turkey
42 D2 Osmaniye Turkey
54 F2 Os'mino Rus. Fed.
59 G2 Ösmo Sweden
54 C2 Osmussaar i. Estonia
72 D3 Osnabrück Germany
76 C3 Osno Lubuskie Poland
124 E4 Oso r. Zaire
112 D3 Osogovske Planine mountain range Bulgaria/Macedonia
107 H2 Osoppo Italy
107 J4 Osor Croatia
167 B6 Osório Brazil
172 A6 Osorno Chile
99 F2 Osorno Spain
171 B5 Osorno, Vol. volcano Chile
136 F5 Osoyoos B.C. Canada
58 A1 Osøyri Norway
159 E5 Ospino Venezuela
106 E3 Ospitaletto Italy
15 F2 Osprey Reef reef Coral Sea Islands Terr. Pacific Ocean
68 D3 Oss Netherlands

100 C2 Ossa h. Portugal
114 D3 Ossa mt. Greece
101 H2 Ossa de Montiel Spain
13 F5 Ossa, Mt mt. Tasmania Australia
93 C5 Osse r. France
123 F5 Osse r. Nigeria
148 B3 Osseo Wisconsin U.S.A.
108 A4 Ossi Sardegna Italy
81 E4 Ossiacher See l. Austria
149 F3 Ossineke Michigan U.S.A.
147 H3 Ossipee Lake l. New Hampshire U.S.A.
58 D1 Ossjøen l. Norway
139 H3 Ossokmanuan Lake l. Newfoundland Canada
45 S4 Ossora Rus. Fed.
93 B5 Ossun France
53 E2 Ostap"ye Ukraine
52 B2 Ostashevo Rus. Fed.
52 A1 Ostashkov Rus. Fed.
76 G1 Ostaszewo Poland
72 C3 Ostbevern Germany
55 B4 Østbirk Denmark
72 E2 Oste r. Germany
107 F4 Ostellato Italy
Ostend see Oostende
72 E1 Ostenfeld (Husum) Germany
52 A2 Oster r. Rus. Fed.
52 A2 Oster Rus. Fed.
53 D1 Oster Ukraine
55 A3 Øster Agger Denmark
75 J4 Osterbach r. Germany
73 G3 Osterburg Germany
74 E3 Osterburken Germany
59 G1 Österbybruk Sweden
59 F3 Österbymo Sweden
57 D3 Österdalälven l. Sweden
57 C3 Østerdalen v. Norway
59 G1 Österfärnebo Sweden
59 H3 Östergarnsholm i. Sweden
59 F2 Östergötland div. Sweden
72 D1 Osterhever Germany
75 J4 Osterhofen Germany
72 D2 Osterholz-Scharmbeck Germany
55 C3 Øster Hurup Denmark
55 A2 Østerild Denmark
80 D2 Ostermiething Austria
82 C2 Ostermundigen Switzerland
81 E4 Osternig mt. Austria/Italy
72 F4 Osterode am Harz Germany
56 D3 Östersund Sweden
59 G1 Östervåla Sweden
55 C2 Øster Vrå Denmark
73 F4 Osterwieck Germany
58 B1 Østese Norway
74 E4 Ostfildern Germany
58 D2 Østfold div. Norway
72 B2 Ostfriesische Inseln is Germany
72 C2 Ostfriesland reg. Germany
59 H1 Östhammar Sweden
74 D3 Osthofen Germany
106 E3 Ostiano Italy
107 F3 Ostiglia Italy
93 A6 Ostiz Spain
80 C3 Östliche Karwendelspitze mt. Austria/Germany
59 E1 Östmark Sweden
107 H5 Ostra Italy
83 E1 Ostrach r. Germany
74 E5 Ostrach Germany
59 G2 Östra Ed Sweden
59 F2 Östra Löa Sweden
59 E3 Östra Nedsjön l. Sweden
59 E2 Östra Silen l. Sweden
79 H2 Ostrava Czech Rep.
79 J3 Ostredok mt. Slovakia
114 B1 Ostren Albania
72 C2 Ostrhauderfehn Germany
69 B4 Ostricourt France
53 E3 Ostriv Dzharylhach i. Ukraine
53 D3 Ostriv Tendrivs'ka Kosa spit Ukraine
77 H2 Ostróda Poland
51 F5 Ostrogozhsk Rus. Fed.
53 B1 Ostroh Ukraine
77 K3 Ostrołęka div. Poland
78 E1 Ostroměř Czech Rep.
76 E3 Ostroróg Poland
78 B1 Ostrov Czech Rep.
112 G2 Ostrov Romania
54 F3 Ostrov Rus. Fed.
52 F1 Ostrovskoye Rus. Fed.
76 D2 Ostrowice Poland
77 K5 Ostrowiec Świętokrzyski Poland
77 L4 Ostrów Lubelski Poland
77 K3 Ostrów Mazowiecka Poland
76 F4 Ostrów Wielkopolski Poland
77 K4 Ostrożeń Poland
76 F4 Ostrzeszów Poland
73 J1 Ostseebad Binz Germany
73 G2 Ostseebad Boltenhagen Germany
73 H1 Ostseebad Dierhagen Germany
73 J1 Ostseebad Göhren Germany
73 H1 Ostseebad Graal-Müritz Germany
73 G1 Ostseebad Kühlungsborn Germany
73 H1 Ostseebad Prerow am Darß Germany
73 G1 Ostseebad Rerik Germany
73 J1 Ostseebad Sellin Germany
73 H1 Ostseebad Wustrow Germany
80 D4 Osttirol reg. Austria
111 G2 Ostuni Italy
52 A1 Osuga r. Rus. Fed.
140 B1 O'Sullivan Lake l. Ontario Canada
113 C4 Osum r. Albania
112 E3 Osŭm r. Bulgaria
28 C8 Ōsumi Hantō pen. Japan
27 O5 Ōsumi-shotō is Japan
123 E5 Osun div. Nigeria
101 E3 Osuna Spain
168 C4 Osvaldo Cruz Brazil
54 F3 Osveyskoye, Oz. l. Belarus
65 G3 Oswaldkirk England U.K.
147 F2 Oswegatchie New York U.S.A.
147 E3 Oswego r. New York U.S.A.
148 C5 Oswego Illinois U.S.A.
146 E3 Oswego New York U.S.A.
62 C2 Oswestry England U.K.
77 H5 Oświęcim Poland
53 G3 Osypenko Ukraine
100 B1 Ota r. Portugal
29 G5 Ōta Japan
28 D6 Ōta-gawa r. Japan
9 B6 Otago div. New Zealand
9 C6 Otago Harbour harbour New Zealand
9 C6 Otago Peninsula pen. New Zealand
108 A4 Ossi Sardegna Italy
8 E4 Otaki New Zealand
56 G2 Otanmäki Finland
47 J4 Otar Kazakhstan
28 H2 Otaru Japan
9 B7 Otatara New Zealand
78 C2 Otava r. Czech Rep.
162 B3 Otavalo Ecuador
128 B2 Otavi Namibia
29 H5 Ōtawara Japan
102 B2 Oteiza Spain
112 D2 Oţelu Roşu Romania
9 C6 Otematata New Zealand
54 E2 Otepää Estonia
114 B2 Oteševo Macedonia
87 E3 Othain r. France
152 C2 Othello Washington U.S.A.
113 B5 Othonoi i. Greece
114 D3 Othrys mt. Greece
123 E5 Oti r. Ghana/Togo
22 D2 Oti Indonesia
87 H4 Ötigheim Germany
156 D3 Otinapa Mexico
9 C5 Otira New Zealand
147 E3 Otisco Lake l. New York U.S.A.
139 F3 Otish, Monts mts Québec Canada
101 G4 Otívar Spain
128 B3 Otjiwarongo Namibia
128 A2 Otjovasandu waterhole Namibia
128 B2 Otjozondjupa div. Namibia
52 F3 Otkhozheye Rus. Fed.
65 G4 Otley England U.K.
76 F5 Otmuchów Poland
28 H3 Otobe Japan
104 E3 Otočac Croatia
28 J2 Otofuke Japan
28 J2 Otofuke-gawa r. Japan
30 D5 Otog Qi China
28 J1 Otoineppu Japan
104 F3 Otoka Bos.-Herz.
8 E3 Otorohanga New Zealand
126 B2 Otoro, Jebel mt. Sudan
138 C3 Otoskwin r. Ontario Canada
28 D7 Ōtoyo Japan
58 B2 Otra r. Norway
158 □2 Otrabanda Curaçao Netherlands Ant.
52 C3 Otradinskiy Rus. Fed.
111 H2 Otranto Italy
109 E2 Otricoli Italy
45 T3 Otrozhnyy Rus. Fed.
148 E4 Otsego Michigan U.S.A.
148 E3 Otsego Lake l. Michigan U.S.A.
147 F3 Otsego Lake l. New York U.S.A.
147 F3 Otselic New York U.S.A.
29 E6 Ōtsu Japan
57 C3 Otta Norway
108 B4 Ottana Sardegna Italy
69 E5 Ottange France
141 H4 Ottawa airport Ontario Canada
141 F3 Ottawa r. Québec Canada
148 C5 Ottawa Illinois U.S.A.
150 E4 Ottawa Kansas U.S.A.
146 A4 Ottawa Ohio U.S.A.
141 H4 Ottawa Ontario Canada
138 D2 Ottawa Islands is Québec Canada
73 J4 Ottendorf-Okrilla Germany
81 G2 Ottenschlag Austria
81 F2 Ottensheim Austria
81 G2 Ottenstein Stausee l. Austria
62 C4 Otter r. England U.K.
67 F5 Otterburn England U.K.
155 G2 Otter Creek Reservoir Utah U.S.A.
75 G5 Otterfing Germany
140 B2 Otter I. i. Ontario Canada
72 D2 Otterndorf Germany
140 E1 Otter Rapids Ontario Canada
72 E2 Ottersberg Germany
59 E2 Otterstad Sweden
87 H4 Ottersweier Germany
66 □2 Otterswick Scotland U.K.
55 C4 Otterup Denmark
62 B4 Ottery r. England U.K.
69 C4 Ottignies Belgium
81 E2 Ottnang am Hausruck Austria
74 F5 Ottobeuren Germany
75 G4 Ottobrunn Germany
135 K1 Otto Fjord inlet N.W.T. Canada
22 D4 Ot Tongo mt. Indonesia
131 E3 Ottosdal South Africa
131 E2 Ottoshoop South Africa
148 A5 Ottumwa Iowa U.S.A.
74 C3 Ottweiler Germany
123 F5 Otukpa Nigeria
123 F5 Otukpo Nigeria
170 D2 Otumpa Argentina
6 □5 'Otu Tolu Group is Tonga
164 A1 Otuzco Peru
13 E4 Otway, C. c. Victoria Australia
76 D4 Otyń Poland
53 A2 Otyniya Ukraine
80 B3 Ötztal v. Austria
80 B4 Ötztaler Alpen mountain range Austria
151 E5 Ouachita r. Arkansas U.S.A.
151 E5 Ouachita, L. l. Arkansas U.S.A.
151 E5 Ouachita Mts mts Arkansas U.S.A.
120 B4 Ouadâne Mauritania
124 D2 Ouadda Central African Rep.
118 D5 Ouaddaï div. Chad
118 C4 Ouadi Achim watercourse Chad
118 D4 Ouadi Archeï watercourse Chad
118 D5 Ouadi Bahaguibi watercourse Chad
118 D4 Ouadi Bao watercourse Chad
118 D5 Ouadi Bitea watercourse Chad
118 D5 Ouadi Doy watercourse Chad
118 C5 Ouadi Enné watercourse Chad
118 C5 Ouadi Haddad watercourse Chad
118 D5 Ouadi Hamra watercourse Chad
118 D4 Ouadi Howa watercourse Chad/Sudan
118 D5 Ouadi Kadja watercourse Chad/Sudan
118 C4 Ouadi Karma watercourse Chad
118 D4 Ouadi Oum Hadjer watercourse Chad
118 C5 Ouadi Rime watercourse Chad
118 D4 Ouadi Sala watercourse Chad
124 D1 Ouadi Séifou watercourse Chad
118 C5 Ouadi Tornoy watercourse Chad
124 C1 Ouadi Zérab watercourse Chad
122 D4 Ouagadougou Burkina
122 D4 Ouahigouya Burkina
124 D2 Ouaka div. Central African Rep.
124 D2 Ouaka r. Central African Rep.
120 C5 Oualâta Mauritania
123 E4 Ouallam Niger
121 E4 Ouallene Algeria
163 G3 Ouanary French Guiana
124 D2 Ouanda-Djallé Central African Rep.
124 C2 Ouandago Central African Rep.
124 D2 Ouandja-Vakaga, Réserve de Faune de la res. Central African Rep.
124 E2 Ouando Central African Rep.
124 D3 Ouango Central African Rep.
122 C5 Ouangolodougou Côte d'Ivoire
90 B1 Ouanne France
163 G3 Ouaqui French Guiana
124 D2 Ouara r. Central African Rep.
120 C4 Ouarâne reg. Mauritania
141 H3 Ouareau, Lac l. Québec Canada
121 F2 Ouargla Algeria
123 E3 Ouarissibitil well Mali
120 D2 Ouarkziz, Jbel ridge Algeria/Morocco
123 E4 Ouarogou Burkina
89 G3 Ouarville France
120 C2 Ouarzazate Morocco
130 E6 Oubergpas pass South Africa
90 C1 Ouche r. France
68 C3 Oud-Beijerland Netherlands
68 B3 Ouddorp Netherlands
68 D2 Oudemirdum Netherlands
69 B4 Oudenaarde div. Oost-Vlaanderen Belgium
69 B4 Oudenaarde Belgium
68 C3 Oudenbosch Netherlands
69 B3 Oudenburg Belgium
68 F1 Oude Pekela Netherlands
68 C2 Oude Rijn r. Netherlands
68 D2 Oudeschild Netherlands
68 C1 Oudeschild Netherlands
68 C2 Oudewater Netherlands
68 C3 Oud-Gastel Netherlands
89 E4 Oudon r. France
88 D4 Oudon France
130 D6 Oudtshoorn South Africa
121 E4 Oued Adjelman watercourse Algeria
121 E3 Oued Aguemour watercourse Algeria
121 E4 Oued Amded watercourse Algeria
120 C2 Oued Beth r. Morocco
121 D2 Oued Charef watercourse Morocco
120 B3 Oued Chbika watercourse Morocco/Western Sahara
120 D3 Oued Chenachane watercourse Algeria
120 C2 Oued Dadès watercourse Morocco
121 E3 Oued Djaret watercourse Algeria
121 E4 Oued Djoûdem watercourse Algeria
120 B3 Oued Drâa watercourse Morocco
121 E2 Oued el Attar watercourse Algeria
121 D2 Oued el Korima watercourse Algeria
121 F3 Oued El Melah watercourse Algeria
121 E2 Oued El Rharbi watercourse Algeria
121 D2 Oued En Namous watercourse Algeria
121 E2 Oued er Retem watercourse Algeria
123 G2 Oued er Roui watercourse Niger
120 C2 Oued Grou r. Morocco
120 D2 Oued Guir watercourse Algeria/Morocco
121 E4 Oued Ihirène watercourse Algeria
121 E4 Oued Ilaferh watercourse Algeria
121 F3 Oued Imirhou watercourse Algeria
121 E4 Oued In Takoufi watercourse Algeria
121 F3 Oued Irharrhar watercourse Algeria
96 D5 Oued Laou Morocco
121 E4 Oued I-n-Ouzzal watercourse Algeria
121 E2 Oued Mehaïguène watercourse Algeria
121 D3 Oued Messaoud watercourse Algeria
100 D5 Oued Mharhar r. Morocco
120 D2 Oued Moulouya r. Morocco
121 E3 Oued Mya watercourse Algeria
121 E2 Oued M'zab watercourse Algeria
121 D3 Oued Saoura watercourse Algeria
120 C2 Oued Sebou r. Morocco
121 E2 Oued Seggeur watercourse Algeria
121 E4 Oued Tadjeraout watercourse Algeria
121 F4 Oued Tadjettaret watercourse Algeria
121 F4 Oued Tafassasset watercourse Algeria/Niger
121 F4 Oued Takalous watercourse Algeria
121 G4 Oued Takisset watercourse Algeria/Libya
121 E4 Oued Tamanrasset watercourse Algeria
121 E4 Oued Tasendjanet watercourse Algeria
121 E4 Oued Tekouiat watercourse Algeria
120 C2 Oued Tensift r. Morocco
120 B3 Oued Tigzerte watercourse Morocco
121 E3 Oued Tilia watercourse Algeria
121 E4 Oued Tin Amzi watercourse Algeria
121 F4 Oued Tin Tarabine watercourse Algeria
121 E4 Oued Tirahart watercourse Algeria
121 F4 Oued Tiririne watercourse Algeria
121 G4 Oued Tourndo watercourse Algeria/Niger
121 F4 Oued Zazir watercourse Algeria
120 C2 Oued Zem Morocco
120 D2 Oued Ziz r. Morocco
121 D2 Oued Zousfana watercourse Algeria
6 □2 Ouegoa New Caledonia Pacific Ocean
122 C4 Ouéléssébougou Mali
123 E5 Ouémé r. Benin
6 □2 Ouen i. New Caledonia Pacific Ocean
122 D4 Ouessa Burkina
88 A3 Ouessant, Île d'i. France
124 C3 Ouésso Congo
124 B2 Ouest div. Cameroon
120 C2 Ouezzane Morocco
69 D4 Ouffet Belgium
67 D2 Oughter, Lough l. Rep. of Ireland
82 A1 Ougney France
124 C2 Ouham div. Central African Rep.
124 C2 Ouham r. Central African Rep./Chad
124 C2 Ouham Pendé div. Central African Rep.
123 E5 Ouidah Benin
120 D3 Ouinardene Mali
156 C3 Ouiriego Mexico
89 E2 Ouistreham France
120 C5 Oujâf well Mauritania
120 D2 Oujda Morocco
120 B5 Oujeft Mauritania
56 G2 Oul div. Finland
120 C2 Oulad Teïma Morocco
56 G2 Oulainen Finland
86 C3 Oulchy-le-Château France
69 E4 Oulder Belgium
120 B5 Ould Yenjé Mauritania
121 F2 Ouled Djellal Algeria
121 E1 Ouled Farès Algeria
121 E2 Ouled Naïl, Monts des mts Algeria
121 E3 Ouled Saïd well Algeria
90 C3 Oullins France
63 H2 Oulton England U.K.
56 G2 Oulu Finland
56 G2 Oulujärvi l. Finland
56 G2 Oulujoki r. Finland
56 G2 Oulunsalo Finland
106 B3 Oulx Italy
118 D4 Oum-Chalouba Chad
122 C5 Oumé Côte d'Ivoire
121 F1 Oum el Bouaghi Algeria
118 C5 Oum-Hadjer Chad
122 D2 Oumm el A'sel well Mali
121 F3 Ounane, Djebel mt. Algeria
120 C2 Ounara Morocco
56 G2 Ounasjoki r. Finland
63 F2 Oundle England U.K.
118 D4 Ounianga Kébir Chad
118 D4 Ounianga Sérir Chad
69 D4 Oupeye Belgium
69 E4 Our r. Luxembourg
114 E2 Ouranopoli Greece
29 □2 Oura-wan b. Japan
153 F4 Ouray Colorado U.S.A.
155 H1 Ouray Utah U.S.A.
86 D4 Ource r. France
86 C3 Ourcq r. France
166 C1 Ourém Brazil
100 B2 Ourém Portugal
98 C2 Ourense Orense Spain
166 D2 Ouricuri r. Brazil
166 D2 Ouricuri Brazil
168 D5 Ourinhos Brazil
100 B3 Ourique Portugal
166 C3 Ouro r. Brazil
98 C1 Ouro r. Spain
169 E5 Ouro Fino Brazil
169 G4 Ouro Prêto Brazil
90 C2 Ouroux-sur-Saône France
69 D4 Ourthe r. Belgium
69 E5 Our, Vallée de l' v. Germany/Luxembourg
89 F2 Ourville-en-Caux France
65 H4 Ouse r. England U.K.
63 G4 Ouse r. England U.K.
88 C4 Oust r. France
93 D6 Oust France
122 B5 Outamba Kilimi National Park nat. park Sierra Leone
139 G3 Outardes r. Québec Canada
86 B4 Outarville France
120 D2 Outat Oulad el Haj Morocco
130 C6 Outeniekwaberg mountain range South Africa
66 A3 Outer Hebrides is Scotland U.K.
148 B2 Outer I. i. Wisconsin U.S.A.
154 C5 Outer Santa Barbara Channel chan. California U.S.A.
120 C5 Outfene well Mauritania
128 B3 Outjo Namibia
56 H3 Outokumpu Finland
98 C2 Outomuro Spain
86 A2 Outreau France
66 □2 Out Skerries is Scotland U.K.
63 G2 Outwell England U.K.
6 □2 Ouvéa i. New Caledonia Pacific Ocean
91 D4 Ouvèze r. France
33 F3 Ouyang Hai Sk. resr China
13 E3 Ouyen Victoria Australia
63 F2 Ouzel r. England U.K.
89 G4 Ouzouer-le-Marché France
89 H4 Ouzouer-sur-Loire France
108 B3 Ovace, Pte d' mt. Corse France
42 C2 Ovacık İçel Turkey
42 D2 Ovacık Tunceli Turkey
43 B1 Ovacık Bur pt Turkey
106 C4 Ovada Italy
6 □8 Ovalau i. Fiji
172 B1 Ovalle Chile
128 B2 Ovamboland reg. Namibia
124 B3 Ovan Gabon
98 B4 Ovar Portugal
172 E2 Oveja mt. Argentina
72 D2 Ovelgönne Germany
124 B3 Oveng Cameroon
13 F4 Ovens r. Victoria Australia
74 C2 Overath Germany
66 F1 Overbister Scotland U.K.
68 F2 Overdinkel Netherlands
69 C4 Overijse Belgium
68 E2 Overijssel div. Netherlands
68 E2 Overijssels Kanaal canal Netherlands
55 B4 Over Jerstal Denmark
56 F2 Överkalix Sweden
17 A5 Overlander Roadhouse Western Australia Australia
59 E3 Överlida Sweden
69 D3 Overpelt Belgium
155 E3 Overton Nevada U.S.A.
62 D2 Overton Wales U.K.
56 F2 Övertorneå Sweden
59 G3 Överum Sweden
131 G1 Overysel South Africa
148 E4 Ovid Michigan U.S.A.
53 D3 Ovidiopol' Ukraine
112 G2 Ovidiu Romania
98 E1 Oviedo Spain
109 F2 Ovindoli Italy
108 B4 Ovodda Sardegna Italy
30 E3 Ovoot Mongolia
30 B3 Övör-Hangay div. Mongolia
56 G1 Øvre Anarjåkka Nasjonalpark nat. park Norway
58 B1 Øvre Ardal Norway
56 E1 Øvre Dividal Nasjonalpark nat. park Norway
58 C2 Øvrella Norway
57 C3 Øvre Rendal Norway
53 C1 Ovruch Ukraine
30 B3 Övt Mongolia
9 B7 Owaka New Zealand
124 C4 Owando Congo
29 F6 Owase Japan
150 E2 Owatonna Minnesota U.S.A.
39 E2 Owbeh Afghanistan
147 E3 Owego New York U.S.A.
67 D3 Owel, Lough l. Rep. of Ireland
126 B4 Owen Falls Dam dam Uganda
175 H3 Owen Fracture sea feature Indian Ocean
9 □1 Owenga Chatham Is New Zealand
67 B2 Owenmore r. Rep. of Ireland
9 D4 Owen, Mt mt. New Zealand
9 D4 Owen River New Zealand
154 C3 Owens r. California U.S.A.
144 C4 Owensboro Kentucky U.S.A.
154 D3 Owens Lake l. California U.S.A.
140 E4 Owen Sound inlet Ontario Canada
140 E4 Owen Sound Ontario Canada
6 □1 Owen Stanley Range mountain range P.N.G.
123 F5 Owerri Nigeria
8 E3 Owhango New Zealand
136 D4 Owikeno L. l. B.C. Canada
146 B5 Owingsville Kentucky U.S.A.
147 J2 Owls Head Maine U.S.A.
123 F5 Owo Nigeria
149 E4 Owosso Michigan U.S.A.
152 C3 Owyhee r. Oregon U.S.A.
152 C3 Owyhee Nevada U.S.A.
152 C3 Owyhee Mts mts Idaho U.S.A.
164 A2 Oxapampa Peru
56 M6 Öxarfjörður b. Iceland
147 J1 Oxbow Maine U.S.A.
137 J5 Oxbow Saskatchewan Canada
115 C4 Oxeia i. Greece
59 G2 Oxelösund Sweden
63 E3 Oxford England U.K.
149 F4 Oxford Michigan U.S.A.
151 F5 Oxford Mississippi U.S.A.
147 F3 Oxford New York U.S.A.
146 A5 Oxford Ohio U.S.A.
147 F5 Oxford Pennsylvania U.S.A.
9 D5 Oxford New Zealand
137 K4 Oxford House Manitoba Canada
137 K4 Oxford L. l. Manitoba Canada
63 E3 Oxfordshire div. England U.K.
13 F3 Oxley New South Wales Australia
13 G2 Oxleys Pk mt. New South Wales Australia
Ox Mtns h. see Slieve Gamph
154 C4 Oxnard California U.S.A.
63 F3 Oxted England U.K.
141 F4 Oxtongue Lake Ontario Canada
114 F4 Oxylithos Greece
56 D2 Øya Norway
29 F5 Oyabe Japan
29 G5 Oyama Japan
163 G3 Oyapock r. French Guiana
163 G3 Oyapock, Baie d' b. French Guiana
124 B3 Oyem Gabon
58 D1 Øyer Norway
58 D2 Øyeren l. Norway
118 C4 Oyé Yeska well Chad
30 A2 Oygon Mongolia
66 D3 Oykel r. Scotland U.K.
58 D2 Oy-Marksjøen l. Norway
123 E5 Oyo div. Nigeria
124 C4 Oyo Congo
123 E5 Oyo Nigeria
164 A2 Oyón Peru
99 H2 Oyón Spain
90 D2 Oyonnax France
13 G5 Oyster B. b. Tasmania Australia
24 A2 Oyster I. i. Myanmar
72 E2 Oyten Germany
37 E1 Oytograk China
43 B1 Oyuklu D. mt. Turkey
98 B1 Oza Spain
29 J4 O-zaki pt Japan
42 E2 Özalp Turkey
23 B4 Ozamiz Philippines
89 G3 Ozanne r. France
145 C6 Ozark Alabama U.S.A.
148 E2 Ozark Michigan U.S.A.
151 E4 Ozark Plateau plat. Missouri U.S.A.
150 E4 Ozarks, Lake of the l. Missouri U.S.A.
77 K5 Ożarów Poland
39 D2 Ozbagū Iran
113 F6 Özbaşı Turkey
51 H5 Oz Baskunchak l. Rus. Fed.
79 K3 Ózd Hungary
77 K6 Ożenna Poland
52 A2 Ozerishche Rus. Fed.
52 G2 Ozerka r. Rus. Fed.
52 H3 Ozerki Rus. Fed.
52 G3 Ozerki Rus. Fed.
53 A1 Ozerne Volyns'ka Oblast' Ukraine
53 C1 Ozerne Zhytomyrs'ka Oblast' Ukraine
45 R4 Ozernovskiy Rus. Fed.
52 G4 Ozernoye Rus. Fed.
46 D2 Ozernoye Rus. Fed.
52 E1 Ozernyy Rus. Fed.
52 A2 Ozernyy Rus. Fed.
46 F2 Ozernyy Rus. Fed.
Ozero Sevan l. see Sevana Lich
54 C4 Ozersk Rus. Fed.
52 D2 Ozery Rus. Fed.
31 J2 Ozeryane Rus. Fed.
47 H4 Özgön Kyrgyzstan
52 D2 Ozherel'ye Rus. Fed.
45 Q3 Ozhogino Rus. Fed.
108 B4 Ozieri Sardegna Italy
51 J5 Ozinki Rus. Fed.
86 B4 Ozoir-le-Ferrière France
54 C3 Ozolnieki Latvia
151 C6 Ozona Texas U.S.A.
77 H4 Ozorków Poland
28 D7 Ōzu Japan
28 C6 Ozuki Japan
51 G7 Ozurget'i Georgia
55 H3 Oz. Yanis'yarvi l. Rus. Fed.
77 N5 Ozyutychi Ukraine

P

122 D4 Pâ Burkina
6 □2 Paama i. Vanuatu
135 O3 Paamiut Greenland
24 B3 Pa-an Myanmar
130 B6 Paarl South Africa
54 E2 Paasvere Estonia
66 A3 Pabbay i. Scotland U.K.
66 A4 Pabbay i. Scotland U.K.
172 B1 Pabellón Chile
77 H4 Pabianice Poland
108 A5 Pabillonis Sardegna Italy
173 H4 Pablo Acosta Argentina
37 G4 Pabna Bangladesh
81 F2 Pabneukirchen Austria
54 D4 Pabradė Lithuania
36 A4 Pab Range mountain range Pakistan
88 B3 Pabu France
165 D2 Pacaás Novos, Parque Nacional nat. park Brazil
168 C4 Pacaembu Brazil
130 D7 Pacaltsdorp South Africa
162 B5 Pacasmayo Peru
162 B5 Pacaya Samiria, Reserva Nacional res. Peru
88 D3 Pacé France
110 B5 Paceco Sicilia Italy
172 C1 Pachaco Argentina
153 E6 Pacheco Chihuahua Mexico
156 E3 Pacheco Zacatecas Mexico
171 B7 Pacheco, I. i. Chile
52 F3 Pachelma Rus. Fed.
113 E6 Pachia i. Greece
115 G7 Pachia Ammos Greece
111 E6 Pachino Sicilia Italy
164 A1 Pachitea r. Peru
36 D5 Pachmarhi India
114 F1 Pachni Greece
36 D5 Pachore India
157 F4 Pachuca Mexico
108 E1 Paciano Italy
154 B2 Pacific California U.S.A.
23 C4 Pacijan i. Philippines
22 C3 Pacinan, Tg pt Indonesia
22 B4 Pacitan Indonesia
81 F4 Packsattel pass Austria
98 B3 Paços de Ferreira Portugal
78 E2 Pacov Czech Rep.
166 B1 Pacoval Brazil
169 F2 Pacuí r. Brazil
89 G2 Pacy-sur-Eure France
76 F5 Paczków Poland
23 C5 Padada Philippines
22 B2 Padang Indonesia
20 D7 Padang Indonesia
22 E3 Padang Indonesia
20 D7 Padangpanjang Indonesia
22 B2 Padangtikar i. Indonesia
22 B2 Padangtikar Indonesia
50 E2 Padany Rus. Fed.
77 N3 Padarosk Belarus
163 E3 Padauiri r. Brazil
24 A3 Padaung Myanmar
55 B5 Padborg Denmark
164 D4 Padcaya Bolivia
136 F3 Paddle Prairie Alberta Canada
79 K6 Padej Yugoslavia
146 C5 Paden City W. Virginia U.S.A.
72 D4 Paderborn Germany
100 B3 Paderne Portugal
65 F4 Padiham England U.K.
164 D3 Padilla Bolivia
112 F2 Padina Romania
52 H3 Padishchevo Rus. Fed.
56 E2 Padjelanta National Park nat. park Sweden
37 G5 Padma r. Bangladesh
107 F3 Padova div. Veneto Italy
107 F3 Padova Italy
125 B5 Padrão, Pt pt Angola
37 F4 Padrauna India
168 D1 Padre Bernardo Brazil
151 D7 Padre Island i. Texas U.S.A.
169 H2 Padre Paraíso Brazil
108 A4 Padria Sardegna Italy
108 A2 Padro, Mte mt. Corse France
98 B2 Padrón Spain
131 F6 Padrone, Cape c. South Africa
108 B4 Padru Sardegna Italy
62 B4 Padstow England U.K.
54 E4 Padsvillye Belarus
38 C2 Pādua India
Padua see Padova
144 B4 Paducah Kentucky U.S.A.
151 C5 Paducah Texas U.S.A.
101 G3 Padul Spain
109 H4 Padula Italy
109 G3 Paduli Italy
36 D2 Padum India
7 □11 Paéa French Polynesia Pacific Ocean
31 J4 Paegam North Korea
31 J4 Paekdu San mt. North Korea
31 H5 Paengnyŏng-do i. North Korea
8 E2 Paeroa New Zealand
106 B4 Paesana Italy
107 G3 Paese Italy
23 B3 Paete Philippines
43 B2 Pafos Cyprus
131 H1 Pafuri r. South Africa
129 E3 Pafúri Mozambique
107 J4 Pag i. Croatia
104 E3 Pag Croatia
166 B1 Paga Conta Brazil
23 B5 Pagadian Philippines
20 D7 Pagai Selatan i. Indonesia
20 D7 Pagai Utara i. Indonesia
21 M3 Pagan i. Northern Mariana Is Pacific Ocean
83 G2 Paganella mt. Italy
108 D2 Paganico Italy
172 D1 Paganzo Argentina
22 A2 Pagaralam Indonesia
114 D3 Pagasitikos Kolpos b. Greece
22 C2 Pagatan Indonesia
22 D2 Pagatan Indonesia
155 G3 Page Arizona U.S.A.
54 B4 Pagėgiai Lithuania
22 A2 Pagerdewa Indonesia
171 □ Paget, Mt mt. S. Georgia Atlantic Ocean
63 F4 Pagham England U.K.
54 D4 Pagiriai Kedainiai Lithuania
54 D4 Pagiriai Vilnius Lithuania
108 D2 Paglia r. Italy
7 □13 Pago Pago American Samoa Pacific Ocean
153 F4 Pagosa Springs Colorado U.S.A.
123 E5 Pagouda Togo
37 G4 Pagri China
140 C2 Pagwachuan r. Ontario Canada
140 C1 Pagwa River Ontario Canada
153 □2 Pahala Hawaii U.S.A.
25 C7 Pahang div. Malaysia
9 A7 Pahia Pt pt New Zealand
8 E4 Pahiatua New Zealand
83 G1 Pähl Germany
153 □2 Pahoa Hawaii U.S.A.
145 D7 Pahokee Florida U.S.A.
39 E2 Pahra Kariz Afghanistan
155 E3 Pahranagat Range mts Nevada U.S.A.
77 M2 Pahranichny Belarus
36 D4 Pahuj r. India
154 D3 Pahute Mesa plat. Nevada U.S.A.
24 B3 Pai Thailand
167 A4 Paiaguás Brazil
54 D2 Paide Estonia
6 □2 Paita New Caledonia Pacific Ocean
62 C4 Paignton England U.K.
57 G3 Päijänne l. Finland
37 F3 Paiku Co l. China
172 A5 Paillahueque Chile
93 D5 Paillhès France
25 C4 Pailin Cambodia
172 A6 Paillaco Chile
153 □2 Pailolo Chan. chan. Hawaii U.S.A.
54 C1 Paimio Finland
88 B3 Paimpol France
172 B2 Paine Chile
169 F3 Paineiras Brazil
146 C4 Painesville Ohio U.S.A.
169 F4 Pains Brazil
63 E3 Painswick England U.K.
155 G3 Painted Desert desert Arizona U.S.A.
155 F5 Painted Rock Reservoir res. Arizona U.S.A.
75 G4 Painten Germany
137 K3 Paint Lake Provincial Recr. Park res. Manitoba Canada
146 B6 Paintsville Kentucky U.S.A.
140 E4 Paisley Ontario Canada
66 D5 Paisley Scotland U.K.
99 H1 País Vasco div. Spain
162 A5 Paita Peru
23 A5 Paitan, Tk b. Malaysia
98 C4 Paiva r. Portugal
33 F2 Paizhou China
56 F2 Pajala Sweden
162 A4 Pajan Ecuador
97 □ Pájara Canary Is Spain
71 J3 Pajęczno Poland
166 E2 Pajeú r. Brazil
81 H4 Páka Hungary
25 C6 Paka Malaysia
163 E2 Pakaraima Mountains mountain range Guyana
37 F4 Pakaur India
31 H5 Pakch'ŏn North Korea
140 E4 Pakesley Ontario Canada
45 S3 Pakhacha Rus. Fed.
52 C2 Pakhomovo Rus. Fed.
52 C2 Pakhra r. Rus. Fed.
47 H4 Pakhtaabad Uzbekistan
130 B6 Pakhuispas pass South Africa
123 F4 Paki Nigeria
18 H7 Pakistan country Asia
109 J1 Pakleni Otoci i. Croatia
Paknampho see Muang Nakhon Sawan
24 A2 Pakokku Myanmar
76 G3 Pakość Poland
8 D1 Pakotai New Zealand
36 C3 Pakpattan Pakistan

25 C6 Pak Phayun Thailand
104 F3 Pakrac Croatia
54 C4 Pakruojis Lithuania
79 H5 Paks Hungary
39 G2 Paktīkā Afghanistan
22 A2 Paku, Tg pt Indonesia
25 D4 Pakxé Laos
124 B2 Pala Chad
25 B4 Pala Myanmar
22 A3 Palabuhanratu Indonesia
22 A3 Palabuhanratu, Tk b. Indonesia
173 G1 Palacios Argentina
159 F5 Palacios Venezuela
98 D2 Palacios del Sil Spain
98 D2 Palacios de Sanabria Spain
91 D3 Paladru, Lac de l. France
102 G3 Palafrugell Spain
111 G2 Palagiano Italy
110 D5 Palagonia Sicilia Italy
109 J2 Palagruža i. Croatia
107 E5 Palaia Italy
115 H7 Palaikastro Greece
115 E7 Palaiochora Greece
114 C2 Palaiochori Greece
115 F5 Palaiopoli Greece
114 C3 Palaiopyrgos Greece
114 B4 Palairos Greece
86 B4 Palaiseau France
Palakkat see Palghat
131 G1 Palala r. South Africa
131 G2 Palala South Africa
37 F5 Pāla Laharha India
25 A5 Palalankwe Andaman and Nicobar Is India
114 D3 Palamas Greece
102 G3 Palamós Spain
36 C4 Palana India
45 R4 Palana Rus. Fed.
23 B2 Palanan Philippines
23 B2 Palanan Point pt Philippines
103 C5 Palancia r. Spain
39 E3 Palangān, Kūh-e mountain range Iran
22 C2 Palangkaraya Indonesia
38 B4 Palani India
36 C4 Palanpur India
39 F4 Palantak Pakistan
23 C3 Palapag Philippines
128 D3 Palapye Botswana
38 B3 Palar r. India
36 C2 Palas Pakistan
22 E1 Palasa Indonesia
37 G4 Palasbari India
98 C2 Palas de Rei Spain
54 F4 Palata r. Belarus
45 R3 Palatka Rus. Fed.
4 E4 Palau country Pacific Ocean
23 B2 Palaui i. Philippines
23 A3 Palauig Philippines
25 B4 Palauk Myanmar
7 □12 Palauli B. b. Western Samoa
176 E5 Palau Tr. sea feature Pacific Ocean
91 B5 Palavas-les-Flots France
25 B4 Palaw Myanmar
23 A4 Palawan i. Philippines
23 A4 Palawan Passage str. Philippines
23 B3 Palayan Philippines
110 D5 Palazzolo Acreide Sicilia Italy
106 D3 Palazzolo sull'Oglio Italy
108 A2 Palazzo, Pta pt Corse France
109 J4 Palazzo San Gervasio Italy
54 D2 Paldiski Estonia
52 E1 Palekh Rus. Fed.
22 A2 Palembang Indonesia
173 G3 Palemon Huergo Argentina
171 B5 Palena r. Chile
171 B5 Palena Los Lagos Chile
109 G3 Palena Italy
171 B5 Palena, L. l. Chile
99 F2 Palencia div. Castilla y León Spain
99 F2 Palencia Spain
157 G5 Palenque Mexico
159 E3 Palenque, Pta pt Dominican Rep.
110 C5 Palermo div. Sicilia Italy
110 C4 Palermo Sicilia Italy
110 C4 Palermo, Golfo di b. Sicilia Italy
110 C4 Palermo Pta Raisi airport Sicilia Italy
77 J6 Paleśnica Poland
164 C4 Palestina Chile
43 C4 Palestine reg. Israel
151 E6 Palestine Texas U.S.A.
109 E3 Palestrina Italy
24 A2 Paletwa Myanmar
38 B4 Palghat India
17 A4 Palgrave, Mt h. Western Australia Australia
128 A3 Palgrave Point pt Namibia
36 C4 Pali India
79 J5 Palić Yugoslavia
54 F4 Palik Belarus
23 C5 Palimbang Philippines
90 C2 Palinges France
109 H4 Palinuro Italy
109 H4 Palinuro, Capo c. Italy
114 E3 Paliouri Greece
114 C3 Paliouria Greece
155 H2 Palisade Colorado U.S.A.
69 D5 Paliseul Belgium
36 B5 Palitana India
54 C2 Palivere Estonia
38 B4 Palk Bay b. Sri Lanka
54 F3 Palkino Rus. Fed.
38 C2 Palkohda India
38 B3 Palkonda Range mountain range India
38 B4 Palk Strait str. India/Sri Lanka
114 G1 Palladio Greece
111 F3 Pallagorio Italy
164 B2 Pallapalla mt. Peru
100 D2 Pallarés Spain
93 D6 Pallaresa r. Spain
67 C4 Pallas Green Rep. of Ireland
51 H5 Pallasovka Rus. Fed.
38 C3 Pallavaram India
38 B2 Palleru r. India
17 B7 Pallinup r. Western Australia Australia
127 B4 Pallisa Uganda
9 E4 Palliser Bay b. New Zealand
9 E4 Palliser, Cape c. New Zealand
7 □10 Palliser, Îles is French Polynesia Pacific Ocean
36 C3 Pallu India
92 A2 Palluau France
166 C3 Palma r. Brazil
127 D7 Palma Mozambique
100 B2 Palma Portugal
109 G4 Palma Campania Italy
99 H3 Palmaces, Emb. de resr Spain
101 E3 Palma del Río Spain
103 F5 Palma de Mallorca airport Spain
103 F5 Palma de Mallorca Mallorca Spain
110 C5 Palma di Montechiaro Sicilia Italy
97 □ Palma, La i. Canary Is Spain
107 H3 Palmanova Italy
103 F5 Palma Nova Spain
164 C2 Palmares Acre Brazil
166 E2 Palmares Pernambuco Brazil
167 B7 Palmares do Sul Brazil
106 D4 Palmaria, Isola i. Italy
162 C2 Palmarito Venezuela
109 E4 Palmarola, Isola i. Italy
141 F2 Palmarolle Québec Canada
173 L3 Palmar, Punta del pt Uruguay
167 B6 Palmas Paraná Brazil
166 C3 Palmas Tocantins Brazil
122 C6 Palmas, Cape c. Liberia
166 D3 Palmas de Monte Alto Brazil
108 A5 Palmas, Golfo di b. Sardegna Italy
158 D2 Palma Soriano Cuba
145 D7 Palm Bay Florida U.S.A.
145 D7 Palm Beach Florida U.S.A.
154 C4 Palmdale California U.S.A.
168 D6 Palmeira Brazil
167 B6 Palmeira das Missões Brazil
166 E2 Palmeira dos Indios Brazil
166 D2 Palmeirais Brazil
166 C3 Palmeiras r. Brazil
166 D3 Palmeiras Brazil
168 D2 Palmeiras de Goiás Brazil
125 B5 Palmeirinhas, Pta das headland Angola
100 B2 Palmela Portugal
179 B2 Palmer U.S.A. Base Antarctica
15 E3 Palmer r. Queensland Australia
14 C5 Palmer watercourse Northern Terr. Australia
134 D3 Palmer Alaska U.S.A.
179 B2 Palmer Land reg. Antarctica
9 C6 Palmerston New Zealand
15 G4 Palmerston, C. c. Queensland Australia
176 J7 Palmerston Island i. Cook Islands Pacific Ocean
8 E4 Palmerston North New Zealand
147 F4 Palmerton Pennsylvania U.S.A.
15 F2 Palmerville Queensland Australia
145 E7 Palmetto Pt pt The Bahamas
111 E4 Palmi Italy
157 F4 Palmillas Mexico
162 B3 Palmira Colombia
168 B6 Palmital Paraná Brazil
168 C5 Palmital São Paulo Brazil
173 J2 Palmitas Uruguay
154 D5 Palm Springs California U.S.A.
15 G5 Palm Tree Cr. r. Queensland Australia
14 C5 Palm Valley v. Northern Terr. Australia
148 B6 Palmyra Missouri U.S.A.
146 E3 Palmyra New York U.S.A.
148 C4 Palmyra Wisconsin U.S.A.
Palmyra see Tadmur
176 J5 Palmyra I. i. Pacific Ocean
37 F5 Palmyras Point pt India
101 G2 Palo h. Spain
154 A3 Palo Alto California U.S.A.
162 B2 Palo de las Letras Colombia
109 J3 Palo del Colle Italy
126 B2 Paloich Sudan
56 F1 Palojärvi Finland
56 F1 Palojoensuu Finland
56 G1 Palomaa Finland
164 C2 Palomani mt. Peru
157 G5 Palomares Mexico
100 D3 Palomares del Río Spain
154 D5 Palomar Mt mt. California U.S.A.
100 D2 Palomas Spain
109 E2 Palombara Sabina Italy
100 D2 Palomilas r. Spain
155 G6 Palominas Arizona U.S.A.
38 C2 Paloncha India
83 G3 Pałoń, Cima mt. Italy
22 E2 Palopo Indonesia
170 E2 Palo Santo Argentina
103 C7 Palos, Cabo de c. Spain
100 D3 Palos de la Frontera Spain
159 □3 Palo Seco Trinidad and Tobago
168 B6 Palotina Brazil
155 F5 Palo Verde Arizona U.S.A.
155 E5 Palo Verde California U.S.A.
164 A2 Palpa Peru
15 E5 Palparara Queensland Australia
59 F2 Pålsboda Sweden
58 C1 Pålsbufjorden l. Norway
56 G2 Paltamo Finland
112 F1 Păltiniș Romania
54 F1 Pal'tsevo Rus. Fed.
52 B3 Pal'tso Rus. Fed.
22 D2 Palu r. Indonesia
22 D2 Palu Indonesia
42 E2 Palu Turkey
159 G5 Palúa Venezuela
23 B3 Paluan Philippines
93 A5 Palue r. France
89 F2 Paluel France
107 H2 Paluzza Italy
46 F5 Pal'vart Turkmenistan
36 D3 Palwal India
77 O1 Palyatskishki Belarus
45 T3 Palyavaam r. Rus. Fed.
69 E5 Palzem Germany
124 C3 Pama r. Central African Rep.
162 C4 Pamar Colombia
38 B4 Pamban Channel chan. India
13 G4 Pambula New South Wales Australia
22 C3 Pamekasan Indonesia
22 A3 Pameungpeuk Indonesia
81 H3 Pamhagen Austria
38 B3 Pamidi India
93 D5 Pamiers France
47 H5 Pamir r. Afghanistan
47 H5 Pamir reg. Tajikistan
145 E5 Pamlico Sound chan. N. Carolina U.S.A.
151 C5 Pampa Texas U.S.A.
164 C3 Pampa Aullagas Bolivia
171 C6 Pampa Chica Argentina
164 B2 Pampachiri Peru
172 C5 Pampa del Agua Amarga plain Argentina
172 C4 Pampa de la Matanzilla plain Argentina
172 D1 Pampa de la Salinas salt pan Argentina
172 D3 Pampa de la Varita plain Argentina
171 C6 Pampa del Castillo h. Argentina
172 C3 Pampa del Diamante plain Argentina
164 D3 Pampa Grande Bolivia
22 C3 Pampanua Indonesia
172 E3 Pampas reg. Argentina
164 B2 Pampas Peru
172 D3 Pampa Seca plain Argentina
173 K1 Pampeiro Brazil
52 E4 Pampelonne France
43 A1 Pamphylia reg. Turkey
130 E3 Pampierstad South Africa
98 C4 Pampilhosa da Serra Portugal
127 □4 Pamplemousses Mauritius
162 C2 Pamplona Colombia
23 B4 Pamplona Philippines
102 B2 Pamplona Spain
73 G2 Pampow Germany
22 D2 Pamukan, Tk b. Indonesia
113 F5 Pamukçu Turkey
146 E6 Pamunkey r. Virginia U.S.A.
52 G1 Pamyat' Parizhskoy Kommuny Rus. Fed.
36 D2 Pamzal Jammu and Kashmir
144 B4 Pana Illinois U.S.A.
124 B4 Pana Gabon
157 H4 Panabá Mexico
23 C5 Panabo Philippines
155 E3 Panaca Nevada U.S.A.
114 C4 Panachaïko mts Greece
114 F2 Panagia i. Greece
114 F2 Panagia Anatoliki Makedonia kai Thraki Greece
23 A4 Panagtaran Point pt Philippines
112 E3 Panagyurishte Bulgaria
22 A3 Panaitan i. Indonesia
114 C4 Panaitoliko mts Greece
38 A3 Panaji India
133 K9 Panama country Central America
156 L7 Panamá Panama
156 L7 Panamá, B. de b. Panama
156 L7 Panama Canal canal Panama
145 C6 Panama City Florida U.S.A.
156 L8 Panamá, Golfo de g. Panama
153 C4 Panamint Range mountain range California U.S.A.
154 D3 Panamint Range mts California U.S.A.
154 D3 Panamint Springs California U.S.A.
154 D3 Panamint Valley California U.S.A.
164 A1 Panao Peru
23 C4 Panaon i. Philippines
37 F4 Panar r. India
111 E4 Panarea, Isola i. Italy
25 E7 Panarik Indonesia
114 B2 Panarit Albania
107 F4 Panaro r. Italy
93 C5 Panassac France
23 B4 Panay i. Philippines
23 C3 Panay i. Philippines
23 B4 Panay Gulf b. Philippines
92 D3 Panazol France
131 H3 Panbult South Africa
155 E2 Pancake Range mts Nevada U.S.A.
169 H3 Pancas Brazil
112 C2 Pančevo Yugoslavia
112 F2 Panciu Romania
99 G2 Pancorbo Spain
102 B4 Pancrudo r. Spain
129 E3 Panda Mozambique
23 C3 Pandan Philippines
23 B4 Pandan Philippines
23 B4 Pandan B. b. Philippines
25 □ Pandan Res. resr Singapore
37 E5 Pandaria India
173 K3 Pan de Azucar Uruguay
23 A3 Pandeglang Indonesia
169 F1 Pandeiros r. Brazil
54 D3 Pandėlys Lithuania
38 A2 Pandharpur India
36 D5 Pandhurna India
12 D1 Pandie Pandie S. Australia Australia
83 E3 Pandino Italy
164 C2 Pando div. Bolivia
173 K3 Pando Uruguay
36 A3 Pandran Pakistan
55 B2 Pandrup Denmark
62 D3 Pandy Wales U.K.
99 F1 Panes Spain
54 D4 Panevėžys Lithuania
53 D1 Panfyly Ukraine
31 G1 Pang r. China
124 E3 Panga Zaire
6 □5 Pangai Tonga
6 □3 Pangaimotu i. Tonga
114 E2 Pangaio mt. Greece
22 B3 Pangandaran Indonesia
127 C6 Pangani Tanzania
22 D2 Pangean Indonesia
24 B2 Panghsang Myanmar
125 E4 Pangi Zaire
37 H3 Pangin India
36 C2 Pangi Range mountain range Pakistan
22 D3 Pangkajene Indonesia
22 B2 Pangkalanbuun Indonesia
20 C6 Pangkalansusu Indonesia
22 A2 Pangkalpinang Indonesia
21 H7 Pangkalsiang, Tg pt Indonesia
24 B1 Panglang Myanmar
135 M3 Pangnirtung N.W.T. Canada
125 B5 Pango Aluquém Angola
44 J3 Pangody Rus. Fed.
124 D2 Pangonda Central African Rep.
36 D2 Pangong Tso l. India
22 A3 Pangrango volcano Indonesia
172 A5 Panguipulli Chile
172 A5 Panguipulli, L. l. Chile
155 F3 Panguitch Utah U.S.A.
23 B5 Pangutaran i. Philippines
23 B5 Pangutaran Group is Philippines
151 C5 Panhandle Texas U.S.A.
125 E5 Pania-Mwanga Zaire
108 E1 Panicale Italy
6 □2 Panié, Mt mt. New Caledonia Pacific Ocean
36 B5 Pānikoita i. India
52 B1 Panino Rus. Fed.
52 E4 Panino Rus. Fed.
36 D3 Panipat India
90 C3 Panissières France
23 A4 Panitan Philippines
39 G1 Panj Tajikistan
39 F2 Panjāb Afghanistan
47 G5 Panjakent Tajikistan
25 E7 Panjang i. Indonesia
22 A3 Panjang Indonesia
Panjang I. i. see West I.
39 F4 Panjgur Pakistan
36 C5 Panjhra r. India
Panjim see Panaji
36 B3 Panjnad r. Pakistan
56 H3 Pankakoski Finland
47 J2 Pankrushikha Rus. Fed.
123 F5 Pankshin Nigeria
36 D4 Panna India
36 E4 Panna India
16 B4 Pannawonica Western Australia Australia
90 B1 Pannesière-Chaumard, Barrage de dam France
69 D3 Panningen Netherlands
168 C4 Panorama Brazil
115 F7 Panormos Greece
47 H1 Panovo Rus. Fed.
52 E3 Panovy Kusty Rus. Fed.
38 B4 Panruti India
31 G4 Panshan China
31 H4 Panshi China
63 G3 Pant r. England U.K.
102 F2 Pantà de Boadella l. Spain
102 F3 Pantà de Susqueda l. Spain
22 D2 Pantai Indonesia
167 A4 Pantanal de São Lourenço marsh Brazil
167 A4 Pantanal do Rio Negro Brazil
167 A4 Pantanal do Taquari marsh Brazil
167 A4 Pantanal Matogrossense, Parque Nacional de nat. park Brazil
115 D6 Pantanassa Greece
112 F2 Pantelimon Romania
110 A6 Pantelleria Italy
110 B6 Pantelleria, Isola di i. Italy
21 H8 Pantemakassar Indonesia
114 A3 Pantokratoras h. Greece
102 D3 Pantorrillas h. Spain
23 C5 Pantukan Philippines
157 F4 Pánuco r. Mexico
157 F4 Pánuco Veracruz Mexico
38 A2 Panvel India
32 D3 Pan Xian China
33 F4 Panyu China
53 G2 Panyutyne Ukraine
154 B4 Panza Range, La mts California U.S.A.
81 E5 Panzaro, Golfo di b. Italy
125 C5 Panzi Zaire
157 H6 Panzos Guatemala
166 E2 Pão de Açúcar Brazil
111 F3 Paola Italy
111 □ Paola Malta
144 C4 Paoli Indiana U.S.A.
7 □11 Paopao French Polynesia Pacific Ocean
124 C2 Paoua Central African Rep.
47 H4 Pap Uzbekistan
78 G4 Pápa Hungary
114 E4 Papades Greece
115 D6 Papadianika Greece
Papagaio r. see Sauêruiná
169 F3 Papagaios Brazil
170 C3 Papagayos Argentina
8 E2 Papakura New Zealand
109 H4 Papa, Monte del mt. Italy
157 F4 Papantla Mexico
162 B5 Papa Playa Peru
7 □11 Papara French Polynesia Pacific Ocean
38 C2 Pāparhāhandi India
8 E2 Paparoa New Zealand
9 C5 Paparoa Range mountain range New Zealand
66 □2 Papa Stour i. Scotland U.K.
8 E2 Papatoetoe New Zealand
9 B7 Papatowai New Zealand
7 □11 Papava French Polynesia Pacific Ocean
66 F1 Papa Westray i. Scotland U.K.
7 □11 Papeete French Polynesia Pacific Ocean
72 C2 Papenburg Germany
68 C3 Papendrecht Netherlands
7 □11 Papenoo r. French Polynesia Pacific Ocean
7 □11 Papenoo French Polynesia Pacific Ocean
7 □11 Papetoai French Polynesia Pacific Ocean
114 G1 Papikio mt. Greece
141 H3 Papineau-Labelle, Réserve faunique de res. Québec Canada
155 E3 Papoose L. l. Nevada U.S.A.
170 B2 Paposo Chile
75 F4 Pappenheim Germany
77 L3 Paprotnia Poland
66 B5 Paps of Jura h. Scotland U.K.
67 B4 Paps, The h. Rep. of Ireland
6 □1 Papua, Gulf of g. P.N.G.
4 F5 Papua New Guinea country Australasia
172 B2 Papudo Chile
24 B3 Papun Myanmar
14 B4 Papunya Northern Terr. Australia
39 C3 Pa Qal'eh Iran
62 B4 Par England U.K.
166 B1 Pará div. Brazil
169 F3 Pará r. Brazil
52 E3 Para r. Rus. Fed.
111 H2 Parabita Italy
17 B4 Paraburdoo Western Australia Australia
23 B3 Paracale Philippines
169 G5 Paracambi Brazil
163 F4 Paracari r. Brazil
169 F2 Paracatu r. Brazil
169 E2 Paracatu Brazil
20 F3 Paracel Islands is South China Sea
12 D2 Parachilna S. Australia Australia
36 B2 Parachinar Pakistan
112 C3 Paraćin Yugoslavia
166 E1 Paracuru Brazil
79 K4 Parád Hungary
98 C4 Parada Portugal
115 D5 Paradeisia Greece
114 F1 Paradeisos Greece
169 F3 Pará de Minas Brazil
158 □1 Paradera Aruba Caribbean
141 G2 Paradis Québec Canada
154 B2 Paradise California U.S.A.
148 E2 Paradise Michigan U.S.A.
163 F2 Paradise Guyana
137 H4 Paradise Hill Saskatchewan Canada
145 □2 Paradise I. i. The Bahamas
154 D2 Paradise Peak summit Nevada U.S.A.
139 J3 Paradise River Newfoundland Canada
77 J4 Paradyż Poland
151 F4 Paragould Arkansas U.S.A.
165 D2 Paragua r. Bolivia
163 E2 Paragua r. Venezuela
166 D3 Paraguaçu r. Brazil
168 C5 Paraguaçu Paulista Brazil
165 E3 Paraguai r. Brazil
162 C1 Paraguáipoa Venezuela
162 D1 Paraguaná, Pen. de pen. Venezuela
165 E5 Paraguarí Paraguay
161 F5 Paraguay country South America
165 E5 Paraguay r. Argentina/Paraguay
39 E4 Parahadab Pakistan
166 E2 Paraíba div. Brazil
166 E2 Paraíba r. Brazil
169 H4 Paraíba do Sul r. Brazil
169 G5 Paraíba do Sul Brazil
168 B3 Paraíso Brazil
157 G5 Paraíso Mexico
166 C3 Paraíso do Norte Brazil
169 F5 Paraisópolis Brazil
52 H2 Parakino Rus. Fed.
123 E5 Parakou Benin
39 D4 Parākūn Iran
12 D2 Parakylia S. Australia Australia
38 D2 Paralākhemundi India
115 D6 Paralia Peloponnisos Greece
115 D4 Paralia Stereá Ellás Greece
115 D5 Paralia Tyrou Greece
115 E4 Paralimni l. Greece
38 C2 Paralkot India
38 B4 Paramakkudi India
163 F2 Paramaribo Surinam
162 B2 Paramillo mt. Colombia
162 B2 Paramillo, Parque Nacional nat. park Colombia
172 C2 Paramillos, S. de los mountain range Argentina
166 D3 Paramirim r. Brazil
166 D3 Paramirim Brazil
98 D2 Páramo del Sil Spain
98 E2 Páramo Leonés reg. Spain
52 C3 Paramonovo Rus. Fed.
147 F4 Paramus New Jersey U.S.A.
45 R4 Paramushir, O. i. Rus. Fed.
114 B3 Paramythia Greece
43 C4 Paran watercourse Israel
166 B6 Paraná div. Brazil
166 C3 Paranã r. Brazil
173 G2 Paraná r. South America
173 G1 Paraná Argentina
166 C3 Paranã Brazil
168 D6 Paranaguá Brazil
168 D6 Paranaguá, Baia de b. Brazil
168 C3 Paranaíba r. Brazil
168 C3 Paranaíba Brazil
173 H2 Paraná Ibicuy r. Argentina
168 C3 Paranaiguara Brazil
165 E1 Paranaita r. Brazil
168 C5 Paranapanema r. Brazil
167 C4 Paranã, Sa do h. Brazil
168 A1 Paranatinga r. Brazil
168 B5 Paranavaí Brazil
39 B2 Parandak Iran
114 F1 Paranestio Greece
22 B3 Parang i. Indonesia
23 B5 Parang Philippines
38 B4 Paranigipettai India
168 A5 Paranhos Brazil
36 C5 Parantij India
7 □10 Paraoa i. French Polynesia Pacific Ocean
169 F3 Paraopeba r. Brazil
169 F3 Paraopeba Brazil
101 G3 Parapanda, Sierra de mountain range Spain
9 E4 Paraparaumu New Zealand
114 B3 Parapotamos Greece
151 D7 Paras Mexico
37 G5 Parashunam Bangladesh
169 F5 Parati Brazil
38 B1 Paratwada India
166 B2 Parauapebas r. Brazil
163 F5 Parauari r. Brazil
168 C2 Paraúna Brazil
90 C2 Paray-le-Monial France
36 D5 Parbati r. India
37 G4 Parbatipur Bangladesh
38 B2 Parbhani India
103 C6 Parcent Spain
73 G2 Parchim Germany
76 F1 Parchowo Poland
77 L4 Parczew Poland
148 C4 Pardeeville Wisconsin U.S.A.
112 G2 Pardina Romania
37 G2 Parding China
169 F1 Pardo r. Brazil
168 B4 Pardo r. Brazil
173 H4 Pardo Argentina
102 B3 Pardos, Sierra de mountain range Spain
78 E1 Pardubice Czech Rep.
22 C3 Pare Indonesia
77 N2 Parechcha Belarus
165 E2 Parecis r. Brazil
166 A3 Parecis Brazil
98 B3 Paredes Portugal
98 B3 Paredes de Coura Portugal
99 F2 Paredes de Nava Spain
172 C2 Pareditas Argentina
157 E3 Paredón Mexico
172 B3 Paredones Chile
42 F2 Pareh Iran
99 H4 Pareja Spain
166 E2 Parelhas Brazil
93 E4 Pareloup, Lac de l. France
92 B4 Parempuyre France
8 D1 Parengarenga Harbour harbour New Zealand
141 H3 Parent Québec Canada
93 A4 Parentis-en-Born France
141 G2 Parent, Lac l. Québec Canada
9 C6 Pareora New Zealand
22 D3 Parepare Indonesia
172 E3 Parera Argentina
50 D3 Parfino Rus. Fed.
114 B3 Parga Greece
57 F3 Pargas Finland
111 E4 Parghelia Italy
86 D4 Pargny-sur-Saulx France
54 G1 Pargolovo Rus. Fed.
163 E2 Pariaguán Venezuela
163 E1 Paria, Gulf of b. Venezuela
159 □3 Paria, Gulf of g. Trinidad Trinidad and Tobago
163 E1 Paria, Peninsula de pen. Venezuela
155 F3 Paria Plateau plat. Arizona U.S.A.
22 E2 Parigi Indonesia
89 F4 Parigné-l'Évêque France
163 F2 Parika Guyana
57 H3 Parikkala Finland
163 D3 Parima-Tapirapecó, Parque Nacional nat. park Venezuela
162 A4 Pariñas, Pta pt Peru
83 E3 Parino r. Italy
166 A1 Parintins Brazil
146 A5 Paris Kentucky U.S.A.
140 E5 Paris Ontario Canada
145 B4 Paris Tennessee U.S.A.
151 E5 Paris Texas U.S.A.
86 B4 Paris France
140 C3 Parisienne, Île i. Ontario Canada
93 D4 Parisot France
156 K8 Parita Panama
25 C6 Parit Buntar Malaysia
39 C3 Pārīz Iran
67 D2 Park Northern Ireland U.K.
39 D4 Parkā Bandar Iran
38 B2 Parkal India
57 F3 Parkano Finland
139 J3 Parke Lake l. Newfoundland Canada
47 G4 Parkent Uzbekistan
155 E4 Parker Arizona U.S.A.
155 E4 Parker Dam dam Arizona U.S.A.
137 K2 Parker Lake l. N.W.T. Canada
27 □ Parker, Mt h. Hong Kong
148 A4 Parkersburg Iowa U.S.A.
146 C5 Parkersburg W. Virginia U.S.A.
13 G3 Parkes New South Wales Australia
148 B3 Park Falls Wisconsin U.S.A.
148 D5 Park Forest Illinois U.S.A.
159 □7 Parkham Antigua Caribbean
140 D3 Parkinson Ontario Canada
150 E2 Park Rapids Minnesota U.S.A.
80 D2 Parkstetten Germany
136 E5 Parksville B.C. Canada
147 F4 Parksville New York U.S.A.
47 J5 Parkutta Jammu and Kashmir
36 D2 Parkutta Pakistan
99 G4 Parla Spain
38 D2 Parla Kimedi India
159 □2 Parlatuvier Tobago Trinidad and Tobago
38 B2 Parli Vaijnath India
106 E4 Parma div. Emilia-Romagna Italy
106 E4 Parma r. Italy
152 C3 Parma Idaho U.S.A.
146 C4 Parma Ohio U.S.A.
106 D4 Parma Parma Italy
163 D2 Parmana Venezuela
166 D1 Parnaíba r. Brazil
166 B3 Parnaíba r. Brazil
166 C2 Parnaíba r. Brazil
166 D1 Parnaíba Brazil
166 C2 Parnaibinha r. Brazil
166 E2 Parnamirim Brazil
166 D2 Parnarama Brazil
114 D4 Parnassos mt. Greece
114 D4 Parnassos nat. park Greece
9 D5 Parnassus New Zealand
12 D3 Parndana S. Australia Australia
81 H3 Parndorf Austria
148 A5 Parnell Iowa U.S.A.
115 E4 Parnitha mts Greece
115 E4 Parnitha nat. park Greece
115 D5 Parnon mts Greece
54 D2 Pärnu r. Estonia
54 D2 Pärnu Estonia
54 D2 Pärnu-Jagupi Estonia
37 G4 Paro Bhutan
86 C4 Paron France
13 F2 Paroo watercourse New South Wales Australia
13 E2 Paroo Channel watercourse New South Wales Australia
39 E2 Paropamisus mountain range Afghanistan
115 G5 Paros i. Greece
115 G5 Paros Greece
159 □1 Parottee Pt pt Jamaica
155 F3 Parowan Utah U.S.A.
91 E4 Parpaillon mts France
173 K3 Parque del Plata Uruguay
172 B4 Parral Chile
147 F6 Parramore I. i. Virginia U.S.A.
156 E3 Parras Mexico
173 J4 Parravicini Argentina
62 D3 Parrett r. England U.K.
156 J7 Parrita Costa Rica
139 H4 Parrsboro Nova Scotia Canada
134 F2 Parry, Cape pt N.W.T. Canada
134 G2 Parry Islands is N.W.T. Canada
135 L2 Parry, Kap c. Greenland
159 □3 Parrylands Trinidad and Tobago
140 E4 Parry Sound Ontario Canada
75 G3 Parsberg Germany
80 B3 Parseierspitze mt. Austria
76 E2 Parsęta r. Poland
52 E3 Parskiy Ugol Rus. Fed.
151 E4 Parsons Kansas U.S.A.
146 D5 Parsons W. Virginia U.S.A.
73 J3 Parsteiner See l. Germany
37 E5 Partabpur India
110 B5 Partanna Sicilia Italy
80 B4 Partenen Austria
74 E2 Partenstein Germany
92 B2 Parthenay France
110 C4 Partinico Sicilia Italy
79 H3 Partizánske Slovakia
63 G1 Partney England U.K.
67 B3 Partry Rep. of Ireland
67 B3 Partry Mts h. Rep. of Ireland
52 F2 Partsa r. Rus. Fed.
53 F3 Partyzany Ukraine
163 G4 Paru r. Brazil
163 F3 Paru de Oeste r. Brazil
53 D3 Parutyne Ukraine
38 C2 Parvatipuram India
36 C4 Parvatsar India
36 D4 Parwan r. India
37 E3 Paryang China
54 F5 Parychy Belarus
59 F3 Påryd Sweden
131 F3 Parys South Africa
77 K4 Parysów Poland
77 H4 Parzęczew Poland
99 G1 Pas r. Spain
154 C4 Pasadena California U.S.A.
151 E6 Pasadena Texas U.S.A.
113 F4 Paşalimanı Adası i. Turkey
22 D2 Pasangkayu Indonesia
24 B3 Pasawng Myanmar
145 B6 Pascagoula Mississippi U.S.A.
151 F6 Pascagoula Mississippi U.S.A.
141 G2 Pascalis Québec Canada
112 F1 Pașcani Romania
81 F2 Pasching Austria
152 C2 Pasco Washington U.S.A.
169 J2 Pascoal, Monte h. Brazil
15 E2 Pascoe r. Queensland Australia
14 D3 Pascoe Inlet inlet Queensland Australia
Pascua, Isla de i. see Easter I.
23 B3 Pascual Philippines
86 B2 Pas-de-Calais div. France
Pas de Calais str. see Strait of Dover
86 B2 Pas-en-Artois France
73 K2 Pasewalk Germany
137 H3 Pasfield Lake l. Saskatchewan Canada
50 E2 Pasha Rus. Fed.
47 K1 Pashino Rus. Fed.
52 F3 Pashkovo Rus. Fed.
31 J2 Pashkovo Rus. Fed.
107 H2 Pasiàn di Prato Italy
77 K3 Pasieki Poland
23 B3 Pasig Philippines
37 H3 Pasighat India
42 E2 Pasinler Turkey
25 □ Pasir Gudang Malaysia
22 C4 Pasirian Indonesia
25 C6 Pasir Mas Malaysia
25 □ Pasir Panjang Singapore
25 C6 Pasir Putih Malaysia
59 G3 Påskallavik Sweden
154 A2 Paskenta California U.S.A.
39 E4 Paskūh Iran
77 H1 Pasłęk Poland
77 H1 Pasłęka r. Poland
17 C7 Pasley, C. c. Western Australia Australia
39 E4 Pasni Pakistan
157 H5 Paso Caballos Guatemala
172 B6 Paso Chacabuco Argentina
171 C5 Paso de Indios Argentina
173 H1 Pasode la Laguna Argentina
156 J7 Paso del Cascal summit Nicaragua
170 C2 Paso del Inca pass Argentina/Chile
172 B6 Paso del Limay Argentina
172 C5 Paso de los Indios Argentina
170 E2 Paso de los Libres Argentina
173 J2 Paso de los Toros Uruguay
173 J2 Paso del Palmar, Lago Artificial de resr Uruguay
165 E5 Paso de Patria Paraguay
170 C2 Paso de Peña Negra Chile
170 C2 Paso de San Francisco pass Argentina
172 B6 Paso Flores Argentina
172 E2 Paso Grande Argentina
24 A2 Pasok Myanmar
173 K2 Paso Pereira Uruguay
171 B6 Paso Río Mayo Argentina
154 B4 Paso Robles California U.S.A.
137 J4 Pasquia Hills h. Saskatchewan Canada
39 C3 Pasrūdak Iran
147 J2 Passadumkeag Maine U.S.A.
88 C2 Passage de la Déroute str. Channel Is./France
88 B4 Passage de la Teignouse str. France
88 A3 Passage du Fromveur str. France
148 C1 Passage I. i. Michigan U.S.A.
81 G3 Passail Austria
89 E3 Passais France
169 F4 Passa Tempo Brazil
75 J4 Passau Germany
179 □ Passe Royale chan. Kerguelen Indian Ocean
81 E3 Pass Gschütt Austria
23 B4 Passi Philippines
108 E1 Passignano sul Trasimeno Italy
107 F2 Passirio r. Italy
173 J1 Passo da Guardia Brazil
173 J1 Passo de las Caretas Uruguay
167 B6 Passo Fundo Brazil
169 E4 Passos Brazil
73 K2 Passow Germany
80 D3 Paß Thurn Austria
90 E3 Passy France
54 E4 Pastavy Belarus
162 B4 Pastaza r. Peru
173 F3 Pasteur Argentina

137 J4 **Pas, The** *Manitoba* Canada
162 B3 **Pasto** Colombia
155 H3 **Pastora Peak summit** *Arizona* U.S.A.
166 D2 **Pastos Bons** Brazil
99 H4 **Pastrana** Spain
79 M5 **Pasul Vârtop pass** Romania
23 B2 **Pasuquin** Philippines
22 C3 **Pasuruan** Indonesia
54 D3 **Pasvalys** Lithuania
79 J4 **Pásztó** Hungary
23 B5 **Pata i.** Philippines
124 D2 **Pata** Central African Rep.
122 B4 **Pata** Senegal
164 B4 **Patache, Pta pt** Chile
171 B6 **Patagonia reg.** Argentina
155 G6 **Patagonia** *Arizona* U.S.A.
22 A3 **Patah, G. mt.** Indonesia
37 G4 **Patakata** India
39 E3 **Patambar** Iran
36 C5 **Patan** India
Patan *see* **Somnath**
36 D5 **Patan** India
37 F4 **Patan** Nepal
170 D2 **Patay** Argentina
89 G3 **Patay** France
13 E3 **Patchewollock** *Victoria* Australia
62 D3 **Patchway** *England* U.K.
8 E3 **Patea r.** New Zealand
8 E3 **Patea** New Zealand
123 F5 **Pategi** Nigeria
127 D5 **Pate I. i.** Kenya
65 G3 **Pateley Bridge** *England* U.K.
37 G5 **Patenga P. pt** Bangladesh
130 E6 **Patensie** South Africa
103 C5 **Paterna** Spain
100 E4 **Paterna de Rivera** Spain
81 E4 **Paternion** Austria
110 D5 **Paternò** *Sicilia* Italy
109 H4 **Paterno** Italy
75 H3 **Patersdorf** Germany
147 F4 **Paterson** *New Jersey* U.S.A.
13 G3 **Paterson** *New South Wales* Australia
131 E6 **Paterson** South Africa
9 B7 **Paterson Inlet inlet** New Zealand
37 E5 **Pathalgaon** India
36 C2 **Pathankot** India
Pathein *see* **Bassein**
152 F3 **Pathfinder Res. resr** *Wyoming* U.S.A.
25 B5 **Pathiu** Thailand
38 B2 **Pathri** India
25 C4 **Pathum Thani** Thailand
22 B3 **Pati** Indonesia
162 B3 **Patía r.** Colombia
36 D3 **Patiala** India
163 G3 **Patience** French Guiana
23 □2 **Pati Pt pt** *Guam* Pacific Ocean
22 E3 **Patiro, Tg pt** Indonesia
37 H4 **Pātkai Bum mountain range** India
113 F6 **Patmos i.** Greece
64 D2 **Patna** *Scotland* U.K.
37 F4 **Patna** India
37 E5 **Patnagarh** India
23 B3 **Patnanongan i.** Philippines
42 E2 **Patnos** Turkey
76 G4 **Pątnów** Poland
171 B6 **Pato, C. mt.** Chile
36 E3 **Paton** India
113 B4 **Patos** Albania
166 E2 **Patos** Brazil
169 E3 **Patos de Minas** Brazil
159 □3 **Patos, I. i.** *Trinidad* Trinidad and Tobago
167 B7 **Patos, Lagoa dos lag.** Brazil
173 F1 **Patos, L. de los l.** Argentina
168 D1 **Patos, R. dos r.** Brazil
170 C3 **Patquía** Argentina
115 C4 **Patra** Greece
115 C4 **Patraïkos Kolpos b.** Greece
50 G1 **Patrakeyevka** Rus. Fed.
112 F1 **Pătrăuţi** Romania
56 K6 **PatreksfjörZur** Iceland
171 A6 **Patricio Lynch, I. i.** Chile
168 D3 **Patrimônio** Brazil
65 J4 **Patrington** *England* U.K.
165 G3 **Patrocínio** Brazil
115 E5 **Patroklou i.** Greece
56 H1 **Patsoyoki r.** Rus. Fed.
108 B4 **Pattada** *Sardegna* Italy
25 C6 **Pattani r.** Thailand
25 C6 **Pattani** Thailand
25 C4 **Pattaya** Thailand
147 J2 **Patten** *Maine* U.S.A.
72 E3 **Pattensen** Germany
65 F3 **Patterdale** *England* U.K.
146 D5 **Patterson r.** *W. Virginia* U.S.A.
154 B3 **Patterson** *California* U.S.A.
154 C3 **Patterson Mt mt.** *California* U.S.A.
136 C2 **Patterson, Mt mt.** *Yukon Terr.* Canada
148 E3 **Patterson, Pt pt** *Michigan* U.S.A.
Patteson Pass. chan. *see* **Lolvavana, Pass.**
110 D4 **Patti** *Sicilia* Italy
37 E4 **Patti** India
56 G2 **Pattijoki** Finland
56 F1 **Pättikkä** Finland
38 B3 **Pattikonda** India
9 □1 **Pattison, C. c.** *Chatham Is* New Zealand
136 D3 **Pattullo, Mt mt.** *B.C.* Canada
37 G5 **Patuakhali** Bangladesh
137 H3 **Patuanak** *Saskatchewan* Canada
156 J6 **Patuca r.** Honduras
156 J6 **Patuca, Pta pt** Honduras
146 E5 **Patuxent r.** *Maryland* U.S.A.
179 B3 **Patuxent Ra. mountain range** Antarctica
157 E5 **Pátzcuaro** Mexico
93 B5 **Pau** France
169 J1 **Pau-Brasil** Brazil
164 B2 **Paucarbamba** Peru
164 B2 **Paucartambo** Peru
166 C2 **Pau d'Arco r.** Brazil
166 C2 **Pau d'Arco** Brazil
81 G2 **Paudorf** Austria
92 B3 **Pauillac** France
165 D2 **Pauini r.** Brazil
164 C1 **Pauini** Brazil
24 A2 **Pauk** Myanmar
24 A3 **Paukkaung** Myanmar
24 A2 **Pauktaw** Myanmar
98 C4 **Paúl** Portugal
107 H2 **Paularo** Italy
134 F3 **Paulatuk** *N.W.T.* Canada
155 F4 **Paulden** *Arizona* U.S.A.
146 A4 **Paulding** *Ohio* U.S.A.
92 E3 **Paulhac** France
91 B4 **Paulhac-en-Margeride** France
91 B3 **Paulhaguet** France
91 B5 **Paulhan** France
108 A4 **Paulilatino** *Sardegna* Italy
139 H2 **Paul Island i.** *Newfoundland* Canada
166 D2 **Paulistana** Brazil
166 E2 **Paulo Afonso** Brazil
168 D4 **Paulo de Faria** Brazil
131 H3 **Paulpietersburg** South Africa
131 F4 **Paul Roux** South Africa
147 F2 **Paul Smiths** *New York* U.S.A.
151 D5 **Pauls Valley** *Oklahoma* U.S.A.
112 F1 **Păunesti** Romania
24 A3 **Paungde** Myanmar
36 D3 **Pauri** India
75 H2 **Pausa** Germany
162 C2 **Pauto r.** Colombia
93 B5 **Pau-Uzein airport** France
86 D3 **Pauvres** France
169 H2 **Pavão** Brazil
42 F3 **Pāveh** Iran
52 D3 **Pavelets** Rus. Fed.
106 D3 **Pavia div.** *Lombardia* Italy
98 C4 **Pavia r.** Portugal
106 D3 **Pavia** Italy
100 B2 **Pavia** Portugal
89 F2 **Pavilly** France
54 B3 **Pāvilosta** Latvia
50 H3 **Pavino** Rus. Fed.
77 L1 **Pavištyčio kalnas h.** Lithuania
77 N4 **Pavitstsye** Belarus
114 D4 **Pavliani** Greece
112 E3 **Pavlikeni** Bulgaria
52 A2 **Pavlinovo** Rus. Fed.
53 A1 **Pavlivka** *Volyns'ka Oblast'* Ukraine
53 F1 **Pavlivka** Ukraine
47 J2 **Pavlodar div.** Kazakhstan
47 J2 **Pavlodar** Kazakhstan
53 F2 **Pavlohrad** Ukraine
53 F3 **Pavlopillya** Ukraine
114 E4 **Pavlos** Greece
47 H2 **Pavlovka** Kazakhstan
52 H3 **Pavlovka** Rus. Fed.
52 F2 **Pavlovo** Rus. Fed.
51 G5 **Pavlovsk** Rus. Fed.
47 K2 **Pavlovsk** Rus. Fed.
51 F6 **Pavlovskaya** Rus. Fed.
52 D2 **Pavlovskiy Posad** Rus. Fed.
52 E1 **Pavlovskoye** Rus. Fed.
51 H4 **Pavlovka** Rus. Fed.
53 E2 **Pavlysh** Ukraine
162 C3 **Pavon** Colombia
107 E4 **Pavullo nel Frignano** Italy
54 F4 **Pavul'skaye, Vozyera reg.** Belarus
22 B2 **Pawan r.** Indonesia
36 E3 **Pawayan** India
76 F2 **Pawłówek** Poland
148 E4 **Paw Paw** *Michigan* U.S.A.
147 H4 **Pawtucket** *Rhode Island* U.S.A.
25 B4 **Pawut** Myanmar
115 H7 **Paximada i.** Greece
115 F7 **Paximadia i.** Greece
114 B3 **Paxoi i.** Greece
114 B3 **Paxoi** Greece
148 C5 **Paxton** *Illinois* U.S.A.
65 F2 **Paxton** *Scotland* U.K.
37 E4 **Payagpur** India
20 D7 **Payakumbuh** Indonesia
25 □ **Paya Lebar** Singapore
162 C3 **Paya, Parque Nacional la nat. park** Colombia
81 G3 **Payerbach** Austria
82 B2 **Payerne** Switzerland
152 C2 **Payette** *Oregon* U.S.A.
31 J2 **Paykan** Rus. Fed.
44 H3 **Pay-Khoy, Khrebet h.** Rus. Fed.
100 C3 **Paymogo** Spain
138 F2 **Payne, Lac l.** *Québec* Canada
154 B1 **Paynes Creek** *California* U.S.A.
17 B6 **Payne's Find** *Western Australia* Australia
100 D2 **Payo, Sierra h.** Spain
93 D4 **Payrac** France
173 J2 **Paysandú div.** Uruguay
173 H2 **Paysandú** Uruguay
93 A5 **Pays Basque reg.** France/Spain
89 F2 **Pays d'Auge reg.** France
93 A4 **Pays de Born reg.** France
89 G2 **Pays de Bray reg.** France
89 F2 **Pays de Caux reg.** France
89 E4 **Pays de la Loire div.** France
88 A3 **Pays de Léon reg.** France
88 C4 **Pays de Retz reg.** France
86 C4 **Pays d'Othe** France
89 F3 **Pays d'Ouche reg.** France
155 G4 **Payson** *Arizona* U.S.A.
155 G1 **Payson** *Utah* U.S.A.
172 C4 **Payún, Co volcano** Argentina
39 B3 **Pāzanān** Iran
42 E1 **Pazar** Turkey
112 E3 **Pazardzhik** Bulgaria
113 G5 **Pazarlar** Turkey
156 C3 **Paz, B. de la b.** Mexico
162 C2 **Paz de Ariporo** Colombia
162 C2 **Paz de Rio** Colombia
107 H3 **Pazin** Croatia
93 E6 **Paziols** France
80 B4 **Paznauntal v.** Austria
98 B1 **Pazo de Irixoa** Spain
98 B2 **Pazos** Spain
166 B2 **Paz, R. da r.** Brazil
112 C3 **Pčinja r.** Macedonia
25 B4 **Pe** Myanmar
6 □4 **Pea** Tonga
168 B5 **Peabiru** Brazil
136 G3 **Peace r.** *B.C./Yukon* Canada
63 F4 **Peacehaven** *England* U.K.
136 F3 **Peace River** *Alberta* Canada
155 F4 **Peach Springs** *Arizona* U.S.A.
63 E1 **Peak District National Park** *England* U.K.
12 C2 **Peake watercourse** *S. Australia* Australia
139 G4 **Peaked Mt. h.** *Maine* U.S.A.
23 A4 **Peaked Point pt** Philippines
13 G3 **Peak Hill** *New South Wales* Australia
15 G4 **Peak Ra. h.** *Queensland* Australia
128 □1 **Peak, The summit** *Ascension* Atlantic Ocean
101 G3 **Peal de Becerro** Spain
155 H2 **Peale, Mt mt.** *Utah* U.S.A.
155 H6 **Pearce** *Arizona* U.S.A.
14 B2 **Pearce Pt pt** *Northern Terr.* Australia
151 F6 **Pearl r.** *Mississippi* U.S.A.
140 A2 **Pearl** *Ontario* Canada
153 □1 **Pearl City** *Hawaii* U.S.A.
153 □1 **Pearl Harbor harbour** *Hawaii* U.S.A.
151 D6 **Pearsall** *Texas* U.S.A.
145 D6 **Pearson** *Georgia* U.S.A.
173 G2 **Pearson** Argentina
135 J2 **Peary Channel chan.** *N.W.T.* Canada
135 P1 **Peary Land reg.** Greenland
16 B4 **Peawah r.** *Western Australia* Australia
138 C2 **Peawanuck** *Ontario* Canada
129 F2 **Pebane** Mozambique
162 C4 **Pebas** Peru
171 E7 **Pebble I. i.** Falkland Is.
22 E2 **Pebengko** Indonesia
112 C3 **Peć** Yugoslavia
169 G3 **Peçanha** Brazil
167 C6 **Peças, I. das i.** Brazil
83 D2 **Peccia** Switzerland
107 E5 **Peccioli** Italy
56 H1 **Pechenga** Rus. Fed.
53 G2 **Pechenihy** Ukraine
53 A2 **Pechenizhyn** Ukraine
52 D2 **Pecherniki** Rus. Fed.
44 G3 **Pechora r.** Rus. Fed.
44 G3 **Pechora** Rus. Fed.
54 E3 **Pechory** Rus. Fed.
112 G3 **Pecineaga** Romania
122 A4 **Pecixe, Ilha de i.** Guinea-Bissau
149 F4 **Peck** *Michigan* U.S.A.
75 L2 **Pečky** Czech Rep.
108 A5 **Pecora, Capo pt** *Sardegna* Italy
151 C6 **Pecos r.** *Texas* U.S.A.
151 C6 **Pecos** *Texas* U.S.A.
79 H5 **Pécs** Hungary
79 H5 **Pécsvárad** Hungary
158 B6 **Pedasí** Panama
131 F6 **Peddie** South Africa
54 E3 **Pededze r.** Latvia
54 E3 **Pededze** Latvia
172 B2 **Pedegua** Chile
159 E3 **Pedernales** Haiti
156 D2 **Pedernales** Mexico
159 G5 **Pedernales** Venezuela
168 D5 **Pederneiras** Brazil
107 F3 **Pederobba** Italy
56 F3 **Pedersöre** Finland
12 C1 **Pedirka** *S. Australia* Australia
125 B7 **Pediva** Angola
37 E3 **Pedo La pass** China
169 H1 **Pedra Azul** Brazil
98 B3 **Pedrada mt.** Portugal
98 C2 **Pedrafita do Cebreiro** Spain
103 C5 **Pedralba** Spain
98 D2 **Pedralba de la Pradería** Spain
122 □ **Pedra Lume** Cape Verde
100 C1 **Pedra, Monte da** Portugal
168 A2 **Pedra Preta** Brazil
166 B2 **Pedras r.** Brazil
169 F1 **Pedras de Maria da Cruz** Brazil
162 C2 **Pedraza La Vieja** Venezuela
162 C1 **Pedregal** Venezuela
168 E4 **Pedregulho** Brazil
166 D1 **Pedreiras** *Maranhão* Brazil
169 E5 **Pedreiras** *São Paulo* Brazil
102 F3 **Pedres h.** Spain
156 E3 **Pedriceña** Mexico
99 G3 **Pedro r.** Spain
101 F3 **Pedro Abad** Spain
166 C2 **Pedro Afonso** Brazil
173 K2 **Pedro Aramendia** Uruguay
158 C3 **Pedro Bank sea feature** Caribbean
99 F4 **Pedro Bernardo** Spain
159 C3 **Pedro Cays i.** Caribbean
158 C3 **Pedro Chico** Colombia
164 C4 **Pedro de Valdivia** Chile
98 B5 **Pedrógão** Portugal
98 B5 **Pedrógão Grande** Portugal
168 A3 **Pedro Gomes** *Mato Grosso do Sul* Brazil
167 B4 **Pedro Gomes** *Mato Grosso do Sul* Brazil
156 L7 **Pedro González, I. i.** Panama
162 D3 **Pedro II, Ilha reg.** Brazil
165 E4 **Pedro Juan Caballero** Paraguay
169 F3 **Pedro Leopoldo** Brazil
166 D1 **Pedroll** Brazil
173 F5 **Pedro Luro** Argentina
156 B2 **Pedro Mártir, Sa S. mountain range** Mexico
101 H1 **Pedro Muñoz** Spain
170 F3 **Pedro Osorio** Brazil
159 □1 **Pedro Pt pt** Jamaica
38 C4 **Pedro, Pt pt** Sri Lanka
98 B3 **Pedroso** Portugal
168 E6 **Pedro Toledo** Brazil
66 E5 **Peebles** *Scotland* U.K.
145 E5 **Pee Dee r.** *S. Carolina* U.S.A.
147 G4 **Peekskill** *New York* U.S.A.
13 G2 **Peel r.** *New South Wales* Australia
134 E3 **Peel r.** *N.W.T.* Canada
64 D3 **Peel** *Isle of Man*
73 J2 **Peene r.** Germany
73 J1 **Peenemünde** Germany
69 D3 **Peer** Belgium
136 F4 **Peers** *Alberta* Canada
13 E2 **Peery L. salt flat** *New South Wales* Australia
9 D5 **Pegasus Bay b.** New Zealand
73 H4 **Pegau** Germany
81 G3 **Peggau** Austria
106 C4 **Pegli** Italy
75 G3 **Pegnitz r.** Germany
75 G3 **Pegnitz** Germany
103 C6 **Pego** Spain
100 B2 **Pego do Altar, Barragem do resr** Portugal
24 A3 **Pegu div.** Myanmar
24 B3 **Pegu** Myanmar
22 A2 **Pegunungan Barisan mountain range** Indonesia
22 C1 **Pegunungan Iran mountain range** Indonesia
22 C1 **Pegunungan Kapuas Hulu mountain range** Indonesia/Malaysia
21 L7 **Pegunungan Maoke mountain range** Indonesia
22 C2 **Pegunungan Meratus mountain range** Indonesia
22 C1 **Pegunungan Muller mountain range** Indonesia
22 C2 **Pegunungan Schwaner mountain range** Indonesia
21 L7 **Pegunungan Van Rees mountain range** Indonesia
24 A3 **Pegu Yoma mountain range** Myanmar
63 H3 **Pegwell Bay b.** *England* U.K.
50 J2 **Pegysh** Rus. Fed.
113 F4 **Pehlivanköy** Turkey
173 G3 **Pehuajó** Argentina
173 G5 **Pehuén-Có** Argentina
33 H4 **Peikang** Taiwan
72 F3 **Peine** Germany
107 E2 **Peio** Italy
Peipsi Järve l. *see* **Peipus, Lake**
54 E2 **Peipus, Lake l.** Estonia/Rus. Fed.
115 E5 **Peiraias** Greece
82 B3 **Peisey-Nancroix** France
74 H4 **Peißen** *Sachsen-Anhalt* Germany
73 G4 **Peißen** *Sachsen-Anhalt* Germany
75 G5 **Peißenberg** Germany
75 F5 **Peiting** Germany
73 K4 **Peitz** Germany
168 D2 **Peixe r.** Brazil
166 C3 **Peixe** Brazil
168 B2 **Peixe, R. do r.** Brazil
169 G4 **Peixes r.** Brazil
168 B1 **Peixes, R. dos r.** Brazil
33 G1 **Pei Xian** China
33 G1 **Pei Xian** China
165 E3 **Peixo de Couro r.** Brazil
165 E2 **Peixoto de Azevedo r.** Brazil
68 E1 **Peize** Netherlands
22 A1 **Pejantan i.** Indonesia
22 B3 **Pekalongan** Indonesia
25 C7 **Pekan** Malaysia
52 E3 **Pekhlets** Rus. Fed.
148 C5 **Pekin** *Illinois* U.S.A.
Peking *see* **Beijing**
52 A3 **Peklino** Rus. Fed.
52 D1 **Peksha r.** Rus. Fed.
25 C7 **Pelabuhan Kelang** Malaysia
105 D7 **Pelagie, Isole is** Italy
114 C1 **Pelagonija plain** Macedonia
22 C2 **Pelaihari** Indonesia
114 D4 **Pelasgia** Greece
91 E4 **Pelat, Mont mt.** France
106 A4 **Pelat, Mt mt.** France
131 G4 **Pelatsoeu mt.** Lesotho
22 D1 **Pelawanbesar** Indonesia
76 D2 **Pelczyce** Poland
54 E3 **Pelēči** Latvia
140 D6 **Pelee I. i.** *Ontario* Canada
159 □4 **Pelée, Montagne volcano** *Martinique* Caribbean
140 D6 **Pelee Pt pt** *Ontario* Canada
23 □1 **Peleliu i.** Palau
21 H7 **Peleng i.** Indonesia
115 D5 **Peleta** Greece
78 E2 **Pelhřimov** Czech Rep.
134 E4 **Pelican** *Alaska* U.S.A.
15 E3 **Pelican Cr. r.** *Queensland* Australia
148 A1 **Pelican Lake l.** *Minnesota* U.S.A.
148 C3 **Pelican Lake l.** *Wisconsin* U.S.A.
137 J3 **Pelican Narrows** *Saskatchewan* Canada
53 B3 **Pelinia** Moldova
91 D5 **Pélissanne** France
114 C2 **Pelister mt.** Macedonia
114 C2 **Pelister nat. park** Macedonia
104 F4 **Peljeŝac pen.** Croatia
56 G2 **Pelkosenniemi** Finland
114 C1 **Pella div.** Greece
130 B4 **Pella** South Africa
111 E4 **Pellaro** Italy
137 H1 **Pellat Lake l.** *N.W.T.* Canada
173 F4 **Pellegrini** Argentina
172 D5 **Pellegrini, L. l.** Argentina
106 D4 **Pellegrino Parmense** Italy
93 C4 **Pellegrue** France
106 B4 **Pellice r.** Italy
107 E2 **Pellizzano** Italy
148 C4 **Pell Lake** *Wisconsin* U.S.A.
56 F2 **Pello** Finland
172 A3 **Pelluhue** Chile
72 D1 **Pellworm i.** Germany
136 B2 **Pelly r.** *Yukon Terr.* Canada
135 K3 **Pelly Bay** *N.W.T.* Canada
136 B2 **Pelly Crossing** *Yukon Terr.* Canada
137 J1 **Pelly Lake l.** *N.W.T.* Canada
136 C2 **Pelly Mountains mountain range** *Yukon Terr.* Canada
69 E4 **Pelm** Germany
22 D3 **Pelokang is** Indonesia
115 D5 **Peloponnisos div.** Greece
111 E5 **Peloritani, Monti mts** *Sicilia* Italy
111 E4 **Peloro, Capo c.** Italy
9 D4 **Pelorus Sd chan.** New Zealand
170 F3 **Pelotas** Brazil
173 L2 **Pelotas, Punta pt** Uruguay
167 B6 **Pelot, R. das r.** Brazil
76 G2 **Pelplin** Poland
119 F1 **Pelusium** Egypt
Pelusium, B. of b. *see* **Khalig el Tîna**
91 C3 **Pélussin** France
91 E4 **Pelvoux** France
91 E4 **Pelvoux, Mt mt.** France
52 G2 **Pelya-Khovanskaya** Rus. Fed.
147 J2 **Pemadumcook Lake l.** *Maine* U.S.A.
22 B3 **Pemalang** Indonesia
22 B1 **Pemangkat** Indonesia
25 B7 **Pematangsiantar** Indonesia
127 D7 **Pemba** Mozambique
125 E7 **Pemba** Zambia
127 D7 **Pemba, Baia de b.** Mozambique
127 C6 **Pemba Channel chan.** Tanzania
127 C6 **Pemba I. i.** Tanzania
17 A7 **Pemberton** *Western Australia* Australia
136 F4 **Pembina r.** *Alberta* Canada
150 D1 **Pembina** *N. Dakota* U.S.A.
62 B3 **Pembrey** *Wales* U.K.
62 D2 **Pembridge** *England* U.K.
147 K2 **Pembroke** *Maine* U.S.A.
141 G4 **Pembroke** *Ontario* Canada
62 B3 **Pembroke** *Wales* U.K.
62 B3 **Pembroke Dock** *Wales* U.K.
9 A6 **Pembroke, Mt mt.** New Zealand
62 A3 **Pembrokeshire div.** *Wales* U.K.
62 A3 **Pembrokeshire Coast National Park** *Wales* U.K.
22 C2 **Pembuanghulu** Indonesia
63 G3 **Pembury** *England* U.K.
75 H3 **Pemfling** Germany
22 B2 **Pemuar** Indonesia
172 A4 **Pemuco** Chile
24 A2 **Pen r.** Myanmar
38 A2 **Pen** India
53 G1 **Pena r.** Rus. Fed.
164 C4 **Pena Barrosa** Bolivia
172 B1 **Peña Blanca** Chile
99 H2 **Peñacerrada** Spain
102 C2 **Peña Collarada mt.** Spain
99 E2 **Peña Corada mt.** Spain
98 B4 **Penacova** Portugal
98 D4 **Peña de Francia mt.** Spain
99 G1 **Peña del Aro mt.** Spain
102 C2 **Peña de Oroel mt.** Spain
98 B3 **Penafiel** Portugal
99 F3 **Peñafiel** Spain
101 E3 **Peñaflor** Spain
99 H1 **Peña Gorbea mt.** Spain
159 □3 **Penal** Trinidad and Tobago
99 G4 **Peñalara mt.** Spain
102 C3 **Peñalba** Spain
166 C1 **Penalva** Brazil
98 C4 **Penalva do Castelo** Portugal
98 C4 **Penamacor** Portugal
157 F4 **Peñamiller** Mexico
98 D2 **Peña Negra mt.** Spain
157 F4 **Peña Nevada, Co mt.** Mexico
168 C4 **Penápolis** Brazil
99 F1 **Peña Prieta mt.** Spain
99 E4 **Peñaranda de Bracamonte** Spain
99 G3 **Peñaranda de Duero** Spain
101 E2 **Peñarroya-Pueblonuevo** Spain
101 H2 **Peñarrubia** Spain
62 C3 **Penarth** *Wales* U.K.
99 F1 **Peña Santa mt.** Spain
172 D4 **Peñas Blancas** Argentina
156 J7 **Peñas Blancas** Nicaragua
98 E1 **Peñas, Cabo de c.** Spain
156 B2 **Peñasco, Pto** Mexico
101 H2 **Peñascosa** Spain
103 B6 **Peñas de San Pedro** Spain
171 A6 **Penas, Golfo de g.** Chile
159 G5 **Peñas, Pta pt** Venezuela
98 D1 **Peña Treisa mt.** Spain
98 E1 **Peña Ubiña mt.** Spain
38 B1 **Pench r.** India
179 D5 **Penck, C. c.** Antarctica
22 C2 **Pendadahian** Indonesia
124 C2 **Pendé r.** Central African Rep.
62 A4 **Pendeen** *England* U.K.
122 B5 **Pendembu** Sierra Leone
16 C3 **Pender B. b.** *Western Australia* Australia
113 G4 **Pendik** Turkey
123 E4 **Pendjari, Parc National de la nat. park** Benin
65 F4 **Pendle Hill h.** *England* U.K.
152 C2 **Pendleton** *Oregon* U.S.A.
136 D4 **Pendleton Bay** *B.C.* Canada
22 A2 **Pendopo** Indonesia
152 C1 **Pend Oreille r.** *Washington* U.S.A.
152 C2 **Pend Oreille L. l.** *Idaho* U.S.A.
37 E5 **Pendra** India
98 B3 **Peneda Gerês, Parque Nacional da nat. park** Portugal
98 C4 **Penedono** Portugal
98 B4 **Penela** Portugal
123 E5 **Pénessoulou** Benin
141 F4 **Penetanguishene** *Ontario* Canada
32 D2 **Peng'an** China
38 B2 **Penganga r.** India
27 □ **Peng Chau i.** Hong Kong
33 H3 **P'eng-chia Hsü i.** Taiwan
131 H2 **Penge** South Africa
125 D5 **Penge** Zaire
33 G4 **P'eng-hu Lieh-tao is** Taiwan
33 G4 **Peng-hu Tao i.** Taiwan
22 B1 **Pengiki i.** Indonesia
25 □ **Peng Kang h.** Singapore
31 G5 **Penglai** China
32 C2 **Pengshan** China
32 E2 **Pengshui** China
32 D2 **Pengxi** China
33 G2 **Pengze** China
88 A3 **Penhir, Pte de pt** France
131 F5 **Penhoek Pass pass** South Africa
100 A1 **Peniche** Portugal
66 E5 **Penicuik** *Scotland* U.K.
22 C4 **Penida h.** Indonesia
50 E2 **Peninga** Rus. Fed.
25 D7 **Peninsular Malaysia pen.** Malaysia
111 E5 **Penisola della Maddalena pen.** *Sicilia* Italy
111 E5 **Penisola Magnisi pen.** *Sicilia* Italy
166 C2 **Penitente, Sa do reg.** Brazil
42 F3 **Penjwin** Iraq
62 D2 **Penkridge** *England* U.K.
73 K2 **Penkun** Germany
89 G2 **Penly** France
88 A4 **Penmarch** France
88 A4 **Penmarc'h, Pte de pt** France
107 G5 **Pennabilli** Italy
109 G2 **Penna, Pta della pt** Italy
109 F2 **Penne** Italy
93 C4 **Penne-d'Agenais** France
179 A5 **Pennell Coast coastal area** Antarctica
111 G2 **Penne, Punta pt** Italy
38 B3 **Penner r.** India
12 D3 **Penneshaw** *S. Australia* Australia
65 F3 **Pennines h.** *England* U.K.
147 F5 **Pennsville** *New Jersey* U.S.A.
146 D4 **Pennsylvania div.** U.S.A.
146 E3 **Penn Yan** *New York* U.S.A.
66 B4 **Pennyghael** *Scotland* U.K.
135 M3 **Penny Icecap ice cap** *N.W.T.* Canada
137 H2 **Pennylan Lake l.** *N.W.T.* Canada
179 B4 **Penny Pt pt** Antarctica
52 A1 **Peno** Rus. Fed.
147 J2 **Penobscot r.** *Maine* U.S.A.
147 J2 **Penobscot Bay b.** *Maine* U.S.A.
12 E4 **Penola** *S. Australia* Australia
103 D6 **Peñón de Ifach pt** Spain
12 C2 **Penong** *S. Australia* Australia
156 K7 **Penonomé** Panama
62 B2 **Penrhyn Mawr pt** *Wales* U.K.
65 F3 **Penrith** *England* U.K.
62 A4 **Penryn** *England* U.K.
145 C6 **Pensacola** *Florida* U.S.A.
179 B3 **Pensacola Mts mts** Antarctica
165 D2 **Pensamiento** Bolivia
13 E4 **Penshurst** *Victoria* Australia
114 C4 **Pentalofo** Greece
114 C2 **Pentalofos** Greece
6 □2 **Pentecost I. i.** Vanuatu
Pentecôte, Î. i. *see* **Pentecost I.**
88 C3 **Penthièvre reg.** France
136 F5 **Penticton** *B.C.* Canada
62 B4 **Pentire Point pt** *England* U.K.
15 F4 **Pentland** *Queensland* Australia
66 E2 **Pentland Firth chan.** *Scotland* U.K.
66 E5 **Pentland Hills h.** *Scotland* U.K.
66 F2 **Pentland Skerries is** *Scotland* U.K.
64 D4 **Pentraeth** *Wales* U.K.
62 C1 **Pentrefoelas** *Wales* U.K.
148 D4 **Pentwater** *Michigan* U.S.A.
22 A2 **Penuba** Indonesia
38 B3 **Penukonda** India
24 B3 **Penwegon** Myanmar
53 F1 **Peny** Rus. Fed.
62 C2 **Penybont** *Wales* U.K.
62 C2 **Pen-y-bont-fawr** *Wales* U.K.
62 C1 **Penycae** *Wales* U.K.
62 C2 **Penygadair h.** *Wales* U.K.
65 F3 **Pen-y-Ghent h.** *England* U.K.
52 F3 **Penza div.** Rus. Fed.
52 G3 **Penza** Rus. Fed.
62 A4 **Penzance** *England* U.K.
75 G5 **Penzberg** Germany
45 S3 **Penzhinskaya Guba b.** Rus. Fed.
45 S3 **Penzhino** Rus. Fed.
91 E4 **Péone** France
155 F5 **Peoria** *Arizona* U.S.A.
148 C5 **Peoria** *Illinois* U.S.A.
173 J1 **Pepe Nuñez** Uruguay
69 C4 **Pepingen** Belgium
69 D4 **Pepinster** Belgium
170 F2 **Pepiri Guaçú r.** Argentina/Brazil
114 A1 **Pëqin** Albania
79 G4 **Pér** Hungary
115 D4 **Perachora** Greece
15 E2 **Pera Hd headland** *Queensland* Australia
25 C6 **Perai** Malaysia
114 C2 **Peraia** Greece
25 C6 **Perak div.** Malaysia
25 B6 **Perak i.** Malaysia
25 C6 **Perak r.** Malaysia
100 E2 **Peraleda del Zaucejo** Spain
102 B4 **Peralejos de las Truchas** Spain
102 C4 **Perales del Alfambra** Spain
98 D4 **Perales del Puerto** Spain
102 B2 **Peralta** Spain
102 C2 **Peraltilla** Spain
114 B3 **Perama** *Ipeiros* Greece
115 F7 **Perama** *Kriti* Greece
38 B4 **Perambalur** India
56 F2 **Perämeri Bottenviken g.** Finland/Sweden
100 C3 **Peramora r.** Spain
57 F3 **Peräseinäjoki** Finland
139 H4 **Percé** *Québec* Canada
90 E3 **Percée, Pointe mt.** France
81 H2 **Perchtoldsdorf** Austria
16 D4 **Percival Lakes salt flat** *Western Australia* Australia
147 H2 **Percy** *New Hampshire* U.S.A.
88 D3 **Percy** France
172 E6 **Percy H. Scott** Argentina
15 G4 **Percy Is is** *Queensland* Australia
141 G4 **Percy Reach l.** *Ontario* Canada
108 B5 **Perdasdefogu** *Sardegna* Italy
131 G3 **Perdekop** South Africa
173 H2 **Perdices** Argentina
172 C2 **Perdida r.** Brazil
173 H4 **Perdido r.** Argentina
165 E4 **Perdido r.** Brazil
102 D2 **Perdido, Monte mt.** Spain
102 D2 **Perdiguère, Pic mt.** Spain
114 B3 **Perdika** Greece
114 C2 **Perdikkar** Greece
168 E3 **Perdizes** Brazil
169 F4 **Perdões** Brazil
79 M3 **Perechyn** Ukraine
98 D3 **Peredo** Portugal
44 H3 **Peregrebnoye** Rus. Fed.
162 B3 **Pereira** Colombia
168 C4 **Pereira Barreto** Brazil
100 C3 **Pereiro** Portugal
98 C2 **Pereiro de Aguiar** Spain
50 D3 **Perekhoda r.** Rus. Fed.
53 E1 **Perekopivka** Ukraine
51 G5 **Perelazovskiy** Rus. Fed.
46 D2 **Perelyub** Rus. Fed.
148 D4 **Pere Marquette r.** *Michigan* U.S.A.
179 C6 **Peremennyy, C. c.** Antarctica
52 F2 **Peremilovskiye Gory h.** Rus. Fed.
53 G2 **Peremoha** *Kharkivs'ka Oblast'* Ukraine
53 D1 **Peremoha** *Kyyivs'ka Oblast'* Ukraine
52 C2 **Peremyshl'** Rus. Fed.
53 A2 **Peremyshlyany** Ukraine
164 A2 **Perene** Peru
17 B6 **Perenjori** *Western Australia* Australia
98 E3 **Pereruela** Spain
53 F2 **Pereshchepyne** Ukraine
52 D1 **Pereslavl' Zalesskiy** Rus. Fed.
52 F3 **Pereshypkino Pervoye** Rus. Fed.
81 H3 **Pereszteg** Hungary
107 F5 **Peretola airport** Italy
Pereval Bedel pass *see* **Bedel Pass**
Pereval Torugart pass *see* **Turugart Pass**
79 M2 **Pereval Uzhots'kyy h.** Ukraine
52 F3 **Perevesinka** Rus. Fed.
53 E1 **Perevid r.** Ukraine
46 D2 **Perevolotskiy** Rus. Fed.
52 G2 **Perevoz** Rus. Fed.
31 K3 **Pereyaslavka** Rus. Fed.
53 D1 **Pereyaslav-Khmel'nyts'kyy** Ukraine
108 A4 **Perfugas** *Sardegna* Italy
81 F2 **Perg div.** Austria
81 F2 **Perg** Austria
173 G2 **Pergamino** Argentina
43 A1 **Perge** Turkey
107 F2 **Pergine Valsugana** Italy
107 G5 **Pergola** Italy
53 B1 **Perha** Ukraine
25 C6 **Perhentian Besar i.** Malaysia
56 G3 **Perho** Finland
141 J2 **Péribonca** *Québec* Canada
141 K1 **Péribonca, Lac l.** *Québec* Canada
170 C1 **Perico** Argentina
156 D3 **Pericos** Mexico
112 F1 **Perieni** Romania
88 D2 **Périers** France
92 C4 **Périgord reg.** France
92 C3 **Périgord Blanc reg.** France
93 C4 **Périgord Noir reg.** France
92 C3 **Périgueux** France
162 C2 **Perijá, Parque Nacional nat. park** Venezuela
114 E3 **Peristera i.** Greece
114 C2 **Peristera** Greece
115 E4 **Peristerio** Greece
114 E1 **Perithorio** Greece
171 B6 **Perito Moreno** Argentina
171 B6 **Perito Moreno, Parque Nacional nat. park** Argentina
166 D1 **Peritoró** Brazil
114 B3 **Perivoli** Greece
148 D3 **Perkins** *Michigan* U.S.A.
53 B2 **Perkivtsi** Ukraine
74 B3 **Perl** Germany
156 K6 **Perlas, Laguna de lag.** Nicaragua
156 K6 **Perlas, Pta de pt** Nicaragua
73 G2 **Perleberg** Germany
77 L3 **Perlejewo** Poland
75 J4 **Perlesreut** Germany
52 D4 **Perlevka** Rus. Fed.
25 C6 **Perlis div.** Malaysia
77 N1 **Perloja** Lithuania
77 K1 **Perły** Poland
44 G4 **Perm'** Rus. Fed.
50 H3 **Permas** Rus. Fed.
114 B2 **Përmet** Albania
52 G2 **Permisi** Rus. Fed.
107 J4 **Permuda i.** Croatia
54 E1 **Pernå** Finland
166 E2 **Pernambuco div.** Brazil
78 C2 **Pernarec** Czech Rep.
12 D2 **Pernatty Lagoon salt flat** *S. Australia* Australia
81 G3 **Pernegg an der Mur** Austria
91 D5 **Pernes-les-Fontaines** France
114 F1 **Perni** Greece
112 D3 **Pernik** Bulgaria
54 C1 **Perniö** Finland
68 C3 **Pernis** Netherlands
81 G3 **Pernitz** Austria
83 E3 **Pero** Italy
91 B5 **Pérols** France
90 D2 **Péronne** France
14 B2 **Peron Is is** *Northern Terr.* Australia
90 D2 **Péronnas** France
86 B3 **Péronne** France
17 A5 **Peron Pen. pen.** *Western Australia* Australia
106 B4 **Perosa Argentina** Italy
157 F5 **Perote** Mexico
90 D3 **Pérouges** France
93 E6 **Perpignan** *Pyrénées-Orientales* France
93 E6 **Perpignan-Rivesaltes airport** France
172 B4 **Perquilauquén r.** Chile
62 A4 **Perranporth** *England* U.K.
90 C2 **Perrecy-les-Forges** France
90 C2 **Perreux** France
154 D5 **Perris** *California* U.S.A.
100 D4 **Perro, Pta del pt** Spain
88 B3 **Perros-Guirec** France
145 D6 **Perry** *Florida* U.S.A.
145 D5 **Perry** *Georgia* U.S.A.
150 E3 **Perry** *Iowa* U.S.A.
151 D4 **Perry** *Oklahoma* U.S.A.
146 B4 **Perrysburg** *Ohio* U.S.A.
151 C4 **Perryton** *Texas* U.S.A.
151 F4 **Perryville** *Missouri* U.S.A.
86 B3 **Persan** France
81 G2 **Persenbeug** Austria
8 □2 **Perseverance Harbour inlet** *Campbell I.* New Zealand
165 D2 **Perseverancia** Bolivia
59 G2 **Pershagen** Sweden
53 E2 **Pershe Travnya** Ukraine
62 D2 **Pershore** *England* U.K.
53 G2 **Pershotravens'k** Ukraine
53 G3 **Pershotravneve** *Donets'ka Oblast'* Ukraine
53 C1 **Pershotravneve** *Zhytomyrs'ka Oblast'* Ukraine
Persia *see* **Iran**
Persian Gulf g. *see* **Gulf,The**
59 E3 **Perstorp** Sweden
42 D2 **Pertek** Turkey
141 G4 **Perth** *Ontario* Canada
66 E4 **Perth** *Scotland* U.K.
13 F5 **Perth** *Tasmania* Australia
17 A6 **Perth** *Western Australia* Australia
147 F4 **Perth Amboy** *New Jersey* U.S.A.
147 K1 **Perth-Andover** *New Brunswick* Canada
69 C5 **Perthes** *Champagne-Ardenne* France
86 B4 **Perthes** *Île-de-France* France

150 D3 Pipestone Minnesota U.S.A.
173 J3 Pipinas Argentina
8 E3 Pipiriki New Zealand
141 K2 Pipmuacan, Réservoir resr Québec Canada
88 D4 Pipriac France
47 K4 Piqanlik China
146 A4 Piqua Ohio U.S.A.
99 H2 Piqueras, Pto de pass Spain
169 F5 Piquete Brazil
168 A2 Piquiri r. Brazil
168 D3 Piracanjuba r. Brazil
168 D2 Piracanjuba Brazil
169 G3 Piracicaba r. Brazil
168 E5 Piracicaba Brazil
168 E4 Piraçununga Brazil
166 D1 Piracuruca Brazil
168 D6 Piraí do Sul Brazil
168 D5 Piraju Brazil
168 D3 Pirajuba Brazil
168 D4 Pirajuí Brazil
42 G1 Pirallahı Adası Azerbaijan
36 C5 Piram I. i. India
107 H3 Piran Slovenia
170 E2 Pirané Argentina
169 G4 Piranga r. Brazil
169 G4 Piranga Brazil
168 C2 Piranhas r. Brazil
168 C2 Piranhas Goiás Brazil
169 G4 Pirapetinga Brazil
168 C5 Pirapó r. Brazil
169 F2 Pirapora Brazil
168 C5 Pirapozinho Brazil
168 D6 Piraquara Brazil
173 K2 Pirarajá Uruguay
170 F3 Piratini r. Brazil
170 F3 Piratini Brazil
169 E1 Piratininga r. Brazil
169 D5 Piratininga Brazil
170 F2 Piray r. Argentina
77 N1 Pirčiupiai Lithuania
168 D1 Pirenópolis Brazil
168 D2 Pires do Rio Brazil
114 B2 Pirg Albania
37 G4 Pirganj Bangladesh
166 C1 Piriá r. Brazil
88 C4 Piriac-sur-Mer France
173 K3 Piriápolis Uruguay
114 E1 Pirin Bulgaria
169 H1 Piripá Brazil
166 D1 Piripiri Brazil
162 D1 Píritu Venezuela
167 A4 Pirizal Brazil
81 G3 Pirka Austria
74 C3 Pirmasens Germany
75 J2 Pirna Germany
64 C2 Pirnmill Scotland U.K.
99 F3 Pirón r. Spain
8 E2 Pirongia volcano New Zealand
8 E2 Pirongia New Zealand
112 D3 Pirot Yugoslavia
36 C2 Pir Panjal Pass pass India
36 C2 Pir Panjal Range mountain range India
21 J7 Piru Indonesia
107 E5 Pisa div. Toscana Italy
77 K2 Pisa r. Poland
106 E5 Pisa Italy
164 B3 Pisagua Chile
9 B6 Pisa, Mt mt. New Zealand
147 F4 Piscataway New Jersey U.S.A.
81 G3 Pischelsdorf in der Steiermark Austria
109 H4 Pisciotta Italy
164 A2 Pisco r. Peru
164 A2 Pisco Peru
164 A2 Pisco, B. de b. Peru
172 B1 Pisco Elqui Chile
147 F3 Piseco Lake l. New York U.S.A.
78 D2 Písek Czech Rep.
9 C6 Pisgah, Mt mt. New Zealand
47 J5 Pishan China
77 M4 Pishcha Ukraine
53 C2 Pishchana Ukraine
53 D2 Pishchane Ukraine
53 C2 Pishchanka Ukraine
39 E4 Pīshīn Iran
36 A3 Pishin Pakistan
36 A3 Pishin Lora r. Afghanistan/Pakistan
53 C1 Piskivka Ukraine
114 C2 Pisoderi Greece
165 D2 Piso Firme Bolivia
106 E3 Pisogne Italy
93 B4 Pissos France
157 H4 Pisté Mexico
114 C3 Pistiana Greece
109 J4 Pisticci Italy
107 E5 Pistoia div. Italy
107 E5 Pistoia Italy
52 E1 Pistsovo Rus. Fed.
99 G1 Pisueña r. Spain
99 F3 Pisuerga r. Spain
77 K2 Pisz Poland
77 M4 Piszczac Poland
152 B3 Pit r. California U.S.A.
122 B4 Pita Guinea
139 G3 Pitaga Newfoundland Canada
157 H5 Pital Mexico
162 B3 Pitalito Colombia
168 C6 Pitanga Brazil
168 D4 Pitangueiras Brazil
169 F3 Pitangui Brazil
13 E3 Pitarpunga L. l. New South Wales Australia
7 □14 Pitcairn Island territory Pacific Ocean
159 □3 Pitch Lake Trinidad Trinidad and Tobago
56 F2 Piteå Sweden
56 E2 Piteälven r. Sweden
52 E2 Pitelino Rus. Fed.
51 H5 Piterka Rus. Fed.
112 E2 Pitești Romania
38 C2 Pithapuram India
17 B6 Pithara Western Australia Australia
86 B4 Pithiviers France
36 E3 Pithoragarh India
23 □2 Piti Guam Pacific Ocean
108 D2 Pitigliano Italy
93 A6 Pitillas Spain
153 D6 Pitiquito Mexico
12 B1 Pitjantjatjara Lands Aboriginal Land nat. park S. Australia Australia
50 D2 Pitkyaranta Rus. Fed.
66 E4 Pitlochry Scotland U.K.
6 □6 Pitman Reefs reef Fiji
124 B2 Pitoa Cameroon
78 G6 Pitomača Croatia
127 □5 Piton de la Fournaise mt. Réunion Indian Ocean
127 □4 Piton de la Petite R. Noire r. Mauritius
127 □5 Piton des Neiges mt. Réunion Indian Ocean
156 J6 Pito Solo Honduras
101 G4 Pitres Spain
172 A5 Pitrufquén Chile
131 E2 Pitsane Siding Botswana
66 F4 Pitscottie Scotland U.K.
131 G4 Pitseng Lesotho
63 F2 Pitsford Res. resr England U.K.
69 B4 Pittem Belgium
66 D3 Pittentrail Scotland U.K.
66 F4 Pittenweem Scotland U.K.
136 D4 Pitt I. i. B.C. Canada
9 □1 Pitt I. i. Chatham Is New Zealand
162 □ Pitt, Pta pt Galapagos Is Ecuador
151 E4 Pittsburg Kansas U.S.A.
146 D4 Pittsburgh Pennsylvania U.S.A.
148 B6 Pittsfield Illinois U.S.A.
147 J2 Pittsfield Maine U.S.A.
147 G3 Pittsfield Massachusetts U.S.A.
147 H3 Pittsfield New Hampshire U.S.A.
147 G3 Pittsfield Vermont U.S.A.
9 □1 Pitt Strait str. Chatham Is New Zealand
15 G5 Pittsworth Queensland Australia
14 D4 Pituri Cr. watercourse Queensland Australia
79 K5 Pitvaros Hungary
137 K2 Pitz Lake l. N.W.T. Canada
80 B3 Pitztal v. Austria
169 F4 Piuí Brazil
166 C3 Pium Brazil
162 A5 Piura Peru
54 E3 Piusa r. Estonia
154 C4 Piute Peak summit California U.S.A.
37 E3 Piuthan Nepal
140 D1 Pivabiska r. Ontario Canada
77 N1 Pivašiūnai Lithuania
53 D3 Pivdennyy Buh r. Ukraine
162 C1 Pivijay Colombia
107 J3 Pivka r. Slovenia
107 J3 Pivka Slovenia
53 F3 Pivostriv Chonhar pen. Ukraine
77 J6 Piwniczna Poland
36 D1 Pixa China
157 H5 Pixoyal Mexico
164 C3 Pizacoma Peru
101 F4 Pizarra Spain
83 E2 Piz Bernina mt. Italy/Switzerland
83 F2 Piz Buin mt. Austria/Switzerland
83 E2 Piz d'Anarosa mt. Switzerland
83 E2 Piz Duan mt. Switzerland
83 E2 Piz Ela mt. Switzerland
123 F5 Pizhi Nigeria
50 J3 Pizhma r. Rus. Fed.
50 H3 Pizhma Rus. Fed.
83 E2 Piz Kesch mt. Switzerland
83 D2 Piz Medel mt. Switzerland
83 E2 Pizol mt. Switzerland
83 F2 Piz Pisoc mt. Switzerland
83 E2 Piz Platta mt. Switzerland
83 E2 Piz Varuna mt. Italy/Switzerland
106 D3 Pizzighettone Italy
111 F4 Pizzo Italy
83 E3 Pizzo Arera mt. Italy
83 F3 Pizzo della Presolana mt. Italy
106 E2 Pizzo di Coca mt. Italy
109 G3 Pizzoferrato Italy
109 F2 Pizzoli Italy
83 D2 Pizzo Rotondo mt. Switzerland
23 □1 Pkurengei pt Palau
88 A3 Plabennec France
139 K4 Placentia Newfoundland Canada
139 K4 Placentia B. b. Newfoundland Canada
23 B4 Placer Philippines
23 C4 Placer Philippines
154 B2 Placerville California U.S.A.
155 H2 Placerville Colorado U.S.A.
164 C2 Plácido de Castro Brazil
173 L2 Plácido Rosas Uruguay
64 C2 Pladda i. Scotland U.K.
82 C2 Plaffeien Switzerland
91 C5 Plage de Piémanson beach France
87 G2 Plaidt Germany
87 G4 Plaine d'Alsace v. France
89 E2 Plaine de Caen plain France
124 D1 Plaine de Garar plain Chad
87 E3 Plaine de la Woëvre plain France
127 □4 Plaine des Roches plain Mauritius
120 D2 Plaine de Tamlelt plain Morocco
90 C3 Plaine du Forez plain France
121 E3 Plaine du Tidikelt plain Algeria
87 E4 Plaine Lorraine plain France
90 B2 Plaines de la Loire et de l'Allier plain France
92 C2 Plaines et Seuil du Poitou plain France
87 G4 Plainfaing France
147 H4 Plainfield Connecticut U.S.A.
148 C5 Plainfield Illinois U.S.A.
148 C3 Plainfield Wisconsin U.S.A.
88 C3 Plaintel France
148 A3 Plainview Minnesota U.S.A.
150 D3 Plainview Nebraska U.S.A.
151 C5 Plainview Texas U.S.A.
93 C5 Plaisance France
93 D5 Plaisance-du-Touch France
147 J1 Plaisted Maine U.S.A.
22 A2 Plaju Indonesia
114 G3 Plaka Greece
43 C2 Plakoti, C. pt Cyprus
45 T3 Plamennyy Rus. Fed.
136 G4 Plamondon Alberta Canada
22 D4 Plampang Indonesia
78 B2 Planá Czech Rep.
154 B3 Planada California U.S.A.
168 E1 Planaltina Brazil
169 H1 Planalto Brazil
166 E2 Planalto da Borborema plat. Brazil
166 B3 Planalto de Mato Grosso plat. Brazil
169 H2 Planalto do Brasil plat. Brazil
168 A1 Planalto do Mato Grosso plat. Brazil
166 B1 Planalto Maracanaquará plat. Brazil
129 F2 Planalto Moçambicano plat. Mozambique
102 C3 Planas de Elena plain Spain
82 B1 Plancher-Bas France
172 B3 Planchón, P. de pass Argentina
88 C3 Plancoët France
91 D4 Plan-de-Baux France
73 H3 Plane r. Germany
80 C2 Planegg Germany
162 B2 Planeta Rica Colombia
84 E2 Planèze reg. France
75 J3 Plánice Czech Rep.
172 D4 Planicie de la Loma Negra plain Argentina
91 D5 Planier, Île de i. France
81 F5 Planina Slovenia
81 G4 Planina Slovenia
150 D3 Plankinton S. Dakota U.S.A.
148 C5 Plano Illinois U.S.A.
151 D5 Plano Texas U.S.A.
83 F1 Plansee l. Austria
159 □1 Plantain Garden Jamaica
172 B2 Planta Los Queltehues Chile
145 D7 Plantation Florida U.S.A.
93 D6 Plantaurel, Montagnes du h. France
168 D4 Planura Brazil
151 F6 Plaquemine Louisiana U.S.A.
98 D4 Plasencia Spain
77 M2 Płaska Poland
104 E3 Plaški Croatia
59 E1 Plassen Norway
46 F2 Plast Rus. Fed.
147 K1 Plaster Rock New Brunswick Canada
131 H2 Plaston South Africa
79 H3 Plášťovce Slovakia
78 C2 Plasy Czech Rep.
162 A4 Plata, I. la i. Ecuador
110 C5 Platani r. Sicilia Italy
114 E3 Platania Greece
111 F3 Platania Italy
115 F4 Platanistos Greece
115 C5 Platanos Dytiki Ellas Greece
115 E7 Platanos Kriti Greece
115 F7 Platanos Kriti Greece
130 B5 Platbakkies South Africa
131 G4 Platberg mt. South Africa
73 G2 Plate Germany
123 F5 Plateau div. Nigeria
118 D4 Plateau de Basso plat. Chad
91 D3 Plateau de Chambaran plat. France
123 E5 Plateau de Danyi plat. Togo
92 E3 Plateau de Gentioux plat. France
90 D1 Plateau de Haute-Saône plat. France
125 E6 Plateau de la Manika plat. Zaire
90 C1 Plateau de Langres plat. France
69 C5 Plateau de l'Ardenne plat. Belgium
92 D3 Plateau de Millevaches plat. France
91 E5 Plateau de Valensole plat. France
87 E4 Plateau du Barrois plat. France
91 C4 Plateau du Coiron plat. France
123 G2 Plateau du Djado plat. Niger
121 F3 Plateau du Fadnoun plat. Algeria
123 G2 Plateau du Manguéni plat. Niger
121 E3 Plateau du Tademaït plat. Algeria
123 G2 Plateau du Tchigaï plat. Niger
121 F3 Plateau du Tinrhert plat. Algeria
87 F4 Plateau Lorrain plat. France
Plateau of Tibet plat. see Xizang Gaoyuan
124 C4 Plateaux div. Congo
125 B4 Plateaux Batéké plat. Congo
92 D2 Plateaux de la Marche plat. France
92 D3 Plateaux du Limousin plat. France
77 L3 Platerów Poland
75 L1 Platerówka Poland
112 B2 Platičevo Yugoslavia
134 B4 Platinum Alaska U.S.A.
162 C2 Plato Colombia
47 M2 Plato Alash reg. Rus. Fed.
46 D4 Plato Kendyrli-Kayasanskoye plat. Kazakhstan
46 E4 Plato Ustyurt plat. Uzbekistan
131 G3 Platrand South Africa
150 C3 Platte r. Nebraska U.S.A.
148 B4 Platteville Wisconsin U.S.A.
75 H4 Plattling Germany
147 G2 Plattsburgh New York U.S.A.
150 E3 Plattsmouth Nebraska U.S.A.
114 D2 Platy Greece
114 D3 Platykampos Greece
115 F6 Platys Gialos Greece
73 H2 Plau Germany
75 F2 Plaue Germany
75 H2 Plauen Germany
73 H2 Plauer See l. Germany
112 B3 Plav Yugoslavia
54 D3 Pļaviņas Latvia
52 E3 Plavitsa r. Rus. Fed.
107 J4 Plavnik i. Croatia
52 C3 Plavsk Rus. Fed.
97 □ Playa Blanca Canary Is Spain
100 D3 Playa de Castilla beach Spain
153 E6 Playa Noriega, L. l. Mexico
162 A4 Playas Ecuador
25 E4 Plây Cu Vietnam
14 D3 Playford watercourse Northern Terr. Australia
137 K4 Playgreen L. l. Manitoba Canada
156 C3 Playón Mexico
101 F2 Plaza del Judío mt. Spain
172 C5 Plaza Huincul Argentina
147 J4 Pleasant Bay b. Massachusetts U.S.A.
155 G1 Pleasant Grove Utah U.S.A.
155 F5 Pleasant, Lake l. Arizona U.S.A.
155 H5 Pleasanton New Mexico U.S.A.
151 D6 Pleasanton Texas U.S.A.
9 C6 Pleasant Point New Zealand
155 H3 Pleasant View Colorado U.S.A.
147 F5 Pleasantville New Jersey U.S.A.
144 C4 Pleasure Ridge Park Kentucky U.S.A.
92 E3 Pleaux France
78 C3 Plechý mt. Czech Rep.
88 C3 Plédran France
25 D4 Plei Doch Vietnam
88 D3 Pleine-Fougères France
75 F3 Pleinfeld Germany
75 H2 Pleiße r. Germany
88 C4 Plélan-le-Grand France
88 C3 Plélan-le-Petit France
88 C3 Plélo France
88 C3 Plémet France
88 C3 Plénée-Jugon France
88 C3 Pléneuf-Val-André France
14 D4 Plenty watercourse Northern Terr. Australia
8 F2 Plenty, Bay of b. New Zealand
152 F1 Plentywood Montana U.S.A.
88 C3 Plérin France
52 G3 Ples Rus. Fed.
52 E1 Ples Rus. Fed.
50 G2 Plesetsk Rus. Fed.
52 D1 Pleshcheyevo, Oz. l. Rus. Fed.
47 G1 Pleshkovo Rus. Fed.
88 D4 Plessé France
141 K3 Plessisville Québec Canada
88 B3 Plestin-les-Grèves France
76 F4 Pleszew Poland
139 F3 Plétipi L. l. Québec Canada
72 C4 Plettenberg Germany
130 D7 Plettenberg Bay South Africa
81 F3 Pletzen mt. Austria
88 B3 Pleubian France
88 D3 Pleudihen-sur-Rance France
88 B3 Pleumeur-Bodou France
88 A4 Pleuven France
112 E3 Pleven Bulgaria
88 B3 Pleyben France
88 B3 Pleyber-Christ France
103 B7 Pliego Spain
79 J3 Pliešovce Slovakia
83 F2 Plima r. Italy
9 E4 Plimmerton New Zealand
73 K3 Pliszka r. Poland
104 E3 Plješevica mountain range Croatia
112 B3 Pljevlja Yugoslavia
108 A4 Ploaghe Sardegna Italy
88 A4 Plobannalec France
87 G4 Plobsheim France
104 F4 Ploče Croatia
77 H3 Płock div. Poland
77 H3 Płock Poland
107 G2 Plöckenpass pass Austria/Italy
104 F4 Pločno mt. Bos.-Herz.
54 G1 Plodovoye Rus. Fed.
69 A4 Ploegsteert Belgium
88 B4 Ploemeur France
88 C4 Ploeren France
88 C4 Ploërmel France
88 C3 Plœuc-sur-Lié France
88 A4 Plogastel-St-Germain France
88 A3 Plogoff France
73 J1 Plogshagen Germany
112 F2 Ploiești Romania
113 F5 Plomari Greece
92 E3 Plomb du Cantal mt. France
87 F5 Plombières-les-Bains France
88 A4 Plomeur France
88 A3 Plomodiern France
72 F1 Plön Germany
137 H3 Plonge, Lac la l. Saskatchewan Canada
73 L2 Płonia r. Poland
77 J3 Płońsk Poland
112 F2 Plopeni Romania
52 D3 Ploskosh' Rus. Fed.
50 G3 Ploskoye Rus. Fed.
77 J2 Płośnica Poland
76 D2 Ploty Poland
73 H3 Plötzin Germany
88 C3 Plouagat France
88 B3 Plouaret France
88 A3 Plouarzel France
88 B4 Plouay France
88 C3 Ploubalay France
88 B3 Ploubazlanec France
88 B3 Ploubezre France
78 D1 Ploučnice r. Czech Rep.
88 A3 Ploudalmézeau France
88 A3 Ploudiry France
88 A3 Plouescat France
88 C3 Plouézec France
88 C3 Ploufragan France
88 B3 Plougasnou France
88 A3 Plougastel-Daoulas France
88 A3 Plougonvelin France
88 B3 Plougonven France
88 B3 Plougrescant France
88 C3 Plouguenast France
88 A3 Plouguerneau France
88 B3 Plouguernével France
88 B3 Plouguiel France
88 B3 Plouguin France
88 C3 Plouha France
88 A3 Plouhinec Finistère France
88 B4 Plouhinec Morbihan France
88 B3 Plouigneau France
88 B3 Ploumilliau France
88 A3 Plounévez-Lochrist France
88 B3 Plounévez-Moëdec France
88 A3 Plouvien France
88 A3 Plouzané France
88 A3 Plouzévédé France
114 F1 Plovdiv div. Bulgaria
112 E3 Plovdiv Bulgaria
148 C3 Plover r. Wisconsin U.S.A.
148 C3 Plover Wisconsin U.S.A.
27 □ Plover Cove Res. resr Hong Kong
88 A4 Plozévet France
157 F6 Pluma Hidalgo Mexico
88 C4 Plumelec France
88 C4 Pluméliau France
88 C4 Plumergat France
147 G4 Plum I. i. New York U.S.A.
152 C2 Plummer Idaho U.S.A.
128 D3 Plumtree Zimbabwe
88 C4 Pluneret France
54 B4 Plungė Lithuania
88 B4 Pluvigner France
112 B3 Plužine Yugoslavia
54 E4 Plyeshchanitsy Belarus
24 B3 Ply Huey Wati, Khao mt. Myanmar/Thailand
62 C4 Plym r. England U.K.
154 B2 Plymouth California U.S.A.
62 B4 Plymouth England U.K.
148 D5 Plymouth Indiana U.S.A.
147 H4 Plymouth Massachusetts U.S.A.
159 G3 Plymouth Montserrat Caribbean
147 H3 Plymouth New Hampshire U.S.A.
144 F3 Plymouth Pennsylvania U.S.A.
159 □2 Plymouth Tobago Trinidad and Tobago
148 D4 Plymouth Wisconsin U.S.A.
147 H4 Plymouth Bay b. Massachusetts U.S.A.
62 B4 Plympton England U.K.
62 B4 Plymstock England U.K.
62 C2 Plynlimon h. Wales U.K.
53 C2 Plyskiv Ukraine
53 E1 Plysky Ukraine
54 F2 Plyussa r. Rus. Fed.
54 F2 Plyussa Rus. Fed.
78 C2 Plzeň Czech Rep.
77 K3 Pniewo Poland
76 E3 Pniewy Poznań Poland
77 J4 Pniewy Radom Poland
107 G4 Po r. Italy
122 D4 Pô Burkina
175 L8 Pobeda Ice Island ice feature Indian Ocean
75 H3 Poběžovice Czech Rep.
76 F3 Pobiedziska Poland
98 E2 Pobladura del Valle Spain
76 D2 Pobrzeże reg. Poland
76 F1 Pobrzeże Koszalińskie reg. Poland
53 D2 Pobuz'ke Ukraine
151 F4 Pocahontas Arkansas U.S.A.
146 C5 Pocatalico r. W. Virginia U.S.A.
152 D3 Pocatello Idaho U.S.A.
81 G1 Počátky Czech Rep.
126 B3 Pochala Sudan
53 A1 Pochayiv Ukraine
52 A3 Pochep Rus. Fed.
52 G2 Pochinki Rus. Fed.
52 A2 Pochinok Rus. Fed.
81 G2 Pöchlarn Austria
172 E1 Pocho, Sa de mountain range Argentina
172 A4 Pocilla Chile
101 F1 Pocito, Sierra del mountain range Spain
67 B5 Pocket, The h. Rep. of Ireland
75 J4 Pocking Germany
65 H4 Pocklington England U.K.
166 D3 Poço r. Brazil
166 D2 Poco r. Brazil
169 H1 Poções Brazil
169 F4 Poço Fundo Brazil
147 F5 Pocomoke City Maryland U.S.A.
147 F6 Pocomoke Sound b. U.S.A.
167 A4 Poconé Brazil
147 F4 Pocono Mountains h. Pennsylvania U.S.A.
147 F4 Pocono Summit Pennsylvania U.S.A.
169 E4 Poços de Caldas Brazil
114 D1 Podareš Macedonia
79 J2 Podbiel Slovakia
78 C1 Podbořany Czech Rep.
81 E4 Podbrdo Slovenia
81 G4 Podčetrtek Slovenia
76 G4 Poddębice Poland
50 D3 Poddor'ye Rus. Fed.
78 E1 Poděbrady Czech Rep.
93 B4 Podensac France
76 E2 Podgaje Poland
112 C3 Podgorac Yugoslavia
51 F5 Podgorenskiy Rus. Fed.
112 B3 Podgorica Montenegro Yugoslavia
81 F4 Podgorica Slovenia
114 B2 Podgorie Albania
77 L2 Podgórze Poland
107 J3 Podgrad Slovenia
38 B3 Podile India
107 G3 Po di Levante r. Italy
53 C3 Podisul Moldavei Centrale plat. Moldova
112 G1 Podișul Moldovei Centrale reg. Moldova
53 B2 Podișul Moldovei de Nord plat. Moldova
81 H2 Podivín Czech Rep.
45 L3 Podkamennaya Tunguska r. Rus. Fed.
52 D2 Podkhozheye Rus. Fed.
114 G1 Podkova Bulgaria
51 H5 Podlesnoye Rus. Fed.
162 B4 Podocarpus, Parque Nacional nat. park Ecuador
114 F2 Podochori Greece
114 C4 Podogora Greece
112 F1 Podoleni Romania
52 C2 Podol'sk Rus. Fed.
122 B3 Podor Senegal
52 E1 Podozerskiy Rus. Fed.
50 E2 Podporozh'ye Rus. Fed.
78 G5 Podravina reg. Croatia
104 F3 Podravska Slatina Croatia
81 G4 Podsreda Slovenia
81 H4 Podturen Croatia
112 C3 Podujevo Yugoslavia
79 H2 Podvysoká Slovakia
50 G2 Podyuga Rus. Fed.
73 G1 Poel i. Germany
129 F4 Poelela, Lagoa lag. Mozambique
130 B4 Pofadder South Africa
140 E3 Pogamasing Ontario Canada
52 A3 Pogar Rus. Fed.
73 J1 Poggendorf Germany
81 F4 Poggersdorf Austria
111 H2 Poggiardo Italy
107 F5 Poggibonsi Italy
108 C2 Poggio Ballone h. Italy
109 E2 Poggio Bustone Italy
108 D2 Poggio Lecci h. Italy
108 B2 Poggio-Mezzana Corse France
109 E2 Poggio Moiano Italy
107 F4 Poggio Renatico Italy
109 J4 Poggiorsini Italy
107 F4 Poggio Rusco Italy
81 G2 Pöggstall Austria
108 A4 Poglina, Pta di pt Sardegna Italy
112 F2 Pogoanele Romania
114 B3 Pogoniani Greece
52 B1 Pogoreloye-Gorodishche Rus. Fed.
76 F4 Pogorzela Poland
52 C4 Pogozheye Rus. Fed.
114 B2 Pogradec Albania
168 A2 Poguba r. Brazil
31 J5 P'ohang South Korea
54 C1 Pohja Finland
56 H3 Pohjois-Karjala div. Finland
4 G4 Pohnpei i. Fed. States of Micronesia
78 F3 Pohořelice Czech Rep.
81 G4 Pohorje mountain range Slovenia
53 E2 Pohreby Ukraine
53 C2 Pohrebyshche Ukraine
36 D4 Pohri India
79 H3 Pohronská pahorkatina mts Slovakia
112 D3 Poiana Mare Romania
79 M6 Poiana Ruscă, Munții mountain range Romania
112 E1 Poiana Stampei Romania
125 D4 Poie Zaire
52 F3 Poim Rus. Fed.
6 □2 Poindimié New Caledonia Pacific Ocean
179 C6 Poinsett, C. c. Antarctica
154 A2 Point Arena California U.S.A.
134 C2 Point Barrow c. Alaska U.S.A.
12 D3 Point Broughton S. Australia Australia
154 B4 Point Buchon pt California U.S.A.
141 H3 Point-Comfort Québec Canada
158 D3 Pointe-à-Gravois pt Haiti
159 □3 Pointe-à-Pierre Trinidad Trinidad and Tobago
159 □5 Pointe-à-Pitre Guadeloupe Caribbean
140 E4 Pointe au Baril Sta. Ontario Canada
141 J2 Pointe-Bleue Québec Canada
172 C2 Pointe del Inca Argentina
125 B4 Pointe-Noire Congo
159 □3 Point Fortin Trinidad and Tobago
9 □1 Point Gap pt Chatham Is New Zealand
134 B3 Point Hope c. Alaska U.S.A.
134 B3 Point Hope Alaska U.S.A.
12 C3 Point Kenny S. Australia Australia
136 G1 Point Lake l. N.W.T. Canada
62 C1 Point of Ayr pt Wales U.K.
140 D6 Point Pelee National Park nat. park Ontario Canada
147 F4 Point Pleasant New Jersey U.S.A.
146 B5 Point Pleasant W. Virginia U.S.A.
154 A2 Point Reyes pt California U.S.A.
159 □3 Point Rouge pt Trinidad Trinidad and Tobago
106 B4 Poirino Italy
90 B1 Poiseux France
141 H4 Poisson Blanc, Lac du l. Québec Canada
16 B3 Poissonnier Pt pt Western Australia Australia
87 E4 Poissons France
92 C2 Poitiers France
92 C2 Poitiers-Biard airport France
27 □ Poi Toi I. i. Hong Kong
92 B2 Poitou reg. France
92 B2 Poitou-Charentes div. France
89 G2 Poix-de-Picardie France
86 D3 Poix-Terron France
83 F2 Poja r. Italy
114 B2 Pojan Albania
76 C3 Pojezierze Lubuskie reg. Poland
77 J2 Pojezierze Mazurskie reg. Poland
76 F2 Pojezierze Pomorskie reg. Poland
76 F3 Pojezierze Wielkopolskie reg. Poland
164 D3 Pojo Bolivia
166 E3 Pojuca Brazil
36 C2 Pokal Pakistan
36 B4 Pokaran India
13 G2 Pokataroo New South Wales Australia
37 E3 Pokhara Nepal
46 D2 Pokhvistnevo Rus. Fed.
163 F3 Pokigron Surinam
124 E3 Poko Zaire
76 F5 Pokój Poland
36 A4 Pokran Pakistan
52 B2 Pokrov Rus. Fed.
52 D2 Pokrov Rus. Fed.
47 J4 Pokrovka Kyrgyzstan
47 J1 Pokrovka Rus. Fed.
31 J4 Pokrovka Rus. Fed.
31 G1 Pokrovka Rus. Fed.
53 D3 Pokrovka Ukraine
45 O3 Pokrovsk Rus. Fed.
52 G3 Pokrovskaya Archada Rus. Fed.
52 D3 Pokrovskoye Rus. Fed.
51 F6 Pokrovskoye Rus. Fed.
52 C3 Pokrovskoye Rus. Fed.
77 M4 Pokrówka Poland
77 K3 Pokrzywnica Poland
52 E1 Poksha r. Rus. Fed.
50 G2 Pokshen'ga Rus. Fed.
23 B3 Pola Philippines
155 G4 Polacca Arizona U.S.A.
155 G4 Polacca Wash r. Arizona U.S.A.
101 J4 Polacra, Pta de la headland Spain
98 D1 Pola de Allande Spain
98 E1 Pola de Laviana Spain
98 E1 Pola de Lena Spain
98 E1 Pola de Siero Spain
98 D1 Pola de Somiedo Spain
82 B1 Polaincourt-et-Clairefontaine France
76 E3 Połajewko Poland
99 F5 Polán Spain
79 J3 Poľana mt. Slovakia
79 J3 Poľana mts Slovakia
173 K2 Polanco Uruguay
48 G3 Poland country Europe
147 F3 Poland New York U.S.A.
76 E5 Polanica-Zdrój Wałbrzych Poland
76 E1 Polanów Poland
138 D3 Polar Bear Provincial Park Ontario Canada
43 D1 Polateli Turkey
42 C2 Polatlı Turkey
54 F4 Polatsk Belarus
54 E4 Polatskaya Nizina lowland Belarus
38 C2 Polavaram India
74 C2 Polch Germany
56 F2 Polcirkeln Sweden
76 G1 Połczyno Poland
76 E2 Połczyn Zdrój Poland
50 H2 Poldarsa Rus. Fed.
63 G4 Polegate England U.K.
39 E1 Pole-Khatum Iran
39 G2 Pol-e-Khomrī Afghanistan
102 C3 Poleñino Spain
75 K2 Polepy Czech Rep.
39 C1 Pol-e Safid Iran
107 F4 Polesella Italy
107 F4 Polesine reg. Italy
107 G4 Polesine, Isola di i. Italy
77 M4 Poleski Park Narodowy nat. park Poland
54 B4 Polessk Rus. Fed.
52 E4 Poletayevo Rus. Fed.
52 C4 Polevaya Rus. Fed.
46 F1 Polevskoy Rus. Fed.
22 D2 Polewali Indonesia
112 D4 Polezhan mt. Bulgaria
79 L4 Polgár Hungary
79 H4 Polgárdi Hungary
124 B2 Poli Cameroon
111 F4 Polia Italy
114 B2 Poliçan Berat Albania
114 B2 Poliçan Gjirokastër Albania
171 C7 Policarpo Argentina
111 E3 Policastro, Golfo di b. Italy
76 C2 Police Poland
113 F5 Polichnitos Greece
78 F2 Polička Czech Rep.
111 F2 Policoro Italy
77 K4 Policzna Poland
92 G2 Polientes Spain
111 G2 Polignano a Mare Italy
90 D2 Poligny France
23 B3 Polillo i. Philippines
23 B3 Polillo Islands is Philippines
23 B3 Polillo Strait chan. Philippines
159 □1 Polink Pt pt Jamaica
43 B2 Polis Cyprus
53 C1 Polis'ke Kyyivs'ka Oblast' Ukraine
53 B1 Polis'ke Rivens'ka Oblast' Ukraine
86 D4 Polisot France
111 F4 Polistena Italy
50 J1 Politovo Rus. Fed.
52 D2 Polivanovo Rus. Fed.
110 D5 Polizzi Generosa Sicilia Italy
81 F4 Poljane Slovenia
81 G4 Poljčane Slovenia
54 E3 Polkorona Latvia
76 E4 Polkowice Poland
109 H4 Polla Italy
38 B4 Pollachi India
58 A1 Pollatind h. Norway
72 E4 Polle Germany
103 G5 Pollença Spain
80 C2 Pollenfeld Germany
90 D2 Polliat France
110 D5 Pollina Sicilia Italy
75 G5 Polling Germany
111 F3 Pollino, Monte mt. Italy
9 B6 Pollux mt. New Zealand
56 H1 Polmark Norway
92 E4 Polminhac France
65 E2 Polmont Scotland U.K.
78 E2 Polná Czech Rep.
54 F2 Polna Rus. Fed.
53 G1 Polnaya r. Rus. Fed.
148 C5 Polo Illinois U.S.A.
56 H2 Polo Finland
6 □4 Poloa i. Tonga
53 G3 Polohy Ukraine
50 J3 Polom Rus. Fed.
52 G1 Polom Rus. Fed.
23 C5 Polomoloc Philippines
173 L3 Polonio, C. c. Uruguay
38 C5 Polonnaruwa Sri Lanka
53 B1 Polonne Ukraine
81 H4 Pölöske Hungary
52 B2 Polotnyanyy Zavod Rus. Fed.
47 G2 Polovinnoye Rus. Fed.
112 D2 Polovragi Romania
172 B2 Polpaico Chile
62 B4 Polperro England U.K.
81 F3 Pöls r. Austria
81 F3 Pöls Austria
80 B2 Polsingen Germany
78 E5 Polskava r. Slovenia
112 E3 Polski Trŭmbesh Bulgaria
152 D2 Polson Montana U.S.A.
50 G1 Polta r. Rus. Fed.
79 J3 Poltár Slovakia
53 E2 Poltava div. Ukraine
53 F2 Poltava Ukraine
47 H2 Poltavka Rus. Fed.
31 J3 Poltavka Rus. Fed.
54 D2 Põltsamaa Estonia
44 H3 Polunochnoye Rus. Fed.
44 E2 Poluostrov Rybachiy pen. Rus. Fed.
45 L2 Poluostrov Taymyr pen. Rus. Fed.
44 H2 Poluostrov Yamal pen. Rus. Fed.
73 L3 Połupin Poland
54 E2 Põlva Estonia
172 C2 Polvaredos Argentina
56 H3 Polvijärvi Finland
52 D2 Polya r. Rus. Fed.
115 F6 Polyaigos i. Greece
79 M3 Polyana Ukraine
54 F1 Polyany Rus. Fed.
56 J2 Polyarnye Zori Rus. Fed.
56 J1 Polyarnyy Rus. Fed.
45 T3 Polyarnyy Rus. Fed.
114 E2 Polygyros Greece
114 C2 Polykastano Greece
114 D2 Polykastro Greece

176 H6 Polynesia is Pacific Ocean
81 G4 Polzela Slovenia
164 A1 Pomabamba Peru
9 B7 Pomahaka r. New Zealand
107 E5 Pomarance Italy
93 B5 Pomarez France
57 F3 Pomarkku Finland
167 D5 Pomba r. Brazil
166 B2 Pombal r. Brazil
166 E2 Pombal Paraíba Brazil
98 B5 Pombal Portugal
168 B4 Pombo r. Brazil
91 D5 Pomègues, Île i. France
67 E2 Pomeroy Northern Ireland U.K.
146 B5 Pomeroy Ohio U.S.A.
131 H4 Pomeroy South Africa
109 E3 Pomezia Italy
130 D2 Pomfret South Africa
53 D2 Pomichna Ukraine
77 J3 Pomiechówek Poland
6 □1 Pomio P.N.G.
90 C1 Pommard France
154 D4 Pomona California U.S.A.
128 B4 Pomona Namibia
172 E5 Pomono Argentina
112 F3 Pomorie Bulgaria
50 E1 Pomorskiy Bereg Rus. Fed.
73 L3 Pomorsko Poland
43 B2 Pomos Pt pt Cyprus
Pomo Tso l. see Puma Yumco
50 K2 Pomozdino Rus. Fed.
92 B2 Pompaire France
145 D7 Pompano Beach Florida U.S.A.
109 G4 Pompei Italy
168 C5 Pompéia Brazil
169 F3 Pompeu Brazil
87 F4 Pompey France
129 E2 Pompuè r. Mozambique
50 H3 Ponazyrevo Rus. Fed.
151 D4 Ponca City Oklahoma U.S.A.
145 □3 Ponce Puerto Rico
153 F4 Poncha Springs Colorado U.S.A.
141 G1 Poncheville, Lac l. Québec Canada
90 D2 Poncin France
38 B4 Pondicherry India
135 L2 Pond Inlet N.W.T. Canada
131 G5 Pondoland reg. South Africa
139 J3 Ponds, Island of i. Newfoundland Canada
156 J6 Poneloya Nicaragua
6 □2 Ponérihouen New Caledonia Pacific Ocean
98 D2 Ponferrada Spain
124 A3 Pongara, Pte pt Gabon
8 F4 Pongaroa New Zealand
80 E3 Pongau v. Austria
124 E2 Pongo watercourse Sudan
131 J3 Pongola r. South Africa
131 H3 Pongola South Africa
131 J3 Pongolapoort Dam dam South Africa
77 L4 Poniatowa Poland
77 H2 Poniatowo Poland
76 E4 Poniec Poland
22 E2 Ponindilisa, Tg pt Indonesia
53 B1 Poninka Ukraine
38 B3 Ponnaivar r. India
38 A4 Ponnani India
24 A2 Ponnyadaung Range mountain range Myanmar
136 G4 Ponoka Alberta Canada
53 E1 Ponornytsya Ukraine
22 B3 Ponorogo Indonesia
50 F1 Ponoy r. Rus. Fed.
50 G1 Ponoy Rus. Fed.
92 B3 Pons France
107 E5 Ponsacco Italy
100 C1 Ponsul r. Portugal
93 B5 Pontacq France
169 J2 Ponta da Baleia pt Brazil
169 F5 Ponta de Juatinga pt Brazil
100 □ Ponta Delgada Azores Portugal
131 J2 Ponta de Macaneta pt Mozambique
169 J3 Ponta de Monsarás pt Brazil
166 C1 Ponta de Pedras Brazil
169 F5 Ponta do Boi pt Brazil
163 G3 Ponta dos Índios Brazil
122 □ Ponta do Sol Cape Verde
168 C6 Ponta Grossa Brazil
90 D1 Pontailler-sur-Saône France
91 D4 Pontaix France
166 D2 Pontal r. Brazil
168 D2 Pontalina Brazil
86 C2 Pont-à-Marcq France
87 F4 Pont-à-Mousson France
167 A5 Ponta Porã Brazil
62 C3 Pontardawe Wales U.K.
92 D3 Pontarion France
90 E2 Pontarlier France
107 F5 Pontassieve Italy
89 F2 Pont-Audemer France
86 B4 Pontault-Combault France
92 E3 Pontaumur France
88 B4 Pont-Aven France
106 B3 Pont-Canavese Italy
91 E3 Pontcharra France
151 F6 Pontchartrain, L. l. Louisiana U.S.A.
88 C4 Pontchâteau France
88 A3 Pont-Croix France
90 D2 Pont-d'Ain France
69 C4 Pont-de-Loup Belgium
90 D2 Pont-de-Poitte France
90 E1 Pont-de-Roide France
93 E4 Pont-de-Salars France
102 D2 Pont de Suert Spain
90 C2 Pont-de-Vaux France
90 C2 Pont-de-Veyle France
91 B4 Pont-d'Hérault France
89 E3 Pont-d'Ouilly France
90 B3 Pont-du-Château France
90 D2 Pont-du-Navoy France
98 B3 Ponte Portugal
166 C3 Ponte Alta do Norte Brazil
98 B2 Ponteareas Spain
107 H2 Pontebba Italy
168 B2 Ponte Branca Brazil
98 B2 Ponte Caldelas Spain
98 B2 Ponte-Ceso Spain
109 F3 Pontecorvo Italy
98 B3 Ponte da Barca Portugal
98 B3 Ponte de Lima Portugal
106 D4 Ponte dell'Olio Italy
168 A2 Ponte de Pedra Mato Grosso Brazil
165 E2 Ponte de Pedra Mato Grosso Brazil
107 E5 Pontedera Italy
100 B1 Ponte de Sor Portugal
98 B1 Pontedeume Spain
107 G3 Ponte di Piave Italy
169 E3 Ponte Firme Brazil
65 G4 Pontefract England U.K.
80 C4 Ponte Gardena Italy
65 G2 Ponteland England U.K.
109 G3 Pontelandolfo Italy
108 B2 Ponte-Leccia Corse France
80 D4 Ponte nelle Alpi Italy
83 E3 Ponte Nossa Italy
169 G4 Ponte Nova Brazil
80 C4 Ponte Nova Italy
91 D3 Pont-en-Royans France
106 D3 Pontenure Italy
93 A4 Pontenx-les-Forges France
83 E3 Ponte San Pietro Italy
165 E3 Pontes-e-Lacerda Brazil
98 B2 Ponte Valga Spain
98 B2 Pontevedra div. Galicia Spain
98 B2 Pontevedra Spain
90 C3 Pont-Évêque France
83 F3 Pontevico Italy
89 D3 Pont-Farcy France
86 D3 Pontfaverger-Moronvilliers France
92 E3 Pontgibaud France
89 D2 Pont-Hébert France
86 A2 Ponthieu reg. France
148 C5 Pontiac Illinois U.S.A.
149 F4 Pontiac Michigan U.S.A.
22 B2 Pontianak Indonesia
115 E7 Pontikonisi i. Greece
109 F3 Pontinia Italy
88 C3 Pontivy France
88 A4 Pont-l'Abbé France
90 C1 Pont, Lac de l. France
90 E1 Pont-les-Moulins France
89 F2 Pont-l'Évêque France
89 G4 Pontlevoy France
163 F3 Pontoetoe Surinam
86 B3 Pontoise France
17 C6 Ponton watercourse Western Australia Australia
137 K4 Ponton Manitoba Canada
93 B5 Pontonx-sur-l'Adour France
67 B3 Pontoon Rep. of Ireland
88 D3 Pontorson France
151 F5 Pontotoc Mississippi U.S.A.
106 D4 Pontremoli Italy
62 C2 Pontrhydfendigaid Wales U.K.
88 B3 Pontrieux France
62 D3 Pontrilas England U.K.
141 K3 Pont-Rouge Québec Canada
102 E3 Ponts Spain
86 D4 Pont-Ste-Marie France
86 B3 Pont-Ste-Maxence France
91 C4 Pont-St-Esprit France
106 B3 Pont-St-Martin Italy
86 C4 Pont-sur-Yonne France
89 F4 Pontvallain France
62 B3 Pontyberem Wales U.K.
62 C3 Pontycymer Wales U.K.
141 F4 Pontypool Ontario Canada
62 C3 Pontypool Wales U.K.
62 C3 Pontypridd Wales U.K.
52 C3 Ponyri Rus. Fed.
109 E4 Ponza Italy
109 E4 Ponza, Isola di i. Italy
109 E4 Ponziane, Isole is Italy
106 C4 Ponzone Italy
12 C3 Poochera S. Australia Australia
12 D1 Poolanna L. salt flat S. Australia Australia
63 E4 Poole England U.K.
63 E4 Poole Bay b. England U.K.
66 C3 Poolewe Scotland U.K.
65 F3 Pooley Bridge England U.K.
12 D1 Poolowanna L. salt flat S. Australia Australia
Poona see Pune
13 E3 Pooncarie New South Wales Australia
13 F2 Poopelloe, L. salt lake New South Wales Australia
164 C3 Poopó, Lago de l. Bolivia
8 E1 Poor Knights Is is New Zealand
122 D4 Pô, Parc National de nat. park Burkina
162 B3 Popayán Colombia
54 B3 Pope Latvia
30 D1 Poperechnoye Rus. Fed.
69 A4 Poperinge Belgium
112 F2 Popeştii-Leordeni Romania
45 M2 Popigay r. Rus. Fed.
53 C2 Popil'nya Ukraine
12 E3 Popiltah New South Wales Australia
12 E3 Popilta L. l. New South Wales Australia
53 E1 Popivka Ukraine
137 K4 Poplar r. Manitoba Canada
152 F1 Poplar Montana U.S.A.
151 F4 Poplar Bluff Missouri U.S.A.
146 C6 Poplar Camp Virginia U.S.A.
145 B6 Poplarville Mississippi U.S.A.
151 F6 Poplarville Mississippi U.S.A.
52 E3 Poplevino Rus. Fed.
52 D3 Poplevinskiy Rus. Fed.
157 F5 Popocatepetl volcano Mexico
22 B4 Popoh Indonesia
125 C5 Popokabaka Zaire
109 F2 Popoli Italy
6 □1 Popondetta P.N.G.
104 F3 Popovača Croatia
112 F3 Popovo Bulgaria
76 G4 Popów Poland
73 F4 Poppenberg h. Germany
107 F5 Poppi Italy
79 K2 Poprad Slovakia
112 F1 Popricani Romania
108 C2 Populonia Italy
36 A4 Porali r. Pakistan
8 F4 Porangahau New Zealand
166 C3 Porangatu Brazil
77 N3 Porazava Belarus
36 B5 Porbandar India
136 C4 Porcher I. i. B.C. Canada
80 D5 Porcia Italy
86 D3 Porcien reg. France
169 G4 Porciúncula Brazil
166 C3 Porcos r. Brazil
79 M4 Porcsalma Hungary
101 F3 Porcuna Spain
134 E3 Porcupine r. Yukon Terr. Canada
139 J3 Porcupine, Cape c. Newfoundland Canada
137 J4 Porcupine Hills h. Saskatchewan Canada
148 C2 Porcupine Mts mts Michigan U.S.A.
137 J4 Porcupine Plain Saskatchewan Canada
137 J4 Porcupine Prov. Forest res. Saskatchewan Canada
107 G2 Pordenone div. Italy
107 G3 Pordenone Italy
88 C3 Pordic France
162 C2 Pore Colombia
77 K3 Poręba-Kocęby Poland
107 H3 Poreč Croatia
168 C5 Porecatu Brazil
52 B2 Porech'ye Rus. Fed.
52 D1 Porech'ye-Rybnoye Rus. Fed.
52 H2 Poretskoye Rus. Fed.
81 E4 Porezen mt. Slovenia
57 F3 Pori Finland
9 E4 Porirua New Zealand
54 F3 Porkhov Rus. Fed.
163 E1 Porlamar Venezuela
107 D2 Porlezza Italy
62 C3 Porlock England U.K.
99 E2 Porma r. Spain
75 G4 Pörnbach Germany
88 C4 Pornic France
88 C4 Pornichet France
23 C4 Poro i. Philippines
27 Q2 Poronaysk Rus. Fed.
172 D1 Porongo, Co mt. Argentina
115 E5 Poros i. Greece
115 E5 Poros Attiki Greece
115 B4 Poros Ionioi Nisoi Greece
79 M3 Poroshkove Ukraine
50 E2 Porosozero Rus. Fed.
50 K2 Porozhsk Rus. Fed.
107 J3 Porozina Croatia
179 C6 Porpoise Bay b. Antarctica
128 □1 Porpoise Pt pt Ascension Atlantic Ocean
91 E5 Porquerolles, Île de i. France
140 E2 Porquis Junction Ontario Canada
82 C1 Porrentruy Switzerland
107 E4 Porretta Terme Italy
98 B2 Porriño Spain
56 G1 Porsangen chan. Norway
57 C3 Porsgrunn Norway
88 A3 Porspoder France
82 B2 Porsuk r. Turkey
93 D5 Porta France
172 B5 Portada Covunco Argentina
67 E2 Portadown Northern Ireland U.K.
9 B7 Port Adventure b. New Zealand
67 F2 Portaferry Northern Ireland U.K.
147 J1 Portage Maine U.S.A.
148 E4 Portage Michigan U.S.A.
148 C4 Portage Wisconsin U.S.A.
137 K5 Portage la Prairie Manitoba Canada
150 C1 Portal N. Dakota U.S.A.
136 E5 Port Alberni B.C. Canada
13 F4 Port Albert Victoria Australia
100 C1 Portalegre div. Portugal
100 C1 Portalegre Portugal
153 F5 Portales New Mexico U.S.A.
136 C3 Port Alexander Alaska U.S.A.
131 F6 Port Alfred South Africa
136 D4 Port Alice B.C. Canada
146 D4 Port Allegany Pennsylvania U.S.A.
151 F6 Port Allen Louisiana U.S.A.
15 G4 Port Alma Queensland Australia
152 B1 Port Angeles Washington U.S.A.
159 □1 Port Antonio Jamaica
153 D3 Port-à-Piment Haiti
114 E2 Portaria Greece
67 D3 Portarlington Rep. of Ireland
13 F5 Port Arthur Tasmania Australia
151 E6 Port Arthur Texas U.S.A.
Port Arthur see Lüshun
98 C2 Portas, Emb. das resr Spain
66 B5 Port Askaig Scotland U.K.
12 D3 Port Augusta S. Australia Australia
159 D3 Port-au-Prince Haiti
149 F3 Port Austin Michigan U.S.A.
139 J3 Port aux Choix Newfoundland Canada
67 F2 Portavogie Northern Ireland U.K.
88 D2 Portbail France
130 C7 Port Beaufort South Africa
127 B4 Port Bell Uganda
25 A5 Port Blair Andaman and Nicobar Is India
141 F4 Port Bolster Ontario Canada
102 G2 Portbou Spain
14 D2 Port Bradshaw b. Northern Terr. Australia
140 E5 Port Burwell Ontario Canada
37 G5 Port Canning India
141 F4 Port Carling Ontario Canada
9 C6 Port Chalmers New Zealand
145 D7 Port Charlotte Florida U.S.A.
63 E4 Portchester England U.K.
147 G4 Port Chester New York U.S.A.
136 C4 Port Clements B.C. Canada
146 B4 Port Clinton Ohio U.S.A.
147 J3 Port Clyde Maine U.S.A.
141 F5 Port Colborne Ontario Canada
136 E5 Port Coquitlam B.C. Canada
141 F5 Port Credit Ontario Canada
91 E5 Port-Cros, Île de i. France
91 E5 Port-Cros, Parc National de nat. park France
179 □ Port Curieuse Kerguelen Indian Ocean
103 F5 Port d'Andratx Spain
14 B2 Port Darwin b. Northern Terr. Australia
13 F5 Port Davey b. Tasmania Australia
91 C5 Port-de-Bouc France
159 D3 Port-de-Paix Haiti
103 G5 Port de Pollença Spain
92 A3 Port-des-Barques France
103 F5 Port de Sóller Spain
93 C6 Port de Venasque pass France/Spain
25 C7 Port Dickson Malaysia
15 F3 Port Douglas Queensland Australia
146 C3 Port Dover Ontario Canada
148 D3 Porte des Morts chan. Wisconsin U.S.A.
136 C4 Port Edward B.C. Canada
131 H5 Port Edward South Africa
148 C3 Port Edwards Wisconsin U.S.A.
169 G1 Porteirinha Brazil
166 B1 Portel Brazil
100 C2 Portel Portugal
100 B3 Portela das Corchas pass Portugal
168 B2 Portelândia Brazil
140 E4 Port Elgin Ontario Canada
131 E6 Port Elizabeth South Africa
66 B5 Port Ellen Scotland U.K.
173 F1 Portena Argentina
89 E2 Port-en-Bessin-Huppain France
64 D2 Portencross Scotland U.K.
170 E2 Porteño r. Argentina
64 D3 Port Erin Isle of Man
137 H2 Porter Lake l. N.W.T. Canada
136 C3 Porter Landing B.C. Canada
154 C3 Porterville California U.S.A.
130 B6 Porterville South Africa
91 C4 Portes-lès-Valence France
159 □1 Port Esquivel Jamaica
12 E4 Port Fairy Victoria Australia
8 E2 Port Fitzroy New Zealand
124 A4 Port-Gentil Gabon
12 D3 Port Germein S. Australia Australia
151 F6 Port Gibson Mississippi U.S.A.
66 D5 Port Glasgow Scotland U.K.
91 E5 Port Grimaud France
131 G5 Port Grosvenor South Africa
62 C3 Porth Wales U.K.
123 F6 Port Harcourt Nigeria
136 D4 Port Hardy B.C. Canada
Port Harrison see Inukjuak
139 H4 Port Hawkesbury Nova Scotia Canada
62 C3 Porthcawl Wales U.K.
16 B4 Port Hedland Western Australia Australia
159 □1 Port Henderson Jamaica
147 G2 Port Henry New York U.S.A.
100 B2 Porthino da Arrábida Portugal
62 A4 Porthleven England U.K.
62 B2 Porthmadog Wales U.K.
115 B5 Porthmos Zakynthou chan. Greece
62 B2 Porth Neigwl b. Wales U.K.
141 F5 Port Hope Ontario Canada
139 J3 Port Hope Simpson Newfoundland Canada
149 F4 Port Huron Michigan U.S.A.
27 □ Port I. i. Hong Kong
179 □ Port, I. du i. Kerguelen Indian Ocean
42 G2 Port-Iliç Azerbaijan
99 F1 Portilla de la Reina Spain
172 B2 Portillo Chile
100 B3 Portimão Portugal
62 B4 Port Isaac Bay b. England U.K.
62 D3 Portishead England U.K.
147 G4 Port Jefferson New York U.S.A.
147 F4 Port Jervis New York U.S.A.
88 C5 Port-Joinville France
159 □1 Port Kaiser Jamaica
163 F2 Port Kaituma Guyana
13 G3 Port Kembla New South Wales Australia
66 F3 Portknockie Scotland U.K.
Port Lairge see Waterford
159 □1 Portland div. Jamaica
148 E5 Portland Indiana U.S.A.
147 H3 Portland Maine U.S.A.
152 B2 Portland Oregon U.S.A.
12 E4 Portland Victoria Australia
8 E1 Portland New Zealand
159 □1 Portland Bight b. Jamaica
136 D3 Portland Canal inlet B.C. Canada
8 F3 Portland I. i. New Zealand
62 D4 Portland, Isle of pen. England U.K.
128 □1 Portland Pt pt Ascension Atlantic Ocean
159 □1 Portland Pt pt Jamaica
159 □1 Portland Ridge mt. Jamaica
91 B5 Port-la-Nouvelle France
67 D3 Portlaoise Rep. of Ireland
151 D6 Port Lavaca Texas U.S.A.
67 D4 Portlaw Rep. of Ireland
66 F3 Portlethen Scotland U.K.
93 F6 Port-Leucate France
12 C3 Port Lincoln S. Australia Australia
122 B5 Port Loko Sierra Leone
159 □5 Port Louis Guadeloupe Caribbean
88 B4 Port-Louis France
127 □4 Port Louis Mauritius
12 E4 Port MacDonnell S. Australia Australia
13 H2 Port Macquarie New South Wales Australia
67 A5 Portmagee Rep. of Ireland
103 C7 Portman Spain
139 H2 Port Manvers harbour Newfoundland Canada
159 □1 Port Maria Jamaica
64 B4 Portmarnock Rep. of Ireland
127 □3 Port Mathurin Rodrigues I. Mauritius
14 D2 Port McArthur b. Northern Terr. Australia
136 D4 Port McNeill B.C. Canada
139 H4 Port-Menier Québec Canada
152 B1 Port Moody B.C. Canada
159 □1 Port Morant Jamaica
159 □1 Portmore Jamaica
6 □1 Port Moresby P.N.G.
64 C3 Portmuck Northern Ireland U.K.
15 E1 Port Musgrave b. Queensland Australia
66 C4 Portnacroish Scotland U.K.
66 B2 Portnaguran Scotland U.K.
66 B5 Portnahaven Scotland U.K.
12 D3 Port Neill S. Australia Australia
158 D2 Port Nelson The Bahamas
141 K3 Portneuf Québec Canada
141 J3 Portneuf, Réserve faunique de res. Québec Canada
66 B2 Port Nis Scotland U.K.
130 A4 Port Nolloth South Africa
Port-Nouveau-Québec see Kangiqsualujjuaq
98 B3 Porto airport Portugal
98 B3 Porto div. Portugal
108 A2 Porto Corse France
98 B3 Porto Porto Portugal
166 D1 Pôrto Brazil
164 C1 Pôrto Acre Brazil
164 C1 Pôrto Alegre Amazonas Brazil
166 B1 Porto Alegre Pará Brazil
167 B7 Porto Alegre Rio Grande do Sul Brazil
168 B4 Pôrto Alegre Brazil
125 B6 Porto Amboim Angola
166 A3 Pôrto Artur Brazil
108 C2 Porto Azzurro Italy
167 C6 Pôrto Belo Brazil
156 L7 Portobelo Panama
108 B3 Porto Cervo Sardegna Italy
111 G2 Porto Cesareo Italy
115 E5 Portocheli Greece
103 G5 Porto Colom Spain
103 G5 Porto Cristo Spain
98 C1 Porto da Cesta pass Spain
100 B3 Pôrto de Lagos Portugal
166 B1 Pôrto de Mós Brazil
100 B1 Pôrto de Mós Portugal
98 C2 Porto de Piedrafita pass Spain
169 H1 Pôrto de Santa Cruz Brazil
98 C1 Porto do Barqueiro Spain
166 B3 Pôrto dos Meinacos Brazil
98 A2 Porto do Son Spain
110 C5 Porto Empedocle Sicilia Italy
108 D2 Porto Ercole Italy
165 E3 Pôrto Esperidião Brazil
107 E3 Portoferraio Italy
168 E4 Porto Ferreira Brazil
108 A4 Porto Ferro b. Sardegna Italy
106 D4 Portofino Italy
169 G4 Pôrto Firme Brazil
166 C2 Pôrto Franco Brazil
159 □3 Port of Spain Trinidad and Tobago
107 G4 Porto Garibaldi Italy
163 G3 Pôrto Grande Brazil
107 G3 Portogruaro Italy
168 B5 Pôrto Guareí Brazil
122 □ Porto Inglês Cape Verde
167 A4 Pôrto Jofre Brazil
154 B2 Portola California U.S.A.
110 D4 Porto Levante Sicilia Italy
107 G3 Porto Levante Italy
107 F4 Portomaggiore Italy
98 C2 Portomarín Spain
129 G2 Porto Mocambo b. Mozambique
96 □ Porto Moniz Madeira Portugal
165 E4 Pôrto Murtinho Brazil
166 C3 Pôrto Nacional Brazil
123 E5 Porto-Novo Benin
122 □ Porto Novo Cape Verde
Porto Novo see Parangipettai
111 E6 Portopalo di Capo Passero Sicilia Italy
103 G5 Porto Petra Spain
115 F5 Porto Rafti Greece
107 H5 Porto Recanati Italy
152 A3 Port Orford Oregon U.S.A.
125 B5 Porto Rico Angola
109 F1 Porto San Giorgio Italy
108 B4 Porto San Paolo Sardegna Italy
166 B1 Pôrto Santana Brazil
107 H5 Porto Sant'Elpidio Italy
96 □ Porto Santo Madeira Portugal
96 □ Porto Santo, Ilha de i. Madeira Portugal
108 D2 Porto Santo Stefano Italy
168 B5 Pôrto São José Brazil
108 A5 Portoscuso Sardegna Italy
169 J2 Pôrto Seguro Brazil
107 G4 Porto Tolle Italy
108 A4 Porto Torres Sardegna Italy
108 B3 Porto-Vecchio Corse France
164 D1 Pôrto Velho Brazil
107 D4 Portovenere Italy
162 A4 Portoviejo Ecuador
66 C6 Portpatrick Scotland U.K.
9 A7 Port Pegasus b. New Zealand
141 F4 Port Perry Ontario Canada
14 C2 Port Phillip Bay b. Victoria Australia
93 D6 Port, Pic du mt. France/Spain
12 D3 Port Pirie S. Australia Australia
67 E3 Portrane Rep. of Ireland
62 A4 Portreath England U.K.
66 B3 Portree Scotland U.K.
136 E5 Port Renfrew B.C. Canada
8 □1 Port Ross inlet Auckland Is New Zealand
140 E5 Port Rowan Ontario Canada
146 E5 Port Royal Virginia U.S.A.
159 □1 Port Royal Jamaica
67 E1 Portrush Northern Ireland U.K.
119 F1 Port Said Egypt
145 C6 Port St Joe Florida U.S.A.
131 G5 Port St Johns South Africa
64 D3 Port St Mary Isle of Man
67 D1 Portsalon Rep. of Ireland
6 □2 Port Sandwich Vanuatu
149 F4 Port Sanilac Michigan U.S.A.
81 F4 Pörtschach am Wörther See Austria
102 D4 Ports de Beseit mountain range Spain
141 F4 Port Severn Ontario Canada
27 □ Port Shelter b. Hong Kong
131 H5 Port Shepstone South Africa
136 C4 Port Simpson B.C. Canada
63 E4 Portsmouth England U.K.
147 H3 Portsmouth New Hampshire U.S.A.
146 B5 Portsmouth Ohio U.S.A.
147 E6 Portsmouth Virginia U.S.A.
159 G4 Portsmouth Dominica
127 □3 Port South East inlet Rodrigues I. Mauritius
66 F3 Portsoy Scotland U.K.
93 C4 Port-Ste-Marie France
13 H3 Port Stephens b. New South Wales Australia
171 D7 Port Stephens Falkland Is.
67 E1 Portstewart Northern Ireland U.K.
91 C5 Port-St-Louis-du-Rhône France
119 G4 Port Sudan Sudan
145 B6 Port Sulphur Louisiana U.S.A.
90 E1 Port-sur-Saône France
62 C3 Port Talbot Wales U.K.
Port Taufiq see Bûr Taufiq
56 G1 Porttipahdan tekojärvi l. Finland
48 E5 Portugal country Europe
99 G1 Portugalete Spain
162 D2 Portuguesa r. Venezuela
67 C3 Portumna Rep. of Ireland
93 F6 Port-Vendres France
6 □2 Port-Vila Vanuatu
56 J1 Port Vladimir Rus. Fed.
8 E2 Port Waikato New Zealand
12 D3 Port Wakefield S. Australia Australia
148 D4 Port Washington Wisconsin U.S.A.
66 D6 Port William Scotland U.K.
148 B2 Port Wing Wisconsin U.S.A.
173 F3 Porvenir Argentina
171 B7 Porvenir Chile
54 D1 Porvoo Finland
54 D1 Porvoonjoki r. Finland
54 D1 Porvoon mlk Finland
52 F1 Porzdni Rus. Fed.
101 F1 Porzuna Spain
108 B4 Posada r. Sardegna Italy
108 B4 Posada Sardegna Italy
98 E1 Posada de Llanera Spain
170 E2 Posadas Argentina
101 E3 Posadas Spain
53 E3 Posad-Pokrovs'ke Ukraine
112 A2 Posavina reg. Bos.-Herz./Croatia
83 F2 Poschiavo Switzerland
115 F5 Poseidonia Greece
52 H3 Poselki Rus. Fed.
149 F3 Posen Michigan U.S.A.
102 D2 Posets mt. Spain
50 F3 Poshekhon'ye Rus. Fed.
39 D3 Posht watercourse Iran
39 C2 Posht-e Badam Iran
80 C5 Posina r. Italy
56 H2 Posio Finland
109 G4 Positano Italy
22 E2 Poso r. Indonesia
22 E2 Poso Indonesia
51 G7 Posof Turkey
31 H6 Posŏng South Korea
47 K2 Pospelikha Rus. Fed.
107 F3 Possagno Italy
166 C3 Posse Brazil
86 D4 Possesse France
179 A5 Possession Is is Antarctica
75 G2 Pößneck Germany
151 C5 Post Texas U.S.A.
112 F2 Poşta Călnău Romania
109 H3 Posta Piana Italy
75 H4 Postau Germany
138 E2 Poste-de-la-Baleine Québec Canada
127 □4 Poste, R. du r. Mauritius
69 E3 Posterholt Netherlands
109 H4 Postiglione Italy
130 D4 Postmasburg South Africa
166 B3 Posto Alto Manissaua Brazil
81 F5 Postojna Slovenia
77 K3 Postoliska Poland
75 J2 Postoloprty Czech Rep.
76 D3 Postomia r. Poland
76 E1 Postomino Poland
148 B4 Postville Iowa U.S.A.
139 J3 Postville Newfoundland Canada
121 E4 Post Weygand Algeria
104 F4 Posušje Bos.-Herz.
31 J4 Pos'yet Rus. Fed.
22 E4 Pota Indonesia
115 D6 Potamia Greece
114 F1 Potamoi Greece
115 D6 Potamos Attiki Greece
114 A3 Potamos Ionioi Nisoi Greece
52 F2 Potap'yevo Rus. Fed.
131 F3 Potchefstroom South Africa
169 H2 Poté Brazil
151 E5 Poteau Oklahoma U.S.A.
76 F1 Potęgowo Poland
51 H5 Potemkino Rus. Fed.
109 H4 Potenza div. Italy
107 H5 Potenza r. Italy
109 H4 Potenza Italy
107 H5 Potenza Picena Italy
9 A7 Poteriteri, L. l. New Zealand
99 F1 Potes Spain
130 E5 Potfontein South Africa
22 B1 Po, Tg pt Malaysia
131 G2 Potgietersrus South Africa
151 D6 Poth Texas U.S.A.
138 F2 Potherie, Lac La l. Québec Canada
166 D2 Poti r. Brazil
51 G7 P'ot'i Georgia
115 D4 Potidania Greece
89 E3 Potigny France
38 C2 Potikal India
169 J1 Potiraguá Brazil
123 G4 Potiskum Nigeria
53 C1 Potiyivka Ukraine
52 F2 Pot'ma Rus. Fed.
52 G3 Pot'ma Rus. Fed.
152 D2 Pot Mt. mt. Idaho U.S.A.
6 □2 Potnarvin Vanuatu
164 C2 Poto Peru
146 E5 Potomac r. U.S.A.
146 D5 Potomac South Branch r. W. Virginia U.S.A.
164 C4 Potosí div. Bolivia
150 F4 Potosi Missouri U.S.A.
164 C3 Potosí Bolivia
155 E4 Potosi Mt mt. Nevada U.S.A.
23 B4 Pototan Philippines
156 J6 Potrerillos Honduras
172 C2 Potrerilos Argentina
81 E3 Pötschenpass Austria
147 F2 Potsdam New York U.S.A.
73 J3 Potsdam Germany
81 H3 Pottendorf Austria
81 H3 Pottenstein Austria
75 G3 Pottenstein Germany
62 D3 Potterne England U.K.
63 F3 Potters Bar England U.K.
6 □2 Pott, Île i. New Caledonia Pacific Ocean
75 G4 Pöttmes Germany
23 □2 Potts Junction Guam Pacific Ocean
147 F4 Pottstown Pennsylvania U.S.A.
147 E4 Pottsville Pennsylvania U.S.A.
38 C5 Pottuvil Sri Lanka
77 J4 Potworów Poland
89 D4 Pouancé France
136 E3 Pouce Coupe B.C. Canada
139 K4 Pouch Cove Newfoundland Canada
6 □2 Pouébo New Caledonia Pacific Ocean
147 G4 Poughkeepsie New York U.S.A.
90 B1 Pougny France
90 B1 Pougues-les-Eaux France
86 D4 Pougy France
82 A1 Pouilley-les-Vignes France
93 B5 Pouillon France
90 C1 Pouilly-en-Auxois France
90 C2 Pouilly-sous-Charlieu France
92 E1 Pouilly-sur-Loire France
90 D1 Pouilly-sur-Saône France
67 B5 Poulgorm Bridge Rep. of Ireland
115 D5 Poulithra Greece
147 G3 Poultney Vermont U.S.A.
65 F4 Poulton-le-Fylde England U.K.
90 D2 Poupet, Mont h. France
91 D5 Pourcieux France
90 B1 Pourrain France
90 E3 Pourri, Mt mt. France
173 G4 Pourtalé Argentina
169 F5 Pouso Alegre Brazil
87 F4 Poussay France
7 □12 Poutasi Western Samoa
25 C4 Poŭthĭsăt Cambodia
87 F4 Pouxeux France
93 C5 Pouyastruc France
93 B5 Pouydesseaux France
92 B2 Pouzauges France
89 F4 Pouzay France
52 C1 Povarovo Rus. Fed.
79 H2 Považská Bystrica Slovakia
50 E2 Povenets Rus. Fed.
8 F3 Poverty Bay b. New Zealand
107 E4 Poviglio Italy
100 C2 Póvoa Portugal
100 □ Povoação Azores Portugal
98 B3 Póvoa de Lanhoso Portugal
98 B3 Póvoa de Varzim Portugal
51 G5 Povorino Rus. Fed.
31 G1 Povorotnaya Rus. Fed.
154 D5 Poway California U.S.A.
152 F2 Powder r. Montana U.S.A.
152 F3 Powder River Wyoming U.S.A.
146 B6 Powell r. Kentucky/Tennessee U.S.A.
152 E2 Powell Wyoming U.S.A.
15 E5 Powell Cr. watercourse Queensland Australia
155 G3 Powell, Lake l. Arizona/Utah U.S.A.
154 C2 Powell Mt mt. Nevada U.S.A.
128 □2 Powell Pt pt St Helena Atlantic Ocean
158 C1 Powell Pt pt The Bahamas
136 E5 Powell River B.C. Canada
148 D3 Powers Michigan U.S.A.
146 E6 Powhatan Virginia U.S.A.
62 D2 Powick England U.K.
32 B1 Powo China
62 C2 Powys div. Wales U.K.
168 A1 Poxoreu Brazil
6 □2 Poya New Caledonia Pacific Ocean
33 G2 Poyang Hu l. China
25 □ Poyan Res. resr Singapore
31 J2 Poyarkovo Rus. Fed.
148 C3 Poygan, Lake l. Wisconsin U.S.A.
64 B3 Poyntz Pass Northern Ireland U.K.
81 H2 Poysdorf Austria
54 C1 Pöytyä Finland
165 E3 Pozama Bolivia
43 C1 Pozantı Turkey
112 C2 Požarevac Yugoslavia
157 F4 Poza Rica Mexico
31 J2 Pozdeyevka Rus. Fed.
112 C3 Požega Yugoslavia
77 K1 Pozezdrze Poland
31 K3 Pozharskoye Rus. Fed.
76 E3 Poznań div. Poland
76 E3 Poznań Poznań Poland
101 H3 Pozo Alcón Spain
164 C4 Pozo Almonte Chile
101 H1 Pozoamargo Spain
99 E3 Pozoantiguo Spain
101 F2 Pozoblanco Spain
103 B6 Pozo Cañada Spain
165 E4 Pozo Colorado Paraguay
173 F2 Pozo del Molle Argentina
170 D2 Pozo Hondo Argentina

53 C3 Râbniţa Moldova
50 E1 Rabocheostrovsk Rus. Fed.
39 D3 Rābor Iran
52 G1 Rabotki Rus. Fed.
118 D3 Rabyānah oasis Libya
111 H3 Racale Italy
79 H4 Rácalmás Hungary
110 C5 Racalmuto Sicilia Italy
81 E4 Raccolana r. Italy
106 B4 Racconigi Italy
146 B5 Raccoon Creek r. Ohio U.S.A.
81 G4 Rače Slovenia
139 K4 Race, C. c. Newfoundland Canada
147 H3 Race Pt pt Massachusetts U.S.A.
151 D7 Rachal Texas U.S.A.
155 E3 Rachel Nevada U.S.A.
52 C1 Rachevo Rus. Fed.
25 D5 Rach Gia Vietnam
77 J3 Raciąż Poland
76 G5 Racibórz Poland
73 K2 Racimierz Poland
148 D4 Racine Wisconsin U.S.A.
140 D2 Racine Lake l. Ontario Canada
79 H4 Ráckeve Hungary
148 E2 Raco Michigan U.S.A.
112 E1 Racoş Romania
77 L2 Raczki Poland
59 E1 Råda Sweden
126 D2 Radā' Yemen
54 E4 Radashkovichy Belarus
112 E1 Rădăuti Romania
78 C2 Radbuza r. Czech Rep.
52 C1 Radchenko Rus. Fed.
144 C4 Radcliff Kentucky U.S.A.
31 J2 Radde Rus. Fed.
110 D5 Raddusa Sicilia Italy
58 D2 Rade Norway
73 J4 Radeberg Germany
73 J4 Radebeul Germany
73 J4 Radeburg Germany
81 G4 Radeče Slovenia
91 E5 Rade d'Hyères harbour France
53 A1 Radekhiv Ukraine
81 H4 Radenci Slovenia
81 E4 Radenthein Austria
72 C4 Radevormwald Germany
76 E1 Radew r. Poland
146 C6 Radford Virginia U.S.A.
36 B5 Radhanpur India
107 F5 Radicondoli Italy
52 H4 Radishchevo Rus. Fed.
138 E3 Radisson Québec Canada
52 B3 Raditsa-Krylovka Rus. Fed.
131 G2 Radium South Africa
136 F4 Radium Hot Springs B.C. Canada
81 G4 Radizelj Slovenia
53 G1 Rad'kovka Rus. Fed.
76 E5 Radków Poland
81 G4 Radlje ob Dravi Slovenia
112 E3 Radnevo Bulgaria
78 C2 Radnice Czech Rep.
162 B3 Rado de Tumaco inlet Colombia
74 D5 Radolfzell am Bodensee Germany
77 K4 Radom div. Poland
77 K4 Radom Poland
124 D2 Radom Sudan
77 H2 Radomin Poland
114 E1 Radomir mt. Bulgaria/Greece
112 D3 Radomir Bulgaria
53 E1 Radomka Ukraine
124 D2 Radom National Park nat. park Sudan
77 H4 Radomsko Poland
53 C1 Radomyshl' Ukraine
77 K5 Radomyśl Wielki Poland
75 J2 Radonice Czech Rep.
77 J4 Radoszyce Poland
76 D3 Radoszyn Poland
112 F4 Radovets Bulgaria
112 D4 Radoviš Macedonia
52 D2 Radovitskiy Rus. Fed.
81 F4 Radovljica Slovenia
76 D2 Radowo Małe Poland
58 A1 Radøy i. Norway
81 E3 Radstadt Austria
80 E3 Radstädter Tauern mts Austria
81 E3 Radstädter Tauern pass Austria
62 D3 Radstock England U.K.
12 C3 Radstock, C. headland S. Australia Australia
112 F1 Răducăneni Romania
53 D1 Radul' Ukraine
77 N1 Radun' Belarus
53 E3 Radushne Ukraine
54 C4 Radviliškis Lithuania
119 G3 Radwá, J. mt. Saudi Arabia
76 D4 Radwanice Poland
77 L6 Radymno Poland
53 A1 Radyvyliv Ukraine
77 J3 Radzanów Poland
77 J4 Radzice Duże Poland
76 G3 Radziejów Poland
73 K3 Radzików Poland
77 L2 Radziłów Poland
77 K3 Radzymin Poland
76 G2 Radzyń Chełminski Poland
77 L4 Radzyń Podlaski Poland
36 E4 Rae Bareli India
136 F2 Rae-Edzo N.W.T. Canada
7 □10 Raeffsky, Îles is French Polynesia Pacific Ocean
136 F2 Rae Lakes N.W.T. Canada
69 E4 Raeren Belgium
72 B4 Raesfeld Germany
17 C6 Raeside, Lake salt flat Western Australia Australia
8 E3 Raetihi New Zealand
119 G2 Rāf h. Saudi Arabia
173 G1 Rafaela Argentina
173 G3 Rafael Obligado Argentina
43 C4 Rafah Gaza
124 D3 Rafaï Central African Rep.
53 B1 Rafalivka Ukraine
110 C5 Raffadali Sicilia Italy
66 E3 Rafford Scotland U.K.
119 H2 Rafḩā Saudi Arabia
115 F4 Rafina Greece
59 E1 Råforsen Sweden
39 D3 Rafsanjān Iran
124 E2 Raga Sudan
124 D1 Ragag Sudan
54 D3 Ragana Latvia
23 C5 Ragang, Mt volcano Philippines
23 B3 Ragay Gulf b. Philippines
73 H2 Rägelin Germany
147 J3 Ragged I. i. Maine U.S.A.
158 D2 Ragged I. i. The Bahamas
17 C7 Ragged, Mt h. Western Australia Australia
159 □9 Ragged Pt pt Barbados Caribbean
36 D4 Rāghogarh India
126 D1 Raghwān, W. watercourse Yemen
62 D3 Raglan Wales U.K.
8 E2 Raglan New Zealand
73 H3 Ragösen Germany
73 H4 Raguhn Germany
110 D6 Ragusa div. Sicilia Italy
110 D6 Ragusa Sicilia Italy
32 C1 Ra'gyagoinba China
21 H7 Raha Indonesia
95 K1 Rahachow Belarus
119 G5 Rahad r. Sudan
118 D4 Rahad Wahal well Sudan
Rahaeng see Tak
72 D3 Rahden Germany
42 E3 Raḩḩālīyah Iraq
38 A2 Rahimatpur India
38 B3 Rahimyar Khan Pakistan
90 E1 Rahin r. France
39 B2 Rāhjerd Iran
8 D3 Rahotu New Zealand
172 B5 Rahué Argentina
38 A2 Rahuri India
39 E2 Rahzanak Afghanistan
7 □10 Raiatea i. French Polynesia Pacific Ocean
Raibu i. see Air
38 B2 Raichur India
37 G4 Raiganj India
37 E5 Raigarh India
6 □3 Raihifahifa i. Tonga
155 E2 Railroad Valley v. Nevada U.S.A.
37 G5 Raimangal r. Bangladesh
139 G3 Raimbault, Lac l. Québec Canada
75 F4 Rain Germany
81 F2 Rainbach im Mühlkreis Austria
155 G3 Rainbow Bridge Nat. Mon. nat. park Utah U.S.A.
136 F3 Rainbow Lake Alberta Canada
15 F1 Raine Entrance chan. Queensland Australia
15 E1 Raine I. i. Queensland Australia
146 C6 Rainelle W. Virginia U.S.A.
152 B2 Rainier, Mt volcano Washington U.S.A.
36 B4 Raini N. r. Pakistan
138 B4 Rainy r. Minnesota U.S.A.
143 H2 Rainy Lake l. Canada/U.S.A.
138 B4 Rainy River Ontario Canada
36 C4 Raipur India
37 E5 Raipur India
37 F5 Rairangpur India
72 F1 Raisdorf Germany
36 D5 Raisen India
36 C3 Raisinghnagar India
57 F3 Raisio Finland
110 C4 Raisi, Pta pt Sicilia Italy
86 C2 Raismes France
80 C1 Raitenbuch Germany
177 K7 Raivavae i. French Polynesia Pacific Ocean
36 C3 Raiwind Pakistan
54 E2 Raja Estonia
22 A3 Rajabasa, G. volcano Indonesia
37 F5 Rajagangapur India
38 C2 Rajahmundry India
56 H1 Raja-Jooseppi Finland
36 D4 Rajakhera India
36 C3 Rajaldesar India
54 D1 Rajamäki Finland
38 B3 Rajampet India
22 C1 Rajang r. Malaysia
36 B3 Rajanpur Pakistan
38 B4 Rajapalaiyam India
38 A2 Rajapur India
36 C4 Rajasthan India
37 F4 Rajauli India
37 G5 Rajbari Bangladesh
79 H2 Rajec Slovakia
36 D4 Rajgarh India
36 C3 Rajgarh India
77 L2 Rajgród Poland
81 H1 Rajhrad Czech Rep.
78 F2 Rajhradice Czech Rep.
22 A2 Rajik Indonesia
37 E5 Rajim India
78 G3 Rajka Hungary
36 B5 Rajkot India
37 F4 Rajmahal India
37 F4 Rajmahal Hills h. India
36 E5 Raj Nandgaon India
36 C5 Rajpipla India
36 D4 Rajsamand India
37 G4 Rajshahi div. Bangladesh
37 G4 Rajshahi Bangladesh
38 B2 Rajura India
37 F3 Raka China
5 L5 Rakahanga atoll
127 B5 Rakai Uganda
9 C5 Rakaia r. New Zealand
39 E4 Rakan, Ra's pt Qatar
36 C1 Rakaposhi mt. Pakistan
37 F3 Raka Zangbo r. China
31 J5 Rakdong r. South Korea
81 F5 Rakek Slovenia
112 E1 Rakhiv Ukraine
53 E3 Rakhmanivka Ukraine
36 B3 Rakhni Pakistan
39 F4 Rakhshan r. Pakistan
6 □8 Rakiraki Fiji
22 B3 Rakit i. Indonesia
53 F1 Rakitnoye Rus. Fed.
54 E2 Rakke Estonia
58 D2 Rakkestad Norway
36 B3 Rakni r. Pakistan
76 E3 Rakoniewice Poland
79 M3 Rakoshyn Ukraine
78 C1 Rakovník Czech Rep.
112 E3 Rakovski Bulgaria
52 E3 Raksha Rus. Fed.
58 D1 Rakskiftet h. Norway
46 D3 Rakusha Kazakhstan
54 E2 Rakvere Estonia
145 E5 Raleigh N. Carolina U.S.A.
74 B3 Ralingen Germany
22 D3 Ralla Indonesia
179 □ Rallier du Baty, Péninsule pen. Kerguelen Indian Ocean
148 D2 Ralph Michigan U.S.A.
136 E2 Ram r. N.W.T. Canada
43 C5 Ram Jordan
77 M5 Rama r. Ukraine
43 C3 Rama Israel
110 D5 Ramacca Sicilia Italy
164 C4 Ramaditas Chile
139 H2 Ramah Newfoundland Canada
155 H4 Ramah New Mexico U.S.A.
99 G1 Ramales de la Victoria Spain
173 G2 Ramallo Argentina
38 B3 Ramanagaram India
38 B4 Ramanathapuram India
37 E5 Ramanuj Ganj India
38 A3 Ramas, C. c. India
52 A3 Ramasukha Rus. Fed.
131 E2 Ramatlabama r. Botswana/South Africa
131 E2 Ramatlabama Botswana
87 F4 Rambervillers France
103 B6 Rambla del Judío r. Spain
103 B6 Rambla del Moro r. Spain
89 G3 Rambouillet France
69 D5 Rambrouch Luxembourg
87 E4 Rambucourt France
6 □1 Rambutyo I. i. P.N.G.
38 A3 Ramdurg India
37 F4 Ramechhap Nepal
62 B4 Rame Head headland England U.K.
131 G5 Rame Head pt South Africa
64 A2 Ramelton Rep. of Ireland
129 H1 Ramena Madagascar
52 D2 Ramenki Rus. Fed.
52 D2 Ramenskoye Rus. Fed.
52 C1 Rameshki Rus. Fed.
38 B4 Rameswaram India
36 D3 Ramganga r. India
37 G5 Ramgarh Bangladesh
36 B4 Ramgarh India
37 F5 Ramgarh India
39 G2 Ramgul reg. Afghanistan
39 C3 Rāmhormoz Iran
69 C4 Ramillies Belgium
81 E3 Ramingstein Austria
126 D3 Ramis Shet' r. Ethiopia
42 C4 Ram, Jebel mt. Jordan
43 C4 Ramla Israel
118 C3 Ramlat al Wīgh sand dunes Libya
119 H4 Ramlat Dahm sand dunes Saudi Arabia/Yemen
118 D3 Ramlat Rabyānah desert Libya
55 A3 Ramme Denmark
87 G3 Rammelsbach Germany
80 B2 Rammingen Germany
131 F3 Rammulotsi South Africa
Ramnad see Ramanathapuram
36 C2 Ramnagar India
36 D3 Ramnagar India
59 G2 Ramnäs Sweden
112 F2 Râmnicu Sărat Romania
112 E2 Râmnicu Vâlcea Romania
52 D4 Ramon' Rus. Fed.
154 D5 Ramona California U.S.A.
82 B1 Ramonchamp France
173 K2 Ramón Trigo Uruguay
93 D5 Ramonville-St-Agne France
140 E2 Ramore Ontario Canada
67 D3 Ramor, Lough l. Rep. of Ireland
83 F2 Ramosch Switzerland
128 D3 Ramotswa Botswana
65 E3 Rampside England U.K.
36 D3 Rampur India
36 D3 Rampur India
36 D3 Rampur India
36 C4 Rampura India
Rampur Boalia see Rajshahi
37 F4 Rampur Hat India
24 A3 Ramree Myanmar
24 A3 Ramree I. i. Myanmar
59 F2 Ramsberg Sweden
65 F4 Ramsbottom England U.K.
56 E3 Ramsele Sweden
83 D1 Ramsen Switzerland
63 F2 Ramsey England U.K.
140 D3 Ramsey Ontario Canada
64 D3 Ramsey Isle of Man
64 D3 Ramsey Bay b. Isle of Man
62 A3 Ramsey Island i. Wales U.K.
140 D3 Ramsey Lake l. Ontario Canada
63 H3 Ramsgate England U.K.
37 G4 Ramshai Hat India
87 G3 Ramstein Germany
36 D5 Ramtek India
43 D3 Ramtha Jordan
6 □1 Ramu r. P.N.G.
159 □4 Ramville, Îlet i. Martinique Caribbean
54 D4 Ramygala Lithuania
52 F3 Ramza Rus. Fed.
98 D1 Rañadoiro, Sierra de mountain range Spain
37 G5 Ranaghat India
22 E4 Ranakah, P. mt. Indonesia
36 C5 Ranapur India
23 A5 Ranau Malaysia
22 A3 Ranau, D. l. Indonesia
172 B3 Rancagua Chile
88 C3 Rance r. France
69 C4 Rance Belgium
168 C5 Rancharia Brazil
37 F5 Ranchi India
173 H3 Ranchos Argentina
172 A6 Ranco, L. de l. Chile
13 F3 Rand New South Wales Australia
67 E2 Randalstown Northern Ireland U.K.
90 B2 Randan France
110 D5 Randazzo Sicilia Italy
55 C3 Randers Denmark
55 C3 Randers Fjord inlet Denmark
147 H3 Randolph Massachusetts U.S.A.
147 G3 Randolph Vermont U.S.A.
73 K2 Randow r. Germany
58 D1 Randsfjorden l. Norway
56 D3 Randsjö Sweden
131 G3 Randvaal South Africa
56 F2 Råneå Sweden
122 B3 Ranérou Senegal
89 E3 Rânes France
9 C6 Ranfurly New Zealand
25 C6 Rangae Thailand
37 H5 Rangamati Bangladesh
37 H4 Rangapara North India
22 D2 Rangas, Tg pt Indonesia
22 D2 Rangas, Tg pt Indonesia
9 □1 Rangatira I. i. Chatham Is New Zealand
8 D1 Rangaunu Bay b. New Zealand
147 H2 Rangeley Maine U.S.A.
147 H2 Rangeley Lake l. Maine U.S.A.
155 H1 Rangely Colorado U.S.A.
140 D3 Ranger Lake Ontario Canada
37 G4 Rangia Patharughat India
9 D5 Rangiora New Zealand
8 F2 Rangipoua mt. New Zealand
7 □10 Rangiroa i. French Polynesia Pacific Ocean
8 F3 Rangitaiki r. New Zealand
9 C5 Rangitata r. New Zealand
8 E4 Rangitikei r. New Zealand
8 D4 Rangitoto Is is New Zealand
22 A3 Rangkasbitung Indonesia
47 H5 Rangkŭl Tajikistan
24 B3 Rangoon r. Myanmar
Rangoon see Yangon
37 G4 Rangpur Bangladesh
25 C7 Rangsang i. Indonesia
73 J3 Rangsdorf Germany
38 A3 Ranibennur India
37 F5 Raniganj India
37 E5 Ranijula Pk mt. India
36 D3 Ranikhet India
36 B4 Ranipur Pakistan
36 C4 Raniwara India
14 D4 Ranken watercourse Northern Terr. Australia
151 C6 Rankin Texas U.S.A.
137 L2 Rankin Inlet inlet N.W.T. Canada
137 L2 Rankin Inlet N.W.T. Canada
131 F2 Rankin Pass South Africa
13 F3 Rankin's Springs New South Wales Australia
80 A3 Rankweil Austria
54 E2 Ranna Estonia
15 G5 Rannes Queensland Australia
66 D4 Rannoch, L. l. Scotland U.K.
66 D4 Rannoch Moor moorland Scotland U.K.
36 B4 Rann of Kachchh marsh India
123 F4 Rano Nigeria
129 G2 Ranobe r. Madagascar
129 H3 Ranohira Madagascar
7 □16 Rano Kito h. Easter I. Chile
129 H3 Ranomena Madagascar
6 □2 Ranon Vanuatu
25 B5 Ranong Thailand
6 □1 Ranongga i. Solomon Is.
7 □16 Rano Raraku h. Easter I. Chile
25 C6 Ranot Thailand
52 D3 Ranova r. Rus. Fed.
172 C4 Ranquilcó, S. salt pan Argentina
172 C4 Ranquil del Norte Argentina
39 B2 Rānsa Iran
59 E1 Ransby Sweden
21 K7 Ransiki Indonesia
56 H3 Rantasalmi Finland
22 C2 Rantau Indonesia
22 C2 Rantaupanjang Indonesia
20 D6 Rantauprapat Indonesia
22 D2 Rantemario, G. mt. Indonesia
81 F3 Ranten Austria
22 D2 Rantepao Indonesia
148 C5 Rantoul Illinois U.S.A.
52 B1 Rantsevo Rus. Fed.
56 G2 Rantsila Finland
56 G2 Ranua Finland
55 B3 Ranum Denmark
112 B4 Ranxë Albania
42 F2 Rānya Iraq
31 K3 Raohe China
87 F4 Raon-l'Étape France
33 G4 Raoping China
8 □4 Raoul I. i. Kermadec Is New Zealand
177 K7 Rapa i. French Polynesia Pacific Ocean
106 D4 Rapallo Italy
36 B5 Rapar India
39 D4 Rapch watercourse Iran
172 B2 Rapel r. Chile
172 B3 Rapel, Emb. resr Chile
67 D2 Raphoe Rep. of Ireland
146 E5 Rapidan r. Virginia U.S.A.
12 D3 Rapid Bay S. Australia Australia
150 C2 Rapid City S. Dakota U.S.A.
141 F3 Rapide-Deux Québec Canada
141 F3 Rapide-Sept Québec Canada
148 D3 Rapid River Michigan U.S.A.
54 E2 Rāpina Estonia
54 D2 Rapla Estonia
109 H4 Rapolla Italy
100 B1 Raposa Portugal
146 E5 Rappahannock r. Virginia U.S.A.
22 D2 Rappang Indonesia
83 D1 Rapperswil Switzerland
81 G2 Rappottenstein Austria
37 E4 Rapti r. India
36 B5 Rapur India
23 C3 Rapurapu i. Philippines
147 F2 Raquette r. New York U.S.A.
147 F3 Raquette Lake l. New York U.S.A.
147 F3 Raquette Lake New York U.S.A.
129 F2 Raraga r. Mozambique
7 □10 Raraka i. French Polynesia Pacific Ocean
86 B3 Raray France
147 F4 Raritan Bay b. New Jersey U.S.A.
7 □10 Raroia atoll French Polynesia Pacific Ocean
82 C2 Raron Switzerland
177 J7 Rarotonga i. Cook Islands Pacific Ocean
119 G3 Ra's Abū Madd headland Saudi Arabia
119 G3 Ras Abu Shagara pt Sudan
120 A4 Râs Agâdîr pt Mauritania
42 A4 Râs 'Alam el Rûm c. Egypt
43 C2 Ra's al Basīţ c. Syria
118 D1 Ra's al Hilāl pt Libya
126 D2 Ra's al Kathīb pt Yemen
39 C4 Ra's al Khaymah U.A.E.
118 E1 Ra's al Muraysah pt Libya
43 C5 Ras al Qaşbah pt Saudi Arabia
173 F6 Rasa, Pta pt Argentina
119 H4 Ra's aţ Ţarfā pt Saudi Arabia
118 D1 Ra's at Tīn pt Libya
119 G3 Ras Banâs pt Egypt
119 G3 Ra's Barīdī headland Saudi Arabia
126 D2 Ras Bir pt Djibouti
43 B4 Râs Burûn pt Egypt
112 F1 Râşca Romania
99 G4 Rascafría Spain
53 B3 Râşcani Moldova
75 H2 Raschau Germany
126 C2 Ras Dashen mt. Ethiopia
43 B5 Râs Dib pt Egypt
54 C4 Raseiniai Lithuania
43 A4 Râs el Barr pt Egypt
43 B5 Râs el Gineina mt. Egypt
119 E1 Râs el Kenâyis pt Egypt
122 D3 Râs el Mâ Mali
43 C5 Râs el Nafas mt. Egypt
43 B5 Râs el Sudr pt Egypt
119 F2 Râs Ghârib Egypt
30 C3 Rashaant Mongolia
126 B2 Rashad Sudan
119 G3 Râs Hadarba pt Sudan
43 C4 Rashādīya Jordan
64 B3 Rasharkin Northern Ireland U.K.
119 G3 Ra's Ḩāţibah pt Saudi Arabia
119 F1 Rashid Egypt
39 F3 Rashid Qala Afghanistan
53 E1 Rashivka Ukraine
39 C2 Rashm Iran
39 B1 Rasht Iran
43 C2 Ras Ibn Hāni' pt Syria
81 F5 Rašica Slovenia
111 □ Ras Id-Dawwara pt Malta
111 □ Ras l-Irqieqa pt Malta
111 □ Ras il-Dwejra pt Malta
111 □ Ras il-Qala pt Malta
111 □ Ras il-Qammieh pt Malta
111 □ Ras il-Wahx pt Malta
111 □ Ras il-Wardija pt Malta
112 C3 Rasina r. Yugoslavia
99 G1 Rasines Spain
38 B4 Rasipuram India
111 □ Ras ir-Raheb pt Malta
126 D1 Ra's 'Īsā pt Yemen
39 E4 Rāsk Iran
112 C3 Raška Yugoslavia
47 J5 Raskam mountain range China
119 G4 Ras Kasar pt Sudan
126 □ Ra's Kattānahan pt Socotra Yemen
127 C6 Ras Kizimkazi pt Tanzania
39 F3 Raskoh mountain range Pakistan
36 A3 Ras Koh mt. Pakistan
118 C1 Ra's Lānūf pt Libya
43 B5 Râs Mal'ab pt Egypt
43 B5 Râs Matarma Egypt
127 C6 Ras Mkumbi pt Tanzania
126 □ Ra's Momi pt Socotra Yemen
119 F2 Râs Muhammad c. Egypt
135 J3 Rasmussen Basin b. N.W.T. Canada
120 A4 Râs Nouâdhibou c. Western Sahara
112 E2 Râşnov Romania
127 C6 Ras Nungwi pt Tanzania
171 C5 Raso, C. pt Argentina
171 C5 Raso, Cabo Argentina
166 E2 Raso da Catarina reg. Brazil
17 D6 Rason L. salt flat Western Australia Australia
54 F4 Rasony Belarus
42 A4 Râs Qattâra Egypt
102 D3 Rasquera Spain
37 E4 Rasra India
43 B5 Râs Ruahmi pt Egypt
121 G2 Ras Ajdir Tunisia
111 □ Ras San Dimitri pt Malta
126 D2 Ras Shakhs pt Eritrea
126 □ Ra's Shu'ab pt Socotra Yemen
43 B5 Râs Shukheir Egypt
105 C7 Rass Jebel Tunisia
52 E3 Rasskazovo Rus. Fed.
39 B4 Ras Tannurah Saudi Arabia
96 D5 Ras Targa Morocco
74 D4 Rastatt Germany
55 B3 Råsted Denmark
72 D2 Rastede Germany
81 G2 Rastenfeld Austria
126 D2 Ras Terma pt Eritrea
120 A5 Ras Timirist pt Mauritania
80 C3 Rastkogel mt. Austria
73 G2 Rastow Germany
99 E3 Rasueros Spain
39 C4 Rasul watercourse Iran
43 B6 Râs Umm 'Omeiyid h. Egypt
59 F2 Råsvalen l. Sweden
76 F4 Raszków Poland
52 C4 Rat' r. Rus. Fed.
36 C3 Ratangarh India
56 D3 Rätansbyn Sweden
77 M3 Rataychytsy Belarus
25 B4 Rat Buri Thailand
52 D3 Ratchino Rus. Fed.
81 E4 Rateče Slovenia
73 F2 Ratekau Germany
130 B5 Ratelfontein South Africa
36 D4 Rath India
67 E3 Rathangan Rep. of Ireland
64 B4 Rathcoole Rep. of Ireland
64 B4 Rathcor Rep. of Ireland
67 D4 Rathdowney Rep. of Ireland
67 E4 Rathdrum Rep. of Ireland
24 A2 Rathedaung Myanmar
73 H3 Rathenow Germany
67 E2 Rathfriland Northern Ireland U.K.
67 C4 Rathkeale Rep. of Ireland
67 E1 Rathlin Island i. Northern Ireland U.K.
67 C4 Rathluirc Rep. of Ireland
64 B4 Rathmolyon Rep. of Ireland
64 A4 Rathowen Rep. of Ireland
67 E4 Rathvilly Rep. of Ireland
72 B4 Ratingen Germany
81 F4 Ratitovec mt. Slovenia
36 C3 Ratiya India
36 C5 Ratlam India
38 A2 Ratnagiri India
38 C5 Ratnapura Sri Lanka
53 A1 Ratne Ukraine
64 B4 Ratoath Rep. of Ireland
36 B4 Rato Dero Pakistan
153 F4 Raton New Mexico U.S.A.
75 F2 Rattelsdorf Germany
81 G3 Ratten Austria
80 C3 Rattenberg Austria
65 E1 Rattray Scotland U.K.
66 G3 Rattray Head headland Scotland U.K.
59 F1 Rättvik Sweden
73 F2 Ratzeburg Germany
73 G3 Rätzlingen Germany
136 C3 Ratz, Mt mt. B.C. Canada
25 C7 Raub Malaysia
75 H5 Raubling Germany
173 H4 Rauch Argentina
58 C1 Raudbergskarvet mt. Norway
42 F4 Raudhatain Kuwait
54 C4 Raudondvaris Lithuania
56 N6 Raufarhöfn Iceland
8 G2 Raukumara mt. New Zealand
8 F3 Raukumara Range mountain range New Zealand
169 G4 Raul Soares Brazil
57 F3 Rauma Finland
9 E4 Raumati New Zealand
54 D3 Rauna Latvia
58 B1 Raundalselvi r. Norway
63 F2 Raunds England U.K.
22 C4 Raung, G. volcano Indonesia
8 E3 Raurimu New Zealand
80 D3 Rauris Austria
37 F5 Raurkela India
28 K1 Rausu Japan
53 B3 Răut r. Moldova
56 H3 Rautavaara Finland
57 H3 Rautjärvi Finland
107 G2 Ràut, Monte mt. Italy
7 □10 Ravahéré i. French Polynesia Pacific Ocean
152 D2 Ravalli Montana U.S.A.
104 G3 Ravan mt. Bos.-Herz.
39 D4 Rāvang Iran
39 F4 Ravānsar Iran
110 C5 Ravanusa Sicilia Italy
39 D3 Rāvar Iran
77 M5 Rava-Rus'ka Ukraine
109 G4 Ravello Italy
164 C3 Ravelo Bolivia
69 C3 Ravels Belgium
81 G2 Ravelsbach Austria
59 F3 Rävemåla Sweden
147 G3 Ravena New York U.S.A.
65 E3 Ravenglass England U.K.
107 F4 Ravenna div. Italy
107 G4 Ravenna Italy
74 E5 Ravensburg Germany
15 F3 Ravenshoe Queensland Australia
68 D3 Ravenstein Netherlands
17 C7 Ravensthorpe Western Australia Australia
15 F4 Ravenswood Queensland Australia
146 C5 Ravenswood W. Virginia U.S.A.
36 C3 Ravi r. Pakistan
93 E5 Raviège, Lac de la l. France
107 J3 Ravna Gora Croatia
81 F4 Ravne na Koroškem Slovenia
46 F5 Ravnina Turkmenistan
47 G3 Ravnina Dar'yalyktakyr plain Kazakhstan
135 Q3 Ravn, Kap pt Greenland
46 E4 Ravshan Uzbekistan
42 E3 Rāwah Iraq
5 K5 Rawaki i. Kiribati
36 C2 Rawalpindi Pakistan
77 J4 Rawa Mazowiecka Poland
42 F2 Rawāndiz Iraq
36 C3 Rawatsar India
126 D1 Rawdah Yemen
141 J3 Rawdon Québec Canada
43 D5 Rawghah watercourse Saudi Arabia
76 E4 Rawicz Poland
146 D5 Rawley Springs Virginia U.S.A.
17 D6 Rawlinna Western Australia Australia
152 F3 Rawlins Wyoming U.S.A.
17 D5 Rawlinson, Mt h. Western Australia Australia
17 E5 Rawlinson Ra. h. Western Australia Australia
173 G3 Rawson Buenos Aires Argentina
171 D5 Rawson Chubut Argentina
65 F4 Rawtenstall England U.K.
32 B2 Rawu China
81 G3 Raxalpe mts Austria
37 F4 Raxaul India
38 B3 Rayachoti India
38 B3 Rayadurg India
38 C2 Rāyagarha India
139 J4 Ray, C. headland Newfoundland Canada
31 J2 Raychikhinsk Rus. Fed.
126 D1 Raydah Yemen
46 D2 Rayevskiy Rus. Fed.
63 G3 Rayleigh England U.K.
136 G5 Raymond Alberta Canada
147 H3 Raymond New Hampshire U.S.A.
152 B2 Raymond Washington U.S.A.
151 D7 Raymondville Texas U.S.A.
91 E5 Rayol-Canadel-sur-Mer France
25 C4 Rayong Thailand
146 D4 Raystown Lake l. Pennsylvania U.S.A.
43 D5 Rayth al Khayl watercourse Saudi Arabia
119 G3 Rayyis Saudi Arabia
39 B2 Razan Iran
112 C3 Ražanj Yugoslavia
Razdan see Hrazdan
31 J4 Razdol'noye Rus. Fed.
30 B1 Razdol'ye Rus. Fed.
81 F5 Razdrto Slovenia
39 B2 Razeh Iran
92 D2 Razès France
112 E3 Razgrad div. Bulgaria
112 F3 Razgrad Bulgaria
77 N2 Razhanka Belarus
112 G2 Razim, L. lag. Romania
112 D4 Razlog Bulgaria
36 B2 Razmak Pakistan
54 E3 Rāznas r. Latvia
88 A3 Raz, Pte du pt France
53 G1 Razumnoye Rus. Fed.
62 D2 Rea Brook r. England U.K.
63 F3 Reading England U.K.
147 F4 Reading Pennsylvania U.S.A.
159 □1 Reading Jamaica
148 B4 Readstown Wisconsin U.S.A.
131 F2 Reagile South Africa
166 E3 Real r. Brazil
173 H4 Real Audiencia Argentina
164 C3 Real, Cord. mts Bolivia
172 D3 Real de Padre Argentina
101 E4 Reales mt. Spain
172 E3 Realicó Argentina
93 E5 Réalmont France
25 C4 Reăng Kesei Cambodia
157 E3 Reata Mexico
121 F2 Rebaa Algeria
86 C4 Rebais France
17 C6 Rebecca, L. salt flat Western Australia Australia
69 C4 Rebecq Belgium
93 E6 Rébenty r. France
Rebiana Sand Sea desert see Ramlat Rabyānah
76 G1 Rębiechowo airport Poland
173 K3 Reboledo Uruguay
101 F2 Rebollera mt. Spain
98 C3 Rebordelo Portugal
28 H1 Rebun-suidō chan. Japan
28 H1 Rebun-tō i. Japan
173 G4 Recalde Argentina
107 H5 Recanati Italy
53 C3 Recea Moldova
67 B3 Recess Rep. of Ireland
90 C1 Recey-sur-Ource France
17 C7 Recherche, Archipelago of the is Western Australia Australia
87 F4 Réchicourt-le-Château France
36 C3 Rechna Doab lowland Pakistan
69 E4 Recht Belgium
51 D4 Rechytsa Belarus
6 □2 Récif de la Gazelle reef New Caledonia Pacific Ocean
6 □2 Récif des Français reef New Caledonia Pacific Ocean
6 □2 Récif Durand reef New Caledonia Pacific Ocean
166 F2 Recife Brazil
131 E7 Recife, Cape c. South Africa
127 □1 Recif I. i. Seychelles
6 □2 Récif Petrie reef New Caledonia Pacific Ocean
6 □2 Récifs de l'Astrolabe reef New Caledonia Pacific Ocean
6 □2 Récifs d'Entrecasteaux reef New Caledonia Pacific Ocean
172 B4 Recinto Chile
72 C3 Recke Germany
72 C4 Recklinghausen Germany
73 H1 Recknitz r. Germany
107 F3 Recoaro Terme Italy
170 E2 Reconquista Argentina
91 D4 Recoubeau-Jansac France
165 E1 Recreio Mato Grosso Brazil
169 G4 Recreio Minas Gerais Brazil
170 C2 Recreo Catamarca Argentina
173 G1 Recreo Santa Fé Argentina
76 D2 Recz Poland
77 H4 Ręczno Poland
151 E6 Red r. Louisiana U.S.A.
137 K5 Red r. Canada/U.S.A.
76 G1 Reda Poland
58 D1 Redalen Norway
25 C6 Redang i. Malaysia
69 D5 Redange Luxembourg
147 F4 Red Bank New Jersey U.S.A.
145 C5 Red Bank Tennessee U.S.A.
139 J3 Red Bay Newfoundland Canada
154 A1 Red Bluff California U.S.A.
155 F4 Red Butte summit Arizona U.S.A.
65 G3 Redcar England U.K.
137 G4 Redcliff Alberta Canada
129 D2 Redcliff Zimbabwe
15 H5 Redcliffe Queensland Australia
17 C6 Redcliffe, Mt h. Western Australia Australia
13 E3 Red Cliffs Victoria Australia
150 D3 Red Cloud Nebraska U.S.A.
137 G4 Red Deer r. Alberta Canada
137 J4 Red Deer r. Saskatchewan Canada
136 G4 Red Deer Alberta Canada
137 J4 Red Deer L. l. Manitoba Canada
147 F5 Redden Delaware U.S.A.
131 F4 Reddersburg South Africa
152 B3 Redding California U.S.A.
63 E2 Redditch England U.K.
65 F2 Rede r. England U.K.
73 G2 Redefin Germany
130 B6 Redelinghuys South Africa
166 D2 Redenção Brazil
121 F2 Redeyef Tunisia
147 F3 Redfield New York U.S.A.
150 D2 Redfield S. Dakota U.S.A.
159 □3 Redhead Trinidad and Tobago
63 F3 Redhill England U.K.
155 H4 Red Hill New Mexico U.S.A.
12 D3 Redhill S. Australia Australia
128 □1 Red Hill, Mt h. Ascension Atlantic Ocean
151 D4 Red Hills h. Kansas U.S.A.
78 F5 Rédics Hungary
139 J4 Red Indian L. l. Newfoundland Canada
148 E5 Redkey Indiana U.S.A.
52 C1 Redkino Rus. Fed.
138 B3 Red L. l. Ontario Canada
155 E4 Red L. l. Arizona U.S.A.
138 B3 Red Lake Ontario Canada
150 E1 Red Lakes lakes Minnesota U.S.A.
152 E2 Red Lodge Montana U.S.A.
63 E4 Redlynch England U.K.
152 B2 Redmond Oregon U.S.A.
75 G3 Rednitz r. Germany
150 E3 Red Oak Iowa U.S.A.
127 C5 Redojari waterhole Kenya
88 C4 Redon France
98 B2 Redondela Spain
100 C2 Redondo Portugal
Red River r. see Song Hông
140 A2 Red Rock Ontario Canada
147 E4 Red Rock Pennsylvania U.S.A.

17 D7 Red Rocks Pt pt Western Australia Australia
62 A4 Redruth England U.K.
119 G3 Red Sea sea Africa/Asia
136 D2 Redstone r. N.W.T. Canada
136 E4 Redstone B.C. Canada
137 L4 Red Sucker L. l. Manitoba Canada
Red Volta r. see Nazinon
136 G4 Redwater Alberta Canada
62 B1 Red Wharf Bay b. Wales U.K.
139 H3 Red Wine r. Newfoundland Canada
148 A3 Red Wing Minnesota U.S.A.
154 A3 Redwood City California U.S.A.
150 E2 Redwood Falls Minnesota U.S.A.
152 B3 Redwood Nat. Park California U.S.A.
154 A2 Redwood Valley California U.S.A.
148 E4 Reed City Michigan U.S.A.
154 C3 Reedley California U.S.A.
148 C4 Reedsburg Wisconsin U.S.A.
152 A3 Reedsport Oregon U.S.A.
147 E6 Reedville Virginia U.S.A.
179 B4 Reedy Gl. gl. Antarctica
Reef Islands is see Rowa
9 C5 Reefton New Zealand
67 D3 Ree, Lough l. Rep. of Ireland
72 B4 Rees Germany
73 G2 Reetz Germany
42 D2 Refahiye Turkey
43 D3 Refa'i, T. mt. Jordan/Syria
171 B5 Refugio i. Chile
151 D6 Refugio Texas U.S.A.
76 D2 Rega r. Poland
110 D5 Regalbuto Sicilia Italy
81 E3 Regau Austria
75 H3 Regen r. Germany
75 J4 Regen Germany
169 J3 Regência Brazil
75 H3 Regensburg Germany
83 D1 Regensdorf Switzerland
75 H3 Regenstauf Germany
168 C5 Regente Feijó Brazil
121 E3 Reggane Algeria
68 E2 Regge r. Netherlands
107 F5 Reggello Italy
111 E4 Reggio di Calabria div. Italy
111 E4 Reggio di Calabria Italy
107 E4 Reggio Emilia div. Italy
107 E4 Reggiolo Italy
107 E4 Reggio nell'Emilia Italy
112 E1 Reghin Romania
137 J4 Regina Saskatchewan Canada
163 G3 Regina Brazil
163 G3 Régina French Guiana
39 F3 Registan reg. Afghanistan
168 E6 Registro Brazil
168 C1 Registro do Araguaia Brazil
59 F2 Regna Sweden
56 H2 Regozero Rus. Fed.
55 D4 Regstrup Denmark
98 B2 Reguengo Spain
100 C2 Reguengos de Monsaraz Portugal
75 H2 Rehau Germany
72 E3 Rehburg Germany
72 D3 Rehden Germany
36 D5 Rehli India
80 B2 Rehling Germany
74 B3 Rehlingen-Siersburg Germany
75 J2 Řehlovice Czech Rep.
73 G2 Rehna Germany
155 H4 Rehoboth New Mexico U.S.A.
128 B3 Rehoboth Namibia
147 F5 Rehoboth Bay b. Delaware U.S.A.
147 F5 Rehoboth Beach Delaware U.S.A.
43 C4 Rehovot Israel
115 E6 Reicheia Greece
81 G3 Reichenau an der Rax Austria
75 H2 Reichenbach Germany
82 C2 Reichenbach Switzerland
81 F3 Reichenfels Austria
80 D3 Reichenspitze mt. Austria
75 G4 Reichertshofen Germany
87 G4 Reichshoffen France
82 C1 Reiden Switzerland
6 □7 Reid Reef reef Fiji
145 E4 Reidsville N. Carolina U.S.A.
63 F3 Reigate England U.K.
92 A2 Ré, Île de i. France
155 G5 Reiley Peak summit Arizona U.S.A.
91 D5 Reillanne France
86 D3 Reims Marne France
82 D1 Reinach Aargau Switzerland
82 C1 Reinach Basel Switzerland
148 A4 Reinbeck Iowa U.S.A.
72 F2 Reinbek Germany
137 J3 Reindeer r. Saskatchewan Canada
137 K4 Reindeer I. i. Manitoba Canada
137 J3 Reindeer Lake l. Saskatchewan Canada
56 D2 Reine Norway
58 C1 Reineskarvet mt. Norway
72 F2 Reinfeld (Holstein) Germany
8 D1 Reinga, Cape c. New Zealand
74 D3 Reinheim Germany
99 F2 Reinosa Spain
90 C3 Reins r. France
69 E5 Reinsfeld Germany
58 B2 Reinsnosi mt. Norway
58 D1 Reinsvoll Norway
56 L2 Reiphólsfjöll mt. Iceland
56 F1 Reisaelva r. Norway
75 H4 Reisbach Germany
80 D2 Reischach Germany
56 G3 Reisjärvi Finland
72 B2 Reitdiep r. Netherlands
110 D5 Reitano Sicilia Italy
131 G3 Reitz South Africa
131 F3 Reitzburg South Africa
59 F2 Rejmyre Sweden
77 M4 Rejowiec Fabryczny Poland
163 D3 Rejunya Venezuela
72 C4 Reken Germany
36 A3 Rekgwash Pakistan
28 J2 Rekifune-gawa r. Japan
77 N5 Reklynets' Ukraine
112 C3 Rekovac Yugoslavia
58 C1 Reksjåeggi mt. Norway
137 H2 Reliance N.W.T. Canada
121 E1 Relizane Algeria
72 E2 Rellingen Germany
121 G2 Remada Tunisia
72 C3 Remagen Germany
89 F3 Rémalard France
9 □3 Remarkable Arch arch Antipodes Is New Zealand
12 D3 Remarkable, Mt mt. S. Australia Australia
22 B3 Rembang Indonesia
172 F4 Remecó Argentina
98 A2 Remedios, Pta dos pt Spain
39 D4 Remeshk Iran
69 E5 Remich Luxembourg
163 G3 Rémire French Guiana
87 F4 Remiremont France
36 D2 Remo Gl. gl. India
102 B3 Remolinos Spain
51 G6 Remontnoye Rus. Fed.
91 C5 Remoulins France
22 A1 Rempang i. Indonesia
74 E4 Rems r. Germany
72 C4 Remscheid Germany
88 C4 Remungol France
148 E4 Remus Michigan U.S.A.
91 D4 Rémuzat France
32 E1 Ren r. China
58 D1 Rena r. Norway
58 D1 Rena Norway
100 E1 Rena Spain
172 A4 Renaico Chile
90 B2 Renaison France
38 B2 Renapur India
89 D4 Renazé France
87 H4 Renchen Germany
111 F3 Rende Italy
144 B4 Rend L. l. Illinois U.S.A.
6 □1 Rendova i. Solomon Is.
72 E1 Rendsburg Germany
99 G1 Renedo Spain
82 B2 Renens Switzerland
68 B3 Renesse Netherlands
141 G4 Renfrew Ontario Canada
66 D5 Renfrew Scotland U.K.
66 D5 Renfrewshire div. Scotland U.K.
172 B3 Rengo Chile
74 C2 Rengsdorf Germany
33 F2 Renheji China
33 F3 Renhua China
32 D3 Renhuai China
53 C3 Reni Ukraine
54 D1 Renko Finland
Renland reg. see Tuttut Nunaat
12 E3 Renmark S. Australia Australia
31 H3 Renmin China
6 □1 Rennell i. Solomon Is.
74 D2 Rennerod Germany
75 G4 Rennertshofen Germany
88 D3 Rennes Ille-et-Vilaine France
58 A2 Rennesøy i. Norway
179 B5 Rennick Gl. gl. Antarctica
137 H2 Rennie Lake l. N.W.T. Canada
74 D4 Renningen Germany
81 E3 Rennweg Austria
107 F4 Reno r. Italy
154 C2 Reno Nevada U.S.A.
72 F2 Renön Italy
108 B2 Rénoso, Monte mt. Corse France
130 C6 Renoster r. South Africa
131 F3 Renoster r. South Africa
146 E4 Renovo Pennsylvania U.S.A.
31 F5 Renqiu China
32 D2 Renshou China
148 D5 Rensselaer Indiana U.S.A.
147 G3 Rensselaer New York U.S.A.
102 B1 Rentería Spain
114 C3 Rentina Greece
152 B2 Renton Washington U.S.A.
37 E4 Renukut India
86 D3 Renwez France
9 D4 Renwick New Zealand
122 D4 Réo Burkina
22 E4 Reo Indonesia
78 F4 Répce r. Hungary
129 E3 Repembe r. Mozambique
77 L3 Repki Poland
54 F2 Repolka Rus. Fed.
8 F3 Reporoa New Zealand
72 F2 Reppenstedt Germany
168 C3 Represa Agua Vermelha resr Brazil
168 D5 Represa Barra Bonita resr Brazil
168 C5 Represa Capivara resr Brazil
165 E5 Represa de Acaray resr Paraguay
163 F4 Represa de Balbina resr Brazil
168 E3 Represa de Emborcação resr Brazil
168 A6 Represa de Itaipu resr Brazil
168 D5 Represa de Jurumirim resr Brazil
168 D3 Represa de São Simão resr Brazil
168 D5 Represa de Xavantes resr Brazil
169 E4 Represa Furnas resr Brazil
168 B5 Represa Ilha Grande resr Brazil
168 C4 Represa Ilha Solteira resr Brazil
168 C4 Represa Jupiá resr Brazil
169 E4 Represa Peixoto resr Brazil
168 B4 Represa Pôrto Primavera resr Brazil
168 D4 Represa Promissão resr Brazil
168 C4 Represa Três Irmãos resr Brazil
169 F3 Represa Três Marias resr Brazil
166 C1 Represa Tucuruí Brazil
152 C1 Republic Washington U.S.A.
150 D3 Republican r. Nebraska U.S.A.
15 G4 Repulse B. b. Queensland Australia
135 K3 Repulse Bay N.W.T. Canada
162 C5 Requena Peru
103 B5 Requena Spain
172 B3 Requinoa Chile
93 E4 Réquista France
42 D1 Reşadiye Turkey
22 A3 Resag, G. mt. Indonesia
114 C1 Resen Macedonia
169 F5 Resende Brazil
98 C3 Resende Portugal
168 C6 Reserva Brazil
52 F1 Reshetikha Rus. Fed.
53 C1 Reshetnikovo Rus. Fed.
53 E2 Reshetylivka Ukraine
52 F1 Reshma Rus. Fed.
39 D1 Reshteh-ye Esfarayen mountain range Iran
107 E2 Resia, Lago di l. Italy
80 B4 Resia, Passo di pass Austria
170 E2 Resistencia Argentina
112 C2 Reşiţa Romania
76 D2 Resko Poland
135 J2 Resolute N.W.T. Canada
135 M3 Resolution Island i. N.W.T. Canada
9 A6 Resolution Island i. New Zealand
169 H3 Resplendor Brazil
52 B2 Ressa r. Rus. Fed.
52 B3 Resseta r. Rus. Fed.
86 B3 Ressons-sur-Matz France
159 □1 Rest Jamaica
164 B1 Restauracão Brazil
101 E5 Restinga Morocco
169 G5 Restinga de Marambaia beach Brazil
65 F2 Reston Scotland U.K.
110 D5 Resuttano Sicilia Italy
53 E1 Ret' r. Ukraine
157 H6 Retalhuleu Guatemala
172 C2 Retamito Argentina
25 □ Retan Laut, P. i. Singapore
172 B2 Retén Atalaya Chile
172 A3 Retén Llico Chile
123 E5 Retenue de Nangbéto res. Togo
63 F1 Retford England U.K.
86 D3 Rethel France
72 E3 Rethem (Aller) Germany
86 B3 Rethondes France
115 F7 Rethymno div. Greece
115 F7 Rethymno Greece
69 D3 Retie Belgium
88 D4 Retiers France
100 D2 Retin r. Spain
100 E4 Retín, Sierra de mountain range Spain
172 B4 Retiro Chile
79 L3 Rétköz reg. Hungary
91 C3 Retournac France
79 J4 Rétság Hungary
83 F1 Rettenberg Germany
102 B4 Retuerta mt. Spain
81 G2 Retz Austria
73 H3 Reuden Germany
89 H4 Reuilly France
117 K8 Réunion i. Indian Ocean
102 C3 Reus Spain
69 D3 Reusel Netherlands
83 D1 Reuss r. Switzerland
53 F1 Reut r. Rus. Fed.
87 G4 Reute Germany
73 H2 Reuterstadt Stavenhagen Germany
74 E4 Reutlingen Germany
83 E1 Reutte div. Austria
80 B3 Reutte Austria
69 E3 Reuver Netherlands
46 E1 Revda Rus. Fed.
154 D3 Reveille Peak summit Nevada U.S.A.
93 E5 Revel France
74 F4 Revelganj India
91 F4 Revello Italy
136 F4 Revelstoke B.C. Canada
162 A5 Reventazón Peru
90 D2 Revermont reg. France
85 G2 Revigny-sur-Ornain France
136 C3 Revillagigedo I. i. Alaska U.S.A.
156 □ Revillagigedo, Islas is Mexico
86 D3 Revin France
43 C4 Revivim Israel
52 B3 Revna r. Rus. Fed.
75 K3 Řevnice Czech Rep.
73 C1 Řevničov Czech Rep.
107 F2 Revò Italy
101 H2 Revolcadores mt. Spain
129 E2 Revúboè r. Mozambique
79 K3 Revúca Slovakia
129 E2 Revuè r. Mozambique
52 C2 Revyakino Rus. Fed.
6 □8 Rewa r. Fiji
37 E4 Rewa India
76 D1 Rewal Poland
36 D3 Rewari India
152 E3 Rexburg Idaho U.S.A.
139 H4 Rexton New Brunswick Canada
53 C1 Reya Ukraine
124 B2 Rey Bouba Cameroon
56 N6 Reyðarfjörður b. Iceland
164 C2 Reyes Bolivia
154 C4 Reyes Peak summit California U.S.A.
43 D1 Reyhanlı Turkey
156 L7 Rey, Isla del i. Panama
56 L6 Reykir Iceland
174 H2 Reykjanes Ridge sea feature Atlantic Ocean
56 L7 Reykjanestá pt Iceland
56 L6 Reykjavík Iceland
14 C4 Reynolds Ra. mountain range Northern Terr. Australia
157 F3 Reynosa Mexico
92 D2 Reyssouze r. France
88 D4 Rezé France
54 E3 Rēzekne r. Latvia
54 E3 Rēzekne Latvia
106 E3 Rezzato Italy
156 D2 R.F. Magón Mexico
112 D2 Rgotina Yugoslavia
83 E1 Rhätikon mts Switzerland
87 G3 Rhaunen Germany
62 C2 Rhayader Wales U.K.
72 D4 Rheda-Wiedenbrück Germany
72 B4 Rhede Germany
72 C2 Rhede (Ems) Germany
62 C2 Rheidol r. Wales U.K.
68 E3 Rhein r. Germany/Switzerland
74 C4 Rheinau Germany
87 G2 Rheinaugebirge h. Germany
74 B2 Rheinbach Germany
72 B4 Rheinberg Germany
87 G3 Rheinböllen Germany
69 F4 Rheinbreitbach Germany
72 C3 Rheine Germany
83 E1 Rheineck Switzerland
82 C1 Rheinfelden Switzerland
82 C1 Rheinfelden (Baden) Germany
74 C3 Rheinhessen-Pfalz div. Germany
74 B2 Rheinisches Schiefergebirge h. Germany
74 C3 Rheinland-Pfalz div. Germany
73 H2 Rheinsberg Germany
74 D4 Rheinstetten Germany
83 E2 Rheinwaldhorn mt. Switzerland
106 B3 Rhêmes-Notre-Dame Italy
82 C3 Rhêmes-St-Georges Italy
120 D3 Rhemilès well Algeria
68 D3 Rhenen Netherlands
66 D2 Rhiconich Scotland U.K.
74 C5 Rhin r. France
Rhin r. Germany/Switzerland see Rhein
Rhine r. France see Rhin
Rhine r. Netherlands see Rijn
147 G4 Rhinebeck New York U.S.A.
148 C3 Rhinelander Wisconsin U.S.A.
73 H3 Rhinkanal canal Germany
73 H3 Rhinluch marsh Germany
126 B4 Rhino Camp Uganda
73 H3 Rhinow Germany
73 H3 Rhinowes Berge h. Germany
120 C2 Rhir, Cap pt Morocco
69 C4 Rhisnes Belgium
106 D3 Rho Italy
147 H4 Rhode Island div. Rhode Island U.S.A.
Rhodes i. see Rodos
152 D2 Rhodes Pk summit Idaho U.S.A.
62 C3 Rhondda Wales U.K.
62 C3 Rhondda Cynon Taff div. Wales U.K.
90 C3 Rhône div. France
91 C5 Rhône r. France/Switzerland
91 D3 Rhône-Alpes div. France
68 C3 Rhoon Netherlands
80 D3 Rhordorf Germany
62 C1 Rhosllanerchrugog Wales U.K.
62 C1 Rhos-on-Sea Wales U.K.
62 B3 Rhossili Wales U.K.
121 F1 Rhoufi Algeria
62 C1 Rhuddlan Wales U.K.
92 E3 Rhue r. France
Rhum i. see Rum
102 B1 Rhune, La h. Spain
88 C4 Rhuys, Presqu'île de pen. France
Rhydaman see Ammanford
62 C1 Rhyl Wales U.K.
124 A3 Riaba Equatorial Guinea
111 F4 Riace Italy
166 C2 Riachão Brazil
166 D3 Riachão das Neves Brazil
166 E3 Riachão do Jacuípe Brazil
166 D2 Riacho r. Brazil
169 H3 Riacho Brazil
166 D3 Riacho de Santana Brazil
169 G1 Riacho dos Machados Brazil
173 F6 Riachos, I. de los i. Argentina
171 D5 Riachos, Is de los i. Argentina
98 B2 Ría de Arousa est. Spain
98 B4 Ria de Aveiro est. Portugal
98 E1 Ría de Avilés inlet Spain
98 B1 Ría de Betanzos est. Spain
98 A2 Ría de Corcubión b. Spain
98 A2 Ría de Corme e Laxe b. Spain
98 A1 Ría de Lires b. Spain
98 A2 Ría de Muros e Noia est. Spain
98 D1 Ría de Navia inlet Spain
98 B2 Ría de Pontevedra est. Spain
98 B2 Ría de Vigo est. Spain
99 E1 Ría de Villaviciosa inlet Spain
98 C1 Ría de Viveiro est. Spain
100 C4 Ria Formosa lag. Portugal
88 D4 Riaillé France
98 B2 Rial Spain
102 E2 Rialb de Noguera Spain
168 D1 Rialma Brazil
22 B2 Riam Indonesia
22 C2 Riamkanan, D. l. Indonesia
99 F2 Riaño Spain
168 D1 Rianópolis Brazil
91 D5 Rians France
101 G1 Riansáres r. Spain
88 B4 Riantec France
92 B2 Rianxo Spain
36 C2 Riasi India
22 A1 Riau div. Indonesia
99 G3 Riaza r. Spain
99 G3 Riaza Spain
99 G1 Riba Spain
98 B2 Ribadavia Spain
98 D2 Ribadelago Spain
98 C1 Ribadeo Spain
99 H4 Riba de Saelices Spain
99 E1 Ribadesella Spain
168 B4 Ribas do Rio Pardo Brazil
39 G1 Ribat Afghanistan
100 B1 Ribatejo reg. Portugal
129 F1 Ribáuè Mozambique
65 F4 Ribble r. England U.K.
65 F3 Ribblesdale reg. England U.K.
55 A4 Ribe div. Denmark
55 A4 Ribe r. Denmark
55 A4 Ribe Denmark
87 G4 Ribeauvillé France
86 B3 Ribécourt-Dreslincourt France
168 D6 Ribeira r. Brazil
168 D6 Ribeira Brazil
98 B3 Ribeira Portugal
96 □ Ribeira Brava Madeira Portugal
98 C3 Ribeira de Pena Portugal
100 □ Ribeira Grande Azores Portugal
168 D6 Ribeirão Branco Brazil
169 F3 Ribeirão das Neves Brazil
168 C5 Ribeirão do Pinhal Brazil
168 E4 Ribeirão Prêto Brazil
86 C3 Ribemont France
110 C5 Ribera Sicilia Italy
92 C3 Ribérac France
100 D2 Ribera del Fresno Spain
164 C2 Riberalta Bolivia
102 B2 Ribera Navarra reg. Spain
103 C4 Ribesalbes Spain
102 F2 Ribes de Freser Spain
91 D4 Ribiers France
81 F5 Ribnica Slovenia
81 G4 Ribnica Slovenia
73 H1 Ribnitz-Damgarten Germany
164 C4 Rica Aventura Chile
111 E4 Ricadi Italy
78 D2 Říčany Czech Rep.
109 G3 Riccia Italy
107 G4 Riccione Italy
155 E4 Rice California U.S.A.
148 A2 Rice Lake l. Minnesota U.S.A.
140 D3 Rice Lake l. Ontario Canada
141 F4 Rice Lake l. Ontario Canada
148 B3 Rice Lake Wisconsin U.S.A.
148 A4 Riceville Iowa U.S.A.
146 D4 Riceville Pennsylvania U.S.A.
87 F4 Richardménil France
131 J4 Richards Bay South Africa
170 B2 Richards Deep depth Chile
137 G3 Richardson r. Alberta Canada
151 D5 Richardson Texas U.S.A.
147 H2 Richardson Lakes l. Maine U.S.A.
134 E3 Richardson Mts mountain range N.W.T. Canada
9 B6 Richardson Mts mountain range New Zealand
6 □3 Richards Patches reef Tonga
122 A3 Richard Toll Senegal
127 □4 Riche en Eau Mauritius
68 D1 Richel i. Netherlands
89 F4 Richelieu France
155 F2 Richfield Utah U.S.A.
147 F3 Richfield Springs New York U.S.A.
147 E3 Richford New York U.S.A.
147 G2 Richford Vermont U.S.A.
64 B3 Richhill Northern Ireland U.K.
148 B5 Richland Iowa U.S.A.
148 B4 Richland Center Wisconsin U.S.A.
146 C6 Richlands Virginia U.S.A.
146 E6 Richmond airport Virginia U.S.A.
65 G3 Richmond England U.K.
148 E6 Richmond Indiana U.S.A.
146 A6 Richmond Kentucky U.S.A.
131 H4 Richmond KwaZulu-Natal South Africa
147 J2 Richmond Maine U.S.A.
149 F4 Richmond Michigan U.S.A.
13 G3 Richmond New South Wales Australia
130 D5 Richmond Northern Cape South Africa
141 H4 Richmond Ontario Canada
141 J4 Richmond Québec Canada
15 E4 Richmond Queensland Australia
147 G2 Richmond Vermont U.S.A.
146 E6 Richmond Virginia U.S.A.
159 □1 Richmond Jamaica
9 D4 Richmond New Zealand
141 F5 Richmond Hill Ontario Canada
9 D4 Richmond, Mt mt. New Zealand
13 H2 Richmond Ra. h. New South Wales Australia
9 D4 Richmond Range mountain range New Zealand
73 H1 Richtenberg Germany
130 A4 Richtersveld National Park nat. park South Africa
83 D1 Richterswil Switzerland
146 B4 Richwood Ohio U.S.A.
146 C5 Richwood W. Virginia U.S.A.
82 C1 Rickenbach Germany
102 B3 Ricla Spain
155 H3 Rico Colorado U.S.A.
98 E3 Ricobayo, Emb. de resr Spain
170 E2 Rico, Pto Argentina
68 C3 Ridderkerk Netherlands
82 C2 Riddes Switzerland
14 C4 Riddock, Mt mt. Northern Terr. Australia
141 H4 Rideau r. Ontario Canada
141 G4 Rideau Lake l. Ontario Canada
154 D4 Ridgecrest California U.S.A.
146 D4 Ridgway Pennsylvania U.S.A.
79 J5 Ridica Yugoslavia
137 J4 Riding Mountain Nat. Park nat. park Manitoba Canada
131 F6 Riebeek-Oos South Africa
130 B6 Riebeek Wes South Africa
88 B4 Riec-sur-Belon France
80 C2 Ried Germany
83 F1 Riedbergerhorn mt. Germany
75 G4 Riedenburg Germany
81 E2 Ried im Innkreis div. Austria
81 E2 Ried im Innkreis Austria
80 B3 Ried im Oberinntal Austria
90 F1 Riedisheim France
74 B3 Riegelsberg Germany
81 G3 Riegersburg Austria
82 C1 Riehen Switzerland
131 F2 Riekertsdam South Africa
83 D1 Rielasingen-Worblingen Germany
69 D4 Riemst Belgium
58 B2 Rienshornhei mt. Norway
107 G2 Rienza r. Italy
73 J4 Riesa Germany
171 B7 Riesco, Isla i. Chile
110 D5 Riesi Sicilia Italy
73 G4 Riestedt Germany
130 E4 Riet r. South Africa
130 C5 Riet r. South Africa
54 B4 Rietavas Lithuania
72 D4 Rietberg Germany
130 D6 Rietbron South Africa
130 C3 Rietfontein South Africa
130 C7 Riethuiskraal South Africa
109 E2 Rieti div. Lazio Italy
109 E2 Rieti Italy
131 G2 Rietkolk South Africa
131 G3 Rietkuil South Africa
73 K4 Rietschen Germany
130 C5 Riet se Vloer salt pan South Africa
80 C3 Rietz Austria
93 D5 Rieumes France
93 E4 Rieupeyroux France
91 B4 Rieutort-de-Randon France
88 C4 Rieux Bretagne France
93 D5 Rieux Midi-Pyrénées France
91 E5 Riez France
153 F4 Rifle Colorado U.S.A.
56 M6 Rifstangi pt Iceland
127 C5 Rift Valley div. Kenya
37 H3 Riga India
54 D3 Rīga Latvia
54 C3 Riga, Gulf of g. Estonia/Latvia
114 D3 Rigaio Greece
39 D3 Rīgān Iran
Rīgas Jūras Līcis see Riga, Gulf of
141 H4 Rigaud Québec Canada
152 C2 Riggins Idaho U.S.A.
93 E4 Rignac France
109 F2 Rignano Flaminio Italy
86 C4 Rigny-le-Ferron France
90 C2 Rigny-sur-Arroux France
139 J3 Rigolet Newfoundland Canada
118 B5 Rig-Rig Chad
66 E5 Rigside Scotland U.K.
39 D2 Rīgū Iran
37 E5 Rihand r. India
Riia Laht see Riga, Gulf of
57 G3 Riihimäki Finland
179 D4 Riiser-Larsenhalvøya pen. Antarctica
179 C3 Riiser-Larsenisen pen. Antarctica
179 D3 Riiser-Larsen Sea sea Antarctica
54 D2 Riisipere Estonia
153 D5 Riito Mexico
123 F4 Rijau Nigeria
107 J3 Riječki Zaliv b. Croatia
107 J3 Rijeka airport Croatia
107 J3 Rijeka Croatia
68 C3 Rijen Netherlands
69 D3 Rijn r. Netherlands
68 C2 Rijnsburg Netherlands
69 C3 Rijsbergen Netherlands
68 E2 Rijssen Netherlands
68 C2 Rijswijk Netherlands
119 H3 Rikā, W. ar watercourse Saudi Arabia
28 J2 Rikubetsu Japan
29 H4 Rikuzen-takata Japan
112 D3 Rila mts Bulgaria
152 C3 Riley Oregon U.S.A.
69 C3 Rilland Netherlands
90 C3 Rillieux-la-Pape France
102 C4 Rillo Spain
123 F4 Rima watercourse Niger/Nigeria
119 H2 Rimah, W. al watercourse Saudi Arabia
5 M7 Rimatara i. French Polynesia Pacific Ocean
22 A2 Rimau r. Indonesia
79 J3 Rimava r. Slovakia
79 K3 Rimavská Sobota Slovakia
136 G4 Rimbey Alberta Canada
59 H2 Rimbo Sweden
59 F2 Rimforsa Sweden
107 G4 Rimini Italy
69 C5 Rimogne France
93 D6 Rimont France
139 G4 Rimouski Québec Canada
74 E3 Rimpar Germany
66 D2 Rimsdale, Loch l. Scotland U.K.
39 F2 R i Musa Qala r. Afghanistan
37 G3 Rinbung China
22 D4 Rinca i. Indonesia
168 D4 Rincão Brazil
75 J4 Rinchnach Germany
158 □3 Rincon Bonaire Netherlands Ant.
145 □3 Rincon Puerto Rico
101 F1 Rinconada, Sierra de la mountain range Spain
164 C4 Rincon, Co del mt. Chile
103 B4 Rincon de Ademuz reg. Spain
172 C3 Rincón del Atuel Argentina
101 F4 Rincón de la Victoria Spain
170 E3 Rincón del Bonete, L. Artificial de resr Uruguay
173 J2 Rincón de Palacio Uruguay
156 E4 Rincón de Romos Mexico
56 C3 Rindal Norway
115 G5 Rineia i. Greece
110 D4 Rinella Italy
13 F5 Ringarooma B. b. Tasmania Australia
59 G2 Ringarum Sweden
36 C4 Rīngas India
37 G2 Ring Co salt lake China
55 C4 Ringe Denmark
57 C3 Ringebu Norway
83 E2 Ringelspitz mt. Switzerland
64 D3 Ringford Scotland U.K.
6 □6 Ringgold Isles is Fiji
24 B1 Ringhkung Myanmar
123 F4 Ringim Nigeria
55 A3 Ringkøbing div. Denmark
55 A3 Ringkøbing Denmark
55 A4 Ringkøbing Fjord lag. Denmark
63 G4 Ringmer England U.K.
64 B2 Ringsend Northern Ireland U.K.
59 E4 Ringsjön l. Sweden
59 G2 Ringsön i. Sweden
58 D1 Ringsrudåsen h. Norway
55 D4 Ringsted Denmark
56 E1 Ringvassøy i. Norway
63 E4 Ringwood England U.K.
172 A5 Riñihue Chile
172 A5 Riñihue, L. l. Chile
172 A6 Riñinahué Chile
22 D4 Rinjani, G. volcano Indonesia
59 F4 Rinkaby Sweden
64 C3 Rinns of Galloway, The pen. Scotland U.K.
64 B2 Rinns of Islay pen. Scotland U.K.
64 B2 Rinns Point pt Scotland U.K.
72 E3 Rinteln Germany
148 C4 Rio Wisconsin U.S.A.
115 C4 Rio Greece
167 A4 Rio Alegre Brazil
162 B4 Riobamba Ecuador
155 H2 Rio Blanco Colorado U.S.A.
172 B2 Río Blanco Chile
169 G5 Rio Bonito Brazil
164 C2 Rio Branco Brazil
173 L2 Río Branco Uruguay
168 D6 Rio Branco do Sul Brazil
163 E3 Rio Branco, Parque Nacional do nat. park Brazil
168 A4 Rio Brilhante Brazil
172 A6 Río Bueno Chile
159 □1 Rio Bueno Jamaica
163 E1 Río Caribe Venezuela
169 G4 Rio Casca Brazil
172 E1 Río Ceballos Argentina
159 F5 Río Chico Venezuela
168 E5 Rio Claro Brazil
159 G5 Rio Claro Trinidad and Tobago
159 E5 Río Claro Venezuela
159 □1 Rio Cobre r. Jamaica
172 E5 Río Colorado Argentina
122 B4 Rio Corubal r. Guinea-Bissau
172 E2 Río Cuarto Argentina
166 C3 Rio das Balsas r. Brazil
169 F4 Rio das Mortes r. Brazil
166 B3 Rio das Mortes r. Brazil
169 G5 Rio de Janeiro div. Brazil
169 G5 Rio de Janeiro Brazil
156 K8 Río de Jesús Panama
173 J3 Río de la Plata chan. Argentina/Uruguay
170 E4 Río de la Plata est. Uruguay
164 B2 Río de las Piedras r. Peru
100 E1 Rio de la Vid r. Spain
98 D3 Rio de Onor Portugal
120 A4 Río de Oro, B. de b. Western Sahara
166 C1 Rio do Para r. Brazil
168 C5 Rio do Peixe r. Brazil
167 C6 Rio do Sul Brazil
156 K7 Río Frio Costa Rica
98 D3 Riofrío de Aliste Spain
171 C7 Río Gallegos Argentina
122 B4 Rio Gêba r. Guinea-Bissau/Senegal
101 F4 Riogordo Spain
159 □1 Rio Grande r. Jamaica
156 J6 Río Grande r. Nicaragua
166 D2 Rio Grande Piauí Brazil
170 F3 Rio Grande Rio Grande do Sul Brazil
171 C7 Río Grande Argentina
156 E4 Río Grande Mexico
151 D7 Rio Grande City Texas U.S.A.
166 E2 Rio Grande do Norte div. Brazil
167 B6 Rio Grande do Sul div. Brazil
174 G8 Rio Grande Rise sea feature Atlantic Ocean
162 C1 Riohacha Colombia
162 B5 Rioja Peru
157 H4 Río Lagartos Mexico
166 E2 Rio Largo Brazil
107 F4 Riolo Terme Italy
90 B3 Riom France
100 B1 Rio Maior Portugal
172 B3 Río Malo Chile
168 B1 Rio Manso r. Brazil
108 C2 Rio Marina Italy
92 E3 Riom-ès-Montagnes France
164 C3 Río Mulatos Bolivia
124 B3 Río Muni reg. Equatorial Guinea
93 B5 Rion-des-Landes France
172 D5 Río Negro div. Argentina
173 J2 Río Negro div. Uruguay
168 A3 Rio Negro Mato Grosso do Sul Brazil
167 C6 Rio Negro Paraná Brazil
172 A6 Río Negro Chile
98 D2 Rionegro del Puente Spain
109 H4 Rionero in Vulture Italy
51 G7 Rioni r. Georgia
169 G4 Rio Novo Brazil
169 H4 Rio Novo do Sul Brazil
167 B6 Rio Pardo Brazil
169 G1 Rio Pardo de Minas Brazil
170 D1 Río Pescado Argentina
170 D2 Río Piedras Argentina
169 G4 Rio Pomba Brazil
169 G5 Rio Prêto Brazil
172 F1 Río Primero Argentina
153 F5 Rio Rancho New Mexico U.S.A.
155 G6 Rio Rico Arizona U.S.A.
98 C3 Ríos Spain
98 E2 Rioseco de Tapia Spain
172 F1 Río Segundo Argentina
99 G4 Riosequillo, Emb. de resr Spain
162 B2 Riosucio Colombia
173 H2 Río Tala Argentina
172 E2 Río Tercero Argentina
172 E2 Río Tercero, Emb. resr Argentina
162 B4 Río Tigre Ecuador
98 B3 Rio Tinto Portugal
23 A4 Rio Tuba Philippines
91 D5 Riou, Île de i. France
168 C2 Rio Verde Brazil
171 B7 Río Verde Chile
157 F4 Río Verde Mexico
168 A3 Rio Verde de Mato Grosso Brazil
154 B2 Rio Vista California U.S.A.
90 E1 Rioz France
165 E3 Riozinho r. Brazil
166 B2 Riozinho r. Brazil
106 A4 Ripa r. Italy
112 C2 Ripanj Yugoslavia
107 E5 Riparbella Italy
109 F2 Ripatransone Italy
107 H5 Ripe Italy
53 D1 Ripky Ukraine
65 G3 Ripley England U.K.
63 E1 Ripley England U.K.
146 B5 Ripley Ohio U.S.A.
145 B5 Ripley Tennessee U.S.A.
146 C5 Ripley W. Virginia U.S.A.
102 F2 Ripoll Spain
102 F2 Ripolles reg. Spain
154 B3 Ripon California U.S.A.
65 G3 Ripon England U.K.
148 C4 Ripon Wisconsin U.S.A.
111 E5 Riposto Sicilia Italy
62 C3 Risca Wales U.K.
93 B5 Riscle France
172 C3 Risco Plateado mt. Argentina
55 B3 Risgårde Bredning b. Denmark

100 C3 Sanlúcar de Guadiana Spain
100 D3 Sanlúcar la Mayor Spain
156 B3 San Lucas Baja California Sur Mexico
156 C4 San Lucas Baja California Sur Mexico
164 C4 San Lucas Bolivia
156 C4 San Lucas, C. c. Mexico
111 F3 San Lucido Italy
172 D2 San Luis div. Argentina
155 E5 San Luis Arizona U.S.A.
155 G5 San Luis Arizona U.S.A.
172 D2 San Luis Argentina
156 H5 San Luis Guatemala
156 D3 San Luis Mexico
159 E5 San Luis Venezuela
173 L2 San Luis al Medio Uruguay
157 E4 San Luis de la Paz Mexico
170 E2 San Luis del Palmar Argentina
156 B2 San Luisito Mexico
164 D2 San Luis, Lago de l. Bolivia
154 B4 San Luis Obispo California U.S.A.
154 B4 San Luis Obispo Bay b. California U.S.A.
157 E4 San Luis Potosí div. Mexico
157 E4 San Luis Potosí Mexico
154 B3 San Luis Reservoir resr California U.S.A.
156 B1 San Luis Río Colorado Mexico
170 C3 San Luis, Sa de mountain range Argentina
108 A5 Sanluri Sardegna Italy
80 D4 San Maddalena Vallalta Italy
98 C2 San Mamede, Serra do mountain range Spain
173 H4 San Manuel Argentina
107 E4 San Marcello Pistoiese Italy
110 C5 San Marco, Capo c. Sicilia Italy
108 A5 San Marco, Capo pt Sardegna Italy
109 G3 San Marco dei Cavoti Italy
109 H3 San Marco in Lamis Italy
151 D6 San Marcos Texas U.S.A.
172 B1 San Marcos Chile
157 H6 San Marcos Guatemala
157 F5 San Marcos Mexico
107 G5 San Marino country Europe
107 G5 San Marino San Marino
165 D2 San Martín r. Bolivia
172 C2 San Martín Argentina
170 C2 San Martín Argentina
162 C3 San Martín Colombia
99 G4 San Martín de la Vega Spain
172 B6 San Martín de los Andes Argentina
99 F5 San Martín de Pusa Spain
99 F4 San Martín de Valdeiglesias Spain
171 B6 San Martín, L. l. Argentina/Chile
83 G3 San Martino Buon Albergo Italy
107 F2 San Martino di Castrozza Italy
108 B2 San-Martino-di-Lota Corse France
83 G2 San Martino in Passiria Italy
154 A3 San Mateo California U.S.A.
102 C3 San Mateo de Gállego Spain
165 E3 San Matías Bolivia
171 D5 San Matías, Golfo g. Argentina
162 D2 San Mauricio Venezuela
109 J4 San Mauro Forte Italy
82 C3 San Mauro Torinese Italy
33 H2 Sanmen China
109 H3 San Menaio Italy
33 H2 Sanmen Wan b. China
33 E1 Sanmenxia China
155 H2 San Miguel r. Colorado U.S.A.
164 D2 San Miguel r. Bolivia
162 B3 San Miguel r. Colombia
156 C2 San Miguel r. Mexico
155 G6 San Miguel Arizona U.S.A.
154 B4 San Miguel California U.S.A.
165 D3 San Miguel Bolivia
156 H6 San Miguel El Salvador
156 L7 San Miguel Panama
164 B2 San Miguel Peru
23 B3 San Miguel Bay b. Philippines
157 E4 San Miguel de Allende Mexico
99 F3 San Miguel de Arroyo Spain
164 C3 San Miguel de Huachi Bolivia
173 H3 San Miguel del Monte Argentina
103 C7 San Miguel de Salinas Spain
170 C2 San Miguel de Tucumán Argentina
166 B3 San Miguel do Araguaia Brazil
156 L7 San Miguel, G. de b. Panama
154 B4 San Miguel I. i. California U.S.A.
23 A5 San Miguel Is. is Philippines
164 C2 San Miguelito Bolivia
156 L7 San Miguelito Panama
157 F5 San Miguel Sola de Vega Mexico
99 G2 San Millán mt. Spain
99 H2 San Millán de la Cogolla Spain
33 G3 Sanming China
107 E5 San Miniato Italy
23 B3 San Narciso Philippines
131 F4 Sannaspos South Africa
111 □ Sannat Malta
106 C3 Sannazzaro de'Burgondi Italy
36 A3 Sanni Pakistan
109 H3 Sannicandro Garganico Italy
111 H2 Sannicola Italy
111 F3 San Nicola dell'Alto Italy
173 G2 San Nicolas de los Arroyos Argentina
100 E2 San Nicolás del Puerto Spain
97 □ San Nicolás de Tolentino Canary Is Spain
154 C5 San Nicolas I. i. California U.S.A.
79 K5 Sânnicolau Mare Romania
108 B5 San Nicolò Gerrei Sardegna Italy
131 E3 Sannieshof South Africa
77 H3 Sanniki Poland
122 C5 Sanniquellie Liberia
29 H3 Sannohe Japan
77 L6 Sanok Poland
164 C4 San Pablo Potosí Bolivia
165 D3 San Pablo Santa Cruz Bolivia
172 A6 San Pablo Chile
157 F4 San Pablo Mexico
23 B3 San Pablo Philippines
83 G2 San Pancrazio Italy
111 G2 San Pancrazio Salentino Italy
83 F3 San Paolo, Isola i. Italy
155 G5 San Pedro r. Arizona U.S.A.
158 C2 San Pedro r. Cuba
172 A4 San Pedro Biobío Chile
173 H2 San Pedro Buenos Aires Argentina
170 D1 San Pedro Jujuy Argentina
170 F2 San Pedro Misiones Argentina
172 B2 San Pedro Santiago Chile
172 E1 San Pedro Argentina
157 J5 San Pedro Belize
165 D3 San Pedro Bolivia
122 C6 San-Pédro Côte d'Ivoire
156 C4 San Pedro Mexico
165 E4 San Pedro Paraguay
23 B3 San Pedro Philippines
154 C5 San Pedro Channel California U.S.A.
101 F4 San Pedro de Alcántara Spain
162 C3 San Pedro de Arimena Colombia
164 C4 San Pedro de Atacama Chile
99 F4 San Pedro del Arroyo Spain
163 E2 San Pedro de las Bocas Venezuela
156 E3 San Pedro de las Colonias Mexico
99 E3 San Pedro de Latarce Spain
103 C7 San Pedro del Pinatar Spain
159 E3 San Pedro de Macorís Dominican Rep.
100 D2 San Pedro de Mérida Spain
100 C1 San Pedro, Sierra de mountain range Spain
156 H6 San Pedro Sula Honduras
106 D3 San Pellegrino Terme Italy
79 K5 Sânpetru Mare Romania
110 D4 San Piero Patti Italy
111 E4 San Pietro Italy
107 E3 San Pietro in Cariano Italy
107 F4 San Pietro in Casale Italy
108 A5 San Pietro, Isola di i. Sardegna Italy
111 H2 San Pietro Vernotico Italy
106 E4 San Polo d'Enza Italy
42 G1 Sanqaçal Azerbaijan
66 E5 Sanquhar Scotland U.K.
162 B3 Sanquianga, Parque Nacional nat. park Colombia
102 D3 San Quilez mt. Spain
156 B2 San Quintín Mexico
156 A2 San Quintín, C. c. Mexico
155 G2 San Rafael r. Utah U.S.A.
154 A3 San Rafael California U.S.A.
172 C3 San Rafael Argentina
165 D3 San Rafael Bolivia
172 B3 San Rafael Chile
162 C1 San Rafael Venezuela
155 G2 San Rafael Knob summit Utah U.S.A.
154 C4 San Rafael Mts mts California U.S.A.
164 D2 San Ramón Beni Bolivia
165 D3 San Ramón Santa Cruz Bolivia
172 D1 San Ramon Argentina
173 K3 San Ramon Uruguay
106 B5 San Remo Italy
173 G5 San Román Argentina
162 C1 San Román, C. c. Venezuela
99 F4 San Román de los Montes Spain
101 E4 San Roque Andalucía Spain
98 B1 San Roque Galicia Spain
170 E2 San Roque Argentina
109 H4 San Rufo Italy
151 D6 San Saba Texas U.S.A.
172 E1 San Salano Argentina
122 B4 Sansalé Guinea
158 D1 San Salvador i. The Bahamas
173 J2 San Salvador r. Uruguay
173 H1 San Salvador Argentina
156 H6 San Salvador El Salvador
99 F2 San Salvador de Cantamunda Spain
170 C1 San Salvador de Jujuy Argentina
162 □ San Salvador, I. i. Galapagos Is Ecuador
106 C4 San Salvatore Monferrato Italy
109 G2 San Salvo Italy
122 C4 Sansanding Mali
123 E4 Sansanné-Mango Togo
36 D5 Sansar India
98 B2 San Sebastián h. Spain
156 B2 San Sebastian i. Mexico
San Sebastián see Donostia-San Sebastián
171 C7 San Sebastián Argentina
145 □3 San Sebastián Puerto Rico
171 C7 San Sebastián, B. de b. Argentina
97 □ San Sebastián de la Gomera Canary Is Spain
99 G4 San Sebastián de los Reyes Spain
107 G5 Sansepolcro Italy
108 D2 San Severa Italy
107 H5 San Severino Marche Italy
109 H3 San Severo Italy
33 H3 Sansha China
33 F4 Sanshui China
159 E5 San Silvestre Venezuela
104 F3 Sanski Most Bos.-Herz.
99 H2 Sansol Spain
111 F3 San Sosti Italy
108 B5 San Sperate Sardegna Italy
159 □5 Sans Toucher mt. Guadeloupe Caribbean
32 E3 Sansui China
25 D4 San, T. r. Cambodia
112 E1 Şanţ Romania
164 A1 Santa r. Peru
164 A1 Santa Peru
168 D4 Santa Adélia Brazil
100 D1 Santa Amalia Spain
154 D5 Santa Ana California U.S.A.
164 C3 Sta Ana Bolivia
164 C2 Santa Ana Bolivia
162 A4 Santa Ana Ecuador
157 H6 Sta Ana El Salvador
156 C2 Santa Ana Mexico
159 F5 Sta Ana Venezuela
173 H2 Sta Anita Argentina
151 D6 Santa Anna Texas U.S.A.
101 H3 Santa Bárbara mt. Spain
154 C4 Santa Barbara California U.S.A.
169 G3 Santa Bárbara Brazil
172 A4 Sta Bárbara Chile
162 B2 Sta Bárbara Colombia
156 H6 Sta Bárbara Honduras
156 D3 Santa Bárbara Mexico
102 D4 Sta Bárbara Spain
159 G5 Sta Bárbara Venezuela
153 B5 Santa Barbara Chan. chan. California U.S.A.
154 B4 Santa Barbara Channel chan. California U.S.A.
100 C3 Santa Bárbara de Casa Spain
154 C5 Santa Barbara I. i. California U.S.A.
167 B5 Sta Bárbara, Sa de h. Brazil
173 J2 Santa Bernardina Uruguay
156 C3 Sta Catalina i. Mexico
172 E2 Sta Catalina Argentina
170 C2 Sta Catalina Chile
158 D5 Sta Catalina Colombia
156 K7 Sta Catalina Panama
98 B1 Santa Catalina de Armada Spain
154 D5 Santa Catalina, Gulf of b. California U.S.A.
154 C5 Santa Catalina I. i. California U.S.A.
167 B6 Santa Catarina div. Brazil
156 B2 Sta Catarina Baja California Mexico
157 E3 Sta Catarina Nuevo León Mexico
167 C6 Sta Catarina, Ilha de i. Brazil
108 A4 Sta Caterina di Pittinuri Sardegna Italy
110 D5 Sta Caterina Villarmosa Sicilia Italy
158 □2 Sta Catharina Curaçao Netherlands Ant.
111 H2 Sta Cesarea Terme Italy
102 C2 Santa Cilia de Jaca Spain
7 □15 Santa Clara i. Juan Fernandez Is Chile
154 B3 Santa Clara California U.S.A.
155 F3 Santa Clara Utah U.S.A.
162 D4 Santa Clara Colombia
158 C2 Sta Clara Cuba
156 D2 Sta Clara Mexico
100 B3 Santa Clara-a-Velha Portugal
100 C3 Santa Clara de Louredo Portugal
173 K2 Santa Clara de Olimar Uruguay
173 G1 Sta Clare de Saguier Argentina
154 C4 Santa Clarita California U.S.A.
162 C4 Santa Clotilde Peru
102 F3 Sta Coloma de Farners Spain
102 F3 Sta Coloma de Gramanet Spain
102 E3 Santa Coloma de Queralt Spain
98 D2 Santa Colomba de Somoza Spain
98 B4 Santa Comba Dão Portugal
98 E2 Santa Cristina de la Polvorosa Spain
110 D6 Sta Croce Camerina Sicilia Italy
111 E5 Sta Croce, Capo c. Sicilia Italy
107 E5 Santa Croce sull'Arno Italy
171 B6 Santa Cruz div. Argentina
165 D3 Santa Cruz div. Bolivia
102 B3 Santa Cruz mt. Spain
153 E5 Santa Cruz r. Arizona U.S.A.
171 C7 Santa Cruz r. Argentina
166 A1 Santa Cruz r. Brazil
154 A3 Santa Cruz California U.S.A.
166 B1 Santa Cruz Pará Brazil
165 D3 Santa Cruz Bolivia
166 E2 Sta Cruz Brazil
170 B3 Sta Cruz Chile
159 □1 Sta Cruz Jamaica
156 C2 Sta Cruz Mexico
23 B3 Santa Cruz Philippines
23 A3 Sta Cruz Philippines
23 B2 Santa Cruz Philippines
100 A1 Sta Cruz Portugal
157 H6 Sta Cruz Barillas Guatemala
169 J2 Santa Cruz Cabrália Brazil
100 □ Santa Cruz das Flores Azores Portugal
168 D2 Santa Cruz de Goiás Brazil
97 □ Sta Cruz de la Palma Canary Is Spain
100 E1 Santa Cruz de la Sierra Spain
99 G5 Santa Cruz de la Zarza Spain
157 H6 Sta Cruz del Quiché Guatemala
99 F4 Santa Cruz del Retamar Spain
158 C2 Santa Cruz del Sur Cuba
103 B5 Santa Cruz de Moya Spain
101 G2 Santa Cruz de Mudela Spain
97 □ Sta Cruz de Tenerife Canary Is Spain
168 D5 Santa Cruz do Rio Pardo Brazil
167 B6 Santa Cruz do Sul Brazil
154 C4 Santa Cruz I. i. California U.S.A.
162 □ Santa Cruz, I. i. Galapagos Is Ecuador
176 G6 Santa Cruz Is is Solomon Is.
159 □1 Sta Cruz Mts mts Jamaica
171 C7 Santa Cruz, Pto Argentina
108 A5 Santadi Sardegna Italy
111 E3 Sta Domenica Talao Italy
110 D5 Sta Domenica Vittoria Sicilia Italy
173 H1 Sta Elena Argentina
162 A4 Santa Elena Ecuador
163 E3 Sta Elena Venezuela
162 A4 Sta Elena, B. de b. Ecuador
156 J7 Sta Elena, C. headland Costa Rica
101 F3 Santaella Spain
173 F2 Sta Eufemia Argentina
101 F2 Santa Eufemia Spain
111 F4 Sta Eufemia, Golfo di g. Italy
98 B2 Santa Eugenia Spain
100 C1 Santa Eulália Portugal
102 B4 Santa Eulalia Spain
103 E6 Sta Eulalia del Río Spain
173 G1 Santa Fé div. Argentina
153 F5 Santa Fe New Mexico U.S.A.
173 G1 Santa Fé Argentina
101 G3 Santa Fe Spain
169 F2 Santa Fé de Minas Brazil
168 C4 Santa Fé do Sul Brazil
162 □ Santa Fé, I. i. Galapagos Is Ecuador
110 D4 Sant'Agata di Militello Sicilia Italy
156 C4 Sta Genovéva mt. Mexico
108 A5 Santa Giusta Sardegna Italy
80 D4 Santa Giustina Italy
166 C1 Santa Helena Maranhão Brazil
168 A6 Santa Helena Paraná Brazil
168 C2 Santa Helena de Goiás Brazil
32 D2 Santai China
171 B7 Sta Inés, Isla i. Chile
6 □1 Santa Isabel i. Solomon Is.
172 D4 Sta Isabel Argentina
173 G2 Santa Isabel Argentina
165 D2 Sta Isabel Brazil
145 □3 Santa Isabel Puerto Rico
164 B3 Sta Isabel de Sihuas Peru
168 B5 Santa Isabel do Ivaí Brazil
172 A4 Sta Juana Chile
168 E3 Santa Juliana Brazil
170 D2 Sta Justina Argentina
102 D2 Sta Liestra y San Quílez Spain
36 B5 Santalpur India
107 E5 Santa Luce Italy
170 E2 Sta Lucía Argentina
164 B4 Sta Lucía Chile
162 B4 Sta Lucía Ecuador
157 H6 Sta Lucía Guatemala
173 J3 Sta Lucía Uruguay
111 E4 Sta Lucia del Mela Sicilia Italy
97 □ Sta Lucía de Tirajana Canary Is Spain
173 F2 Sta Lucía, L. l. Argentina
153 B4 Santa Lucia Range mountain range California U.S.A.
167 B4 Sta Luísa, Sa de h. Brazil
122 □ Santa Luzia i. Cape Verde
100 B3 Santa Luzia Portugal
103 D4 Santa Magdalena de Pulpís Spain
172 F3 Sta Magdelena Argentina
112 F1 Santa Mare Romania
102 E3 Sta Margarida de Montbui Spain
156 C3 Sta Margarita i. Mexico
103 G5 Sta Margarita Spain
110 C5 Sta Margherita di Belice Sicilia Italy
106 D4 Sta Margherita Ligure Italy
100 □ Santa Maria i. Azores Portugal
103 C5 Santa María mt. Spain
169 E1 Santa Maria r. Brazil
173 K1 Santa Maria r. Brazil
153 F6 Sta María r. Mexico
163 F4 Santa Maria Amazonas Brazil
154 B4 Santa Maria California U.S.A.
166 B1 Santa Maria Pará Brazil
167 B6 Santa Maria Rio Grande do Sul Brazil
170 C2 Sta María Argentina
122 □ Santa Maria Cape Verde
156 D3 Sta María Mexico
162 C4 Santa María Peru
83 F2 Santa Maria Switzerland
173 K3 Santa Maria, C. c. Uruguay
100 C4 Santa Maria, Cabo de c. Portugal
129 E4 Santa Maria, Cabo de pt Mozambique
109 G3 Sta Maria Capua Vetere Italy
166 E2 Santa Maria da Boa Vista Brazil
98 B4 Santa Maria da Feira Portugal
166 C2 Santa Maria das Barreiras Brazil
166 D3 Santa Maria da Vitória Brazil
99 G1 Santa María de Cayón Spain
99 H3 Sta María de Huertas Spain
163 D2 Sta María de Ipire Venezuela
99 G2 Santa María del Campo Spain
101 H1 Santa María del Campo Rus Spain
111 E3 Sta Maria del Cedro Italy
98 E2 Santa María del Páramo Spain
157 E4 Sta María del Río Mexico
162 C4 Sta Maria de Nanay Peru
103 B7 Santa María de Nieva Spain
109 G4 Sta Maria di Castellabate Italy
111 H3 Sta Maria di Leuca, Capo c. Italy
169 H2 Santa Maria do Salto Brazil
169 G3 Santa Maria do Suaçuí Brazil
162 □ Santa María, I. i. Galapagos Is Ecuador
172 A4 Santa María, I. i. Chile
6 □2 Santa Maria I. i. Vanuatu
99 F3 Sta María la Real de Nieva Spain
169 G4 Santa Maria Madalena Brazil
106 C2 Sta Maria Maggiore Italy
108 B5 Sta Maria Navarrese Sardegna Italy
83 E2 Sta Maria Rezzonico Italy
158 D2 Sta Marie, Cape c. The Bahamas
110 D4 Sta Marina Salina Italy
108 D2 Santa Marinella Italy
101 H1 Santa Marta Castilla - La Mancha Spain
100 D2 Santa Marta Extremadura Spain
162 C1 Santa Marta Colombia
125 B6 Santa Marta, Cabo de c. Angola
98 C3 Santa Marta de Penaguião Portugal
98 E4 Santa Marta de Tormes Spain
167 C6 Sta Marta Grande, C. de c. Brazil
154 C4 Santa Monica California U.S.A.
154 C5 Santa Monica Bay b. California U.S.A.
22 D2 Santan Indonesia
168 C3 Santana r. Brazil
166 D3 Santana Bahia Brazil
167 B7 Santana da Boa Vista Brazil
100 B3 Santana da Serra Portugal
166 E2 Santana do Ipanema Brazil
173 K1 Santana do Livramento Brazil
109 G4 Sant'Anastasia Italy
102 B3 Santander Colombia
99 G1 Santander Spain
99 G1 Santander, Bahía de b. Spain
108 B5 Sant' Andrea Frius Sardegna Italy
111 G2 Sant'Andrea, Isola i. Italy
110 D4 Sant'Angelo di Brolo Sicilia Italy
107 G5 Sant' Angelo in Lizzola Italy
106 D3 Sant Angelo Lodigiano Italy
110 B5 Sta Ninfa Sicilia Italy
155 G5 Santan Mt mt. Arizona U.S.A.
108 A5 Sant' Anna Arresi Sardegna Italy
108 A5 Sant' Antioco Sardegna Italy
108 A5 Sant' Antioco, Isola di i. Sardegna Italy
108 A5 Sant' Antonio di Santadi Sardegna Italy
103 G5 Santanyí Spain
99 F4 Santa Olalla Spain
100 D3 Santa Ollala del Cala Spain
111 E5 Sta Panagia, Capo c. Sicilia Italy
154 C4 Santa Paula California U.S.A.
103 C6 Sta Pola Spain
103 C6 Santa Pola, Cabo de pt Spain
166 D1 Santa Quitéria Brazil
107 G4 Santarcangelo di Romagna Italy
173 F3 Sta Regina Argentina
100 B1 Santarém div. Portugal
100 B1 Santarém Santarém Portugal
166 B1 Santarém Brazil
158 C2 Santaren Channel chan. Cuba
23 □2 Santa Rita Guam Pacific Ocean
166 F2 Sta Rita Brazil
165 E1 Santa Rita Brazil
162 C3 Santa Rita Colombia
162 C1 Sta Rita Venezuela
166 D3 Santa Rita de Cassia Brazil
168 B2 Santa Rita do Araguaia Brazil
169 F5 Santa Rita do Sapucaí Brazil
154 B3 Santa Rita Park California U.S.A.
164 B1 Santa Rosa Acre Brazil
164 C2 Santa Rosa Beni Bolivia
164 C2 Santa Rosa Beni Bolivia
154 A2 Santa Rosa California U.S.A.
172 E4 Santa Rosa La Pampa Argentina
153 F5 Santa Rosa New Mexico U.S.A.
167 B6 Santa Rosa Rio Grande do Sul Brazil
172 D6 Santa Rosa Río Negro Argentina
172 C2 Sta Rosa Argentina
162 B4 Sta Rosa Ecuador
157 H5 Sta Rosa Mexico
164 B2 Sta Rosa Peru
156 H6 Sta Rosa de Copán Honduras
165 D3 Sta Rosa de la Roca Bolivia
172 F1 Sta Rosa del Río Primero Argentina
168 E4 Santa Rosa de Viterbo Brazil
154 B5 Santa Rosa I. i. California U.S.A.
156 B3 Sta Rosalia Mexico
152 C3 Sta Rosa Ra. mountain range Nevada U.S.A.
155 G5 Santa Rosa Wash r. Arizona U.S.A.
111 F3 Sta Severina Italy
107 F5 Santa Sofia Italy
100 B2 Santa Sofia Portugal
100 B2 Santa Susana Portugal
170 D2 Santa Sylvina Argentina
166 C3 Santa Teresa r. Brazil
14 C5 Santa Teresa Northern Terr. Australia
173 G2 Sta Teresa Argentina
169 H3 Santa Teresa Brazil
159 F5 Sta Teresa Venezuela
108 B3 Sta Teresa di Gallura Sardegna Italy
111 E5 Sta Teresa di Riva Sicilia Italy
98 E4 Sta Teresa, Embalse de resr Spain
173 J4 Sta Teresita Argentina
170 C1 Sta Victoria, Sierra mountain range Argentina
168 C3 Santa Vitória Brazil
173 L2 Sta Vitória do Palmar Brazil
108 B5 Sta Vittoria, Monte mt. Sardegna Italy
102 F3 Sant Boix de Llobregat Spain
102 D4 Sant Carles de la Ràpita Spain
88 A3 Santec France
145 E5 Santee r. S. Carolina U.S.A.
154 D5 Santee California U.S.A.
109 G3 Sant' Elia a Pianisi Italy
156 A2 San Telmo Mexico
100 D3 San Telmo Spain
156 E5 San Telmo, Pta pt Mexico
107 H5 Sant Elpidio a Mare Italy
108 B4 San Teodoro Sardegna Italy
111 F2 Santeramo in Colle Italy
107 F4 Santerno r. Italy
86 B3 Santerre reg. France
102 B1 Santesteban Spain
102 G3 Sant Feliu de Guíxols Spain
102 F2 Sant Feliu de Palterols Spain
106 C3 Santhià Italy
172 B2 Santiago div. Chile
162 B4 Santiago r. Peru
156 C4 Santiago Baja California Sur Mexico
156 D3 Santiago Durango Mexico
167 B6 Santiago Brazil
172 B2 Santiago Chile
159 E3 Santiago Dominican Rep.
156 K7 Santiago Panama
23 B2 Santiago Philippines
98 B2 Santiago Spain
157 G5 Santiago Astata Mexico
171 A7 Santiago, C. headland Chile
156 K7 Santiago, Co mt. Panama
100 C1 Santiago de Alcántara Spain
101 F3 Santiago de Calatrava Spain
162 B5 Santiago de Cao Peru
164 A2 Santiago de Chocorvos Peru
164 A1 Santiago de Chuco Peru
98 B2 Santiago de Compostela airport Spain
158 D2 Santiago de Cuba Cuba
101 H2 Santiago de la Espada Spain
170 D2 Santiago del Estero div. Argentina
100 B2 Santiago do Cacém Portugal
100 B2 Santiago do Escoural Portugal
156 D4 Santiago Ixcuintla Mexico
124 A3 Santiago, Pta pt Equatorial Guinea
165 E3 Santiago, Sa de h. Bolivia
172 F1 Santiago Temple Argentina
156 D3 Santiaguillo, L. de l. Mexico
137 N2 Santianna Point pt N.W.T. Canada
99 F2 Santibáñez de la Peña Spain
98 E4 Santibáñez de la Sierra Spain
98 D2 Santibáñez de Vidriales Spain
22 E1 Santigi Indonesia
99 F1 Santillana Spain
99 G4 Santillana, Emb. de resr Spain
83 E1 Säntis mt. Switzerland
101 G2 Santisteban del Puerto Spain
99 F3 Santiuste de San Juan Bautista Spain
102 D4 Sant Jordi, Golf de g. Spain
93 D6 Sant Julià de Lòria Andorra
102 E2 Sant Llorenç de Morunys Spain
100 C2 Santo Aleixo Portugal
166 E3 Santo Amaro Brazil
169 H4 Santo Amaro de Campos Brazil
168 C4 Santo Anastácio r. Brazil
168 C4 Santo Anastácio Brazil
169 E5 Santo André Brazil
100 B2 Santo André Portugal
100 B2 Santo André, Lagoa de lag. Portugal
167 B6 Sto Angelo Brazil
122 □ Santo Antão i. Cape Verde
169 G3 Sto Antônio r. Brazil
166 E3 Sto Antônio, C. c. Brazil
168 C2 Santo Antônio da Barra Brazil
168 C5 Santo Antônio da Platina Brazil
166 E3 Sto Antônio de Jesus Brazil
167 A4 Sto Antônio de Leverger Brazil
169 G4 Santo Antônio de Pádua Brazil
162 D4 Santo Antônio do Içá Brazil
169 F4 Santo Antônio do Monte Brazil
100 A2 Sto Antonio dos Cavaleiros Portugal
169 J2 Santo Antônio, Pta pt Brazil
165 E3 Santo Corazón Bolivia
107 G2 Santo Croce, Lago di l. Italy
159 E5 Sto Domingo r. Venezuela
156 B2 Sto Domingo Baja California Mexico
156 C3 Sto Domingo Baja California Sur Mexico
97 □ Sto Domingo Canary Is Spain
157 E4 Sto Domingo San Luis Potosí Mexico
159 E3 Santo Domingo Dominican Rep.
157 H6 Santo Domingo Guatemala
156 J6 Sto Domingo Nicaragua
164 C2 Santo Domingo Peru
99 H2 Sto Domingo de la Calzada Spain
162 B4 Sto Domingo de los Colorados Ecuador
99 G3 Santo Domingo de Silos Spain
100 B2 Santo Estêvão Portugal
169 F3 Santo Hipólito Brazil
168 C5 Santo Inácio Brazil
166 D3 Sto Inácio Brazil
73 L3 Santok Poland
99 G1 Santoña Spain
166 D3 Sto Onofre r. Brazil
108 B2 Santo-Pietro-di-Tenda Corse France
Santorini i. see Thira
169 E5 Santos Brazil
169 G4 Santos Dumont Brazil
101 E2 Santos, Sierra de los h. Spain
106 D4 Sto Stefano d'Aveto Italy
80 D4 Santo Stefano di Cadore Italy
110 D4 Sto Stefano di Camastra Sicilia Italy
106 D4 Sto Stefano di Magra Italy
80 D5 Santo Stino di Livenza Italy
98 B3 Sto Tirso Portugal
156 A2 Sto Tomás Baja California Mexico
156 D2 Sto Tomás Chihuahua Mexico
156 J6 Sto Tomás Nicaragua
164 B2 Santo Tomás Peru
170 E2 Santo Tomé Corrientes Argentina
173 G1 Santo Tomé Santa Fé Argentina
101 G2 Santo Tomé Spain
98 E3 Santovenia Spain
68 C2 Santpoort Netherlands
108 A4 Santu Lussurgiu Sardegna Italy
99 G1 Santurtzi Spain
155 F3 Sanup Plateau plat. Arizona U.S.A.
171 B6 San Valentín, Co mt. Chile
109 E2 San Venanzo Italy
80 D5 San Vendemiano Italy
108 A4 San Vero Milis Sardegna Italy
99 F4 San Vicente mt. Spain
173 H3 San Vicente Buenos Aires Argentina
173 G1 San Vicente Santa Fe Argentina
172 B3 San Vicente Chile
156 H6 San Vicente El Salvador
156 A2 San Vicente Mexico
23 B2 San Vicente Philippines
100 C1 San Vicente de Alcántara Spain
164 A2 San Vicente de Cañete Peru
99 F1 San Vicente de la Barquera Spain
162 C3 San Vicente del Caguán Colombia
103 C6 San Vicente del Raspeig Spain
99 G1 San Vicente de Toranzo Spain
173 H1 San Victor Argentina
111 E4 San Vincenzo Sicilia Italy
108 C1 San Vincenzo Italy
108 B5 San Vito Sardegna Italy
107 G3 San Vito al Tagliamento Italy
110 B4 San Vito, Capo c. Sicilia Italy
109 G2 San Vito Chietino Italy
111 G2 San Vito dei Normanni Italy
110 B4 San Vito lo Capo Sicilia Italy
109 E3 San Vito Romano Italy
109 F1 San Vittoria in Matenano Italy
38 A1 Sanwer India
98 B2 Sanxenxo Spain
33 E5 Sanya China
129 D2 Sanyati r. Zimbabwe
33 E1 Sanyuan China
109 H4 Sanza Italy
125 C5 Sanza Pombo Angola
125 □ São Antônio Sao Tome and Principe
169 H2 São Antônio do Jacinto Brazil
168 E2 São Bartolomeu r. Brazil
100 B3 São Bartolomeu de Messines Portugal
163 F5 São Benedito r. Brazil
166 D1 São Benedito Brazil
164 C1 São Bento Amazonas Brazil
166 D1 São Bento Maranhão Brazil
168 C6 São Bento do Amparo Brazil
166 D1 São Bernardo Brazil
167 C5 São Bernardo do Campo Brazil
167 A6 São Borja Brazil
100 C3 São Brás Portugal
100 C3 São Brás de Alportel Portugal
167 B6 São Carlos Santa Catarina Brazil
168 E5 São Carlos São Paulo Brazil
100 B2 São Cristóvão Portugal
166 D3 São Desidério r. Brazil
166 D3 São Desidério Brazil
168 B3 São Domingos r. Brazil
169 E1 São Domingos r. Brazil
166 C3 São Domingos Brazil
100 B3 São Domingos Portugal
166 B3 São Félix Mato Grosso Brazil

73 J3 Schöneiche Berlin
73 J2 Schönermark Germany
75 F5 Schongau Germany
73 H3 Schönhausen Germany
73 F3 Schöningen Germany
72 F1 Schönkirchen Germany
74 E3 Schöntal Germany
73 J4 Schönwalde Brandenburg Germany
76 B3 Schönwalde Brandenburg Germany
73 F1 Schönwalde am Bungsberg Germany
80 B3 Schönwies Austria
147 J2 Schoodic Lake l. Maine U.S.A.
148 E4 Schoolcraft Michigan U.S.A.
69 B3 Schoondijke Netherlands
68 E2 Schoonebeek Netherlands
68 C3 Schoonhoven Netherlands
68 E2 Schoonoord Netherlands
68 C2 Schoorl Netherlands
74 C5 Schopfheim Germany
74 F3 Schopfloch Germany
73 F3 Schöppenstedt Germany
68 F2 Schöppingen Germany
73 J3 Schorfheide heath Germany
74 E4 Schorndorf Germany
72 C2 Schortens Germany
74 E2 Schotten Germany
13 G5 Schouten I. i. Tasmania Australia
6 □1 Schouten Islands is P.N.G.
74 D2 Schramberg Germany
80 C3 Schrankogel mt. Austria
140 B2 Schreiber Ontario Canada
81 G2 Schrems Austria
73 H3 Schrepkow Germany
74 D3 Schriesheim Germany
75 G4 Schrobenhausen Germany
81 F3 Schröder Austria
147 G3 Schroon Lake l. New York U.S.A.
74 E3 Schrozberg Germany
80 A3 Schruns Austria
83 D1 Schübelbach Switzerland
72 E1 Schuby Germany
155 F5 Schuchuli Arizona U.S.A.
67 B5 Schull Rep. of Ireland
137 K2 Schultz Lake l. N.W.T. Canada
73 K3 Schulzendorf Germany
73 J3 Schulzendorf bei Eichwalde Germany
82 D2 Schüpfheim Switzerland
154 C2 Schurz Nevada U.S.A.
74 E5 Schussen r. Germany
80 C2 Schutter r. Germany
74 C4 Schutterwald Germany
72 C3 Schüttorf Germany
147 G3 Schuylerville New York U.S.A.
73 H2 Schwaan Germany
75 G3 Schwabach Germany
75 F4 Schwaben div. Germany
80 C2 Schwabhausen Germany
74 E4 Schwäbische Alb mts Germany
74 E4 Schwäbisch Gmünd Germany
74 E3 Schwäbisch Hall Germany
75 F4 Schwabmünchen Germany
72 D3 Schwaförden Germany
74 E3 Schwaigern Germany
87 F3 Schwalbach Germany
74 E2 Schwalmstadt-Treysa Germany
74 E2 Schwalmstadt-Ziegenhain Germany
81 G4 Schwanberg Austria
83 E1 Schwanden Switzerland
75 H3 Schwandorf Germany
73 G4 Schwanebeck Germany
81 E2 Schwanenstadt Austria
72 D2 Schwanewede Germany
75 F5 Schwangau Germany
72 E1 Schwansen reg. Germany
72 E3 Schwarmstedt Germany
73 H2 Schwarz Germany
75 G2 Schwarza r. Germany
75 H4 Schwarzach Germany
80 E3 Schwarzach im Pongau Austria
81 G3 Schwarzau im Gebirge Austria
73 J4 Schwarze Elster r. Germany
75 G3 Schwarze Laber r. Germany
72 F2 Schwarzenbek Germany
75 H2 Schwarzenberg Germany
82 C2 Schwarzenburg Switzerland
75 H3 Schwarzenfeld Germany
80 C3 Schwarzenstein mt. Austria/Italy
74 B2 Schwarzer Mann h. Germany
75 H3 Schwarzer Regen r. Germany
73 K4 Schwarzer Schöps r. Germany
73 J4 Schwarzheide Germany
83 G1 Schwarzhorn mt. Austria
82 D2 Schwarzhorn mt. Switzerland
128 B4 Schwarzrand mts Namibia
74 D4 Schwarzwald mts Germany
80 C3 Schwaz div. Austria
80 C3 Schwaz Austria
81 H2 Schwechat Austria
73 K2 Schwedt Germany
74 D3 Schwegenheim Germany
74 B3 Schweich Germany
74 F2 Schweinfurt Germany
73 J4 Schweinitz Germany
73 H2 Schweinrich Germany
131 E3 Schweizer-Reneke South Africa
72 C4 Schwelm Germany
81 C3 Schwendau Austria
80 A2 Schwendi Germany
74 D4 Schwenningen Germany
73 J4 Schwepnitz Germany
73 G2 Schwerin Germany
73 G2 Schweriner See l. Germany
72 C4 Schwerte Germany
74 D3 Schwetzingen Germany
73 J2 Schwichtenberg Germany
73 K3 Schwielochsee l. Germany
72 E2 Schwinge r. Germany
82 C1 Schwörstadt Germany
72 F3 Schwülper Germany
83 D1 Schwyz div. Switzerland
83 D1 Schwyz Schwyz Switzerland
110 C5 Sciacca Sicilia Italy
110 D6 Scicli Sicilia Italy
89 G2 Scie r. France
82 B2 Sciez France
111 E4 Scilla Italy
63 □1 Scilly, Isles of is England U.K.
76 E4 Ścinawa Poland
90 E2 Scionzier France
146 B5 Scioto r. Ohio U.S.A.
155 F2 Scipio Utah U.S.A.
152 F1 Scobey Montana U.S.A.
110 D6 Scoglitti Sicilia Italy
63 H2 Scole England U.K.
13 G3 Scone New South Wales Australia
106 C3 Scopello Italy
92 C2 Scorbé-Clairvaux France
111 E4 Scordia, Monte mt. Italy
110 D5 Scordia Sicilia Italy
135 Q2 Scoresby Land reg. Greenland
135 Q2 Scoresby Sund chan. Greenland
Scoresbysund see Ittoqqortoormiit
88 B4 Scorff r. France
112 E2 Scornicești Romania
107 G3 Scorzè Italy
65 G3 Scotch Corner England U.K.
179 B1 Scotia Ridge sea feature Atlantic Ocean
174 G9 Scotia Sea sea Atlantic Ocean
60 E3 Scotland div. U.K.
140 E5 Scotland Ontario Canada
141 K4 Scotstown Québec Canada
141 K3 Scott Québec Canada
179 B5 Scott Base N.Z. Base Antarctica
131 H5 Scottburgh South Africa
136 D4 Scott, C. c. B.C. Canada
14 B2 Scott, C. c. Northern Terr. Australia
150 C4 Scott City Kansas U.S.A.
179 B5 Scott Coast coastal area Antarctica
146 D4 Scottdale Pennsylvania U.S.A.
179 B4 Scott Gl. gl. Antarctica
179 A5 Scott I. i. Pacific Ocean
135 L2 Scott Inlet inlet N.W.T. Canada
137 H3 Scott Lake l. Saskatchewan Canada
179 D4 Scott Mts mountain range Antarctica
8 D1 Scott Pt pt New Zealand
16 C2 Scott Reef reef Western Australia Australia
150 C3 Scottsbluff Nebraska U.S.A.
145 C5 Scottsboro Alabama U.S.A.
144 C4 Scottsburg Indiana U.S.A.
153 E5 Scottsdale Arizona U.S.A.
13 F5 Scottsdale Tasmania Australia
154 A3 Scotts Valley California U.S.A.
148 D4 Scottville Michigan U.S.A.
154 D3 Scotty's Junction Nevada U.S.A.
66 C2 Scourie Scotland U.K.
66 □2 Scousburgh Scotland U.K.
66 E2 Scrabster Scotland U.K.
146 F4 Scranton Pennsylvania U.S.A.
66 B4 Scridain, Loch inlet Scotland U.K.
65 H4 Scunthorpe England U.K.
82 F2 Scuol Switzerland
17 B6 Seabrook, L. salt flat Western Australia Australia
147 F5 Seaford Delaware U.S.A.
63 G4 Seaford England U.K.
140 E5 Seaforth Ontario Canada
15 G4 Seaforth Queensland Australia
159 □1 Seaforth Jamaica
23 A4 Seahorse Bank sand bank Philippines
137 K3 Seal r. Manitoba Canada
13 E3 Sea Lake Victoria Australia
128 □3 Seal Bay b. Tristan da Cunha Atlantic Ocean
130 D7 Seal, Cape c. South Africa
159 E2 Seal Cays is Turks and Caicos Is Caribbean
147 J3 Seal I. i. Maine U.S.A.
139 H3 Seal Lake l. Newfoundland Canada
130 E7 Seal Point pt South Africa
155 E3 Seaman Range mts Nevada U.S.A.
65 H3 Seamer England U.K.
155 E4 Searchlight Nevada U.S.A.
151 F5 Searcy Arkansas U.S.A.
154 D4 Searles Lake l. California U.S.A.
148 E4 Sears Michigan U.S.A.
147 J2 Searsport Maine U.S.A.
65 E3 Seascale England U.K.
154 B3 Seaside California U.S.A.
152 B2 Seaside Oregon U.S.A.
62 C4 Seaton England U.K.
65 E3 Seaton England U.K.
65 G2 Seaton Delaval England U.K.
152 B2 Seattle Washington U.S.A.
63 E4 Seaview England U.K.
15 F3 Seaview Ra. mountain range Queensland Australia
147 F5 Seaville New Jersey U.S.A.
9 D5 Seaward Kaikoura Ra. mountain range New Zealand
147 H3 Sebago Lake l. Maine U.S.A.
22 D2 Sebakung Indonesia
22 C2 Sebangan, Tk b. Indonesia
22 A1 Sebangka i. Indonesia
147 J2 Sebasticook r. Maine U.S.A.
23 A5 Sebatik i. Indonesia
131 G1 Sebayeng South Africa
92 E4 Sébazac-Concourès France
123 E4 Sebba Burkina
55 B3 Sebbersund Denmark
121 D2 Sebdou Algeria
122 C4 Sébékoro Mali
112 D2 Sebeș Romania
22 A3 Sebesi i. Indonesia
149 F4 Sebewaing Michigan U.S.A.
54 F3 Sebezh Rus. Fed.
128 D3 Sebina Botswana
42 D1 Şebin Karahisar Turkey
79 M5 Sebiș Romania
121 E3 Sebkha Azzel Matti salt pan Algeria
120 B4 Sebkhet Chemchâm salt lake Mauritania
121 G1 Sebkhet de Sidi El Hani salt pan Tunisia
120 B4 Sebkhet Oumm ed Drous Guebli salt lake Mauritania
120 A5 Sebkhet Te-n-Dghâmcha salt marsh Mauritania
120 B3 Sebkra Oum el Drouss Telli salt flat Mauritania
75 K2 Sebnitz Germany
147 J2 Seboeis Lake l. Maine U.S.A.
147 J2 Seboomook Maine U.S.A.
147 J2 Seboomook Lake l. Maine U.S.A.
145 D7 Sebring Florida U.S.A.
22 D2 Sebuku i. Indonesia
22 B1 Sebuyau Malaysia
106 E4 Secchia r. Italy
126 C3 Seccia Mts mts Ethiopia
52 G2 Sechenovo Rus. Fed.
162 A5 Sechura Peru
162 A5 Sechura, Bahía de b. Peru
74 E3 Seckach Germany
81 F3 Seckau Austria
81 F3 Seckauer Alpen mts Austria
86 C2 Seclin France
102 D4 Seco r. Spain
119 F3 2nd Cataract rapids Sudan
122 D6 Secondi Ghana
92 B2 Secondigny France
147 H2 Second Lake l. New Hampshire U.S.A.
15 E2 2nd Three Mile Opening chan. Queensland Australia
140 C5 Secord Lake l. Michigan U.S.A.
79 L3 Sečovce Slovakia
9 A6 Secretary Island i. New Zealand
131 G3 Secunda South Africa
38 B2 Secunderabad India
164 C3 Sécure r. Bolivia
79 K5 Secusigiu Romania
100 C1 Seda r. Portugal
54 D3 Seda Latvia
54 C3 Seda Lithuania
150 E4 Sedalia Missouri U.S.A.
38 B2 Sedam India
12 D3 Sedan S. Australia Australia
86 D3 Sedan France
99 G2 Sedano Spain
65 F3 Sedbergh England U.K.
9 E4 Seddon New Zealand
9 C4 Seddonville New Zealand
42 A1 Seddülbahir Turkey
43 C4 Sede Boqer Israel
39 D2 Sedeh Iran
91 D4 Séderon France
43 C4 Sederot Israel
65 G3 Sedgefield England U.K.
147 J2 Sedgwick Maine U.S.A.
122 A4 Sédhiou Senegal
107 G2 Sedico Italy
108 A4 Sedilo Sardegna Italy
78 D2 Sedlčany Czech Rep.
75 K3 Sedlec Prčice Czech Rep.
75 J3 Sedlice Czech Rep.
53 A1 Sedlyshche Ukraine
53 D1 Sedniv Ukraine
43 C4 Sedom Israel
155 G4 Sedona Arizona U.S.A.
105 A7 Sédrata Algeria
22 D1 Sedulang Indonesia
54 C4 Šeduva Lithuania
77 K5 Sędziszów Małopolski Poland
89 D3 Sée r. France
87 H4 Seebach Germany
73 K2 Seebad Heringsdorf Germany
81 F4 Seeberg Austria/Slovenia
81 E4 Seeboden Austria
80 D3 Seebruck Germany
73 F2 Seedorf Germany
80 C2 Seefeld Germany
80 C3 Seefeld in Tirol Austria
67 B4 Seefin h. Rep. of Ireland
75 F5 Seeg Germany
73 J2 Seehausen Brandenburg Germany
73 G3 Seehausen Sachsen-Anhalt Germany
83 G1 Seehausen am Staffelsee Germany
128 B4 Seeheim Namibia
74 D3 Seeheim-Jugenheim Germany
80 E3 Seekirchen am Wallersee Austria
130 D6 Seekoegat South Africa
130 E5 Seekoei r. South Africa
155 E5 Seeley California U.S.A.
179 B3 Seelig, Mt mt. Antarctica
73 K3 Seelow Germany
72 E3 Seelze Germany
83 D1 Seerücken v. Switzerland
89 F3 Sées France
72 F4 Seesen Germany
75 G5 Seeshaupt Germany
81 F3 Seetaler Alpen mountain range Austria
81 E3 Seethal Austria
72 F2 Seevetal Germany
81 E3 Seewalchen am Attersee Austria
81 H3 Seewinkel marsh Austria
90 E3 Sééz France
122 B5 Sefadu Sierra Leone
113 F5 Seferihisar Turkey
39 B2 Sefīd Dasht Iran
129 D3 Sefophe Botswana
120 D2 Sefrou Morocco
93 E4 Ségala reg. France
122 B4 Ségala Mali
93 E4 Ségala du Quercy reg. France
58 D1 Segalstad Norway
23 A5 Segama r. Malaysia
25 C7 Segamat Malaysia
96 E5 Segangane Morocco
112 D2 Segarcea Romania
102 E3 Segarra reg. Spain
123 E4 Ségbana Benin
22 D3 Segeri Indonesia
59 G2 Segersäng Sweden
50 E2 Segezha Rus. Fed.
39 G1 Seghnān Afghanistan
88 B3 Séglien France
83 E2 Segl, Lago da l. Switzerland
109 F3 Segni Italy
92 B3 Segonzac France
103 C5 Segorbe Spain
122 C4 Ségou div. Mali
122 C4 Ségou Mali
99 F3 Segovia div. Castilla y León Spain
162 C2 Segovia Colombia
99 F4 Segovia Spain
50 E2 Segozerskoye, Oz. l. Rus. Fed.
102 D3 Segre r. Spain
89 E4 Segré France
89 E4 Segréen reg. France
102 D3 Segrià reg. Spain
123 G2 Séguédine Niger
122 C5 Séguéla Côte d'Ivoire
122 C5 Séguélon Côte d'Ivoire
173 G2 Seguí Argentina
151 D6 Seguin Texas U.S.A.
173 F1 Segundo r. Argentina
103 C6 Segura r. Spain
98 D5 Segura Portugal
101 H2 Segura de la Sierra Spain
100 D2 Segura de León Spain
102 C4 Segura de los Baños Spain
101 H2 Segura, Sierra de mountain range Spain
99 F4 Segurilla Spain
128 C3 Sehithwa Botswana
72 E3 Sehnde Germany
36 D5 Sehore India
36 A4 Sehwan Pakistan
98 C4 Seia Portugal
88 D4 Seiche r. France
89 E4 Seiches-sur-le-Loir France
75 K2 Seifhennersdorf Germany
90 B1 Seignelay France
82 B1 Seignelégier Switzerland
93 E4 Seigne, Mt mt. France
24 A2 Seikpyu Myanmar
64 C1 Seil i. Scotland U.K.
56 F1 Seiland i. Norway
92 D3 Seilhac France
151 D4 Seiling Oklahoma U.S.A.
90 D2 Seille r. France
69 D4 Seilles Belgium
56 F3 Seinäjoki Finland
138 B4 Seine r. Ontario Canada
89 F2 Seine r. France
89 E2 Seine, Baie de b. France
86 B4 Seine-et-Marne div. France
89 F2 Seine-Maritime div. France
86 C4 Seine, Val de v. France
112 D1 Seini Romania
88 A3 Sein, Île de i. France
22 C2 Seipinang Indonesia
93 C6 Seira Spain
93 C5 Seissan France
81 F2 Seitenstetten Austria
93 D6 Seix France
100 A2 Seixal Portugal
100 B3 Seixe r. Portugal
55 D4 Sejerø i. Denmark
55 D4 Sejerø Bugt b. Denmark
77 M1 Sejny Poland
22 B1 Sekadau Indonesia
22 A2 Sekanak, Tk b. Indonesia
23 A6 Sekatak Bengara Indonesia
22 A2 Sekayu Indonesia
29 F6 Seki Japan
130 D2 Sekoma Botswana
52 G3 Sekretarka Rus. Fed.
39 E3 Sekūheh Iran
22 A3 Sekura Indonesia
126 C3 Sela Dingay Ethiopia
152 B2 Selah Washington U.S.A.
22 B1 Selakau Indonesia
25 C7 Selangor div. Malaysia
108 B5 Selargius Sardegna Italy
21 K8 Selaru i. Indonesia
22 D4 Selat Alas chan. Indonesia
22 C3 Selatan, Tg pt Indonesia
22 C4 Selat Bali chan. Indonesia
22 A2 Selat Bangka chan. Indonesia
22 A2 Selat Berhala chan. Indonesia
21 K7 Selat Dampir chan. Indonesia
22 A2 Selat Gaspar chan. Indonesia
25 □ Selat Johor chan. Malaysia/Singapore
25 □ Selat Jurong chan. Singapore
22 B2 Selat Karimata str. Indonesia
22 C2 Selat Laut chan. Indonesia
22 C4 Selat Lombok chan. Indonesia
22 C3 Selat Madura chan. Indonesia
25 □ Selat Pandan chan. Singapore
22 E3 Selat Salayar chan. Indonesia
22 D4 Selat Sape chan. Indonesia
22 D4 Selat Sumba chan. Indonesia
22 A3 Selat Sunda chan. Indonesia
62 C2 Selattyn England U.K.
21 L7 Selat Yapen chan. Indonesia
134 B3 Selawik Alaska U.S.A.
75 H2 Selb Germany
56 C3 Selbekken Norway
80 D3 Selbhorn mt. Austria
75 G2 Selbitz Germany
58 A2 Selbjørnsfjorden chan. Norway
56 C3 Selbu Norway
65 G4 Selby England U.K.
150 C2 Selby S. Dakota U.S.A.
107 J3 Selce Croatia
113 F6 Selçuk Turkey
79 L5 Selcuș Romania
109 H4 Sele r. Italy
128 D3 Selebi-Phikwe Botswana
114 C1 Selečka Planina mountain range Macedonia
108 B4 s'Elema r. Sardegna Italy
115 G7 Selena mt. Greece
Selencia see Silifke
113 G5 Selendi Turkey
30 C2 Selenduma Rus. Fed.
30 C1 Seleng r. Rus. Fed.
30 C2 Selenge div. Mongolia
30 B2 Selenge Mongolia
124 C4 Selenge Zaire
30 C2 Selenge Mörön r. Mongolia
30 C2 Selenginsk Rus. Fed.
113 B4 Selenicë Albania
72 F1 Selenter See l. Germany
87 G4 Sélestat France
25 □ Seletar Singapore
25 □ Seletar, P. i. Singapore
25 □ Seletar Res. resr Singapore
47 H2 Seletinskoye Kazakhstan
47 H2 Selety r. Kazakhstan
47 H2 Seletyteniz, Oz. salt lake Kazakhstan
Seleucia see Silifke
Seleucia Piera see Samandağı
54 F1 Seleznevo Rus. Fed.
150 C2 Selfridge N. Dakota U.S.A.
50 J2 Selib Rus. Fed.
120 B5 Sélibabi Mauritania
52 B3 Selichnya Rus. Fed.
74 D2 Seligenstadt Germany
52 A1 Seliger, Oz. l. Rus. Fed.
155 F4 Seligman Arizona U.S.A.
119 E3 Selīma Oasis oasis Sudan
22 C1 Selimbau Indonesia
113 F6 Selimiye Muğla Turkey
43 A1 Selimiye Turkey
122 C4 Sélingué, Lac de l. Mali
115 D4 Selinous r. Greece
149 J5 Selinsgrove Pennsylvania U.S.A.
52 A1 Selishche Rus. Fed.
52 A1 Selishchi Rus. Fed.
51 H6 Selitrennoye Rus. Fed.
52 A1 Selizharovo Rus. Fed.
58 C2 Seljord Norway
58 C2 Seljordsvatnet l. Norway
73 G4 Selke r. Germany
137 K4 Selkirk Manitoba Canada
66 F5 Selkirk Scotland U.K.
136 F4 Selkirk Mountains mountain range B.C. Canada
65 E3 Sellafield England U.K.
109 E2 Sellano Italy
115 D5 Sellasia Greece
89 G4 Selles-St-Denis France
89 G4 Selles-sur-Cher France
115 F7 Sellia Greece
111 F4 Sellia Marina Italy
90 D2 Sellières France
63 G3 Sellindge England U.K.
55 C3 Selling Denmark
68 F2 Sellingen Netherlands
Sellore I. i. see Saganthit Kyun
80 C3 Sellrain Austria
155 G6 Sells Arizona U.S.A.
72 C4 Selm Germany
145 C5 Selma Alabama U.S.A.
154 C3 Selma California U.S.A.
145 B5 Selmer Tennessee U.S.A.
73 F2 Selmsdorf Germany
89 G4 Selommes France
82 B1 Seloncourt France
52 D4 Selong Indonesia
90 D1 Selongey France
91 E4 Selonnet France
131 G2 Selonsrivier South Africa
122 B4 Sélouma Guinea
127 C6 Selous Game Reserve res. Tanzania
39 E3 Selseleh-ye-Pīr Shūrān mountain range Iran
65 F3 Selset Res. resr England U.K.
63 F4 Selsey England U.K.
63 F4 Selsey Bill headland England U.K.
74 C2 Selters (Westerwald) Germany
52 B3 Sel'tso Rus. Fed.
87 H4 Seltz France
89 E3 Sélune r. France
102 B2 Selva mt. Spain
102 F3 Selva reg. Spain
111 G2 Selva Italy
172 A5 Selva Obscura Chile
168 C4 Selvíria Brazil
137 J3 Selwyn Lake l. N.W.T. Canada
136 C2 Selwyn Mountains mountain range Yukon Terr. Canada
14 D4 Selwyn Range h. Queensland Australia
53 A3 Selyatyn Ukraine
53 G2 Selydove Ukraine
74 D3 Selz r. Germany
81 F3 Selzthal Austria
113 B4 Seman r. Albania
22 A3 Semangka, Tk b. Indonesia
22 B3 Semarang Indonesia
22 B1 Sematan Malaysia
22 C2 Semayang, D. l. Indonesia
23 A6 Sembakung r. Indonesia
25 □ Sembawang Singapore
124 B3 Sembé Congo
93 C5 Séméac France
22 C4 Semenanjung Blambangan pen. Indonesia
125 C4 Semendua Zaire
52 D1 Semendyayevo Rus. Fed.
51 E4 Semenivka Chernihivs'ka Oblast' Ukraine
53 E2 Semenivka Poltavs'ka Oblast' Ukraine
50 H3 Semenov Rus. Fed.
50 H3 Semenovo Rus. Fed.
52 D1 Semibratovo Rus. Fed.
50 G3 Semigorodnyaya Rus. Fed.
52 G3 Semiley Rus. Fed.
52 F2 Semilovo Rus. Fed.
52 D4 Semiluki Rus. Fed.
78 E1 Semily Czech Rep.
111 E4 Seminara Italy
90 D2 Semine r. France
152 F3 Seminoe Res. resr Wyoming U.S.A.
151 C5 Seminole Texas U.S.A.
145 C6 Seminole, L. l. Georgia/Florida U.S.A.
47 L2 Seminskiy Khrebet mountain range Rus. Fed.
52 E2 Semion Rus. Fed.
46 F2 Semiozernoye Kazakhstan
30 D2 Semiozer'ye Rus. Fed.
47 K2 Semipalatinsk Kazakhstan
23 B3 Semirara i. Philippines
23 B4 Semirara Islands is Philippines
39 B3 Semīrom Iran
22 B1 Semitau Indonesia
47 J2 Semiyarka Kazakhstan
47 H2 Semiz-Bugu Kazakhstan
73 F3 Semmenstedt Germany
81 G3 Semmering pass Austria
39 C2 Semnān div. Iran
39 C2 Semnān Iran
30 B5 Sêmnyi China
69 D5 Semois r. Belgium
69 C5 Semois, Vallée de la v. Belgium/France
131 G4 Semonkong Lesotho
82 D1 Sempach Switzerland
82 D1 Sempacher See l. Switzerland
23 A5 Semporna Malaysia
22 C4 Sempu i. Indonesia
166 B1 Sem Tripa Brazil
52 A3 Semtsy Rus. Fed.
90 C1 Semur-en-Auxois France
90 C2 Semur-en-Brionnais France
92 B3 Semussac France
50 H1 Semzha Rus. Fed.
164 C2 Sena Bolivia
79 L3 Seňa Slovakia
102 C3 Sena Spain
168 D2 Senador Canedo Brazil
166 E2 Senador Pompeu Brazil
23 A5 Senaja Malaysia
107 E2 Senales Italy
164 C1 Sena Madureira Brazil
38 C5 Senanayake Samudra l. Sri Lanka
125 D7 Senanga Zambia
22 B1 Senaning Indonesia
89 G2 Senarpont France
91 D5 Sénas France
53 E1 Sencha Ukraine
81 F4 Šenčur Slovenia
29 H4 Sendai Japan
28 C8 Sendai Japan
28 C8 Sendai-gawa r. Japan
74 F4 Senden Germany
98 D3 Sendim Portugal
131 G1 Sending South Africa
32 A2 Sêndo China
88 C4 Séné France
25 C7 Senebui, Tanjung pt Indonesia
78 G3 Senec Slovakia
155 G5 Seneca Arizona U.S.A.
148 C5 Seneca Illinois U.S.A.
152 C2 Seneca Oregon U.S.A.
146 E3 Seneca Falls New York U.S.A.
146 E3 Seneca Lake l. New York U.S.A.
146 D5 Seneca Rocks W. Virginia U.S.A.
146 C5 Senecaville Lake l. Ohio U.S.A.
69 C4 Seneffe Belgium
116 C4 Senegal country Africa
122 B3 Sénégal r. Mauritania/Senegal
108 A4 Seneghe Sardegna Italy
131 F4 Senekal South Africa
148 E2 Seney Michigan U.S.A.
91 E5 Senez France
81 G2 Senftenberg Austria
73 K4 Senftenberg Germany
127 B6 Senga Hill Zambia
36 D4 Sengar r. India
22 D1 Sengata Indonesia
80 C1 Sengenthal Germany
127 B5 Sengerema Tanzania
50 J4 Sengiley Rus. Fed.
111 □ Senglea Malta
93 C6 Sengouagnet France
81 F3 Sengsengebirge mts Austria
171 B6 Senguerr r. Argentina
129 D2 Sengwa r. Zimbabwe
166 D3 Senhor do Bonfim Brazil
78 G3 Senica Slovakia
107 H5 Senigallia Italy
172 C5 Senillosa Argentina
107 F4 Senio r. Italy
108 A5 Senis Sardegna Italy
109 J4 Senise Italy
107 J4 Senj Croatia
56 E1 Senja i. Norway
122 C5 Senko Guinea
53 G2 Sen'kove Ukraine
36 D2 Senku India
130 D2 Senlac South Africa
86 B3 Senlis France
25 D4 Senmonorom Cambodia
29 E6 Sennan Japan
119 F5 Sennar Sudan
119 F5 Sennar Dam dam Sudan
108 A4 Sennariolo Sardegna Italy
72 D4 Senne reg. Germany
90 C2 Sennecey-le-Grand France
62 A4 Sennen England U.K.
141 G2 Senneterre Québec Canada
108 A4 Sennori Sardegna Italy
52 H3 Sennoy Rus. Fed.
83 E1 Sennwald Switzerland
62 C3 Sennybridge Wales U.K.
86 C4 Sénonais reg. France
87 F4 Senones France
171 D7 Seno Otway b. Chile
108 B5 Senorbì Sardegna Italy
91 B3 Senouire r. France
81 G4 Senovo Slovenia
81 F5 Senožeče Slovenia
131 F5 Senqu r. Lesotho
131 G4 Senqunyane r. Lesotho
86 C4 Sens France
86 C2 Sensée r. France
156 H6 Sensuntepeque El Salvador
79 K6 Senta Yugoslavia
102 D2 Senterada Spain
81 G4 Šentilj Slovenia
155 F5 Sentinel Arizona U.S.A.
136 E3 Sentinel Pk summit B.C. Canada
179 B3 Sentinel Ra. mountain range Antarctica
81 G5 Šentjernej Slovenia
81 G4 Šentjur pri Celju Slovenia
25 □ Sentosa i. Singapore
131 F2 Sentrum South Africa
22 D1 Senyiur Indonesia
42 E2 Şenyurt Turkey
28 D7 Sen-zaki pt Japan
28 C6 Senzaki Japan
82 D1 Seon Switzerland
36 D5 Seoni India
37 E5 Seorinarayan India
Seoul see Sŏul
93 C4 Séoune r. France
22 C3 Sepanjang i. Indonesia
8 D4 Separation Pt pt New Zealand
22 D1 Sepasu Indonesia
22 B1 Sepauk Indonesia
167 D5 Sepetiba, Baía de b. Brazil
39 B3 Sepīdān Iran
6 □1 Sepik r. P.N.G.
22 D1 Sepinang Indonesia
109 G3 Sepino Italy
76 F2 Sępólno Krajeńskie Poland
165 E3 Sepotuba r. Brazil
82 C1 Seppois-le-Bas France
92 E2 Septaine reg. France
91 D5 Septèmes-les-Vallons France
89 G3 Septeuil France
93 D4 Septfonds France
88 B3 Sept-Îles, Les is France
139 G3 Sept-Îles Québec Canada
82 A2 Septmoncel France
99 G3 Sepúlveda Spain
22 A3 Seputih r. Indonesia
107 G2 Sequals Italy
173 J1 Sequeira Uruguay
98 D4 Sequeros Spain
99 E3 Sequillo r. Spain
154 C3 Sequoia National Park nat. park California U.S.A.
51 G5 Serafimovich Rus. Fed.
86 D3 Seraincourt France
69 D4 Seraing Belgium
39 E1 Serakhs Turkmenistan
21 J7 Seram i. Indonesia
21 J7 Seram Sea g. Indonesia
90 D3 Séran r. France
22 A3 Serang Indonesia
25 □ Serangoon Harbour harbour Singapore
25 □ Serangoon, P. i. Singapore
91 B5 Séranne, Montagne de la ridge France
91 E5 Séranon France
25 E7 Serasan i. Indonesia
106 E5 Seravezza Italy
25 E7 Seraya i. Indonesia
25 □ Seraya, P. i. Singapore
43 B5 Serbâl, G. mt. Egypt
Serbia div. see Srbija
106 E4 Serchio r. Italy
156 D2 Serdán Mexico
126 D2 Serdo Ethiopia
52 G3 Serdoba r. Rus. Fed.
52 G3 Serdobsk Rus. Fed.
47 K3 Serebryansk Kazakhstan
52 D2 Serebryanyye Prudy Rus. Fed.
79 G3 Sered' Slovakia
52 E1 Sereda Rus. Fed.
52 B2 Seredeyskiy Rus. Fed.
54 F2 Seredka Rus. Fed.
52 D2 Serednikovo Rus. Fed.
52 B3 Seredyna-Buda Ukraine
79 M3 Seredyne Ukraine
42 C2 Şerefli-koçhisar Turkey
79 H4 Seregélyes Hungary
106 D3 Seregno Italy
90 B1 Serein r. France
25 C7 Seremban Malaysia
127 B5 Serengeti National Park nat. park Tanzania
127 C5 Serengeti Plains plain Kenya
127 B7 Serenje Zambia
166 C2 Sereno r. Brazil
88 C4 Sérent France
126 B4 Serere Uganda
53 A2 Seret r. Ukraine
52 F2 Serezha r. Rus. Fed.
80 B3 Serfaus Austria
115 F5 Serfopoula i. Greece
52 G2 Sergach Rus. Fed.
30 E2 Sergelen Mongolia
30 D3 Sergelen Mongolia
47 G2 Sergeyevka Kazakhstan
86 C4 Sergines France
166 E3 Sergipe div. Brazil
114 G2 Sergitsi i. Greece
52 D1 Sergiyev Posad Rus. Fed.
46 D2 Sergiyevsk Rus. Fed.
52 C3 Sergiyevskoye Rus. Fed.
52 D3 Sergiyevskoye Rus. Fed.
83 E3 Sergnano Italy
53 E1 Serhiyivka Chernihivs'ka Oblast' Ukraine
53 D3 Serhiyivka Odes'ka Oblast' Ukraine
53 D3 Serhiyivka Odes'ka Oblast' Ukraine
20 F6 Seria Brunei
22 B1 Serian Malaysia
83 E3 Seriate Italy
89 G2 Sérifontaine France
115 F5 Serifos i. Greece
115 F5 Serifos Greece
91 B5 Sérignan France
91 C4 Sérignan-du-Comtat France
139 G2 Sérigny, Lac l. Québec Canada
42 B2 Serik Turkey
47 J5 Serikbuya China
16 C2 Seringapatam Reef reef Western Australia Australia
131 G2 Seringkop South Africa
109 G4 Serino Italy
106 D3 Serio r. Italy
12 D2 Serle, Mt h. S. Australia Australia
86 D4 Sermaize-les-Bains France
108 B2 Sermano Corse France
107 F4 Sermide Italy
109 F3 Sermoneta Italy
54 D3 Sērmūkši Latvia
98 C4 Sernancelhe Portugal
79 M3 Serne r. Ukraine
50 J3 Sernur Rus. Fed.
46 E5 Sernyy Zavod Turkmenistan
77 K3 Serock Poland
158 □1 Seroe Colorado Aruba Caribbean
51 H6 Seroglazovka Rus. Fed.
101 H3 Serón Spain
99 H3 Serón de Nájima Spain
128 C2 Seronga Botswana
68 B3 Serooskerke Netherlands
102 D3 Seròs Spain
121 F4 Serouenout well Algeria
44 H4 Serov Rus. Fed.
128 D3 Serowe Botswana
100 C3 Serpa Portugal
12 B2 Serpentine Lakes salt flat S. Australia Australia
163 E2 Serpent's Mouth chan. Venezuela
52 B2 Serpeysk Rus. Fed.
103 C6 Serpis r. Spain
53 C3 Serpneve Ukraine
52 E3 Serpovoye Rus. Fed.
52 C2 Serpukhov Rus. Fed.
89 F2 Serquigny France
169 H4 Serra Brazil

28 H2 Shikotsu-ko l. Japan
28 H2 Shikotsu-Tōya National Park Japan
65 G2 Shilbottle England U.K.
65 G3 Shildon England U.K.
50 H1 Shilega Rus. Fed.
37 G4 Shiliguri India
33 F2 Shilipu China
Shiliu see Changjiang
31 F1 Shilka r. Rus. Fed.
31 F2 Shilka Rus. Fed.
67 E4 Shillelagh Rep. of Ireland
140 E2 Shillington Ontario Canada
37 G4 Shillong India
51 J5 Shil'naya Balka Kazakhstan
147 F5 Shiloh New Jersey U.S.A.
30 D5 Shilou China
52 E2 Shilovo Rus. Fed.
52 D3 Shilovo Rus. Fed.
28 C7 Shimabara Japan
28 C7 Shimabara-wan b. Japan
29 G6 Shimada Japan
28 D6 Shimane div. Japan
28 D6 Shimane-hantō pen. Japan
31 H1 Shimanovsk Rus. Fed.
126 E2 Shimbiris mt. Somalia
127 D4 Shimbirre waterhole Kenya
33 E2 Shimen China
32 C2 Shimian China
29 G6 Shimizu Japan
36 D3 Shimla India
29 G6 Shimoda Japan
29 G5 Shimodate Japan
38 A3 Shimoga India
28 H3 Shimokita-hantō pen. Japan
28 B8 Shimo-Koshiki-jima i. Japan
127 C5 Shimoni Kenya
28 C7 Shimonoseki Japan
52 F2 Shimorskoye Rus. Fed.
47 J5 Shimshal Jammu and Kashmir
36 C1 Shimshal Pakistan
50 D3 Shimsk Rus. Fed.
33 E4 Shinan China
29 G5 Shinano-gawa r. Japan
39 E2 Shindand Afghanistan
63 F3 Shinfield England U.K.
24 B1 Shingbwiyang Myanmar
24 B1 Shing-gai Myanmar
36 B3 Shinghar Pakistan
36 C1 Shinghshal P. pass Pakistan
148 D2 Shingleton Michigan U.S.A.
27 □ Shing Mun Res. resr Hong Kong
36 D2 Shingo P. pass India
47 K3 Shingozha Kazakhstan
29 F7 Shingū Japan
131 H1 Shingwedzi r. South Africa
131 H1 Shingwedzi South Africa
62 D1 Shining Tor h. England U.K.
140 E3 Shining Tree Ontario Canada
28 D6 Shinji-ko l. Japan
29 H4 Shinjō Japan
39 F3 Shīnkāy Afghanistan
66 D2 Shin, Loch l. Scotland U.K.
29 F5 Shinminato Japan
28 C6 Shin-nanyō Japan
147 J1 Shin Pond Maine U.S.A.
43 D2 Shinshār Syria
28 J2 Shintoku Japan
127 B5 Shinyanga div. Tanzania
127 B5 Shinyanga Tanzania
29 H4 Shiogama Japan
29 F5 Shiojiri Japan
29 E7 Shiono-misaki c. Japan
29 H5 Shioya-zaki pt Japan
158 C1 Ship Chan Cay i. The Bahamas
52 D1 Shipilovo Rus. Fed.
32 C4 Shiping China
36 D3 Shipki Pass pass India
65 G4 Shipley England U.K.
139 H4 Shippegan New Brunswick Canada
146 E4 Shippensburg Pennsylvania U.S.A.
155 H3 Shiprock New Mexico U.S.A.
155 H3 Shiprock Peak summit New Mexico U.S.A.
63 E2 Shipston on Stour England U.K.
62 D2 Shipton England U.K.
33 H2 Shipu China
47 K2 Shipunovo Rus. Fed.
32 E3 Shiqian China
36 E2 Shiquan r. China
32 E1 Shiquan China
Shiquanhe see Ali
32 E1 Shiquan Sk. resr China
47 M2 Shira Rus. Fed.
29 E7 Shirahama Japan
28 H3 Shirakami-misaki pt Japan
29 H5 Shirakawa Japan
29 F5 Shirakawa Japan
29 G5 Shirane-san volcano Japan
28 K2 Shiranuka Japan
28 H2 Shiraoi Japan
179 D4 Shirasebreen gl. Antarctica
179 A4 Shirase Coast coastal area Antarctica
28 J2 Shirataki Japan
39 C3 Shīrāz Iran
43 A4 Shirbîn Egypt
129 E2 Shire r. Malawi
30 E3 Shireet Mongolia
28 K2 Shiretoko-hantō pen. Japan
28 K1 Shiretoko-misaki c. Japan
46 F4 Shirikrabat Kazakhstan
36 A3 Shirinab r. Pakistan
52 F3 Shiringushi Rus. Fed.
28 H3 Shiriya-zaki c. Japan
46 E3 Shirkala reg. Kazakhstan
147 G4 Shirley New York U.S.A.
147 J2 Shirley Mills Maine U.S.A.
29 H5 Shiroishi Japan
29 G5 Shirone Japan
123 F5 Shiroro Reservoir resr Nigeria
29 F6 Shirotori Japan
36 C5 Shirpur India
30 A4 Shirten Hōloy Gobi desert China
39 D1 Shīrvān Iran
31 H2 Shisanzhan China
33 F2 Shishou China
33 G2 Shitai China
33 H2 Shitang China
29 F6 Shitara Japan
42 E3 Shithāthah Iraq
36 B4 Shiv India
144 C4 Shively Kentucky U.S.A.
36 D4 Shivpuri India
43 C4 Shivta Israel
155 F3 Shivwits Plateau plat. Arizona U.S.A.
39 G1 Shiwal l. Afghanistan
32 D4 Shiwan Dashan mountain range China
127 B7 Shiwa Ngandu Zambia
33 F3 Shixing China
33 E1 Shiyan China
32 E2 Shizhu China
32 C3 Shizong China
29 H4 Shizugawa Japan
30 C5 Shizuishan China
29 G6 Shizuoka div. Japan
29 G6 Shizuoka Japan
42 E1 Shkhara mt. Rus. Fed.
77 M6 Shklo Ukraine
50 D4 Shklow Belarus
112 B3 Shkodër Shkodër Albania
113 B4 Shkumbin r. Albania
53 G1 Shlyakhovo Rus. Fed.
45 T3 Shmidta, M. Rus. Fed.
15 G4 Shoalwater B. b. Queensland Australia
28 D6 Shōbara Japan
28 E6 Shōdo-shima i. Japan
29 F5 Shō-gawa r. Japan
46 E5 Shoghlābād Iran
28 H2 Shokanbetsu-dake mt. Japan
50 E1 Shomba r. Rus. Fed.
46 E3 Shomishkol' Kazakhstan
50 J2 Shomvukva Rus. Fed.
24 D2 S. Hông r. Vietnam
37 G4 Shongar Bhutan
43 A4 Shôni Egypt
52 D1 Shopsha Rus. Fed.
36 D2 Shor India
38 B4 Shoranur India
36 A4 Shorap Pakistan
39 F3 Shorawak reg. Afghanistan
46 E4 Shor Barsa-Kel'mes salt marsh Uzbekistan
63 F4 Shoreham-by-Sea England U.K.
36 C3 Shorkot Pakistan
6 □1 Shortland Is is Solomon Is.
28 H1 Shosanbetsu Japan
52 B1 Shosha r. Rus. Fed.
152 E2 Shoshone r. Wyoming U.S.A.
154 D4 Shoshone California U.S.A.
152 D3 Shoshone Idaho U.S.A.
152 E2 Shoshone L. l. Wyoming U.S.A.
153 C4 Shoshone Mts mountain range Nevada U.S.A.
128 D3 Shoshong Botswana
152 E3 Shoshoni Wyoming U.S.A.
53 E1 Shostka Ukraine
64 E2 Shotts Scotland U.K.
31 F5 Shouguang China
33 G3 Shouning China
33 G1 Shou Xian China
30 E5 Shouyang China
32 E1 Shouyang Shan mt. China
37 E3 Shovo Tso salt lake China
119 G5 Showak Sudan
155 G4 Show Low Arizona U.S.A.
44 F3 Shoyna Rus. Fed.
52 E4 Shpikulovo Rus. Fed.
53 D2 Shpola Ukraine
53 C2 Shpykiv Ukraine
53 E1 Shramkivka Ukraine
151 E5 Shreveport Louisiana U.S.A.
62 D2 Shrewsbury England U.K.
38 A2 Shrigonda India
36 B4 Shri Mohangarh India
63 E3 Shrivenham England U.K.
62 D2 Shropshire div. England U.K.
114 B2 Shtërmen Albania
33 G1 Shu r. China
32 C3 Shuangbai China
31 H3 Shuangcheng China
32 D2 Shuanghechang China
31 J2 Shuanghedagang Rus. Fed.
32 B4 Shuangjiang China
31 G4 Shuangliao China
33 E3 Shuangpai China
31 H4 Shuangyang China
31 J3 Shuangyashan China
46 E3 Shubarkuduk Kazakhstan
46 E3 Shubarshi Kazakhstan
43 D2 Shubayţ, J. ash h. Syria
52 G2 Shubino Rus. Fed.
119 H3 Shubrāmīyāh well Saudi Arabia
33 G2 Shucheng China
37 H4 Shuganu India
52 H2 Shugurovo Rus. Fed.
Shuicheng see Liupanshui
33 G3 Shuiji China
30 B5 Shuiquanzi China
32 C2 Shuituo r. China
36 D5 Shujalpur India
39 B3 Shūl watercourse Iran
31 H3 Shulan China
47 J5 Shule China
52 E3 Shul'gino Rus. Fed.
31 E5 Shulu China
134 C4 Shumagin Islands is Alaska U.S.A.
53 G1 Shumakovo Rus. Fed.
46 E4 Shumanay Uzbekistan
28 J1 Shumarinai-ko l. Japan
128 D2 Shumba Zimbabwe
112 F3 Shumen Bulgaria
52 H2 Shumerlya Rus. Fed.
46 F1 Shumikha Rus. Fed.
54 F4 Shumilina Belarus
53 B1 Shums'k Ukraine
155 G4 Shumway Arizona U.S.A.
50 E4 Shumyachi Rus. Fed.
43 C4 Shuna Jordan
33 G3 Shunchang China
33 F4 Shunde China
52 E1 Shunga Rus. Fed.
134 C3 Shungrak Alaska U.S.A.
31 F4 Shunyi China
32 D4 Shuolong China
30 E5 Shuo Xian China
36 C2 Shupiyan India
126 E2 Shuqrah Yemen
39 C3 Shūr r. Iran
39 C3 Shūr r. Iran
39 D2 Shur r. Iran
39 C3 Shūr r. Iran
39 C4 Shūr watercourse Iran
39 D3 Shūr Āb r. Iran
39 C2 Shūrāb Iran
39 B2 Shūr Āb Iran
39 B2 Shurâb Iran
39 D2 Shūrāb Iran
47 G5 Shurchi Uzbekistan
39 D3 Shūr Gaz Iran
29 □2 Shuri Japan
39 C3 Shūrjestān Iran
50 J3 Shurma Rus. Fed.
129 E2 Shurugwi Zimbabwe
39 E3 Shusf Iran
39 B2 Shūsh Iran
Shusha see Şuşa
114 B1 Shushicë Albania
50 G3 Shushkodom Rus. Fed.
39 B2 Shushtar Iran
52 B4 Shustovo Rus. Fed.
136 F4 Shuswap L. l. B.C. Canada
39 F2 Shutar Khun P. pass Afghanistan
52 G2 Shuvary Rus. Fed.
52 E1 Shuya Rus. Fed.
33 G1 Shuyang China
24 A3 Shwebandaw Myanmar
24 A2 Shwebo Myanmar
24 A3 Shwedaung Myanmar
24 A1 Shwedwin Myanmar
24 B3 Shwegun Myanmar
24 B3 Shwegyin Myanmar
24 B2 Shweli r. Myanmar
24 B2 Shweudaung mt. Myanmar
53 B2 Shybena Ukraine
47 G4 Shymkent Kazakhstan
36 D2 Shyok r. India
53 G2 Shypuvate Ukraine
53 E3 Shyroke Dnipropetrovs'ka Oblast' Ukraine
53 F2 Shyroke Dnipropetrovs'ka Oblast' Ukraine
53 D3 Shyrokolanivka Ukraine
53 D3 Shyryayeve Ukraine
53 F2 Shyshaky Ukraine
54 E5 Shyshchytsy Belarus
21 K8 Sia Indonesia
36 D2 Siachen Gl. gl. Jammu and Kashmir
91 E5 Siagne r. France
39 E4 Siahan Range mountain range Pakistan
42 F2 Sīah Chashmeh Iran
39 F2 Siah Koh mountain range Afghanistan
39 C2 Sīāh Kūh mountain range Iran
39 F3 Siah Sang P. pass Afghanistan
36 C2 Sialkot Pakistan
Sian see Xi'an
76 E1 Sianów Poland
25 D7 Siantan i. Indonesia
39 E3 Sīāreh Iran
23 C4 Siargao i. Philippines
23 B5 Siasi i. Philippines
23 B5 Siasi Philippines
114 C2 Siatista Greece
23 B4 Siaton Philippines
54 C4 Šiauliai Lithuania
Siazan' see Siyäzän
39 E4 Sib Iran
111 F3 Sibari Italy
47 L3 Sibati China
23 B4 Sibay i. Philippines
46 E2 Sibay Rus. Fed.
131 J3 Sibayi, Lake l. South Africa
179 B5 Sibbald, C. c. Antarctica
104 E4 Šibenik Croatia
18 L3 Siberia reg. Rus. Fed.
20 C7 Siberut i. Indonesia
36 A3 Sibi Pakistan
126 C4 Sibiloi National Park nat. park Kenya
125 B4 Sibiti Congo
112 E2 Sibiu Romania
63 G3 Sible Hedingham England U.K.
22 E1 Siboa Indonesia
20 C6 Sibolga Indonesia
22 E1 Siboluton Indonesia
131 H3 Sibowe r. Swaziland
37 H4 Sibsagar India
63 G1 Sibsey England U.K.
20 F6 Sibu Malaysia
23 B5 Sibuco Philippines
23 B5 Sibuguey r. Philippines
23 B5 Sibuguey Bay b. Philippines
124 C2 Sibut Central African Rep.
23 A5 Sibutu i. Philippines
23 A5 Sibutu Passage chan. Philippines
23 B3 Sibuyan i. Philippines
23 B3 Sibuyan Sea sea Philippines
23 B2 Sicapoo mt. Philippines
12 D2 Siccus watercourse S. Australia Australia
32 C2 Sichuan div. China
32 C2 Sichuan reg. China
32 D2 Sichuan Pendi basin China
91 D5 Sicié, Cap c. France
110 C5 Sicilia div. Sicilia Italy
110 B5 Sicilia i. Italy
110 B5 Sicilian Channel chan. Mediterranean Sea
Sicily i. see Sicilia
164 B2 Sicuani Peru
110 C5 Siculiana Sicilia Italy
112 B2 Šid Yugoslavia
123 F3 Sidaouet Niger
114 A3 Sidari Greece
62 C4 Sidbury England U.K.
63 G3 Sidcup England U.K.
68 E1 Siddeburen Netherlands
36 C5 Siddhapur India
38 B2 Siddipet India
Side see Selimiye
122 D4 Sidéradougou Burkina
111 F4 Siderno Italy
130 D6 Sidesaviwa South Africa
37 E4 Sidhi India
121 E1 Sidi Ali Algeria
118 E1 Sidi Barrani Egypt
121 D1 Sidi Bel Abbès Algeria
120 C2 Sidi Bennour Morocco
121 F1 Sidi Bouzid Tunisia
120 B3 Sidi Ifni Morocco
120 C2 Sidi Kacem Morocco
121 E2 Sidi Khaled Algeria
122 C4 Sidikila Guinea
121 D3 Sidi Mannsour well Algeria
120 B4 Sidi Mhamed well Western Sahara
121 F2 Sidi Okba Algeria
114 E1 Sidirokastro Kentriki Makedonia Greece
115 C5 Sidirokastro Peloponnisos Greece
43 A4 Sidi Sâlim Egypt
66 E4 Sidlaw Hills h. Scotland U.K.
63 G4 Sidley England U.K.
179 A4 Sidley, Mt mt. Antarctica
62 C4 Sidmouth England U.K.
136 E5 Sidney B.C. Canada
152 F2 Sidney Montana U.S.A.
150 C3 Sidney Nebraska U.S.A.
147 F3 Sidney New York U.S.A.
146 A4 Sidney Ohio U.S.A.
145 D5 Sidney Lanier, L. l. Georgia U.S.A.
122 C4 Sido Mali
22 E1 Sidoan Indonesia
22 C3 Sidoarjo Indonesia
93 E5 Sidobre reg. France
24 A2 Sidoktaya Myanmar
Sidon see Saïda
77 M2 Sidra Poland
168 A4 Sidrolândia Brazil
131 H3 Sidvokodvo Swaziland
73 L4 Siecieborzyce Poland
77 L3 Siedlce div. Poland
77 L3 Siedlce Poland
73 L2 Siedlice Poland
76 E3 Siedlisko Poland
77 M4 Siedliszcze Poland
74 C2 Sieg r. Germany
74 C2 Siegburg Germany
74 D2 Siegen Germany
80 C2 Siegenburg Germany
81 H3 Sieggraben Austria
81 H2 Sieghartskirchen Austria
75 H5 Siegsdorf Germany
76 D4 Siekierczyn Poland
77 L3 Siemiatycze Poland
77 L4 Siemień Poland
25 C4 Siĕmréab Cambodia
73 L1 Siemyśl Poland
107 F5 Siena div. Toscana Italy
107 F5 Siena Siena Italy
77 L5 Sieniawa Poland
88 D3 Sienne r. France
77 K4 Sienno Poland
76 G4 Sieradz div. Poland
76 G4 Sieradz Poland
76 E3 Sieraków Poland
77 H3 Sierakówek Poland
76 F1 Sierakowice Poland
87 F3 Sierck-les-Bains France
90 F1 Sierentz France
81 H2 Sierndorf Austria
81 F2 Sierning Austria
77 H3 Sierpc Poland
151 B6 Sierra Blanca Texas U.S.A.
172 D6 Sierra Colorada Argentina
102 C2 Sierra de Luna Spain
163 E2 Sierra del Zamuro mountain range Venezuela
162 C2 Sierra de Perija mountain range Venezuela
101 F3 Sierra de Yeguas Spain
155 F5 Sierra Estrella mts Arizona U.S.A.
164 C4 Sierra Gorda Chile
172 E1 Sierra Grande mountain range Argentina
162 D2 Sierra Guanay mts Venezuela
117 C5 Sierra Leone country Africa
174 H5 Sierra Leone Basin sea feature Atlantic Ocean
174 H5 Sierra Leone Rise sea feature Atlantic Ocean
157 G5 Sierra Madre mountain range Mexico
23 B2 Sierra Madre mt. Philippines
157 E5 Sierra Madre del Sur mountain range Mexico
154 C4 Sierra Madre Mts mts California U.S.A.
156 C2 Sierra Madre Occidental mountain range Mexico
157 E3 Sierra Madre Oriental mountain range Mexico
163 D2 Sierra Maigualida mountain range Venezuela
156 E3 Sierra Mojada Mexico
153 B4 Sierra Nevada mountain range California U.S.A.
162 C2 Sierra Nevada del Cocuy mt. Colombia
162 C1 Sierra Nevada de Santa Marta nat. park Colombia
162 C2 Sierra Nevada, Parque Nacional nat. park Venezuela
172 E6 Sierra Pailemán Argentina
155 F5 Sierra Pinta summit Arizona U.S.A.
171 D5 Sierra, Pta pt Argentina
154 B2 Sierraville California U.S.A.
155 G6 Sierra Vista Arizona U.S.A.
156 B3 Sierra Vizcaíno mountain range Mexico
82 C2 Sierre Switzerland
54 D4 Siesartis r. Lithuania
165 E4 Siete Puntas r. Paraguay
73 H2 Sietow Germany
107 F5 Sieve r. Italy
73 H3 Sieversdorf Germany
56 G3 Sievi Finland
77 H5 Siewierz Poland
32 D4 Sifang Ling mountain range China
31 H3 Sifangtai China
59 F1 Sifferbo Sweden
115 F5 Sifnos i. Greece
6 □8 Sigatoka r. Fiji
6 □8 Sigatoka Fiji
93 E5 Sigean France
111 □ Siggiewi Malta
112 D1 Sighetu Marmației Romania
112 E1 Sighișoara Romania
107 G5 Sigillo Italy
25 □ Siglap Singapore
35 J9 Sigli Indonesia
56 M6 Siglufjörður Iceland
23 B4 Sigma Philippines
74 E4 Sigmaringen Germany
74 E4 Sigmaringendorf Germany
107 F5 Signa Italy
75 H3 Signalberg h. Germany
69 E4 Signal de Botrange h. Belgium
91 B4 Signal de Mailhebiau mt. France
91 B4 Signal de Randon mt. France
92 E3 Signal du Luguet mt. France
92 D3 Signal du Pic h. France
89 E3 Signal du Viviers h. France
101 □ Signal Hill h. Gibraltar
155 E5 Signal Peak summit Arizona U.S.A.
59 H1 Signilskär i. Finland
179 B1 Signy U.K. Base Antarctica
86 D3 Signy-L'Abbaye France
86 D3 Signy-le-Petit France
92 B3 Sigogne France
148 A5 Sigourney Iowa U.S.A.
52 A1 Sig, Oz. l. Rus. Fed.
59 G2 Sigtuna Sweden
156 J6 Siguatepeque Honduras
99 H3 Sigüenza Spain
102 B2 Sigües Spain
122 C4 Siguiri Guinea
54 D3 Sigulda Latvia
25 C5 Sihanoukville Cambodia
83 D1 Sihlsee l. Switzerland
33 G1 Sihong China
36 E5 Sihora India
164 A1 Sihuas Peru
33 F4 Sihui China
56 G2 Siikajoki Finland
56 G3 Siilinjärvi Finland
42 E2 Siirt Turkey
20 D7 Sijunjung Indonesia
36 B5 Sika India
136 E3 Sikanni Chief r. B.C. Canada
136 E3 Sikanni Chief B.C. Canada
36 C4 Sikar India
39 G2 Sikaram mt. Afghanistan
122 C4 Sikasso div. Mali
122 C4 Sikasso Mali
24 B2 Sikaw Myanmar
114 E2 Sikea Greece
151 F4 Sikeston Missouri U.S.A.
27 P3 Sikhote-Alin China/Rus. Fed.
115 G6 Sikinos i. Greece
115 G6 Sikinos Greece
37 G4 Sikkim India
79 H6 Siklós Hungary
56 E2 Siksjö Sweden
23 A5 Sikuati Malaysia
98 C2 Sil r. Spain
23 C4 Silago Philippines
54 C4 Šilalė Lithuania
107 E2 Silandro Italy
22 B1 Silantek, G. h. Indonesia/Malaysia
108 A4 Silanus Sardegna Italy
23 B4 Silay Philippines
107 J4 Silba i. Croatia
107 J4 Silbanski Kanal chan. Croatia
72 E2 Silberberg h. Germany
37 H4 Silchar India
58 B1 Sildefjorden chan. Norway
54 E4 Silene Latvia
83 D2 Silenen Switzerland
69 C4 Silenrieux Belgium
131 F2 Silent Valley South Africa
38 C2 Sileru r. India
101 H2 Siles Spain
121 E4 Silet Algeria
36 E3 Silgarhi Nepal
37 H4 Silghat India
127 □1 Silhouette I. i. Seychelles
121 F1 Siliana Tunisia
42 C2 Silifke Turkey
108 A4 Siligo Sardegna Italy
37 G3 Siling Co salt lake China
36 D4 Silipur India
108 A5 Siliqua Sardegna Italy
7 □12 Silisili mt. Western Samoa
Silistat see Bozkır
112 E2 Siliștea Nouă Romania
112 F2 Silistra Bulgaria
113 G4 Silivri Turkey
59 F1 Siljan l. Sweden
58 C2 Siljan Norway
55 B3 Silkeborg Denmark
80 C3 Sill r. Austria
103 C5 Silla Spain
164 C3 Sillajhuay mt. Chile
54 E2 Sillamäe Estonia
91 E5 Sillans la Cascade France
107 F4 Sillaro r. Italy
98 B2 Silleda Spain
89 E3 Sillé-le-Guillaume France
86 D3 Sillery France
80 D4 Sillian Austria
36 C5 Sillod India
88 B3 Sillon de Talbert pen. France
65 E3 Silloth England U.K.
76 E2 Silnowo Poland
37 G3 Silong China
102 F3 Sils Spain
83 E2 Sils Switzerland
151 E6 Silsbee Texas U.S.A.
56 G1 Siltaharju Finland
54 E1 Siltakylä Finland
118 C4 Siltou well Chad
22 B1 Siluas Indonesia
123 F5 Siluko r. Nigeria
123 F5 Siluko Nigeria
39 E4 Sīlūp r. Iran
54 B4 Šilutė Lithuania
169 G5 Silva Jardim Brazil
42 E2 Silvan Turkey
168 D2 Silvânia Brazil
83 E2 Silvaplana Switzerland
83 E2 Silvaplaner See l. Switzerland
98 C4 Silvares Portugal
36 C5 Silvassa India
100 B2 Silveiras Portugal
159 E2 Silver Bank sea feature Turks and Caicos Is Caribbean
159 E2 Silver Bank Passage chan. Turks and Caicos Is Caribbean
148 B2 Silver Bay Minnesota U.S.A.
153 E5 Silver City New Mexico U.S.A.
140 A2 Silver Islet Ontario Canada
154 D4 Silver Lake l. California U.S.A.
148 D2 Silver Lake l. Michigan U.S.A.
152 B3 Silver Lake Oregon U.S.A.
67 C4 Silvermine Mts h. Rep. of Ireland
154 D3 Silver Peak Range mts Nevada U.S.A.
146 E5 Silver Spring Maryland U.S.A.
154 C2 Silver Springs Nevada U.S.A.
63 E2 Silverstone England U.K.
130 D4 Silver Streams South Africa
62 C4 Silverton England U.K.
12 E2 Silverton New South Wales Australia
140 D4 Silver Water Ontario Canada
100 B3 Silves Faro Portugal
163 F4 Silves Brazil
109 G2 Silvi Italy
157 H5 Silvituc Mexico
83 F2 Silvretta Gruppe mountain range Switzerland
80 B3 Silz Austria
46 E2 Sim r. Rus. Fed.
46 E2 Sim Rus. Fed.
52 D1 Sima Rus. Fed.
99 F3 Simancas Spain
22 B1 Simanggang Malaysia
53 C1 Simanichy Belarus
114 E2 Simantra Greece
32 C4 Simao China
166 E3 Simão Dias Brazil
23 B3 Simara i. Philippines
141 F3 Simard, Lac l. Québec Canada
42 F3 Sīmareh r. Iran
37 F4 Simaria India
42 B2 Simav Turkey
113 G5 Simav Dağları mountain range Turkey
124 D3 Simba Zaire
75 H4 Simbach Germany
75 J4 Simbach am Inn Germany
111 F4 Simbario Italy
50 J4 Simbirsk Rus. Fed.
Simbor i. see Pānikoita
140 E5 Simcoe Ontario Canada
141 F4 Simcoe, Lake l. Ontario Canada
37 F5 Simdega India
126 C2 Simēn Mountains mountain range Ethiopia
111 F4 Simeri r. Italy
112 D2 Simeria Romania
110 D5 Simeto r. Sicilia Italy
20 C6 Simeuluë i. Indonesia
51 E6 Simferopol' Ukraine
91 D5 Simiane-la-Rotonde France
37 E3 Simikot Nepal
83 F2 Similaun mt. Austria/Italy
79 K2 Siminy mt. Slovakia
162 C2 Simití Colombia
112 D4 Simitli Bulgaria
154 C4 Simi Valley California U.S.A.
153 F4 Simla Colorado U.S.A.
79 M4 Şimleu Silvaniei Romania
82 C2 Simme r. Switzerland
82 C2 Simmental v. Switzerland
74 B2 Simmerath Germany
74 C3 Simmern (Hunsrück) Germany
154 C4 Simmler California U.S.A.
155 F4 Simmons Arizona U.S.A.
145 F7 Simms The Bahamas
145 □2 Simms Pt pt The Bahamas
54 C4 Simnas Lithuania
56 G2 Simojärvi l. Finland
136 F4 Simonette r. Alberta Canada
137 J4 Simonhouse Manitoba Canada
79 L3 Šimonka mt. Slovakia
141 H4 Simon, Lac l. Québec Canada
59 G2 Simonstorp Sweden
130 B7 Simon's Town South Africa
79 H5 Simontornya Hungary
115 C5 Simopoulo Greece
93 C5 Simorre France
114 C4 Simos Greece
22 A2 Simpang Indonesia
69 D4 Simpelveld Netherlands
166 D2 Simplício Mendes Brazil
82 D2 Simplon Switzerland
82 D2 Simplon Pass pass Switzerland
171 B6 Simpson r. Chile
14 D5 Simpson Desert desert Northern Terr. Australia
12 D1 Simpson Desert Conservation Park res. S. Australia Australia
14 D5 Simpson Desert Nat. Park nat. park Queensland Australia
17 D5 Simpson Hill h. Western Australia Australia
140 B2 Simpson I. i. Ontario Canada
154 D2 Simpson Park Mts mts Nevada U.S.A.
59 F4 Simrishamn Sweden
22 B1 Simunjan Malaysia
23 A5 Simunul i. Philippines
45 R5 Simushir, O. i. Rus. Fed.
38 A2 Sina r. India
81 G3 Sinabelkirchen Austria
126 E3 Sina Dhaqa Somalia
43 C6 Sināfir i. Saudi Arabia
119 F2 Sinai pen. Egypt
112 E2 Sinaia Romania
86 D3 Sinai, Mont h. France
42 E2 Şınak Turkey
156 C3 Sinaloa div. Mexico
108 D1 Sinalunga Italy
32 E3 Sinan China
31 H5 Sinanju North Korea
46 F1 Sinara r. Rus. Fed.
114 A3 Sinarades Greece
118 B1 Sīnāwin Libya
24 A3 Sinbaungwe Myanmar
24 B1 Sinbo Myanmar
24 A2 Sinbyugyun Myanmar
42 D2 Sincan Turkey
162 B2 Sincé Colombia
162 B2 Sincelejo Colombia
86 C3 Sinceny France
145 D5 Sinclair, L. l. Georgia U.S.A.
136 E4 Sinclair Mills B.C. Canada
130 A2 Sinclair Mine Namibia
66 E2 Sinclair's Bay b. Scotland U.K.
36 D4 Sind r. India
Sind see Thul
55 C2 Sindal Denmark
23 B4 Sindañgan Philippines
22 A3 Sindangbarang Indonesia
124 B4 Sindara Gabon
36 B4 Sindari India
74 D4 Sindelfingen Germany
38 B2 Sindgi India
36 B4 Sindh Pakistan
38 B3 Sindhnur India
54 D2 Sindi Estonia
108 A4 Sindia Sardegna Italy
113 G5 Sındırgı Turkey
38 B2 Sindkhed India
36 C5 Sindkheda India
50 J2 Sindor Rus. Fed.
114 D2 Sindos Greece
37 F5 Sindri India
36 B3 Sind Sagar Doab lowland Pakistan
50 J3 Sinegor'ye Rus. Fed.
123 E4 Sinendé Benin
100 B3 Sines Portugal
100 B3 Sines, Cabo de pt Portugal
56 G2 Sinettä Finland
52 B3 Sinezerki Rus. Fed.
122 C5 Sinfra Côte d'Ivoire
24 B2 Sing Myanmar
119 F5 Singa Sudan
36 E3 Singahi India
32 B4 Singaingmyo Myanmar
31 H4 Sin'galp'a China
36 D2 Singa P. pass India
19 M9 Singapore country Asia
25 C7 Singapore Singapore
22 A1 Singapore, Str. of chan. Indonesia/Singapore
22 C4 Singaraja Indonesia
25 C4 Sing Buri Thailand
74 D5 Singen (Hohentwiel) Germany
140 E4 Singhampton Ontario Canada
87 G2 Singhofen Germany
127 B6 Singida div. Tanzania
127 B5 Singida Tanzania
24 A1 Singkaling Hkamti Myanmar
22 E3 Singkang Indonesia
22 B1 Singkawang Indonesia
22 A2 Singkep i. Indonesia
13 G3 Singleton New South Wales Australia
14 B4 Singleton, Mt h. Northern Terr. Australia
17 B6 Singleton, Mt h. Western Australia Australia
59 H1 Singö i. Sweden
36 C4 Singoli India
Singora see Songkhla
24 A2 Singu Myanmar
131 J1 Singuedeze r. Mozambique
112 E2 Singureni Romania
22 D2 Sinio, G. mt. Indonesia
108 B4 Siniscola Sardegna Italy
104 F4 Sinj Croatia
22 E3 Sinjai Indonesia
112 B3 Sinjajevina Planina mountain range Yugoslavia
42 E2 Sinjār Iraq
42 E2 Sinjār, Jabal mt. Iraq
119 G4 Sinkat Sudan
Sinkiang Uighur Aut. Region div. see Xinjiang Uygur Zizhiqu
86 C2 Sin-le-Noble France
31 H5 Sinmi i. North Korea
74 D2 Sinn Germany
108 B5 Sinnai Sardegna Italy
163 G2 Sinnamary French Guiana
43 B5 Sinn Bishr, G. h. Egypt
Sinneh see Sanandaj
111 F2 Sinni r. Italy
43 A5 Sinnûris Egypt
112 G2 Sinoie, L. lag. Romania
54 E3 Sinole Latvia
42 C1 Sinop Turkey
31 J4 Sinp'o North Korea
31 H5 Sinp'yŏng North Korea
83 D1 Sins Switzerland
31 H5 Sinsang North Korea
74 D3 Sinsheim Germany
22 B1 Sintang Indonesia
79 M4 Şinteu Romania
158 □1 Sint Nicolaas Aruba Caribbean
151 D6 Sinton Texas U.S.A.
100 A2 Sintra Lisboa Portugal
162 B2 Sinú r. Colombia
31 H5 Sinŭiju North Korea
126 E3 Sinujiif Somalia
54 F3 Sinyaya r. Rus. Fed.
87 H4 Sinzheim Germany
74 C2 Sinzig Germany
75 H4 Sinzing Germany
79 H5 Sió r. Hungary
102 D3 Sió r. Spain
23 B5 Siocon Philippines
125 D7 Sioma Ngwezi National Park nat. park Zambia
82 C2 Sion Switzerland
67 D2 Sion Mills Northern Ireland U.K.
90 B2 Sioule r. France
150 D3 Sioux Center Iowa U.S.A.
150 D3 Sioux City Iowa U.S.A.
150 D3 Sioux Falls S. Dakota U.S.A.
138 B3 Sioux Lookout Ontario Canada
157 H6 Sipacate Guatemala
23 B4 Sipalay Philippines
163 F3 Sipaliwini r. Surinam
104 F4 Šipan i. Croatia
22 B1 Sipang, Tg pt Malaysia
159 □3 Siparia Trinidad and Tobago
24 B2 Sipein Myanmar
31 H4 Siping China
137 K3 Sipiwesk Manitoba Canada
137 K3 Sipiwesk L. l. Manitoba Canada
179 B4 Siple Coast coastal area Antarctica
179 A4 Siple, Mt mt. Antarctica
83 E1 Sipplingen Germany
36 C5 Sipra r. India
145 C5 Sipsey r. Alabama U.S.A.
20 C7 Sipura i. Indonesia
126 □ Siqirah Socotra Yemen
168 D5 Siqueira Campos Brazil
23 B4 Siquijor i. Philippines
23 B4 Siquijor Philippines
39 G4 Sir r. Pakistan
58 B2 Sira r. Norway
38 B3 Sira India
58 B2 Sira Norway
39 C4 Şīr Abū Nu'āyr i. U.A.E.
91 E4 Sirac mt. France
111 E5 Siracusa reg. Sicilia Italy
111 E5 Siracusa Sicilia Italy
37 G4 Sirajganj Bangladesh
136 E4 Sir Alexander, Mt mt. B.C. Canada
92 E4 Siran France
36 A4 Siranda L. l. Pakistan
123 E4 Sirba r. Burkina/Niger
39 C4 Şīr Banī Yās i. U.A.E.
58 B2 Sirdalsvatn l. Norway
14 D2 Sir Edward Pellew Group is Northern Terr. Australia
122 B5 Sirekude Sierra Leone
148 A3 Siren Wisconsin U.S.A.
112 F1 Siret Romania
39 E4 Sīrgān Iran

16 D2 **Sir Graham Moore Is** is Western Australia Australia
36 D3 **Sirhind** India
79 L5 **Şiria** Romania
24 C3 **Siri Kit Dam** dam Thailand
36 B3 **Siritoi** r. Pakistan
39 C3 **Sīrīz** Iran
136 D2 **Sir James McBrien, Mt** mt. N.W.T. Canada
39 C3 **Sīrjan salt flat** Iran
Sīrjan see **Sa'īdābād**
12 D3 **Sir Joseph Bank's Group** is S. Australia Australia
39 D4 **Sirk** Iran
107 E3 **Sirmione** Italy
83 E1 **Sirnach** Switzerland
90 E2 **Sirod** France
38 C2 **Sironcha** India
36 D4 **Sironj** India
120 C2 **Siroua, Jbel** mt. Morocco
38 B2 **Sirpur** India
154 C4 **Sirretta Peak** summit California U.S.A.
37 E4 **Sirsa** Madhya Pradesh India
36 C3 **Sirsa** Haryana India
136 F4 **Sir Sanford, Mt** mt. B.C. Canada
131 F2 **Sir Seretse Khama airport** Botswana
36 D3 **Sirsi** Uttar Pradesh India
38 A3 **Sirsi** Karnataka India
38 B2 **Sirsilla** India
Sirte see **Surt**
Sirte, Gulf of g. see **Khalīj Surt**
12 B1 **Sir Thomas, Mt** h. S. Australia Australia
101 E2 **Siruela** Spain
38 A2 **Sirur** India
54 D4 **Širvintos** Lithuania
42 F3 **Sīrwān** r. Iraq
136 F4 **Sir Wilfred Laurier, Mt** mt. B.C. Canada
15 E2 **Sir W. Thompson** h. Queensland Australia
Sis see **Kozan**
104 F3 **Sisak** Croatia
25 D4 **Sisaket** Thailand
39 B3 **Sīsakht** Iran
157 H4 **Sisal** Mexico
101 H1 **Sisante** Spain
98 B1 **Sisargas, Illas** is Spain
130 D3 **Sishen** South Africa
42 F2 **Sisian** Armenia
122 D4 **Sisili** r. Burkina/Ghana
135 N3 **Sisimiut** Greenland
148 C2 **Siskiwit Bay** b. Michigan U.S.A.
25 C4 **Sisŏphŏn** Cambodia
154 B4 **Sisquoc** r. California U.S.A.
82 C1 **Sissach** Switzerland
150 D2 **Sisseton** S. Dakota U.S.A.
147 K1 **Sisson Branch Reservoir** resr New Brunswick Canada
86 C3 **Sissonne** France
39 E3 **Sistan** reg. Iran
39 E3 **Sīstān va Balūchestān** div. Iran
91 D4 **Sisteron** France
25 A5 **Sisters** i. Andaman and Nicobar Is India
128 ◻1 **Sisters Pk** h. Ascension Atlantic Ocean
9 ◻1 **Sisters, The** is Chatham Is New Zealand
127 ◻1 **Sisters, The** is Seychelles
37 F4 **Sitamarhi** India
36 C5 **Sitamau** India
129 H2 **Sitampiky** Madagascar
23 A5 **Sitangkai** Philippines
36 E4 **Sitapur** India
115 H7 **Siteia** Greece
131 H3 **Siteki** Swaziland
102 E3 **Sitges** Spain
114 E2 **Sithonia** pen. Greece
169 E1 **Sítio da Abadia** Brazil
166 D3 **Sítio do Mato** Brazil
136 B3 **Sitka** Alaska U.S.A.
37 E4 **Sitlaha** India
112 C3 **Sitnica** r. Yugoslavia
79 H3 **Sitno** mt. Slovakia
54 F2 **Sitnya** r. Rus. Fed.
24 B3 **Sittang** r. Myanmar
69 D4 **Sittard** Netherlands
24 A1 **Sittaung** Myanmar
72 E2 **Sittensen** Germany
83 E1 **Sitter** r. Germany
81 F4 **Sittersdorf** Austria
63 G3 **Sittingbourne** England U.K.
24 A2 **Sittwe** Myanmar
22 C3 **Situbondo** Indonesia
73 H4 **Sitzenroda** Germany
27 ◻ **Siu A Chau** i. Hong Kong China
7 ◻12 **Siumu** Western Samoa
156 J6 **Siuna** Nicaragua
54 D1 **Siuntio** Finland
37 F5 **Siuri** India
38 B4 **Sivaganga** India
38 B4 **Sivakasi** India
31 H1 **Sivaki** Rus. Fed.
39 C3 **Sīvand** Iran
42 D2 **Sivas** Turkey
42 B2 **Sivaslı** Turkey
42 D2 **Siverek** Turkey
54 G2 **Siverskiy** Rus. Fed.
52 F2 **Sivin'** r. Rus. Fed.
52 G2 **Sivin'** Rus. Fed.
42 B2 **Sivrihisar** Turkey
69 C4 **Sivry** Belgium
87 E3 **Sivry-sur-Meuse** France
131 G3 **Sivukile** South Africa
118 E2 **Siwa** Egypt
22 E2 **Siwa** Indonesia
36 D3 **Siwalik Range** mountain range India
37 F4 **Siwan** India
36 C4 **Siwana** India
118 E2 **Siwa Oasis** oasis Egypt
91 D5 **Six-Fours-les-Plages** France
33 G1 **Si Xian** China
30 A5 **Sixin** China
148 E4 **Six Lakes** Michigan U.S.A.
67 D2 **Sixmilecross** Northern Ireland U.K.
90 E2 **Sixt-Fer-à-Cheval** France
131 G2 **Siyabuswa** South Africa
33 G1 **Siyang** China
131 G3 **Siyathemba** South Africa
42 G1 **Siyäzän** Azerbaijan
30 D4 **Siyitang** China
39 C2 **Sīyunī** Iran
100 A1 **Sizandro** r. Portugal
31 H2 **Sizhan** China
30 A2 **Sizim** Rus. Fed.
30 D4 **Siziwang Qi** China
88 A3 **Sizun** France
55 D4 **Sjælland** i. Denmark
55 D4 **Sjællands Odde** pen. Denmark
112 C3 **Sjenica** Yugoslavia
59 E4 **Sjöbo** Sweden
55 B3 **Sjørup** Denmark
59 E2 **Sjötorp** Sweden
56 E1 **Sjøvegan** Norway
59 F3 **Sjunnen** Sweden
55 E1 **Sjuntorp** Sweden
53 E3 **Skadovs'k** Ukraine
55 D4 **Skælsør** Denmark
55 A4 **Skærbæk** Denmark
135 R2 **Skærfjorden** inlet Greenland
59 E4 **Skævinge** Denmark
56 M6 **Skaftafell** nat. park Iceland
56 M7 **Skaftárós** b. Iceland
55 C2 **Skagen** Denmark
59 F2 **Skagern** l. Sweden
58 C3 **Skagerrak** str. Denmark/Norway
152 B1 **Skagit** r. Canada/U.S.A.
136 B3 **Skagway** Alaska U.S.A.
56 G1 **Skaidi** Norway
54 D4 **Skaidiškės** Lithuania
115 D6 **Skala** Greece
56 E1 **Skaland** Norway
115 E4 **Skala Oropou** Greece
53 B2 **Skala-Podil's'ka** Ukraine
53 A2 **Skalat** Ukraine
77 J5 **Skalbmierz** Poland
59 E3 **Skälderviken** b. Sweden
55 A4 **Skallingen** pen. Denmark
56 D2 **Skalmodal** Sweden
114 F1 **Skaloti** Greece
55 B3 **Skals** r. Denmark
55 B3 **Skals** Denmark
55 B3 **Skanderborg** Denmark
147 E3 **Skaneateles Lake** l. New York U.S.A.
148 C2 **Skanee** Michigan U.S.A.
59 E4 **Skåne-Tranås** Sweden
59 F2 **Skänninge** Sweden
59 E4 **Skanör med Falsterbo** Sweden
114 F3 **Skantzoura** i. Greece
76 D3 **Skąpe** Poland
59 E2 **Skara** Sweden
59 E2 **Skaraborg** div. Sweden
107 J4 **Škarda** i. Croatia
15 E1 **Skardon** r. Queensland Australia
36 C2 **Skardu** Jammu and Kashmir
58 B2 **Skare** Norway
59 J2 **Skärgårdshavets Nationalpark** nat. park Finland
55 D2 **Skärhamn** Sweden
58 D1 **Skarnes** Norway
55 C4 **Skarø** i. Denmark
59 G1 **Skärplinge** Sweden
76 G1 **Skarszewy** Poland
55 C4 **Skårup** Denmark
77 K4 **Skaryszew** Poland
53 B2 **Skarzhyntsi** Ukraine
77 J4 **Skarżysko-Kamienna** Poland
59 E1 **Skasbegert** h. Norway
59 E2 **Skattkärr** Sweden
59 F1 **Skattungbyn** Sweden
54 C4 **Skaudvilė** Lithuania
56 F2 **Skaulo** Sweden
54 E3 **Škaune** Latvia
55 A3 **Skave** Denmark
77 H6 **Skawa** r. Poland
77 H6 **Skawina** Poland
120 A4 **Skaymat** Western Sahara
59 H2 **Skebobruk** Sweden
59 F3 **Skede** Sweden
59 F2 **Skedevi** Sweden
58 D2 **Skee** Sweden
136 D3 **Skeena** r. B.C. Canada
136 D3 **Skeena Mountains** mountain range B.C. Canada
56 M6 **Skegafjörður** b. Iceland
63 G1 **Skegness** England U.K.
128 A2 **Skeleton Coast Game Park** res. Namibia
56 F2 **Skellefteå** Sweden
56 E2 **Skellefteälven** r. Sweden
56 F2 **Skelleftehamn** Sweden
67 A5 **Skellig Rocks** i. Rep. of Ireland
65 F4 **Skelmersdale** England U.K.
62 D3 **Skenfrith** Wales U.K.
77 H3 **Skępe** Poland
67 E3 **Skerries** Rep. of Ireland
77 L6 **Skhidni Beskydy** mountain range Poland/Ukraine
77 M6 **Skhidnytsya** Ukraine
58 D2 **Ski** Norway
114 E3 **Skiathos** i. Greece
114 E3 **Skiathos** Greece
67 B5 **Skibbereen** Rep. of Ireland
55 D4 **Skibby** Denmark
56 F1 **Skibotn** Norway
77 N2 **Skidal'** Belarus
65 E3 **Skiddaw** mt. England U.K.
54 D4 **Skiemonys** Lithuania
58 C2 **Skien** Norway
77 J3 **Skierniewice** div. Poland
77 J4 **Skierniewice** Poland
121 F1 **Skikda** Algeria
59 F3 **Skillingaryd** Sweden
59 F2 **Skinnskatteberg** Sweden
36 D2 **Skio** India
64 C2 **Skipness** Scotland U.K.
65 H4 **Skipsea** England U.K.
130 C7 **Skipskop** South Africa
65 F4 **Skipton** England U.K.
13 E4 **Skipton** Victoria Australia
55 B3 **Skive** Denmark
55 B3 **Skive Fjord** b. Denmark
56 M6 **Skjálfandafljót** r. Iceland
56 M6 **Skjálfandi** b. Iceland
58 D2 **Skjeberg** Norway
58 D1 **Skjellbreidfjellet** mt. Norway
58 B2 **Skjerkeknuten** mt. Norway
55 A4 **Skjern** r. Denmark
55 A4 **Skjern** Denmark
57 B3 **Skjolden** Norway
114 D3 **Sklithro** Greece
52 C1 **Sknyatino** Rus. Fed.
59 H1 **Skoby** Sweden
76 G6 **Skoczów** Poland
58 B3 **Skodje** Norway
131 E7 **Skoenmakerskop** South Africa
81 F4 **Škofja Loka** Slovenia
81 F5 **Škofljica** Slovenia
56 G1 **Skog** Sweden
56 G1 **Skoganvarre** Norway
59 G2 **Skogstorp** Sweden
62 A3 **Skokholm Island** i. Wales U.K.
76 F3 **Skoki** Poland
148 D4 **Skokie** Illinois U.S.A.
58 C2 **Skollenborg** Norway
59 F2 **Sköllersta** Sweden
62 A3 **Skomer Island** i. Wales U.K.
131 F3 **Skoonspruit** r. South Africa
115 G4 **Skopelos** i. Greece
114 E3 **Skopelos** i. Greece
114 E3 **Skopelos** Thessalia Greece
114 E3 **Skopelou, D.** chan. Greece
114 G3 **Skopia** h. Greece
52 D3 **Skopin** Rus. Fed.
112 C4 **Skopje** Macedonia
55 ◻1 **Skopun** Faeroes
55 ◻1 **Skopunarfjørður** chan. Faeroes
76 G2 **Skórcz** Poland
58 C2 **Skornetten** h. Norway
53 G1 **Skorodnoye** Rus. Fed.
52 D1 **Skoropuskovskiy** Rus. Fed.
55 B3 **Skørping** Denmark
77 L3 **Skórzec** Poland
59 E2 **Skotterud** Norway
114 E1 **Skoutari** Kentriki Makedonia Greece
115 D6 **Skoutari** Peloponnisos Greece
59 E2 **Skövde** Sweden
55 A4 **Skovlund** Denmark
27 M1 **Skovorodino** Rus. Fed.
147 J2 **Skowhegan** Maine U.S.A.
114 D1 **Skra** Greece
59 F1 **Skräddrabo** Sweden
58 D1 **Skreia** Norway
58 C2 **Skrimfjell** h. Norway
54 D3 **Skrīveri** Latvia
81 E4 **Škrlutica** mt. Slovenia
54 C3 **Skrunda** Latvia
76 G6 **Skrzyczne** mt. Poland
58 A2 **Skudeneshavn** Norway
136 B2 **Skukum, Mt** mt. Yukon Terr. Canada
154 D3 **Skull Peak** summit Nevada U.S.A.
130 A5 **Skulpfonteinpunt** pt South Africa
76 G3 **Skulsk** Poland
59 E2 **Skultorp** Sweden
59 G2 **Skultuna** Sweden
148 B5 **Skunk** r. Iowa U.S.A.
54 B3 **Skuodas** Lithuania
59 E4 **Skurup** Sweden
78 E2 **Skuteč** Czech Rep.
59 G1 **Skutskär** Sweden
77 N6 **Skvaryava** Ukraine
53 C2 **Skvyra** Ukraine
76 D3 **Skwierzyna** Poland
114 D2 **Skydra** Greece
66 B3 **Skye** i. Scotland U.K.
58 B2 **Skykula** h. Norway
114 F4 **Skyropoula** i. Greece
114 F4 **Skyros** i. Greece
114 F4 **Skyros** Greece
179 B3 **Skytrain Ice Rise** ice feature Antarctica
54 E4 **Slabodka** Belarus
79 G3 **Sládkovičovo** Slovakia
55 D4 **Slagelse** Denmark
68 E2 **Slagharen** Netherlands
56 E2 **Slagnäs** Sweden
64 E2 **Slamannan** Scotland U.K.
22 B3 **Slamet, G.** volcano Indonesia
79 K3 **Slaná** r. Slovakia
67 E3 **Slane** Rep. of Ireland
79 L3 **Slanec** Slovakia
67 E4 **Slaney** r. Rep. of Ireland
55 E4 **Slangerup** Denmark
112 E2 **Slănic** Romania
112 F1 **Slănic Moldova** Romania
79 L3 **Slanskévrchy** mountain range Slovakia
54 F2 **Slantsy** Rus. Fed.
78 D1 **Slaný** Czech Rep.
54 C4 **Šlapaberžė** Lithuania
78 F2 **Šlapanice** Czech Rep.
51 G5 **Slashchevskaya** Rus. Fed.
52 G4 **Slastukha** Rus. Fed.
59 G2 **Slätbaken** inlet Sweden
140 B2 **Slate Is** is Ontario Canada
112 E2 **Slatina** Romania
114 B1 **Slatino** Macedonia
53 G1 **Slatyne** Ukraine
137 G2 **Slave** r. N.W.T. Canada
123 E5 **Slave Coast** coastal area Africa
136 G3 **Slave Lake** Alberta Canada
47 J2 **Slavgorod** Rus. Fed.
53 F2 **Slavhorod** Dnipropetrovs'ka Oblast' Ukraine
53 F1 **Slavhorod** Sums'ka Oblast' Ukraine
54 F3 **Slavkovichi** Rus. Fed.
75 H2 **Slavkovský les** h. Czech Rep.
78 F2 **Slavkov u Brna** Czech Rep.
52 C1 **Slavnoye** Rus. Fed.
78 E3 **Slavonice** Czech Rep.
104 F3 **Slavonija** reg. Croatia
104 F3 **Slavonska Požega** Croatia
104 G3 **Slavonski Brod** Croatia
79 K3 **Slavošovce** Slovakia
53 B1 **Slavuta** Ukraine
53 D1 **Slavutych** Ukraine
47 G4 **Slavyanka** Kazakhstan
31 J4 **Slavyanka** Rus. Fed.
112 E3 **Slavyanovo** Bulgaria
51 F6 **Slavyansk-na-Kubani** Rus. Fed.
76 E4 **Sława** Poland
77 M4 **Sławatycze** Poland
76 E1 **Sławno** Poland
76 D2 **Sławoborze** Poland
76 E1 **Sławsko** Poland
65 F2 **Sleaford** England U.K.
12 C3 **Sleaford B.** b. S. Australia Australia
67 A4 **Slea Head** headland Rep. of Ireland
66 C3 **Sleat** pen. Scotland U.K.
66 C3 **Sleat, Sound of** chan. Scotland U.K.
68 E2 **Sleen** Netherlands
138 E2 **Sleeper Islands** is Québec Canada
148 D3 **Sleeping Bear Dunes National Seashore** res. Michigan U.S.A.
148 D3 **Sleeping Bear Pt** pt Michigan U.S.A.
65 H3 **Sleights** England U.K.
51 H7 **Sleptsovskaya** Rus. Fed.
77 F2 **Ślesin** Bydgoszcz Poland
76 G3 **Ślesin** Konin Poland
179 C3 **Slessor Glacier** gl. Antarctica
151 F6 **Slidell** Louisiana U.S.A.
68 C3 **Sliedrecht** Netherlands
111 ◻ **Sliema** Malta
67 A4 **Slievanea** h. Rep. of Ireland
67 D2 **Slieve Anierin** h. Rep. of Ireland
67 D4 **Slieveardagh Hills** h. Rep. of Ireland
67 C3 **Slieve Aughty Mts** h. Rep. of Ireland
67 D2 **Slieve Beagh** h. Rep. of Ireland/U.K.
67 C4 **Slieve Bernagh** h. Rep. of Ireland
67 D3 **Slieve Bloom Mts** h. Rep. of Ireland
67 B4 **Slievecallan** h. Rep. of Ireland
67 B2 **Slieve Car** h. Rep. of Ireland
67 F2 **Slieve Donard** h. Northern Ireland U.K.
67 B3 **Slieve Elva** h. Rep. of Ireland
67 C4 **Slievefelim Mts** h. Rep. of Ireland
67 B2 **Slieve Gamph** h. Rep. of Ireland
67 C2 **Slieve League** h. Rep. of Ireland
67 B4 **Slieve Mish Mts** h. Rep. of Ireland
67 A5 **Slieve Miskish Mts** h. Rep. of Ireland
67 A2 **Slieve More** h. Rep. of Ireland
67 D3 **Slieve na Calliagh** h. Rep. of Ireland
67 D4 **Slievenamon** h. Rep. of Ireland
67 D1 **Slieve Snaght** mt. Rep. of Ireland
66 B3 **Sligachan** Scotland U.K.
Sligeach see **Sligo**
67 C2 **Sligo** div. Rep. of Ireland
67 C2 **Sligo** Rep. of Ireland
67 C2 **Sligo Bay** b. Rep. of Ireland
63 F3 **Slinfold** England U.K.
68 E2 **Slinge** r. Netherlands
59 H3 **Slite** Sweden
112 F3 **Sliven** Bulgaria
112 F3 **Slivo Pole** Bulgaria
76 G2 **Śliwice** Poland
53 C3 **Slobidka** Ukraine
50 H2 **Sloboda** Rus. Fed.
50 J2 **Slobodchikovo** Rus. Fed.
52 B2 **Slobodka** Rus. Fed.
50 J3 **Slobodskoy** Rus. Fed.
53 C3 **Slobozia** Moldova
112 F2 **Slobozia** Romania
136 F5 **Slocan** B.C. Canada
68 E1 **Slochteren** Netherlands
77 J5 **Słomniki** Poland
77 O2 **Slonim** Belarus
53 G1 **Slonovka** Rus. Fed.
76 D2 **Słonowice** Poland
76 C3 **Słońsk** Poland
68 D2 **Slotermeer** l. Netherlands
6 ◻1 **Slot, The** chan. Solomon Is.
63 F3 **Slough** England U.K.
52 A4 **Slout** Ukraine
48 G4 **Slovakia** country Europe
53 C1 **Slovechne** Ukraine
48 G4 **Slovenia** country Europe
81 G4 **Slovenj Gradec** Slovenia
81 G4 **Slovenska Bistrica** Slovenia
81 G4 **Slovenske Gorice** h. Slovenia
81 G4 **Slovenske Konjice** Slovenia
79 K3 **Slovenské Rudohorie** mountain range Slovakia
79 K3 **Slovenský kras** mountain range Slovakia
79 K3 **Slovenský raj** nat. park Slovakia
77 N6 **Slovita** Ukraine
53 G2 **Slov"yanohirs'k** Ukraine
53 G2 **Slov"yans'k** Ukraine
53 C1 **Slovyechna** r. Belarus
76 F1 **Słowiński Park Narodoway** nat. park Poland
77 H3 **Słubice** Płock Poland
76 C3 **Słubice** Zielona Gora Poland
54 E5 **Sluch** r. Belarus
53 B1 **Sluch** r. Ukraine
83 F2 **Sludrno** Italy
69 B3 **Sluis** Netherlands
69 B3 **Sluiskil** Netherlands
78 D1 **Šluknov** Czech Rep.
78 G2 **Slunečná** h. Czech Rep.
104 E3 **Slunj** Croatia
76 F3 **Słupca** Poland
77 J4 **Słupia** Kielce Poland
77 H4 **Słupia** Skierniewice Poland
77 H3 **Słupno** Poland
76 F1 **Słupsk** div. Poland
76 F1 **Słupsk** Poland
56 E2 **Slussfors** Sweden
76 G4 **Słuszków** Poland
54 E5 **Slutsk** Belarus
54 C4 **Šlyna** r. Lithuania
67 A3 **Slyne Head** headland Rep. of Ireland
30 B2 **Slyudyanka** Rus. Fed.
92 B2 **Smagne** r. France
55 D4 **Smålandsfarvandet** chan. Denmark
59 E3 **Smålandsstenar** Sweden
147 J3 **Small Pt** pt Maine U.S.A.
139 H3 **Smallwood Reservoir** resr Newfoundland Canada
77 N3 **Smalyanitsa** Belarus
54 F4 **Smalyavichy** Belarus
54 E4 **Smarhon'** Belarus
81 G4 **Šmarje pri Jelšah** Slovenia
81 G5 **Šmarjeta** Slovenia
130 D5 **Smartt Syndicate Dam** resr South Africa
92 C2 **Smarves** France
137 J4 **Smeaton** Saskatchewan Canada
75 L2 **Směda** r. Czech Rep.
112 C2 **Smederevo** Yugoslavia
112 C2 **Smederevska Palanka** Yugoslavia
59 F1 **Smedjebacken** Sweden
112 F2 **Smeeni** Romania
67 A4 **Smerwick Harbour** harbour Rep. of Ireland
146 D4 **Smethport** Pennsylvania U.S.A.
31 K2 **Smidovich** Rus. Fed.
76 E3 **Śmigiel** Poland
53 D2 **Smila** Ukraine
54 F5 **Smilavichy** Belarus
68 E2 **Smilde** Netherlands
53 E1 **Smile** Ukraine
54 D3 **Smiltene** Latvia
52 G2 **Smirnovo** Rus. Fed.
146 C6 **Smith** r. Virginia U.S.A.
136 G3 **Smith** Alberta Canada
154 C2 **Smith** Nevada U.S.A.
173 G3 **Smith** Argentina
134 F3 **Smith Arm** b. N.W.T. Canada
136 D4 **Smithers** B.C. Canada
145 E5 **Smithfield** N. Carolina U.S.A.
152 E3 **Smithfield** Utah U.S.A.
131 F5 **Smithfield** South Africa
179 A3 **Smith Glacier** gl. Antarctica
25 A4 **Smith I.** i. Andaman and Nicobar Is India
147 E5 **Smith I.** i. Maryland U.S.A.
179 B2 **Smith I.** i. S. Shetland Is Antarctica
147 F6 **Smith I.** i. Virginia U.S.A.
146 D6 **Smith Mountain Lake** l. Virginia U.S.A.
136 D3 **Smith River** B.C. Canada
141 G4 **Smiths Falls** Ontario Canada
135 L2 **Smith Sound** str. Canada/Greenland
13 F5 **Smithton** Tasmania Australia
154 C1 **Smoke Creek Desert** desert Nevada U.S.A.
136 F4 **Smoky** r. Alberta Canada
150 C4 **Smoky** r. Kansas U.S.A.
12 C3 **Smoky Bay** S. Australia Australia
13 H2 **Smoky C.** headland New South Wales Australia
140 D1 **Smoky Falls** Ontario Canada
150 D4 **Smoky Hills** h. Kansas U.S.A.
136 G4 **Smoky Lake** Alberta Canada
56 B3 **Smøla** i. Norway
76 F1 **Smołdzino** Poland
52 A2 **Smolensk** div. Rus. Fed.
52 A2 **Smolensk** Rus. Fed.
52 A2 **Smolenskaya Vozvyshennost'** reg. Rus. Fed.
47 K2 **Smolenskoye** Rus. Fed.
114 B2 **Smolikas** mt. Greece
52 F1 **Smolino** Rus. Fed.
59 E2 **Smolmark** Sweden
79 K3 **Smolník** Slovakia
113 E4 **Smolyan** Bulgaria
140 E2 **Smooth Rock Falls** Ontario Canada
138 C3 **Smoothrock L.** l. Ontario Canada
137 H4 **Smoothstone Lake** l. Saskatchewan Canada
56 G1 **Smørfjord** Norway
53 B2 **Smotrych** Ukraine
112 F3 **Smyadovo** Bulgaria
59 E4 **Smygehamn** Sweden
53 A1 **Smyha** Ukraine
77 J4 **Smyków** Poland
179 B3 **Smyley I.** i. Antarctica
147 F5 **Smyrna** Delaware U.S.A.
145 C5 **Smyrna** Georgia U.S.A.
146 C4 **Smyrna** Ohio U.S.A.
147 J1 **Smyrna Mills** Maine U.S.A.
53 G3 **Smyrnove** Ukraine
64 D3 **Snaefell** h. Isle of Man
56 N6 **Snæfell** mt. Iceland
136 A2 **Snag** Yukon Terr. Canada
65 H3 **Snainton** England U.K.
65 G4 **Snaith** England U.K.
152 D3 **Snake** r. Idaho U.S.A.
155 E2 **Snake Range** mts Nevada U.S.A.
152 D3 **Snake River Plain** plain Idaho U.S.A.
158 C2 **Snap Pt** pt The Bahamas
55 C4 **Snaptun** Denmark
136 G2 **Snare Lake** N.W.T. Canada
8 ◻3 **Snares Is** is New Zealand
56 D2 **Snasa** Norway
55 A3 **Snedsted** Denmark
68 D1 **Sneek** Netherlands
68 D1 **Sneekermeer** l. Netherlands
67 B5 **Sneem** Rep. of Ireland
130 E5 **Sneeuberg** mts South Africa
139 H3 **Snegamook Lake** l. Newfoundland Canada
54 B3 **Snēpele** Latvia
59 H1 **Snesslinge** Sweden
63 G2 **Snettisham** England U.K.
55 A4 **Sneum** r. Denmark
44 K3 **Snezhnogorsk** Rus. Fed.
107 J3 **Snežnik** mt. Slovenia
77 K2 **Śniadowo** Poland
164 A3 **S. Nicolás, Bahía** b. Peru
76 D5 **Sněžka** mt. Czech Rep./Poland
53 E3 **Snihurivka** Ukraine
79 M3 **Snina** Slovakia
66 B3 **Snizort, Loch** b. Scotland U.K.
58 B2 **Snjoheii** mt. Norway
55 ◻2 **Snogebæk** Denmark
152 B2 **Snohomish** Washington U.S.A.
58 B2 **Snønuten** mt. Norway
152 B2 **Snoqualmie Pass** pass Washington U.S.A.
56 D2 **Snøtinden** mt. Norway
53 D1 **Snov** r. Ukraine
53 D2 **Snova** r. Rus. Fed.
54 E5 **Snow** Belarus
137 J2 **Snowbird Lake** l. N.W.T. Canada
62 B1 **Snowdon** mt. Wales U.K.
9 B6 **Snowdon** mt. New Zealand
62 B1 **Snowdonia National Park** Wales U.K.
155 G4 **Snowflake** Arizona U.S.A.
147 F5 **Snow Hill** Maryland U.S.A.
145 E5 **Snow Hill** N. Carolina U.S.A.
137 J4 **Snow Lake** Manitoba Canada
12 D3 **Snowtown** S. Australia Australia
152 D3 **Snowville** Utah U.S.A.
13 G4 **Snowy** r. Victoria Australia
141 H5 **Snowy Mt** mt. New York U.S.A.
13 G4 **Snowy Mts** mountain range New South Wales Australia
54 E4 **Snudy, Vozyera** l. Belarus
158 D2 **Snug Corner** The Bahamas
139 J3 **Snug Harbour** Newfoundland Canada
140 E4 **Snug Harbour** Ontario Canada
25 D4 **Snuŏl** Cambodia
53 A2 **Snyatyn** Ukraine
151 D5 **Snyder** Oklahoma U.S.A.
151 C5 **Snyder** Texas U.S.A.
130 C5 **Snydersspoort** pass South Africa
129 G2 **Soahany** Madagascar
64 B1 **Soa Island** i. Scotland U.K.
98 B3 **Soajo** Portugal
9 A6 **Soaker, Mt** mt. New Zealand
129 H2 **Soalala** Madagascar
129 G3 **Soalara** Madagascar
98 B3 **Soalhões** Portugal
129 G3 **Soamanonga** Madagascar
82 C3 **Soana** r. Italy
129 H2 **Soanierana-Ivongo** Madagascar
28 A6 **Soan kundo** i. South Korea
107 F3 **Soave** Italy
129 H2 **Soavinandriana** Madagascar
66 ◻1 **Soay** i. Scotland U.K.
126 B3 **Sobat** r. Sudan
74 C3 **Sobernheim** Germany
78 D2 **Soběslav** Czech Rep.
21 M7 **Sobger** r. Indonesia
77 K4 **Sobolew** Poland
28 C7 **Sobo-san** mt. Japan
76 E5 **Sobótka** Poland
75 L2 **Sobotka** Czech Rep.
76 F4 **Sobótka** Poland
168 E1 **Sobradinho** Brazil
166 D3 **Sobradinho, Barragem de** resr Brazil
166 D1 **Sobral** Brazil
100 A1 **Sobral de Monte Agraço** Portugal
79 M3 **Sobrance** Slovakia
102 D2 **Sobrarbe** reg. Spain
98 C5 **Sobreira Formosa** Portugal
99 G2 **Sobrón, Emb. de** resr Spain
55 C5 **Søby** Denmark
53 E1 **Sobych** Ukraine
81 E4 **Soča** r. Slovenia
173 K3 **Soca** Uruguay
77 J3 **Sochaczew** Poland
90 E1 **Sochaux** France
51 F7 **Sochi** Rus. Fed.
77 J3 **Sochocin** Poland
114 E2 **Sochos** Greece
Society Islands is see **Archipel de la Société**
112 C2 **Socol** Romania
164 C4 **Socompa** Chile
153 F5 **Socorro** New Mexico U.S.A.
169 E5 **Socorro** Brazil
162 C2 **Socorro** Colombia
156 C5 **Socorro, I.** i. Mexico
Socotra i. see **Suqutra**
103 B6 **Socovos** Spain
25 D5 **Soc Trăng** Vietnam
101 H1 **Socuéllamos** Spain
154 D4 **Soda Lake** l. California U.S.A.
56 G2 **Sodankylä** Finland
36 D2 **Soda Plains** plain China/Jammu and Kashmir
152 E3 **Soda Springs** Idaho U.S.A.
59 G3 **Söderåkra** Sweden
59 H1 **Söderboda** Sweden
59 H2 **Söderby-Karl** Sweden
59 G1 **Söderfors** Sweden
57 G3 **Söderhamn** Sweden
59 G2 **Söderköping** Sweden
59 G2 **Södermanland** div. Sweden
59 G2 **Södertälje** Sweden
119 E5 **Sodiri** Sudan
130 D5 **Sodium** South Africa
126 C3 **Sodo** Ethiopia
57 E3 **Södra Kvarken** str. Finland/Sweden
81 F5 **Sodražica** Slovenia
118 D4 **Soéka well** Chad
131 G1 **Soekmekaar** South Africa
54 C2 **Soela Väin** chan. Estonia
72 D4 **Soest** Germany
68 D2 **Soest** Netherlands
72 C3 **Soeste** r. Germany
114 D3 **Sofades** Greece
129 E2 **Sofala** div. Mozambique
129 E3 **Sofala, Baia de** b. Mozambique
Sofia see **Sofiya**
115 E5 **Sofiko** Greece
52 F4 **Sof'ino** Rus. Fed.
112 D3 **Sofiya** div. Bulgaria
112 D3 **Sofiya** Bulgaria
53 E2 **Sofiyivka** Ukraine
56 H2 **Sofporog** Rus. Fed.
52 C1 **Sofrino** Rus. Fed.
162 C2 **Sogamoso** Colombia
31 K2 **Sogda** Rus. Fed.
72 C3 **Sögel** Germany
58 B1 **Sogndalsfjøra** Norway
58 B2 **Søgne** Norway
58 A1 **Sognefjorden** inlet Norway
58 A1 **Sognesjøen** chan. Norway
58 A1 **Sogn og Fjordane** div. Norway
23 C4 **Sogod** Philippines
30 B4 **Sogo Nur** l. China
50 H2 **Sogra** Rus. Fed.
32 C1 **Sogruma** China
37 H3 **Sog Xian** China
119 F2 **Sohâg** Egypt
36 D5 **Sohagpur** India
63 G2 **Soham** England U.K.
36 C2 **Sohan** r. Pakistan
6 ◻1 **Sohano** P.N.G.
69 D4 **Soheit-Tinlot** Belgium
37 E5 **Sohela** India
36 D3 **Sohna** India
74 C3 **Sohren** Germany
69 C4 **Soignies** div. Belgium
69 C4 **Soignies** Belgium
32 B2 **Soila** China
79 M5 **Şoimi** Romania
82 A1 **Soing-Cubry-Charentenay** France
56 G3 **Soini** Finland
86 D2 **Soire-le-Château** France
86 C3 **Soissons** France
172 D3 **Soitue** Argentina
86 C4 **Soizy-aux-Bois** France
28 D6 **Sōja** Japan
36 C4 **Sojat** India
23 B4 **Sojoton Point** pt Philippines
78 F5 **Söjtör** Hungary
46 D2 **Sok** r. Rus. Fed.
53 A1 **Sokal'** Ukraine
31 J5 **Sokch'o** South Korea
42 A2 **Söke** Turkey
47 H5 **Sokh** Tajikistan
30 D2 **Sokhondo, G.** mt. Rus. Fed.
51 G7 **Sokhumi** Georgia
112 C3 **Sokobanja** Yugoslavia
123 E5 **Sokodé** Togo
27 ◻ **Soko Islands** is Hong Kong
50 G3 **Sokol** Rus. Fed.
104 G4 **Sokolac** Bos.-Herz.
53 D2 **Sokolivka** Cherkas'ka Oblast' Ukraine
77 N5 **Sokolivka** L'vivs'ka Oblast' Ukraine
77 M2 **Sokółka** Poland
77 L1 **Sokółki** Poland
81 H1 **Sokolnice** Czech Rep.
52 B1 **Sokol'niki** Rus. Fed.
52 D2 **Sokol'niki** Rus. Fed.
122 C4 **Sokolo** Mali
53 F3 **Sokolohirne** Ukraine
78 B1 **Sokolov** Czech Rep.
81 H4 **Sokolovac** Croatia
52 G4 **Sokolovyy** Rus. Fed.
77 L5 **Sokołów Małopolski** Poland
77 L3 **Sokołow Podlaski** Poland
52 F1 **Sokol'skoye** Rus. Fed.
77 L3 **Sokoły** Poland
122 A4 **Sokone** Senegal
29 ◻2 **Sokoniya** Japan
123 F4 **Sokoto** div. Nigeria
123 E4 **Sokoto** watercourse Nigeria
123 F4 **Sokoto** Nigeria
52 G4 **Sokur** Rus. Fed.
53 B2 **Sokyryany** Ukraine
77 H6 **Sola** r. Poland
173 H2 **Sola** Argentina
36 D3 **Solan** India
100 D2 **Solana de los Barros** Spain
101 F2 **Solana del Pino** Spain
9 A7 **Solander I.** i. New Zealand
58 C1 **Sølandsfjellet** mt. Norway
173 H4 **Solanet** Argentina
110 B4 **Solanto, Pta di** pt Sicilia Italy
38 A2 **Solāpur** India
111 E5 **Solarino** Sicilia Italy
112 E1 **Solca** Romania
83 F2 **Solda** r. Italy
83 F2 **Solda** Italy
53 C3 **Şoldăneşti** Moldova
80 C4 **Sölden** Austria
93 D6 **Soldeu** Andorra
76 G2 **Solec Kujawski** Poland
154 B3 **Soledad** California U.S.A.
173 G1 **Soledad** Argentina
162 C1 **Soledad** Colombia
163 E2 **Soledad** Venezuela
157 F5 **Soledad de Doblado** Mexico
167 B6 **Soledade** Brazil
51 G6 **Solenoye** Rus. Fed.
63 E4 **Solent, The** str. England U.K.
108 B3 **Solenzara** Corse France
173 F3 **Solesino** Italy
86 C2 **Solesmes** France
111 H2 **Soleto** Italy
93 B4 **Solférino** France
83 F3 **Solferino** Italy
56 D2 **Solfjellsjøen** Norway
59 F3 **Solgen** l. Sweden
50 G2 **Solginskiy** Rus. Fed.
42 E2 **Solhan** Turkey
107 E4 **Soliera** Italy
50 G3 **Soligalich** Rus. Fed.
91 B4 **Solignac-sur-Loire** France
80 D5 **Soligo** r. Italy
63 E2 **Solihull** England U.K.
44 G4 **Solikamsk** Rus. Fed.
46 D2 **Sol'-Iletsk** Rus. Fed.
163 E4 **Solimões** r. Brazil
72 C4 **Solingen** Germany
173 K3 **Solís** Uruguay
173 K3 **Solís de Mataojo** Uruguay
81 F3 **Solker Tauern** pass Austria
59 E2 **Sollebrunn** Sweden
56 E3 **Sollefteå** Sweden
81 H3 **Sollenau** Austria
59 G2 **Sollentuna** Sweden
103 F5 **Sóller** Spain
59 F1 **Sollerön** Sweden
55 D5 **Søllested** Denmark
73 H4 **Söllichau** Germany
91 E5 **Solliès-Pont** France
72 E4 **Solling** h. Germany
74 D2 **Solms** Germany
52 C1 **Solnechnogorsk** Rus. Fed.
53 G1 **Solntsevo** Rus. Fed.
22 B3 **Solo** r. Indonesia
53 B2 **Solobkivtsi** Ukraine
109 G4 **Solofra** Italy
89 G4 **Sologne** reg. France
157 H6 **Sololá** Guatemala
93 C5 **Solomiac** France
53 B2 **Solomna** Ukraine
4 H5 **Solomon Islands** country Pacific Ocean
6 ◻1 **Solomon Sea** sea P.N.G./Solomon Is.
31 G3 **Solon** China
53 G2 **Solona** r. Ukraine
46 F3 **Solonchak Ghalkarteniz** salt marsh Kazakhstan
46 E4 **Solonchak Goklenkuy** depression Turkmenistan
46 D4 **Solonchak Kendyrlisor** l. Kazakhstan
46 E5 **Solonchakovyye Vpadiny Unguz** salt flat Turkmenistan
46 E4 **Solonchak Shorkozakhly** depression Turkmenistan
53 F2 **Solone** Ukraine
52 E1 **Solonitsa** r. Rus. Fed.
166 E2 **Solonópole** Brazil
148 B2 **Solon Springs** Wisconsin U.S.A.
58 D1 **Solør** reg. Norway
99 F4 **Solosancho** Spain
54 F3 **Solot"** r. Rus. Fed.
52 D2 **Solotcha** Rus. Fed.
82 C1 **Solothurn** div. Switzerland
82 C1 **Solothurn** Switzerland
53 A2 **Solotvyn** Ukraine
50 E1 **Solovetskiye Ostrova** Rus. Fed.
52 E3 **Solovoye** Rus. Fed.
77 N4 **Solovychi** Ukraine
31 E2 **Solov'yevsk** Mongolia
102 E3 **Solsona** Spain

152 D3 Spruce Mt. mt. Nevada U.S.A.
111 F3 Spulico, Capo c. Italy
65 J4 Spurn Head c. England U.K.
136 E5 Spuzzum B.C. Canada
77 K2 Spychowo Poland
136 E5 Squamish B.C. Canada
147 H3 Squam Lake l. New Hampshire U.S.A.
147 J1 Squapan Lake l. Maine U.S.A.
147 J1 Square Lake l. Maine U.S.A.
111 F4 Squillace Italy
111 F4 Squillace, Golfo di g. Italy
111 H2 Squinzano Italy
17 D5 Squires, Mt h. Western Australia Australia
22 B3 Sragen Indonesia
112 C3 Srbija div. Yugoslavia
112 B2 Srbobran Yugoslavia
25 C5 Srê Âmbĕl Cambodia
104 G3 Srebrenica Bos.-Herz.
45 R4 Sredinnyy Khrebet mountain range Rus. Fed.
81 H4 Središče Slovenia
112 F3 Sredishte Bulgaria
112 D3 Sredna Gora mountain range Bulgaria
31 H2 Sredne-belaya Rus. Fed.
45 R3 Srednekolymsk Rus. Fed.
52 C2 Sredne-Russkaya Vozvyshennost' reg. Rus. Fed.
45 M3 Sredne-Sibirskoye Ploskogor'ye plat. Rus. Fed.
50 D1 Sredneye Kuyto, Oz. l. Rus. Fed.
112 E3 Srednogorie Bulgaria
51 H5 Srednyaya Akhtuba Rus. Fed.
112 B2 Srem reg. Yugoslavia
76 F3 Śrem Poland
25 D4 Srêpok, T. r. Cambodia
31 F1 Sretensk Rus. Fed.
53 E1 Sribne Ukraine
38 C3 Sriharikota I. i. India
38 D2 Srikakulam India
38 B3 Sri Kālahasti India
18 K9 Sri Lanka country Asia
36 C2 Srinagar Jammu and Kashmir
36 D3 Srinagar Himachal Pradesh India
38 B4 Srirangam India
24 C3 Sri Thep Thailand
38 B4 Srivaikuntam India
38 A2 Srivardhan India
38 B4 Srivilliputtur India
104 F3 Srnetica mts Bos.-Herz.
76 E4 Środa Śląska Poland
76 F3 Środa Wielkopolska Poland
79 K6 Srpska Crnja Yugoslavia
38 C2 Srungavarapukota India
52 D3 Sselki Rus. Fed.
130 C3 Staansaam South Africa
15 E3 Staaten r. Queensland Australia
15 E3 Staaten River Nat. Park nat. park Queensland Australia
81 H2 Staatz Austria
73 G1 Staberhuk c. Germany
69 C3 Stabroek Belgium
55 A3 Staby Denmark
78 C2 Stachy Czech Rep.
72 E2 Stade Germany
69 B4 Staden Belgium
55 A3 Stadil Fjord lag. Denmark
68 E1 Stadskanaal canal Netherlands
68 E2 Stadskanaal Netherlands
74 E2 Stadtallendorf Germany
75 F4 Stadtbergen Germany
72 E3 Stadthagen Germany
75 G2 Stadtilm Germany
74 B2 Stadtkyll Germany
74 F2 Stadtlauringen Germany
72 B4 Stadtlohn Germany
72 E4 Stadtoldendorf Germany
75 G2 Stadtroda Germany
81 H3 Stadtschlaining Austria
83 D1 Stäfa Switzerland
66 B4 Staffa i. Scotland U.K.
55 F4 Staffanstorp Sweden
83 G1 Staffelsee l. Germany
75 F2 Staffelstein Germany
106 D4 Staffora r. Italy
62 D2 Stafford England U.K.
146 E5 Stafford Virginia U.S.A.
62 D2 Staffordshire div. England U.K.
22 D2 Stagen Indonesia
108 A5 Stagno di Cabras l. Sardegna Italy
54 D3 Staicele Latvia
81 F3 Stainach Austria
65 G3 Staindrop England U.K.
63 F3 Staines England U.K.
81 G4 Stainz Austria
111 F6 Staiti Italy
79 M2 Stakčín Slovakia
66 D5 Stake, Hill of h. Scotland U.K.
51 F5 Stakhanov Ukraine
62 D4 Stalbridge England U.K.
82 C2 Stalden Switzerland
63 H2 Stalham England U.K.
58 B1 Stalheim Norway
Stalingrad see Volgograd
136 E3 Stalin, Mt mt. B.C. Canada
59 G2 Stallarholmen Sweden
59 F2 Ställdalen Sweden
77 L5 Stalowa Wola Poland
112 F2 Stâlpu Romania
108 A3 Sta-Maria-Siché Corse France
147 G4 Stamford Connecticut U.S.A.
63 F2 Stamford England U.K.
147 F3 Stamford New York U.S.A.
15 E4 Stamford Queensland Australia
65 H4 Stamford Bridge England U.K.
65 G2 Stamfordham England U.K.
75 G4 Stammham Germany
Stampalia i. see Astypalaia
128 B3 Stampriet Namibia
80 B3 Stams Austria
56 D1 Stamsund Norway
150 E3 Stanberry Missouri U.S.A.
131 G3 Standerton South Africa
65 F4 Standish England U.K.
149 F4 Standish Michigan U.S.A.
144 C4 Stanford Kentucky U.S.A.
130 B7 Stanford South Africa
59 H3 Stånga Sweden
59 F3 Stångån r. Sweden
109 H4 St'Angelo a Fasanella Italy
109 H4 St'Angelo dei Lombardi Italy
131 H4 Stanger South Africa
65 F3 Stanhope England U.K.
158 C1 Staniard Ck The Bahamas
112 G1 Stănileşti Romania
77 L4 Stanin Poland
112 B2 Stanišić Yugoslavia
53 E3 Stanislav Ukraine
77 K3 Stanisławów Poland
112 D3 Stanke Dimitrov Bulgaria
78 C2 Staňkov Czech Rep.
65 G3 Stanley England U.K.
152 D2 Stanley Idaho U.S.A.
150 C1 Stanley N. Dakota U.S.A.
147 K1 Stanley New Brunswick Canada
65 E1 Stanley Scotland U.K.
13 F5 Stanley Tasmania Australia
148 B3 Stanley Wisconsin U.S.A.
171 E7 Stanley Falkland Is.
27 Stanley Hong Kong
13 E5 Stanley, Mt h. Tasmania Australia
126 A4 Stanley, Mt mt. Uganda/Zaire
38 B4 Stanley Reservoir resr India
65 G2 Stannington England U.K.
114 C4 Stanos Greece
45 R3 Stanovaya Rus. Fed.
47 H1 Stanovka Rus. Fed.
52 D3 Stanovoye Rus. Fed.
45 N4 Stanovoye Nagor'ye mts Rus. Fed.
45 O4 Stanovoy Khrebet mountain range Rus. Fed.
52 C3 Stanovoy Kolodez' Rus. Fed.
83 D2 Stans Switzerland
16 E4 Stansmore Ra. h. Western Australia Australia
63 G3 Stansted airport England U.K.
63 G3 Stansted Mountfitchet England U.K.
15 G6 Stanthorpe Queensland Australia
63 G2 Stanton England U.K.
146 B6 Stanton Kentucky U.S.A.
148 E4 Stanton Michigan U.S.A.
52 D3 Stantsiya Babarykino Rus. Fed.
80 B3 Stanzach Austria
68 E2 Staphorst Netherlands
63 G3 Staplehurst England U.K.
150 C3 Stapleton Nebraska U.S.A.
77 J4 Stąporków Poland
178 Stappen c. Bjørnøya Arctic Ocean
52 B3 Star' Rus. Fed.
53 D1 Stara Basan' Ukraine
77 J4 Stara Błotnica Poland
77 K4 Starachowice Poland
75 K3 Stará Huť Czech Rep.
78 E1 Stara Kamienica Poland
76 G2 Stara Kiszewa Poland
77 L3 Stara Kornica Poland
76 E2 Stara Łubianka Poland
79 K2 Stará L'ubovňa Slovakia
79 J6 Stara Moravica Yugoslavia
107 J4 Stara Novalja Croatia
112 C2 Stara Pazova Yugoslavia
112 D3 Stara Planina mountain range Bulgaria/Yugoslavia
81 H5 Stara Plošćica Croatia
76 C3 Stara Rudnica Poland
77 L6 Stara Sil' Ukraine
52 B3 Stara Synyava Ukraine
53 B2 Stara Ushytsya Ukraine
114 C1 Staravina Macedonia
53 A1 Stara Vyzhivka Ukraine
51 H1 Staraya Rudka Rus. Fed.
50 D3 Staraya Russa Rus. Fed.
47 J2 Staraya Tumba Rus. Fed.
52 E1 Staraya Vichuga Rus. Fed.
112 E3 Stara Zagora Bulgaria
95 J3 Stara Zagora Bulgaria
5 M5 Starbuck Island i. Kiribati
53 G3 Starchenkove Ukraine
112 F2 Starchiojd Romania
62 C4 Starcross England U.K.
76 C2 Stare Czarnowo Poland
76 D2 Stare Dąbrowa Poland
77 L2 Stare Dolistowo Poland
77 L2 Stare Juchy Poland
76 G3 Stare Miasto Poland
53 E3 Stare, Ozero l. Ukraine
77 N6 Stare Selo Ukraine
76 E4 Stare Strącze Poland
76 D2 Stargard Szczeciński Szczecin Poland
77 N4 Stari Koshary Ukraine
52 B1 Staritsa Rus. Fed.
145 D6 Starke Florida U.S.A.
9 Star Keys is Chatham Is New Zealand
151 F5 Starkville Mississippi U.S.A.
75 G5 Starnberg Germany
75 G5 Starnberger See l. Germany
47 K2 Staroaleyskoye Rus. Fed.
51 F5 Starobil's'k Ukraine
54 E5 Starobyn Belarus
52 A3 Starodub Rus. Fed.
73 L2 Starogard Poland
76 G2 Starogard Gdański Poland
53 B2 Starokostyantyniv Ukraine
53 C3 Starokozache Ukraine
52 D2 Staroletovo Rus. Fed.
51 F6 Starominskaya Rus. Fed.
53 G3 Staromlynivka Ukraine
112 F3 Staro Oryakhovo Bulgaria
53 G1 Starooskol'skoye Vdkhr. resr Rus. Fed.
112 F3 Staro Selo Bulgaria
52 E3 Staroseslavino Rus. Fed.
76 C4 Starosiedle Poland
46 E2 Starosubkhangulovo Rus. Fed.
53 F2 Starovirivka Ukraine
77 H4 Starowa Gora Poland
52 H2 Staroye Drozhzhanoye Rus. Fed.
52 A2 Staroye Istomino Rus. Fed.
52 G2 Staroye Shaygovo Rus. Fed.
52 G2 Staroye-Sindrovo Rus. Fed.
52 G3 Staroye Slavkino Rus. Fed.
52 E3 Staroyur'yevo Rus. Fed.
77 H3 Staroźeby Poland
52 D2 Starozhilovo Rus. Fed.
109 H4 St'Arsenio Italy
62 C4 Start Bay b. England U.K.
62 C4 Start Point pt England U.K.
77 M4 Stary Brus Poland
77 H2 Stary Dzierzgoń Poland
76 D4 Stary Kisielin Poland
77 H3 Stary Kobrzyniec Poland
77 K3 Stary Lubotyń Poland
77 K4 Stary Mirów Poland
75 J3 Starý Plzenec Czech Rep.
79 K2 Starý Smokovec Slovakia
77 K3 Stary Szelków Poland
53 G1 Starytsya Ukraine
54 F5 Staryya Darohi Belarus
31 E2 Staryy Chindant Rus. Fed.
52 H3 Staryy Chirchim Rus. Fed.
52 H2 Staryye Aybesi Rus. Fed.
53 G3 Staryy Krym Ukraine
31 F1 Staryy Olov Rus. Fed.
53 G1 Staryy Oskol Rus. Fed.
53 B2 Staryy Ostropil' Ukraine
77 L6 Staryy Sambir Ukraine
73 G4 Staßfurt Germany
77 K5 Staszów Poland
146 E4 State College Pennsylvania U.S.A.
145 D5 Statesboro Georgia U.S.A.
145 D5 Statesville N. Carolina U.S.A.
58 C2 Stathelle Norway
119 F3 Station No. 6 Sudan
81 G2 Statzendorf Austria
73 J4 Stauchitz Germany
74 D2 Staufenberg Germany
74 C5 Staufen im Breisgau Germany
80 B2 Staufersberg h. Germany
146 D5 Staunton Virginia U.S.A.
83 F2 Stausee Gepatsch l. Austria
80 D3 Stausee Mooserboden l. Austria
58 A2 Stavanger Norway
63 E1 Staveley England U.K.
69 D4 Stavelot Belgium
112 E3 Stavertsi Bulgaria
53 D3 Stavkove Ukraine
77 N4 Stavky Ukraine
55 C4 Stavns Fjord b. Denmark
68 D2 Stavoren Netherlands
55 C4 Stavreshoved headland Denmark
115 E5 Stavronisi i. Greece
51 G6 Stavropol' Rus. Fed.
51 G6 Stavropol' div. Rus. Fed.
51 G6 Stavropol'skaya Vovyshennost' reg. Rus. Fed.
114 E2 Stavros Greece
114 F1 Stavroupoli Greece
59 H2 Stavsnäs Sweden
53 D2 Stavyshche Ukraine
15 E4 Stawell r. Queensland Australia
13 E4 Stawell Victoria Australia
77 J2 Stawiguda Poland
77 L2 Stawiski Poland
76 G4 Stawiszyn Poland
52 B3 Stayki Rus. Fed.
131 G4 Steadville South Africa
154 C2 Steamboat Nevada U.S.A.
152 F3 Steamboat Springs Colorado U.S.A.
114 B1 Steblevë Albania
53 D2 Stebliv Ukraine
77 M6 Stebnyk Ukraine
111 F4 Steccato Italy
75 K3 Štěchovice Czech Rep.
83 D1 Steckborn Switzerland
68 E1 Stedum Netherlands
80 B3 Steeg Austria
130 E3 Steekdorings South Africa
140 B2 Steel r. Ontario Canada
179 B2 Steele I. i. Antarctica
131 G2 Steelpoort r. South Africa
131 H2 Steelpoort South Africa
11 Steel's Pt pt Norfolk I. Pacific Ocean
146 E4 Steelton Pennsylvania U.S.A.
68 C3 Steenbergen Netherlands
131 H2 Steenkampsberg mts South Africa
136 F3 Steen River Alberta Canada
152 C3 Steens Mt. mt. Oregon U.S.A.
135 N2 Steenstrup Gletscher gl. Greenland
86 B2 Steenvoorde France
68 E2 Steenwijk Netherlands
62 C3 Steep Holm i. England U.K.
65 G4 Steeton England U.K.
81 H5 Štefanje Croatia
179 D4 Stefansson Bay b. Antarctica
134 H2 Stefansson I. i. N.W.T. Canada
53 C3 Ştefan Vodă Moldova
82 C2 Steffisburg Switzerland
52 D3 Stegalovka Rus. Fed.
55 E4 Stege Bugt b. Denmark
81 H3 Stegersbach Austria
68 E2 Steggerda Netherlands
79 M5 Stei Romania
81 G3 Steiermark div. Austria
74 F3 Steigerwald forest Germany
131 G1 Steilloopbrug South Africa
131 G1 Steilwater South Africa
73 G3 Stein Germany
69 D4 Stein Netherlands
82 C1 Stein Switzerland
83 D1 Steina r. Germany
75 G2 Steinach Germany
80 C3 Steinach am Brenner Austria
81 G2 Steinakirchen am Forst Austria
83 D1 Stein am Rhein Switzerland
74 E2 Steinau an der Straße Germany
137 K5 Steinbach Manitoba Canada
87 H2 Steinbach Germany
81 E3 Steinbach am Attersee Austria
75 G2 Steinbach am Wald Germany
81 F4 Steindorf am Ossiacher See Austria
74 C5 Steinen Germany
80 D3 Steinernes Meer mts Austria
80 E4 Steinfeld Austria
87 H3 Steinfeld Germany
72 D3 Steinfeld (Oldenburg) Germany
69 D5 Steinfort Luxembourg
72 C3 Steinfurt Germany
75 F5 Steingaden Germany
73 H1 Steinhagen Mecklenburg-Vorpommern Germany
72 D3 Steinhagen Nordrhein-Westfalen Germany
128 B3 Steinhausen Namibia
72 E4 Steinheim Germany
80 D2 Steinhöring Germany
72 E3 Steinhuder Meer l. Germany
56 C2 Steinkjer Norway
87 H2 Steinkopf h. Germany
130 A4 Steinkopf South Africa
155 H5 Steins New Mexico U.S.A.
56 C2 Steinsdalen Norway
73 K3 Steinsdorf Germany
58 A1 Steinsland Norway
130 D5 Stekaar South Africa
69 C3 Stekene Belgium
52 F2 Steksovo Rus. Fed.
130 E3 Stella South Africa
127 5 Stella Matutina Réunion Indian Ocean
72 F2 Stelle Germany
130 B6 Stellenbosch South Africa
68 C3 Stellendam Netherlands
108 B2 Stello, Monte mt. Corse France
106 E2 Stelvio, Parco Nazionale dello nat. park Italy
106 E2 Stelvio, Passo dello pass Italy
59 G3 Stenåsa Sweden
76 F3 Stęnava r. Poland
87 E3 Stenay France
55 A3 Stenbjerg Denmark
59 G3 Stenbo Sweden
73 G3 Stendal Germany
54 C3 Stende Latvia
55 A4 Stenderup Denmark
59 G2 Stenhamra Sweden
12 D3 Stenhouse Bay S. Australia Australia
27 Stenhouse, Mt h. Hong Kong
66 E4 Stenhousemuir Scotland U.K.
107 E2 Stenico Italy
114 E4 Steni Dirfios Greece
55 D4 Stenlille Denmark
55 E4 Stenløse Denmark
66 E2 Stenness, Loch of l. Scotland U.K.
115 D5 Steno Greece
115 E7 Steno Antikythiro chan. Greece
115 D6 Steno Elafonisou chan. Greece
115 B4 Steno Ithakis chan. Greece
115 F5 Steno Kafireos chan. Greece
113 F6 Steno Karpathou chan. Greece
113 F7 Steno Kasou chan. Greece
115 F5 Steno Keas chan. Greece
115 F6 Steno Kimolou-Sifnou chan. Greece
115 F5 Steno Kythnou chan. Greece
115 E5 Steno Petasi chan. Greece
115 F6 Steno Polyiagou-Folegandrou chan. Greece
115 F5 Steno Serifou chan. Greece
115 F5 Steno Sifnou chan. Greece
59 F4 Stenshuvuds Nationalpark Sweden
55 E5 Stensved Denmark
58 D2 Stenungsund Sweden
77 N5 Stenyatyn Ukraine
77 N5 Stenzharychi Ukraine
53 B1 Stepan' Ukraine
Stepanakert see Xankändi
114 C1 Stepanci Macedonia
53 B1 Stepanivka Khmel'nyts'ka Oblast' Ukraine
53 F1 Stepanivka Sums'ka Oblast' Ukraine
53 F3 Stepanivka Persha Ukraine
52 E1 Stepantsevo Rus. Fed.
73 G2 Stepenitz r. Germany
80 D2 Stephansposching Germany
137 K5 Stephen Minnesota U.S.A.
8 D4 Stephens, Cape c. New Zealand
8 D4 Stephens I. i. New Zealand
148 D3 Stephenson Michigan U.S.A.
136 C3 Stephens Passage chan. Alaska U.S.A.
139 J4 Stephenville Newfoundland Canada
151 D5 Stephenville Texas U.S.A.
52 A3 Stepne Ukraine
76 C2 Stepnica Poland
47 H2 Stepnogorsk Kazakhstan
53 F3 Stepnohirs'k Ukraine
51 H5 Stepnoye Rus. Fed.
112 C2 Stepojevac Yugoslavia
47 G4 Step' Shaidara plain Kazakhstan
7 13 Steps Pt pt American Samoa Pacific Ocean
52 B1 Stepurino Rus. Fed.
77 L3 Sterdyń Osada Poland
114 D4 Sterea Ellas div. Greece
131 G2 Sterk r. South Africa
131 G4 Sterkfontein Dam dam South Africa
131 G2 Sterkrivierdam dam South Africa
131 F5 Sterkspruit South Africa
131 F5 Sterkstroom South Africa
131 G2 Sterkwater South Africa
77 K1 Sterławki-Wielkie Poland
152 G3 Sterling Colorado U.S.A.
148 C5 Sterling Illinois U.S.A.
150 C2 Sterling N. Dakota U.S.A.
155 G2 Sterling Utah U.S.A.
130 C5 Sterling South Africa
151 C6 Sterling City Texas U.S.A.
149 F4 Sterling Hgts Michigan U.S.A.
46 E2 Sterlitamak Rus. Fed.
73 G2 Sternberg Germany
78 G2 Šternberk Czech Rep.
115 F7 Sternes Greece
72 E1 Sterup Germany
76 E3 Stęszew Poland
78 D1 Štětí Czech Rep.
136 G4 Stettler Alberta Canada
148 D2 Steuben Michigan U.S.A.
146 C4 Steubenville Ohio U.S.A.
63 F3 Stevenage England U.K.
8 D4 Stevens, Mt mt. New Zealand
12 C1 Stevenson Cr. watercourse S. Australia Australia
137 K4 Stevenson L. l. Manitoba Canada
148 C3 Stevens Point Wisconsin U.S.A.
64 D2 Stevenston Scotland U.K.
134 D3 Stevens Village Alaska U.S.A.
55 E4 Stevns Klint cliff Denmark
136 B2 Stewart r. Yukon Terr. Canada
136 D3 Stewart B.C. Canada
14 C1 Stewart, C. headland Northern Terr. Australia
136 B2 Stewart Crossing Yukon Terr. Canada
171 B7 Stewart, I. i. Chile
9 A7 Stewart Island i. New Zealand
135 K3 Stewart Lake l. N.W.T. Canada
66 D5 Stewarton Scotland U.K.
159 1 Stewart Town Jamaica
148 A4 Stewartville Minnesota U.S.A.
72 E3 Steyerberg Germany
131 F3 Steynrus South Africa
131 E5 Steynsburg South Africa
81 F3 Steyr r. Austria
81 F2 Steyr Austria
81 F3 Steyr-Land div. Austria
130 E6 Steytlerville South Africa
76 F1 Stężyca Poland
107 F5 Stia Italy
79 H3 Štiavnické Vrchy mts Slovakia
62 B4 Stibb Cross England U.K.
68 D1 Stiens Netherlands
109 J4 Stigliano Italy
136 C3 Stikine r. Canada/U.S.A.
136 C3 Stikine Ranges mountain range B.C. Canada
130 C7 Stilbaai South Africa
131 F3 Stilfontein South Africa
65 G3 Stillington England U.K.
64 B4 Stillorgan Rep. of Ireland
148 A3 Stillwater Minnesota U.S.A.
154 C2 Stillwater Nevada U.S.A.
151 D4 Stillwater Oklahoma U.S.A.
153 C4 Stillwater Ra. mountain range Nevada U.S.A.
111 F4 Stilo Italy
111 F4 Stilo, Punta pt Italy
63 F2 Stilton England U.K.
112 C3 Štimlje Macedonia
108 A4 Stintino Sardegna Italy
112 D4 Štip Macedonia
87 F3 Stiring-Wendel France
66 D4 Stirling div. Scotland U.K.
12 D3 Stirling S. Australia Australia
66 E4 Stirling Scotland U.K.
154 B2 Stirling City California U.S.A.
14 B3 Stirling Cr. r. Northern Terr. Australia
17 B6 Stirling, Mt h. Western Australia Australia
17 B7 Stirling Ra. mountain range Western Australia Australia
17 B7 Stirling Range Nat. Park nat. park Western Australia Australia
106 D4 Stirone r. Italy
56 C3 Stjørdalshalsen Norway
66 D4 Stob Choire Claurigh mt. Scotland U.K.
78 C1 Stochov Czech Rep.
75 G2 Stockach Germany
59 E4 Stockamöllan Sweden
73 F2 Stockelsdorf Germany
81 H2 Stockerau Austria
75 G2 Stockheim Germany
59 G2 Stockholm div. Sweden
147 J1 Stockholm Maine U.S.A.
59 H2 Stockholm Sweden
82 C2 Stockhorn mt. Switzerland
13 F3 Stockinbingal New South Wales Australia
131 F1 Stockport South Africa
65 F4 Stockport England U.K.
65 F3 Stocks Res. resr England U.K.
74 D3 Stockstadt am Rhein Germany
63 G3 Stocks, The England U.K.
154 B3 Stockton California U.S.A.
150 D4 Stockton Kansas U.S.A.
155 F1 Stockton Utah U.S.A.
148 B2 Stockton I. i. Wisconsin U.S.A.
151 E4 Stockton L. l. Missouri U.S.A.
65 G3 Stockton-on-Tees England U.K.
147 J2 Stockton Springs Maine U.S.A.
77 K4 Stoczek Łukowski Poland
78 C2 Stod Czech Rep.
57 E3 Stöde Sweden
25 C4 Stœng Sângke r. Cambodia
25 D4 Stœng Sên r. Cambodia
25 D4 Stœng Trêng Cambodia
66 C2 Stoer, Point of pt Scotland U.K.
131 G2 Stoffberg South Africa
114 B1 Stogovo Planina mountain range Macedonia
55 B3 Stoholm Denmark
62 D1 Stoke-on-Trent England U.K.
62 C4 Stoke St Mary England U.K.
62 D2 Stokesay England U.K.
65 G3 Stokesley England U.K.
9 E4 Stokes, Mt mt. New Zealand
13 E5 Stokes Pt pt Tasmania Australia
14 B2 Stokes Ra. h. Northern Terr. Australia
53 A1 Stokhid r. Ukraine
56 L7 Stokkseyri Iceland
56 D2 Stokkvågen Norway
56 D1 Stokmarknes Norway
81 E4 Stol mt. Slovenia
104 F4 Stolac Bos.-Herz.
73 F4 Stolberg Germany
74 B2 Stolberg (Rheinland) Germany
76 F2 Stołczno Poland
79 K3 Stolica mt. Slovakia
53 B1 Stolin Belarus
75 H2 Stollberg Germany
76 G2 Stolno Poland
128 3 Stoltenhoff I. i. Tristan da Cunha Atlantic Ocean
68 C3 Stolwijk Netherlands
72 E3 Stolzenau Germany
114 D3 Stomio Greece
62 D2 Stone England U.K.
62 D3 Stone England U.K.
141 G3 Stonecliffe Ontario Canada
147 F5 Stone Harbor New Jersey U.S.A.
66 F4 Stonehaven Scotland U.K.
15 E5 Stonehenge Queensland Australia
64 E2 Stonehouse Scotland U.K.
136 E3 Stone Mountain Prov. Park res. B.C. Canada
155 H3 Stoner Colorado U.S.A.
147 F4 Stone Ridge New York U.S.A.
128 2 Stone Top B. b. St Helena Atlantic Ocean
137 K4 Stonewall Manitoba Canada
146 C5 Stonewall Jackson Lake l. W. Virginia U.S.A.
140 D5 Stoney Point Ontario Canada
60 K1 Stongfjorden Norway
147 J2 Stonington Maine U.S.A.
154 A2 Stonyford California U.S.A.
159 1 Stony Hill Jamaica
128 3 Stonyhill Pt pt Tristan da Cunha Atlantic Ocean
147 E3 Stony Pt pt New York U.S.A.
137 H3 Stony Rapids Saskatchewan Canada
77 J5 Stopnica Poland
55 B5 Stör r. Germany
55 A3 Stora r. Denmark
59 F2 Stora Åby Sweden
59 G2 Stora Ålö i. Sweden
59 G3 Stora Alvaret i. Sweden
59 G3 Stora Askö i. Sweden
59 E3 Stora Färgen l. Sweden
59 E2 Stora Gla l. Sweden
55 E2 Stora Horredssjön l. Sweden
56 E2 Stora Inlevatten l. Sweden
59 G3 Stora Karlsö i. Sweden
58 D2 Stora Le l. Sweden
59 H2 Stora Nassa skärgård is Sweden
56 E2 Stora Sjöfallets National Park nat. park Sweden
56 E2 Storavan l. Sweden
58 A2 Stord i. Norway
55 C4 Store Bælt chan. Denmark
58 A1 Storebø Norway
55 E5 Store Damme Denmark
58 B1 Store Grananutane mt. Norway
58 B1 Store Grånosi mt. Norway
55 E4 Store Heddinge Denmark
58 C1 Store Jukleeggi mt. Norway
59 E3 Store Moss Nationalpark nat. park Sweden
56 C3 Støren Norway
58 B2 Store Nup mt. Norway
58 B1 Store Shrekken mt. Norway
58 A1 Store Sotra i. Norway
58 B2 Store Urevatnet l. Norway
58 A1 Storfjellet mt. Norway
56 G1 Storfjordbotn Norway
178 3 Storfjorden inlet Svalbard Arctic Ocean
58 C1 Storfjorden l. Norway
57 F2 Storfors Sweden
56 D2 Storforshei Norway
81 E5 Štorje Slovenia
56 D2 Storjord Norway
59 G1 Storjungfrun i. Sweden
59 E1 Stor Kallberget h. Sweden
58 B2 Storkarshei h. Norway
73 J3 Storkow Germany
13 F5 Storm Bay b. Tasmania Australia
131 F5 Stormberg mt. South Africa
131 F5 Stormberg mt. South Africa
131 F5 Stormberg r. South Africa
131 F5 Stormberg South Africa
150 E3 Storm Lake Iowa U.S.A.
130 D6 Stormsrivier South Africa
141 K4 Stornoway Québec Canada
66 B2 Stornoway Scotland U.K.
107 E3 Storo Italy
50 K2 Storozhevsk Rus. Fed.
53 A2 Storozhynets' Ukraine
63 F4 Storrington England U.K.
147 G4 Storrs Connecticut U.S.A.
66 B3 Storr, The h. Scotland U.K.
56 E2 Storseleby Sweden
58 D1 Storsjøen l. Norway
59 G1 Storsjön l. Sweden
56 D3 Storsjön l. Sweden
58 B1 Storskavlen mt. Norway
57 C3 Storskrymten mt. Norway
56 F1 Storslett Norway
55 D5 Storstrøm div. Denmark
55 D5 Storstrømmen chan. Denmark
63 G3 Stort r. England U.K.
68 D1 Stortemelk chan. Netherlands
56 E2 Storuman l. Sweden
56 E2 Storuman Sweden
59 G1 Storvik Sweden
55 C2 Storvorde Denmark
59 G2 Storvreta Sweden
63 F2 Stotfold England U.K.
75 F5 Stötten am Auerberg Germany
55 B4 Stouby Denmark
148 C4 Stoughton Wisconsin U.S.A.
69 D4 Stoumont Belgium
63 H3 Stour r. England U.K.
63 G3 Stour r. England U.K.
63 E2 Stour r. England U.K.
62 D2 Stourbridge England U.K.
62 D2 Stourport-on-Severn England U.K.
138 B3 Stout L. l. Ontario Canada
55 B3 Støvring Denmark
66 F5 Stow Scotland U.K.
54 E5 Stowbtsy Belarus
147 F4 Stowe Pennsylvania U.S.A.
63 G2 Stowmarket England U.K.
63 E3 Stow-on-the-Wold England U.K.
77 N5 Stoyaniv Ukraine
107 G3 Stra Italy
73 H4 Straach Germany
131 F2 Straatsdrif South Africa
67 D2 Strabane Northern Ireland U.K.
64 C1 Strachur Scotland U.K.
77 N1 Stračiūnai Lithuania
76 E2 Strączno Poland
67 D3 Stradbally Rep. of Ireland
63 H2 Stradbroke England U.K.
106 D3 Stradella Italy
63 G2 Stradishall England U.K.
64 A4 Stradone Rep. of Ireland
63 G2 Stradsett England U.K.
72 B4 Straelen Germany
13 F5 Strahan Tasmania Australia
155 G3 Straight Cliffs cliff Utah U.S.A.
69 D5 Straimont Belgium
108 A3 Strait of Bonifacio str. France/Italy
63 H4 Strait of Dover str. France/U.K.
136 E5 Strait of Georgia chan. B.C. Canada
111 H2 Strait of Otranto str. Mediterranean Sea
158 B2 Straits of Florida str. The Bahamas/U.S.A.
78 C2 Strakonice Czech Rep.
112 F3 Straldzha Bulgaria
81 G3 Stralleqq Austria
73 J1 Stralsund Germany
82 C3 Strambino Italy
69 D3 Stramproy Netherlands
130 B7 Strand South Africa
56 B3 Stranda Norway
58 B1 Strandavatnet l. Norway
145 E7 Strangers Cay i. The Bahamas
67 F2 Strangford Northern Ireland U.K.
67 F2 Strangford Lough inlet Rep. of Ireland
59 G2 Strängnäs Sweden
14 C2 Strangways r. Northern Terr. Australia
64 B2 Stranocum Northern Ireland U.K.
67 D2 Stranorlar Rep. of Ireland
66 C6 Stranraer Scotland U.K.
110 B5 Strasatti Sicilia Italy
87 G4 Strasbourg Bas-Rhin France
87 G4 Strasbourg-Entzheim airport France
146 D5 Strasburg Virginia U.S.A.
73 J2 Strasburg Germany
112 G1 Străşeni div. Moldova
53 C3 Străşeni Moldova
81 F4 Straßburg Austria
69 E5 Strassen Luxembourg
81 G3 Straßengel Austria
81 H2 Strasshof an der Norbahn Austria
80 E3 Straßwalchen Austria
140 E5 Stratford Ontario Canada
151 C4 Stratford Texas U.S.A.
13 F4 Stratford Victoria Australia
148 B3 Stratford Wisconsin U.S.A.
8 E3 Stratford New Zealand
63 E2 Stratford-upon-Avon England U.K.
12 D3 Strathalbyn S. Australia Australia
66 D5 Strathaven Scotland U.K.
66 D4 Strathblane Scotland U.K.
66 F3 Strathbogie reg. Scotland U.K.
66 D3 Strathcarron v. Scotland U.K.
136 D5 Strathcona Prov. Park nat. park B.C. Canada
66 D3 Strathconon v. Scotland U.K.
66 D3 Strath Dearn v. Scotland U.K.
65 E1 Strath Earn v. Scotland U.K.
66 D2 Strath Fleet v. Scotland U.K.
66 D3 Strathglass v. Scotland U.K.
66 E2 Strath Halladale v. Scotland U.K.
66 D2 Strathmore r. Scotland U.K.
136 G4 Strathmore Alberta Canada
66 D2 Strathnaver v. Scotland U.K.
136 E4 Strathnaver B.C. Canada
66 E2 Strath of Kildonan v. Scotland U.K.
140 E5 Strathroy Ontario Canada
66 E3 Strathspey v. Scotland U.K.
65 E1 Strath Tay v. Scotland U.K.
66 E2 Strathy Scotland U.K.
66 D2 Strathy Point pt Scotland U.K.
66 D4 Strathyre Scotland U.K.
114 E2 Stratoni Greece
114 E2 Stratoniki Greece
114 C4 Stratos Greece
62 B4 Stratton England U.K.
147 H2 Stratton Maine U.S.A.
63 E3 Stratton St Margaret England U.K.
75 H4 Straubing Germany
56 L6 Straumnes pt Iceland
73 K4 Straupitz Germany
73 J3 Strausberg Germany
73 F4 Straußfurt Germany
114 B2 Stravaj Albania
148 B4 Strawberry Point Iowa U.S.A.
155 G1 Strawberry Reservoir resr Utah U.S.A.
112 E3 Strazhitsa Bulgaria
81 F1 Stráž nad Nežárkou Czech Rep.
75 J3 Strážov Czech Rep.
79 L3 Strážske Slovakia
12 C3 Streaky Bay b. S. Australia Australia
12 C3 Streaky Bay S. Australia Australia

155 F2 Swasey Peak summit Utah U.S.A.
140 E2 Swastika Ontario Canada
36 C2 Swat r. Pakistan
36 C2 Swat Kohistan reg. Pakistan
64 B3 Swatragh Northern Ireland U.K.
63 E4 Sway England U.K.
117 H8 Swaziland country Africa
128 □1 S. W. Bay b. Ascension Atlantic Ocean
48 G2 Sweden country Europe
152 B2 Sweet Home Oregon U.S.A.
152 E3 Sweetwater r. Wyoming U.S.A.
145 C5 Sweetwater Tennessee U.S.A.
151 C5 Sweetwater Texas U.S.A.
130 C7 Swellendam South Africa
14 D3 S. Wellesley Is is Queensland Australia
15 G3 S. West I. i. Coral Sea Islands Terr. Pacific Ocean
77 J2 Świątki Poland
76 G1 Świbno Poland
76 E5 Świdnica Wałbrzych Poland
76 D4 Świdnica Poland
77 L4 Świdnik Poland
76 D2 Świdwin Poland
76 E5 Świebodzice Poland
76 D3 Świebodzin Poland
76 G2 Świecie Poland
76 E4 Święciechowa Poland
76 G2 Świekatowo Poland
76 D5 Świeradów-Zdrój Poland
77 J3 Świercze Poland
76 D4 Świerzawa Poland
77 M4 Świerże Poland
76 E1 Świerzenko Poland
76 C2 Świerzno Poland
77 L1 Świętajno Suwałki Poland
77 K2 Świętajno Poland
77 K5 Świetokrzyski Park Narodowy nat. park Poland
147 H2 Swift r. Maine U.S.A.
137 H4 Swift Current Saskatchewan Canada
137 H5 Swiftcurrent Cr. r. Saskatchewan Canada
68 D2 Swifterbant Netherlands
136 C2 Swift River Yukon Terr. Canada
67 D1 Swilly, Lough inlet Rep. of Ireland
63 E3 Swindon England U.K.
63 F2 Swineshead England U.K.
67 C3 Swinford Rep. of Ireland
76 C2 Świnoujście Szczecin Poland
66 F5 Swinton Scotland U.K.
83 F2 Swiss National Park nat. park Switzerland
48 F4 Switzerland country Europe
73 K2 Swobnica Poland
67 C3 Swords Rep. of Ireland
15 E4 Swords Ra. h. Queensland Australia
77 N3 Syalyets Belarus
77 N3 Syalyets Vodaskhovishcha resr Belarus
50 D2 Syamozero, Oz. l. Rus. Fed.
50 G2 Syamzha Rus. Fed.
54 F4 Syanno Belarus
77 N2 Syarednenemanskaya Nizina plain Belarus/Lithuania
50 E2 Syas'troy Rus. Fed.
67 A4 Sybil Point pt Rep. of Ireland
148 C5 Sycamore Illinois U.S.A.
76 E1 Sycewice Poland
52 B2 Sychevka Rus. Fed.
52 C2 Sychevo Rus. Fed.
76 F4 Syców Poland
13 G3 Sydney New South Wales Australia
139 H4 Sydney Nova Scotia Canada
11 □1 Sydney B. b. Norfolk I. Pacific Ocean
138 B3 Sydney L. l. Ontario Canada
139 H4 Sydney Mines Nova Scotia Canada
51 F5 Syeverodonets'k Ukraine
72 D3 Syke Germany
115 D6 Sykea Greece
114 E3 Syki Greece
50 J2 Syktyvkar Rus. Fed.
145 C5 Sylacauga Alabama U.S.A.
56 D3 Sylarna mt. Norway/Sweden
37 G4 Sylhet Bangladesh
72 D1 Sylt i. Germany
145 D5 Sylvania Georgia U.S.A.
146 B4 Sylvania Ohio U.S.A.
136 G4 Sylvan Lake Alberta Canada
145 D6 Sylvester Georgia U.S.A.
14 C3 Sylvester, L. salt flat Northern Terr. Australia
136 E3 Sylvia, Mt mt. B.C. Canada
115 □ Symi i. Greece
115 □ Symi Greece
156 E3 Symon Mexico
58 C2 Syndle I. Norway
53 F2 Synel'nykove Ukraine
58 C1 Synhovd mt. Norway
58 C1 Synnfjell mt. Norway
62 B2 Synod Inn Wales U.K.
52 E2 Syntul Rus. Fed.
53 D2 Synyukha r. Ukraine
179 D4 Syowa Japan Base Antarctica
147 E3 Syracuse airport New York U.S.A.
150 C4 Syracuse Kansas U.S.A.
147 E3 Syracuse New York U.S.A.
Syracuse see Siracusa
47 G4 Syrdar'ya r. Kazakhstan
47 G4 Syrdar'ya Uzbekistan
18 E6 Syria country Asia
24 B3 Syriam Myanmar
Syrian Desert desert see Bādiyat ash Shām
113 F6 Syrna i. Greece
115 F5 Syros i. Greece
59 G3 Syrsan I. Sweden
52 D3 Syrskiy Rus. Fed.
57 G3 Sysmä Finland
50 J2 Sysola r. Rus. Fed.
52 E3 Sysoy Rus. Fed.
63 E2 Syston England U.K.
53 C2 Sytkivtsi Ukraine
50 J3 Syumsi Rus. Fed.
46 D1 Syun r. Rus. Fed.
53 F3 Syvas'ke Ukraine
114 B3 Syvota Greece
55 C2 Syvsten Denmark
50 J4 Syzran' Rus. Fed.
79 J5 Szabadszállás Hungary
79 M3 Szabolcsbáka Hungary
79 M3 Szabolcs-Szatmár-Bereg div. Hungary
71 J3 Szadek Poland
79 H5 Szakály Hungary
79 H6 Szalánta Hungary
79 F2 Szamocin Poland
79 M3 Szamos r. Hungary
79 M3 Szamosköz reg. Hungary
76 E3 Szamotuły Poland
78 G4 Szany Hungary
79 K5 Szarvas Hungary
76 D3 Szczaniec Poland
77 J6 Szczawnica Poland
77 L5 Szczebrzeszyn Poland
76 D2 Szczecin div. Poland
76 C2 Szczecin Szczecin Poland
76 E2 Szczecinek Poland
76 G2 Szczecińskie reg. Poland
77 H5 Szczekociny Poland
77 H4 Szczerców Poland
77 K4 Szczucin Poland
77 L2 Szczuczyn Poland
77 J1 Szczurkowo Poland
77 H3 Szczutowo Poland
79 J2 Szczyrk Poland
77 J2 Szczytno Poland
Szechwan div. see Sichuan
79 J3 Szécsény Hungary
79 H5 Szederkény Hungary
79 K5 Szeged Hungary
79 L4 Szeghalom Hungary
79 H4 Székesfehérvár Hungary
79 K5 Székkutas Hungary
79 H5 Szekszárd Hungary
76 G1 Szemud Poland
79 K3 Szendrő Hungary
79 J4 Szentendre Hungary
79 K5 Szentes Hungary
78 F5 Szentgotthárd Hungary
79 G5 Szentlászló Hungary
79 J4 Szentmártonkáta Hungary
81 H3 Szentpéterfa Hungary
78 F5 Szepetnek Hungary
77 L3 Szepietowo Poland
79 L3 Szerencs Hungary
77 K3 Szestno Poland
77 L1 Szeszka Góra h. Poland
79 H4 Szigetcsép Hungary
79 G5 Szigetvár Hungary
79 L3 Szikszó Hungary
78 G4 Szil Hungary
76 F4 Szkaradowo Poland
76 D5 Szklarska Poręba Poland
76 E4 Szlichtyngowa Poland
79 H4 Szob Hungary
79 K4 Szolnok Hungary
78 F4 Szombathely Hungary
79 H4 Szomód Hungary
76 D4 Szprotawa Poland
77 J5 Szreniawa r. Poland
76 D5 Szrenica mt. Czech Rep.
77 J2 Szreńsk Poland
77 M2 Sztabin Poland
77 H2 Sztum Poland
77 H1 Sztutowo Poland
76 F2 Szubin Poland
77 M2 Szudziałowo Poland
77 J4 Szydłowiec Poland
76 E2 Szydłowo Poland
77 K2 Szymonka Poland
76 G4 Szynkielów Poland
77 M1 Szypliszki Poland

T

122 C5 Taabo, Lac de l. Côte d'Ivoire
126 D3 Taagga Duudka reg. Somalia
43 C3 Taalabaya Lebanon
23 B3 Taal, L. l. Philippines
7 □11 Taapuma French Polynesia Pacific Ocean
79 H5 Tab Hungary
23 B3 Tabaco Philippines
119 H2 Tābah Saudi Arabia
22 D1 Tabang Indonesia
131 G5 Tabankulu South Africa
42 D3 Ţabaqah Syria
159 □3 Tabaquite Trinidad and Tobago
98 E3 Tábara Spain
6 □1 Tabar Is is P.N.G.
105 B7 Tabarka Tunisia
39 E2 Ţabas Iran
39 D2 Ţabas Iran
54 D2 Tabasalu Estonia
157 G5 Tabasco div. Mexico
39 D3 Tabāsin Iran
139 J3 Tabatière Québec Canada
168 D4 Tabatinga Brazil
162 D4 Tabatinga Colombia
23 B2 Tabayoo, Mt mt. Philippines
120 D3 Tabelbala Algeria
137 G5 Taber Alberta Canada
59 F3 Taberg Sweden
101 H3 Tabernas Spain
125 B5 Tabi Angola
124 E3 Tabili Zaire
4 J5 Tabiteuea i. Kiribati
54 E2 Tabivere Estonia
23 B3 Tablas i. Philippines
172 B1 Tablas, C. c. Chile
101 G5 Tablas de Daimiel, Parque Nacional de las nat. park Spain
23 B3 Tablas Strait chan. Philippines
8 F3 Table Cape c. New Zealand
127 □5 Table, Pointe de la pt Réunion Indian Ocean
151 E4 Table Rock Res. resr Missouri U.S.A.
15 F3 Tabletop, Mt h. Queensland Australia
123 E5 Tabligbo Togo
101 F2 Tablillas r. Spain
101 E4 Tablon, Sierra del mountain range Spain
98 C2 Taboada Spain
165 E3 Taboco r. Brazil
24 B1 Tabong Myanmar
78 D2 Tábor Czech Rep.
127 B6 Tabora div. Tanzania
127 B6 Tabora Tanzania
47 G4 Taboshar Tajikistan
173 H1 Tabossi Argentina
122 C6 Tabou Côte d'Ivoire
123 E3 Tabrichat well Mali
42 F2 Tabrīz Iran
98 B4 Tábua Portugal
98 C3 Tabuaço Portugal
5 M4 Tabuaeran i. Kiribati
102 B3 Tabuenca Spain
119 G2 Tabūk Saudi Arabia
13 H2 Tabulam New South Wales Australia
47 J2 Tabuny Rus. Fed.
6 □2 Tabwémasana mt. Vanuatu
59 H2 Täby Sweden
163 G3 Tacalé Brazil
157 E5 Tacámbaro Mexico
158 C5 Tacarcuna, Co mt. Panama
47 K3 Tacheng China
75 H4 Tacherting Germany
118 A2 Tachiumet well Libya
78 B2 Tachov Czech Rep.
22 E3 Tacipi Indonesia
23 C4 Tacloban Philippines
164 B3 Tacna Peru
152 B2 Tacoma Washington U.S.A.
164 C3 Tacopaya Bolivia
170 D2 Taco Pozo Argentina
164 C3 Tacora, Vol. volcano Chile
173 K2 Tacuarembó div. Uruguay
173 K1 Tacuarembó r. Uruguay
173 K1 Tacuarembó Uruguay
173 L2 Tacuarí r. Uruguay
156 C2 Tacupeto Mexico
168 A5 Tacuru Brazil
76 F4 Taczanów drugi Poland
29 G5 Tadami-gawa r. Japan
65 G4 Tadcaster England U.K.
Tademaït Plateau plat. see Plateau du Tademaït
6 □2 Tadine New Caledonia Pacific Ocean
121 E3 Tadjmout Algeria
126 D2 Tadjoura Djibouti
126 D2 Tadjoura, Golfe de b. Djibouti
121 E2 Tadjrouna Algeria
63 E3 Tadley England U.K.
42 D3 Tadmur Syria
137 K3 Tadoule Lake l. Manitoba Canada
139 G4 Tadoussac Québec Canada
54 C2 Taebla Estonia
31 H5 Taech'ŏn South Korea
31 H5 Taedong man b. North Korea
31 J6 Taegu South Korea
31 H6 Taehŭksan Do i. South Korea
31 H5 Taejŏn South Korea
31 J5 T'aepaek South Korea
62 B3 Taf r. Wales U.K.
5 K6 Tafahi i. Tonga
102 B2 Tafalla Spain
130 C6 Tafelberg mt. South Africa
82 C2 Tafers Switzerland
62 C3 Taffs Well Wales U.K.
39 C3 Tafīhān Iran
42 C4 Tafila Jordan
170 C2 Tafi Viejo Argentina
120 C3 Tafraoute Morocco
39 B2 Tafresh Iran
154 C4 Taft California U.S.A.
39 E3 Taftān, Kūh-e mt. Iran
25 A6 Tafwap Andaman and Nicobar Is India
7 □12 Taga Western Samoa
119 F4 Tagab Sudan
29 H4 Tagajō Japan
51 F6 Taganrog Rus. Fed.
51 F6 Taganrogskiy Zaliv b. Rus. Fed./Ukraine
120 B5 Tagant div. Mauritania
24 B2 Tagaung Myanmar
28 C7 Tagawa Japan
50 H4 Tagay Rus. Fed.
23 B3 Tagaytay City Philippines
123 F3 Tagaza well Niger
23 B4 Tagbilaran Philippines
58 A1 Tagelt h. Norway
123 F3 Taggart Tegguet well Niger
106 B5 Taggia Italy
121 D2 Taghit Algeria
122 D2 Taghmanant well Mali
67 E4 Taghmon Rep. of Ireland
136 C2 Tagish Yukon Terr. Canada
109 F2 Tagliacozzo Italy
107 G2 Tagliamento r. Italy
107 G3 Taglio di Po Italy
86 D3 Tagnon France
23 C4 Tagoloan r. Philippines
23 B4 Tagolo Point pt Philippines
103 E5 Tagomago i. Spain
168 D1 Taguatinga Distrito Federal Brazil
166 C3 Taguatinga Tocantins Brazil
123 F3 Taguedoufat well Niger
6 □1 Tagula I. i. P.N.G.
23 C5 Tagum Philippines
Tagus r. Spain see Tajo
Tagus r. Portugal see Tejo
7 □10 Tahaa i. French Polynesia Pacific Ocean
136 F4 Tahaetkun Mt. mt. B.C. Canada
101 H3 Tahal Spain
121 E4 Tahalra reg. Algeria
7 □10 Tahanéa i. French Polynesia Pacific Ocean
25 C6 Tahan, Gunung mt. Malaysia
29 F6 Tahara Japan
Tahat mt. see Tahat, Mt
121 F4 Tahat, Mt mt. Algeria
31 H1 Tahe China
8 D1 Taheke New Zealand
30 A3 Tahilt Mongolia
7 □11 Tahiti i. French Polynesia Pacific Ocean
39 E3 Tahlab r. Iran/Pakistan
151 E5 Tahlequah Oklahoma U.S.A.
154 B2 Tahoe City California U.S.A.
154 B2 Tahoe, Lake l. California/Nevada U.S.A.
134 H3 Tahoe Lake l. N.W.T. Canada
151 C5 Tahoka Texas U.S.A.
123 F3 Tahoua div. Niger
123 F4 Tahoua Niger
39 D3 Tahrūd r. Iran
119 F2 Tahta Egypt
136 D4 Tahtsa Pk summit B.C. Canada
164 C2 Tahuamanu r. Bolivia
23 C6 Tahuna Indonesia
122 C5 Taï Côte d'Ivoire
37 G4 Taiabpur India
27 □ Tai a Chau i. Hong Kong
31 F5 Tai'an China
32 D1 Taibai Shan mt. China
Taibei see T'ai-pei
101 H2 Taibilla r. Spain
101 H2 Taibilla, Sierra de mountain range Spain
80 D4 Taibòn Agordino Italy
31 E4 Taibus Qi China
33 H3 T'ai-chung Taiwan
9 C6 Taieri r. New Zealand
30 E5 Taigu China
30 E5 Taihang Shan mountain range China
8 E3 Taihape New Zealand
33 F1 Taihe China
33 F3 Taihe China
29 □2 Taiho Japan
33 H2 Tai Hu l. China
33 G2 Taihu China
29 E7 Taiji Japan
32 E3 Taijiang China
33 F1 Taikang China
24 A3 Taikkyi Myanmar
31 G3 Tailai China
27 □ Tai Lam Chung Res. resr Hong Kong
12 D3 Tailem Bend S. Australia Australia
91 D3 Taillefer mt. France
27 □ Tai Long Bay b. Hong Kong
33 H3 T'ai-lu-ko Taiwan
39 E2 Taimani reg. Afghanistan
27 □ Tai Mo Shan h. Hong Kong
66 D3 Tain Scotland U.K.
Tainan see T'ai-nan
33 H4 T'ai-nan Taiwan
33 H4 Tainan Taiwan
33 G3 Taining China
91 C3 Tain-l'Hermitage France
27 □ Tai O Hong Kong
83 G2 Taio Italy
169 G1 Taiobeiras Brazil
22 E2 Taipa Indonesia
54 E1 Taipalsaari Finland
122 C5 Taï, Parc National de nat. park Côte d'Ivoire
33 H3 T'ai-pei Taiwan
33 E4 Taiping China
32 D2 Taiping China
25 C6 Taiping Malaysia
30 B5 Taipingbao China
31 G3 Taipingchuan China
33 G3 Taiping Ling mt. China
27 □ Tai Po Hong Kong
37 H4 Taipudia India
29 □2 Taira Japan
28 H3 Tairadate-kaikyō chan. Japan
28 G2 Taisei Japan
28 J2 Taisetsu-zan mountain range Japan
28 J2 Taisetsu-zan National Park nat. park Japan
28 D6 Taisha Japan
33 F4 Taishan China
33 E5 Taishan China
33 G3 Taishun China
120 B3 Taïssa, Jbel mt. Morocco
86 D3 Taissy France
9 D5 Taitanu New Zealand
171 B6 Taitao, Península de pen. Chile
171 A6 Taitao, Pta pt Chile
33 H4 T'ai-tung Taiwan
56 H2 Taivalkoski Finland
56 G1 Taivaskero h. Finland
54 B1 Taivassalo Finland
19 O7 Taiwan country Asia
Taiwan Haixia str. see Taiwan Strait
33 H4 Taiwan Shan mountain range Taiwan
33 G3 Taiwan Strait str. China/Taiwan
33 H1 Tai Xian China
33 H1 Taixing China
33 G3 Taiyuan China
30 E5 Taiyue Shan mountain range China
Taizhong see T'ai-chung
33 G1 Taizhou China
33 H2 Taizhou Wan b. China
126 D2 Ta'izz Yemen
36 B4 Tajal Pakistan
118 B3 Tajarḥī Libya
22 A2 Tajem, G. h. Indonesia
18 H6 Tajikistan country Asia
29 G5 Tajima Japan
29 F6 Tajimi Japan
156 B2 Tajito Mexico
100 D1 Tajo r. Spain
99 H4 Tajuña r. Spain
24 B3 Tak Thailand
39 A1 Takāb Iran
126 D4 Takabba Kenya
22 E3 Taka'Bonerate, Kep. atolls Indonesia
29 H5 Takahagi Japan
28 D6 Takahashi Japan
28 D6 Takahashi-gawa r. Japan
8 D4 Takaka New Zealand
36 D5 Takal India
127 C6 Takaloi well Tanzania
127 □2 Takamaka Seychelles
28 E6 Takamatsu Japan
29 H3 Takanosu Japan
29 F5 Takaoka Japan
8 F4 Takapau New Zealand
7 □10 Takapoto i. French Polynesia Pacific Ocean
8 E2 Takapuna New Zealand
7 □10 Takaroa i. French Polynesia Pacific Ocean
28 E6 Takasago Japan
29 G5 Takasaki Japan
28 B7 Taka-shima i. Japan
128 C3 Takatokwane Botswana
29 E6 Takatsuki Japan
28 D7 Takatsuki-yama mt. Japan
24 B2 Ta-Kaw Myanmar
29 F5 Takayama Japan
25 C6 Tak Bai Thailand
29 F6 Takefu Japan
28 D6 Takehara Japan
28 C7 Takeo Japan
59 F2 Tåkern l. Sweden
39 B1 Takestān Iran
28 C7 Taketa Japan
25 D5 Takêv Cambodia
42 F4 Takhādīd well Iraq
46 E4 Takhiatash Uzbekistan
25 D5 Ta Khmau Cambodia
46 F5 Takhta-Bazar Turkmenistan
47 G2 Takhtabrod Kazakhstan
46 F4 Takhtakupyr Uzbekistan
39 F3 Takhta Pul Post Afghanistan
36 B3 Takht-i-Sulaiman mt. Pakistan
137 G1 Takijuq Lake l. N.W.T. Canada
28 H2 Takikawa Japan
28 J1 Takinoue Japan
22 C2 Takisung Indonesia
9 A6 Takitimu Mts mts New Zealand
136 D3 Takla Lake l. B.C. Canada
136 D3 Takla Landing B.C. Canada
Takla Makan desert see Taklimakan Shamo
47 K5 Taklimakan Shamo desert China
122 D6 Takoradi Ghana
37 H3 Takpa Shiri mt. China
79 L3 Takta r. Hungary
136 C3 Taku r. B.C. Canada
28 C7 Taku Japan
123 F5 Takum Nigeria
7 □10 Takumé i. French Polynesia Pacific Ocean
36 C2 Tal Pakistan
43 A4 Tala Egypt
173 K3 Tala Uruguay
172 C1 Talacasto Argentina
50 D4 Talachyn Belarus
36 C2 Talagang Pakistan
36 B4 T Alahyar Pakistan
38 B4 Talaimannar Sri Lanka
92 A3 Talais France
38 A1 Talaja India
31 G2 Talakan Rus. Fed.
31 K2 Talakan Rus. Fed.
53 E1 Talalayivka Ukraine
108 D2 Talamone Italy
31 J2 Talandzha Rus. Fed.
22 A2 Talangbatu Indonesia
22 A2 Talangbetutu Indonesia
172 F1 Tala Norte Argentina
37 H4 Talap India
162 A4 Talara Peru
39 E4 Talar-i-Band mountain range Pakistan
101 E1 Talarrubias Spain
47 H4 Talas div. Kyrgyzstan
47 H4 Talas r. Kazakhstan
47 H4 Talas Kyrgyzstan
47 H4 Talas Ala-Too mountain range Kyrgyzstan
6 □1 Talasea P.N.G.
52 A2 Talashkino Rus. Fed.
Talas Range mountain range see Talas Ala-Too
43 B4 Talata Egypt
43 D2 Ţal 'at Mūsá mt. Lebanon
100 D1 Talaván Spain
99 F5 Talavera de la Reina Spain
100 D2 Talavera la Real Spain
14 E3 Talawanta Queensland Australia
24 B1 Talawgyi Myanmar
45 R3 Talaya Rus. Fed.
23 C5 Talayan Philippines
98 E5 Talayuela Spain
103 B5 Talayuelas Spain
36 D4 Talbehat India
135 L2 Talbot Inlet b. N.W.T. Canada
13 G3 Talbragar r. New South Wales Australia
172 B3 Talca Chile
172 D6 Talcahuala Argentina
172 A4 Talcahuano Chile
172 B2 Talca, Punta pt Chile
37 F5 Talcher India
52 C1 Taldom Rus. Fed.
47 J3 Taldykorgan div. Kazakhstan
47 J4 Taldykorgan Kazakhstan
47 H5 Taldyk P. Kyrgyzstan
47 G3 Taldysayskiy Kazakhstan
Taldysu see Taldy-Suu
47 J4 Taldy-Suu Kyrgyzstan
39 B2 Taleh Zang Iran
6 □5 Taleki Tonga i. Tonga
6 □5 Taleki Vavu'u i. Tonga
88 D3 Talensac France
103 C5 Tales Spain
39 B1 Tālesh Iran
47 J4 Talgar Kazakhstan
62 C3 Talgarth Wales U.K.
98 B4 Talhadas Portugal
21 H7 Taliabu i. Indonesia
91 E4 Taliard France
23 C4 Talibon Philippines
38 B2 Talikota India
47 G5 Talimardzhan Uzbekistan
38 A3 Taliparamba India
126 B3 Tali Post Sudan
23 B4 Talisay Philippines
22 D1 Talisayan Indonesia
23 C4 Talisayan Philippines
42 G2 Talış Dağları mts Azerbaijan/Iran
172 E2 Talita Argentina
50 H3 Talitsa Rus. Fed.
52 D3 Talitsa Rus. Fed.
52 E3 Talitskiy Chamlyk Rus. Fed.
52 F1 Talitsy Rus. Fed.
22 D4 Taliwang Indonesia
43 A4 Talkha Egypt
107 F5 Talla Italy
145 C5 Talladega Alabama U.S.A.
42 E2 Tall 'Afar Iraq
145 C6 Tallahassee Florida U.S.A.
13 F4 Tallangatta Victoria Australia
145 C5 Tallassee Alabama U.S.A.
119 G4 Talla Talla Seghir I. i. Sudan
17 A6 Tallering Pk h. Western Australia Australia
42 E3 Tall Fadghāmī Syria
54 D2 Tallinn Estonia
42 D3 Tall Kalakh Syria
42 E2 Tall Kayf Iraq
90 E3 Talloires France
67 C4 Tallow Rep. of Ireland
151 F5 Tallulah Louisiana U.S.A.
42 E2 Tall 'Uwaynāt Iraq
112 E2 Tălmaciu Romania
90 D1 Talmay France
47 K2 Tal'menka Rus. Fed.
43 D3 Tal Misma h. Jordan
92 B3 Talmont France
92 A2 Talmont-St-Hilaire France
53 D2 Tal'ne Ukraine
36 C5 Talod India
126 B2 Talodi Sudan
23 □2 Talofofo Guam Pacific Ocean
24 B2 Ta-long Myanmar
139 G2 Talon, Lac l. Québec Canada
39 G1 Tāloqān Afghanistan
108 B4 Talora r. Sardegna Italy
36 C2 Tal or Shohi P. pass Pakistan
53 E2 Talova Balka Ukraine
46 D2 Talovaya Kazakhstan
51 G5 Talovaya Rus. Fed.
135 J3 Taloyoak N.W.T. Canada
30 A3 Talshand Mongolia
54 C3 Talsi Latvia
170 B2 Taltal Chile
137 G2 Taltson r. N.W.T. Canada
42 F3 Talvar r. Iran
107 F2 Talvera r. Italy
56 F1 Talvik Norway
15 G6 Talwood Queensland Australia
53 D2 Tal'yanky Ukraine
13 E3 Talyawalka r. New South Wales Australia
Talyshskiye Gory mts see Talış Dağları
50 K1 Talyy Rus. Fed.
148 A4 Tama Iowa U.S.A.
24 A2 Tamadaw Myanmar
52 F3 Tamala Rus. Fed.
162 C2 Tamalameque Colombia
122 D5 Tamale Ghana
22 C2 Tamalung Indonesia
98 D4 Tamames Spain
28 C7 Tamana Japan
173 H5 Tamanqueyú Argentina
118 B2 Tamanhint Libya
28 D6 Tamano Japan
121 F4 Tamanrasset Algeria
24 A1 Tamanthi Myanmar
162 C2 Tama, Parque Nacional el nat. park Venezuela
147 F4 Tamaqua Pennsylvania U.S.A.
62 B4 Tamar r. England U.K.
127 □4 Tamarin Mauritius
112 F1 Tămăşeni Romania
77 M4 Tamashowka Belarus
79 H5 Tamási Hungary
112 F1 Tamaşi Romania
157 F3 Tamaulipas div. Mexico
126 C3 Tama Wildlife Reserve res. Ethiopia
156 D3 Tamazula Mexico
157 F5 Tamazulápam Mexico
157 F4 Tamazunchale Mexico
127 C4 Tambach Kenya
75 F2 Tambach-Dietharz Germany
122 B4 Tambacounda Senegal
37 F4 Tamba Kosi r. Nepal
22 E3 Tambalongang i. Indonesia
22 B2 Tambangmunjul Indonesia
168 E4 Tambaú Brazil
123 E4 Tambawel Nigeria
22 A1 Tambelan Besar i. Indonesia
17 B7 Tambellup Western Australia Australia
172 C1 Tamberías Argentina
39 B3 Tambiān Iran
172 C2 Tambillo, Co mt. Argentina
23 A5 Tambisan Malaysia
13 F4 Tambo r. Victoria Australia
164 B3 Tambo r. Peru
15 F5 Tambo Queensland Australia
162 A4 Tambo Grande Peru
129 G2 Tambohorano Madagascar
22 D4 Tambora, G. volcano Indonesia
173 J1 Tambores Uruguay
166 D1 Tamboril Brazil
124 E2 Tambura Central African Rep.
52 E3 Tambov div. Rus. Fed.
52 E3 Tambov Rus. Fed.
31 J2 Tambovka Rus. Fed.
98 B2 Tambre r. Spain
22 D2 Tambulan Indonesia
124 E2 Tambura Sudan
22 D1 Tambu, Tk b. Indonesia
25 C6 Tambuyukon, G. mt. Malaysia
120 B5 Tâmchekket Mauritania
46 F4 Tamdybulak Uzbekistan
162 C2 Tame Colombia
98 C3 Tâmega r. Portugal
123 E3 Tamesna reg. Niger
157 F4 Tamiahua Mexico
157 F4 Tamiahua, L. de lag. Mexico
38 B4 Tamil Nadu div. India
22 C2 Taminglayang Indonesia
83 E2 Tamins Switzerland
30 B3 Tamirin Gol r. Mongolia
112 C2 Tamiš r. Yugoslavia
166 B3 Tamitatoala r. Brazil
50 F1 Tamitsa Rus. Fed.
43 A5 Tāmiya Egypt
25 D4 Tam Ky Vietnam
109 G3 Tammaro r. Italy
54 C1 Tammela Finland
59 G1 Tämnaren l. Sweden
98 C1 Tâmoga r. Spain
145 D7 Tampa Florida U.S.A.
145 D7 Tampa Bay b. Florida U.S.A.
22 A3 Tampang Indonesia
39 D4 Tamp-e Gīrān Iran
57 F3 Tampere Finland
157 F4 Tampico Mexico
25 □ Tampines Singapore
31 F3 Tamsagbulag Mongolia
30 B4 Tamsag Muchang China
54 E2 Tamsalu Estonia
162 C4 Tamshiyacu Peru
81 E3 Tamsweg div. Austria
81 E3 Tamsweg Austria
24 A1 Tamu Myanmar
157 F4 Tamuín Mexico
23 □2 Tamuning Guam Pacific Ocean
37 F4 Tamur r. Nepal
63 E2 Tamworth England U.K.
13 G2 Tamworth New South Wales Australia
127 C5 Tana r. Kenya
29 E7 Tanabe Japan
168 D4 Tanabi Brazil
56 H1 Tana bru Norway
132 D3 Tanacross Alaska U.S.A.
56 H1 Tanafjorden chan. Norway
111 E2 Tanagro r. Italy
126 C2 T'ana Hāyk' l. Ethiopia
22 D2 Tanahgrogot Indonesia
22 E3 Tanahjampea i. Indonesia
23 A6 Tanahmerah Indonesia
25 C6 Tanah Merah Malaysia
22 B3 Tanah, Tg pt Indonesia
22 D3 Tanakeke i. Indonesia
36 E3 Tanakpur India
22 D2 Tanambung Indonesia
15 B3 Tanami Northern Terr. Australia
14 B3 Tanami Desert desert Northern Terr. Australia
25 D5 Tân An Vietnam
134 C3 Tanana Alaska U.S.A.
91 C4 Tanargue, le mt. France
106 C4 Tanaro r. Italy
62 C2 Tanat r. Wales U.K.
23 C4 Tanauan Philippines
6 □8 Tanavuso Pt pt Fiji
15 E5 Tanbar Queensland Australia
29 □2 Tancha Japan
33 G1 Tancheng China
31 J4 Tanch'ŏn North Korea
122 D5 Tanda Côte d'Ivoire
37 E4 Tanda India
59 E1 Tandådalen Sweden
23 C4 Tandag Philippines
112 F2 Țăndărei Romania
125 C7 Tandaué Angola
23 A5 Tandek Malaysia
80 C2 Tandern Germany
36 D2 Tandi India
173 H4 Tandil Argentina
173 H4 Tandil, Sa del h. Argentina
124 C2 Tandjilé div. Chad
36 B4 Tando Adam Pakistan
36 B4 Tando Muhammmad Khan Pakistan
13 E3 Tandou L. l. New South Wales Australia
59 E1 Tandövarn h. Sweden
67 E2 Tandragee Northern Ireland U.K.
38 B2 Tandur India
8 F3 Taneatua New Zealand
29 H3 Taneichi Japan
121 F3 Tan Emellel Algeria
24 B3 Tanen Taunggyi mountain range Thailand
77 L5 Tanew r. Poland
146 E5 Taneytown Maryland U.S.A.
121 D4 Tanezrouft reg. Algeria
121 E4 Tanezrouft Tan-Ahenet reg. Algeria
64 A4 Tang Rep. of Ireland
127 C6 Tanga div. Tanzania
118 C4 Tanga well Chad
30 D2 Tanga Rus. Fed.
127 C6 Tanga Tanzania
8 E2 Tangaehe New Zealand
37 G4 Tangail Bangladesh
129 H3 Tangainony Madagascar
6 □1 Tanga Is is P.N.G.
38 C5 Tangalla Sri Lanka
127 A5 Tanganyika, Lake l. Africa
39 C1 Tangar Iran
124 C2 Tangaray Chad
38 B4 Tangasseri India
32 C3 Tangdan China
Tangdan see Dongchuan
39 C1 Tangeli Iran
58 D1 Tangen Norway
179 D4 Tange Prom. headland Antarctica
120 C1 Tanger Morocco
22 A3 Tangerang Indonesia
73 G3 Tangerhütte Germany
73 G3 Tangermünde Germany
55 B3 Tange Sø l. Denmark
32 C1 Tanggor China
37 G2 Tanggula Shan mountain range China
37 G2 Tanggula Shankou pass China
33 F1 Tanghe China
Tangier see Tanger
147 E6 Tangier I. i. Virginia U.S.A.
22 A3 Tangkittebak, G. mt. Indonesia
37 G4 Tangla India
25 □ Tanglin Singapore
32 A2 Tangmai China
29 E6 Tango Japan
37 F3 Tangra Yumco salt lake China
31 F5 Tangshan China
23 B4 Tangub Philippines
123 E4 Tanguieta Benin
31 J2 Tangwanghe China
31 E5 Tang Xian China
33 F2 Tangxianzhen China
32 E2 Tangyan r. China
24 B2 Tang-yan Myanmar
33 F1 Tangyin China
31 J3 Tangyuan China
56 G2 Tanhua Finland
25 D5 Tani Cambodia
32 A2 Taniantaweng Shan mountain range China
90 E2 Taninges France
Tanintharyi see Tenasserim
23 B4 Tanjay Philippines
Tanjore see Thanjavur
22 C2 Tanjung Indonesia
22 A1 Tanjungbalai Indonesia
25 B7 Tanjungbalai Indonesia
22 A1 Tanjungbatu Indonesia
22 D1 Tanjungbuaya i. Indonesia
22 D2 Tanjunggaru Indonesia
22 A3 Tanjungkarang Telukbetung Indonesia
22 A2 Tanjungpandan Indonesia
22 A1 Tanjungpinang Indonesia
22 A2 Tanjungraja Indonesia
21 G6 Tanjungredeb Indonesia
22 B2 Tanjungsaleh i. Indonesia
22 B2 Tanjungsatai Indonesia
21 G6 Tanjungselor Indonesia
36 B2 Tank Pakistan
30 C2 Tankhoy Rus. Fed.
122 B4 Tankon mt. Guinea
36 D2 Tankse India
130 C6 Tankwa r. South Africa
130 B6 Tankwa-Karoo National Park nat. park South Africa
90 C1 Tanlay France
75 H4 Tann Germany
6 □2 Tanna i. Vanuatu
66 F4 Tannadice Scotland U.K.
57 D3 Tannäs Sweden
90 B1 Tannay Bourgogne France
86 D3 Tannay Champagne-Ardenne France
58 D1 Tannfjell h. Norway
80 B2 Tannhausen Germany
80 B3 Tannheim Austria
55 C2 Tannis Bugt b. Denmark
26 F1 Tannu Ola, Khrebet mountain range Rus. Fed.
122 D5 Tano r. Ghana
23 B4 Tañon Strait chan. Philippines

36 B4 Tanot India
123 F4 Tanout Niger
120 C2 Tanout-ou-Fillali Morocco
73 K2 Tanowo Poland
156 E3 Tanque Alvarez Mexico
37 E4 Tansen Nepal
33 H3 Tan-shui Taiwan
119 F1 Tanta Egypt
24 B3 Tantabin Myanmar
24 A2 Tantabin Myanmar
120 B3 Tan-Tan Morocco
157 F4 Tantoyuca Mexico
31 G3 Tantu China
38 C2 Tanuku India
58 D2 Tanumshede Sweden
75 L2 Tanvald Czech Rep.
117 H6 Tanzania country Africa
32 C1 Tao r. China
31 G3 Tao'an China
31 G3 Tao'er r. China
33 F2 Taojiang China
30 C5 Taole China
25 □ Tao Payoh Singapore
111 E5 Taormina *Sicilia* Italy
153 F4 Taos *New Mexico* U.S.A.
122 D2 Taoudenni Mali
120 D2 Taounate Morocco
123 D2 Taounnant well Mali
121 D2 Taourirt Morocco
120 D2 Taouz Morocco
33 G3 Taoxi China
33 E2 Taoyuan China
33 H3 T'ao-yuan Taiwan
Taoyuan *see* T'ao-yuan
54 D2 Tapa Estonia
23 B5 Tapaan Passage chan. Philippines
157 G6 Tapachula Mexico
165 E2 Tapaiuna r. Brazil
163 F4 Tapajós r. Brazil
173 G4 Tapalqué Argentina
163 F3 Tapanahoni r. Surinam
157 G5 Tapanatepec Mexico
162 D5 Tapauá r. Brazil
163 E5 Tapauá Brazil
9 D4 Tapawera New Zealand
167 B6 Tapera Brazil
167 B7 Tapes Brazil
122 C5 Tapeta Liberia
80 B2 Tapfheim Germany
36 C5 Tāpi r. India
98 D1 Tapia de Casariego Spain
23 B5 Tapiantana i. Philippines
165 E3 Tapia, Sa de h. Bolivia
22 B2 Tapinbini Indonesia
148 C2 Tapiola *Michigan* U.S.A.
169 E3 Tapira *Minas Gerais* Brazil
168 B5 Tapira *Paraná* Brazil
166 B3 Tapirapé r. Brazil
25 C6 Tapis mt. Malaysia
78 F4 Táplánszentkereszt Hungary
37 F4 Taplejung Nepal
27 □ Tap Mun Chau i. Hong Kong
78 G5 Tapolca Hungary
146 E6 Tappahannock *Virginia* U.S.A.
36 D3 Tappal India
22 D2 Tappalang Indonesia
146 C4 Tappan Lake l. *Ohio* U.S.A.
39 B2 Tappeh, Kūh-e h. Iran
28 H3 Tappi-zaki pt Japan
9 D4 Tapuaenuku mt. New Zealand
23 B5 Tapul Philippines
23 B5 Tapul Group is Philippines
163 D4 Tapurucuara Brazil
126 D2 Taqar mt. Yemen
167 B6 Taquarí r. Brazil
165 E3 Taquari r. Brazil
168 B2 Taquari Brazil
168 D4 Taquaritinga Brazil
168 D5 Taquarituba Brazil
168 B4 Taquaruçu r. Brazil
172 B4 Taquimilán Argentina
67 D4 Tar r. Rep. of Ireland
47 J1 Tara r. Rus. Fed.
112 B3 Tara r. Yugoslavia
15 G5 Tara *Queensland* Australia
123 G5 Taraba div. Nigeria
123 G5 Taraba r. Nigeria
164 D3 Tarabuco Bolivia
118 B1 Ţarābulus Libya
53 C3 Taraclia Moldova
162 D3 Taracua Brazil
8 F3 Taradale New Zealand
118 B2 Tarāghin Libya
36 B4 Tar Ahmad Rind Pakistan
36 E4 Tarahuwan India
37 G4 Tarai reg. India
23 A6 Tarakan i. Indonesia
23 A6 Tarakan Indonesia
39 F2 Tarakki reg. Afghanistan
28 L2 Taraku-shima i. Rus. Fed.
36 D5 Tarana India
36 C3 Tārānagar India
8 E3 Taranaki div. New Zealand
Taranaki, Mt volcano *see* Egmont, Mt
99 G4 Tarancón Spain
127 C5 Tarangire Nat. Park nat. park Tanzania
111 F2 Taranto div. *Puglia* Italy
111 G2 Taranto *Taranto* Italy
111 G2 Taranto, Golfo di g. Italy
164 C3 Tarapacá div. Chile
162 D4 Tarapacá Colombia
162 B5 Tarapoto Peru
90 C3 Tarare France
173 J3 Tarariras Uruguay
8 E4 Tararua Range mountain range New Zealand
91 C5 Tarascon France
93 D6 Tarascon-sur-Ariège France
112 F1 Tarashany Ukraine
53 D2 Tarashcha Ukraine
39 D2 Tarasht Iran
50 H1 Tarasovo Rus. Fed.
121 F3 Tarat Algeria
164 B3 Tarata Peru
162 C5 Tarauacá r. Brazil
164 B1 Tarauacá Brazil
7 □11 Taravao *French Polynesia* Pacific Ocean
108 A3 Taravo r. France
8 F3 Tarawera New Zealand
8 F3 Tarawera, L. l. New Zealand
8 F3 Tarawera, Mt mt. New Zealand
102 B3 Tarazona Spain
103 B5 Tarazona de la Mancha Spain
30 C2 Tarbagatay Rus. Fed.
47 K3 Tarbagatay, Khrebet mountain range Kazakhstan
66 E3 Tarbat Ness pt *Scotland* U.K.
103 C6 Tárbena Spain
66 B3 Tarbert *Scotland* U.K.
66 C5 Tarbert *Scotland* U.K.
66 C5 Tarbert *Scotland* U.K.
67 B4 Tarbert Rep. of Ireland
64 B2 Tarbert, Loch inlet *Scotland* U.K.
93 C5 Tarbes France
64 D2 Tarbolton *Scotland* U.K.
145 E5 Tarboro *N. Carolina* U.S.A.
107 H2 Tarcento Italy
12 C2 Tarcoola *S. Australia* Australia
13 F2 Tarcoon *New South Wales* Australia
77 J4 Tarczyn Poland
88 D3 Tard r. France
99 G2 Tardajos Spain
86 C3 Tardenois reg. France
92 E2 Tardes r. France
93 B5 Tardets-Sorholus France
102 C3 Tardienta Spain
92 C3 Tardoire r. France
13 H2 Taree *New South Wales* Australia
126 B2 Tareifing Sudan
123 E3 Tarenkat well Mali
82 B3 Tarentaise reg. France
45 L2 Tareya Rus. Fed.
43 A5 Tarfa, W. el watercourse Egypt
120 B3 Tarfaya Morocco
123 F3 Targa well Niger
31 H3 Targan China
152 E2 Targhee Pass pass *Idaho* U.S.A.
93 B4 Targon France
112 E2 Târgovişte Romania
112 F2 Târgu Bujor Romania
112 D2 Târgu Cărbuneşti Romania
112 F1 Târgu Frumos Romania
112 D2 Târgu Jiu Romania
112 D1 Târgu Lăpuş Romania
112 E1 Târgu Mureş Romania
112 F1 Târgu-Neamt Romania
112 F1 Târgu Ocna Romania
112 E2 Târgu Secuiesc Romania
118 B1 Tarhūnah Libya
6 □1 Tari P.N.G.
30 D5 Tarian Gol China
39 C4 Tarif U.A.E.
100 E4 Tarifa Spain
100 E5 Tarifa o Marroqui, Pta de pt Spain
164 D4 Tarija div. Bolivia
164 D4 Tarija Bolivia
21 L7 Tariku r. Indonesia
47 K4 Tarim r. China
41 G6 Tarīm Yemen
Tarim Basin basin *see* Tarim Pendi
127 B5 Tarime Tanzania
47 K5 Tarim Pendi basin China
39 F2 Tarīn Kowt Afghanistan
47 K4 Tariskay Shan mt. China
131 E6 Tarka r. South Africa
131 F6 Tarkastad South Africa
123 F4 Tarka, Vallée de watercourse Niger
150 E3 Tarkio *Missouri* U.S.A.
44 J3 Tarko-Sale Rus. Fed.
122 D5 Tarkwa Ghana
23 B3 Tarlac Philippines
65 F4 Tarleton *England* U.K.
77 K4 Tarłów Poland
55 A4 Tarm Denmark
164 A2 Tarma Peru
72 E2 Tarmstedt Germany
93 E5 Tarn div. *Midi-Pyrénées* France
93 D4 Tarn r. France
79 K4 Tarna r. Hungary
56 D2 Tärnaby Sweden
39 F2 Tarnak r. Afghanistan
79 K3 Tarnalelesz Hungary
112 E1 Târnăveni Romania
77 L5 Tarnawa Duża Poland
93 D4 Tarn-et-Garonne div. France
77 K5 Tarnobrzeg div. Poland
77 K5 Tarnobrzeg Poland
77 L5 Tarnogród Poland
50 G2 Tarnogskiy Gorodok Rus. Fed.
93 A5 Tarnos France
77 M5 Tarnoszyn Poland
77 J5 Tarnów div. Poland
76 C3 Tarnów *Gorzów* Poland
77 J5 Tarnów *Tarnów* Poland
76 E2 Tarnówka Poland
76 G5 Tarnowskie Góry Poland
106 E4 Taro r. Italy
37 F3 Tarok Tso l. China
39 C3 Ţārom Iran
53 F2 Taroms'ke Ukraine
15 G5 Taroom *Queensland* Australia
98 C3 Tarouca Portugal
120 C2 Taroudannt Morocco
55 A4 Tarp Denmark
72 E1 Tarp Germany
77 M1 Tarprubežiai Lithuania
158 C1 Tarpum Bay The Bahamas
39 B2 Tarq Iran
108 D2 Tarquinia Italy
108 D2 Tarquinia Lido Italy
102 D3 Tarragona div. Spain
102 E3 Tarragona Spain
56 E2 Tårrajaur Sweden
9 B6 Tarras New Zealand
102 E3 Tàrrega Spain
80 B3 Tarrenz Austria
55 C2 Tårs *Nordjylland* Denmark
55 D5 Tårs *Storstrøm* Denmark
111 F3 Tarsia Italy
118 C3 Tarso Emissi mt. Chad
32 B1 Tarsumdo China
43 C1 Tarsus r. Turkey
42 C2 Tarsus Turkey
55 D5 Tårs Vig b. Denmark
170 D1 Tartagal *Salta* Argentina
170 E2 Tartagal *Santa Fé* Argentina
77 N5 Tartakiv Ukraine
42 F1 Tärtär r. Azerbaijan
107 F3 Tartaro r. Italy
47 J1 Tartas r. Rus. Fed.
93 B5 Tartas France
54 E2 Tartu Estonia
43 C2 Ţarţūs div. Syria
42 C3 Ţarţūs Syria
169 H3 Tarumirim Brazil
28 C8 Tarumizu Japan
51 H6 Tarumovka Rus. Fed.
24 B1 Tarung Hka r. Myanmar
52 C2 Tarusa r. Rus. Fed.
52 C2 Tarusa Rus. Fed.
53 C3 Tarutyne Ukraine
107 H2 Tarvisio Italy
111 □ Tarxien Malta
30 A2 Tarys-Arzhan Rus. Fed.
39 D3 Tarz Iran
43 A1 Taşağıl Turkey
59 E1 Tåsan r. Sweden
47 G4 Tasbuget Kazakhstan
141 F2 Taschereau *Québec* Canada
38 A2 Tasgaon India
52 E2 Tashchilovo Rus. Fed.
Tashi Chho *see* Thimphu
37 G4 Tashigang Bhutan
42 F1 Tashir Armenia
39 C3 Tashk Iran
47 G4 Tashkent Uzbekistan
46 F5 Tashkepri Turkmenistan
47 H4 Tash-Kömür Kyrgyzstan
46 D2 Tashla Rus. Fed.
140 B1 Tashota *Ontario* Canada
Tāshqurghān *see* Kholm
47 L2 Tashtagol Rus. Fed.
47 L2 Tashtyp Rus. Fed.
138 F2 Tasiat, Lac l. *Québec* Canada
135 P3 Tasiilaq Greenland
22 B3 Tasikmalaya Indonesia
43 C3 Tasīl Syria
55 C4 Tåsinge i. Denmark
139 G2 Tasiujaq *Québec* Canada
123 G4 Task well Niger
43 B1 Taşkent Turkey
123 G3 Tasker Niger
47 K3 Taskesken Kazakhstan
42 C1 Taşköprü Turkey
115 □ Taşlıca Turkey
42 E2 Taşlıçay Turkey
9 D4 Tasman div. New Zealand
175 P6 Tasman Basin sea feature Pacific Ocean
9 D4 Tasman Bay b. New Zealand
13 F5 Tasmania div. Australia
9 D4 Tasman Mountains mts New Zealand
175 O7 Tasman Plateau sea feature Pacific Ocean
11 L6 Tasman Sea sea Pacific Ocean
79 M4 Tăşnad Romania
42 D1 Taşova Turkey
154 B3 Tassajara Hot Springs *California* U.S.A.
123 F3 Tassara Niger
90 C1 Tasselot, Mont h. France
139 F2 Tassialujjuaq, Lac l. *Québec* Canada
121 F4 Tassili du Hoggar plat. Algeria
121 F3 Tassili n'Ajjer reg. Algeria
90 C3 Tassin-la-Demi-Lune France
55 E4 Tåstrup Denmark
47 G4 Tasty Kazakhstan
47 G2 Tasty-Taldy Kazakhstan
43 B1 Taşucu Turkey
42 F2 Tasūj Iran
45 N3 Tas-Yuryakh Rus. Fed.
79 H4 Tata Hungary
120 C3 Tata Morocco
7 □11 Tataa, Pte pt *French Polynesia* Pacific Ocean
21 H7 Tataba Indonesia
79 H4 Tatabánya Hungary
52 E3 Tatanovo Rus. Fed.
121 G2 Tataouine Tunisia
112 G2 Tatarbunary Ukraine
54 F5 Tatarka Belarus
47 J1 Tatarsk Rus. Fed.
27 Q1 Tatarskiy Proliv Rus. Fed.
52 H3 Tatarskiy Sayman Rus. Fed.
50 J4 Tatarstan div. Rus. Fed.
7 □11 Tatatua, Pte pt *French Polynesia* Pacific Ocean
30 C1 Tataurovo Rus. Fed.
42 F2 Tatavi r. Iran
15 F3 Tate r. *Queensland* Australia
29 F6 Tateishi-misaki pt Japan
29 F5 Tate-yama volcano Japan
29 G6 Tateyama Japan
136 F2 Tathlina Lake l. *N.W.T.* Canada
119 H4 Tathlīth Saudi Arabia
119 H3 Tathlīth, W. watercourse Saudi Arabia
120 B5 Tâtîlt well Mauritania
137 K2 Tatinnai Lake l. *N.W.T.* Canada
52 G4 Tatishchevo Rus. Fed.
24 B2 Tatkon Myanmar
152 A1 Tatla Lake *B.C.* Canada
136 D3 Tatlatui Prov. Park res. *B.C.* Canada
79 K2 Tatranský nat. park Slovakia
77 H6 Tatry mts Poland/Slovakia
77 H6 Tatrzański P. N. nat. park Poland
136 B3 Tatshenshini r. *B.C.* Canada
51 G5 Tatsinskiy Rus. Fed.
28 E6 Tatsuno Japan
36 A4 Tatta Pakistan
47 H4 Tatty Kazakhstan
168 E5 Tatuí Brazil
136 E4 Tatuk Mtn mt. *B.C.* Canada
153 G5 Tatum *New Mexico* U.S.A.
42 E2 Tatvan Turkey
7 □13 Tau i. *American Samoa* Pacific Ocean
6 □4 Tau i. Tonga
58 A2 Tau Norway
166 D2 Taua Brazil
163 E5 Tauariã Brazil
169 F5 Taubaté Brazil
74 E3 Tauber r. Germany
74 E3 Tauberbischofsheim Germany
73 H4 Taucha Germany
46 D4 Tauchik Kazakhstan
73 K4 Tauer Germany
7 □10 Tauére i. *French Polynesia* Pacific Ocean
75 G4 Taufkirchen *Bayern* Germany
80 D2 Taufkirchen *Bayern* Germany
75 H4 Taufkirchen (Vils) Germany
74 E2 Taufstein h. Germany
6 □3 Taula i. Tonga
88 B3 Taulé France
37 E4 Taulihawa Nepal
8 E3 Taumarunui New Zealand
130 E3 Taung South Africa
24 A2 Taungdwingyi Myanmar
24 B2 Taung-gyi Myanmar
24 B2 Taunglau Myanmar
24 B4 Taungnyo Range mountain range Myanmar
24 A2 Taungtha Myanmar
7 □11 Taunoa *French Polynesia* Pacific Ocean
24 A3 Taunqup Myanmar
36 B3 Taunsa Pakistan
62 C3 Taunton *England* U.K.
147 H4 Taunton *Massachusetts* U.S.A.
74 D2 Taunus h. Germany
9 □1 Taupeka Pt pt *Chatham Is* New Zealand
8 F3 Taupo New Zealand
8 E3 Taupo, Lake l. New Zealand
54 C4 Tauragė Lithuania
54 B4 Tauralaukis Lithuania
8 F2 Tauranga New Zealand
141 J3 Taureau, Réservoir resr *Québec* Canada
111 F4 Taurianova Italy
92 D3 Taurion r. France
111 H3 Taurisano Italy
Tauriuiná r. *see* Verde
8 D1 Tauroa Pt pt New Zealand
Taurus Mts mountain range *see* Toros Dağları
102 B3 Tauste Spain
7 □14 Tautama pt *Pitcairn I.* Pacific Ocean
88 D2 Taute r. France
7 □11 Tautira *French Polynesia* Pacific Ocean
6 □1 Tauu or Mortlock Is is P.N.G.
92 E3 Tauves France
Tauz *see* Tovuz
107 H2 Tavagnacco Italy
79 J5 Tavankut Yugoslavia
82 C1 Tavannes Switzerland
42 B2 Tavas Turkey
90 D1 Tavaux France
98 B4 Taveiro Portugal
91 C4 Tavel France
63 H2 Taverham *England* U.K.
111 F3 Taverna Italy
90 C1 Tavernay France
91 E5 Tavernes France
103 C5 Tavernes de la Valldigna Spain
86 B3 Taverny France
6 □6 Taveuni i. Fiji
115 D5 Tavgetos mountain range Greece
111 H3 Taviano Italy
108 B2 Tavignano r. *Corse* France
100 C3 Tavira Portugal
100 C3 Tavira, Ilha de i. Portugal
62 B4 Tavistock *England* U.K.
108 B4 Tavolara, Isola i. *Sardegna* Italy
98 C3 Távora r. Spain
25 B4 Tavoy Myanmar
Tavoy I. i. *see* Mali Kyun
25 B4 Tavoy Pt pt Myanmar
47 H2 Tavricheskoye Rus. Fed.
53 E3 Tavriys'k Ukraine
42 B2 Tavşanlı Turkey
6 □8 Tavua i. Fiji
6 □8 Tavua Fiji
107 G5 Tavullia Italy
62 B4 Tavy r. *England* U.K.
62 B3 Taw r. *England* U.K.
9 E4 Tawa New Zealand
149 F3 Tawas Bay b. *Michigan* U.S.A.
149 F3 Tawas City *Michigan* U.S.A.
23 A5 Tawau Malaysia
62 C3 Tawe r. *Wales* U.K.
69 E5 Tawern Germany
23 A5 Tawitawi i. Philippines
24 B1 Tawmaw Myanmar
33 H4 T'a-wu Taiwan
157 F5 Taxco Mexico
80 D3 Taxenbach Austria
47 J5 Taxkorgan China
66 E4 Tay r. *Scotland* U.K.
136 C2 Tay r. *Yukon Terr.* Canada
23 B3 Tayabas Bay b. Philippines
22 B1 Tayan Indonesia
56 J1 Taybola Rus. Fed.
126 D4 Tayeeglow Somalia
66 F4 Tay, Firth of est. *Scotland* U.K.
30 A3 Taygan Mongolia
66 C5 Tayinloan *Scotland* U.K.
53 D3 Tayirove Ukraine
17 C7 Tay, L. salt flat *Western Australia* Australia
66 D4 Tay, Loch l. *Scotland* U.K.
155 G4 Taylor *Arizona* U.S.A.
136 E3 Taylor *B.C.* Canada
149 F4 Taylor *Michigan* U.S.A.
148 B6 Taylor *Missouri* U.S.A.
150 D3 Taylor *Nebraska* U.S.A.
151 D6 Taylor *Texas* U.S.A.
9 C5 Taylor, Mt mt. New Zealand
147 E5 Taylors Island *Maryland* U.S.A.
144 B4 Taylorville *Illinois* U.S.A.
119 G2 Taymā' Saudi Arabia
45 L3 Taymura r. Rus. Fed.
45 M2 Taymyr, O. Mal. i. Rus. Fed.
45 M2 Taymyr, Ozero l. Rus. Fed.
25 D5 Tây Ninh Vietnam
66 C4 Taynuilt *Scotland* U.K.
66 F4 Tayport *Scotland* U.K.
23 B3 Taytay Philippines
23 A4 Taytay Philippines
23 A4 Taytay Bay b. Philippines
22 B3 Tayu Indonesia
31 H2 Tayuan China
64 C1 Tayvallich *Scotland* U.K.
39 E2 Tayyebād Iran
43 C5 Ţayyib al Ism Saudi Arabia
44 K3 Taz r. Rus. Fed.
120 D2 Taza Morocco
42 F3 Tāza Khurmātū Iraq
29 H4 Tazawa-ko l. Japan
24 A2 Taze Myanmar
42 F2 Tazeh Kand Azerbaijan
146 B6 Tazewell *Tennessee* U.S.A.
146 C6 Tazewell *Virginia* U.S.A.
137 H2 Tazin r. *N.W.T.* Canada
137 H3 Tazin Lake l. *Saskatchewan* Canada
118 D2 Tāzirbū Libya
118 D2 Tazirbu Water Wells' Field well Libya
112 F1 Tazlău Romania
44 J3 Tazovskaya G. chan. Rus. Fed.
121 F4 Tazrouk Algeria
51 H7 T'bilisi Georgia
51 G6 Tbilisskaya Rus. Fed.
124 B2 Tchabal Mbabo mt. Cameroon
123 E5 Tchamba Togo
123 E5 Tchaourou Benin
125 B4 Tchibanga Gabon
123 F3 Tchidoutene watercourse Niger
118 C4 Tchié well Chad
125 B6 Tchindjenje Angola
123 F3 Tchin-Tabaradene Niger
124 B2 Tcholliré Cameroon
76 G1 Tczew Poland
98 B2 Tea r. Spain
156 D4 Teacapán Mexico
17 C5 Teague, L. salt flat *Western Australia* Australia
7 □11 Teahupoo *French Polynesia* Pacific Ocean
9 A6 Te Anau New Zealand
9 A6 Te Anau, L. l. New Zealand
109 G3 Teano Italy
157 G5 Teapa Mexico
8 G2 Te Araroa New Zealand
8 E2 Te Aroha New Zealand
7 □11 Teavaro *French Polynesia* Pacific Ocean
8 E3 Te Awamutu New Zealand
101 F4 Teba Spain
22 B1 Tebas Indonesia
65 F3 Tebay *England* U.K.
22 B1 Tebedu Malaysia
51 G7 Teberda Rus. Fed.
137 K2 Tebesjuak Lake l. *N.W.T.* Canada
121 F1 Tébessa Algeria
165 E5 Tebicuary r. Paraguay
25 B7 Tebingtinggi Indonesia
105 B7 Tébourba Tunisia
121 F1 Téboursouk Tunisia
156 A1 Tecate Mexico
46 F1 Techa r. Rus. Fed.
122 D5 Techiman Ghana
112 G2 Techirghiol Romania
114 C3 Techniti Limni Arachthos resr Greece
114 C4 Techniti Limni Kastrakiou resr Greece
114 C4 Techniti Limni Kremaston resr Greece
115 D5 Techniti Limni Ladonos resr Greece
114 D4 Techniti Limni Mornos resr Greece
115 C5 Techniti Limni Pineiou resr Greece
114 C3 Techniti Limni Tavropou resr Greece
114 F1 Techniti Limni Thissavros resr Greece
171 B5 Tecka r. Argentina
171 B5 Tecka Argentina
72 C3 Tecklenburger Land reg. Germany
157 F4 Tecolutla Mexico
156 E5 Tecomán Mexico
154 D4 Tecopa *California* U.S.A.
156 D3 Tecoríchic Mexico
156 C2 Tecoripa Mexico
157 E5 Técpan Mexico
112 F2 Tecuci Romania
149 F5 Tecumseh *Michigan* U.S.A.
126 D4 Ted Somalia
118 C3 Tédogora watercourse Chad
39 E2 Tedzhen r. Iran/Turkmenistan
46 F5 Tedzhen Turkmenistan
39 E1 Tedzhenstroy Turkmenistan
155 H3 Teec Nos Pos *Arizona* U.S.A.
130 C6 Teekloof Pass pass South Africa
47 M2 Teeli Rus. Fed.
65 G3 Tees r. *England* U.K.
65 G3 Tees Bay b. *England* U.K.
65 F3 Teesdale reg. *England* U.K.
65 G3 Tees-side airport *England* U.K.
163 D4 Tefé r. Brazil
121 F4 Tefedest mts Algeria
163 E4 Tefé, Lago l. Brazil
115 G7 Tefeli Greece
42 B2 Tefenni Turkey
22 B3 Tegal Indonesia
73 J3 Tegel airport Germany
69 E3 Tegelen Netherlands
75 G5 Tegernsee Germany
109 H4 Teggiano Italy
62 C2 Tegid, Llyn l. *Wales* U.K.
123 F4 Tegina Nigeria
22 A3 Tegineneng Indonesia
106 E2 Teglio Italy
80 C4 Tegnàs r. Italy
6 □2 Tégua i. Vanuatu
156 J6 Tegucigalpa Honduras
123 F3 Teguidda-n-Tessoumt Niger
97 □ Teguise *Canary Is* Spain
154 C4 Tehachapi *California* U.S.A.
153 C5 Tehachapi Mts mountain range *California* U.S.A.
154 C4 Tehachapi Pass pass *California* U.S.A.
137 K2 Tehek Lake l. *N.W.T.* Canada
Teheran *see* Tehrān
122 D5 Téhini Côte d'Ivoire
39 B2 Tehrān div. Iran
39 B2 Tehrān Iran
Tehri *see* Tikamgarh
36 D3 Tehri India
157 F5 Tehuacán Mexico
157 G6 Tehuantepec, Golfo de g. Mexico
157 G5 Tehuantepec Ridge ocean feature Pacific Ocean
177 N5 Tehuantepec, Istmo de isth. Mexico
157 F5 Tehuitzingo Mexico
97 □ Teide, Pico del mt. *Canary Is* Spain
62 B2 Teifi r. *Wales* U.K.
62 C4 Teign r. *England* U.K.
62 C4 Teignmouth *England* U.K.
93 E5 Teillet France
29 □2 Teima Japan
75 H5 Teisendorf Germany
75 H3 Teisnach Germany
64 D1 Teith r. *Scotland* U.K.
112 D1 Teiuş Romania
166 E2 Teixeira Brazil
169 J2 Teixeira de Freitas Brazil
169 G4 Teixeiras Brazil
98 B1 Teixeiro Spain
98 C4 Teixoso Portugal
22 C4 Tejakula Indonesia
97 □ Tejeda *Canary Is* Spain
123 F4 Tejira well Niger
55 □2 Tejn Denmark
100 B1 Tejo r. Portugal
154 C4 Tejon Pass pass *California* U.S.A.
8 D1 Te Kao New Zealand
9 C6 Tekapo r. New Zealand
9 C5 Tekapo, L. l. New Zealand
37 F4 Tekari India
8 E2 Te Kauwhata New Zealand
157 H4 Tekax Mexico
46 F3 Tekeli Kazakhstan
47 J4 Tekeli Kazakhstan
47 H2 Teke, Oz. salt lake Kazakhstan
47 K4 Tekes r. China
126 C2 Tekezē Wenz r. Africa
36 E1 Tekiliktag mt. China
31 K2 Tekin Rus. Fed.
113 F4 Tekirdağ div. Turkey
42 A1 Tekirdağ Turkey
38 D2 Tekkali India
37 H5 Teknaf Bangladesh
148 E4 Tekonsha *Michigan* U.S.A.
8 D2 Te Kopuru New Zealand
8 E3 Te Kuiti New Zealand
37 E5 Tel r. India
156 J6 Tela Honduras
121 D2 Télagh Algeria
77 L3 Telaki Poland
123 E3 Télataï Mali
51 H7 T'elavi Georgia
43 C3 Tel Aviv Yafo Israel
78 E2 Telč Czech Rep.
157 H4 Telchac Puerto Mexico
52 C3 Tel'ch'ye Rus. Fed.
112 E1 Telciu Romania
124 D3 Tele r. Zaire
22 C2 Telegapulang Indonesia
52 G3 Telegino Rus. Fed.
136 C3 Telegraph Creek *B.C.* Canada
90 C1 Télégraphe, Le h. France
168 C6 Telêmaco Borba Brazil
58 C2 Telemark div. Norway
22 D1 Telen r. Indonesia
172 E4 Telén Argentina
53 C3 Teleneşti Moldova
112 E2 Teleorman r. Romania
121 F4 Telertheba, Djebel mt. Algeria
154 D3 Telescope Peak summit *California* U.S.A.
159 □8 Telescope Pt pt *Grenada* Caribbean
109 G3 Telese Italy
165 E1 Teles Pires r. Brazil
47 L2 Teletskoye, Ozero l. Rus. Fed.
62 D2 Telford *England* U.K.
80 C3 Telfs Austria
79 K3 Telgárt Slovakia
72 C4 Telgte Germany
156 J6 Telica Nicaragua
122 D2 Telîg well Mali
122 B4 Télimélé Guinea
118 E5 Teljo, Jebel mt. Sudan
42 E2 Tel Kotchek Syria
136 D4 Telkwa *B.C.* Canada
87 E3 Tellancourt France
110 D5 Tellaro r. *Sicilia* Italy
134 B3 Teller *Alaska* U.S.A.
42 E3 Tell es Suwar Syria
38 A4 Tellicherry India
69 D4 Tellin Belgium
72 E1 Tellingstedt Germany
53 D3 Tellodar Ukraine
46 E4 Tel'mansk Turkmenistan
30 A2 Telmen Nuur salt lake Mongolia
81 H1 Telnice Czech Rep.
25 □ Telok Blangah Singapore
157 F5 Teloloapán Mexico
171 C5 Telsen Argentina
54 C4 Telšiai Lithuania
108 B4 Telti *Sardegna* Italy
73 J3 Teltow Germany
23 A5 Telukan Labuk b. Malaysia
23 A5 Telukan Lahad Datu b. Malaysia
25 C6 Teluk Anson Malaysia
23 A5 Telukan Tawau b. Malaysia
22 B2 Telukbatang Indonesia
21 K7 Teluk Berau b. Indonesia
22 E3 Teluk Bone b. Indonesia
21 L7 Teluk Cenderawasih b. Indonesia
22 E1 Teluk Dondo b. Indonesia
21 K7 Teluk Kamrau b. Indonesia
22 D2 Teluk Mandar b. Indonesia
22 B2 Telukpakedai Indonesia
22 E2 Teluk Poso b. Indonesia
22 D4 Teluk Saleh b. Indonesia
22 E2 Teluk Tomini g. Indonesia
21 H7 Teluk Towori b. Indonesia
52 C3 Telyazh'ye Rus. Fed.
122 E5 Tema Ghana
141 F3 Temagami *Ontario* Canada
141 F3 Temagami Lake l. *Ontario* Canada
22 B1 Temaju i. Indonesia
22 B3 Temanggung Indonesia
8 E3 Te Mapou h. New Zealand
157 H4 Temax Mexico
131 G2 Temba South Africa
131 J3 Tembe r. Mozambique
131 J3 Tembe Elephant Park res. South Africa
22 A2 Tembilahan Indonesia
131 G2 Tembisa South Africa
101 G1 Tembleque Spain
125 C5 Tembo Aluma Angola
131 G5 Tembuland reg. South Africa
62 D2 Teme r. *England* U.K.
154 D5 Temecula *California* U.S.A.
30 A2 Temenchula, G. mt. Rus. Fed.
115 D4 Temeni Greece
122 D3 Téméra Mali
112 B2 Temerin Yugoslavia
25 C7 Temerloh Malaysia
46 E3 Temir Kazakhstan
47 G4 Temirlanovka Kazakhstan
47 H2 Temirtau Kazakhstan
47 L2 Temirtau Rus. Fed.
141 F3 Temiscaming *Québec* Canada
141 F3 Témiscamingue, Lac l. *Ontario/Québec* Canada
139 G4 Témiscouata, L. l. *Québec* Canada
22 A1 Temiyang i. Indonesia
52 B2 Temkino Rus. Fed.
13 F5 Temma *Tasmania* Australia
56 G2 Temmes Finland
52 F2 Temnikov Rus. Fed.
108 A4 Temo r. *Sardegna* Italy
13 F3 Temora *New South Wales* Australia
156 D2 Temósachic Mexico
155 G5 Tempe *Arizona* U.S.A.
22 D3 Tempe, D. l. Indonesia
14 C5 Tempe Downs *Northern Terr.* Australia
73 J3 Tempelhof airport Germany
22 A2 Tempino Indonesia
108 B4 Tempio Pausania *Sardegna* Italy
148 E3 Temple *Michigan* U.S.A.
151 D6 Temple *Texas* U.S.A.
15 E2 Temple B. b. *Queensland* Australia
62 B2 Temple Bar *Wales* U.K.
63 H3 Temple Ewell *England* U.K.
67 D4 Templemore Rep. of Ireland
64 B3 Templepatrick *Northern Ireland* U.K.
23 A4 Templer Bank sand bank Philippines
65 F3 Temple Sowerby *England* U.K.
14 D4 Templeton watercourse *Queensland* Australia
62 B3 Templeton *Wales* U.K.
67 D4 Templetuohy Rep. of Ireland
69 B4 Templeuve France
73 J2 Templin Germany
64 A3 Tempo *Northern Ireland* U.K.
157 F4 Tempoal Mexico
125 C6 Tempué Angola
51 F6 Temryuk Rus. Fed.
51 F6 Temryukskiy Zaliv b. Rus. Fed.
69 C3 Temse Belgium
172 A5 Temuco Chile
9 C6 Temuka New Zealand
162 B4 Tena Ecuador
154 D1 Tenabo, Mt mt. *Nevada* U.S.A.
122 D4 Ténado Burkina
54 C1 Tenala Finland
38 C2 Tenali India
157 F5 Tenancingo Mexico
25 B4 Tenasserim div. Myanmar
25 B4 Tenasserim r. Myanmar
25 B4 Tenasserim Myanmar
102 C2 Tena, Valle de reg. Spain
82 A3 Tenay France
68 E1 Ten Boer Netherlands
62 D2 Tenbury Wells *England* U.K.
62 B3 Tenby *Wales* U.K.
140 D3 Tenby Bay *Ontario* Canada
91 C3 Tence France
126 D2 Tendaho Ethiopia
91 F4 Tende France
25 A5 Ten Degree Channel chan. *Andaman and Nicobar Is* India
119 F5 Tendelti Sudan
29 H4 Tendō Japan
121 D2 Tendrara Morocco
82 B2 Tendre, Mont mt. Switzerland
53 D3 Tendrivs'ka Zatoka b. Ukraine
42 E2 Tendürük Daği mt. Turkey
122 D4 Ténenkou Mali
165 E2 Tenente Marques r. Brazil
123 G3 Ténéré reg. Niger
123 G2 Ténéré du Tafassâsset desert Niger
97 □ Tenerife i. *Canary Is* Spain
121 E1 Ténès Algeria
112 F3 Tenevo Bulgaria
22 D3 Tengah, Kep. is Indonesia
32 B3 Tengchong China
25 □ Tengeh Res. resr Singapore
74 D5 Tengen Germany
22 D2 Tenggarong Indonesia
30 C5 Tengger Shamo desert China
25 C6 Tenggul i. Malaysia
47 G2 Tengiz, Oz. salt lake Kazakhstan
122 C4 Tengréla Côte d'Ivoire
52 F2 Ten'gushevo Rus. Fed.
33 G1 Teng Xian China
33 E4 Teng Xian China
59 F3 Tenhult Sweden
91 E4 Ténibre, Mt mt. France/Italy
165 D4 Teniente Enciso, Parque Nacional nat. park Paraguay
172 E6 Teniente General E. Frías Argentina
179 B2 Teniente Jubany Argentina Base Antarctica
173 F5 Teniente Origone Argentina
179 B2 Teniente Rodolfo Marsh Chile Base Antarctica
74 C4 Teningen Germany
125 E6 Tenke Zaire
45 Q2 Tenkeli Rus. Fed.
122 D4 Tenkodogo Burkina
109 F1 Tenna r. Italy
14 C3 Tennant Creek *Northern Terr.* Australia
87 H4 Tennenbronn Germany
81 E3 Tennengau v. Austria
146 B6 Tennessee div. U.S.A.
145 C5 Tennessee r. *Alabama* U.S.A.
153 F4 Tennessee Pass pass *Colorado* U.S.A.
69 D4 Tenneville Belgium
56 E1 Tennevoll Norway
172 B3 Teno r. Chile
172 B3 Teno Chile
56 G1 Tenojoki r. Finland
157 H5 Tenosique Mexico
120 C3 Tenouchchad watercourse *Western Sahara*
29 F6 Tenryū r. Japan
29 F6 Tenryū Japan
152 F2 Ten Sleep *Wyoming* U.S.A.
22 E2 Tenteno Indonesia
63 G3 Tenterden *England* U.K.
13 H2 Tenterfield *New South Wales* Australia
145 D7 Ten Thousand Islands is *Florida* U.S.A.
100 D2 Tentudia mt. Spain
88 D5 Tenu r. France
173 G3 Teodelina Argentina
168 B5 Teodoro Sampaio Brazil
172 A5 Teodoro Schmidt Chile
169 H2 Teófilo Otoni Brazil
53 B2 Teofipol' Ukraine
23 B5 Teomabal i. Philippines

97 Tinajo *Canary Is* Spain
118 B3 Tin Alkoum Algeria/Libya
123 E3 Ti-n-Azabo well Mali
120 C4 Ti-n-Bessaïs well Mauritania
89 E3 Tinchebray France
123 D2 Ti-n-Didine well Mali
38 B3 Tindivanam India
120 C3 Tindouf Algeria
79 L5 Tinea Romania
122 D3 Ti-n-Echeri well Mali
91 E4 Tinée r. France
98 D1 Tineo Spain
123 E3 Ti-n-Essako Mali
120 C3 Tinfouchy Algeria
33 G3 Ting r. China
25 D7 Tinggi i. Malaysia
13 G2 Tingha *New South Wales* Australia
122 B5 Tingi Mts mts Sierra Leone
55 B5 Tinglev Denmark
164 A1 Tingo María Peru
37 F3 Tingri China
59 F3 Tingsryd Sweden
59 H3 Tingstäde Sweden
170 B3 Tinguiririca, Vol. volcano Chile
58 B2 Tingvatn Norway
56 C3 Tingvoll Norway
66 E1 Tingwall *Scotland* U.K.
166 E3 Tinharé, I. de i. Brazil
98 C3 Tinhela r. Portugal
24 D3 Tinh Gia Vietnam
21 M4 Tinian i. *Northern Mariana Is* Pacific Ocean
107 H3 Tinjan Croatia
22 A3 Tinjil i. Indonesia
122 C4 Tinkisso r. Guinea
58 C2 Tinne r. Norway
58 C2 Tinnsjo l. Norway
170 C2 Tinogasta Argentina
115 G5 Tinos i. Greece
115 G5 Tinos Greece
101 F3 Tiñosa mt. Spain
103 B7 Tiñoso, Cabo headland Spain
86 C3 Tinqueux France
121 E4 Ti-n-Rerhoh well Algeria
37 H4 Tinsukia India
62 B4 Tintagel *England* U.K.
120 B5 Tînţâne Mauritania
123 E3 Ti-n-Tékouffé well Mali
88 D3 Tinténiac France
62 D3 Tintern Parva *Wales* U.K.
69 D5 Tintigny Belgium
170 D2 Tintina Argentina
12 E3 Tintinara *S. Australia* Australia
66 E5 Tinto h. *Scotland* U.K.
100 D3 Tinto r. Spain
9 F4 Tinui New Zealand
123 E3 Ti-n-Zaouâtene Mali
146 E4 Tioga r. *Pennsylvania* U.S.A.
25 D7 Tioman i. Malaysia
140 D2 Tionaga *Ontario* Canada
83 F3 Tione r. Italy
107 E2 Tione di Trento Italy
146 D4 Tionesta Lake l. *Pennsylvania* U.S.A.
147 E3 Tioughnioga r. *New York* U.S.A.
149 J4 Tioughnioga r. *New York* U.S.A.
121 E1 Tipasa Algeria
156 J6 Tipitapa Nicaragua
148 D5 Tippecanoe r. *Indiana* U.S.A.
148 E5 Tippecanoe Lake l. *Indiana* U.S.A.
67 C4 Tipperary div. Rep. of Ireland
67 C4 Tipperary Rep. of Ireland
37 F4 Tiptala Bhanjyang pass Nepal
148 D5 Tipton *Indiana* U.S.A.
148 B5 Tipton *Iowa* U.S.A.
155 E4 Tipton, Mt mt. *Arizona* U.S.A.
140 B2 Tip Top Hill h. *Ontario* Canada
63 G3 Tiptree *England* U.K.
164 C3 Tipuani Bolivia
162 D3 Tiquié r. Brazil
157 H6 Tiquisate Guatemala
43 C6 Tīrān i. Saudi Arabia
39 B2 Tīrān Iran
Tirana *see* Tiranë
114 A1 Tiranë Albania
114 A1 Tiranë-Rinas airport Albania
106 E2 Tirano Italy
53 C3 Tiraspol Moldova
43 A4 Tir'at el Ismâ'îlîya canal Egypt
8 E2 Tirau New Zealand
128 B4 Tiraz Mts mts Namibia
42 A2 Tire Turkey
66 B4 Tiree i. *Scotland* U.K.
121 E4 Tirek well Algeria
123 E2 Tirest well Mali
66 B3 Tirga Mor h. *Scotland* U.K.
36 B1 Tirich Mir mt. Pakistan
111 F4 Tiriolo Italy
120 C4 Tiris Zemmour div. Mauritania
38 B2 Tirna r. India
80 D4 Tirol div. Austria
99 G2 Tirón r. Spain
169 F3 Tiros Brazil
124 D2 Tiroungoulou Central African Rep.
75 H3 Tirschenreuth Germany
108 A5 Tirso r. *Sardegna* Italy
55 C3 Tirstrup Denmark
101 F2 Tirteafuera r. Spain
38 A3 Tirthahalli India
37 F5 Tirtol India
172 A5 Tirúa Chile
38 B4 Tiruchchendur India
38 B4 Tiruchchirāppalli India
38 B4 Tiruchengodu India
38 B4 Tirunelveli India
164 A1 Tiruntán Peru
38 B3 Tirupati India
38 B3 Tiruppattur India
38 B4 Tiruppur India
38 B4 Tirutturaippundi India
38 B3 Tiruvannamalai India
54 E3 Tirza r. Latvia
38 B4 Tisaiyanvilai India
59 F2 Tisaren l. Sweden
112 F2 Tisău Romania
62 D3 Tisbury *England* U.K.
137 J4 Tisdale *Saskatchewan* Canada
75 K2 Tišice Czech Rep.
43 D3 Ţisīyah Syria
58 C1 Tisleifjorden l. Norway
59 G2 Tisnaren l. Sweden
78 F2 Tišnov Czech Rep.
79 J3 Tisovec Slovakia
38 C5 Tissamaharama Sri Lanka
121 E1 Tissemsilt Algeria
55 D4 Tissø l. Denmark
37 G4 Tista r. India
55 E3 Tisvilde Denmark
79 K4 Tisza r. Europe
79 J5 Tiszaalpár Hungary
79 M3 Tiszabecs Hungary
79 K5 Tiszaföldvár Hungary
79 K4 Tiszafüred Hungary
79 K4 Tiszajenő Hungary
79 K5 Tiszakécske Hungary
79 K5 Tiszalök Hungary
79 K5 Tiszántúl reg. Hungary
79 K4 Tiszaörs Hungary
79 L4 Tiszaújváros Hungary
79 L4 Tiszavasvári Hungary
121 E3 Tit *Adrar* Algeria
121 F4 Tit *Tamanrasset* Algeria
103 B5 Titaguas Spain
179 B4 Titan Dome ice feature Antarctica
114 D3 Titarisios r. Greece
45 Q2 Tit-Ary Rus. Fed.
112 C2 Titel Yugoslavia
164 C3 Titicaca, Lago l. Bolivia/Peru
82 D1 Titisee Germany
37 E5 Titlagarh India
83 D2 Titlis mt. Switzerland
109 H4 Tito Italy
104 E3 Titova Korenica Croatia
104 F3 Titov Drvar Bos.-Herz.
52 F3 Titovo Rus. Fed.
112 B3 Titovo Užice Yugoslavia
14 C4 Ti Tree *Northern Terr.* Australia
149 E4 Tittabawassee r. *Michigan* U.S.A.
80 C2 Titting Germany
75 J4 Tittling Germany
75 H4 Tittmoning Germany
112 E2 Titu Romania
99 G4 Titulcia Spain
145 D6 Titusville *Florida* U.S.A.
146 D4 Titusville *Pennsylvania* U.S.A.
36 C4 Tivari India
112 B3 Tivat Yugoslavia
59 F2 Tiveden Nationalpark nat. park Sweden
62 C4 Tiverton *England* U.K.
140 E4 Tiverton *Ontario* Canada
102 D3 Tivissa Spain
109 E3 Tivoli Italy
157 H4 Tixkokob Mexico
157 F5 Tixtla Mexico
43 D2 Tiyās Syria
156 E4 Tizapán el Alto Mexico
120 C3 Tizi Mighert Morocco
157 H4 Tizimín Mexico
120 C2 Tizi-n-Test Morocco
120 C2 Tizi-n-Tichka Morocco
121 E1 Tizi Ouzou Algeria
47 J5 Tiznap r. China
120 C3 Tiznit Morocco
156 E3 Tizoc Mexico
59 F2 Tjällmo Sweden
56 E2 Tjappsåive Sweden
58 A1 Tjeldstø Norway
68 D2 Tjeukemeer l. Netherlands
58 D2 Tjøme Norway
58 B2 Tjorhom Norway
58 D2 Tjörn i. Sweden
Tkibuli *see* Tqibuli
Tkvarcheli *see* Tqvarch'eli
157 F5 Tlacolula Mexico
157 G5 Tlacotalpán Mexico
151 C7 Tlahualilo Mexico
157 F5 Tlalnepantla Mexico
157 F5 Tlapa Mexico
157 F5 Tlaxcala div. Mexico
157 F5 Tlaxcala Mexico
157 F5 Tlaxiaco Mexico
121 D2 Tlemcen Algeria
96 D5 Tleta des Beni Yder Cherki Morocco
96 D5 Tleta Rissana Morocco
131 G4 Tlholong South Africa
128 D3 Tlokweng Botswana
77 H3 Tłuchowo Poland
53 A2 Tlumach Ukraine
77 K3 Tłuszcz Poland
51 H7 Tlyarata Rus. Fed.
42 F1 Tlyarata Rus. Fed.
52 B1 T'ma r. Rus. Fed.
121 C2 Tmassah Libya
120 B4 Tmeïmîchât Mauritania
136 D3 Toad River *B.C.* Canada
23 Toagel Mlungui chan. Palau
129 H2 Toamasina div. Madagascar
129 H2 Toamasina Madagascar
7 11 Toanoano *French Polynesia* Pacific Ocean
7 10 Toau i. *French Polynesia* Pacific Ocean
119 G3 To Awai well Sudan
172 E4 Toay Argentina
32 B2 Toba China
29 F6 Toba Japan
36 A3 Toba & Kakar Ranges mountain range Pakistan
159 2 Tobago i. Trinidad and Tobago
103 B6 Tobarra Spain
21 J6 Tobelo Indonesia
64 B3 Tobermore *Northern Ireland* U.K.
14 D4 Tobermory *Northern Terr.* Australia
140 E4 Tobermory *Ontario* Canada
15 E5 Tobermory *Queensland* Australia
66 B4 Tobermory *Scotland* U.K.
28 H2 Tōbetsu Japan
29 1 Tobishi-hana c. Japan
135 Q2 Tobin, Kap c. Greenland
137 J4 Tobin L. l. *Saskatchewan* Canada
154 D1 Tobin, Mt mt. *Nevada* U.S.A.
147 K1 Tobique r. *New Brunswick* Canada
29 G4 Tobi-shima i. Japan
22 A2 Toboali Indonesia
44 H4 Tobol r. Kazakhstan
47 G1 Tobol r. Kazakhstan/Rus. Fed.
46 F2 Tobol Kazakhstan
44 H4 Tobol'sk Rus. Fed.
25 E4 Tô Bong Vietnam
23 B4 Toboso Philippines
166 C2 Tocantinópolis Brazil
166 C3 Tocantins div. Brazil
166 C1 Tocantins r. Brazil
166 C3 Tocantinzinha r. Brazil
145 D5 Toccoa *Georgia* U.S.A.
106 C3 Toce r. Italy
98 B4 Tocha Portugal
36 B2 Tochi r. Pakistan
29 G5 Tochigi div. Japan
29 G5 Tochio Japan
58 D2 Töcksfors Sweden
159 3 Toco Trinidad and Tobago
164 C4 Toconao Chile
164 B4 Tocopilla Chile
162 D1 Tocuyo r. Venezuela
14 C5 Todd watercourse *Northern Terr.* Australia
173 G3 Todd Argentina
63 E3 Toddington *England* U.K.
21 H7 Todeli Indonesia
83 D2 Todi mt. Switzerland
109 E2 Todi Italy
65 F4 Todmorden *England* U.K.
29 J4 Todoga-saki pt Japan
28 H3 Todohokke Japan
164 C3 Todos Santos Bolivia
156 C4 Todos Santos Mexico
154 D6 Todos Santos, Bahía de b. Mexico
74 C5 Todtmoos Germany
74 C5 Todtnau Germany
67 B5 Toe Head headland Rep. of Ireland
98 C2 Toén Spain
9 B7 Toetoes Bay b. New Zealand
136 G4 Tofield *Alberta* Canada
136 D5 Tofino *B.C.* Canada
66 2 Toft *Scotland* U.K.
148 B2 Tofte *Minnesota* U.S.A.
58 D2 Töftedal Sweden
59 F2 Toften l. Sweden
55 B4 Toftlund Denmark
6 5 Tofua i. Tonga
6 2 Toga i. Vanuatu
37 E2 Togatax China
126 E3 Togdheer div. Somalia
83 E1 Toggenburg reg. Switzerland
29 F5 Togi Japan
75 H4 Töging am Inn Germany
117 E5 Togo country Africa
148 A2 Togo *Minnesota* U.S.A.
28 C7 Tōgō Japan
30 D4 Togtoh China
29 2 Toguchi Japan
47 K1 Toguchin Rus. Fed.
47 L2 Togul Rus. Fed.
36 C3 Tohana India
155 H4 Tohatchi *New Mexico* U.S.A.
22 C1 Tohenbatu mt. Malaysia
7 11 Tohiea mt. *French Polynesia* Pacific Ocean
56 G3 Toholampi Finland
30 C4 Tohom China
30 D3 Töhöm Mongolia
29 G6 Toi Japan
25 A5 Toibalewe *Andaman and Nicobar Is* India
57 F3 Toijala Finland
54 C1 Toijala Finland
28 C8 Toi-misaki pt Japan
57 G3 Toivakka Finland
154 D2 Toiyabe Range mts *Nevada* U.S.A.
22 E2 Toja Indonesia
114 C1 Tojaci Macedonia
28 D6 Tōjō Japan
46 D2 Tok r. Rus. Fed.
134 D3 Tok *Alaska* U.S.A.
28 J2 Tokachi-gawa r. Japan
29 F6 Tōkai Japan
79 L3 Tokaj Hungary
29 G5 Tōkamachi Japan
8 B7 Tokanui New Zealand
119 G4 Tokar Sudan
27 N6 Tokara-rettō is Japan
52 E4 Tokarevka Rus. Fed.
52 E2 Tokarevo Rus. Fed.
42 D1 Tokat Turkey
31 H5 Tŏkchŏktŏ i. South Korea
31 H5 Tŏkch'ŏn North Korea
5 K5 Tokelau territory Pacific Ocean
Tokkuztara *see* Gongliu
47 J4 Tokmak Kyrgyzstan
53 F3 Tokmak Ukraine
8 G3 Tokomaru Bay New Zealand
29 F6 Tokoname Japan
8 E3 Tokoroa New Zealand
28 J2 Tokoro-gawa r. Japan
122 C5 Tokounou Guinea
131 G3 Tokoza South Africa
Toksu *see* Xinhe
26 E3 Toksun China
28 C5 Tok-tō i. Japan
47 H4 Toktogul Kyrgyzstan
47 H4 Toktogul Suu Saktagychy resr Kyrgyzstan
28 E7 Tokushima div. Japan
28 E6 Tokushima Japan
28 C6 Tokuyama Japan
29 G6 Tōkyō div. Japan
29 G6 Tōkyō Japan
29 G6 Tōkyō-wan b. Japan
39 F2 Tokzār Afghanistan
8 G3 Tolaga Bay New Zealand
129 H3 Tôlañaro Madagascar
170 C2 Tolar, Co mt. Argentina
52 G2 Tolba Rus. Fed.
46 E2 Tolbazy Rus. Fed.
68 E1 Tolbert Netherlands
52 E1 Tolbukhino Rus. Fed.
52 H1 Tolbuzino Rus. Fed.
156 K7 Tolé Panama
172 F4 Toleant Mexico
99 F5 Toledo div. Spain
148 A5 Toledo *Iowa* U.S.A.
146 B4 Toledo *Ohio* U.S.A.
99 F5 Toledo Spain
168 B6 Toledo Brazil
151 E6 Toledo Bend Res. resr *Louisiana/Texas* U.S.A.
107 H5 Tolentino Italy
172 B5 Tolhuaca, Parque Nacional nat. park Chile
129 G3 Toliara div. Madagascar
129 G3 Toliara Madagascar
Toling *see* Zanda
22 E1 Tolitoli Indonesia
22 E1 Tolitoli, Tk b. Indonesia
44 K3 Tol'ka Rus. Fed.
59 E3 Tolken l. Sweden
77 H1 Tolkmicko Poland
59 E4 Tollarp Sweden
68 D2 Tollebeek Netherlands
73 J2 Tollense r. Germany
73 J2 Tollensesee l. Germany
63 G3 Tollesbury *England* U.K.
55 D4 Tølløse Denmark
54 F2 Tolmachevo Rus. Fed.
107 H2 Tolmezzo Italy
81 E4 Tolmin Slovenia
79 H5 Tolna div. Hungary
79 H5 Tolna Hungary
79 H5 Tolnai-hegyhát h. Hungary
125 C4 Tolo Zaire
27 Tolo Channel chan. Hong Kong
27 Tolo Harbour harbour Hong Kong
99 H1 Tolosa Spain
31 H6 Tolsan Do i. South Korea
140 D5 Tolsmaville *Ontario* Canada
66 B2 Tolsta Head headland *Scotland* U.K.
172 A5 Toltén r. Chile
172 A5 Toltén Chile
162 B2 Tolú Colombia
157 F5 Toluca Mexico
56 H2 Tolvand, Oz. l. Rus. Fed.
109 J4 Tolve Italy
50 J4 Tol'yatti Rus. Fed.
46 F2 Tolybay Kazakhstan
93 C4 Tolzac r. France
47 L2 Tom' r. Rus. Fed.
31 J2 Tom' r. Rus. Fed.
122 D4 Toma Burkina
148 B4 Tomah *Wisconsin* U.S.A.
148 C3 Tomahawk *Wisconsin* U.S.A.
28 H2 Tomakomai Japan
22 E2 Tomali Indonesia
28 H1 Tomamae Japan
6 8 Tomanivi mt. Fiji
100 B1 Tomar *Santarém* Portugal
163 E4 Tomar Brazil
28 H2 Tomari Japan
114 B3 Tomaros mt. Greece
53 G1 Tomarovka Rus. Fed.
42 C2 Tomarza Turkey
164 C3 Tomás Barron Bolivia
173 J1 Tomás Gomensoro Uruguay
53 B1 Tomashhorod Ukraine
53 C2 Tomashpil' Ukraine
77 M5 Tomaszów Lubelski Poland
77 J4 Tomaszów Mazowiecki Poland
66 E3 Tomatin *Scotland* U.K.
156 D5 Tomatlán Mexico
168 D5 Tomazina Brazil
28 D6 Tombara Japan
93 C4 Tombebœf France
145 B6 Tombigbee r. *Alabama* U.S.A.
125 B5 Tomboco Angola
169 G4 Tombos Brazil
122 D3 Tombouctou div. Mali
122 D3 Tombouctou Mali
155 G6 Tombstone *Arizona* U.S.A.
125 B7 Tombua Angola
131 G1 Tom Burke South Africa
172 A4 Tomé Chile
59 E4 Tomelilla Sweden
101 G1 Tomelloso Spain
141 F3 Tomiko *Ontario* Canada
13 G3 Tomingley *New South Wales* Australia
122 D4 Tominián Mali
66 E3 Tomintoul *Scotland* U.K.
29 H5 Tomioka Japan
104 F4 Tomislavgrad Bos.-Herz.
12 B1 Tomkinson Ranges mountain range *S. Australia* Australia
55 A2 Tommerby Fjord l. Denmark
56 D2 Tømmerneset Norway
55 C4 Tommerup Denmark
45 O4 Tommot Rus. Fed.
162 D2 Tomo r. Colombia
162 D3 Tomo Colombia
30 E4 Tomortei China
131 G2 Tompi Seleka South Africa
22 D2 Tompo Indonesia
45 P3 Tompo Rus. Fed.
16 B4 Tom Price *Western Australia* Australia
44 K4 Tomsk Rus. Fed.
59 F3 Tomtabacken h. Sweden
45 Q3 Tomtor Rus. Fed.
43 C1 Tömük Turkey
28 J2 Tomuraushi-yama mt. Japan
Tomur Feng mt. *see* Pik Pobedy
51 G6 Tomuzlovka r. Rus. Fed.
102 F3 Tona Spain
157 G5 Tonalá Mexico
155 G4 Tonalea *Arizona* U.S.A.
83 F2 Tonale, Passo di pass Italy
29 F5 Tonami Japan
162 D4 Tonantins Brazil
108 B4 Tonara *Sardegna* Italy
152 C1 Tonasket *Washington* U.S.A.
163 G2 Tonate French Guiana
63 G3 Tonbridge *England* U.K.
21 J6 Tondano Indonesia
98 B4 Tondela Portugal
55 A5 Tønder Denmark
62 C4 Tone r. *England* U.K.
178 3 Tonefjellet h. *Svalbard* Arctic Ocean
29 H6 Tone-gawa r. Japan
107 F3 Tonezza del Cimone Italy
5 K7 Tonga country Pacific Ocean
13 E2 Tonga *Queensland* Australia
131 H4 Tongaat South Africa
33 G3 Tong'an China
5 M5 Tongareva atoll *Cook Islands* Pacific Ocean
8 E3 Tongariro mt. New Zealand
8 E3 Tongariro National Park nat. park New Zealand
6 4 Tongatapu i. Tonga
6 4 Tongatapu Group is Tonga
176 H7 Tonga Tr. sea feature Pacific Ocean
33 F1 Tongbai China
33 F1 Tongbai Shan mountain range China
33 G2 Tongcheng China
33 F2 Tongcheng China
33 E1 Tongchuan China
33 E3 Tongdao China
32 C1 Tongde China
31 H5 Tongduch'ŏn South Korea
69 D4 Tongeren div. Belgium
69 D4 Tongeren Belgium
33 F2 Tonggu China
33 E1 Tongguan China
33 E5 Tonggu Jiao China
31 J5 Tonghae South Korea
32 C3 Tonghai China
31 J3 Tonghe China
31 H4 Tonghua China
31 K3 Tongjiang China
32 D2 Tongjiang China
31 H3 Tongken r. China
32 D4 Tongking, Gulf of g. China
32 D2 Tongliang China
31 G4 Tongliao China
33 G2 Tongling China
33 G2 Tongling China
33 G2 Tonglu China
32 D2 Tongnan China
6 2 Tongoa i. Vanuatu
129 G3 Tongobory Madagascar
172 B1 Tongoi, Bahía b. Chile
172 B1 Tongoy Chile
23 B5 Tongquil i. Philippines
33 E3 Tongren China
32 C1 Tongren China
37 G4 Tongsa r. Bhutan
37 G4 Tongsa Bhutan
33 F2 Tongshan China
Tongshan *see* Xuzhou
32 A1 Tongtian r. China
152 F2 Tongue r. *Montana* U.S.A.
66 D2 Tongue *Scotland* U.K.
66 D2 Tongue, Kyle of inlet *Scotland* U.K.
158 C1 Tongue of the Ocean chan. The Bahamas
32 D1 Tongwei China
31 F5 Tong Xian China
30 C5 Tongxin China
33 G2 Tongyanghe China
31 G3 Tongyu China
32 D2 Tongzi China
148 C5 Tonica *Illinois* U.S.A.
156 C2 Tónichi Mexico
124 E2 Tonj watercourse Sudan
124 E2 Tonj Sudan
36 C4 Tonk India
39 B1 Tonkābon Iran
24 D2 Tonkin reg. Vietnam
50 H3 Tonkino Rus. Fed.
25 D5 Tônle Basăk r. Cambodia
25 C4 Tônlé Sab l. Cambodia
92 B3 Tonnay-Boutonne France
92 B3 Tonnay-Charente France
93 C4 Tonneins France
90 B1 Tonnerre France
90 C1 Tonnerrois reg. France
72 D1 Tönning Germany
29 H4 Tōno Japan
154 D2 Tonopah *Nevada* U.S.A.
28 E6 Tonoshō Japan
156 K8 Tonosí Panama
58 D2 Tønsberg Norway
58 B2 Tonstad Norway
172 C1 Tontal, Sa mountain range Argentina
130 C5 Tontelbos South Africa
155 G5 Tonto National Monument nat. park *Arizona* U.S.A.
6 5 Tonumea i. Tonga
24 A2 Tonzang Myanmar
15 G6 Toobeah *Queensland* Australia
122 C5 Toobli Liberia
152 D3 Tooele *Utah* U.S.A.
64 B3 Toomebridge *Northern Ireland* U.K.
15 F5 Toompine *Queensland* Australia
13 G2 Tooraweenah *New South Wales* Australia
130 E6 Toorberg mt. South Africa
24 B3 To or China Bakir r. Myanmar
15 G5 Toowoomba *Queensland* Australia
126 F2 Tooxin Somalia
155 G6 Topawa *Arizona* U.S.A.
154 C2 Topaz *California* U.S.A.
127 3 Topaze B. b. *Rodrigues I.* Mauritius
47 K2 Topchikha Rus. Fed.
65 G3 Topcliffe *England* U.K.
150 E4 Topeka *Kansas* U.S.A.
156 D3 Topia Mexico
52 D2 Topkanovo Rus. Fed.
47 L1 Topki Rus. Fed.
79 L3 Topľa r. Slovakia
136 D4 Topley Landing *B.C.* Canada
112 C3 Toplica r. Yugoslavia
79 M6 Toplița Romania
112 E1 Toplița Romania
73 H3 Töplitz Germany
172 A3 Topocalma, Pta pt Chile
155 E4 Topock *Arizona* U.S.A.
112 C2 Topola Yugoslavia
114 C1 Topolčani Macedonia
79 H3 Topoľčany Slovakia
76 G3 Topólka Poland
156 C3 Topolobampo Mexico
112 G2 Topolog Romania
79 L6 Topolovătu Mare Romania
112 E2 Topoloveni Romania
112 F3 Topolovgrad Bulgaria
73 L3 Toporów Poland
53 B1 Topory Ukraine
50 D1 Topozero, Oz. l. Rus. Fed.
152 B2 Toppenish *Washington* U.S.A.
147 K2 Topsfield *Maine* U.S.A.
62 C4 Topsham *England* U.K.
155 F3 Toquerville *Utah* U.S.A.
126 B3 Tor Ethiopia
102 E3 Torá de Riubreós Spain
98 D2 Toral de los Vados Spain
42 A2 Torbalı Turkey
39 D2 Torbat-e-Heydarīyeh Iran
39 E2 Torbat-e Jām Iran
62 C4 Tor Bay b. *England* U.K.
52 F2 Torbeyevo Rus. Fed.
52 B2 Torbeyevo Rus. Fed.
107 G3 Torcello Italy
52 E1 Torchino Rus. Fed.
148 E3 Torch Lake l. *Michigan* U.S.A.
53 A1 Torchyn Ukraine
99 F5 Torcón r. Spain
102 F3 Tordera Spain
99 F3 Tordesillas Spain
102 B4 Tordesilos Spain
109 F2 Tordino r. Italy
56 F2 Töre Sweden
59 F2 Töreboda Sweden
59 E3 Torekov Sweden
109 G3 Torella del Sannio Italy
103 C6 Torellano Spain
102 F2 Torelló Spain
68 D2 Torenberg h. Netherlands
98 D2 Toreno Spain
30 C2 Torey Rus. Fed.
62 C3 Torfaen div. *Wales* U.K.
73 H4 Torgau Germany
73 K2 Torgelow Germany
109 E1 Torgiano Italy
51 H5 Torgun r. Rus. Fed.
59 F3 Torhamn Sweden
69 B3 Torhout Belgium
89 E2 Torigni-sur-Vire France
99 G4 Torija Spain
156 C3 Torin Mexico
106 B3 Torino div. *Piemonte* Italy
106 B3 Torino *Torino* Italy
4 F2 Tori-shima i. Japan
126 B4 Torit Sudan
168 B2 Torixoreu Brazil
98 E4 Tormes r. Spain
79 K3 Tornaľa Slovakia
98 E4 Tornavacas Spain
65 H4 Torne r. *England* U.K.
56 F2 Torneälven r. Sweden
101 F1 Torneros, Sierra de los mountain range Spain
72 E2 Tornesch Germany
56 E1 Torneträsk l. Sweden
56 E1 Torneträsk Sweden
82 C2 Tornette, La mt. Switzerland
139 H2 Torngat Mountains mountain range *Newfoundland* Canada
56 G2 Tornio Finland
106 D3 Torno Italy
173 F5 Tornquist Argentina
79 M3 Tornyospálca Hungary
59 G2 Torö i. Sweden
123 F4 Toro Nigeria
99 E3 Toro Spain
170 C2 Toro, Co del mt. Chile
123 E4 Torodi Niger
118 C4 Toro Doum well Chad
108 A6 Toro, Isola il i. *Sardegna* Italy
79 K4 Törökszentmiklós Hungary
141 F5 Toronto airport *Ontario* Canada
13 G3 Toronto *New South Wales* Australia
141 F5 Toronto *Ontario* Canada
81 H3 Torony Hungary
50 D3 Toropets Rus. Fed.
154 D5 Toro Pk summit *California* U.S.A.
172 B2 Toro, Punta pt Chile
127 B4 Tororo Uganda
43 B1 Toros Dağları mountain range Turkey
42 C2 Toros Dağları mountain range Turkey
99 F3 Torozos, Montes de reg. Spain
108 B4 Torpè *Sardegna* Italy
66 F3 Torphins *Scotland* U.K.
62 B4 Torpoint *England* U.K.
173 K1 Torquato Severo Brazil
62 C4 Torquay *England* U.K.
62 F2 Torquemada Spain
108 A4 Torralba *Sardegna* Italy
99 E5 Torralba de Oropesa Spain
154 C5 Torrance *California* U.S.A.
100 B2 Torrão Portugal
59 E1 Tørrberget Norway
98 C4 Torre mt. Portugal
109 G4 Torre Annunziata Italy
103 B4 Torrebaja Spain
103 D4 Torreblanca Spain
103 G3 Torreblascopedro Spain
99 F4 Torrecaballeros Spain
101 F2 Torrecampo Spain
111 G2 Torre Canne Italy
111 H2 Torre Cavallo, Capo di pt Italy
101 F4 Torrecilla mt. Spain
99 H2 Torrecilla en Cameros Spain
100 E1 Torrecillas de la Tiesa Spain
102 E2 Torre de Cadí mt. Spain
98 C3 Torre de Dona Chama Portugal
101 G2 Torre de Juan Abad Spain
100 D3 Torre de la Higuera o Matalascañas Spain
98 D2 Torre del Bierzo Spain
99 G4 Torre del Burgo Spain
101 G3 Torre del Campo Spain
109 G4 Torre del Greco Italy
111 F4 Torre del Mar Spain
102 E3 Torredembarra Spain
98 C3 Torre de Moncorvo Portugal
109 F2 Torre de'Passeri Italy
101 G3 Torredonjimeno Spain
98 D5 Torrejoncillo Spain
99 H4 Torrejoncillo del Rey Spain
99 G4 Torrejón de Ardoz Spain
98 E5 Torrejón el Rubio Spain
98 E5 Torrejón-Tajo, Emb. de resr Spain
98 E5 Torrejón-Tiétar, Emb. de resr Spain
102 B4 Torrelacarcel Spain
99 G4 Torrelaguna Spain
102 B3 Torrelapaja Spain
99 F1 Torrelavega Spain
99 E3 Torrelobatón Spain
99 G4 Torrelodones Spain
109 H3 Torremaggiore Italy
100 D2 Torremegía Spain
109 H3 Torre Mileto Italy
100 D1 Torremocha Spain
102 B4 Torremocha de Jiloca Spain
101 F4 Torremolinos *Málaga* Spain
15 F4 Torrens Cr. watercourse *Queensland* Australia
15 F4 Torrens Creek *Queensland* Australia
12 D2 Torrens, Lake salt flat *S. Australia* Australia
103 C5 Torrent Spain
102 D3 Torrente de Cinca Spain
101 G2 Torrenueva Spain
106 D5 Torre Nuovo Scalo Italy
156 E3 Torreón Mexico
109 H4 Torre Orsaia Italy
103 C7 Torre-Pacheco Spain
101 F3 Torreparedones h. Spain
106 B4 Torre Pellice Italy
101 G3 Torreperogil Spain
101 G3 Torres r. Spain
167 C6 Torres Brazil
156 C2 Torres Mexico
111 H3 Torre San Giovanni Italy
111 G2 Torre Sta Susanna Italy
98 E1 Torres, Cabo pt Spain
171 B7 Torres del Paine, Parque Nacional nat. park Chile
6 2 Torres Islands is Vanuatu
100 B1 Torres Novas Portugal
11 H1 Torres Strait str. Australia/P.N.G.
100 A1 Torres Vedras Portugal
103 C7 Torrevieja Spain
155 G2 Torrey *Utah* U.S.A.
111 G2 Torricella Italy
83 D2 Torricella Taverne Switzerland
107 E3 Torri del Benaco Italy
62 B4 Torridge r. *England* U.K.
66 C3 Torridon *Scotland* U.K.
66 C3 Torridon, Loch inlet *Scotland* U.K.
106 D4 Torriglia Italy
103 C4 Torrijas Spain
99 F5 Torrijos Spain
55 B4 Torring Denmark
147 G4 Torrington *Connecticut* U.S.A.
152 F3 Torrington *Wyoming* U.S.A.
108 D1 Torrita di Siena Italy
100 B2 Torroal Portugal
102 G2 Torroella de Montgrí Spain
101 G4 Torrox Spain
101 G4 Torrox, Punta de pt Spain
37 G4 Torsa r. Bhutan
59 E1 Torsby Sweden
55 1 Tórshavn Faeroes
59 J1 Torsholma Finland
55 A3 Torsminde Denmark
59 E2 Torsö i. Sweden
110 C5 Torto r. *Sicilia* Italy
145 3 Tortola i. *Virgin Is* Caribbean
170 C2 Tórtolas, Co Las mt. Chile
99 F3 Tórtoles de Esgueva Spain
108 B5 Tortolì *Sardegna* Italy
106 C4 Tortona Italy
111 E3 Tortora Italy
109 F2 Tortoreto Italy
110 D4 Tortorici *Sicilia* Italy
102 D4 Tortosa Spain
173 G2 Tortugas Argentina
156 B3 Tortugas, Bahía Mexico
42 E1 Tortum Turkey
39 C2 Ţorūd Iran
42 D1 Torul Turkey
77 H2 Toruń div. Poland
76 G2 Toruń Poland
59 E3 Torup Sweden
54 D2 Tõrva Estonia
109 E3 Tor Vaianica Italy
101 G4 Torvizcón Spain
67 C1 Tory Island i. Rep. of Ireland
79 L2 Torysa r. Slovakia
67 C1 Tory Sound chan. Rep. of Ireland
52 B1 Torzhok Rus. Fed.
76 D3 Torzym Poland
28 D7 Tosa Japan
83 F2 Tosa, Cima mt. Italy
28 D7 Tosashimizu Japan
28 D7 Tosa-wan b. Japan
56 D2 Tosbotn Norway
130 D2 Tosca South Africa
107 E5 Toscana div. Italy
107 E3 Toscolano-Maderno Italy
29 H3 Tōshima-yama mt. Japan
50 D3 Tosno Rus. Fed.
30 A2 Tosontsengel Mongolia
83 D1 Töss r. Switzerland
102 F3 Tossa Spain
102 E2 Tossal de l'Orri mt. Spain
93 A5 Tosse France
59 E2 Tösse Sweden
170 D2 Tostado Argentina
54 C2 Tõstamaa Estonia
72 E2 Tostedt Germany
98 A1 Tosto, Cabo pt Spain
28 C7 Tosu Japan
42 C1 Tosya Turkey
76 G5 Toszek Poland
58 B2 Totak l. Norway
103 B7 Totana Spain
89 G2 Tôtes France
81 E3 Totes Gebirge mts Austria
79 K5 Tótkomlós Hungary
63 E4 Totland *England* U.K.
50 G3 Tot'ma Rus. Fed.
62 C4 Totnes *England* U.K.
163 F2 Totness Surinam
157 F5 Totolapan Mexico
157 G4 Totonicapán Guatemala
164 C3 Totora Bolivia
172 D1 Totoral Argentina
170 B2 Totoral Chile
173 G2 Totoras Argentina
122 C5 Totota Liberia
6 7 Totoya i. Fiji
179 C6 Totten Glacier gl. Antarctica
13 F3 Tottenham *New South Wales* Australia
63 E4 Totton *England* U.K.
28 D6 Tottori div. Japan
28 E6 Tottori Japan
123 F2 Touâret well Niger
122 C5 Touba Côte d'Ivoire
122 A4 Touba Senegal
120 C2 Toubkal, Jbel mt. Morocco
124 C2 Touboro Cameroon
98 C3 Touça Portugal
93 D5 Touch r. France
90 B1 Toucy France
30 C5 Toudaohu China
120 B4 Toueïrma well Mauritania
122 D3 Touérât well Mali
122 D2 Toufourine well Mali
122 D4 Tougan Burkina
121 F2 Touggourt Algeria
122 D4 Tougouri Burkina
122 B4 Tougué Guinea
6 2 Touho *New Caledonia* Pacific Ocean
120 C5 Touijinet well Mauritania
120 B5 Touil Mauritania
122 C4 Toukoto Mali
87 E4 Toul France
122 C5 Toulépleu Côte d'Ivoire
91 D5 Toulon *Var* France
90 B2 Toulon-sur-Allier France
90 C2 Toulon-sur-Arroux France
93 E6 Toulouges France
93 D5 Toulouse *Haute-Garonne* France
93 D5 Toulouse-Blagnac airport France
123 F3 Toumbélaga well Niger
123 G2 Tournmo well Niger
122 C5 Toumodi Côte d'Ivoire
123 F3 Tounfaminir well Niger
123 G5 Toungo Nigeria
24 B3 Toungoo Myanmar
33 E3 Toupai China
89 F2 Touques r. France
89 F2 Touques France
89 F4 Touraine reg. France
24 C3 Tourakom Laos
124 C1 Tourba Chad
86 C2 Tourcoing *Nord* France
98 A1 Touriñán, Cabo c. Spain
88 D2 Tourlaville France
69 B4 Tournai div. *Hainaut* Belgium

163 F2 Tumatumari Guyana
114 D1 Tumba mt. Bulgaria/Greece
59 G2 Tumba Sweden
125 D4 Tumba Zaire
124 C4 Tumba, Lac l. Zaire
22 C2 Tumbangsamba Indonesia
22 B2 Tumbangtiti Indonesia
23 C5 Tumbao Philippines
13 G3 Tumbarumba New South Wales Australia
162 A4 Tumbes Peru
172 A4 Tumbes, Punta pt Chile
136 E3 Tumbler Ridge B.C. Canada
52 F2 Tumbotino Rus. Fed.
12 D3 Tumby Bay S. Australia Australia
30 D4 Tumd Youqi China
30 D4 Tumd Zuoqi China
31 J4 Tumen r. China/North Korea
31 J4 Tumen China
30 B5 Tumenzi China
163 E2 Tumeremo Venezuela
163 E2 Tumereng Guyana
23 A5 Tumindao i. Philippines
169 H3 Tumiritinga Brazil
38 B3 Tumkur India
66 E4 Tummel r. Scotland U.K.
66 E4 Tummel, Loch l. Scotland U.K.
118 B3 Tummo, Mts of mts Libya
23 □2 Tumon Bay b. Guam Pacific Ocean
39 E4 Tump Pakistan
22 C2 Tumpah Indonesia
100 D1 Tumuja r. Spain
13 G3 Tumut New South Wales Australia
47 J4 Tumxuk China
59 F1 Tuna-Hästberg Sweden
145 □3 Tuna, Pta pt Puerto Rico
159 □3 Tunapuna Trinidad and Tobago
158 C2 Tunas de Zaza Cuba
173 F3 Tunas, L. l. Argentina
39 C4 Tunb al Kubrā i. Iran
39 C4 Ṭunb aṣ Ṣughrā i. Iran
63 G3 Tunbridge Wells, Royal England U.K.
42 D2 Tunceli Turkey
33 E5 Tunchang China
13 H3 Tuncurry New South Wales Australia
119 E4 Tundubai well Sudan
123 F4 Tundun-Wada Nigeria
127 C7 Tunduru Tanzania
112 F3 Tundzha r. Bulgaria
170 B3 Tunel la Cumbre tunnel Chile
123 F5 Tunga Nigeria
38 B3 Tungabhadra r. India
38 A3 Tungabhadra Reservoir resr India
37 H3 Tunga Pass India
126 B2 Tungaru Sudan
23 B5 Tungawan Philippines
27 □ Tung Chung Wan b. Hong Kong
56 M6 Tungnaá r. Iceland
136 D2 Tungsten N.W.T. Canada
6 □5 Tungua i. Tonga
45 L3 Tunguska, Nizh. r. Rus. Fed.
27 □ Tung Wan b. Hong Kong
178 □2 Tunheim Bjørnøya Arctic Ocean
36 B4 Tuni r. India
38 C2 Tuni India
87 H4 Tuningen Germany
140 E2 Tunis Ontario Canada
121 G1 Tunis Tunisia
121 G1 Tunis, Golfe de g. Tunisia
116 E2 Tunisia country Africa
162 C2 Tunja Colombia
30 B2 Tunka Rus. Fed.
30 B2 Tunkinskiye Gol'tsy mountain range Rus. Fed.
30 E5 Tunliu China
93 C6 Tunnel de Bielsa tunnel France/Spain
Tunnel du Fréjus see Fréjus Tunnel
Tunnel du Mont Blanc see Mont Blanc Tunnel
59 F2 Tunnerstad Sweden
58 C1 Tunnhovdfjorden l. Norway
56 D2 Tunnsjøen l. Norway
55 C4 Tunø i. Denmark
52 E1 Tunoshna Rus. Fed.
63 H2 Tunstall England U.K.
56 H2 Tuntsa Finland
56 H2 Tuntsayoki r. Rus. Fed.
139 H2 Tunungayualok Island i. Newfoundland Canada
172 D2 Tunuyán r. Argentina
172 C2 Tunuyán Argentina
Tunxi see Huangshan
33 G1 Tuo r. China
32 D2 Tuo r. China
31 G5 Tuoji Dao i. China
25 D5 Tuŏl Khpos Cambodia
154 B3 Tuolumne California U.S.A.
154 C3 Tuolumne Meadows California U.S.A.
32 D3 Tuoniang r. China
32 D2 Tuotuo r. China
37 H2 Tuotuoyan China
168 C4 Tupã Brazil
168 D3 Tupaciguara Brazil
Tupai i. see Motu Iti
173 K2 Tupambaé Uruguay
167 B6 Tupanciretã Brazil
151 F5 Tupelo Mississippi U.S.A.
163 F4 Tupinambarama, Ilha i. Brazil
168 C4 Tupi Paulista Brazil
166 C2 Tupiratins Brazil
54 F2 Tupitsyno Rus. Fed.
164 C4 Tupiza Bolivia
76 C4 Tuplice Poland
147 F2 Tupper Lake l. New York U.S.A.
147 F2 Tupper Lake New York U.S.A.
170 C3 Tupungato volcano Argentina
172 C2 Tupungato Argentina
172 C2 Tupungato, Co volcano Argentina
42 F4 Tuqayyid well Iraq
31 G3 Tuquan China
162 B3 Túquerres Colombia
33 E5 Tuqu Wan China
37 G4 Tura India
45 M3 Tura Rus. Fed.
119 H3 Turabah Saudi Arabia
8 E4 Turakina New Zealand
9 E4 Turakirae Head headland New Zealand
39 D2 Turan Iran
30 B2 Turan Rus. Fed.
31 J2 Turana, Khrebet mountain range Rus. Fed.
8 E3 Turangi New Zealand
46 E5 Turanskaya Nizmennost plain Asia
76 G5 Turawa Poland
119 G1 Turayf Saudi Arabia
54 D2 Turba Estonia
162 B1 Turbaco Colombia
77 J6 Turbacz mt. Poland
126 D1 Turbah Yemen
39 E4 Turbat Pakistan
83 D1 Turbenthal Switzerland
53 C2 Turbiv Ukraine
162 B2 Turbo Colombia
80 E3 Türchlwand mt. Austria
98 E2 Turcia Spain
79 H3 Turčianske Teplice Slovakia
87 G4 Turckheim France
112 G2 Turcoaia Romania
112 D1 Turda Romania
52 C3 Turdey Rus. Fed.
90 C3 Turdine r. France
17 B4 Turee Cr. r. Western Australia Australia
99 F3 Turégano Spain
76 G3 Turek Poland
54 D1 Turenki Finland
Turfan see Turpan
46 F3 Turgay r. Kazakhstan
46 F3 Turgay Kazakhstan
47 G2 Turgay div. Kazakhstan
47 H2 Turgay Kazakhstan
46 F3 Turgayskaya Dolina v. Kazakhstan
46 F2 Turgayskaya Stolovaya Strana reg. Kazakhstan
52 E2 Turgenevo Rus. Fed.
141 F2 Turgeon, Lac l. Québec Canada
112 F3 Tŭrgovishte Bulgaria
46 F1 Turgoyak Rus. Fed.
42 A2 Turgutlu Turkey
113 F6 Turgutreis Turkey
42 D1 Turhal Turkey
164 C4 Turi Chile
54 D2 Türi Estonia
111 G2 Turi Italy
103 C5 Turia r. Spain
166 C1 Turiaçu r. Brazil
166 C1 Turiaçu Brazil
Turin see Torino
44 H4 Turinsk Rus. Fed.
103 C5 Turís Spain
53 A1 Turiya r. Ukraine
31 J3 Turiy Rog Rus. Fed.
53 A1 Turiys'k Ukraine
26 J1 Turka Rus. Fed.
77 M6 Turka Ukraine
126 C4 Turkana, Lake salt lake Ethiopia/Kenya
113 F4 Türkeli Adası i. Turkey
80 C2 Türkenfeld Germany
47 G4 Turkestan Kazakhstan
47 G5 Turkestan Range mountain range Tajikistan
79 K4 Túrkeve Hungary
18 E6 Turkey country Asia
148 B4 Turkey r. Iowa U.S.A.
16 E3 Turkey Creek Western Australia Australia
75 F4 Türkheim Germany
52 F4 Turki Rus. Fed.
42 B2 Türkmen Daği mt. Turkey
18 G6 Turkmenistan country Asia
39 E1 Turkmen-Kala Turkmenistan
46 D5 Turkmenskiy Zaliv b. Turkmenistan
42 D2 Türkoğlu Turkey
133 L8 Turks and Caicos Islands territory Caribbean
159 E2 Turks I. Pass. chan. Turks and Caicos Is Caribbean
159 E2 Turks Is is Turks and Caicos Is Caribbean
59 J1 Turku r. Finland
57 F3 Turku Finland
54 B1 Turku-Pori div. Finland
126 C4 Turkwel r. Kenya
154 B3 Turlock California U.S.A.
154 B3 Turlock L. l. California U.S.A.
169 G2 Turmalina Brazil
119 H2 Turmus, W. at watercourse Saudi Arabia
8 F4 Turnagain, Cape c. New Zealand
79 K3 Turňa nad Bodvou Slovakia
81 G3 Turnau Austria
66 D5 Turnberry Scotland U.K.
155 G5 Turnbull, Mt mt. Arizona U.S.A.
157 J5 Turneffe Is is Belize
16 B4 Turner r. Western Australia Australia
149 F3 Turner Michigan U.S.A.
69 C3 Turnhout div. Antwerpen Belgium
69 C3 Turnhout Belgium
81 G3 Türnitz Austria
137 H3 Turnor Lake l. Saskatchewan Canada
78 E1 Turnov Czech Rep.
112 E3 Turnu Măgurele Romania
47 L2 Turochak Rus. Fed.
13 G3 Turon r. New South Wales Australia
101 F4 Turón r. Spain
77 L4 Turów Poland
26 E3 Turpan China
26 E3 Turpan Pendi depression China
158 C3 Turquino mt. Cuba
108 A5 Turri Sardegna Italy
66 F3 Turriff Scotland U.K.
42 F3 Tursāq Iraq
109 J4 Tursi Italy
77 N4 Turs'kyy Kanal canal Ukraine
46 F4 Turtkul' Uzbekistan
148 B2 Turtle Flambeau Flowage resr Wisconsin U.S.A.
137 H4 Turtleford Saskatchewan Canada
15 H3 Turtle I. i. Coral Sea Islands Terr. Pacific Ocean
23 A5 Turtle Islands is Philippines
122 B5 Turtle Islands is Sierra Leone
148 A3 Turtle Lake Wisconsin U.S.A.
47 J4 Turugart Pass pass China/Kyrgyzstan
44 K3 Turukhansk Rus. Fed.
163 F3 Turuna r. Brazil
30 C1 Turuntayevo Rus. Fed.
168 C2 Turvo r. Brazil
167 B6 Turvo r. Brazil
167 C6 Turvo Brazil
77 N5 Turynka Ukraine
77 J2 Turza Wielka Poland
110 D5 Tusa r. Sicilia Italy
110 D5 Tusa Sicilia Italy
155 F4 Tusayan Arizona U.S.A.
145 C5 Tuscaloosa Alabama U.S.A.
108 D2 Tuscania Italy
146 C4 Tuscarawas r. Ohio U.S.A.
146 E4 Tuscarora Mts h. Pennsylvania U.S.A.
148 C6 Tuscola Illinois U.S.A.
151 D5 Tuscola Texas U.S.A.
39 D2 Tusharīk Iran
52 C4 Tuskar' r. Rus. Fed.
145 C5 Tuskegee Alabama U.S.A.
80 B2 Tussenhausen Germany
146 D4 Tussey Mts h. Pennsylvania U.S.A.
77 H4 Tuszyn Poland
39 D3 Tūtak Iran
42 E2 Tutak Turkey
52 D1 Tutayev Rus. Fed.
62 E2 Tutbury England U.K.
38 B4 Tuticorin India
166 D1 Tutóia Brazil
112 F2 Tutrakan Bulgaria
150 D4 Tuttle Creek Res. resr Kansas U.S.A.
74 D5 Tuttlingen Germany
135 Q2 Tuttut Nunaat reg. Greenland
7 □13 Tutuila i. American Samoa Pacific Ocean
128 D3 Tutume Botswana
157 F5 Tututepec Mexico
75 G5 Tutzing Germany
30 C2 Tuul Gol r. Mongolia
54 D1 Tuulos Finland
31 H4 Tuun, Mt mt. North Korea
56 H3 Tuupovaara Finland
56 H3 Tuusniemi Finland
54 D1 Tuusula Finland
7 □16 Tuutapu h. Easter I. Chile
30 A2 Tuva div. Rus. Fed.
4 J5 Tuvalu country Pacific Ocean
6 □7 Tuvuca i. Fiji
6 □8 Tuvutau h. Fiji
22 D1 Tuwau r. Indonesia
43 D4 Tuweiyil esh Shiqāq mt. Jordan
80 C3 Tuxer Gebirge mountain range Austria
63 F1 Tuxford England U.K.
156 E5 Tuxpan Jalisco Mexico
157 F4 Tuxpan Veracruz Mexico
157 G5 Tuxtla Gutiérrez Mexico
25 D4 Tuy Đưc Vietnam
24 D2 Tuyên Quang Vietnam
25 E4 Tuy Hoa Vietnam
46 D2 Tuymazy Rus. Fed.
39 B2 Tūysarkān Iran
42 C2 Tuz Gölü salt lake Turkey
50 H3 Tuzha Rus. Fed.
112 B3 Tuzi Yugoslavia
155 F4 Tuzigoot National Monument nat. park Arizona U.S.A.
42 F3 Tuz Khurmātū Iraq
Tuz, L. salt lake see Tuz Gölü
42 E2 Tuzla r. Turkey
43 C1 Tuzla Adana Turkey
104 G3 Tuzla Bos.-Herz.
112 G3 Tuzla Romania
51 F6 Tuzlov r. Rus. Fed.
81 H4 Tužno Croatia
118 C3 Tuzugu well Libya
59 E3 Tvååker Sweden
81 H1 Tvarožná Czech Rep.
58 C2 Tvedestrand Norway
58 C2 Tveit Norway
58 A1 Tveitakvitingen mt. Norway
52 B1 Tver' div. Rus. Fed.
52 B1 Tver' Rus. Fed.
55 C2 Tversted Denmark
52 B1 Tvertsa r. Rus. Fed.
55 □1 Tvøroyri Faeroes
112 E3 Tvŭrditsa Bulgaria
76 F4 Twardogóra Poland
66 E1 Twatt Scotland U.K.
65 F2 Tweed r. England/Scotland U.K.
141 G4 Tweed Ontario Canada
65 E2 Tweeddale v. Scotland U.K.
68 E2 Tweede Exloërmond Netherlands
65 F2 Tweedmouth England U.K.
65 E2 Tweedsmuir Scotland U.K.
136 D4 Tweedsmuir Prov. Park res. B.C. Canada
131 G3 Tweeling South Africa
130 B2 Twee Rivier Namibia
130 C3 Twee Rivierene South Africa
131 F4 Tweespruit South Africa
68 E2 Twello Netherlands
68 E2 Twente reg. Netherlands
68 E2 Twentekanaal canal Netherlands
154 D4 Twentynine Palms California U.S.A.
139 K4 Twillingate Newfoundland Canada
152 D2 Twin Bridges Montana U.S.A.
151 C6 Twin Buttes Res. resr Texas U.S.A.
152 D3 Twin Falls Idaho U.S.A.
139 H3 Twin Falls Newfoundland Canada
16 D4 Twin Heads h. Western Australia Australia
136 F3 Twin Lakes Alberta Canada
147 H2 Twin Mountain New Hampshire U.S.A.
146 C6 Twin Oaks N. Carolina U.S.A.
154 B2 Twin Peak summit California U.S.A.
12 C2 Twins, The S. Australia Australia
72 C3 Twist Germany
72 D3 Twistringen Germany
13 G4 Twofold B. b. New South Wales Australia
155 G4 Two Guns Arizona U.S.A.
148 B2 Two Harbors Minnesota U.S.A.
137 G4 Two Hills Alberta Canada
152 D1 Two Medicine r. Montana U.S.A.
148 D3 Two Rivers Wisconsin U.S.A.
76 G5 Tworóg Poland
63 F3 Twyford England U.K.
77 D1 Tyachiv Ukraine
37 H5 Tyao r. India
53 E2 Tyasmyn r. Ukraine
28 L1 Tyatya mt. Rus. Fed.
76 E2 Tychówko Poland
76 E2 Tychowo Poland
77 L6 Tyczyn Poland
56 C3 Tydal Norway
59 F1 Tyfors Sweden
146 D5 Tygart Lake l. W. Virginia U.S.A.
146 D5 Tygart Valley v. W. Virginia U.S.A.
31 H1 Tygda Rus. Fed.
58 C1 Tyin l. Norway
58 C1 Tyinkrysset Norway
113 F4 Tykhero Greece
53 E1 Tykhonovychi Ukraine
77 K6 Tylawa Poland
151 E5 Tyler Texas U.S.A.
151 F6 Tylertown Mississippi U.S.A.
145 B6 Tylertown Mississippi U.S.A.
53 D3 Tylihul r. Ukraine
59 G2 Tyllinge Sweden
55 B2 Tylstrup Denmark
53 E2 Tymchenky Ukraine
114 B2 Tymfi mts Greece
53 F3 Tymoshivka Ukraine
115 F7 Tympaki Greece
45 O4 Tynda Rus. Fed.
136 A2 Tyndall Gl. gl. Alaska U.S.A.
66 D4 Tyndrum Scotland U.K.
66 F5 Tyne r. Scotland U.K.
65 G3 Tyne and Wear div. England U.K.
75 L2 Týnec nad Labem Czech Rep.
78 D2 Týnec nad Sázavou Czech Rep.
65 G2 Tynemouth England U.K.
59 E1 Tyngsjö Sweden
53 D2 Tynivka Ukraine
78 D2 Týn nad Vltavou Czech Rep.
53 B1 Tynne Ukraine
57 C3 Tynset Norway
77 L6 Tyrawa Wołoska Poland
Tyre see Sour
13 E3 Tyrell, L. l. Victoria Australia
137 H2 Tyrell Lake l. N.W.T. Canada
59 H2 Tyresö Sweden
58 D1 Tyrifjorden l. Norway
58 D1 Tyristrand Norway
80 D2 Tyrlaching Germany
31 J2 Tyrma r. Rus. Fed.
31 K2 Tyrma Rus. Fed.
56 G2 Tyrnävä Finland
114 D3 Tyrnavos Greece
52 D2 Tyrnovo Rus. Fed.
Tyrol div. see Tirol
67 D2 Tyrone div. Northern Ireland U.K.
146 D4 Tyrone Pennsylvania U.S.A.
13 E3 Tyrrell r. Victoria Australia
13 E3 Tyrrell, L. l. Victoria Australia
108 C4 Tyrrhenian Sea sea Italy
112 D1 Tysa r. Romania/Ukraine
53 D2 Tyshkivka Ukraine
53 A2 Tysmenytsya Ukraine
58 B2 Tysnesøy i. Norway
58 A1 Tysse Norway
58 A1 Tyssebotnen Norway
58 B1 Tyssedal Norway
59 G2 Tystberga Sweden
55 D4 Tystrup Sø l. Denmark
77 M5 Tyszowce Poland
45 Q3 Tyubelyakh Rus. Fed.
47 H1 Tyukalinsk Rus. Fed.
46 D4 Tyulen'i, O-va i. Kazakhstan
46 E2 Tyul'gan Rus. Fed.
47 G1 Tyumen' Rus. Fed.
44 H4 Tyumen' Rus. Fed.
47 G4 Tyumen'-Aryk Kazakhstan
47 K2 Tyumentsevo Rus. Fed.
45 N3 Tyung r. Rus. Fed.
Tyuratam see Leninsk
56 J1 Tyuva-Guba Rus. Fed.
53 C2 Tyvriv Ukraine
73 K2 Tywa r. Poland
62 B3 Tywi r. Wales U.K.
62 B2 Tywyn Wales U.K.
68 E1 't Zandt Netherlands
131 H1 Tzaneen South Africa
131 H1 Tzaneen Dam dam South Africa
68 D1 Tzummarum Netherlands

U

163 E3 Uacauyén Venezuela
7 □12 Uafato Western Samoa
125 D7 Uamanda Angola
163 D4 Uarini Brazil
163 F4 Uatumã r. Brazil
166 E2 Uauá Brazil
162 D3 Uaupés r. Brazil
162 D4 Uaupés Brazil
157 H5 Uaxactún Guatemala
112 C2 Ub Yugoslavia
47 K2 Uba r. Kazakhstan
169 G4 Ubá Brazil
123 G4 Uba Nigeria
69 E4 Übach-Palenberg Germany
47 F2 Ubagan r. Kazakhstan
169 F2 Ubaí Brazil
118 E5 Ubaid well Sudan
166 E3 Ubaitaba Brazil
46 E4 Ubal Karabaur h. Uzbekistan
124 C3 Ubangi r. Central African Rep./Zaire
53 C1 Ubarts r. Belarus
162 C2 Ubate Colombia
169 F5 Ubatuba Brazil
126 D2 Ubaydīyah Yemen
91 E4 Ubaye r. France
42 E4 Ubayyia, Wādī al watercourse Iraq/Saudi Arabia
42 E3 Ubayyid, Wādī al watercourse Iraq
55 D4 Ubby Denmark
28 C7 Ube Japan
101 G2 Úbeda Spain
168 D3 Uberaba r. Brazil
168 E3 Uberaba Brazil
165 E3 Uberaba, Lagoa l. Brazil
168 D3 Uberlândia Brazil
75 G5 Überlingen Germany
83 E1 Überlinger See l. Germany
75 H5 Übersee Germany
25 □ Ubin, Pulau i. Singapore
47 J1 Ubinskoye Rus. Fed.
47 K1 Ubinskoye, Ozero l. Rus. Fed.
168 B6 Ubiratã Brazil
24 C3 Ubolratna Res. resr Thailand
131 J3 Ubombo South Africa
25 D4 Ubon Ratchathani Thailand
53 B1 Ubort' r. Ukraine
101 E4 Ubrique Spain
74 D3 Ubstadt-Weiher Germany
124 E4 Ubundu Zaire
172 F2 Ucacha Argentina
42 F1 Ucar Azerbaijan
43 B1 Uçarı Turkey
162 C5 Ucayali r. Peru
69 C4 Uccle Belgium
99 G3 Ucero r. Spain
39 E1 Uch-Adzhi Turkmenistan
46 E2 Uchaly Rus. Fed.
39 B1 Üchān Iran
47 K3 Ucharal Kazakhstan
28 D7 Uchiko Japan
28 C8 Uchinoura Japan
52 C1 Uchinskoye Vdkhr. resr Rus. Fed.
28 H2 Uchiura-wan b. Japan
164 A1 Uchiza Peru
46 F4 Uchkuduk Uzbekistan
39 F1 Uchkyay Uzbekistan
46 E4 Uchsay Uzbekistan
73 G3 Uchte r. Germany
72 D3 Uchte Germany
36 A4 Uchto r. Pakistan
99 F2 Ucieza r. Spain
73 K1 Ückeritz Germany
73 J2 Uckermark reg. Germany
63 G4 Uckfield England U.K.
99 H5 Uclés Spain
136 D5 Ucluelet B.C. Canada
155 H3 Ucolo Utah U.S.A.
152 F2 Ucross Wyoming U.S.A.
30 D1 Uda r. Rus. Fed.
53 G2 Uda r. Ukraine
46 C3 Udachnoye Rus. Fed.
45 N3 Udachnyy Rus. Fed.
38 B4 Udagamandalam India
36 C4 Udaipur India
37 G5 Udaipur India
36 D5 Udaipura India
37 F4 Udaipur Garhi Nepal
37 H4 Udalguri India
37 E5 Udanti r. India/Myanmar
173 H4 Udaquiola Argentina
79 M2 Udava r. Slovakia
53 E1 Uday r. Ukraine
38 B3 Udayagiri India
59 E1 Uddeholm Sweden
58 D2 Uddevalla Sweden
66 D5 Uddingston Scotland U.K.
64 E2 Uddington Scotland U.K.
56 E2 Uddjaure l. Sweden
68 D3 Uden Netherlands
38 B2 Udgir India
36 C2 Udhampur India
50 H2 Udimskiy Rus. Fed.
107 H2 Udine div. Friuli - Venezia Giulia Italy
107 H2 Udine Udine Italy
139 J2 Udjuktok Bay b. Newfoundland Canada
50 E3 Udomlya Rus. Fed.
24 C3 Udon Thani Thailand
76 F1 Udorpie Poland
45 P4 Udskaya Guba b. Rus. Fed.
38 B4 Udumalaippetai India
38 A3 Udupi India
6 □6 Udu Pt pt Fiji
53 G1 Udy Ukraine
45 P4 Udyl', Ozero l. Rus. Fed.
Udzhary see Ucar
73 J2 Uecker r. Germany
73 K2 Ueckermünde Germany
29 G5 Ueda Japan
22 E2 Uekuli Indonesia
124 D3 Uele r. Zaire
134 B3 Uelen Rus. Fed.
134 A3 Uel'kal Rus. Fed.
68 E2 Uelsen Germany
73 F3 Uelzen Germany
131 J2 Uembje, Lagoa l. Mozambique
29 F6 Ueno Japan
124 E3 Uere r. Zaire
82 C2 Uetendorf Switzerland
72 E2 Uetersen Germany
74 E3 Uettingen Germany
72 F3 Uetze Germany
46 E1 Ufa r. Rus. Fed.
46 E2 Ufa Rus. Fed.
126 B2 Uffat r. Sudan
74 F3 Uffenheim Germany
75 G5 Uffing am Staffelsee Germany
128 B3 Ugab watercourse Namibia
54 C3 Ugāle Latvia
127 B6 Ugalla r. Tanzania
127 B6 Ugalla River Game Reserve res. Tanzania
117 H5 Uganda country Africa
172 C2 Ugarteche Argentina
30 E1 Ugdan Rus. Fed.
55 B5 Uge Denmark
111 H3 Ugento Italy
58 A1 Uggdal Norway
55 C2 Uggerby r. Denmark
111 H2 Uggiano la Chiesa Italy
123 F5 Ughelli Nigeria
131 G5 Ugie South Africa
101 G4 Ugíjar Spain
90 E3 Ugine France
27 Q2 Uglegorsk Rus. Fed.
52 D1 Uglich Rus. Fed.
104 E3 Ugljan i. Croatia
31 J2 Uglovoye Rus. Fed.
47 K2 Uglovskoye Rus. Fed.
45 Q3 Ugol'naya Zyryanka Rus. Fed.
45 T3 Ugol'nyye Kopi Rus. Fed.
52 B2 Ugra r. Rus. Fed.
52 B2 Ugra Rus. Fed.
79 M3 Uh r. Slovakia
79 G2 Uherské Brod Czech Rep.
78 G2 Uherské Hradiště Czech Rep.
74 E4 Uhingen Germany
78 C2 Úhlava r. Czech Rep.
74 E5 Uhldingen Germany
130 A1 Uhlenhorst Namibia
75 L3 Uhlířské Janovice Czech Rep.
77 M5 Uhniv Ukraine
146 C4 Uhrichsville Ohio U.S.A.
53 F1 Uhroyidy Ukraine
73 K4 Uhyst Germany
106 B3 Uia di Ciamarella mt. Italy
Uibhist a' Deas i. see South Uist
Uibhist a' Tuath i. see North Uist
66 B3 Uig Scotland U.K.
125 C5 Uíge div. Angola
125 C5 Uíge Angola
6 □5 'Uiha i. Tonga
31 H5 Ŭijŏngbu South Korea
31 H4 Ŭiju North Korea
46 E3 Uil r. Kazakhstan
46 D3 Uil Kazakhstan
51 G7 Uilpata mt. Rus. Fed.
56 H3 Uimaharju Finland
155 F3 Uinkaret Plateau plat. Arizona U.S.A.
142 D3 Uinta Mts mts Utah U.S.A.
28 B6 Ŭiryŏng South Korea
128 A3 Uis Mine Namibia
31 J5 Ŭisŏng South Korea
131 E6 Uitenhage South Africa
68 C2 Uithoorn Netherlands
68 E1 Uithuizen Netherlands
139 H2 Uivak, Cape headland Newfoundland Canada
76 G5 Ujazd Poland
79 L4 Újfehértó Hungary
36 D4 Ujhani India
29 E6 Uji Japan
28 B8 Uji-guntō is Japan
127 A5 Ujiji Tanzania
36 C5 Ujjain India
78 F4 Újkér Hungary
76 E2 Ujście Poland
79 K4 Újszász Hungary
78 F5 Újudvar Hungary
22 D3 Ujung Pandang Indonesia
29 □2 Uka Japan
123 F4 Ukata Nigeria
127 B5 Ukerewe I. i. Tanzania
119 H4 Ukhdūd Saudi Arabia
52 E3 Ukholovo Rus. Fed.
77 N4 Ukhovets'k Ukraine
37 H4 Ukhrul India
50 K2 Ukhta Rus. Fed.
52 E1 Ukhtokhma r. Rus. Fed.
54 F4 Ukhvala Belarus
154 A2 Ukiah California U.S.A.
152 C2 Ukiah Oregon U.S.A.
135 N2 Ukkusissat Greenland
76 D2 Ukleja r. Poland
54 D4 Ukmergė Lithuania
49 H4 Ukraine country Europe
53 D1 Ukrayinka Ukraine
79 M3 Ukraynis'ki Karpaty mountain range Ukraine
104 F3 Ukrina r. Bos.-Herz.
50 J2 Uktym Rus. Fed.
125 B6 Uku Angola
28 B7 Uku-jima i. Japan
128 C3 Ukwi Pan salt pan Botswana
36 D2 Ul r. India
54 F4 Ula r. Belarus
54 F4 Ula Belarus
113 G6 Ula Turkey
30 C3 Ulaanbaatar Mongolia
30 D3 Ulaan-Ereg Mongolia
26 F2 Ulaangom Mongolia
30 C3 Ulaanhudag Mongolia
30 B3 Ulaan Nuur l. Mongolia
30 D3 Ulaan-Uul Mongolia
53 C2 Uladivka Ukraine
13 G3 Ulan New South Wales Australia
34 J3 Ulan China
Ulan Bator see Ulaanbaatar
47 H4 Ulanbel' Kazakhstan
30 C4 Ulan Buh Shamo desert China
30 C1 Ulan-Burgasy, Khr. mountain range Rus. Fed.
51 H6 Ulan Erge Rus. Fed.
Ulanhad see Chifeng
Ulanhot see Horqin Youyi
53 C2 Ulaniv Ukraine
77 L4 Ulan-Majorat Poland
52 B4 Ulanove Rus. Fed.
30 D4 Ulansuhai Nur l. China
30 B4 Ulan Tohoi China
30 C2 Ulan-Ude Rus. Fed.
37 G2 Ulan Ul Hu l. China
172 D1 Ulapes Argentina
42 D2 Ulaş Sivas Turkey
113 F4 Ulaş Tekirdağ Turkey
108 A4 Ula Tirso Sardegna Italy
6 □1 Ulawa I. i. Solomon Is.
47 K2 Ul'ba Kazakhstan
55 B3 Ulbjerg Denmark
66 E2 Ulbster Scotland U.K.
31 J5 Ulchin South Korea
112 B4 Ulcinj Yugoslavia
130 E4 Ulco South Africa
30 D2 Uldz r. Mongolia
30 D2 Uldz Mongolia
58 C2 Ulefoss Norway
54 E2 Ulenurme Estonia
30 E2 Ulety Rus. Fed.
55 A3 Ulfborg Denmark
68 E3 Ulft Netherlands
31 F3 Ulgain Gol r. China
47 G2 Ul'gili Kazakhstan
38 A2 Ulhasnagar India
30 A3 Uliastay Mongolia
79 M3 Ulič Slovakia
124 E4 Ulindi r. Zaire
21 L4 Ulithi i. Fed. States of Micronesia
46 F3 Ul'kayak r. Kazakhstan
98 B2 Ulla r. Spain
13 G3 Ulladulla New South Wales Australia
66 C3 Ullapool Scotland U.K.
59 E3 Ullared Sweden
56 F3 Ullava Finland
102 D4 Ulldecona Spain
55 C4 Ullerslev Denmark
99 H2 Ullívarri, Emb. de resr Spain
65 F3 Ullswater l. England U.K.
31 J5 Ullŭng South Korea
31 J5 Ullŭng do i. South Korea
74 E4 Ulm Germany
31 J2 Ul'ma r. Rus. Fed.
13 H2 Ulmarra New South Wales Australia
100 B1 Ulme r. Portugal
74 B2 Ulmen Germany
112 F2 Ulmeni Călărași Romania
112 D1 Ulmeni Maramureș Romania
104 G4 Ulog Bos.-Herz.
129 E1 Ulongue Mozambique
12 D1 Uloowaranie, L. salt flat S. Australia Australia
59 E3 Ulricehamn Sweden
81 E2 Ulrichsberg Austria
59 F2 Ulrika Sweden
68 E1 Ulrum Netherlands
31 J6 Ulsan South Korea
56 C3 Ulsberg Norway
66 □2 Ulsta Scotland U.K.
67 C2 Ulster div. Rep. of Ireland/U.K.
67 D2 Ulster Canal canal Rep. of Ireland/U.K.
55 C4 Ulstrup Vestsjælland Denmark
55 B3 Ulstrup Viborg Denmark
13 E3 Ultima Victoria Australia
113 G4 Ulubat Gölü l. Turkey
42 B2 Uluborlu Turkey
42 B1 Uludağ mt. Turkey
47 H5 Uluggat China
6 □6 Uluiqalau mt. Fiji
25 C7 Ulu Kali, Gunung mt. Malaysia
42 C2 Ulukışla Turkey
131 H4 Ulundi South Africa
47 L3 Ulungur Hu l. China
25 □ Ulu Pandan Singapore
Uluru h. see Ayers Rock
14 B5 Uluru Nat. Park nat. park Northern Terr. Australia
51 E7 Ulus Turkey
66 B4 Ulva i. Scotland U.K.
Ulvéah i. see Lopévi
65 E3 Ulverston England U.K.
13 F5 Ulverstone Tasmania Australia
59 F2 Ulvettern l. Sweden
58 B1 Ulvik Norway
56 D3 Ulvsjön Sweden
52 C1 Ul'yanikha Rus. Fed.
50 H4 Ul'yankovo Rus. Fed.
53 D2 Ul'yanovka Ukraine
52 B3 Ul'yanovo Rus. Fed.
52 H3 Ul'yanovsk div. Rus. Fed.
Ul'yanovsk see Simbirsk
47 H2 Ul'yanovskiy Kazakhstan
31 F2 Ulyatuy Rus. Fed.
151 C4 Ulysses Kansas U.S.A.
47 G3 Ulytau Kazakhstan
47 G3 Ulyzhilanshik r. Kazakhstan
31 G1 Uma Rus. Fed.
107 H3 Umag Croatia
157 H4 Umán Mexico
53 D2 Uman' Ukraine
170 C2 Umango, Co mt. Argentina
36 A3 Umarao Pakistan
36 E5 Umaria India
38 B2 Umarkhed India
38 C2 Umarkot India
36 B4 Umarkot Pakistan
23 □2 Umatac Guam Pacific Ocean
152 C2 Umatilla Oregon U.S.A.
50 E1 Umba Rus. Fed.
131 H2 Umbabat Game Reserve res. South Africa
147 H2 Umbagog Lake l. New Hampshire U.S.A.
124 D2 Umbelasha watercourse Sudan
62 C4 Umberleigh England U.K.
107 G5 Umbertide Italy
6 □1 Umboi i. P.N.G.
9 B6 Umbrella Mts mts New Zealand
159 □1 Umbrella Pt pt Jamaica
109 E2 Umbria div. Italy
111 F3 Umbriatico Italy
129 D2 Ume r. Zimbabwe
56 F3 Umeå Sweden
56 D2 Umeälven r. Sweden
43 C3 Um ed Daraj, J. mt. Jordan
52 F3 Umet Rus. Fed.
52 F2 Umet Rus. Fed.
131 J4 Umfolozi r. South Africa
131 H4 Umfolozi Game Reserve res. South Africa
131 H4 Umgeni r. South Africa
80 B3 Umhausen Austria
131 H4 Umhlanga South Africa
98 B2 Umia r. Spain
136 H3 Umingmaktok N.W.T. Canada
138 E2 Umiujaq Québec Canada
131 H5 Umkomaas r. South Africa
131 H5 Umkomaas South Africa
131 H4 Umlazi South Africa
119 G3 Umm al Birak Saudi Arabia
39 C4 Umm al Qaywayn U.A.E.
73 J1 Ummanz i. Germany
119 H2 Umm at Qalbān Saudi Arabia
39 B4 Umm Bāb Qatar
119 E5 Umm Bel Sudan
43 B5 Umm Bugma Egypt
80 A2 Ummendorf Germany
118 C2 Umm Farud Libya
119 F3 Umm Gerifat waterhole Sudan
119 E5 Umm Keddada Sudan
119 G2 Umm Lajj Saudi Arabia
43 C5 Umm Mafrūd, G. mt. Egypt
43 C5 Umm Nukhaylah well Saudi Arabia
42 F4 Umm Qasr Iraq
119 E4 Umm Qurein well Sudan
119 F5 Umm Rimtha well Sudan
119 F5 Umm Ruwaba Sudan
118 E1 Umm Sa'ad Libya
119 F5 Umm Saiyala Sudan
43 D5 Umm Shajtiya waterhole Saudi Arabia
43 B5 Umm Shomar, G. mt. Egypt
119 E4 Umm Sunaita well Sudan
43 B5 Umm Tināṣṣib, G. mt. Egypt
119 G2 Umm Urūmah i. Saudi Arabia
43 B5 Umm Zanatir mt. Egypt
132 B4 Umnak I. i. Alaska U.S.A.
129 F1 Umpilua Mozambique
152 A3 Umpqua r. Oregon U.S.A.
125 C6 Umpulo Angola
36 D5 Umred India
38 A1 Umreth India
131 G5 Umtamvuna r. South Africa
131 G5 Umtata r. South Africa
131 G5 Umtata South Africa
131 G5 Umtata Dam resr South Africa

V

98 B3 Valongo Portugal
101 G4 Válor Spain
99 F3 Valoria la Buena Spain
54 E4 Valozhyn Belarus
98 C3 Valpacos Portugal
102 C2 Valpalmas Spain
141 F2 Val-Paradis *Québec* Canada
172 B2 Valparaíso div. Chile
148 D5 Valparaiso *Indiana* U.S.A.
168 C4 Valparaíso Brazil
172 B2 Valparaíso Chile
156 E4 Valparaíso Mexico
106 B3 Valpelline v. Italy
82 C3 Valpelline Italy
104 G3 Valpovo Croatia
107 F2 Val Pusteria v. Italy
91 C4 Valréas France
101 F1 Valronquillo mt. Spain
131 F3 Vals r. South Africa
83 E2 Vals Switzerland
36 C5 Valsād India
82 C3 Valsavarenche v. Italy
106 B3 Valsavarenche Italy
99 F3 Valseca Spain
83 F2 Val Senales v. Italy
90 D2 Valserine r. France
109 J4 Valsinni Italy
112 C2 Valška Yugoslavia
91 C4 Vals-les-Bains France
130 E3 Valspan South Africa
131 G4 Valsrivier South Africa
107 F3 Valstagna Italy
21 L8 Vals, Tg c. Indonesia
107 E2 Valsura r. Italy
90 C1 Val-Suzon France
50 H1 Val'tevo Rus. Fed.
81 H2 Valtice Czech Rep.
97 G3 Valtiendas Spain
102 B2 Valtierra Spain
56 H3 Valtimo Finland
127 □4 Valton Mauritius
114 C3 Valtou mountain range Greece
106 B3 Valtournenche Italy
6 □8 Valukoula Fiji
107 J4 Valun Croatia
52 A3 Valuyets Rus. Fed.
51 F5 Valuyki Rus. Fed.
107 E2 Val Venosta v. Italy
97 □ Valverde *Canary Is* Spain
99 H5 Valverde de Júcar Spain
100 D3 Valverde del Camino Spain
100 D2 Valverde de Leganés Spain
98 D4 Valverde del Fresno Spain
83 F3 Valvestino, Lago di l. Italy
59 F1 Våmån r. Sweden
78 F1 Vamberk Czech Rep.
25 D5 Vam Co Tay r. Vietnam
55 B4 Vamdrup Denmark
127 D7 Vamizi, Ilha i. Mozambique
57 F3 Vammala Finland
55 B3 Vammen Denmark
115 F7 Vamos Greece
79 H4 Vámosmikola Hungary
79 L4 Vámospércs Hungary
54 C1 Vampula Finland
38 C2 Vamsadhara r. India
114 E1 Vamvakofyto Greece
42 E2 Van Turkey
42 F1 Vanadzor Armenia
54 D1 Vanajavesi l. Finland
59 E1 Vanån r. Sweden
86 D4 Vanault-les-Dames France
45 M3 Vanavara Rus. Fed.
141 J3 Van Bruyssel *Québec* Canada
151 E5 Van Buren *Arkansas* U.S.A.
147 K1 Van Buren *Maine* U.S.A.
25 E4 Văn Canh Vietnam
147 K2 Vanceboro *Maine* U.S.A.
146 B5 Vanceburg *Kentucky* U.S.A.
136 E5 Vancouver *B.C.* Canada
152 B2 Vancouver *Washington* U.S.A.
17 B7 Vancouver, C. c. *Western Australia* Australia
136 D5 Vancouver Island i. *B.C.* Canada
136 B2 Vancouver, Mt mt. *Alaska/Yukon Territory* Canada/U.S.A.
8 □3 Vancouver Rock i. *Snares Is* New Zealand
144 B4 Vandalia *Illinois* U.S.A.
146 A5 Vandalia *Ohio* U.S.A.
80 A3 Vandans Austria
55 B4 Vandel Denmark
102 D3 Vandellós Spain
90 B2 Vandenesse France
131 F3 Vanderbijlpark South Africa
148 E3 Vanderbilt *Michigan* U.S.A.
146 D4 Vandergrift *Pennsylvania* U.S.A.
136 E4 Vanderhoof *B.C.* Canada
14 D2 Vanderlin I. i. *Northern Terr.* Australia
155 H4 Vanderwagen *New Mexico* U.S.A.
55 A2 Vandet Sø l. Denmark
14 B1 Van Diemen, C. c. *Northern Terr.* Australia
14 D3 Van Diemen, C. c. *Queensland* Australia
14 C1 Van Diemen Gulf b. *Northern Terr.* Australia
87 F4 Vandœuvre-lès-Nancy France
107 F2 Vandoies Italy
54 D2 Vändra Estonia
141 J3 Vandry *Québec* Canada
131 G3 Vandyksdrif South Africa
59 E2 Vänerborgsviken b. Sweden
59 E2 Vänern b. Sweden
59 E2 Vänersborg Sweden
132 J2 Vaneteze r. Mozambique
146 E3 Van Etten *New York* U.S.A.
129 H3 Vangaindrano Madagascar
54 D3 Vangaži Latvia
42 E2 Van Gölü salt lake Turkey
58 C1 Vangsmjøsi l. Norway
58 B1 Vangsvatnet l. Norway
6 □1 Vangunu i. Solomon Is.
151 B6 Van Horn *Texas* U.S.A.
141 H4 Vanier *Ontario* Canada
82 C2 Vanil Noir mt. Switzerland
6 □1 Vanimo P.N.G.
27 Q2 Vanino Rus. Fed.
38 B3 Vanivilasa Sagara resr India
38 B3 Vaniyambadi India
112 D2 Vânju Mare Romania
134 A3 Vankarem Rus. Fed.
141 H4 Vankleek Hill *Ontario* Canada
Van, L. salt lake *see* Van Gölü
56 E1 Vanna i. Norway
56 E3 Vännäs Sweden
86 C4 Vanne r. France
88 C4 Vannes France
47 H4 Vannovka Kazakhstan
107 F2 Vanoi r. Italy
91 E3 Vanoise, Parc National de la nat. park France
131 G4 Van Reenen South Africa
130 B5 Vanrhynsdorp South Africa
130 B5 Vanrhyns Pass pass South Africa
15 E3 Vanrook *Queensland* Australia
15 E3 Vanrook Cr. r. *Queensland* Australia
59 F1 Vansbro Sweden
16 D2 Vansittart B. b. *Western Australia* Australia
135 K3 Vansittart I. i. *N.W.T.* Canada
131 F4 Vanstadensrus South Africa
57 G3 Vantaa Finland
6 □7 Vanua Balavu i. Fiji
6 □2 Vanua Lava i. Vanuatu
6 □6 Vanua Levu i. Fiji
6 □8 Vanua Levu Barrier Reef reef Fiji
4 H6 Vanuatu country Pacific Ocean
146 A4 Van Wert *Ohio* U.S.A.
130 C6 Van Wyksdorp South Africa
130 C5 Vanwyksvlei l. South Africa
130 C5 Vanwyksvlei South Africa
24 D2 Văn Yên Vietnam
130 D3 Van Zylsrus South Africa
6 □2 Vao *New Caledonia* Pacific Ocean
93 D4 Vaour France
53 C2 Vapnyarka Ukraine
91 E5 Var div. *Provence-Alpes-Côte-d'Azur* France
91 F5 Var r. France
106 D4 Vara r. Italy
54 E2 Vara Estonia
59 E2 Vara Sweden
38 A3 Varada r. India
89 D4 Varades France
91 D5 Varages France
93 D4 Varaire France
106 B4 Varaita r. Italy
54 E3 Varakļāni Latvia
122 D5 Varalé Côte d'Ivoire
106 C3 Varallo Italy
39 B2 Varāmīn Iran
37 E4 Varanasi India
56 H1 Varangerfjorden chan. Norway
56 H1 Varangerhalvøya i. Norway
106 D4 Varano de'Melegari Italy
109 H3 Varano, Lago di lag. Italy
54 E4 Varapayeva Belarus
101 F2 Varas r. Spain
78 F5 Varaždin Croatia
81 H4 Varaždinske Toplice Croatia
106 C4 Varazze Italy
59 E3 Varberg Sweden
54 C2 Varbla Estonia
91 D3 Varces France
39 B2 Varcheh Iran
115 C4 Varda Greece
38 B2 Vardannapet India
112 C4 Vardar r. Macedonia
55 A4 Varde r. Denmark
55 A4 Varde Denmark
42 F1 Vardenis Armenia
59 J1 Vårdö Finland
56 H1 Vardø Norway
114 D4 Vardousia mts Greece
52 D1 Varegovo Rus. Fed.
72 D2 Varel Germany
172 D3 Varela Argentina
77 N1 Varėna Lithuania
89 F2 Varengeville-sur-Mer France
106 D2 Varenna Italy
89 G2 Varenne r. France
141 J4 Varennes *Québec* Canada
87 E3 Varennes-en-Argonne France
90 D2 Varennes-St-Sauveur France
90 B2 Varennes-sur-Allier France
90 B1 Varennes-Vauzelles France
104 G3 Vareš Bos.-Herz.
106 C3 Varese div. *Lombardia* Italy
106 C3 Varese *Varese* Italy
83 D3 Varese, Lago di l. Italy
106 D4 Varese Ligure Italy
79 M5 Vârful Bihor mt. Romania
112 E1 Vârful Bivolu mt. Romania
112 E2 Vârful Cozia mt. Romania
53 A3 Vârful Harghita-Mădăra mt. Romania
112 C2 Vârful Leordișu mt. Romania
79 M5 Vârful Malului h. Romania
112 E2 Vârful Moldoveanu mt. Romania
79 M6 Vârful Padeșu mt. Romania
53 B3 Vârful Șandru Mare mt. Romania
79 M5 Vârful Vlădeasa mt. Romania
79 M5 Vârfurile Romania
59 E2 Vårgårda Sweden
172 C3 Vargas Argentina
166 E2 Vargem r. Brazil
169 E4 Vargem Grande do Sul Brazil
169 F4 Varginha Brazil
59 E2 Vargön Sweden
58 A2 Varhaug Norway
93 D5 Varilhes France
164 B4 Varillas Chile
59 F2 Väringen l. Sweden
44 D3 Varkaus Finland
59 E2 Varmeln l. Sweden
59 E2 Värmland div. Sweden
59 E2 Värmlandsnäs i. Sweden
112 F3 Varna div. Bulgaria
112 F3 Varna Bulgaria
80 C4 Varna Italy
46 F2 Varna Rus. Fed.
59 F3 Värnamo Sweden
59 E1 Värnäs Sweden
52 G1 Varnavino Rus. Fed.
54 C4 Varniai Lithuania
54 E2 Varnja Estonia
78 D1 Varnsdorf Czech Rep.
43 B2 Varosia Cyprus
78 F3 Varoška Rijeka Bos.-Herz.
79 G4 Városlőd Hungary
56 G3 Varpaisjärvi Finland
79 H4 Várpalota Hungary
91 E4 Vars France
39 G1 Varsaj Afghanistan
53 E3 Varska Estonia
68 E3 Varsseveld Netherlands
59 G2 Vårsta Sweden
Vartashen *see* Oğuz
54 G1 Vartemyagi Rus. Fed.
115 C5 Vartholomio Greece
42 E2 Varto Turkey
112 D2 Vârtop Romania
37 E4 Varuna r. India
53 E1 Varva Ukraine
172 B4 Varvarco Campos, L. l. Argentina
112 C3 Varvarin Yugoslavia
53 G1 Varvarivka *Kharkivs'ka Oblast'* Ukraine
53 B1 Varvarivka *Khmel'nyts'ka Oblast'* Ukraine
146 D3 Varysburg *New York* U.S.A.
39 C2 Varzaneh Iran
42 F2 Varzaqān Iran
167 B6 Várzea r. Brazil
169 F2 Várzea da Palma Brazil
169 F1 Várzelândia Brazil
106 D4 Varzi Italy
106 C2 Varzo Italy
51 F1 Varzuga Rus. Fed.
90 B1 Varzy France
78 F4 Vas div. Hungary
166 E3 Vasa Barris r. Brazil
79 M3 Vásárosnamény Hungary
100 C3 Vascão r. Portugal
79 M5 Vașcău Romania
54 D2 Vaselemma Estonia
50 H1 Vashka r. Rus. Fed.
53 A2 Vashkivtsi Ukraine
Vasht *see* Khāsh
54 B2 Vashtëmi Albania
50 H2 Vasilevo Rus. Fed.
114 B4 Vasiliki Greece
115 B5 Vasilikos Greece
77 N2 Vasilishki Belarus
115 C6 Vasilitsi Greece
52 H1 Vasil'sursk Rus. Fed.
52 B1 Vasil'yevskiy Mokh Rus. Fed.
52 G1 Vasil'yevskoye Rus. Fed.
52 F1 Vasil'yevskoye Rus. Fed.
54 E2 Vasknarva Estonia
53 C1 Vas'kovychi Ukraine
112 F1 Vaslui Romania
149 F4 Vassar *Michigan* U.S.A.
92 D3 Vassivière, Lac de l. France
59 G3 Vassmolösa Sweden
79 F4 Vas-Soproni-síkság h. Hungary
169 G5 Vassouras Brazil
89 E3 Vassy France
54 C1 Västanfjärd Finland
54 E2 Vaste-Kuuste Estonia
56 E3 Väster div. Sweden
59 G2 Västerås Sweden
56 E1 Västerdalälven r. Sweden
56 E2 Västerfjäll Sweden
59 H2 Vasterhaninge Sweden
59 G3 Västervik Sweden
59 F2 Västmanland div. Sweden
109 G2 Vasto Italy
59 F3 Västra Silen l. Sweden
54 E3 Vastseliina Estonia
78 F4 Vasvár Hungary
53 E2 Vasylivka *Kirovohrads'ka Oblast'* Ukraine
53 F1 Vasylivka *Sums'ka Oblast'* Ukraine
53 F3 Vasylivka *Zaporiz'ka Oblast'* Ukraine
53 D1 Vasyl'kiv Ukraine
53 B2 Vasyl'kivka Ukraine
53 B2 Vasyutyntsi Ukraine
79 M5 Vața de Jos Romania
89 G4 Vatan France
Vaté i. *see* Éfaté
59 H3 Väte Sweden
114 C2 Vatero Greece
66 A4 Vatersay i. *Scotland* U.K.
75 G4 Vaterstetten Germany
38 A2 Vathar India
115 D6 Vathia Greece
115 E4 Vathy Greece
114 C2 Vathylakkos Greece
6 □8 Vatia Pt pt Fiji
109 E3 Vatican City country Europe
111 E4 Vaticano, Capo c. Italy
115 □ Vatio Greece
56 M6 Vatnajökull ice cap Iceland
6 □7 Vatoa i. Fiji
114 C2 Vatolakkos Greece
129 H2 Vato Loha mt. Madagascar
129 H2 Vatomandry Madagascar
112 E1 Vatra Dornei Romania
112 E1 Vatra Moldoviței Romania
79 K4 Vatta Hungary
59 F2 Vättern l. Sweden
59 G1 Vattholma Sweden
6 □8 Vatu-i-Ra Channel chan. Fiji
6 □8 Vatu-i-Thake i. Fiji
6 □8 Vatulele i. Fiji
53 D2 Vatutine Ukraine
6 □6 Vatu Vara i. Fiji
89 E2 Vaubadon France
86 C4 Vauchassis France
90 B1 Vauclaix France
91 D4 Vaucluse div. France
91 D4 Vaucluse, Monts de mts France
90 D1 Vauconcourt-Nervezain France
87 E4 Vaucouleurs France
82 B2 Vaud div. Switzerland
153 F5 Vaughn *New Mexico* U.S.A.
90 C3 Vaulx-en-Velin France
162 C3 Vaupés r. Colombia
91 D5 Vauvenargues France
91 C5 Vauvert France
87 F5 Vauvillers France
89 F4 Vaux du Loir, Les v. France
86 B4 Vaux-le-Pénil France
92 A3 Vaux-sur-Mer France
69 D5 Vaux-sur-Sûre Belgium
129 H2 Vavatenina Madagascar
6 □3 Vava'u Group is Tonga
122 C5 Vavoua Côte d'Ivoire
38 C4 Vavuniya Sri Lanka
54 E4 Vawkalata Belarus
77 N2 Vawkavysk Belarus
77 N2 Vawkavyskaye Wzvyshsha h. Belarus
59 H2 Vaxholm Sweden
59 F3 Växjö Sweden
38 B3 Vāyalpād India
44 G2 Vaygach, O. i. Rus. Fed.
92 D4 Vayrac France
169 E2 Vazante Brazil
50 H1 Vazhgort Rus. Fed.
52 B2 Vazuza r. Rus. Fed.
52 B2 Vazuzskoye Vdkhr. resr Rus. Fed.
159 □7 V.C. Bird airport *Antigua* Caribbean
81 F2 Včelná Czech Rep.
47 K1 Vdovino Rus. Fed.
25 C4 Veal Vêng Cambodia
59 E4 Veberöd Sweden
91 B4 Vebron France
72 F3 Vechelde Germany
68 E2 Vecht r. Netherlands
72 D3 Vechta Germany
72 B3 Vechte r. Germany
98 F4 Vecinos Spain
72 E4 Veckerhagen Germany
79 J4 Vecsés Hungary
78 E2 Vectec h. Czech Rep.
54 D3 Vecumnieki Latvia
38 B4 Vedaranniyam India
59 E3 Veddige Sweden
112 E2 Vedea r. Romania
112 E3 Vedea *Giurgiu* Romania
91 C5 Vedène France
59 F2 Vedevåg Sweden
42 F2 Vedi Armenia
173 G3 Vedia Argentina
50 E2 Vedlozero Rus. Fed.
91 B3 Védrines-St-Loup France
148 D5 Veedersburg *Indiana* U.S.A.
68 E1 Veendam Netherlands
68 D2 Veenendaal Netherlands
68 D1 Veenwouden Netherlands
68 B3 Veere Netherlands
68 B3 Veerse Meer resr Netherlands
56 C2 Vega i. Norway
151 C5 Vega *Texas* U.S.A.
145 □3 Vega Baja Puerto Rico
98 D2 Vega de Espinareda Spain
98 C1 Vegadeo Spain
98 D2 Vega de Valcarce Spain
58 C2 Vegar l. Norway
98 D2 Vegarienza Spain
58 C2 Vegarshei Norway
58 C1 Veggli Norway
68 D3 Veghel Netherlands
114 C2 Vegoritis, L. l. Greece
89 E4 Vègre r. France
137 G4 Vegreville *Alberta* Canada
57 G3 Vehkalahti Finland
36 B3 Vehoa r. Pakistan
75 F2 Veilsdorf Germany
166 B1 Veiros Brazil
100 C2 Veiros Portugal
39 G4 Veirwaro Pakistan
77 M1 Veisiejis Lithuania
74 E3 Veitshöchheim Germany
108 E2 Vejano Italy
55 E3 Vejby Denmark
55 B4 Vejen Denmark
100 E4 Vejer de la Frontera Spain
55 B4 Vejle div. Denmark
55 B4 Vejle *Vejle* Denmark
55 B4 Vejle Fjord inlet Denmark
75 J3 Vejprnice Czech Rep.
75 J2 Vejprty Czech Rep.
55 D4 Vejrø i. Denmark
55 C4 Vejrø i. Denmark
55 C5 Vejsnæs Nakke pt Denmark
39 E1 Vekil'-Bazar Turkmenistan
162 C1 Vela, Cabo de la pt Colombia
99 F5 Velada Spain
104 F4 Vela Luka Croatia
38 B4 Velanai I. i. Sri Lanka
162 □ Velasco Ibarra *Galapagos Is* Ecuador
170 C2 Velasco, Sa de mountain range Argentina
91 D5 Velaux France
91 B3 Velay reg. France
173 K3 Velázquez Uruguay
72 C4 Velbert Germany
80 C1 Velburg Germany
130 B6 Velddrif South Africa
75 H4 Velden Germany
69 E3 Velden Netherlands
81 F4 Velden am Wörther See Austria
69 D3 Veldhoven Netherlands
104 E3 Velebit mountain range Croatia
104 E3 Velebitski Kanal chan. Croatia
72 B4 Velen Germany
79 H4 Velence Hungary
79 H4 Velencei-tó l. Hungary
81 G4 Velenje Slovenia
112 C4 Veles Macedonia
81 F2 Velešín Czech Rep.
114 B1 Velešta Macedonia
52 F2 Velet'ma Rus. Fed.
104 F4 Velež mts Bos.-Herz.
101 F4 Vélez r. Spain
162 C2 Vélez Colombia
101 H3 Vélez-Blanco Spain
101 G4 Vélez de Benaudalla Spain
101 F4 Vélez-Málaga Spain
101 H3 Vélez-Rubio Spain
73 H1 Velgast Germany
169 E3 Velhas r. Brazil
51 H6 Velichayevskoye Rus. Fed.
53 A2 Velika Berezovytsya Ukraine
81 H5 Velika Gorica Croatia
53 A1 Velika Hlusha Ukraine
104 E3 Velika Kapela mountain range Croatia
112 C3 Velika Kruša Yugoslavia
81 H5 Velika Mlaka Croatia
53 B1 Velika Ozera Ukraine
112 C2 Velika Plana Yugoslavia
50 J3 Velikaya r. Rus. Fed.
50 E2 Velikaya Guba Rus. Fed.
81 F5 Velike Lašče Slovenia
53 A2 Veliki Birky Ukraine
112 C3 Veliki Jastrebac mts Yugoslavia
107 J3 Veliki Risnjak mt. Croatia
50 D3 Velikiye Luki Rus. Fed.
53 A2 Velikiy Hlybochok Ukraine
53 D1 Velikiy Lystven Ukraine
77 M6 Velikiy Lyubin' Ukraine
50 H2 Velikiy Ustyug Rus. Fed.
53 B2 Velikiy Zhvanchyk Ukraine
52 E2 Velikodvorskiy Rus. Fed.
112 C2 Veliko Gradište Yugoslavia
38 B3 Velikonda Ra. h. India
52 A1 Velikooktyabr'skiy Rus. Fed.
112 E3 Veliko Tŭrnovo Bulgaria
52 D1 Velikoye Rus. Fed.
52 C1 Velikoye, Oz. l. Rus. Fed.
52 E2 Velikoye, Oz. l. Rus. Fed.
99 F2 Velilla del Río Carrión Spain
101 G3 Velillas r. Spain
107 J4 Veli Lošinj Croatia
93 C4 Vélines France
122 B4 Vélingara *Kolda* Senegal
122 B3 Vélingara *Louga* Senegal
112 D3 Velingrad Bulgaria
109 F2 Velino r. Italy
109 F2 Velino, Monte mt. Italy
50 D4 Velizh Rus. Fed.
78 F2 Velká Bíteš Czech Rep.
75 K2 Velká Dobrá Czech Rep.
79 J2 Velká Fatra mts Slovakia
78 F2 Velká Haná r. Czech Rep.
79 G3 Veľká Javořina mt. Czech Rep./Slovakia
79 L2 Veľká Javořina mt. Slovakia
79 J3 Veľ'ká nad Ipľom Slovakia
81 H2 Velké Bílovice Czech Rep.
79 M3 Veľké Kapušany Slovakia
81 J2 Veľké Leváre Slovakia
78 F2 Velké Meziříčí Czech Rep.
81 H2 Velké Němčice Czech Rep.
81 H2 Velké Pavlovice Czech Rep.
54 B1 Velkua Finland
79 J3 Veľký Krtíš Slovakia
79 G4 Veľký Meder Slovakia
6 □1 Vella Lavella i. Solomon Is.
38 B4 Vellar r. India
80 A1 Vellberg Germany
109 E3 Velletri Italy
82 B1 Vellevans France
59 E4 Vellinge Sweden
38 B3 Vellore India
93 C6 Vellos r. Spain
115 E6 Velopoula i. Greece
69 D5 Velosnes France
69 C4 Velp r. Belgium
68 D3 Velp Netherlands
73 F3 Velpke Germany
50 G2 Vel'sk Rus. Fed.
73 J3 Velten Germany
78 D1 Veltrusy Czech Rep.
68 D2 Veluwe reg. Netherlands
68 D2 Veluwemeer l. Netherlands
68 D2 Veluwezoom, Nationaal Park nat. park Netherlands
137 J5 Velva *N. Dakota* U.S.A.
75 K2 Velvary Czech Rep.
52 C2 Vel'yaminovo Rus. Fed.
53 E2 Velyka Bahachka Ukraine
53 F3 Velyka Bilozerka r. Ukraine
53 E2 Velyka Burimka Ukraine
53 D3 Velyka Korenykha Ukraine
53 E3 Velyka Lepetykha Ukraine
53 C3 Velyka Mykhaylivka Ukraine
53 G3 Velyka Novosilka Ukraine
53 E3 Velyka Oleksandrivka Ukraine
53 F1 Velyka Pysarivka Ukraine
53 F2 Velyka Rublivka Ukraine
53 B1 Velyka Tsvilya Ukraine
77 N6 Velyka Tur"ya Ukraine
53 D2 Velyka Vys' r. Ukraine
53 D2 Velyka Vyska Ukraine
79 M3 Velyki Kom"yaty Ukraine
53 C2 Velyki Korovyntsi Ukraine
53 E2 Velyki Krynky Ukraine
53 A1 Velyki Mosty Ukraine
53 E1 Velyki Sorochyntsi Ukraine
53 E2 Velykiy Khutir Ukraine
53 D3 Velykodolyns'ke Ukraine
53 G3 Velykomykhaylivka Ukraine
79 M3 Velykyy Bereznyy Ukraine
53 G1 Velykyy Burluk Ukraine
112 E1 Velykyy Bychkiv Ukraine
174 G5 Vema Fracture sea feature Atlantic Ocean
175 J4 Vema Trough sea feature Indian Ocean
55 A3 Vemb Denmark
38 B4 Vembanād L. l. India
59 E4 Ven i. Sweden
59 F3 Vena Sweden
66 D4 Venachar, Loch l. *Scotland* U.K.
108 B2 Venaco *Corse* France
173 G2 Venado Tuerto Argentina
109 G3 Venafro Italy
92 A2 Venansault France
90 C1 Venarey-les-Laumes France
106 B3 Venaria Italy
91 F5 Vence France
168 D5 Venceslau Brás Brazil
77 N1 Venčiūnai Lithuania
169 H4 Venda Nova Brazil
100 B2 Vendas Novas Portugal
92 A3 Vendays-Montalivet France
92 A2 Vendée div. *Pays de la Loire* France
92 B2 Vendée r. France
92 C2 Vendeuvre-du-Poitou France
86 D4 Vendeuvre-sur-Barse France
111 E6 Vendicari, Isola i. *Sicilia* Italy
50 H2 Vendinga Rus. Fed.
89 G4 Vendôme France
55 B2 Vendsyssel reg. Denmark
53 B2 Vendychany Ukraine
91 D5 Venelles France
93 E5 Vénès France
107 G3 Veneta, Laguna lag. Italy
115 C6 Venetiko i. Greece
107 F3 Veneto div. Italy
50 F4 Venev Rus. Fed.
107 G3 Venezia div. *Veneto* Italy
107 G3 Venezia *Venezia* Italy
107 G3 Venezia, Golfo di g. Italy
160 F3 Venezuela country South America
162 C1 Venezuela, Golfo de g. Venezuela
38 A3 Vengurla India
68 D2 Venhuizen Netherlands
98 E3 Venialbo Spain
145 D7 Venice *Florida* U.S.A.
Venice *see* Venezia
83 E2 Venina r. Italy
90 C3 Vénissieux France
59 E1 Venjan Sweden
59 F1 Venjanssjön l. Sweden
38 B3 Venkatagiri India
38 C2 Venkatapuram India
69 E3 Venlo Netherlands
114 G1 Venna Greece
58 B2 Vennesla Norway
58 C1 Vennisfjellet mt. Norway
55 A3 Venø Bugt b. Denmark
109 H4 Venosa r. Italy
109 H4 Venosa Italy
90 B1 Venoy France
69 D3 Venray Netherlands
7 □10 Vent, Îles du is *French Polynesia* Pacific Ocean
7 □10 Vent, Îles sous le is *French Polynesia* Pacific Ocean
54 B3 Venta r. Latvia/Lithuania
99 F3 Venta de Baños Spain
98 E1 Venta de las Ranas Spain
101 G2 Venta de los Santos Spain
170 D4 Ventana, Sa de la mountain range Argentina
173 F5 Ventana, Sa de la mts Argentina
98 D1 Venta Nueva Spain
101 G3 Ventas de Huelma Spain
101 F4 Ventas de Zafarraya Spain
91 D4 Ventavon France
131 F4 Ventersburg South Africa
131 F3 Ventersdorp South Africa
131 F3 Venterskroon South Africa
131 E5 Venterstad South Africa
106 B5 Ventimiglia Italy
171 B5 Ventisquero mt. Argentina
63 E4 Ventnor *England* U.K.
109 F4 Ventotene, Isola i. Italy
91 D4 Ventoux, Mont mt. France
31 J3 Ventselevo Rus. Fed.
54 B3 Ventspils Latvia
163 D3 Ventuari r. Venezuela
154 C4 Ventucopa *California* U.S.A.
154 C4 Ventura *California* U.S.A.
13 F4 Venus B. b. *Victoria* Australia
7 □11 Vénus, Pte pt *French Polynesia* Pacific Ocean
107 H2 Venzone Italy
81 H3 Vép Hungary
170 D2 Vera Argentina
103 B7 Vera Spain
157 F4 Veracruz div. Mexico
164 C1 Vera Cruz Brazil
157 F5 Veracruz Mexico
102 B1 Vera de Bidasoa Spain
165 E5 Verá, L. l. Paraguay
36 B5 Veraval India
53 A1 Verba *Rivens'ka Oblast'* Ukraine
77 N5 Verba *Volyns'ka Oblast'* Ukraine
106 C3 Verbania Italy
86 B3 Verberie France
111 E3 Verbicaro Italy
82 C2 Verbier Switzerland
52 C1 Verbilki Rus. Fed.
53 F3 Verbove Ukraine
53 A2 Verbovets' Ukraine
52 E2 Verbovskiy Rus. Fed.
53 F3 Verby Ukraine
83 E2 Verceia Italy
106 C3 Vercelli div. *Piemonte* Italy
106 C3 Vercelli *Vercelli* Italy
90 E1 Vercel-Villedieu-le-Camp France
141 J4 Verchères *Québec* Canada
91 D4 Vercors reg. France
52 E3 Verda r. Rus. Fed.
91 E4 Verdaches France
56 C3 Verdalsøra Norway
155 G4 Verde r. *Arizona* U.S.A.
171 C5 Verde r. Argentina
168 C3 Verde r. Brazil
168 C2 Verde r. Brazil
169 F4 Verde r. Brazil
168 D3 Verde r. Brazil
168 D1 Verde r. Brazil
170 E1 Verde r. Paraguay
101 G3 Verde r. Spain
169 G2 Verde Grande r. Brazil
159 F3 Verde, Isla del airport Puerto Rico
23 B3 Verde Island Pass. chan. Philippines
72 E3 Verden (Aller) Germany
173 F5 Verde, Pen. pen. Argentina
171 D4 Verde, Pen. pen. Argentina
169 G1 Verde Pequeno r. Brazil
151 E4 Verdigris r. *Kansas* U.S.A.
114 C3 Verdikoussa Greece
168 C2 Verdinho r. Brazil
91 E5 Verdon r. France
114 B2 Vërdovë Albania
87 E3 Verdun France
93 D5 Verdun-sur-Garonne France
90 D2 Verdun-sur-le-Doubs France
110 C5 Verdura r. *Sicilia* Italy
131 G3 Vereeniging South Africa
53 E2 Veremiyivka Ukraine
131 G2 Verena South Africa
138 E4 Vérendrye, Réserve faunique La nat. park *Québec* Canada
141 G3 Vérendrye, Réserve faunique La *Québec* Canada
79 J4 Veresegyház Hungary
52 C2 Vereya Rus. Fed.
93 D5 Verfeil France
122 B4 Vergara, Cap pt Guinea
173 L2 Vergara Uruguay
107 F4 Vergato Italy
130 E2 Vergelee South Africa
15 E4 Vergemont Cr. watercourse *Queensland* Australia
147 G2 Vergennes *Vermont* U.S.A.
102 G2 Verges Spain
86 C5 Vergigny France
91 B3 Vergongheon France
92 C3 Vergt France
52 D1 Verigino Rus. Fed.
98 C3 Verín Spain
54 E2 Veriora Estonia
168 D3 Veríssimo Brazil
131 F4 Verkeerdevlei South Africa
53 F2 Verkhivtseve Ukraine
46 E2 Verkhne-Avzyan Rus. Fed.
52 A2 Verkhnedneprovskiy Rus. Fed.
44 K3 Verkhneimbatskoye Rus. Fed.
50 H3 Verkhnespasskoye Rus. Fed.
56 H1 Verkhnetulomskiy Rus. Fed.
52 D4 Verkhneturovo Rus. Fed.
46 E2 Verkhneural'sk Rus. Fed.
45 O3 Verkhnevilyuysk Rus. Fed.
52 A1 Verkhnevolzhskoye Vdkhr. resr Rus. Fed.
52 G2 Verkhneye Talyzino Rus. Fed.
51 H5 Verkhniy Baskunchak Rus. Fed.
53 G2 Verkhniy Byshkyn Ukraine
51 J5 Verkhniy Kushum Rus. Fed.
52 F1 Verkhniy Landekh Rus. Fed.
52 F3 Verkhniy Lomov Rus. Fed.
53 F3 Verkhniy Rohachyk Ukraine
30 E2 Verkhniy Ul'khun Rus. Fed.
50 E1 Verkhniy Vyalozerskiy Rus. Fed.
53 F2 Verkhn'odniprovs'k Ukraine
53 D2 Verkhnyachka Ukraine
52 C4 Verkhnyaya Grayvoronka Rus. Fed.
47 K2 Verkhnyaya Irmen' Rus. Fed.
52 D4 Verkhnyaya Khava Rus. Fed.
31 E2 Verkhnyaya Khila Rus. Fed.
56 J2 Verkhnyaya Pirenga, Oz. l. Rus. Fed.
50 H2 Verkhnyaya Toyma Rus. Fed.
52 C1 Verkhnyaya Troitsa Rus. Fed.
50 J3 Verkhoshizhem'ye Rus. Fed.
50 G2 Verkhovazh'ye Rus. Fed.
52 C3 Verkhov'ye Rus. Fed.
53 A2 Verkhovyna Ukraine
45 P3 Verkhoyansk Rus. Fed.
45 O2 Verkhoyanskiy Khrebet mountain range Rus. Fed.
52 H3 Verkhozim Rus. Fed.
30 D2 Verkh. Shergol'dzhin Rus. Fed.
46 F1 Verkh. Ufaley Rus. Fed.
31 E1 Verkh-Usugli Rus. Fed.
56 H2 Verkneye Kuyto, Oz. l. Rus. Fed.
50 H2 Verkola Rus. Fed.
131 G3 Verkykerskop South Africa
69 D4 Verlaine Belgium
130 C7 Vermaaklikheid South Africa
86 C3 Vermand France
86 C3 Vermandois reg. France
168 C1 Vermelho r. Brazil
166 C2 Vermelho r. Brazil
166 C2 Vermelho r. Brazil
90 B1 Vermenton France
148 C5 Vermilion r. *Illinois* U.S.A.
137 G4 Vermilion *Alberta* Canada
155 F3 Vermilion Cliffs cliff *Utah* U.S.A.
148 A2 Vermilion Lake l. *Minnesota* U.S.A.
148 A2 Vermilion Range h. *Minnesota* U.S.A.
150 D3 Vermillion *S. Dakota* U.S.A.
138 B4 Vermillion Bay *Ontario* Canada
114 C2 Vermio mt. Greece
147 G3 Vermont div. U.S.A.
52 F3 Vernadovka Rus. Fed.
83 F2 Vernago, Lago di l. Italy
152 E3 Vernal *Utah* U.S.A.
91 F4 Vernante Italy
89 F4 Vernantes France
82 C2 Vernayaz Switzerland
140 E3 Verner *Ontario* Canada
75 K2 Vernéřice Czech Rep.
93 D5 Vernet France
93 E6 Vernet-les-Bains France
89 F3 Verneuil-sur-Avre France
130 C4 Verneuk Pan l. South Africa
82 B2 Vernier Switzerland
58 D2 Verningen Norway
107 F4 Vernio Italy
93 D5 Verniolle France
111 H2 Vernole Italy
155 H4 Vernon *Arizona* U.S.A.
136 F4 Vernon *B.C.* Canada
147 G4 Vernon *Connecticut* U.S.A.
151 D5 Vernon *Texas* U.S.A.
155 F1 Vernon *Utah* U.S.A.
89 G2 Vernon France
89 G3 Vernouillet France
91 C4 Vernoux-en-Vivarais France
88 D3 Vern-sur-Seiche France
87 F3 Verny France
145 D7 Vero Beach *Florida* U.S.A.
114 D2 Veroia Greece
83 F3 Verolanuova Italy
109 F3 Veroli Italy
107 E3 Verona div. *Veneto* Italy
107 E3 Verona *Verona* Italy
173 J3 Veronica Argentina
90 C2 Verosvres France
79 K4 Verpelét Hungary
106 B3 Verres Italy
86 B4 Versailles France
94 D2 Versailles France
90 D2 Vers-en-Montage France

33 F3 Xingan China
33 E3 Xing'an China
31 G4 Xingcheng China
33 F3 Xingguo China
30 A6 Xinghai China
30 E4 Xinghe China
33 G1 Xinghua China
33 G3 Xinghua Wan b. China
31 K3 Xingkai China
31 K3 Xingkai Hu l. China/Rus. Fed.
31 H2 Xinglong China
31 F4 Xinglong China
31 H3 Xinglongzhen China
33 F3 Xingning China
33 F2 Xingou China
32 E1 Xingping China
32 D3 Xingren China
32 C1 Xingsagoinba China
33 E2 Xingshan China
30 E5 Xingtai China
30 E5 Xingtang China
166 B1 Xingu r. Brazil
32 D2 Xingwen China
30 D5 Xing Xian China
33 F1 Xingyang China
32 D3 Xingyi China
33 G2 Xingzi China
47 K4 Xinhe China
31 E5 Xinhe China
33 E3 Xinhua China
30 B5 Xinhuacun China
33 E3 Xinhuang China
33 F4 Xinhui China
30 B5 Xining China
33 F2 Xinjian China
30 D6 Xinjiang China
47 J4 Xinjiang Uygur Zizhiqu div. China
37 D1 Xinjiang Uygur Zizhiqu China
30 D5 Xinjie China
32 B3 Xinjie China
32 C2 Xinjin China
31 G5 Xinjin China
31 J3 Xinkai r. China
31 H2 Xinlitun China
32 C2 Xinlong China
31 G4 Xinmin China
33 E3 Xinning China
32 C3 Xinping China
31 J2 Xinqing China
33 G3 Xinquan China
31 F6 Xintai China
33 F3 Xintian China
33 F2 Xin Xian China
30 E5 Xin Xian China
33 F1 Xinxiang China
33 F4 Xinxing China
33 F1 Xinyang China
33 F1 Xinyang China
33 H1 Xinyang Gang r. China
33 G1 Xinye r. China
33 F1 Xinye China
33 G1 Xinyi China
33 E4 Xinyi China
33 F5 Xinying China
33 F3 Xinyu China
47 K4 Xinyuan China
30 E5 Xinzhou China
Xinzhu see Hsin-chu
98 C2 Xinzo de Limia Spain
31 G4 Xiongyuecheng China
33 E1 Xiping China
33 F1 Xiping China
32 C1 Xiqing Shan mountain range China
166 D3 Xique Xique Brazil
114 E4 Xiro mt. Greece
32 D2 Xishui China
33 F2 Xishui China
98 C1 Xistral, Serra do mountain range Spain
122 B4 Xitole Guinea-Bissau
31 F3 Xi Ujimqin Qi China
33 G2 Xiuning China
33 E2 Xiushan China
33 F2 Xiu Shui r. China
33 F2 Xiushui China
32 D3 Xiuwen China
33 F1 Xiuwu China
31 G4 Xiuyan China
33 E5 Xiuying China
32 B1 Xiwu China
37 F3 Xixabangma Feng mt. China
33 E1 Xixia China
33 F1 Xi Xian China
30 D5 Xi Xian China
32 D1 Xi Xiang China
32 D4 Xiyang r. China
33 H3 Xiyang Dao i. China
37 F2 Xizang Gaoyuan plat. China
37 F3 Xizang Zizhiqu China
31 G5 Xizhong Dao i. China
126 E2 Xjis Somalia
37 H3 Xoka China
131 F6 Xolobe South Africa
25 D5 Xom An Lôc Vietnam
25 D5 Xom Dưc Hanh Vietnam
87 F4 Xonrupt-Longemer France
33 G2 Xuancheng China
33 E2 Xuan'en China
32 D2 Xuanhan China
30 C5 Xuanhepu China
31 E4 Xuanhua China
25 D5 Xuân Lôc Vietnam
32 D3 Xuanwei China
33 F1 Xuchang China
42 G1 Xudat Azerbaijan
126 D4 Xuddur Somalia
126 E3 Xudun Somalia
33 E3 Xuefeng Shan mountain range China
37 H2 Xugui China
Xulun Hobot Qagan Qi see Zhengxiangbai Qi
Xulun Hoh Qi see Zhenglan Qi
32 B1 Xümatang China
33 E1 Xun r. China
33 E4 Xun r. China
31 J2 Xun r. China
32 C3 Xundian China
37 E2 Xungba China
37 F3 Xungru China
31 H2 Xunhe China
31 J2 Xunke Rus. Fed.
33 F3 Xunwu China
30 E6 Xun Xian China
33 E1 Xunyang China
32 E1 Xunyi China
33 E3 Xupu China
37 F3 Xuru Co l. China
31 E5 Xushui China
33 E4 Xuwen China
33 G1 Xuyi China
32 D2 Xuyong China
33 G1 Xuzhou China
114 G2 Xylagani Greece
115 D4 Xylokastro Greece
114 E2 Xylopoli Greece

Y

32 C2 Ya'an China
13 E3 Yaapeet Victoria Australia
124 A3 Yabassi Cameroon
126 C4 Yabēlo Ethiopia
126 C4 Yabēlo Wildlife Sanctuary res. Ethiopia
112 E3 Yablanitsa Bulgaria
112 F3 Yablanovo Bulgaria
52 E3 Yablonovets Rus. Fed.
30 D2 Yablonovyy Khrebet mountain range Rus. Fed.
53 A2 Yabluniv Ukraine
123 F4 Yabo Nigeria
30 B5 Yabrai Shan mountain range China
30 B5 Yabrai Yanchang China
43 D3 Yabrūd Syria
145 □3 Yabucoa Puerto Rico
31 J3 Yabuli China
53 C1 Yabunets' Ukraine
162 D2 Yacambu, Parque Nacional nat. park Venezuela
6 □6 Yacata i. Fiji
Yacha see Baisha
33 E5 Yacheng China
13 F4 Yackandandah Victoria Australia
164 C2 Yacuma r. Bolivia
38 B2 Yadgir India
34 G5 Yadong China
52 H2 Yadrin Rus. Fed.
6 □6 Yadua i. Fiji
118 B1 Yafran Libya
122 D4 Yagaba Ghana
29 □2 Yagaji-jima i. Japan
Yagda see Erdemli
44 J3 Yagel'naya Rus. Fed.
28 H1 Yagishiri-tō i. Japan
52 B3 Yagodnoye Rus. Fed.
45 Q3 Yagodnoye Rus. Fed.
124 C1 Yagoua Cameroon
37 E3 Yagra China
32 A1 Yagradagzê Shan mt. China
173 K2 Yaguari r. Uruguay
25 C6 Yaha Thailand
29 F6 Yahagi-gawa r. Japan
124 D3 Yahuma Zaire
42 C2 Yahyalı Turkey
39 G3 Yahya Wana Afghanistan
29 G5 Yaita Japan
97 □ Yaiza Canary Is Spain
29 G6 Yaizu Japan
32 C2 Yajiang China
124 C3 Yaka Central African Rep.
31 G2 Yakeshi China
39 F3 Yakhehal Afghanistan
52 C1 Yakhroma Rus. Fed.
152 B2 Yakima r. Washington U.S.A.
152 B2 Yakima Washington U.S.A.
39 C2 Yakinish Iran
39 E3 Yakmach Pakistan
122 D4 Yako Burkina
136 B3 Yakobi I. i. Alaska U.S.A.
124 D3 Yakoma Zaire
112 D4 Yakoruda Bulgaria
52 H3 Yakovlevka Rus. Fed.
53 G1 Yakovlevo Rus. Fed.
28 H2 Yakumo Japan
134 E4 Yakutat Alaska U.S.A.
134 E4 Yakutat Bay b. Alaska U.S.A.
45 O3 Yakutsk Rus. Fed.
53 F3 Yakymivka Ukraine
25 C6 Yala Thailand
12 B2 Yalata Abor. Reserve res. S. Australia Australia
149 F4 Yale Michigan U.S.A.
124 D3 Yaleko Zaire
6 □7 Yalewa Kalou i. Fiji
52 G2 Yalga Rus. Fed.
17 B6 Yalgoo Western Australia Australia
113 F6 Yalıkavak Turkey
124 D2 Yalinga Central African Rep.
54 F5 Yalizava Belarus
157 H4 Yalkubul, Pta pt Mexico
159 □1 Yallahs Jamaica
15 F5 Yalleroi Queensland Australia
124 C2 Yaloké Central African Rep.
32 C3 Yalong r. China
124 D3 Yalongwe Zaire
42 B1 Yalova Turkey
53 G3 Yalta Donets'ka Oblast' Ukraine
51 E6 Yalta Respublika Krym Ukraine
51 F6 Yalta Ukraine
53 B2 Yaltushkiv Ukraine
31 G3 Yalu r. China
31 H4 Yalu r. China/North Korea
31 H5 Yalujiang Kou river mouth North Korea
47 G1 Yalutorovsk Rus. Fed.
42 B2 Yalvaç Turkey
29 H4 Yamada Japan
29 G4 Yamagata div. Japan
29 H4 Yamagata Japan
28 C8 Yamagawa Japan
29 C6 Yamaguchi Japan
28 C6 Yamaguchi Japan
29 G6 Yamanashi div. Japan
30 D2 Yamarovka Rus. Fed.
29 H5 Yamatsuri Japan
13 H2 Yamba New South Wales Australia
13 E4 Yambacoona Tasmania Australia
137 G2 Yamba Lake l. N.W.T. Canada
124 E3 Yambio Sudan
52 F3 Yambirno Rus. Fed.
112 F3 Yambol Bulgaria
162 B5 Yambrasbamba Peru
44 J3 Yamburg Rus. Fed.
4 E5 Yamdena i.
28 C7 Yame Japan
37 G3 Yamenzhuang China
24 B2 Yamethin Myanmar
23 B1 Y'ami i. Philippines
29 H5 Yamizo-san mt. Japan
54 F2 Yamm Rus. Fed.
15 E5 Yamma Yamma, L. salt flat Queensland Australia
43 C4 Yammit Egypt
122 C5 Yamoussoukro Côte d'Ivoire
152 E3 Yampa r. Colorado U.S.A.
53 B2 Yampil' Khmel'nyts'ka Oblast' Ukraine
52 A4 Yampil' Sums'ka Oblast' Ukraine
53 C2 Yampil' Vinnyts'ka Oblast' Ukraine
36 E4 Yamuna r. India
36 D3 Yamunanagar India
47 J2 Yamyshevo Kazakhstan
37 G3 Yamzho Yumco l. China
30 D5 Yan r. China
45 P3 Yana r. Rus. Fed.
122 B5 Yana Sierra Leone
12 E4 Yanac Victoria Australia
164 A2 Yanachaga-Chemillen, Parque Nacional nat. park Peru
29 □2 Yanaha-jima i. Japan
30 D7 Yanai Japan
38 C2 Yanam India
30 D5 Yan'an China
164 B2 Yanaoca Peru
46 E1 Yanaul Rus. Fed.
32 C3 Yanbian China
119 G3 Yanbu'al Baḩr Saudi Arabia
119 G3 Yanbu' an Nakhl reg. Saudi Arabia
33 H1 Yancheng China
17 A6 Yanchep Western Australia Australia
30 C5 Yanchi China
30 D5 Yanchuan China
13 F2 Yanda watercourse New South Wales Australia
12 E2 Yandama Cr. watercourse S. Australia Australia
6 □1 Yandina Solomon Is.
124 C4 Yandja Zaire
24 A3 Yandoon Myanmar
122 C4 Yanfolila Mali
31 E4 Yang r. China
124 D2 Yangalia Central African Rep.
124 D3 Yangambi Zaire
37 H3 Ya'ngamdo China
122 C4 Yangasso Mali
37 G3 Yangbajain China
32 B3 Yangbi China
33 F1 Yangcheng China
33 E4 Yangchun China
31 H5 Yangdok North Korea
30 E4 Yanggao China
31 E5 Yanggu China
36 D2 Yangi Davan China
39 B1 Yangi Kand Iran
47 G4 Yangirabad Uzbekistan
47 G4 Yangiyul' Uzbekistan
33 E4 Yangjiang China
24 B3 Yangon div. Myanmar
24 B3 Yangon Myanmar
32 E3 Yangping China
33 F5 Yangquan China
33 F3 Yangshan China
33 E3 Yangshuo China
32 C3 Yangtouyan China
Yangtse, Mouth of the river mouth see Changjiang Kou
Yangtze r. see Jinsha
Yangtze r. see Chang Jiang
99 H2 Yanguas Spain
126 D2 Yangudi Rassa National Park nat. park Ethiopia
32 D1 Yang Xian China
30 E4 Yangyuan China
33 G1 Yangzhou China
32 E2 Yanhe China
37 E2 Yanhuqu China
31 J4 Yanji China
32 D2 Yanjin China
32 B2 Yanjing China
123 G5 Yankara Nat. Park nat. park Nigeria
54 F4 Yankavichy Belarus
150 D3 Yankton S. Dakota U.S.A.
45 Q2 Yano-Indigirskaya Nizmennost' lowland Rus. Fed.
52 A2 Yanovo Rus. Fed.
44 K3 Yanov Stan Rus. Fed.
38 C4 Yan Oya r. Sri Lanka
32 E3 Yanqi China
31 E4 Yanqing China
33 F1 Yan Shan mountain range China
31 F5 Yanshan China
33 G2 Yanshan China
32 D4 Yanshan China
32 H2 Yanshiping China
31 J3 Yanshou China
31 P2 Yanskiy Zaliv g. Rus. Fed.
13 F2 Yantabulla New South Wales Australia
31 G5 Yantai China
34 A4 Yantarnyy Rus. Fed.
31 H4 Yantongshan China
112 E3 Yantra r. Bulgaria
6 □8 Yanuca i. Fiji
6 □6 Yanuca reef Fiji
119 H3 Yanūfi, J. al h. Saudi Arabia
6 □8 Yanuya i. Fiji
32 B3 Yanwa China
47 G4 Yany-Kurgan Kazakhstan
32 C3 Yanyuan China
31 F6 Yanzhou China
32 C3 Yao'an China
124 B3 Yaoundé Cameroon
33 E1 Yao Xian China
31 H2 Yaoxiaoling China
21 L5 Yap i. Fed. States of Micronesia
21 L7 Yapen i. Indonesia
15 E3 Yappar r. Queensland Australia
176 E5 Yap Tr. sea feature Pacific Ocean
163 F3 Yapukarri Guyana
6 □6 Yaqaga i. Fiji
6 □8 Yaqetu i. Fiji
156 C2 Yaqui r. Mexico
50 K3 Yar Rus. Fed.
15 F5 Yaraka Queensland Australia
52 H1 Yaransk Rus. Fed.
12 C3 Yardea S. Australia Australia
42 B2 Yardımcı Burnu pt Turkey
42 G2 Yardımlı Azerbaijan
Yardymly see Yardımlı
63 H2 Yare r. England U.K.
50 K2 Yarega Rus. Fed.
53 A2 Yaremcha Ukraine
50 J2 Yarensk Rus. Fed.
162 C3 Yari r. Colombia
29 F5 Yariga-take mt. Japan
126 D2 Yarīm Yemen
163 G3 Yaripo Brazil
162 D1 Yaritagua Venezuela
47 J5 Yarkant r. China
Yarkant see Shache
141 G4 Yarker Ontario Canada
36 C1 Yarkhun r. Pakistan
37 H3 Yarlung Zangbo r. China
65 G3 Yarm England U.K.
53 B2 Yarmolyntsi Ukraine
63 E4 Yarmouth England U.K.
139 G5 Yarmouth Nova Scotia Canada
147 H4 Yarmouth Port Massachusetts U.S.A.
155 F4 Yarnell Arizona U.S.A.
52 E3 Yarok Rus. Fed.
53 E1 Yaroslavets' Ukraine
52 C1 Yaroslavl' div. Rus. Fed.
52 C1 Yaroslavl' Rus. Fed.
13 F4 Yarram Victoria Australia
15 G5 Yarraman Queensland Australia
17 A6 Yarra Yarra Lakes salt flat Western Australia Australia
15 F5 Yarronvale Queensland Australia
15 F4 Yarrowmere Queensland Australia
37 H3 Yartö Tra La China
52 A2 Yartsevo Rus. Fed.
162 B2 Yarumal Colombia
32 B2 Yarzhong China
125 C4 Yasa Zaire
6 □7 Yasawa i. Fiji
6 □8 Yasawa Group is Fiji
112 F3 Yasenkovo Bulgaria
123 F4 Yashi Nigeria
123 E5 Yashikera Nigeria
47 H5 Yashikül l. Tajikistan
28 D7 Ya-shima i. Japan
29 H4 Yashima Japan
28 D7 Yashiro-jima i. Japan
51 H6 Yashkul' Rus. Fed.
112 F3 Yasna Polyana Bulgaria
52 C2 Yasnogorsk Rus. Fed.
31 E2 Yasnogorsk Rus. Fed.
53 D1 Yasnohorodka Ukraine
46 E2 Yasnyy Rus. Fed.
13 G3 Yass New South Wales Australia
28 D6 Yasugi Japan
39 B3 Yāsūj Iran
53 G2 Yasynuvata Ukraine
123 G2 Yat well Niger
124 D2 Yata r. Central African Rep.
42 B2 Yatağan Turkey
127 C5 Yata Plateau plat. Kenya
62 D3 Yate England U.K.
6 □2 Yaté New Caledonia Pacific Ocean
151 E4 Yates Center Kansas U.S.A.
9 A6 Yates Pt pt New Zealand
137 K2 Yathkyed Lake l. N.W.T. Canada
124 D3 Yatolema Zaire
29 G6 Yatsuga-take volcano Japan
28 C7 Yatsushiro Japan
28 C7 Yatsushiro-kai b. Japan
43 C4 Yatta Israel
62 D3 Yatton England U.K.
145 □3 Yauco Puerto Rico
164 A2 Yauli Peru
162 C4 Yauna Maloca Colombia
164 B2 Yauri Peru
27 □ Yau Tong Hong Kong
164 A2 Yauyos Peru
162 C4 Yavari r. Brazil
156 C3 Yavaros Mexico
52 F2 Yavas r. Rus. Fed.
52 F2 Yavas Rus. Fed.
36 D5 Yavatmāl India
163 D2 Yaví, Co mt. Venezuela
53 E3 Yavkyne Ukraine
77 M6 Yavora Ukraine
53 A2 Yavoriv Ivano-Frankivs'ka Oblast' Ukraine
77 M6 Yavoriv L'vivs'ka Oblast' Ukraine
28 D7 Yawatahama Japan
47 K5 Yawatongguz r. China
47 K5 Yawatongguzlangar China
32 B3 Yawng-hwe Myanmar
122 B5 Yawri Bay b. Sierra Leone
157 H5 Yaxchilan Guatemala
Yaxian see Sanya
24 D2 Yayladağı Turkey
52 G2 Yaz Rus. Fed.
24 A2 Yazagyo Myanmar
39 C3 Yazd div. Iran
39 C3 Yazd Iran
39 E2 Yazdān Iran
39 C3 Yazd-e Khvāst Iran
151 F5 Yazoo r. Mississippi U.S.A.
151 F5 Yazoo City Mississippi U.S.A.
52 H2 Yazykovo Rus. Fed.
52 H2 Yazykovo Rus. Fed.
81 F2 Ybbs r. Austria
81 G2 Ybbs an der Donau Austria
81 F3 Ybbsitz Austria
55 B4 Yding Skovhøj h. Denmark
115 E5 Ydra i. Greece
115 E5 Ydra Greece
Y Drenewydd see Newtown
25 B4 Ye r. Myanmar
24 B4 Ye Myanmar
13 F4 Yea Victoria Australia
62 C4 Yealmpton England U.K.
118 C3 Yebbi-Bou Chad
118 C3 Yebbi-Souma Chad
101 F1 Yébenes, Sierra de mountain range Spain
47 J5 Yecheng China
103 B6 Yecla Spain
156 C2 Yécora Mexico
24 B3 Yedashe Myanmar
50 H2 Yedoma Rus. Fed.
118 C3 Yedri well Chad
145 D7 Yeehaw Junction Florida U.S.A.
12 C3 Yeelanna S. Australia Australia
52 F2 Yefanovo Rus. Fed.
50 E3 Yefimovskiy Rus. Fed.
52 D3 Yefremov Rus. Fed.
123 G3 Yeggueba well Niger
42 F2 Yeghegnadzor Armenia
47 J3 Yegindybulak Kazakhstan
51 G6 Yegorlykskaya Rus. Fed.
52 A2 Yegor'ye Rus. Fed.
31 H2 Yegor'yevka Rus. Fed.
52 D2 Yegor'yevsk Rus. Fed.
101 F2 Yeguas r. Spain
101 E3 Yeguas, Sierra de las h. Spain
123 E5 Yégué Togo
124 F2 Yei r. Sudan
126 B4 Yei Sudan
122 D5 Yeji Ghana
33 F2 Yejiaji China
46 F1 Yekaterinburg Rus. Fed.
31 J2 Yekaterinoslavka Rus. Fed.
52 G3 Yekaterinovka Rus. Fed.
52 D3 Yekaterinovka Rus. Fed.
Yekhegnadzor see Yeghegnadzor
118 C4 Yékia well Chad
52 A2 Yekimovichi Rus. Fed.
24 A3 Ye Kyun i. Myanmar
46 D1 Yelabuga Rus. Fed.
52 F4 Yelan' r. Rus. Fed.
51 G5 Yelan' Rus. Fed.
53 D3 Yelanets' Ukraine
15 G6 Yelarbon Queensland Australia
52 H1 Yelasy Rus. Fed.
52 E2 Yelat'ma Rus. Fed.
46 F5 Yelbarsli Turkmenistan
52 B3 Yelenskiy Rus. Fed.
52 D3 Yelets Rus. Fed.
122 B3 Yélimané Mali
52 D2 Yelino Rus. Fed.
45 R4 Yelizovo Rus. Fed.
50 J4 Yelkhovka Rus. Fed.
66 □2 Yell i. Scotland U.K.
38 C2 Yellandu India
38 A3 Yellapur India
148 B3 Yellow r. Wisconsin U.S.A.
146 D4 Yellow Creek Pennsylvania U.S.A.
134 G3 Yellowknife N.W.T. Canada
13 F3 Yellow Mt h. New South Wales Australia
Yellow River r. see Huang
31 G6 Yellow Sea sea Asia
152 F2 Yellowstone r. Montana U.S.A.
152 E2 Yellowstone L. l. Wyoming U.S.A.
152 E2 Yellowstone Nat. Park Wyoming U.S.A.
152 E2 Yellowtail Res. resr Montana/Wyoming U.S.A.
66 □2 Yell Sound chan. Scotland U.K.
52 F2 Yel'niki Rus. Fed.
52 A2 Yel'nya Rus. Fed.
47 G1 Yeloshnoye Rus. Fed.
46 F5 Yeloten Turkmenistan
53 C1 Yel'sk Belarus
98 D4 Yeltes r. Spain
47 L2 Yel'tsovka Rus. Fed.
53 G3 Yelyseyivka Ukraine
53 E2 Yelyzavethradka Ukraine
46 F2 Yemanzhelinsk Rus. Fed.
18 F8 Yemen country Asia
47 G1 Yemets r. Rus. Fed.
50 G2 Yemetsk Rus. Fed.
53 B1 Yemil'chyne Ukraine
50 G2 Yemtsa Rus. Fed.
50 J2 Yemva Rus. Fed.
56 H2 Yena Rus. Fed.
123 F6 Yenagoa Nigeria
53 F2 Yenakiyeve Ukraine
24 A2 Yenangyat Myanmar
24 A2 Yenangyaung Myanmar
24 A3 Yenanma Myanmar
24 D2 Yên Bai Vietnam
122 D5 Yendi Ghana
125 B4 Yénéganou Congo
24 B2 Yengan Myanmar
39 A1 Yengejeh Iran
122 B5 Yengema Sierra Leone
47 J5 Yengisar China
124 C3 Yengo Congo
30 B2 Yengorboy Rus. Fed.
113 F5 Yenice Çanakkale Turkey
43 C1 Yenice İçel Turkey
42 C2 Yeniceoba Turkey
113 F6 Yenihisar Turkey
113 G5 Yeniköy Turkey
113 G6 Yenipazar Turkey
113 F5 Yenişakran Turkey
26 F1 Yenisey r. Rus. Fed.
44 L4 Yeniseysk Rus. Fed.
45 L4 Yeniseyskiy Kryazh h. Rus. Fed.
44 J2 Yeniseyskiy Zaliv b. Rus. Fed.
32 B1 Yeniugou China
24 D2 Yên Minh Vietnam
90 D3 Yenne France
51 H6 Yenotayevka Rus. Fed.
62 C4 Yeo r. England U.K.
17 D5 Yeo L. salt flat Western Australia Australia
36 C5 Yeola India
Yeotmal see Yavatmāl
13 G3 Yeoval New South Wales Australia
62 D4 Yeovil England U.K.
Yeo Yeo r. see Bland
156 C2 Yepachic Mexico
52 D3 Yepifan' Rus. Fed.
15 G4 Yeppoon Queensland Australia
52 E2 Yerakhtur Rus. Fed.
46 D4 Yeraliyev Kazakhstan
42 F1 Yerevan Armenia
51 H6 Yergeni h. Rus. Fed.
17 C6 Yerilla Western Australia Australia
154 C2 Yerington Nevada U.S.A.
42 C2 Yerköy Turkey
38 A2 Yerla r. India
47 J2 Yermak Kazakhstan
31 H1 Yermakovo Rus. Fed.
47 H2 Yermentau Kazakhstan
52 F2 Yermish' Rus. Fed.
154 D4 Yermo California U.S.A.
151 B7 Yermo Mexico
52 E1 Yermolino Rus. Fed.
52 C2 Yermolino Rus. Fed.
27 M1 Yerofey-Pavlovich Rus. Fed.
43 C4 Yeroham Israel
89 G3 Yerre r. France
86 C4 Yerres r. France
69 C3 Yerseke Netherlands
52 B2 Yershi Rus. Fed.
53 A3 Yershichi Rus. Fed.
51 J5 Yershov Rus. Fed.
50 G2 Yertsevo Rus. Fed.
164 A2 Yerupaja mt. Peru
Yerushalayim see Jerusalem
51 H5 Yeruslan r. Rus. Fed.
89 F2 Yerville France
102 B2 Yesa Spain
24 A2 Yesagyo Myanmar
31 H5 Yesan South Korea
52 B1 Yesenovichi Rus. Fed.
47 G2 Yesil' Kazakhstan
43 B1 Yeşildere Turkey
42 C2 Yeşilhisar Turkey
42 D1 Yeşilırmak r. Turkey
42 B2 Yeşilova Turkey
173 H1 Yeso Argentina
172 B3 Yeso, Co mt. Chile
51 G6 Yessentuki Rus. Fed.
45 M3 Yessey Rus. Fed.
62 B4 Yes Tor h. England U.K.
13 G2 Yetman New South Wales Australia
24 A2 Yeu Myanmar
88 C5 Yeu, Île d' i. France
47 H1 Yevgashchino Rus. Fed.
Yevlakh see Yevlax
52 C3 Yevlanovo Rus. Fed.
42 F1 Yevlax Azerbaijan
51 E6 Yevpatoriya Ukraine
92 E1 Yèvre r. France
31 J2 Yevreyskaya Avtonomnaya Oblast' div. Rus. Fed.
31 F5 Ye Xian China
33 F1 Ye Xian China
51 F6 Yeya r. Rus. Fed.
37 E1 Yeyik China
51 F6 Yeysk Rus. Fed.
47 L4 Yeyungou China
50 H1 Yezhuga r. Rus. Fed.
50 D4 Yezyaryshcha Belarus
Y-Fenni see Abergavenny
88 C3 Yffiniac France
92 E2 Ygrande France
168 A6 Yguazú r. Paraguay
33 F1 Yi r. China
173 J2 Yí r. Uruguay
43 B4 Yi'allaq, G. mt. Egypt
31 H3 Yi'an China
119 H4 Yibā, W. watercourse Saudi Arabia
32 D2 Yibin China
37 F2 Yibug Caka salt lake China
33 E2 Yichang China
33 E2 Yichang China
30 D6 Yicheng China
33 F2 Yicheng China
30 D6 Yichuan China
33 F3 Yichun China
31 J3 Yichun China
31 F5 Yidu China
33 E2 Yidu China
32 B2 Yidun China
33 F2 Yifeng China
23 □2 Yigo Guam Pacific Ocean
33 G3 Yihuang China
33 E1 Yijun China
31 H2 Yilaha China
31 J3 Yilan China
112 F4 Yıldız Dağları mountain range Turkey
42 D2 Yıldızeli Turkey
43 A1 Yıldızı D. mt. Turkey
31 G2 Yilehuli Shan mountain range China
32 D3 Yiliang China
32 C3 Yiliang China
32 D2 Yilong China
31 H3 Yilong China
32 C4 Yilong Hu l. China
32 C3 Yimen China
31 J3 Yimianpo China
31 F2 Yimin r. China
31 F6 Yinan China
30 C5 Yinchuan China
17 C6 Yindarlgooda, L. salt flat Western Australia Australia
33 F1 Ying r. China
33 F2 Yingcheng China
31 H4 Yingchengzi China
33 F3 Yingde China
32 B3 Yingjiang China
31 G4 Yingkou China
31 G4 Yingkou China
30 C5 Yingpanshui China
32 D2 Yingshan China
33 F2 Yingshan China
33 G1 Yingshang China
33 G2 Yingtan China
30 E5 Ying Xian China
47 K4 Yining China
32 E3 Yinjiang China
31 H3 Yinma r. China
24 A2 Yinmabin Myanmar
30 D4 Yin Shan mountain range China
Yin Xian see Ningbo
32 A2 Yi'ong Zangbo r. China
32 C3 Yipinglang China
169 F5 Yira Chapeu, Monte mt. Brazil
126 C3 Yirga Alem Ethiopia
126 C3 Yirga Ch'efē Ethiopia
37 G2 Yirna Tso salt lake China
126 B3 Yirol Sudan
31 F3 Yirshi China
31 F5 Yi Shan mountain range China
32 E3 Yishan China
31 F6 Yishui China
25 □ Yishun Singapore
31 H3 Yitong r. China
31 H4 Yitong China
31 G2 Yitulihe China
32 C4 Yiwu China
26 F3 Yiwu China
33 G2 Yi Xian China
31 G4 Yi Xian China
33 G2 Yixing China
33 G2 Yiyang China
33 F2 Yiyang China
31 F5 Yiyuan China
33 F3 Yizhang China
54 F1 Ylämaa Finland
57 F3 Yläne Finland
56 F3 Ylihärmä Finland
56 G2 Yli-Ii Finland
56 G2 Yli-Kärppä Finland
56 G2 Ylikiiminki Finland
56 H2 Yli-Kitka l. Finland
56 F3 Ylistaro Finland
56 F2 Ylitornio Finland
56 G2 Ylivieska Finland
62 C2 Y Llethr h. Wales U.K.
57 F3 Ylöjärvi Finland
59 G2 Yngaren l. Sweden
59 F2 Yngen l. Sweden
47 H3 Yntaly Kazakhstan
151 D6 Yoakum Texas U.S.A.
118 D4 Yóa, Lac well Chad
123 G4 Yobe div. Nigeria
28 H2 Yobetsu-dake volcano Japan
126 D2 Yoboki Djibouti
28 B7 Yobuko Japan
28 D6 Yodoe Japan
54 E4 Yody Belarus
22 B4 Yogyakarta div. Indonesia
22 B3 Yogyakarta Indonesia
136 F4 Yoho Nat. Park nat. park B.C. Canada
28 E6 Yōka Japan
124 C3 Yokadouma Cameroon
29 F6 Yokkaichi Japan
124 B2 Yoko Cameroon
29 G6 Yokohama Japan
28 H3 Yokohama Japan
29 G6 Yokosuka Japan
28 D6 Yokota Japan
29 H4 Yokote Japan
28 H3 Yokotsu-dake mt. Japan
123 G5 Yola Nigeria
157 F5 Yoloxochitl Mexico
29 □2 Yomitan Airport Japan
122 C5 Yomou Guinea
92 A2 Yon r. France
23 □2 Yona Guam Pacific Ocean
29 □2 Yona Japan
29 □2 Yonabaru Japan
28 D6 Yonago Japan
29 □2 Yonaha-dake summit Japan
29 H5 Yonezawa Japan
28 A6 Yŏng-am South Korea
33 G3 Yong'an China
30 B5 Yongchang China
33 G1 Yongcheng China
31 J6 Yŏngch'ŏn South Korea
32 D2 Yongchuan China
33 G3 Yongchun China
30 B5 Yongdeng China
31 F5 Yongding r. China
33 G3 Yongding China
31 J5 Yŏngdŏk South Korea
33 E3 Yongfu China
37 H3 Yonggyap India
30 D5 Yonghe China
31 H5 Yŏnghŭng North Korea
31 H5 Yŏnghŭng-man b. North Korea
31 H4 Yongji China
33 E1 Yongji China
33 H2 Yongjia China
30 B6 Yongjing China
31 J5 Yŏngju South Korea
33 H2 Yongkang China
32 B3 Yongkang China
30 E5 Yongnian China
32 E4 Yongning China
32 B3 Yongping China
32 C3 Yongren China
31 H6 Yŏngsan'o South Korea
32 C2 Yongshan China
32 C3 Yongsheng China
32 E2 Yongshun China
33 G3 Yongtai China
33 F3 Yongxin China
33 F3 Yongxing China
33 F2 Yongxiu China
33 E3 Yongzhou China
31 H4 Yŏnhwa, Mt mt. North Korea
122 B5 Yonibana Sierra Leone
147 G4 Yonkers New York U.S.A.
86 C5 Yonne div. Bourgogne France
86 C4 Yonne r. France
24 A2 Yonzingyi Myanmar
123 G3 Yoo Baba well Niger
162 C2 Yopal Colombia
32 B3 Yopurga China
65 G4 York England U.K.
150 D3 York Nebraska U.S.A.
146 E5 York Pennsylvania U.S.A.
145 D5 York S. Carolina U.S.A.
17 B6 York Western Australia Australia
15 E1 York, C. c. Queensland Australia
12 D3 Yorke Pen. pen. S. Australia Australia
12 D3 Yorketown S. Australia Australia
135 M2 York, Kap c. Greenland
65 F3 Yorkshire Dales National Park nat. park England U.K.
65 H4 Yorkshire Wolds h. England U.K.
16 D2 York Sound chan. Western Australia Australia
137 J4 Yorkton Saskatchewan Canada
146 E6 Yorktown Virginia U.S.A.
65 G3 York, Vale of v. England U.K.
156 J6 Yoro Honduras
30 C2 Yöröö r. Mongolia
122 D4 Yorosso Mali
154 C3 Yosemite National Park nat. park California U.S.A.
154 C3 Yosemite Village California U.S.A.
28 E6 Yoshii-gawa r. Japan
29 E6 Yoshino r. Japan
28 D6 Yoshino-gawa r. Japan
29 F6 Yoshino-Kumano National Park nat. park Japan
52 H1 Yoshkar-Ola Rus. Fed.
31 H6 Yŏsu South Korea
43 C5 Yotvata Israel
126 C3 Yoube well Ethiopia
32 D4 Youg r. China
67 D5 Youghal Rep. of Ireland
67 C5 Youghal Bay b. Rep. of Ireland
146 D5 Youghiogheny River Lake Pennsylvania U.S.A.
122 B4 Youkounkoun Guinea
13 G3 Young New South Wales Australia
173 J2 Young Uruguay
9 □1 Young, C. c. Chatham Is New Zealand
12 D2 Younghusband, L. salt flat S. Australia Australia
12 D3 Younghusband Pen. pen. S. Australia Australia
179 A6 Young I. i. Antarctica
7 □14 Young' Rock rock Pitcairn I. Pacific Ocean
146 C4 Youngstown Ohio U.S.A.
120 C2 Youssoufia Morocco
122 D3 Youvarou Mali
33 G3 Youxi China
33 F3 You Xian China
32 E2 Youyang China
47 L3 Youyi Feng mt. China/Rus. Fed.
30 E5 Youyu China
47 G5 Yovon Tajikistan
42 C2 Yozgat Turkey
165 E4 Ypané r. Paraguay
114 D4 Ypati Greece
165 E4 Ypé-Jhú Paraguay
89 F2 Yport France
Ypres div. see Ieper
114 A3 Ypsos Greece
115 D5 Ypsous Greece
152 B3 Yreka California U.S.A.
Yr Wyddfa mt. see Snowdon
123 G4 Ysdseram watercourse Nigeria
86 B2 Yser r. France
91 C3 Yssingeaux France
59 E4 Ystad Sweden
62 C3 Ystalyfera Wales U.K.
62 C2 Ystwyth r. Wales U.K.
47 J4 Ysyk-Köl salt lake Kyrgyzstan
47 J4 Ysyk-Köl Kyrgyzstan
66 F3 Ythan r. Scotland U.K.
58 B2 Ytre Vinje Norway
59 H3 Ytterholmen i. Sweden
59 E1 Yttermalung Sweden
45 P3 Ytyk-Kyuyel Rus. Fed.
33 E4 Yu r. China
33 H4 Yüalin Taiwan
32 C4 Yuan r. China
33 E2 Yuan'an China

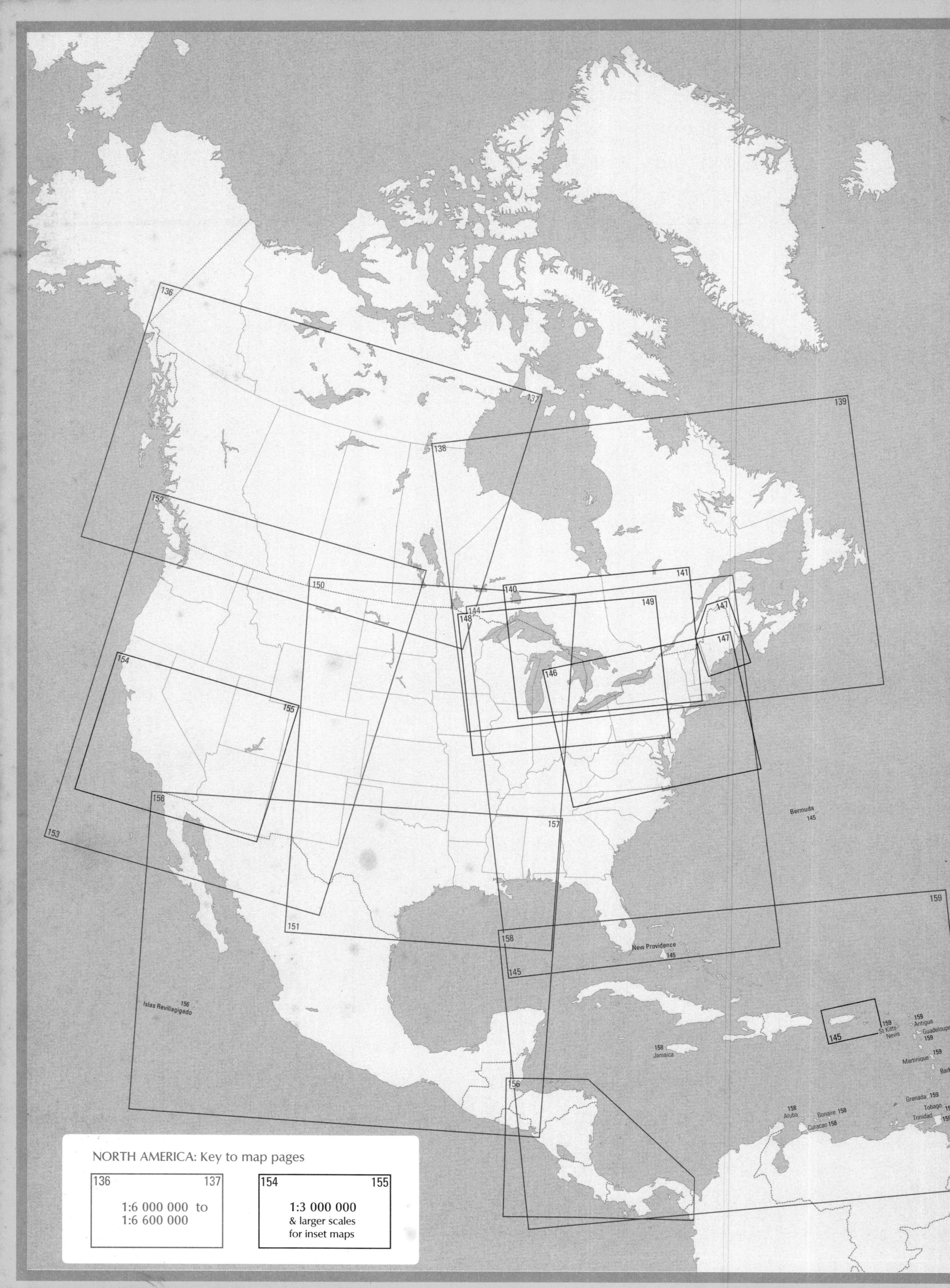

NORTH AMERICA: Key to map pages

136	137
1:6 000 000 to	
1:6 600 000	

154	155
1:3 000 000	
& larger scales	
for inset maps	

Bermuda
145

New Providence
145

Islas Revillagigedo 156

St Kitts-
Nevis 159
159
Antigua
Guadeloupe
159

159
145

Martinique 159

158
Jamaica

Grenada 159

158
Aruba Bonaire 158
Curaçao 158

Tobago
Trinidad 159